PSYCHOLOGY

FOURTH EDITION

PSYCHOLOGY

John M. Darley

Sam Glucksberg

Ronald A. Kinchla

Princeton University

PRENTICE HALL

Englewood Cliffs, New Jersey 07632

Library of Congress Cataloging-in-Publication Data
Darley, John M.
  Psychology.

  Includes bibliographies and indexes.
  1. Psychology. I. Glucksberg, Sam. II. Kinchla,
Ronald A. III. Title.
BF121.D26 1988   150   87-32884
ISBN 0-13-733650-0

Acquisition Editor: Susan Finnemore
Art Director: Florence Dara Silverman
Interior Design: Judith A. Matz-Coniglio
Page Layout: Jack Meserole
Cover Design: Judith A. Matz-Coniglio
Photo Editor: Lorinda Morris-Nantz
Photo Research: Pamela Degnan
New Line Art: Network Graphics
Manufacturing Buyer: Ray Keating
Cover Art: Lyonel Feininger, "The Grain Tower at Treptow on the Rega."
Courtesy Hessis ches Landesmuseum Darmstadt.

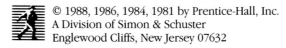
Printed in the United States of America

10 9 8 7 6 5 4 3 2 1

ISBN 0-13-733650-0

Prentice-Hall International (U.K.) Ltd., London
Prentice-Hall of Australia Pty. Limited, Sydney
Prentice-Hall Canada Inc., Toronto
Prentice-Hall Hispanoamericana S.A., Mexico
Prentice-Hall of India Private Limited, New Delhi
Prentice-Hall of Japan, Inc., Tokyo
Simon & Schuster Asia Pte. Ltd., Singapore
Editora Prentice-Hall do Brasil, Ltda., Rio de Janeiro

Overview

Contents

3   Sensation   80

4   Perception   118

5 States of Consciousness   154

6 Conditioning and Learning   186

7 Memory 220

8 Language 254

Preface

With great delight, we find ourselves writing the fourth edition of this textbook. Although the years have passed quickly, it is now over a decade since we began the first edition. Throughout each edition, our purpose has remained constant: we have tried to show how psychology attempts to provide scientific explanations for human thoughts, feelings, and actions. As in the previous editions, we remain committed to presenting a balanced view of the whole of modern psychology, including a detailed examination of the biological and physiological underpinnings of human functioning, in-depth coverage of perceptual and cognitive processes, and a comprehensive discussion of personality and the interpersonal dynamics that determine who we are and how we behave.

The three of us who continue as authors approach this revision with considerable enthusiasm, knowing that the previous editions have been well received and widely adopted. We feel that one reason for the success of our text is the number of years each of us has taught introductory psychology. Indeed, we have often team-taught the "Psych One" course at Princeton University. While the diversity of our individual areas of research allows us to bring some expertise to each of the areas that we cover, our common experiences in teaching have meant that we share a common sense of the discipline. This has helped us to integrate the various divisions of the text.

The basic content of this book is consistent with that of most introductory psychology courses. The table of contents, therefore, should look comfortably familiar to those who have taught such courses. Our book is designed to compete primarily in terms of the clarity of presentation, our choice of examples and illustrations, and coverage that is in-depth and comprehensive.

Psychology is a diverse discipline and those who teach it are normally more sophisticated in some areas than in others. Some texts are written with the assumption that there will be additional explanation for each chapter in lectures. Our text doesn't require this. If an instructor wishes to emphasize only certain areas in lectures, he or she can be sure that all the chapters are clear and without need of further explanation. We don't introduce technical terms without adequate illustration and explanation. This may seem like an obvious maxim that every introductory text would follow. However, with the enormous amount of technical information to be dealt with in such books it is tempting to introduce terms that are not fully defined. One of our basic goals has been to avoid this. Perhaps the most gratifying reports we have received from those using our earlier editions is that students find the book both interesting and clear. Instructors are free to choose the areas they wish to cover in lectures without having to explain the text.

In earlier editions of this textbook, professor Leo Kamin participated as one of the authors. While he no longer joins us in writing this book, we would like to again acknowledge our debt to him for his previous contributions.

We have made a number of changes in the textbook between the last edition and this one, and we would like to call the reader's attention to the most significant of these.

In Chapter 1 we have tried to document the complex interplay between the development of research techniques (i.e. neural staining, statistical data-integrative techniques such as sophisticated scaling methods, and experimental control and data recovery techniques made possible by the computer) and the scientific advances made in the substantive fields of psychology. In doing so, we have attempted to convey to the student some of the excitement and sense of discovery that is characteristic of psychological research.

Chapter 2 (The Biological Framework) includes updates on the rapidly evolving body of relevant biological research. We have also added a section entitled "From superstition to science," which provides a richly illustrated historical perspective on the study of the nervous system.

Chapter 3 (Sensation) has been updated to include a discussion of the principles of signal detection theory and spatial frequency analysis. The sections on "Seeing" and "Hearing" contain new material on visual and auditory impairments that not only focuses on the practical consequences of research in these fields, but also involves the student in a rapid review of the basic components of each sensory system. Chapter 4 (Perception) contains important new material relating work on computer pattern recognition to human pattern recognition.

Chapter 5 (States of Consciousness) begins with a new discussion on ways on characterizing states of consciousness.

Chapter 6 (Conditioning and Learning) has been completely rewritten for this edition. It now provides a more concise introduction to the traditional topics of instrumental and classical conditioning, and an expanded treatment of recent research on cognitive components in animal learning.

Chapter 7 (Memory) has been extensively updated. It also includes a highlight explaining how the recent exciting work on massively parallel connectionist systems can explain the classic neurological puzzle of how knowledge is registered and distributed in the brain.

Chapter 8 (Language) includes updated material on discourse and on machine comprehension. Chapter 9 (Thinking, Reasoning, and Problem Solving) contains new material on reasoning and artificial intelligence. Chapter 10 (Intelligence) incorporates material based on new theories of intelligence: notably, Sternberg's theory of componential intelligence, and Gardner's model of multiple intelligences.

Chapter 11 (Biological Bases of Motivation) presents recent studies on biological mechanisms of motivation. Chapter 12 (Human Motivation and Emotion) reviews the cognitive theory of emotions in light of recent research, and presents the results of important new studies on the basic categories of emotional experiences.

Chapter 13 (Childhood) has been expanded to include new material on attachment and social development. Chapter 14 (Adolescence, Adulthood, and Aging) emphasizes life-span development and incorporates recent research on the ongoing processes of development that characterize people as they grow older.

Chapters 15 through 18 focus on the human personality. Undeniably, the

major shift that has taken place in this field in the last few years has been in the development of our understanding of the biological determinants of personality. Research workers are now able to trace and document the neurochemical workings of several disorders with psychological components. The action mechanisms of some psychotropic medications, previously little understood, are becoming clearer. To those working in the field, the cumulative weight of these findings is enormously exciting; to the textbook writer, the task of presenting these developments while explaining the possible limits of the biological perspective is a challenging one.

In Chapter 15 (Personality), material on the implications of the biological perspective for the study of human personality has been updated and is presented along with the more standard perspectives. The discussion of the cognitive (representational) perspective has been expanded to include new research that strengthens the foundation of the cognitive model of personality.

Chapter 16 (Stress and Coping) has been reorganized to provide expanded coverage of new developments in the field. The physiological effects of stress on the human body are becoming better understood, and the new field of "psychoneuroimmunology" is tracing the relationships between stressful life events and the failure of the body's protective systems. At the same time, it is becoming clearer that, at the psychological level, feelings of loss of control are at the core of the experience of stress.

Chapter 17 (Abnormal Psychology) includes updated research on the genetic origins of several types of abnormalities.

Chapter 18 (Therapy) updates the discussion of the rise of problem-focused therapeutic interventions that draw on personality theories to treat specific personality dysfunctions. The sad continuing story of the "deinstitutionalization movement," now even clearer than it was three years ago, is discussed.

The major addition to Chapter 19 (Social Behavior) includes a convergence of developments in social psychology with theoretical trends in personality psychology. There is an updated discussion of attribution and attitude formation theory. Chapter 20 (Social Influence and Group Processes) contains coverage of recent research done on individuals in romantic and other close relationships.

Supplements

The fourth edition of *Psychology* is accompanied by the most complete package of supplementary aids ever. The **Test Item File,** prepared by James Evans, contains over 2,500 questions, each of which is designated either applied, conceptual, or factual. All items are page-referenced into the text. Two testing services are available for your convenience: Our computerized **Test Generator,** designed for Apple or IBM computers, allows you to add and edit your own questions, to print multiple versions of each test, and to randomly generate tests. This system is fully integrated with a **computerized gradebook** and **calendar,** as well as a **practice test package** for your students. Prentice Hall's **Telephone Testing Service** will prepare your test for you—simply call our toll free number and request any questions from our test bank in any order, and they will have a master test and answer key in the mail within 24 hours. The **Instructor's Resource and Activity Manual,** prepared by Janet Proctor, includes suggested activities, demonstrations, and

audiovisual materials. Over 100 quality **Transparencies** or over 160 **Slides,** most in full color, and most of which come from sources outside the text, are available to qualifying adopters.

For your students, **PSYCHOLOGY ON A DISK** consists of nine interactive experiments for Apple or IBM computers. Created and extensively class-tested by Charles Catania and Eliot Shimoff, these can enhance the effectiveness of your teaching of some basic psychological principles. A **Study Guide with Practice Tests,** by Gordon Hodge, provides students with key names, terms and concepts, study questions, a page-by-page fill-in-the-blanks review of each chapter, and practice tests. The practice tests are also available in the form of an **Interactive Study Guide** for the microcomputer.

Acknowledgments

We continue to be grateful to all of those whose help on earlier editions has allowed this text to enjoy continued growth and success. We are particularly indebted to several of our colleagues who have been most generous and helpful with suggestions for improving the fourth edition.

Lauren B. Alloy
Northwestern University

Barney Beins
Ithaca College

Nathan Brody
Wesleyan University

George A. Cicala
University of Delaware

Lynn Clemow
Robert Wood Johnson Medical School

Robert J. Contreras
University of Alabama/ Birmingham

Faye Crosby
Smith College

Joseph Farley
Princeton University

Robert Fox
Vanderbilt University

Dedre Gentner
University of Illinois/Urbana

Anne E. Harris
Arizona State University

Jack F. Heller
Franklin and Marshall College

James Jenkins
University of South Florida

Freda Rebelsky
Boston University

Steven L. Schandler
Chapman College

Thomas R. Scott
University of Delaware

Robert D. Sorkin
Purdue University

W. Scott Terry
University of North Carolina/ Charlotte

We would especially like to thank four people for their contributions to this edition: Richard Gerring (Chapters 8 and 9), Judith Harris (Chapters 10 and 13), Thane Pittman (Chapter 12), and Peggy Thoits (Chapter 16).

Our colleagues in the Psychology Department at Princeton University have grown used to our appearances in their doorways, requesting answers to questions in their areas of expertise. We are grateful for their patient help.

Finally, we would like to thank several people from Prentice Hall, including Susan Finnemore and John Isley, who helped to define the audience and structure of the book; Colette Conboy, whose hours of dedication saw this

book through the production cycle in a miraculously timely way; and to Marcia Rulfs, whose persistence, patience, and attention to every detail of the revision was critical to completing this edition of the text. We would also like to thank Judy Matz-Coniglio for creating the design for the fourth edition, Pamela Degnan for her photographic research, and Carol Carter for coordinating the advertising and marketing programs. We are grateful to Martha Masterson for developing the supplements and to the authors of those supplements: Janet Proctor for the Instructors Manual, Gordon Hodge for the Study Guide, and James Evans for the Test Item File. We appreciate their contribution toward creating an effective package for instruction to complement our text.

We cannot end without restating two more acknowledgments. The first is to the readers—teachers and students—of the first three editions who made so many genuinely worthwhile suggestions for revision.

Writers of textbooks discover that they have committed themselves to keeping track of new developments in research psychology. After reviewing developments of the past few years, we have a sense of how far and how fast psychology has moved in that time. What we present in this text is the product of the labor and the insights of hundreds, perhaps thousands, of research psychologists. Our largest debt is to them, and we gratefully acknowledge it. The reader must think of our index of authors as a set of heartfelt acknowledgments, as we do.

Finally, although we are grateful to all these people for their positive contributions to this book, we take full responsibility for any errors in fact.

J.M.D.

S.G.

R.A.K.

1 Introduction to Psychology

T here are very many people who are called psychologists, and what they have in common may not be immediately obvious. Psychologist A, for example, is a clinical psychologist. He works with people who have "psychological problems." A student comes to the college's counseling center, complaining that she feels depressed and lethargic. Perhaps also she has had some difficulty in sleeping and some loss of appetite. Another student is suffering from a far more pervasive psychological disturbance. Perhaps he has recently begun to act strangely. He is often silent and withdrawn but occasionally bursts into almost incoherent speech. He believes that there is a widespread plot against him: His professors are spying on him and reporting slanderous information to the college authorities and the police. Recently he has noticed that the food served to him in the college cafeteria tastes peculiar, and he believes that "they" are trying to poison him. He has been referred to the psychologist after creating a disturbance in the cafeteria. The clinical psychologist is an expert—as expert as the present state of knowledge will allow—in the understanding and treatment of the sorts of problems we have described. He works with patients in such places as mental health clinics, state hospitals, community centers, or private offices.

Psychologist B seems to be a very different kind of psychologist. She is a physiological psychologist and she has never done counseling in her life. She spends most of her working hours in a laboratory, surrounded by complex (and expensive) pieces of apparatus. She wants to understand more about

A clinical psychologist counseling a client. (Michal Heron/Monkmeyer Press)

The study of what it is to be human can be approached from many perspectives. In addition to the natural science perspective offered by this text, literature and art also provide insight into human life, as can be seen in this sixteenth-century glimpse of peasant life, "Die Kornernte," by Pieter Brueghel. (The Metropolitan Museum of Art)

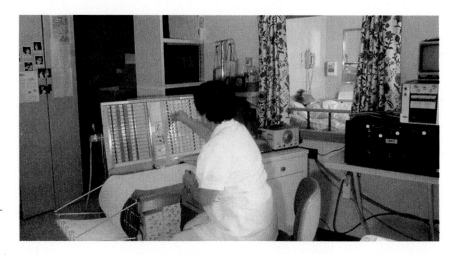

A physiological psychologist monitoring someone's electrophysiological patterns. (Peter Arnold, Inc.)

how the brain controls and influences human behavior and feelings. To acquire such understanding, she has had to learn neuroanatomy (the physical structure of the nervous system and brain) and biochemistry. She is studying rats—she can perform many experiments on them that, for obvious reasons, cannot be performed on human subjects. Psychologist B probably holds a university professorship and is thus teaching as well as performing research. Or she may be working full-time at research, perhaps in a government laboratory devoted to health problems or in the laboratories of a private drug manufacturer.

Psychologist C is also a college teacher, but at the moment he is in a courtroom, where he is about to appear as an expert witness for the defense. He has conducted research on human cognitive processes, particularly on human memory. He knows a great deal about the way in which the "memories" reported by eyewitnesses can be influenced by changes in the wording of questions. The defense hopes that his testimony will help to discredit earlier testimony elicited from an eyewitness by the prosecution.

Psychologist D is employed as a researcher in a government laboratory. She is designing visual displays that mimic or simulate what an astronaut would see when landing a craft on a planet with an atmosphere very different from that of earth. The safety of future space flights is increased considerably by such practice under simulated conditions here on earth.

This is a flight simulator. It is designed to mimic the controls found in airplane cockpits. Psychologists test for the optimal design of control systems by having actual pilots "fly" these simulators (John J. Bangma/Photo Researchers)

The activities of the psychologists we have described give some indication of the scope of modern psychology. There are some psychologists whose interests seem very close to those of biologists or biochemists. There are others whose interests seem close to those of sociologists, anthropologists, and social philosophers. The reason for this wide scope should be obvious. Psychology is concerned with human thought and action, and humans are both biological and social creatures. To ignore either our biological or our social nature is to guarantee defeat in any effort to truly understand ourselves. To understand how our biological and social natures interact and unite would be the crowning achievement of human thought. The task set out for modern psychology—to become nothing less than the integrator of the biological and social sciences—is as exciting as it is difficult. Psychologists specialize at some point in their careers, but they must remain sensitive to, and informed about, the many different areas of psychology. Despite their inevitable specialization, psychologists do talk to one another, and they tend to share a common point of view. This chapter is concerned with that common point of view—how it developed, what it includes, and what it excludes.

HISTORICAL PERSPECTIVES

The origins of psychology can be found in philosophy, in medicine, and in physiology. For philosophers concerned with how the state should be governed, it was useful to have a view of human nature; their concern would now be recognized as one addressed by psychologists. In every society healers were concerned with the plight of people whom we would now regard as having thought or personality disorders. Physiologists, who concerned themselves with the workings of the human nervous system, frequently speculated on the connections between the nervous system and the mind.

Wundt and Titchener: Structuralism

The first group of people who regarded themselves as scientific psychologists flourished in Germany in the second half of the nineteenth century, around the pioneer figure of Wilhelm Wundt (1832–1920). Their interest and activities seem, from today's perspective, surprisingly narrow. They were chiefly concerned with the problem of how the mind constructs sensations and perceptions out of the raw nerve messages delivered to the brain by the sense organs. They had been trained in the physiology of the sense organs and the nervous system. Their unique contribution was to be an analysis of the contents of the mind itself, made in an effort to understand the relations between physiological events and conscious mental experience.

Wilhelm Wundt, generally regarded as the founder of psychology.

E. B. Titchener was a particularly influential advocate of Wundt's thinking for the English-speaking world, though historians of psychology now realize that many of what Titchener presented as Wundt's ideas were really his own. Titchener argued that in order to analyze the content of conscious experience into its component parts, the appropriate experimental method was **introspection.** The first experimental psychologists sat in a quiet laboratory and examined their own mental experiences. They exposed themselves to controlled sensory stimulation of various sorts—perhaps a complex sound or a film of color on a textured surface—and then carefully analyzed the conscious experience produced by such stimuli and reported what "elementary sensations" combined to produce the complex experience, or perception, evoked by the stimulus. This method assumed the existence of a kind of "mental chemistry." The basic notion was that, through the sense organs, the mind contained a fixed number of basic sensations. These sensations were analogous to the elements in chemistry. Complex conscious mental experience might ultimately be understood as the result of various recombinations of these basic mental elements. These recombinations were analogous to compounds. It was quite in keeping with such a viewpoint to ask a conscientious and patient introspecting subject to describe in detail the sensations created by the complex experience of being tickled—perhaps some pressure, a little pain, and just a touch of warmth.

Clearly these early psychologists regarded their subject matter as the mind itself and felt that the life of the mind could be revealed by the technique of careful introspection. In emphasizing "direct access" to the mind, however, they paid a price. First, many minds—such as those of animals, young children, and mentally disturbed people—were simply inaccessible. Second, even in the well-trained, normal, adult human subject some mental operations might not be reflected in consciousness. It is noteworthy that these early workers seem to have been rather unconcerned with the actual

E.B. Titchener, wearing his academic robes. Every lecture, flanked by his teaching assistants, he would march into the classroom in full academic regalia. (*Both:* Courtesy Archives of the History of American Psychology, University of Akron)

behavior of their subjects. What do people *do* with the sensations and perceptions that are forever cluttering up their minds? How do perceptions and experience influence behavior? How are they used to help the individual adjust to the vicissitudes of living on this earth?

Functionalism

Reactions to the structuralist tradition soon began to develop, and in North America they had a particularly down-to-earth "American character." In 1890 William James (1842–1910) published his highly influential *Principles of Psychology*. James was not as concerned with the introspectionist's task of describing the exact content of a thought or perception as he was with understanding the *functions* of thought and perception. Influenced by a Darwinian evolutionary perspective, he argued that human consciousness had evolved because it made possible the thinking and decision processes that helped humankind survive. John Dewey (1859–1952) brought functional perspectives to bear on the field of education, seeking the best ways of teaching children to be independently functioning problem solvers. Functionalist perspectives have continued to shape the work of psychologists, particularly in the fields of education and industrial psychology.

Behaviorism

A second movement in North American psychology reflected even more strongly the down-to-earth, practical aspects of the American character.

In the United States a kind of revolution took place in experimental psychology early in the twentieth century. The major figure, at least in terms of popular impact, was John B. Watson (1878–1958). To Watson it seemed that early psychologists had attempted to study something that was too vague and subjective—perhaps even too "unreal"—to be a proper subject for scientific study. What is this thing called "mind"? How can we rely on the reports of introspectors about what is going on in their (to us) unobservable minds? What do we do when different introspectors give contradictory reports about the same stimulus? For psychology to become a genuine science, Watson argued, it had better concentrate on a definite subject matter that could be directly observed by all interested investigators. The proper study of psychology then, is, **behavior.** We can all observe the behavior of a subject and agree that it occurred in a particular way at a definite time and place. We ought to discover what the determinants of behavior are. What stimuli produce what observable responses? How do the relations between stimuli and responses change with experience? This kind of program, as Watson noted, could profoundly extend the scope of experimental psychology. The *behavior* of animals, infants, and the "insane"—unlike their "minds"—could be directly studied.

For a period, at least, Watson's arguments had enormous force, not so much because of their logic, perhaps, as because of the vast expansion of

(Top) William James. His two-volume textbook on psychology appeared in 1890. (New York Public Library)

(Center) John Dewey, like James, often adopted a functionalist perspective. His writings on education influenced developments in the American school system. (Library of Congress)

(Left) John Watson, the leader of the "behavioral revolution" in American psychology. (Courtesy Archives of the History of American Psychology)

psychological research the behaviorist perspective encouraged. Then, too, there was disillusionment with the meager results of early introspectionism. Whatever the reason, it seems correct to say that at least until 1950 the vast majority of American psychologists agreed that psychology is the science of behavior. The mind, consciousness, and mental processes tended to be—so far as possible—ignored in psychological research. The behaviorists made no attempt to argue that the mind did not exist or that it was of no interest. They simply stressed the methodological simplicity of studying observable behavior.

Gestalt Psychology

Though Watson's behaviorism tended to dominate the American scene, a vigorous dissenting point of view was that of **Gestalt** psychology, a school founded by Max Wertheimer (1880–1943). Quickly becoming part of the Gestalt movement—and movement it was, since it gained much of its energy from its opposition to the principles of structural psychology—were two younger men, Wolfgang Köhler (1887–1967) and Kurt Koffka (1886–1941). These two were students of Wertheimer, as well as subjects in his earliest experiments. Excited by the research demonstrations, and convinced of the Gestalt perspective by the results, the pair went on to become his professional colleagues. The Gestalt psychologists, whose leaders immigrated to the United States from Germany before World War II, objected both to the "atomism" of behavioristic psychology and to the short shrift it gave to perceptual processes. The Gestalt principles of perceptual organization led these psychologists to argue that complex psychological wholes could not be reduced to a mere sum of separate parts and that many forms of psychological organization—contrary to Watson's emphasis—were unlearned and innate.

The Gestalt psychologists did much of their work in the field of visual perceptions. Their frequently vivid and dramatic demonstrations of Gestalt phenomena (see Figure 1–1) did much to draw the attention of psychologists to the fascinating and complex processes of perception that are described in Chapter 4. In time, they also turned their attention to learning and memory processes, and the role of insight in problem solving.

Modern Behaviorism

Watson did not argue that mental processes did not exist, only that it was unnecessary to include them in theories designed to explain behaviors. However, some experimental psychologists always felt that the facts of behavior

(Top) Max Wertheimer, the founder of the Gestalt psychology movement.

(Center) Kurt Koffka was another of the trio of psychologists who pioneered the development of Gestalt psychology. Of the three, he was most responsive to the needs of other psychologists to have Gestalt psychology explained to them. It was his book that gave many American psychologists their first complete introduction to these theories. (*Both:* Courtesy Archives of the History of American Psychology)

(Right) Wolfgang Köhler, one of the foremost Gestalt psychologists. Köhler's background was in physics, and he continued to relate the fields of psychology and physics. Kept on the island of Tennirife for four years, he passed the time resourcefully by studying the action patterns of a colony of apes there, devoping the Gestalt perspective on problem solving from his observations. After emigrating from Germany, he taught for many years at Swarthmore College in Pennsylvania. (Courtesy Swarthmore College)

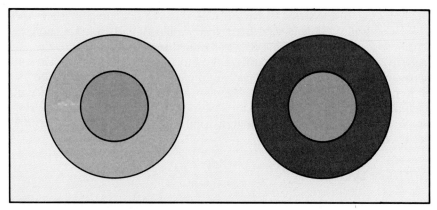

a. Gestalt figure

Figure 1–1

(a) Look at the gray centers of the two circles. The one on the right looks darker than the one on the left. But it's not; it's the same color. (You can test this by covering over the two surrounding circles.) Why does it look different? Gestalt psychologists used this to illustrate how the perception of the whole can influence the perception of its parts. **(b)** Now look at this etching of a waterfall by M. C. Escher. Study it carefully until you see what is wrong or paradoxical about it. **(c)** Finally, look at the "Street" figure (named for the person who first designed this type of picture). Can you determine what this picture is supposed to be? See if a cue helps you: It is a picture of a dog. Generally, once people know what they are looking for, they can "see" the dog.

b. M. C. Escher's "Waterfall"

c. "Street" figure of a dog

had to be interpreted in terms of mental processes. Behaviorism stressed simple, straightforward connections between stimuli and responses (it was often called S-R psychology). Some stimuli and responses were simply and reliably related in this reflexlike way. With many stimuli, and with some kinds of subjects, however, it seemed obvious that the stimulus input was operated upon, transformed, processed, or mulled over before it was responded to. That kind of internal processing—events taking place within the organism between the stimulus input and the response output—is what we mean when we talk about thinking or about mental processes. The existence of those internal events made it necessary to replace a simple S-R psychology with a more complex S-O-R psychology, where O stands for the

organism that interposes its internal processes between observable stimuli and responses. Those internal events, of course, are not directly observable. They must be *inferred*—and they are inferred from the relations that we observe between stimuli and responses. Psychology in this respect is like any other science. To understand the phenomena that we directly observe, we have to construct "models" of *un*observable structures and processes that make sense out of our observations. Models and inferences constructed to explain one set of observations may have to be revised (or even abandoned) in the face of later and different observations. The goal is to collect those kinds of observations that seem to demand interpretation in terms of a particular model of mental processes. Psychologists, as later chapters will indicate, have been reasonably successful in devising experimental procedures that seem to reveal some of the properties of internal mental processes. The structure of the mind, and mental processes, are thus very much part of the subject matter of scientific psychology, along with the analysis of behavior.

Psychoanalytic Theory

We should note that mental processes inferred in the way described above do not necessarily correspond to the results of introspection, for these mental processes may be entirely unobservable even to the organism in which they are occurring. This was, in fact, a central belief of the extremely influential (and nonexperimental) branch of psychology founded by Sigmund Freud (1856–1939). **Psychoanalytic theory** was developed by Freud to account for the often bizarre behaviors exhibited by neurotic patients who came to him seeking relief from their problems and symptoms. The behaviors and symptoms could be understood, Freud believed, in terms of the operation of powerful mental forces of which patients themselves were entirely unaware. According to the Freudian model, **unconscious** impulses, wishes, and symbolisms profoundly affect the behavior of all of us. The techniques Freud used to infer and argue for such unconscious mental processes were, if not entirely convincing, at least stunningly original and ingenious. We shall examine Freud's model in some detail in Chapter 15.

Sigmund Freud, the founder of psychoanalytic theory. (WHO/Photo)

The Current Consensus

For the first century of its development, psychology struggled with the question, What do psychologists study? The discipline as a whole seems to have arrived at a sensible resolution of that question, one that is shared by most psychologists. The things that psychologists *directly* study are the things that we can observe. These include the actions and reactions of other people, their decisions, what they can tell us about their decisions, their linguistic behaviors, their body movements, and many, many other observable events. As in many other sciences, what we can observe is not static. Psychologists have been enormously ingenious in working out techniques and devices to enable them to observe processes or entities that previously were unobservable. From the patterns we find in what we can observe, and with the best intuitions that we can muster, we construct our best guesses about the processes underlying, and perhaps causing, the events and actions that we have seen. We then organize these guesses into a **theory.** A theory is a formal statement of principles that are proposed to explain certain phenomena that scientists have observed.

Generally, a theory begins with a set of interlocking postulates. For in-

This young boy is working with a mathematics learning system. Psychologists have been involved in the research and design of many such systems. (Jim Cartier/Photo Researchers)

This is an "open plan" office. Researchers study the needs and communication patterns of people who work in offices and attempt to design office layouts that maximize work productivity and also respond to people's needs for privacy. (Courtesy Steelcase Inc.)

stance, as you will see in Chapter 13, Jean Piaget had a theory about the cognitive development of children. He suggested that development proceeds in a set of stages. In the first or the sensorimotor stage, children learn to distinguish between themselves and objects that are not part of themselves. Connected with this, Piaget postulated that children learn that objects have permanence. Piaget's theory contained many examples of specific instances of object permanence, and his research demonstrated how we can tell whether an individual child has such a notion or not.

Psychologists, depending on their interests, form theories about widely different topics. Some theorize about the workings of the human nervous system, others about how children learn a language, others about the emotions that are basic to all humans. As you will see in the following chapters, the theories of psychology range across many aspects of human thought and action. However, once psychologists have developed a theory, they proceed in much the same general ways, regardless of the exact content of the theory. They subject the theory to **empirical tests.** They predict in advance what sorts of observable actions should occur when certain variables are changed. By testing to see whether their predictions describe the actual research outcomes, they find out whether their laboriously constructed theories are correct.

THE RESEARCH METHODS OF PSYCHOLOGY

A general agreement is emerging among many, if not all, psychologists about the ordering of research methods within the field. First, it is important to make a distinction between how psychologists arrive at a theory that might fit the beginning and fragmentary observations that they have made, and how they conduct research to test the theory. (The first stage is often called the "context of discovery," while the second is the "context of justification.")

Most psychologists, most scientists, and perhaps most importantly, most people who study how actual scientists work would agree that the first process—the **context of discovery**—is an intuitive and creative one. Although rules for it can be given, the rules are open-ended and inductive, rather than formal and deductive. The scientist observes the data, makes guesses about what might be causing the patterns into which the data fall, and talks to other scientists to get their guesses. In fact, the scientist trying to generate a theory uses all the methods that an ordinary person employs when attempting to figure out how some complex process or piece of machinery works.

Once the story of what is causing the observed events has been developed, scientists turn to a second, more constrained and disciplined set of processes to evaluate the theory. This is called the **context of justification.** Like all scientists, psychologists have worked out a good many methods of first finding evidence for various theories, and second of assessing the degree of support that the evidence provides for the theory being tested. The ways of finding the evidence are referred to as **research methods.**

Psychologists have a strong predilection for the **experimental method** in acquiring reliable knowledge, and there are good and sufficient reasons for this preference. It is not always possible to use this method, however, so students of psychology should be aware not only of the virtues and

weaknesses of the experimental method but also of the virtues—and pitfalls—of other methods.

Correlational Research

The starting point for all knowledge about the world is the observation of some regularity in the flow of events. Thus people long ago observed the movements of the planets and calculated their orbits. They were regular, and this discovery made possible the development of the science of astronomy. We came to understand the movements of the planets long before it was possible to perform experiments on the orbits of bodies in space. In psychology, too, we make systematic observations about events with which we cannot interfere experimentally. Suppose, for example, you were interested in discovering what factors produce successful marriages. Perhaps people who are alike should marry one another—or perhaps not. You cannot force people to marry one another for your experimental convenience, but you can measure the personality characteristics of people who are already married. Then if you can devise an accurate measure of the "success" of a marriage, you can observe whether couples with very similar personalities tend to have more or less successful marriages than average. This kind of correlational technique is often used in psychological research.

The major drawback of this technique is that the facts and regularities observed are often open to many different interpretations. Suppose you discovered that couples with very similar personalities did enjoy more successful marriages. Would you then feel confident in advising young people to select mates with similar personalities? That would be rash counsel. Perhaps people who are happily married tend *as a result of that fact* to become like each other in personality. The mere observation that two things (similar personalities and successful marriages) occur together does not tell us which causes which, or even if one causes the other at all.

The facts revealed by this study of marriage are basically correlational: We merely observed that some things tended to occur together in the real world. But though successful marriages correlated with similar personalities in both spouses, the existence of this correlation may suggest many different interpretations. For instance, as we pointed out, either of the correlated events could have caused the other; or a third event, unmeasured, could have caused both of the correlated events that we observed. To take another example, assume for a moment that we see a correlation between the viscosity (softness) of blacktop roads and an increase in death rates from certain respiratory diseases. This might lead us to speculate that blacktop roads are emitting some life-threatening chemical. But it is more likely that heat waves are the cause of both road viscosity *and* the breathing difficulty that is life threatening to those with certain respiratory diseases.

It is, after all, too easy to leap from the fact of a correlation to the interpretation of one, without realizing such a leap has been made. For instance, many surveys have demonstrated that college graduates earn considerably larger incomes than other people. This has often been interpreted to mean that college equips you with the skills and habits of mind that are necessary to earn a good income. Perhaps, consciously or not, knowledge of this fact had something to do with your deciding to attend college. But the truth is that nobody knows how, if at all, what you learn in college affects your ultimate income level. The people who attend college tend to come from certain backgrounds and to possess certain abilities and personality characteris-

tics. Thus it is entirely possible that those same people, if turned loose in the real world at age 18, might earn the same relatively high incomes without ever attending college. Further, it is also possible that a college degree is an irrelevant "credential" that serves as a passport to better job opportunities. That is, what one *learns* in college might be irrelevant to the economic benefits that flow from merely possessing a college degree.

There are several research methods that are essentially correlational in nature. (More about the meanings of correlations, and the methods by which they are calculated, can be found in the statistics appendix.) Each has its genuine uses, and all share the problem of being unable to establish causality unequivocally.

Surveys, often administered on a statewide or national level, ask people to respond to a set of standardized questions. A familiar example is the polling of the electorate before national elections. Sometimes such polls result in remarkably accurate predictions of voting outcomes. Other times they badly miss. Major determinants of survey accuracy are of two general kinds. The first arises from the fact that in a survey we are not so interested in exactly how the respondents as individuals answer any given question. Instead, the respondents are selected to represent certain segments of the population at large, with the hope that their answers will closely reflect the opinions, habits, or interests of the targeted segment of the population. Political surveys are often used to help determine how the electoral population will vote or to find out how the public feels about some new foreign policy initiative. Major corporations invest millions of dollars in marketing surveys that attempt to discern the potential response to a new advertising campaign or product. Great care is taken to see that there will be a high correlation between the responses of the sample group and the larger population. The ability of a survey to predict a general public response depends on both how carefully participants are chosen (or how well they actually represent the larger population) and how well the survey is administered (how carefully the questions are composed and how many of the target respondents actually complete the survey). Survey researchers have developed highly sophisticated sampling procedures to ensure that the group being surveyed (the *sample*) is statistically representative of the population about which the survey takers wish to generalize. Upon examination, many of the more notorious survey failures of the past can be blamed on mistakes in assembling a representative sample. One famous failure was the survey that predicted the victory of Dewey over Truman in the 1948 presidential election. Since the survey was conducted exclusively by telephone, it improperly sampled only those voters who could afford to own a phone. Thus the survey based its prediction on a sample of relatively well-to-do voters, completely ignoring the possibility that many poorer people, not included in the sample because they didn't own telephones, might vote for the other candidate.

The second difficulty with surveys is harder to see. As pointed out before, the survey is a specific type of correlational research—it relates two or more entities to each other. When we ask people how they are going to vote, the first entity is their response to the survey, that is, the candidate whom they *say* will get their vote. The second entity is harder to see, but it is there. It is how the person will actually vote on election day. At times polls have failed because they assumed a high correlation between these two entities when, in fact, the high correlation did not exist. For instance, the number of people who will vote for "fringe" or "deviant" political candidates is often underestimated. This is probably because some voters are embarrassed to tell a specific other person, the poller, that they will vote for an offbeat candidate.

Thus, they report themselves as "undecided," or even say that they intend to vote for one of the more conventional candidates, occasionally causing startling upsets on election day.

Surveys can be administered by telephone or in the form of written questionnaires. **Interviews,** in other ways much like surveys, are usually conducted face-to-face. This is quite an expensive means of gathering information, and is usually done only when the interviewer's particular skills are needed. Instead of following a fixed set of questions, the interviewer is free to deviate from the format and to ask further questions exploring aspects of the interviewee's opinions or personality. Interviews are used for many of the same purposes as surveys, polls, and marketing surveys. However, an interview allows a more in-depth analysis of the variables that may affect the interviewee's future behavior. More information about the general structure of interviews will be given in Chapter 15, when we discuss personality assessment procedures. For now, the important thing to understand is that a lengthy questionnaire or interview is administered because the researcher is interested in the relationship between the different kinds of information collected in the interview. Thus a poller might simply be interested in whether individuals who identify themselves as political conservatives report a preference for a particular candidate or public policy. Sometimes the researcher is also interested in the relationships among the many patterns of responses that emerge in the interview, as well as the future actions and behaviors of the respondent. For example, the poller might be searching for the patterns of responses (or overall political opinions) of those respondents who later fail to vote at all.

Within some areas of psychology the **case-study** method has been an invaluable technique for gaining important information and drawing hypotheses. The case study may be regarded as a special form of the interview method. The number of subjects surveyed (one) is, of course, very much smaller than in the usual survey, but the number of possibly relevant facts collected about that individual is very large. The case study involves very detailed knowledge about a single individual. Thus if you observed some striking behavior in that person, you could sift through your knowledge of his or

The newly elected Harry Truman holds up a newspaper headline announcing his "loss" to Dewey. This famous picture is often shown to illustrate the fact that polls can go wrong. (UPI/Bettmann Newphotos)

The case study involves only a single subject, but the amount of information gathered about that subject is much more than can be gathered through the broader survey method.
(Mimi Forsyth/Monkmeyer Press)

her history and make guesses about the causes of that behavior. Your guesses might be wrong, but you could test them by studying new and additional cases. For example, if you knew the detailed life history of a certain person with a severe stuttering problem, you might be struck by the fact that he had an unusually domineering father who often punished him severely. Perhaps your intuition would suggest that people with domineering fathers have trouble expressing themselves and may thus become severe stutterers. This is just the sort of hunch or tentative hypothesis that psychologists derive from a case study. Recall that we said that creativity and intuitive leaps were entirely appropriate when working in the "context of discovery." Thus, developing a hypothesis or theory is a valid use of the case-study method. In this case, though, the hunch is wrong; there is no indication that stutterers have more domineering parents than do nonstutterers. So you can see that the danger of the case-study method is that it may confuse a striking coincidence with a true relationship. Later in the text we will show you that people who draw hypotheses out of a limited number of instances tend to become convinced of the general validity of those hypotheses. So the further danger of the case-study method is that the scientist who made the original observations may be overly committed to the truth of the hypothesis and not notice that the weight of the later evidence is for its disconfirmation.

Controlled Experimental Intervention

To illustrate the advantages of the experimental method, we shall first describe an experiment that, although it can never be performed, could answer an important question. Then we shall describe some actual examples of how a straightforward experimental approach has helped to clarify interesting psychological problems. Finally, we shall introduce a few useful technical terms that will help you understand the basic structure of psychological experiments.

The available survey data establish beyond all doubt that cigarette smokers tend to die young—from lung cancer, heart disease, and many other illnesses. The data are so clear and overwhelming that no one can seriously question that fact that cigarette smoking is hazardous to health. There is not, however, any *experimental* evidence that smoking causes cancer, heart disease, or anything else in humans. What other interpretation of the survey data is possible?

There is an apparent psychological component in many diseases, as is discussed in Chapter 16. There is good reason to suppose that smokers and nonsmokers differ in their psychological makeup. The heavy smoker is often a tense and "nervous" individual. Possibly, then, tense and nervous individuals tend to die young from various diseases that are the result of their psychological traits. The correlation between cigarette smoking and early death might be nothing more than that—a correlation, and not a cause-and-effect relationship.

This line of reasoning seems more clever than wise, but it is hard to find fault with the logic. What about the fact, established by surveys, that heavy smokers who give up the habit improve their chances of living a long life? That can easily be explained away by asking who *are* the heavy smokers who give up the habit. Possibly they are previously tense and nervous people who at last have learned to live more comfortable and relaxed lives, and thus have improved their health.

The point by now may seem repetitious, but it is an important one:

Without an *experimental* analysis, correlational data are open to many different interpretations. Theoretically, we could provide an unambiguous interpretation of the connection between cigarette smoking and early death by performing a simple experiment. Take 1,000 children ten years old. Force half of them, selected at random, to smoke three packs a day for as long as they live. Forbid the other half to ever smoke. Then observe how long each subject in this experiment lives and also observe the cause of death of each subject. Presuming that the smokers die younger (it seems a safe bet), we would *know* that it is smoking—and not psychological traits correlated with smoking—that causes early death. We could also safely conclude that those causes of death that occur excessively in the smokers are the result of their smoking. Theoretically, it is possible that *some* of the causes of death now associated with heavy smoking might not occur excessively among the subjects who had been experimentally forced to smoke.

The ethical sense of anyone seriously proposing such an experiment would be grossly defective, but the experimental analysis outlined does have the simplicity and definiteness to which science aspires. We want clear and certain answers to our questions. We are much more likely to obtain such answers if, rather than passively observing what occurs in nature, we actively arrange an experiment.

Experimenters intervene, arrange, prepare, manipulate, and plan. Thus in a sense they are in control of what is about to occur, and they are especially prepared to record accurately both what has happened and the circumstances that were in effect when it happened. They can—within ethical and practical limits—vary those circumstances at will and observe how, if at all, the phenomenon in which they are interested is affected. That, in essence, is what the celebrated experimental method is all about. Wherever it can be applied, it provides a certainty of knowledge that cannot be duplicated by any other technique.

The purpose of conducting experiments is not merely to control and to predict phenomena but also to understand them. To achieve an understanding of behavior, psychologists, like other scientists, use the results of experiments to construct theories. Theories—which are stated in general terms— explain many different and individual phenomena as the result of the operation of a small set of general principles. They enable us to see regularity and order in what would otherwise be an unending flow of unique events. Thus they make our world more understandable.

Research Instrumentation in Psychology

Psychologists, like other scientists, have developed a wide variety of laboratory and research instruments to conduct their investigations. You may learn about some of these devices first-hand if there is a laboratory component to your course, or your instructor may discuss some of them in lectures. The many applications of these different instruments will become more apparent as the course progresses. However, for now, it is useful to understand something about the history of such devices and the role they have played in psychological experimentation.

The most basic function of a research instrument is to make visible some entity or process that was previously invisible. One of the earliest examples of a research instrument was the *microscope,* invented by the seventeenth-century Dutch naturalist Anthony Van Leeuwenhoek (see Figure 1–2). Its combination of optical lenses made visible the "microscopic" world of

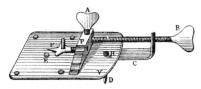

a: Leeuwenhoek's microscope. (Mary Evans Picture Library/Photo Researchers)

b: Here are several drawings of various organisms and tissues made by earlier observers using microscopes. Slowly, painstakingly, they developed an understanding of the structures of biological materials, and in the process, created drawings of great beauty. (The New York Academy of Medicine Library)

c: The electron microscope. A modern invention that shows finer detail than earlier optical microscopes. (Stan Levy/Photo Researchers)

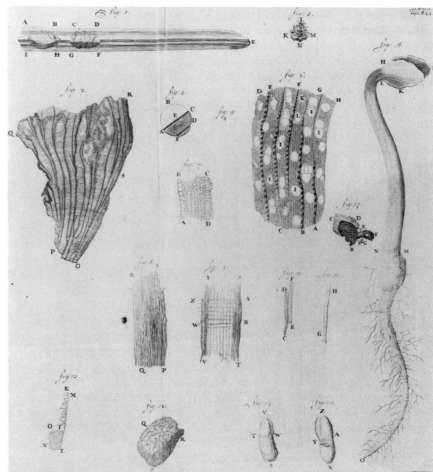

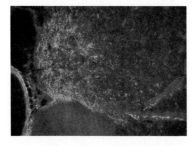

d: An example of the kind of detail that an electron microscope can show. This is a photo of axons and axon terminals. (See Chapter 2 for an explanation of axon terminal functions.) (Dr. J. F. McGinty/Peter Arnold, Inc.)

Figure 1–2

single-celled plants and tiny bodily organisms (e.g., muscle fibers, capillaries, and neural pathways), as well as paved the way for Leeuwenhoek's discovery of bacteria.

Over the years microscopes have become more powerful and sophisticated. Allied discoveries enabled the microscope to make the "invisible" visible in more complex ways. For example, the discovery that certain chemicals stained certain neurons differently helped nineteenth-century neuroanatomists to trace the workings of individual neurons in the brains of laboratory animals (see Figure 2–9). As a result of continual advances in the field, modern neuropsychologists have been able to plot specific neural connections in the human brain, such as those that connect the eye and the brain (see Chapter 3).

The *reaction time device* (see Figure 1–3) was one of the first instruments to be used extensively in psychology. By means of a clock-driven mechanism, the reaction time device was used as early as the nineteenth century to measure the time that elapsed between two or more events that occurred in close succession. Using this instrument, John Dewey was able to test his theories about the speed of various mental processes, and Hermann von Helmholtz (1821–1894) was able to measure the speed of a nervous impulse.

Other researchers developed controlled environments to study learning processes in humans and animals. The maze is a simple example of such an environment (see Figure 1–4), and is still widely used in experimentation today. B. F. Skinner, one of the leading psychologists of the twentieth century, realized that quite complicated forms of conditioning and learning could be studied in very simple environments. He and his students worked out the design of the *Skinner box* (see Figure 1–5). Originally, it consisted of a bare box, with a bar or lever and a food tray. A laboratory rat or a pigeon could be placed in the box and learn to press the bar to receive a food pellet. This allowed Skinner to study the effects of different schedules of reinforcement—or the effect of various independent variables—on the response behavior of animals. (We will say more about Skinner's discoveries in Chapter 6.)

Skinner and his group also made an important contribution to the process of recording the responses of experimental subjects. They designed the *cumulative recorder,* a direct descendant of the reaction time apparatus. This device provided a pen that traced a mark on a moving strip of paper each time the rat pressed the bar.

Another descendant of the reaction time device is the *chart plotter,* developed in the 1950s by researchers who wanted to study the characteristics of human dreams (see Figure 1–6). They had already discovered that

Figure 1–3 An early reaction time apparatus. A clockwork drive would rotate the cylinder and the "pens" that rested on the cylinder drum would leave marks on the smoke-stained piece of paper that was wrapped around the drum. The distance between the tracings revealed the time between the events that caused the pens to move.

It is difficult to convey in a photo the wonderful beauty and skilled craftsmanship of these instruments. They were made by the same individuals who made the elegant, decorative burnished brass clocks of the 19th century. The field of psychology in which these instruments were originally employed is known to this day as "brass instrument psychology." (Courtesy of the History of American Psychology, University of Akron, Ohio)

Figure 1–4 During the 17th and 18th centuries, it became fashionable for the landed gentry and nobility of England to amuse themselves by turning their estates into mazes, constructed of carefully cultivated garden hedges. Psychologists drew on the designs of these mazes to test the learning skills and capabilities of small animals. One of the first mazes used in psychological research was a copy of the Hampton Court Maze. It is interesting, if a little strange, to think of psychologists watching rats scurrying along paths that replicate those traveled by royalty in a previous century. (A: Georg Gerster/Photo Researchers; B: Ken Karp)

Figure A: The Hampton Court Maze

Figure B: A modern version of the psychological mazes modeled after the Hampton Court Maze.

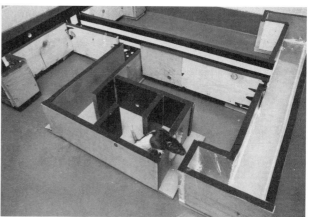

Figure 1–5 A Skinner Box. On the right side, the rat is shown pressing the bar. The reward, a food pellet, is delivered to the tray behind the rat. The equipment controls, normally covered, are shown on the left side of the box. (Walter Dawn/Photo Researchers)

Figure 1–6 Electrical signals generated by this man's breathing are received by sensors placed on his chest and recorded by the chart plotter in the foreground. (*Photo:* Nat Laurendi; *courtesy:* Sleep-Wake Disorders Center, Montefiore Hospital)

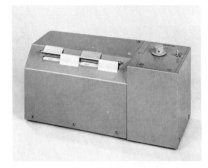

Figure 1–7 A Memory Drum. Changing sets of words for the subject to memorize are presented in the two slots at the top of the drum. (Lafayette Instrument Company)

dreams seemed to occur in one particular stage of sleep, and that one way this stage could be identified was by the distinct patterns of electrical activity generated by the brain during dreaming. When they realized that the brain's electrical activity could be used to drive the movements of a recording pen that left a trace on a moving sheet of paper, the chart plotter was born.

In addition to data-recording devices, timing devices were developed to standardize the process of actually conducting experiments. Researchers wanted to ensure that they were presenting stimuli to subjects in some set sequence on a set time schedule, whether they were experimenting with human memory processes or conditioning monkeys. These timing devices became a component of many experimental instruments, and allowed researchers to control experiments more precisely. One such instrument, the **memory drum** presents a series of words for a human subject to memorize, one at a time at designated intervals (see Figure 1–7).

More sophisticated technology allowed researchers to control more complex experiments. An electronic device known as the *logic chip* could be used to control rewards that depended on simultaneous responses from two subjects. For example, a logic chip might function as an "and gate." If one wanted to study cooperation among children, the logic chip could be hooked up so that if two children pushed their switch at the same time, both would receive bits of candy. If only one child pushed the switch, neither would receive a reward.

More recently, it has been the *computer* that has held the greatest promise for psychological experimenters (see Figure 1–8). Excitement in the field grew when it was realized that the computer could serve not one, but two functions. First, the computer can carry out the same set of logical operations repeatedly, and timing elements can easily be built into a program. This means that experiments can be carried out more reliably than by previous methods. Since the computer never gets bored or tired, as a human researcher might, the same experiment can be conducted over and over again in a uniform way. Second, the computer can be programmed to analyze the data. Since this function eliminates much of the tedium of the research process, it allows researchers more time to manipulate data and to ask more creative and sophisticated questions about the meaning of what they have observed. As computer technology has developed, more and more sophisticated applications are being found by psychologists. For example, the new graphics capabilities of computers make it possible to observe a three-dimensional picture of an intact human brain as it processes a math problem, or even an emotionally charged bit of information.

As you can see, with instrumentation, psychologists have made great strides in learning how to make previously "invisible" processes visible. They have also developed increasingly sophisticated ways to measure and record the responses of laboratory subjects, be they human or animal. And they have learned how to control experiments in more precise ways, so that studies can be more easily replicated (an important factor in any kind of scientific research). Many of the discoveries that we will report throughout the text have been made utilizing such devices.

Experiments on Thought and Behavior

We turn now to some actual examples of experimental analysis applied to psychological problems. The experiments noted here are not described because we want you to know the results in detail. The full meanings of these

experiments will be explained in successive chapters as we take them up again. Our purpose here is to show you how researchers have been able to make the experimental method work in a wide variety of contexts, including some that initially would not seem adaptable to such treatment.

Do Fish Get Jealous?   We will first use the experimental method to investigate the emotional life of a fish. The subject is the three-spined stickleback, a fish richly endowed with numerous "instinctive" or "species-specific" behaviors, as we will discuss in Chapter 11. The work of Tinbergen (1951) with this fish serves as a brilliant example of how a patient and ingenious experimental analysis can help to clarify what might otherwise appear to be a mysterious problem.

The male stickleback tends to stake out a patch of water as his own territory. Within that territory, during the mating season, he courts the female. The courtship behavior is quite complicated, and it follows a stereotyped and highly predictable pattern. When another male stickleback intrudes during the mating season, the owner of the territory will attack and fight with the intruder. The attack and fighting behavior, like the courtship behavior, is stereotyped and predictable. The question is: What makes the male stickleback attack other males at this time? Those of us who have felt savage passions stir in our own breasts might be tempted to believe that the fish is in a jealous rage. To saddle a stickleback with an Othello complex, however, seems a bit extreme. Tinbergen's careful analysis of the problem followed more prosaic lines.

To answer the question, Tinbergen isolated the male stickleback in a special laboratory tank. The experimenter had provided himself with a number of wooden models of sticklebacks, and he proceeded to drop these into the tank one at a time. The models differed in various ways, as shown in Figure 1–9. Some were lifelike representations of male sticklebacks, while others were chunks of wood with little resemblance to a fish. The point was to discover what properties a model must have in order to elicit attack from the live fish. The result was clear: Any model with red paint on its bottom side tended to be attacked, but even very lifelike models without red paint on the underside were not attacked. The stickleback is so constructed that during the mating season it attacks things with a red underside that drift into its territory. That is, red-on-the-underside is a "releasing stimulus" for stereotyped and instinctive attack behavior. This may seem strange, but perhaps not so strange when you learn another fact about sticklebacks: Glandular changes that take place in the male at the beginning of the mating season turn his belly red. To design the fish so that it attacks red-on-the-underside means that in its natural environment it will be attacking other males during the mating season.

The experiment, of course, does not answer all questions about this striking behavioral adjustment. We have no idea how the visual system of the fish is hooked up to its brain and its motor system in such a way as to produce this result. Physiologists, biochemists, psychologists, and others will be working for a very long time before we can begin to provide answers to such questions. This kind of experiment has in the meantime provided real clarification and has helped to "demystify" instinctive behavior. We may wonder how widely the implications of such studies can be generalized. In many other species the releasing stimuli for various instinctive behaviors have been discovered in a similar manner. We might wonder—and investigate—whether humans too are so constructed that certain stimuli tend automatically to trigger certain emotional reactions.

a: The PDP 8 laboratory computer was the first to have widespread use in research laboratories. It contained 8000 bits of recordable memory, which was a large amount at the time. The personal computers today have between 10 and 1000 times the amount of memory. (Digital Equipment Corporation)

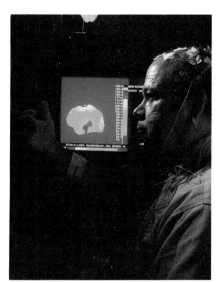

b: One type of research made possible by the computer is shown here. The subject is experiencing pain produced by mild electrical shock. The red area at the top of the brain scan shows the site that is generating the greatest electrical activity in response to the pain stimulus. (Alexander Tsiaras/Science Source/Photo Researchers)

Figure 1–8

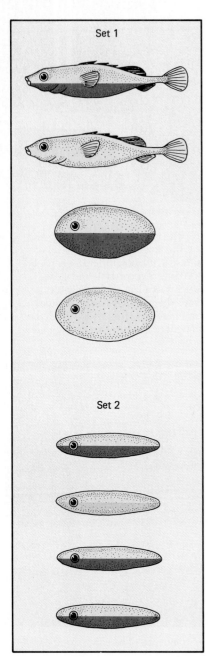

Set 1

Set 2

Figure 1–9   Look at the four figures displayed. Think about how a researcher might approach the task that Tinbergen faced—determining the "releasing stimulus" for the attack response of the male stickleback fish. Notice first that the four models present stimuli that differ in two ways: closeness to the stickleback shape and redness of the underside. How would you go about figuring which property of the model causes the real fish to fight?

An experimenter might first display the top model—the one that most closely resembles the stickleback itself—to a real stickleback. If the fish reacts with an attack, the experimenter would begin to conclude that she could successfully elicit the behavior that she wants to study using a "fake stickleback." Next she might try the second figure, which is similar in shape to the first, but without the red markings on the underside. If it fails to provoke an attack, the experimenter would conclude that shape similarity to the stickleback is not the releasing stimulus for fighting behavior. If the third figure (which is dissimilar in shape but carries the red markings) provokes an attack, it would suggest that it is the red markings that are the stimulus for fight.

Finally, if the stickleback does not respond to the fourth figure, the researcher could be reassured that certain complex explanations, such as the stickleback's aversion to any roundish figures in its tank, can be ruled out. The researcher might then go on to test a second set of figures all with red undermarkings, but vary the range of redness to determine just how "red" the stimulus must be to elicit a fight response from the stickleback. (After Tinbergen, 1951)

Probing Human Memory Processes.   Of course, the experimental method can be used to analyze the behavior and mental processes of more complex organisms than fish. Since so many experimental psychologists work in a university setting, college students—who are easily accessible and often cooperative—have served as subjects in many significant psychological studies. One such study, on human memory, was done by Sternberg (1966). It is worth our attention both because of its results and because it developed a new experimental method that has been used in hundreds of studies since. What Sternberg did was deceptively simple, and very elegant. He first gave a subject a small set of letters or numbers. (for instance, 6, 8, 3, 9) called the "memory set." Next he showed the subject one "probe" number and observed the length of time it took the subject to decide whether or not it had appeared as a member of the memory set. He found a strong relationship between the number of items in the memory set and the time it took subjects to respond to the probe. Thus we have evidence for a serial scanning process in memory. The process is also a high-speed one; the data suggest that each item is scanned in the remarkably rapid time of 38 milliseconds. These and other specific conclusions arising from the research will be discussed in Chapter 7. The point here is that by bringing to bear an ingenious adaptation of the reaction time technique, Sternberg gave us an experimental window into otherwise inaccessible memory processes.

Are City Dwellers Heartless?   We shall briefly describe one more experiment, which deals with a distinctively human problem and some very complicated social behavior. We include it to illustrate that the experimental method is fruitfully employed in all the various branches of psychology, including social psychology.

The interest of social psychologists in "bystander intervention" was spurred by a brutal incident that occurred in New York City in 1964 and was very widely reported in the press. A young woman was stabbed to death in the courtyard of her apartment building during the early morning hours. She screamed for help, and the loud and protracted disturbance awakened many

neighbors. Police investigation later established that at least 38 people had observed part or all of the murderous attack, many watching from their windows. However, not one person went to the aid of the victim. Perhaps even more remarkable, not one bothered to telephone the police!

This apparently heartless and inhumane behavior provoked much editorializing and philosophizing. The incident was said to reveal the dehumanizing effect of modern urban living and our callous lack of concern for our fellow beings. Some observers thought that episodes of this sort signaled the breakdown of modern civilization. Two social psychologists, however, Darley and Latané (1968), decided to subject "bystander intervention" (or lack of it) to experimental test.

The subjects in the Darley and Latané study regarded themselves as participants in an experiment to test how human subjects go about solving problems under conditions of controlled communication. The "rules" of the experiment were explained to each participant individually upon arrival at the laboratory. Everyone was to take part in a collective discussion on urban problems. Some participants were to be part of a two-person group; others, a three-person group; others, a six-person group. Each person was then escorted to an isolation booth and at no point saw the other "members" of his or her group. The booths were interconnected so that discussion could be held between participants from one booth to another.

The critical point of the experiment came when, as a subject sat alone in the booth, a dramatic message from a "fellow group member" suddenly passed through an audio channel into the booth. The caller explained that he was not feeling well, that he really felt quite badly, that he sometimes had severe seizures, that one seemed to be coming on, wouldn't someone please go get help? The dramatic message, though real-sounding, was acted. The question of interest in this experiment was whether the subject would do anything about the caller's appeal for help. The obvious thing to do would be to leave the booth and search for the caller's booth. The measurement being recorded by the experimenter was a simple one: How many subjects emerged from the booth to act after hearing the simulated appeal for help?

The results of this part of the study are indicated in Table 1–1. The variable manipulated by the experimenter was the number of people whom the subject believed to be in his or her "group." The table shows that the subject was most likely to act and act quickly if told that he or she was the only other member of the group. The subjects who believed they were part of three- or six-member groups had a lower response rate. By extension, the larger the number of bystanders when an emergency takes place, the less likely is a given subject to intervene. The theoretical analysis of bystander intervention has been advanced well beyond this first study, as we will discuss in Chapter 20. For the moment, the point is how an ingenious application of the experi-

Would you intervene or would you look the other way? Why? (Jan Halaska/Photo Researchers)

Table 1–1: Effect of Group Size on Likelihood and Speed of Response.

Size of Group	Number of Subjects	% Response	Mean Time (Sec)
2 (subject and "victim")	13	85	52
3 (subject, "victim," and 1 other)	26	62	93
6 (subject, "victim," and 4 others)	13	31	166

Adapted from Darley and Latané (1968).

mental method to even very complex human social behaviors can produce orderly and theoretically significant results.

The Nature of Psychological Experiments

Independent and Dependent Variables. We stated earlier that psychologists prefer the experimental method. It should be obvious by now that they agree that this method can be usefully applied to the whole range of phenomena with which they are concerned. The basic features of the experimental method are identical, regardless of the subject matter to which it is applied. Two terms that are very useful in understanding the structure of any experiment are *independent variable* and *dependent variable.*

The **independent variable** is something that there is reason to suppose might affect the dependent variable and that can be manipulated by the experimenter. Thus the makeup of the models dropped into the fish tank and the number of bystanders in the discussion group are both independent variables. In each of these experiments two or more values of each independent variable were subjected to deliberate study by the experimenter. The goal in each case was to observe whether different values of the independent variable produced different effects on the behavior of subjects.

The **dependent variable** is always some measurable aspect of the behavior of a subject, be it fish or human. Thus whether the stickleback attacks a model, how quickly a subject responds to a memory probe, and whether a subject emerges from the booth to get help are dependent variables. The dependent variable cannot be manipulated by the experimenter in the same direct fashion as the independent variable can. The question that interests the experimenter is whether the value of the dependent variable is determined by the value of the independent variable arbitrarily chosen for a given subject. The purpose of the experiment is in fact to discover whether such relations between the independent and dependent variables exist. In the experiments we discussed, the dependent variable was clearly related to the independent variable. Since the values of the independent variable were manipulated by the researcher while other possible causes of the dependent variable were held constant, we can be sure that the independent variable played a causal role in altering the value of the dependent variable.

There is often—thank goodness—a clear functional relationship between the values of the independent and dependent variables studied in a psychological experiment. For example, in the study of bystander intervention the time subjects took to emerge from their booths was smoothly related to the number of other subjects present. The data showing this relationship are clear and orderly. The probability of an individual bystander's intervening *is a function of* the number of other bystanders who are present. We would like, obviously, to discover many such functional relationships. Whenever such functional relationships are established, we accumulate information to guide us in the construction of models and theories about the underlying processes that account for the relationships. If the theories are good ones, they will not only account for the data already obtained but will also suggest the existence of functional relationships that have not yet been established. Thus theory and experiment depend very much on each other. Without experimental facts, we have precious little to theorize about. Without theories, we would have no clear idea of how or where to find important experimental facts, what they mean when we find them, or how to relate them to other facts.

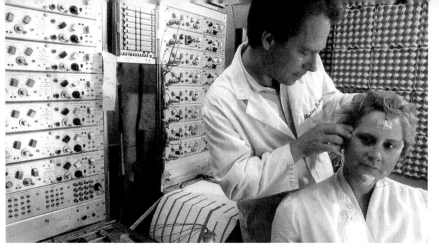

The Necessity for Control Groups.

This description of the structure of an experiment suggests that the carrying out of a meaningful experimental study is simple. Unfortunately it is not. Psychologists must often cudgel their brains in order to include in their studies appropriate **control groups.** We can best illustrate the logic of, and the necessity for, control groups by describing a hypothetical example—which is, by the way, not at all farfetched.

Psychologist X wondered whether a particular drug really made people feel cheerful. To test this possibility, he recruited a large number of volunteer subjects. The subjects were asked to rate how cheerful they felt on a scale ranging from 1 ("abysmally depressed") to 7 ("ecstatically delighted"). The average self-rating of the subjects was 4.3—just a trifle more toward the cheerful end of the scale than the neutral scale value of 4. Then the subjects were each given a standard dose of the drug being tested. Psychologist X waited a long enough time to be certain that the drug had been absorbed into the subjects' bloodstream, then asked them to rate their cheerfulness once again. The subjects now reported an average rating of 6.1—a little short of ecstasy, but evidently much more cheerful than they had been. With appropriate statistical formulas (see the statistical appendix), Psychologist X demonstrated that so large a change in average self-rating could not reasonably be attributed to mere chance. Thus he concluded that, just as the drug manufacturer had asserted, the drug really does make people feel cheerful. Psychologist X is either in the pay of the drug manufacturer or he knows very little about how to design a psychological experiment.

The same experiment was performed in a different way by Psychologist Y. The subjects studied were randomly divided into two different groups. One group was treated exactly the same as Psychologist X had treated all his subjects. First they rated their moods, then they took the same drug dosage, then they rated their moods once again. The results were virtually identical to those obtained by Psychologist X. The cheerfulness ratings increased from about 4.3 to about 6.1. The subjects in the second group were also treated in the same way, with one very important difference. They were given the same instructions and made the same mood ratings before and after receiving a pill. However, the pill did not contain the drug being tested—it contained only inactive ingredients. The cheerfulness ratings of this group *also* increased from about 4.3 to about 6.1. Thus Psychologist Y properly concluded that the drug does *not* affect cheerfulness. The second group served as a check or control over the interpretation of the results. This control group demonstrated a truism known to psychologists and physicians: People often respond to drugs and treatments in the way they think they "should." The bitter taste of a worthless patent medicine may convince some people that it

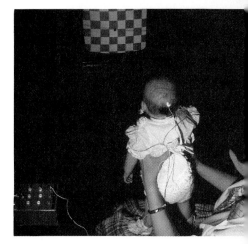

The photos on this page show some experimental psychologists and their subjects at work: *(Top left):* a graduate student monitors equipment at a sleep-wake research center; *(top right):* a primate communicates with a human through learned signs; *(middle & lower):* the developing perceptual abilities of infants are tested. *(In order:* Michael Nichols/Magnum; Vic Cox/Peter Arnold; Enrico Ferorelli/DOT; Hank Morgan/Photo Researchers)

is good for them, and they may then report that their symptoms are much improved.

The necessity for appropriate control groups, as the following chapters will repeatedly demonstrate, applies to all areas of psychology. The point of a control group should be clear. We are often unaware of the effects that we, or unsuspected features of the experimental treatment, may exert upon our subjects. We are conscious of manipulating one thing deliberately, but we may well be inadvertently manipulating other things at the same time. Thus, in our example, the important aspect of the experimental treatment was not the contents of the pill but the suggestion to subjects that the thing they swallowed might make them feel better. To guard against such possibilities, it is essential that a control group and an experimental group be treated identically in *every respect but one*. Then if the behavior of the two groups differs significantly, we can logically attribute the difference to the one respect (the independent variable) in which they differed.

We might note that the purposes of a control group are sometimes accomplished in an experiment without designating any particular group of subjects as the control group. Suppose the drug experiment had been carried out with subjects randomly divided into four experimental groups, all of which received the same- size pill and the same instructions. The pills contained, for different groups, either 1, 2, 3, or 4 grams of the drug substance. If there were significant differences in the mood ratings of the four groups, we could conclude that the drug did affect cheerfulness. However, the inclusion of a **placebo** control—a group that receives a zero dosage of the real drug—would obviously provide a clearer picture of the drug's effect.

Experimental psychologists must also be extraordinarily rigorous in the use of a variety of procedural controls. With a drug study of the sort described, it would not be gilding the lily to insist that the experimenter, like the subject, not know which subjects receive the real drug and which the placebo. There are several nasty possibilities here. The experimenter, without realizing it, might treat those subjects who are to receive the drug in a more pleasant and caring way. This could easily influence those subjects' moods in a way that might affect their cheerfulness rating. The experimenter might also mishear, misread, or miscalculate the responses of the subjects in such a way as to bias the results systematically.

Do these possibilities strike you as farfetched, even paranoid? Psychologists wish that were so, because including the proper controls for them complicates experimental designs considerably. However, there is good evidence—good experimental evidence—that these possibilities are very real indeed. In a thorough and convincing set of studies Rosenthal (1967) documented the pervasive workings of the **experimenter expectancy effect**. He did a set of studies that varied greatly in specifics but were tied together by the choice of independent variable, which was the expectation of the experimenter about how different groups of subjects would behave. In other words, experimenter expectation itself became the independent variable, and the tests were designed to determine how this would affect the dependent variable—the subject's performance.

Rosenthal sorted his subjects into the various experimental groups at random. Therefore he had groups of subjects among whom, on average, no real differences existed. Yet the experimenters were given to believe that there were in fact differences among the groups, and further, that these differences could be expected to cause differences in the dependent variables. In a variety of tests, using both animals and human beings, Rosenthal found that the expectations of the experimenter affected the outcomes of the experi-

ment. Several discrete differences were noted in the experimenters' behavior that led to this effect.

In the case of rats running a maze, those thought to be "maze bright" were set carefully in the maze and perhaps launched on their way. "Maze dulls" were likely to get a more abrupt introduction to the start box, perhaps being dropped in, and perhaps in a way that oriented them away from the first turn. People expected to show positive mood states were dealt with in a tone of voice and with nonverbal communication patterns that somehow elicited higher mood ratings from them, and so on. Errors were sometimes made in transcribing data—copying it from the experimental protocols to the summary pages—and these errors were likely to be in the direction that would confirm the experimenter's expectation. For example, in any experiment trials get botched by experimenters' errors in procedures or equipment failure. Rosenthal's experimenters were much more likely to conclude that a trial was botched—and exclude its data from the final analysis—if the data from that trial came out in a direction opposite from the one expected.

So for all these reasons, psychologists take the possibility of experimenter expectancy effects seriously. Sometimes psychologists have even irritated their colleagues in the physical sciences by urging them to review their work for such biases because the Rosenthal research shows that biasing effects are by no means limited to research within the psychological domain. To guard against this kind of thing, many studies are now conducted with a **double-blind** procedure. That is, the experimenter who actually deals with the subject (like the subject himself) is unaware of which experimental group the subject has been assigned to.

Other techniques to guard against the experimenter expectancy effect include automating data-collection efforts to reduce the possibility of transcription biases, ensuring that the individuals who code the data do not know from which experimental group they originated, and enforcing rigorous rules for the exclusion of botched trials.

In psychology the word **artifact** is shorthand for a differing result between experimental groups caused by some other reason than the one the researchers thought they were manipulating via the independent variable. A psychologist who discovers that she has an artifact in her experimental design feels the same embarrassment that an ordinary person might experience upon discovering a piece of spinach stuck between his teeth at an important dinner meeting. Previously we said that proper experimental design requires considerable ingenuity. Now you can see why a good deal of this ingenuity must be directed toward seeing that the experimenters themselves do not bias the experimental process. This task requires discipline, but good experimental researchers develop it.

Ethical Issues in Research

The "raw material" of psychology comes from observations of the behaviors of humans and sometimes animals. Some experimental conditions may create *stress* for the individual. In other experiments a degree of *deception* is involved, in that the participant is misled or at least not fully informed about the purposes of the experiment. Questionnaires on personality issues may ask individuals to disclose material they would not want widely known about themselves; thus they need to be reassured about the *confidentiality* of their answers. Interviews following traumatic experiences can rearouse some of the emotions experienced in the original situation. In all these cases the

researcher must strike a careful balance between science's need for reliable information and the research participant's integrity and humanity.

At universities and other research institutions there are Institutional Review Boards that review research proposals involving human subjects. The IRB has the difficult task of estimating the trade-offs between the potential adverse effects on the subjects and the usefulness of the proposed research. For each study the IRB must ask some hard questions that will determine its decision. If the study stresses individuals, is that stress within tolerable ranges? Is there a way of identifying in advance individuals who might be unduly stressed by the experience and who therefore should be excluded from the research? Is what might be learned from the experiment of sufficient importance to warrant putting people through it? If some of the true purposes of the experiment are kept obscure from the subject initially, will a full explanation be provided immediately afterward? Just how is the anonymity of subjects to be maintained and guaranteed?

Few now believe that there are simple rules that enable us to easily attain the balance between the need for reliable information and the welfare of subjects. However, the American Psychological Association has developed a set of principles governing research, involving, first, the informed consent of the research subjects to their participation; second, their understanding that they can terminate any study if it is causing them discomfort; and third, the confidential character of the responses participants provide.

Recently, the ethics of research with animals has also become a controversial issue. One of the motives for using animals in research is to trace the movement of information along neural or brain pathways in ways that cannot be done with human beings. Many of the important discoveries about the visual system, for instance, have been made using procedures involving brain implants in monkeys. Here ethical standards require that the research animals be well cared for, kept in clean and hygienic surroundings, and not made to experience needless pain or suffering. But just as in research with humans, some people vociferously protest against animal research on the grounds that much or all of it is ethically unwarranted.

The ethical issues raised by psychological research are complex and constantly being debated. Many, but not all, of the people involved in the debate think that the quality and importance of research discoveries should be taken into consideration. As you study psychology this term, you will be learning about the discoveries made, and you can assess these ethical questions in the light of what you learn.

Basic and Applied Research

Within all sciences there are two research traditions: one emphasizing basic or "pure" research, and the other emphasizing applied or "practical" research. Basic research assumes that discovering knowledge for its own sake is an appropriate and justifiable enterprise, while applied research is concerned with the immediate usefulness of experimental results. Although various subfields of psychology may emphasize either basic or applied research, in general the distinction between the two is not at all neat. In fact, much research bridges both orientations. Nonetheless, the basic-versus-applied-research distinction has created some tensions in the field. Basic research has been criticized as producing a body of literature that is of interest only to other psychologists. Particularly when public funds have been used, basic research has been criticized for wasting time and money to

Lately, you may have noticed that fire engines are changing their colors. As you can imagine, it is important that fire engines are painted in an eye-jarring color. Red is such a color, but only during the daytime. At night, because of the ways in which color receptors work (more on this in Chapter 4), red "shifts" to appear black. Yellow, however, retains its vivid character at night. This understanding of how the human visual system works has been applied to practical use and many fire departments are now painting their fire engines yellow. (*Top:* Eunice Harris; *bottom:* Wesley Bocxe; both Photo Researchers)

answer far-out questions that do not seem to be linked to pressing human problems. Within academic circles applied research has often been criticized for its lack of theory, and thus its lack of general applicability.

Kurt Lewin (1951), a distinguished social psychologist, struggled to amalgamate theoretical and applied interests in psychology. He argued that psychology should not only increase the scientific understanding of human behavior but should also improve the quality of human life. By the late 1960s, in the subfield of social psychology, many were ready to follow Lewin by conducting theory-oriented research in real-world settings. There was a general call to take psychology "out of the laboratory" and into the social world. Some recent examples of "social-action" research in the Lewinian tradition are a study by McClelland and Cook (1980) of energy conservation in an apartment building when financial incentives are used; Kassin and Wrightsman's (1980) construction of "mock" juries to test the Supreme Court's assumption that jurors do not allow a forced confession to influence their decisions; and a study conducted by Maniscalco, Doherty, and Ullman (1980) to discover whether applicants to graduate school were discriminated against because of a physical handicap. More recently, the National Institute of Mental Health realized that depression was a significant and widespread social problem (as you will see in Chapter 17). It was also recognized that a number of treatments had been developed to alleviate depression, and that a massive experimental comparison of these methods was appropriate. With leadership and funding from NIMH, a large-scale experiment on the efficacy of various methods of treating depression was carried out. The study utilized therapists specially trained in several standardized methods of intervention, and examined treatment outcomes for patients from different cities and seen in various settings (Elkin et al., 1986). While the results will be described later, at this point it is useful to understand that when an applied problem is of sufficient importance, one can attack it with sound experimental research. These kinds of studies, as Lewin noted in 1951, occur when and "if the theorist does not look toward applied problems with highbrow aversion or with a fear of social problems, and if the applied psychologist realizes that there is nothing so practical as a good theory" (p. 169).

Kurt Lewin (1890–1947) studied in Berlin with the Gestalt psychologists. Influenced by their thinking but interested in more complex human processes than perception, he went on to found modern social psychology. We will talk about that field in Chapters 19 and 20.

Field and Natural Experiments

As the preceding examples make clear, not all experiments need to be carried out within the confines of the laboratory. Because of the advantages of experiments in establishing causal relationships, many researchers carry them out in larger-scale settings as well. Suppose, for example, that you were superintendent of a large school system and were interested in trying out a new method of teaching geometry. You could simply direct that the new teaching method be instituted in all geometry classes throughout the system. But if it proved ineffective, that would be a costly and embarrassing failure. You might think to try out the new method in half the geometry classes. Then you could compare the average performance of classes under the new and old methods to see which was better, and by how much. You could also begin to answer more sophisticated questions, such as: Does the new method do a better job of teaching below-average students than the old method? This sort of approach has come to be known as "field experimental" research.

Take another example. Suppose a researcher had a theory about the long-lasting mental effects of a sudden severe stress. Obviously, the researcher is

not going to inflict sudden severe stress on a group of individuals to test the theory. However, nature at times does something quite close to that, inflicting disasters such as tornadoes, floods, or hurricanes. The researcher could study the people in a disaster-stricken area, selecting, as a "control," a set of people nonafflicted areas that were geographically and otherwise matched to the stricken area. This general approach is sometimes referred to as "the natural experiment": Nature provides the "experimental manipulation," and human ingenuity retrospectively identifies individuals or groups that can serve as control groups for purposes of testing a theory.

The idea of a society that guides social innovation by the reasoned use of such large-scale experimental findings is an interesting one. Certainly many recent examples document the usefulness of field experiments in discovering nonobvious and important findings. For instance, in a study done on preventing adolescent smoking, researchers (Murray, Luepker, Johnson, and Mittelmark, 1984) discovered that "a program which teaches specific skills to resist social pressures to begin smoking and which teaches students about the short-term physiological consequences of smoking is more effective than a program which concentrates on long-term health consequences" (p. 274). Interestingly, too, the programs that worked best, in the sense of causing a high percentage of adolescents to avoid smoking, were those led by same-age peers.

Another interesting example is an automobile seat-belt campaign conducted near the Canadian capital. Canadian police repeatedly set up a checkpoint in a particular location to see whether drivers and passengers were wearing seat belts, and to ticket them if they were not. Similar locations in which no seat-belt checkpoints were established provided control-group comparisons. Is this a field experiment or a natural experiment? It depends. If the researchers had arranged in advance with the police to set up checkpoints at certain locations and to avoid certain otherwise matched locations, then it would be a field experiment. However, if the police had just set up the checkpoints without thought of cooperating in an experiment, and the researchers had scrambled to find appropriate control sites, then it would be a natural experiment. In any event, the researchers (Jonah and Grant, 1985) found that seat-belt usage two years after the first campaign was still above its previous baseline, and that subsequent campaigns raised it up to 84 percent. Driver casualties actually declined by 14 percent.

As these examples suggest, policy-relevant field experiments are often extremely valuable. But experience has taught psychologists that their implementation is rarely easy and the interpretation of the results seldom simple. A few examples will illustrate this. Think back to our example of implementing a new method of teaching geometry. Suppose a teacher assigned to continue teaching with the old method independently decided that the new method was better and "bootlegged" Xeroxed versions of it into her classes. From some perspectives, this is an admirable action, but it certainly harms the experiment—certain control groups are now receiving the experimental treatment. Or suppose that some parents hear that a new teaching method is being used, but not in their children's classes. Their protests cause the school board to suddenly install the new method in the control classrooms. Any possibility of a control comparison is destroyed—and so is the experiment.

These sorts of real-world phenomena intrude on the scientific purity of field experiments frequently enough to cause field researchers considerable worry. But often such intrusions can be avoided by hard work and planning

by the researcher. For instance, if a new teaching method is shown in an experiment to work better, it can later be used on students in the former control group as an enhancement of what they have already been taught.

A second set of flaws may creep into the field experiment if the experimenter is not rigorous in following good experimental procedure, taking care to avoid experimenter bias. Suppose, for instance, that the school superintendent had decided to let the teachers who were most enthusiastic about the new geometry teaching method be the ones to try it out. From many perspectives, this seems a sensible decision, but it markedly changes the conclusions that can be drawn from the experiment. Suppose the experiment came out as we suspect the superintendent anticipated: The students taught by the new method do better on a final test of geometry than those taught by the old method. What can be concluded? Not that students taught by the new method learn better, but rather that students taught by the new method learn better *when taught by teachers who are enthusiastic about that method.* As a result, one cannot conclude that it is a good idea to impose the new teaching method on teachers who favor the old teaching method. The action implications of the research have becomed blurred.

Thus the effects observed in field and naturalistic studies are subject to a variety of related concerns. Although such studies have potentially important social applications, they do not provide easy or unequivocal answers to questions of social policy or psychological causality.

RESISTANCE TO PSYCHOLOGICAL UNDERSTANDING

The attempt to develop a science of psychology sometimes meets with considerable skepticism, if not downright resistance. One type of objection seems largely theological. That is the argument that some aspects of human behavior and of the human spirit are outside the grasp of science. That may or may not be true, but the argument is not relevant to what psychologists are trying to do. Psychologists want to understand as much as they can as definitely as they can. To do this, they use the techniques and principles that have helped expand human understanding of the natural world. The use of these techniques and principles has helped us to make progress in understanding human behavior. We do not know how far we can progress—after all, in historical perspective, we have not been practicing the science of psychology very long. Perhaps the most we can ever achieve is very partial understanding. Even so, to replace ignorance with partial understanding seems to us worthwhile. Psychologists do, however, acknowledge that there are ways of coming to understand humanity outside of science: There is no danger that the advance of psychological science will cancel Shakespeare's worth as an illuminator of the human condition.

Another common objection to psychology can be answered more simply. This argument is that human behavior is too "spontaneous" or unpredictable to be captured by scientific laws. This is just plain wrong. In many areas of human behavior highly accurate predictions are made by all of us every day. When the traffic light in front of you turns green, you can be reasonably certain that if you drive ahead, drivers from your left and right will not ram into you. There is little doubt that if it were stated here that on page 118 of this book there is a vivid account of the sexual problems of college students,

many of you would stop reading this dreary argument and turn at once to page 118. The odds are very high that nobody you know has engaged in incestuous sexual relations but that most of the people you know have had incestuous dreams. There are innumerable examples of human behavior that is both predictable and controllable—the task is to understand why and how.

Still another common objection to experimental psychology is that despite its high-flown promises, much of it turns out to be trivial. The facts and the data may be true enough, but they are neither interesting nor important. The experiments often involve animal subjects rather than humans. The problems analyzed frequently seem small-scale and unrelated to real human problems. Why perform experiments that you know cannot provide answers to the truly significant questions?

There is a very good reason for performing "simple" experiments that seem artificial and contrived. To discover the laws that govern falling bodies we do not stand passively at the foot of the Empire State Building waiting for whatever happens to drop down. Instead we set up a quiet corner of a laboratory and deliberately roll balls down inclined planes. The advantages are obvious. We are prepared to make particular observations at a particular time, with as many disturbing influences as possible eliminated. We deliberately isolate, and then manipulate, a *simple system.* There is too much going on in the real world all at once for us to grasp the relations between events. We are thus better off observing a simple system, with only a few variables at work, so that we can systematically make one thing happen after another. The history of science indicates that the general principles unearthed by the observation of artificially simple systems also operate in the wider world. The same principles that account for the motions of billiard balls in the laboratory also explain the grander movements of the planets in the heavens. The "simple" experiments described throughout this text are attempts to isolate principles that can be applied to the understanding of many phenomena. We shall point to as many such applications as we can. We should repeat, however, that even the "simple" systems studied by psychologists are extraordinarily complex. To understand the movements of a white rat through a maze is doubtless easier than to understand the movements of a person through life, but still, it is not easy. And the complexity of nervous tissue in the human brain makes balls and planes look like a child's playthings.

Despite resistance to the psychological perspective and the difficulty of the tasks, it is certain that the work of psychologists will continue, for at least two obvious reasons. First, the subject matter of psychology is enormously interesting. There is little likelihood that people will ever lose interest in trying to understand "what makes them tick," and that is what psychology is about. Second, the results of psychological inquiry and speculation are relevant both to public policy and to the more private concerns of our personal lives. If we are to live better, we *need* to know more about psychology than we do now.

Psychologists do not yet know everything about human behavior; but what we already know is of interest, and it is also useful. There are a number of widespread beliefs about psychology that have little or no basis in fact but have considerable impact and influence on many people. We hope that reading this book will help you to distinguish between valid and invalid claims about psychology. To use psychology effectively, it is necessary not only to know the facts, but also to have enough understanding to reject unfounded assertions. We hope and believe that the knowledge you acquire from the study of psychology will help you to better understand both yourself and others.

THE SCIENCE AND PROFESSION OF PSYCHOLOGY

Psychology is unquestionably a vast field. Psychological research ranges from the processes involved in neural transmission and perception to decision making and the complex functioning of humans in organizations. In some other sciences the practitioners are separated off as engineers; psychology keeps its practitioners within the field. Psychologists do research on basic theoretical questions, and on many social policy issues as well. Many also "practice" psychology, in the sense that they use psychological principles in the service of various individuals or groups.

In 1985 the American Psychological Association had about 62,000 members. (And this organization by no means includes all psychologists.) As you might expect, specializations abound; but it is possible to group psychologists into a few major subfields.

Theoretical Specialists

Many psychologists work solely or primarily on the development and advancement of psychological theory. They are divided as follows:

1. *Physiological psychologists.* Physiological psychologists (also called neuroscientists) are concerned with the workings of the human body, particularly the human brain, as a biological and neurological system. They study perception, thought, and behavior in relation to underlying neurological activity. Topics investigated by physiological psychologists include the role of brain chemicals in human thought processes; the neural organization of the visual system, the auditory system, and other sensory systems; and the neurological bases of hunger, feeding, and reward. Many of these researchers work in university settings, in medical schools as well as in psychology departments. Others are found in private companies, particularly in the pharmaceutical industry.

2. *Sensory and perceptual psychologists.* The work of psychologists who study the sensory system (e.g., the vision system) often resembles that of physiological psychologists. They examine the particular neural and physiological systems that are the physical substrata of the sensory system under study. For instance, they trace the pathways of nerves that connect the auditory receptors in the ears with specific parts of the brain. Sensory psychologists also take the next step of relating the flow of neural information to the reported sensory experiences of the sensing individual. (Thus their field of study is often called "psychophysics.") Perceptual psychologists continue one step further, and study how various sensations of sound, light, and other sensory information are centrally integrated into perceptions of complex entities such as persons, events, and shapes. These sorts of researchers are characteristically found in universities, but also increasingly in private corporations and working for the federal government.

3. *Conditioning and learning psychologists.* These are the psychologists who have made the discoveries represented in Chapter 6. For some years theirs was the dominant experimental field in psychology, and discoveries in this area are among the most important ones made in psychology to date. Conditioning and learning psychologists are also fre-

quently found in universities, but in addition, they also make important contributions to the pharmacological and other industries.

4. *Cognitive psychologists.* This group of psychologists takes the natural next step in studying the complexity of the human mind. They concern themselves with the processes by which the various perceptual entities that we register are processed into judgments, or prototypes of real-world categories, and how these representations are encoded, stored, and retrieved in the human mind. This is the group of psychologists most concerned with human thinking processes and memory.

5. *Comparative psychologists.* We have been able to represent the previous three sets of psychologists along a single continuum of complexity of the processes they study, but comparative psychologists do not fit into this continuum. Their concerns are frequently of an evolutionary variety. For example, many species of animals have a system that "hears," in the sense that it processes sound waves. However, it turns out that these hearing systems evolved in different species from fascinatingly different bodily structures. The comparative psychologist often brings two messages to the rest of us. The first is the functional message that if a characteristic such as hearing conveys evolutionary advantage to the species, systems to bring about hearing are likely to evolve in many species. Second, by examining the ways in which auditory mechanisms have evolved in different species to bring about hearing, they remind us of the many different ways in which functionally similar effects can be brought about.

6. *Developmental psychologists.* The developmental psychologist focuses on the human life span: infancy, childhood, adolescence, adulthood, and old age. Specific issues that developmental psychologists study include the acquisition of language and reasoning skills; the development of altruistic behavior and moral reasoning; the development of social skills and perceptions of self and others; and issues of adjustment in adulthood and old age.

7. *Social psychologists.* Social psychologists study the interactions between people, their perceptions of one another, and the effects that groups have on the behavior of the individual. Some of the topics studied by social psychologists are: social perception and impression formation; aggression and violence; the formation and change of attitudes; sex roles; and conformity and social influence.

   Most social psychologists hold positions in colleges and universities; some hold research positions at private foundations and government agencies.

8. *Personality psychologists.* The field of personality psychology overlaps with both social and developmental psychology. Personality psychology is both a research area and an area of concentration in educational and clinical psychology. Personality psychology is the study of individual differences—how people differ in terms of characteristics such as authoritarianism or emotional stability.

   More than half of all personality psychologists hold positions in universities, where they teach and conduct research. Other personality psychologists are employed by the government and private foundations.

9. *Psychometric psychologists.* Psychometric psychologists develop testing instruments that evaluate intellectual, personality, educational, or social characteristics and adapt or develop statistical techniques for the analysis of such test data. They also evaluate testing instruments to

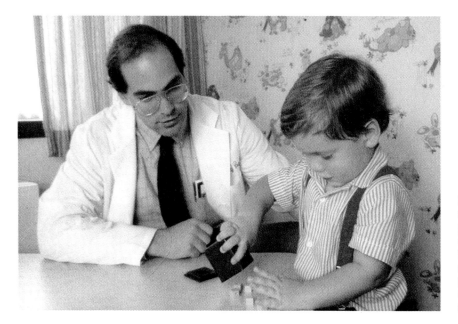

Psychometricians develop testing instruments that evaluate intellectual, personality, educational, or social characteristics. These tests may then be administered by any one of several different types of psychologists: school, educational, clinical, counseling, developmental, or personality. (SIU Biomedical Communications)

determine if they are consistent and valid indicators of what is measured. The field of psychometrics overlaps many of the other areas of psychology; for example, a psychometrician may construct measuring instruments in clinical, personality, or developmental psychology. Psychometric psychologists frequently supply the quantitative theory and techniques that enable other psychologists to test their theories or carry out their practices.

Applied Specialists

In addition to the theoreticians are those psychologists who work in "applied" settings. Applied specialists concern themselves with the applications of psychological theory to a variety of real-world problems. The best known of the applied group are clinicians, who help people resolve problems of everyday living. However, practitioners apply psychological theory in many other settings as well:

1. *Clinical psychologists.* The clinician diagnoses and treats individuals suffering from emotional or adjustment problems. The clinician may conduct psychotherapy in private practice; in a state or private institution, such as a Veterans Administration hospital; or in a number of varied settings such as juvenile courts, probation offices, prisons, or institutions for the mentally retarded. The clinician may also be a member of the psychology faculty of a university, teaching courses, training clinical graduate students, and perhaps also conducting therapy.

2. *Counseling psychologists.* Counseling psychologists are similar to clinicians in both their academic training and the problems they address. However, they are more likely to be employed in high school or college settings, and to deal with people who generally have different, and perhaps less severe, problems than the individuals seen by many clini-

The American Psychological Association (Woods, 1976) conducted a survey aimed at locating trained psychologists engaged in unusual or nontraditional careers. The range of such occupations was found to be very wide, indicating that psychological skills are useful in a great variety of employment settings. The complete range is only suggested by the samples mentioned here.

In occupations concerned with social issues, psychologists were employed as: consultant to a public defender's office; legislative assistant to a United States senator, focusing on health-care legislation; developmental psychologist working as a consultant for children's television programming; president of a nonprofit environmental research foundation; psychologist in accident research; psychologist in social-urban planning; editor for a feminist publishing house, concerned with sex-role stereotypes; and warden at a center for young offenders.

In the clinical-counseling areas psychologists were working as: administrator and consultant in the criminal justice system; assistant commissioner of public welfare; child psychologist consultant for day-care centers; vocational counselor in a rehabilitation agency; and rehabilitation psychologist. Trained educational and school psychologists were employed as evaluator of children's television programs; private consultant to schools, colleges, and state departments of education; and guidance specialist for foreign students. In the industrial field, psychologists worked as: consultant to management-development programs; researcher in the insurance industry; researcher on human-computer interactions; and engineering psychologist for the military.

Still other psychologists built careers as: researcher for a drug company in the treatment of psychiatric disorders; developer of curriculum materials and specialized learning devices for insurance underwriters; researcher in human fertility issues; psychologist-editor for a medical publishing company; government researcher in highway safety; researcher and consultant for museums on visitor behavior; private practitioner concerned with animal behavior problems; social psychologist organizer of volunteer work; and nursing-home consultant.

Recently there has been an explosion of growth in computational processing and computer use, and many psychologists are employed in those settings. Some assist in making computers "user-friendly;" that is, easily understood and operated. Others interrogate expert decision makers, such as oil-prospecting geologists or medical diagnosticians, and turn their discoveries into "expert systems"—computerized sets of rules for others to follow in making decisions.

The comments offered by the individuals who responded to this survey made it clear that the broad training in basic psychological principles that they had received had made it possible for them to enter these careers and had also been useful in guiding their day-to-day work. There seem to be few, if any, areas of human concern to which psychological training is irrelevant.

---

cians. For instance, they might counsel a college student about some anxieties he is feeling about his grades, or a high-school student about careers that make sense for her. (The latter case indicates why many counseling psychologists receive training in vocational psychology, an area in which many other clinicians are not trained. In fact, this subgroup of psychologists are sometimes referred to as "vocational counselors.")

3. *Engineering psychologists.* The majority of engineering psychologists are employed in industry, where they aid in the design of equipment and training devices that are appropriate to human capacities. They also design and implement training programs to ensure the efficient functioning of human-machine systems. Other engineering psychologists work in governmental agencies or in private consulting firms.

4. *Computational psychologists.* These psychologists could be regarded as a subset of engineering psychologists because they are involved with human-machine interaction—in this case, interactions between humans and computers. However, computational psychology is such an active and rapidly developing specialty that it calls for further distinction. Some computer psychologists are well versed in theories of human learning and are working to develop teaching methods that make use of the computer's vast potential. Others concentrate on the industrial and societal implications of the computer and the expanded work possibilities it

creates. For instance, a secretary or stockbroker can now theoretically work entirely from home, and still have his or her work completely monitored. What are the human implications of this? Still other computer psychologists focus on making computers more accessible and usable by human operators.

5. *Industrial and organizational psychologists.* Industrial psychology is considered both an applied and a theoretical field. Many industrial and organizational psychologists teach in university settings, schools of management, or business schools. They work on organizational theory, manpower selection theory, and ways of improving industrial productivity. Others specialize in drawing organizational implications from theories of learning, or social-psychological theory. Still others do psychometric work on the development of tests for use in industrial settings. Finally, some in this field are practitioners who apply psychological principles to the work setting, though they may also conduct research to solve on-the-job problems.

Industrial psychologists are concerned with the "human factor" in the technological setting—how satisfied workers are with their jobs, how to increase morale and productivity, how to increase the quality of the industry's services, and how to develop better training and placement procedures. Industrial psychologists must be able to translate psychological knowledge and skills to practical settings, and also to communicate psychological principles to an audience with little or no background in the field.

6. *School and educational psychologists.* School psychologists are concerned with problems of adjustment, mental health, and academic achievement in schoolchildren. They may also administer intelligence and proficiency tests to students; assess problem behaviors and refer affected children to counseling agencies; and design and evaluate special-education projects.

Educational psychologists are primarily concerned with the application of psychological principles and techniques to problems in education. They analyze educational needs, develop curriculum and teaching materials, and evaluate instructional programs.

SUMMARY

1. Early psychologists were concerned with elementary sensations and consciousness; their chief method was introspection. Wilhelm Wundt was a pioneer in this field.

2. William James argued for the importance of a *functional perspective.* According to James, we should be less concerned with the exact form of thought content than with the functional uses human beings make of that thought.

3. In the United States John B. Watson revolutionized experimental psychology with his claim that psychology is the study of behavior.

4. The Gestalt psychologists and others, however, stressed the role of perceptual and other mental processes, both innate and learned.

5. At approximately the same time as Wundt, Freud developed his theories of psychoanalysis, in which the unconscious mind was a prominent idea.

6. Methods used by psychologists to acquire data vary, just as the various disciplines within psychology vary. Among the various methods are *experimental method, survey method, interviews,* and *case studies.*

7. The experimental method involves beginning with a hypothesis and then testing it. Experiments must be carefully planned and repeated so that coincidence and accidental occurrences will not be misinterpreted as proof of the hypothesis.

8. Psychologists have utilized various kinds of instruments to help them with their research. These devices include: the *microscope, reaction time devices, the*

Skinner box, the *cumulative recorder,* the *chart plotter,* the *memory drum, logic chips,* and the *computer.* In general, these devices help make "invisible" entities or processes visible, and are used for many different types of experiments. Some facilitate the researcher's ability to measure, record, and—in the case of the computer—even analyze data. Others provide a means to control experiments more accurately, and make studies easier to replicate in other settings.

9. In an experiment the *independent variable* is the factor being tested; it is under the direct control of the experimenter. The *dependent variable* is some measurable aspect of a subject's behavior that may be affected by the independent variable. The purpose of an experiment is to discover whether such relations between the independent and dependent variables exist.

10. In an experiment the control group—which should be as similar as possible to the experimental group—experiences all of the same conditions as experimental subjects *except* for the independent variable. Control groups are necessary for the correct interpretation of the experimental results: Because the control group and the experimental group are treated identically in every way except for the independent variable, it is logical to conclude that any differences in behavior are a result of the independent variable being tested.

11. Ethical principles governing research have been instituted to assure subjects of their rights to informed participation, minimum discomfort, and confidentiality. Ethical standards govern research with animals as well, to ensure careful treatment and the avoidance of unnecessary pain.

12. Basic research is conducted for the sake of knowledge, whereas applied research is concerned with putting the results to immediate and practical use. In recent years psychologists have attempted to bridge the gap by conducting theory-oriented research in real-world settings.

13. Field and natural experiments, although complicated in execution and interpretation, may provide an opportunity to study the actual effects of social innovations, or of stresses and pressures far beyond those that are possible in laboratory settings.

14. Experimenters must be very careful not to bias the outcome of their research. In psychology an *artifact* refers to a differing result (or dependent variable) between experimental groups caused by some reason other than the one the researchers thought they were manipulating via the independent variable. Experimental controls are designed to eliminate artifacts. Some examples of experimental controls are: placebo control, procedural control, and the double-blind procedure.

15. The practice of psychology falls into theoretical and applied specialities. Theoretical specialities include: physiological psychology, sensory and perceptual psychology, conditioning and learning psychology, cognitive psychology, comparative psychology, developmental psychology, social psychology, personality psychology, and psychometric psychology. Applied specialities include: clinical psychology, counseling psychology, engineering psychology, computational psychology, industrial and organizational psychology, and school and educational psychology.

SUGGESTED READINGS

ARONSON, E., CARLSMITH, J. M., and ELLSWORTH, P. C. (1976). *Methods of research in social psychology.* Reading, Mass.: Addison-Wesley. More than most method books, this one explores the creative and inventive side of research design, particularly when the research uses human subjects.

BORING, E. E. (1950). *A history of experimental psychology* (2nd ed.). Englewood Cliffs, N.J.: Prentice-Hall. This is considered the classic overview of experimental psychology. The book begins with the rise of scientific psychology in the early nineteenth century and continues through to the modern period with a discussion of such areas as behavioral and Gestalt psychology.

DEMENT, W. (1976). *Some must watch while some must sleep.* New York: Norton. This is a charmingly written work in which Dement, one of the world's leading sleep researchers, weaves a fine account of what we know about the patterns and functions of sleep into a narrative of his own life in research.

DETHIER, V. (1962). *To know a fly.* San Francisco: Holden-Day. Dethier's research life has involved genetic structures, behaviors, and their interconnections in the fruit fly. In this wonderfully engaging book, he makes clear the fascination of scientific study.

EVANS, R. I. (1976). *The making of psychology: Discussions with creative contributors.* New York: Knopf. This book consists of dialogues with prominent psychologists representing the major areas of psychology. The interviews introduce the reader to the contributor's major ideas and the historical antecedents of his or her field.

The psychologists interviewed include B. F. Skinner, Jean Piaget, Gordon Allport, Konrad Lorenz, Carl Rogers, Leon Festinger, C. G. Jung, and Erik Erikson.

GUTHRIE, R. V. (1976). *Even the rat was white: A historical view of psychology.* New York: Harper & Row. The first half of this book explores the social antecedents of psychology by outlining the relationship between psychology and anthropology. The author reviews early research approaches to black/white differences. The second half of the book discusses the impact of psychology on the education of black people and the contributions of black American psychologists.

SCHULTZ, D., and SCHULTZ, S. (1987). *A history of modern psychology.* San Diego: Harcourt Brace Jovanovich. This book begins its coverage in the mid-1800s, and gives a good detailed presentation of the various movements within psychology, such as functionalism and structuralism.

SHERMAN, R. (1965). *A career in psychology.* Washington, D.C.: American Psychological Association; WOODS, P. J. (Ed.) (1976). *Career opportunities for psychologists.* Washington, D.C.: American Psychological Association; WOODS, P. J. (1979). *The psychology major: Training and employ-* *ment strategies.* Washington, D.C.: American Psychological Association. These three books discuss career opportunities and educational requirements in all areas of psychology. In addition, the American Psychological Association has several pamphlets on careers in psychology, which can be obtained by writing the APA, 1200 17th St. N. W., Washington, D.C. 20036.

WATSON, R. I (1978). *The great psychologists.* Philadelphia: Lippincott. An examination of the historical unfolding of psychology through the works of its chief proponents. Drawing heavily on original sources, the book discusses the writings of Plato and Aristotle, Descartes, Kant, Wundt, Binet, James, Cattell, Watson, French, and contemporary American and European psychologists.

WERTHEIMER, M. (1979). *A brief history of psychology.* New York: Holt, Rinehart & Winston. A very readable little book that traces the emergence of psychology from the writings of the ancient Greeks and other philosophical traditions to the evolution of psychology as a separate field in the nineteenth and twentieth centuries. This is a good source to launch the reader on a historical exploration of psychology.

2 *The Biological Framework*

I n this chapter we consider basic human biological mechanisms, particularly that incredible network of communicating cells called our nervous system, which makes us supreme among living things in our ability to acquire and utilize knowledge. While much of what we shall consider reflects work outside psychology, in fields such as biology, physiology, and neurology, it also reflects the work of physiological psychologists and neuroscientists trained in psychology. Their work represents a type of psychology that focuses on biological processes. Other psychologists, whose work will be considered in subsequent chapters, draw most of their inferences about the mind from the way people behave. However, the common goal of both approaches is to understand fully the nature of human thought and feeling.

FROM SUPERSTITION TO SCIENCE

Accidents and battles undoubtedly provided even prehistoric man with an occasional glimpse inside the human head. Reference to the brain can be found in Egyptian hieroglyphics as early as 1600 B.C., in which a physician tells of reaching into a shattered skull and feeling the brain "throbbing and fluttering" under his fingers. Yet he did not recognize the brain as the organ of mind. Egyptians carefully preserved the bodies of their kings for life after death, especially the heart and bowels, which they saw as the seat of mental life. The brain was simply spooned out through the nose and discarded.

In Western civilization the idea of the brain as the organ of mind can be traced back to Greek scholars of the sixth and fifth century B.C.: Hippocrates, the father of medicine, and his contemporary, Plato. Later, Plato's student, Ar-

A self-portrait by Leonardo da Vinci, one of the first to directly study the brain. (Biblioteca Nationale)

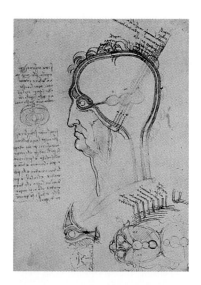

Figure 2–1 In 1490 Leonardo da Vinci depicted the mind as three spherical chambers into which tube-like nerves fed "animal spirits" from the senses. This view was hardly more sophisticated than the mental plumbing envisioned by Aristotle almost 2,000 years earlier. [Fincher, J. (1981) *The Human Body.* The Brain: Mystery of Mind and Matter. U.S. News Books.]

istotle, opted for the heart. These differing views were gradually reconciled by succeeding generations, who hypothesized an elaborate plumbing system in which "natural spirits" formed in the liver and then mixed with blood from the heart and air from the lungs to form *pneuma*. According to the theory, this substance spread through a system of vessels into the *ventricular* cavities of the brain, where it controlled mental life. Variants of this conception persisted for almost 2,000 years, so that its influence can still be seen in a drawing done by Leonardo da Vinci in A.D. 1490. (see Figure 2–1). The three spherical ventricular cavities shown in Leonardo's drawing owe more to Aristotle's conception of the sphere as an ideal form than to any real knowledge of anatomy. However, 14 years later Leonardo's curiosity led him to inject molten wax into the brain cavities (ventricles) of a dead ox. When the cooled wax had hardened, Leonardo cut away the brain to reveal the wax forms. This simple experiment allowed him to accurately depict the ventricles in later drawings (see Figure 2–2).

While the Church strongly opposed the dissection of human cadavers by Leonardo, less than 40 years later an anatomist named Andreas Vesalius had artists drawing detailed pictures of the dissected heads of executed criminals (see Figure 2–3).

Direct observation gradually replaced philosophical and religious speculation as a basis for knowledge, and in the seventeenth-century a French philosopher, René Descartes, fully separated the scientific study of mind from the theological study of soul. Descartes' *dualism* represents the two pursuits as essentially separate. This distinction allowed him to view the brain and body as an elaborate machine to be studied like any other machine, by careful examination of its parts and functions (see Figure 2–4). Conveniently, it left matters of the soul to the Church. The scientific study of the nervous system had begun in earnest.

Figure 2–2 Leonardo injected hot wax into the brain cavities (ventricles) of a dead ox. Cooled and removed, the hardened wax revealed the true shape of the cavities. This is reflected in a drawing Leonardo did 14 years after the one shown in Figure 2–1. [Fincher, J. (1981)]

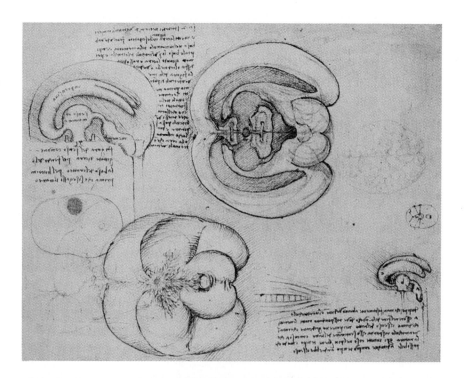

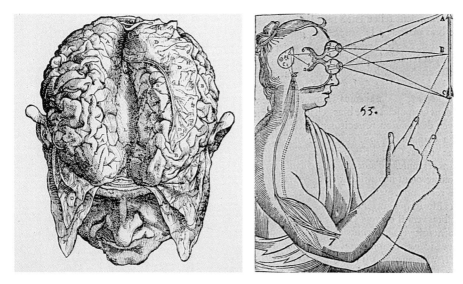

Figure 2–3 (left) In 1543 anatomist Andreas Vesalius published a major work entitled *De Humani Corporis Fabrica (Structure of the Human Body)*. It contained detailed drawings like this one, based on his dissections of executed criminals. [Fincher, J. (1981)]

Figure 2–4 (right) The seventeenth-century French philosopher René Descartes used this drawing to illustrate his mechanistic view of the nervous system. Light entering the eye stimulates animal spirits to flow through tubular "nerves" to the pineal gland, where it is then directed into other nerves to activate muscles in the arm. While anatomically unsophisticated, the drawing reflects Descartes' view of the mind as a machine. [Fincher, J. (1981)]

THE NERVOUS SYSTEM

In everyday language, "nervous" means "anxious" or "excitable," and "nerves" are what you're a bundle of when you're particularly anxious (not to be confused with "nerve," which is what you have a lot of when you're not anxious *enough*). Physiologically speaking, however, "nervous" simply means "having to do with nerves," the parts of the body that specialize in transmitting information. You may have dissected a frog or a cat in a biology lab and isolated long stringy gray strands of tissue that were called nerves. These are really bundles of individual cells too small to be seen by the naked eye. Even under a microscope it is difficult to make out individual cells because their boundaries are so indistinct. In fact, it wasn't until 1875 that an Italian anatomist named Carrillo Golgi found a way to see the individual nerve cells.

The Discovery of Neurons

Golgi discovered that certain chemicals completely stained a small number of cells while leaving the rest completely unstained. The structure of the stained cells could then be clearly seen under a microscope (Figure 2–5). What Golgi saw were **neurons,** the basic message-carrying cells of the ner-

Figure 2–5 Golgi-stained neurons from the cortex of a monkey. The approximate 1 out of 100 cells that take up the stain stand out dark against the unstained ones. This is a microscopic view in which the cells are magnified 500 diameters. The long needlelike object is a microelectrode thinner than a human hair. (Fritz Goro)

Figure 2–6 An idealized diagram of a typical neuron. Actual neurons vary tremendously in shape and size. Neurons receive stimulation through their dendrites or the cell body; the message is transmitted along the axon, which may be as much as a meter in length.

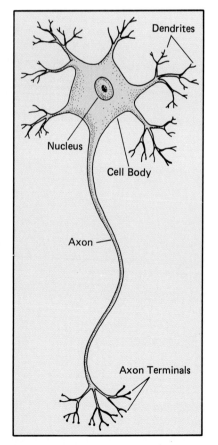

vous system. The unstained cells were both nonneural cells and other neurons (only about 1 out of 100 neurons absorb the Golgi stain, for reasons that are still not completely understood).

A schematic diagram of a common type of neuron is shown in Figure 2–6. Its major components are: the **cell body** (which contains the nucleus of the cell), short limblike structures called **dendrites** extending from the cell body, and a longer thinner extension called an **axon.** (Actual neurons differ considerably in size, number of dendrites, and length of axon as seen in Figure 2–7.) Through a process we will consider later, neurons receive messages at the dendrite or cell body and relay them out along the axon to other neurons.

A Spanish contemporary of Golgi named Santiago Ramon y Cajal used Golgi's methods to study the nervous system. (His drawing of neural structure, made in 1888, is shown in Figure 2–8.) Cajal demonstrated that neurons were discrete, well-defined cells whose interconnections seemed highly organized and specific. While many other staining methods have since been developed (see Figures 2–9 and 2–10), Cajal's use of Golgi's methods revealed much of the basic structure of our nervous system. (In 1906 the two researchers were awarded a Nobel prize for their work.)

There are three basic types of neurons: sensory neurons, motor neurons, and interneurons. **Sensory neurons** are connected to receptor cells located in the skin, in muscles and joints, in internal organs, and in the sense organs. They carry information from these receptors toward the spinal cord (the neurons within the bones of the spine) or brain. **Motor neurons** carry information away from the spinal cord or brain, and many form synapses with muscle cells. **Interneurons** receive signals from sensory neurons, and send signals to other interneurons or to motor neurons.

Neurons developed quite early in the course of evolution; animals as primitive as jellyfish have sensory and motor neurons. Neurons haven't even changed very much. A squid or a leech has basically the same kind of neu-

rons as a human. In fact, much of our knowledge of neural functioning has come from studies of the nervous system of the squid.

In simple animals like the jellyfish sensory neurons transmit their signals directly to motor neurons. But only a little higher on the evolutionary ladder—for example, in *Ascaris,* a parasitic roundworm—interneurons appear. These intermediate neurons process the signals sent to them by sensory neurons and by other interneurons. Then, on the basis of all the information they receive, they may or may not send a signal to the motor neurons for transmission to the muscles. Clearly, this three-stage system is capable of producing more complex forms of behavior than a two-stage system.

In *Ascaris* and other invertebrates bunches of interneurons form clumps called **ganglia.** In general, both the proportion of neurons in the interneuron class and the total number of cells in the nervous system are greater in the more highly developed species.

By the time we get to the vertebrates (fish, amphibians, reptiles, birds, and mammals), the ganglia have become a full-fledged brain. We like to believe that the brain has reached its highest state of development in the human species—and perhaps it has, judging by some of our achievements. But it is well to remember that humans have neither the largest brains in the animal

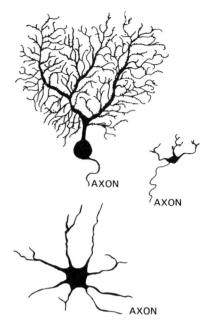

Figure 2–7 Some of the wide variety of neurons from different parts of the body as they can be seen using a Golgi stain. [Afifi, A.K, & Bergman, R.A. (1980) *Basic Neuroscience,* Baltimore, Munich: Urban & Scwarzenberg.]

Figure 2–8 (left) In 1888 Cajal sketched this view of the Golgi-stained neurons in a rat's visual cortex. Using Golgi's methods, Cajal was able to demonstrate the existence of a complex network of interconnections between neurons. (*Scientific American,* September 1979)

Figure 2–9 (right) One way of tracing neural pathways is to inject a substance called horseradish peroxidase into living nervous tissue. It enters neurons and is carried through their axons by a process called axonal transport. This photograph shows a slice of cat brain in which horseradish peroxidase appears white. It was originally injected into the cat's visual cortex, then spread along axons, revealing the pathways connecting that area of cortex to the lateral geniculate. (Carl Olsen and Henry Hall, Princeton University)

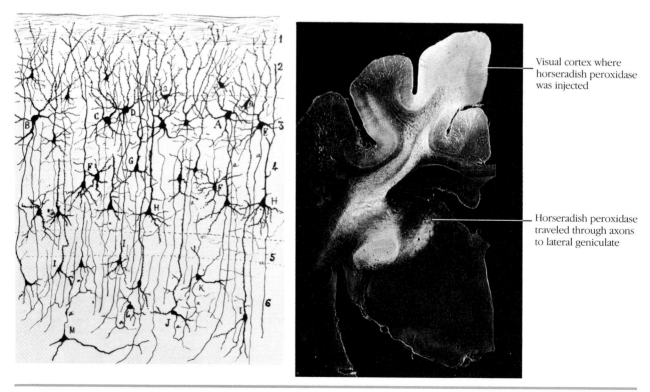

Visual cortex where horseradish peroxidase was injected

Horseradish peroxidase traveled through axons to lateral geniculate

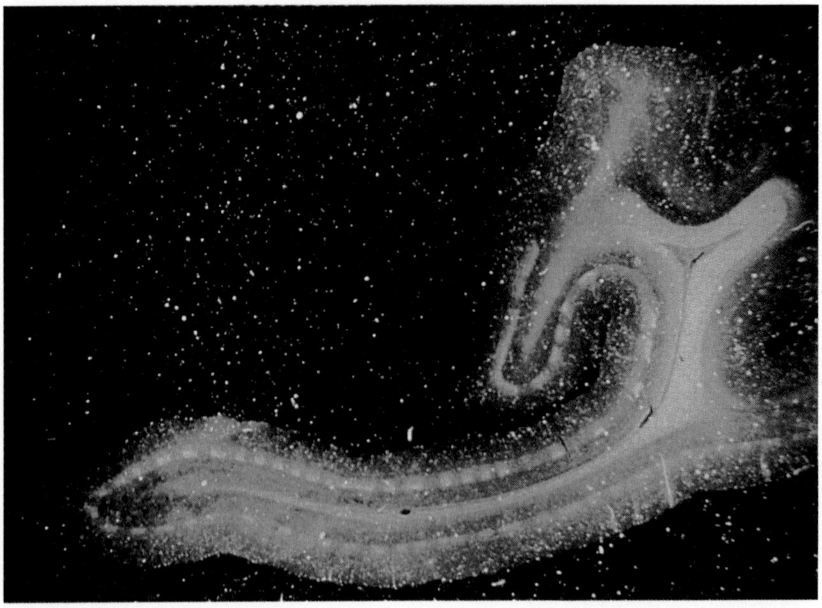

Figure 2–10 Radioactive amino acid injected into a monkey's right eye traveled through neurons to his visual cortex. A slice of this cortex was placed on photographic film for several months to produce this autoradiograph. The lighter bands indicate neurons containing the radioactive amino acids from the right eye, which affected the film. The alternate dark bands indicate neurons associated with the left eye. (Courtesy Dr. David H. Hubel, Harvard Medical School)

kingdom (elephants and porpoises have larger brains) nor even the highest brain-weight-to-total-weight ratio (it is about 1:50 in humans, but 1:20 in certain monkeys). There is no need, though, to feel overly humble. The human brain has somewhere between 10^{10} and 10^{11} neurons, or between 10 billion and 100 billion—as many as there are stars in our galaxy!

Development of the Nervous System

Even more remarkable, just about all these neurons are present in the human brain at birth—and all grow from the single cell that is the fertilized ovum. That means that brain-cell formation during the nine months of fetal life must proceed at an average rate of 250,000 per minute! Of course, the rate of cell formation is not the same throughout development, because cells increase in number geometrically rather than arithmetically—one cell becomes two, two become four, and so on. Looking at it this way, it only takes about 36 generations of neurons to complete the human brain, or one division every seven or eight days during gestation.

In recent years it has been discovered that in many regions of the brain far more neurons are originally generated than eventually survive. Many seem to die during critical periods of development. Furthermore, there is evidence that sensory input to the developing brain determines in part which particular neurons survive. For example, certain cells in a mouse's brain have been shown to receive sensory input from certain whiskers on its nose. These brain cells develop differently depending on the stimulation received by the whiskers (Figure 2–11). The more a particular whisker is stimulated, the more brain cells associated with that whisker will survive. The survival of cells in the developing visual system has also been shown to depend partially on visual stimulation (Hirsch & Spenelli, 1970).

This sort of evidence has led to a growing belief that the kind of stimulation—or lack of stimulation—newborns and infants receive can affect the development of their nervous systems. For example, children whose

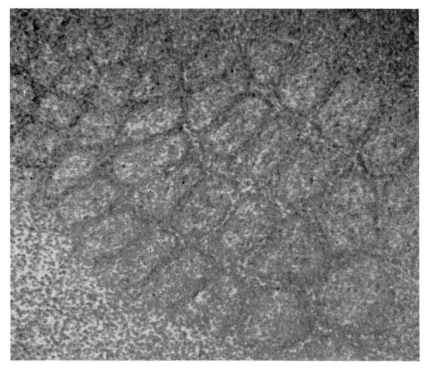

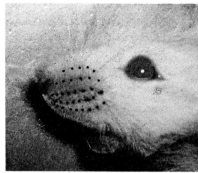

Figure 2–11 The photo of a mouse's snout shows how the animal's whiskers are arranged in rows. The blue-green stained tissue from the sensory area of a mouse's brain reveals corresponding rows of brain cells. The same thing (rows of whiskers and clusters of brain cells) is shown in drawing (a). Drawing (b) shows how removal of one row of whiskers from a newborn mouse's snout results in a subsequent loss of a row of cortical cells as the mouse develops. (Photos: Blakemore, C. *Mechanics of the mind.* Cambridge, Eng.: Cambridge University Press, 1977.)

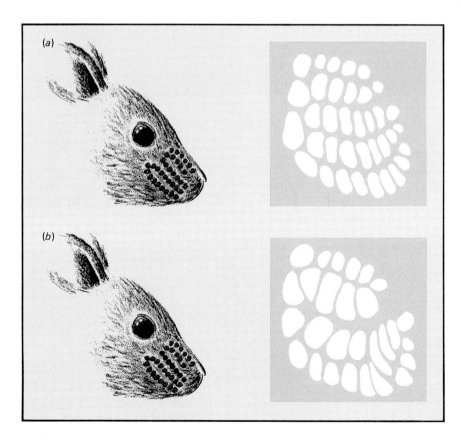

hearing mechanism doesn't work properly early in life may suffer irreversible damage to those areas of their brain that process sounds, even if the hearing mechanism itself is repaired later in life. This is why surgeons have begun to perform certain types of corrective ear (and eye) surgery on infants, when previously they preferred to wait until the children were older and more sturdy. This is also the reason for growing concern about providing adequate stimulation for institutionalized infants who might spend too much time alone in a crib.

Growth of the Brain After Birth. Approximately nine months after conception, neurons in the human nervous system lose their ability to divide. Unlike most other cells in the body, neurons that die are not replaced. (Outside the central nervous system, however, an axon that is severed may be regenerated if the cell body remains intact.) Despite the fact that no new neurons are formed after birth, the brain continues to grow from about 350 grams in a newborn infant to about 1,400 grams at puberty. This quadrupling in weight is partly due to an increase in the size of individual cells. In addition, the axons of many cells gradually grow a multilayered jacket of insulation made up of fatty cells called **myelin.** Since the transmission of neural impulses is as much as 20 times faster in myelinated fibers, the process of myelination is essential to the maturation of the nervous system. About half the cells in the nervous system eventually acquire a myelin sheath.

Probably the most important factor in the brain's growth in size during childhood is the proliferation of a second kind of brain cell, the **glial cell.** Unlike neurons, glial cells continue to divide; by adulthood they are ten times as numerous as neurons. When a neuron dies, a glial cell grows to fill the gap.

Glial cells were once thought to serve primarily to hold the neurons together ("glial" comes from a Greek word meaning "sticky oil"). Now it is known that they have several other functions. They are responsible for the myelination of axons in the brain; they direct the growth of neuronal pathways or interconnections; and they play a general role in nervous system metabolism.

We have said that no new neurons are formed after fetal development. But parts of them are continuously being replaced as they wear out or are used up. In a neuron all replacement parts are manufactured in the cell body and must be transported from there to wherever they are needed. A slow-moving system known as **axonal transport** carries the new cellular components down the axon to their destination. Cells in the brain are no more than a few centimeters in length, but in the peripheral nervous system—where an axon may extend more than a meter from its cell body—it may take weeks for the replacement parts to reach their intended site.

How Neurons Work

The most important property of neurons is their ability to carry information from one place to another. This information is in the form of **nerve impulses,** which travel along the neuron, normally from the dendrite or cell body out to the ends of the axon. The passage of nerve impulses can be recorded by inserting a tiny, needlelike electrical contact (microelectrode) into the liquid-filled interior of the neuron. Since only the tip of the needle is not insulated, we can measure the difference in electrical potential between the inside and outside of the cell. The electrical potential is meas-

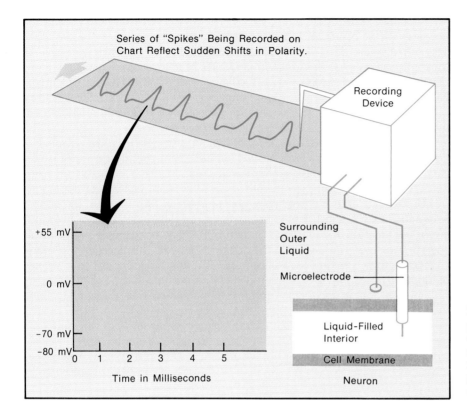

Series of "Spikes" Being Recorded on Chart Reflect Sudden Shifts in Polarity.

Recording Device

Surrounding Outer Liquid

Microelectrode

Liquid-Filled Interior

Cell Membrane

Neuron

+55 mV

0 mV

-70 mV
-80 mV

0   1   2   3   4   5

Time in Milliseconds

Figure 2–12 Recording nerve impulses. Detail shows the specific sequence of voltage changes of one nerve impulse over time. Each nerve impulse appears as a "spike" on the graph produced by the recording device.

ured in millivolts (mV). Figure 2–12 shows how the normally negative (about −70 mV) interior of the neuron periodically goes positive (about 55 mV). The normal negative state is called the neuron's **resting potential,** while each brief reversal of electric charge or *polarity* is a nerve impulse or **action potential.** One of the action potentials in Figure 2–12 is shown spread out in time to reveal more of its detail. Notice that after each positive phase or "spike" the potential of the interior of the neuron falls, becoming even more negative (about −80 mV) before returning to the resting potential.

What causes the sequence of electrical changes during an action potential? Basically, the successive opening and closing of microscopic channels in the "skin" or membrane of the neuron allow electrically charged ions to flow in and out. Ions are molecules that have lost (positive ions) or gained (negative ions) electrons. Large negative ions called *organic anions* (A^-) are produced within the neuron and remain there because they are too big to pass out through the membrane. Other smaller ions, such as the positive sodium (Na^+) and the positive potassium (K^+), can sometimes pass through the membrane. Normally a process called the *ionic pump* keeps the inside of the neuron about ten times richer in potassium (K^+) ions than sodium (Na^+) ions, with this ratio just about reversed on the outside. A neuron's resting potential reflects the distribution of ions produced by the ionic pump, as well as the negative anions (A^-) trapped inside. (The inside is about −70 mV with respect to the outside.)

An action potential is triggered at a particular point on the membrane if the resting potential is sufficiently reduced at that point (e.g., by direct electrical stimulation). The action potential begins when microscopic sodium channels in the membrane suddenly open for about 1 millisecond. This al-

lows *positive sodium (Na⁺) ions to flow in,* quickly reversing the polarity of the neuron (the inside becomes about + 55 mV with respect to the outside). This immediately causes other potassium channels to open for 1 or 2 milliseconds, allowing *positive potassium (K⁺) ions to flow out,* leaving the interior even more negative (−80 mV) than it was at first. Finally, with both types of channels closed, the ionic pump restores the normal resting potential (−70 mV) by pushing sodium (Na⁺) ions out and potassium (K⁺) ions inside. The whole sequence takes only 4 or 5 milliseconds.

An important feature of the action potential is its **all-or-none property:** Once the sodium channels open, the entire electrochemical sequence occurs. Furthermore, when the sodium channels close and the potassium channels open, it is impossible to initiate a second action potential (at that point on the neuron) until the potassium channels close. This is called the **absolute refractory period.** It is possible, but more difficult, to trigger a second action potential during the period when both types of channels have closed and the ionic pump is restoring the resting potential. This is called the **relative refractory period** (see Figure 2–13). These refractory periods limit the number of nerve impulses a neuron can transmit in a fixed period of time (i.e., pulses per second), since some minimum time must elapse between successive pulses.

Why do nerve impulses seem to travel along a neuron? If an action potential occurs at one point, it triggers off another action potential next to itself, which in turn triggers another one next to itself, and so on. The whole series moves like a wave along the neuron. A new action potential is triggered only

Figure 2–13 The electrical changes that occur during an action potential (top) correspond to chemical changes (bottom) as shown here. The beginning of a spike occurs when the interior of the neuron abruptly becomes positive (+ 55mV), with respect to the outside. This corresponds to a sudden influx of sodium (Na) ions. This in turn triggers an outflow of potassium (K) ions, which causes the interior to become even more negative (−80mV) than it was at first. Finally, the interior returns to its original negative resting potential (−70mV) as the normal balance of ions is restored by the ionic pump. (Adapted from McFarland, R. A. *Physiological psychology.* Palo Alto, Calif.: Mayfield, 1981.)

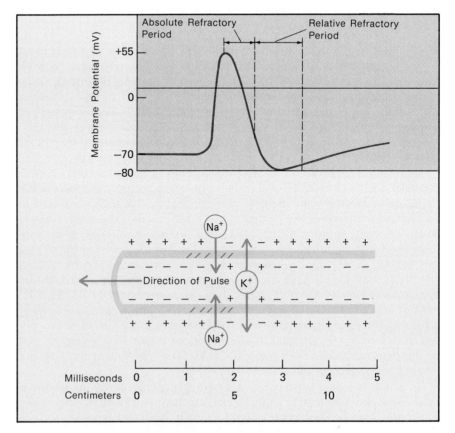

in front of the traveling nerve impulse because the region just behind it is still in its absolute refractory period. This, then, is how information, in the form of nerve impulses (waves of action potentials), is carried along a neuron.

While nerve impulses travel faster along thicker axons, really rapid travel occurs only along axons that are partially enclosed and insulated by a fatty substance called myelin. Action potentials on myelinated neurons only occur at unenclosed junctions called **nodes,** between these fatty cells. Nodes are found every 1 or 2 millimeters along the axon. When an action potential occurs at one junction (node), it quickly triggers one at the next junction, instead of moving continuously along the axon, as it does in the absence of the myelin (see Figure 2–14). This rapid jumping from node to node along a myelinated neuron is called **saltatory conduction** (*saltation* means "leaping"). Thus, depending on the thickness and myelination of a neuron, its speed of information transmission varies from about ⅓ to 120 meters per second.

Until now we have considered only how a nerve impulse, once triggered, moves along a neuron. We shall now consider how this triggering normally occurs and how the information traveling along one neuron is carried over to another.

Synaptic Transmission

Nerve impulses traveling along one neuron affect the activity of other neurons at points of interaction called **synapses.** These normally occur where the axon of one neuron terminates on the dendrite or cell body of another. Here a nerve impulse (action potential) reaching the end of its axon can trigger an impulse in another neuron. In this way, information can be relayed from neuron to neuron. However, this is really too simple a picture of the interactions between neurons. Although they can relay information in this simple fashion, they often do far more. They combine, modify, transform, and process information in ways that we are only just beginning to understand and that are far more complex than the internal mechanism of the most advanced electronic computer. While much of this complexity need not be considered in a course on introductory psychology, some appreciation of it seems appropriate. In particular, we should be aware of the variety of ways in which one neuron can affect another and of the chemical nature of this interaction.

Figure 2–15 shows how the axons of many neurons (sometimes hundreds) can form synapses with a single neuron. Each point where the knobby ending of an axon (*synaptic knob*) contacts the neuron is an individual synapse. Between each synaptic knob and the other neuron is a very narrow (about 2 billionths of a meter), fluid-filled gap called the **synaptic cleft.** The arrival of an action potential causes the synaptic knob to release chemicals into the synaptic cleft. Those chemicals that are taken up by the other neuron so as to directly increase (*excitatory synapse*) or decrease (*inhibitory synapse*) the likelihood of an action potential are called **neurotransmitters.**

While at first it was believed that there was only one kind of neurotransmitter, *acetylcholine,* it is now clear that there are many. Most neurons manufacture a particular type of neurotransmitter that is stored within each synaptic knob in microscopic containers called *vesicles.* Figure 2–16 shows

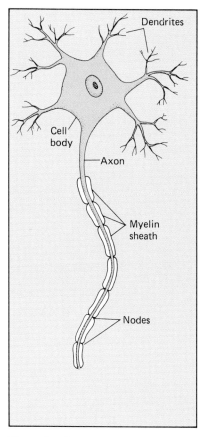

Figure 2–14 Segments of a fatty substance called myelin enclose and electrically insulate most axons. Within the myelinated segments the nerve impulse travels as fast as an electric current. Only at the gaps between myelin segments (nodes of Ranvier) does the slower action potential occur. Thus the action potential seems to jump (saltate) from node to node along the axon.

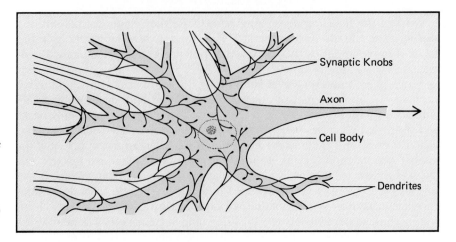

Figure 2–15 Synapses between the axons of many other neurons and the cell body and dendrites of a single neuron. The numerous synaptic knobs are the terminals of the axons of other neurons. Note that the axon of this single neuron (shown at right) will in turn synapse with another neuron.

how an action potential causes some vesicles to release neurotransmitters into the synaptic cleft. These can be taken up at specific *receptor sites* on the other neuron and affect that neuron's activity. Each neurotransmitter fits like a "key" into a specific receptor site "lock." This whole process is called **synaptic transmission.**

Synaptic transmission occurs in less than half a millisecond at some "fast synapses," with any excess neurotransmitter quickly broken down or reabsorbed into the synaptic knob (a process known as *reuptake*). The entire sequence can occur again within a few milliseconds. Thus many action potentials can be evoked by repeated synaptic transmission in a very short time. In contrast, synaptic transmission between some neurons may take a second or more to occur, with a slow breakdown and reabsorption of excess neurotransmitter. These "slow synapses" provide another means of communication between neurons that is not completely understood.

Our bodies also produce chemicals that can influence synaptic transmission without actually serving as neurotransmitters. These chemicals are

Figure 2–16 A single synaptic knob of an axon is shown on the dendrite of another neuron prior to synaptic transmission. Inside the synaptic knob are vesicles or sacs containing neurotransmitter. During an action potential some of these vesicles release neurotransmitter into the synaptic cleft. The detail shows how a filled vesicle successively (1) makes contact with the presynaptic membrane, (2) empties its neurotransmitter into the cleft, and (3) moves back into the synaptic knob, where it can again become filled with neurotransmitter.

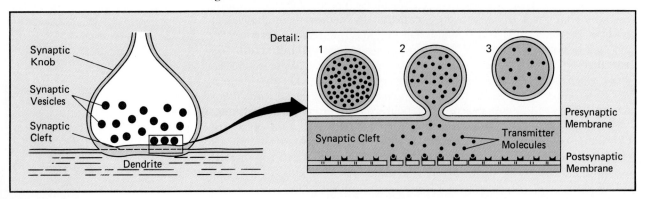

called **neuromodulators** (some of which may also serve as neurotransmitters in certain locations). Neuromodulators are sometimes produced outside the nervous system and carried to it by the blood—for example, the hormones estrogen and testosterone produced by the endocrine system. Others are released by neurons but act as neuromodulators rather than neurotransmitters. For example, enkephalins released by interneurons in our spine seem to block the transmission of pain signals at certain synaptic junctions (see the Highlight on endorphins).

Our knowledge of neurotransmitters and neuromodulators has grown rapidly in the last ten years, yet we are still a long way from fully understanding their complex role. What is clear is the degree to which these complex neurochemical processes can be altered by subtle changes in our body chemistry.

Effects of Chemicals on Neurotransmission

Chemicals can influence neurotransmission in a wide variety of ways. Those that block or inhibit the normal effect of synaptic transmission are called *antagonists,* those that facilitate it are called *agonists.* (The Greek word *agon* means "contest.")

Every synapse between an axon and the cell membrane of a muscle employs the neurotransmitter **acetylcholine (ACh).** Thus a substance that interferes with the action of ACh (an antagonist) can prevent nerve impulses from crossing these synapses and therefore can produce paralysis. If the paralysis involves the muscles used in breathing, the results can be fatal. The deadly effects of *Botulinus* toxin come about in precisely this way, by blocking the release of ACh. (Botulinus toxin is sometimes present in improperly canned foods; it can be destroyed if the food is boiled for 5 minutes before eating.)

Other poisons block the uptake of ACh by the postsynaptic membrane; these include curare and cobra venom. Still others, such as the venom of the black widow spider and certain nerve gases developed for chemical warfare (agonists), prevent the breakdown of ACh, prolonging its action and causing convulsions.

Norepinephrine (NE) is a neurotransmitter released by neurons whose firing causes a general activation of various body systems. The stimulant *amphetamine* is an agonist since it stimulates the release of NE and blocks its breakdown in the synaptic cleft, as does the stimulant *cocaine.* Thus both drugs produce a highly activated, wide-awake state. In contrast, the drug *reserpine* is an antagonist since it causes the vesicles to "leak" norepinephrine before the action potential, allowing the NE to be broken down. It is often used as a relaxant to combat hypertension (high blood pressure).

Dopamine is a neurotransmitter closely related to norepinephrine and is affected in a similar fashion by the drugs reserpine and amphetamine. Abnormalities in neurons releasing dopamine are related to Parkinson's disease (see Highlight on neurotransmitters, brain disorders, and brain grafts). They may also be involved in the serious mental illness schizophrenia. The antipsychotic *chlorpromazine* seems to block dopamine receptors in the brain (it is a dopamine antagonist) and reduces symptoms of schizophrenia.

Serotonin is the neurotransmitter that seems to be affected by the "mind-bending" (hallucinogenic) drug LSD (*lysergic acid*). LSD acts as an antagonist of serotonin by increasing the activity of neurons in the brain that are normally inhibited by that neurotransmitter.

HIGHLIGHT _____

Endorphins: The Body's Own Painkillers

Over the last decade it was determined that chemicals produced within the body, called **endorphins,** are intimately involved with our sensitivity to pain. The manner in which successive findings led to this conclusion is a kind of scientific detective story that illustrates the often rapid and exciting interplay of experimentation and conjecture in modern neuroscience.

In 1973 several researchers (e.g., Pert & Snyder, 1973) published studies showing that certain regions of the brain and spinal cord are particularly sensitive to opiates such as morphine, the analgesic (painkilling) drug derived from the opium poppy. Fragments of neural tissue taken from

these regions were shown to bind with (take up) radioactively labeled opiate compounds. Thus these regions of the nervous system appeared to be *opiate receptor sites*—that is, regions where opiates were taken up or received by the system. It was also noted that many of these same regions were known to be involved in the perception of pain by humans and other mammals.

Why should the nervous system have receptor sites for exotic foreign **(exogenous)** substances such as the opiate morphine? Suspicion grew that these sites normally function as receptors for internally produced **(endogenous)** chemicals similar to the exogenous opiates. Supporting this conjecture was evidence that electrical stimulation of certain sites in the brain reduced the perception of pain in ways quite similar to that of opiates. For example:

1. Both electrical stimulation and opiates caused neural signals to be

sent along the same pathways from the brain to the spinal cord, where they blocked the transmission of pain signals.
2. Sites where electrical stimulation reduced pain were also found to be opiate receptor sites (Pert, Kuhar, & Snyder, 1976).
3. The analgesic effect of electrical stimulation is at least partially blocked by the *opiate antagonist* naloxone.

All this could readily be explained if the electrical stimulation caused the release of endogenous opiates that were then picked up by the same receptors that picked up morphine. Sure enough, in 1975 scientists in Scotland isolated endogenous brain chemicals that would bind tightly to opiate receptors and could be blocked by naloxone (Hughes, Smith, Kosterlitz, Fothergill, Morgan, & Morris, 1975). They named these chemicals *enkephalins* (based on Greek words meaning "in the head"). Within a year other scientists had identified another group of endogenous, opiatelike substances they named *endorphins* (a contraction of *endogenous* and *morphine*). Most people now think of enkephalin as simply a particular type of endorphin.

Once the existence of these endogenous opiatelike substances was established, the next question was whether they had analgesic effects similar to those of morphine. The first answers to this question came from experiments on rats. The tail-flick test is a commonly used measure of pain sensitivity in rats. It measures the speed with which a rat will move or flick its tail when a hot beam of light is focused on the tail. Even low dosages of morphine cause measurable decreases in the speed of tail flicking. This seems to reflect the analgesic effect of the morphine. Several experiments established that injections of endorphins—either directly into the brain (Jacquet & Marks, 1976) or into

The light spots on this autoradiograph of a rat's brain indicate opiate receptors.

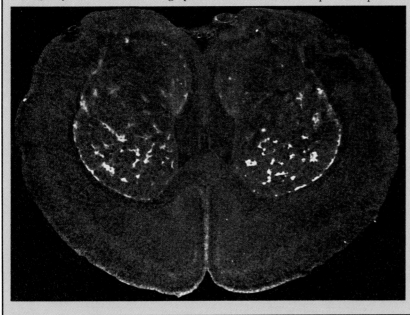

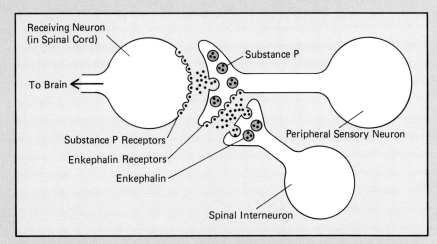

Receiving Neuron (in Spinal Cord)

To Brain

Substance P

Substance P Receptors

Enkephalin Receptors

Enkephalin

Peripheral Sensory Neuron

Spinal Interneuron

Regulation or "gating" of pain information takes place at synapses in the spinal cord. The neurotransmitter *substance* P is carried in the axon of pain neurons. At the synapse these axons encounter *enkephalin,* the neurotransmitter released by interneurons. Enkephalin appears to control or modulate the release of substance P, so that the receiving neuron that sends pain impulses to the brain actually is receiving less substance P and therefore less pain information. Thus enkephalin acts as a *neuromodulator*.

the bloodstream (Tseng, Loh, & Li, 1976)—produced similar analgesic effects on rats and that this analgesia could be blocked by the opiate antagonist naloxone. Furthermore, the analgesic effect of the endorphins was reduced in rats that had earlier developed tolerance to morphine.

Endorphins seem to play a role in regulating the transmission of pain information from peripheral pain receptors to the brain. This regulation or "gating" of pain information occurs in the spinal cord, as illustrated in the figure. Peripheral pain neurons send signals into the spinal cord; there they form synapses with neurons leading upward toward the brain. The excitatory neurotransmitter at these synapses is believed to be a chemical known as *substance P*. It has been shown that endorphin can block the release of substance P from sensory neurons. It has been demonstrated that endorphin is present in interneurons (neurons intervening between sensory and motor neurons)

that form synapses with the axon terminals of the peripheral pain neurons. We saw above that both morphine and electrical brain stimulation cause neural signals to be sent from the brain to the spinal cord, where they block transmission of pain signals to the brain. It appears that they do this through the release of endorphins, which bock the release of substance P from the peripheral pain axon—that is, endorphins act as *neuromodulators*.

While there is much current speculation concerning the exact role of the endogenous opiates in normal body function, the picture is far from complete. They sometimes function quite locally at specific synaptic junctions as neurotransmitters or neuromodulators, and other times more globally, affecting whole systems of neurons. One of the most interesting conjectures is that they reduce our sensitivity to pain so that we can continue to function in highly stressful circumstances. One research

strategy employed to test this idea has been to see whether experimentally induced "stress" produces temporary analgesia. For example, Madden and colleagues (1977) reported that after 30 minutes of discontinuous electric shock, rats showed increased levels of endogenous opiates and slower responses on the tail- flick test of analgesia. Similarly, Miller (1981) showed that humans exposed to repeated foot shocks had temporarily higher pain thresholds and that this temporary analgesia could be blocked by naloxone. Yet the results of other studies have been mixed. This may be because something as complex as "stress" is difficult to define and also because some "painful" stimuli may involve nonopiate pain-control systems (Watkins & Mayer, 1982).

In any case, research on this fascinating topic continues, along with conjecture. For example, it has been shown that a runner's endorphin level rises during a long-distance race (Colt, Wardlaw, & Frantz, 1981). Also, it appears that strenuous exercise increases endorphin levels and that this increase is even greater with regular physical training. Does this mean that the exhilaration and freedom from pain reported by long-distance runners, the so-called runner's high, is caused by the release of endogenous opiates? Do runners become "addicted" to this "high," needing more and more endogenous opiates as their tolerance to them increases? Do they experience something akin to "withdrawal symptoms" when they are unable to run? Given what we know now, these are reasonable and intriguing questions.

It seems likely that some other endogenous chemicals also act much like familiar drugs. In the Highlight on endogenous benzodiazepines in Chapter 5, for example, we will examine endogenous chemicals that seem to act like the tranquilizers Librium and Valium.

Organization of the Nervous System

It is useful to consider the nervous system in terms of the hierarchical organization shown in Figure 2–17. The first major division is between the **central nervous system** (CNS), which consists of all those neurons completely within the brain or spinal cord; and the **peripheral nervous system,** which consists of all the other neurons.

The sensory neurons of the peripheral system carry information toward the CNS, which is why they are sometimes called *afferent neurons* (from the Latin *ad,* or "toward," and *ferre,* or "to carry"). The motor neurons carry information away from the CNS and are sometimes called *efferent neurons* (from the Latin *ex,* or "away from," and *ferre*).

The peripheral nervous system can be further divided into the **somatic nervous system,** whose sensory and motor components control the movements of our skeletal muscles—for example, the movements of our arms and legs. Other sensory components of the somatic system carry information to the CNS from receptor organs throughout our body.

The **autonomic nervous system** controls *smooth muscles* (so named to distinguish them from the "striated" or striped skeletal muscles). These include muscles in the stomach, heart, blood vessels, and gut. The autonomic nervous system itself has two major components: the **parasympathetic nervous system,** whose actions generally conserve energy; and the **sympathetic nervous system,** whose generally opposite actions tend to expend energy. (We shall discuss the autonomic nervous system in some detail later in this chapter.)

Figure 2–17 A schematic drawing of the hierarchical organization of the nervous system. The first division is between the central nervous system and the peripheral nervous system. The peripheral nervous system divides further into sensory and motor classes of neurons. Interneurons can be found connecting neurons in all parts of the nervous system, particularly the central nervous system.

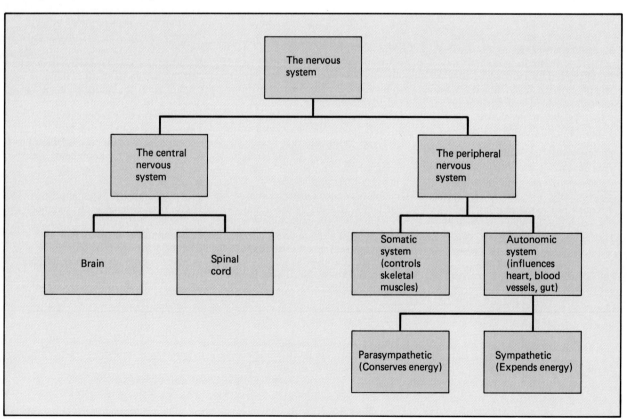

Outside the central nervous system neurons are generally collected into **nerves,** which are bundles of parallel fibers covered by membrane. Nerves from the head and neck enter the central nervous system directly into the brain; these are the 12 pairs of *cranial nerves.* Those from below the neck enter the spinal cord as *spinal nerves.* Perhaps the best known nerve is the one that rudely announces its presence when you hit your so-called funny bone. It is the ulnar nerve, which passes close to the surface at the outside of the elbow.

Most nerves contain a mix of sensory and motor fibers. However, the fibers of the spinal nerves are sorted out before they enter the spinal cord. Sensory fibers enter from the back or dorsal side, forming the *dorsal root;* motor fibers enter from the front or ventral side, forming the *ventral root.*

Peripheral nerves are composed primarily of axons. A somatic motor neuron, for example, has its cell body within the spinal cord and sends out one extremely long axon that may reach all the way to the toe. In the autonomic motor system, on the other hand, the (generally shorter) journey is made in two or three stages: One axon leaves the spinal cord and forms a synapse with another cell, which either goes the rest of the way or synapses with a third cell. The many neurons that make up an autonomic nerve all have their cell bodies in the same place—within a ganglion, visible as a bulge on the nerve. Peripheral sensory nerves have their cell bodies clustered in ganglia located just outside the spinal cord.

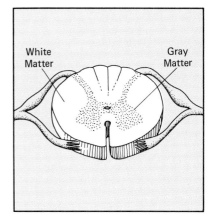

Figure 2–18 The drawing shows a cross section of the spinal cord, indicating the white and gray matter.

The Spinal Cord

This column of neural tissue, only about 2 centimeters in diameter, runs downward from the brain through the hollow bones of the spine like a thread through a string of beads. A cross section of the **spinal cord** (see Figure 2–18) shows two areas that differ somewhat in appearance: a butterfly-shaped area of "gray matter" in the middle, surrounded by "white matter." The grayish area consists mostly of cell bodies; the whitish area, of myelinated axons that carry neural impulses upward, downward, or across the cord.

The spinal cord has two major jobs: to carry information back and forth between the body and the brain and to provide the necessary connections between the sensory and motor neurons involved in **spinal reflexes.** These are automatic motor responses to stimulation that don't involve neurons in the brain.

During a physical examination your leg may be struck with a rubber hammer just below the kneecap. Unless you inhibit it by tensing your muscles, your leg swings up in the familiar "knee-jerk" reflex. This is a good example of the simplest kind of reflex: the *monosynaptic reflex arc.* The doctor's hammer strikes a tendon that pulls a muscle and causes it to stretch. The movement fires sensory neurons that go from the muscle all the way to the spinal cord. In the spinal cord the sensory neurons synapse directly onto motor neurons, which lead back to the knee. Thus the impulses received in the spinal cord are "reflected" right back to the muscle, causing it to contract. Figure 2–19 shows the neural pathway of the knee-jerk reflex.

Because the knee-jerk reflex is so easily tested, it serves as a ready, if rough, measure of nervous system health. It is one of a large number of reflexes that make it possible to stand and walk erect. Such reflexes enable you to keep your balance when, for example, someone pushes down unexpectedly on your shoulders or knocks you sideward.

Figure 2–19 The neural pathway through the spinal cord of the knee-jerk reflex, a monosynaptic reflex arc.

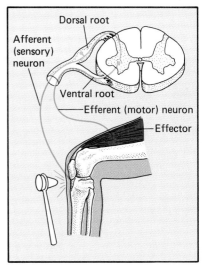

Few reflexes, however, are as simple as the knee-jerk. Most involve at least one additional neuron, an interneuron. For instance, when you touch something that is hot and your hand withdraws automatically, the sensory neurons from the finger carry the message to the spinal cord. The message to the arm to withdraw the hand comes out of a *different* level of the spinal cord. To transmit the signal from the sensory neuron at one level to the motor neuron on another, at least one more neuron—and one more synapse—are required. Interneurons are also needed whenever the reflex crosses the spinal cord to the opposite side of the body. If you're barefoot and you step on something sharp, not only does the hurt foot withdraw, but the *other* leg stiffens so that you won't fall down.

The signals from the burnt hand or the hurt foot do not stop at the spinal cord. They continue upward to the brain. Only when the message gets to the brain do you become aware of the sensation of pain—by which time your hand or foot has already jerked back. A person whose spinal cord is severed in an accident cannot feel any stimulation from the areas of the body innervated (supplied with nerves) by the part of the spinal cord below the break. Yet many reflexes remain intact because they do not involve neurons in the brain.

THE BRAIN

Although the brain makes up only 2 or 2.5 percent of the weight of an adult human body, its rich supply of blood vessels furnishes it with about a fifth of the body's circulating blood. It uses a fifth of the body's supply of glucose (blood sugar), and a fifth of its oxygen. If the supply of oxygen is cut off for only 7 or 8 seconds, unconsciousness results; after 1 minute neurons start to degenerate. The same results follow if the supply of glucose is cut off—for example, by an overdose of insulin.

The interior portions of the brain have an additional circulatory system. This is the series of interconnected hollows (ventricles) that are filled with *cerebrospinal fluid,* a plasmalike liquid that aids in the nourishment of brain tissue and the disposal of wastes. The fluid also surrounds the CNS, supporting and protecting it. For example, it usually keeps the brain from hitting against the bones of the skull when you receive a blow to the head. However, very strong or repeated blows, such as those received by a boxer, produce brain damage.

Removed from its protective bony case and deprived of its blood supply, the surface of the brain is grayish in color. This is the **gray matter** or **cerebral cortex,** which forms a coating 2 or 3 millimeters thick over most of the outside of the human brain. It is composed chiefly of cell bodies. Underneath is the **white matter,** composed primarily of myelinated axon fibers.

Almost everything that is visible in the intact brain is **cerebrum** (see Figure 2–20). The two hemispheres of the cerebrum, with their wrinkled wrapping of cerebral cortex, resemble the two connected halves of a walnut meat. Poking out from beneath the rear of the cerebrum is the **cerebellum,** with an even more heavily convoluted surface.

Extending downward from between the **cerebral hemispheres** is the lower portion of the **brain stem,** which continues through a hole in the base of the skull and becomes the spinal cord. There is no clear-cut separation between the top of the spinal cord and the bottom of the brain; as in many other brain areas, the transition is gradual. But something very important is happening during that transition. Most of the fibers coming from the

Neurotransmitters, Brain Disorders, and Brain Grafts

When it comes to synaptic transmission in the brain, the neurotransmitter situation is incredibly complicated. Dozens of substances are involved, with different transmitters used in different brain areas and for different functions.

In order for the brain to function normally, the proper neurotransmitter must be produced in the proper synapse at just the right time; this substance must be received by the postsynaptic cell and then be inactivated soon enough so that it will not interfere with the next transmission, but not *too* soon. Given the complexity of the process, it is not surprising that things sometimes go wrong.

Two neurological disorders that have been traced to malfunctions of neurotransmission are Parkinson's disease and Huntington's chorea. **Parkinson's disease** is characterized by tremors and muscular rigidity (especially of the face) and by difficulty in making voluntary movements. This disorder has been traced to a deficiency of dopamine in certain parts of the brain.

Huntington's chorea is a hereditary disease that first appears in middle age. It is characterized by jerky, uncoordinated motions of the face and body and by progressive mental deterioration. A deficiency of the neurotransmitter GABA is believed to be responsible. Huntington's chorea is carried by a dominant gene, so that each child of an affected individual has a 50 percent chance of developing the disease.

You might think that such disorders can be treated simply by supplying the missing substances. This is not always possible, however, because of the **blood-brain barrier.** Nature has evolved a system for protecting the brain from toxic substances that might reach it through its rich supply of blood vessels. Blood vessels in the brain are less permeable than in other parts of the body; in addition, they are closely surrounded by glial cells. Only certain substances, such as oxygen, carbon dioxide, and glucose (blood sugar), can pass through this mesh. Large molecules are generally not able to get through, unless they are soluble in the fatty membranes of the glial cells. Thus neither dopamine nor GABA can enter the brain directly from the bloodstream. For dopamine, an alternative has been found: A chemical called L-DOPA, which is metabolized into dopamine in the brain, does pass through the blood-brain barrier. L-DOPA has been used successfully in the treatment of Parkinson's disease. (Unfortunately, no metabolic precursor of GABA has yet been found that will penetrate the brain; thus there is still no effective treatment for Huntington's chorea.)

An even more exciting way of increasing dopamine production may now be possible using a technique based on earlier work with rats (Wuerthele, Freed, Olson, Morihisa, Spoor, Wyatt, & Hoffer, 1981) In 1980, Swedish neurologists transplanted dopamine-producing cells from the adrenal glands of elderly Parkinsonian patients into the dopamine-deficient area of their brains (Bjorkland, Dunnet, Stenevi, Lewis, & Ivenson, 1980) (Wyatt & Freed, 1985). Because the body's immune system works through the bloodstream, the blood-brain barrier prevented the transplanted brain tissue from being rejected by the body. It was hoped that the transplanted tissue would produce enough dopamine in its new site to relieve the patient's symptoms. The observations were not completely successful but the results were encouraging. Very recently, a team of Mexican doctors (Madrazo, Drucher-Colin et al., 1987) performed several operations similar to the ones done by the Swedes. However, there were two major differences in their procedure: the patients were considerably younger; and they grafted the cells onto a slightly different brain location where they are bathed in cerebrospinal fluid. This latter difference may be important in distributing the effects of the dopamine. The Mexican team has reported dramatic initial success. Two patients who had been previously confined to wheel chairs and had little ability to speak were both walking and speaking clearly a few months after their operations. If these results are long-lasting and can be repeated, they open up a whole realm of new possibilities. Since so much of the brain's activity is chemical in nature, it may be possible to transplant specific chemical-producing cells without concern for the precise synaptic connections. This would be, in effect, a kind of **brain graft.**

This autoradiograph (see Figure 2–10) shows how a neuron (pale yellow-green) from a rat embryo has begun to grow branching fibers after being transplanted into the brain of an adult rat.

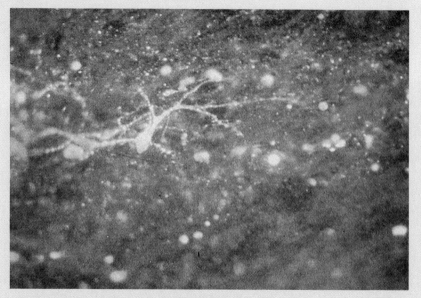

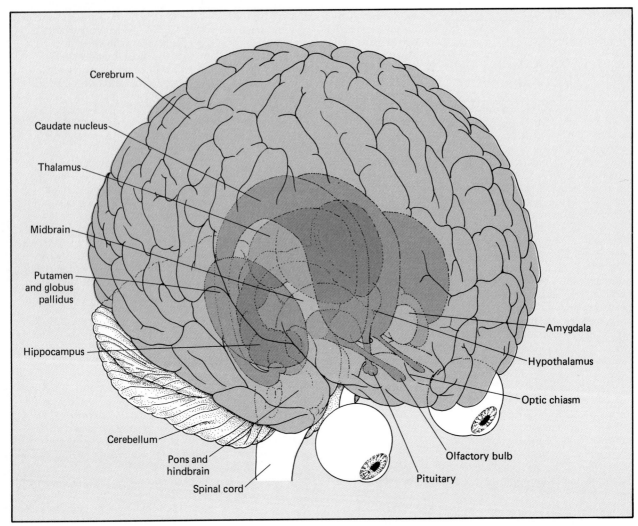

Cerebrum

Caudate nucleus

Thalamus

Midbrain

Putamen
and globus
pallidus

Hippocampus

Cerebellum

Pons and
hindbrain

Spinal cord

Amygdala

Hypothalamus

Optic chiasm

Olfactory bulb

Pituitary

Figure 2–20 An interior view of the basic components of the human brain. The cerebrum is split visibly into two hemispheres. The corpus callosum, which connects the two hemispheres, is located just above the thalamus at the base of the crevice between the two hemispheres.

(From Nauta, W.J.H., & Feirtag, M. The organization of the brain. Copy © 1979 by Scientific American, Inc. All rights reserved.)

left side of the spinal cord are crossing over to the right, and vice versa. The left side of the spinal cord serves the left side of the body, but in the brain there is a reversal of this pattern. For reasons that may always remain a mystery, *the left side of the brain controls the right side of the body, and the right side controls the left side of the body.* Thus when a person suffers a stroke and develops paralysis in the left hand or the left side of the face, physicians know that the damage (usually caused by a blocked blood vessel) occurred in the right side of the brain. Fortunately, some recovery of function is usually possible, since unaffected brain areas may take over certain functions of the dead neurons.

The Organization of the Brain

Neuroanatomists generally divide the brain into three parts: hindbrain, midbrain, and forebrain. In the adult human being, however, this division makes little sense because almost everything is forebrain, and most of the rest is hindbrain (see Figure 2–21 and Table 2–1 on the next page). The three divisions arose from structures that serve separate functions in simpler ver-

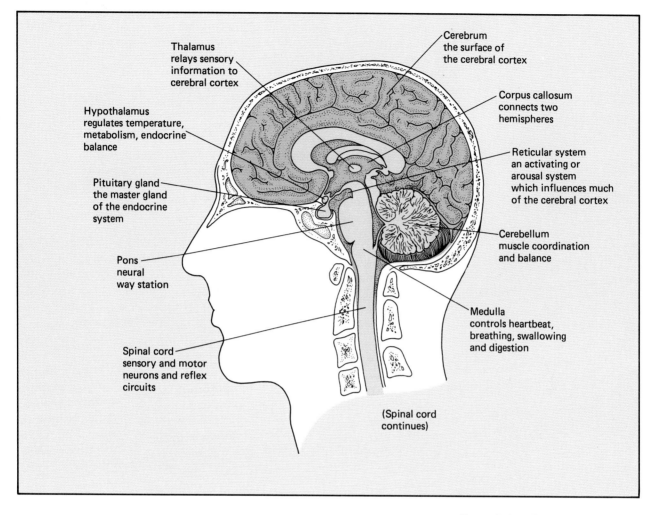

Thalamus
relays sensory
information to
cerebral cortex

Hypothalamus
regulates temperature,
metabolism, endocrine
balance

Pituitary gland
the master gland
of the endocrine
system

Pons
neural
way station

Spinal cord
sensory and motor
neurons and reflex
circuits

Cerebrum
the surface of
the cerebral cortex

Corpus callosum
connects two
hemispheres

Reticular system
an activating or
arousal system
which influences much
of the cerebral cortex

Cerebellum
muscle coordination
and balance

Medulla
controls heartbeat,
breathing, swallowing
and digestion

(Spinal cord
continues)

Figure 2–21   Cross section of the brain.

Table 2–1:   Divisions of the Brain

The brain has three major divisions: the hindbrain, midbrain, and forebrain. (The brain stem includes the medulla, pons, and midbrain).

Hindbrain
  Medulla
  Pons
  Reticular activating system (extends into midbrain)
Midbrain
  Tracts to and from upper portions of brain and clusters of cell bodies (nuclei), which are way stations for sensory and motor information.
Forebrain
  Cerebral cortex
  Cerebrum
  Corpus callosum
  Olfactory bulb
  Thalamus
  Hypothalamus
  Pituitary gland
  Limbic system

tebrates: the hindbrain for balance and coordination of movement, the midbrain for vision, and the forebrain for smell. Although the organization of the human brain is considerably different and markedly more complicated, the three divisions can still be seen in the human embryo, arising as three separate lumps at the head end of the developing nervous system.

The Hindbrain

The **hindbrain** consists of the **medulla,** the **pons,** and the cerebellum. The medulla and the pons are two adjacent swellings of the brain stem, just above the spinal cord. The medulla controls some very important involuntary functions such as breathing, heartbeat, and digestion. In addition, several of the cranial nerves enter the brain at this point. Other cranial nerves enter at the pons, which serves mainly as a way station for neural pathways going to other brain areas.

The cerebellum (the name means "little cerebrum") is in charge of body equilibrium, muscle tone, and particularly the regulation of smoothly coordinated movements. Disorders of this brain area, sometimes seen in elderly people, lead to a characteristic kind of tremor that is most noticeable when the hand is making (or attempting to make) a purposeful movement.

The Midbrain

In the submammalian vertebrates the **midbrain** is the primary area for processing sensory information from the eyes and ears. In mammals this function is largely taken over by the cerebral cortex, and the midbrain shrinks in relative size and importance. Some visual and auditory fibers still travel to the midbrain, however. In primates, including humans, the midbrain's role in vision involves the control of eye movements; it sends out three pairs of cranial nerves to the eye muscles.

The midbrain possesses one other characteristic worthy of note. Many of the neurons that use the neurotransmitter dopamine originate in this area and send their projections upward to the forebrain. These pathways have been implicated in the regulation of complex movements and of emotional responses.

The hindbrain and the midbrain together make up the brain stem.

The Reticular Formation

Scattered through the brain stem is an intricate network of cells known collectively as the **reticular formation.** These cells receive inputs from several sensory systems; they send outputs upward to the forebrain. The reticular formation plays an important role in sleep and arousal. When the reticular formation of a sleepy animal is given a small electric shock through an electrode implanted in its brain, the animal immediately becomes alert and attentive.

The Forebrain

The forebrain is composed of two parts: the *diencephalon* and the cerebrum *(telencephalon)*. The diencephalon contains the **thalamus,** a fairly large bilobed area at the midline of the brain. In mammals, whose cerebral cortex is

the main locus for sensory processing, the thalamus is an important way station for receiving information from the various sense organs and relaying it—in an orderly fashion—to the cortex. For example, 80 percent of the axons of the optic nerve go directly to the *lateral geniculate nucleus* in the thalamus. (A **nucleus** is a ganglion located in the brain.) There these optic fibers form synapses with other neurons that project to the visual area of the cortex. Other nuclei in the thalamus receive information from the ears and from the sensory fibers that come up the spinal cord. This area also receives inputs from the reticular formation and from feedback fibers coming down from the cortex. Clearly, this is a major center for collecting and integrating sensory information.

The other part of the diencephalon is the **hypothalamus,** located (as its name implies) below the thalamus. This is an extremely important part of the brain because of its role in the regulation of many of the body's systems. For example, damage to the hypothalamus can disrupt temperature regulation, resulting in death from fever. Another important function of the hypothalamus is the regulation of motivated behavior (such as eating, drinking, and sexual activity) and of emotional responses. The hypothalamus has been somewhat irreverently described as being in charge of the four F's: fleeing, fighting, feeding, and mating.

Hanging from the hypothalamus like an apple from a tree is the **pituitary gland.** Although this organ is an endocrine gland and not really part of the nervous system, it receives neural inputs from the hypothalamus. Thus there is a connection between neural and hormonal mechanisms in the brain.

The Cerebrum

From a human evolutionary view, the most dramatic change in our central nervous system has been the increase in the size of our cerebrum. The human cerebrum is composed of two heavily wrinkled hemispheres, which are (in appearance) almost perfect mirror images of each other. The gray carpet of **cortex**—a layer of cells roughly 2 millimeters thick—extends into the fissures and down the two flat facing sides of the hemispheres, until it is stopped by the **corpus callosum,** a wide band of white matter that connects the two halves (see the Highlight on split brains).

Under the cortex are several brain areas, known collectively as the *basal ganglia,* that are primarily concerned with the regulation of movement. One of these areas, the **corpus striatum,** receives dopamine-containing fibers from the midbrain. It is the corpus striatum that is affected by a deficiency of dopamine, thus causing Parkinson's disease, as we saw in the earlier Highlight on neurotransmitters, brain disorders, and brain grafts.

The remainder of the cerebrum can be subdivided into the **limbic system** and the **neocortex.** The limbic system is an oddly assorted set of structures (including the hippocampus, the amygdala, and the septum) that are grouped together on the basis of function rather than anatomy. These structures are responsible for the coordination and control of emotional responses.

The limbic system receives dopamine-containing fibers from the midbrain; abnormally high levels of dopamine have been found in this area in the brains of deceased schizophrenics (Iverson, 1979). There are also close neural ties between the limbic system and the hypothalamus. In fact, on a strictly functional basis, parts of the hypothalamus can be considered part of the limbic system.

CAT, PET, and NMR: Making Pictures of the Living Brain

While it is possible to dissect, stain, and microscopically examine the brain of a dead person, X-ray photographs have provided one of the few ways to look inside the living brain. Recently three new methods of "seeing" inside the brain of a living person have been developed: CAT, PET, and NMR. They rely heavily on the enormous information-processing capabilities of modern high-speed computers and provide heretofore inaccessible views of the living brain.

Figure A is a conventional X-ray photograph of a person's head. To make this sort of X ray, called an *angiogram,* a special dye that blocks X rays is injected into the patient's carotid artery. This dye shows up black in the final picture. Thus both the bone structure of the head and the vascular system (blood vessels containing the dye) are clearly visible. Unfortunately, the soft tissue of the brain is virtually invisible because X rays pass through it so easily.

In 1961 an American scientist, Allan M. Cormack, had an idea for a new way of taking X rays. Soon afterward, an engineer in England, Geoffrey N. Hounsfield, constructed an initial model of the device. (They shared a

Nobel prize for their work in 1979.) In their process an X-ray source sends a single narrow beam of X-rays through the patient's head to a detector on the other side; then both the X-ray source and the detector are rotated one degree clockwise and another beam is sent through. As the X-rays proceed in this way around the head, the amount of X-ray absorbed along each of 180 paths is sent to a computer. Using this information, the computer is able to calculate the total amount of X-ray absorbed *at each point* along each path and to produce a picture of the sort shown in Figure B. The picture reveals the detailed structure of a narrow slice of brain tissue cut across the X-ray device's axis of rotation. This is why the technique is called **computerized axial tomography,** or **CAT,** for short (*tomo* is from a Greek word meaning "cut" or "slice"). Pictures of additional brain "slices" can be made in the same fashion, by simply sliding the patient along the axis of rotation.

While the CAT scan has already become an important medical and research tool, it has one important limitation. It reveals only the *structure* of the brain—not its neural activity. Another computerized method for generating pictures of narrow brain slices has recently been developed that does reveal aspects of neural activity. This method is called **positron emission tomography,** or **PET,** because it is based on the release (emission) of positively charged

particles (positrons) during neural activity. The emission occurs because some chemical involved in the neural activity has been radioactively tagged and introduced into the patient (e.g., by injection or inhalation). Each positron emitted as the chemical is used in neural action immediately collides with an electron, emitting *two gamma-ray photons that travel off in exactly opposite directions.* Photon detectors arrayed in a ring around a patient's head feed into a computer, which calculates sites of high neural activity based on the simultaneous detection of photons by particular pairs of detectors. Using such information, the computer constructs images like the one shown in Figure C.

The major difference between CAT scans and PET scans is illustrated by Figures B and C. Both are images of a stroke patient's brain. The patient had recently suffered a stroke that blocked the blood flow to the left hemisphere of the brain. The CAT scan reveals no perceptible structural alteration. The blood blockage was too recent for such changes to have occurred. However, it had already caused major changes in neural activity, as revealed in the PET scan.

Perhaps the most exciting new development in this field is a technique of computer imaging based on the tiny magnetic fields produced by the spinning nuclei of atoms. Placing a patient in an extremely strong magnetic field causes the spinning nuclei to have parallel axes of

The role of the limbic system in emotionality has been revealed by recent experiments performed with animals. Such experiments have shown that electrical stimulation of the amygdala or of certain parts of the hypothalamus (by electrodes permanently implanted in an animal's brain) produces all the signs of rage in laboratory animals. A cat, for example, hisses and bares its teeth and claws. Destruction of the amygdala has a taming effect in most species, resulting in an animal that is totally lacking in aggressiveness. Lesions in the septal area, on the other hand, tend to produce an increase in fear and anger reactions. Sexual disturbances, either hypersexuality or reduced sexuality, are also associated with damage to various parts of the limbic system.

Consistent with the limbic system's role in emotion is the fact that it contains so-called pleasure centers. These are sites that when stimulated electrically seem to produce "pleasant" sensations for laboratory animals. They were discovered accidentally when rats were allowed to press a lever that

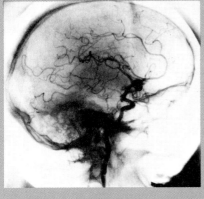

A. Angiogram

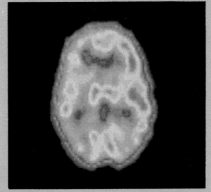

B. CAT Scan

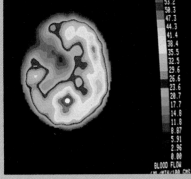

C. PET Scan

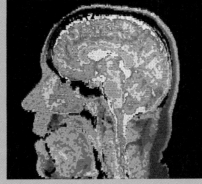

D. NMR

out tiny radio signals that can be detected and localized when the oscillating field is turned off. Since each element has its own *resonant frequency,* choosing the proper frequency of oscillation allows one to detect the presence and location of particular elements. This method of testing for the presence of particular elements is called **nuclear magnetic resonance (NMR).**

The inventors of NMR, Felix Bloch and Edward Purcell, won a Nobel prize for their work in 1952. Yet it was not until 1973 that Paul Lauterbur was able to produce an actual image based on NMR. He did this by processing the NMR information in a computer, which used it to construct an image.

In principle, NMR imaging could selectively portray every element and therefore every chemical process and structure in our bodies. However, at present the imaging of hydrogen atoms has proved most successful. Such an image is shown in Figure D. See Figure 2–21 for identification of the different parts of the brain.

The recent NMR images surpass in quality those from either X rays, CAT, or PET, and do so *without exposing a patient to any harmful radiation,* which is not the case for the others. Someday NMR imaging may allow one to literally "see" both the detailed structure of the living brain and the chemical processes occurring in it.

rotation. If another, weaker magnetic field is introduced, oscillating at a given frequency, it causes the nuclei of certain atoms to wobble about their axes (much as tops wobble before they fall). The "wobbling" atoms send

(A. Courtesy Dr. Fred J. Hodges, III, Washington University of Medicine. B. National Institute of Health. C. Courtesy Dr. Michel M. Ler-Pogossian. D. Science Photo Library/Photo Researchers, Inc.)

produced a weak electric current in a permanently implanted brain electrode. Rather than avoiding the lever, the rats pressed it more and more frequently (Olds & Milner, 1954). It was noticed that some male rats actually ejaculated following such electrical brain stimulation. Were the rats treating themselves to an orgasm each time they pressed the lever? Subsequent research (e.g., Deutsch, 1960; Gallistel, 1983) has revealed a less colorful story. Electrical stimulation of the pleasure centers seems to produce various effects analogous to feeding a hungry rat, giving water to a thirsty one, and so on. In other words, the only consistent definition of a pleasure center is that its stimulation produces effects similar to a variety of rewards.

Efforts have been made to produce similar effects in patients whose brains could be electrically stimulated (e.g., during an operation). While there were some indications that this stimulation caused pleasurable sensations, the sensations were mild compared to what the animal research might lead one to expect.

THE NEOCORTEX

At last we come to the part of the brain that is responsible for all the things that distinguish humans from animals. The neocortex (often called simply the "cortex") is the outer layer of the cerebrum. This part of the brain began as a thin layer of cells in rodents, developed a few wrinkles in carnivores such as cats, expanded dramatically in the primates, and then suddenly swelled to tremendous proportions—pushing out the walls of the skull in the process—in human beings. The human neocortex has been estimated to contain "no fewer than 70 percent of all the neurons in the central nervous system" (Nauta & Feirtag, 1979). Neuroanatomists divide the neocortex of each hemisphere into four regions or *lobes* (see Figure 2–22); these lobes are separated from one another by landmarks such as the *central fissure* (which goes over the top of the head, cutting across both hemispheres) and the *lateral fissure* (on the side of each hemisphere).

Our knowledge of the functions of the neocortex has been greatly expanded by modern techniques of brain surgery. The Canadian neurosurgeon Wilder Penfield perfected a technique in which the patient remains conscious during the operation. The surgeon can then "map" areas of the cortex by applying a small electric current and noting what the patient reports or what movements occur.

Sensory and Motor Areas of the Neocortex

The human neocortex, like that of other mammals, is partly taken up by sensory and motor functions. Two areas that have been extensively mapped are the **somatosensory area** and the **motor area.** These lie in a band that goes over the top of the brain, just behind and just in front of the central fissure.

Figure 2–22 The figure shows the four lobes of the neocortex and the major fissures that separate them.

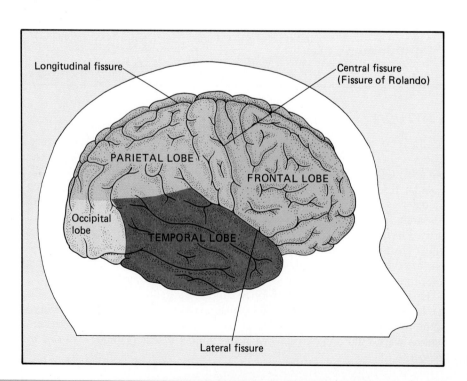

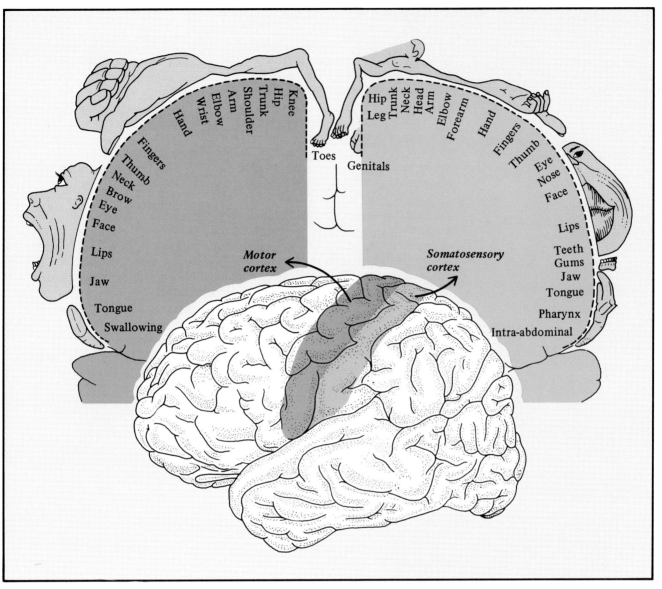

The Motor Cortex. Mild electrical stimulation of a specific point on the motor cortex causes a movement of a specific part of the body. If a point on the right hemisphere is stimulated, a body part on the left side will respond, and vice versa. Moving the electrode to a different spot produces movement of another part of the body. Penfield found that some regions of the body—for instance, the fingers and the face—are represented by relatively large areas of the motor cortex, whereas other parts—the trunk and the legs—are allotted relatively small areas. The left side of Figure 2–23 is a graphic depiction of the resulting map of the motor cortex. In this picture, called a **motor homunculus,** each part of the body is shown in proportion to how much motor cortex is devoted to it. This is an approximate index of how many neurons serve that body part, which reflects the precision with which it can be controlled.

The Somatosensory Cortex. A similar mapping procedure on the posterior side of the central fissure produces a **somatosensory homunculus,** shown

Figure 2–23 *(Green)* A cross section of the human somatosensory cortex, and a somatosensory homunculus.

(Brown) A cross section of the human motor cortex and a motor homunculus. The sizes of the body parts reflect the amount of cortex area devoted to them. (After Penfield & Rasmussen, 1950)

on the right side of Figure 2–23. In this case, the result of the electrical stimulation is a sensation somewhere in the body (again, on the opposite side). The two homunculi are quite similar—the parts of the body, such as the face and the hands, that take up a lot of motor cortex also take up a lot of somatosensory cortex. *All* somatosensory information is represented in this brain area: warmth, cold, pressure, pain, and awareness of location and motion of body parts. This information comes from the somatosensory neurons of the spinal cord and of the cranial nerves, and assembles in the thalamus before reaching the cortex. The neural pathways that serve the sense of taste also end up on the somatosensory cortex.

The Auditory Cortex.   Auditory information from the ears is projected to the auditory cortex, which is just below the lateral fissure. The auditory cortex on each hemisphere receives inputs from *both* ears; however, each hemisphere gets more of its information from the ear on the opposite side of the head. Most neurons in the auditory cortex are "tuned" to sounds of a particular frequency or pitch. That is, a given neuron fires rapidly when sounds of a certain frequency are heard; it fires at slower rates to higher or lower frequencies.

The Visual Cortex.   Information from the eyes is carried to the brain by the two optic nerves and ultimately reaches the occipital lobe, in the very back of the head. Information from both eyes reaches both hemispheres, but it is divided up in a rather peculiar way: Neural signals from the right side of each eye (the left half of the visual field) reach the right side of the brain, those from the left side of each eye (the right half of the visual field) go to the left side of the brain. If you stare at the crease between the left- and right-hand pages of this book, the left-hand page is represented on your *right* occipital lobe, the right-hand page on your *left!* In order to accomplish this partition, each optic nerve has to split in half, with the two halves nearest the nose crossing over to go to the opposite side of the brain. The point where they cross is known as the **optic chasm.** (This is considered in more detail in Chapter 3.)

Association Areas of the Neocortex

If we subtract all sensory and motor areas from the neocortex, the parts that remain are called **association areas.** It is to these areas that we owe our ability to speak, to read, to think, and to laugh. The association areas receive no direct inputs from the outside world; nor do they produce any outputs that result directly in motor responses. As the British brain biochemist Steven Rose (1975) has put it, "Neurons of the association areas talk only to one another and to other cortical neurons."

Speech Area.   The first part of the neocortex to be correctly assigned a specific function was a region known as **Broca's area,** located near the part of the motor cortex that controls movements of the mouth and jaws (see Figure 2–24). The discovery that this area plays an important role in the production of speech was made in 1861 by the French neurologist Paul Broca. One of Broca's patients was a man called "Tan," who totally lacked meaningful speech, although he was able to communicate with gestures. After Tan's death Broca examined his brain and found a lesion just above the lateral fissure, on the left hemisphere.

The disorder from which Tan had suffered is called **aphasia.** People with Broca's aphasia are able to understand speech and to use their vocal apparatus in other ways (they can sing, for instance); but they speak—if at all— only with great difficulty. Words are wrested out one by one and do not form complete sentences.

A second kind of aphasia was described by Carl Wernicke in 1874. It is associated with a brain area called **Wernicke's area,** located on the lower side of the lateral fissure near the auditory cortex. Damage to Wernicke's area produces a type of language difficulty in which both comprehension and speech are affected. People with Wernicke's aphasia speak fluently and in recognizable sentences, but the content of their speech is often bizarre or nonsensical.

The kind of brain damage that produces Broca's or Wernicke's aphasia usually involves only one hemisphere—the left, in most cases. Injuries to the same areas on the right side generally do not affect language ability. This fact, noted by Broca himself, was the first indication that the two hemispheres are not identical in function. We will now take a closer look at the differences between the two sides of the brain.

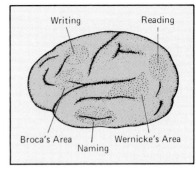

Figure 2–24 The usual brain locations that serve language functions such as writing, reading, and naming are shown on the left cerebral hemisphere. The locations of these language centers vary somewhat from person to person. In some individuals they are located on the right hemisphere.

Right and Left Brain

The connection between speech and handedness has been known for over a century; it was too obvious to miss. When a person suffers a massive injury to the **left hemisphere** of the brain (most often because of a stroke), there are usually two results: paralysis of all or part of the right side of the body and a loss of the use of language. Perhaps a double-edged tragedy of this kind served as the inspiration for the Psalmist, who wrote: "If I forget thee, O Jerusalem, let my right hand forget her cunning. If I do not remember thee, let my tongue cleave to the roof of my mouth" (Psalm 137). Most people use the left side of the brain to process language, and the right hand—which is controlled by the left side of the brain—to perform tasks that require skill. A little more than 90 percent of humans are right-handed. This preponderance has prevailed for at least 5,000 years (Coren & Porac, 1977) and probably goes back to the earliest hominids (Dart, 1949). Apes, however, like subprimate vertebrates, do not tend to right-dominance. In most animal species individual members may favor one paw over the other, but the favored side is as likely to be the left as the right (Corballis & Beale, 1976).

The fact that the left side of the brain generally controls both the dominant hand and the ability to speak led some to dub it the "dominant hemisphere" and to wonder whether the right side might be just another one of those useless parts that we have inherited from our animal ancestors. For two reasons this view has been discarded. First, there is the problem of left-handers. Second, there is the fact, recognized only in recent years, that the right side of the brain has its uses too. (Also see Highlight on split brain patients.)

Left-Handed People. If right-hand, left-brain dominance is characteristically human, how do we account for left-handers? One possibility is that they were simply formed backward, like "mirror-image" twins. There *are* sets of twins whose hair and fingerprints whorl in opposite directions, but the overwhelming majority of twins—and of left-handed people—have their insides formed just like everybody else's: The asymmetrical locations of the heart, the stomach, and the intestines are normal. There are very, very few truly "mirror-image" people, and they are not necessarily left-handed.

HIGHLIGHT

Split Brains: Two Brains in One Body?

Normally, the two cerebral hemispheres communicate directly through the bundles of connecting neurons that form the corpus callosum. What would happen if these connections were cut? It has been reported (Miller, 1983) that in 1908 a woman was hospitalized for bizarre behavior in which her left hand seemed out of control, throwing and breaking things, fighting with her right hand for objects, and even trying to choke her. It was as if each hand were controlled by a different brain. After her death, an autopsy revealed damage to her corpus callosum. Were her two hemispheres acting like separate brains—with her left hemisphere controlling her right hand and speech, and her right hemisphere controlling her runaway left hand? In retrospect, this appears to be a plausible explanation for the poor woman's plight, but at the time physicians had no way to prove such a theory.

An experimental approach to this issue was undertaken in 1953 by two scientists at the California Institute of Technology. Ronald Meyers and Roger Sperry severed the corpus callosum of a cat, producing a split-brain feline. They also cut the cat's optic nerve, so that each eye sent neurons to only one hemisphere. After training the cat to discriminate certain visual patterns with a cap over one eye, they found that there was no sign of the prior learning when the cap was removed and placed on the other eye. This seemed remarkable, as either eye was capable of the original learning. A variety of such studies indicated that the two hemispheres of a cat's brain could function like two independent brains.

The study of human split-brain subjects became possible because of efforts to control epilepsy. In addition to providing for routine communication between two sides of the brain, the corpus callosum allows the abnormal electrical discharges that cause epileptic seizures to spread from one hemisphere to another. In an attempt to control this disability and confine the seizures to one hemisphere, a daring surgical procedure was carried out in 1961 by P. J. Vogel and J. E. Bogen. They severed the corpus callosum and one or two other smaller commissures (nerve bundles) that link the two sides of the cerebrum together.

The split-brain operation served the purpose it was designed for; in fact, it eliminated almost all epileptic attacks, even those confined to one hemisphere. More remarkably, the small group of people who underwent this surgery appeared to the casual observer to be completely normal. These **split-brain subjects** showed no noticeable changes either in intelligence or in personality. One patient awoke after the operation and, still drowsy from the anesthetic, joked that he had a "splitting headache" (Gazzaniga, 1967).

It took some fairly subtle psychological testing to reveal the strange kinds of deficits that the surgery produced. A series of experiments reported by Gazzaniga (1985) demonstrated these deficits. When an object such as a pencil was placed in the right (dominant) hand of the split-brain subjects, they easily identified it by touch and said "pencil." But if the pencil was placed in their left hands and the subjects couldn't see it, they could not say what the object was. Yet there was nothing wrong with the hand itself: The subjects could identify the object by pointing (with their left hands) to a card on which the word *pencil* was printed, or they could use their left hands to pick out a pencil from among a group of objects hidden from view behind a screen. Information from the left hand was being delivered to the right hemisphere, but the right hemisphere could not speak. Because the corpus callosum had been severed, the information in the right hemisphere could not cross over to the speech centers in the left hemisphere. The left hemisphere didn't have the slightest idea what the left hand was holding!

Similar results were found when words or pictures were shown to only one hemisphere. This experiment made use of the fact that the visual field is split down the middle, with half going to the left hemisphere and half to the right. If a normal person

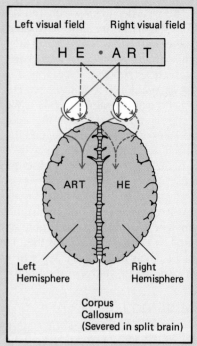

Figure A

looks at a point on a screen and a picture is flashed on the screen too briefly to allow eye movements, the part of the picture to the right of the point goes to the left hemisphere; the part to the left goes to the right hemisphere. This technique was used with the split-brain subjects.

One way of studying split-brain subjects is to send different visual information to each hemisphere. This is possible because of the way the eyes normally send information to our brains. Information about the left half of our visual field goes to the right hemisphere, and information about the right half goes to the left hemisphere (this is described in more detail in Chapter 3). Normally each hemisphere quickly shares its visual information with the other through the connecting neurons of the corpus callosum. Since the corpus callosum is severed in a split-brain subject, the normal sharing cannot occur. Each hemisphere only has information about one-half of the visual field.

For example, consider the experiment illustrated in Figure A. Split-brain subjects were asked to gaze at a dot in the center of the screen. Then, too briefly for them to move their eyes, large printed letters spelling the word "heart" were

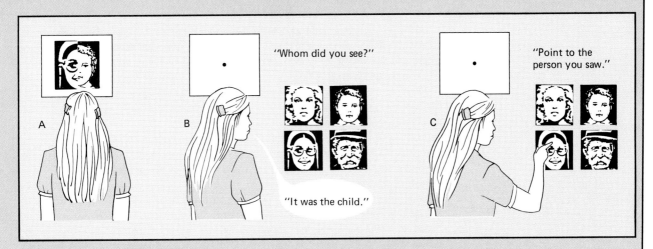

Figure B

projected onto the screen, positioned so that the dot fell between the letters "e" and "a." The letters "he" in the left half of their visual field were projected onto the right rear of their eyes, from where neural signals were sent to the right hemisphere. Just the opposite occurred for the letters "art" in the right visual field, which were signaled to the left hemisphere. If the subjects were asked to *say* what they saw, they said "art"—the part of the word transmitted to the left (speaking) side of the brain. But if they were asked instead to point with their left hand to the word they had seen, they pointed to a card that said "he." Notice that neither hemisphere knew that the word had been "heart." Notice also that although the right hemisphere was unable to speak, it was able to read and to understand spoken commands.

In another experiment (Levy, Trevarthen, & Sperry, 1972) split-brain patients were shown composite photographs combining the left half of one face with the right half of another (Figure B). These photographs are often called **chimeric stimuli** after the mythical chimera, whose appearance kept changing. They were flashed briefly on a screen positioned in the subjects' view so that their left hemispheres received the right half of the image and their right hemispheres the left half. The subjects were then shown four normal faces, among which were the two contributing to the composite, and were asked which one they had seen. While they seemed totally unaware of the chimeric or conflicting nature of the briefly flashed

image, their answer typically depended on how they were told to report. If they were told to *vocalize* their answer, they chose the face containing the half "seen" by the left hemisphere (the right half of the composite image). If told to *point* (using either hand), they chose the face whose half had gone to the right hemisphere (the left half of the composite). It was *as if* the verbal response was controlled by the left hemisphere and the pointing by the right (although fine control of each hand is governed by the opposite hemisphere, gross movements can be controlled by either hemisphere).

The split-brain patient seems in the curious position of having two separate minds in a single body. The left mind has language and can readily communicate its experiences. The right mind, though not as verbal, can perform many acts independently. It can actually do some things better than the left mind. For instance, it seems to be better at arranging blocks to match a given pattern and at drawing pictures of figures such as cubes. The drawings made with the left hand are clumsy but fairly accurate; the drawings made with the right hand are neater but wrong.

The two minds of a split-brain patient are each capable of learning and remembering, but the memories of each are not accessible to the other side. Experiments with split-brain animals have made this apparent. When the corpus callosum of an animal is severed, the result is two approximately equal hemispheres. If the right hemisphere of such an animal is taught to discriminate (with

its left paw) between two different shapes, it turns out that the left hemisphere has learned nothing. It takes the left hemisphere just as long to learn the discrimination as it took the right hemisphere (Sperry, 1964).

The fact that split-brain animals and people have two independent minds should not be taken to mean that everybody else also has. In the intact brain there is complete, immediate, and constant communication between the two hemispheres. Learning and memories are shared. Each side has full access to the special talents and abilities of the other. That is why consciousness in a person with a complete corpus callosum is unitary.

Michael Gazzaniga (1985), who has been a major figure in split-brain research, believes that many functions of the right hemisphere are nonverbal, although the left hemisphere is constantly attempting to verbalize and rationalize these right-hemispheric functions. He points out how glibly the left hemisphere of a split-brain subject will provide a verbal explanation for actions of the right hemisphere. For example, if a picture of someone coughing is presented in the left visual field of a split-brain subject, he might *actually* cough, while the left hemisphere might say, "I saw nothing." However, if asked "Why did you cough?" the left hemisphere might quickly say, "I was out in the rain yesterday and feel like I'm coming down with a cold."

(B: Adapted from Levy, J., Trevarthen, C., & Sperry, R. W. Perception of bilateral chimeric figures following hemispheric disconnection. *Brain*, 1972, *95*, fig. 4, p. 68,)

Another puzzle is that although the speech centers of right-handers are almost invariably in the left hemisphere, in left-handers these centers are not always in the **right hemisphere.** As Table 2–2 shows, most left-handers process language with the hemisphere associated with their *non*dominant hand. Still more perplexing, a considerable proportion have speech centers on *both* sides of the brain.

Some psychologists have proposed that these atypical cases are the results of early brain injuries: If the left side of the brain is injured (at birth, say), the right takes over some of its duties. That this can happen is unquestionable. As we have seen, stroke victims often regain many of their abilities, as cells surrounding the damaged tissue, or in the same location on the opposite hemisphere, take over some of the functions of the dead neurons. If an injury to the left hemisphere occurs early enough—in the first year or two of life—there is often no language deficit. However, there is. no evidence that brain damage is responsible for left-handedness. Quite the contrary: Left-handers are known to recover their language abilities after a stroke more rapidly than right-handers, and this would not be likely if part of the brain had already been damaged. People who are right-handed but have close relatives who are left-handers also have a more favorable prognosis for recovery of speech after a stroke.

A theory to account for all of these findings was first proposed by Annett (1972) and later elaborated by Corballis and Beale (1976). According to this theory, two factors are involved in the lateralization (sidedness) of the hand and brain: an inherited component and a random component. You inherit either a tendency toward lateralization or a tendency toward symmetry. In the former case, you are right-handed and have your speech centers on the left hemisphere. In the latter case, you have no innate tendency toward lateralization, and the random component takes over: Both handedness and lateralization of the brain are determined by chance.

What the Other Hemisphere Does. An ordinary right-handed person with speech centers in the normal place on the left hemisphere *does* suffer deficits if damage occurs to the right side of the brain. For example, there is an impairment of the ability to perceive the emotional responses of other people (Geshwind, 1979). An ordinary person with a lesion on the language side of the brain may not understand the meaning of what someone else is saying but will understand that the speaker is angry, or is joking. In contrast, a person with a lesion on the right hemisphere will understand the words but may be unable to recognize the emotional tone. This person may show further signs of emotional impairment, such as unconcern about any other disabilities that resulted from the brain injury.

Table 2–2: The Location of the Brain Area Devoted to Speech, and Its Relationship to Handedness[a]

	Right-Handed People	Left-Handed and Ambidextrous People
Speech on left hemisphere	92%	69%
Speech on right hemisphere	7%	18%
Speech on both hemispheres	1%	13%

[a]Based on the effects of accidental lesions to the left or right hemisphere.
From Milner, Branch, and Rasmussen (1966).

Many other specialized functions are believed to be represented primarily on the right hemisphere: for example, perception of melody, of nonverbal patterns, and of spatial relationships (Springer & Deutsch 1985). However, the two sides of the brain normally work together, and there are usually no signs of their differing roles. Information is carried freely back and forth between the two hemispheres by the wide band of tissue known as the corpus callosum.

THE AUTONOMIC NERVOUS SYSTEM

Earlier we said that the peripheral nervous system has two parts: somatic and autonomic. So far we have concentrated primarily on the somatic system, which innervates striated (skeletal) muscles. Now we return to the autonomic system, which innervates two kinds of muscles: the smooth muscles of the glands and internal organs and the specialized cardiac muscles of the heart. It is because these muscles generally function without voluntary control (although voluntary control can be imposed upon some of them) that we call this system *autonomic* ("self-governed").

The autonomic system itself has two divisions: **sympathetic** and **parasympathetic.** Most organs and glands are innervated by both the sympathetic and the parasympathetic systems, which have opposing effects on them. The sympathetic system is concerned, to a large extent, with emergency situations and stress, whereas the parasympathetic system maintains the routine "vegetative" functions such as digestion. Another way of putting it is that the sympathetic system is associated with activation and expenditure of energy, while the parasympathetic system tends to conserve energy.

Inputs to the autonomic nervous system come from a number of areas of the central nervous system. In general, such inputs do not come directly but make many connections along the way. One important pathway starts in the sensory areas of the neocortex and filters downward through the association areas, the limbic system, the hypothalamus, the reticular formation, and the spinal cord. This pathway would be used when, for example, you see or hear something frightening. The physiological responses that accompany the feeling of fear—accelerated heart rate and breathing, increase in blood pressure, inhibition of digestion, and so on—are produced by the action of the sympathetic nervous system. These physiological responses are counteracted by the opposing effects of the parasympathetic nervous system, which tends to return the activity of the organs to their normal levels.

Anatomy of the Autonomic Nervous System

Sympathetic.   Neurons of the sympathetic system exit from the central portion of the spinal cord, below the neck and above the small of the back. Each of these neurons synapses immediately within one of the ganglia of the *sympathetic chains.* There are two of these long chains of ganglia, one lying along each side of the spinal cord.

Some of the axons that leave the sympathetic chain go directly to the organs they innervate. Others travel to secondary ganglia and synapse with another set of neurons that go the rest of the way. A secondary sympathetic ganglion is known as a *plexus;* the best known of these is the solar plexus, located behind the stomach.

Because all the neurons of the sympathetic system come together in the

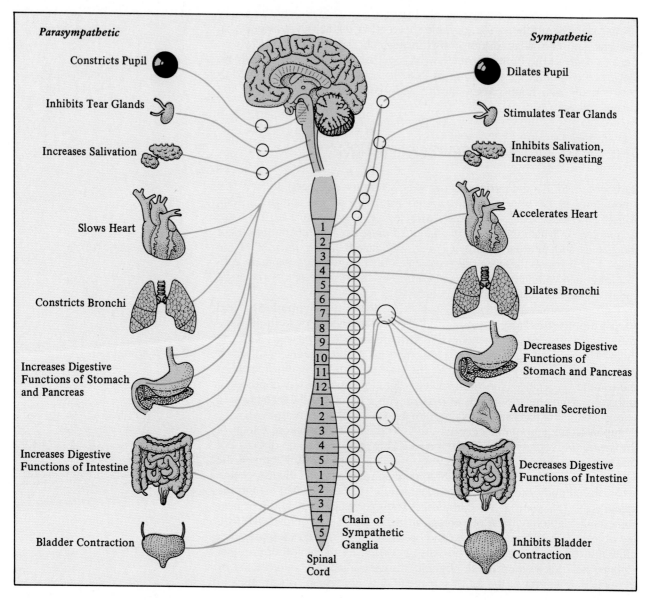

Figure 2–25 The parasympathetic (left) and sympathetic (right) divisions of the autonomic nervous system. Parasympathetic nerves arise from the brain and from the base of the spinal cord, sympathetic nerves from the remainder of the spinal cord. The two sets of nerves serve the same organs but, as is shown, in opposing ways.

sympathetic chain, they tend to work in unison. The effects produced by this system and by the parasympathetic system are shown in Figure 2–25.

Parasympathetic. Parasympathetic motor fibers leave the central nervous system from one of two locations: from the very bottom of the spinal cord, or directly from the brain in a cranial nerve. One of the cranial nerves, the *vagus* nerve, is the only exception to the rule that cranial nerves serve the head and neck. Some of the axons in this nerve provide the parasympathetic innervation of the heart, the lungs, and the digestive system.

Parasympathetic neurons also form ganglia, but these are generally located near the organs they help control. Because the parasympathetic system has no unifying structure like the sympathetic chain, the parasympathetic ganglia are more independent of one another than the sympathetic ganglia, and do

not necessarily act in concert. Moreover, some parts of the body receive sympathetic innervation but not parasympathetic—the sweat glands, the hair follicles, and the smaller blood vessels.

THE ENDOCRINE SYSTEM

Our nervous system processes and carries information throughout our bodies via neurons. There is another bodily messenger service that carries information outside the nervous system. It is the **endocrine system,** whose messages are carried throughout the body as chemicals secreted into the bloodstream by glands.

The glands of the endocrine system interact closely with one another and with the autonomic nervous system to regulate a number of vital metabolic and physiological functions. **Endocrine glands** are *ductless*—that is, they secrete their **hormones** or "chemical messengers" directly into the bloodstream, which carries the hormones all over the body. A list of the major endocrine glands and their principal hormones is given in Table 2–3.

Each hormone exerts its effects on a target organ somewhere in the body. In some cases, the target organs themselves are other endocrine glands. Hormones that control the secretion of other hormones are described as *tropic.*

Table 2–3:   Major Glands and Hormones of the Endocrine System

Gland	Hormone	Main Effect
Pituitary		
Anterior lobe	Adrenocorticotropic hormone (ACTH)	Stimulates adrenal cortex to produce steroids
	Growth hormone	Stimulates growth
	Thyrotropin	Stimulates thyroid to produce thyroxin
	Follicle-stimulating hormone (FSH)	Development of ova and sperm
	Luteinizing hormone (LH)	Maturation of ova and sperm; ovulation
	Prolactin	Production of milk in nursing female
Posterior lobe	Antidiuretic hormone (Vasopressin)	Prevents excess loss of fluids through urination
	Oxytocin	Uterine contractions, release of milk during nursing
Adrenal		
Cortex	Steroids (e.g., Cortisol)	Increase of blood glucose; maintenance of metabolism and level of minerals in body
Medulla	Epinephrine (Adrenalin)	Increases blood pressure, heart rate, blood glucose, and perspiration; stimulates production of ACTH
	Norepinephrine	Increases blood pressure, slows heart rate; stimulates production of ACTH
Thyroid	Thyroxin	Increases metabolism
Pancreas		
Alpha cells	Glucagon	Increases blood glucose
Beta cells	Insulin	Enables body cells to use glucose (thereby decreasing blood glucose)
Parathyroid	Parathormone	Maintains level of calcium in blood
Ovaries (in female)	Estrogens	Development of female reproductive organs, secondary sex characteristics, and sexual behavior
	Progesterone	Thickening of lining of uterus and maintenance of pregnancy
Testes (in male)	Androgens (e.g., Testosterone)	Development of male reproductive organs, secondary sex characteristics, and sexual behavior

The primary secretor of tropic hormones is the *pituitary gland,* located at the base of the brain and attached by a stalk to the hypothalamus. Because of its influence on many of the other endocrine glands, this tiny organ is often called the *master gland.*

The pituitary consists of two parts, the *anterior* and the *posterior.* The anterior pituitary puts out several tropic hormones that regulate the functions of other glands. It, in turn, is regulated by the hypothalamus. For example, if the blood level of the hormone *thyroxin* becomes too low, the hypothalamus reacts by stimulating the anterior pituitary to secrete the hormone *thyrotropin.* Thyrotropin, released into the bloodstream, reaches the thyroid gland (located in the neck) and causes it to secrete more thyroxin. Thyroxin is important in the maintenance of the body's rate of metabolism. Too little thyroxin produces a condition known as **hypothyroidism,** which is associated with depression and fatigue. Hypothyroidism is particularly dangerous in childhood, when it causes a serious retardation of growth and mental development. Too much thyroxin also has ill effects: It produces **hyperthyroidism,** which leads to irritability, restlessness, and weight loss.

The anterior pituitary puts out several other important hormones. One of these is the *growth hormone,* too much of which results in a giant, too little in a dwarf. The *gonadotropic hormones* stimulate the ovaries to secrete the female sex hormones, the testes to secrete the male sex hormones.

Stress Hormones. Two endocrine glands act with the autonomic nervous system to generate the body's reaction to fear and other forms of stress. The hormonal response to stress begins when the hypothalamus triggers the anterior pituitary to release **adrenocorticotropic hormone (ACTH).** The target of this hormone is the other surface (cortex) of the **adrenal glands,** located on top of the kidneys. In response to stimulation by ACTH, the adrenal cortex secretes hormones called *steroids,* which regulate the blood levels of glucose and of certain minerals (sodium, potassium, and chloride). In addition, the hypothalamus acts through the sympathetic nervous system to stimulate the inner part of the adrenal gland—the adrenal medulla—to secrete **epinephrine** (also called **adrenalin**) and **norepinephrine.** These hormones complement the action of the sympathetic nervous system. For example, they increase glucose levels and raise blood pressure. Their effects will be examined in more detail in Chapter 11, Human Motivation and Emotion, in the section on emotion.

We have already discussed norepinephrine in its role as a neurotransmitter in the brain. The same substance, secreted by the adrenal medulla instead of by the presynaptic membrane, acts as a hormone. The two functions of norepinephrine are kept separate by the blood-brain barrier, which prevents most of the circulating norepinephrine from entering the brain.

We are only beginning to understand the complex relationships between hormones and neurotransmitters, between chemistry and behavior. Research in this field is currently very active and likely to produce exciting results.

HEREDITY AND BEHAVIOR

The instructions for building a car—including the "recipes" for the steel of the axles, the plastic of the dashboard, and the glass of the headlights—fill several thick volumes. Yet the instructions for making the infinitely more complex human body—including the "recipes" for the hard surface of the

teeth, the flexible fibers of the muscles, and the transparent surface of the eye—can be fit into the microscopic area of a single cell. These instructions are contained in the **genes.** Your own genes are a randomly determined combination of genes from your mother and father—your genetic inheritance, or **heredity.**

Genes determine physical traits. These include visible traits such as whether you have blue eyes or brown, curly hair or straight. Genes also provide the directions for the construction of the nervous system, the endocrine system, the sense organs, the muscles. We sometimes think of genes as being primarily involved in producing *differences* among people; it is important to remember that they are also responsible for the many things that all humans have in common.

Genes and Chromosomes

Located within the nucleus of every cell in the body of an organism are genes composed of DNA (deoxyribonucleic acid). This complex molecule, shaped like a spiral staircase, has the remarkable ability to break in half lengthwise and form two new molecules identical to the first (see Figure 2–26). The information in each gene is coded within the structure of the long

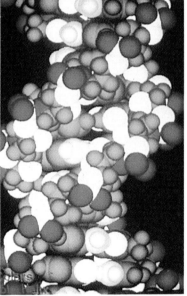

Figure 2–26 *(Below)* This colored model of a DNA molecule shows its double-helix form. *(Left)* This diagram shows how DNA duplicates itself by splitting down the middle. Each base in the chain of bases defining the molecule attracts a specific base from the surrounding medium, thereby forming two identical molecules: Ademine (A) attaches to thyamine (T); cytosine (C) attaches to guamine (G). (*Photo:* NIH/Science Source/Photo Researchers)

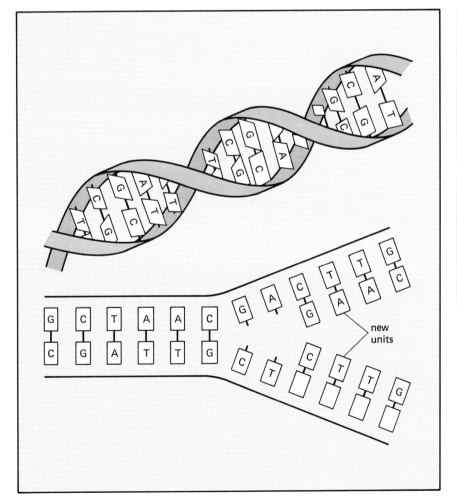

new units

helical DNA molecule by the precise ordering of its four organic bases (adenine, guanine, cytosine, and thymine). This code determines which of the 20 amino acids will be used, and in what order, in forming the protein that is synthesized by the cell. The kinds of protein that are consequently produced determine, in turn, the course of development. In other words, the information coded within the gene determines whether development results in a grasshopper, a sea anemone, a cow, or a human.

A large number (a thousand or more) of genes grouped together in a specific order form a **chromosome.** With the exception of the cells for reproduction, chromosomes are found in pairs in the nuclei of the cells of the body. The number of chromosomes in a nucleus varies from species to species—fruit flies have 8, frogs 26, rats 42, chimpanzees 48, and chickens, oddly enough, have 78. Humans have a relatively modest number: 46 (23 pairs). In each of these pairs one chromosome is inherited from the father and one from the mother.

When a human reproductive cell is formed, it receives just one chromosome from each pair, the particular one being determined by chance. Thus an ovum (egg cell) and a sperm cell each contain only 23 chromosomes instead of 46. When a sperm cell unites with an ovum at the moment of conception, the chromosomes from the mother join with those from the father, giving the fertilized ovum the full complement of 46. The chances are equal of getting either member of the mother's 23 pairs of chromosomes and either member of the father's 23 pairs. Thus a given couple could theoretically produce 2^{23} times 2^{23} different combinations of chromosomes. Despite this genetic diversity, a child still tends to resemble its parents, for the simple reason that half of its genes are shared with its mother and half with its father.

Figure 2–27 shows the 23 pairs of chromosomes of the normal male and female. Genetic sex is determined by the so-called sex chromosomes—the

Figure 2–27 This figure shows the result of a process known as karyotyping, in which a dividing cell is flattened and stained, and a magnified photograph is taken of the chromosomes. The picture of each individual chromosome is then cut out, and they are arranged and numbered according to a standardized system. The result is as shown—23 pairs of chromosomes with the 23rd pair indicating sex: XX (female) or XY (male).

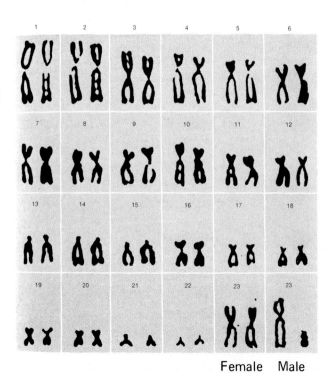

Female Male

23rd pair. There are two sorts of sex chromosomes, X chromosomes and Y chromosomes. Every fertilized egg contains one **X chromosome** that is contributed by the mother. The second member of the pair, contributed by the father, may be either another X chromosome—in which case a female is formed—or a **Y chromosome**—which produces a male. Since only males have the Y chromosome, the genetic sex of a child is entirely determined by which one of the father's two sex chromosomes the child inherits. Occasionally something goes wrong with this process and a child is produced with only one X chromosome, or two X's and a Y, or two Y's and an X. At other times hormonal abnormalities may cause a child whose genetic sex is male to appear female and be reared as a girl, or vice versa. (Such cases are discussed in Chapter 11, Biological Bases of Motivation.)

The 44 other chromosomes normally occur in matched pairs, although here again there are occasional genetic errors. In the most common of these there are 3 chromosomes instead of 2 in the 21st set; the result is a child born with **Down's syndrome** (formerly called "mongolism"), which consists of mental deficiency combined with various physical abnormalities.

Although the transmission of information from one generation to the next via the genes usually works very well, on occasion something goes awry. In a process called **mutation** one or more genes in an ovum or sperm cell is altered. Mutations can affect the structure and development of an organism in ways that may be beneficial or harmful; or they may have no significant effect on the organism. The causes of mutations are varied and include exposure to X rays and certain chemicals.

Although chromosomes are large enough to be visible through a good microscope, this is not the case with genes. No one knows exactly how many genes there are in a human cell (the total number has been estimated to be somewhere between 20,000 and 125,000) or in exactly what order they are arranged on the chromosomes. Most of what is known about genetic action is derived by inference from breeding experiments, such as those that Gregor Mendel performed on pea plants more than a century ago. Nowadays geneticists often use fruit flies for their experiments, partly because it is possible to produce three or four generations of fruit flies in the time it takes for one pea plant to mature.

Single-gene Traits.   The genes for any particular trait are believed to be from the same part of each of the two chromosomes that make up a normal pair. At a given location, a gene might occur in any one of several different forms, called **alleles.** Consider, for example, a trait that is controlled by a single gene, such as eye color in the fruit fly. We'll assume that two alleles are possible: one for red eyes (which we'll call *E*) and one for white eyes *(e).* If a fly has two of the same kind of allele, either *EE* or *ee,* it is *homozygous* for the trait. If allele *E* appears at the eye-color locus on one chromosome and *e* on the other, then the fly is *heterozygous* for the trait. In the latter case, the fly will have red eyes, because the red gene is **dominant,** and the white **recessive.** The recessive version of a trait (white eyes, in this example) only appears when an individual is homozygous *(ee)* for the recessive gene.

If we mate a pair of red-eyed fruit flies that are each heterozygous for eye color *(Ee),* half of the offspring (on the average) will be heterozygous for the eye-color gene and will have red eyes. Half will be homozygous. A quarter will have the *EE* combination and will have red eyes; the remaining quarter will have the *ee* combination and will have white eyes (see Figure 2–28). Of course, two white-eyed flies (both *ee*) can only produce white-eyed offspring,

Figure 2–28   Eye color in the fruit fly is a single-gene trait. The gene for red eyes (E) is dominant over the gene for white eyes (e). Each offspring fly represents one-quarter of the offspring. Of course, since genes pair randomly, the offspring of any given pair of flies may deviate considerably from the expected proportions.

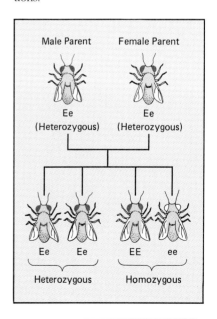

just as two homozygous red-eyed flies (both *EE*) can only produce red-eyed offspring.

A number of human traits are believed to be controlled in this way by single pairs of genes. For example, albinism appears to be a single-gene recessive trait: Two normally pigmented parents who are each carrying the albinism gene have one chance in four of producing an albino (unpigmented) child. An albino who marries a person without the albinism gene will produce only normally pigmented children; half of them, however, will be heterozygous carriers of the trait. On the other hand, the mutant gene that produces achondroplasia, the most common form of dwarfism, is dominant. If an achondroplastic dwarf marries a normal-size individual, half of their children would probably be dwarfs (although none or all could be, depending on chance).

Sex-linked Traits. The situation becomes more complicated when the gene for a trait is located on the sex chromosomes. In that case, it is known as a **sex-linked trait,** and the chances of having it generally depend on whether you're male or female. The two best-known examples of sex-linked traits are color blindness and hemophilia (the condition in which the blood does not clot normally). The genes for these abnormalities are located on the X chromosome. A female has *two* X chromosomes, and if either one contains a normal gene for these traits, the abnormalities will not be expressed because they are recessive. A female can only be color blind or hemophiliac in the unlikely event that she inherits one gene for the defect from each parent. But a male lacks a second X chromosome, so if the single X chromosome contains a gene for hemophilia, there is no allele to dominate it, and the child is born with the condition. Both color blindness and hemophilia can be inherited by a son only from the *mother,* since a male always receives his X chromosome from his female parent. The female is a *carrier* of the sex-linked recessive gene.

Polygenic Traits. Very few human traits are fully controlled by a single pair of genes; most of a person's characteristics, such as height and skin color, are **polygenic traits**—determined by the action of more than one gene pair. Even human eye color, although following fairly well the pattern of a single-gene trait (brown dominant, blue recessive), is probably a polygenic trait. Two blue-eyed parents *can,* on rare occasion, produce a brown- eyed child.

The Study of Heredity

Breeding experiments have been used to study polygenic traits in animals. Tryon (1942) performed a classic experiment. He started with an unselected sample of laboratory rats. These original rats differed considerably in the number of errors they made while learning to negotiate a complex maze for a food reward. Afterward, the rats were separated into a "bright" group and a "dull" group on the basis of their maze-running performance. Then they were selectively bred: bright females were mated with bright males, dull females with dull males. In the second generation this procedure was repeated, and so on for several generations. Tryon found that by the eighth generation of **selective breeding** there were two distinct strains of rats, "brights" and "dulls," with hardly any overlap between the two. Just about every member of the group that was bred for "brightness" was better at

maze running than an average rat of the first generation; just about every member of the group bred for "dullness" was worse.

The Tryon study demonstrated clearly that differences in the number of errors made while running the maze were somehow determined by inheritance. But is it really the case that Tryon's two strains of rats differed in *general* "brightness" or "dullness"? No, later studies showed that even small changes in the particular makeup of Tryon's maze were enough to eliminate all differences in maze running between his two strains. It is possible, for example, that Tryon's groups differed in their willingness to leave safe corners for open spaces—and that different mazes differed in the arrangement of corners and open spaces. We do know that selective breeding experiments have been performed—with results similar to Tryon's—using active versus inactive rats, emotional versus phlegmatic rats, and even alcoholic versus sober rats!

Heredity and Environment. Tryon's rats were presumably treated alike— they all lived in the same kinds of cages, ate the same type of food, and had the same amount of maze-running experience. Thus any systematic differences in the scores made by the two groups of rats can be confidently attributed to differences in heredity. More commonly, experimenters use rats or mice that have been inbred (by breeding sisters to brothers for a number of generations) until genetic variations among them are minimized and the individual members of the strain are practically carbon copies of one another. Then differences in environment are introduced—for example, one subgroup is raised in bare cages, the other in an "enriched" environment. Any nonrandom differences that are found between the two subgroups can therefore be safely attributed to differences in environment.

In fact, differences in maze performance as large as those between Tryon's "bright" and "dull" strains of rat can be produced in either strain, simply by varying the complexity of their early environment (Cooper & Zubek, 1958). Thus it is important to distinguish between the specific genetic makeup of an organism, its **genotype,** and the manner in which these genes are expressed in a particular organism's development, its **phenotype.** The same genotype may yield quite different phenotypes, depending on the organism's environment.

Such techniques cannot, of course, be used with human beings. A perennial question asked of psychologists is: How much of human behavior is inherited and how much is due to the effects of environment? Often it is impossible to answer this question because there is generally no way to hold environment constant and vary only heredity (as Tryon did), or to hold heredity constant and vary only environment (as experimenters with inbred rats do).

Nature, however, occasionally provides us with the perfect opportunity to view heredity held constant: two people with exactly the same genes (the same genotype). In the United States 1 out of every 86 births results in twins. Of these, the major proportion—about three-quarters—are **fraternal twins.** Fraternal twins are conceived when a woman's ovaries release two ova instead of one, and each ovum is fertilized separately by a different sperm. Thus fraternal twins are no more closely related than ordinary siblings—on the average, they share 50 percent of their genes with each other (the same proportion that they share with each of their parents). Fraternal twins do not even have to have the same father: There are several authenticated cases of twins fathered by two different men. The other quarter of twins are **identi-**

cal. Sometimes a fertilized egg, for unknown reasons, splits in two and forms two embryos instead of one. The genetic material in these two twins is identical—they have 100 percent of their genes in common—so any differences between them must be due to environment. Bear in mind, though, that "environment" includes what happens *before* birth as well as after. One member of a pair of twins is often more favorably situated in the uterus than the other; birth weights of twins often differ considerably. There is also an advantage to the baby born first—the second-born may suffer the ill effects of having been deprived of oxygen for a longer period of time.

The Study of Nature and Nurture

Many human characteristics have been studied with the goal of determining the relative contributions of heredity and environment. The methods employed are, of course, necessarily less direct than the technique of selective breeding—and the results, accordingly, are sometimes ambiguous. **Family studies** often indicate that a particular trait occurs more frequently among parents, siblings, and other relatives in some family lines than in the population at large. However, such data do not make clear whether the cause of such "running in families" is the genetic similarity of close relatives, or the fact that their environments are similar, or both. **Twin studies** try to provide an answer by comparing, for the trait in question, the similarity of identical twins with the similarity of fraternal twins. Since identical twins have 100 percent of their genes in common, while fraternal twins have only about 50 percent, identical twins should be more alike than fraternals if the trait is genetically determined. However, since it is known that identical twins experience more similar environments than do fraternals, environment is not in fact held constant when the two types of twins are compared. Finally, **adoption studies** focus upon children given up for adoption at a very early age and thus reared without contact with their biological relatives. The aim of an adoption study is to *separate* genetic from environmental variables; such studies depend upon the assumption that the placement of children into adoptive homes has been essentially random. Complications arise if, for example, the biological children of "superior" parents tend to be placed into equally "superior" adoptive homes.

Twin and adoption studies have focused on a number of physical, mental, and behavioral traits. The results of such studies will be reported and critically evaluated where they are relevant throughout this book.

SUMMARY

1. There are three basic types of neurons. *Sensory neurons* are connected to receptor cells located in the skin, muscles and joints, internal organs, and sense organs. They carry information from these receptors toward the spinal cord or brain. *Motor neurons* carry information away from the spinal cord or brain, and many form synapses with muscle cells. *Interneurons* receive signals from sensory neurons and send signals to other interneurons or motor neurons.

2. A neuron is a cell that transmits information in the form of *nerve impulses;* these normally travel from a *dendrite* or the *cell body* out to the tips of the axon *(axon terminals),* where they can affect other neurons.

3. The inside of a neuron is normally electrically negative with respect to its outside. This is called its *resting potential.* When a nerve impulse reaches a particular point on the neuron, the interior becomes momentarily positive at that point. This reversal of polarity, called an *action potential,* is caused by the opening and closing of microscopic channels in the membrane, thereby allowing electrically charged ions to move in and out of the neuron.

4. The transfer of information between two neurons takes place at a junction called the *synapse;* for a message to cross the synaptic space, a substance called a *neurotransmitter* is released, to be taken up at specific receptor sites on the other neuron. This whole process of sending a chemical signal from one neuron to another is called *synaptic transmission.*

5. *Internally produced chemicals called neuromodulators* can affect neurotransmission without actually serving as neurotransmitters. An example is enkephalins, which seems to block the transmission of pain signals at certain synapses.

6. The action of neurotransmitters (e.g., *norepinephrine, acetylcholine, dopamine,* and *serotonin*) can be affected by chemical substance in a wide variety of ways. Substances that inhibit normal effects are called *antagonists;* those that facilitate them are called *agonists.*

7. The nervous system can be considered in terms of a hierarchical organization. The *central nervous system* consists of all those neurons completely within the brain or spinal cord, while the *peripheral nervous system* consists of all the other neurons.

8. The spinal cord carries information between the brain and the body and also provides the connections between the sensory and motor neurons involved in spinal reflexes.

9. The hindbrain consists of the *medulla,* the *pons,* and the *cerebellum;* the cerebellum is in charge of equilibrium, muscle tone, and coordination. The hindbrain and the midbrain make up the *brain stem.*

10. Scattered throughout the brain stem is an intricate network of cells known as the *reticular formation;* this system has a role in sleep and arousal.

11. The forebrain consists of the *thalamus,* the *hypothalamus,* and the *cerebrum.* The thalamus is an important collection and integration center for sensory information; the hypothalamus regulates motivated behavior and maintains a balance in many body systems.

12. The cerebrum includes the *limbic system,* which plays a major role in emotional behavior, and the *neocortex,* which contains about 70 percent of all neurons in the central nervous system.

13. Some areas of the neocortex have specialized functions; these areas include the *motor cortex,* the *visual cortex,* the *auditory cortex,* and the *somatosensory cortex* (which receives sensory information from the skin, joints and muscles, and internal organs). Such abilities as thinking, speaking, and reading are localized in the *association areas* of the cortex.

14. The cerebrum consists of a right hemisphere and a left hemisphere; the left hemisphere controls the right side of the body. Language abilities are generally localized in the left hemisphere; the right hemisphere may function in abilities such as spatial relationships and perception and nonverbal patterns.

15. The peripheral motor system has two divisions: *somatic* and *autonomic.* The somatic motor system innervates skeletal muscles. The autonomic system is composed of two subdivisions, the *sympathetic* and the *parasympathetic.* The sympathetic system is associated with activation and expenditure of energy (especially in stress situations), and the parasympathetic system is associated with the maintenance of routine functions such as digestion.

16. The *endocrine system* consists of glands that secrete hormones into the bloodstream. These hormones regulate a number of vital metabolic and physiologic functions and interact closely with the autonomic nervous system.

17. A person's heredity is determined by the *genes,* located on the *chromosomes* in the nuclei of body cells.

SUGGESTED READINGS

CARLSON, N. R. (1986). *Physiology of behavior* (3rd ed.). Boston: Allyn & Bacon. A comprehensive introduction to neuroscience.

KOLB, B., & WHISHAW, I. Q. (1985). *Fundamentals of human neuropsychology* (2nd ed.). New York: Freeman. A comprehensive review of the field, with considerable information regarding brain disorders.

RESTAK, R. M. (1984). *The brain.* New York: Bantam Books. A richly illustrated explanation of the nervous system based on the PBS series of the same name.

SACKS, O. (1985). *The man who mistook his wife for a hat and other clinical tales.* New York: Summit. In this book written for the layman, a neurologist explores the extraordinary life stories of twenty patients affected by a variety of neurological disorders.

SPRINGER, S. P., & DEUTSCH, G. (1985). *Left brain, right brain* (rev. ed.). New York: Freeman. A good overview of the work on hemispheric specialization.

THOMPSON, R. F. (1985). *The brain: An introduction to neuroscience.* New York: Freeman. An excellent introduction to current knowledge about the brain for the nonscientist.

3 Sensation

A|ll our lives our brains remain in total darkness, insulated from the outside world by layers of tissue and bone. Knowledge of that world is carried into the brain through the sensory systems. These systems respond to certain aspects of the environment to produce sensations such as light, sound, and taste. This chapter considers exactly how this is done by each sensory system.

Sensations are private or subjective events. You may describe your sensations to others, but no one else can directly experience them. Nevertheless, if a particular change in the physical environment evokes similar reports from many different people, it seems reasonable to assume that they experienced similar sensations. For example, turning up the volume control on a phonograph causes most listeners to describe the sound as growing louder. This shows a consistent relationship between a *physical stimulus* (the amount of energy coming from the loudspeaker) and the listeners' *sensations* (or at least their descriptions of what they hear). Relations of this sort are often referred to as **psychophysical relations,** since they seem to relate physical and psychological variables (stimuli and sensations).

Each of the body's sensory systems is sensitive to some form of physical energy. Our auditory system responds to rapid variations in air pressure (sound), while our visual system responds to specific forms of electromagnetic energy (light). Yet we don't respond to every stimulus in our environment; there are limits to our sensitivity. First, we can only sense forms of energy for which we have "receivers" or **receptor organs** (eyes, ears, etc.) and to which we are "attuned." (For example, we are surrounded by electromag-

Charles Jervis's portrait of Sir Isaac Newton (1642–1727). Newton did much of the original research on the nature of light and color. (Royal Society)

netic energy in the form of radio and television waves, yet unless we have a radio or television turned on, we sense none of it.) Second, the energy itself must be intense enough to produce a noticeable sensation: A source of light must be strong enough for us to see it; a source of sound must be intense enough for us to hear it.

Some of the earliest work in experimental psychology was aimed at assessing our sensory limits. By varying the strength or intensity of a stimulus, psychologists found that they could determine the minimum level capable of evoking a sensation. This level, called the **absolute threshold,** marks the boundary between energy levels strong enough to evoke a noticeable sensation and those too weak to do so (see Table 3–1). Another kind of sensory limit is defined by our ability to notice a change in sensation. For example, a source of light has to be increased or decreased a minimum amount for someone to notice that change. Again, early experimental psychologists tried to measure exactly how small a difference in a physical stimulus would be noticed. They referred to this as the **difference threshold.**

The methods developed to measure absolute and difference thresholds were among the earliest attempts at precise measurement in psychology. They are still of interest, not only on historical grounds, but also because they are simple and adequate as rough measures.

MEASURING SENSORY CAPACITIES

Absolute and Difference Thresholds

You can obtain a rough measure of an absolute threshold simply by asking a subject to adjust the intensity level of a stimulus until it just begins to evoke a sensation. For example, "Slowly increase the energy level of this light source by turning this knob until you just begin to see the light." Generally, the **method of adjustment** is a perfectly good procedure and leads to a reasonably consistent measure of the absolute threshold. Yet certain problems arise when you attempt to be more precise. First of all, subjects won't be entirely consistent if asked to repeat this procedure; they will set the threshold intensity at a slightly different value each time. The same thing happens when subjects are asked to reverse the procedure—that is, to begin with a high intensity and slowly reduce it until the sensation disappears.

In an attempt to obtain more consistent measures, the **method of con-**

Table 3–1:   Absolute Thresholds

These estimates of absolute thresholds indicate the incredible sensitivity of the various receptor organs.	
Sense	Absolute Threshold
Vision	A candle flame can be seen from 30 miles away on a clear, dark night.
Hearing	A watch can be heard ticking from 20 feet away in a quiet room.
Taste	A teaspoon of sugar can be tasted in 2 gallons of water.
Smell	A drop of perfume can be smelled when circulated into 6 large rooms.
Touch	A fly's wing can be felt falling onto one's cheek from a height of 1 centimeter.

After Galanter (1962).

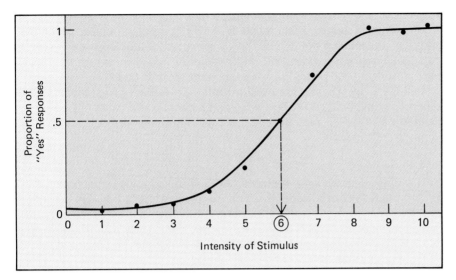

Figure 3–1 The absolute threshold of a stimulus is the intensity that has a 50 percent chance of evoking a sensation. A smooth curve has been fitted to the data points, and it appears that a stimulus intensity of about 6 will evoke a "yes" response about 50 percent of the time. Thus the absolute threshold is about 6.

stant stimuli was developed. A fixed set of stimulus intensities is repeatedly presented, in a randomly determined sequence, over a series of test trials. On each trial one intensity is presented and subjects report whether or not they experience any sensation; for example, "Yes, I saw the light that time," or "No, I didn't hear a sound that time." This would be simple if the method revealed an intensity level above which subjects always reported a sensation, and below which they never did. Unfortunately, things are not quite that simple. Between the high intensities, which almost always evoke a "yes" report, and the very low intensities, which almost never do, there is a middle range where the proportion of reported sensations gradually increases with the intensity. Stimuli in this range sometimes evoke a sensation and at other times do not. What, then, determines the absolute threshold? It seems reasonable to call the absolute threshold the intensity that has a 50 percent chance of evoking a sensation. Figure 3–1 shows how this threshold is calculated.

Measuring difference thresholds involves a similar procedure. Here, instead of presenting a single intensity of the signal on each trial, a pair of intensities is presented and the subject reports on his or her ability to discern a difference between the two sensations ("Did the second light seem brighter than the first?" "Is this sound louder than that sound?") As before, a general pattern of results emerges. There is a range of intensity differences so small they almost never evoke a reported difference in sensation, a range of large differences that almost always do, and a middle range in which the proportion of noticeable differences increases slowly with the size of the stimulus intensity difference. Thus the graph in Figure 3–1 is also characteristic of difference threshold data, only here the units would refer to the size of the stimulus intensity difference. The best measure of the difference threshold seems to be the physical difference that is noticed 50 percent of the time. This difference threshold is often called the **just noticeable difference (JND).**

A very general feature of difference thresholds was apparent long before the formal measurement techniques just described were developed: People are usually more sensitive to changes in weak stimuli than they are to similar changes in stronger or more intense stimuli. For example, if you were listening to two voices in an otherwise quiet room, you would readily notice the addition of a third voice. Yet the addition of one voice to the chatter of many

Table 3–2: Some Typical Values of Weber's Constant for Various Types of Stimuli.

Type of Stimulus	Weber's Constant
Electric shock	.01
Heaviness	.02
Length	.03
Vibration	.04
Loudness	.05
Brightness	.08

After Teghtsoonian (1971).

voices at a large cocktail party would probably go unnoticed. Similarly, you would probably notice a difference in weight between an empty paper cup and one containing a penny, yet you wouldn't notice a difference between a cup containing 100 pennies and one containing 101, even though the difference in weight (one penny) is exactly the same in both cases.

In 1834 a German psychophysicist named Ernst Weber suggested that the difference threshold (JND) for each type of stimulus is a constant fraction or proportion (k) of the stimulus intensity (I) being changed; that is,

$$JND = kI$$

This is often referred to as **Weber's law,** and the constant of proportionality (k) is called **Weber's constant.** For example, Weber's constant for lifted weights, or heaviness, is about .02. This means that the JND for a 50 gram weight is .02 times 50 grams, or 1 gram, while the JND for a 500 gram weight is .02 times 500 grams, or 10 grams. Table 3–2 indicates some typical values of Weber's constant for other types of stimuli.

More recent research indicates that Weber's law should be viewed as only a rough characterization of our sensitivity to changes in stimulation. It fails in the case of very weak or very intense stimuli and is only approximately true for the middle range of stimuli. Nevertheless, it is a useful, general approximation of human sensitivity to stimulus differences.

Psychophysical Scaling

Determining sensory thresholds is only one of the ways in which we can measure our sensory capacities. Another is deciding how the strength or quality of a sensation changes as the physical stimulus is changed. For example, how rapidly does loudness grow with increases in the physical energy of a sound? How fast does brightness grow as the energy level of a light source is increased? Attempts to answer such questions have produced measurement techniques called **psychophysical scaling.** The value of such techniques can be shown by the following practical problem.

Suppose you were asked to design a volume control for a phonograph to produce a subjectively constant increase in loudness as the control knob is turned clockwise for one full revolution (360 degrees); that is, each degree of rotation should seem to increase the loudness by the same amount. You might consider building the control so that the sound energy coming from the loudspeakers increased at a constant rate as the knob turned (each degree of rotation produced exactly the same increase in energy). If you did this, you would be disappointed, for the same amount of rotation (the same increase in energy) would produce much larger changes in loudness at the lower volume settings than at the higher ones. A more satisfactory system—and the one actually used in most volume controls—is indicated in Figure 3–2. Only if a given rotation produces progressively larger increases in sound energy as the knob is turned will listeners hear a constant growth in loudness.

You might argue, as Gustav Fechner did in 1860, that the relation between sound energy and loudness could be predicted from Weber's study of difference thresholds. The argument goes something like this: If the JND is the smallest noticeable difference in sensation, then larger differences could be considered the sum of many JNDs. Since Weber's law states that the size of a JND increases as stimulus intensity increases, progressively larger increases

Figure 3–2 Only if equal rotations of the knob produce progressively larger increments in sound energy (E) will loudness (L) increase at a constant rate.

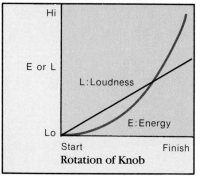

in intensity should be required to produce the same difference in sensation. Fechner showed that this argument implies that the relation between physical stimulus intensity (I) and the strength of sensation (S) is logarithmic; specifically,

$$S = c \log I$$

where c is simply a constant that depends on your unit of intensity. This logarithmic relation, often referred to as **Fechner's law,** implies that an increase in weight from 50 to 100 grams, for example, should produce the same increase in the sensation of heaviness as an increase from 25 to 50 grams, or from 100 to 200. The same *ratio* of stimulus intensities produces the same difference in sensation.

Fechner's law has proved to be less generally applicable than he hoped. This is partly because Weber's law is itself only a rough approximation (it tends to fail at extreme intensity levels), and partly because more direct ways of measuring the relations between physical stimulus variables and sensation have since been devised.

In 1956 S. S. Stevens showed that you could ask subjects to specify the strength of a sensation simply by assigning it a number. He called this method **magnitude estimation.** For example, you could present a stimulus of a certain light intensity and tell subjects that it has a brightness of 10, then present another light intensity and ask them to assign it a number indicating its relative brightness. If subjects believe the second light is twice as bright as the first, they should assign it the number 20; if they think it is only half as bright, they should give it the number 5; and so on. You could repeat this procedure with many different light intensities until you had a clear picture of the average number assigned to each. The black line in Figure 3–3 shows the type of relation defined in this way. Increases in light intensity produce progressively smaller changes in perceived brightness—the same general conclusion Fechner drew from Weber's law. However, Stevens argued that this is true only for certain types of stimulation. For example, magnitude estimation of the sensation evoked by electrical shock grows slowly at first, and then more rapidly as the shock is increased (the color line in Figure 3–3)—the opposite of the result predicted by Fechner's law.

Stevens proposed a more general way of characterizing such relations. This is referred to as **Steven's power law,** since it asserts that sensation (S) is proportional to stimulus intensity (I) raised to some power (b):

$$S = kI^{b}$$

where k is simply a constant that depends on the unit of measurement being used. The three curves in Figure 3–3 follow this rule, with b equal to .33 for brightness, 1 for apparent length, and 3.5 for electrical shock. When b is less than 1, as it is for brightness, sensation grows progressively more slowly as intensity increases, but when b is greater than 1, as it is for shock, sensation grows progressively more rapidly as intensity increases. When b equals 1, as it does for apparent length, sensation is directly proportional to intensity.

Signal Detection Theory

While the traditional techniques for measuring sensory thresholds and sensitivity to changes in sensation are generally adequate, there are some problems. Underlying the concept of a "threshold" or a "JND" is the idea that

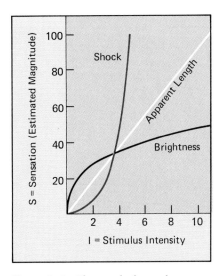

Figure 3–3 The graph shows the average estimated magnitude of sensation (S) for various intensities (I) of light, line length, and electric shock. These curves can be described by Stevens's power law, S = kI^b, with the exponent b equal to .33 for brightness, I for apparent length, and 3.5 for shock. (After Stevens, 1961)

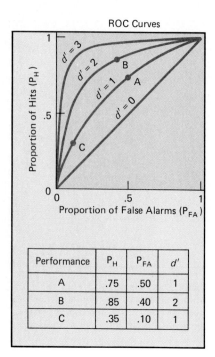

ROC Curves

Performance	P_H	P_{FA}	d'
A	.75	.50	1
B	.85	.40	2
C	.35	.10	1

Figure 3–4 Plotting ROC Curves. Performance of a detection task can be summarized by the proportion of times the subject reports signals when they are presented, "hits" (P_H), and the proportion of times a signal is erroneously reported when none was presented, "false alarms" (P_{FA}). Any performance can be represented as a point on the type of graph shown here. For example, point A indicates a performance in which P_H equals .75 and P_{FA} equals .50. It has been found that instructing a subject to be more or less conservative in reporting signals shifts the performance point along a curve called a *receiver operating characteristic* (ROC). Thus, giving subjects "conservative instructions" might shift their performance from point A to point C along the same ROC curve labeled *d' = 1*. In contrast, increasing signal intensity slightly might shift performance from point *A* to point *B*, which lies on another ROC curve, labeled *d' = 2*. Notice that the higher the value of *d'*, the closer the subject can come to perfect discrimination (the upper left corner of the graph where P_H equals 1 and P_{FA} equals 0. Thus *d'* is a measure of sensitivity or discriminability. It is independent of the subject's tendency to be "liberal" or "conservative," since this only shifts performance along a particular ROC curve.

Figure 3–5 This is a typical waveform of the speech sound "ah." Even as simple a speech sound as this one involves a complex variation in air pressure over time. (From Denes & Pinson, 1963)

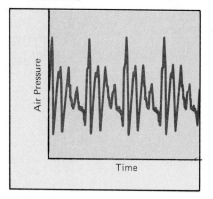

people either do, or do not, detect a test stimulus each time it is presented. Yet subjects often say they are uncertain whether they detected anything; for example, "I thought I might have heard something that time, but I'm really not sure." If subjects are instructed to report a detection even when they are uncertain *("liberal instructions"),* they tend to report more detections, and this liberal reporting *lowers* the measured threshold. On the other hand, if subjects are discouraged from reporting a detection when they are uncertain *("conservative instructions"),* they tend to report fewer detections, and this *raises* the measured threshold. Such changes in the measured threshold seem to reflect shifts in subjects' judgmental standards rather than any real change in their sensitivity to the test stimuli. What was needed was a measure of sensitivity to a stimulus that isn't influenced by instructional effects. Such a measure, termed *d',* is provided by the **signal detection theory** (Green & Swets, 1966). The way in which this measure is obtained is illustrated in Figure 3–4. The central idea is that sensations evoked by very weak test stimuli may also occur in their absence. Thus subjects must decide whether the sensations were really evoked by a test stimulus or were simply a product of irrelevant "background noise" in their own sensory system.

To understand the sorts of things that can influence such reasoning, suppose you are spending the night in an old house. Such houses spontaneously generate a variety of sounds as they expand or contract with the temperature, old pipes rattle in their fittings, or loose shingles and shutters are tossed by the wind. Lying in bed, you hear a sound. Is it a prowler or simply part of the normal background noise? Your decision will be influenced by at least two factors: how unusual the sound is compared to the usual noises of the house, and your estimate of how likely it is that a prowler would be there. This is often referred to as your **expectancy.** If you know there has been a recent series of burglaries in the neighborhood, you would be far more likely to investigate the noise that you would otherwise. Thus the cost or *consequence* of an erroneous decision is also an important consideration. While such judgmental factors may also influence your interpretation of weak stimuli, they do *not* affect the *d'* measures of sensitivity shown in Figure 3–4. (For a comprehensive review of psychophysical measurement, see Falmangne, 1986.)

HEARING

Auditory Stimuli

The type of environmental stimulus that normally produces the sensation of sound is a rapid variation in air pressure next to your ears. This is usually caused by a similar variation introduced into the air some distance away and slightly earlier in time. If you were high in the stands watching the half-time show at a football game, you would see the bass drum being struck a few moments before you heard the sound. The rapid variations in air pressure produced by the vibrating surface of the drum spread through the air at about 1,100 feet per second, so that a similar, but weaker, pattern of variation is eventually produced next to your ears. If the drummer were 1,100 feet away, the sound would take 1 second to reach your ear. You would see the drum being hit before this, since light travels much faster than sound (186,000 miles per second). Other sources of sound (horns, cheering fans, a plane overhead) produce additional patterns of pressure variation that could reach your ears at the same time as those from the drum, mixing with and adding to them to produce an even more complex pattern of variation. Even a single human voice is a very complex pattern of pressure variations. Figure 3–5 shows the variations produced by a speaker making the sound "ah."

Pure Tones. It is possible to consider complex patterns of the sort shown in Figure 3–5 as being made up of much simpler patterns called *pure tones.* Figure 3–6 illustrates particular pure tones. They consist of a rapid increase and decrease of air pressure over time in a regular pattern called a *sine wave.* All pure tones have this general form, although they differ in frequency and in amplitude. The **frequency** of a pure tone is defined as the number of complete cycles of pressure variation occurring in 1 second. (A complete cycle is the sequence of change from the highest pressure down to the lowest pressure and back to the highest pressure again.) Frequency is usually expressed in cycles per second or **hertz (Hz).** The **amplitude** of a pure tone is the greatest change from normal air pressure level produced during the cyclic variation in pressure. Figure 3–6 shows pure tones that differ in frequency and amplitude. Roughly speaking, the sensation of **pitch** is determined by the frequency of a tone, and its loudness by the amplitude. For example, the higher-pitched notes on a piano are produced by shorter strings that vibrate more rapidly, while the lower-pitched tones are produced by longer strings that vibrate more slowly. The harder a particular key is struck, the more the string vibrates back and forth, producing a higher-amplitude tone, which sounds louder.

Most people can only hear tones whose frequencies are between 20 and 20,000 Hz, and people vary in their sensitivity to tones within this range. Figure 3–7 illustrates the range of pure tones we normally hear. The lower curve is known as an **audiometric function.** It shows the lowest audible (threshold) energy for each frequency. The upper curve shows the highest tolerable energy (anything higher causes pain and damage to the ear). Notice that sound energy is expressed in bels. The **bel,** or **decibel, scale** (1 bel equals 10 decibels) is named in honor of Alexander Graham Bell. One bel represents a tenfold (10^1) increase in energy, two bels a hundredfold (10^2) increase, and three bels a thousandfold increase (10^3). Zero on the bel scale corresponds to the normal threshold energy for a 1,000 Hz tone. The threshold energy of a 20 Hz tone is over 80 dB or (8 bels); thus the threshold en-

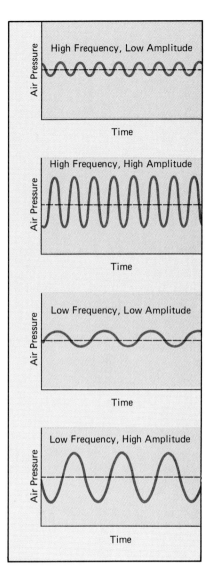

Figure 3–6 The graph shows four pure tones that differ in how rapidly the cycles of air pressure variation occur (frequency) and in the magnitude of that variation (amplitude).

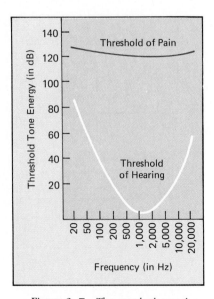

Figure 3–7 The graph shows the range of pure tones we normally hear. The white curve is the normal audiometric function.

Figure 3–8 (Top) A pure tone of 128 Hz produced by an oscillator contains only that frequency. (Bottom) The note C (middle C) on a piano has the same fundamental frequency (128 Hz) but also contains other overtones.

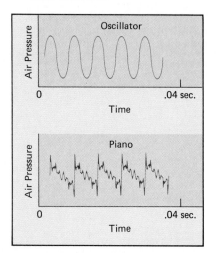

ergy for a 20 Hz tone is more than 10^8 times as great as that for a 1,000 Hz tone.

The average energy level of the sound frequencies we hear in normal conversation is about 60 dB or 6 bels. This means it is 10^6 or 1,000,000 times the threshold level of a 1,000 Hz tone. Prolonged exposure to sounds above 80 or 90 dB can produce permanent hearing loss. The sounds at a rock music concert may be as high as 150 dB for those standing near the speakers.

Combinations of Pure Tones. We rarely hear a single pure tone under normal circumstances, although the sound of a single note played on a flute comes close to it. Pure tones can be produced electronically for such purposes as tests of hearing or the composition of "electronic music." (If you have ever heard electronic music, you probably noticed the unnatural purity of the individual notes.) A single note played on most other musical instruments is really a mixture of pure tones. This can be seen in Figure 3–8, which shows the same note **(middle C)** produced by an *oscillator* (an electronic device capable of producing a pure tone) and a piano. The piano produces several tones at once—the fundamental tone (128 Hz for middle C) and several overtones. The **fundamental tone** is the basic frequency of the note and sounds the loudest. The **overtones** are multiples of the fundamental and sound softer than the fundamental. On the piano you can hear as many as 15 overtones besides the fundamental tone. These overtones (also called **harmonics**) blend with the fundamental tone to give the note its characteristic quality or **timbre**. The timbre, or pattern of overtones, varies with each instrument. It is determined by the material the instrument is made of, its design, and the way it is played. It is the timbre that makes the same note sound different when it comes from a tuba, a piano, or a human voice.

Most of the sounds we hear contain a wide range of frequencies. In fact, the sound of a shower running in an empty bathtub includes approximately equal amounts of all the audible frequencies. Such a sound is often called *white noise.* Since we are not equally sensitive to all frequencies, the loudness of a sound made up of many frequencies depends on the specific amount of energy at each frequency. In fact, most sounds are complex and constantly shifting mixture of tones. The sounds of speech, as recorded by use of a **sound spectrogram** or *voice print,* provide an excellent example (see Figure 3–9).

The Ear

The ear is made up of three major structural components: the outer ear, the middle ear, and the cochlea. The outer ear, or *pinna,* is essentially a funnel that channels the air pressure variations into the head, where they are forced against the surface of a flexible membrane called the **eardrum,** causing it to vibrate (see Figure 3–10). These movements of the eardrum are then transmitted through the **middle ear** by a series of three small bones: the *hammer,* the *anvil,* and the *stirrup.* The hammer connects the eardrum to the anvil, which, in turn, is connected by the stirrup to another flexible membrane covering a small opening in the **cochlea,** or inner ear. This membrane, called the **oval window,** is much smaller than the eardrum. The bones connecting the two cause movements in the eardrum to produce smaller but more powerful movements of the oval window.

It is in the cochlea that the movements begun by pressure variations

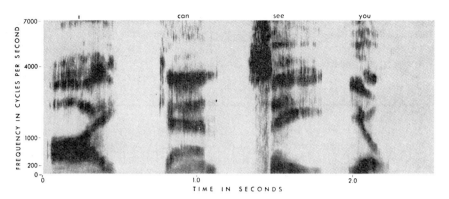

Figure 3–9 A sound spectrogram (or "voice print") of the simple sentence: "I can see you." The darkened regions show which tone frequencies were present (from 0 to 7,000 Hz on the ordinate) during each moment in time (0 to 2.5 seconds along the abcissa). (From McBurney/Collings, *Introduction to Sensation Perception*, 2nd Ed., 1984, p. 170.).

against the eardrum are changed into patterns of neural activity that produce the sensation of hearing. The amplified pressure variations on the oval window are transmitted through fluid-filled channels within the cochlea. When the fluid in the channel moves, it causes wavelike movements of the **basilar membrane,** which is the wall of one channel. Hair cells in the basilar membrane are attached to neurons that fire (transmit a neural impulse) when the hair cells are bent by the movement of the membrane. Figure 3–11A shows the snail-shaped cochlea; a better view of the fluid-filled channels within the cochlea is shown in Figure 3–11B, which is an "uncoiled" drawing of the normally coiled structure. Notice how the pressure vibrations enter by the oval window, pass through a fluid-filled channel to the end of the cochlea, and pass back through another channel to the **round window,** where they are absorbed.

Figure 3–10 A diagram of the ear, showing the outer ear, the middle ear, and the cochlea.

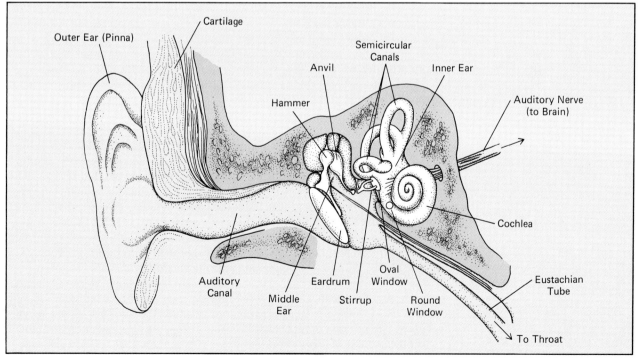

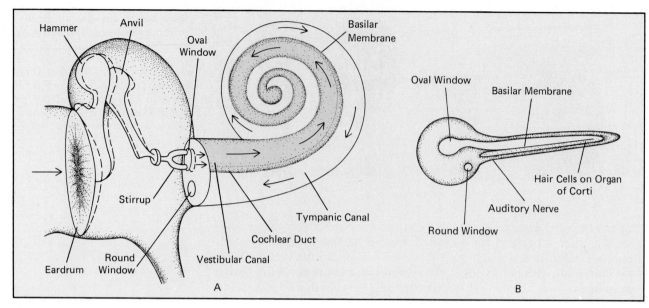

Figure 3–11 A. The cochlea, or inner ear, is a coiled, snail-shaped canal; it is the part of the ear that contains the organ of hearing, called the organ of Corti. B. An "uncoiled" drawing of the normally coiled structure of the cochlea. It is easier to see here how the pressure vibrations enter through the oval window, pass through a fluid-filled channel to the end of the cochlea, and pass back through another channel to the round window.

Theories of Hearing

Neural impulses are transmitted to the brain from neurons in the hair cells of the basilar membrane. The main question about hearing is how these neural impulses are coded to give different kinds of information—for instance, how do we know that a tone is a certain pitch (how do we tell middle C from a note an octave below)?

One theory of pitch perception, called the **place theory,** is based on the idea that different sound frequencies (different pitches) actually trigger different neurons. It has been found that the frequency of vibrations determines which portion of the basilar membrane is moved or pushed about most (Békésy, 1955). Thus pitch information could correspond to the stimulation of particular neurons on a specific section of the membrane. Electrophysiological studies have, in fact, shown that individual neurons in the cat's auditory nerve are "tuned" (most sensitive) to specific frequencies (see Figure 3–12).

One problem with this theory is that not all frequencies seem to cause more movement in the basilar membrane in one place than another. In fact, only high and (to some extent) middle frequencies seem to do this; pitch information about low frequencies must be transmitted in another way.

An alternative theory is that neural activity is coded in terms of the rate (rather than the place) at which neurons are triggered. This is called the **frequency theory** of pitch perception (Wever & Bray, 1937). In fact, it can be shown that the rate or frequency of pulses traveling up the auditory nerve to the brain matches that of a tone over a wide range of frequencies. This is not too surprising for low frequencies, since individual nerves can respond over and over at these low rates. Yet it is impossible for a single nerve to fire, recover, and fire again as fast as would be necessary to follow a high-frequency tone. However, such high firing rates could be the product of several different sets of nerve fibers, each firing in turn at a lower rate, but combining to produce the higher overall rate (just as when you listen to ten carpenters hammering, you hear many more hammer blows per minute than any one

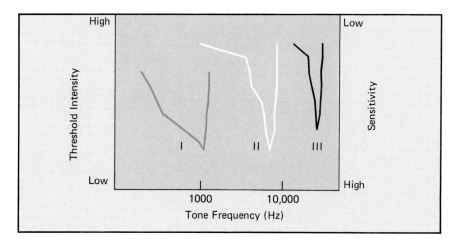

Figure 3–12 Tuning curves for three neurons in a cat's auditory nerve are consistent with the place theory of hearing. Each curve indicates the sensitivity of a single neuron to various frequencies of tone as registered by a microelectrode inserted into the neuron. Measures are taken of the minimal (threshold) intensity of tone that, at each frequency, increases neuronal activity. The lower the threshold intensity, the greater is that neuron's sensitivity to that frequency. Notice that neurons, I, II, and III are "tuned" (most sensitive) to progressively higher frequencies, as if they were carrying information from a particular place on the basilar membrane. (Adapted from Kiang, Watanabe, Thomas, & Clark, 1962)

carpenter could make). This is often referred to as the **volley principle,** being named for the way in which rows of soldiers in the Revolutionary War loaded, fired, and reloaded one after another to produce more frequent volleys than would have been possible if all the rows fired at the same time.

While pure-tone stimuli are adequate to measure basic properties of human hearing, most of the sounds we hear are more complex. Of special interest are the shifting combinations of tones that make up human speech. In fact, certain regions of our sensory cortex may respond only to such stimuli (Lieberman & Studdart-Kennedy, 1978). These same regions may also be involved in speech production. For example, electrical stimulation of certain points in a person's brain can simultaneously alter perception of speech *and* cause speechlike movements in facial muscles (Ojemann & Mateer, 1979). We are really just beginning to explore these complex aspects of hearing. (Speech perception will be considered further in Chapter 8.)

Hearing Loss and Treatment

There are a number of ways in which the hearing mechanism can break down, starting with the eardrum and working inward. Damage to the eardrum itself can occur in many ways, the most common being the effect of external pressure, such as that caused by a blow to the ears, a nearby explosion, or extreme water pressure during a scuba dive. Ordinarily the pressure within the middle ear is matched to the external air pressure by means of the air entering the *Eustachian tube,* a small channel that runs from the rear of the mouth to the middle ear (see Figure 3–10). However, a difference in external air pressure may puncture the eardrum if changes in pressure occur too rapidly, or if the Eustachian tube is blocked because of a heavy cold or a failure to swallow frequently enough during changes in pressure—as in a scuba dive or when an airplane takes off or lands. This damage can usually be repaired surgically, but the scar tissue in the repaired eardrum may produce permanent changes in the ear's response to various frequencies.

In a common form of deafness the tiny bones in the middle ear fuse because of calcium deposits, and this fusion effectively blocks the mechanical transmission of sound to the cochlea. Delicate surgical techniques can break the calcium deposits and restore the flexibility of the bones. This surgery produces a dramatic and almost complete return of normal hearing.

APPLICATION

The Bionic Ear

Ordinarily, the bending of hair cells attached to neurons at various points along the basilar membrane triggers the nerve impulses we experience as sound. When these hair cells are missing or badly damaged, the result is a profound form of deafness—the fate of nearly a quarter of a million Americans. Conventional hearing aids that amplify sounds are ineffective, since there are no hair cells to trigger nerve impulses. Fortunately, there is now greater promise for treating this form of deafness. It involves the construction of the first truly artificial sense organ, what could be called a "bionic ear."

The purpose of the bionic ear is to trigger nerve impulses electrically (rather than mechanically by bending hair cells). The basic strategy is to implant tiny electrodes at various points along the basilar membrane.

These electrodes are activated only when a sound is present that would ordinarily affect hair cells at that point on the basilar membrane.

The figure below shows a schematic representation of the components of the bionic ear. A complex sound wave is picked up by a microphone worn on the ear like a normal hearing aid. Filters separate the frequency components in the sound wave into three bands: low, medium, and high. These separate components of the sound are amplified, converted to radio signals, and then transmitted through the skin to three permanently implanted receivers, one for each frequency band. Each receiver activates a particular electrode implanted at the point on the basilar membrane ordinarily affected by that range of frequencies. The electrode can then trigger impulses electrically whenever its particular range of frequencies is present in a sound, and the brain receives at least a rough approximation of the normal pattern of neural activity produced along the basilar membrane.

Devices have been developed that can separate the sound components into as many as 10 frequency ranges, thereby activating 10 separate electrodes at various points along the basilar membrane. While, in theory, increasing the number of electrodes should improve the range of hearing, the spread of electrical activity from each electrode poses some practical limits. Each electrode triggers nerve impulses in neurons spaced over some distance along the basilar membrane, including some already triggered by adjacent electrodes. Thus until some way can be found to mimic the highly specific action of each hair cell on particular neurons, the bionic ear will yield only a rough approximation to the quality of normal hearing. Nevertheless, there is already evidence that patients with implants of this sort can distinguish many sounds. Some patients have even attained word recognition as high as 70 percent correct (Loeb, 1985; Tyler et al., 1986). Thus the device offers at least some hope for people who would otherwise be totally deaf.

The components of the bionic ear.

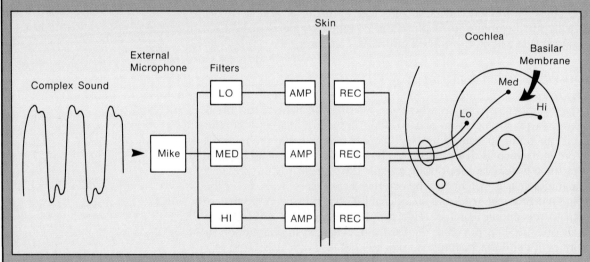

The basilar membrane is susceptible to damage in a number of ways. First of all, there is the progressive deterioration due to age, which seems to affect the high-frequency regions of the membrane first. This produces heightened thresholds for the higher frequencies. A *hearing aid* designed to amplify the higher frequencies can restore normal hearing to many elderly people.

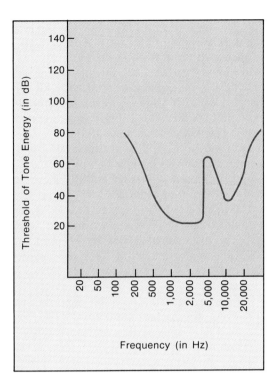

Figure 3–13 Prolonged exposure to very loud sounds of a particular frequency can cause loss of hearing at that frequency, or a *tonal gap*. For example, prolonged exposure to a 5,000 Hz tone could produce the sort of audiometric function shown here. Note the heightened threshold indicating loss of sensitivity around 5,000 Hz.

A very similar pattern of hearing loss occurs if a patient is given extensive doses of the drug **mycine,** which seems to cause progressive damage to the hair cells in the basilar membrane similar to the degeneration caused by age. Again, a hearing aid may restore normal hearing if the damage is not too extensive. (Extensive damage to the hair cells results in profound hearing loss. See the Application, The Bionic Ear, for a report on a new type of hearing aid specially developed to compensate for this damage.)

Exposure to very intense sounds can also cause damage to the basilar membrane. If the sound is primarily of one frequency, there may be damage to only one region, producing a *tonal gap;* that is, a loss of sensitivity to a narrow range of tones (see Figure 3–13). If the damage is not too great, a special hearing aid that amplifies only those frequencies to which sensitivity is reduced may restore normal hearing. Fortunately, there is tremendous redundancy in most sounds, which means that the ability to hear only a small part of the total frequency range may be all that is necessary for comprehension. People with tonal gaps are often unaware of any problem because their brain automatically compensates for the lost frequencies.

There are also various forms of nerve damage in the acoustic pathways or in the auditory projection areas in the cortex. These may be caused by a variety of factors, including birth defects, disease, blows to the head, and tumors. Nerve damage may result in profound deafness.

It is hard to make up for total loss of hearing. One way is to use another sensory system that provides the same information in a different form. For example, deaf people become quite adept at interpreting speech from lip movement. While normal people also rely on lip movements to some extent, it is only when hearing is lost that most people fully use the redundant visual information to interpret speech.

Sound Localization

Slight differences in the way a sound affects your two ears provide cues for localizing its source. For example, a sound coming from your left arrives both slightly earlier—and slightly stronger—at your left ear than at your right. The *time difference* is most useful for lower-frequency sounds (less than about 2,000 Hz); a *difference in intensity* is more useful for high-frequency sounds. This is because a time difference is more noticeable with low frequencies, while high frequencies lose more energy as they travel around the head. The time difference can be as large as .6 msec when a sound comes from your far left or far right. As it moves in front or behind you, this difference diminishes. Amazingly, even when a sound is only 3 degrees to the right or left of straight ahead, the .03 msec difference in time of arrival at each ear can be heard as a difference in apparent position. Since there is no difference in the arrival time or intensity at each ear, people have difficulty distinguishing whether a sound is directly in front or directly behind them. Normally this confusion can easily be resolved by simply moving your head so that the two ears are no longer equally distant from the source.

Two types of sound recording have been used to mimic normal localization cues (Figure 3–14). In *stereophonic recording* two microphones are placed much farther apart than your ears to exaggerate the localization cues. The sounds picked up by each microphone can then be played back through separate speakers placed well apart. If during the recording an instrument is closer to one microphone, it will be reproduced more loudly and earlier from one speaker than the other. However, this only mimics some aspects of normal localization cues—primarily the intensity difference. Notice in Figure 3–14 that a listener hears sounds from both loudspeakers in *both* ears. If a stereophonic recording is heard through earphones, each ear only hears the sounds picked up by one microphone. However, since the two recording microphones were much farther apart than normal ears, the localization cues are highly exaggerated.

In order to truly mimic normal localization cues, two things are necessary. First, recording must be done with two microphones separated by the normal distance between the ears; and then second, the recording must be listened to over earphones, so that the sounds picked up by each microphone go only to the corresponding ear. *Binaural recordings* made in this way accurately reproduce the time delay and intensity differences normally occurring at each ear (so long as you don't move your head while you listen). If you play a binaural tape through separated speakers, the time and intensity differences are too small to notice. Furthermore, the sounds from both speakers reach both ears.

Even though stereophonic recording doesn't mimic localization cues as accurately as binaural recording, it is more widely used. It can be enjoyed by one or more people without earphones; and it produces a highly exaggerated, but vivid, three-dimensional effect with earphones.

Figure 3–14 (opposite) Placement of the two microphones and speakers in stereophonic (L, R) and binaural (L′, R′) recording and playback systems. Notice the widely separated microphones in the stereophonic method of recording. This method causes large differences in the intensity of sound produced during playback by each loudspeaker. In the binaural method the microphones are separated by the normal distance between the ears. This causes an exact mimicking of time and intensity of sound differences in each ear during playback through earphones.

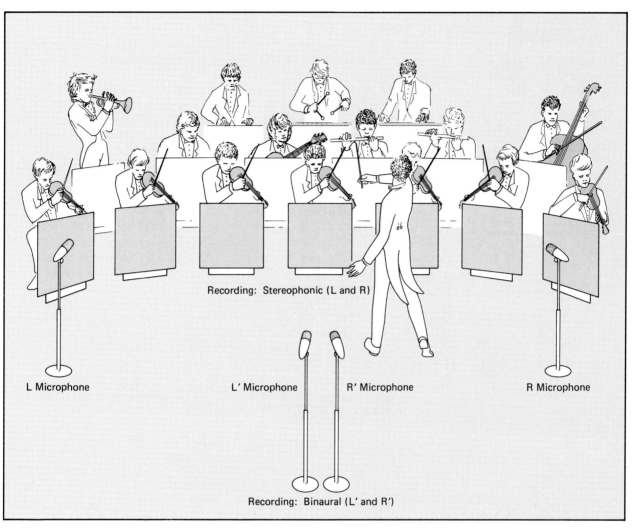

Recording: Stereophonic (L and R)

L Microphone   L' Microphone   R' Microphone   R Microphone

Recording: Binaural (L' and R')

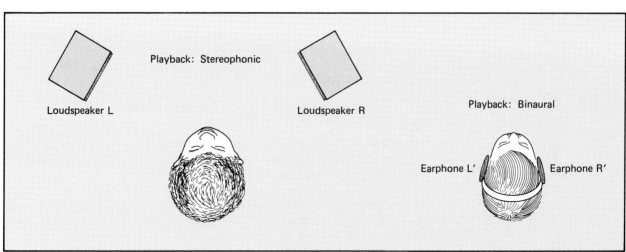

Playback: Stereophonic

Loudspeaker L   Loudspeaker R   Playback: Binaural

Earphone L'   Earphone R'

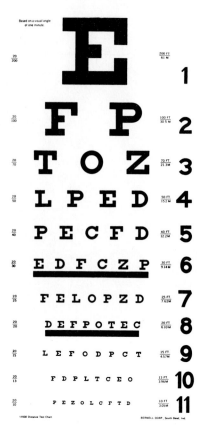

Figure 3–15 A Snellen chart is a standard set of letters of various sizes used to measure visual acuity. If the smallest row of letters a subject can read at 20 feet corresponds to the smallest row someone with normal (average) vision can read at 20 feet, the subject has "20/20 vision," or normal acuity. However, if the smallest row of letters the subject can read at 20 feet corresponds to the smallest row a person with normal vision can read at an even greater distance (e.g., 50 feet), the subject would have "20/50 vision," or below-average acuity. A subject with better than normal vision ("20/10") could see the letters as clearly at 20 feet as a normal person at only 10 feet.

SEEING

Visual Stimuli

Our eyes are sensitive to a narrow range of electromagnetic energy, wavelengths between 400 and 760 nanometers. This range is referred to as the **visible spectrum,** or, more simply, *light.* Particular sources of light vary in their brightness and color, depending on (among other things) the amount of energy present from each part of the spectrum—the light's spectral composition. Furthermore, most of our visual experience involves complex patterns of light—spatial patterns defined by variations in light across our field of view, and temporal patterns defined by variations in light over time. There are limits to our ability to discern both sorts of patterns. You've probably taken an eye test (called a *Snellen test*) that determined your ability to read rows of progressively smaller letters (see Figure 3–15). Such tests measure **visual acuity,** the ability to discern fine details in spatial patterns of light. Your acuity is best in the very center of your field of view, and much poorer everywhere else. You normally don't notice this, since you can easily shift your eyes to gaze directly at any detail of interest (as you do when you read). Your ability to discern rapid variations in light in temporal patterns, **temporal acuity,** is also limited (Watson, 1986). For example, an ordinary fluorescent bulb isn't really on all the time; it is actually flickering off and on 60 times a second. You may notice this flicker if the light is viewed from the side, because temporal acuity is better with side vision than it is with an object that is in the center of your view. The light projected onto a motion picture screen is actually flickering off and on about 64 times a second, yet the picture seems to be illuminated continuously. This phenomenon is called *flicker fusion.* Note that flicker is *not* what makes a motion picture seem to move. Fusion is the apparent continuity of illumination when in fact the screen is alternatively dark and illuminated. (The illusion of smooth movement will be discussed in the next chapter under the heading Stroboscopic Motion.)

What light in your visual environment reaches your eyes? If you stood in the center of a large circle, the combined field of view from both eyes—your **visual field**—would include over 200 degrees of the circle's 360 degree circumference. The size of an object as it appears in this visual field depends on both its physical size and its distance from you. This is why it is often useful to describe the size of an object by how much of your visual field it occupies; that is, by how many degrees of the imaginary surrounding circle's circumference it would cover. This is referred to as an object's size in **degrees visual angle.** A convenient reference is that your fingernail seen at arm's length has a width of about 1 degree visual angle (whereas the moon is only half a degree).

Sinusoidal Gratings. In recent years interest has developed in a type of visual stimulus that may be as useful in the study of vision as pure tones have been in the study of hearing. In fact, the two types of stimuli have much in common. Where a pure tone is a regular cyclical variation in air pressure over time, the visual stimulus is a regular cyclical variation in brightness across space. Because the formal mathematical name for such cyclical variation is a **sine wave,** the patterns are often referred to as **sinusoidal gratings.** An example is shown in Figure 3–16.

Just as a pure tone can be described or specified in terms of its frequency and amplitude, a grating has two corresponding properties called spatial fre-

quency and contrast. **Spatial frequency** refers to how rapidly the brightness variations occur across space, and **contrast** refers to the difference in brightness between the lightest and darkest parts of the grating.

We can see certain spatial frequencies better than others, just as we can hear certain frequencies of tone better than others. We require less amplitude in order to hear some tones, and we require less contrast in order to see some spatial frequencies. This aspect of vision is immediately apparent when you look at the pattern of brightness variations shown in Figure 3–17. This pattern consists of sinusoidal gratings whose frequency increases as you go from left to right and whose contrast increases as you go from bottom to top. Thus the higher up on the pattern you must go to see each frequency of grating, the more contrast you need in order to see it (i.e., the less sensitive you are to that spatial frequency).

For most people, the boundary between those gratings they can see at a normal reading distance and those they can't is shaped like the curve shown in Figure 3–17. Notice that this is a sort of threshold curve much like the audiometric function shown in Figure 3–7, only here it indicates sensitivity to various spatial frequencies. Traditional measures of acuity, such as the Snellen chart, only indicate our limited ability to see fine detail (high spatial frequencies). The curve shown in Figure 3–17 also indicates our limited ability to see brightness variations that occur too slowly (low spatial frequencies).

Just as complex sounds can be interpreted as combinations of many pure tones, complex spatial patterns of brightness variation can be interpreted as combinations of many sinusoidal gratings. (See the Highlight on Adaptation to Spatial Frequencies).

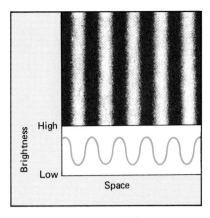

Figure 3–16 A sinusoidal grating is shown above, with a curve below showing how brightness varies in a regular, cyclical (sinusoidal) fashion across space. Other gratings can differ in frequency and contrast.

Figure 3–17 The stimulus pattern (left) contains sinusoidal gratings that increase in frequency from left to right and in contrast from bottom to top. For most people, the boundary between the gratings they can see and those they can't is shaped like the curve shown on the graph (below). This indicates sensitivity to each spatial frequency: the less contrast required to make it visible, the greater the sensitivity. Compare this to the audiometric function shown in Figure 3–7. (From Cornsweet, T. N. *Visual perception.* New York: Academic Press, 1970.)

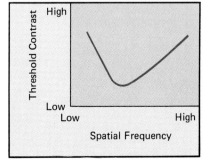

HIGHLIGHT _____
Adaptation to Spatial Frequencies

In the section on sinusoidal gratings in the text we saw evidence that our visual system is primarily "tuned" (sensitive) to particular spatial frequencies. Related studies have shown that it is possible to reduce one's sensitivity to a particular spatial frequency by prolonged viewing of that frequency (just as your sensitivity to a particular pure tone is reduced by prolonged exposure to that tone). Such adaptation to a particular spatial frequency is illustrated in the following example.

Figure A presents three high-contrast *adaptation gratings,* labeled *high, medium,* and *low,* to indicate their relative spatial frequencies. Next to these gratings is a column of five low-contrast *test gratings,* which are just barely discernible. Notice that the spatial frequencies of these test gratings range from high to low.

To selectively adapt your vision to a particular spatial frequency, look at one of the adaptation gratings under a fairly bright light for about 30 seconds. During this time slowly move your gaze around the small circle in the center of the grating. After this adaptation period look briefly at each of the five test gratings. Most people find that the test grating that is least discernible is the one whose frequency matches that of the adaptation grating just viewed. This indicates a loss of sensitivity (that is, *adaptation*) to that spatial frequency.

Careful experimentation has clearly demonstrated adaptation to specific spatial frequencies (Blakemore & Campbell, 1969). It has also been shown that adaptation depends on the orientation of a grating (e.g., vertical or horizontal) as well, suggesting that certain visual channels are tuned to both the frequency and the orientation of gratings.

Adaptation to specific spatial frequencies was recently used to test a theory of visual illusions (Carasco et al., 1987). The theory's author, Arthur Ginzburg, argued that many illusions are due primarily to the low spatial-

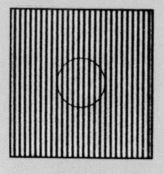

high

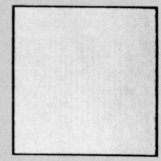

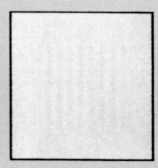

medium

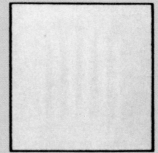

low

Figure A

frequency components of an image (Ginzburg, 1978). For example, Figure B shows the classic Müller-Lyer illusion, in which a line seems longer when it terminates in two "arrowheads" rather than two "wings." Figure C shows a somewhat blurred representation of the same stimuli in which only the low spatial frequency components of Figure B are present. Notice that these low-frequency representations of the two stimuli actually *do* differ in length.

A test of Ginzburg's theory was recently conducted in which subjects first adjusted the length of Müller-Lyer patterns (Figure B) to make them look equal in length. This indicated the magnitude of their normal illusion. Next they viewed either a high- or low-frequency adaptation grating for 4 minutes and afterward readjusted the Müller-Lyer stimuli.

Ginzburg's theory would seem to imply that adaptation to the low-frequency grating would reduce the Müller-Lyer illusion more than would adaptation to the high-frequency grating, because he argues that it is primarily the low-frequency components that produce the illusion. Figure D shows the results, which clearly support Ginzburg's theory. The magnitude of the illusion doesn't differ before and after adaptation to a high-frequency grating, but it is sharply diminished after adaptation to a low-frequency grating. Other factors that may contribute to the Müller-Lyer illusion are discussed in Chapter 4.

(From John Frisby: *Seeing.* After Blakemore, C., & Campbell, F. W., 1969, On the existence of neurons in the human visual system selectively sensitive to the orientation and size of retinal images. *Journal of Physiology,* Vol. 203, pp. 237–60.)

Figure B

Figure C

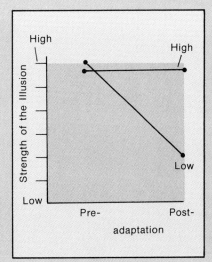

Figure D

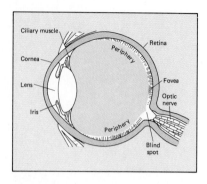

Figure 3–18 A cross section of the eye.

The Eye

In 1637 the philosopher-scientist René Descartes removed an eye from a dead bull, carefully scraped away the covering from the rear of the eyeball, and replaced it with a thin paper film. He then held a lighted candle in front of the eye. Clearly visible on the paper at the rear of the eye was an upside-down image of the candle. Since then, scientists have learned considerably more about the eye, but its basic property was clear to Descartes: It projects an image of the scene in front of it onto its rear wall. On this rear wall is a complicated inner lining of tissue called the **retina.** It is in the retina that light-sensitive cells convert the projected image (i.e., pattern of light) into pattern of neural activity.

Figure 3–18 is a schematic cross section of the eye, showing some of its major parts. The optical system at the front of the eye that projects the image onto the retina consists of a slightly protruding, clear outer cap called the **cornea** and an inner component called the **lens.** Fine adjustment in the shape of the lens is required to focus either near or far objects onto the retina. These fine adjustments are termed **accommodation** and are produced by changes in the tension of small muscles, the *ciliary muscles,* connected to the lens. Between the cornea and the lens is a richly pigmented structure called the **iris** (from the Greek word for rainbow). The pigments in the iris determine whether the eye is blue, black, brown, or hazel. A small, ringlike opening in the iris forms the round, blackish **pupil.** The size of this circular opening controls the amount of light entering the eyes and varies as a function of the level of illumination. The diameter of the pupil is greatest in a dimly lighted environment and smallest in a brightly lighted environment. Inside the pupil the light passes through the lens, which focuses it onto the retina, the inner lining of the back of the eyeball.

There are two major landmarks on the retina: the fovea and the blind spot (see Figure 3–19). The **fovea** is a tiny spot on the retina positioned behind

Figure 3–19 A view of the retina as seen through an opthalmoscope, a device invented by Helmholtz and now used in most medical examinations to inspect the blood vessels in patients' eyes. Two major landmarks are the fovea (the dark area in the center) and the blind spot where the optic nerve leaves the eyes (the large circle at left from which blood vessels radiate). The circular area of the retina in this view has a diameter of about 10 mm or 36 degrees visual angle. (Courtesy Dr. Francis A. L'Esperance, Jr.)

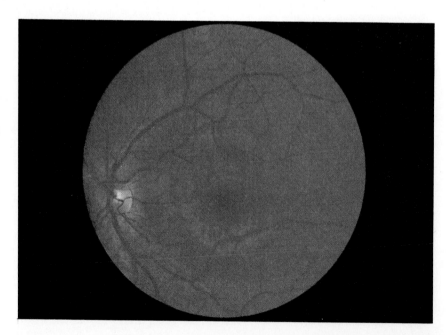

the lens. It corresponds to the center of your field of view, where your visual acuity is highest. The **blind spot,** the center of a radiating web of blood vessels, is the point where blood vessels and neurons pass out through the wall of the eye. The blind spot is totally insensitive to light. (You aren't normally aware of this because the blind spot is at a different point in the visual field of each eye, so that what one eye misses, the other eye sees.)

Rods and Cones

There are approximately 120 million rods and 6 to 8 million cones on the retina (see Figure 3–20). Most of the cones are on the fovea, which is the center of the field of vision, where acuity is highest. **Cones** are primarily responsible for the ability to see fine detail; they function best in daylight or bright light and are also responsible for the ability to see color.

While **rods** are distributed over most of the retina (except for the fovea and blind spot), they are concentrated most heavily a few degrees off the fovea. As we will see shortly, rods are more sensitive to light than cones—thus we depend on them for our ability to see at night or in dim light. You may have noticed that at night you are better able to see a very weak light (for example, a faint star) by looking just to one side of it, where the image falls on the heaviest concentration of rods. Rods, though sensitive to light, have no ability to distinguish colors. This is why at night you do not see colors, only black and white and gray.

It is in the rods and cones that light energy triggers a complex photochemical process that results in the neural activity we experience as vision. The critical step in this process seems to be the breaking down or bleaching of photosensitive pigment in these cells by light. This chemical activity stimulates the neurons attached to the rods or cones, and the firing of the neurons is signaled to the brain. The chemicals then recombine to form new pigment.

Visual Adaptation.   Rods and cones differ in their sensitivity to light and in the rate at which the bleaching and recombination of pigment takes place. This difference is important in *visual adaptation,* the adjustment in visual

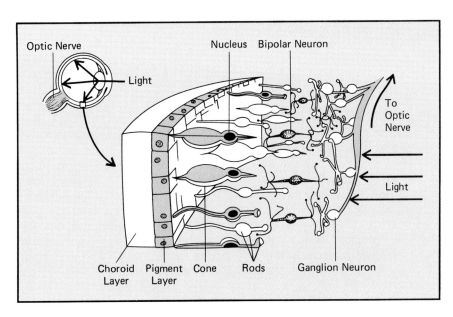

Figure 3–20   A cross section of the retina. Note that light has to pass through blood vessels and nerve cells before reaching the rods and cones, which are named for their shapes. Indeed, it has been said that the rods and cones have their backs to the light. (Adapted from *The Psychology of Being Human,* Second Edition by Zick Rubin and Majorie McNeil, p. 73. Copyright © 1977 by Majorie McNeil and Zick Rubin. Reprinted by permission of Harper & Row, Pub., Inc.)

HIGHLIGHT

Receptive Fields

In 1875 Camillo Golgi first saw the complex networks of neurons revealed by his stains (see Chapter 2). He might have wondered how these myriad nerve cells communicated with each other: What were the messages passing through this incredible loom? Just about a century later, David Hubel and Tørsten Wiesel received the Nobel prize in medicine for partially answering this question in relation to neurons in the visual system. Their basic strategy was rather simple: Insert a tiny electrode into a single cell in the visual cortex (the primary visual sensory area on the occipital lobe) and listen in on the messages the cell received as different stimuli were

presented to the eye. Achieving this goal took years of painstaking research. But in the end they began to understand how what we see is represented in the neural networks of our visual system.

Figure A shows the basic experimental setup used by Hubel and Wiesel. A tiny microelectrode is slowly inserted into the visual cortex of an anesthetized cat until the pattern of electrical activity shows that the tip of the electrode is situated inside a single neuron. This activity is amplified and shown on an oscilloscope, where each neural action potential produces a single vertical *spike*.

The cat's eye is held open so that light stimuli, projected onto a screen in front of the cat, are focused onto its retina. Most cells typically show a slow random pattern of firing. Various stimuli are presented to determine

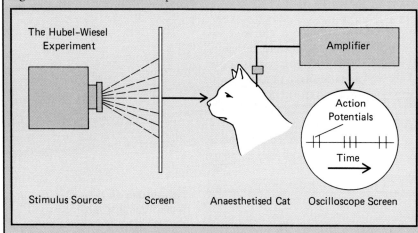

Figure B   Three types of receptive field

their effect on the cell's activity. These effects include facilitation (increase), inhibition (decrease), or no effect on the rate of firing. For example, a dot of light may increase firing (+) at some points and decrease it (−) at others. The exact pattern of these effects can be recorded by marking the screen on which the stimuli are projected with a plus (+) or minus (−) to indicate the effect of the white dot at each location. This pattern of responsiveness defines the cell's **receptive field.**

The cluster of pluses and minuses labeled Neuron A in Figure B indicates one type of receptive field that Hubel and Wiesel were able to "map" in this manner. Notice that light in the center of the cluster tended to increase neural firing, whereas light on the periphery tended to reduce firing (dots of light presented further away had no effect). This common type of simple receptive field is often called a *center-on field.* The type of stimulus that would evoke the most activity in

Figure A   The Hubel-Wiesel Experiment

sensitivity in response to changes in the level of illumination. On a clear dark night we can see a single candle flame over 50 kilometers away. We can also see quite well on a sunny, snow-covered ski slope, where the levels of light energy affecting our eyes may be more than a trillion times greater than that of the candle flame. However, to function effectively in both situations, our visual system needs time to adjust its sensitivity to the level of illumination. This process of adjustment is called adaptation. **Dark adaptation** begins when you leave a brightly lighted environment and enter a darkened one; for example, when you leave a sunny street to enter a darkened movie theater. **Light adaptation** begins when this sequence is reversed; for example, when you leave the theater and step back into the sunlight. Your sensitivity to light is often so low on entering a darkened theater that you find it difficult to locate a seat. Yet gradually, over a period of minutes, your sensitivity increases

the neuron was a small dot of light falling in the facilitating (+) center of the receptive field, surrounded by darkness so that no light fell on the inhibiting (−) peripheral regions. Thus this neuron could be thought of as a sort of *small-white-dot detector*. A dot of light that is too large would fall onto *both* + and − regions of the field, with inhibiting effects canceling out some or all of the facilitating effects.

The receptive fields of two other neurons, labeled B and C, are also shown. Before reading further, see whether you can deduce the type of stimulus pattern that would evoke the most activity in each neuron.

Neuron B should respond most actively to the vertical boundary, or "edge," between a lighted area on the left and a dark area on the right, positioned so that the light fell only on the + regions of the field, and dark only on the − regions. This would produce the maximum facilitation with no inhibition. Thus Neuron B could be thought of as a *vertical-edge-detector*. In contrast, Neuron C could be considered a *horizontal-white-bar detector,* since a horizontal white bar (of an appropriate thickness) could be positioned to fall on all the + regions of the field but not on the − regions. Many other types of fields have been mapped in this fashion, including some that seem designed to detect certain patterns of light *moving* in specific directions (e.g., a vertical white bar moving from left to right). In general, neurons in the visual cortex have the largest and most complex receptive fields, with neurons closer to

the retina having simpler and smaller fields (such as Neuron A).

By carefully mapping the receptive fields of neurons at various points in the visual cortex, Hubel and Wiesel have revealed much about its organization. For example, Figure C shows how an electrode can be inserted at right angles to the cortex (I) or diagonally (II). The small dashes next to the path of each electrode show the type of stimulus that neurons positioned at that point seem designed to detect. It seems as if the neurons are organized in columns. Within a column, the neurons seem to detect stimuli having one orientation (I), with the particular orientation changing gradually from one column to the next (II).

Figure C Electrodes inserted along the path indicated by arrow I encounter neurons that detect stimuli of the same orientation. Those inserted along the path of arrow II encounter neurons that detect progressively rotated stimuli, revealing an organization in columns.

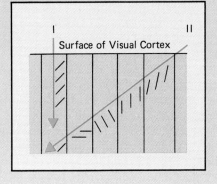

Figure 3–21 Two things happen as your eyes adapt to the dark. They gradually become more sensitive to light (the threshold becomes lower) and their sensitivity to various wavelengths of light (spectral sensitivity) shifts from the pattern typical of cones to that typical of rods. The process shown below takes approximately 40 minutes, with the break in the curve occurring after approximately 13 minutes. This represents the point at which the early cone adapation levels off while the rods continue to adapt.

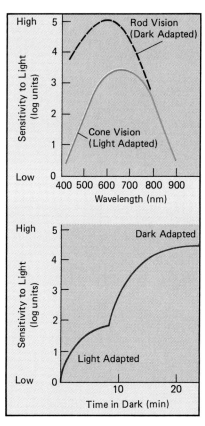

until even the faces of the audience are clearly visible. When you eventually emerge from the theater, your eyes are so sensitive to the previously comfortable sunlight that you may squint for a few moments until you adapt to the light.

How does this take place? As we have seen, the basic process of vision is a photochemical one—the breaking down or bleaching of chemical pigments in rods and cones. It seems possible to account for much (but not all) of light and dark adaptation in terms of the balance between the bleaching and reconstitution of pigments in the rods and cones.

Pigment in the rods is much more sensitive to light than pigment in the cones. This means that it takes a less intense light stimulus to start the breaking down of the pigment in rods than it does in cones (see Figure 3–21). In fact, when you are light-adapted you are relying primarily on the less-

Figure 3–22 First stare continuously for about 10 seconds at the black dot in the center of the upper triangle. Then shift your gaze to the black dot in the lower rectangle and hold it steady. Within a moment or so you should see an illusionary vertical gray area against a white background. This negative afterimage occurs because the region of your retina previously exposed to the white region in the upper rectangle has slightly light-adapted (become less sensitive), while the parts of your retina previously exposed to the black regions in the upper rectangle, have slightly dark-adapted (become more sensitive). When you shifted your gaze to the lower rectangle, the central part of your retina, which was less sensitive, produced a "grayer" sensation than the more sensitive areas on either side.

Figure 3–23 Cells, 1, 2, and 3 converge on a single cell (cell A). Because of this convergence, there is no way of knowing whether activity at cell A was initiated by cell 1, 2, or 3—or any combination of the three.

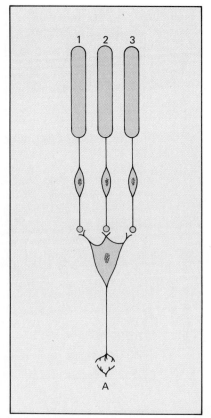

sensitive cones for vision, because most of the highly sensitive pigment in the rods is depleted. Only when you remain in a dimly illuminated environment long enough to dark-adapt completely does the highly sensitive pigment in the rods reach its highest concentration. This allows you to see very dim stimuli that are too weak to affect the less-sensitive cones.

Exposing parts of your retina to different amounts of light for even a few seconds produces differences in their level of light adaptation. If you then look at an evenly illuminated screen, that part of your retina made less sensitive to light causes you to see an illusionary darker region on the screen, called a **negative afterimage.** You can experience this for yourself by looking at Figure 3–22. The part of your retina exposed to the vertical white bar becomes locally light-adapted—that is, less sensitive to light. When you then look at the all-white rectangle, you "see" an illusionary vertical gray bar. This is because the less sensitive (more light-adapted) part of your retina sends weaker sensations to the brain, as if there were actually less light reflected from that part of the image.

Neural Activity in the Retina. The firing of a single rod or cone is not communicated to the brain in a simple one-retinal-cell-to-one-brain-cell fashion. Considerable interaction in neural activity occurs in the network of cells lying just above the rods and cones in the retina. Rods and cones connect to *bipolar cells,* which in turn connect to *ganglion cells* whose axons exit the eye through the optic nerve. There are also horizontal interconnections between these cells, as shown in Figure 3–20. This network of cells is really a sort of peripheral brain that carries out the first steps in the analysis of the visual image. Two important types of neural interaction that take place in the retina are convergence and lateral inhibition. **Convergence** is the flowing together of neural activity into common paths, much as automobiles leave their driveways to go into a common street. An example of this would be several rods or cones all influencing the same ganglion cell (see Figure 3–23). The firing of any one or more of these receptor elements could trigger activity in the same ganglion cell, so that the ganglion cell would respond to stimulation over a wider region of the retina than could a single rod or cone, and in that sense would be more sensitive. However, this increase in area of sensitivity would be accompanied by a loss in spatial information, since firing of the ganglion cell wouldn't identify which of the converging rods or cones had been stimulated. Thus neural convergence involves a loss of the type of spatial information most important for acuity. It is clear that there is considerable convergence of retinal elements; although there are about 120 million rods and 6 to 8 million cones, only 1 million neurons leave the eye in the optic nerve. Convergence occurs primarily in the periphery of the retina and

mostly in the rods; there is hardly any convergence of the cones on the fovea. This is consistent with the high degree of acuity found in the center of our visual field, and the lower acuity that exists on the periphery.

Another basic form of neural interaction on the retina is **lateral inhibition.** Here the firing of one neuron inhibits (reduces) activity in adjacent neurons. This difference in firing rate is experienced as a contrast in brightness between the stimulated cell and its neighbor. Thus lateral inhibition makes the contours of an image appear sharper, aiding acuity. Not surprisingly, lateral inhibition is most characteristic of the interaction of the cones in the fovea, where acuity is highest. (See the Highlight on Receptive Fields for another approach to studying neural activity in the visual system.)

Optic Pathways to the Brain

Figure 3–24 shows the optic pathways between the retina and the brain. A major feature of this system is that signals from the left half of each retina are transmitted to the left hemisphere of the brain, while signals from the right half of each retina project to the right hemisphere of the brain. Half of the neurons in each optic nerve cross over at a point called the *optic chiasm* and come together with neurons carrying information from the corresponding half of the retina in the other eye. There they join with new nerve bundles to carry the information to the visual cortex. However, this does not mean that each cortical hemisphere receives information from only one half of the visual field. The two hemispheres have many interconnections through which information can be transferred from one side of the brain to the other, as we discussed in Chapter 2.

Color Vision

There are three dimensions used to describe our sensation of color: brightness, hue, and saturation. **Brightness** refers mainly to the amount of visible energy present in the light source. As the amount of energy or intensity increases, a stimulus appears brighter. But brightness also depends to some extent on the context in which we see the stimulus, the general level of illumination, and other perceptual elements, to be discussed in Chapter 4.

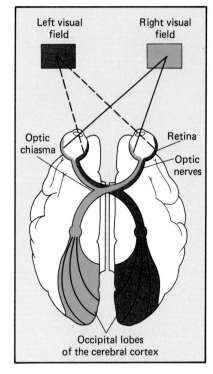

Figure 3–24 This diagram shows how information from the eyes is transmitted to the brain. The left side of the visual field falls on the right side of the retina of each eye. The nerves from the right side of each retina project, to a relay station, and then to the right hemisphere of the brain. Similarly, the right side of the visual field falls on the left side of the retina, whose neurons project to the left hemisphere.

Figure 3–25 The Color Spectrum   The color spectrum can be produced by passing white light through a prism. The fact that different wavelengths bend at different angles as they pass through glass causes white light to be broken up into its component colors, as shown above. The rainbow appears in the sky when sunlight passes through droplets of water falling from rain clouds, producing the same prismatic effect.

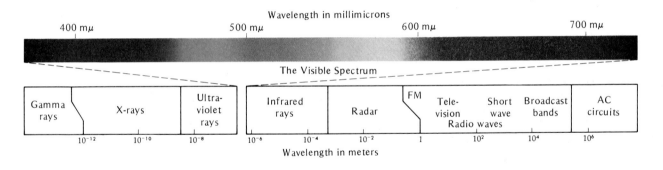

Hue corresponds to our names for colors. When we differentiate between red and blue, for example, we are talking about two different hues. As the wavelength varies on the visual spectrum, we see different hues (see Figure 3–25). But hue and wavelength are not interchangeable—any hue can be produced either by a single wavelength or by a mixture of quite different wavelengths (see color circle in Figure 3–26). "Light rays of different wavelength can be mixed together in infinite variations without affecting each other—when 'red light' and 'green light' add together to form 'yellow,' the yellow is in us, not in the light, which remains unchanged by the mixing" (Hochberg, 1978, p. 30).

The third dimension is **saturation** or purity of color. This quality is based on how much one wavelength predominates in the stimulus. If all energy is concentrated at a single wavelength, the hue seems very pure; as other wavelengths are added, the hue becomes grayer, more diluted.

While it is possible to distinguish only about 150 hues, various levels of brightness and saturation combine to yield more than 300,000 different color sensations (Hochberg, 1978). The three separate dimensions that describe our sensation of color are illustrated in the color solid shown in Figure 3–27.

Figure 3–26 The Color Circle The colors on this circle are laid out in the identical order in which they appear in the visible spectrum, and a few nonspectral colors are added. The distance (along the circumference) between each of the colors is such that colors opposite one another are complementary. A mixture of two complements will produce a neutral gray. Mixing noncomplementary colors will produce a color midway between the two along the circumference of the circle.

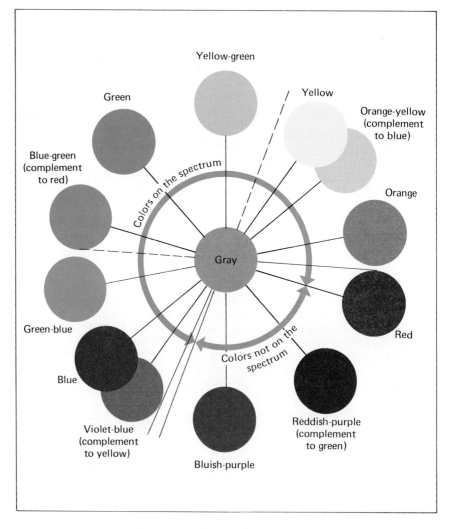

Figure 3–27 **The Color Solid** The color solid contains all of the distinguishable sensations of color. Hue varies as one travels around the circumference of the solid. The horizontal dimension depicts brightness and the vertical dimension depicts saturation. A complete solid would contain about 350,000 patches of discriminable colors. (Courtesy of Inmont Corporation)

Mixtures of Wavelengths. Most of what we see is a mixture of many wavelengths. The particular mixture, or **energy spectrum,** is determined first of all by the original source of light, since each source emits a particular amount of energy at each wavelength. The particular mixture of light can be further modified by **filtering** or **reflection** of some light source (see Figure 3–28). For example, only the wavelengths we see as green are transmitted through the green part of a stained glass window; the rest are filtered out. Green grass reflects only those wavelengths we see as green; the rest are absorbed (converted to heat energy).

There are basically two ways to produce a particular mixture of wavelengths. You can *add* sources of light to produce an **additive mixture,** or you can reflect light off various pigments that *subtract* or absorb specific wavelengths to produce a **subtractive mixture.** For example, an additive mixture occurs if you project two colored light sources onto the same area of a white screen; a subtractive mixture occurs when you mix paints together. The general laws of color mixing are shown in Figure 3–29.

Theories of Color Vision

How is the sensation of color produced in the brain? One clue to this puzzle is that we see colors quite well in very bright light, when only the cones are responding, whereas we don't distinguish colors under very weak illumination, when only the rods are sensitive enough to respond. For example, a person whose eyes have dark-adapted could recognize forms in a color photograph by the light of the moon, but they would only appear in shades of gray. This suggests that the cones are primarily responsible for translating spectral (wavelength) information into the neural patterns (codes) that signal colors to the brain.

It has been known since at least the time of Isaac Newton that it is possible to create virtually all colors by mixing blue, green, and red light. The British scientist Sir Thomas Young speculated in 1802 that only three types of color receptors are required to see all colors: one primarily sensitive to blue, one to green, and one to red. According to this theory, the stronger each of the three colors is in the visual stimulus, the more strongly each type of receptor

Figure 3–28 The spectral composition of white (a) and a green (b) light. All wavelengths are present in white light, while mostly green wavelengths are present in a green light. White light can be made green by passing it through a green filter, or reflecting it off a green surface, to remove certain wavelengths.

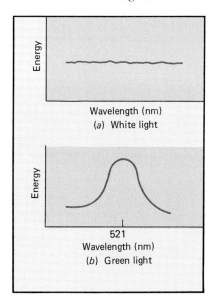

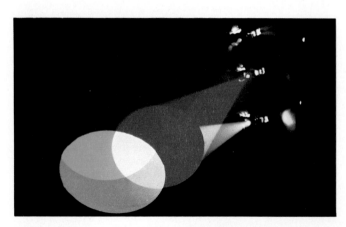

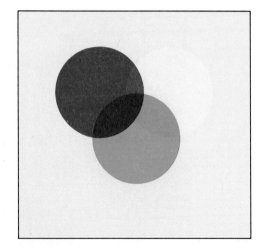

Figure 3–29 Color Mixing **A.** The area of overlap of the red, green, and blue lights shows what happens when the three primaries are *additively* mixed: All three lights together yield white. **B.** Since paint pigments absorb most wavelengths and reflect only a few, a mixture of the three primaries of paint is *subtractive* and all wavelengths are absorbed, producing black. (A: Fritz Goro, Life Magazine, © Time Inc.)

reacts. Thus if the visual stimulus contains a lot of blue light, the blue receptors will respond strongly; if it contains mostly red or green light, the red or green receptors will react. The resulting *pattern* of neural responses is interpreted by the brain as color. If the stimulus contains energy from all parts of the spectrum, all three types of receptors respond and the sensation of white is evoked. If only the green and red receptors are stimulated, the sensation is

Normally a mixture of paints is subtractive (each pigment absorbs or "subtracts" wavelengths). However, in the technique used in pointillist paintings, such as the one shown, the colors reflected by each daub of paint (see detail) mix in an additive fashion when the viewer is too far away to see the individual dots of color (the light reflected from adjacent daubs of color blurs together).

yellow. Any visual stimulus that produces the same *pattern* of activity in the three types of receptors is seen as the same color.

This provides an explanation of negative-color afterimages of the sort illustrated in Figure 3–30. As you stare at the black dot in rectangle *a,* the red bar will primarily light-adapt (make less sensitive) your red receptors, whereas your green and blue receptors are less affected. When you then shift your gaze to stare at the dot in the center of the white rectangle *b,* you will soon "see" an illusionary green bar. (Be warned, however, that the color will be pale.) This negative- (opposite-) color afterimage occurs because the red receptors don't respond as strongly as the blue and green receptors, having just been partially light-adapted (made less sensitive). This produces a *pattern* of activity in the three types of receptors that mimics the pattern produced by a real green bar. Just the opposite explanation can be made for the illusionary afterimage that you can "see" after staring at the green bar in rectangle *c.*

Young's three-receptor theory was elaborated some 50 years ago by Helmholtz and became known as the **Young-Helmholtz theory.** To this day, it is one of the two most influential theories of color vision. In fact, modern measuring techniques have shown that there actually are three types of cones, each primarily sensitive to a different part of the spectrum (see Figure 3–31).

Hurvich (1978) has provided an elaboration of another theory of color vision originally proposed by a contemporary of Helmholtz named Ewald Hering. This **opponent-process theory** is illustrated in Figure 3–32. It accepts Helmholtz's idea that there are three types of cones, each primarily sensitive to light from a different part of the spectrum. It goes on to propose

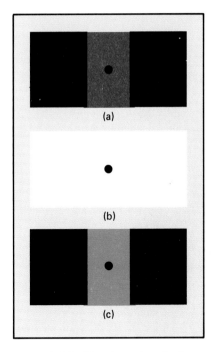

Figure 3–30 Negative-color afterimages can be seen by first staring continuously at the black dot in the center of the red or green bar for about 10 seconds, then shifting your gaze to the black dot in the center of the all-white rectangle. In a second or so you should see an illusionary bar in the color of the opposite side of the color circle (Figure 3–26). In terms of the Young-Helmholtz theory (Figure 3–31), prior stimulation of one (or primarily one) of the three types of cones reduces it sensitivity. The remaining types of cones are then more stimulated when you look at the white rectangle.

Figure 3–31 (left) The Young-Helmholtz theory of color vision is based on the existence of three types of cones, each type primarily sensitive to wavelengths on a different part of the spectrum, as shown here.

Figure 3–32 (right) The Young-Helmholtz theory suggests that there are three types of cones (α, β, γ) in the retina, each primarily sensitive to light from a different part of the spectrum (around 440, 530, and 570 nm, respectively). The opponent-process theory says that the outputs from these three types of cones feed into other neural networks, which then calculate differences between outputs and send this information on toward the brain. The figure shows light from the three parts of the spectrum (A) affecting the three types of cones (B) whose outputs are compared by opponent-process systems (C). This sort of system represents blue-yellow, or red-green, color blindness as a failure of one of the opponent-process systems at level C. (Based on Hurvich & Jameson, 1957)

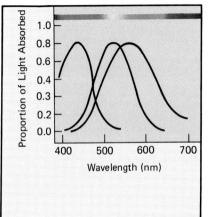

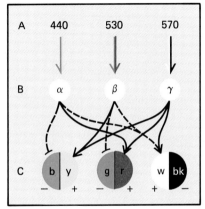

Figure 3–33 A photograph of balloons and two chips used to test for color blindness are shown as they would appear to four types of people. (*a*) A *normal person* sees all the colors in the photograph and can make out the snakelike form in the chip on the right and the number 48 in the chip on the left. (*b*) A *red-green blind person* cannot distinguish red from green in the photograph and cannot see the number 48 in the left chip. (*c*) A *yellow-blue blind person* cannot distinguish yellow from blue in the photograph and cannot see the snakelike form in the right chip. (*d*) A totally color-blind person cannot see any colors in the photograph or the forms in the chips. Notice how each type of color blindness could be interpreted as a failure of either the red-green or blue-yellow opponent-process system (see Figure 3–32) or, in the case of total color blindness, of both.

(Photo © Douglas Faulker/Photo Researchers, Inc. Color chips courtesy of Scientific Publishing Co.)

(a) Photo and chips as seen by normal person

(b) Photo and chips as seen by red-green blind person

(c) Photo and chips as seen by yellow-blue blind person

(d) Photo and chips as seen by totally colorblind person

opponent-process systems that calculate *differences* in the firing rate of these three types of cones. These differences determine which colors we see. Thus if the system that calculates the red-green differences fails, we cannot distinguish red from green; a failure of the system that calculates blue-yellow differences produces a similar loss of blue-yellow discrimination. People with either form of **color blindness** are called **dichromats,** since they can still distinguish one pair of colors. By far the most common form is red-green color blindness (about 7 percent of all males and 1 percent of all females have this problem). When both the red-green and blue-yellow systems fail, people are totally color-blind. These **monochromats** see the world only in shades of gray (see Figure 3–33).

Visual Impairment and Treatment

One way of appreciating how the eye normally works is to consider some of the possible defects in vision and how they can be treated. For example, the cornea, which accomplishes about 70 percent of the focusing of the eye, is normally very clear. However, various injuries and diseases can leave it so scarred or clouded that vision may be lost or seriously impaired. Fortunately, a damaged cornea can be replaced with a clear one taken from the eye of a donor. And while most implants are subject to attack and even rejection by antibodies in the blood, the cornea is normally not susceptible because it contains no blood vessels.

A somewhat more common defect is an irregular shape of the cornea that makes it impossible to bring all parts of an image into focus on the retina at the same time. This condition, called *astigmatism,* can be corrected by eyeglasses ground to compensate for the cornea's irregular shape.

In a progressive condition called *presbyopia,* the lenses of the eyes stiffen with age until the ciliary muscles can no longer adjust their shape to focus on near or far objects. Some forms of presbyopia require bifocals (invented by Benjamin Franklin), eyeglasses having one part that corrects for near vision and one for distant vision. Not all presbyopes need bifocals, however. Depending on the degree of stiffening of the lens, glasses worn for certain activities, such as reading, may solve the problem.

Even if the lens in the eye is naturally flexible, it can't alter its shape enough to compensate for an eyeball that is too long or too short. In the normally shaped eye, the focus falls directly on the retina. Figure 3–34 illustrates what happens to the focus when the eyeball is too long (resulting in *myopia* or *nearsightedness*), and when the eyeball is too short (resulting in *hyperopia* or *farsightedness*). Nearsightedness, in which the focus falls in front of the retina, makes it difficult to see objects that are distant. Farsightedness, in which the focus falls behind the retina, makes it difficult to see objects that are close. Both conditions can be corrected with eyeglasses or contact lenses that adjust the focal point to a more accommodating range for the eyeball.

A disease called *glaucoma* results from an increase in the internal fluid pressure on the eyeball. This growing pressure may eventually destroy the retina and cause total blindness. (Surprisingly, one of the most successful drugs for controlling this pressure increase is marijuana. In 1976 someone suffering from glaucoma became the first person in the United States to use marijuana legally on a prescription basis.)

There can also be visual problems resulting from physical damage to the retina itself. Sometimes a blow to the face or head detaches a small part of

Figure 3–34 The top drawing shows the normally shaped eye with the focus falling directly on the retina. The middle figure shows the focus falling in front of the retina when the retina is too long (nearsightedness). The bottom figure shows the focus falling behind the retina when the retina is too short (farsightedness). Nearsightedness causes a problem in focusing on distant objects; farsightedness causes a problem in focusing on near objects.

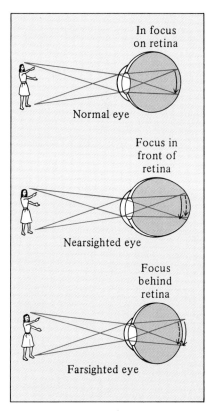

In focus on retina

Normal eye

Focus in front of retina

Nearsighted eye

Focus behind retina

Farsighted eye

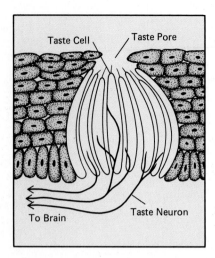

Figure 3–35 The diagram shows the structure of a taste bud, the main receptor for taste. Each bud consists of about a dozen individual taste cells clustered together.

the retina from the rear surface of the eyeball (the *sclera*). A number of surgical techniques are currently used to repair retinal detachment. One recently developed procedure involves briefly focusing a tiny, high-intensity laser beam on the retina, causing a minute burn. The resulting spot of scar tissue reconnects the retina to the sclera, much like a tiny thumbtack.

OTHER SENSES

Taste

The physical stimuli for taste are chemical substances (mostly food) that touch the surface of the tongue or, to some extent, the soft palate, the pharynx, and the larynx. Yet the sensation of taste produced by these substances is heavily influenced by various other factors, including color, texture, temperature, and smell. (This explains why margarine is colored yellow and some fruits are dyed before being put on sale.) What is popularly meant by "taste" is really a complex response involving other senses as well; nonetheless, it is possible to study taste alone. There appear to be four primary taste qualities: sweet, sour, salt, and bitter. Békésy (1966) applied various substances to very tiny areas of the tongue and found that each area responded primarily to one of the four basic sensations. Normally the substances are spread over the whole surface of the tongue and we experience combinations of these basic tastes, which may seem quite different from any one of them. Furthermore, some tastes arise more slowly than others. For example, a wine taster might describe a sip of wine as "first fruity, followed by a huskier mellow flavor, and finally a golden aftertaste."

Taste buds contain the receptors for taste. There are about 9,000 of these tiny structures, located mostly on the tip, sides, and rear of the tongue. Each bud consists of about a dozen individual taste cells clustered together (see Figure 3–35). Liquids, or substances dissolved in saliva, affect the individual taste cells and trigger impulses in neurons attached to each bud. By recording the electrical activity in an individual cell, it is possible to determine which of the four taste qualities it mainly responds to. Although two cells on the same taste bud may be "tuned" to respond primarily to different tastes, the cells on the tip of the tongue are mainly sensitive to sweet and salt tastes, those on the sides to sour, and those at the back to bitter. These cells are constantly dying and being replaced, so that a whole new set of cells is produced over any seven-day period. If you temporarily lose part of your taste sense by burning some of your taste buds with hot coffee, you can count on recovery within seven days as new buds replace the injured ones. However, as we age, some of our taste buds die and aren't replaced, and a permanent change occurs in our sense of taste.

Smell

The basic stimuli for the sense of smell **(olfaction)** are airborne molecules that enter our nasal cavities. In order to produce a sensation of odor, these molecules must be soluble in the water or fat found in our nasal passages. Although many people have tried to set up categories of odor, there is no generally accepted classification scheme. One such attempt was a seven-category system—camphoraceous, pungent, ethereal, floral, pepperminty, putrid, and musty (Amoore, 1964). However, even these odors may be broken

down into more categories. At present the variety of classification schemes serves mainly to illustrate the complexity of odors.

The olfactory receptors are located on the *olfactory epithelium.* It consists of surfaces located deep inside our two nasal cavities. The basic receptor units are cells buried in and under the epithelium that project their tips (bulbs), along with small hairlike cilia, into the layer of mucus covering the epithelium. It is the reaction of the bulbs and cilia to the soluble molecules trapped in the mucus that triggers the nervous impulse. The actual coding of the smell information is not well understood.

One reason so little is definitely known about the olfactory system is that it is difficult to reach or electrically record from the receptor cells in the epithelium. Furthermore, it is difficult to control the presentation of stimuli (airborne, soluble molecules), although there have been elaborate attempts to do so. The movement of air in our nasal passages is very complicated. It is known that the act of sniffing alters the shape of the cavities so that more air passes over the olfactory epithelium, thereby exposing it to molecules of matter in the air that stimulate the odor sense. Congestion of the nasal passages makes it harder for the soluble molecules to reach the sense bulbs, which is why your sensitivity to odors is reduced when you have a cold.

In perhaps the largest study ever conducted on the sense of smell (Doty et al., 1984), the smelling abilities of almost 2,000 people ranging in age from 5 to 99 years were evaluated using an ingeniously designed test booklet. Each page of the test booklet contained a "scratch-and-sniff" patch that released a particular odor. Odors tested included those of peanuts, onion, motor oil, lilacs, and pizza. The results clearly showed that our sense of smell diminishes dramatically in old age. It is strongest between the ages of 30 and 60, then diminishes slightly until, around age 80, it finally begins to deteriorate rapidly. In fact, a majority of subjects over 80 displayed virtually no sense of smell. (This can't be attributed to failing memory, since the researchers found no correlation between the elderly subjects' smelling abilities and their scores on a standard test of memory.)

Comparing odors in an olfaction experiment. (Sybil Shackman/Monkmeyer Press Photo Service.)

Skin Sensations

Many different types of physical stimuli cause sensations in the skin. For scientific purposes, the sensation of pressure may be evoked by pressing the tip of a tiny hair against the skin. Warmth or cold may be evoked by touching the skin with a tiny metal point of a certain temperature. Pain may be evoked by intense application of either pressure or temperature stimuli. (There are so specific receptors for pain—see the following section.) It is possible to "map" **skin sensitivity** by drawing a small grid on the skin and then systematically applying each type of stimulus to each square of the grid. Figure 3–36 shows a typical distribution of sensitivity for each sensation. If enough pressure, heat, or cold is applied at one point, its effect will be distributed over a wider area, so these maps are based on low levels of stimulation. A curious property of these spots of sensitivity is that stimulation of a cold spot with a warm metal tip evokes the sensation of cold, while stimulation of a warm spot with a cold tip evokes the sensation of warmth (this is known as *paradoxical cold* or *warmth,* respectively). Very warm water will cause both cold *and* warmth receptors to fire, producing a sensation of "hot." Of course, under most circumstances our skin is stimulated over large areas, so that whole populations of these spots are stimulated in unison or in rapid succession.

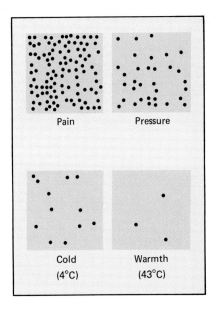

Figure 3–36 The diagrams above show a map of the typical distribution of skin sensitivity to pain, pressure, cold, and warmth.

The distribution of sensitivity spots varies considerably from one part of the body to another. For example, there are many more pressure-sensitive spots on your lips and fingertips than on your back. This can be demonstrated by measuring how far apart two stimulated points must be for you to notice that two points, rather than only one, are being applied to the skin. It turns out that the smallest discernable separation is more than 35 times as great on your back as it is on your fingertips.

Neurons in the skin have a variety of endings: Some are attached to the base of hair follicles, some have a type of enclosed or encapsulated ending, and some have free endings. At one time it was believed that specific sensitivity (warmth, cold, or pain) was determined by the type of nerve ending. But close examination of the skin tissue identified as a cold, warmth, or pain spot failed to reveal any consistent association between the type of nerve ending and sensitivity. It is clear that the neurons attached to hair follicles generally respond to light pressure. However, we are also sensitive to light pressure on skin areas that have no hair, such as the lips or fingertips.

Most of the skin sensations we experience should be thought of as complex patterns of stimulation involving multiple receptor systems. For example, the successive stimulation of adjacent pressure spots produces the sensation of being tickled. (For a recent comprehensive review of the skin senses, see Sherrick & Cholewaik, 1986.)

Sensations of Pain

Unlike the other sensations, each of which has its own sensory system, pain has no specific receptors. Rather, it appears that the sensation of pain can be evoked by intense stimulation of almost any sort, including extremes of temperature, intense light or sound, pressure on the skin, or electrical shock to almost any part of the body. Normally pain is experienced whenever a physical stimulus is intense enough to cause bodily damage (for example, the swelling of blood vessels in the head that can result in a headache).

While it would seem that a life totally free of pain would be ideal, people born without a sense of pain usually die young because they aren't sufficiently aware of dangerous stimuli (Manfredi et al., 1981). Pain is often a signaling device: It normally triggers reflexes that withdraw our limbs from dangerous stimuli; it keeps us from exercising until sprained or damaged muscles have healed; it causes us to seek medical aid for toothaches or intestinal pain.

There seem to be two distinct types of pain. One is a sharp, well-localized "bright" pain; the other is a dull, diffuse, "deep" pain, often described as a vague burning, aching, or throbbing (such as that of a headache or stomachache). Bright pain seems to be associated with the action of myelinated neurons, which rapidly carry pain signals to the brain (such as those involved in withdrawal reflexes). Deep pain signals, on the other hand, seem to be carried to the brain much more slowly by smaller, unmyelinated neurons.

There also seems to be an important distinction between controlling the physical sensation of pain and controlling the emotional response it produces. For example, aspirin or morphine seem to actually block the experience or sensation of pain, while tranquilizers such as Valium (see Chapter 5) seem to reduce the aversiveness of pain. Patients on Valium, for example, often say they still experience the pain—"it just doesn't bother me as much."

While most pain is transient in nature, about one out of three people ex-

perience extended or *chronic pain* during their lifetime (Wallis, 1984). This can be caused by conditions as diverse as back problems, arthritis, migraine headache, or cancer. The control of chronic pain is a major medical concern. Aspirin is far and away the most commonly used drug for pain relief. Its exact physiological action is not completely understood, but it appears to slow the production of prostaglandins, chemicals normally released by neurons at points of intense stimulation. (The more powerful painkillers such as morphine and other opium derivatives are discussed at length in Chapter 5.)

Sensations of Bodily Position

As you move about in the world your body is influenced by gravity and inertia. Your muscles constantly flex and relax in relation to these forces. For example, you hold your body erect against the pull of gravity, or you put an arm in motion and then brake it as your fork approaches a plate. Considering the number of cooperative muscles involved, it is truly amazing that you can bring a fork to rest precisely under several peas, let alone perform a back somersault on a narrow balance beam. While vision is an important part of these processes, two other sensory systems cooperate in feeding your brain the information required to perform these complex acts: the **kinesthetic sense** and the **equilibratory sense.**

Kinesthesis.   Sense organs in the joints and muscles send signals to the brain that indicate the position of the joints and the degree of tension in the muscles. These sensors are responsible for our kinesthetic sense. Ballet dancers unconsciously use these sensors to monitor the position of their limbs, just as you do when you perform the more mundane acts of walking, sitting, or lifting. A rare form of disease called *tabes dorsalis* robs its victims of the kinesthetic sense in their legs. They compensate for this by visually monitoring their position in order to walk. Their slow, oddly shuffling gait is a vivid illustration of the importance of kinesthesis. Most people become aware of the important of kinesthesis only when temporarily robbed of it: for example, when the dentist anesthetizes your tongue with a shot of Novocaine and your speech becomes slurred, or when your leg "goes to sleep" because you sit on it too long.

Equilibratory Sense.   Two sensory organs located next to the cochlea in the inner ear are responsible for our general sense of equilibrium or balance. They are the semicircular canals and the vestibular sacs.

The **semicircular canals** are three ringlike structures, each oriented in a different plane at right angles to the other, like the three surfaces forming the corner of a box. They are filled with fluid that moves in the canals when they are rotated, just as the water in a glass will rotate with respect to the glass when the glass is turned. The movement of the liquid twists small hair cells, triggering neurons attached to these cells. Any bodily movement influences the three separate semicircular canals in a specific way, and the pattern of neural activity signals the direction of motion to the brain.

The **vestibular sacs** are located between the cochlea and the semicircular canals. These sacs are filled with a jellylike substance containing small bones called **otoliths.** Hair cells embedded in the jellylike substance are twisted by the gravitational pull on the otoliths, producing nerve impulses. While the semicircular canals only respond to movement or shifts in position, gravitational pull on the otoliths in the vestibular sacs continuously signals the head's position even when the head is motionless. Disease or infec-

A windsurfer demonstrates the same kinesthetic and equilibratory senses we all possess. The ability to keep one's balance while skiing or windsurfing may take a long time to acquire, but it is based on the same sensory systems which a baby employs when it learns to walk. (Richard D. Wood/Taurus Photos)

tion of the middle ear can produce an almost constant sense of *vertigo* (dizziness) because this signaling function is interrrupted.

The emphasis in this chapter has been on the sensory systems that constantly send information about the outside world and other parts of our bodies back to the brain. It is in the brain that this information is integrated and interpreted. It is here that warmth, pressure, odor, and visual sensations become your experience of being held by your mother, and that a pattern of light and dark contours on the retina becomes the words of a novel. This is the process of *perception,* to which we turn in the next chapter.

SUMMARY

1. All knowledge of the world is carried into the brain through the various sensory systems; activity in these systems is highly correlated, or *redundant* (e.g., the sound of a person's voice and the sight of that person's lips moving are highly correlated or redundant).

2. Before we can sense any form of energy, the stimulus must be at or above the *absolute threshold.* Before we can sense a stimulus change, the stimulus must be greater than the *difference threshold.*

3. Three basic *psychophysical relations* that characterize the association between changes in sensation and changes in stimulus intensity are *Weber's law,* JND = kI; *Fechner's law,* S = c log I; and *Steven's power law,* S = kI^b.

4. Auditory stimuli are complex patterns of variations of air pressure; in the auditory system stimuli are converted into patterns of neural activity that we experience as sound. An *audiometric function* indicates the absolute threshold for each frequency of tone.

5. The sensation of *pitch* is determined primarily by the *frequency* of a tone; *loudness* is determined by the *amplitude* of the tone.

6. The *place theory* of pitch perception is based on the idea that different sound frequencies (different pitches) actually trigger different neurons. An alternative way in which pitch information could be coded into neural activity is in terms of the rate at which neurons are triggered; this is the *frequency theory* of pitch perception.

7. The *visible spectrum,* or *light,* is the range of wavelengths of electromagnetic radiation between 400 and 760 nanometers (for normal vision).

8. *Sinusoidal gratings* are cyclical variations in brightness across space. *Spatial frequency* refers to how rapidly these brightness variations occur, and *contrast* refers to the difference in brightness between the lightest and darkest parts of the grating.

9. The optical system at the front of the eye—consisting of the *cornea* and the *lens*—projects an image onto the *retina.* The eye's receptors are the *rods* and the *cones* of the retina.

10. When the *rods* and *cones* receive light energy, this triggers a complex photochemical process, resulting in neural activity that we experience as sight.

11. The *Young-Helmholtz theory of color vision* assumes that there are three types of cones, each primarily sensitive to a different part of the spectrum. Hering's *opponent-process theory* identifies three antagonistic pairs of color systems in the retina or along the optic pathways. It seems likely that a combination of these theories explains color vision.

12. The physical stimuli for taste are chemical substances (generally food) that touch the *taste buds* on the tongue.

13. Some other factors that influence the sense of taste are color, texture, temperature, and smell.

14. The basic stimuli for smell (*olfaction*) are airborne molecules that enter the nasal cavities; the olfactory receptors are buried in and under the *olfactory epithelium,* located deep inside the nasal cavities.

15. Many different types of physical stimuli evoke skin sensations; these sensations include pressure, warmth, cold, and pain.

16. There are no specific receptors for pain. Intense stimulation of almost any sort seems to evoke the sensation of pain.

17. Two sensory systems that provide the brain with information needed for the body to move properly are the *kinesthetic sense* and the *equilibratory sense.*

18. Sense organs in the joints and muscles define the kinesthetic sense; *semicircular canals* and *vestibular sacs* in the inner ear are responsible for equilibrium (balance).

SUGGESTED READINGS

Boff, K., Kaufman, L., & Thomas, J. (Eds.) (1986). *The handbook of perception and human performance.* Vol. 1. New York: Wiley. An advanced, comprehensive, and detailed reference source for work in sensory process and perception. Each chapter is written by experts in the particular area of research.

Coren, S., Porak, C., & Ward, L. (1984). *Sensation and perception* (2nd ed.). New York: Academic Press. A comprehensive and exceptionally well-written introduction to these topics suitable for undergraduate courses in sensation and perception.

Gescheider, G. A. (1985). *Psychophysics: Method, theory and application* (2nd ed.). Hillsdale, N.J.: Erlbaum. An excellent review of psychophysical methods and signal detection theory.

Levine, M. W., & Shefner, J. M. (1981). *Fundamentals of sensation and perception.* Reading, Mass.: Addison-Wesley. A fairly advanced but very clearly written book that emphasizes sensory process but also deals with perception.

Ludel, J. (1978). *Introduction to sensory processes.* San Francisco: W. H. Freeman. A detailed treatment of basic sensory processes, including physics and biochemistry relevant to these processes.

McBurney, D., & Collings, V. (1977). *Introduction to sensation and perception.* Englewood Cliffs, N.J.: Prentice-Hall. A clearly written and concise general introduction to sensation and perception.

Schiffman, H. R. (1982). *Sensation and perception* (2nd ed.). New York: Wiley. A well-written introduction to a broad range of topics in sensation and perception.

Sekuler, R., & Blake, R. (1985). *Perception.* New York: Knopf. An excellent textbook on sensation and perception, suitable for a first college course in these subjects.

4 Perception

In the last chapter we saw how various stimuli act on sense receptors and cause patterns of neural activity to be sent to our brains. Yet we are seldom aware of this sensory activity as isolated sensations. We don't see "gradients of brightness" or "shifts in spectral composition" on our retina—we see things, people, faces, a sentence, a sunset, a touchdown. We don't hear shifts in the distribution of energy along our basilar membrane—we hear an airplane, guitar music, thunder, a baby's cry, a friend's voice. These experiences, called **perceptions,** usually depend as much on our prior experiences and knowledge of the world as they do on the immediate sensory information reaching our brain. For example, consider what is happening as you read these words. The sensory messages being sent from your retina to your brain indicate patterns of lines we call letters and words. Yet you immediately experience them as "meaning." Certainly this perceptual experience depends as much on prior knowledge as it does on the neural cues traveling between retina and brain. If you hadn't already learned to read English, you certainly couldn't understand what the patterns of lines on this page are saying to you. These patterns, which so easily evoke meaning for you, are a meaningless jumble of lines to an illiterate.

VIEWS OF PERCEPTION:
HELMHOLTZ AND GIBSON

A view of perception that has been more or less dominant over the last 100 years holds that our experiences teach us how to draw broad inferences about the world from very limited sensory information; and that most per-

This engraving entitled "Fish," by the Dutch engraver M. C. Escher, can be seen in a variety of ways as the mind attempts to organize a coherent perception. (© M. C. Escher Heirs, c/o Cordon Art-Baarn, Holland)

ceptions are made up, or *synthesized,* from combinations of more elementary sensations. It also maintains that these perceptual inferences are usually so accurate, highly practiced, and practically automatic that you are almost totally unaware of making them. This is why one of the early proponents of the view, Hermann von Helmholtz (1925, 1962), referred to them as *unconscious inferences.*

This view of perception has been challenged by the work of James J. Gibson (1966, 1972) and others. Gibson argued that traditional perceptual research failed to consider the active, information-seeking interaction between organisms and their natural environments. Rather than simply supplying sensations from which our brain subsequently draws inferences, our sensory systems have evolved to be perceptual systems in their own right. These systems are sufficiently sensitive to complex aspects of our environment to evoke immediate perceptual experience without any intervening inferential process.

Proponents of Gibson's view (Neisser, 1967, 1976; Shaw & Bransford, 1977; Turvey & Shaw, 1978, 1979) have called for more *ecologically valid* experiments in perception, experiments that involve the complex patterns of stimulation encountered as we move about in normal environments, rather than those that have traditionally been used in sensory research. For example, consider Figure 4–1. Although A and B are different pictures, they share one feature in common: a gradual shift in the average size of objects or detail as you go from bottom to top. Gibson referred to such shifts as **texture gradients,** and he pointed out that they are virtually invariant features of scenes in which surfaces recede from us, whether the surface is a field of flowers or a shore covered with rocks. Gibson argued that our visual system has evolved so as to be sensitive to such texture gradients. Thus they act as powerful cues for depth, evoking the perception of a receding surface as directly as our experience of hue or pitch, without any intervening process of synthesis or interpretation.

Gibson's concern with the natural occurrence of cues in our environment has led to a greater appreciation of how complex stimulus properties can be picked up directly by our sensory systems and evoke an immediate perception, rather than one built up from a combination of simpler component sensations. Yet there are types of stimuli that do seem to evoke perception through a rather slow, inferential process. Figure 4–2 shows a drawing that is perceived at first as a normal building. Only after you have taken some time to examine components of the building closely do you perceive it as an impossible structure, one whose component parts couldn't really fit together.

Whether one takes a Gibsonian or Helmholtzian view, there is little question that perceptions are evoked by cues in the environment and depend to a

Figure 4–1 These pictures have in common a texture gradient that is a strong cue for depth: the average size of details diminishes as a surface recedes from the viewer. (*Left:* Alec Duncan/Taurus Photos)

Figure 4–2 M. C. Escher's drawing *Belvedere* is usually seen at first as a normal building. Only upon closer examination is it perceived to be an impossible structure, one whose component parts cannot really fit together. Notice, for example, the ladder that begins on the inside of the building and ends up outside, and the pillars that cross from back to front. Can you spot other impossible features? (Copyright © M.C. Escher, Heirs, c/o Cordon Art-Baarn, Holland)

large extent on prior experience. The major goals of this chapter are to make you more aware both of how cues evoke perception and of the distinction between such cues and what we perceive. To begin, we will consider some general principles of perception.

SOME GENERAL PRINCIPLES

Redundancy and Perception

If one part of a message repeats what is conveyed in another part, the parts are said to be redundant (just as a lecturer is redundant when she repeats herself). There is considerable repetition of information, **redundancy,** in the sensory messages sent to our brain, and this plays a major role in perception.

Figure 4–3 Even though only half the normal cues for a face are present in the top and bottom views, each is capable of evoking virtually the same perception of a whole face. Again, note the distinction between the cues and the perception they evoke. This perception depends as much on your familiarity with the normal features of faces as it does on the immediate sensory cues. (Broadbent, 1958)

A newborn infant does not immediately understand the relationship between the sound of its mother's voice, the sight of her face, and the feel of her bodily warmth, but it rapidly learns that these are all closely related aspects of a single thing, "mother." Soon one sensation becomes a reliable signal or cue for the experience of the others. For instance, the sound of the mother's voice often comes just before the sight of her face above the crib, or the sensation of being held. Almost every aspect of our experience involves relationships of this sort. As these relationships are learned, they begin to color every experience we have.

As another example, suppose a friend approached you in the subbasement of the library one night and, as water dripped from his raincoat onto your term paper, announced that it was "really raining out." In this case you would have received three highly redundant messages: his spoken words, his manner of dress, and your soggy paper. All three would tell you that it was raining outside. As you come to learn that redundant things tend to occur together, they all tend to evoke the same, or similar, perceptions.

Figure 4–3 shows how your knowledge of the structural redundancy (the relationships among its parts) in a familiar object such as a face allows you to perceive a whole face when only half of the contours are acting as cues.

Our language itself is highly redundant—for example, you can often finish a sentence in your mind after hearing or seeing only part of it. This feature of language will be discussed later in the chapter in the section on reading and also in the chapters on memory and language (Chapters 7 and 8).

Attention: Selectivity in Perception

Another basic principle of perception is that we seem unable to cope with all potentially perceptible aspects of our environment at the same time; our tendency is to deal with incoming information selectively. The study of how we selectively perceive one environmental aspect or another is the study of **attention.** For example, you are probably sitting as you read this. Without moving, shift your attention to the sensations produced by the pressure of your body against the surfaces supporting it. Exactly where is the chair pressing against your back? Which parts of your left foot are pressing against something? As you attempt to answer questions of this sort, you selectively attend to sensory activity that was present earlier but unnoticed.

Have you even been at a party gazing with apparent interest into the eyes of someone speaking to you, only to realize that you're really listening to a conversation going on behind you? Both voices, your partner's and the one you're really attending to, are entering your ears and evoking patterns of sensory activity. Yet you selectively perceive only one of them, finding it difficult to listen closely to both conversations at the same time. You may occasionally need to switch your full attention back to your partner in order to keep the conversation going.

This "cocktail-party problem" has been studied experimentally. Subjects hear two voices speaking at the same time (usually one voice in the right ear and a different voice in the left). They are sometimes instructed to listen primarily to one voice, sometimes to the other, and sometimes to try to listen to both simultaneously. In general, there is a "trade-off" between the comprehension of one voice and the other: Increased comprehension of one voice is generally associated with reduced comprehension of the other (see Figure 4–4). To explain this negative relationship, an English psychologist named Donald Broadbent (1958) proposed that people only have the capa-

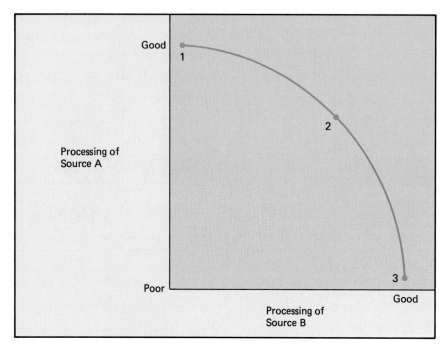

Figure 4–4 The figure shows the sort of trade-off often found in processing two alternate sources of information (A and B): Better (faster, more accurate) processing of one source can only be achieved by poorer (slower, less accurate) processing of another source. Such trade-offs underlie the concept of *attention.* For example, if the two sources of information were the two voices in the "cocktail-party problem," instructions to "attend" to one voice (A) or the other (B) would produce comprehension levels consistent with points 1 or 3, respectively. Instructions to "attend equally" to both voices would probably produce comprehension levels consistent with point 2. Trade-off functions of this sort have been called *attention operating characteristic* (AOC) functions (Kinchla, 1969) and *performance operating characteristic* (POC) functions (Norman & Bobrow, 1975). They have been used to analyze a variety of attentional problems in vision and audition (see Kinchla, 1980; or Shiffrin, 1985).

city to listen to one voice at a time. When they try to follow two voices at the same time they must *switch* attention back and forth. The negative relationship between the comprehension of each voice reflects the proportion of time subjects spend listening to each voice.

This sort of trade-off between attending to one voice or another can also be explained as a simultaneous *sharing* of attention rather than switching. That is, you may attend primarily to one voice, but at the same time allocate some small portion of your attention to the other. This view, sometimes referred to as the *filter theory,* was advanced by Anne Triesman (1964) to account for subjects' apparent sensitivity to certain kinds of information spoken by the unattended voice. For example, they were likely to notice the unattended voice if it said their own name.

Another view of attention (Norman, 1979) is that selection occurs not by selectively blocking or filtering sensory information, but by selectively *processing* information already evoked or activated in memory by incoming sensory information. Highly practiced and familiar stimuli (such as your own name) often seem to be perceived so automatically that it is almost impossible to ignore them (Schneider & Shiffrin, 1977). A good example of such automaticity in perception is the so-called *Stroop effect* (Stroop, 1935). Subjects are shown words that are printed in different colors of ink. They are told to ignore the words and just name the ink colors. They have little difficulty doing this, except when the words are names of different colors. For example, if the word "red" is printed in green ink, subjects often hesitate or stumble in saying "green," as if they have difficulty ignoring the word's meaning. Normally, the highly practiced and almost automatic perception of word meaning facilitates reading. However, this same automaticity makes it difficult to ignore meaning and pay attention only to certain other aspects of the stimulus. Thus the Stroop effect is a failure of selective perception (see Figure 4–5).

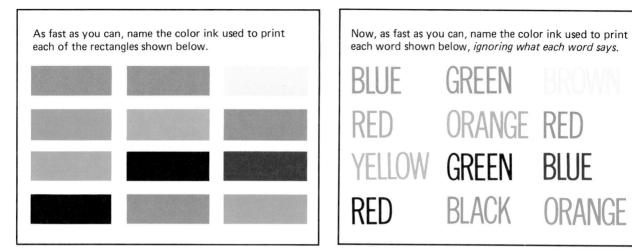

As fast as you can, name the color ink used to print each of the rectangles shown below.

Now, as fast as you can, name the color ink used to print each word shown below, *ignoring what each word says*.

BLUE   GREEN   BROWN
RED   ORANGE   RED
YELLOW   GREEN   BLUE
RED   BLACK   ORANGE

Figure 4–5 It is easy to name the color inks used to print the rectangles in the box at left. But notice how difficult it is to ignore what the words say when you try to name the color inks used to print the words in the box at right. This is called the *Stroop effect* after the experimenter who devised this demonstration of automatic perception.

Figure 4–6 Organization into meaningful forms is highly dependent on experience. While today most of us would recognize the planet Saturn (top photograph) as a sphere surrounded by a ring, the ever-changing appearance of Saturn puzzled early astronomers such as Hevelius. Hevelius, who didn't know anything about Saturn, couldn't "see" it correctly, as his drawings (bottom left) indicate. Similarly, without some kind of clue (man on horseback), you may have the same problem "seeing" a meaningful form in the figure at bottom right.

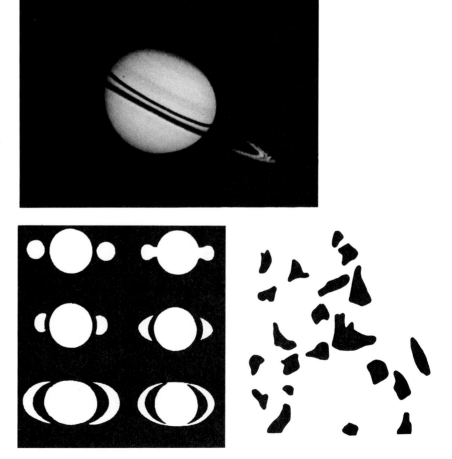

At present there is no general agreement concerning the mental processes that control attention. It seems likely that many different processes are responsible for selectivity in perception (Kinchla, 1980).

Organization

As we have seen, we are seldom aware of isolated sensations. Our minds constantly organize sensory activity to perceive *things*. Complex sequences of auditory stimulation are perceived as speech, or a car motor, or water running. Complex patterns of visual stimulation are seen as people, cars, printed words. Much of our ability to organize or structure complex patterns of sensory activity into meaningful forms depends on experience (see Figure 4–6 and 4–7A). However, certain kinds of perceptual organization seem so universal and natural that it has been proposed they are innate rather than the product of earlier experience.

Gestalt Principles of Organization. The **Gestalt** psychologists (Koffka, 1935; Köhler, 1940) believed that a number of innate organizational tendencies influence the way we see. (While many contemporary psychologists feel that even these tendencies are the result of experience and learning, all agree that they are strong and virtually universal tendencies.)

Examples of such apparently universal organizational tendencies are called *Gestalt principles of grouping*. These refer to the human tendency to organize sets of isolated stimuli into groups on the basis of *proximity* (closeness), *similarity, closure, continuity,* and *symmetry*. These principles are illustrated and explained in Figure 4–8.

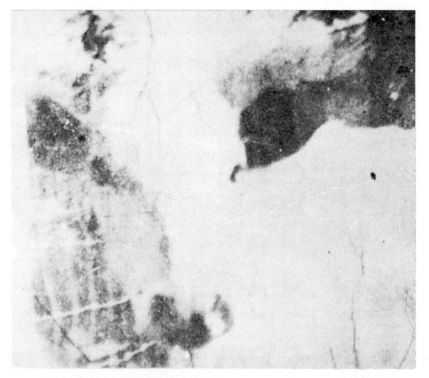

Figure 4–7A Try and organize the pattern shown at left into a recognizable form. Most people take a long time to do this because the visual cues aren't powerful enough to evoke an immediate perception. Perhaps this additional verbal cue will help: Moo! If you are still stumped, turn the page to where the familiar form is outlined in Figure 4–7B.

Figure 4–7B Here an additional cue (the outline of the cow's head) has been added to help you "see" the head of a cow. Turn back to 4–7A and note how easy it is to recognize the cow now that you have seen its head outlined here.

Figure 4–8 The Gestalt principles of grouping: *proximity, similarity, closure, continuity,* and *symmetry.*

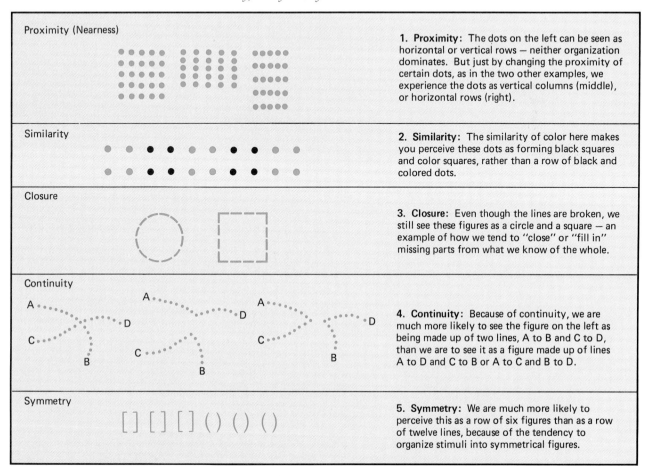

Figure-ground Organization. Another basic organizational tendency that the Gestalt psychologists argued is innate is referred to as **figure-ground organization**—the tendency to perceive things (figures) standing out against a background (ground). For example, as you read this page, the words are black *figures* standing out against the white back*ground* of the paper. Normally, this type of organization is so efficient and automatic that it occurs unnoticed. However, consider the pattern shown in Figure 4–9. Here the normal figure-ground organization suggested by the generally white background of the page encourages you to see the black regions as "figure" and the white regions as "ground." Only after some time and effort can you reverse this usual organization and see the word "house" as a white figure against a black background.

A more complex example of this phenomenon is seen in Figure 4–10. At first glance most people see the figure as a white triangle in front of three black circles; that is, the triangle and circles are seen as figures against a white ground. The three black "Pacmen," with their "mouths" agape, act as strong cues for the perception of a white triangle. Most observers even claim to see the "edges" of the triangle between the circles—so-called *illusionary contours*—which are not really there at all.

While figure-ground organization has traditionally referred to visual perception, there also seem to be similar organizational processes in hearing. For example, the "cocktail-party problem" can be interpreted as a choice of which voice to hear as the "figure" standing out against a background of another voice (or voices). Similarly, the particular stream of notes one chooses to hear as a single melodic line in a Bach fugue also seems to be a "figure" heard against a background of the other notes.

Bistable or Reversible Stimulus Patterns. One of the most convincing ways to illustrate the importance of organizational processes in perception is to consider stimulus patterns that are perceived in very different ways depending on your choice of organization. If there are only two alternative organizations, the stimulus patterns are often referred to as *bistable* or *reversible* patterns. Each organization produces a stable perception, although it is impossible to experience both simultaneously. One organization must be changed or reversed in order to experience the other perception. Figure 4–11 presents some examples of stimuli susceptible to more than one organization. Each of these patterns could be described as *ambiguous,* that is, each stimulus pattern can be thought of as a cue for two very different perceptions and it is unclear which organization is appropriate. Fortunately, most of the things we see occur in contexts that provide additional cues that help resolve such ambiguity.

Figure 4–9 By reversing the normal figure-ground organization (black letters against white ground), you will eventually see the word "house" as white letters (figures) against a black ground. (Murich, 1973, p. 146)

Figure 4–10 This figure is usually seen as a white triangle in front of three black circles, in front of a white "ground." Notice that perceptually you even divide the white area of the stimulus into two distinct regions: the white triangle in front and the white ground behind. The white triangle even appears brighter than the white of the ground, producing an "illusionary contour."

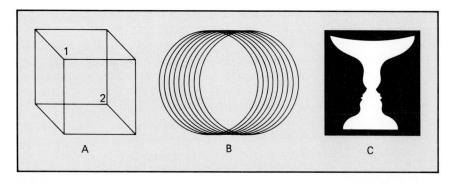

Figure 4–11 These are three examples of reversible, or bistable, patterns. In Pattern A you can see a cube with either corner 1 or corner 2 closer to you. Pattern B can be seen as a cylinder lying on its side with its closer end on the left or on the right. Pattern C looks like a goblet if the white area is seen as "figure," or like two faces in profile if organized as "ground."

VODKA TODAY

Figure 4–12 Experimenters briefly presented these words with colored letters and asked subjects to report the color of particular letters (Prinzmetal, Treisman, & Rho, 1986). Subjects erroneously reported the "D" in "VODKA" more often as green, while they reported the "D" in "TODAY" more often as red. These and other results suggest that such conjunction errors occur more often between letters in the same syllable than between letters in different syllables (for example, in "VODKA" between the "D" and "VO," rather than between the "D" and "KA").

Illusionary Conjunctions: Organizing Color and Form. Suppose you glanced quickly at a table top and "saw" a green cup next to a blue glass; then on closer examination, you realized that it was really a blue cup next to a green glass. This type of erroneous organization of color and form has been called an *illusionary conjunction* (Treisman, 1987). Such errors may occur because color and form are sensed through different visual systems and only later combined. Normally, this is done successfully and automatically. However, when objects are seen only briefly (or when you aren't paying close attention), such failures of organization are more likely to happen. Figure 4–12 shows how the occurrence of conjunction errors can even be influenced by linguistic factors in reading.

Constancies: Invariance Amid Change

Although sensory cues may vary enormously from moment to moment, you perceive many aspects of the world as stable and invariant. For example, a person seen from different angles or distances produces different patterns of stimulation on your retina, yet you still "see" the same person. Different cues evoke much the same perception. This provides a stability or constancy to your perceptions of the world despite great changes in sensory activity. We will discuss this phenomenon, **perceptual constancy,** in regard to size, shape, and color.

Size Constancy. If a person walking away from you casts a smaller and smaller image onto your retina, why do you see that person's size as remaining constant? One explanation is that your perception of an object's size depends both on the size of its image on your retina and on distance cues (see Figure 4–13). Two objects casting the *same* size image onto your retina would be perceived as different in size if they appeared to be at different distances. The object that looks farther away from you would seem to be larger. Thus **size constancy** is the almost automatic tendency to compensate for changes in the size of the retinal image caused by changes in viewing distance.

Some psychologists argue that this process of compensation is unnecessary to explain size constancy. They say that size constancy occurs because both the object and its surroundings change together as the distance of the object changes. In other words, your friend at a distance looks smaller, but so do the buildings around her, and the trees and the cars. When close up, all of

Figure 4–13 Your perception of an object's size must be based on more than the size its image casts on the retina. For example, a shorter tree could cast exactly the same-size retinal image as a taller one if the shorter tree were closer, as shown in the diagram. Thus, if distance cues indicated the tree was standing farther away (Distance A), it would be perceived as larger than if distance cues indicated it was closer (Distance B). Given a particular retinal size, perceived size will increase with perceived distance.

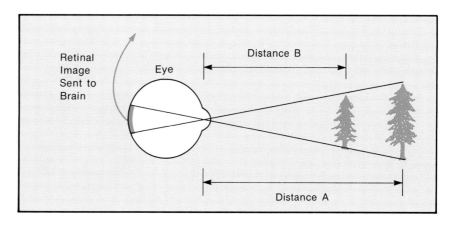

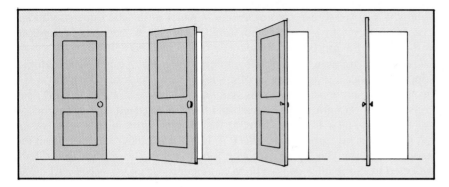

Figure 4–14   The figure shows an example of shape constancy. The opening door is actually many different shapes, yet we still see it as basically a rectangular door. The different retinal images evoke an unchanging (constant) perception of shape. Only your perspective seems to change.

these—your friend and her surroundings—look larger, but they are in the same *relationship* to one another. In other words, size remains constant because the relationship between the object and its surroundings stays the same.

Shape Constancy.   **Shape constancy** is the tendency to perceive objects as having the same shape in spite of variations in the shape they cast onto your retina (see Figure 4–14). As you watch a door opening, your view of it may change from a rectangle to a trapezoid. However, your past experience with doors causes you to infer or understand automatically that it is not the door itself that is changing shape, but only your particular view of it.

Shape constancy depends on both familiarity with the shapes of objects and knowledge of their position in space relative to you. You may have had the experience of sitting far to one side in a movie theater and being keenly aware of the distortion produced by your perspective of the screen. However, you are capable of rapidly accommodating to the situation, and before long you were probably able to follow the movie without even noticing the distortion.

Another example of how retinal image depends on your perspective is the following: As you walk through an art gallery, you may first view many of the paintings from the side before viewing them directly from the front. Yet as your view of a particular painting shifts from side to front, you tend to perceive it as remaining constant, even though its pattern on your retina changes considerably. The magnitude of this change is illustrated by the sixteenth-century painting shown in Figure 4–15. The face as actually painted is highly distorted, but in a way that is exactly canceled out by the normal distortion that occurs when you view the painting from one side. Thus the face in the side view seems oddly normal, as if you weren't viewing it from the side. In fact, it almost seems to be floating out of the painting at right angles to your line of sight. This painting should make you aware of how much the pattern cast on your retina can change depending on the angle at which you view something, yet your perception normally remains constant.

Color Constancy.   The light reflected into your eyes from a familiar object, such as a person's skin, varies considerably with the type of illumination in the room (firelight, sunlight, moonlight, fluorescent light), yet the color of the skin does not seem to change. This illustrates the principle of **color constancy**, another perceptual process that lends stability to our perceptions.

Learning and expectation have a lot to do with color constancy. If you are shown an orange or a banana under hidden colored lights that distort the natural color, you still tend to perceive the orange as orange or the banana as

Figure 4–15   This painting of Edward VI (top) was done in 1546 by an Englishman named William Scrots. He distorted the face so that it would only look normal when viewed from the side (bottom): The distortion normally produced by side viewing exactly canceled out the distortion in the painting. In this way Scrots made the viewer aware of how different a painting normally appears when viewed from the side, even though our brain automatically "sees" the correct perception.

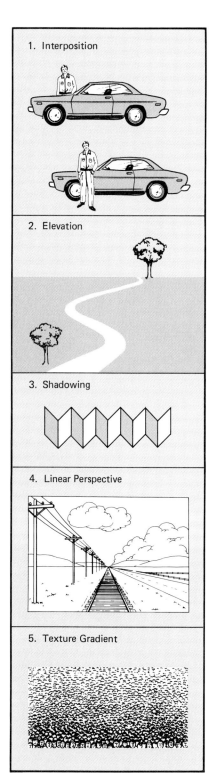

1. Interposition

2. Elevation

3. Shadowing

4. Linear Perspective

5. Texture Gradient

yellow. If you are shown colored pieces of paper under the same conditions, even if you are told what colors they are "supposed" to be, your perceptions will probably be more highly influenced by the colored lights.

There are times when color constancy does not operate. For example, suppose that after developing a color snapshot you took of a friend, you notice a strange greenish tinge to his skin on the left side of his face. Only after considerable thought do you recall that he standing next to a green hedge that doesn't appear in the picture. At the time, your brain compensated for the predominantly green light reflected onto the left side of his face from the hedge; you "saw" his whole face as normally colored even though the light reflected from the left side contained more energy from the green part of the spectrum. When you saw the color print, your brain couldn't make the automatic adjustment for the green light coming from the hedge and there was a failure of normal color constancy. The point here is that the light reaching your eyes from an object depends both on the light falling on it (its illumination) and on the way it reflects some wavelengths and absorbs others (its color). Our brain is usually able to take illumination into account when judging an object's color, even though changes in illumination cause large changes in the light reflected into our eyes.

Having considered some general principles of perception (redundancy, attention, organization, and constancy), we will now consider how these principles apply in four important problems of visual perception: depth perception, picture perception, movement perception, and reading. At the end of the chapter we will discuss computer pattern recognition.

DEPTH PERCEPTION

How do we make inferences about a three-dimensional world on the basis of the two-dimensional patterns of light projected onto each retina? We use depth (distance) cues: **monocular cues** that are available from the retina of a single eye and **binocular cues** that depend on combining information from both eyes. For some interesting examples involving both monocular and binocular cues, see the Highlights on the Ames demonstrations and experience and perception.

Monocular Cues for Depth

Cover one of your eyes with your hand and look about you with the other eye. You still have a clear sense of seeing things at different distances, although perhaps not quite so vividly. Now hold one finger out in front of the uncovered eye. Notice that when you focus on the finger, the background is out of focus and blurred, and when you focus on the background, the reverse is true. Thus focusing, or **accomodation,** produces a strong monocular depth cue: differences in the sharpness of objects at different distances.

Figure 4–16 1. *Interposition:* If one object seems to be covering another, it will be perceived as being closer. 2. *Elevation:* The higher the object in the horizontal plane, the farther away it seems to be. 3. *Shadowing:* Shadows or shading tend to give an impression of depth. 4. *Linear perspective:* Parallel lines seem to converge at a point in the distance, which is what gives the illusion of depth to this drawing. 5. *Texture gradient:* As distance increases, the average size of surface details diminishes. This variance in texture is a strong cue to depth.

Figure 4–17 (Top) If you rotate your eyes inward toward your nose (converge them) so as to see the nearer point A, its image will fall on the fovea (F) of each retina, while the image of the more distant point B will fall on other parts of each retina. (Bottom) If you converge your eyes to see the more distant point B, the reverse is true. Thus the differences in convergence required to see objects at different distances is a cue for depth.

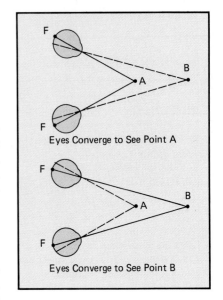

Eyes Converge to See Point A

Eyes Converge to See Point B

Although an artist could paint what you saw given a particular accommodation, the blurred and unblurred parts of the painting would remain constant if you refocused your eye. This is probably why artists seldom use this as a major cue for depth. Monocular cues that *are* often used to represent depth in paintings are **interposition, elevation, shadowing, linear perspective,** and **texture gradient** (see Figure 4–16).

Binocular Cues for Depth

Since your eyes are separated by a few centimeters, the view from one is almost never exactly the same as the view from the other. The left eye sees more of the left side of an object, and the right eye sees more of the right side. These two monocular views are automatically combined into a single subjective view, sometimes called the **cyclopean view** after the mythical one-eyed Cyclops.

Both the disparities (differences) and the similarities in the two monocular views produce unique effects in the cyclopean view. If a line or edge is projected onto the same part of the retina in each eye, the contour will be seen clearly and vividly in the combined cyclopean view, a process called **binocular fusion.** Exactly which contours will be fused depends on the **convergence** of the eyes—their rotation inward toward the nose (see Figure 4–17). Ordinarily, you constantly adjust the convergence of your eyes to produce fusion of those aspects of a scene you wish to see clearly. However, when one set of contours is fused by the appropriate convergence, other contours will fall on noncorresponding parts of the retina in each eye. These differences, called **binocular disparities,** can produce a double image in the cyclopean view or a fluctuating competition, called **binocular rivalry,** in which one or the other part of the double image is alternately represented in the cyclopean view (see Figure 4–18).

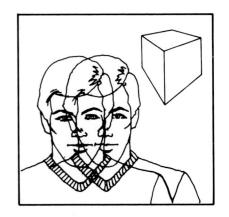

The primary reason that we aren't more aware of binocular disparity and rivalry is because we usually fuse the details that we are interested in. When you attend to a particular detail, you rotate your eyes to minimize binocular disparity for that detail, thereby producing fusion. You also aim and focus (accommodate) your eyes so that the detail of current interest is clearly projected onto each fovea. If this detail is some distance away, the two eyes may be pointing virtually straight ahead. However, when you attend to something closer, it is necessary to converge the eyes (Figure 4–17). As you successively attend to details at different distances, you shift convergence, successively producing fusion and disparity for details at each distance. The brain automatically interprets the shifts in convergence, fusion, and disparity as binocular cues indicating relative distance. The whole process, termed binocular

Figure 4–18 (Top) Convergence is such that the near object, the man, is fused in the cyclopean view and the distant object, the block, is not fused, producing a double image. (Bottom) Convergence is such that the distant object is fused, and the nearer object, which is not fused, produces a double image.

One of the more intriguing figures in the history of perceptual research was an amateur psychologist named Adelbert Ames II. Ames was over 50 before he began his work in perception; he never held a university position, and he wrote little. Yet there is hardly an introductory psychology or perception text that fails to refer to his work. He was characterized by the famous mathematician and philosopher Alfred North Whitehead as a "true genius" and by the philosopher John Dewey as doing "the best work by far in the physiological-philosophical world during this century" (Cantril, 1960, p. 231).

Ames's reputation is based almost exclusively on a series of visual demonstrations he developed at Dartmouth College around 1938. Several years earlier he had abandoned a successful law career to study painting and optics at Dartmouth. While he made some important contributions to visual optics, Ames's true fascination was with the "correspondence" between the sensations that "exist in consciousness and the . . . objects, qualities, etc. that exist externally" (Cantril, 1960, p. 11). This interest led Ames to the study of *visual illusions:* instances where one confidently perceives something that isn't really there. To Ames these failures of the normal correspondence between perception and objective reality seemed to hold the key to an understanding of visual perception—

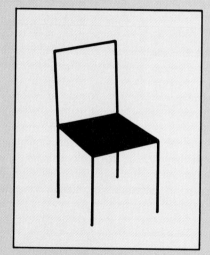

Figure A

a   b

Figure B

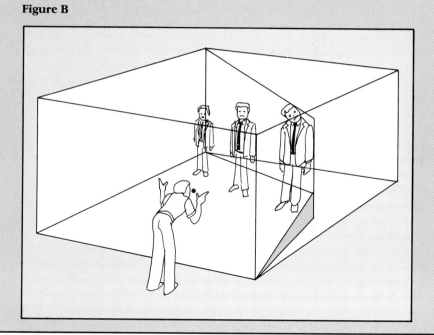

perception or **stereopsis,** is a major part of our sense of a third dimension (depth) in vision.

PERCEPTION OF PICTURES

Most of the characteristics of perception that we have discussed can be demonstrated in terms of how we look at pictures (paintings, drawings, or photographs). As with all perception, we draw as much from our earlier experiences (what we expect to see) as we do from the actual signals our eyes send to our brain. This process of interpretation is so automatic that we are

indeed to the way one comes to understand the world.

Ames designed a series of visual illusions, first at Dartmouth and then at Princeton University, which are collectively referred to as the *Ames Demonstrations.* One of these, the *Chair Demonstration,* is illustrated in Figure A. Ames first directed a viewer to look into a large box through a small peephole just big enough for one eye. Inside the box the viewer "saw" a simple white kitchen chair suspended against a black background ([a] of Figure A). Ames then opened the top of the box and again asked the viewer to look inside. From this new perspective the viewer saw only a jumbled collection of white cardboard and wooden sticks suspended by invisible black threads ([b] of Figure A). Only when viewed through the peephole did these things seem to be a chair. The point of the demonstration is to clearly distinguish between the pattern cast on the retina and the perception of seeing a chair.

Another demonstration is the *Ames Room.* This room is so constructed that if one looks into it through a particular peephole the image cast onto the retina is that of a normally shaped room. Just like the chair, however, it looks normal only from one perspective. The rear wall appears to be at right angles to the viewer's line of sight, when in reality it slants sharply away (see Figure B).

Figure C shows a photograph taken in the type of Ames Room first constructed at Princeton University around 1948. One woman appears much taller than the others because from this perspective you "see" a normally shaped room. In fact, because the rear wall is slanted, the "shorter" women is much farther away from you than the "taller" one. The corners of the room seem equally far away because the wall doesn't appear to be tilted. Thus, by the laws of size constancy, the difference in size of the retinal image cast by the two people automatically evokes the perception of "short" and "tall."

One person who often visited the Ames Room at Princeton was Albert Einstein, who worked at the nearby Center for Advanced Studies. He, too, was fascinated by the work of this lawyer-turned-psychologist whose demonstrations, contributed to our understanding of perception.

Figure C (William Vandernert)

usually unaware of what is happening. In this section we shall slow down the process to show exactly what happens when you look at a picture.

Eye Movements

When you look at a photograph or a painting you may think that you take in the whole image at once, but actually you build up a perception of the whole picture based on a series of separate looks. These are produced by successively moving your eye, then briefly holding it still for about one- to three-tenths of a second. Each movement of the eye is called a **saccade;** holding it still is a **fixation.** Almost the whole image of the picture is cast onto some

HIGHLIGHT _____

Experience and
Perception: An Example

The pygmies of the Congo inhabit a kind of densely foliated tropical rain forest. Anthropoligist Colin Turnbull has described these people and their way of life. Many pygmies never leave this world. Turnbull describes what happened when a pygmy man named Kenge took his very first trip out of the dense mountain forest into the valley.

> Then he saw the buffalo, still grazing lazily several miles away, far down below. He turned to me and said, "What insects are those?" At first I hardly understood; then I realized that in the forest the range of vision is so limited that there is no great need to make an automatic allowance for distance when judging size. Out here in the plains, however, Kenge was looking for the first time over apparently unending miles of unfamiliar grasslands, with not a tree worth the name to give him any basis for comparison.
>
> When I told Kenge that the insects were buffalo, he roared with laughter and told me not to tell such stupid lies. Kenge still did not believe, but he strained his eyes to see more clearly and asked what kind of buffalo were so small. I told him they were sometimes nearly twice the size of a forest buffalo, and he shrugged his shoulders and said we would not be standing out there in the open if they were. I tried telling him they were possibly as far away as from Epulu to the village of Kopu, beyond Eboyo. He began scraping the mud off his arms and legs, no longer interested in such fantasies. . . .
>
> The road led on down to within about half a mile of where the herd was grazing, and as we got closer the "insects" must have seemed to get bigger and bigger. Kenge, who was now sitting on the outside, kept his face glued to the window, which nothing would make him lower. I even had to raise mine to keep him happy. I was never able to discover just what he thought

> was happening—whether he thought that the insects were changing into buffalo, or that they were miniature buffalo growing rapidly as we approached. His only comment was that they were not real buffalo, and he was not going to get out of the car again until we left the park. (From *The Forest People* by Colin M. Turnbull. Copyright © 1961 by Colin M. Turnbull. Reprinted by permission of Simon & Schuster, Inc.)

part of the retina during each fixation. Yet, as we discussed in Chapter 3, the ability to see fine detail lies only in the fovea—acuity falls off very rapidly on the periphery of the eye. Thus you move your eyes over the picture so that the fovea can pick up the details. This series of fixations is like making a pic-

Figure 4–19 The network of lines on the right is a pattern of eye movements made by someone looking at a photograph of a piece of sculpture of Egyptian Queen Nefertiti (on the left). The pattern was recorded by bouncing a beam of light off a tiny mirror attached to the eye as the person looked at the photograph for two minutes. The pattern indicates that most fixations were on the face; other parts of the head and neck were sampled infrequently. (From Yarbus, A. L. *Eye movements and vision.* Fig. 116. Copyright 1967 by Plenum Publishing Corporation. Reprinted by permission.)

How limited Kenge's perceptions seem to us! He was apparently so used to viewing objects at very close range in the dense underbrush of the tropical rain forest that he couldn't maintain size constancy when viewing objects at the unfamiliar distances he encountered in the valley. But are our perceptions any less limited?

Almost everyone has seen a full moon close to the horizon and marveled at how much larger it seemed than when viewed directly overhead. In fact, there isn't any real difference in the size of the moon—it always subtends a visual angle of about one-half degree. Rather, this *moon illusion* seems to be a failure of size constancy. We seem to judge its size as if it were closer to us when seen overhead than when near the horizon (as shown in the photograph and in the figure). One explanation for this (Kaufman & Roch, 1962) is that the outlines of objects near the horizon are powerful depth cues indicating that the moon is even farther away than the horizon. These depth cues are missing when the moon is overhead, so it seems closer (and therefore smaller, since its visual angle is the

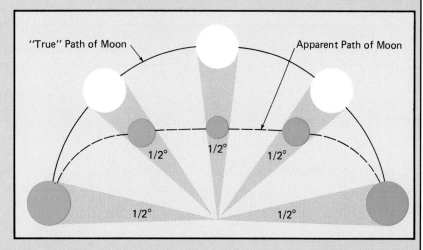

same). This interpretation is consistent with the fact that viewing the moon through a rolled-up magazine or other tube eliminates these depth cues—and the moon illusion.

The size illusions experienced in the Ames Room (see the earlier Highlight) also show how experience affects our perception. Even after you are told the true shape of the room,

the illusion tends to persist. However, if you are allowed to move about in the room, to explore its shape actively, to reach into one corner after another with a long stick, the illusion gradually disappears. No doubt Kenge's lack of size constancy would also slowly disappear as he gained more experience outside the rain forest.

---

ture from a series of snapshots, each of which shows most of the image but with only a small part in sharp focus.

Fixations are not random. They seem to concentrate on parts of the picture that are particularly informative and only rarely on highly redundant parts that can easily be inferred from the rest of the image. For example, in Figure 4–19 most of a subject's fixations were on details of the face; parts of the head and the neck, which could easily be guessed from the rest of the image, were sampled infrequently. This is an example of the sort of dynamic information-seeking interaction between the person and the environment that was emphasized by Gibson (1966).

The fact that it takes time to see a picture, even though you feel you took it all in in a single look, is clearly shown in the way you "see" impossible figures, such as the one in Figure 4–20. The various parts of such figures seem to make sense until you try to put them together. Note how reasonable each part of the picture appears at first. Each separate fixation by your eyes takes in a seemingly logical detail of the figure; it is only when you put them all together, or try to, that you realize there are impossible contradictions in the separate parts.

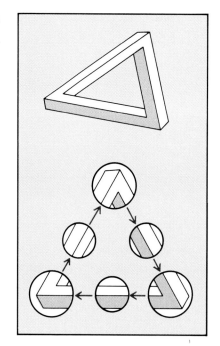

Figure 4–20 If you make separate fixations on the details of the triangle shown above, each separate fixation (shown in the circles below) would be entirely acceptable alone. But it would be impossible to put them together to form an acceptable perception of the whole object. (After Lindsay & Norman, 1972, p. 25) (After Lindsay, P.H., & Norman, D. A. *Human information processing* (2nd ed.). New York: Academic Press, 1977. Reprinted with permission.)

Three Dimensions from Two

When you think about it, it is amazing that a pattern of light-and-dark pigments on a flat two-dimensional surface can evoke the perception of a three-dimensional world. Indeed, this was a process that puzzled painters for centuries. While the modern sense of *perspective* was probably first realized in the fifteenth century, artists have become more and more sophisticated in evoking three-dimensional perceptions with two-dimensional surfaces. To do this, painters use a number of the depth cues mentioned earlier in the chapter.

M. C. Escher, a Dutch engraver, wanted to portray the different levels of psychological space that could be evoked by two-dimensional images. In Figure 4–21 you first perceive the representation of a three-dimensional world containing some objects on a table top: a bottle, a drawing pad, and a book on which some lizards appear to be crawling. Follow the lizards as they climb a geometrically shaped object and down over a cup onto the drawing tablet. They appear to merge into the drawing page, becoming flat figures drawn onto it. As you scan the drawing, one of the flat lizards suddenly becomes three-dimensional, and another climbs up onto the book. The lizards exist in three distinct levels of psychological space. First, you're obviously aware that Figure 4–21 is a flat figure in your own book. Second, you see in that figure another three-dimensional world containing the table top on which are located the drawing pad, the book, and the lizards. Finally, there is a third world represented in the drawings on the pad. By having the lizards move in and out of the normally isolated worlds, Escher provokes the viewer into an appreciation of their separate psychological existence.

Figure 4–21 M. C. Escher's *Reptiles* is an example of the representation of a three-dimensional world by means of two-dimensional images. (Copyright © M. C. Escher, Heirs, c/o Cordon Art-Baarn, Holland)

(Above left) M.C. Escher, *Puddle*. Here, the artist represents the three-dimensional surface of the muddy road as well as the sky and trees reflected in what the mind automatically interprets as the flat surface of a puddle. (Above right) M.C. Escher, *Three Worlds*. Notice the texture gradients of the leaves. The "three worlds" of the title are, according to Escher, "the autumn leaves which show the receding surface of the water, the reflection of three trees in the background and in the foreground, the fish seen through the clear water." (Copyright © M. C. Escher, Heirs, c/o Cordon Art-Baarn, Holland)

Illusions Induced by Two-Dimensional Depth Cues

The mind's ability to use two-dimensional cues for three-dimensional space is so automatic and deeply ingrained that it can produce strong illusionary effects. For example, suppose you were asked to judge the length of each man in Figure 4–22 as a ruler laid on the page would measure them. Naturally, you should ignore the converging lines, since they are irrelevant to your judgment. However, such lines normally serve as strong linear perspective cues for depth. Even though you try to ignore them, it is almost impossible not to "see" the man on the right as longer than the other two. In fact, all three men measure exactly 26 mm. Thus they all project exactly the same-size image onto your retina (subtend the same visual angle). However, when you perceive the representation as a three-dimensional space (a perception strongly suggested by the linear perspective), the figure on the right will be seen as farthest away. Thus, according to the "automatic" rules of size constancy, the figure on the right must be much larger than those on the left, since it projects the same-size retinal image.

Two other illusions that have been explained in a similar fashion (Gregory, 1973) are shown here. The *Ponzo illusion* (Figure 4–23) seems to involve linear perspective cues much like those in Figure 4–22. The *Müller-Lyer illusion* (Figure 4–24) may also be interpreted as involving linear perspective cues—in one case, those seen in the corner of a room, and in the

Figure 4–22   The converging straight lines in the figure above serve as strong linear-perspective cues for depth, suggesting a three-dimensional space. This in turn produces the illusion that the figure on the right is farther away and thus larger than the figures on its left. In fact, though, all three figures are exactly the same size.

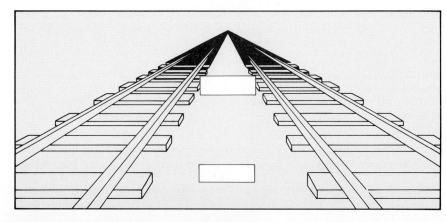

Figure 4–23 The kind of linear perspective that operates in real life (top photo) is responsible for the Ponzo illusion in the drawing. The linear perspective cues make it seem as if one rectangle is farther away and hence larger than the other, although both are exactly the same size. (*Photo:* Bill Longcore/Photo Researchers)

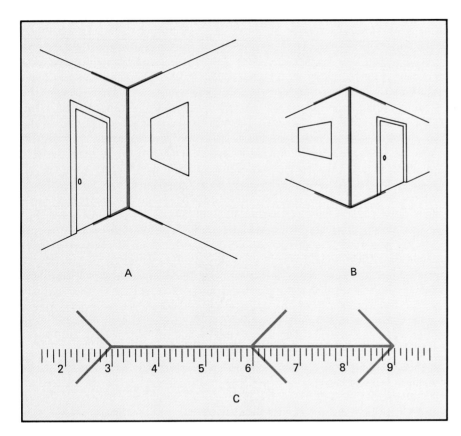

A

B

C

Figure 4–24 The Müller-Lyer illusion is shown in two different ways here. In both cases, the line between the arrows is exactly the same length, although in each case one looks visibly longer than the other. Notice that in c, even though the figures appear against a ruler, quite clearly showing that the two lines are the same length, the illusion persists.

other, those seen on the outside corner of a building. In each case, these two-dimensional cues may automatically evoke an unconscious perception of a three-dimensional space. The illusionary appearance of differing lengths would then be consistent with the rules of size constancy. (An alternative interpretation of the Müller-Lyer illusion is discussed in the Highlight on adaptation to spatial frequencies in Chapter 3.)

MOVEMENT PERCEPTION

The images cast onto your retina constantly shift and change as you shift the direction of your gaze or move about, and yet your brain is remarkably good at maintaining **location constancy.** A room doesn't seem to move just because you move or look about. There is an invariance or constancy in your perception of where things are, even though their representation on your retina changes considerably. Your mind constantly takes into account changes in the direction of your gaze and the position of your body. Only when these two factors seem insufficient to account for changes in the location of objects in your visual field do you perceive them as moving.

Absolute and Relative Retinal Movement

It is useful to distinguish between the absolute and relative position of objects within your visual field (on your retina). For example, as you read this line of text, a word's absolute position within your visual field changes each

time you move your eyes. However, the relative position of (separation between) words doesn't change, since the words all shift across the field (retina) together. You don't perceive the words as moving simply because their absolute position within your visual field changes. You automatically interpret these changes as due to eye movements. Since your brain initiates the efferent (motor) commands that move your eyes, it can compare that movement with the absolute movement of objects across your retina. Only if the two differ do you perceive movement. You can demonstrate this for yourself: Close one eye and slightly move the other one by pressing it from the side with your finger. Since your brain didn't send out any efferent command to move your eye, the absolute movement of the image across your retina is perceived as movement of the scene "out there," almost as if you were seeing movements of a huge photograph that filled your whole visual field.

Another situation in which a misperception of absolute movement occurs is when you watch a small *stationary* point of light in an otherwise totally dark room. After a while you tend to see the light as slowly moving about, even though it really remains stationary. This is the so-called **autokinetic effect.** It can be shown that the primary cause of this illusion is your inability to keep track of exactly where your eyes are pointing. You believe your eyes are stationary, but they really have shifted position slightly. This produces absolute movement of the light across your retina, which is erroneously interpreted as movement of the light rather than of your eyes. Why isn't your lack of perfect control over the position of your eyes a problem in other situations—for instance, in a well-lighted room? This is probably because interpreting absolute movement of the image on your retina as movements of the room is so implausible (in the absence of sounds and other sensations

Figure 4–25 Notice how your successive views of the man, house, and tree change as you drive past them. The tree seems to move from left to right behind the house, while the man moves from right to left in front of the house. This relative movement is a strong cue for motion and depth perception. (Adapted from William Schiff: *Perception: An Applied Approach,* p. 245. Copyright © 1980 by Houghton Mifflin Company.)

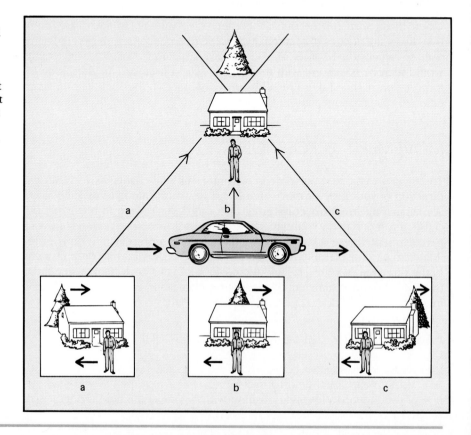

suggesting something like an earthquake) that you automatically attribute the image motion to small eye movements (Kinchla & Allan, 1969).

There is another situation in which you may misperceive (misinterpret) relative retinal movement, the so-called *train illusion*. Sitting next to the window in a train you may perceive an adjacent train slowly begin to move. Then suddenly you realize that it is really your train that is beginning to move. You erroneously attributed the clearly visible relative movement of the two trains to the other train's movement. Ordinarily, you don't make mistakes like this, since other cues (kinesthetic, tactile, auditory) clearly indicate your own body motion. However, when a train starts up very slowly and smoothly, these cues may not be available.

Fortunately, you rarely (if ever) have to rely solely on absolute retinal motion. Objects are ordinarily seen to move in well-illuminated visual fields against complex backgrounds. Thus the relative motion of object and background within your visual field is a strong cue for motion. The advantage of such cues is evident if you have ever tried to discern the movement of a small cloud high overhead in an otherwise clear blue sky. If the cloud is moving slowly, its movement may be hard to see. However, if you can view the cloud in reference to some stationary point, such as the edge of a roof, its motion may be easily discerned. In addition to changes in the separation between cloud and roof (relative movement), the cloud may actually pass slowly behind the edge of the roof. This progressive covering up of one object by another is another strong cue for motion that arises whenever objects move against clearly visible backgrounds. Relative motion, or **motion parallax,** is a monocular cue for both depth and motion perception (see Figure 4–25).

People often misperceive relative retinal movement when a small spot of light is projected onto a large screen. If the screen is suddenly moved slightly, people often perceive the spot as moving. This is called *induced motion*. However, in most environments we have little difficulty in discerning stationary reference points when interpreting relative retinal movement.

Stroboscopic Motion

An important aspect of visual perception is that a succession of still (static) images can produce the perception of smooth continuous motion. Called the **phi illusion** or **stroboscopic motion** (Figure 4–26), this is what makes a string of successively illuminated lights on a theater marquee appear to move. It also causes us to perceive smooth motion when watching a movie, though we are looking at a series of still photographs flashed in rapid succession on a screen.

The succession of images must be sufficiently fast to produce the phi illusion. You probably have seen early films in which the movement is jerky. This is because only 16 pictures a second were taken. Modern films show as many as 24 separate pictures a second to produce the illusion of smooth motion. Television presents up to 30 separate images a second.

Blur Cues for Movement

When you fixate on one part of a scene, images of other moving objects may shift across your retina so rapidly that you essentially experience them as a blur. Figure 4–27A uses a still photo to show how everything but a motorcyclist is blurred when you move your eyes to follow his motion. Another pat-

Figure 4–26 If after just the right delay (50 to 100 msec) form 1 is replaced by form 2 in A, B, or C, stroboscopic motion will be perceived as indicated by the dotted line. In A this will be a horizontal motion of the bulb from left to right. In B it will be a smooth tipping of the bar from vertical to horizontal. In C the top angular bar will appear to flip over. These effects reveal the cognitive aspect of stroboscopic motion: In each case you perceive the most "reasonable" movement.

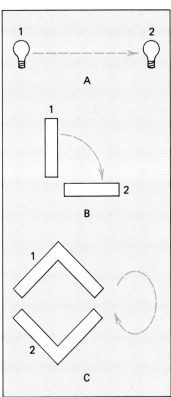

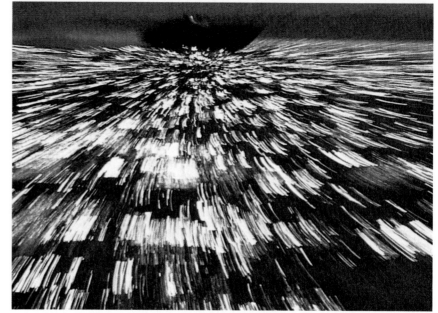

Figure 4–27A When you move your eyes to watch a moving figure, such as the motorcyclist in the photograph, the figure remains fixed on your retina while the background is a blur of horizontal streaks.
(O. Callaud/Photo Researchers)

B An example of peripheral streaming. As you speed toward the boat (at the top of the photo), the sunlight sparkling on the water becomes blurred lines (streams) that spread out toward the edge (periphery) of your view. (Alastair Black/Kodak/Time Life)

tern of blurring called **peripheral streaming** is shown in Figure 4–27B. This often occurs as you move rapidly toward something. Objects outside the center of your view tend to shift their position toward the edge or periphery of your retina. This happens so rapidly, in fact, that they become blurs radiating out from the center of your gaze. Photographers produce this sort of motion cue in a still photograph by zooming their telephoto lens in on an object as they expose the film. Notice how the peripheral streaming cues in Figure 4–27B tend to evoke a perception of motion. Gibson (1966) argued that our visual systems may have an *affordance* (built-in sensitivity) to patterns of peripheral streaming as an invariant cue for certain sorts of motion (just as texture gradients are invariant cues for depth).

READING

Reading is clearly one of our most important, efficient, and highly practiced information-processing skills. Just as with most forms of perception, you are unconscious of the many components of this skill because the process has

become so automatic. In this section we will examine these complex components. We begin with an earlier view of the reading process, which grew out of research on eye movements during reading and is still advanced by many companies selling speed-reading courses. We shall then raise some questions about it, presenting an alternative view and the modern research that supports it.

Early Ideas About Reading

One of the first people to study eye movements was G. T. Buswell (1922). He recorded these movements by bouncing a light from a tiny mirror on the edge of a subject's contact lens onto a photographic film. He found that the eye successively makes a quick (1 or 2 msec) move (a saccade), then briefly (150 to 200 msec) holds still (a fixation). Figure 4–28 shows the patterns of eye movements he recorded during silent reading of both slow and fast readers. Buswell's slow readers usually made many fixations per line of text and often went back over parts of the line they had already passed. Such right-to-left shifts in fixation he called *recursions*.

In contrast, Buswell's fast readers usually made only three or four fixations per line in an orderly left-to-right sequence without going back over the line. This suggested to early investigators that fast readers have learned to move their eyes in a more efficient manner, taking in more information during each fixation than poor or slow readers. They also discovered that when fast silent readers read out loud, their pattern of eye movements become more like that of slow silent readers; that is, there are many more fixations per line and more recursions. Maybe, investigators thought, slow readers simply haven't learned to read silently and are still trying to voice each word as they read. In fact, many slow silent readers could be seen to move their lips as they read, just as beginning readers often do. If this were the problem, then slow readers might be helped by teaching them not to vocalize during silent reading and to move their eyes in the more efficient pattern adopted by fast readers, taking in more information during each fixation.

But how much information does a good reader take in during a single fixation? To answer this question, early investigators used a device called a **tachistoscope,** which flashes printing onto a screen for precise periods of time. For example, a test subject could be asked to fixate on a particular part

Figure 4–28 Eye movements by a fast reader (left) and a slow or beginning reader (right) during silent reading. The center of each fixation is shown by a vertical slash; the number above shows the order in which the fixation occurred. The slow reader makes many more fixations per line and often moves back over the line. The fast reader makes only four or five fixations per line and few recursions. (Buswell, G. T. Fundamental reading habits: A study of their development. *Supplementary Educational Monographs, No. 21,* 1922.)

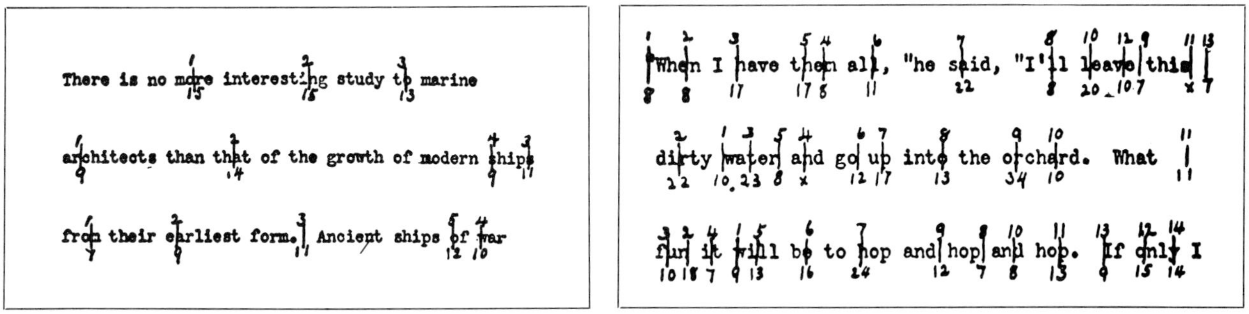

of the screen and then a sentence could be projected onto the screen for perhaps 100 msec. This was sufficiently fast to ensure that the subject held only a single fixation while the sentence was on the screen. The experimenters were amazed to find that, with practice, subjects seemed able to read almost a whole sentence during a single presentation. Perhaps, then, subjects could be trained to read whole lines of text with a single 100-msec fixation. Since the rapid eye movement between fixations takes only 2 or 3 msec, subjects might be trained to read up to 10 lines a second. This is the basic strategy behind many "speed-reading" courses. Students are encouraged to break old reading habits and to absorb a whole line of text in a single fixation. This is done first by tachistoscopic presentation and then by training students to fix their gaze briefly on the center of each line of text during regular reading. To make this easier, students are often told to slowly run the tip of their finger down the center of each page, fixating briefly on each line as the tip of the finger passes that line. In addition, they are encouraged to pick out key words and main ideas. To assess the effectiveness of such training, students are given comprehension tests to determine how well they understood the material they read. In fact, prospective customers of speed-reading courses are often asked to read something at their normal reading speed, and are then given a comprehension test. For example, they might read eight pages in 10 minutes and correctly answer 80 percent of the questions on the comprehension test. They are then given an initial speed-reading lesson. Afterward they are asked to "speed-read" the same number of pages in a comparable text. They may then read eight pages in only 5 minutes and correctly answer 75 percent of the questions on a subsequent comprehension test. This usually convinces prospective students they have "doubled their reading speed" (eight pages in 5 minutes instead of 10 minutes) with "virtually no loss of comprehension" (75 percent correct instead of 80 percent).

Some Questions and a Modern View

This approach to speed reading seems based on rather convincing evidence. However, let's examine this evidence in the light of modern reading research (Carver, 1972; Carpenter & Just, 1977; Just & Carpenter, 1987: Smith, 1970). Can we really read a whole line of text during a 100-msec tachistoscopic exposure? There are really two questions here: When do we actually read the material? How much do we actually read?

Modern research on the perception of tachistoscopically presented stimuli has shown that an **iconic image** of the stimulus may persist in the visual system for up to a second after a stimulus has been presented (e.g., Sperling, 1960). This means that reading may continue after a tachistoscopic stimulus has be presented. Furthermore, if a second line of text is presented immediately after the first and in the same position on the screen, it will normally block or *mask* perception of the first line. Again, this indicates that reading normally continues beyond the time a tachistoscopic stimulus is presented on the screen. Thus early investigators were wrong to conclude that a sentence was read in 100 msec simply because the sentence was on the screen for only 100 msec.

The second question about speed reading is how much we actually read in a single look. What do we mean by this? Suppose you were reading a story

about farmers. Consider the following sentence, in which some letters have been replaced by a capital letter X:

XXX XARMER PLOWED THE FIXXX.

Can you guess the missing parts of the sentence from the parts you can see? Most people quickly guess that the complete sentence is: The farmer plowed the field. How about the following sentence?

XXX XRACTOR WAS IN THE BXXX.

Again, given the context, you would quickly read it as: The tractor was in the barn. Because language is redundant, you can infer a great deal about the missing parts of the sentence from the parts you can see. Early tachistoscopic studies that seemed to show that a person could read a whole line of text with only one fixation could be explained quite differently. Subjects may have actually read only a very small part of the line, and then made the same sort of inferences about the rest as you made when "reading" the partially obscured sentences shown above.

Recent research has made use of highly accurate computer-based systems to measure eye movements during reading (Just & Carpenter, 1987). These studies provide a rather different view of the reading process than Buswell's less accurate measurements and early tachistoscopic studies. First of all, most readers actually fixate directly on up to 70 percent of the words in a sentence (depending on the complexity of the material). The words most likely to be skipped are short *function words* such as *a, of, two,* and so on. (This is probably why one fails to notice the extra phrases in Figure 4–29). *Content words* (adjectives, nouns, verbs, pronouns) are usually viewed directly (fixated) for a period of two- to six-tenths of a second, depending on the frequency with which the word occurs in normal English (infrequently occurring words are viewed the longest, as illustrated in Figure 4–30). There is reason to believe that only a directly fixated word is truly processed or read (see, for example, McKonkie et al., 1982), although there is some evidence that an adjacent word may have an effect on comprehension (Balota, Pollatsek, & Rayner, 1985). Faster reading occurs because a reader has learned to comprehend the meaning of words more rapidly. Thus, in summary, it seems as if comprehension of most words involves looking directly at them for two-tenths to six-tenths of a second—a far cry from the speed-reading companies claims of being able to teach people to read a whole line of text with a single one-tenth-of-a-second fixation.

Finally, what about the rather impressive "improvement in reading speed" with "little loss in comprehension" that was produced by the initial speed-reading lesson? The high degree of redundancy in most written material makes it difficult to design accurate measures of comprehension. For exam-

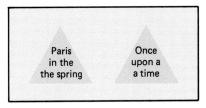

Figure 4–29 Read the phrases in the two triangles. Did you notice that there is an extra word in each phrase? In reading, people only fixate directly on up to 70 percent of the words in a sentence; the words most likely to be skipped are short function words such as *the* and *a*.

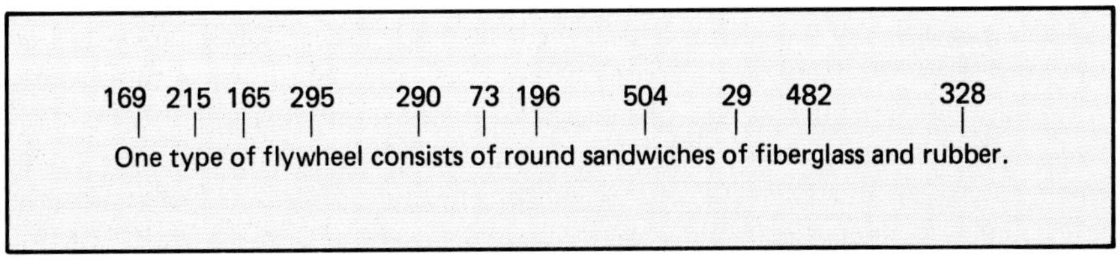

Figure 4–30 This record shows the location and duration (in msec) of the series of eye fixations that occurred when an average adult read the sentence to the left (Carpenter & Just, 1980). Virtually all the words were fixated (except "and"), although there was considerable variability in the duration of fixation.

| 169 | 215 | 165 | 295 | 290 | 73 | 196 | 504 | 29 | 482 | 328 |

One type of flywheel consists of round sandwiches of fiberglass and rubber.

ple, a comprehension test to assess your understanding of the story about farmers might contain the following question:

The farmer wore _____ when he worked.
(a) a suit (c) a dress
(b) overalls (d) shorts

While the correct answer might have been stated explicitly in the story, you could also make an educated guess based on other knowledge you had gained from the story (or from just the word "farmer" in the question). It is very difficult to devise comprehension questions whose answers could *not* be deduced from only partial knowledge of the material. Simply by guessing on all of the questions of a multiple-choice test with four alternatives for each question, you should get about 25 percent correct. If you had any knowledge at all of the material, you could do appreciably better.

Learning to read eight pages in 5 minutes instead of 10 minutes with a drop in comprehension of only 5 percent (from 80 percent to 75 percent) seems impressive. However, suppose someone who hadn't even read the material took the comprehension test and got 70 percent of the answers correct. That would change the interpretation of the earlier evidence completely. In fact, many of the comprehension tests used in speed-reading courses are not well designed, and people who haven't even read the material could do as well as 70 percent correct answers. Notice that the poorer the design of the speed-reading comprehension test, the easier it would be to impress prospective customers. Since such courses are a lucrative business, we would expect the salespeople to encourage prospective students.

A recent study by psychologists Marcel Just, Patricia Carpenter, and Michael Masson (Carpenter & Just, 1987) seems to support our view of speed-reading. They had three groups of subjects read both easy and difficult passages. One group applied recently learned speed-reading techniques, another group was instructed to "skim," and the third group was told to read at their normal pace. The speed-readers averaged almost 700 words per minute, the skimmers about 600, and the normal readers about 240. Both the speed-readers and the skimmers fixated on about one-third of the words for approximately 230 msec each, while the normal readers fixated on about two-thirds of the words for 330 msec each.

After reading the material, all subjects were asked to briefly summarize the passages and answer ten general and ten detailed questions about each one. There were two principal findings: first, reading faster reduced comprehension; and second, the skimmers performed just about as well as the speed-readers. The results of the study were consistent for both the easy and difficult material and the general and specific questions. For example, the normal readers correctly answered about 80 percent of the general questions concerning the easy material, while the other groups scored only about 65 percent.

Does this mean that speed-reading courses are a sham and don't really teach you anything? No—simply that these courses might better be described as *speed-skimming courses* (Carver, 1972). They train you to skim rapidly and remember the major features of the text, key ideas, terms, and concepts. This is a very useful skill. Many people don't realize how much they can get out of many books and articles merely by skimming them. This level of reading is adequate and even desirable for much material, and slower, more careful reading would be a waste of time. For people who do not vary their speed of

reading to fit the material and the goals they have in mind, a course that shows how to skim material rapidly could be very helpful.

COMPUTER PATTERN RECOGNITION AND HUMAN PERCEPTION

The field of **artificial intelligence** (AI) is concerned with machines (e.g., computers) that can do intelligent things—things once considered to require human intelligence. One area of AI where there has been substantial progress is called *computer pattern recognition*. Today computers routinely and rapidly recognize specially designed labels on products at the grocery checkout counter or numbers printed on the bottom of checks. Progress has also been made on having computers recognize much more complex patterns such as written and spoken words, human faces, and three-dimensional scenes. The work of perceptual psychologists has significantly enhanced the research in this field, and the exchange of information with computer scientists has had a major influence on the study of psychology.

Characterizing Pattern Structure

An important achievement in computer pattern recognition has been finding ways to represent the structure of a pattern. For example, Figure 4–31 shows

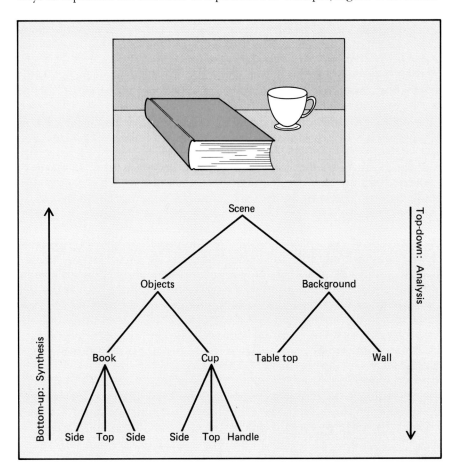

Figure 4–31 Syntactic scene analysis represents the structure of a scene by parsing it into a hierarchy of components.

Figure 4–32 Look at the picture above, then turn the picture upside down. Notice how your knowledge of facial features misleads you. The eyes and mouth are right-side-up in an upside-down head. Only when you turn the picture around do you realize how grotesque this face appears.

how the structure of a simple scene can be represented as a hierarchy of components. This type of representation is called **syntactic scene analysis.** The scene is parsed into components in much the way you parse a sentence into its grammatical (*syntactic*) components. As you go from the *top-down* through the hierarchy, the scene is successively decomposed (*analyzed*) into progressively lower-order forms. Going from the *bottom-up* shows how components are combined (*synthesized*) into progressively higher-order forms.

The relationships between different levels of structure in most natural scenes are highly predictable or redundant. This sort of *structural redundancy* was illustrated earlier with the face in Figure 4–3. It showed how one part of a face is a fairly good predictor (or **cue**) for another part, although you can sometimes be fooled (see Figure 4–32).

Computer scientists have used both top-down and bottom-up methods of pattern recognition. For example, a top-down method for sorting mail begins with a television image of an envelope. Higher-order forms such as "stamp," "return address," and "destination" are identified first. Next, the "destination" is analyzed into lower-order forms, such as "name," "address," and "ZIP code." Each step of this process is guided by the predictable relationships (structural redundancy) between the different levels of form common to an envelope. The computer program knows that "destination" is usually found in the center of the envelope, and that the "ZIP code" is usually below, or at the lower right, of the "address."

Other pattern recognition schemes utilize a bottom-up method. One such scheme recognizes geometric forms. It first identifies low-level features, such as "lines" and various types of "intersections," and then synthesizes these into higher-order forms, such as "edges" and "surfaces" (Guzman, 1969). Again, each phase of the process is guided by knowledge of structural relationships. Methods have even been developed that allow the computer to acquire (learn) such information through its experience with a variety of patterns (Rosenberg, 1987; Winston, 1970).

As indicated earlier in this chapter, the dominant Helmholtzian view in psychology has been that perception is primarily a bottom-up process: Elementary *sensations* are synthesized into progressively higher-order *percepts*. This view has also been encouraged by work in receptive fields (see Chapter 3). Simple feature detectors on the retina seem to feed into progressively more complex receptive fields as one moves to higher visual centers (Marr, 1982).

However, other researchers have proposed a top-down view of perception. We noted earlier that Gibson, in contrast to Helmholtz, believed our sensory systems could pick up high-level aspects of stimulus patterns directly (e.g., receding surfaces). There are also many examples of visual patterns in which the higher-order components seem to be perceived first. In the impossible structure in Figure 4–2 (as well as in Figure 1–1) one sees the higher-order structure before realizing that the lower-order details are entirely contradictory. Thus it would appear that higher-order structures do exert strong **context effects** on our perception of lower-order forms (see Figure 4–33).

Developments in computer pattern recognition have led modern perceptual psychologists to view perception as having both top-down and bottom-up components. This can be made clear by considering the history of work on a representative problem: computer recognition of letters and words.

Figure 4–33 The small red detail in this image can be seen as either an ear or an eye. If the higher order form is that of a young woman with her head turned to one side, the detail is seen as an ear. If the higher order form is an old woman with her chin buried in her fur collar, the same detail is seen as an eye.

Computer Recognition of Letters and Words

One of the earliest methods used to recognize letters was called *template matching*. Letters were recognized by the computer if they matched one of a set of model letters (templates). The problem with this approach was the variability in size, exact shape, and orientation of normal letters (Figure 4–34).

A more powerful approach was to use a *structural description* of the letters: for example, two vertical lines connected at their midpoints by a horizontal line form an "H." An early bottom-up method of this sort was called **Pandemonium** (Selfridge, 1959) because it could be thought of as a collection of shouting demons. Naturally, there were really no noisy demons—only parts of a computer program designed to detect particular features (e.g., "vertical line") and then signal ("shout to") other parts of the program. One demon might shout only if it detected a vertical line in the pattern being processed. Another higher-order demon might shout "T" only if it heard the cries of both a "vertical line" and a "horizontal line" demon. This sort of pattern recognition begins by detecting very low-order features, which are then combined or synthesized into higher-order forms (letters or words). The higher-order forms are essentially defined by the lists of features required in their construction.

A major advance over purely bottom-up schemes like Pandemonium was called **analysis-by-synthesis** (Halle & Stevens, 1963; Neisser, 1967). The basic idea was simple but very powerful: A tentative synthesis of a higher-order form can aid in analyzing one of its components. This is illustrated in Figure 4–35.

Modern theories of letter and word recognition employ even more elaborate forms of interaction between different levels of structure (Carr, 1987).

(a) 5 7 6 3 4 6
(b) A 4 A A A B B B 13 B

Figure 4–34 Template matching can be used to reorganize (a) the very regular numerals found on most bank checks but not (b) the highly varied letter forms one encounters in everyday life.

Figure 4–35 A tentative synthesis of the word "CAR" helps analyze the last letter as fragments of an "R." Other possible words (CAT, CAP, CAN) suggest last letters inconsistent with these fragments. This combination of bottom-up and top-down process (termed analysis-by-synthesis) takes advantage of the redundant information in the context (CA-).

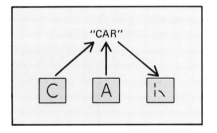

Seeing the Forest or the Trees: Which Level of Structure Do We See First?

The sixteenth-century painting by Giuseppe Arcimboldi (Figure A) is a somewhat grotesque example of an image having two virtually unrelated levels of structure: a human bust composed of various types of sea life. Artists' fascination with such images stems from this violation of the usual structural redundancy found in most images. Normally, recognition of one level of structure aids in the recognition of other levels. However, in this picture seeing the bust probably interferes with seeing the sea life, and vice versa. Which level does one see first?

In a paper entitled "The Forest Before the Trees: The Precedence of Global Features in Visual Perception," a psychologist named David Navon argued that perception involves an invariant "global-to-local" (top-down) process (Navon, 1977). He based this claim on an experiment involving stimulus patterns similar to the one seen in Figure B: a large letter made up of smaller letters. It had been suggested earlier (Kinchla, 1974) that *letter-letters* of this sort were useful experimentally because they define familiar forms at two levels of structure. (Unlike Arcimboldi's painting, with letter-letters one can easily vary the form defined at either level.) Navon had subjects view a series of letter-letter patterns under two conditions: In a *global-directed condition* they were to ignore the *local* (small) letters and identify the *global* (large) one; in a *local-directed condition* they were to ignore the global letter and identify the local ones. The letters defined at each level were sometimes the same and sometimes different, but always an "E" or an "H." Subjects responded by pressing either an E-button or an H-button as "quickly as they could without making errors." Navon found that his subjects could successfully

Figure A

ignore the small letters in the global-directed condition and respond independently of them. But in the local-directed condition they responded faster if the large letter was the same as the small ones and slower if it wasn't. Navon saw this inability to ignore the large letter as implying an inevitable global-to-local (top-down) perceptual sequence. Responses to the large letter were apparently made before recognition of the smaller ones could produce any effect. On the other hand, earlier recognition of the large letter interfered with responses to the small letters (similar to the Stroop effect illustrated earlier in Figure 4–5).

Kinchla and Wolf (1979) questioned Navon's conclusion. They noted that his stimulus patterns were never larger than about 5.5 degrees visual angle in height (about the size of a playing card viewed at arm's length). If the stimuli had been larger, would the smaller letters have been perceived before the larger one? Kinchla and Wolf devised an experimental approach to this question. Each of a series of test trials began when a subject heard the name of a *target letter* for that trial, either "E," "H," or "S." A letter-letter pattern then appeared on a screen in front of the subject. He or she was told to quickly press a yes-button if either the large or the small letters in the pattern corresponded to the target letter. Otherwise, the subject was to press a no-button. For example, if the pattern

Figure B A stimulus pattern with two levels of structure: higher-level (global) letter "H," and lower-level (local) letters "E."

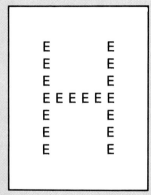

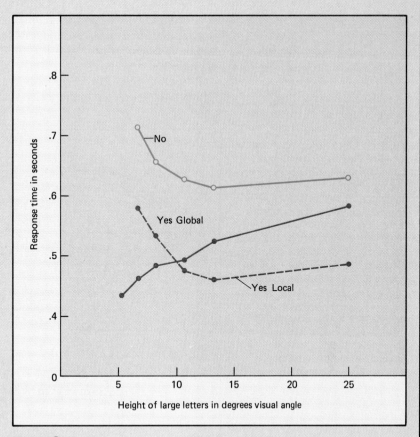

Figure C

in Figure B was presented and the target letter was an "H," the subject should have responded yes. If the target letter was an "S," the response should have been no. Of principal interest was the fact that the pattern's angular size affected the relative speed with which a subject could recognize a target letter at each level of structure. The graph in Figure C shows how targets were recognized faster at the "global" level when the letter-letter patterns were as small as those in Navon's study (5.5 degrees). However, targets were recognized faster at the "local" level once the patterns were taller than about 9 degrees. Notice that even the largest pattern used in the study was not taller (25 degrees) than a standard sheet of 8½-by-11-inch paper seen at arm's length. At the largest size, local targets were perceived about a tenth of a second faster than global ones, just

the opposite of the order for the smallest (5.4 degrees) patterns.

Thus it would seem that the order in which we perceive different levels of structure is neither consistently top-down nor consistently bottom-up. Instead, forms at some optimal angular size and position in our visual field are seen first. This can then influence the perception of forms at both higher and lower levels of structure—what Kinchla and Wolf termed *middle-out processing*. Of course, other factors such as the clarity of a form (Hoffman, 1979), our relative familiarity with what we are seeing, and what we expect (or want) to see (Kinchla, 1977) should affect the speed of perception. Nevertheless, if you view Arcimboldi's painting first from 4 or 5 inches and then from arm's length, you can see how visual angle affects the relative perceptibility of the two levels of structure.

For example, McClelland and Rumelhart (1981) have characterized human word perception with the neural-like network of interconnected nodes shown in Figure 4–36. (Also see the Highlight on Distributed Memory in Chapter 7.)

It seems clear that there will continue to be a productive interplay between work on computer pattern recognition and perceptual psychology.

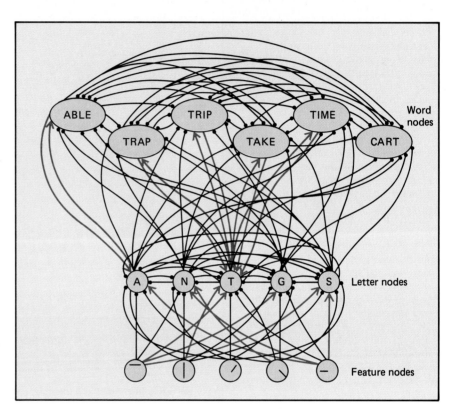

Figure 4–36 McClelland and Rumelhart (1981) proposed a neural-like pattern recognition network in which the "activation" of "nodes" at various structural levels influences each others activity. Nodes corresponding to consistent information facilitate each other (red lines), while inconsistent nodes inhibit each other (black lines). In the example shown here "feature" nodes activated by viewing the *first letter of a word* influence both higher-order "letter" and "word" nodes. These nodes in turn feed back to influence the activity of the letter nodes, much as in analysis-by-synthesis. (See the Highlight on Distributed Memory and Connectionist Systems in Chapter 7.)

SUMMARY

1. One sensation can be a reliable cue for the experience of other sensations; because sensory data are *redundant,* we can make inferences from limited sensory input.

2. *Attention* is what allows us to selectively focus on certain sensory information while we tune out other information.

3. According to Gestalt principles of organization, we tend to organize visual stimuli into groups on the basis of *proximity, similarity, symmetry, closure,* and *continuity.*

4. Another Gestalt organization principle is *figure-ground organization,* the tendency to perceive things (figures) standing out against a background (ground).

5. *Bistable* or *reversible figures* are stimulus patterns that have two alternative organizations. *Ambiguous figures* are those open to multiple organizations.

6. Although sensory activity may vary enormously from moment to moment, we perceive many aspects of the world as stable and invariant because of *perceptual constancy,* which includes *size constancy, shape constancy,* and *color constancy.*

7. Monocular cues for depth perception include *accommodation, interposition, elevation, shadowing, relative size,* and *texture gradients.*

8. The left eye and the right eye see slightly different versions of the same object, because each sees it from a slightly different angle. These differences are called

binocular disparity. Convergence of the eyes may reduce this disparity enough to cause *fusion,* a single *cyclopean* view.

9. *Binocular perception* or *stereopsis* is the process by which the brain automatically interprets the shifts in convergence, fusion, and disparity as cues indicating relative distance.

10. Perception of pictures involves eye movements (*saccades*) and *fixations;* the eyes move over the picture so that the fovea can pick up the details. These eye movements are concentrated on the most informative parts of the picture.

11. The *autokinetic effect* and *induced motion* are two examples of misperception of retinal movement. In the *phi illusion* a succession of static images produces the perception of continuous motion.

12. Fast readers seem able to comprehend the meanings of words faster than slow readers, allowing them to fixate more briefly on each word.

13. *Syntactic scene analysis* yields a hierarchical representation of *image structure,* which, like parsing a sentence, reveals the relationships among its parts.

14. *Analyses-by-synthesis* was an early attempt to use the synthesis of a higher-order form as an aid to analyzing a lower-order form.

SUGGESTED READINGS

BOFF, K., KAUFMAN, L., & THOMAS, J. (1987). *Handbook of perception and human performance.* Vols. I and II. New York: Wiley. A detailed and technical review of various areas of research on sensation and perception written by experts in each area.

CARPENTER, M., & JUST, P. (1987). *The psychology of reading and language comprehension.* New York: Allyn and Bacon. A general review of research on reading.

CROWDER, R. G. (1982). *The psychology of reading.* New York: Oxford University Press. An introduction to a wide range of reading research.

GIBSON, J. J. (1966). *The senses considered as perceptual systems.* Boston: Houghton Mifflin. Gibson's influential and controversial refutation of traditional perception research.

GREGORY, R. L. (1970). *The intelligent eye.* New York: McGraw-Hill. A lively introduction to some fascinating aspects of visual perception, including a number of stereographic illustrations.

GREGORY, R. L. (1973). *Eye and brain: The psychology of seeing.* New York: McGraw-Hill. A beautifully illustrated and highly readable introduction to visual perception.

HABER, R. N., & HERSHENSON, M. (1980). *The psychology of visual perception* (2nd ed). New York: Holt, Rinehart & Winston. An advanced text covering a wide range of experimental work on visual perception.

HOCHBERG, J. (1978). *Perception* (2nd ed.). Englewood Cliffs, N.J.: Prentice-Hall. A detailed discussion of past and current theories of perception; includes a chapter on social perception and communication.

KERAS, D. E., & JUST, M. A. (1984). *New methods in reading comprehension research.* Hillsdale, N.J.: Erlbaum. An up-to-date series of edited papers on reading research by the leading researchers in this field.

LACHMAN, R., MISTLER-LACHMAN, J., & BUTTERFIELD, E. C. (1979). *Cognitive psychology and information processing: An introduction.* Hillsdale, N.J.: Erlbaum. An advanced and comprehensive review of the modern information-processing approach to human perception.

SEKULAR, R., & BLAKE, R. (1985). *Perception.* New York: Knopf. An excellent, clearly written, and detailed introduction to research on perception.

SCHIFF, W. (1980). *Perception: An applied approach.* Boston: Houghton Mifflin. A Gibsonian approach to perception, emphasizing the function (utility) of natural human perception.

5 States of Consciousness

A t the beginning of the twentieth century the distinguished American psychologist William James had this to say about the variety of conscious states:

> Our normal waking consciousness is but one special type of consciousness, whilst all about it, parted from it by the filmiest of screens, there lie potential forms of consciousness entirely different. We may go through life without suspecting their existence, but apply the requisite stimulus, and at a touch they are all there in all their completeness, definite types of mentality which probably somewhere have their field of application and adaptation. No account of the universe in its totality can be final which leaves these other forms of consciousness quite disregarded. How to regard them is the question—for they are so discontinuous with ordinary consciousness. Yet they may determine attitudes though they cannot furnish formulas, and open a region though they fail to give a map. At any rate, they forbid a premature closing of our accounts with reality. (James, 1890).

What would you consider a **normal state of consciousness?** Could you describe it? Perhaps it is being wide awake but not highly excited, alert but not unusually tense, aware of things happening around you and reacting to them in a normal manner. Your description might be somewhat different, but you would probably agree that this definition is generally correct. In fact, there is no precise definition of a normal state of consciousness. Nevertheless, it seems clear that there are states of consciousness that would *not* be described as normal—for example, when you are sound asleep, intoxicated, highly agitated, or under hypnosis. These have been described as **altered states.** In this chapter we will consider some of these altered states, both be-

"The Dream" by deChavannes is an attempt to capture the strange form of consciousness we experience in our dreams. (The Louvre, Paris)

155

cause they are of interest in their own right, and because by way of contrast they help define what we mean by a normal state.

CHARACTERIZING STATES OF CONSCIOUSNESS

For many years the study of consciousness was very unpopular in psychology. While early psychologists like William James were very interested in the subject, behaviorists like J. B. Watson (1919) believed that the subjective study of inner experience was not a worthy pursuit for behavioral scientists. The study of mental processes became less important as various experimental approaches to the study of actual human behavior came to dominate the study of psychology. During the late 1950s and the 1960s the study of consciousness again began to attract the attention of researchers. Even though psychologists must still rely to some degree on subjects' reports of their mental experiences, it is now possible to measure the physiological activity that accompanies various states of consciousness.

Although there is no single definition of consciousness, psychologists generally describe it as one's *awareness* of external stimuli and internal mental events (Natsoulas, 1983; Ornstein, 1977). By nature, consciousness is selective and intimately related to the concept of attention discussed in Chapter 4. Right now you are reading this book (and are perhaps conscious of the fact that you have an exam tomorrow), but you may also be conscious of people talking in the next room—even if you can't hear exactly what they are saying. However, you may be totally ignoring the rain outside your window or the gentle hiss of the radiator.

There is also the dilemma of differing states of consciousness. Various physiological and emotional factors influence our state of mind and may affect our awareness of events or stimuli occurring around us. After a car accident someone in a "state of shock" may be awake, or "conscious," but totally unaware of the events that led to the accident. On the other hand, people on amphetamines may be hyperaware of their surroundings and even hear their own hearts beating. What sorts of things are important in characterizing or contrasting states of consciousness? While there is no definite answer to this question, we might consider three aspects of consciousness: responsiveness, cognitive capacity, and personality. None of these aspects alone defines consciousness, but each describes some element of the processes collectively referred to as consciousness.

Responsiveness

Certainly one of the most obvious aspects of consciousness is responsiveness to stimulation. Someone in a coma, under deep anesthesia, or with severe brain damage may show virtually no responsiveness to stimuli. A loud voice, a shake, even a pinprick on the toe will produce no response. In contrast, a sleeping person shows some responsiveness. Touch someone who is asleep, or softly call his or her name, and the person may shift position slightly without waking. Speak loudly to a sleeping person, or shake him or her, and the person will usually wake up. Once awake, a normal person responds to the full range of stimulation considered in the last two chapters. Of course, there are intermediate states. Some people take a long time to wake up, appearing groggy and unresponsive until after a shower or a cup of coffee.

Someone who is very tired or intoxicated may show a reduced, or slower, responsiveness to stimuli.

Even when you are fully awake, your responsiveness to a particular stimulus may depend on your *focus of attention*. You may be quite responsive to a televised football game without hearing the doorbell ring, or suddenly realize that you haven't been listening to your partner at a party because you were eavesdropping on another couple talking behind you (the cocktail-party phenomenon described in Chapter 4).

Here it seems important to distinguish between physical responsiveness and mental awareness. While you are often aware of the stimuli to which you respond, this isn't always true. Many highly practiced responses are essentially *automatic,* occurring with little conscious awareness of the stimuli that trigger them. For example, you might have a spirited conversation with someone while driving a car, yet have little awareness of the road signs and scenery, the road's twists and turns, or the traffic, all of which clearly influence your driving. Thus responsiveness to stimuli alone isn't a clear indicator that you are conscious of those stimuli.

Cognitive Capacity

People have a whole range of basic cognitive (thinking) abilities. They can speak clearly, remember quite a bit, imagine the future, and make reasonable plans. The study of cognition has contributed much to the study of consciousness, and will be discussed in more detail in subsequent chapters. The point here is simply that one aspect of consciousness is the degree to which one's normal cognitive abilities are present or impaired. If following a knockdown a fighter tells his manager that the boxing ring is in Chicago when it is really in New York, the manager may suspect that the fighter is experiencing an altered state of consciousness. Slurred speech, poor memory, and seeing little green men can all be signs of an unusual state of consciousness. Such states may be normal in the very young, the retarded, or the mentally ill, but most adults exhibit a fairly predictable range of basic cognitive abilities (at least when fully awake, sober, and free of drugs).

One of the normal cognitive abilities is *self-awareness,* an ability to describe one's own thought processes. People possess a range of ability in this area, but just as we may automatically respond to familiar stimuli with little conscious awareness, certainly none of us are fully aware of our cognitive processes. Sigmund Freud's concept of *unconscious motivation* saw much of our adult thinking and behavior as due to events occurring early in life— events about which we may have little memory or awareness. Freud argued that while we can retrieve many memories into consciousness from what he termed our *preconscious,* many other desires, fears, or socially unacceptable feelings and wishes (often sexual in nature) are *repressed* or held in our *unconscious,* where they exert a powerful effect on our thoughts and behavior. Freud's views are controversial and will be considered in more detail in Chapter 15; however, most psychologists would agree that our thought processes are only partly conscious.

Personality

Subtle differences in consciousness are often distinguished in the same way that we characterize differences in personality. These *personality factors* are typically nonintellectual attributes. Rather than basic cognitive abilities, they

refer to attitudes, values, feelings, and emotions that influence our normal consciousness. A person generally responds to events and situations in a predictable way consistent with his or her personality, yet certain factors may alter the personality and can be said to alter a person's state of consciousness. Someone who is normally quite timid and holds rather orthodox values and political views may undergo a dramatic change after a few drinks at the office Christmas party. Someone who is normally pleasant and easygoing may become irritable and demanding after staying awake for 48 hours. Someone who is normally cheerful and optimistic may become gloomy and pessimistic for several weeks or months following the death of a parent or close friend.

An interesting example of shifts in personality causing changes in consciousness can be found in people who exhibit *multiple personalities*. It is *as if* there were several people inside one body, each with his or her own personality and typical form of consciousness. The highly acclaimed movie *The Three Faces of Eve* portrayed the three distinct personalities of a woman named Chris Sizemore: "Eve White," "Eve Black," and "Jane." As she describes in her autobiography (Sizemore & Pitello, 1977), each of these alternately emerging personalities dramatically altered Ms. Sizemore's state of consciousness. There have even been reports of people with a dozen or more distinct personalities (Spanos, Weeks, & Bertrand, 1985).

SLEEP AND DREAMING

People spend about one-third of their lives sleeping. For most of us, that means about 25 years will be spent in an unconscious state. Why do people sleep? There are several theories, but ultimately these are only guesses. One view, the *adaptation theory* (Cohen, 1979), is that our sleep-wake cycle had survival value during our early evolution as a species: Primitive humans were simply more likely to survive if they stayed quiet at night, hidden from predators, conserving their energy for the next day's hunt. Another closely related view could be called the *energy conservation theory:* We sleep to conserve our energy. This view is supported by studies that compared the energy needs of various species and how much they sleep. Species that have a hard time supporting the energy requirements of their waking state (e.g., because of metabolism rates or food shortages) tend to sleep more (Allison & Cicchetti, 1976). In any case, one should not suppose that the whole body is less active during sleep. The brain is very active, and in fact, cerebral blood flow and oxygen consumption are actually greater during sleep.

Emotional problems, drugs (for example, caffeine, alcohol), or simply erratic sleeping habits may disrupt normal sleep patterns, causing insomnia. **Insomnia,** the chronic inability to sleep, is known to affect many people at one time or another during their lives (see the Application: Insomnia and How to Avoid It). Normally, the longer one is deprived of sleep, the harder it is to stay awake. Most people report this as a very troubling problem. Surprisingly, however, researchers have found that if sleep-deprived individuals are properly motivated, they perform both physical and cognitive tasks as well as ever (e.g., Webb, 1975).

It is likely that sleep has always been a source of fascination, but scientific investigation of the subject has developed rapidly only in the last 30 years. Most of this work is conducted in "sleep laboratories," where volunteers agree to spend the night (or nights) hooked up to various electronic devices that measure changes in brain activity throughout the sleep cycle: the **EEG (electroencephalogram),** which records the patterns of brain waves; the

EOG (electrooculogram), which measures eye movements; and the **EMG (electromyogram),** which measures muscle tension or electrical activity in the muscles.

The actual moment of sleep onset can be determined. This is usually best measured by the optical reaction to light. In a typical experiment a bright light is repeatedly flashed into subjects' eyes, which are taped open. The subjects are instructed to press a button whenever they see the light, and at some point the pressing stops: that is the moment at which sleep begins. (What is really amazing in this demonstration is sleep's power to overcome what seem to be overwhelming odds. Do you think you could fall asleep with someone flashing a light in your taped-open eyes?)

Stages of Sleep

Everyone has experienced some variation in the depth of sleep. You may experience a head-nodding drowsiness, barely distinguishable from relaxed wakefulness, or a heavy slumber from which it is difficult to awaken. Sleep researchers have distinguished four basic stages of sleep in terms of characteristic brain-wave (EEG) patterns. Figure 5–1 shows the rapid, erratic variations in voltage characteristic of *alert wakefulness;* the slower, more regular variations of *relaxed wakefulness,* and the progressively slower and more

Figure 5–1 Brain Waves During Sleep. The figure shows how brain waves change systematically from when a person is awake (right) through drowsiness and the stages of sleep. Brain waves are measured in cycles per second (cps), which generally decrease with deeper sleep. However, notice that the brain waves of REM (dreaming) sleep resemble those of the waking state. (*Right:* After Hauri, 1977; *left:* Bart Bartholomew/Black Star)

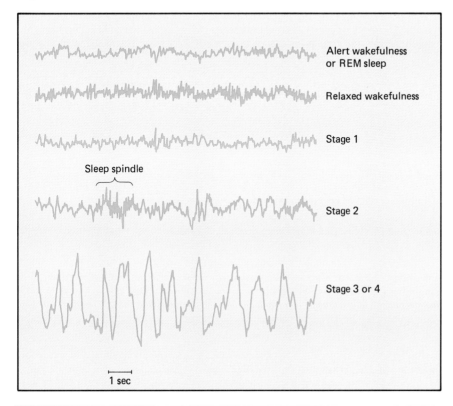
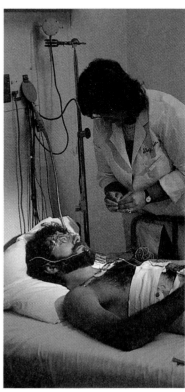

Insomnia and How to Avoid It

Most people sleep well and wake up refreshed most of the time. Most people also experience occasional difficulty in falling asleep. Such episodes usually have a simple explanation: You are worrying about some problems; you are trying to sleep at an unusual time or in a strange setting; you aren't feeling well; the bed is uncomfortable; and so on. Difficulties of this sort shouldn't trouble you because they are usually temporary or easily rectified.

Those who suffer more serious and persistent difficulty in getting to sleep are said to have *insomnia*. Either they experience consistent difficulty in getting to sleep, or they wake up in the middle of the night and are unable to get back to sleep. There are many possible reasons for insomnia: stress, poor health, depression, and disruptive patterns of activity, to name only a few. According to one government study on sleep (U.S. Department of Health and Human Serivces, 1980), as many as 25 million Americans (over one-sixth of the population) suffer from insomnia at some time in their lives. Kripke and Gillin (1985) report that 6 percent of all adult males and 14 percent of adult females have difficulty falling or staying asleep.

There are other sleep problems that affect only a few people. For example, some people actually tend to stop breathing when they fall asleep, which causes them to reawaken repeatedly. This problem, called *sleep apnea*, may be caused by obstructions in the throat due to obesity or abnormal development, or it may be due to a malfunction of breathing mechanisms in the brain. (Sleep apnea is one suspected cause of the "sudden crib deaths" of otherwise healthy infants.)

Ironically, the habitual use of prescription sleeping pills (often, but not always, barbiturates) usually makes insomnia worse. While such pills may be useful under special circumstances, they are frequently habit-forming and over time lose their effectiveness. People addicted to sleeping pills are unable to sleep without them and require progressively higher dosages—dosages high enough to cause morning grogginess and even the risk of a fatal overdose, especially if taken with alcohol. People caught in this cycle are amazingly resourceful in obtaining pills, often getting prescriptions from several doctors at once. Unfortunately, the many varieties of nonprescription sleep remedies have little real effect (Webb & Bonnet, 1979).

Those who suffer serious insomnia should consult a physician, but most people can be helped by changing certain bad habits that interfere with sleep (Coleman, 1986). The following hints should prove helpful:

1. Don't try to sleep when you are highly excited or worried. Try to make the period before you go to bed as relaxing as possible.
2. Don't keep irregular hours. Try to get to bed at the same time most nights so that your body can adjust to one schedule.
3. Don't drink a lot of alcohol before going to bed. It may "knock you out" at first, but you tend to wake up as soon as the alcohol's effect wears off. A light snack or a hot milk drink tends to put you to sleep for the whole night.
4. Don't try to sleep in a noisy, brightly lit room. Our ancestors tended to sleep when it grew dark and to wake up when they heard strange noises. It is unlikely that you can overcome centuries of biological evolution and sleep while your roommate is having a party.
5. Don't use your bed as a place to watch television, do homework, or (except under appropriate circumstances) socialize. Use it primarily as a place to sleep, so that getting into bed becomes a conditioned stimulus for sleep (see Chapter 6).
6. Don't neglect exercise. Physical fatigue is a great old-fashioned sedative.
7. Finally, don't worry about occasional restlessness or not getting enough sleep. Your body can adjust to some variation in sleep patterns, if you let it. Provide the proper situation for sleep, think of pleasant things, and let sleep come in its own time.

regular variations characteristic of the *four stages of sleep: Stages 1, 2, 3,* and *4.* EEG patterns in Stages 3 and 4 are very similar, although variations are somewhat slower in Stage 4. In contrast to this, Stage 2 is characterized by occasional bursts of rapid voltage variations called "sleep spindle."

"Falling asleep" usually means passing from a state of relaxed wakefulness into Stage 1 sleep. This is followed in slow succession (10 to 20 minutes a stage) by the progressively deeper stages of sleep—Stages 2, 3, and 4. It is in Stage 4, the deepest stage of sleep, that one becomes hardest to wake up and episodes of sleepwalking, night terrors, and bed-wetting are most likely to occur (Dement, 1971). Rather than remaining in Stage 4 for the rest of the night, a normal sleeper cycles back and forth between Stages 1 and 4 several times a night, as shown in Figure 5–2.

About 30 years ago two investigators, Aserinsky and Kleitman (1953), no-

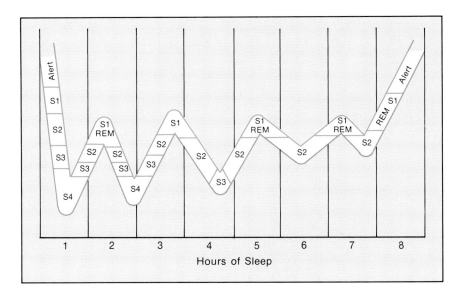

Figure 5–2 Successive cycles through the various stages of sleep shown by a normal sleeper. Note how rapid eye movements (REM) often occur during a return to Stage 1 (S1) sleep. Adapted from *The Human Body.* (U.S. News Books)

ticed that something strange occurred when a sleeper returned to Stage 1 sleep: the bumps visible beneath a sleeper's closed eyelids often moved rapidly back and forth, indicating **rapid eye movement (REM).** Furthermore, while the subject otherwise seemed to continue sleeping, the EEG pattern became more like that seen in alert wakefulness. Aserinsky and Kleitman suspected that the periods of REM, marked by the change in brain-wave pattern, signaled a special stage of sleep. They called this *REM sleep* to distinguish it from the four basic non-REM stages they called *NREM sleep.* Others have referred to REM sleep as **D-Sleep,** since the EEG suggests highly *dysynchronus* underlying neural activity during this stage. The other four stages are termed **S-Sleep,** since the underlying neural activity appears more *synchronized* (leading to a slower EEG pattern).

REM Sleep

Electrical recordings of eye movements (electroooculargraphs, or EOGs) reveal that normal sleepers spend about 25 percent of their night (1 1/2 to 2 hours) in REM sleep. Periods of REM sleep occur about every 90 minutes or so with various stages of NREM sleep in between (see Figure 5–2).

During REM sleep the muscles become relaxed to the point of paralysis, as measured by an electromyogram (EMG). REM sleep is sometimes referred to as "paradoxical sleep" because the brain-wave pattern is similar to that of someone awake, but the sleeper is deep in sleep with no tension in the muscles and no response to outside stimuli.

The amount of normal sleep and the percentage of daily REM sleep change throughout our lives. Figure 5–3 shows this. A week-old baby sleeps about 16 hours a day, with 50 percent of that being REM sleep. By age 5, the amount of REM sleep is about the same as in adulthood, 20 percent. The total sleep time continues to decline throughout life.

Soon after the discovery of REM sleep, Dement and Kleitman (1957) proposed that rapid eye movements indicate that dreaming is taking place, whereas dreaming does not take place during NREM sleep. To prove this, they tried waking subjects each time the EOG indicated a pattern of rapid eye movements: About 85 percent of the subjects were able to recall a dream

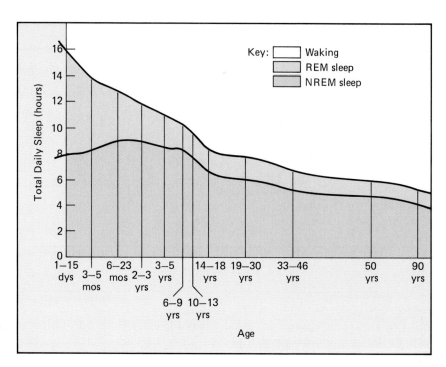

Figure 5–3 The average amount of sleep and the percent of it that is REM sleep changes over the life cycle. In the first few weeks of life babies sleep about 16 hours a day, and half of that is REM sleep. By middle age, adults sleep a bit less than 7 hours a night, with about one-quarter of it being REM sleep. (Rolfwarg et al., 1966)

when they were awakened during a REM period. However, it is also known that not all REM sleep is associated with dreams—and some dreams occur during NREM periods.

There have been several theories to account for rapid eye movements. One was that they are actually attempts by the sleeper to visually follow the course of a dream—much like watching a movie; however, it now seems more likely that rapid eye movements are simply indications of the intense brain activity occurring during these periods of sleep. It is not known what function REM sleep serves in humans, but it is clear that it is very important. If people are deprived of REM sleep by being awakened as soon as they enter the REM period, they become irritated and uncomfortable. Sleepers will tend to compensate for REM deprivation in one night by increasing the number of REM periods on the next night or nights (a phenomenon called *REM rebound*). In one experiment a volunteer was awakened four succesive nights each time he entered a REM period. On the fifth night his sleep pattern showed 30 REM periods, over four times what the normal amount would be (Dement, 1974). A similar effect does not occur with NREM sleep.

Another important aspect of REM sleep is the accompanying loss of muscle tone, which acts to inhibit motor activity. This has been interpreted as a protective process to prevent the actions one takes in dreams from spilling out into real movements. This is consistent with the fact that sleepwalking and talking in your sleep are more likely to occur in NREM sleep, even though one would expect them to occur during dreams. There are some movements during REM sleep, but these tend to be only small, quick motions, unlikely to cause a person harm (Chase & Morales, 1983). In recent experiments investigators have found a way to remove much of the motor inhibition that normally accompanies REM sleep in cats. Cats with lesions in their pons will move about (sluggishly, at least) during REM sleep, perhaps pawing an empty chair or appearing to stalk an invisible prey. It is as if their dreams were spilling out into real activity (Morrison, 1983).

Why We Dream

To Sigmund Freud (1900/1953), dreams were the "royal road to the unconscious." He believed that during sleep the conscious mind is, for the most part, not active. As a result, it is not an effective monitor during sleep and many of those disturbing ideas, feelings, and recollections that we try to avoid thinking about when we are awake spill over when we are asleep. Nevertheless, even during sleep we defend against threatening thoughts by disguising them, often in fantastic images. These images make up our dreams, and an interpretation of dreams can provide insight into the hidden, repressed corners of the mind. (Freud's theories on dream interpretation are discussed in greater detail in Chapter 18.)

Some sleep and dream researchers are not receptive to Freud's view. McCarley, for example, suggests that dreams do not indicate "a process of disguise or concealment, but a process of activation" (1978, p. 72). He feels that this might explain why so many dream reports mention strenuous activity such as running, climbing, and so on.

There are also theories proposing that dreaming is a way of processing stored memories of daytime experiences (Evans, 1984; Palumbo, 1978). So many events impinge on us daily that if we were to stop and consider each one at the time we would become confused and overwhelmed. Nevertheless, much of this information is needed for our adequate functioning and should be examined. As these waking events come crowding in on us, they are held, many unevaluated, in a limited memory system. The experiences remain in the system until we fall asleep, when they are released. According to these theorists, we need to dream in order to sort out the events and solve some of the problems that may have arisen during the day.

Consistent with this idea is the finding that dreams show an alternating pattern: a buildup of emotional tension followed by a release of tension. The number of buildup-release cycles appears to depend on the amount of tension present during the waking period (Cartwright, 1978).

Finally, a controversial theory proposed by Crich and Mitchison (1983) sees dreams as meaningless noise generated as neural networks are purged of irrelevant information during sleep—a far cry from Freud's "royal road to the unconscious."

Dream Content

Whatever the function of the dream, its content can be dazzling. Yet as vivid and strange as the content may be, it still contains glimpses of the commonplace. The setting might be your home or somewhere near it, and the characters might be friends, relatives, and your pet dog—even though in the dream the dog might be dancing to the latest disco tune. The point is that we draw on familiar material to stock the content of our dreams.

Our dreams can also be influenced by stimuli occurring during sleep. For example, suppose there is an audible sound in the background, though not one loud enough to awaken the sleeper. Will that sound be fed into the dream? Certainly this sometimes happens. For example, most people have had the experience of integrating the sound of the alarm clock into an ongoing dream. Some sleep-laboratory research has addressed this issue.

In one experiment various stimuli were presented to 4-year-old children during REM sleep. The stimuli might be a few drops of water, a puff of air, or the like. The children were then awakened and asked to describe their

dreams. One girl reported, after the air puff was administered, that she dreamed of sailing in a boat with the wind blowing in her face. The drops of water resulted in a dream about being sprayed with a hose; and when a ball of cotton was rubbed lightly on her skin, she dreamed of her sister playing with a cuddly toy lion (Foulkes, Larson, Swanson, & Rardin, 1969). In a similar demonstration, 5 to 10 minutes after the onset of REM sleep, adults were presented with the first name of a person. Though the names were not always integrated into a dream, in a substantial number of cases they influenced the dream.

Remembering Dreams

One of the most striking observations about dreams is that they may be difficult to remember after only a short period of wakefulness. Results from the sleep laboratory do indicate that about 80 to 85 percent of dreams from REM sleep, and fewer from NREM sleep, are recalled. But this high proportion of recollection occurs only if the individual reports the dream immediately upon awakening and if he or she is awakened while in the midst of the dream or directly after it has ended. With delays, the memory for dreams deteriorates rapidly (Goodenough, 1978). (See Chapter 7 for a further discussion on recalling dreams.) This also helps explain why, when dreams are recalled, it is usually the last dream of the night that is remembered best. Of course, as Cartwright (1978) points out, the last dream of the night tends to be the longest, strangest, and most exciting—factors that are likely to make it more memorable.

Perhaps because dreams are so fascinating in their origins and content, psychologists continue to explore them. More recent dream research has been done on a phenomenon referred to as *lucid dreaming* (LaBerge, 1985). LaBerge defines a lucid dream as one where the dreamer is conscious that he or she is dreaming. Many people have an occasional awareness that they are dreaming, which often causes them to awaken. However, the lucid dreamers in LaBerge's experiments sought to develop control of their dreams. Subjects typically used eye-movement signals or clenched their fists to alert observers that a dream had begun. As in regular dream research, various instruments continued to monitor brain waves and other vital signs for changes. While dreaming, subjects have been able to control their breathing or remember to sing a simple nursery rhyme. Such experiments suggest that there may as yet be much to learn about the differences and similarities between sleeping and waking consciousness.

HYPNOSIS

Hypnosis is another condition in which people seem to lose normal consciousness. In the hypnotic-trance state people are thinking, perceiving, and often acting out their perceptions, but, as in sleep, they appear to be unaware of the world around them. The term *hypnosis* comes from the Greek word *hypnos,* meaning sleep. Despite the derivation, and contrary to popular belief, the similarities between hypnosis and sleep are largely superficial. These two conditions differ in some important respects. A basic difference is that a hypnotized person does not show the same brain-wave pattern as a sleeping person—the pattern in hypnosis resembles that of a person who is awake.

What Is Hypnosis?

Hypnosis has been defined as "that state or condition in which subjects are able to respond to appropriate suggestions with distortions of perception and memory" (Orne, 1977, p. 19). The psychological characteristics of someone under hypnosis include increased suggestibility, limited attention to a very small stimulus field, and the acceptance of illusionary perceptions and irrational arguments.

Actually, entering the hypnotic trance itself is not as dramatic as many people believe. Swinging pendants and whirling disks are not necessary to induce a trance; all that is required is a responsive person and some simple suggestions from the hypnotist—your arm is getting heavy, your eyes are closing, you are finding it difficult to move your hands, and so on.

Early researchers believed that subjects in a hypnotic trance would be able to perform tasks that they would normally find impossible, and that the deeper the trance, the more profound the differences in performance. (See the Highlight: Hypnotism—Its Checkered Past). Another common but false belief is that hypnotized people will do things that they wouldn't ordinarily do—jump out of windows, for example, or shoot themselves in the foot (Orne, 1977). A hypnotized person is neither lacking in perception nor out of control, though the nature of the control may shift somewhat. For example, an otherwise voluntary act, such as brushing one's hair, might come to feel much more involuntary—brushing one's hair when a certain word is heard. Nonetheless, the person is still in contact with reality and is still able to make judgments. If someone under hypnosis is told to stare at a blank wall and it is suggested that there is a picture of a house there, the person will be able to "see" and describe the picture. But he or she will also know that the picture being "seen" is not real. It might appear to be floating around in the

A subject undergoing hypnosis. (Bart Bartholomew/Black Star)

This is a painting of an early class in hypnosis given by Charcot, a highly respected French clinician and a teacher of Sigmund Freud. It was because of Charcot that the French Academy of Sciences finally recognized hypnotism as a legitimate form of treatment. (The Bettmann Archive, Inc.)

air or to be transparent, as if it were an apparition. Similarly, hypnotized people are unlikely to dive from a 20-story window ledge under the mistaken impression that they are plunging into the backyard swimming pool. They know that the window ledge is not a diving board.

Hypnotic Responsiveness

The great variation in the degree to which people respond to hypnotism is one of the most important discoveries in hypnosis research. In general, about 15 percent of the population show a high degree of hypnotic responsiveness, while 5 to 10 percent show no effect at all (they seem unable to be hypnotized). The rest of the population falls somewhere between these extremes.

A mistaken generality is that hypnotic susceptibility rises in childhood to a maximum in the preteenage years, then declines slowly thereafter. In fact, susceptibility to hypnosis is essentially stable over time. An individual who is highly responsive to hypnotism today will usually be highly responsive 10 years from now; and a person who shows low responsiveness is not likely to develop high responsiveness in the future.

High responsiveness to hypnotism, however, is not indicative of a general personality trait of suggestibility: The person who is responsive to hypnotism is not likely to be more suggestible or compliant than other people in nonhypnotic situations (Orne, 1977). Evans (1977) has found that people who are highly susceptible to hypnotism are more likely to be able to control sleep. That is, they can fall asleep easily and in different locations, take daytime naps, and so on. These individuals may have a general ability to control their level of consciousness. For example, people who are highly susceptible to hypnotism also learn meditation techniques rapidly. People who seem to be easily hypnotized are often those who like to daydream and who tend to have vivid imaginations (Crawford, 1982).

Pain Reduction Through Hypnosis

Probably the best example of a practical application of hypnosis is its use in reducing the pain response. Hypnosis has proved to be a remarkably effective **anesthetic;** indeed, its wide spread use as a medical anesthetic in the nineteenth century was halted only by the introduction of ether and chloroform as more acceptable substitutes.

Two types of pain have been studied extensively in the laboratory. In research into *ischemic pain,* a blood pressure cuff or tourniquet is attached to the subject's arm and tightened; the subject is then told to exercise the hand and fingers. There is almost no pain at first, but then very severe pain starts, becoming almost intolerable by 10 to 20 minutes from the time the tourniquet is applied. Ischemic pain produced in this way resembles the pain that follows surgery (Hilgard, 1975). In research into *cold-pressor pain,* the person's hand and arm are placed in ice water. The pain is severe and intensifies very rapidly; 30–45 seconds are as much as most people can tolerate.

Under hypnosis it is suggested to subjects that they will feel no pain from either of these two procedures. There is some positive effect for all subjects, regardless of the individual level of responsiveness. With the cold-pressor test, 67 percent of subjects who are highly responsive to hypnotism show substantial pain reduction. Of subjects who have medium or low responsiveness, 17 and 13 percent, respectively, experience significant pain reduction

(Hilgard, 1975). Tests with ischemic pain have yielded comparable results. Moreover, in ischemic pain tests, when the pain disappears, the corresponding blood-pressure rise is also eliminated (Hilgard, 1975).

Of course, other agents can be administered for the relief of pain, such as aspirin or morphine. How does hypnosis compare to these drugs? Stern and his colleagues compared the effects of hypnosis, acupuncture, morphine, diazepam (the main ingredient in the tranquilizer Valium), aspirin, and a placebo (Stern, Brown, Ulett, & Sletten, 1977). In both the cold-pressor and ischemic tests, the greatest reduction of pain occurred in the hypnotic condition; morphine was second, and acupuncture was a close third. Diazepam, aspirin, and the placebo were ineffective in reducing the type of pain produced in these experiments. Once again, the superiority of hypnosis in pain reduction was more prominent among those individuals who were highly responsive. Hypnosis is also useful in reducing the *fear* of pain, with its accompanying hypersensitivity. If we think something is going to hurt, it is likely to hurt all the more; anxiety is often our worst enemy. In surgical procedures anesthesia is often administered not so much to prevent pain (except in the first incision of the knife) as to reduce anxiety and prevent shock (Barber, Spanos, & Chaves, 1974).

Psychological factors are an important element in the perception of pain, and we have all witnessed at one time or another how powerful and unpleasant they can be. In one case, a man with an intense neurotic fear of dental pain consulted a psychotherapist for help. Hypnotic suggestions that his mouth would be anesthetized and that he would feel no pain seemed to do no good, so the therapist tried a different approach. Placing the patient in a hypnotic trance, the therapist suggested that it would be the patient's left hand that would be "excruciatingly hypersensitive." No mention was made of mouth pain at all. The patient was assured that the dentist would be extremely careful not to touch his left hand. It worked: The overwhelming fear of dental pain was shifted to the hand, and the dentist was able to complete "extensive dental work . . . *without* any direct suggestions of anesthesia or use of chemical agents" (Beahrs, 1971, pp. 83–84).

Why is it that hypnosis works so well in reducing pain? A theory to account for the effects has been proposed by Ernest Hilgard, one of the most active researchers in the field. The theory has two components. The first simply involves waking suggestion—we just try to tell ourselves that the pain will be reduced, or we try not to think about it, depending instead on a "diversion of attention, relaxation, and reduced anxiety" (Hilgard, 1977). This approach is open to anyone, whether of high, medium, or low responsiveness to hypnosis, and it can be used by people who are not hypnotically responsive at all. At best, however, this waking suggestion will reduce the perception of pain by about 20 percent. The second component accounts for the remaining 80 percent reduction, and it seems to be available only to those individuals who have high hypnotic responsivity. Hilgard describes it as an "amnesic-like" process in which hypnosis prevents the perception of pain from entering the person's awareness (Hilgard, 1977). Hypnosis may help reduce pain simply by helping the person to shift attention elsewhere. Many programs for treating chronic pain have used hypnosis in this fashion (Moore & Chaney, 1985).

While hypnosis has been used successfully to reduce pain, certain other claims, especially those asserting its effectiveness as a treatment for obesity, cigarette smoking, or alcoholism, seem to have little foundation in fact (Wadden & Anderton, 1982). For example, someone may be told that he or she will no longer have a desire to smoke after coming out of the hypnotic state.

HIGHLIGHT _____

Hypnotism—Its Checkered Past

The early history of hypnotism is a checkered one, filled with intrigue, drama, and generally garbled thinking clarified by occasional flashes of legitimate scientific insight. Unfortunately, its early notoriety threw hypnotism into disrepute and delayed the development of our current knowledge.

The story begins with Friedrich Anton Mesmer (1734–1815), the Viennese physician who lent his name to the technique of mesmerism, now called hypnotism. Through an unlikely combination of medical ingenuity, sheer egotism, and showmanship, Mesmer stumbled onto a process for inducing a trancelike state.

Mesmer believed that magnets could influence the functioning of the human body. He also believed, quite sincerely, that he possessed an above-normal amount of "magnetic fluid," and that this could be channeled toward his patients to relieve them of long-standing paralyses and other symptoms. Seating his patients—up to 30 of them at a time—around a tub filled with iron fragments.

> Mesmer, wearing a coat of lilac silk, walked up and down carrying a long iron wand, with which he touched the bodies of the patients, and especially those parts that were diseased. Often laying aside the wand, he magnetized them with his eyes, fixing his gaze on theirs. (Binet & Frere, 1901, quoted in Sarbin, 1962, pp. 753–754)

Our present knowledge of mental disorders suggests that Mesmer's patients were probably suffering from hysterical conversion disorders, and thus their symptoms had a predominantly psychological cause. Hence the power of suggestion was very effective. Indeed, his patients' belief that Mesmer could cure them in this fashion was an important element in his success. Likewise, the trappings of the chamber that housed the iron-filled tub, and Mesmer's flamboyant dress and manner (he probably resembled a medieval wizard) all helped to enhance the strong effects of suggestion.

Mesmer's results were clearly impressive, and it wasn't long before word of them reached the established scientific community. In 1784 a royal commission was convened in Paris, the city where Mesmer conducted most of his healing sessions. The American ambassador, Benjamin Franklin, presided. The commission found no evidence of actual magnetic powers and therefore supposed the means of cure to be a secret of Mesmer's. The French government is said to have offered him 20,000 francs to disclose the secret. Mesmer reportedly refused the money—presumably because there was no secret to reveal. After the investigation Mesmer gradually fell into disrepute and was eventually denounced as an imposter. He withdrew to Switzerland, where he died in 1815.

The confusion and notoriety that initially surrounded hypnotism stemmed from the disorganized way its results were first described and the questionable behavior of Mesmer and other early practitioners. When later investigators dealt with the subject more soberly, the real advances in the field began. Braid, in the mid-nineteenth century, proposed two basic ideas about hypnosis that have since proved to be correct. One was that concentration on a particular idea could be so intense that memories would not carry over from the hypnotic to the normal state. The other was that suggestion was basic to hypnotism (Sarbin, 1962).

Some years later Charcot, an eminent clinician and a teacher of Freud, correctly understood the effect of hypnotic suggestion in relieving conversion reactions (see Chapter 17) brought on by psychological stresses. Largely because of Charcot's work, the French Academy of Sciences finally recognized hypnotism as a legitimate technique. The study of hypnotism and the hypnotic state was well on the way to respectability and genuine accomplishment.

Some of Mesmer's patients seated around a tub filled with iron fragments. (The Bettmann Archive, Inc.)

While such suggestions do carry over, the effect is usually only for a short time, and the person may experience the desire to smoke again in a few hours or a few days (Coleman, Butcher, & Carson, 1984).

Posthypnotic Effects

In **posthypnotic suggestion** a person is given a suggestion during hypnosis that is to be acted on only when the person is no longer hypnotized. For example, someone might be told that an ear will itch whenever the hypnotist says "dog." The idea is that the effects of the suggestion will carry over from the hypnotic to the normal state. Since this is often an undesired outcome, most hypnotists make it a point to tell subjects that they will not remember suggestions made in the trance state when they come out of it. After all, the stage hypnotist does not want a woman to leave the theater still hallucinating that there is a hippopotamus standing next to her, nor would the psychotherapist in the case mentioned earlier want the patient to leave the dentist's office continuing to believe that his left hand is hypersensitive. It is believed that the signal to cancel the prior suggestion does prevent this from happening, and when it doesn't, there is usually some simple explanation, as in the following example:

> Evans likewise suggested amnesia to the number 6 to a group of subjects. He intended this amnesia to last for the duration of the session, but one subject misunderstood the instruction to mean that the amnesia for the number 6 was to last until a later scheduled session. The subject was a high school mathematics teacher, who proceeded to experience great teaching difficulty in the classroom during the interim. (Perry, 1977, p. 264)

Suppose the hypnotist forgets to cancel the suggestion or the subject misinterprets the instruction—will the subject continue to respond to it for days, years, a lifetime? Actually, there seems to be little or no risk that this dire outcome will occur. In most cases, the trance effects simply disappear by themselves. It is as if subjects give themselves a signal to cancel the suggestion. In some cases, subjects actually instruct themselves to remove the suggestion.

MEDITATION

Meditation seems to be a way in which someone can limit reception of multiple stimuli by directing attention to a single unchanging or repetitive stimulus. It often creates a sense of harmony between the meditator and his or her surroundings and may evoke a sense of expanded awareness. Meditation resembles some forms of self-hypnosis, but differs in having no "goal" and in the fact that self-suggestions are not given during the meditative state. Also, many people who are "unhypnotizable" by standard measures are able to learn meditation easily (Morse, 1977).

Meditation is usually practiced seated, in a quiet environment. Each of the various forms of meditation—Zen, yoga, Sufi, Transcendental Meditation are among the best known—focuses the meditator's attention in a slightly different way. The object of the meditator's attention may be at mentally repeated sound (*mantra*), the breath, or any other appropriate focal point. When attention wanders, the mediator is directed to bring it back to the attentional object in an easy, unforced manner.

HIGHLIGHT _____

Meditation and Stress Management

_____

Can some form of meditation, practiced daily, help to improve health and reverse stress-related illness? If so, are there limitations on the range of meditation's potential effects? These questions are more pointed than they sound, given widely held beliefs about the effects of meditation and its growing use—personally and professionally—in stress management.

On the positive side, research has shown that meditation may indeed have an effect on certain components of stress-related illnesses (Carrington et al., 1980). The practice of meditation has been correlated, for example, with improvement in the breathing patterns of patients with bronchial asthma (Honsberger & Wilson, 1973); decreased blood pressure in hypertensive patients (Benson, 1977; Patel, 1973, 1975); reduced premature ventricular contractions in patients with ischemic heart disease (Benson et al., 1975); reduction of abnormally elevated serum cholesterol levels (Cooper & Aygen, 1979); reduced sleep-onset insomnia (Woolfolk et al., 1976; Mishkiman, 1978); amelioration of stuttering (McIntyre et al., 1974); and reduction of symptoms of psychiatric illness (Glueck & Stroebel, 1975). Those for whom meditation brings improvement of a medical condition must keep on meditating regularly to maintain their gains, however. In such cases, meditation is like a change of diet that eliminates symptoms only as long as the diet is faithfully followed.

In terms of the actual, measurable physiological effects of meditation, evidence indicates that during meditative states the individual consumes less oxygen (10 to 20 percent lower than during wakefulness), breathes more slowly, and has a slower heart rate—all signs of a lower than normal rate of metabolism. (See the accompanying figure.) Further, these changes appear to be related to decreased activity of the sympathetic nervous system, the

system that arouses the body in times of stress. The galvanic skin response (GSR) also rises and shows less spontaneous fluctuation, indicative of a calm bodily state. Moreover, brain-wave patterns of meditators indicate a preponderance of alpha waves, which are typical of presleep or relaxed, drowsy states.

If, as hypothesized, incessant stimulation of the sympathetic nervous system is largely responsible for the incidence of stress-related illness, then the quiescence of the nervous system during meditation may well be a step toward reduced stress and improved health. (In Chapter 16 we will discuss the connection between stress and illness in greater detail.)

However, meditation may not be any more effective than other relaxation methods, such as progressive relaxation, in reducing arousal of the nervous system (West, 1985). If various methods can accomplish the same goals, then despite the claims made for meditation, it is not unique. Holmes

(1985) claims that there is no experimental evidence that the measurable bodily responses in meditation (for example, heart rate, blood pressure, skin temperature, respiration rate, oxygen consumption) are different from what one would obtain simply by resting.

What, then, accounts for the greater popularity of meditation over other methods? Perhaps the distinguishing feature of meditation is that it is the most readily learned of all relaxation techniques and, according to many people, the easiest and most pleasant to practice. Meditation may simply possess a special appeal that tends to keep people practicing it more faithfully than other self-help relaxation methods (Carrington, 1978). From that standpoint, meditation possesses some important practical advantages for clinical application. And it is possible that with different types of stressors and/or different measures of bodily arousal, future research will be able to pinpoint the effects of meditation on stress.

Graph showing the lowered rate of metabolism during meditation, as measured by reduced oxygen absorption in the blood. (Wallace et al., 1972)

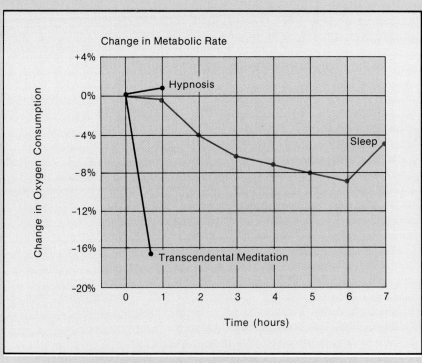

Change in Metabolic Rate

Change in Oxygen Consumption

Hypnosis

Transcendental Meditation

Sleep

Time (hours)

170

This basically simple procedure has been practiced in numerous societies throughout recorded history to alter consciousness in a way that has generally been perceived as deeply beneficial. Traditionally, the benefits of meditation have been defined as spiritual in nature, and it is considered an integral part of many religious practices. Recently, however, modern forms of meditation, simplified and divested of mystery and religious overtones, have been used for stress management, and this use has had promising results (see the accompanying Highlight: Meditation and Stress Management). Such adaptations of meditation are increasingly being used along with other forms of therapy to effect desired personality changes (Carrington, 1977).

Among the new "Westernized" forms of meditation, the most extensively studied to date is Transcendental Meditation (TM). Perhaps more transitional than transcendental, TM retains certain ancient features such as the *puja* (a Hindu religious ceremony) and is taught by an organization that does not permit mental-health practitioners to assume an active role in its clinical management (unless they are TM teachers). So, despite its popularity with the general public, the TM method has not been widely used in clinical settings.

Of the clinically oriented techniques, Clinically Standardized Meditation (CSM) (Carrington, 1978) and the Respiratory One Method (ROM) (Benson, 1975) are the best known. Both these techniques were originated with clinical objectives in mind and are noncultic. The two methods differ from each other in several respects. CSM is more permissive in its instructions and, unlike ROM, does not link the internally repeated sound to breathing. Each method seems to appeal to a somewhat different sort of person, and often the client is given a choice between them.

Jusy why is limiting attention to a repetitive stimulus basic to meditation? One reason may be that regularly repeated sounds or rhythmic movements are inherently soothing. Parents the world over, for example, pick up an agitated infant and rock it with an intuitive awareness of the soothing effects that these rhythmic actions have on the child. The tranquilizing properties of rhythm may be a key to some of meditation's effects, for rhythm is a basic component of meditation. The rhythm of the mantra is obvious, but in addition, the more subtle rhythms of breathing and heartbeat may come sharply into awareness during the inner stillness of any type of meditation. Some people have likened the experience of meditating to being rocked dreamily, "as though one were in a small boat bobbing at anchor in a gentle sea." The feeling of well-being that typically results from meditation may thus be related to its rhythmical nature.

What all forms of meditation have in common is that they seek to limit attention to all normal distractions, while the meditator focuses his or her consciousness on inner thoughts or experience. Some psychologists have even used **sensory deprivation** in therapy for problems like obesity and smoking (Suedfeld, 1980). For example, subjects may lie in a dark, quiet space, or even float in water at body temperature in a totally soundproof box. This in effect mimics the purpose of meditation by allowing the person to think quietly about his or her problem in an environment devoid of outside stimuli.

The ancient meditative practices of Indian yogis have today been adapted to nonreligious forms of meditation for the control of stress. (Bottom: The Bettmann Archive, Inc.)

"DRUGS" AND SUBSTANCE USE

In Chapter 2 we saw how minute quantities of certain chemicals can dramatically change the function of the nervous system through their effects on neu-

Table 5–1 Classification of Psychoactive Substances (Drugs) Discussed in This Chapter.

I. Stimulants
   Nicotine
   Caffeine
   Cocaine
   Crack
   Amphetamines
     Amphetamine
      (Benzedrine)
     Dextroamphetamine
      (Dexedrine)
     Methamphetamine
      (Methadrine)
II. Depressants
   Alcohol
   Opioids (Narcotics)
     Opium
     Morphine
     Heroin
     Codeine
     Methadone
   Sedative-Hypnotics
     Barbiturates
     Benzodiazepines (minor
      tranquilizers)
     Diazepam (Valium)
     Chlordiazepoxide
      (Librium)
III. Halucinogens
   Lysergic acid diethylamide
    (LSD)
   Mescaline (peyote)
   DOM (STP)
   Dimethyltryptine (DMT)
IV. Marijuana and Other Forms of Cannabis
V. Phencylidine (PCP or "Angel Dust")

rotransmission. These changes in functioning are often accompanied by altered states of consciousness. We will consider some of these effects in this section. (Chapter 17 provides a discussion of substance abuse and addiction.)

Technically, any substance other than food that alters our bodily or mental functioning is a **drug.** Many people mistakenly believe the term *drug* refers only to some sort of medicine or an illegal chemical taken by drug addicts. They don't realize that familiar substances such as alcohol, caffeine, and tobacco are also drugs. This is why the more neutral term *substance* is now used by many physicians and psychologists. The phrase "substance abuse" is often used instead of "drug abuse" to make clear that substances such as alcohol and tobacco can be just as harmfully misused as heroin and cocaine.

We live in a society in which the medicinal and social use of substances (drugs) is pervasive: an aspirin to quiet a headache, some wine to be sociable, coffee to get going in the morning, a cigarette for the nerves, perhaps even a tranquilizer to deal with periods of extreme stress. When do these socially acceptable uses of a substance become misuse? First of all, most substances taken in excess will produce negative effects such as intoxication or intense perceptual distortions. Repeated use of a substance can also lead to physical addiction or **substance dependence.** Dependence is marked first by an increased tolerance, with more and more of the substance required to produce the desired effect, followed by the appearance of unpleasant withdrawal symptoms when the substance is discontinued.

Drugs (substances) that affect the central nervous system and alter perception, mood, and behavior are known as **psychoactive substances.** Psychoactive substances are commonly grouped according to whether they are stimulants, depressants, or hallucinogens. Stimulants initially speed up or activate the central nervous system, whereas depressants slow it down ("uppers" and "downers," in street parlance). Subsequent effects of substances in these categories may be more complex, however. For example, a stimulant may activate some part of the central nervous system (CNS) that then inhibits or depresses activity in another part. Hallucinogens have their primary effect on perception, distorting and altering it in a variety of ways that sometimes produce hallucinations. These substances are often called *psychedelic* (from the Greek word meaning "mind-manifesting") because they seem to radically alter one's state of consciousness. They have also been called *psychotomimetic,* since they can produce behavioral effects that mimic a severe form of mental illness called *psychosis.*

Some substances don't fit into the preceding three categories, seeming to require a special category of their own. Two that we shall consider are marijuana (and other forms of cannabis) and PCP or "angel dust." Table 5–1 presents a summary of the substances we will consider in each category. You may be surprised at the way some drugs are categorized. For example, many people think of alcohol as a stimulant, whereas it is actually a depressant; or they think of nicotine as a depressant, whereas it is actually a stimulant. The drugs we shall consider in most detail are those that are often abused. We do this partly because it's important to understand the dangers of such drugs (many of which are illegal), and partly because many of these drugs have been studied more extensively than those that seem less dangerous.

Stimulants

Stimulants act to energize the central nervous system. Some, like the nicotine in cigarettes or the caffeine in coffee, are so common and relatively

mild in action that we hardly think of them as stimulants at all. Others, such as amphetamines and cocaine, produce a high level of psychological dependence and are more likely to be seriously abused.

In moderate amounts, stimulants increase alertness and reduce fatigue. In stronger doses, they can produce anxiety and irritability. People who take stimulants often experience a short-term feeling of inexhaustible energy and become excited and euphoric; in physiological terms, the pupils dilate, the pulse rate and blood pressure increase, and appetite is suppressed because the blood sugar level is raised. However, when the initial effect of the stimulant wears off, the user often experiences a letdown or "crash," with accompanying depression, anxiety, and fatigue.

Cocaine. Since prehistoric times, the natives of such South American countries as Peru and Bolivia have chewed the bark of the coca plant as a source of energy and refreshment. **Cocaine,** the active ingredient in the plant, was first extracted in 1865. This odorless, white, fluffy powder, although illegal, is now widely used by millions of people and is the most powerful known natural stimulant.

Cocaine is usually taken by sniffing it up the nose ("snorting"), after which it passes into the bloodstream through the mucous membranes. Other users prefer the more powerful effects obtained either by injecting it intravenously or by smoking a concentrated form ("base") in a pipe or cigarette. Recently an even more powerful and addictive form of concentrated cocaine, called *crack,* has become a best-selling street drug. This crystalized form of cocaine is usually smoked.

The initial effect of cocaine is a euphoric rush of pleasure and well-being as it begins to stimulate the central nervous system. Its specific action is to block the natural breakdown of the neurotransmitter norepinephrine so that synapses involving this neurotransmitter become more active. The user feels excited, talkative, and energetic. As more cocaine is taken, lower areas of the central nervous system are affected (the thalamus, hypothalamus, and reticular formation). The heart beats faster, blood pressure goes up, breathing becomes faster and deeper, and the person feels even more aroused and alert. More cocaine can lead to a state of *cocaine intoxication,* with confusion, anxiety, distorted speech, paranoia, and even hallucinations. If no more cocaine is taken, these effects subside, to be followed by a letdown that may include headache, dizziness, or even fainting, and extreme fatigue leading to heavy and prolonged sleep. Usually the person awakes within 24 hours with few or no residual effects, unless the dose of cocaine was excessive (or unless it was mixed with some other drug, such as alcohol or heroin; in such cases, the sleep may lead to coma and even death). Cocaine also affects temperature-regulating mechanisms in the brain and the ability to perspire. This is why overdosage sometimes leads to death from elevated temperature.

Extended use of cocaine produces increased tolerance and, according to some, physical dependence. There is no question that rising numbers of people have developed strong psychological dependence on cocaine; however, there is some controversy as to whether physical addiction actually occurs. There is little doubt that heavy users of cocaine find withdrawal a very unpleasant process.

Although the cost of cocaine has dropped, it is costly enough that most people can't afford to use it regularly. On the other hand, the very expense adds to its glamour and desirability. Cocaine is clearly gaining in popularity (Johnston, O'Malley, & Zachman, 1986), with its use by high-school seniors up from 1.9 percent in 1979 to 6.2 percent in 1986 (see Table 5–2).

Table 5–2:   High-School Students and Drug Use
Over the last 12 years about 15,000 seniors in 130 high schools filled out a confidential questionnaire indicating which drugs they had used during the last month.

	'75	'76	'77	'78	'79	'80	'81	'82	'83	'84	'85	'86
Marijuana	27.1	32.2	35.4	37.1	36.5	33.7	31.6	28.5	27.0	25.2	25.7	23.4
Cocaine	1.9	2.0	2.9	3.9	5.7	5.2	5.8	5.0	4.9	5.8	6.7	6.2
Alcohol	68.2	68.3	71.2	72.1	71.8	72.0	70.7	69.7	69.4	67.2	65.9	65.3

Source: University of Michigan Institute for Social Research Study for the National Institute on Drug Abuse. From an unpublished study by L.D. Johnston, J. Bachman, & P. O'Malley. University of Michigan Institute of Social Research, Ann Arbor. Funded by the U.S. Department of Health and Human Services; Public Health Service; Alcohol, Drug Abuse, and Mental Health Administration; National Institute of Drug Abuse.

Amphetamines.   These synthetic stimulants are manufactured in the laboratory. Some common **amphetamines** are *amphetamine,* trade-named Benzedrine; *dextroamphetamine,* trade-named Dexedrine; and *methamphetamine,* trade-named Methedrine. Most amphetamines are taken as pills or capsules, but some heavy users inject the drug directly for a faster and more powerful effect. Although amphetamines have much the same effect as cocaine, they cause it by increasing the release of the neurotransmitter norepinephrine (rather than blocking its breakdown, as cocaine does). In low dosages, this causes an increase in alertness and energy and a reduction in appetite. For this reason, amphetamines until quite recently were widely used for weight reduction. As the dangers of amphetamine use became better understood, this practice was largely abandoned. People who take amphetamines soon develop a tolerance, requiring more and more pills to produce the same effect. Chronic abusers ("speed freaks") may come to need 200 times or more the initial dosage. They also "crash" into deep depression and fatigue, similar to that experienced by people who stop using cocaine. Just as with cocaine, excessive use of amphetamines produces intoxication with paranoia, confusion, and hallucination. Overdosage can lead to death through respiratory failure or uncontrolled variation in body temperature.

Depressants

Depressants actually reduce or "depress" the activity of the central nervous system, although their initial effects sometimes seem stimulating because they suppress some of the normal processes of social inhibition. While there are numerous depressants, here we shall consider only three of the most important types: alcohol; opiates and similar substances; and sedative-hypnotics.

Alcohol.   Archaeological evidence suggests that humans began drinking one form of **alcohol** or another before 6000 B.C. In moderation, drinking seems to make most people feel relaxed, sociable, and easygoing. In excess, however, it leads to dullness of sensation, degraded sensory motor performance, impaired thought processes, sleep, and in extreme cases, even coma and death.

All alcoholic beverages contain the ingredient *ethyl alcohol,* but they don't all pack the same "punch." Hard liquors, for example, have much higher concentrations of alcohol than beer and wine. When an alcoholic drink is consumed, it enters the stomach, where about 20 percent of the alcohol passes through the stomach lining and is absorbed directly into the

bloodstream (food present in the stomach before drinking begins tends to slow this process). Later the remaining alcohol is absorbed into the bloodstream as it passes through the small intestine.

The bloodstream carries the alcohol to the central nervous system, where it has its psychoactive effect. Although many people think that alcohol is a stimulant, it really acts to slow down the central nervous system: It is a *CNS depressant*. The first CNS centers to be affected seem to be those controlling judgment and inhibition. Thus the drinker often becomes less inhibited, more talkative, and more outgoing. Reduced social inhibitions may lead to relaxation and a sense of well-being (although some people react by becoming morose or even aggressive). Notice that while a person may appear more stimulated and active, this is really the result of a reduction in inhibition (i.e., a disinhibition) produced by *depressing* certain regions of the central nervous system.

The extent of alcohol's effect on the body and behavior is primarily dependent on the proportion, or percentage, of it in the bloodstream. For example, 2 ounces of alcohol in the bloodstream of a large person will have less effect than 2 ounces in a small person. The percentage of blood alcohol depends not only on body size and how much is drunk, but also on how rapidly the person drinks. Alcohol is not chemically broken down by digestion. About 90 percent of it is converted into carbon dioxide and water by the liver, while the remaining 10 percent is eliminated directly through breathing, perspiring, or urinating. The liver can only deal with about ⅓ to ½ ounce of alcohol per hour (the equivalent of about 2 ounces of hard liquor, 6 ounces of wine, or 12 ounces of beer). If alcohol is consumed more rapidly than this, the concentration in the bloodstream builds up (and the liver is overburdened and abused). As the percentage of alcohol increases, its negative effects as a CNS depressant become more apparent: Coordination is lost; the perception of sensations such as temperature and pain is dulled; speech is slurred; thought processes are impaired; and vision becomes hazy. Larger doses lead to general sedation, sleep, coma, and sometimes death (see Table 5–3). The exact relation between blood alcohol level and these behavioral changes depends on many factors, including age, familiarity with drinking, physical health, and length of time since previous drinking. The legal definition of "drunk" varies from state to state. In Utah you are legally drunk

Table 5–3:   The Relationship Between Percentage of Blood Alcohol and Behavior

Percent Blood Alcohol Level	Behavioral Effects
0.05	Lowered alertness, usually good feeling, release of inhibitions, impaired judgment
0.10	Slowed reaction times and impaired motor function, less caution
0.15	Large, consistent increases in reaction time
0.20	Marked depression in sensory and motor capability, decidedly intoxicated
0.25	Severe motor disturbance, staggering, sensory perceptions greatly impaired, smashed!
0.30	Stuporous but conscious—no comprehension of the world around them
0.35	Surgical anesthesia; minimal level causing death

The "breathalyzer" test is used by law enforcement agencies to identify drunken drivers. The concentration of alcohol in the blood can be accurately estimated from breath analysis. (Roger Sandler/Black Star)

if more than 0.08 percent of your blood volume is alcohol, while some states allow up to 0.15 percent before classifying you as drunk.

Alcohol's effect on emotional behavior is inconsistent, varying from one person to another. Some become friendly or silly; others become sad or uncommunicative. Apparently, these large individual differences involve a complex interaction of such factors as the basic personality of the drinker, the social setting, the reason for drinking, and so on. For example, it has been noted that alcohol tends to remove inhibitions. But one individual might be more inhibited than another before drinking, and therefore the behavioral effect of drinking will vary. Also, one person may normally inhibit aggression, exposing it only when drinking, while another may normally inhibit positive social activities and become more gregarious and friendly when drinking.

Most people who use alcohol keep their drinking within reasonable limits, usually having only one or two drinks in social settings, with very occasional overindulgence leading to intoxication.. Others, however, fall into a pattern of alcohol abuse; they regularly drink to excess and feel they "need" alcohol in order to handle certain situations. Their drinking may interfere with their social and occupational activities. They have frequent arguments because of their drinking, and they begin to be absent from work and may even lose their jobs. Extended alcohol abuse **(alcoholism)** usually leads to actual alcohol dependence, in which unpleasant withdrawal symptoms occur when no alcohol is taken: Within hours, people dependent on alcohol may begin to shake, experience extreme fatigue, become nauseated, and vomit. Their hearts beat faster, and their blood pressure increases. They feel anxious and depressed and are easily irritated. In extreme cases, they may experience what is formally called *alcohol withdrawal delirium,* also known as *delirium tremens* or the *DTs.* They become mentally confused and suffer frightening visual hallucinations, such as being attacked by small animals or insects. All these withdrawal symptoms disappear within a week if the person does not drink during that time.

Chronic alcohol abuse can cause enlargement and scarring (cirrhosis) of the liver, which is often fatal. Since alcohol has no food value, alcoholics are often undernourished and fall easy prey to other diseases. Ray (1972) found that 70 percent of the males killed in car accidents were legally intoxicated, and Chafetz (1975) estimates that almost half of the murders, assaults, and rapes committed in this country involve excessive use of alcohol. The average adult alone consumes nine quarts of pure alcohol annually, and more than 18 million people in the United States are heavy drinkers, consuming alcohol almost every day. Although alcohol is legal, highly accessible, and alluringly advertised (sales amount to $20 billion to $30 billion per year), in many ways it is the most dangerous drug in our society.

What leads some people to alcohol abuse and alcoholism, while others remain modest social drinkers? Many factors may be involved, among them anxiety, work pressures, and numerous opportunities to drink. Some people maintain that alcoholism is an illness. Still others, citing twin studies and other evidence, believe that there is a genetic predisposition toward alcoholism. At present, however, this evidence is too sketchy, and it is accompanied by too many obvious social factors, to either accept a purely biological explanation or rule out a purely environmental explanation of alcoholism. It has also been suggested that there is a particular personality type, the "addictive personality," that is prone to abuse many substances, including food and cigarettes as well as alcohol.

Opioids. Natural products of the opium poppy, together with similar but synthetic substances such as methadone, are classified as **opioids.** The best-known natural opioids are opium, the least-processed form, and its derivatives, heroin, morphine, and codeine. **Opium** has been used for thousands of years. It is produced from the dried milk-like fluid that comes from the seedpods of the poppy. Smoking opium produces a warm, disembodied-feeling euphoria. While early physicians used it to reduce stomach cramps and ease the physical and emotional pain of patients, many people took it simply to escape into euphoria. In either case, users rapidly developed a physical dependence on the drug: If they stopped taking it, they experienced extreme discomfort.

In 1804 a new substance called **morphine** was derived from opium. (We owe its name to Morpheus, the Greek god of dreams.) Morphine appeared to have all of opium's painkilling properties, quickly calming patients and helping them to sleep, and best of all, it did not seem to be addictive. This is why it was used extensively during the Civil War to relieve pain. Unfortunately, it soon became apparent that morphine was just as addictive as opium.

Further efforts to produce a nonaddictive form of opium led in the late 1800s to a derivative named **heroin.** Again, however, early enthusiasm and wide usage gave way to frustration: Heroin also proved to be highly addictive. Finally, in 1917 it was concluded that there were *no nonaddictive forms of opium,* and all were made illegal in the United States for other than medical uses. Since then, other derivatives of opium have been found (e.g., *codeine*), and synthetic opioids have been developed. The latter are artificially synthesized drugs (e.g., *methadone*) that seem to act on the nervous system in much the same fashion that natural opium and its derivatives do. Both the natural and the synthetic opioids are now referred to as **narcotics.**

Although illegal and extremely dangerous, heroin is used illicitly by many people for the euphoria it produces. They introduce it into their bodies in a variety of ways: smoking it with tobacco, inhaling it ("snorting"), or injecting it just under the skin ("skin popping") or directly into the bloodstream ("mainlining"). Unfortunately, the initial highly pleasurable "rush" (particularly intense with injection) and subsequent few hours of euphoric "high" lead almost inevitably to heroin addiction, with increased tolerance and physical dependence, including exceedingly painful withdrawal symptoms. It is estimated that today there are about half a million heroin addicts in the United States alone.

During the few hours of euphoric high, when centers of emotion in the central nervous system are depressed, the heroin user is almost lethargic. The pupils constrict to tiny points; there are no pains or anxieties; neither food nor sex holds much interest. Then, as this stage passes, the person once again returns to reality. Not only do addicts require extremely large doses of heroin because of their increased tolerance, but they also experience unpleasant withdrawal symptoms almost as soon as they come down from their high. They feel anxious, perspire heavily, breath rapidly, and show many of the symptoms of a bad head cold. Most of all, they start to worry about obtaining their next dose of heroin ("fix"). Life for many addicts is a constant cycle of brief highs interspersed with desperate efforts to obtain more heroin. Not only do they run the risk of arrest for purchasing an illegal drug, but their increased tolerance may force them to spend up to several hundred dollars a day to support their habit. Often this money can only be obtained through burglary, prostitution, or other criminal activities.

Heroin can kill if taken in excess. An overdose depresses the respiratory

centers in the central nervous system to a point where breathing actually stops. A user who remains awake can fight this to some extent by making a conscious effort to breathe. But a user who falls asleep simply dies. Because the drug is obtained illegally, it is often difficult to determine how much the heroin has been "cut" (mixed with other substances). Many overdoses occur because the user obtains an unusually pure form of heroin. The user is also vulnerable to toxic impurities in the drug and to unsterile injections that may transmit disease. This last issue has received considerable attention recently because of the increase of AIDS (acquired immune deficiency syndrome) among intravenous drug users. Some doctors advocate providing free disposable syringes to addicts to help prevent the spread of this disease. It is estimated that 2 percent of all heroin addicts die from their addiction, usually from an overdose (Dupont, 1971).

One promising new form of treatment of heroin addiction seems worth mentioning here. Clinical use of a substance called *naltraxone* has recently been approved by the Food and Drug Administration. It seems to be taken up at the same receptor sites as opiates, thereby blocking the uptake of heroin, while producing no "high" or new addiction (U.S. Department of Health and Human Services, 1984). Thus a heroin addict may be able to take naltraxone at the beginning of each day, when he or she is under little stress (or have it administered daily at a treatment center), and never be able to get high on heroin. It is too soon to know if this type of treatment will really be successful, but it illustrates the interplay between basic research in neurochemistry and clinical treatment of addiction.

Sedative-Hypnotics.   In general, sedative-hypnotic substances induce a state of relaxed drowsiness. At low dosages they simply calm the user and are called **sedatives.** At higher dosages they induce sleep and are called **hypnotics.**

The most widely employed sedative-hypnotic substances are called **barbiturates.** Since their development in the late nineteenth century they have been widely used, both to induce calm and to induce sleep. In recent years, however, because of the development of tranquilizers, the barbiturates have been used primarily as hypnotics (sleep inducers). Taken in pill or capsule form, they depress CNS centers in much the same way that alcohol does. Low dosages calm and relax the user. Higher dosages inhibit the activity of neurons entering arousal centers in the reticular formation and thus induce sleep. At still higher dosages barbiturates can cause respiratory failure.

Doctors did not begin to appreciate the dangers of barbiturates until the 1950s. Not only is there the risk of death through accidental or suicidal overdose, but barbiturates are also physically addictive. Chronic use leads to increased tolerance and to unpleasant withdrawal symptoms much like those experienced with alcohol withdrawal (e.g., nausea, vomiting, fatigue, anxiety, and depression). A particularly dangerous aspect of the increased tolerance is that more and more of the substance is required to induce sleep. Thus, to achieve sleep, the chronic user eventually needs a dose that is almost lethal. Given the often groggy and confused state of the user, this may lead to accidental death. Such accidents and suicidal overdoses cause approximately 5,000 deaths in the United States each year (Seymour, 1979). Illegal (nonprescription) use of barbiturates and other sedative-hypnotics (e.g., *methaqualone,* trade-named Quaalude) has become a major substance-abuse problem. Often such abuse begins with the legal (prescription) use of a barbiturate, or other sedative-hypnotic, such as a sleeping pill. The user, finding

that the pill also produces a pleasant and very relaxed state if taken during the day, turns to illegal sources of supply to maintain a growing dependence on the drug.

In the 1950s a group of sedatives called **benzodiazepines** were developed to treat anxiety. These include *diazepam,* trade-named Valium, and *chlordiazepoxide,* trade-named Librium. They are often referred to as *antianxiety drugs* or **minor tranquilizers** (the "major tranquilizers" were the phenothiazenes, such as *thorazine,* now referred to as *antipsychotic drugs* rather than as tranquilizers). As antianxiety drugs, the minor tranquilizers (benzodiazepines) seem superior to barbiturates in several respects: First, they reduce anxiety without making the person drowsy; second, they act at very low dosages and are less likely to produce addiction; and third, they have less of an effect on respiratory centers, reducing the risk of a fatal overdose. In part, they have these unique properties because they act on CNS sites that are unaffected by barbiturates, although they do also affect some of the same sites as both barbiturates and alcohol (indeed, excessive use can lead to markedly similar patterns of intoxication). Identification of receptor sites for benzodiazepines has led to speculation that our bodies may produce substances that are chemically similar to the minor tranquilizers, providing a natural way of controlling anxiety (see the Highlight on endogenous benzodiazepines). The wide and enthusiastic prescription of Librium and Valium that began in the 1950s has now been sharply curtailed as their addictive properties and potential for abuse have become more apparent. Nevertheless, they remain the most widely used antianxiety drugs.

Hallucinogens

Hallucinogens are substances that are capable of producing hallucinations; they can alter our sensations and perceptions to the extent that we experience both our inner and outer worlds in radically different ways. Perhaps the best-known and most powerful hallucinogen.is **LSD (lysergic acid diethylamide),** which was discovered in 1938 by a chemist named Albert Hoffman. Here is his own description of what happened after he unknowingly consumed a tiny amount of the new substance:

> In the afternoon of 16 April 1943, when I was working on this problem I was seized by a peculiar sensation of vertigo and restlessness. Objects, as well as the shape of my associates in the laboratory appeared to undergo optical changes. I was unable to concentrate on my work. In a dream-like state I left for home where an irresistible urge to lie down overcame me. I drew the curtains and immediately fell into a peculiar state similar to drunkenness characterized by an exaggerated imagination. With my eyes closed, fantastic pictures of extraordinary plasticity and intensive color seemed to surge toward me. After two hours this state gradually wore off. (Hoffmann, quoted in Goodman & Gilman, 1975)

Later experiments revealed that Hoffman had probably consumed no more than 0.1 milligram of LSD, an amount that would barely cover the head of a pin. We now know that such minute doses can produce bizarre alterations of consciousness. Within an hour of ingesting the drug, perceptions, especially visual ones, become highly intensified. Colors seem more intense. Previously insignificant parts of a scene leap out in incredibly fine detail. Inanimate objects move and alter their form. Hallucinations may occur, such as rapidly moving geometric forms that appear and disappear. In addition to these visual distortions, other senses are affected as well: There are strange

Endogenous Benzodiazepines—Does the Body Produce Its Own Tranquilizers?

In Chapter 2 we considered evidence that our bodies produce a substance that acts like the opiates to kill pain (see the Highlight on endorphins in that chapter). More recently, researchers have begun to suspect that another internally produced (endogenous) substance may control anxiety in much the same fashion as the benzodiazepine tranquilizers (e.g., Valium and Librium). The way in which research has led to this speculation resembles the story of the endogenous opiates.

In 1977 research groups in Denmark (Mohler & Okada, 1977) and Switzerland (Squires & Braestrup, 1977) discovered binding sites in the brain for benzodiazepines—that is, specific brain tissue that takes up benzodiazepines in a lock-and-key fashion (other sedatives, such as barbiturates, did not bind to these sites). Furthermore, the degree to which specific benzodiazepines were taken up reflected their relative effectiveness as tranquilizers (Mohler & Okada, 1977).

It was also noticed that the location of the benzodiazepine binding sites was generally consistent with the effects of tranquilizers (Young & Kuhar, 1980). For example, many of these sites were found in parts of the brain known to be involved in regulating emotions.

Just as the discovery of opiate receptors in the central nervous system led to a search for endogenous opiates, the discovery of benzodiazepine receptors (binding sites) seemed to imply the existence of some internally produced tranquilizer (i.e., an endogenous benzodiazepine).

Benzodiazepines seem to interact in some complicated way with GABA (gamma aminobutyric acid), the inhibitory neurotransmitter released by about 30 percent of the neurons in the brain. Anxiety is believed to be associated with excessive firing (hyperexcitability) of certain neural pathways, or to the activity of so-called anxiety peptides at receptor sites in specific regions of the brain. (This new evidence is discussed in Chapter 15.) This may trigger an increase in the release of GABA to produce a compensatory inhibition. The binding of benzodiazepines seems to facilitate the uptake of GABA at its closely associated receptor sites. Thus both GABA and some as yet undiscovered endogenous benzodiazepine may act in conjunction as tranquilizers.

Chronic use of tranquilizers may produce tolerance because GABA production diminishes as its effects are magnified. Withdrawal symptoms may occur because the sudden reduction in benzodiazepines takes place when GABA production is low, leaving little inhibition of the anxiety-evoking neural activity. In fact, a drug has been found that blocks the effects of GABA. It produces profound anxiety, just what one would expect if theories regarding benzodiazepine are correct (Dorrow, Horowski, Paschelke, & Braestrup, 1983).

The major point to be made here is *not* that we know exactly how tranquilizers affect the brain. It is, rather, that psychoactive drugs affect our minds in a complicated fashion. Recent research on brain chemistry and neurotransmitters seems to be opening the door to an understanding of these processes (Snyder, 1986).

The lightest areas in this autoradiograph show sites where benzodiazephine tranquilizers were taken up in a rat's brain.

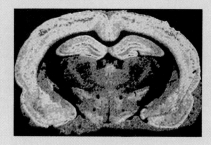

sensations of hot and cold, as well as amplified sounds, both real and totally imagined. *Synesthesia,* a crossover in one's sensations, may occur: Sounds are "seen" and colors "heard." Time may crawl, with minutes seeming to pass like hours.

While the emotional effects of LSD can be euphoric, many people feel depersonalized and detached, and they may even suffer extreme anxiety or panic. Such "bad trips" can lead to serious accidents as the frightened user flees or fights off imagined danger.

The psychoactive properties of LSD are still not well understood. Early interest centered on its apparent ability to induce a schizophrenic distortion of reality. In the 1950s and 1960s counterculture spokesman Timothy Leary and others maintained that LSD produced profound new insights into one's self. Others have argued that the risk of "bad trips," lingering aftereffects, and even genetic damage make it a highly dangerous drug. In any case, it remains a potent hallucinogen, capable of profoundly distorting one's sense of reality in a highly unpredictable fashion, even at tiny dosages.

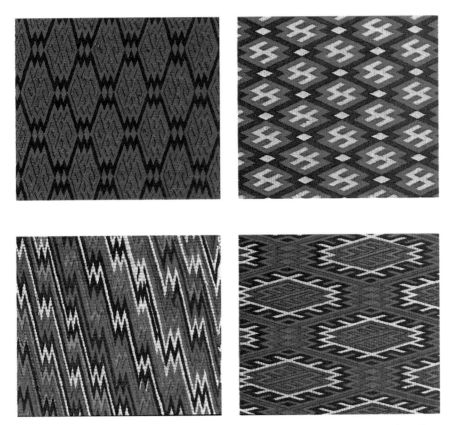

Mexico's Huichol Indians used geometric patterns in their weaving that were based on visions commonly seen during peyote rituals.

There are many other hallucinogenic drugs, both naturally occurring and synthetic. **Mescaline** is the active ingredient of the **peyote** cactus. For centuries Indians in Mexico and the southwestern United States have chewed peyote to induce hallucinations ("visions") during certain religious ceremonies. **DOM (dimethoxy-4-methylamphelamine)** is a long-lasting (12 hours) hallucinogen originally developed by the Dow Chemical Company and now illegally traded on the street as STP. A much more short-term hallucinogen is **DMT (dimethyltryptine),** the effects of which last only about an hour.

It is now finally clear (Jacobs, 1987) that *all hallucinogenic drugs have the same site of action* in the brain: receptor cells that normally pick up the neurotransmitter serotonin. Systems of serotonin-releasing neurons begin in the brain stem and project from there to virtually all areas of the brain. The various hallucinogens are apparently picked up by certain serotonin receptor cells (5-HT$_z$ receptors) in the brain, producing effects similar to those of one type of naturally released serotonin (Trulson, Ross, & Jacobs, 1976). Slight variations in the molecular structure of the different hallucinogens apparently account for each one's individual effects. However, all hallucinogens produce *cross-tolerance* (use of one reduces the effect of another) and all are blocked in their action by the same drugs that are known to block the effects of serotonin.

Marijuana and Other Forms of Cannabis

Marijuana is a mixture of the crushed leaves and flowering tops of the hemp plant (*Cannabis sativa*). The plant contains a substance called *THC* (tetrahydrocannabinal) that has a combination of psychoactive properties which defy simple categorization. It produces the euphoria and release from inhibition of the depressant alcohol; the relaxation or even fatigue of a sedative; and the hypnotic, sensory, and perceptual distortions of a mild hallucinogen (which ordinarily increases wakefulness). This is why marijuana and other cannabis drugs are treated as a unique category of psychoative substance in the latest revision of the *Diagnostic and Statistical Manual of Mental Disorders,* or *DSM III* (1980). The various forms of cannabis differ chiefly in their concentration of THC. Of the natural forms of cannabis, marijuana is the least potent, and **hashish** (pure plant resin) the most potent. Recently an almost pure form of THC has been artificially synthesized in the laboratory.

Cannabis is most frequently taken by smoking it in a cigarette or pipe. It can also be eaten (Alice B. Toklas, a friend of the poet Gertrude Stein, is said to have baked delicious marijuana brownies). At low dosages, most users quickly develop a feeling of relaxed euphoria. Some become more talkative, while others become quiet and contemplative. Many describe their perceptions and sensory experiences as intensified and unusual. Previously unnoticed colors and sounds become vivid and important. Space and forms may appear distorted, and time slows. However, while many people feel only pleasant or interesting effects, others become anxious and irritable. The particular pattern of one's reactions depends a great deal on the particular situation and the behavior of those who are nearby.

There are physical symptoms as well. The eyes redden as blood vessels dilate, the mouth dries as saliva flow is inhibited, and the heart beats faster; appetite often increases.

As more THC enters the bloodstream, the user feels more and more drowsy. Speech may become slurred and thinking distorted. Things may seem hysterically funny and inspire long spells of giggling. Finally, the user falls into a deep sleep.

For many centuries cannabis was used in Asia as an anesthetic and medication for maladies ranging from insomnia to rheumatism. In the mid-nineteenth century Western European doctors began to prescribe it for neuralgia, menstrual pain, and migraine headaches. In the early twentieth century its medical use was widely promoted in the United States by the drug company Parke-Davis. By the 1930s, however, doctors were prescribing such other drugs as morphine, aspirin, and barbiturates instead. Marijuana began to be used simply for pleasure and was distributed illegally. This period was marked by progressively harsher antidrug laws, and by 1937 marijuana, incongruously lumped with opium and heroin, was completely outlawed. During the 1960s marijuana use underwent a resurgence, with growing recognition that the harsh legal penalties seemed inconsistent with its apparent low level of danger. The *National Survey of Drug Abuse* (1979) reported that during 1979 more than 26 million Americans used cannabis at least once, including 31 percent of adolescents under 18 (10 percent of all high-school seniors), 68 percent of individuals between 18 and 25, and 20 percent of those over 26. However, this report may have underestimated actual drug use among adolescents. Answers to a confidential questionnaire on drug use given to high-school seniors for the last 12 years (see Table 5–2) suggest a different picture. From a 1978 high (we mean maximum) of 37.1 percent

who reported using marijuana within the preceding 30 days, use has gradually dropped to 23.4 percent in 1986 (coupled with an increase in cocaine use).

It is clear that earlier efforts to characterize cannabis as a "killer weed" were counterproductive exaggerations. Concerning its safety, however, real doubts still remain. Nearly a quarter of all drivers involved in accidents were using marijuana alone or with alcohol (Jones & Rovinger, 1985). Some evidence suggests that it is addictive. Chronic users may develop tolerance (Nowland & Cohen, 1977) and experience withdrawal symptoms such as loss of appetite, running nose, diarrhea, and sweating (Jones, 1977). Also, the potency of illegally obtained cannabis has increased, and there are more instances of accidents related to cannabis intoxication (Marijuana Research Findings, 1980). Longer-term dangers may include susceptibility to lung disease (Tashkin, Calvarese, & Simmons, 1978) and reduced fertility (Hembree, Nabias, & Huang, 1979).

PCP or "Angel Dust"

In 1959 a substance named **phencyclidine (PCP)** was developed for use as a powerful painkiller and an alternative to the highly addictive opiates. It seemed to control pain, not so much by eliminating it as by producing a state of detachment from bodily sensations so that the pain could be ignored. PCP is chemically distinct from all the other drugs we have discussed, and it produces a sufficiently distinctive pattern of effects to warrant its own special category in *DSM III*.

In 1967, only four years after it first appeared on the market as a prescription drug, certain negative aspects of PCP had become so apparent that its use by humans was made illegal. Nevertheless, it soon began to be sold illegally on the street, where it is often referred to as "angel dust." It comes in a variety of forms, including pills, powder, rock crystals, and liquid. It can be swallowed, inhaled injected, or even sprayed on tobacco and smoked. In fact, since it is cheaply and easily produced, it is often secretly added to other illicit drugs such as marijuana or cocaine to increase their apparent potency.

Shortly after taking PCP, many users feel mildly euphoric, while others become nervous and agitated. Moods swing rapidly: The user may feel elated and powerful one moment and fearful the next. Judgment is impaired, and the person may grow aggressive and start fights. Perception, including the sense of time, may be distorted. Physical changes include uncontrolled movement of the eyes, loss of pain sensitivity, increased blood pressure and heart rate, and loss of muscular control.

Larger doses of PCP produce even more negative effects. The user often feels detached from reality. Hallucinations occur and thought processes are seriously disturbed to the point of delirium. Paranoia and outbursts of violence are common. Strangely, these negative symptoms may occur either shortly after the PCP is taken or days later, after the user seems to have totally recovered.

Not surprisingly, the irrational thought processes, insensitivity to pain, paranoia, and outbursts of violence produced by high doses of PCP have led to numerous instances of severe injury, suicide, and accidental death (Siegal, 1978; Burns & Lerner, 1976). Sufficiently high doses of PCP have even led directly to coma and death through a depression of respiratory centers.

In spite of its dangers, PCP has become an increasingly popular illicit drug. It does produce some pleasant sensations, and its very unpredictability may appeal to some. It is inexpensive and easy to manufacture and, as yet, does not appear to produce tolerance or withdrawal symptoms.

SUMMARY

1. *NREM Sleep* has four stages, which differ in terms of brain-wave patterns and muscular changes. *REM sleep,* characterized by rapid eye movements and *dreaming,* usually occurs at 90-minute intervals throughout the sleep cycle.

2. There are a number of theories about why people dream. Freud believed that a dream is the expression of unconscious impulses and thoughts when a person's conscious defenses are lowered during sleep. Other theorists believe that dreams are a way of processing daytime memories. Still others think dreams are a way of purging the neural networks of irrelevant information.

3. *Hypnosis* can be defined as a condition in which subjects are able to respond to appropriate suggestions with distortions of perception and memory.

4. There are individual differences in responsiveness to hypnotism; about 15 percent of the population can be greatly affected by hypnotic suggestion, while about 5 to 10 percent show no effect at all; the rest fall somewhere between these two extremes.

5. Pain reduction through hypnosis has been tested with both *ischemic* and *cold-pressor pain;* those who are highly responsive to hypnotism show substantial pain reduction, while the results are less dramatic with those who are of medium or low responsiveness.

6. *Meditation* is concentration on one thought or word in order to block out all other sensations and thoughts. Adaptations of meditation are being used in the practice of stress management.

7. Drugs affecting behavior or consciousness are called *psychoactive drugs;* they include stimulants, depressants, and hallucinogens, as well as other substances such as cannabis and PCP.

SUGGESTED READINGS

BOWERS, K. (1983). *Hypnosis for the seriously curious* (2nd ed.). Monterey, Calif.: Brooks/Cole. An extensive review of experimental studies of hypnosis.

CARRINGTON, P. (1977). *Freedom in meditation.* New York: Doubleday. A demystified, practical approach to meditation as a means of reducing tension.

CARTWRIGHT, R. A. (1978). *A primer of sleep and dreaming.* Reading, Mass.: Addison-Wesley, A simple, readable introduction to research on sleep and dreaming.

COLEMAN, R. (1986). *Wide awake at 3:00 a.m.* New York: Freeman. A highly readable book for the layman on sleep and dreaming, dealing with topics as far-ranging as jet lag and the effects of working nights.

DEMENT, W. (1978). *Some must watch while some must sleep.* New York: Norton. A more advanced treatment of modern experimental methods of studying sleep.

GOLEMAN, D., & Davidson, R. J. (Eds.). (1979). *Consciousness: Brain, states of awareness, and mysticism.* New York: Harper & Row. A collection of articles about consciousness, ranging from neuroscience to mysticism in approach.

GRINSPOON, L., & Hedblom, P. (1975). *The speed culture: Amphetamine use and abuse in America.* Cambridge, Mass.: Harvard University Press. An extensive and technical review of the use of stimulants.

HILGARD, E. R. (1977). *Divided consciousness.* New York: Wiley. An excellent introduction to hypnosis and altered states of consciousness by one of the foremost investigators in the field.

JAYNES, J. (1977). *The origin of consciousness in the breakdown of the bicameral mind.* Boston: Houghton Mifflin. A fascinating, if controversial. view of consciousness as a relatively recent development in human history.

JOUVET, M. (1967). The states of sleep, *Scientific American, 216,* 62–72. A brief highly readable, and well-illustrated introduction to sleep research.

KAPPELL, H., Glaser, M., & Israel, Y., et al. (1986). *Research advances in alcohol and drug problems.* Vol. 9. New York:

Plenum Press. A technical and comprehensive review of current research in the causes and treatment of substance abuse.

MAYES, A. (Ed.) (1983). *Sleep mechanisms and functions.* Cambridge, England: Van Nostrand Reinhold (UK). A review of methodology and findings on the function and pathology of sleep in man and animals.

NARANJO, C., & ORNSTEIN, R. E. (1977). *On the psychology of meditation.* New York: Penguin, An introduction to meditation, its history and current practice.

SPRINGER, S., & DEUTSCH, G. (1985). *Left brain, right brain* (rev. ed.). New York: Freeman. A summary of research on hemispheric specialization.

UNDERWOOD, G., & STEVENS, R. (1979–86). *Aspects of consciousness.* Vols. 1–5. New York: Academic Press. A series of volumes containing chapters written by experts on various aspects of consciousness.

WALLACE, B. (1979). *Applied hypnosis: An overview.* Chicago: Nelson-Hall. Applied uses of hypnosis are described in a very readable manner.

6 Conditioning and Learning

The behavior of people, and of animals, is continually changed by the experiences they have in the world. To be once bitten is to be twice shy; and the burnt child avoids the flame. Practice, we are told, makes perfect—and experience is the great teacher. We can define **learning** as the relatively permanent changes in behavior that result from past experience. Those changes, for the most part, serve to adjust us to the world in which we live. We can and do learn some maladjustive behaviors, but most of us profit from experience most of the time. The obvious function of learning is to enable us to go about the business of living in an effective way. The newborn mammal knows nothing about the world and depends for its survival on parental care. Through learning—as well as through growth—it is transformed into a knowledgeable and effective adult creature.

If you had attended college in the 1940s or 1950s, you might have taken a very different course in introductory psychology. This period was the high-water mark of strict behaviorism in psychology when psychologists sought to avoid the pitfalls of the older philosophical mentalism by studying lower organisms. It often seemed as if every laboratory was studying rats and pigeons. They were clearly capable of learning; and this learning could be studied from a purely behavioral point of view, without any reference to "mental processes." More importantly, most behaviorists believed that the basic principles of learning were the same for humans and other animals. Why not discover these principles by studying animals in a laboratory where it was possible to control and manipulate every aspect of their environment?

Psychology has evolved considerably since this earlier behavioristic

Long before there was a science of learning conditioning, hunters knew how to train animals to help them hunt, as in this medieval view of a hunter with a dog, a horse, and a falcon. (University Library, Heidelberg)

period. Most psychologists today would agree that *some* principles of learning apply to both humans and lower organisms. However, humans with their unique linguistic skills and highly evolved brain structure seem to have very different thought processes. To understand these processes one must study humans. The nature of humans' more complex learning processes will be considered in later chapters. However, this "higher" learning does not simply take the place of the more primitive processes we share with other animals.

In this chapter we consider two basic types of learning initially studied in lower organisms: classical conditioning and operant conditioning. In classical conditioning, organisms learn about *contingencies between stimuli:* If a certain stimulus occurs, another is likely. For example, a flash of lightning is normally followed by the sound of thunder. In operant conditioning, organisms learn about *contingencies between their behavior and certain consequences:* A certain response is usually followed by a certain consequence. For example, touching a lighted match is likely to cause pain. While these two forms of learning are relatively simple, they are of fundamental importance, and, as we shall see, occur in humans in much the same way as in the more humble creatures commonly studied in experimental psychology. These studies are useful in their own right, allowing us to better understand animal behavior. Furthermore, they reveal aspects of learning that are clearly relevant to human behavior.

CLASSICAL CONDITIONING

The learning process called **classical conditioning** normally involves the *consistent pairing of two stimuli* so that a **response** originally evoked by only one of the stimuli is eventually evoked by the other as well. For example, a loud noise usually causes an animal to freeze or cringe, while turning on a weak light does not. Yet consistently turning on the light just before the loud noise will eventually cause the animal to cringe as soon as the light comes on, even when the noise is not present. (The possible neurological effects of such pairings are discussed later in the Application: The Biological Basis of Learning.)

The Work of Ivan Pavlov

The basic phenomena of classical conditioning were first identified and analyzed by a Russian physiologist named Ivan Pavlov (1849–1936) who had previously won a Nobel prize (1904) for his research on the digestive system. During that work he had studied the flow of saliva in a dog's mouth. Placing food in the dog's mouth normally produced an immediate increase in the flow of saliva. Pavlov assumed that this stimulus-response relation was *reflexive,* that is, naturally built into a dog's nervous system. However, he also noticed that after a dog had been in the laboratory for a few weeks, it began to produce more saliva whenever it heard or saw things that usually preceded feeding: for example, when the dog heard its food bowl clattering as it was being filled, or when the animal caught sight of the attendant who normally fed it. Pavlov's curiosity was aroused by this apparently learned or **conditioned reflex,** a stimulus-response relation acquired through experience.

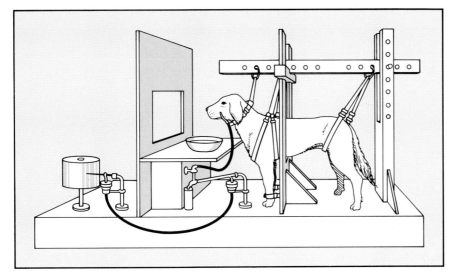

Figure 6–1 Pavlovian dog, surgically prepared for measurement of salivary flow, restrained in a conditioning chamber.

Basic Principles of Classical Conditioning

Pavlov began to systematically study the conditioned reflex using the experimental setup shown in Figure 6–1. A dog, new to the laboratory, was restrained with a harness in a soundproof chamber. A surgically implanted tube in the dog's mouth collected saliva, and the flow was recorded on a revolving drum. Pavlov first determined that placing food powder in the dog's mouth increased the flow of saliva. He called the food the **unconditioned stimulus (US),** and the dog's salivary response he termed the **unconditioned response (UR).** Then, on several occasions, he sounded a bell in the chamber. While the dog clearly heard the bell, perking up its ears each time it sounded, there was no change in the flow of saliva. Finally, Pavlov began to follow each sounding of the bell with a presentation of food powder. Gradually, the dog's saliva flow began to surge as soon as the bell sounded, even before the food powder had been presented. Pavlov considered the bell to be a learned or **conditioned stimulus (CS),** and the increase in salivation at the sound of the bell a **conditioned response (CR).** Each pairing of the CS and US was called a **reinforcement** since it strengthened the tendency of the CS to evoke the CR. Thus the basic Pavlovian, or classical, conditioning process typically involves repeated pairings of the CS and the US (reinforcements), which eventually condition the CS to evoke a CR similar to the UR (see Figure 6–2).

Acquisition and Extinction. The course of one of Pavlov's experiments is shown in Figure 6–3. In *Phase I* an initially untrained dog gradually increased his salivary response (CR) through repeated pairings of the bell and food (CS + US). Pavlov called this process **acquisition.** In *Phase II* he continued to present the CS but without the US, and he found that the CR evoked by the CS gradually disappeared. He called this gradual loss of the CR (when the CS is repeatedly presented alone) **extinction.** Following Phase II, the animal was removed from the testing chamber and returned to its kennel for a night's rest. The next day it was brought back to the laboratory, where *Phase III* consisted of further extinction training (CS presented alone). Pavlov noted

Figure 6–2 The relations between stimuli and responses before, during, and after the establishment of a conditioned response. In this example the salivary reflex is used, but the basic diagram could apply to other conditioned reflexes as well.

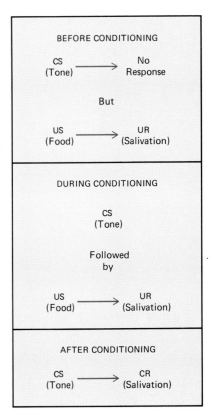

BEFORE CONDITIONING

CS (Tone) ⟶ No Response

But

US (Food) ⟶ UR (Salivation)

DURING CONDITIONING

CS (Tone)

Followed by

US (Food) ⟶ UR (Salivation)

AFTER CONDITIONING

CS (Tone) ⟶ CR (Salivation)

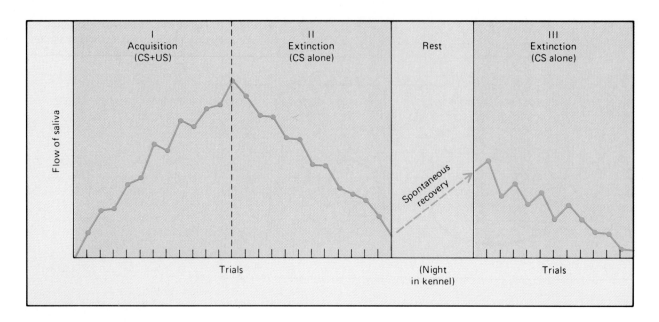

Figure 6-3 The acquisition (Phase I) and extinction (Phases II and III) of a conditioned salivary response. Although the conditioning seems almost totally extinguished by the end of Phase II, spontaneous recovery during the night is indicated by the initially high level of conditioning present in Phase III.

that instead of the very weak CRs observed at the end of Phase II, the first few presentations of the CS in Phase III evoked fairly strong CRs. Pavlov termed this partial restoration of the learning after a period of rest **spontaneous recovery.** This is characteristic of previously extinguished classically conditioned responses. Furthermore, the animal will usually relearn very rapidly if reinforcement (pairing the CS and the US) is begun again. Spontaneous recovery and rapid relearning *(reacquisition)* indicate how hard it is to completely eliminate the effects of conditioning. In fact, animals have shown signs of conditioning many years after a conditioned response was originally acquired and extinguished.

Pavlov found that the rate of acquisition depended on a number of factors, such as the amount of food powder presented at each reinforcement and the loudness of the bell used as the CS. However, the most important factor was the *temporal relation between the CS and the US.* Conditioning occurs most rapidly when the CS slightly precedes the US **(forward conditioning).** Simultaneous presentation **(simultaneous conditioning)** produces less conditioning, while presenting the CS after the US **(backward conditioning)** is least effective of all.

The most effective CS-to-US interval in forward conditioning depends on both the specific animal and the stimuli involved. In most cases, a delay of about *half a second is best,* as there appears to be little or no learning at delays of more than a second or two (a dramatic exception to this will be discussed later).

Generalization and Discrimination. When a conditioned response has been established to a particular CS, stimuli *similar* to that CS will also tend to elicit the response. This phenomenon is called **generalization.** The more similar the new stimulus is to the original CS, the greater will be the strength of the response. A simple example by Pavlov clearly illustrated the nature of generalization. The CS was a mechanical scratching of the dog's skin that had been paired with meat powder (the US). Once the conditioned response (salivation) had been firmly established, the dog was tested with scratches on

different parts of its body: The closer the scratch was to the point at which the original CS had been applied, the more the dog salivated.

Though conditioning normally generalizes to stimuli similar to the CS, it is possible to train an animal *not* to respond to similar stimuli while continuing to respond to the CS itself. This is referred to as **discrimination** training. For example, Pavlov first conditioned a dog to salivate to a 1,000 Hz tone. When this conditioning was firmly established, the dog would also salivate (though not as much) to tones with a similar frequency—the greater the similarity, the more salivation. (This sort of **generalization gradient** is illustrated in Figure 6–4a.) Discrimination training consisted of more pairings of the 1,000 Hz tone and food, randomly interspersed with presentations of 900 and 1,100 Hz tones *without food*. This training gradually sharpened the generalization gradient until the dog only salivated to the 1,000 Hz tone (CS), as seen in Figure 6–4b. (With further training using tones even closer to

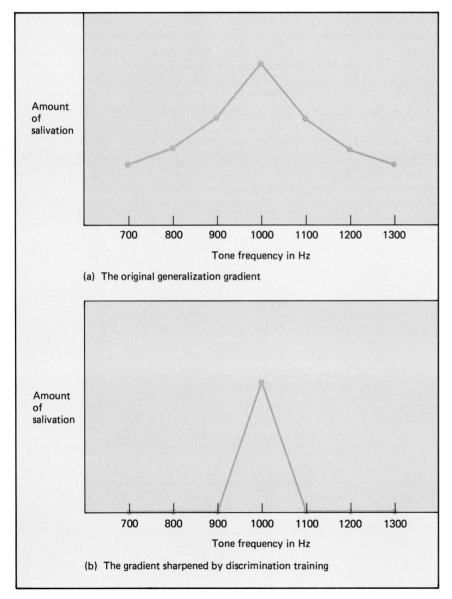

(a) The original generalization gradient

(b) The gradient sharpened by discrimination training

Figure 6–4 The effect of discrimination training. (a) After repeated pairings of a 1,000 Hz tone (CS) and food, a dog shows a typical generalization gradient. (b) This figure shows a sharpened generalization gradient after discrimination training consisting of more pairings of 1,000 Hz tones and food, along with randomly interspersed presentations of 900 and 1,100 Hz tones with *no* food.

1,000 Hz, Pavlov was able to show that the dog could discriminate between tones of 1,000 Hz and 1,012 Hz.)

Conditioned Reinforcers. Through conditioning, the CS and the US come to evoke a similar response (the CR and the UR). Pavlov wondered whether the two stimuli might have become similar in other respects as well. He found that the CS also acquired some of the **reinforcing properties** of the US. Pavlov began with a dog conditioned to salivate to the sound of a bell (CS). He found he could then condition another stimulus, such as a light (CS′), to also evoke salivation by repeatedly pairing it with the bell, *even though food was never presented.* Pavlov went even further. He showed that it was possible to condition a third stimulus (CS″), such as touching the dog, so that it also evoked salivation simply by pairing it with the light, again without presenting any food (see Figure 6–5). He called this **higher-order conditioning.** Stimuli such as the bell and the light, which acquired their reinforcing properties through conditioning, were termed **conditioned** or **secondary reinforcers.** This was to distinguish them from **unconditioned** or **primary reinforcers** such as food and water, whose reinforcing properties seemed to be built into the organism (i.e., not acquired through conditioning). There seems to be a natural limit to most forms of higher-order conditioning because conditioned reinforcers eventually extinguish if they are no longer paired with any primary reinforcer.

Up to this point we have only considered unconditioned stimuli, such as food or water, that might be regarded as "desirable" or "pleasant" for the animal. Another important class of unconditioned stimuli are those that might be regarded as "painful" or "unpleasant." Pavlov called these **aversive stimuli.** They are defined by the characteristic pattern of unconditioned responses they evoke and depend somewhat on the animal involved. For ex-

Figure 6–5 The sequence of events in progressively higher-order conditioning. There seems to be a natural limit to this process, since presentations of a conditioned stimulus without the US also produce extinction.

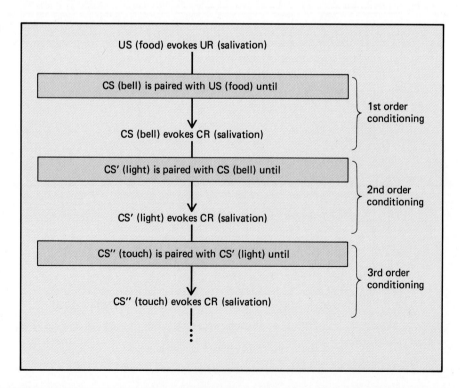

HIGHLIGHT

The Biological Basis of Learning

Today a major focus of investigations of animal learning is the attempt to pinpoint those physical changes in the nervous system that underlie conditioning and associative learning. The complexity of the mammalian nervous system poses enormous technical problems for researchers interested in tracing out the physical and chemical changes presumed to underlie the learning of new behaviors. Thus in recent years some have turned to the study of very simple organisms—especially those whose nervous systems contain relatively few, and manipulable, cells. The marine snail *Hermissenda crassicornis* is one such organism, and it has served as a subject in a series of pathbreaking studies (Alkon, 1983).

First, it has been shown that this small animal can acquire (and extinguish) a Pavlovian form of associative learning. *Hermissenda* is positively phototaxic; that is, it tends to approach a source of light. (In *Hermissenda's* normal environment, moving upward toward sunlit water brings it into contact with its food supply.) With laboratory apparatus, the speed with which the animal moves toward a light source can be precisely measured. Now, if presentation of a light is repeatedly paired with rotation of the animal on a turntable, the snail will, as a consequence, be much less likely to approach light. (Again, in its natural environment, turbulence of the sea causes the snail to move to solid surfaces in deeper and darker water.) The important point is that the laboratory-induced inhibition of light-approaching behavior is a consequence of light-rotation *pairings*. Neither exposure to light alone, nor to rotation alone, nor to noncontingent presentations of light and rotation produces such inhibition.

This associative learning not to approach light has been correlated with measurable changes in the activity of the three "Type B" photoreceptors located in the snail's small eye.

Hermissenda Crassicornis.

Following the conditioning treatment, the Type B cells fire more vigorously when exposed to light. That increased activity of the Type B cells inhibits the firing of the two Type A cells in the animal's eye; and since the firing of Type A cells normally excites motor neurons that trigger the movement toward light, the net result is inhibition of positive phototaxis.

In addition, detailed microelectrode studies reveal that the light-rotation pairings produce a cumulative depolarization and increased input resistance of the Type B photoreceptors. However, these electrophysiological changes occur only when light and rotation are presented in a paired, Pavlovian fashion. What happens when we mimic this "natural" outcome of light-rotation pairings by directly injecting depolarizing current into a Type B cell of an anesthetized snail while presenting it with light? The results of five such light-current pairings were clear. When the animals were tested following recovery from the anesthesia, those that had received pairings displayed significantly more inhibition of phototaxis than did snails that received light and current injections unpaired (Farley, Richards et al., 1983). This ability to produce an apparent "conditioned response" by artificially inducing cellular changes normally observed in the course of conditioning clearly suggests that investigators are close to identifying important physical and chemical substrates of associative learning.

---

ample, when you shock a rat or expose it to a very loud noise, the animal usually exhibits a variety of emotional responses such as crying out, cringing, momentarily freezing, urinating, defecating, engaging in primitive escape behavior such as leaping or running about, or even exhibiting aggression. Other animals have different **species-specific patterns of response:** A cat may arch its back, a dog may bark, or a pigeon may flap its wings. Pairing an aversive stimulus such as shock (US) with some neutral stimulus like light (CS) will normally cause the light to evoke a response (CR) similar to that evoked by the shock (UR). The light becomes a **conditioned aversive stimulus.** A feature of such aversive conditioning is that it may take only a single pairing of CS and US to produce a strong conditioned response (sometimes called a **conditioned emotional response**) that is highly resistant to extinction. Furthermore, conditioned aversive stimuli can function as conditioned reinforcers, so other stimuli may become aversive simply

by being paired with them. As we shall see, this sort of emotional conditioning seems to occur quite readily in humans and is often difficult to fully understand or extinguish.

The manner in which animals learn to avoid certain foods **(conditioned food aversions)** offers a particularly interesting example of aversive conditioning. We said earlier that conditioning rarely occurs if the delay between the CS and a subsequent US extends beyond 1 or 2 seconds. Yet Garcia and Koelling (1966) have shown that rats will learn to avoid a food (CS) even though they are not made ill (US) until several hours after they eat. (The illness is actually induced by a process that is imperceptible to the rats, such as exposure to X rays.) This extraordinarily long delay between CS and US seems consistent with a wild animal's need to avoid foods that may not make them ill for several hours. Similar long delays between CS and US have been used to condition food aversions in birds. However, birds are highly visual animals and have been shown to condition much more readily to the color of a food than to its taste (Wilcoxin, Dragoin, & Kral, 1971).

Classical Conditioning of Humans

Perhaps the most widely cited example of classical conditioning in humans is the story of how a little boy named Albert was conditioned to fear rats by two psychologists, the famous behaviorist James B. Watson and Rosalie Raynor (Watson & Raynor, 1920). Poor little Albert enjoyed playing with the white laboratory rats until he received one pairing of a white rat (CS) with a sudden very loud noise behind him (US). After that, the sight of a white rat evoked a response (CR) very similar to the crying and fear (UR) typically evoked in a young child by a sudden loud noise. Albert is also said to have generalized this conditioned emotional response—showing fear of other small white animals and even a piece of white fur.

Many other examples of generalized emotional responses can be found in humans. The **Galvanic skin response (GSR),** a change in the electrical resistance of the skin related to sweating, is an unconditioned emotional reaction (see Chapter 12). When human subjects receive an electric shock (US), one of their emotional reactions (UR) is a marked GSR. The GSR is easily conditioned: If a pure tone is sounded shortly before the subjects receive a shock, after only one or two trials they show a pronounced GSR to the tone alone. When human subjects were conditioned to a particular tone, higher and lower tones also elicited a GSR. The GSR was greater when the test tone was close to the tone used as a CS during conditioning (Hovland, 1937). Both the generalization gradient and the effect of discrimination training are similar to those shown in Figure 6–4.

With people, the similarity of one stimulus to another may depend critically on higher-order learning such as language and symbolization. Thus Diven (1936) conditioned human subjects to make a GSR in response to the word "barn" embedded in a list of recited words. This was easily accomplished by following the word "barn" with an electric shock. When conditioning had been established, the subjects also displayed GSRs to such rural words as "cow" or "hay"—but not to neutral words like "table" or "chair." The generalization in this case obviously depended on the meanings of the words.

Another basic human emotional response is an increase in blood pressure (UR) following electric shock (US). Bykov (1957) paired a light (CS) with a shock until he could evoke a change in his subject's blood pressure (CR)

Drug Addiction and Classically Conditioned Tolerance

Siegel's (1976) application of a classical conditioning model to some of the phenomena of drug tolerance appears to have profound medical significance. When people use a drug such as morphine or heroin, they rapidly develop a tolerance for it. That is, larger and larger drug doses are required to produce the same (or any) effect on behavior and feeling. The physiological basis for such tolerance effects is beginning to be understood, but Siegel's studies suggest that classical conditioning may play a large role.

The immediate effect of a drug on our nervous system often triggers a *compensatory response, or opponent process,* which tends to counterbalance or cancel out the effect of the drug itself. Thus stimuli that precede the injection of a drug may become conditioned (act as a CS), not only to the immediate effects of the drug, but to the compensatory response as well. For example, the sight of the needle and preparation of a vein for injection may not only produce conditioned responses similar to the desired effect of a drug, but may also trigger conditioned compensatory processes before the drug is actually injected, thus reducing its ultimate effects.

Siegel (1977) tested this idea by giving rats morphine for several days until they showed signs of tolerance. One group of these rats simply rested for 12 days, while the rest were injected with a saline solution each day. Siegel reasoned that part of the tolerance was a conditioned opponent process triggered by the prick of the needle (CS). Thus repeated injections of the saline solution would serve as extinction trials (that is, the pinprick, the CS, is *not* followed by the injection of the drug, the US). Sure enough, the rats who had 12 days of saline injections subsequently showed less tolerance than the rats who simply rested for 12 days.

More recently, Siegel, Hinson, and their colleagues reported a study (1982) in which groups of rats were made tolerant of heroin by being given gradually larger injections every other day. Following a series of 15 such increasing doses, all animals were suddenly given a very much larger dose. The "overdose," enough to kill almost all rats without previous heroin experience, was given to half of the experimental animals in the *same*

(Alan Mercer/Stock, Boston)

room in which they had received their earlier injections. The other group of rats received their overdose in a *different room.* The overdose produced rapid death in many of the experimental rats—but death occurred twice as often in the group tested in the different room. The conditioned tolerance mechanism evidently failed to function when the environmental cues were drastically changed.

The general implications of Siegel's work is that at least part of the tolerance drug users develop should be considered a conditioned compensatory response triggered by the setting and preparation for drug use. This effect can be so strong that drug users with high tolerance might actually die from using their normal amount of heroin in an unusual setting where the conditioned compensatory response would be weaker.

simply by turning on the light. Similar sorts of conditioning may cause a business executive's blood pressure to rise whenever he goes into the office.

You can probably recall a number of conditioning examples from your own experience. Going to sleep in your own bed (US) as a little child normally evoked warm, relaxed feelings (UR). Repeated pairings of some favorite stuffed toy (CS) with this US made it likely that the toy would help you relax and go to sleep (CR) in a strange house or hospital room. The tension (CR) evoked by the sound (CS) of a dentist's drill owes much to previous pairings of that sound with actual drilling (US) and the resulting pain (UR).

Figure 6–6 By pairing the image of a slender, attractive body with a particular brand of yogurt, the advertiser hopes to condition an association between eating the yogurt and having such a body. (Dannon Co., Inc./Marstellar, Inc.).

You may have experienced a negative emotional response to someone and only later realized that he simply looked like a person who had hurt you long ago. Advertisers constantly seek to evoke a pleasurable (even sexual) response to the sight of their products by repeatedly pairing them with stimuli that already produce such responses: for example, a particular brand of perfume or designer jeans paired with highly erotic scenes (or for another example see Figure 6–6).

Many methods for helping people with emotional fears or aversions (phobias), or just bad habits, are based on studies of classical conditioning (see the Application: Drug Addiction and Classical Conditioned Tolerance). While these will be discussed more fully in our chapter on therapy (Chapter 18), some examples will be useful here.

Mourer and Mourer (1938) developed a treatment for children who wet their beds. They felt that the bed-wetter needed help in waking up when his or her bladder was full. They designed a special pad with an alarm bell to lay under the child during sleep. The moment any moisture reached the pad, the alarm bell was triggered. The feeling of a full bladder (CS) was then automatically paired with the alarm (US) that woke the child (UR). After many such pairings the full bladder (CS) woke the child (CR) in time to go to the bathroom.

People who have had violent or painful experiences may later have strong emotional responses to any stimuli associated with the traumatic event. For example, someone who has been involved in a severe car accident may be terrified to drive again or even to walk near a car. Extinction of this conditioned emotional response can be achieved by a process called **systematic desensitization.** For the accident victim afraid to drive, this process would consist of extinguishing the emotional response in situations progressively closer to actual driving: viewing pictures of cars, looking out the window at them, walking near them, touching them, and so on. This is much like discrimination training (see Figure 6–4) since the patient must learn to discriminate between simply being near or driving a car, and life-threatening driving situations where fear is appropriate. Another desensitization technique is called **flooding.** Here the patient is promptly reintroduced to driving but with a therapist present to give constant reassurance and support (Agras, 1985). This method immediately begins to train the patient to discriminate between ordinary driving and really dangerous situations. While this may produce faster discrimination learning, some patients are too frightened of actual driving to begin with that task.

OPERANT CONDITIONING

In the discussion of classical conditioning we saw how one stimulus can come to evoke a response similar to that evoked by another stimulus through repeated pairings of the two stimuli. The animal that came into the world with nothing but a Pavlovian learning mechanism might learn to salivate and to jerk its paw in response to a great many previously neutral stimuli, but it would not be capable of doing much else. There must, one might speculate, be a learning mechanism that works in a more direct way to change and to shape responses. The question becomes: How are new responses learned? Many appear to be learned because of their consequences. For example, an animal repeatedly returns to a particular place because it finds food or water there; it finds other reliable places to escape the

Circuses featured trained animal acts long before formal theories of conditioning and learning. (Seurat: *Le Cirque.* Paris, Jeu de Paume; Art Resource)

cold or avoid predators. Since the animal learns to *operate* on its world in ways that produce certain desired consequences, this sort of learning has been called **operant conditioning.** (It is also sometimes called **instrumental conditioning,** since the animal's behavior is instrumental in producing a certain outcome.)

The Pavlovian kind of experiment is performed on a basically passive animal, generally kept under rather severe restraints. The sequence of CS followed by US is continually repeated, and the animal begins to make a reflexlike response to the CS. In operant conditioning, on the other hand, the animal quite literally operates actively on its environment. The animal must itself push the lever, or peck the key, before its response can be followed by reinforcement. Without activity on the animal's part—often motivated by a strong drive state such as hunger—there could be no operant conditioning.

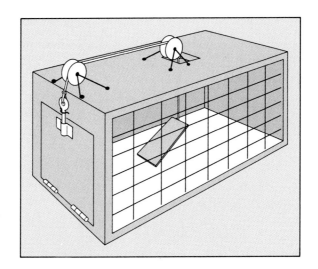

Figure 6–7 One of Thorndike's puzzle boxes. A cat could only escape from the box by pressing down on the treadle, which pulled the string, releasing the bolt holding the door closed. (After Thorndike, 1911)

The Work of Edward Thorndike and B. F. Skinner

Just a few years before Pavlov began his study of conditioned reflexes in Russia, the first studies of what would eventually be called operant conditioning were done in the United States by Edward L. Thorndike. In his doctoral dissertation Thorndike criticized the largely anecdotal evidence for animal intelligence advanced by many naturalists, including Charles Darwin. Stories of how animals reasoned solutions to problems much like humans were not convincing to Thorndike. His careful study of how cats escaped from various puzzle boxes (see Figure 6–7) suggested something more like **trial-and-error learning:** a blind attempt at one possible means of escape after another, until one just happens to work. Thorndike believed that the *satisfying effect* of a successful response made it more likely to occur the next time the cat was placed in the box. He called this the **law of effect.** Thorndike repeatedly placed the cat back in the puzzle box, each time recording how

Figure 6–8 Thorndike's record of the time it took a cat to escape from the puzzle box (see Figure 6–7) on successive trials. The gradual, if erratic, reduction in the time required to escape suggested a kind of trial-and-error learning process, not the sudden "insight" or thoughtful solution some naturalists would have expected.

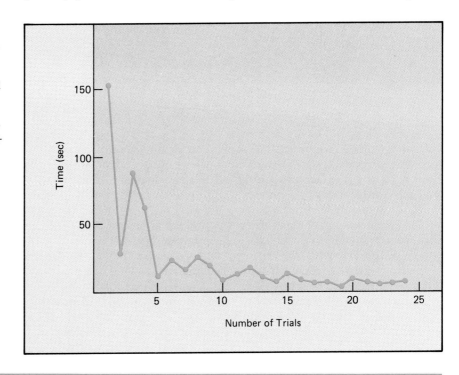

long it took the animal to escape on that trial. (Figure 6–8 shows how long it took one cat to escape on each of a series of such trials.) Thorndike argued that such learning curves suggested no sudden insight or understanding, but simply a gradual, if erratic, increase in speed. A cat might seem very intelligent if one only saw it perform after it had many learning trials. However, the learning process seemed to require no more than blind trial-and-error plus the law of effect.

The person most closely identified with the study of operant conditioning, in fact the man who first suggested the term, is B. F. Skinner (1904–   ). Skinner began his work in the late 1930s, committed to a program of strict behaviorism. He saw Thorndike's concern with the satisfying or desirable nature of an effect as needlessly mentalistic. It was only necessary to show that when a response was followed by a certain outcome or consequence, it was more likely to occur in the future.

In operant conditioning, the sequence of a response and a subsequent event that makes the response more likely is called **reinforcement.** (Note: Reinforcement has a different meaning in operant conditioning than it does in classical conditioning.) Sometimes the event involves the *presentation* of a stimulus, such as food or water. These stimuli are called **positive reinforcers.** Other times the event involves the *removal or cessation* of a stimulus such as an electric shock or an extremely loud noise. These stimuli are called **negative reinforcers.** Whether the experimenter presents a positive reinforcer or removes a negative one, reinforcement always makes the response more likely to occur.

Basic Principles of Operant Conditioning

Much of Skinner's research dealt with the operant conditioning of laboratory rats. The rat was typically isolated in a so-called **Skinner box** (Figure 6–9) where the experimenter had total control of the rat's environment and the consequences of its behavior. For example, the equipment could be programmed to give the rat a pellet of food each time the animal pressed a lever. At first, an untrained rat might go for some time before accidently pressing the lever and receiving food. However, if the food acted as a positive reinforcer, the rate of pressing would gradually increase, with each reinforcement making the next press more likely. Skinner recorded bar presses on a moving sheet of paper, with each press moving the recording pen one

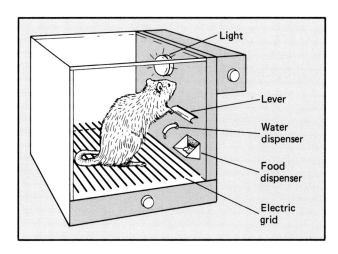

Figure 6–9 A Skinner box for rats. The animal could be observed for long periods of time with automatic recording of such responses as pressing a bar on the side of the cage. Stimuli such as lights, tones, electric shocks, food pellets, and water were all under experimental control.

Light

Lever

Water dispenser

Food dispenser

Electric grid

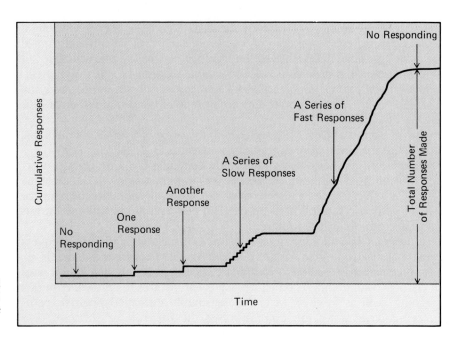

Figure 6–10 The cumulative record made by a rat reinforced with a small food pellet for each lever press made in a Skinner box.

step higher. Figure 6–10 shows the sort of **cumulative record** this provided. The rat might remain in the box an hour or so each day, gradually obtaining its fill of food more rapidly until acquisition of the bar press response was complete. If at this point the apparatus was reprogrammed so that a bar press no longer produced food, extinction would gradually occur: The rat would make fewer and fewer presses until the behavior was no more likely to occur than before the first reinforcement.

Acquisition of operant conditioning proceeds faster with larger reinforcements—just as Pavlovian conditioning is a function of the strength of the US. There is also a critical time interval that profoundly affects operant conditioning. To maximize operant conditioning, the reinforcement must be delivered immediately after the response occurs. The time (if any) between a

If in the past a vending machine has always delivered each time you put in coins, once the machine stops paying off, one of your reactions will probably be to stop feeding it coins. Even stronger reactions to the lack of reinforcement may soon follow. (Irene Springer)

response and the subsequent reinforcement is referred to as the **delay of reinforcement.** Even short delays of reinforcement—on the order of 5 or 10 seconds—are often enough to prevent operant conditioning from taking place at all with animals; and any delay, no matter how short, slows down the rate of acquisition (Figure 6–11).

Shaping.   One might have to wait a long time before an untrained rat made its first lever press. Since no learning occurs until a reinforcement is given, this is essentially wasted time. To speed things up, Skinner used a technique called **shaping.** Watching the rat closely, he could manually trigger delivery of a food pellet each time the rat began to approach the bar. Reinforcing this likely response made it that much more likely to occur again. Once the rat had learned to spend most of its time near the lever, Skinner could demand a closer approximation to an actual lever press. Only if the rat touched the wall near the lever would a food pellet be delivered. Again, this would occur quickly, be reinforced, and then be even more likely to occur. Skinner found that this method of **successive approximations** usually resulted in a lever press sooner than simply waiting for the first response to occur without such shaping.

Shaping is most useful when the desired operant might never occur at all without shaping. For example, Skinner is reputed to have entertained guests at a lawn party by conditioning a dog to climb a stepladder. Since this was unlikely to occur spontaneously, he employed a gradual shaping process. First he gave the dog a small piece of food each time it even moved in the general direction of the ladder. Once this began to occur more often, he would only give the dog food when it moved within 10 feet of the ladder, then only when it moved within 5 feet, then only when it touched the ladder, and so on, until the dog actually climbed the ladder. At each stage he was able to reinforce, and thereby increase the likelihood of, the operant response defined for that stage. This, in turn, made it feasible to move on to the next stage.

An interesting variant of regular shaping is called **autoshaping.** In studies of operant conditioning of pigeons it was often necessary to first shape them to peck a lighted key in the pigeon version of a Skinner box (see Figure 6–12). This was a time-consuming process since someone, usually a graduate student, had to closely watch the pigeon in order to deliver food at the right moments. One graduate student tried something different (Brown & Jenkins,

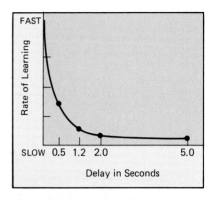

Figure 6–11   A delay-of-reward gradient observed in operant conditioning in rats. Note that even a very small delay between responding and the subsequent reinforcement can drastically slow down the rate of learning.

Figure 6–12   A Skinner box for pigeons in which the birds typically pecked lighted keys to obtain food and water (rather than the rats' bar press, Figure 6–9).

1968). He put a hungry but totally untrained pigeon in a box where, once a minute, the key light came on for a few seconds. *Each time the light went off, a food hopper opened briefly, regardless of what the bird did.* Within a short time the bird approached the key, and began to peck at it. This allowed the experimenter to begin automatically recording and reinforcing pecks without ever needing to shape the bird by hand. Autoshaping seems to occur because of *classical conditioning:* The pairing of a lighted key (CS) and food (US) eventually conditions the bird to peck the key (CR) much as he pecks food (UR). This view is consistent with observations that pigeons peck the key as if they were eating when food is the reinforcer, but peck it with beaks open, as if drinking, when water is the reinforcer (Figure 6–13).

Partial Reinforcement. Skinner found that a rat will respond even more rapidly if only some of its lever presses produce food. Furthermore, following a **partial reinforcement** schedule of this sort the rat will continue to respond much longer during extinction (when no reinforcement occurs). These *partial reinforcement effects* can be obtained by reducing the proportion of trials that are reinforced. However, it is crucial that the proportion of reinforced responses be reduced slowly at first, to avoid extinguishing the response. The animal will eventually respond very rapidly for only an occasional reinforcement (some pigeons have made thousands of pecks an hour for only a few reinforcements) and will continue to respond for a very long time without any extinction. Skinner investigated several other types of partial reinforcement schedules: for example, only reinforcing responses made at least 30 seconds apart (a **fixed-interval schedule**). The characteristics of many different reinforcement schedules have been described in detail by Ferster and Skinner (1957). The most interesting fact is that the same schedule has very much the same effect, no matter what response, what reinforcer, and what species are involved. The cumulative record produced by a pigeon pecking a key for grain under a certain kind of schedule cannot be distinguished from the cumulative record produced by a person pulling a plunger for cigarette rewards under the same schedule.

Discrimination, Generalization and Conditioned Reinforcers. The phenomena known as discrimination and generalization found in classical conditioning are also present in operant conditioning. Animals can be trained to *discriminate* the presence or absence of a certain stimulus by only reinforcing a response when the stimulus is present. A rat might only be given food for a bar press when a tone is sounded, or a pigeon given food for pecking a key when the key is lighted. Eventually, the rat will press the lever only when the tone is sounded, and the pigeon peck the key only when it is lighted. Note that the stimulus appears to control the behavior, since (if the animal is sufficiently hungry or thirsty) presenting the stimulus evokes the response. The animal will also show evidence of *generalization* by responding to stimuli that are simply similar to the one that preceded reinforcement in the past.

Animals can be trained to discriminate between two very similar stimuli using the same basic procedure. For example, suppose a rat had been trained to respond when a 1,000 Hz tone was sounded, and you then occasionally presented 500 Hz tones with no reinforcement. At first the rat would generalize, responding at least sometimes to the 500 Hz tone. However, responding to that tone would gradually extinguish. Proceeding in this fashion, one could determine exactly how small a difference in pitch the rat

Figure 6–13 A pigeon will peck the key differently after autoshaping (see text), depending on whether food or water is used as the CS. The pecks are (a) similar to eating (head down, beak more closed) when food is used, and (b) similar to drinking (head up, beak open) when water is used. It is as if the CR is similar to the UR (approach and consume) evoked either by food or by water, depending on the CS. Once pecking is established through classical conditioning, it can be automatically reinforced in an operant conditioning procedure. (Courtesy B. Moore, Dalhousie University)

Using the Visual Abilities of Pigeons

Humans use animals for food and beasts of burden. But what about using their senses and minds? At least a few examples come readily to mind: seeing-eye dogs, bloodhounds, sheep dogs. You can probably think of others. In this application we will consider three efforts to use the extraordinary visual abilities of pigeons—abilities that cannot yet be matched by the best modern computer vision system. The pigeon, unlike the computer, can learn to recognize a form regardless of its size and orientation, just as it recognizes a tree seen from any distance or angle. Furthermore, the pigeon has a wider field of view than a human, with excellent acuity and color vision over most of the field rather than the two or three degrees afforded by the human fovea. Using techniques of conditioning, pigeons have been successfully trained to perform useful visual tasks.

Early in World War II Harvard professor B. F. Skinner began a secret military project aimed at teaching a pigeon to fly a missile. The idea was to mount the pigeon in the missile so that it could steer by pecking at a viewing screen on which the forward course of the missile was optically projected. If the missile was headed directly toward a target (e.g., a ship or a building), the target's image would appear in the center of the screen: A peck there would not alter the missile's course. However, if the missile moved off course, the target's image would drift to one side of the screen. Pecks there would electrically trigger a change in the missile's course such that the image would move back toward the center of the screen. In this way the valiant (but doomed) pigeon would guide the missile to its target. All Skinner had to do was to train pigeons to peck at a target *wherever* it appeared on the screen.

To train his pigeons Skinner mounted the front of a missile on a motor-driven framework that could be moved across the floor of his laboratory. Pictures of targets were attached to the laboratory wall and projected onto the pigeon's viewing screen, just as they would be in the air. At first training was very simple: Any peck on the screen was *reinforced* (rewarded with food). When pecking occurred frequently enough, the next stage of training began. The apparatus was placed close to the wall and the image of a target alternately presented and removed. The new reinforced response, or *operant,* was a peck anywhere on the screen *with the target present.* If the pigeon pecked in the absence of a target, there was a *time-out* (a brief period of total darkness with no food). Gradually, the animal learned to peck when the target was present and not peck when it was absent (i.e., it learned to *discriminate*). Next the target was slowly moved about so that its image shifted on the screen, and the operant was now defined as a peck *directly on the target.* Shaped in this way, the bird came to control the course of the simulated missile as it was wheeled across the laboratory toward the mock target on the wall.

Notice that in the laboratory Skinner could tell whether each peck should be reinforced or not, but of course this would not be possible in combat. Thus in order to keep the pigeon pecking without reinforcement, Skinner gradually altered the laboratory *reinforcement schedule* so that the bird only occasionally received a reinforcement for a correct response. This *partial reinforcement schedule* not only made the pigeon's conditioning more resistant to *extinction* (it would continue pecking without reinforcement), but also caused it to peck more rapidly, improving its control of the missile.

Alas, even though Skinner's pigeons were demonstrably successful pilots, they never flew a mission. The Air Force, never too enthusiastic about feathered pilots, chose to use newly developed electronic control systems instead.

There is a sequel to the story. After the war one of Skinner's assistants, Thom Verhave, went to work for a drug company. There he saw a way of using what Skinner's team had learned from the wartime project. The drug company employed a team of "quality control" personnel who watched pills pass by on a conveyor belt. Each time they noted a misshapen or discolored pill they picked it out. Verhave wondered whether pigeons couldn't do the job just as well or better. First he constructed a tubular system that presented pills, one at a time, in a window in front of a pigeon. He then gradually shaped the pigeon's pecking behavior: first reinforcing any peck; next reinforcing only pecks given a misshapen or discolored pill (with a "time-out" for inappropriate pecks); and finally shifting to a partial reinforcement schedule so that the pigeon would continue to peck without reinforcement. After such training the birds demonstrated better quality control (detection of defective pills) than their human counterparts.

Perhaps you can guess what happened when Verhave presented his results to the drug company. First of all, management felt customers might be a little nervous if they learned quality control was being handled by pigeons. Second, the workers' union was outraged. How could anyone be cruel enough to rob workers of a job in this way? It was bad enough to be replaced by a machine, but a pigeon! (Although one wonders how kind it was to use human workers to do a job a pigeon could do.)

Thus in spite of demonstrated ability, pigeons have been rejected as pilots and quality controllers. Is there no clear application for their extraordinary visual skills? Navy psychologist Jim Simmons may finally have found one. Over the past few years tests have been conducted in which pigeons mounted in a plexiglass station beneath a helicopter have participated in air-sea rescue missions. They were trained to peck a key only if they saw a red, yellow, or orange object in the ocean below (the colors of most life rafts). The pigeons proved to be almost twice as accurate in detecting life rafts as the human observers (Stark, 1981). Pigeons' superior visual abilities make them ideal searchers. Furthermore, by using three birds at a time and having each monitor a third of the horizon, it is possible to simultaneously search in all directions.

Thus Skinner's World War II idea of training pigeons to provide useful visual services for humans may at last be realized—only in ways that can save lives rather than destroy them.

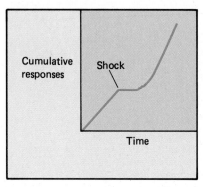

Figure 6–14 A shock (see arrow) temporarily suppresses the bar pressing of a rat, but after a while, pressing resumes at an even faster rate, so that the total number of responses is eventually the same as if no shock had been given.

could discriminate. Similarly, one could train a pigeon to discriminate progressively smaller differences in key light color in order to determine the limits of its color discrimination. *Animal psychophysics* of just this sort has been used to determine the sensory capacities of lower organisms (see the Application: Using the Visual Abilities of Pigeons).

As indicated earlier in our discussion of classical conditioning, repeatedly pairing a stimulus with a primary reinforcer tends to endow the stimulus with similar reinforcing properties. Stimuli that consistently precede positive reinforcement in discrimination learning become *conditioned positive reinforcers*. For example, if a pigeon's pecks produce food only when the key is lighted, lighting the key eventually becomes a conditioned reinforcer. Some other response, such as lifting a foot, will occur more frequently if it is consistently followed by illumination of the key.

Punishment, Escape, and Avoidance. You may recall that negative reinforcers, such as shock or a very loud noise, are often called aversive stimuli in classical conditioning. In operant conditioning, the presentation of a negative reinforcer is referred to as **punishment** (its removal is reinforcing).

Skinner distinguished between the temporary suppression of responding produced by punishment and the reinforcing effect of the cessation of punishment. Figure 6–14 shows how a rat, previously conditioned to press a lever to obtain food, temporarily stopped pressing after being shocked. After a while, the animal not only resumed pressing but increased its rate, so that it eventually made as many responses as it would have if it hadn't been shocked. Skinner suggested that the only real conditioning produced by punishment was the classical conditioning of such emotional responses as agitation and aggression. These responses may actually interfere with subsequent operant conditioning. Hitting an animal that is not housebroken may produce such severe emotional responses that it will not learn to scratch the front door in order to go out. The best way to get rid of a response is simply not to reinforce it (so the response will extinguish) and to reinforce incompatible responses (so they will occur instead). If you want to extinguish your dog's habit of begging from the dining room table, you should never feed it there. However, you can also reinforce an alternative response of staying in the kitchen by making sure that you place food there for the dog. Nevertheless, punishment is a quick way of halting undesirable behavior and may also allow responses to occur that can be reinforced.

The primitive emotional and escape behavior initially evoked by punishment can be modified through the conditioning of a specific **escape response.** For example, a rat can learn to escape (or turn off) shock by jumping over a barrier, turning clockwise, or even pressing a lever. In each case, the response terminates punishment (a negative reinforcer), which constitutes reinforcement.

Avoidance learning is an elaboration of simple escape training. Here the animal can respond to a stimulus presented prior to the punishment, and thereby totally *avoid* it. For example, Solomon, Kamin, and Wynne (1953) trained dogs in a shuttle box like that shown in Figure 6–15. When one side of the box was lighted, the dog had a few seconds in which to jump over the middle barrier to the darker side before the floor was electrified on the lighted side. The dogs quickly learned to avoid receiving a shock by jumping over the barrier each time their side of the box was illuminated. After enough training a dog might *calmly* jump over the barrier each time the light came on, avoiding any shocks for thousands of trials.

There has been considerable theoretical debate as to exactly what would cause the persistence of avoidance responses for so long when the animal is never shocked. One explanation is that the warning stimulus itself, by virtue of its previous pairing with shock, becomes a conditioned aversive stimulus (Mourer, 1947). Thus the animal's avoidance response serves to diminish, distance, or terminate the warning stimulus. For example, Kamin (1956) terminated a warning buzzer as soon as the animal made what would ordinarily be the avoidance response. *But he then shocked the animal anyway.* Even so, the animal learned to make the response. The termination of the warning buzzer apparently functioned as a *conditioned negative reinforcer.* As indicated earlier, conditioned aversions or emotional responses seem particularly resistant to extinction and escape from a warning stimulus may support avoidance responses for a very long time with no shocks.

What happens when an animal can neither avoid nor escape highly aversive stimuli such as electric shock? Seligman and Meier (1975) exposed two groups of dogs to occasional shocks. Both groups were restrained in harnesses and received the same number of shocks, but the dogs in the *escape group* could turn off the shock (escape from it) by pressing a lever with their noses. The dogs in the *helpless group* had no control whatsoever over the shocks. Each dog in the helpless group was paired ("yoked") with a dog in the escape group, receiving exactly the same shocks. The dogs from each group were then compared in their ability to learn a conventional shock-avoidance task. While dogs from the escape group learned the new task, the dogs from the helpless group tended to simply cower and take their shocks without learning to avoid. Seligman termed this behavior **learned helplessness.** We will consider this phenomenon again later in the chapter when we discuss the cognitive aspects of learning.

Finally, it should be pointed out that in both escape and avoidance training, animals learn faster if the required response is similar to a *species-specific defense response* or the natural defense response of the animals' species (Bolles, 1970). For example, a pigeon might learn to escape or avoid shock very quickly if this involved flapping its wings, whereas a dog might learn most rapidly if it was required to bark. This is still another example of the predispositions toward learning certain tasks that each species carries in its genes (see the Highlight: Ethology and Learning).

Figure 6–15 A shuttle box similar to that used by Solomon, Kamin, and Wynne (1953). A shock was presented on one side of the box a few seconds after a light went on. Dogs learned to jump over the central barrier each time one side of the box was illuminated in order to avoid a shock.

Gold medals in gymnastics, won by the U.S. team at the 1984 Summer Olympics, are a good example of a secondary reinforcer. (Duhamel/ Mega/Photo Researchers)

Operant Conditioning of Humans

Humans also learn behaviors that either gain them positive reinforcers or remove (or avoid) negative reinforcers (i.e., remove or avoid punishment). While some of these reinforcers seem "built-in" rather than learned (food, water, painful stimuli), most people seem to be conditioned by *secondary reinforcers* (a grade of A or F, compliments or criticisms, a friend's smile or frown, an Olympic Gold Medal). Again, as with animals, reinforcement is most effective if it closely follows the response. This is clearly why humans acquire a number of secondary reinforcers that can be used more conveniently than primary ones: "Good work!" or "Thanks for your help. How about letting me buy you dinner next week?"

In fact, a variety of child-rearing and educational techniques have been based on the principles of operant conditioning initially studied with laboratory animals. For those who wish to modify behavior through the systematic application of reinforcement, **Premack's principle** (Premack, 1965) provides an invaluable rule of thumb. Premack reported that he could train thirsty rats to increase their running in a rotating cage if running were followed by access to drinking; at the same time, he could train exercise-deprived rats to increase their drinking if drinking were followed by access to running. The general principle suggested by Premack's study was that a more preferred activity could be used to reinforce a less preferred activity. The parent who tells a shy but athletic child, "You can play ball after you go to the dance," while telling his sociable but nonathletic sibling, "You can go to the dance after you play ball," has understood Premack's principle.

Despite the argument that punishment only suppresses behavior temporarily, it does have a place in controlling human behavior. If a child runs into the street without looking or plays with matches, the immediate suppression of that behavior may be lifesaving. Nevertheless, positive reinforcement of an alternative response remains the best hope of permanently changing a given behavior. Otherwise the bad habit may simply return, or the child may learn to discriminate those situations where a parent is watching and avoid punishment by only behaving badly at other times. What seems crucial is for the parent to watch for good behavior, such as stopping at the curb or looking both ways before entering the street, and to provide some immediate positive reinforcement. Unfortunately, some parents are more likely to punish bad behavior than to reinforce good behavior.

Skinner is particularly critical of the use of punishment in the classroom. Too often, he says, children who fall behind in some class receive so much punishment (criticism by the teacher, taunting and laughter from other students, and low grades) that they develop conditioned emotional responses to school. These emotional responses interfere with future learning and are difficult to extinguish.

Aside from the many applications of operant conditioning in child rearing and education, much everyday human behavior is under considerable stimulus control. Your ability to drive a car is a good example: stopping at traffic signs or red lights, starting on the green, staying within your lane, and varying your speed as you pass schools or enter highways. Social stimuli are particularly important. The response of others to our behavior in social situations often dictates our responses. For example, a young man who noticed that his conversation was producing yawns and little eye contact from a pretty companion might learn to modify his behavior so as to gain a desired social goal.

With just a little planning, and without any apparatus at all, it should be possible for you to demonstrate some of the basic phenomena of operant conditioning while apparently engaging in casual conversation with a friend. The following experiment was reported by Verplank (1955), and can easily be repeated by anyone.

The basic rule of operant conditioning is to follow a particular response with the delivery of a reinforcer. The response that Verplank selected for reinforcement was any statement of opinion made in the course of conversation. That is, whenever the subject uttered a sentence beginning with "It seems to me" or "I think" or "I believe," the experimenter reinforced the statement. The reinforcer was verbal agreement, perhaps given with a nod of smiling approval. Thus whenever the subject expressed an opinion, the experimenter responded with some such remark as "That's true," or "I agree," or "How right you are!" The delivery of such verbal reinforcement had a marked effect on the subject's behavior. There was a clear increase in the frequency with which the subject made statements of opinion. To clinch matters, the experimenter went on to demonstrate that extinction could be brought about simply by withholding further reinforcement. When this happened, the statements of opinion decreased markedly.

Two notes of caution must be sounded for readers who wish to attempt this experiment. First, you may have to wait some time before your subject utters a first statement of opinion (recall that in operant conditioning a response must occur before it can be reinforced). Second, it is possible that your subject may "catch on" to what you are doing.

Partial-reinforcement effects are both powerful and widespread in human learning. Perhaps the most direct example can be found in the behavior of hardened slot machine players in a gambling casino. They will rapidly and continuously deposit coins and pull levers, sometimes using two machines at a time, with only a small proportion of these responses paying off. However, there are many practical training situations in which partial-reinforcement effects seem to be totally ignored. Imagine a little girl who cries each night when put to bed. The parents come to realize that they have unknowingly reinforced this behavior by picking her up and comforting her. To break her now bothersome habit, they adopt a psychologically sound principle: The habit will no longer be reinforced. When she cries on future nights, they will no longer comfort her. This withholding of reinforcement should gradually eliminate the habit. The difficulty arises when after a few nights of listening to the child cry herself to sleep, her parents relent and—just this once—pick her up and comfort her. The child has now experienced partial reinforcement of her bedtime crying and the habit will be harder than ever to extinguish.

Suppose that you wish to train a child to perform a socially desirable behavior. While common sense suggests that this can best be done by rewarding the behavior each time it occurs, the partial-reinforcement effect suggests otherwise. We usually want to "build in" desirable behaviors in our children: The behavior should persist even when it is no longer followed by the immediate rewards that seem right for children. To build in such *persistence* and resistance to extinction, partial reinforcement seems a better bet than continuous reinforcement. Praising children each time they clean their rooms, might be all right at first. However, only occasional praise (partial reinforcement) might be more appropriate in preparing them for living at college, where that and other socially desirable behaviors should persist without praise.

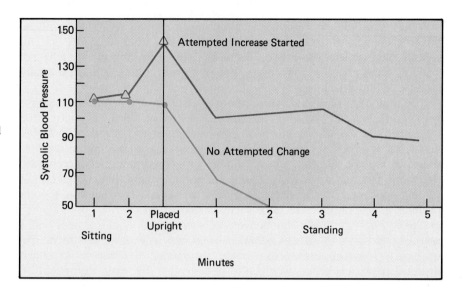

Figure 6–16 A patient whose blood pressure dropped precipitously whenever he stood up, learned to voluntarily increase his blood pressure using biofeedback. The feedback was a tone that sounded whenever his blood pressure increased. The graph shows how this learned behavior could maintain blood pressure when the patient stood up (was placed upright). (After Miller & Brucker, 1979)

The following case study, taken from Ayllon (1963), illustrates an ingenious and systematic use of basic operant conditioning concepts in a mental hospital setting. The patient was a schizophrenic woman who wore enormous amounts of clothing—many sweaters, shawls, dresses, underclothes, and even sheets and towels wrapped around her body. The total weight of her clothing was 25 pounds. To get the patient to give up this odd symptom, Ayllon made effective use of the shaping technique, with food as a reinforcer. To get into the hospital dining room, the patient had to step on a scale and was required to weigh less than a target weight selected by the experimenter. Thus, at first, the patient had to reduce the weight of her clothing to 23 (rather than 25) pounds. When this limit was met, a stricter limit was used, and so on. Although the patient missed a few meals during this shaping process, in a few months she was wearing only 3 pounds of clothing. The systematic use of food as a reinforcer had gradually eliminated a bizarre psychiatric symptom. The conditioning treatment in no way "cured" the patient of her schizophrenia and its many other symptoms. However, as Ayllon pointed out, once the odd symptom was eliminated, other patients in the hospital were more likely to talk to and interact with the woman. In fact, her family took her home for a visit for the first time in nine years, relieved that the patient no longer looked like a "circus freak."

Biofeedback also employs the basic principle of operant conditioning. **Biofeedback** can be defined as a procedure that gives subjects information about their own internal processes, allowing them to monitor and modify a number of normally involuntary responses. Working with paralyzed hospital patients, Miller and Brucker (1979) have reported some fascinating results concerned with the voluntary control of blood pressure. They worked first with a man whose spinal cord had been severed by a gunshot wound and who, although he had strong arms and shoulders, had been unable to walk with crutches and braces. The man's problem, a consequence of his injury, was severe postural hypotension. That is, whenever he was placed in an upright position, his blood pressure fell so low that he promptly fainted. To combat the hypotension, an apparatus was hooked up to the patient in such a way that whenever his blood pressure increased slightly, an audible tone was produced. With practice, the patient learned to produce very large increases

in his blood pressure. This in turn made it possible for him to boost his blood pressure high enough so that he did not faint when placed upright. The remarkable results are illustrated in Figure 6–16, which shows the patient's blood pressure in the first few minutes after being placed in a standing position. When he did not try to control his blood pressure, it fell to a dangerously low level within 2 minutes; but by producing a voluntary increase just before standing, he was able to maintain normal blood pressure. This facilitated his learning to walk with crutches and braces, and at last report he had been doing so for more than three years.

To assure themselves that the spectacular result with their first paralyzed patient was not a fluke or an artifact, Miller and Brucker then worked with ten additional patients, all paralyzed by severe spinal injuries. During practice sessions without biofeedback, none of the patients learned to raise their blood pressure. However, when feedback was provided, nine out of ten patients learned to produce large increases in their blood pressure within 25 practice sessions. Moreover, the changes in pressure observed over the course of the 25 sessions produced a typical Thorndike-like learning curve.

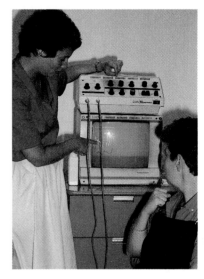

Experiments have shown that when subjects are given knowledge of their bodily states (biofeedback) in the form of audible tones, moving graphs, or dials, they can learn to control such bodily responses as brain-wave pattern, blood pressure, and muscle tension. Here a subject learns biofeedback techniques as an adjunct to treatment for chronic headaches. (Harriet Newman/Monkmeyer Press)

COGNITIVE ASPECTS OF ANIMAL LEARNING

Most of the early work in the conditioning of animals was highly behavioristic and any consideration of an animal's cognitive processes was strictly taboo. Pavlov's approach was that of a physiologist interested solely in objective phenomena. Skinner and his contemporaries intentionally avoided speculations concerning cognitive processes. They wanted to break with the older philosophical mentalism, which they felt had kept psychology from becoming a true natural science. Today, inferences about mental processes based on objective phenomena are part of the natural science of psychology. While no one believes the cognitive processes of lower organisms are the same as those found in humans, it does seem useful to make some inferences about them.

Early Studies of Animal Cognition

Both prior to and during the period of extreme behaviorism in psychology there were attempts to study cognitive aspects of animal learning. We shall consider three such areas of study: insight, learning sets, and latent learning.

Insight.   Some of the most vigorous criticisms of early conditioning studies came from the Gestalt psychologists (see Chapter 4). They argued that the learning observed by Pavlov and Thorndike only seemed blind and mechanical because the experimental situations employed in such studies offered little opportunity for the animal to exhibit truly creative or insightful behavior. Gestalt psychologists felt that to study **insight** (a form of learning and problem solving that depends on complex cognitive abilities), one must choose a suitable experimental situation. A Gestalt psychologist named Wolfgang Köhler (1927) conducted a classic study of insight learning by chimpanzees. The kind of procedure he used can best be seen in the *two-stick problem* (see Figure 6–17). The chimp was in its cage; easily visible on the floor outside the cage was a tempting banana. There was a short stick on the floor of the cage, and a longer stick on the floor just outside the cage. When first

The early behavioristic view of learning in psychology saw the choice of a conditioned stimulus in classical conditioning, or of a response in operant conditioning, as essentially arbitrary. So long as the organism was sensitive to the stimulus and could physically manage the response, learning could take place. However, it has become increasingly clear that animals, including humans, have *instinctual predispositions to learn* some things and not others. We have pointed out a number of these genetically based predispositions in our disucssions of classical and operant conditioning. For example, rats have a species-specific tendency to develop food aversions on the basis of taste, while pigeons develop food aversions on the basis of color. This makes ecological sense since rats are nocturnal animals that must depend heavily on taste and smell, whereas pigeons are diurnal animals with highly developed visual abilities.

Our growing appreciation of the role of genetically based factors in learning has led psychologists to look more closely at the field of ethology—the study of instinct (genetically based behavioral tendencies). In Chapter 1 we discussed how an ethologist named Nikolas Tinbergen (1951) studied the fighting behavior of the stickleback fish. He showed that a male stickleback attacks any object that vaguely resembles another fish so long as it has red on its underside (see Figure 1–11). In the language of ethology, the red underside (common to male sticklebacks during mating season) is a **sign** (or *releasing*) **stimulus** that triggers the **motor program** of attack. Both the sign stimulus and the motor program are instinctual. Another example of this comes from the work done by Konrad Lorenz (1966), whose ethological research on wild geese won him the Nobel prize. Geese build their nests on the ground and sit on them to incubate their eggs. If an egg accidentally rolls out of the nest, the bird cranes its neck, eyes the errant egg, rises, and slowly rolls the egg back into the nest with its bill. Is this something that the goose learned from its parents? Or is it creative problem solving? Neither. Lorenz was able to show that virtually any convex object placed near the nest would serve as a *sign stimulus* for the instinctual *motor program* of egg rolling. Such sign stimuli are not always effective in evoking motor programs; often they work only when the animal is in a certain biological **drive state.** For example, Lorenz found that egg rolling was only evoked during a drive state that arose two weeks before egg laying and persisted for two weeks after the eggs were hatched. (Biologically based drive states are discussed further in Chapter 11.)

Instincts represent knowledge about the world carried from one generation to the next by genes. Organisms also acquire knowledge during their lifetimes through learning (e.g., classical and operant conditioning processes). The point we wish to emphasize here is that these two sources of knowledge interact: *What is learned is often influenced by instinct.* For example, Lorenz found that during a certain *drive state* arising shortly after birth young goslings will follow almost any receding object that emits a particular "kum-kum" call. The call is a *sign stimulus* for the *motor program* of following a receding object. Furthermore, if the goslings once follow an object in this manner, they tend to follow it in the future—a process Lorenz called **imprinting.** Normally, of course, the receding object imprinted upon the baby gosling is its mother. However, Lorenz found that almost any receding object would do, including himself (see Figure A). Since the imprinted "object to be followed" depends on the gosling's experience, it is not fully defined by the genes, it is also learned.

Notice that one could consider the sign stimulus (the "kum-kum" call) as an unconditioned stimulus (at least during the drive state), the motor

presented with this problem the chimp typically reached between the cage bars in a futile effort to obtain the banana. When this failed, the chimp would fly into a temper tantrum. After calm returned, the eye of the chimp was suddenly drawn to the stick inside its cage. Then, very quickly, the chimp picked up the short stick, ran to the front of the cage, and tried to rake the banana in with the stick. The stick, however, was not long enough. This failure would produce a real temper tantrum. To shorten the story, a bright chimp would eventually notice the long stick just outside the cage. Then, quick as a flash— we talk of the "flash of insight"—the chimp would rake in the long stick with the short stick, and immediately use the long stick to rake in the banana. (The same kind of insightful solutions occurred when the banana was suspended out of reach from the cage ceiling and three boxes were scattered about the cage floor. After sizing up the situation, the chimp would stack the three boxes into a kind of tower, climb the tower, and obtain the banana.)

In Köhler's view, these problem solutions depended on the chimp's ability to restructure cognitive elements into a new and purposeful whole. The chimp seemed to be thinking much as you and I do. Köhler stressed that this

program (the following behavior) as an unconditioned response, and the receding object as a particularly suitable conditioned stimulus. A single pairing of US and CS conditions the gosling to follow (CR) the object in the

future. Viewed in this way, imprinting is a special form of classical conditioning highly determined by instinct.

Something like imprinting occurs between a mother bird and her newly hatched chicks. The cuckoo takes advantage of this when it lays its eggs in other birds' nests. The unsuspecting mother bird feeds the newly hatched cuckoo because it emits the proper sign stimuli ("begging calls") to evoke the motor program of feeding. In fact, the learning or imprinting that takes place is so strong that it persists even if the cuckoo's growth far exceeds the size of the surrogate mother (see Figure B). Again, the mother bird

learns to accept this monstrous offspring because of the interplay between instinct and experience.

Lorenz and Tinbergen, along with Karl von Frisch (1967), whose work on "bee language" is considered in Chapter 8, are generally considered the founders of ethology. Their work and that of other ethologists has had a growing influence on psychology. While some of this influence is controversial (see the Highlight on sociobiology in Chapter 11), other influences have been clearly constructive, leading to better understanding of how instincts and learning interact to determine behavior.

insight was not the result of blind, Thorndikeian trial and error. When the chimp got the point, the insight came very suddenly—and irreversibly. Köhler argued that when an animal (or person) learns something insightfully rather than by rote (repetitive drill), the solution is less likely to be forgotten. He suggested that there was a basically arbitrary nature to the associations that experimenters imposed upon their subjects in early conditioning studies. Köhler tried to employ elements in his insight studies that the animal could relate to one another to form a meaningful whole and a sensible cognitive structure.

Critics of Köhler pointed out that his chimps had lived in the wild before he studied them and had undoubtedly learned quite a bit about how sticks could be used and how objects could be stacked and climbed upon. Perhaps their "insights" were possible only because of previous, and lengthy, trial-and-error learning in the wild. This would appear likely and, in fact, animals trained in laboratories to perform certain tasks do appear to exhibit sudden insights when faced with new problems that can utilize their previously acquired skills. Recently, a study was done in which pigeons were trained

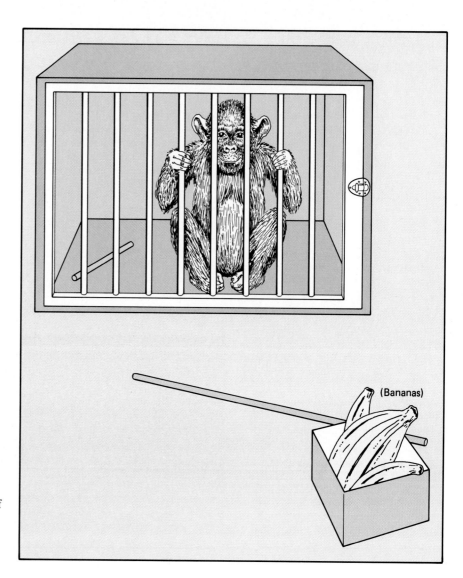

Figure 6–17 Köhler's (1927) two-stick problem could only be solved if the chimp used the shorter stick in the cage to reach the larger stick, which could then be used to reach the box of bananas.

separately to perform two tasks: push boxes, and climb on boxes to obtain suspended food (they were also trained *not* to use their wings to reach the food). After such training each pigeon was then placed in a cage with a box and suspended food, where for the first time it had the opportunity to combine the two skills. The birds quickly learned to push the box under the food and then climb on it to reach the food (Epstein et al., 1984). This clearly demonstrates how prior learning may set the stage for "sudden insights."

Learning Set. Harlow (1949) repeatedly trained monkeys to make a simple two-stimulus discrimination: food under one stimulus (a square box) nothing under the other (a round box). As described in Figure 6–18, each time a monkey mastered this task with one pair of stimuli, a new pair was introduced (e.g., a black triangular box and a white triangular box). At first learning was fairly slow, as the monkeys made a number of mistakes with each pair of stimuli before mastering the discrimination. However, the monkeys tended to master each new discrimination faster than the one before. After learning to discriminate hundreds of different pairs of stimuli, the animals

developed a **learning set** that allowed them to quickly master each new stimulus pair: *If food is found under one stimulus, look under it the next time that pair is presented; otherwise look under the other stimulus.* This type of phenomenon is sometimes called *learning to learn,* and is yet another example of how previous, gradual learning may set the stage for quick, "insightful" solutions to later problems. Nevertheless, it is important to note that Harlow's monkeys learned a general *concept* (the learning set) rather than a response to two specific stimuli. Thus it seems reasonable to infer some sort of *cognitive representation* of this concept that is sufficiently abstract to be applied to any pair of stimuli.

Latent Learning. The maze studies done by Edward C. Tolman and his followers are a persuasive demonstration of cognitive factors in animal learning. The kind of multiple-entry maze used in such studies can be seen in Figure 6–19. The hungry rat must work its way from the start box to a goal box, containing food. There are many blind alleys along the way. When the rat is first put in the maze, it will enter a number of these blind alleys (make many errors) as it goes from the start box to the goal box. With more trials, learning is shown by a steady decrease in the number of errors. Though it is possible to theorize that the food in the goal box stamps in a particular sequence of right-turning and left-turning responses, Tolman argued that this was not the case. What the rat learns, according to Tolman, is a kind of **cognitive map,** or mental picture, of the maze. Since this kind of learning—the storing of information about the world—takes place even when there is no

Figure 6–18 In this discrimination task food is under the square box, but not under the round box. When the discrimination is mastered, two new stimuli would be used: for example, food under a black triangular box, but no food under a white triangular box. (Harlow, 1949)

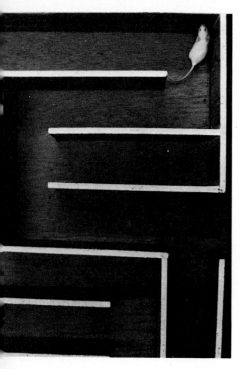

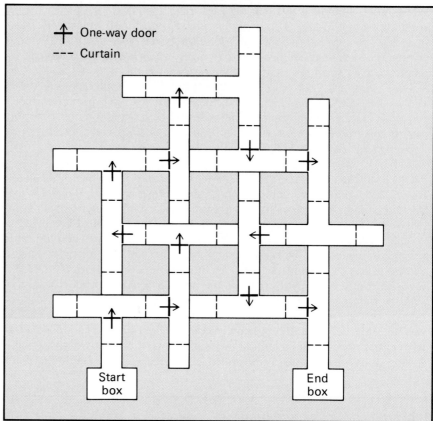

Figure 6–19 Photo and floor plan of the type of maze used in the study of latent learning in rats. (Tolman & Honzik, 1930)

apparent reinforcement and no immediate demonstration of the learning, Tolman called it **latent learning.**

The outcome of a classic study of latent learning by Tolman and Honzik (1930) is shown in Figure 6–20. Three different groups of rats were run through the same maze. The first group received a food reward in the goal box on each trial. These animals gradually reduced their number of errors to a near-zero level. The second group of rats received no reinforcement in the goal box. Though their errors declined slightly over time, they continued to make many more errors than did the reinforced group. The interesting result is that found with the third group. These rats received no reinforcement during the first 10 days. On the 11th day, food was given in the goal box for the first time. When placed into the maze on the next (12th) day, these animals made almost no errors. The single reinforcement brought about a dramatic improvement in their performance, so that they ran the maze about as well as the first group, which had been rewarded on all the previous days. The rats had shown latent learning. Their early days of wandering through the maze without reinforcement had led to the building up of a cognitive map of the maze (Tolman, 1948).

In addition to pointing toward the operation of cognitive factors in animal learning, the latent learning studies force us to make a clear distinction between *learning* and *performance*. The performance of an animal may not change much from trial to trial, but that does not necessarily mean that the animal is not learning. The learning may involve cognitive restructuring that remains latent until some event—such as the sudden introduction of a reinforcement—prompts the animal to use what information it has already

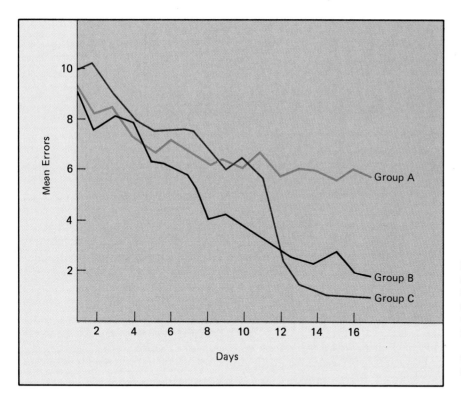

Figure 6–20 The results of the classic study of latent learning. Group A never received a food reward in the maze, while Group B was rewarded on each day. The reward was given to Group C for the first time on Day 11. Note the immediate change in Group C's behavior on Day 12. (Tolman & Honzik, 1930)

learned. This distinction between learning and performance is often made by students who do poorly on an exam. A student may argue that a poor exam performance does not accurately reflect what the student insists he or she learned from the course. School grading systems are geared to performance, however, not to latent learning.

Cognitive Aspects of Classical Conditioning

During the preceding discussion of classical conditioning you may have wondered why we didn't say the animal learned to "expect" the US to follow the CS, or that the CS "signaled" the animal that the US was about to occur. We didn't because Pavlov didn't describe things that way, nor did most of the staunchly behavioristic psychologists who first studied classical conditioning. They regarded such terms as needlessly mentalistic. However, as strict behaviorism declined during the 1950s and 1960s, the use of such cognitive terminology became more acceptable. There were also specific studies that seemed to require an interpretation in cognitive terms.

The Study of Blocking. A purely mechanical view of conditioning would suggest that simply pairing a stimulus with a US would be sufficient to produce conditioning. That this is *not* the case was clearly demonstrated by a psychologist named Leon Kamin, who discovered a phenomenon he called **blocking** (Kamin, 1969). Kamin first conditioned a rat by repeatedly pairing a tone (CS) and a shock (US), until the tone alone evoked a strong conditioned emotional response (fear). He then continued to pair the tone with the shock, but also turned on a light (CS′) each time the tone was sounded. Remarkably, even though this meant the light (CS′) and the shock (US) were

repeatedly paired, the rat showed no conditioning to the light. The light alone evoked no CR; conditioning to the light was blocked *as if* the rat had "not attended to it." This seems perfectly reasonable if one views the tone as a signal that allows the rat to "predict" the shock. The rat has no need to learn anything about the light, since the previously conditioned tone carries the same *information* about the shock.

The Study of Stimulus Contingencies. The idea that conditioning depends on the *information* carried by a stimulus was confirmed in a subsequent study by a psychologist named Robert Rescorla (1967). Using dogs as his subjects, Rescorla varied the *predictive* or *informational value* of the CS (a tone) by varying the proportion of times a US (a shock) immediately followed the tone. The animals were divided into two basic experimental groups: a *contingent group,* for whom shocks were more likely following a tone; and a *noncontingent group,* for whom shocks were no more likely to occur after a tone than at any other time (Figure 6–21). Thus tones carried information about the shocks in the contingent group, but were totally uninformative in the noncontingent group. Rescorla also arranged that the total number of tone-shock pairings was the same in both groups. In this way any difference between the groups in the conditioned aversiveness of the tone could not be due to the absolute number of CS-US pairings. The results support an *informational or predictive interpretation of classical conditioning.* The noncontingent group showed no sign of conditioning, while the contingent group clearly did. Other groups, in which the CS was a progressively poorer predictor of shocks (containing progressively less informational value), showed progressively less conditioning. Subsequent studies have confirmed these results (Rescorla, 1972, 1978; Fontino & Logan, 1979). Notice that these results imply animals can learn something, not only when the CS (a tone) and US (a shock) are paired (the traditional view), but also when either stimulus occurs alone. This seems perfectly reasonable from a cognitive point of view. For example, you learn whether to believe a weatherman's predictions not only by counting how often he predicted it would rain and it did, but also by noting how often he predicted it would rain and it didn't. There are a variety of views concerning the explanation of both Kamin and Rescorla's results (e.g., Wagner & Rescorla, 1972; Schwartz, 1984). However, there is little doubt that the informational value of a stimulus is an important consideration in classical conditioning.

Seligman (1968) has pointed out an important function of a CS in emotional or aversive conditioning. Rats that experienced shocks immediately following tones became quite agitated each time they heard the tone, but seemed relatively calm following shocks. It was as if they learned to expect

Figure 6–21 Illustrative periods of time during which tones (blue lines) and shocks (red lines) were occasionally presented in Rescorla's study of stimulus contingencies (1967). The tone and shock are paired (occur in immediate succession) equally after in each period, as indicated by the black triangle (▼). However, the tone serves as a good predictor of shock only in the upper, *contingent* presentation schedule, where shocks only occur immediately after a tone. In the lower, *noncontingent* schedule shocks are no more likely to occur following a tone than at any other time. Dogs learn to use the tone as a signal for shock in the contingent condition, but *not* in the noncontingent condition. Thus it is the *information* a CS carries concerning the US that determines conditioning, not simply the number of CS-US pairings.

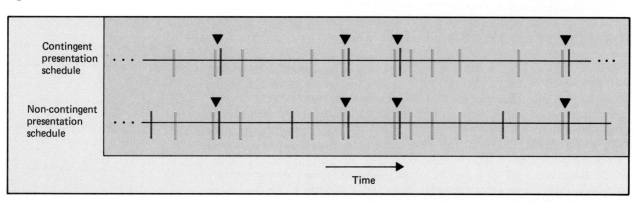

shocks after a tone, but could "feel safe" in the absence of a tone. In contrast, rats that received exactly the same pattern of shocks without any warning tone tended to develop stomach ulcers (a sign of chronic anxiety in humans discussed in Chapter 16). Seligman (1975) and others (e.g., Schwartz, 1978) argue that humans experience *fear* when specific stimuli signal punishment and can relax when such stimuli are absent. However, a history of totally unpredictable punishment produces a state of *chronic anxiety* that may be much more destructive than transient fears.

Cognitive Aspects of Operant Conditioning

A cognitive view of classical conditioning sees animals as expecting one stimulus to follow another. A similar view of operant conditioning sees animals as *expecting* their responses to have certain consequences: A lever press should produce food; jumping a barrier should avoid shock; and so on. Animals may also be able to operate on the mental representations of such knowledge, to perform a sort of mental trial-and-error learning. Thus Köhler's chimps may have simply thought about various manipulations of the objects in their environment, recognized when certain steps would lead to a solution, and only then taken overt action. Harlow's work on *learning sets* also implies that the mental representation of response expectancies may be fairly abstract, that is, sufficiently general to apply to a wide range of particular actions.

Seligman (1975) has interpreted the *learned helplessness* he produced in dogs as the dogs learning that *all* responses are useless in avoiding shock. When the animals are later in a situation where escape or avoidance is possible, they simply give up. (Seligman has gone on to suggest that humans may also learn to be helpless through repeated unavoidable punishment, so that they fail to avoid or escape when such options later become possible.) This way of thinking about animal thinking has encouraged a variety of new work on animal cognition.

Spatial Maps.   Recent work on how animals know where to find rewards has extended Tolman's earlier work on latent learning (Roberts, 1984). One study employed a maze in which several paths (arms) radiated out from a central area. Rats could obtain food at the end of each path only once. The rats quickly learned to avoid paths they had already run as if they had developed a mental representation of the maze that allowed them to remember where they had been already (Olton & Samuelson, 1976; Olton 1978, 1979). Similar results have been obtained using pigeons (Roberts & Van Veldhuizen, 1985).

Learning Concepts and Manipulating Symbols.   Premack (1976) trained chimps to make one response when two stimuli (pictured objects) were the same, and another when they were different. Just as Harlow's monkeys acquired a general learning set, these chimps learned a general *concept* (same/different) rather than a response to particular stimuli.

Chimps have also been taught to manipulate objects that are used to represent other objects, that is, manipulate *symbols* (Premack, 1985). Later, in the chapter on language (Chapter 8), we will consider studies in which chimps seem to manipulate symbols very much as humans use language. However, at this point we will return to our central interest—that animal whose linguistic and cognitive abilities are unsurpassed, the human.

SUMMARY

1. Pavlov's basic experiment is a clear example of what has come to be known as the law of classical conditioning. Whenever a previously neutral stimulus (CS) is *consistently* paired with an unconditioned stimulus (US), a response like the one made to the US will come to be made to the CS.

2. The basic rule followed by the experimenter during acquisition is: Whenever the CS is presented, follow it with the US. That procedure—CS followed by US—is called *reinforcement*. If the CS is no longer reinforced, the conditioned response disappears—this is known as *extinction*. *Spontaneous recovery* of a response occurs after extinction, indicating that extinction does not completely erase the conditioned response.

3. When a conditioned response has been established to a particular conditioned stimulus, stimuli similar to that CS will also tend to elicit the response, in a process called *generalization*. In *discrimination*, the subject learns not to respond to similar stimuli while continuing to respond to the CS itself.

4. Pavlov noted that a CS established in one series of trials could then, on its own, act as a US in a second series of trials. This is called *higher-order conditioning*. Much human learning depends on such conditioning.

5. In operant conditioning, the *presentation* of a *positive reinforcer* increases the likelihood that a particular response will be repeated. The *termination* of a *negative reinforcer* also increases the likelihood that the response will be repeated.

6. *Shaping* is the technique used to modify or change responses. In shaping, one reinforces the successive approximations of a particular response until the desired behavior is performed.

7. In general, reinforcing every correct response is less effective than some type of *partial reinforcement*, which leads to learning that is more resistant to extinction. Schedules of reinforcement can be based on either the number of responses or the time elapsed between responses.

8. *Punishment* is the presentation of a negative reinforcer. There are a number of serious drawbacks to punishment: It tends to generally suppress and inhibit responding; it causes the person or animal to become fearful of the situation in which it occurred and of the person who administered it; and it does not tell a person or animal what to do, it merely says what *not* to do, without presenting satisfactory alternatives.

9. A *primary reinforcer* is one that is rewarding by itself, without any association with other reinforcers. The value of a *secondary* or *conditional reinforcer* must be learned by associating it with primary reinforcers.

10. *Insight,* a form of learning and problem solving that depends on cognitive activity, was studied by Köhler, who described it as the ability to restructure cognitive elements into new and purposeful wholes.

11. Trial-and-error learning and insightful learning can be combined in learning how to learn—that is, in acquiring a *learning set,* which was studied by Harlow.

12. *Latent learning* may occur without any change in performance, until that learning becomes useful. Thus a *cognitive map* may be learned but not used until a previously successful path to food is blocked.

13. *Blocking* occurs when the previous conditioning to one stimulus in some way blocks conditioning to a second stimulus. It is as if the information in the first stimulus is sufficient, so there is no reason for attending to the second stimulus.

14. When the CS has predictive value about the US, there is *contingency* between them. *Positive contingency* exists when the probability of US occurrence is higher immediately after CS presentation than at other times. When the probability is lower, there is *negative contingency*. Such contingencies appear to be learned in classical conditioning.

SUGGESTED READINGS

DICKINSON, A. (1980). *Contemporary animal learning theory.* New York: Cambridge University Press. A brief and readable account of recent theoretical developments, with a stress on animal cognition.

DOMJAN, M., & BURKHARD, B. (1982). *The principles of learning and behavior.* Monterey, Cal.: Brooks/Cole. A solid entry-level text, especially strong on examples and applications to human behavior.

HILGARD, E. R., & BOWER, G. H. (1981). *Theories of learning,* 5th ed. Englewood Cliffs, N.J.: Prentice-Hall. As implied by the title, the emphasis is on theory, not data. Much material of historical interest.

HONIG, W. K., & STADDON, J. E. R. (Eds.). (1977). *The handbook of operant behavior*. Englewood Cliffs, N.J.: Prentice-Hall. Individual chapters by different authorities, covering a wide range of subject matters, each in considerable detail.

KÖHLER, W. (1927). *The mentality of apes*. London: Routledge & Kegan Paul.

MACKINTOSH, N.J. (1983). *Conditioning and associative learning*. New York: Oxford University Press. A comprehensive survey of cognitive learning research employing animal subjects.

PAVLOV, I. (1927). *Conditioned reflexes* (G. V. Anrep, trans.). London: Oxford University Press. The famous original work on classical conditioning.

SCHWARTZ, B. (1984). *Psychology of learning and behavior* 2nd ed. New York: Norton. A thorough and wide-ranging review of learning research, placed on its full psychological and scientific context.

SCHWARTZ, B., & LACY, H. (1982). *Behaviorism, science and human nature*. New York: Norton. A brief summary of basic conditioning phenomena, with an emphasis on operant techniques and some of their applications. Includes a thoughtful critique of the philosophy underlying behavior theory, and of its limitations.

SKINNER, B. F. (1953). *Science and human behavior*. New York: Macmillan. A lucid exposition of Skinner's approach to operant conditioning.

SKINNER, B. F. (1971). *Beyond freedom and dignity*. New York: Knopf. A view of "free will" as a dangerous conceit. Skinner challenges some basic social beliefs.

7 Memory

Afterr you make an appointment with someone, you may simply hope you will remember it, or you may jot it down on your calendar. That is, you either rely on your own internal **memory** or use some sort of external memory. Fortunately, given the enormous amount of information that we wish to retain and the limits of our internal memory, there are many forms of external memory systems, ranging from a string tied to a finger to huge computer memories. A **memory system** is simply an aid to the retention of information over time. Thus a book, a tape recording, and a photograph are all external memory systems. Each preserves information in a particular form, and each is best suited to preserving certain types of information.

DESCRIBING MEMORY SYSTEMS

Psychological ideas about internal memory are often expressed as analogies with external forms of memory. For this reason, although our central interest in this chapter is internal human memory, it is useful to begin by considering some external memory systems and some of the terminology used to describe them. Next we will consider how people perform a variety of memory tasks and some factors that lead to forgetting. Finally, we will consider theories of human memory and discuss some ways of improving memory suggested by these theories.

Salvador Dali's "Memory" gives his surrealistic impression of the vast mental space that holds our recollections. (The Museum of Modern Art, New York)

(Rhoda Sidney/Monkmeyer)

External Memory Systems

The terms *encoding, retention,* and *retrieval* are often used to describe three basic aspects of memory systems. **Encoding** refers to the way information is first stored or represented in a system. **Retention** refers to the way the information is preserved in a system over time. And **retrieval** refers to the way the information is finally recovered from a system. The three aspects can be illustrated in terms of that most familiar external memory system, a book. Information is first *encoded* into patterns of ink in the form of words when the book is printed. It is *retained* over time by the persistence of this pattern, although information can be lost if the ink or paper is of poor quality, or if the book is physically damaged (by water or fire, etc.). Finally, the information in the book is *retrieved* or recovered when it is read.

The same distinctions can also be made in terms of another external memory system, a tape recording. Here information—for example, a lecturer's voice—is encoded in the form of magnetic patterns laid down on the tape as it moves past the recording head. Retention of the information depends on the persistence of this pattern over time. Again, information can be lost if the tape is physically damaged or exposed to strong magnetic fields, or if another recording is made over the first. Finally, information is retrieved from the tape by playing it back.

We will use the phrase *information loss* in a very general way to refer to anything that interferes with the accurate retrieval of information. Information loss can occur during encoding, retention, or retrieval. For example, a tape recorder could lose information because of improper recording (encoding), accidental erasure during retention, or a broken playback system that prevents retrieval. Note that if the defective playback system were repaired, it would then be possible to recover the information on the tape. Thus while failure to recover information from a memory system is an instance of information loss, the information is not necessarily permanently beyond retrieval. This point can be illustrated in another way. Suppose you consulted a card catalog in a library and then went to the place where the book should be shelved. If it wasn't there, and hadn't been checked out, you couldn't retrieve the information in the book. The book could have been permanently lost or simply misplaced. You might make an exhaustive search of the stacks for the missing book—another retrieval process. But even if this failed, the book might eventually turn up, or you might be able to locate another copy in another library or bookstore. So you couldn't consider the loss permanent. Later we shall consider similar instances pertaining to human memory, when it is difficult to decide whether information is permanently lost or only temporarily irretrievable.

Notice that information is represented in different ways in each of the memory systems we have considered (printed letters, magnetic patterns). Each of these representations or **codes** has its special properties, such as the ease and speed with which you can code (encode) various forms of information and the sorts of things that will interfere with retention. For example, a person's voice is normally easier to store on magnetic tape than on the printed page, although a good writer may describe a voice quite accurately. Also, the retention of printed words is uninfluenced by magnetic fields, but a tape recording can be completely erased by such fields.

Different codes may be used in the same memory system. For example, a novel printed in different languages would be an encoding of the same information in the same form of memory system (a book) using a different code

Table 7–1: Examples of codes.

The same information can be represented in many different forms or codes. For example, the concept of *hat* can be represented by the four codes shown here: English, French, Samuel Morse's telegraphic code of dots and dashes, and the system of raised dots invented for blind readers by Louis Braille.

English: hat
French: chapeau
Morse code: · · · · , · — , —
Braille: ●○   ●○   ○●
        ●●   ○○   ●●
        ○○, ○○, ●○

(e.g., French and English). Table 7–1 illustrates how different codes can represent the same concept.

Information held in a memory system may also be **recoded,** either by retrieving the information from that system and coding it into another system, or by recoding it into the same system. Suppose you had a friend make a tape recording of a lecture you had to miss. You might listen to that tape that evening and then either write a summary of the main ideas into another memory system, your notebook, or simply make another tape recording of your summary. In either case, there are two important aspects of this recoding process: information reduction and reorganization. **Information reduction** occurs because there is less information about the lecture in the recoded summary than there was on the original tape. Even if the lecture were typed out verbatim, some reduction would be inevitable because the typed pages wouldn't contain the sounds of the lecturer's voice. In any case, many details of the lecture (jokes, illustrations, etc.) are purposely left out of a summary. Organization of information can also be changed during the recoding process. The information on the tape is in the exact sequence in which the lecturer presented it. You might choose to summarize the principal points in a very different sequence if such a **reorganization** seemed simpler.

It should be emphasized that recoding doesn't always involve information reduction. In fact, some coding processes involve **elaborative** processes that may actually add to the retrieved information (see Figure 7–1). For example, when you rewrite lecture notes, you might expand on a point made by the lecturer with an example drawn from your own experience. **Reconstructive** or **reintegrative** processes allow you to fill in text in an old manuscript that had been partly destroyed, or to bridge gaps caused by static on a tape recording of a human voice. In each case you reconstruct the missing information through educated guessing based on the information that wasn't lost and your knowledge of linguistic redundancy. This is the same sort of inferential process that occurs so automatically in perception, as we discussed in Chapter 4. For example, you often infer parts of a scene or printed sentence that you don't gaze at directly from those you do.

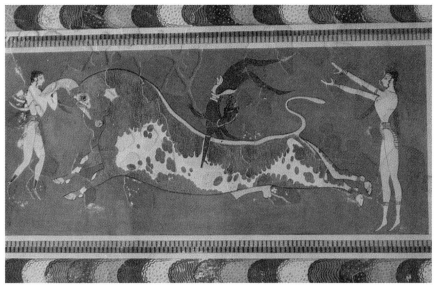

Figure 7–1 This ancient wall painting from Crete is a kind of memory system because it retains information about how things looked centuries ago. The ravages of time have interfered with retention, producing some loss of information. It was possible in this case to restore or reconstruct much of what was lost based on what was left and the restorer's knowledge of the normal relationship (redundancy) between different parts of an age. (Robert Caputo/Stock, Boston)

Magnetic tape (left) was an early form of mass storage memory for computers. (Courtesy Control Data Corp.)

A neuron (right) seen against the miniaturized circuitry of a modern computer. While computer circuits are very small, they are much less complicated than neural circuits. (Hewlett Packard)

Memory systems can also be described in terms of their *capacity*. For example, a sales rep might use a small pocket notebook to record appointments during the day, then at the end of the day transfer those appointments to a larger notebook in her office. The pocket notebook has a lower capacity for storing information than the large office notebook. However, the pocket notebook has compensating advantages, such as its physical size and transportability, that make it easier and faster to use during the day. The office notebook has a greater capacity, but in order to retrieve information from it during the day, the sales rep must return to, or at least phone, her office. Thus the two memory systems differ in ease of encoding and retrieval as well as in capacity.

Perhaps the richest source of ideas about external memory systems has been computer science. Computers are distinguished in terms of their memory (e.g., random access, disk, tape). Information is represented and organized in a variety of ways and elaborate strategies have been developed for information retrieval. Computer scientists are continuing to explore alternative means of representing knowledge in memory with new forms of computer architecture (Rumelhart, McClelland, et al., 1986). An example of this is presented in the Highlight: Distributed Memory and Connectionist Systems. Computer programs have been designed to simulate "experts" in such fields as geology and medicine—that is, they can respond to questions about the field much like a real expert. Later in the chapter you will see how storage and retrieval of knowledge by such **expert systems** are regarded by some (e.g., Anderson, 1983) as similar to human memory.

Human Memory Systems

As we have seen, it is possible to describe external memory systems in terms of such properties as their capacity, codes, speed of encoding and retrieval, susceptibility to interference, and so on. Even though the human memory system is an internal one, it can be described in similar terms. We can often *infer* quite a bit about a memory system from the way it functions or behaves. In the next section we will examine some of the ways in which human memory has been studied. Careful observation of how humans perform various memory tasks has suggested a variety of theoretical conjectures about the nature of human memory. Many of these theoretical approaches involve analogies between human memory and external memory systems, in particular, computer-based systems for storing and retrieving knowledge.

MEMORY TASKS: ASSESSING HUMAN MEMORY

The first systematic experiments on human memory were conducted around 1876 by a German named Hermann Ebbinghaus (Ebbinghaus, 1885). He developed a number of simple memory tasks and carefully observed how people performed them. Similar tasks have since been employed in hundreds of memory experiments. We will look briefly at three different types of tasks: recall, recognition, and relearning.

Recall

One of the simplest ways to test human memory is to allow subjects to study a list of words, and then to ask them to **recall** as many as possible, either by naming them or by writing them down. Take a minute to study the list of words in Figure 7–2. Now cover the list and write out as many of the items as you can remember. Not surprisingly, the longer you take to study a list of this sort, the more words you can recall. However, the longer you study, the more study time is required to recall one additional word (a "diminishing return"). Furthermore, items that aren't recalled in the first minute of recall may still be recalled if you are given enough time.

Some common recall tasks are naming each state in the United States, or answering such questions as "What is her name?" or "What is your phone number?" The more you use or study an item of information, the more likely you are to recall it. However, recall often takes some time, even when you are quite confident that it will occur promptly. How often have you felt that the correct answer is on the tip of your tongue, and not been able to produce it? This **tip-of-the-tongue (TOT) phenomenon** suggests that recall is an active process that requires both time and concentration. Sometimes you may have the TOT experience and finally give up trying to recall some fact, only to find a few moments later that the fact pops into your mind without any further conscious effort on your part.

In order to control more precisely the amount of time each word in a recall list is available for study, experimenters often present the words serially (one after another), so that subjects see each word for the same length of time. With this kind of presentation, words at the beginning and end of the list are more likely to be recalled than those in the middle. This is called the **serial position effect** and is illustrated in graph form in Figure 7–3. The higher recall of the words at the beginning of the list is referred to as a **primacy effect**; the higher recall of words at the end of the list (the most recently presented words) is called a **recency effect.**

Distribution of practice also has a very strong effect on recall. For example, suppose you were trying to learn a list of Spanish vocabulary words. You would probably recall more words after four separate (spaced) 30-minute study sessions (perhaps one session a day for four days) than after a single concentrated (massed) 2-hour session, even though you had a total of 2 hours' practice in each case. This effect is often referred to as the *advantage of distributed* (spread out) *over massed* (close together or concentrated) *practice.* Figure 7–4 shows the results of a recent study that clearly demonstrated the advantage of distributed practice. English-speaking subjects studied a list of Spanish vocabulary words and their English meanings during two

house
tree
car
grass
coin
candle
barn
bus
gun
soup

Figure 7–2 Study this list for a minute, then cover it and see how many words you can recall.

Figure 7–3 This graph shows the serial position effect: The position of the words in the list, which determines the order in which they are presented, affects recall. Higher recall of words at the beginning of the list is called the primacy effect, and higher recall of words at the end of the list (the most recently presented words) is called the recency effect.

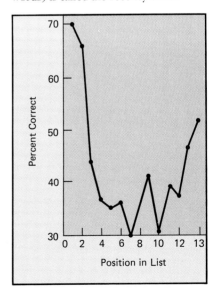

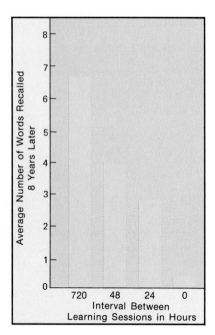

Figure 7–4 Bahrick and Phelps (1987) gave a Spanish vocabulary test to people who had studied the vocabulary eight years earlier. This earlier studying was done during two practice sessions separated by either 720, 48, 24, or 0 hours (i.e., 720 hrs. equals 30 days and 0 hrs. indicated immediately consecutive sessions). Even after eight years, recall was significantly better the greater the distribution of practice. This illustrates the advantage of spaced over massed practice.

sessions, which were separated by various intervals. Even eight years later subjects recalled more English meanings when the interval between the two study sessions was greater; immediately consecutive study sessions were less useful for recall than widely spaced ones. This is one reason why studying all night just before an exam (massed practice) is less useful than studying a little bit each week all through the term (distributed practice).

The ability to recall something can be strongly influenced by other stimuli presented at the time of recall. Such stimuli are often referred to as **recall cues.** For example, your ability to recall someone's name might be aided by such recall cues as hearing his or her voice or seeing a picture of the person. In fact, simply asking someone to recall something can be considered a recall cue. There is no doubt that such stimuli as "What is your address?" or "What items were on the list you just read?" influence what you remember. Stimuli present at the time you learn something are likely to be good recall cues, a phenomenon Tulving (1978) called **encoding specificity.**

The fact that contiguous or repeatedly paired stimuli make each one a good recall cue for the other explains a phenomenon called **state-dependent learning.** Things learned in a particular environment (indoors, outdoors, a noisy dormitory, a quiet library) or in a particular room, physiological state (happy, sad, tired, intoxicated, cold, warm) are often recalled better in the same environment or state (e.g., Bower, 1981). For instance, if you studied for an exam in a cold, small room, you might not recall the information as well in a warm, large room as you would in a cold, small one. Similarly, the bodily sensations associated with mild intoxication could serve as recall cues for things learned in that state.

In some of the earliest recall experiments Ebbinghaus used **nonsense syllables** such as DAK, MIF, BIP, and RUC. Because these had virtually no prior associations or meaning for his subjects, almost everything they·learned about them could be introduced in the laboratory. In studies of cued recall subjects were first shown two nonsense syllables at a time (e.g., DAK–VOP, BIP–TIF, ZOX–VAM) and then later shown only the first member of each pair and asked to recall the second (e.g., if they were shown DAK, they should respond VOP). Thus the first member of each pair served as a recall cue for the second member. By repeatedly pairing the two associates, then testing the ability of one to evoke recall of the other, Ebbinghaus was able to measure the gradual growth of associations.

In one of his studies Bartlett had subjects read a short but strange and complicated story, "The War of the Ghosts." Then, after some time had elapsed, he had them recall as much of the story as they could (see Figure 7–5). "The War of the Ghosts" is a legend told by nineteenth-century Indians on the northwest coast of Canada. Bartlett purposely chose a tale that would not only be unfamiliar to his English subjects, but that also came from a quite different culture. He wondered whether the cultural differences would affect his subjects' recall of the story. He found that subjects had a systematic tendency to forget, distort, and add details in a way that made the recalled story less strange and unusual to them. For example, the subject whose recall is shown in Figure 7–5 changed "hunt seals" to "went fishing," "war cries" to "a cry," and "arrows are in the canoe" to 'arrows are in the boat." For other subjects, "something black came out of his mouth" became "frothed at the mouth" or simply "vomited." Bartlett used the term **schemas** to characterize the familiar way of thinking about things common to each culture. Since the English students had different schemas than the Indians who wrote the legend, they tended to remember details as being more like their own schemas.

(a) Original Indian Myth	(b) Typical recall by a student in England
The War of the Ghosts	**The War of the Ghosts**
One night two young men from Egulac went down to the river to hunt seals, and while they were there it became foggy and calm. Then they heard war-cries, and they thought: "Maybe this is a war-party." They escaped to the shore, and hid behind a log. Now canoes came up, and they heard the noise of paddles, and saw one canoe coming up to them. There were five men in the canoe, and they said:	Two men from Edulac went fishing. While thus occupied by the river they heard a noise in the distance.
"What do you think? We wish to take you along. We are going up the river to make war on the people."	"It sounds like a cry," said one, and presently there appeared some in canoes who invited them to join the party of their adventure. One of the young men refused to go, on the ground of family ties, but the other offered to go.
One of the young men said, "I have no arrows."	"But there are no arrows," he said.
"Arrows are in the canoe," they said.	"The arrows are in the boat," was the reply.
"I will not go along. I might be killed. My relatives do not know where I have gone. But you," he said, turning to the other, "may go with them."	He thereupon took his place, while his friend returned home. The party paddled up the river to Kaloma, and began to land on the banks of the river. The enemy came rushing upon them, and some sharp fighting ensued. Presently someone was injured, and the cry was raised that the enemy were ghosts.
So one of the young men went, but the other returned home.	
And the warriors went on up the river to a town on the other side of Kalama. The people came down to the water, and they began to fight, and many were killed. But presently the young man heard one of the warriors say: "Quick, let us go home; that Indian has been hit." Now he thought: "Oh, they are ghosts." He did not feel sick, but they said he had been shot.	The party returned down the stream, and the young man arrived home feeling none the worse for his experience. The next morning at dawn he endeavoured to recount his adventures. While he was talking something black issued from his mouth. Suddenly he uttered a cry and fell down. His friends gathered round him.
So the canoes went back to Egulac, and the young man went ashore to this house, and made a fire. And he told everybody and said: "Behold I accompanied the ghosts, and we went to fight. Many of our fellows were killed, and many of those who attacked us were killed. They said I was hit, and I did not feel sick."	But he was dead.
He told it all, and then he became quiet. When the sun rose he fell down. Something black came out of his mouth. His face became contorted. The people jumped up and cried.	British college students tended to systematically forget, distort, and revise details of a North American Indian myth in ways that made the recalled story less unusual to them.
He was dead.	

Figure 7–5 "The War of the Ghosts," a nineteenth-century North American Indian myth, and its recall by one of Bartlett's subjects. (Bartlett, 1932, p. 65)

Recognition

Another way to test memory is to use a **recognition** task. Consider the list of the words in Figure 7–6. Some of these terms were in the list in Figure 7–2; others are new or *distractor* items. Check those items you remember seeing in the earlier list.

Notice that in this case a word is presented and you must decide whether or not you recognize it from a previous list. This is similar to asking someone "Is that Mary?" or "Is your phone number 621-7753?" rather than "Who is that?" or "What is your phone number?" as in the recall task. In this task the answer to the recall question is actually there, and you must say whether or not you recognize it.

In general, people are more likely to recognize an item than to recall it. This may be simply because presentation of the item is itself a good recall cue. This idea was explored by Tulving and Watkins (1973), with the results shown in Figure 7–7. They varied how much of an item was present at the time of recall by varying the number of its letters shown to the subject. When no letters were shown, as in a simple recall task, recall was low. The more letters shown, the better the recall, indicating that presentation of even part of an item serves as a recall cue. Finally, when the whole item was presented, as in a conventional recognition task, subjects were most likely to recall seeing the item earlier. So recognition may be thought of as a special case of recall in which the item itself serves as a recall cue.

Figure 7–6 Study this new list of words for a minute. How many do you recognize from the list in Figure 7–2?

grass	heart	gun
bike	car	bus
phone	soup	bridge
coin	tree	cliff
house	door	barn
boat	bat	rifle

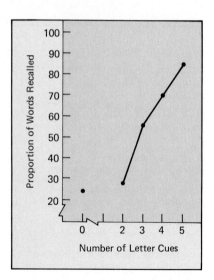

Figure 7–7 In this experiment Tulving and Watkins varied how much of an item (a 5-letter word) was presented to subjects to see how it would affect recall of the item. Their results are shown in the graph above: When no letters are shown, as in a simple recall task, recall is low; the more letters shown, the better the recall; and when the whole item is presented, as in a recognition task, recall is highest. (Tulving & Watkins, 1973)

Relearning

Even when people seem to have totally forgotten something they learned earlier, **relearning** it may take less time than the original learning. This reduction in time to learn, or **savings,** suggests that they actually had some memory of the material before they began to relearn it. Suppose subjects study a list of 20 items for successive 1-minute periods with a recall test following each study period. Proceeding in this way, it might take 15 study periods (minutes) before all 20 items can be recalled on the following test. Several weeks later the subjects might claim they can't recall any of the words.

Now suppose they relearn the words, using exactly the same procedure as before. A perfect performance on the recall test might occur after only 10 study periods, a savings score of 5 minutes (time for the original learning minus time for relearning). The savings score in this case is one-third of the total original study time, or 33⅓ percent. This savings suggests that the subjects actually did remember something from the original learning, even though they couldn't recall any of the items before the relearning session. Figure 7–8 shows how Ebbinghaus charted the course of forgetting over a 31-day period using a *percent savings score.*

FORGETTING: INFORMATION LOSS IN HUMAN MEMORY

We saw earlier that information is lost in external memory systems in ways that are characteristic of each system. Of course, information loss or forgetting also occurs in human memory. The ways in which this occurs, and the factors that influence it, have led to a variety of theories concerning the nature of human memory, which we will examine later in this chapter.

Figure 7–8 The most obvious factor in forgetting is the passage of time, as shown in this graph. Note that retention decreases very rapidly at first, then much more slowly after the first 9 hours. (Ebbinghaus, 1885)

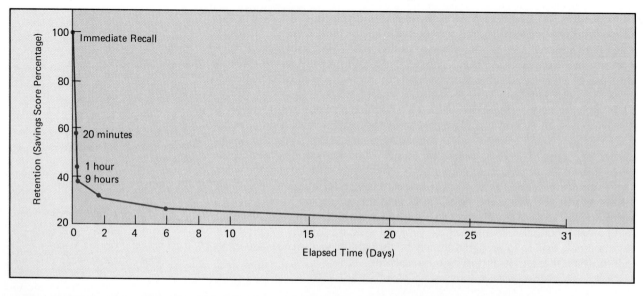

The Effect of Retention Time

The most obvious factor in forgetting is the passage of time. In general, the longer the interval between learning and recall (the retention interval), the less likely it is that we will remember something (see Figure 7–8). Yet there are many exceptions to this general rule. You often remember events that occurred during a time of crisis, such as the death of a friend or a moment of personal peril, even though they took place many years ago. It is remarkable, in fact, how clearly most people can remember things of this sort. On the other hand, you may forget the name of someone just introduced to you before you finish shaking hands. Thus the passage of time alone is not a reliable indicator of whether something will be remembered. More important, it seems, is how well the information was learned or encoded originally, what happens to the person during the retention period, and the situation in which retrieval is attempted.

Distraction and Attentional Problems

You are unlikely to remember people's names if you don't pay attention when they are introduced. Nor will you find it easy to remember the details of your last psychology lecture while driving at high speed through heavy traffic. There is a difference between these two examples. Distractions that occur while you are trying to retrieve information usually affect your memory only temporarily (you probably will remember the lecture once you are safely home). But if your attention is distracted when information is first presented, you may never be able to remember it; it is as if it was not even encoded. In Chapter 4 we considered a number of attentional problems, such as being unable to attend closely to more than one person's voice at a time. if someone else is speaking simultaneously, you neither perceive nor remember much of what that person says. Thus an important determinant of what you remember is what you attend to.

Even if you do attend to information as it is presented, distraction immediately afterward may produce information loss. You may, for instance, have noticed that you're more likely to forget someone's name if you are distracted right after being introduced. An experiment by Peterson and Peterson (1959) illustrates this effect. Their subjects heard 3-consonant trigrams, such as P-T-K or L-C-J, which they were then asked to recall after retention intervals ranging from 3 to 18 seconds. If allowed to attend solely to this task, the subjects could perform it perfectly. However, if they had to perform a distracting task during the retention interval (counting backwards by threes from a number seen right after hearing the trigram), recall was hindered until there was almost no recall after 18 seconds (see Figure 7–9). It is clear that attending to information as it is presented *and* not being distracted immediately afterward are both required to avoid forgetting.

Interference from Other Memories

Your ability to remember something may be impaired, or interfered with, by memories of other things, particularly things that are quite similar or conceptually related. Suppose you have been shown through several homes by a real estate agent. Thinking back, you might have difficulty recalling which homes had which features, sometimes erroneously remembering a feature of one house as belonging to another, or sometimes being unsure whether you

Figure 7–9 In this experiment, subjects who heard 3-consonant trigrams (such as P-T-K) were asked to recall them after retention intervals ranging from 3 to 18 seconds. Subjects performed a distracting task during the retention interval (counting backward). The letters were rapidly forgotten, with almost no recall after 18 seconds. (Peterson & Peterson, 1959)

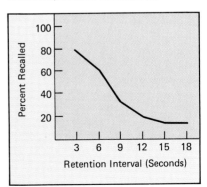

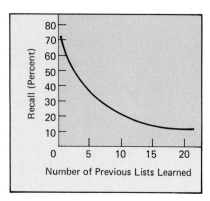

Figure 7–10 When subjects are shown a series of word lists and then asked to recall items from a particular list, the more lists they are shown, and the more similar the words in the lists, the more poorly they perform.

Figure 7–11 The graph shows evidence of a release from interference if there is a distinct category shift in the fourth word presented in the list. That is, there is less proactive interference if the item is unrelated to the words already retained in memory. (Wickens, 1972)

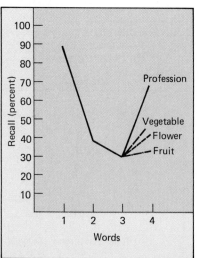

really saw a particular feature at all, since you saw so many. The more similar the houses and the more of them you saw, the more likely you would be to experience confusions of this sort.

Phenomena very much like this have been studied experimentally. Subjects are shown several word lists and then asked to recall items from a particular list. The more lists they are shown, and the more similar the words in the lists, the more poorly the subjects perform (see Figure 7–10). The simplest form of this experiment requires three groups of subjects and two lists of words. Two groups of subjects learn only one list, either list A or list B. The third group learns both lists, first A and then B. The 2 list group is typically poorer at recalling either list than the corresponding 1 list group. This indicates both that learning list A interferes with recall of B, and that learning list B interferes with recall of A. The interference of A with recall of B is termed **proactive interference,** since A was learned before B. The interference of B with recall of A is called **retroactive interference** since B was learned after A. Both types of interference depend on the similarity of the words on each list. For example, there will be more interference if both lists are vegetable names than if one is vegetables and the other is fruit.

These effects can be demonstrated in even simpler form. Wickens (1972) presented subjects with a series of words and then tested their recall. While the list was much longer, only recall of the first 4 words is of interest here. The first 3 words on each subject's list were names of fruits; the fourth word varied for different groups of subjects—it was the name of either a fruit, a vegetable, a flower, or a profession. The rest of the list was identical for all subjects. Figure 7–11 shows how recall gradually falls off for the first 3 words as proactive interference increases the primacy effect shown earlier in Figure 7–3. However, the amount of proactive interference indicated on the fourth item clearly depends on its similarity to the first three. It is as if there is a *release from interference* when there is a distinct *category shift.*

It seems, then, that the likelihood of forgetting something because of interference from other information in memory depends on the item's relation to that information.

Emotional Factors

We seem to remember most vividly an event to which we have had a strong emotional response. Moments of great elation or excitement, grief or sorrow, are often sharply etched in our memories. Every detail seems to stand out. Of course, these are the types of events we also tend to discuss often. Each time we describe the event or someone mentions it, we have another opportunity to encode information about it. This is surely one reason we remember such events better than others. Another reason is that things we feel strongly about usually command our attention and make us less likely to be distracted by other things. For example, a difference of opinion between family members can cause them to focus attention on the issue and on their interactions, and prevent them from being distracted by other events. This may be why we remember quarrels so vividly.

Of course, while our attention is focused on our emotions, we are likely to pay little attention to other kinds of information. For example, great anxiety can distract you from listening to a lecture. You may spend your time looking nervously about the classroom at your fellow students, or gazing out the window thinking about your problems.

Freud (1933) argued that many of the seemingly innocent failures of memory that occur in everyday life are the product of unconscious motives

and emotions. Forgetting your car keys may be caused by an unconscious desire to stay home from work. Forgetting someone's name or an appointment may be an expression of unconscious anger. Freud called such unconsciously purposeful forgetting **repression** and made the gradual uncovering of such repressed memories, particularly those associated with traumatic experiences, a central goal of psychoanalysis. He argued that when patients finally remember such events, they are freed from feelings of anxiety and maladaptive behavior caused by the repressed memories, a process he called **catharsis.**

Emotional problems can produce almost total failure of memory for even recent events that are too painful for a person to deal with. A mother may be unable to remember anything that happened on the day her child drowned. A man may leave his home for work one day, then find himself in a distant city months later with no memory of what has happened to him since he left home. Such **fugue states** seem to satisfy some psychological or emotional need. They are discussed in more detail in Chapter 17.

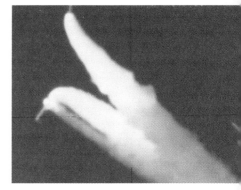

An event to which we have a strong emotional response is often sharply etched in memory. What were you doing when you first saw this picture on January 28, 1986? (NASA)

Organic Causes of Forgetting

Some causes of forgetting have a clear organic basis. These **organic amnesias** are usually caused by some sort of damage to the brain resulting from disease, injury to the head, or brain surgery. For example, in **Alzheimer's disease,** which affects some older people, gradual reduction in the brain's oxygen supply and general atrophy of the brain produce an overall reduction in cognitive function, including memory.

More specific effects on memory may be produced by other types of brain damage, in particular damage to the frontal or temporal lobes, or to the hippocampus (see Chapter 2). If the damage causes loss of memory only for events occurring *after* it, it is termed **anterograde amnesia.** If it affects events occurring *before* it, it is termed **retrograde amnesia.** Combinations of retrograde and anterograde amnesia also occur.

Korsakoff's syndrome is a disease associated with chronic alcoholism and the resulting malnutrition; it causes permanent brain damage. While victims of this disease have some retrograde amnesia, they can remember most of their earlier life. However, they don't remember new information for more than a few minutes. People with this chronic anterograde amnesia can meet someone, or read a magazine, and a few minutes later fail to recognize the person, or read the magazine as if it were new. Each day they start afresh with memories only of their early life. Similar chronic patterns of anterograde amnesia can be produced by damage to the hippocampus. Milner (1970) studied a patient, H. M., whose hippocampus was surgically lesioned to reduce epileptic seizures. The patient had a normal IQ but seemed unable to remember new information for more than a few minutes. Recent studies (e.g., Graf, Squire, & Mandler, 1984; Schacter & Graf, 1986) have revealed a more complex picture of such patients and suggest that they may only reveal longer-term retention if carefully tested on just the right tasks. Furthermore, it has been shown that patients like H.M. can learn new skills, such as reading inverted writing or tracing along a line seen in a mirror. These skills improve with daily practice, although each day the patients typically assert that they have no memory of performing the task before. Nevertheless, once they acquire such skills, these patients retain them for long periods and can perform the tasks quite well after several weeks without practice (Baddeley, 1982; Moscovitch, 1982).

Retrograde amnesia is often caused by a blow to the head. Depending on the severity of the blow, the amnesia may extend back a few moments or a few weeks. The rider in this accident may not later remember any of the events leading up to it. (Philippe Hulin/Agence Vandystadt/Photo Researchers)

Retrograde amnesias are usually temporary and often caused by a blow to the head. (They can also be caused by electroconvulsive shock, which is sometimes used to treat severely depressed mental patients.) These amnesias may extend back a few moments, days, or even weeks, depending on the severity of the blow to the head. As time passes, the older events are usually recalled first, until finally there is no amnesia. Sometimes, however, memory of events that occurred during the last few minutes before the injury (or electroconvulsive shock) seems to be permanently lost. It is almost as if these events were never completely encoded.

There is considerable debate over just how clearly the loss of specific memory functions can be linked with damage to a specific area of the brain (Mayer, 1984; Squire & Cohen, 1984; Corkin et al., 1985). In the Highlight: Distributed Memory and Connectionist Systems we consider how the same knowledge might be stored redundantly in many parts of the brain, thereby preventing damage to any one part from preventing recall of that information.

THEORIES OF HUMAN MEMORY

Some Early Ideas

Early ideas about memory were closely related to ideas about learning. Plato likened human memory to soft wax on which experiences produce imprints or traces; forgetting occurs as successive traces gradually obliterate earlier ones. Plato's conception was elaborated by Aristotle to include associations of these traces: Retrieving one memory could lead to others through an organized network of associations.

The conception of learning as the formation of associations has been central to many theories of learning up to the present day. Formation of associations was often attributed to simple **temporal contiguity.** Things that happen at the same time tend to become associated; memory of one will then evoke a memory of the other. This was the view of Ebbinghaus (1885), whose methods for studying human memory we considered earlier in this chapter.

Some theorists thought of the associations between memory traces as "neural paths." Like footpaths across a field, neural paths were supposed to become more defined through repeated use; if not used, they would gradually decay or fade away. Notice the difference between the idea of forgetting as simple decay through disuse and Plato's conception of new impressions overlying and obscuring old ones. Arguments as to whether forgetting occurs because of decay or simply the interfering effects of new memories have continued to this day.

The concept of associated neural traces was elaborated in **consolidation theory** (Müller & Pilzecker, 1900). According to this theory, the neural paths "reverberate" or remain active for some time after they are formed, and this continued activity is necessary for them to "consolidate" or become permanent. An explanation of retrograde amnesia is offered by consolidation theorists in support of their view: The traumatic event (a blow to the head or electroconvulsive shock) that causes the amnesia prevents consolidation of the traces laid down by immediately preceding events, causing a loss of memory for such events. Similar effects have been shown in lower animals given electroconvulsive shock immediately after learning.

Multiprocess Theories of Human Memory

Early learning theorists hoped to account for all learning by both humans and lower organisms in terms of a few basic models—for example, by association based on contiguity, or by reinforcement, as in Pavlovian or operant conditioning. It was hoped that memory could be accounted for in the same way. However, by the 1950s many psychologists had grown pessimistic about achieving a unified theory. Influenced by work on communication theory, decision making, and computer science, they began to develop models for specific aspects of human information processing. Some concentrated on how humans retain information for intervals as brief as a few minutes or even seconds. Others, less interested in short-term memory, studied how people retain and retrieve information over periods of days, weeks, and even years. Still other psychologists focused on how people remember visual images or sounds, how they remember particular experiences or episodes rather than facts, and so on.

Out of this varied work emerged a picture of human memory, *not* as a single memory system, but as a number of interrelated memory systems, each with its own special properties. This multiprocess view of human memory is reflected in the highly influential theory proposed by Atkinson and Shiffrin (1971, 1977), which attempted to integrate earlier work on both short-term and long-term memory systems (see Figure 7–12). They suggested that sensory information is briefly retained in **sensory memory systems.** Some of it is then recoded into **short-term memory,** where it may be maintained through a process called **rehearsal.** According to Atkinson and Shiffrin, the longer the information resides in short-term memory, the more likely it is to be finally recoded or transferred into **long-term memory.** Retention in long-term memory is assumed to be virtually permanent, although effective strategies are required for retrieval.

Let's consider this and other multiprocess theories of memory and some of the phenomena they were designed to explain.

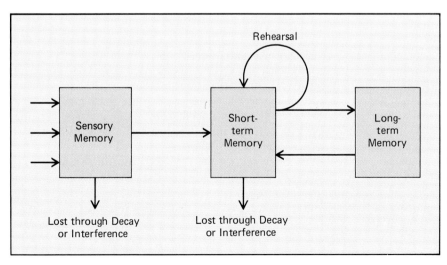

Figure 7–12 Atkinson and Shiffrin's multiprocess view of human memory is shown in this model. Sensory information is briefly retained in some type of sensory memory system; some of it is then recoded into short-term memory, where it may be retained through rehearsal. The longer it remains in short-term memory, the more likely it is to be transferred into long-term memory. While information can be lost from sensory and short-term memories through decay or interference, retention in long-term memory is assumed to be virtually permanent.

Distributed Memory and Connectionist Systems

Where is knowledge stored in the brain? Is each thing that we learn stored in its own memory location, the way facts are stored in computers? Carl Lashley, a famous physiological psychologist, spent most of his life trying to answer such questions. His basic strategy was to train an animal to make a simple discrimination, then to destroy a small part of the animal's brain. The idea was that if the animal still showed evidence of its training, then the memory trace of that training (what Lashley called an *engram*) must have been stored somewhere else in its brain. After many years of research Lashley concluded:

It is not possible to demonstrate the isolated localization of a memory trace anywhere within the nervous system. Limited regions may be essential for learning or retention of a particular activity, but within such regions the parts are functionally equivalent. The engram is represented throughout the region. (1950, p. 478)

In other words, the same knowledge is *distributed* throughout an entire region of the brain and destroying any one part doesn't fully destroy the knowledge.

Most computers represent knowledge (information) as numbers stored in specific memory locations. Information is processed by operating on these numbers one at a time (serially) in a single, central processing unit. *Serial processing computers* of this sort don't seem to have the kind of distributed memory described by Lashley; however, certain newer *parallel processing computers* do. These are called *massively parallel connectionist systems.* They consist of many interconnected processing units that operate simultaneously (in parallel).

Figure A shows the processing *units* (circles) and *connections* (lines) of an illustrative connectionist system. Each unit has some level of *activation,* and each connection a positive or negative *strength*. The more positive the connection between two units, the

Figure A   A simple illustration of a connectionist system.

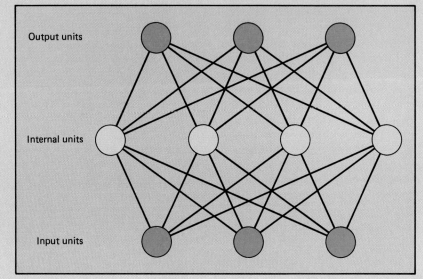

Sensory Memory

A simple example of visual persistence can be seen when a brightly glowing cigarette is moved rapidly back and forth in the dark. It seems to have a tail behind it, indicating that you continue to see light a short time after it has ceased falling on a particular part of the retina. Is this persistence in visual sensation a form of memory? Certainly information about an image is being retained over time, even though that time is very brief, so it would seem to meet the basic definition of a memory system.

This and other evidence has led to the idea of an **iconic memory system** (an *icon* is an image or pictorial representation) that can retain at least some information about visual images for periods up to 1 or 2 seconds. Such information appears to be in a form or code quite similar to the original sensation. It also seems susceptible to disturbance by other visual stimuli. For example, as we pointed out in Chapter 4, while subjects can read short sentences presented on a screen for only 100 milliseconds, reading can be

more they mutually facilitate each other's activity; the more negative the connection, the more they mutually inhibit each other (much as neurons can facilitate or inhibit each other's activity). Information to be processed is entered into the system by fixing the activation levels of *input units* (the blue circles in Figure A). This, in turn, facilitates or inhibits the activity of every other unit, depending on the strengths of the various connections. Processed information is represented by the activity level of certain *output units* (the green circles in Figure A). The rest of the units are referred to as *internal units* (the yellow circles in Figure A).

Sejnowski and Rosenberg (1986) developed a connectionist system called NETtalk that essentially reads text aloud. It is similar to the simple system shown in Figure A except that it involves many more units. The system accepts input consisting of 7 letters at a time through 7 groups of 26 input units (one unit is activated in each group to define each letter). One of 55 output units is then activated by the system, indicating the proper pronunciation of the middle letter (one of 55 phonetic codes). Entering groups of 7 letters in an appropriate sequence (see Figure B) and using the resulting phonetic codes to trigger a sound synthesizer, one can actually hear the system reading text.

How does a system of this sort

1. THE REPRESENTATION OF KNOWLEDGE
2. THE REPRESENTATION OF KNOWLEDGE
3. THE REPRESENTATION OF KNOWLEDGE

Figure B Seven letters of text are successively input (blue) and the system outputs (red) the phonetic code for the middle letter.

"learn" to produce the correct output (sound) for each input (letters), and how is such knowledge represented in the system? While a number of specific learning processes have been developed for such computers (Rumelhart, Hinton, & Williams, 1986), they all operate on the same general principle: *If a specific input doesn't produce the right output, slightly modify the strength of every connection, so that the correct output is more likely the next time that input is given.* After sufficient "training" with a variety of inputs, the system tends to produce the desired output for each input. The "knowledge" it has acquired is simply the total pattern of connection strengths. Furthermore, since during training each input influenced the value of *every* strength,

the knowledge is *distributed*. The system's "memory" of each input-ouput association isn't stored in any one place, it is partially represented in every connection strength. Thus destroying any small set of connections, or arbitrarily changing their strengths, wouldn't completely eliminate the effects of training, just as Lashley's animals showed evidence of prior training no matter which part of their brains he destroyed.

This is but one example of why massively parallel connectionist systems may provide better models of the neural basis of cognition than the more traditional serial computers. (For further discussion and more examples, see Rumelhart, Hinton, & Williams, 1986).

prevented (or at least reduced) by highly contoured patterns presented up to 1 second after the sentence. Since reading can be disrupted by a *subsequent* "masking" pattern, it must occur at least partly *after* the exposure. It is as if subjects continue to read from an iconic memory of the sentence. This effect has been interpreted as a form of retroactive interference that produces information loss in the iconic memory system.

A now-classic experiment on iconic memory was conducted by George Sperling (1960), who was interested in how much people could "see" in a briefly presented visual image. In what he termed a *whole-report procedure,* subjects were shown a 3-by-3 array of 9 letters for only 50 milliseconds and asked to name as many of the letters as they could. While they could usually name only about 4 or 5 of the letters, they reported "seeing" all 9 of them. Sperling surmised that their problem wasn't "seeing" the letters but simply *remembering* them long enough to report them (just as you would have difficulty repeating back a list of 9 letters someone read aloud to you). He devised a *cued partial-report procedure* (Figure 7–13) in which the subject was required to report only 1 of the 3 rows of letters. The particular row was

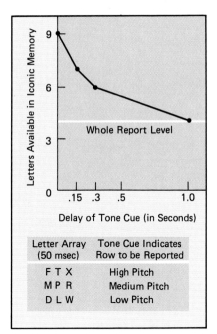

Figure 7–13 Sperling's Cued Partial Report Procedure Sperling (1960) visually presented a 3-by-3 array of letters for 50 milliseconds, followed by an auditory tone cue indicating which row of letters the subject was to report. Sperling estimated the total number of *letters available in iconic memory* by multiplying the number of letters correctly reported from the cued row by the number of rows (3). The results suggest a large-capacity iconic memory that "fades away" (decays) in about 1 second. (From Sperling, 1960)

indicated by a tone cue sounded *after* the letter array had been presented: A high, medium, or low tone indicated, respectively, that the top, middle, or bottom row of letters was to be reported.

Sperling's reasoning went like this: If an iconic memory persisted until the tone cue sounded, the subject need only "read out" and remember for report the 3 letters in the cued row, a relatively easy memory task. Even if only some of the 9 letters remained available in iconic memory when the cue sounded, the subject could at least report these. Thus if you multiplied the average number of letters reported from the cued row times the number of rows (3), you would have an estimate of the total number of letters available in iconic memory when the cue sounded. For example, if the average was 2 letters correctly reported from the cued row, this would imply that 2 × 3 (that is, 6) letters were, on average, available in iconic memory when the cue sounded.

Figure 7–13 shows how Sperling's estimate of the "letters available in iconic memory" depended on the timing of the tone cue. If the cue was sounded immediately after the letters were shown (0 delay), all 3 letters in the cued row were usually reported correctly (the "letters available" equaled 3 × 3 or 9). However, as the delay of the tone cue increased, the estimate of available letters diminished. For example, when the tone occurred 0.3 second after the letters were shown, only about 2 letters in the cued row were reported (the available letters equaled 2 × 3 or 6). At delays of 1 second or more, the subjects reported no more letters from the cued row than would be expected from their whole-report performance.

Sperling's results were seen as supporting the idea of a *high-capacity, rapidly decaying, iconic memory system* in which information is coded in a form similar to the original stimulus (since other visual stimuli would produce interference of "masking").

While the persistence of an iconic memory may be important in tachistoscopic perception, it may not be important in normal vision. Haber (1983) points out that in normal vision most fixations last long enough for the information in view to be processed, without any need for iconic memory. This is exactly what Just and Carpenter (1984) concluded from their studies of eye movements in reading (their results were described in Chapter 4).

Certain characteristics of hearing may be evidence of an **echoic memory system** (Neisser, 1967). As with iconic memory, the information retained seems to be in a form or code quite similar to the original sensation and susceptible to disturbance by other auditory stimulation. For example, the ability to discriminate the pitch of a briefly presented tone can be reduced by the subsequent presentation of an auditory masking tone (Massaro, 1970). This retroactive masking effect occurs at delays of up to a quarter of a second. It should be pointed out that this does not prove that the echoic memory system retains information for only a quarter of a second; it may simply be that pitch recognition is completed in a quarter of a second, so that longer retention doesn't affect pitch judgments.

Iconic and echoic memory systems represent what many theorists, including Atkinson and Shiffrin, have referred to as **sensory memory systems.** Such systems have been suggested for other senses besides vision and hearing. They seem to briefly retain a representation of sensory information in a code quite similar to the original sensation and are susceptible to disturbance by subsequent stimulation of the same sort. These systems may hold sensory information until it can be selectively processed and recoded into a short-term memory system. For example, Sperling interpreted the limit of 4

or 5 letters reported in his whole-report procedure as the capacity of a short-term verbal memory system rather than as the capacity of iconic memory.

Evidence for Two Kinds of Code. Errors made by subjects in the Sperling (1960) study (see Figure 7–13) seemed to reflect the existence of two types of memory representation or code: visual and acoustic. Subjects sometimes reported a letter that wasn't in the display but *looked* like one that was presented—for example, reporting a Y when an X was present, or reporting D when Q was present. Such errors suggest a **visual code.** They also tended to erroneously report letters that *sounded* like letters in the display—for example, reporting T for D, or K for A. These errors seemed more like confusions between some sort of sound representation or **acoustic code.**

Conrad (1964) briefly showed subjects a list of 6 consonants and then asked them to write out the list of letters in the same sequence. Errors were primarily acoustic confusions, such as B instead of T *as if* the sound *tee* had been replaced by the similar sound *bee*. A more recent study by Zhang and Simon (1985) also suggests the existence of an acoustic code. They had Chinese subjects perform a variant of Conrad's task using a list of 6 Chinese characters. If the 6 characters had different acoustic representations in Chinese, the subjects were virtually perfect. However, if the 6 characters shared the same acoustic representation (not uncommon in the Chinese language), subjects could write out only about half the characters correctly. It was *as if* the absence of a different acoustic code forced the subjects to rely on a less persistent visual code.

While acknowledging the existence of visual codes, both Sperling and Conrad interpreted acoustic confusions as evidence for acoustic (verbal) forms of representation as well. They believed that these acoustic codes were maintained in a limited-capacity, short-term memory.

Short-Term Memory

The idea that short-term memory has a capacity of only a few items goes back at least to Ebbinghaus, who reported that the longest list of nonsense syllables we can recall perfectly after only one presentation is about 6 or 7. Similarly, the number of digits **(digit span)** a normal adult can successfully recall immediately after hearing them spoken is about 7 or 8. A variety of evidence suggesting that the capacity of short-term memory is somewhere between 5 and 9 is discussed in a famous paper by George Miller (1956) entitled "The Magical Number Seven Plus or Minus Two." Miller pointed out that these 5 to 9 items should be thought of as "chunks" of information rather than individual units. For example, Figure 7–14 illustrates how subjects can be taught to "chunk" sets of 3 binary digits (1's or 0's) into a single octal digit (0 through 7). The subjects' immediate memory for the binary digits was originally about 7; after training on the chunking or recoding procedure, they could remember almost 7 octal digits, which correspond to about 21 binary units. Thus recoding into more parsimonious "chunks" can effectively increase short-term memory capacity.

Baddeley and Hitch (1974) have suggested that short-term memory might also be thought of as **working memory:** a kind of work space that is used to manipulate and combine information as well as simply hold it. They report several studies in which subjects were asked to remember a short string of digits while simultaneously answering "True" or "False" to a simple logical

<table>
<tr><th colspan="2">Three-Digit
Binary Code</th><th>One-Digit
Octal Code</th></tr>
<tr><td>000</td><td>=</td><td>0</td></tr>
<tr><td>001</td><td>=</td><td>1</td></tr>
<tr><td>010</td><td>=</td><td>2</td></tr>
<tr><td>011</td><td>=</td><td>3</td></tr>
<tr><td>100</td><td>=</td><td>4</td></tr>
<tr><td>101</td><td>=</td><td>5</td></tr>
<tr><td>110</td><td>=</td><td>6</td></tr>
<tr><td>111</td><td>=</td><td>7</td></tr>
</table>

Binary Number:	110	101	111	001	100	110	111
Recoded into Octal Number:	6	5	7	1	4	6	7

Figure 7–14 Subjects can be taught to recode sets of 3 binary digits into a single octal digit. Original memory for binary digits was about 7; after training in the "chunking" procedure, subjects could remember 7 octal digits, or 21 binary digits.

question, such as; "Does L precede T in TL? (The correct answer is "False.") Remembering strings of 1 or 2 digits had little effect on how fast subjects answered the questions. However, as the string of digits increased to 6, their answers became appreciably slower. It was *as if* the logical operations required to answer the question competed for a place in short-term (working) memory with the digits. Just and Carpenter (1980, 1987) suggest that such competition for space in working memory is reflected in normal reading. Readers tend to fixate longer on the last word of a sentence or a long clause, as if they are "wrapping up" their interpretation of its meaning. At this same point readers also tend to lose information about the exact wording of the sentence or clause, often retaining only its general meaning as they continue to read (Jarvella, 1971). Thus the cognitive operations involved in extracting the meaning of a sentence or clause may exhaust the capacity of short-term (working) memory, thereby displacing information about the specific sequence of words.

Retrieval from Short-Term Memory. Sternberg (1966) devised an experimental method for studying how fast people can retrieve information from short-term memory. This method, often referred to as Sternberg's *memory-scanning procedure,* is a simple form of recognition task. On each of a series of trials subjects are shown a small set of items, called the *memory set;* then, a few moments later, another item, called a *probe.* The subject's task is to decide as quickly as possible whether or not the probe is in the memory set shown on that trial. For example, in Sternberg's original experiments each

Table 7–2:   Examples of Test Trials.

Example	Memory Set	Probe	Correct Response
A	2,5	5	yes
B	8	3	no
C	6,8,5,9,2,0	2	yes
D	9,3,6	0	no
E	2,1,9,4,7	2	yes

memory set consisted of from 1 to 6 digits, shown one after another. The probe was also a digit, shown 2 seconds after the last digit of the memory set. Subjects were to quickly press one button if the probe was also in the memory set, a "yes" response; or another button if it wasn't, a "no" response. Both types of trials occurred equally in a random order.

Table 7–2 gives several examples of such trials. Notice that the number of digits in the memory set ranges from 1 in Example B to 6 in Example C. Sternberg wondered how the variation in the size of the memory set would influence the speed of a subject's response. He speculated that the more items a subject had to retain in short-term memory, the longer it would take the subject to retrieve or "scan" those items and decide if one matched the probe.

Figure 7–15 shows the approximately linear relation Sternberg found between the number of items in the memory set and average response time. Each additional item in the memory set added about 38 milliseconds to that time. This suggested to Sternberg that subjects "scanned or compared the items in a short-term memory one after another (serially), with each item taking about 38 milliseconds—a *high-speed, serial-scanning process.*"

A surprising feature of Sternberg's results was the fact that both "yes" and "no" responses could be described by linear functions with the same slope. This is not what one would expect if the serial-scanning process ended as soon as an item in the memory set was found to match the probe.

A *self-terminating process* of this sort would require you to scan all the items to decide "no," but (on average) only half the items to decide "yes." Thus the slope of the "yes" response function in Figure 7–15 should be only half that of the "no" response function. This led Sternberg to propose that *all* items are scanned before either a "yes" or "no" decision is made, an *exhaustive process.*

Although it is now clear that there are other ways of interpreting Sternberg's data, his interpretation is elegantly simple and difficult to disprove. It remains a fine example of the interplay between theory and data in the study of human memory.

Rehearsal and Transfer. Atkinson and Shiffrin (see Figure 7–12) believed that information could be retained in short-term memory through a process of *rehearsal*—repeating it over and over. The longer the rehearsal period, the more likely that the information would be transferred to long-term memory. This theory provides an interpretation of the Peterson and Peterson (1959) experiment we described earlier (see Figure 7–9). Distracting subjects immediately after they heard a trigram prevents rehearsal, so the trigram is rapidly lost and unlikely to enter long-term memory.

A similar explanation can be given for the shape of the serial position curve (see Figure 7–3) in recall. Rundus (1971) conducted an experiment in which subjects were slowly shown a list of words, one word at a time. They were instructed to "rehearse out loud" any words they wished as the list was presented. This allowed Rundus to count how often each word was rehearsed. The primacy effect can be explained by the more frequent rehearsal of early items, thereby (according to Atkinson and Shiffrin) allowing them more opportunity to transfer into long-term memory. The recency effect can be attributed to late items remaining in short-term memory after the list is presented.

The rehearsal explanation is an alternative to consolidation theory's interpretation of retrograde amnesia caused by trauma. It proposes that trauma causes loss of information from short-term memory before it can be

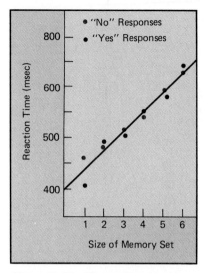

Figure 7–15 The average time to answer "yes" (black circles) or "no" (red circles) for memory sets. (Sternberg, 1966)

rehearsed and transferred to long-term memory. This loss, rather than the failure to consolidate a memory trace, causes retrograde amnesias.

The pattern of memory in patients who have Korsakoff's syndrome also seems consistent with the idea of separate short- and long-term memory systems. Perhaps these patients have normal short-term memories but have lost the ability to transfer new information into long-term memory.

Notice how closely related the idea of short-term memory is to the concept of consciousness (see Chapter 5). Information in short-term memory seems readily accessible. It is information we are currently working with, transforming, rehearsing, recoding. In fact, it is the almost immediate accessibility of information in working memory that distinguishes it from the larger store of information in longer-term memory systems, which seem to involve lengthier retrieval processes.

Long-Term Memory

Consider how long it can take you to recall what you did three summers ago, or the way your bedroom looked when you were in high school. Are you retrieving information from a separate **long-term memory system,** with a much greater capacity than short-term memory, but requiring lengthier and more complicated retrieval processes? Many psychologists believe so. Some also believe that there are different types of long-term memory, specialized for different types of knowledge. For example, one distinction is that between propositional (declarative) knowledge and procedural knowledge (Ryle, 1949; Anderson, 1976). **Propositional** or **declarative knowledge** is factual knowledge, such as "5 is larger than 4," "I walked to school," or "Ice is cold." Each statement is a *proposition,* a relation between two or more concepts (for example, the relation "larger than" between the concepts "5" and "4"). Each proposition is a declaration of fact and is either true or false. Such knowledge can often be acquired through a single experience and represented in a purely symbolic form (as by the words on this page). In contrast, **procedural knowledge** is knowledge of how to do something, whether tying your shoes or programming a computer. Such knowledge is usually gained slowly, through repeated experience or practice, and is evidenced by how well (or poorly) you perform some task.

Propositional or Declarative Knowledge. Tulving (1972) argued that there are really two forms of propositional or declarative knowledge, episodic and semantic, each represented in its own memory system. **Episodic knowledge** consists of propositions regarding specific experiences or episodes in your past, such as "I walked to school this morning," "I spoke to John last night," or "We talked until midnight." In contrast, the propositions of **semantic knowledge** are declarations of facts independent of *when* you learned or experienced them, such as "5 is larger than 3," "A pelican is a bird," or "Hartford is in Connecticut."

An incident involving a neurologist and a brain-damaged patient (Clarparede, 1911) is sometimes cited as evidence of separate semantic and episodic memory systems. The doctor once hid a sharp pin in his hand before shaking hands with the patient. He wanted to see how the pain of the pinprick would affect her memory for the event. Later when the doctor again offered his hand to her, she refused, saying only that "doctors sometimes hide pins in their hands." It was as if she had forgotten the specific painful

episode (a failure of episodic memory) but remembered a general fact (semantic memory).

Tulving (1972) also pointed out that the verbal learning research of Ebbinghaus was really the study of episodic rather than semantic memory. Subjects recalled such things as "DAX was one of the nonsense syllables I just read" or "*Crystal* was one of the words in the first list you read to me." The subject was *not* concerned with the (semantic) meaning of DAX and *crystal,* but simply with whether or not they had been presented at a particular time (episodic knowledge). Thus, much of the research on verbal learning discussed earlier in this chapter could be considered research on episodic rather than semantic memory.

The study of semantic memory is more in the tradition of Bartlett. It is concerned with the *meanings* of words and with memory for progressively larger meaningful units such as sentences (Anderson & Paulson, 1977), paragraphs (Kintsch & Bates, 1977), and stories (Rumelhart, 1977; Bower, Black, & Turner, 1979).

Many theoretical ideas about semantic memory stem from the gradual (step-by-step) way we often retrieve information from long-term memory. The desired information isn't recalled immediately, but is remembered only after we first recall related information. Aristotle referred to this gradual process of recall as "recollection" and argued that it reflected a sequence of associations between ideas. The recollection of one idea leads through association to the next, and so on, until you finally recall the desired information. Put another way, *each recalled idea in turn becomes a recall cue for another idea.*

The idea of knowledge as a *network of associations* has a long history in psychology. A modern version of this view is that human memory should be thought of as a *network of interrelated propositions* (Anderson & Kintsch, 1974; Norman & Rumelhart, 1975). This stems in large part from computer scientists' use of such networks to represent knowledge in computer programs, especially those designed to process language or recognize forms (see the discussion of computer pattern recognition in Chapter 4). A simple illustration of knowledge represented by a propositional network can be made in terms of the following sentence:

Mattingly hit a high pop-up to Carter, the catcher for the Mets.

The information (knowledge) in this sentence could be broken down into three simpler propositions:

A. Mattingly hit a pop-up to Carter.
B. The pop-up was high.
C. Carter was the catcher for the Mets.

The network of interrelations among these three propositions is represented graphically in Figure 7–16. Again, each proposition specifies a relation between two or more concepts; for example, Proposition C specifies that the concept "Carter" (the player) has the relation "catcher for" with the concept "Mets" (the baseball team). Other aspects of each proposition, such as tense (time), subject, object, or recipient of an action, are indicated next to the arrows in Figure 7–16. The psychological reality of such representations is suggested by experiments in which people were asked to recall sentences (e.g., Anderson, 1976). They were much better at recalling the information represented in individual propositions than at recalling the actual sequence

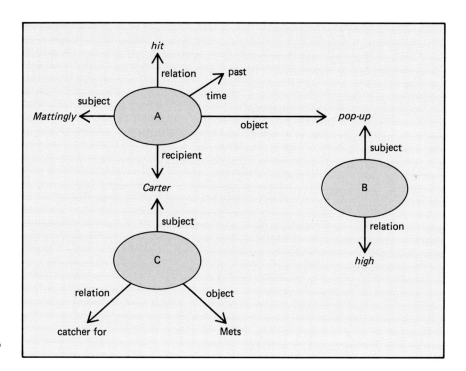

Figure 7–16 A graphic representation of the network of interrelated propositions (A, B, C) in the statement "Mattingly hit a high pop-up to Carter, the catcher for the Mets."

of words *(surface form)* of the sentences. For example, they might remember the full sentence represented in Figure 7–16, but in this form:

The high pop-up hit by Mattingly went to the Mets' catcher, Carter.

The information in the individual propositions (A, B, and C) would have been recalled, but not the surface form.

Recall of information from a propositional network is often described in terms of *activating* particular propositions, thereby making them easier to recall. It is assumed that a proposition is activated either by some external event (cue) or by the earlier activation of a related proposition. In other words, there is a **spread of activation** from an activated proposition to closely related propositions. A good *recall cue* either activates the desired information directly or activates it indirectly by first activating related information. This is one explanation for the tip-of-the-tongue (TOT) phenomenon discussed earlier: Closely related information is activated first, with activation finally spreading to the desired word.

Spread of activation would also explain a phenomenon called **priming:** Information is often recalled more easily (rapidly) if closely related information has recently been recalled or activated (primed). For example, Meyer and Schvaneveldt (1971) asked subjects to decide as quickly as possible whether the items in pairs of letter strings were *both* words (e.g., first–truck) or not (e.g., roast–frist; flact–brive). Subjects recognized a pair of words faster if the two items were closely related (e.g., bread–butter; farm–barn) than if they weren't (e.g., rope–crystal; nurse–steak). It was as if the first word the subjects processed activated or primed knowledge that was closely related, thus making a closely related word easier to recognize.

It has been argued that knowledge can be represented in long-term memory by images or pictures as well as by propositional or verbal codes. This **dual-coding** view (Paivio, 1971) was encouraged by experiments of the

Table 7–3: Examples of Two Productions.
Each production consists of conditions (IF) and a procedure (THEN) to be followed when the conditions are met. Anderson's ACT theory represents human procedural knowledge as a combination of propositional networks and procedures of this sort.

Production:	One way to make a noun plural.
IF	the goal is to generate a plural noun and the noun ends in a hard consonant,
THEN	generate the noun with an "s" on the end.
Production:	Changing from first to second gear in one kind of car.
IF	the car is in first gear and the car is going faster than 10 mph and there is a clutch and there is a stick shift,
THEN	depress the clutch and move the stick to the upper right and release the clutch.

Adapted with permission from *Cognitive Psychology and Its Applications* by John R. Anderson. Copyright © 1980, W. H. Freeman and Company.

sort described in the Highlight: Visual Memory. An alternative view (e.g., Anderson, 1978) is that information in long-term memory is always represented in a propositional code. We may simply construct a "mental image" as we retrieve this information, just as we visualize a scene described verbally in a novel.

Procedural Knowledge. We learn how to do things, and we can remember (or forget) how to do them. Thus we have some sort of memory for procedural knowledge. Applied psychologists have long been interested in how we learn such perceptual-motor skills as aiming a rifle or hitting a golf ball (see Keele & Summers, 1976, for a review of such work). More recently, cognitive psychologists have become interested in cognitive skills such as adding two numbers, playing chess, or running a meeting. How is such procedural knowledge represented in memory?

A theory of procedural knowledge has recently been proposed (Anderson, 1980, 1983). Called ACT theory, it combines a propositional network of the sort we considered earlier with the step-by-step procedures, resulting in a *production* (Newell, 1973; Simon, 1978). Some examples of productions are shown in Table 7–3. Notice that each procedure is to be carried out when certain conditions (indicated by propositions) are met. *Production systems* have been used quite successfully in the programming of "expert systems." As mentioned earlier in this chapter, such efforts to simulate the way an "expert" stores and retrieves knowledge may provide a theory of human memory.

Procedural knowledge can also be represented as a **script** (Schank & Abelson, 1976), a generalized program that outlines how to do something and that we can modify to fit particular circumstances. For example, subjects were asked to describe the 20 most important steps in "eating in a restaurant" (Bower et al., 1979). While there were many individual differences, most agreed on several basic steps or "scenes" (see Table 7–4). Each scene also tended to have a typical internal structure: For example, in Scene 5 the main course is eaten before dessert. This basic script could be modified to fit special circumstances such as "eating at a cafeteria." One can easily think of

Table 7–4: The Restaurant Script.

Scene 1
Enter restaurant.
Scene 2
Be seated.
Scene 3
Look over menu.
Scene 4
Order meal.
Scene 5
Eat meal.
Scene 6
Pay bill.
Scene 7
Leave restaurant.

scripts for other activities, such as making an airline reservation, getting dressed, or going to a party.

Earlier we pointed out that some chronic anterograde amnesiacs can learn new *skills* and retain them for several months even though they can't retain new facts for more than a few minutes (Baddeley, 1982; Moscovitch, 1982). This has been cited as clinical evidence for the existence of a separate procedural memory system.

Depth of Processing: An Alternative to the Multiprocess View

The multiprocess view of human memory sees knowledge as represented in a number of interacting memory systems. For example, according to the Atkinson and Shiffrin model (Figure 7–12), transfer of information from short-term to long-term memory depends only on the length of time it remains in short-term memory. Thus transfer is more likely to occur if the subject maintains the information in short-term memory through rehearsal.

It seems clear, however, that one does many things to information in short-term memory beyond the simple rehearsal process suggested by Atkinson and Shiffrin. First of all, information may be combined with other information to form more complex representations or codes, the process we referred to earlier as *elaboration*. For example, on hearing the word *boat,* you might encode it into short-term memory. You might then retrieve information held in long-term memory and visualize a boat you had previously sailed on. Thus you would now have a representation of a word just spoken, plus information of an earlier experience. The more you thought about boats, the more complex the representations you might develop. Any of these may be encoded and available for retrieval later. The question arises: Is it simply the amount of time an item spends in short-term memory that increases its long-term retention, or is retention enhanced by the multiplicity and complexity of representations that the item evokes as you continue to think about it?

Craik and Lockhart (1972) proposed the latter view as an alternative to Atkinson and Shiffrin's multiple memory system. They argued that we ignore most of the information available in our ongoing sensory experiences, so it is never elaborated into more complex representations. This is why it is unlikely to be remembered. For example, as you drive down a street, many signs are projected onto your retina. Some you attend to and think about to varying degrees, others go totally unnoticed. A stop sign usually requires only a small amount of attention or thought, while a sign advertising a movie you recently saw could evoke a complex series of thoughts drawing on a large amount of associated information in memory. Thus it could be argued that the **depth of processing** we give any experience determines the number and complexity of its encodings and therefore how likely we are to recall it in the future.

Craik and Tulving (1975) conducted an experiment to evaluate depth of processing. They presented a series of words to subjects, along with questions asking something about each word. Some questions—such as "Is the word in capital letters?"—only required a surface analysis of the word. Other questions required deeper processing—for example, "Would the word fit in the sentence 'The boy played the ———'?" Later, when subjects were given an unexpected recognition test, their ability to recognize a word was directly related to the depth of processing required by the earlier question about that word.

One's "depth of processing" of various parts of this scene (and therefore, your memory of the scene) would differ considerably depending on whether you were hungry, wanted to buy gasoline for your car, or a new stereo system for your home. (Lynn Johnson/Black Star)

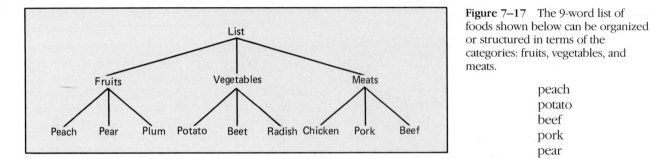

Figure 7–17 The 9-word list of foods shown below can be organized or structured in terms of the categories: fruits, vegetables, and meats.

peach
potato
beef
pork
pear
beet
plum
radish
chicken

A closely related aspect of depth of processing is the organization and structuring that occur during elaboration. This can involve reordering material from the sequence in which it was experienced into a sequence more consistent with some logical structure. You often do this when abstracting or summarizing a lecture, particularly when the lecturer's organization of the material seems less satisfactory than your own. Note that such recoding or reorganization of information is one way in which our general world knowledge (general rules or principles, facts, etc.) may derive from our ongoing experience. Memory for particular sequences of our own experiences (episodic memory) and memory for general knowledge (semantic memory) may simply reflect different levels or forms of organization rather than different memory systems.

We mentioned earlier that stimuli that were present when something was originally learned (encoded) may later serve as effective recall cues, a phenomenon Tulving (1978) called *encoding specificity*. If as you originally learned something you organized it into categories and thought about those category names, the names might later serve as useful recall cues. For example, suppose you were asked to remember the list of foods in the margin of this page (see Figure 7–17). After looking at the list for a few moments, you would probably notice that it contains the names of three fruits, three vegetables, and three meats. Thus you could reorganize it to reflect this structure, as shown in Figure 7–17. In attempting to recall the list, you could first retrieve a category name, which then, according to encoding specificity, would serve as a cue for the recall of items in the category.

Your understanding of a story's structure (see Figure 7–18) might aid recall in a very similar fashion. In thinking about the story structure, you could develop more elaborate codes *(schemas, scripts)* to characterize the story— for example: "There were four main scenes in the story—the setting, crisis, solution, and reward." This code, which would probably be easier to recall than the details of the story, could serve as a cue for recalling these details, just as the category names (fruits, vegetables, and meats) did in the preceding examples.

Constructive Memory

In Chapter 4 we emphasized the role of stimulus redundancy in perception. Because different aspects of a stimulus are often correlated (redundant), we can infer things about one aspect from another (e.g., linear perspective is a strong cue for depth). It appears that the same sort of thing happens when information is retrieved from human memory. Suppose, for example, you were asked to describe someone you met only briefly a year ago. You might

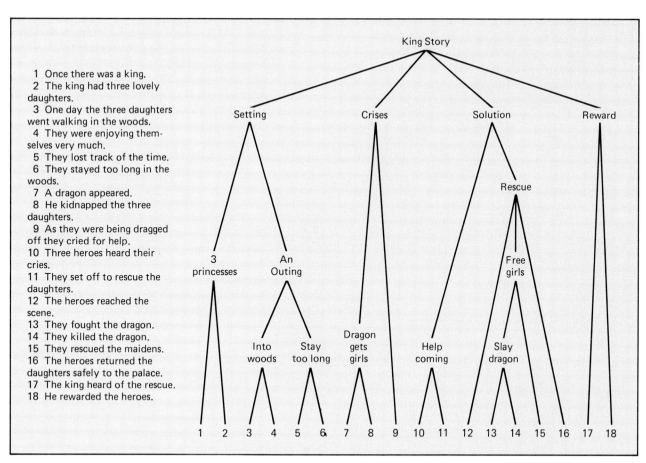

Figure 7-18 Understanding a story's structure can aid recall. In thinking about the structure of the king story shown here, you might develop more elaborate codes to characterize the story; these codes would serve as cues for recalling details of the story. (Pollard-Gott, McCluskey, & Todres, 1979)

first recall that the person was an automobile salesman. You might then recall that he had an outgoing personality, was quite verbal, and argued persuasively. But wait! Is this information based on your actual experience with this man or on your *stereotype* of car salesmen (that is, on what you believe to be the typical personality characteristics of car salesmen)? Certainly people's choice of occupation is often correlated with their personality. It would be possible, but very surprising, to find an introverted, inarticulate car salesman who couldn't argue persuasively. Thus remembering a person's occupation often allows us to make useful inferences about his or her personality. In fact, we make such inferences so often and so automatically that we may not even be sure whether we are recalling our actual experiences with people or inferring what their behavior was like on the basis of what we remember about their occupation. Inferences of this sort can sometimes distort our recollection of people so that we treat them unfairly, just as our perceptions can sometimes be biased because of inappropriate inferences. (Our ways of interpreting events and people, and some inherent biases in the process, will be discussed at length in Chapter 19.) However, most such inferences aid retrieval, just as they do perception. Even if you can recall only a few major details of some past event, you can often fill in or construct details you can't recall on the basis of your knowledge of redundancy.

In her book *Eyewitness Testimony,* Elizabeth Loftus (1979) considers how witnesses recall a crime or accident. In one experiment all subjects were shown a filmed auto accident. Half of the subjects were then asked, "How fast

Take about 2 minutes to simultaneously recall as many names as you can from the following two categories: *Category* A, names of males you knew in high school; *Category* B, names of Asian countries. Most people feel they can't "search their memory for" or "recall items from" both categories at the same time. Instead they seem to recall names from one category for a while, then the other, switching back and forth as they run out of names in each (Kinchla, 1985). In other words, they seem to have an *attentional problem* similar to those discussed earlier in Chapter 4: Two sources of information can't both be processed optimally at the same time. Only here the two competing "sources of information" are categories of knowledge in memory, rather than external sources of information (such as the two simultaneous voices in the cocktail party problem).

Not all categories of knowledge produce the same attentional problem. For example, suppose the two categories to be recalled were: A, names of males you knew in high school; and B, names of females you knew in high school. Here the cognitive processes involved in recalling the two categories seem much more compatible. In fact, the recall of a name from one category may even facilitate recall of one from the other. For example, a subject might report: "Bill Howard was in my math class, and ahh . . . , he was always talking to that girl who sat in front of him. What was her name? Oh yes, Joan

Peters!" Clearly the degree of *recall compatibility* between two categories of knowledge seems to reflect something about the way knowledge is organized in memory. Closely related categories should show more recall compatibility than totally unrelated categories.

It is possible to show trade-offs in recalling two categories from memory, similar to the trade-offs referred to as *attention operating characteristic* (AOC) *functions* in perception (see Chapter 4). Kinchla (1985) gave subjects 3-minute periods to simultaneously recall items from two categories of knowledge. For example, during one 3-minute period Category A would be *"famous people from the John F. Kennedy administration,"* while Category B was *"famous people from the Richard M. Nixon administration."* Furthermore, during each 3-minute recall period the two categories were each given a "point value" to indicate the relative importance of recalling an item from that category. Items from Category A were worth either 6, 4, 3, 2, or 0 points while items from B were worth, respectively, either 0, 2, 3, 4, or 6 points. Kinchla found that the average number of items recalled from each category varied with the point value, revealing a processing trade-off. Subjects could recall more items from a category worth more points only at the cost of recalling fewer items from the other category. This is *not* simply due to limits on writing speed since subjects spent only about 20 percent of the recall period writing words. The rest of the time was spent in ruminating.

Thus, just as in the processing of external sources of information, processing (recalling) information

from memory can involve selective or attentional problems. Processing one source faster (more accurately, etc.) often precludes optimal processing of another source.

Of course not all recall is as slow as the examples we have just considered. When one is shown the symbol (cue) "DOG," it evokes an almost automatic recall of both the sound of the word and semantic knowledge one has about dogs. Note that this automaticity is essentially the same as that illustrated by the Stroop effect (see Chapter 4): One can't ignore what a word says, even when only the color of ink is relevant. Looked at in this way, the concepts of attention and automaticity in cued recall are very similar to those in perception. Indeed it seems possible to think of perception as a kind of cued recall, usually involving many redundant and powerful cues capable of evoking nonvolitional, rapid, and highly accurate ("automatic") recall of knowledge.

It may seem strange to think of perception as cued recall. Don't we sometimes see something for the first time? How does one recall something one never saw before? Yet any normal scene is filled with elements we have seen before, or at least similar things (chairs, trees, hills, etc.). Just as we can "see" a scene described in a novel, we may see actual scenes as a combination of things (or classes of things) we *recall* based on the visual cue present, a cued recall process. Some of these cues evoke virtually automatic recall, while the effect of other cues is susceptible to volitional control much like any other form of recall. This selective form of recall may be what we think of as attention in perception.

were the cars going when they *smashed into* each other?" The other subjects were asked, "How fast were the cars going when they *hit* each other?" The "smashed into" phrasing elicited much higher speed estimates than the "hit" phrasing. Furthermore, this effect on the subjects' memories was still evident a week later when they were asked (among other questions), "Did you see any broken glass?" Almost twice as many of the "smashed into" subjects remembered broken glass, even though no broken glass was shown in the film. It was as if the verbs in the original question colored their reconstruction of the event, with "smashed into" evoking a memory of a more violent accident than "hit."

One interesting aspect of constructive processes in memory is the difficulty they produce in interpreting the recall of dreams. Suppose you are trying to recall a dream you had the night before. You remember dreaming that you were sitting in your kitchen and then, a short while later, driving your car. Now, in the real world it would be impossible to get from your kitchen to your car without leaving the house and walking to your car. In other words, the two events you do remember—sitting in your kitchen and driving a car—are almost perfectly correlated with the intermediate event of moving from the kitchen to the car (they are among the scripts or schemas that you have for traveling). If you were recalling these events from real life instead of from a dream, you would be quite safe in assuming you had moved from the kitchen to the car. In fact, you might find it hard to tell whether you really remember walking to the car or have simply inferred it from events you do recall. You probably make such automatic inferences during your attempts to recall dreams, but in the dream world events aren't constrained by the rules of physical reality. Therefore we have no way of determining how much people really remember about their dreams and how much they automatically infer during reconstruction on the basis of inappropriate physical laws.

IMPROVING MEMORY

Methods for improving memory are called **mnemonic techniques** or simply **mnemonics.** They can be as trivial as tying a string around your finger, or highly elaborate strategies that take considerable time to learn. Many of these techniques were developed hundreds of years ago by actors, politicians, scholars, magicians, and priests. While the originators of these techniques weren't familiar with modern theories of human memory, most mnemonics can be understood in terms of these theories, and they seem to involve only a few basic principles.

Mnemonics may help in learning your lines in a play. (Susan McCartney/ Photo Researchers)

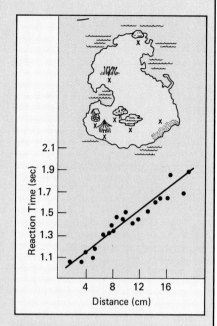

HIGHLIGHT

Visual Memory: When Remembering Seems Like Seeing

Can you remember how many right turns you normally make when walking from one campus building to another? Or how many windows there are in the front of your house? Many people say they would answer such questions by taking an imaginary walk across the campus and noticing how often they turned right, or by creating a mental image of their house and "looking at it" to count the windows. This suggests that remembering may sometimes be like seeing. Although this is a controversial issue, there are a number of studies that seem to support this view.

The work on iconic memory described earlier in the text suggests that we have very short-term visual memory systems (1 to 2 seconds). Other experiments imply that retrieval of information over much longer retention intervals may also have "visual" properties.

Paivio (1978) asked subjects to recall how clocks looked at various times and to compare the angles formed by the hour and minute hands. For example, he asked, "Is the angle larger at 4:25 or 9:10?" As can be seen in Figure A, the angle in this case is larger at 9:10. The graph in Figure A indicates how the average reaction time (time to decide) decreased as the *difference* between the two angles increased. Thus when the angles are similar in size (for example, 12:05 and 1:10), answers are given more slowly than when the angles are very different (for example, 4:25 and 9:10).

The important point is that this pattern of results is similar to that obtained when the subjects are actually shown two clock faces and asked to compare the angles. Thus when asked to compare how two times would look from memory, subjects act *as if* they were seeing a mental image.

Kosslyn, Ball, and Reiser (1978) had subjects memorize a map similar to the one shown in Figure B. They then asked them to "visualize" the map from memory, focusing on a particular object such as the "hut" in the lower left corner of the island. The subjects were then told to "imagine a black dot moving from that object to another point on the map"; for example, to the "marsh" in the upper left of the island. As indicated on the graph in Figure B, the time it took to visualize the dot moving from one point to another was a linear function of the actual distance on the map. Again, it was as if subjects

Figure A When asked to mentally compare the angles formed by the two hands of a clock at different times, the reaction time to decide which was larger decreased as angular differences increased. (Paivio, 1978)

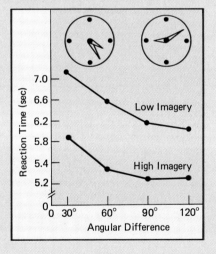

Figure B If asked to visualize a dot moving from one point (X) to another in a previously memorized map, subjects' visualization time was a linear function of distance on the map (Kosslyn et al., 1978)

were actually seeing a dot move across a remembered image of the map, since the farther it had to move, the longer it took.

If remembering how something looked is really like seeing it again, such visualization may interfere with normal vision. Segal and Fusella (1970) asked subjects to form either a visual image (for example, the image of a horse) or an auditory image (for example, the sound of a doorbell). They found that when subjects formed visual images they were poorer at detecting visual signals than when they imagined sounds. Similar *modality-specific interference* during visualization has been demonstrated by Brooks (1968) and Byrne (1974).

Basic Principles

It seems clear that the more you think about something, the more likely you are to remember it. However, as we have seen, this usually means more than simple repetitive rehearsal of the information. It also involves elaboration and reorganization of the information, which produce multiple encodings

APPLICATION

Unusual Memories

It is popularly believed that some people are born with an extraordinary ability to remember things, a sort of supermemory. Actually, there is very little hard evidence to support this belief, even though psychologists have long been interested in studying such people.

Many of those who claim to have supermemories make their living on the stage, and are referred to as *mnemonists*. Like magicians, many mnemonists are quite secretive about their methods. However, there is little reason to believe they actually have supermemories. Like magicians, many simply employ outright deception, such as a confederate in the audience or a hidden radio system. Others use mnemonic techniques that, with sufficient practice, could be used just as effectively by anyone. Of course, such mnemonists would like their audiences to believe they are using extraordinary mental powers rather than elaborations of the basic mnemonic techniques described in this chapter.

One interesting case of someone who actually seemed to combine mnemonic techniques with unusual mental abilities is presented in the book *The Mind of a Mnemonist* by the Russian neurophysiologist Alexander Luria (1920/1968). Luria's subject seemed to have an unusually well-developed capacity for visualization, which he used to recall information. He reported being able to associate information with visual experience quite easily. In fact, his subjective experiences could be described as synesthetic. *Synesthesia* refers to experiences in one sensory mode evoked by stimulation of another. Luria's subject had intense visual associations to nonvisual stimuli. Thus he often described auditory tones as having a vivid color. He also wasn't very good at remembering certain things, particularly aspects of a stimulus that didn't lend themselves to visualization. Other interesting studies of mnemonists have been reported by Aitkin (1962), Hunt and Love (1972), and Coltheart and Glick (1974).

Another type of supermemory is **eidetic imagery** or, as it is more commonly called, **photographic memory.** This is an ability to remember how something looked in such vivid detail that it is like actually seeing it again. Strangely, considering how many people claim to know, or have heard of, or be related to, someone who has this ability, there is very little evidence that such an ability exists. Early studies of eidetic imagery used such questionable methods that it is difficult to draw any clear conclusions from them. More recently, Leask, Haber, and Haber (1969) tested 500 schoolchildren and classified only about 7 percent as eidetic, and even these children could have been described as simply having very good imagery rather than a photographic memory.

What appeared to be the first really convincing evidence of true eidetic imagery was reported by Stromeyer and Psotka in 1973. Their subject was shown one member of a pair of random-dot stereograms on one day, and then saw the second a day later. The two patterns were such that, when fused stereoptypically, a viewer would see a digit standing out against a background. Each pattern by itself consisted of thousands of tiny black-and-white squares arranged in a totally random pattern. It would seem impossible for subjects to identify the digit unless they had a virtually photographic memory of the first pattern, which they could then "fuse" with the pattern seen a day later. The apparent ability of one subject to do this has been cited as finally proving the existence of eidetic imagery. Unfortunately, that subject subsequently refused to demonstrate her skill, and the study has never been successfully repeated. Thus it is still questionable whether true eidetic imagery exists.

and useful recall cues. The importance of such cues is obvious if you consider how information is usually retrieved from long-term memory. The process can take some time and often has discernible stages. Each retrieved piece of information aids the retrieval of more information—thus the retrieval process may require several steps to recover information gradually. If you can't immediately recall a particular fact, you may find it possible to recall something that will serve as an effective recall cue for what you want to remember. Thus a common feature of most mnemonic techniques is the use of recall cues that are easier to retrieve than the information they subsequently help you to remember.

How does one select appropriate cues and how does something come to function as a cue? First of all, a cue will serve no useful purpose unless it can be recalled. Second, it is of no use to recall the cue if it isn't an effective one. For example, a string tied around your finger is an external memory cue that may help you remember something. It has the advantage of being easily retrieved, but it may not be an effective recall cue: You may be aware that the knot on your finger was put there to remind you of something, but be totally unable to remember what that something was.

The phenomenon of encoding specificity suggests one principle for making cues effective. The cue should be present at the time you originally encoded the information. For example, you were thinking about something when you tied the string around your finger; thus, according to the principle of encoding specificity, seeing the string may be a good cue for remembering those thoughts. This principle should apply not only to physical, contextual cues but also to cognitive cues. Visiting the house you grew up in may be an effective cue for many childhood memories, but simply visualizing the house may also serve to evoke these early memories.

Something may also serve as a cue if it is closely related to the information you want to remember. This relation may be as simple as "rhymes with" or "has the same first letter"; or as complex as a category name. For example, you might remember that your shopping list included "vegetables," which, in turn, would help you recall specific members of this category. Similarly, suppose you want to remember the information in a chapter or story. The title of a specific section or structural component of the material could serve as a recall cue for information in that component. For example, the structure of the king story was illustrated earlier in Figure 7–18. The terms *setting, crisis, solution,* and *reward* could serve as recall cues for various major parts of the story (e.g., *crises* for the information in sentences 7, 8, and 9). Outlining material helps you remember it, partly because the phrases you use to characterize each section can function as recall cues.

Mnemonics

One of the oldest mnemonics was used by ancient Greek orators to help them remember the sequence of points they wanted to make in a speech. The technique is called the **method of loci.** The basic idea is to use some well-learned sequence of locations as a series of cues for the information you want to remember. For example, suppose you wanted to remember the following shopping list: milk, cereal, eggs, and bread. You could use the familiar sequence of locations encountered on entering your own house as an easily recalled sequence of cues: your front porch, the hallway inside the front door, the living room, and the kitchen. Then you would associate each location with one of the items to be remembered by clearly visualizing each location cue and the associated grocery item. You might imagine milk covering your front porch and dripping down the steps. Next you might visualize your front hall ankle deep in cereal, crunching underfoot as you waded through it. Your living room could be completely covered with eggs—splattered against the wall, breaking under your feet. Finally, you would visualize your kitchen full of loaves of bread, fluffy loaves piled one upon the other, pouring out of your oven and filling the whole kitchen. Then when you reached the store, you could take a mental walk through your house, using each location as a cue for a particular item.

A related mnemonic involves learning an ordered series of **peg words.** You start with an easily recalled series, the numbers 1 to 10. These numbers will be the cues for words that rhyme with each number. These words, in turn, will be cues for things you wish to remember. For example, the numbers can be used to recall the list of rhyming words in Figure 7–19. After only a few moments of practice each number should become an effective cue for its rhyming word. In order to use these words as cues for the items you wish to remember, you must somehow associate them in your memory. This can be done in much the same fashion as in the method of loci: Each item to

Figure 7–19 In this mnemonic technique the numbers serve as cues for the rhyming *peg words* beside them. The peg words can be used as cues for things one wishes to remember, such as items on a shopping list.

one	bun
two	shoe
three	tree
four	door
five	hive
six	sticks
seven	heaven
eight	date
nine	vine
ten	hen

be remembered is visualized in conjunction with the cue word. For example, suppose you wanted to use this method to remember the same shopping list (milk, cereal, eggs, bread). You could first visualize a bun with milk; perhaps an overturned milk bottle with a soggy bun in a puddle of milk. Next a shoe filled with cereal. Then a green tree growing up through an enormous pile of pure white eggs, or a tree with eggs in place of fruit. And finally, a loaf of bread caught in a closing door. Now, to retrieve the four grocery items, you could use the numbers as cues for the rhyming words, which would, in turn, cue recall of the visualizations and the grocery items.

Many techniques for remembering take advantage of the fact that certain stimuli are presented to you when you need to recall something; thus such stimuli are particularly useful as recall or retrieval cues. Consider the **key word method** developed by Atkinson and Raugh (1975) for learning foreign languages. At first foreign words may not be good direct cues for their English equivalent. However, they can often be used as an indirect recall cue. Many foreign words are good cues for English words that rhyme with them. For example, the word *maison* in French corresponds to *house* in English. *Maison* approximately rhymes with the English word *mason,* and it is easy to visualize a stonemason building a house. Thus *maison* would be a cue for *mason,* which would be a cue for *house.* Naturally, in the later stages of learning a language the use of key words should become unnecessary. However, studies have shown that initial use of key words speeds the learning of a foreign language (e.g., Pressley, Revin, & Delaney, 1982).

A generally useful sort of cue is an abbreviation or reductive coding of a more complex phrase. An **acronym** is a word made up from parts of the words in a more complex phrase—a type of "chunking" procedure. Comsat, for example, is an abbreviation of "communications satellite." Not only is it an abbreviation, but it is a good cue for the longer title.

How to Remember

The preceding mnemonic techniques may be useful in special instances. More importantly, however, they illustrate general strategies that may be applied whenever you want to remember something. Here are some things you can do to aid your memory:

1. Think about the information you want to remember as long, and as often, as possible. (Remember, spaced practice is better than massed practice.)
2. Don't just repeat the information over and over. Try to elaborate, rephrase, and reorganize it.
3. If possible, ask questions about the material you wish to remember. In addition to giving you more time to think about it, this also forces you to consider different aspects and details of the material.
4. Think of ways in which you might use recall cues. What do you associate with the material that may be easier to recall and could then act as recall cue? Are there key words you could learn to recall through rhyming or visualization? They would serve as good recall cues.
5. Outline or think about the structure of the information. Is there a way of naming or describing major components of the structure so that these names might serve as recall cues?

6. Is the information redundant? Could you recode or reduce it to a simpler form from which it would be easy to reconstruct the rest? In other words, what are the key ideas? Can you summarize or abbreviate?

7. Practice retrieval. Don't just study material; put it aside occasionally and practice remembering it. Can you remember things in sequence so that one thing serves as a recall cue for the next? Practice going through these sequences, and try to devise better ones.

SUMMARY

1. *Encoding* is the way information is first stored in a memory system; *retention* is the way information is preserved over time; and *retrieval* is the way information is recovered from memory.

2. Three basic types of memory tasks are *recall, recognition,* and *relearning.* People are often able to relearn a task faster than they originally learned it; the reduction in learning time is called *savings.*

3. In general, people are better at recognition tasks than at recall tasks; the items used in recognition tests seem to act as *recall cues.*

4. Factors involved in forgetting include passage of time, distraction and attentional problems, interference from other memories, emotional factors, and organic causes.

5. Multiprocess theories of memory assume that knowledge is represented in a variety of interacting memory systems. For example, the Atkinson and Shiffrin model proposes three systems: *sensory memory, short-term memory,* and *long-term memory.*

6. Different kinds of knowledge may be retained in different memory systems. Two kinds of knowledge are *procedural* ("knowing how") and *propositional* or *declarative* ("knowing that"). Propositional knowledge, in turn, may be either *semantic* or *episodic.*

7. *Depth of processing* is essentially a "single-process" view of memory: Differences in the way we remember things arise because we process them differently, not because they are held in different memory systems. As we process things more "deeply," we may *associate, organize, structure, visualize,* and *elaborate* them, thereby making them easier to recall.

8. Memory appears to involve *reconstructive* processes that cause us to fill in gaps in our recall with what seems reasonable or likely.

9. Mnemonic techniques involve the effective use of recall clues. Some effective methods include the *method of loci, peg words,* the *key word method,* and the use of reductive coding or *acronyms.*

SUGGESTED READINGS

ANDERSON, J. R. (1985). *Cognitive psychology and its implications* (2nd ed.). San Franciso: W. H. Freeman and Co. An introduction to modern theories of how knowledge is represented in memory.

ANDERSON, J. R. (1983). *The architecture of cognition.* Cognitive Science Series No. 5. Cambridge, Mass: Harvard University Press. A theoretical view of human memory that draws on some of the work done in computer science, in particular the production systems used in "expert system" programs.

GLASS, A., & HOLYOAK, K. (1986). *Cognition* (2nd ed.). New York: Random House. A general introduction to cognition with a particularly lucid treatment of research on memory.

HIGBEE, K. L. (1977). *Your memory: How it works and how to improve it.* Englewood Cliffs, N.J.: Prentice-Hall. A practical guide to better memory, which also clearly relates mnemonic methods to basic research on memory.

KIHLSTROM, J., & EVANS, F. (1979). *Functional disorders of memory.* Hillsdale, N.J.: Erlbaum. The authors approach the study of human memory through an examination of failures of normal memory.

KLATZKY, R. (1980). *Human memory: Structures and processes* (2nd ed.). San Francisco: W. H. Freeman & Co. An excellent and widely used undergraduate text in human memory.

LOFTUS, E. F. (1979). *Eyewitness testimony.* Cambridge, Mass.: Harvard University Press. A survey of memory research bearing on eyewitness testimony.

LURIA, A. R. (1968; originally published in 1920). *The mind of a mnemonist.* New York: Basic Books. A fascinating and detailed account of a mnemonist by a famous Russian scientist.

STERN, L. (1985). *The structures and strategies of human memory.* Homewood, Ill.: Dorsey. An excellently written undergraduate text on memory.

8 Language

H olding an ordinary conversation with a friend seems as easy and natural to us as breathing or walking. But if you look carefully at the mental activities that must take place whenever you speak or listen to speech, the complexity of the process will become apparent. Imagine, for example, that you are Participant B in this brief interchange:

A: Would you like to go to the movies tonight?

B: I have to dust my record collection.

To understand what Participant A is saying, you must first recognize English words in the stream of sounds. You must then determine the meanings of the individual words in the context of the sentence they make up. In this case, you also have to realize that A's utterance has more than one level of meaning. The question means not only "Do you wish to go to the movies?" (to which your answer may be Yes), but also "Do you wish to go with A?" (to which your answer may be "no"). Once the listener has understood the various levels of meaning, he or she must formulate an appropriate reply. When you produce the hypothetical response "I have to dust my record collection," you indirectly communicate the response "No!" by suggesting that you lack one of the conditions necessary to attend a movie— free time. This particular reply, however, is so blatantly sarcastic that A ought to feel rebuffed (and ought never ask you to the movies again).

These mental processes and social adjustments take place in seconds. As we describe the activities involved in language use, keep in mind all that you accomplish unconsciously and quickly every time you have a converstion.

The biblical "Tower of Babel" as envisioned by the sixteenth-century painter Pieter Brueghel. (Art Resource)

THE NATURE OF HUMAN LANGUAGE

Language Universals

On the surface, languages such as Chinese and Turkish seem quite different from one another. They sound different, seem to have different grammatical rules, and, to a native English speaker, may not even sound like languages at all. The stream of speech coming from someone speaking a totally unfamiliar language sometimes appears to be a continuous rush of sound rather than separate words.

Beneath the surface differences however, all natural human languages (languages that arose naturally in human society as contrasted with artificially constructed ones such as computer programming languages) share fundamental properties. The most important of these is *productivity*. Natural languages are productive in two senses.

First, in every human language there is no upper limit to the number of novel sentences that can be created. (See the upcoming section on phrase-structure rules for an illustration of how a very simple artificial grammar can generate an amazing number of different sentences.) The capacity of hundreds of thousands of words and complex grammatical rules to generate an infinite number of different sentences should not be surprising. Just consider the possibilities we have for composing new melodies and musical compositions from the few notes of the ordinary musical scale.

The second way in which all languages are productive is that the same ideas or thoughts can be expressed in any language. What can be said in English can also be said in French, in Hebrew, or in Swahili. Of course, if a language doesn't have a word for a particular concept, then several words may be needed to express the concept. Children who are learning to talk provide clear and often humorous examples of how easily this is accomplished, as when a 3-year-old, noticing her father's bald spot for the first time, said, "Daddy has a hole in his hair!" Lacking the word *bald,* she could express the idea, nonetheless, much to her father's chagrin.

Underlying the productivity of languages are certain shared fundamental

Natural languages can seem very different on the surface, but they share some fundamental properties. (Burt Glinn/Magnum Photos)

features of design. Roger Brown (1965) has summarized these features quite nicely. First, all languages use a limited number of speech sounds, called **phonemes.** Most languages use fewer than 100 phonemes. English, for example, has about 45 phonemes, while Hawaiian manages with even fewer, about 13. (With so few phonemes, a language such as Hawaiian has to render the English "Merry Christmas" as "Melly Kalikamaka.") Each of the speech sounds of a language is meaningless on its own. For example, the consonant that we represent by the letter *k* has no meaning. These meaningless units can be combined to form meaningful units such as words in virtually limitless ways—the 45 phonemes of English can be combined and recombined to form hundreds of thousands of words, just as the 13 phonemes of Hawaiian can.

A second way in which all languages are alike in design is that they all have a small number of meaningless speech units that can be combined to form a virtually infinite number of *meaningful* speech units. This property—having both meaningless and meaningful language units—is technically known as *duality of structure.*

Third, in all languages most meanings are assigned to words arbitrarily. That is, a word does not have to sound like the thing it refers to. Of course, some words *do* sound like the thing they refer to, such as *gurgle* (of a brook) or *coo* (of a pigeon). But such examples are rare, and fortunately so. If words always had to sound like what they mean, then how could we have words to express abstract concepts such as justice, envy, or imagination? Because we are not constrained by a word's physical features (either its sound or its spelling), we are free to coin new words, to change the meanings of old words, and in general to build a vocabulary that suits our communicative and symbolic needs.

Fourth and finally, all languages combine words in systematic ways to form sentences. In principle, the number of sentences that can be generated, starting with a small set of phonemes, is infinite. Every language spoken on earth has the characteristics just outlined, and so every language has the capacity to create an unlimited set of sentences that can be used to express any conceivable set of ideas. (Note the Application: Are Some Languages Better Than Others?)

The universality of these four features extends to languages such as American Sign Language (ASL) that are gestural rather than spoken (Klima & Bellugi, 1979). The words of ASL, *signs,* are constructed from a small number of meaningless hand positions, placements, and motions. Also, with a small number of exceptions, the pairings of signs and meanings are arbitrary. Although some signs look like their referents (for example, nonsigners are often able to guess the meaning of the ASL sign for *tree*), it is as difficult to have a word that *looks* like justice or envy as it is to have a word that *sounds* like those concepts. Finally, all the ideas that can be expressed in spoken languages can also be expressed in ASL and other signed languages. Although we focus on spoken languages in this chapter, once we move beyond the level of speech perception our observations will apply to all human languages, including sign languages.

An idea or concept that can be expressed in one language can also be expressed in any other language—one sense in which languages are productive. (Tom McHugh/Photo Researchers)

Phonemes and Speech Perception

The basic unit of speech sound is the *phoneme.* As we mentioned above, English has about 45 phonemes. Does this mean that people who speak English make only 45 different speech sounds? Obviously not. All English speakers use the 45 basic speech sounds, but with differences in pronunciation. For

example, a New Yorker, a Texan, an Iowan, and a Vermonter can all say the word *ball* and can be understood perfectly well by one another. Yet because of regional accents, the precise sound of the vowel represented by the letter *a* will be different in each case. Similarly, the sounds represented by the letter *p* in the words *pin* and *spin* are also different, yet we tend to hear those two *p* sounds as identical (You can feel this difference by holding your hand in front of your mouth as you pronounce the two words.) In each of these two examples a single phoneme—the vowel sound in *ball* in one case, the sound of the letter *p* in the other—is heard and recognized correctly, despite marked differences in the physical sound itself. This poses an intriguing question: When are two speech sounds functionally the same, and when are they different?

For any specific language, two speech sounds are different phonemes if substituting one for another actually changes the meanings of the words in which they appear. For example, changing the sound of *r* to the sound of *l* in the word *rip* changes the word itself. In contrast, changing the quality of the sound of *r* from the typical English pronunciation to the trilling Scots pronunciation does not change the word *rip* into another word. Therefore *r* and *l* are considered two separate and distinct phonemes in English, while the trilled and untrilled *r*'s are merely variants **(allophones)** of the same phoneme.

Are the sounds of *r* and *l* inherently more "different" or more discriminable than the two variants of *r?* Not to speakers of Japanese, a language that does not treat *r* and *l* as two separate phonemes. This does not, of course, indicate defective hearing among Japanese. We who speak English do not hear some of the differences between the phonemes of other languages. For example, the sounds represented by the letteres *k* and *c* in the phrase "keep cool" sound exactly alike to us, yet they are actually different sounds and are treated as such in Arabic. (Note the placement of the tongue for the sound of *k* in *keep,* where it touches the roof of the mouth toward the front, and the placement further back for the sound of *c* in *cool.*) When we learn a language, one of the first things we learn is to categorize differences among those speech sounds that are specifically important in *that language.* We also learn to categorize certain physically different speech sounds as the same. For example, the *d* sounds in the syllables *dee* and *do* sound exactly alike to us, even though the physical stimuli for these two sounds are quite different (see Figure 8–1).

Figure 8–1 The *d* sounds in *dee* and *doo* sound exactly alike, but the physical stimuli for these two sounds are quite different.

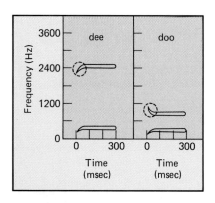

People use not only the stimulus information in the sounds themselves, but the context as well. We are better able to recognize speech sounds when they form words than when they form nonsense syllables (Stevens & House, 1972). Common words are heard more clearly than uncommon ones (Pollack, Rubenstein, & Decker, 1959), and grammatical and meaningful sentences are heard more clearly than nonsensical sentences (Miller & Isard, 1963).

As we discussed in Chapter 4, most computerized pattern-recognition devices—like the kind that recognizes the computer-patterned letters and numerals on bank checks—can use only the physical stimuli they are given, and must rely completely on them. People can tolerate a remarkable amount of variability and distortion by using their knowledge of the language and of the world to identify accurately the sounds that occur in ordinary conversation. Specifically, we do this by combining the information in the sounds themselves with other information that may be available in the situation. We do this so automatically that we are seldom aware of it, and are often

surprised when such phenomena are called to our attention. One common example involves our perception of *where* a sound is coming from. The speech sounds we hear in movies rarely originate at the mouth of a character on the screen, although with careful stereo recording and reproduction they can be made to seem so. More important, however, is what our eyes tell us about a sound source. Even if a sound actually originates elsewhere, we "hear" the sound as coming from what appears to be its visual source. An easy experiment to try at home is to tune in to a television broadcast that is being simultaneously broadcast over the radio. Even though the radio (or stereo speakers) may be some distance from the television screen, you will hear the sound as coming from that screen as long as you look at and pay attention to the television. If you look away, or close your eyes, you will then hear the sound as coming from its actual source. This phenomenon is known as *visual capture.*

The same kind of information-integration process can strongly influence *what* you hear, not just where you hear it coming from. In one of the more compelling demonstrations of visual effects on speed perception, people watched a film of a person repeating the syllable *ga,* while the sound track presented the syllable *ba* synchronized with the lip movements for *ga.* People heard neither *ba* nor *ga,* but a fusion of the two, *da.* Apparently, fusing the visual and auditory stimuli resolves the conflict between the two (McGurk & McDonald, 1976).

This sort of phenomenon is one reason you sometimes find foreign-language movies that are inexpertly dubbed into English so unpleasant and uncomfortable to watch. You continue to experience unresolved conflict between the visual and auditory sources of information, so both the facial expressions of the actors and the dubbed speech sounds seem strained and unnatural. Dubbing that is done with skill and precision resolves the conflict by maximizing the match between what the actors appear, visually, to be saying and what is being heard on the sound track.

Ventriloquists take advantage of visual capture. If the dummy's mouth is made to move, and the ventriloquist can keep his or her own mouth from moving too much, then the sound of the ventriloquist's voice seems to be coming from the dummy. What people often think of as the "throwing" of the ventriloquist's voice into and out of the dummy is really an illusion. (Laima Druskis)

Morphemes, Words, and Meanings

The smallest unit of speech that has meaning is the **morpheme.** A morpheme may be a word or a part of a word. Common prefixes and suffixes, as in the words *a*typical, *non*sense, jump*ed,* and lesson*s,* are one type of morpheme. These morphemes must always be used with at least one other morpheme to form a word, so they are called *bound* morphemes. *Free* morphemes correspond roughly to words: Words like *man* and *page* are simultaneously single morphemes and words. Finally, many words consist of several morphemes put together, both free and bound.

Morphemes and words are made by combining phonemes according to the morphophonemic rules of the language. The phonological rules of English describe our implicit knowledge of the sound system of our language. For example, most native English speakers would agree that *spall* is a possible sound sequence, whereas *sball* is not. The particular rule, in this case, says that a voiced consonant such as *v* may not follow the sound represented by the letter *s.*

A voiced consonant is sounded with vocal chord vibration, called *voicing.* Voiceless consonants do not include such vibration. You can appreciate this difference by putting your fingers on your Adam's apple (the larynx) while you alternate pronouncing *zzzz* and *ssss.* The former is voiced; the latter is not. For consonants such as *b,* the "buzz" of voicing starts about 35 mil-

liseconds (thirty-five thousandths of a second) after the onset of the consonant when it is voiced, as in *boo,* but not until the following vowel when it is unvoiced, as in *poo.* Among the voiced consonants of English are *v* as in *voo* and *d* as in *do.* Their unvoiced counterparts are *f* as in *foo* and *t* as in *too.* Because of the phonological rule that an *s* sound may not be followed by a voiced consonant, not only *svall* but also *sdall* is not possible in English. We know this intuitively, although few of us can state the rule explicitly.

The grammar of a language contains rules for the allowable sequences of sounds and for morpheme combinations, but, as we mentioned earlier, there are essentially no rules for assigning meanings to words. With a very few exceptions, the meanings of words are assigned arbitrarily—the words bear no physical resemblance to the things they name. Because meanings are assigned arbitrarily, we can have as many words as we need.

Aspects of Meaning: Denotative and Connotative.   Words such as *and, or, on,* and *of* are function words. Their function is to specify relations among things, and they are the parts of speech known as prepositions and conjunctions. Nouns, verbs, adjectives, and adverbs are content words. Content words symbolize at least two different kinds of meanings, denotative and connotative.

The **denotative** meaning of a word is usually defined as the thing or class of things that the word can label. This meaning is like a dictionary definition of a word. But dictionary definitions are, at best, only rough guides to what a word denotes. For a dictionary to be useful, one must already have a good command of the language and a reasonable knowledge of one's physical and social world. For example, a partial dictionary definition of the word *"chaste"* is "innocent of unlawful sexual intercourse." A third-grader who had been assigned this word to look up in a dictionary did so and, when asked to use the word in a sentence, wrote: "The amoeba is a chaste animal" (Deese, 1967). Clearly, one aspect of the word's denotative meaning had been understood, but not several other important aspects, such as that the word can sensibly be applied only to adult human beings. If we include this kind of knowledge of what words mean, then the meanings of words would look more like encyclopedia entries than dictionary entries. For example, a dictionary entry for the work *dog* is "a carnivorous domesticated mammal probably descended from the common wolf" (Merriam-Webster, 1973). An encyclopedia would provide the additional information that dogs are furry, that they make excellent pets, that some dogs are used for hunting and others for herding, that they come in a variety of sizes and shapes, and so on. The denotative meaning of the word *dog,* then, is really the sum total of the ideas shared by people in our culture of what a dog is—namely, our concept of "dog."

When the word *dog* is used in a conversation, one or more aspects of our conception of what a dog is may be appropriate to the intended meaning of the sentence. For example, if someone says that her dog eats only prime beef, then the word "dog" clearly refers to a pet. However, if someone says that the movie he went to last week was a real dog, then the word *dog* refers to a particular property or attribute of dogs—in this case, a rather negative property. These examples illustrate one of the primary characteristics of word meanings in isolation. Virtually any word, when considered out of context, can be interpreted in many ways. Clearly, when we refer to a word's meaning, we can only refer to a range or set of meanings that the word may have when used in sentences or conversational contexts.

A second aspect of words is their **connotative,** or emotional, meanings.

This emotional (sometimes called **affective**) meaning of a word essentially reflects how we feel about the thing that the word represents. This meaning is measured by the **semantic differential,** a technique devised by Osgood, Suci, and Tannenbaum (1957). The semantic differential is a set of rating scales. Each scale has a pair of opposite adjectives, as shown in Figure 8–2. The word to be rated is put at the top of the scale, and people are asked to rate that word on each of the scales below it. Because the ratings on some scales tend to go together (that is, they *correlate* with one another), the ratings of the ten scales can be summarized in terms of three general scales, or *dimensions,* of connotative meaning. These three summary scales are the good-bad scale, the active-passive scale, and the strong-weak scale, representing the three major dimensions of connotative meaning, respectively: *evaluation, activity,* and *potency.*

Just as the denotative meanings of words will vary with context, so will the connotative meanings. Sometimes even a small change in context will have a sizable effect. For example, the evaluative and activity connotations of the word *inventive* would be quite different in the phrases "an inventive assassin" and "an inventive poet."

Are the three dimensions of connotative meaning—evaluation, activity, and potency—unique to the English language, or do they also characterize the connotative meanings of words in other languages? Obviously, the connotative meaning of any particular word may vary considerably from one language and culture to another. For example, *peasant* may be rated as bad, passive, and weak by Americans, and good, active, and strong by the Chinese. This is to be expected when peoples differ in culture, ideology, and experience. However, extensive cross-cultural research by Osgood and his colleagues (1957) has revealed a striking universality in the structure of connotative meaning. Using the semantic differential in many different cultures and languages, including American English, Dutch, French, Finnish, and Japanese, the same three major dimensions of connotative meaning appear again and again. Of the world's peoples that have been tested so far, all seem to judge the connotative meanings of words in similar ways, using the same three dimensions of evaluation, activity, and potency.

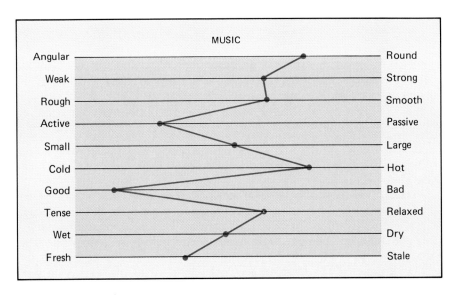

Figure 8–2 How one person rated the word *music* on the semantic differential. How would you rate *music* on these scales? (Glucksberg & Danks, 1975)

Sentences and Messages

In every language words are combined into sentences according to rules. These word-combining rules form the **syntax** of a language, and they can be used to generate all the grammatical sentences of a language. To date, no such complete grammar has been written for any language, but theoretical linguists such as Noam Chomsky (1957) have argued convincingly that any such grammar would need at least two types of rules—phrase-structure rules and transformational rules.

Phrase-structure Rules and Transformational Rules. **Phrase-structure rules** govern the organization of the various parts of a sentence. To illustrate how phrase-structure rules can be used to generate the sentences of a language, let us assume that there is a language with just four types of words: nouns, verbs, articles, and adjectives. Using the symbol → to mean "can be rewritten as," we can represent the lexicon (vocabulary) of this language as follows:

$$\begin{array}{rl}
\text{Nouns:} & \text{N} \rightarrow \text{man, woman, horse, dog} \ldots \\
\text{Verbs:} & \text{V} \rightarrow \text{saw, heard, hit} \ldots \\
\text{Articles:} & \text{Art} \rightarrow \text{a, the} \ldots \\
\text{Adjectives:} & \text{Adj} \rightarrow \text{happy, sad, fat, timid} \ldots
\end{array}$$

Thus wherever the symbols [N → man] appear, we can substitute the word *man* for the symbol *N*. Phrase-structure or rewrite rules such as this one can refer to parts of sentences, such as noun phrases and verb phrases, as well as to single words. The sentence "A fat man hit the dog" can, under the rewrite rules of this partial grammar, be described in terms of its parts: The first three words are a noun phrase (NP), the last three words are a verb phrase (VP).

These parts can be further broken down. The noun phrase consists of an article, an adjective, and a noun. The verb phrase consists of a verb plus a noun phrase. These relationships can be summarized in two ways. One way is in terms of a tree structure diagram, as in Figure 8–3. The other way, which is equivalent to the diagram, is in the form of a set of phrase-structure (grammatical) rules for rewriting:

Rule 1. S → NP + VP. This rule states that a sentence (S) consists of, or can be rewritten as, a noun phrase (NP) plus a verb phrase (VP).

Rule 2. NP → Art + [Adj] + N. This rule states that a noun phrase (NP) consists of an article (Art) plus, optionally, an adjective (Adj) plus a noun (N).

Rule 3. VP → V + NP. This rule states that a verb phrase (VP) consists of a verb (V) plus a noun phrase (NP).

This grammar, which was devised for illustrative purposes by Victoria Fromkin (1976), can, with just the lexicon listed above, generate 4,800 sentences.

Notice, however, that these 4,800 sentences represent a tiny fraction of the kinds of sentences that could occur in English. For example, all the verbs are in the simple past tense. All the nouns are in singular form, and they refer only to animate beings. Only simple declarative sentences can be generated—this small grammar does not generate questions, commands, or any of the many other kinds of sentences we normally use. Yet, with very

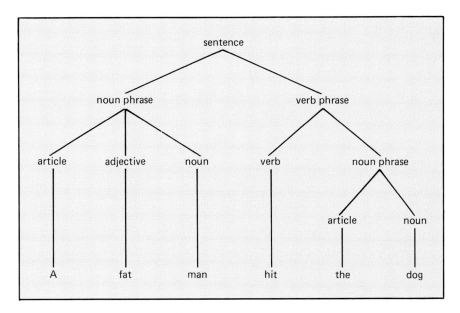

Figure 8–3 Phrase-structure analysis of the sentence, "A fat man hit the dog."

small additions to the rules, the number of sentences that can be generated increases enormously. Merely by allowing each verb to appear in present as well as past tense, we double the number of verb phrases and so double the number of different sentences we can have. If we also double the number of available nouns by allowing each to appear in both singular and plural form, we could then generate 38,400 different sentences (80 different NPs multiplied by 480 different VPs). How many sentences could we generate if we once again double the number of available nouns by simply adding four new ones in both singular and plural form?*

Phrase-structure rules not only tell us how sentences can be constructed, they also provide a description of those sentences. For example, the sentences

John saw Mary.
Peter heard Sally.

strike us as being quite similar to each other, even though the words are different. One way they are similar is that they have the same grammatical structure—they have both been generated by the same phrase-structure rules (in this case, S → NP + VP; NP → N; VP → V + NP). However, some sentences that appear similar to one another have quite different structures. Consider the following two sentences:

John saw Mary.
Mary was seen by John.

Here we have two sentences with different phrase structures, yet they are obviously related; indeed, they mean roughly the same thing. In each case, John is the person who saw someone and Mary is the person who was seen. The grammatical rules that describe the relationships *between* sentences are called **transformational rules.** These are rules that specify how various

*This would give us 160 NPs and 960VPs, which can yield 153,600 different sentences.

types of sentences are related to one another. They do this by showing how one string (sequence) of words can be rewritten or transformed into another. For example, one set of transformational rules allows us to rewrite

Mary hit the ball.

into

The ball was hit by Mary.

Surface Structure and Deep Structure   These types of phrase-structure and transformational rules make explicit some of the intuitions we have about our language. For example, most of us feel intuitively that the two sentences

John is easy to please.
John is eager to please.

are similar to and yet different from one another. They share a surface similarity in that they differ by just one word—*eager* versus *easy*. They have the same **surface structure.** However, they differ quite markedly in terms of their underlying organization and intent, that is, their **deep structure.** This intuition of ours, that these two sentences are really basically different, can be demonstrated by applying the same transformation to each sentence.

John is easy to please.   It is easy to please John.
John is eager to please.   It is eager to please John.

The difference between the original two sentence types is now obvious and explicit. The first can be transformed in this way and still make sense, but the second cannot. Therefore the original two sentences have different deep structures; they are basically different sentence types.

Certain types of ambiguity can be better understood when their surface and deep structures are compared. A sentence is syntactically ambiguous when it can be paraphrased in two different ways. For example, the sentence

Visiting relatives can be boring.

is really two different sentences that happen to have the same surface structure. The two sentences can be paraphrased as either

Relatives who visit can be boring

or

To visit relatives can be a boring thing to do.

Can you see the ambiguity in these sentences?

They were charming snakes.
They were charming young women.

In each of the sentences, who or what does the pronoun *they* refer to? Who *is* charming? Who *is doing* the charming?

Speech Acts and How to Make a Promise

According to speech-act theorists such as John Searle (1979), language is used in five general ways: to tell people how things are; to get people to do things; to express feelings and attitudes; to commit ourselves to something; and to accomplish things directly (as in making a declaration such as "I now pronounce you husband and wife"). Whenever we interpret an utterance, we must decide which of these five things the speaker is trying to do: tell us something, get us to do something, and so on. The surface form of the sentence is usually not enough to let us know just what speech act is being performed. For example, the simple declarative sentence "It is raining" can be a descriptive act, or it can be a request to shut a window, or an expression of lack of confidence in the weather-forecasting system.

Listeners must use their knowledge of the person who is talking and the context of the conversation to interpret correctly even the simplest of utterances. Both listeners and speakers must also follow the implicit rules of speech-act theory if they are to understand one another. The rules of speech-act theory specify the conditions for well-formed speech acts. Consider the conditions that must be satisfied when someone wants to make a promise.

1. The promise must be spoken in the presence of a listener, unless it is a promise to oneself.
2. The utterance describes a future action by the speaker.
3. The listener would prefer that the speaker take that action, and the speaker assumes that this is indeed so.
4. Neither the speaker nor the listener expects that the promised action would normally have been taken without this promise.
5. The speaker sincerely intends to perform the action.
6. By promising, the speaker takes on an obligation to carry out the promised action.
7. The speaker intends to inform the listener that the speaker is taking on that obligation.

Searle suggests that these "rules" for how to make a well-formed promise are, like the rules of syntax, implicitly known by all adult members of the language community.

Searle's is a philosophical theory that can be tested by psychological research. In real life people's use of promises departs somewhat from Searle's ideal (Gibbs & Delaney, 1987). In particular, rule 4 is not consistently upheld. Speakers often make promises that confirm—rather than create—obligations. A statement like "I promise to pay you back the twenty-five dollars" only gives verbal confirmation of an expectation dictated by societal norms; the speaker is under obligation to repay the loan whether or not the explicit promise is made. Thus a promise often serves only to acknowledge what is already held to be true.

Researchers in many disciplines create theories of language. Psychologists are largely responsible for assessing the reality of those theories in terms of day-to-day language use.

Form and Meaning.   The surface structure of a sentence is known as its surface *form*. We have already seen how the same meaning can be expressed in different surface forms. What do people remember about a sentence—its form, its meaning, or both? Under most circumstances people tend to forget the verbatim form of sentences and remember only the meaning. Jaqueline Sachs (1967) asked people to listen to short stories and then tested to see if they could remember the exact wording of selected sentences in those stories. If the test came immediately after hearing the original sentence, then people could easily recognize any changes in wording, as in:

Original sentence: He sent a letter about it to Galileo.
Test Sentence: A letter about it was sent to Galileo.

However, if the test came a mere 27 seconds after hearing the sentence, then people could not tell whether it was the same as the original. In contrast, people could easily tell when the meaning had been changed as in:

Galileo sent him a letter about it.

even after longer delays, when memory for exact wording becomes particularly poor (Anderson & Paulson, 1977).

Memory for exact wording can be quite good when the exact wording is important for one reason or another. Memorized prose, poetry, and song lyrics can be retained verbatim for years, often for a lifetime (Rubin, 1977). Similarly, the intent of jokes or insults often depends upon the exact words that are used, and we all too often remember such material verbatim. People also tend to remember the surface form of statements with personal significance, such as sarcasm, personal criticism, and humorous remarks (Gibbs, 1986; Keenan et al., 1977; Kintsch & Bates, 1977). Since such statements are exactly the kind that cannot survive paraphrasing, it is not surprising that the original wording is usually remembered.

Literal, Intended, and Conveyed Meanings. The grammatical rules of a language could, in principle, be used to specify the literal meanings of all the sentences of that language. But would such a set of rules enable a computer to interpret the meanings of ordinary language? (See the Highlight: Language Processing by Computer for a discussion of what language skills have been programmed into computers already.) Unfortunately, it would not, because people often go beyond the *literal* meanings of sentences in order to understand what a speaker intends to convey. This meaning is the *intended* or *conveyed* meaning of an utterance. For example, the literal meaning of the question "Can you pass the salt?" is, roughly, "Are you physically or otherwise capable of passing the salt?" In most ordinary contexts, such as when people are sitting around a table eating lunch, the literal meaning of that question makes no sense. The intended meaning—"Please pass the salt" —does. Similarly, if you say to someone who is standing by a closed window, "Gee, it's hot in here," it would probably be understood that you are not merely commenting on the temperature but are asking that a window be opened.

These examples illustrate the **pragmatics** of language use: how people combine the information they have about the language, about the situation they are in, and about other people to arrive at the meaning of the speech they hear or read. The information that people have about their language is their *linguistic competence*. The information about the situation and about the people involved in the conversation is *contextual knowledge*.

Both linguistic competence and contextual knowledge are necessary for understanding, but they are not enough. Grice (1975) was among the first philosophers of language to point out that people who participate in conversations act in accordance with the *Cooperative Principle*. To be cooperative, speakers must attempt at all times to be informative, truthful, relevant, and concise. Listeners assume that speakers are trying to fulfill this obligation. (Note the Highlight: Speech Acts and How to Make a Promise for an examination of the role of speaker and listener in this speech act.) The expectation of cooperation is an important aspect of our implicit linguistic knowledge. For example, when a speaker's utterance appears to violate expectations of cooperation, then the listener will often "cooperate" by seeking some alternative interpretation of the utterance. This is known as a *conversational implicature*. For example, if someone remarks, "Seems to be raining a bit," in the midst of a torrential downpour, this would be a violation of the maxim to be informative, so the remark would be interpreted as irony or sarcasm rather than as a mere description of the weather. The question "Can you pass the salt" is hardly relevant as a question about ability, so it is interpreted as a request. Similarly, a statement such as "My aunt Sarah is a baby" is not likely to be literally true; therefore, on the assumption that the speaker is trying to

All languages have a large number of conventional words—such as *dog, walk,* and *dastardly*—that are sufficient to express a great range of ideas. On many occasions, however, speakers move beyond the somewhat limited repertory of stored meanings to create their own *innovative* meanings (Clark & Clark, 1979). Suppose, for example, you are taking a picture of a group of friends and you would like to get them all to stand with their hands tucked inside their jackets. Because this is a pose associated with Napoleon, you could say, "Please *do a Napoleon* for the camera." *Do a Napoleon* is an example of an *eponymous verb phrase* (Clark & Gerrig, 1983). Such verb phrases based on people's names can be used to describe any action or property that is generally attributed to the individual. Of course, *do a Napoleon* could also mean "invade Russia in winter" or "go into exile," but these would not be typical interpretations of the phrase. (You might consider what a verb phrase with your name after "do a" would mean. What actions might your friends think sufficiently characteristic of you to encode in this fashion?) People use eponymous verb phrases, and other types of innovations, to describe categories of experience that are not covered by the conventional words of their language.

Metaphors also serve to capture experiences and impressions that cannot be adequately described by the conventional lexicon. Some metaphors are masterful, as the Shakespearean lines, "Shall I compare thee to a summer's day? Thou art more lovely and more temperate" (Sonnet 18). Others are more mundane, as when a restaurant advertises itself as "The Picasso of Italian Cuisine," ignoring the fact that Picasso was Spanish. Often without realizing it, people create their own metaphors in everyday life, as when a young child describes traffic descending a steep hill as "a waterfall." To what extent is a listener inconvenienced when a speaker creates a metaphorical meaning? In one experiment sentences like "Regardless of the danger, the troops marched on" were preceded by two types of contexts. One context induced a literal interpretation of the sentence (the story described an endangered group of soldiers); the second induced a metaphorical reading (the story described some boisterous school children and an irritated adult). When contexts were appropriate, readers found it equally easy to understand the sentence as a literal or a metaphorical utterance (Ortony, Schallert, Reynolds, & Antos, 1978). This result suggests that, as listeners, we possess the appropriate mental abilities to allow speakers to indulge their creativity.

be truthful, it is interpreted metaphorically—Aunt Sarah behaves childishly. (See the Highlight: Creating New Meanings for further discussion of this aspect of speech.)

People also go beyond both the literal and conveyed meanings of utterances to draw inferences about matters that are related to an utterance. If someone were to say to you, "Peter forgot to close the door," you would get far more information than is contained in the literal interpretation of that sentence. For example, you would probably be left with the following beliefs, among others: that Peter was supposed to or intended to close the door; that Peter was able to do so; that the door was open at some time; that something undesirable might have happened or did happen because the door was left open; that the undesirable consequences of Peter's forgetfulness might have been a robbery, or rain soaking the floor, or the escape of a canary or a dog, and so on. And, just as important, you would be learning something about Peter's reliability as well as, of course, about the speaker's attitudes and feelings about poor old Peter. Whenever we deal with speech in meaningful ways, we bring to bear our knowledge of the language and the world, and, perhaps most of all, our beliefs about ourselves and other people.

It is just this characteristic of everyday language use that prompted George Bernard Shaw to offer this advice to an actress friend: "Get out the words from which an audience can guess the rest; . . . the others . . . are useful only for rhythm" (Shaw, 1985).

LEARNING A FIRST LANGUAGE

Most children utter their first words toward the end of their first year (see Table 8–1). By the time they are 2, most children have an active vocabulary of more than 250 words and can speak in short simple sentences. By 3 to 4 years of age, children have acquired the basic grammar of their language. The apparent ease and speed of first-language learning has led some theorists to postulate an innate **language-acquisition device,** or **LAD** (Chomsky, 1975). The LAD can be defined as some characteristic property of the hu-

Table 8–1: Average Age at Which Linguistic Advances First Occur.

Age in Months*	Milestone
0.25	Infant makes some response to sound
1.25	Smiles in response to stimulation
1.6	Coos; makes long vowel sounds
4	Turns toward speaker
	Says "ah-goo"
	Makes razzing sound
5	Turns toward ringing bell
6	Babbles
7	Looks up sideways toward ringing bell
8	Says "dada" and "mama" indiscriminately
9	Plays gesture games like peek-a-boo
	Looks directly at ringing bell
	Understands word "no"
11	Uses "dada" and "mama" as names
	Responds to one-step command and gesture indicating activity[1]
	Says first word
12	Says gibberish "sentences" without using real words
	Says second word
13	Says third word
14	Responds to one-step command without gesture[2]
15	Says 4 to 6 words
17	Says gibberish sentence with some real words
	Can point to 5 body parts
	Says 7 to 20 words
19	Forms 2-word combinations
21	Forms 2-word sentences
	Has 50-word vocabulary
24	Uses pronouns (*I, me, you*) indiscriminately
30	Uses pronouns (*I, me, you*) discriminately
36	Uses all pronouns discriminately
	Has 250-word vocabulary
	Uses plurals
	Forms 3-word sentences

*After age 2 months, ages have been rounded off to nearest month.

1. For example, "Give it to me" with hand extended.

2. For example, "Give it to me," without hand extended.

Source: Brody, J. (1987) Child development: language takes on new significance. *The New York Times,* May 5, 1987, p. C1, C11. From Capute, A.J., Palmer, F.B., Shapiro, B.K., Wachtel, R.C., Schmidt, S., Ross, A. (1986). Clinical linguistic and auditory milestone scale: Prediction of cognition in infancy. *Developmental Medicine & Child Neurology, 28,* 762-771.

man mind that is uniquely and specially tuned for language acquisition. As we describe the various steps children go through on their way to full language competence, we shall see that there may be many LADs, each consisting of a specific characteristic of the human organism that helps in learning one or another aspect of language (Wanner & Gleitman, 1982; Pinker, 1984).

Is Language Learned or Innate?

Until Noam Chomsky revolutionized linguistics with his theory of transformational generative grammar, people believed that language was learned in the same ways that other simpler skills and habits are learned. Speech sounds were learned by **imitation.** Word meanings were learned by associating the sound of a word with the thing that the word named. Finally, syntax—the set of rules for combining words to form sentences—was learned by forming associations between words. Thus the expression "the red ball" would be learned by associating *the* with *red,* and *red* with *ball.*

This simple form of learning undoubtedly does occur during language acquisition. Some aspects of word meanings can be acquired by classical (Pavlovian) conditioning (described in Chapter 6). For example, if a word or nonsense syllable is repeatedly paired with an unpleasant event, then the word itself can become unpleasant (Staats & Staats, 1957). Operant-conditioning techniques (also described in Chapter 6) have been used to teach simple word meanings to such special types of people as autistic children and the mentally retarded. If a child is positively reinforced for making an appropriate sound (for example, the word *truck* in the presence of a toy truck), then the child could gradually learn to associate the word and its referent—the thing it names.

Chomsky's contribution to the psychology of language acquisition was to demonstrate convincingly that some aspects of language could not, in principle, be learned by conditioning or by imitation. The mistakes young children make illustrate that they are learning rules, and not just imitating the speech they hear. When children say "Daddy runned" or "This is my bestest color," they are not imitating the speech that they have heard; they are using a rule that they have somehow discovered (Ervin, 1964).

Rules are involved at every level of language learning, from the sounds of language to the grammar. The sounds of a language are not merely composed of a set of independent, discrete sounds. Instead, the sounds of a language form a phonological system, obeying the kinds of rules we described earlier. Word meanings, while arbitrary, are not just labels for things but also represent complex concepts. For example, knowing the word *dog* implies that one knows what dogs are, how they differ from cats, and how they differ from everything else we know about in the world (Murphy & Medin, 1985). Finally, learning the syntax of a language must involve rule-discovery procedures. The syntactic rules of a language are not transparent—they are not given explicitly in speech. Indeed, few of us can readily describe the rules we use to form grammatical sentences, but the fact that we can form grammatical sentences is an incontrovertible sign that the rules are there. If the rules are not explicitly laid out in the speech that a child hears, and if parents don't teach the rules explicitly, then how can imitation and reinforcement learning work?

Chomsky and his followers believe that children are born with an **innate** knowledge of the general form of linguistic rules. Some evidence for this hypothesis comes from the study of *pidgin* and *creole* languages (Bickerton,

1983). Pidgin languages arise in areas of the world in which groups of people with different native languages are forced to communicate with each other. In Hawaii, for example, a pidgin developed so that speakers of diverse languages such as Visayan, Ilocano, and Tagalog could converse in a rudimentary fashion as they labored in the sugarcane fields. Pidgins generally represent some compromise among the native tongues of the speakers, and are highly impoverished with respect to vocabulary and grammatical structure. When pidgin speakers begin to have children, something remarkable happens. The children acquire a native language that is far more sophisticated than the pidgin; this is the process of *creolization*. This process supports the existence of innate knowledge of linguistic rules in at least three ways:

1. The creole language that the children speak has far more complex grammatical structures than those that were present in their parents' pidgin.
2. The syntax of the creole does not necessarily parallel the syntax of the languages that originally gave rise to the pidgin.
3. Creole languages from diverse regions of the world are highly similar in their syntactic structure.

It does seem as if there is an innate *language acquisition device* that leads children to develop the same kinds of grammatical forms all over the world, as well as makes it possible for children to acquire all the known languages of the world. Yet whatever the universal component of language learning, children still must learn a particular language by virtue of growing up in some particular language community. These particular and specific aspects of language cannot be innate. Children learn the particulars of their native language by hearing it spoken around them.

From Prespeech to Speech

From the moment they are born, infants are prepared for learning language by learning many of the prerequisites for language. They learn to distinguish between speech and nonspeech sounds—between words and the sneezes, coughs, grunts, and other noises that people make. They learn how to produce the speech sounds of their native language. They learn to differentiate between self and others, and they learn concepts of objects. And, of course, they learn that things have names. Infants also learn, even if only in the crudest of terms, about communicative *intentions*—that when their mother or father makes speech sounds, some meaning or communication is intended (Bruner, 1974/75). Once this idea has been grasped, children can begin to figure out *what* meanings are being expressed (Macnamara, 1972).

Infant Perception and Vocalizations. Until quite recently very little was known about newborns' perceptual abilities or about the development of their vocal abilities. In the early 1970s scientists started to investigate these two aspects of language development, with surprising results.

It had long been believed that the newborn's auditory sensitivity is quite poor, and that the ability to distinguish among minimally different speech sounds could develop only with learning and experience. This is undoubtedly true for many speech sounds, but human infants have a head start in being able to discriminate among *some* important speech sounds virtually at birth. Eimas and his colleagues (1971) discovered that infants between 1 and

4 months discriminate between the syllables *[ba]* and *[pa]* exactly as adults do. This was also true of children who had only had experience with Kikuyu, a language that does not make a distinction between these two sounds—even stronger evidence that the discrimination is not a function of learning (Streeter, 1976). This early ability to hear at least some of the important speech sounds, especially those that are common to most human languages, is surely helpful to children as they begin to pick up the sound patterns of speech. Furthermore, the infant brain seems to be especially prepared to acquire language. As you may recall from Chapter 2, for most right-handed adults, speech is localized in the left hemisphere. Infants as young as 35 weeks after conception already display this hemispheric asymmetry. Speech-like sounds evoked more cortical (brain) responses from the left than from the right hemispheres in these infants (Molfese & Molfese, 1980), suggesting that brain specialization for speech develops quite early indeed. Of course, such early specialization would not be particularly useful if infants did not hear much speech, but they do. Both male and female adults talk incessantly to infants, even newborns, providing them with early and extensive speech experience (Rheingold & Adams, 1980).

In contrast to the very early appearance of speech-perception abilities, the human infant's ability to produce speech sounds at birth is very poor indeed. The major reason for this is the shape and structure of the baby's vocal tract (see Figure 8–4). At birth, it is more like the vocal tract of a chimpanzee than the vocal tract of an adult human. The larynx is relatively high, and the tongue takes up virtually all the space in the oral cavity. These two factors provide a very small resonance chamber that cannot be adjusted very much to produce differences in vowel sounds. This means that the infant simply does not have the vocal machinery to produce speech sounds at birth (Oller & Warren, 1976).

While this vocal tract structure is not well suited for speech, it is perfectly suited for sucking and drinking without gagging or choking. This configuration of tongue, larynx, and epiglottis virtually guarantees that the infant can breathe only through the nose, and that the epiglottis will protect the breathing passages from any liquids or solids taken by mouth. It is as if Mother Nature intended the infant to eat first, talk later.

From birth to 6 weeks, infant vocalizations are mostly reflexive. The baby cries, fusses, spits, sneezes, and coughs. From 6 weeks to about 4 months, the baby begins to combine these vocalizations with the speechlike sounds of cooing and gurgling. These sounds somewhat resemble consonant-vowel syllables, and are usually addressed to the caretaker. By about 4 months, the shape and structure of the baby's vocal tract have matured, and the baby begins to produce a variety of speechlike sounds.

Babies seem to practice one or two types of sounds at a time. For example, an infant might spend 4 weeks producing "raspberries," then 2 days of high-pitched squealing, usually making these sounds while looking at people or at interesting objects. This vocal play appears to serve two functions. First, it obviously attracts attention and plays a role in communication between the infant and other people. Second, it enables infants to learn what they can do with their vocal apparatus, preparing for the learning that will occur between 6 months and 1 year.

By the sixth month, infants can voluntarily control some consonant sounds, and they engage in a characteristic form of baby talk called **reduplicated babbling.** Typically, this consists of a consonant and a vowel, such as *da-da-da-da-da* or *ma-ma-ma-ma-ma*. It may not be coincidental that the words that children use for father and mother in many human languages

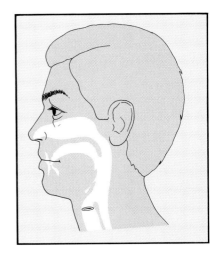

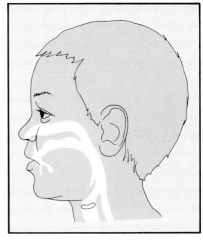

Figure 8–4 (Top) The typical vocal tract of a human adult. The oral cavity is relatively large and its shape and size can be varied rather extensively by moving the tongue around. (Bottom) The typical vocal tract of a human infant at birth. The infant's oral cavity is quite small because the tongue takes up so much space and because the larynx is high up in the throat. This vocal tract cannot be varied much at all, and so cannot produce a variety of speech sounds.

sound like this babbling—virtually all infants, regardless of the language spoken in their home, say things like this. Almost as soon as infants have achieved control of simple consonant-vowel sounds, they stop making them, and begin to use **expressive jargon.** This involves a variety of syllables, with far less repetition than reduplicated babbling, and with a surprising similarity to the intonation patterns of adult speech. Indeed, it sounds very much like normal adult speech, but not a bit of it is intelligible. It is almost as if infants have learned the broad characteristics of the sounds of the language, including many of the vowels, consonants, and the intonation patterns, and are now practicing their newfound vocal skills.

Social and Cognitive Development.   During this first year of life other prerequisites to language learning become established. Babies begin to *imitate* adult actions. Nonverbal communication occurs in a variety of settings—play, feeding, dressing, bathing, bedtime. Baby and parent begin to understand one another's intentions, motivations, and behaviors. This interpersonal understanding is a necessary step toward learning the meanings of words. It is much like visiting a foreign country and figuring out the names of things. The most common way is to notice that someone is talking about, say, bread or cheese, and then associate the words you hear with the appropriate things. This requires that you know what a person is talking about *before* you understand the language. Similarly, young children "learn their language by first determining, independent of language, the meaning which a speaker intends to convey to them, and by then working out the relationship between the meaning and the language. To put it another way, the infant uses meaning as a clue to language, rather than language as a clue to meaning" (Macnamara, 1972, p. 1).

The behaviors of parents and infants seem designed to maximize the chances of their understanding one another before they can rely on spoken language alone. A parent will try to capture an infant's attention when naming things. Infants, by their fourth month, will tend to look at what their parent is looking at, thus ensuring that when infant and parent interact, they are paying attention to the same thing (Bruner, 1974/75). In these as well as in other, more subtle ways, an infant can find out what the parent is saying and talking about and so can begin to learn the meanings of the words that the parent uses.

Acquiring a Vocabulary

When children utter their first words, they do so one at a time. For example, a child might say "Doggie," or "Milk," or "Mama." What could each of these utterances mean? During this stage of one-word utterances the child may often use a single word to express a whole message. For example, the word *milk* could mean "I want more milk" or "Where is the milk?" These one-word utterances cannot be interpreted without considering the specific situation the child is in, and what the child and others are doing at the moment. They are called **holophrastic** utterances because just one word can express a whole message.

Single words can also be used by young children to refer to several different things. The word *dog,* for example, may be used to refer to other furry, four-legged animals, such as cats, horses, or sheep. This kind of **overextension** of a word's meaning is quite common. Sometimes such an

overextension is a sign that the child has not yet learned the precise referent of a word. At other times it could simply be a child's way of talking about something whose name isn't yet known. In the latter case, the word *dog* would be used holophrastically to express the meaning "an animal that is like a dog."

At first, new words are learned rather slowly. Gradually, the rate of learning increases, and then accelerates quite rapidly, so that by 24 months an average working vocabulary of almost 300 words is not unusual, with many of the words having been learned toward the end of the second year (see Figure 8–5).

By the time children are about 3 years old, they display a characteristic and efficient pattern of word learning. Carey and Bartlett (1983) studied the ways that 3-year-olds learned the meaning of a single new word, *chromium*. They used *chromium* to refer to the color olive and introduced this new word by saying to children, "You see those two trays over there. Bring me the chromium one. Not the red one, the chromium one." The children could easily follow this direction by picking out the tray that wasn't red, and virtually all of them did so. More interestingly, virtually all gave clear indications that they had heard a new word by repeating the word *chromium*. Noticing that a new word has been spoken is the first important aspect of children's word-learning strategies. After this single exposure, about half the children realized that the new word was the name of a color, but did not seem to know that the color was olive. This is the second efficient strategy for word learning: knowing the general category of the word. Once children realize that *chromium* is a color word, then the next time it is used they can discover what specific color it refers to. After a total of only five exposures to this new word over a period of ten weeks, about 70 percent of the children seemed to understand that it referred to the color olive. Apparently, young children can learn the meanings of new words with only minimal exposure to them, provided that the new words are used meaningfully in natural, conversational settings (See also Heibeck & Markman, 1987).

What do children talk about during the early part of language acquisition? Katherine Nelson watched 18 children as they spoke their first 50 words. Her observations suggest that children do not learn words passively, nor by merely imitating what their parents say. Instead, they tend to talk about what interests them (Nelson, 1973).

Among the first 10 words used by every child were the names for animals, food, and toys. Not once in the first 50 words did *diaper, pants, sweater,* or *mittens* appear, even though parents must have used these words quite often. In general, young children seem to name the things that they handle or play with directly, and the things that do something, like move or make noises. They do not name things that just sit there, like furniture, grass, or stores.

During this naming and learning period parents prepare the way for the next advance—two-word and three-word utterances. In addition to talking in short sentences themselves, parents will often expand a child's short utterances. If a child says "Milk," a parent might say "Does Tommy want more milk?" This reply is based on the parent's best guess about the child's communicative intent. If the parent has guessed correctly, the reply can serve as a model for an expanded utterance. If the parent has guessed incorrectly, the reply tells the child that his or her one-word utterance is inadequate and ambiguous. In either case, children can get useful information about language and communication.

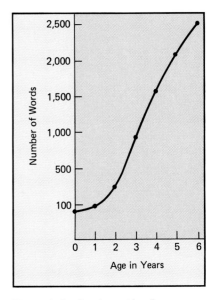

Figure 8–5 Starting with a few words at the age of 1 year, children learn, on the average, about 270 words by age 2, and by age 6 have a vocabulary of over 2,500 words. (Smith, 1926; Lenneberg, 1967)

From Words to Sentences

Sometime around the middle of the second year the one-word utterances of holophrastic speech begin to be replaced by the child's first sentences—two-word utterances. The particular words that children put together in these early and primitive sentences are carefully chosen. In many respects they resemble the kinds of word choices we make when we compose telegrams. We leave out relatively unimportant words, and include only those we absolutely need to get our message across.

Young children who put together no more than two- or three-word sentences are using **telegraphic speech.** They do not, of course, deliberately decide which words to omit. They do, however, use the few words and limited grammar they have to good effect. Like the single-word utterances of holophrastic speech, two-word utterances are used to express a wide variety of meanings. Thus the sentence "Mommy lunch" might be used to express any one of several different meanings: "That lunch belongs to Mommy," "Mommy is eating lunch," and so on (Bloom, 1970, 1973).

Children throughout the world, in different cultures and in different language communities. behave in pretty much the same ways during this stage of language development. They all proceed from holophrastic speech to telegraphic speech, and they talk about the same kinds of things (Slobin, 1971). All children name things and people. All children have a way of announcing that they have noticed something (for instance, "Hi, doggie!"). All children have simple ways of expressing important things such as the hoped-for-reappearance of something like "More milk," or the equally important facts of disappearance, like "Cookie allgone." The kinds of semantic relations and functions of language expressed by children are the same the world over (see Table 8–2).

Once children have mastered two-word utterances, they begin to learn the syntax of the language. One of the more sensitive measures of a child's level of language development is the number of words (or morphemes) used per utterance. This measure, devised by Roger Brown at Harvard, is called MLU—mean length of utterance (1973). With increasing cognitive and linguistic sophistication, children's utterances tend, on average, to get longer (see Figure 8–6). This reflects at least two kinds of developmental changes. First, it reflects the child's capacity to organize and produce longer sequences of words, irrespective of the grammatical complexity of those sequences. Second, it reflects the child's learning of more complex grammatical forms. In early speech a child might say "Go home?" Later the same meaning will be expressed in the adult form, "Can we go home now?"

Children's acquisition of syntax involves more than learning how to string more and more words together. It also involves learning the syntactic rules that make it possible to produce new sentences, as well as to make some revealing mistakes. Sometimes when children first learn to express the past tense in English, they will use the standard form, as in *walk-ed,* and sporadically also use irregular forms, like *went.* When they really learn the rule—adding the suffix *-ed* to a verb stem—they apply it to all verbs and say things like *goed* instead of *went, breaked* instead of *broke,* and so on. It then takes them several years to learn the exceptions to the rule. This pattern of rule learning, then overgeneralizing the rule, and finally learning the exceptions to the rule has been observed in every language that has these kinds of rules and exceptions (Ervin, 1964).

The rules of grammar, even though they may lead to some mistakes, greatly simplify the task of language learning. Once we have a rule, we need

Table 8–2: Two-Word Sentences in Children's Speech from Several Languages.

Function of Utterance	Language				
	English	German	Russian	Finnish	Samoan
Locate, Name	There book That car See doggie	Buch da [Book there] Gukuk wauwau [See doggie]	Tosya tam [Tosya there]	Tuossa Rina [There Rina] Vettä siinä [Water there]	Keith lea [Keith there]
Demand, Desire	More milk Give candy Want gum	Mehr milch [More milk] Bitte apfel [Please apple]	Yeshchë moloko [More milk] Day chasy [Give watch]	Anna Rina [Give Rina]	Mai pepe [give doll] fia moo [Want sleep]
Negate	No wet No wash Not hungry Allgone milk	Nicht blasen [Not blow] Kaffee nein [Coffee no]	Vody net [Water no] Gus' tyu-tyu [Goose gone]	Ei susi [Not wolf] Enää pipi [Anymore sore]	Le 'ai [Not eat] uma mea [allgone thing]
Describe Event or Situation	Bambi go Mail come Hit ball Block fall Baby highchair	Puppe kommt [Doll comes] Tiktak hängt [Clock hangs] Sofa sitzen [Sofa sit] Messer schneiden [Cut knife]	Mama prua [Mama walk] Papa bay-bay [Papa sleep] Korka upala [Crust fell] Nashla yaichko [Found egg] Baba kresio [Grandma armchair]	Seppo putoo [Seppo fall] Talli 'bm-bm' [Garage 'car']	pa'u pepe [fall doll] tapale 'oe [hit you] tu'u lalo [put down]
Show Possession	My shoe Mama dress	Mein ball [My ball] Mamas hut [Mama's hat]	Mami chashka [Mama's cup] Pup moya [Navel my]	Täti auto [Aunt car]	lole a'u [candy my] polo 'oe [ball your] paluni mama [balloon mama]
Modify, Qualify	Pretty dress Big boat	Milch heiss [Milk hot] Armer wauwau [Poor dog]	Mama khoroshaya [Mama good] Papa bol'shoy [Papa big]	Rikki auto [Broken car] Torni iso [Tower big]	fa'ali'i pepe [headstrong baby]
Question	Where ball	Wo ball [Where ball]	Gde papa [Where papa]	Missä pallo [Where ball]	fea Punafu [where Punafu]

From Slobin (1971).

not memorize every form of every word in the language. We can even generalize the grammar to words that don't exist. In an ingenious experiment Jean Berko (1958) taught nonsense names to 5- and 6-year-old children. A child would be shown a drawing of an unfamiliar animal (see Figure 8–7), and told, "This is a wug." then Berko would point to a second picture and say, "There are two of them. "There are two———." The children then completed the sentence by saying "Wugs," indicating that they indeed knew the rule for pluralization in English.

Knowing a rule does not necessarily mean that we are conscious of that knowledge or that we can describe the rule. Even literate adults know rules of grammar without being aware of them. For example, what rules do we follow to produce *tag questions,* such as "John went home yesterday, didn't he?" or "John didn't go home yesterday, did he?" What are the rules that

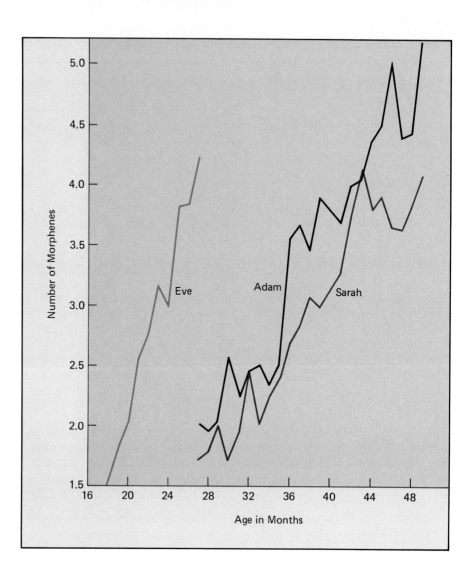

Figure 8–6 Mean length of utterance increases with age. This increase is shown for three children studied by Brown (1973).

Figure 8–7 A test used to assess children's knowledge of pluralization rules. (Berko, 1958)

This is a wug.

Now there is another one.
There are two of them.
There are two_____.

specify that the phrase "a large red Turkish truck" is correct, while the phrase "A Turkish red large truck" is incorrect? We must know these rules, because we follow them when we speak, but we don't know them consciously.

From Sentences to Conversation

A telephone rings and a 3-year-old child answers. The caller asks, "Is your mommy home?" The child immediately puts the phone down and calls for Mother to answer the phone. This child has understood the *intent* of the caller—to speak to Mother. At this age, most children use the immediate situation to help them interpret what people say. They very often ignore the details of the speech they hear. Somewhat older children may go to the other extreme. They will rely completely on the literal meaning of a sentence and ignore the social or conversational context. Thus a 4-year-old who is asked, "Is your mommy home?" may very well answer, "Yes," and wait for the conversation to continue.

From about 3 to 6 years, children learn a great deal about conversational

behavior. This includes learning how to tell whether to take a statement literally or not, as in our telephone example. It also includes the development of awareness and sensitivity to other people's feelings and their needs for information. Young children tend to ask for things or tell people to do things directly. They will say "Swing me," or "I want a cookie." Older children, starting at about 4 to 5 years of age, will use adultlike, indirect requests. They will say "Do you want to swing me?" or "Can I have a cookie?" They will also provide reasons for requests, such as "Gimme the hammer—I *need* it."

This shift away from direct requests to indirect statements that are justified reflects an increasing understanding of social and interpersonal factors in communication. When adults talk to one another, they routinely tailor their speech to suit their listeners. For example, when two strangers are given a communication problem that involves talking about unusual geometric forms (as in Figure 8–8), they begin by using long descriptive phrases, and then gradually shorten those phrases as they tacitly develop a two-person code (Krauss & Glucksberg, 1977). When nursery- school children are given a version of this task (Figure 8–9), they behave as if a tacit code had already been

Figure 8–8 In the adult communication task the speaker had to describe each of six novel designs on a paper in front of him and give the number that went with each; a listener on the other side of an opaque barrier had to assign the correct number to copies of the same designs. Adult speakers communicated successfully by giving detailed descriptions the first time a design was used; when the same form appeared in later trials, speakers shortened their descriptions (for example, "The spaceman's helmet," and then just "helmet"), and continued to be well understood by listeners. (*Krauss & Glucksberg, 1977*)

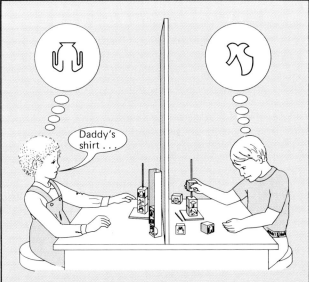

Figure 8–9 In the children's version of the task, the speaker had to describe the design on blocks appearing at the base of a dispenser and then stack the blocks on a peg. The listener's task was to select the correct blocks from a randomly ordered collection and stack them in the same order. The youngest speakers gave noncommunicative descriptions that were usually misunderstood. (*Krauss & Glucksberg, 1977*)

277

developed. The descriptions they give to one another are short, idiosyncratic, and virtually uninformative to the listeners (Glucksberg, Krauss, & Weisberg, 1966).

With further development of their language and social skills, children learn when and how to adjust what they say and how they say it, depending on who their listeners are. Most 4-year-olds know how to adjust their speech in some obvious situations. For example, they will use longer sentences and more complex grammatical constructions when talking to adults than when talking to 2-year-olds (Shatz & Gelman, 1973). Further elaboration and development of these social-linguistic skills will enable them to make the same subtle and fine-tuned adjustments that adults make during ordinary conversation (Asher, 1979).

LANGUAGE AND THOUGHT

Can animals other than humans learn a humanlike language? Can animals who have no such language reason or solve problems? Is there any connection between being able to talk and being able to think?

Nonhuman Language

All animals communicate with one another. A honey bee returning from a food source will perform a dance in the hive that informs the other bees where food can be found (von Frisch, 1967). Wolves, lions, and other pack-hunting animals communicate with one another when coordinating a hunt. Until recently, however, no animal learned even the rudiments of a human language.

People have always wondered whether animals, particularly chimpanzees, could be taught a humanlike language. Early attempts to teach chimpanzees to talk were complete failures (Kellogg & Kellogg, 1933; Hayes, 1951). Allen and Beatrice Gardner of the University of Nevada suspected that chimps could not talk because they lacked the necessary vocal apparatus, not because they weren't smart enough. Acting on this hunch, they decided to teach a drastically simplified version of American Sign Language to a young female chimp, Washoe. Washoe learned a small repertory of signs, and after about two years she began to combine signs into short simple sequences—much like the early sentences of human children (Gardner & Gardner, 1969).

Washoe, like a human child, was able to produce word combinations that could be interpreted quite readily. Her combinations seemed to express the same semantic relations that are expressed universally in young children's utterances (see Table 8–2). Furthermore, Washoe used virtually all of her combinations spontaneously, without having them taught to her or having any opportunity to imitate them.

Since the Gardners' pioneering work with Washoe, several other chimpanzees—and at least one gorilla—have been taught fairly complex communication systems. Some of these were based on signs adapted from ASL, others on artificial signing systems. David Premack (1976) taught the chimpanzee Sarah to make symbol strings by placing magnetized plastic forms on a magnetic board (see Figure 8–10). Duane Rumbaugh (1977) taught a chimpanzee named Lana to use a computerlike keyboard with illuminated push buttons to communicate in a system he called *Yerkish*. In each of these cases, it was claimed that the chimpanzee had mastered an

Figure 8–10 David Premack (1976) taught a chimpanzee named Sarah to use this symbol system.

HIGHLIGHT

Language Processing by Computer

As the debate rages on about whether nonhuman animals can truly learn language, our linguistic uniqueness is being challenged on a second front: Researchers in the discipline of *Artificial Intelligence* (AI) have been trying to instill computers with language-processing capabilities. In the last chapter the Highlight on distributed memory described how computers could be taught to read text aloud. Computers have also been programmed to understand other aspects of language. Early researchers in this area were able to show that a computer can be made *to appear* to have sophisticated linguistic abilities.

Joseph Weizenbaum (1965), for example, created a program named ELIZA that simulated a client-centered therapist. This type of therapist spends a good part of the therapeutic session eliciting feelings and reflecting them back to the client (see Chapter 18). Weizenbaum's program gave a powerful illusion of understanding by checking the input for critical words (relevant to issues that might arise in therapy) and by responding to these words with a large repertory of preplanned phrases. This is what a conversation might look like (from Winston, 1977):

CLIENT: I do not like computers.
THERAPIST (The computer): Do machines frighten you?
CLIENT: Not like my mother.
COMPUTER: Tell me more about your family.

CLIENT: Yes.
COMPUTER: Please do not be so short with me.

ELIZA was quite adept at convincing people that they were interacting with another human being. But researchers in AI were interested in creating computer programs that were more than mere parrots. They hoped to create a system that could truly be said to understand language—and in doing so, to illuminate some of the properties of language processing in humans.

One area in which these researchers have been particularly successful is in identifying the knowledge structures that both computers and humans must have to make language comprehension possible. Consider this brief text:

Arthur was having lunch at his favorite Chinese restaurant. He ordered Won Ton soup and Chicken Chow Mein. He ate the food quickly and hurried back to his office.

After reading this story, we would be quite willing to make a number of inferences about what else occurred during Arthur's lunch. We would assume that Arthur had ordered his meal from a waiter or waitress, that he paid for the food before he left, and that he left a tip. When a computer program was written to understand such brief stories, it incorporated the notion of *scripts* (see Chapter 7) to facilitate this type of inferencing (Schank & Abelson, 1977). Recall that scripts are structures that record information about stereotypical situations like visits to restaurants and doctors' offices. The computer

program needed to have such information in memory to infer what was left unstated. Research has confirmed that humans do have knowledge structures of this sort (Bower, Black, & Turner, 1979). Further research in AI has identified many types of knowledge that are necessary for computers—and by implication, humans—to process language (see Schank & Birnbaum, 1984). For example, we store extensive knowledge about people's typical goals and how those goals are implemented by plans. Such stored information enables us to understand many conversational interchanges:

CHRIS: I could really go for some pizza.
SANDY: I'm not going to lend you my car.

Sandy's response shows that he is aware of the plans relevant to Chris's goal: (1) To get pizza Chris must get to the pizza parlor; (2) to get to the pizza parlor, he needs to find a vehicle; (3) to get a vehicle, he may ask Sandy to lend him his car. Sandy's response acknowledges this hierarchy of plans. A computer system with this same sort of goal-and-plan knowledge would also be able to appreciate the connection between these two utterances.

Although no one has yet created a computer system that can carry on a conversation, the study of language processing by computer has yielded insight into how people converse. By asking, "What sort of knowledge is necessary to allow a computer to comprehend language?" researchers in AI have discovered a number of interesting knowledge structures that apply to people as well.

---

essential component of natural language, the ability to create a sentence. There is however, some question about two aspects of the language use exhibited by the animals in these studies. First, there is considerable doubt that apes can proceed beyond two-sign utterances of any complexity. Second, the apes who have learned these skills have not yet shown any evidence of using their communication systems conversationally, either with people or with other apes. In general, their spontaneous communications consist primarily of requests and, occasionally, casual object naming.

Herbert Terrace (1979) has reported the results of an intensive study of a chimpanzee named Nim Chimpsky (the pun was intended). Over a period of

Duane Rumbaugh (1977) taught a chimpanzee named Lana to use a computerlike keyboard to communicate. (Paul Fusco/Magnum Photos)

several years Nim made more than 19,000 multiple-sign utterances in the version of ASL that Terrace taught him. These utterances were then carefully analyzed for evidence of syntactic regularities. According to Terrace, most of the multiple-sign utterances were either simple repetitions, like "Tickle me tickle" or "Hug me Nim," or they were inadvertently cued by a human teacher. Terrace analyzed the film records of other chimpanzees who had been taught ASL, including Washoe, and concluded that they did not clearly demonstrate that the chimpanzees had mastered even an elementary form of syntax. Terrace concluded that "apes can learn many isolated symbols (as can dogs, horses, and other nonhuman species), but they show no unequivocal evidence of having mastered the conversational . . . or syntactic organization of language" (Terrace, Petitto, Sanders, & Bever, 1979, p. 901).

The key word in this quotation is *unequivocal*. The Gardners strongly disagree with Terrace's conclusion. They argue that Washoe did use languagelike rules, and that she did show "conversational give-and-take" between herself and human companions (Gardner & Gardner, 1980). Can an ape learn to create a sentence? Maybe. The evidence is equivocal. We will have to see more complete studies of chimpanzees' learning to "talk" before the final answer is in.

Leaving aside the question about creating sentences, can an ape learn arbitrary linguistic reference? Sue Savage-Rumbaugh and her colleagues (Savage-Rumbaugh et al., 1983) taught two young chimpanzees the meanings of two labels—one for edibles (foods), the other for nonedibles (tools). The chimpanzees were then tested to see if they could categorize novel objects and novel labels as foods or as tools on the basis of the previously learned "names." They clearly could, suggesting that chimps are capable of learning at least this aspect of humanlike language—arbitrary symbolic reference.

The latest efforts of Savage-Rumbaugh and her colleagues (1986) to teach language to great apes have involved two pygmy chimpanzees, Kanzi and his sister, Mulika. Remarkably, these two animals did not need explicit training to use the symbols of their artificial language in an appropriate fashion—they *spontaneously* used the symbols to communicate with people. What is even more striking is that these two chimpanzees appear to understand *spoken* English. For example, when faced with a choice of three alternatives, Kanzi and Mulika can readily select a picture of what their trainer names.

These linguistic abilities far outstrip what has been demonstrated in other animals. Savage-Rumbaugh argues that what sets Kanzi and Mulika apart is that they are pygmy chimpanzees rather than common chimpanzees: Pygmy chimpanzees may be closer to humans in their capacity to learn and use linguistic-like symbols. When the results from Savage-Rumbaugh's work are contrasted with earlier studies, we get a strong sense of how the cognitive capabilities necessary for language may have developed across species. Although Kanzi and Mulika may never develop a syntactically complex language, they have demonstrated that there is a smaller linguistic gap between apes and humans than we had previously believed.

Concepts

A concept is our knowledge about a category of objects or events. When we have a concept of, say, *chairs,* we can recognize something as a chair even if we have never seen it or one just like it before. We would also know that it belongs to a larger category of things called *furniture*. Having such concepts

is enormously useful and efficient. Most of the things and events we encounter every day are examples of well-known categories, even though the specific examples may be new to us in many ways. By having a concept of what a thing or event is, we can classify something new as an instance of a familiar category.

For example, my concept of *cats* allows me to recognize any one of an infinite number of different animals as cats, and to classify accurately almost any animal I might see as being a cat or not. I also know where cats fit in the animal kingdom, and I can compare them with other animals such as dogs, elephants, or fish. I know pretty much what to expect from any cat I might meet, and therefore I would know what to do if I should meet one.

How do we acquire such concepts? One way is to learn a set of rules that defines a category. In an influential study of concept formation, Heidbreder (1947) found that people learn classification rules based on concrete ideas more easily than rules based on abstract properties such as numbers (see Figure 8–11). The relative difficulty of concrete and abstract concepts can also be seen in the developing child. Children's early concepts are primarily concrete, including such things as dogs, people, toys and candy. Later concepts like *living things* come in, as well as such concepts as *fairness, honesty,* and *truth*. At first, these abstract concepts are quite simple: *Truth* may be defined as "not lying." In adulthood the concept of *truth* is far more complex, and few of us would even try to define it.

Concepts can also be easy or difficult to learn, depending on the types of rules that define them. When a single rule defines a concept, it is a *simple* concept. In this sense, all of the concepts shown in Figure 8–11 are *simple* concepts, whether they are abstract or concrete. When the rules become more complicated, then the concepts become more difficult to learn. Bruner and Goodnow (1956) used arbitrary concepts to see what kinds of classification rules were hardest to learn. When classification decisions had to be based on two or more rules, it took longer to learn the concept than when only one rule was required. When something must have two or more features or characteristics in order to qualify as a member of the category, it is called a **conjunctive concept.** The concept of *registered voter* is a conjunctive concept. In order to qualify as a registered voter, a person must be 18 years old, a citizen, and a resident of a particular district, and must also have his or her name entered on a particular roster of names.

Even more difficult are **disjunctive concepts.** These involve "either-or" rules. For example, the category *U.S. citizen* is defined as someone (1) who was born in the United States; *or* (2) either of whose parents was a United States citizen; *or* (3) who was naturalized in a U.S. District Court. If any one of these conditions is met, then the person is a citizen.

When the rules for classifying examples of a concept can be stated explicitly, then that concept is well defined. Many everyday concepts (for example,

Examples of cat and noncats. What properties do cats have that the noncats don't have?

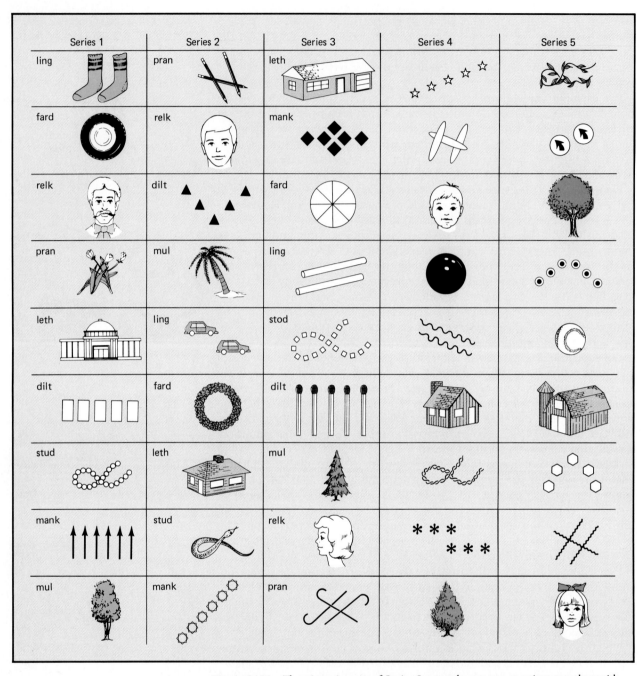

Figure 8–11 The nine pictures of Series I were shown one at a time together with their labels. This was followed by Series 2, then 3, 4, and 5, and people had to learn which labels went with which pictures. Concrete object concepts, such as *faces,* were learned most quickly. Spatial form and pattern concepts, such as *circle,* were more difficult. Most difficult were concepts based on number, such as *two objects.* Can you provide the correct labels for the pictures in Series 4 and 5? If you can, then you have learned the concepts that are labeled *ling, fard,* and so on. (Edna Heidbreder, 1947)

citizen and *voter*) are well defined, but many others are not. In fact, there is good reason to believe that most natural concepts—those that people develop spontaneously and have discrete names for—are not at all well defined (Rosch, 1978). Instead, the members of most natural categories, such as *furniture* or *games,* bear something like a family resemblance to one another. For example, the category of things that we call *games* includes such activities as chess, football, gin rummy, poker, solitaire, charades, frisbee, and hopscotch. What do all these activities have in common? If we think of games as being members of the same family, then they can resemble one another as people do. For example, chess and gin rummy are alike in that they involve two competing players, gin rummy and poker are alike in that they both use playing cards, football and frisbee are alike in that they can involve teams, hopscotch and frisbee are alike in that they both involve physical activity, and so on. As the philosopher Wittgenstein (1953) pointed out, the concept of *game* cannot be defined exactly because there is no set of features or conditions that precisely describes what it is to make a game of something. Technically, there is no set of features that is individually necessary and jointly sufficient to define something as a game.

If we don't use precise definitions or precise rules to classify things, then what do we use? Instead of rules we classify things in terms of their similarity to the most typical examples of that category. Consider the category of things we call *birds*. All birds share certain characteristics: They all have wings and feathers. However, it would not bother us to learn that someone had discovered a wingless bird, or that someone had managed to breed a wingless and featherless bird for the domestic poultry market. This means that wings and feathers are not necessary or defining features of birds, although they are certainly characteristic of them. Other features that we associate with birds are their abilities to fly, sing, build nests, and so on.

Our concept of *bird,* then, consists of what we expect birds to look and act like. On this basis, people agree that robins and sparrows are highly typical birds. Chickens and turkeys are not quite as typical, and penguins and ostriches are highly atypical (Rosch, 1977). Similarly, our concept of *fruit* enables us to classify things as fruits and also to know that apples, pears, and oranges are typical fruits, while watermelons, papayas, and blueberries are atypical. Atypical fruits differ from typical fruits in one or more ways. Watermelons are larger than most fruits, papayas have an unusual texture and taste, and blueberries are small and, of course, blue (how many other blue fruits are there?). Notice that we do not use the technical definition of fruit in our everyday life, so tomatoes and cucumbers are not included in the fruit category despite the fact that they are technically fruits.

How do we learn everyday concepts like these if we do not learn a set of defining rules? Rosch (1977) has suggested that after extensive experience with members of a category, such as birds, we gradually learn what most birds are like. This includes things such as their average size, their most usual coloring, their common behavior patterns, and everything else about them that is *birdlike*. It would *not* include such things as having two eyes or warm blood, because lots of other kinds of animals have these features, too. In other words, we learn what most birds have in common with one another, and what most birds have that other kinds of animals do not. This enables us to distinguish between birds and all the other animals that are not birds, and also gives us a notion of what a typical bird is like. Our concept of *bird,* then, is the sum total of what we have learned about birds and about other kinds of animals.

Another way of saying this is that our concepts are based on our knowledge of the world, and on our theories or ideas about what the world is like. For example, because we know that most birds can fly and that most fish cannot, we are far more likely to note in describing a penguin that it *cannot* fly, than if we were describing a salmon (Murphy & Medin, 1985). In so doing, we are making use of our knowledge of the implicit contrasts among things that are most important. To say that a salmon cannot fly is not especially informative because virtually all fish cannot fly; this statement adds nothing new about salmon. However, to say that a penguin cannot fly *is* informative—because it specifies how penguins differ from other birds. Our concepts, then, are based on two general classes of knowledge: what we know about the entity in question, and in what ways other entities are to be contrasted or compared to it.

The Functions of Language in Thought

The chimpanzees who have learned language-like communication systems provide striking illustrations of some of the noncommunicative uses of language. Obviously, languages and language-like signs or symbol systems are designed primarily for communicative functions. But the ability to express ideas, urges, or concepts in words or in signs can also have profound effects on other behaviors. For example, people can express aggression or anger either physically (by hitting someone) or verbally. Can chimpanzees who have learned language-like communications systems express their emotions in similar fashions? When Nim Chimpsky was being trained, he would sometimes threaten and bite people. After he had learned the sign for "bite," he seldom actually threatened or bit—he simply signed "Bite" and that seemed enough to do two things. First, it told people that he was angry; second it seemed to vent his anger. The chimp seldom bit people after symbolically expressing his anger (Terrace, 1979). This was particularly surprising because Terrace and his colleagues had used the results of their work with Nim to challenge the contention that chimps could learn sentences.

Nevertheless, Nim's language-like abilities finally did serve him well. When the research program at Columbia ended, Nim was sent to a primate research laboratory in Oklahoma. He was then donated to a medical research laboratory in New York, where he was kept in a small cage and was scheduled to receive hepatitis virus and other potentially painful treatments. Terrace and others who knew of his plight protested vigorously. Nim, after all, had grown up in social contact with people. He even knew some "words," and apparently protested vigorously himself by signing "Out! Out!" to the medical laboratory personnel. After his case was publicized in the newspapers, he was released and sent back to Oklahoma, where he is living out his life with other chimpanzees in relative peace and freedom. Having a language, even a minimal one, can help when one is in trouble.

Having a language can also help in solving conceptual problems. One problem that is difficult for chimpanzees to solve is *cross-modal matching*—deciding whether two objects are the same or different when one of the objects can be seen but not touched and the other can be touched but not seen. Lana, the chimp who was taught a computer-based sign system, could solve such problems easily when the objects involved were ones that she had names for. She had much more difficulty with objects that she had no names for (Rumbaugh et al., 1979).

Children, too, display changes in their abilities to solve certain kinds of

Besides its communicative functions, language can be useful in thinking and problem solving. (L.L.T. Rhodes/Taurus Photos)

problems when they learn how to use language. One such problem is the *far transposition* test. A child is first taught that to find a toy or a piece of candy, he or she must choose the smaller of two boxes. After learning this, the child is given two new boxes, both of which are quite different in size from the original training pair. Children who could not express the original learning in words—"Pick the smaller one"—generally could not succeed in transferring the knowledge they had gained in the first test to the second test. Most of the children who could express the answer verbally did succeed (Kuenne, 1946).

Language, then, does more than serve communicative functions. It can help us to control and guide our behavior, and it can be useful in thinking and problem solving.

Linguistic Relativity

In the late nineteenth century and the early part of this century, linguists and anthropologists worked primarily with exotic cultures and languages—for example, American Indian, Samoan, tribal African, and Eskimo people. The languages that they studied were strikingly different from the familiar European languages, and the people's modes of thinking and action also seemed strikingly different. Did the culture influence the development of the language, or could it be that modes of thought and conceptualization are prisoners of the language—that what and how people think depend on the particular language they speak?

This idea—that the particular language a person speaks determines how that person perceives and conceptualizes the world—is known as the Whorfian hypothesis, after Benjamin Whorf (1940), who with Edward Sapir (1912/58) was among the early proponents of **linguistic relativity.**

There is ample evidence that the way we describe things can affect how we perceive, remember, or think about those things. The labels we give to ambiguous stimuli will influence how we see and remember them. Look at

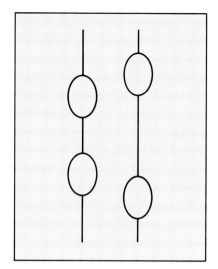

Figure 8–12 What is this a picture of? See the text for an explanation.

Figure 8–12. It can be seen either as two strings with beads on them, or as a bear cub climbing the far side of a tree. In a classic experiment people were shown drawings that could be named in either of two ways (see Figure 8–13). The names given to the drawings substantially influenced the drawings that subjects later reproduced from memory (Carmichael, Hogan, & Walter, 1932).

These kinds of experiments suggested a way to test the Whorfian hypothesis. If different languages provide different sets of names for, say, colors, then people who speak different languages should show differential color memory. For example, in ordinary English we have about six basic color terms—red, orange, yellow, green, blue, and violet (plus, of course, black and white). In the language of the Dani, a tribe in Western New Guinea, there are only two color words. One term refers to all the dark, cool colors, the other to all the light, warm colors. Do English speakers conceptualize colors differently from speakers of Dani?

Eleanor Rosch Heider and Daniel Olivier (1972) tested Dani natives and American college students for their ability to remember and discriminate among colors. The Americans and the Danis were equal in their ability to discriminate shades of difference among colors. The Americans were slightly better at remembering which one of 40 different color chips had been shown to them 30 seconds before. However, these two groups of very different people fundamentally perceive and conceptualize color in identical ways. Both Danis and Americans link together the same colors. Colors that are only somewhat similar to Americans are also only somewhat similar to the Danis. The colors that Americans confuse in memory are the same ones that the Dani confuse in memory. In other words, the perceived degrees of similarity and difference among colors are the same in these two language groups. The color names available to these two groups of people have not influenced their basic aspects of perception and knowledge of colors.

These findings, as well as many others, offer no support for the Whorfian hypothesis, at least with respect to naming practices. But Whorf was not so much interested in vocabulary differences between languages as in syntactic differences. For Whorf, it was chiefly the grammar of the language that shaped thought, not the words that are available. This argument was en-

Figure 8–13 The drawings in the center column were shown to people, together with the labels of List 1 or the labels of List 2. When asked to draw the original pictures from memory, people tended to make the pictures more like their labels than the original was. (Carmichael, Hogan, & Walter, 1932)

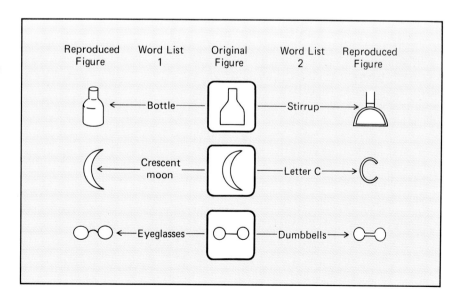

APPLICATION

Are Some Languages Better Than Others?

Is English better than French? Is Portuguese better than Hungarian? Except for a snob or a chauvinist, the answer to both these questions is no. All known languages, from the Dani of Western New Guinea to the English of the Court of St. James's, are equally complex and equally grammatical. There are no general criteria that would enable us to judge whether any one language is better or worse than any other.

Of course, the vocabulary of one language may be better suited to some purposes than the vocabulary of another. The many different Eskimo words for snow make the Eskimo language more efficient for talking about snow than English is. But vocabulary can easily be expanded, and English-speaking skiers have developed a specialized vocabulary for different kinds of snow conditions (e.g., *powder, corn,* and *ice*) that affect skiing. In the same way, people in specialized occupations develop "buzz words" or technical jargon to make communication among themselves more efficient (and sometimes to exclude outsiders). In the business world, for example, people might say "The new project needs a *haircut,*" or "That's a *candy store problem.*" In these contexts, *haircut* means to reduce or cut back costs without endangering a project; a *candy store problem* is a situation that presents a wide choice of options, with no good reason to pick one over another.

The grammars of different languages can also differ in terms of what is obligatory and what is optional. In all languages it is obligatory to provide information about number. Every language distinguishes between singular and plural. English simply distinguishes between one (singular) and more than one (plural), but other languages go further and distinguish grammatically among one, two, and more than two. Sometimes these distinctions are quite complex.

For example, a near-extinct dialect spoken by the Inuvialuit of Canada's Arctic region uses verb declensions (different forms of a verb) to distinguish number (Wren, 1985):

Utaqqiyara:
  I am waiting for him.
Utaqqiyakka:
  I am waiting for two of them.
Utaqqiyatka:
  I am waiting for three or more of them.
Utaqqiyaqquka:
  Two of us are waiting for him.
Utaqqiyaqqut:
  Three or more of us are waiting for him.
Utaqqiyavuk:
  We are waiting for two of them.

Although in a sense this language is far more precise than English, it is also more burdensome. There are many situations where such precise information is not called for. This points to an inherent trade-off in languages between precision and specificity on the one hand, and simplicity on the other. A language presumably develops in ways that are maximally efficient for the communicative needs of the society that uses it. When those needs change, then the language changes—first in vocabulary, then, more slowly, in grammar. But our conclusions about the relative merits of one language over another remain the same: No one language is better than any other in the abstract; all languages are adapted to the needs of the people who use them.

What about language dialects? Are some versions of English, for instance, better than others? Is a Vermont or Maine accent better than a Texas or Louisiana accent? Are all of these regional accents inferior to "standard English"? If so, what is "standard English," and who speaks it?

In England, the standard was once defined by the type of people who spoke it. In 1931 an English linguist wrote this definition of the "best" English:

> Every one knows that there is a kind of English which is neither provincial nor vulgar, a type which most people would willingly speak if they could, and desire to speak if they do not. . . . It is the type spoken by members of the great Public* Schools, and by those classes in society which normally frequent these. . . . This is the best kind of English . . . because it is spoken by those often very properly called "the best people." (Wyld, 1931, p. 605)

What is the American equilvalent of this? Perhaps the kind of radio and television broadcast English that bears no trace of a regional accent. The more obvious the regional accent, the less standard the speech. Obviously, this criterion is as arbitrary as the social-class criterion used by Mr. Wyld in 1931. Ultimately, our feelings about regional and ethnic accents reflect our feelings about the people themselves. If a particular group has high status, then its members' accents are acceptable (for example, an upper-class British or sophisticated French accent). If a group has low status, then its members' accents are judged as unacceptable.

---

*The public schools of England are expensive and exclusive private schools.

---

dorsed by an American psychologist, Alfred Bloom (1981), who proposed that Chinese people think differently from Western people because the Chinese language has no grammatical way to express counterfactuals. Counterfactuals in English are expressed by the subjunctive: for example, "If I *were* king, I *would* make you queen." In Chinese this idea can only be expressed with an if-then construction: "If I am king, then I will make you

queen." Thus, Bloom hypothesized, Chinese people should inevitably have difficulty in understanding and, of course, in describing counterfactuals. When he tested this idea, he found some evidence for it. However, a more extensive and careful set of experiments conducted by Terry Au, a Chinese-American psychologist at Harvard, discovered no support at all for this claim. Au (1983) found that even monolingual Chinese (who did not know English or any language other than Chinese) had no trouble understanding a counterfactual story. Au therefore concluded that mastery of the English subjunctive is irrelevant to the ability to reason counterfactually.

The idea that thinking and language might be independent of one another can be demonstrated by looking at a hypothetical language that encodes concepts in one way, while the people who speak that language think in quite a different way. Consider the following example, taken from a novel about an exotic river people:

> The speech of the river people posed philosophical as well as linguistic problems. . . . The tenses divided time into two great chunks, a simple past and a continuous present. . . . A future tense was created by adding various suffixes indicating hope, intention and varying degrees of probability and possibility to the present stem. (Carter, 1972, p. 91)

If language shapes thought, then it seems these river people must conceive of time quite differently from the way we English speakers do. Their future cannot be thought of as a pure and simple counterpart of the past because their language lacks a future tense that is a simple counterpart of the past tense. But if English grammar reveals how we think about time, then we think just like the river people because English does not have a simple future tense. A future tense is created by adding various modal *auxiliaries* "indicating hope, intention and varying degrees of probability and possibility to the present" form of the verb: for example, I *might* go, I *could* go, I *should* go, I *will* go, I *shall* go. Unlike the simple past tense, as in "I went," English grammar does not permit us to express a future action without simultaneously expressing probability, possibility, or intention. Does this mean that we cannot conceive of a simple future? Few would argue that. The influence of language upon thought may be pervasive, but the differences among human languages do not seem to cause important differences in how people perceive and conceptualize the world (Glucksberg & Danks, 1975).

SUMMARY

1. All languages share certain features: (a) a limited number of speech sounds, called *phonemes:* (b) combinations of phonemes to form countless words; (c) meanings assigned arbitrarily to words; (d) words combined in systematic ways to form a theoretically infinite number of sentences. Because all languages share these features, any idea or concept that can be expressed in one language can also be expressed in any other language.

2. The *morpheme* is the smallest unit of speech that has meaning. The *denotative meaning* of a word is the thing or class of things the word can label; the *conno-*

tative meaning reflects how we feel about the thing the word stands for.

3. Words are combined into sentences according to rules, which form the *syntax* of a language. *Phrase-structure rules* govern the organization of various parts of a sentence; *transformational rules* specify the relationships between sentences and spell out how one type of sentence can be transformed into another. Sentences have both a *surface structure* (particular words and phrases) and a *deep structure* (underlying organization or meaning).

4. Language understanding is guided by implicit knowledge of *linguistic rules, context,* and the *pragmatics* of language use.

5. Chomsky believes that children are born with an innate *language-acquisition device* (LAD). Others believe that children discover basic linguistic rules as part of growing up in a speaking community.

6. By the sixth month, infants engage in *reduplicated babbling.* In the next phase they use *expressive jargon,* vocalizations that sound like adult speech but are unintelligible.

7. The one-word utterances of children are called *holophrastic* utterances because just one word can express a whole phrase or sentence. A child's first sentences, which are two-word utterances, are *telegraphic* in the use of words—only the most important words are included.

8. One of the noncommunicative uses of language is to help solve conceptual problems; being able to label things and to express what we have learned in words helps in thinking and problem solving.

9. Whorf's *linguistic-relativity hypothesis*—that differences in languages cause important differences in the way people perceive and conceptualize the world—has not been borne out by recent experiments.

SUGGESTED READINGS

CLARK, H. H., & CLARK, E. V. (1977). *Psychology and language: An introduction to psycholinguistics.* New York: Harcourt Brace Jovanovich. A comprehensive survey of linguistics and psychology, with particular attention to the mental processes people use to comprehend language.

GLUCKSBERG, S., & DANKS, J. H. (1975). *Experimental psycholinguistics.* Hillsdale, N.J.: Erlbaum. A clear introduction to the concepts of speech perception, semantics, and syntax in the context of the experimental psychology of language.

MILLER, G. A. (1981). *Language and speech.* San Francisco: W. H. Freeman & Co. An introduction to the science of language by an eminent scholar in the field.

ROSCH, E., & LLOYD, B. B. (Eds.). (1978). *Cognition and categorization.* Hillsdale, N.J.: Erlbaum. Reviews the literature on categorization and concept formation, bringing together a representative set of essays from various disciplines and approaches.

SMITH, E. E., & MEDIN, D. L. (1981). *Categories and concepts.* Cambridge, Mass.: Harvard University Press. Surveys the psychological literature on concept formation during the last ten years.

WANNER, E., & GLEITMAN, L. R. (1982). *Language acquisition: The state of the art.* Cambridge: Cambridge University Press. A collection of essays on children's language growth, with a clear and balanced discussion of the innateness vs. learning controversy.

9 Thinking, Reasoning, and Problem Solving

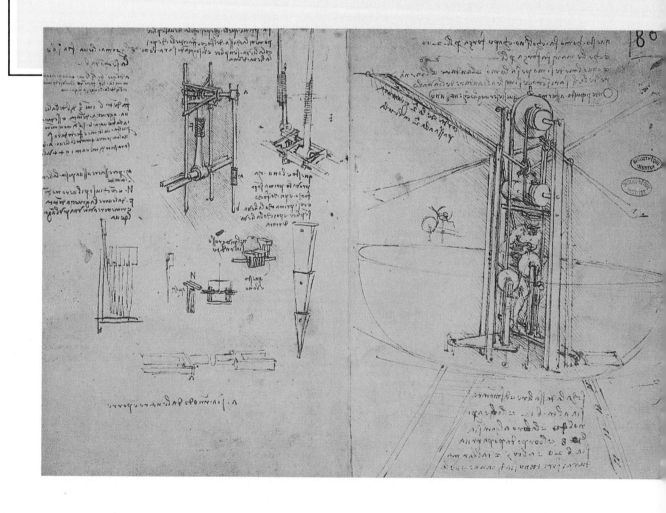

I n the chapter on perception (Chapter 4) we discussed how information from the world is encoded. In our discussion of memory we described how that coded information is stored for later retrieval. Thinking can be defined as the use and manipulation of the information that is coded in long-term memory.

THINKING

Using and manipulating coded information can take many different forms. At one extreme is the conscious, idle daydreaming that we all do occasionally. At the other is the creative thought, usually unconscious, of scientists, writers, and artists—thought that produces new ideas, inventions, literature, and art. While the complexity and the products of these two kinds of thinking are quite different, they do have something in common with all thought: the manipulation of coded information in memory. The coded information is a symbolic representation of a past experience, of a state of the world, or even of an imaginary state of the world. These **symbolic representations** are the contents of thought.

These contents can take several different forms. They can be verbal, and in that form thinking is like talking. For example, if you're planning to go to the beach next weekend, you might talk silently to yourself, listing all the things you need to pack. When the content of thought consists of imagery, then thinking can be like perceiving. For example, you may have coded the loca-

The sketch of a flying machine by Leonardo da Vinci was inspired by his observations and analyses of how birds fly. (Art Resource)

tion of objects in your room in terms of visual imagery. If you are then asked whether the door is to the right or left of your bed, you can generate a visual image of the room, inspect it in your mind's eye, and then know the answer.

There is a third kind of coding that is neither verbal nor imaginal. This is the code we use when we think but are not consciously aware of thinking in either words or images. Indeed, when we think in this abstract mode, we are unable to describe exactly what is going on. All that we are usually aware of is beginning to work on some problem or another, and then suddenly coming up with an idea or a solution. This kind of thinking is the most difficult to study because it is not open to introspection or conscious report. Nevertheless it is an important mode of information processing—perhaps the most important—because it is not limited to a particular form of coding. This "language of the mind" may be the basis for the more concrete manifestations of thought in words and images. Before we consider this kind of thinking, we will describe the roles of language and imagery in thinking.

Thinking in Words

We are all aware that we *sometimes* use speech to aid in thinking, as when we talk to ourselves while working on a difficult problem. John Watson (1925), however, suggested that speech is implicated in *all* thinking. Watson, one of the founders of the behaviorist movement that dominated American psychology in the first half of this century, wanted to discard all traces of mentalism from the science of psychology. He claimed that the only thing that could be studied scientifically was overt behavior that could be objectively observed and measured. Thinking was clearly not such a behavior, but it was nonetheless something that people did. The behaviorist solution to this thorny problem was simple and straightforward: Thinking was defined as nothing but implicit speech. When you thought, you silently talked to yourself; the muscle movements of subvocal speech were the behavior of thinking.

Is this really true? Do we think in words, and if so, can we think only in "spoken" words? Most of us would agree that sometimes we consciously think in words: We talk to ourselves about problems, about plans for the summer, about things we should remember to do. But is this the only way we think?

To try to answer this question, experimenters asked people to imagine counting, telling the date, and doing other mental tasks while sensitive electrodes monitored the tiny muscle movements of the lips, tongue, and larynx. The idea was to demonstrate that during thinking the speech muscles were active, and indeed they were. Thinking is very often accompanied by covert, silent speech (Jacobson, 1932). When this same experiment was repeated with deaf people who used American Sign Language instead of spoken language, implicit motor movements were detected in the muscles that control hands and fingers. This gave further support to the notion that thought is accompanied by silent speech (Max, 1937).

These studies, however, did not tell us whether implicit speech is *necessary* for thinking. What was required was some way to make it impossible for people to "talk" silently to themselves, and then to determine if they could still think. An intrepid psychologist named Smith (Smith et al., 1947) found a way by administering the paralyzing drug *curare* to himself. Smith's voluntary muscles were completely paralyzed. He was kept alive during the experiment by artificial respiration. When the drug wore off, Smith could recall

everything that had happened during his paralysis. He reported doing mental arithmetic, and he answered questions that had been put to him while he was paralyzed; in general, he demonstrated that he had experienced no impairment in mental functioning while he was unable to move a muscle. Smith's experiment proved that at least the motor activity part of speech is not necessary for thought.

What about the symbolic role of language in thought? Must we have a name or a label in order to have a concept, or can we have a concept without having a specific word for it? The English language has words for such concepts as *floor, wall, ceiling, room,* and *window* (see Chapter 8). But English has no single word for "interior surfaces of a room." Can we nevertheless have this concept? Clearly we can. Our language has single words for those concepts that are talked about frequently; if there is no social need to talk about a concept, then that concept will not be *lexicalized,* that is, given a one-word name. Thus we can say that we will paint the living room, and it will be understood that we mean to paint the walls and ceiling, not the floor and not the window glass. Having a single word for all of the interior room surfaces would not be useful, either for thought or for communication. But that doesn't mean we can't have the concept, and given the productivity of language (see Chapter 8), concepts that are not lexicalized can still be described—in several words, if not in a single word.

Thinking in Imagery

Many people experience thinking in terms of visual images, using visual coding (see Chapter 7). The content of thought can be "like" pictures, and we can use these pictures in the mind's eye in much the same ways that we can use actual pictures or scenes. But visualization is not limited to our memories of what we have seen. We can also construct images and then use those images to obtain new information. For example, most people have no trouble with the following problem:

Imagine a rectangle that is three times as high as it is wide.
Next, imagine drawing two lines parallel to the base so that the rectangle is divided into three equal parts.
Now draw (in your mind) two diagonals, one from each corner of the original rectangle to the opposite corner.
Question: How many segments are now in the rectangle?

People report that they can do this problem by mentally inspecting their finished imagined figure, and then counting the number of segments that they "see." (Figure 9–1 shows the finished figure.)

Not only can we mentally construct and scan visual images, we can also manipulate them. In a pioneering study, Shepard and Metzler (1971) asked people to judge whether two geometric figures displayed on a card were the same shape or different shapes (see Figure 9–2). The time to make a "same" judgment was directly related to the difference in orientation between the two shapes. This is exactly what we would expect if people mentally rotated one picture until it was aligned with the other, and then decided if the two were matched. The greater the angle of rotation, the longer it takes to decide.

There are individual differences in the ability to generate visual imagery and to use it in thinking. Some people are faster than average at doing men-

Figure 9–1 How many segments are produced in the "imaginary drawing"? (See text for terms of the problem.)

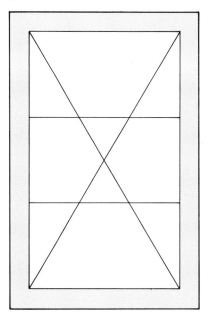

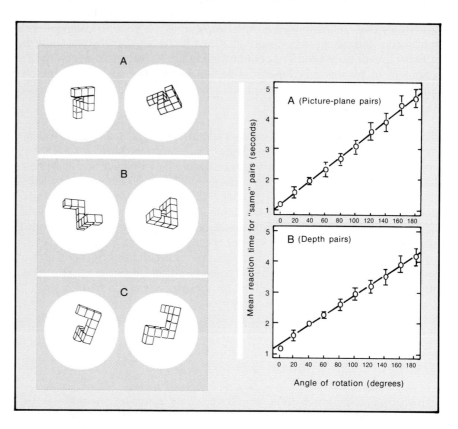

Figure 9–2 (Left) Examples of pairs of perspective drawings used by Shepard and Metzler (1971) to demonstrate mental rotation of visual images: A is a "same" pair, which differ by an 80° rotation in the picture plane; B is also a "same" pair, which differ by an 80° rotation in depth; and C is a "different" pair, which cannot be brought into alignment by any rotation. (Right) Time taken to decide that two drawings are the "same" as a function of angular difference in orientation: A plots times for pairs differing by a rotation in the picture plane only; and B plots times for pairs differing by a rotation in depth.

tal rotation; others seem unable to manipulate mental images at all (Shepard & Cooper, 1982). Still, most people take advantage of this ability when they can. For example, how would you go about classifying each of the following breeds of dogs as to whether (a) ears project above the head or (b) ears don't project above the head: German shepherd, French poodle, cocker spaniel, Labrador retriever, dachshund, beagle, fox terrier, bulldog, Doberman pinscher. The usual way of deciding is through some form of visual image, because it is very unlikely someone has memorized the fact that German shepherds have ears that point up above their heads, while beagles have ears that point down.

Thinking in Abstract Codes

Thinking in words (verbal codes) and thinking in imagery (visual codes) tend to be concrete; both are also generally conscious forms of thinking. But thinking can also occur in abstract form, using what cognitive psychologists refer to as *propositions* (Anderson, 1980). A proposition is a form of coding that is neither verbal nor perceptual. How might we conceive of such a code—the "language of thought" (Fodor, 1975)? Consider the difference between a standard long-playing record and a laser-beam compact disk. The standard record has tiny grooves with waves that are strictly analogous to sound waves. The playback stylus on the record player follows these waves and vibrates according to the frequency and amplitude of the recorded sound waves. The coding for this playback device thus has an analog in nature—the sound wave—and can be considered a form of auditory image. Contrast this with the coding of music on a compact disk. Here there is no

analog to natural sound waves. Instead, the information is coded in digital form and read by a laser beam that translates the coded information into musical sounds for playback. This is analogous to the process whereby information stored in the brain can be used to generate an auditory or visual image—or, for that matter, language itself.

To process certain kinds of information, we seem to use such abstract codes directly, without prior translation into words or images. For example, if asked which is bigger, a rat or a hamster, we would probably first have to generate two visual images and then compare them for size. However, if asked the same question about an elephant and a mouse, we could answer immediately without using imagery (Kosslyn, 1980). We "know" that an elephant is bigger than a mouse in a way that is different from our knowing the relative difference in the sizes of rats and hamsters. This "knowing" is not in words, although we can express it verbally. Other such "knowing" includes our knowledge of the grammar of our language, of basic arithmetic, and, in all likelihood, our functional knowledge of the world.

Information that is coded in abstract form enables us to translate freely and quickly between different surface forms of thought. For example, pictures of objects and names of objects both represent the same concepts: The word *table* and a picture of a table both represent our concept of the natural category *table*. Similarly, if a person knows the name for *table* in three different languages, then those three different words are different verbal codes for the same concept of "table" (Glucksberg, 1984; Snodgrass, 1984).

REASONING

Do kangaroos have livers? Even if you have never learned this fact directly (and it's most unlikely that you have), you can still answer the question correctly. The answer is not recalled or remembered, but generated by **reasoning.** In **deductive reasoning** the steps are explicit and the conclusions firm. In order to answer the kangaroo question deductively, we could transform it into a syllogism (a three-term reasoning format):

All kangaroos are mammals.
All mammals have livers.
Conclusion: Kangaroos have livers.

We could also answer the question by using **inductive reasoning:**

Many animals that I know have livers.
The kangaroo resembles these animals in many ways.
Therefore it is more than likely that kangaroos have livers. But I wouldn't bet my life on it.

In both cases, information that we already have permits us to generate additional information. This is one of the more important functions of reasoning.

We also use reasoning to judge the validity of arguments. In general, college students are quite good at detecting logical flaws in syllogisms. For example, many students would agree that this argument is false:

All Xs are Y.
All Zs are Y.
Therefore all Xs are Zs.

This same logic problem, however, can be made either easier or more difficult by changing the particular terms used. For example, it is most clearly recognized as false if we already know that the conclusion is, in the real world, false:

All Israelis are people.
All Egyptians are people.
Therefore all Israelis are Egyptians.

In contrast, if we tend to agree with the conclusion, then it is more difficult to detect the logical flaw:

Welfare is giving to the poor.
Charity is giving to the poor.
Therefore welfare is charity.

These examples illustrate how our knowledge and our biases can interfere with our ability to use deductive logic (Wason & Johnson-Laird, 1972).

Rules and Mental Models

When we solve logical reasoning problems such as the syllogisms illustrated above, what kinds of thinking are we doing? One possibility is that we are using propositions in the form of **inference rules.** An inference rule states that a particular proposition must be true when certain other propositions are true (Braine, 1978). For example, if these two propositions are true:

Either Reagan won or Mondale won.
Mondale did not win.

Then the conclusion follows immediately.

Reagan won.

The general form or *schema* for this rule is:

p or q.
Not p.
Therefore q.

Another kind of inference rule can be used to judge whether syllogisms of the following form are valid:

Some A are B.
Some B are C.
Therefore some A are C.

The rule here is very simple: Whenever the premises contain two "some" statements, no conclusion follows. When the abstract problem is stated in concrete terms, the possibility of contradiction is made explicit:

Some men are teachers.
Some teachers are women.
Therefore some men are women.

We have all had extensive experience with moving objects. Living things, such as people, dogs, cats, and birds, are self-powered and move in predictable ways. Nonliving things that require outside forces for motion, such as sleds, bicycles, tennis balls, and frisbees, also move in fairly predictable ways. From our observations of these different sorts of moving things, we develop mental models of how things

move, and along with these models, a naive or intuitive theory about why things move as they do. Given our considerable experience with moving objects, we might expect that these beliefs about motion would be fairly accurate. However, despite this experience, and even with formal education, we tend to have striking misconceptions about how objects move. Michael McCloskey and his colleagues (1980) at The Johns Hopkins University first noticed these rather systematic misconceptions about the laws of motion when they tested college students with some simple problems. They showed students diagrams such as those in Figure A.

Figure A

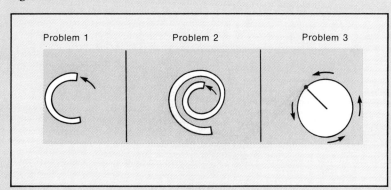

For Problems 1 and 2, the students were told:

A tube is laid flat on a horizontal surface, such as a large table. In the diagrams you are looking down on the tube. A metal ball is put into the end of the tube indicated by the arrow. The ball is then shot out of the other end of the tube at high speed. Your task is to draw the path the ball will follow after it comes out of the tube. . . . In drawing the path of the ball ignore air resistance.

For Problem 3, they were told:

Imagine that someone has a metal ball attached to a string and is twirling it at high speed in a circle above his head. In this diagram you are looking down on the ball. The circle shows the path followed by the ball and the arrows show the direction in which it is moving. The line from the center of the circle to the ball is the string. Assume that when the ball is at the point shown in the diagram, the string breaks where it is attached to the ball. Draw the path the ball will follow after the string breaks. Ignore air resistance.

Before looking at the correct answers on the next page, try doing these three problems yourself.

Why should concrete verbal materials such as *men, teachers,* and *women* be easier to comprehend than abstract ones such as *A, B,* and *C?* One reason may be that people don't generally use inference rules, but instead employ mental models of the problem in order to solve it. One kind of mental model makes use of visual imagery. For example, consider this problem:

All the artists are beekeepers.
All the beekeepers are chemists.

What conclusions can you draw? One way to handle this sort of problem is to set up an imaginary scene, or cast of characters, based on the two premises. Using the first premise—All the artists are beekeepers—we can set up the following cast of characters:

Artist 1 = Beekeeper 1
Artist 2 = Beekeeper 2
Artist 3 = Beekeeper 3
       (Beekeeper 4)
       (Beekeeper 5)

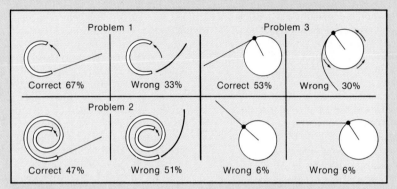

Figure B

Shown in Figure B are the correct and some of the most common incorrect answers to the problems.

The correct answers follow from Newton's first law of motion: In the absence of an externally applied force, an object in motion will travel in a straight line. The ball leaving the tube will move in a straight line in the direction of its instantaneous velocity when it leaves the tube. The ball leaving the string in Problem 3 will fly off in a straight line along the tangent to the circle at the point of the breaking string.

Two other problems—the airplane problem and the cliff problem—also revealed common misconceptions of motion:

Figure C shows a side view of a cliff. The top of the cliff is frictionless (in other words, perfectly smooth). A metal ball is rolling along the top of the cliff at a constant speed of 50 miles per hour. Draw the path the ball will follow after it goes over the edge of the cliff. Ignore air resistance.

The correct answer for the cliff problem shown in (a), is similar to that for the airplane problem, Figure D. After the ball goes over the edge of the cliff, it will continue to travel horizontally at a constant speed of 50 mph. However, the ball will acquire a constantly increasing downward velocity, and consequently will fall in a parabolic arc.

Newton's laws are one form of representation of physical forces and motions. These laws are stated in words (as above) and in mathematical equations, as in the law relating force, mass, and acceleration, $F = ma$.

Ordinary people's representations of physical forces and motions are not necessarily in these forms. Instead, much of our "knowledge" of physical motion is in the form of a mental model, a distillation of what we've seen and experienced.

In our everyday experience friction, air resistance, and the way we perceive motion can combine to give us a

misleading mental model—misleading if we take Newtonian mechanics as accurate. For example, imagine that you are walking at a moderate pace and you drop your keys straight down on the sidewalk, which is analogous to the ball dropping from the airplane in the airplane problem. The subjective impression is that the keys hit the ground behind you as you walk on. This is an illusion, but a powerful one—and it contributes to our mental model of moving objects.

In addition to such perceptual illusions, we have misconceptions about the causes of motion. These beliefs are similar to the impetus theory of motion, the prevalent idea during the fourteenth through sixteenth centuries, until Newton formulated the laws of motion. The intuitive impetus theory that people still seem to hold assumes that setting an object in motion gives that object some force, or "impetus," that keeps it going after it is no longer in contact

Figure C The Cliff Problem   Correct response (a) and most common incorrect responses (b) and (c).

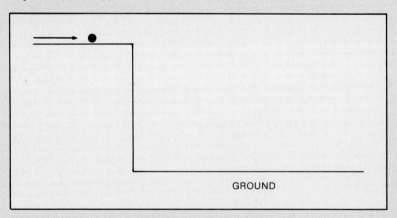

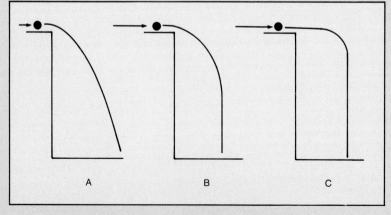

with, or influenced by, the original mover. This impetus gradually dissipates, and the object comes to a stop. What we "know" of moving objects pretty much fits with this belief. When we push a toy car, it rolls for a while and then stops because of friction and air resistance. When we throw a ball in the air, it slows, stops, and then falls down because of gravity. These observations and beliefs, however, are at odds with classical physics. No force is required to keep an object at rest, and no force is required to keep an object in motion.

The incompatibility between the laws of classical physics and people's mental models of moving objects may be one reason why teaching physics is difficult and very often unsuccessful. Many of McCloskey's subjects had taken college courses in physics, and yet they still made errors on the simple motion problems illustrated above. This suggests that the naive impetus theory is not easily changed by classroom instruction. It may be useful for physics instructors to be aware of the naive theories of motion held by their students, and to demonstrate explicitly how they are incompatible with the views of classical physics (McCloskey, 1983).

If our mental models of motion are so mistaken, how is it that we generally get along so well in the world? Fortunately, we only appear to reason with our mental models when we are put in unfamiliar situations. For example, subjects in an experiment were shown a physical realization of the apparatus in Problem 2 (Figure A). They were asked to imagine what path both flowing water and a metal ball would take after passing through the tube (Kaiser, Jonides, & Alexander, 1986). Many of the students had probably had the experience of watching water emerge on a straight path from a tangled garden hose; 66 percent gave the correct response for that problem. The very same respondents were correct only 39 percent of the time for the ball version of the same problem. With the water, many subjects could evoke specific memories; with the ball, most subjects could only reason from their faulty mental models. In general, the inaccuracy of our mental models will be most problematic when we must reason outside our normal realm of experiences.

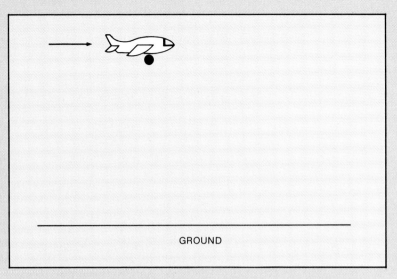

GROUND

Figure D The Airplane Problem   In the top diagram an airplane is flying along at a constant speed. The plane is also flying at a constant altitude, so that its flight path is parallel to the ground. The arrow shows the direction in which the plane is flying. When the plane is in the position shown in the lower diagram, a large metal ball is dropped from the plane. The plane continues flying at the same speed in the same direction and at the same altitude. Draw the path the ball will follow from when it is dropped until it hits the ground. Ignore wind or air resistance. Also show as well as you can the position of the plane at the moment the ball hits the ground. (Correct response A and incorrect responses B-D.)

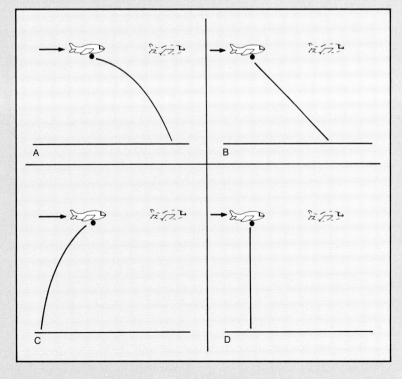

In this scene the first three characters play joint roles: Each is both artist and beekeeper. Two other characters (4 and 5) are beekeepers, but not artists. Using the second premise, we can then set up a more elaborate cast of characters:

Artist 1 = Beekeeper 1 = Chemist 1
Artist 2 = Beekeeper 2 = Chemist 2
Artist 3 = Beekeeper 3 = Chemist 3
        (Beekeeper 4 = Chemist 4)
        (Beekeeper 5 = Chemist 5)
                    (Chemist 6)

Now if you were to be asked, "Are all the artists chemists?" you could inspect your mental model and answer, "Yes." You could also answer other questions correctly, such as "Are all the beekeepers artists?" ("No".) Are all the chemists artists? ("No".). Note that if you hadn't bothered to add Chemist 6 to your cast of characters, then you would still answer this last question correctly, but you would answer the question "Are all the chemists beekeepers?" incorrectly. Using a cast of characters *without* Chemist 6, you'd inspect the model and say "Yes."

This way of solving syllogistic reasoning problems is not perfect, but it usually works (Johnson-Laird, 1983). It also helps explain individual differences in reasoning ability. Good reasoners build more complete models than poor reasoners do. In the example above, a poor reasoner might not add Chemist 6 to the cast of characters, and so would get the question about all chemists being beekeepers wrong. People also differ in the reasoning processes that they have learned to use. Expert reasoners usually rely primarily on inference rules; most people without formal training in logic tend to rely on mental models (Galottii, Baron, & Sabini, 1986). (See the Highlight: Mental Models of Motion for a discussion of how people's mental models often go contrary to the laws of physics.)

Hypothesis Testing

When people are asked to test a simple **hypothesis** or proposition, they usually look for evidence in favor of the hypothesis instead of evidence to disconfirm or falsify it. This tendency is called the *confirmatory bias*. The bias is stronger with relatively abstract material, as illustrated by a study of hypothesis testing and reasoning by Johnson-Laird and Wason (1977). College students were given the problem of testing a simple hypothesis about letters and numbers that were printed on file cards. Four cards were placed on a table, as shown in Figure 9–3. The students were told that each of the four cards had a letter on one side and a number on the other. The hypothesis to be tested was:

If a card has a vowel on one side, then it has an odd number on the other side.

In formal terms, this hypothesis can be stated as:

If p, then q,

where p represents any vowel and q represents any odd number. This hypothesis can be tested by turning over those cards that would provide the

Problem Form	Test the Hypothesis: If *p*, then *q*			
Formal	*p*	*not-p*	*q*	*not-q*
Abstract	A	B	5	2

Figure 9–3 Hypothesis-Testing Problem

relevant information. The problem is: What is the minimal number of cards that must be turned over, and which cards are they?

Most people either turn over more cards than necessary or the wrong ones. Everyone turns the *p* card, with the vowel *A* on one side, to see if it has an odd number *(q)* on the other side. Should the *q* card, with a 5 on it, also be turned over? Most people do, but this card provides no useful information at all. If the 5 card has a vowel on the other side, then it is consistent with the hypothesis. If the 5 card does *not* have a vowel on the other side, then it is still consistent with the hypothesis. Remember that the hypothesis, or rule, does not say that *only* cards with vowels have odd numbers on the other side, so it really makes no difference what letter is on cards with odd numbers on them. The only other informative card is the card with an even number on it (*not-q*—that is, the card with a 2 on it). If that card has a vowel on the other side, then the hypothesis (if vowel, then odd number) is false. However, very few people spontaneously choose just these two informative cards, the *p* (vowel) card and the *not-q* (even number) card.

The poor performance of most people on the abstract form of this problem should not lead to the general conclusion that human beings are poor reasoners. Rather, our reasoning ability reflects the regularities we have observed in concrete, real-world situations. Instead of abstract reasoning principles, we seem to use *pragmatic reasoning schemas* (See the Application: Learning to Think.) (Cheng & Holyoak, 1986; Cheng, Holyoak, Nisbett, & Oliver, 1986). We reason successfully when a hypothesis-testing situation evokes (reminds us of) one of these schemas. For example, we have been in many situations in which *permission* has been granted in a conditional form: "If you want dessert, you must finish your lima beans." From these many permission situations, we have induced an abstract set of rules that can be applied to particular situations (see Table 9–1). For example, as children, we may have learned about Rule 4 when we were punished for taking dessert without finishing our lima beans. When we reason about the consequences of our actions in a permission situation, we do so based on this schema. The years of experiences abstracted in the schema guarantee efficient hypothesis testing.

Our use of the permission schema can be demonstrated with the same type of conditional problem that stumps people in its abstract version. Consider this rule (see Figure 9–4):

If an envelope is sealed, then it must have first-class postage (a 22-cent stamp) on it.

Table 9–1: Pragmatic Reasoning Schema for Permission

Abstract Rule	Concrete Instantiation
1. If the action is to be taken, the precondition must be satisfied.	If you want dessert, you must finish your lima beans.
2. If the action is not to be taken, then the precondition need not be satisfied.	If you do not want dessert, then you need not finish your lima beans.
3. If the precondition is satisfied, then the action may be taken.	If you finish your lima beans, then you may have dessert.
4. If the precondition is not satisfied, then the action must not be taken.	If you do not finish your lima beans, you may not have dessert.

After Cheng & Holyoak, 1986.

In formal terms, this is the same as the vowel and number problems, "if *p*, then *q*." When this type of rule is unfamiliar, people perform relatively poorly when asked which envelopes ought to be turned over. However, when a rationale is offered that evokes the permission schema—for example, a foreign country's postal regulations that require that this rule be followed—people reason quite effectively (Cheng & Holyoak, 1986); turning over the 14-cent envelope *(not-q)* conforms to testing Rule 4. The permission schema—and other reasoning schemas—capture important regularities about what we have learned concerning the causes and consequences of our behaviors. We assess the truth of a current hypothesis using reasoning rules derived from what has been true in the past.

In other real-life circumstances we must judge the relative merits of a range of different hypotheses. Suppose, for example, that you are a detective who must determine which of a number of likely suspects actually committed a murder. Robinson and Hastie (1985) placed groups of students in exactly that situation: While listening to a murder mystery, the students were asked to assess the probable guilt of a range of suspects. Clues along the way provided strong evidence about the guilt or innocence of individual suspects. As you would expect, ratings of probable guilt were associated with these clues. However, the subjects failed to adjust the probable guilt of the other suspects in the face of this information. In formal terms, if one suspect becomes more (or less) likely to be the guilty party, then all other suspects must be less (or more) probable; evidence about one hypothesis should have complex effects. The subjects, however, did not follow this formal rule. Rather, they simplified the situation by treating all suspects as independent

Figure 9–4 Hypothesis-Testing Problem

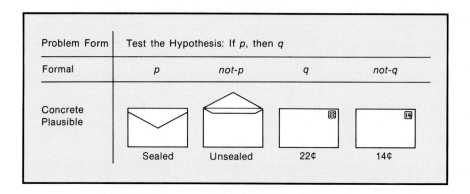

Problem Form	Test the Hypothesis: If *p*, then *q*			
Formal	*p*	*not-p*	*q*	*not-q*
Concrete Plausible	Sealed	Unsealed	22¢	14¢

entities; evidence about one hypothesis had little or no effect on their assessments of other hypotheses. This study demonstrates some limitations of our hypothesis-testing abilities. When situations become too complex to handle, we simplify them.

PROBLEM SOLVING

Problems are novel situations that require people to respond with novel behaviors. They pose situations in which prior learning may provide methods for coping, but the solution is not immediately available: We cannot simply remember what to do. Games such as chess or checkers provide problems every time we play them. Aside from the small set of opening moves, we have to figure out what move to make every time. Other games, such as tic-tac-toe, pose problems only to those who have not learned the *algorithm* for playing. An **algorithm** is a precise prescription of what to do given any conceivable situation. The game of tic-tac-toe is simple enough for people to easily memorize a small set of rules that dictate exactly what to do at each turn of the game (see Figure 9–5). If the number of alternatives is not

(Paul Conklin, Monkmeyer Press)

Figure 9–5 Heuristic and algorithm for playing tic-tac-toe. A useful general strategy, or *heuristic,* is: Never allow opponent two simultaneous lines of two (because only one can be blocked). Following this heuristic, the algorithm illustrated here will guarantee a draw. Other algorithms, based on different initial moves, will also guarantee a draw. When two players play optimally, neither can ever win (or lose).

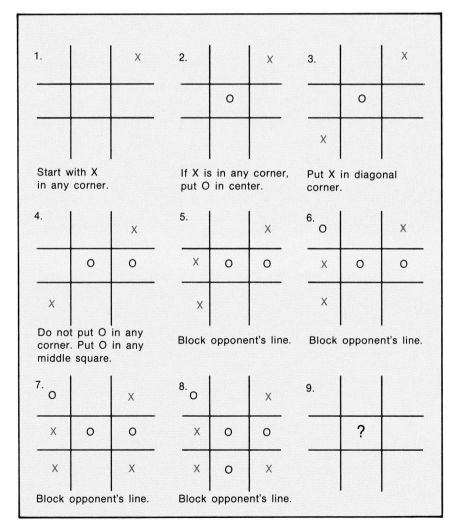

1. Start with X in any corner.

2. If X is in any corner, put O in center.

3. Put X in diagonal corner.

4. Do not put O in any corner. Put O in any middle square.

5. Block opponent's line.

6. Block opponent's line.

7. Block opponent's line.

8. Block opponent's line.

9.

too great, both people and computers can use algorithms. If, however, the number of alternatives is too many to handle, even for very large and fast computers, then strategies, or *heuristics,* are more useful than algorithms. A **heuristic** is a strategy or mode of approach to a problem that doesn't dictate every specific move, but instead guides the search for what to do. A heuristic is flexible and depends on the outcome at each stage of problem solution. (See the Highlight: Artificial Intelligence: How Computers Think for a comparison of the problem-solving abilities of people and computers.)

Problem Representation

One useful heuristic when presented with problems of any kind is: Consider alternative ways to describe the problem. A problem's description consists of four parts; these four parts make up the problem space:

> *Initial state:* How the starting conditions are described.
> *Goal state:* How the final state or goal conditions are described.
> *Operators:* Moves or operations to change from one state to the next.
> *Intermediate problem states:* Any states that are generated by applying an operator to a state on the way to a final goal state.

Your internal representation (or mental model) of these four aspects of a problem is your **problem space.** Obviously, one person's problem space will not necessarily be the same as another's, and neither may be identical to an ideal problem space (Simon, 1978). In the artists-beekeepers-chemists syllogism used above, one person's problem space (mental model) would include Chemist 6; someone else, with poorer reasoning ability, might omit Chemist 6, so that person's problem space would be less than ideal.

The initial state of a problem (how the problem is formulated to begin with) is often critical. One initial state can lead to an efficient problem space; another to a space that is unnecessarily complex. Consider the following fairly simple problem:

> Two train stations are 50 miles apart. At 2 P.M. one Saturday afternoon two trains start toward each other, one from each station. Just as the trains pull out of the stations, a bird springs into the air from the front of the first train and flies ahead to the front of the second train. When the bird reaches the second train, it turns back and flies toward the first train. The bird continues to do this until the trains meet.
>
> If both trains travel at the rate of 25 miles per hour and the bird flies at 100 miles per hour, how many miles will the bird have flown before the trains meet?

You can solve this problem (see Figure 9–6) by figuring out how far the bird flies on each trip between trains, taking into account the changing distances between the trains on each trip. This method will work, but it is tedious. If you try to do it in your head, you will probably find it impossible to keep track of the calculations you must make. In terms of the problem space, if the initial state of the problem is left unchanged, then the series of operators is simply too cumbersome and detailed for most people to handle. However, we can move from that initial state to a more manageable intermediate state by applying a simple operator—putting the question in another form. Instead of asking: How far must the bird fly? we can ask: For how long a time must the bird fly? The next intermediate state is the answer to this question,

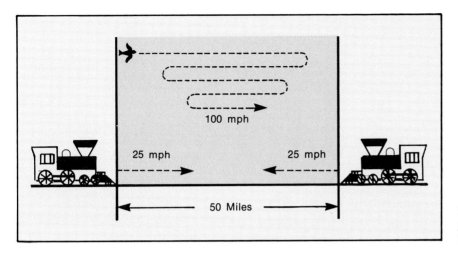

Figure 9–6 The train and bird problem. How far must the bird fly? (See text.)

namely, one hour. The sequence of moves (or train of thought) for this problem might then be:

1. The trains are 50 miles apart.
2. Since they travel at the same speed, each must travel 25 miles before they meet.
3. They travel at 25 miles per hour, so one hour passes until they meet.
4. The bird flies at 100 miles per hour.
5. If one hour elapses, then the bird must have flown 100 miles.

Thus a difficult problem has become an easy one.

Consider a second problem that involves a similar symbolic transformation of a particular problem element.

> At 6 A.M. one morning a monk starts out from the bottom of a mountain. He follows a well-worn trail up the mountain, stopping occasionally to rest and to meditate. Sometime during the evening of the same day he reaches the top and goes to sleep. The next morning at 6 A.M. he starts down the same trail, again stopping to rest when tired. He reaches the bottom sometime after sundown of the same day. Can you prove that the monk will reach a point on the trail on the way down that is the exact point he had reached on the way up at precisely that same time of day? This can be proved without making any assumptions about rates of walking up or down.

At first glance, it seems highly unlikely that such a coincidence should occur, yet such a coincidence *must* occur. Again, as in the flying bird problem, a change in some part of the problem space provides an intuitively clear answer. For the moment, assume that the problem is changed so that instead of one monk going up one day and coming down the next, we have two monks. One monk starts at the bottom and the other starts at the top at 6 A.M. *on the same day*. It is clear that these two monks will pass each other on the trail at some time during the day, regardless of how often either stops to rest and regardless of their walking rates. The point at which they meet is analogous to the point at which our first monk finds himself at the same time of day that he was there the day before.

Yet another way to represent this problem is graphically, as in Figure 9–7. Putting a problem in graphic form often leads to the answer.

Figure 9–7 The Monk and Mountain Problem Drawing a graph to represent the problem state can be useful. The problem is solved when you realize that the two graph lines—one representing the ascent, the other the descent—must cross, no matter how the monk's rate of walking changes from moment to moment.

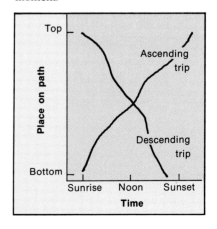

Imagine that you are in a room with two computer terminals. One of them is hooked up to a computer in another room, the other to a person, who is also out of view. You can communicate with both by typing messages and questions on the terminals, and by getting answers back on a video screen. Your job is to discover which terminal is connected to the computer and which to the person. The person will try to answer all questions as honestly and directly as possible; the computer is programmed to simulate a person, so that if you ask on each terminal: "Are you a person?" both will answer: "Yes." If you can't tell the difference between the computer and the person, then the computer has passed the *Turing test,* named after the mathematician Alan Turing, who first proposed it in answer to the question: Can machines think? (1950).

A principled answer to the question of whether machines can think is based on the definition of thinking as manipulation of symbols or of information. Machines can certainly manipulate symbols, and so by that definition they think. Whether they can be programmed to think in the same ways that people do is still an open question, but in some domains machines can be programmed to manipulate symbols and to solve problems. Some computer scientists create *artificial intelligence* by designing programs that solve specific problems in the most efficient way possible. Others attempt to create programs that mimic human thinking: *computer simulations.* These

simulations are often an important tool in psychology because they force researchers to be sufficiently precise about the details of their theories— with respect to knowledge structures and mental operations—to enable a programmer to implement them on a computer. (See Highlight: Language Processing by Computer in Chapter 8.)

How are machines programmed to think? There are two approaches to this task: *algorithms* and *heuristics* (see text). Algorithms are rules that automatically generate correct answers. For example, the set of rules for doing long division is an algorithm. Heuristics are general plans or strategies that do not guarantee a correct answer, but are often the optimal approach to a problem or task. For example, the game of chess is far too complex to be played with algorithms. For any given board position, there are simply too many possibilities for the problem space to be searched completely. Novice players, however, will rely on algorithms—set moves in particular situations—partly because their memory for board positions is fairly limited. Experts have memorized approximately 50,000 chess configurations, and so can supplement their stock of set moves with heuristically guided novel moves in novel situations (Chase & Simon, 1973). Experts in physics behave in the same general way: They employ general heuristics or strategies to decide which equations to use for solving a particular problem. Novices, on the other hand, most often start writing equations with no particular plan in mind (Larkin et al., 1980).

The simplest way to program a computer to deal with a problem resembles the novice's approach to a physics problem—*random trial and error.* The Tower of Hanoi problem

(facing page), can be solved this way by a computer; but this method is terribly inefficient, particularly if the computer cannot learn from past mistakes. The illustration shows the problem space from the initial state (1) to the goal state (8), with the optimal intermediate states (2–7) and other states that can be used to get from the initial state to the goal state. A completely random trial-and-error approach to this problem will eventually reach State 8, but could take an enormous amount of time.

A second heuristic, *hill climbing,* is more sophisticated. In hill climbing you always take the move that gets you closer to the goal. For many problems this is an efficient strategy. However, there are times where this strategy fails because some problems *require* detours—steps that move temporarily away from the goal. In the Tower of Hanoi problem a hill-climbing strategy might take you from State 4a to State 4b, rather than to the more optimal State 4. Worse yet, hill climbing can strand you at an intermediate goal, with moves away from that goal seeming to take you further from the final goal state. For example, a strict hill-climbing strategy might strand you at 7a because moving any of the discs on the third peg moves you away from the final goal state. Hill climbing, then, is severely limited as a strategy because it does not look more than one move ahead.

A third heuristic, *means-end analysis,* does look ahead, and sets up *subgoals* to be reached on the way to a final goal. An example in the Tower of Hanoi problem would be to recognize that State 4 is an optimal subgoal, and to make those moves that can attain that subgoal. When people are given this problem, they often begin by random trial and error. They learn from their mistakes and begin to use

Negative Set

A **set** is a tendency to continue doing something in a particular way. A **negative set** is the tendency to continue doing something in the same way, but without success: Whatever it is you're doing, it's the wrong thing for the circumstances. Such negative sets are often hard to break. For example, in the bird problem and in the monk-mountain problem, the initial problem state

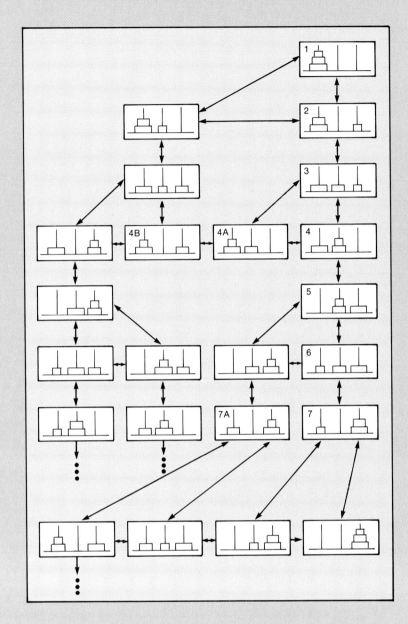

Problem Space for the Tower of Hanoi Problem

hill climbing; eventually they apply means-end analysis to set up efficient subgoals. This is one critical way that people and machines differ. People learn from past experience; so far, one of the more difficult problems in computer science is to develop computer programs that enable the machines to learn (However, as we saw in the Highlights on distributed memory on computers in Chapter 7, there seems to be progress in this area.)

A second way that people and machines differ is in the kinds of things each does extremely well. Computers are greatly superior to people at rapid sequential calculations: For well-defined problems, with appropriate algorithms, computers far outperform people. However, people are greatly superior whenever the information to be dealt with is unclear or noisy. For example, instructions to a computer must always be letter-perfect: people, on the other hand, can tolerate all kinds of mistakes, including the error in this sentence (repetition of the word *can*). People are also very good at making inductive leaps—at seeing analogies between disparate domains (e.g., the atom is like the solar system), and at making connections between seemingly disparate ideas. For ill-defined problems and noisy input, then, people far outperform computers.

Researchers in artificial intelligence are diligently trying to overcome these computer limitations. As they discover how to simulate increasingly complex types of thought, they are certain to shed light on how we humans are able to carry out these tasks with such apparent ease.

tends to lead people astray. In Luchins's water jar problems (see Table 9–2) people have to figure out how to get a specified amount of water from three jars with different capacities (in cups). An incorrect or negative set can easily be established. Problem 1 is easy. To obtain 20 cups of water, fill Jar A and remove 9 cups, using the 3-cup jar three times: $29 - 3 - 3 - 3 = 20$. In terms of the notation used, the answer is obtained by the formula $A - 3B$. Problem 2 is slightly more difficult, but still can be done simply. Fill the 127-cup jar, then remove 21 cups, then 3 cups twice: $127 - 21 - 3 - 3 = 100$.

Table 9–2:   Luchins's Water Jar Problems

How do you measure out the right amount of water using Jars A, B, and C?

Problem No.	Jars Available for Use			Required Amount (Cups)
	A	B	C	
1	29	3		20
2	21	127	3	100
3	14	163	25	99
4	18	43	10	5
5	9	42	6	21
6	20	59	4	31
7	23	49	3	20
8	15	39	3	18
9	28	76	3	25
10	18	48	4	22
11	14	36	8	6

After Luchins, 1942.

Again, following the notation, the answer is given by the formula: $B - A - 2C$. Now try to solve the remaining nine problems as quickly as you can.

You may have found that Problems 3–11 are all soluble by the same method ($B - A - 2C$), except for Problem 9. However, many people who are not aware of the phenomenon of set overlook a simpler solution method for Problems 7–11. Each of these last five problems, including problem 9, can be solved by using only two jars.

People who have learned to solve Problems 2–6 in one particular way tend to continue using that way. People who are given just Problem 1 followed by Problems 7–11 solve them in the simpler way. Given set-inducing problems, practice makes perfect only if variations do not occur in subsequent problems. Here, practice actually interferes with efficient problem solving.

The interference that can be obtained may even prevent problem solution. A fair number of people fail to solve Problem 9 because of their incorrect set. Yet had they not had that set, none would have had difficulty in measuring out 25 cups of water from a number of jars, two of which hold 28 and 3 cups, respectively.

Set can also lead someone into ridiculously inefficient behavior. One variation of Luchins's experiment required people to measure out 5 cups of water after solving a series of set-inducing problems. They were given three containers: 10 cups, 25 cups, and 5 cups. Many subjects maintained the set, solving the problem in the $B - A - 2C$ manner: $25 - 10 - 5 - 5$. Others solved it using the method $A - B$, or $10 - 5$. Why didn't they use the 5-cup container in the first place?

Max Wertheimer, in his book *Productive Thinking* (1945/59), describes a classroom example of this kind of negative set. He observed teachers explaining how the area of a parallelogram is obtained, and also observed students practicing calculating parallelogram areas. The children had already been taught how to find the area of a rectangle: They had learned that the area of a rectangle is the product of two sides. When they were first shown a parallelogram, one student incorrectly assumed that the area was the product of the two sides. The teacher then explained the formal procedure for finding the area of a parallelogram. The students were told to drop a perpen-

dicular from each upper corner and then to extend the base line and label the two new points *e* and *f*. The customary proof of the method was then given: The area is equal to the product of base and altitude (Area = *ef* × *cf* = *dc* × *de;* see Figure 9–8). The students were then given several problems to solve with parallelograms of various bases, sides, and angles. By the end of one class hour, the class had solved all the problems and was given ten more for homework.

The next day a student was called upon to demonstrate how to find the area of a parallelogram. He succeeded and the teacher was pleased. Wertheimer, observing all this, was not pleased, despite the class's success on a written quiz. He wished to know precisely what the students had learned. To find out, he gave the class the problem of finding the area of the parallelogram shown in Figure 9–8B. Two general kinds of solution attempts were obtained. The first kind, Figure 9–8C, indicated a virtually complete lack of understanding. Just like the people in Luchins's water jar experiment, these students blindly applied a procedure even when it was no longer appropriate. Other students displayed understanding and applied the procedure they had learned in an appropriate manner (see Figure 9–8D.)

The students who had blindly applied a learned procedure were operating under a set that had been successful, but that now required a change in a new situation. Their behavior was analogous to the behavior of Luchins's subjects solving the water jar problems. This raises the general question of transfer of training. There is no doubt that the way people behave in new situations is related to the way they have behaved in previous situations. What people have learned to do may be useful in a new problem or it may interfere with successful problem solving. Negative set is a specific case of negative transfer of training. An old approach or behavior pattern, learned earlier, is no longer applicable, but the new situation is sufficiently like the old one that the older, inappropriate approach is used anyway. An inappropriate approach thus competes with a more useful one.

Functional Fixedness

Habitual ways of thinking about ordinary objects can lead to a kind of negative set called *functional fixedness* (Duncker, 1945). One such problem is shown in Figure 9–9. When people are asked to mount a candle on the wall, given only tacks in a box and a book of matches, as many as 50 percent fail to notice that the tack box can be used as a candle holder. However, when the tack box is presented empty and the tacks left loose on the table, the solution becomes easy. These two forms of the problem—tack box full and tack box empty—lead people to represent the initial state of the problem differently. The tack box full leads to a problem space in which the box is simply not available psychologically. The tack box empty leads to a more appropriate problem space in which the box is available psychologically and is used to solve the problem.

One way to make the full tack box available psychologically is to label it as such. When the box is explicitly labeled as a *box,* everyone tested solved the problem in less than a minute (Glucksberg & Weisberg, 1966). Thus explicit labeling can lead to an appropriate representation of the problem.

Would just being more motivated by some promised reward help us solve more difficult kinds of problems? In these kinds of cases, where people have to break a negative set and change their initial representation, such extrinsic motivation (see Chapter 12) can actually hurt. College students who were of-

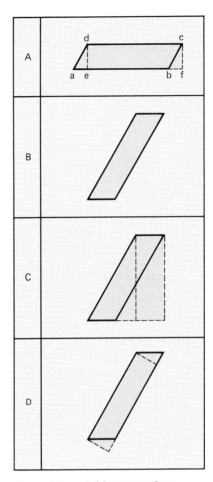

Figure 9–8 Children were first taught to find the area of parallelograms, using the diagram shown in A. They were then given the parallelogram shown in B and asked to find the area. One kind of solution attempt, C, indicated a complete lack of understanding. The solution method illustrated in D demonstrated that the child understood the nature of the problem and the solution. (Wertheimer, 1945/1959)

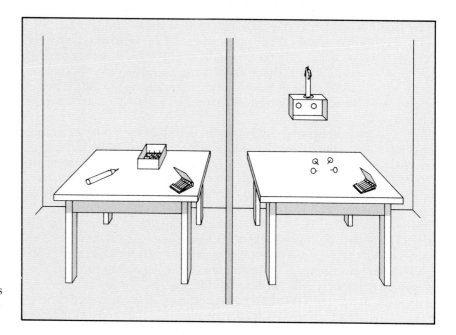

Figure 9–9 The Candle Problem Using only the materials on the table, how can the candle be mounted on the wall? The solution is shown on the right. (Glucksberg & Weisberg, 1966)

fered no reward for solving the candle problem solved it much more quickly than students who were offered $20, which was a fairly large sum of money 25 years ago (Glucksberg, 1962).

Transfer of Learning

Negative sets are all too easy to establish. Is it just as easy to establish positive sets, so that doing one problem makes it easier to solve others of the same kind? Unfortunately, positive sets are more difficult to establish than negative sets. In one study of positive transfer of learning, Weisberg and his colleagues (1978) trained people toassociate the box and candle with one another and then gave them the candle problem to solve. The prior association of *box* with *candle* did not help at all unless the subjects had been informed that what they had learned earlier might be useful in the problem situation.

This result is all too typical. Even when the solution to one problem is exactly analogous to that of a previous problem, people may not notice the relationship, and so not benefit from prior experience. Consider the following problem: A cancer patient with an inoperable stomach tumor can be treated with X rays. Unfortunately, X rays that are powerful enough to destroy the tumor would also destroy the surrounding healthy tissue, including the stomach. How can radiation be used to destroy the tumor without harming any healthy tissue that surrounds it? When the German psychologist Karl Duncker (1945) first tried out this problem on college students, he found that it gave them a great deal of difficulty. The students tried to solve it in various ways (see Figure 9–10 for a typical subject's solution attempts). The best solution calls for either a lens to focus the rays, or a circle of low-intensity X-ray guns to beam weak rays at the tumor. Each individual ray is too weak to do any harm, but at the point of concentration, they work together to destroy the tumor.

Would solving an analogous problem help people to find this solution?

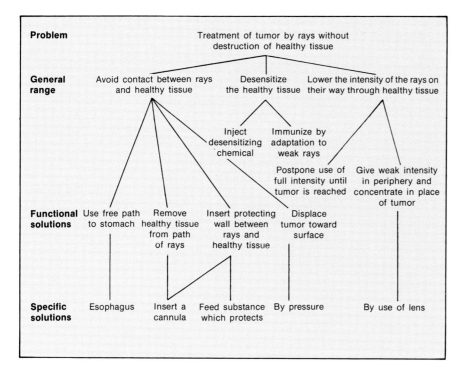

Problem	Treatment of tumor by rays without destruction of healthy tissue		
General range	Avoid contact between rays and healthy tissue	Desensitize the healthy tissue	Lower the intensity of the rays on their way through healthy tissue

Inject desensitizing chemical — Immunize by adaptation to weak rays

Postpone use of full intensity until tumor is reached — Give weak intensity in periphery and concentrate in place of tumor

Functional solutions Use free path to stomach — Remove healthy tissue from path of rays — Insert protecting wall between rays and healthy tissue — Displace tumor toward surface

Specific solutions Esophagus — Insert a cannula — Feed substance which protects — By pressure — By use of lens

Figure 9–10 One subject's solution attempts for Duncker's tumor and X-ray problem. This way of describing solution attempts is called a *solution tree*. It shows the organization of the attempts and their relationships. It does not, however, necessarily correspond with how the person actually went through the problem, or the order in which each particular idea was thought of. (From Duncker, 1945)

Figure 9–11 The Nine-Dot Problem Connect the dots by drawing only four straight lines. Do not retrace any lines, and do not lift your pencil from the paper.

College students were given a problem just like the radiation problem, only the particular form was changed (Gick & Holyoak, 1980).

> A general wishes to capture a fortress. There are many roads radiating out from the fortress, but all have been mined so that only small groups of soldiers can pass over the roads without being blown up. The general knows that he will eventually need a large group of soldiers to take the fortress, so he sends small groups down each of the roads, timed to meet at the fortress at the same time.

Both the radiation and fortress problems involve central objects that must be affected by a strong force, yet are surrounded by things that must be preserved. Do people who are first given the fortress problem notice this similarity and use it to solve the radiation problem? Hardly ever, unless they are explicitly informed that the first problem can help them solve the second. These results help explain why teaching people problem-solving strategies is so difficult. Practical problem-solving and thinking programs can improve people's performance, but only for the specific kinds of problems that were used in training, and only when people are aware of the similarity between the novel problems and the ones they learned to do during training (Mayer, 1983).

Insight

We can solve many of the problems we face on a day-to-day basis by recalling how we dealt with similar situations in the past. However, some problems require an entirely new type of solution—they can only be solved if we have an appropriate *insight*. Consider the problem given in Figure 9–11. The object is to connect all nine dots by drawing only four straight lines. To solve this problem, you must have the insight that the lines must extend outside the

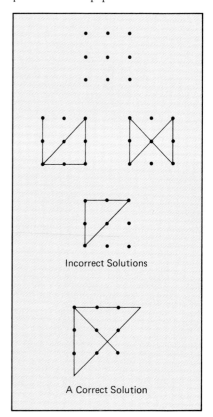

Incorrect Solutions

A Correct Solution

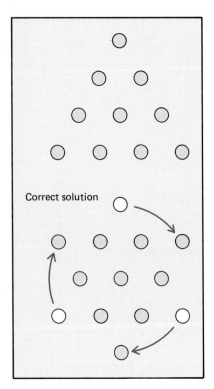

Figure 9–12 Move three circles so that the triangle points toward the bottom of the page.

bounds of the imaginary square formed by the nine dots. There is no way to solve this problem by steadily working at it over a long period of time, as you might a physics or calculus problem—the insight that accompanies this solution has a special sudden feeling to it.

The suddenness of insight has been demonstrated in experimental settings (Metcalfe, 1986a, 1986b). Students were asked to solve a series of insight problems, such as the problem shown in Figure 9–12. The object here is to make the triangle point toward the bottom of the page by moving only three circles. Students were not accurate at predicting how likely it was that they would be able to solve this type of problem. Furthermore, they could not judge how close they were to a solution while they tried to solve the problems: At 10-second intervals the students were asked to give a *feeling-of-warmth* rating for how likely they thought it was that they were approaching the solution. The pattern of these ratings was striking. The problem solvers gave higher feeling-of-warmth ratings before giving incorrect solutions than before giving correct solutions; the feeling-of-warmth ratings suggested that they had no sense at all that a correct solution was about to emerge.

Because insight is characterized by this feeling of a sudden breakthrough, some researchers have hypothesized that insight is a special process unlike other problem-solving activities; others have suggested that insight is merely an impressive extension of our normal processes. A compromise position identifies three separate skills that, when performed in novel and imaginative ways, lead to insightful thinking (Davidson, 1986; Davidson & Sternberg, 1984):

1. *Selective Encoding.* When we are trying to solve a new problem, we are often overwhelmed by large amounts of useless information. An insight arises when we determine which information is relevant for further consideration.

Sir Alexander Fleming discovered penicillin through selective encoding. Fleming's attempts to grow bacteria had been disrupted by the appearance of a mold in his culture. Rather than dismissing this mold as irrelevant to his original experiments, he realized that the mold's bacteria-killing ability was relevant to a greater medical concern: The need for antibiotics to kill disease-causing organisms.

2. *Selective Combination.* When we have a problem to solve, we often have all the pieces of the solution, but we don't know how to put them together. An insight arises when we discover a novel way of combining the elements of the solution.

Darwin's construction of the theory of evolution involved selective combination. The various facts about natural history had been available to him for a long time. What Darwin did was to combine this information into an innovative and coherent theory.

3. *Selective Comparison.* When we solve a problem, we often use a model solution we have encountered in the past. Insight occurs when we discover that a more novel comparison leads to unforeseen consequences.

Kekulé's discovery of the structure of the benzene ring involved selective comparison. In a dream Kekulé saw a snake curl back on itself and catch its own tail. Upon waking, he realized that this was the structure he had been seeking. His insight was to discern the underlying similarity between his dream image and the benzene ring.

Because insights arise as a consequence of these processes, you should try to make use of them when you are faced with a new problem to solve. You can ask yourself: Am I treating the correct facts as relevant and irrelevant? Am

Many programs have been developed to teach people how to be more efficient in their thinking, reasoning, and problem solving. These programs must take into account the kinds of factors we have been describing in this chapter: To the extent that we know how people carry out these activities—and why difficulties arise—we can create teaching techniques to improve their performance (Nickerson, Perkins, & Smith, 1985). In particular, we'd like to be able to develop classroom lessons that will be carried into everyday life. Here are two examples of successful improvement of thinking skills:

1. *The Law of Large Numbers.* Consider this problem:

A traveling businesswoman often returns to restaurants where she had an excellent meal on her first visit. However, she is usually disappointed because subsequent meals are rarely as good as the first. Why would this happen? (Fong, Krantz, & Nisbett, 1986)

An appropriate answer to this question requires some knowledge of the law of large numbers, which states that as the size of a random sample increases, the sample distribution is more likely to get closer and closer to the actual (population) distribution. For the restaurant problem, imagine that the restaurant serves meals that differ somewhat in quality, but on the average are pretty good. The businesswoman's first sample from this distribution was unusually excellent—and therefore uncharacteristic of the population. If she eats at the same restaurant regularly, it is likely that over time her average meal will just be "pretty good."

Fong and his colleagues suggested that people have intuitive knowledge of the law of large numbers—and that even minimal training could perfect it for ready use. Accordingly, they invented a variety of different training tasks to acquaint students with the properties of this statistical rule. Some of the methods were abstract: In one example, subjects were shown how sampling worked with urns filled with colored gumballs. Others were more concrete: Subjects read specific examples of real-life situations that were analyzed in terms of the law of large numbers. On the whole, all the types of training were very effective.

If you take the time now to understand this statistical rule and how it applies to the businesswoman's situation, you can easily improve this one aspect of your reasoning.

2. *Pragmatic Reasoning Schemas.* In the text we described how pragmatic reasoning schemas can lead to successful reasoning. Cheng and her colleagues (1986) designed a training program to show that reasoning could be easily improved if people were taught to access these schemas more reliably in appropriate situations. Consider this problem:

If a steel support is intended for the roof, then it must be rustproof.

Subjects were asked to select which conditions they must check to see if this rule was followed:

1. Support A is intended for the roof.
2. Support B is intended for the foundation.
3. Support C is rustproof.
4. Support D is not rustproof.

This problem is formally similar to the vowel-and-number and postage problems described in the text. Cheng and her colleagues suggested that the problem can best be solved by assimilating the circumstances to an *obligation* schema. Like the *permission* schema, this schema enables reasoners to make use of all their prior experience with obligation situations. Cheng and her colleagues demonstrated that subjects who were given training on recognizing situations as fitting the obligation schema were much more successful at solving these problems.

Again, if you try to analyze situations in everyday life as conforming to *permission* or *obligation* situations, you should be able to improve your reasoning ability. By doing so, you can make use of your prior experience when you are faced with new problems.

I combining the right aspects of the problem? Can I find an analogy that will cast new light on the problem? Use of these strategies should allow you to have better insights.

JUDGMENT AND DECISION MAKING

Most of the problems that we have been discussing up to now involve certainties. They contain the full information needed for a solution, and each has a single correct answer. In daily life, however, we encounter problems where we must make decisions under conditions of uncertainty (Kahneman, Slovic, & Tversky, 1982). We do not have full information, and there may be no single, correct answer. Instead, the information that we have is probabilistic, and the decisions that we make are really our best bets about the future. How good are we at making such decisions?

Framing Effects

In general, people seem to get along quite well amidst the uncertainties of daily life. At the same time, we are susceptible to subtle biases. Too often, the way a situation is worded, or *framed,* can have significant biasing effects. Assume that you have just entered a theater lobby and discover that you've lost your ticket, for which you had paid $25. Would you buy another ticket for $25 to see the show? Many people decide that they would not do so, possibly on the grounds that the show is not worth $50. Now consider a slight variant of this situation. You have just entered a theater lobby to buy a $25 ticket. You discover that you have lost $25 sometime during the day. Would you still buy a ticket for $25? In this context, most people say that they would. Notice that the only difference in the two situations is the subjective impression that in one case it costs $50 to see the show, but only $25 in the other. But in both cases you are $50 out of pocket. The different decisions, then, are not rational in any economic sense, but they do seem to make intuitive psychological sense.

Other framing effects can be understood in terms of the problem spaces that people construct. Consider this problem:

> A man buys a horse for $10, then sells it to his brother for $20. The following week he realizes that he needs the horse, so he buys it back for $30. After a while he decides that he doesn't really need a horse, so he sells it to a stranger for $40. How much money did the man gain or lose on this horse?

Most people judge that the man came out even, neither gaining nor losing any money. Do you agree? Now consider a different version of the same problem.

> A man buys a horse for $10, then sells it to his brother for $20. The following week he realizes that he needs a cow, so he buys one for $30. After a while he decides that he doesn't really need the cow, so he sells it to a stranger for $40. How much money did the man gain or lose with the horse and the cow?

Now, most people say that the man made $20. He made $10 on his first transaction, buying the horse for $10 and selling it for $20, making a $10 profit. Then he made a $10 profit on the cow, having bought it for $30 and sold it for $40. What's different about the first version? People are misled into thinking that the man *lost* $10 because he paid $30 for a horse that he'd originally sold for $20.

Kahneman and Tversky (1982) were among several psychologists to demonstrate the power of such framing effects—the effects of how a problem is worded. These effects can be particularly pronounced when decisions involve serious risks. Consider this problem:

> Imagine that the government is preparing for an outbreak of a rare disease that is expected to kill 600 people. Two programs are available. If program A is adopted, then 200 people will be saved. If Program B is adopted, then there is a one-third chance that 600 people will be saved, and a two-thirds chance that nobody will be saved. Which program should be adopted?

When the issue is framed this way, most people prefer Program A over Program B. This avoids the two-thirds risk that nobody will be saved. Now consider a similar problem involving the same disease and the same expectation that if nothing is done, 600 people will die:

Two programs are available. If Program C is adopted, then 400 people will die. If Program D is adopted, then there is a one-third chance that nobody will die, and a two-thirds chance that 600 people will die:

When the issue is framed this way, most people prefer Program D over Program C, avoiding the certain consequence that 400 people will die. This might seem reasonable to you until you realize that Programs A and C have precisely the same outcomes: Of the original 600 people at risk, 200 will live and 400 will die. Programs B and D are also precisely the same: A one-third chance of 600 people being saved is the same as a one-third chance of nobody dying. We may be too easily swayed by how such problems are worded!

Heuristics

Decisions are often based on our beliefs about the relative likelihood of things happening—the price of real estate next year, the availability of jobs for engineers in the year you expect to graduate, whether the romance of the moment will last through marriage, and so on. As mentioned earlier, people estimate the likelihood of such things by relying on rather general and useful strategies called **heuristics.**

In one of these strategies, the *representativeness heuristic,* we use the similarity among objects or events to help us estimate probabilities. For example, we might be told that "George is quiet and shy. He likes to be helpful to others but is generally uninterested in people or in daily events. He is very concerned with tidiness, order, and neatness in every detail." What is the likelihood that George is a librarian rather than a farmer? Most people would guess that George is a librarian because he matches our stereotype of librarians. This would be a perfectly valid inference in this case, if the stereotype were in fact true. Nevertheless, this heuristic can lead us astray by diverting our attention from other important factors, such as the laws and principles of probability. Imagine that you were given the description of George and then were told: "George belongs to a club that has 5 librarians and 20 farmers. What is the likelihood that George is a librarian?" This additional information about the relative number of librarians and farmers in George's club should influence your answer, but unfortunately, it rarely does. This information about *prior probability* is simply ignored by most people, even though it is important and informative.

The representativeness heuristic is also respsonsible for another common type of error. Suppose you tossed a coin six times in a row. Which of the following sequences would be more likely to occur, A or B:

A: Head, Head, Head, Tail, Tail, Tail.
B: Head, Tail, Tail, Head, Tail, Head.

Most people choose B because it looks more like our stereotype of a random sequence than does A. A moment's reflection, however, should convince you that A and B are equally likely. With any given proportion of heads and tails, any one sequence is just as likely as any other.

The respresentativeness heuristic is partly responsible for another common error. Suppose that you and a friend are tossing coins, and you can bet on each coin toss. Assume that the coin is fair, and so over the long run will come down evenly: 50 percent heads, 50 percent tails. During one run of tosses the coin has come down heads 20 times in a row. What's your bet on

The Uses of "Irrationality"

I've about decided that my new car will be a Volvo. I've read what the automobile magazines have to say, kept track of frequency-of-repair, recall, and resale-value statistics, and looked up the latest *Consumer's Reports*, which cites highly reassuring statistics to the effect that the Volvo is a safe, reliable, good-handling, and adequately powered car. On the basis of these well-researched facts, I am on my way out the door to the Volvo dealership when my next-door neighbor drops by. He tells me in vivid detail about his new Volvo, and ends his report by saying, "It's a lemon"! I immediately change my mind about the Volvo and buy another car instead. Have I made a rational decision?

By a number of accounts, no. Nisbett and Ross, in their book *Human Inference: Strategies and Shortcomings of Social Judgment* (1980), cite many such examples of what they consider poor judgment. They attribute such errors in judgment to two tendencies: "the overutilization of certain generally valid, intuitive, inferential strategies, and the underutilization of certain formal, logical, and statistical strategies" (p. 15). In the Volvo example, my decision not to buy the car flies in the face of statistics: I take a single bad report at face value, in opposition to several other reports, including at least one with data from a large sample (the frequency-of-repair

and other statistics). This violates a principal maxim of inferential decision making: Large samples are more reliable than small ones. My decision is also overly influenced by the vividness of the negative evidence. My neighbor's report is clearly more immediately compelling than a published report, but this is not a good reason to give it more weight. My decision is also influenced by the *availability heuristic* (see explanation in text). My neighbor's report is the most recent and the most available one in my memory, and so, again, is given undue weight.

Nisbett and Ross document other weaknesses in judgment to which we are prone:

1. As intuitive thinkers, we are overly influenced by prior beliefs. This is apparent in McCloskey's research on intuitive physics and people's beliefs about the laws of motion (see the Highlight: Mental Models of Motion). We show the same naive tendency when we accept invalid conclusions in syllogistic reasoning problems because we agree with those conclusions; when we ignore sample size; and when we are biased toward confirming rather than disconfirming hypotheses (see the hypothesis-testing problem illustrated in Figures 9–3 and 9–4).

2. We are unduly influenced by the vividness of real-life examples. Statistics on the incidence of rectal-colon cancer were widely known in 1985, before President Reagan's surgery for polyps removal, but were largely ignored. The president's operation, however, produced a flood of calls and visits to clinics and physicians around the country. The highly publicized event "reminded" people of the risk. It also incited many

to action, including deciding on having polyps removed immediately instead of waiting.

3. We tend to persevere in our beliefs even when evidence is available that should convince us to the contrary. For example, a woman sends away to a correspondence school for an appraisal of her artistic talent. She receives a glowing report, and is now convinced that she has talent. She then hears that three of her friends answered the same advertisement and got the same glowing report. She should, on the basis of this evidence, reconsider her initial evaluation of her talent, but she does not. She still believes that she has talent, and may even decide that her friends' reports are mistakes.

Nisbett and Ross further document how people fail to understand fundamental statistical principles and principles of causal analysis. In short, as Miller and Cantor (1982) put it: "We educated citizens of this advanced industrial society are not nearly as rational as we think we are." The picture is dismal indeed if we accept this portrayal of human irrationality as being *prescriptive* rather than simply *descriptive*. A descriptive account merely describes. A prescriptive account not only describes, it also states what people *ought to* do. Should people behave "more rationally"? Should we always take sample size into account, ignore vivid examples, abandon the availability and representativeness heuristics?

Perhaps not. Let's look at the Volvo example again, but from a somewhat different perspective. Was the decision not to buy a Volvo really such a bad one? From a normative viewpoint, yes, but only if the *sole* purpose or goal was to buy the seemingly best car for

the 21st toss: Is it more likely to come down heads or tails? Most people feel strongly that tails is far more likely because of the "law of averages": Because the chances of heads and tails in the long run are equal, we expect a shift after a long run so that things will balance out. But the long-run averages have nothing to do with any one particular event. Just because heads came up 20 times in a row, the 21st toss is still an independent event, with a 50-50 chance of being heads or tails. This error is known as the *gambler's fallacy*—the belief that a forthcoming event will turn out a particular way because, in the long run, it's past due.

the money. In the social context, however, there are other considerations (Miller & Cantor, 1982). How would I feel if I went ahead and bought the Volvo and it turned out to be a lemon? I'd feel pretty foolish, especially if I value my neighbor's opinion. Other considerations may also be involved, including a generalized distrust of published reports as opposed to a friend's advice. Given the fact that my neighbor's tastes are much like mine and so forth, I could easily rationalize not buying a Volvo. I might even make some informal calculations: Let's say that 1 out of every 20 cars turn out to be a lemon, and that Volvos have a better record than most—only 1 in 30. Still, is that worth the risk of appearing foolish in front of my neighbor?

So, at the cost of a slightly increased risk of getting an inferior car, I minimize the risk of social discomfort. Seen from this point of view, my decision not to buy a Volvo is cost-efficient. I am saving face by doing something (buying another car) that can still be satisfying, and I am following an important principle of choice behavior: minimizing regret.

Departures from normative or optimal models of choice behavior are also prevalent in gambling situations, where people often make decisions that seem irrational. In a recent study of how people play the game of blackjack, systematic violations of optimal card playing were routinely observed. The rules of the game are fairly simple. Optimal decisions can not only be calculated in theory, but are also relatively easy for players to learn and use if they wish to.

The game of blackjack, or "21," involves a dealer and from one to seven players. Before any cards are dealt, each player places his or her bet. The dealer then deals two cards to each player and one to himself, with all cards up. The object of the game is to total as close to 21 as possible without exceeding 21 ("busting"). The numerical value of the cards are their face value, with picture cards (jacks, queens, kings) counting as 10 and the ace counting either as a 1 or an 11. After the initial cards have been dealt, each player in turn can draw additional cards. If a player draws a card, then he or she remains in the game unless the new total exceeds 21, whereupon he or she immediately loses. After all players have drawn as many cards as they wish, the dealer takes a second card. He must draw again if his total is 16 or less; he may not draw again if his total is 17 or higher. If the dealer busts, then all players still remaining in the game win. If the dealer gets "blackjack" (exactly 21), then all players lose. If the dealer gets under 21, the dealer must pay those players whose total is higher than his, and collect from those whose total is lower than his.

Keren and Wagenaar (1985) observed experienced players in an Amsterdam casino for several months. They saw several departures from optimal play. One such departure consisted of players staying with small totals when they should have drawn an additional card. For example, assume your hand totals 15 and the dealer's up card is an 8. According to the optimal strategy described by Keren and Wagenaar, players should draw an additional card in this situation. Yet 78 percent of the time players did not draw that additional card. While theirs was not the optimal strategy in terms of long-term wins and losses, it did minimize regret—the chance of a player busting and losing and then seeing the dealer exceed 21 and paying off those who had stayed with low hands. A second good reason to stay with a low hand is that it postpones bad news. If you bust, you lose immediately. If you wait until the end, you lose if the dealer gets a higher total—but the bad news is delayed. Finally, drama is involved. Busting is a dramatic event, so players may concentrate on avoiding that instead of carefully evaluating all other alternatives.

Should we conclude that experienced blackjack players play suboptimally? Not unless we assume that their *sole* goal in playing is to maximize financial gain (or minimize financial loss). Keren and Wagenaar point out that the optimal strategy for playing blackjack in casinos is not to play at all! The optimal strategy for playing will, if followed perfectly, end up in an eventual *loss* of .4 percent of total investment (excluding the strategy of counting cards). Thus, if the overriding goal is to minimize loss, players should not play at all. So why do they play? For the excitement of risk and for the enjoyment of the game. If they followed the optimal strategy, the game would be boring indeed.

Other considerations are involved as well, but the main point is clear. What people *should* do, including casino blackjack players, cannot be *prescribed* unless we know what all the relevant goals are. What may appear irrational or suboptimal, given one set of assumptions, may turn out to be rational and adaptive after all. The safest course of action for psychologists studying "irrationality" is to be *descriptive*, not *perscriptive*.

There are innumerable corny jokes that turn on this common error in thinking. In one such joke a woman anxiously asks her doctor if she should risk having a sixth child because she had read that every sixth child born into the world is malformed, and she already has five children. In another a man plants a bomb on an airplane for five weeks in a row. He is caught, and he explains that he is planning to take an airplane trip the next week, and he figures that an airplane bombing couldn't possibly occur for more than five weeks in a row, so the plane he plans to take must be safe. Both the anxious mother and the concerned traveler share the belief that things must come

out even in the long run, and they let this belief influence their expectation of a single event.

This general belief that things *must* come out even in the long run was used most effectively by Tom Stoppard in his play *Rosencrantz and Guildenstern Are Dead.* The drama is set in the Denmark of Shakespeare's *Hamlet,* and the two courtiers, Rosencrantz and Guildenstern, appear in the opening scene tossing a coin. Rosencrantz exclaims that it has just come down heads for the 250th time in a row, and he takes this as a sign that something is indeed rotten in the state of Denmark.

The gambler's fallacy is an example of people treating a single event as if it were representative of a larger number of events. A similar phenomenon can be seen when people ignore sample size. If, for example, we want to know the average height of 20-year-old men in California, we would not be able to measure every single 20-year-old male Californian. Instead, we would measure a *sample* of that population, and then use the average obtained as our best estimate of the true average. A best estimate based on a sample size of, say, 2,000 men would be more trustworthy than one based on a sample size of just 5 men. Obviously, the larger the sample size, the more trustworthy the estimate of the population value.

People are usually aware of this, though they also make incorrect assumptions about sample size. For example, suppose you polled five Californians and found that all five drank ginger ale for breakfast. Would you then believe that most Californians drink ginger ale in the morning? Probably not, but when the problem is somewhat more subtle, then sample size tends to be ignored. Tversky and Kahneman (1974) demonstrated people's insensitivity to sample size with a problem like this one:

> A town has two hospitals, a large one and a small one. About 50 babies are born every day in the large hospital, and 10 babies every day in the small hospital. As everyone knows, about 50 percent of all babies born are boys, but of course the exact percentage will fluctuate from day to day, sometimes being higher than 50 percent, sometimes lower. In one particular year both hospitals kept a record of the days on which more than 60 percent of the babies born were boys. Which hospital was more likely to record such days?

About half of the college students who were given this problem judged that the likelihood was the same for both hospitals, while the other half split evenly between choosing the larger and the smaller hospitals. The correct judgment is that the smaller hospital is more likely to have such deviant days. This becomes crystal clear in the extreme case of a really small hospital that records just one birth a day. If half the babies born in a year are boys, then on half of the days of the year this hospital would record 100 percent boys! If a hospital had two babies born a day, then on one-quarter of the days of a year it would record 100 percent boys (on half of the days of the year, on average, one boy and one girl would be born; on the other half, two boys or two girls). These examples illustrate the general principle: Small samples are deviant far more often than large samples. Yet people often assume that small samples are just as representative as large ones.

The *availability heuristic* is another method people use to estimate the relative frequency of events or things. If you are asked which is more common in small towns, American or foreign cars, how would you decide? One way is to try to remember specific instances of American and foreign cars in small-town settings. If you can think of more American instances than foreign, you would infer that American cars are more frequent. In this way,

we can make a frequency estimate without actually counting. Because more frequent or common events are more available in memory, this is generally a useful and informative strategy. However, this heuristic can also lead us astray if availability of instances does not accurately reflect true frequency.

Imagine that you are sampling words that are four or more letters long from a book written in English. After sampling several hundred at random, will you have more words that start with the letter *r* or more words with *r* as the third letter? Most people judge that there are more words with *r* as first letter than words with *r* as third letter (e.g., more words such as *road* than *cartoon*). This is because it is easier to think of words that begin with *r* than to think of words that have *r* in the third-letter position. The availability heuristic leads to the judgment that words with initial letter *r* are relatively frequent. But just the opposite is true. There are far more words with *r* in third position than in first. This last sentence, for example, had no words starting with *r*, but four with *r* in third position—*far, more, words,* and *first.*

These examples may suggest that people in general do not think clearly, particularly under conditions of uncertainty. We tend to overuse such generally valid but intuitive strategies as the representativeness and availability heuristics, and to underuse formal logical, and statistical strategies (Nisbett & Ross, 1980). Still, the occasions and situations in which we are led astray may actually be relatively rare. (See the Application: The Uses of "Irrationality.")

CREATIVITY

The kinds of laboratory puzzles we have been dealing with bear little overt resemblance to the problems faced by scientists, engineers, or artists. They do, however, share one important property with real-world problems: The person begins either by not knowing at all what to do, or by going off on the wrong track. Both the laboratory puzzles and the real-world problems require novel behavior—a change of habitual modes of acting and thinking.

The Creative Process

Many creative problem solutions and discoveries seem to occur in four stages: preparation, incubation, illumination, and verification. Gutenberg's invention of the printing press illustrates these stages. The **preparation stage** consisted of several substages. The first was his explicit goal—to reproduce the Bible economically. The second substage consisted of learning about and considering several ways to print letters. He considered and thought about how woodblock printing is done by rubbing paper or material on a carved, inked block. Because carving a page of letters in wood is laborious and slow, he searched for alternatives that would allow individual letters to be reused. He got the idea of type-casting from coin stampings and seals. In his own words, "Do you not see that you can repeat as many times as necessary the seal covered with signs and characters?" (Gutenberg, in Koestler, 1964, p. 123).

Many, if not all, of the elements of the printing press were now available in Gutenberg's mind. However, he was still stuck with the notion of rubbing to make an imprint—he was on the wrong track. The idea of making an imprint by pressure did not occur to him until after a period of **incubation**—a period of time during which no progress seemed to be made, and during

Creativity consists of making new combinations of previously known ideas. Gutenberg wanted to produce an affordable Bible to replace costly handwritten versions. His invention of movable and reusable type drew on familiar elements from woodblock printing and coin casting; the printing press itself owed a debt to the winepress then widely in use. In this bas-relief from the pedestal of a statue of Gutenberg in the German city of Mainz, we see the printer reading a proof sheet while an assistant turns the press to ink another proof. On a line strung across the print shop, proofs hang to let the ink dry.

which little conscious thought seemed to be applied to the problem. The moment of **illumination** came to Gutenberg when, as he described it, "I took part in the wine harvest. I watched the wine flowing, and going back from the effect to the cause, I studied the power of this press. . . ." Suddenly the idea occurs—put together the seal and the winepress, and the letterpress is created! The **verification** follows: Will the idea actually work?

Many firsthand accounts of important discoveries follow this pattern. A goal is clearly set, and then potentially relevant information is gathered. This preparation done, a period of apparent inactivity follows. This period of incubation often involves a great deal of unconscious mental activity. Sometimes this leads to a flash of illumination or insight. Finally, if the idea is promising, it can be tested and verified.

The moment of illumination itself often involves the coming together of familiar elements in new ways. The gifted mathematician Henry Poincaré wrote: "To create consists of making new combinations of associative elements that are useful" (1929). A psychologist who devised a test of creativity described creative thinking as "the forming of associative elements into new combinations which either meet new requirements or are in some way useful" (Mednick, 1962, p. 221).

Conditions for Creative Behavior

What are the necessary prerequisites for creative behavior? First, creative people must have a "prepared mind." Throughout the history of human thought, apparently accidental discoveries have been made. A chance observation presumably led to the discovery of X rays, penicillin, and a host of other phenomena. Discovery by accident even has a word to describe it—*serendipity.* Serendipity is the art of finding something that you were not

looking for or expecting. Finding something and recognizing its potential importance are, however, two different things. Pavlov was surely not the first person to observe that dogs salivate in response to food-associated stimuli. He was the first, however, to recognize the relation between conditioned salivation and the study of mental processes. His accidental observation of anticipatory salivation led him to shift his attention from the digestive system to the study of conditioning and learning (see Chapter 6). He, as well as many other scientists with prepared minds, had an appropriate store of ideas and knowledge with which to integrate a new observation.

Second, the prepared mind may need to have a goal or purpose. Archimedes would probably not have discovered how to measure the volume of an irregular solid had he not been given the task of deciding if the king's crown was made of gold or of some baser metal. He was not permitted to take a sample nor was he permitted to melt it down. Since the crown was intricately carved, he could not make a simple measurement of its total volume. He could, of course, weigh it. If he could only measure its volume, he could then calculate its density and thus determine if it were made of gold.

He discovered how to measure its volume when two things happened at once. He was, legend has it, sitting in his bath and thinking of the problem when suddenly an idea struck—the volume of any object is equal to the volume of water it displaces! While he was sitting in his bath, the two necessary components of the answer to his problem were available: the goal he had in mind and the means to achieve that goal. While thinking of the problem, he saw the water rise as his body sank into the tub.

This was, presumably, not the first time Archimedes had taken a bath and had seen water rise as a solid object was immersed in it. Neither was it the first time that he had thought of the problem. But it was the first time that both occurred simultaneously. The prepared mind, in this case, consisted of knowledge of the elements of a problem (i.e., a measurement of volume was needed), knowledge of what happens when objects are immersed in water, and the ability to recognize the relevance of one thing to another. It is this last quality of the prepared mind—the ability to see remote connections—that is least understood. Poorly understood though it is, we do know that people differ with respect to this ability.

Individual Differences in Creative Ability

There is no single accurate measure of creative ability other than actual creative performance. Intelligence, for example, is not an accurate measure of creativity. As we will see in the next chapter, IQ score and high creativity do not necessarily go together. A person can be creative and yet not score any higher on intelligence tests than a noncreative person. But creative people do tend to be more accepting and understanding of other people's ideas than noncreative people (MacKinnon, 1965). This quality may be related to the ability to suspend critical judgment when trying to generate new (and often wild) ideas. The technique of *brainstorming,* where groups of people work together to solve a problem, relies critically on this. All ideas, no matter how outlandish, are accepted without criticism. Later in the process, of course, each idea is carefully and critically evaluated, but evaluation is postponed so as not to inhibit the free flow of ideas.

High scores on creativity tests also are not necessarily related to college grades. In one case, students with low grades scored higher on a creativity

test than students with high grades. Creativity—or at least originality as measured by tests—may not be rewarded by high grades. Perhaps the problem is in the creative person's attitudes. Einstein had this to say about the physics that he was taught in the classroom: "For the examinations one had to stuff oneself with all this rubbish, whether one wanted to or not . . . after my finals the consideration of any scientific problems was distasteful to me for a whole year" (Seelig, 1954, p. 26).

One source of friction between creative students and their less creative teachers may be the particular needs that creative people have. In general, people who score high on creativity tests tend to seek novelty and to prefer the unexpected. Low-scoring people, on the other hand, tend to prefer the familiar (Houston & Mednick, 1963). This finding may be related to the possibility that creative people are particularly open to new ideas (Jones, 1957). This openness often leads to extreme acceptance of new ideas and a gullibility that we wouldn't expect of highly creative minds. For example, Johann Sebastian Bach firmly believed in the mystical properties of numbers. Copernicus believed that circular motion was an expression of the perfection of the Divine Creator. Even that archetype of Yankee common sense, Benjamin Franklin, was a member of a mystic sect that believed in reincarnation and the transmigration of souls, and thus he practiced vegetarianism for fear of eating a reincarnation of a human being. Such examples of credulity could be multiplied many times (see Koestler, 1964, for example).

The evidence for gullibility among the creative is, however, anecdotal. We still do not know if gullibility is, in fact, a characteristic more pronounced in creative people than in others. If it is, it is a small price to pay for the delights of novelty and discovery and for the fruits of creative labor.

SUMMARY

1. Thinking is the manipulation of symbolic representations. These representations may be verbal (words), imaginal, or abstract.

2. Our knowledge and biases can interfere with reasoning performance. If we agree with a conclusion, then it is harder for us to detect a flaw in the logical argument.

3. People can reason by using *inference rules, mental models,* or *pragmatic reasoning schemas.*

4. People are better able to test hypotheses when the situation matches a pragmatic reasoning schema. They also must simplify complex situations.

5. People's representation of a problem is their *problem space.* Different problem spaces can make a problem either easier or more difficult to solve.

6. Some problems are difficult because their initial states set us off on the wrong track. Such problems induce *negative set.* One kind of negative set is *func-*

tional fixedness, in which habitual ways of thinking block solution.

7. *Insights* occur when problem solving is carried out in a novel or imaginative fashion.

8. Just as with logical reasoning, people can be biased in their decision making by the way a problem is posed or *framed.*

9. People use *heuristics* to make decisions and judgments under conditions of uncertainty. Two widely used heuristics are the *representativeness heuristic* and the *availability heuristic.*

10. Creativity is often a four-stage process: *preparation, incubation, illumination,* and *verification.*

11. Two conditions are necessary for creative behavior: (1) availability of elements that can be combined in novel ways; and (2) a clear goal or purpose. These two conditions characterize the *prepared mind.*

SUGGESTED READINGS

ANDERSON, J. R. (1980). *Cognitive psychology and its implications*. San Francisco: W. H. Freeman. An introduction to the field of cognitive psychology, with excellent treatment of problem solving, reasoning, and artificial intelligence.

BRANSFORD, J. D., & STEIN, B. (1984). *The ideal problem solver*. San Francisco: W. H. Freeman. One of the more sensible and entertaining guides to improving your strategies for solving various kinds of problems and puzzles.

GARDNER, M. (1978). *AHA! Insight*. San Francisco: W. H. Freeman. If you enjoy doing puzzles and problems of the kinds illustrated in this chapter, this little book is for you. A collection from Martin Gardner's classic columns in *Scientific American*.

JOHNSON-LAIRD, P. N. (1983). *Mental models*. Cambridge, Mass.: Harvard University Press. A theory of reasoning and thinking that stresses concrete mental representation and imagery.

KAHNEMAN, D., & TVERSKY, A. (1982). The psychology of preferences. *Scientific American,* 246 (1), 160–173. A readable summary of research on how people's choices may be biased.

MAYER, R. E. (1983). *Thinking, problem solving, and cognition*. New York: W. H. Freeman. An up-to-date survey of research and theory in thinking and problem solving.

NISBETT, R., & ROSS, L. (1980). *Human inference: Strategies and shortcomings of social judgment*. Englewood Cliffs, N.J.: Prentice-Hall. A controversial book that claims that people "lack the inferential machinery for bringing the relevant facts into conscious view" and so are doomed to error and irrationality.

10 Intelligence

F
ew applications of psychology have had as much impact on students'
lives as the intelligence test. That you are a college student reading this book
makes it almost certain that your score on a standardized intelligence test is
higher than average—and the fact that you were known to have a higher than
average score may be responsible for your being in college at all. The kinds
of courses you were encouraged to take in high school were very likely
influenced by teachers' knowledge of your intelligence-test score. The college you are attending almost certainly examined your score on a "scholastic
aptitude" test—a kind of intelligence test—before deciding to admit you. The
results of intelligence tests have deeply affected the personal lives and
careers of millions of people.

The data collected by intelligence testers have also played a prominent
role in influencing our ideas about education and about social policy in general. We know, for example, that intelligence-test scores tend to run in families. That is, parents with high test scores tend to have children with high test
scores—just as parents with low test scores tend to have children with low
test scores. Furthermore, there are quite large average differences in measured intelligence among social classes and ethnic and racial groups. These
differences are also somehow passed on from one generation to the next. Do
these facts mean, as some have suggested, that differences in intelligence are
largely a matter of heredity? Or do they mean, as others have argued, that
intelligence-test scores are largely determined by environment, which in turn
is shared by members of the same family, social class, or race? Are individual
differences *within* a race largely determined by heredity, while differences in

Rembrandt's painting of "Aristotle Contemplating the Bust of Homer." (The Metropolitan Museum of Art, New York)

the average test scores *between* races largely determined by environment? If differences in test scores are mostly determined by the genes, would that mean that education and other environmental influences cannot increase intelligence beyond some genetically fixed level? These are obviously important and controversial questions, which we will address in this chapter.

THE CONCEPT OF INTELLIGENCE

Most of us have an intuitive notion of what it means for someone to be "intelligent." In everyday terms, we consider some people we know "bright," and others not so bright. Just what is the intuitive understanding that people have of "intelligence"?

Research indicates that people have a fairly cohesive idea about what intelligence is. We tend to agree about who is smart and who is not; we also tend to agree about the components of intelligence. Robert Sternberg of Yale University conducted a study in which people were asked about their idea of intelligence. Both laypeople and experts were asked to list characteristics of intelligence and then to rate various kinds of people on these characteristics. Sternberg and his colleagues (Sternberg, Conway, Ketron, & Bernstein, 1981) found that laypeople think of intelligence as consisting of three very general sets of abilities: practical problem solving, verbal ability, and social competence.

In laypeople's view, *practical problem solving* includes such abilities as being able to reason logically, to identify connections among ideas, to see all aspects of a problem, and to keep an open mind. This kind of intelligence corresponds to the theoretical concept of **fluid intelligence** (Horn, 1968; Cattell, 1971). *Verbal ability* includes skills such as speaking clearly and articulately, conversing well, being knowledgeable about a particular field, studying hard, reading widely, and having a good vocabulary. This kind of intelligence corresponds to the theoretical concept of **crystallized intelligence** (Cattell, 1971). These two kinds of intelligence, as conceived by nonexperts, correspond nicely with the views of experts in the field, who also distinguish between verbal ability and problem solving and define them similarly.

Where laypeople and experts differed in Sternberg's study was with respect to a third kind of intelligence. Laypeople consider *social competence* a major component of intelligence. This includes a variety of competencies such as being able to accept others for what they are and to admit mistakes, having a social conscience, and being sensitive to other people's needs and desires. Experts—psychologists who have studied intelligence and intelligence testing—cited practical intelligence rather than social competence as their third factor. *Practical intelligence* consists of such abilities as being able to size up situations well, knowing how to achieve goals, and displaying an interest in the world at large.

Despite this difference over the third kind of intelligence, experts and laypeople shared a common conception of the *contents* of intelligence. The two groups also agreed on the *structure* of intelligence: There exists such a thing as *general* intelligence, and also such a thing as *factors* or different kinds of intelligence.

This last issue—whether intelligence is a unitary quality of mind or a set of independent factors—differentiates competing formal theories of intelligence. At one extreme is Spearman's (1923) *minimum factors theory*. For

Spearman, intelligence consists of two kinds of factors. The first is a general factor, termed "g" for general intelligence. The higher the value of "g," the more intelligent a person is. The second factor is specific to a particular domain of knowledge, such as verbal ability, spatial ability, or quantitative ability. These two factors are consistent with what we ordinarily expect of people. We generally expect that someone who scores high on one test of intelligence, such as vocabulary, will also score high on another, such as analogical reasoning. However, we are not surprised when someone who scores high on the vocabulary portion of a test scores somewhat lower on the arithmetic reasoning portion, though we would be surprised were the high and low scores to be very wide apart: Scoring in the 99th percentile on vocabulary and in the 5th percentile on arithmetic reasoning would violate our expectations. Indeed, some theorists believe that such unevenness in intellectual performance is a sign of underlying pathology. For example, Rapaport (1946) suggested that a person who scores high on the verbal but low on the performance portion of an intelligence test may be suffering from depression. This expectation that people should perform consistently across different types of tests reflects our belief in a general quality of mind, akin to Spearman's "g." At the same time, we recognize, as did Spearman, that people can be better at some things than at others—hence the notion of specific factors.

At the other extreme from Spearman, Guilford (1967, 1982) argued that there is no such thing as general intelligence. Instead, people can be very good or very bad at any number of different things, and there is no necessary relationship among these abilities. A person can be adept at dealing with some kinds of content, such as visual and symbolic, but inept with others, such as auditory. Similarly, a person may be skillful at tasks requiring memory, but poor at tasks requiring evaluation of materials. Guilford proposed 120 different mental abilities, all theoretically independent of one another.

A moderate position between Spearman's "g" and Guilford's 120 components is that of Thurstone (1938; Thurstone & Thurstone, 1962), who believed that intelligence consisted of seven primary mental abilities. These abilities, with examples of how they are measured, are:

1. *Verbal comprehension:* estimated by vocabulary tests.
2. *Verbal fluency:* measured by how quickly people are able to produce words that begin, say, with the letter *d*.
3. *Number:* measured by arithmetic reasoning problems.
4. *Spatial visualization:* reflected in the ability to do such tasks as pattern matching.
5. *Memory:* tested by performance on recall tasks.
6. *Reasoning:* measured by performance on analogy problems (for example, apple:tree :: raspberry:_____).
7. *Perceptual speed:* measured by tests that ask for rapid performance in, say, crossing out all the *t*'s in a string of letters.

Current views on intelligence lean toward the several-different-abilities approach rather than to the unitary-quality-of-mind outlook. Like Thurstone, Gardner (1983) proposes that intelligence consists of seven different qualities: linguistic intelligence (possessed most obviously by the writer or poet), musical intelligence (characteristic of the musician and composer), logical-

mathematical intelligence (essential in science, mathematics, and philosophy), spatial intelligence (manifested in art, navigation, and blindfold chess), bodily-kinesthetic intelligence (dancing, athletics, and using tools), and two "personal intelligences"—sensitivity to other people and knowledge of self. According to Gardner (1983), these seven intelligences are independent, yet they "interact with, and build upon, one another from the beginning of life" (p. 278).

The latest contribution to this field is the "triarchic" theory of Robert Sternberg (1985). Sternberg has a three-part view of intelligence: contextual, experiential, and componential. *Contextual intelligence* involves adaptation to the environment. If the environment is not tolerable, then intelligent people will either modify that environment or select a better one.

Sternberg's *experiential intelligence* reflects the idea that the intelligence required for a given task or situation may be more or less, depending on its novelty or familiarity. Intelligence is measured most clearly at two points along the novelty-familiarity continuum: when a task or a situation is fairly (but not completely) novel, and when performance in that task is beginning to become automatic. Thus an ability to cope with novel task-demands is one aspect of this type of intelligence. A second, equally important, aspect is the ability to automatize task performance and information processing: "Complex tasks can feasibly be executed only because many of the operations involved in their performance have been automatized. . . . Intellectual operations that can be performed smoothly and automatically by more intelligent individuals are performed only haltingly and under conscious control by less intelligent individuals" (Sternberg, 1985, p. 71). For example, poor readers are people who have failed to automatize the operations involved in reading.

Componential intelligence corresponds roughly to what other theorists have labeled simply *intelligence:* "It specifies the structures and mechanisms that underlie intelligent behavior" (Sternberg, 1985, p. xii). There are three subcomponents: metacomponents, which are involved in planning and monitoring performance and in making decisions; performance components, which carry out the plans of action formulated by the metacomponents; and knowledge-acquisition components, which selectively encode new information and combine or compare it with old information. The first component is required for identifying what the problem is and deciding how to solve it, the second is required for information processing and responding, and the third is used in selectively gaining new knowledge and integrating it into a cohesive whole. Performance on intelligence tests depends heavily on all three aspects of componential intelligence—in fact, this type of intelligence is what intelligence tests are designed to measure.

MEASURING INTELLIGENCE

Whether intelligence is assumed to consist of a single general factor or of 120 separate factors, the various tests of intelligence look pretty much alike. (See, for example, the sample questions from the Wechsler Adult Intelligence Scale in Table 10–3 later in this chapter. This test is used to obtain a measure of general intelligence.) The major reason for this similarity among tests is that they are all based on the same simple idea. This idea is that we cannot really define what intelligence is; rather, the best we can do is to

identify at least two groups of people—an intelligent group and a less intelligent group—and then see how these two groups differ.

The first step in devising both a theory and a test of intelligence, then, is to agree on who is smart and who isn't. (See the Highlight: The Search for a Simple Measure of Intelligence for some early scientific notions on the subject.) Once we have done that, we can give both the smart and the not-so-smart groups an assortment of test questions. If a test question can be answered by both groups, we throw that question away because it does not discriminate between the two groups. If a question doesn't discriminate between people differing in intelligence, then it is not a test of intelligence. If, however, a question is answered by the smart people but not by the not-so-smart, we keep it because it does discriminate between the two groups and is therefore, by definition, a test of intelligence. This is the logic behind the work of the great French psychologist Alfred Binet, who wisely chose chronological age as the criterion for selecting people who differ in intellectual attainment and abilities.

The Background of Binet's Test

The first useful intelligence test was devised in France by Alfred Binet and his collaborator, Theophile Simon. This test, published in 1905, marked a radical departure from earlier efforts to measure intelligence or mental ability. The first impetus toward the development of "mental tests" came from Charles Darwin's cousin, Francis Galton. In Galton's view, differences among people were largely caused by heredity. To support this view, he demonstrated that "eminence" in British life tended to run in families. For example, the sons and grandsons of eminent judges were more likely than the average person to themselves become eminent judges. This and other such facts suggested to Galton the importance of the genes in propelling a given person to eminence. There were also, he noted, racial differences in the frequency of eminent people or people of genius—many such superior individuals were to be found among the British, but he believed there were virtually none in Africa or India.

Throughout his life Galton maintained an active interest in measuring and testing human "specimens," recording, cataloging, and calculating the differences among them. The quantitative "mental tests" used by Galton and his early followers, however, were very simple. Perhaps because of his strong biological leanings, Galton concentrated on such laboratorylike tests as simple reaction time and measures of sensory thresholds and capacities. Not only could these be measured with precision, but there were large differences among individuals on such tests. The difficulty was that performance on such tests did not seem to be related to what most people would recognize as signs of real intelligence or mental ability. For example, an excellent student did not necessarily react more quickly to the sound of a buzzer than did an inferior student.

The task that faced Binet was much more down-to-earth and practical than Galton's concern with eugenics. The school authorities in the city of Paris had asked him to develop a testing procedure that could help to pick out students with low academic aptitude—that is, those who would not profit much from the regular school curriculum, and for whom special classes should be set up. That meant, of course, that the test Binet made had to be related to—had to be able to *predict*—a child's performance in school.

The Concept of Mental Age

Binet's point of departure was a simple but powerful idea: Normally, as children grow older, their mental powers increase. We do not expect a normal 2-year-old to learn the multiplication tables, no matter how often they are recited in his or her presence. However, if the same child has failed to learn the multiplication tables by the age of 12, we might well be concerned that the child is not very intelligent. (That assumes, of course, that the child has been exposed to and drilled in the multiplication tables at school or elsewhere.)

The normal growth of mental power with age suggested to Binet the concept of **mental age.** A 9-year-old of average intelligence was assumed to have the mental age of 9, a 6-year-old was thought to have a mental age of 6, and so forth. The knowledge, problem-solving ability, and other intellectual skills possessed by a hypothetical 9-year-old define the mental age of 9. Thus 6-year-olds should have difficulty solving problems or answering questions that the average 9-year-old can handle, and older children should find such problems or questions very easy.

Binet set about interviewing and examining Paris schoolchildren, trying to find out precisely what intellectual accomplishments were characteristic of children of different ages. From his point of view, a good item for inclusion in his test was one that most (but not all) children of a given age could answer correctly. Further, the proportion of children younger than that age who could answer the item should be small, while the proportion of older children answering successfully should be large. In practice, Binet selected items that about three-fourths of children of a given age could answer. If one found, as Binet did, a number of such items for 9-year-olds, the child who could answer those items was said to have a mental age of 9. That same child usually could answer the items that Binet had placed on his scale measuring 8-year-olds, but he or she would have difficulty with items on the scale for 10-year-olds.

Table 10–1: Intelligence Test Items at Three Different Age Levels of Binet's Test, 1911 Version.

Year 3
1. Point to eyes, nose, and mouth
2. Repeat 2 digits
3. Identify objects in a picture
4. Repeat a sentence of 6 syllables

Year 7
1. Show right hand and left ear
2. Describe a picture
3. Carry out 3 commands given simultaneously
4. Count the value of 6 coins

Year 15
1. Repeat 7 digits
2. Find 3 rhymes for a given word in 1 minute
3. Repeat a sentence of 26 syllables
4. Interpret a set of given facts

The kinds of items that Binet included in his scales dealt directly with knowledge, thinking, reasoning, and judgment—the intellectual factors involved in successful school performance. Table 10–1 lists a number of representative tasks that Binet's test required children of different ages to perform.

Any child who could answer the items on the scale for 10-year-olds was assigned a mental age of 10. To fully assess the child's brightness or dullness, however, the child's mental age had to be compared to his or her chronological age. For an 8-year-old to have a mental age of 10 means one thing; for a 12-year-old to have a mental age of 10 means something else. The first child seems to be obviously bright, while the second child may seem to be dull. This led to the concept of mental age relative to chronological age: the *intelligence quotient,* or *IQ.*

The Concept of the Intelligence Quotient

For Binet, it was enough simply to compare the child's mental and chronological ages. His original concern was to be able to pick out, for special education classes, children who would not profit from the regular school curriculum. (The Application: An Abuse of Testing offers a modern example of how such efforts can go astray.) To Binet, it seemed clear that a young child whose mental age lagged behind his or her chronological age by as much as two years was backward and needed special education attention.

The concept of **intelligence quotient,** or IQ, was introduced by a German psychologist, William Stern. The IQ, as proposed by Stern, represented the *ratio* of a child's mental age to his or her **chronological age.** To be rid of fractions, the ratio was multiplied by 100. This meant that, for any chronological age, the average IQ was arbitrarily set at 100. Obviously, if a child's mental age was greater than the chronological age, the child's IQ would be above 100. If the mental age was lower than the chronological age, the child's IQ would be below 100. For a 10-year-old child with a mental age of 12, the formula for calculating IQ gives the following result:

$$\text{IQ} = \frac{\text{Mental age}}{\text{Chronological age}} \times 100 = \frac{12}{10} \times 100 = 120$$

If the same 10-year-old had a mental age of 8, the IQ would be calculated as 80.

The Stanford-Binet Test

The **Stanford-Binet test,** a translated and modified version of Binet's original scale, was introduced into the United States by Lewis Terman, a professor at Stanford University, in 1916. The standardization of Binet's test items—determining what items corresponded to what mental ages—had, of course, to be revised, using a standardization sample of American children. A **standardization sample,** at least in theory, is representative of the entire population, and thus provides the norms, or standards of performance, with which the performance of any individual can be compared. The Stanford-Binet test was modified and restandardized on new samples of children in 1937, 1960, and 1972. Note that with the passage of time any intelligence test must be restandardized. When given the same test items that had been used in 1937, American children of 1972 performed at a considerably higher level than

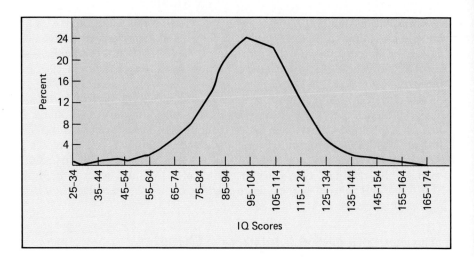

Figure 10–1 The approximate distribution of IQs in the population.

their 1937 predecessors. This might reflect changed schooling conditions or the impact of exposure to television. Whatever the cause, it is important to understand that an IQ score is always a relative, not an absolute, measure. It expresses an individual's standing relative to the performance of other people of the same age in the standardization sample. Thus 5-year-olds in the 1972 sample could answer harder questions than 5-year-olds in the 1937 standardization sample, but the 1972 5-year-olds still have an average IQ of 100.

The Stanford-Binet test has retained the basic Binet procedure of using separate items for each mental age; the items themselves are also similar to those originated by Binet. For each age level there is a scale consisting of six different items. To determine a child's IQ, the first step is to discover his or her *basal* mental age—that is, the highest mental age level at which the child can pass all six items. When the basal age level has been established, the tester proceeds to items from the next highest mental age level. This continues until a mental age level is reached at which the child can pass no items at all. The child's mental age is the basal age plus some credit for each item passed in scales above the basal age level. Since each mental age scale contains six items, each correct answer above the basal mental age level is worth two more months of mental age.

With earlier versions of the Stanford-Binet test, an intelligence quotient was actually calculated by dividing a child's mental age by his or her chronological age. This is no longer done, however. The performance of the children in the standardization sample has now been scored in such a way that the average score at every age is set equal to an IQ of 100, and the higher or lower scores are assigned higher or lower IQs in a symmetrical fashion, according to how far they fall from the mean. Thus IQ scores near 100 are defined as very common in the population; whereas scores above 135 or below 65 are relatively rare. The approximate distribution is shown in Figure 10–1.

Criteria for Useful Tests: Reliability and Validity

For a test to be useful, it must yield *consistent* measures. One index of consistency is called *test-retest reliability:* the degree to which we can expect to get approximately the same score for the same individual when he or she is

HIGHLIGHT

The Search for a Simple Measure of Intelligence

A major goal of science is to further understanding by uncovering simplicity and unity in the natural world. In modern physics, for instance, the discovery that energy and matter are different forms of the same thing simplified physical theory and led to a deeper understanding of the universe. In the realm of intelligence and intelligence testing, however, the search for a simple measure has often led us astray.

No less a figure than the renowned French neurologist and surgeon Paul Broca (1824–1880) believed that brain size determined intelligence: The greater the size of one's brain, the greater one's intelligence. *Craniometry*—the use of skull measurements to infer mental traits—was then quite popular and respectable. At a meeting of the Anthropological Society of Paris, Broca (1861, p. 188) claimed: "There is a remarkable relationship between the development of intelligence and the volume of the brain" (cited in Gould, 1981). Biologist Stephen Gould reports that Broca not only believed that high intelligence depends on having a large brain, but also had very firm opinions on what kind of people possessed these advantageous traits: "In general, the brain is larger in mature adults than in the elderly, in men than in women, in eminent men than in men of mediocre talent, [and] in superior races than in inferior races" (1861, p. 304). In other words, Broca felt that people just like *him* were blessed with the largest brains—and, of course, the greatest intelligence.

Does it make intuitive sense for brain size to be related to intelligence? From an evolutionary perspective, increasing brain size is somewhat related to mental capacity. However, it is not brain size per se but rather the size of the brain relative to total body size that seems to be important. For example, elephants have larger brains than do domestic dogs and cats, but it is not at all clear that elephants are smarter than cats, and few would claim that Saint Bernards are more intelligent than miniature poodles, or that ostriches are smarter than hummingbirds. With respect to people, brain size has no relation whatsoever to intelligence level, at least within normal ranges. It is true that a person with an abnormally small brain will most likely be mentally retarded, as in a condition known as microcephaly, in which abnormal skull growth severely constrains normal brain growth. But apart from such abnormalities, brain size, brain weight, and other simple measures such as skull circumference are worthless as indices of general intelligence.

Even so careful a scientist as Alfred Binet once believed that the larger the skull, the brighter the person. Binet wrote at the close of the last century: "The relationship between the intelligence of subjects and the volume of their head . . . has been confirmed by all methodical investigators, without exception" (Binet, 1898, pp. 294–295). But as he pursued craniometric methods of measuring intelligence, Binet gradually began to doubt not only the reports of others, but even his own findings. He recognized the danger of a scientist being unconsciously biased by prior beliefs, and reminded himself of the importance of double-blind controls (see Chapter 1). He set about repeating some earlier measurements, wherein he had obtained consistently higher values than had his colleague Simon, in the expectation that they should be smaller. Binet found that the second set of measurements were indeed smaller.

Binet's response to his failure was characteristically candid. His studies had "ended with the discouraging conclusion that there was often not a millimeter of difference between the cephalic measures of intelligent and less intelligent students. The idea of measuring intelligence by measuring heads seemed ridiculous" (1900, p. 403, cited in Gould, 1981). By 1904, Binet had abandoned the simplistic anatomical measures of craniometry to concentrate on measures that were, as we have seen, correlated with school success and with age.

Still another simple measure of intelligence was current at the time— *speed of response*. As early as the 1880s, pure speed of response had been proposed as an index of intelligence (Galton, 1883; Cattell, 1890). The rationale was both straightforward and intuitively plausible. People who can react quickly to a stimulus (e.g., the onset of a light or the sound of a buzzer) would appear to have more efficient nervous systems than people who react more slowly. Therefore we would expect quickness and slowness to be indicative of intelligence. We even use these terms metaphorically in describing intellectual level: A "quick" person is one who is clever; a "slow" person is one who is not.

Unfortunately, pure speed of response happens not to be correlated with measures of intelligence such as IQ scores (Wissler, 1901; Jensen, 1982). Decision reaction time would seem to be a better choice. In this kind of task, both pure response speed and decision speed are involved—for example, in moving your hand from a resting point to the one light out of a possible five or six that turns on. But here, too, the data are not encouraging. Jensen (1982), one of the most optimistic supporters of decision reaction time as a measure of intelligence, reports correlations anywhere from zero to $-.30$ in different samples.

Speed of reasoning and speed of performing various intellectual tasks do correlate with IQ test scores, but this is only because the ability to think fast is one of the qualities that IQ tests are designed to measure. Since IQ tests are generally timed, people who do well on them are those who are able to answer the test questions within the allotted time. The fact that the makers of IQ tests believe that speed is important does not mean that the issue is settled. Isn't it possible that there are people who consider their responses carefully, and whose answers are slow but brilliant?

tested on the same test more than once. Test **reliability** is measured by the agreement between two sets of scores, such as between an individual's scores on two separate test-taking occasions. This agreement is expressed in terms of a correlation coefficient. For a perfectly consistent test this correlation coefficient would be 1.00—everyone taking the test got exactly the same relative scores on both occasions. For a totally inconsistent test the correlation coefficient would be 0.00—that is, there would be no relationship between the scores on the two separate occasions. In practice, no tests are perfectly reliable, but well-designed tests come pretty close. For example, the 1937 version of the Stanford-Binet had a short-term reliability of .91, the correlation between scores on two forms of the test when they were administered to the same individuals a few days apart (Terman & Merrill, 1937).

But even with as high a correlation coefficient as this one, any individual's scores on a test can change appreciably. For example, the average change in children's scores on the Stanford-Binet was 5.9 for children with measured IQs of 130. This means that a child who scores 130 on one day might score as much as 14 points lower a few days later (Cronbach, 1960). On average, however, people tend to perform at the same level on different occasions when the same test is used.

A test can be quite reliable—that is, yield consistent scores—yet not have **validity.** For a test to be valid, it should measure what it was intended to measure. This is estimated by the extent of agreement between test scores and some other criterion. For example, if a test is intended to measure academic ability or aptitude, then an individual's test scores should enable us to predict the person's academic achievement as evidenced by, say, school grades. It is therefore perfectly possible to have an extremely reliable test—one that yields nearly the same scores for the same people over and over again—that is useless because it is not valid. For example, Galton's early attempts to assess intelligence used such measures as simple reaction time—the time taken by an individual to react to a buzzer. This response can be measured quite accurately and reliably. Unfortunately, differences in reaction time are totally unrelated to school performance. So speed of reaction, though it can be *reliably* measured, is not a *valid* test of academic aptitude or ability.

The opposite, of course, cannot be true. We cannot have a valid test that is not reliable. For a test to be valid, it must first be reliable. Then, if the test scores agree with some criterion—for example, if the scores accurately predict school grades or job performance—the test is a valid estimator of the abilities required for academic or job success.

Stability of IQ

Do children's IQs remain stable as they grow older? That is, will bright 5-year-olds (compared to other 5-year-olds) be equally bright when, 7 years later, they are compared to other 12-year-olds? The answer is that they are quite likely to remain relatively bright, but that there are many individual exceptions.

There is a clear tendency for IQs measured early in childhood to be highly correlated with IQs measured in later childhood or in adulthood. The correlations in IQ scores of the same individuals tested at different ages are illustrated in Table 10–2. IQ at any age is obviously correlated with IQ at any other age; but it is also the case (sensibly enough) that the correlations are smaller when many years separate the two tests.

Table 10–2: Correlations Among IQ Scores at Different Test Ages and Retest Intervals.

Test Age (Years)	Retest Age (Years)				
	5	7	10	14	18
2	.32	.46	.37	.28	.31
5		.73	.71	.61	.56
7			.77	.75	.71
10				.86	.73
14					.76

After Honzik, Macfarlane, Allen (1948).

The fact that, for the most part, IQ remains relatively stable throughout life should not obscure the equally obvious fact that many dramatic changes in IQ—clearly involving more than measurement error—do take place. For example, Honzik, Macfarlane, and Allen (1948) tested a group of children repeatedly between the ages of 2 and 18 and reported that 37 percent of the children showed IQ differences of at least 20 points between testings. Hindley and Owen (1978) report that about half of the children tested changed IQ by at least 10 points between the ages of 3 and 17. Figure 10–2 illustrates two examples of IQs changing progressively, and dramatically, over time. These examples should serve as a caution against premature labeling and pigeonholing of children with low (or high) IQs. Clearly there are individual cases in which IQ does change markedly.

The Test Defines Intelligence

For practical purposes, what psychologists mean by the world "intelligence" has been pretty well defined by the content of the Stanford-Binet and other widely used intelligence tests. In other words, you are an intelligent person if you do well on the sorts of questions asked by intelligence tests. This may seem to be an empty statement, but it is not entirely so. The validity of the test was originally established by the fact that scores on the test correlated reasonably well with other criteria—in this case, school grades and teachers' judgments of the brightness or dullness of their students. Children who did well on the test also tended to do well in their school subjects. Ever since Binet's time, revised or new tests of intelligence have been validated by their correlation with school grades—or by their correlation with Binet's test. Thus it is no accident that a child's IQ score can be used to predict his or her performance in school. The magnitude of the correlation varies with a number of conditions, but as a general rule, correlations in the range of .40 to .60 are found between IQ and school grades. This substantial but far from perfect correlation means that school performance is influenced by other qualities and conditions than those that are (or can be) measured on IQ tests.

The Test as Diagnostic Instrument

The original purpose that Binet had in mind for his IQ test was to use it as a diagnostic instrument, to identify those children who would do poorly in school. The problem with these children, Binet believed, was that their intelligence had not yet been developed enough. The task of the educator, once the test had located such backward children, was to *develop and increase* their intelligence by special educational procedures. Thus Binet definitely did not think of the test as measuring some fixed or unchangeable quantity. He argued that the right instruction—a form of "mental orthopedics"—could increase the intelligence of children who lagged behind their peers. This optimistic attitude about test scores and the possibility of training children to become more intelligent has not been very common since Binet (Cronbach, 1984). To the degree that IQ tests serve a diagnostic purpose, they are usually used to help assign children to classes thought right for their measured level of intelligence. The basic assumption is that the children's IQs will remain constant, that classroom experience will neither increase nor decrease their IQs.

Recently, however, the beneficial effects of early-intervention programs

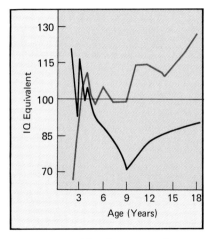

Figure 10–2 The changes in IQ over time of two different children, who were tested repeatedly from age 2 to age 18. (After Honzik, Macfarlane, & Allen, 1948)

such as Head Start and television programs such as *Sesame Street* have begun to challenge this assumption. Both IQ scores and classroom performance can be significantly enhanced, provided that the educational program is tailored to the individual and is continued over a reasonable period of time (Zigler & Berman, 1983). Interestingly, the children directly involved in such programs as Head Start are not the only ones to benefit. Many parents who participate find it challenging and afterwards choose to take part in other forms of community work (Adams, 1976, cited in Zigler & Berman, 1983). Even the younger siblings of Head Start children seem to benefit. In one study of Head Start families significant gains in IQ were found not only in the target children, but also in their younger brothers and sisters who had not been directly involved in the program (Gray & Klaus, 1970). One likely explanation for these gains is that the program's emphasis on parent participation changed parent's behaviors in ways that extended to all their children, not just to the child in the program.

These kinds of results underscore the misconception that IQ scores reflect some fixed, immutable capacity. Such thinking is misleading, and potentially harmful. Test scores can be used as Binet envisioned—to provide teachers and other professionals with diagnostic information to help them design educational and remedial programs.

Aptitude and Achievement

We live in a society that uses many different kinds of tests for many different purposes. It is important to understand both the purpose of a particular test and the assumptions that underlie its use. There are, at one extreme, **achievement tests.** Their purpose is to measure, as accurately as possible, how much you have learned before taking the test. Thus when you finish a college course, you usually take an exam. The purpose of the exam is to assess how much of the course content you have learned. Though it is possible that students with high IQs will receive higher exam grades, they get no special credit for having a high IQ. The slower, plodding student who works hard may receive a higher grade than the brilliant student who does not study. This is wholly appropriate since the only purpose of the exam, as an achievement test, is to measure how much of the tested material has in fact been learned.

There are other occasions, however, when tests are used to *predict* some future performance. For example, the military wants to predict the likelihood that a given candidate for aircraft pilot training will successfully complete the complicated and expensive course of training. To fly a plane well requires, among other things, good physical coordination and a good sense of mechanical matters. Thus all candidates for pilot training are normally given a battery of **aptitude tests,** including tests of mechanical aptitude and of eye-hand coordination, which are used to predict how well they'll do in the training program. People with poor scores on such tests tend to fail pilot training.

The distinction between an achievement test and an aptitude test thus depends on the purpose to which the test is put. It is impossible to distinguish between the two types of tests on other grounds. The very same item can be—and often is—included in both achievement and aptitude tests. Think back to the entrance examination you took before being accepted by your college. The college thought of that exam as an aptitude test, from which it predicted that you would do well in college. That is, your "scholastic

aptitude" was found to be high. The questions you answered, however, were very similar to questions that you had earlier answered in high-school course examinations. The same questions were then regarded as part of an achievement test. When you did poorly on such an achievement test in high school, you might have argued that the test did not reflect your **aptitude**—only the fact that you had not studied enough for it. Those who do poorly on a test of scholastic aptitude can just as reasonably argue that the test reflects nothing more than their failure to study enough—but in this instance the failure to study would have occurred over a long time span. The failure to have studied, it should be obvious, does not necessarily mean that that person *could* not have mastered the material on the aptitude test.

The fundamental equivalence of aptitude and achievement tests is best seen in tests that serve both purposes simultaneously—that is, they can be used either as an achievement test or as an aptitude test. Driving tests are used not only to assess how well a person has learned to drive (achievement), but also to predict whether that person will be able to drive a car safely on public highways (aptitude). Medical licensing exams, the bar exam for lawyers, and licensing examinations for clinical psychologists all play the same dual role: They are used to assess how much people have learned about their profession, and also whether they will be able to function at some reasonable level in that profession. Indeed, it is hard to think of an achievement test that is not used, or is not at least usable, as an aptitude test to predict either future performance or future ability to learn or improve a skill. If one did not want to make such predictions, they why bother to test achievement in the first place?

An important point to remember about aptitude tests is that people—including psychologists—often make the mistake of thinking that such tests can somehow measure a person's *capacity* to learn. The assumption is made that everyone has some fixed limit to his or her learning ability, and that the limit is at least partly determined by heredity. This may be a plausible assumption, but it is clearly wrong to believe that any test can directly measure a person's hereditary potential or capacity. The results of *all* tests necessarily depend upon a person's past experiences, present motivation, and many other factors. There is not and cannot be any direct test of "innate intelligence." These points have been made clearly by a distinguished committee of mental-test specialists appointed by the American Psychological Association (Cleary, Humphreys, Kendrick, & Wesman, 1975). These authorities pointed out that the assumption that all members of our society had an "equal opportunity" to learn the materials presented in IQ tests is incorrect. Of course, it is possible to argue that *most* people have had *almost* equal opportunities, and that tests are therefore more or less *approximate* indicators of mental capacity. But when language is this imprecise, the potential for misinterpretation and controversy is obvious.

Intelligence and Aging

It is obvious that intellectual capability continues to increase throughout childhood. For that reason, different kinds of items must be introduced into the scales that are used to measure the IQs of children of different ages. The items for older children are, of course, more complex and difficult than those for younger children. What, however, happens to intellectual capability beyond childhood, as people pass through adulthood and old age?

To answer this question, it is necessary to compare the performances of

adults of differing ages when tested with the same material. The early studies of intelligence and aging (for example, Jones & Conrad, 1933) suggested that intellectual abilities decline gradually during adult life, beginning when people are in their early 20s, and that the average decline by the age of 60 is very great. We know now, however, that at least part of this apparent decline was an effect produced by the cross-sectional method of studying the aging process. In a **cross-sectional study** the subjects are groups of individuals who differ in age. For example, the experimenters might test a group of 20-year-olds, a group of 40-year-olds, and a group of 60-year-olds, all at about the same time. Then the performances of the different age groups are compared. The trouble is that when we compare the performances of the younger and older people, we are observing not only the effects of chronological age; we are also comparing groups of subjects born at different times and exposed to different educational experiences and cultural conditions. It is impossible to determine whether the observed differences are due to age alone or to the differing experiences of the groups. (This issue is discussed more fully in the Chapter 13 Highlight: Two Ways to Study Development.)

A more satisfactory way of studying the effects of age on intelligence is with **longitudinal studies,** in which the *same* people are repeatedly tested as they grow older. The difficulty is that such studies take a long time to carry out. A longitudinal study of changes in intellectual performance from age 20 to age 80 would take 60 years just to collect the data. In addition, there is the problem of dropouts. A certain number of people involved in a longitudinal study will drop out for various reasons: Some will move away, others will die, still others will decide that they no longer wish to be tested. To the extent that the tendency to drop out is not completely random, the results of the study could be biased. For example, smarter people might drop out because they are more likely to be busy or to move away, or duller people might drop out because they do not enjoy being tested. Thus the people who remain in the study may not be representative of the original sample. This can affect the results, perhaps misleadingly.

In an effort to overcome these problems, techniques have been developed that enable us to compare cross-sectional with longitudinal samples. The one most commonly used is a compromise between the two methods called the *overlapping longitudinal design.* This kind of study uses several groups of people of different ages, and follows each group for a number of years. Thus one group might be followed from age 20 through 30, another from age 25 through 35, and so on.

Figure 10–3 shows the results of a comparison between two studies of changes in intellectual functioning with age. The cross-sectional study shows an apparent decline with age, but this is misleading. If we compare today's 25-year-olds with today's 50-year-olds, the 25-year-olds will probably do better on the test—not because they are younger, but because, on the average, they have had more education than the 50-year-olds, as well as greater access to modern communication devices such as television. (Recall that American children of 1972 were able to answer more questions on the Stanford-Binet IQ test than children of the same ages in 1937.) The overlapping longitudinal study, which followed groups of people over a period of 14 years, shows no decline with age until the participants reach their early 70s, when ill health and advancing age begin to take their toll.

The best data now available suggest that performance on tests of general ability may actually increase up to age 60 in healthy, active, people. Thereafter, some people may show some decline, but this is certainly not true for all. Whatever declines do occur are most likely attributable to illness,

Figure 10–3 Trends Over Time in General Ability The graph shows the results of a study combining cross-sectional and longitudinal methods. The results show minimal decline when the appropriate longitudinal method is used. (Cronbach, 1984; data from Schaie, 1979)

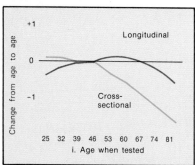

primarily ailments that affect the brain, such as strokes, tumors, Korsakoff's syndrome (a loss of mental functioning and memory caused by alcoholism), and a number of other drug- and alcohol-related impairments.

On the average, the decline of intellectual capability with age is slight. One study of active and healthy people showed no average decline until age 75 (Botwinick & Siegler, 1980). Highly educated people, who tend to maintain intellectual interests and activities throughout life, are the least likely to experience a decline. When declines do occur, all mental abilities are not likely to be equally affected. Vocabulary and verbal skills may actually improve with age, whereas skills involving spatial visualization and deductive reasoning are more likely to diminish. In general, tasks that require quick responding are especially vulnerable to aging.

Children with Low IQs

The original purpose of Binet's test was to identify students who lagged behind their agemates. The test, and others based on it, is still used in an effort to diagnose the "mentally retarded." For someone to be so diagnosed, an IQ below 70 is usually regarded as a necessary—but not sufficient—condition. Only when a low IQ is coupled with inadequate social and occupational adjustment should a label of retardation be applied. Many low-IQ children appear retarded in the classroom, but not on the playground or in their home environments. After leaving school these children are usually able to find productive employment and to function successfully and independently. They merge imperceptibly into the rest of the normal population, and so are not really retarded.

Typically, distinctions are made among various degrees of **mental retardation.** Mild retardation, with IQs ranging from about 55 to 69, occurs in about 2 percent of the population; among such people, prospects for successful adaptation to independent adult life are reasonably good. Moderate retardation, with IQs between 40 and 54, occurs in about .1 percent of the population. Severe retardation—with IQs below 40—is much rarer, occurring in some .003 percent of the population. The severely retarded usually need institutional care throughout their lives. With appropriate training, they can be taught self-help skills and the quality of their lives can be improved.

For most mentally retarded people, no clear physical cause can be found. This type of relatively mild retardation is often called "familial-cultural." Those so diagnosed are generally born to parents with low IQs and have been reared in depressed and deprived conditions. The other type of retardation is biologically caused, or "organic." This type is likely to be more severe and may be accompanied by other problems, such as motor disabilities, deafness, or blindness. The cause of organic mental retardation may be brain injury, prenatal infection, a lack of oxygen during birth, or various genetic or chromosomal defects. The moderate to severe retardation associated with **Down's syndrome** (once called *mongolism*) is caused by the presence of an extra chromosome in the cells of the affected child (three instead of two of the twenty-first chromosome). This extra chromosome is not "inherited" in the ordinary sense, but results from a biological accident whose mechanisms are not clearly understood. The risk of having a Down's syndrome child is much higher for women in their 40s than for younger women. The extra chromosome produces a number of characteristic physical signs as well as mental retardation. Recent advances in education and health

This child was born with Down's syndrome, which is caused by the presence of an extra, 47th chromosome in the cells. This extra chromosome produces a number of physical abnormalities, as well as mental retardation. (Richard Hutchings/Photo Researchers)

care have greatly improved the potential attainments and the physical health of people with Down's syndrome.

A rare form of retardation known as **phenylketonuria (PKU)** results from the inheritance of a particular pair of recessive genes. It was first noted in 1934 that a few retarded children, some of whom were siblings, excreted phenylpyruvic acid in their urine. We now know that the mental retardation of such children is produced by the overaccumulation of that amino acid in their brains, caused by an inherited defect in metabolism. Happily, there is a successful treatment for this genetic defect: The child must be fed a diet very low in phenylalanine. The dietary treatment, if begun early enough, prevents the accumulation of the responsible amino acid, and the child develops with a normal IQ. It should be stressed that PKU is quite uncommon. Unfortunately, there are no similarly successful treatments—and no clearly understood physical causes—for most forms of retardation, including Down's syndrome.

There is an important lesson to be learned here. PKU is known to be an inherited defect, yet it can be successfully treated. Down's syndrome is known *not* to be inherited, yet it cannot be successfully treated, at least not yet. Thus the fact that a trait is inherited or not inherited tells us nothing about our chances of modifying that trait by environmental intervention. What matters is whether we understand the causes of a particular defect. If we understand what causes it, there is a good chance that we will learn how to treat it, whether it is inherited or not.

Children with High IQs

In 1925 Lewis Terman began to study a large group of California schoolchildren with very high IQs, averaging about 150. The original children, numbering over a thousand, have now been followed for more than 50 years. Terman often referred to the project as a study of "genius," but "people with high IQs" seems to be a more accurate description of these subjects. These people, selected at a young age because of their outstandingly high IQs, for the most part went on to live productive and successful lives. Many of them earned advanced degrees, and many became doctors, lawyers, professors, or novelists. They wrote many books and scientific papers. They earned good incomes. As adults they seemed to be socially well-adjusted members of their communities and to be content with the way they lived their lives.

As children, these people tended to be taller and healthier than their age-mates throughout childhood; even at birth they weighed more than the average newborn. Their social adjustment was good and, of course, most of them did very well in school. These findings clearly disprove the notion that high-IQ children are in some way unbalanced or freakish. They also indicate that if all we know about a schoolchild is that he or she has a very high IQ, it is a good bet that he or she will go on to lead the kind of "successful" life described above—though, it should be said, not *all* of Terman's subjects were successful. There is also no indication that these very-high-IQ children produced works of genuinely creative genius. There is really no proof, either, that their successes were *caused* by their very high IQs. Almost all of Terman's subjects had been born into professional and well-to-do families. This kind of family background might well be responsible for their good childhood health and for much of their adult success—quite apart from their high IQs. We do not know, for example, whether the lower-IQ sisters and brothers of Terman's selected subjects were any less successful than the sub-

jects themselves. Though Terman would doubtless have expected such a difference, we do not in fact have the necessary data to prove or disprove it.

TYPES OF INTELLIGENCE TESTS

The benchmark against which more recently developed IQ tests were measured was the Stanford-Binet test. When new tests were proposed, their validity as IQ tests was often demonstrated by showing that they were highly correlated with Stanford-Binet scores. The Stanford-Binet test does have scales that can be used with adults, but it was basically designed to test children. To measure adult intelligence, some awkward assumptions had to be made—for instance, that mental growth stops at the age of 16. In order to translate an adult's performance on the Stanford-Binet into an IQ score, a "chronological age" of 16 must be assumed.

Testing Individuals: The Wechsler Scale

The measurement of adult IQ was greatly advanced by the development of the **Wechsler Adult Intelligence Scale (WAIS).** Introduced in 1939, this test was revised in 1955 and most recently restandardized in 1981. The success of his adult scale prompted Wechsler to develop the **Wechsler Intelligence Scale for Children (WISC–R),** revised in 1974 and designed for children aged 6–16. Most recently, the Wechsler Preschool and Primary Scale of Intelligence has been developed for even younger children.

The various Wechsler scales, although designated for different age groups, are very much alike in their basic form and types of content. They are all substantially correlated with the Stanford-Binet, with which they have much in common, but from which they differ in some important ways. The outstanding similarity is that both the Stanford-Binet and Wechsler tests are designed to be administered by a trained examiner to one person at a time. The examiner must use judgment in deciding whether the answer to a given item is correct. The one-on-one testing session takes about an hour in each case, and a skilled examiner can note not only the child's answers but also his or her mannerisms, emotional state, cooperativeness, and so on.

Deviation IQ. The Wechsler scales were the first to use the concept of a **deviation IQ.** The decision was made that the average test score for people of any age should be 100, and that the standard deviation of these IQs should be 15 at every age. (This and other statistical concepts are explained in the Appendix.) This result is accomplished by statistical adjustment of the actual raw scores obtained in the standardization samples among people of different ages. That is, one's IQ is determined by comparing one's performance to that of people one's own age in the standardization sample for the test. To have a Wechsler IQ of 130 means that you have done better on the test than about 97.5 percent of people *your age* in the standardization sample. Thus if you have recently taken the WAIS, you are being compared to a standardization sample studied shortly before 1981. The deviation-IQ procedure also means that if you are 18 years old and your 65-year-old grandparent has done about as well as you in answering the test questions; your grandparent will have a considerably higher IQ than you. That is because in the standardiza-

The various Wechsler scales, though intended for different age groups, are very much alike in basic form and types of content. At top, a child is working on the Object Assembly portion of the test. She has before her the separate pieces of an object and must put them together to form the complete object (in this case, a horse). At bottom, an adult works on the Block Design portion of the test. She has been shown a pattern and must now try to arrange the small colored cubes in the same pattern. (*Top:* Lew Merrim; *bottom:* Mimi Forsyth; both Photo Researchers)

Table 10–3:   Sample Questions from the Wechsler Adult Intelligence Scale.

Verbal Scale	
Information	What is steam made of? What is pepper?
Comprehension	Why is copper often used in electrical wires? Why do some people save sales receipts?
Arithmetic	It takes 3 people 9 days to paint a house. How many would it take to do it in 3 days? An automobile goes 25 miles in 45 minutes. How far would it go in 20 minutes?
Digit Repetition	Repeat the following numbers in order: 1, 3, 7, 2, 5, 4 Repeat the following numbers in reverse order: 5, 8, 2, 4, 9, 6
Similarities	In what way are a circle and a triangle alike? In what way are an egg and a seed alike?
Vocabulary	What is a hippopotamus? What does "resemble" mean?

Performance Scale	
Picture Arrangement	A story is told in 3 or more cartoon panels placed in the incorrect order; put them together to tell the story.
Picture Completion	Point out what's missing from each picture.
Block Design	After looking at a pattern or design, try to arrange small colored cubes in the same pattern.
Object Assembly	Given pieces with part of a picture on each, put them together to form such objects as a hand or a face.
Digit Symbol	Learn a different symbol for each number and then fill in the blank under the number with the correct symbol.

tion sample the average 65-year-old could answer fewer questions than the average 18-year-old.

The Wechsler scales differ from the Stanford-Binet by breaking down the total IQ into two separate components—a verbal IQ and a performance IQ. The Stanford-Binet contains many different kinds of testing materials mixed together, and provides a single "global" IQ score. The WAIS, however, separates its material into 11 different subscales, as shown in Table 10–3. The first 6 scales are combined to yield a verbal IQ, and the last 5 scales yield a performance IQ. The total IQ is basically the average of the two. Verbal and performance IQs are substantially correlated with each other, and each is correlated with the Stanford-Binet IQ—the verbal IQ somewhat more so. There are individual cases, however, in which the verbal and performance IQs are very different. This can be informative, and might indicate language or reading difficulties or perceptual disabilities. One researcher (Rapaport, 1946) went so far as to suggest that a person who scores high on the verbal portion but low on the performance portion might be suffering from depression. However, such diagnoses should be made with great caution. Many people who are normal in every respect can score quite differently on the two sets of scales. It might be better simply to view the two types of items as

testing two kinds of abilities. In general, abilities tend to go together, but there is nothing inherently wrong with people who are good in some things but poor in others.

Testing Groups

Group tests of intelligence sacrifice the detail and the kinds of intimate personal knowledge available from an individual testing session, but they are obviously necessary if very large groups of people are to be examined. The first impetus for group tests came at the time of World War I, when the United States Army decided to test draftees. Two group tests—the Alpha and the Beta—were quickly developed; sample items from each are shown in Figure 10–4. Typically, group tests are administered simultaneously to large numbers of people, with paper, pencil, and multiple-choice answer blanks. Though some of the items included in the Alpha test seem amusing and unfair today, the basic form of the Alpha test is very similar to that of many verbal paper-and-pencil tests in use today. The Army General Classification Test of World War II and its more recent replacements are more sophisticated than the old Alpha, as are most of the group tests now used in school systems and in industry. The Beta test of World War I is rather unusual. It was designed as a *performance* test. To measure accurately the IQs of illiterate or foreign-born draftees, the test had to be "nonverbal"—it couldn't depend on reading skill or familiarity with the English language. The kinds of material shown in Figure 10–4 were made up with that aim in mind. The test, however, had to be given to large groups of men. The instructions were thus conveyed in "pantomime." Readers may decide for themselves whether this performance test fairly measured the intellectual capabilities of people who could not understand English and who were ignorant of American culture. It

Figure 10–4 Specimen items from the Army Alpha and Beta tests of World War I.

From the Alpha Test

Disarranged Sentence: property floods life and destroy (True or False)

If you save $7 a month for 4 months, how much will you you save?

Revolvers are made by: Smith & Wesson   Armour & Co.   Ingersol   Anheuser-Busch

Why is tennis good exercise?

The Battle of Gettysburg was fought in: 1863   1813   1778   1812

From the Beta Test

What is missing from the picture below?

From the Beta Test

Rearrange the three pictures below in the correct order:

World War I recruits taking the U.S. Army Alpha test, the first mass test to determine individual differences in intelligence. (Signal Corps/National Archives)

is really not surprising that scores on the World War I Army tests showed dramatic differences betwen native-born American soldiers and newly arrived immigrants. It is also not surprising that the longer a person had been in the United States, the higher his score tended to be. Obviously, performance tests do not test "pure" mental ability isolated from specific knowledge or familiarity. This is an important fact to keep in mind when we consider the issue of culture fairness in testing.

Performance Tests and "Culture Fairness"

To say that one has measured "intelligence" rather than what people happened to have learned, it is necessary that the test be fair in allowing people to *use* their intelligence. Much verbal material is highly specialized knowledge, not available to all. Thus an item such as "Wundt is to Werthei-mer as Watson is to _____?" might be a fair test of the intelligence of someone who has studied psychology, but clearly not for anybody else. The item "Sunday is to Monday as January is to _____?" would probably be regarded as fairer by most test makers, at least for people who speak English. They assume that everyone has been exposed over and over to the names and sequences of the days and the months. That is, if material is "equally" familiar to everyone, it is appropriate for an IQ test. The other approach to fairness, in theory, is to use material with which everybody is equally *un*familiar; for example, people may be asked to see relationships among groups of unusual geometric forms.

Performance tests of IQ try to avoid some of the more obvious biases of

APPLICATION

An Abuse of Testing

The limits of intelligence tests as measures of learning ability are clearly understood in theory, but are sometimes ignored in practice. This can lead to serious injustices, as the following case history makes clear.

Alicia P. was 4 ½ years old when she came, with her parents, from Puerto Rico to an industrial state in the Northeast. Placed in a nursery school at the age of 5, Alicia, who spoke very little English, was given the Stanford-Binet IQ test with the help of a Spanish-speaking interpreter. The examining psychologist did not assign a specific IQ score to Alicia but wrote into her record that she was a "Potentially Severe Learning Disability Case." The next year, when she was to enroll in the first grade, another psychologist tested her, again with the Stanford-Binet, but this time in English. The IQ score assigned to Alicia was 47—though the examiner noted that she was "well-poised and socially responsive" and gave "an impression of mental alertness not borne out by the testing." The psychologist wrote that an IQ of 47 "places Alicia in the category of moderately retarded mentally, usually accepted as trainable." The recommendation was made, and accepted, that she be placed into a special class for trainable mental retardates.

Within two weeks the teacher of the special class for retardates had written to the school superintendent to point out that Alicia was incomparably in advance of all other students in her class and did not seem at all retarded. The decision was then made to place her in a slightly higher-level class for "educable mental retardates." Three years later, under state law, it was necessary to test Alicia once more. This time, in an attempt to get around language problems, she was tested with the performance scale only of the WISC–R. Her performance IQ was now 76. The psychologist wrote that since three years in a class for retardates had increased her IQ from 47 to 76, the class had obviously been good for her!

By this time, Alicia's Spanish-speaking parents, who had noticed that she seemed to be learning very little at school, had become aware that she had been placed in a class for retardates. They demanded that their child be tested by a Spanish-speaking psychologist, who employed a specially translated version of the WISC–R. This test indicated that Alicia's IQ was an entirely normal 95. The school authorities, now in some doubt, had her tested yet again, by still another psychologist. That tester reported that Alicia stated that she preferred to be tested in English. Her IQ, again on the WISC–R, was now said to be 73—with a verbal IQ of 86. The Child Study Team in charge of Alicia's case met to consider all these apparently contradictory findings. They concluded that since the Spanish-speaking psychologists had not had access to Alicia's past records (did not know of her earlier IQ score of 47), they would be guided by the opinion of the tester who said that her present IQ was 73. That tester called her a borderline case and suggested that she remain in the class for retardates.

Some years later, prodded by a lawyer hired by Alicia's parents, the child was tested once again with the WISC–R, by the same school psychologist who had reported her IQ to be 73. This time, however, the psychologist's report stated that she "preferred to have this examination administered in the Spanish language." Her IQ was now 103—with a verbal IQ of 96 and a performance IQ of 110. The psychologist now wrote that "the classification of educable mentally retarded can no longer be sustained . . . I am at a loss to explain the wide discrepancy between the two IQ evaluations." It is hard to believe that this tester failed to recognize the role of language difficulties in Alicia's test scores—but the stigmatizing effect of a scientific-looking IQ number like 47 can blind even sophisticated people to the obvious.

Finally, after ten long years, Alicia was placed for the first time in an ordinary classroom. She was far behind her classmates, however. When her parents asked for special tutoring for her, they were told that such help was available only for retarded pupils—which the test now showed she was not! Testing clearly was not of much help to Alicia, nor can it be to other children like her if the tests are so blatantly misused and misinterpreted.

---

verbal materials by concentrating on materials such as making designs from blocks, completing incomplete drawings, fitting the right peg into the right hole, seeing relations among geometric forms, and so on. Cattell (1949) called his version of such a test "culture free." Perhaps the most widely used such test is Raven's Progressive Matrices (1947), which depends entirely on seeing relationships among different groups of geometric figures.

To call any test "culture free" is obviously an exaggeration. To begin with, instructions must be communicated in some way. Further, members of some cultures find the very idea of being tested strange or offensive. The best that might be hoped for is that tests might be devised that are relatively more "culture fair" than others. The differences among human cultures, however, are enormous, complex, and subtle. We cannot be sure that by reducing the verbal content of a test we are making it fair to all cultures and subcultures. The attempt to develop **culture-fair tests** seems on the whole to have been

disappointing. Within the United States, at least, results obtained with them have not differed greatly from those obtained with more traditional tests. Perhaps, in view of the substantial correlation between the verbal and performance scales in Wechsler's tests, this is not surprising.

More recently, test makers have been concerned with the question of whether tests are *biased* against members of minority groups. Bias, in this technical usage of the term, refers to whether or not the same test score, earned by members of two different groups, predicts the same academic (or other) performance. For college students at least, tests do not seem to be biased in this sense against minority groups (Jensen, 1980). For example, black and white students with the same scores on the Scholastic Aptitude Test tend to receive about the same grades in college courses. The lack of bias, however, does not necessarily mean that the test score is a fair assessment of the academic *potential* of minority students. The difference between groups in average score on an "unbiased" test may reflect an unfair distribution of educational and other resources in society at large. The test score is being used merely to predict college grades of high-school graduates in society as it now exists. Those students who have high SAT scores are somewhat more likely to receive better grades—whether they are black or white.

Just how well do SAT scores predict grades? If we could use only one predictor for freshman grades in college, the best single one would be high-school grades. The median correlation between high-school and freshman grade average in a sample from 312 colleges was .50. In contrast, the median correlation between SAT verbal scores and grades was only .38; between SAT quantitative scores and grades, .34 (Linn, 1982). When high-school grades and SAT scores were combined, the prediction improved only slightly, yielding a correlation of .59 between the combined predictors and freshman grades. This suggests that the SAT and school grades measure pretty much the same thing—the ability to do well in school.

Tests of Divergent Thinking

The intelligence tests we have discussed up to now were designed to measure one kind of thinking, *convergent* thinking. Test items that require convergent thinking are those that have a single correct answer. Getting the answer often requires a logical narrowing down among possible alternatives in order to converge finally on the one correct answer. This is the kind of thinking that was involved in Spearman's two-factor theory of intelligence, described earlier in this chapter. Recall that Spearman postulated a general factor, "g," that was not specific to any one domain of knowledge, plus a small number of specific factors such as verbal or mathematical ability. All of Spearman's tests were based on convergent thinking; he used **factor analysis** (also mentioned earlier) to support his theory by "extracting out" various factors from his data.

J. P. Guilford, whose 120-factor theory was contrasted with Spearman's in the first section of this chapter, likewise used factor analysis to support *his* theory. One reason why Spearman and Guilford each found support for their very different theories from the same mathematical procedure is that they each began with a different assortment of items and tests. In addition to tests of convergent thinking, Guilford also used tests of *divergent* thinking. These tests use questions that do not have a single correct answer. Instead, the solutions to divergent-thinking questions depend on being able to let one's thoughts roam creatively along different or divergent pathways. This type of

thinking results in original and surprising ideas—not necessarily in one predetermined answer. To test divergent-thinking ability—which has sometimes been identified with creativity—Guilford and Hoepfner (1971) used such items as: "Name as many uses as you can think of for a toothpick," or "Imagine all of the things that might possibly happen if all national and local laws were suddenly abolished." To do well on such a test, the subject must respond not with one correct answer but with many novel ideas.

Though a number of tests of divergent thinking have been developed, it has turned out that, at least to some degree, scores on such tests are correlated with scores on "convergent" IQ tests. The average correlation between tests of divergent thinking and more traditional intelligence tests is about .30. However, the correlation fluctuates widely, depending on the sample of people being tested. One possibility is that high general intellectual ability is required for creativity, but is not sufficient in itself. Hypothetically, then, people who score low on tests of intelligence should also score low on tests of divergent thinking. This premise should lead to a substantial correlation between intelligence and divergent-thinking performance. However, because intelligence is a necessary but not sufficient condition for creativity, people who score high on intelligence tests need not also score high on tests of divergent thinking. In general, the available evidence is consistent with this view (Barron & Harrington, 1981).

We do not know to what degree, if any, people with high scores on divergent-thinking tests are creative in real life. There are, no doubt, many factors involved in real-life creativity that are not captured by simple divergent-thinking tests. We do know that divergent-thinking scores are not as highly correlated with school grades as IQ scores are. The relations among IQ, genuinely creative thinking, school grades, and accomplishment are obviously complex. Thus, for example, Albert Einstein had an indifferent school career, and James Watson, who solved the riddle of the DNA molecule, had an unspectacular measured IQ of 115. Yet there are school counselors who advise students not to attempt college unless they have an IQ of 120! The prediction from IQ or from school grades to actual accomplishment clearly cannot be made with any degree of certainty.

NATURE, NURTURE, AND IQ SCORES

There are some people with high IQs, many people with average IQs, and some people with low IQs. That is to say, there is much variation among people in IQ test scores. What accounts for these differences among people? To what extent are they produced by the different genes that people inherit? To what extent are they produced by the different environments that people experience as they grow up? These questions, having to do with the relative importance of nature and nurture, have been the source of passionate controversy ever since the birth of IQ testing.

Everyone agrees, of course, that human genes are a necessary precondition for the development of human intelligence and of IQ. There is no environment that can raise the intellectual level of a fish, a bird, or a monkey to that of a normal human being. Everyone also agrees that exposure to human language and society is an absolute necessity for the development of those skills measured by IQ tests. Without this exposure, people, no matter how normal their genes, cannot achieve a normal IQ score. Thus it is obviously correct to state that *both* genes *and* environment are inextricably involved in the development of IQ—or, for that matter, in the development of any trait.

The controversy has to do with the differences in IQ among normal human beings, all of whom possess normal sets of human genes. Within these limits there are great differences in the sets of genes that all of us inherit from our parents. The question is: Are the IQ differences among us closely related to these differences in genes, or is the relationship between genes and IQ only a weak one?

The Concept of Heritability

The **heritability ratio** is one effort to give a quantitative answer to this question. In theory, the heritability of IQ can be estimated by comparing the IQ correlations of various types of biological relatives. For example, we know that parents and children have 50 percent of their genes in common. Grandparents and grandchildren have only 25 percent of their genes in common. Put very simply, if the heritability of IQ were very high, we would expect the IQ correlation between parent and child to be about .50, and that between grandparent and grandchild to be about .25. The actual procedures used in calculating heritability are quite complex, but the basic idea is to see how closely the resemblance in IQ of relatives corresponds to their resemblance in genetic makeup (that is, the proportion of genes they have in common).

Arthur Jensen, in an influential 1969 article, summarized a number of studies of IQ correlations among relatives within the white population. The data, Jensen argued, indicated that the heritability of IQ among whites is about .80. That figure, if correct, would indicate that 80 percent of the variance in IQ among individuals is due to the fact that they have different genes. **Variance,** as a statistical measure, is simply the square of the standard deviation (see the Appendix for a discussion of these concepts). The standard deviation of IQ scores is 15 points, so the variance in IQ is 225, or 15 squared. A standard deviation of 15 means that about 95 percent of the population have IQs between 70 and 130. To say that the heritability of IQ is .80 is to imply that if all people were brought up in exactly the same environment, the variance in IQ would be .80 times 225, or 180. The standard deviation of IQ scores would thus be reduced from 15 to 13.4, so that 95 percent of the population would then fall between about 73 and 127. This large remaining variation in IQ scores would be *entirely* the product of genetic differences among people, since, in our hypothetical example, everyone was reared in exactly the same environment. A similar calculation indicates that if the heritability of IQ were only .20, rearing everyone in the same environment should compress the range of IQs so that 95 percent of scores would fall in the narrow region between 87 and 113.

We must note, however, that very great difficulties are involved in calculating the heritability of a human trait. The basic problem is that close biological relatives not only have many genes in common, they also tend to have highly similar environments. The more closely related people are biologically, the more similar their environments are likely to have been. This **co-variance** of genes and environment, together with other difficulties, has convinced at least some authorities (Layzer, 1974; Feldman & Lewontin, 1975) that accurate or meaningful heritability estimates cannot be made for human populations. (With animals or plants, no such problem exists. The breeding of individual plants or animals can be controlled, and offspring can be assigned at random to strictly controlled environments.)

The paragraphs that follow will examine the data from which Jensen and

many others have tried to calculate the heritability of IQ. We shall not be concerned, however, with attempting to estimate a precise heritability ratio. We shall ask—more modestly, but more realistically—do the available data suggest that genetic differences are responsible for a large, moderate, or small proportion of the differences in IQ among people? These terms may seem very imprecise, but—as we shall see—so are the available data. Throughout our examination of the relevant research studies we shall try to focus on a critical question: Does this study effectively separate the effects of heredity from those of environment? To the extent that genes and environment are allowed to covary in any study, a meaningful answer about the relative importance of each cannot be obtained.

Genetic Relatedness and IQ

The simplest way—in theory, at least—of studying the genetic basis of IQ is to study identical twins who have been brought up apart from each other. Pairs of identical twins are the only individuals in the world whose genes are entirely the same. Thus if IQ is largely determined by inheritance, pairs of identical twins ought to resemble each other greatly in IQ scores. This should be true even if the twins have been reared in entirely different environments. Most twin pairs, of course, grow up in the same household and share very similar environments. There are, however, a few rare cases of identical twins who have been separated very early in life and brought up in different families. Those rare cases make up a kind of natural experiment on heredity and environment. The basic logic is simple. Two separated identical twins have their heredity in common, but not their environments. Thus if their IQs are very similar, that similarity must be due to the one factor they have in common—their heredity.

Studies of Separated Identical Twins. Because such cases are rare, there have been few studies of separated identical twins. Four investigators, however, have gathered large enough samples to make some statistical analysis possible. The largest and apparently most impressive study was made in England by the late Sir Cyril Burt (1966) (see the accompanying Highlight). The Burt study, said to be based on 53 pairs of separated twins, reported a very high IQ correlation between twins. Further, Burt indicated that there was no correlation at all in the socioeconomic status levels of the households in which the separated twins had been reared. Twins reared in households with vastly different socioeconomic levels resembled each other greatly in IQ—just as did twins reared in very similar households. Taken at face value, Burt's study appeared to provide very strong evidence for an overwhelming genetic effect on IQ. However, it has now become clear that Burt's study cannot be taken at face value. There is clear evidence that much of his published work was fraudulent, and much of his data invented. Psychologists are now unanimous—regardless of their views about heredity and environment—in rejecting Burt's discredited data.

The second largest study was also done in England by Shields (1962), who managed to test 40 pairs of separated twins. The IQ correlation obtained by Shields was .77—not as high as Burt's, but still very substantial. The difficulty, however, is that in the Shields study most of the twins seem to have been reared in quite similar environments. Some were not separated at all until they were 7 or 8 years old, and 27 of the 40 pairs were actually brought up in related branches of the same family. The twins had usually been born into

Separated at birth, the Mallifert twins meet accidentally. (Drawing by Chas. Addams; © 1981 The New Yorker Magazine, Inc.)

poor families, and the mother had felt unable to take on the burden of two more infants at the same time. The most common pattern was for the mother to keep one child and to give the other to her sister (or to the father's sister) to rear. This, of course, tended to result in the "separated" twins having similar environments. Thus Shields says of one pair: "The paternal aunts decided to take one twin each, and they have brought them up amicably, living next-door to one another in the same Midlands colliery village. . . . They are constantly in and out of each other's houses" (p. 164). This kind of close contact and highly similar environment also occurred even when the twins were brought up by unrelated families. Shields writes of another pair: "Brought up within a few hundred yards of one another. . . . Told they were twins after the girls discovered it for themselves, having gravitated to one another at school at the age of 5 . . . they were never apart, wanted to sit at the same desk . . . " (p. 189).

For the 27 Shields pairs reared in related branches of the same family, the IQ correlation was .83. For the 13 pairs reared in unrelated families, the correlation was a significantly lower .51. That is clear evidence that "separated" identical twins resemble each other more if the environments in which they have been reared are similar. We cannot deduce what the IQ correlation would be if—as Burt falsely claimed—there were *no* systematic similarities in the environments of separated pairs. The correlation, if such an ideal experiment could in fact be performed, might conceivably be .00, though few psychologists would expect this outcome. There is some reason to suppose that the correlation might be lower than the .51 observed among the Shields pairs reared by unrelated families. We have seen that even among these pairs there were substantial similarities in environment.

The two remaining studies reported results basically similar to those of Shields. The 19 pairs studied in the United States by Newman, Freeman, and Holzinger (1937) correlated .67, while the 12 pairs studied in Denmark by Juel-Nielsen (1965) correlated .62. These correlations seem substantial, but

HIGHLIGHT _____

Cyril Burt: Science, Fraud, and Policy

The late Sir Cyril Burt(1883–1971) was doubtless England's most distinguished psychologist—he was knighted by his monarch and given a medal by the American Psychological Association. Burt served for many years as a school psychologist of the London County Council. He was the first person in the English-speaking world to hold such a position.

Throughout his long life Burt conducted research on the inheritance of mental ability. He reported that he had managed to locate 53 pairs of separated identical twins. With the assistance of two collaborators, J. Conway and Margaret Howard, all the twins' IQs had supposedly been tested. Though the twins were said to have been reared in wholly unrelated environments, they resembled one another dramatically in IQ.

Burt was also the only investigator who was able to test, in the same population, large numbers of pairs of biological relatives of every sort—grandparents and grandchildren, second cousins, uncles and nieces, etc. The IQ correlations that he reported for various kinds of relatives corresponded with remarkable precision to the values one would expect if IQ were almost entirely determined by the genes. Professor Arthur Jensen (1972b) spoke for many when he wrote that Burt's work was "the most satisfactory attempt" to estimate the heritability of IQ; and that Burt's "larger, more representative samples than any investigator had ever assembled" would "secure Burt's place in the history of science."

Things began to unravel when it was first pointed out (Kamin, 1973) that in later published papers, as the size of Burt's twin samples gradually increased, the IQ correlations remained identical to the third decimal place. That is so unlikely an outcome as to be unbelievable! Many other contradictions and inconsistencies were revealed by cross-checking of Burt's many published papers. There was also a disturbing ambiguity in Burt's research reports—no details were given about what IQ tests had been used, or when or where the testing had been carried out. By 1974, Jensen was ready to agree that Burt's data were "useless for hypothesis testing." But Jensen maintained that Burt had been merely careless, not fraudulent—and that data other than Burt's ("the most satisfactory") also supported the idea of a high heritability of IQ.

In 1976 Oliver Gillie, a reporter for the *London Sunday Times,* charged in a front-page article that Burt had perpetrated the most sensational scientific fraud of the century. Burt's "collaborators" and "coauthors"— J. Conway, Margaret Howard, and others—appeared never to have existed. Testimony was available that Burt himself had written papers using their names, and that they were unknown to anybody and clearly were not in England during the time when they were supposedly testing twins! This frank labeling of Burt as a fraud was attacked by some as "unfounded defamation" (Jensen, 1976) and

(Courtesy Mrs. Gretl Archer)

"McCarthyism . . . character assassination" (Eysenck, 1977).

The argument about whether Burt was careless or a fraud was put to rest when the authorized Burt biography by Leslie Hearnshaw was published in 1979. With Burt's private papers and documents available to him, Hearnshaw was reluctantly forced to conclude that much of Burt's data was the result of systematic fraud.

With the disappearance of Burt's "data," the case for high heritability of IQ has been substantially weakened. But the unhappy story of Cyril Burt raises some troublesome questions. *Why* did he invent false data? Throughout his life Burt was interested in—and had great influence on—educational policy in England. He argued that the "11-plus exam," a form of IQ test taken at age 11, should be given to all schoolchildren in order to measure their "innate intelligence." Thus, in Burt's view, it was proper to use this test result as the basis for "streaming" children, irreversibly, into one of three educational channels. Only the children who scored very high on the test would enter the channel that led to a university education. Because of Burt's great influence, this policy was in fact adopted. Burt (1943) also argued that the limited resources in the school system should go primarily to the gifted. His rationale was that the majority were genetically too inferior to profit much from academic training, and he used the "data" he invented to support his policy recommendations.

There have been celebrated frauds in almost all of the sciences. Perhaps more disturbing than the fact that a distinguished psychologist could lie is the fact that so many people accepted Burt's data at face value. This demonstrates how preconceived strong ideas about what is true can prevent scientists from exercising their normally critical judgments. With hindsight, the embarrassing flaws and discrepancies in Burt's work are painfully obvious. Unfortunately, this flawed and fradulent work was accepted by a whole generation of psychologists, educators, and geneticists as serious science.

they cannot be attributed entirely to heredity. The twins in these studies, like those observed by Shields, tended to be reared in quite similar environments and often had considerable contact with each other. Further, there is reason to believe that the particular IQ tests used in these studies were not accurately standardized for age and for sex (Kamin, 1974). Since a pair of identical twins is always of the same age and same sex, any tendency for the test to favor a particular age group or sex will tend to make the twins appear more similar in IQ than they really are.

To sum up, the actual studies of separated identical twins have produced results much less conclusive than might have been obtained in an ideal—but in practice impossible-to-perform—experiment. The twins who have been studied do resemble each other in IQ, but—once Burt's data are rejected—they have also experienced quite similar environments. Thus there is no way of knowing how much of the observed IQ correlation is due to identical genes and how much to similar environments. There is obviously much room for disagreement in interpreting these data; if there were not, the argument about heredity, environment, and IQ would long since have ended.

Studies of Adopted Children.   The practice of adoption makes possible other kinds of studies that, in principle, might be able to unravel the combined effects of heredity and environment on IQ. A number of interesting and relevant questions can be asked about the IQs of adopted children. First, we might ask: Do adopted children tend to have normal IQs? The answer is clearly no: The average IQ of adopted children is distinctly superior. This tends to be the case even when the biological parents of the adopted children have very low IQs. For example, 100 adoptees in Iowa had an average IQ of 117 (Skodak & Skeels, 1949). The biological mothers of the same children had an average IQ of only 87. We can safely conclude that the source of the superior IQs of the adopted children must have been the excellent environment that most adoptive parents give their children. Those families that choose to adopt children—and that are selected by adoption agencies as suitable parents—tend to be highly advantaged. Thus they can provide environments that foster the development of high IQ in their children.

The beneficial effect of an adoptive environment has been dramatically illustrated in a more recent French adoption study (Schiff, Duyme, Dumaret, & Tomkiewicz, 1982). The authors located a number of children whose biological parents were unskilled workers and who had been adopted shortly after birth into upper-middle-class families. The adopted children, however, had biological siblings or half-siblings who were reared by their natural parents. There is no reason to expect any systematic genetic difference between the adopted children and their siblings, or half-sibs. Nevertheless, the adoptees, at school age, averaged 14 points higher on IQ tests than their sibs. Perhaps of more social importance, the adopted children had had to repeat one or more school grades only one-fourth as often as did the sibs reared by their own parents. These facts tell us that environment can have a large effect on IQ and school performance. They tell us little, however, about the *relative* importance of heredity and environment. The results do tell us that we could reduce the school-failure rates and increase the IQs of the children of unskilled workers by providing them with the kinds of environments typical of middle-class adopting families.

There have been a number of attempts to compare the IQ correlation between adopted parents and adopted children with that between ordinary, biological parents and children. Biological children living in normal families receive both their genes and their environment from their parents. Adopted

children, however, receive only their environment from their adoptive parents. Thus, to the extent that genes are important determinants of IQ, one would expect the correlation between biological parent-child pairs to be larger than that between adoptive parent-child pairs.

The earliest studies of adopted children showed clearly that the IQ correlation between adoptive parent and child was relatively small—and clearly smaller than that observed between parent and child in ordinary biological families (Burks, 1928; Leahy, 1935). This kind of comparison, however, may be misleading. We have already noted that adoptive parents, having been rigorously selected by adoption agencies, are a very special group of people. There is relatively little variation among them in IQ, and relatively little variation in the excellence of the environments they provide for their adopted children. When there is little variation in a measurement, correlations involving that measure tend to be low. Thus the special and unique characteristics of adoptive families make it hazardous to compare them to ordinary families.

Many adoptive families, however, contain not only an adopted child, but also a *biological* child of the same parents. These families seem especially suited for investigating the nature-nurture problem. They are all "special" families, all having wished to adopt a child and all having been selected as suitable by an adoption agency. Within each family the adopted child has received only the environment from the parents, and the biological child has received both genes and environment from the very same parents. To the degree that IQ is passed on through the genes, within such families the correlation between parent and biological child should be larger than that between parent and adopted child.

In two adoption studies data were collected from a reasonably large number of these special families. The correlations between the mother and her two kinds of children, in each of the studies, are given in Table 10–4 (top). There is obviously no significant difference between the two correlations within either study. The child's IQ resembles the mother's IQ to the same degree, whether or not the child and mother are genetically related. This result clearly does not support the idea that IQ is a very heritable trait. The study by Scarr and Weinberg (1977), it might be noted, has one rather unusual feature. The adopted children are black, and the adoptive parents—as well as the biological children of those parents—are white.

The picture seems rather different, however, when the correlations between the father and his two kinds of children are considered. These data, given in Table 10–4 (bottom), show that the father more closely resembles his biological than his adopted child. That is especially the case in Scarr and Weinberg's transracial adoption study. There is no obvious reason why the data for fathers and for mothers should differ in this way, although it is possible to invent plausible reasons. For example, fathers in these special families might tend to interact more with their biological children than with their adopted children, and this is why their biological children resemble them more in IQ than their adopted children do. If this is true, then the resemblance in IQ between biological child and father reflects the contribution of environment to IQ. Another possibility is that the fathers in these families tend not to interact with their children at all, whether the children are biologically or adoptively related. If this is so, then the resemblance in IQ between the biologically related fathers and children would reflect the contribution of heredity to IQ. Until more detailed studies are done, we cannot decide between these (or other) plausible explanations.

We can also look at correlations between various types of siblings in these two studies. The families contain some pairs of biological siblings. That is,

Table 10–4: Mother-Child and Father-Child IQ Correlations in Adoptive Families with Biological Children.

	Texas Adoption Project (Horn Et Al., 1979)	Transracial Adoption (Scarr and Weinberg, 1977)
Correlation of mother and biological child	.20 (N = 162)	.34 (N = 100)
Correlation of mother and adopted child	.22 (N = 151)	.29 (N = 66)
Correlation of father and biological child	.28 (N = 163)	.34 (N = 102)
Correlation of father and adopted child	.12 (N = 152)	.07 (N = 67)

(From Horn, Loehlin, & Willerman, 1979)

the parents have had two or more biological children of their own. Within each of these families there are also one or more adopted children. There are therefore two kinds of biologically unrelated sibling pairs. There are some pairs of genetically unrelated adopted children reared by the same parents; and there are some genetically unrelated pairs consisting of one biological child and one adopted child of the same parents. The correlations for all three types of sibling pairs, in each study, are given in Table 10–5. The samples are in some cases relatively small, and the correlations fluctuate somewhat. What is clear, however, is that there is no tendency for the biologically related pairs to be more highly correlated than the unrelated pairs. Within the Scarr and Weinberg study, the biological pairs are all white, the adopted pairs are all black, and the biological-adopted pairs consist of one white and one black child each.

The Texas Adoption Project was able to obtain the IQ scores of the biological mothers of the adopted children. Their average IQ was lower, by about six points, than that of the adoptive mothers. Despite this, the adopted children and the biological children of the adoptive parents each had the same average IQ of 112. Thus it is clear that the adoptive parents were able to transmit high IQs equally to *all* their children—whether or not they shared genes with them. These IQ averages, according to the authors of the Texas Project, suggest "a heritability of IQ that is close to zero" (Horn, Loehlin, & Willerman, 1979). From a consideration of all the correlational data in their

Table 10–5: Sibling IQ Correlations in Adoptive Families with Biological Children.

	Texas Adoption Project (Horn Et Al., 1979)	Transracial Adoption (Scarr and Weinberg, 1977)
Biological-biological (related) pairs	.35 (N = 46)	.37 (N = 75)
Adopted-adopted (unrelated) pairs	———	.49 (N = 21)
Biological-adopted (unrelated) pairs	.29 (N = 197)	.30 (N = 134)

Sex Differences. Two large groups of considerable interest to most people are the male and female sexes. The answer to the question of whether the two sexes differ in measured IQ is straightforward: No, they do not. But this might be simply because test makers do not believe that males and females *should* differ in IQ. The tests of general intelligence in common use have all been standardized so as to do away with, or at least to minimize, possible sex differences.

Recall how IQ tests are designed in the first place. The first step is always to designate groups of people that are assumed to differ in intellectual ability, such as different age groups. The next step is to try out test items, retaining those that differentiate between the different intelligence-level groups. Two types of items are then always eliminated when making up tests: items that everyone answers in the same way, and items that are answered more easily by the *lower* intelligence group. The items that everyone can answer are clearly useless because they do not discriminate between people of different intellectual abilities. The items that are answered more often by the people with presumably lower ability are worse than useless, they are misleading; so these, too, are eliminated from the test.

If we assume, as most test makers have assumed, that men and women do not differ in intellectual ability, then standard test-construction practice would be to eliminate from the tests items that disproportionately favor one sex or the other. Where this has not been done, items favoring one sex have been deliberately balanced by items favoring the other. The equality of the sexes in IQ may thus be more a fact of test construction than a fact of nature. The point is that it would be easy to construct a test with all the surface characteristics of an IQ test to make *either* sex look more "intelligent." For example, Willerman (1979) has reported that among a Texas sample of husbands and wives, one item was successfully passed by 70 percent of males but only 30 percent of females. The item is included in the Wechsler test, and it asks what is the temperature at which water boils.

When specialized tests have not been deliberately standardized to remove sex differences, there is some suggestion that males may do a little better on quantitative items, and females a little better on verbal items. These are not large differences, however, and they are not consistently found in all studies. The most consistently found sex difference—at least after early childhood—is on tasks involving spatial visualization, on which males tend to do better. We do not know to what extent the sex difference in spatial abilities is genetic and to what extent it is cultural. The fact that women are less knowledgeable than men about the temperature at which water boils should not be taken to indicate the intellectual inferiority of females! We might also note from this example that inability to answer an IQ test question does not necessarily imply a handicap in adjusting to the demands of the real world. The Texas wives were probably at least as adept as their husbands in the constructive use of boiling water in the kitchen.

Social-Class Differences. There are large and clear differences in the average IQs of members of different social classes and occupations, and they are not surprising ones. Put most simply, people who work with their heads—especially professional people—generally do very well on IQ tests. People who work with their hands do less well, and unskilled workers have still lower scores than skilled workers. The World War II testing program of the United States Army, using the Army General Classification Test, found different average IQs across a wide range of civilian occupations. These are il-

lustrated in Figure 10–5. Note that there is a considerable range of IQs *within* a given occupation—enough of a range, in fact, that the most intelligent teamsters and farmhands easily outscore the least intelligent engineers and accountants. This means that we can't assume that people are "smart" or "dumb" merely by knowing their occupations. Nor, as it happens, can we predict how well they will do in their occupations on the basis of where they fall in the range of IQs. For example, a recent study of horse-racing handicappers (Ceci, 1986) found no relation between IQ scores and the ability to perform the complex cognitive tasks required by the unusual occupational pursuit.

The differences in average IQ among people in various occupations or in various socioeconomic classes is also found among the children of these people, although the differences are not so large as in the parent generation. The 1937 restandardization of the Stanford-Binet test found substantial differences among children whose parents had been grouped into seven occupational classes. These data are given in Table 10–6. The same kind of social-class differences were again observed when the WISC–R test was restandardized in 1974 (Kaufman & Doppelt, 1976). The 6- to 16-year-old children of "professional and technical workers" had an average IQ of 109.4, compared to 92.1 for the children of "laborers, farm laborers, and farm foremen."

The existence of IQ differences among adults in various occupations and social classes says nothing at all about the genetic or environmental basis of these differences. People with high IQs, no matter how they got them, tend to end up in the more prestigious and better-paid occupations. On the other hand, we do not know whether high or low IQ is really the *cause* of entering a given occupation. Possibly, for example, family background or traditions, a university degree, or social sophistication is more important than IQ in determining occupational choice (Jencks, 1972). In particular, the influence of education should not be ignored. Among Terman's (1954) sample of grownups who had been judged gifted as children, 70 percent were college

Figure 10–5 The averages and ranges of IQs in a number of different occupations. There are distinctly different average IQs across the range of occupations, and there is also considerable variation within any given occupation. (Harrell & Harrell, 1945)

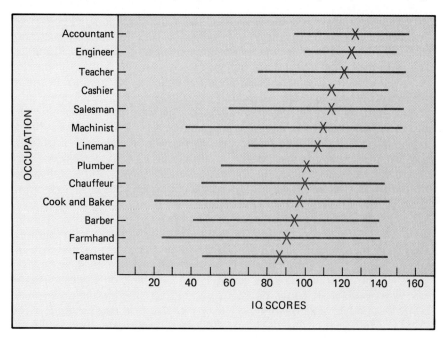

Table 10–6: Average IQ of Children, Ages 2–18, According to Father's Occupation.

Father's Occupation	Children's Average IQ
Professional	115.9
Semiprofessional and managerial	111.9
Clerical, skilled trades, and retail business	107.1
Semiskilled, minor clerical, and minor business	104.4
Slightly skilled	99.1
Day laborers, urban and rural	96.3
Rural owners	94.2

(After McNemar, 1942)

graduates and 90 percent had at least some college. According to Cronbach (1984): "The key to adult achievement seems to have been amount of education. . . . Among equally educated adults in the sample, the early test scores had no relation to the level of career achievement" (p. 242).

That children born into different social classes have different IQs can be—and, as we might expect, has been—interpreted in various ways. There is no doubt that the environments of children differ widely across social classes, and it seems reasonable to believe that this is the source of the observed IQ differences. However, social-class differences in children's IQs appear before they are 5 years old. This implies that the relevant environmental differences must begin to exert their effects even before the child has entered school.

The alternative interpretation is to assume that social classes differ genetically, and that genes making for high IQ occur more often in the upper social classes. This idea was argued vigorously by the early American translators of Binet's test (Terman, 1916; Goddard, 1920; Yerkes & Foster, 1923). The same notion has been proposed somewhat more recently by Herrnstein (1973), who argued that in a free society, people born with "good" genes tend to rise in social class and to transmit their good genes to their offspring. This must result, according to Herrnstein, in a "meritocracy"—a society in which the upper classes are genetically gifted, and in which the genetically superior children of upper-class parents necessarily (and justifiably) remain in the upper class. This idea and variants of it are as old as civilization. Plato, for example, argued that slaves were by nature born to be slaves, and that Athenians were born to be free men. The evidence to support the hereditary basis of social-class membership has not become much more convincing since Plato's time.

We can note that the 1937 restandardization of the Stanford-Binet test also indicated (Table 10–7) that children born in farm areas had much lower average IQs than children born in cities. This seems an obvious consequence of the greater educational and environmental opportunities available in cities (at least in 1937). The argument has also been made, however, that genetically bright people tended to migrate to the stimulating and rewarding cities, leaving a residue of duller folk, who have genetically dull children, in rural areas. This hypothetical argument is not likely to convince many farmers; further, by the time the WISC–R was restandardized in 1974, the urban-rural difference in average IQ had sunk to a mere 2 IQ points. That, as Kaufman and Doppelt (1976) suggested, might well be attributed to the increasing im-

Table 10–7: Average IQ of Children (Ages 2–18) in Urban, Suburban, and Rural Areas.

Type of Area	Children's Average IQ
Urban	106.2
Suburban	104.9
Rural	96.6

(After McNemar, 1942)

pact of the mass media on rural families and to improved educational facilities in these areas.

Black-White Differences.   The most inflamed arguments about the heritability of IQ have involved the fact that, in the United States, black people on average tend to score some 10 to 15 points lower in IQ than do white people. This fact has been known for a long time. The Army testing program of World War I indicated such a difference—and it also indicated that black people in some northern states had a higher average IQ than whites in some southern states. To some, the data proclaimed that black people were genetically inferior to white people. To others, the data indicated that IQ was determined by educational and environmental opportunities.

The influential article by Jensen (1969), already cited, not only argued that the heritability of IQ among white people was .80, but it also maintained that the difference in average IQ between black people and white people was probably of genetic origin. Further, in Jensen's view, attempts at compensatory education of underprivileged children—such as Head Start and other interventions aimed at increasing the children's intellectual competence—had failed, and were bound to fail. That was so, said Jensen, because of the high heritability of IQ. Since then, of course, the effectiveness and success of such early-intervention programs have been well documented (Zigler & Berman, 1983).

There are few more obvious social facts than the overwhelming discrimination to which black people have been exposed throughout American history. The clear environmental differences between black people and white people seem, to most social scientists, obviously related to the difference in average IQ. The fact is, however, that black people and white people do inherit somewhat different genes, which affect, among other things, skin color and hair texture. Thus it is difficult to *disprove* the idea that genetic differences between the races *might* be responsible for the IQ difference. (*Why* one would want to prove or disprove such an idea is another question—perhaps better left untouched in this textbook.)

There seems little point in attempting to summarize in detail the multitude of research studies on black-white IQ differences. (see the Highlight: Race and IQ). The topic seems almost an obsession among some American researchers, which in view of the importance of race in American society, seems scarcely surprising. For example, there are studies to show that light-skinned black people have higher IQs than dark-skinned black people. This has been interpreted as indicating that degree of black ancestry is a predictor (genetically) of IQ. The same result, however, has also been interpreted as a consequence of the lesser discrimination against light-skinned black people. Other studies have focused on regional differences among blacks. The fact that northern blacks have higher IQs than southern blacks (and than southern whites in some states) has been interpreted as a result of better educational opportunity—but it has also been interpreted as a consequence of selective migration of genetically bright black people from the South to the North, or as a result of greater black-white intermarriage in the North. The point should be obvious: Until and unless black people have the same environmental experiences as white people, those who wish to argue about the basis of the observed IQ difference will be free to do so. Yet, while their arguments may be ingenious, they will be without convincing evidence. The pity is that in a society that supposedly treats people as individuals, and not as nameless representatives of particular groups, so much time and energy

There are many kinds of studies that make it very implausible to suggest that the black-white difference in average IQ is genetically determined. Lee (1951) studied black children who had arrived in Philadelphia with their migrating parents from the South. When first tested, the children had very low IQs, but after enrolling in the Philadelphia schools and living in the city for some time, their IQs increased steadily, by an average of about 6 points. There was no such increase in IQ over time observed among a control group of black children who had been born in Philadelphia. This result indicates that superior educational and cultural opportunities in the city (at least at the time of Lee's study) served to elevate the environmentally depressed IQ scores of southern black children.

There is clearly no support for a genetic interpretation in a study by Eyferth (1961) conducted in Germany. The children in this study were all born out of wedlock to white German mothers. The fathers were American servicemen, some black and some white. The race of the father made no overall difference in the average IQs of the children. Other researchers (Willerman, Naylor, & Myrianthopoulos, 1974) studied 101 white women who had borne children by black fathers, and 28 black women who had borne children by white fathers. There is no genetic reason to suppose that the IQs of these two types of interracial children should be different, and there were no significant differences between the two sets of parents in socioeconomic status. But the average IQ of interracial children born to white mothers was 102, compared to 93 for equally interracial children born to black mothers.

This outcome makes no genetic sense, but it is open to a number of environmental interpretations—for instance, the mother is the main "teacher" of the child, and white mothers had not experienced racial prejudice while growing up.

The effects of transracial adoption (at least on IQ) have been studied by Scarr and Weinberg (1976). The average IQ of 99 black and interracial children adopted before they were 1 year old by advantaged white families was a very high 110. That average score is considerably higher than would have been observed if the children had not been adopted. The families adopting these children were obviously able to endow them with high IQs by nongenetic means. That is not to say that the adoption of black children by white families is necessarily a good policy; and it is not to say that being reared in a *white* family increased and adopted children's IQs. If the same children had been adopted into advantaged *black* families, the same IQ result would presumably have occurred. We have no information about what would happen if white children were adopted into black families, since such adoptions are very rare in our society.

Those studies that have most directly examined whether there might be a genetic black-white IQ difference have consistently failed to find supporting evidence. We cannot prove the nonexistence of such a difference, but we cannot prove the nonexistence of unicorns either. We should be aware that our persistent interest in this question may well have nonscientific roots.

have been wasted on an irrelevant and, strictly speaking, unanswerable question.

Most present-day psychologists believe that there is no evidence that clearly supports a genetic interpretation of black-white IQ differences. Many also believe that what is known about environmental and cultural differences between the races seems adequate to explain the observed IQ difference.

Although Jensen (1969) asserted that the heritability of IQ among whites is .80, our own review has indicated that this number is unrealistically high. The fact is that even if IQ heritability *were* very high, within both the white and the black populations, this would *not* necessarily mean that a difference between the two races in average IQ had any genetic basis. The concept of heritability is relevant only to *differences* among individuals in some measured trait, not to the average level of that trait. Thus, for example, any environmental treatment that immediately increased everyone's IQ would have no effect on the heritability of IQ. Those who had average IQs before the new environmental treatment would still have average IQs, but the average itself would be higher.

The fact that the heritability of a trait is high does not imply that it cannot be profoundly affected by appropriate environmental intervention. To see this clearly, imagine two sacks of seeds, each containing the same mixture of many different genetic varieties of corn. The seeds from the white sack are planted in a field with good soil, given plenty of fertilizer and water, and kept

free of weeds. The seeds from the black sack are planted in a field with poor soil and given no special care. *Within* each of these two fields some plants will grow taller than others, and these differences will be entirely determined by genetics (the different strains of corn). But there will also be a difference in average heights *between* the two fields: The corn in the "advantaged" field will grow taller, on the average, than the corn in the "disadvantaged" one. The difference between the two fields will be entirely a result of environment. This example should make it clear how fruitless—or even absurd—it is to ask whether heredity or environment is responsible for differences between human groups.

IQ TESTING AND SOCIAL HISTORY

The controversy surrounding the use and interpretation of IQ tests has a long history. Perhaps hindsight makes ethical judgments easier than they appeared at the time, but the social biases and racism of the early mental-testing movement in the United States seem shocking by today's standards. When Lewis Terman first published his Stanford-Binet test in 1916 he wrote confidently that black and Mexican children *would* be found to have lower average IQs than whites, and that such differences could never be eradicated by educational or cultural changes. He argued that such children "should be segregated in special classes. . . . They cannot master abstractions, but they can often be made efficient workers. . . . There is no possibility at present of convincing society that they should not be allowed to reproduce. . . . They constitute a grave problem because of their unusually prolific breeding" (p. 92). Writing later of children in the low-IQ ranges, Terman (1917) urged society to "curtail the increasing spawn of degeneracy" (p. 165).

The major social involvement of the early IQ testers, however, was with the long national debate over immigration policy that took place before and after World War I. The United States Public Health Service in 1912 invited Henry Goddard to apply the new mental tests to samples of European immigrants arriving at Ellis Island, New York. The tests, Goddard reported, showed that 83 percent of Jews, 80 percent of Hungarians, 79 percent of Italians, and 87 percent of Russians were "feeble-minded." There was no problem, Goddard believed, posed by the fact that immigrants did not know English. The verbal tests could be translated, and they could be supplemented with "culture-fair" performance tests. The use of mental tests "for the detection of feeble-minded aliens," Goddard proudly reported (1917), had greatly increased the number of would-be immigrants deported from Ellis Island.

Those who opposed immigration from the countries of southeastern Europe were greatly encouraged by the IQ data collected by the United States Army during World War I (Yerkes, 1921). The first mass mental testing in history took place during the war, when people drafted into the Army were given one of two specially developed group IQ tests. The Alpha test was a typical paper-and-pencil verbal test, while the Beta test was a performance test specially designed for those who were illiterate or who could not understand English-language instructions. The data indicated clearly that the highest IQs were scored by immigrants from England, Scotland, Canada, and the countries of northern and western Europe. The lowest IQs were those of immigrants from southeastern Europe—Italians, Russians, Poles, and Jews. The psychologists who summarized these findings wrote simply: "The Latin and Slavic countries stand low" (Yerkes, 1921).

Instructions for part of the Beta test during World War I. (The New York Public Library)

The Army immigrant data were analyzed in great detail by Carl Brigham in his book *A Study of American Intelligence* (1923). Those immigrants who had lived in America for 20 years or more before being tested in the Army, Brigham reported, had IQs every bit as high as native-born Americans. The immigrants who had lived in the country fewer than 5 years tended, with alarming frequency, to be "feeble-minded." These facts might have suggested that IQ scores were heavily influenced by familiarity with American culture and language, even when "nonverbal" performance tests were used. That was not Brigham's interpretation. "We must assume," Brigham declared, "that we are measuring native inborn intelligence." The explanation, according to Brigham, was that immigrants who had arrived in the country 20 years earlier were mostly from northern and western Europe, with much "Nordic blood." The more recent immigrants from southeastern Europe contained inferior "Alpine" and "Mediterranean" blood.

Brigham's book is a profound embarrassment today, but in its time—only six decades ago—it was taken as serious and responsible science. The genetically inferior, Brigham wrote, were reproducing their poor stock at an alarming rate. Further, " we are incorporating the negro into our racial stock, while all of Europe is comparatively free from this taint. . . . The steps that should be taken . . . must of course be dictated by science and not by political expediency. . . . The really important steps are those looking toward the prevention of the continued propagation of defective strains in the present population" (p. 210). The "prevention" of reproduction by defective stocks already in the country, Brigham urged, should be coupled with a law designed to reduce the number of inferior Alpine and Mediterranean immigrants.

The Army data and Brigham's book were cited repeatedly when Congress debated the new immigration law of 1924. The new law did in fact dramatically reduce the proportion of immigrants from southeastern Europe. This was done by assigning each European country an annual quota of allowable immigrants—and by basing the quotas on the United States census of 1890,

before the massive influx of southeastern Europeans had begun. The naive genetic interpretation of the Army IQ data, widely accepted at the time, helped in some measure to pass a racist immigration law that had lasting effects on American Society.* This early episode in the history of IQ testing is obviously relevant to today's concerns over racial or ethnic differences. As experience has taught us, overconfident and ethnocentric interpretations of IQ data can have profound consequences.

*At a later date (1930) Brigham retracted his earlier analysis of the Army data, admitting that he had been wrong and "pretentious." By that time the new immigration law had already been in effect for 6 years, and Brigham had become secretary of the College Entrance Examination Board. There he developed a test with which many students are familiar, the Scholastic Aptitude Test.

SUMMARY

1. Theories of intelligence generally agree that there are two types of factors: a general intellectual ability; and specific abilities, such as verbal, mathematical, and spatial. Theorists do disagree on the numbers of factors, ranging from 2 (Spearman) to 120 (Guilford).

2. Alfred Binet set out to devise a test that would predict a child's performance in school. He used the concept of *mental age (MA)* to assess the child's mental ability as compared to his or her *chronological age (CA)*. Stern developed the concept of the *intelligence quotient (IQ)*, the ratio of MA to CA multiplied by 100; at any given chronological age the average IQ is 100.

3. The Stanford-Binet test was a revised version of Binet's test, which was introduced into the United States by Lewis Terman in 1916. Since then, the test items have been modified and restandardized in 1937, 1960, and 1972.

4. *Achievement tests* measure how much one has learned before taking the test; *aptitude tests* are used to predict some future performance. The difference between the two lies more in the purpose to which the test is put than in the types of questions asked.

5. People are considered mentally retarded if they have an IQ below 70 coupled with inadequate social and occupational adjustment. For the great majority of retarded persons, no physical cause can be specified; some cases of severe retardation are related to biological accidents or genetic disorders such as *Down's syndrome*.

6. A 50-year study begun by Terman in 1922 showed that people with very high IQs tend to live productive and successful lives, disproving the notion that such people are somehow "freakish."

7. Both the Stanford-Binet test and the Wechsler Intelligence Scales are individual tests, designed to be administered by a trained examiner to one person at a time. The Wechsler scales were the first to use the concept of a *deviation IQ*, comparing a person's score to the scores of others of the same age in the standardization sample.

8. The Army Alpha and Beta tests are examples of group tests; they were developed to test draftees in World War I. The Alpha test is a verbal paper-and-pencil test; the Beta test was designed as a performance test for illiterate or foreign-born draftees.

9. Guilford proposed 120 factors of intelligence, each representing a different intellectual ability. Guilford and his followers developed radically different mental tests, some of the most interesting of which tested *divergent* rather than *convergent thinking*.

10. Whether intelligence is inherited or is a function of environment is the subject of much controversy. The *heritability ratio* is one effort to answer the question quantitatively.

11. Various ways of trying to control for one factor or the other include studying identical twins raised apart; comparing adopted children's IQs to those of both their adoptive and their biological parents; and studying adopted children in families that also have biological children. There are difficulties in all these approaches, and we can only say that heritability appears to be somewhere between moderate and low.

12. Researchers have also examined differences among groups in average IQ scores based on sex, race, and social class. There are such differences, but we cannot say whether they are genetically or environmentally based.

SUGGESTED READINGS

BLOCK, N. J., & DWORKIN, G. (1976). *The IQ controversy*. New York: Pantheon. A well-selected and broad set of relevant readings, some old and some new.

BRODY, E. B. & BRODY, N. (1976). *Intelligence: Nature, determinants, and consequences*. New York: Academic Press. An advanced and thorough review, with balanced coverage of the nature-nurture controversy.

EYSENCK, H. J., vs. KAMIN, L. (1981). *The intelligence controversy*. New York: John Wiley. A debate, complete with rebuttals, between two protagonists with very different views.

GLASER, R. & BOND, L. (Eds.) (1981). Testing: Concepts, policy, practice and research. *American Psychologist 36*, 997–1199. This is a special issue devoted entirely to psychological testing. The topics range from a primer on testing to issues involved in testing children, minority groups, job applicants, and those seeking licensure and professional certification. This is an excellent single source on a broad range of important testing-related topics, with a broad spectrum of opinion on the uses and limitations of psychological testing.

GOULD, S. J. (1981). *The Mismeasure of Man*. New York: Norton. An articulate history and critique of the biological approach to measuring intelligence, from craniometry to the hereditary claims of IQ testing. Gould argues that the concept of general intelligence, "g," is an erroneous one, the result of arbitrary interpretations of factor analysis.

The viewpoint is environmentalist, the writing lively and informative.

JENSEN, A. R. (1972). *Genetics and education*. New York: Harper & Row. Reprints several of the author's articles, including the 1969 *Harvard Educational Review* article that rekindled the nature-nurture debate.

KAMIN, L. J. (1974). *The Science and politics of I.Q.* Hillsdale, N.J.: Erlbaum. Reviews much of the same material covered by Eysenck and Kamin's book, but with a clear environmental emphasis.

LOEHLIN, J. C., LINDZEY, G., & SPUHLER, J. N. (1975). *Race differences in intelligence*. San Francisco: W. F. Freeman. Though focused on data relevant to race differences, this book is also broadly concerned with the heritability of IQ.

SAMUDA, R. J. (1975). *Psychological testing of American minorities: Issues and consequences*. New York: Dodd, Mead. Testing from a minority perspective.

STERNBERG, R. J. (1985). *Beyond IQ: A Triarchic Theory of Human Intelligence*. Cambridge: Cambridge University Press. An attempt to synthesize and integrate the various theories of intelligence. Sternberg presents a new theory that incorporates the ideas of both general and independent factors theories. The history of intelligence testing and of theories of intelligence is presented clearly and insightfully.

11 Biological Bases of Motivation

I t is clear that much of human behavior is purposeful or designed to attain some goal. The study of such purposes and goals is the study of **motivation.** You press a series of digits on your phone *because* you want to speak to a friend. You open the refrigerator door *because* you are hungry and want a snack. You go to college *because* you want to become a doctor. These reasons for behavior are often referred to as **motives,** which seem to explain why the behavior occurred.

As simple as the concept of motivation may seem, it has proved very difficult to analyze experimentally. Part of the problem is that the same actions or behaviors may be consistent with very different motives. A salesman may laugh because your joke amused him or because he wants to sell you something. Guests may accept a glass of wine at a party because they like its taste or the relaxing effect of the alcohol, because they are simply thirsty, or even because they don't want to appear different from the other guests. In fact, their motives may actually be a mixture of several of these possibilities.

Another problem in studying motivation is distinguishing primary from secondary motives. For example, you might say a man works at a job because he needs to earn a salary; that is, his motivation is to earn money. But is this his primary motivation, or only a secondary one? Is the primary source of motivation a need for food and shelter, things that are purchased with the salary?

Finally, a third problem in studying motives is that people may not be fully aware of the underlying reasons for their actions and may even believe they are doing something for one reason when, in fact, their true motive is quite

The most basic of our biological needs, food and drink, are lovingly depicted by Paul Cézanne in "Natura Morta." (Art Resource)

different. *Unconscious motives* of this sort were central to Sigmund Freud's theory of human motivation. A woman might consciously believe that she sought the presidency of a business concern because of a desire to maximize her income, when her real motive was to show a long-dead father that she could be just as successful as he was. Even someone's motives for the simple act of eating may be difficult to discern. Is the adult who orders an ice-cream sundae simply hungry? Or is he compensating himself for his loneliness with the sort of "treat" his mother used to give him when he was a child?

In this chapter we will consider the motivations arising from basic needs that are common to both humans and animals, such as the needs for food, liquids, and sexual gratification. The beauty of this body of work is that it deals with motivation at both a biological and a behavioral level. It also reveals how much these basic motives are overlaid by social and psychological factors in humans. In the next chapter we will consider the uniquely human aspects of motivation.

THEORIES OF MOTIVATION

Historical Theories

People have always been interested in the question of what makes us do what we do. The prevalent belief from the time of Plato and Aristotle through the Middle Ages, and probably even today, is that the mind controls behavior and that people are free to choose what they will do. Although their decisions may be influenced by outside stimuli and by internal needs and desires, their actions are controlled by human reason. This view is referred to as the doctrine of **free will.**

Even in Plato's time there were some who argued against the idea of free will. The Greek philosopher Democritus believed that all events in nature are the results of inflexible chains of cause and effect. If we knew all the laws of cause and effect, we would be able to predict the behavior of people as well as we can the motions of inanimate objects. This doctrine is called **determinism.**

The deterministic viewpoint became increasingly popular after the publication of Charles Darwin's *On the Origin of Species* (1859). If humans and animals have the same ancestral origins and are closely related biologically, it seems reasonable to assume that human behavior—like animal behavior—is subject to the laws of cause and effect. From the behavioristic viewpoint of someone like B. F. Skinner, once one specifies how the environment determines behavior, there is nothing more to say about motivation. For most people, the idea of "free will" seems more humanistic than determinism. How many of us want to feel that our actions are determined solely by the environment? Yet in his book *Beyond Freedom and Dignity* (1971), Skinner argues that it is really the myth of free will that is most dangerous to a full development of the human potential. According to Skinner, only when we accept the fact that much of our behavior is controlled by politicians, advertisers, and other social manipulators will we begin to democratically devise laws that limit such selfish manipulation.

A very important concept that Darwin did not originate, but one that he did help to bring into prominence, was that of **instincts,** genetically based behavioral tendencies. To Darwin, an instinct was something like a complicated reflex: an innate pattern of behavior that is emitted in response to

some stimulus. Natural selection, he held, operated in the same way on instincts as on any other innate characteristic. Slight variations of a given instinct occur in a population, and the variation that is most successful is preserved (because its possessor is more likely to survive) and is passed on.

Some later theorists believed that instincts provided not only the behavior itself but also the *motivation* behind the behavior. For example, William James (1890) assumed that a hen possesses the innate behavior pattern for sitting on eggs, as well as the more important innate tendency to *want* to sit on eggs. In James's own words:

> To the broody hen the notion would probably seem monstrous that there should be a creature in the world to whom a nestful of eggs was not the utterly fascinating and precious and never-to-be-too-much-sat-upon object which it is to her. (p. 210)

James felt that "man has a far greater variety of impulses than any lower animal," so, therefore, man must possess more instincts.

The belief that the motivation behind human behavior is provided chiefly by instincts reached its height in the second decade of the twentieth century. Unconscious instincts, such as repressed sexual desire, played a central role in the theories of Sigmund Freud (see Chapter 15). In the United States some psychologists drew up lists of "instincts" such as curiosity, pugnacity, and gregariousness. Almost every kind of human behavior could then be attributed to the motivating force of some instinct or other: A man who washed his hands was impelled by the Instinct of Cleanliness; a woman who bought a pencil was responding to the Instinct of Acquisitiveness. The problem was that saying a behavior was motivated by an instinct didn't help at all in understanding the behavior—saying that people have an instinct of cleanliness doesn't tell us any more than saying that they generally keep themselves clean. Ethologists generally use the term *instinct* in a more restricted sense, identifying specific *motor programs* that are evoked by particular *sign* or *releasing* stimuli: for example, the aggressive behavior of the stickleback fish evoked by the sight of a red underbelly (see Chapter 1), or the egg-rolling behavior of geese evoked by the sight of a round object outside the nest (see the Highlight: Ethology and Learning in Chapter 6). While these instinctual patterns are often modified by experience, they may also express themselves only when an animal is in a specific biological state (e.g., hormonal condition during the mating season). Thus tendencies to behave in certain ways, both instinctual and learned, are clearly related to shifts in biological states. The study of how various biological processes influence behavior has been a central concern in the study of motivation.

Homeostasis and Drive Theory

The idea that replaced the concept of instinct was based on the notion of **homeostasis.** The physiologist Walter Cannon (1939) introduced this term to describe the way the body maintains a balance or equilibrium in its internal environment. For instance, if the temperature of the body drops just a little, the blood vessels in the skin constrict so that less heat escapes into the air (see Figure 11–1). If body temperature goes up, the blood vessels in the skin dilate and the sweat glands begin to function. Thus the temperature of a healthy person normally remains within narrow limits, thanks to the body's internal "thermostat." In a similar way, if the amount of water in the tissues is

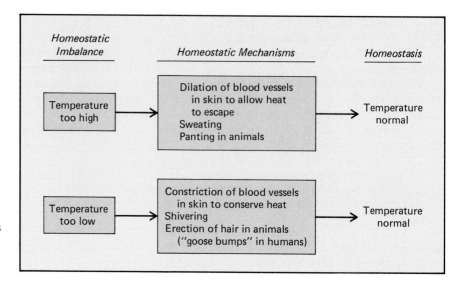

Figure 11–1 This chart shows how temperature regulation in humans and animals can be seen as a process that maintains homeostasis. Normal temperature is a balance between heat gain and loss.

too high, the excess is excreted as urine; if it is too low, the person becomes thirsty and will drink the necessary amount of fluids. In general, whenever the body deviates too far in one direction or another from its ideal state, a response is triggered that restores it to equilibrium. The term *homeostasis* is used to mean both the ideal balanced state and the process by which the state is maintained; the bodily functions that accomplish this are called **homeostatic mechanisms.**

What does homeostasis have to do with motivation? The clearest statement of the theory came from Clark Hull (1943). To Hull, any deviation from homeostatic balance produces a **need.** A need, in turn, produces a **drive.** A drive is a biological state that acts as motivational force, an inciter of action. For example, an animal deprived of nourishment for a day or two has a need for food. The need creates a drive; in this case the drive is called *hunger.* The drive motivates the animal to search for food and to eat when it is found. Eating the food soon restores the animal to a state of homeostasis. The result is what Hull called **drive reduction.** Drive reduction, according to this theory, is what gives positive reinforcers (such as food) their power to increase the probability of a response in operant conditioning (see Chapter 6).

Needs do not result solely from a *lack* of something. Pain or any strong stimulus is assumed to produce a deviation from homeostasis as well. The result is a drive to escape the stimulus. Thus the cessation of pain is a highly effective primary reinforcer.

Problems with Drive Theory. One problem with drive theory is that not all needs produce drives. For example, a person exposed to carbon monoxide might be dying for lack of oxygen, but oxygen deprivation creates no drives. The recent popularity of hot tubs has provided some additional tragic evidence of homeostatic imbalance without a drive. People have died while immersed to the neck in hot water because their bodies gave them no signal that they were becoming dangerously overheated. (The usual physiological mechanisms for controlling body temperature don't work under water.)

There can be needs without drives; there also can be drives without needs. Motivation sometimes seems to arise as a result of external stimuli, instead of from some internal physiological imbalance. An external stimulus of this sort, one that has the capacity to motivate behavior even if a drive was

apparently not present initially, is called an **incentive.** The presence of an incentive is likely to arouse a drive that was previously quiescent. One incentive, to most humans and to animals of many species, is anything that tastes sweet, whether it reduces the hunger drive or not. Rats will press a lever to receive a drop of saccharin solution and will continue to do so over months of testing. Moreover, sweet foods retain their incentive value even in the absence of a need for nutrition. You might have just finished a big meal and be not the least bit hungry, but when offered a tempting dessert you may be unable to resist it.

Even when the drive-inducing qualities of external stimuli are added, there is a great variety of human and animal behavior that cannot be explained in terms of the kinds of drives we have been discussing. Drive theorists assumed that if the organism is not suffering from a physiological deprivation or motivated to escape from a strong stimulus, it will do nothing at all. But that is not the case. Animals act as though they *want* to be stimulated, want novelty, want to explore. Monkeys will learn to solve mechanical puzzles even if they are never rewarded for it (Harlow, Harlow, & Meyer, 1950), and they will perform work in order to see interesting things—a toy train, for example—through a window (Butler, 1957). Even rats will learn to press a lever just to make the illumination in their cages increase and decrease (Roberts, Marx, & Collier, 1958) or to gain access to a running wheel (Collier & Hirsch, 1971). And human beings do all sorts of bizarre things that drive theory can't account for: They scare themselves with ghost stories and roller-coaster rides, eat foods spicy enough to stimulate the pain receptors in the mouth, and go to movies designed to arouse the sexual drive but not to satisfy it. Many psychologists believe that organisms are born with an "exploratory drive," that they have an innate need for a certain amount of stimulation, and that the lack of stimulation is what makes solitary confinement a universally dreaded punishment.

The instinct theorists of the 1920s spoke of an "instinct of curiosity." Are we any further along when we speak of an "exploratory drive?" The concept

What "need" produces this man's "drive" to build a giant ball of twine?
(UPI/Bettmann Newsphotos)

of drive has one theoretical advantage over the concept of instinct. Instincts are assumed to provide the energy or motivation behind a given action and, in addition, to specify the action itself. Drives are assumed only to provide the energy for action. Thus a given sample of behavior can be analyzed into two components: the action itself (say, pressing a lever) and the motivation behind the action (say, the hunger drive produced by a certain period of food deprivation).

The concept of drives has often been useful. It is most useful when we are talking about relatively clear-cut states of physiological deprivation, such as hunger and thirst. However, even in these cases there are difficulties with the traditional view of drive as a product of homeostatic imbalance. We will discuss some of these difficulties in the next sections of this chapter, where specific drives are covered in greater detail.

HUNGER

Everyone has felt hunger. It is a universal source of motivation. Because it is easily produced in the laboratory and easily satisfied, and because an organism does not quickly die if its food needs are not met, hunger has been studied more thoroughly than any other motivation. Yet there is still much that we do not understand about it. One problem is that mechanisms that regulate food intake appear to differ in different species. Thus we cannot be sure that experimental results found with dogs will hold true for rats, or that results found with rats will hold true for people. Humans, of course, are the most difficult species to study. Their eating behavior is controlled by social and cognitive factors as well as by physical ones. And many of the experiments that have been most helpful to our understanding of hunger and feeding behavior in animals cannot, for obvious reasons, be performed on humans.

Physiological Mechanisms and Food-Intake Regulation

Organisms must regulate their food intake both on a day-to-day basis, to meet their immediate physiological requirements, and on a long-term basis, to maintain a stable (adult) body weight. A large animal, such as a horse or a cow, that eats food low in caloric value (such as grass) must eat almost continuously to get enough nutrition. But humans and most animals that have been studied in the laboratory (mainly dogs, cats, rats, mice, and guinea pigs) eat *meals.* That is, they eat for a while, and then they stop eating. After a lapse of time they eat again. The number of meals taken a day (when allowed free access to food) varies: Humans generally take 2 to 4, cats 9 to 10, rats 12 to 15, guinea pigs 22 to 25. The basic questions here are: What makes an organism start eating? What makes it stop? What determines the size of a meal?

The Stomach and the Mouth. An obvious place to look for the origin of hunger and satiety is the stomach. Surprisingly, though, the stomach does not seem to play an important role in regulating food intake. People whose stomachs have been removed for medical reasons still get hungry and eat normal amounts of food. And rats that have had all the nerves from the stomach to the brain cut also maintain their normal food intake (Morgan & Morgan, 1940).

Additional information about the stomach's role in food-intake regulation comes from experiments with rats in which a plastic tube is surgically inserted into the stomach or the esophagus (the passageway from the mouth to the stomach). It is then possible to place food or liquid directly into a rat's stomach, bypassing its mouth. In one experiment, (Miller & Kessen, 1952) milk or a saline solution was injected directly into rats' stomachs. The rats learned to go to the place where they received the milk injections (in preference to the place where they received the saline), even though they were never able to taste or swallow the milk. However, tasting or swallowing did seem to produce an effect on the rat's behavior. Rats that received a quantity of milk directly into their stomachs drank more additional milk than rats that had taken the same quantity by mouth (Berkun, Kessen, and Miller, 1952). Similarly, hospitalized people maintained on intravenous feeding still report feeling hungry, although they do not actually eat much if offered food.

Monitoring of Blood Sugar.   One plausible way for the body to regulate food intake would be through the level of glucose (blood sugar) in the circulatory system, since most foods are at least partially reduced to glucose after digestion. The mechanism has to be a fairly complex one, though—not one that simply equates hunger with low glucose levels and satiety with high levels. Diabetics have elevated glucose levels, yet they tend to eat more, not less, than healthy people. A mechanism postulated by Mayer (1953, 1955) would keep track of the *rate* at which glucose is being used by the body's cells: A low rate would produce hunger; a high rate, satiety. If this were true, then injection of a chemical that blocked the use of glucose by the cells should produce hunger. In fact, a chemical called Z-deoxy-D-glucose (Z-DG) does exactly this, causing hunger in rats and monkeys (Smith & Epstein, 1969), as well as in humans (Thompson & Campbell, 1977). This would also explain why diabetics tend to overeat. They lack insulin, which is required for the passage of glucose into the body's various cells. Thus even though diabetics have high levels of glucose in their blood, their cells can't use it. Mayer hypothesized that "glucostats" somewhere in our bodies monitor the rate of glucose uptake by the cells and thereby control hunger. Some studies suggest that these glucostats may be located in the liver (Campbell & Davis, 1974; Stricker et al., 1976), although Mayer himself believed they were located in the brain.

There apparently are other substances in the blood besides glucose that help to regulate intake of food. If blood from a satiated rat is transfused into a hungry one, the hungry rat eats much less than usual. Transfusions in the opposite direction, however, have no effect: The satiated rat does not begin to eat again after receiving blood from a hungry animal (Davis, Gallagher, & Ladlove, 1967). One candidate for this mysterious "satiety factor" is a hormone called cholecystokinin (CCK), which is produced by the small intestine soon after a meal. This hormone temporarily inhibits eating in both animals (Gibbs, Young, & Smith, 1973) and humans (Pi-Sunyer, Kissileff, Thornton, & Smith, 1982; Carlson, 1985).

Perhaps, given the variety of factors that can produce hunger, there is no simple hunger but rather a variety of *specific hungers.* Rozin (1968) allowed rats to freely select their diet from a variety of foods, some rich in protein, others in carbohydrates, and others in fats or certain vitamins, and so on. The rats selected a well-balanced diet from this "cafeteria"—even, for example, increasing their ingestion of a protein solution when it was diluted, as if to maintain a constant consumption of protein.

Figure 11–2 This rat's ventromedial nucleus has been damaged, causing it to overeat. The result is that it has gained so much weight that it now weighs three times what a normal rat would weigh. (Courtesy Dr. Neal E. Miller)

The Role of the Hypothalamus. The search for mechanisms that control hunger and satiety has led most often to the part of the brain known as the **hypothalamus** (see Chapter 2). The hypothalamus itself is composed of a number of subareas that can be distinguished anatomically and on the basis of their functions. One of these subareas is the *lateral hypothalamus,* or lateral nucleus. This part of the brain has been identified as an excitatory area for eating and drinking. When a rat's lateral hypothalamus is destroyed, it will at first neither eat nor drink, and it will die unless it is force-fed (Teitelbaum & Epstein, 1962). If kept alive, it will eventually resume eating and drinking, but it will only eat foods that taste good. Electrical stimulation of the lateral hypothalamus causes a previously satiated rat to become hungry and thirsty. If food is not immediately available, the rat will press a lever to obtain it (Hoebel, 1971).

If the electrode is located in a different part of the hypothalamus, the ventromedial nucleus, stimulation will cause a hungry rat to *stop* eating. The *ventromedial hypothalamus* (VMH for short) has been called the satiety center—that is, the center where "glucostats" (the blood-sugar monitors) are believed to be located.

If a rat's VMH is damaged or destroyed, the animal will eat more food at each meal and will soon weigh two or three times as much as a normal rat (see Figure 11–2 and Table 11–1). What's interesting is that the rat won't continue to eat in excess and gain weight indefinitely. At some point its weight will level off and it will eat just enough to maintain itself at that new weight (Teitelbaum, 1961). Moreover, although this rat eats more than a normal rat, in some ways it seems *less* hungry: It is more finicky about what it eats and it won't work as hard to get food (Miller, Bailey, & Stevenson,1950; Teitelbaum, 1957).

A rat with brain lesions in the VMH will maintain itself at a higher weight than before its surgery; similarly, a rat with lesions in the lateral hypothalamus will eventually maintain itself at a new, lower weight (Keesey & Porvley, 1975). In both cases it looks as if the homeostatic "thermostat" is still working but the setting has been changed. This is the **set-point theory** of food regulation (Nisbett, 1972). According to this theory, the feeding-regulation mechanisms of the obese rat and the obese human are not out of order—they are just at a higher set point. As long as the weight is below the set point, the person or animal will be hungry. Like rats with VMH lesions, many obese people tend to eat more, eat faster, be less active, and be more

Table 11–1: The Effects of Activating or Destroying Each Part of the Hypothalamus Suggest the Normal Role of Each Part in the Control of Eating.

Part of Hypothalamus	Destroyed (By Lesioning)	Activated (By Electrical Stimulation)
Ventromedial nucleus	Animals overeat (hyperphagia)	Hungry animals won't eat; if eating when activated, they stop immediately
Lateral nucleus	Animals stop eating entirely (aphagia)	Animals start eating immediately, even if they have just eaten

After McNemar (1942).

finicky about what they eat. We will return to the problem of human obesity shortly.

Criticism of Homeostatic Theories of Eating.   From the homeostatic viewpoint, an animal is assumed to begin a meal whenever some physiological mechanism signals a certain level of depletion or need. Some psychologists have presented strong arguments against this view (Collier, Hirsch, & Hamlin, 1972; Collier, Hirsch, & Kanarek, 1977). For example, when food is readily available, the amount taken in a meal is not related to the length of time since the last meal, and perhaps not even to the amount taken in the last meal (Panksepp, 1973). Mealtimes seem to depend not on the level of depletion but on the time of day (cats and rats do most of their eating at night) and on the availability of alternative activities, such as running in wheels. Collier believes that healthy animals in natural environments have developed behavior that assures an adequate intake of food—they *anticipate* their need rather than respond to them. An example is the behavior of large ruminants such as cows. These animals have a tremendous storage capacity and it takes them a long time to digest their food. They must continually take in food to provide the raw material for the fermentation process. If they waited until their previous meal was digested and assimilated before they began to eat again, they would be in trouble. And animals such as wolves and lions, which must expend large amounts of energy to procure food, could scarcely afford to wait until their supply of energy was depleted before they began to look for more food. Thus, according to Collier, through the course of evolution each species has evolved feeding patterns that are suited to its ecological niche and flexible enough to be modified if the environment changes. A good example of this kind of flexibility is the hyena's hunting pack. If the available game is small and a successful hunt results in only the dominant animals eating well while the rest go hungry, the pack splits up into smaller packs. When large game again becomes available, so that a kill will feed many animals, the packs reassemble into larger units (Kruuk, 1972).

Human Obesity

One rarely sees an overweight animal in a natural environment (unless it is getting ready to hibernate). Only humans and a few of the species that humans have domesticated seem to have the capacity to become obese under normal conditions. What causes the normal eating control mechanism to go wrong?

Defining Obesity.   In humans **obesity** is often defined as being more than about 15 percent over the "ideal" weight, given a person's height and overall body build. But what is that "ideal weight?" Certainly cultural issues have a tremendous bearing on this question (see Figure 11–3). Another factor in determining obesity is the proportion of body fat to muscle tissue. Mayer (1955) has pointed out that a 6-foot-tall-football player weighing 200 pounds is "overweight" according to the charts, yet may have very little body fat. On the other hand, a very inactive person whose weight is at or even below the "ideal" weight may be so lacking in muscle tissue that an abnormally high percentage of that weight consists of fat. Mayer has defined obesity as the condition that is present "when the fat content reaches 30 percent of the body weight." The size of fat deposits can be roughly determined by measuring the thickness of a skin fold, or by measurements of body density. It

Animals in natural environments may have developed behaviors, such as storing food, that anticipate their food needs rather than just respond to them. (M. J. Altimus/Photo Researchers)

Figure 11–3 Social standards for an ideal weight vary considerably from one era to another, as well as from one society to another. (*Left:* Rubens, *Helen Fourment coi figli*/Art Resource; *right:* Tonia Carlson Clay/Photo Researchers)

Table 11–2: Some Shared Characteristics of Obese Humans and Rats with VMH Lesions.

1. Eat more when good-tasting food is available.
2. Eat less when the food tastes bad.
3. Are less willing to work for food.
4. Eat faster.
5. Eat fewer meals per day (but more per meal).
6. Tend to be more emotionally reactive.
7. Are generally less active.

From Schachter (1971).

should be noted that the proportion of body fat increases in normal animals as they age, and it is usually higher in females than in males at any age.

Characteristics of Obese People. As we mentioned earlier, there are some interesting parallels between the behavior of obese humans and that of rats that overeat because of lesions in their ventromedial hypothalamus. Schachter (1971) has spelled out these similarities in detail. First, both obese humans and VMH rats are more sensitive than their normal counterparts to the taste of food. When food or drink is adulterated with quinine, a harmless substance with a bitter taste, obese humans and rats take less of it than normal subjects. When the food tastes good, the obese eat more.

Obese subjects are also less willing to work for food than the nonobese. When rats are rewarded with a pellet of food for each lever press, VMH rats press more than normal rats. But when they have to press a number of times for each pellet, they press *less* than normal rats (Teitelbaum, 1957). Schachter (1971) found a similar result with humans. In a cleverly designed experiment subjects were invited to help themselves to a bagful of almonds. The almonds were either shelled or unshelled. Nonobese people accepted the offer and ate some nuts about half the time, whether they were shelled or unshelled. Obese subjects almost always accepted the offer of nuts without shells but almost never accepted when the nuts had to be shelled.

Other reported similarities include general activity level (the obese are less active), emotional responsiveness (the obese react more emotionally), number of meals eaten per day (the obese eat fewer), and speed of eating (the obese eat faster). Some of Schachter's comparisons are summarized in Table 11–2.

A Theory of Obesity. Schachter's theory about these VMH rats and obese humans is that they differ from normal-weight organisms not so much in their mechanisms for food-intake regulation as in their general level of responsiveness to all external stimuli: "When a food-relevant cue is present the obese are more likely to eat and to eat a great deal than are normals. When

such a cue is absent, the obese are less likely to try to eat or complain about hunger." The reason they are less willing to work for their food, says Schachter, is simply because food that has to be worked for is more remote and therefore provokes less of a food-acquiring response.

There is evidence for this hypothesis from human subjects. Overweight and normal-weight people had to lift weights with their fingers to get food. There were four conditions: They worked for sandwiches wrapped either in clear plastic or in opaque white paper, and they either did or did not get a sample piece of sandwich. Figure 11–4 shows that when there were two food cues (transparent wrapper plus sample sandwich), obese subjects worked almost twice as hard as the nonobese. With no food cues, the nonobese subjects worked harder (Johnson, 1971). While Schachter's theory has been quite influential, it has also been criticized. For example, Rodin (1981) claimed that her review of research on human obesity failed to support Schachter's view. (But see Schacter, 1982, where he supports his view).

The Set-Point Theory. Earlier we mentioned Nisbett's theory that overweight people and VMH rats have a higher set-point weight. The assumption is that when they are below this set point, they are in a state of deprivation or homeostatic imbalance, even if their weight is above normal levels. Nisbett believes that it is this state of deprivation that is responsible for the distinctive characteristics of obese people, and not the obesity itself or the mechanisms that caused the obesity.

This theory has been tested in a series of experiments reported by Herman and his colleagues (Herman & Mack, 1975; Herman & Polivy, 1975; Hibscher & Herman, 1977). The experimenters divided their subjects into two categories on the basis of their answers to a series of questions: "restrained eaters" (dieters) and "nonrestrained eaters" (nondieters). They assumed that restrained eaters, whether they are obese or of normal weight, weigh less than their set-point weight and are therefore in a state of chronic deprivation. Nonrestrained eaters, whether obese or nonobese, were assumed to be at or near their set-point weights.

The experimental results supported the set-point theory. College men and women who were concerned about their weight and restrained their eating (dieters) showed many of the same traits that Schachter had found in his obese subjects, even if they were of normal weight at the time of the experiment. Conversely, obese subjects who didn't care about their weight and ate as much as they wanted (nondieters) behaved more like Schacter's nonobese subjects. For example, both obese and nonobese dieters ignored internal cues and ate a lot of ice cream after they had been given two milkshakes to drink as part of a "rating experiment." The milkshakes evidently broke down the dieter's normal restraint, because dieters who hadn't had the milkshakes ate less of the ice cream (as shown in Figure 11–5). This was exactly the opposite of what was found with nondieters (both obese and normal weight).

Another experiment showed that normal-weight subjects who are dieters show the same kind of emotional responsiveness that had previously been linked with obesity. Hibscher and Herman (1977) even showed that both obese dieters and nonobese dieters have elevated blood levels (compared with nondieters) of certain substances known as "free fatty acids." The free-fatty-acid content of the blood has been shown to go up in response to food deprivation (Gordon, 1960).

Fat-Cell Theory. According to Nisbett's theory, the set-point weight determines whether a person can maintain a socially acceptable weight without

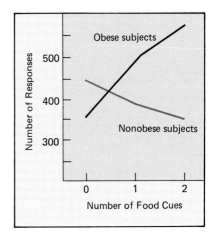

Figure 11–4 When a number of food cues are present, obese subjects will work almost twice as hard as nonobese subjects to get food. When no foods cues are present, nonobese subjects work harder. (From Johnson, 1971)

Figure 11–5 In one of a series of experiments done by Herman and his colleagues, the set-point theory was upheld—both obese and nonobese subjects who were dieters (restrained eaters) ate more ice cream after consuming two milkshakes than similar subjects who weren't dieters (unrestrained eaters). (From Hibscher & Herman, 1977)

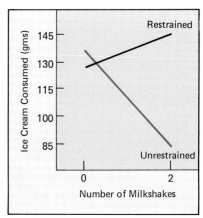

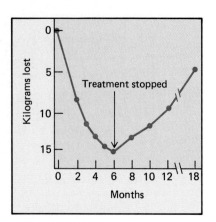

Figure 11–6 While pursuing a variety of weight loss treatments for six months, patients showed a steady loss in their average weight. Unfortunately, once the treatments were halted, this lost weight was steadily regained. (From Brownell, 1982)

being hungry all the time. But what determines the set-point weight? Nisbett claims that it is the number of fat cells in the body. In one study fat cells were found to be three times as numerous in obese subjects as in nonobese subjects (Knittle & Hirsch, 1968). Knittle (1975) believes that the number of fat cells in the body is pretty well fixed by the age of 2; it is determined partly by heredity and partly by eating habits in infancy. According to this theory, overeating simply causes the fat cells to increase in size and dieting causes them to shrink, but the number of these cells stays approximately the same. Thus when an obese person loses weight, the fat cells are supposedly "starved," which accounts for the state of chronic deprivation found in habitual dieters.

Not all psychologists believe in the fat-cell theory. Some who *do* believe in it think that it only accounts for a certain kind of obesity—the kind that produces a moderately overweight child who becomes a moderately overweight adult. There are many other types of obesity. Undoubtedly we will eventually find that there are a number of different causes for obesity, some primarily emotional, some primarily physiological, and some primarily social or environmental. In a society where almost everyone has a car and no one walks, lack of exercise may be an important factor. This idea has led Mayer (1955) to wonder "whether there is not a direct relationship between recent improvements in transportation and increased prevalence of overweight."

Weight Control. Both the set-point and fat-cell theories imply that people are predisposed to maintain a certain weight. Furthermore, the body seems to resist fat loss by slowing down its metabolism (Garrow, 1978). Fat people often need surprisingly few calories to maintain their weight (Spitzer & Rodin, 1981). The data shown in Figure 11–6 are depressingly consistent with this pessimistic view. However, these results may be misleading. They reflect the behavior of people who voluntarily submitted to a supervised program of weight loss and may not be representative of the whole population, nor of all weight-loss programs. Many people *do* lose weight, by themselves, under a physician's supervision, or through an organized program. Among the most promising programs of weight control are those, such as Weight Watchers International, that employ behavior-modification techniques to alter basic eating habits. Their focus is on learning to eat properly, eating more slowly, and encouraging patience with the weight-loss process. Coupled with exercise, which alters body metabolism as well as burns calories (Thompson, Jarvie, Lakey, & Cureton, 1982), and appropriate social supports, such programs may produce permanent weight change rather than the typically transient loss produced by a "diet" (Brownwell & Venditti, 1983; Stunkard, 1983). People who have successfully lost weight through these or other programs do not show the symptoms of depression or irritability that might be expected from the set-point theory. On the contrary, weight loss has been associated with favorable changes in emotional and social adjustment (Wilson, 1978).

THIRST

People who have suffered from severe water deprivation describe extreme thirst as a much more excruciating sensation than extreme hunger. It is also much more life threatening: We can survive for weeks without food, but only for a few days without water.

We lose water all the time. An average 2½ liters passes from out bodies each day in urine, feces, and exhaled air. This water must all be replaced by

drinking liquids or eating foods with a high moisture content. Under normal conditions, organisms do not experience extreme thirst because their patterns of water intake (like their patterns of food intake) *prevent* severe depletion from occurring.

What Starts Drinking?

Most of us would immediately claim that thirst is equivalent to the sensation of a dry mouth and throat. During dehydration there is usually a reduced salivary flow, and that makes the mouth feel dry. But dryness of the mouth does not play an essential role in the regulation of water intake. This has been shown in several ways. People given drugs that cause dryness of the mouth and those who were born without salivary glands drink more frequently, but their total intake is about normal. The same is true of dogs that have had their salivary glands tied off (Montgomery, 1931).

The Hypothalamus.   We saw in the previous section that the mechanisms that produce hunger are located primarily in the hypothalamus and not in the stomach. The situation is similar for thirst: The mechanisms are again located primarily in the hyopthalamus rather than in the mouth or throat. Several hypothalamic areas have been implicated; one of these is the lateral hypothalamus, which was previously mentioned in connection with hunger. Lesions in this region interfere with drinking as well as eating—in fact, the effect on drinking seems to be more severe and more persistent. The *preoptic area,* at the very front of the hypothalamus, has also been shown to be involved in thirst. Electrical stimulation of the preoptic area, or the injection of minute quantities of salty water, causes goats to drink excessively (Andersson, 1952; Andersson & McCann, 1955).

In order for the hypothalamus to regulate water intake, it must have some way of obtaining information about the body's need for fluids. This is accomplished by two independent mechanisms, one based on **osmoreceptors,** the other on **volumetric receptors.** These are sometimes called, respectively, the *intracellular mechanism* and the *extracellular mechanism.* The first kind responds to the amount of fluid inside the body's cells, the second to the fluid outside the cells, especially that contained in the circulatory sys-

tem. Thirst can be triggered by either system. This is sometimes referred to as the **double-depletion hypothesis:** Depletion of *either* intracellular or extracellular water can cause thirst.

Osmoreceptors.   The fluids in the body, both within the cells and outside of them, normally contain about 0.9 percent salt (sodium chloride). When an organism has been deprived of water for a while, the extracellular fluid becomes more concentrated (in other words, saltier). Now there are different concentrations of salt on the two sides of the cell wall, and the result is **osmosis**—the movement of fluids through a semipermeable membrane. In this case, water moves through the cell wall from inside the cell to outside, decreasing the saltiness of the extracellular fluid but at the same time depleting the cell of water. It is believed that certain cells in the hypothalamus, the osmoreceptors, are sensitive to this depletion. When water moves out of these cells, a response is triggered, and signals are sent to other cells in the brain. One result is that the organism becomes thirsty. Another is that the hypothalamus stimulates the pituitary gland to release a hormone (the *antidiuretic* hormone) that causes the kidneys to produce more highly concentrated urine. This means that less water is lose through excretion.

The functioning of the osmoreceptors has been demonstrated experimentally by injecting salty water (more than 0.9 percent salt) into the stomachs or blood vessels of animals. This has the same effect as water deprivation: Because the extracellular fluid becomes saltier than that within the cells, the cells lose water. Such injections cause animals to become thirsty, even if they were previously satiated with water. The same thing happens to people who drink seawater or eat salty foods.

Volumetric Receptors.   People who do not get *enough* salt also become thirsty. In this case, the fluid outside of the cells is less salty than that within, and osmosis causes extracellular water to enter the cells. Now the quantity of extracellular fluid (mainly blood) is depleted. The mechanism that responds to this depletion, called a *volumetric receptor,* is the same one that produces intense thirst in wounded people who have lost a lot of blood. Although, in the case of blood loss, there has been no change in the body's concentration of salts, the total *volume* of extracellular fluid has decreased. The result is a drop in blood pressure.

Where are the receptors that detect a drop in blood volume and pressure? Apparently they are in several places. For example, if the blood supply to the kidneys or the heart is reduced, there is an increase in drinking (Fitzsimmons, 1972). It seems that there are pressure receptors in the left ventricle of the heart and in the blood vessels leading to the kidneys (Carlson, 1980).

When a drop in blood volume or pressure is detected, it triggers the release of an enzyme called *renin* from the kidneys. Renin is responsible for the production of a substance called *angiotensin.* Angiotensin reaches the brain through the bloodstream and stimulates thirst receptors. While there is some debate about the exact location of these receptors (Carlson, 1980), injections of angiotensin into the brain of an experimental animal is the surest way to produce drinking behavior (Epstein, Fitzsimmons, & Rolls, 1970).

What Stops Drinking?

The mechanisms we have described initiate drinking when either intracellular or extracellular fluids, or both, get low. What stops it? A stomach-load of

water is only 25 percent absorbed in 15 minutes; yet dogs (for example) are able to replace their water deficits quite accurately, in one or two short bouts of drinking (Adolph, 1939). What tells them when they have had enough?

A number of experiments have been performed in attempts to answer this question (e.g., Blass & Hall, 1976). Many of these experiments have made use of the technique in which a plastic tube is surgically inserted into an animal's esophagus. Water can be put directly into the animal's stomach through the tube, or water that the animal drinks can be prevented from reaching its stomach. It is also possible to tie off an animal's intestines so that water in the stomach is not absorbed into the body through the intestinal walls. These studies indicate that while the swallowing of water and the subsequent filling of the stomach play some role in the cessation of drinking, *drinking stops primarily because of an increase in intracellular fluids* (Mook, 1987).

SEXUALITY AND MATING

The motivations we have studied so far in this chapter have an important element in common: If the needs that underlie them are not met, the organism dies. The sex drive is different. As far as we know, no one has ever died for lack of sex. In fact, it might be described as a drive without a need because it involves no deviation from homeostasis and is to a certain extent independent of deprivation and satiation. Deprivation and satiation play *some* role, but not nearly so great as with hunger and thirst.

Although it is not necessary to the survival of the individual, the sex or mating drive is essential to the survival of the species. The drive is maintained by the process of natural selection: Organisms endowed with little or no desire to mate are unlikely to bear young. In the human species the expression of the drive is somewhat fettered by social laws and customs, but it remains a powerful source of motivation. Some evidence of this is provided by TV and magazine advertisements, which use sex to sell everything from cars to toothpaste.

Sexual Differentiation

Genetic Sex. Nature has happily provided almost every species with two sexes, male and female. Usually an organism's sex is determined at the time of conception. In humans and other mammals, as we saw in Chapter 2, an egg carrying an X chromosome unites with a sperm carrying an X chromosome to produce a genetic female, or with a sperm carrying a Y chromosome to produce a genetic male. Thus a cell from a normal female contains two X chromosomes, and a cell from a normal male contains one X chromosome and one Y.

Not all humans, however, fall into the simple XX or XY classification. For example, there are men with an XXY pattern. These people have underdeveloped but clearly male genitals. As adults they prove to be sterile and have a somewhat feminine body build. There are also men with an XYY pattern. They are taller than average, and sometimes have genital abnormalities. It was at first thought that this chromosomal pattern is associated with a higher degree of impulsiveness or aggressiveness because prison populations have a higher incidence of XYY individuals. However, XYY men in the nonprison population do not seem to be anymore aggressive than normal XY

men (Owen, 1972). Both the XYY and the XXY patterns are associated with an increased risk of mental retardation.

People with only a single X chromosome are identified as female, but they lack ovaries and so do not mature sexually unless hormones are given artificially. They are likely to have other birth defects as well, and they tend to be quite short.

Hormones. Whether they will ultimately develop into males or females, all human embryos are at first the same. Each possesses a pair of primitive sex glands that can become either ovaries or testes. At seven or eight weeks after conception these glands begin to develop into ovaries if the sex-chromosome pattern is XX, into testes if it is XY. These sex glands or **gonads** each produce a characteristic type of hormone. The ovaries produce the set of related female hormones called **estrogens,** and the testes produce the male hormones called **androgens,** of which the most important is **testosterone.** The hormones secreted by the embryo's gonads determine its **primary sex characteristics**: its internal and external reproductive organs. If the gonads secrete testosterone, the fetus will develop the characteristics of a male. Otherwise it will develop the characteristics of a female, whether or not its gonads secrete estrogen. In mammals both male and female embryos are subjected to the influence of the mother's female hormones, so a female is produced unless there is opposition from testosterone. It is interesting that the situation is just the opposite in bird embryos, which are encased in a shell and not exposed to the mother's hormones. A bird embryo will develop into a male unless estrogen is present at the critical stage of development (Wilson & Glick, 1970).

The hormones also control the development of the **secondary sex characteristics,** which appear at puberty. In humans these include breast and hip enlargement in females, beard growth and voice change in males. Puberty is marked by a great increase in the output of sex hormones. The pituitary gland, located in the brain, produces hormones called *gonadotropins,* which stimulate the gonads to produce androgen and estrogen. Oddly enough, both kinds of hormones (which are closely related in biochemical structure) are produced by both sexes, but the testes tend to produce more androgen, the ovaries more estrogen.

Hormonal sex can override genetic sex more or less completely, depending on how early in development the hormonal influence occurs. There is a condition that occurs in humans called the **androgen-insensitivity syndrome.** In this condition the testes of a genetic male fetus secrete testosterone, but for some reason—probably an enzyme deficiency—the testosterone is not used by the body cells and the fetus develops into what appears to be a normal female. The individual is raised as a girl and at puberty the secretion of estrogen is sufficient to cause the development of female secondary sex charactertistics. However, menstruation does not occur because there are no ovaries and the uterus is incompletely formed. Although these people cannot become pregnant, they are in most respects unquestionably female. Some have had successful careers as fashion models; many have married and have adopted and parented children (Money, 1970; Money & Ehrhardt, 1972).

Genetic females may also develop malelike characteristics if subjected to male hormones early in fetal life. When injections of testosterone were given to pregnant female monkeys, their female offspring were born with sex organs that were partly male and partly female, a condition known as **hermaphroditism.** These baby monkeys had a small but otherwise well-developed

Rough and tumble play is less common among girls than among boys; it is also less accepted by parents. However, as more young girls are encouraged to compete in various sports, the differences in skill between the two sexes seem to be diminishing. (Four by Five)

penis. On the other hand, they also had the internal organs (ovaries, uterus) of a normal female (Goy, 1968).

A synthetic hormone called **progestin,** formerly used to prevent miscarriage in pregnant women, was later discovered to have masculinizing effects on unborn female children. Some of these girls were born with an enlarged clitoris and partially fused labia. The condition was corrected surgically, and they were reared as females (Money & Ehrhardt, 1972). (The Highlight: Sex Role Behavior and Personality in Chapter 15 describes the childhood behavior and development of some of these girls.)

Maleness and Femaleness.   The differences in behavior between "normal" boys and "normal" girls are relative rather than absolute: A particular kind of behavior will occur more often, *on the average,* in boys than in girls, or in girls than in boys. That such statistical differences *do* exist in many species is unquestionable. For example, young male rhesus monkeys engage in more "rough and tumble" play than do young females (Rosenblum, 1977). What is not clear is how much these differences depend on genetic and hormonal influences, and how much they depend on the way the individual is treated by parents and others. Even in nonhuman species different parental treatment for male and female offspring has been observed. Rhesus monkey mothers with female offspring restrain their infants almost three times as often as mothers of male offspring (Mitchell, 1968). *Restraining* was defined as "active interference with the infant's attempts to leave the mother." The importance of social and parental influences on the development of "maleness" and "femaleness" is clearly greatest in the human species, as we will discuss further in Chapter 13.

Even when genetic, hormonal, and environmental factors are all (as far as we know) in agreement, there are people who feel that they have been "assigned" to the wrong sex—men who feel that they "should have been" women, and women who feel that they "should have been" men. These people are called transsexuals. A number of such individuals have requested and received surgical and hormonal treatments that produce a change in apparent sexual identity. However, a recent study (Meyer, 1980) has found that these operations may not produce any long-term beneficial effects on the lives of the people who undergo them. On the basis of this study, some hospitals have stopped performing this type of surgery.

Mating Behavior

Mating behavior begins, in all species, with some preliminaries called *courtship behavior.* The male sniffs, nuzzles, or otherwise expresses interest in the female; the female either rejects or accepts these advances. If she is receptive to them, she will eventually allow the male to mount. In virtually all mammals except humans the female always has all four feet firmly on the ground. The male gets on top and *intromission* (entry of the penis into the female's vagina) is from behind and above. The female must cooperate by standing still, by arching her back somewhat, and by holding her tail (if she has one) to the side; this response is called *lordosis.*

What follows next differs in its details from species to species, although the outcome is the same. The rat, for instance, will mount the female a number of times and achieve 8 to 15 intromissions, each lasting less than a second. During the final intromission the male will *ejaculate* semen (the fluid containing the sperm) into the female's vagina.

Mating behavior in all species begins with preliminaries called *courtship behavior.* An example is the male peacock's display of plummage. (Tom McHugh/Photo Researchers)

The behavior just described evidently has drive-reducing (or incentive) value not only for the male, but for the female as well. It has been shown that receptive female rats will press a lever to gain access to a male rat (Bermant, 1961).

The Influence of Hormones on the Female. All mammalian females show cyclical variations in hormonal state, called the **menstrual cycle** in primates, the **estrus cycle** in lower mammals. In most species ovulation occurs automatically at some specific point in the cycle, and at that time the female becomes both sexually attractive and sexually receptive to the male. One exception to this rule is the rabbit, which is virtually always receptive and which ovulates only upon mating. The other chief exception occurs in those primate species, including humans, in which females ovulate on a cyclical basis but show little or no (there is still some debate on this question) cyclical change in receptivity or sexual attractiveness.

If the ovaries of a nonhuman female mammal are removed (which is done when female dogs and cats are "spayed"), the animal's hormonal cycle ceases, and so do the periods of sexual receptivity and sexual attractiveness. These functions can be restored by the administration of the ovarian hormones estrogen and progesterone (Money & Erhardt, 1972). Removal of the ovaries in human females sometimes lowers sexual drive, but sometimes it increases it (perhaps because fear of pregnancy is removed), and often it has no effect at all.

The Influence of Hormones on the Male. In the male cyclical variations in hormonal level occur in such animals as deer, which confine their sexual activities to a certain season of the year. In most species hormonal production is constant, and the male is able and willing to engage in sexual activity at anytime.

The effects of castration (surgical removal of the testes) depend on the age at which the operation is performed. A male that is castrated before puberty will never reach sexual maturity and will never show normal sexual behavior unless the hormones normally secreted by the testes are supplied artificially by injection. Castration after puberty has a variable effect, depending on the species and the amount of previous sexual experience. A male rat will usually cease to attempt to mount a receptive female within two or three months of castration. An experienced male dog might attempt to mount for a year or more after castration. In humans castration has an unpredictable effect, sometimes resulting in an immediate loss of potency (probably due to psychological factors) and sometimes in a slow decline over a period of years. In both humans and animals sexual desire and ability are restored by the administration of testosterone. By the way, *additional* testosterone administered to a male who already has an adequate supply has little effect on sexual activity (Bermant & Davidson, 1974, Walker, 1978).

The Role of Experience. In many animals the ability to engage in normal sexual activity depends on their having been reared with others of their kind. Guinea pigs raised in isolation do not show sexual behavior (Valenstein, Riss, & Young, 1955). Isolated male rats do mount receptive females, but it takes them much longer (Zimbardo, 1958). Male beagles raised alone attempt to mount as frequently as normally reared dogs, but they often fail because their attempts are directed toward the female's head or side (Beach, 1968).

In monkeys reared in isolation, neither males nor females show normal sexual responses. A group of monkeys was reared in separate cages where

HIGHLIGHT

Sociobiology and Altruistic Behavior

Sociobiology (Wilson, 1971) is an evolutionary view of social processes. The basic idea is that many aspects of social behavior have a genetic basis and were shaped by the evolutionary process of natural selection. However, sociobiologists believe such selection is not simply survival of the fittest individual, but survival of the fittest group. For example, the tendency for humans, or animals, to sacrifice themselves in order to protect their young does not seem consistent with survival of the fittest. Yet such *altruistic* (self-sacrificing) *behavior* is consistent with the survival of the genes that characterize the group.

According to this theory:

> Individuals can afford to sacrifice their own personal genetic fitness if they make up for the loss by increasing the fitness of their relatives. Since many of their own genes are shared with the relatives by common descent, helping the relatives actually multiplies part of their own genetic structure. (Wilson, 1974, p. 9)

In other words, sociobiologists believe that survival value benefits not the individual or even the species, but the genetic material within the chromosomes. In this view the rest of the organism is just an elaborate device for assuring the survival of its genes!

Wilson argues that human altruism has the same genetic basis. In fact, he defines sociobiology as the "systematic study of the biological basis of all (animal and human) social behavior" (1975b). Human religion, ethics, tribalism, warfare, conformity, and competition can all be explained as genetically determined "human nature" (Wilson, 1978). There are now at least three scientific journals devoted to sociobiology, as well as many collections of edited papers (e.g., De Vore, 1979). It has also been widely discussed in the popular press, where it has been used to explain everything from the free-market system (*Business Week,* 1978) to the Kent State massacre (Beck, 1979).

Sociobiology is an essentially "instinctual" or hereditarian view of human behavior and, as such, appeals to those who would justify the status quo. For example, Wilson himself argues that because of our genes,

> even in the most free and egalitarian of future societies . . . even with identical education and equal access to all professions, men are likely to continue to play a disproportionate role in political life, business, and science. (1975a, p. 47)

Arguments of this sort have led some people to criticize sociobiology as rationalizing inequitable features of our society as the products of genetically determined "human nature." They argue that this view discourages progressive social reforms (Geertz, 1980; Sahlins, 1976; Washburn, 1978). Thus the conflict between sociobiologists and their critics is yet another battle in the long war between those who see human behavior as primarily determined by our genes and those who see it as primarily determined by our environment.

(K. Ammann/Bruce Coleman, Inc.)

maladjusted monkeys unable to have normal relationships—either social or sexual. If a female monkey raised on a cloth surrogate became pregnant, she never treated her infant with the tender care shown by a normally reared monkey mother. She refused to nurse the infant and either neglected or abused it.

We conclude that successful parenting of a young monkey or a young human (by mother, father, and/or other adults) must necessarily include cuddling. But cuddling is not enough. Infancy is a time of rapid learning as well as of rapid physical growth. One of the most important things an infant must learn is how to get along with other members of its species. That cannot be taught by wire or terrycloth "mothers."

Figure 11–8 Harlow (1959) found that a monkey separated from its mother at birth and raised with "surrogate mothers" would invariably choose a terrycloth mother over a bare wire mother. (Courtesy Harry F. Harlow, University of Wisconsin Primate Laboratory)

Motherlessness in Monkeys. What exact function does parenting serve? What aspect of parenting is most important to the offsrping? In an attempt to answer these questions, newborn monkeys were taken from their mothers and raised with "surrogate mothers" of various kinds (Harlow, 1959). It was found that the most important thing for the monkeys was to have something soft to cling to. Given a choice of a surrogate mother made out of wire or one covered with several layers of terrycloth, infant monkeys invariably chose the terrycloth mother (see Figure 11–8.) They spent much of their time climing on or clinging to the cloth-covered object and, when frightened, would run to it for reassurance. Monkeys raised without any mother at all, or with only a wire-covered surrogate mother, withdrew in terror from a strange object, but a monkey with a cloth "mother" would soon gain enough courage to release the soft cloth and investigate the object.

The results were the same for baby monkeys that were fed from a bottle attached to the wire mother. Even though they got their milk from the wire mother, they spent most of their time clinging to the cloth one. Thus nourishment alone does not seem to form the basis for the emotional attachment between a primate infant and its mother.

Warmth appears to play some role, but not a major one. An infant monkey would readily abandon a warm heating pad in favor of its unheated cloth mother. In a later experiment, though, newborn infant monkeys given a choice between warm wire mothers and cool cloth ones favored the warm mother (Harlow, 1971). However, after the age of 20 days they began to prefer the cloth mother.

In the subprimate mammals warmth may be of greater importance than contact comfort. Puppies given the choice of a fur surrogate mother and a wire one chose the fur mother. But when the fur mother was cooled and the metal one heated, the puppies spent almost all of their time with the metal mother (Jeddi, 1970).

It should be noted, finally, that Harlow's infant monkeys "reared" by cloth mothers did not fare so well in the long run. Although they behaved normally as long as their cloth mother was available, they grew up to be very

(Gregory G. Dimijian/Photo Researchers)

As an example, consider the threespine stickleback, a small fish that has successfully colonized almost all the coastal waters of the northern hemisphere (Hartmann, 1979). In this species the male provides the parental care. He carefully builds a nest out of bits of plants and covers it with a mixture of sand and a sticky substance secreted by his kidneys. A receptive female is then enticed into the nest, where she lays her eggs. The male fertilizes the eggs by emitting sperm over them and then guards them until they hatch, meanwhile ventilating the nest by fanning water through it. When the young fish hatch, the father continues to guard them and will even retrieve those that stray from the nest. None of the other things this animal can do—obtaining food, fleeing from enemies—is as complex and demanding as the behavior just described.

In most nonhuman mammals the father plays a relatively minor role; nearly all parental care is given by the mother. In the rat and the dog maternal behavior begins before the birth of the young, in the form of nest building. When the young are born, the mother bites off the umbilical cords and cleans off the pups. Almost immediately after the last pup is born, the mother begins to nurse, by lying or crouching in such a way that the pups can reach her nipples. She will keep the pups warm, guard them against predators, and retrieve any that wander away or are removed from the nest. During the first day or so a mother dog will leave her litter for only a minute or two at a time, and only for the purpose of relieving bowel and bladder. A female rat that has been separated from her pups is so motivated to return to them that, in order to reach them, she will cross an electrified grid more readily than a hungry or thirsty rat seeking food or water (see Figure 11–7).

These innate patterns of behavior are elicited by a complex combination of hormonal states and external stimuli. For example, in many species nesting can be induced by progesterone injections, or by presenting a female with a ready-made litter of pups. Most animals—mammalian and nonmammalian—do not appear to recognize their own young but will respond appropriately to any infant member of their species. (Animals will even respond to the young of a different species. Cowbirds and cuckoos lay their eggs in the nests of other species, where their offspring are fed and cared for by the foster mother and father, often to the detriment of their own less-demanding young!)

Figure 11–7 A female rat will cross an electrified grid to reach her pups more readily than a hungry or thirsty male or female rat seeking food, water, or sex. (From Warden, 1931)

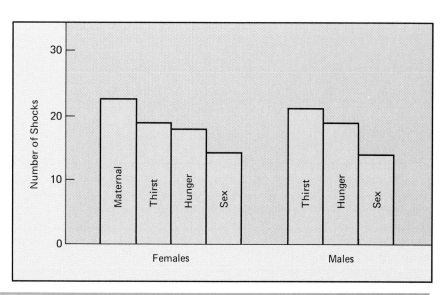

The normal human sexual response described by Masters and Johnson (see text) can be appreciably altered by the use of drugs. For example, *alcohol* is widely used in our society and has a complicated effect on the sexual response. Social inhibitions, self-consciousness, and other forms of anxiety clearly interfere with sexual responsiveness in men and women. The disinhibiting effects of moderate drinking often reduce these sources of anxiety and facilitate the sexual response. This is probably why 45 percent of the males and 68 percent of the females polled by *Psychology Today* felt that alcohol increased their sexual responsiveness (Athanasiou, Shaver, & Tavris, 1976). Furthermore, since many people drink in social situations that may lead to sexual activity, they may simply become conditioned to associate sexuality and alcohol (Briddell & Wilson, 1976; Wilson & Lawson, 1976). Nevertheless, alcohol is a physiological depressant (see Chapter 5), and any appreciable

use of it will eventually reduce or interfere with the sexual response. In the male this is reflected in a suppression or slowing of penile erection during the initial excitement stage (Farkas & Rosen, 1976), while in the female vaginal lubrication is inhibited (Wilson & Lawson, 1976). Thus those who mix alcohol and sex may experience failures of normal sexual function, which in turn increase their anxiety about sexual performance, thereby further reducing their natural sexual response. Chronic use of alcohol may also lead to renal (kidney) and vascular diseases, which can reduce or prevent normal sexual function.

While there is some evidence that moderate use of *marijuana* enhances feelings of sexuality (Goode, 1969), little is known about its effect on the sexual response. There is reason to believe that, like alcohol, heavy use of marijuana both reduces sexual feelings and inhibits the natural sexual response (Koff, 1974).

Heroin and other opiates are generally believed to interfere with the sexual response, slowing or reducing erections in males (Cicero et al.,1975) and vaginal lubrication in females. However, opiates also seem to delay ejaculation, which may be seen as

enhancing sexual performance under certain circumstances (DeLeon & Wexler, 1973).

Cocaine, amphetamines, and other strong stimulants seem to facilitate penile erection and delay ejaculation (Kaplan, 1974), as well as produce a feeling of power and exhilaration. Thus, in contrast to depressants, stimulants may actually enhance the sexual response.

In addition to the legal and illegal "recreational" drugs we have just considered, many people take prescription drugs that may influence their sexual responses. While there are few really satisfactory studies, there is reason to suspect that some reduction in sexual response may be produced by taking *antipsychotic drugs,* such as the major tranquilizers (Kotin et al., 1976), *antidepressant drugs,* (Segraves, 1977), or *antihypertensive drugs* (Carver & Oaks, 1976). However, one of the problems with evaluating the effects of such drugs is that it is difficult to find adequate control subjects. Many people who are given such drugs are older and in poorer health than the general population. Thus their reduced sexual function may be due to these other factors rather than to the drugs themselves.

the body contract. Physiologically, the female's orgasm is quite similar to the male's. No differences were found between orgasms produced through clitoral stimulation and those produced through vaginal stimulation.

4. **Resolution.** A rapid decrease in physiological arousal follows orgasm in males. In females one or several orgasms may occur before resolution.

Since this description is, of course, rather cold and clinical, perhaps we should add that the whole sequence is usually considered highly pleasurable by both of the parties involved.

PARENTING

In virtually all species the period immediately following birth is a dangerous time, associated with a high rate of mortality that declines as the organism matures. If the offspring are nurtured and protected by the adult members of a species, more of them are likely to survive. Thus parental care is clearly important to the success of the species as a whole. For this reason, care of the young has evolved in a great variety of species, including those as primitive as insects, spiders, and fish.

they could see and hear—but not touch—other monkeys. In adulthood these animals failed to mate even when a male and female were caged together for as long as seven years. When paired with normally reared monkeys, none of the isolated males ever achieved a normal mount, and only one female became pregnant. These effects seem to be due not to the infant monkey's lack of a mother, but to its lack of social interactions with other young monkeys. Infant monkeys raised without mothers but allowed to play with one another for only 20 minutes a day later showed perfectly normal sexual behavior (Harlow, 1962).

Homosexuality. **Homosexuality,** a sexual preference for one's own biological sex, shows up in all human societies and in most animal species. In animals mounting is frequently seen in females as well as males, and males will attempt to mount other males. Often this behavior is associated with dominance rather than with sexuality. However, mounting by female rats and by female monkeys is increased if they are exposed to testosterone early in development. Male rats that are castrated at birth will exhibit the female sexual response as adults if they are given estrogen and progesterone.

In humans male or female homosexual behavior often shows up as isolated episodes in the lives of otherwise heterosexual individuals. In some societies homosexual behavior is considered normal during adolescence. Later most people in these societies marry and show normal **heterosexuality** (Money & Erhardt, 1972). Another type of homosexuality involves people (male or female) who *never* engage in heterosexual behavior. It has been estimated that about 4 percent of males and 3 percent of females are exclusively homosexual during their adult years (Paul et al., 1982).

Many attempts have been made to link homosexuality to physical factors such as chromosomal errors or hormonal abnormalities. It is true that the incidence of homosexual experience is somewhat higher in men with an XXY or XYY chromosomal pattern. However, the number of such cases is so small that these genetic errors account for a negligible proportion of homosexuals. It is the same with hormonal disorders: They are found in some small proportion of homosexuals, but not in most (Money, 1970). There is also some evidence that levels of the gonadotrope hormone LH, released by the pituitary gland, may be lower in homosexuals (Gladue, Green, & Hellman, 1984).

The Human Sexual Response.   In 1966 Masters and Johnson published the results of their pioneering study of human sexuality. In this study volunteer subjects engaged in sexual activity to the point of orgasm, while sophisticated devices monitored a number of their physiological responses. Four different stages of the human sexual pattern were defined:

1. **Excitement.** The stage is characterized by vaginal lubrication, thickening of the vaginal walls, and elevation of the clitoris in the female. In the male it involves erection of the penis and elevation of the testes. Nipple erection may also occur in both males and females.

2. **Plateau.** In both sexes heart rate, respiration, and muscle tension increase. The male testes increase in size and are pulled up very high in the scrotum. In the female the outer vaginal wall swells and the clitoris retracts.

3. **Orgasm.** In the male the penis throbs in rhythmic contractions and semen is expelled. The female experiences rhythmic contractions of the muscles of the vagina and uterus. In both sexes muscles throughout

HIGHLIGHT

Mating and Parental Behavior in the Ring Dove

The ring dove is a small relative of the domestic pigeon. It gets its name from the semicircle of black feathers that "rings" the back of its neck. These birds breed freely under laboratory conditions and have been used extensively for detailed studies of parental behavior (Lehrman, 1964).

When a male and a female ring dove are placed together in a cage, courtship begins almost at once: The male begins to strut about, bowing and cooing. After several hours the birds choose a nesting site; in the laboratory this consists of a shallow glass bowl put in the cage for that purpose. Nest building takes about a week and is shared by both sexes. During this week the birds also mate. The female lays the first egg about nine days after the beginning of the courtship period, and a second egg two days later. The parent birds take turns incubating the eggs, with the female doing most of the sitting and the male relieving her for about 6 hours of each day.

The eggs hatch in two weeks, and the newly hatched squabs are fed with a substance called "crop milk," a liquid secreted in the crops of both male and female birds. (The *crop* is a pouchlike enlargement of a bird's esophagus.) The squabs leave the nest when they are about 11 days old, but the parents continue to feed them— with increasing reluctance—for another 10 days. Then courtship begins again, and the cycle repeats itself.

What determines the performance of the actions described above and the physiological changes that accompany them? Experiments have shown that hormonal factors play an important role, and so do visual and auditory stimuli. (The sense of smell does not seem to be involved; birds are not very sensitive to odors.)

When adult ring doves are caged separately they never make a nest, no matter how much nesting material is available. If these single birds are offered nests with eggs in them, they ignore them. If a male and a female bird are put together and immediately presented with a nest and eggs, they will not incubate them. They will do so, however, if the eggs are presented six or seven days later, even though the female has not yet laid her own eggs. Similarly, if the eggs are removed from a nesting pair and baby birds are substituted, the parents will feed the squabs at once, even if their own eggs were not due to hatch for another week. They will have to feed the squabs on regurgitated seeds at first, but very soon (sooner than usual) their crops will start to produce crop milk.

Lehrman and his collaborators showed that a female ring dove that is prevented from mating will lay (infertile) eggs if she can see and hear a male ring dove bowing and cooing in an adjacent cage behind a glass partition. If the male has been castrated, he will not bow and coo, and the female will not lay eggs. The growth of the oviduct and the laying of eggs are dependent on two hormones: estrogen first, then progesterone. Evidently, visual and auditory stimuli from the normal male are enough to stimulate the female's ovaries to produce these hormones. The same hormones determine incubation behavior: If a male and a female that have each been injected with progesterone are put together in a cage and offered a nest with eggs, they will incubate them almost immediately, instead of after six or seven days. Estrogen injections cause them to incubate the eggs after a delay of two or three days.

Growth of the crop and production of crop milk has been shown to depend on the hormone *prolactin,* secreted by the pituitary gland. (Prolactin is also responsible for milk production in female mammals.) Injections of prolactin will cause either single male or single female ring doves to feed baby birds that are put into their cages. Secretion of this hormone (like that of estrogen and progesterone) is affected by external stimuli: Male birds separated from their mates early in the nesting period will fail to produce prolactin and their crops will not grow. But if they are placed in an adjacent cage and can still see the female sitting on the eggs, their crops will grow just as if they were sharing in the incubation. The presence of squabs also stimulates prolactin production and crop growth.

The conclusion is that the visual and auditory stimuli that appear at different stages of the breeding cycle produce changes in hormonal activity. These hormonal changes produce changes in behavior. The changes in behavior may, in turn, be a source of new visual and auditory stimuli.

(Animals Animals)

The behavior just described evidently has drive-reducing (or incentive) value not only for the male, but for the female as well. It has been shown that receptive female rats will press a lever to gain access to a male rat (Bermant, 1961).

The Influence of Hormones on the Female. All mammalian females show cyclical variations in hormonal state, called the **menstrual cycle** in primates, the **estrus cycle** in lower mammals. In most species ovulation occurs automatically at some specific point in the cycle, and at that time the female becomes both sexually attractive and sexually receptive to the male. One exception to this rule is the rabbit, which is virtually always receptive and which ovulates only upon mating. The other chief exception occurs in those primate species, including humans, in which females ovulate on a cyclical basis but show little or no (there is still some debate on this question) cyclical change in receptivity or sexual attractiveness.

If the ovaries of a nonhuman female mammal are removed (which is done when female dogs and cats are "spayed"), the animal's hormonal cycle ceases, and so do the periods of sexual receptivity and sexual attractiveness. These functions can be restored by the administration of the ovarian hormones estrogen and progesterone (Money & Erhardt, 1972). Removal of the ovaries in human females sometimes lowers sexual drive, but sometimes it increases it (perhaps because fear of pregnancy is removed), and often it has no effect at all.

The Influence of Hormones on the Male. In the male cyclical variations in hormonal level occur in such animals as deer, which confine their sexual activities to a certain season of the year. In most species hormonal production is constant, and the male is able and willing to engage in sexual activity at anytime.

The effects of castration (surgical removal of the testes) depend on the age at which the operation is performed. A male that is castrated before puberty will never reach sexual maturity and will never show normal sexual behavior unless the hormones normally secreted by the testes are supplied artificially by injection. Castration after puberty has a variable effect, depending on the species and the amount of previous sexual experience. A male rat will usually cease to attempt to mount a receptive female within two or three months of castration. An experienced male dog might attempt to mount for a year or more after castration. In humans castration has an unpredictable effect, sometimes resulting in an immediate loss of potency (probably due to psychological factors) and sometimes in a slow decline over a period of years. In both humans and animals sexual desire and ability are restored by the administration of testosterone. By the way, *additional* testosterone administered to a male who already has an adequate supply has little effect on sexual activity (Bermant & Davidson, 1974, Walker, 1978).

The Role of Experience. In many animals the ability to engage in normal sexual activity depends on their having been reared with others of their kind. Guinea pigs raised in isolation do not show sexual behavior (Valenstein, Riss, & Young, 1955). Isolated male rats do mount receptive females, but it takes them much longer (Zimbardo, 1958). Male beagles raised alone attempt to mount as frequently as normally reared dogs, but they often fail because their attempts are directed toward the female's head or side (Beach, 1968).

In monkeys reared in isolation, neither males nor females show normal sexual responses. A group of monkeys was reared in separate cages where

penis. On the other hand, they also had the internal organs (ovaries, uterus) of a normal female (Goy, 1968).

A synthetic hormone called **progestin,** formerly used to prevent miscarriage in pregnant women, was later discovered to have masculinizing effects on unborn female children. Some of these girls were born with an enlarged clitoris and partially fused labia. The condition was corrected surgically, and they were reared as females (Money & Ehrhardt, 1972). (The Highlight: Sex Role Behavior and Personality in Chapter 15 describes the childhood behavior and development of some of these girls.)

Maleness and Femaleness. The differences in behavior between "normal" boys and "normal" girls are relative rather than absolute: A particular kind of behavior will occur more often, *on the average,* in boys than in girls, or in girls than in boys. That such statistical differences *do* exist in many species is unquestionable. For example, young male rhesus monkeys engage in more "rough and tumble" play than do young females (Rosenblum, 1977). What is not clear is how much these differences depend on genetic and hormonal influences, and how much they depend on the way the individual is treated by parents and others. Even in nonhuman species different parental treatment for male and female offspring has been observed. Rhesus monkey mothers with female offspring restrain their infants almost three times as often as mothers of male offspring (Mitchell, 1968). *Restraining* was defined as "active interference with the infant's attempts to leave the mother." The importance of social and parental influences on the development of "maleness" and "femaleness" is clearly greatest in the human species, as we will discuss further in Chapter 13.

Even when genetic, hormonal, and environmental factors are all (as far as we know) in agreement, there are people who feel that they have been "assigned" to the wrong sex—men who feel that they "should have been" women, and women who feel that they "should have been" men. These people are called transsexuals. A number of such individuals have requested and received surgical and hormonal treatments that produce a change in apparent sexual identity. However, a recent study (Meyer, 1980) has found that these operations may not produce any long-term beneficial effects on the lives of the people who undergo them. On the basis of this study, some hospitals have stopped performing this type of surgery.

Mating Behavior

Mating behavior begins, in all species, with some preliminaries called *courtship behavior.* The male sniffs, nuzzles, or otherwise expresses interest in the female; the female either rejects or accepts these advances. If she is receptive to them, she will eventually allow the male to mount. In virtually all mammals except humans the female always has all four feet firmly on the ground. The male gets on top and *intromission* (entry of the penis into the female's vagina) is from behind and above. The female must cooperate by standing still, by arching her back somewhat, and by holding her tail (if she has one) to the side; this response is called *lordosis.*

What follows next differs in its details from species to species, although the outcome is the same. The rat, for instance, will mount the female a number of times and achieve 8 to 15 intromissions, each lasting less than a second. During the final intromission the male will *ejaculate* semen (the fluid containing the sperm) into the female's vagina.

Mating behavior in all species begins with preliminaries called *courtship behavior*. An example is the male peacock's display of plummage. (Tom McHugh/Photo Researchers)

AGGRESSION

The term **aggression** refers to the kinds of behavior that lead to the damage or destruction of something—either another organism or an inanimate object. (In humans, as we shall see in Chapter 19, aggression also may refer to pain-inflicting behaviors.) A coyote killing a lamb, a stallion attacking another stallion, a cat slashing out at a dog, a human destroying an automobile with a sledgehammer—all these actions fall under the definition of aggression. Clearly we are not referring to a single type of behavior: There are many different kinds of aggressive responses, and they are elicited by a wide variety of internal and external stimuli (Moyer, 1976). Seven categories of aggressive behavior are described below. It should be noted, however, that it is not always possible to distinguish these types of behavior in practice because they overlap. Thus a given aggressive act may be the result of two or three factors acting together.

Kinds of Aggressive Behavior

1. **Angry aggression.** This is the classical variety, the type most people think of when they hear the word "aggression." It is generally accompanied by the signs of emotional arousal (see the section on emotion in the next chapter) and is often produced by pain or frustration. For example, two rats put together in a cage and given brief, intermittent electric shocks will attack each other when the shock comes on. Under these circumstances a rat will even attack a doll or a stuffed animal if another rat is not available. A monkey or a mouse whose tail is pinched will bite its tormentor or (if that is impossible) any other object.

   Frustration of goal-directed behavior—for example, preventing a hungry animal from reaching a food reward that it has worked for—generally produces an aggressive response. A pigeon that has been taught to peck a key to obtain grain will attack another pigeon if the grain is withheld (Azrin, Hutchinson, & Hake, 1965). However, frustration does not *invariably* have this kind of effect. A theory relating frustration to aggression, as well as other theories of the origins of human aggressive behavior, will be discussed in Chapter 19.

2. **Predatory aggression.** Quite different from the aroused state associated with angry aggression is the dispassionate stalking of its prey by a carnivorous animal such as a fox, a wolf, or any member of the cat family. One would hesitate to call this behavior "aggressive" and would label it "food-seeking" instead, were it not for the fact that the hunger drive need not be present—the response seems to be elicited simply by the presence of the prey and may occur even when the predator is totally satiated.

   An interesting finding about predatory behavior is that in some animal species it is partly learned through imitation. A kitten learns to kill rats by the age of 4 months if it is normally reared and allowed to see its mother killing rats. If a kitten is raised in isolation, however, the chances are that it will *not* kill a rat if it is presented with one when it is 4 months old. It can soon learn to do so if it is given the opportunity to watch other cats kill (Kuo, 1930).

3. **Fear-induced aggression.** This is exemplified by the usually meek animal that, when cornered by a predator, turns on it and attacks it. More

generally, any fearful animal is likely to bite when approached too closely by the object of its fear.

4. **Operant aggression.** An organism may perform an aggressive act simply because it is rewarded for doing so, or punished for not doing so. For example, the tendency of a rat to attack another animal or an object when it is given an electric shock can be strengthened if the shock is turned off whenever the rat attacks. Human adults (Loew, 1967) and children (Lovaas, 1961) who are praised for making hostile remarks tend to become more aggressive. The hired killer, who kills because he is paid to do so, is a good example of this class of aggression.

As in other forms of operant conditioning (discussed in Chapter 6), the reinforcement for aggressive behavior need not follow every response. Once the behavior is learned, an occasional reward (or punishment) is enough to maintain it. This is particularly clear in what is known as **obedient aggression.** A guard dog that attacks on command, or a person who harms someone because he or she is "ordered" to do so, is committing obedient aggression.

5. **Territorial aggression.** This category of behavior has been studied more thoroughly by ethologists (such as Konrad Lorenz, 1966) than by psychologists. Animals of many different species will stake out a territory, frequently mark it in some way (by spraying the boundaries with urine, for instance), and then threaten to attack any unfamiliar member of its species that intrudes within its borders. Note that this behavior is confined to the territory itself: If the animal is taken out of its own territory, its territorial aggressiveness vanishes. Some people see parallels in human territorial conflict.

6. **Altruistic aggression.** The aggressiveness of a bird or mammal guarding its young, and of a "soldier" bee or ant defending its hive or nest, are examples of altruistic aggression. Moyer (1976) has used the term **maternal aggression** to describe the fierce behavior of a female mammal whose nestful of pups is threatened. For example, male rats who approach young rat pups are often attacked and driven off by the pups' mother, who at other times would never challenge a male (Svare, 1983). In some species, however—notably humans—the same kind of behavior may be shown by the father, or even by unrelated individuals.

7. **Intermale aggression.** In many species the normal reaction of a full-grown male to another, unfamiliar adult male is a hostile one. Frequently the animal will attack without provocation. This behavior is distinguished from territorial aggression because it can occur in any location. Studies of intermale aggression in mice and rats have shown that the stimulus that elicits the attack is the scent of the other male. If the animals' odors are masked by an artificial scent, or if their sense of smell is surgically destroyed, they are unlikely to fight (Ropartz, 1968). Furthermore, in many species such as dogs and wolves (Lorenz, 1966), and even bison (Barash, 1977), the fight will not occur if one animal assumes a stereotyped position of submissiveness.

The male hormone testosterone is of critical importance in intermale aggression. Immature or castrated animals do not show this behavior, but if they are injected with testosterone, the aggressiveness appears (Levy & King, 1953). It is also clear that intermale aggression is closely connected with the competition for females. In species that breed only in certain seasons, notably the hoofed mammals, almost all aggressive behavior takes place during the mating season.

Physiological Factors in Aggression

Parts of the brain seem to play a major role in aggressive behavior. These are the limbic system and associated areas of the hypothalamus (see Chapter 2). Damage to one of these brain areas, or stimulation of them through implanted electrodes, is likely to affect one or more of the types of aggressive behavior—especially predatory, angry, and fear-induced aggression. Particularly interesting to psychologists and physiologists are those cases in which only a single kind of aggressive behavior is affected. For example, mild electrical stimulation of one part of a cat's hypothalamus will cause it to attack a rat. Stimulation of another area within the hypothalamus, on the other hand, causes it to ignore the rat and instead launch an enraged attack on the experimenter (Wasman & Flynn, 1962; Egger & Flynn, 1963).

The amygdala, which is part of the limbic system, appears to be of particular importance in aggressiveness. Surgical destruction of all or part of this brain structure generally results in an animal that is docile, unaggressive, and unfearful. In humans there have been reports of abnormal aggressiveness resulting from tumors in the region of the amygdala. In 1966 a young man named Charles Whitman shot and killed 14 people from the observation tower at the University of Texas before he himself was shot down by police bullets. In autopsy a walnut-sized tumor was found in his amygdala (Beck 1983).

Another factor that has been linked to aggressiveness is the level of glucose in the blood. Ralph Bolton, an American anthropologist, lived for two years among the Qolla, a tribe of Indians in the Andes Mountains of Peru (Bolton, 1976). These people have been described as among the most aggressive on earth—their homicide rate is extremely high, and they are constantly embroiled in arguments and brawls. Bolton found, first of all, that the individuals within this group that were rated most aggressive were likely to be suffering from a moderate degree of hypoglycemia (low blood glucose). The people with normal blood glucose levels were less aggressive, and so were those with *severe* hypoglycemia, doubtless because of the weakening effects of this condition.

Which of the types of aggression described in the text do these photos illustrate? (*Left:* Tom Branch; *above:* Richard Hutchings; both Photo Researchers)

Second, Bolton found that the overall proportion of hypoglycemics in the Qolla population was far greater than in other populations studied: 55 percent had mild or severe hypoglycemia. (In the United States the proportion has been estimated at between 2 percent and 30 percent, but most researchers believe the 30 percent figure to be very exaggerated.) Bolton attributed the remarkable hypoglycemia rate found among the Qolla to three factors: (1) the effects of living at a high altitude; (2) poor nutrition; and (3) the effects of chewing coca leaves, which contain cocaine. Coca (not to be confused with cocoa, which comes from the bean of the cacao tree) deadens hunger pangs and makes its users feel better temporarily, but its long-term effects on the body's metabolism are harmful. Bolton hypothesized that fighting, too, may have temporary beneficial effects: By increasing the secretion of epinephrine by the adrenal glands, it may produce a rise in blood glucose that, though short-lived, results in an increased feeling of well-being while it lasts. Indeed, Qolla individuals sometimes mentioned to Bolton that fighting "makes one feel better."

From as early as 2 or 3 years of age, human males behave in a more aggressive fashion than human females (Pederson & Bell, 1970). The same sex difference has been noted in rhesus monkeys (Harlow, 1971) and in a wide variety of mammalian species. This aggressiveness includes not only intermale aggression, but also angry aggression, territorial aggression, and perhaps even operant aggression (male dogs are used as guard dogs more often than females).

In adult male animals castration greatly reduces all kinds of aggressive behavior. A gelded horse or steer is considerably more tractable and slower to anger than a stallion or bull. The same effect is produced by the administration of estrogens and progesterone to a male animal (Moyer, 1971). Injections of testosterone restore the aggressiveness of castrated animals.

Human motivation is, of course, influenced by many factors other than physiological ones. As we will see in Chapter 12, cognitive, social, and emotional factors are as important considerations in human motivation as the biological ones we have discussed in this chapter.

SUMMARY

1. In motivation theory James emphasized concepts of impulses and instincts; Cannon put forth the idea of *homeostasis,* or the way the body maintains an equilibrium in its internal environment.

2. The concept of *drives* and *drive reduction* was introduced by Hull. The concept of drives is most useful when we are talking about relatively clear-cut states of physiological deprivation, such as hunger and thirst.

3. Hunger is one of the most universal sources of *motivation.* Regulation of food intake seems to depend on gastric secretions, a sensation of bulk in the small intestine, blood sugar level, and signals from the hypothalamus.

4. Some experiments support the *set-point theory* and suggest that obese poeple have a higher set point than nonobese people. When obese people are below their set point, they are in a state of deprivation or homeostatic imbalance, even if their weight is above normal levels.

5. *Osmoreceptors* in the brain seem to respond to dehydration in the cells by causing the organism to be thirsty and by triggering the release of a hormone, causing the kidneys to excrete less water. *Volumetric receptors* respond to a change in the total volume of extracellur fluid by stimulating the thirst receptors in the brain.

6. Sexual behavior apparently has *drive-reducing* (or positive *incentive*) value for both males and females of the species; hormones also play a role in both sexual behavior and the development of secondary sex characteristics.

7. The innate patterns of behavior that are part of mothering or parenting in many organisms are elicited by a complex combination of hormonal states and external stimuli.

8. Psychologists have identified at least ten classes of aggressive behavior; the motivations for *aggression* are diverse, including pain, fear, predatory behavior, and maternal behavior.

SUGGESTED READINGS

BECK, R. C. (1983). *Motivation: Theories and principles* (2nd ed.). Englewood Cliffs, N.J.: Prentice-Hall. Thorough coverage of historical and present-day motivation theories. Also deals with specific motivations such as aggression.

HARLOW, H. (1971). *Learning to love.* San Francisco: Albion. The effects of parental care and peer-group interactions on young monkeys. Describes the development of social, sexual, and aggressive behavior in these animals.

LORENZ, K. (1966). *On aggression.* M. K. Wilson, trans. New York: Harcourt Brace Jovanovich. Here Lorenz argues that humans as well as animals have an innate drive to be aggressive.

MAHONEY, B. K., ROGERS, T., STRAW, M. K., et al. (1983). *Human obesity: Assessment and treatment.* Englewood Cliffs, N.J.: Prentice-Hall. A comprehensive review of modern research on obesity and methods of weight reduction.

MASTERS, W. H., JOHNSON, V. E., & KOLODNY, R. C. (1985). *Human sexuality* (2nd ed.). Boston: Little Brown. A classic review of human sexuality by the leading researchers in the field.

MONEY, J., and EHRHARDT, A. A. (1972). *Man and woman, boy and girl.* Baltimore: Johns Hopkins Press. Chromosomal and hormonal factors in human sexual identity and behavior.

MOOK, D. G. (1987). *Motivation: The organization of action.* New York: Norton. An addition to providing a review of traditional topics in motivation, this book integrates a cognitive approach to motivation as well.

STUNDKARD, A. J. (Ed.)(1983). *Obesity.* Philadelphia: Saunders. A collection of papers by experts on obesity.

12 Human Motivation and Emotion

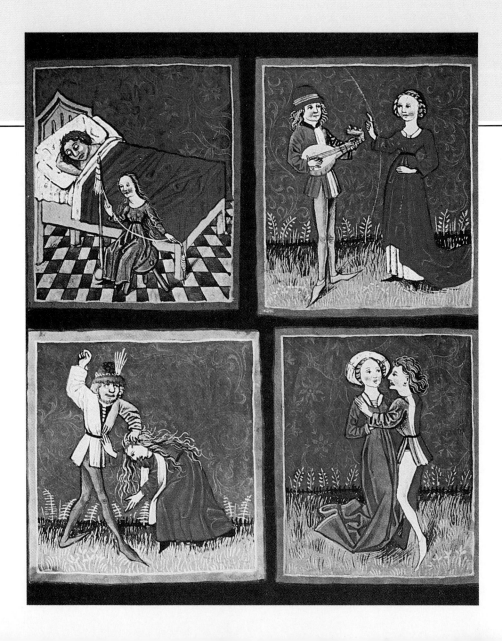

T he previous chapter was concerned with the biological bases of **motivation.** We discussed motives and drives that are common to a wide variety of species: human beings, monkeys, dogs, rats, and even honeybees. In this chapter the focus will be on the factors involved in human motivation.

Why do people do what they do? What motivates us to behave at all? And why, of all the things we are capable of doing, do we do a certain thing in a certain situation? Answers to these questions concern the very core of human nature. The answers are, as you might expect, quite complex.

Human motivation ranges from basic physiological drives (such as hunger) through drives for stimulation that are part of our ability to know and understand our environment (such as curiosity) to socially based drives that we acquire from our culture (such as the desire to achieve).

In this chapter we will also consider the related topic of emotion. Motivation and emotion are closely linked—indeed, as we shall see, it is often hard to distinguish between them. Emotions can act as motivators, and motivations can produce emotion. We will begin by distinguishing between primary and secondary motivation.

SOURCES OF NEEDS AND MOTIVES

Primary Motivation: Biological Needs

In the previous chapter we reviewed some of our biological needs: We need food and water to survive. We also require air and an appropriate tempera-

A common medieval belief was that people were controlled or motivated by four humors: (clockwise from top left) *melancholic*—which corresponded to an excess of black bile; *phlegmatic*—which corresponded to an excess of phlegm; *sanguine*—which corresponded to an excess of blood; and *choleric*—which corresponded to an excess of yellow bile. (Central Library, Zurich/Art Resource)

ture range. When we encounter deficiencies in any of our basic needs, we typically take action to correct them.

If you think about your typical daily activities, however, you will realize that much of your behavior seems to have little or nothing to do with these basic biological needs. At first glance it is hard to see that reading this book, riding a bicycle, talking with friends, or watching television has anything to do with hunger or thirst. But some of these behaviors may have originally been motivated by basic biological needs, through complex conditioning and learning processes.

Secondary Motivation and Conditioning

In Chapter 6 we saw how Pavlov was able to give previously neutral stimuli the ability to elicit behaviors through the process of *classical conditioning*. A dog will normally salivate when it sees food, but it will not normally salivate when it hears a tone. After repeated pairings of the tone with the sight of food, Pavlov found that the tone alone could elicit salivation. Furthermore, through higher-order conditioning, the tone could be used to create a link between another stimulus, such as a light, and salivation. Seeing a dog salivate when a light flashes would seem very strange unless you knew the dog's conditioning history.

Skinner has also shown that through *operant conditioning* previously neutral stimuli can become secondary reinforcers and can then cause learning of new behaviors. When a rat learns that pressing a bar leads to food, the bar acquires the properties of a secondary reinforcer and can be used to reinforce other behaviors. A rat will learn to run a maze to get at the bar, will then learn to open a door to get into the maze, and so on until a complex chain of behavior is formed. An uninformed observer looking at several rats who had received such training might mistakenly conclude that rats have a built-in fondness for mazes.

Human beings, of course, are able to learn even more complex sequences of behaviors. Some of our behaviors that seem to have little relationship to basic biological needs may in fact be the result of such complex chainings of behaviors. One very common secondary motivator in our society is money. Money serves the same function for us as the bar or lever does for the rat—it gets us the food, drink, clothing, and shelter that we need. We are all familiar with the numerous things people will do to acquire money.

Functional Autonomy of Motivation

With both classical and operant conditioning, previously neutral stimuli eventually lose their acquired reinforcing power if they are not, at least some of the time, paired with the original reinforcer (such as food, in the case of hunger). Humans, however, appear to have many "secondary" reinforcers that do not seem to be paired with primary reinforcers. Color preferences or desires for certain kinds of friends, music, and clothing do not seem to need association with primary reinforcers. This observation has led some motivation theorists to believe that acquired motives can have a "life of their own," independent of any association with the satisfaction of basic biological needs.

Perhaps the clearest example of such a learned or acquired motive comes from the work of Neal Miller and others on fear and anxiety. Miller (1948) demonstrated the motivating power of learned fear in rats. The animals were placed in a box that contained a white compartment and a black compart-

ment with a door between them. First, the rats were given several shocks on the white side of the box through an electrified floor. The animals soon learned to run from the white compartment through the open door into the black compartment. Following this training period, the animals were placed in the white compartment with the door between the compartments closed. Even though the shock was never turned on again, the rats learned to turn a wheel so that they could get out of the white compartment. Later, when the wheel was disconnected so that it no longer opened the door, the rats learned to press a bar instead to open the door. The bar pressing persisted for hundreds of trials, even though the rats were never shocked again.

Behavior motivated by learned fear, then, can continue indefinitely without the organism ever reexperiencing the pain that originally created the fear. Several theorists have taken this kind of analysis one step further and argued that many acquired motives can become **functionally autonomous** (Woodworth, 1918; Allport, 1937). This means that motives that were originally conditioned to basic biological needs can, through repeated use, become motives in their own right. The behavior of the hoarder who collects money for the sheer pleasure of having larger and larger piles of it, and who does not want to spend it even to provide adequate food and clothing, is an example of functional autonomy of motivation.

The behavior of someone who collects money for the sheer pleasure of having more of it is an example of functional autonomy of motivation. (The Bettmann Archive)

Acquired Motivation or Innate Need?

Many of the complex motives that we see displayed by the people around us are the result of complex learning involving secondary reinforcement. Some of these acquired motives may eventually become functionally autonomous. All of them have their origins in basic biological needs. Some psychologists, indeed, believe that all human motivation can be explained in this way. Others, however, think that there are some innate or built-in motives that do not stem from tissue deficits or physiological imbalances. Such motives are assumed to be part of "human nature." Curiosity is one example of a motive that may reflect built-in characteristics of human nature rather than being acquired through learning. In the next section we will examine several examples of motives that have been studied extensively by psychologists and that appear to involve fundamental aspects of human nature. These include curiosity, affiliative, and competence needs. Our discussion will also suggest that the expression of all human motives is strongly influenced by learning. This will be particularly clear when we discuss two other human motivations: sexual and achievement motivation. Finally, we will consider motivation in the workplace, a setting in which the variety and complexity of human motivation are expcessed.

THE MAJOR HUMAN MOTIVES

Curiosity and the Need for Stimulation

All animals are equipped with means of gathering and processing information, and human beings are particularly well equipped for these tasks. We routinely gather a wide variety of information through our senses. Through sight, hearing, touch, smell, and taste sensors we take in, organize, interpret, and use information about ourselves and our environment. This enables us to understand our world and to take effective action. But in addition to having the ability to process information, we also have a need to use that ability.

Human information-processing capabilities can be likened to a fine piece of machinery. An automobile engine, for example, can be efficient, powerful, and smooth, but if it is left unused for six months, it will probably be balky, dirty, and unreliable. Similarly, if our information-processing abilities are to work well, they need exercise. Unlike an automobile engine, however, we do not need an outside force to "turn us on." Humans and animals have a built-in need for stimulation that motivates them to seek out sensory stimulation from the environment.

A Theoretical Account of Curiosity. The fact that we seek stimulation, and exhibit preferences for and interest in certain degrees of complexity in that stimulation, is explained by the concept of an *optimal level of stimulation* (Hunt, 1965). According to this theory, we tend to pay attention to stimuli that deviate from our standards of comparison (Miller, Galanter, & Pribram, 1960). We develop standards of comparison through experience. The first time you see an object, it interests you and holds your attention. However, as you continue to be exposed to that object, you become used to it or adapt to it, and it is less likely to command your attention. For example, if you are used to seeing birds with two legs, another two-legged bird will not be as likely to arouse your interest as a four-legged bird would be. Standards of comparison are also called *adaptation levels* (Helson, 1964). For any given stimulus, the adaptation level is the level of stimulation perceived as average or normal. Stimuli that fall within the average or expected range are not likely to capture our attention; stimuli that fall outside the average range or are exceptional (such as four-legged birds) probably will.

Using the concepts of adaptation level and focus of attention on incongruous stimuli, Hunt (1965) theorized that there are optimal levels of stimulation. If all incoming stimuli are average, or within our adaptation levels, we become bored. On the other hand, excessive stimulation can be very unpleasant. But stimuli that are somewhat unusual are of interest to us. Optimal levels of stimulation, then, contain enough surprises to keep our interest alive and allow us to exercise our information-processing abilities, but are not so different from our experience and expectations that they frighten or overwhelm us. For example, a crowded shopping mall or a museum exhibit with large jostling crowds can be unpleasant because they provide too much stimulation. In contrast, jobs, lectures, or other daily routines that contain no surprises can become unpleasantly boring.

Experiments on Sensory Deprivation. If people need stimulation and prefer it to be mildly different from their adaptation levels, then we would expect a complete absence of stimulation to be very unpleasant and to have negative effects on people's efficiency at processing information. In an early experiment on sensory deprivation reported by Bexton, Herm, and Scott (1954), college student volunteers were paid for each day they participated in a study of the effects of reduced sensory input. The subjects spent their time lying on a cot in a sound-deadened room with a constant background noise. They wore translucent goggles, cardboard tubes around their arms, and gloves. This experience was very unpleasant, and most of the subjects refused to continue after a few days. In this experiment and others like it, subjects have experienced visual hallucinations, rapid changes in mood, and an inordinate interest in normally boring material, such as old stock-market reports. After a period of sensory deprivation, subjects also showed reduced competence on a variety of visual, manual dexterity, and abstract-reasoning tasks (Bexton, Heron, & Scott, 1954; Held & White, 1959; Vernon, McGill, Gulick, & Cand-

Humans have a built-in need for stimulation. This, in conjunction with a tendency to focus attention on incongruent stimuli, may cause exploration of novel elements in the environment—hence curiosity.
(Michael Kagan/ Monkmeyer Press)

land, 1959). Rodgers and Jones (1980) have also shown that the longer people are deprived of sensory input, the stronger their desire for new information becomes. Taken together, these studies of sensory deprivation underscore the importance of our need for stimulation.

Affiliation

Wherever people are found, whether in a high-rise office building, along the banks of a tropical river, around a desert oasis, or in a crowded disco, one clear fact of human existence is that we spend a great deal of our time with other people. We work together, eat together, and play together. We have developed extremely complex languages for the purpose of communicating with one another. At birth we are completely dependent on other people to satisfy our biological needs, and this dependence lasts longer in humans than in any other species. Stories of hermits who live in isolated caves and shun all human contact capture our interest because such behavior is so unusual. For these and other reasons, the human being is often called a social animal.

In the previous chapter we saw that a monkey that is reared alone (or with a terrycloth "mother" instead of a real one) is likely to be permanently impaired in its ability to form normal relationships with other monkeys. Not surprisingly, the deficits caused by lack of proper parental care and attention are even more serious in humans.

Effects of Lack of Parenting. Human babies need more than milk and a warm blanket. They need what is usually called "mothering," but which we will call "parenting," since it can be equally well provided by a father—or, for that matter, any caring adult. Case studies of children who have been subjected to early social deprivation show that it can have very serious ill effects on human development. When infants are reared in institutions in which they receive food and medical care but little social stimulation, they show striking deficits in emotional, intellectual, and even physical development (Goldfarb, 1944, 1945; Spitz, 1946). Provence and Lipton (1962) observed institutionalized infants, aged 4 days to 8 months, whose main contact with other humans was limited to the changing of bottles (which were propped in their cribs) and diapers. Even by 4 months of age these infants acted differently from children raised in normal family settings. They vocalized less, were less interested in manipulating objects, and were very passive. H. Gardner (1982) described a group of infants who required hospitalization and had to be removed temporarily from their parents. These infants became listless, showed signs of depression, and failed to gain weight. When they returned to their homes they quickly began to thrive.

It is difficult to pinpoint the specific aspects of social deprivation that led to impaired development in these human infants. It is quite clear, though, that some close human contact is necessary for normal development; humans need far more than merely food and shelter. However, while some instances of extreme early social deprivation seem to cause irreversible damage, several investigators have discovered that human beings have a remarkable resilience even to severe deprivation. Koluchova (1972) studied the effects of early deprivation on a pair of identical twin boys who were subjected to severe deprivation for the first six years of their lives. When they were discovered, they had almost no language and appeared to be severely retarded. By age 14, however, their IQs were average, their speech was normal, and they were doing well in school. This and other examples of rehabilita-

tion give some hope that the negative effects of early social deprivation may be at least partially reversible. (See the Application: Severe Early Isolation—Feral Children for a description of several children raised in the wild.)

Need For Affiliation in Adults. Fortunately, most of us do not encounter severe social deprivation. Anyone reading this book is already deeply involved in human society and experiences contact with others as a common, daily fact of life. We all spend time with others and time by ourselves, and we all have some control over our social lives. Sometimes we want to be with others: When Saturday evening approaches, dates, parties, and other social activities are often uppermost in our minds. At other times, we want to be alone: A quiet evening with a book or a solitary stroll is sometimes quite appealing. Because we seem to need both socializing and solitude, questions about *when* we seek out social contact and *why* we do so become important.

In one of the first systematic investigations of people's changing desires for **affiliation,** Schachter (1959) did a series of studies of the relationship between anxiety and the desire to affiliate. On the basis of several case studies of college students' reactions to social isolation, he theorized that an increase in anxiety would lead to an increased desire to be with others. In his initial experiment female college students who volunteered for a psychology experiment were divided into two groups. The subjects were met by a person who introduced himself as "Dr. Gregor Zilstein in the Medical School's Departments of Neurology and Psychiatry," who told them that the experiment involved the use of electric shock. Subjects in the high-anxiety condition were told that the shocks would be quite intense and painful, though they were "reassured" that there would be no "permanent damage" and were shown the alleged shock-delivering equipment. This description was, of course, designed to be frightening: No one was ever actually shocked. Subjects in the low-anxiety condition were met by a less ominous "Dr. Zilstein" who, adhering to a reassuring script, told them that the shocks would be extremely mild and that at most they would feel a tickle. Next, all subjects were informed that a number of people were waiting to take part in the experiment and that they too would have to wait. Each subject was asked to indicate

Humans of all ages are motivated to seek social contact. (Bonnie Freer/Photo Research)

APPLICATION

Severe Early Isolation—Feral Children

From time to time we hear reports of children who have been living in the wild from a very early age with little or no human contact. Often these *feral children* are living with, and appear to have been reared by, wild animals.

Sargent and Stafford (1965) reviewed a number of these cases. One of the earliest feral children described in some detail was the Wild Boy of Aveyron, discovered by hunters in southern France in 1799. Apparently he had been foraging for himself for some time (he was about 11 years old). Dr. Jean Itard attempted to socialize and teach the boy. Although he did develop some affection for his caretaker and learned a few simple things, the boy never approached normality.

A pair of girls about 2 and 9 years of age were found living with wolves in India in 1920. The younger girl died soon after she was discovered. The older girl, Kamala, had developed wolflike mannerisms: She howled, lapped up liquids, and bared her teeth at anyone who came too close (Gesell, 1941). An even more recent case of a child being thoroughly socialized by an animal community is that of the Gazelle-boy of the Sahara Desert (Armen, 1974). He ran with a heard of gazelle, had gazellelike mannerisms, and generally seemed to be an accepted part of the gazelle community.

Attempts to resocialize these feral children have met with varied degrees of success. Itard had very limited success with the Wild Boy of Aveyron. Kamala, the wolf girl, was originally completely hostile toward other humans, but eventually she came to like her playmates and learned to use about 100 words. She did not, however, become a normal person. In contrast, Tamasha, the "Wild Boy of Salvador," who was found in the jungle, progressed quite rapidly. He acquired language fairly easily, as well as other habits of human culture, and was able to talk about his experiences in the wild.

It is difficult to compare these children because their experiences and situations varied considerably, but it seems that the longer the period of time away from human contact and society, and the earlier such separation begins, the more difficult it is for the person ever to become integrated into human society.

It is tempting to think that these difficulties of adjustment result from social isolation—that is, to assume that human contact is necessary for normal development and that the absence of such contact is the major source of the feral children's difficulties. There are, however, other possible explanations. For example, how did these feral children get into the wilderness in the first place? One plausible guess is that they were retarded or defective in some other way at birth, and that their parents abandoned them for that reason (Sargent & Stafford, 1965). Another possibility is that the severe malnutrition that most of these children must have experienced caused some central nervous system damage, and that this, rather than their social isolation, was the major problem.

It is because of these ambiguities in the interpretation of isolated cases that the laboratory work on animals by Harlow and others cited in the text is so valuable in trying to understand the effects of extreme social isolation.

---

whether she would prefer to wait in a room with other people or by herself. Only 33 percent of the low-anxiety subjects asked to wait with other people; almost twice as many (63 percent) of the high-anxiety subjects asked to wait with others. In subsequent experiments Schachter found that anxiety increased the desire to affiliate, even when the subjects knew that they would not be allowed to talk with the people with whom they would be waiting.

Schachter's studies showed that when people experience anxiety, their desire to be with others increases. Schachter believed he was studying the effects of anxiety on affiliative behavior, but later researchers pointed out that fear might have caused the affiliation pattern he observed. Explanations for the results of these and other experiments point to two factors. First, simply being with others often causes a reduction in fear (Wrightsman, 1960). Second, when people are frightened, they want to find out how others in the same situation are reacting, so they can compare their own reactions with those of similar others (Schachter, 1959; Gerard & Rabbie, 1961). The experiments on fear and affiliation thus uncovered two of the most important aspects of social contact: emotional support from others, and the provision of standards of correctness through social comparison (Festinger, 1954). (See Chapter 19 for a discussion of social-comparison theory.)

Affiliation Avoidance. There are, of course, times when we do *not* wish to be around others. While people may be motivated to confide their feelings to

others when they are under stress, they may avoid affiliation if the stressful situation is an embarrassing one (Fish, Karabenick, & Heath, 1978). When we are embarrassed, the last thing we want is to be around our peers. Our most fervent desire when we have just tripped over a small crack in an otherwise smooth sidewalk, or have just dropped a melting ice-cream cone in our lap, is to be unnoticed by others. When Sarnoff and Zimbardo (1961) told subjects that they would be participating in a study of oral needs and would be sucking on pacifiers, baby bottles, and breast shields, a clear preference to wait alone was expressed. And just as some people typically desire to be around others, chronically shy individuals often take great pains to avoid social contact (Zimbardo, 1977).

Human Sexual Expression

One of the major reasons for affiliating with others is sexual attraction. We will discuss the general question of why we like or dislike others in Chapter 19; the physiology of sexual motivation was described in Chapter 11. In this section we will examine some of the tremendous variability in the expression of our basic sexual needs. Although human sexual behavior has a common physiological basis, its expression varies widely. This variability can be seen in comparisons among different cultures, in historical changes within particular societies, and in differences among subgroups of society at any given time. Such variability attests to the powerful influence of socialization on the expression of our basic sexual needs.

Differences and Changes in Sexual Behaviors. The overwhelming influence of socially transmitted standards can be seen clearly in variations in sexual behavior among cultures. In some cultures, for example, homosexuality is approved, but in others it is not (Davenport, 1965); some cultures expose children to their parents' sexual activities and encourage adolescent sexual experimentation, while others make these kinds of behaviors taboo (Marshall, 1971). Cultural standards produce rates of adult sexual intercourse that vary widely (Marshall, 1971). In Mangaia, a South Pacific culture, adolescents have sex every night and average three orgasms per night (Hyde, 1979). On the island of Ines Beag, off the Irish coast, married couples wear undergarments during intercourse, and the women report that they never have orgasms (Messinger, 1971).

Within our own society sexual behavior appears to have changed dramatically in this century. The evidence for these changes comes from surveys in which people are asked to report on their attitudes toward various sexual practices and on their own sexual behaviors. The results of such surveys need to be interpreted with some caution. Differences in the reported frequency of particular sexual behaviors between surveys taken in the 1950s and those done in the 1970s, for example, might be due to real changes in behavior, or they might be due to changes in the willingness to admit to such behaviors. It is also possible that the people who are willing to participate in such surveys are not representative of the population as a whole, and that generalizations from these surveys to the nation are therefore questionable. This problem is particularly acute with surveys conducted by popular magazines, in which the respondents are (1) only people who read such magazines, and (2) only those readers who are motivated to voluntarily respond.

Keeping these cautions in mind, it is still fairly clear from the more carefully conducted surveys that substantial changes in sexual attitudes and prac-

Table 12–1:   Percentage of White High-School and College Students Reporting Premarital Intercourse in Three Historical Periods.

Period	High School		College	
	Males	Females	Males	Females
1925–1965	25	10	55	25
1966–1973	35	35	85	65
1974–1979	56	44	74	74

From Dreyer (1982), p. 575.

tices have taken place in the last few decades. Comparisons between the Kinsey studies, which were the first systematic surveys (Kinsey, Pomeroy, & Martin, 1948; Kinsey, Pomeroy, Martin, & Gebhard, 1953), and the study by Hunt (1974) two decades later reveal considerable liberalization of both sexual attitudes and behaviors. Attitudes toward premarital sex, masturbation, oral sex, and homosexuality have all become more tolerant. Among adolescents and young adults, Dreyer's (1982) review of a large number of surveys shows a clear increase in premarital sexual intercourse in the period from 1966 to 1973. This increased sexual activity continued during the 1974 to 1979 period (see Table 12–1). More recent surveys of college freshmen (Astin, 1977, 1979, 1980, 1983) indicate that attitudes toward premarital sex have remained relatively constant since 1975 (see Figure 12–1). Recent events such as the sexually-transmitted disease AIDS, may bring about changes both in sexual practices and attitudes toward various sexual practices.

The Effects of Erotica on Sexual Behavior.   A topic of current interest and concern is the increasing availability of sexually explicit materials, or *erotica,* in North American society. Psychologists have recently examined similarities and differences in individuals' responses to erotica and have been exploring the possible links between exposure to erotica and the likelihood of subsequent aggression.

In general, erotic material (stories, photographs, and movies) causes physiological arousal in both males and females (Schmidt, Sigush, & Meyberg, 1969; Schmidt & Sigush, 1970) and increases the likelihood of sexual activity for short periods following exposure (Mosher, 1973). There are, however, a

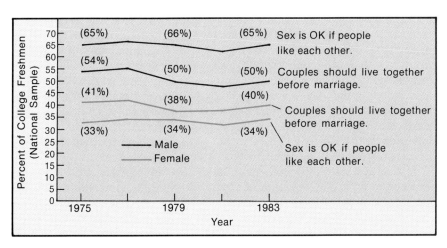

Figure 12–1   Percent of College Freshmen (Males and Females) "Agreeing Strongly" or "Agreeing Somewhat" with Sex-Related Statements, from 1975 to 1983. Survey research indicates that attitudes among college freshmen toward premarital sex have remained relatively constant since 1975. (From Lloyd, 1985; based on data from Astin, 1979; 1980; 1983)

number of differences in individuals' responses to erotica, just as there are individual differences in other aspects of sexual behavior. Even though erotica can be arousing for everyone, this experience can be either positive or negative in emotional tone. Females, for example, tend to find explicit or "hard-core" sexual materials more disturbing than males do (Sapolsky & Zillman, 1981). Individuals classified as sexual liberals or conservatives (based on questionnaire responses to a liberalism-conservatism scale) are equally aroused by sexual material, but while liberals find the most arousing material to be the most entertaining, conservatives find the most arousing material to be the most offensive and least entertaining (Wallace & Wehmer, 1972). And individuals classified as high in sex guilt are less likely to view erotic materials than those low in sex guilt. Schill and Chapin (1972), for example, found that males low in sex guilt tended to look at issues of *Playboy* and *Penthouse* while seated in a waiting room, but males high in sex guilt look at *Outdoor Life* and *Newsweek*.

Erotica, Violence, and Aggression. The increased availability of erotic material in North America has produced heated and continuing debates about censorship and personal freedoms, morality, and the debasement of women. One issue that has been the subject of recent psychological research is the potential link between erotica and crimes of violence such as rape. Rape cannot be studied in the laboratory, of course, but some experiments have produced evidence that bears on this issue. Aggression in the form of verbal abuse or the willingness to deliver shocks to another subject has been studied in the laboratory (see Chapter 19). In the typical study subjects view erotica, and their subsequent behavior is measured for aggressiveness and compared to the behavior of subjects who have not viewed erotic stimuli. One general finding is that erotic material by itself does not increase aggression (Sapolsky & Zillman, 1981). But when subjects have been angered before viewing erotic materials (usually by being insulted and/or aggressed against by an experimenter or a confederate posing as another subject), subsequent aggressive behavior increases.

The results of some of these studies seem to be contradictory: Some find that erotica increases the aggressiveness of provoked subjects (e.g., Cantor, Zillman, & Einsiedel, 1978), while others find that erotica reduces aggression (e.g., Baron & Bell, 1977). More recent studies have clarified this contradiction by defining more carefully the nature of erotic content. Erotica can vary in its explicitness and in the extent to which it contains themes of violence. The portrayal of sexually violent erotic scenes has been increasing in both the print and electronic media (Malamuth & Spinner, 1980), and this kind of material does appear to increase subsequent aggression of males against females. Donnerstein and Berkowitz (1981), for example, exposed provoked males to either a neutral movie, an erotic movie with no violent themes, or to a movie portraying a sexual attack. The ending of the violent movie was also varied. In the "positive-ending" film the woman became a willing participant; in the "negative-ending" film she was shown to be suffering. As you can see in Figure 12–2, none of these movies affected aggression toward a male target. The female target, however, was given shocks of higher intensity when subjects had viewed either of the violent films.

In a related study Malamuth and Check (1981) found that males previously exposed to an erotic depiction of a rape showed little sympathy toward the victim of a more realistic rape when it was described to them, and an increase in self-reported willingness to commit rape themselves. The most recent evidence, then, suggests that materials portraying sexual violence do

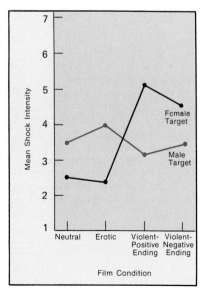

Figure 12–2 Mean shock intensity as a function of sex of target and film condition. (From Donnerstein & Berkowitz, 1981, p. 716)

tend to increase subsequent aggression toward women. These effects appear to result because some depictions imply that rape is "acceptable" to potential victims (as in the "positive-ending" film in Donnerstein and Berkowitz's study), and because women are presented to angry persons as potential targets for their wrath (Berkowitz, 1974).

Competence

Imagine trying the following observational exercise: For one day you pretend to be a visitor from another world. You know nothing at all about humans, so you watch them to find out what they are like. One of the most obvious things that you notice, the most accurate description of the humans you saw, would be that they are almost always *doing* something. Except for periods of sleep, and excluding a few abnormal cases of coma or catatonia, people spend nearly all their time *behaving*. They handle machinery, jog around tracks, fly airplanes, ski, scratch their noses, doodle, and tap their feet. What inspires all this activity? Some behaviors clearly serve basic biological needs; hunger, for example, provides the motivation for moving the forkful of spaghetti from the plate to the mouth. But even when all the basic needs are satisfied, people still talk, drive autos, work crossword puzzles, and do many other things.

This incessant activity has led a number of psychologists to argue that humans *need* to behave. We saw earlier that people need to exercise their information-processing abilities; we now turn to the related notion that they need to exercise their ability to behave. Woodworth (1958), for example, believed that the great variety of behavior that seems to be completely incidental to any primary needs (such as doodling in a notebook) cannot be adequately explained by the theories of secondary motivation reviewed at the beginning of this chapter. He hypothesized that the need to deal with the environment is itself a primary drive. Similarly, Goldstein (1939) gave self-actualization the status of a **primary drive.** His hypothesis, not unlike Woodworth's, was that humans have a basic tendency to actualize or bring into being their inherent abilities, to do things merely because they are capable of doing them.

After reviewing these and other ideas, White (1959) suggested that people are motivated to develop and exercise **competence** in interacting with their environment. According to this hypothesis, interacting effectively with the environment produces feelings of competence or efficacy. The feeling that you have when you do something perfectly, whether it be making a basketball swish through the net, completing a difficult crossword puzzle, or knitting a row of even stitches in a sweater, is an example of the feeling of efficacy. This urge to manipulate the environment, to make effective use of capabilities, was termed **effectance motivation.** Some of White's most interesting examples concerned the play of children. Although dropping a cookie from a highchair might teach a toddler about gravity, and this knowledge might prove useful later in life, White believed that the child is motivated by the desire to create an effect on the environment. He argued that because we need to interact effectively with the environment, effective interaction can be its own reward.

Harter (1978) has proposed a revision of White's model that includes a three-stage analysis of the development of effectance motivation (see Figure 12–3). In infancy the effectance motive is thought to be an inherent, biologically based striving to affect the environment. Striking at a rattle, pulling on a

Figure 12–3 Harter's three stages of effectance motivation

1. Infancy	Innate desire to affect the environment
2. Early childhood	Imitation of the effective behaviors of others
3. Adolescence and adulthood	Internalized social values channel innate effectance desires through socially approved outlets

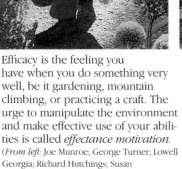

Efficacy is the feeling you have when you do something very well, be it gardening, mountain climbing, or practicing a craft. The urge to manipulate the environment and make effective use of your abilities is called *effectance motivation.*
(*From left:* Joe Munroe; George Turner; Lowell Georgia; Richard Hutchings; Susan McCartney—all Photo Researchers; Laimute Druskis)

string, and biting on a squeaky toy are some examples of this kind of behavior. These sorts of things will happen naturally; they do not require any urging from parents. As children grow older, however, they begin to imitate the behavior of other people and to choose behaviors that are shaped by the reinforcements that others give for particular kinds of mastery attempts. As children are given chemistry sets or books and are reinforced for using them, or as they see friends and family members engaged in sports, the arenas in which they express effectance motivation are shaped. The third stage emerges as people internalize values and begin to reward themselves or set goals for themselves based on their own acquired values. As you can see, this theory emphasizes the influences of learning on effectance motivation and the ways in which it is expressed.

Bandura (1979) has proposed a theory of **self-efficacy** that focuses on expectations of efficacy rather than on feelings of efficacy. According to this theory, the decision about whether or not to try a particular behavior, and the likelihood of succeeding if the attempt is made, depend on the person's belief that he or she will be successful (Collins, 1982; Bandura, 1984). For example, your decision about trying the crossword puzzle in the Sunday newspaper depends on your belief about your ability to complete the puzzle. Expectations of efficacy will also affect how long a person persists at an activity. For instance, once you begin a crossword puzzle, how long you continue to work on it will depend on your beliefs about your ability to finish it. If you decide that it is too hard for you, you will probably quit after a short time. But if you think that you have a good chance of completing it, you might work on it all morning.

There are four sources of efficacy expectations. One is *past performance accomplishments.* If you have solved a number of crossword puzzles in the past, your expectations will be high. If you have not had much success in the past, your expectations will be low. Expectations are also affected by *vicarious experience.* Seeing other people succeed or fail will influence your own expectations of success. If your roommate solves a lot of crossword puzzles, and you think your verbal skills are equally good, you will be tempted to try one. Another source of expectations comes from *verbal persuasion.* Pep talks from friends or teachers can encourage you to try tasks that you might otherwise avoid. Finally, *emotional arousal* influences efficacy expectations. Positive emotions make expectations of success more likely, while negative

moods cause us to lower our expectations of success (Kavanagh & Bower, 1985).

Negative Effects of Loss of Competence.   As you can see, competence is a fundamental aspect of human nature. This becomes dramatically apparent when people are deprived of their feelings of competence. Seligman (1975) has shown in a number of studies what happens when people are put through experiences in which they are unable to control their environment. Such experiences lead them to become depressed at the time and to become passive and unresponsive in later settings in which they do have control (Miller & Seligman, 1975; Roth & Kubla, 1975; see Chapter 16 for a further discussion of loss of control). The more that people expect to have control, the more adversely they are affected by experiences in which they have no control (Pittman & Pittman, 1979; Moore, Strube, & Lacks, 1984). This kind of evidence underscores the vital importance of feelings of competence and efficacy.

Efficacy expectations are affected by vicarious experience. For example, if your friends are good players of video games, you will probably be influenced to try your skills at them, too. (Michael Kagan/Monkmeyer Press)

Two Sources of Competence Motivation—Intrinsic and Extrinsic. As we have seen, much of an infant's behavior appears to be directed toward producing an effect on the environment. This behavior might seem to be a fairly pure example of effectance motivation. But as a person grows older and becomes socialized, the reasons for a given behavior become more complicated. We might do some things for the pure satisfaction of doing them; many games and other forms of entertainment probably serve this function. But other activities are done with an eye toward gaining something else. We may wash the family car on a Saturday morning motivated more by the thought of next week's allowance than by the sheer joy of seeing a clean automobile. These two kinds of reasons for behaving are called **intrinsic** and **extrinsic motivation** (Deci & Ryan, 1985; Pittman & Heller, 1987). When we act from intrinsic motivation, we do things because they are fun, or are ends in themselves. When we act from extrinsic motivation, we do things in order to get something else, as a means to an end (Kruglanski, 1975). For many people, these two kinds of motives represent the basic difference between their approaches to play and work.

These definitions of intrinsic and extrinsic motivation imply that activities that lead to other rewards (such as money or candy or other valued possessions) are extrinsically motivated. A clear demonstration of the truth of this idea was provided by Lepper, Greene, and Nisbett (1973). In their study nursery-school children who liked to draw for the sheer fun of it were asked to draw some pictures under one of three sets of circumstances. Some of the children were told that they would win an attractive Good Player Award if they drew some pictures. This should have encouraged them to think of drawing as an extrinsically motivated activity ("I did it for the reward"). Other children did not find out about the reward until after they had finished drawing. Those children would not have been thinking of the reward as they drew pictures, so they should have continued to think of drawing as intrinsically motivated ("I did it because I like to draw"). The third group of children simply drew the pictures and were never told about any reward. When all the children were observed during free play periods two weeks later, the children who had drawn in order to get the reward were much less interested in drawing as a free-choice-time activity than were the children from the other two groups (see Figure 12–4).

This study shows that the addition of a reward to an initially interesting activity causes a shift from an intrinsic to an extrinsic motivational orientation. Once this shift in orientation occurs, we tend to think of the activity (in this case, drawing) as being more like work than play, and therefore we are less likely to choose it as something to do in our free time. Shifting to an extrinsic orientation can mean that competence motivation becomes a less important influence, and this in turn leads to decreased creativity (Amabile, 1979) and a preference for the least challenging versions of an activity (Pittman, Emery, & Boggiano, 1982).

Our interactions with other people can also be either intrinsically or extrinsically motivated (Pittman, 1982; Pittman & Heller, 1987). This has been shown in a number of different kinds of interactions. Couples who were reminded of the rewards that their partners provided reported less love than couples who were not encouraged to think about those rewards (Seligman, Fazio, & Zanna, 1980). People who were paid for helping others felt less like helping later on (Kunda & Schwartz, 1983). People who were paid for talking to each other were later less likely to converse (Pittman, 1982), and children who were given extrinsic reasons for playing with another child were later less likely to play with that child again (Boggiano, Klinger, & Main, 1986).

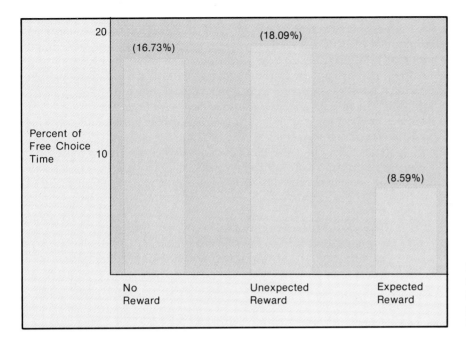

Figure 12–4 Mean percentage of free-choice time chosen by three subject groups to engage in the target activity. (Lepper, Greene, & Nisbett, 1973)

Some of the interaction rules that apply to friendships (e.g., "Don't lend money to friends") may have developed to prevent the shift from intrinsic to extrinsic motivation (Clark & Mills, 1979; Clark, 1984).

Achievement

The need for **achievement** involves competence needs that include the desire to excel, to complete difficult tasks, to meet high standards, and to outperform others. People differ, of course, in the extent to which they express competence motivation in these ways. Those who have a great need for achievement, called high-need achievers, differ from low-need achievers in a number of ways. For example, they tend to do better on problem-solving tasks and show better performance and more rapid improvement on verbal problems (Raynor & Entin, 1982). They also tend to set realistic but challenging goals for themselves (McClelland, 1985). (See Chapter 16 for a discussion of a related personality distinction, the Type-A and Type-B behavior pattern.) McClelland (1958) showed this with 5-year-old children who played a game in which they tried to toss rings onto a peg standing on the floor. They were allowed to stand as far away from the peg as they liked. McClelland found that the children who had a high need for achievement typically chose to stand at an intermediate distance from the peg, neither so close that the game was very simple, nor so far away that it was almost impossible. Children who had a low need for achievement did just the opposite. Either they stood so close that they were assured of some success, or they stood unrealistically far away. The same findings have been obtained with college students who played the ring-toss game (Atkinson & Litwin, 1960).

How do children come to have high or low achievement needs? Parental attitudes and child-rearing practices in middle childhood appear to play an important role in the development of achievement motivation (McClelland & Pilon, 1983). Winterbottom (1953) interviewed the mothers of 8- to 10-year-old boys and found that boys who scored high in achievement motivation

had mothers who were more likely to encourage early independence and to reward successful performance with physical affection (such as hugging) than were mothers of boys whose achievement motivation was low. Rosen and D'Andrade (1959) gave young boys a difficult and frustrating task to perform while their parents watched. The mothers of boys who scored high in achievement need were more encouraging and supportive than the mothers of low-achievement boys. Fathers of low-achievement boys were most likely to interfere and become irritated when their sons were having difficulty with the task. Notice that, characteristically for the times, these studies all involved the role parents play in the development of achievement needs in their sons. While we might assume that parents play a similar role with children of both genders, more research needs to be done in this area to confirm that this is so.

Atkinson's Theory of Achievement Motivation. What determines a person's achievement orientation toward a specific task? Atkinson and Feather (1966) theorized that orientation results from two separate motives: to achieve success, and to avoid failure. The motive to achieve success is determined by three things: (1) the need to succeed, or need achievement (nAch); (2) the person's estimate of the likelihood of success in performing the particular task; and (3) the incentive for success—that is, how much the person wants to succeed in that particular task. The motive to avoid failure is determined by three similar considerations: (1) the need to avoid failure, which, like the need to achieve success, varies among individuals; (2) the person's estimate of the likelihood of failure at the particular task; and (3) the incentive value of failure at that task, that is, how unpleasant it would be to fail. The relative strengths of the motives to succeed and to avoid failure determine the level of task difficulty people will prefer. When the motive to succeed is stronger, as it is for people who have a high need to achieve, the preferred tasks are those intermediate in difficulty, in which the likelihood of success is reasonable and the pride in accomplishment fairly high. When the motive to avoid failure is dominant, however, people prefer either very simple tasks in which the probability of failure is low, or very difficult tasks in which the shame in failing is low. As we have already seen, high and low achievers have shown this pattern of preferences in risk-taking studies. Atkinson has recently expanded this theory to take account of changes in achievement behavior over time (Atkinson & Birch, 1970; Atkinson, 1977). One such change is that people progressively choose more and more difficult tasks (Kuhl & Blankenship, 1979).

With such a wide range of needs, can we predict what people will do in a specific setting at a specific time? Unless we have some way of knowing when particular needs are actively influencing current behavior and when they are not, we will have a difficult time figuring out which of the many possible needs are the important or dominant ones at any moment. These kinds of problems have been addressed by psychologists who study motivation in the workplace.

Motivation in the Workplace

What motivates people in their jobs? What need or needs are fulfilled or frustrated in the workplace? As we have seen in this selective review of some prominent needs, human motivation is complex and varied. Organizational psychologists interested in work motivation and job satisfaction have

developed a number of theories of work motivation. Each has implications for establishing working conditions to enhance both productivity and human satisfaction.

Schein (1980) has identified three major theoretical approaches to work motivation. The *rational-economic* approach assumes that workers are primarily motivated by economic incentives and that the principles of learning through reinforcement discussed in Chapter 6 are the main determinants of workers' behavior. If workers are primarily motivated by the need to satisfy basic needs, such as for food, clothing, and shelter, then specific worker behaviors can be controlled through the application of appropriate rewards. One technique this approach suggests is the use of pay incentives for achieving the desired quantity or quality of productivity.

The *social* approach, while recognizing that incentives do have some importance, focuses mainly on the social needs that may be fulfilled in the work environment. As we have seen, people need to affiliate for self-evaluation, social interaction, and acceptance. To fulfill these needs, they must be able to form social groups and have the opportunity for social interaction. Changes in the work environment that ignore or disrupt the fulfillment of social needs can reduce productivity and job satisfaction (Roethlisberger & Dickson, 1939; Schrank, 1978). This approach emphasizes that work motivation can be enhanced in an environment that fosters the formation of work groups so that affiliative needs can be met. Ouchi and Jaeger (1978) report that attention to the social needs of workers is characteristic of Japanese organizations, which have high productivity and high-quality products.

The *self-actualization* approach focuses on fulfilling curiosity, competence, and achievement needs. We have seen that people need to be stimulated, to feel effective, and to have opportunities to improve and to advance. Whether or not these needs will be fulfilled for a given individual depends on the nature of the work that person does. Boring, repetitive tasks clearly will not satisfy self-actualization needs. This approach asserts that job enrichment can increase worker motivation and satisfaction (Ford, 1973; Robey, 1974) and therefore improve productivity. Job enrichment can be accomplished by making work tasks varied instead of repetitive, by allowing workers to participate in setting goals, and by making opportunities for advancement available. In this way, personal growth is encouraged.

Each of these three approaches has been used with some success to improve job performance and satisfaction, but no single approach by itself will increase motivation for all workers in all work environments. *All* human needs are important, and programs focused on one need may fail if the workers are unfulfilled in other areas. This points to a general problem with using our knowledge about human motivation. At a particular time, in a particular situation, for a particular person, how can we predict which of the rather sizable set of human needs will be most important? One potential answer to this question that has been influential in psychology in general and in organizational psychology in particular is Maslow's (1954, 1970) concept of a need hierarchy—the idea that some needs come first and must be satisfied before other needs gain attention.

Organizational psychology draws upon various theories of work motivation to help improve job performance and satisfaction. (Tim Davis/Photo Researchers)

Maslow's Hierarchy of Needs. Imagine that you are swimming underwater and you accidentally come up under a large raft where there is no air. As you struggle to reach open water before your lungs burst, do you wonder about what you will have for dinner that evening? Or suppose you are on a summer camping trip in a national forest, become separated from your companions, and it is now five days since you last ate. You are tired and cold, and you

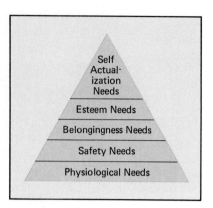

Figure 12–5 Maslow's hierarchy of needs

keep hearing noises at night that sound like bears and wolves. Do you think you would be most concerned about food, about safety, or about a need for achievement? Finally, try this more pleasant scene: You have just finished an excellent meal of all your favorite foods and you feel very satisfied, but not stuffed. You are rested, feel somewhat energetic but relaxed, and have no commitments. You can do whatever you like. What would you do? Your answer may reveal something about yourself; it will also reveal something about the nature of needs. In the first two examples, needs for air, food, and safety become paramount when a deficit exists. The third example illustrates that once a need is satisfied, it is a much less demanding motive. Whether a particular need will motivate behavior seems to depend on two things: (1) whether that need has been satisfied recently; and (2) how strong other, more fundamental needs may be. For example, no matter how hungry we are, the need to breathe will take precedence over the need to eat. This idea—that some needs come first and must be satisfied before other needs gain attention—is basic to Maslow's theory.

Maslow (1970) believed that there are five categories of needs and that these categories form a sequence or **hierarchy of needs** (see Figure 12–5). For a particular need to guide the person, all the more basic needs must be satisfied first. The most basic needs are *physiological;* these must be met if we are to survive, and they include oxygen, food, water, shelter, and sex (although not necessary to the survival of the individual, sex is essential to the survival of the species). When basic physiological needs are satisfied, then and only then do needs higher in the hierarchy become dominant. *Safety* needs form the next category. Again, these needs are often routinely satisfied, but they can become preoccupations if we live in a high-crime neighborhood or near a defective nuclear power plant, or have a hazardous job. Next come needs for *love and belongingness,* the affiliative needs. Maslow believed that people need to give and receive affection; they also need to feel that they belong to a group or a society. The need to belong has become increasingly difficult to satisfy as society becomes more mobile. Changing homes, jobs, and schools may frustrate an individual's need to belong. Maslow thought that the growth of encounter groups in the 1960s could be attributed to widespread frustration of this need. Once the needs for love and belongingness are satisfied, then needs for *esteem* can arise. These include the desire to think highly of yourself **(self-esteem)** and to have others think highly of you. We need to respect ourselves and to have others respect us. Esteem is what makes us feel confident and worthy; without it we feel inferior and worthless.

You might think that someone who has no worries about food, clothing, or safety, who feels loved and accepted by others, and who commands respect from others and has high self-esteem would be very content. Maslow, however, found such people to be tense and restless, because when all the other needs are satisfied, the need for **self-actualization** becomes dominant. Self-actualization is the realization of our potential, the exercise of our talents to the fullest. A person with musical talents needs to make music; someone with a logical, inquisitive mind devoted to science needs to be a scientist. Most of us do not reach the self-actualization level because most of us never fully satisfy our needs for love and esteem. Those who do become self-actualizers seem to have certain characteristics and talents that set them apart, as we will see in Chapter 15.

Maslow's ideas have been particularly influential for organizational psychologists who have a self-actualization perspective (e.g., McGregor, 1960;

Argyris, 1964). However, the research support for the need hierarchy concept is weak at best (Wahba & Bridwell, 1976). There are two problems with the specific assumptions of Maslow's theory: (1) an individual's needs do not always follow the hierarchical order (for example, a person might be guided by esteem needs even though belongingness needs were not met); and (2) different needs come to the fore as time on a job increases. Although some of the specifics of Maslow's theory have had to be modified in practice, the general strategy of distinguishing need categories, determining which are paramount, and making appropriate changes in the work environment has proved useful in increasing work motivation.

EMOTION

As we mentioned at the beginning of the chapter, motivation and emotion are very closely intertwined. We usually consider hunger, thirst, and sex to be needs or drives; typical emotions are anger, disgust, fear, happiness, sadness, surprise (Ekman & Friesen, 1975). But what about pain? A painful stimulus produces both an emotional response and a drive to escape the pain. In the same way, fear is an emotion but also a motivator—for example, in the Miller (1948) experiment described earlier the rats that received electric shocks in the white cage presumably became afraid when they were put into that cage again and were motivated to escape. So an unpleasant emotion can serve as a motivator—the organism is motivated to terminate that feeling.

Drives and needs can produce emotions, too. Consider the example of the person swimming underwater who comes up under a raft. The need for air will produce not only a struggle to reach the edge of the raft, but also intense fear. Extreme hunger or thirst is also likely to result in emotional responses such as grief, anger, or fear.

Buck (1985) has suggested that emotions can be viewed as indications or *readouts* of motivational potential. For example, in response to a dangerous situation, a heightened readiness to flee or fight would be represented through the emotion of fear. This emotional readout (see Figure 12–6) could be represented simultaneously through physiological changes (e.g., through activation of the sympathetic nervous system), changes in expressive behavior (facial expressions and postural attitudes), and changes in basic cognition (subjective experience or awareness of the situation). Current views of emotion emphasize the complexity of emotional representation, and research has been conducted on all of these levels of emotional expression (Lazarus, Kanner, & Folkman, 1980; Scherer, 1984).

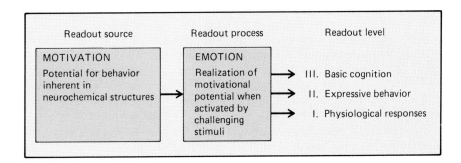

Figure 12–6 Emotions can be viewed as readouts or representations of motivational potential that are expressed at several different levels (After Buck, 1985)

Dimensions of Emotional Expression

Physiological Responses. Perhaps the most important characteristic of an emotional response is its physiological component. Many—perhaps all—emotions are associated with some change in the body's condition. The most clear-cut and well-known changes are those that accompany the feeling of fear. Everyone has experienced fear. When you've narrowly escaped an automobile accident, when you think you hear someone breaking into your home, even when you are called upon to answer a difficult question in front of a large audience, you've probably noticed your heart pounding, your knees shaking, your palms sweating, or your mouth feeling dry.

The bodily reactions to a fearful stimulus result from the action of the sympathetic nervous system and from the effects of the hormone *epinephrine* (popularly known as *adrenaline*) secreted by the adrenal glands. These reactions occur:

1. The rate and depth of breathing increase.
2. There is an increase in heart rate and in the amount of blood pumped out with each beat.
3. Blood pressure goes up.
4. Less blood goes to the internal organs, more to the muscles.
5. The liver releases extra blood sugar to supply energy.
6. Production of saliva in the mouth, and of mucus in the respiratory passages, decreases.
7. The pupils of the eyes dilate, letting in more light.
8. The galvanic skin response or GSR (changes in the electrical resistance of the skin) goes up. The GSR is related in a complex way to the functioning of the sweat glands in the skin.

The fact that many of these changes are quite easy to measure provides the basis for the ordinary lie detector, or **polygraph.** This device generally measures heart rate, breathing rate, blood pressure, and GSR. The idea behind the polygraph, as with the voice-stress analyzer, is that most people cannot tell a lie without feeling at least a little uncomfortable—consciously or unconsciously—and this discomfort is often reflected by a change in one or more of the measured functions. These changes must be compared with the baseline measurements obtained when neutral questions (such as "What's your name?") are asked.

One trouble with the polygraph—and this is a problem with the voice-stress analyzer, too—is that some people *don't* get anxious when they tell a lie, and others get anxious under questioning even when they're not telling one. In addition, it may be somewhat easier to produce a false outcome on the polygraph simply because it is possible to voluntarily increase some or all of the measurements—by breathing faster, tensing one's body, or thinking about something emotionally arousing. If a person understands the principles underlying polygraph testing and uses these methods when neutral questions are asked, the baseline is raised, and it is often impossible to tell when a lie has actually been told.

Many of the bodily changes that occur with fear also accompany anger, but there are some physiological differences between the two emotions (Ax, 1953). Epinephrine is secreted with anger as well as with fear, but anger involves an additional adrenal hormone, *norepinephrine* (see Chapter 2).

Norepinephrine also increases blood pressure, but it does so not by increasing heart rate but by constricting the blood vessels that supply the muscles. In fact, injections of norepinephrine *slow* the heart. Ekman, Levensen, and Friesen (1983) also found that anger increases skin temperature but fear does not.

Attempts to differentiate other emotions on the basis of different physiological responses have been less successful. Averill (1969) had one group of subjects watch a sad movie, while another group watched a funny movie. The resulting differences in bodily responses were not statistically significant. In fact, it is likely that a given individual produces a characteristic pattern of physiological responses to almost *any* form of emotional arousal. The physiological reactions of a given subject to different sources of stress are quite similar; the reactions of different subjects to the *same* stimulus are quite different (Lacey & Lacey, 1958). For these reasons, various physiological changes are considered to be associated with emotional change in general, but they cannot be used as the sole indicators of particular kinds of emotion (Grings & Dawson, 1978).

Excessive Behavior.   In 1872 Charles Darwin published a book entitled *The Expression of the Emotions in Man and Animals.* In it he described in minute detail the facial expressions of emotion in humans and animals—even naming the particular muscles that come into play in each instance. The principles that Darwin wished to establish were that facial expressions of emotions in humans are innate, not learned; that they are universal in all races of humanity; and that they have their origins in the facial expressions of animals. He pointed out that a human snarl of anger closely resembles the teeth-baring grimace of angry dogs and cats. Young chimpanzees, when tickled under the arms, make a response that looks and sounds very much like human laughter. Darwin's observations were so thorough and so careful that they are still informative today. We still believe that facial expressions of emotions are not learned. Children blind from birth, who have never even seen a smile or a frown on another person's face, are nonetheless able to smile or frown as well as children with normal vision.

In fact, there has been a good deal of research into the universality of facial expressions and, in particular, the ability of people from various cultures to correctly decode the emotion that lies behind a facial expression. Ekman and Friesen (1968) photographed people portraying various emotions such as grief, happiness, fear, surprise, and disgust. They showed these photographs to subjects in the United States, Brazil, Chile, Japan, and Borneo. All the subjects tended to identify the same faces with the same emotions.

In another experiment Ekman and Friesen (1971) showed their pictures to the Fore of New Guinea, a people who had had little or no contact with Western or Eastern literate cultures. With the aid of a translator, the experimenters read a simple story to the subjects—for example, "She is just now looking at something which smells bad"—and asked the subject to pick which of three faces best agreed with the story. The Fore subjects picked the "correct" picture almost all the time; the main exception was that fear and surprise proved hard to tell apart.

Generally, the recent research on the communication of emotion through facial displays shows that while facial expressions are universal, the understanding or decoding of those expressions is not always completely accurate (Friedlund, Ekman, & Oster, 1987; Russell & Bullock, 1986). For example, Wagner, MacDonald, and Manstead (1986) found that of the six emotions represented in facial expressions (anger, disgust, fear, happiness, sadness,

Darwin was the first to observe that facial expression of emotion is innate, is universal, and has its origins in the facial expressions of animals. (George Goodwin/Monkmeyer; Edward Lettan/Photo Researchers; Charles Harbutt & Burk Uzzle, Archive Pictures)

and surprise), their subjects were only able to reliably identify three (happiness, anger, and disgust).

It is important to distinguish between *facial* expressions of emotions—which are unlearned and universal—and *gestures*—which are culturally determined. Morris, Collett, Marsh, and O'Shaughnessy (1979) made an extensive survey of hand and head gestures in many parts of the world. They reported that a given gesture might mean one thing in one place and something quite different somewhere else. For instance, the "thumb up" sign means either "everything's okay" or "hitching a ride" in most countries studied. But in parts of Greece and Sardinia it is unwise to try to hitch a lift with an upraised thumb. There it is an insult, equivalent to the raised third finger in the United States!

There are three other kinds of expressive behavior that characterize emotion. The first is postural—a happy person stands and walks erect, a sad person slumps, and an angry or fearful one assumes a tense position.

The second is a rapid, automatic motor response. A sudden loud noise or any intense and unexecpted stimulus produces a predictable pattern of involuntary actions called the *startle pattern:* The head moves forward, the eyes blink and the mouth may open, the muscles of the neck stand out, and the arms and legs may jerk.

Third are voluntary behavioral actions. People express their feelings by clapping or "jumping for joy," or by running away from something they are afraid of. The most interesting and complex of these behavioral indications are those that result from anger, which were discussed in the section on aggression in Chapter 11.

Basic Cognitive Representation. Emotions are also represented in subjective awareness or consciousness. We "know" and can think and talk about the emotions we are experiencing. In fact, often the easiest way to find out what a person is feeling is by asking. When someone says "I'm delighted" or "Ugh, that's disgusting," that person is presumably giving us a description of some internal state that otherwise we might have no way of determining.

People learn to make these statements about private aspects of their consciousness in two ways. From childhood, we use given words or labels that help us identify the emotions we feel. For example, parents judge a child's emotion by the situation (Did she just fall down? Did someone take her toy away?) and by the child's facial expression. The parent then says to the child, "You're sad, aren't you?" or "Don't be angry." The child learns to associate the words "sad" and "angry" with a particular internal state. Of course, there is no way of knowing whether that child is *really* sad or angry, or whether her anger or grief feels the same as yours!

The other way we learn to talk about our emotions is by *metaphor.* We often hear and use terms that liken inner feelings to some objective event in the outside world: "I was crushed," "He suffered a stab of regret," "I'm walking on air."

Finally, we often think we can tell what another person is feeling through the process of *empathy,* or imagining ourselves in that person's shoes. You can imagine how someone who has just been told that she won the state lottery feels. Similarly, you can guess the emotions of a person after he has been informed of his mother's death, or after he has slipped on the ice and fallen heavily on his knees. We know how *we* would feel in these situations, and we assume that the other person feels the same way. In addition, we often assume—with less justification—that we know the emotional state of *animals* on the same basis. For example, we might guess that a horse being

The startle pattern: The head moves forward, the mouth is open, the muscles of the neck stand out, and the arms and legs jerk. (Laimute Druskis)

whipped feels anger or fear, even if there are no outward signs of these emotions.

What Produces an Emotional Response?

Innate vs. Learned Emotions. Human beings, as well as animals, have a number of built-in emotional responses. For example, any sudden intense stimulus is likely to evoke the startle pattern and the emotion of fear. Restraint of motion or the sudden withdrawal of a proffered reward generally leads to anger. An infant's smile elicits feelings of love and delight from its parents. The death of a close relative usually results in grief. Human babies of a certain age are afraid to cross from a table onto a pane of glass 3 or 4 feet above the floor—a deviced called the **visual cliff,** which will be discussed in Chapter 13.

Other stimuli produce emotional reactions that are clearly acquired through experience. This phenomenon was discussed at length in the learning and conditioning chapter (Chapter 6). Recall that if we administer an electric shock to a rat each time we sound a buzzer, the rat begins to act afraid whenever the buzzer goes on. Rats that became ill after eating a certain food reacted with apparent disgust when offered that food at a later time—they scooped it out of the food dish with their paws and scattered it on the floor of the cage. The delight that some people feel when they listen to a Mozart concerto or when they hear the bell of the ice-cream wagon is another example of acquired, or secondary, emotional responses.

Also relevant here is the case study of little Albert (Watson & Rayer, 1920) previously cited in Chapter 6. Albert's conditioning led him to be afraid, not only of rats, but also of other furry things: a white toy rabbit, a Santa Claus beard. In fact, a great deal of time and effort has gone into attempts to determine whether the human emotional response to a certain stimulus is a primary (innate) or a secondary (learned or acquired) response. For example, is the fear of snakes innate or learned? Some psychologists have said "innate" and pointed to the fact that chimpanzees raised in the laboratory are innately afraid of snakes (Hebb, 1946). Others have shown that children under 2 years of age often seem to have no fear of snakes. Neither of these arguments is very persuasive, however: That chimpanzees are innately afraid of snakes doesn't mean that humans are; and that a fear develops after infancy does not mean that it is learned. Indeed, only two stimuli seem to elicit fear in a newborn: a loud noise and a sudden loss of support.

Preparedness. Martin Seligman (1972) has proposed a new approach to the old problem of innate vs. learned emotional responses. He asks why it was so easy to make little Albert become afraid of furry animals. Other experimenters (English, 1929; Bregman, 1934) tried to repeat Watson's experiment using wooden blocks, wooden ducks, or curtains. They were not able to condition fear at all, even after pairing these objects many times with loud noises. Seligman describes an occasion in his own life when he came down with a violent stomach flu a few hours after eating filet mignon with sauce Béarnaise. After that he couldn't stand sauce Béarnaise, although previously it was a favorite of his. But, as he says, "neither the filet mignon, nor the white plates off which I ate the sauce, nor *Tristan und Isolde,* the opera that I listened to [in the time between the meal and the onset of the illness], nor my wife, Kerry, became aversive. Only the sauce Béarnaise did" (Seligman & Hager, 1972, p. 8). Even though Seligman *knew* the sauce was not responsi-

ble (because others had eaten it and had not gotten sick, or had gotten sick without eating it), this knowledge did not affect his feelings—what we might call his "gut reaction."

Seligman accounted for his acquired disgust by a concept he called **preparedness:** Organisms are more prepared to associate a given emotional response with one kind of stimulus, and less prepared to associate it with another kind. An experiment by Garcia and Koelling (1966) illustrates this principle. Rats were given water sweetened with saccharin and then made sick by exposure to radiation. Afterward they didn't want to drink saccharin-flavored water. When the sweetened water was paired with a visual and an auditory stimulus (a light and a clicking sound), the rats showed no tendency later to avoid either the light or the sound. But when rats were given electric shocks after drinking water, they avoided water associated with the light and sound but didn't object to the saccharin-flavored water. The conclusion is that rats are *prepared* to associate illness with a taste, or electric shock with a visual or auditory stimulus. They are not prepared—or, rather, are *less* prepared—to associate illness with light or sound, or shock with a taste. Consistent with this analysis, Lanzetta and Orr (1980) and Ohman and Dinsberg (1978) have shown that angry faces are more easily conditioned to electric shock than happy faces: When angry faces are paired with electric shocks, subjects' autonomic arousal levels indicate conditioning after fewer trials than are necessary for those subjects who experience happy faces paired with shocks.

Preparedness is not a yes-or-no, all-or-none situation; it is a continuum. Each possible association of a stimulus and an emotional response can be given a position on this continuum by asking: How many pairings of this stimulus with this response are necessary in order to condition the association? On the extreme "prepared" end of the continuum, the answer may be *none*—some stimuli elicit the emotional response the very first time they are presented. On the "unprepared" end of the continuum, the answer is an infinite number—some emotional responses may *never* become linked to a specific stimulus. In between are all the associations that are more or less easy to condition.

Determinants of Emotional Experience

We have reviewed some of the ways that emotions are expressed and how they can be measured, and we have discussed whether they are learned or innate. But how do emotions arise? What is the relationship between physiological changes and emotion? What role does cognitive interpretation play? Theories of emotion have been developed to answer these kinds of questions.

The James-Lange Theory.   If you are walking home in the dark and someone jumps out at you from behind a tree, two things happen. One is that you feel afraid. The other is that your adrenal glands stimulate the sympathetic nervous system (see Chapter 2), your heart starts to pound, and so on. The question is: Which comes first? It may seem obvious to you that first you become afraid and then your body responds to your fear, but this did not seem so obvious to the Harvard psychologist William James or the Danish physiologist Carl Lange. A century ago these two scientists both came to the same conclusion: that the bodily changes come *first,* and then—as a result of these changes—you become afraid. In James's words:

Common-sense says, we lose our fortune, are sorry and weep; we meet a bear, are frightened and run; we are angry and strike. . . . The more rational statement is that we feel sorry because we cry, angry because we strike, afraid because we tremble. . . . Without the bodily states following on the perception, the latter would be purely cognitive in form, pale, colorless, destitute of emotional warmth. We might then see the bear and judge it best to run, receive the insult and deem it right to strike, but we should not actually *feel* afraid or angry. (1890, pp. 449–450)

In 1927 the influential physiologist Walter Cannon published an attack on the James-Lange theory. He pointed out, first of all, that the bodily changes that are associated with emotional states occur too slowly to be the cause of emotion. When the bear appears, fear is felt immediately, too quickly to be a byproduct of the physiological reactions.

Second, the physiological changes that occur with emotions take place in other situations too, *without* producing the emotions. Many of the same bodily responses that accompany fear—the increases in heart rate, breathing rate, blood pressure, GSR, and so on—can be produced simply by exercising violently. Yet exercise does not have any noteworthy effect on the state of the emotions. These same physiological changes can also be induced artificially, by injections of stimulants, without resulting in a feeling of fear.

Still, recent evidence seems to provide some support for the **James-Lange theory.** A psychologist (Hohmann, 1966) interviewed a group of patients who had suffered serious spinal cord injuries and were unable to feel any sensations in the parts of their bodies below the level of the injury. Some of these people had spinal cord injuries at the neck (cervical) level and therefore could not feel anything from the neck down; in others the injury was at the lower part of the spine (sacral); the rest were somewhere in between. These patients were asked how the emotions they felt since their accidents differed from the emotions they remembered feeling before they were injured. Were they the same as before, or more intense or less intense? The people with sacral injuries (who felt no sensations in their legs) reported only minor changes in emotional feelings, but the people with cervical injuries (affecting the entire body) reported a decrease in feelings of fear, anger, grief, and sexual drive (see Figure 12–7). Only the emotion that the experimenter labeled "sentiment" was unaffected. The people with intermediate injuries gave mixed reports—some reported decreases in certain emotions, others did not. From these results, Hohmann concluded that in order to experience strong emotions, it is necessary to have some feedback from the body—some indication of the physiological reactions going on. When the sensations produced by these reactions are absent, the emotions may be felt less intensely. If you hear some very sad news and do not cry, you might wonder whether you are really sad, or perhaps whether you really care. Similarly, if you are about to give a speech and you do not feel your heart pounding or "butterflies" in your stomach, you might marvel at how calm you are.

The Cannon-Bard Theory. The theory of emotion that Cannon (1927/72) proposed and that Bard (1934) elaborated was based on what was known about the brain at the time. Cannon placed the source of emotions in the thalamus, which is located in the center of the brain. According to the **Cannon-Bard theory,** when an emotionally arousing stimulus is perceived, the thalamus sends out impulses to the sympathetic nervous system, which produces the physiological reactions. *At the same time,* the thalamus also

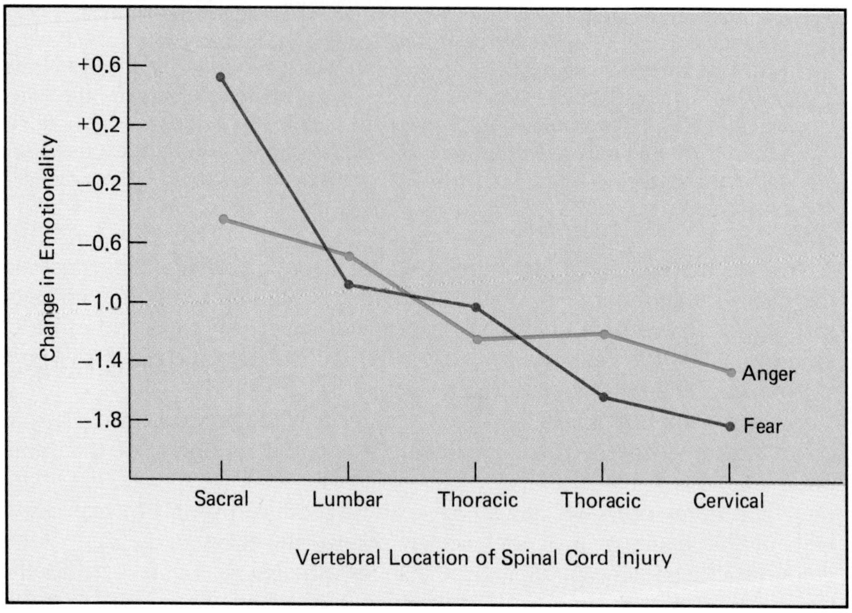

Figure 12–7 According to research by Hohmann, the greater the degree of incapacity resulting from spinal cord injury, the greater the decrease in feelings of anger and fear. Those with sacral injuries (who felt no sensation in their legs) reported only minor changes in emotional feelings, but those with cervical injuries (affecting the entire body) reported a significant decrease in feelings of emotions like anger and fear. (After Hohmann, 1966)

sends out impulses to the cerebral cortex, producing the conscious feeling of emotion. This hypothesis implies that the bodily changes and the emotional feelings occur simultaneously.

Modern neurophysiology does not support the involvement of the thalamus in emotion. It is now believed that the *hypothalamus* and the *limbic system* are the brain parts involved in emotional response (see Chapter 2). It has, for example, been found that lesions in certain parts of these areas produce permanent changes in emotional behavior in animals: They become passive and unreactive, or they become overactive and fly into a rage with little or no provocation, depending on the location of the brain injury. Neurophysiologists have also investigated the limbic system by implanting electrodes in the brains of animals and giving tiny electric shocks to various areas. Depending on the location of the electrode, the shock may produce fear, rage, passivity, or even pleasure.

Activation Theory. Moruzzi and Magoun (1949) studied the **reticular activating system (RAS),** which consists of pathways in the brain extending from the brain stem upward to the thalamus and the cerebral cortex. Inputs to the RAS come from all the senses except smell. This system controls **arousal:** When an animal's RAS is damaged, it goes into a coma and is unresponsive to stimulation. Drugs such as amphetamines increase RAS activity, while barbiturates depress it.

In a normal individual the reticular system works "something like a fire alarm that gets people into action but does not really say where the fire is" (Beck, 1983, p. 104). At moderate levels of activity it makes a person alert and attentive; but when incoming stimuli are too intense or numerous, the reticular system produces too much arousal or excitement, and behavior becomes disorganized. This is presumably what happens to people who "lose their heads" in an emergency, or to soldiers who panic under enemy fire. The **activation theory** states that there is some optimal level of emotional arousal—too little produces sleepiness or apathy, too much produces aimless activity and emotional disturbance.

As you read earlier in this chapter, one of the ways we can tell what emotions others are experiencing is by observing their nonverbal behaviors, such as their facial expressions and body posture. Smiles and upright postures can indicate happiness or confidence, while frowns and a slumped posture with drooping shoulders tell us that the person is feeling sad or depressed. These kinds of nonverbal behaviors are *expressive* because we reveal or express our emotions through them. The basic idea is that emotions include expressive behavior. Recently, however, psychologists studying emotion have found that this relationship also works the other way around—expressive behaviors can affect emotions.

The idea that nonverbal behaviors can affect the experience of emotions was suggested by Charles Darwin in 1872: "The free expression by outward signs of an emotion intensifies it. On the other hand, the repression, as far as possible, of all outward signs softens our emotions" (p. 22). The hypothesis is that, for example, smiling can make you feel happy and frowing can make you feel sad. To test this *facial feedback hypothesis,* Laird (1974) had subjects hold either smiles or frowns on their faces while rating the humor of a series of cartoons. Subjects thought the cartoons were funnier when they were smiling than when they were frowning, and also reported being in a better mood when smiling than when frowning. Lanzetta, Cartwright-Smith, and Kleck (1976) had their subjects try either to hide or to exaggerate their facial expressions while they were receiving electric shocks. Their subjects reported that the shocks were less painful when they were hiding their facial expressions than when they were exaggerating them. More interestingly, actual physiological responses to the electric shocks (measured by changes in galvanic skin conductance) were reduced when facial expressions were suppressed, and increased when facial expressions were exaggerated. Facial expressions, then, serve both as indicators and determinants of emotion.

Recently, this analysis has also been tested with body postures. Riskind and Gotay (1982) and Riskind (1984) reported a number of studies in which they assessed the effects of assuming different body postures on subsequent

Nonverbal behaviors such as facial expression and body posture can affect our emotions. (Sepp Seitz/Woodfin Camp & Associates)

emotional reactions. In one of these studies subjects first posed in either a slumped (sitting bent forward with the head down) or an upright posture for 8 minutes. After posing, subjects went to another room and were given a task that has been used to measure susceptibility to learned helplessness. Subjects who had previously posed in the slumped position gave up much more quickly than subjects who had posed in the upright position.

These research findings indicate that expressive behaviors are an integral part of the emotional experience. More than simple indicators or readouts of emotion, they serve to intensify and perhaps even to initiate emotional experiences.

Cognitive Factors and the Jukebox Theory. This theory is based on an experiment performed by Schachter and Singer (1962); the term **jukebox theory** was coined by Mandler (1962). In Schachter and Singer's experiment subjects were injected with epinephrine (which, as we know, produces the symptoms of fear: increased blood pressure, heart rate, GSR, and so on). They were told that these injections were a new vitamin compound and that the purpose of the experiment was to study the effects of this compound on visual perception. After the injection each subject was sent into another room to wait with a second subject until the compound "took effect." In fact, epinephrine works very quickly, and the 20-minute "waiting period" was really the experiment itself and the "second subject" was really a confederate of the experimenters.

Some subjects had been told the truth about the effects of the injection— that it would produce a slight hand tremor, increased heart rate, and a flushed feeling in the face. Subjects in a second group were misinformed— they was told that the drug would cause numbness in the feet, itching sensations, and a slight headache. A third group of subjects was told nothing at all.

Soon after the real subject entered the waiting room, the confederate be-

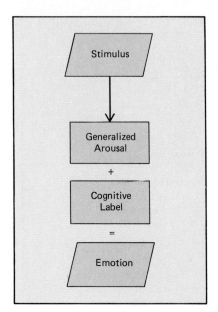

Figure 12–8 The jukebox theory of emotion.

gan to behave in a bizarre manner. He made paper airplanes and flew them around the room, made a ball of paper and played basketball with the wastepaper basket. He even hula-hooped with a piece of equipment left in the room! During this display of feigned euphoria the confederate invited the real subject to participate in his games.

The experimenters found that the subjects who had been *correctly* informed about the effects of the injection behaved normally and did not accept the confederate's invitation to play. But the subjects who had been given the wrong information or no information at all often participated in the games, sometimes behaving as foolishly as the confederate. In a variation of the experiment, the confederate feigned anger and aggression instead of euphoria, and again, the subjects who had been correctly informed about the effects of the epinephrine behaved normally, whereas those who had not been informed were affected by the put-on emotion. Thus the same drug given to different groups of subjects made them happy, made them angry, or had no effect at all on their emotions—depending on their understanding of the situation.

The conclusion drawn from these experiments is that the physiological arousal produced by a drug can set the basis for an emotion, but it is not enough. When subjects *know* what reactions to expect, they correctly interpret their physiological changes as resulting from the injection; when they have no explanation for the effects they are feeling, they interpret these effects in terms of the situation (see Figure 12–8). This is where the name *jukebox* comes in. The injection of the drug—like the coin you drop into a jukebox—starts things going, provides the energy. But the tune played—or the emotion experienced—depends on which button is pushed.

In the years since Schachter and Singer's experiment, a number of similar experiments have been performed. Although some have failed to substantiate the jukebox theory (Maslach, 1979), many have provided support. Some results that are consistent with Schachter and Singer's hypothesis were provided by an experiment in which physiological arousal was induced in some subjects by having them view a sex movie (Zillman, 1971). When the subjects later had a chance to express anger toward a person who had insulted them, the ones who had seen the sex movie were more aggressive than those who hadn't. Even physiological arousal produced by fast pedaling on an exercise bicycle has, under some conditions, produced an enhanced emotional response (Cantor, Zillman, & Bryant, 1975).

Note the contrast between this situation, in which physiological arousal appears to produce emotional arousal, and the situation we examined earlier, that people with severed spinal cords are likely to feel emotions less strongly than before they were injured (Hohmann, 1966). It seems, then, that emotion-producing stimuli affect us in two ways: We have a cognitive awareness of the meaning of the stimuli, and we make a variety of physiological responses. In order for emotion to be deeply felt, the physiological responses must occur and must be perceived. But the nature of these responses is sometimes vague and generalized, and signs of physiological arousal often can be attributed to several different emotions. The emotion to which they *are* attributed is the emotion that is appropriate to the person's cognitive awareness of the situation.

The Opponent-Process Theory. The last theory of emotion we will discuss is compatible with any of the previous theories because it does not attempt to specify where emotion comes from or what it consists of. This theory, in-

stead, is designed to explain the motivation behind such potentially self-destructive human behaviors as thrill-seeking, masochism, and addiction.

The **opponent-process theory** (Solomon & Corbit, 1973, 1974; Solomon, 1980) begins with several assumptions about emotional states:

1. Whenever a stimulus causes an emotional response, it also causes another emotional response that is opposite to, or the opponent of, the initial response. Thus if the sight of a bear causes the emotion of fear (state A), it will also activate the opponent emotion, which in this case might be relief (state B).

2. The opponent process (state B) is aroused more slowly, and decays more slowly, than the initial response (state A). In the example, the emotion of relief will lag behind the emotion of fear when the bear is sighted. Similarly, when the bear goes away, the feeling of relief will linger after the feeling of fear has left us.

3. With repeated experience, states A and B slowly change character. For example, with repeated sightings of the bear, fear may change to alert tension, while relief may change to joy. To indicate such changes we could relabel the two states A′ and B′.

4. This implies that with repeated experience the B (or B′) state gets stronger, but the A (or A′) state does not. In the example, moderate relief (B) turns into strong joy (B′).

These four assumptions explain a very common sequence of emotional reactions: When the eliciting stimulus is presented (the bear appears from behind a tree), a very strong emotional response occurs (stark, petrifying fear). As the exposure to the stimulus continues (the bear continues to stand there), the emotion is reduced a bit and remains steady (plain old fear). Solomon and Corbit explain that this reduction occurs because the opponent process (relief), as it is slowly activated, subtracts from and thus reduces state A. When the stimulus is withdrawn (the bear leaves), a very different emotion is experienced. This happens because state A (fear) disappears rapidly when the stimulus is withdrawn, but state B goes away much more slowly. Therefore when the stimulus is removed, the person experiences state B (relief). This pattern of emotions has repeatedly been found in experiments; it also agrees with many experiences that people report and that we all have had.

The operation of opponent-process theory is clearly illustrated in a recent study of the emotions associated with blood donation. Piliavin, Callero, and Evans (1982) measured the emotions of a large number of blood donors both before and after donation. First-time donors reported feeling uptight, fearful, and jittery (the A state). After donation, they felt carefree, playful, and warmhearted (the B state). The researchers found that the stronger the A state was, the more intensely the B state was experienced after donation, just as the theory would predict. Furthermore, for veteran donors, the A state became less intense as the number of prior donations increased (because an increasingly strong B state was subtracted from it). Over time, then, blood donors' emotional reactions appear to be dominated by the pleasant post-donation B state, while the negative predonation A state becomes progressively weaker.

Solomon and Corbit (1974) have made a similar analysis of the thrill-seeking sport of parachute jumping based on Epstein's (1967) reports of the changes in emotions of veteran jumpers. With repeated experience, prejump anxieties (the A state) weaken, and postjump exhilaration (the B state) in-

Schachter's cognitive theory of emotion explains that what we think can determine how we feel. Recent research shows the converse is also true: that what we *feel* affects what we *think*. When we are in a positive mood, we find it easier to remember positive things. When we are in a negative mood, we tend to remember negative things. Several investigators have shown how positive mood affects memory. Isen, Shalker, Clark, and Karp (1978), for example, found that college students who had just succeeded (by winning a Star Trek video game) were better at remembering positive words they had learned than at remembering neutral or negative words they had learned at the same time. Bartlett and Santrock (1979) found that 5-year-old children best remembered words they had learned when they were in a happy mood when they were again put into a happy mood, and worse when they were put into a sad mood at time of recall. Bower (1981) hypnotized his subjects, put them into happy and sad moods by having them imagine appropriate scenes, and then had them learn lists of words in each mood. Later, subjects were put into happy or sad moods and asked to recall what they had learned. Subjects were best able to recall words they had learned while in a happy mood when they were again put into a happy mood.

It appears that positive mood facilitates the recall of positive material. It also appears that information learned while in a positive mood is best remembered later when again in a positive mood. This phenomenon is called *state-dependent memory*: Memory is best when the mood that is in effect during recall matches the mood that was in effect during learning.

The most recent evidence indicates that moods can elicit a wide variety of mood-congruent responses about past experiences. Kavanagh and Bower (1985) had two groups of subjects recall either a romantic success or a romantic failure, thereby inducing either a positive or a negative mood. A third group served as controls (neutral mood) and were not asked to recall any such incidents before questioning. When subsequently asked how competent or self-efficacious they were, negative-mood subjects said they were generally less self-efficacious than neutral-mood subjects, while positive-mood subjects judged themselves to be more self-efficacious than neutral-mood subjects. These differences emerged not only when subjects were questioned about other romantic experiences, but also when they were asked about interpersonal and athletic competence.

How do these effects of mood on memory work? Emotions appear to serve as organizing points or *nodes* in memory, and pieces of information are associated and stored with related moods. When a mood is activated or experienced, the information associated and stored with that mood becomes more accessible and is more readily remembered. You can see how the association of information with moods can intensify an emotion: When you become depressed, you then find it easy to recall things that happened when you were depressed in the past; and since those things are likely to be unpleasant, you become even more depressed. The concept of state-dependent memory may also provide a key to remembering information that is difficult to recall: Such material will be more likely to be remembered if we can reconstruct the mood we were in at the time we learned it in the first place.

creases. This pattern of reactions can explain much thrill-seeking behavior. The increasingly pleasant aftereffects, together with the decreasing aversiveness of the initial anxiety reaction, motivate people to keep taking risks.

Masochistic (self-punishing) behavior can be explained in the same way: The person submits to painful or unpleasant abuse in order to experience the positive opponent process afterward. In sexual masochism, for example, the positive B state associated with the cessation of pain apparently enhances the pleasure of orgasm for some people.

Of course, just as unpleasant initial reactions are followed by a positive opponent process, so will pleasant initial reactions be followed by an unpleasant opponent process. This sequence of reactions appears to be involved in various kinds of addictions.

The opponent-process theory seems to explain a number of emotional phenomena very well. But why are emotional reactions arranged this way? What is the reason for the existence of opponent processes? According to Soloman and Corbit, opponent processes allow the organism to damp down emotional reactions, to keep them from becoming too strong or too removed from neutral. Since severe emotional reactions can be debilitating and can interfere with new learning (Spence & Spence, 1966), such an emotional cooling-off system appears to have adaptive survival value.

SUMMARY

1. Human *motivation* ranges from basic physiological needs through needs for stimulation (such as curiosity) to socially based needs.

2. Secondary motivations associated with physiological needs may be acquired through conditioning; these acquired motivations, according to some theorists, can become *functionally autonomous*.

3. Some prominent human needs are *curiosity, affiliation, competence,* and *achievement*.

4. The optimal level of stimulation theory attempts to explain curiosity motives: Stimuli outside the adaptation level allow people to exercise their information-processing abilities and fulfill curiosity needs. Sensory-deprivation studies underscore humans' needs for stimulation.

5. Infants reared in institutions in which they receive food and medical care but little social stimulation show striking deficits in emotional, intellectual, and even physical development.

6. Sexual expression varies among cultures and across time, owing to different learning experiences. Reactions to erotica, for example, may vary according to gender, degree of liberalism or conservatism, and sex guilt.

7. Among the theories of *competence motives* are White's theory of *effectance motivation* and Bandura's theory of *self-efficacy*. Many physiologists believe that loss of competence leads to depression or passivity.

8. *Achievement motives* are related to the desire to excel, to complete difficult tasks, to meet high standards, and to outperform others.

9. Theories based on rational-economic, social, or self-actualization assumptions emphasize different sets of workers' needs. Maslow's hierarchy of needs (physiological, safety, love and belongingness, esteem, and self-actualization) is one of several approaches that attempt to guide the design of the workplace to enhance worker productivity and motivation.

10. Emotional states are represented in physiological responses, expressive behavior, and cognitive awareness.

11. The question of whether emotions are innate or learned is still not absolutely resolved. Seligman's concept of *preparedness* theorizes that organisms may be more prepared to associate a given emotional response with a particular stimulus.

12. The *James-Lange theory* of emotion asserts that bodily changes are experienced first, then emotion; the *Cannon-Bard theory* maintains that bodily changes and emotions occur simultaneously.

13. Modern neurological research focuses on the *limbic system* and the *hypothalamus* as the parts of the brain that play the major role in emotion.

14. The *activation theory* emphasizes the *reticular activation system (RAS)* and its effects on arousal, including the idea that there is some optimal level of emotional arousal.

15. According to the *jukebox theory,* physiological arousal provides the basis or energy for emotion, but the emotion experienced depends on cognitive factors.

16. *Opponent-process theory* states that for every emotion, there is a paired opponent or opposite emotion.

SUGGESTED READINGS

BUCK, R. (1985). Prime theory: An integrated view of motivation and emotion. *Psychological Review, 92,* 389–413. A recent review and integration of current research on theories of emotion.

DECI, E. L., & RYAN, R. M. (1985). *Intrinsic motivation and self-determination in human behavior.* New York: Plenum. The book covers most of the research on intrinsic and extrinsic motivation.

McCLELLAND, D. C., (1985). *Human motivation.* Glenview, Ill.: Scott, Foresman. This book contains a comprehensive review of the research on achievement motivation.

PITTMAN, T. S., & HELLER, J. F. (1987). Social motivation. In M. Rosenzweig & L. Porter (Eds.), *Annual Review of Psychology,* Vol. 38. Palo Alto, Cal.: Annual Reviews, Inc. A review of recent advances in motivation and emotion in the social realm.

SCHACHTER, S. (1959). *The psychology of affiliation.* Stanford, Cal: Stanford University Press. This is a research monograph in which the original studies on affiliation are reported. It is a good example of how a set of studies build upon one another.

SELIGMAN, M. E. P. (1975). *Helplessness: On depression, development, and death.* San Francisco: Freeman. A readable and provocative presentation of the relationship between lack of control and depression.

SOLOMON, R. L. (1980). The opponent-process theory of acquired motivation: The costs of pleasure and the benefits of pain. *American Psychologist, 35,* 691–712. This is the latest comprehensive statement of the opponent-process theory of acquired motivation.

13 Childhood

T he study of development is the study of how people change as they get older, and of the causes of such changes. The fact that we do change from conception to childhood to old age is obvious enough. But exactly *how* do younger and older people differ from one another? And what causes these changes to occur as people move from one age and stage to another? These two questions form the basic subject matter of **developmental psychology.**

Answering the first question requires accurate descriptions of people at various ages and stages of development. For example, most adults see the world as a colorful, three-dimensional place, filled with a variety of solid objects. But do newborns also see the world this way, or is it for them a "blooming, buzzing confusion," as William James (1890) believed? One of the most challenging problems for developmental psychologists has been to devise methods for answering such questions. (We will discuss this in the Application: Studying Visual Perception in Infants that appears later in this chapter.)

The second question concerns the mechanisms, or sources, of developmental change. How does a fertilized ovum develop into an embryo, then a fetus, then a baby, and ultimately an adult? The unborn child is obviously very different from you and me; the infant is not quite so different; the child still less different. What mechanisms are at work to change the unborn child into an infant, the infant into a child, and the child into an adult? We can point to two general sources of these changes: **maturation** and **experience.**

Concepts of childhood are different in different times and in different places. This painting, "Maids of Honor" by Diego Velázquez depicts the seventeenth-century European view of children as miniature adults. (Art Resource)

SOURCES OF DEVELOPMENTAL CHANGE

Maturation

One important way that changes come about is through the physical growth and differentiation of the body and the nervous system. For the unborn child, genetic programming guides the maturation of muscles, glands, bones, neurons, and sensory organs. These structural changes allow the growing fetus to do things in a later stage that it couldn't do in an earlier one. For example, five or six months after conception the fetus begins to hear and respond to sounds in its environment. Although this kind of development is programmed by the genes, unfavorable environmental factors may prevent it from occurring. If the mother contracts German measles during the first trimester (first three months) of pregnancy, the virus is likely to infect the fetus and may cause deafness, mental retardation, or even fetal death. Malnutrition in the mother, or her use of alcohol, tobacco, or other drugs, can also interfere with fetal development. Smoking cigarettes, for instance, contributes to infant mortality by increasing the chances that the fetus will be abnormally small at birth. Maturation, then, is not independent of environmental influences—an appropriate environment must be present if such development is to occur.

A classic experimental demonstration of maturation was Leonard Carmichael's (1927) study of the development of swimming ability in frog and salamander embryos. In the period that begins a day or two after the eggs are fertilized and ends when the embryos become free-swimming tadpoles, these embryos become capable of increasingly coordinated swimming movements. Are the movements that occur during the embryonic stage necessary for the development of full-fledged swimming? In other words, is practice necessary? To answer this question, Carmichael allowed one group of embryos to develop in ordinary tap water. A second group of similar embryos was kept in water containing an anesthetic that allowed them to grow but prevented them from moving. When the first group had begun to swim in a coordinated way, the second was removed from the anesthetic and put into fresh water. As soon as the anesthetized tadpoles had revived (in less than half an hour), they were swimming as well as the tadpoles reared normally. Carmichael concluded that swimming in the tadpole results from maturation alone and that practice or experience is not necessary.

Since human babies obviously cannot be kept under long-term anesthesia, it is not so easy to demonstrate the effects of maturation in our own species. However, different cultures follow different methods of child rearing, and these differences can sometimes shed light on the question of maturation versus practice. For example, a traditional practice among the Hopi Indians of Arizona was to wrap babies in cloth and fasten them to a stiff support called a *cradleboard*. One study found that a group of Hopi babies restrained in this manner for most of their first year learned to walk at about the same age as other Hopi babies whose parents had never used the cradleboard (Dennis & Dennis, 1940).

Human motor development is, in this sense, dependent primarily on maturation. Virtually all normal babies will progress through the same sequence of motor skills and abilities—from sitting to crawling to walking—whether they are given special practice or not. An early experiment by Gesell and Thompson (1929) clearly demonstrated this point. One of a pair of identical twin girls was given extensive training and practice in climbing stairs. The

This child has fetal alcohol syndrome, a developmental abnormality characterized by wide-apart eyes, flat bones, a thin upper lip, and mental retardation. (Health Service Center for Educational Resources, University of Washington)

A cradleboard, typically used by many American Indians, to bind a child during the infant stage of development. (Harold Hoffman/Photo Researchers)

Developmental psychology is concerned with identifying and understanding the many kinds of changes that occur as people grow older—the ways in which 5-year-olds differ from 2-year-olds, or 10-year-olds differ from 5-year-olds. There are two ways of making such comparisons: the **cross-sectional** method and the **longitudinal** method.

With the cross-sectional method we can select a sample of people of different ages, administer appropriate tests, and then compare the performances of subjects of various ages. This type of study is relatively easy to do, but there are some problems with it. The most serious of these problems is that it is extremely difficult to disentangle age effects from **cohort** effects. A cohort is a group of people born in a given year or period of time—for example, all the people born in 1920. If you compare people born in 1920 with people born in 1940, the groups do not differ only in age; they have also had an entirely different set of cultural and historical experiences. Therefore, if the two groups respond differently to a specific test, it is virtually impossible to say whether the differences are due to age or to these cohort effects.

An alternative approach is to use the *longitudinal* method, in which the same people are tested periodically over a span of time. This type of study avoids the entanglement of age and cohort effects, but it has difficulties of its own. For one thing, longitudinal studies are time-consuming and expensive to carry out. For another, some of the people in the study may die, drop out, or move away before the project is completed. Moreover, the researcher cannot take advantage of new techniques that become available but is restricted to those that were in use when the study began.

Various compromise techniques—such as longitudinal sequences within cross-sequential designs—have been proposed. Such mixtures tend to combine the advantages of both methods with the disadvantages of both methods. There is no perfect solution; methodological concerns will continue to be a problem in the study of age-related changes. Thus the data obtained in studies of development must always be interpreted with caution. (For a specific example, see the different conclusions drawn about aging and intelligence using these two methods as reported in Chapter 10.)

other twin received no practice. When the trained twin was a little over a year old and had become quite adept in stair climbing, her sister was allowed to try it on her own. She was able to crawl up the stairs in her very first test session, and within a week or two could climb as swiftly as her far more experienced twin sister.

Of course, once maturation has taken place, practice and training can have dramatic effects on the further development of a skill. There is a world of difference between the running ability of an ordinary person and that of an Olympic-class runner. Part of the difference is due to the talented athlete's superiority in physical structure, and part to a learned mastery of technique and style. But even the athlete's physical structure is highly dependent on experience and training—the degree of muscle development is very much a function of how much (and how strenuously) the muscles have been used.

Experience and Learning

Maturational changes occur naturally if the environment of the developing person is within normal ranges. Other developmental changes depend more directly on a person's particular experiences. To take one simple example, children growing up in the United States learn to speak English, and children growing up in modern Egypt learn to speak Arabic. While we accept this as the logical consequence of a child's experience, the reason for this phenomenon was not always so obvious. One of the first recorded experiments in history, reported by the Greek scholar Herodotus, was performed by King Psammetichus of Egypt in the seventh century B.C. Psammetichus wanted to demonstrate that Egyptian was the most ancient language in the world—the original tongue of the human race. He decided to rear some chil-

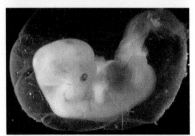

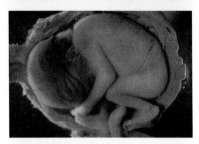

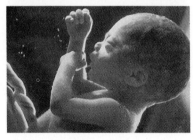

Certain types of development can only occur during specific, or critical, periods of an organism's life. (*Top, second, fourth:* Petit Format, Nestle, Science Source/Photo Researchers; *third:* Biophoto Associates/Photo Researchers)

A gosling's mother is determined during the gosling's critical period of imprinting. (Nina Leen, Life Magazine © Time Inc.)

dren without ever letting them hear human speech so that he could prove that their first spoken word would be in Egyptian! Here is Herodotus' description of Psammetichus' experimental method:

> He took two children of the common sort, and gave them over to a herdsman to bring up at his folds, strictly charging him to let no one utter a word in their presence, but to keep them in a sequestered cottage, and from time to time introduce goats to their apartment, see that they got their fill of milk, and in all other respects look after them. His object herein was to know, after the indistinct babblings of infancy were over, what word they would first articulate. (Herodotus, quoted in R. Watson, 1968)

As it turned out, the results of this experiment were not at all what Psammetichus had hoped for. The first distinct word the children uttered sounded like "becos," which happened to mean "bread" in a language called Phyrigian. Psammetichus reluctantly concluded that Phyrigian was a more ancient language than Egyptian.

Although this ancient experiment makes an amusing anecdote, one cannot ignore the fact that its two human subjects were exposed to extreme deprivation. Unfortunate children in every era have sometimes been reared under similarly deprived conditions, with a minimum of human interaction and stimulation. As we saw in Chapter 12, babies reared under such conditions are likely to show striking deficits in physical, emotional, and intellectual development (Spitz, 1946). Normal development—from the acquisition of simple motor skills to the ability to reason or to care about others—cannot occur in the absence of certain essential experiences.

Critical Periods

There are some types of development that can take place only during a specific time in an organism's life; otherwise, they will not occur at all. The interval of time during which such development must take place is referred to as a **critical period.** For instance, during the development of the human embryo there is a certain period of time (lasting only a few days) when the arms are formed. If something happens during that brief period to prevent the formation of arms, the baby will be born without arms. The drug thalidomide has this effect on the developing fetus. In the early 1960s, many European mothers who took thalidomide during their first trimester of pregnancy gave birth to armless or legless babies. The drug had this effect only if it was taken during the critical period for arm or leg formation.

In some species of animals there are certain kinds of learning that can occur only during a specific stage of the animal's life—the critical period for that type of learning. The phenomenon of **imprinting,** described in Chapter 6 in the Highlight: Ethology and Learning, is a good example. As you may recall, the Austrian ethologist Konrad Lorenz (1937) discovered that a gosling can become imprinted upon virtually any moving object it sees during the first day or so after hatching. In the normal course of events, the first moving object that a gosling sees after hatching is its mother. Thus the tendency to become imprinted is highly adaptive—it keeps the young bird from straying from its mother. However, the object doesn't have to look much like a goose—in fact, it can even look like an Austrian ethologist.

The critical period for imprinting lasts only a little more than 24 hours. Once this period has passed, a gosling's tendency to become imprinted quickly disappears (see Figure 13–1). A gosling that is kept alone in an empty

room for 36 hours after hatching will never become imprinted at all (Hess, 1959; Hoffman, 1978).

In people such strictly delimited time periods with such specific effects are not readily apparent. In human development it is more accurate to say that there are *sensitive periods* for learning, when various traits and abilities may be more readily acquired. Even a second language, which at one time did seem to require a critical period (Lenneberg, 1967), can be learned at any time in the life span, from early childhood to old age (McLaughlin, 1978). For many years people believed that languages were best acquired before the onset of puberty. This seemed reasonable because of the striking contrast between how easily children learn to talk and how difficult it seems for older students to learn foreign languages in school. This view, however, may well be peculiar to North Americans, where few people other than bilingual Canadians and Hispanic Americans learn any language other than English. In countries where bilingualism or second-language learning is expected, people of all ages learn languages without any apparent difficulties. Indeed, the observable age differences seem to favor adult rather than childhood language learning. Among a group of English speakers learning Dutch in the Netherlands, adults and teenagers progressed more quickly and achieved greater mastery than did prepubescent or younger children (Snow & Hoefnagel-Höhle, 1978). The advantages of the older learners included vocabulary, grammar, and even pronunciation. The important factors seem to be motivation and the opportunity to learn and to practice the language in natural as opposed to classroom settings.

Figure 13–1 Although the critical period for imprinting for goslings lasts from hatching to 36 hours, it is most effective within 13 hours of hatching. (Hess, 1959)

INFANCY

Newborn infants give the impression of being quite helpless and ignorant. To the casual observer, they seem to be capable of doing little else than sleeping, feeding, and crying. In the last few years, however, developmental psychologists have discovered that newborns (or *neonates*) have a number of abilities that were previously unsuspected. Infants in their first week of life appear to be able to tell what direction a sound is coming from (Muir & Field, 1979), to discriminate their mother's voice from the voices of other women (DeCasper & Fifer, 1980), and even to notice the difference between two objects and three objects (Antell & Keating, 1983; see the Application: Studying Visual Perception in Infants). There is also evidence that 1-week-old infants can imitate simple facial gestures, such as sticking out their tongues when they see an adult doing the same thing (Bower, 1977; Meltzoff & Moore, 1983). These infants appear to be perceptually "tuned in" to the sights and sounds of their environment at a remarkably early age.

(Four By Five)

Perceptual Capabilities

As these findings indicate, the basic machinery for perceiving the world is pretty much ready at birth. Day-old infants will gaze at nearby objects and people, and can track a slowly moving object with the eyes, even turning the head to keep the object in view. The eye movements, however, are imprecise and irregular, in contrast to the smooth and accurate eye movements of older people (Banks & Salpatek, 1983). A more serious disadvantage is the young infant's inability to adjust the eyes to focus on near or far stimuli. Infants can see things reasonably well at distances between 7 and 15 inches (18–38 cm);

APPLICATION

Studying Visual Perception in Infants

Back in 1890, when William James described the perceptual world of the infant as a "blooming, buzzing confusion," he was really just guessing. How could he know what the world looked like to a newborn baby? He obviously couldn't ask the baby! But asking the baby is just what developmental psychologists eventually learned to do. They know now that if a question is presented in just the right way, the baby is perfectly capable of answering it.

For example, if 1-week-old infants are shown two dissimilar pictures, they will usually gaze at one picture longer than at the other. This behavior does not depend on position: If we switch the pictures around, they still spend more time looking at the same picture. These results lead us to two conclusions: first, that the infants can tell the difference between the two

An infant being tested on pattern perception. (Enrico Ferorelli/DOT)

pictures (they can *discriminate* between them); and second, that they prefer one to the other. This **visual-preference** technique has provided striking evidence that even the youngest infants are capable of discriminating among various visual patterns. For example, within 48 hours of birth infants prefer pictures of faces to uniformly colored disks (Fantz, 1963).

The problem with the visual-preference method is that sometimes infants will show no preference for either of two stimuli, and there's no way of knowing whether they like them equally well or are unable to tell them apart. For this reason, the **habituation** technique is often used instead. With this method, one stimulus is displayed repeatedly: When the infant grows tired of it and stops looking at it, the baby is said to be *habituated* to it. At this point, the infant is given a choice between the old stimulus and a fresh one. Like everyone else, babies prefer something new and interesting to something old and boring, and they will invariably look longer at the new stimulus. If they do not, it implies that they cannot tell the stimuli apart. But even a newborn is able to detect fairly subtle differences between stimuli. For example, newborns who were habituated to one checkerboard pattern showed a preference for gazing at a new one with a different number and size of squares (Friedman, 1972).

The habituation technique provides a remarkably sensitive tool for studying infant perception, cognition, and even memory. The habituated stimulus can be put aside for a period of time, and a month or two later infants can be presented with the choice between the new stimulus and the old one. If they prefer the one they have never seen before, then they must remember (or, more precisely, recognize) the original stimulus. In fact, the habituation technique has demonstrated many sophisticated abilities of perception and discrimination in young infants. One study showed that 1-week-old babies could tell the difference between sets

The visual cliff. (DOT Photography)

of two dots and sets of three, regardless of how the dots were arranged or which number of dots they were habituated to (Antell & Keating, 1983). At this age, however, the infants were unable to discriminate between four and six dots. The habituation method has also been used with auditory stimuli. Newborn infants who have been habituated to a recording of a word such as "beagle" spoken over and over again will listen with renewed interest when a different word, such as "tinder," is played (Brody, Zelazo, & Chaika, 1984).

Still other perception studies make use of physiological measures. Infants' heart rates, for example, have proved useful in the study of depth perception. When placed on a *visual cliff* (see text), a platform of clear glass over what looks like a sharp drop, infants' heart rates slow down when they are placed on the deep side. This reaction is typical of infants when they stop to orient themselves to something new, in this case the noticed difference between the deep and the shallow side (Campos, Langer, & Krowitz, 1970). This suggests that infants as young as 1½ months have depth perception.

434

at other distances, objects appear blurred. The ability to focus improves rapidly and reaches near-adult levels within two or three months (Aslin & Dumais, 1980), by which time infants are able to see the world in color (Teller, 1981).

By age 3 or 4 months, infants have some depth perception and can judge, to some extent, how far away objects are. In fact, by 4 or 5 months of age, they can usually reach with some accuracy for a nearby toy, though they are not yet likely to succeed in grasping it (von Hofsten & Fazel-Zandy, 1984). They are able to use binocular vision (or stereopsis—see Chapter 4) to judge distances; however, unlike older children, their ability to judge when a toy is within reach virtually disappears when one of their eyes is covered (Granrud, Yonas, & Pettersen, 1984).

By the time they reach crawling age, at 9 or 10 months, they have acquired a healthy respect for heights. Rudimentary depth discrimination is present by about 1½ months of age. When such a young infant is placed on the deep side of a visual-cliff apparatus (see the Application: Studying Visual Perception in Infants), its heart rate *decelerates* (slows down) compared to when it is placed on the shallow side. This deceleration indicates that the infant notices a difference between the two sides; it does *not* indicate fear of the deep side. The heart rate *accelerates* (speeds up) in fear situations, and this is just what happens when older children (who have already had crawling experience) are placed on the deep side of the visual cliff (Campos, Hiatt, Ramsay, Henderson, & Svejda, 1978). Children 7 months or older show heart rate acceleration when placed on the deep side, suggesting that they fear the apparent drop. They also avoid crawling out over the deep side, even when encouraged to do so by their mothers. But 7-month-olds who have not yet begun to crawl do not show a fear response—accelerated heart rate—to the deep side. This suggests that human infants with **depth perception** have to *learn* to fear and to avoid sharp drops. They can learn either from their own painful experience of falling, or from the fright reactions shown by their parents when they are in danger of falling (Campos et al., 1978; Walk, 1966). Not surprisingly, many young animals show the same developmental progression. Very young kittens and rabbits do not avoid the deep cliff; older ones do (Walk, 1966). Yet other animals, such as goats, avoid the deep cliff from the very beginning (Walk & Gibson, 1961). Apparently, what may require learning and experience in one species may, in other species, be present at birth. In humans learning and experience almost invariably play crucial roles.

More complex types of perception also appear at an early age. For example, 3- and 4-month-old infants seem to perceive an object as a solid, unitary thing rather than as a patch of color or brightness. In one experiment (Kellman & Spelke, 1983) infants of this age range were shown a rod moving back and forth behind another object in such a way that the middle of the rod was blocked from view and only its top and bottom were visible. Using a habituation procedure, the experimenters were able to show that the infants perceived the rod as a unitary whole.

Perhaps the most surprising of the recent discoveries have involved infants' learning about intermodal perceptions—their ability to associate perceptions in one sense (or modality) with those in another. In several experiments infants of 4 or 5 months have been shown two videotapes side by side, while the soundtrack from only one of the films was played in their ears. The question was: Would the babies tend to look at the film that matched the soundtrack, or would they look at either one at random? The answer was clear—the babies looked significantly more often at the appropriate picture.

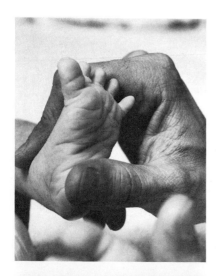

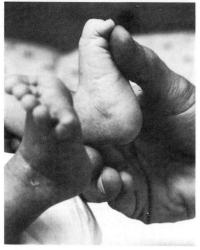

The Babinski reflex is pictured here—the immature form in the top photo, the mature form in the bottom photo. (J. da Cunha/Photo Researchers)

They looked at the video of the woman's face whose lip movements matched the speech sounds they heard (Spelke & Cortelyou, 1981). They looked at the happy-looking woman when they heard a happy-sounding voice, and at the angry-looking one when an angry voice was played (Walker, 1982). And they even looked at the picture of a car driving away when the soundtrack played car sounds getting dimmer, and at the approaching car when the car sounds grew louder (Walker-Andrews & Lennon, 1985).

Indeed, by 6 months, babies seem to experience the world pretty much as adults do; the world is no longer, as William James put it, a "blooming, buzzing confusion."

Motor Development

Human and animal neonates come into the world equipped with a number of built-in responses called **reflexes.** Many of these are essential to life; among these are the reflexes that control breathing and include coughing, sneezing, and yawning. Other important reflexes are those that have to do with feeding: sucking, swallowing, and *rooting* (which means turning the head in the direction of a touch on the cheek or on the side of the mouth, as happens when a nipple is placed near an infant's mouth). Other reflexes, such as the *Babinsky reflex* (in which the toes flare outward in response to the foot being stroked), serve no obvious purpose.

A number of reflexes, especially those connected with breathing and temperature regulation, are present all through life. But others disappear in the first few months of life, often to be replaced by voluntary movements. The clumsy rooting motions of the newborn disappear; the older infant recognizes the bottle or breast by sight, reaching out for it when hungry and pushing it away when satiated.

Motor development in infancy is **cephalocaudal:** that is, it starts at the head and progresses toward the feet. Infants gain control of their eyes and head before they gain control of their hands; they learn to reach for things with their hands before their legs are capable of crawling or walking. Progress is also **proximodistal:** it proceeds from the center of the body to the extremities, from the large muscles to the small. Arm motions are controlled before hand motions, hand motions before finger motions.

Most normal infants go through the same basic sequence in their acquisition of motor skills—sitting, crawling, standing, and walking (see Table 13–1 and Figure 13–2). However, the timing of this development may vary considerably. Some babies walk at 10 months; others not until 16 or 18 months. Studies of the effects of practice on the acquisition of any of these motor abil-

Table 13–1: Motor Milestones in Infancy

Motor Skill	Mean Age in Months	Usual Range in Months
Sits with support	2.3	1–5
Sits alone	6.6	5–9
Stands up with support	8.6	6–12
Stands alone	11.0	9–16
Walks alone	11.7	9–17

a   b   c

d   e   f

Figure 13–2 These photos represent some of the more visible stages in the sequence of motor development. Every baby goes through the same sequence, but some go at a faster rate than others. Lags of a few weeks in early infancy and of a few months in later infancy are normal. The stages shown here are: (a) lift head up (1 month), (b) roll over (2½–4 months), (c) creep (7–10 months), (d) pull to stand (7–8 months), (e) climb stair steps (10 months), and (f) getting ready to stand alone (11 months). (*a:* C. Vergara; *b:* Susan McCartney; *c:* Townsend P. Dickinson; *d:* Herb Levart—all Photo Researchers; *e:* Renate Hiller/Monkmeyer Press; *f:* Suzanne Szasz/Photo Researchers)

ities show little if any permanent effects. A baby given practice might be able to do something slightly earlier than usual, but such early practice seems to confer no permanent advantage (Stone, Smith, & Murphy, 1973). The role of special experience in motor development is skill-specific and rather small. This is not true for other important developmental processes, including early social attachments.

Social Attachments

According to Erikson (1963), the first year of life is important for the formation of a person's basic sense of trust in others and faith in the future. Of the many experiences that contribute to the development of these feelings, perhaps the most important are those that take place between infant and mother (or other primary caregiver) in the first year of life. Infants whose mothers respond to their needs in a reliable and sensitive way are likely to be happier and to cry less in the long run than those whose mothers often ignore their cries (Bell & Ainsworth, 1972).

Newborn infants are not much concerned about who feeds them and changes their diapers, as long as the care is administered in a reasonably

kind, consistent, and competent way. But by the time infants are 7 or 8 months old, they have usually begun to develop an **attachment** to their mother, and perhaps to one or two other familiar people as well. They may demonstrate this attachment by crying when mother leaves or clinging to her when frightened or hurt. The tendency to form attachments of this kind is a universal characteristic of human infants: every normal child becomes attached to someone by the age of 12 or 13 months, if there is anyone at all to become attached to. Even a child who has been physically abused by the mother will become attached to her (Schneider-Rosen, Braunwald, Carlson, & Cicchetti, 1985).

Not all attachments are equally satisfactory, however. Mary Ainsworth and her collaborators (Ainsworth, Blehar, Waters, & Wall, 1978) have distinguished between *secure* and *insecure* attachments. The security of an infant's attachment to the mother is judged in the "strange situation" test. In this test a 12- to 15-month-old infant is brought into an unfamiliar room with the mother and is allowed to play with some toys. The mother then leaves the room for two brief periods and returns again. An infant who has formed a secure attachment to the mother is likely to play happily while she is in the room, glancing at her from time to time to check on her whereabouts. When she leaves, the infant will probably stop playing and start to cry, or at least look grave. When she returns, the infant will greet her joyfully, perhaps going to her for reassurance.

The behavior of insecurely attached children is more variable. Some cry and refuse to play even when their mother is present; some pay no attention to her and appear unconcerned when she leaves. But the most important indication is what happens when the mother returns after her brief absence. Insecurely attached children will not greet their mothers with enthusiasm: such a child might simply ignore his or her mother, or might cling to her and continue to cry in an angry way, or might even push her away if she offers comfort.

Around 70 percent of babies from middle-class American homes are judged to be securely attached to their mothers at age 12 months. Children are less likely to be securely attached if their mother has abused them or neglected them, or if she has failed to meet their needs in a consistent and responsive way (Belsky, Rovine, & Taylor, 1984; Schneider-Rosen et al., 1985). But an insecure attachment cannot be blamed solely on the mother since some infants are more difficult to care for than others from birth on. In one study hospital nurses rated 2-day-old infants on various characteristics such as alertness and irritability. The newborns who were less alert and more irritable than average were less likely to be securely attached to their mothers at age 12 months (Egeland & Farber, 1984).

Security of attachment also has implications for a child's future. A child who was insecurely attached at 12 months runs a greater than average risk of having a number of problems later on. Securely attached infants are more likely to turn into friendly, cooperative preschoolers. Insecurely attached ones are more likely to become aggressive, impulsive, or overly dependent and clingy (Erickson, Sroufe, & Egeland, 1985; Sroufe, Fox, & Pancake, 1983).

Changes in Family Structure. In the past decade there have been major changes in the structure of the American family and, consequently, in child-care practices. One notable change has been the increasing tendency of mothers of young children to work outside the home. Among women with children under the age of 3, over half are now employed (Easterbrooks & Goldberg, 1985). Fortunately, this trend does not seem to have had harmful

effects. Children of working mothers are no less secure in their attachments than the children of mothers who stay at home (Owen, Easterbrooks, Chase-Lansdale, & Goldberg, 1984). In some respects, the children of employed mothers may even have some advantages. For example, daughters of employed mothers may be more self-confident and do better in school (Scarr & Hall, 1984).

Another trend that seems to have favorable effects is the father's increasing participation in child care. Infants are likely to develop an attachment to their fathers, as well as to their mothers, if the father shares some of the feeding, diapering, and bathing chores (Zelazo, Kotelchuck, Barber, & David, 1977).

On the other side of the coin, many American children are growing up without a father at all. Because of the current high rates of divorce and single parenthood, over half of American children will spend part of their childhood in a single-parent home. The great majority of these homes are headed by a woman. Somewhat surprisingly, a child who is reared in such a fatherless home is less likely to form a secure attachment to his or her *mother,* possibly because the pressures of single parenthood—rearing a child without assistance—are stressful for both parent and child (Egeland & Farber, 1984).

EARLY CHILDHOOD

By the age of 2½ or 3, children's attachments to their caregivers have become less intense; they are no longer so dependent on their parents. They have acquired a fair amount of language and are able to communicate many of their needs and thoughts (see Chapter 8). Now they must learn the many behaviors and skills expected of members of their society, including those that pertain to sex and gender. Early childhood is an important period for social, personality, and sex-role development.

Psychosexual and Psychosocial Development

One of the most influential approaches to personality development has been Sigmund Freud's **psychoanalytic theory.** Freud revolutionized our thinking about childhood and adult personality with his views on **psychosexual development.** Later, Erik Erickson modified Freud's theory; his approach focuses more on social influences than on sexual ones and is thus referred to as **psychosocial.** Both of these theorists view development as a series of stages. Each stage has its own conflict or crisis, which may or may not be resolved successfully. Individuals who have failed to deal successfully with a conflict at one stage may carry that problem with them into adulthood.

Psychosexual development involves the gradual acquisition of one's identity as a woman or man, as well as basic ways of relating to people and to the world. For Freud (1920/1955), the determinants of adult personality are rooted in early childhood, and the ways that children deal with sexual energy (or in Freud's terms, their **libido**) determine how they will cope with life as adults.

We will give here only a bare outline of the theory of psychosexual development, which is discussed in more detail in Chapter 15. The central idea is that a person's drives are focused on various parts of the body during different stages of development, and that experiences during each stage will affect adjustment to the next stage, as well as needs and attitudes in later life. For example, the first psychosexual stage is the **oral stage** (see Table 13–2).

Table 13–2: Stages of Psychosexual and Psychosocial Development

Approximate Age Range	Freudian Stages	Eriksonian Crises and Their Successful Resolutions
Birth to 1½	Oral	Basic trust vs. mistrust Experiences with reliable caregivers lead children to develop a basic attitude of trust in the world and in other people.
1½ to 3	Anal	Autonomy vs. shame and doubt Development of a sense of independence and self-control.
3 to 5½	Phallic	Initiative vs. guilt Development of the ability to initiate activities and see them through.
5½ to 12	Latency	Industry vs. inferiority Successful testing of self against peers, in neighborhood and school, leads to a feeling of industry.
Adolescence	Genital	Identity vs. role confusion Various roles (son or daughter, sibling, friend, student, etc.) are integrated into one identity.
Young adulthood	—	Intimacy vs. isolation Development of close relationships; commitments are made to others and to a career.
Middle adulthood	—	Generativity vs. stagnation Feeling that one is being productive—family and work are basic ways to do this and they are the focus at this time.
Late adulthood	—	Ego integrity vs. despair Feeling that life has been worthwhile.

Adapted from Erikson (1963).

According to Freud, if oral needs such as sucking are not met or are overindulged during this stage, the long-term outcome may be an adult with an "oral" personality. There will be an excessive desire for oral satisfactions such as food or cigarettes: other people will not be trusted because of the original betrayal by a mother who perhaps weaned a child from the breast too abruptly.

The transition from one psychosexual stage to another is partly maturational. As our bodies mature and grow, we acquire new drives, needs, and satisfactions. At around 18 months, with the onset of the **anal stage,** the focus of libidinal energy shifts to the organs of elimination. Then, at around age 3, the focus shifts again, this time to the sexual organs. During this stage, the **phallic stage,** girls and boys must deal with their sexual feelings for the parent of the opposite sex. According to psychoanalytic theory, a little boy desires his mother and fears his father's jealous wrath; this is the **Oedipal conflict.** Girls are presumed to have a parallel experience, the **Electra conflict.** Both sexes eventually resolve their conflicts by giving up their hopes for the opposite-sex parent and achieving **identification** with the same-sex parent. This means that they take on the standards, behaviors, and moral values of the parent of the same sex.

Next comes the **latency stage,** which lasts from about age 5 to the beginning of adolescence. During this time sexual feelings are suppressed, and en-

ergies are focused on social and intellectual achievements. The final stage in Freudian theory is the **genital stage,** during which sexual feelings reemerge and, if all goes well, are now directed at an appropriate partner, so that the person can marry and have children.

For the young child, the changes from the oral to the anal to the phallic stages, while partly maturational, are also very heavily influenced by the social demands of growing up. Erikson (1963) views each stage as a time in a person's life when certain basic psychosocial crises must be resolved. During the first 1½ years, infants must resolve their feelings of trust versus mistrust of the important people in their world. During this period, if their parents care for them in a reliable and consistent manner, they learn to place basic trust in others.

During the second stage infants must begin to cope with the world around them and with their own feelings of unworthiness. If this stage is successfully negotiated, children will develop a sense of autonomy and will have confidence in their ability to control their own fate.

The years 3 through 5 are considered critical for acquiring initiative and for minimizing feelings of guilt and dismay (Erikson, 1963). The final stage of childhood is the latency period, during which children work to acquire many of the specific skills required by their society. A lack of confidence in their ability to perform these skills may result in feelings of inferiority. The fifth stage occurs during adolescence and focuses on the **identity crisis.** Erikson believes that development continues all through the life span; accordingly, he provides three additional stages to cover the adult year (see Table 13.2).

During each stage of childhood the parents' behavior—whether they encourage or discourage their children's development of trust, attempts to control things, and efforts to initiate activities—is crucial in determining how children will resolve these basic conflicts and how they will cope with later crises.

For both Freud and Erikson, a central factor in the process of development is children's identification with the parent of the same sex. One product of this identification is the **superego,** or conscience, which tells them what is right and what is wrong, and makes them feel guilty if they do something they know they shouldn't. Another consequence of identification is sex-role development. Boys' identification with their fathers leads them to act as males do in their society, and girls' identification with their mothers leads them to act as females do in that same society. (An expanded discussion of sex roles can be found in the Highlight in Chapter 15.)

But sex-role identifications and expectations are apparent even earlier than the age that Freud and Erikson specify for the end of the phallic stage. Children as young as 2 or 3 have already absorbed many of society's stereotypes about the behaviors expected from each sex. In one study (Kuhn, Nash, & Brucken, 1978) children were introduced to a pair of paper dolls named "Michael" and "Lisa," and asked which doll had made various statements. Both boys and girls believed that Lisa liked to help her mother, talked a lot, was the one who said "I need some help," and stated that she would be a nurse and clean the house when she grew up. And both girls and boys believed that Michael liked to help his father, was the one who said "I can hit you," and stated that he would be a boss when he grew up. Apparently, both boys and girls learn at an early age what is expected not only of themselves, but also of the other gender. Such shared expectations make stereotypes and habitual ways of thinking about sex and gender roles extremely resistant to change.

The power of societal expectations and stereotypes should not be un-

Social-learning theorists suggest that environmental influences are the key shapers of sex roles. Accordingly, as the traditional sex roles played by men and women in our society start to change, this will affect the way children view themselves. (Four By Five)

derestimated. In a study of children's beliefs about sex roles and occupations, one 4-year-old girl firmly maintained that only boys could become doctors; she said that girls had to become nurses (Maccoby & Jacklin, 1974). This little girl could not possibly have gotten such an idea from her parents—her own mother was a doctor!

Social-learning theory. Identification theorists such as Freud and Erikson attribute the development of "good" behavior—behavior that conforms to society's rules—to the formation of the superego, resulting from identification with the same-sex parent. This means that the parent's moral values and standards of behavior are adopted as a whole, and that henceforth the superego will tell the child what to do (and what not to do) in a variety of situations.

In contrast, social-learning theorists (such as Bandura, 1986) propose that rules of behavior are not adopted as a unit. Instead, a child learns, one by one, each of the many behaviors and attitudes that his or her society demands. This learning is accomplished partly through imitation of **role models,** and partly through reinforcement and punishment (see Chapter 6). The model can be anyone—parents, friends, siblings, teachers, characters seen on TV or read about in books. And the reinforcements and punishments do not have to be experienced directly: **vicarious reinforcements** and **punishments** (those that the child sees another person receive) are also effective.

Because they believe that any learned behavior can be modified, learning theorists do not view behaviors as fixed, even sex-role behaviors. Moreover, they view the same-sex parent as only one of many shapers of sex roles. Reinforcement by nursery-school teachers, for example, may help to shape this kind of behavior. Serbin and O'Leary (1975) found that nursery-school teachers unintentionally rewarded different behaviors in boys and in girls, encouraging boys to be aggressive and to tackle difficult tasks, while encouraging girls to be dependent. Such stereotypes are further reinforced by many children's books and television programs. Fortunately, this appears to be changing somewhat in recent years.

Cognitive Development

Just as children must ultimately develop adult personalities and an adult understanding of social relationships, so must they eventually acquire adult forms of thinking, reasoning, and comprehending the world. One of the major theorists of cognitive and conceptual development was the Swiss psychologist Jean Piaget. According to Piaget (1954; Piaget & Inhelder, 1968), children progress through a series of cognitive stages, beginning at birth with the **sensorimotor stage** of cognitive development (see Table 13–3).

In Piaget's view, infants are born with no sense of self, no conception of the difference between themselves and the other objects in their environment, and no understanding that these other objects have a permanent existence in the world—that they continue to exist even when the infant isn't looking at them or touching them. Infants develop these ideas gradually, through their explorations and experiences of the environment. They learn, for example, that some things (their fingers) are always there, whereas others (their parents) come and go. They learn how to produce interesting effects on their environment, as when they shake a rattle in order to hear the noise. And they learn that if they drop a toy, it hasn't disappeared forever but

Table 13–3: Piagetian Stages of Cognitive Development

Approximate Age Range	Stage	Description
Birth to age 2	Sensorimotor Stage	Children develop the concept of object permanence and the ability to form mental representations.
Age 2 to 7	Preoperational Stage	Children's thought is egocentric; they lack the concept of conservation and the ability to decenter.
Age 7 to 11	Period of Concrete Operations	Children can decenter; they acquire the concept of conservation; but they cannot reason abstractly or test hypotheses systematically.
Starts at age 11 or 12	Period of Formal Operations	Children begin to reason abstractly.

Adapted from Piaget & Inhelder (1968).

can be found by looking down at the floor. This is one of the early steps in the development of **object permanence,** the understanding that objects (and people) have a permanent existence in the world, independent of oneself. A 6-month-old infant might reach for an attractive toy, but if the toy is covered with a cloth, he instantly forgets it: It is "out of sight, out of mind." But a 20-month-old will search for a hidden toy until he finds it, because he understands that the toy still exists even if he can't see it. A newly developed skill that permits him to do this is his ability to form **mental representations**—visual images or symbols (such as words) that represent objects or ideas. Mental representations enable the child to envision the consequences of his actions, to make plans, to have insights. In other words, they enable the child to think.

The next Piagetian stage, beginning around age 2, is the **preoperational stage.** According to Piaget, the thought of preoperational children is **egocentric;** that is, they see everything from their own point of view. Preoperational children also tend to **center** (focus their attention) on one aspect of a situation, which leads them to make errors on a test that Piaget invented, the **conservation** problem (see Figure 13–3). For example, we might show a 5-year-old child two identical glasses of juice, both filled to the same level. We then ask, "Is there the same amount of juice in the two glasses?" "Yes," the child replies. Then we pour the contents of one glass into a tall, narrow glass cylinder. Of course, the level of the juice in the cylinder is much higher than the level in the glass. Now we ask again, "Is there the same amount of juice?" and this time the child replies, "No, this one [the narrow cylinder] has more." According to Piaget, preoperational children center on the height of the liquid and ignore the width. They lack the concept of *conservation of liquid volume.*

The preoperational stage gives way to the **concrete operational stage,** which starts at around age 7 and lasts until 11 or 12. Concrete operational children understand the principle of conservation: They realize that the amount of liquid stays the same, regardless of the shape of the container it is poured into. They are able to **decenter**—to consider more than one aspect of a situation at a time. For example, they can consider both the height of the liquid in the container and its width or diameter. By the end of this period,

Figure 13–3 One test of conservation is to pour water from a short, wide glass into a tall, narrow one and ask if the amount of water is the same. Preoperational children will say that there is more water in the taller glass; concrete operational children will say that the amount of water has not changed. (Mimi Forsyth/Monkmeyer)

they can not only judge that, say, an amount of water poured from a tall, narrow glass into a short, wide one does not change, but can also explain how they know it did not change. This kind of logical thinking is the beginning of **formal operations,** which develop during adolescence in Piaget's last stage of cognitive development, the **formal operational stage.** (We will discuss formal operations again in Chapter 14.)

How does the child move from one level of cognitive ability to the next? According to Piaget, progress from one stage to another depends on two fundamental instruments of cognitive change, **assimilation** and **accommodation.** When people encounter something only a little different from what they have experienced before, it is *assimilated* into their previous experience or knowledge. The "learning" in this case involves interpreting the new information to fit preexisting patterns of understanding. Whenever we interpret new things in terms of their similarity to what we are familiar with, we are using the process of assimilation.

But sometimes we encounter situations or concepts that are so different from the familiar that they cannot be assimilated. Such events are rare in adult life. When they do occur, either they are totally ignored or they force us to change our way of thinking—to *accommodate* what we already know to something new and important. Great and pervasive new ideas, such as Darwin's theory of evolution, Freud's theory of the unconscious, Einstein's theory of relativity, and the emergence of nuclear power, have forced people to change their basic conceptions of the biological, social, and physical worlds.

For young children, events and situations that require accommodation are commonplace. Those that a child cannot yet cope with are ignored. Those that are just beyond the present level of the child, and that cannot be assimilated, force accommodation: They force changes in the way the child views reality, as well as changes in the way the child thinks.

Learning about language involves the process of accommodation. Every child must, at some point in normal development, get the idea that words represent things—that words "mean" something. This is an important accommodation, usually lost to our memory. But in at least one instance a person was later able to remember that flash of insight, that moment of accommodation. Helen Keller lost her sight and hearing in infancy before she learned to speak. When she was almost 7, her tutor, Anne Sullivan, began to teach her a language transmitted by taps of the fingers. One day, during a session with her tutor, Keller (1903) suddenly understood the concept of naming, and, as she later put it, "The mystery of language was revealed to me. . . . Everything had a name, and each name gave birth to a new thought."

The Roots of Language

In Chapter 8, we discussed language and language acquisition at some length. Here we return to the topic briefly in the context of early childhood development. Understanding the nature of words and the use of language as a medium of communication are major breakthroughs that have enormous consequences for children's learning (Sinclair-de Zwart, 1973). The social ties between child and parents, and between child and other children, are also important for the growth of language. From early infancy children's behavior during social interactions facilitates their acquisition of communication skills. As early as 3 or 4 months of age, a baby playing with mother will look at the same things she looks at—mother and child usually pay attention

Shared attention patterns between mother and child help set the stage for language learning. (Matuson/ Monkmeyer)

to the same things simultaneously (Bruner, 1974/1975). At about the same age, the mother begins to name things when she's showing them to her child or when she's aware that the child's looking at them (Reich, 1986). Thus social attachment and shared attention patterns between mother and child set the stage for language learning.

More complicated ideas than simple naming must also be communicated between parent and child.

Mothers help by speaking in "motherese," a simplified form of language that is carefully tailored to the child's linguistic and cognitive levels. For example, a mother might say to her 2-year-old, "That's a lion. And the lion's name is Leo. Leo lives in a *big* house. Leo goes for a walk every morning. And he always takes his cane along" (Snow, 1972). It would be a rare mother indeed who would tell her 2-year-old, "That is a lion named Leo who lives in a large house and goes for a walk every morning invariably taking his cane along." Parents make sure that the child is listening to them; they use questions both to test the child and to continue the conversation, and rarely make the mistake of talking about things the child doesn't understand (Gleason & Weintraub, 1978). Children, for their part, give clear signals when they do not understand—they simply turn off. Babies either fuss or go to sleep; young children fidget and look away. The sensitivity of most people to these conservational signals greatly facilitates early language development (Shatz, 1978). When children are deprived of such important and sensitive social interactions, as in some institutional settings, language development can be delayed and even permanently impaired (Spitz & Wolf, 1946).

Children's growing cognitive ability provides another support for their acquistion of language. During the late sensorimotor and early preoperational stages of development, children become able to deal with increasingly complex ideas and relationships. Early in this period, between 1 and 2 years, they classify assortments of objects by dealing with one kind of object at a time. For example, if children are given four plates and four blocks to play with, they might pick up one plate after another, grouping them together in one pile. Children at this age use language in a similar way, talking about one thing at a time by saying "Plate, plate, plate, plate" (Sugarman, 1982, 1983).

Between 2½ and 3 years of age, children become able to consider two classes of objects simultaneously and to talk about the relationships between classes of objects. A child might pick up a plate and put it in one pile, then pick up a block, say "Not plate," and put it in a different pile. These conceptual advances are reflected both in the child's increasingly complex use of language and in other cognitive abilities such as counting (Gelman & Gallistel, 1978).

The Development of Moral Reasoning

As children learn to talk and to think about their world, they inevitably encounter problems of interpretation. One area of great importance to people and to society is the concept of morality: decisions about "good" and "bad," and the attribution of responsibility.

The most direct way of deciding whether people's actions are worthy of praise or blame is to consider the outcome of their actions. This simplistic way of thinking relies entirely on observables and completely ignores *intentions*. Children in the preoperational stage of cognitive development often judge people this way (Piaget, 1932). Someone who breaks a plate while trying to be helpful (a bad consequence but a good intention) is blamed as much as someone else who broke a plate deliberately (a bad intention as well as a bad consequence). However, it is not clear whether this tendency is a consequence of immature moral reasoning or merely a reflection of common adult behavior. Consider what adults usually do when a child happens to break a treasured vase or spill ice cream on the linen tablecloth—they usually get angry, despite the child's plea, "It was an accident!" Thus young children may simply be imitating their elders in attributing guilt to the well-meaning breaker of plates, even though they may already be capable of taking intentions into account.

On the other hand, a very young child may not find it so easy to distinguish between a person's intentional actions and those that are unintentional. Smith (1978) found that children 3½ to 4½ years old tend to describe any action performed by another person as intended, even sneezing. However, by age 4½, children clearly recognize that some actions are intended and others are not. Furthermore, they are able to recognize that an action might have been intended (that is, voluntary), but that a consequence of that action could be unintentional. Such thinking is fairly sophisticated, since it involves an interpretation of what might be going on in another person's mind. When it comes to their *own* behavior, even 3-year-olds appreciate the difference between "an accident" and something done "on purpose." Shultz (1980) reported that when one child, age 3, accidentally hurt another, he refused to apologize because he had not done it "on purpose." It doesn't take long before children learn to use this same kind of logic in interpreting the behavior of others and in making moral judgments (Flavell, 1985).

Making moral judgments of others is only one aspect of moral development, and perhaps not the most important one at that. Of far greater concern is the development of our own morality and the ways in which we judge ourselves and control our own behavior. Lawrence Kohlberg (1963, 1971, 1981) proposed a theory of moral development based on Piaget's view of cognitive development. According to Kohlberg, children in the sensorimotor and preoperational stages are in the **preconventional stage** of moral development (see Table 13–4 for a summary of the stages). Their behavior is governed by rewards and punishments, rather than by higher principles. It is bad to hurt

Table 13–4: Kohlberg's Stage Theory of the Development of Moral Reasoning

I. Preconventional Level

Rules are set down by others.

Stage 1. Punishment and Obedience Orientation

Consequences of an action (rewards or punishments) determine its goodness or badness. Rules are followed in order to avoid punishment.

Stage 2. Instrumental Hedonistic Orientation.

"Right" is defined in terms of satisfying one's own needs or attaining rewards. Will do things for others in order to get favors in return: "You scratch my back and I'll scratch yours."

II. Conventional Level

Individual takes on the rules and standards of the family, group, or nation. Rules and laws are viewed as valuable in themselves, taking precedence over the needs of individuals.

Stage 3. "Good Boy"–"Good Girl" Orientation

"Right" is whatever pleases others and is approved of by them. Emphasis is on being considered "nice" and avoiding disapproval.

Stage 4. Law and Order Orientation.

"Right" is doing one's duty, showing respect for authority, and maintaining the social order for its own sake.

III. Postconventional Level

"Right" is defined in terms of general ethical principles that the individual has chosen.

Stage 5. Social Contract Orientation

Rules and laws are considered generally beneficial because they preserve the rights of individuals and the welfare of society. If a particular law is unjust, it should be changed.

Stage 6. Universal Ethical Principle Orientation.

"Right" is defined according to self-chosen ethical principles, which are abstract (such as the Golden Rule) rather than specific and concrete (such as the Ten Commandments).

Stage 7. Cosmic Ethical Principle Orientation

What's right is defined in terms of a sense of cosmic unity.

Adapted from Kohlberg (1969, 1981). Stage 7 was added later to provide for a morality that conforms to religious beliefs beyond those of one's personal conscience.

---

puppies, for example, because you will be punished if you do it. However, many young children are capable of compassion and empathy in such matters, and it is a rare child indeed whose actions are as completely dominated by rewards and punishments as Kohlberg's theory would have us believe. Nonetheless, Kohlberg's stage theory is of interest; it does capture what children often *say* about morality, although not necessarily what they do.

As is the case with some of the Piagetian tests, there is often a wide gap between what children say to an experimenter and what they are actually capable of doing (Gelman, 1978). Preschool children are not very good at describing their thoughts and ideas; in fact, one of the aims of schooling is to produce articulate children who can talk about their own mental lives and social beliefs (Flavell, 1978).

Self-Control

The relationship between what one says and what one does has another aspect: the use of language to control behavior. In the first year or two of life children gradually acquire the ability to follow instructions. Soon parents can exert some control over their children's behavior just by talking to them. For example, at about 1 year of age, a child can be asked to pick up a toy truck from a nearby table. Most 1-year-olds have no trouble carrying out this request. Children of this age can also get the truck if it is across the room. However, if there is another toy between themselves and the truck, children will often be distracted and bring the other toy instead. A 1-year-old is not yet able to sustain an action in the face of external distractions, whereas an older child is better able to concentrate on the goal and ignore distractions.

One way that children remind themselves about what they are supposed to do (or not do) is by talking to themselves. Sometimes they even sound like their own parents, saying things like "Mustn't touch, Daddy spank" when tempted by forbidden objects. Alexander Luria, a Russian psychologist who studied the development of self-control in children, described this development as a shift from control by others to control by oneself. He pointed out that speech, which starts out as a means of communication between a child and an adult, "later becomes a means of organizing the child's own behavior. . . . The function which was previously divided between two people later becomes an internal function of human behavior" (1959, p. 341). Children first learn to act on the basis of instructions given by other people, then learn to talk to themselves, and eventaully can think silently to themselves about what to do and what not to do.

Verbal instructions can also be used to teach preschool children how to resist an immediate temptation in order to gain a larger reward later on. Young children often seem to go for immediate gratification, even in cases where a short delay will bring them a much better prize. For example, children between the ages of 3 and 5 years were told that if they finished a simple task, such as copying letters of the alphabet, they would be allowed to play with some really terrific toys. If they didn't finish, then they could play only with some uninteresting, broken ones. While they were working, a toy clown would pop up from a jack-in-the-box and say things like "Ho ho ho, I love to play with children. Come push my nose and see what happens." Without instructions about how to resist this temptation, most children stopped working to play with the distracting clown. However, children could easily be taught simple strategies for resisting the temptation. They were told: (1) to tell the clown "No, I can't; I'm working"; (2) to say to themselves, "I'm going to keep working so I can play with the fun toys and Mr. Clown later"; or (3) to pretend that there was a wall between themselves and the distractor. Giving children these simple ways of dealing with temptation proved to be an effective method of teaching them self-control (Mischel & Patterson, 1978). Such learning is an essential part of socialization in cultures such as ours, where people are expected to be able to postpone gratification.

THE SCHOOL-AGE CHILD

In our society children enter school around the age of 5 or 6. They are then faced with a wider social and intellectual world than they knew at home, and are more exposed to influences from adults other than their parents. They are also more exposed to influences from other children, especially from

HIGHLIGHT

Nativist and Empiricist Traditions

Throughout history there have been two contrasting views of what shapes human personality and behavior. The first, **nativism,** emphasizes our biological and physical structure, and relies on heredity and maturation to account for most human characteristics and abilities. The second, **empiricism,** emphasizes learning, experience, and the power of the environment to shape development. The seventeenth-century French philosopher René Descartes championed the nativist view when he maintained that the human mind was innately capable of thinking and reasoning. The seventeenth-century English philosopher John Locke represented the opposing side: He held that the mind starts out as a piece of blank paper, empty until it is written upon by experience:

> Let us suppose the mind to be, as we say, white paper void of all characters, without any ideas—How come it to be furnished? . . . To this I answer, in one word, from EXPERIENCE. In that all our knowledge is founded; and from that it ultimately derives itself. (1690/1973, p. 23)

It has been three centuries since Locke wrote those words, but the controversy still goes on. Sometimes it is labeled "nature versus nurture," sometimes "heredity versus environment." Sometimes one side seems to be winning, but then the pendulum swings the other way again. Charles Darwin was a nativist; he attributed a great deal of animal and human behavior to instincts, which are innate. For many years after Darwin, nativism was in vogue; a favorite saying was "The apple doesn't fall far from the tree." The pendulum swung back again when behaviorism became the dominant voice in psychology. There has probably never been a clearer statement of the empiricist view than this famous quote from the first

René Descartes (Frans Hals/Giraudon/Art Resource)

John Locke (The Bettmann Archive)

popularizer of behaviorism, John B. Watson:

> Give me a dozen healthy infants, well-formed, and my own specified world to bring them up in and I'll guarantee to take any one at random and train him to become any type of specialist I might select—doctor, lawyer, artist, merchant-chief, and, yes, even beggar-man and thief, regardless of his talents, penchants, tendencies, abilities, vocations, and race of his ancestors. (1924, p. 104)

Of course, neither extreme view can be true or the argument would have ended long ago. Both nature and nurture interact continually. Yet theorists sometimes ignore this critical fact and lean heavily toward one or the other position, each of which has its counterparts in other aspects of psychology, as well as in theories of education and social policy. *Nativists* will weigh the role of instinct more heavily than the role of learning in describing animal behavior; *empiricists* have the opposite bias. In discussions of heredity and nature versus environment and nurture, nativists lean to nature, empiricists to nurture. Nativists thus tend to weigh genetic determinants of behavior quite heavily, while empiricists see the causes of behavior in the past and present environments of organisms.

The philosophical orientation of nativists is typically conservative. If the primary source of development is innate, then what point is there in attempting to change the environment? For just the opposite reasons, empiricists tend to be advocates of social engineering, social change and activism. After all, if we are primarily the products of our environments, then we should design our environments to improve human nature. Of course, we should keep in mind that these parallels between political and psychological beliefs are not necessarily true in every case. A committed geneticist might well be in favor of social engineering, while a committed learning theorist could easily be conservative about such programs.

When political arguments arise over the possibilities of changing or modifying human conditions—as, for example, over the efficacy of Head Start or other early enrichment programs—the debate often hinges on basic beliefs about human nature. Is it pliable and susceptible to change (the basic tenet of empiricism), or is it fixed and determined at birth (as an extreme nativist would argue)? Neither position is useful to a scientist, however much either may enhance a political argument. We are interested in how nature and nurture interact to guide development.

Beginning at about the age of 5, children start to assess their own skills and abilities by comparing them with those of other children. (Mimi Forsyth/Monkmeyer Press)

their agemates, or peers. Indeed, the **peer group** soon becomes a major factor in shaping attitudes, beliefs, and behavior.

Becoming a Unique Person

In Freud's scheme of psychosexual development, the years 6 through 12 are the latency period. On the surface there seems to be no interest in the opposite sex, and little or no interest in sexual matters in general. Boys play with boys and shun little girls; girls play with girls and despise little boys. Friendships are almost exclusively between children of the same sex.

For Erikson, psychosocial growth centers on the development of basic competences; the neighborhood and the school are the major areas of activity. Progress is unspectacular but steady, and broad in scope. Children learn how to behave in a variety of social situations. They begin to understand political concepts such as nations, states, and government, and to appreciate individual points of view (H. Gardner, 1982).

As they grow older, children turn more and more to their agemates for information, approval, and models of behavior. The school-age child is a conformist through and through. Tastes in music, books, games, movies, television programs, and even clothing seem to be arrived at by consensus, with little or no deviance tolerated. There are inexorable rules for what to do and when to do it. One spring day it's time to play baseball. In the fall, just as suddenly, it's soccer; and woe unto the child who makes the mistake of carrying a baseball mitt during soccer season!

Interest in assessing one's own skills and abilities, especially in comparison with other children in the same classroom, increases during this period. Younger children show little interest in comparing themselves with others and tend not to use such information in evaluating their own performance. For example, 3- and 4-year-olds who observe that others scored 10 in a game in which they scored 5 would still rate their own performance as quite good (Ruble, Parsons, & Ross, 1976). Older children use such comparisons to lower their estimates of their own performance. (We will discuss the topic of social comparisons further in Chapter 19.)

This time of conformity is also a time for the emergence of individual differences in important personal characteristics. Differences in such characteristics as creativity, impulsiveness or reflectivity, achievement motivation, and intellectual curiosity become more noticeable at this stage. Such differences tend to persist over the life span and to have important effects on a child's achievements, both in school and outside of it.

Cognitive Advances

Some of the most obvious changes between the ages of 5 and 13 take place in the intellectual domain. Reading and writing skills improve enormously, and children's language becomes more complex, subtle, and rich. As compared with preschoolers, school-age children are less likely to be misled by appearances—they understand the distinction between the way something looks and what it really is (Flavell, 1986). They have also acquired an understanding of other important matters, such as the differences between living things and inanimate objects (Tumner, 1985), and the concepts of death (Speece & Brent, 1984) and of time (Levin, Wilkening, & Dembo, 1984).

According to Piaget, children enter the period of concrete operations at about the time they begin second grade. One of the questions that Piaget was inevitably asked when he visited the United States (in fact, he came to

refer to it as "the American question") was: Can cognitive development be speeded up? Is it possible to teach concepts such as conservation to children who, according to their age, should still be in the preoperational period? Piaget's own answer to that question was: "It is probably possible to accelerate, but maximal acceleration is not desirable. There seems to be an optimal time" (quoted in Elkind, 1973, p. 172). Whether or not Piaget was justified in his fears that "maximal acceleration" might do more harm than good, it is quite clear that acceleration *is* possible, and that the specific experiences of an individual child will affect his or her understanding of various concepts. For example, a child who has never experienced the death of a pet or a relative is less likely to understand that death is permanent and irreversible than one who has had some experience with death. Similarly, children who are given specialized training in the concept of conservation can be taught to understand this concept as early as age 4 (Field, 1981). The acquistion of specific knowledge plays a major role in the cognitive advances that occur during childhood.

Learning and Memory.   Acquiring specific knowledge is something that goes on all through life. But many people assume that the ability to learn and to remember is greatest in infancy and declines steadily as one gets older. This is not the case; In fact, these abilities improve steadily during childhood. Very young children are rather incompetent at any kind of memorization task. For example, if you show a group of preschoolers a small set of objects and ask them to look at the objects until they think they can remember them, they perform very poorly. They gaze at the objects for a short time and say they're ready, but when the objects are removed, they can remember only a few of them. In contrast, school-age children will study the objects for a longer period and then remember them all (Flavell, 1985).

An important source of this difference in performance is the preschoolers' lack of *metacognitive* skills. **Metacognition** is knowledge and understanding about one's own mental processes. Learning and memorizing are cognitive skills; knowing how to learn and memorize things, and being able to judge how well you are doing it, are *meta*cognitive skills. Preschool children often don't know good strategies for learning and remembering, they don't tend to use these strategies even if they are taught them, and they don't seem to realize that they are failing to learn as much as they could. (You will recall that in Chapter 7 we discussed memory at length. In this section we will focus on the developmental aspects of memory in children.)

Preschoolers greatly overestimate their own ability to remember things—some will even deny that they ever forget *anything* (Kreutzer, Leonard, & Flavell, 1975). In contrast, school-age children have acquired a considerable store of metacognitive understanding. For example, they are aware of the uses of *rehearsal*—of repeating something over and over again to themselves so they won't forget it. In a classic experiment (Flavell, Beach, & Chinsky, 1966) children were shown a set of seven pictures and the experimenter pointed to three of the pictures in a particular order. Then the children's eyes were covered for 15 seconds. Their task was to point to the same three pictures, in the same order, as soon as their eyes were uncovered. Most of the older children in this experiment (age 10) used rehearsal to remember the pictures: During the 15-second delay they would repeat to themselves, for instance, "Ball, cup, flower . . . ball, cup, flower." But the younger children (age 5) seldom did this, so they didn't remember as much as the older ones. In a second experiment (Keeney, Cannizzo, & Flavell, 1967) a group of 7-year-olds who didn't use rehearsal on their own were taught to do so.

Their performance on the picture test immediately improved. But as soon as the experimenters stopped reminding them to rehearse, they stopped doing so and their performance declined again. Evidently, the failure of younger children to use metacognitive strategies is not due simply to their ignorance of these techniques.

On the other hand, it does not seem to be age alone that makes the difference. A study of the Kpelle people of Africa, done at a time when some Kpelle children were attending European-style schools and others were not, indicates that schooling itself is an important source of metacognitive skills (Cole, Gay, Glick, & Sharp, 1971). Two groups of Kpelle adolescents, comparable in every respect except for the fact that one group had attended school and the other had not, were given lists of words to memorize. The schooled group used far more sophisticated memorization strategies and, as a consequence, performed much better on the memory test than the unschooled group. Note that this result does not indicate that people who don't go to school have terrible memories. It simply means that schooling helps people to acquire techniques for memorizing relatively meaningless material, such as lists of words.

As children progress through school, their knowledge and use of memorization strategies becomes more sophisticated. But metacognitive development is only one of the reasons for the continued improvement in learning and memorizing ability throughout the grade-school and high-school years. It appears that *all* aspects of memory improve over this time period: In addition to metacognitive advances, the *short-term memory* span lengthens (Case, Kurland, & Goldberg, 1982), there is an improvement in *retention* and *retrieval* efficiency (Brainerd, Howe, Kingma, & Brainerd, 1984), and even *recognition* memory continues to develop (Sophian & Stigler, 1981). A final factor in the increase in learning ability is a gradual improvement in selective attention (see Chapter 4). Older children are better than younger ones at focusing their attention on a given task as well as at maintaining that focus for longer periods of time (Higgins & Turnure, 1984).

Monitoring Cognitive Processes. As they grow older, children also develop the ability to reflect upon, and monitor the progress of, their own mental processes. They acquire an appreciation, for example, of the factors that make it easier or harder for them to pay attention to something (Miller & Weiss, 1982). They are better able to judge whether or not they understand something, and why. When two people converse, it often happens that one person doesn't understand what the other is saying. Generally, this is due to the speaker's failure to communicate clearly and unambiguously. But research indicates that younger children tend to assume that their failure to understand something must be *their* fault, even when the speaker's words were purposely made confusing or ambiguous (Speer, 1984). In fact, unlike older children, preschoolers often do not even realize that they have failed to understand what was said (Krauss & Glucksberg, 1977; Flavell, Speer, Green, & August, 1981). The ability to monitor one's own comprehension—to recognize whether or not one has understood something—is an important component of metacognitive development during childhood.

By the end of the preadolescent years, children have acquired a considerable amount of knowledge about the workings of their own cognitive processes, including information about how they compare to others in this respect. They have also acquired a comfortable familiarity with their social, cultural, and physical worlds. They are now ready for the next step in the pathway from childhood to adulthood.

SUMMARY

1. The changes that a person undergoes throughout the life cycle are of central importance in the study of psychological development.

2. An important source of developmental change is *maturation,* the ability to do something one couldn't do before, through physical growth and development. In order for maturation to proceed normally, the environment and experiences must also be within normal ranges.

3. The second source of developmental change is learning from *experience.*

4. Some learning must take place at a specific time during development; this specific development time is called a *critical period.* In human development it is more accurate to say that there are *sensitive periods* for learning, when various traits and abilities are most readily acquired.

5. In the course of perceptual development the infant acquires *object constancy,* and by about 6 months seems to perceive the physical world very much as adults do. The rate and sequence of motor development is orderly and is controlled almost exclusively by rate of maturation.

6. Freud theorized that people pass through five *psychosexual stages*—(oral, anal, phallic, latency, and genital)—as they develop from infancy through adulthood.

7. Erikson described development in terms of *psychosocial stages,* periods during which basic crises arise and must be resolved.

8. Learning about oneself involves *identification,* including sex-role identification, which is greatly affected by society's expectations. *Social-learning theory* is an explanation of sex-role development based on concepts of reinforcement and imitation.

9. Jean Piaget identified various stages in a child's awareness of the world, or cognitive development. In childhood one passes through the *sensorimotor, preoperational, concrete operation,* and *formal operational stages.* Development from one cognitive level or stage to another involves the processes of *assimilation* and *accommodation.*

10. Language development is dependent to a certain extent on the child's early social interactions with parents.

11. Development of moral reasoning progresses from simple ideas of morality, based almost entirely on consequences of an action, to more complicated ideas that take in to account such things as principles and *intentions.*

12. Preschool children must learn to control their own actions. First children learn to follow their parents' instructions. Next they tell themselves what to do as if they were their parents. Finally, children learn to think silently about what to do when. Preschool children can also be shown how to delay gratification in order to gain larger rewards later.

13. During the school years children are faced with a wider social and intellectual world, and the peer group becomes a major factor in shaping attitudes, beliefs, and personality. Cognitive abilities develop. Basic skills of reading, writing, numbers, and knowledge of the physical, cultural, and social world, are acquired.

14. Older children not only learn certain skills, they also develop *metacognition,* or knowledge and understanding of their own mental processes.

SUGGESTED READINGS

CHUKOVSKY, K. (1968). *From two to five.* Los Angeles: University of California Press. A poet's observations and reflections on preschool children's language, thought, and imagination.

FLAVELL, J. H. (1985). *Cognitive development.* Englewood Cliffs, N.J.: Prentice-Hall. Piaget's work is somewhat difficult for people just entering the field. This contains a clear and concise introduction to his work.

GARDNER, H. (1982). *Developmental psychology: An introduction* (2nd ed.). Boston: Little, Brown. A readable introduction to the major concepts of developmental psychology, providing lucid introductions to the major views in the field, such as those of Piaget, Freud, and Darwin.

GARDNER, J. K. (1982). *Readings in developmental psychology* (2nd ed.). Boston: Little, Brown. A diverse and tasteful selection of articles and essays on the many phases and aspects of child development. The pieces from literary sources are particularly well chosen.

PIAGET, J. (1960). *The child's conception of the world.* Totowa, N.J.: Littlefield, Adams. A very readable account of children's spontaneous explanations of natural phenomena, with detailed observations by Piaget. This is a good introduction to Piaget's way of looking into the child's mind first-hand.

14 Adolescence, Adulthood, and Aging

Twenty years ago the previous chapter (perhaps with some additional comments on adolescence) would have been all the standard introductory psychology textbook had to say on the subject of human development. There were various reasons for this. First, most developmental studies were of children; few studies had been done of adults in various stages of life. Second, developmental psychologists were mostly concerned with plotting the ways in which children "developed" into full-grown adults—a task once thought to be finished by the time physical maturity was attained. A few psychologists studied old people, but that effort seemed mainly committed to a sad mapping of what was seen as the inevitable decline of people's physical and mental powers. Third, with the exception of Erikson, psychological theorists paid little if any, attention to possible changes in people once they had become adults. In fact, the opposite was true. Some of the most exciting theories developed in the first half of this century, such as Freudian and learning theory, purposefully shifted attention away from adulthood to early childhood.

In more recent times the approach to developmental study has changed. *Life-span developmental psychologists* have pointed out that development, properly conceived of, continues throughout life—it does not stop at age 18 or 21. Newer research studies have looked at the ongoing processes of development and the developmental issues people face as they grow older. Introductory psychology textbooks (written by authors who are getting older) increasingly reflect these life-span perspectives.

Rembrant painted many self-portraits from his vigorous youth to his old age. This painting clearly reflects the difficulties of his later years, which were marred by the death of his children and his mounting indebtedness. (The Metropolitan Museum of Art, Bequest of Benjamin Altman)

Table 14–1: Levinson's Stages of Adult Development.

Age	Stage
17–22	Early Adult Transition
22–28	Entering the Adult World
28–33	Age 30 Transition
33–40	Settling Down
40–45	Midlife Transition
45–50	Entering Middle Adulthood
50–55	Age 50 Transition
55–60	Culmination of Middle Adulthood
60–65	Late Adult Transition
65+	Late Adulthood

After Levinson et al., 1978, p. 57.

In this chapter we will first consider the traditional developmental topic of adolescence, then go on to discuss some of the later stages of development that have been the focus of much recent research and theory. Perhaps the most influential view has been the idea of distinct, age-related *stages* proposed by Erik Erikson (1950, 1968), which are summarized in Table 13–2 in Chapter 13. Variations of this view are expressed in the *stages of adult life* proposed by Daniel Levinson (1978), shown in Table 14–1, and in the best-selling book *Passages* by Gail Sheehey (1977).

Other theorists have emphasized the *type of adjustment* or *transition* one has to make when entering a new stage, regardless of the specific age at which this occurs (e.g., Helson, Mitchell, & Moane, 1984; Schlossberg, 1984). For example, the transition to being a parent involves many similar adjustments whether this happens when you are 20, 30, or 40 years old. Adjusting to marriage, being away from your parents, holding a job, or retiring, are all important transitions that can occur at different ages and in various sequences. Some of these transitions can be anticipated and planned for, while others are unexpected, such as a serious illness, the death of a parent, or forced retirement. There are also the transitions that Schlossberg (1984) calls *nonevents;* for example, adjusting to the fact that you won't become president of the company, won't find a spouse in time to have a family, or won't have enough money to live as you had hoped upon retirement.

Thus, while we will use Erikson's age-related stages as a general framework for our discussion in this chapter, you should keep in mind that many life transitions occur unexpectedly, or in unpredictable sequences, rather than in an orderly age-determined sequence of developmental events.

ADOLESCENCE

The term **adolescence** derives from the Latin word *adolescere*, meaning "to grow into maturity." In our culture adolescence is the period between childhood and adulthood during which the individual learns the skills needed to flourish as an adult. As this implies, relative to earlier stages, adolescence is a culturally rather than a biologically defined phase of development. Many other cultures have no developmental stage that corresponds to our adolescence; postpubescent individuals are regarded as adults (see the Highlight: Rites of Passage). In our society, and in Western society in general, adolescence begins with the onset of puberty, and ends, somewhat indefinitely,

As we said in the text, in our culture puberty signals the beginning of adolescence; in some other cultures it marks the transition to adulthood. In cultures where the change from the status of child to adult is abrupt, this transition may be highlighted with an initiation ceremony that specifically signals the attainment of adult status. The ceremony is usually highly symbolic, signaling that some very explicit and dramatic event is needed to establish for the community, no less than for the initiate, the fact that he or she is now an adult. In some cultures boys' initiation rites involve a display of courage and skill—qualities required by adult men (Benedict, 1934; Brown, 1969; Munroe & Munroe, 1975). Thus boys may be beaten, thrown into icy waters, circumcised, or scarified. In other societies the initiation rites for boys involve the teaching of ideas considered important for their culture (Whiting, Klucholm, & Anthony, 1958). Among the Zuñi Indians of New Mexico, during initiation rites boys learn that the sacred Kachina, who appear at seasonal festivals, are really masked adult members of the community, and that "they as mortals, must exercise all the functions which the uninitiated ascribed to the supernaturals themselves" (Benedict, 1934, p. 70).

For girls, initiation rites frequently involve a period of isolation or seclusion from other people. For example, the girl may go to a hut outside the village, where women teach her the skills needed to be a lover, wife, and mother, including information on lovemaking, contraception, and childbirth. The isolated girl may also undergo certain hardships: She may be subjected to genital mutilation; her skin may be tatooed or scarred; and her teeth may be filed and blackened (Ford & Beach, 1951). When the girl emerges from seclusion, she is usually honored with great ceremony. She often signals her change of status by a change of hairstyle and by putting on the clothing of an adult woman. All of this announces that she is eligible for marriage.

To us, in our complex and less communal culture, these rites of passage may sound naive or "barbaric." But perhaps they aren't. In cultures in which such rites are carried out, children have often had the opportunity to witness adult functions and adult roles. The initiation rites at puberty exist to explicitly teach them certain aspects of these functions and roles so that they will be better prepared to fulfill them. The rite of passage simply declares that now is the appropriate time for the individual to begin acting as an adult. Anthropological studies suggest that in cultures with initiation rites, individuals quickly master the skills needed for adult life and make an easier transition from childhood to adulthood.

The Papua New Guinean skin cutting (left) and the Bar Mitzvah of a Jewish youth (right) are both traditional rites of passage that mark initiation into adulthood. (Malcolm Kirk; Miro Vintoniv, The Picture Cube)

with the transition to young adulthood. This passage to adulthood is marked by a number of small changes in status during or near the end of adolescence. Graduating from high school and attaining the right to vote, drink liquor, and drive a vehicle are all events that, to some degree, signify adult status. These events frequently occur at different times and may or may not coincide with the independence and self-sufficiency usually associated with adulthood. This lack of consistency in the laws and customs signaling the attainment of adult status may be a source of conflict and anxiety for many adolescents in our society (Conger, 1977).

Physical Development

Puberty is marked by dramatic physical changes in both growth rate and sexual characteristics. The initial adolescent growth spurt and the first signs of the developing secondary sex characteristics signal the onset of a period of

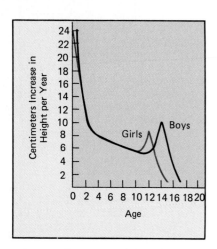

Figure 14–1 Typical growth curves for males and females during the first 18 years. Notice that the growth spurt during adolescence occurs one or two years earlier for females. (Adapted from Tanner, Whitehouse, & Takaish, 1966)

Figure 14–2 Growth rates and sexual development during puberty. The bars represent the average age at onset and completion of the events of puberty. (Tanner, 1973)

rapid physical growth that is second only to the rate of growth during infancy and early childhood (see Figure 14–1). For boys, active acceleration in growth and the development of coarse pubic hair and facial hair usually precede such other signs of puberty as voice change. For girls, rapid growth in height usually begins about two and a half years before **menarche** (the start of menstruation). The growth spurt generally begins at age 12 or 13 for boys and at 10 or 11 for girls; it is however, normal for puberty to occur several years later in both boys and girls (see Figure 14–2). In both sexes it takes about four and a half years from the first appearance of secondary sex characteristics to the development of the adult configuration of sexual characteristics (Marshall & Tanner, 1969, 1970; Conger, 1977; Peterson & Taylor, 1980; Goldhaber, 1986).

The age at which puberty occurs varies across individuals and groups. For example, it is clear that better-nourished children reach sexual maturity before those who are undernourished (Tanner, 1970). Genetic factors are also influential (Tanner, 1962, 1970). And the beginning of puberty sometimes varies across time in the same culture. In the United States, for example, menarche has been occurring at younger ages than in the past. The average girl reached menarche at age 14 in 1910, at 13.4 in 1930, at 13.3 in 1940, and at 12.8 in 1955 (Cagas & Riley, 1970; Malina, 1979). The mean age of menarche decreased by six months between 1940 and 1955. However, since the mid 1950s the mean age of menarche has been stable; in a national sample of American girls in the 1960s, the median age of menarche was 12.8

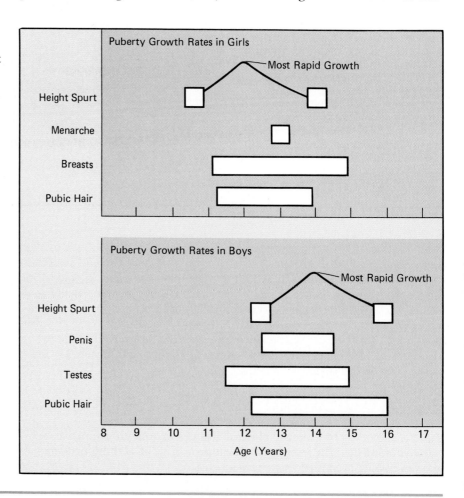

(12.5 for black girls, 12.8 for white girls) (MacMahon, 1973). Perhaps nutrition and general health have risen to such a high level among American girls that the average age for menarche will not decrease in the future, or perhaps it will continue to decrease.

Neuroendocrinal mechanisms stimulate these growth patterns that change boys and girls into men and women (see the discussion of sexual differentiation in Chapter 11). In brief, these changes are triggered hormonally in both sexes (see Figure 14–3). The onset of puberty is precipitated by activity in the hypothalamus, which stimulates the production of hormones in the anterior pituitary gland. These hormones affect other glands, which secrete other hormones, some of which stimulate the development of certain systems such as the one that causes ovulation in the female. Both *androgens* (male hormones) and *estrogens* (female hormones) are released by the sex glands in the developing child; the predominance of one over the other causes the physical differentiation between the sexes, but both are needed for the normal development of either sex. Once this hormonal sequence of sexual maturation is under way, its order of progression is fairly predictable (Peterson & Taylor, 1980). The sequence of changes has both emotional and psychological effects upon the developing young person of either sex.

The Effects of Being an Early or a Late Bloomer. The age at which children go through the dramatic physical changes associated with puberty and later adolescence varies greatly, and these variations appear to have an effect on the adolescent's personality. According to an intensive study of boys aged 14 to 17, early-maturing boys are at an advantage over late-maturing boys. Both their peers and adults tend to see them as superior (Conger, 1977). Early maturers were more reserved, self-assured, displayed more socially appropriate behavior, and were better able to laugh at themselves. Boys who were late bloomers were seen as less attractive physically, less poised, more prone to attention-getting behavior, more tense, more eager and expressive, and less popular with their peers (Jones & Bayley, 1950; Jones, 1958). The late bloomers also reported more feelings of inadequacy and rejection and held more negative self-concepts (Mussen & Jones, 1957). Furthermore, the effects of being an early or a late maturer were long-term. When the boys were studied again at age 33, those who had matured later were relatively less responsible, dominant, and self-controlled, and were more dependent on others than the

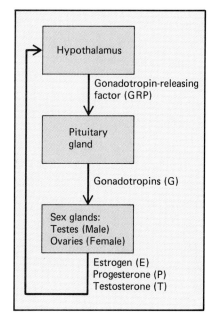

Figure 14–3 In puberty chemical messengers or hormones are released by the hypothalamus (GRP), which causes the pituitary to release others (G), which finally trigger the release of sex hormones (E, P, or T) from the sex glands (ovaries or testes). These cause the development of secondary sexual characteristics and "feedback" to the hypothalamus, which alters the output of its chemicals (GRP).

The age at which children go through the dramatic physical changes associated with puberty and later adolescence can vary greatly. Moreover, the effects of being an early or late maturer appear to be long-term in both sexes. (The Bettmann Archive)

early maturers. However, early and late maturers did not differ in marital status, family size, or educational level (Jones, 1957; Levson & Peshkin, 1980).

The picture for girls is more complicated. According to a 1960 study by Faust, girls who matured early tended to be at a social disadvantage in late elementary school, but in junior high school and high school they had more prestige than the late maturers. According to another study, early bloomers tended to be more adjusted, self-assured, relaxed, and secure, and they displayed more adequate thought processes in adolescence, although they were sometimes uncomfortably aware of the physical differences between them and their peers (Jones & Mussen, 1958). Other studies indicate that early-maturing girls tend to make better adjustments in adulthood, perhaps because they had to confront growing up somewhat earlier (Papalia & Olds, 1986).

Cognitive Development

At about age 11 or 12, children enter into Piaget's final stage of cognitive development—the stage of formal operations. During this stage they acquire several important cognitive capacities they did not have in early childhood (Inhelder & Piaget, 1958; Piaget, 1972).

During the stage of concrete operations, which we discussed in Chapter 13, children can do mental operations in their head, but only if they concern concrete material objects or actions already performed. The most basic change in the **formal operational stage** is adolescents' newfound ability to think about the possible and the abstract. In contrast to children at the concrete operational stage, adolescents can consider that which has not yet occurred, and they can imagine all the diverse possible relationships and outcomes in a given situation. For instance, they can reason about contrary-to-fact situations (e.g., if coal were white) and consider all the ramifications of such a situation. Further, adolescents at the formal operational stage often display what is called **hypothetico-deductive reasoning.** This is the ability to systematically test a set of possibilities for correctness by using logic and experimental methods. Scientists who test a hypothesis by systematically examining each alternative explanation are using hypothetico-deductive thinking (Inhelder & Piaget, 1958; Flavell, 1963).

Adolescents can also manipulate thoughts and systems of thought mentally. This ability to reason about verbal statements and abstractions is called **propositional thinking.** It enables adolescents to think systematically about the future and about abstract ideology and philosophy.

The development of formal operational thinking makes the adolescent's thought richer and far more flexible than the child's. Adolescents can consider and explore the realms of the impossible and the improbable, as well as the realm of reality. And they can systematically evaluate the many possibilities in their own lives, as well as the validity of others' assertions and hypotheses (such as political candidates' platforms and ideological claims). This acquisition of the ability to think more abstractly is reflected in the educational system's curriculum. In junior high and high school, students are generally required to apply propositional and hypothetico-deductive thinking in their classwork. The ability to think abstractly also gives adolescents more analytic and planning capabilities. For instance, they are able to project plans into the future and figure out ahead of time how these plans could change (Neimark, 1982). They can work out the relationship between the courses they choose to take in high school, the grades they get, and the kind of col-

The ability to test a formula for correctness by using experimental methods (as in this high-school chemistry lab) is called hypothetico-deductive reasoning and is an ability that adolescents gain as part of formal operational thinking. (Paul Conklin/Monkmeyer Press)

According to the famous research done by Kinsey and his colleagues, only 8 percent of females born before 1900 had premarital intercourse before the age of 20; in contrast, 21 percent of the mothers of people now in their 30s had premarital intercourse by the same age (Kinsey, Pomeroy, & Martin, 1953). The figures for intercourse among adolescents in a study published in 1973 were 72 percent for boys and 57 percent for girls by age 19 (Sorenson, 1973). Another study (Zelnich & Kantner, 1980) found that the percentage of 15-year-old females reporting intercourse rose from 11 to 23 percent, while among unmarried 14-year-old females living in metropolitan areas, the percentage increased from 45 to 70 percent. Although studies may overstate the percentages—in another study only 33 percent of males and 55 percent of females in their senior year had had sexual intercourse (Jessor & Jessor, 1975)—there has indeed been a dramatic change in sexual behavior during adolescence over the past century.

In contrast to behavior, adolescents' attitudes regarding sex have not changed as much as many people believe. Most adolescents strongly oppose sex solely for physical enjoyment, exploitation in sexual relationships, and sex among people too young to know what they are doing. In one survey, for example, over 80 percent of all adolescents disagreed with the statement that the most important thing in a relationship is sex. And when adolescents rated the relative importance of different goals such as learning about themselves, having fun, and being independent, having sex with different people and "making out" were ranked as among the *least* important goals (Sorenson, 1973). So while contemporary adolescents are relatively sexually active, they have not renounced all traditional values relating to sex.

Although sexual activity has increased, it should be noted that the overall number of births by women under the age of 19 has fallen steadily since 1958. What has increased for adolescent women is the rate of child bearing outside marriage. By 1980, more than one-fourth of the babies born to white teenagers, and 80 percent of those born to black teenagers, were born to unmarried women (National Center for Health Statistics, 1983). The problems this poses for both the teenage mother and society are obvious and severe.

Finally, it should be noted that fears about a spread of acquired immune deficiency syndrome (AIDS) among heterosexuals may have a profound impact on teenage sexuality. Health concerns may sharply reduce the sexual activity of all segments of our population and place an even greater emphasis on monogamy and/or marriage.

Moral Development

Moral development continues from childhood into adolescence. As discussed in the last chapter (see Table 13–4), most children reason in what Kohlberg calls a preconventional manner. Young children are concerned with obedience to authority, avoidance of punishment, and hedonistic gains for themselves and the people important to them. Around adolescence most people enter Kohlberg's (1969, 1971) conventional level of moral judgment, which contains two stages—Stages 3 and 4. In contrast to the preconventional moral reasoning of children, which is essentially nonmoral, individuals reasoning at the conventional level have accepted the moral values and standards of their culture. At the conventional level of moral reasoning, an act is seen as right if it is in accordance with the established rules of society.

As already noted, the adolescent is developing the cognitive capacities to reason abstractly and to consider the effects of personal actions on future

HIGHLIGHT _____

When Adolescence Goes Wrong

Problems of early childhood are often first expressed in adolescence, when for the first time children are given more freedom and the resulting opportunity to make their own decisions. Of course, it is not surprising that some of these decisions are unwise ones, and that an adolescent may not know how to use his or her newfound freedom from parental authority. Certainly temptations and risks are available throughout one's life; however, adolescence marks the first real test of one's ability to deal with them. We shall briefly consider a few ways in which adolescence can go terribly wrong.

Deliquency. About 43 percent of all serious crimes are committed by people under 18, and 20 percent by those under 15 (Robertson, 1977). Minor acts of vandalism, petty theft, and pot smoking may occur more frequently in the early teens, with more serious crimes such as assault and robbery peaking for most adolescents around age 16 (Gold & Petronio, 1980). Most of these offenders gradually improve their behavior, although some eventually go on to adult prisons. Statistics suggest that the majority of these crimes are

(John C. Pitkin)

committed by children from the more deprived socioeconomic groups. However, this may be a biased view since many affluent children can escape arrest or conviction through the intercession of their parents.

Runaways. About one out of 12 children runs away from home by age 18—the average age of the runaway being 15. Most (70 percent) stay within 50 miles of home and return within a week. Girls are as likely to run away as boys; however, they usually claim that their parents were too strict, while boys claim they didn't receive enough supervision (Borbino, 1985). Some teens run away to escape abusive parents, but far more seem to be escaping from their whole social situation. They are looking for excitement, love, or new friends. Unfortunately, they risk falling prey to those who would use them as prostitutes or as partners in crime, and who lure them with food, money, or simply attention and affection—all of which the runaway usually needs.

Unwanted Pregnancy. Almost 30 percent of all teenage girls will become pregnant, most without the benefit of marriage. About half of these pregnancies will result in births, and in most cases the baby will be kept by the mother. These figures represent the highest rate of teenage pregnancy of any industrialized country (Brozan, 1985; Senderowitz & Paxman, 1985). The long-term impact on the young mother's life is obvious, particularly if she is poor. She is usually unable to work and is trapped into a life on welfare. However, the problem is not confined to the poor; it is evident at all socioeconomic levels. Despite these statistics, there is considerable resistance to educating young people about birth control in this country (clearly one way of reducing unwanted pregnancies). There is an even stronger resistance to the idea of abortion. Thus the problem remains: Adolescents are sexually active, and one of the greatest risks they face is that of an unwanted pregnancy.

Eating Disorders. The eating disorders of anorexia nervosa and bulimia most often strike young women while they are still adolescents. The typical victim is a well-behaved child from a comfortable socioeconomic background. Both the anorexic and the bulimic have an obsessive desire to be slender. But while anorexics may actually starve themselves to death, bulimics go on eating binges, then vomit and/or take laxatives to avoid gaining weight.

(John Running/Stock, Boston)

(Russ Kinne/Comstock)

466

Some psychiatrists feel the adolescent girl is trying to control her body development (particularly secondary sexual characteristics), starving herself to a prepubescent shape to avoid her fears of sexuality. Others see these conditions as extreme manifestations of the socially imposed ideal of slenderness (Chernic, 1981). A Highlight in Chapter 17 explores the eating disorder anorexia nervosa at some length.

Teenage Suicide. Periodically a cluster of suicides occurs among teenagers from the same town. While these multiple suicides receive national media coverage, individual teenage suicides often go unnoticed by the press. Unfortunately, all such incidents are occurring more often today than ever before. After accidental death and homicide, suicide is the third leading cause of death among adolescents (Smith, 1985). However, since many "accidental deaths" may really be suicides, it is likely that the problem is underreported (Cohen-Sandler, Berman, & King, 1982). The suicide rate for teenagers has more than doubled in the last 20 years, with almost 2,000 adolescent suicides now reported each year. Among young people 15 to 24 years of age (see Figure A), suicide increased 150 percent between 1961 and 1981, from a rate of 5.1 per 100,000 to 12.8 per 100,000 (Klerman, 1986).

Sometimes such deaths are preceded by signs of depression, or talk of wanting to end it all, or even more seriously by schizophrenic symptoms (these are discussed in Chapter 17). But often parents and friends are reported to be at a loss to explain a young victim's motivations. Many teenagers who try suicide appear quite normal, particularly since some signs of stress and emotional variability are common to the teenage years. In fact, many adolescents who unsuccessfully attempt suicide subsequently describe it as a passing impulse and are glad that they failed. This is why it is crucially important to take seriously any statement by a teenager (or an adult) regarding a desire to end his or her life as a "call for help." Many parents or friends of a victim sadly report denying the problem, either because they were embarrassed by it or simply because they didn't know what to do. The first steps in helping are bringing the problem out into the open by talking about it, suggesting alternative methods of solving the problems confronting the potential suicide, and encouraging him or her to seek professional counseling.

Drug and Alcohol Abuse. Experimentation with drugs and alcohol are common in adolescence, despite the fact that the teenager may

(T.C. Fitzgerald/The Picture Cube)

be too young to drink legally and that drug use is obviously against the law. Because they want to feel accepted by the crowd, desire to act more like adults, or feel a need to escape the multiple pressures of schoolwork and social activities, teens are especially vulnerable to alcohol and drug abuse. As you will recall, we discussed the effects of various substances on the brain and consciousness in Chapter 5. We refer you to Chapter 17 for a more detailed description of substance use and abuse.

Most adolescents struggle to develop a strong sense of self-worth, to become independent of their parents, and to integrate themselves into society as young adults. The overwhelming majority succeed. However, some fail in ways that, if not fatal, may at the least seriously jeopardize the rest of their lives.

Figure A Percent change in suicide rate for three age groups.

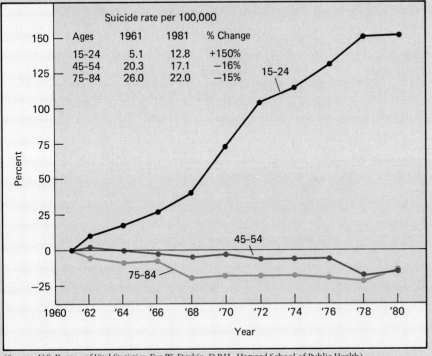

Suicide rate per 100,000

Ages	1961	1981	% Change
15–24	5.1	12.8	+150%
45–54	20.3	17.1	−16%
75–84	26.0	22.0	−15%

(Source: U.S. Bureau of Vital Statistics. Eva W. Deykin, D.P.H., Harvard School of Public Health)

events. Kohlberg, who was influenced by Piaget, argued that this sets the stage for more advanced moral thinking. Others (e.g., Elkind, 1967) remind us that adolescent self-preoccupation, often described as "adolescent egocentrism," can lead to flaws in formal operational thought. Adolescents spend a great deal of time thinking about themselves. This is understandable. Their near-adult selves are new and much in need of self-analysis. But their self-absorption leads them to believe that others are thinking of them as well and constantly judging them. This "imaginary audience," before whom they feel painfully on display, creates a real burden for adolescents trying to gain perspective on their new intellectual processes and developing sexuality. Self-absorption gets in the way of objective reasoning, biasing the adolescent's conclusions. Adolescent egocentrism is worth keeping in mind as we review the two adolescent stages of moral thought.

Stage 3 is frequently called the "interpersonal concordance" or "good boy–nice girl" orientation. The individual conforms to stereotypic conceptions of a "good boy" or a "nice girl." Good behavior is that which fulfills the demands of the roles society provides. Acts that help others or lead to their approval are moral (Kohlberg, 1976, 1978; Colby, 1979).

During Stage 4, the "law-and-order" orientation, norms and values of the society become more internalized. Stage 4 individuals are oriented toward duties, defined responsibility, fixed rules, and maintenance of the social order. Right behavior consists of showing respect to authorities, doing one's duty, and maintaining the social order for its own sake.

EARLY ADULTHOOD

As we have seen, in some societies puberty heralds the beginning of adulthood; in others the child does not become an adult until much later. In the United States it is not clear when an adolescent becomes an adult. Is it at graduation from high school, or when the person becomes self-supporting, or moves out of the parental home?

In recent years the question of when an adolescent attains adult status has become even less clear. For example, many college students live with their parents, and many marry while still financially dependent on their parents. Many people today spend long periods first searching for and then training for a career.

Because so many people in their late teens and early 20s are caught in limbo between adolescence and adult status, Keniston (1970) proposed that a new stage of life, called "youth," has appeared in our culture. According to Keniston, people in this stage are deeply involved in working out the conflict between maintaining personal integrity and achieving effectiveness in society. Since they realize the potency of societal forces that conflict with their self-identity, youths may refuse to be socialized into the predominant adult society. They may become estranged from the dominant culture and identify with a distinctive "youth culture" instead.

Keniston developed his theory of a "youth" stage to explain the unrest among young people in the 1960s, but the theory makes a worthwhile point about the ambiguous status of young people in our society today. An adult is generally seen as responsible, mature, self-supporting, and well integrated into adult society, but people may not develop all these attributes and characteristics simultaneously. Thus there is disagreement among both social scientists and people in general as to when an individual becomes an adult.

Social Development

Theory. According to a number of theorists, the major social task in early adulthood is to establish intimate relationships. Freud believed that successful development during the genital stage meant the ability to "lieben and arbeiten" (to love and to work). Therefore he thought that a heterosexual loving relationship was a major component of adult development. Similarly, Erikson's (1963) sixth stage of development, which occurs during early adulthood, is called *intimacy versus isolation*. During this stage,

> the young adult, emerging from the search for and the insistence on identity, is eager and willing to fuse his identity with that of others. He is ready for intimacy, that is, the capacity to commit himself to concrete affiliations and partnerships and to develop the ethical strength to abide by such commitments, even though they may call for significant sacrifices and compromises. (Erikson, 1963, p. 58)

Empirical research has supported Freud's and Erikson's claims that the establishment of intimate relationships is a major developmental task during early adulthood (Gould, 1974, 1978; Levinson, Darrow, Klein, Levinson, & McKee, 1978), though some have suggested that Freud's and Erikson's descriptions of the task are male-oriented. If one grants equal validity to the experiences of young women, their task is also to develop and deepen relationships, and to abide by commitments to established goals.

According to Erikson (1963, 1980), intimacy is not synonymous with sexuality, The mutual respect and caring that create an intimate situation may be expressed in close friendships as well as in sexual relationships. If the young adult does not form some sort of intimate relationship, however, he or she will develop a deep sense of isolation and consequent self-absorption.

Marriage and Parenting

For many people, the quest for intimacy results in marriage and children. Today marriage is certainly not the enduring institution it once was. However, relationships between parents and children are usually not dissolved by divorce, and children remain both a major source of concern and joy throughout most of their parents' lives.

Marriage. Over 90 percent of the adults in our society marry at least once. During the last 25 years there has been a consistent increase in the average age at first marriage (Cherlin, 1980; U.S. Bureau of the Census, 1982), as well as an increase in the number of marriages that end in divorce (Norton, 1983). People typically marry for the first time at age 25 to 28, with about 40 percent of all marriages ending in divorce (although most of these people try marriage again).

A number of factors contribute to the current tendency to delay marriage. Young adults are generally more concerned with their careers and financial security than they were in the 1960s and 1970s (Astin et al., 1987), and many more go on to college before marrying (see the Highlight: Twenty Years of American Freshmen). In particular, there has been a significant rise in the numbers of young women attending college as the role of the female in our society changes. Young women are joining young men in the quest for a career outside the home. Also, more people are choosing not to marry at all. Norton (1983) estimates that as many as 8 percent of our population now makes this choice compared to only half as many 20 years ago.

One of the tasks of early adulthood is the choice of career. Many young people have access to vocational or career conselors in high school and college. Some of the methods used by these counselors to gather information about individuals have been developed by psychologists.

Vocational interest inventories are frequently used to provide a basis for advising young adults about careers. Two of the most popular are the Kuder Personal Preference Inventory and the Strong-Campbell Interest Inventory. Persons taking the inventory are typically presented with pairs of activities to do or events to watch, and they then report which of the pair they would prefer. The inventory also asks people to report which they prefer from a large number of pairs of school subjects, activities, amusements, and types of people. Sample items include: geometry or physiology; writing reports or pursuing a bandit in a sheriff's posse; skiing or organizing a play; and ballet dancers or business people. An individual's pattern of preferences is then analyzed. One person may generally prefer active outdoor activities that are done alone, a second may prefer sedentary, problem-solving activities, and a third person may enjoy working with groups of people.

To correlate preference patterns with career options, the inventory developers administered the inventory to groups of people already engaged in a wide range of occupations. These criterion groups were used to create a composite profile of the interest patterns of, for instance, doctors, accountants, or forest rangers.

Research has shown that many (although not all) occupations do have characteristic interest patterns. Thus counselors are able to suggest those careers associated with an interest profile most matched to that of the person being counseled.

Certain problems with vocational interest batteries are worth pointing out. First, no test can magically produce career interests where none exist. Those who are most likely to be confused about careers may not have many interests or like many activities, so vocational preference batteries are not likely to find many careers to suggest for them. Second, we are today concerned about avoiding sex bias in career choices. But the criterion groups used to create the occupational keys on these tests consisted of people who chose their careers years ago, before the fairly recent changes in occupational patterns of women. As a result, the standardized career profiles may tend to steer women and men away from careers that have recently been opened to them. The psychologists who create and administer the inventories are aware of these problems but have not yet completely overcome them.

A third difficulty with career inventories results from the way in which the occupational keys are constructed. If a large number of surgeons are interested in building small-scale models, that interest may well be linked to a particular component of surgeons' professional tasks. But some interests that may be shared by many members of an occupational group may have no connection to their career tasks. Suppose, for instance that bankers were at one time largely recruited from wealthy families and that "polo" showed up as an interest of many members of that group. While it is true that people who didn't play polo might have received a cold reception in

banking at one time, it is quite clear that the sport has no relationship to banking tasks. We should be concerned that the various social-class and ethnic biases historically associated with certain occupations might be perpetuated as a result of such accidental associations during construction of career inventories.

Aptitude tests (discussed in Chapter 10) are also used in career counseling. Obviously, people will do best at jobs for which they possess the requisite skills, and employers certainly seek as potential employees those who have the needed skills. Aptitude testing, therefore, is useful if two sets of conditions are met: First, the aptitude test reliably measures an actual aptitude; and second, that aptitude is central and indispensable to the job.

These are not always easy conditions to meet in practice. Probably a plumber should have a reasonable degree of mechanical aptitude, an electronics technician good spatial-relations skills, and an airline pilot good eye-hand coordination. But what aptitudes are required for success as a social worker or college teacher? They are remarkably hard to define. Is there such a thing as a single aptitude called "teaching ability"? Probably not. Careers like these seem to require somewhat different bundles of competencies, not necessarily connected, and they should not necessarily be thought of as utilizing single aptitudes.

For these reasons, as well as for others, there is some question whether aptitude test batteries can precisely determine people's fitness for various careers. Therefore industries that use tests to choose workers should demonstrate that the skills and aptitudes for which they are testing are directly relevant to the jobs in question.

Campbell (1981) summarizes over 20 years of surveys as follows:

> The basic source of social support among adult Americans is marriage. The need for human relationships can undoubtedly be met in various ways and countless individuals live what they regard as very satisfactory lives outside of marriage. But on the average no part of the unmarried population—never-married, separated,

divorced, widowed—described itself as happy and contented with life as that part which is presently married. This may seem curious in light of the probability that a sizable fraction of those married will eventually terminate their marriages in divorce. But the evidence is consistent and substantial: Married people see their lives more positively than unmarried people. Despite the fact that attitudes towards marriage are changing in this country, especially among young people, the marriage pattern continues to contribute something uniquely important to the feelings of well-being of the average man and woman. (pp. 226–227)

Those who are successful in marriage see their partners as fair, honest, appreciative, reasonably optimistic and cheerful, and willing to communicate about their feelings (Schafer & Keith, 1981; White, 1983; Laur & Laur, 1985). While such attributes might be found in partners from any socioeconomic level, it is clear that severe financial difficulties can be very destructive to a family. In addition to the obvious strains imposed by economic problems, such couples may also experience conflict involving complex social factors that may not be easily resolved. For example, the necessity for the wife to work may be inconsistent with one or both partners' expectations regarding the roles of husband and wife (Campbell, 1981).

Interestingly enough, Cleary and Mechanic (1983) found less depression among married women who worked than among those who didn't. There is evidence that the stress of being a housewife has been underestimated, perhaps because male psychologists associate stress with the workplace (Baruch, Beiner, & Bennett, 1987).

Parenting. Figure 14–4 is a whimsical "advertisement" suggesting how little training or preparation is required for perhaps the most demanding, and rewarding, "occupation" in our society—parenting. Not surprisingly, since young people are marrying later, they are also beginning families later and having fewer children. This is probably due to many of the same reasons that cause people to delay marriage. From 1960 to 1980 the number of childless women between the ages of 20 and 24 rose from 24 percent to 43 percent. During the same period the percentage of childless women aged 25 to 29 went from 13 percent to 23 percent (U.S. Bureau of the Census, 1982).

Becoming a parent can be one of the most difficult and stressful transitions of a young adult's life (Feshbach, 1985), even though it is usually accompanied by the gratification of intimacy and love for the child (Bolsky,

EMPLOYMENT OPPORTUNITIES

> One couple to procreate and raise a child. No experience necessary. Applicants must be available 24 hours per day, 7 days per week, and must provide food, shelter, clothing, and supervision. No training provided. No salary; applicants pay $140,000 over the next 18 years. Accidental applications accepted. Single people may apply but should be prepared for twice the work.

3,500,000 people successfully applied for this job in 1979 (U.S. Department of Commerce Bureau of the Census, 1980)

Figure 14–4 This "advertisement" (Polster & Dangel, 1984) can be compared with the required credentials and job descriptions for other "occupations." Of course, the ad doesn't mention the "compensations," which for most parents are priceless.

HIGHLIGHT _____

20 Years of American Freshmen

In the fall of 1966 America was still recovering from the assassination of a popular young president, the war in Vietnam ground on, and in San Francisco an antimaterialistic "hippie" counterculture had reached its zenith. Timothy Leary, a defrocked Harvard professor and hippie guru, proposed a religion based on LSD-fueled explorations of inner space. He called on young people to "drop out, turn on, and tune in." Many older people then saw college students as too concerned with social issues and not interested enough in educating themselves for a productive future. Street demonstrations, radical proposals for social change, and a disdain for "money-grubbing" careers seemed to typify the 1960s college student. This appalled many parents, who were only a generation or so removed from the Great Depression, when simply getting a steady job was a major goal in life.

That year, 1966, was also the first year that over 300,000 representative American college freshmen were given a questionnaire regarding their values and goals in life. Recently, The Higher Education Institute at UCLA published a report entitled *The American Freshman: Twenty Year Trends* (Astin, Green, & Korn, 1987) that summarizes student answers to that questionnaire between 1966 and 1985.

One of the most striking trends is illustrated in the accompanying graph based on data from 1967 to 1985. In 1967 more than 80 percent of the college freshmen queried felt that "developing a meaningful philosphy of life" was a major life goal, while less than 50 percent felt that "being well off financially" was equally important. Twenty years later these values appear to be almost reversed (see Figure A). Developing a meaningful philosophy of life is apparently less important to today's average freshman than making a good living. This is also suggested by the more than one in four students who now plan to major in business or economics, almost double the number 20 years ago (with progressively fewer

majoring in the humanities and physical sciences). While many students still prepare for postgraduate work in professions such as medicine and the law, the general trend is for students to be less interested in those careers that require years of unpaid, and costly, postgraduate study. Most students apparently want to start earning a salary and building their careers as soon as possible. Furthermore, as we point out elsewhere in this chapter, many are willing to defer, or even give up, starting a family for the benefit of a career.

The shift in values suggested by the questionnaire results seems to validate a view held by many observers of

college students. The antimaterialistic hippie generation of 20 years ago seems to have given way to a more materialistic, career-oriented one, one the press has dubbed the *yuppie generation* (*yuppie* being an abbreviation for "young urban professional").

Like most gross generalizations, this one is only partly correct. Today's students are concerned with social issues such as apartheid, environmental pollution, and nuclear disarmament. Most do plan to have families, and aspire to do more with their lives than simply make money. Nevertheless, it is important for today's students to realize how values and goals can change in 20 years.

Figure A *The American Freshman Twenty Year Crisis,* 1966–1985 Cooperative Institutional Research Program, American Council on Education, University of California, Los Angeles.) (Astin, A. W., Green, K. C. Kornlos (1987)

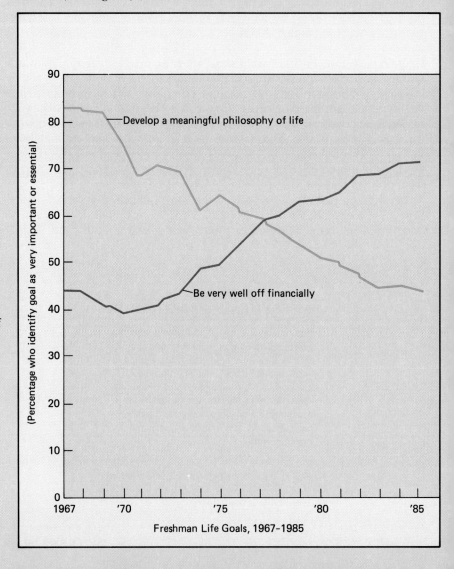

Freshman Life Goals, 1967–1985

Spaier, & Rovine, 1983). One source of stress is the loss of time—time for sleep, for recreation, even for sex (La Rossa, 1983). A first child also signals the need for the parent to acquire a host of new skills in order to deal with the details of parenting: for example, changing diapers, feeding, and caring for various minor illnesses. (This author recalls the alarm he felt when his first child had the hiccups. Would they go on forever? Should the doctor be called?) While there are a number of excellent books on such details of parenting, the general rule is "on the job" training. Since even good marriages are tested by these problems, marriages that are already under stress may dissolve under the pressure of additional problems encountered in parenting (LaRossa & LaRossa, 1981; Bernard, 1982).

Despite the stress associated with parenting, it provides a unique opportunity for growth and satisfaction. Erikson sees it as one of the primary ways of successfully dealing with his sixth stage of development. It is for many people the purest and most enduring form of intimacy and love.

Moral Development

Moral development usually continues into adulthood. While many people attain the highest level of moral judgment during adolescence, others keep on developing their moral reasoning into their 20s and perhaps even later (Kohlberg & Kramer, 1969; Kohlberg, 1976).

During early adulthood a relatively small percentage of people achieve Kohlberg's third level of moral development, the *postconventional level* (Kohlberg, 1969, 1971). Previously in Kohlberg's theory this level consisted of two stages—Stages 5 and 6, although Kohlberg (1978) later acknowledged that these stages may not be distinct. At Stage 5, the *social-contract orientation*, right behavior is defined in terms of general individual rights and standards that have been critically examined and agreed upon by members of a society. The Stage 5 individual has a clear awareness of the relativism of personal values and opinions, emphasizes procedural rules for reaching consensus in a group, and believes that laws should be changed in accordance with rational considerations. Aside from what is democratically agreed upon by the group, right is considered a matter of personal value.

In Stage 6, the *universal ethical principle orientation*, right is defined by a decision of conscience in accordance with self-chosen ethical principles that are logically comprehensive, universal to all people, and consistent. These principles are abstract, such as ideas of justice, equality of human rights, and respect for the dignity of individual human beings (Kohlberg, 1971). In a recent modification of his theory Kohlberg (1981) added Stage 7, in which moral choices are suffused with a sense of the oneness of the universe, a cosmic rather than a people- or world-oriented perspective.

THE MATURE YEARS

In the last decade or so the attitude of both psychologists and people in general toward middle age has undergone a radical transformation. Previously, middle age was regarded as a period in which nothing much happened. Life "ended at forty and there was nothing to do but wait around for retirement and death" (Brim, 1976). However, it is fashionable now to regard middle age as a time of considerable conflict and growth, the time of *midlife crisis*. Yet there is considerable debate concerning the nature of this crisis. Clearly

many transitions may be required between 40 and 60: Children are likely to leave home, the limits of a career may become apparent, health problems may arise, and so on. Stage theorists such as Erikson (1968) and Levinson (1978) see these changes as inevitably linked to age. Others such as Schlossberg (1984) see them as probable, but not inevitable. Certainly the vigor and continued career growth of someone like Ronald Reagan alters one's perceptions of middle age. However, some changes are highly likely in the middle years and, in some people, may produce enough stress for these years to be considered a time of crisis.

Physical Changes

Although individuals vary in the rate at which these changes occur, virtually all middle-aged people notice signs of deterioration in some aspects of their physical functioning.

In the 40s, for example, there is usually a decline in near vision, a condition known as presbyopia. The lens of the eye becomes less elastic and loses its ability to accommodate to objects at close range. Reading glasses or bifocals may be required for the first time. The individual may also notice increased sensitivity to glare—on the windshield of the car, for example, or in brightly lit stores. In their 50s people often find that it takes their eyes longer to adapt to the change in illumination when they enter a darkened theater or when they go outside on a bright, sunny day. Some degree of hearing loss is also found in many people over 50.

Changes in outward appearance also occur. Hair thins or grays noticeably, facial wrinkles become more pronounced, the physique alters (as one individual noted ruefully, "The sand shifts"). Weight gain is common, and the ratio of muscle to fat in the body declines. People may also notice a decline in their ability to engage in strenuous activities.

These and other physical changes clearly signal to the individual that he or she is growing older. Both sexes are affected by this realization, but there is some evidence that men are more concerned with health and physical prowess, and women with physical appearance. A study by Carol Nowak (1977) found that middle-aged women were less able than women of other ages to separate their assessment of their appearance from their assessment of their other qualities. Developing wrinkles was often equated with being less interesting or less active. In judging the attractiveness of other women, middle-aged women were more likely than those of other ages and all men to equate a youthful appearance with looking attractive and to minimize the attractiveness of other middle-aged women. On the other hand, Neugarten (1968) found in her study of 100 people between the ages of 40 and 60 that men were more likely than women to make such spontaneous comments as "Mentally, I still feel young, but suddenly one day my son beat me at tennis," or "It was the sudden heart attack in a friend that made the difference. I realized that I could no longer count on my body as I used to" (p. 96).

People adapt to these physical changes on at least two levels. At the physical level, they may pay more attention to diet and exercise and stop smoking in order to slow down the rate of deterioration. At the psychological level, theorists such as Robert Peck (1968) suggests that middle-aged people shift from valuing physical power to valuing wisdom, a term Peck uses for the mental skills that are derived from life experience.

One specific physical change that occurs in women has been the subject of much research on the psychological impact of aging. Women typically ex-

perience **menopause** sometime in their mid to late 40s or early 50s. Menopause marks the shutting down of the female reproductive system and the end of a woman's capacity to have children. Usually, women's menstrual periods start to become irregular at this time, and over the next year or so cease entirely.

Like menarche, menopause is a neuroendocrinally controlled event, and other bodily changes may accompany it. Some women experience such physical symptoms as "hot flashes," headaches, nausea, dizziness, and heart palpitations. In a sizable minority of women these symptoms may cause real physical incapacity. The vast majority of women, however, experience only minor discomfort. There may also be negative psychological effects. A woman may become depressed over the loss of her ability to bear children or worry about the effects of menopause on her sexuality. She may become moody and feel less in control of herself. However, the experience of menopause is usually less difficult than its anticipation (Kraenes & Loomes, 1963; Nathenson & Lorenz, 1982). Most women seem to adjust quite readily to the loss of reproductive ability (Severne, 1982).

In men there is no obvious counterpart to menopause. Most men undergo a gradual decline in fertility during middle and old age, although there are reports of men as old as 94 fathering children (Talbert, 1977).

Middle age and the loss of reproductive capacity need not mean the end of sexual functioning for either sex. Although, for example, a middle-aged man may take longer to attain an erection, and a postmenopausal woman may experience some irritation of the vaginal wall during intercourse, the primary barriers to full sexual enjoyment are not physical but psychological. They include tension at home and at work, boredom, and acceptance of the myth that sexual waning is an inevitable part of the aging process (Masters & Johnson, 1966, 1970). In fact, the majority of individuals 40 to 60 continue to engage in regular, satisfying sexual activity (Pfeiffer, Verwoerdt, & Davis, 1974; Adams & Turner, 1985).

Vocational Changes

A woman who has not previously worked outside the home sometimes decides to return to work after her children leave home. This decision may carry with it several difficulties. She may find that she no longer has the skills necessary for successful competition in the work world. The jobs that are available to her may be low-paying and monotonous and provide little of the satisfaction she seeks in this new phase of her life. A return to work may also mean a shift in the woman's relationship with her husband, both because she has less time available for household chores and because she is making a greater economic contribution to the family.

Many middle-aged men and women who have been employed throughout their adult life experience increased dissatisfaction with their work. In her book on midlife career changes, Paula Robbins (1978) identifies several sources of this dissatisfaction. Although her research focused primarily on middle- and upper-middle-class men, several of the issues she raises seem equally pertinent to working women and to men in blue-collar occupations. Among the most important complaints were:

1. *"Being put on the shelf"* or *"topping out."* At some point in their careers most men must face the fact that they have advanced as far as they are likely to. Although they may view their current position, in and of itself,

as satisfying, they may find the loss of potential mobility hard to accept (Tamir, 1982).

2. *Lack of challenge.* Once the demands of a particular job are thoroughly mastered, boredom may set in and the individual may seek new challenges.

3. *Change in values.* Middle-aged people may find that they no longer want to pursue the goals that were important to them earlier in life. The reasons for this shift are varied. It may be the result of exposure to new ideas. For example, many of the men in Robbins's study cited experiences with the antiwar and civil rights movements of the late 1960s and early 1970s as contributing to their changed outlook. It may also reflect a shift in orientation. Several authors (Jung, 1933; Gutmann, 1977) have suggested that in middle age men and women reclaim underutilized parts of themselves. Men become more oriented toward nurturance, women toward competitive interaction. Both sexes may seek occupations that allow freer expression of these new interests. Or the shift in values may grow out of a resurgence of interest in early dreams that were pushed aside (Levinson et al., 1978).

4. *Lack of autonomy.* People's desire to have more control over their work lives is an important motivator for change during the middle years.

5. *Income level.* At middle age, individuals often realize that they are earning about as much as they ever will. Many middle-aged people realize that they will never have certain possessions or worry that they will be unable to prepare adequately for their retirement.

Despite all these possible difficulties, the middle years can be a time of considerable satisfaction vocationally. People are likely to be at their peak in terms of income, status, and responsibility. In a survey of 100 middle-class and upper-middle-class men and women, Neugarten (1968) found that the majority felt that they had the maximum capacity to handle the demands of their job in middle age. To quote a participant:

> I know now exactly what I can do best, and how to make best use of my time. . . . I know how to delegate authority, but also what decisions to make myself. . . . I know how to buffer myself from troublesome people. . . . (p. 98)

Marriage at Middle Age

Several studies (Burr, 1970; Rollins & Feldman, 1970; Campbell, 1975; Thurnher, 1976) show that marital satisfaction, particularly for women, is relatively low at the beginning of this period, until just before the children leave home. Couples report that they are less likely than in the early days of their marriage to confide in each other (Pineo, 1961), to laugh together, or to have a stimulating exchange of ideas (Rollins & Feldman, 1970). A study of midlife marriages by Majda Thurnher (1976) found that couples put greater stress on whether or not the spouse lives up to role expectations (e.g., is a "good mother" or "good provider") and much less stress on personality attributes than do younger or older couples. She suggested that couples may be particularly "out of sync" during this period of life, because each partner is preoccupied with the changes in his or her own life. She quotes a male participant in her study:

Now I go my way and she goes hers and they don't seem to coincide that much. I think one of these days we'll come to a closer understanding. When I stop being so tense about things at work, we should be able to get back on the beam. (p. 132)

This man's optimism about the future is justified, at least for marriages in general. With the departure of the children from the family center, and perhaps also as the couple comes to terms with the issues of the midlife period, marital satisfaction begins to rise (Thurnher, 1976; Skolnick, 1981). Many, if not most, couples share more activities and strengthen the emotional bond between them in the later years of this period.

Groups such as the Gray Panthers have worked to alter the conception of what being "old" means in our society. (Freda Leinwand)

OLD AGE

Just when "old age" begins is not easily determined. Traditionally, researchers in the field of aging have used age 65 as the point at which an individual may be considered "old." However, being old is seen as undesirable in American society, so many people continue to think of themselves as middle-aged until they are well into their 70s. Several studies suggest that it is not until people have experienced many of the changes that we associate with aging (retirement, loss of spouse and friends, poor health) that they are willing to apply the label "old" to themselves.

The relative status of the old in our society, as well as people's willingness to think of themselves as old, may be changing. Organizations such as the Gray Panthers have worked hard to increase the visibility and political power of the elderly. The media have also focused more attention on this age group. In part, these changes reflect changing demographic patterns. Increased life expectancy and a declining birthrate have resulted not only in greater numbers of people over 65 in the United States, but also in a greater proportion of people in that age range. In 1980 over 40 percent of the people over 50 in the United Staes had a living parent (Schaie & Willis, 1986). Figure 14–5 shows how this trend should lead to more than 18 percent of the population being over 65 by the year 2020—a substantial gain and one likely to lead to increased power and status for the elderly in our society.

Whether or not they label themselves as "old," individuals in their 60s and 70s encounter new changes in their functioning and in their environment. As in earlier periods of life, these changes require adjustment, which may sometimes be easy and sometimes difficult.

Physical Changes

Many of the physical changes of middle age become more marked in the later years of life. Visual and auditory capacities generally show further decline. Decreases in muscle strength, reaction time, and stamina continue to occur. Outward appearance continues to alter.

Health becomes an increasingly important issue during this period. Acute (temporary) problems such as injuries and influenza actually tend to decline with age. However, chronic (long-term) problems increase significantly. It has been estimated that approximately 80 percent of all older people have one or more chronic conditions, including arthritis, rheumatism, hypertension, heart disease, and cancer (Ward, 1979). In 1974, according to the U.S. Public Health Service (1974), 39 percent of people over 65 experienced limi-

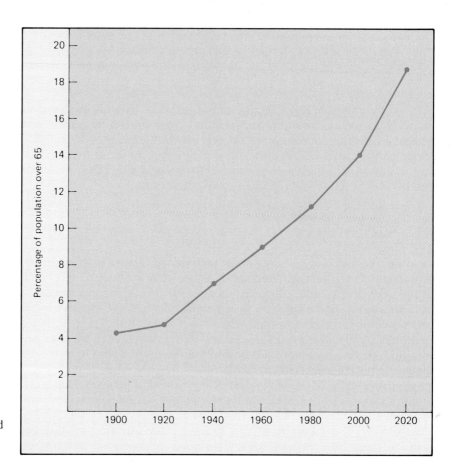

Figure 14–5 The percentage of people in the United States over 65 years of age is increasing steadily and is projected to exceed 18 percent by the year 2020.

tations on major activities (defined as the ability to work, keep house, or engage in school activities) and another 7 percent experienced less serious limitations.

Research suggests that older people learn to live with and accept many of these conditions as an inevitable part of aging. Consequently, self-ratings of health decline less than objective ratings (Riley & Foner, 1968). Nevertheless, perceived and actual health are clearly related to each other—actual health cannot decline too far before perceived health is affected. The importance of this is illustrated in a study by Palmore and Luikart (1972), which found that self-rating of health was the variable most related to life satisfaction among middle-aged and older men and women.

While the human "physical plant" naturally declines with age, it is important to realize that not all the health complaints of the elderly lack medical causes. In fact, advocates for the elderly are worried about a tendency among medical, psychiatric, and psychological practitioners to attribute true disease symptoms shown by old people to the irreversible process of aging and therefore fail to prescribe treatments that could greatly benefit the elderly and enhance the quality of their lives.

Related to physical changes are questions about sexuality. The traditional view is that older people are not and should not be sexually active. It is difficult to obtain reliable data on sexual activity in old age, partly because different studies focus on different aspects of sexuality. Sexual functioning has been variously defined as coitus once a week or more, successful coitus

at least once a year, or regular orgasmic release through any means including coitus, masturbation, or nocturnal emission. Further, most research has focused on males. Given these limitations, the evidence suggests that even in the 70s the majority of men continue to function sexually (Kahn & Fisher, 1967; Botwinick, 1973). The evidence further suggests that loss of responsiveness is not an inevitable part of aging but is due instead to factors such as chronic physical problems, lack of an available partner, and the belief that sex after 60 is somehow unusual or immoral (Botwinick, 1973).

Cognitive Changes

It used to be considered common knowledge that cognitive ability declined with age. Today this view is highly debatable. First of all, one must separate the effects of neurological disease from the effects of aging. Diseases that affect the flow of blood to the brain, or that destroy brain tissue, are not inevitable consequences of aging. For example, we now know that many of the supposedly "senile" elderly are actually suffering from Alzheimer's disease. Recent studies of the healthy elderly, or at least those whose health problems don't affect their brains, show no general decline in cognitive ability (Bates, Dittman-Kohli, & Dixon, 1984).

This may be one reason why earlier studies of cognition and aging drew a distinction between crystallized and fluid intelligence. As discussed earlier in Chapter 10, *crystallized intelligence* was seen as the accumulation of facts and knowledge that seemed to grow with age. *Fluid intelligence* referred to the processing of new information, a function that seemed particularly vulnerable to the effects of age—or neurological disease. Recent research on neurologically healthy elderly people revealed no consistent evidence of a reduced ability to learn (Schaie & Willis, 1986). In one study (Reder, Wible, & Martin, 1986) elderly subjects were asked to recall either the exact wording or the "gist" of a short story. They didn't do as well as younger subjects on the exact wording (which one rarely needs to recall), but did just as well on the "gist" (the more useful cognitive function).

It has become increasingly clear that much of the earlier work on this topic failed to consider the motivation of the elderly subjects. They may simply lack the same motivation that younger subjects have to both attend to and persist in solving the problems presented by experimenters (Craik & Bird, 1982). Furthermore, one must consider how long it has been since the elderly subjects have been asked to perform the types of cognitive tasks used in the laboratory. Willis (1985) has shown that very little practice may be required to substantially improve an elderly person's ability to perform some cognitive task. Dearmond (1984) concluded from her study of mentally active people in their 80s that loss of cognitive ability stemmed more from intellectual apathy and boredom than from biological deterioration.

Retirement

Retirement is one of the most important, and most studied, changes associated with old age. Some people see it as a quite negative change, a separation from an important source of satisfaction and self-esteem. Those who take this point of view have been active in the movement to raise or even abolish mandatory retirement ages. But others view retirement as a positive shift to a life with more free time and more opportunity to pursue non-work–related interests. Over two-thirds of the adults interviewed in one

Many people view retirement as a positive shift to a life with more free time and more opportunity to pursue outside interests. (Richard Hutchings/ Photo Researchers)

study reported that they had little difficulty adjusting to a rewarding retirement life (Szinovacz, 1982). Some labor unions have demanded "30 and out" plans, allowing workers to retire on full pension after 30 years of service. At present, only about 20 percent of males and 8.5 percent of females continue to work after age 65 (Kalish, 1982).

Why someone retires and how that person perceives retirement are among the most important predictors of later adjustment and satisfaction (Kimmel, Price, & Walker, 1978; Crowley, 1984). Some other factors that affect adjustment are:

1. *Health.* Continued good health is one of the most important predictors of postretirement satisfaction (Kimmel 1978).
2. *Voluntary vs. involuntary retirement.* It is not easy to define "voluntary"—for example, is retiring before a mandatory time because one is in poor health voluntary? But the more voluntary the retirement, the better the adjustment (Kimmel et al., 1978).
3. *Adequate income.* Many people face a sharp drop in income upon retirement. Several studies indicate that "the money it brings in" is the most missed aspect of work (Harris poll, 1975) and that the expectation of a reasonable standard of living is a major factor in making a positive adjustment to retirement (Eisdorfer, 1972; Glamzer, 1976).

Overall, most people seem to adjust well to retirement and find it a relatively satisfying experience (Newton, Lazurus, & Weinberg, 1984).

Marriage and Widowhood

The upswing in marital happiness that begins in middle age continues into this period of life. Although an increase in tension may occur just before the husband's retirement, the necessary adjustments in the marriage are usually made smoothly, and the majority of older couples report high levels of satisfaction (Dressler, 1973; Thurnher, 1976; Kalish, 1982).

The death of a spouse, however, is common during this period. While only 15 percent of the males over 65 years old in the United States are widowers, more than 50 percent of the women over 65 are widows.

Lopata (1973, 1975) found three general patterns of adaptation. The "self-initiating woman" is both aware that she has to make behavioral and relational adjustments and flexible enough to do so. She selects those aspects of her previous life that can be continued and discards those it would be impossible to maintain. She modifies her relationships with friends and children, builds a life-style suited to her individual needs, and attempts to match available resources and personal goals. The second pattern, generally found in widows in lower-class ethnic communities, involves relatively little change after a husband dies. "Being immersed in kin relations, a very close peer group, or a network of neighbors, such a woman may continue many of her involvements with little modification after becoming a widow." Lopata suggests that a similar pattern may be found in some suburbanites. The third pattern is that of the "social isolate," the woman who was never highly engaged in the broader society, whose life was centered on her husband, and who lacks the resources to develop new roles as her old ones fall away.

Other studies have focused on specific factors that affect the adjustment to widowhood. Among the variables found to affect morale are income level, mobility, health, age (older widows tend to adjust more easily), and availabil-

ity of alternative roles such as employment or family involvement (Newton, Lazurus & Weinberg, 1984; Morgan, 1976). In general, the data suggest that most people cope adequately, although widows and widowers are somewhat less satisfied with their lives than older people who are still married (Campbell, 1975).

Establishment of Ego Integrity

We have focused so far on specific areas requiring adjustment in old age. In his classic description of the stages of life, Erik Erikson (1963) identified what he felt was the crucial broad task confronting individuals who are approaching death—the establishment of a sense of *ego integrity*. They must evaluate their lives, affirm that their years have been meaningful, and accept that various outcomes were "meant to be." The alternative is despair, a sense that one's life has been wasted and that it is now too late to find fulfillment.

In a similar vein, Robert Butler (1968) suggests that the older individual engages in a "life review" and that an inability to handle this process may lead to depression. Like Erikson, Butler argues that a possible and ideal outcome is the further evolution of such characteristics as candor, serenity, and wisdom.

DEATH AND DYING

Although death has traditionally been a taboo subject in American culture, interest in this "final stage of development" is currently on the rise. Partly this reflects a recognition that death is "the most mysterious, most threatening, and most tantalizing of all human phenomena" (Shneidman, 1973, p. 23) and that understanding life and development requires coming to terms with death. It also reflects concern that avoidance of the topic leads to dehumanization of the dying (Kübler-Ross, 1969).

Elisabeth Kübler-Ross has been a pioneer in the study of the dying. On the basis of intensive interviews with over 200 terminally ill patients in a Chicago hospital, she outlined five stages that people go through as they approach death (Kübler-Ross, 1969).

The first stage is *denial and isolation*. The initial response by most patients is "No, not me, it cannot be true." *Anger* is the next stage and occurs when denial can no longer be maintained. The question becomes "Why me? Why not someone else, who is older or meaner or of less use to society?" The anger usually subsides and people may move on to the third stage, *bargaining*. Now they attempt to reach some sort of agreement, usually with God. "I will be good"—e.g., I will live a life in the service of the church or eventually give my body to science—"if only I am allowed to live." The fourth stage is *depression*. (Kübler-Ross distinguishes two different types of grief that may be experienced during this time. The first is what she calls *reactive* depression, in which patients respond to current and past losses—the disfigurement caused by the disease, the inability to care for their family because they are ill, the wrongs they committed that cannot be righted. The second is a *preparatory* depression, a reaction to impending losses, the separation from life and loved ones. At last, given sufficient time and support, people may reach the final stage, *acceptance*, in which they are able to contemplate death with some degree of quiet expectation, without fear or despair. (Kübler-Ross emphasizes that this is neither a happy time nor a time of hopelessness and resignation. It is a period of peace.

Subsequent research has not fully confirmed Kübler-Ross's idea of stages

(Perlmutter & Hall, 1985). Even she has acknowledged that the stages may not occur in the sequence that she described (Kübler-Ross, 1974).

Care of the Terminally Ill   Though the terminally ill are usually hospitalized, some people believe that the modern hospital, with its emphasis on aggressive therapy and the prolongation of life by every means possible, does not and cannot provide the right kind of support for either the dying person or that person's family (Holden, 1976).

One alternative to hospitalization of the terminally ill is the hospice, which originated in its modern form in England. The term **hospice** is generally used to describe centers established for the care of patients dying of such diseases as cancer. It can also refer to a community of volunteers and professionals who provide support for dying patients and their families, both at the center and in the patients' homes. Although hospices differ, most share certain aims (Holden, 1976; DuBois, 1980; Smith, 1985):

1. *Adequate pain control.* The first goal is to free the patient from pain and from the fear that pain will return. Movement leaders point out that many hospitals fail to control pain adequately, partly because of the pharmacological ignorance of many doctors, and partly because of concern about addiction and side effects (which makes little sense when the patient is dying).

2. *The avoidance of high-technology attempts to prolong life.* Treatments that would only postpone death, prolong suffering for the patient and the patient's family, and financially burden both patients and their families are shunned.

3. *Psychological support for the patient.* "Support" in this sense means doing whatever will give the dying person the greatest comfort and peace. This may mean getting the person's house in order and making plans for the children. It may mean providing opportunities for the patient to be with family and friends as much as possible. Or it may mean giving the person an opportunity to see and talk with other dying patients.

4. *Support for the bereaved, both before and after the death.* Although some family members will need little follow-up, others will need considerable aftercare. The latter may return to the hospice at any time for further help.

The hospice concept is still too new in the United States to gauge its impact on medical care. There is resistance from traditional health-care providers, as well as some concern that hospices will become simply another type of nursing home (Holden, 1976). So far, there are few reports on how well the hospice meets the needs of the dying and their families. However, the hospice concept appears to be a potentially valuable tool in the effort to make the process of dying less frightening and dehumanizing.

In any case, advances in medical technology have given us new techniques for prolonging life. Inevitably, this forces us to consider decisions and consequences that we did not have to face before. Kübler-Ross has alerted us to the dehumanizing aspects of this application of modern medical science to the prolongation of life; there are probably equally dehumanizing aspects to many well-meaning attempts to force people through her stages of dying. This whole area is an emotionally charged one that will be handled by different individuals in vastly different ways.

SUMMARY

1. *Adolescence* is the period between childhood and adulthood during which the individual learns the skills needed to survive as an adult; it is a socially rather than a biologically determined phase of development that begins at puberty.

2. *Puberty* is marked by dramatic changes in growth rate and the development of primary and secondary sex characteristics.

3. At about age 12, the child enters Piaget's final stage of cognitive development—*formal operations*. The most basic change in this stage is the ability to deal with abstract concepts and use both *hypothetico-deductive reasoning* and *propositional thinking*.

4. According to Freud, during adolescence the sexual energy of libido, repressed during the latency period, reemerges, and the adult stage of development begins. Erikson called the search for *self-identity* the key crisis in need of resolution during the adolescent years.

5. Keniston suggested the term *youth* for the stage between adolescence and adulthood when people spend long periods training for a career while still financially dependent on their parents.

6. According to a number of theorists, the major task in early adulthood is the establishment of intimate relationships.

7. A major event of the middle years is the departure of children from the home. This is also the time when many women are able to reenter the job market.

8. Physical changes during the midlife years may cause some people to experience self-doubts or stress; in women the *menopause* is characterized by physical changes that may be accompanied by psychological effects.

9. Among the major changes occurring in old age are physical and cognitive changes, retirement, and widowhood.

10. Erikson has described the crucial task confronting the person entering old age as the establishment of a sense of *ego integrity*. Butler suggests that old age is a time in which "life review" is essential.

11. Kübler-Ross has outlined five stages of dealing with death: denial, anger, bargaining, depression, and acceptance.

SUGGESTED READINGS

ATCHLEY, R. C. (1985). *The social forces in later life* (4th ed.). Belmont, Cal.: Wadsworth. The role of family and society in growing old.

GOETHALS, B. W., & KLOS, D. S. (1976). *Experiencing youth: First person accounts* (2nd ed.). Boston: Little, Brown. Autobiographical studies of adolescents with focus on interpersonal problems and personality development.

GOLDHABER, D. (1986). *Life-span human development*. New York: Harcourt, Brace, Jovanovich. An excellent review of the full range of developmental research.

SARASON, S. G., (1977). *Work, aging, and social change*. New York: Free Press. An examination of our current expectations about professional careers, with suggestions for social policy to facilitate career change.

SKOLNICK, A. S. (1986). *The psychology of human development*. New York: Harcourt, Brace, Jovanovich. A thorough review of the research in human development, written to be fully comprehensible to the undergraduate student.

SMITH, W. J. (1985). *Dying in the human life cycle*. New York: Holt, Rhinehart & Winston. A detailed review of research on dying, ranging from the death of infants to the hospice movement for elderly patients.

WOODRUFF, D. W., & BIRREN, J. E. (1983). *Aging: Scientific perspectives and social issues* (2nd. ed.). Belmont, Cal.: Wadsworth. Considers the social aspects of scientific studies of aging.

15 Personality

There is no single definition of personality. Uniting many definitions, however, is the idea that **personality** is the organized and distinctive pattern of behavior that characterizes an individual's adaptation to an environment and endures over time. The study of personality concerns ideas, motives, attitudes, emotions, life crises, beliefs, and values, as well as the processes by which people try to understand their own behavior, that of others, and the world. The study of personality is rich with theories about what makes us think, feel, behave, and experience life as we do. Each theory views the inherent nature, personality structure, and outward functioning of human beings differently, and offers a different perspective on their relationship to their environment.

Personality theories have traditionally attempted to deal with several classes of questions.

1. What is the structure of personality? What are its more stable aspects and in what ways are they interrelated?
2. What motivates human action? What external events or internal changes set the person in motion?
3. Although people are in many ways alike, there are remarkable differences among them. How do we account for these differences?
4. How does personality develop? Once developed, in what ways can it change and how deep and lasting can these changes be?
5. How are personality dysfunction and psychopathological behavior to be interpreted? How are they to be treated?

This painting by Frans Hals, "The Laughing Cavalier," is a finely drawn impression of an ebullient personality. (The Wallace Collection, London)

The four chapters in this section on personality and clinical psychology explore the theories that attempt to deal with these questions. Several of the personality theories that we shall discuss in this chapter have their origins in theories already covered in earlier chapters or in material that will be explored more fully in later chapters. In order to show you the relationship between the different areas of psychology, we will make reference to these chapters when appropriate. For example, the discussion on conditioning and learning in Chapter 6 has some relevance to personality, as does perception (see Chapter 4), memory (see Chapter 7), and thought (see Chapter 9). Many of the questions that we address in the study of personality are similar to the issues raised in the study of human motivation covered in Chapters 11 and 12. Cognitive personality theory represents one of the most exciting recent developments in the study of personality. This theory draws on the attributional principles of social psychology, which will be discussed more thoroughly in Chapter 19.

Students might sometimes feel that all this complexity is introduced for the express purpose of confusing them, but it isn't. One of the goals of personality theory is to account for how human beings function—a formidable task given the intricacies of the human mind. In order to do this, it stands to reason that personality theories must draw on other theories that explain some of the more simple aspects of human functioning and behavior. For instance, a theory of personality that didn't contain some sections about human memory would be hopelessly incomplete. While theories that explain the personality are complex and ambitious, human beings by nature are complicated and their behavior must be modeled by complicated theories before it is completely understood. In order to help your comprehension, we will review or preview related theories as we go along in our discussion.

We will begin the chapter with a discussion of traits, the place where most people seem to begin their understanding of the human personality. Next, we will unfold alternatives to the various trait theories. Throughout our discussion, we will give you a sense of how each theory goes about assessing the personality of any given individual. As you will see, different theories have quite different perceptions about what is important to measure, and thus quite different techniques are used by the various methods of personality assessment. At the end of the chapter, we will focus specifically on assessment measures, and offer some insight into what discriminates good ones from bad ones.

TRAIT THEORIES

You know someone who is introverted. She is quiet. Particularly when confronted with stress or conflict, she tends to retreat into herself. Another friend is extroverted; he's always the life of any party. You call a third friend domineering, possibly because you are tired of being told what to do by him or her. These examples reflect one of the oldest and most compelling observations about human behavior—that it seems to flow from the underlying dispositions, or traits, of the individual. **Trait theories** categorize people on the basis of their distinctive attributes and traits.

One of the most ancient theories of personality that we know about is a trait theory. The Greek physician Hippocrates suggested that people could be categorized as falling into one of four types: melancholic (in modern terms, depressive), choleric (touchy and irritable), sanguine (cheerful and optimistic), and phlegmatic (calm, but perhaps tending to listlessness). These were

thought to correspond to the four elements—that is, earth, fire, air, and water. As a good personality theory ought to do, Hippocrates' theory explained how people came to have one personality or another, how people came to be abnormal, and how abnormality could be treated or cured. The Greeks thought that the four fluids they observed in the body were expressed as personality types, and a particular personality type was caused by an excess of one fluid over the others (see Figure 15–1). So, for instance, a choleric personality was found in a person who had an excess of yellow bile, while phlegmatic people were characterized by an excess of phlegm. Treatments for personality problems involved diet alterations and other procedures that sought to improve the balance of fluids.

While we no longer believe that personality is a manifestation of the four fluids in the body, we do continue to believe that people can be sorted out in terms of the personality traits they possess. Modern trait theories attempt to make more scientific observations based on ideas similar to those of the ancient Greeks.

The earliest approaches to personality accounted for human behavior in terms of people's innate characteristics or dispositions. **Traits** were said to be stable, enduring, and consistent. Actions followed from these underlying traits. Thus an honest person would display honest behavior in a variety of situations in which there were temptations to lie or cheat. According to some trait theories, traits existed relatively independently of one another. In other theories, the traits were somehow linked into an overarching structure.

Nomothetic Personality Theories: Cattell

Trait theories in personality psychology have traditionally been **nomothetic** in character—that is, based on the belief that all traits are equally applicable to all individuals. In this view, every person occupies some position with regard to every trait. An individual's personality, then, is the sum total of his or her rankings on each of the traits. For example, John may be *very* independent, Jane *moderately* independent, and Ralph *not at all* independent, but the relative independence of each individual is measurable on the same scale. Within this framework there has been some disagreement over the number or kinds of traits that exist (Eysenck, 1977), but the idea that traits are universal is common to most traditional views of personality.

Some theorists who used the nomothetic approach tried to reduce the potentially vast number of traits to a more manageable and efficient list. Raymond Cattell, a leading trait theorist, set out to identify a reasonable number of traits that could be used to describe all individuals and predict their behavior. To accomplish this empirical "mapping of the personality," he used a sophisticated statistical technique known as *factor analysis*. This procedure makes it possible to analyze data for a large number of variables simultaneously and to group together those variables that are associated with one another. Two or more characteristics that correlate highly are assumed to reflect the existence of one underlying trait. For example, think of "warm" and "sociable." These two characteristics seem to go together and to manifest an underlying trait of "friendliness." Cattell initially collected data on people's judgments of a vast number of possible traits and then used factor analysis to sort out the patterns. He eventually concluded that 16 dimensions were sufficient to convey the important underlying differences in personalities.

For Cattell, this approach to personality "permits a prediction of what a

Figure 15–1 The Four Temperaments. The first frame *(top left)* represents the choleric personality associated with the element fire. The second frame *(top right)* represents the sanguine personality associated with the element air. The third frame *(bottom left)* represents the melancholic personality associated with the element earth. And the fourth frame *(bottom right)* represents the phlegmatic personality associated with the element water. (The Bettmann Archive)

Table 15–1: Cattell's 16 Source Traits, as Measured by His 16 PF (Personality Factor) Test.

Notice that Cattell has frequently used unfamiliar words to identify his traits. This was deliberate. He wanted to emphasize that his distinctions were not exactly those captured by ordinary, imprecise words. Still, psychologists and other readers alike are helped by the ordinary-language descriptions that appear in the table.

Source Trait Index	Low-Score Description	High-Score Description
A	SIZIA Reserved, detached, critical, aloof, stiff	AFFECTIA Outgoing, warmhearted, easygoing, participating
B	LOW INTELLIGENCE Dull	HIGH INTELLIGENCE Bright
C	LOW EGO STRENGTH At mercy of feelings, emotionally less stable, easily upset, changeable	HIGH EGO STRENGTH Emotionally stable, mature, faces reality, calm
E	SUBMISSIVENESS Humble, mild, easily led, docile, accommodating	DOMINANCE Assertive, aggressive, competitive, stubborn
F	DESURGENCY Sober, taciturn, serious	SURGENCY Happy-go-lucky, gay, enthusiastic
G	WEAKER SUPEREGO STRENGTH Expedient, disregards rules	STRONGER SUPEREGO STRENGTH Conscientious, persistent, moralistic, staid
H	THRECTIA Shy, timid, threat-sensitive	PARMIA Venturesome, uninhibited, socially bold
I	HARRIA Tough-minded, self-reliant	PREMSIA Tender-minded, sensitive, clinging, overprotected

person will do in a given situation" (1950, p. 2). Once he could position a person according to the 16 dimensions, he would attempt to predict many of the person's behaviors. The method involves several steps. Cattell called the 16 first-order dimensions the **source traits** (see Table 15–1). These formed the underlying personality structure. But Cattell also knew that many variables besides source traits were involved. People's motives needed to be considered, along with their mood states (such as depression, curiosity, or anxiety) and the specific settings and roles in which they act. (This makes sense. Anger is differently expressed in classroom settings than in sports arenas, or by students than by sports fans.)

Idiographic Personality Theories: Allport

Attempts like Cattell's to predict behavior from underlying traits have met with mixed success. Moreover, the assumption that traits are universal characteristics or dispositions has not gone unchallenged. **Idiographic**

Source Trait Index	Low-Score Description	High-Score Description
L	ALAXIA Trusting, accepting conditions	PROTENSION Suspicious, hard to fool
M	PRAXERNIA Practical, "down-to-earth," concerned	AUTIA Imaginative, bohemian, absentminded
N	ARTLESSNESS Forthright, unpretentious, genuine, but socially clumsy	SHREWDNESS Astute, polished, socially aware
O	UNTROUBLED ADEQUACY Self-assured, placid, secure, complacent, serene	GUILT PRONENESS Apprehensive, self-reproaching, insecure, worrying, troubled
Q1	CONSERVATISM OF TEMPERAMENT Conservative, respecting traditional ideas	RADICALISM OF TEMPERAMENT Experimenting, liberal, free-thinking
Q2	GROUP ADHERENCE Group-dependent, a "joiner" and sound follower	SELF-SUFFICIENCY Self-sufficient, resourceful, prefers own decisions
Q3	LOW SELF-SENTIMENT INTEGRATION Undisciplined, self-conflict, follows own urges, careless of social rules	HIGH STRENGTH OF SELF-SENTIMENT Controlled, exacting willpower, socially precise, compulsive, following self-image
Q4	LOW ERGIC TENSION Relaxed, tranquil, torpid, unfrustrated, composed	HIGH ERGIC TENSION Tense, frustrated, driven, overwrought

From Cattell and Kline, 1937, p. 44.

models of personality are based on the assumption that traits are concrete (i.e., based on specific situations) and unique to particular individuals. Personality is seen as the sum of an individual's experiences. In this view, the same trait may mean different things to different individuals. For example, for John, independence may mean being aggressive with peers and unwilling to take advice; Jane's idea of independence may include unorthodox political views and socially outgoing behavior at parties; Ralph, on the other hand, may not think of himself in terms of independence at all. The unique experiences of these three individuals have given them ideas of independence that may overlap but are by no means identical.

One of the first personality psychologists to attempt to approach personality in this idiographic way was Gordon Allport. According to Allport, no two people are alike; no two individuals respond in the same way even to identical stimuli. To study personality, then, one must study the combination of traits as they appear in single individuals. Traits direct action and motivate us to behave the way we do. However, some traits are more impelling than others. Allport distinguished three levels of traits according to the degree to which they govern personality:

Figure 15–2 The dramatist Ben Jonson created memorable characters in his plays based on the model of cardinal traits: One character represents greed, another lust, and so on. This drawing by Beardsley depicts Jonson's greedy Volpone adoring his treasure. (Princeton University Library)

1. *Cardinal traits.* These are the most powerful and pervasive traits; they dominate a person's life. Actually, few people possess cardinal traits. When they do, we are likely to think of them chiefly in terms of those traits. Playwrights and novelists sometimes create characters with cardinal traits (Figure 15–2), and we may think of certain figures in history as possessing such traits. If we describe someone as "a Machiavellian," then we are saying that we think this person's actions are manipulative, and further, that we perceive that the manipulative characteristic marks everything this person says, does, and thinks.

2. *Central traits.* Most people are not so single-minded as to be characterized by one or two traits. Still, we do not need every trait listed in the dictionary to adequately describe another personality. Allport (1961) did an important study in which he asked people to describe other people. (He arranged it so that the subjects knew each other well enough to be confident about doing so.) He found that people required a limited number of traits to give what they felt was a reasonably complete characterization of others. For instance, someone might first describe a friend as "thoughtful of others." New information might be added by saying that he or she was either "lively and outgoing" or "shy and quiet." And so on. But not forever. Allport found that just over seven traits were thought sufficient to describe the central attributes of other people.

3. *Secondary traits.* These are the most limited in frequency and least crucial to an understanding of the dynamics of an individual's personality. They include particular attitudes and preferences, for example, the kind of music or food one likes.

Allport's theory allows for situational differences in an individual's behavior. This is possible because there are many traits, many are active at the same time, traits overlap, and they are organized in a different way for each individual. For instance, two people may both be accurately described as possessing the trait of "honesty," but for the first, honesty may extend to a prohibition even of "white lies" (telling people that you like their expensive new clothes even though you actually think they are tasteless), while for the second, an apparently harmless deception is acceptable.

Allport's theory has some clear strengths. First, it deals directly with the question of what causes behavioral consistencies by explaining that they flow from underlying traits. Second, it leaves room for human uniqueness and accounts for the fact that some people can be described in terms of one or two traits, while most of us require more.

Allport's theory also has problems, several of which are common to trait theories in general. For instance, people do behave in seemingly contradictory ways. How is this to be explained within a trait system that emphasizes consistency.

Other personality researchers have also questioned the strength of trait theory's evidence for the consistency of a person's actions. Clearly, if actions are not consistent across situations, as most personal observations suggest, then one of the central arguments of trait theories is in trouble. As we will see, this controversy over whether or not behavior is consistent across situations is an active one in personality psychology.

A second problem is that trait theories do not tell us why traits develop and whether or not there are underlying structures of the personality that produce them. It sometimes seems as if they are explaining why a person acts "honestly" by saying that the person has the trait of honesty. This kind of

circular reasoning leaves much to be desired, and points to something missing in the explanation of the relationship between behavior and any given trait supposed to exist as part of the personality.

THE BIOLOGICAL MODEL OF PERSONALITY

Many people seeking the underlying causes of personality traits have suggested that the answer lies in the physiological and biological nature of the human body and brain. We observe that people are born with different hair color, grow to different heights, and have different body types. It is natural to assume that the different traits that people possess come from the same underlying forces that cause these physical differences. This is the guiding assumption behind many of the biological approachs to human personality. The biological approach to the study of personality holds that physical constitution, genetic endowment, and other physiological characteristics determine at least some basic features of personality. Older theories claim that almost all the important elements of personality are biological in origin, while more modern versions state that only some personality characteristics originate in biological factors and that biological and other factors interact in complex ways that affect personality.

The Constitutional Approach: Sheldon

The **constitutional approach** holds that the structure of the body, or body type, determines personality and behavior. Some stereotypes that we all have heard express this view. For instance, all fat people are jolly; thin, frail people are scholarly and ascetic. William Sheldon thought that there was a great deal of truth to these everyday generalizations even though they were given short shrift by psychologists. He commented, "It is the old notion that structure must somehow determine function. In the face of this expectation it is rather astonishing that in the past so little relation has been discovered between the shape of man and the way he behaves" (1942, p. 4). After analyzing more than 4,000 photographs, Sheldon concluded that there are three basic body structures or **somatotypes** (see Figure 15–3): **Endomorphs** are usually fat and have underdeveloped musculature; **mesomorphs** are generally muscular and of medium build; and **ectomorphs** tend to be slender and fragile and to have a light muscle structure.

Sheldon also did an extensive analysis of over 500 trait words, using intuitive procedures and correlational methods. He found three major groups of traits that make up the primary components of "temperament." He also found that each somatotype was strongly associated with one of the three primary temperaments. The chubby endomorph was likely to have an easygoing, sociable temperament; the athletic-looking mesomorph would probably be a risk-taking, assertive type; and the physically fragile ectomorph often was withdrawn and restrained.

Modern researchers tend to discount such facile correlations. They have been particularly critical of the fact that ratings of temperament were made by people (Sheldon and his associates) who had set out to find a body type–temperament correlation. In other words, the high degree of correlation found may reflect a bias in the eye of the beholder. When such studies are done in a methodologically more sophisticated way, the connections between body type and temperament are much less strong.

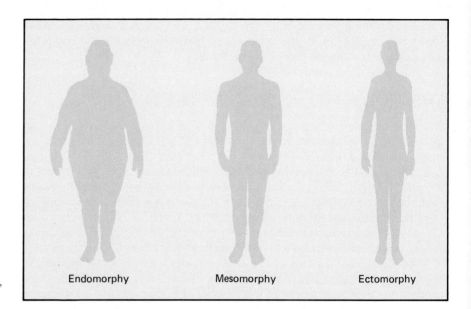

Figure 15–3 This diagram shows examples of the three body types described by Sheldon: endomorphy, mesomorphy, and ectomorphy.

Endomorphy   Mesomorphy   Ectomorphy

Still, there *is* a correlation, and Sheldon must be given credit for calling attention to the connection between physique and temperament. Nor did he argue that all of a person's temperamental characteristics mysteriously flowed from that person's physique at birth. He discussed the ways in which a person's physique might cause interactions with other people that could shape temperamental development. For instance, he pointed out that mesomorphs were likely to be recruited for sports because of their physiques and could further develop their competitive temperaments in this setting.

Genetic Theories of Personality Characteristics

As the modern study of genetics and inheritance has developed, a number of psychological researchers have investigated the idea that at least some human characteristics, including traits and behavior patterns, are, in whole or in part, genetically determined. Thus there are a number of studies (methodologically similar to some of the IQ studies we discussed in Chapter 10) that are aimed at discovering the degree to which various measurable personality traits and patterns are determined by an individual's genetic makeup. Many investigators have been struck by the continuities in behavior from infancy to later life. For instance, in their study of temperament, Thomas Chess, and Birch (1970) followed the development of 150 children for almost a decade, gathering information from interviews with parents and home observation. They concluded that there are evident temperamental patterns in children at birth and that these patterns endure. For example, "moody" babies are likely to become "moody" children and to have more behavior problems later in life than even-tempered babies.

Introversion/extroversion is a temperamental pattern that has also been suggested to have a genetic component. Whether as adults people are shy and anxious, or friendly and outgoing, correlates with expressions of these orientations at birth: Friendly infants tend to become friendly teenagers, while cold infants are also somewhat unfriendly as adolescents (Schaeffer & Bayley, 1963). Babies also appear to differ at birth in the way

they prefer to be calmed when they are upset: Some like to be held, others want to be left alone. The names "cuddlers" and "noncuddlers" have been applied to these two types (Schaffer & Emerson, 1964a). Cuddlers are described by their mothers as snuggling, loving to be held, and cuddling back; mothers of noncuddlers say their children don't like to be held, resist all attempts to do so, and fret and wriggle until they are put down.

Of course, it is also important to assess environmental influences. A child who at first doesn't seek attachment with the parent may be perceived and treated by the parent as more independent; continued noncuddling behavior could be the product of interaction with a parent who expects the baby to avoid warm behavior. Similarly, friendly, extroverted babies may draw reinforcing responses from their parents that encourage further development of that pattern. Thomas, Chess, and Birch (1970) observed parental reactions to children's temperamental displays such as moodiness, and saw how these reactions could support the temperamental patterns that were first exhibited by the child.

Genetic theories of personality, then, may actually be genetic-environmental theories of development. These theories suggest that the influence of genetics will be greatest when the first signs of a predisposition draw from the environment some reaction that supports the continuation of that predisposition. It should also be pointed out that even behaviors that appear extremely early in life are not necessarily genetic in origin. They can be very quickly learned reactions, and there is evidence that some learning can take place soon after birth.

For the reasons discussed in the intelligence chapter (Chapter 10), identical twins reared apart are generally regarded as ideal subjects for separating the roles of environment and heredity in the development of various characteristics or behaviors. Personality researchers at the University of Minnesota (Bouchard et al., 1981; Bouchard & McGue, 1984) have undertaken the laborious process of tracking down cases of identical twins reared apart since early childhood. (The twins in this particular study were separated at an average age of 6 weeks.) Among the relatively few such cases they were able to locate, the researchers have found some interesting results and there have been some striking similarities between several sets of twins. For example, one pair of twins both appeared wearing wire-rimmed glasses and sporting mustaches. The two men, who were reared in different countries, also exhibited similar mannerisms. A number of tests have been given to all these twin pairs, and early research reports indicate a high similarity in brain-wave patterns and what might be descirbed as energy activity levels. The research also reports a high correspondence on sociability and ability test levels. While its ultimate impact on modern personality theory is yet to be determined, this research does suggest that genetics may have a greater influence on personality than was previously acknowledged.

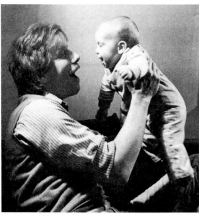

Do we encourage an infant's fretfulness by picking up the baby when he or she cries? Traditional learning theory would say yes. Smiling and laughing can also be encouraged by a parent's smile. (Barbara Rios/Photo Researchers; Joan Menschenfreund/Taurus Photos)

Modern Directions in Biological Theories of Personality

In the past, although many psychologists believed that various personality patterns were due to different patterns of brain functioning, we did not understand enough about brain functioning to be able to say much about how this was so. For those convinced of the inherited nature of some personality traits, the evidence hinted that different brain mechanisms con-

trolled different behaviors, but relatively little was known about exactly how those brain mechanisms operated.

Recently, through our rapid increase in knowledge about brain functioning, we have learned enough to generate some interesting, if often frustratingly incomplete, stories about how different patterns of activity in the brain might lead to different thoughts and actions in a given individual. Technological developments have created the possibility of much more specific and focused interventions and facilitated measurements of more precisely targeted areas of the brain. These discoveries have given new excitement to modern biological theories of personality and personality disorders, and made a significant contribution to treatment efforts in these areas. In later chapters we will discuss theories of schizophrenia and depression that relate these disorders to brain chemical imbalances, and we will review what has been learned about such disorders from tracing the effects of drugs that alter brain functioning.

However, here it is useful to illustrate one of the many possible applications of modern neuropsychological thinking to the study of personality—the study of anxiety. Anxiety is a common human experience and one that theorists regard as central to personality functioning. Scientists have been tracing the workings of what they informally call the "anxiety peptide" (Marx, 1985). Peptides are neurotransmitters. When this particular peptide is transmitted to certain areas of the brain, such as the hypothalamus of a human or an animal, anxiety-linked behaviors result. The peptide has its anxiety-producing effect in regions of the brain that are known to control emotion. It is in these same brain areas that the newly available drug alprazolam (a benzodiazepine) has its anxiety-reducing effects. For reasons that are not yet understood, certain people may be deficient in the neurotransmitter that is the naturally produced equivalent of the synthetic drug alprazolam. Unlike the rest of us, they do not have the natural mechanism for slowing or blocking the uptake of the anxiety peptide, and they experience extreme anxiety as a result of minor external events.

This research has obvious implications for the study of personality. For example, there may be times, given natural hormonal fluctuations, that any individual is much more likely to have a panic reaction to a fixed level of external stimulation. Thus the case of the anxiety peptide is a useful example of the state of physiological research into human thought and personality. Yet while much has already been learned, much more remains to be discovered before we can complete our understanding of the biological underpinnings of personality functioning.

THE PSYCHOANALYTIC MODEL OF PERSONALITY

Psychoanalytic theory is the most comprehensive and influential of all the personality theories. Given Freud's undeniable genius, and his willingness to make intuitive leaps in his theorizing, his theories will strike you as rather different from anythng that you have yet encountered. However, it is useful to see Freud in the historical context of his time. Since he began with a biological orientation to personality, we will begin our account of his discoveries there.

Freud was trained as what we would now call a medical researcher. More specifically, he was trained at the University of Vienna as a neurologist. He

had a medical degree, but his plan was to stay in the university setting and carry out neurological research. In making this plan, Freud showed a very good sense of where the scientific action was. During the late 1800s, exciting discoveries were being made about the human nervous system. Much, but by no means all, of what you learned in Chapter 2 about the nervous system and the neural transmission of electrical impulses was first discovered at this time.

Freud was not allowed to fulfill his plan to be a university-based scientist. For a number of reasons, including the anti-Semitic climate of Vienna at the time, Freud's professor informed him that his prospects for a long-term job at the university were bleak to nonexistent. Without much money, and needing a steady means of support so that he could marry his long-waiting fiancée, Freud reluctantly decided to open a private practice in neurology.

What kind of patients was a young, not socially well-connected new doctor likely to treat? Not surprisingly, those who were annoying or puzzling to the more established neurologists. Freud saw patients other doctors suspected of malingering, or those who had problems that could not be understood according to the newly developing knowledge of the human nervous system. So, in effect, if Freud wanted to treat his patients' problems as real, he would have to reject current neurological explanations of their difficulties.

An example will make this more clear. A patient might show up in Freud's consulting room with a "glove paralysis." The patient's hand would be numb under roughly the area that would be covered by a glove. The problem was quite real, in the sense that the patient would show no response to what ordinarily would be painful pokes and prods in the area of "paralysis." Furthermore, the patient would have normal responsiveness higher up in the arm. The problem with this condition is that the way the nerves in the arm interconnect, no sensible neurological cause could be found for such a disorder.

So slowly, as Freud faced more and more cases in which neurological reasoning seemed inadequate, he was moved to create psychological explanations for these disorders. Thus we need to realize that the origins of psychoanalytic theory are far removed from the scientific laboratory. Freud's discoveries stemmed from his attempts to treat patients suffering from mysterious ailments that could not be cured by more orthodox approaches.

Psychoanalytic theory strongly reflects its origins. It is *holistic,* in that it insists on recognizing the relationship between various components of the personality and the observed behavior. For related reasons, it emphasizes multiple determinants of actions rather than single causes. And, as many have pointed out, because Freud's subjects were patients in distress, it focuses on maladaptive rather than adaptive behavior. It uses standards of evidence that have their origins in single case studies rather than experimental procedures.

According to Freud's psychoanalytic theory, we are at the mercy of a strict psychic determinism, primiarily motivated by "drives" or "instincts" over which we have little control and of which we are only dimly aware. In this view, human personality is like an iceberg: The tip above the water, a small fraction of the total iceberg, represents our conscious awareness, while the vast mass below represents our unconscious life. Thus the primary motivation for our actions is not always directly accessible to us.

One of the fundamental conceptual discoveries of psychoanalytic theory is the role of the unconscious mind. To Freud, several different things point toward the existence of unconscious thought processes. Slips of the tongue, memory errors, and other apparently trivial phenomena, which are produced without conscious awareness, often can be shown to be connected by some systematic and very revealing links. Dreams show the same connectedness.

Freud at his writing table, perusing the *Abriss der Psychanalyse. (Mary Evans/Picture Library)*

Though they contain apparently disconnected leaps and illogical gaps, on analysis the psychological connections between dream elements are clear. From these observations Freud was led to postulate the existence of the unconscious mind, in which the continuity of thought processes unfolds, blocked from the awareness of the thinker. The unconscious, unknown to consciousness, fundamentally affects the thoughts, feelings, and behavior of the individual; from it spring many of the forces that govern people's behavior.

After a brief early commitment to hypnosis as a method of uncovering unconscious material, Freud later developed his psychoanalytic method of *free association.* He instructed patients to simply say what came to mind, without censoring any material or attempting to impose any order on their thoughts. (You might want to try this for a few minutes. It's not all that simple a task to render a completely accurate report of every thought as it comes into consciousness.) In contemporary psychoanalysis, patients are sometimes shown ambiguous shapes (known as *Rorschach* test) and asked to free-associate to them.

Freud's Structure of Personality

We can get a clearer picture of Freud's concept of the unconscious and how it exerts its influence by looking more closely at his three-part structure of personality: the id, ego, and superego. Remember, these concepts refer to processes, not actual physical locations in the brain. And although they are interrelated, each of the three processes has its own operating principles and functions. Personality and behavior are the products of the interaction of these three systems.

Id.   The **id** is the most basic of the three personality systems. The ego and the superego develop out of the id; throughout life they rely on the id as the source of psychic energy for their activities. In a sense, then, their dependence on the id never ceases. The id is formed by the instincts, or *drives,* that an infant possesses at birth. Freud divided the instincts into two broad categories: life instincts **(eros)** and death instincts **(thanatos).** In terms of drives, these are frequently expressed as sex and aggression. The human organism, Freud believed, simultaneously wants to live and die, create and destroy.

Many psychologists have since wished that Freud had not attached the label "sexual" to the first class of instincts, for many of the needs he placed in this category—affection, warmth, nourishment—are not what most people would term "sexual." But as we will see shortly, Freud was attempting to make clear the underlying unity of these needs and their connection with the sexual drive. This general class of sexual or life instincts enables the individual organisms of a species to survive and the species as a whole to perpetuate itself. Freud called the energy that fuels the life instincts **libido.**

The death or destructive instincts are less apparent in their operation. Indeed, Freud did not originally include them in his system. Only after the apparently senseless slaughter of World War I did he decide that his theory required some such concept. In a famous dictum, "The goal of all life is death" (1920/1955, p. 38), he pessimistically expressed his view of the relationship between life and death.

According to Freud, the human system is continually experiencing tension caused by both internal and external pressures. The goal of the id is immediate tension reduction. When a person experiences a need, such as hunger, this is felt as an uncomfortable state of tension. The id automatically strives to reduce this tension and return to a low energy level. Freud called this the **pleasure principle.**

The id seeks immediate gratification without resort to objective reality. For example, if the organism is hungry, the id will create a mental image of "food" or a mother's breast. Creating an image of the desired object is called **wish fulfillment.** This obviously does not enable an organism to survive—an image of food cannot satisfy hunger—so the organism has to evolve a mode of thinking that can relate its needs to the external or objective world, where real, material food exists. This mode of thinking, which is based on logic and reason, Freud called **secondary-process thinking,** as opposed to the id's **primary-process thinking.** This secondary process, which developed out of the id and became differentiated from it, is the ego.

Ego. The **ego,** in contrast to the id, is concerned with, and aware of, objective reality. The ego seeks actual food, not an image of it. In general, the ego attempts to "match" objects in the external world as closely as possible to the images created by the id. The ego is devoted primarily to protecting the organism and to coping with the real world.

The ego will not allow the organism to release tension until it has located the object in the external world that will satisfy the instinctual need. Because the ego resorts to external reality to satisfy needs, it is said to obey the **reality principle** (as against the id's pleasure principle). If necessary, the ego will delay the organism's attempts at immediate gratification and pleasure, either because these attempts are unlikely to be successful or because greater gratification can be gained by waiting. The ego, therefore, is concerned with what is good and bad for the organism on the basis of objective criteria.

The ego is not the "enemy" of the id. In the most fundamental sense, it exists to serve the id's needs, to work in its behalf. The ego and id only come into conflict over the best way to do this. The ego seeks to pospone gratification until a real object in the external world has been found to satisfy an instinctual need. The id, on the other hand, demands immediate gratification and has no awareness of or concern about external reality—it is unsocialized and unconscious.

Superego. The last personality system to be differentiated from the id is the **superego.** Often referred to as the "conscience" or "moral arm" of the personality, the superego is concerned with moral ideals. These ideals are originally conveyed to the child by the parents; later, other authority figures and the rewards and punishments imposed by society also play a part in shaping the growing child's development of self-control.

The superego deals in absolute rules. Unlike the ego, which seeks compromise, the superego strives for perfection. It does not function merely to postpone id impulses, as the ego does; it seeks to block them permanently. In this effort it is as persistent and unyielding as the id. Many of the people Freud saw as patients could be described as being in unbearable conflict between the strong demands laid down by their ids and the absolute prohibitions on fulfilling those demands laid down by their superegos. Their egos were so weakened in the attempt to cope with this psychic conflict that they were no longer able to meet the day-to-day demands of ordinary life.

Jean Cocteau's drawing of Sigmund Freud. The set of eyes peering out from the body is Cocteau's way of symbolizing Freud's emphasis on the effects of the id on human behavior.

Defense Mechanisms

Defense mechanisms are automatic and unconscious reactions in response to intrapsychic conflict. They are used to ward off anxiety and serve to allow a compromise between the demands of the id and society. A defense mechanism works in one of two ways: (1) It blocks a sexual or aggressive impulse, and thus relieves the anxiety and guilt caused by such impulses; or (2) it changes the nature of the impulse itself, and both relieves the guilt and anxiety and permits some gratification of the now-transformed impulse.

Freud and his followers identified several strategies that people use to cope with stress or anxiety stemming from intrapsychic conflict.

Repression. People who use this coping method exclude their unacceptable drives, thoughts, and feelings from their consciousness. Evidence of **repression** is underreaction to a relevant situation and indirect indications that the repressed tendencies are actually present. For example, a woman feels angry at having to pay taxes, but blocks that feeling from her awareness. That her anger is actually present is shown indirectly—she forgets to sign or enclose the check with her tax return.

Displacement. Repression can lead directly to **displacement** because the most common type of repressive barricade is to focus attention on a substitute—to displace attention. If you have ever been angry at a boss or a professor and were unable to express that anger to that person, you may have found yourself lashing out at your roommate or a stranger in the street. Because you could not show anger at the person who provoked it, you displaced that anger onto a more acceptable target.

Projection. One way to block unacceptable thoughts and feelings is to attribute them to another person. This is called **projection.** A person who feels guilty about aggressive business practices may attribute to competitors the same practices and claim that their actions made it necessary to retaliate. Projection locates the responsibility for one's behavior outside oneself and removes the guilt and conflict that the behavior would otherwise cause.

Reaction Formation. In **reaction formation** we reverse our unacceptable feelings. For example, a man may hate his mother because she nags him and makes extraordinary demands on him. The conflict between his angry impulses and his superego's command to honor and love his parents causes him anxiety and guilt. To relieve those feelings, he unconsciously converts his hatred into exaggerated love and devotion and acts like a model son. We sometimes hold a number of deeply felt attitudes that are the direct opposites of our repressed attitudes.

Negation. This is another way of refusing to acknowledge unacceptable feelings. In **negation** the feeling is expressed, but with a "negative sign" next to it. Take the example of the man who hates his mother. If his method of coping is reaction formation, he will say, "I love my mother." If he uses negation to cope, he will state, emphatically, "I don't hate my mother." And often he will make this statement out of the blue, when no one has been questioning or challenging his feelings about his mother. If he states his love negatively, he will be able to get rid of the anger he is feeling without acknowledging its unacceptable source.

Intellectualization. This is simply an exaggerated preference for thought over feeling. A person who uses **intellectualization** will talk about sexual or aggressive matters in a very cool, detached way. This prevents that person from experiencing any of the feelings most of us have when discussing these subjects. Teenagers often use this defense mechanism in "bull sessions" in which sexual matters are discussed in the abstract. Intellectualization helps them get through many of the conflicts that are inevitable in growing up.

Undoing. **Undoing** means following an unacceptable act with one that negates it, thus relieving the guilt and anxiety that resulted from the first act. It is the only defense mechanism that is an "after-the-fact" response. The other defense mechanisms operate to prevent unacceptable thoughts or feelings from occurring. A husband who habitually argues with his wife in the morning and then brings her flowers when he comes home from work is using the undoing defense. He would be quite surprised if you confronted him with this pattern, though, and would deny that that was what he was doing.

Regression. In **regression** a person flees anxiety by retreating into behavior appropriate to an earlier, seemingly safer stage in life. A little girl going through the stress of entering school for the first time may begin to act in a very babyish way: She may suck her thumb, wet her bed, or insist on being carried by her mother or father instead of walking.

Sublimation. **Sublimation** is the channeling of unacceptable urges and feelings into acceptable activities. Freud interpreted the madonnas painted by the great Léonardo da Vinci as an example of sublimation of Oedipal feelings—in other words, he believed Leonardo dealt with an unresolved Oedipal conflict by transforming his feelings about his mother into art. Sublimation might also allow an individual to express repressed, sadistic urges in constructive activities such as surgery. Freud believed that the intellectual curiosity of adults was a sublimation of childhood sexual curiosity. Thus the inhibition of creativity that Freud saw in some adults seemed to him to derive from the strong repression of childhood sexual curiosity.

Defense mechanisms are very much a part of normal behavior. But, according to Freud, their overuse is a symptom of neurosis. Overuse means either carrying a defense to an extreme (such as marked regression to a childish state) or habitually resorting to the same defense (such as a lifelong repression of sexual feelings).

The Development of Personality

Freud's model of personality assumes that individuals develop in discrete, observable stages. Successful progression from one stage to the next is a critical determinant of adult mental health. As a physician, Freud investigated these developmental stages by observing the behavior of his patients. He believed that the regularity of the stages of personality development could be best understood by examining those individuals in whom the normal progression had been interrupted or subverted. One of Freud's greatest discoveries was that the roots of his adult patients' difficulties could be traced to their early childhood experiences. According to Freud, the basic patterns of behavior are established at an early age, and later development and growth are consistent with or constrained by these patterns.

One major source of these basic behavior patterns is the person's adaptation to each of the four psychosexual stages of development through which we all pass (see Chapter 13 for a summary of these stages). Freud believed that people who do not resolve the developmental challenges and problems of any one of these stages fixate at that stage. They then fail to solve properly the problems posed by later stages, and as adults they have neurotic problems reflecting the stage at which the **fixation** occurred.

A person can also return to an earlier stage of development when experiencing conflict later in life. These individuals regress, or proceed backward, to the stage at which the fixation occurred. For example, a child experiencing unresolved conflict may return to an oral stage, with infantile behaviors such as thumb sucking; later, that child, now an adult with other problems, may seek refuge in drinking, another type of oral activity.

A person rarely fixates or regresses totally. These are relative conditions. Under a similar set of stresses, one individual may regress to an oral stage, another to a later stage, and a third person may not regress at all.

Freud thought that particular personality problems or behaviors were due to problems in progressing through specific psychosexual stages. For example, a problem in the oral stage, in which the mouth is the primary source of pleasure, can lead to problems with dependency or aggression in the adult. Clinging to authority figures and attempting to draw strength from them can be an oral-stage attempt to solve a problem. Similarly, a "biting," aggressive style of wit can represent a return to the biting, aggressive aspects of the later oral stage. It is important to recognize here that, for Freud, these stages represent a very general and even metaphorical way of coping with the world. The oral stage, for instance, involves some very general impulses of dependency.

Regression to the anal stage would be signaled by a person's being obstinate, overly concerned with orderliness, or parsimonious. Misers and, more generally, people who are unable to "let go" of control may be fixated at the anal stage. Attitudes toward authority and sexual activity are determined by the manner in which the conflicts of the phallic stage (in which the genitals becomes the center of pleasure) are resolved. Little personality development takes place during the latency period, but it is critical to pass through latency to reach the genital stage. in which more altruistic, less self-centered motives become possible. The final resolution of the genital stage allows the individual to function as a mature, well-adjusted member of society.

Jungian Analysis

Carl Jung was a contemporary of Freud's who became a convert to psychoanalytic theory. Freud initially was terribly impressed by Jung, and arranged for him to be elected president of the Psychoanalytic Society, which Freud had founded. However, Jung soon began to deviate from orthodox analytic theory, and as this happened, the relationship between Freud and Jung, originally so warm and intimate, became strained and more distant, and finally ruptured entirely. This was quite characteristic of Freud's relationships with those who came into theoretical disagreement with him.

Jung developed his own theory, called *analytic psychology*. It shared with psychoanalysis an emphasis on personality as a "battlefield" of unconscious urges in conflict with the other systems of the personality. However, Jung argued that Freud's sexually motivated unconscious coexisted with a **collec-**

tive unconscious containing **archetypes** (see Figure 15–4). The collective unconscious is the "memory trace" of our ancestral history, including our animal origins, which exists in each individual and is essentially the same for everyone. It is independent of anything personal in the life of the individual, and at times it can overwhelm both the ego and the personal unconscious (our repressed thoughts, forgotten experiences, and so on). It is likely to surface in dreams, but also in literature, and particularly in cultural myths and in art.

One of the useful points of comparison between psychoanalytic personality theories is their degree of past versus present and future orientation. As we have seen, Freud's theory places heavy emphasis on the past as a determinant of present conflict. Job conflicts with a boss, for example, are likely to have their origins in some unresolved conflict with parental authority formed during a psychosexual stage. Jung, on the other hand, assigned a much more major role to a person's future aims and goals. He argued that a person first attempts to develop certain aspects of his or her personality—a process he called *individuation*—before attempting to integrate them into some more unified whole. Although this unity is rarely achieved, it remains a major goal of human activity. Thus Jung's theory, more than Freud's, suggests the possibility of genuine growth and change.

Jung, like Freud, relied on the free association of patients during therapy sessions; he developed the word associations test to provide clues to his patients' unconscious thought processes. Quite simply, he would say a word to the patient, and the patient was instructed to respond with the first word that came to mind. Jung often included in the test words that he thought might evoke a reaction to the material he was attempting to uncover. So, for example, if horses were thought to be a source of anxiety, Jung might include the word "horse" on the list. Clues to the unconscious were thought to be provided by the association given, the time it took to produce an association, and changes in the patient's demeanor in response to a certain word.

Figure 15–4 Jung's collective unconscious consists of archetypes—primary ideas shared by the human race. According to Jung, archetypes such as the sun god, tree of life, and earth mother were likely to surface in various forms, but particularly in cultural myths and in art. This ancient stone carving is a representation of the winged sun-moon disc and tree of life.

Neo-Freudian Theorists

Both because of his training in the biological sciences and because of the intellectual climate of the time, Freud believed that psychological processes are tied to the biological inheritance of the human being. He considered such concepts as the libido, the stages of development, and the Oedipus complex as essentially biological in nature.

There were two important intellectual consequences of this emphasis on biology. First, it meant that an individual's development has a fixed, immutable character. Second, since humans are biologically the same in all cultures, Freud felt that his theory was universal and did not require serious modification for peoples of other cultures. Put another way, Freud did not think that the specifics of the culture in which one was reared had an important effect on the psychodynamic unfolding of personality development in the early childhood years.

Certain intellectual developments of the early twentieth century challenged this biologically based conceptualization of human nature. About the same time that Freud was formulating and developing psychoanalytic theory, sociology and anthropology were changing people's conception of human nature and the factors that influence behavior. The vivid descriptions of cultural anthropologists were making Westerners aware that other cultures existed with social systems and patterns that were dramatically different from

those of Europe and the United States. And in at least some of these cultures such Freudian "universals" as the latency period simply did not occur. Individuals and their personalities did not grow in splendid isolation during which biological patterns dictated a single sequence of development, but rather in a cultural context that had its own sequences of growth and development, and its own standards of "normal" behavior and desirable personality.

The implications of this cross-cultural perspective for psychoanalytic theory were there for Freud's younger colleagues to contend with. As they absorbed the thinking of the times and substituted sociocultural for biological determinants, this "second generation" of Freudian thinkers modified Freudian theory in interesting and important ways.

Neo-Freudians such as Alfred Adler and Karen Horney took issue with Freud and Jung's insistence on the role of instinct in determining behavior. They emphasized social rather than biological determinants of personality motivation, and believed that anxiety and conflict result from the social conditions in which people find themselves rather than from the preordained unfolding of biological needs. Adler (1930) suggested that instead of being motivated by sexual and aggressive instincts, people were motivated to "strive for superiority." This was not seen as superiority over other people, but as a quest for self-improvement and perfection. Interestingly, Adler also suggested that people are motivated to strive for the public good. In other words, as we mature, we begin to direct our social commitments toward specific social ends as a way of attaining feelings of superiority.

The opposite of superiority is inferiority, so it will not surprise you that it was Adler (1931) who developed the concept of the *inferiority complex*. This has its origins in the childhood discovery that there are things we cannot do that others (perhaps because they are adults) can do. Not unnaturally, we feel inferior. Most of us successfully overcome these feelings of inferiority; those who do not usually manage to convey the appearance of competence but retain internal feelings of inferiority. To such individuals, every success seems to be achieved by the narrowest of margins. Every new situation presents not a challenge but the occasion for disastrous failure. Unless one returns to childhood patterns as the source of these internal feelings and attempts to work them out, the inferiority complex will prevail.

Karen Horney also differed from Freud in regarding the basic sources of conflict as social in origin. According to Horney, every child feels *basic anxiety* about being small and helpless in a demanding world. Dependable parents allay this anxiety by providing security for the child. Erratic, rejecting, or nonresponsive parents add to a child's feelings of basic anxiety. These feelings are experienced by all children at some time, and by neglected children much of the time. Basic anxiety leads to feelings of *basic hostility* toward the parents, though, of course, these hostile feelings cannot be expressed directly because the child needs and depends on the parents.

Horney believed that how the anxiety-hostility conflict is managed later in life is the key to adult personalities. A maladjusted person almost always copes with anxiety by relating to people solely in one of three ways: by "moving toward others," "moving against others," or "moving away from others." The choice of one of these coping styles is made in childhood. One child copes with anxiety-hostility by figuratively moving toward the powerful other, perhaps by showing affection to gain nurturance. Later in life this might manifest itself as a tendency toward subjugation, or a willingness to curry favor. Another child might move against others by hitting or bullying people. As an adult, this type of person deals with the fear of losing control

by seizing control. Still another child might habitually cope with anxiety-hostility by moving away from people. As an adult, this person will keep isolated and withdrawn in order to protect him- or herself, giving up the possibilities of real human relationships.

According to Horney, a well-adjusted individual copes with anxiety by choosing whichever of the three modes is appropriate to the situation. Also, he or she will exhibit a reasonably mature form of coping response. A well-adjusted person will not usually assert power by hitting another person but by assertively stating his or her own needs or wishes. A mature response to an untrustworthy individual would be to withdraw from that individual, but not from people in general.

Horney's emphasis on social determinants also led her to take issue with Freud's view of female personality development. Freud held that women failed to achieve much in society and become strong leaders because they did not develop mature superegos (Freud believed that penis envy during the resolution of the Oedipus complex was responsible for this arrested development). Horney disagreed sharply. She argued that it was not the inevitable workings of the Oedipus complex, but rather the ways in which society defines women's dependency, the ways women are taught to cope with dependency, and particularly men's stereotyped attitudes toward women that explain women's lower performance. Changes in women's status in society since Freud, and their noticeably greater level of achievement, suggest that Horney was correct in her assessment.

Ego Psychology

A second group of theorists shared with Freud and Jung a belief in the importance of the unconscious, but they gave a more independent role to the ego. Because of this emphasis, they have been called "ego psychologists." In suggesting that the ego had its own powers independent of the id, the ego psychologists were in effect saying that people are capable of a wider sphere of rational activity than orthodox psychoanalytic theory granted. As compared to Freud's deterministic approach, they saw people as freer—at least potentially—to choose their own fates.

Erik Erikson, a prominent ego psychologist, concentrated on the personality development of the individual through successive stages of life. His theory, like Freud's, suggests that the early stages of development are those in which a child is required to integrate biological needs with the demands of society. Unlike Freud, who maintained that the personality was permanently laid down during early childhood, Erikson maintained that personality continued to grow and develop throughout the life span. At each stage a person could fail to meet the challenge that society sets. The person's development could then be arrested at that stage, causing problems in moving beyond it. For example, a child whose parents fail to generate trust and support at the oral stage may well have difficulty trusting others throughout life. An adolescent whose relationships with peers do not allow her to properly solve her identity conflicts may suffer from role confusion throughout successive stages.

Like Jung and others, Erikson suggests that a person strives toward developing an integrated sense of self. Achieving this can be more difficult in some societies than others. In the more traditional societies young people know, with a fair degree of certainty, how they will live. Other societies

present more transitional crises for an individual. In our own society, for instance, adolescents are faced with such a variety of career and value choices that they experience what Erikson was first to term an *identity crisis.*

THE HUMANISTIC-EXISTENTIAL MODEL OF PERSONALITY

The common emphasis of humanistic and existential theories is on the total personality as opposed to the separate behaviors that make up that personality. This is a radically antideterministic view that minimizes not only the effects of environment but also those of biology. The emphasis is on choice and the personal responsibility that being able to make choices implies.

The **humanistic-existential model** stresses personal experience and what that experience means to the individual as the basis of human personality and behavior. In order to understand the behavior of another person, we must first understand the way that person constructs his or her world.

As we mentioned before, the psychoanalytic model of personality is basically one of *conflict* between the pleasure-seeking id and a restrictive society. Existential psychologists deemphasize conflict and favor a model that emphasizes *striving:* awareness of one's own actions, understanding and acceptance of their consequences, and eagerness to embrace future choices. This condition of striving is known as being *authentic.* Being authentic includes being aware of the fear that one's choices may be wrong. This fear, or *ontological anxiety,* must be accepted as a part of being if an individual is to be authentic. A person who ignores or hides from this fear, or refuses to accept responsibility for his or her actions, becomes inauthentic and riddled with guilt. Since every choice we make involves giving up all the other choices available to us at that moment, all choices involve some pain because they mean forgoing other possibilities.

Nonetheless, particularly among the American practitioners of humanistic-existential psychology such as Maslow and Rogers, a more optimistic theme emerges. The basic force motivating human behavior is the need for growth and self-direction. People are seen as continually striving for increased awareness, self-actualization, and the fulfillment of their human potential.

Motives for Growth: Goldstein and Maslow

Abraham Maslow developed his approach to personality from the study of healthy, creative people. In general, he objected to the usual emphasis of personality theories on neurosis and maladaptive behavior, which he argued derived from the fact that most personality theorists were therapists who worked with disturbed individuals. Maslow believed that in every person "there is an active will toward health, an impulse toward growth, or toward the actualization of human potentialities" (1967, p. 153). This view stands in sharp contrast to Freudian and other theories that claim we have impulses, instincts, urges, or traits that stand in opposition to society and that need to be repressively socialized through training and education.

Maslow drew on the work of Kurt Goldstein, a neuropsychiatrist who had developed a theory about positive motives for behavior. In Goldstein's theory any need motivates us to satisfy it. But underlying all our needs is one real drive, one true motive: to self-actualize, to continuously realize our own po-

tential by whatever means we can. The drive for **self-actualization** gives unity and organization to the personality. The tasks we perform to satisfy a need are the way we work toward self-actualization.

We may all have the same drive for self-actualization, but the means and ends we seek vary. This is because, according to Goldstein, we have different inherent preferences and potentialities. These not only help define our means and ends, they also influence our individual development.

According to Goldstein, our drive for self-actualization comes from within, and the healthy individual can overcome "the disturbance arising from the clash with the world, not out of anxiety but out of the joy of conquest" (1939, p. 305). The individual has the possibility of *mastery* or *control* of the environment. However, if the realities of the environment are too inconsistent with the goals of the individual, the individual will break down or redefine his or her goals.

An environment, then, must allow an individual to be in a state that is normal or adequate to his or her nature. If the environment is too unstable, the constancy and identity of the individual are threatened. If, during childhood development, the environment is too stressful or inconsistent with the needs of the individual, Goldstein says, the child will develop behavior patterns that deter the process of self-actualization.

Maslow's need hierarchy, which we discussed Chapter 12, can be used to clarify the conditions under which this occurs. Maslow divides his need hierarchy into two groups, one based on deficiency, the other on growth. The former (for example, the need for food) Maslow calls **basic needs;** the latter (for example, the desire for beauty, justice, and goodness) are called **meta-needs.** Basic needs, according to Maslow, are basic in the sense that if they are unfulfilled, people give them priority over other needs. A starving person seeks food and has no time or energy for appreciating works of art. For Maslow, self-actualization is the final concern of the person: It can receive attention only after the physiological, safety, belonging and love, and esteem needs have been met.

If the physical and social environments do not provide fulfillment of these basic needs, the person will seek to satisfy them by whatever means possible. Thus the environment can either temporarily or permanently block or thwart the natural drive for self-actualization. A person who sees the world as threatening or unpredictable may pursue safety or security needs to the exclusion of self-actualization. Maslow believed in the possibilities of personal growth and thought it worthwhile to urge people to self-actualize. He described in detail the characteristics of the self-actualized person (see Table 15–2).

Self Theory: Rogers

Like Goldstein and Maslow, Carl Rogers, in his **person-centered personality theory,** viewed the individual as a whole being composed of complex cognitive, emotional, biological, and other processes and capable of self-actualization. Like Jung and Adler, Rogers also emphasized the role of the **self** and conscious awareness in the life of the individual. Like many other personality theorists, he constantly tried to help people with their problems. Perhaps because many of the people he saw were college students, Rogers reached a more optimistic conclusion about personal growth than did other theorists.

In keeping with the humanistic-existential tradition, Rogers placed great

Table 15–2: The Characteristics of Self-Actualized Individuals.

1. Are able to perceive reality accurately.
2. Are able to accept reality readily.
3. Are natural and spontaneous.
4. Can focus on problems rather than on themselves.
5. Have a need for privacy.
6. Are self-sufficient and independent.
7. Are capable of fresh, spontaneous, nonstereotyped appreciation of objects, events, and people that they encounter.
8. Have peak experiences, and attain transcendence.
9. Identify with mankind, and experience shared social bonds with other people.
10. May have few or many friends, but will have deep relationships with at least some of these friends.
11. Have a democratic, egalitarian attitude.
12. Have strongly held values and do not confuse means with ends.
13. Have a broad, tolerant sense of humor.
14. Are inventive and creative, and able to see things in new ways.
15. Resist the pressures of conformity to society.
16. Are able to transcend dichotomies, bring together opposites.

From Maslow (1967).

emphasis on the individual's total experience at a given moment. This unique personal experience, the **phenomenal field** of the individual, cannot be directly known by another. Rogers believed that knowing how people interpret their experiences is the first step in understanding their personality and behavior. But he also pointed out that elements of people's experience may be incorrectly represented by them, or not represented at all. A healthy, mature condition of adjustment exists, he said, when people accurately symbolize to themselves their phenomenal field. Maladjustment arises when there is a gap between people's actual experience and their awareness of it—in other words, when they deny or distort parts of their experience.

The self-image is particularly important in the development of personality. Each of us has an image of our real self (the self as it is) and of an ideal self (the self we'd like to be). The self-image develops from interaction with others. Our parents reward "worthy" actions and feelings and punish "unworthy" actions and feelings. If children are forced to give up or deny the "unworthy" actions or feelings (rather than learn to express them in more acceptable ways), they are compelled to deny a part of their existence. Their self-image then becomes inconsistent with their actual experience. Because their behavior is regulated not just by their own perceptions and feelings, but also by values they have incorporated from their parents and others, their personality is in effect divided.

The condition for self-actualization, therefore, is trusting one's own experience in the evaluation of oneself rather than evaluating oneself on the basis of the needs and interests of others. According to Rogers, a period of positive regard from parents and others in our lives helps us to do this.

It is difficult in this preliminary discussion to explain fully all the differences between the humanistic-existential theories and all other theories of personality. In Chapters 17 and 18, where we discuss the humanistic perspective on abnormal psychology and the existential modes of therapy, other distinctions will become clear. In brief, the humanistic-existential approaches assert that people have the freedom to choose the actions they take; because

they do so, they have the capacity to grow and develop. But the other side of the coin is that they may use that same freedom to choose actions that limit or diminish their lives.

THE LEARNING MODEL OF PERSONALITY

The learning and conditioned-response theories of personality are based on findings and theories described in Chapter 6. Learning theorists believe that human beings, like rats and pigeons, respond to stimuli presented by other people or by the external world. The environment controls our behavior through the reinforcement contingencies it delivers. Learning theorists hold that the human personality is a set of patterns of learned behaviors. A set of stimulus conditions is presented, the person responds to it, and reinforcement may follow. If it does, the response will be repeated if the stimulus conditions recur.

A problem that all personality theories must address is the development of uniqueness. Learning theorists believe that people's personalities differ because of childhood differences in stimulus patterns, reinforcement contingencies, and punishment patterns. If we know someone's reinforcement history, we should be able to predict that person's present behavior patterns. Even though the human personality is complex, it is based on simple learning principles.

Conditioned Anxiety: Dollard and Miller

One of the important contributions of learning theory to personality dynamics is the theory of conditioned anxiety conceived of by John Dollard and Neil Miller (1950). As we saw in our discussion of conditioning in Chapter 6, a tone originally may be a neutral stimulus, but if it is frequently followed by an electric shock, the tone becomes a cue for fear responses originally produced by the shock. Further, animals have been able to learn new responses to escape from or terminate an anxiety cue. Two properties of conditioned anxiety make it a particularly important concept in learning theories of personality. First, anxiety may be conditioned to a previously neutral stimulus by just a few pairings, and sometimes by a single pairing. Given the normal hurts and harms of an ordinary childhood, we probably all have many conditioned fears. Second, because people learn responses that get them out of an anxiety situation, they may never discover that the original reason for the anxiety—the physical or emotional pain that once followed the cue—is no longer present. The child who avoids the swing from which he or she once fell may not discover that with a little practice the swing is easy to manage. Conditioned anxiety theory gives us an insight into why many people continue to engage in patterns of action that seem to be useless or even self-defeating: They do so because these patterns remove them from anxiety cues and do not allow them to discover that the original source of the fear is gone.

Operant Conditioning: Skinner

Skinner's learning principles (see Chapter 6) proved useful in specifying the ways in which a person's history of reinforcements determines that person's behavior. The simplest kind of learning is based on *classical conditioning,* in

which an initially neutral stimulus is paired with an unconditioned stimulus that causes an unconditioned response. Pavlov's famous demonstration of a dog being conditioned to salivate at the sound of a tone is an example of this, as is the conditioning of fear to a previously neutral stimulus, which Dollard and Miller used as the basis of conditioned anxiety.

Skinner, however, was most concerned with reinforcement in *operant conditioning*. In this type of conditioning, the likelihood that a response will be emitted is affected by whether that response was followed by reinforcement in the past. Reinforcement is the primary way in which people learn responses and control the responses of others.

In the course of personality development a child learns to respond to certain stimuli with certain responses and to give very different responses to other stimuli. This learning takes place through stimulus generalization and discrimination. A child cuddles a furry toy and is reinforced by its pleasing texture and the parents' smiles. Because of stimulus generalization, the child will at first respond to a real furry cat by cuddling it—it looks like the furry toy and therefore elicits the response given to the toy. The scratches of the squashed cat teach the child stimulus discrimination: The child learns to discriminate between two physically similar stimuli because the environment rewards the response to one and not the other.

Is it possible to use this model to account for the acquisition of behavior that is maladaptive, harmful, or abnormal? Skinner and other learning theorists have proposed several mechanisms to explain such behavior. The first we have already mentioned: Conditioned anxiety can cause a person to try to escape from a once-threatening stimulus situation in which no real reasons for fear remain. Skinner suggests three other mechanisms that may produce maladaptive behavior.

The first is "random" or chance reinforcement. Occasionally the environment delivers a reward to people that is quite independent of their actions. Nonetheless, the reinforcement increases the probability that a person will repeat whatever action he or she was emitting when the reward was delivered. This type of reinforcement, where there is no cause-and-effect relation between action and reward, can lead to "superstitious" behavior. For example, a person who wore a particular shirt just before winning a big game may wear it again because it "brought luck." While this example is fairly harmless, accidental or random reinforcement can result in continued self-destructive behavior, as when depressive symptoms are accidentally rewarded by winning a lottery. The likelihood of future depressive behavior is increased by the simple chance pairing of a reinforcement (winning the lottery) with past depressive episodes.

Sometimes, of course, the reinforcement is not produced at random. For example, a friend may deliberately increase the care and attention given to a depressed individual. While this might temporarily help the depressed person in certain ways, conditioning theorists would argue that it also reinforces depression, and thus increases its likelihood. There is an interesting parallel here with the psychoanalytic concept of *secondary gains*. Psychoanalytic theorists point out that people suffering with phobias, depression, and other personality difficulties are also benefiting from their symptoms. Other people do things for them, give them attention, and so forth. Thus a force is set in motion that works to sustain their symptoms. For the conditioning theorist, that force is explained by the reinforcing properties of the secondary gains.

Skinner's second reward mechanism for producing unwanted behaviors centers on ambiguities about what exactly is reinforcing. Tired or preoccu-

pied parents may not pay attention to their children until the children get out of hand. The attention may then take the form of scolding, but it may also have rewarding elements. Sadly, some people get so little attention that they find almost any form of it rewarding. A patient in a mental hospital, for instance, gradually became too uncoordinated to eat and had to be fed by an attendant. The few words the harassed but kindly attendant addressed to her while feeding her were the only pleasant human interactions the patient had all day and led her to behave in ways that demanded more and more of the attendant's time.

Skinner's third conditioning mechanism accounting for maladaptive behavior was provided by his discovery of schedules of reinforcement. For any of the reasons we just discussed, undesirable behavior may have been at least occasionally reinforced in a person's past. The problem is why that behavior does not cease in the present, when it is obviously maladaptive. The answer, for reinforcement theorists, lies in their observations of the effects of intermittent schedules of reinforcement on responding. You will recall that responses learned under conditions of intermittent reinforcement are not only much more resistant to extinction than responses that are always reinforced, but are also often emitted at higher rates. This has clear implications for maladaptive behaviors. Consider dependent behaviors as a case in point. During childhood such behaviors may have been appropriate and thus reinforced. In adulthood they are inappropriate and generally cause difficulties with other people. Still, they may occasionally produce positive results, or accidentally be coincident in time with positive results. Thus the person continues to make childish responses, sometimes at quite a high rate.

Social-Learning Theory: Bandura

Bandura and other **social-learning theorists** agree that personality consists of patterns of human responses that are learned, and they acknowledge the validity of the learning mechanisms as defined by Dollard and Miller and by Skinner in conditions of direct reinforcement. Their major contribution has been to point out that there is a second kind of learning that is very important for personality development: They show that people can learn through **observational learning,** by observing the responses of others.

In fact, it can be argued that most of our learning is of this indirect, observational kind. Children, for example, can learn a new response just by watching others, without ever having made that response themselves and without having been reinforced themselves or even having seen anyone else being reinforced for the response. In one study (Bandura, Ross, & Ross, 1961) some nursery-school children watched adults behave aggressively toward an oversized doll, while other children watched nonaggressive adults sit quietly, ignoring the doll. The children were later placed in a room with the doll, and their behavior toward it was observed. Those who had watched the more aggressive adult models were more aggressive toward the doll than the children who had observed nonaggressive models.

It has been found that observational learning can take place when the model is presented symbolically, as in films or on TV, as well as in real-life situations. Models in films and TV are very influential—children who watched a model behave aggressively on TV or in a film were just as likely to imitate that behavior as children who observed a model who was physically present (Bandura, Ross, and Ross, 1963b).

Observing models may help to reduce inhibitions, especially if the model

Models seen on TV can be as influential as those who are physically present. There has been a great deal of concern over the effect that the violence shown on TV has on the children who watch it. (Renate Hiller/Monkmeyer Press)

is doing something that is not socially acceptable. In this case the observer may not so much be learning a new response as gaining the nerve to make a response that before was only imagined (Walters & Thomas, 1963). Again, imitation may depend on the observer's ability to discover the reinforcement structure of the situation. A model who is not punished for an action may be particularly effective in removing inhibition of a similar action in the observer.

Certain aspects of the modeling situation affect the influence of the model:

1. *Whether the model being observed is rewarded or punished.* Although people may imitate a model who is not rewarded, they are much more likely to imitate models who have been rewarded for their behavior than those who have been punished or have not received any reward (Bandura, Ross, & Ross, 1963a). However, even when a model has been punished, people may still imitate the model's behavior if the threat of punishment is subsequently removed (Bandura, 1965).

2. *Characteristics of models.* These characteristics include age, sex, and social status, but most important is whether or not the model is seen as powerful or weak. Children are much more likely to imitate a model who seems powerful to them than one who seems weak (Jakubczak & Walters, 1959). Thus for a young child, the most commonly imitated model is likely to be the same-sex parent, although the effectiveness of models presented through the mass media, particularly television, cannot be overlooked (Liebert, Neale, & Davidson, 1973).

According to Bandura, people do not merely learn to imitate specific behaviors; they are also capable of generalizing from one situation to another. However, the degree to which the generalization occurs has not been entirely spelled out by empirical research. In addition, there is still a great deal of disagreement concerning the conditions under which imitation will occur. For example, empirical research into the effects of television violence on aggressive behavior in children has yielded mixed findings. In some situations viewing aggressive behavior led to more aggression (Liebert & Baron, 1972; Parke, Berkowitz, Leyens, West, & Sebastian, 1977); in others viewing an aggressive sequence decreased viewers' levels of aggressive behavior (Feshback & Singer, 1971); still other studies indicate that the degree of imitation of aggressive behavior may be a function of individual personality characteristics of the viewer (Stein & Friedrich, 1972).

Although a large body of research in social learning deals with the imitation of aggression, it is important to note that aggressive behavior is not the only kind of behavior that can be learned. Research has also shown that with the right models, individuals can learn to imitate altruistic behavior such as sharing (Midlarsky, Bryan, & Brickman, 1973) or helping (Bryan & Test, 1967). Thus, whether or not imitation will occur does not seem to depend on the *type* of behavior being observed, but rather on characteristics of the models themselves and the situation in which they are presented.

Bandura and Rosenthal (1976) pointed out another type of learning that is important in social-learning theory, and that is vicarious learning of classically conditioned emotional responses. For example, if a person observes a model reacting with extreme fear and repugnance to a stimulus, the next time that stimulus is presented, the observer may react the same way. For example, small children, before they are toilet-trained, often play with their fecal material with no signs of disgust. But their parents react to these activities

with expressions of repugnance. Soon, even in the parents' absence, the child responds to his feces with disgust. Through vicarious conditioning the child has learned the accepted social response.

Fears, particularly, are easily learned this way. Bandura has shown that the conditioned anxiety-avoidance sequence described by Dollard and Miller may begin not as the person's *own* anxiety experience, but as a second-hand fear acquired from observing another. This other may even be a character in a drama. It is interesting to speculate about how many of our anxieties are acquired from the overcharged excitements of television and the movies.

Social-learning theorists have made important additions to a learning theory of personality: People can learn indirectly by observing the actions of others and the consequences of those actions.

More recently, Bandura (1977, 1978) has been considering the influence of the goals people set for themselves and their evaluations of their success or failure in meeting those goals. People's self-evaluation standards affect their reactions to their own performance. They gain self-respect by living up to their standards and experience disappointment from not reaching them. These self-standards, Bandura points out, are an important part of all our experience, and "to ignore the influential role of self-evaluation reactions in the self-regulation of behavior is to disavow a uniquely human capacity" (1978, p. 351).

Bandura has explored self-evaluation in a therapeutic context as well, in developing the concept of **self-efficacy** (Bandura, 1977). A sense of self-efficacy refers to a person's expectation of having the power to control specific situations and influence events in a positive way. Achieving a sense of self-efficacy is a little like becoming "authentic" in the existential sense. The difference between them lies in the grounding of self-efficacy in actual behavior. According to social-learning theory, one can *learn* to be efficacious through imitation of others. People who lack a sense of self-efficacy may be fearful, depressed, or unable to cope with certain stressful situations. Indeed, Bandura suggests that such mental health problems as phobias can be alleviated by giving sufferers a sense of mastering these particular situations. This sense of competence would then generalize to competence, or at least more effective coping, in other problem areas.

Therapists can teach people to feel more efficacious by allowing them to interact with efficacious models. In this technique, known as *participant modeling,* the model is gradually phased out as the individual takes a larger and more positive role in a series of tasks (Bandura, Jeffery, & Wright, 1974). This approach was tried with individuals who feared snakes. Snake phobics became less fearful (as measured by their willingness to approach snakes) after being exposed to an efficacious model and taught to feel efficacious themselves (Bandura, Adams, & Beyer, 1966).

THE BEHAVIORAL CONSISTENCY CONTROVERSY

By now, you will have noticed that the theories we have been discussing have moved away from the trait approach with which we began the chapter. Recall that trait approaches state that internal, relatively stable forces of personality have a consistent effect on behavior. Trait theorists hold that persons should therefore exhibit consistent trait-linked patterns of behavior across many situations. A different view is that individual responses in any situation do not reflect consistent traits but instead vary according to the situation.

The classic study in this area was conducted by Hartshorne and May (1928) on honesty in children. Children were put in a number of situations in which they had a chance to be dishonest and believed they would not be detected. For example, they were given money to play with that they could have kept, they were asked to report about work done at home, or they were observed taking tests to see who would cheat and who would not. The children were neither consistently honest nor consistently dishonest. Rather, their behavior seemed specific to the situation.

Walter Mischel (1968, 1976), a leading proponent of the situationalist view, argues for a shift in focus away from the characteristics of the person to the characteristics of the situation. Personality theories cannot be based on traits, he argues, because people do not show the consistency of behavior across situations that trait theory requires them to. Instead, theories of personality must be *situationalist:* They must include descriptions of situations since these situations control people's responses.

We have just reviewed the learning theory approach to personality development, and it is clear that this view is compatible with a situationalist perspective. In fact, Mischel uses the stimulus-discrimination principle of learning as a basis for his argument: People can learn to make very different responses to similar stimuli if past reinforcement contingencies have led them to do so. More recently, Mischel has drawn on cognitive and attributional theories of human action that make a similar point in a different way. These theories hold that it is necessary to take into account a person's perceptual and cognitive processes—how someone uniquely perceives, organizes, and interprets the social environment—before deciding how that person will respond.

Mischel also argues that research should determine when situational variables are more important and when personality variables are more important. This depends on the strength or weakness of the situation. When a situation leads everyone to make the same interpretation, induces uniform expectancies, and requires skills that everyone can perform, situational variables are more important. A red light is an example of a strong situational variable—it is perceived uniformly by nearly everyone and leads to predictable patterns of behavior. On the other hand, if you ask how someone will behave at a cocktail party, the answer will be far less certain. When situations are ambiguous, personality variables exert a greater influence on behavior.

Mischel's recent research (1985) suggests one class of situations in which people do show consistent behaviors. He has found that people do exhibit consistent modes of responding—for example, aggressively or dependently—in circumstances where other skills do not help them cope adequately with the situational demands. This implies that consistency appears in situations when the person is performing inadequately.

There have been remarkably few studies of persons that span long periods in their lives. Perhaps this is not surprising when you consider the enormous patience and financial support such studies require, not to mention the difficulties of keeping track of people in our highly mobile culture. The investigators from one of the few such projects undertaken have found evidence for consistency in personality across the life span of their subjects (Block, 1971, 1981). Respondents were first tested in junior high school, and follow-up was conducted at intervals into their 40s. Certain characteristics for males seemed relatively stable over time. Males who were seen by raters as being dependable and responsible continued to be seen that way through life. Similar consistency was observed for those who were seen as undercontrolled, impulsive, and unable to delay gratification. Self-defeating behaviors

were also seen as continuing through life. For females, submissiveness, gregariousness, and rebelliousness were all characteristics that were seen by raters as persisting over time. (The first two seem to be stereotypical female characteristics that now may be changing, so perhaps it is important to point out that these traits were characteristic of females who were born at a particular time into the American culture.)

In this study some individuals changed more over time than others. The researchers report that these individuals had adolescences characterized by stress, tension, and conflict, both within themselves and with those around them. From this description, in contrast to the description of better adjustment in those adolescents who changed less later in life, we can surmise that changes were precipitated by the difficulties that the "changers" experienced in their insecure earlier years.

Other contemporary theorists argue that there is reasonable evidence for personality consistency and that we need not adopt Mischel's situationalist perspective. For instance, a more sophisticated mathematical analysis of the Hartshorne and May (1928) data reveals patterns of consistent behavior. More recently, Epstein (1979) has demonstrated that when several measurements of a person's behavior are taken rather than a few, there is more evidence for consistency. Mischel and Peake (1983) reply that the type of consistency Epstein has shown is one that they have never denied—consistent behavior across repeated instances of the same situation. But this is not the kind of consistency suggested by trait theory, which is consistency across different situations that all measure a specific trait such as honesty.

Still other researchers have suggested that consistency in behavior across situations varies among individuals. Bem and Allan (1974), for instance, have shown that people are capable of identifying the traits on which they are consistent, and are in fact rated as consistent across situations on those traits by parents and friends. Further, some people identify themselves as consistent on many traits, while others report only a few consistent traits. Two implications follow from this. First, if we study consistency of behavior on a specified trait across many persons, we will find low estimates of consistency because inevitably we will include in the study people for whom it is not important to be consistent on that trait. Second, it begins to sound as if what is important here is not some stimulus-response patterns, but the person's image of him- or herself. These sorts of findings have led to what is frequently called the *interactionalist* approach to personality.

Researchers who favor the interactionalist approach (Magnusson & Endler, 1977) maintain that behavior is best predicted not from traits or situations alone, but rather from some combination (interaction) of the two. It is not enough for a person to report being independent-minded; we would need to know what situations that person thought should count as requiring a show of independence. A number of theories (Cantor & Kihlstrom, 1983) now being developed take the interactionalist approach.

To understand this interactionalist approach, we need to consider one last class of personality theories, the *social-cognitive* model of personality.

THE SOCIAL-COGNITIVE MODEL OF PERSONALITY

Cognitive theories draw on what psychologists have learned about the information-processing strategies of human beings—namely, that people construct internal representations of persons, events, and situations, and act

in terms of these internal representations. For the cognitive psychologist, personality is made up of people's particular and unique representations of the interpersonal and physical situations in which they find themselves: Their actions flow from their perspectives. By taking this as their working principle, cognitive personality theorists have made central and explicit a principle toward which other personality theories are converging.

Personal Construct Theory

Kelly (1955), for example, focuses on how people make sense out of, or construe, experience. In his view, people create their own picture, or **personal construct,** of reality by actively perceiving, evaluating, and organizing their own experience. Kelly suggests that it is useful to think of ourselves as scientists, going about making sense out of our own world in the same way that scientists make sense out of their field of study. Not only do we construe events and objects, but we also try to find cause-and-effect relationships. We use our understanding of these to predict future events and to intervene in the world in effective ways, trying to control events and produce outcomes that we desire.

People constantly try to make more accurate predictions about their world, and to Kelly, this is the primary motivating force in personality. Our ability to predict may improve with experience, because experience changes our anticipations (predictions), according to whether or not it fulfills them. Like scientists, we change our hypotheses as we acquire new information; consequently, learning from experience that one of our anticipations was wrong is a particularly important opportunity for growth.

The Interactionalist Perspective

Cognitive models have redefined the debate between nomothetic and idiographic theories of personality. Research using a cognitive perspective has produced a variety of theories about the ways in which people construct their social worlds. Common to these theories is the idea that the thoughts and feelings that are "in the head" of perceivers interact with the situations in which perceivers find themselves and the needs and purposes they bring to those situations.

The debate surrounding the relative strength of the person—in terms of traits and dispositions—and the situation has led to attempts to assess empirically the ways in which certain situations are differentially represented by different individuals, and thus lead these individuals to react in particular ways.

This kind of interactionalist view has been described by Walter Mischel in the realm of person perception:

> Structure, I believe, exists neither "all in the head" of the perceiver nor "all in the person" perceived: it is instead a function of an interaction between the beliefs of observers and the characteristics of the observed. . . . Perceivers surely go beyond the information they are "given," but they just as surely do not invent regularly the information itself. Information in the head of the perceiver and in the world of the perceived interacts in the course of person perception. (1981, p. 15)

What kinds of structures exist "in the head" of the perceiver? Recently, these structures have been given several names: *prototypes* (Cantor & Mischel, 1977), *schemas* (Markus, 1977), and *exemplars* (Medin & Smith,

1985). Generally, these words are used to refer to categories that people form to group things together. As you will recall from previous chapters, categories like "bird" group together chickens, sparrows, and other winged creatures in a person's mind. Other categories, such as "foods not to eat on a diet" (Barsalon, 1982), may link together things like chocolate cake and butter, even though these substances do not resemble one another in the concrete visual ways that birds do. For a claustrophobic, telephone booths, closets, and other small spaces may be linked together in the anxiety-producing category of "enclosed spaces." As the last example suggests, these sorts of categories may produce strong emotions, such as fear, anger, or love, and the emotion may determine the person's response to something or someone that belongs to the category. "Person categories" are often very important elements in an individual's internal map of the world. Someone who has an early memory of a parent who died in the hospital might grow up to have an intense dislike of doctors.

What is important to realize here is that our reactions to an individual or a situation can be governed by the category into which we place them, and our emotional reactions to that category. We will see this again in the chapter on stress and coping (Chapter 16), where it is argued that it is a person's cognitive definition of the meaning of an event that determines how stressfully that person will experience the event.

In addition to concepts of people and situations, individuals also have representations of stereotyped patterns of events they carry through time. These are called *scripts* (Schank & Abelson, 1976). For instance, each of us carries around a "restaurant script," which includes such things as finding a table, selecting a meal from the menu, paying the bill, and calculating the tip (see also Chapter 7). Different people will have learned different scripts for various activities, which they then use to govern their behavior. Though the behavior may be carried out in an automatic and unthinking way, other people are likely to take that behavior as revealing the performer's personality. For example, a person whose restaurant script omits the tipping event will be judged "stingy."

Other cognitive theorists suggest that our cognitive representations of ourselves are as important in determining our actions as our representations of events and other people. Bandura (1986) has coined the phrase **self-efficacy expectancies** to refer to one's conceptualizations of his or her abilities to carry out actions required to master and control different situations. As you would expect, people who expect that they can master a task are willing to attempt it and will persist in the face of initial failures. They will also do so independently of their actual skill at the task. Researchers (Marcus & Smith, 1981) have shown that the dimensions that people use to describe themselves are also the dimensions they use to analyze the behavior of others. Other psychologists (Cantor & Kihlstrom, 1987) have made the interesting suggestion that **social intelligence**—the skills and strategies that we all have about how to behave on the job or how to solve problems in personal affairs—should be recognized as a part of people's personalities. This makes sense since people clearly do have different skills in different settings and set about solving personal dilemmas in various ways. Furthermore, when we think about differences between people, these various ways in which people evaluate options or go about planning their actions seem to be both characteristic of them and important in our descriptions of them. For example, one person may maintain a meticulous office and keep to a carefully detailed daily schedule. Another may not be able to find anything under piles of papers and prefer a spontaneous approach to organizing daily activities. Such

Sex-Role Behavior and Personality

The search for stable, enduring traits in personality is nowhere more clearly defined than in the area of sex roles. Many researchers have attempted to catalog masculinity and femininity and to characterize differences in behavior as a function of the fundamental personality differences they see as inherent in men and women (Murdock, 1965). It has been argued that this emphasis on *differentiation* has led to an exaggeration of the number of differences between the sexes that cannot be attributed to situational factors.

Using an entirely different perspective, Maccoby and Jacklin (1974) conducted an extensive review of the sex-role literature in an attempt to discover which of the many alleged behavioral differences between men and women really exist. Their research yielded only four basic distinctions: Females have better verbal ability; males have better spatial judgment; males are better at mathematics; females are less aggressive.

This disagreement concerning the nature of sex-role behaviors is also reflected in the ongoing debate concerning how individuals develop their particular sex-role identity. Research has shown that sex-role identity is an early component of the child's self-concept; even children who are younger than 2 years old can reliably identify themselves as male or female (Thompson, 1975). Where does this knowledge come from? The most radical biological view suggests that sex-role identity is largely determined by an individual's genetic identity (Daly & Wilson, 1978). In this view, a "masculine" or "feminine" personality grows out of the individual's response to his or her own sex-linked behavior. In the psychoanalytic tradition, on the other hand, Freud cited case studies of his patients as proof that all individuals are born with the potential for both sex-role identities. His often quoted assertion that "anatomy is destiny" refers to his notion that normal sex-role development is centered around proper resolution of the conflicts associated with an individual's first awareness of his or her sex organs. The goal of this resolution—identification with the same-sex parent—ensures that the individual will adopt sex-appropriate behavior and personality traits.

Because sex differences are associated with a large number of obvious and directly observable biological differences, some researchers have sought biological explanations for observed behavioral differences between the sexes. The sex hormones are obvious targets for such research. Among lower animals, there is a great deal of evidence that sexual differentiation in behavior is an adaptive function of the gonadal hormones—androgens in males and estrogen in females (see Daly & Wilson, 1978, for a review). In laboratory experiments, for example, female rhesus monkeys injected with the male hormone testosterone at various stages of prenatal development exhibit alterations not only of sexual behavior but in such areas as aggressiveness, play, and interest in babies (Phoenix, 1974). It is extremely tempting to generalize from the behavior of monkeys to that of humans, especially since we obviously cannot perform the same kinds of experiments on humans. But while such experiments are suggestive, they are not sufficient evidence. We have to rely on different kinds of evidence in searching for sex differences in human personality.

Most of the biological evidence that has been examined has been the result of abnormality or medical malpractice. One such study involved genetic females with a clinical condition called *adrenogenital syndrome* (AGS), in which the adrenal glands wrongly produce an androgen. At birth, AGS girls show some genital masculinization; with hormone treatments and minor surgery, however, these girls can have normal lives and even bear children. AGS girls are normally raised as girls; the only obvious difference between AGS girls and normal girls is their exposure to

characteristic behavioral styles often find their way into our descriptions of people's personalities.

Social-cognitive theories can easily assimilate an interactionalist perspective. Interactionalist theories of personality also help us understand another common observation made by researchers. For example, the various people in John's life can all confidently describe his personality. The problem is that all do so in different and even contradictory terms. The interactionalist cites several different reasons for this. First, John's life, like our own, is likely to be divided into *roles*. For instance, if John is a graduate student, he probably takes classes from faculty members, teaches a discussion section to undergraduates, and perhaps has a relationship with a woman friend. To the faculty, he appears quiet, respectful, and docile—and as one who has a great deal to learn. To his students, he seems confident, enormously knowledgeable, and dominant. To his friend, he is a warm and caring companion. While people all have different images of John's personality, the various images are

male hormones before birth. Erhardt and Baker (1974) conducted extensive interviews with AGS girls and their families, in which they discovered that both the subjects and their families saw the AGS girls as more "tomboyish" than other girls.

Similar results were found in an earlier study (described in Chapter 11) of children whose mothers had been injected with androgens to prevent miscarriage (Money & Erhardt, 1972). The daughters of these women, like the AGS girls, preferred "boyish" games to more traditional female occupations and thought of themselves as tomboys. Even though the behavior of these girls was well within the range of "acceptable" feminine behavior, their "masculine" tendencies were taken as evidence for the effect of fetal hormones on the development of sex-typed behavior. A final example, also described by Money and Erhardt, concerns the strange case of a pair of identical male twins. When they were being circumcised, the penis of one of the twins was accidentally mutilated. The child's parents decided to raise the child as a girl, and genital surgery was performed before the child's second birthday. Money and Erhardt report that the twins' mother made every effort to make her daughter "quiet and ladylike" (p. 122) and to differentiate her from her twin brother. Even though the child did exhibit some "tomboyish" behavior, she did on the whole accept her girlhood completely, while her brother was seen as a normal male. These results were seen as evidence that socialization could sometimes override genetic tendencies.

However, such studies do not really clarify the effects of biological factors on personality development. They are not controlled experiments, and thus their outcomes may be due to interacting multiple factors. For example, in the studies mentioned here, the parents knew of the abnormalities in their children's development. The differences found may have been due to differential treatment by the parents, or to some other aspect of the children's environments. Also, most of these children received hormone therapy after birth, which may have had additional behavioral effects. For instance, Money and Erhardt's "feminized" twin presumably received large amounts of estrogen to facilitate development of appropriate secondary sex characteristics at puberty. Biology and the environment clearly could interact in complex ways in such cases.

Both social-learning and cognitive models of personality assert that sex-role development is the result of experience, but each model places a different interpretation on that experience. As one psychologist put it:

The social-learning syllogism is: "I want rewards, I am rewarded for doing boy things, therefore, I want to be a boy." In contrast, a cognitive theory assumes this sequence: "I am a boy, therefore I want to do boy things, therefore the opportunity to do boy things (and to gain approval for doing them) is rewarding." (Kohlberg, 1966, p. 89)

Learning theory, then, argues that sex-role identity is learned in much the same way as other kinds of behavior. For example, if a male child is rewarded for displaying aggressive, masculine behavior, he will continue to act in a way that will allow observers to categorize him as a "masculine" personality. Cognitive theories, however, assume that the child is aware of himself as a boy or herself as a girl and uses this awareness to interpret the social world. According to this view, the male child in the example sees himself as masculine and uses that category to give meaning to his behavior. Expanding this view, recent research (Bem, 1981) has suggested that sex-role differences in personality may be the result of individual differences in the range of circumstances in which gender is used by individuals to categorize behavior.

Thus the development of sex-role identity—and the search for masculinity, femininity, and androgyny—are rich, relevant topics for the student of personality. Biological, psychoanalytic, learning, and social-cognitive models of personality all have their own unique perspective on these important questions.

equally valid in the sense that they reflect his personality in certain situations. Yet none of these images can be generalized to describe John's personality in other roles or situations.

Aside from the fact that certain situations are likely to bring out different personality attributes, people tend to devote more of their energies to some tasks than to others. We have different definitions of various situations and are not always equally committed to the many challenges that life presents. For example, Rob, who is an amateur director, displays a remarkable ability to coordinate the myriad details that go into a theatrical production. Still, he can't seem to organize himself to complete his academic projects on time. Those who know him from his theater activities might describe Rob as a real go-getter, while his teachers believe him to be an underachiever. Other people exhibit more proficiency in their work than in simple everyday tasks of living. For example, Mary, who edits a newspaper, has no trouble managing the complex process of getting a daily edition to press. However, when she

invites her parents to dinner, the meat invariably gets cold as she waits for the other dishes to finish cooking. Mary's co-workers might describe her as an inspiring leader, yet her mother finds her incompetent.

Identification of individual differences in the way people structure the social world, and the effects these differences have on behavior, have become an important focus for cognitive personality psychology. Traditional measures of memory, like recognition, recall, and reaction time, are being used to investigate the nature of these differences and their implications for personality theories. Cognitive personality researchers are also using self-reports to see how people describe their personalities and skills. In addition, they employ observational techniques to determine how people attack conceptual or interpersonal problems. Researchers not only watch what happens in certain situations, they also notice what self-interpretations are made when a subject's initial solution to a problem doesn't work. As a result of the research done in the field of social cognition, the interactionalist approach has created a new perspective on the study of personality.

SUMMARY: THE CENTRAL THEMES OF PERSONALITY THEORY

Unlike some other areas of psychology, it is clear that the study of personality has not arrived at any single representation of "personality." Given the nature of personality theory, and its bearing on issues in which we all have an emotional investment, this lack of convergence is not surprising. Still, some shared perspectives are emerging, and we suspect the reader will be grateful for a characterization of them.

First, the psychoanalytic, humanistic, learning, and cognitive theories all share the conclusion that people act not so much in terms of "objective" pictures of the world as it "really is," but according to their internal representations of the world. One of the central ideas emerging in the field of psychology is that events take the shape of mental representations, and that those representations in the mind are not necessarily the same "shape" as the real events they represent. Instead, the mental representations tend to be abstractions and simplifications of real events. Personality theorists of varying schools of thought had long been talking about such representation, although in different terms such as phobias about certain frightening animals or sexually arousing objects. But now personality theory is converging with a modern trend in experimental psychology. Modern psychological researchers are much more comfortable than past generations of psychologists in speculating about people's mental structures. This is because they now have the empirical techniques and skills necessary to subject their theories to rigorous experimental tests and they can draw on what experimental psychology is discovering about mental representations.

Of course, the various personality theories differ as to what events in the past shape these representations.

Freudian and Neo-Freudian theorists emphasize the importance of the success or failure of certain past events, such as weaning, toilet training, and other events that bring about transitions to different stages, in the shaping of present reactions to events.

For the learning theory of personality, it is the past reinforcement history of individuals that is the important determinant of their response to stimuli in the present.

For cognitive theorists, it is the interpretations that people store of past events that are critical in determining their reactions to present events.

Psychoanalytic and cognitive theory agree that many representations are not readily accessible to a person's conscious awareness. According to psychoanalytic theory, the material is kept in an unconscious state by the active process of repression. In cognitive theory, subjective representation is, like many other things a person does (such as constructing a grammatically correct sentence), not immediately accessible to conscious analysis. Speaking in terms of reinforcement and secondary gains, humanistic theorists are likely to emphasize how difficult these patterns are to change.

Theories are also converging on the recognition that regardless of what specific past events have contributed to a person's present mental representations, it is the representations themselves that determine present actions and thoughts. As we will see in Chapter 18, therapists concerned with altering self-defeating behavior will often seek to make their patients aware of their interpretative patterns. The theory is that by recognizing those patterns that cause difficulty a person can change them, and that more healthy behaviors can flow from altered definitions of the meanings of present events. Classical Freudian theorists still hold that this process must include an exploration of past events that brought about the way one looks at the world. Social-cognitive theorists, on the other hand, are more optimistic that significant changes can be fostered by focusing on the present. However, among all personality theorists there has been an increased emphasis on understanding the ways in which people represent various aspects of the physical or interpersonal world, and the influence these representations have on their actions and personalities.

The biological perspective on personality stands outside the others for the obvious reason that much of what it is concerned with is on a different level of explanation. Perhaps biological theory's eventual role will be to help meld an integrated psychological theory of personality.

THE ASSESSMENT OF PERSONALITY

All the models of personality we have looked at—the biological, psychoanalytic, humanistic-existential, learning, and social-cognitive—require some means of identifying and locating the various characteristics, traits, and other personality dimensions they are studying. This is true for two reasons. First, practical decisions may hinge on it. One would not want to put a paranoid schizophrenic in charge of a missile-testing base, nor a psychopathic deviant in a police uniform. More positively, it is desirable to match people with jobs that suit their personalities. Some people enjoy stress and ought to have jobs in which they will be presented with challenging tasks; others would fall apart if they had to endure constant stress on the job, no matter how challenging.

A second reason for assessing personality is scientific—it is useful for testing personality theories. For instance, according to Maslow's theory, there should be a distinct group of people who are self-actualized. These people should share certain qualities or characteristics described by Maslow—a broad and tolerant sense of humor, the tendency to stand by their friends, and so on. But we cannot prove that there are such people unless we measure people's sense of humor, tendency to back their values in the face of pressure to conform, and other qualities that Maslow hypothesized for self-actualized individuals.

Reliability and Validity

Tests used for personality assessment, like any effective test instruments, must possess both reliability and validity. A personality test should give the same result each time it is administered to the same person, assuming there is no reason to believe that his or her personality has changed between tests. This is **reliability.** In general, there are two ways to check a test for reliability. For a test with a relatively straightforward output such as "true/false" or "agree/disagree" answers, reliability is assessed by comparing equivalent parts or versions of the test. Thus we might judge the correlation between two halves of the same test (split-half method), two versions of the same test (alternate-forms method), or two successive versions of the same test (test-retest method). For a test whose outcome consists of ratings made by an observer or judge, interrater reliability is used: The person being tested is rated by a second, equally qualified observer, and the correlation between the two judges' ratings is calculated.

Validity determines whether the test actually measures those factors it is intended to measure. Psychologists distinguish different kinds of validity. **Predictive validity** is of concern when an assessment is being made for a practical purpose—when, for instance, the object is to predict how well a person will do in college, or as an airplane pilot, or in another job. The future performance being predicted is called the **criterion,** and the purpose of the test is to predict it as accurately as possible. Therefore if the maximum correlation ($+1$ or -1) between the test instrument and the criterion could be obtained, the test would be considered wildly successful because it would predict without error whether a person would do well ($+1$) or poorly (-1) at the criterion. The predictive validity of a test instrument, then, is the degree of correlation between that instrument and the future performance that is being predicted. Establishing the predictive validity of a test can have important practical consequences. For example, equal employment opportunity legislation now requires that all tests used to screen job applicants have a measurable degree of predictive validity. This was done to ensure that individuals are hired on the basis of their ability to perform the actual tasks of a job (the criterion) and not on the basis of extraneous or irrelevant variables such as sex, age, or race.

Construct validity is generally of interest when personality assessment is being done for theoretical rather than practical purposes. It is possible to think of a theory as a set of constructs or ideas and the relationships among them. There is a difference between the construct itself (which is always hypothetical) and measures or ways to identify the construct. Constructs, although they can be defined, described, and discussed, are not directly observable—but measures are. A construct whose presence cannot be inferred by some measure is useless in psychology, which takes an empirical approach to knowledge. Thus a measure must be related to the constructs it is supposed to identify; this is *construct validity.*

There is no direct empirical way to assess the relevance of a given measure to a given construct. Relevance can only be assessed indirectly, by using other, related constructs.

Suppose that a psychologist has developed the construct for "test anxiety," defined as a tendency to become anxious in test situations and thus to perform more poorly than would otherwise be the case. What kind of measure would assess this construct? What pattern of correlations with other behaviors should the measure show? To demonstrate construct validity, the researcher must be able to specify what the relationship *should be* between

Table 15–3:   The Construct Validation of a Test.

Person	Math Ability 1 = Low, 10 = High	Test Anxiety 1 = Low, 10 = High	Math Test Performance 1 = Low, 10 = High
1	8	1	8
2	8	9	6
3	4	2	4
4	4	8	2
5	7	5	6
6	2	7	1

Table 15–4:   Performance Scores as a Function of Test Anxiety.

Person	Test Anxiety 1 = Low, 10 = High	Math Test Performance 1 = Low, 10 = High
1	1	8
3	2	4
5	5	6
6	7	1
4	8	2
2	9	6

$r = -.41$

the construct under scrutiny and other constructs. From this relationship, the researcher can infer what the relationship should be between the *measure* of this construct and the measures of other constructs. If these measures are related in ways expected by the theory, the measure of the experimental construct has construct validity. In the construct of "test anxiety," we would look for an assessment instrument (measure) that would show *moderate* correlations with a number of other measures. (Contrast this to the predictive validity requirement of a *high* correlation with some single-criterion measure.) As an example, consider the factors that determine performance on a math test. Certainly anxiety about taking the test is one such factor, but so is mathematical ability and how much time the person has spent studying for the test.

Now imagine six individuals who have the test anxiety, math ability, and math test scores shown in Table 15–3. Notice that the people with low test anxiety tend to work at the level of their abilities, whereas people who are highly "test-anxious" do a bit worse than their ability alone would lead us to expect. But what about the correlation between performance on the math test and test-anxiety measure? In Table 15–4 the test-anxiety scores are listed in ascending order and the math scores are listed in the right-hand column. The correlation is −.41, indicating that there is a negative relationship between test anxiety and test performance. (Recall that a negative correlation is just as useful as a positive one—it simply indicates that scoring at the high end of one scale correlates with scoring at the low end of the other scale.) This is a moderate and not a perfect correlation. To understand why, consider Person 2, who did fairly well on the math test, even though she was highly test anxious, because she had a high level of mathematical ability. Now you can see why the first requirement for construct validity is a moderate

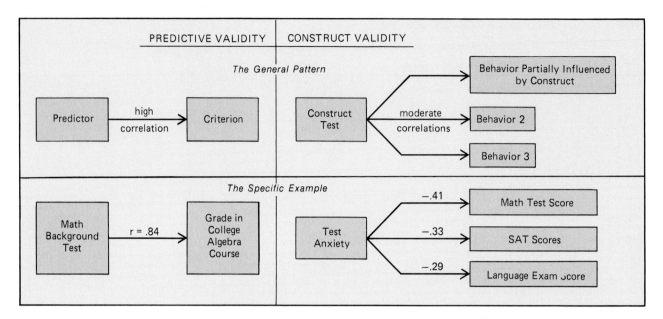

Figure 15–5   The Different Correlational Patterns Desirable in Predictive and Construct Validation.

Notice that in our specific example the correlations differ in two ways. Only one difference is important. The math background test–algebra grade correlation is a high one, indicating a strong association between the test and the grade, while the set of correlations between the measure of test anxiety and the various behaviors are all much lower. This is exactly what is desired: high correlations when predictive validity is at issue, moderate ones for construct validity. Note the second difference. The predictive validity correlation is positive, while the construct validity correlations are negative. This is not important. It simply reflects the fact that a high score on the test anxiety measure goes with lower scores on the other tests, which is exactly what one would expect. (See the Appendix for more on the mathematics of correlations.)

rather than a high correlation between the construct measure and some other measure that we expect to be influenced by that construct.

The second requirement for validation is that the construct show not just a single correlation but a pattern of correlations with a number of other behaviors. This is because a construct that is theoretically useful should have general implications. If our measure of test anxiety correlated only with people's scores on a single test of math performance, then we could not be sure that we had a general measure of test anxiety. A general measure ought to correlate with performances on English and social studies tests, written and oral tests, and so on. Figure 15–5 diagrams the different correlational patterns that are desirable in predictive versus construct validation.

There are many other kinds of validity. Indeed, Bringborg (1981) actually described as many as 40! To illustrate the variety of special kinds of validity, we will conclude our discussion by describing two variations of construct validity.

A measure has **convergent validity** when other measures that purport to measure the same construct correlate well with the target measure. Thus if I am trying to measure "intelligence" by asking subjects to interpret inkblots, I would expect that individuals who achieved high scores on my measure would have high scores on other measures of intelligence as well. Conversely, I would also expect low scorers on my inkblot measure to have low

scores on other measures of intelligence. Thus several measures would converge in evaluating intelligence.

Is it sufficient for an assessment device to have convergent validity? Can I safely conclude that my inkblot measure is a valid measure of intelligence? Before I apply for the copyright, I must also make sure that my inkblot test measures the construct of "intelligence" *at least as well* as it measures other things. The **discriminant validity** of my inkblot test depends on the specificity with which it measures intelligence. For example, if my inkblot scores correlate highly with IQ but also correlate equally well with social class, salary earned, and prestige of occupation, I cannot be sure whether my test is measuring intelligence or some other construct in which intelligence plays a role. If my measure fails to discriminate between intelligence and other constructs, it lacks discriminant validity.

To introduce our discussion of personality assessment we have presented the measurement (sometimes called psychometric) characteristics of assessment devices. To summarize, a successful assessment device must be *reliable*—it must give approximately the same result when applied repeatedly to the same individual. This is a precondition for *validity,* the second requirement for a successful assessment device. Validity requirements differ according to the purpose of the test. A test designed to predict a person's performance on some practical task should have predictive validity; a test designed to measure an individual's disposition or style should have construct validity.

We now turn to different kinds of procedures used to assess personality: observational techniques (including interviews), self-reports and self-ratings, projective tests, and personality inventories.

Observational Techniques

As we observe other people, we come to certain conclusions about their personalities. If we write these observations in list form, a sort of personality assessment emerges. Personal observation is perhaps the oldest assessment technique, and it is still in use today. But different observers may have seen different samples of the person's behavior and may have different questions in mind when they write their assessments. For these and other reasons, personal assessments have often proved unreliable (and therefore a low validity). Consequently, psychologists have come up with ways to make such judgments more precise and systematic. These include structuring the assessment techniques, either by structuring the rating system itself or by structuring the methods of gathering the information on which the assessment is based or the setting in which the observations are carried out.

Structuring the Ratings.   Instead of making a general summary of someone's characteristics, observers can rate the person on certain specific, defined dimensions. This assures that every observer will rate the same qualities. Sometimes observers are given a set of adjectives and asked to select those that apply to the person they are evaluating. The adjectives can describe various personality characteristics or can refer to the person's moods, skills, or physical appearance, depending on the purpose of the assessment (see Figure 15–6). For statistical reasons, adjectival ratings are usually done using the **q-sort technique.** Here the observer is given a large set of cards with an adjective or phrase printed on each. The observer then sorts the cards into nine groups, Group 1 being those statements that best describe the person, and Group 9 those that are false about the person. Sometimes the judge is

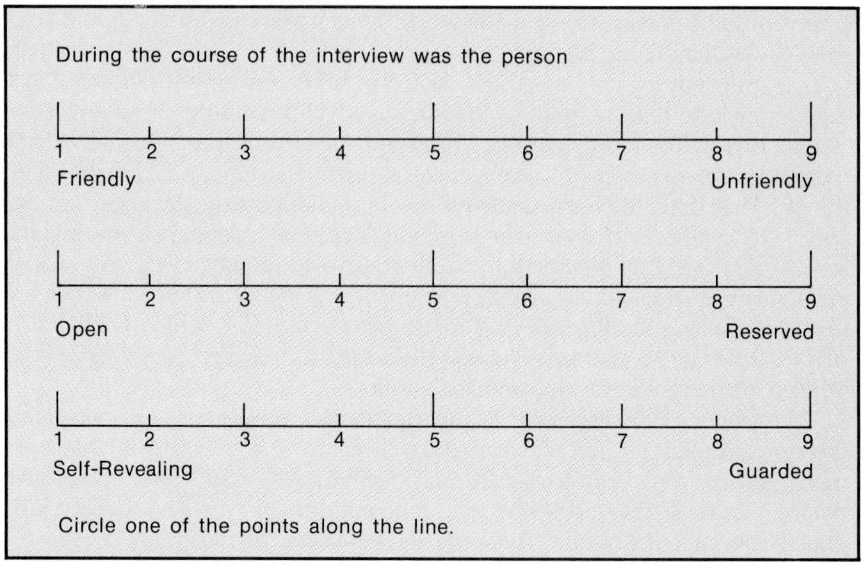

During the course of the interview was the person

| 1 | 2 | 3 | 4 | 5 | 6 | 7 | 8 | 9 |
| Friendly | | | | | | | | Unfriendly |

| 1 | 2 | 3 | 4 | 5 | 6 | 7 | 8 | 9 |
| Open | | | | | | | | Reserved |

| 1 | 2 | 3 | 4 | 5 | 6 | 7 | 8 | 9 |
| Self-Revealing | | | | | | | | Guarded |

Circle one of the points along the line.

Figure 15–6 An example of adjectival ratings. Depending on what is being evaluated, the adjectives could refer to various personality characteristics or to specifics such as moods, skills, or personal appearance. (Hathaway, S.R. & McKinley, J.C. *Minnesota Multiphasic Personality Inventory Revised 1967.* New York: The Psychological Corporation. Copyright 1970, reproduced with permission.)

told to make the distribution of items conform to a normal distribution (see Appendix), with the fewest cards in Groups 1 and 9, and the most in Groups 3–5. Conforming with this direction facilitates comparisons among individuals because exactly the same number of adjectives are reported as most or least typical of each individual.

Structuring the Observations. Another way to make observations more reliable and valid is to structure the information on which they are based. In the interview setting this would involve structuring the kinds of questions asked of the person.

An interview in which the observer talks to a person and follows the conversation wherever it leads is called an **unstructured** or **open-ended interview.** In a **structured interview** everyone is asked the same questions in the same order. This makes it easier to sort, rate, and analyze the answers. It is also more reliable in that the same results are likely if the interview is repeated. With the open-ended interview, very different outcomes may result the second time (or with a different interviewer). A compromise format, often called a *semistructured* or *structured/open-ended interview,* sets out a prearranged schedule of questions, but allows the interviewer to explore in depth any of the respondent's answers that seem particularly revealing or important.

Structuring the Settings or Situations. Observers sometimes form impressions of others by watching their behavior rather than by interviewing them. A clinical or developmental psychologist, for instance, may gain impressions of a child by observing that child interact with parents in the home, teachers in the classroom, and other children on the playground.

This kind of observation is more reliable if the situations in which the person performs are structured. In addition, research shows that the predictive validity of observations increases as the test situation more closely resembles the situation for which one is attempting to predict behavior.

One of the most extensive attempts at arriving at personality data from structured settings was made by American Army Intelligence during World War II. At several secret locations in the United States elaborate training

centers were built to simulate some of the situations in which undercover agents sent into Nazi-occupied Europe might find themselves. The primary function of these centers was training, but their secondary function was to enable observers to make behavioral assessments of the future agents, focusing on testing their behavior under stress.

Some of these test situations were quite ingenious. For instance, posing as another trainee, an observer would strike up conversations with acquaintances at an after-hours bar in an attempt to extract information that trainees had been told individually and instructed to keep secret. The unsuspecting trainees' reactions when an acquaintance tried to extract secret information from them were thought to be revealing of how they would behave in a similar future situation in which their lives might depend on avoiding just such an unguarded reaction.

Two general principles of test construction are demonstrated, in a somewhat romanticized fashion, by this army test procedure. First, the test is constructed to be as similar to actual work conditions as possible. Second, on the premise that a particularly important component of every job is decision making under stress, stress-producing incidents are included in the test.

The end of the story is less romantic. The validity of the army testing methods was studied: Teams of observers rated the future agents at the training centers; then, overseas, their superior officers and colleagues rated them again in actual situations. Unfortunately, the observers' ratings did not reliably predict success in the field. There were many reasons for this, but the major one was that most of the actual war situations differed from the test situations in unpredictable ways.

Self-Reports and Self-Ratings

Often people are asked to report on their own personalities. As Allport pointed out, the easiest way to find out about a person is to ask that person. There are many aspects of our own personalities that we are quite aware of and capable of reporting on. The same rating scales and adjective cards that we described for observational techniques are used when people make observations about themselves. The reliability of the self-rating is assessed by test-retest correlations, and the predictive and construct validity of the self-report is assessed in the same way that these validities are assessed for observers' judgments.

The problem with this procedure is that people sometimes do not wish to reveal certain things about themselves that they feel are embarrassing or socially undesirable. When asked whether they are "flexible or rigid," or "organized or disorganized," many people report that they are flexible and organized because they believe these are the socially desirable answers. So researchers working with **self-reports** have found it wise to try to balance their scales so that neither end of the scale is the "good" or "bad" end. This is surprisingly difficult to do because many words used to describe people carry positive or negative connotations.

One way around this difficulty is to ask people to rate their behavior patterns rather than their personalities. Instead of asking them whether they are "dependable," for instance, the tester would ask questions about missed appointments, forgotten meetings, and tasks left incomplete. Again, though, because it is not socially desirable to respond "frequently" to questions about missed meetings, people may falsely report that they act in socially desirable ways (much as they would, in a personality test, report that they are socially desirable people).

Another problem with this technique is that people have certain personality characteristics and behavior patterns they are unaware of. In an effort to uncover underlying problems, conflicts, or qualities that people are unaware of (or are unwilling to report), psychologists have used indirect ways to gain information. For example, they may ask questions about some seemingly harmless thought or act that they believe correlates with or reveals an underlying conflict or difficulty. These types of tests are divided into two groups on the basis of how the correlation between test question and characteristic is established. **Projective tests** generally rely on theoretically determined correlations, **personality inventories** on empirical correlations.

Projective Tests

The typical projective test presents an ambiguous visual stimulus, which a subject is asked to describe. Interpretation of the test is based on the assumption that respondents reveal something about their internal psychological processes by the structure or content of their answers.

Rorschach Test. The **Rorschach inkblot test** is one of the oldest of the projective tests. Each inkblot is a pattern that can look like many things: animals, people, devils, masks, birds.

Rorschach tested thousands of inkblots for years before choosing the ten that are still in use today. He tested the blots both on mental patients who had been classified by disorder and on normal people. The final ten were those that Rorschach felt discriminated reactions of mental patients from those of normal people, and also showed some discriminatory tendency among patients according to disorder.

The ten inkblots are on cards. Most are black; others contain one or more colors. The cards are presented one at a time in a certain order. The person being tested can make one interpretation or many. After showing all the inkblots, the tester goes back over the cards, asking why the person saw what he or she did in the card, what part of the blot gave that appearance, and so on.

As in some other testing procedures, the tester observes the person's behavior and style of answering as well as actual answers. The answers are

At left, a sample Rorschach inkblot. Some of the inkblots are in one or more colors, but most are black, like this one. At right, a young girl taking the Rorschach test. (Courtesy University of Florida Clinical Psychology Department; Mimi Forsyth/Monkmeyer Press)

The psychologist shown here is administering the Thematic Apperception Test (TAT). In this test the person being interviewed is asked to tell what is happening in the scene shown, what led up to it, and what the outcome will be. (Van Bucher/Photo Researchers)

scored in several ways. Does a subject see the whole blot or just parts? What is the subject matter or content? To what qualities does the subject respond (color, shape, etc.)? In all of this, the tester is looking for consistencies in patterns of responding.

From the answers, the tester makes inferences about the underlying personality structure of the respondent, in accordance with psychoanalytic principles: Recurring themes across pictures are thought to hint at recurring underlying conflicts; sequential responses to the same images reveal material that is causally linked in the unconscious. Stylistic characteristics of the response may also be meaningful: A person who consistently focuses on a part rather than the whole inkblot may be revealing an obsessional concern with detail; someone who persistently sees movement in the figures may be revealing something important about his or her internal functioning.

The Thematic Apperception Test. Henry Murray (1943) developed the **Thematic Apperception Test (TAT)** in an attempt to find out more about an individual's functioning with other people. Murray collected a set of photographs and sketches of people, often shown in some ambiguous relationship with other people, and asked the respondent to make up a story based on the picture.

The person is asked to tell what led up to the scene on the card, what is happening in the scene, and what the outcome will be. Basically the tester is interested in several elements of respondents' stories: which character on the card is seen as central to the story, which character respondents identify; with, what needs and drives are expressed in their story, and what seems to be helping or hindering the achievement of them. By interpreting the themes of the stories, the details the respondent uses to illustrate them, and the pattern of consistent themes and images that recur across stories, a skilled interpreter can arrive at a surprisingly rich and detailed interpretation of the respondent's character.

But these are still only interpretations. Both the Rorschach and the Thematic Apperception Test result in a complex and free-form mix of descriptive and evaluative statements by the interpreter about the respondent, and, like any other test result, they require validation. If the clinician interprets the fussy, orderly way an individual organizes the TAT answers as re-

vealing an underlying trait of anal compulsivity, this interpretation requires checking. The respondent may simply have been attempting to live up to perceived demands of the test situation. Hundreds of studies have attempted to validate elements of projective interpretations, and while they are far too numerous to review in detail here, it is fair to say that many psychologists are highly skeptical about the validity of results from projective testing. To develop better test instruments, a new system of test construction was adopted.

Personality Inventories

One of the best known personality tests is the **Minnesota Multiphasic Personality Inventory (MMPI).** The psychologists who constructed the MMPI started with several hundred statements or test items that were thought to be useful in diagnosing and detecting serious behavior disorders such as depression, paranoia, and hysteria. The test consists of statements to which the person answers "true," "false," or "cannot say." These include statements on the person's past experiences, attitudes, physiological and psychological symptoms, and views of the world. For example:

I daydream a little.
People are following me.
My mother often made me obey even when I thought it was unreasonable.

A test for a specific characteristic is constructed in the following way: The items on the inventory are treated as a source pool. First, the test constructor decides what the test will be used for. For instance, it could be used to identify people who perform poorly in highly stressful situations. Then the test constructor identifies a group of people who actually have the characteristic for which the test is being developed. It may, for example, be a group of students who "fall apart" under the pressure of timed tests, or a group of workers who have been identified as poor performers under stress. The test is given to these *criterion groups* and their pattern of answers is compared to the answers given by the normal population. The questions that the criterion and normal groups answer differently (the "discriminating items") are the ones selected to go on the test for poor performance under stress. So research reports developing this kind of test often contain such lists as "25 +" and "37 −." This means that a true (+) answer to Question 25 on the MMPI is characteristic of (for example) a poor performer under stress, and a false (−) answer to Question 37 is also characteristic of that pattern. The set of questions that proves to discriminate the criterion from the normal group, not only on the first application, but through successive sets of trial with different specific criterion groups, becomes the scale for the factor or characteristic in question. For instance, the depression scale of the MMPI has between 40 and 50 items that have been shown to discriminate between depressed people and the rest of the population, and also between depressed people and people with other behavior disorders. Answers are not expressed as raw scores; they are plotted as deviations from the general patterns of answers given by thousands of previous respondents.

The initial use of the MMPI was in diagnostic settings, such as mental hospitals, and this is reflected in the scales that appear on the standard MMPI report form. For instance, the "Hy" scale is the "hysteria scale" and was developed with a criterion group of patients in mental hospitals reported to be high on hysterical symptomatology. But suppose someone else taking the

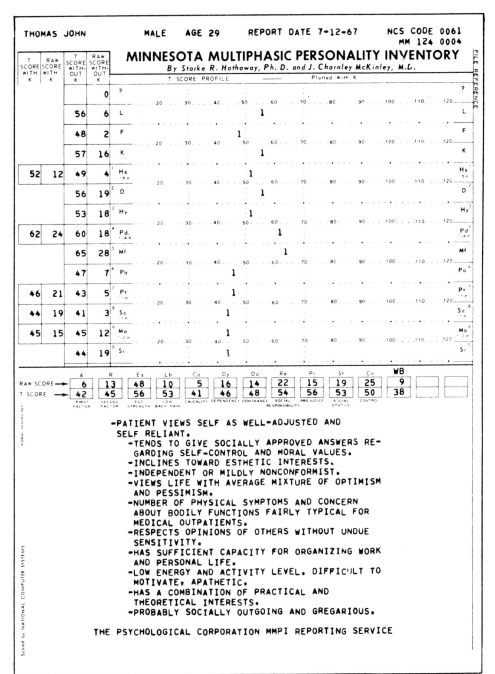

Figure 15–7 This is a computer printout of a profile and its interpretation for the Minnesota Multiphasic Personality Inventory (MMPI). (Hathaway, S.R. & McKinley, J.C. *Minnesota Multiphasic Personality Inventory Revised 1967.* New York: The Psychological Corporation. Copyright 1970, reproduced with permission.)

test comes out with a high "Pa" ("paranoia scale") score. Does this mean that person is a raving paranoid who is or ought to be hospitalized? Certainly not. Many normally functioning individuals have MMPI profiles that are elevated on one or more scales. On the MMPI a tendency to anticipate dangers in order to avoid them might be indicated by an elevated psychasthenia (Pt) scale score, since this scale contains items that reflect a tendency to worry. The MMPI is fruitfully used to characterize the personality profiles of normal individuals (see Figure 15–7). It has also been used to identify some characteristic that we do not ordinarily think of as personality traits. For instance, it

has been keyed to identify individuals who will be relatively successful salespersons and college teachers (Welsh & Dahlstrom, 1965).

Since the development of the MMPI, other multiphasic inventories have been contructed on the same principles. (*Multiphasic* means that a test measures many aspects of personality, in contrast to a test that measures only one construct—neurotic anxiety, for instance.) These new tests focus less on behavior disorders and more on normal personality characteristics. For instance, the California Psychological Inventory contains scales measuring such attributes as self-acceptance, sociability, and several kinds of achievement strivings. The content of the items and the labels of the scales of these inventories make them less threatening to respondents, but the developers of the MMPI would point out that research with these new inventories produces dimensions that are quite similar to those included in the MMPI. Apparently, empirical scale construction is a powerful technique for identifying subgroups of individuals whose personality elements differ from those of the population at large.

Test Construction and Personality Theory

We have been discussing various methods of personality assessment in the abstract. But in practice, it is the tester's theory of personality that should determine the design of a personality test. A behavioral personality theorist who believes that a child's reinforcement history determines his current behavior will wish to observe and measure how that child's parents interact with and punish and reward the child. On the other hand, a cognitive personality theorist would wish to give the child a list of situations and have the child judge which ones are similar. Then the cognitive theorist would try to determine the dimensions along which the child grouped the situations together.

Psychoanalytic theorists would be more inclined to use projective testing, feeling that responding to ambiguous stimuli allows the individual's unconscious concerns to manifest themselves (although in a disguised fashion that would require psychodynamic interpretation to decipher). Biologically oriented psychologists, on the other hand, might begin by observing someone for signs of psychological dysfunction, but go on to gather results of physical testing for genetic damage, hormonal imbalance, brain damage, or other physical impairment. The biological psychologist would view these as underlying the observed behavior.

SUMMARY

1. *Personality* refers to an organized and distinctive pattern of behavior that shows endurance over time and characterizes a person's adaptation to a situation.

2. The earliest ideas about personality attempted to account for a person's behavior in terms of innate *traits*.

3. In the *biological model* of personality, genetic endowment and biological features are assumed to be the determinants of personality. Sheldon's constitutional theory classifies personality types according

to body type: endomorphy, mesomorphy, and ectomorphy.

4. The *psychoanalytic model of personality* assumes that we are primarily motivated by drives and instincts over which we have little control; these motivations exist, for the most part, in our unconscious. Personality is made up of three processes, or systems—the *id,* the *ego,* and the *superego.* A person's behavior is the product of the interaction, and often conflict, among these three systems.

5. According to Freud, personality development takes place during four psychosexual stages: oral, anal, phallic, and genital.

6. Jungian analysis conceived of the *collective unconscious* coexistent with the Freudian personal unconscious. The collective unconscious is the same for everyone and contains *archetypes*.

7. The Neo-Freudians substituted social for biological determinants of personality, thereby modifying Freudian theory. Adler put forth the concept of the *inferiority complex*. Horney emphasized the management of anxiety-hostility and challenged Freud's view of female personality development.

8. Ego psychologists generally assign a more independent role to the ego in the unconscious. Erikson maintained that the personality continues to develop throughout successive stages of the life span.

9. *Humanistic-existential* models of personality focus on the total personality as opposed to separate behaviors that make up personality. Biology and the environment are minimized as determinants, and personal choice is emphasized.

10. Maslow emphasizes the drive for self-actualization, whereas Rogers emphasizes the role of the self and conscious awareness in the life of the individual.

11. According to *learning theorists,* personality is a set of patterns of behavior that we learn to make in response to specific stimuli, according to how such responses have been reinforced in the past.

12. *Social-learning theory* points out that a second type of learning—imitation based on observation of others—also affects behavior and thus personality.

13. *Cognitive models* view personality as being the result of a person's unique cognitive organization of the world; in other words, a person's actions flow from his or her perspective. *Personal construct theory* focuses on how people make sense of their experience.

14. Effective test instruments used for personality assessment must be carefully constructed so that they possess *reliability* and *validity*. Reliability may be assessed by comparing equivalent parts or versions of the test or by comparing the ratings of two equally qualified observers. Psychologists distinguish different kinds of validity: *predictive validity, construct validity, convergent validity,* and *discriminant validity*.

15. Among the methods used in assessing personality are: *q-sort technique, open-ended interviews, projective tests,* and *personality inventories*.

SUGGESTED READINGS

BANDURA, A. (1986). *Social conditions of thought and action: A social-cognition theory*. Englewood Cliffs, N.J.: Prentice-Hall. An influential theorist's perspective on the rapidly developing social-cognitive field.

CANTOR, N., & KIHLSTROM, J. (Eds.) (1981). *Personality, cognition, and social interaction*. Hillsdale, N.J.: Earlbaum. An influential presentation of recent trends in cognitive personality therapy.

FREUD, S. (1933). *New introductory lectures on psychoanalysis*. W. J. H. Sproutt, trans. New York: Norton. An introduction to the psychodynamic approach to personality. Included is Freud's most concise explanation of id, ego, and superego provinces and functioning; anxiety; and the development of the female psyche. In the final lectures the implications of psychoanalysis for religion and social order are presented.

HALL, C. S., LINDZEY, G., LOEHLIN, J. C., & MANOSEUITZ, M. (1985) An introduction to *theories of personality*. New York: John Wiley. Concise and detailed digest of the major theories of personality. Presents each theorist's conceptualization of the human being, the structure of personality, mechanisms of development and change, assessment, and (when applicable) therapeutic procedure.

HUESMANN, L., & MELAMUTH (Eds.) (1986). Media violence and antisocial behavior. *Journal of Social Issues,* Vol.42, No.3.

MASLOW, A. H. (1968). *Toward a psychology of being* (2nd ed.) New York: Van Nostrand. Describes the humanistic approach to personality, exploring the fundamental motive of growth and the characteristics of the self-actualized personality. Contrasts the humanistic model with the psychodynamic model and makes comparisons with other humanistic, existential, and neo-Freudian theories.

PERVIN, L. (1985). *Current controversies, issues, and directions*. In Rosenzweig, M., and Porter, L. (Eds.), *Annual Review of Psychology, 36,* 1985 Annual Research Issue, Palo Alto, Ca A current review of active controversies in personality theory and research. It focuses particularly on the person-situation controversy and the development of cognitive theories of personality.

ROGERS, C. R. (1961). *On becoming a person*. Boston: Houghton Mifflin. There is really no substitute for reading Rogers in the original. This is a wise introduction to his views on human personality and the possibilities of growth.

SKINNER, B. F. (1953). *Science and human behavior*. New York: Macmillan. Details an approach to personality based on a functional analysis of cause-and-effect relationships and the application of the principles of operant conditioning to the study of personality and behavior.

WILSON, G. T., & FRANKS, C. (Eds.) (1982). *Contemporary behavior therapy: Conceptual and empirical foundations*. New York: Guilford. A modern presentation of learning perspectives on therapy, which shows the convergence of the learning perspective with the cognitive one.

16 Stress and Coping

S tress is a universal human experience. Unpleasant experiences can bring on stress—getting fired, having an illness in the family, or failing an important exam are all potentially stressful. But even generally pleasant events and experiences can have stressful components—a sudden promotion, going away to college, or the purchase of a new house may also be stressful. The common element among these experiences, pleasant and unpleasant alike, is that they require some kind of **adjustment** or **adaptation.** Sometimes people are able to adapt to stressful situations fairly easily; at other times they may have more difficulty adjusting. Certain people react badly to certain kinds of stresses but cope well with other kinds; other people have different coping patterns.

Stress can be defined as a state that occurs when people are faced with demands from the environment that require them to change in some way. One question this definition raises is whether stress is the environmental demand itself or rather a person's response to that demand. It is helpful to think of stress as including both environmental demands, or **stressors,** and the person's reactions to them, the **stress responses.** In this chapter we will discuss stress, its causes and consequences, and the methods people use to cope with it. All of us at one time or another experience many of these sources of stress and show many, if not all, of the reactions that we will discuss.

Edvard Munch vividly captures the torture of chronic fear in "Anxiety." (Oslo Kuntstsamlinger, Munich-Museet)

SOURCES OF STRESS

According to our definition, stress arises from demands placed on the person by the environment. That environmental demand, or *stressor,* can be physical or psychological, intrinsic to a situation or attributed to it by the person involved, universal or unique to one person's experience. Some specific stressors are physical in nature, stressors like sleep deprivation, hunger, and noise. Others are psychosocial such as traumatic events, life events, chronic difficulties, daily hassles, and conflict.

Traumatic Events

Perhaps the most easily understood sources of stress are traumatic events. These are situations of exceptional danger generally outside the range of usual experience. Examples of traumatic events are natural disasters (floods, earthquakes), disasters caused by other human beings (being held hostage, military combat, air-raid attack), catastrophic accidents (car accidents, airplane crashes), and physical assaults (torture, attempted murder, rape). These extreme situations produce severe symptoms of stress in nearly everybody and require extensive and prolonged adaptive efforts (see the Highlight: Extreme Situational Stress). Adjusting to traumatic events can be very costly in physical and psychological terms. We will talk about the consequences of adapting to such severe stressors later in the chapter.

Life Events, Chronic Difficulties, and Daily Hassles

Although most people do not experience traumatic events, they do go through many eventful changes and encounter persistent difficulties in the course of their lives. Such events and difficulties can pose considerable challenge or even hazard to an individual. Major changes that disrupt or threaten to disrupt people's usual activities are called *life events.* These include normal and even happy life-stage transitions such as graduation, marriage, birth of a first child, and retirement. They also include more unexpected life changes such as divorce, illness or injury, job promotion or demotion, and change in career. Life events, both positive and negative, require substantial readjustments in behavior, and these readjustments can be quite stressful (Holmes & Rahe, 1967). Think, for example, of the myriad adjustments new parents must make to take care of their first baby. Career plans and work schedules are disrupted, sleeping patterns are altered, schedules and responsibilities must be rearranged, and social activities typically decrease. Even more readjustment is required by such negative events as the loss of a job or the death of a spouse.

Major life events can produce chronic difficulties as well, although events and difficulties can exist independently. Chronic difficulties are problems that cause individuals to make adjustments more or less continually in the course of daily life. Poverty, marital troubles, crowded living conditions, urban noise, job and academic pressures, continuous ill health—all of these and many other situations pose problems requiring daily adaptation. The wear and tear on individuals experiencing such demands can be considerable, especially when they have no control over those conditions.

Recently, psychologists have used the term *daily hassles* to describe the irritating, frustrating, and distressing minor demands that individuals face in their everyday lives (Kanner, Coyne, Schaefer, & Lazarus, 1981). This term

HIGHLIGHT _____

Extreme Situational Stress

Situations of exceptional tension—war, catastrophe, physical assault—often produce characteristic stress reactions. One of the most common of these stress reactions is combat fatigue. First described during World War I by a British pathologist who called it "shell shock," combat fatigue is characterized by psychic numbing or diminished responsiveness to the external world, and also by severe depression, hypersensitivity, sleep disturbance, nightmares, anxiety, and tremors. It can result from prolonged exposure to battle conditions or from some traumatic experience during combat, such as the death of a comrade. Sometimes combat fatigue strikes well after the battle is over. A minor stress may suddenly trigger the stress symptoms the soldier managed to suppress in the field.

One study conducted during the Yom Kippur War in Israel (Merbaum & Hefez, 1976) indicated that wounded soldiers were less likely to experience combat fatigue than the unwounded. In fact, according to this study, the more seriously wounded men tended to have the least anxiety of all. The researchers suggested that wounded soldiers had less anxiety because they were removed from the stress of battle, at least temporarily, and seriously wounded men knew they probably would never have to return to the field. The unwounded not only anticipated future combat, but also wondered, sometimes guiltily, why they had been spared while their buddies had fallen.

In civilian life catastrophic events can produce a stress reaction not unlike combat fatigue. The victims may show a wide range of symptoms, depending on the nature and severity of the catastrophe, its degree of unexpectedness, and their own unique personalities. The common behavior pattern following a catastrophic event has been called the **disaster syndrome** (Lifton, 1968; Erikson, 1976). It consists of three stages: In the shock stage victims appear to be unaware of their injuries or of danger. They are stunned, dazed, and apathetic. In extreme cases, they may be disoriented or show signs of partial amnesia. In the suggestible stage victims continue to be passive. They will take orders readily but are often unable to perform even the simplest tasks. In the recovery stage, which is the final stage, victims are anxious, tense, apprehensive. They may have difficulty sleeping or concentrating and may repeat the story of the catastrophe over and over. But in this final stage psychological equilibrium is gradually attained.

Like combat fatigue and other extreme stress reactions, the disaster syndrome may not occur immediately after the trauma but, instead, may be brought on by some minor stress several weeks or even months later. The newest edition of the *Diagnostic and Statistical Manual of Mental Disorders* (DSM–III) (American Psychiatric Association, 1980) terms this syndrome "post-traumatic stress disorder" and distinguishes among acute, chronic, and delayed types. In the acute type symptoms occur within six months of the trauma but are not prolonged beyond six months, as they are in the chronic type. Delayed post-traumatic stress disorder is diagnosed if symptoms begin at least six months after the crisis situation.

Post-traumatic stress disorder was introduced into DSM–III in part through the lobbying efforts of veterans and psychiatric professionals following the Vietnam War. Although data cannot be considered conclusive, veterans of Vietnam seemed especially likely to experience this syndrome because of the unusual aspects of waging this war: absence of clear front and back lines, unpredictable attacks in dense jungle conditions, an inability to distinguish easily between Vietnamese allies and enemies, the horrors of napalm bombing, and the lack of unified support at home. Vietnam vets, like other victims of extreme stress, complain of reexperiencing traumatic events in painful, recurrent memories or dreams. In rare instances, they relive the events for a few minutes or hours, behaving as though experiencing the crisis situation at that moment; this may occur in response to circumstances that are similar to or symbolize the original traumatic events.

Other responses associated with post-traumatic stress disorder are feelings of estrangement from previously significant persons and activities, severe depression (often brought on by guilt for having survived when others did not), and occasional unpredictable explosions of rage or aggression with little provocation. Aggressive reactions are particularly characteristic of war veterans; death-camp survivors more often experience failing memory and an impaired ability to concentrate.

Methods of treatment for post-traumatic stress disorder are still being devised. It does appear that among soldiers in battle, removal to back lines or a return home can be counterproductive, stabilizing the disorder rather than relieving it (Glass, 1953). Rest and care behind front lines, coupled with the expectations of a quick return to combat, appear more successful at preventing chronic disorder from developing. In cases of civilian survivors of disaster, participation in volunteer community clean-up and rebuilding efforts can speed recovery (Barton, 1969). Much remains to be learned, however, regarding effective treatment for the effects of extreme situational stress.

---

encompasses a wide range of common experiences, such as exposure to an inconsiderate smoker or having unexpected company, worries about the rising costs of food and housing, concerns about one's future, feelings of loneliness, and fear of rejection by others. Daily hassles are transitory, minor experiences that nonetheless are viewed by the individual as memorable and

distressing. They, too, can produce demands that tax a person's abilities to cope. We will examine the physical as well as the psychological consequences of life events, chronic difficulties, and daily hassles at some length later in the chapter.

Conflict

Another kind of demand that results in stress is **conflict,** which occurs when a person must choose between incompatible, contradictory, or mutually exclusive goals or courses of action. Two goals are mutually exclusive when the action needed to achieve one automatically prevents the person from reaching the other. Conflict can occur when two inner needs are in opposition, when two external demands pull the person in different directions, or when an inner need is incompatible with an external demand. Psychologists who have described and studied conflict (Lewin, 1931; Miller, 1944) have categorized some basic forms of conflict according to the person's tendency to approach or to avoid a goal.

Approach-Approach Conflict.   In **approach-approach conflict** people are faced with two equally attractive but mutually exclusive goals, a situation in which choosing one automatically means giving up the other. This is bound to make people more discontented than if they faced only one attractive goal. Someone who receives two good job offers, for example, may agonize over the decision and feel doubts after making the choice; this stress probably would not have occurred with only one job offer.

Approach-Avoidance Conflict.   Here the person is confronted with a single goal that has both positive and negative consequences. If you have ever tried to feed a wild animal, you have seen **approach-avoidance conflict**—the animal wants the food, yet is naturally afraid to come close to a human for it. People generally experience this sort of stress when they want to do something but know that some of the consequences will be unpleasant. Many people approach marriage with these feelings—love for the other person leads them to approach marriage, but uneasiness about new responsibilities and loss of freedom makes them want to avoid it.

One child seems to be experiencing a form of approach-avoidance conflict: The desire to touch the dog conflicts with a natural fear of getting too close. (Bill Anderson/Monkmeyer Press)

Avoidance-Avoidance Conflict. This type of stressful situation involves an inescapable choice between two equally unattractive goals or outcomes. A baseball player caught between two bases is faced with **avoidance-avoidance conflict:** Going forward or going back will result in being tagged out. A middle-aged man may hate the thought of spending the rest of his working years in a job that he finds boring. At the same time, he knows the problems of changing careers at his age, and he probably has family responsibilities that make it hard for him to start over. The response to this type of conflict is often to avoid making any decision at all.

Double Approach-Avoidance Conflict. In this complex situation two possible courses of action each present an approach-avoidance conflict. Think of a college senior attempting to choose between two job offers, each of which has both desirable and undesirable components. One job, for example, promises challenging work (approach) but low pay (avoidance). The other promises a good deal of tedium (avoidance) but a lucrative salary (approach). The student in this situation is in a **double approach-avoidance conflict** and, quite understandably, may respond with stress.

The runner caught between two bases is a classic example of avoidance-avoidance conflict: Moving ahead or going back will both result in the negative outcome of being tagged out. (Focus on Sports)

CONSEQUENCES OF STRESS

It is now widely believed that exposure to severe or prolonged environmental stress can produce physical and even mental illness. Stress has been linked to a variety of disorders—high blood pressure, heart disease, ulcers, even cancer and schizophrenia. But exactly how these illnesses are produced by stress is not yet understood, although studies of physiological reactions to stress suggest important answers, especially with respect to physical illness.

The Biological Perspective

Psychologists who assert a physiological basis for behavior consider stress a biological event. In this view, stress is a set of physiological responses to demands placed upon the individual. (Indeed, physiological change is one of the most widely used indicators of stress reactions because it is concrete and measurable.) Most psychologists who take a biological approach to stress believe that physiological reactions to external demands overwhelm the body's resistance to disease or impair the ability of body organs to function.

Much of our understanding of the physiology of stress comes from the pioneering work of Hans Selye (1956), an endocrinologist and biochemist. In the mid-1920s Selye's experiments on animals showed that physical reactions repeatedly occurred in response to a variety of noxious stimuli—heat, cold, X rays, forced exercise, injections, and so on. This gave Selye the idea that there might be a general pattern of reaction to stress that did not differ according to the source of the stress. He called this pattern the **General Adaptation Syndrome.**

The General Adaptation Syndrome. This syndrome is described by Selye (1956) as a three-stage response. It begins with an *alarm reaction* characterized by a number of physical changes: increases in heart rate, respiratory activity, endocrine secretions, sweat-gland activity, temperature, and blood

pressure, as well as muscle tension. You may have observed many of these reactions in yourself when you were under stress.

In the *stage of resistance* people recover from the initial alarm and try to cope with the stressful situation. The external physical symptoms of stress disappear and the internal responses to stress—hormone activity, heart rate, and blood pressure—become normalized. In this stage everything appears to be under control, but the appearance is deceptive. In fact, the person's emotional and physical resources are being consumed by his or her efforts to control the stress. If the stressful condition continues, the person will enter the third stage—*exhaustion*. If a new stress arises during the stage of resistance, a person will often break down and enter the exhaustion phase immediately.

Selye's (1956) biochemical studies showed that the adrenal glands play a major role in the General Adaptation Syndrome. The adrenal medulla is controlled by the sympathetic nervous system (see Chapter 2). When it is stimulated in response to some form of excitement, it secretes quantities of epinephrine and norepinephrine into the blood. These hormones increase metabolism and help the body to release energy stores, which causes the physical reactions described as part of the alarm reaction.

The stage of resistance is characterized by increased activity of the adrenal cortex. In order to function, the adrenal cortex must be stimulated by the hormone ACTH, which is produced by the pituitary gland. When an organism is subjected to stress, the pituitary secretions increase. This, in turn, causes the adrenal cortex to produce more hormones. Some of the effects of these hormones on other parts of the body are maintenance of blood pressure, manufacture of red blood cells, blocking of the inflammatory response, and increased blood sugar level.

It is not surprising that with all these physiological responses to stress, people who are exposed to stress over a long period of time often become ill. In the next section we will look at some of these stress-linked disorders.

Psychosomatic Illiness.   Psychosomatic illnesses are real physical illnesses that require medical attention. Examples are ulcers, migraine headaches, asthma, eczema, and high blood pressure. These are illnesses that appear to be caused, at least in part, by psychological stress. It is important to note that the term *psychosomatic* is often misused. Quite often it is applied to types of neurotic physical symptoms that exist primarily in the patient's mind. Psychosomatic illnesses have true physical symptoms.

Scientists who have studied these stress-linked disorders have been confronted with a number of questions. Why, for example, do some people become ill from stress while others do not? Why does stress cause a physical illness instead of an emotional one? Why does one person get ulcers from stress while another has a heart attack?

Many theories have been developed to answer these questions. One, the *specific-reaction theory,* says that psychosomatic illnesses depend on the particular stressor experienced by a person (Alexander, 1950; Mason, 1971). For example, Alexander argued that particular unconscious emotional conflicts (types of stress) produce particular psychosomatic disorders. Others have pointed to possible variations in illness outcomes that occur with acute versus chronic stress (Mahl, 1952), or with certain emotional reactions (Mason, 1971), or with particular perceptions of the stressful situation (Lazarus & Launier, 1978). However, specific-reaction theory does not explain why some people who experience a particular stressor become ill, while others do not.

Diathesis-stress theory, on the other hand, suggests that specific disorders

HIGHLIGHT

Stress and the Immune System

Quite recently, some exciting developments have come from research on the immune system's response to stress. The immune system manufactures antibodies to fight against invasions of bacteria, viruses, allergens, and even cancerous cells. Researchers previously believed that the immune system worked independently of other bodily systems—not responding to changes in the nervous system, the sympathetic or parasympathetic systems, or the brain, for example. There is now considerable new evidence that the immune system does respond to bodily changes. In particular, studies show that when a person is experiencing a reaction to stress, the functioning of the immune system is impaired. This, in turn, leaves the person more vulnerable to disease (Jemmott & Locke, 1984).

For example, in one study periods of high academic stress were associated with low secretion rates of immunoglobulin A (IgA), an antibody that defends against upper respiratory infections. Students with low IgA had more respiratory infections during midterm and final examination weeks than they had during periods of lower academic stress (Jemmott et al., 1983). Similarly, a study of bereaved men whose wives had died of breast cancer showed that the men's white blood cells (T lymphocytes) were less responsive to an activating substance during the two months following their wives' deaths (Schleifer et al., 1979). In some of the men low immunological responsiveness persisted for a year. Low T lymphocyte responsiveness leaves widowers more susceptible to disease. This immunological response may help explain why so many widowers die soon after their wives do (Stroebe & Stroebe, 1983). Notice that these studies are consistent with Selye's stress-response model. One of the consequences of the stage of exhaustion is lowered resistance to infection, which increases the likelihood of the occurrence of disease.

Impaired immune functioning may eventually help explain why stress is related to such diseases as tuberculosis, mononucleosis, allergies, recurrences of herpes simplex, and even cancer. For example, Sklar and Anisman (1981) compared the tumor development of mice that had been implanted with cancer cells. Those that were exposed to inescapable shocks developed larger tumors rapidly than mice given escapable shocks or receiving no shock at all. Since inescapable shocks are more stressful than escapable shocks, this research again suggests that stress interferes with immune functioning— in this case, reducing the proliferation of T lymphocyte cells necessary to fight cancer. Even patients' attitudes toward their disease can make a difference in immune activity. In one study breast cancer patients who suppressed their anger, lacked good social support, and were generally apathetic had lower killer cell activity and a greater spread of cancer through their lymph nodes (Morris et al., 1981). Although it is not clear at this time whether the women's attitudes were a result or a cause of the spread of their cancers, these findings raise the exciting possibility that increased immunological activity might be stimulated by training patients to take a more aggressive attitude toward their disease. At a minimum, studies such as these point to the importance of psychosocial factors for explaining disease onset. Interventions designed to prevent disease may also be developed as the relationships between stress experiences and immunological functioning become better understood.

are produced by a combination of stressors and biological predisposition (Sternbach, 1966; Schwartz, 1977; Gannon, 1981). According to this model, both a diathesis, or predisposing organic condition, and precipitating stressful events are necessary to produce psychosomatic symptoms. Some theorists hold that any stressor can generate a reaction similar to Selye's General Adaptation Syndrome (Levi, 1965; Lazarus, 1977). The type of illness that develops depends upon the person's weakest or most vulnerable body system. For example, people whose lungs have been weakened by smoking may be predisposed to asthma when they experience prolonged stress.

Other theorists suggest that people develop disorders in the system in which they show the greatest responsiveness to stress (Engel, 1960). In this view, the illness is not due to a weak body system; instead, the system is overreactive to stress. One individual, for example, experiences rapid acceleration of heartbeat under stress. Another produces excessive stomach acid. These unique reactions, which may be genetically determined, may help predict which system of the body will be prone to a stress-linked disorder. Diathesis-stress theory explains, in part, why different people exposed to the same stressor develop different symptoms. Future work may pinpoint combinations of specific stressors with specific body weaknesses (or

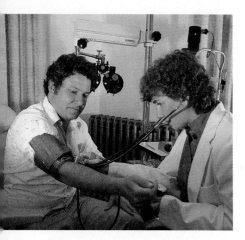

High blood pressure, or hypertension, has been repeatedly linked to stress. The disorder is known to affect more men than women at present, but women's rates of hypertension are on the rise. (Linda K. Moore/Rainbow)

Table 16–1: Social Readjustment Rating Scale

Life Event	Mean LCU Value
Death of spouse	100
Divorce	73
Marital separation	65
Jail term	63
Death of close family member	63
Personal injury or illness	53
Marriage	50
Fired at work	47
Marital reconciliation	45
Retirement	45
Change in health of family member	44
Pregnancy	40
Sex difficulties	39

overreactivities) to further explain the development of particular psychosomatic disorders. Environmental, psychological, and physiological factors undoubtedly interact, but exactly how these factors work together has yet to be determined (Weiner, 1977; Lazarus, 1977). We turn now from theories of physiological stress processes to describe specific psychosomatic disorders.

Hypertension, or high blood pressure, is one disorder that has been linked to stress. *Essential hypertension* is chronic high blood pressure that cannot be traced to an organic cause. Acceleration of the heartbeat, often experienced under stress, has something to do with high blood pressure. More important, experts feel, is the constriction of the walls of the arteries, a phenomenon that also occurs under stress, which forces the heart to work harder to drive the blood through the narrowed arteries.

Much research has been done on the link between stress and hypertension. Numerous studies show an association between stress and a short-term rise in blood pressure (Hokanson, DeGood, Forrest, & Britton, 1971; Dembroski, MacDougall, Herd, & Shields, 1979). These studies consistently demonstrate that people respond to the threat of shock or to challenge with increased blood pressure. However, the blood pressure returns to normal after a short time. Long-term or chronic hypertension has been found in people who have lost their jobs (Kase & Cobb, 1970), people who experience daily traffic congestion while commuting (Stokols, Novaco, Stokols, & Campbell, 1978), and even people who are undergoing the stressful experience of hospitalization (Volicer & Volicer, 1978). How these episodic environmental stressors translate into chronic hypertension has not yet been established.

Ulcers.   Another set of physiological responses to stress occurs in the *gastrointestinal* system. The body reacts to a stressor by secreting certain hormones that increase the flow of the stomach's acidic digestive juices as well as engorge the stomach with blood. As a result, the mucous lining of the stomach is stretched out and the entire gastrointestinal system is subjected to excessive amounts of gastric acid. After prolonged exposure to such acids, the mucous layer is eaten through, resulting in ulceration of the stomach or small intestine (producing *gastric ulcers* or *duodenal ulcers,* respectively). The most common ulcers are duodenal (Walker & Sandman, 1981), which have been clearly related to excess hydrochloric acid secretion. Gastric ulcers, on the other hand, may be due less to excess acid than to inadequate secretions of protective mucus in the stomach lining. Certain individuals seem predisposed to produce high levels of gastric acid (Weiner, 1977). If these people are exposed to prolonged stress, they have an increased likelihood of developing an ulcer.

Probably the best-known experiments showing a relationship between stress and gastrointestinal activity were performed by Brady and his colleagues (Brady, 1958; Porter et al., 1958). They placed two monkeys who had initially been trained to avoid shock in situations where only one of them (the "executive monkey") could turn off the shock for both of them after a warning signal had been given. The executive monkey had to press a lever at least every 20 seconds to prevent a shock to itself and the control monkey. The executive monkey died, and at autopsy it was found to have both gastric and duodenal ulcers. Brady and his co-workers suggested from these studies that ulcers are related to responsibility for decision making. Although several studies have failed to replicate the "executive monkey effect" (Foltz & Millett, 1964; Natelson, 1977; Weiss, 1977), subsequent research suggests that the combination of low situational control and a high number of required responses will predict severe ulceration (Weiss, 1977).

Stress Measurement

In order to study the effects of stress on health, researchers have had to devise ways to measure exposure to stressful demands. Because major life events are common stressors, they have been a special focus of attention. One scale, the Social Readjustment Rating Scale, developed by Holmes and Rahe (1967), has proved to be a valuable tool in examining the number and magnitude of stressful events people experience.

Holmes and Rahe (1967) asked people to judge 43 life events according to the degree of social readjustment each required. All comparisons were made against marriage, which was assigned an arbitrary value; judges were supposed to decide whether each event listed called for more or less readjustment than marriage. Ratings did not depend on the desirability of the event—it could be positively or negatively viewed—but only on the amount of readjustment required. Consensus was high among participants in the first rating study, and has continued high in subsequent studies, even among adolescents, who presumably have not themselves experienced a number of these life changes (Holmes, 1979).

These readjustment ratings were averaged to yield a value for each life event. These were called Life Change Units (LCUs). The more stressful an event, the higher its LCU value. But again, the emphasis is on change rather than on the psychological meaning or social desirability of the event. The events ranged in stressfulness from death of a spouse down to a vacation or a minor law violation.

The resulting Social Readjustment Rating Scale has proved to be a useful tool in examining the relationship between life change and health change (see Table 16–1). In the typical study using the Social Readjustment Rating Scale, people are asked to indicate which of the events listed on the questionnaire happened to them over a fixed time period, either six months to one year ago or one year to two years ago. The stress value for each event is multiplied by the number of times the event occurred and the values for all events are totaled to produce a score in Life Change Units for the specific time period. Researchers then look at the relationship between Life Change Units, a quantified amount of required readjustment, and health changes in the individual.

In one study, for example, 100 college athletes filled out a special version of the scale, called the Social and Athletic Readjustment Rating Scale (Bramwell et al., 1975), before the start of the football season. At the end of the season the researchers collected data about injuries. Seventy percent of those players in the high-risk group (with 300 or more Life Change Units) had had at least one injury during the three-month season. Of those in the medium-risk group (200 to 300 LCUs), about 50 percent had been injured. And only about a third of those in the low-risk group (100 to 200 LCUs) had been hurt. Furthermore, of the 11 players who had multiple injuries during the season, 9 were in the high-risk group.

Since its publication in 1967, literally hundreds of studies have utilized the Social Readjustment Rating Scale. Scores on the scale have been positively associated with sudden cardiac death, onset of heart disease, fractures, diabetes, leukemia, and influenza as well as minor illnesses such as colds (Holmes & Masuda, 1974). Scores on the Social Readjustment Rating Scale (and other life-events scales developed subsequently) have also been associated with neurosis, depression, schizophrenia, and symptoms of serious psychological distress (Dohrenwend & Dohrenwend, 1974; Barrett, 1979). Psychological disorders are particularly likely to follow from negative life

Table 16–1: (cont.)

Life Event	Mean LCU Value
Gain of new family member	39
Business readjustment	39
Change in financial state	38
Death of close friend	37
Change to different line of work	36
Change in number of arguments with spouse	35
Mortgage over $10,000	31
Foreclosure of mortgage or loan	30
Change in responsibilities at work	29
Son or daughter leaving home	29
Trouble with in-laws	29
Outstanding personal achievement	28
Wife begins or stops work	26
Begin or end school	26
Change in living conditions	25
Revision of personal habits	24
Trouble with boss	23
Change in work hours or conditions	20
Change in residence	20
Change in schools	20
Change in recreation	19
Change in church activities	19
Change in social activities	18
Mortgage or loan less than $10,000	17
Change in sleeping habits	16
Change in number of family get-togethers	15
Change in eating habits	15
Vacation	13
Christmas	12
Minor violations of the law	11

From Holmes and Rahe (1967), p. 216.

For several reasons, we should be cautious in interpreting the findings of studies based on the Holmes and Rahe (1967) Social Readjustment Rating Scale (SRRS) and other life-events scales. First, the SRRS may not adequately measure the extent of life change for most people. Many common stressful life events are not listed on the scale—for example, being the victim of a crime, going on strike, receiving a promotion or demotion, having a traffic accident, obtaining an abortion. You can probably think of many others as you examine the scale (see Table 16–1). The SRRS tends to underrepresent events that happen to the poor, to students, to women, and to various ethnic and specific occupational groups.

Second, ratings of the amount of readjustment required by each event, averaged into Life Change Unit (LCU) scores, can vary depending upon the sex, age, race, ethnicity, and nationality of the raters (Miller et al., 1974; Rosenberg & Dohrenwend, 1975; Hough et al., 1976). Notice, too, that

the most socially undesirable, or negative, events (death of spouse, divorce, etc.) have the highest LCU values. This suggests that rather than measuring the amount of life *change,* the SRRS may be measuring the amount of *negative* change in a person's life. In fact, numerous studies do suggest that negative changes are more predictive of ill health than either total change or positive change (Vinokur & Selzer, 1975; Glass, 1977; Mueller et al., 1977; Sarason et al., 1978).

Third, studies using the SRRS often rely on retrospective reports that may not be highly accurate. The longer the time period for which people are asked to report, the less accurate may be their recall. (What has happened to *you* in the last five years?) On the other hand, people who are trying to explain their illness may recall more events, especially undesirable ones, in an "effort after meaning" (Brown, 1974). Such biased recall may inflate the associations between LCU scores and illness. For this reason, many life-events researchers have designed prospective studies (Holmes & Masuda, 1974). That is, they collect data on the SRRS at one point in time, and several months to a year later they assess their subjects' health status. In this way, bias from retrospective reporting can be avoided.

But finally, even prospective studies must be viewed cautiously: The SRSS contains many items that are changes in health (personal illness and injury) or may be symptoms of health change (change in eating habits, change in sleeping habits, sex difficulties). A researcher who thinks he or she is examining the relationship between *life* changes and future illness may simply be finding a relationship between *health* changes and future illness (Thoits, 1981). The SRRS contains items that are contaminated by the outcomes that they are intended to explain. This problem affects both prospective and retrospective life-events studies.

In short, it pays to be a critical consumer of life-events research. Many flaws may undermine the significance of many of the findings thus far. However, those researchers who have carefully controlled for these problems (cf. Tausig, 1982) still report that there are indeed associations between life changes, especially negative ones, and physical and psychological disorders. The SRRS has served as a useful springboard for research in this area. More recent life-events scales (e.g., Dohrenwend et al., 1978) have advanced beyond the SRRS, reflecting a wider range of people's life experiences, while also controlling for contaminating items.

events rather than from the total number of events, both positive and negative. Depression is especially associated with negative, uncontrollable events (such as deaths, being laid off, and sudden illness). Although there have been numerous criticisms of life-events studies in general and the Social Readjustment Rating Scale in particular, the bulk of the evidence does suggest that the cumulative effects of adapting to environmental demands lowers the body's resistance to disease.

More recently, attention has turned to the measurement of daily hassles (as well as uplifts). Recall that hassles are transitory experiences and concerns that nevertheless are appraised as stressful. Uplifts, on the other hand, are passing experiences perceived as positive or favorable for one's well-being (e.g., a good night's rest, making a friend, receiving a compliment). Kanner and his colleagues (1981) have created a 117-item Hassles Scale and a 135-item Uplifts Scale (see Table 16–2). Subjects are asked to indicate how often each hassle or uplift on these scales occurred in the past month and also to rate how intensely each experience affected them (somewhat, moderately, or extremely). Simple frequency scores for hassles and for uplifts are computed from the number of items checked on each scale. Intensity scores are the average intensity ratings for all items checked on each scale.

In one study (DeLongis et al., 1982) 100 adults in the San Francisco Bay area were asked to fill out the Hassles and Uplifts Scales every month for a total of nine months. They were also asked to report the number and intensity of major life events experienced over that time. Finally, their health status was assessed at the end of that period with a questionnaire about physical symptoms, physical disabilities, and overall energy level. Interestingly, ill health in these adults was more strongly associated with the frequency and intensity of hassles than with the number and severity of life events. (Uplifts were not associated with ill health at all.) In other words, the minor stresses of daily life appeared to predict illness better than major life changes did. These and similar findings (Kanner et al., 1981) have led some researchers to argue that the cumulative difficulties of daily life are more important than major events in affecting one's health. But at present such claims must be viewed cautiously. Daily-hassles research is plagued by the same problems as life-events research (see the Highlight: A Cautionary Note on Life-Events Research). In addition, a personality factor such as pessimism may cause some subjects to report both more hassles and more health problems, in effect inflating the association between hassles and illness. So, although the findings do suggest that accumulated minor stresses lower resistance to disease, additional research will be needed to verify this and to rule out other possibilities.

So far we have been concerned with the consequences of stress for the physical and psychological health of individuals. Although illness or disturbance often follows from severe or prolonged stress exposure, such consequences are far from inevitable. This is because people often successfully cope with the stressors in their lives, thus eliminating or reducing their harmful physiological effects. We turn now to consider the different ways that people cope with environmental demands.

COPING WITH STRESS

Many coping patterns that we will discuss are used to eliminate a general psychological response elicited by most stressors—**anxiety.** Anxiety is a term with many connotations. It is used to refer to symptoms of psychopathology, to realistic fears, to irrational emotional states, and to normal reactions experienced by everyone. We will see that while anxiety is a fearful psychological *reaction* to stressful events, it often becomes itself a *source* of stress to which the individual must adjust. That is, anxiety may be so intense that the person must cope with it first before turning attention to its causes. Some coping patterns, then, may be used to reduce (or avoid) anxiety itself, while others are used to adapt to external stressors. In either case, anxiety serves to motivate coping attempts.

The Learning Perspective

Learning theorists suggest that the various methods people use to cope with stress are the result of learning specific response-reinforcement relationships. In this view, the reduction of anxiety or fear is reinforcing. To describe this perspective, we must include both classical and operant conditioning processes.

You will recall from our discussion in Chapter 6 that an organism can be conditioned to fear a neutral stimulus through *classical conditioning* tech-

Table 16–2: Example Items from the Hassles and Uplifts Scales.

Hassles

Misplacing or losing things
Troublesome neighbors
Concerns about owing money
Too many responsibilities
Planning meals
Having to wait
Being lonely
Too many things to do
Too many meetings
Gossip
The weather
Difficulties with friends
Silly practical mistakes
Difficulties with getting pregnant
Auto maintenance
Filling out forms
Unchallenging work
Concern about the meaning of life
Declining physical abilities
Problems with your lover

Uplifts

Getting enough sleep
The weather
Not working (on vacation, laid-off, etc.)
Staying or getting into good physical shape
Quitting or cutting down on smoking
Sex
Spending time with family
Shopping
Making a friend
Looking forward to retirement
Being complimented
Going someplace that's different
Giving love
Being "one" with the world
Flirting
Fixing/repairing something (besides at your job)
Having good ideas at work
Getting a present
Having fun
Socializing (parties, being with friends, etc.)
Good news on local or world level

From Kanner, Coyne, Schaefer, & Lazarus, 1981.

niques. In one experiment (Miller, 1948), for example, rats were shocked repeatedly while a tone was sounded; after many trials the rats showed fear at the sound of the tone alone. The tone had become a conditioned stimulus for the fear response.

The rats also learned new responses to avoid the sound of the tone (the conditioned stimulus), and thus they learned new responses to avoid fear (the conditioned response). This part of the learning model uses the principles of *operant conditioning*. The new response was rewarded by a reduction of the fear caused by a previously conditioned stimulus, the tone. The interesting point here is that the rats learned new behavior to avoid a stimulus that in itself was harmless—the tone didn't hurt them, and yet to escape the tone was reinforcing.

Learning theory suggests, then, that coping behaviors are learned avoidance responses that alleviate anxiety. Such behaviors will be used repeatedly unless they subsequently fail to reduce anxiety. An interesting extension of this idea can be found in the work of Martin Seligman (1975) and his colleagues. They discovered that dogs exposed to uncontrollable and inescapable shock later failed to try to escape, even in situations where escape was possible. What is most interesting about these studies is that the animals appear to give up—they stop responding entirely and endure the shocks passively. Seligman has labeled this state "learned helplessness" because what the animals are learning is that no response they make will affect the outcome or change what happens to them.

Learned helplessness has also been demonstrated in humans (Hiroto & Seligman, 1975; Garber & Seligman, 1980). In the typical study subjects are exposed to bursts of uncontrollable noise or to puzzles they cannot solve. In a subsequent situation when control *is* possible, these subjects fail to try—they react helplessly. They have learned that their responses do not affect the outcome of events, and their learned expectation prevents them from acquiring other knowledge or behavior patterns that would help them to gain control over their environment. Learned helplessness is not necessarily an inappropriate or negative response in some situations. It is at times a beneficial strategy, since giving up can be accompanied by reduced anxiety (Gatchel & Proctor, 1976).

While learning theorists see learned helplessness as an entirely learned mode of responding, recent research disputes this. The inability to control a situation is a key factor in the experience of helplessness, and the expectation of control depends in part on a person's perceptions and attributions. Thus it is the individual's *interpretation* of the situational demand that determines the stress reaction. Recently, learned-helplessness theory has been reformulated to take these interpretational or attributional factors into account. This reformulation leads us to another approach to stress and anxiety, the cognitive approach.

The Cognitive Perspective

So far, we have been concerned with how individuals respond to anxiety that results from environmental demands. But individuals also differ widely in their perception of what is or is not stressful, and this perception determines the degree of anxiety they experience as well as the types of coping responses they use. For this view, we will turn to the cognitive model.

From a cognitive perspective, the stress experience is more than the sum total of the stressors to which one is exposed. A cognitive psychologist ac-

In our society transportation delays are certainly a common source of daily hassles. (John Huber)

APPLICATION

Type-A Behavior and Coronary Heart Disease

Most discussions of coping imply that making an active effort to solve problems is a good way to combat or reduce stress in our lives. However, one particular kind of coping response calls this idea into question. This response is called Type-A or coronary-prone behavior pattern (Friedman, 1969).

You have probably observed many Type-A people in your own life. They tend to be impatient, aggressive, competitive individuals who are filled with a sense of urgency. A traffic jam

Ten Easily Spotted Signs of Type-A Behavior

- Moving, eating, or walking rapidly
- Hurrying the ends of sentences
- Impatience
- Feeling guilty about relaxation
- Thinking about work while vacationing
- Doing several things at once; e.g., shaving and driving
- Trying to increase work over ever-shorter time periods
- Not listening to the opinions of others
- Acquiring objects rather than enjoying them
- Relating success to time; i.e., speed is everything

Adapted from Richard D. Lyons, "Stress addiction: 'Life in the fast lane' may have its benefits." *New York Times*, July 26, 1983, p. C9.

can send a Type-A person into a fit of anger; Type-A people cannot stand to be kept waiting even for a few minutes. Type-B people, in contrast, tend to be more relaxed and accepting of events and occurrences.

Does the Type-A behavior pattern fit you? If so, then watch out. There is a considerable amount of evidence that Type-A behavior is related to heart disease. One study followed more than 3,000 employed, college-educated, middle-aged California men over an eight-and-a-half-year period (Rosenman et al., 1975; Brand et al., 1976). These men were interviewed in 1960 and classified as Type A or Type B. At regular intervals over the next eight years, Rosenman and his colleagues assessed blood pressure, serum cholesterol, weight, cigarette smoking, and other measures of risk for heart disease. They found that the rate of coronary heart disease among Type A men was *twice* that of Type Bs, even when standard risk factors were controlled.

Recent studies have reported a weaker relationship between Type A and coronary disease (Matthews, 1984). However, this change may be due to altered methods of measuring Type-A behavior or to changes in the health practices of people at high risk for the disease. Type-A behaviors such as rapid speech, impatience, and especially hostility are still highly related to coronary trouble (Dembroski et al., 1985).

Although Type-A behavior is strongly associated with coronary heart disease, the mechanisms by which this behavior brings about illness have yet to be established. One hypothesis suggested by Glass (1977) is that Type-A individuals overrespond to

stress, and in particular, to loss of control.

In a series of studies Glass showed that when confronted by a stressful situation in which they feel they do not have control, Type-A individuals struggle to assert their control. They work faster, strive harder, and become more aggressive. After extended exposure to situations that they feel unable to control, however, Type-A people show a dramatic decline in their attempts to manage the situation. In contrast, when Type-B people encounter uncontrollable situations, their reactions are calmer and more even. They show neither frantic attempts to gain control in the beginning nor a lack of assertive energy when stress is prolonged.

Physiological comparisons of Type-A and Type-B people indicate that extreme blood pressure elevations characterize Type-A individuals under stress but not Type Bs (Goldband et al., 1979). Blood pressure, then, may represent the physiological link between the Type-A behavior pattern, uncontrollable stress, and coronary heart disease. These self-destructive coping responses may be amenable to change. In a recent study a sample of men who had had heart attacks were trained to relax. They were encouraged to practice behaviors incompatible with Type-A responses: driving in slow highway lanes, standing in the longest line at the bank, playing games to lose, taking time off to do nothing. Compared to a control group of heart attack victims, the men who changed their behaviors suffered only half as many subsequent heart attacks over a three-year period (Friedman & Ulmer, 1984).

knowledges the role that the individual plays in the experience of stress. Lazarus and Folkman (1984) describe stress as a transaction between people and their environments in which the critical mediating variable is people's *perception* of a demand and of their own ability to cope with it. Stress in this view is composed of three elements. First, there is a set of environmental events that may or may not be potentially stressful. Second, there is the individual's cognitive appraisal of the degree to which those environmental events represent serious harm, threat, or challenge to well-being *(primary appraisal)*. And finally, there is the individual's appraisal of the adequacy of his or her resources and abilities to cope with that threat or challenge

(secondary appraisal). Secondary appraisal helps determine the type of coping response the person will use in the face of stress.

The crucial importance of appraisal was demonstrated in an early set of studies by Lazarus and his colleagues (Lazarus & Alfert, 1964; Speisman et al., 1964). They showed subjects a silent film of Australian Aboriginal puberty rites. The film focused on the crude surgical operations performed on the genitals of male adolescents (subincision). The film's graphic depiction of pain and genital mutilation elicited strong physiological stress reactions and self-reports of stress among a group of control subjects (Lazarus et al., 1962), so the film was clearly highly threatening. Three different sound tracks were then superimposed upon the film. In one sound track, the "trauma" track, the commentary emphasized the pain, mutilation, and health hazard to the boys. The "denial" track emphasized the happiness of the boys at becoming fully accepted members of the tribe and denied the harm of the operation. The "intellectualization" track took a detached, unemotional, anthropological view of these strange rites.

As measured by skin conductance and heart rate, the trauma track significantly increased the stress reactions of experimental subjects compared to controls. The denial and intellectualization tracks both significantly reduced subjects' distress. Moreover, the effectiveness of the denial and intellectualization tracks in decreasing stress was enhanced for subjects with denying and intellectualizing personality dispositions, respectively (see Figure 16–1).

These findings, which have been replicated in subsequent studies (Alfert, 1964; Lazarus et al., 1965), are important for two reasons. First, they show that people's *interpretations* of an event alter the amount of anxiety they will feel in response to it. The same threatening event evoked different amounts of stress in subjects who differed only in their appraisals of its meaning. Second, these findings suggest that the use of defense mechanisms can be beneficial for individuals, a theme usually underemphasized by psychoanalytical theorists. From Lazarus's cognitive approach, intrapsychic defense mechanisms can be viewed as ways of interpreting environmental stressors rather than as potentially neurotic responses to internal conflict (see Chapter 17).

Cognitive theorists typically classify coping responses into two broad types: *emotion-focused* and *problem-focused coping* (Lazarus & Folkman, 1984). Emotion-focused responses are attempts to control the anxiety or distress produced by threatening environmental demands: Examples are the use of drugs, alcohol, relaxation techniques, and reinterpretations of the meaning of environmental demands. Problem-focused coping responses are efforts to alter the stress situation itself. The person may actively seek more information, change the situation, or pursue the skills needed to meet environmental demands. A recent study shows that people typically use several coping responses to handle each stressor (Folkman & Lazarus, 1980). For example, a person facing life-threatening surgery may put his or her financial affairs in order (problem-focused coping), try not to think about the upcoming operation (emotion-focused coping), and take tranquilizers (emotion-focused coping).

Recently, attention has turned to ways of measuring people's coping responses. Folkman and Lazarus (1980) have devised a Ways of Coping Checklist that consists of 63 items. The checklist measures many problem-focused and emotion-focused techniques that people may use when attempting to handle a stressful episode. Problem-focused techniques include "made a plan of action and followed it," "stood your ground and fought for what

Cognitive researchers typically classify coping responses into two broad types: emotion-focused and problem-focused. The threat to home and family posed by a natural disaster such as an earthquake would very likely elicit both. (Peter Marlow/Magnum Photos)

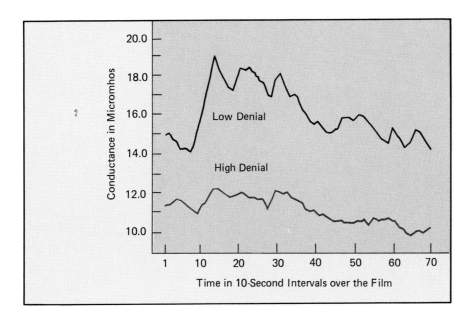

Figure 16–1 Effects of the subincision film on skin conductance for subjects high and low in denial disposition. (Lazarus & Alfert, 1964, p. 201)

you wanted," and "got the person responsible to change his or her mind." Emotion-focused techniques include "looked for the 'silver lining,'" "accepted sympathy and understanding from someone," and "tried to forget the whole thing." Recently, Stone and Neale (1984) have discovered that people may use the same coping technique for very different purposes. For example, people might engage in hard physical exercise in order to relax, to distract themselves from a problem, or to release their emotions. Consequently, Stone and Neale have devised a shorter instrument to measure the purposes, or functions, of people's coping efforts (see Table 16–3). As more research on coping efforts is done using these instruments, we may better understand which coping techniques and which coping functions are most effective for reducing stress in specific situations.

Perception of Control

Recent research has begun to focus on a key cognitive factor that affects anxiety: **perceived control,** or the degree to which people believe they have some control over a stressor. When they think they can escape it, avoid it, or even just predict it, people have a milder reaction to a threatening environmental demand. This reduction of stress often is based entirely on people's *perception* of their control, not on how much control they actually have.

Several studies have demonstrated that perceptions of control over avoidance responses can actually reduce stress responses (Glass & Singer, 1972). For example, Hokanson and his colleagues (1971) assigned two groups of college students to a learning task. Students who failed to achieve a good score received an electric shock. One group was given the option of asking for "time-out" from the stress of learning. The other group received the same number and length of rest periods as the first group, but these students had no control over when the "time-outs" occurred. The students' blood pressure levels were measured to indicate their stress levels. Students who believed that they could control their escape from the shock showed less stress (had lower blood pressure) than those who did not (see Figure 16–2).

Table 16–3: Coping Efforts and Function.

1. Diverted attention away from the problem by thinking about other things or engaging in some activity.
2. Tried to see the problem in a different light that made it seem more bearable.
3. Thought about solutions to the problem, gathered information about it, or actually did something to try to solve it.
4. Expressed emotions in response to the problem to reduce tension, anxiety, or frustration.
5. Accepted that the problem had occurred, but that nothing could be done about it.
6. Sought or found emotional support from loved ones, friends, or professionals.
7. Did something with the implicit intention of relaxing.
8. Sought or found spiritual comfort and support.

From Stone & Neale (1984).

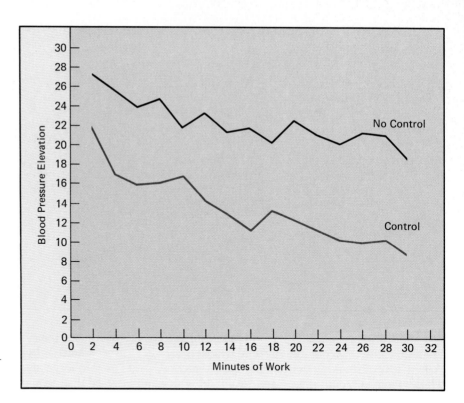

Figure 16–2 The graph shows the results of a study by Hokanson et al. (1971). Students who perceived that they had control over when they escaped the shock showed less stress (had lower blood pressure) than students who perceived that they had no control.

It is useful to distinguish between three types of control (Thompson, 1981). *Behavioral control* is an action or response that can eliminate an aversive stimulus. When we can press a button to signal the dentist to stop drilling, we have behavioral control. Information that allows us to anticipate and get ready for an experience, or information that explains the causes and probable outcomes of a stressful experience, gives us *informational control.* When the doctor warns us that "This will hurt a little bit," or explains how long it might take to recover from an illness, we have informational control. *Cognitive control* is the ability to reduce stress by thinking in a certain way. When we deliberately distract our attention from the discomfort of long-distance running by listening to loud music, we have cognitive control.

It is important to recognize that when a situation is truly uncontrollable, attempts to achieve behavioral control may be less effective in reducing stress than other means of coping (Folkman, 1984). A study of reactions to the accident in the nuclear energy plant at Three Mile Island offers a useful example. Although the Three Mile Island disaster in 1979 was a short-term life event in the lives of residents in the area (the immediate danger ended when the reactor was stabilized), the accident has created long-term, chronic strain. Local residents continue to worry about the possible future effects of radiation on themselves and their children—effects such as sterility and leukemia.

Baum, Fleming, and Singer (1983) interviewed a sample of Three Mile Island residents after the accident and another sample living near an undamaged nuclear plant more than 100 miles away. They administered the Ways of Coping Checklist to both groups (Folkman & Lazarus, 1980), assessed people's stress symptoms (e.g., dizziness, nightmares, headaches, nervousness), and also collected physiological measures of stress (levels of epinephrine and norepinephrine in the urine). Three Mile Island residents who

had attempted to gain behavioral control (by attending investigatory hearings, by bringing suit against the plant, and so on) had higher stress levels than residents who had engaged in cognitive control (a type of emotion-focused coping). Because there was little that residents could actually do to make the situation safer, controlling their thoughts and emotions about the accident and its aftermath was more effective in reducing stress than trying to act.

Some studies have directly compared the effectiveness of informational control and cognitive control for reducing stress. In one study Langer, Janis, and Wolfer (1975) worked with patients who were scheduled for elective surgery in a large hospital. One group of patients was taught to concentrate only on the favorable aspects of their upcoming surgery (e.g., it was a chance to rest, to take stock of your life, or to lose unwanted pounds). In essence, these patients learned how to control their thoughts about the situation. A second group was told in some detail about the upcoming operation and the recovery period. The information was intended to make the experience more understandable and therefore less stressful. A third group was given a combination of cognitive control and informtion. A fourth group, the control group, received no special instructions. The most effective coping method turned out to be cognitive control, although information control was also effective. Patients who had learned to avoid thoughts about the negative aspects of the situation had the least amount of pre- and postoperative stress. Moreover, 93 percent of the control patients requested both pain relievers and sedatives at least once; 73 percent of the information-control patients made such requests; but only 50 percent of the cognitive-control patients requested medicine.

In some situations, increasing behavioral control can also reduce stress. This has been shown with one group that is especially vulnerable to stress, the institutionalized aged. The inevitable stressors of aging (bereavement, compulsory retirement, declining income and mobility, ill health) and the effects of institutionalization itself can contribute to feelings of loss, anxiety, and dependency in the aged.

Langer and Rodin (1976) demonstrated that these stresses could be reduced by increasing feelings of control among residents of a nursing home. They divided their subjects into two groups. Members of one group were encouraged by the staff to take more control over their daily lives. They were given choices about where to see their visitors, how their rooms would be arranged, what night they would go to a movie. In addition, they were each offered a plant to care for. Those who decided to take a plant had to choose the one they wanted. Members of the second group were encouraged to let the staff help them and look after them. They were told where they would be allowed to see visitors and what night they were scheduled to attend the movies. They were given plants and told that the nurses would water and care for them.

The attitudes and behaviors of the two groups were studied as these treatments continued over a three-week period. The staff and the residents were interviewed, and the activity levels of the residents were monitored. The group that was encouraged to be independent showed an improvement in several areas of behavior. They were more active, happy, and alert than before. The dependent group, in only 3 weeks' time, had become generally more debilitated, less active, and more withdrawn.

Eighteen months later Rodin and Langer (1977) returned to the nursing home to do a follow-up study of their subjects. Using the same methods of interviewing and observation, they discovered that the level of health, happi-

The institutionalized aged are especially vulnerable to stress created by loss of control. In one study researchers found that encouraging elderly residents of a nursing home to take more control over their daily lives helped moderate feelings of loss, anxiety, and dependency. (Langer & Rodin, 1976. *Photo:* James H. Karales/Peter Arnold, Inc.)

ness, activity, and involvement continued to be higher for the subjects in the independence-induced group. Also, only 15 percent of the independence-induced group had died during the 18-month interval, while 30 percent of the dependency-induced group had died. These results were replicated in another study of nursing-home patients (Pohl & Fuller, 1980). Clearly, a sense of control over one's life is important to happiness and health.

Perceived Control as a Personality Resource.   Perceived control not only varies from situation to situation, it exists as an enduring personality characteristic. Some people are high in perceived control as a general outlook on life, others feel a general lack of control. It is believed that people high in perceived control are more likely to engage in problem-focused coping and therefore to experience less stress. Unfortunately, to date the relationship between perceptions of control and the use of problem-focused coping has rarely been examined. However, considerable research indicates that this personality characteristic does reduce reactions to stressful experiences in general.

How is perceived control assessed? The most popular measure, called the Locus of Control Scale, was developed by Rotter (1966). It consists of 23 sets of contrasting belief statements between which people are asked to choose. For example, people could agree with one of these two statements: "Many of the unhappy things in people's lives are partly due to bad luck" versus "People's misfortunes result from the mistakes they make." Other choices were: "What happens to me is my own doing" versus "Sometimes I feel that I don't have enough control over the direction my life is taking." People who believe that things are due to luck and that events are uncontrollable are characterized as having an *external locus of control orientation*. That is, they see their lives as governed primarily by outside forces. People who believe what happens to them is due primarily to their own efforts are characterized as having an *internal locus of control orientation*. These control orientations significantly predict people's reactions to stress.

For example, in a study of Marine Corps recruits, only 1 percent of those with an internal locus of control orientation (high perceived control) dropped out of basic training, compared to 17 percent of those with an external locus of control orientation (low perceived control) (Cook et al., 1980). Similarly, among small businessmen whose stores had been extensively damaged in a flood in a small Pennsylvania town, those who had high perceived control over life (as measured by the Rotter scale) reacted to their misfortune with much lower emotional distress than businessmen with an external locus of control orientation (Anderson, 1977). Moreover, an independent national credit rating agency assessed the business performance of the high-control owners as significantly better than that of the low-control owners over a two-and-a-half-year recovery period. From these and many other studies (Lefcourt, 1983), it is clear that this personality characteristic acts as an important *stress buffer*, lowering the impact of major life stressors on physical and emotional health.

The hardy personality.   In addition to perceived control, two other personality characteristics make it easier for a person to handle stress: commitment and challenge. Kobasa (1979) has described this triad of traits as *hardiness*. Kobasa studied 837 middle- and high-level executives in a large Chicago utility company. She divided the executives who had experienced stressful life events over a three-year period into two groups: those who had become physically ill following the events, and those who had not. The hardy executives

possessed three characteristics that the others did not: They had a strong feeling of control over their lives; they had a strong sense of commitment to specific goals; and they viewed changes as challenges rather than as threats.

Once again, we see the importance of people's perceptions of demands placed upon them. Those who have somehow learned to view themselves as active determinants of the outcomes of change can more easily overcome the objective difficulties and stressful reactions that change produces.

Attributional factors. How do people learn to see themselves as in control of their lives? Recall that lack of control over situational outcomes was an important factor leading Seligman's dogs to exhibit helpless and passive behaviors. Although helplessness could also be produced in human subjects, research indicated that human responses to uncontrollable outcomes were much more complex and variable. This observation led Seligman and his colleagues to incorporate cognitive or attributional factors into their theory of learned helplessness (Abramson et al., 1978). They argued that when people find they are unable to control outcomes, they ask themselves *why* this is so. If they attribute their helplessness to external factors ("This is an unfair math test"), they are much less likely to become passive and depressed. However, if people attribute lack of control to their own personal inadequacies ("I'm just no good at math"), especially to enduring, general inadequacies ("I'm no good at anything"), they are much more likely to give up, suffer a serious loss of self-esteem, and stay depressed. In short, when we attribute stress to our permanent personal failings, we have a much more difficult experience than when we attribute it to some external uncontrollable factor or to some internal controllable factor.

As you might expect, people's history of coping experiences and their attributions about those experiences affect coping efforts in later situations. People who believe they are unable to control environmental demands will not attempt to meet those demands in later situations. In an interesting series of studies Dweck and Goetz (1978) show this to be so. They selected a group of fourth- to sixth-graders who exhibited severe symptoms of helplessness and obtained an estimate of the children's baseline performance on a set of math problems. The next day the researchers administered another math set. Embedded halfway through the set were a few unsolvable problems. Every child showed a severely impaired performance on the solvable problems that followed the unsolvable ones. In other words, the children very quickly gave up trying after a relatively mild failure experience. This failure affected their performance on math problems for several days afterward.

Then Dweck and Goetz set up two treatment situations. Half of the children received only *success* experiences on math problems. The other half received "attribution retraining"—success experiences interspersed with a few failure trials. At each failure the experimenter reminded the child of his or her rate of prior successful solutions and explicitly attributed the child's failure to a lack of effort rather than a lack of ability. Note that this attribution training emphasized an internal and controllable factor: effort. These treatments continued over 25 daily sessions.

At the end of the treatments the experimenters administered another problem set with unsolvable items placed in the middle. Children in the attribution retraining condition showed no impairment in performance after failure and, unexpectedly, most showed improvement compared to their baseline level. In contrast, children in the success-only condition showed deteriorated performances after failure. This study indicates that success experiences alone are not sufficient to encourage future problem-focused cop-

ing efforts. Rather, continued attempts to master problems depend upon success experiences *and* the attributions one makes about one's occasional failures.

In sum, cognitive factors appear to affect the amount of stress one feels as well as the types of coping one will attempt. This may explain why some people develop physical or psychological disorders in the face of stress while others do not. However, one other factor can make a crucial difference—social support.

Social Support as a Coping Resource

Recently, a good deal of interest has been stimulated among behavioral scientists by the apparent stress-buffering properties of social support. Social support can be viewed as a coping resource. If a person can obtain emotional concern, material aid, useful information, and/or helpful feedback from significant others, that person has *social support* (House, 1981).

Early interest in social support as a buffer of stress derived from research with animals. One study found that a young goat subjected to a monotonous conditioning situation while isolated developed signs of experimental neurosis. In another box the goat's twin, subjected to the same stimulus, but with its mother goat present, did not (Liddell, 1950). Similarly, Henry and Cassell (1969) produced hypertension in mice by placing them in boxes all linked to a common feeding place, thus creating a persistent state of territorial conflict. Hypertension only occurred, however, when the mice were "strangers" to one another. When the other mice were litter mates, high blood pressure did not result. More recently, a study showed that if rabbits on a high-fat diet were cuddled, petted, and talked to by their handlers, they were less likely to develop heart disease, while rabbits on the same diet who were not given such special attention usually developed arteriosclerosis (Nerem et al., 1980).

Does social support protect people in the same ways? The answer appears to be a resounding "yes." Berkman and Syme (1979) showed that among roughly 5,000 adults randomly sampled in Alameda County, California, the presence or absence of four types of social ties in 1965—marriage, friends, church participation, and formal and informal group membership—strongly affected the probability of the person dying over the next nine years, even when factors such as age, sex, income, and diet were controlled. People lacking social ties were from 30 to 300 percent more likely to die than those with each kind of relationship. Nuckolls and her colleagues (1972) studied 170 pregnant army wives. Wives who experienced stressful events *and* who lacked social support during pregnancy were three times more likely to develop medical complications during childbirth than those who experienced little stress or had high amounts of support. In a major study of 1,809 men working in a large manufacturing plant, House and his colleagues (1981) found that support was extremely important in reducing the psychological and physical effects of chronic job strains. In general, workers who reported high amounts of job dissatisfaction, many conflicts between job and nonjob demands, too many job responsibilities, and work overload were much more likely to report symptoms of emotional distress and to have developed psychosomatic disease (e.g., angina pectoris, ulcers, rashes, and persistent coughs). But workers who felt they could rely on their supervisors, co-workers, and wives for emotional and practical support were significantly less likely to have symptoms of emotional and psychosomatic illness. In par-

ticular, support from the men's supervisors reduced psychosomatic illness, and support from their wives reduced emotional distress (see Figure 16–3).

These studies and many others clearly indicate that social support is an important stress buffer. In fact, support appears to protect health in two major ways (Cohen & Wills, 1985; Kessler & McLeod, 1985). First, the more social ties or social contacts people have, the less likely they are to develop physical or psychological disorders, independent of the stressors in their lives. This is commonly termed the *main effect* of social support—it protects people regardless of whether they are currently experiencing stress or not. Second, the more people perceive that support is available to them, the less likely they are to develop disorders when they are experiencing stress or strain. This is called the *buffering effect* of social support—that is, support reduces the physical and psychological impacts of stress exposure. The simplest and strongest indicator of social support appears to be whether a person has an intimate, confiding relationship with someone, such as a spouse or close friend. A confiding relationship is a major stress buffer.

It is important to emphasize that *how* social support operates to protect health is still poorly understood. Do caring others remind people to engage in good health habits? Does support increase people's self-confidence or self-esteem under stress? Does it give people a sense of control? Does it help them use more effective coping methods? There is still a good deal that we must discover about this important coping resource.

Figure 16–3 Summary of significant buffering effects of social support on relationships between perceived stress and health.

| Perceived Stress | Health Outcome | | | | |
	Angina Pectoris	Ulcers	Itching and Rash	Cough and Phlegm	Neurosis
Job Satisfaction	Wife	Supervisor Total	Wife		Wife
Work Self-Esteem	Wife	Supervisor Total	Supervisor	Total	Coworker Total
Job versus Nonjob Conflict		Supervisor Friend and Relative Total			
Role Conflict		Supervisor Total	Supervisor		Supervisor Wife Total
Quality Concern					Wife
Responsibility				Supervisor	Wife Total
Workload		Coworker Friend and Relative Total		Supervisor	Wife

Note: Cell entries indicate sources of support that significantly buffer each health-stress relationship. "Total" means support from all sources: supervisor, co-workers, friends, relatives, and wife.

(From House, 1981, Table 4.3, p. 77. Reprinted by permission.)

Perceived control and social support have been found to reduce the negative health impacts of stress and strain. These findings have practical implications for medicine in general and have led to the development of a new area of specialization within psychology.

Health Psychology

Researchers and medical practitioners alike have become increasingly aware of the importance of psychosocial factors in the development course, treatment, and prevention of disease. The contribution of psychosocial factors to health and illness is the focus of *health psychology* (Taylor, 1978; Stone, Cohen, & Adler, 1979; Matarazzo, 1980).

We have already discussed a number of studies that implicate psychosocial forces in the development of disease. Life events (particularly negative and loss events) and ongoing difficulties (especially occupational strains and daily hassles) have been linked to a variety of physical and psychological disorders (Glass & Singer, 1972; Glass, 1977; Kaplan, 1983).

Research in health psychology is contributing importantly to medical knowledge of factors that influence people's resistance or vulnerability to disease. Personality dispositions, such as the aggressive, striving Type-A behavior pattern have been associated with coronary heart disease (see the Application: Type-A Behavior and Coronary Heart Disease). Continued exposure to stress has been linked to impaired functioning of the immune system, leaving a person more prone to infection (see the Highlight: Stress and the Immune System). And the possibility of an association between feelings of helplessness and hopelessness and the development of cancer has even been raised (Sklar & Anisman, 1981).

Psychological studies are also contributing to improving stress-management techniques to help patients cope with hospitalization and recovery from illness. Recall that Langer, Janis, and Wolfer (1975) were able to reduce patients' postoperative anxiety and pain by teaching them techniques of cognitive control. These results stimulated a number of similar studies, which indicate that very simple interventions can be designed to help patients better cope with and recover from unpleasant medical procedures. For example, patients do better when they have been taught relaxation techniques, when they have been given specific information about surgery, when they have received hypnotic suggestion for reduced pain, and when they have voiced their fears and concerns in a small group led by a nurse (Mumford et al., 1982). Psychosocial interventions are valuable not only because they make patients feel cared for, but also because by speeding recovery they can reduce the total cost of hospital care.

In addition to coping interventions, social support interventions have been used to prevent patient relapses once they have left the hospital, and also to prevent the onset of physical or psychological disturbances among highly stressed groups, such as the newly bereaved and families caring for a severely ill member (Wortman & Conway, 1985). Support interventions have also been used to reduce the isolation that many patients feel when dealing with their own terminal illness. In one study women who were slowly dying of breast cancer gathered weekly for supportive group sessions led by a mental health professional (Spiegel et al., 1981). These groups met for over one year. Compared to a control group of women who simply received medical care, support group members were significantly less emotionally distressed, less fearful about death, and less likely to deny their illness and their

families' concerns. The effectiveness of social support for improving health and psychological well-being is encouraging health psychologists to develop and test a variety of supportive interventions.

Another major challenge for health psychology is improving the relationships between patients and medical personnel. One area of special concern has been patient noncompliance with doctors' orders. As many as 50 percent of all patients fail to take prescribed medications as instructed. Psychological studies of communications between patients and physicians have identified factors that may lead to noncompliance: Physicians fail to use terms that are familiar to the patient, to give concrete and clear instructions, and to convey warmth and concern (Davis, 1968; Kirsht & Rosenstock, 1979).

Finally, psychological studies may in time suggest more effective ways of promoting public health. One ambitious longitudinal study focused on reducing the risk for cardiovascular disease. The project, conducted by Stanford researchers (Meyer et al., 1980), involved three California communities. In one town an intensive mass-media campaign warned residents about the harmful effects of smoking, overweight, and hypertension. In a second town the media campaign was combined with intensive counseling and behavior modification sessions for a sample of residents at high risk for coronary heart disease. The third town served as a control; no special communications about heart disease were made to the general public. The media campaign and the counseling program had significant effects. The media messages improved people's knowledge about cardiac risk and changed their dietary preferences toward foods lower in cholesterol and saturated fats. Fewer fatty foods were consumed on a community-wide basis in the towns exposed to the media campaigns. When the media campaign was combined with intensive counseling, significantly more smokers cut down or quit altogether.

Similar interventions are being devised for use elsewhere on a smaller scale. Psychologists have utilized learning and cognitive approaches to design more effective programs for smoking cessation, weight control, and alcoholism (Henderson, Hall, & Lipton, 1979).

Thus the new field of health psychology may someday contribute substantially to our ability to alleviate stress, change destructive coping or health ha-

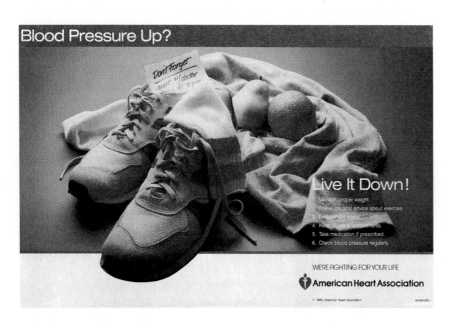

Learning and cognitive approaches have been applied to designing more effective programs to promote public health. (Copyright 1985, American Heart Association)

bits, prevent disease, and improve treatment experiences and outcomes for patients (Taylor, 1978).

Stress, Coping, and Disease: Toward an Integrated Model

The term *health psychology* suggests an integration of psychology with the disciplines of medicine, physiology, and biology. This is indeed occurring, not only in research, but also in medical practice, where psychologists are increasingly being hired by medical schools and general hospitals to work in collaboration with medical practitioners (Matarazzo, 1980). Nowhere in the field of health psychology is the integration of disciplines clearer than in research on stress, coping, and disease.

As we reviewed the biological, learning, and cognitive approaches to stress and coping, it may have struck you that no one of these approaches seemed adequate to explain why some people become ill under stress while others do not, or why a person develops one psychosomatic disease rather than another. To explain these phenomena, a combination of perspectives appears necessary.

For example, biological theory alone seems unable to identify the conditions under which reactions to prolonged or severe stress will overwhelm the body's defenses and lead to particular physical or psychological disorders. Rather, some knowledge of people's past learning histories, their perceptions of stress, and their coping resources seems necessary. Cognitions, coping responses (both problem-focused and emotion-focused), and social support resources seem to mediate the stress-disease relationship.

These considerations suggest that a more elaborate model of stress, coping, and illness is required, one that incorporates learning, cognitions, and psychological processes. For example, people's past reinforcement history may determine the kinds of skills they have available to meet environmental demands. More importantly, past learning may determine people's expectations for successful coping with those demands. These learned behavioral and cognitive responses in turn should influence the degree to which new environmental demands are perceived as threatening. The intensity of physiological stress reactions should vary directly with the degree of perceived threat. Physiological reactions may be dampened or eliminated as the person utilizes learned skills to actively master the situation or successfully reduces anxiety to manageable levels. To the degree that these learned coping mechanisms fail and individuals lack social support, prolonged or recurrent physiological stress reactions may weaken genetically vulnerable body systems and produce illness. In short, disease is quite likely the end product of a multiplicity of factors, both psychological and physiological.

To understand the extremely complex interrelationships between the mind and the body, we clearly require a combination of theoretical perspectives and interdisciplinary efforts. But many difficult questions remain to be answered. Why do some people become psychologically disturbed while others become physically ill in response to stress? What is the mechanism by which stress reactions weaken the body? How can we change people's environments, particularly work settings, to reduce their stressfulness? What types of coping mechanisms and what types of support are most effective in reducing what types of stress?

Much still has to be done to increase our knowledge of the relationships among stress, coping, and disease, but these questions are exciting ones, rich

in potential payoffs for significantly improving the lives and the health of many.

Coping and Adaptation

Because we are confronted with psychological stress in some form every day of our lives, we become adept at coping with it. If we are continually confronted with a certain stressor, our coping results in *adaptation,* or decreased reactivity to stress. The pressure of a new job, for example, is stressful to a person who has just taken on added responsibility, but he or she will rise to the challenge and gradually adapt to the pressure. Adaptation is indicated by a return to equilibrium levels of functioning.

The ability to adapt to the environment has been one key to the success and survival of the human species. Adaptation has made it possible for people to thrive in a wide range of climates. It has made it possible for people to endure and emerge from the horrors of war, concentration camps, and natural disasters. On a personal level, it helps us to overcome the pains of surgery, the trauma of a loved one's death, the noise and overcrowding of cities. But we pay a price for our adaptability.

When people adapt to demands, their stress responses seem to be minimized. Noise, for example, that might once have disturbed them is hardly noticed. Crowds that might once have made them feel panicky no longer arouse their fears. This adaptation, however, may only be superficial. Continued exposure to a stressor may cause a buildup of stress effects that explode when the stressor is removed. When the period of coping is over, a double dose of reaction may set in, both to the stressor *and* to the strain of coping (Glass & Singer, 1972).

One study of men who had just completed a stressful and demanding army training course bears this out. Although the men adapted successfully to the training, they experienced severe anxiety right after graduation. In accord with Selye's General Adaptation Syndrome, Glass and Singer conclude that "adaptive effort may leave the individual less able to cope with subsequent environmental demands and frustrations, and this reduction in coping ability can be described as the psychic cost of adaptation to stressful events" (p. 11). Sooner or later, then, the effects of stress are felt. Coping may help for the moment, but then an aftershock may hit.

The Benefits of Stress. However, the phenomenon of stress does have a positive side. Some research has shown that laboratory animals and children who experience stress early in life function better as adults than do their nonstressed peers. They outperform them and are more adaptable to novel or stressful situations. For example, an experiment done in the late 1950s showed that rat pups exposed to stress in the first few weeks of life (during the critical period of development) were tamer, less emotional, and physically larger as adults than rats unexposed to stress early in life. More recently, Landauer and Whiting (1978) reported similar evidence of stress benefits in humans. They first compared societies that customarily subject infants to stressful practices and those that carefully protect infants in their first few years of life. Societies categorized as stress-inducing followed ritual practices such as circumcision, body scarring, piercing of the nose, lips, or ears, and physical separation from the mother. Landauer and Whiting later obtained data on growth rates in these societies. Even when differences in diet, genetic makeup, and geographic location were controlled, adult stature was

on average 2.6 inches greater in stress-inducing societies than in more protective ones. Earlier work by Landauer and Whiting (1964) had suggested that not only physical growth was enhanced by stress exposure, but cognitive development was, too.

Similarly, Elder (1974) reconstructed data from psychological studies begun during the Great Depression by the Institute of Human Development at Berkeley. These studies were designed to measure the psychological and social development of younger children and adolescents during the Depression and in later years (one follow-up was done 40 years later). Elder found that adolescents from income-deprived families had actually been affected positively by the stressful experiences of the Depression. As a group, they were more independent, resourceful, and responsible than peers from less deprived families. And they were more successful in later life—they more often attended college, attained career success, and enjoyed happier marriages. Younger children, however, showed more negative signs of stress. Being more dependent on their parents, they were also more vulnerable to parental tension, unpredictability, and hostility during the stressful time. Thus, whether stress exposure has positive or negative results may depend both on the stressor and on one's stage of development at the time of exposure.

Further work in the area of stress and coping may enable social scientists to do more than merely warn people to avoid stressful lives. New studies may show us how to develop the characteristics and coping skills that can aid in a productive and healthy life.

SPECIAL ISSUES IN STRESS AND ADJUSTMENT

Victimization and Coping

Attention has turned recently to the special problems victims face in coping with their experiences. A "victim" is anyone who suffers from intentional or accidental harm caused by others or by external factors. Particular attention has been paid to victims of rape, incest, physical abuse, criminal assault, cancer, and disabling accidents. One interesting and counterintuitive finding is that victims who blame themselves for causing these negative events cope better and recover more quickly (Bulman & Wortman, 1977). Psychologists have often assumed that self-blame increases guilt feelings, damages self-esteem, and causes depression (Abramson et al., 1978). Why, then, should blaming oneself for an accident or injury caused by someone or something else be adaptive?

First, most people believe in a just world—the notion that people get what they deserve and deserve what they get (Lerner, 1980). Severe victimization shatters the assumption that the world is a meaningful, orderly place—the sudden loss of perceived predictability is deeply anxiety-producing. One way for victims to reduce this anxiety is to accept blame for their fate. By doing so, they are able to preserve the belief that bad things do not happen by chance, even to themselves (Janoff-Bulman & Frieze, 1983).

Second, consistent with the humanistic-existential model, people seem to need to find meaning or purpose in significant events, even in ones that are random and unjust (Silver & Wortman, 1980). One way to make sense of otherwise incomprehensible events is to accept blame for them.

Third, people need to feel that they have control over their lives (Bulman

& Wortman, 1977). We have seen in this chapter that perceived lack of control can be highly stressful. One way to maintain the perception of control and reduce stress is to accept responsibility for a victimizing event.

It is important here to distinguish between types of self-blame (Janoff-Bulman, 1979). People who blame some aspect of their character or personality for negative events may be less able to cope and recover than people who blame some aspect of their behavior (e.g., "I would not have been raped if I hadn't been out late at night"). Attributing causality to a behavior gives the victim some hope that changing the behavior will prevent another such event in the future.

There appears to be another important distinction between types of self-blame, and that is between accepting responsibility for a problem and accepting responsibility for its solution (Brickman et al., 1982). Victims of undesirable events may cope more effectively if they believe that they are not responsible for causing something to happen, but that they are responsible for handling its consequences (e.g., "This is God's way of testing me").

Some victimizing events are so socially undesirable or unacceptable that individuals are reluctant to discuss them with anyone. Many victims of rape, incest, spouse or child abuse, and marital infidelity hide their experience from others. Recently, Pennebaker (1985) found an association between suppressed mention of traumatic victimization and the occurrence of psychosomatic disease. Individuals who have never discussed a traumatic experience with others are much more likely to have long-term health problems such as ulcers, hypertension, and allergies. Pennebaker argues that inhibiting the mention or discussion of trauma causes a person to think about that trauma obsessively, sometimes for many years. Prior studies have indicated that actively inhibiting discussion of a trauma and obsessively thinking about it can cause strong physiological arousal—and prolonged or repeated arousal can culminate in psychosomatic disease. To test this reasoning, Pennebaker conducted an experiment. He asked undergraduates to write either an extremely personal essay on something they had not told anyone about before or an essay describing the events of the day. The subjects' heart rates were monitored continuously both during and after the essay writing. During the writing, the heart rates of the personal-event group were higher than those of the day's-event group. But after completing the essays, the heart rates of the personal-event group dropped below those of the day's-event group. This and subsequent experiments have led Pennebaker to suggest that "confession is good for the body." The energy needed to keep a traumatic experience secret and to cope with it alone is released when the secret is confided. Confiding may reduce the long-term wear and tear on the body produced by inhibition.

The Burdens of Caring

We have seen that social support can buffer the ill effects of exposure to stress. Recently, interest has turned to *support providers* and how they are affected by giving support to others during a crisis. Despite the old adage that it is better to give than receive, new evidence suggests that supporting others can be highly distressing, at least in the long run.

After a number of years of dealing with troubled clients, professional support providers, such as clinical psychologists, social workers, and counselors, frequently complain of emotional exhaustion, depersonalization, and a sense of reduced accomplishment. This syndrome of complaints has been termed

burnout (Maslach, 1982). Because support providers sometimes become overwhelmed by the demands imposed by people who need help, they begin to distance themselves from others' problems, and therefore feel more and more ineffective at their jobs. Without a vacation or a chance to let off steam with sympathetic co-workers, burnout can cause support providers to leave their professions.

Such emotional exhaustion is not limited to professional supporters. Those who care for an aging or severely ill family member are particularly vulnerable to this syndrome. The burdens of caring for an Alzheimer's patient offer a good example. Alzheimer's disease is a degenerative brain disease that usually occurs in the elderly. It erodes patients' abilities to remember, to process information, to make appropriate decisions, and, eventually, to care for themselves. It often causes a loss of control over bodily functions as well. A family with a member afflicted with Alzheimer's disease must monitor that person's behavior and safety virtually 24 hours a day. The patient must be dressed, fed, helped in the bathroom, and quieted when emotional outbursts occur. Dispiritingly, the patient might not even remember who the caregiver is. The daily burdens of caring for such a patient can exhaust the provider both physically and emotionally. Consequently, caregivers are themselves in need of social support—both material and emotional.

Not surprisingly, women are frequently the ones upon whom such burdens of caring and support giving fall. Recent evidence indicates that women are more likely than men to report major life events that happen to their loved ones; women are more likely than men to become support providers during their loved ones' crises; and women are more emotionally upset than men by their loved ones' crises (Kessler et al., 1985). Thus caring and supporting have their costs. Although additional research will be needed to weigh the relative costs and benefits of supporting others, these findings suggest that support giving is one reason why rates of psychological distress are so much higher among women than men (Kessler et al., 1985).

SUMMARY

1. *Stress* occurs when a person is faced with environmental demands, whether pleasant or unpleasant, that require some kind of *adjustment* or *adaptation*. Traumatic events are extremely stressful situations involving grave physical risk. Life events are major changes that disrupt people's usual activities. Daily hassles are transitory, minor stressors.

2. *Approach-approach conflict* occurs when a person is faced with two equally attractive but mutually exclusive goals. In *approach-avoidance conflict* the person faces a single goal that has both positive and negative consequences. *Avoidance-avoidance conflict* is the situation in which a person faces an unavoidable choice between two equally unattractive goals. The final category, *double approach-avoidance conflict,* occurs when a person is faced with two goals that each presents an approach-avoidance conflict of its own.

3. In the biological perspective, stress is a set of physiological responses (such as increased heart-rate or sweat-gland activity) that occur because of demands placed on the individual. Selye observed a general pattern of physiological reactions that occurs no matter what demands are involved; this is called the *General Adaptation Syndrome.*

4. Physical disorders linked to stress (such as hypertension or ulcers) are known as *psychosomatic*

illnesses. Among the theories devised to explain these illnesses are the *specific-reaction theory* and the *diathesis-stress theory.*

5. According to the learning perspective, coping behaviors are learned avoidance responses that alleviate anxiety. *Learned helplessness* occurs when animals and humans learn that there is no connection between their responses and what happens to them, which leads to a reduced rate of active coping.

6. In the cognitive perspective, the definition of stress includes three elements: the set of environmental demands that are potentially stressful; one's cognitive appraisal of the demands; and one's appraisal of one's abilities to cope with those demands. Coping responses have been classified into two types: emotion-focused and problem-focused.

7. Studies by cognitive researchers indicate that stress is based on people's *perception* of their control rather than on how much control they actually have.

When people attribute their lack of control to their personal inadequacies, they are less able to cope effectively.

8. Social support consists of emotional concern, material aid, information, and/or helpful feedback from others. Studies have shown that support is a coping resource that buffers or reduces the harmful effects of stress situations.

9. *Health psychology* is a new field of study that examines the importance of psychosocial factors in the development, course, treatment, and prevention of disease.

10. Continually being confronted with and having to cope with a certain stressor results in adjustment, or *adaptation,* the process of becoming less sensitive to a particular stressor. However, researchers note aftereffects of adaptation, including illness, anxiety, and a possible inability to cope with later environmental demands.

SUGGESTED READINGS

COELHO, G. V., HAMBURG, D. A., ADAMS, J. E. (Eds.) (1974). *Coping and adaptation.* New York: Basic Books. A collection of theoretical articles on coping, including discussions of the development of coping competence in children and coping with real-life crises.

COHEN, S., & SYME, S. L. (Eds.) (1985). *Social support and health.* New York: Academic Press. Chapters review the impressive effects of social support as a stress buffer. Special topics include social support and children, the health of the elderly, and community support groups.

DOHRENWEND, B. S., & DOHRENWEND, B. P. (Eds.) (1974). *Stressful life events: Their nature and effects.* New York: John Wiley. Papers by leading researchers in the field discuss the ways in which stress can be measured in terms of life events, and the connection between stress and physical illness.

FRASER, M. *Children in conflict.* (1973). Garden City, N.Y.: Doubleday. Deals with the way children in Northern Ireland have learned to cope with the immensely stressful conflict between Catholics and Protestants.

GARBER, J., & SELIGMAN, M. E. P. (Eds.) (1980). *Human helplessness: Theory and applications.* New York: Academic Press. Presents the reformulation of learned helplessness theory and its applications to depression, anxiety, intellectual achievement, Type-A behavior, and aging.

GLASS, D. C., & SINGER, J. E. (1972). *Urban stress: Experiments on noise and social stressors.* New York: Academic Press. This book presents an interesting series of experiments on human responses to noise as a function of predictability and control.

HOUSE, J. S. (1981). *Work stress and social support.* Reading, Mass.: Addison-Wesley. An extremely readable review of social support findings, plus the results of an important study of job strains and how they are buffered by support.

LAZARUS, R. S., & FOLKMAN, S. (1984). *Stress, appraisal, and coping.* New York: Springer. Presents a detailed theory of stress and coping, with extensive supporting research. *The* sourcebook on coping.

MECHANIC, D. *Students under stress* (1978). Madison: University of Wisconsin Press. An engrossing in-depth study of how students cope with the stresses of preparing for a major exam that can make or break their careers.

SELYE, H. *The stress of life* (1956). New York: McGraw-Hill. Selye's autobiographical account of his discovery of the General Adaptation Syndrome and a very readable explanation of the physiological processes involved.

SELYE, H. (Ed.) (1980). *Selye's guide to stress research,* Vol. 1. New York: Van Nostrand Reinhold. First in an annual series on current topics in stress research, this volume covers such topics as stressful life-events research, the effects of learning on physical symptoms, and hormones and stress.

STONE, G. C., COHEN, F., & ADLER, N. E. (Eds.) (1979). *Health psychology.* San Francisco: Jossey-Bass. This collection of articles examines psychology's contributions to the development, course, and treatment of disease and to the maintenance of health. There is special focus both on the health-care delivery system and on trends and new directions in health psychology as a field.

17 Abnormal Psychology

He had a theory about what we would now call the personality, and a notion of how the personality was connected to underlying bodily processes. He also had a theory of abnormality: When the underlying bodily processes got out of balance, the person's behavior became correspondingly "unbalanced." Someone who was constantly enraged, for example, had a predominance of yellow bile; a person we might think of as a "depressive" had an excess of phlegm. Second, although Hippocrates' notion of humoral imbalance does not stand up under modern scrutiny, it was one of the first *somatogenic* theories of abnormal behavior (Davison & Neale, 1982). Somatogenic theories of abnormality hold that disturbances of thought are caused by disturbances of the physical body. They are thus closely related to the biological and constitutional theories of personality discussed in Chapter 15.

By the Middle Ages much of the scientific knowledge of the classical era had been lost. As you may recall from medieval history, warfare and social upheaval were frequent. Bad diet and malnutrition were common, and famines were ever threatening. Plagues swept through Europe, sickening and killing vast numbers of people. In these uncertain times abnormal behavior came to be associated with demonic possession. Medieval "classification systems" were concerned with showing how various kinds of demonic possession led to different sorts of abnormal behavior. Demonic possession was thought to be at the root of a wide range of inexplicable occurrences: from what we now would call insanity, to the inability to conceive children, to strange physical illnesses and death. People who were dangerously insane, or conspicuously unable to take care of themselves, were called "lunatics." The afflicted were given minimal care in the towns from which they came, or else driven outside town limits to become the responsibility—and expense—of a nearby town. Sometimes ship captains were paid to deposit the insane in foreign ports. Eventually the port cities refused to allow these types of passengers to disembark; the legend of the "ship of fools" grew up around stories of ships sailing from port to port, unable to unload their cargo of lunatics.

During the fifteenth and sixteenth centuries asylums were opened in which lunatics, along with beggars and other destitute people, were confined in squalid conditions and given minimal rations. In these asylums the insane were sometimes subjected to treatments we would now consider crackpot, such as copious bleeding in the belief that insanity was caused by an excess of blood in the brain. Most were kept in close confinement, even shackled to walls year after year.

Even during the periods when these views prevailed, the somatogenic view of abnormal behavior never entirely disappeared. In the seventeenth and eighteenth centuries there was a growing understanding of the nervous system and its functioning, as well as of the diseases that could make it malfunction. During the 1860s and 1870s Pasteur proposed the germ theory of physical disease and other scientists began to gather evidence for it. The notion that mental illness also was caused by an underlying physical disorder gained popularity. In fact, it is likely that this is the model that most of us, at some level or other, currently accept. However, modern researchers generally suggest that there are a number of perspectives from which the causes of abnormal behavior can be analyzed. These are basically the same models used to describe personality theory in Chapter 15. Each personality theory provides an analysis of the general and specific causes of abnormal behaviors.

In a scene from William Hogarth's *The Rake's Progress*, high society pays a visit to London's Bethlem Royal Hospital, an insane asylum. (The Bettmann Archive)

A young man confined to a padded cell at Ward's Island hospital (anonymous German engraving). (The Bettmann Archive)

MODELS OF ABNORMAL BEHAVIOR

The *psychoanalytic model* generally views abnormal behavior as evidence of unresolved conflicts among the id, ego, and superego. Somehow we have to harmonize the instinctual and unreasoning desires of the id, the rational and realistic requirements of the ego, and the moral and restrictive demands of the superego. Because conflicts among them can lead to unpleasant and anxious feelings, we develop defense mechanisms to help us avoid such feelings. Defense mechanisms (see Chapter 15) may reduce our anxiety by staving off the conscious awareness of conflicts that would be too painful for us to acknowledge. Defense mechanisms do not actually reduce the conflicts, however; they merely hide them from us. Abnormal behavior can result from faulty defense mechanisms that allow conflict and anxiety to break through, or from overuse of defense mechanisms.

In the *humanistic-existential model* abnormal behaviors are caused by failure to fulfill one's personal potential. These failures may occur when people lose sight of or distort their real emotions and thoughts, cut themselves off from those around them, or come to view their lives as totally meaningless.

The *biological model* argues that abnormal behaviors can be traced to physical disorders. The link between the mind and the body can work in two directions: (1) Biological abnormalities can affect mind and behavior; or (2) emotional stress can have a physical effect, setting the stage for yet a further impact on our behavior. According to the biological model, it makes no sense to separate the mind from the body in explaining abnormal behavior. To do so obscures the critical role played by physical factors.

According to the *learning model,* abnormal behaviors are learned in the same way that all behaviors are learned. People acquire them through either classical conditioning, operant conditioning, or modeling. Abnormal behaviors can be understood in terms of stimulus, response, and reinforcement.

The *cognitive model* finds the roots of abnormal behavior in the way we think about and perceive the world. People who distort or misinterpret their experiences, the intentions of those around them, and the kind of world they live in are bound to act abnormally.

Classification of Abnormal Behavior

We now have five perspectives that we can take on abnormal behavior. Our next task is to examine some specific kinds of abnormality from the standpoints of these five theories. The procedure seems simple—we can just list all the various abnormal behaviors and then give each of the five perspectives a chance to show its strengths by explaining them.

Soon that is exactly what we will do. But first we need to look at some problems in the classification of abnormal behavior patterns, for this is not as simple a task as it first appears. Some history will give us an orientation. In 1883 Emil Kraepelin, a German psychiatrist, developed a classification system that is influential to this day. His effort was a most comprehensive one in that he attempted to include all mental disorders, and to distinguish them on the basis of their *symptoms, origin, course,* and *outcome.* The classification system was squarely within the somatogenic tradition, in which each disorder was thought to have an organic origin.

Since Kraepelin's time others have attempted to establish comprehensive diagnostic schemes. In 1952 the American Psychiatric Association issued a

classification system called the *Diagnostic and Statistical Manual of Mental Disorders,* known as the DSM. The current and third version, (1980), is referred to as DSM-III. In 1987 a revision of DSM-III, was issued, referred to as DSM-III-R. Unlike DSM-III, it was not a complete reworking of the diagnostic system. Mainly, it added a few new diagnostic categories. The major changes to focus on, therefore, are the ones introduced in DSM-III.

The authors of DSM-III wanted it to be reliable, meaning that if two different clinicians using the system are faced with patients presenting the same or similar symptoms, then they ought to make similar diagnoses. The reasoning is obvious: A diagnostic system that doesn't foster consistent diagnoses does not serve clinicians or patients well. No previous system had achieved an acceptable consistency. Researchers even found that the same observer presented with virtually identical descriptions of a patient on two different occasions would often give different diagnoses (Beck, 1962; Wilson & Meyer, 1962). In their pre–DSM III review of studies of the reliability of psychiatric diagnoses, Spitzer and Fleiss (1974) concluded that only a few broad categories (such as mental retardation or alcoholism) were reliable.

Those constructing the DSM-III attempted to achieve better diagnostic reliability in several ways. First, they eliminated or redefined diagnostic terms that had been used inconsistently. Second, they used the results of reliability studies to decide which categories should be retained. Third, they specified in much greater detail the behavioral elements that were to be taken as signs of each diagnostic category. Fourth, they broke down vague or broad categories into more precise categories. Finally, in an attempt to eliminate hidden theoretical biases in the system, they decided not to identify the origins, or *etiology,* of each mental condition. Those working on DSM-III essentially concluded that for most of the disorders being defined, the etiology is unknown. This omission was a radical departure for a diagnostic system. Since Kraepelin, virtually all systems had tried to establish an etiology for each disorder.

If this omission surprises you, it might help to recall the five classes of personality theories and how each makes different claims about the origins of many disorders. For instance, Freudian theorists hold that phobic disorders are generated by a displacement of anxiety, resulting from the breakdown of defensive operations for keeping internal conflict out of conciousness. Learning theorists, on the other hand, regard phobias as learned-avoidance responses to conditioned anxiety. In order to generate diagnostic categories on which clinicians could agree—a major goal in revising the DSM system—it was necessary to eliminate most etiological claims from the diagnostic process.

In keeping with the goal of achieving more reliable diagnoses, DSM-III attempts to be more descriptive than previous diagnostic systems. The manual lists both the essential features of each disorder and those frequently associated with it. It indicates which features must be present for the diagnostic category to be used, and describes how to distinguish a particular disorder from other disorders with which it may be confused.

The DSM-III and III-R Category System

A central change in DSM-III is the use of five axes for clinical diagnosis. Whereas its predecessors had required clinicians to find one label to define a person's problem, DSM-III provides the diagnostician with five different dimensions on which to evaluate functioning. Axis I is called the *clinical*

psychiatric syndrome. This is a statement of the presenting client's most central problem, usually the one that caused the person to seek or be referred for help. More specifically, the first axis is a statement of the specific psychiatric syndrome that the individual displays, such as depression or phobic disorder. The second axis outlines *personality or developmental disorders* in adults or children. It focuses on any long-term personality disorder that the client has shown, such as a compulsive personality disorder. Axes I and II specify all the mental disorders and together provide what most people consider a complete index to diagnosis (see Table 17–1). Axis II describes *physical disorders.* Here attention is called to the possibility of some physical syndrome that may be a factor in the presenting condition. Axis IV (see Table 17–2) asks the diagnostician to rate the observed *severity of psychosocial stress.* This implies a recognition of the main point of our chapter on stress—namely, that stress can play a considerable role in exacerbating internal conflicts and precipitating abnormal behaviors. Axis V (see Table 17–3) is concerned with the person's *highest level of adaptive functioning in the past year.* Both Axis IV and Axis V are useful in planning treatments for the diagnosed individual and predicting the success of such treatments. For example, a person who is experiencing psychological problems after several deaths in the family, but who functioned very well in the preceding year, would have a better prognosis than someone who usually functioned poorly and was experiencing moderate life stresses.

Unresolved Problems with DSM-III.   In several ways the multiaxial diagnostic system of DSM-III represents a considerable gain over previous systems. For one, field trials (Spitzer, Forman, & Nee, 1979) on the first two axes show that diagnostic agreement is quite high on a number of categories. While more research is needed, the reliability results are generally promising. Second, making the system more acceptable to theoreticians of various persuasions enhances its utility. Third, providing more detailed and careful descriptions of various diagnostic categories makes it more comprehensive clinically. However, there are many criticisms of the system, and it is important to acknowledge them, for they shed light on the expected functions of a diagnostic system as well as on its limitations.

Some critics have complained that the new system is sometimes political rather than scientific. For example, in DSM-II homosexuality was classified as a personality problem; in DSM-III it is classified as a personality problem only if it is "ego dysfunctional"—that is, if it causes problems for the individual. Homosexuality may or may not be a personality problem, say the critics, but its classification shouldn't have been changed because of social pressure or the votes of various influential psychiatrists. DSM-III-R introduces several new diagnostic categories that feminists, among others, find objectional. Thus the "politics of diagnosis" remains a very vexing issue.

Another problem is that often the diagnosis of a condition necessarily contains some implicit assumptions about its cause. Clinicians of various schools make different assumptions about the origins of various syndromes. Therefore, even though DSM-III is more descriptive and less theoretical than its predecessors, its users may still be influenced by their different theories as to cause. Some critics argue that because the factors causing a condition can be important in determining its treatment, a completely nontheoretical diagnostic system might not be desirable.

Critics also argue that the new system retains a pervasive medical and psychiatric bias. Some kinds of mental retardation fit well with a medical approach, but what about "developmental arithmetical disorder"? Or fear of

Table 17–1: Psychological Disorders as Classified in DSM-III, Axes I–II

Axis I. CLINICAL PSYCHIATRIC SYNDROMES

1. Disorders Usually First Evident in Infancy, Childhood, or Adolescence
   A. Mental retardation
   B. Attention deficit disorder
   C. Conduct disorder
   D. Anxiety and other disorders of childhood or adolescence: separation anxiety and avoidant disorders, . . . , elective mutism, . . .
   E. Eating disorders: anorexia nervosa, bulimia, pica, rumination disorder of infancy
   F. Stereotyped movement disorders: tics, Tourette's disorder
   G. Other disorders with physical manifestations: stuttering, enuresis, encopresis, sleepwalking disorder, sleep terror disorder
   H. Pervasive development disorders: infantile autism, childhood-onset pervasive developmental disorder.

2. Organic Mental Disorders
   A. Organic brain syndromes: delirium, dementia, amnestic, delusional, hallucinosis, affective, personality
   B. Organic mental disorders: dementias arising in the senium and presenium, substance-induced organic mental disorders

3. Substance Use Disorders
   A. Substance abuse: alcohol, barbiturate, opioid, cocaine, amphetamine, phencyclidine, hallucinogen, *Cannabis*
   B. Substance dependence: alcohol, barbiturate, opioid, amphetamine, *Cannabis,* tobacco

4. Schizophrenic Disorders
   A. Disorganized
   B. Catatonic
   C. Paranoid
   D. Undifferentiated
   E. Residual

5. Paranoid Disorders

6. Psychotic disorders Not Elsewhere Classified
   A. Schizophreniform disorder
   B. Brief reactive psychosis
   C. Schizoaffective disorder

7. Affective Disorders
   A. Major affective disorders: bipolar disorder, major depression
   B. Other specific affective disorders: cyclothymic and dysthymic disorders

8. Anxiety Disorders
   A. Phobic disorders
   B. Anxiety states: panic disorder, generalized anxiety disorder, obsessive-compulsive disorder
   C. Post-traumatic stress disorder

9. Somataform Disorders
   A. Somatization disorder
   B. Conversion disorder
   C. Psychogenic pain disorder
   D. Hypochondriasis

10. Dissociative Disorders
    A. Psychogenic amnesia
    B. Psychogenic fugue
    C. Multiple personality
    D. Depersonalization disorder

11. Psychosexual Disorders
    A. Gender identity disorders: transsexualism, gender identity disorder of childhood
    B. Paraphilias: fetishism, transvestism, pedophilia, exhibitionism, voyeurism, sexual masochism, sexual sadism, atypical
    C. Psychosexual dysfunctions: inhibited sexual desire; inhibited sexual excitement; inhibited female, male orgasm; premature ejaculation; functional dyspareunia; functional vaginismus
    D. Ego-dystonic homosexuality

12. Factitious Disorders

13. Disorders of Impulse Control Not Elsewhere Classified

14. Adjustment Disorder

15. Psychological Factors Affecting Physical Condition

16. Conditions Not Attributable to a Mental Disorder That Are a Focus of Attention or Treatment: malingering, borderline intellectual functioning, antisocial behavior, academic and occupational problems, uncomplicated bereavement, . . . , marital problem, parent-child problem, . . .

Axis II.

1. Specific Developmental Disorders
   A. Developmental reading disorder
   B. Developmental arithmetic disorder
   C. Developmental language disorder
   D. Developmental articulation disorder

2. Personality Disorders: paranoid, schizoid, schizotypal, histrionic, narcissistic, antisocial, borderline, avoidant, dependent, compulsive, passive-aggressive

Table 17–2: Axis IV: Scale for Rating Severity of Psychosocial Stressors.*

1 None—no apparent psychosocial stressor.
2 Minimal—minor violation of the law; small bank loan.
3 Mild—argument with neighbor; change in work hours.
4 Moderate—new career; death of close friend; pregnancy.
5 Severe—serious illness in self or family; major financial loss; marital separation; birth of child.
6 Extreme—death of close relative; divorce.
7 Catastrophic—concentration camp experience; devastating natural disaster.
0 Unspecified—no information, or not applicable.

*Compare this scale with the life-change scale presented in Chapter 16.

Adapted from American Psychiatric Association (1980), p. 27.

crowds and open spaces? Or frequent shoplifting? Or setting fires? Many clinicians do not think that these are medical conditions like fevers or flus, best "treated" according to standard medical practice. Humanists and existentialists, as well as cognitive and learning theorists, worry about the somatic bias of the system.

Other critics wonder why therapists are in the business of diagnosis at all since an agreed-upon diagnosis hardly ensures an effective treatment. Learning theorists, for instance, begin by eliciting careful descriptions of the behaviors that their clients want to modify. Next they analyze what patterns of reinforcement are maintaining these behaviors. To these specialists, elaborate diagnoses seem beside the point.

Finally, at a societal level, it is important to realize that any diagnosis of a "mental disorder" attaches a label to an individual that can have serious negative effects. For example, once committed to a diagnosis, a clinician may be less likely to recognize signs indicating that the label does not fit the client. Then, too, the label often becomes a permanent part of a person's records. It may frighten off potential friends or employers; it may also damage the individual's self-image. If a diagnostic label leads to genuinely helpful treatment, then these negative consequences may be outweighed; but it is important to be aware of them just the same.

Table 17–3: Axis V: Scale for Rating Level of Functioning.

Levels	Adult Examples
1. *Superior*—Unusually effective functioning in social relations, occupational functioning, and use of leisure time.	Single parent living in deteriorating neighborhood takes excellent care of children and home, has warm relations with friends, and finds time for pursuit of hobby.
2. *Very Good*—Better than average functioning in social relations, occupational functioning, and use of leisure time.	A 65-year-old retired widower does some volunteer work, often sees old friends, and pursues hobbies.
3. *Good*—No more than slight impairment in either social or occupational functioning.	A woman with many friends functions extremely well at a difficult job, but says "the strain is too much."
4. *Fair:* Moderate impairment in either social relations or occupational functioning, or some impairment in both.	A lawyer has trouble carrying through assignments; has several acquaintances, but hardly any close friends.
5. *Poor:* Marked impairment in either social relations or occupational functioning, or moderate impairment in both.	A man with one or two friends has trouble keeping a job for more than a few weeks.
6. *Very Poor:* Marked impairment in both social relations and occupational functioning.	A woman is unable to do any of her housework and has violent outbursts toward family and neighbors.
7. *Grossly Impaired:* Gross impairment in virtually all areas of functioning.	An elderly man needs supervision to maintain minimal personal hygiene and is usually incoherent.
0. *Unspecified*	No information.

Adapted from American Psychiatric Association (1980), pp. 29–30.

We will now review several specific categories of abnormality cited in the DSM-III. The review will be a selective one—it will not include all the disorders that were listed in Table 17–1. You will note that not every one of the five perspectives is applied to each disorder reviewed. In some cases, a very complicated story needs to be told in order to make the given theory fit a specific disorder. In other cases, a perspective has very little application to a specific disorder. As you might imagine, in therapy the perspective of the individual clinician greatly influences the treatment as well as the diagnosis of a specific disorder. We will learn more about this in Chapter 18.

ANXIETY DISORDERS

This heading in DSM-III includes conditions in which anxiety is either the major symptom in itself or accompanies attempts to overcome another symptom. We will look first at phobic, anxiety, and panic disorders, and then at obsessive-compulsive disorders. In each of these categories anxiety is manifested in different, but very dysfunctional, ways.

Phobic, Anxiety, and Panic Disorders

Phobic disorders involve a persistent and irrational fear of a particular object or situation, a fear far out of proportion to the actual threat present. For example, it is quite natural to be afraid of a snarling dog that lunges at you; it is not natural to be afraid of any dog in any situation. Examples of phobic disorders include simple phobias such as **claustrophobia** (fear of closed spaces) and **acrophobia** (fear of heights), and more complex phobias such as **agoraphobia** (a fear of being alone, particularly in public places). The usual defense against this type of fear is to avoid the source of it. Most of us have some irrational fears. We may, for instance, feel uncomfortable in the presence of strange dogs. But unless we are suddenly appointed the local dog catcher, such a fear won't prevent us from functioning normally most of the time. A phobia like agoraphobia is more serious because if we see the outside world as continually threatening, we are forced to seriously restrict our ordinary activities. Often agoraphobic people refuse to venture out of the house without a friend or relative at their side.

Generalized anxiety disorder produces the same kind of discomfort as phobic disorders, but the anxiety is not clearly linked to a specific object or situation. It has sometimes been called "free-floating anxiety" because the feeling is present in so many different situations. Signs of the disorder include tenseness, autonomic system hyperactivity, general apprehensiveness, and continual scanning of the external environment for dangers. Sufferers feel that their lives are out of control and that disaster is imminent. They may find it difficult to make decisions or to pursue relationships with other people. Physical manifestations may include excessive sweating, nausea, fatigue, and muscular tension.

The essential features of a **panic disorder** are recurrent panic attacks that occur unpredictably, although they may happen more frequently in certain situations such as riding an elevator or flying in an airplane (see the Case History: Panic Disorder). The essential feelings are of overwhelming terror or impending doom, with physical sensations of pain, choking, dizziness, and vertigo. Normally these attacks last for minutes, occasionally for hours.

The *psychoanalytic model* suggests that phobic, anxiety, and panic disorders can be traced to an unresolved clash between the id and the ego and su-

Mathew (1980) conducted a study in Houston of what has been tentatively referred to as "traffic phobia." This disabling fear—and what may well be a new phobia—is most often associated with freeway driving. It has become a problem in big cities where freeway, thruway, or expressway driving is a major part of everyday life.
(Photo: Georg Gerster/Photo Researchers)

perego. If the id's drive for sexual or aggressive expression is harshly punished in childhood, these early punishments result in the development of a rigid, overcontrolling superego. This is experienced by the person as ill-understood internal prohibitions that would be terrible to violate. Therefore the individual comes to fear either the person who meted out the punishment or his or her own id impulses.

People who fear their punisher are likely to develop phobic or panic disorders. Typically, the fear of the punisher is displaced to a more neutral object or situation, perhaps something that only symbolizes the punisher. In this way people manage to avoid fearing the punisher, who is often very important to them—for instance, their mother or father.

People who are afraid of their own id impulses live in constant fear, since such impulses are always fighting for expression. These people will have free-floating anxiety in all kinds of situations. Their egos constantly struggle to contain their impulses. Since this is a losing battle, these people see danger in every kind of situation.

The *learning model* does not make a clear distinction among phobic, anxiety, and panic disorders. A phobia is viewed as a conditioned fear reaction followed by a learned avoidance response. For example, as a child you were frightened one night by the loud noises of a thunderstorm. Afterward you developed an intense fear of the color blue—the color of the bedroom in which you spent that frightening night. The color blue (conditioned stimulus), which just happened to be present at the same time as the loud noises of thunder (unconditioned stimulus), now brings about the same intense fear reaction. According to Mowrer (1947), this classically conditioned fear is reinforced by a reduction in fear as you avoid the color blue over and over again. Constant avoidance prevents you from realizing that what you are avoiding is really quite harmless.

The learning model goes on to say that a pattern of anxiety can be explained in essentially the same way. The only difference is in the number of conditioned stimuli that come to cause the fear reaction. To go back to the thunderstorm example, in addition to fearing the color blue, you may also

Richard Benson, age 38, applied to a psychiatrist for therapy because he was suffering from severe and overwhelming anxiety which sometimes escalated to a panic attack. During the times when he was experiencing intense anxiety, it often seemed as if he was having a heart seizure. He experienced chest pains and heart palpitations, numbness, and shortness of breath, and he felt a strong need to breathe in air. He reported that in the midst of the anxiety attack, he developed a feeling of tightness over his eyes and he could only see objects directly in front of him (tunnel vision). He further stated that he feared that he would not be able to swallow.

As the anxiety symptoms became more severe and persistent, the client began to worry about when another acute attack would occur and this apprehension made him more anxious still. He expressed a general concern about his physical well-being, and he became extremely sensitive to any fluctuations in his breathing or difficulties in swallowing. He began to note the location of doctors' offices and hospitals in whatever vicinity he happened to be, and he became extremely anxious if medical help was not close by.

Mr. Benson stated that he could not fight off his constant feelings of anxiety, and he was unable to control his behavior when the anxiety symptoms occasionally spiralled to a panic attack. He could not sit still when he felt acutely and painfully anxious, and the only way he could find relief from his symptoms was to go home and pace back and forth in his yard. Gradually, he stopped perspiring and the rapid heart rate and other somatic symptoms subsided as well. He went back into the house as soon as he felt calmer, but after a half hour the symptoms often reappeared and the anxiety episode started all over again. At that point, the only way he could bring the anxiety attack under control was to contact his physician for a tranquilizer injection.

(From Leon, 1977, pp. 113–118)

fear many other stimuli present on the night of the storm (that is, the fear is conditioned to other stimuli). Quite possibly the fear has also been conditioned to the clothes on the chair in the bedroom, to the bedroom itself, to the toys illuminated by the sudden flash of lightning, to dreams in progress just before the storm—even to sleep itself. If you were conditioned in this way, you would be likely to show fear in so many settings that your condition would look like an anxiety that is general and free-floating—that is, has nothing to do with a particular stimulus. To a learning theorist, however, with a thorough enough search the anxiety could be traced to a set of specific fears triggered by specific stimuli.

The *humanistic-existential model* attributes phobic and anxiety disorders to a failure to fulfill one's potential. You may recall from Chapter 15 that Carl Rogers believed we all have a need for unconditional positive regard. However, not everyone receives unconditional regard from others—some were criticized a great deal as children and in turn become intensely self-critical. These people later find it very hard to accept themselves and their actions because everything they do falls far short of their strict standards of self-evaluation. They come to perceive their experiences in a selective fashion, denying or distorting any experiences that are contrary to or threaten their self-concept. Constant denial and distortion require a lot of energy and leave no room for self-actualization. According to this model, anxiety, panic, and phobic disorders are the consequences of comparing one's actual behaviors to an unrealistically high standard of performance. This causes people to fear and avoid situations in which they might otherwise grow.

Existentialists would alter this explanation somewhat. They would stress the need to act in an authentic fashion in a world that often requires inauthentic behavior. People who are too aware of the degree to which their actions fail to correspond to their desired authentic selves experience anxiety and panic.

The *cognitive model* explains phobic, anxiety, and panic disorders as problems that can be traced to troublesome thought processes. Albert Ellis (1958, 1973, 1975) argues that such disorders develop because of people's ir-

rational assumptions. Many people believe that if they receive any disapproval at all, they must be totally worthless. Thus they try to avoid disapproval in all their interactions, and they die a thousand deaths whenever they are criticized. Other people assume they must do everything perfectly. Such an assumption leads to expectations that are impossible to fulfill, and assures the very high level of anxiety and dysfunction that characterizes phobic and anxiety disorders. Research has indeed suggested that such irrational assumptions are related to anxiety disorders. For example, Newmark, Frerking, Cook, and Newmark (1973) found that people classified as having anxiety disorders endorse extreme beliefs or assumptions significantly more often than other people.

The *biological model,* naturally enough, looks for organic causes of anxieties and phobias and, at least initially, searches for evidence of an inherited pattern. There is no clear evidence for such heritability at present. However, researchers have found physiological contingencies for some types of problems. For instance, a person may have an autonomic nervous system or a reticular activating system that is easily aroused by stressful or negative events. This may come from inherited tendencies (Lacey, 1967) or chronic stress (Seligman, 1971). Either of these sensitivities could produce an individual who "overreacts" to stressful or negative events, and whose overreactions, according to learning principles, might become attached to different real-world stimuli.

With chronic anxiety patients it has long been known that panic attacks can be brought about by injections of sodium lactate. The linkage between sodium lactate and anxiety goes back to an earlier observation that exercise intensified the symptoms of chronically anxious persons; it was then discovered that these persons also showed higher lactic acid levels in the blood following exercise than did nonanxious individuals. More recently, it has been discovered that inhaling small amounts of carbon dioxide has the same panic-inducing effect on anxious individuals (Carr, 1985). Researchers suggest that when the oxygen concentrations in the bloodstream are getting dangerously low, the body has sensing mechanisms that are automatically set off. This natural biological reaction is experienced as a panic attack. In people who experience frequent panic attacks these mechanisms may be overly sensitive, and thereby produce "inappropriate" panic attacks. Or in susceptible individuals an increase in lactic acid concentrations might trigger the sensors. Through conditioning principles, the situation in which these attacks occur becomes associated with panic, perhaps producing one of the phobias discussed earlier.

There is also growing evidence that biological and learning factors are jointly involved in the development of certain anxieties. Conditioning researchers have found that it is much easier to condition certain stimulus-response pairings than others. Recall that in Chapter 6 discussion of *aversive conditioning* that a rat learned in just one trial to associate the taste of a certain food with sickness that occurred several hours later, and thereafter avoided the food. No such rapid learning took place in response to other stimuli, a fact that argues for a biological predisposition to certain types of learning. Such responses, moreover, are extremely difficult to extinguish.

The application of this idea to phobias is clear enough. Because the human organism appears biologically predisposed to certain connections, a single pairing of certain stimuli with certain frightening or punishing experiences may result in an instantly formed phobia. Like the rat in the lab, many people have strongly expressed food aversions:"———makes me so sick I can't stand the sight of it." The likely root of the reaction is the experience of

having eaten some food and, either because of food poisoning or some coincidental occurrence of illness, becoming sick soon after.

A similar biological predisposition may underlie phobic reactions to snakes. To test this, researchers conditioned fear responses in subjects by pairing electric shocks with slides of houses, faces, or snakes (Ohman, Erixon, & Lofberg, 1975). The fear conditioned to slides of snakes was much more difficult to extinguish than the others. Further research showed that people with chronically high levels of arousal were particularly susceptible to fear responses, and these fear responses are difficult to extinguish. Thus a biological perspective on why certain fears are conditioned seems likely to add to our understanding of phobias.

Obsessive-Compulsive Disorders

Obsessive-compulsive disorders are shown by people who feel forced to repeat unwanted thoughts or ideas over and over, or to repeat certain actions or rituals again and again. Examples are the need to count every step when you walk, or to wash your hands every time you touch a doorknob. A minor example that most of us have experienced is having a tune or part of an advertising jingle repeat itself in our heads in spite of our attempts to get rid of it. Such an experience is usually no more than mildly annoying. For people with an obsessive-compulsive disorder, however, the intrusion may be so severe and constant that they find it almost impossible to function normally.

Obsessions and compulsions represent different aspects of a disorder. **Obsessions** are thoughts that repeatedly intrude against one's will and defy one's efforts to ignore them. They may occur in various forms. For example, there are obsessive doubts, such as "Did I turn off the stove before I left the house?" There are also obsessive impulses, which may range from whimsical ideas like winking at passers-by to the thought of violent acts such as stabbing one's child. Other people are plagued by obsessive fears, such as "I am going to shout something in church" (Akhter, Wig, Varma, Pershad, & Verma, 1975).

In the vast majority of cases such obsessive thoughts never translate into action. However, they often are so dramatic and unpleasant that they cause very high levels of anxiety. Many people who obsess worry most about the possibility that they will someday act out their terrible obsessive thoughts.

Compulsions are acts or rituals that are repeated against a person's will. There are minor compulsions that most people have and that fall well within the realm of normal behavior—for example, stepping over cracks in the sidewalk. Also, it is common to have daily rituals—for example, many people go through their morning routines without variation day after day and are quite upset if something forces them to change the routine.

A note to the reader is useful here. All of us have rituals, and it is quite within the realm of normal behavior to practice them. Be reassured, even the author of this chapter occasionally surreptitiously arranges to step on a sidewalk crack with his left foot if he stepped on the last two with his right foot. It is only when compulsive actions become extremely frequent, intense, unyielding, and disruptive to a person's life that they are no longer within the realm of normal behavior. For example, people who feel compelled to take 10 showers a day or to wash their hands 50 times a day are displaying significant compulsive patterns. Table 17–4 reveals the aspects of rituals that cross the boundary from normal to abnormal. People who are obsessive and compulsive carry out their rituals even though they regard them as absurd.

Table 17–4: Obsessive-Compulsives Rate Aspects of Their Rituals.

Is there resistance to carrying out the rituals?	Definitely Yes 32%	Somewhat 22%	Definitely No 46%
How sensible do you consider the rituals?	Sensible 22%	Rather Silly 13%	Absurd 65%
Does reassurance from others reduce the occurrence of the rituals?	Definitely Yes 27%	Some 15%	Definitely No 68%
Does the presence of others affect the rituals?	Occurs When Alone 20%	Company Irrelevant 76%	Occurs in Company 4%
Amount of family distress caused by the rituals.	Little or None 29%	Moderate 22%	A Great Deal 49%

Adapted from Stern and Cobb (1978).

They also can't stop themselves from carrying them out when others are present, even when to do so causes distress to others and they are aware of that distress.

People may have obsessive thoughts without performing compulsive acts, or may act compulsively without experiencing much obsessive thinking. However, the two often occur together in the same person—in fact, one is frequently a response to the other. Someone who compulsively checks the locks on doors and windows is often yielding to an obsessive fear of burglars. And sometimes compulsive acts are used to control obsessive thoughts: People may recite certain words or phrases over and over again to keep an obsessive and frightening image from occupying their minds.

The *psychoanalytic model* regards obsessive-compulsive disorders as inappropriate defenses against the anxiety produced by unconscious aggressive conflicts. Freudians suggest that the difficulty begins with id impulses that were dealt with too harshly in childhood. Take, for example, id impulses that were severely punished during the toilet-training period of the anal stage. Because these impulses could not be expressed during that stage, they demand expression later in life. They may come to the surface in the form of obsessive thoughts; or they may be prevented or overcome by counter-thoughts or actions. In short, the id and the ego's defense mechanisms are in a seesaw battle. For example, the id impulse to partake in a forbidden sexual encounter (obsessive thought) may be countered by repeatedly thinking other thoughts or by engaging in purifying rituals (compulsive acts) that help the person deny the obsessive idea.

The *learning model* views obsessions and compulsions as learned reactions reinforced by their ability to reduce anxiety. For example, compulsively washing one's hands many times a day might be regarded as an escape mechanism from obsessive fears of disease. It is not even necessary that the fear be so specific. As long as general anxiety is regularly reduced or avoided by such activity, the person will tend to repeat it in the face of danger, real or imagined.

It is possible that some obsessional actions originally are learned by a process Skinner (1948) described for the acquisition of what he called *supersti-*

tious behaviors. He observed that if a reinforcer is delivered at a random time to a pigeon, the bird will frequently continue to emit whatever response it was making just before the reinforcer was delivered. Suppose a man feels anxious and these feelings come and go. One day, just before the anxiety feelings naturally dissipated, he was washing his hands. Because of this fortuitous reinforcement, he increases the frequency of hand washing when he becomes anxious, without becoming particularly aware of it. This in turn increases the probability that hand washing will be followed by a decrease in anxiety, which in turn, reinforces the behavior. Furthermore, if hand washing does not always alleviate anxiety, it can be said to be only a partial reinforcement, which is known to produce a high rate of responding.

The *cognitive model* views at least some forms of obsessive-compulsive disorders as an attempt to assure order and predictability. People who perceive the world as highly threatening may become obsessed with a ritual of meticulous orderliness, arranging their personal environment in exacting ways to maintain their sense of order and control. When the smallest detail becomes disarranged—say, the handle of a cup points the wrong way—their entire sense of order is threatened, and they have to repeat the ritual in order to relieve the anxiety once again.

DISSOCIATIVE DISORDERS

The behaviors that fall under this heading are quite dramatic. Rarely does a year go by in which a multiple personality, an amnesiac protagonist, or a mysterious sleepwalker fails to appear in a book, movie, or television drama. However, although it may be dramatically disappointing, it is scientifically correct to state that such disorders are rare and represent only a very small proportion of the abnormal behaviors seen by clinicians.

Dissociative disorders are characterized by sudden, temporary changes in consciousness, activity, or identity. They include amnesia, fugue, somnambulism, and multiple personality. We will discuss each of these in turn, presenting where possible both the modern clinical perspective and the more classical theories.

As you may recall from Chapter 7, **amnesia** is a partial or total loss of memory for a period lasting from several hours to several years. Although people with amnesia usually retain the ability to communicate and reason, they may forget who they are or where they live; they generally fail to recognize relatives and friends. The forgotten material is sometimes but not always irretrievable; it may reappear spontaneously or under hypnosis.

Fugue (from the Latin word meaning "to flee") is amnesia accompanied by actual physical flight—a person in a state of amnesia may simply wander away for several hours, or even move to another area and set up a new life. Years later the amnesia may suddenly reverse. The person then "awakens" in a strange place with a full memory of his or her original identity, but with amnesia now about the fugue period.

Somnambulism, or sleepwalking, has been traditionally viewed with *psychoanalytic theory* as a dissociative disorder because the individual's body movements are apparently being controlled without the knowledge or participation of the conscious mind. As researchers have learned more about sleep, a different picture of what is now called "sleepwalking disorder" has emerged. It usually occurs during stage 3 or stage 4 sleep (see Chapter 5) and involves the carrying out of what looks like purposive sequences of

behavior—walking, dressing, or going to the bathroom. Its major danger is that sleepwalkers may accidentally injure themselves during their excursions. Up to 15 percent of children show isolated instances of sleepwalking; clinicians estimate that between 1 and 6 percent of children do it often enough to be labeled as having this condition. For the great majority of children, the condition disappears in a few years (American Psychiatric Association, 1980). The conservative course of treatment is no treatment at all aside from protecting the person against injury during the course of the sleepwalking episode.

Multiple personality means the presence of two or more separate personalities in the same person. These personalities compete for access to consciousness, as discussed in Chapter 5. Often they alternate, with one personality being in control for a few hours or days and then the other. The most famous accounts of multiple personalities are the books *Three Faces of Eve* (Thigpen & Cleckley, 1954) and *Sybil* (Schreiber, 1974).

Because dissociative disorders are relatively rare, well-documented literature on the subject is scarce. These disorders therefore remain among the least clearly understood patterns. Nevertheless, the psychoanalytic and learning models have offered some explanations.

The *psychoanalytic model* suggests that the cause of the appearance of a second personality is a massive repression that actually splits off part of consciousness. In this view, the person becomes so upset and threatened by his or her own thoughts or acts that the only way to resolve the resulting conflict is to separate that part of consciousness completely and become totally unaware that it ever existed. The second personality, the one with the unacceptable wishes, seems to be formed with a more flexible superego so that it can more readily carry out the wishes forbidden to the first personality, which has a more "tender conscience."

The *learning model* regards these denials as avoidance responses. This model does not use such concepts as unconsciousness or split consciousness. Rather, people are seen as ignoring or not thinking about significant dimensions of themselves because this allows them to escape or avoid anxiety. While the avoidance pattern in dissociative disorders is quite extreme, it is nevertheless due to basic learning principles. In the person's past such behaviors were reinforced by the immediate reduction of anxiety they brought about. It may be true that other less extreme behaviors would also reduce anxiety, but the individual has not learned such alternative behaviors. The dissociative responses have become the ones used by the individual to cope with certain anxiety-arousing situations.

The *biological model* has not yet had much to say about multiple personality, although a group of researchers at the National Institute of Mental Health has made a preliminary but interesting finding (Patman, 1982). It has long been known that every human being has a distinct set of brain-wave responses (evoked potentials) to stimuli such as flashes of light. Your averaged evoked potentials, like your fingerprints, are characteristic of you and distinct from those of any other person. The researchers had normal subjects create imaginary personalities for themselves and practice those personalities. They found that whatever "new" personalities those in the normal group displayed, their evoked potentials retained their original and characteristic patterns. People with multiple personalities, on the other hand, showed significant shifts of their evoked potential pattern as their different personalities appeared. This suggested that the different personalities were basically disconnected, and, that they processed sensory information in quite different ways.

SOMATOFORM DISORDERS

DSM-III distinguishes several **somatoform disorders,** or physical symptoms that have no apparent organic cause. In **conversion disorders** the person develops symptoms in response to some stressful event (see the Case History: Conversion Disorder). A symptom serves a twofold purpose: It gains sympathy for the individual from others, and it makes it possible for the person to avoid the stress-producing situation. The physical disabilities that appear in conversion disorders may take many forms:

1. *Sensory symptoms:* partial or complete loss of sight or hearing, insensitivity to pain, and unusual tactile sensations, such as itchiness or tingling.
2. *Motor symptoms:* paralysis, tremors, rigid joints, and inability to talk above a whisper.
3. *Visceral symptoms:* chronic coughing, headaches, nausea, and shortness of breath.

Freud believed that people transformed or converted their unacceptable desires or psychological conflicts into a bodily symptom that was tangible and socially acceptable. The *psychoanalytic model* begins its explanation of conversion disorders by focusing on id impulses (for example, sexual desires) that were dealt with too harshly during childhood. For instance, during the oedipal stage children come to desire the parent of the opposite sex. If this desire is not resolved adequately in the form of identification with the same-sex parent, children may feel threatened and anxious about such sexual impulses. Later in life, when these or similar id impulses emerge in a particularly strong manner, the individual may convert them into a physical channel. Of course, a conversion disorder need not involve sexual impulses. Abse (1959) described a case in which a man's desire to kill his wife and her lover was so threatening to him that he repressed it and instead developed paralysis of the legs. In this case, as in others, the conversion to the physical channel helps protect people from their disturbing impulses.

The *learning model* does not see a conversion process in such physical disabilities. Instead, it views them as learned behaviors that are reinforced by their role in helping the individual avoid stressful situations. This does not mean that such people are pretending. Rather, their physical difficulties have in the past been reinforced by serving to reduce or avoid the anxiety of key stressful events. So their illness may serve to protect them from social, occupational, or family pressures and may be further reinforced by the attention and comfort elicited from others. The similarities between such disorders and actual, organic-based disorders indicate that the person may have had some experience with a relative or acquaintance who had a real physical disease that served as a model.

As in the case of dissociative disorders, the empirical evidence for these explanations of conversion disorders is rather sparse. Indeed, DSM-III states that a case of true conversion disorder is rare and that numerous other explanations must be tested before this diagnosis can be made.

AFFECTIVE DISORDERS

Affect is the term used by psychologists to refer to the expression of emotion. (Affect does not refer to the emotion itself, but to the signs of feelings that people show to others.) **Affective disorders** are patterns of behavior in

CASE HISTORY
Conversion Disorder

A young woman of 22 was referred [to the clinic] with a 6-year history of total incapacity from continuous generalized shaking and trembling movements. Extensive and exhaustive investigations at a number of previous hospitals had effectively excluded structural damage or disease. The history of the complaint was that she had begun to fall helpless to the ground, and to lie there twitching, when she was 16, shortly after her parents had refused to allow her to continue for another year at school, since she was required to earn money for the family. At about the same time their own chronic and severe marital disharmony had become increasingly apparent to her and to the rest of the family. Within a year, her attacks of falling had been followed by increasing periods of disability due to the jerking, twitching, and trembling movements, until after 2 years, she had become totally helpless and disabled.

On examination, the generalized twitching, jerking, and trembling of all her limbs, head, and body effectively prevented her from reading, writing, feeding herself, or indeed looking after herself in any way whatever. She was helpless and bedridden, and her sole recreation was listening to the radio.

(From Stafford-Clark & Smith, 1978, p. 145)

which an individual expresses emotional states excessively, inappropriately, or inadequately.

Depression

In contrast to a disorder like multiple personality, which we are more likely to encounter in movies or television than in real life, we are all likely to know a person, a friend, or family member who experiences **depression** at some time. Approximately 5 to 10 percent of men and 10 to 20 percent of women in our society will suffer at least one bout of serious depression during their lives (Woodruff, Goodwin, & Guze, 1974; Weissman & Myers, 1978). In addition to feelings of sadness, depression often involves a change in appetite, sleeping difficulties, and a decrease in activities, interests, and energy (see Table 17–5). Severely depressed people think of themselves negatively and self-reproachingly. Their sex drive is low, and they experience either insomnia or an increased need for sleep. They avoid social contact and may consider suicide. (Not all depressed persons have all these symptoms, nor are these symptoms unique to depression.)

There seem to be different kinds of depression. For example, there is a range of severity from relatively mild symptoms of depression to patterns so severe as to make daily functioning all but impossible. DSM-III differentiates between *major depression*, which seems to arise from within the individual, and depression caused by adjustment to a stressful life situation. *Adjustment disorder with depression* is precipitated by some external event, usually a loss such as death, illness, or departure of a family member, but it may also be caused by such stresses as divorce, job loss, or change in work conditions (Paykel, 1973). Theorists (Bowlby, 1973) have suggested that the present loss or stress connects with earlier loss of a parent to cause the current feelings of depression. Evidence shows that people who suffered the death of a parent during childhood are more likely to experience depression as adults (Heinicke, 1973).

Major depression is not a response to an external situation. It is characterized by long-lasting and overwhelming sadness of mood, with many of the behaviors described above. Those who are psychotically depressed have delusions or hallucinations, or may be mute and unresponsive. Classically, such pervasive depressions were thought to be biological in origin, but many modern depression researchers do not agree. They also believe that major

(David M. Grossman/Photo Researchers)

Table 17–5:   Changes from Normal to Depressed States.

Items	Normal State	Depressed State
Stimulus	*Response*	
Loved object	Affection	Loss of feeling, revulsion
Favorite activities	Pleasure	Boredom
New opportunities	Enthusiasm	Indifference
Humor	Amusement	Mirthlessness
Novel stimuli	Curiosity	Lack of interest
Abuse	Anger	Self-criticism, sadness
Goal or Drive	*Direction*	
Gratification	Pleasure	Avoidance
Welfare	Self-care	Self-neglect
Self-preservation	Survival	Suicide
Achievement	Success	Withdrawal
Thinking	*Appraisal*	
About self	Realistic	Self-devaluating
About future	Hopeful	Hopeless
About environment	Realistic	Overwhelming
Biological and Physiological Activities	*Symptom*	
Appetite	Spontaneous hunger	Loss of appetite
Sexuality	Spontaneous desire	Loss of desire
Sleep	Restful	Disturbed
Energy	Spontaneous	Fatigued

From Beck (1974).

depression may be rarer than previously thought, because situationally depressed individuals may repress, forget, or minimize the external circumstances that triggered their depression.

The *psychoanalytic model* generally regards major depression as anger turned inward. Freud believed that the tendency toward depression starts in early childhood, specifically during the first phase of development, the oral period. If our infantile needs during this time are over- or undergratified, a fixation occurs that results in overdependence on others. Later in life, after the loss of a loved one through separation or death, our overdependent ego identifies with this lost person. We "introject" or incorporate the person and essentially make the person part of ourselves. According to Freud, we all have unconscious feelings of hate toward those we love, and we now turn those feelings against ourselves so that depression results.

There are several problems with the psychoanalytic formulation, some of them theoretical. If we incorporate the loved one within us, why do feelings of hate rather than love dominate? Also, many people who did not experience the death of a loved one during childhood become depressed. Why? The psychoanalytic answer is that it is possible to feel depressed without actually losing a loved one. A person may experience a "symbolic loss" in which some action or event creates a trauma equivalent to actual loss of a

loved one—a father may be drafted into the military and called away; a mother may enter the work force; or a father may do something the child interprets as rejection. But if these sorts of events, which occur in nearly everybody's life, are considered losses of a loved one, the Freudians must tell us why they cause depression in only some people.

There is also some evidence against the Freudian view of depression. Researchers (Beck & Ward, 1961) find images of loss and failure in the dreams of depressed people, not the anger and hostility Freudians would expect to be present, given their view that unconscious material is represented in dreams. Despite the psychoanalytic view that depression is anger turned inward, researchers have found that depressed people are quite capable of expressing rage and hostility at other people (Weissman, Klerman, & Paykel, 1971).

Learning and *cognitive models* combine to form an account of depression that more clearly fits the empirical results. Learning theorists (Lewinsohn, 1974; Eastman, 1976) suggest that depressed feelings are produced when the reinforcers a person is receiving from the outside world drop to a low rate(see Figure 17–1). Because of this decrease in reinforcement (which may be caused by some external event such as the loss of a job or the death of a spouse), activities that would have called forth positive responses in the past decrease, leading to an even further loss of reinforcers and further dejection. Thus a vicious circle begins.

For example, a woman's husband may die, leading to a major reduction in the pleasures and reinforcers she receives. Without her husband, she is less rewarded for being active, initiating conversations, dressing attractively, or acting cheerfully. Her range of behaviors becomes more limited and depressive in nature. Such behaviors make it difficult for others to be around her, converse with her, have fun with her, and reward her. This causes further isolation, which makes her feel more depressed.

A related viewpoint is that of Seligman's helplessness model. Seligman proposes that depressed people have developed a **learned helplessness** from earlier experiences and now believe themselves unable to influence and control events. Thus they develop negative symptoms, including helplessness and passivity, as well as depressed and negative expectations when faced with stressful situations. An experiment by Miller and Seligman (1975) demonstrated that depressed subjects, unlike nondepressed subjects, did not expect success in performing a skilled task even after they had done it successfully several times. In other words, even success did not give them faith in their abilities; helplessness, once learned, apparently does not dissipate easily.

Notice that the research on reinforcement and learned helplessness was done to clarify the *learning perspective* on depression, but that the results recognize a very important *cognitive component*. Both are concerned with the reinforcement patterns the individual experiences and the mental representations of the world the individual constructs from these patterns of reinforcement.

In an influential modification of the theory of learned helplessness (Abramson, Seligman, & Teasdale, 1978), the cognitive components were made even more explicit. They found that the interpretations people make about the causes of their failure will determine both whether they become depressed by that failure and what effects that failure will have in the future. Thus attribution is part of this cognitive process. (See Chapter 19 for a further discussion of theories of attribution.) If I believe that the reasons for my failure are global, stable, and internal to me, then depression and loss of

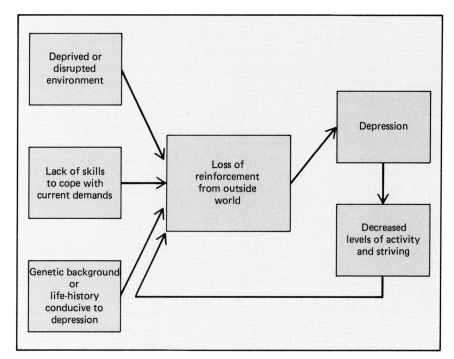

Figure 17.1 Lewinshohn's Model of Depression The diagram indicates several possible causes for a person experiencing fewer reinforcements from the physical or interpersonal world and its relationship to depression. For example, a high-school student who was relocated with his family (disrupted environment) has no friends in his new school (loss of reinforcement in his interpersonal world). This could lead to a depression, which in turn causes him to spend a lot of time alone in his room (decreased levels of activity). A decreased level of activity lessens the likelihood of further reinforcements and thus strengthens the depression. So if the student does not make any efforts, he will continue to experience a lack of reinforcement from his social world.

self-esteem are likely to result, and I will feel helpless as well. I may then decide that I will not try similar tasks in the future, since I will only fail at them. For instance, if I fail a high-school math test and decide that I failed because I lack intelligence, I will be very depressed indeed.

A more specific attribution, although still internal and stable, would be that I lacked math ability. An even more specific attribution, and a correspondingly less depressing one, would be that I perform poorly on high pressure, multiple-choice tests. Note the difference in the consequences that I expect to follow from each attribution. If I really believe that I'm unintelligent, then I am likely not to aspire to college and a whole set of "intellectual" careers. If I believe that I'm poor at math, the effects, while still general, are less so. I may well go to college, and simply stay away from mathematics courses. Finally, if my interpretation of my failure is simply that I am bad at a certain kind of test-taking skill, then I might even take college math courses, provided I am sure the tests will be of the take-home variety.

Researchers postulate that some people have a *depressive attributional style*; such people attribute frequently poor outcomes to global, stable, internal causes. Research (Seligman, Abramson, Semmel, & von Baeyer, 1979) supports the notion that depressed students are more likely to attribute failure in this way. Other research (Metalsky, Abramson, Seligman, Semmel, & Peterson, 1982) showed that students who indicated a depressive attributional style on a beginning-of-term questionnaire became more depressed if they received a lower-than-expected midterm grade. Peterson and Seligman (1984) identified a group of college students who were mildly depressed. Those who manifested a depressive attributional style were found later to become more severely depressed by subsequent events than those who had other coping styles.

Aaron Beck has developed an exceedingly influential *cognitive* model of

depression. According to Beck (1967), depression is one point on a continuum that includes ordinary forms of everyday "blues" and sadness, rather than some special state. Beck sees depression as the result of a series of logical errors made by depressed people in interpreting the causes of events that happen to them. These "negative schemas" converge to produce negative self-evaluation.

Depressed people show consistent tendencies of self-deprecation and self-blame, and these tendencies are evidenced in several ways. Negative self-evaluations are reached on the basis of insufficient evidence, by wildly overgeneralized conclusions from a few and possibly unimportant events. For instance, one poorly received lecture causes a lecturer to be depressed about his teaching abilities and self-worth. The negativity of small events, such as an ill-considered remark, is maximized, while positive outcomes are minimized. We all know that many events in life have multiple causes, but depression prone people abstract from this multiplicity of causes the ones that support their feelings of low self-worth. They regularly draw conclusions without evidence, attend to only certain aspects of a situation (usually the wrong ones), and overgeneralize from specific occurrences to their whole lives. These kinds of repeated cognitive distortions seem quite reasonable and natural to depressed people and add strength to their negative self-view and world view. This negative view flavors decisions, behaviors, emotions, and interactions, thus locking in a pattern of depression.

There is evidence that depressed individuals do show the thought patterns Beck describes (Beck, 1967; Beck, Weissman, Lester, & Trexler, 1974; Nelson, 1977). However, Beck's theory postulates more than this correlational finding; it postulates that the negative reasoning processes should be the cause of depression. Studies need to be done that first assess individuals' negative thought patterns and then see whether these individuals become depressed when negative events occur in their lives. Some of the studies by Seligman and his associates already seem to point to this. But other studies of hospitalized individuals show that a depressive attributional style accompanies depressions in this population while the patients are hospitalized, yet doesn't seem to persist after release (Hamilton & Abrahmson, 1983; Fennell & Campbell, 1984). Since we know that depressed people are subject to subsequent bouts of depression, this is a puzzling finding and one that may suggest the causal sequence of depression is more complicated. Perhaps some external events or internal processess reactivate the depressive attributional style first; and then because later negative events are interpreted in terms of the depressive style, these events produce the depression.

Seasonal Affective Disorder.   One more kind of depression is recognized in the new DSM-IIIR. It is called *seasonal affective disorder* and consists of a general feeling of listlessness and depression that is experienced by some individuals during the winter months. Like most depressives, people suffering from this condition have a reduced interest in sex and show feelings ranging from irritability to lethargy. However, unlike most depressives, such people gain rather than lose weight and report an intense desire for sleep. Initial suggestions about causes of this condition are that the sufferers are showing an exaggerated tendency that is found in all of us, which at one time was useful in an evolutionary sense—that is, the tendency for bodily processes to slow down during the winter months to conserve energy and possibly scarce food supplies. (Sooner or later somebody is going to call this "human hibernation disorder.")

HIGHLIGHT _____

Abnormality and You

Physicians teaching in medical schools have identified a condition that they informally call *medical student's disease*. This term describes the tendency of some medical students to discover that they have one or another of the diseases being discussed in a class. Sometimes the students' self-diagnoses are accurate; they really do have a disease that they have recently learned about. However, the teachers feel that most of their students with medical student's disease are basically healthy but suggestible. The giveaway is when the students find that they have each and every disorder mentioned by the clinical professor.

Just like medical students, those who study psychology are prone to recognize that some symptoms of various disorders apply to themselves. Indeed, some of the symptoms are necessarily vague and may seem to describe the feelings of loneliness, sorrow, rage, or euphoria that we all do, and should, feel at appropriate times. They become true symptoms only if they are sufficiently severe and persistent in nature.

Therefore be warned: We are about to describe many disorders that are of a strongly psychological nature. Not surprisingly, many have symptoms that may resemble states that you have been in at one time or another. Don't assume that you are clinically depressed, schizophrenic, or otherwise a victim of any other disorder discussed in this chapter just because you have a shock of recognition while reading your textbook.

On the other hand, we don't want to say that this sort of recognition is always meaningless. People have accurately realized that they do have some identifiable abnormal condition by reading about it in a textbook. How do you know which of these possibilities fits when you find the description of a particular disorder hitting uncomfortably close to home? Several points can be made. First, is the condition persistent and bothersome? And did you find yourself often worrying about it well before you encountered the textbook description? Second, is it getting in the way of your life? Are you prevented from doing things that you really care about because, for instance, you are afraid of being in crowds? If you are concerned about some possible psychological difficulty that you are currently experiencing, look back at Table 17–3. How much impairment of functioning is the problem causing you? The more problems it is causing in your daily life, the more it would make sense for you to think about getting help.

Just what exactly does it mean to "think about getting help"? What sorts of help are available and useful? At the conclusion of the therapy chapter (Chapter 18), we try to say something about modern trends in therapy. The conclusion that we come to is an optimistic one. We say optimistic because many more specific forms of therapy are being developed, each one is focused on a specific class of problems, and each one shows some evidence of being effective for these specific problems. However, often problems are initially ill-defined and unclear; the first issue for the person seeking psychological help is typically to decide what exactly the problem is. This in itself is not an easy task, and it may require the guidance of a trained professional. If you are experiencing some significant problem, it is usually sensible to start with the resources that your college provides for students. Most colleges have a counseling service or a psychological branch of the health service. This is where you will find people trained to help others assess and define their problems. Often this is a good place to begin if you feel that you have serious and persistent problems of living that keep you from being what you could be.

A biological triggering mechanism is being sought for this disorder. One possibility involves the human hormone melatonin, which is produced at a greater rate in humans who do not receive much sun. A simple treatment is to spend more time outside in the winter (during those scarce sunny hours when most of us are indoors at work or in class). Unwittingly, "modern" lighting conditions may be contributing to this disorder. Ordinary fluorescent lights contain only a limited range of the wavelengths of natural light. Therefore, as more and more people work in environments illuminated by fluorescent lights, increasing numbers may be susceptible to this condition. Thus another therapy for this disorder is to spend time under special artificial lights that contain more of the spectrum of wavelengths found in natural light.

All of this, of course, represents the initial best guesses about a disorder that has only recently been identified. Much more will need to be discovered before we have a clear picture of how many people actually suffer from this disorder and exactly how to best treat it.

Bipolar Disorders

Bipolar disorders add manic behavior to the symptoms of depression. A person with this type of disorder will at times go through periods of intense depression and at other times be energetic and excessively lively.

Manic behavior may at first appear to be simply a very positive and enthusiastic approach to life. But it soon becomes clear that the behavior and reactions of people in a manic period are extreme and inappropriate. Often they have feelings of great joy or elation, show great agitation, become involved in many different undertakings, and show a heightened pace of activity and thinking, extreme impatience, poor concentration, and poor judgment. In some cases, they will make expensive and extravagant plans that are totally unrealistic. Most people think of manic behavior as happy behavior, but this is not always so. Sometimes people in a manic pattern are quite irritated and unpleasant. They may be quite aggressive or may become confused, incoherent, disoriented, or even violent.

The periods of depression and mania are of varying duration—sometimes they go on for months at a time—and seem unrelated to particular situational factors or changes. For this reason, bipolar disorders have often been analyzed in biological terms. Since Pavlov, researchers have characterized the nervous system as having an excitatory, action-producing component and an inhibitory, action-suppressing component. It has been suggested that depressive disorders are caused by a neurophysiologically produced activation of the inhibitory system, and that bipolar disorders are produced by some cyclical neurophysiological process that involves first the relative dominance of the excitatory system, then the inhibitory system.

Most neuroscientists now regard this as an oversimplification, but several more sophisticated versions of neurophysiological explanations for bipolar disorders are being investigated. As we discussed in Chapter 2, neurotransmitters regulate the transmission of impulses across synapses between neurons in the brain. This suggests that excesses or deficiencies of *norepinephrine* (a neurotransmitter) are the cause of manic or depressive behavior (Schildkraut, 1965). That many of the drugs that affect bipolar disorders also affect norepinephrine levels is taken as evidence for this.

Again, further research (Barchas, Akil, Elliott, Holman, & Watson, 1978; Berger, 1978) tells a more complicated story. A second neurotransmitter, *serotonin*, has also been linked to depression (Prange, Wilson, Lynn, Lacoe, & Strikeleather, 1974). The current tentative formulation is that lowered levels of serotonin predispose an individual to bipolar disorders. Given a serotonin deficiency, a high or low level of norepinephrine leads to manic or depressive behavior, respectively. Alternatively, there is some evidence (Bunney & Garland, 1983) that the swing from depression to mania may not be due so much to shifts in neurotransmitter levels as to shifts in the sensitivity of neurotransmitter receptors.

The Genetics of the Manic-Depressive Disorder. One important area of research in the study of abnormality has been the field of genetics. As you will recall from Chapter 15, there is some scientific speculation about the role of genetics in personality. In Chapter 10 you learned a great deal about the controversy over the respective roles of heritability and environment in intelligence. There is also a great deal of interest in what role genetics plays in disorders such as manic-depression.

Recent advances in research techniques for identifying genetic defects

have created a whole new field called *reverse genetics*. One of the early subjects of inquiry in this field has been the manic-depressive disorder. We will use this case to illustrate the general approach of reverse genetics. You should extract two points from this discussion: first, what has been discovered about manic-depression; and second, how a scientist using these techniques would search for the origins of many mental disorders.

In reverse genetics scientists begin by identifying a disease or condition that they think has a genetic component. They then observe groups of families in whom that disease occurs with some frequency and identify its inheritance patterns. This process is easier if the researchers can find large families that all still live in one geographically contiguous area, and, even better, if they can locate families whose lives do not subject them to significant amounts of other stressors that might lead to the disease. Once a set of people who share many genes has been found, researchers identify those who have the disease and those who do not. They then can microscopically inspect chromosome samples from each group, and by laborious and time-consuming procedures of comparison and elimination, figure out at least the approximate chromosomal location of the defective gene.

A favorite research population of reverse geneticists has been a group of Amish families who still carry on traditional farming lives in and around Lancaster, Pennsylvania. (It is not that the Amish people have a higher rate of manic-depression than the general population; it is simply that they fulfill the requirements for a study group just described.) One group of researchers (Egeland et al., 1986) determined that, among Amish families, the gene that produced the tendency to manic-depressive episodes was found on the short arm of chromosome 11. Almost simultaneously, another group of researchers (Baron et al., 1987), working with a sample of families in Jerusalem, found that the manic-depressive tendency in this group was associated with a defect on the sex-linked X chromosome.

The most likely conclusion from this discrepancy between the two studies is that there are at least two different genetic flaws that can cause a propensity to the manic-depressive disorder. Further research can examine the ways in which the disorder manifests itself in the two different populations. It may be that the manic-depressive disorder, once thought to be a single condition, will now be found to fall into two separate conditions. Further, the structural or neurological deficiencies underlying the two may also be different. From our previous discussion about neurotransmitters, it is clear that the researchers will be attempting to discover how these specific genetic deficiencies might express themselves as flaws in serotonin or norepinephrine production or reception.

Finally, even the researchers pursuing the genetic linkages of the manic-depressive disorder have been very careful to point out that this disorder has an environmental component as well (Egeland et al., 1986; Baron et al., 1987; Hodgkinson et al., 1987). Some individuals who—given their genetic makeups—"should" show manic-depressive behaviors do not do so. Therefore these researchers continue to argue for the joint, and perhaps interactive, effects of heredity and environment in producing the manic-depressive disorder, as well as abnormal disorders in general.

Over the next few years we can expect to read a number of similar discoveries about the genetic determinants of many physical disorders and some mental ones. What we will probably come to understand more slowly are the possibilities for treating these genetic defects once they have been identified.

SCHIZOPHRENIA

When we turn to a discussion of **schizophrenia,** we are confronted with the most controversial and puzzling of mental disorders. The diagnosis of schizophrenia has been applied to such a wide variety of behaviors that many professionals argue that it is a wastebasket category. Still, there are some characteristics that most persons diagnosed as schizophrenic do seem to share: a distortion of reality in some significant way, social withdrawal, and prominent disturbances in thought, perception, motor activity, or emotionality. Schizophrenia always involves a deterioration from a previous level of functioning. To family, friends, or work colleagues, schizophrenics seem not to be doing (or thinking) as well as they once did.

Disturbances of Thought, Perception, Emotion, and Motor Abilities

The thought disturbances of schizophrenia are centered on the person's inability to organize ideas coherently. Often such people have trouble sticking to one topic at a time (loose associations). The ends of their statements are only distantly related to the beginnings. For some, the only rule is that key words in their statements rhyme (clang associations). Yet others are so unaffected by the usual rules of communication that they use their own private words (neologisms) that have meaning to no one else.

Sometimes it is not the organization of thought but its content that is disturbed. This is best illustrated by the delusions that often form part of schizophrenic thinking, beliefs that seem totally unfounded and are frequently bizarre. People with delusions of grandeur view themselves as magnificent or powerful persons such as Christ, Einstein, or Joan of Arc. Those who have delusions of influence or control may believe that others are trying to contact them by radar, television, or other means. And those with delusions of persecution imagine that others are trying to hurt them.

The perceptual disturbances of schizophrenia center on individuals' inability to selectively filter out the millions of stimuli surrounding them at any given moment and to give order and meaning to their world. The result is that schizophrenics often pay great attention to seemingly irrelevant stimuli and ignore important stimuli. Distraction is a way of life for them.

Often the perceptual difficulties extend to **hallucinations,** the perception of things that are not actually there. People with visual hallucinations may see imaginary persons or objects. Those with auditory hallucinations may hear imaginary voices that command, advise, criticize, or praise them. Other senses may also be involved in hallucinations, as in the case of people who feel millions of insects crawling on their skin or taste poison in their food.

There can be other sorts of emotional disturbances. Some schizophrenics show extremely inappropriate emotional reactions—for example, laughing at the death of someone dear to them. Others show ambivalent reactions, repeatedly expressing both intensely positive and negative emotions toward the same person or object. And yet others show virtually no reaction at all, no matter what the situation.

The motor activities of a schizophrenic are often quite disturbed. Some spend hour upon hour gesturing in systematic ways—for example, bending each finger of each hand in succession, or raising and lowering an arm over

This painting has appeared on the cover of *Schizophrenia Bulletin*, which features art done by current or former mental hospital patients. The artist provided the following description of his work: "This was the 'ghost' I used to see all the time. It was my other self that I was always talking to. The deep eyes represent that mysteriousness of the self; and the background shows all the different kinds of thoughts a person experiences. It shows a lot of energy." (Mark C. Blumenthal)

and over again. Some schizophrenics move about with much excitement, waving, and activity. Others show virtually no movement at all. They stay in the same position for long periods of time, whether sitting, squatting, or lying. Such people often have a "wavy flexibility"—their hands, arms, and legs can be molded into any position by another person, and they will maintain that position. (See the Case History: Schizophrenia for a description of one man's symptoms.)

Different Types of Schizophrenia

Because schizophrenia is characterized by such a wide range of behavioral and perceptual disturbances, it can be considered to have a number of subtypes based on the predominant symptoms. For example, if the person has delusions of grandiosity or of persecution, has unfocused anxieties, or tends to be argumentative or aggressive, the diagnosis is likely to be **paranoid schizophrenia**. **Catatonic schizophrenics** are generally immobile and resistant to instructions or attempts to move them; they occasionally have bursts of purposeless excited motor activity. The number of subtypes of schizophrenia has alternately grown and decreased over the years in line with contemporary thinking. Some clinicians have questioned the usefulness of distinguishing so many subtypes.

Research has indicated, however, that it is useful to distinguish schizophrenics according to at least a few dimensions. Paranoid schizophrenics, for example, have been found to be distinctly more alert than nonparanoid schizophrenics, and more coherent in their thoughts and statements. One may not agree with their view of things, but they are capable of stating it quite coherently. Another useful distinction is between chronic schizophrenics, whose symptoms emerge gradually and last a long time, and acute schizophrenics, whose symptoms emerge rapidly and improve rapidly. The prior social adjustment (called premorbid adjustment) of schizophrenic persons has also proved to be an important variable. A schizophrenic with a "good premorbid adjustment" tends to improve significantly faster.

Models of Schizophrenia

The explanations of schizophrenia vary greatly. Psychoanalytic theorists are themselves divided in their interpretations. One *psychoanalytic* perspective, that proposed by Freud, views schizophrenia as regression to a pre-ego stage, that very early period in childhood when self-absorption ruled the day. To function without an ego is to function without reality testing (understanding that something exists outside of you), which is certainly consistent with the separation from reality that is so typical of schizophrenia.

An alternative psychoanalytic perspective sees schizophrenia as an ego-defense strategy. According to this interpretation, schizophrenic persons are coping with their early and ongoing traumatic experiences by relying strongly on a wide range of ego-defense mechanisms. For example, delusions and hallucinations are said to be exaggerated uses of such defenses as projection, fantasy, and wish fulfillment. Delusions of influence are simply the projections of blame onto others for one's own unacceptable thoughts, behaviors, and failures. Delusions of grandeur represent extreme fantasy and wish fulfillment. And hallucinations enable one to tolerate one's own negative thoughts and ideas by externalizing them as "voices" outside oneself.

Two months before commitment the patient began to talk about how he had failed, how he had "spoiled" his whole life, and how it was now "too late." Note here the point we stressed earlier about deterioration of functioning. He spoke of hearing someone say, "You must submit." One night his wife was awakened by his talking. He told her of having several visions but refused to describe them. He stated that someone was after him and trying to blame him for the death of a certain man. He had been poisoned, he said. Whenever he saw a truck or a fire engine, the patient stated that someone in it was looking for him in order to claim his assistance to help save the world. He had periods of laughing and shouting and became so noisy and unmanageable that it was necessary to commit him.

On arrival at the hospital the patient . . . lay down on the floor, pulled at his foot, made undirected, violent striking movements . . . struck attendants, grimaced, assumed rigid, attitudinized postures, refused to speak, and appeared to be having auditory hallucinations. Later in the day, he was found to be in a stuporous state. His face was without expression, he was mute and rigid, and paid no attention to those about him or to their questions. His eyes were closed and the lids could be separated only with effort. . . .

For five days he remained mute, negativistic, and inaccessible, at times staring vacantly into space, at times with his eyes tightly closed. He ate poorly and gave no response to questions but once was heard to mutter to himself in a greatly preoccupied manner, "I'm going to die—I know it—you know it." On the evening of the sixth day he looked about and asked where he was and how he came there. When asked to tell of his life, he related many known events and how he had once worked in an airplane factory, but added that he had invented an appliance pertaining to airplanes, that this had been stolen and patented through fraud and that as a result he had lost his position. He ate ravenously, then fell asleep, and on awaking was in a catatonic stupor, remaining in this state for days. . . .

(Kolb, 1973, pp. 334–335)

Learning theorists also offer more than one explanation for schizophrenia, although all involve reinforcement principles. One account (Ullman & Krasner, 1975) suggests that schizophrenics are people who were not reinforced for responding to the social stimuli that most of us learned to respond to, because of disturbed contact with their families while growing up. The result is that in social situations schizophrenics do not "pay attention" to the cues. They are then ostracized or punished for their inappropriate behavior, which can contribute to their "paranoid" beliefs that people are talking about them. Actually, their peers probably do talk about their weird behavior and may even be cruel to them.

Since they are deprived of normal reinforcement, these people are particularly in need of whatever few reinforcements the environment does provide, and these may come from the attention or sympathy they receive when they make schizophrenic responses. In other words, in the reward-deprived worlds of schizophrenics, crazy behavior may produce most of the reinforcements that they receive. Support for this view comes from research that shows that schizophrenic talk can be reduced by systematic efforts to ignore it and to reward "normal" talk.

Yet a third learning perspective suggests that schizophrenic individuals learn their behaviors by imitating other schizophrenic people in their environment. Some studies suggest that sometimes the parents of schizophrenics are schizophrenic themselves, thus providing an influential model. This perspective does not account for that vast number of schizophrenics who did not have schizophrenic parents or other such models; nor does it explain why so many children of schizophrenic parents are apparently normal.

The leading spokesperson for the *humanistic-existential* point of view on schizophrenia is the British psychiatrist R. D. Laing (1964). Laing's position is that schizophrenia is a sane response to a social world gone mad. To be successful and "normal" in our society, Laing claims, requires accepting false, depersonalizing, trivial, or destructive goals and modes of behavior. Because schizophrenic individuals have suffered intolerable pressures and contradic-

tory demands from their environment, they react in an appropriately negative fashion to all of society. People who become schizophrenic may have had exceptionally difficult family situations, which simply made them more sensitive to societal contradictions than the rest of us. Their schizophrenia is a withdrawal from others to make an inward search. This search, if allowed to continue, will result in a strong, well-adjusted person who has come appropriately to terms with living authentically in a world that frequently demands less-than-authentic behavior. Laing believes that the standard, well-meaning efforts of family members, therapists, and others to alleviate schizophrenic symptoms actually interfere with this constructive process. Such interventions suspend the person in an endless journey and prevent the natural positive outcome of the search.

Not surprisingly, Laing's theory has raised a great deal of controversy. The main difficulty is his notion that schizophrenic symptoms are constructive. Critics point to the apparent suffering and limited lives of schizophrenic persons and ask how these can be viewed as positive. Laing responds that the suffering and limitations result from the environment's inappropriate interference with the natural growth process.

The *biological approach* to schizophrenia has generated high excitement for various physiological or biochemical explanations. Unfortunately, many of these that suggest a simple link between some biochemical imbalance and schizophrenia have not held up when subjected to more tightly controlled scientific scrutiny.

Research into the biological bases of schizophrenia is now focusing on an approach generally familiar to you—neurotransmitter system dysfunctions. Some chromosomal abnormalities may cause these neurotransmitter imbalances. At the 1987 American Psychiatric Association convention preliminary evidence was presented suggesting that the gene that produces schizophrenia exists on chromosome 5 in humans (Meltzers: Kane, 1987). Recall that in discussing the possible physiological causes of bipolar disorders, we raised the possibility that manic and depressive disorders were caused by certain complex patterns of neurotransmitter imbalances. Similarly, it has been suggested that schizophrenics have too much of the neurotransmitter *dopamine* at certain brain centers. Dopamine, among other functions, plays a key role in our ability to attend to, perceive, and integrate information. It may help us to link sensations such as a smell or a color with our memories or internal feelings. If a person had too much dopamine, almost every smell, color, or other perception would trigger a distinct memory or feeling until the person was overloaded with sensations demanding attention. How upsetting and confusing this would be—and how similar this experience is to schizophrenic symptoms.

The support for this theory is indirect but intriguing. For example, *phenothiazines* (antipsychotic medications such as thorazine) not only remove schizophrenic symptoms, but also bring on the Parkinsonian symptoms of extreme muscle tremors. We know that Parkinsonian symptoms are caused by too little dopamine in the brain. Antipsychotic medications apparently reduce schizophrenic symptoms by severely reducing dopamine, perhaps from a level that was much too high in the first place.

It has also been observed that chronic amphetamine abuse often leads to the appearance of schizophrenic symptoms, and amphetamines are now kown to stimulate dopamine production. In fact, schizophrenic persons who take even small dosages of an amphetamine show more intense symptoms. At this point, high dopamine levels do seem to be involved in schizophrenia. But as with much other physiological research, the complete explanation is

probably more complex. In general, it is unlikely that any complex psychological syndrome will have any simple correlation to simple patterns of neurotransmitter surpluses or deficiencies. Second, even when the links between neurotransmitter patterns of acitivity and personality disorders are known, we will still need to understand the events that produce these neurotransmitter dysfunctions. Those events may well be psychological in nature, including the events specified in the psychodynamic, learning, cognitive, and humanistic models.

The possibility may be illustrated by considering one interesting *cognitive model* of schizophrenia. In a sense, it begins its explanation where the biological model leaves off. Maher (1970) argues that there is nothing wrong with the thinking processes of schizophrenics. Rather, such people have a very real biochemical problem that leads them to experience sensory distortions such as odd sensations, visions, or sounds. Their apparent delusions result from their efforts to make sense of these unusual experiences. Since everyone around them denies that they could be experiencing such sensations, they learn to ignore or discount the opinions of others. Thus schizophrenic individuals apply their logical processes to their unique but real experiences, and they apply them in relative isolation.

In trying to explain these experiences, the person may well decide that such odd sounds are coming from a source that other people apparently cannot hear. The individual may further believe that he or she is a special person to be receiving such communications. Or the person may feel that others are lying about not hearing these sounds or are even secretly sending the sounds and voices. Either way, a delusional system emerges, all from trying to logically understand events that cannot be logically explained within the person's framework of knowledge.

PERSONALITY DISORDERS

All people show characteristic patterns of behavior and ways of thinking about and perceiving the environment and other people. When these characteristic patterns become maladaptive, causing individuals distress or impairing their normal functioning in occupational or social situations, these individuals are characterized as having a **personality disorder** (American Psychiatric Association, 1980). We will discuss the antisocial personality disorder as an example of this group of disorders.

Antisocial Personality Disorder

In a society in which criminal behavior is increasing, many people take advantage of others, and many behave unethically and immorally. Society often looks to psychology for reasons why this is so. Is antisocial behavior (including behavior by seemingly respectable persons) a form of abnormality? What accounts for some people's indifference to the moral standards of their society? One answer provided by psychology is the **antisocial personality disorder,** previously called the psychopathic or sociopathic personality.

Many psychologists have felt uncomfortable about even considering such behaviors as a form of abnormal functioning. Clearly, such patterns are deviant, but "deviant" does not necessarily equal abnormal. Perhaps it is because the kinds of behavior involved are so harmful to society that clinicians strug-

gle to understand the antisocial personality disorder. Researchers are well aware that this investigation involves some complex legal, moral, and societal problems.

Certainly not everyone who is a criminal should be categorized as having an antisocial personality disorder. The label has been applied to those individuals whose personality characteristics include pervasive unsocialized behavior in conflict with society: inability to display loyalty to others; gross selfishness, callousness, irresponsibility, and impulsiveness; inability to feel guilt or to learn from experience; and low tolerance of frustration. Obviously, these characteristics fit many people at various times in their lives. It is important to know, therefore, that the label of antisocial personality disorder is applied only to those whose whole life-style is typified by such characteristics—the essential feature of the disorder is a *history* of chronic antisocial behavior. Antisocial behavior characteristically emerges during the person's teenage years. It affects on-the-job performance, and generally, these people are unable to sustain genuinely close friendships or loving relationships with other people.

A brief look at the history of psychological perspectives on antisocial behavior will help us to understand the current theories about this disorder. Throughout most of history people who committed crimes were generally treated as criminals and subjected to the standard punishments inflicted in their era. During the nineteenth century, however, it was noticed that some criminals seemed different from the others, and observers began to describe what we now call the antisocial personality disorder. Because the scientific thinking of the time was dominated by a hereditarian perspective, the disorder was originally thought to be genetic in origin. Later observers suggested that the origins of the syndrome lay in an early breakdown in the individual's relations to society, particularly to his family. (The "his" in the previous sentence is not inappropriate. DSM-III estimates that the disorder is about three times as likely to appear in males as in females: less than 1 percent of females, but 3 percent of males would be labeled antisocial personalities. However, our Case History: Antisocial Personality Disorder does discuss the story of a young female patient.)

In the 1950s and 1960s the tendency was for many clinicians to view all antisocial acts as the product of an antisocial personality disorder. Broadly stated, the view was that all people who committed crimes were "sick" or "mentally ill" and probably had been made so "through no fault of their own"—in other words, by a failure of their families or of society in general. Current diagnostic practice requires the clinician to be more discriminating. We now distinguish between crimes committed by antisocial personalities and those committed by normal individuals for motives such as gain or revenge.

Theories and research into antisocial personality patterns have centered on two areas: (1) socialization and family backgrounds, and (2) biological factors. The *biological* factor first proposed, as in almost every other case, was genetic inheritance. It was, for example, suggested that a tendency to commit crimes was inherited. Later, it was suggested that a rare chromosomal abnormality—carrying an extra male chromosome—is a cause of criminality (Jacobs, Branton, & Melville, 1965), but after much empirical research the conclusion was that the extra Y chromosome is not a predictor of criminal behavior. However, this conclusion does not demonstrate a general failure of the biological approach to the disorder. Several researchers (Crowe, 1974; Cadoret, 1978) have suggested that there is a genetic component to the

CASE HISTORY

Antisocial Personality Disorder

"I can't understand the girl, no matter how hard I try," said the father, shaking his head in genuine perplexity. "It's not that she seems bad or that she means to do wrong. She can lie with the straightest face, and after she's found in the most outlandish lies she still seems perfectly easy in her own mind."

He had related . . . how Roberta at the age of 10 stole her aunt's silver hairbrush, how she repeatedly made off with small articles from the dime store, the drug store, and from her own home. . . .

Neither the father nor the mother seemed a severe parent. . . . [However], there was nothing to suggest that this girl had been spoiled. The parents had, so far as could be determined, consistently let her find that lying and stealing and truancy brought censure and punishment.

As she grew into her teens [she] began to buy dresses, cosmetics, candy, perfume, and other articles, charging them to her father. He had no warning that these bills would come. . . . For many of these things she had little or no use; some of them she distributed among her acquaintances. . . . As a matter of fact, the father, previously in comfortable circumstances, had at one time been forced to the verge of bankruptcy.

In school Roberta's work was mediocre. She studied little and her truancy was spectacular and persistent. No one regarded her as dull, and she seemed to learn easily when she made any effort at all. (Her IQ was found to be 135.) . . .

"I wouldn't exactly say she's like a hypocrite," her father said. "When she's caught and confronted with her lies and other misbehavior she doesn't seem to appreciate the inconsistency of her position. Her conscience seems still untouched. . . . "

Having failed in many classes and her truancy becoming intolerable to the school, Roberta was expelled from the local high school. . . .

Roberta was sent to 2 other

boarding schools from which she had to be expelled. . . . Employed in her father's business as a bookkeeper, she used her skill at figures and a good deal of ingenuity to make off with considerable sums.

[Eventually she was hospitalized for psychiatric observation.] During her hospitalization she . . . discussed her mistakes with every appearance of insight. She spoke like a person who had been lost and bewildered but now had found her way. . . . (Roberta returned home but her old behavior patterns continued.)

Despite her failures she would, in her letters . . . write as if she had been miraculously cured: "This time we have got to the very root of my trouble and I see the whole story in a different light. . . . If, in your whole life you had never succeeded with one other patient, what you have done for me should make your practice worthwhile. . . . I wish I could tell you how different I feel. How different I am! . . . "

(Abridged from Cleckley, 1976)

---

disorder. This hints at the possibility of neurotransmitter system dysfunction, but as of yet little is known about what specific neurotransmitter might be involved in the disorder.

Other theories of the causes of antisocial personality disorder have cut across the psychoanalytic, learning, and cognitive models and focused on such variables as identification, modeling, poor value acquisition, and attitude development. *Psychoanalytic theory* suggests that the disorder is shown by people who have not developed superego control of their behavior. Without these superego controls, the person is much more likely to succumb to some of the id's demands for immediate gratification, regardless of the moral dictates of the situation. Developing an adequate superego, you will recall, involves absorbing parental standards at an early stage. As researchers (Greer, 1964; Robins, 1966) have in fact found, the absence of a parent, because of death, separation, or desertion, is a rather common factor in the background of antisocial individuals.

Learning theorists suggest, first, that antisocial responses are learned through imitation of parents, peers, and even of the violence in the entertainment media. Second, parents of well-socialized children have been found (Snyder, 1977) to reinforce cooperative behavior and to punish or not reinforce antisocial behavior. In contrast, parents of antisocial children frequently punish their children and rarely reinforce them; and their punishments, at least from the child's point of view, are arbitrary rather than tied to antisocial actions. *Cognitive theorists* suggest that such children are likely to realize that

the moral rules of conduct they hear preached do not really govern who gets punished and who gets rewarded, and that they might as well act as their impulses direct them.

As will be apparent from this discussion, psychologists have many questions about the exact nature of this disorder, and investigation continues.

OTHER DIMENSIONS OF ABNORMALITY

During the past few decades we have seen an enormous increase in the discovery and manufacture of mind-affecting drugs. As you may recall from our discussion in Chapter 5, we increasingly recognize that many of these substances—new and old—can have rather complex negative effects. For example, many of these substances can cause brain damage. Chronic consumption of alcohol can lead to an amnesia syndrome called Korsakoff's disease; other substances can lead to strong states of dependency, the maintenance of which may dominate an addict's life. DSM-III signals an awareness of current drug problems by including many more drug-related disorders than did the previous diagnostic systems.

In general, a diagnosis of **organic mental disorder** is made when the substance use has acute or chronic effects on the central nervous system. **Substance-use disorders** are diagnosed from the maladaptive behavior patterns that users show. These behaviors generally include impairment in social and occupational functioning, inability to control or limit use of the substance, and withdrawal symptoms. In some cases, these two diagnoses are interrelated; frequently someone who has an alcohol-produced organic mental disorder of intoxication and withdrawal will have an alcohol-abuse and -dependence disorder.

The list of abuse and dependence characteristics of substance-use disorders is depressingly long. In other words, there are a variety of addictions. Alcoholism is certainly an addiction, though many people do not think of alcohol as a drug because it is legal and accessible. Narcotics addiction (addiction to opium, heroin, and morphine) is a major problem and is linked to crime because narcotics are relatively inaccessible and illegal in our society. Another very serious addiction is to barbiturates (certain kinds of sedatives and sleeping pills). Amphetamine, cocaine, and the cocaine derivative "crack" have more recently been added to the list. PCP and various hallucinogens clearly provoke abusive behavior, but physiological dependence has not yet been shown for these substances. Tobacco, oddly, is not generally thought of as producing abusive behaviors (apparently death by cancer is not an abuse), but it does result in acute physiological dependency. However, given recent discoveries about "passive smoking" (the effects of cigarette smoking on the health of people around the smoker), more and more smokers may become aware of and forced to deal with their addiction.

Substance-Use Disorders

We will focus in the next few pages on those disorders that are classified as addictions. **Addiction** or **substance dependence** typically involves increasing physical tolerance, psychological dependence, and severe withdrawal symptoms, both physical and psychological, when use of the substance is discontinued.

It is difficult to capture in a textbook the dynamics of drug or alcohol addiction. While some people are able to carry on a fairly normal life despite their substance dependency, others show disturbing effects fairly soon. At first people get pleasurable effects from the drug, but often they come to need greater and greater amounts to achieve the same pleasurable effects. In fact, they come to need greater and greater amounts to reach even the basic level of comfort they originally had without any drugs. If they try to stop taking the drug, they experience painful physical symptoms (**withdrawal** symptoms), including hypertension, severe cramps, and restlessness. (See Chapter 5 and also the Application: Drug Addiction and Classically Conditioned Tolerance in Chapter 6.) People who are dependent on drugs are running around a vicious circle—they must take more and more of the drug just to keep going. If they stay off the drug long enough, they can break out of this circle; but withdrawal is a most painful and feared experience among the addicted.

In an attempt to understand substance dependence, it is useful to describe three related aspects of the problem: the *host* (mental or physical makeup of the individual); the *environment*; and the *agent* or nature of the substance involved.

Host. Although psychologists have been unable to come up with a personality profile that leads inevitably to dependency, studies suggest that certain characteristics are fairly consistent. Among these are emotional immaturity, a low tolerance for frustration or tension, and a strong tendency to avoid reality. Because addicts or problem drinkers often seem to run in families, a genetic influence has long been suspected. One study by Goodwin, Schulsinger, Hermansen, Guze, and Winokur (1973) showed a higher than normal rate of drinking problems among adopted children whose biological parents were alcoholics, even though the children were unaware of their background. However, there are also circumstances under which drug use leading to dependence does not seem to be related to any particular "addiction personality pattern." A wounded soldier might be treated for real pain with morphine and later develop a dependence. During the 1950s and 1960s a number of people who experienced occasional anxieties or depressions were rather casually prescribed tranquilizers that were later found to have addictive properties.

Environment. Social acceptability plays a major role in substance dependence. As might be expected, both drug and alcohol abuse are more prevalent in sociocultural environments where these substances are readily available. It is easier for a susceptible individual to become dependent on drugs that are considered "normal," as alcohol is in our culture. Economic factors may also be influential. In times of prosperity money is available to spend on drugs and alcohol. Conversely, during a financial depression these substances provide an eagerly sought escape mechanism.

Agent. Obviously people become dependent on some drugs more easily than on others. Users of the opiates (heroin in particular) or barbiturates may become dependent in a relatively short time, no matter how psychologically stable they are. Other drugs, including amphetamines, may become addictive through conditioned response to their tension-releasing properties.

Alcoholism. **Alcoholism** is an easy dependence to drift into because alcohol is both readily available and socially acceptable in our society. Alcoholism affects a wide range of age groups and cuts across all levels of occupation, wealth, and religion. Male alcoholics have traditionally outnumbered female alcoholics, but the gap seems to be narrowing.

The destructiveness of alcoholism is pervasive and dramatic. Alcoholics

Alcohol dependence, although more socially acceptable, can be as damaging as other drug dependencies—and as depressing. Alcohol has been associated with over half the deaths and major injuries suffered in automobile accidents each year, and with about 50 percent of all murders, 40 percent of all assaults, 35 percent or more of all rapes, and 30 percent of all suicides. About one out of every three arrests in the United States results from the abuse of alcohol.

(Joseph Szabo/Photo Researchers)

Diet and Abnormal Behavior

Many people believe that diet affects mental health. For instance, many parents have been led to believe that sugar and some food additives cause hyperactivity in children or criminality in adults. There are several problems with these contentions. For one, the evidence so far is more anecdotal than experimental. For another, the mechanisms by which the food additives are postulated to affect activity patterns have generally not been specified. Finally, those proposing such relationships between food additives and human actions were highly committed to their claims and therefore not in the best position to be objective about them.

Recently, scientists studying the behavioral effects of diet have met in order to assess the state of the art. Their conclusions are tentative but potentially intriguing. Many researchers in this area have done studies with animals because the high precision of measurement and control obtainable in these circumstances has been most valuable. Their results (Kolata, 1982) demonstrate that the presence or absence of various nutrients in the diet alters the rate of synthesis of various neurotransmitters, including serotonin, dopamine, norepinephrine, and acetylcholine. (See Chapter 2 for a description of the role of these neurotransmitters in brain functioning.) For instance, high-carbohydrate meals cause an increased release of insulin, which in turn triggers a differentially high concentration of tryptophan in the bloodstream, which in turn facilitates the production of serotonin. Serotonin, as you will recall, has sleep-inducing effects.

In human beings the effects of diet are much more subtle than popular accounts would have us believe, at least as they can be measured in research. Even though the body's only source of tryptophan is dietary protein, it is high-carbohydrate diets, rather than high-protein diets, that differentially increase the amount of tryptophan in the blood, and therefore the amount of serotonin produced. Hartmann (reported in Kolata, 1982) concludes that a high-carbohydrate meal makes mildly insomniac patients fall asleep more quickly, but not normal sleepers or serious insomniacs.

There are a number of possible reasons for this complex pattern, and further research is needed to clarify the entire area, but several cautionary points can be extracted: The effects of diet on behavior are likely to be complex and subtle. There is no reason to believe that neurochemically produced changes will lead to an increase in *abnormal* behaviors, as opposed to complex shifts in many behaviors. As we recognized at the beginning of the chapter, abnormality is a category with societally imposed elements in its definition, and the connections between shifting patterns of neurotransmitters in the brain and increasing patterns of deviant or socially condemned behavior are generally going to be remote and complex. It certainly looks as though researchers are on to a generally exciting area of inquiry, but much of the story remains to be discovered.

can cause themselves grave bodily damage (including liver damage, malnutrition, hypertension, and endocrine gland and heart problems), psychological damage (for example, overdependence, poor social judgment, and loss of self-respect), and damage to the quality and purposefulness of their lives (loss of job, friends, others' trust, and sense of accomplishment).

The family and friends of alcoholic people suffer greatly as they observe loved ones destroying their lives. Family and friends are themselves often subjected to abuse, embarrassment, frustration, and financial instability in the course of their relationships with individuals dependent on alcohol.

Alcoholics also inflict suffering on members of society whom they have never met. The number of crimes and accidents related to alcohol is staggering.

Because alcoholism is so prevalent, there have been numerous efforts to understand its causes and cures. The *psychoanalytic model* provides several viewpoints. One of the more common is that alcoholics are fixated at the oral stage of development—their needs as infants during the oral stage either were not met or were met excessively. In either case, oral fixation may later take the form of alcoholism under a particular set of life events and circumstances. In the 1980s it is safe to say that most experts in alcoholism research find the psychoanalytic theory tells only a small part of the story. Attention has shifted to an approach mixing components of the learning and biological models.

The *learning model* sees the use of alcohol as a learned method of reduc-

Anorexia Nervosa

Sometime recently you may have seen a young woman or girl whose extreme thinness shocked you. Broomstick arms and legs, elbow and knee joints clearly visible beneath the skin, a skeletal face—all made you wonder whether she was a famine victim or a terminal cancer patient.

More likely the person you observed was suffering from a puzzling emotional disorder called **anorexia nervosa,** which is seen with increasing frequency in North America. DSM-III defines anorexia as an emotional disorder in which "the essential features are intense fear of becoming obese . . . severe weight loss, and refusal to maintain a minimal normal body weight" (p. 67). Anorexics maintain their state of severely reduced weight in the most obvious way possible—they simply avoid eating an adequate supply of food. People with a closely related disorder—**bulimia**—eat considerably more; instead of constantly starving themselves, their pattern is one of fasting, followed by binge eating of junk foods, followed by self-induced vomiting. In both disorders, as more weight is lost and eating is further

restricted, bodily processes are adversely affected. Blood pressure becomes abnormally low, and the effects of vitamin deficiencies begin to appear; in women menstruation becomes irregular or ceases altogether. The condition is serious. Some researchers estimate that 2 to 6 percent of anorexics die from the condition (Agras & Kraemer, 1983).

The disorder appears in both sexes, but many more anorexics are women. It is a condition that characteristically affects girls of upper-middle-class families, usually beginning somewhere between ages 10 and 20. Further, it is seen most often in girls or young women who have a history of being well-behaved and cooperative within the family and achievement-oriented at school. This is obviously not a group at risk for physical illnesses; therefore something else must be the source of this problem.

What causes anorexia? The evidence suggests that family and cultural factors trigger a psychological process in certain susceptible individuals. The person is motivated to lose weight and, if carried far enough, the dieting begins to have biological consequences. The biological effects of low weight and semistarvation may in turn reinforce the psychological process, promoting a circular pattern that keeps the disorder going (Garfunkel & Garner, 1982).

The origins of anorexia are also believed to be at least partially cultural. As anyone who sees television or magazine ads knows, there is a tremendous emphasis on being attractive, which in our society means being slender. These cultural stereotypes measurably affect women's perceptions of their bodies. In a recent study (Fallon & Rozin, 1985) women at the University of Pennsylvania reported that the body weight they believed men found most attractive was lower than their own body weight; further, what they themselves considered the "ideal" body weight was lower still. In other words, young women are likely to see themselves as overweight both in terms of what is considered attractive to men and of some feminine ideal.

Many researchers conclude that anorexia begins when teenage girls with a history of being obedient are pressured to conform to body stereotypes and decide to diet. Often the dieting begins innocently enough—perhaps in response to a casual comment about appearance from a family member or friend (Garfunkel & Garner, 1982). It is even likely that the dieting is praised and encouraged at first; only belatedly is its severity noticed by family and friends. At this point the anorexic frequently begins an even more restrictive diet and drops below a caloric intake

ing stress. At first glance, this theory seems at odds with the obvious punishment and increased stress that ultimately result from long-term usage. One explanation for this seeming contradiction is provided by the concept of a *delay-of-reward gradient* (Dollard & Miller, 1950). Rewards and punishments decrease in value the farther off they seem; the alcoholic individual prefers the immediate gratification of temporary tension relief. Alcohol also seems to deaden some anxieties. Early reports of agoraphobics indicated that they frequently drank when anticipating a particularly stressful exposure to crowds or public spaces (Thorpe & Burns, 1983).

The *biological model* also points to the withdrawal symptoms that occur when a chronic drinker suddenly stops as evidence that some physiological changes are involved in alcoholism. A group of withdrawal symptoms that occurs in many chronic drinkers is called *delerium tremens (DTs)*. A sudden drop in the blood's alcohol level can cause profuse sweating, eye pupil irregularity, delirious experiences, and hallucinations of the most disturbing sort. Of course, such withdrawal reactions do not prove that alcoholism is primarily a physical event that causes psychological dependency, but there is a lot of interest in this possibility. Many people have proposed that alcohol-

sufficient to sustain even minimal day-to-day activity. A striking feature of the disorder is that while others see the anorexic as frighteningly thin, she herself does not. In fact, she often dresses in ways that call attention to her thinness. She also denies that she feels any loss of physical energy and may bolster this denial with impressive expenditures of energy in athletics or class work.

Just how far anorexics can go is illustrated by the accompanying photograph. As you can see, they can go very far indeed. Some die from the condition, and others contract serious diseases in their weakened state. Depressive thoughts accompany anorexia, and suicide is not uncommon.

The treatment of anorexia is a subject of some controversy. A recent review provides a list of treatments that fill a page (Garfunkel & Garner, 1982). Given what we have said so far in this chapter, it will not surprise you that the reviewers concluded that treatments "have been largely based on the theoretical orientation of the physician and the mechanisms presumed to be responsible for the illness" (Garfunkel & Garner, 1982). There is general agreement that the initial imperative is to get the anorexic to gain weight, because otherwise there is a danger of death from starvation. Then agreement on

treatment begins to break down. Recommendations range from providing love from parent surrogates to implanting hormone-generating calves' organs in the anorexic. Many programs try multiple treatments, hoping that one will work.

The disagreements about treatment stem from disagreements about the causes of anorexia. *Cognitive* therapists blame cultural pressures toward thinness and the resulting one-sidedness of an anorexic's cognitions: She doesn't see what the mirror tells her; she simply cannot conceive that she is too thin. *Behavior* therapists emphasize the effect of reinforcements received during the early phases of dieting. *Psychoanalysts* suggest that unresolved sexual conflicts are the source of the problem: Fasting prevents the young girl from developing an adult body and thereby having to confront the sexual issues of womanhood. The accompanying prevention of menarche or cessation of menstruation is central to this analysis. The *biologically* oriented therapist looks for possible organic causes such as hormonal deficiencies.

Although further investigation is needed, each of these theories offers significant insight into anorexia. It seems likely that an initial factor is the individual's cognitive interpretation of the cultural stereotype of slenderness. The encouragement first received for

embracing the stereotype may be reinforcing to someone who has a difficult role in the family structure or excessive concern about her sexuality. As the biological effects of extreme dieting become acute (dangerously low blood pressure, loss of appetite, and so on), they sustain the psychological process that keeps the disorder going.

The singer Karen Carpenter suffered from anorexia. (Paul Fusco/Magnum Photos)

ism is primarily a physical event that causes psychological dependency, but there is a lot of interest in this possibility. Many people have proposed that alcoholism is indeed a problem "caused" by biological predispositions, metabolic or organic weaknesses, genetic factors, and the like (Williams, 1959; Segovia-Riguelma, Varela, & Mardones, 1971; Goodwin et al, 1973).

Genetics is also making a contribution to the biological study of alcoholism. New evidence based on the now familiar twin and adopted children studies (Cloninger, 1987) suggests that we need to distinguish between the propensity to seek alcohol, the susceptibility to loss of control under the influence of alcohol, and dependence on the sedative or antianxiety effects of alcohol. Future research developing this analysis may clear up some questions that puzzle people who work with alcoholics. "Alcoholism" may not be simply a single condition; instead, it may contain a number of different patterns of disorder, each with different genetic and environmental influences.

Drug Dependence.   Other forms of addiction, though unique in some ways, basically involve the same dimensions as alcoholism. For example, in narcotic addiction and barbiturate addiction there are significant physiological

addiction, bodily and psychological damage, personal damage, family and social impact, and societal implications. And the explanations offered by the various models parallel those offered for alcoholism.

Narcotic dependence has stirred a great deal of attention in recent years because of some critical research findings that may point to a clear understanding of what dependence is all about, at least in biological terms. More than a decade ago researchers (Pert & Snyder, 1973) discovered that the body had certain receptor sites for opiates, including sites in the brain, intestines, and other locations. Apparently opiates affect a person through their impact on these receptor sites. For example, there is a high number of opiate receptors in the area of the brain that regulates pupil dilation. One effect of opiates is constriction of the pupils, which indicates an impact on these particular receptor sites in the brain.

Researchers were able to map the opiate receptor sites throughout the body. They then asked why we have receptor sites in our bodies for foreign substances like opium, morphine, and heroin. A possible answer was that perhaps our bodies have naturally occurring opiates that regularly operate on these receptor sites in all people. The search was on for the body's natural opiates, and indeed, natural opiatelike substances called *endorphins* were found in the bodies of human beings and other animals. Endorphins are apparently naturally produced substances that help us cope with pain and stress (see the Highlight: Endorphins: The Body's Own Painkillers in Chapter 2). Our bodies automatically produce them, use them, and need them at certain times.

Putting this startling discovery together with what is known about narcotic dependence, researchers think that dependence may operate in the following way. When first taken, opiates relieve pain or give an extra push to the emotions by filling those receptor sites that have not yet been filled by the body's natural opiates—endorphins. But if a person takes opiates too often, these receptor sites get overloaded and the body's own production of endorphins is decreased or cut off because these substances simply aren't needed as much. At this point, the opiates are needed not just for an extra push but to *make up for* the decreases in normal bodily production of endorphins. Thus the dependent person needs to take more and more opiates to fill this increasing number of empty receptor sites.

This explanation is certainly consistent with the increasing tolerance we noted earlier. If opiates are withheld from the dependent person, the receptor sites will remain empty for a period of time because endorphin production has been cut off. With no opiates—foreign or natural—at these sites, the body has no tools to fight pain or stress or to perform certain regulatory functions. The person will feel and react in a most uncomfortable and debilitated manner. This explanation is consistent with the experience of withdrawal. Withdrawal symptoms will continue until the body renews its production of endorphins.

Research in this area is now moving at a rapid pace. As our insights into the biological mechanisms involved in narcotic dependence grow, so should the implications for treating dependence. Possible connections with other forms of dependence may also emerge in the near future.

Abnormal Categories: A Perspective

What can we say about the reasons for abnormal behavior? In the past researchers, clinicians, and theoreticians assumed that most disorders could

500,000	reported cases of child abuse per year (1.5 million cases are estimated to go unreported).[1]
27,300	deaths from suicide per year.[2]*
1,200,000	individuals are actively schizophrenic.[3]
16,000,000	individuals suffer from anxiety, phobia or other related disorders.[3]
18,000,000	individuals suffer from major depression and other affective disorders.[3] (300,000 persons are hospitalized each year for disabling depressive disorders.[4])
2,200,000	individuals suffer from drug dependence.[3]
13,000,000	individuals suffer from alcohol abuse, including 10,000,000 adults and 3,000,000 teenagers. (Alcohol abuse includes both alcoholism and problem drinking.)[3]
10,200,000	individuals are arrested per year in connection with serious crimes.[5] (315,000 individuals are in state and federal prisons.[6]*)
29,000	children in the United States are estimated to be afflicted by some form of psychosis. (From 2 to 5 college students out of every 1,000 will develop psychosis while they are in college.[7])
3,500,000	elementary school children in the U.S. have moderate to severe emotional problems requiring some kind of mental health care.[7]
34,000,000	persons are affected by a mental disorder each year.[8]

*The incidence of suicide attempts and serious crimes may be much higher because of the large number that are not reported.

[1]Michael de Courcy, "Child-Abuse Parley Deplores Fund Cuts," *The New York Times,* April 8, 1981, III, 1:3.

[2]U.S. Bureau of the Census, *Statistical Abstract of the United States* (Washington, D.C.: U.S. Government Printing Office, 1981), table 113, p. 74.

[3]U.S. Public Health Service, *The Alcohol, Drug Abuse, and Mental Health National Data Book* (Alcohol, Drug Abuse and Mental Health Administration, DHEW Publication No. (ADM) 80-938) (Washington, D.C.: U.S. Government Printing Office, 1980), p. 19.

[4]Judith Norback, *The Mental Health Yearbook/Directory* 79–80. (New York: Van Nostrand Reinhold, 1979), p. 745.

[5]*Sourcebook of Criminal Justice Statistics* 1981, table 4.1, p. 338.

[6]*Statistical Abstract of the U.S.,* table 336. p. 191.

[7]*The Mental Health Yearbook/Directory* 79–80, p. 745: *Statistical Abstract of the U.S.,* table 31, pp. 28–29.

[8]*The Mental Health Yearbook/Directory* 79–80, p. 746.

be explained with one theoretical structure; we no longer believe that is possible. For some disorders, biological explanations are relevant; for other problems, the psychoanalytic, learning, cognitive, and humanist-existential explanations clearly provide more insight into their causation. Research has sometimes provided clarification of a particular type of abnormal functioning, but more often it has simply given us further clues. Few disorders are completely understood. It is clear, though, that the psychoanalytic explanations are not the whole story.

In the 1980s a stream of new developments in the understanding of abnormal behavior has been coming from the biological perspective. More specifically, our increased understanding of the role of neurotransmitters in brain functioning has been shown to have implications for abnormal behavior. (Since many people think that neurotransmitters are affected by diet, the Highlight on diet and abnormal behavior is relevant to this discussion.) In fact, new developments have been coming out so fast that writing this chapter has occasionally reminded us of those old movies about newspaper reporters in which somebody is constantly yelling, "Hold the presses." These discoveries are genuinely exciting, but they are often incomplete. One major gap in the story involves how a neurotransmitter dysfunction actually brings about (or is brought about by) the thought patterns associated with a particular disorder. How, for instance, do the joint workings of seritonin and norepinephrine lead to depressive affect? A second limit on the biological story about abnormality comes from the cumulative impact of recent discoveries about the action patterns of brain neurotransmitters. It was originally thought that there were relatively few substances functioning as neurotransmitters and that their action patterns were fairly simple. One neuron released one—and only one—neurotransmitter; and that transmitter—acting alone—activated other connecting neurons. Now we know that there are upwards of 60 substances that function as neurotransmitters (and more are still being discovered). Further, we know that a single neuron may emit different neurotransmitters, and that receptor neurons may have action sites for several neurotransmitters. The prior reception of one neurotransmitter may make a neuron more receptive to firing when it is stimulated by another neuron, or it may block its receptor activity entirely. So the picture of brain functioning grows steadily more complicated, and thus the story about abnormal brain functioning must grow correspondingly more complicated as well.

Society is presenting us with an urgent set of questions here. Clearly, abnormal functioning in its various forms is a major problem in our society. People are increasingly seeking the services of mental health personnel and facilities. This rise in numbers may be due in part to the lessening of the stigma associated with emotional and behavioral problems, but it probably also reflects an increase in the actual prevalence of such problems. The estimated incidence of major maladaptive behavior patterns in the United States is summarized in Table 17–6.

As we have given up the search for simple causes of abnormal benaviors, we have come to better comprehend the different and multiple causes of specific abnormal syndromes. In the past decade great strides have been made in our understanding of brain functioning, particularly the role of neurotransmitters. Many of these discoveries have implications for understanding abnormal brain functioning and the behaviors that result. Many, though by no means all, of the conditions we have discussed will be illuminated by these new biological discoveries.

SUMMARY

1. Defining normal and abnormal behavior in statistical, cultural, or ideal terms has proved difficult. Instead, it has been found useful to establish criteria that, taken together, give a picture of abnormal behavior. These criteria are bizarre and extreme behaviors; disturbance of others; inappropriate or excessive emotional display; and behavior that interferes with daily functioning.

2. The *Diagnostic and Statistical Manual of Mental Disorders (DSM-III)* is the official classification system

of the American Psychiatric Association. In contrast to previous systems, it is multiaxial—that is, it requires evaluation of a person on five different dimensions. This procedure is designed to give a more complete picture of the individual. DSM-III also uses highly explicit and detailed descriptions in order to achieve high diagnostic reliability. In 1987, a revised version of the manual, DSM-III R, was published.

3. *Phobic disorders* involve a persistent, disproportionate fear of a particular object or situation, such as a fear of heights (acrophobia). *Generalized anxiety disorders* involve the same fear and discomfort as in phobic disorder, but are not linked to a specific stimulus. A *panic disorder* consists of recurrent panic attacks that occur unpredictably.

4. *Obsessive-compulsive disorders* are those that compel a person to repeat unwanted thoughts over and over or to repeat certain actions or rituals.

5. *Dissociative disorders* involve problems of memory and consciousness, such as amnesia, fugue, somnambulism, and multiple personality. *Conversion disorders* are a subdivision of *somatoform disorders*, in which people develop physical symptoms, such as blindness, body aches, or paralysis, with no apparent physical cause.

6. *Depression* describes a wide range of complaints from mild sadness to a highly disabling state. The various schools of thought differ as to the cause of depression. For example, the cognitive theorists suggest that depression results from a person making uniquely personal and broad-reaching interpretations of negative events that happen to us all.

7. *Bipolar disorders* occur when the "lows" of depression alternate with the "highs" of a manic phase, which is characterized by euphoria and energetic activity.

8. *Schizophrenia* is a term that is applied to a wide range of disorders; schizophrenia includes disturbances of thought, perception, emotion, and motor abilities. Thoughts may be disorganized or their content may be delusional. Disturbances of perception can range from distraction to *hallucinations*. Emotional disturbances may include inappropriate reactions or ambivalent reactions; motor disturbances may include systematic gesturing or catatonic states.

9. The *antisocial personality disorder* has been a difficult one for psychologists and psychiatrists to come to terms with, and theories about its causes have changed as society's thinking about criminality has changed.

10. *Substance-use disorders* involve both impaired functioning (such as poor social or occupational functioning), and withdrawal symptoms when the drug is withheld. Neuroscientists are making promising discoveries about the workings of drugs on the chemicals in the brain. The three interconnected areas of influence in drug dependence have been described as the *host*, the *environment*, and the *agent*.

SUGGESTED READINGS

BECK, A. T. (1976). *Cognitive therapy and emotional disorders*. New York: International Universities Press. A thoughtful statement of the cognitive theory of depression and other disorders by one of its leading proponents.

BECKER, J. (1977). *Affective disorders*. Morristown, N.J.: General Learning Press. Provides an overview of the problem of depression, citing theories and research from the various models.

FADIMAN, J., and KEWMAN, D. (Eds.) (1973). *Exploring madness: Experience, theory, and research*. Monterey, Cal.: Brooks/Cole. Looks at abnormal functioning through an interesting mixture of personal and literary accounts, research, and theoretical perspectives, including both traditional and radical perspectives.

LEON, G. R. (1977). *Case histories of deviant behavior* (2nd ed.). Boston: Holbrook. Interesting case histories are presented, along with interpretations and discussions reflecting the behavioral and cognitive models.

MCNEIL, E. G. (1967). *The quiet furies*. Englewood Cliffs, N.J.: Prentice-Hall. Presents interesting case histories in detail from a psychodynamic perspective.

ORNSTEIN, R., and THOMPSON, R. (1985). *The Amazing Brain*. New York: Houghton Mifflin. An up-to-date account of the implications of recent discoveries about brain functioning for abnormal thought and behavior.

SACKS, O. (1985). *The man who mistook his wife for a hat*. New York: Summit. A sensitive and literate clinical neurologist describes various patients with strikingly abnormal behavior.

SELIGMAN, M. E. P. (1975). *Helplessness*. San Francisco: W. H. Freeman. Offers the learned-helplessness interpretation of depression, a cognitive-behavioral view that has stirred a great deal of research in recent years.

SZASZ, R. (1960). The myth of mental illness. *American Psychologist*, 15, 113–118. Presents a controversial position on the nature and definition of mental illness by one of the field's most interesting figures.

18 Therapy

W ho is an "abnormal" person? Is it someone who exhibits "abnormal behavior"? Most of us recognize how difficult it is to define abnormal behavior. It might, then, be simpler to ask: What are the differences between normal and abnormal behavior? But this means defining normal behavior, also a hard task. Is normal behavior simply behavior that is predictable and socially acceptable? Or is it behavior that the individual considers acceptable, even though others regard it as bizarre?

In this chapter we are going to look at some of the answers that have been proposed to these basic questions. We will also examine models of abnormality and describe some patterns of abnormal behavior.

NORMAL VS. ABNORMAL BEHAVIOR

Theorists have used various criteria to distinguish between the normal and the abnormal. Some have tried a statistical approach: Normal behavior is simply behavior that is typical of most people. Thus all people who stray from the statistical average are behaving abnormally. Others argue that such a definition is too broad and too vague. It would result in the abnormal category including, for example, very intelligent people and nearsighted people.

Others have tried to define normal and abnormal behavior in terms of cultural boundaries and expectations. In this view, behavior can only be judged in the context of the culture in which it takes place—there are no absolutes. Behavior that is abnormal in some cultures may be acceptable, and

This self-portrait by Vincent van Gogh clearly reveals the onset of the mental illness that, soon after, drove him to suicide. (The Louvre, Paris)

563

thus normal, in others. Heavy drug use or constant aggression are accepted as normal in some cultures. In ours they are not.

Normal behavior can also be thought of in absolute or ideal terms. You might define a normal person as someone who is happy, effective with other people, sincere, and free of anxiety. But this describes an ideal rather than a real person. If normal behavior is an ideal, and we define abnormality as the absence of the ideal, just about everyone would be abnormal.

Since it has proved so difficult to define abnormal behavior in statistical, cultural, or ideal terms, we will try to be guided by the characteristics people generally associate with abnormal behavior. The following four divisions are ones that ordinary people use to sort out abnormal from normal behavior. The more divisions the behavior fits, the more certain we generally are that the behavior is "abnormal."

1. *Bizarre and extreme behaviors.* Typical examples would be hallucinations, delusions, and uncontrolled violence. Some normal and even ordinary behaviors, such as handwashing, could fall into this category if performed dozens of times a day.

2. *Disturbance of others.* Unusual behavior that interferes with the well-being of others is generally considered abnormal. Drunken driving, molesting a child, and talking incoherently to strangers on a bus are examples of such disturbances. (Some of these acts we regard as "abnormal" in the sense of mentally disturbed. Other, more calculating, harmful acts we regard as criminal.)

3. *Inappropriate or excessive emotional display.* People with obvious outward manifestations of distress, panic, overwhelming happiness, or uncontrollable depression when circumstances don't seem to warrant such a display, are often regarded as abnormal.

4. *Behavior that interferes with daily functioning.* When people are unable to meet society's standards of daily functioning and personal relationships, they often are considered abnormal. Disheveled dress and chronic self-destructive tardiness are two examples.

These are some of the behaviors that ordinary people regard as abnormal. They give us enough understanding of what is meant by abnormality to continue our discussion of it. By now, though, you probably appreciate the problems of trying to classify and diagnose abnormal behavior. To give you a better perspective on this issue, a brief history of the diagnosis of abnormality is in order.

A History of Clinical Diagnosis

From ancient times down to the present, numerous attempts have been made to classify abnormal behavior. Different individuals have tried to make sense of what they observed about others' behavior; understandably, then, classification systems often reflected personal views of what causes abnormality. Recall from the previous chapter that the Greek physician Hippocrates believed that a person's temperament and behavior were related to the relative properties and balance among four humors (liquids) found in the body.

Two things are noteworthy about Hippocrates' system. First, it was shaped by his idea of how the bodily system worked and affected mental functioning.

T herapy can be defined as a set of procedures designed to improve the psychological problems of individuals. Guided by one or more theories of personality (discussed in Chapter 15), a therapist attempts to help a person (or sometimes a group of people) change aspects of his or her life, usually because the person is experiencing one of the problems or disorders that we examined in Chapter 17. *Change,* then, is the key element in therapy. The change may be cognitive, behavioral, or emotional—that is, therapy may change the way a person thinks, behaves, or feels—or it may be all three.

As we have seen, there are many theories about the probable causes of abnormal behavior. And, as you might expect, there is a correspondingly vast choice of therapies, dependent on the presumed cause of the disorder being treated. At least one broad distinction is between **psychotherapies** (talk therapies) and **drug therapies.** The talk therapies characteristically involve a client "talking through" problems with a therapist, seeking to gain insight into their causes. Generally, these therapies are guided by *psychoanalytic, humanistic* and *existential,* or *learning* and *cognitive* thinking. Drug therapy involves prescribing medications that affect mood, thought, or behavior by altering underlying physiological states.

More recently, other techniques have emerged. A therapist who uses principles of learning theory may set up mechanisms to selectively reinforce or discourage certain behaviors of the client. Another may have clients reenact old scenes of conflict in their lives, or realistically role-play new social skills modeled by other people. Recently, too, many therapists have become more

Shortly after the French revolution, Philippe Pinel received charge of a hospital for the insane in Paris. "Pinel Unchaining the Inmates" depicts his successful effort to make the institution more humane. (The National Library of Medicine)

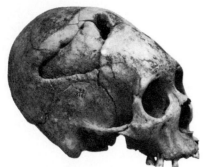

Three examples of trephining. (The American Museum of Natural History)

eclectic, drawing on several theories and using a mix of therapeutic techniques to deal with clients' problems. In this chapter we will look at various theories and approaches to therapy, their intended purposes, and their demonstrated effectiveness.

THE HISTORY OF THERAPEUTIC PROCEDURES

In every age the dominant influence in the choice of therapy has been the particular model of abnormality in use by the therapist. The first known attempt at treatment of what we now call emotional disorder took place roughly half a million years ago, during the Stone Age (Coleman, Butcher, & Carson, 1984). There is archaeological evidence from the period of a practice known as *trephining,* which involved chipping a round hole in the skull with a stone tool, presumably to allow an evil spirit, or demon, to escape. Some of these unearthed skulls show evidence of healing around the hole, so at least some "patients" survived this drastic remedy and lived for several years afterward (see the bottom skull on this page).

Early recorded history shows a similar belief among the ancient Chinese, Hebrews, Egyptians, and Greeks that mental abnormalities were the result of possession by demons. The accepted mode of treatment was *exorcism* (expulsion of demons), involving rites of prayer and assorted attempts to make the body a most undesirable place for evil spirits. These included drinking vile liquids that were then regurgitated, presumably along with the offending demon. Other approaches, perhaps reserved for more stubborn cases, included flogging and starvation.

Some centuries later, Hippocrates (*c.* 450–*c.* 377 B.C.), the Greek physician, rejected the prevailing idea of possession and formulated an early medical model. He divided mental illness into three categories: mania, melancholia, and phrenitis (brain fever). All three, he thought, arose from natural disturbances of the body. Treatment was therefore aimed at the body and, depending on the category, included vegetarianism, exercise, sexual abstinence, and bleeding.

Medieval treatment of abnormal behavior sometimes involved surgical practices that were variations on the practice of trephining. (The Bettmann Archive)

By the Middle Ages, however, the belief in demons had been revived. Priests took over the treatment of abnormal behavior, first with prayers and sprinklings of holy water, and later with more violent forms of exorcism. Starting in the fifteenth century, abnormal behavior was thought to be due to witchcraft. Treatment consisted of torturing "witches" until they confessed, and then burning them to death.

Witchcraft was still an offense punishable by both church and state in the early sixteenth century. Persecution of witches was not, however, without strong opposition. One of the leading attackers, Johann Weyer, published a book based on a humanitarian model, arguing that witches were mentally ill rather than "possessed." He advocated treatment based on understanding and helping rather than on torturing and burning at the stake. Although Weyer is regarded as the founder of modern psychopathology, his ideas were met at the time with scathing criticism.

Mentally disturbed people who escaped the more horrific treatments for witchcraft were usually confined to monasteries or prisons. From the sixteenth century onward, special asylums, or mental hospitals, gradually took over this responsibility. Patients in institutions were usually treated like animals or prisoners, and were often chained down and given little in the way of food, light, or fresh air. Then, in 1792, there came a turning point. A Frenchman, Philippe Pinel, was put in charge of a hospital for the insane near Paris. Pinel made some radical changes. He removed the patients' chains; he moved them from dark dungeons to sunny rooms; and he allowed them to work and exercise outdoors. The results were almost miraculously beneficial.

About the same time, reforms were taking place in similar types of institutions in America. One notable advocate of the humanitarian approach was Benjamin Rush, later known as the father of American psychiatry. Another energetic reformer was a retired schoolteacher from New England named Dorothea Dix. Dix took her humanitarian crusade throughout the country (and several other countries as well) and is credited with the establishment or reform of more than 30 mental hospitals.

Throughout the nineteenth century many more state mental hospitals were founded—all on the optimistic belief that proper treatment in proper surroundings would lead to recovery. The result was a dramatic increase in admissions: by midcentury this had reached such proportions that the institutions were forced to shift their priority from curing mental illness to providing custodial care. Bars reappeared on windows, doors were locked, and the atmosphere once more resembled a prison rather than a hospital. Private mental hospitals were usually superior to public ones. Better financed and with a lower staff-to-patient ratio, they were often able to provide the quiet therapeutic atmosphere and patient attention that could lead to improvement. However, private hospitals were usually available only to the wealthy. Most people requiring hospitalization went to the inadequate public facilities.

As knowledge of abnormal functioning improved, it became clear that many people who needed treatment did not have to be hospitalized. *Outpatient treatments* (treatments that do not require the recipient to stay in the hospital) proved helpful to many people. Again, the therapy was available only to those who could afford it. Others in need tended to receive no outpatient treatment or were hospitalized even though outpatient treatment may have proved to be more beneficial.

Thus effective outpatient and inpatient care was available only to a small number of people with emotional and behavioral problems. Those less well off received inadequate custodial care or no care at all. This situation contin-

In this painting, "witches" are being tortured with violent forms of exorcism. (The Bettmann Archive)

An engraving by Tardieu of a Bedlam mental patient named William Morris, who has been chained upright to a post. (National Library of Medicine)

ued until after World War II, when major developments brought about changes. First, psychoactive drugs were developed in the 1950s. These drugs provided an easier way to control violent patients and to reduce anxiety and depression. Such drugs generally lowered the incidence of "crazy" behavior on the hospital wards, in turn facilitating other kinds of patient therapy. The drug-moderated decrease in symptoms of mental disturbance also helped create a more favorable climate for a second major development—what is called the **deinstitutionalization movement:** the return of mental patients to care provided by the local community.

Deinstitutionalization. The deinstitutionalization movement began with the recognition that hospitalization is a major step: It removes people from their jobs, from their patterns of daily life, and from the social support of their family and friends. It is also a major expenditure for the individual, the family, and, increasingly, the medical plan. For all these reasons, "reentry" into society is difficult following hospitalization.

Recognizing these social and financial costs of hospitalization, some mental-health policy experts urged that many mental hospital patients be discharged. The hope was that these people would be treated in other settings, particularly **community mental-health centers.** The concept of community health centers appeared in the 1960s, partly in response to dissatisfaction with mental institutions. The community mental-health movement was formed to deal with problems on a local level, if possible before hospitalization was needed (see Figure 18–1).

Services at community mental-health centers were tailored to the needs of the local population and might include: ongoing psychotherapy; hotlines phones so that anyone with a problem could find a ready listener; public

Figure 18–1 This chart shows the percentage of patients treated in a number of different facilities in 1955 *(left)* and 1983 *(right)*. Note the increase in patients treated by community mental-health centers and the increase in outpatient treatment in general by 1983. (National Institute of Mental Health, 1983)

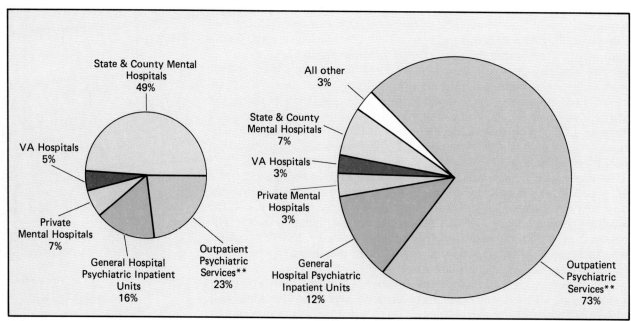

education on problems like drug abuse; and active participation in projects, such as upgrading poor housing, that might affect the emotional stability of the community.

For many deinstitutionalized patients, the community mental-health center, along with help from their families and the continued use of psychoactive drugs, worked adequately. These people reentered normal life with some success. But for many others, deinstitutionalization worked poorly. To begin with, many discharged patients had no homes or communities to go to. Others did not always get the help they needed to function successfully outside the hospital. Many, for instance, lost access to the medications that had moderated their abnormal behaviors. There is an extremely unfortunate effect of deinstitutionalization almost every reader of this text is likely to be aware of—the growing number of homeless "street people" in towns and large cities. Some of these people, who stand on corners shouting their anger or carrying on lengthy conversations with imaginary others, are discharged mental patients.

The increasing visibility of the homeless, particularly in large cities, as well as the media coverage of their plight, has created greater public awareness and concern about the deinstitutionalization movement. (Note that not all the homeless are suffering from some sort of mental disorders. Surveys indicate that many have simply lost their jobs, or in some other way have lost hold of a stable life situation.) Since a large proportion of the homeless also suffer from mental disorder, the situation raises some important issues about the effectiveness of mental-health care and services. Researchers are attempting to determine the factors that help predict which patients will return to a productive life in society and which patients are likely to end up in the streets (Avison & Speechley, 1987). Coordination between mental hospitals and community mental-health centers has been poor. The homeless create an especially difficult problem for community outpatient clinics, which are generally mandated to serve client populations with verifiable addresses in a certain *catchment area* (Bachrach, 1984). For those without a permanent address, what sort of services are available?

Naturally, there is tension between people of the community and the "street people." Many people are frightened by seeing such people on city streets and public places, such as bus stops and train stations. Their fears are intensified when they spot such people drifting through residential neighborhoods. Important ethical issues arise from attempts to solve the problem. If such people are not making a successful readjustment to society, should they be involuntarily committed? If so, what safeguards to their rights need to be built into the commitment proceedings (Bloom & Faulkner, 1987; Stromberg & Stone, 1983)? Some suggest that no legal action is warranted unless a person is proved dangerous to others. But what if the person appears more dangerous and self-destructive to himself than dangerous to others? Once hospitalization has been justified, the dilemma of how to uphold the individual's human rights continues. For example, if a patient has been determined to be schizophrenic, should he or she be forced to accept chemotherapeutic treatment? You might strongly believe that such treatment would benefit the patient and answer with a resounding "yes." However, your response might be tempered if you recall the enthusiasm shown by the proponents of some earlier "treatments" of mental illness that we now judge barbaric.

These complex issues have not yet been resolved. However, it is clear that the deinstitutionalization movement was poorly planned and poorly implemented.

For some discharged mental patients, release has resulted in homelessness and street living, not in the community support and professional care that were intended. (Geoffrey Gove/Rapho/ Photo Researchers)

WHO PRACTICES THERAPY?

Anyone who attempts to help resolve the psychological problems of another individual can be said to be doing therapy. Psychoanalytic therapy, which was originally guided by Freudian theory, was first practiced early in this century by Freud and his followers.

Today practitioners of psychotherapy fall into four groups, largely on the basis of the type of training they have undergone: clinical psychologists, psychiatrists, psychiatric social workers, and counselors. The type of training is also likely to have a strong influence on the model used by a particular therapist.

Clinical psychologists do four to five years of graduate work in a clinical psychology program and obtain a Ph.D. Their training includes laboratory work, research design, and specialized training in abnormal behavior and therapy techniques, usually followed by an internship in which candidates work with clients under professional supervision.

Psychiatrists must attend medical school and earn an M.D. degree, after which they undertake a residency program in psychiatry. Psychiatrists are the only psychotherapists who are permitted to prescribe psychoactive drugs and electroshock treatment. Because psychiatrists are medical doctors, they are often thought of as being more extensively trained in psychotherapy than other kinds of therapists. This is not necessarily true, because the initial four-year period of medical training involves little psychiatry.

Psychiatric social workers study for two years to earn a master's degree in social work, which includes a year's internship in social work. The number of social workers involved in psychotherapy is growing rapidly in this country. This growth reflects our society's increasing use of psychotherapy services, as well as the heightened degree of training and professionalism now available in the field of social work.

Counseling psychologists and **counselors** earn graduate degrees in psychology or counseling and then do internships in a counseling setting. Often their training and attention are concentrated in specific areas such as student, marriage, or family counseling. Yet, in the process of doing specialized counseling, such professionals often find it necessary to deal with other emotional aspects of the client's life as well. Thus many counseling professionals practice something that is much like psychotherapy.

It is not uncommon for these different groups of mental health practitioners to practice similar kinds of therapy or focus on similar problems. For example, marriage and couple counseling is a field of specialization practiced not only by counselors but also by psychiatrists, psychologists, social workers, and other professionals in the course of performing other functions. As another example, psychiatric nurses not only carry out the medication orders of staff psychiatrists but also interact with patients in psychotherapeutic ways. And, while the main function of school psychologists and social workers is the assessment of emotional and behavioral difficulties, they often engage in therapeutic interactions with students. As a result, there is an increasing trend to include therapeutic training techniques in the training of these individual professionals.

Increasingly, there is a tendency for mental health professionals to function as a team dealing with clients' problems. A psychiatrist prescribes psychoactive medications for a client and monitors their effectiveness; a psychologist sees the same client in individual or group psychotherapy; and a social worker monitors the home environment of the client.

Thus there are many different types of therapists operating in many different settings. There are also different approaches to therapy, which we shall look at next. The five basic approaches are the same ones we discussed in relation to abnormal behavior (Chapter 17): the biological, psychoanalytic, humanistic-existential, learning, and cognitive models. In addition, we will discuss a family of approaches that draw on theories of social interaction for their theoretical foundations.

THE BIOLOGICAL MODEL OF THERAPY

According to the biological model, abnormal behavior is due to a malfunction of the body. Treatment is thereby designed to bring about a particular change in the person's biological functioning. As you read in the first part of this chapter, the biological model of abnormal behavior generated the earliest therapies designed to treat mental disorders. For example, Hippocrates sought to cure mental disorders by treating the body. If imbalances in bodily fluids were the cause of abnormal behavior, then diet (controlling the intake of certain fluids) and expulsive procedures (getting rid of excess fluids causing the problem) were the appropriate cures. In Chapter 17 you also learned about some of the more recent research into the biological roots of abnormal behavior. Clearly this approach is one in which exciting discoveries are being made, and rapid advances in knowledge are helping to increase our understanding of mental disorders. Interestingly enough, it is also the approach that stands in greatest contrast to other methods of therapy. For all these reasons, we discuss the biological model first.

Mental Disorders as Symptoms of Physical Illness

In some cases, a mental disorder is just one manifestation of a physical illness or condition. For example, most of us have experienced the disordered thought patterns and the mild hallucinations characteristic of a high fever. Once the cause of the illness—germ, virus, or bacterium—is treated (or the illness runs its course), the fever subsides and the disordered thoughts cease along with the other symptoms. It is also known that neurological damage to the brain results in wild grandiosity and freewheeling thought during the last stage of syphilis. Only if the initial stages of syphilis are treated with the appropriate antibiotics can the otherwise irreversible brain damage be prevented and the psychological symptoms avoided. The characteristic memory impairments and mood patterns in Korsakoff's syndrome are the results of brain damage caused by chronic consumption of alcohol. Unfortunately, while the psychological symptoms have a biological origin, such damage is often irreversible even if the patient stops drinking.

Among health-care providers, it is the clinical neurologist who is trained to determine whether a patient's symptoms of mental disorder are related to some physical illness. Of course, it often proves to be the case that the patient's mental disturbance does not have its origins in physical disease per se. Even so, in some of these cases, the biological perspective has things to say about the causes of the condition (e.g., a neurological or genetic abnormality) and thus may suggest a biologically based therapy. Historically, biological interventions fall into two groups: (1) chemotherapy and (2) shock therapy and psychosurgery.

Chemotherapy

Chemotherapy, the treatment of abnormal behavior with drugs, is the most widespread biological therapy. What is most interesting about such treatments is that many were discovered by chance. For example, one antidepressant called a monoamine oxidase (MAO) inhibitor was originally tested as a possible cure for tuberculosis. Although it failed as a cure, it seemed to elevate the mood of those who took it. The treatment was then adopted for mental patients with depressive disorders.

The dangers of this practice should be pointed out here. First, given the accidental nature of many initial discoveries, it is often unclear why a particular drug has the psychological effect that it does. Lacking a theory about the reasons for a drug's beneficial effects, scientists may be uncertain about its potential negative side effects as well. Thus many drugs have been widely prescribed before there was adequate empirical evidence about their safety. As we proceed in our discussion, we will illustrate both the positive and the negative effects of the drugs in question.

Most psychoactive drugs can be classified as antianxiety, antidepressant, or antipsychotic. As the names imply, each type of drug is aimed at treating a specific type of abnormal functioning. Antianxiety drugs are essentially tranquilizers that calm people who are tense or anxious. Antidepressant drugs are designed to lift the mood of a depressed person, and antipsychotic drugs modify the severe manifestations of psychosis.

The treatment of anxiety with antianxiety drugs is widely practiced, not only by therapists, but also by medical doctors who give their patients something to "calm their nerves" and by individuals who swallow a tranquilizer whenever they feel emotionally upset. The popularity of these drugs is due, in large part, to the speed with which they work. (They are also less expensive than psychotherapy.) When they do work, they seem almost to be an instant cure. The "instant cure," however, may be little more than a temporary alleviation of symptoms. There is growing evidence that the so-called minor tranquilizers, such as Librium, Miltown, and Valium, are physically and psychologically addictive when used consistently in high doses over a long period of time. They are even more addictive and dangerous (sometimes fatally so) when used with alcohol.

Antidepressant drugs are the most common biological treatment for depression. The two main types of antidepressants are *tricyclics* and *monoamine oxidase (MAO) inhibitors,* both of which were discovered by accident. The tricyclics were being tested as a treatment for schizophrenia, and although they proved to be ineffective, researchers noted that subjects showed an unexpected increase in positive mood. As mentioned earlier, the same result was found when MAO inhibitors were administered as a treatment for tuberculosis.

Tricyclic drugs are usually preferred over MAO inhibitors for depressed persons, first because they have been proved more effective, and second because the MAO inhibitors sometimes have very dangerous side effects, including brain and liver damage, when mixed with certain foods.

The tricyclics, in those cases where they do help, start lifting a person's spirits after a period of approximately ten days. Further adjustments in dosage are then made until a maintenance level is reached.

The number of antidepressant medications is growing, largely because no single drug has proved uniformly effective in treating depression. A given person may be helped significantly by one kind of drug, yet be virtually unaf-

fected by another. One form of depressed functioning that is relatively unresponsive to antidepressant medications is the manic-depressive pattern. As you will recall from the chapter on abnormal psychology, this form of depression, with its dramatic manic phase, is distinctly different from other forms. In recent years a different type of drug, not an antidepressant, has been found to significantly reduce the manic-depressive symptoms of people who have experienced them for many years without relief. This drug, *lithium*, must be taken at just the right level to be effective. Below the necessary level, it offers little therapeutic value; above that level, it can be quite toxic and dangerous. For this reason, careful monitoring of people on lithium is critical.

It is not yet clear why lithium works with manic-depressives. One notion is that the problem itself reflects an imbalance of intracellular sodium and potassium, and that lithium, which has properties similar to those of sodium, corrects this imbalance (Coppen, 1967). Since the net effect of lithium is to produce a marked reduction in intracellular sodium, it is not surprising that taking too much lithium can be very dangerous.

Chemotherapy has rapidly become the most effective form of treatment for schizophrenia, largely because of the *phenothiazines*, a group of drugs introduced in the 1950s. Because of their success in relieving schizophrenic symptoms, the phenothiazines and related drugs became known as antipsychotic drugs. Before these drugs were discovered, the populations of schizophrenic persons in mental hospitals had been increasing, with no end in sight. With these drugs, however, there has been a reversal in this trend, and in the past few decades the number of schizophrenics in mental hospitals has been reduced dramatically. In fact, many state hospitals have closed altogether. New philosophies of treatment have helped bring about change, but the antipsychotic medications have been the single most important factor (see Figure 18–2).

In fact, there is every indication that advances in drug therapies for mental disorders will continue to alter the treatment and care of the mentally ill. New discoveries are being made so rapidly that it is difficult to keep pace. Even as we were completing work on the latest revision of this chapter, an announcement at the 1987 meetings of the American Psychiatric Association caused a good deal of excitement in the field. It concerned the results of the first clinical trials of a drug called *clozapine*, which was found to induce improvements in patients suffering from a severe form of schizophrenia previously unresponsive to chemotherapy (Meltzer, 1987). Now available only on an experimental basis, clozapine has potentially life-threatening side effects. In some patients the drug destroys white blood cells and would ultimately leave the patient with a fatal inability to fight off infections. While the side effects are reversible if detected in time, patients taking the medication must be monitored closely. Since mental patients receive variable levels of medical care, this necessity may be a significant drawback of clozapine.

Not only is chemotherapy influencing treatment options, research in this area has caused clinicians to reexamine their diagnostic categories. At times disorders thought to be fundamentally the same in their cause have been discovered to be significantly different in the way they respond to chemotherapy. Chemotherapy for anxiety provides an excellent example. Drugs known to be useful for the treatment of more long-term anxieties were found to be ineffective for dealing with the sudden onsets of anxiety that we call *panic attacks*. In investigating the reasons for this lack of efficacy, researchers discovered that a specific neurotransmitter seemed to be in-

Figure 18–2 The use of antipsychotic drugs (phenothiazines and related drugs) since their discovery in the 1950s has led to a dramatic reduction in the number of hospitalized schizophrenics in the United States. (National Institute of Mental Health, 1975)

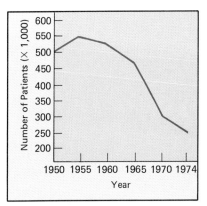

volved in the production of panic attacks. Thus the findings suggest that panic attacks may fall into their own diagnostic category, distinct from other types of anxiety disorders.

There is no doubt that chemotherapeutic intervention has revolutionized the care of the mentally ill, yet it will continue to present ethical dilemmas for caregivers, patients, and their families.

Criticisms of Chemotherapy

Several of the problems with chemotherapy are ones we have alluded to earlier in our discussion. For instance, the reliance upon antipsychotic medications is not wholly warranted. Psychotics released from hospitals often end up as homeless derelicts, wandering city streets. Moreover, those individuals who have improved enough on these drugs to be discharged often show high readmission rates. This has led to what is called the *revolving-door syndrome*—patients improve enough to be released, but return to the hospital because they are incapable of coping with the outside world. Thus chemotherapy cannot be said to be a "cure." Drugs often produce more normal functioning temporarily, but behavior and functioning can lapse to pretreatment rates when the drugs are discontinued. Of course, sometimes temporary alteration is sufficient. An individual going through a period of situationally induced anxiety or depression, such as that caused by the death of a close relative, may have only a temporary need for the kind of help a tranquilizer or antidepressant can provide.

Summarizing the general value of chemotherapy is a very difficult task. First, research has repeatedly demonstrated the effectiveness of these medications (Casey, Bennett, & Lindley, 1960; Cole, 1964; Freedman, 1977). As those who have experienced schizophrenic or severe depressive episodes will attest, the targeted use of psychoactive medications seems justified. However, research also shows that some people experience uncomfortable and even serious side effects that must be dealt with, such as tremors and problems in motor control. As more information comes to light about the undesirable side effects of all medications, not just psychoactive ones, it seems increasingly clear that both prescriber and user must be sure the improvement is worth the side effects that are risked.

Difficult questions exist here for both the clinician prescribing the treatment and the patient taking the medication. On the one hand, maintenance doses of chemotherapy may prevent subsequent episodes of abnormal behavior in susceptible individuals. If this is so, and the side effects are not life-threatening or exceptionally harmful, then the clinician may well decide to prescribe the drug and the individual may agree to take it. On the other hand, there is often no easy way to determine whether those patients now being maintained on chemotherapy are in any danger of further outbreaks of abnormal behavior. Thus it is possible that such persons may actually be risking the side effects of various drugs unnecessarily.

For many psychoactive drugs, the exact effects on the brain are still not well understood (but remember that the exact effects of aspirin are not well understood either, and it is one of the most frequently used drugs of all). However, modern neuroscience is developing theories of brain functioning, and we are learning more and more about the systems of neurons and neurotransmitters that make up the brain. This research is compatible with the interest in chemotherapy, since these drugs frequently have their effects on various concentrations of neurotransmitters. As these two areas of research

overlap and inform one another, it is likely that chemotherapy will become more popular. However, because of the complexities of brain functioning, and the intricate connections between brain functioning and thought processes, chemotherapy will never be a complete cure for all the human difficulties discussed in these chapters.

Genetic Therapy and Genetic Counseling

The biological approach suggests interventions that are not "therapeutic" in any normal sense of the word, yet are aimed at circumventing abnormal behavior. Exciting possibilities exist for what can be called *human genetic therapy*. This involves the insertion of a normal gene to correct a genetic deficit. One procedure involves linking the new gene to be implanted into a "viral vector" that will invade the normal cells (Marx, 1987). These experiments are still in the stage of animal studies, and the genes transferred by these methods have not had their expected normal effects.

Recently, preliminary reports (Madrazo, 1987) suggest that certain dopamine-producing cells transplanted into a particular location of the brain within the same individual might be successful in correcting deficits in the functioning of neurotransmitter systems caused by Parkinson's disease. (Since Parkinson's is a physical disease that has mental manifestations, it falls into a special class of mental disorders.) Apparently, the transplanted cells have dopamine-producing systems. This makes sense as it is known that Parkinson's disease involves a deficiency in dopamine; however, the finding is so new that we do not yet know exactly how the genetic transplant works. Furthermore, some patients benefited from the operation while others did not, and there is no understanding of why these differences occurred. We also do not know whether initially encouraging effects of the operation on these patients' symptoms will persist over time.

Still, this discovery holds forth hope for those afflicted by Parkinson's disease. How many other seemingly miraculous genetic implantation cures can we expect? We quote a leading expert in the field: "Gene therapy techniques are becoming increasingly efficient. Their future application in human beings should result in at least partial correction of a number of genetic disorders. However, the safety of the procedures must still be established . . . before human clinical trials would be ethical" (Anderson, 1984, p. 401). Furthermore, the best prospects for this kind of genetic therapy involve physical rather than mental defects. Genetic therapy is a promising therapeutic technique for the future, but it is not yet a reality for any of the mental disorders described in this chapter—even the ones with the most clear genetic causes. And we cannot assume that genetic repair will inevitably be possible for all diseases with genetic causes. Over the course of a disease certain neurotransmitter systems may decay or die, and it may be impossible to reverse such effects with later implantation procedures. In fact, one reason the operation to reverse Parkinsonism described above sometimes worked while previous attempts failed is that the subjects in the most recent study were younger and in earlier stages of the disease.

In cases where it is not possible to repair genetic material, it is sometimes possible to predict when genetic defects will be passed down from parents to children. (See the Highlight: Genetic Screening and Ethical Controversy for a discussion of the ethical issues involved.) **Genetic counseling** is designed to provide prospective parents with such information. It begins by identifying certain diseases that are inherited. Next, prospective parents are

Genetic Screening and Ethical Controversy

Scientific discoveries can create ethical dilemmas. As we discover techniques for predicting future happenings, we can intervene to make those happenings more or less likely. Nowhere is this ethical dilemma more apparent than in recent discoveries made by genetic researchers. As you saw in the abnormal psychology chapter (Chapter 17), new methods of genetic research have made it possible to identify the chromosomal locations of various genetic defects that cause certain physical or mental diseases. It is now feasible to test a fetus for a rapidly lengthening list of genes, which when damaged, are known to cause physical deformities, disease, or impaired brain functioning. In the future, as this chapter makes clear, we may have the skills to repair or replace the damaged genetic material, and so prevent dysfunctions from occurring.

Since we don't presently have such skills, one possibility for parents faced with the news that their child will be less than perfect is to abort the fetus. (Alternatively, some couples, after learning of the danger of inherited disease, might avoid parenthood altogether.) Everyone who reads this is already aware of the vast moral controversy that surrounds the topic of abortion, but the new scientific discoveries are destined to sharpen the focus of that debate. We now can say that a particular fetus is genetically damaged in a way that will lead to, for instance, malformations of bodily organs that would cause the newborn terrible pain and result in death soon after birth. Many would find that grounds for abortion.

Yet what if a fetus has the genetic abnormality associated with susceptibility to manic-depression? Here it is likely, but not certain, that the fetus would ultimately develop the manic-depressive disorder (see Chapter 17). Should it be aborted? Certainly parents who decide against abortion would be influenced in their behavior toward a child that faces such a grim possibility. Should such a child be told of the problem? At the moment, aside from the common sense advice to avoid stress, we do not know a great deal about how to avert the manic-depressive disorder. Thus receiving news that one has genetic damage of this kind only causes fear and offers little hope of avoiding the disorder. Still, a case can be made that a person has the right to such information.

What if a fetus has the genetic structure identified in a physical disease that causes severe psychological symptoms, such as Alzheimer's disease? This condition is sometimes called *premature senility,* and it leads to memory losses so severe that eventually the person cannot function in life and, although apparently physically healthy, must be

interviewed about the incidence of these diseases in their families. Sometimes this information is supplemented by information from physical examination of the individuals. Particularly as electromicroscopic techniques become more sophisticated, even direct examination of chromosomes may be used to provide information. Fitting this information into the available models of genetic inheritance, the genetic counselor attempts to give the prospective parents some estimate of the odds that their offspring will be born with or develop certain physical conditions. Decisions about having children can then be made in light of that information.

Many of the disorders identified in this manner are physical ones, such as Tay-Sachs disease, an inherited metabolic disorder. However, at least some of these physical disorders will have among their symptoms various kinds of mental disorganization. This may well motivate potential parents to avoid conceiving a child. Amniocentesis, the testing of the fluid in the womb after the fetus is conceived, is one direct means of detecting genetic abnormalities, and it may lead to a decision to abort the fetus.

All of these are grim possibilities, involving wrenching decisions for the people involved. And there is some possibility that genetically damaging agents are more insidious than has been realized. In the first half of this century there was an incredible proliferation in the manufacture and use of complex chemicals, many of them in the workplace. Many scientists now suspect that overexposure to some of these chemicals or certain manufacturing processes may cause chromosomal damage and that damage may be genetically passed on to descendants: There is good evidence that this occurs in nonhuman mammals (National Academy of Sciences, 1983). Although the evidence is indirect, because the transmission mechanisms are similar it is

kept under constant observation. However, the onset of this condition generally does not occur until age 50 or 60. Although Alzheimer's disease is the subject of a crash program of research being sponsored by the National Institutes of Health, there is still no known cure. Would one abort a fetus because of something that would happen decades after birth? If not, would one tell such a person of the genetic defect so that he or she would worry whenever a normal lapse of memory occurred?

Now you can see why many people are ambivalent about scientific discoveries. In a classical Greek legend Pandora rashly opened a mysterious chest and let loose a swarm of evils on humankind. People have applied the "Pandora's box" analogy to the discovery of atomic power, and many now feel the same way about the exploration of genetic factors in disease and mental disorders. Just like the unwitting Pandora, scientists often create dilemmas where none existed before.

Two things need to be said about this. First, while it is true that scientific discoveries have created ethical dilemmas, they have done so as a byproduct of making enormously valuable discoveries. As we learn more about genetics, and how genetic messages are transformed into patterns of physical development and neurological functioning, we may be able to ameliorate or eliminate various diseases that are caused by genetic damage. Second, even when knowledge is painful—as knowledge that one has a dread disease surely is—it is still often better than ignorance. On April 8, 1987, a National Institutes of Health panel recommended that all babies be tested for sickle cell disease. Since sickle cell disease is incurable, health policy specialists had long thought there was no point in screening the entire population for it. However, a recent NIH-sponsored clinical trial found that there are preventive treatments that are often effective in avoiding the bacterial infections that cause children

with sickle cell disease to die in the first few years of life. The report (Kolata, 1987) also notes that the panel heard from several mothers who had not known their children had the condition when the children showed the fever, swollen joints, and joint pain that is the crisis stage of the disease. These children were incorrectly diagnosed by the hospital, and in one case the mother was accused of child abuse! Given this experience, it is hard to argue that the parents, and eventually the children, shouldn't have been told that they had sickle cell disease. Even for incurable diseases, various secondary measures can be taken that may prevent some of the worst effects. While it is difficult to predict what impact such screening may have on those faced with the prospect of various mental disorders, it does raise vexing and compelling ethical issues for parents, researchers, and society.

likely that this occurs in humans as well. In the future genetic counselors are likely to add questions about chemical hazards at the workplace to their lists of interview questions.

Some other forms of biologically based interventions are less bleak. Today it is sometimes possible to compensate for a genetic deficiency with drugs or control of diet. For instance, phenylketanuria (PKU) is a genetically transmitted disease that was often fatal; the underlying cause involves an abnormal buildup of amino acids when elimination mechanisms malfunction. This buildup can be avoided by conrol of diet.

Electroshock Treatment and Psychosurgery

One of the more controversial biological treatments for depression is **electroshock (ECT).** It is generally used only with people for whom other forms of therapy have not been effective. Therapists have resorted to it less frequently since the antidepressant drugs became available. In electroshock therapy, introduced in the 1930s, a brief electric current is sent through the brain by means of electrodes placed on either side of the forehead.

Before receiving electroshock, people generally are given a sedative and a muscle relaxant, which reduce the risk of injury and seem to minimize the discomfort. A standard course of treatment would consist of two or three weeks of treatments of three electroshocks a week. The result of the shock is a convulsive seizure that lasts for about a minute, following which the person loses consciousness for several minutes. The treatment is often accompanied by a memory loss of unpredictable length, ranging from a few minutes to several hours.

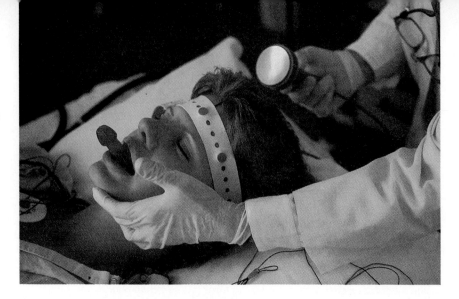

One of the more controversial biological treatments is electroshock. Once used to reduce symptoms of severe depression, it is currently used only when other therapies have failed. (Will McIntyre/Photo Researchers)

There is still no certainty about how ECT works. It causes so many changes in brain activity that it is difficult to figure out which ones cause the reduction in depression. Some experimenters think that ECT temporarily stimulates the synthesis of norepinephrine in the brain (Kety, 1974). Others (Sackheim, 1985) note that the right frontal cortex is overactive during depression and that it shows reduced activity levels following ECT. Physiological conceptualizations are being developed of how ECT might both produce improvement in depressive behaviors and affect memory (Lerer, 1985). However, much remains to be discovered about the mechanisms that produce the ECT effects (Malitz and Sackheim, 1986, Small, Small, and Milstein, in press), and its possible harmful effects (Weiner, 1984).

Recently a panel of scientists advising the National Institutes of Health guardedly approved ECT for short-term treatment of severe episodes of depression that have not responded to medication (Holder, 1985). But ECT is not an absolute cure—the depression often recurs later in the person's life. Vexing questions remain about the possibility of memory loss caused by using shock. In some cases, ECT has caused long-term, severe effects. But less than 1 percent of patients who receive ECT report memory impairment. Nonetheless, ECT is a treatment that, not surprisingly, is now used sparingly and with great caution.

Psychosurgery is the attempt to cure psychological disorders by surgical intervention. The first known attempts at psychosurgery are illustrated by the skulls shown in the opening pages of this chapter. Our guess is that the skulls were opened to let evil spirits escape from the head. As this suggests, psychosurgery is always based on some theory about the connections between brain or body functioning and disordered thoughts or actions. Obviously, psychosurgery can only be successful when the theories about brain functioning are correct. Sadly, one major example of psychosurgery, the **prefrontal lobotomy,** was based on an inadequate theory—the notion that the frontal lobes of the brain strengthen or increase emotional responses, which actually arise in the limbic system and hypothalamus. Thus it was thought that cutting the connections between the frontal lobes and these other brain regions would help in such problems as schizophrenia and depression. In the 1940s and 1950s an enormous number of lobotomies were performed with claims of great success. Subsequent research, however, found that people who had had lobotomies showed very bad side effects,

such as seizures, stupor, and extreme listlessness, to say nothing of impaired mental functioning. This Nobel Prize–winning procedure fell into disfavor when it became evident that the theory upon which it was based was grossly oversimplified and wrong, and when it became apparent that it caused many unanticipated and destructive side effects. As a result, all forms of psychosurgery are now treated with great caution by both the professional community and the public at large.

Criticisms of Electroshock Treatment and Psychosurgery

Many of the difficulties with electroshock and psychosurgery have already been discussed. The pattern of discovery with both treatments guaranteed problems. Each was discovered accidentally when procedures done for other purposes were found to have some unexpected positive effects on mood or behavior. "Theories" were then developed about why these initially unexpected effects were actually predictable, and advocates proceeded to implement these theories. In practice, this meant that if a powerful person in a mental hospital came to believe in the efficacy of a certain procedure, the procedure was performed on many patients confined to that institution. Families of patients were induced to grant permission for the procedures with wildly overblown claims about their desirability and even their necessity. Sometimes the procedures were simply inflicted on patients without permission. As we know, terrible harm was inflicted on many mental patients.

Does this mean that such techniques should never be used? No. Recently we have learned enough about how the brain works so that we may be able to design a complex surgical intervention or procedure like electroshock that has some hope of success with certain disorders. (For example, the brain implantation procedure for Parkinson's disease described earlier is most definitely "psychosurgery.") By using scientifically acceptable means of clinical investigation and experimentation, we can measure what effects the operations actually produce rather than optimistically overstating the case on the basis of preliminary findings. We can also stay alert for signs of unexpected negative side effects, since all of our past experience suggests that there will be some.

THE PSYCHOANALYTIC MODEL OF THERAPY

The **psychoanalytic model,** formulated by Freud, locates the origin of abnormal functioning in emotionally painful childhood experiences or events that have resulted in arrested personality development. As an adult, the person is unable to resolve unconscious conflicts and impulses except by maladaptive defense mechanisms such as excessive repression.

Psychoanalytic therapy—or **psychoanalysis,** as it is called—is based on verbal techniques. Its basic purpose is to solve psychological problems by bringing the unconscious conflicts into the conscious mind, where they may be confronted and resolved. The focus is on underlying ways of experiencing things and thinking about them rather than on behavior. Psychoanalysis aims to change the client's personality rather than just certain behaviors. In Freudian terms, psychoanalysis is designed to strengthen the ego, increase the awareness of the id, and bring the superego under control (see Chapter 15).

Psychoanalysis is usually an involved process that takes years to complete. The role of the psychoanalyst is largely passive, more that of a guide and interpreter than a teacher. One of the major problems the analyst must deal with is the emotional resistance of the client to the painful awareness that an emotional problem exists. Therefore analysis must do more than uncover the emotional origins of problems; if therapy is to be effective, it must enable the person to acknowledge and confront these problems.

Techniques of Psychoanalysis

Psychoanalysis uses several techniques—most of them originated by Freud—as part of the therapeutic process. One of the best known is **free association,** in which the patient is encouraged to say whatever thoughts come to mind, regardless of how illogical, irrelevant, or embarrassing they seem. Freud said that free association should be like someone viewing scenes smoothly flowing by a train window. The theory is that by disregarding intellectual judgment and interpretation, the person will bypass the ego's defenses and produce clues to the unconscious source of problems. Of course, it rarely happens this easily. What gets in the way is the person's own **resistance,** which occurs in the form of blanks, obviously contrived associations, or disputes with the therapist. The form or source of this resistance is regarded as significant by the psychoanalyst and a possible opportunity for insight and interpretation because it is a clue that the person is getting close to the source of a problem.

Interpretation is another technique used by the psychoanalyst to make the unconscious conscious. When the person seems ready to face underlying problems, the analyst suggests possible hidden meanings or defense mechanisms revealed by the person's actions or statements. The analyst points out connections and associations the client may not have seen—connections between belief and actions, or between current attitudes and something that happened in the past. When an analyst offers an interpretation, it may be accepted or denied by the client. Sometimes the client's denial is interpreted by the analyst as resistance. To the analyst, this means that the interpretation is correct but the patient is not yet ready to accept it.

In addition to interpreting a person's resistance, psychoanalysts engage in dream interpretation. In the client's dreams the psychoanalyst seeks clues about the true nature of the client's problem. Recall from the discussion of

A group psychotherapy session. (Ken Karp)

Freud's theory of dreams in Chapter 5, why this should be possible. When we are asleep, the ego and superego are not as much in control as when we are awake, and as a result unconscious impulses surface. Thus the analyst is able to see more clearly where problems might lie. But this is not an easy process because the ego still exercises some control over the dream content, thus disguising the real conflicts represented in the dream. According to Freud, dreams have two levels of content. One is the **manifest content,** which involves the overt and concrete happenings of the dream. This is the dream as dreamers experience and remember it. The other level is the **latent content,** the hidden and symbolic meaning of the dream, the disguise that the impulse appears in. It is the latent content that the psychoanalyst helps people to understand and use to gain insight into their hidden conflicts.

As psychoanalysis progresses, a special relationship, called **transference,** develops between patient and analyst. Patients begin to form irrational expectations of the analyst. They may feel that the analyst is angry with them, bored by them, disappointed in them, trying to seduce them, or expecting too much of them. Their own reaction may be anger, fear, love, or an effort to dominate the analyst. According to Freud, these unrealistic interpretations are a result of transferring past relationships with important adults (usually parents) onto the analyst, relating to the analyst as if he or she were the parent figure. Unconsciously, patients expect the analyst to react the way their parents would, so they reenact repressed wishes and experiences. A patient with a stern, demanding mother, for example, might express the fear that the analyst is displeased with the progress of the therapy. A patient who was emotionally abandoned by an unresponsive father might feel that the analyst is not really interested in helping with the problem (that is, is abandoning the patient again). By recognizing the role in which a client casts them, and observing the ways a client acts toward them, alert analysts are able to understand a good deal about the client's early relationship with parents—a likely source of psychological difficulties.

There are many different forms of therapies, which take place in many different settings. This is Freud's study in London, containing the patients' couch. (Mary Evans/Sigmund Freud Copyrights)

Psychoanalysis Since Freud

Psychoanalysis as a therapeutic approach has been modified by many people over the years. Just as different psychoanalytic theorists have attached greater importance to social drives (as opposed to sexual drives) or to the ego (as opposed to the id), different psychoanalytic therapists following those theorists have emphasized interpersonal relationships or insights into the role of the ego. Thus there may be significant differences among psychoanalytic therapies, though all share the belief that intrapsychic conflict is at the core of the problem and that insight is essential to improvement.

Psychoanalysis has also undergone some significant changes in technique. Sessions five days a week in which the patient lies on a couch—once the hallmark of this approach—still take place, but are less common. More common are sessions once a week in which the patient and the therapist sit face to face. In some psychoanalytic circles there are efforts to shorten the duration of psychotherapy or to have the therapist play a much more active role. The goals also differ somewhat from Freud's. Today there is more emphasis on resolving immediate problems and less on building a psychodynamic history of the person. Techniques are also more flexible, and the therapist may vary techniques to deal with different individuals' problems, or even to deal with one individual's different needs at various points in the therapy.

APPLICATION

Psychoanalysis

THERAPIST: It sounds as if you would like to let loose with me, but you are afraid of what my response would be *(summarizing and restating).*

PATIENT: I get so excited by what is happening here. I feel I'm being held back by needing to be nice. I'd like to blast loose sometimes, but I don't dare.

THERAPIST: Because you fear my reaction?

PATIENT: The worst thing would be that you wouldn't like me. You wouldn't speak to me friendly; you wouldn't smile; you'd feel you can't treat me and discharge me from treatment. But I know this isn't so, I know it.

THERAPIST: Where do you think these attitudes come from?

PATIENT: When I was 9 years old, I read a lot about great men in history. I'd quote them and be dramatic. I'd want a sword at my side; I'd dress like an Indian. Mother would scold me. Don't frown, don't talk so much. Sit on your hands, over and over again. I did all kinds of things. I was a naughty child. She told me I'd be hurt. Then at 14 I fell off a horse and broke my back. I had to be in bed. Mother then told me on the day I went riding not to, that I'd get hurt because the ground was frozen. I was a stubborn, self-willed child. Then I went against her will and suffered an accident that changed my life, a fractured back. Her attitude was, "I told you so." I was put in a cast and kept in bed for months.

THERAPIST: You were punished, so to speak, by this accident.

PATIENT: But I gained attention and love from mother for the first time. I felt so good. I'm ashamed to tell you this. Before I healed I opened the cast and tried to walk to make myself sick again so I could stay in bed longer.

THERAPIST: How does that connect up with your impulse to be sick now and stay in bed so much? *(The patient has these tendencies, of which she is ashamed.)*

PATIENT: Oh . . . *(pause)*

THERAPIST: What do you think?

PATIENT: Oh, my God, how infantile, how ungrown-up *(pause).* It must be so. I want people to love me and be sorry for me. Oh, my God. How completely childish. It is, *is* that. My mother must have ignored me when I was little, and I wanted so to be loved. *(This sounds like insight.)*

THERAPIST: So that it may have been threatening to go back to being self-willed and unloved after you got out of the cast *(interpretation).*

PATIENT: It did. My life changed. I became meek and controlled. I couldn't get angry or stubborn afterward.

THERAPIST: Perhaps if you go back to being stubborn with *me,* you would be returning to how you were before; that is, active, stubborn but unloved.

PATIENT: *(excitedly)* And, therefore, losing your love. I need you, but after all you aren't going to reject me. But the pattern is so established now that the threat of the loss of love is too overwhelming with everybody, and I've got to keep myself from acting selfish or angry.

(Wolberg, 1977, pp. 560–561)

Criticisms of Psychoanalysis

Psychoanalytic approaches have received a great deal of criticism—this after an extended period during which psychoanalysis was almost the only approach to therapy available. Some of the criticisms are about the scientific status of the underlying theory. Most research-trained psychologists are disturbed by the relative lack of research evidence supporting psychoanalytic theory. Others are at a loss to say exactly what sort of evidence would count as scientific support. Today, many years after the initiation of psychoanalysis, that debate continues (Greenbaum, 1984). Similar criticisms can be made about psychoanalysis in practice. Perhaps you thought of this when you read about resistance earlier. If the patient accepts an interpretation by the analyst, then the interpretation is true. If the patient does not accept the interpretation, then this indicates resistance and therefore the interpretation is true.

Other critics accept that psychoanalysis may be an effective treatment, but argue that it simply takes too long and costs too much money for most people. Still others point out that the techniques and complexities of psychoanalysis make it helpful only to people who are basically in touch with reality and who possess verbal abilities and verbal interaction skills. Schofeld summarized this critique by remarking that the typical analytic client must be a YAVIS—a *y*oung *a*dult, *v*erbally skilled, *i*ntelligent, and *s*ophisticated.

The requirement of coherence is particularly troubling when it comes to

treating people whose major symptom is a lack of coherence. It is not surprising, therefore, that psychoanalytic approaches have been regularly applied to problems of anxiety and depression, where the person's intellectual ability is intact, and less often to cases of psychosis, such as schizophrenia. Many psychoanalysts, including Freud, have admitted that psychoanalysis is not an effective therapy for schizophrenia. Beyond the issue of coherence and reality testing, one of the major problems with the psychoanalytic approach is the necessity for establishing a bond of trust between therapist and patient. This can be discouragingly difficult to achieve with certain classes of the mentally disturbed and further restricts the applicability of psychoanalysis.

Finally, there is the criticism that psychoanalysis may be a good way to get at the source of the patient's problem, but not necessarily to solve it. It may be that the quickest and most effective way to solve present problems is to focus on the problems themselves rather than on what caused them. That, at least, is the viewpoint behind many of the recent developments that have taken place in therapy.

THE HUMANISTIC-EXISTENTIAL MODEL OF THERAPY

Like the analytically based therapies, humanistic and existential therapies attempt to increase a person's awareness of underlying motivational confusions, thought processes, and emotional conflicts. Thus, like analytic therapies, their general goal is to produce insight. Also like analytic therapies, these therapies are usually talk-centered: The typical analytic session involves a therapist and a "client" (to use Carl Rogers's term) in a room together for an hour, with the client talking and the therapist listening. (But we will see that the Gestalt therapists break this mold with some interesting therapeutic techniques.)

Despite the similarities just outlined, humanistic and existential therapists locate the source of clients' problems in a very different set of causes than do psychoanalysts.

For humanistic and existential therapists, abnormal functioning results from a failure to reach or strive toward one's full potential. In humanistic theories, this is often called a failure to self-actualize: that is, a failure to move toward the fulfillment of one's natural potential as a human being and to be in close touch with who one is, how one feels, and what one actually thinks. In existential theories, too, abnormality represents a failure to reach one's full potential, but this failure is rooted in one's inability to overcome the sources of anxiety built into the existential situation of life; this is an inability to meet life assertively, give it meaning, and take responsibility for one's life. Both theories define abnormal functioning as a failure to be and fulfill oneself, and the humanistic-existential approach to therapy seeks to help people get in touch with their real selves, and then to make deliberate choices regarding their lives and behaviors, rather than letting outside events determine their behavior.

Many therapy approaches fall under the humanistic or existential heading. We will examine two that are quite different in everything but their overall humanistic orientation and goals—Carl Rogers's client-centered therapy and Fritz Perls's Gestalt therapy. Each works toward enhanced self-awareness in a different way.

CLIENT: Well, it happened again yesterday. I got back that exam in American Lit.

THERAPIST: I see.

CLIENT: Just like before. I got an A all right—me and 8 others. But on the third question the instructor wrote a comment that I could have been a little clearer or else could have given more detail. The same old crap. I got an A all right, but it's pretty damn clear that I'm like a machine that can generate correct answers without ever understanding. That's it. I memorize, but there's no spark, no creativity. Boy!

THERAPIST: What else can you tell me about the exam?

CLIENT: Well, it was like we talked about before. I'm doing OK, but I just don't feel like I really measure up. I remember my brother bringing home a paper in high school. It was a C, but the instructor said John had real potential. I just don't think I've got it.

THERAPIST: Even though you got an A you are not satisfied.

CLIENT: I know I should be satisfied with an A. Other guys would be. They'd be glad to get an A.

THERAPIST: Mm-hmm.

CLIENT: But I can't. No wonder the folks are so proud of John. He got decent grades, and he was satisfied—not like me. It's a wonder they don't get fed up with my moping around.

THERAPIST: So even with good grades your unhappiness is enough to turn people off.

CLIENT: Sure. But somehow I've got to get rid of this defeatist attitude. I've got to think about the good side.

THERAPIST: Mm-hmm.

CLIENT: A lot of times I've tried to forget my lack of potential. Just go on and plug along.

THERAPIST: Yeah, I guess you really felt people put you down because of this lack of potential?

CLIENT: Boy, did they! Especially my folks. They never really said so, but I could tell them from the way they acted.

THERAPIST: Mm-hmm.

CLIENT: They'd say that John really has a head on his shoulders, or *(pause)* . . . he can think his way out of anything.

THERAPIST: And this made you feel sort of worthless—not hearing things like that about yourself.

CLIENT: That's right!

(Phares, 1979, pp. 360–361)

Client-Centered Therapy

You will recall from Chapter 17 (Abnormal Psychology) that Carl Rogers believed people may come to accept the negative evaluations others have imposed on them and as a result develop a negative and limited self-concept. Thus they do not feel the positive self-regard that everyone needs. Over time they have developed a style of self-distortion, selectively perceiving events and behaviors in a way that is consistent with their self-view. Their inaccurate self-view and the energy invested in this constant self-deception make it impossible for them to fulfill their potential.

The idea underlying Rogers's **client-centered therapy** is that therapy must create a totally nonthreatening atmosphere in which people can honestly look at and accept themselves and make relevant decisions. This follows from Rogers's assumption that all people are naturally good and effective and will function in an effective and moral way if given the freedom to do so. More accurate self-awareness and acceptance will in turn lead to the more functional and productive life-style of self-actualization.

Thus the humanistic technique created by Rogers (1950, 1961, 1970) allows the client a large role in directing the course of the therapy. For therapy to be effective, the client must perceive the therapist as showing unconditional positive regard, empathy, and genuineness.

Unconditional positive regard is essential to the concept of client-centered therapy. The therapist must consider the client a worthy human being, without qualification. No judgment should be passed, either against or in support of the client's viewpoint or actions. (Rogers referred to this as AT&T, or Attitude of Tentativeness and Tolerance.) The therapist must, however, show a deep faith in the ability of the client to discover the right path to follow. As a result of this unconditional positive regard, clients begin to accept

themselves, partly because even when they reveal bizarre or seemingly terrible thoughts, they still feel accepted by their therapist.

Unlike psychoanalysis, in which the therapist attempts to observe and analyze the patient's conception of reality, the client-centered therapist *empathizes* with the client's world by trying to enter it and experience it from the same viewpoint as the client. When listening to their clients, therapists make remarks reflecting the emotional content of what is being said. They do this to make sure they understand it, but also to make sure that clients recognize all that they are saying, or the implications of what they're saying. This has been described as "mirroring" clients' feelings so that they will see all that is there.

Genuineness means that the therapist must establish a human-to-human relationship with the client, not one that could be interpreted by the client as doctor-patient, expert-amateur, or savior-sinner. For Rogers, the therapist must *feel* a genuine concern and empathy for the client in order for therapy to be effective.

Gestalt Therapy

Another humanistic approach, **Gestalt therapy,** is largely the work of Frederick (Fritz) Perls (1969, 1970). Like Rogers, Perls believed all people are innately good. Abnormal functioning originates in the denial of this goodness and the blocking of its expression. Ordinarily, in whatever we perceive, whether it be ideas, events, or emotions, we concentrate on only part of our whole experience. We focus on the figure, or *foreground,* and largely ignore the *background* against which the figure appears. If we are holding a conversation with a professor who has rejected a term paper, for example, we concentrate our attention on the conversation and our efforts to defend our work (the foreground) and are only partly aware of our anger and frustration against which this conversation is taking place (the background). Perls wanted people to perceive the wholeness, or **Gestalt,** of their experiences. (The concept of Gestalt or whole perception was discussed in Chapter 4.)

The purpose of Gestalt therapy is to help people become aware of this wholeness by bringing more of the background into the foreground experience. Great importance is placed on the *here and now.* Therapy encourages people to recognize the immediate experience in its entirety, which means knowing what they are feeling as well as thinking, so that their behavior is in harmony with their whole being. To achieve this goal, they must free themselves from trying to live up to the expectations of others. They must be responsible for their own behavior and recognize their capabilities for self-improvement.

Among the techniques practiced by Gestalt therapists, role playing and projection are used to bring out problems caused by expectations or rules of behavior that were originally applied by parents and other authority figures and that people have internalized. The purpose is to show that these problems are really self-imposed, that they do not result from universal rules that everyone must follow.

In the empty-chair technique, for example, clients are asked to imagine that some person with whom they have an emotionally charged relationship (father, mother, spouse) is sitting in the empty chair opposite them. They then talk to this person about the problems in their relationship and their specific feelings toward that person. Then the client switches chairs and talks

as if he or she were the other person speaking—this brings out how clients think other persons see them. The empty-chair technique may also be used to encourage clients to talk to different parts of themselves—to their fears, desires, dreams—and to try to confront their feelings and accept them as part of their total makeup.

Another Gestalt technique is to ask clients to act out the opposite of what they feel. People who feel emotionally unresponsive, for example, would be instructed to react as if they were extremely sensitive and emotionally uninhibited. Through this exercise, Perls felt, clients could discover a very real part of their being that had never been allowed open expression.

In Gestalt therapy an effort is made to experience feelings, to acknowledge them and let them guide actions. Further, Gestalt therapy encourages concentrating on the here and now rather than on the past or future, and on what is present rather than absent.

Criticisms of Humanistic-Existential Therapies

The humanistic and existential therapies, as compared to psychoanalytic ones, emphasize the role of present experiences, and even future purposes, in determining human actions. As a result, the Gestalt and client-centered therapists have a much more optimistic perspective on the possibilities for change. One criticism of these therapies is similar to that voiced about psychoanalytic therapies: primarily, what many consider to be a disturbing lack of evidence for the underlying theory. How, for instance, would one test Rogers's grand assumption that people are intrinsically good? Second, it is recognized that these therapies are likely to work best with select problems, such as depression or low self-esteem. For many seeking therapy, particularly college students, these more optimistic orientations may, in fact, be ideally suited to their needs. But how would client-centered or Gestalt therapies deal with a catatonic schizophrenic or a drug addict, for instance?

Although we have criticized these theories for providing little evidence of their validity, we should point out that Carl Rogers and his students, frequently working in university counseling centers, pioneered research in therapeutic processes. For instance, by analyzing tape recordings of therapy sessions (made with the knowledge and permission of the clients), it was discovered that therapists who were perceived by the clients as warm, genuine, and empathetic caused their clients to feel that the therapy was more successful. In many kinds of therapy, treatment begins with the client making a good many statements that present or restate symptoms or problems, and progress is later indexed by the emergence of client statements that show insight into or understanding of these problems. While it may be difficult to scientifically measure the value of insight or self-understanding, many people do report finding such therapy a positive and helpful experience.

LEARNING MODELS OF THERAPY

The next two models of therapy we will discuss—learning and cognitive models—have their origins in the research laboratories of experimental psychology. Learning-based therapies, generally called **behavioral therapies,** draw on the principles of learning and conditioning discussed in Chapter 6. Cognitive therapies draw on the cognitive learning principles discussed in the second part of Chapter 6, the principles of thought discussed in

Chapter 9, and the attributional principles that we will discuss in Chapter 19. In contrast to the learning (or behavioral) therapies, which attempt to alter people's behaviors, the cognitive therapies attempt to alter perceptual interpretative styles and thought patterns, particularly their interpretations of the meaning of negative events. Both kinds of therapies, in contrast to insight therapies, adhere to what has been called a *modernistic ideology* (Woolfolk & Richardson, 1984). Along with specifying therapeutic techniques that produce measurable results, their concern is that these techniques be geared to goals set by the client rather than the therapist. The behaviorists often objected to what they viewed as a tendency on the part of insight therapists to substitute their own goals for the goals that brought clients to therapy in the first place.

We will begin with a description of the behavioral therapist's techniques, and then go on to present those used by cognitive therapists. But you need to know that most therapists working within this tradition now use a mix of both cognitive and behavioral techniques to get at different aspects of the client's problem. The term for this is *cognitive-behavioral therapy*.

The first step in behavioral therapy is to listen carefully to the client's statement of the problem. A client comes to a therapist wanting to change something—what is that something? Is it a fear of heights, of uncontrolled drinking? The initial task is to define the problem clearly and make it into a set of specific therapeutic objectives. If, for example, a person wants to overcome feelings of helplessness, the therapist will begin by working with the person to better describe these feelings and to pinpoint what behaviors are affected by these feelings. Helpless to do what? To get to work on time? To complete assignments? To quit drinking? Once the specific behaviors in need of change are defined, treatment programs using conditioning techniques are worked out. In this way the therapist chooses the treatment method according to the particular problem, rather than using the same method with all problems.

Systematic Desensitization

Certain situations lend themselves to easy analysis on learning and conditioning terms—for example, the problems of people with identifiable anxieties and phobias. The standard approach to these situations is **systematic desensitization.** The client is first trained to make a response that is incompatible with the anxiety response—namely, the *relaxation response.* This response is trained by giving the person cues to relax deeply. The next step is to make up a hierarchy of the anxiety-producing situations, which are ranked from extremely mild to extremely tense and anxiety-filled. The client is then asked to relax and experience or imagine each step in the hierarchy, starting at the lower or mild end. (It is best if the person actually undergoes the experience, but that is not always possible. The alternative method is to imagine or visualize it.)

An example may make all this more clear. You know someone who is afraid of snakes. Suppose that through some weird combination of circumstances that person is offered a job as the snake handler in a children's zoo. Within a month he needs to be able to calmly handle (harmless) snakes to show to children. And he wants the job! So he seeks the help of a behavioral therapist.

First, the therapist teaches the person the relaxation response. Next, therapist and patient construct the anxiety hierarchy. It is obvious what the objec-

tive of the hierarchy is—calmly handling a harmless snake in front of a group of children. Arousing very little fear, and thus at the lower end of the anxiety hierarchy, would be visualizing a distant massive wall, behind which is, one tiny snake in a pen. A scene that would provoke a moderate level of anxiety, and therefore be an intermediate step in the hierarchy, would be imagining standing 10 feet away from a clearly glassed off cage containing one harmless snake.

The therapist would start by having the client imagine this low-anxiety situation while practicing the relaxation response. When this was successfully accomplished, the client would be instructed to imagine the next anxiety-provoking step in the hierarchy, and so on. The training might also include slides or pictures and even active contact with snakes. Thus through repeated short exposures while using the relaxation technique, the person learns to imagine each step without feelings of anxiety. As each step in the hierarchy is "conquered," the person moves on until he is able to experience or imagine the most disturbing level without anxiety. The final step is for the person to carry the learned relaxed responses into the feared environment.

In order for systematic desensitization to work, it is obviously necessary that people be able to identify what they are afraid of. For this reason the approach has been most successfully applied to **phobias** (such as specific fears of animals or heights) and **anxieties** that can be broken down into basic elements (such as the fear of performing in public).

Implosion Therapy

Rather than beginning with the least anxiety-provoking event of the hierarchy, therapists who employ **implosion therapy** have clients imagine the most anxiety-provoking events first. They also ask them to experience the event as fully and realistically as they can. The anxieties that the client experiences in this treatment are often so massive that this is sometimes called a *flooding* technique. While the method may seem counterintuitive, the principle at work here is that the patient experiences the feared event without experiencing any of the normal harms that would accompany that event. Through the normal processes of extinction, the internal explosion (or implosion) of anxiety becomes disconnected from the stimuli that originally provoked it. For reasons readily apparent even to the layperson, this technique is typically used with clients who are generally strong but suffer isolated phobias, obsessions, or compulsions. A client who compulsively washes his hands, for instance, can be asked to imagine situations where he is restrained from doing so. Obviously his anxieties will be aroused by this imagined prevention of what he considers to be a necessary action, but no bad things will happen to him as a consequence. Thus one would expect his compulsive behavior to fade.

Aversive Counterconditioning

Undesirable habits such as smoking, overeating, or excessive drinking are hard for many people to break. In such cases it can be more helpful to develop a negative response to the stimulus rather than attempt to eliminate the response entirely. The behavioral approach called **aversive counterconditioning** seeks to help people extinguish undesirable positive responses to a stimulus by repeatedly pairing it with an unpleasant consequence, such as verbal ridicule, nausea-producing drugs, or electric shock.

For example, a chronic smoker is repeatedly offered a cigarette, and then given a mild electric shock with each puff. In conditioning terms, the attractive stimulus, the cigarette, is the conditioned stimulus. It is paired with the unattractive stimulus, the shock, which is the unconditoned stimulus. This pairing conditions a new response to the attractive stimulus, the response of fear or revulsion. When the cigarette comes to elicit fear (or nausea or whatever), its attraction no longer exits—it is no longer tempting. It is important, however, to replace the smoking with a more desirable response that meets the needs or desires originally fulfilled by smoking. Otherwise, relapse rates in this kind of treatment are high.

Aversive counterconditioning is more promising in theory than in actuality. Research has shown that its effects are short-lived in many cases. There is also the problem that the learned negative reaction will generalize too much. For instance, an aversively conditioned smoker may become anxious when anyone else takes out a cigarette.

Operant Conditioning

Operant approaches to therapy borrow from Skinner's (1953) demonstrations that desired behaviors can be shaped by rewarding them and by not rewarding undesirable behaviors. One of the best-known operant conditioning therapies is the use of an incentive system called **token economy.** Positive behavior is reinforced by the reward of tokens that can be exchanged later for special privileges. Thus behavior is reinforced right away by the token. This approach has been used with such problems as schizophrenic disorders, retardation, and school misbehavior.

Token-economy programs are often practiced in controlled environments such as mental hospitals or psychiatric wards. (Notice an interesting relationship here. These are the typical settings for exactly the sorts of problems not easily corrected by talk-therapy techniques.) For instance, in the Allyon and Azrin (1968) study done in a mental hospital ward, tokens could be used to buy such privileges as listening to records, going to the movies, or "renting" a space in which to be alone. In other studies tokens have been exchangeable for "grounds passes," candy, cigarettes, and other goodies at the canteen, as well as television time. It is a simple system, which is its big

Behavioral therapies are quite effective in helping people overcome specific anxieties and phobias—for example, a fear of heights. (Jacques M. Chenet/Woodfin Camp & Associates)

In a "token economy" program at Camarillo State Hospital, a patient is rewarded for positive behavior with tokens that can be exchanged for special privileges. (David Gonzales, Camarillo State Hospital)

advantage—even severely retarded children quickly catch on to the use of tokens.

The therapist (and sometimes also the client) controls the choice of specific behaviors that are to be reinforced and the items or privileges for which the tokens may be exchanged. An advantage of using tokens is that with one item you can reinforce many different people having many different needs or desires.

Good results have been shown for token-economy programs used to improve behavior within institutions (Goldfried & Davison, 1976; Hersen, 1976; Paul & Lentz, 1977). However, the results need to be carefully assessed. First, consider how socially impoverished these institutions were in the first place. Unlike most other human-contact situations, ward life gave patients no positive feedback for making socially acceptable responses. Also, before the token economy was instituted, there were very few things within the hospital that patients wanted to do. Introduction of a token economy often had to be preceded by an effort to discover what patients did want to do, and what new reinforcers could be made available. (Stop and think for a moment how strange and difficult a hospital environment must be if a chance to be alone for a few minutes is so much desired that a patient will be eager to purchase it.) A second problem is predicted by conditioning theory: Once the reinforcements are ended—that is, once the tokens are no longer supplied—the desired behaviors gradually cease to be performed (extinction). This is certainly a problem when patients are discharged into the outside world and their behavior is no longer affected by the direct token-reward relationship. Therapists have begun to work on this problem by trying to shift gradually from tokens to social approval (which *can* be obtained outside the institution) and from delivering the rewards every time a patient performs the desired action to some kind of partial reinforcement schedule. These schedules both are more resistant to extinction and better model the reinforcement patterns that will be delivered in the outside world.

Finally, recall the discussion in Chapter 12 about the effect of rewards on shifting task motivation from an intrinsic to an extrinsic basis. This has relevant implications for the use of token economies. Look at the examples in Table 18-1. Does a patient learn that the reason she talks to other people is not because she wants to hear what they have to say, but because she earns a token for doing so? In the light of intrinsic-extrinsic research, it makes sense

Table 18–1:   Token Economy: A Sample Treatment Program.

Behavior	Reinforcer	Schedule	Control Stimuli
Smiling	Tokens	Each time detected	As part of greeting
Talking to other patients	Tokens	Each time detected	
Sitting	Tokens	Each time detected	Patients must be with others; not alone
Reading (patient looking at printed material)	Tokens	Each time detected	Appropriate time and place: especially not in group meetings or at medications
Grooming—hair	Tokens or praise	Each time detected	
Completion of specific assignment	Tokens or free trip out-of-doors	Each time detected	Prior to reinforcement patient must say something positive about the job she completed

From Schaefer & Martin (1969).

to redesign token economies to avoid reinforcing certain actions that would be better done for intrinsic reasons.

Do token economies produce "cures"? Behavior therapists are not particularly fond of the concept of "cure," which they feel is too closely associated with the medical model of illness. What they would claim for token economy is this: First, the wards where it is installed become more normal and more human places to live. Second, many patients on the system can relearn enough normal behaviors so that they can return to life outside the institution, although their behavior is likely to retain many odd and impaired characteristics. Third, some patients may relearn enough normal behaviors to be candidates for insight therapies. While these are not perfect achievements, therapists using token economies are entitled to ask what other methods produce better results with mental patients.

A good deal of imaginative behavioral therapy has been done with children. Among other things, it illustrates that an operant approach need not actually use tokens. It may use more direct means of reinforcement, as Lovaas (1977) has in treating autistic children. Lovaas developed an intensive behavior modification program to condition appropriate behaviors in psychotic children. His approach focused on speech training, which was carried out six days a week for as long as 7 hours a day. The children were rewarded with food for imitating the sounds produced by the trainer. Lovaas also used punishment in the form of shouting and spanking to suppress undesirable behaviors such as self-destructive acts. Some children took as many as 7,000 trials to learn their first words. As the program progressed, they learned at a faster rate. Treatment lasted 12–14 months, after which the children were transferred to a state hospital. A follow-up study showed that their behavior deteriorated discouragingly over the next four years. Better results were achieved with the next group by training the parents to continue the program's reinforcement schedules at home after the child's initial training was completed. In terms of operant conditioning theory, the intent is to alter the reinforcement contingencies available to the child by altering the actions of the parents. Behavioral therapists increasingly realize that altering the patient's "reinforcement environment" may be one of their most important tasks.

Modeling

Another behavioral approach is modeling. In this relativley new technique, a person who fears a certain object repeatedly observes another person—the model—interacting with the object. For example, a person who fears snakes watches a model handling a snake. After the observer sees that the model survives the experience with no bad consequences, he or she comes to believe there is no basis for an anxiety response (Bandura, 1968; Bandura, Blanchard, & Ritter, 1969). This is a kind of social learning. The person learns something by observing rather than by experiencing it.

Modeling is very effective in overcoming fears and anxieties (Wilson & O'Leary, 1980) because it gives the person a chance to see someone else go through the anxiety-producing situation without getting hurt. Usually people avoid such situations entirely and therefore never learn that they are not harmful.

Modeling is very likely to be combined with guided rehearsal in a treatment program. The model and the client progress through a graded hierarchy of tasks in order to ensure that the client will actually learn the skill demonstrated by the model. The therapist functions much like an acting coach, demonstrating to the client how to act at a job interview, for instance, or what to say when asking for a date.

Social-Skills Training

Recently therapists have developed a set of techniques that are designed to help clients perform more skillfully in social situations. They reason, for instance, that a child may become socially isolated because he or she does not have the interaction skills necessary to draw forth reinforcing actions from other children or teachers. This may lead not only to increased social isolation, but also to depression, a failure to learn more advanced social skills, and a tendency to seek attention by destructive or disruptive actions. Therapists are increasingly willing to teach social skills. They begin with behavioral-rehearsal procedures (Lazarus, 1971) in which the therapist coaches the client in appropriate ways to behave in a specific, concrete social setting. They then move on to role-playing techniques in which the therapist takes the part of a teacher, peer, or potential date and coaches the client through a set of responses that will be socially effective.

Within conditioning theory, this process can be conceptualized as training new responses to stimulus situations in which clients previously made immature or self-defeating responses. It is especially useful if the two responses are incompatible. This technique is based on the observation that even after bad responses are extinguished or suppressed through punishment, they are likely to reappear because they occasionally get rewarded. The key to extinction, then, is learning novel responses to a given stimulus situation that will produce a high frequency of desired reward from the environment. Some of the techniques that we have previously discussed (e.g., aversive conditioning) are used to lower the frequency of maladaptive responses so that the individual has the opportunity to produce new responses that his or her social world will reinforce. For example, if a woman responds to unreasonable demands from her boss by giving the kind of submissive responses that she learned as a child, the therapist would not only seek to extinguish these self-

defeating responses, but would also try to train her in new ones. In fact, assertiveness training works on exactly this principle.

Assertiveness training is a recently developed therapy that seeks to train a selected set of social skills. Assertiveness therapists believe that many people suffer because they have problems making their own needs and desires clear; unassertive people may feel that all too often they "give in to" or are "pushed around by" their fellow workers, friends, or family. Assertiveness trainers try to teach their clients to express their needs and desires in a way that is straightforward and forceful, but not seen by others as threatening or hostile.

Behavioral Techniques for Self-Regulation

Clients meet with therapists infrequently (e.g., once a week for an hour) in the privacy of a consulting room that is totally removed from the reward and punishment contingencies of the client's natural environment. Because behavioral therapists realize that they cannot control everyday events in a client's life, they have recognized that it is often valuable, and occasionally necessary, to alter the behavior of significant others who interact with the client. For example, behavioral therapists attempting to alter the behavior of a child will often spend considerable time with the child's parents, teaching them the principles of reinforcement and alerting them to the often subtle ways that they provide partial reinforcements for their child's maladaptive behavior. Reinforcement theorists have also made many suggestions for how teachers can more effectively run their classrooms on good conditioning principles.

In addition to working closely with parents and teachers of young clients, behavioral therapists also teach clients to administer their own rewards and punishments. One of the most interesting extensions of learning therapy involves the concept of **self-regulation:** The client is challenged to take responsibility for altering his or her own behaviors, and for restructuring the environment in which these behaviors occur. According to learning and conditioning principles, the client is first trained to keep a careful record of the stimulus situations that give rise to a specific maladaptive behavior. If the client has a weight problem, what are the circumstances that prompt eating between meals or overindulging at meals? If the student fails to study until late at night, what are the factors in the environment that promote this self-defeating behavior? Together the client and therapist study the record of such behaviors, and the therapist points out possible environmental contingencies controlling the undesirable behavior.

One technique that we discussed before is developing incompatible responses. The client with a weight problem might learn to go to the company exercise rooms for a workout instead of out to a nearby restaurant where the menu is filled with tempting high-calorie foods. The student with the poor study habits might learn to head to the library at a certain time each night, rather than stopping to check out what's on television in the dorm TV room. Next the client is encouraged to develop self-reinforcement habits. After studying well for a few hours, the student might do something rewarding like visit with a friend for a time-limited study break. Self-punishments may also be part of the process. If the student fails to make it to the library at the nightly appointed hour, he might self-administer a negative task like cleaning his room, or give up a positive reward like watching a favorite TV

program. By putting all of these principles into practice, people can gain control of behaviors that are maladaptive and adopt new behaviors that better serve their life goals.

COGNITIVE MODELS OF THERAPY

As has perhaps occurred to you, some of the therapeutic techniques we have described, although they make good sense, have gotten some distance away from the exact principles of instrumental and classical conditioning. Another set of therapists, drawing on other psychological principles have developed a different set of therapeutic techniques. Rather than starting with maladaptive behaviors, they focus on maladaptive thought.

Cognitive therapies start with the assumption that emotional upsets or abnormal patterns of behavior result from what we think (content) and how we think (process). Even if the problem appears to be one of emotion, behavior, or circumstance, it is our cognitive mediation—our thoughts—that plays the most critical role. Our depressed feelings or inappropriate behaviors are important, but they are products of our inappropriate patterns of thought. If we change our inappropriate ways of thinking and reasoning, our behaviors and feelings will automatically change. Thus cognitive theorists are less concerned with the symptoms than with the thinking process that led to them, and they try to change these thoughts or thinking processes in therapy. The cognitive therapies that are best known are the rational-emotive therapy of Albert Ellis and the cognitive therapy of Aaron Beck.

Ellis: Rational-Emotive Therapy

Ellis's **rational-emotive therapy (RET)** focuses primarily on thought content: that is, on specific irrational thoughts or assumptions that Ellis says lie at the core of abnormal functioning. This approach, which has been most often applied to problems in anxiety and disturbed functioning, argues that therapy should be directed at pointing out the false beliefs people hold that lead to their feelings of anxiety. Some of the more common false beliefs at the root of abnormal functioning are the following (Ellis, 1962):

1. I must be loved or approved of by virtually every significant other person around me.
2. I must be thoroughly competent, adequate, and achieving in all possible respects or I can't consider myself worthwhile.
3. Certain people are bad, wicked, or villainous . . . they should be severely punished for it.
4. It is awful and catastrophic when things are not the way I want them to be.

Rational-emotive therapy tries to show clients how to separate rational from irrational thoughts and accept reality. Ellis emphasizes tolerance of oneself, of others, and of inevitable frustration in the real world. Instead of irrationally thinking "I ought to succeed" or "I must succeed," the client learns to accept the more rational thought, "It would be better to succeed," or "I may fail at this one thing, but that doesn't mean I'm a total failure."

CLIENT: I had another anxiety attack yesterday. I was having lunch with some friends in this really nice restaurant in North Dallas. I felt like I couldn't finish my meal. It was just terrible.

THERAPIST: Okay: Now think back to when you were in the restaurant yesterday, and tell me what you experienced. You know, how you felt and what you were thinking.

CLIENT: Okay. . . . Well, the waiter had just served the main course. I noticed I was really tense. I remember thinking . . . What if I have another panic attack, right here? I might not be able to continue eating. I might even faint. That would be terrible.

THERAPIST: Well, you said that you've never actually fainted in situations like this before. And so my guess is you won't . . . but what if you did? How would it be terrible? Do you mean that you would injure yourself physically or something like that?

CLIENT: No . . . not really. I think I imagine myself, you know, slumped over in my chair. And my friends and everybody else are looking at me, just staring.

THERAPIST: And what are those people thinking?

CLIENT: *(Her eyes begin to tear)* That . . . I can't even have lunch without making an ass of myself . . . that I'm incompetent . . . worthless.

THERAPIST: Okay. Now it looks to me like you think the worst thing that could happen would be that you'd faint. First, that's pretty unlikely, right?

CLIENT: Sure, but what if I *did*?

THERAPIST: Suppose you were in a restaurant and you saw somebody else faint. What would you think about them? Would you judge them to be incompetent and worthless?

CLIENT: I guess I'd think they were, you know, sick. . . . I'd probably try to help them. No . . . I wouldn't think they were . . . bad . . . or worthless. I see what you mean. Maybe they wouldn't ridicule me.

THERAPIST: I think they wouldn't. But *suppose* they did. There you are, slumped in your chair, and you are just regaining consciousness. And everyone in the restaurant . . . your friends . . . everyone . . . they are jeering at you . . . making fun of you. We just agreed that isn't likely to happen, but suppose everybody in the restaurant just happened to behave like purple meanies?

CLIENT: That would be awful . . . I couldn't stand it. I'd just wither up and die.

THERAPIST: You'd literally, physically wither up and die?

CLIENT: Well, when you put it that way. . . . I guess not.

(Rim & Masters, 1979, pp. 383–384)

This requires, in many cases, big changes in the client's basic values and beliefs. In leading clients to this change, RET therapists tend to be more actively involved than therapists who use other approaches. Unlike Rogers's client-centered therapists, for example, RET therapists openly challenge statements they consider irrational: They don't wait for clients to discover irrationality on their own. They give their own personal opinion when asked by clients, and often when not asked. Instead of occasionally interpreting, like psychoanalysts, or restating, like Rogerians, they spend a good deal of time telling their clients the way things are and what is wrong with their thinking.

Among the techniques used by RET therapists are role playing and modeling. Both of these techniques may be used in individual sessions or in groups to show clients in what ways their thinking is unrealistic and what the consequences of this irrationality are for their relationships with others and their own self-perceptions.

RET therpaists also try to show unconditional acceptance of their clients. Unlike Rogerian therapists, who strive to give unconditional acceptance in a nonjudgmental way, RET therapists will criticize their clients for faulty thinking but still demonstrate that they accept them unconditionally, even with their flaws. The hope is that clients can learn to accept themselves even when they are not living up to their self-imposed rules.

Beck: Cognitive Therapy

Aaron Beck's **cognitive therapy** (1972, 1973, 1975) has been most often applied to the problems of depression. Beck traces depressed patterns to both problematic thoughts and distorted thinking processes. He argues that depressed persons have basic "rules," not unlike Ellis's irrational thoughts or

assumptions, that underlie their depression. For example, "It would be terrible if someone else had a low opinion of me," or "Anything less than total success would be a disaster." While Beck does not describe these rules as irrational, he does see them as very limiting because of their arbitrary, extreme, and unyielding nature. These rules give rise to "automatic thoughts"—negative self-verbalizations that pop into a person's head continually throughout the day.

In addition to problematic thoughts (such as the rules and automatic thoughts just described), Beck is concerned with distorted thinking processes, which he says characterize depressed functioning. These distortions in thinking include jumping to conclusions without having enough evidence and drawing too many and too general negative conclusions from a single event. Usually these distorted thinking processes help to lock in a negative self-view and view of the future.

This is a summary and expansion of Beck's cognitive theory of depression that was presented in Chapter 17 (Abnormal Psychology). In light of Beck's theory, the therapy he developed seems a little unexpected. Beck's therapeutic approach is a two-stage one. (Ursnao & Hales, 1986) He deals first with alleviating the depressed state. Therapy begins with some tasks that can lead the person to experience the joy of success—a pleasure that typically escapes very depressed people. Clients are assigned a series of tasks within their range of ability. The series starts with something very simple, such as buying some items at a nearby supermarket, and moves on to harder tasks. As the person's mood becomes somewhat more elevated in the face of undeniable accomplishment, the therapy becomes more cognitive. The therapist begins to probe the disturbed thought processes that underlie the depressed state. Clients are helped to evaluate and challenge these processes rather than accept them automatically. Next they are taught to further identify and challenge the assumptions and style of thinking attached to these automatic thoughts.

A very similar set of therapeutic procedures is currently being developed from ideas implicit in Seligman's learned helplessness theory. His point is that we all draw conclusions from the events that happen to us. For instance, someone who has done poorly at a new task might conclude that this proves he has no ability at the skill measured by the task. Therefore he would be likely to avoid similar tasks in the future. Another person might believe that her failure on a task was due to not trying hard enough. Thus the same failure that the first person experienced as having no ability simply caused the second person to work harder. Therapists are designing "attribution therapy" programs to help people reinterpret the occasional failures that we all experience in more constructive, less defeating ways.

Criticisms of Behavioral and Cognitive Therapies

Both these forms of therapy grew out of experimental traditions. Each laudably employed research to determine whether its technique, elegant in theory, really worked in practice. While those who observe the field agree that these types of therapists are more likely to do outcome studies than colleagues with other theoretical orientations, this type of research is terribly difficult and time-consuming if done well. Thus certain theories may not as yet be adequately tested in the field, despite the willingness of practitioners to submit their work to such evaluations.

In addition, as you may have noticed, both perspectives seem incomplete. For example, the learning perspective doesn't come to terms with the rapid-fire leaps of the schizophrenic's tortured internal logic, or the heavy, almost hopeless, cognitive patterns of the person experiencing a depression. On the other hand, the cognitive therapist doesn't seem to acknowledge that sometimes a person who feels bad about some failure is right—the behavior is maladaptive and the client needs some social-skills training to perform in ways that would be positively reinforced by others.

Cognitive-Behavioral Therapy.   Many therapists working exclusively with either the behavioral or cognitive tradition recognized this incompleteness. Originally, cognitive therapists added behavioral techniques; later some clinicians who began with the learning approach added cognitive methods. As its name implies, **cognitive-behavioral therapy** represents a fusion of these two approaches.

Many behavioral therapists have moved away from complete reliance on the manipulation of reinforcement contingencies. More and more, these therapists have recognized that people's learning can be enhanced by an explicit focus on the generalizations they draw from their experiences or by observing the behavior of other people. In short, a good many behaviorists have become more cognitive in their therapeutic perspective.

In a similar fashion, many cognitive therapists have found that they need to turn their attention to their clients' various maladaptive behaviors in order to fully deal with their problems. They have discovered that paying attention to the reinforcements that their clients receive for certain actions is necessary, and that techniques such as social-skills training and self-regulation are useful.

NEW DEVELOPMENTS IN THERAPY: PROBLEM-CENTERED APPROACHES

Thus far we have presented therapies that are derived from theoretical models of personality and abnormality (see Chapters 15 and 17). However, recall that therapists are faced with making a psychological theory fit the complex problems of a real individual in distress. Many therapists borrow strategies from other perspectives. For example, many clinicians have taken techniques from the well-publicized learning and cognitive therapies and adapted them to their own modality.

Realizing that often no one theory deals successfully with all aspects of a problem, more and more modern therapists have decided to specialize not in theories, but in problems. For example, one group of clinicians specializes in alcoholism, learning all that they can about the range of causes and possible treatments for that condition. They seek information about the genetic underpinnings of alcohol dependency, as well as insight into the personality types that are likely to be prone to alcohol abuse. They also investigate the social milieus that promote alcoholism. They become knowledgeable about the psychochemical effects of the various drugs that are marketed as treatments for alcoholism, and about the relative success rates of other forms of therapy as well. In other words, they learn everything there is to know about alcoholism, and then they look at various therapeutic systems to see what techniques they can apply to the problems of alcoholics.

Other researcher-therapists specialize in anxiety, depression, suicide, or

sexual dysfunction. These therapists recognize that problems in the real world have complex origins—and even more complex forces sustaining them—and they do not think that they can be solved by any single theoretical approach. Within therapeutic circles this combined approach to treatment is common enough to have a name—the *eclectic* or *problem-centered approach.* In this section we will briefly look at some problem-centered approaches to therapy to see how the combined approach works in practice.

Biofeedback

Elevated blood pressure is a problem affecting many people to a greater or lesser degree. One specific problem-centered approach that actually cuts across the biological, learning, and humanistic models to cope with this problem is called *biofeedback training.* The basic premise is that high blood pressure (as well as certain other physiological responses that may be caused by stress) can be lessened if a person can learn to control the bodily responses involved. Experiments have shown that when subjects are given feedback of their present bodily states in the form of audible tones, moving graphs, or dials, they can in turn learn to voluntarily control such bodily reactions as brain-wave pattern, blood pressure, and muscle tension. Since heart rate normally increases as a reaction to fear, for example, people who can learn to control their heart rate can control their fear (see also the biofeedback highlight in Chapter 6).

Biofeedback procedures have been used effectively to deal with hypertension, heart rate arrhythmia, epilepsy, and tension migraine headaches (Runck, 1980). However, it has not always been easy to transfer biofeedback techniques to the world outside the laboratory, where people are subject to the normal tensions of life and cannot be hooked up to the biofeedback device. Amid the activity and stress of a normal workday, for instance, a person may find it hard to remember and to practice the exact techniques used in the laboratory to reduce heart rate. Also, a person who is not hooked up to the feedback device may be unable to tell whether attempts to reduce heart rate and muscle tension have been effective. Perhaps for these reasons, general relaxation training has often proved to be about as effective as more elaborate biofeedback procedures.

One of the most promising future applications of biofeedback is to compensate for accident- or disease-induced neuromotor disability where there has been deterioration of muscle and motor functioning. It has been suggested that the deterioration occurs because the central nervous system cannot sense the signals that flow back to it from the muscles. The use of biofeedback to amplify the faint signals and to bypass damaged signal pathways may enable the victim to bring muscle movements under voluntary control once again. It is possible to leave miniature feedback devices permanently in place to provide a constant source of feedback information.

Clearly, the biofeedback approach employs techniques from the biological, learning, and humanistic models. The biological perspective is represented by the focus on the bodily functions as the center of the problem. The learning approach is at the heart of the training program, in which direct control over involuntary processes is learned by observation and feedback. The function of biofeedback training as a technique that enables people to get in touch with hidden dimensions of their bodily responses has sometimes led to its classification as a humanistic therapy.

Therapy for Sexual Dysfunction

Some of the problems our society considers important and valid are particularly resistant to a therapeutic approach based on a single theory. One such example is *sexual dysfunction*. In their book *Human Sexual Inadequacy* Masters and Johnson (1970) suggest that for sexual dysfunctions, two causes are predominant: a person's tendency to adopt a spectator role during intercourse, and a person's fear of performing inadequately. When someone focuses undue attention on *performance* during intercourse, either of these problems can create inhibitions about enjoying the normal sensations that lead to sexual satisfaction.

Even a transitory case of sexual dysfunction can lead to long-term sexual dysfunction in couples. Suppose a male executive is going through a particularly anxious period in his life and uses tranquilizers to help him deal with the stress. The medication dulls his sexual arousal and, coupled with whatever effect the job anxieties are having on him, makes it difficult for him to maintain an erection. (Here we see a physiological or biological component of the problem. Because sexual dysfunction may be linked to a drug's side effects, the sex therapist must be knowledgeable to some degree about pharmacology.) The result is that after a few failures, the man's performance anxieties build up. Because his attention has been focused on his performance, and more particularly on his performance failure, the man now steps outside himself and begins to examine his sexual performance. (This is not conducive to any improvement in the near future!) This scenario exemplifies the *vicious circle* characteristic of many psychological problems in the real world. Anxiety inhibits good performance, and a failed performance leads to more anxiety and therefore an increased prospect of future failure.

Next an interpersonal component contributes to the problem. Unfortunately, almost any way the man's wife responds may contribute to his problem. If she continues to be physically affectionate, her husband may interpret her manner as a demand for sexual intercourse, a demand he fears he cannot satisfy. His anxieties cause him to give his wife cues to keep her distance. He may develop avoidance patterns—for instance, working so late that his wife is asleep before he comes to bed. Or, if his wife is less affectionate physically out of a desire not to make demands on him, the anxious husband may defensively interpret her behavior as a rejection of his sexually inadequate self.

One can see how these problems might persist long after the specific events that started them have disappeared. Depending on a therapist's perceptions of the background causes of sexual dysfunction, the therapeutic techniques used will vary. The difficulties that many couples experience when talking directly about sex may exacerbate the situation; in these cases, sex therapists often seek first to improve the couple's communication skills about sexual matters. Because of a psychosexual trauma or a set of religious, ethnic, or cultural beliefs, a person may fear sexual intercourse or believe that it is wrong, evil, or not pleasurable. Because of inadequate instruction, a man or a woman may not know how the rather complicated human reproductive system works. Excessive intake of alcohol or physiological problems may hamper sexual performance. Once the therapist identifies what conditions are contributing to the couple's problems, an eclectic set of therapeutic techniques is available to deal with them.

One element in almost all treatments of sexual dysfunction is anxiety reduction. The visualization techniques of desensitization hierarchies

(Wolpe, 1958) are used, but the therapist also usually arranges desensitization experiences in real sexual encounters between the couple. These real-life anxiety-reduction techniques are often effective in reducing sexual dysfunction, as one might anticipate from the central role of performance anxiety in causing sexual dysfunction. Information about the human reproductive system and the physical aspects of sexual intercourse is also frequently given by sex therapists. Education can be very helpful, particularly if it teaches the range of experiences and feelings that are normal aspects of the process. People who have sexual dysfunction problems often have a limited knowledge of the body's system of sexual responsiveness (Lo Piccolo & Hogan, 1978). Many other standard therapeutic techniques, often of a cognitive-behavioral sort, are used to explore whatever negative feelings or attitudes might be contributing to the sexual dysfunction. Couples may also need help in learning to communicate their sexual needs to each other without embarrassment and misinterpretations. Finally, a medical consultation might be suggested to explore any physiological conditions contributing to the problem.

Sexual dysfunction therapy seems to work. Although evidence from tightly controlled outcome studies is scarce, a great deal of clinical evidence supports this conclusion (Lo Piccolo & Lo Piccolo, 1978). It is interesting to note, too, that sex therapists draw on all the perspectives we have discussed, although the cognitive-behavioral and biological approaches are most central to this type of therapy.

GROUP THERAPIES

Most of the forms of treatment that we have described thus far involve a one-to-one relationship between client and therapist: that is, a client meets privately with his or her therapist. An alternative form of increasing popularity is **group therapy,** in which several clients simultaneously meet with a therapist. Obviously such a format is an efficient use of the therapist's time and is usually cheaper for clients. Moreover, group therapy seems to have certain therapeutic advantages over individual therapy. For one thing, members of a group may learn from one another's difficulties. It is sometimes easier to observe oneself by looking at and listening to others. Also, people whose problems have a distinct interpersonal dimension often find the group setting the ideal place to develop the interpersonal skills they sorely need.

Group therapies, like individual therapies, differ in the theories that underlie them. Some depend on the models we have discussed so far, and use group settings as an efficient and powerful means of achieving desired ends. The goals of the therapist are to influence individually each member of the group, but not primarily to have group members influence one another. For instance, several group therapies have been derived from learning and conditioning principles. In a *group desensitization session* people who share snake phobias or anxieties about tests may be led together through a desensitization hierarchy. In *social-skills training* a group of shy or unassertive individuals may be coached by a therapist in a set of shyness-overcoming actions. As in theatrical acting classes, individuals may learn not only from the therapist's response to their performance, but also from the therapist's response to the performance of others.

The protagonist in a psychodrama is walled in symbolically by a chair held by another group member. The material produced by this directed role playing is then interpreted psychodynamically by the therapist. (George S. Zimbel/Monkmeyer Press)

Other group procedures are derived from the psychoanalytic perspective. *Psychodrama* is a form of insight-oriented group therapy. Here a person is surrounded by other individuals who, at the direction of the director-therapist, play roles in the person's life. For example, a man may be instructed to play a scene requesting something from his mother. Using the material thus produced, the therapist can make psychodynamic interpretations about the sources of the man's underlying conflicts. Here the people in the group are not present because they have the same problem. Their function is to serve as "actors" who can take on the roles of another group member's punishing parent, inconsiderate boss, or any other person in the member's life who may have had an important influence on his or her current problem. Thus the experience of the interaction and associated feelings is made more vivid for the individual whose personal problem is the subject for the session's psychodrama. Remaining group members serve as an audience that later comments on the action and discusses its meaning for their own personal experience.

All of the theories discussed above derive from individual perspectives on abnormality. The function of the group is to assist the individual in developing interactional skills, or to offer another avenue to personal insight—empathy with another's problem. Another type of therapy involving a so-called group is *family therapy* or *family systems therapy*. This modality brings together parents, children, and sometimes even grandparents to work on problems. The family, not the patient, is seen as the unit in need of assistance (Minuchin & Fishman, 1981). Drawing on theories of social interaction, the guiding theory suggests that when an individual has a problem, he or she is actually expressing a problem that is shared by the entire family or "system." More specifically, the person who appears to have the problem—the "identified patient" or "scapegoat"—may not even be the major source of the family's difficulties. For example, a little girl might be afraid to go to school—a condition known as *school phobia*. The family therapist would explore beneath the surface of the child's behavior and find perhaps that the parents are experiencing marital difficulties, and what the child fears is not going to school, but rather what will happen when she leaves home. In fact, family therapy is often used in working with children. While working with children alone can seem futile, working with them in the context of their families enables a therapist to deal with their problems in a more comprehensive and successful way.

This is so, family therapists would assert, because the problems presented (e.g., anorexia nervosa; see Chapter 17) are being *shown* by the child but are a *product* of the tensions within the family system. This is particularly true of families that do not acknowledge conflicts: The anorexia of a daughter or the delinquent behavior of a son deflects attention from more basic conflicts. Family therapy, to be successful, must turn attention back to those conflicts and show how the identified disorder is due to these underlying conflicts rather than to the pathology of a single family member.

Family therapists tend to assume that conflict within family relationships is inevitable (Schwartz & Schwartz, 1980), but that many couples or families refuse to acknowledge this because they believe in the cultural stereotype that suggests conflicts do not occur in "good families." Family therapists directly focus on addressing conflicts, developing communication skills, and negotiating strategies among family members (Hsu, 1986).

In sessions family members work together on such matters as communication and interaction patterns. As members become better able to relate to

one another, the initial presenting problem and others that surface in the course of treatment improve significantly.

CRISIS PREVENTION AND COMMUNITY PSYCHOLOGY

The model of suicide-prevention centers has led to the development of **crisis-intervention** programs for a wide range of difficulties. These take different forms, but all serve to make a trained person available, either over the phone or in personal interviews, to help people faced with a crisis. All sorts of problems may be encountered—from floods, accidents, or illness to crises such as desertion by a spouse, sexual anxieties, or abuse of some sort.

Not all crises are equally dramatic, and the range of problems suggests the lack of any easy system of classification. One person may call in reference to a psychotic family member and thus present a family problem. Another caller may be on the verge of suffering a cascading series of interrelated problems because the plant where she works is closing and she is about to lose her job. A mother may call to report that her son is dealing drugs because easy money is available that way and there are no legitimate job prospects.

Suicide.   One of society's most serious yet least understood problems is suicide. A major difficulty is that there are a great many myths that tend to lull relatives, friends, and even professionals into a false sense of security about the likelihood of someone committing suicide. The recent increase in suicide attempts and actual suicides has led to the establishment of suicide-prevention centers around the country. They provide around-the-clock hot-line telephone services for people in distress.

A telephone worker at such a center will seek to (1) establish a relationship with the caller and obtain information; (2) clarify the central problem; (3) assess the potential for suicide; (4) assess the person's strengths and resources; and (5) develop with the person a constructive plan of action, including involvement in an appropriate treatment program.

Suicide-prevention centers typically provide in-person treatment services and personnel for longer-term intervention in addition to the hotline, assessment, and referral service. These centers are staffed by psychiatrists, psychologists, social workers, other professionals, and trained nonprofessionals (paraprofessionals).

Community Psychology.   The problems of everyday living, such as those discussed at length in the chapter on stress (Chapter 16), defy easy classification and often are not "psychological" in nature. However, thoughtful psychologists realize that if these early problems are not solved, then psychological problems may indeed ensue. For example, a father loses his job because the plant closes. He is frustrated and feels diminished, problems that are compounded by his lack of training and poor job-seeking skills. He stays home, watches television, drinks, and falls into a pattern of spouse or child abuse to vent his anger. Now let's say that the wife's elderly mother becomes disabled as a result of Alzheimer's disease and comes to live with them. They cannot cope with the bureaucratic maze that might provide funds for home care or doctor visits, so they pay for all her bills themselves. As time goes on, the grandmother needs more and more care. The teenagers in the family be-

come embarrassed to bring friends home. In addition, they are now increasingly required to assist in the grandmother's care when the parents are out, which keeps them from participating in age-appropriate afterschool activities. Their schoolwork suffers. One child in particular becomes moody, depressed, and withdrawn. The message of community psychology is that this hypothetical family is an example of how real psychological problems often develop for real people. A community psychologist would advocate early intervention at the first major sign of family distress—for example, counseling for the father to assist him in finding new work. Early intervention is likely to be more economical than waiting until the problems are magnified in scope.

Community psychologists distinguish among three types of intervention. **Primary prevention** is concerned with eliminating chronic social problems such as inadequate housing or unemployment, and attempts to reduce the incidence of new cases of mental disorder. Not surprisingly, the goals of primary prevention are long-range and very difficult to realize. **Secondary prevention** aims to identify problems early on, before they become chronic. For example, one might arrange for a visiting nurse to medicate an aging family member each day, before her forgetfulness puts too much stress on other family members. **Tertiary prevention** deals with the immediate aftereffects of personal crises and thus includes many of the therapeutic techniques described in this chapter. Community psychologists approve of these techniques and often practice them, but strongly recommend that more effort, and more money, be put into the earlier forms of prevention.

In summary, the message of community psychology is that a focus on prevention could avoid many problems (Caplan, 1964). Far less costly and drastic efforts, applied earlier in time, can stem the progress of abnormal functioning. Thus community psychologists continue to emphasize primary and secondary, along with tertiary, prevention efforts.

THE EFFECTIVENESS OF THERAPY

Over the past few decades, with the emergence of many new approaches to therapy, there has also emerged a debate in which the effectiveness of therapy itself has been questioned. This debate involves not only the effectiveness of therapy in general, but also how the different forms of therapy compare in terms of effectiveness.

The issue of general therapy effectiveness is a very difficult one for several reasons. First of all, how are we to define success? Is our criterion to be partial change or total change? Change in the behavioral, emotional, or cognitive spheres? Change seen by the person, the therapist, a friend, or a relative? Second, there are so many forms of therapy that we cannot properly speak of "therapy" as if it represents a general process. Moreover, there are many different kinds of problems in abnormal functioning, so it is impossible to talk about the general effectiveness of psychotherapy. Furthermore, many other life events have an impact on people while they are involved in therapy. How can we sort out these factors in evaluating the role of therapy?

When we seek to compare the effectiveness of particular therapies, we run into these same questions, plus additional difficulties. A major problem is that the various forms of psychotherapy differ in their definitions of psychotherapy success and goals. Then we are faced with the fact that every therapist practices his or her orientation in at least a slightly different manner. For example, there are many differences in technique and interpretation among psychoanalytic psychotherapists. Similarly, there are many vari-

ations among behavioral therapists. How, then, can we confidently compare the effectiveness of psychoanalysis to that of behavioral therapy? Are we comparing processes or therapists? Furthermore, there are many different variables and factors that bear on therapy outcome: different settings, formats, personality factors, and so on. Certainly these will complicate our comparison of the effectiveness of various therapies.

It is not surprising, therefore, that despite a great deal of research over the past few decades, our conclusions about the effectiveness of psychotherapy are still tentative. Here are some of the things we do seem to know:

1. Psychotherapy can be a helpful and effective process for certain problems and individuals (Bergin, 1971; Smith & Glass, 1977).
2. Sometimes psychotherapy will provide no help or even have a negative effect (Eysenck, 1952).
3. Often a spontaneous remission will occur after a period of time whether or not the person has been in therapy. Such improvements may be due to factors in the individual's personal life or to some internal factors.
4. In direct comparisons the major psychotherapy approaches (psychoanalytic, behavioral, humanistic) often demonstrate similar overall rates of effectiveness (Luborsky, Singer, & Luborsky, 1975; Smith & Glass, 1977).
5. At the same time, some therapy approaches seem superior for specific difficulties (Luborsky & Spence, 1971). For example, the behavioral approach seems most effective with phobias, and the biological approach of antipsychotic medications seems most effective with schizophrenic disorders (May, 1968).

Recognizing the difficulties of therapy outcome studies, and realizing that any such study, to be useful and valid, would have to include multiple therapists and multiple research sites, the National Institutes of Mental Health organized one such large-scale therapy outcome study. The mental disorder that they chose to study was depression.

Why did they choose depression? First, because it is one of the most prevalent mental disorders, and thus any treatment that is found to be successful will benefit large numbers of people. Second, it is a disorder for which several competing forms of clinical treatment have been developed. Various psychoactive drugs have been thought to help depression, and several forms of "talk therapy" are available as well.

Three forms of therapy were selected for the research. The first involved the prescription of modern antidepressive drugs. The second involved a standardized version of Beck's cognitive therapy for depression. The third focused on an anlaysis of the interpersonal relations of the depressed person. Notice that these therapies were well chosen. The drug treatment is based on biological approaches, Beck's theory is both a good representative of cognitive theories and one for which there was previous evidence of effectiveness (Rush, Beck, Kovacs & Hollon, 1977), and the interpersonal relations theory was one generally based on moden insight procedures.

The research was conducted by several universities located in several cities across the country. Clinicians were trained to give somewhat standardized versions of one of the two talk therapies. Only the initial results are in, and they have not yet been completely analyzed at this writing. However, the early results indicate that all three forms of therapy are effective, in that they produce more improvement than is found in untreated persons. Further,

there is some evidence that the cognitive therapy gains are slightly better maintained at time of first follow-up.

As these studies show, research efforts on the outcomes of various forms of therapy are accelerating, and should lead to more effective therapy. We are becoming increasingly aware of the strengths and weaknesses, the similarities and differences as well as the key variables of the various forms of therapy.

A cautious note needs to be struck here. The research on the treatment of many disorders is at a very early stage. For instance, alcoholism has been regarded as a unitary disease, and a single treatment has been sought for it. As it becomes increasingly clear (Holden, 1987; Cloninger, 1987) that alcoholism is not a unitary disease, it makes sense to consider the possibility that different treatments will be effective, depending on the connection of the alcoholism to either personality disorders or affective disorders like anxiety and depression, and factors in the patient's life such as job stability and the stability of interpersonal relationships. Until research recognizes the existence of these complexities, no very clear picture about effective treatments is likely to emerge, and exactly as this suggests, no clear picture of effective treatments for alcoholism has yet emerged. On other disorders, our understanding of effective treatments appears to be more advanced. But it is entirely possible that new research will eventually make certain treatments widely favored today seem as unenlightened as those practices from the early days of institutional care for the mentally ill.

FUTURE DIRECTIONS FOR THERAPY

Therapy is in large part a "user-driven" activity. The problems that therapists treat are the ones people choose to bring to them (and, to be realistic, the ones regarded as legitimate claims for payment by medical benefit plans). Thus to a large extent social trends help define the types of problems for which one can and should seek therapy. For example, consider the recent growth and popularity of therapies for sexual dysfunction. Is it really the case that lately there has been a great increase in sexual dysfunction? Probably not—it is simply a problem that people are more willing to talk about in the 1980s. This greater frankness, and the favorable publicity surrounding the careful and reassuringly "medical" approach of Masters and Johnson, among others, have combined to create a clientele for that form of therapy. In the future we can expect to see more new therapies developed as our society's "notion" of what constitutes a serious problem evolves.

This tendency will probably be strengthened by a trend within the therapeutic community itself—namely, to show greater concern for the specific problems brought to therapy, rather than viewing them as manifestations of other, underlying problems. For example, if a pregnant woman, knowing the dangers of smoking to the fetus, comes to therapy to stop smoking, the therapist will need to work on that specifically. Giving the client insight into why she smokes is beside the point, unless it helps brings about a reduction or cessation of smoking.

All this suggests that an increase in problem-centered therapies is likely, with a corresponding decrease in exclusively insight-oriented therapies (Woolfolk, 1984). In effect, a more "consumerist" orientation is likely to emerge. The newer versions of consumer-oriented, problem-centered therapies are expected to be eclectic in nature, drawing on various models for

whatever techniques can be shown to be most effective. This new orientation is also likely to have implications for the way therapy is carried out. It may move away from office talk sessions into settings closer to the context of the client's problem. For example, sexual dysfunction therapists eventually deal with their clients' problem by coaching them in what to do in actual sexual encounters. Similarly, therapists are likely, whenever possible, to help clients confront phobias and anxieties in feared real-life situations. Thus more and more therapists will be leaving the confines of offices and clinics to accompany their clients into the real world (Davison & Neale, 1986).

The trend to move therapy toward serious consideration of clients' goals is converging with the trend to tackle those goals in a problem-centered, eclectic way. However, it would be inappropriate to conclude this section without briefly considering some fundamental concerns for the practice of therapy at present and in the future. As we have seen, most therapies seek to adjust individuals to what is happening around them and to help the individual become a smoothly functioning member of society. If this means helping a college professor reduce stage fright before lecturing, or a college student reduce anxiety before taking exams, it is hard to raise any objections. But what if the therapist is helping a racist police officer adjust to keeping blacks "in their place"? Worse still, what if the therapist is dealing with an SS soldier in Hitler's Germany (as actually happened)? Admittedly, such extreme examples may oversimplify complex issues. Nonetheless, they call attention to moral and ethical questions that must be considered by the client, the therapist, and society.

SUMMARY

1. *Therapy* can be defined as a set of procedures designed to produce positive change in an individual's cognitions, emotions, or behaviors, or all three. It involves applying various theories of personality in an effort to reduce or eliminate abnormal behavior.

2. In the 1960s the community health movement introduced such practices as public education about mental health, crisis hotlines, ongoing psychotherapy services, and community treatment centers offering free or inexpensive care. The deinstitutionalization movement has not been well implemented, resulting in both a rising homeless population and readmissions to institutions.

3. In the biological model of therapy the role of treatment is to change the person's biological functioning. This may be done through *chemotherapy* (drugs), *electroshock treatment,* or *psychosurgery.*

4. Psychoactive drugs, discovered in the 1950s, had a major effect on the quality of care in public hospitals by making possible outpatient treatment and reduced inpatient population, and also by improving treatment prognoses. Some of the possible gains here were lost when patients were discharged to streets rather than community care facilities.

5. *Psychoanalysis* uses verbal techniques and attempts to solve problems by bringing unconscious conflicts into consciousness, where they may be confronted and resolved by the person. Techniques include *free association, interpretation,* and *transference.*

6. The humanistic-existential approach to therapy involves attempting to help people get in touch with themselves and subsequently take charge of their lives and behaviors. Among the various kinds of humanistic-existential therapies are Carl Rogers's *client-centered therapy* and Fritz Perls's *Gestalt therapy.*

7. The behavioral model of therapy involves extinguishing maladaptive patterns and learning more appropriate ones. Techniques include *systematic desensitization, implosion therapy, aversive counterconditioning, token economies,* and *modeling* and *social-skills training.*

8. In cognitive therapies the focus is on thoughts and thinking processes and how they must be changed. Ellis's *rational-emotive therapy (RET)* attempts to show the client how to separate rational from irrational thoughts and to accept reality through the use of role-playing and modeling techniques. Beck's cognitive therapy attempts to reveal a person's basic "rules" and

distorted thinking processes and, subsequently, to change the "rules."

9. Cognitive-behavioral therapy emphasizes the multiple influences on human thinking and behaviors. This approach combines several perspectives and uses a variety of techniques.

10. Problem-centered therapies focus on distinct problems and may take an eclectic approach. Therapy for sexual dysfunction is one example of this type of therapy.

11. Group therapies bring clients together to work on individual problems. Drawing on social-interactional approaches, *family systems therapy* sees the entire family as the unit in need of treatment.

12. Community psychologists emphasize the prevention of problems. They distinguish between *primary prevention* (or eliminating chronic social problems affecting many families), *secondary prevention* (early identification of a potential problem), and *tertiary prevention* (crisis intervention).

13. Producing change in another person inevitably raises moral and ethical questions. These questions must be considered by the client, the therapist, and society.

SUGGESTED READINGS

BELKIN, G. S. (1980). *Contemporary psychotherapies*. Chicago: Rand McNally. Offers an overview of the many forms of psychotherapy practiced in the United States today and includes a wide range of clinical case studies.

BRODSKY, A., & HARE-MUSTIN, R. (Eds.) (1980). *Women and psychotherapy*. New York: Guilford Press. A book with the general purpose of drawing together the research literature on women and psychotherapy. Topics include gender differences in rates of experiencing various disorders, gender differences in therapeutic process and outcome, and some alternatives to traditional therapeutic approaches to "the problems of women."

ELLIS, A., & GREIGER, R. (Eds.) (1977). *Handbook of rational-emotive therapy*. New York: Springer. A compendium of chapters on rational-emotive therapy, its uses, and its successes. This book includes a chapter by Ellis on the clinical theory underlying the therapy.

GARFIELD, S. L., & BERGIN, A. E. (Eds.) (1978). *Handbook of psychotherapy and behavior change* (2nd ed.). New York: John Wiley. Good appraisal of the research in the field of psychotherapy, with leading theorists focusing on such issues as methodology, psychotherapeutic processes, outcomes, various approaches, and new developments in the field.

HOFFMAN, L. *Foundations of family therapy* (1981). New York: Basic Books. This book gives a thoughtful presentation of the systems approach to family therapy, often from a historical perspective.

LICHTENSTEIN, E. (1980). *Psychotherapy: Approaches and applications*. Monterey, Cal.: Brooks/Cole. A broad look at psychotherapy, including economic, social, and political influences, with an evaluative framework.

PERLS, F. T. (1969). *Gestalt therapy verbatim*. Monterey, Cal.: Real People Press. Provides a good introduction to Gestalt therapy by the intriguing theorist and therapist who developed this approach.

ROGERS, C. R. (1951). *Client-centered therapy*. Boston: Houghton Mifflin. A comprehensive introduction to the client-centered approach by the originator of this form of therapy.

VALENSTEIN, E. S. (1986). *Great and desperate cases: The rise and decline of psychosurgery and other radical treatments for mental illness*. New York: Basic Books. A detailed and fascinating account of how desires for scientific prestige, and quick and "efficient" biologically based cures, made dangerous psychosurgery briefly popular.

19 Social Behavior

In this chapter and the next we will be discussing how individuals interact with each other and with groups—the content of **social psychology.** Social psychology studies the ways in which people influence and are influenced by those around them. Social psychologists focus on such topics as liking and loving, conformity, communication, and prejudice. It probably strikes you that many of the topics studied by social psychologists are also studied by personality and developmental psychologists. But the approach social psychologists take is quite different. If we can make that difference apparent here, then you will have an easier time grasping the essence of social psychology.

Social psychology emphasizes present rather than past influences on a person's behavior. It also attempts to predict human behavior by understanding the cognitive representations that people construct of their situations. An example may make this more clear. Suppose a man in a group *conforms,* in the sense of supporting a certain opinion held by others around him. A personality psychologist would focus on the particular elements in this man's personality that led him to conform. A Freudian thinker, on the other hand, might infer childhood events that caused this man to have a dependent personality. In contrast, a social psychologist would first look closely at the man's circumstances. Were the other group members unanimous in their opinion or were there some dissenters? If some members dissented from a group opinion in the past, how were they treated? Second, the social psychologist would attempt to understand the conforming individual's thoughts about the

This painting by Auguste Renoir, "Luncheon Boating Party," evokes the colorful and complex nature of social processes. (The Phillips Collection, Washington, D.C.)

matter. Did he truly agree with the view held by the other people in his group, or did he conform because he believed they were more powerful than he?

We can now introduce some terms that summarize the points made in the example and that will be useful through these final two chapters. Social psychologists work from a *situationalist perspective:* Their first source of explanation for a behavior is the ongoing factors inherent in the situation. Also, the social-psychological perspective is *phenomenological,* in that it begins by taking into account the world view presently held by the person performing the behavior. This view does not discount past actions. Obviously, people's past experiences can lead them to a certain set of interpretations of events in the present. For instance, if your past experiences have led you to expect other people to be hostile, then you will very likely see a crowd of people who surround you in a busy public place as hostile. You will feel threatened and respond with fear, fight, or flight. The point the social psychologist insists on is that it is the way you *represent* past experiences to yourself in the present that determines your present action.

This chapter begins with a discussion of how people as "social actors" form their definitions of the situations they find themselves in and, more particularly, how they come to conceptualize the intentions, motivations, and personalities of those they interact with.

ATTRIBUTION

The processes of interpersonal perception are similar to the general processes of perception discussed in Chapter 4. Like object perception, person perception is a categorical process. That is, the details we perceive about other people—their clothes, their body postures, and the like—lead us to make inferences about the categories to which they belong. The middle-aged person in the coat and tie standing in front of the classroom is the teacher, the young person in blue jeans talking to the teacher is obviously a student, and so on.

Person perception, like object perception, is done by making rapid inferences from fragments of information received by the senses. As with all guessing processes, the perceptual inferencing process can "go wrong" and lead the perceiver to make incorrect categorical decisions. The middle-aged person in the coat and tie may suddenly sit down with the other students, and the person in blue jeans may start lecturing.

In one way, person perception is obviously different from object perception. Unlike rocks, trees, and other inanimate objects, people have intentions, plans, and personalities. This means that part of the task of perceiving other people is "looking behind" their actions to discover what they are "really like." **Attribution theories** describe the ways in which we go about developing explanations for and interpretations of the actions of others.

The process of attributing characteristics and motives to another person is a complex one, involving interpretation and judgment. Consequently, different perceivers will see a certain person in different and even contradictory ways because different observers have (1) different experiences with the person, (2) different impressions of the person, (3) different beliefs about the nature of personality, (4) different rules for making attributions, (5) different opportunities to observe the person, or (6) different perspectives on the situation in which they encounter the person. In the following sections we will consider each of these factors in turn.

Experience and Attribution

People may have different experiences with another person because they meet that person in different roles or settings. Students who see a professor only in a large lecture class may attribute some of the inevitably formal nature of that situation to the character of the professor and perceive her as distant, ironic, witty, and pedantic. But the professor's children may see her as close, warm, and relaxed. Her colleagues may have yet a third view of her. The point is that these different perspectives are held by people who have had systematically different experiences with that person and have thereby been led to systematically differing attributions of her personality.

First Impressions and Attribution

It can be expected that the first impressions we form of others will be highly influential in our final impressions of their personalities. An experiment by Luchins (1942) vividly illustrates this. Read the following description and see what impressions you draw about Jim:

> Jim left the house to get some stationery. He walked out into the sun-filled street with two of his friends, basking in the sun as he walked. Jim entered the stationery store, which was full of people. Jim talked with an acquaintance while he waited for the clerk to catch his eye. On his way out, he stopped to chat with a school friend who was just coming into the store. Leaving the store, he walked toward school. On his way out he met the girl to whom he had been introduced the night before. They talked for a short while, and then Jim left for school.
>
> After school Jim left the classroom alone. Leaving the school, he started on his long walk home. The street was filled with brilliant sunshine. Jim walked down the street on the shady side. Coming down the street toward him, he saw the pretty girl whom he had met on the previous evening. Jim crossed the street and entered a candy store. The store was crowded with students, and he noticed a few familiar faces. Jim waited quietly until the counterman caught his eye and then gave his order. Taking his drink, he sat down at a side table. When he had finished his drink he went home.

Why do you think Jim crossed the street? Why did he sit by himself? When Luchins showed subjects these paragraphs, they usually said that Jim crossed the street not to avoid the girl, but to buy something at the store, and that he then sat by himself not because he wanted to be alone, but because he had some work to do. But these interpretations of Jim's actions were caused by the subjects' first impression of Jim as a gregarious person. The first paragraph does indeed describe actions that seem characteristic of an outgoing, extroverted individual. However, the actions described in the second paragraph are those of a withdrawn, introverted person. Indeed, when Luchins reversed the order of these two paragraphs, subjects thought him was a shy person who avoided contact with other people.

Often, as in this example, the first information received has more influence than information received later, a phenomenon known as the **primacy effect.** First impressions of people do tend to stay with us. Still, under certain circumstances, the last information carries more weight, a phenomenon known as the **recency effect** (see Chapter 7).

Either Primacy or Recency can make some thoughts more salient, or "prime" them. If you had just been thinking about money, for example, you might interpret the word *bank* differently than if you had just been thinking

about rivers. This is because one sense of the word has, by virtue of being recently thought about, become easier to imagine. The technical term for this is **construct accessibility.** As an example, recite the following words as many times as it takes to say them five times in a row correctly without looking at the page.

Reckless   Conceited   Aloof   Stubborn

Now read the following paragraph.

> Donald spent a great amount of his time in search of what he liked to call excitement. He had already climbed Mt. McKinley, shot the Colorado rapids in a kayak, driven in a demolition derby, and piloted a jet-powered boat—without knowing very much about boats. He had risked injury, even death, a number of times. Now he was in search of new excitement. He was thinking that perhaps he would do some skydiving or maybe cross the Atlantic in a sailboat. By the way he acted, one could readily guess that Donald was well aware of his ability to do many things well. Other than business engagements, Donald's contact with people was rather limited. He felt that he really did not need to rely on anyone. Once Donald made up his mind to do something, it was as good as done, no matter how long it might take or how difficult the going might be. Only rarely did he change his mind, even when it might well have been better if he had.

Do you like Donald? If you do not like him, you may have been affected by construct accessibility. Some subjects in a study memorized the same words that you did, and they didn't like Donald very much at all (Higgins, Rholes, & Jones, 1977). A natural reaction, you say? Not for some other subjects, who memorized a different set of words. They had to recite the words *adventurous, self-confident, independent,* and *persistent.* When they read about Donald's sensation-seeking, they saw it in a more positive light than you have—as adventurous rather than reckless. When he stuck to his guns in the face of adversity, they saw him as persistent rather than stubborn, and so on. Their overall impression of Donald was positive rather than negative, even though they read the same story. This is probably because they were using the positive connotations that were easily brought to mind from the memory part of the study.

Implicit Personality Theories

Social psychologists have recognized that we all have our own implicit personality theories that we apply to people we meet. An implicit personality theory consists of our beliefs about the traits that are likely to occur together in people; for example, some people believe that musical ability and a sense of humor go hand in hand, or that someone who does not look you straight in the eye is bound to be untrustworthy.

So, different people can make very different judgments about the same individual, for two reasons: either their first impressions differ, or their different implicit personality theories cause them to come to different conclusions on the basis of the same first impression.

Attribution Rules

Sometimes our implicit personality theories don't help us—for instance, when we are able to observe only one action of another person and yet need to make a judgment about what that person is like from this scanty informa-

tion. When, for example, do we conclude that a kind action means that the person who committed that action is kind? Jones and Davis (1965) pointed out that we learn relatively little from the socially desirable actions of a person. We cannot tell if someone who makes cheerful conversation when we meet him or her for the first time really likes us or is just fulfilling social norms of politeness. However, an unusual, unexpected, or inappropriate behavior is assumed to reflect an intention by an individual to act in that way. We infer that the person had an intention that corresponded to the choice of behavior.

In order to infer the intention that lies behind another's behavior, we analyze the social circumstances that surround the action. These interpretations are called **attributions** (Jones & Davis, 1965). One important element of the circumstances, and therefore one that people frequently use, has to do with the *status* of the actor relative to the perceiver. This is why an unmarried heiress (the perceiver) doubts the flattery of the penniless suitor (the actor) more than she would if he were a rich man. To demonstrate the effect of status on our inferences, Thibaut and Riecken (1955) had male college students try to persuade two other students (actually confederates of the experimenter) to donate blood. In each subject's hearing one of the confederates described himself as a graduate law student, while the other confederate described himself as a freshman. Since the subjects were predominantly sophomores and juniors, they had lower status than the graduate student and higher status than the freshman.

Both confederates let the subjects persuade them to give blood, at which point the subjects believed that the "experiment" was over. But at the last minute the experimenter just happened to ask subjects why they thought that each of the confederates had agreed to give blood. Subjects typically said that the graduate law student agreed because he was that kind of person—warm, likable, generous, and so on. In other words, they drew the conclusion that his behavior *corresponded* with, or was an accurate reflection of, his underlying personality. This is called a "correspondent inference." As for the lowly freshman, his compliance earned him nothing in the eyes of subjects. Subjects generally said that the freshman was most likely pressured into giving blood by the experimental situation, and that he had probably agreed to please them and the experimenter. Like the heiress with the impoverished suitor, they discounted his good intentions as an explanation for his actions because they thought he had sufficient other reasons for behaving generously.

Another factor affecting our attributions is that people tend to look for information confirming their initial hypotheses and expectations in a situation. This *confirmatory bias* (see Chapter 9) or *biased hypothesis testing* leads us to search for facts to support our hypotheses rather than facts that could show our hypotheses are incorrect—a discovery that should be equally useful. In one study college students each planned to interview a second student (Snyder & Swann, 1978b). The subjects were divided into two groups. The experimenter asked subjects in the first group to choose some questions that would allow them to determine whether the other student was an extrovert. The second group was asked to discover whether the other student was an introvert. Both groups were presented with the same possible list of interview questions. On the list were items that would bring out someone's extroverted tendencies (e.g., "What do you like about lively parties?" or "Why do you enjoy being with other people?"), as well as items that would elicit more introverted qualities (e.g., "At what times do you feel like being alone?" or "How do you enjoy yourself without involving other people?"). Students who

had been asked to find out whether the other student was an extrovert chose predominantly questions of the extrovert kind—leading questions that would probably confirm the hypothesis. They did not seem to realize that they could get at least as much helpful information by giving the interviewed student a chance to *disconfirm* the hypothesis through answers to the introvert questions. As might be expected, those asked to determine if the interviewed student was an introvert chose predominantly the introvert questions and avoided the extrovert questions. Thus subjects, regardless of which hypothesis they set out to test, behaved as though they somehow wanted their hypothesis to be confirmed—as though they were motivated to prove an initial guess true.

Attributions from Multiple Observations

The attribution rules we have just discussed are those we use to infer a person's momentary intentions and enduring personality characteristics from a single action. But we are able to learn a lot more about other people by observing not one but many of their actions. Kelley (1967) has proposed a set of rules that people use in determining the meaning of a set of observations of another person's actions. When, for example, we observe changes in a person's behavior, we ask ourselves what changes in circumstances might be the cause.

Suppose that you see John laughing at a certain comedian. What sorts of information will help you understand *why* John laughed? Kelley (1967) suggests three dimensions around which we organize new information—the actor, the entity or stimulus, and time—and illustrates them with the following example:

Observations of John's behavior over a long period of time give us information about the *consistency* of his response. If John laughs at this comedian every time he sees him, this highly consistent information helps us judge that John really likes the comedian. If John laughs one time but not the next, this inconsistency may lead us to different conclusions.

Distinctiveness information refers to a person's reaction to similar entities or stimuli. Does John laugh at all comedians? If he does, then his behavior shows low distinctiveness, because it does not vary from one comedian to the next. His reaction, then, would not be distinctive to this comedian.

Figure 19–1 Kelley's Theory of Attribution from Multiple Observations The combination of high-consistency, low-distinctiveness, and low-consensus information usually leads to an attribution of internal causality—an attribution about the actor. High consistency, high consensus, and high distinctiveness lead to an attribution of external causality—an attribution about the entity or stimulus. (After Kelley, 1974)

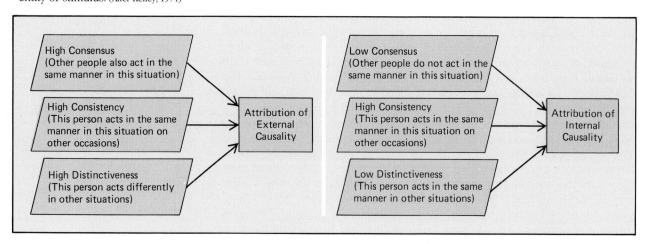

Consensus information refers to a similar reaction by many actors to one entity. If John laughs at the comedian and everyone else does too (high-consensus information), then we conclude that John's reaction is not unique; the comedian is genuinely funny.

Kelley next suggested that certain patterns of these three kinds of information lead naturally to certain kinds of conclusions. For instance, the combination of high-consistency, low-distinctiveness, and low-consensus information leads to an attribution about the actor (see Figure 19–1). If John always (high consistency) laughs at any and all comedians (low distinctiveness), even when other people don't (low concensus), then we know something about John—namely, that he is a fool for comedians. On the other hand, high-consistency and high-consensus information lead to another type of attribution. That is, if everybody (high consensus) always (high consistency) laughs at a particular comedian, especially if there are some other comedians at whom they don't laugh (high distinctivenss), then we know that the comedian (the entity) is indeed very funny—but this tells us nothing in particular about John. The results of several studies (McArthur, 1972; Karaz & Perlman, 1975; Ruble & Feldman, 1976) generally confirm Kelley's suggestions about the attribution rules used by most of us, with some interesting quirks we will discuss below.

As an example of the use of Kelley's (1967) attribution rules in everyday life, consider the factors that might influence you to give a large or a small tip to a pizza delivery man. If you were convinced that how fast the pizza got delivered was determined by something about the delivery man, you would tip him more when it was early than when it was late. If you were convinced that delivery time was beyond his control (a situational rather than dispositional attribution), you would tip him the same whether the pizza was early or late. A group of researchers (Seligman, Finegan, Hazlewood, & Wilkinson, 1985) set up an experiment using this everyday experience. Customers who called for a pizza were first told that it would be delivered in 45 minutes. Some customers were phoned back and told that the pizza would be early or late, either because of something about the driver ("He's been doing a fine job of keeping up" or "He's having trouble keeping up with the delivery load tonight") or because of the situation ("traffic conditions are better/worse than anticipated"). With the situational explanation, the driver got an average tip of 27 cents when it was early and 29 cents when it was late. With the personal explanation, the driver got an average tip of 46 cents when it was early, but only 16 cents when it was late.

Individual Perspectives and Attribution

Sometimes a difference in the perspective from which people view an interpersonal exchange leads them to make systematically different attributions about the role of the participants in the exchange. For instance, Taylor and Fiske (1975) showed that the physical perspective from which an observer witnessed a discussion led to different attributions of the contributions to the discussion of the different participants (see Figure 19–2). Apparently, the focus of our attention in a situation determines to some extent the attributions we make about the participants.

As this experiment shows, perspective can and often does influence people's attributional interpretations of a situation. "Perspective" can mean the physical position from which an observer witnesses an interaction, but it can also have the more general meaning of "point of view." In one experi-

Figure 19–2 Observers watched Speaker A and Speaker B in conversation. Observers of A, who paid more attention to Speaker A because of the location of their seats, believed that Speaker A set the tone of the conversation and chose the conversational topics. Observers of B, whose field of vision was focused on Speaker B, thought B had more to do than A with choosing the topics and setting the tone. In actuality, both speakers were following a script that gave each equal conversational control. The results of this experiment suggest that one's physical point of view determines one's causal attributions. (Adapted from Taylor & Fiske, 1975)

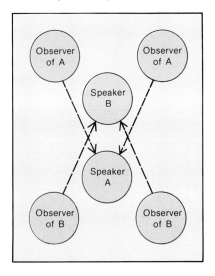

ment subjects were told they would perform a task as workers or as supervisors. While waiting for the task to be assigned, they witnessed an incident in which a "supervisor" bumped into a table, which tipped over an elaborate construction built by a "worker." As a consequence, the worker would not get paid for his efforts. Subjects who anticipated taking the job of worker blamed the supervisor for the accident. But subjects who believed they would be supervisors blamed the experimenter for having a setup so flimsy that it led to accidents (Chaikin & Darley, 1973).

Distorted and Biased Attributions

As might be expected, people are not perfectly accurate "attributors." Indeed, the attribution process has been found to be skewed by several different kinds of misperceptions. These systematic biases are of practical significance as well as being theoretically intriguing.

The Fundamental Attribution Error. After reviewing many studies, Jones (1979) concluded that when people judge others' behavior, they generally attribute the causes of the behavior to the actors rather than to the situations in which the actors are involved. Since this error occurred in experiments in which there was an independent definition of the accurate attribution, this person-attribution bias is clearly an attribution *error*. Because of its central theoretical character, it is called the **fundamental attribution error** (Ross, 1977).

Consider the following circumstances: A college student is asked to write a speech that happens to be contrary to his true beliefs. He might be personally in favor of establishing coeducation at a men's college, but a coin toss has determined that he is to write a speech in favor of maintaining the present all-male student body. But (and this is the important part) he is given plenty of good reasons for taking this position—it is necessary to have speeches on both sides of the issue, the topic assignment was fairly made by a coin toss, and so on. In these circumstances, people are usually willing to write a speech that goes against their own beliefs. But even when observers are told that the position advocated in the speech was assigned by a coin flip, and also told the reasons that compelled the student to go along with his assignment, the observers will still falsely believe that the speaker's true underlying opinion is reflected in his speech, and will rate him as holding beliefs consistent with the speech.

Ross, Anabile, and Steinmetz (1977) have given a dramatic demonstration of the fundamental attribution error. They staged a quiz game in which one person in a pair, as decided by a coin flip, invented and asked tough questions of the other person. In the experiment the person quizzed did poorly, being unable to answer very many of the questions. Observers of the quiz game judged that the questioner was very knowledgeable and the answerer much less so. In other words, they made the fundamental attribution error of not recognizing that we all have a store of idiosyncratic items of knowledge with which we can at times stump other people. The observers equally overlooked the fact that the questioner was chosen at random.

The social implications of the fundamental attribution error are interesting to contemplate. It is as if we attempt to control our complex world by overestimating people's ability to determine their own behavior and the outcomes of their acts. A primary-school teacher, for instance, may decide that a child's poor performance on an arithmetic quiz indicates poor arithmetic

ability rather than considering the possibility that the child is temporarily distracted by some event taking place at home, such as the birth of a new sibling. Or a person observing the angry response of a worker may, without knowing the cause of her anger, conclude that she is a hostile and cantankerous person.

Actor-Observor Differences. We are more apt to make a fundamental attribution error when thinking about someone else's behavior than about our own. This is primarily because we have more *information* about the circumstances that contribute to our own actions. The primary-school teacher in the example above might have made some arithmetic mistakes himself in grading his students' tests, but if his wife had just given birth he would attribute the mistakes to this distracting event rather than to his own incompetence. Granted, he may not know that the failing student has a new baby brother or sister. We might presume that if he did know, he would give the youngster the benefit of the doubt. In the real world, however, we are more likely to give ourselves the benefit of the doubt than others. For example, imagine that you were just treated unfairly by your boss, and then you snapped at the next co-worker who asked you to do something. You would in all likelihood judge yourself as "having a bad day," rather than as being generally "cantankerous." Yet if that same co-worker snapped at you, your tendency would be to think that she was revealing her underlying hostility, rather than to search for reasons why she behaved rudely in the situation.

One study attempted to demonstrate these actor-observer differences. College men were asked why they chose their particular major in preference to other concentrations and why they chose their girlfriend in preference to other women (Nisbett, Caputo, Legant, & Maracek, 1973). They explained their *own* preferences by referring to characteristics of the major or of the girlfriend. For example, "Engineering pays well" or "She's very affectionate." These explanations implied that they liked what anyone else would like, whether good pay or personal warmth. But when asked why their roommate chose his major or his girlfriend, the answers had a different slant. "He chose engineering because he's the type of person who thinks in terms of monetary rewards. As for his girlfriend, he's the kind of person who is attracted to 'clinging vines.' It may be a sign of his basic insecurity. . . . " As actors, we believe that we respond as any rational person would to the environment, but as observers, we interpret overt behaviors as revealing underlying personality traits.

Not all of these actor-observer differences are caused by differences in information, however. Another important determinant of actor-observer attributional differences is *visual salience.* Consider the work on individual perspectives described earlier, in which a subject's physical point of view determined his or her causal attributions. Subjects saw the person who commanded their visual field as more in charge of the situation and more apt to impose his or her personality on the conversation. In the same way, we are able to actually observe another, whereas we cannot actually see ourselves in action. Subjects who are asked about reasons for choosing a major might naturally assume that the person in the center of their everyday field of vision (in this case the roommate) is expressing his underlying personality, whereas the person who is seldom seen in action (themselves) is merely responding to the demands of the situation. It has been shown, in fact, that conversationalists who are allowed to watch a videotape of their own part in a conversation make attributions that are more like those of observers (Storms, 1973). Relative to situational demands, they come to see their own

behavior as more of an expression of their own personalities, even though they have no greater information about the circumstances than they did before. In everyday life, it is the combination of informational differences and visual salience that makes us imagine that others are imposing their own personalities on a situation, while we tend to see ourselves as making normal responses to a certain need.

False Consensus. A common thread that runs through a number of these attributional biases is our unawareness that we are looking at the world from just one point of view—our own—and that not everyone shares this unique perspective. Like the subject who believes that any rational person would respond positively to engineering or to his affectionate girlfriend, we often overestimate the extent to which everyone else would make the same choices that we would. The *false consensus* bias was illustrated vividly in a study in which college students were asked to walk around campus wearing a large sandwich board sign with the word "REPENT!" painted on it in garish red letters (Ross, Greene, & House, 1977). The experimenter explained that he would appreciate the subjects' compliance, but that he could still ask them some questions and obtain valuable data even if they refused to wear the sign. Imagine what you would do if you were in this experiment. Would you agree to wear the sign around campus, or would you refuse? What percentage of other students do you think would agree, and what percentage would refuse? How would you describe the other students who agreed? How would you describe the other students who refused? Think about these questions before you read the next paragraph.

In the actual study, which was performed at Stanford University, about half the students agreed to wear the sign and half refused. The hypothesis was that each half would falsely believe that they were in the majority. As predicted, the half who agreed estimated that 62 percent of their peers would do it and only 38 percent would refuse, whereas the half who refused estimated that 37 percent of their peers would do it and 63 percent would refuse. In addition, both groups felt that they could make much more confident attributions about the personality of other subjects who made the choice opposite to their own. A subject who refused to wear the sign, for example, concluded that any rational person would refuse and that those who agreed were "weird." Obviously, those who agreed to do it in the interests of science were just as convinced about the "oddball" qualities of those who refused. As mentioned above, we feel that we learn relatively little from a person's socially desirable or "expected" actions, but we assume that unusual or unexpected actions reveal a person's true character. What false consensus adds to this attribution rule is that the terms *unusual* and *unexpected* are often defined in terms of our own point of view.

Egocentric Biases. This tendency to see everything from our own point of view, or our own *egocentric biases,* can lead to disagreements about who contributed what to a joint venture. In one study husbands and wives were asked what percentage of time they performed various chores around the house (Ross & Sicoly, 1977). The two estimates on any one chore often totaled more than 100 percent! For example, when asked how often he took out the garbage, the husband might estimate that he performed this chore approximately 80 percent of the time and that his wife did so 20 percent of the time. The wife, who was interviewed separately, might claim that her husband took out the garbage about 40 percent of the time and that she did it 60 percent of the time. Clearly, they could not both be correct, but why were

their estimates so discrepant? As in so many attributional biases, the discrepancy probably arose from taking a self-centered view of the world, not out of a malicious intent to deny the partner's contribution. Differences in information and visual salience often create perceptual differences of which we are largely unaware. The husband most likely wasn't around on many occasions when his wife took out the garbage—that's why she had to do it herself. However, that is also the reason why he lacked the necessary information to make a correct estimate. As for the wife, she presumably had better things to do than sit around and watch out the window as her husband lugged out the garbage cans, so his actions were not visually salient to her. In time, the results of such discrepancies can be disastrous. Husbands and wives who do not realize how much the odds are stacked against knowing about, and attending to, a spouse's contributions often find their marriages on the rocks.

The "Just World" Belief.   Another general tendency that leads to attributional bias is our desire to believe in a just world. We want, for instance, to believe that victims of horrible events must have done something to deserve their fate because such explanations preserve our faith in the proposition that people generally receive fair and equitable treatment in life (Lerner, Miller, & Holmes, 1975). This tendency to see the world as we would like it to be may explain the "blame the victim" phenomenon. Thus poor people are often categorized as "shiftless," and women who have been raped are frequently said to have acted enticingly. In some cases, this is a form of the general attribution error; the causality for the event is attributed to the person rather than to the surrounding situation. In other cases, though, it is more than that. Since both victim and attacker are persons, the fundamental attribution error does not suggest to whom causality will be assigned. But the "just world" rule does: It assigns causality to some past bad action or enduring negative characteristic of the victim so that the rest of us can continue believing that such things will not happen to us.

Attribution and Coping

Attribution styles have an effect on how people cope with unexpected traumatic or victimizing events. For example, people who suffer traumatic accidents and sustain severe injury generally undergo stunning changes in their lives. Before the accident they are functioning normally and naturally; afterwards they may have to cope with permanent injury or even paralysis. Some people handle this type of injury better than others in that they accept its reality instead of denying it, and they work at rehabilitating themselves rather than waiting to get better naturally (Bolman & Wortman, 1977). Those who cope better make internal attributions for their injuries: That is, they attribute responsibility for their injuries to themselves. Initially, this conclusion is counterintuitive because it seems that self-blame would cause a geat deal of guilt and self-hatred. However, further investigations (Lanoff-Bulman, 1979; Miller & Porter, 1983) have clarified how internal attribution works in these cases. Two types of self-blame are possible: behavioral and dispositional. Take the case of a woman who has been attacked and raped. If she thinks something like "I shouldn't have been walking in that neighborhood at that time of night," she is saying that a particular set of behaviors explained what happened to her, and thus asserting the possibility of control: By avoiding these actions in the future, she can avoid similar negative consequences. If,

on the other hand, she thinks, "It happened to me because I'm such a stupid person that I deserved it," she is implying dispositional self-blame: The events were not under her control, and will happen again and again. Taking behavioral self-responsibility for negative events leads to better coping, dispositional self-responsibility to poorer coping. Not surprisingly, women who get raped in their habitual environments, for which it is hard to think of behaviors that would avert similar events in the future, have greater difficulty coping.

Efficient Decision Making and Heuristics

We have seen that a person's perception of others is guided by implicit theories of personality and subjected to several biases. If the perceiver is completely rational, as objective as a scientist, taking all the time necessary to draw a perfectly accurate picture of others—even then, various studies imply that perceptions are bound to be inaccurate. And the perfect perceivers who wait until all the information is in before making a decision are likely to find life's events passing them by and the time for making the decision long past. Increasingly, social psychologists are realizing that people do not need to be *perfect* decision makers but *efficient* ones. Viewed from this perspective, the existence of personal biases does not necessarily mean that people are poor judges of the world around them. Indeed, quite the opposite is generally true.

As we learned in the chapter on thought (Chapter 9), people have many useful strategies for estimating the various elements in a situation and making a decision. These strategies are called *heuristics.* Recall from the earlier discussion that one such heuristic is referred to as the *representativeness heuristic:* We estimate probabilities by using our previous attributions about objects, events, or people. Thus we might categorize librarians as people who like to read in their spare time, and professors as absentminded, and so on. Sometimes, however, the representativeness heuristic leads people to make attribution errors—for example, you just might meet the one librarian in 50 states whose hobby is race car driving.

The *availability heuristic* is another strategy previously discussed: We judge the likelihood of a fact or event by how easily it comes to mind. Read the list of names in Figure 19–3. Now, without looking back, can you remember how many men and women were on the list? As a hint, there were 20 names in all. If you said that there were more women than men, you were probably using the availability heuristic, a strategy that doesn't work in this particular situation. Since the women on the list are much more famous, their names are easier to remember. In memory, the men fade into the background. Actually, the men on the list include a Nobel Prize winner, a chief justice of the Supreme Court, the father of the H-bomb, a World Series baseball manager, a director of the Federal Reserve, and a vice president of the United States.

It is wise to remember that representativeness and availability are rules of thumb that normally serve us quite well. If they did not, we would stop using them. Most times, we can prepare for meetings with people about whom we know very little by using the representativeness heuristic, and we can be prepared to encounter the same events and people tomorrow that we have most frequently in our past, and thus are easiest to call to mind. Like perceptual illusions (see Chapter 4), the examples of the librarian who races and the famous women are designed to show the cognitive strategies that we use

Figure 19–3: Read this list of names. When you have finished reading the list, return to the text.

Queen Elizabeth
Herbert Simon
William Casey
Mother Theresa
Margaret Thatcher
Alben Barclay
Madonna
William Rehnquist
Edward Teller
Cyndi Lauper
Brooke Shields
Jackson Pollack
Nancy Reagan
Earl Weaver
Elizabeth Taylor
Alan Greenspan
Malcolm Forbes
Cory Aquino
Barbara Walters
Larry Nelson

habitually because they are so often efficient and so frequently lead to correct answers.

One possibility, in fact, is that cognitive heuristics may be employed selectively so as to reach conclusions that we *want* to be true. We may construct one set of hypotheses if we want a particular proposition to be true, and an entirely different set of hypotheses if we want its opposite to be true. We may then use biased, or confirmatory, hypothesis testing in the service of theories that make us feel good. One example is that, although the divorce rate in this country is 50 percent, almost every newly married couple feels that they are among the 50 percent who will stay married. How do they convince themselves that their marriage is one of those likely to defy the odds? Recent research evidence shows that they believe that their own attributes are the very ones that are characteristic of happily married couples, and they do this regardless of what their own attributes happen to be (Kunda, in press). Women who have had a number of romantic relationships prior to marriage are convinced that this experience gives them an understanding of men that will make it easier to establish a stable relationship with their spouse. Women who have had no prior romantic relationships are just as convinced that the absence of experience is an advantage because it allows them to enter marriage without the "baggage" of prior assumptions or hostility left over from earlier relationships. Men invent just as convincing causal scenarios to tell themselves that theirs will be a happy marriage. No matter what people's attributes are, they come to believe that those attributes will help them achieve desired outcomes and avoid feared ones (Kunda, in press).

Self-Fulfilling Prophecies

As we have already seen, our initial attributions about other people can cause us to have certain expectations about them. For instance, many people expect mental patients to behave in weird and hostile ways. Suppose a person with these expectations discovers that a co-worker with whom he is on friendly terms was briefly hospitalized for mental illness. Whereas before he acted friendly toward this co-worker, even inviting her to lunch, he now becomes guarded and distant because of his expectations about people labeled mentally ill. When his co-worker reciprocates his lunch invitation, he panics and makes up excuses not to go. The co-worker becomes aware that this person has begun to act differently toward her and becomes quite angry, for as far as she can see, she has done nothing to deserve his sudden cold treatment. She may respond in kind, and the situation may escalate, perhaps until harsh words are exchanged.

So the interaction ends. But notice how it ends from the perspective of the first individual. He is convinced that he is right about former mental patients, and he now has one more case to prove it. But in fact it was his own expectations, translated into actions, that caused his "prophecy" to be "fulfilled."

These sorts of effects seem to be of two kinds. One process involves expecting certain behaviors from others and seeing those expectations as being confirmed. This we will call *perceptual confirmation process*. In the second process, as in our example of the co-workers, a person who expects another to behave in certain ways acts toward that person in a manner that elicits the expected behaviors. These behaviors are then interpreted as proof that the other person has the personality that was expected (Darley & Fazio, 1980).

Perceptual Confirmation Effects. When we make judgments about a person over whom we have power, we assign that person to the treatments that our judgments imply are correct. We punish a child, hire or fire a worker, or make a friend miserable according to our attributions of their behaviors. To the extent that our judgments are inaccurate because they are based on biases in the attribution process, our treatments of those individuals will be flawed.

One researcher (Rist, 1970), who observed the treatment of children when they entered school for the first time, has provided poignant documentation of this. In the first few days the kindergarten teacher assigned each child to one of three tables. The table groupings were apparently based on such things as the children's grooming and the cleanliness of their clothes, whether they were from "intact" or "broken" homes, and whether their families were on welfare. With no test results in the children's files, the teacher used their appearances and caseworker reports to make attributions about their maturity and ability to learn.

As you might surmise, Table 1 children got more of the teacher's attention and more intensive training in reading and mathematics than Table 2 or 3 children. For example, when the teacher was working at Table 1, children from Table 3 worked in workbooks or on assignments. If they had a question, the teacher kept them waiting until she finished with Table 1, but when she was working with the Table 3 children, she was more likely to accept interruptions by Table 1 students.

Follow-up observations showed that as those students moved through the school system, they continued to be grouped and treated on the basis of their initial table assignments: Most of the Table 1 children were at Table A in the first grade and the "tiger's table" in the second grade, whereas the children from Table 3 went to Table C and then to the "clown's table." It is important to realize that the teachers in this study were not being malicious. They were simply applying the perceptual biases and heuristics discussed in previous sections. They started with tentative hypotheses about the children, and they probably felt that they were open-minded and willing to revise these preliminary estimates on the basis of actual classroom performance. They then, without realizing it, attended more to information that would confirm than to

Rist (1970) demonstrated that teachers' erroneous attributions about young pupils' maturity and ability to learn can have serious and long-term social effects. (Photo: Michal Heron/ Monkmeyer Press)

information that would disconfirm these hypotheses; they probably accepted their subsequent conclusions as unbiased validation of their earlier estimates.

This is likely to be what happened to subjects in one study on perceptual biases (Darley & Gross, 1983). One group of subjects saw a videotape of a fourth-grade girl playing in a playground surrounded by parklike grounds and expensive homes, presumably where she lived. A second group of subjects saw the same little girl playing in a ghetto playground. When asked how well the girl probably did on school achievement tests, did the groups' estimates differ? Not at all. Both groups thought that she performed at about the appropriate fourth-grade level. In other words, they were unwilling to draw any conclusions about the girl's school ability from her home background. But had they formed any tentative hypotheses that might be confirmed by the biased cognitive processes we have been discussing? Apparently they did because both groups then watched the same videotape of the girl taking an oral school achievement test and estimated her performance. Those who had initially seen her in the wealthy neighborhood thought that she had performed at a level between grades 4 and 5, whereas those who had initially seen her in the ghetto thought that she had performed at a level between grades 3 and 4. Both groups "read into" the videotaped test performance an ability level that confirmed their tentative hypothesis. Obviously, if the subjects had been the child's teachers, their different perceptions of her would have led them to take different actions toward her—perhaps the same kind observed in the actual classroom study above.

In our society judgments about people that can have lifelong effects on them are made every day. A judge decides which delinquent is a prospect for rehabilitation and which one is "incorrigible," and then sentences them accordingly. A psychiatrist decides which mentally ill patients will benefit from psychotherapy as outpatients and which are to be confined to a state hospital. The attributor has the power to assign the perceived individual to a treatment that may make the first impressions come true. These are the processes that sociologists discuss under the heading of "labeling effects" (Gove, 1975) and are akin to the behavioral confirmation effects, which we will discuss in the following section.

Behavioral Confirmation Effects

In the course of our own interactions, it seems to us that we are simply responding to the actions of others; it is hard for us to see that our expectations about them can channel the interaction. A careful and important experiment demonstrated this effect (Snyder, Tanke, & Berscheid, 1977). Men students who were to have a get-acquainted telephone conversation with a woman student were first shown a photograph of her. The researchers had arranged that some of the men would see a picture of an attractive woman, while others would see a plain-looking woman. Questioning revealed that the men who expected to talk to the attractive woman thought she would be poised, humorous, and socially adept, while those who expected to talk to the unattractive woman thought she would be awkward, serious and socially inept. In fact, the women the men actually spoke to were not those whose photos they had seen and were of varying degrees of attractiveness.

Those men who thought they were talking to an attractive woman carried on animated, warm, friendly, and humorous conversations with her. Not surprisingly, she responded in a similar way. But those men who believed

While we generally believe that we are simply responding to others' behavior in the course of our interactions with them, Snyder, Tanke, and Berscheid (1977) vividly demonstrated how our initial expectations of others can shape our interactions. (*Top:* Freda Leinwand; *bottom:* Paul Conklin; both Monkmeyer Press)

they were conversing with a plain woman were colder, less interesting, and more reserved, and the women to whom they spoke gave cool, aloof, and distant responses. Thus the men's stereotypes were confirmed: Those women thought to be attractive indeed acted more socially adept, but not because they were so by nature. They seemed more poised and sociable because the men's conversations created the opportunities for them to be so. But the men emerged from the conversations convinced that the women were as they seemed to be. Interestingly, observers agreed with them. People who listened to taped recordings of the women's side labeled as attractive were more socially adept then those who were originally identified by a less attractive photograph.

Other researchers have shown that women's stereotypes of men can also shape an interaction (Anderson & Bem, 1981). Also, studies in the workplace have demonstrated that workers labeled at random as having high aptitude learn faster and perform better on objective tests after being trained by instructors with these originally false expectations. These and similar studies confirm the wide influence of self-fulfilling prophecies on our daily lives.

Self-fulfilling prophecies are neither mysterious nor automatic. If we analyze the goals of the participants in an interaction, we can better understand the circumstances in which self-fulfilling prophecies may occur. Suppose I think that you know nothing about classical music. If the two of us are talking together pleasantly at a party, I will not steer the conversation toward classical music, though it is a favorite topic of mine, because I think it might embarrass you. But if I need to find people for a team I am forming to be on a music quiz show, my goal would prompt me to probe the topic rather than avoid it, even though my expectation is that you are probably too ignorant about classical music to make a good team member. In the first case, by avoiding the topic, I will not discover whether in fact you are ignorant about classical music. My expectancy—that you probably know nothing about the subject—will remain intact; I may even hold it more strongly because I expended effort to stay away from my favorite topic during our conversation. On the other hand, if I probe the topic, what I end up thinking about you depends on your answers. If you reveal a knowledge of classical music, then my expectancy will be contradicted. Given that it was the expectancy that triggered the search that eventually led to its disconfirmation, we might call this a *self-disconfirming prophecy* (Miller & Tarnbull, 1986).

An interesting question is whether behavioral confirmation has any effect on social interactions other than the one in which they initially occur. This possibility was tested in a study in which two college men sat in separate rooms and played a game (Snyder & Swann, 1978b). During the game they were allowed to try to disrupt the other player's concentration by using a "noise weapon"—a loud blast in the other person's ears just when he was trying to think of an answer. Analogous to the photographs in the earlier telephone study, subjects were given brief personality descriptions of the other player. In one condition the second subject described himself as a competitive and somewhat hostile sort who enjoyed playing rough. In the other condition he described himself as sensitive, cooperative, and fair-minded.

As expected, subjects used the noise weapon much more often to disconcert the person they thought was hostile than to disrupt the performance of the person they thought was not hostile. The subject in the other room, of course, knew nothing about any personality description. He only knew whether he was getting "blasted" or not, and he retaliated in kind. Up to this point, the study simply demonstrated a self-fulfilling prophecy effect, in which the first subject's expectations caused him to treat the second subject

as though those expectations were valid, and the second subject responded in a way that made the first subject look as though he had been "right all along." But then a new wrinkle was introduced. The first subject was dismissed, and a new subject was brought in to play the "noise weapon" game with the original second subject—the one who had acted in a hostile or nonhostile way strictly according to how he had been treated himself. Would this second subject continue to act aggressively or nonaggressively toward the third subject? He did. Thus self-fulfilling prophecies are not limited to the social interaction in which they originally occur, but can "spread" to other social interactions.

Stereotypes and Prejudice

Expectations, then, can have major effects on people's interactions. **Stereotypes** are one of the most frequent and pervasive ways in which these expectations take shape. Stereotypes are assumptions we make about people on the basis of their membership in a group. For example, a stereotyped view of women is that they are emotional, talkative, prone to hysteria, and drive badly. Negative stereotypes can obviously be quite damaging. First, they are usually excessively negative. Second, they are often erroneously attributed to people who are members of the stereotyped group, without regard for their individuality.

One source of stereotypes is our tendency to pay more attention to the similarities between ourselves and members of groups to which we belong and more attention to the differences between ourselves and members of groups to which we do not belong (Wilder & Allen, 1978). This tendency to focus on the dissimilarity of outgroup members probably encourages the formation of negative stereotypes.

A second source of stereotypes comes from our tendency to form illusory correlations (Chapman, 1967). Two things are correlated when they appear or occur together, and most stereotypes are actually assumed correlations. For example, the stereotyped belief that the Welsh are good singers implies that if a man is of Welsh descent, he is probably a good singer. In forming such correlations, we are disproportionately influenced by distinctive or unusual events. Unusual personal characteristics such as skin color or physical deformity draw our attention (Langer, Taylor, Fiske, & Chanowitz, 1976). Unusual behaviors, particularly negative ones, also draw our attention. Hamilton and Gifford (1976) found that people overestimate the extent to which unusual group membership and unusual behavior go together. Even when such pairings are actually quite infrequent, the combination of unusual personal characteristics and unusual behavior is so memorable that it is difficult to avoid overestimating the extent to which they go together and thus to avoid forming a negative stereotype. In a sense, then, stereotypes are implicit personality theories "run wild," formed on the basis of limited evidence and too frequently applied to broad groups of individuals.

Just like any attributions, stereotypes can become the basis for self-fulfilling prophecies that can further damage the stereotyped individual. If a school system tester believes that Mexican Americans are not intelligent, she may assign a Mexican-American child to a lower grade level than the child's age would suggest. Pushed only as fast as the rest of the children in that grade, the child may never catch up with his age group. Moreover, if the teacher shares the stereotype, the Mexican-American child may get relatively little of the teacher's teaching energies. Bored and frustrated, he may be-

Word, Zanna, and Cooper (1974) demonstrated experimentally the ways in which racial stereotypes can lead to damaging self-fulfilling prophecies in a situation such as a job interview. (David Schaefer/Monkmeyer Press)

come a behavior problem and his education may further suffer. To others, the child will certainly end up looking like a person of low abilities and intelligence. As we will see later, such a child may even come to believe that about himself or herself.

ATTITUDE FORMATION AND CHANGE

As we have seen, attributional theories are concerned with the ways in which we make inferences about other people's behavior. Social psychologists have also been concerned with another, similar, problem: how people form attitudes about objects, groups (such as political parties), issues (such as capital punishment), and events. An **attitude** is a broad general disposition to react in a certain way to categories of events, objects, or persons.

Classically, attitudes have been thought to have several components. The first is **evaluation.** We are all generally able to say how favorably or unfavorably disposed we are toward things, how good or bad we think certain politicians, are, and so on. A second component involves our cognitions or beliefs about the facts pertaining to the person, event, or object—for instance, what we think are the planks of the 1984 Democratic Party platform or the sequence of events that led up to a favored team losing the big game. The third component is the set of actions that we believe are appropriate toward the attitudinal object. Two people may have the same favorable evaluation of a political candidate, but have very different guidelines for acting in regard to that candidate. One may feel obliged, if the weather isn't too bad, to go to the polls to vote for the candidate. The other may feel obliged to help campaign for the candidate.

Attitude Change

Attempts to change people's attitudes are widespread in modern life. Millions of dollars are spent on attempting to convince us that Brand X is better, more fashionable, and more effective than Brand Y or Brand Z. In a depressingly similar way millions more are spent to convince us that Candidate X is better, more fashionable, and more effective than Candidate Y or Candidate Z. What factors about a communication cause changes in attitudes? The first investigators to systematically study attitude change (Hovland et al., 1949; Hovland, Janis, & Kelley, 1953) formulated a remarkably succinct categorization of these factors: "*Who* says *what* to *whom* via *what channel* and with what effect? In other words, the factors that cause attitude change fall into four categories: aspects of the person doing the communicating, aspects of the communication itself, aspects of the channel through which the communication is delivered (e.g., radio or TV), and aspects of the audience receiving the communication.

TV news is brought to us by attractive, trustworthy-looking individuals. (Michal Heron/Woodfin Camp & Associates)

Aspects of the Communicator.   Attractive, prestigious, trustworthy, expert communicators are more persuasive. One reason may be that we find what they have to say more credible than when it comes from someone who lacks these characteristics. In one early study of communicator credibility subjects read a persuasive message about the feasibility of this country building atomic submarines. Some subjects thought that the message had been written by Robert Oppenheimer, the eminent American physicist. Other subjects read the same message, but thought it was an editorial from the Soviet news-

paper *Pravda*. They were far less persuaded by its argument than those who thought it had been written by the American physicist (Hovland & Weiss, 1952; see also Hastie, Penrod, & Pennington, 1984). Credibility, though, has its limits. Had Oppenheimer disagreed with an average sports fan about the relative merits of pro football quarterbacks, it seems unlikely that his opinion would carry any additional weight because of his prestige in nuclear physics.

Aspects of the Communication. As you might expect, more logical and comprehensible messages are more persuasive (Wyer & Goldberg, 1970; Eagly, 1974), as are messages that are forcefully delivered (McGuire, 1985). Persuasive messages are also somewhat more effective when they present only one side of an issue, unless the particular audience happens to know about the counterarguments. Then it is best to present the counterarguments and refute them (McGuire, 1985).

Aspects of the Communication Channel. Would you rather have your persuasive message on television, on radio, or in written form? The available evidence suggests that the various communication channels are equally effective, but that none has as much effect as one might suppose (McGuire, 1985), especially given the enormous sums of money spent on them by politicians and product marketers.

Aspects of the Audience. Is it easier to persuade a person of low intelligence than a person a high intelligence? Surprisingly, it is not (Hovland & Janis, 1959; Hovland & Mandell, 1952). But people with different educational backgrounds are differentially susceptible to different kinds of messages (Hovland et al., 1949). This was discovered when the Army prepared two different radio scripts to persuade American soldiers that World War II might not be over as soon as they thought—that they might have to keep fighting Japan for two more years. One of these scripts only presented reasons for expecting two more years of war (one-sided). The other presented some reasons for thinking that Japan might capitulate sooner, but followed these with the reasons for believing that this view was overly optimistic (two-sided). The one-sided message was more effective in molding the attitudes of less educated soldiers, but the two-sided message worked better for those with more education, presumably because their schooling had instilled skepticism and the ability to generate counterarguments on their own (Miller & Buckhout, 1973).

One reason for the limited impact of the media is that people expose themselves to messages that support their current beliefs (McGuire, 1985). This is known as the *audience-selection effect.* When a Republican commercial comes on television, many Democrats may take that as an opportunity to visit the refrigerator for a snack. The Republican viewers might well make their trip to the kitchen when a Democratic commercial appears. In general, the very audience that persuasive speakers are trying to reach are the ones who "tune them out."

In a time when we are keenly aware of gender biases and interested in what differences may actually exist between the sexes, we might also ask if the listener's gender affects the impact of a communication. Early research suggested that women were more easily persuaded than men (Janis & Field, 1959), presumably because men are raised to be independent thinkers, whereas women are raised to be submissive and cooperative. More recent evidence has shown that women are only more readily persuaded in experi-

The audience-selection effect describes the tendency of listeners to attend to messages they agree with and to shun persuasive arguments for the other side. In all likelihood the people attending this disarmament rally came predisposed to support the issue, while those in disagreement stayed home. (Freda Leinwand/ Monkmeyer Press)

ments conducted by male experimenters, not in experiments conducted by female experimenters (Eagly & Carli, 1981). Although the reason for this is not clear at present, one possibility is that the male experimenters *expected* their women subjects to be more easily persuaded, and treated the two sexes so differently as to bring about a self-fulfilling prophecy effect. (Note, of course, that the research question was framed "Are women more easily persuaded than men?" One might wonder what would have happened if the hypothesis to be tested was "Are men more easily persuaded than women?")

One caution in interpreting the work on persuasive communications is that the vast majority of experiments have studied attitude change in social isolation. A subject reads, listens to, or watches a persuasive communication, and her attitude is recorded. She has discussed it with no one. Outside the psychology laboratory attitudes are quite homogeneous across social groups. People tend to vote the same way their family, friends, or fellow employees vote, and they often get their attitudes toward an election or any other issue from "opinion leaders" in their immediate social environment (Katz & Lazarsfeld, 1955). When new information on a topic comes to light, the group discusses the information (usually informally) and seems to arrive at a consensus as to whether it should change its attitudes or not. That consensus often centers around the interpretations of one member of the group, even though the member "in charge" may vary from one issue to the next. Thus there is a two-step process by which information is spread in a population. Ideas flow from the media and other sources to opinion leaders, and from opinion leaders to the less active sections of the population (Katz & Lazarsfeld, 1955).

Do Attitudes Cause Behavior?

It seems logical to assume that attitudes do guide behavior, and that if we know a person's attitudes, we can predict how that person will behave. But this logical assumption was called into question by one of the earliest attitude-behavior studies. In fact, a number of experiments over the years have shown that in some instances attitudes and behaviors have little or nothing to do with each other. In the first of these failures to find a consistent relationship between attitudes and behaviors, LaPiere (1934) reported on his experiences traveling through the United States with a young Oriental couple. In the course of their travels LaPiere and his companions stopped at a large number of restaurants and hotels. In only one case was the couple not treated hospitably because of their race. However, when LaPiere later measured the racial attitudes of the owners of the places they had visited, over 90 percent of those who responded were negative, saying that as a matter of policy Orientals would not be served in their establishment. Their reported attitudes and their actual behavior seemed to be completely unconnected. The LaPiere study contains many procedural flaws—for example, it is quite likely that the people who answered the attitude questionnaire (i.e., owners) were not the same people who had actually provided service (i.e., waiters, hostesses, and desk clerks). But a number of subsequent investigators have found similar discrepancies between attitudes and behavior. Most recently, Nisbett and Wilson (1977) reported a series of experiments that seem to show that even when people think they have acted on their attitudes, they may really have acted in response to outside influences of which they are completely unaware.

Somewhat surprised by these and other findings of a lack of consistency

between attitudes and behavior, psychologists have recently reexamined their thinking and carried out more research on the problem (Ajzen & Fishbein, 1980; Fazio & Zanna, 1981). From their research, the following generalizations can be made.

First, in some circumstances it is inappropriate or undesirable to express certain attitudes. For instance, I may intensely dislike Shakespeare's *Henry IV*, but when my son excitedly tells me that he has been selected to play the lead role in it, I will not announce my feelings about the play. Researchers have generally found that constraints imposed by social norms inhibit the expression of inappropriate attitudes (Warner & DeFleur, 1969).

Second, individuals who value being consistent show a greater tendency to guide their behaviors by their attitudes (Snyder & Tanke, 1976; Zanna, Olson, & Fazio, 1980).

Third, if the action one wants to predict is very specific, it is better to predict it from attitudes specifically related to that action (Ajzen & Fishbein, 1979). Thus, if you want to know whether a person will vote for a particular Democratic candidate, it would be more to the point to ask about the voter's attitudes toward Democrats in general, but it would help even more to ask about his or her attitudes toward that candidate. On the other hand, if you want to predict general behavior patterns, then measure general attitudes: To determine a person's voting pattern in regard to all Democratic candidates, ask about the rater's attitudes toward the Democratic party.

Fourth, in what may well be the converse of the previous point, attitudes may be general dispositions to react in a certain way to categories of objects, events, or persons. However, the attitude only applies in situations where the specific object, event, or person fits our stereotype. This phenomenon is referred to as an **attitude prototype.** LaPiere's (1934) proprietors had very hostile attitudes toward Orientals, but they probably never pictured "Orientals" as anything like the smiling, well-educated, impeccably dressed couple who accompanied LaPiere on his travels. Another research study (Lord, Lepper, & Mackie, 1984) found that subjects' attitudes toward homosexuals could only predict their behavior toward a specific homosexual if he matched their attitude prototype of homosexuals. If the homosexual seemed atypical (according to that subject), the general attitude did not predict the subject's willingness to interact with him.

Fifth, attitudes that are based on direct experience relate more closely to behavior than attitudes that are based on indirect experience (Fazio & Zanna, 1981). In one study college students were asked for their attitudes toward a campus housing shortage that had some students sleeping on cots in hallways and lounges. Were their attitudes reflected in the actions they took? Did their attitudes predict whether they would sign a petition protesting the situation, or whether they would write letters to the university housing office? They did, but primarily for the students whose attitudes had been formed on the basis of direct experience—who were themselves assigned to a cot in the lounge (Regan & Fazio, 1977). In another study student attitudes toward participation in psychological research were excellent predictors of whether they would volunteer for a specific study, but much more so for those who had previously taken part in a number of studies (Fazio & Zanna, 1978). One reason for these results may be that direct experience allows us to form a more accurate prototype or best exemplar of a category, whether it be knowing what a homosexual is actually like or knowing what a psychology experiment actually entails.

Finally, attitudes are more apt to guide behavior if they have been recently and frequently acted on, or at least thought about (Fazio, in press). Presum-

ably a voter who had on several occasions reviewed his preference for candidate X over candidate Y would be less likely to change his mind in the voting booth than one who had only thought about his attitude once. In the same way, subjects in a recent study completed a questionnaire in which they were asked about their attitude toward capital punishment either on one item or on five items. They then reviewed mixed empirical evidence, some of it showing that the death penalty deters potential murderers, some of it showing the opposite, and evaluated that evidence. Consistent with previous research (Lord, Ross, & Lepper, 1979), they found the studies supporting their own attitude better done in a scientific sense than the studies that contradicted their general attitude, but this relationship between attitude and biased interpretation was found only for subjects who had previously been asked about, and expressed, their attitudes five times (Fazio & Houston, 1986).

What these recent studies have in common is a new emphasis on the *process* rather than merely the content of attitudes (Fazio, in press). Researchers are increasingly interested in the cognitive processes through which attitudes are formed and applied, and this new attention to process is already reaping rewards by showing that attitudes guide behavior much more closely than earlier nonprocess research seemed to indicate.

Behavior Affects Attitudes: Cognitive Dissonance Theory

We have just examined some situations in which attitudes do, or do not, influence a person's behavior. The time has come to put the question in reverse: What effect does behavior have on attitudes?

Much of the research on this question has been stimulated by Leon Festinger's (1957) theory of **cognitive dissonance,** which attempts to explain what happens when people behave in ways that are contrary to their beliefs or attitudes. The basic elements in Festinger's theory are **cognitions,** or bits of knowledge that we have about the world. When two cognitions are inconsistent—that is, when one thought or cognition contradicts another—a dissonant relationship is said to exist between the two. For example, knowledge that one is a Democrat is dissonant with knowledge that one has just voted for a Republican. According to Festinger, this state of cognitive dissonance produces a psychological tension that a person is motivated to reduce. In other words, having two inconsistent cognitions is unpleasant, and people will find a way to get rid of that unpleasant dissonant feeling.

How can dissonance be reduced? One way would be to change one or both cognitions to make them less dissonant. Voters, for instance, might convince themselves that they are not rigidly loyal to the Democrats, after all. This strategy had been proposed by others before Festinger (Heider, 1946; Newcomb, 1953). Festinger's contribution, and the real hallmark of cognitive dissonance theory, was to state more explicitly the process by which cognitions are made to become less dissonant, and to express it in terms that could be experimentally tested.

Festinger proposed that certain of our cognitions are more resistant to change than others. For instance, cognitions based on reality, such as the knowledge that ice is cold or that you have just eaten spinach, will be particularly difficult to alter. In contrast, cognitions based on opinions and attitudes ("I dislike spinach") are more open to change. Festinger believed that dissonance can be reduced by altering those cognitions that are *least* resistant to

change. It is through this process that your behaviors may come to influence your attitudes. Suppose that your behavior (eating spinach) is dissonant with your attitude ("I dislike spinach"). It is difficult to deny that the behavior has occurred; the easier course of action is to bring the attitude into line with the behavior ("Spinach isn't so bad, after all"; "I really do like spinach").

Support for these notions came from a now-classic experiment conducted by Festinger and Carlsmith (1959). They recruited subjects for what was supposedly an experiment on task performance. When individual subjects arrived, they were given a series of exceedingly dull, boring tasks to occupy their time. For example, they were required to turn each peg along a number of rows on a pegboard, first a quarter turn to the left, then a quarter turn to the right. After the tasks were finished, the experimenter explained that the actual experiment had to do with mental sets or expectations. The subjects were informed that other subjects would be met by a confederate of the experimenter before they performed the tasks and convinced that the tasks were going to be interesting and fun.

Subjects were then told that they were in the *control* condition of the experiment—that is, the condition that assessed task performance without the confederate raising any expectations. At this point the subjects assumed that they had completed the experiment, but in fact the crucial part was yet to come. Acting somewhat perplexed, the experimenter stated that the confederate had yet to arrive for the next subject, who was to be in the "positive expectation" condition. The experimenter then had what appeared to be a flash of insight: Perhaps the present subject could help by filling in as the confederate. All that was required was to convince the next "subject" (actually the real confederate of the experimenter) that the tasks were in fact interesting and fun. For this, subjects were offered $1. (A second group of "controls" were offered $20 to do the same thing). After complying with the experimenter's request, subjects then indicated on a questionnaire their own "true" attitudes toward the tasks.

Festinger and Carlsmith had created a situation ripe for dissonance arousal. The subjects' behavior in attempting to influence the confederate was clearly dissonant with their original attitudes about the tasks. Moreover, the $1 inducement does not seem to have been enough to justify the behavior (that is, to serve as a supportive cognition). It is unlikely that subjects would change their cognitions about the behavior (they could hardly be persuaded that they hadn't performed the tasks). Dissonance theory would predict a change in the least resistant cognitions (the attitudes toward the tasks), so that they would no longer be inconsistent with the behavior. In other words, subjects would be expected to rate the tasks as having actually been interesting. In fact, compared to the second group of subjects (who were paid $20 for attempting to influence the confederate) and an actual control group (who simply rated the tasks after completing them), subjects in the $1 condition brought their attitudes into line with their behavior and rated the tasks as more interesting. Subjects in the $20 condition experienced little dissonance in the first place, since the $20 (at least in 1959) provided a ready self-explanation for their behavior.

This finding of greater attitude change with lower incentive has come to be known as the **induced compliance effect,** and has been repeated in numerous other experiments (Cohen, 1962; Zimbardo, Weisenberg, Firestone, & Levy, 1965).

The general principle seems to be that those who wish to change attitudes ought to use just enough of a reward or punishment to induce compliance, and no more. In what are known as the "forbidden toy" studies (Aronson &

Anyone who has ever been a zealous jogger will probably have a good intuitive understanding of effort justification. (Maureen Fennelli/Photo Researchers)

Carlsmith, 1963; Freedman, 1965), children were brought into a room full of toys and allowed to play with them. The experimenter "had to leave the room" for a few moments and cautioned the child that he or she could play with any of the toys except one—the forbidden toy. In one condition he said something mild like "I'd be upset if you played with that toy" and in the other condition something severe like "I'd be very mad and take all these toys away and never let you play with them again."

While the experimenter was gone, none of the children played with the forbidden toy. In other words, they behaved no differently regardless of what the experimenter had said. Later they were given a chance to rate the attractiveness of the toys, as well as an opportunity to play with any toy they wanted. Those who had been threatened with only mild punishment said that the forbidden toy was not very attractive and 71 percent of them disdained playing with it. The severe-threat children liked the toy, and 67 percent of them played with it. The experimenters reasoned that dissonance was aroused when children in the mild-threat condition found themselves not playing with the toy in the experimenter's absence. The mild threat didn't seem a sufficient justification for not playing with the toy, so these children concluded (whether unconsciously or consciously) that they must not have liked the toy very much in the first place.

A second line of research has also provided support for cognitive dissonance theory. This is in the area of **effort justification,** which is perhaps best captured by the idea that we learn to like what we have suffered to achieve. The basic notion is that when we expend a great deal of effort for little or no reason, we will experience dissonance. The cognition that we are working hard is dissonant with the knowledge that we are not gaining anything worthwhile by doing it. As with induced compliance, we can reduce the dissonance by bringing our attitude into line with our behavior. In this case, the positive benefits of the activity being undertaken can be elevated to justify the expenditure of effort.

A recent interesting application of effort justification has been in evaluating the effectiveness of psychotherapy. Many theorists have speculated that part of the reason people recuperate is that therapy is so costly both financially and emotionally. Patients may justly conclude, "If I'm paying all this money and suffering all this anguish, then it *must* be worth it—I must be getting better." In a convincing demonstration of this effort-justification aspect of psychotherapy, some snake phobics were given a traditional type of psychotherapy, while others were asked to perform strenuous and demanding physical tasks (like winding a yo-yo with a 5-pound weight attached). Although these physical tasks had nothing to do with snakes, they were depicted as a respectable form of therapy and were found to be just as effective in reducing fear of snakes as the traditional therapy (Cooper, 1980).

Self-Perception and Attitude Change

Perceiving Our Own Behavior. Cognitive dissonance theory helps us to understand what happens when we act in ways that are inconsistent with our attitudes. But what about those occasions when our actions are consistent with our attitudes? Or when we don't have a particular attitude in the first place? Darryl Bem (1965, 1977) has suggested that we frequently form our beliefs about ourselves, about what we prefer and what our attitudes are, by observing our own behavior in the same way that other people observe us.

If, for example, you find yourself doing things that don't require the company of others, you might conclude that you are a "loner."

Of course, others' attributions about our behavior can influence our perceptions of ourselves as well. A comment such as, "You must be a history buff—you keep taking history courses," may make us conclude that what we previously thought of as a pastime is instead a major concern in our life. This is, in fact, the way we learn about ourselves during our growing-up years. If as children we didn't hesitate to greet strangers, our parents might have said, "What a friendly child you are!" and we might then have said to ourselves, "I must be a friendly person—Mother said so."

Self-perception theory provides an alternative explanation for the results of many dissonance experiments. The major difference between the two theories is that cognitive dissonance theory postulates a state of tension that is critical in producing attitude change. Research (Zanna & Cooper, 1974) suggests that this state of tension is an important determinant of attitude change, and that dissonance is therefore the better explanation, at least for some classes of attitude change. The researchers (Fazio, Zanna, & Cooper, 1977) went on to suggest the domains to which each of the theories best applied. Basically, they propose that when an action we commit is only mildly discrepant from our attitude, we observe our behavior and decide that our attitude is more in line with it than it really was. In these cases, the self-perception theory best explains the data. It is only when we are induced to perform actions, apparently of our own free choice, that seem strongly counter to our beliefs that we experience the tension of dissonance. An interesting fact about human beings is revealed here. By applying various pressures, researchers are able to cause people to behave in a way that is counter to their attitudes, yet people apparently do not find the pressure itself sufficient explanation for their actions. Apparently, human beings have a persistent *illusion of choice,* a feeling that their actions are less controlled than, objectively, they seem to be. This illusion is often central to dissonance-produced attitude change.

Perceiving Our Abilities and Competences.   Most of us are quite concerned with discovering our true abilities. How intelligent are we? How good-looking? How socially adept? Much of the information we have about ourselves is acquired through making comparisons with others. Festinger's **social-comparison theory** (1954) addresses this important source of self-knowledge. Two of the central points of this theory have to do with social reality and appropriate sources of comparison. In many ways, we depend on others to help us determine what is right and wrong, correct and incorrect, good and bad. Particularly in new or ambiguous circumstances, the actions of others help us to define what is real. A student transferring to a new high school learns, by the reaction of other students to his clothes, what are the "right" things to wear to signal the appropriate "cool" personality. But even in school or employment settings, where our performance is evaluated explicitly and such evaluations are communicated in the unmistakable form of grades and salaries, the meaning of such evaluations is not clear until we have compared ourselves with others. For example, a salary increase of 10 percent can be taken as a reward or a punishment, depending on whether your co-workers' raises were generally larger or smaller.

With whom are we most interested in comparing ourselves? Whom do we seek out as comparison others? One answer (Darley & Goethals, 1980) is that we seek comparison with people who match us on relevant background factors. For instance, if you want to know how well you performed on a

psychology quiz, you compare your score with the scores of other introductory students, not faculty. If a college teacher does the 100-yard dash at the annual picnic, he compares his time to the times of other equally out-of-shape faculty, not members of the college track team. These sorts of comparisons enable us to come to some conclusions about our own abilities, uncluttered by such factors as the degree of practice we have had or our physical condition.

Of course, this assumes that people are motivated to learn the true degree of their abilities. And often they are. But people are also strongly motivated to discover that their abilities are quite high. Self-esteem is better served, and the good opinion of others is more easily gained, if one possesses high levels of abilities. Recently, social psychologists have turned their attention to this side of the coin—the conditions under which people avoid comparing themselves to others in order to preserve their favorable images of themselves.

Jones and Berglas (1978) have coined the term **self-handicapping** to describe some of the ways that individuals strive to protect their self-concepts from negative information. Do you really want to know *for certain* that 40 percent of the people around you are smarter than you are? Would you like to know *exactly* how much other people like you? Jones and Berglas have argued that most of us don't really care to receive unequivocal feedback that might destroy some of our favorite illusions about ourselves. One good way to avoid such unpleasant information is to give ourselves handicaps that can be used as excuses. For example, if you don't study for an examination, then a poor grade does not imply that you are stupid. Or if you have a hangover or a sore leg when you play tennis, your losses don't have to be taken as an indication of physical inferiority. And if, with such handicaps, you should happen to do well, so much the better. If you played reasonably well under a handicap, then your true, unhandicapped level of ability must be high indeed.

Weiner (1971, 1974) has offered a useful system for classifying the kinds of explanations that people give for their own performances and the performances of others. To illustrate this system, imagine that you have just learned you received a grade of C on your psychology midterm exam. How might you explain your performance? According to Weiner, you would probably use one or more of the following types of explanations:

1. *Ability:* "I am not too good at this psychology stuff."
2. *Effort:* "I knew I should have studied last night instead of partying."
3. *Task difficulty:* "That exam was ridiculous—I'll bet most of those psych professors couldn't have done better than a C."
4. *Luck:* "What rotten luck—that professor emphasized all the things I didn't know and didn't ask anything about the stuff I studied."

Later studies have shown that these are the categories people appeal to when they generate spontaneous explanations for their own behavior or the behavior of others. In the face of failure, most of us avoid the first of these attributions: ability. The other three—the self-handicapping strategies—are designed to allow us to attribute our bad performances to causes that are not damaging to our self-esteem. Lack of effort, task difficulty, and bad luck are all plausible excuses for a poor performance, though they become implausible as explanations for a whole set of poor performances. After a series of poor performances our self-esteem might be expected to drop, along with (supposedly) the opinions that others have of us.

DESTRUCTIVE RELATIONSHIPS— AGGRESSION

Social perceptions turn into social actions, and it is important to consider how the process works. We begin with one all-too-frequent form of interpersonal interaction that involves the injury (physical and/or psychological) of one person by another. The term **aggression** (when applied to humans) refers to attempts by one individual to inflict pain or injury on another. Almost any daily newspaper or television newscast is sufficient to remind us that many relationships are destructive. Human aggression takes many forms, ranging from verbal insults and individual mayhem and murder to the numerous wars throughout human history.

Originally the psychological theories of human aggression were drawn from the conditioning and learning theories discussed in Chapter 6. These were then broadened by the social-learning perspectives of Bandura and others, which recognized that many aggressive actions are learned by observation. Finally, it was realized that attributions are also important determinants of human aggressions.

Instinct Theories of Aggression

Why is aggression so common? What makes one person want to harm another? The frequency and persistence of violence in human history have led some to believe that we possess an aggrressive instinct. Freud, for example, assumed that aggression resulted from displacement of a universal urge to return to an inert state. Because our death instinct is usually kept in check by our instinct for self-preservation, it finds expression in hostile actions toward others rather than toward ourselves.

Naturalistic observations of a number of animal species led Lorenz (1966) to argue that an aggressive instinct is the natural product of evolution, in which the strong and ruthless tend to weed out the weak and passive. This is so, Lorenz suggested, for several reasons. First, a male animal that uses aggressive acts to dominate other males of the same species will have the opportunity to impregnate more females. This increases the number of animals in subsequent generations that possess the genes of aggressive forebears. Second, among carnivorous animals that prey on animals of other species for their food, successful aggressiveness has obvious survival value, and thus provides an evolutionary advantage.

Most psychologists who study human aggressive behavior would assign relatively little causal role to instinctive or innate processes. From a human perspective, there are a discouragingly large number of ways in which aggression is learned and rewarded, so it is usually not necessary to resort to instinct to explain acts of human aggression.

The Frustration-Aggression Theory

We all seem to have an occasional urge to harm another person. One attempt to explain this, first formulated by Dollard, Doob, Miller, Mower, and Sears (1939), was the **frustration-aggression hypothesis.** These researchers believed that **frustration** (the blocking of the path to a goal) always leads to aggression, and that aggression is always the result of frustration.

It has become clear that the initial form of this hypothesis is wrong. Frustration does not *always* lead to aggression; it can, for example, cause depres-

sion and lethargy instead (Seligman, 1975). Likewise, aggression is not *always* the result of frustration; soldiers and executioners, for example, engage in aggression when they are ordered to do so. There is, however, considerable support for a more modest form of the hypothesis. Frustration does, under certain circumstances, tend to increase the likelihood of aggression.

One determinant of the frustration-aggression link is the nature of the frustration. *Arbitrary* frustrations do lead to aggression, but nonarbitrary frustrations (those that seem to have an acceptable reason for occurring) do not (Zillman & Cantor, 1976). Capricious or inexplicable sources of frustration thus appear to be most likely to provoke aggressive reactions.

One implication of the frustration-aggression analysis is that each new frustration will increase the instigation to aggress, until the person finally "blows up." After this, the person's arousal level is presumably lowered, until new frustrations begin to build it up again. This view implies that if aggressive impulses could be drained off in some harmless, socially acceptable way, then the negative effects of uncontrolled aggression could be eliminated. The process of draining off aggressive impulses is called **catharsis.** The most obvious form of catharsis would be aggression directed toward the source of frustration. Aggression against a person not related to the original source of frustration may also reduce aggressive arousal. A more controversial notion is that *vicarious catharsis* (such as the observation of someone else aggressing) serves to reduce the tendency to aggress. A large number of studies testing the validity of the catharsis hypothesis lead to the conclusion that catharsis only occurs when the person actually aggresses against the source of frustration (Doob & Wood, 1972; Konecni & Doob, 1972). Aggressing against some other person, or watching someone else aggress, does not produce a cathartic effect. In fact, as we shall see in the next section, watching someone else agress can *increase* the likelihood of subsequent aggression from the observer.

The Aggression-Cues Theory

Berkowitz (1973, 1974) has suggested a reformulation of the frustration-aggression hypothesis. Frustration, in his theory, leads to the emotional response of anger. Anger creates a readiness for aggressive acts, but those acts do not actually take place unless cues to aggressive actions are present. For example, Berkowitz and LePage (1967) first had a confederate make subjects angry. The subjects were then given the opportunity to aggress against the confederate by giving him electric shocks. When no aggressive cues were present, subjects engaged in little aggression against the confederate. When aggressive cues were present, in the form of a shotgun and a revolver lying on a table next to the subject, the confederate was much more likely to be given powerful electric shocks. (The confederate was not actually shocked in this and similar experiments. For a description of the device used in such studies, see Chaper 20.)

The classic frustration-aggression hypothesis holds that frustration can be reduced by committing an act of aggression against *any* person that is similar, but not identical, to the act that instigated the aggression. Berkowitz rejects this and instead suggests that the frustrated individual's anger will not be reduced unless harm is inflicted directly on the instigator.

Berkowitz and his students have generated an impressive body of research supporting his theory (Berkowitz, 1974), but controversy remains (see, for

instance, Feshback & Fraczek, 1979). One area of disagreement involves the sources of aggression. According to social-learning theory (which we will examine below), the sources of aggression are multiple. In contrast, according to Berkowitz, frustration first instigates anger, but cues associated in the past with aggression must be present for aggressive acts to occur in the present. Here the controversy may be more apparent than real. Sources of frustration are frequent in our culture, and cues associated with aggression are also plentiful. So, in a sense, the "sources" of aggression in Berkowitz's theory may be multiple. Moreover, the original frustration-aggression theory suggests that the aggressive tension produced by frustration can be reduced when it is directed against something or someone other than the source of the frustration. In contrast, the aggression-cues theory suggests that the cause of the frustration must be the target of the aggression. The evidence reviewed earlier suggesting that catharsis does not necessarily reduce aggression supports the aggression-cues theory. On the other hand, there is evidence that activities other than aggression can reduce the arousal produced by frustration. Further research is needed to clarify this issue.

The Instrumental Theory of Aggression

While the frustration-aggression hypothesis, in its recently modified form, has some validity, there is a second explanation for aggressive behavior that is also clearly valid in our society. Aggression is learned and practiced because it leads to rewards for the aggressing person **(instrumental aggression).** According to the leading proponents of this **social-learning theory** (Bandura & Walters, 1963; Bass, 1971), the laws of operant learning that we discussed in Chapter 6 provide good explanations for much of the aggression that we see around us.

One "good" reason for attacking another person is that such aggression will lead to a reward. In the case of mugging or armed robbery, the potential reward is obvious. The rewards can, of course, be more subtle, involving feelings of power and control or social approval. In street gangs or military organizations, aggressive behavior may be explicitly or implicitly approved by group members. Geen and Stonner (1971), for example, found that verbal approval is very effective in increasing aggression.

The other major ways in which we learn aggressive behavior is through imitating others. An excellent demonstration that aggression can be learned by imitating the behavior of others was provided by Bandura, Ross, and Ross (1963b) in their "Bobo doll" experiment. Young children were shown either a live or filmed adult model or a cartoon figure hitting an inflatable punching-bag doll. Children who saw any of the three kinds of models displayed more aggression toward the Bobo doll than did children who had not been exposed to an aggressive model.

Aggression, then, can be learned either directly or by observation. But, as you will remember, learning theory suggests that aggressive action will continue to be committed only if there are reinforcing contingencies that maintain it. This does, unfortunately, often seem to be the case (Baron, 1977). Bullies sometimes get their way, or the best position on the team, or the best toys in the preschool, and their adult equivalents sometimes get the adult equivalents of such rewards. First, aggression is sometimes rewarded. Second, recall (from Chapter 6) that partial reinforcements have particularly strong sustaining effects on responses. Reward does not need to occur after *every* aggressive act for aggressive behavior to be maintained. It has been

The best explanation for why aggression occurs is that, like most other human behavior, it is learned and its performance is rewarded. (Philip Jon Bailey/The Picture Cube)

shown, rather, that partial reinforcement can maintain a high rate of responding (see Chapter 6). There seem to be three kinds of rewards that the real world offers aggressors. First, as in the above examples, there are tangible rewards in the form of commodities such as toys or scarce supplies of food. Second, approval and other social rewards are often available to aggressors. The calls of "kill the quarterback" from crowds, even at children's football games, are a convincing example of this. And in neighborhood gangs the "toughest kid" often gains status and power. Third, self-reward mechanisms that maintain aggressive action may develop. When "toughness" becomes a part of one's self-image, living up to it through aggressive acts may bring self-satisfaction.

Situational Determinants of Aggression

We have seen that such environmental conditions as the presence of weapons and the viewing of violence can increase the likelihood of aggression. A number of other precipitating factors have also been studied. Perhaps the most obvious instigator of aggression is aggression itself. For example, if someone gives you a shove, it is quite likely that you will shove back (Taylor & Pisano, 1971). Laboratory studies have often made use of aggression as an instigator of aggression. This calls to mind the attributional perspective mentioned earlier. If another person intentionally aggresses against you, then the circumstances entitle you to aggress back. Counteraggression in self-defense is an action that most people consider justified.

High levels of arousal, even arousal from a source that has nothing to do with frustration or aggression, also facilitate aggression. Geen and O'Neal (1969), for example, found that subjects aroused by loud noise were more affected by an aggression-laden film than subjects who had not been exposed to noise. Zillman (1971) believes that heightened, generalized arousal can lead to aggressive behavior when an inducement to aggress is present. Zillman (1971) also found that increased sexual arousal made subsequent aggression more likely when subjects were irritated by a confederate. Malar-

Perhaps the most common instigator of aggression is aggression itself. If someone gives you a shove, the chances that you will shove back are high. The knowledgeable sports fan will recognize still another situational factor of aggression at work here. The owners of professional hockey (and some other sports) teams are convinced that fans pay to see aggression, so they tend to reinforce players who commit it. (Michael Hayman/Photo Researchers)

muth and Donnerstein (1983) have pointed out the possible connection between erotic stimulation caused by pornography and later aggression, particularly when the pornographic material contains aggression-laden content. (Note the similarities between these theories of aggression and Schachter's general theory of emotion presented in Chapter 12.)

States of Awareness and Aggression

The likelihood that people will act aggressively appears to be closely related to their *state of awareness*. Evidence for this assertion comes from research inspired by Duval and Wicklund's (1972) theory of **objective self-awareness.** The central idea of this theory is that we can be either *objectively* or *subjectively* self-aware. In a state of subjective self-awareness, attention is focused outward. For example, if we are driving down a twisting road at high speed, most of our attention will be concerned with staying on the road. Subjective awareness is probably the most typical state of consciousness.

When we are objectively self-aware, however, we turn our full attention onto ourselves. Seeing yourself in a mirror or on closed circuit television would make you consider yourself as an object of attention. When we focus on ourselves, we tend to evaluate ourselves compared to the standards and values that we hold and that are salient or relevant at the time.

There is a third state of awareness, one in which the self is completely caught up in concerns of the moment, with no thought of what others or oneself might think of one's behavior. In the state of *deindividuation* (Zimbardo, 1969), one loses all concern for oneself as an individual, and instead focuses on the present environment with little thought of the past or future. In this state the normal self-controls (such as values, concerns about the reactions of others, and feelings such as shame and guilt) are disconnected. In a sense, deindividuation is the opposite of objective self-awareness and is more like an extreme form of subjective self-awareness.

Deindividuation often occurs in crowds. One thinks of the mobs of people who occasionally gather under building ledges on which would-be suicides are perched, agonizing about whether to jump. One person in the crowd calls out "Jump," and suddenly others pick up the chant as well. When people are in a deindividuated state, their behavior tends to be vigorous, repetitive, and difficult to stop. Behaviors that are normally inhibited may occur, and the person may not respond to cues that normally would trigger self-control mechanisms. This means that the behavior of a person who begins to aggress while in a deindividuated state may be of high intensity, difficult to stop, and indiscriminate in its choice of targets. This description fits that of someone who has "gone beserk." It may explain the violent crimes one hears of in which victims are stabbed scores or even hundreds of times.

The social-learning model of aggression and its offshoots have been substantially supported by empirical evidence in recent years (Baron, 1977). What, then, are its implications? First, unlike instinctive or drive theories, learning theory suggests that aggressive behavior has multiple causes. Second, there seem to be a large number of ways in which aggressive actions are directly learned or indirectly modeled. For this reason, learning theorists see aggression as deeply rooted in our society. But, unlike drive and instinct theorists, they do not view aggression as an inevitable and inescapable human behavior. They do not see human aggression as the product of an ever-filling internal reservoir of aggressive energy, or as an automatic response to

Does Violence on Television Cause Violent Behavior?

Like many of us, George Gerbner and his colleagues at the Annenberg School of Communication watch a great deal of television. Unlike the rest of us, they keep careful records of what they watch. They find that they watch a great deal of physical violence. Seventy percent of prime-time shows contain one or more episodes of physical violence, and children's programs contain even more (Gerbner & Gross, 1976). On the basis of estimates of the numbers of hours children spend watching television, Walters and Malmud (1975) figured that the average 16-year-old has "witnessed" 13,000 television murders, while heavy television watchers have viewed many more.

Parents and other citizens, observing the barrage of television violence, have become concerned about its effects on children's development. Does viewing violent acts on television lead to violent behavior? For ethical and practical reasons, this is a very difficult question on which to gather proof. We cannot perform true long-term controlled experiments, sentencing some children, chosen at random, to watch only violent shows for months or years and others to watch only nonviolent shows. Only field studies are possible. (We can, of course, set up a short-term experiment in which we control what children watch for the duration of the experiment and test immediately for its effects. However, it is the long-term effects of television viewing that have caused concern, and we cannot have 24-hour-a-day control over children's viewing habits.)

Some researchers have watched the development of children's viewing patterns over time (e.g., Huesmann, 1982). Often, but not always, these studies have found that children who watch a great deal of television, or who prefer to watch violent television shows, do display higher levels of violent behavior later in childhood. Obviously, this finding is consistent with the interpretation that watching violence provokes violence, but it does not prove it. It could be that some children are predisposed toward violence, and that they therefore tend to watch more violent television shows at an early age and to behave violently as they get older. The watching of violent television, then, may be a symptom of a violence-disposed personality rather than a cause of violence.

Another research approach is to look at the world views of people—including children—who are heavy television viewers. By extensive analyses of random samples of shows, researchers can determine the rates at which fictional crimes happen to television people. Government statistics, of course, document the real-life incidences of various crimes. As you might expect, the crime rate is higher on television than in real life. (It is higher still on children's cartoon shows: Just watch some weekend morning and observe the crashing, bashing, and crushing typical of the "kiddy ghetto" programs!) When asked about the rates at which various events happen in the real world, heavy television viewers tend to overestimate the likelihood that they will be crime victims, whereas light viewers have a more accurate perspective (Gerbner et al., 1979). How do you think this affects the relationships of heavy television viewers with their neighbors, acquaintances, and strangers, or their votes for public officials?

frustration or some other innate releasing mechanism. In fact, from a social-learning perspective, human aggression can be reduced by eliminating the conditions under which it is learned and reducing the reinforcements by which it is maintained. The message of social-learning theory contains components of both pessimism and optimism: pessimism at the number of elements in our social system supporting violence, and optimism that these can be changed and violence decreased.

CONSTRUCTIVE RELATIONSHIPS— ATTRACTION

After the consideration of aggression and harmful acts against others, it is something of a relief to turn to the more positive question of how people come to like each other. The study of liking also provides a useful bridge to social-interaction questions. Liking begins with social perceptions, but soon involves social exchanges.

What causes people to like each other? Why do we like some people very much and dislike others? Whenever two or more people interact, they form attitudes and opinions about each other. These evaluations combine to determine how much attraction they feel toward each other. In between the ex-

tremes of passionate love and hatred lies a range of positive and negative evaluations that have pervasive consequences for all of us. Where do these evaluations come from?

Liking and Propinquity

There are thousands—perhaps millions—of people in the world we could like. Which ones we *do* come to like depends on which ones we meet. Thus our physical proximity or *propinquity* to other people is an important precondition for future liking because it makes possible the encounter that may begin the liking process. People can come to like one another after encounters due to accidents as various as being assigned to the same section of a course or being placed next to one another in a state police training program in which seating was by alphabetical order (Segal, 1974). Even racial barriers to friendship have crumbled under the propinquity effect (Deutsch & Collins, 1951).

Studies have shown that all of the essentially accidental reasons that bring people together can lead to liking relationships. Why is this so? Propinquity doesn't always work, but when it does, it is often because it gives people a chance to discover they have shared interests, matching opinions, and similar values. As you will read immediately below, these are important determinants of liking. A second reason for the effects of propinquity is more subtle. When people are presented with new situations or conditions, they at first react negatively and with feelings of strangeness, but gradually, as they become more familiar with the material, they become more positively disposed toward it. Think, for example, of what often happens when you hear a new song. At first it seems strange, and perhaps you don't care for it; but after you have heard it a few times, you begin to like it.

Liking and Similarity

Conventional wisdom says that birds of a feather flock together. This particular bit of conventional wisdom has been proved correct by a number of experimental studies. As the degree of similarity of attitudes and values held by two people increases, so does the attraction between them (Byrne & Rhamey, 1965). Most of these investigations have been conducted in laboratory settings, in which the degree of apparent similarity can be controlled and manipulated, but there is also evidence of a relationship between similarity and attraction in such varied settings as marriage (Kerckhoff & Davis, 1962) and bomb shelters (Griffitt & Veitch, 1974).

Why do we tend to like similar others? One major explanation employs the principle of cognitive consistency. As we have seen, Festinger's (1957) theory of cognitive dissonance makes it clear that people try to reduce or eliminate inconsistency, and a number of other theorists have observed that people prefer consistency (e.g., Heider, 1958). Newcomb (1956, 1971) has applied the principle of cognitive consistency to interpersonal relationships. According to this **balance theory,** we tend to like relationships that are consistent or balanced. If we are very similar to another person, it "makes sense" (is consistent or balanced) to like that person (see Figure 19–4).

Still another reason why we tend to like similar others is that they reinforce and validate our opinions and values. It is always reassuring and rewarding to discover that another person agrees with you or has similar values (Lott & Lott, 1968, 1974; Byrne & Clore, 1970).

Figure 19–4 Balanced and Unbalanced Triads So strong is the effect of the balance principle that people often use it as a predictive guide. If I (P) like one person (O), and that person likes another (X), I guess that probably I will like X also (see *a*). If I like O, and O dislikes X, what am I likely to guess about whether I will like or dislike X? Balance theory suggests, and research shows, that I will expect to dislike X (see *b*). Extensions of balance theory are also possible: If I disagree violently with the political opinions of person O, and if all I know about candidate X is that he is endorsed by person O, what am I likely to suspect about candidate X's political views? And, therefore, am I likely to vote for candidate X (see *c*)?

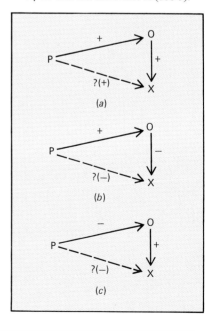

While we have a general tendency to like people who are like us, there are a number of exceptions to this rule. One obvious one is implied by another piece of conventional wisdom: "Opposites attract." Although we may like people who are like us, we may get along better with people who have complementary characteristics. For example, a person who talks a lot is likely to have some friends who are listeners; a dominant person needs someone to dominate and therefore might be disposed to like submissive acquaintances; a sadist is a natural partner for a masochist. Need complementarity is primarily important in long-term relationships. Kerckhoff and Davis (1962), for example, found that couples in the early stages of a relationship were more likely to move toward forming a permanent relationship when they had similar needs; later in the relationship, however, complementary needs became more important.

The Reciprocation of Liking

A second major determinant of our attraction for another comes from our belief about whether or not that person likes us. Liking tends to be reciprocated. If people obviously like you, then you will probably like them. If people clearly dislike you, you will probably dislike them (Byrne & Rhamey, 1965; Sigall & Aronson, 1969; Tagiuri, Blake, & Bruner, 1953). Being liked by others makes you feel good, but being disliked makes you feel bad. It is not surprising that both liking and disliking are reciprocated (Byrne & Clore, 1970).

You might expect, then, that the more good things Tom says about Bill, the more Bill will like Tom. Similarly, the more critical or disparaging remarks Ann makes about Sue, the less Sue should like Ann. However, a study by Aronson and Linder (1965) makes it clear that such predictions must be qualified. They found that the *sequence* of liking information can be as important as its positive or negative quality. To become liked by someone who formerly disliked you, or to lose the approval of someone who formerly liked you, has a greater impact than sustained liking or disliking by another person (see Table 19–1).

Table 19–1: Liking the Confederate.

Experimental Condition	Mean
Gain (Negative-positive)	+7.67
(Positive-positive)	+6.42
(Negative-negative)	+2.52
Loss (Positive-negative)	+0.87

Aronson and Linder (1965).

Physical Attractiveness and Liking

Anyone who has watched television, leafed through a popular magazine, or looked at billboard advertisements knows that our culture values physical attractiveness very highly. Manufacturers spend millions of dollars advertising products that are designed to make us look good, and we spend billions buying those products. The popularity of diets, exercise clubs, and the latest fashions attests to our interest in improving our appearance. There is good reason for this great interest in our appearance: A large number of investigations all point to the conclusion that the more physically attractive a person is, the more he or she is liked by others (Berscheid, 1985).

Walster, Aronson, Abrahams, and Rottman (1966) measured liking for various partners at a "computer dance," at which each participant was matched with a series of partners of the opposite sex by a computer. A number of personal characteristics of the dance participants were measured in an attempt to discover which ones would influence liking. The researchers found, however, that the only one that mattered was physical attractiveness. The more physically attractive the partner was, the more he or she was liked.

In addition to being liked, physically attractive people are generally as-

Is romantic love simply a deeper, more extreme form of liking, or does it have different characteristics altogether? Probably most of us feel that the two emotions differ importantly in kind, and a set of research studies by Rubin (1973) tends to bear this out. First, Rubin assembled a large number of statements that could describe one person's feelings toward another. He then had subjects sort these into two categories: those characteristic of loving relationships and those characteristic of liking relationships. There was general agreement as to which statements belonged in each category; relatively few items were judged by subjects to be descriptive both of loving and of liking relationships. This suggests, first, that people generally agree on descriptions of loving and liking; and second, that these two feelings are described—and experienced—quite differently. Loving seems to involve feelings of attachment, caring for the

welfare of the other, and intimacy; while liking implies affection, respect, and a favorable evaluation of the other on such positive characteristics as good judgment and maturity and on what Rubin refers to as "associated tendency to view the other person as similar to oneself" (1973, p. 217). (Recall our earlier discussion about opinion similarity and liking.)

Rubin brought together couples who reported being deeply in love with each other (as measured by the Rubin scale; see table). They made more eye contact with each other than did members of pairs who were not as much in love, and the more deeply in love they reported being, the more likely they were six months later to report that their relationship had progressed. Interestingly, this last finding was true only for those respondents who believed that love should "conquer all." For those who held a less romantic ideology and who felt that economic gain and social status should be considered in choosing a marriage partner, there was no association between depth of love and progress of the relationship toward marriage. Apparently, the effects of love on one's relationships

are tempered by one's ideology about the importance of love for marriage.

Selected Love-Scale and Liking-Scale Items

Love Scale

1. I would do almost anything for _____.
2. I would forgive _____ for practically anything.
3. I feel resposible for _____'s well-being.
4. It would be hard for me to get along without _____.

Liking Scale

1. I think that _____ is unusually well adjusted.
2. I have great confidence in _____'s good judgment.
3. I think that _____ is one of those people who quickly win respect.
4. _____ is one of the most likable people I know.

Adapted from Rubin, 1973, p. 219.

sumed to have a number of more positive qualities than their more average-looking counterparts. For example, when Dion, Berscheid, and Walster (1972) showed photographs of attractive and ordinary-looking people to their subjects, the subjects attributed more positive personality traits, greater occupational success, and higher marital competence to the physically attractive people.

The Development of Long-Term Relationships

As you have probably noticed, most of the causes of liking that we have been discussing are those most likely to determine only our initial reactions to other people. Once we have gained a favorable first impression and decided that we like someone, how do we move into short-term early relationships, and then how do such acquaintances develop into long-term, close relationships? A number of psychologists (Levinger & Snoek, 1972; Levinger, 1974; Murstein, 1976) have watched the actual course of long-term relationships as they develop and have reported on the processes they observed. Levinger (1974) identified three levels of relationships, each distinguished from an earlier level by an increasing degree of interdependence between the participants.

The first level is one of *unilateral awareness* of each other. At this stage the other variables we have discussed have their effects. Proximity creates the possibility of contact. Brief contact, perhaps not even involving the exchange of words, creates the possibility of an assessment of the other's behavior,

(Paul Conklin/Monkmeyer Press)

manners, and looks. Other cues, such as the absence of an engagement ring, signal availability: Manner of dress—trendy or conventional—can tell much about attitudes. At this level of awareness the attraction one person feels toward another depends largely on the image projected by the other person. Our perceptions of another's image, in turn, depend on the visible characteristics of the other's appearance, filtered through our own conceptualizations of the desirability or attractiveness of those characteristics.

The second level of a relationship is that of *surface contact*. Many of the initial contacts between two people are likely to take place in the setting in which they first encountered each other, and so, quite naturally, their conversation will be formed by this setting and the social role played by each within it. Two people who meet at a political club will begin talking to each other about their candidates and issues. Even when these early conversations are relatively superficial, they create chances for the discovery of similarities—both may, for instance, agree on which issues are more relevant at the time.

It is at this second level that *self-disclosure* begins. Psychologists (Jourard, 1968) have noted that a key component of the process that leads to intimacy involves the sharing of increasingly important and intimate personal information. Generally (Jourard, 1968), one individual tells the other some fact that he considers important about himself, and the other responds by telling a similar confidence about herself that is equally or a little more revealing. In this way, the two people may discover that they have important similar experiences, likes, and dislikes that could not be discovered from the superficial impressions of the first stage. (Or, of course, they may discover that although their superficial similarities drew them together, the more important things they learn about each other through self-disclosure suggest they are mismatched. In this case, the relationship may go no further.)

Self-disclosure between two people marks the beginning of a relationship that sets them apart from others. All of us have had this experience—and it is a quite wonderful one—of discovering that there is another person who thinks, feels, and experiences the world "just as I do." So people in this stage are generally motivated to continue their relationship. Each will seek to discover if the other's time and other commitments permit a deepening of the relationship.

Mutuality characterizes the third stage of close relationships. Deeper self-disclosures create greater feelings of intimacy. The two partners, who previously discovered shared attitudes, now come to work out a joint position on new topics. Empathy develops between them; they each become highly aware of how the other feels. Each adapts his or her behavior to decrease actions that might hurt or dissatisfy the other person. In this state people experience a "we" rather than an "I" identification.

The major theme that runs through the three stages in the development of a relationship is *interdependence*. As relationships grow and deepen, the participants come to depend on each other more, and in a greater number of ways; for need gratification, for confirmations of the ways each sees the world, for reward, and for the experiences of being secure and unthreatened within a relationship and of providing that security for another (Burgess & Huston, 1979). This sequence describes the development of romantic relationships, but it is true of intimate friendships as well.

Social Exchange in Long-Term Relationships

One theory of long-term relationships suggests that two people with attitudinal similarity are able to supply something—in this case, confirmation of

ideas and attitudes—that is of value to one another. Obviously one reason for liking another is that the other provides one with rewards. One reason people stay together is that they continue to provide rewards for each other. These social-exchange principles, which will be discussed further in Chapter 20, are at work in most interpersonal relationships. In the traditional marriage, for example, the husband was thought to give economic and emotional security to the wife, who because of her dependence valued these commodities. Meanwhile, she gave domestic services, children, and sexual favors to the male. This is an example of an exchange in which the participants have complementary resources that allow for a satisfactory exchange of rewards. In other words, different people need different things, and exchange relationships can become successful and endure because one person can relatively easily give what another person needs. The example also makes it clear that the traditional image of marriage relies on social diagnoses of the needs of men and women that are not valid for many people today and that, indeed, are currently much argued about.

Changes in a person's view of marriage can lead to dissatisfaction. For example, if a once-traditional wife becomes more concerned about intellectual and professional goals than about homemaking, she may begin to be less satisfied in her traditional marriage. In such a case, she views her situation less favorably because her set of expectations or *comparison level* has changed (Thibaut & Kelley, 1959; Kelley & Thibaut, 1978). If both partners can change together, a new satisfactory relationship may be established on a new basis. However, if one party cannot or will not change, or if the resources available to the other person prevent the kind of change desired by the partner, then the relationship may dissolve.

Dissolution of marital relationships is much more common now than in the past. One reason may be that changes in traditional male and female roles and expectations have created new stresses in marriages that are difficult to resolve. But there is another important consideration. If the outcomes in a relationship fall below a person's minimum requirements, or comparison level, the person will not be satisfied. This does not necessarily mean that the relationship will end, because the alternatives must be considered. If the satisfactions obtainable from other relationships seem even lower than the few satisfactions gained from the existing relationship, then the person will seek to preserve the present relationship even though it is unsatisfactory in an absolute sense. The phrase "the lesser of two evils" contains this idea; if the relationship you are in is better than any of your alternatives, then you will stay in it even though you are dissatisfied.

Kelley and Thibaut (1978) point out that leaving a relationship also has *exit costs*. Exit costs include whatever negative events the former partner inflicts, such as tears and recriminations. They can also include any guilt the person ending the relationship feels. Finally, they can include whatever costs society inflicts on the terminator. In the past divorce entailed all these costs. A man divorcing a woman who had been a good wife, for instance, could expect bitter recriminations from his wife, guilty feelings, and severe condemnation from society. Today these exit costs, although still substantial, have been reduced. The increased frequency of divorce has coincided with a more lenient public attitude toward such behavior. In addition, many states have liberalized divorce laws, further reducing the social cost of ending an unsatisfactory relationship.

It is clear that viewing marriage as an exchange relationship is a useful analytic approach. It is also clear, however, that participants in such long-term relationships as marriage, or even close friendships, do not like to view

their behavior in such an analytical way. Indeed, a person would probably feel rejected if a friend or spouse kept a balance sheet of favors rendered and received, and immediately returned every kindness with a similar favor of equal value. Clark and Mills (1979) argue that relationships are thought of in two different categories. In *exchange* relationships, such as business transactions, it is appropriate and fair to keep close track of the benefits that accrue to each participant, and to be concerned with the equity of reward distribution. In *communal* relationships, such as marriage, these concerns are not so appropriate. In these relationships favors are given as affirmations of attraction or to satisfy the needs of the other; they need not and should not be returned "tit-for-tat." In a series of studies Clark and Mills demonstrated that in exchange relationships requests for favors and unreturned favors are viewed negatively. In communal relationships, however, requests for favors are viewed favorably, and promptly returning the favor of the other is taken as a rebuff.

Other research suggests that love may not be as concerned with the give-and-take or barter-and-exchange aspects of social interaction as it has been depicted in many studies. According to Shakespeare (Sonnet 116), "Love is not love which alters when it alteration finds . . . it is an ever-fixed mark that looks on tempest and is never shaken"—a far cry from the calculation of comparison levels, exit costs, and "favors rendered" balance sheets. Some psychologists have reasoned that subjects in psychology experiments describe their relationships in such economic exchange terms because the experimental setting induced them to provide logical reasons. A different approach is through imagination. When asked to make up fantasy stories about ambiguous scenes, people who describe themselves as deeply in love invent fantasies that differ from those of people who are not in love, and differ in ways akin to what Shakespeare had in mind (McAdams, 1980). The "lovers" invent scenarios in which the characters display need for harmony, union, commitment, and intimacy. McClelland (1986) has speculated that this is because self-reports on questionnaires elicit logical, rational reasons, whereas fantasies tap emotions, feelings, and motives. Not all theorists would agree with the speculation, but it raises an issue that may well affect future perspectives on liking and loving.

SUMMARY

1. *Attribution* is the process by which we perceive people and make judgments about what they are like. It can be influenced by a number of factors, including experience with the person, first impressions, accessible constructs, implicit personality theories, attribution rules, and different opportunities to observe the person.

2. There are three dimensions around which we can organize information about a person's behavior: the actor, the entity, and time. The *fundamental attribution error* is a tendency to attribute behavior to actors rather than to the situations they are in.

3. *Actor-observer differences* in attribution occur because we tend to see our own actions as reasonable responses to the environment, and the actions of other

persons as manifestations of their inner selves or true personalities.

4. We also believe that other persons would react to situational pressures in the same way that we would, thus sometimes perceiving a *false consensus* that does not actually exist. This tendency to see everything from our own point of view is sometimes given the general label of *egocentric bias*.

5. Various decision-making *heuristics* or rules of thumb, including *representativeness* and *availability*, can also bias our reasoning about other people.

6. Our attributions produce our conceptualizations of others, and we then act toward others on the basis of these conceptualizations. If our attributions are initially incorrect, then interactions with others may

serve to correct them. But our interactions may also reflect a *self-fulfilling prophecy,* in which we make an originally false expectation "come true."

7. Psychologists have long attempted to determine how attitudes influence behavior. Present thinking holds that the relationship is complex. Attitudes that closely relate to the behaviors in question are the best predictors of future behavior, and this is particularly true for attitudes based on previous experience with the attitude object.

8. Some characteristics of a communicator that make a communication more effective are expertise or credibility, trustworthiness, and similarity to the receiver. Aspects of a communication that make it more persuasive include clarity and, oftentimes, presentation of both sides of an issue. Aspects of the listener also plan an all important role in the effectiveness of a communication.

9. We experience *cognitive dissonance* when two or more of our beliefs or attitudes (cognitions) are contradictory or inconsistent (dissonant). According to Festinger's theory, we are so uncomfortable in a state of cognitive dissonance that we alter one or more of our cognitions to make them more compatible with another.

10. Explanations of the causes of aggression include instinct theories, the *frustration-aggression hypothesis,* and *social-learning theory.* The situational determinants of aggression are also important in understanding its occurrence. Social-learning theory suggests that just as aggression is learned, nonaggressive behaviors can also be learned.

11. Proximity generally encourages the development of liking relationships. In the early stages of a relationship relatively superficial characteristics, such as physical attractiveness and similarity, determine whether we like another person. Later on, considerations of social exchange come into play.

12. In intimate relationships, social exchange considerations seem to diminish, and considerations of harmony, union and commitment increase.

SUGGESTED READINGS

BARON, R. A. (1977). *Human aggression.* New York: Plenum Press. An excellent introduction to theories of human aggression and the empirical evidence for these theories.

BERSCHEID, E. (1985). Interpersonal Attraction. In G. Lindsey and E. Aronson (Eds.), *The handbook of social psychology* (3rd ed.). New York: Random House. An excellent and up-to-date review of both interpersonal attraction, and via attraction, into the rapidly developing field of attraction in close relationships.

BURGESS, R., and HUSTON, T. (Eds.) (1978). *Social exchange in developing relationships.* New York: Academic Press.

KAHNEMAN, D., SLOVIC, and TVERSKY, A. (1982). *Judgment under uncertainty: Heuristics and biases.* Cambridge: Cambridge University Press. People face the constant necessity for making decisions when the information on which to base these decisions is incomplete and jumbly erroneous. These authors report their research and the research of others on how people go about this task.

NISBETT, R. E., and ROSS, L. (1980). *Human inference: Strategies and shortcomings of social judgment.* Englewood Cliffs, N.J.: Prentice-Hall. The authors present a recent, readable summary of findings on our strengths and weaknesses as intuitive psychologists.

PETTY, R. E., and CAPIOPPO, J. T. (1981). *Attitudes and persuasion: Classic and contemporary approaches.* Dubuque, Iowa: Brown. An up-to-date, thoughtful summary of classic and recent perspectives on attitudes and attitude change.

ROSS, M. and FLETCHER, G. (1985). Attribution and Social Perception. In G. Lindzey and E. Aronson (eds.) *The handbook of social psychology* (3rd ed.) New York, Random House. An integrative review of current research and theory on the important topics of person perception, attribution, and stereotypes.

SHAVER, K. G. (1975). *An introduction to attribution processes.* Cambridge, Mass.: Winthrop. A thoughtful orientation to attribution theories.

WICKLUND, R. A. and BREHM, J. W. (1976). *Perspectives on cognitive dissonance.* Hillsdale, N.J.: Erlbaum. The huge amount of dissonance research is summarized in this comprehensive review.

20 Social Influence and Group Processes

T he previous chapter was concerned primarily with the way we think about and act toward other people, with how we draw inferences about what they do and what they say, with how we form and maintain our impressions of and attitudes toward them, and with what makes us aggress against, like, and sometimes love them. The present chapter, in contrast, is concerned with the ways in which people influence each other's behavior, the ways in which individuals affect groups, and the ways in which groups affect individuals. It is also concerned with what happens in general when people get together in groups.

SOCIAL INFLUENCE: ONE SOURCE AFFECTING MANY TARGETS

We begin with a general framework that describes social influence (Latané, 1981). Figure 20–1 represents in pictorial form the way in which one person (a source of influence) can affect others (the targets of influence). Although this is only a useful metaphor, one can imagine the source as analogous to the sun in our solar system, and the targets as the planets. The rays emanating from the source are rays of social influence, akin to the sun's heat.

Three factors seem important here: the strength of the source, the immediacy of the source, and the number of targets. Just as a larger sun will bestow more heat on its attendant planets than a smaller sun, so will a stronger or more potent source of social influence have more effect than one

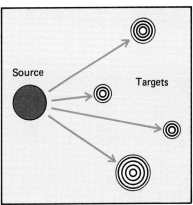

Figure 20–1 Leadership: One source affecting many targets. (After Latané, 1981)

Pieter Brueghel's "Flemish Country Festival" captures the social world of a peasant village in the sixteenth century. (Art Resource)

less powerful. A president will get more compliance from his cabinet, for example, than will a vice president. In addition, the closer or more immediate the source, the greater its effect, as reflected in the popular saying "When the cat's away the mice will play." Finally, although here the analogy to a sun and planets breaks down, the number of social targets makes a difference in that it is usually easier for a source to influence 2 targets than 20, because with 20 targets the influence has to be "spread thin." We shall see all of these principles—strength, immediacy, and number—in action as we discuss various forms of social influence.

Leadership

The above discussion brings us neatly to the study of **leadership,** which is, after all, the influence of an individual on a group. Over half a century's research has been devoted to the study of leadership. Originally, these studies took a *trait-centered approach*—that is, they searched for people who possessed the **trait** of "leadership" or who had traits that were thought to constitute leadership, such as "dominance" or "extroversion." It was assumed that these traits would guarantee their selection as leaders, regardless of the groups in which they found themselves or the tasks faced by these groups. This approach had very limited success, however (Stodgill, 1948; Mann, 1959). Very few traits that were supposed to predict leadership were found in more than one study. Worse, a trait that was positively related to leader effectiveness (for example, sensitivity) in one study was found to be negatively related in another.

Components of Leadership. Pressed by this evidence to rethink their models of leadership, many organizational psychologists turned to the study of leadership behavior to see if they couldn't come to a better understanding of the phenomenon itself before attempting to predict that a particular individual would be a success at it. A useful distinction that has stood up well over the years is that much of leadership behavior has two components: consideration and initiation (Fleishman, 1957; Halpin & Winer, 1957). Acts of *consideration* generally are supportive acts that show concern for other group members. Examples include praising the work other group members do or listening attentively to their opinions. Leaders show consideration by being friendly or helpful to subordinates, listening to their suggestions, being concerned for their welfare, going to bat for them with the company, and so on.

Acts of *initiation* involve undertaking the tasks of the group and structuring the group to achieve its goals most effectively. A group member who volunteers to do one part of the group's task is demonstrating initiating behavior. In a business setting a superior who sets deadlines, assigns tasks, sets quotas, coordinates the production of subordinates, and criticizes poor performance is fulfilling an initiating role (Wexley & Yukl, 1977).

Contingency Model of Effective Leadership. Theories of leadership have grown much more complicated since their beginnings with the simple trait approach. It has become increasingly clear that a leader's success depends not only on his or her personal qualities, but also on numerous situational factors such as the skills necessary to accomplish the task, the existing rules by which the group operates, the resources and skills available in the group, the competition, and often sheer luck.

Having the right skills is important for a leader. Successful leadership skills may vary greatly with the purposes for which the group comes together. For example, very different skills are called for in coaching an athletic team, commanding a military unit, and heading a government. (*Top:* Alec Duncan/Taurus; Joseph Lawton/DOT; *bottom:* Paul Conklin/Monkmeyer)

Fiedler (1967, 1972) has demonstrated that the effectiveness of a given leadership style depends on the acceptance of the leader by the group and on the kinds of problems the group must deal with. Fiedler used an ingenious method to identify two different types of leadership styles. Subjects are asked to think of the person they would most like to work with and the person they would least like to work with in the future. They then rate these two workers negatively or positively on a number of dimensions (for example, intelligence and determination). Typically, there is little difference among people's ratings of their most preferred co-worker, who is generally highly positively rated. On the other hand, there is some divergence in the way people rate their *least preferred co-worker (LPC)*. Some people give this person relatively positive ratings, while others give him or her sharply negative ratings. Those who give high ratings turn out to be people who are concerned with having good interpersonal relations and with being well regarded by people with whom they work **(relation-oriented leaders).** Those who give negative ratings to their least preferred co-worker tend to be people who are concerned with successfully completing tasks, even if they must risk poor interpersonal relations with their co-workers **(task-oriented leaders).**

As might be expected, these two different kinds of orientations lead to two different styles of leadership, each of which can be effective, depending on the setting. For instance, when the group's human relationships are of primary importance, the successful leader is one who is oriented toward developing good interpersonal relations; a task-oriented leader would be ineffective and resented. If, however, the group's relationships are going well and pressure to complete the task successfully is high, then the task-oriented leader would be more successful. Successful leadership depends on complex relationships between leaders and group members and is strongly affected by the nature of the task the group faces (Fiedler, 1972; Hollander, 1985).

Communication Networks. Sometimes people may become leaders simply by virtue of their position in an organization's communication network. Leavitt (1951), for example, studied the four kinds of communication networks shown in Figure 20–2. The figure indicates in what directions communication can flow (that is, who can talk to whom). In the *circle* no position conveys an advantage. In the *chain* those at each end are at a disadvantage since they can talk to only one other person. In both the *Y* and *wheel* arrangements there is one position where communications tend to concentrate. Leavitt found that the person occupying such a central position was most likely to become the group leader. This study illustrates how particular roles, no matter who occupies them, tend to produce leaders.

Understanding conformity pressures and leadership qualities and styles is clearly important when assigning groups to perform various tasks. For example, relation-oriented leaders are generally better for groups that are either very poorly or very well organized and integrated; task-oriented leaders do better with groups that are intermediate on these dimensions. It has also been found that when a group faces a complex task, a decentralized communication network is more effective in transmitting essential information, whereas centralized networks function well for simple group tasks (Leavitt, 1951; Shaw, 1954).

By way of summary, the initial work on leadership looked to interpersonal strength as the deciding factor in what makes a good leader. Consistent with the framework that we established at the start of the chapter, researchers thought that a stronger leader would be able to exert a greater influence on the group. Subsequent research revealed, however, that one could define

Figure 20–2 These are the communication networks studied by Leavitt. The circle configuration is the most decentralized: Everyone can talk directly to the person on either side. The wheel is the most centralized: All communicaitons must go through the person in the center or hub position. (Leavitt, 1951)

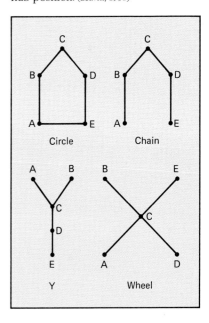

"strong" in many ways. (Note that in the Highlight: Obedience to Authority the experimenter was seen as a "strong leader" by virtue of his "expert" status.) Some leaders had an influence because they were strong in keeping group members concentrated on the group task, but others had an influence because they were strong in maintaining good interpersonal relations. The research thereby shifted to an emphasis on immediacy. Some kinds of communication arrangements within groups gave the leader better access to each of the group members, whereas other, more hierarchical arrangements were organized so that a leader's influence was not as directly felt by group members who were a step or two down in the hierarchy. Finally, although studies of leadership have not specifically addressed the number of group members that the leader tries to influence, evidence from other lines of research suggests that workers may not work quite as hard in situations where the leader's influence has to be spread across many group members.

Social Loafing

Have you ever participated in a tug-of-war? How hard did you try? Do you think it possible that you might have pulled harder on the rope if you had 2 teammates than if you had 20? That is just what has been found in many studies. As the old saying goes, "Many hands make light the work."

In one study college men were asked to stand in the middle of the football stadium at Ohio State University and make as much noise as they could (Latané, Williams, & Harkins, 1979). They were allowed to shout, scream, clap their hands, beat their chests, or whatever—anything to get the decibel level as high as possible. A machine measured how much noise they made. Some of the men were alone when they did this, some were in pairs, and some were in groups of six. Naturally, the larger groups made more noise, but did they make as much noise as they should have? In other words, did six men make six times the noise of one man? Far from it. Two men making noise together made less than 80 percent of the combined noise of two men making noise separately, and six men yelling and screaming together made only 36 percent of the combined noise of six men yelling and screaming separately. Part of the result may be attributed to the fact that sound waves cancel each other out, but not all of it. In another version of the study subjects were alone but were led to believe that some number of other subjects were making noise at the same time. Subjects who thought they had the sole responsibility for making noise made the most noise, subjects who thought they were accompanied by another noisemaker made less noise themselves, and subjects who thought they were accompanied by five other noisemakers made the least noise.

The point is to picture a leader trying to get one, two, or six workers to perform. The more the leader has to spread his or her influence around, the less that influence is exerted on each worker.

Helping

Imagine a ship at sea sending out distress signals. In terms of Figure 20–1, the ship would be the source, the rays the distress signals, and the targets the other ships that might or might not come to the rescue. A more interpersonal example would be the case of a crime victim who needs help. The victim would probably send out distress signals in the way of screams or cries, and research shows that the more potential helpers are present to receive

those signals, the less likely it is that any one of them will help (see the Highlight: Bystander Intervention). One explanatory mechanism involves diffusion of responsibility. The source's (in this case, the victim's) distress signals do not have as much impact on any one of the targets when they spread across many targets.

By way of summary, studies of leadership, social loafing, and helping all fit well within the framework of social influence emanating from one source toward several targets, as depicted in Figure 20–1. But what of the case where several sources of influence converge on one target? That situation, depicted in Figure 20–3, follows the same rules. Strength, immediacy, and number are still the important factors in determining how much or how little that target person will be affected by the others. Quite simply, when the sources are powerful, nearby, and many, they will have more effect than when they are weak, far away, and few.

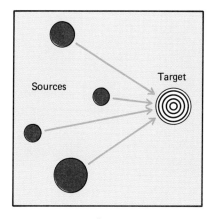

Figure 20–3 Influence: Many sources affecting one target. (After Latané, 1981)

MANY SOURCES AFFECTING ONE TARGET

From its inception, social psychology has been concerned with the impact of others on an individual's behavior. Sometimes other people make us feel good and perform better, and sometimes they have just the opposite effect. Sometimes they can get us to do things that we might not have done without their influence. Sometimes we defy their influence, or even influence them back by instituting some innovation that the group adopts. It is important to discover the circumstances under which we will and will not be influenced by others.

Social Facilitation and Impairment

Could you run faster if running all by yourself against the clock or running against someone of about your own speed? Intuitively, most of us believe that the keen competition would spur us to run slightly faster than we think ourselves capable of running, so we think we would run faster in competition. That is exactly what was found in several early studies (e.g., Tripplett, 1897.) Interestingly, the same sorts of "social-facilitation" effects were found when other people just sat and watched the subject perform. Performance on several kinds of tasks was facilitated by performing in front of an audience as opposed to performing alone. Not only that, but more prestigious audiences (strength), audiences in the same room with the performer (immediacy), and larger audiences (number) produced greater social facilitation.

One problem with this early work, however, was that every now and then it was found that an audience had the opposite effect—it impaired performance. Stutterers, for example, stutter on more words when reading a passage aloud before an audience than when reading a passage aloud alone; the larger the audience, the more they stutter (Porter, 1939). In other work normal college students were asked to imagine reciting a poem before an audience, and to say how tense it made them. The larger and more prestigious the audience, the more tense they felt (Latané & Harkins, 1976). So it looked as though strength, immediacy, and number of sources affected a target person's performance in one way on some tasks and in exactly the opposite way on other tasks. What was the difference?

A careful analysis of these studies led to **social-facilitation theory** (Zajonc, 1965). It appeared that only simple, automatic, overlearned behaviors

HIGHLIGHT _____

Bystander Intervention

Some years ago, in a case that attracted national attention, a woman returning home late at night was attacked and repeatedly stabbed until she was dead, while other people watched from their apartment windows. The onlookers neither directly intervened to help nor called the police. This was a shocking but not an isolated case. In numerous situations witnesses have failed to help people in trouble, even when there was relatively little danger to themselves in offering help. Research on bystander responses to emergencies illustrates some of the social-psychological principles we have discussed.

First, this research illustrates the differences between the theoretical approaches of personality psychologists and social psychologists. Personality theoreticians sought to identify personality traits that might distinguish nonresponders from responders. They suggested that nonresponders would be characterized by apathy and anomie, and perhaps also by hostility that caused them to get secret satisfaction from the suffering of people in distress.

Analyzing such situations from a social-psychological perspective, Latané and Darley (1970) suggested a different set of reasons for failure to help—reasons that affect everyone who witnesses a potential emergency. Among these reasons for failure to help is the information-conformity process discussed in the text.

An event that becomes an emergency may not seem so at the beginning. The observable details may be ambiguous. For instance, suppose that in a big city you see a poorly

dressed, unshaven man reeling along the street. He then sits on a park bench, holding his head in his hands. What is going on? The man could be having a heart attack and need immediate medical attention. Or he could be dazed and drunk. Or he could simply be tired. What, if anything, should you do?

What you decide to do will depend on which of the possible interpretations of the situation you adopt. Suppose other people also witness the incident. You will look to their reactions to determine their interpretations of the event, and their interpretations may influence your own.

To see the effect of information-produced conformity on decisions about emergencies, Latané and Darley (1968) set up an experiment in which an ambiguous but potentially dangerous event was staged. Subjects' reactions would be determined by their interpretation of the event. Students came one at a time to a waiting room to fill out a preliminary information form before taking part in an interview on "urban settings." While each subject filled out the questionnaire, white smoke began to jet through a vent in the wall. The cause of the smoke was not immediately apparent, but one possibility was that it signaled a fire somewhere in the building. Those waiting for the interview generally reacted in terms of this possibility. They didn't panic, but they did walk out and find a person to whom they could report the problem. To that person they said something like, "I don't know if there is anything wrong, but smoke is coming into the waiting room; could you please check?"

Other subjects were presented with the same event but in a different social context: Two strangers were also in the waiting room filling out questionnaires and apparently also

waiting for interviews. Actually, the two other people were confederates of the experimenters who had been instructed to continue filling out their questionnaires even after the smoke appeared.

What did their behavior convey to the subjects? Apparently it indicated that they knew the smoke did not signal a dangerous fire. Perhaps they had had previous experiences with smoke in the building, or perhaps they had figured out something the subjects did not figure out. But they seemed to have concluded that it was safe to stay in the room.

The results of this experiment are shown in Figure A: Most subjects remained in the waiting room, continuing to fill out their questionnaires even as the smoke poured into the room.

It would be easy to condemn these people as "conformers," but it is probably more accurate to say they followed a generally rational process that in this instance led to a less than rational conclusion. The lack of action by the other people in the room conveyed the information that no danger was present. The subjects integrated this information with the other information available to them

Figure A

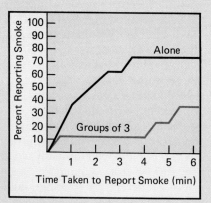

were facilitated by an audience; anything more complex than running, copying prose, or reeling in a fishing line was impaired by having other people watch. Not only that, but in some cases other people seemed to have this effect when they were not actually watching, but merely physically present. This led some theorists to speculate that other members of our species have an "energizing" effect such that they get us aroused and motivated enough to do simple tasks faster, but that this increased level of arousal is counterpro-

and came to their conclusions. Some reported afterward that they thought the smoke signaled the presence of a chemistry lab nearby, or was somehow connected with the heating system or with the changeover from the heating to the cooling system. The inaction of the confederates had given them some cues about the meaning of the smoke, and had caused them to conclude that it was not a sign of danger.

Another study (Darley & Latané, 1968) in this series illuminates a different situational determinant of nonresponding. (This situation was described in Chapter 1 of this text, so only a reminder of it is necessary here.) It concerned the different perceptions of responsibility in an emergency when many people are present. In this situation it seems that each potential responder feels a decrease in his or her responsibility to help.

To test this notion of diffusion of responsibility, an experiment was arranged in which people talked to each other over communications systems. One participant (whose presence was actually simulated by a tape recording) apparently had an epileptic seizure and called for help. Because his call for help preempted the single communications channel, there was no way the other participants could discuss the incident with each other or even know whether others were responding. (The situation was designed in this way to remove the influence of visible behavioral responses, as in the previously described experiment.) Some participants believed that they were in a two-person discussion group, and therefore reasoned that they alone had heard the victim's call for help. Others believed that they were in three-person groups, and still others that they were in six-person groups; therefore there was one other person, or four others, who could help.

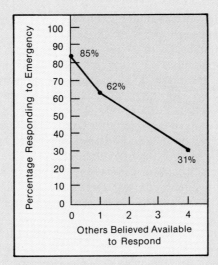

Figure B

As Figure B shows, the more people a subject thought were available, the less likely he or she (both men and women showed the same effect) was to offer help. Apparently the diffusion-of-responsibility notion is an accurate portrayal of how people think during emergencies.

Figure C diagrams the researchers' suggestions about the ways in which the definition and diffusion processes interact. Notice that only if the situation is defined as an emergency does the question of personal responsibility even become relevant. Only one path through the set of decisions leads to a helping response; several paths lead to the response of not helping.

Thus it seems that the influence processes set up by the presence of other observers actually accounts for nonresponding. Why, then, are we so shocked and upset when we read about incidents of nonhelping in the real world, in which not one but many people fail to help? In this and other experiments (i.e., Gergen & Morse, 1971) it has been found that

personality characteristics of participants do not predict their likelihood of responding. Yet many of us, reading reports of emergencies in which spectators do not respond, cannot help but feel that the nonresponders are somehow different from the rest of us normal, helpful people. Does this sound familiar? It should: We have again made the fundamental attribution error, discussed in Chapter 19, attributing to personality a behavior that is actually caused by the situation.

Figure C

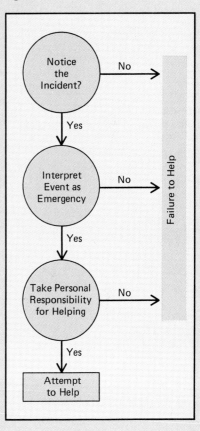

ductive for more complex tasks, where we sometimes find ourselves "all thumbs" when we are trying too hard.

This explanation was thought broad enough to apply to other species as well as our own. An ingenious experiment was devised to demonstrate social-facilitation and impairment effects in cockroaches! As shown in Figure 20–4, the general idea was that the mere presence of other cockroaches would facilitate a roach's performance on a simple task such as running

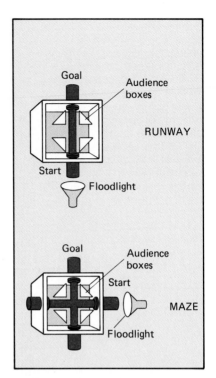

Figure 20–4 Social Facilitation Experiment Diagrams of runways and mazes used in Zajonc's social facilitation experiment with cockroaches. (After Zajonc, 1965)

straight down an alley to get away from a light (roaches hate the light). In one version the roach was placed in the start box and had only to run straight ahead to get to the dark goal box when the light was turned on. Sometimes other roaches were placed in the "audience boxes" at the middle of the maze, and sometimes those boxes were empty. The "subject" roach ran reliably faster with an audience than without one. In a second version the roach had to turn one way or the other at the corner in order to get to the dark goal box—in other words, the simple task of running straight ahead was replaced by a more complicated discrimination task (see Chapter 6). When there were other roaches in the "audience boxes," the "subject" roach was reliably slower in reaching the goal box. If it works for roaches the same as for humans, the argument went, then it must be "built in" to the species that the presence of a species mate is energizing (Zajonc, Heinsartner, & Herman, 1969).

A somewhat different explanation (Cottrell, 1968) is that organisms have *learned* that the presence of others carries the potential for aversive consequences. But what could people possibly fear from other people who are only watching them perform a task? The answer is *negative evaluation*. When we are watched by an audience, they can gauge our progress. We can look bad in front of them, and that is in itself very arousing.

If the audience could not see us, of course, there would be no reason to fear negative evaluation. Acting on this reasoning, some studies have measured human task performance when the audience is blindfolded, and found no evidence of social-facilitation effects (Cottrell et al., 1968; Paulus & Murdock, 1971). In terms of the framework we have been using to explain social influence, one might speculate that a blindfolded audience has been robbed of its strength.

Other explanations of social facilitation and impairment have emphasized the audience's role as a distraction (Sanders, 1981). Performers get frustrated, this version goes, by the conflict between watching the audience and concentrating on the task. The frustration produces arousal, with subsequent facilitation of simple tasks and impairment of complex tasks as described above. Yet other explanations stress the performer's concern with self-presentation and his or her assumption that the audience's evaluations are negative (Bond, 1982). The reason simple tasks are facilitated, this version goes, is that they can easily be performed well. With complex tasks, the performer almost invariably makes some mistakes, assumes a negative audience reaction to those mistakes, and then gets flustered. In support of this position, subjects have been found to perform even complex tasks well when those tasks are embedded in a sequence of tasks on which they are doing very well before an audience, and to perform even simple tasks poorly when those tasks are embedded in a sequence of tasks on which they are doing poorly before an audience (Bond, 1982).

Obviously, the final chapter has yet to be written on social facilitation and impairment, but enough is known to say that other people can exert a powerful influence on our behavior, sometimes without even meaning to, and that this influence seems to wax and wane according to the strength, immediacy, and number of sources of social influence.

Conformity

Social psychology often deals with value-laden issues. **Conformity** is one of these, and it is important to recognize this early in the discussion. *Confor-*

Social-facilitation and impairment effects are nondirective. These are cases when a source (e.g., an audience) is not trying to influence the target person's behavior, and yet somehow does. Of at least as much interest are cases of deliberate social influence—when one person (or more) tries to influence others to do things that they would not normally do.

One of the most disturbing forms of human interaction occurs when a person harms or kills another. Often this happens in response to orders from a third person.

Are people so cowed by a person "in authority" that they will inflict harm on another human being because they are "under orders"? Stanley Milgram (1963, 1965) was determined to find out.

Subjects in Milgram's study thought they were giving a "learner" shocks of increasing intensity for incorrect responses on a memorization task. The learner then called out from an adjoining room begging the subject to stop giving him the shocks. Yet because the experimenter said something as minor as "Please continue," subjects did continue to "administer" electric shocks. (It should be noted that no shocks were ever delivered, and "victims" were experimental confederates.) Many who read Milgram's results concluded that

if concentration camps were established in North America, we would not have to look far for people to staff them.

Milgram later brought the "victim" physically closer to the shock-giving subject. This reduced the likelihood that the subject would deliver the full series of shocks. (But even when the subject was seated right next to the "victim" and told to forceably push the "victim's" hand down on the shock device, giving the maximum shocks, 35 percent of the subjects did so.) The fact that being physically distant from the pain being inflicted makes it easier to continue does remind one of the experience of bomber crews during the Vietnam War. They flew so high above the countryside, and the damage done by their bombs was so distant and remote, that they had trouble conceiving of it at all.

But before we make the generalization that all of Milgram's subjects were revealing latent capacities for evil, we should examine a few more aspects of their behavior. First, when subjects were paired with two peers who defied the experimenter and refused to continue delivering shocks, 90 percent of the subjects refused to obey the experimenter. Second, when the experimenter was "unexpectedly called away" and another participant ordered subjects to continue, they generally refused. Indeed, when this person then stepped forward to administer further shocks himself, subjects frequently forceably restrained him.

This gives us a clue to what is going on in the subject's mind: It is not so much the presence of the *authority* that is critical as it is the presence of the *expert* authority (a strong *source*). When the expert says "Please continue," more is implied. The phrase means something like "I'm the expert here. Even though that other person says he doesn't want to continue, I know he's not really being harmed, so it's O.K. Please continue." Apparently, such an implied assurance was an important determinant of the subjects' continued participation.

Thus it seems that, in the context of a scientific experiment, when there is a convincing rationale for inflicting electric shocks on another person, subjects continue to participate even though the person seems to be in considerable pain. This differs in some ways from prison camp guards and other real-world settings, but it is also in many ways similar. There are striking similarities between a person causing pain for "the good of science" and a person harming another for "the good of the state." The obedience phenomena uncovered by Milgram remain disturbing from a societal perspective. The study of obedience, in fact, can be viewed as just one instance of the more general human tendency to conform with group norms when under social pressure. This work also illustrates a number of other principles discussed in these chapters on social psychology, and demonstrates how group processes can lead to acts of violence.

---

mity is a negative word that calls up images of submissive actions by weak-willed people. But consider the following definition of a conforming response: one that agrees with the response of a group when respondents have insufficient evidence themselves to know that their response is correct. Next consider the following example: You are guiding your sailboat into a harbor in which you have never anchored before. Your charts and the harbor markers show two possible entrances, and you are on course for the nearest one. Then you notice that several other boats near you are choosing the other entrance. From the home port markings on those boats, you realize that this harbor is the home harbor for all of them. What's going on? One obvious explanation is that there is some hidden danger in the near channel—a recent wreck, perhaps, or a shift in the channel depth—that occurred too recently to get on the charts. You don't know, but to be safe you alter course and follow the other boats to the more distant entrance.

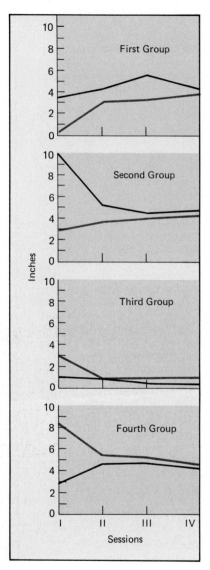

Figure 20–5 In each of the graphs above you can see that when the two subjects independently guessed how far a light had "moved," their guesses varied widely (Session I). However, as soon as the pairs of subjects began making judgments in each other's presence, their guesses began to be influenced by each other. A "group opinion" about an event in the physical world began to develop. (Sherif & Sherif, 1948/1956)

This fits the definition of conformity: You have gone along with the response of the group without having sufficient evidence yourself to judge whether that is the correct response. Yet, because it is so obviously the sensible action to take, it seems wrong to label it "conformity." That is the point: It seems wrong because conformity has negative connotations, but conformity, like other actions, can be good or bad, rational or irrational, depending on the context in which it occurs.

Informational Social Influence. The kind of conformity found in our example—a rational conformity that can be thought of as learning about the world from the actions of others—is called **informational social influence** (Kelley, 1952). It is likely to arise in two cases: when the realities to be learned about are essentially social in nature, and when they have physical components.

In the United States we drive our automobiles on the right-hand side of the road, and in the English language we use the word *chair* to describe a piece of furniture on which a person sits That these are socially agreed on ways of doing or labeling things rather than physically necessary ones is demonstrated by the fact that in England vehicles are driven on the left and the German word for chair is *Stuhl*. People are the best source of information about these social customs. Indeed, they are the only source. Therefore the only sensible way for a person who is new to a group to learn about its customs is by observing the actions of the group members. This is the normal learning process of socialization, without which no child could become a functioning member of a culture. It continues into adult life, producing what could often be called conformity.

Another word for social realities is *conventions,* those social rules about the "right" clothes to wear, the "right" way to address a faculty member, and so on. We learn about social conventions from others. But when what we need to know are not social but *physical* realities—things that can be measured and monitored—we still may look to the opinions of others. In some circumstances direct learning about events or objects might be too time-consuming or costly. Think back, for instance, to the example at the beginning of the section, in which, as the boat owner, you tried to determine whether the channel was clear of obstructions. You could have sailed in and investigated for yourself, but you knew that this was likely to be hazardous and that you were better off simply going along with the decision of the other sailors.

In one of the earliest studies of conformity Musafer Sherif made elegant use of an ambiguous event to demonstrate the ways in which individuals, when making judgments about physical events, are influenced by the judgments of others (Sherif, 1936). To appreciate what he did, you need to know the following: When you look at a stationary, pinpoint source of light in a totally darkened room, the light appears to move, even though it actually doesn't (the **autokinetic effect** discussed in Chapter 4). Furthermore, to each person the "movement" is somewhat different. Sherif realized that this was an excellent experimental context in which to demonstrate how people can be made to conform to a belief about a physical reality.

Sherif had pairs of subjects watch the light, each making an estimation of movement. At first, each member of the pair quite naturally gave a judgment that was different from the other's. One subject might report movement of 12 inches, for instance, while the other might report movement of only 3 inches. As the experiment progressed, however, the estimates of movement came closer and closer together. Each subject was influenced by the judg-

ment of the other, and a joint standard emerged (see Figure 20–5). New people, introduced into the group after the other members had developed a standard, converged in their judgments toward that standard (Jacobs & Campbell, 1961), thus demonstrating the power of a group to influence our interpretations and descriptions of physical realities.

Clearly, other people provide information that we use in making judgments about what is going on in the real world. The Sherif experiment proves that, but it does so in a rather artificial context. Many other studies, however, show conformity effects on judgments of other physical stimuli, thus demonstrating that the informational conformity effect generally occurs. These studies follow a format designed by Solomon Asch (1951, 1955). Imagine yourself in the following position: You volunteer to be in a psychology study, and you and seven other students are waiting for the session to begin. The experimenter has everyone take a seat and then explains that the task is to guess which of three lines is the same length as a comparison or standard line (see Figure 20–6). When you look at the first set of lines, the correct answer is very obvious. The first subject is asked and gives the correct answer; and so does everyone else in the group. The next few sets of lines are just as easy; everyone is correct, and you settle back anticipating a boring experience.

On the next trial the answer is again obvious, but this time the first subject picks a line that is clearly not the same length as the standard. The second person, in a casual tone of voice, makes the same mistake! The third subject agrees with the first two! You look at the lines again, squinting your eyes and moving your head to get a different angle. Everyone else has agreed, and now it is your turn to speak up. What would you do?

Asch placed a number of students in just such a predicament. In his line-judging groups all participants but one were confederates of the experimenter who gave unanimous but incorrect answers on some trials, thereby placing conformity pressure on the one "real" subject. Overall, Asch found that his subjects conformed on about one-third of the trials when there was a unanimous majority.

Experiments done on similar tasks have revealed that the conformity shown by subjects does have an informational component, particularly when the stimuli are ambiguous or difficult to discriminate. However, the conformity is also partially produced by social pressure. Subjects are hesitant to violate what they see as a group rule. This is called *normative social influence*.

Normative Social Influence.   Informational social influence results from using information provided by other people about social conventions or physical realities. **Normative social influence** occurs when people suppress or downplay their own opinions and "go along with" the group because they want to gain the rewards or avoid the punishments that the group has to give. Although it may be rational to give in to social influence for this reason, it is not always admirable; hence the "bad name" conformity has come to have. But certainly this kind of conformity does occur, as was demonstrated in a landmark study by Deutsch and Gerard (1955).

Deutsch and Gerard wanted to demonstrate the existence of both normative and informational social influence. They reasoned that if people were conforming because they were using the judgments of others to help them form their impressions (informational social influence), it should make no difference whether they announced their own judgments publicly. All that should matter is that they hear and conform to the judgments of the others.

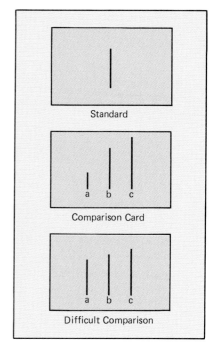

Figure 20–6   Asch (1951) presented subjects with a series of cards like the top one ("standard"). Their task was to select the line from the comparison card that was matched in length to the standard line. Other researchers made the task more difficult by giving the subjects a comparison set in which lines were of similar lengths.

Subject number 6 was the one "real" subject in Asch's experiment. The other group members were previously instructed confederates.
(William Vandivert)

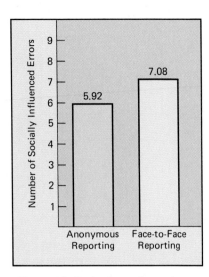

Figure 20–7 As shown here, the number of socially influenced errors in the experiment was a function of whether subjects reported anonymously or in the presence of others.

On the other hand, if people felt pressured to conform because they wanted to avoid looking foolish to the others or because they did not want to be criticized or rejected by them (normative social influence), then it should make a significant difference whether or not they publicly pronounced a judgment. Their deviance would become apparent and punishable only if the others knew their pattern of answers.

The experimenters arranged a social-influence test. First, individuals judged the lengths of a series of lines. The right answers were very obvious, and these subjects made virtually no mistakes. Other subjects were asked to make the same judgments, but only after hearing the responses of a group of people to the same task. Although these subjects were unaware of it, the answers of the others were prearranged: They all gave an identical wrong answer. All experimental subjects faced the same dilemma: Should they trust their own opinion (which was actually correct), or should they conform to the response of the group? One group of subjects knew that their answers would be heard by the other group members. The other group of subjects believed that the people in their group could not hear their answers. If subjects were influenced only by the informational content of the others' answers (if they believed that the others were actually correct), then the conformity rate of the two groups would be alike. However, if subjects were also concerned about violating group norms and the possible sanctions the group might inflict on them for doing so, then the subjects who gave their answers publicly should have a higher conformity rate than those who gave their answers privately. As Figure 20–7 shows, the data support the latter hypothesis. The experiment clearly showed a difference between informational and normative social influence. More precisely, a good deal of the conformity was of an informational variety (the approximately six errors made by the average subject in the anonymous condition). In the face-to-face reporting condition, the increase in conformity was caused by the desire of subjects not to violate group norms.

Deviation

What if people continue to deviate in the face of group pressure to conform because they hold a strong opinion or have a prior public commitment to a particular viewpoint? Research by Schachter (1951) and Newcomb (1953) shows us what happens in this kind of **deviation.** In both experiments an actor was planted among a small group of people who were supposed to reach an agreement about the solution to a problem. The experimenter instructed the actor to oppose the solution of the other group members and to speak out for a different one. For instance, the group was asked to make a decision regarding the future of a juvenile delinquent. They were told that the boy had a terrible and rejecting home environment, and he was committing increasingly harmful crimes. Should the boy be given another chance in a foster home, or should he be sent to a relatively severe house of detention? As instructed, the "plant" deviated from the group opinion. Thus, if the group favored the foster home, the deviant argued for the house of detention, and vice versa.

An interesting pattern emerged in some of the experimental groups. Once the group's position became clear, some group members directed more attention to anyone who disagreed, trying to get them to change their position. The experimenters had instructed the actor in some of the groups to "be-

come convinced" at this point and conform to the group's opinion. This willingness to conform made the former "deviant" acceptable as a group member. Once this person became convinced, the group turned more attention to remaining deviants. In other groups deviants were instructed to stand firm and not conform to the group's opinion. Communication directed toward them dropped off: Previously they had received more attention than the average group member, but now they received less. It seemed as if the other group members gave up on the deviants, and further evidence indicates that this was so.

The experimenters wondered whether the group members wished to punish the deviants or even exclude them. Group members were asked to assign several jobs. As the experimenters predicted, deviants were frequently nominated for the relatively boring and menial tasks. When the experimenters then explained that it might be necessary to have future meetings with a smaller group, deviants were frequently "nominated" to be the ones left out.

Consider what this means in real-life situations for those who deviate from the group. Frequently, they find themselves excluded after their opinions are discovered. Because their opinions have been contradicted, their values have been threatened and are in need of bolstering. An excellent way of doing this is by finding a group of people who think as they do, thereby receiving social support from them. Thus deviants' future associations are likely to include a disproportionate number of people who agree with them on this one opinion. Naturally, they come to spend more time with these other people and less time with the rejecting majority. They become members of an *outgroup*.

Innovation

At this point the fate of deviants seems rather bleak. If people don't conform to the opinions of the groups in which they find themselves, they are rejected; if rejected, they seek out a supporting group, only to find themselves subjected to conformity pressures from this new source. But there is another side to this picture: Sometimes a majority will tolerate views that differ. Sometimes it may even come to adopt the very views it once resisted. Under what conditions will the majority either tolerate or adopt deviant opinions?

Hollander (1958, 1960) demonstrated that high-status individuals can hold deviant opinions and still stay in favor with the group. Such individuals are frequently successful in bringing the group to accept their views and proposals. Low-status group members, on the other hand, are less successful in getting the group to adopt their position. This is not necessarily elitist or irrational, for the person with high status might have gained that status by making a set of suggestions that paid off for the group in the past.

This implies that the group's history of successes may make a difference in its willingness to follow deviant suggestions from group members. Groups that have experienced a recent string of failures may feel that their high-status leaders are discredited and be more open to the apparently radical ideas of low-status members. At the national level, analysts have used this to explain the successes of political extremists. Hitler, for instance, came to power at a time when the prior government had gone through a series of disasters that caused marked deterioration in the quality of the German people's lives.

GROUPS: THEIR DECISIONS AND ACTIONS

What makes a group? We would all agree that a fraternity or sorority is a group. The members get together frequently and usually support each other both socially and intellectually. They are interdependent in that each member's well-being to some extent depends on the success of the group as a whole. In some cases, as in sports teams, the success of the group depends on the lack of success of some other rival group. A *cohesive group* is one in which the members are highly committed to group membership, morale is high, and the group serves the function of "pulling together" in times of crisis. People in such cohesive groups usually feel a sense of belonging, take comfort and support from their membership, and find the other members of the group to be especially nice people.

Functional Groups

The traditional view of a group is that it serves some function; the better it serves that function, the more the group's members will help each other and band together against outsiders. Given this definition of what makes a group, it is obvious that the task of reducing dangerous intergroup rivalries, whether between teenage street gangs or between warring nations, ought best to be accomplished by introducing superordinate goals—goals that will appeal to members of both groups. If two groups have a common objective, and neither can accomplish that objective by itself but could with the other group's help, then the members of the two groups will be forced to cooperate. In the course of that cooperation they will come to see the members of the other group as serving a useful function and as "not such bad guys after all."

The classic study establishing this *function theory* of group formation and maintenance was performed at a boys' summer camp (Sherif et al., 1961). The camp directors first encouraged in-group cohesiveness and out-group rivalry by dividing the boys into groups that were identifiably different and that competed for scarce resources. In no time the members of each group came to admire and respect their fellow group members, and to despise those from the rival group. Just as the altercations between the two groups were getting violent, the directors staged some problems that could be solved only by the two groups cooperating. For example, a supply truck "just happened" to get stuck on its way to a distant site to which the two groups had hiked. Neither group could budge the truck alone, and both wanted the supplies, so they literally had to "pull together." After several experiences of this kind, they came to appreciate the qualities of boys in the other group, the very boys whom they had previously despised.

Minimal Groups

This traditional view of groups has recently been challenged by those who claim that groups need serve no particular function in order to generate in-group favoritism and out-group enmity (Tajfel et al., 1971). They can do that, so these theorists claim, just by being labeled as groups. The argument is akin in some ways to the argument, discussed above, that other people can facilitate or impair performance without doing anything except being there. When we become part of a group, we selectively attend (see Chapter 4) to

the dimensions on which our own group is different from some other group, and fail to notice the similarities.

In fact, an experiment that recalls the perception studies discussed in Chapter 4 was used to explore this phenomenon. The researchers showed subjects pictures of a white background with many small dots and asked them, after only a brief exposure, to estimate how many dots there were in each picture. As you might guess, this is a very difficult task, and one on which the experimenter can provide almost any kind of feedback. If you guess that there are 57 dots on a card after seeing it for a few seconds, the experimenter could probably tell you either that there were actually 55 or that there were actually 59, and both would seem believable to you. Taking advantage of this ambiguity, the investigators told some subjects (selected at random) that they were "overestimators," people who consistently estimated more dots than were actually on the card. They told other subjects (also selected at random) that they were "underestimators," people who consistently estimated fewer dots than were actually on the card.

What kind of group feeling ought to be engendered by being told that you are an overestimator? Should it make you like other overestimators more than underestimators? According to the functional theory of group formation and maintenance, it should not. You have never met these mythical other overestimators, and all you know that you have in common with them is an almost meaningless label. Nonetheless, when subjects in this experiment were asked to distribute rewards to other subjects whom they had never met, some of whom were said to be overestimators and some of whom were said to be underestimators, they consistently gave extra rewards to those "of their own kind" and gave less than their fair share to those "of the other kind." In fact, they did this even when they were explicitly told that assignment to one group or another was totally random (Billig & Tajfel, 1973).

The explanation offered is that the mere act of categorization in and of itself accentuates perceived similarities within a group and perceived differences between groups. It is a purely cognitive phenomenon that is then supplemented by a social-comparison process in which the group is identified with oneself: "I am a nice person. I am also an overestimator. Therefore overestimators are nice people" (see the discussion of balance theory in Chapter 19). "If they prosper, then I prosper" (Tajfel & Turner, 1979).

Thus there are two accounts of what makes a group. One emphasizes the function that groups serve, and the other notes that group cohesiveness and intergroup rivalry can emerge from our natural perceptual inclination to exaggerate the similarities among objects that belong to the same category, and to emphasize the differences among objects that belong to different categories. These two perspectives are not necessarily at odds, however. They may merely address two levels of group formation. Category labels may be sufficient to start a group, but it probably takes functional interaction to keep a group going.

Making Decisions in Groups

One kind of group performance of special significance is the process of group decision making. Many of the most important decisions that affect our lives—such as the size and nature of the federal budget, admissions to college and graduate school, and the marketing and production actions of business organizations—are made by groups. Stoner (1961) made a discovery about group decision making that triggered a great deal of interest. Stoner

- A low ranked participant in a national chess tournament, playing an early match with the top-favored man, has the choice of attempting or not trying a deceptive but risky maneuver which might lead to quick victory if successful or almost certain defeat if it fails.

- A college senior with considerable musical talent must choose between the secure course of going on to medical school and becoming a physician, or the risky course of embarking on the career of a concert pianist.

- A research physicist, just beginning a five-year appointment at a university, may spend the time working on a series of short-term problems which he would be sure to solve but which would be of lesser importance, or on a very important but very difficult problem with the risk of nothing to show for his five years of effort.

Figure 20–8 Wallach, Kogan, and Bem (1962) developed a choice-dilemma questionnaire containing problems such as these. Individuals were asked to read a problem and then report the probability of success that must hold before they would recommend the action. (One person might want to risk a particular course of action if it had even 1 chance in 10 of success. Another might require 5 chances in 10 of success in order to be willing to risk it.) The researchers found that many (but not all) individuals made a more risky recommendation after a group discussion of the problems than they made alone. For example, an individual deciding alone might recommend an action only if it had 9 chances in 10 of succeeding. Following group discussion, the same individual might recommend the action even if there were only 5 or 7 chances in 10 of success. The reasons for this *risky shift* are discussed in the text.

had his subjects read a series of problems and make choices among several recommendations that varied in the risk of failure they carried. Subjects made private decisions, had a group discussion, and then made the decision again. After the group discussions the recommendations tended to become riskier; this phenomenon was termed the *risky shift* (see Figure 20–8). A number of other investigators also found risky shifts following group discussions (Wallach, Kogan, & Bem, 1962). The existence of risky shifts seemed to have obvious importance, since it implied that groups might need to be aware of (and wary of) a tendency to take too many risks (See the Highlight: Groupthink and Group Decisions). However, it soon became apparent that groups often show conservative rather than risky shifts (Zajonc, Wolosin, Wolosin, & Sherman, 1968; Pruitt, 1971). It is now clear that both of these effects can be thought of as specific instances of a more general **group polarization effect.** Group discussion tends to make the average decision of the group members more extreme in one direction or the other. This holds in areas as widely diverse as attitudes, ethical decisions, judgments about other people, and decisions about bargaining and negotiating postures.

Several explanations offer insight into this group polarization phenomenon. **Value theory** emphasizes the kinds of social comparisons that tend to occur in groups (Brown, 1965). By themselves, individuals try to avoid being either too cautious or too risky; thus they avoid making extreme recommendations. When they find out that others have a more extreme inclination, however, individuals may be willing to go with a more extreme decision because of the emerging group support. Since our cultural norms generally favor risk taking, an individual may feel that his or her position is more moderate than the social norm.

Whether a particular private decision leads to a risky or conservative shift will be determined by the average group tendency, which presumably will reflect the dominant cultural value for that kind of problem. **Information-exchange theories** point out that during group discussion persuasive arguments that some members would not have thought of on their own are raised, and these arguments tend to convince people to be more extreme than they would have been otherwise (Vinokur, 1971; Burnstein, Vinokur, & Trope, 1973). In other words, it is not just the awareness of more extreme positions that causes people to change their minds; it is the presentation of new information or arguments that makes them alter their decision.

Diffusion of responsibility theory points out that the responsibility for a potentially bad decision is diffused when decisions are made in a group. This frees some individuals to be more extreme than they would be if making the decision alone (Wallach, Kogan, & Bem, 1962). Examples of extremity shifts have been found in numerous contexts, including bargaining (Lamm & Sauer, 1974) and court decisions (Walker & Main, 1973).

Finally, **social-identification** theory (Wetherell & Turner, 1979) emphasizes the perceptual "edge sharpening" that occurs when one identifies with a group. As described in the discussion of minimal groups above, the idea is that the mere act of categorizing people into groups makes us attend selectively to differences between the groups and ignore similarities. We are especially likely to do this when we identify with a group, or feel that we are part of it. To test this idea, subjects were allowed to listen to a taped group discussion about the use of standardized tests for college admission decisions. They shifted their attitudes toward the group's, but only when they thought they were about to join that group. In addition, they misperceived the group's position as more extreme than it actually was, but again only when it was "their" group. Thus identifying with the group caused subjects to

HIGHLIGHT _____

Groupthink and Group Decisions

Irving Janis (1982) has documented a number of cases in which groups have made disastrous decisions. He reminds us of John Kennedy's decision to invade Cuba (the Bay of Pigs fiasco) and Richard Nixon's decision to suppress evidence of White House complicity in illegal activities (the Watergate coverup). By studying such events as these, Janis discovered a process that he calls **groupthink,** in which a cohesive group lets concerns for unanimity "override their motivation to realistically appraise alternative courses of action" (p. 9).

Through analyses of such materials as the tape-recorded transcripts of meetings of Nixon's close advisers, and the recollections of Kennedy's advisers, Janis has identified a number of symptoms characteristic of thought processes of a group on the way to a disastrous decision. A prime symptom, he reports, is the group's sense of its own invulnerability. The group has an exaggerated sense of its own power to control events, and tends to ignore or minimize cues from the real world that suggest dangers to the group's plan. One of Nixon's key staff members, for example, reported that he was confident that Nixon would avoid any negative political fallout from revelations that White House personnel were linked to the burglary attempt at the Democratic campaign headquarters. He was equally certain that Nixon's power would be sufficient to force staff members to commit perjury. He was, of course, wrong on both counts. But even as more and more negative reactions from the nation became evident, the conspirators reassured one another by belittling their detractors and seizing on any external support as evidence that the "tide of popular sentiment" was about to swing in their favor. The group seemed to engage in some of the defense mechanisms that Freud

identified in individuals. To preserve its internal harmony and collective well-being, it became more and more out of touch with reality.

Janis's analysis of groupthink suggests that group think is likely to occur in socially homogeneous, cohesive groups that are isolated from outsiders, that have no tradition of careful consideration of alternatives, and that face a decision with high costs for failure.

Lest we conclude that group decision making is inevitably disastrous, Janis suggests a number of ways in which groups can be structured to avoid poor decision making. These include encouraging dissent, assigning some members to the task of being "devil's advocates" to advance unpopular alternatives, and holding "second chance" meetings to reexamine the wisdom of the previously accepted decision.

Organizational psychologists have naturally looked into the problem of group decision making, since it is frequently practiced in businesses and other organizations. They point out that if the group can avoid the dangers of groupthink, there are several advantages of making decisions in groups. First, because of differing sources of information, a group will generally have more knowledge than a single individual; this should help both in defining the problem and in generating and assessing alternative solutions. Second, in the course of a group discussion the nature of the problem being solved and the nature of the solution to the problem can become clearer to all participants. Third, each person is likely to feel that he or she participated in making the decision and is, therefore, likely to be more committed to making it work well.

It has been amply demonstrated that groups can come to decisions that are both better and more likely to be successfully implemented than those arrived at by individuals. Yet the phenomenon of groupthink cannot be ignored. How can we integrate these apparently contradictory insights? Janis suggests that a group that is vulnerable

to groupthink, with the resulting likelihood of making poor decisions, is under high stress from its environment. In such a situation members are excessively dependent on one another for support. Unless they have internal traditions and decision-making safeguards, they can be led to suppress dissent and strive for consensus—even when that means consensus on a disastrous decision.

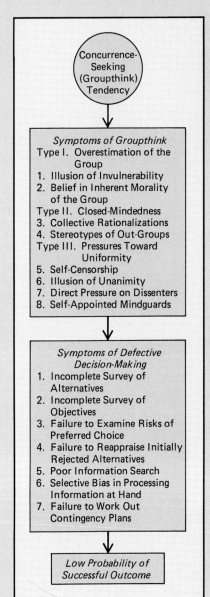

Concurrence-Seeking (Groupthink) Tendency

Symptoms of Groupthink
Type I. Overestimation of the Group
1. Illusion of Invulnerability
2. Belief in Inherent Morality of the Group
Type II. Closed-Mindedness
3. Collective Rationalizations
4. Stereotypes of Out-Groups
Type III. Pressures Toward Uniformity
5. Self-Censorship
6. Illusion of Unanimity
7. Direct Pressure on Dissenters
8. Self-Appointed Mindguards

Symptoms of Defective Decision-Making
1. Incomplete Survey of Alternatives
2. Incomplete Survey of Objectives
3. Failure to Examine Risks of Preferred Choice
4. Failure to Reappraise Initially Rejected Alternatives
5. Poor Information Search
6. Selective Bias in Processing Information at Hand
7. Failure to Work Out Contingency Plans

Low Probability of Successful Outcome

Examples of extremity shifts following group discussion have been found in numerous contexts, including bargaining and court decisions. The photo shows a scene from *Twelve Angry Men,* a famous film about a jury deliberating.
(Culver Pictures)

shift their attitudes toward what they perceived to be the group consensus, but subjects misperceived that group consensus because they were, without realizing it, exaggerating the difference between "their" group and other groups (Mackie & Cooper, 1984).

Various of the explanations cited above have been found to account for the shifts in different contexts, and this makes sense. When an individual is likely to be blamed if a decision goes badly, it helps if others came to the same decision so that any blame can be shared. Members of a group responsible for making a decision need not moderate their true opinions in the interest of avoiding blame if they sense that others hold equally extreme opinions and thus share responsibility for the final decision.

Cooperation and Social Exchanges

We all seek resources, whether they be as simple and tangible as food and money or as complex and intangible as status and power. To gain these resources, we must engage in transactions with other people who have resources to exchange, but who also have their own motives, which may complement or conflict with ours. When people depend on one another for the fulfillment of their needs, they are in a relationship of interdependence. Psychologists have developed their analysis of interdependence in the context of bargaining games (in which subjects compete for shares of limited resources such as points, money, or prizes), but have then applied it very generally to a wide variety of human interactions. (Recall the discussion of social-exchange theory in long-term attraction relationships in Chapter 19.)

Matrix Analysis.   Social scientists use a **matrix** format to show interdependencies between people (Thibaut & Kelley, 1959). This type of analysis can be applied to real and complex social situations, such as the following: Two men have been arrested. There is clear evidence that they have committed a minor crime for which they could receive a year in jail, and there is circumstantial evidence that they may have committed a major crime for which they could receive a 12-year sentence. The police separate the men and offer each a deal: If one immediately confesses to the major crime and provides evidence incriminating the other, then the prosecutor will recommend only a 1-year sentence for that person. Of course, once a confession is obtained from one of the suspects, a second confession adds little to the prosecution's

		Prisoner A	
		Confess	Not Confess
Prisoner B	Confess	Whoever is first gets 1 year; the other gets 12 years	A = 12 years B = 1 year
	Not Confess	A = 1 year B = 12 years	A = 1 year B = 1 year

Figure 20–9 This is a matrix format representing the various choices and outcomes involved in the prisoner's dilemma. Note that outcomes in the matrix format do not depend solely on people's own choice, but on their choice in conjunction with the choice of another. (Thibaut & Kelley, 1959)

case, so only the first person to confess will get a light sentence. The other person will receive the major sentence.

If you were one of the prisoners, what would you choose? This exercise, called the **prisoner's dilemma,** is represented in matrix format in Figure 20–9. Think about it—it's not an easy decision. If neither confesses, then both may get off with minor sentences because there is not enough evidence to sustain a heavier sentence for either. If A confesses first, he is certain to get the light sentence, while B is equally certain to get a 12-year jail term. Meanwhile, B, not knowing whether A will incriminate him, must decide whether *he* should turn state's evidence against A. (The application: a matrix analysis of the arms race explores the global impact of such a dilemma.)

Some of the most general properties of interdependent interaction are shown by this example. One of the key properties is the way in which one's fate—*outcome,* in the matrix format—depends not on one's own choice or action, but on one's choice *in conjunction* with the choice of another. For each prisoner, the choice not to confess may get him off with the light sentence of 1 year—*if* the other doesn't confess. But if the other does confess, then the later-confessing prisoner will get a 12-year sentence. The fate of each rests in the hands of the other.

A second point made by this example is the wide range of human situations that can be represented in the matrix format. Consider a boy who has gone out with a girl for several months and who now feels he is in love with her. Should he tell her? If he does and she responds that she is beginning to love him too, then we can imagine the increase in his happiness that this will produce. On the other hand, she might say that although she likes going out with him, she doesn't feel that she loves him. And no matter how gently and tactfully this is conveyed, it still would hurt. Again, this is a situation in which the consequences of the boy's choice to speak or not to speak depend heavily on the other person's response to his actions.

Social-Exchange Theory. Psychologists, economists, mathematicians, and sociologists have taken seriously the proposition that much of life can be thought of as a series of **social exchanges** in which people provide each other with mutually satisfying rewards. These rewards (Foa & Foa, 1976) can be money or services or goods, but they can also be less tangible commodities such as information, status, or love. All of these diverse entities are desired by or needed by a person at one time or another, and therefore can become the "currencies" people use in social exchanges with one another. Using the matrix-analysis format, scientists have explored the ramifications of this idea in many areas of life. Many social interactions can be thought of as

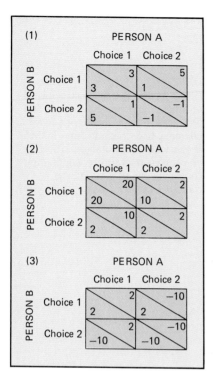

Figure 20–10 Outcomes in three different sets of payoff contingencies shown as gains (positive numbers) or losses (negative numbers). In each case, the number above the diagonal is Person A's outcome, and the number below the diagonal is Person B's. For example, in Matrix 1, if A selects choice 1 and B selects choice 2, then A's outcome is 1 and B's outcome is 5.

exchanges between individuals. When a boy helps his younger brother, he "earns" the brother's gratitude and his father's praise and approval. A worker's successful completion of a task "earns" her the praise of her boss, possible raises, and so on.

Several useful insights arise from this view of social interaction. First, people are unlikely to continue a relationship voluntarily unless both are receiving reasonable "payoffs" from it. This is a useful thing to remember when you are studying human relationships—if you observe a relationship in which one person seems to be receiving no benefits and much grief, dig deeper. Perhaps that person has hidden needs and is receiving some benefits after all.

Social-exchange theory gives us another insight into the way people interact. Our decision as to whether or not we should continue a relationship is based not on the absolute value of the profits we are getting from it, but on the relative magnitude in comparison to what we could get elsewhere (Thibaut & Kelley, 1959). This can be seen, for example, in the way workers will cling to even menial and degrading jobs during a depression because they perceive that no other jobs are available. It also helps us to understand cases in which someone ends a long-term relationship that continues to produce the same level of satisfactions that it always did. The possibility of a new relationship has opened up, holding out the promise of an even higher level of satisfaction.

Cooperation vs. Competition.   Much of the research on social exchange has focused on whether individuals will choose to cooperate or to compete with each other in certain situations. Researchers in this area have found that people govern their behavior according to the contingencies offered by the environment. That is, the pattern of "payoffs"—which can be represented in a matrix as gains or losses—does strongly control people's choices. Consider the three matrices in Figure 20–10.

Assume a pair of individuals will give a set of 10 joint responses. If both choose choice 1 all 10 times, each will make 30 points (10 × 3). However, if person A can select choice 2 even once, person A will make 32 points (9 × 3 + 1 × 5). This will work *unless* person B selects choice 2 at the same time. (What happens to the total payoffs then?) As you might expect, this matrix provokes some complex moves by each player, and they both frequently end up making fewer than the 30 points they could have achieved. Matrices 2 and 3 differ from matrix 1 in that they both, in different ways, almost compel the cooperative response of choice 1 out of both participants. Matrix 2 does this by making choice 1, and only choice 1, highly profitable for any player who makes it. Matrix 3 accomplishes the same result by making choice 2 highly punishing for any participant who chooses it. Research has shown that people are responsive to such changes in payoff contingencies.

Researchers have also come up with another more subtle finding. In many bargaining situations an optimal strategy—which means the greatest gains for both players—can be mapped out. But many times people played the games in such a way that their actual payoffs were far below the maximum levels possible. This was most likely to occur when the possibilities of negative outcomes existed. In many real-life situations participants can cause negative outcomes for each other. Lovers can quarrel, workers can strike and management can lock workers out, faculty can give failing grades and students can give low course evaluations. In such situations the behavior of the participants often seems to take on tones of mistrust and suspicion.

A landmark study of the role of threat in bargaining settings was made in

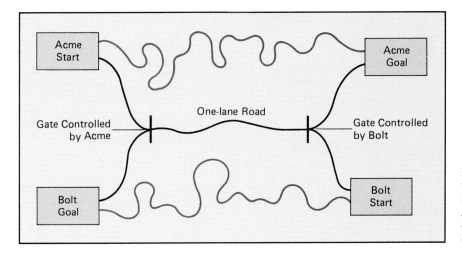

Figure 20–11 This sketch shows the basic layout of the Deutsch and Krauss trucking game. Note that both Acme and Bolt controlled gates that could be used to block the progress of the other.

1960 by Deutsch and Krauss. They developed a realistic situation that contained the possibilities of threat and conflict. Participants found the *trucking game* highly involving. In this game one player is in charge of the Acme Trucking Company and the other is in charge of Bolt. Both are to deliver goods from their own start to their own destination; the more quickly they do so, the more profit they make. Each player could take the slow, winding, alternate route, shown in Figure 20—11, but at a small loss of time. The center route is more direct, so it presented the possibility of greater profit. However, it also contained a one-lane stretch that could accommodate only one truck at a time.

Confronted with this choice, subjects generally arrived at an alternating strategy, taking turns with the long and short routes. Over the 20 trials played, this earned a reasonable payoff for each player. For some subjects, the game was complicated by the addition of weapons, in the form of gates at the points marked in Figure 20–11. One gate was controlled by Acme and therefore could be used to block the progress of Bolt; the other gate was controlled by Bolt and could block the progress of Acme. When both players had the use of gates, the situation became a payoff disaster: Often both trucks would sit at each other's gates while seconds ticked away. The addition of the bilateral threat was actually a hindrance to the players' resolution of their potential conflicts and coming to terms with each other.

For a third set of players, the trucking games was altered so that Acme was given a gate and Bolt was not. This meant that Acme had the unilateral capability to block Bolt's path. Not surprisingly, Acme sometimes used this capacity, and at the end of the game Bolt's payoffs were well below zero, indicating losses rather than profits (although the losses were not as bad as those incurred in the bilateral threat condition). Interestingly, Acme, the high-power participant in the interaction, also had a negative payoff over the 20-trial series, because the one-lane section of the center highway gave Bolt the capacity to block Acme's truck if they met head-on in that lane. This prevented Acme from making a quick and profitable run. This version of the trucking game demonstrated that the person who has relatively more power suffers from its availability because it causes others to use whatever negative sanctions are at their disposal. The results of the trucking games are shown in Table 20–1.

Some psychologists, although impressed with the Deutsch and Krauss studies, suggest that the presence of threats or negative sanctions may not al-

Table 20–1:   Payoffs in the Deutsch and Krauss Trucking Game.

Variable	No Threat	Bilateral Threat (Acme and Bolt Both Control Gates)	Unilateral Threat (Acme Controls Gate)
		Means	
Summed payoffs (Acme and Bolt)	203.32	−875.12	−405.87
Acme's payoff	122.44	−406.56	−118.56
Bolt's payoff	80.88	−468.56	−287.31

Deutsch & Krauss, 1960

ways hinder the resolution of conflict. For instance, Kelley (1965) pointed out that the gate in the trucking game was first an actual block, and only secondarily a threat. That is, the intention to use it in the future (the threat component) had to be communicated by actually using it as a block. Other researchers (Shomer, Davis, & Kelley, 1966) devised a version of the trucking game that gave subjects both a way of signaling a threat and a way of actually blocking the other player. Use of the threat-signaling capability caused participants to increase their gains. This suggests that the ability to communicate a threat is an effective conflict-resolution tool.

Other investigators have found that communication promotes cooperative behavior (Wichman, 1970; Caldwell, 1976), and Nemeth (1972) pointed out that communication between participants was not possible in the original Deutsch and Krauss games. Communication is usually possible in most of the real-world situations to which psychologists wish to apply their findings. However, in later studies that allowed participants to communicate, the course of the bargaining or the payoff outcomes were not necessarily affected (Deutsch & Krauss, 1962). We are not yet sure of the precise conditions under which communication enhances cooperation.

A picture begins to emerge of the complexity of bargaining research and the difficulties of making such general conclusions as "the presence of threat always increases conflict." Each bargaining situation has its own complex characteristics, so that the interrelationship of possibilities of communication, threats, and the balance of alternative causes of action and relative payoffs determines the role of each factor in the bargaining outcome. In addition, there are the bargaining participants, each trying to "decode" the situation in terms of the underlying motives and dispositions of the other player.

One of the conclusions that arises from the social-exchange perspective and matrix analysis is that the *kinds* of situational interdependency can strongly influence the behavior of the individuals involved. Many individuals in interactive situations (such as the prisoner's dilemma) are afraid of unfavorable outcomes if they make the cooperative choice and the other person does not. Thus they may choose not to cooperate, beginning a series of destructive exchanges that each side would prefer to avoid. There are also bargaining exchanges in which an individual chooses a cooperative strategy that is contingent on the opponent cooperating rather than competing. Otherwise one person would react competitively to competitive moves by the opponent. This contingent cooperative strategy does induce cooperative responses in the other person (Rappaport, 1973; Kuhlman & Marshello, 1975).

When we said above that certain situations of interdependency may be destructive by driving participants into "destructive exchanges that each

APPLICATION

A Matrix Analysis of the Arms Race

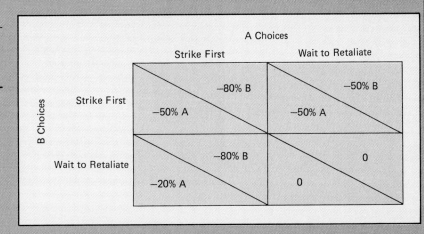

Consider yourself the leader of Superpower A with a decision to make. You have enough missiles to wipe out 50 percent of the major population centers of potentially hostile Superpower B, and it has enough missiles to do the same to you. You know you will never launch a first strike, but you suspect the other side might. You also know that if your opponent attacks first, your retaliatory strike will be able to destroy only 20 percent of its population centers, and vice versa. Assume, too, for the purposes of this exercise, that each nation has 100 missiles and 100 major population centers.

All of this can be represented in a matrix as shown below:

This, then, is your problem: If the other side strikes first, it will thereafter be sufficiently stronger and more likely than you to win the subsequent conflict. (It will have 80 percent of its population left after you retaliate, while you are left with only 50 percent of yours.) So you decide to increase your missiles until you will be able to destroy 50 percent of your opponent's population even after it strikes first. Naturally, your increase in armaments gives you additional first-strike capability as well.

This changes the matrix as shown above:

Notice first that your addition of missiles has done what you want; it has changed the matrix terms so that Superpower B will now lose 50 percent of its population if it strikes first and you retaliate. As the leader of Superpower A, you feel that you have increased the protection of your country, and you are ready to stop adding missiles.

As the leader of Superpower A, you know that your country will never strike first, but the leader of Superpower B, does not know this. Notice the second change in the matrix: If Superpower A strikes first, B loses 80 percent of its population centers, putting it in a hopeless position to fight a subsequent war against A. (This occurs because, by increasing its retaliatory capacity to destroy B's population from 20 percent to 50 percent, A added 30

percent to its first-strike capability as well.) Now what are B's options? Obviously, one option is to increase the number of its missiles. The other is to strike first and gamble on winning the war that follows.

The action A took to increase its stock of missiles to protect the country is perceived by B as sufficiently threatening to require a response. In the real world defense planners are aware of this and attempt to avoid it— for instance, by storing missiles in hidden locations not recognized by potential enemies as first-strike weapons. Still, they could function as first-strike weapons, so they are actually a threat to the other side.

In working through this exercise, you are carrying out in very much oversimplified terms the kind of calculations that any group in charge of national security must consider. As you have done so, you have been thinking rationally about a nearly unthinkable possibility—nuclear holocaust resulting in the deaths of half of the men, women, and children in this and other countries. There is research evidence that merely thinking about a particular outcome increases people's estimate of the likelihood that it will actually occur. How might this "thinking the unthinkable" affect real-world national defense planners who must consider various scenarios for nuclear war? Would they be likely to overestimate the probability that such a war may actually occur? If so, what changes might they make in their analyses?

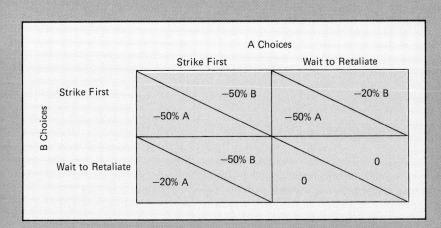

Each bargaining situation has its complexities, and a number of factors can influence the bargaining outcome. Shown here is the 24-foot-diameter peace table at which American and North Vietnamese delegations signed the Vietnam peace accord. The table itself was a factor in the bargaining—it symbolized that the two countries are geographically and ideographyically half a world apart. (Bettmann Newsphotos)

would prefer to avoid," were you reminded of any real-world situations? You should have been, for this type of conflict is reported daily on the front pages of our newspapers in stories about lock strikes or international arms limitation negotiations. The fact that the social-exchange model—and particularly its typical analytic method, matrix analysis—can be fitted to conflicts between groups and between nations as well as between individuals is not coincidental. Much of the original impetus for developing these techniques came from the need to analyze conflicts between groups and nations.

THE CONTEXTS OF GROUP ACTIVITIES

In our discussion of group interactions we hinted that social interactions are affected by the settings in which they take place. The interaction between two people depends on the availability of other interaction partners for each of the individuals. The physical realities of the communication network sometimes make an individual a central communicator link, and that person is likely to emerge as group leader.

Other contexts of group actions affect participants' behavior as well. Groups conduct their activities in physical settings that influence the nature of those activities. Every college student knows this—think of a lecture hall, with rows and rows of chairs, all facing ahead, all bolted to the floor, and imagine trying to have a group discussion in that room. Nobody could face the person with whom he or she was talking. Students in the first rows would be talking to empty air, those in the back row to the backs of heads. At best, the discussion would be awkward to carry out; more likely, it would simply not take place. Clearly, the physical and spatial context within which group interactions occur can foster or inhibit those interactions.

Behavior Settings and Environmental Psychology

Environmental psychology is a branch of social psychology that is concerned with the relationship of behavior to the setting in which it occurs. On a baseball field pitchers, catchers, batters, and fielders carry out their activities. In a bank, tellers, officers, and customers carry out their transactions, watched over by guards. Sometimes the behavior setting is a neighborhood, for example, or a city. Other settings studied by environmental psychologists include college dormitories, inner-city housing projects, and a variety of business organizations.

Institutions can differ in the number and range of the behavior settings they provide, and this makes a great deal of difference to the lives of people in those settings. Roger Barker (1960) and his colleagues painstakingly cataloged all of the behavior settings available to adolescents in a small Kansas town called "Midwest" and in a town about the same size in England called "Yoredale." They found that the two towns differed markedly: Midwest had a larger number of behavior settings than did Yoredale, and it also had a larger number of people acting in each setting. So, for instance, the American adolescents took positions of responsibility in over three times as many behavior settings as did their English counterparts.

This is important, first of all, in what it says about the social-learning experiences of the two sets of adolescents. Compared to their English counterparts, the American teenagers have many more possibilities for learning how to play various roles and for practicing the various skills associated with those roles. The high-school newspaper editor, for instance, learns a whole set of skills concerning clear writing and how to prepare copy for the press. But this person also has the chance to learn skills in working with people, in coordinating their activities, and in being in a position of authority. Such skills originally learned in an adolescent behavior setting may create career possibilities later in life.

Second, behavior settings can generate forces that cause people to want to maintain the settings. A high school wouldn't seem complete without a newspaper, and since a newspaper traditionally requires an editor, a person is needed to serve that function. So arms are twisted and an editor appears in that behavior setting.

Generalizing from this, environmental psychologists realized that the ratio of people needed to people available to fill behavior settings can have very general effects on the social climate of an institution. In underpopulated settings where there are more jobs than people to fill them, one cannot be too strict about the qualifications of potential position fillers, nor demand too much work from them. In overpopulated settings, on the other hand, where there are many applicants for every position, only people with strong skills and a willingness to work very hard at the job need be accepted. The latter situation will produce a more competitive social climate.

Physical settings can create behavior settings that encourage or discourage social interaction, as can be seen in the informal arrangement in a student cooperative and the formal arrangement of pews in a church. (*Top:* Joseph Nettis/Photo Researchers; *bottom:* George Hall/Woodfin Camp & Associates)

Destructive Environments

Some physical surroundings are destructive because they inhibit the development of certain group processes. The rigidly row-organized lecture hall that inhibits group discussion is an example of this. Robert Sommer (1974) has studied interactions in a number of environments and has called attention to some specific settings that have negative consequences for human interactions. Given some of the earlier discussions in this text, you will not be surprised to discover that the mental hospital was the source of many of his examples. The common room of a geriatric ward was remodeled, painted a more cheerful color, carpeted, and decorated with new furniture, in the hope that this would combat some of the apathy and isolation observed among the patients. Long lines of chairs were neatly placed against the walls and in the center of the room, an arrangement that the staff felt was sensible and that the custodial staff found easy to keep clean. Despite the redecoration, patients seldom used the common room, and even when they did, there was little interaction among them. But what are the possibilities for human interaction in such an environment? Picture yourself trying to converse with

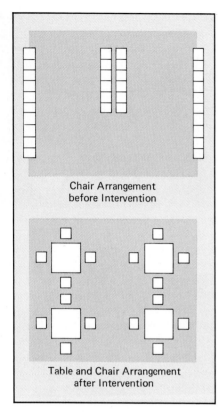

**Chair Arrangement
before Intervention**

**Table and Chair Arrangement
after Intervention**

Figure 20–12 Here are the two seating arrangements in the geriatric ward. Which do you guess would promote social interaction?

Crowding is the term used by environmental psychologists to describe the psychological state of feeling crowded, surrounded, and intruded on by other people. Crowding occurs in high-density environments, but it is not endemic to them. (Robert Frerck/Woodfin Camp & Associates)

a person sitting shoulder to shoulder with you. It's awkward, isn't it? Usually people face one another when they talk, so that they can give the nonverbal signs that enhance conversation. That is not possible when chairs are placed side by side.

Or imagine trying to converse with someone sitting across the room. You can look at each other when you talk, and that helps, but the distance between you is too great. Normal conversations take place at distances between 2 and 4 feet, and intimacy is lost at greater distances (Hall, 1966). Also, other people walking through the room will pass between the two who are conversing, further disrupting their interaction. Such seating layouts are not structured to promote social interaction. In fact, they are structured to inhibit it.

How would you arrange the furniture to encourage social interactions? The researchers convinced the hospital management to add some square tables to the room and to group the chairs in sets of four around these tables. This is the pattern normally seen in dining rooms, office meeting rooms, and other spaces designed to aid communication (see Figure 20–12). The new arrangement worked: The interactions among the patients increased, nearly doubling within a few weeks. The change in the furniture arrangement produced a behavioral setting that encouraged social contact.

Density, Crowding, and Privacy

The **density** of a group of individuals refers to the number of people present in a particular environment, expressed in terms of persons per square foot. For instance, if 10 people are in a room 8 feet wide and 12 feet long (96 square feet), the density is 1 person per 9.6 square feet.

Intuitively, high-density situations feel unpleasant to us, and a great deal of research has attempted to demonstrate this in large-scale urban environments. A number of demographic studies examined the relationship between density indices, such as the number of people who lived in a city block, and the rates of disease, crime, and mental pathology for that area. The results of these studies were confusing, sometimes supporting the existence of a relationship between density and pathology, but sometimes contradicting it. Hong Kong, for instance, has population densities four times as great as even the most crowded American cities, but it has lower rates of hospitalization for mental illness and criminal violence than American cities.

These contradictions led researchers to think more carefully about population density and how it relates to other elements of human experience. They found that high density was not always experienced as negative, and that its effects could be altered by the physical arrangements within which it existed. The concept of **crowding** was developed to describe the psychological state of feeling crowded, surrounded, and intruded on by other people (Stokols, 1972; Altman, 1975). Crowding occurs when there are too many people present or too many activities going on. This excessive stimulation can lead to a feeling of stimulus overload (Milgram, 1970). The feeling of being crowded also occurs when one is subjected to a higher degree of social contact than is desired, so that one feels one's privacy or personal space is being violated.

High density does not always lead to these conditions and therefore will not always be stressful (see the Highlight: Is Crowding Bad for Humans?). Sometimes the potential negative effects of high density can be avoided by changing the interaction space to limit overload and create the possibilities

Is Crowding Bad for Humans?

Is crowding bad for human beings? Is it somehow unnatural to have so many millions of people jammed into our largest cities? Does the enormous population density strip away the veneer of civilization and make people behave like vicious beasts, or does crowding have no effect?

For those who fear that human crowding may elicit barbaric behavior the data from animal studies are less than reassuring. In 1916 a small herd of deer was placed on a 280-acre island in the Chesapeake Bay. By 1955 they numbered about 300, and were in perfect health, but in 1958 over half of them died from no known cause (Christian, Flyger, & Davis, 1960). They had plenty of food and the climate had not changed, so what killed them? Autopsies revealed that the deer were perfectly healthy except in one respect: they had swollen and abnormal adrenal glands, a condition that in many animal species is known to be caused by prolonged stress. After the deer population had plummeted to 80, it leveled off and there were no more unexplained deaths. Could it be that the stress of overcrowding killed the deer, and the sudden deaths returned the population to a less stressful density?

In a laboratory study of population density, rats were placed in pens that could accommodate 40 to 50 adult rats, but the experimenters allowed the population in each pen to reach 80. In the next 16 months the rats started behaving very strangely. They either stopped building nests, or did so ineffectively. Males tried to mount other males and even babies. Mothers abandoned their babies or killed them. Both sexes bit their own tails until the pen was splattered with blood. Females died of pregnancy complications or tumors of the sex organs and mammary glands. The only term that the experimenter could think of to describe these deplorable conditions was a "behavioral sink" (Calhoun, 1962).

Humans are not deer, nor are they rats. Perhaps overly dense conditions would not have the same effect on people. Then again, stress is likely to result from having one's personal space invaded. Researchers have noticed that we try to maintain a certain distance between ourselves and other people. The space varies from culture to culture, with Americans and British keeping much more distance than Arabs or Latin Americans (Stockdale, 1978). In the United States we like to keep about 2 to 3 feet from friends (except lovers), and 4 feet from strangers. Any closer, and we start to feel uncomfortable, and become physiologically aroused (Evans, 1979). After all, when we are packed in with a bunch of strangers they get in our way, frustrate our freedom of movement, and in general cause us to lose personal control of the situation (Schmidt & Keating, 1979)—all consequences that can lead to stress and anxiety.

Correlational studies provide little support for the "crowding is bad for people" hypothesis, but they also do little to argue against it. The usual procedure is to divide a city into its high-density and low-density areas, and examine the crime rates, juvenile delinquency rates, rates of mental illness, and so on. The usual finding is that high-density areas have higher rates of pathological behavior than low-density areas, but they also have lower levels of personal income and education, and personal income and education predict these forms of behavior even within areas that have the same density. Does this mean that crowding has nothing to do with pathological behavior—that personal income and education level are the real culprits? Perhaps, but from these correlations it is also possible to conclude that those who live in high-density areas are so stressed that they perform poorly in life pursuits such as attaining a good education and earning a good income. Correlational evidence cannot identify the underlying cause.

In an attempt to decide whether crowding causes behavioral changes, researchers have performed laboratory studies in which they vary either the number of people in a room or the space available to the same number of people. In general, they have found that crowding has no effect on performing various tasks (Freedman, Klevansky, & Ehrlich, 1971). This is not surprising. Submariners and astronauts perform very well in extremely crowded conditions for extended periods of time. But are they nonetheless bothered by it? Do they experience stress, tension, and negative affect? Do they label their increased arousal as a negative state? Some research suggests that they do (Worchel & Yohai, 1979).

Other research suggests that people label the increased arousal of high-density situations according to what they think they should be experiencing (Freedman, 1975). Crowding simply intensifies their reaction. Situations that would normally be perceived as unpleasant, such as taking a tough exam, will seem all the more unpleasant if the room is crowded. Situations that would normally be perceived as pleasant, such as viewing a football game, will seem all the more pleasant and exhilarating if the stadium is packed.

Finally, there are individual differences in response to crowding. Several studies have compared the reactions of people of the same sex in high-density versus low-density conditions, and found that men become much more aggressive, punitive, and generally obnoxious when jammed in with many other men, whereas women actually become more friendly, forgiving, and cooperative when jammed in with many other women (Freedman, Levy, Buchanan, & Price, 1972; Paulus, 1976). Also, even within the same sex, some men and some women have personalities that lead them to seek stimulation and excitement, whereas others prefer calm and quiet. As you might expect, the latter are more adversely affected by crowding than the former.

In summary, years of research on crowding in humans have revealed that the original question—Is crowding bad for people?—was much too simplistic. We now know that different people perceive crowding differently under different circumstances. Sometimes it's great to be packed in with many other people. If it were not, no one would attend the Super Bowl. At other times having a lot of other people around can seem like sensory overload (Milgram, 1970). It is the task of future research to specify the types of situations that will produce negative effects, but given the diversity of human responses to any type of situation, this will not be an easy task.

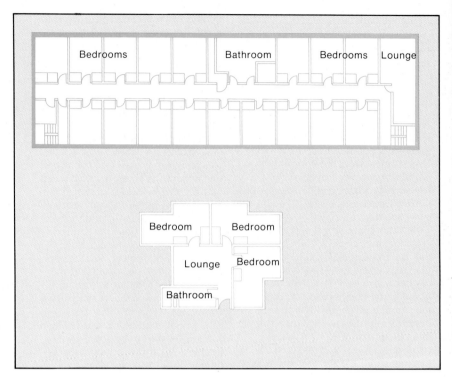

Figure 20–13 The sketch on top is the familiar "long-corridor dormitory" plan that is found on most residential campuses. The sketch underneath it is a newer plan organized by suites, in which the lounge space is shared only by those who have rooms in that suite, not with all the residents on the corridor, as in the older plan. This difference in arrangement leads to different kinds of social interactions. (Baum & Valins, 1977)

of privacy. Researchers have applied these concepts in studies of social interactions in college dormitories. In Figure 20–13 you will certainly recognize the upper floor plan as the familiar "long-corridor dormitory" that exists on nearly every residential campus in the country. The bottom plan is a newer suite floor plan. It can accommodate as many residents as the equivalent amount of space in the corridor arrangement. Its important feature is that the lounge space is shared only by the people who have rooms in the suite. In the long-corridor plan the lounge at the end of the hall is used by all the residents in the hall. Baum and Valins (1977) found that even though both kinds of dorms had the same population density, the long-corridor dorm residents felt more crowded. And they, more than the residents of suite-organized dorms, reported that they felt it was useless to try to change things in their dormitory. To see how far the effects of the dormitories generalized, Baum and Valins set up in a psychology laboratory a task in which rather little information was given to the participants. Participants who lived in long-corridor dorms were more passively accepting of this. They were relatively unlikely to seek out additional information. (Compare this result with the discussion of learned helplessness in Chapters 16 and 17.)

Organizational Settings

So far we have considered the ways people are influenced by and influence the small groups in which they are involved, the ways small groups influence one another, and the ways in which individuals and small groups are influenced by the physical contexts of their activities. We will now look at the ways in which people's activities are influenced by the *organizational* contexts in which their activities take place—the effects of social organizations

on human behavior. Actually, we have already examined some effects of motivation and job design on people's behavior in organizations (Chapter 12). Here we will reconsider some of these themes and bring up new ones in the context of work organizations.

Structuring the Organization. How should work organizations be structured? Initial answers to this question were provided by classical theorists, who saw an organization as essentially a hierarchical authority structure in which superiors controlled the performance of subordinates. Subordinates were to be given a clear, definite, and preferably limited and repetitive set of duties and responsibilities. Each person should have one and only one boss, who would reward or punish the worker on the basis of the worker's productivity. Any problems were to be referred upward, and information was to be passed upward as well. Decisions and orders were to be passed downward. Rules were to be carefully followed.

As critics have pointed out, this classical theory of organizational design has a number of problems. First, it rests on a rather dehumanizing set of assumptions about the worker. The worker is seen as requiring external motivation and as possessing none of his or her own. For modern workers, however, being given a constant stream of orders while doing repetitive work often leads to hostility or withdrawal. Second, today's organizations function in a changing and demanding environment. (An organization's environment includes outside forces, such as competitors and union rules, and internal conditions, such as employee morale and working conditions.) Standard rules cannot be set up to cover every situation because unpredictable events occur frequently. By the time each decision is referred up the hierarchy to a point at which the authority exists to make the decision, it may be too late for an optimal response. Finally, workers who resent rigid organization rules can develop an overprecise way of following them, which actually subverts the goals of the organization.

In response to these kinds of problems, *humanistic theories of organization* were developed in the 1950s and 1960s (Argyris, 1957; McGregor, 1960; Likert, 1967). This new approach saw the organization as a network of supportive relationships, operating through group decision-making processes, with interactions furthered by a free flow of communication. Critics of these organizational theorists (Wexley & Yukl, 1977) have commented that in react-

Organizational structures have changed considerably in this century. Recent research has shown that the key factor in designing an optimal organizational structure is a careful consideration of the organization's external environment and its internal needs. (*Left:* National Archives; *right:* Mimi Forsyth/Monkmeyer Press)

ing to the classical structure, the humanists have gone too far in the other direction. Their assumptions about worker motivations are too idealistic, and their assumption that workers' motivations are always compatible with organizational goals may also be naive. Nor is quick adaptation to a shifting outside environment guaranteed by the sometimes complex and time-consuming process of group decision making.

Other research (Burns & Stalker, 1961; Morse & Lorsch, 1970) suggests that an organization's external environment and its internal needs are the key factors in designing an optimal structure. The contingencies a company must deal with—competitive market, technological innovations, employee characteristics, for example—must be taken into account when establishing its structure. Many organizational structures today include some elements of both the classical and humanistic prescriptions. An organization with stable markets, relatively unchanging production technologies, and low demands for new-product development might well use something close to the classical organizational structure. Companies that need to respond to rapidly changing markets and that are affected by new technologies tend to do better with a more group-centered organization. Of course, it must be a group that is capable of making decisions rapidly. These newer theories of organization, which postulate that an organization's structure must be determined by each company's unique set of external and internal factors, are called *contingency theories of organizational design*. This approach recognizes that no single structure will work for all organizations.

Conflict in Organizations and Its Resolution.   **Conflict** is said to occur when two parties in a dispute begin to interfere intentionally with each other's goal attainment (Wexley & Yukl, 1977). Conflicts occur in all organizations and therefore have been studied intensively by organizational psychologists. As we well know, conflicts also occur between nations, between student organizations, and between individuals; and it is hoped that the analyses of conflict and conflict resolution in organizational settings will have implications for the analysis and resolution of these other conflicts.

A number of causes of conflicts in business organizations have been identified (Walton & Dutton, 1969; Robbins, 1974; Wexley & Yukl, 1977). These include competition for scarce resources, dependence on others for completion of one's own tasks, ambiguous responsibilities, status and power problems, and concerns about promotion or compensation. Generally conflict arises when an individual or a group in an organization is frustrated in pursuit of important goals. When these situations arise, we can expect reactions similar to those we discussed in Chapter 19 in the section on frustration and aggression.

A common source of conflict is poor communication, which often leads to the perception that some frustrating circumstances exist even when they really don't. One of the most frequent research findings is that there is insufficient upward communication in organizations, and managers are often misinformed about workers' motivations as a result. For example, Kahn (1958) discovered that supervisors overestimate the importance of fulfilling such workers' needs as pay and security, and underestimate the importance of the intrinsic satisfaction of doing the job well. Communication problems are frequently exacerbated because workers neither understand nor trust management's goals (Athanassiades, 1973). Meanwhile, managers are sure that they are aware of the real concerns of workers, even though evidence suggests that they are not (Hamann, 1956).

Conflict in an organization can disrupt communication and production and

Table 20–2: Five Modes of Conflict Resolution.

Conflict-Handling Modes	Appropriate Situations	Conflict-Handling Modes	Appropriate Situations
Competing	1. When quick, decisive action is vital—e.g., emergencies. 2. On important issues where unpopular actions need implementing—e.g., cost cutting, enforcing unpopular rules, discipline. 3. On issues vital to company welfare when you know you're right. 4. Against people who take advantage of noncompetitive behavior.	Avoiding	1. When an issue is trivial, or more important issues are pressing. 2. When you perceive no chance of satisfying your concerns. 3. When potential disruption outweighs the benefits of resolution. 4. To let people cool down and regain perspective. 5. When gathering information supersedes immediate decision. 6. When others can resolve the conflict more effectively. 7. When issues seem tangential or symptomatic of other issues.
Collaborating	1. To find an integrative solution when both sets of concerns are too important to be compromised. 2. When your objective is to learn. 3. To merge insights from people with different perspectives. 4. To gain commitment by incorporating concerns into a consensus. 5. To work through feelings that have interfered with a relationship.	Accommodating	1. When you find you are wrong—to allow a better position to be heard, to learn, and to show your reasonableness. 2. When issues are more important to others than to you—to satisfy others and maintain cooperation. 3. To build social credits for later issues. 4. To minimize loss when you are outmatched and losing. 5. When harmony and stability are especially important. 6. To allow subordinates to develop by learning from their mistakes.
Compromising	1. When goals are important, but not worth the effort or potential disruption of more assertive modes. 2. When opponents with equal power are committed to mutually exclusive goals. 3. To achieve temporary settlements to complex issues. 4. To arrive at expedient solutions under time pressure. 5. As a backup when collaboration or competition is unsuccessful.		

Thomas (1977), p. 487.

can cause feelings of hostility among participants. Conflict can also have positive consequences because its resolution can lead to needed changes. For example, college students frequently experience conflict with parents over issues of independence—choice of friends, life patterns, late hours, and so on.

These conflicts are necessary for parents to understand that students are no longer children, and for students to realize that they are responsible for conducting their own lives. The resolution of these conflicts can lead to real growth for both parents and students. It is important to remember that conflict can have positive outcomes.

Often the intervention of third parties is useful in resolving conflict, and standard roles for third parties have been developed. For instance, labor and management can agree to submit a dispute to a respected *arbitrator,* who customarily is given the power to reach a decision that is binding on the disputants. A *mediator* fulfills a similar role but does not have the power to make binding decisions, and so must use persuasion, insight, and conflict-management techniques to achieve a solution. These techniques range from separating the two bargaining parties, in order to eliminate hostilities expressed in face-to-face disputes, to accurately understanding each party's real solution preferences (which they may not have thought through for themselves), from which compromise solutions may be proposed (Pruitt, 1975). Finally, a third-party intervener may focus less on the immediate dispute and more on the *process* by which the parties resolve their disputes.

Thomas (1977) has classified various modes of handling conflicts within organizations (see Table 20–2). His taxonomy is useful for those concerned with resolving disputes between any parties in a conflict—family members, roommates, students and teachers, as well as organizations. The taxonomy contains one important insight, which is that all modes of resolving conflict, including avoiding it, may be appropriate depending on the circumstances.

Conflict resolution relies first on the social-exchange analysis and second on attribution theory. It is vital to recognize that participants in a dispute are making attributions about the attitudes, personalities, goals, purposes, and motives of other disputants, and that flawed communications can cause false attributions about these factors. As you can see, conflict resolution specifically, and organizational psychology generally, rely heavily on the analytic perspectives that they share with social psychology, so it is worth emphasizing these once again. How is the surrounding situation perceived by the actor? What are the motives, goals, and needs of a sibling, a new acquaintance, a possible dating partner, or a boss? What are their personalities? What meanings should be placed on the actions of others? Then through a system of social exchanges and interactions, the perceiver can act in order to reach desired goals.

SUMMARY

1. When discussing the social influence of a leader, three factors are important: the *strength* of the source, the *immediacy* of the source, and the *number* of targets. This same framework can be used to discuss the influence of one source on many targets, or the influence of many sources on one target.

2. Theories of *leadership* include the trait-centered approach, relational theory, and the contingency model of leadership effectiveness.

3. *Social-facilitation theory* is based on the assumption that the presence of others is a source of arousal; depending on the difficulty of the task involved, this can lead to poor or good performance.

4. Three dimensions of the interaction between individuals and groups are conformity, deviation, and innovation.

5. *Conformity* often has a negative connotation, but in some situations it is a sign of rational behavior

rather than weakness. Examples of rational conformity are conforming actions rising from *informational social influence.* Another type of conformity, *normative social influence,* often involves the suppression of one's own opinions.

6. People who deviate from the group opinion are often ostracized and punished by the group; they then may become members of *out-groups.*

7. Status in a group determines how much influence a person will have in getting his or her opinions adopted by the group; this adoption of an opinion not originally held by the majority is called *innovation.*

8. Several theories have been proposed to explain the *group polarization effect:* value theory, information-exchange theories, diffusion of responsibility theory.

9. *Social-exchange theory* analyzes human interaction as a series of exchanges of desired commodities such as money, goods, information, or more intangible commodities such as respect. The *matrix* format is frequently used to analyze the particular nature of the possible exchanges between people and to predict the particular cooperative or competitive relationships that will emerge.

10. *Environmental psychologists* study setting-interaction relationships; the basic unit of their studies is the *behavior setting.*

11. *Density* refers to the number of people present in a particular environment. High-density situations seem to be negative only when they create crowding—the psychological state of feeling crowded, surrounded, and intruded on by other people.

12. Environmental psychologists have shown how space can be manipulated to create the possibilities of privacy and to reduce the potential negative effects of density.

13. Psychologists have tried to understand people's behavior in organizational settings. There is no single organizational structure that seems to work for all organizations.

14. Research on *conflict* and conflict resolution deals with social-exchange analysis and attribution processes.

SUGGESTED READINGS

BAUM, A., & VALINS, S. (1977). *Architecture and social behavior: Psychological studies in social density.* Hillsdale, N.J.: Erlbaum. Contains some good examples of recent developments in ecological research.

DANNETTE, M. (Ed.) (1983). *Handbook of industrial and organizational psychology.* New York: Wiley. This edited volume is an excellent place to begin research into almost any aspect of industrial and organizational psychology.

DAVIS, J. H. (1969). *Group performance.* Reading, Mass.: Addison-Wesley. Interesting but complex findings on group performance variables are reviewed here.

FIEDLER, F. E., & CHEMERS, M. H. (1974). *Leadership and effective management.* Chicago: Scott, Foresman. An excellent review of leadership research; necessary reading for those who wish to pursue the subject further.

FREEDMAN, J. L. (1975). *Crowding and behavior.* San Francisco: W. H. Freeman & Co. This is an award-winning analysis of crowding research that is both readable and entertaining.

KELLEY, H. H. (1979). *Personal relationships: Their structures and processes.* Hillsdale, N.J.: Erlbaum. Using attributional and social exchange principles, Kelley illuminates many of the events that take place in intimate relationships.

KELLEY, H. H., BERSCHEID, E., CHRISTENSEN, A., HARVEY, J., HUSTON, T., LEVINGER, G., McCLINTOCK, E., PEPLAU, A., & PETERSON, D. K. (1983). *Close relationships.* San Francisco: Freeman. This is an excellent introduction to the rapidly developing study of people in close relationships. It is relevant to the material discussed in this and the previous chapter.

KIESLER, C. A., & KIESLER, S. B. (1969). *Conformity.* Reading, Mass.: Addison-Wesley. Well organized and clear, this text reviews the conformity literature in comprehensive but succinct fashion.

LATANÉ, B., & DARLEY, J. M. (1970). *The unresponsive bystander: Why doesn't he help?* Englewood Cliffs, N.J.: Prentice-Hall. This research monograph shows how various social pressures interact when one is faced with the decision to help or not to help in an emergency.

MILGRAM, S. (1974). *Obedience to authority.* New York: Harper & Row. The controversial research on obedience to authority is reported by its author.

STOKALS, D. (1977). *Perspectives on environment and behavior.* New York: Plenum. A thoughtful presentation of many of the issues in environmental psychology, by one of the major figures in the field.

SULS, J., & MILLER, R. J. (Eds.) (1977). *Social comparison processes: Theoretical and empirical perspectives.* Washington, D.C.: Hemisphere/Halsted. This edited volume contains a number of recent papers on social comparison.

WHEELER, L., DECI, E., REIS, H., & ZUCKERMAN, M. (1978). *Interpersonal influence,* 2nd ed. Boston: Allyn & Bacon. This well-written book explores many of the issues discussed in this chapter, e.g., conformity and social facilitation.

Appendix: Statistics

"You haven't told me yet," said Lady Nuttal, "what it is your fiancé does for a living."

"He's a statistician," replied Lamia, with an annoying sense of being on the defensive.

Lady Nuttal was obviously taken aback. It had not occured to her that statisticians entered into normal relationships. The species, she would have surmised, was perpetuated in some collateral manner, like mules.

"But Aunt Sara, it's a very interesting profession," said Lamia warmly.

"I don't doubt it," said her aunt, who obviously doubted it very much. "To express anything important in mere figures is so plainly impossible that there must be endless scope for well-paid advice on how to do it. But don't you think that life with a statistician would be rather, shall we say, humdrum?"

Lamia was silent. She felt reluctant to discuss the surprising depth of emotional possibility which she had discovered below Edward's numerical veneer.

"It's not the figures themselves," she said finally, "it's what you do with them that matters." (K. A. C. Manderville, *The Undoing of Lamia Gurdleneck*)

Psychologists often use numbers to describe behavior—for example, how long it takes for a stimulus to evoke a response, the number of correct answers on a test, a subject's rating of preference on a scale from 1 to 9, and so on. These are all measurement procedures, as are the more familiar procedures for measuring length and weight. In this appendix we will discuss how some aspects of a group of numbers (for example, test scores) can be characterized by other numbers called **statistics** (for example, the average test score), and how inferences can be drawn from such statistics, a process called *statistical inference*.

DESCRIPTIVE STATISTICS

Frequency Distributions

Descriptive statistics is a set of methods for organizing and summarizing numerical data. The data may be any set of measurements of a group of objects, people, or events. For example, if we are interested in the annual incomes of domestic workers, we might conduct a survey by asking some domestic workers what their annual income is. Here the **population** is incomes of all domestic workers, and the **sample** we take is the actual records of incomes we have at the conclusion of the survey. Table 1A gives the incomes reported by each of 17 hypothetical domestic workers. These data could be described as mostly in the $4,000 range, with some much higher and a few lower. A more precise way of characterizing the incomes in the sample is to specify exactly how many there are in the $3,000 range, $4,000 range, $5,000 range, and so on. This is a **frequency distribution.** It can be presented as a table (Table 1B) or as a graph (Figure 1). Notice that

Table 1A: Annual Incomes Sampled from 17 Domestic Workers.

3,000	4,000	6,000
5,000	5,000	4,000
10,000	7,000	10,000
20,000	10,000	4,000
8,000	9,000	4,000
4,000	4,000	

Table 1B: Frequency Distribution of Annual Incomes Grouped in Intervals of $1,000.

Income Interval	Frequency
3,000–3,999	1
4,000–4,999	6
5,000–5,999	2
6,000–6,999	1
7,000–7,999	1
8,000–8,999	1
9,000–9,999	1
10,000–10,999	3
11,000–11,999	0
12,000–12,999	0
13,000–13,999	0
14,000–14,999	0
15,000–15,999	0
16,000–16,999	0
17,000–17,999	0
18,000–18,999	0
19,000–19,999	0
20,000–20,999	1
	17

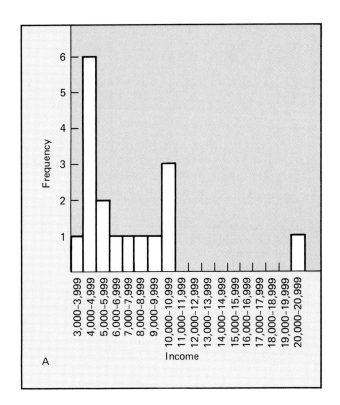

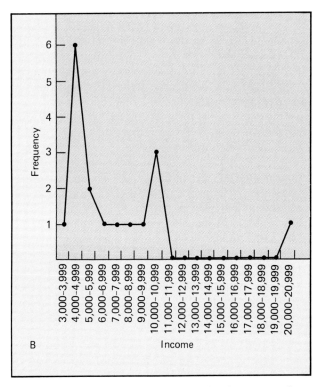

in Table 1 and Figure 1 we have classified incomes into *class intervals* of $1,000.

Two types of graphs are shown in Figure 1: A **histogram,** or bar graph (Figure 1A), indicates the frequency of scores in a class interval by the height of a bar above that interval. A **polygon,** or line graph (Figure 1B), consists of a series of connected points, one above each interval, with each point's height indicating the frequency of scores in that interval.

Tables and graphs are helpful for showing how numbers are distributed. It is also useful to summarize certain characteristics of distributions in terms of a single number. Figure 2 presents three frequency distributions. The centers of distributions A and B are similar, in that each lies in the class interval 50–59. In contrast, the center of distribution C lies above the class interval 70–79. In other words, a "typical" score in both distribution A and B is around 55, whereas it is around 75 in distribution C. This typical value of a distribution is called its **central tendency.**

A second major feature of a distribution is its spread or **variability.** For example, the scores in distribution A are all closely grouped around the center of the distribution, while they are much more spread out or variable in distribution B and C. Thus distribution B is similar to distribution A in central tendency, but similar to distribution C in variability.

Central tendency and variability can be more precisely characterized with specific measures or num-

Figure 1 The data in these frequency distributions are from Table 1. Figure 1A is a histogram or bar graph, and Figure 1B is a polygon or line graph.

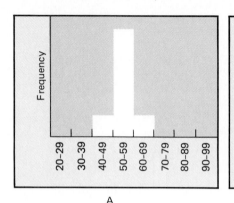
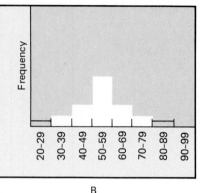
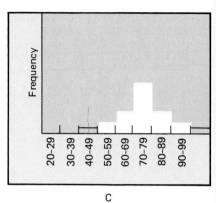

Figure 2 Three frequency distributions. Distribution A has less variability than B but the same central tendency. Distribution C has a higher central tendency than B, but a similar variability.

bers. Such numbers, or statistics, characterize particular aspects of a group of numbers.

Measures of Central Tendency

Three different statistics are commonly used to characterize the central tendency of a distribution. These are the mode, the median, and the mean. The **mode** is the number that occurs most frequently in a distribution. For example, suppose your data consist of these numbers: 11, 7, 7, 10, 11, 8, 11. The mode would be 11, because it occurs more often than any other number. In a frequency distribution graph, the mode would be the interval having the highest bar above it in a histogram, or the highest point in a polygon (for example, the interval from 4,000 to 4,999 in Figure 1). (Exactly which number within that interval you use to denote the mode involves issues we need not consider here.)

The **median** is the middle number in an ascending or descending sequence of numbers. If you order or *rank* the numbers in a distribution, beginning with the largest and ending with the smallest, the median is in the very middle. For example, suppose your data consist of these numbers: 9, 2, 5, 4, 6, 10, 12. If you rank them (12, 10, 9, 6, 5, 4, 2), the number 6 would be the median, because there are as many numbers ranked above it (12, 10, 9) as below it (5, 4, 2). Again, there are some complexities when you use grouped data or when 2 numbers have the same rank.

The third and perhaps most frequently used way of characterizing central tendency is called the arithmetic **mean** or **average.** To calculate the mean, you add all the entries in the distribution and divide by the number of entries. For example, suppose your data consist of 7 numbers: 8, 6, 1, 9, 5, 10, 3. To calculate

the mean, first add all the entries ($8 + 6 + 1 + 9 + 5 + 10 + 3 = 42$). Then divide by the number of entries ($42 \div 7 = 6$). Thus the mean or average of 8, 6, 1, 9, 5, 10, and 3 is 6.

Usually we use different symbols to refer to the mean of a sample and the mean of a total population: $\overline{X}$ stands for the mean of a sample, and the Greek letter μ (mu) stands for the mean of a total population. For example, the mean of the sample of incomes in Table 1 is $6,882; therefore, $\overline{X}$ = $6,882. We would not, however, know the value of μ, the mean of all incomes, unless we were able to determine the income of every domestic worker in the country.

Often the popular press reports an "average" of a frequency distribution without specifying whether it is the mode, the median, or the arithmetic mean. Which of these it is can make a difference. Consider the hypothetical income data we have been discussing: The mode is about $4500; the median is $5500; and the arithmetic mean is $6,882. How well you think domestic workers are paid will certainly depend on which of these "averages" is reported!

Measures of Variability

Three statistics commonly used to characterize the variability of a distribution are the range, the variance, and the standard deviation. The **range** is simply the difference between the largest and smallest number in the distribution. For example, suppose your data consist of the following numbers: 20, 15, 5, 30, 10. The range equals the largest number (30) minus the smallest number (5), or 25. Thus the range is based on the largest and smallest numbers in a distribution.

A more commonly used measure of variability is the **variance,** the average squared *deviation* or difference of each number from the mean of all the numbers. The variance of a sample is called s^2, and the variance of a population is called σ^2, the Greek letter

sigma, squared. As an example of how to compute a variance, say that the data consist of these numbers: 1, 4, 2, 1. First the mean, $\underline{X}$, would be calculated:

$$\overline{X} = \frac{1 + 4 + 2 + 1}{4} = \frac{8}{4} = 2$$

Next, the deviation of each of these numbers from the mean (2) would be squared, as follows:

$$(1 - 2)^2 = 1$$
$$(4 - 2)^2 = 4$$
$$(2 - 2)^2 = 0$$
$$(1 - 2)^2 = 1$$

To compute the variance, you then find the average or mean of these squared deviations, which is their sum divided by 4:

$$s^2 = \frac{1 + 4 + 0 + 1}{4} = \frac{6}{4} = 1.5$$

The variance is just as important as the mean in interpreting data. For example, look at the hypothetical data in Table 2. An object known to weigh 1.5 grams was weighed on a Truway scale and on an Accuway scale on five different occasions. Though the average weight for the two scales is the same, the *Truway scale is more variable* ($s^2 = .5$ grams^2 versus .02 grams^2), and so it is less reliable. Thus, Accuway is clearly the preferred scale, but knowing only the average value of the measurements would not tell you this and, thus, would not help you make the best choice.

The variance of the measurements in Table 2 is shown in grams squared, an awkward kind of quantity to think about. If we take the square root of the variance ($s = \sqrt{s^2}$ and $\sigma = \sqrt{\sigma^2}$), we have another measure of variability, the **standard deviation.** For example, the variance of .5 grams^2 corresponds to a standard

deviation of .71 grams. The standard deviation is easier to use because the units are the same as in the original measurements (grams instead of grams squared).

Position in a Distribution

Two commonly used indices of a number's relative position in a distribution are standard deviation and percentiles. The standard deviation of a distribution of numbers provides a convenient way of expressing how far away any given measurement is from the average of a set of measurements. Look again at the measurements for the Accuway Scale: 1.3, 1.4, 1.5, 1.6, 1.7. The average, $\overline{X}$, is 1.5 grams; the standard deviation is .14 grams. The measurement of 1.7 grams, then, for instance, is 1.4 standard deviation units above the mean ($1.7 = \overline{X} + 1.4s$ or $1.7 = 1.5 + (1.4)(.14) = 1.5 + .20$). Similarly, the measurement of 1.4 grams is .71 standard deviation unit below the mean ($1.4 = \overline{X} - .71s = 1.5 - .1$). Thus we can express any measurement in terms of how many standard deviations it is above or below the mean of the set of measurements. Thus, if we let X be any measurement, we may express X as the mean ($\overline{X}$) plus some multiple (z) of the standard deviation (s): $X = \overline{X} + z(s)$.

As an example, look again at the Truway measurements in Table 2. How many standard deviation units above the mean is the measurement of 2.5? In other words, what is z equal to in $2.5 = 1.5 + z(.71)$? To find out the value of z we first subtract the mean, 1.5, from the measurement, 2.5:

$$2.5 - 1.5 = z(.71)$$

The last set in finding z is to divide both sides of the equation by the standard deviation, or .71:

$$\frac{1}{.71} = \frac{z(.71)}{.71} \qquad 1.41 = z$$

The score of 2.5 is 1.41 standard deviation units above the mean, 1.5. We can do the same thing for measurements below the mean. In Table 2 the Truway Score of .5 is -1.41 standard deviation units *below* the mean, since

$$.5 = 1.5 - (1.41)(.71) \text{ or } Z = \frac{.5 - 1.5}{.71} = -1.41.$$

Table 3 gives each Truway and Accuway measurement and its standard score (how many standard deviations above or below the mean it is). When we reexpress a number in terms of how many standard deviation units it is from the mean, we call that its **standard score,** or **z-score.**

Table 2:   The Results of Five Different Measurements on Truway and Accuway Scales.

	Truway	Accuway
1st weighing	1.5 grams	1.7 grams
2nd weighing	1.0 grams	1.4 grams
3rd weighing	2.0 grams	1.5 grams
4th weighing	2.5 grams	1.3 grams
5th weighing	.5 grams	1.6 grams
	$\overline{X} = 1.5$ grams	$\overline{X} = 1.5$ grams
	$s^2 = .5$ grams^2	$s^2 = .02$ grams^2
	$s = .71$ grams	$s = .14$ grams

Table 3: Truway and Accuway Measurements and Their Standard Scores.

TRUWAY		ACCUWAY	
Raw Score	Standard Score	Raw Score	Standard Score
1.5	0	1.7	+1.43
1.0	− .70	1.4	− .71
2.0	+ .70	1.5	0
2.5	+1.41	1.3	−1.43
.5	−1.41	1.6	+ .71

A second way of expressing a number's relative position in a distribution is in terms of the percentage of numbers that are at the same level or below it—that is, give the number's **percentile rank.** For example, by definition of the median, the percentile rank of the median must be equal to 50. As another example, a score of 80 on a given test is the 40th percentile if 40 percent of the scores are below it. On another test, however, a score of 80 might be at the 90th percentile, because of 90 percent of the scores were at or below 80.

RELATIVE FREQUENCY AND PROBABILITY

Frequencies can be deceiving! University A reports admitting 20 women to graduate school; University B reports admitting 40. Does this indicate a pattern of discrimination on the part of University A as compared to B? Before reaching any conclusions, it would be important at least to determine for each university what proportion or **relative frequency** of admittances were women. Suppose A's total number of admittances is 40 and B's is 80. The picture is now different; it is clear that each university is admitting about 50 percent men and women. Figure 3 shows a relative frequency distribution for the data given in Table 1 and Figure 1.

Suppose we took the incomes in Table 1A, painted each of the numbers on a marble, and then put them all in an urn, which we then shook up. What are the chances that we would draw a marble with a number between 7,000 and 7,999 on it? Since there are 17 marbles and only one is the interval 7,000 to 7,999, we can readily see that the chances are 1 in 17. But what about our original sample of incomes—what were our chances of drawing one income between $7,000 and $7,999? Without knowing the true proportion or *probability* of incomes in this interval in the population, we cannot answer this question. We can, however, say that the true proportion of incomes in the interval $7,000

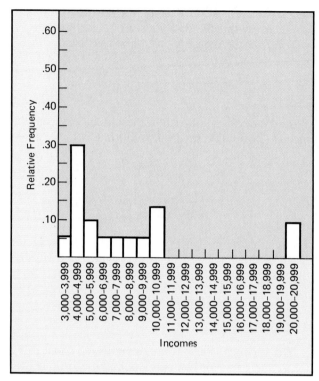

Figure 3 Relative frequency distribution for the scores in Table 1.

to $7,999 is the probability that if we randomly sample one income from the population, then that income will be between $7,000 and $7,999. In a *random sample,* every income in the population has an equal chance of being selected. In a random sample, then, there are no biases that would favor some incomes over others. Such a bias might occur if, for example, we surveyed domestic workers in only one part of the country.

Figure 4 compares a possible true distribution of incomes to the relative frequency distribution of incomes in our sample of 17 incomes. Though we can see that the distribution of incomes in the sample is not exactly the same as the true distribution of incomes, it is very similar. When we don't know the true distribution for the population, we can use the distribution of a random sample as our best guess as to the true proportion in the population. Thus, for example, our best guess as to the true proportion of incomes between $7,000 and $7,999 is .059, the proportion or relative frequency in our sample. When statisticians use quantities or statistics such as relative frequency to guess the true quantity, we say that the sample statistic is used to estimate the population value or *parameter.*

Just as we can use the sample proportion to esti-

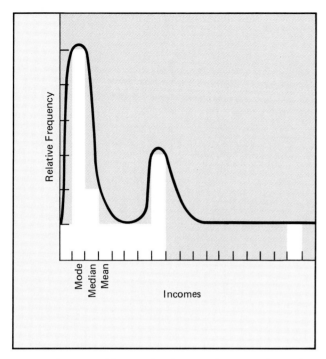

Figure 4 A possible true distribution of incomes (smooth curve) and the relative frequency distribution of the sampled incomes.

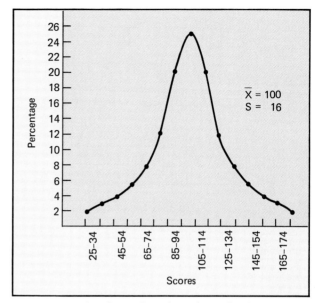

Figure 5 IQ data from a hypothetical sample of 500 tests.

mate the true proportion or probability, we can use the mean of the sample, $\overline{X}$, as an estimate of the population mean, μ. In the income example, we would estimate the average income as the sample average: $6,882. Similarly, we can use the variance of the sample to estimate the variance of the population.

NORMAL DISTRIBUTION

Many kinds of empirical data are distributed in a pattern that is approximately symmetrical, or bell-shaped—as in the sample of IQ data shown in Figure 5. When this occurs, it is often assumed that the true probability distribution is the **normal distribution curve** shown in Figure 6A. In a normal distribution, 68 percent of the numbers are between 1 standard deviation below the mean and 1 standard deviation above the mean ($\mu \pm 1 \sigma$). Looking at the IQ data in Figure 5, we see that the sample mean is 100 and the sample standard deviation is 16 points. The graph shows us that in this sample of IQ scores, 65 percent of the measurements are in the interval from 85 to 114. So for this interval, the proportion of numbers in the sample is similar to a normal distribution. When the sample proportions are so close to the theoretical

probabilities of the normal distribution, we say the normal curve gives a good approximation of the empirical, sample distribution. The theoretical proportion .68 is arrived at by computing the area under the curve and over the interval 1 standard deviation below and above the mean, as shown in Figure 6A. Similarly, the area under the curve and above the interval from $\mu + 1\sigma$ to $\mu + 2\sigma$ is equal to the proportion .136. This is very near the sample proportion in the data of Figure 5A. It is very difficult to compute areas under the normal curve, so statisticians have provided tables of different fractions of areas under this curve. Table 4 gives area under the normal curve as a proportion of the total area.

There are many uses for the proportions given in Table 4. One of them is the interpretation of standard scores and the other is in tests of significance.

Standard Scores and the Normal Distribution

It is often useful to express a measurement in relation to the rest of the measurements—either as a percentile rank or as a standard score. If the population sampled has a normal probability distribution, then the set of standard scores of that population also has a normal distribution. Figure 6B is the normal distribution of standard scores: The mean of the standard scores is 0 (that is, $\mu = 0$), and its standard deviation is equal to 1 (that is, $\sigma = 1$). Standard scores of a distribution are useful for finding the probability that an observation

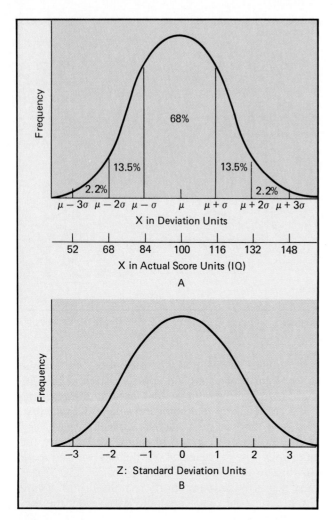

Figure 6 Normal curve: (A) Percent areas from mean to specified distance in deviation units. (B) Standard normal curve.

Table 4: Area under Normal Curve as Proportion of Total Area.

Standard Deviation	(1) Area to the Left of This Value	(2) Area to the Right of This Value	(3) Area Between This Value and the Mean
−3.00	.001	.999	.499
−2.50	.006	.994	.494
−2.00	.023	.977	.477
−1.50	.067	.933	.433
−1.00	.159	.841	.341
− .50	.309	.691	.191
.00	.500	.500	.000
+ .50	.692	.309	.191
+1.00	.841	.159	.341
+1.50	.933	.067	.433
+2.00	.977	.023	.477
+2.50	.994	.006	.494
+3.00	.999	.001	.499

So the chance of sampling a GRE score *below* 450 is .309.

STATISTICAL INFERENCE AND DECISION MAKING

Statistical inference is the process of interpreting sample data. Here we will discuss how to interpret differences among sample means from several groups. First, though, we need to consider just how typical the sample mean really is.

Does the sample mean accurately predict the true population mean? Table 6 gives the results of two dif-

from a normal population will fall in a given interval. For example, the Graduate Record Exam has a mean of 500 and a standard deviation of 100, as shown in Table 5. The probability that a score picked at random will be below −.5 standard deviations (−.5σ below the mean) is given in Table 4 in the row containing −.5; it is .309. The GRE score corresponding to a standard score of −.5 can be computed as follows: We let X denote the unknown GRE score. We know X can be written as

$$X = \overline{X} - (.5)(\sigma)$$

So for the GRE we have

$$X = 500 - (.5)(100) = 450$$

Table 5: Graduate Record Examination Scores and Their Respective Standard Scores.

GRE Scores	Standard Score
200	−3.0
300	−2.0
400	−1.0
500	0.0
600	+1.0
700	+2.0
800	+3.0

Mean = 500
Standard Deviation = 100

Table 6: Raw Scores and Statistics from Two Experiments.

The experiments measured the time it takes a rat to traverse a maze.

	TIME (MIN)		
	Experiment 1		Experiment 2
Rat 1	2.1	Rat 1	2.3
Rat 2	2.4	Rat 2	2.2
Rat 3	1.8	Rat 3	1.9
Rat 4	2.3	Rat 4	1.5
Rat 5	1.9	Rat 5	1.2
	$\overline{X} = 2.1$		$\overline{X} = 1.82$
	$s^2 = .052$		$s^2 = .1736$
	$s = .228$		$s = .417$

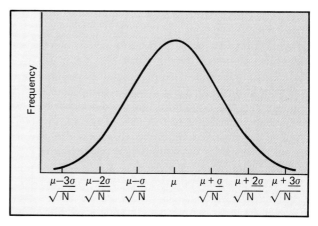

Figure 7 The normal curve distribution of sample means.

ferent experiments on how long it takes rats to complete a maze. The two experiments were conducted under the same procedure, but with different rats. As might be expected, the mean times for the two groups of rats are different. Even if the two groups of rats are from the same population, we would still expect the sample means to be different, because random samples drawn from a population do vary. Thus there is a *distribution of sample means,* whose mean, μ, is the same as the mean of the population from which the samples are drawn. The distribution of sample means can be approximated with the normal curve as shown in Figure 7.

The standard deviation of the distribution of sample means is called the **standard error of the mean,** $\sigma_{\overline{X}}$, since it reflects the accuracy with which the sample means estimates the population mean. The formula for the standard error of the mean is

$$\sigma_{\overline{X}} = \frac{\sigma}{\sqrt{N}}$$

where σ is the population standard deviation and N is the number of measurements added together in computing the sample mean.

The more samples there are, the smaller the size of the standard error. This is just what we would expect; a more reliable (i.e., less variable) estimate of the mean *should* be obtained by taking larger samples. A few sample computations will make this observation clear. First, let's consider the theoretical distribution of IQ scores in Figure 5. Let the standard deviation of the population, σ, be assumed to be 16. Now, suppose we administer an IQ test to a group suspected to differ from the norm in their average IQ. Thus, we wish to estimate their average IQ. Suppose we give the IQ test

to a sample of 64 people in this group. How much variability will there be in our estimate of the group's average IQ? To answer this, we compute the standard error of the mean:

$$\sigma_{\overline{X}} = \frac{\sigma}{\sqrt{N}}$$

For our example,

$$\frac{\sigma}{\sqrt{N}} = \frac{16}{\sqrt{64}} = 2.0$$

Thus, one standard deviation in the distribution of sample means is 2.0 To interpret this, we recall that for the normal probability curve, the chances of being between 1 standard deviation above and below the mean is about 68 percent—in other words, the probability that a sample mean based on 64 test scores is between 98 and 102 is .68. Consider, however, taking a sample mean based on only 16 scores. The standard error of the mean in this case is

$$\frac{\sigma}{\sqrt{N}} = \frac{16}{\sqrt{16}} = 4$$

Thus, the standard error in the mean is twice as great as when N = 64. Now there is a 68 percent chance that the observed sample mean lies between 96 and 104—a much wider interval than when the sample size is 64. Thus, *the smaller the sample size, the less reliable or accurate is the sample mean as an estimator of the population mean.* Furthermore, given the sample size and standard deviation of the population, it is possible to specify the probability that the sample mean will be in a given interval.

Statistical Significance

The interpretation of many experiments in psychology depends on comparisons of measurements made on 2 different populations. Each population is sampled, and the sample mean for each group is computed. Deciding whether the population means differ involves assessing the variability of the sample means to determine if an observed difference between the sample means is reliable, or **statistically significant.** The basic question, then, is whether a difference between two sample means reflects a true difference between population means or is simply the result of the variability inherent in sample means—that is, sampling error.

As an example, let's look at the data from an experiment to test reading comprehension. There are two groups in this experiment. Each group consists of 5 children who were randomly selected from elementary schools in the area. Each group is exposed to a different reading method. At the end of the learning period, a comprehension test is given; the test scores are shown in Table 7. What can be inferred from the data? Is Method I significantly better than Method II? Note that the difference between the means is 12, but the two groups only differ on one score. Thus we would not want to conclude that the groups differ significantly, even though their means differ.

Table 8 shows another set of hypothetical data. Again, the mean difference is the same, but now most of the scores for Method I are higher than most of the scores for Method II. This gives us greater confidence that Method I is better than Method II, but this is just an intuitive judgment—what a test of statistical significance gives us is a precise way to evaluate the reliability of an observed difference between sample means.

The examples comparing reading methods suggest that the reliability of a difference between means depends both on the *size* of the difference in means and on the *variability* of the means. By comparing the

Table 7:   Hypothetical Comprehension Scores for Two Methods for Teaching Reading.

Teaching Method I	Teaching Method II
80	80
85	85
60	60
75	75
90	30
Mean = 78	Mean = 66

Table 8:   A Second Set of Hypothetical Comprehension Scores.

Reading Method I	Reading Method II
70	60
72	58
78	66
84	74
86	72
Mean = 78	Mean = 66

magnitude of the difference between the means to the standard error of the difference between the means, we can evaluate precisely the reliability of the difference between the means. This comparison is done by computing a *test statistic,* which is the ratio of the difference between the means, D, and the standard error of the difference between means, σ_D:

$$\text{test statistic} = \frac{D}{\sigma_D}$$

If the difference in the means is sufficiently larger than σ_D, then the difference, D, is classified as statistically significant or reliable. As a rule of thumb, a ratio of 2.0 or more is considered statistically significant. The formula for the standard error of the difference between means is

$$\sigma_D = \sqrt{\frac{\sigma_1^2}{N_1} + \frac{\sigma_2^2}{N_2}}$$

where $\frac{\sigma_1^2}{N_1}$ is the variance of the first group mean and $\frac{\sigma_2^2}{N^2}$ is the variance of the second group mean.

We will use the data from the reading methods example to illustrate the computation of a test statistic. For the data in Table 7, the difference between the sample means is

$$D = 78 - 66 = 12$$

The estimated standard error of the difference between means, $\hat{\sigma}_D$, is

$$\hat{\sigma}_D = \sqrt{\frac{106}{5} + \frac{394}{5}} = 10$$

Dividing D by $\hat{\sigma}_D$, we find that

$$\text{test statistic} = \frac{12}{10} = 1.2$$

Since this value is smaller than 2.0, we conclude that the difference between the means is not statistically significant. Using the same procedure, we can compute the test statistic for the data in Table 8. The difference between the sample means is

$$D = 78 - 66 = 12$$

The standard error of the difference between means is

$$\hat{\sigma}_D = \sqrt{\frac{40}{5} + \frac{40}{5}} = 4$$

Thus, we compute

$$\text{test statistic} = \frac{12}{4} = 3$$

Because the test statistic is well above 2.0, we may conclude that the difference between the sample means is statistically significant. This confirms our intuition about the data in Table 8.

Notice that the sign of the test statistic could be positive or negative, depending on which mean is subtracted from the other ($78 - 66$ or $66 - 78$). In interpreting the test statistic only the number, not the sign, is relevant.

Why is a test statistic of 2.0 the critical value? Just as the normal curve is the distribution of sample means, it is also the distribution of the *differences* between sample means. Because we can treat the test statistic as a standard score when there is no difference between the population means, the chances of a standard score bigger than 2.0 is .025, and the chances of a standard score smaller than -2.0 is .025. Thus, the total probability of a standard score being more than 2 standard deviations away from the mean is .05, the sum of the 2 probabilities. This means that, on the average, 5 out of 100 times the test statistic will be more than 2 standard deviations from the mean by chance, even though there is no difference between the population means. A test statistic greater than 2.0 is often said to be *significant at the .05 level.*

Correlation

When two measures vary together so that it is possible to predict one measure from the other, the two measures are said to be *correlated.* Height and weight, for example, are correlated, since taller people also tend to be heavier, and vice versa. Similarly, good grades in the freshman year of college tend to go with good grades in the senior year of college. (Of course, there are exceptions. We all know short, heavy people; tall, lightweight people; people who have poor grades as freshmen and good grades as seniors.)

The **correlation coefficient** is a measure of the degree to which two measures are related, or the degree to which one is predictable from the other. For example, weight is a pretty good predictor of height, while parents' IQ is not quite as good a predictor of a child's IQ. In other words, weight is more predictable from height than a child's IQ is from parents' IQ. When two measures are completely *un*related, they are said to be independent or uncorrelated. For example, hair color and IQ are not correlated, and so the correlation coefficient is 0.

Two measures are *positively correlated* when high values of one go with high values of the other (e.g., height and weight). Two measures are *negatively correlated* when high values of one go with low values of the other. For example, there is a negative correlation between the number of cigarettes smoked per day and length of life. A perfect positive correlation is assigned the number $+1$, while a perfect negative correlation is given the number -1. Less than perfect correlations range between -1 and $+1$, with 0 (no correlation) being in the middle.

A rough estimate of the relationship between two measures can be shown in a **scatter diagram.** Figure 8 shows three such diagrams. The points in Figure 8A were obtained by testing the IQ of a number of parents and their children, as shown in Table 9. Thus, each point represents a *pair* of measurements. To plot a point in Figure 8A, we first find the parent IQ on the horizontal axis and the child IQ on the vertical axis and then plot a point where the lines intersect. Notice that in Figure 8A there is a tendency for high parent IQ to go with high child IQ, so the graph indicates a *positive correlation,* Figure 8B illustrates *no correlation* whatsoever between the rated quality of a book and its length. Here the points seem randomly scattered about the graph. Figure 8c illustrates a *negative correlation* between reading time and reading ability—greater reading ability goes with shorter reading time. Figure 9 gives a number of idealized scatter diagram shapes together with an appropriate numerical value of the correlation coefficient.

Product-Moment Correlation

The product-moment method is the most frequently used method for determining the correlation

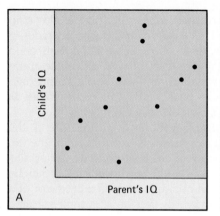
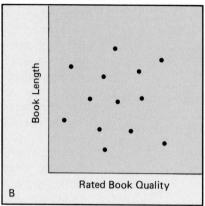
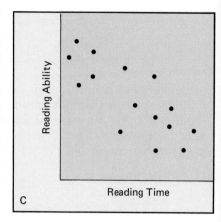

Figure 8 Scatter diagrams for hypothetical data. Each point represents the IQ scores for a given parent-child (left); the book length-rated quality for a given book (middle); and the reading ability-reading time scores for a given student (right).

coefficient (r) of a sample of pairs of measurements. This method provides a way to estimate the true population correlation, which is denoted by the Greek letter ρ (rho).

The formula for computing the sample correlation coefficient is

$$r = \frac{\text{SUM PROD DEV}}{Ns_1s_2}$$

where SUM DEV is the sum of the product of deviation scores, N is the number of pairs of measures, s_1 is the standard deviation of one set of measures, and s_2 is the standard deviation of the other set of measures. To il-

lustrate the computation of r, we will use the data in Table 9. The far right column of this table gives the product of deviation scores for each pair of measurements. The product is obtained by taking the deviation of the parent IQ from the mean parent IQ times the deviation of the child IQ from the mean child IQ. After all these products are computed we add them up to get *SUM DEV*. In Table 9, *SUM PROD DEV* = 1300. Thus

$$r = \frac{\text{SUM PROD DEV}}{N(s_1s_2)} = \frac{1300}{10(15.26 \times 15.33)}$$

$$r = \frac{1300}{2339.36}$$

$$r = .56$$

Table 9: IQ Scores from Pairs of Parents and Children.

Observation Number	Parents' IQ	Child's IQ	Product of Deviations from Mean
1	125	110	$(125 - 100.3)(110 - 100) = 247.0$
2	120	105	$(120 - 100.3)(105 - 100) = 98.5$
3	110	95	$(110 - 100.3)(95 - 100) = -48.5$
4	105	125	$(105 - 100.3)(125 - 100) = 117.5$
5	105	120	$(105 - 100.3)(120 - 100) = 94.0$
6	95	105	$(95 - 100.3)(105 - 100) = -26.5$
7	98	75	$(98 - 100.3)(75 - 100) = 57.5$
8	90	95	$(90 - 100.3)(95 - 100) = 51.5$
9	80	90	$(80 - 100.3)(90 - 100) = 203.0$
10	75	80	$(75 - 100.3)(80 - 100) = 506.0$
	Mean 100.3	100	SUM PROD DEV = 1300
	Variance 232.81	235	
	Standard Deviation 15.26	15.33	

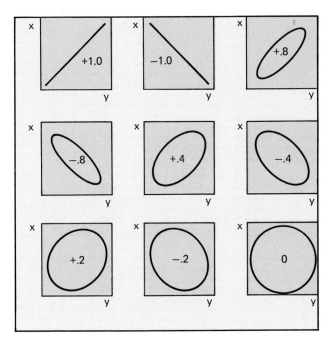

Figure 9 Idealized scatter diagrams and an appropriate correlation coefficient.

Interpretation of the Correlation Coefficient. Since the correlation coefficient tells us how predictable the value of one measure is, given a value of a second measure, it is often tempting to think that a correlation indicates a cause-and-effect relationship. In the case of height and weight there is not much temptation, since it seems silly to say height "causes" weight. We know that both height and weight are the result of a complex of factors—thus they share common causes. In the case of the relation between parent and child IQ it seems more reasonable to infer a cause for the relationship—the child inherits his or her IQ from the parent. However, it is just as reasonable to interpret this correlation the same way we did in the height-weight example: Scores on IQ tests are the result of a complex of factors. Parents and children share a number of environmental as well as heritable factors. As another example, there is a positive correlation between years of education and later income, but this does not mean more education *causes* higher income. Other factors may cause both: People with money are more likely to send their children to college, more intelligent people attend college, and social pressures that select for college attendance versus nonattendance covary with the job opportunities available.

SUGGESTED READINGS

Huff, D. *How to lie with statistics.* New York: Norton, 1954. An excellent introductory book on the use and misuses of statistics.

Kimble, G. A. *How to use (and misuse) statistics.* Englewood Cliffs, N.J.: Prentice-Hall, 1978. A more advanced book on this subject.

Mosteller, F., Rourke, R. E. K., & Thomas, G. B., Jr. *Probability with statistical applications.* Reading, Mass.: Addison-Wesley, 1973. A more advanced introduction to probability and statistics.

Myers, J. L. *Fundamentals of experimental design,* 3rd ed. Boston: Allyn & Bacon, 1979. An advanced book on experimental design for students who have had some elementary statistics.

Welkowitz, J., Ewen, R. B., & Cohen, J. *Introductory statistics for the behavioral sciences,* 3rd ed. New York: Academic Press, 1982. A very elementary introduction to statistics.

Glossary

Absolute refractory period The period during an action potential when it is impossible to initiate a second action potential (at that point on the neuron).

Absolute threshold The minimum amount of stimulus required to produce sensation at least 50 percent of the time.

Accommodation (1) the reshaping of the lens that allows the eye to focus on both near and distant objects; (2) according to Piaget, the child's adjustment to new objects or new stimuli by acquiring new responses.

Acetylcholine A chemical believed to be the major neurotransmitter.

Achievement Expression of competence motivation through the desire to excel, to complete difficult tasks, to meet high standards, and to perform better than others.

Achievement tests Test designed to measure how much material has been previously learned by the testee.

Acoustic code A type of memory representation that creates confusion during recall between two items (e.g., letters) having similar sounds (e.g., B and T).

Acquisition The first part of a learning experiment, during which, as a result of reinforcement, a new response is gradually learned.

Acronym A word made up of parts of a more complex phrase (e.g., the word NASA to denote National Aeronautics and Space Administration).

Acrophobia Fear of heights.

Action potential The rapid change in electrical charge that flows along a neuron and is associated with nerve and muscle activity; this potential is caused by a change in the permeability of the cell membrane.

Activation theory A theory based on the idea that emotional expressions are not unique or independent but exist on a continuum ranging from inactivity (sleep) to maximum activity (violent emotion).

Adaptation Decreased reactivity to environmental stressors. Stress responses are often reduced with coping techniques.

Addiction See **substance dependence.**

Additive mixture A color mixture that is produced by focusing light of different wavelengths on the same spot.

Adjustment Changes in behavior, skills, or personal traits that enable environmental demands upon the individual to be met.

Adolescence In our culture, the period between childhood and adulthood during which a person learns the skills needed to function as an adult.

Adoption studies Studies that examine the behavior of adopted children, especially twins reared apart, to separate the effects of genes (biological parents) and environment (adoptive parents).

Adrenal glands The two endocrine glands situated above the kidneys; the hormones they secrete affect the body's reaction to stress (epinephrine and norepinephrine) and regulate the functions of metabolism and sexual activity (steroids).

Adrenaline A commonly used term for **epinephrine.**

Adrenocorticotropic hormone (ACTH) A hormone that is released by the pituitary gland and causes the adrenal cortex to release **adrenalin (epinephrine).**

Affect The expression of emotion; the signs and feelings of emotion shown to others.

Affective disorders Patterns of behavior in which an individual expresses emotional states to excess, inappropriately, or inadequately.

Affective meaning The emotional connotation of a word. For example, the affective meaning of *sunshine* is generally positive for most people. See **semantic differential.**

Afferent Neuronal impulses that are directed toward the brain or spinal cord.

Affiliation The need or desire to be connected to or to associate with others.

Affordance The built-in sensitivity of our nervous systems to the invariant features of scenes we perceive.

Aggression The kinds of behavior that lead to the damage or destruction of something—either another organism or an inanimate object.

Agoraphobia Fear of open places.

Alcohol A drug that acts as a depressant of the central nervous system and is found in beer, wine, and distilled spirits.

Alcoholism A condition in which dependence on alcohol results in impairment of some significant part of the drinker's life and progressively leads to physical damage.

Algorithm Any special method of solving a certain kind of problem (usually mathematical).

Alleles Pairs of related genes (such as those determining eye color); one allele is usually dominant and the other recessive.

Allophones The different versions of a phoneme (speech sound) that sound different but are equivalent (e.g., the sound of the letter *r* in *bird* can vary depending on the speaker's accent, but these variations are all allophones of the basic phoneme /r/).

All-or-none property The rule that a neuron will always respond with its complete strength (action potential) to a stimulus or will not respond at all, regardless of the stimulus magnitude.

Alpha waves Brain waves produced when the body is in a state of relaxation.

Altered states Those states of consciousness that would not be described as normal.

Altruistic aggression Aggression that is used to protect some other person or thing—a bee protecting its hive, for example.

Altruistic behavior Behavior that helps others and does not result in any personal gain.

Alzheimer's disease A disease that causes rapid aging and loss of cognitive ability.

Amnesia Memory loss caused by head injury or psychological trauma; can be partial or total. See also **anterograde amnesia, retrograde amnesia, organic amnesia,** and **repression.**

Amphetamines Stimulants that affect the central nervous system and can cause edginess, anxiety, and increased heart rate; sometimes prescribed for mood or weight control.

Amplitude The magnitude of a sound or light wave; the main determinants of loudness and brilliance.

Anal stage According to Freud, the second stage of personality development, when retention and elimination of feces become the focus of a child's erotic feelings.

Analysis-by-synthesis The process by which a higher-order form can aid in analyzing one of its component (lower-order) features.

Androgens Hormones that regulate the growth of secondary sex characteristics, principally in males but also in females.

Androgen-insensitivity syndrome Occurs in genetic males whose embryonic testes secrete testosterone, but this testosterone is not used by the body cells, and the fetus develops into what appears to be a normal female.

Anesthetic An agent that blocks the transmittal of nerve impulses so that anesthesia—a loss of sensation and often consciousness—is produced.

Angry aggression The classical type of aggression, one that includes obvious signs of emotional arousal. It is often caused by pain or frustration.

Anorexia nervosa An emotional disorder distinguished by an extreme fear of obesity and by severe weight loss; it can sometimes be fatal.

Anterograde amnesia Following the onset

of amnesia, the inability to learn or retain new information.

Antisocial personality disorder Refers to a wide range of chronic problem behavior patterns which commonly include unsocialized behavior and conflict with society; examples include inability to display loyalty to others, gross selfishness, callousness, irresponsibility, impulsiveness, inability to feel guilt or learn from experience, and low tolerance of frustration. Previously called **psychopathic** or **sociopathic personality disorder.**

Anxiety Emotional arousal similar to fear or apprehension, but lacking a specific object of threat.

Aphasia Impairment or loss of speech production or comprehension, usually because of damage to language areas of the brain.

Approach-approach conflict Occurs when a person confronts simultaneously two attractive but incompatible goals.

Approach-avoidance conflict Occurs when a person is simultaneously attracted to and repelled by the same goal.

Aptitude The capability of learning; aptitude tests are designed to measure a person's ability for future learning.

Aptitude tests Tests designed to predict the future (often academic) performance, of the testee.

Archetypes According to Jung, primary ideas shared by all humans; contents of the collective unconscious.

Arousal A general state of alertness and increased physiological activity following sensory stimulation.

Artifact A differing result between experimental groups caused by some reason other than the independent variable.

Artificial intelligence (AI) The field concerned with creating machines (e.g., computers) that can perform complex tasks formerly considered to require human intelligence.

Assertiveness training Behavioral techniques that help individuals to more effectively and appropriately assert themselves, their needs, and their interests in interactions with others.

Assimilation Interpreting new information in terms of what is already known; fitting new ideas into existing cognitive schema or frameworks.

Association Linking or a response to a stimulus through learning; also, the connection between words, ideas, or concepts in semantic memory.

Association areas Areas of the cerebral cortex believed to serve in integrating the complex flow of information and responses related to learning, memory, speech, and thinking.

Attachment Development of emotional bonds and dependencies between individuals, especially between an infant and its parents.

Attention The process of focusing awareness on a limited set of stimuli.

Attitude A specific and consistent way of reacting to certain people, things, or concepts. Attitudes are learned and have both behavioral and cognitive components.

Attitude prototype The person that we imagine as the best exemplar of a social category—as in picturing Einstein when we think of mathematicians. If we like that individual we have a positive attitude toward members of the class in general; if we dislike that individual we have a negative attitude toward members of the class in general.

Attributions Interpretations people make of the social circumstances that surround others' actions in order to infer the intentions that lie behind those others' behavior.

Attribution theory A theory concerned with the rules people use in attempting to infer the causes of behavior they observe in others.

Audience selection effect The tendency to listen, selectively, to messages and information agreed with and to shun persuasive communications that argue for the other side.

Audiometric function The function relating absolute threshold to the frequency of a pure tone.

Autokinetic effect The illusion that a stationary spot of light is moving when viewed in a darkened room.

Autonomic nervous system That portion of the peripheral nervous system that regulates the mostly involuntary functions of internal muscles and glands.

Autonomy A sense of independence and control over one's own life.

Autoshaping A method of encouraging pigeons to begin pecking at lighted keys in a Skinner box, requiring only that the light (CS) be illuminated just prior to the presentation of food (US).

Availability heuristic The "rule of thumb" that of two events, the more likely to occur is the one that is easier for you to imagine or "call to mind."

Average The arithmetic mean. The calculation of central tendency that involves adding all the entries in a distribution and then dividing by the number of entries.

Aversive counterconditioning By associating an unwanted behavior with negative sensations (pain, discomfort), this kind of therapy attempts to eradicate maladaptive behaviors such as alcoholism and drug abuse.

Aversive stimuli In classical conditioning, those stimuli generally regarded as painful or unpleasant (e.g., shocks or loud noises).

Avoidance-avoidance conflict Occurs when a person is faced with opposing, equally undesirable choices from which there is no escape—a choice must be made.

Avoidance learning A form of operant conditioning in which timely performance of a specified response prevents the occurrence of an otherwise inevitable aversive stimulus.

Axon The extended portion of nerve fiber that carries impulses away from the nerve cell body to other cells and to muscles and glands.

Axonal transport In a neuron, all replacement parts are manufactured in the cell body and carried down the axon to their destination in a slow-moving system called axonal transport.

Backward conditioning Presenting the conditioned stimulus (CS) after the unconditioned stimulus (US) in classical conditioning experiments.

Bait shyness In animal studies, the tendency of the animal to avoid food it once favored if it has been made sick by it. This avoidance often occurs even if the animal does not get sick until hours after eating the food.

Balance theory A cognitive theory that states that people prefer consistency in the relationship between their evaluation of another person and that person.

Barbiturates An hypnotic form of **depressant** often used to induce sleep.

Basic needs According to Maslow, the part of the need hierarchy having to do with *deficiency*; for example, the need for food or the need for shelter.

Basilar membrane A membrane within the cochlea containing sense receptors that, when vibrated, produce the neuronal effects of auditory stimulation.

Behavior All responses or activity of an organism, including thinking, dreaming, and physiological functions; in psychology the emphasis is on behaviors that are observable by others, including cognitive processes related verbally.

Behavioral confirmation One person expects another person to act in a certain way, behaves so as to induce the person to behave that way, and the person does act that way. (As in throwing rocks at a "hostile" new neighbor's dog, and the neighbor reacts in a hostile way.)

Behavioral therapy A type of therapy based on learning theory and focused on problem behaviors themselves. Abnormal functioning is viewed as maladaptive patterns of behavior that are learned; the goal of therapy is to extinguish these patterns and help the client learn new, adaptive ones.

Behavior modification Attempts to alter an individual's behavior through operant-conditioning techniques.

Bel Unit of measurement for the intensity of sound. One bel represents a tenfold (10^1) increase in energy, two bels a hundred-fold (10^2), etc. See also **decibel.**

Bel scale Zero on the bel scale corresponds to the normal threshold energy for a 1,000 Hz tone. Named in honor of Alexander Graham Bell.

Benzodiazepines A group of sedatives developed in the 1950s to treat anxiety. Often referred to as antianxiety drugs or minor tranquilizers.

Binocular cues Visual cues from both eyes, combined through **binocular fusion.**

Binocular disparity The way the same object is seen from two slightly different angles due to the separation of the right and left eyes.

Binocular fusion The combination of both left and right eye perspectives so that they are experienced as one.

Binocular rivalry The competition between disparate monocular views for inclusion in the cyclopian view (e.g., if one eye sees vertical stripes and the other horizontal, then vertical and horizontal views alternate every few seconds in the combined (cyclopian) view.

Biofeedback A technique usually employing physiological sensing devices for providing feedback to an individual, in the form of tones, moving graphs, or dials, on his or her present bodily states. Through these feedback procedures, the individual may learn to monitor and control such functions as brain-wave patterns, blood pressure, muscle tension, and heart rate.

Bipolar disorders Previously known as **manic-depressive** psychosis, bipolar disorders are defined by extreme swings in mood: The individual goes through periods of severe depression and periods of energetic mania of varying durations—from days to months.

Blind spot The region of the retina insensitive to light because the blood vessels and nerves exit there.

Blocking A psychological barrier to acknowledging or remembering an element of reality one fears.

Blood-brain barrier A system for protecting the brain from toxic substances: Blood vessels are less permeable in the brain than in other parts of the body. It has prevented the effective use of some new drugs, which will not pass this barrier (e.g., use of GABA in the treatment of Huntington's chorea).

Brain graft The transplanting of specific chemical-producing cells to parts of the brain without concern for the precise synaptic connections.

Brain stem Lower part of the brain; consists of the hindbrain (medulla, pons, and cerebellum) and midbrain.

Brain transplant Since the normal rejection mechanisms do not operate through the **blood-brain barrier,** it is possible to transplant tissue into the brain without rejection.

Brightness The amount of visible energy present in a light source.

Broca's area A zone in the left cerebral hemisphere that is believed to control speech.

Broca's aphasia A brain disorder that causes a person to have great difficulty in speaking, despite the fact that he or she may understand speech perfectly—and may even be able to sing.

Bulimia An emotional disorder in which a person follows a pattern of fasting, binge-eating of junk foods, and self-induced vomiting. As with *anorexia nervosa,* this pattern results in severe weight loss.

Cannon-Bard theory of emotion States that when an emotionally arousing stimulus is perceived, the thalamus sends out impulses both to the sympathetic nervous system and to the cerebral cortex—thus bodily changes and emotional feelings occur at the same time. See **James-Lange theory; jukebox theory.**

Case study A psychological method in which an exhaustive study is made of an individual's history in an attempt to determine past causes of present behavior.

Cataplexy Immobility following an experience of intense fright or shock; occurs sometimes as a sleep disorder.

Catatonic schizophrenia A severe mental disorder characterized by immobility; resistance to comprehending communication; low levels of coherent verbalization; and occasional outbursts of purposeless, excited motor activity.

Catharsis (1) the process of draining off aggressive impulses; (2) relief from tension associated with repression; obtained by remembering or expressing the experiences that were originally repressed.

Cell body The part of a cell containing its nucleus (which contains **chromosomes**).

Center The tendency of young children to focus their attention exclusively on one aspect of a situation.

Central nervous system The brain and the spinal cord.

Central tendency The "typical" or central value in a distribution characterized by measures such as the mean, median, or mode.

Cephalocaudal Starting at the head and progressing toward the feet, as in motor development in infancy.

Cerebellum The portion of the hindbrain that governs body movement and balance.

Cerebral cortex The deeply folded gray matter that composes the surrounding layer of the cerebrum.

Cerebral hemispheres The two large half-sections of the mammalian brain.

Cerebrum The brain's largest division, consisting of the two cerebral hemispheres and their enveloping layer of cerebral cortex.

Chemotherapy The treatment of abnormal behavior with drugs.

Chimeric stimuli Images made up of incompatible left and right halves (e.g., halves of two different faces) used in research on split-brain patients.

Chromosome Threadlike particle in the cell nucleus that contains genes.

Chronological age A person's age in years.

Classical conditioning In this type of learning, a neutral stimulus (CS) is repeatedly paired with an unconditioned stimulus (US), and the subject comes to respond to the neutral stimulus even when it is presented alone.

Claustrophobia Fear of enclosed spaces.

Client-centered therapy An approach that assumes the client is the most qualified person to identify and solve his or her own problems; the therapist's role is to create a supportive environment and to facilitate the client's self-discovery.

Clinical psychologist A psychologist with a Ph.D. who is trained in the diagnosis and treatment of emotional and behavioral problems.

Cocaine A local anesthetic; produces a state of euphoria, talkativeness, and sometimes muscle tremors.

Cochlea The inner ear structure shaped like a snail's shell in which sound energy is converted into nerve impulses.

Code Any way of representing information.

Cognition A term that encompasses all the kinds of knowing an individual may have, including thoughts, knowledge, interpretations, and ideas.

Cognitive-behavioral therapy A form of **behavioral therapy** in which **cognition**—a person's unique ways of seeing and thinking about the world—is considered to be an important determinant of abnormal behavior.

Cognitive dissonance A situation in which a person perceives fundamental discrepancies between two or more beliefs he or she holds or between beliefs and behaviors; when such cognitive dissonance occurs, it often stimulates action to bring opposing beliefs or beliefs and behaviors back into agreement.

Cognitive map A mental picture of the environment that takes place without reinforcement and facilitates the phenomenon of latent learning described by Tolman.

Cognitive psychology A branch of psychology that focuses on mental processes such as thinking, reasoning, and language.

Cognitive therapy A therapy developed by Aaron Beck and most often applied to problems of depression. It seeks to reveal and change the problematic thoughts and distorted thinking processes that underlie depression.

Cohort Group of people born in a given year or period, as all those born in 1967.

Collective unconscious According to Jung's theory of personality, the part of an individual's unconscious that is inherited and shared by all people; contains the **archetypes.**

Color blindness Having some degree of inability to perceive color. See **dichromats** and **monochromats.**

Color constancy The tendency to perceive a well-known object as being a single color, even if its actual color is modified by changes in illumination.

Community mental-health centers Local mental-health treatment facilities developed to offset the social and financial costs of hospitalization. They provide treatment for discharged hospital patients as well as prehospitalization services and ongoing psychotherapy, hotline phones, public education on problems like drug abuse, and active

participation in projects that affect the community's emotional stability.

Compensation The mechanism of covering up aspects of oneself and substituting more desired traits or behaviors in an exaggerated form.

Competence A person's desire or ability to interact effectively with his or her environment.

Compulsions Acts or rituals that are repeated against a person's will.

Computerized axial tomography (CAT) A method of computing images (e.g., brain "slices") based on a series of X-rays generated as the X-ray source is rotated about the head.

Concrete operational stage The third major stage of Piaget's theory of cognitive development (from 7–11 years), during which children develop logical reasoning abilities and concepts of conservation.

Conditioned aversive stimulus A neutral stimulus paired with an aversive stimulus.

Conditioned emotional response A strong, conditioned response (highly resistant to extinction) typically caused by trauma.

Conditioned food aversion An animal's conditioned response to avoid food previously associated with becoming ill.

Conditioned reflex A stimulus-response relation acquired through experience.

Conditioned reinforcer Stimulus that acquires reinforcing properties through learning (see also secondary reinforcer).

Conditioned response The learned response to a conditioned stimulus (CS).

Conditioned stimulus (CS) A neutral stimulus that is repeatedly paired with an unconditioned stimulus (US) in classical conditioning.

Conditioning An elementary form of learning involving the formation of associations among stimuli, responses, and reinforcers.

Cones Sensory receptors on the retina, primarily responsible for the ability to see fine detail and color; function best in daylight or bright light.

Conflict A state of disturbance or tension resulting from opposing motives, drives, needs, or goals.

Conformity Behavior that goes along with group standards or opinions.

Conjunctive concept A concept that is defined in terms of two or more criteria or rules. For example, the concept of eligible voter defines a person who is both a citizen and at least 18 years of age.

Connotative meaning The emotional or attitudinal component of word meaning. See **denotative meaning.**

Conservation Understanding that changes in the appearance of objects do not change such intrinsic properties as numerosity, total volume, or mass.

Consolidation theory Theory suggesting that for a particular memory to be retained permanently, it must have the benefit of an undisturbed period of consolidation (continued neural activity).

Constitutional approach The biological models of personality that hold that body structure or body type determines personality and behavior.

Construct accessibility In attribution theory, the effect of recently thought-about constructs on subsequent interpretations of events, objects, or people.

Construct validity A determination of whether or not a test actually measures what it proposes to measure.

Context of discovery The initial stage of theory development, in which open-ended, inductive reasoning processes are used to formulate hypotheses about the causes of the phenomenon being studied.

Context effects The influence of higher-order structures on the perception of lower-order forms.

Context of justification The second stage of theory development, in which initial hypotheses are subjected to empirical tests and the evidence to support the theory is assessed.

Contrast A difference in brightness. For example, the difference between the lightest and darkest parts of a sinusoidal grating (akin to the amplitude of a pure tone).

Control group The group of subjects in an experiment who are treated exactly the same as the experimental group(s) except that they are not given the "treatment" under study and thus serve as the basis for comparison.

Convergence (1) In the nervous system, the process in which nerve impulses from many receptor cells are directed toward the same neuron effector cell. (2) Inward rotation of the eyes to produce fusion of the differing views from each eye.

Convergent thinking A term employed by Guilford to describe problem-solving thought processes which involve narrowing down to a single correct solution.

Convergent validity The degree to which a test or measure of a target concept correlates with other measures of that concept.

Conversion disorders The types of **somatoform disorders** in which an individual develops physical symptoms that have no organic basis in response to some traumatic event.

Coping A person's learned behavior for dealing with conflict or stress.

Cornea The slightly protruding clear outer cap over the iris of the eye.

Corpus callosum The thick band of fibrous white matter that connects the cerebral hemispheres to each other and to other parts of the nervous system.

Corpus striatum An area of the cerebrum that receives dopamine-containing fibers from the midbrain. A deficiency of dopamine affects the cells of the corpus striatum, producing Parkinson's disease.

Correlation A relationship or association between two variables.

Correlation coefficient A measure indicating the strength of association (lack of independence) between two variables.

Correspondent inference The attribution that a person's behavior necessarily reflects his or her underlying personality.

Cortex The grayish, thin, unmyelinated covering of the cerebrum; also called **gray matter.**

Counseling psychologist A mental health professional who has been trained to provide student, marriage, family, and other types of counseling.

Counselor A psychologist or other professional who provides counseling.

Covariance A situation in which a change in one variable is associated with a change in another variable.

Creativity Designing, building, or thinking of something that is novel and useful; solving a problem in a unique and clever way.

Crisis intervention Programs that provide a trained person—either over the phone or in person—to help people deal with a personal crisis.

Criterion In personality assessment, the *performance* an assessment instrument is trying to predict.

Criterion groups Groups of individuals thought to exhibit a trait or behavior that is being tested. The answers of criterion groups to test items are compared to "normal" subjects in constructing valid test items.

Critical period A limited time period during development when specific learning must occur if it is to occur at all (e.g., imprinting of ducks or geese).

Cross-sectional studies Studies and surveys that involve comparisons of people from a variety of age groups, backgrounds, etc.

Cross-tolerance If repeated use of substance A produces tolerance for substances A and B, then A and B show cross-tolerance.

Crowding The psychological state of feeling crowded, surrounded, and intruded on by the people around you; occurs in situations in which there are too many people or too many activities for the individual to attend to comfortably.

Crystallized intelligence The kind of intellectual functioning that shows little age-related decline, such as that measured by the verbal subtest of the **Weschler Adult Intelligence Scale.**

Cue A feature that acts as a signal or predictor for the larger scene or structure.

Culture-fair test An IQ test designed to be fair to persons of all backgrounds.

Cumulative record A record of learning trials in operant conditioning provided by a device known as a cumulative recorder.

Cyclopean view The single subjective view that results from the automatic combination of the two monocular views of the left and right eyes.

Dark adaptation The process in which visual sensitivity increases after one enters a dark room as pigment in the rods reaches its highest concentration.

Decenter The ability to consider more than one aspect of a situation at a time.

Decibel A unit of measurement for the intensity of sound; 10 decibels equal 1 **bel.**

Declarative knowledge Another name for **propositional knowledge.**

Deductive reasoning Reaching a conclusion by accepting the premises of an argument and then following formal logical rules. See **inductive reasoning.**

Deep structure In linguistic theory, the underlying organization of a sentence. See **surface structure.**

Defense mechanisms Strategies used by the ego to fight off instinctual outbursts of the id and attacks of the superego; examples include repression, reaction formation, rationalization, and projection.

Degrees of visual angle Used to describe the size of an object in terms of how much of your visual field it occupies—that is, how many degrees of the imaginary surrounding circle's circumference it would cover. This is referred to as an object's size in degrees of visual angle.

Deinstitutionalization movement The mental health industry's attempt (beginning in the 1960s) to use drug therapy and other methods to solve mental-health problems outside of mental hospitals.

Delay of reinforcement The time, if any, between a response and the subsequent reinforcement.

Delusion A false belief that cannot be shaken by presentation of facts or reasoning; examples include delusion of gandeur and delusion of persecution.

DMT Abbreviation for dimethyltryptine, a short-term, synthetic hallucinogen.

Dendrites Fibers with many branches extending from the receptor end of a neuron.

Denotative meaning The conceptual aspect of word meaning—the concept the word refers to. See **connotative meaning.**

Density The number of people present in a specific environment.

Dependent variable In an experiment, the variable that changes or is expected to change when the experimenter manipulates the independent variable.

Depressant A drug that depresses or lowers the activity of the nervous system.

Depression An **affective disorder** of varying degrees of severity, but including common difficulties such as feelings of sadness; a change in appetite; sleeping difficulties; and a decrease in activities, interests, and energy.

Depth of processing The idea that information can be processed (associated, elaborated, recoded, reorganized) to varying degrees (depth); and the more processing, the better recall.

Depth perception The ability to perceive three-dimensional space and objects.

Descriptive statistics Methods of summarizing and describing large amounts of data; for example, the average or mean.

Determinism The theory that all events in

nature (including behaviors) are preceded by specific causes; if the relevant causes are known, an event can be predicted.

Developmental psychology The branch of psychology concerned with physiological and behavioral changes throughout the life span.

Deviation (1) In statistics, the degree to which a measure or measures varies from a particular reference point. (2) In group dynamics, a situation where one person's opinions clash with those of the rest of the group.

Deviation IQ A person's IQ score calculated by comparing his or her test performance to the performance of agemates on the same test.

Dichromats People who are color blind to either yellow-blue or red-green.

Difference threshold The level of stimulus change necessary in order for a person to perceive a difference; also known as just **noticeable difference (JND).**

Diffusion of responsibility theory Emphasizes that in groups people are more likely to make extreme choices because the responsibility for the choice will be shared by many people.

Digit span The number of digits a person can recall immediately after hearing them spoken.

Disaster syndrome A stress reaction to a catastrophic event characterized by three stages: shock, suggestibility, and recovery.

Discriminant validity (also called *divergent validity*) The degree to which a test or measure measures a target concept better than it measures any other concept.

Discrimination In conditioning, the process of being able to distinguish among stimuli, ignore irrelevant stimuli, and respond to a specific stimulus.

Disjunctive concept A category that is defined in terms of an either-or criterion; for example, the category of *citizen* may be defined as someone who is *either* born in a country *or* marries a citizen of that country.

Displacement In psychoanalysis, a defense mechanism in which a person directs an emotional response from its actual object to a safer one.

Dissociative disorders A set of disorders characterized by sudden, temporary changes in consciousness, activity, or identity.

Distance cues Cues that assist a person in perceiving distance, such as relative size of similar objects.

Divergent thinking A term employed by Guilford to describe problem-solving thought processes that involve a set of innovative, original, and alternative possible solutions, rather than a single correct answer.

Dizygotic twins Twins resulting from the fertilization of two separate eggs at the same time; also called **fraternal twins.** See **monozygotic twins.**

DOM A long-lasting, synthetic hallucinogen illegally traded as the street drug STP.

Dominant gene The member of the gene

pair (allele) that takes precedence and determines the particular bodily characteristic.

Dopamine An inhibitory neurotransmitter prevalent throughout the central nervous system and believed to play a part in schizophrenia.

Dorsal Referring to the back.

Double approach-avoidance conflict A complex situation in which two possible courses of action each present an approach-avoidance conflict. A person is faced with both approaching and avoiding two goals simultaneously.

Double blind Studies or experiments in which *neither* the experimenter *nor* the subject knows which condition or group is the control and which condition or group is the experimental.

Double-depletion hypothesis States that depletion of either intracellular or extracellular water can cause thirst.

Down's syndrome (mongolism) A congenital defect characterized by mental deficiency (usually moderate retardation) and some physical abnormalities. Down's Syndrome children have an extra, 47th, chromosome.

Dream Vivid imagery occurring during sleep.

Drive reduction The theory that motivated behavior is the response to a drive and that responses that satisfy drives are reinforced by the subsequent drive reduction.

Drive state The state of arousal or unlearned motivation that occurs when a need is not met.

Drug Any substance other than food that alters our bodily or mental functioning.

Drug abuse See **substance dependence.**

Drug dependence A physiological and/or psychological need for a drug accompanied by increased tolerance of the drug and withdrawal symptoms if the drug is removed.

Drug therapy See **chemotherapy.**

D-sleep An alternative term for REM-sleep, indicating the highly dysynchronous underlying neural activity during this stage of sleep.

Dual coding A theory suggesting that knowledge may be represented in long-term memory by images or pictures as well as by propositional or verbal codes.

Eardrum The thin, flexible membrane separating the middle ear from the outer ear.

Echoic memory system A theoretical human memory system that briefly retains auditory information in a form similar to its initial acoustic code.

Ectomorph In Sheldon's constitutional theory, a person with a thin, fragile build who probably has a corresponding introverted, highly sensitive personality.

Effectance motivation The desire to develop and exercise competence in interacting with the environment.

Efferent Refers to neurons leaving the central nervous system; **motor neurons.**

Effort justification An area of research supporting cognitive dissonance theory that sug-

gests that people learn to like what they have suffered to achieve.

Ego In Freudian terms, the part of the personality that distinguishes between self and the environment and that mediates the demands of the id and the superego.

Egocentric According to Piaget, the tendency of young children to see everything from their own point of view.

Eidetic imagery The ability to retain a mental image of something one has seen for a long period of time; often referred to as **photographic memory.**

Elaboration A recoding of information in an elaborated form (such as adding your own illustration of a point made by a lecturer).

Electra conflict In Freudian terms, a girl's erotic involvement with her father and jealousy of her mother.

Electroencephalogram (EEG) The record of the electrical activity of the brain.

Electroshock therapy (ECT) A controversial therapy in which an electric shock is transmitted to the brain to induce convulsions and unconsciousness. Used in cases of severe and prolonged depression.

Elevation A depth-perception cue operating on the principle that the higher an object appears in the visual plane, the farther away it appears.

EMG (electromyogram) An electronic device that measures muscle tension or electrical activity in the muscles.

Emotion A complex reaction consisting of both physiological change and a subjective experience of feeling.

Empirical tests Laboratory observations or experiments used to substantiate the validity of a theory.

Empiricism In theories of development, the idea that all knowledge is based on experience. In philosophy of science, the reliance on observation and experiment—the empirical method.

Encoding The way information is first stored or represented in a memory system.

Encoding specificity Tulving's view that stimuli present during **encoding** are usually good **recall cues.**

Endocrine gland A ductless gland that secretes hormones directly into the bloodstream.

Endocrine system The bodily system of glands that regulates vital metabolic and physiological functions.

Endogenous Naturally produced within the body.

Endomorph In Sheldon's constitutional theory, a person with a round, heavy build who is likely to have a lethargic, comfort-seeking personality.

Endorphins Naturally produced, opiatelike substances in the body that help people cope with pain and stress.

Energy spectrum The amount of energy from each part of the visible spectrum in a particular source of light.

Enkephalin See **endorphin.**

Environmental psychology A field of scientific inquiry concerned with the interrelationships between the physical environment—the natural or human-made environment—and human behavior.

EOG (electrooculogram) An electronic device that measures eye movement.

Epinephrine A hormone secreted by the adrenal glands; increases blood pressure and heart rate as a response to an emergency.

Episodic knowledge Knowledge of events that occurred at specific times earlier in one's experience. A type of **propositional knowledge.**

Equilibratory sense The sense of balance. **Semicircular canals** and **vestibular sacs** are the sensory organs responsible for this sense.

Erogenous zones Areas of the body associated with sexual pleasure.

Eros According to Freud, the life instincts; love directed toward oneself and others.

Escape response The replication of primitive emotional responses to punishment through operant conditioning.

Estrogens The female hormones that stimulate the development of secondary sex characteristics.

Estrus cycle Cyclical variations in hormonal state in females of the lower mammal species. Ovulation occurs automatically at some specific point in the cycle, and at that time the female becomes both sexually attractive and sexually receptive to the male.

Ethology The study of animal behavior, generally in the animal's own environment.

Evaluation A comparison of a score, object, behavior, or situation with another, and subsequent determination of its relative value.

Excitement The first of Masters and Johnson's four stages of human sexual response.

Existential model A personality theory focusing on individual freedom and responsibility for one's own actions. See also **humanistic model.**

Exogenous Something introduced into the body from outside; not occurring naturally within the body.

Expectancy A person's estimate or belief that a specific behavior will lead to a specific reinforcement or outcome.

Experience In contrast to the concept of maturation, emphasizes the role of specific events and the environment in developmental changes.

Experiential change Behavioral development that is primarily caused by experience, practice, or training. Contrasted with **maturation.**

Experimenter bias A situation in which the scientist performing a particular experiment allows his or her own beliefs to influence the outcome of the experiment.

Experimenter expectancy effect The influence of the experimenter's personal bias in experimental procedures that causes results to be skewed in the direction of the original hypothesis.

Experimental group The group in a scientific observation (experiment) on whom the effect of some particular treatment is observed.

Experimental method A system of testing an idea or theory in a carefully controlled situation involving independent variables and a dependent variable.

Expert system A computer program that simulates an expert in some field (e.g., geology, medicine) such that it can answer questions much like the expert.

Expressive jargon Speech produced by young children that uses adult speech sounds and intonations but is unintelligible. Precedes stage of single-word utterances and disappears when child begins to produce real words.

Extinction The gradual reduction of a conditioned response that occurs because of lack of reinforcement.

Extrinsic motivation Engaging in activities or behaviors because they lead to other rewards; for example, learning course material well in order to win the praise of the professor; a means to an end.

Extroversion An attitude in which a person is more concerned with the outside world than with self.

Extrovert A person who is more concerned with the outside world than with self; an outgoing person.

Factor analysis A statistical procedure for estimating the correlations of several variables with a common factor; a process by which variables can be grouped in categories.

False consensus The belief, sometimes inaccurate, that the vast majority of other people would react to a situation in the same way that you would.

Family studies Studies that examine the occurrence of certain traits within families. Taken alone, they do not clearly separate the effects of a common genetic pool and a common environment.

Family therapy Psychotherapy in which the interactive processes of the family as a group as well as the individual family members are treated.

Fear-induced aggression Aggressive acts taken by an organism to protect itself when threatened.

Feature detectors Systems (neural or electronic) that respond to the presence of a specific stimulus component (e.g., an edge, intersection, or particular speech format).

Fechner's law A law concerning the relationship between a stimulus and a sensation. States that the relation between physical stimulus intensity and the strength of sensation is a logarithmic one, in which a constant ratio of stimulus intensity produces a constant difference in sensation.

Figure-ground organization A basic tendency (which Gestalt physchologists argued is innate) to perceive things (figures) standing out against a background (ground).

Filtering The process whereby certain wavelengths of light are selectively blocked

out as the light passes through a substance (filter).

Fixation In Freudian terms, arrested development characterized by the failure to successfully pass through an earlier psychological stage; a persistent behavior that has outlived its usefulness.

Fixed-interval schedule A schedule of reinforcement in which the animal or person is reinforced for a response only after the passage of a specific interval of time—every three minutes, for example.

Fixed-ratio schedule A schedule of reinforcement in which the animal or person is reinforced after a specific number of correct responses.

Flooding A behavior modification technique by which a patient is reintroduced immediately to the situation that has evoked a conditioned emotional response.

Fluid intelligence The sort of intellectual functioning that shows a decline with age, such as that measured by the performance-oriented subtests of the **Weschler Adult Intelligence Scale.**

Forebrain A large part of the brain that is composed of the diencephalon and the cerebrum.

Formal operations The logical thinking process that begins to develop during adolescence in Piaget's last stage of cognitive development, the formal operant stage.

Formal operational stage The fourth and final major stage of cognitive development (Piaget), during which children and adults become able to think and reason in abstract terms (age 12 and up).

Forward conditioning Presenting the conditioned stimulus (CS) slightly before the unconditioned stimulus (US) in classical conditioning experiments.

Fovea A small area on the retina on which the cones are concentrated; thus, the area of greatest visual acuity.

Framing effects The consequences of the particular way in which a problem is worded, or framed. People can be easily biased by the words used to describe a situation or problem.

Fraternal twins Twins resulting from the fertilization of two separate eggs at the same time; also called **identical** or **monozygotic twins.**

Free association (1) A process in psychoanalysis in which the patient reports whatever thoughts come to mind in a free-floating, nonstructured way; (2) a type of word-association test.

Free recall A type of memory test in which the subject recalls items in a list in any order, rather than in the specific order in which they were presented.

Free will The doctrine that humans are influenced by outside stimulation and bodily states, but are free to choose their actions on rational grounds.

Frequency The number of cycles per second of a sound wave; a primary factor in pitch.

Frequency distribution The frequencies of various values (or ranges of values) occurring in a set of values.

Frequency theory In hearing, the theory that pitch is determined by the rate of firing of sound receptors. The rate of pulses traveling up the auditory nerve to the brain matches that of a tone over a wide range of frequencies.

Frustration The psychological state a person experiences when something prevents him or her from reaching a desired goal. Coleman and Hammen (1974) have identified five sources of frustration: delays, lack of resources, loss, failure, and meaninglessness.

Frustration-aggression hypothesis An explanation of aggression that states that frustration always leads to aggression and that aggression is always a result of frustration.

Fugue states Amnesia accompanied by actual physical flight—the person may wander away for several hours or move to another area and establish a new life.

Functional fixedness An inability to solve a problem because of a perception of only one function (use) of a particular object.

Functionally autonomous motive An acquired motive that is not associated with the satisfaction of any basic biological need; acts as a motive in its own right.

Fundamental attribution error The tendency in people to attribute behavior to internal, dispositional states rather than to external, situational causes.

Fundamental tone The dominant frequency of a note sounded on a musical instrument.

Galvanic skin response (GSR) A response indicated by electrical changes on the skin; common physiological response to fear is a rise in GSR.

Ganglia Clusters of nerve cell bodies found outside the spinal cord and brain.

Gene The basic unit of heredity, located on the chromosomes.

General Adaptation Syndrome Selye's theory of the way people tend to react to stress, beginning with the alarm reaction and progressing through resistance and exhaustion.

Generalization Responding in a similar way to a broad category of stimuli.

Generalization gradient Once a conditioned response (CR) has been established to a particular conditioned stimulus (CS), the range of stimuli that will produce a similar response.

Generalized anxiety disorders Involves the same kind of discomfort as phobic disorders, but the person's anxiety is not clearly linked to a specific object or situation.

Genetics The study of heredity, or how biological traits are passed on from parents to offspring.

Genetic counseling Counseling designed to provide parents with information that can help them predict when genetic defects will be passed down from parents to children.

Genital stage In Freud's theory of psychosexual development, the attainment of firm identification with ones own gender and the capacity for heterosexual love and commitment.

Genotype The specific genetic makeup of an organism.

Gestalt (1) A whole form or figure; (2) a branch of psychology in which behavior is viewed as an integrated whole, greater than the sum of its parts.

Gestalt therapy A humanistic approach, based on the work of Fritz Perls, in which abnormal functioning is viewed as an imbalance in figure-ground perceptions and the denial of one's innate goodness. The goal of Gestalt therapy is to help people become aware of the wholeness of their experiences.

Glial cells Cells of the nervous system that: (1) are responsible for myelination of axons in the brain; (2) direct the growth of neural pathways or interconnections; and (3) play a general role in nervous system metabolism.

Gonads Sex glands: ovaries in females produce estrogen, testes in males produce androgens.

Gray matter See **cortex**

Group polarization effect The finding that members of a group, after discussion of an issue, are likely to take a more extreme position collectively than they would as individuals. A number of explanations exist for this finding, including information-exchange theory and value theory.

Group therapy Psychotherapy involving a number of people working with one another and with a therapist, rather than each person seeing a therapist alone in private or individual sessions.

Groupthink A group decision-making process in which a cohesive group of decision makers lets its concern for group unanimity override making good decisions by carefully appraising alternative courses of action. Obviously, this can, and frequently does, lead to bad decisions.

Habituation In behavior studies, a decrease in the strength of a response as the eliciting stimulus is repeated.

Hallucination A perception that is not based on reality; a false mental image.

Hallucinogen A drug, such as LSD, that causes a person to experience hallucinations.

Harmonic Some multiple of the **fundamental tone.**

Hashish A concentrated form of cannabis or marijuana.

Heredity The passing on of traits from parents to offspring.

Hering's opponent-process theory See **Opponent-process theory of color vision.**

Heritability ratio The ratio depicting the proportion of variability in a trait associated with genetic, as opposed to environment, factors.

Hermaphrodite A person with both male and female sexual organs.

Heroin An **opioid** often used by addicts.

Hertz (Hz) A unit of sound-wave frequency equal to one cycle per second.

Heterosexuality Attraction to persons of the opposite sex.

Heuristics General strategies for solving problems or making decisions.

Hierarchy of needs (Maslow) Maslow's system for categorizing human motivation; ascending from basic, physiological needs that must be satisfied before the higher-level needs such as love, esteem, and finally, self-actualization can be satisfied.

Higher-order conditioning In classical conditioning, the process by which the conditioned stimulus (CS) is paired with additional stimuli (CS′, CS″), which also acquire some of the reinforcing properties of the unconditioned stimulus (US).

Hindbrain A section of the brain that, along with the midbrain, makes up the brain stem. The hindbrain is made up of the medulla, the pons, and the cerebellum; it controls many involuntary body functions and body movement.

Histogram A bar graph indicating a **frequency distribution.**

Holophrastic speech A type of speech used by infants in which one word or phrase stands for a whole idea. *Milk* in this sort of usage can stand for "I want more milk," "Mommy is pouring the milk," or "I spilled the milk."

Homeostatic mechanisms The bodily functions that help maintain **homeostasis.**

Homeostasis The physiological tendency to maintain an internal, bodily state of balance in terms of food, water, air, sleep, and temperature.

Homosexuality Preference for sexual relations with members of the same sex.

Hormones Substances secreted by endocrine glands that activate and/or regulate many bodily processes.

Hospice A center designed for the care of dying patients.

Hue Color

Humanistic model A theory of personality focusing on the worth of the individual and the particular and unique experiences of the individual. (See also **existential model.**)

Huntington's chorea A neurological disorder characterized by jerky, spasmodic movements of the face and body, and by progressive mental deterioration. This disease is hereditary, and the symptoms first appear in middle age. It is believed that a deficiency of the neurotransmitter GABA causes this disease.

Hypertension A chronic condition of high blood pressure. Early stages of hypertension can be caused by stress.

Hyperthyroidism An overactive thyroid causes irritability, restlessness, and weight loss in adults.

Hypnosis An artificially induced, sleeplike state in which the subject is extremely open to the hypnotist's suggestion.

Hypnotics Depressant substances such as barbituates that are used to induce sleep.

Hypothalamus The lower part of the thalamus in the brain; appears to have a regulatory function in motivation and emotion.

Hypothesis An assumption that serves as a possible explanation for some response or phenomenon.

Hypothetico-deductive reasoning The ability to test systematically a set of possibilities for correctness by using logic and experimental methods.

Hypothyroidism An underactive thyroid causes reduced growth and mental retardation in the young and depression and fatigue in the adult.

Iconic image A briefly persisting (1 or 2 seconds) visual memory.

Iconic memory system A kind of short-term memory involving visual images.

Id The most primary of Freud's three-part personality system; the instinctual impulses that supply psychic energy to the system and seek immediate gratification.

Identical twins Twins that develop from the splitting of a single fertilized egg; also called **monozygotic twins.**

Identification The process during psychosexual development by which a child comes to adopt the behaviors, values, and attitudes of significant adults through imitation.

Identity crisis The conflict that arises during an adolescent's quest for an adult identity.

Identity versus role confusion According to Erikson, the crisis occurring in adolescence in which the individual must develop a self-concept, adult role, and adult sexuality.

Idiographic Pertaining to the concrete, the individual, the unique. For example, idiographic approaches to personality are based on the assumption that traits are based on specific situations and are unique to individuals.

Illumination (1) The stage in problem solving or creativity when an idea suddenly comes to mind, as when the light bulb flashes above the head of a cartoon character; (2) the amount of light falling on a surface.

Illusion A mistaken perception or a distortion of perception.

Imitation Mimicking the behavior of another—plays an important role in child development.

Implosion therapy A type of behavioral therapy based on the theory that prolonged exposure to an anxiety-producing stimulus (by imagining it) in the absence of reinforcement (the feared consequences) extinguishes the fear-provoking power of the stimulus.

Imprinting The behavioral responses, such as following, that are learned rapidly and very early in life, and that are not reversible. In ducks and geese the **critical period** for imprinting is from birth to about 36 hours of age.

Incentive An external stimulus that has the capacity to motivate behavior.

Incubation Unconscious problem solving—when not deliberately thinking about a problem, a solution suddenly appears in consciousness.

Independent variable The factor in an experiment that is deliberately varied by the experimenter in order to test its effects on some other factor.

Induced compliance effect The finding in cognitive dissonance research that greater amounts of attitude change can be achieved with lower incentives for change.

Induced motion The apparent motion of one object in the visual field produced by motion of some other object.

Inductive reasoning Drawing a general conclusion from a set of particular instances. See **deductive reasoning.**

Industry vs. inferiority According to Erikson, the developmental crisis that occurs, and should be resolved, during the elementary school years, when children develop basic academic and social competence.

Inference rule Rule that states that a particular proposition must be true when other propositions are true.

Informational social influence A positive form of conformity in which one learns about social realities or conventions from the actions of others.

Information-exchange theory A partial explanation for the group polarization effect that points out how, in the course of group decision making, many persuasive arguments will be raised and will tend to convince group members to be more extreme in their decisions.

Information reduction A loss of information such as that which often occurs in recoding information from one form to another (e.g., lecture notes to a summary).

Initiative vs. guilt According to Erikson, the developmental crisis from ages three to five, when children should acquire the ability to initiate activities and develop a sense of purpose.

Innate Unlearned; present at birth.

Insight (1) Understanding of self and awareness of one's motivations, goals, needs; (2) in thinking or problem solving, the sudden solution to a problem or a sudden flash of understanding.

Insight learning Learning based on a sudden grasp of a problem; frequently involves a novel approach to a situation or problem.

Insomnia A common sleep disorder in which a person has trouble going to sleep initially or wakes up during the night and has trouble going back to sleep.

Instinct An innate, unlearned behavior characteristic of a particular species.

Instrumental aggression Aggression that occurs for the gain of the aggressor rather than to just inflict harm; for example, a mercenary soldier's aggression occurs for money.

Instrumental conditioning Another term

for operant conditioning suggesting that the animal's behavior is instrumental in producing a certain outcome.

Intellectualization A defense mechanism in which one avoids the emotional content of a situation by using abstract, intellectual understandings to explain the situation.

Intelligence quotient (IQ) The ratio of a person's mental age to his or her chronological age. (See **deviation IQ.**)

Intermale aggression A variety of aggression between males of a species in which the mere presence of a second male seems to trigger aggression. This is distinguished from **territorial aggression** because it can occur in any location; it does, however—like territorial aggression—often involve competition for females.

Interneurons Neurons that connect sensory and motor neurons.

Interpretation A psychoanalytic technique used to make the unconscious conscious. The psychoanalyst may either suggest possible hidden meanings or defense mechanisms revealed by a client's actions or statements or seek clues about a client's problem by interpreting his or her dreams.

Interview A meeting of two or more people face to face, usually for the purpose of exchanging information.

Intrapsychic conflict Expressions of the existence of two opposing motivations or impulses within a person.

Intrinsic motivation Engaging in activities or behaviors for the pure satisfaction and pleasure of doing them; for example, learning course material well because it's interesting, challenging, and enjoyable; an end in itself.

Introspection The process of looking inward to one's feelings and attempting to report on what one observes and experiences. Wilhelm Wundt was a pioneering figure in this approach in Germany in the mid-nineteenth century.

Introversion An attitude in which a person is more involved with self than with the outer world.

Introvert A person more involved with self than with the outer world.

IQ See **intelligence quotient.**

Iris The colored portion of the eye; the pigments in the iris determine whether the eye is blue, brown, green, etc.

James-Lange theory A theory of emotion that states that physiological arousal, followed by awareness and labeling of that arousal, is what we experience as emotion.

Jukebox theory A theory of emotion based on the experimental finding that physiological arousal (produced by a drug) can set the basis for an emotion. It is, however, an individual's interpretation or understanding of the arousal that determines the emotional response.

Just noticeable difference (JND) A difference in a stimulus that is noticed 50 percent of the time. Also called **difference threshold.**

Key word method A mnemonic technique in which the meaning of a foreign word is recalled by using an English word (the key word) that rhymes with the foreign word as a **recall cue** for the meaning of the foreign word.

Kinesthetic sense The sense of movement of the body (and its parts—muscles, tendons, and joints) and body position.

Korsakoff's syndrome A disorder of memory and orientation resulting from alcoholism.

Language-acquisition device (LAD) The innate mechanism (posited by Noam Chomsky) that enables children to learn language and language rules as part of their development.

Latency stage According to Freud, the period between the phallic stage and the onset of puberty, in which the Oedipal and aggressive wishes have been repressed.

Latent content (psychoanalysis) The hidden, symbolic meaning of a dream as caused by unconscious wishes and impulses.

Latent learning Learning that occurs but is not necessarily manifested in behavior or performance.

Lateral hypothalamus The portion of the hypothalamus that appears to stimulate eating.

Lateral inhibition A reduction of sensitivity in one neuron produced by stimulation of an adjacent neuron.

Law of effect A term originally used by Thorndike to describe his observation that responses followed by reward (by a "good effect") tended to be repeated.

Leadership Qualities such as intelligence, ambition, skill, and optimism that enable a person to guide, motivate, and control relevant aspects of the behavior of others.

Learned helplessness The idea that an organism may learn to be helpless as a result of the repeated demonstration that its responses have no effect on its surroundings.

Learning A relatively permanent change in behavior as a result of experience or practice.

Learning set The learning of a particular method or approach that can be applied to the solving of a number of similar problems.

Left hemisphere In most persons, the dominant hemisphere of the cerebrum, which controls motor activity and speech.

Lens The transparent part of the eye that focuses light onto the retina.

Libido Freud's term for instinctive sexual energy that drives the personality system; the combination of the life instincts and the death instincts.

Light adaptation The adjustment of the rods and cones in the eye to changes in illumination.

Limbic system Interrelated structures in the brain that appear to play a role in emotions.

Linear perspective A depth-perception cue

based on the apparent converging of two parallel lines at the horizon.

Linguistic relativity A theory that language determines how people think and conceptualize the world, such that people who speak different languages think differently.

Literacy The ability to read and write.

Location constancy A perception of stability in position even though the retinal image is moved about.

Longitudinal studies Studies involving a single group of persons over time (e.g., Terman's study of high-IQ children, which has followed them through life for over 50 years). See **cross-sectional studies.**

Long-term memory The relatively permanent storage of information—storage that continues even when the information is not being used.

Long-term memory system Any memory system capable of retaining information over long periods of time.

LSD (lysergic acid diethylamide) A powerful **hallucinogen** that radically alters sensation and perception with minute doses (e.g., 1 milligram).

Magnitude estimation A psychophysical procedure in which the subject indicates the intensity of a sensation by assigning it a number.

Manic-depression A behavioral disorder characterized by feelings of sadness and lethargy alternating with feelings of ecstasy and excitement.

Manifest content (psychoanalysis) The overt, concrete happenings in a dream.

Marijuana A mild hallucinogen with varying effects on its many users, ranging from mood exaggeration to distorted time sense.

Masochism A pathological desire to inflict pain on oneself, or deriving pleasure from being mistreated or suffering.

Maternal aggression Aggressive acts by the mother to protect her young.

Matrix A table of outcomes arranged in rows and columns to graphically demonstrate interdependencies between and among the participants to the interaction.

Maturation The development of a behavior or an ability solely as a result of physical growth; also, the process of physical development itself.

Mean The average value in a distribution $(\Sigma X/N)$.

Mean length of utterance (MLU) A measurement of sentence length used in language studies of children.

Mechanism A belief that all events in nature (including behaviors) are determined by mechanical causes and that by understanding chemical and physical causes, we can understand the resulting events.

Median The "middle" value in a distribution (as many values exceed it as fall below it.)

Mediation A method of relaxation in which one concentrates one's attention on a single unchanging or repetitive stimulus.

Medulla Swelling of the brain stem just above the spinal cord; controls important

involuntary functions such as breathing, heartbeat, and digestion.

Memory The ability to retain learned information.

Memory drum A timing device that presents a series of words for a human subject to memorize, one at a time at designated intervals.

Memory span The number of items that can be recalled after a single presentation.

Memory system Any system capable of retaining information over time (e.g., a photograph, book, electronic computer, or human memory).

Menarche The start of menstruation in young girls.

Menopause In adult women, the stopping of menstruation and the loss of the ability to reproduce, occurring in the 40s–50s.

Menstrual cycle The regular cycle of discharge of blood and uterine materials in human females.

Mental age A measure of a person's intelligence based on the abilities a person is expected to have at that particular age.

Mental representations Visual images or symbols (such as words) that represent objects or ideas.

Mental retardation Below-normal intelligence; usually an IQ below 70, coupled with social inadequacy.

Mescaline A naturally occurring hallucinogenic drug found as the active ingredient of the peyote cactus.

Mesomorph According to Sheldon's constitutional theory, a person with a muscular, well-developed build who is likely to have an outgoing, risk-taking, athletic personality.

Metacognition Knowledge and understanding of one's own mental processes.

Meta-needs According to Maslow, the "higher" needs, such as beauty, truth and justice.

Method of adjustment A psychophysical method in which the subject simply adjusts a stimulus until it evokes a certain sensation (e.g., until it is as "loud" as some comparison sound or is "just visible").

Method of constant stimuli A psychophysical method in which a fixed set of stimuli is presented in random order to determine the subject's typical response to each one (e.g., the subject "heard it" 20 percent of the times it was presented).

Method of loci A memory-improving technique in which one associates items to be recalled with specific places or locations, such as the various rooms of one's house.

Midbrain The region of the brain containing the reticular activating system.

Middle ear The portion of the ear lying between the eardrum and the cochlea.

Minnesota Multiphasic Personality Inventory (MMPI) A multiphasic personality test originally constructed to diagnose and detect serious behavior disorders such as depression, paranoia, and hysteria. It is used to characterize the personality profiles of normal individuals and to identify some

characteristics not ordinarily considered to be personality traits—for example, to identify individuals who will be successful salespersons and college teachers.

Minor tranquilizers A group of sedatives developed in the 1950s to treat anxiety. Also known as benzodiazepines or antianxiety drugs.

Mnemonics or mnemonic technique Method used to improve one's memory and to aid in remembering something (such as the **method of loci**).

Mode The most frequently occurring value in a distribution.

Modeling A form of behavior training in which a subject learns to make a response by watching others make a response to a particular stimulus.

Mongolism See **Down's syndrome.**

Monochromats People who are missing both color systems and see the world only in shades of gray.

Monocular cues Visual cues from one eye only.

Monozygotic twins Twins that develop from the splitting of a single fertilized egg; also called **identical twins.**

Moral anxiety In psychoanalytic theory, fear of conscience. We feel guilty when we contemplate or do something contrary to our moral code (superego).

Morpheme The smallest linguistic unit that has meaning.

Morphine An **opioid** often used to control pain.

Motion parallax The relative motion of objects at different distances from a moving observer.

Motivation A general term used to describe an internal state that arouses, maintains, and directs an individual's or animal's behavior toward a goal.

Motive An inner drive that moves a person to do something.

Motor area The area of the brain responsible for integrating the responses of the motor neurons, thereby affecting muscular activity.

Motor homunculus A graphic depiction of a map of the motor cortex, in which each part of the body is shown larger or smaller according to how much motor cortex is devoted to it (see Figure 2–20).

Motor neurons Neurons that carry nerve impulses to the muscles.

Motor program An instinctual response to a particular sign or releasing stimulus, which is itself instinctual.

Multiple personality A relatively rare **dissociative disorder** in which two or more distinct personalities are present in one individual. These personalities alternate over a period of hours or days and compete for access to consciousness.

Mutation An alteration in the genetic code (often caused by chemicals or radiation) that results in an alteration of cell growth.

Mycine A drug that, given extensively, seems to cause progressive damage similar to the

degeneration caused by age—to the hair cells in the basilar membrane of the ear.

Myelin The fatty white covering on some axons.

Narcotics Opium and its derivatives, such as heroin and morphine; drugs with pain-killing powers that produce high drug dependence.

Nativism Emphasizes the role of biology and physical structure in the development of human personality and behavior, and relies on heredity and maturation to account for most human characteristics and abilities.

Need A biological or psychological requirement; a state of deprivation that motivates a person to take action toward a goal.

Negation A **defense mechanism,** like **reaction formation,** for refusing to acknowledge unacceptable feelings. The denial of a feeling; for example, I *don't* hate my mother.

Negative afterimage An afterimage that occurs when a person who has been looking at a stimulus looks away; the negative afterimage is perceived in complementary colors to the original stimulus.

Negative reinforcer An event (such as electric shock) that, if stopped when a response is made, increases the likelihood that the response will be repeated.

Negative set A habitual way of approaching a problem that interferes with solving it; a tendency to do things the same old way even when a change of strategy is required.

Neo-cortex The outer layers of the cerebrum.

Neo-Freudian A school of psychological thought based on a modification of Freud's theories: includes such theorists as Horney and Fromm.

Nerve impulse The traveling wave of depolarization that carries information along a neuron.

Nerves Bundles of neurons that are covered by membrane. Nerves usually contain a mix of sensory and motor fibers.

Neuromodulators Chemicals that control the action of **neurotransmitters** at synaptic junctions.

Neuron The basic unit of the nervous system: consists of a cell body, nucleus, axon, and dendrites.

Neurosis A term traditionally used within the Freudian and Neo-Freudian psychodynamic framework to describe an extremely broad pattern of disorders characterized by anxiety, fear, and self-defeating behaviors.

Neurotic anxiety In psychoanalytic theory, fear that an unacceptable id impulse will surface, causing behavior that will be punished.

Neurotransmitter One of several chemical substances that play a role at the synapse in transmitting messages from neuron to neuron.

Nodes Transfer of ions in neurons can only take place at breaks in the myelin sheath, called nodes, that occur every 1 or 2 millimeters along the axon.

Nomothetic Dealing with general statements or laws. For example, nomothetic approaches to personality are based on the belief that all traits are equally applicable to all individuals.

Nonsense syllables Pronounceable, but meaningless, syllables used in memory research; often a consonant, vowel, consonant sequence (CVC trigram).

Norepinephrine A hormone secreted by the adrenal glands; promotes the release of sugar into the blood and also acts as a neurotransmitter; also called noradrenaline.

Normal distribution curve A diagram of scores in which 68 percent of the scores occur between one standard deviation below the mean and one standard deviation above the mean.

Normal state of consciousness A wakeful and alert (but not excited or tense) awareness of external stimuli and internal mental events.

Normative social influence Conformity through social influence; occurs when a person suppresses his or her own opinions and complies with group standards in order to avoid punishment or gain reward from the group.

NREM sleep Sleep during which the physiological processes slow down: consists of four stages of sleep through which the person moves in a regular cycle during the night. For the most part, dreaming does not occur in NREM sleep. See **REM sleep.**

Nuclear magnetic resonance A technique of computer imaging based on magnetic fields and radio frequencies that depicts the presence and location of certain chemical elements (used mostly as a brain scan).

Obedient aggression Aggression that occurs as a response to a command from an authority figure.

Obesity In humans, defined as being more than 15 percent over the "ideal" weight, given the person's height and overall body build.

Objective self-awareness A state in which full attention is focused inward, on oneself, in an evaluative way; contrasted with subjective self-awareness, in which one's attention is directed outward to activities and others.

Object permanence The knowledge that an object that is hidden from view does not cease to exist.

Observational learning A type of indirect learning that results when people observe the responses of others.

Obsessions Thoughts that repeatedly intrude against one's will and defy one's efforts to ignore them. Sometimes used more generally to describe the behaviors that are done repetitively to temporarily terminate these thoughts; for example, excessive hand washing.

Obsessive-compulsive disorders Behavior patterns characterized by a compelling drive to repeat unwanted thoughts or actions over and over again.

Oedipal conflict In Freudian terms, a boy's erotic involvement with his mother and jealousy of his father.

Olfaction The sense of smell.

Open-ended interview An assessment interview in which a judge talks to a person and follows the conversation wherever it leads.

Operant aggression Aggression that causes an organism to perform an aggressive act simply because it is rewarded for doing so or punished for not doing so.

Operant conditioning A type of learning in which specific voluntary behaviors are reinforced.

Opioids Psychoactive derivatives of the opium poppy, or similar but synthetic substances such as methadone.

Opium A natural opioid, produced from the dried, milk-like fluid that comes from the seedpods of the poppy, from which heroin, morphine, and codeine are derived.

Opponent-process theory of color vision One of the two leading theories of color vision. States that there are three separate color systems: red-green, blue-yellow, and black-white. The effect of the two components in each system is opposite, so that each system's signal to the brain indicates how much is in the stimulus.

Opponent-process theory of emotion Formulated to explain the motivation behind some self-destructive behaviors, this theory does not address where emotion comes from or what it consists of. Instead, it hypothesizes that the stimulus that causes an emotion also causes another, opposite, emotional reaction (e.g., fear and relief).

Optic chiasm The point at which the optic nerves cross to go to opposite sides of the brain.

Oral stage In Freudian terms, the first psychosexual stage, during which the infant's sexual pleasure is derived from stimulation of the mouth.

Organic amnesia Amnesia caused by physiological problems such as stroke or disease or by injury.

Organic mental disorders A diagnostic category from DSM-III for the acute or chronic effects of drug use on the central nervous system.

Orgasm The third of Masters and Johnson's four phases of human sexual response, characterized by ejaculation in the man and vaginal contractions in the woman.

Osmoreceptors Receptors, sensitive to the amount of fluid inside the body's cells, that play a role in drinking regulation.

Osmosis The movement of fluids through a semipermeable membrane (e.g., water through the walls of a cell).

Otoliths Small calcium deposits in the inner ear that appear to have a function in maintaining equilibrium.

Oval window The membrane across the opening between the inner ear and the middle ear.

Overextension Stretching the meaning of a word beyond its correct usage, as when young children use the word *dog* to refer to all small, furry four-legged animals.

Overtones Harmonics of the **fundamental tone** that impart a special quality or timbre to notes played on different instruments.

Pandemonium A computer program designed to detect lower-order features (e.g., a vertical line), which are then synthesized into higher-order forms (letters or words).

Panic disorders A type of anxiety disorder in which the essential feature is the unpredictable recurrence of panic attacks. These attacks may occur more frequently in situations such as riding in an elevator or flying in an airplane.

Paranoid schizophrenia A severe psychological disorder in which delusions of persecution play a major role.

Parasympathetic nervous system The branch of the autonomic nervous system that maintains the routine "vegetable" functions such as digestion; tends to conserve energy.

Parkinson's disease A neurological disorder characterized by tremors and incoordination. It is caused by a lack of dopamine in certain parts of the brain.

Partial reinforcement In operant conditioning, the process of gradually reducing the proportion of reinforced responses so that the animal will eventually respond very rapidly for only an occasional reinforcement.

PCP (Phencyclidine or "angel dust") Originally developed as a powerful pain killer, it has become a highly dangerous "street drug" that often produces unpredictable outbursts of violence.

Peer group A group of social and chronological equals.

Peg words A mnemonic technique in which the information to be remembered is associated with specific words (peg words) that are more easily recalled. These peg words then serve as **recall cues** for the associated information (such as *bun* in "one is a bun, two a shoe, etc.").

Perceived control The degree to which people believe they have some control over a stressor.

Percentile rank If a value has a percentile rank of X, it exceeds X percent of the other values in a distribution; e.g., the median is defined as having a percentile rank of 50.

Perception Interpretation of the information provided by one's sensory receptors.

Perceptual constancy The ability, in perception, to draw similar inferences about the world from different patterns of sensory activity (e.g., a person seen from many different angles is still perceived as the same person).

Performance The act of displaying what has been learned or using learned skills.

Peripheral nervous system The entire nervous system outside the brain and spinal cord.

Peripheral streaming The linear "streaming" or movement of stimulus contours toward the periphery of the retina as one

moves through space. A strong cue for motion.

Personal construct A view of reality created by actively perceiving, evaluating, and organizing one's own experience.

Personality An individual's complex and unique patterns of behavior, motives, emotions.

Personality disorders Patterns of behavior, thinking, and perceiving that have become maladaptive, causing distress or impairing normal functioning in the work place or in social situations.

Personality inventories Scales or measures that ask people to report on some thought or behavior that has been empirically shown to correlate with some underlying conflict or difficulty.

Person-centered personality theory Carl Rogers's humanistic personality theory, which emphasizes viewing the individual as a whole being capable of self-actualization as well as the importance of the self and conscious awareness in the life of the individual.

Peyote A natural hallucinogenic substance found in the peyote cactus and chewed by certain Indian tribes in Mexico and the southwestern United States to induce visions.

Phallic stage According to Freud, the developmental stage in which sex urges are directed toward a parent and in which one establishes a sexual identity (usually between ages three to five).

Phenomenal field The boundaries of an individual's awareness and influence.

Phenotype The manner in which an organism's genetic makeup (**genotype**) is expressed as it develops in a particular environment.

Phenylketonuria (PKU) An inherited form of mental retardation caused by a disorder of amino acid metabolism.

Phi illusion An illusion of movement caused by flashing lights off and on one after another, which makes them appear to move.

Phobia A persistent and irrational fear of some class of stimulus objects and events.

Phobic disorders A persistent and irrational fear of a particular object or situation, usually far out of proportion to the actual threat.

Phoneme The smallest functional unit of speech sound in a language.

Photographic memory An ability to remember things as if you were seeing them in full detail. (Also called **eidetic imagery**.)

Phrase-structure rules Rules that govern the organization of the various parts of a sentence (such as nouns, verbs, adjectives, etc.)

Pitch The sensory experience of highness or lowness of a tone corresponding to the frequency of sound waves.

Pituitary gland An endocrine gland located at the base of the brain and attached to the hypothalamus. Secretes tropic hormones, which affect other endocrine glands, causing

them to secrete other hormones. Often called the "master gland" for this reason.

Placebo An inert substance (e.g., an empty pill) that is used as a control in drug experiments.

Place theory The idea that different tone frequencies affect **neurons** located at different places along the **basilar membrane** in the **cochlea.**

Plateau According to Masters and Johnson, the second of four phases of sexual excitation.

Pleasure principle According to Freud, the dominant force in id activity, which calls for immediate reduction of tension through gratification of instinctual impulses.

Polygenic trait A trait determined by more than one gene pair.

Polygon A series of points connected by straight lines indicating a frequency distribution.

Polygraph An apparatus used for measuring and recording various physiological reactions such as GSR. Often referred to as a lie detector.

Pons Part of the hindbrain, just above the spinal cord; acts mainly as a way station for neural pathways going to other brain areas.

Population A clearly defined set of potential measurements from which samples may be drawn.

Positive reinforcer An event (such as food) that, if presented just after a response, increases the likelihood that the response will be repeated.

Positron emission tomography (PET) A computer-generated image of the brain based on the emission of positrons when radioactively tagged chemicals enter into neural activity.

Posthypnotic suggestion A suggestion to take some action, change a way of thinking, or alter behavior. Given to a subject under hypnosis, it takes effect after the subject has come out of hypnosis.

Pragmatics In reference to language, how people combine the information they have about the language, about the situation they are in, and about other people to arrive at the meaning of the speech they hear or read.

Preconventional stage According to Kohlberg, the moral stage of development when children's behavior is governed by rewards and punishments.

Predatory aggression Aggression that occurs for hunting purposes—the action of a predator against its prey.

Predictive validity The determination that a test can accurately predict future results.

Prefrontal lobotomy The surgical removal of the prefrontal part of the frontal lobes in the brain; a controversial form of psychosurgery rarely used today.

Premack's principle Access to a more preferred activity can be used to reinforce a less preferred activity.

Preoperational stage The second major stage of cognitive development (Piaget), during which children begin to use symbols,

including linguistic symbols (words); ages two to seven years.

Preparation stage The first stage of creative thinking, in which an individual absorbs the data and ideas needed to solve a problem creatively.

Preparedness Seligman's theory that organisms are more prepared to associate a given emotional response with one stimulus than another. Has been used to explain why it is more common to develop phobias about some stimuli than others.

Primacy effect Under certain conditions the first item(s) in a series will be remembered better than those that follow.

Primary drive A universal drive based on biological needs.

Primary prevention Intervention that is concerned with eliminating chronic social problems, such as inadequate housing or unemployment, and that attempts to reduce the incidence of new cases of mental disorder.

Primary-process thinking According to Freud, the process in the id by which it gains immediate satisfaction of instinctual wishes. Primary processes are unconscious and often irrational.

Primary reinforcer Stimulus that has its reinforcing properties built into the organism (see also **unconditioned reinforcer**).

Primary sex characteristics Internal and external reproductive organs.

Priming The increased accessibility or retrievability of information in memory produced by the prior presentation of related cues.

Prisoner's dilemma A bargaining game used to illustrate properties of interdependent social interactions; participants can cooperate or compete. The outcome for each individual is dependent on what the other person chooses to do.

Proactive interference Forgetting or memory difficulties caused by interference of information learned earlier.

Problem space The four parts of a problem's description—initial state, goal state, operators, and intermediate problem states—that together indicate how individuals represent problems.

Procedural knowledge "How to" knowledge, such as how to ride a bicycle or tie a shoe. It is usually evidenced by how well you do something (rather than by being right or wrong as in **propositional** or **declarative knowledge**).

Progestin A female sex hormone that has a role in pregnancy and nursing.

Projection The attribution of one's own faults to others.

Projective tests Personality tests in which a person's responses to ambiguous stimuli are analyzed.

Propositional knowledge Knowledge in the form of relations between two or more concepts (propositions); also called **declarative knowledge.** It is a statement of fact that can be true or false.

Propositional thinking The ability to reason about verbal statements and abstractions.

Proximodistal Proceeding from the center of the body to the extremeties, from the large muscles to the small, as in motor development in infancy.

Psychiatric social worker A mental health professional who has earned a master's degree in social work.

Psychiatrist A psychotherapist who has completed both an M.D. degree and a psychiatry residence program. They are the only mental health professionals allowed to prescribe psychoactive drugs and electroshock treatment.

Psychiatry The branch of medicine that deals with mental illness.

Psychoactive substances Drugs (substances) that affect the central nervous system and alter perception, mood, and behavior.

Psychoanalysis (psychoanalytic therapy) A variety of psychotherapies that share the foundational belief that intrapsychic conflict is the cause of abnormality and that insight is essential to improvement.

Psychoanalytic model Model of personality, abnormal functioning, and therapy based on Freud's dynamic system of psychology, which seeks the understanding of behavior in unconscious motivation and conflict.

Psychoanalytic theory Sigmund Freud's theory of human personality, stressing unconscious motives, largely sexual and aggressive in nature.

Psychogenic Something that can be attributed to psychological causes rather than organic.

Psychopathic personality disorders See **antisocial personality disorder.**

Psychophysical relations Relations between physical stimulus variables and the sensations they evoke (as indicated by a subject's responses).

Psychophysical scaling Measurement techniques used to determine how the strength or quality of a sensation changes as the physical stimulus is changed.

Psychosensory Pertaining to sensations not originating in the sense organs.

Psychosexual development Freud's theory of development, in which gratification of sexual energies is focused on various parts of the body during different stages of development.

Psychosis The main difference between neurosis and psychosis is the more extreme or bizarre manifestation of behavior, thought, and emotion shown in psychosis. In psychosis the individual loses contact with reality in some central way, and from this loss a variety of severe problems emerges.

Psychosocial A theory of development based on Erikson's modifications of Freud's theory of psychosexual development. Focuses more on social influences than on sexual ones.

Psychosocial stages Erikson's stages of development in which a person passes through particular social crises at particular ages.

Psychosomatic illness A physical disorder or illness that is psychologically determined and often stress-related.

Psychosurgery Cuts, lesions, and removal of brain sections; based on the biological theory that abnormal behavior is determined by a malfunction in the brain.

Psychotherapy A set of procedures by which one person attempts to change the life of another by using talk-oriented change procedures based on psychoanalytics or other theories.

Puberty The developmental time when people reach physical sexual maturity.

Punishment An aversive (negative) stimulus that follows a response for the purpose of eliminating that response.

Pupil The dark circular opening within the iris of the eye through which light passes into the eye.

Q-sort technique A personality measure in which individuals are given a set of cards containing adjectives or phrases to sort into groups based on the degree to which they describe themselves or a target person.

Range The difference between the largest and smallest value in a numerical distribution.

Rational-emotive therapy (RET) A form of **cognitive therapy** developed by Albert Ellis. RET focuses primarily on thought content; identifying and changing irrational thoughts that lead to anxiety and neurotic functioning are the goals of RET.

Rationalism The philosophical position that assumes that people are born with innate knowledge of the world. Contrasted to **empiricism,** the position that knowledge is acquired through experience.

Rationalization A defense mechanism in which one deceives oneself by giving an acceptable reason to explain an unacceptable outcome or motive.

Reaction formation A defense mechanism in which the way one feels about something is the opposite of the way one behaves toward it.

Reality anxiety In psychoanalytic theory, a reaction of fear to a real danger, physical or psychological, in the external world.

Reality principle According to Freud, the process of the ego mediating the demands of the id and the environment.

Reasoning Drawing conclusions from known or assumed premises, as in deductive reasoning, or making inferences from known or assumed facts, as in inductive reasoning; step-by-step thought processes.

Recall A measure of retention of memory in which a person reproduces or reconstructs the information learned earlier with a minimum of cues.

Recall cues Cues that assist in retaining and retrieving items of memory.

Recency effect Under certain conditions, the last item(s) in a series will be remembered better than the ones preceding them.

Receptive fields If the electrical activity of a neuron in the visual system is affected by a particular type of visual stimulus on a particular part of the retina, the type of stimulus and location on the retina define that neuron's receptive field (e.g., a vertical white bar in the center of the retina).

Receptor organ A body part that receives sensory information; eyes, for example, are the receptor organs of vision.

Recessive gene The member of the gene pair (allele) that carries a weaker characteristic and can determine a trait only when paired with another recessive gene.

Recoding Coding information that was encoded previously in either the same form or a related form.

Recognition A measurement of memory retention in which a person is asked to pick out from a list items that were learned previously.

Reconstruction or redintegration In memory, the process of reconstructing or filling in missing information through educated guessing based on information still available and stimulus redundancy.

Redundancy The idea that activity in one's various sensory receptors is highly correlated, or redundant. For example, when people speak to you, the movement of their lips is highly correlated with the sound of their voice.

Reduplicated babbling Type of vocalization produced by six- to nine-month-old infants, usually consisting of repeated consonant-vowel syllables such as *da da da da.*

Reflection The process whereby light bounces off a surface into a new path.

Reflexes Automatic sequences of stimulus and response, which in some cases may involve only a single synapse between sensory and motor neurons (monosynaptic reflex).

Regression A defense mechanism in which a person returns to less mature levels of behavior when faced with anxiety.

Rehearsal Repeating learned information in one's mind to enhance memory.

Reinforcement In classical conditioning, following the conditioned stimulus with presentation of the unconditioned stimulus. In operant conditioning, following a response by presentation of a reward or by removal of an aversive stimulus. Reinforcement promotes the learning of responses.

Reinforcing properties The characteristics of conditioned stimuli (CS) and unconditioned stimuli (US) that account for their becoming reinforcers.

Relation-oriented leader A leadership style that emphasizes the leader's relationships to the group and relationships within the group; most effective for groups that are either very well or very poorly organized and integrated.

Relative frequency The frequency of a value in a distribution divided by the total number of values (the proportion of such values in the distribution).

Relative refractory period The period fol-

lowing the absolute refractory period when it is more difficult, but not impossible, to trigger a nerve impulse.

Relearning Even when people seem to have forgotten something they learned earlier, relearning will take place faster than the original learning did. This reduction in time to learn, or **savings,** means they actually did retain some of the information from the first time.

Reliability The determination of whether a test will produce consistent results on repeated measurements under the same circumstances.

REM rapid eye movement Rapid movements of the eyes during sleep that seem related to dreaming.

REM sleep One of the two types of sleep, characterized by rapid movements of the eyes; is the period during which dreaming is most likely to occur.

Reorganization A process in which a person orders items of memory and classifies the items into categories to assist in memory.

Repression A defense mechanism in which a person avoids unpleasant thoughts by blocking these thoughts out of consciousness.

Research methods The various means for finding evidence to support scientific theory, including correlational studies, case studies, and controlled experimental interventions.

Resistance In psychoanalysis, the unwillingness or inability to discuss certain painful areas of experience, by preventing these experiences and ideas from becoming part of consciousness.

Resistance to extinction A measure of the ability of a conditioned response to resist being eliminated by later trials with no reinforcement.

Resolution According to Masters and Johnson, the final phase of sexual intercourse; resolution follows orgasm and is the phase in which physiological activity returns to normal.

Response The measurable behavior of an organism, particularly as a reaction to a stimulus.

Resting potential The normal polarity of a neuron in which its interior is about -70 mV negative in respect to its exterior.

Retention The storage of memory; the maintaining of information.

Reticular activating system (RAS) A network of fibers beginning in the spinal cord and extending up through the midbrain into the higher centers; has a role in attention and arousal.

Reticular formation See **reticular activating system (RAS).**

Retina The inside layer of the eye containing the light-sensitive **rods** and **cones.**

Retrieval The process of obtaining memory from storage in the brain.

Retroactive interference The interference of new information with the memory of something learned earlier.

Retrograde amnesia The inability to re-member events and information that were immediately followed by a brain injury or shock.

Right hemisphere The nondominant cerebral hemisphere believed to have a role in spatial perception and artistic interpretation.

Rods Light-sensitive receptor cells found on the retina; sensitive to black and white stimuli but not color.

Role models Those persons (including parents, friends, siblings, teachers, characters on TV or in stories) who serve as examples of proper attitudes and behaviors to the growing child.

Rorschach inkblot test A projective personality test in which a person is asked to describe what images come to mind upon viewing ten ordered inkblots.

Round window The membrane-covered opening on the far end of the **cochlea** that absorbs the waves of energy entering earlier through the **oval window.**

Saccade The rapid rotation of the eye that occurs between successive fixations.

Saltatory conduction The more rapid transmission of a nerve impulse along myelinated neurons where the action potential "leaps" (saltates) from node to node of myelin.

Sample A subset of measurements from some population.

Saturation The purity of a color; as a color becomes less saturated, it becomes progressively whiter.

Savings In relearning, the amount of time saved when seemingly forgotten information or responses are learned again.

Scatter diagram A graph showing pairs of values for two variables as points in a Cartesian coordinate system.

Schedule of reinforcement The schedule determining whether a correct response will be reinforced according to a time interval or after a number of correct responses; the schedule can be fixed or variable.

Schema The conceptual framework that people use to organize their knowledge of the world.

Schizophrenia A term applied to a wide variety of severe abnormal behaviors including distortions of reality, social withdrawal, and prominent disturbances in thought, perception, motor activity, or emotionality. Many professionals argue that the term is no longer a useful diagnostic category.

Script A memory representation of procedural knowledge (e.g., "eating in a restaurant").

Secondary prevention Intervention that aims to identify problems early on, before they become chronic.

Secondary-process thinking In Freudian terms, the activity of the conscious part of the psyche that governs the ego's attempts to meet the id's demands through rational thought and conscious activity directed toward satisfying specific drives.

Secondary reinforcer Stimulus that acquires its reinforcing properties through learning (see also **conditioned reinforcer**).

Secondary sex characteristics Sexually differentiating features that normally emerge at puberty, such as breast and hip enlargement in females and beard growth and voice change in males.

Sedatives Drugs that help people sleep and are highly addictive; **barbiturates** are a class of sedatives.

Selective breeding The breeding of laboratory animals for heredity studies; the animals are selected for specific characteristics and are bred with animals with similar characteristics in an attempt to get as pure a genetic strain as possible.

Self The individual as a unique and conscious being.

Self-actualization According to Maslow, the ultimate goal of human beings and the pinnacle of the hierarchy of needs; self-actualized persons have fulfilled their innate, positive potentials.

Self-efficacy expectancies A person's conceptualizations of his or her ability to carry out actions required to master and control different situations.

Self-esteem A person's own judgment of his or her worth and abilities.

Self-handicapping The strategies that allow one to attribute poor performance to causes that do not damage self-esteem; for example, partying late the night before a final exam provides a "safe" explanation for failing the exam.

Self-monitoring The degree to which an individual attends to the social context in planning his/her behavior.

Self-perception theory A theory proposing that people make judgments about themselves on the basis of qualities they view in other people.

Self-regulation A behavioral therapeutic technique that challenges clients to take responsibility for altering their own behaviors and for structuring the environments in which these behaviors occur.

Self-report An observation and rating of an individual made by that individual.

Self theories Humanistic theories of personality that suggest that people are basically good and have an inborn desire to change for the better and reach self-fullfillment.

Semantic differential Osgood's technique for rating the connotative meanings of words.

Semantic knowledge Factual knowledge that is independent of the individual or when it is learned; another type of **propositional knowledge.**

Semantic memory Our conceptual knowledge, which includes our knowledge of language, the concepts that we have, and general world knowledge. Compare with **episodic memory**—memory for discrete events in our past.

Semicircular canals Three canals in the inner ear that function in the perception of body movement.

Sensation Psychological experience of a stimulus.

Sensorimotor stage The first major stage of cognitive development (Piaget) during which children know the world primarily through their perceptual-motor interactions with the immediate environment and during which they acquire the concept of object **permanence** (also known as object constancy).

Sensory areas Areas of the cerebral cortex that function in the integration of sensory information from each of the various receptor organs.

Sensory codes The specific patterns of neural activity that carry information from the various senses to the brain.

Sensory deprivation The condition characterized by existence in an environment that is devoid of outside stimuli.

Sensory memory A type of short-term memory in which information lasts for only a few seconds.

Sensory memory system A theoretical human **memory system** that briefly retains information in a form similar to its initial sensory code (e.g., **echoic, iconic**).

Sensory neurons Neurons that carry information from receptors to the central nervous system.

Separation anxiety An infant's fear of losing the mother whenever she disappears for even a few moments.

Serial position effect In memory, the tendency for the position of items in a list to affect one's ability to recall them—the first and last items are more easily remembered than the rest of the list.

Serotonin A neurotransmitter found in the midbrain and believed to be affected by hallucinogenic drugs.

Set A tendency to continue doing something in a particular way.

Set-point theory Nisbett's theory that feeding behavior tends to hold weight at a specific value (**set point**); that is, obese rats or humans simply have a higher set point.

Sex-linked trait An inherited trait linked specifically to a sex chromosome.

Sex-related aggression Aggression directly related to sexual potency or sexual rivalry.

Sexual-dysfunction therapy An eclectic set of therapeutic techniques—although primarily cognitive and behavioral that specifically address and try to overcome problems of sexual dysfunction.

Shape constancy The knowledge that even when an object is viewed from a different angle, its shape remains the same.

Shaping An operant-conditioning technique in which behavior is gradually molded into a desired form through reinforcement of successive approximations of the target behavior.

Short-term memory A type of memory with a somewhat limited capacity; items must be consciously rehearsed to be retained in short-term memory.

Sign stimulus An instinctual releasing action that triggers a particular motor program or response.

Signal detection theory A theory that attempts to explain perceptual judgments through analysis of a person's sensitivity to sensory stimuli in addition to the criteria a person uses in decision making.

Simultaneous conditioning A simultaneous presentation of the conditioned stimulus (CS) and the unconditioned stimulus (US) in classical conditioning experiments.

Sine wave A simple pressure wave representing one frequency of sound at one amplitude.

Sinusoidal grating A cyclical (sinusoidal) variation in brightness across the visual field.

Size constancy A tendency to perceive familiar objects as being the same size even when they cast a different-sized image on the retina because of one's distance from them.

Skinner box A chamber containing a lever or some other device that an animal can manipulate to obtain reinforcers (e.g., food or water) during an operant-conditioning experiment.

Skin senses The senses of pressure, pain, hot, and cold.

Skin sensitivity The degree of sensation caused in the skin by various types of physical stimuli.

Social-comparison theory Festinger's theory of how people come to know and understand their own relative abilities, strengths, and weaknesses by comparing themselves with others.

Social exchanges The social and emotional "rewards" exchanged within social interactions; typically participants have complimentary resources to exchange so that one person can fairly easily give what the other needs, and vice versa. The traditional marriage is a good example of the social exchange process.

Social facilitation/impairment Performing a task better or worse as a result of having other people (who *might* be evaluating you) present.

Social identification The tendency when one identifies with a group to attend selectively to differences between that group and other groups, and to ignore similarities between one's own group and other groups.

Social intelligence A term that describes the skills or strategies people apply to various interpersonal situations.

Social-learning theory The theory that people can learn important things about themselves and about others through observation of other people's behaviors, without having to go through trial and error on their own.

Socialization The process in which a person acquires the attitudes and values of his or her culture.

Social-learning theorists Theorists who believe that people can learn important things about themselves and about others through observation of other people's behaviors, without having to go through trial and error on their own.

Social psychology A branch of psychology that studies the interactions between people, with emphasis on the group's effects on behavior.

Sociobiology The study of the biological basis of social behavior in man and animals.

Sociopathic personality disorders See **antisocial personality disorder.**

Somatic nervous system The part of the peripheral nervous system that controls voluntary muscles.

Somatoform disorders Physical symptoms that have no apparent organic cause.

Somatosensory areas Areas of the cerebral cortex that function in the integration of stimuli from the kinesthetic sense and the skin senses.

Somatosensory homunculus Graphic depiction of a map of the somatosensory cortex, in which each part of the body is shown larger or smaller, according to how much somatosensory cortex is devoted to it (see Figure 2–20).

Somatotype Body type.

Somnambulism Sleepwalking.

Sound spectrogram A voice print of recorded speech.

Source trait According to Cattell, one of the basic traits that accounts for a person's behavior and personality.

Spatial frequency The frequency of a sinusoidal variation in brightness across the visual field expressed in cycles per degree of visual angle.

Species-specific response pattern A stimulus-response characteristic of a particular species.

Spinal cord A column of neural tissue that, together with the brain, forms the central nervous system.

Spinal reflexes Also called monosynaptic reflex arc. A reflex that occurs only at the spinal level, which means that the impulses received in the spinal cord are sent right back to the muscle that must respond to those impulses.

Split-brain subjects Subjects who, for medical or for experimental reasons, have had their cerebral hemispheres surgically separated at the corpus callosum and who subsequently have unconnected cerebral hemispheres that appear to function somewhat separately and differently.

Spontaneous recovery The return of a conditioned response after extinction and without further training trials.

Spread of activation The process by which a cue progressively activates (primes, makes accessible) related information in memory.

S-sleep The four stages of sleep other than REM-sleep when the underlying neural activity appears more synchronous.

Standard deviation The square root of the average squared deviation from the mean (a measure of variability).

Standard error of the mean The standard

deviation of sample means about the population mean.

Standard score or z-score The number of standard deviations (σ) between a score (X) and the mean ($\bar{X}$) of the distribution of scores; i.e., $z = (X - X)/\sigma$.

Standardization sample A sample that is representative of the entire population and thus provides the norms, or standards of performance, with which any individual's performance can be compared.

Stanford-Binet test A modified version of Binet's original IQ test used to assess intelligence in children.

State-dependent learning The idea that learning a response in a particular environment or emotional or physical state will enable the person to remember the response much better in a similar environment or state.

Statistically significant A pattern of data that is so unlikely to have occurred by chance (probability less than .01 or .05) that it can be interpreted as a real rather than a random occurrence.

Statistics Mathematical relationships and representations that describe events and other data.

Stereopsis Visual perception of three-dimensional objects.

Stereotype A preconceived notion of how a group or individual will behave.

Steven's power law Assertion that sensation (S) is proportional to stimulus intensity (I) raised to some power (b): $S = kI^b$ where k is a constant that depends on the unit of measurement.

Stimulants Drugs, such as amphetamines, which accelerate brain and nervous system functioning.

Stimulus-response psychology The branch of psychology concerned with behavior as seen through stimulus-response relationships and principles of conditioning and simple learning.

Stress A term that includes demands from the environment requiring the individual to change (stressors) and the state of physiological and psychological tension resulting from those demands (the stress response).

Stressors The environmental demands that lead to a stress response. Stressors can be physical or psychological, universal or unique, intrinsic to a situation or attributed to it.

Stress response A person's reaction to a threatening demand from the environment, including changes in the autonomic nervous system, requiring some kind of adjustment or adaptation.

Stroboscopic motion See **phi illusion.**

Structured interview A personality assessment technique in which an interviewer asks a subject specific questions designed to provide information about particular areas of personality.

Sublimation A defense mechanism in which unacceptable urges and feelings are channeled into acceptable activities.

Substance dependence Addiction typically involving increasing physical tolerance to the substance, psychological dependence, and severe withdrawal symptoms when use is discontinued.

Substance-use disorders Maladaptive behavior patterns shown by chronic drug users: including impaired social and occupational functioning, an inability to control or limit use of the substance, and withdrawal symptoms.

Subtractive mixture A form of color mixing in which pigments absorb part of the spectrum and the result is color produced by a subtraction of a particular color wavelength.

Successive approximations In shaping, the process of gradually coming closer and closer to the desired behavior.

Superego In Freudian terms, the part of the personality that is the conscience and reflects parental and societal codes of morality.

Suppression A defense mechanism in which incompatible ideas are unconsciously inhibited or eliminated.

Surface structure The characteristics and organization of the verbatim form of a sentence. See **deep structure.**

Surface trait According to Cattell, one of the behavioral patterns through which source traits are expressed.

Survey A detailed study that involves gathering information through observations or questionnaires and then analyzing it.

Survey method A method of research involving the collection of data from a large number of individuals.

Symbolic representations The contents of thought, which are comprised of coded information in memory about past experience, a state of the world, or an imaginary state of the world.

Sympathetic nervous system The branch of the autonomic nervous system that functions as the arousal center during emergencies or stress situations.

Synapse The point between neurons where nerve impulses are transmitted from neuron to neuron.

Synaptic cleft The tiny gap between an axon terminal and another neuron into which the axon releases neurotransmitters.

Synaptic transmission Process whereby an action potential in one neuron causes chemicals (neurotransmitters) to be released into the synaptic cleft, where they affect the occurrence of an action potential in the next neuron.

Syntactic scene analysis The structure of a scene represented as a hierarchy of components. Going from top-down, the scene is analyzed into progressively lower-order forms. Going from the bottom-up, the components are synthesized into progressively higher-order forms.

Syntax Grammar; rules for organizing and combining words into phrases and sentences.

Systematic desensitization A type of be-

havior therapy in which the person substitutes for an undesired response a response that is incompatible or competitive with it.

Tachistoscope An instrument used in learning and memory studies; exposes cards or slides for very brief periods of time.

Task-oriented leader A leadership style that emphasizes successful completion of tasks, even at the risk of poor interpersonal relations with group members; most effective for groups that are neither well nor poorly organized and integrated.

Taste buds The receptors on the tongue that respond to substances in your mouth and contribute to your experience of taste.

Telegraphic speech Utterances with the unimportant and the function words left out. Characteristic of an early stage of language and called *telegraphic* because of its resemblance to the way that telegrams are written.

Temporal acuity The ability to discern fine details in spatial patterns of light.

Temporal contiguity Occurring close together in time; a primary cause of association in many theories of learning and memory.

Territorial aggression Aggression that occurs to protect a territory or to let an enemy know which boundaries cannot be crossed.

Tertiary prevention Intervention that deals with the immediate aftereffects of personal crises. It utilizes various therapeutic techniques.

Testosterone One of the androgens (male hormones) that promotes secondary sex characteristics.

Texture gradient Distance cues based on the fact that objects lose definition and detail the farther away they are.

Thalamus A fairly large, bilobed area at the midline of the brain; an important way station for receiving information from the various sense organs and relaying it to the cortex.

Thanatos According to Freud, the death instinct.

Thematic Appperception Test (TAT) A projective personality test in which a person is shown pictures and must make up stories about what he or she feels is going on in the various pictures, what has led up to this situation, and what will come of it afterward.

Theory A formalized statement of particular principles and concepts designed to explain a particular phenomenon or behavior.

Therapy A set of procedures by which one person uses language to change the life of another (Davison and Neale, 1978).

Threshold The minimum stimulus necessary to elicit a response.

Timbre The characteristic quality of a tone produced by the combination of overtones heard along with the pure tone.

Tip-of-the-tongue (TOT) phenomenon When trying to remember something, the feeling that one is just about to recall it, that it is on the "tip of the tongue."

Token economy A behavior therapy technique in which tokens are given to reward desired behavior; the tokens can later be

exchanged for a specific reward that the patient desires, such as specific privileges or candy.

Tolerance The phenomenon in which increasing amounts of a drug are required to produce the same physiological effects.

Traces A hypothetical impression of memory in the nervous system.

Trait A characteristic of a person's behavior/personality that can be measured.

Trait theories Personality theories that categorize people on the basis of their distinctive attributes and traits.

Tranquilizer Drugs that depress nervous system activity and reduce anxiety and tension.

Transference In psychoanalysis, the process in which a patient transfers love or other emotional attachment from another person in his or her past to the therapist.

Transformational rules Rules that specify how one sentence can be "transformed" into another; grammatical rules that spell out the relationships between sentences.

Trial-and-error learning As suggested by Thorndike, an essentially blind trying out of one problem-solving strategy after another until one is successful.

Twin studies Studies that compare the common traits of monozygotic (genetically identical) and dyzygotic (fraternal) twins.

Unconditioned reflex or response A response that is elicited by a stimulus without learning (e.g., a dog's salivation when presented with meat powder is an unconditioned response).

Unconditioned reinforcer Stimulus that has its reinforcing properties built-into the organism (see also **primary reinforcer**).

Unconditioned stimulus A stimulus that provokes a response in the absence of learning or conditioning.

Unconscious That part of one's mental life of which one is unaware and over which one has little or no control.

Undoing A defense mechanism characterized by engaging in a positive act in order to negate a previous, unacceptable act, thus relieving the guilt and anxiety associated with the first act.

Unstructured interview A personality assessment technique in which the interviewer and the subject engage in free-flowing conversation.

Validity The extent to which a test measures what it purports to measure.

Value theory A theory that explains how, in the course of group decision making, social comparison leads members to shift their own position to one that is consistent but more extreme; whether the shift is risky or cautious is determined by the average group tendency, reflecting the dominant cultural value for that type of problem.

Variability The amount of variation among scores in a distribution. Characterized by such measures as the range, variance (σ^2), or standard deviation (σ).

Variable-interval schedule A reinforcement schedule in which the first correct response after unpredictably varying periods of time is reinforced.

Variable-ratio schedule A schedule of reinforcement in which an unpredictably varying number of correct responses must occur before reinforcement occurs.

Variance The mean-square deviation; in other words, the square of the standard deviation. A useful measure of the amount of scatter around the mean or average of a set of numerical observations.

Ventral Pertaining to the abdominal side of the body.

Ventromedial hypothalamus A portion of the hypothalamus believed to have a role in satiation or inhibition of eating.

Verification The part of the creative process in which the person evaluates the results of the illumination (sudden solution to the problem).

Vestibular sacs Bony structures of the head that send sensory stimuli about head movement to the brain.

Vicarious punishments Punishments experienced indirectly, specifically by seeing another person receive them.

Vicarious reinforcements Reinforcements experienced indirectly, specifically by seeing another person receive them.

Visual acuity Ability to discern fine details in spatial patterns of light.

Visual cliff The depth-illusion device developed to determine whether human infants and other species have depth perception.

Visual code A type of memory representation that creates confusion during recall between two different items (e.g., letters) having a similar appearance (e.g., X and Y).

Visual field The three-dimensional space in which all objects are perceived by the eyes at a given time.

Visual preference Refers to the ability of young infants to discriminate among various visual patterns.

Visual preference technique An experimental method that tests whether subjects prefer to look at one visual stimulus rather than another.

Visual spectrum The range of electromagnetic energy to which our eye is sensitive (normally about 400 to 700 nm).

Volley principle The hearing theory based on the idea that hearing receptors respond one after another in rapid succession, signaling pitch of higher frequencies in this way.

Volumetric receptor A body mechanism that responds to a drop in blood volume or pressure.

Weber's constant The constant of proportionality (k) in Weber's law.

Weber's law The principle that the **just noticeable difference (JND)** of a stimulus is a constant fraction of the intensity of the original stimulus.

Wechsler Intelligence Scale for Children (WISC-R) The revised version of Wechsler's Intelligence scale for children. An individual IQ test for children aged 6–16.

Wernicke's aphasia A speech disorder caused by damage to a particular part of the brain. People with Wernicke's aphasia speak in recognizable sentences, but the content of their speech is often nonsensical.

Working memory A mental work space that is used to manipulate and combine information.

Wernicke's area An association area located on the lower side of the lateral fissure, near the auditory cortex. Damage to this area produces Wernicke's aphasia, in which people speak fluently, but with bizarre and nonsensical content.

White matter The fibrous portion of the nervous system; the white appearance is due to the myelin sheath covering the axons.

WISC-R The revised version of Wechsler's intelligence scale for children; an individual IQ test used with children aged 6 to 16.

Wish fulfillment According to Freud, the id's need for immediate gratification causes it to create an image of the desired object. It is up to the ego to actually acquire the object.

Withdrawal A pattern of severe physiological symptoms, such as nausea, intense sweating, muscular cramps, possible coma, as well as psychological effects that occur when one stops taking a drug one has become dependent on (addicted to).

X chromosome The female sex chromosome.

Y chromosome The male sex chromosome.

Young-Helmholtz theory of color vision States that there are three types of cones, each sensitive to a different part of the visual spectrum.

References

Abramsom, L. Y., Seligman, M. E. P., & Teasdale, J. D. (1978). Learned helplessness in humans: Critique and reformulation. *Journal of Abnormal Psychology, 87,* 49–74.

Abse, D. W. (1959). Hysteria. In S. Arieti (Ed.), *American handbook of psychiatry* (Vol. 1). New York: Basic Books, Pp. 272–292.

Adams, C. G., & Turner, B. F. (1985). Reported change in sexuality from young adulthood to old age. *Journal of Sex Research, 21,* 126–141.

Adams, D. (1976). *Parent involvement: Parent development.* Oakland, Cal.: Center for the Study of Parent Involvement. (Cited in Zigler & Berman, 1983.)

Adler, A. (1930). Individual psychology. In C. Murchison (Ed.), *Psychologies of 1930.* Worcester, Mass: Clark University Press, 1930.

Adler, A. (1931). *What life should mean to you.* Boston: Little Brown.

Adolph, E. F. (1939). Measurements of water drinking in dogs. *American Journal of Physiology, 125,* 75–86.

Affifi, et al. (1980). *Introduction to basic neuroscience.* Baltimore, Md.: Urban & Schwarzenberg.

Agras, W. S., & Kraemer, H. (1983). The treatment of anorexia nervosa: Do different treatments have different outcomes? *Psychiatric Annuals, 13,* 928–935.

Ainsworth, M. D. S., Blehar, M. C., Waters, E., & Wall, S. (1978). *Patterns of attachment: A psychological study of the strange situation.* Hillsdale, N.J.: Erlbaum.

Ajzen, I., & Fishbein, M. (1979). Attitude-behavior relations: A theoretical analysis and review of empirical research. *Psychological Bulletin, 84,* 888–918.

Ajzen, I., & Fishbein, M. (1980). *Understanding attitudes and predicting behavior.* Englewood Cliffs, N.J.: Prentice-Hall.

Akhter, S., Wig. N. N., Varma, V. K., Pershad, D., & Verma, S. K. (1975). A phenomenological analysis of symptoms in obsessive-compulsive neurosis. *British Journal of Psychiatry, 127,* 342–348.

Alexander, F. (1950). *Psychosomatic medicine: Its principles and applications.* New York: W. W. Norton.

Alfert, E. (1964). Reactions to a vicariously experienced and a direct threat. Unpublished doctoral dissertation, University of California, Berkeley.

Alkon, D. L. (1983, July). Learning in a marine snail. *Scientific American,* pp. 70–84.

Allison, T., & Cicchetti, D. (1976). Sleep in mammals: Ecological and constitutional corelates. *Science, 194,* 732–734.

Allport, G. W. (1937). *Personality: A psychological interpretation.* New York: Holt, Rinehart & Winston.

Allport, G. W. (1954). *The nature of prejudice.* Reading, Mass.: Addison-Wesley.

Allport, G. W. (1961). *Pattern and growth in personality.* New York: Holt, Rinehart & Winston.

Altman, I. (1975). *The environment and social behavior.* Monterey, Calif.: Brooks-Cole.

Amabile, T. M. (1979). Effects of external evaluation on artistic creativity. *Journal of Personality and Social Psychology, 37,* 221–233.

Amoore, J. E. (1964). Current status of stereochemical theories of odor. *Annals of the New York Academy of Sciences, 116,* 457–476.

Anderson, C. R. (1977). Locus of control, coping behaviors, and performance in a stress setting: A longitudinal study. *Journal of Applied Psychology, 62,* 446–451.

Anderson, J. R. (1976). *Language, memory, and thought.* Hillsdale, N.J.: Erlbaum.

Anderson, J. R. (1978). Arguments concerning representation for mental imagery. *Psychological Review, 85,* 249–277.

Anderson, J. R. (1980). *Cognitive psychology and its implications.* San Francisco: Freeman.

Anderson, J. R. (1983). *The Architecture of Cognition.* Cognitive Science Series: No. 5, Cambridge, MA: Harvard University Press.

Anderson, J. R., & Kintsch, W. (1974). *Human associative memory.* Washington, D.C.: Winston.

Anderson, J. R., & Paulson, R. (1977). Representation and retention of verbatim information. *Journal of Verbal Learning and Verbal Behavior, 16,* 439–451.

Anderson, S. M., & Bem, S. L. (1981). Sex typing and androgyny in dyadic interaction: Individual differences in responsiveness to physical attractiveness. *Journal of Personality and Social Psychology, 41,* 74–86.

Anderson, W. F. (1984). Prospects for human gene therapy. Science, *226,* 401–408.

Andersson, B. (1952). Polydipsia caused by intrahypothalamic injections of hypertonic NaCl solutions. *Experientia, 8,* 157.

Andersson, B., & McCann, S. M. (1955). A further study of polydipsia evoked by hypothalamic stimulation in the goat. *Acta Physiologica Scandinavica, 33,* 333–346.

Annett, M. (1972). The distribution of manual asymmetry. *British Journal of Psychology, 63,* 343–358.

Antell, S. B., & Keating, D. P. (1983). Perception of numerical invariance in neonates. *Child Development, 54,* 695–701.

Argyris, C. (1964). *Integrating the individual and the organization.* New York: Wiley.

Armen, J. C. (1974). *Gazelle-boy: A child brought up by gazelles in the Sahara Desert.* London: Bodley Head.

Arsonson, E., & Carlsmith, J. M. (1968). The effect of severity of threat on the devaluation of forbidden behavior. *Journal of Abnormal and Social Psychology, 66,* 584–588.

Aronson, E., & Linder, D. (1965). Gain and loss of esteem as determinants of interpersonal attractiveness. *Journal of Experimental Social Psychology, 1,* 156–171.

Asch, S. E. (1951). Effects of group pressure upon the modification and distortion of judgment. In H. Guetzkow (Ed.), *Groups, leadership and men.* Pittsburgh: Carnegie.

Asch, S. E. (1955). Opinions and social pressure. *Scientific American, 11,* 32.

Aserinsky, E., & Kleitman, N. (1953). Regularly occuring periods of eye mobility and concomitant phenomena during sleep. *Science, 118,* 273–274.

Asher, S. R. (1979). Referential communication. In G. J. Whitehurst & B. J. Zimmerman (Eds.), *The functions of language and cognition.* New York: Academic Press.

Aslin, R. N., & Dumas, S. T. (1980). Binocular vision in infants: A review and theoretical framework. In H. W. Reese & L. P. Lipsett (Eds.), *Advances in child development & behavior* (Vol. 15). New York: Academic Press.

Astin, A. W. (1979). *The American freshman: National norms for fall 1979.* American Council on Education and University of California at Los Angeles.

Astin, A. W. (1980). *The American freshman: National norms for fall 1980.* American Council on Education and University of California at Los Angeles.

Astin, A. W., Green, K. C., Kern, W. S., & Maier, N. J. (1984), *The American freshman: National norms for 1984,* Los Angeles: American Council on Education.

Astin, A. W., Green, K. C., & Korn, W. S. (1987). *The American freshman: Twenty year trends.* American Council on Education and University of California, Los Angeles.

Astin, H. S., & Kent, L. (1983). Gender roles in transition: Research & policy implications for higher education. *Journal of Higher Education, 54,* 309–324.

Athanasiou, R., Shaver, P., & Tavris, C. (1970). *Sex. Psychology Today, 4*(2), 37–52.

Athanassiades, J. (1973). The distortion of upward communication in hierarchical organization. *Academy of Management Journal, 16*, 207–226.

Atkinson, J. W. (1977). Motivation for achievement. In T. Blass (Ed.), *Personality variables in social behavior*. Hillsdale, N.J.: Erlbaum.

Atkinson, J. W., & Birch, D. (1970). *The dynamics of action*. New York: Wiley.

Atkinson, J. W., & Feather, N. T. (Eds.). (1966). *A theory of achievement motivation*. New York: Wiley.

Atkinson, J. W., & Litwin, G. H. (1960). Achievement motive and test anxiety conceived as motive to approach success and motive to avoid failure. *Journal of Abnormal and Social Psychology, 60*, 27–36.

Atkinson, R. C., & Raugh, M. R. (1975). An application of the mnemonic keyword method to the acquisition of a Russian vocabulary. *Journal of Experimental Psychology: Human learning and Memory, 104*, 126–133.

Atkinson, R. C., & Shiffrin, R. M. (1971). The control of short-term memory. *Scientific American, 225*, 82–90.

Atkinson, R. C., & Shiffrin, R. M. (1977). Human memory: A proposed system and its control processes. In G. H. Bower (Ed.), *Human memory: Basic processes*. New York: Academic Press.

Au, T. K. (1983). Chinese and English counterfactuals: The Sapir-Whorf hypothesis revisited. *Cognition, 15*, 155–187.

Averill, J. R. (1969). Autonomic response patterns during sadness and mirth. *Psychophysiology, 5*, 399–414.

Avison, W. R., & Speechley, K. N. (1987). The discharged psychiatric patient: A review of social, social-psychological, and psychiatric correlates of outcome. *American Journal of Psychiatry, 144*, 10–18.

Ax, A. F. (1953). The physiological differentiation between fear and anger in humans. *Psychosomatic Medicine, 14*, 433–442.

Ayllon, T. (1963). Intensive treatment of psychotic behavior by stimulus satiation and food reinforcement. *Behavior Research and Therapy, 1*, 53–61.

Ayllon, T., & Azrin, N. H. (1968). *The token economy: A motivational system for therapy and rehabilitation*. Englewood Cliffs, N.J.: Prentice-Hall.

Azrin, N. H., Hutchinson, R. R., & Hake, D. F. (1965). Extinction induced aggression. *American Psychologist, 20*, 583.

Bachrach, L. L. (1984). Interpreting research on the homeless mentally ill: Some caveats. *Hospital and Community Psychiatry, 35*, 914–917.

Bachrach, L. L. (1984). Research on services for the homelessly mentally ill. *Hospital and Community Psychiatry, 35*, 910–913.

Baddeley, A. D. (1982). Domains of recollection. *Psychological Review, 89*, 708–729.

Baddeley, A. D., & Hitch, G. J. (1974). Working memory. In G. H. Bower (Ed.). *The psychology of learning and motivation*, Vol. 8. New York: Academic Press.

Bahrick, H. P., & Phelps, E. (1987). Retention of Spanish vocabulary over eight years. *Journal of Experimental Psychology: Learning memory and Cognition 13*, 344–349.

Balota, D., Pollotsek, A., & Rayner, K. (1985). The interaction of contextual constraints and parafoveal visual information in reading. *Cognitive Psychology, 17*, 364–90.

Baltes, P. B., Dittman-Kohl, Freya, and Dixon, Roger A. (1984). New perspectives on the development of intelligence in adulthood: Toward a dual-process conception and a model of selective optimization with compensation. In P. B. Baltes and

D. G. Brim, Jr. (Eds.), *Life-span development and behavior*, Vol. 6. New York: Academic Press.

Bandura, A. (1965). Behavior modification through modeling procedures. In L. Krooner & L. P. Ullman (Eds.), *Research in behavior modification*. New York: Holt, Rinehart & Winston.

Bandura, A. (1968). Social learning interpretation of psychological dysfunctions. In P. London & D. Rosenhan (Eds.), *Foundations of abnormal psychology*. New York: Holt, Rinehart & Winston.

Bandura, A. (1977). *Social learning theory*. Englewood Cliffs, N.J.: Prentice-Hall.

Bandura, A. (1979). Self-efficacy: Toward a unifying theory of behavior change. *Psychological Review, 84*, 191–215.

Bandura, A. (1984). Recycling misconceptions of perceived self-efficacy. *Cognitive Therapy and Research, 8*, 231–255.

Bandura, A. (1986). *Social foundations of thought and action: A social-cognitive theory*. Englewood Cliffs, N.J.: Prentice-Hall.

Bandura, A., Adams, N. E., & Beyer, J. (1966). Cognitive processes mediating behavioral classical conditioning as a function of arousal level. *Journal of Personality and Social Psychology, 3*, 54–62.

Bandura, A., Blanchard, E. B., & Ritter, B. (1969). Relative efficacy of desensitization and modeling approaches for inducing behavioral, affective, and attitudinal changes. *Journal of Personality and Social Psychology, 13*, 173–199.

Bandura, A., Jeffery, R., & Wright, C. (1974). Efficacy of participant modeling as a function of response induction aids. *Journal of Abnormal Psychology, 83*(1), 56–64.

Bandura, A., & Rosenthal, T. L. (1976). Vicarious change. *Journal of Personality and Social Psychology, 35*, 125–139.

Bandura, A., Ross, D., & Ross, S. (1961). Transmission of aggression through imitation of aggressive models. *Journal of Abnormal and Social Psychology, 63*, 575–582.

Bandura, A., Ross, D., & Ross, S. (1963). Imitation of film-mediated aggressive models. *Journal of Abnormal and Social Psychology, 66*, 3–11. (a)

Bandura, A., Ross, D., & Ross, S. (1963). Vicarious reinforcement and imitative learning. *Journal of Abnormal and Social Psychology, 67*, 601–607. (b)

Bandura, A., & Walters, R. H. (1963). *Social learning and personality development*. New York: Holt, Rinehart & Winston.

Banks, M. S. & Salapatek, P. (1983). Infant visual perception. In M. M. Haith & J. J. Campos (Eds.), *Handbook of child psychology* (Vol. 2): *Infancy and developmental psychology*, New York: John Wiley.

Barash, D. P. (1977). *Sociology and behavior*. New York: Elsevier.

Barber, T. X., Spanos, H. P., & Chaves, J. F. (1974). *Hypnosis, imagination, and human potentialities*. New York: Pergamon.

Barchas, J., Akil, H., Elliott, G., Holman, R., & Watson, S. (1978). Behavioral neurochemistry: Neuroregulators and behavioral states. *Science, 200*, 964–973.

Bard, P. (1934). On emotional expression after decortication with some remarks on certain theoretical views. Parts I and II. *Psychological Review, 41*, 309–329 and 424–449.

Barker, R. G. (1960). Ecology and motivation. In M. R. Jones (Ed.), *Nebraska Symposium on Motivation* (Vol. 8). Lincoln: University of Nebraska Press.

Barlett, F. C. (1967). *Remembering. A study in experimental and social psychology*. New York: Cambridge University Press.

Baron, R. A. (1977). *Human aggression*. New York: Plenum Press.

Baron, R. A., & Bell, P. A. (1977). Sexual arousal

and aggression by males: Effects of type of erotic stimuli and prior provocation. *Journal of Personality and Social Psychology, 35*, 79–87.

Barrett, J. E. (Ed.). (1979). *Stress and mental disorder*. New York: Raven.

Barron, F., and Harrington, D. M. (1981). Creativity, intelligence and personality. *Annual Review of Psychology, 32*, 439–476.

Barsalon, L. W. (1982). Context-independent and context-dependent information in concepts. *Memory and Cognition, 10*, 82–93.

Bartlett, J. C., & Santrock, J. W. (1979). Affect-dependent episodic memory in young children. *Child Development, 50*, 513–518.

Bartlett, J. C., & Santrock, J. W. (1981). Affect-dependent episodic memory in young children. *Child Development, 50*, 513–518.

Barton, A. H. (1969). *Communities in disaster*. Garden City, N.Y.: Doubleday.

Baruch, G., Beiner, L., & Barnett, R. (1987). Women and gender in research on work and family stress. *American Psychologist, 42*, 130–136.

Baum, A., Fleming, R. & Singer, J. E. (1983). Coping with victimization by technological disaster. *Journal of Social Issues, 39*, 117–138.

Baum, A., & Valins, S. (1977). *Architecture and social behavior: Psychological studies in social density*. Hillsdale, N.J.: Erlbaum.

Beach, F. A. (1968). Coital behavior in dogs: III. Effects of early isolation on mating in males. *Behavior, 30*, 218–238.

Beahrs, J. O. (1971). The hypnotic psychotherapy of Milton H. Erickson. *American Journal of Clinical Hypnosis, 7*, 223–276.

Beck, A. T. (1962). Reliability of psychiatric diagnosis: A critique of systematic studies. *American Journal of Psychiatry, 119*, 210–216.

Beck, A. T. (1967). *Depression: Clinical, experimental and theoretical aspects*. New York: Harper & Row.

Beck, A. T. (1972). *Depression: Causes and treatment*. Philadelphia: University of Pennsylvania Press.

Beck, A. T. (1973). *Diagnosis and management of depression*. Philadelphia: University of Pennsylvania Press.

Beck, A. T. (1974). The development of depression: A cognitive model. In R. Friedman & M. Katz (Eds.), *Psychology of depression: Contemporary theory and research*. Washington D.C.: Winston.

Beck, A. T. (1975). *Cognitive therapy and emotional disorders*. New York: International Universities Press.

Beck, A. T., & Ward, C. H. (1961). Dreams of depressed patients: Characteristic themes in manifest context. *Archives of Social Psychology, 5*, 462–467.

Beck, A. T., Weissman, A., Lester, D., & Trexler, L. (1974). The measurement of pessimism. *Journal of Consulting and Clinical Psychology, 42*, 861–865.

Beck, H. (1979). The Ocean-Hill Brownsville and Cambodian-Kent State crises: A biobehavioral approach to human sociobiology. *Behavioral Science, 24*(1), 25–36.

Beck, R. C. (1983). *Motivation: Theories and principles* (2nd ed.). Englewood Cliffs, N.J.: Prentice-Hall.

Becker, J. (1977). *Affective disorders*. Morristown, N.J.: General Learning Press.

Békésy, G. von. (1955). Human skin perception of traveling waves similar to those on the cochlea. *Journal of the Acoustical Society of America, 27*, 830–841.

Békésy, G. von. (1966). Taste theories and the chemical stimulation of single papillae. *Journal of Applied Physiology, 21*, 1–9.

Bell, S. M., & Ainsworth, M. D. S. (1972). Infant

crying and maternal responsiveness. *Child Development*, 43, 1171–1190.

Belsky, J., Rovine, R., & Taylor, D. G. (1984). The Pennsylvania infant and family development project. III: The origins of individual differences in infant-mother attachment: Maternal and infant contributions. *Child Development*, 55, 718–728.

Belsky, J., Spanier, G. B., & Rovine, M. (1983). Stability and change in marriage across the transition to parenthood. *Journal of Marriage and the Family*, 45, 567–577.

Bem, D. J. (1965). An experimental analysis of self-persuasion. *Journal of Experimental Social Psychology*, 1, 199–218.

Bem, D. J. (1977). Self-perception theory. In L. Berkowitz (Ed.), *Advances in experimental social psychology* (Vol. 6). New York: Academic Press.

Bem, D. J., & Allen, A. (1974). On predicting some of the people some of the time: The search for cross-situational consistencies in behavior. *Psychological Review*, 81, 506–520.

Bem, S. L. (1981). Gender schema theory: A cognitive account of sex typing. *Psychological Review*, 88, 354–364.

Benedict, R. (1934). *Patterns of culture*. Boston: Houghton Mifflin.

Benson, H. (1975). *The relaxation response*. New York: Morrow.

Benson, H. (1977). Systemic hypertension and the relaxation response. *New England Journal of Medicine*, 296, 1152–1156.

Benson, H., Alexander, S., & Feldman, C. L. (1975). Decreased premature ventricular contractions through use of the relaxation response in patients with stable ischaemic heart disease. *Lancet*, 2, 380.

Berger, P. (1978). Medical treatment of mental illness. *Science*, 200, 974–981.

Bergin, A. E. (1971). The evaluation of therapeutic outcomes. In A. E. Bergin & S. L. Garfield (Eds.), *Handbook of psychotherapy and behavior change: An empirical analysis*. New York: Wiley.

Berkman, L. F., & Syme, S. L. (1979). Social networks, host resistance, and mortality: A nine-year follow-up study of Alameda County residents. *American Journal of Epidemiology*, 102(2), 186–204.

Berko, J. (1958). The child's learning of English morphology. *Word*, 14, 150–177.

Berkowitz, L. (1973). Control of aggression. In B. M. Caldwell & H. M. Ricciutti (Eds.), *Review of child development research* (Vol. 3). Chicago: Chicago University Press.

Berkowitz, L. (1974). Some determinants of impulsive aggression: Role of mediated associations with reinforcements for aggression. *Psychological Review*, 81, 165–176.

Berkowitz, L., & Le Page, A. (1967). Weapons as aggression-eliciting stimuli. *Journal of Personality and Social Psychology*, 1, 202–207.

Berkun, M. M., Kessen, M. L., & Miller, N. E. (1952). Hunger-reducing effects of food by stomach fistula versus food by mouth measured by a consummatory response. *Journal of Comparative and Physiological Psychology*, 45, 550–554.

Bermant, G. (1961). Response latencies of female rats during sexual intercourse. *Science*, 133, 1771–1773.

Bermant, G., & Davidson, J. M. (1974). *Biological bases of sexual behavior*. New York: Harper & Row.

Bernard, J. (1982). *The future of marriage* (1982 ed.). New Haven: Yale University Press.

Berndt, T. J. (1979). Developmental changes in conformity to peers and parents. *Developmental Psychology*, 15, 608–616.

Berry, J. W., & Dason, P. (Eds.). (1974). *Culture and cognition: Readings in cross-cultural psychology*. London: Methuen.

Bexton, W. H., Herm, W., & Scott, T. H. (1954). Effects of decreased variation in the sensory environment. *Canadian Journal of Psychology*, 8, 70–76.

Bickerton, D. (1983). Creole languages. *Scientific American*, 249, 116–122.

Billig, M., & Tajfel, H. (1973). Social categorization and similarity in intergroup behavior. *European Journal of Social Psychology*, 3, 27–52.

Bjorklund, A., Dunnett, S. B., Stenevi, V., Lewis, M. E., & Iverson, D. D. (1980). Reinervation of the denervated striatum by substantia nigra transplants: Functional consequences as revealed by pharmacological and sensorimotor testing. *Brain Research*, 199, 307–333.

Black J. (1971). *Lives through time*. Berkeley: Bancroft.

Blakemore, C. (1977). *Mechanics of the mind*. Cambridge, England: Cambridge University Press.

Blakemore, C., & Campbell, F. W. (1969). On the existance of neurons in the human visual system selectively sensitive to the orientation and size of retinal images. *Journal of Physiology*, 203, 237–260.

Blanchard, E. B., et al. (1981). Social validation of the headache diary. *Behavior Therapy*, 12, 711–715.

Blass, E. M., & Hall, W. G. (1976). Drinking termination: Interactions among hydrational, orgiastic, and behavioral controls in rats. *Journal of Comparative and Physiological Psychology*, 90, 909–916.

Bloom, A. (1981). *The linguistic shaping of thought: A study in the impact of language on thinking in China and the West*. Hillsdale, N.J.: Erlbaum.

Bloom, J. D., & Faulkner, L. R. (1987). Competency determinations in civil commitment. *American Journal of Psychiatry*, 144, 193–196.

Bloom L. (1970). *Language development: Form and function in emerging grammars*. Cambridge, Mass.: MIT Press.

Bloom, L. (1973). *One word at a time*. The Hague: Mouton.

Boggiano, A. K., Klinger, C., & Main, D. S. (1986). Enhancing interest in peer interaction: A developmental analysis. *Child Development*, 57, 852–861.

Bolles, R. C. (1970). Species-specific defense reactions and avoidance learning. *Psychological Review*, 77, 32–48.

Bolton, R. (1976). Aggression and hypoglycemia among the Qolla: A study in psychobiological anthropology. In K. E. Moyer (Ed.), *Physiology of aggression and implications for control*. New York: Raven Press.

Bond, C. F., Jr. (1982). Social facilitation: A self-presentational view. *Journal of Personality and Social Psychology*, 42, 1042–1050.

Botwinick, J. (1973). *Aging and behavior*. New York: Springer.

Botwinick, J., and Siegler, I. C. (1980). Intellectual ability among the elderly: Simultaneous cross-sectional and longitudinal comparisons. *Developmental Psychology*, 16, 49–53.

Bouchard, T. J., Heston, L., Eckert, E., Keyes, M., & Resnick, S. (1981). The Minnesota study of twins reared apart: Project description and sample results in the developmental domain. *Twin research 3: Intelligence, personality and development*. New York: Alan R. Liss.

Bouchard, T. J., & McGue, M. (1981). Familial studies of intelligence: A review. *Science*, 212, 1055–1059.

Bower, G. H. (1981). Mood and memory. *American Psychologist*, 36, 129–148.

Bower, G. H., Black, J. B., & Turner, T. R. (1979). Scripts in memory for text, *Cognitive Psychology*, 11, 117–220.

Bower, T. G. R. (1977). *A primer of infant development*. San Francisco: W. H. Freeman.

Bowlby, J. (1973). *Attachment and loss* (Vol. 1): *Attachment*. New York: Basic Books.

Brady, J. V. (1958, October). Ulcers in "executive monkeys." *Scientific American*, Pp. 95–100.

Braine, M. D. S. (1978). On the relation between the natural logic of reasoning and standard logic. *Psychological Review*, 85, 1–21.

Bramwell, S. T., Masuda, M., Wagner, N. N., & Holmes, T. H. (1975). Psychosocial factors in athletic injuries: Development and application of the Social and Athletic Readjustment-Rating Scale (SARRS). *Journal of Human Stress*, 1(2), 6–20.

Brand, R. J., Rosenman, R. H., Sholtz, R. I., & Friedman, M. (1976). Multivariate prediction of coronary heart disease in the Western Collaborative Group Study compared to the findings of Framingham Study. *Circulation*, 53, 348–355.

Bregman, E. (1934). An attempt to modify the emotional attitude of infants by the conditioned response technique. *Journal of Genetic Psychology*, 45, 169–198.

Brickman, P., Rabinowitz, V. C., Karuza, J., Coates, D., Cohen, E., & Kidder, L. (1982). Models of helping and coping. *American Psychologist*, 37, 368–384.

Bridell, D. W., & Wilson, G. T. (1976). Effects of alcohol and expectancy set on male sexual arousal. *Journal of Abnormal Psychology*, 85, 225–234.

Brigham, C. C. (1923). *A study of American intelligence*. Princeton, N.J.: Princeton University Press.

Brim, O. J. (1976). Theories of the male midlife crisis. *The Counseling Psychologist*, 6(1), 2–9.

Broadbent, D. E. (1958). *Perception and communication*. London: Pergamon.

Brody, L. R., Zelazo, P. R., & Chaika, H. (1984). Habituation-dishabituation to speech in the neonate. *Developmental Pscychology*, 20, 114–119.

Brooks, L. R. (1968). Spatial and verbal components of the act of recall. *Canadian Journal of Psychology*, 22, 349–368.

Brown, G. W. (1974). Meaning, measurement, and stress of life events. In B. S. Dohrenwend & B. P. Dohrenwend (Eds.), *Stressful life events: Their nature and effects*. New York: Wiley.

Brown, J. K. (1969). Adolescent initiation rites among preliterate people. In R. E. Grinder (Ed.), *Studies in adolescence* (2nd ed.). New York: Macmillan.

Brown, P. L., & Jenkins, H. M. (1968). Auto shaping of the pigeon's key peck. *Journal of the Experimental Analysis of Behavior*, 11, 1–8.

Brown, R. (1965). *Social psychology*. New York: Free Press.

Brown R. (1973). *A first language: The early stages*. Cambridge, Mass.: Harvard University Press.

Brownell, K. D. (1982). The addictive disorders. In C. M. Franks, B. T. Wilson, P. C. Kendall, and K. D. Brownell, *Annual review of behavior therapy: Theory and practice* (Vol. 8). New York: Guilford Press.

Brownwell, K., & Venditti, B. (1983). The etiology and treatment of obesity. In W. E. Frann., I. Karacan, A. D. Pokorney, & R. L. Williams (Eds.), *Phenomenology and the treatment of psychophysiologic disorders*. New York: Spectrum.

Bruner, J. S. (1974/75). From communication to language. *Cognition*, 3, 255–287.

Bruner, J. S., & Goodnow, J. J. (1956). *A study of thinking*. New York: Wiley.

Bryan, J. H., & Test, M. A. (1967). Models and helping: Naturalistic studies in aiding behavior. *Journal of Personality and Social Psychology*, 6, 400–407.

Brozen, N. (1985) U.S. leads industrialized nations

in teen-age births and abortions. *New York Times*, p. 1.

Buck, R. (1985). Prime theory: An integrated view of motivation and emotion. *Psychological Review, 92,* 389–413.

Bulman, R. I., & Wortman, C. B. (1977). Attributions of blame and coping in the "real world": Severe accident victims react to their lot. *Journal of Personality and Social Psychology, 35,* 351–363.

Bunney, W. E., & Garland, B. L. (1983). Possible receptor effects of chronic lithium administration. *Neuropharmacology, 22,* 367–372.

Burks, B. S. (1928). The relative influence of nature and nurture upon mental development: A comparative study of foster parent-foster child resemblance and true parent-true child resemblance. *Yearbook of the National Society for the Study of Education, 27* (Part 1), 219–316.

Burns, T., & Stalker, G. M. (1961). *The management of innovation.* London: Tavistock.

Burnstein, E., Vinokur, A., & Trope, Y. (1973). Interpersonal comparison versus persuasive argumentation: A more direct test of alternative explanations for group-induced shifts in individual choice. *Journal of Experimental Social Psychology, 9,* 236–245.

Burr, W. (1970). Satisfaction with various aspects of marriage over the life cycle: A random middle class sample. *Journal of Marriage and the Family, 32*(1), 29–37.

Burt, C. L. (1943). Ability and income. *British Journal of Educational Psychology, 13,* 83–98.

Burt, C. (1966). The genetic determination of differences in intelligence: A study of monozygotic twins reared together and apart. *British Journal of Psychology, 57,* 137–153.

Buswell, G. T. (1922). Fundamental reading habits: A study of their development. *Supplementary Educational Monographs, No. 21.*

Butler, R. A. (1957). Discrimination learning by rhesus monkeys to visual-exploration motivation. *Journal of Comparative and Physiological Psychology, 50,* 239–241.

Butler, R. N. (1968). The life review: An interpretation of reminiscence in old age. In B. L. Neugarten (Ed.), *Middle age and aging.* Chicago: University of Chicago Press.

Bykov, K. M. (1957). *The cerebral cortex and the internal organs.* (W. H. Gantt, trans.). New York: Chemical Publishing Co.

Byrne, B. (1974). Item concreteness vs. spatial organization as predictors of visual imagery. *Memory and Cognition, 2,* 53–59.

Byrne, D., & Clore, G. L. (1970). A reinforcement model of evaluative responses. *Personality: An International Journal, 1,* 103–128.

Byrne, D., & Rhamey, R. (1965). Magnitude of positive and negative reinforcements as a determinant of attraction. *Journal of Personality and Social Psychology, 2,* 884–889.

Cadoret, R. J. (1978). Psychopathology in adopted-away offspring of biologic parents with antisocial behavior. *Archives of General Psychiatry, 135,* 463–466. (a)

Cagas, C. R., & Riley, H. D., Jr. (1970). Age of menarche in girls in a west-south-central community. *American Journal of Diseases of Children, 120,* 303–308.

Caldwell, M. D. (1976). Communication and sex effects in a five-person Prisoner's Dilemma game. *Journal of Personality and Social Psychology, 33,* 273–280.

Calhoun, J. B. (1962). Population density and social pathology. *Scientific American, 206,* 139–148.

Campbell, A. (1975). The American way of mating. Marriage si, children only mabye. *Psychology Today, 8,* 37–41.

Campbell, A. (1981). *The sense of well-being in America.* New York: McGraw-Hill.

Campbell, C. S. & Davis, J. D. (1974). Licking rate of rats reduced by intraduodenal and intraportal glucose infusion. *Physiology and Behavior, 12,* 357–365.

Campos, J. J., Hiatt, S., Ramsay, D., Henderson, C., & Svejda, M. (1978). The emergence of fear on the visual cliff. In M. Lewis & L. A. Rosenblum (Eds.), *The development of affect.* New York: Plenum. Pp. 149–182.

Campos, J. J., Langer, A., & Krowitz, A. (1970). Cardiac responses on the visual cliff in prelocomotor human infants. *Science, 170,* 196–197.

Cannon, W. B. (1927). The James-Lange theory of emotion: A critical examination and an alternative theory. *American Journal of Psychology, 39,* 106–124.

Cannon, W. B. (1939). *The wisdom of the body.* New York: Norton.

Cannon, W. B. (1942). Voodoo death. *American Anthropologist, 44,* 169–181.

Cantor, J. R., Zillman, D., & Bryant, J. (1975). Enhancement of experienced sexual arousal in response to erotic stimuli through misattribution of unrelated residual excitation. *Journal of Personality and Social Psychology, 32,* 69–75.

Cantor, J. R., Zillman, D., & Einsiedel, E. F. (1978). Female responses to provocation after exposure to aggressive and erotic films. *Communication Research, 5,* 395–411.

Cantor, N., & Mischel, W. (1977). Traits as prototypes: Effects on recognition and memory. *Journal of Personality and Social Psychology, 35,* 38–48.

Cantril, Hadley (Ed.). (1960). *The Morning Notes of Adlebert Ames, Jr.* New Brunswick, New Jersey: Rutgers University Press.

Caplan, G. (1964). *Principles of preventive psychiatry.* New York: Basic Books.

Carasco, M., Figueroa, J. G., & Willer, J. D. (1987). A test of the spatial frequency explanation of the Miller-Lyer illusion. *Perception.*

Carey, S., & Bartlett, E. (1983). Acquiring a single new word. *Papers and reports on child language development.* Palo Alto: Stanford University Committee on Linguistics.

Carlson, N. R. (1980). *Psyiology of behavior* (2nd ed.). Boston: Allyn & Bacon.

Carlson, N. R. (1985). *Physiology of Behavior* (3rd ed.) Boston: Allyn & Bacon.

Carmichael, L. (1927). A further study of the development of vertebrates experimentally removed from the influence of external stimulation. *Psychological Review, 34,* 34–47.

Carmichael, L. Hogan, H. P., & Walter, A. A. (1932). An experimental study of the effect of language on the representation of visually perceived form. *Journal of Experimental Psychology, 15,* 73–86.

Carpenter, P. A., & Just, M. A. (1977). Reading comprehension as the eyes see it. In M. A. Just & P. A. Carpenter (Eds.), *Cognitive processes in comprehension.* Hillsdale, N.J.: Erlbaum.

Carr, T. (1987). Perceiving visual language. In Boff, K., Kaufman, L., & Thomas, J. (Eds.), *Handbook of perception and human performance,* Vol. 2. New York: Wiley.

Carrington, P. (1977). *Freedom in meditation.* New York: Anchor Press/Doubleday: Doubleday Paperback, 1978.

Carrington, P. (1978). *Clinically standardized meditation (CSM) instructor's kit.* Kendall Park, N.J.. Pace Educational Systems.

Carrington, P., Collings, G. H., Benson, H., Robinson, H., Wood, L. W., Lehrer, P. M., Woolfolk, R. L., & Cole, J. W. (1980). The use of meditation-relaxation techniques for the management of stress in a working population. *Journal of Occupational Medicine, 22,* 221–231.

Cartwright, R. D. (1978, December). Happy ending for our dreams. *Psychology Today.*

Carver, R. P. (1972). Speed readers don't read: They skim. *Psychology Today.*

Case, R., Kurland, D. M., & Goldberg, J. (1982). Operational efficiency and the growth of short-term memory span. *Journal of Experimental Child Psychology, 33,* 386–404.

Casey, J. S., Bennett, I. F., & Lindley, C. J. (1960). Drug therapy in schizophrenia: A controlled study of the relative effectiveness of chlorpromazine, promazine, phenobarbital and placebo. *Archives of General Psychiatry, 2,* 210–220.

Cattell, J. M. (1890). Mental tests and measurements. *Mind, 15.*

Cattell, R. B. (1949). *The culture free intelligence test.* Champaign, Ill.: Institute for Personality and Ability Testing.

Cattell, R. B. (1950). *A systemic theoretical and factual study.* New York: McGraw-Hill.

Cattell, R. B. (1971). *Abilities; their structure, growth, and action.* Boston: Houghton, Mifflin.

Cattell, R. B., & Kline, P. (1937). *The scientific analysis of personality and motivation.* New York: Academic Press.

Ceci, S. J., Liker, J. K. (1986). A day at the races: A study of IQ, expertise, and cognitive complexity. *Journal of Experimental Psychology: General, 115,* 255–266.

Chafetz, M. E. (1979, May-June). Alcohol and alcoholism. *American Scientist.*

Chaikin, A. L., & Darley, J. M. (1973). Victim or perpetrator?: Defensive attribution of responsibility and the need for order and justice. *Journal of Personality and Social Psychology, 25,* 268–275.

Chapman, L. J. (1967). Illusory correlation in observational report. *Journal of Verbal Learning and Verbal Behavior, 6,* 151–155.

Chase, M. H., & Morales, F. R. (1983). Subthreshold excitatory activity and motoneuron discharge during REM sleep. *Science, 221,* 1195–1198.

Chase, W. G., & Simon, H. A. (1973). Perception in chess. *Cognitive Psychology, 4,* 55–81.

Cheng, P. W., & Holyoak, K. J. (1985). Pragmatic reasoning schemas. *Cognitive Psychology, 17,* 391–416.

Cheng, P. W., Holyoak, K. J., Nisbett, R. E., & Oliver, L. M. (1986). Pragmatic versus syntactic approaches to training deductive reasoning. *Cognitive Psychology, 18,* 293–328.

Cherlin, A. (1980). Postponing marriage: The influence of young women's work expectations. *Journal of Marriage and the Family, 42,* 355–365.

Chomsky, N. (1957). *Synactic structures.* The Hague: Mouton.

Chomsky, N. (1975). *Reflections on language.* New York: Pantheon.

Christian, J. J., Flyger, V., & Davis, D. E. (1960). Factors in mass mortality of a herd of Sika deer (Cerfus nippon). *Chesapeake Science, 1,* 79–95.

Cicero, T. J., Meyer, E. R., Bell, R. D. (1974). Effects of phenoxybenzamine on the narcotic withdrawal system in the rat. *Neuropharmacology, 13,* 601–607.

Cicero, T. J., Wilcox, C. E., Meyer, E. R. (1974). Effect of a-adrenergic blockers on naxolone-binding in brain. *Biochemical Pharmacology, 23,* 2349–2352.

Clark, F. V., & Clark, H. H. (1979). When nouns surface as verbs. *Language, 55,* 767–811.

Clark, H. H., & Gerrig, R. J. (1983). Understanding old words with new meanings. *Journal of Verbal Learning and Verbal Behavior, 22,* 591–608.

Clark, M. S. (1984). Record keeping in two types

of relationships. *Journal of Personality and Social Psychology*, 47, 549–557.

Clark, M. S., & Mills, J. (1979). Interpersonal attraction in exchange and communal relationships. *Journal of Personality and Social Psychology*, 37, 12–24.

Clarparede, E. (1911). La genèse de l'hypothese. *Arch. de Ps.*, 24, 1–154.

Cleary, P. D., & Mechanic, D. (1983). Sex differences in psychological distress among married people. *Journal of Health and Social Behavior*, 24, 111–121.

Cleary, T. A., Humphrey's, L. G., Kendrick, S. A., & Wesman, A. (1975). Educational uses of tests with disadvantaged students. *American Psychologist*, 30, 15–41.

Cleckley. H. (1976). *The mask of sanity* (5th ed.). St. Louis, Mo.: Mosby.

Cohen, A. R. (1962). An experiment on small rewards for discrepant compliance and attitude change. In J. W. Brehm & A. R. Cohen, *Explorations in cognitive dissonance*. New York: Wiley.

Cohen, D. B. (1979). *Sleep and dreaming: Origins, nature and functions*. Oxford: Pergamon Press.

Cohen, S., & Wills, T. A. (1985). Stress, social support, and the buffering hypothesis. *Psychological Bulletin*, 98, 310–357.

Cohen-Sandler, R., Berman, A. L., & King, R. A. (1982). Life stress and symptomatology: Determinants of suicidal behavior in children. *Journal of the American Academy of Child Psychiatry*, 21–2, 178–186.

Cole, J. O. (1964). Phenothiazine treatment in acute schizophrenia: Effectiveness. *Archives of General Psychiatry*, 10, 246–261.

Cole, M., Gay, J., Glick, J. A., & Sharp, D. W. (1971). The cultural context of learning and thinking. New York: Basic Books.

Cole, R., & Stokes, G. (1985). *Sex and the American teenager*. New York: Harper and Row, Colophon Books.

Coleman, J. C., Butcher, J. N., & Carson R. C. (1980). *Abnormal psychology and modern life*. (6th ed.). Glenview, Ill.: Scott, Foresman.

Coleman, J. C., Butcher, J. N., & Carson, R. C. (1984). *Abnormal psychology and modern life*. (7th ed.). Glenview, Ill.: Scot Foresman.

Collier, G., Hirsch, E. (1971). Reinforcing properties of spontaneous activity in the rat. *Journal of Comparative and Physiological Psychology*, 7, 155–160.

Collier, G., Hirsch, E., & Hamlin, P. (1972). The ecological determinants of reinforcement. *Journal of Physiology and Behavior*, 9, 705–716.

Collier, G., Hirsch, E., & Kanarek, R. (1977). The operant revisited in W. K. Honig & J. E. R. Staddor (Eds.), *Handbook of operant behavior*. Englewood Cliffs. N.J.: Prentice-Hall.

Collins, J. (1982). *Self-efficacy and ability in achievement behavior*. Paper presented at the meeting of the American Educational Research Association, New York.

Colt, E. W., Wardlaw, S. L., & Frantz, A. G. (1981). The effect of running on plasma β-endorphin. *Life Sciences*, 28, 1637–1640.

Coltheart, M., & Glick, M. J. (1974). Visual imagery: A case study. *Quarterly Journal of Experimental Psychology*, 26, 438–453.

Conger, J. J. (1977). *Adolescence and youth: Psychological development in a changing world* (2nd ed.). New York: Harper & Row.

Conrad, R. (1964). Acoustic confusions in immediate memory. *British Journal of Psychology*, 55, 75–84.

Cook, T. M., Novaco, R. W., & Sarason, I. G. (1980). *Generalized expectancy, life experience, and adaptations: Marine corps recruit training*. (AR-002). Seattle: University of Washington.

Cooper, J. (1980). Reducing fears and increasing assertiveness: The role of dissonance reduction. *Journal of Experimental Social Psychology*, 16, 199–213.

Cooper, M. J., & Aygen, M. M. (1979). A relaxation technique in the management of hypercholesterolemia. *Journal of Human Stress*, 5, 24–27.

Cooper, R., & Zubek, J. (1958). Effects of enriched and restricted early environments on the learning ability of bright and dull rats. *Canadian Journal of Psychology*, 12, 159–164.

Coppen, A. (1967). The biochemistry of affective disorders. *British Journal of Psychiatry*, 113, 1237–1264.

Corballis, M. C., & Beale, I. L. (1976). *The psychology of left and right*. Hillsdale, N.J.: Erlbaum.

Coren, S., & Porac, C. (1977). Fifty centuries of righthandedness: The historical record. *Science*, 298, 631–632.

Corkin, S., Cohen, N. J., Sullivan, E. V., Clegg, R. A., Rosen, T. J., & Ackerman, R. H. (1985). Analyses of global memory impairments of differant etiologies. In Olton, D. S. and Corkin, S. (Eds.), *Memory dysfunction*. New York: New York Academy of Sciences.

Cottrell, N., Wack, D., Sekerak, G., & Rittle, R. (1968). Social facilitation of dominant responses by the presence of an audience and the mere presence of others. *Journal of Personality and Social Psychology*, 9, 245–250.

Cottrell, R. S. (1968). A study of selected language factors associated with arithmetic achievement in third grade students. *Dissertation Abstracts International*, 28(10b), 4913–4914.

Craik, F. I. M., & Byrd, M. (1982). Aging and cognitive deficits: The role of attentional resources. In F. I. M. Craik and S. E. Thehub (eds.), *Aging and connitive processes*. New York: Plenum.

Craik, F. I. M., & Lockhart, R. S. (1972). Levels of processing: A framework for memory research. *Journal of Verbal Learning and Verbal Behavior*, 11, 671–684.

Craik, F. I. M., & Tulving, E. (1975). Depth of processing and the retention of words in episodic memory. *Journal of Experimental Psychology*, 104, 268–294.

Crawford, H. J. (1982). Hypnotizability, daydreaming styles, imagery vividness, and absorption: A multidimensional study. *Journal of Personality and Social Psychology*.

Crich, F., & Mitchison, G. (1983). The function of dream sleep. *Nature*, 304, 111–114.

Cronbach, L. J. (1960). *Essentials of psychological testing* (2nd ed). New York: Harper and Brothers.

Cronbach, L. J. (1984). *Essentials of psychological testing* (4th ed). New York: Harper & Row.

Crowe, R. R. (1974). An adoption study of antisocial personality. *Archives of General Psychiatry*, 34, 4690–4691.

Crowe, R. R. (1974). An adoption study of antisocial personality. *Archives of General Psychiatry*, 31, 785–791.

Crowley, R. M. (1984). "Unique individuality redeemed": Discussion. *Contemporary Psychoanalysis*, 20 (1), 33–36.

Daley, M., & Wilson, M. (1978). *Sex, evolution, and behavior*. Boston, Mass.: Duxbury Press.

Darley, J. M. & Fazio, R. H. (1980). Expectancy confirmation processes arising in the social interaction sequence. *American Psychologist*, 35, 867–881.

Darley, J. M., & Goethals, G. (1980). People's analyses of the causes of ability-linked performance. In L. Berkowitz (Ed.), *Advances in Experimental Social Psychology*, 13, New York: Academic Press.

Darley, J. M., & Gross, P. H. (1983). A hypothesis-confirming bias in labeling effects. *Journal of Personality and Social Psychology*, 44, 20–33.

Darley, J. M., & Latané, B. (1968). Bystander intervention in emergencies: Diffusion of responsibility. *Journal of Personality and Social Psychology*, 8, 377–383.

Dart, R. A. (1949). The predatory implemental technique of *Australopithecus*. *American Journal of Physical Antropology*, 7, 1–38.

Darwin, C. (1859). *On the origin of species by means of natural selection, or the preservation of favoured races in the struggle for life*. London: Murray.

Davenport, W. (1965). Sexual patterns and their regulation in a society of the Southwest Pacific. In F. A. Beach (Ed.), *Sex and behavior*. New York: Wiley.

Davis, J. D., Gallagher, R. J., & Ladlove, R. F. (1967). Food intake controlled by a blood factor. *Science*, 156, 1247.

Davis, M. S. (1968). Variations in patients' compliance with medical regimens: An empirical analysis of patterns of communication. *American Journal of Public Health*, 58, 274–288.

Davison, G., and Neale, J. (1982). *Abnormal psychology* (3rd ed.). New York: Wiley.

Davison, G. C., & Neale, J. M. (1986). *Abnormal psychology: An experimental clinical approach*, 4th ed. New York: Wiley.

Deese, J. (1967). Meaning and change of meaning. *American Psychologist*, 22, 631–651.

DeCasper, A. J., & Fifer, W. P. (1980). Of human bonding: Newborns prefer their mother's voice. *Science*, 208, 1174–1176.

Deci, E. L., & Ryan, R. M. (1985). *Intrinsic motivation and self-determination in human behavior*. New York: Plenum.

DeLongis, A., Coyne, J. C., Dakof, G., Folkman, S., & Lazarus, R. S. (1982). Relationship of daily hassles, uplifts, and major life events to health status. *Health Psychology*, 1, 119–136.

Dembroski, T. M., MacDougall, J. M., Herd, J. A., & Shields, J. L. (1979). Effects of level of challenge on pressor and heart rate responses in Type A and B subjects. *Journal of Applied Social Psychology*, 9, 209–228.

Dembroski, T. M., MacDougall, J. M. Williams, B., & Haney, T. L. (1985). Components of Type A, hostility, and anger. In: Relationship to angiographic findings. *Psychosomatic Medicine*, in press.

Dement, W. C. (1974). *Some must watch while some must sleep*. San Francisco: Freeman.

Dement, W. C., & Kleitman, M. (1957). The relation of eye movements during sleep to dream activity: An objective method for the study of dreaming. *Journal of Experimental Psychology*, 53, 339–346.

Denes, P. D., & Pinson, E. N. (1963). *The speech chain*. New York: Doubleday.

Dennis, W., & Dennis, M. G. (1940). The effects of cradling practices upon the onset of walking in Hopi children. *Journal of Genetic Psychology*, 56, 77–86.

Deutsch, J. A. (1960). *The structural basis of behavior*. Chicago: University of Chicago Press.

Deutsch, M., & Collins, M. E. (1951). *Interracial housing: A psychological evaluation of a social experiment*. Minneapolis: University of Minnesota Press.

Deutsch, M., & Gerard, H. B. (1955). A study of normative and informational social influences upon individual judgment. *Journal of Abnormal and Social Psychology*, 51, 629–636.

Deutsch, M., & Krauss, R. M. (1960). The effect of threat upon interpersonal bargaining. *Journal of Abnormal and Social Psychology*, 61, 181–189.

De Vore, I. (1979). *Sociobiology and the social sciences*. Chicago: Aldine Atherton.

Diagnostic and statistical manual of Mental Disorders, 3rd ed. (1980). Washington, D.C.: American Psychiatric Association.

Diamond, M. (1984). A love affair with the brain (A conversation). *Psychology Today, 18* (11), November, 62–73.

Dion, K. K., Berscheid, E., & Walster, E. (1972). What is beautiful is good. *Journal of Personality and Social Psychology, 24,* 285–290.

Diven, K. (1936). Certain determinants in the conditioning of anxiety reactions. *Journal of Psychology, 3,* 291–308.

Dohrenwend, B. S., & Dohrenwend, B. P. (Eds.). (1974). *Stressful life events: Their nature and effects.* New York: Wiley.

Dohrenwend, B. S., Krasnoff, L., Askenasy, A. R. & Dohrenwend, B. P. (1978). "Exemplification of a method for scaling life events: The PERI life events scale." *Journal of Health and Social Behavior, 19,* 205–229.

Dollard, J., Doob, L., Miller, N. E., Mower, O., & Sears, R. (1939). *Frustration and aggression.* New Haven: Conn.: Yale University Press.

Dollard, J., & Miller, N. E. (1950). *Personality and psychotherapy.* New York: McGraw-Hill.

Donnerstein, E., & Berkowitz, L. (1981). Victim reactions in aggressive erotic films as a factor in violence against women. *Journal of Personality and Social Psychology, 41,* 710–724.

Doob, A. N., & Wood, L. (1972). Catharsis and aggression: The effects of annoyance and retaliation on aggressive behavior. *Journal of Personality and Social Psychology, 22,* 156–162.

Dorow, R., Horowski, G., Paschelke, M. A., & Braestrup, C. (1983). *Lancet 1983, 11,* 98.

Doty, R. L., Shamon, P., Applebaum, S. L., Giberson, R., Sikorski, L., & Rosenberg, L. (1984). Smell identification ability: Changes with age. *Science, 226,* 1441–1442.

Douvan, E. A., & Adelson, J. (1966). *The adolescent experience.* New York: Wiley.

Dressler, D. M. (1973). Life adjustment of retired couples. *International Journal of Aging and Human Development, 4*(4), 335–349.

Dreyer, P. H. (1982). Sexuality during adolescence. In B. Wolman (Ed.), Handbook of Developmental Psychology. Englewood Cliffs, N.J.: Prentice-Hall.

DuBois, P. M. (1980). *The hospice way of death.* New York: Human Sciences Press.

Duncker, K. (1945). On problem-solving. *Psychological Monographs, 58,* 5(Whole No. 270).

Dupont, R. L. (1971). Profile of a heroin-addiction epidemic. *New England Journal of Medicine, 285*(6), 320–324.

Duval, S., & Wicklund, R. A. (1972). *A theory of objective self-awareness.* New York: Academic Press.

Dweck, C. S., & Goetz, T. E. (1978). Attributions and learned helplessness. In J. H. Harvey, W. Ickes, & R. F. Kidd (Eds.), *New directions in attribution research* (Vol. 2). New York: Wiley.

Eagly, A. H., & Carli, L. L. (1981). Sex of researcher and sex-typed communications as determinants of sex differences in influenceability: A meta-analysis of social influence studies. *Psychological Bulletin, 90,* 1–20.

Eagly, A. H., & Chaiken, S. (1975). An attribution analysis of the effect of communicator characteristics on opinion change: The case of communicator awareness. *Journal of Personality and Social Psychology, 32,* 136–144.

Easterbrooks, M. A., & Goldberg, W. A. (1985). Effects of early maternal employment on toddlers, mothers, and fathers. *Developmental Psychology, 21,* 774–783

Eastman, C. (1976). Behavioral formulations of depression. *Psychological Review, 83,* 277–291.

Ebbinghaus, H. (1885). *MEMORY: A contribution to experimental psychology* (H. A. Ruger & C. E. Bussenius, trans.). New York: Teachers College.

Eckerman, C. O., Whatley, J. L., & Kutz, S. L.

(1975). Growth of social play during the second year of life. *Developmental Psychology, 11,* 42–49.

Egeland, B., & Farber, E. A. (1984). Infant-mother attachment: Factors related to its development and changes over time. *Child Development, 55,* 753–771.

Egger, M. D., & Flynn, J. P. (1963). Effect of electrical stimulation of the amygdala on hypothalamically elicited attack behavior in cats. *Journal of Neurophysiology, 26,* 705–720.

Eimas, P., Siqueland, E. R., Jusczyk, P., & Vigorito, J. (1971). Speech perception in infants. *Science, 171,* 303–306.

Eisdorfer, C. (1972). Adaptation to loss of work. In Frances M. Carp (Ed.), *Retirement.* New York: Behavioral Publications.

Ekman, P., & Friesen, W. V. (1968). The repertoire of nonverbal behavior—categories, origins, usage and coding. *Semiotica, 1,* 49–98.

Ekman, P., & Friesen, W. V. (1971). Constants across cultures in the face and emotion. *Journal of Personality and Social Psychology, 17,* 124–129.

Ekman, P., & Friesen, W. V. (1975). *Unmasking the face.* Englewood Cliffs, N.J.: Prentice-Hall.

Ekman, P., Levenson, R. W. & Friesen, W. V. (1983). Autonomic nervous system activity distinguishes among emotions. *Science, 221,* 1208–1210.

Elder, G. H., Jr., (1974). *Children of the Great Depression.* Chicago: University of Chicago Press.

Elkind, D. (1967). Egocentrism in adolescents. *Child Development, 38,* 1025–1034.

Elkind, D. (1973). Giant in the nursery—Jean Piaget. In *Annual Editions: Readings in Psychology, '72–'73,* Guilford, Conn.: Dushkin Publishing Group.

Ellis, A. (1958). Rational psychotherapy. *Journal of Social Psychology, 59,* 35–49.

Ellis, A. (1962). *Reason and emotion in psychotherapy.* New York: Lyle Stuart.

Ellis, A. (1973). *Humanistic psychotherapy: the rational-emotive approach.* New York: Julian.

Ellis, A. (1975). *A new guide to rational living.* Englewood Cliffs, N.J.: Prentice-Hall.

Engle, B. T. (1960). Stimulus-response and individual-response specificity. *Archives of General Psychiatry, 2,* 305–313.

English, H. B. (1929). Three cases of the "conditioned fear response." *Journal of Abnormal and Social Psychology, 34,* 221–225.

Epstein, A. N., Fitzsimons, J. T., & Rolls, B. J. (1970). Drinking induced by injections of angiotensin into the brain of the rat. *Journal of Physiology* (London), *210,* 457–474.

Epstein, S. (1979). The stability of behavior: I. On predicting most of the people much of the time. *Journal of Personality and Social Psychology, 37,* 1097–1126.

Epstein, S. M. (1967). Toward a unified theory of anxiety. In B. A. Maher (Ed.), *Progress in experimental personality research* (Vol. 4). New York: Academic Press.

Erhardt, A. A., & Baker, S. (1974). Fetal androgens, human CNS differentiation, and behavioral sex differences. In R. C. Friedman, R. M. Richart, & K. L. VandeWiele (Eds.), *Sex differences in behavior.* New York: Wiley.

Erickson, M. F., Sroufe, L. A., & Egeland, B. (1985). The relationship between quality of attachment and behavior problems in preschool in a high-risk sample. In I. Bretherton & E. Waters (Eds.), Growing points of attachment theory and research. *Monographs of the Society for Research in Child Development, 50*(1–2, Serial No. 2·9).

Erikson, E. (1980). *Identity and the life cycle.* New York: Norton.

Erikson, E. H. (1959). Identity and the life cycle. *Psychological Issues, 1.*

Erikson, E. H. (1963). *Childhood and society.* New York: Norton.

Erikson, K. T. (1976). *Everything in its path: Destruction of community in the Buffalo Creek Flood.* New York: Simon & Schuster.

Ervin, S. (1964). Imitation and structural change in children's language. In E. Lenneberg (Ed.), *New directions in the study of language.* Cambridge, Mass.: MIT Press.

Evans, C. (1984). *Landscapes of the night: How and why we dream.* New York: Viking.

Evans, F. J. (1977). Hypnosis and sleep: The control of altered states of awareness. In W. E. Edmonston, Jr. (Ed.), Conceptual and investigative approaches to hypnosis and hypnotic phenomena. *Annals of The New York Academy of Sciences* (Vol. 296), 162–174.

Evans, G. W. (1979). Behavioral and physiological consequences of crowding in humans. *Journal of Applied Social Psychology, 9,* 27–46.

Eyferth, K. (1961). Leistungen verschiedner Gruppen von Besatzungskindern in Hamburg—Wechsler Intelligenztest für Kinder (HAWIK). *Archiv dür die gesamte Psychologie, 113,* 222–241.

Eysenk, H. J. (1952). The effects of psychotherapy: An evaluation. *Journal of Consulting Psychology, 16,* 319–324.

Eysenck, H. J. (1977). The case of Sir Cyril Burt. *Encounter, 48,* 19–24.

Fallon, A., and Rozin, P. (1985). Sex differences in perceptions of desirable body states. *Journal of Abnormal Psychology, 84,* 102–105.

Falmagne, J. C. (1986). Psychophysical measurement and theory. In Boff, K., Kaufman L., & Thomas, J. (Eds.), *Handbook of perception and human performance,* Vol. 1. New York: Wiley.

Fantz, R. L. (1963). Pattern vision in newborn infants. *Science, 140,* 296–297.

Farkas, G. M., & Rosen, R. C. (1976). Effect of alcohol on elicited male sexual response. *Journal of Studies on Alcohol, 37,* 265–272.

Farley, J., Richards, W., Ling, L., Liman, E., & Alkon, D. (1983). Membrane changes in a single photoreceptor cause associative learning in Hermissanda, *Science, 221,* 1201–1203.

Faust, M. S. (1960). Developmental maturity as a determinant in prestige of adolescent girls. *Child Development, 31,* 173–184.

Fazio, R. H. (in press, b). How do attitudes guide behavior? In R. M. Sorrentino & E. T. Higgins (Eds.), *The handbook of motivation and cognition: Foundations of social behavior.* New York: Guilford Press.

Fazio, R. H. (in press, a). On the power and functionality of attitudes: The role of attitude accessibility. In A. R. Pratkanis, S. J. Breckler, & A. G. Greenwald (Eds.), *Attitude structure and function.* Hillsdale, N.J.

Fazio, R. H., & Zanna, M. P. (1978). On the predictive validity of attitudes: The roles of direct experience and confidence. *Journal of Personality, 46,* 228–243.

Fazio, F. H., & Zanna, M. P. (1981). Direct experience and attitude-behavior consistency. In L. Berkowitz (Ed.), *Advances in experimental social psychology* (Vol. 14). New York: Academic Press.

Fazio, R. H., Zanna, M. P., & Cooper, J. (1977). Dissonance and self-perception. *Journal of Experimental Social Psychology, 13,* 464–479.

Fekken, G. C., & Holden, R. R. (1987). Assessing the person reliability of an individual MMPI protocol. *Journal of Personality Assessment, 51,* 123–132.

Feldman, M. W., & Lewontin, R. C. (1975). The heritability hand-up. *Science, 190,* 1163–1168.

Fennell, M. J. V., & Campbell, E. H. (1984). The cognitions questionnaire: Specific thinking errors

in depression. *British Journal of Clinical Psychology, 23*, 81–92.

Ferster, C. B., & Skinner, B. F. (1957). *Schedules of reinforcement.* Englewood Cliffs, N.J.: Prentice-Hall.

Feshbach, N. (1985). Chronic maternal stress and its assessment. In J. N. Butcher & C. D. Speilberger (Eds.), *Advances in personality assessment*, Vol. 5. Hillsdale, N.J.: Erlbaum.

Feshback, S., & Fraczek, A. (1979). *Aggression and behavior change: Biological and social processes.* New York: Praeger.

Feshback, S., & Singer, R. D. (1971). *Television and aggression.* San Francisco: Jossey-Bass.

Festinger, L. A. (1954). A theory of social comparison processes. *Human Relations, 7*, 117–140.

Festinger, L. (1957). *A theory of cognitive dissonance.* Evanston, Ill.: Row, Peterson.

Festinger, K., & Carlsmith, J. M. (1959). Cognitive consequences of forced compliance. *Journal of Abnormal and Social Psychology, 58*, 203–210.

Fiedler, F. E. (1967). *A theory of leadership effectiveness.* New York: McGraw-Hill.

Fiedler, F. E. (1972). Personality, motivational systems, and behavior of high and low LPC persons. *Human Relations, 25*, 391–412.

Field, D. (1981). Can preschool children really learn to conserve? *Child Development, 52*, 326–334.

Fish, B., Karabenick, S., & Heath, M (1978). The effects of observation on emotional arousal and affiliation. *Journal of Experimental Social Psychology, 14*, 251–265.

Fitzsimmons, J. T. (1972). Thirst. *Psychological Review, 52*, 468–561.

Flavell, J. H. (1963). *The developmental psychology of Jean Piaget.* Princeton, N.J.: Van Nostrand.

Flavell, J. H. (1978). Metacognitive development. In J. M. Scandura & C. J. Brainerd (Eds.), *Structural/process theories of complex human behavior.* Alphen a.d. Rijn, The Netherlands: Sijthoff & Noordhoff.

Flavell, J. H. (1985). *Cognitive development* (2nd ed.). Englewood Cliffs, N.J.: Prentice-Hall.

Flavell, J. H., Beach, D. R., & Chinsky, J. M. (1966). Spontaneous verbal rehearsal in memory task as a function of age. *Child Development, 37*, 283–299.

Flavell, J. H., Speer, J. R., Green, F. F., & August, D. L. (1981). The development of comprehension monitoring and knowledge about communication. *Monographs of the Society for Research in Child Development, 46* (5, Serial No. 192).

Fleishman, E. A. (1957). A leader behavior description for industry. In R. M. Stogdill & A. E. Coons (Eds.), *Leader behavior: Its description and measurement.* Columbus: Ohio State University, Bureau of Business Research.

Flotz, E. L., & Millett, F. E. (1964). Experimental psychosomatic disease states in monkeys. I. Peptic ulcer—"Executive monkeys." *Journal of Surgical Research, 4*, 445–453.

Foa, E., & Foa, V. (1976). Resource theory of social exchange. In J. Thibaut, J. Spence, & R. Carson (Eds.), *Contemporary trends in social psychology.* Morristown, N.J.: Social Learning Press.

Fodor, J. A. (1975). *The language of thought.* New York: Crowell.

Folkman, S. (1984). Personal control and stress and coping processes: A theoretical analysis. *Journal of Personality and Social Psychology 46*, 4, 839–852.

Folkman, S., & Lazarus, R. S. (1980). An analysis of coping in a middle-aged community sample. *Journal of Health and Social Behavior, 21*, 219–239.

Ford, C. W., & Beach, F. A. (1951). *Patterns of sexual behavior.* New York: Harper & Row.

Foulkes, D., Larson, J. D., Swanson, E. M., &

Rardin, M. (1969). Two studies of childhood dreaming. *American Journal of Orthopsychiatry, 39*, 627–643.

Freedman, D. X. (1977). Pharmacotherapy. In F. J. Braceland et al. (Eds.), *Year book of psychiatry and applied mental health.* Chicago: Year Book Medical Publishers.

Freedman, J. L. (1965). Long-term behavioral effects of cognitive dissonance. *Journal of Experimental Psychology, 1*, 145–155.

Freedman, J. L., Klevansky, S., & Ehrlich, P. (1971). The effect of crowding on human task performance. *Journal of Applied Social Psychology, 1*, 7–25.

Freedman, J. L., Levy, A. S., Buchanan, R. W., & Price, J. (1972). Crowding and human aggressiveness. *Journal of Experimental Social Psychology, 8*, 528–548.

Freedman, T. (1985). Effects of television violence on aggressiveness. *Psychological Bulletin, 96*, 227–246.

Freud, S. (1933). *New introductory lectures on psychoanalysis* (W. J. H. Sproutt, trans.). New York: Norton.

Freud, S. (1953). The interpretation of dreams. In J. Strachey (Ed. and trans.), *The standard edition of the complete psychological works.* London: Hogarth. (Originally published in 1900.)

Freud, S. (1955). Beyond the pleasure principle. In J. Strachey (Ed. and trans.), *The standard edition of the complete psychological works.* London: Hogarth. (Originally published in 1920.)

Freidhoff, A. J., & Van Winkle, E. (1962). Isolation and characterization of a compound from the urine of schizophrenics. *Nature, 194*, 897–898.

Friedlund, A. J., Ekman, P., & Oster, H. (1987). Facial expressions of emotion. In A. Siegman, & S. Feldstein (Eds.), *Nonverbal communication and behavior* (2nd ed.). Hillsdale, N.J.: Erlbaum.

Friedman, M. & Ulmer, D. (1984). *Treating type A behavior and your heart.* New York: Knopf.

Friedman, M. (Pathogenesis of coronary artery disease. New York: McGraw-Hill.

Friedman, S. (1972). Habituation and recovery of visual response in the alert human newborn. *Journal of Experimental Child Psychology, 13*, 339–349.

Fromkin, V. A. (1976). *Personal communication.*

Gallistel, C. R. (1983). Self-stimulation. In J. A. Deutsch (Ed.), *The Physiological Basis of Memory.* New York: Academic Press.

Galotti, K. M., Baron, J., & Sabini, J. P. (1986). Individual differences in syllogistic reasoning: Deduction rules or mental models? *Journal of Experimental Psychology: General*, in press.

Galton, F. (1983). *Inquiries into human faculty and its development.* London: Macmillan.

Gannon, L. (1981). The psychophysiology of psychosomatic disorders. In S. N. Haynes & L. Gannon (Eds.), *Psychosomatic disorders.* New York: Praeger.

Garcia, J., & Koelling, R. A. (1966). Relation of cues to consequence in avoidance learning. *Psychonomic Science, 4*, 123–124.

Gardner, H. (1982). *Developmental psychology* (2nd ed.). Boston: Little, Brown.

Gardner, R. A., & Gardner, B. T. (1969). Teaching sign language to a chimpanzee. *Science, 165*, 664–672.

Gardner, R. A., & Gardner B. T. (1980). Reply to Terrace. Personal communication.

Garfunkel, P., & Garner, D. (1982). *Anorexia nervosa: A multi-dimensional perspective.* New York: Brunner Mazel.

Gatchel, R., & Proctor, J. D. (1976). Physiological correlates of learned helplessness in man. *Journal of Abnormal Psychology, 85*, 27–34.

Gazzaniga, M. S. (1967). The split brain in man. *Scientific American, 217*(2), 24–29.

Gazzaniga, M. S. (1985). *The social brain: Discovering the networks of the mind.* New York: Basic Books.

Geen, R. G., & O'Neal, E. C. (1969). Activation of cue-elicited aggression by general arousal. *Journal of Personality and Social Psychology, 11*, 287–292.

Geen, R. G., & Stonner, D. (1971). Effects of aggressiveness habit strength on behavior in the presence of aggression-related stimuli. *Journal of Personality and Social Psychology, 17*, 149–153.

Geertz, C. (1980, July 24). Sociosexology. *New York Review of Books*, pp. 3–4.

Gelman, R. (1978). Cognitive development. In L. W. Porter & M. R. Rosenzweig (Eds.), *Annual Review of Psychology* (Vol. 29), Palo Alto, Calif.: Annual Reviews.

Gelman, R., & Gallistel, C. R. (1978). *The child's understanding of number.* Cambridge, Mass.: Harvard University Press.

Gerard, H. B., & Rabbie, J. M. (1961). Fear and social comparison. *Journal of Abnormal and Social Psychology, 62*, 586–592.

Gerbner, G., & Gross, L. (1976). Living with television: The violence profile. *Journal of Communications, 26*, 173–199.

Gerbner, G., Gross, L., Signorielli, N., Morgan, M., & Jackson-Beeck, M. (1979). The demonstration of power: Violence profile No. 10. *Journal of Communication, 29*, 177–196.

Gesell, A. L. (1941). *Wolf child and human child, being a narrative interpretation of the life history of Kamala, the wolf girl; based on the diary account of a child who was reared by a wolf and who then lived for nine years in the orphanage of Midnapore, in the province of Bengal, India.* New York: Harper & Brothers.

Gesell, A. L., & Thompson, H. (1929). Learning and growth in identical twins: An experimental study by the method of co-twin control. *Genetic Psychology Monographs, Vol 6*(1).

Geshwind, N. (1979). Specializations of the human brain. *Scientific American, 241*(3), 180–199.

Gibbs, J., Young, R. C., & Smith, G. P. (1973). Cholecystokinin decreases food intake in rats. *Journal of Comparative and Physiological Psychology, 84*, 488–495.

Gibbs, R. W., Jr. (1986). On the psycholinguistics of sarcasm. *Journal of Experimental Psychological: General, 115*, 3–15.

Gibbs, R. W., Jr., & Delaney, S. M. (1987). Pragmatic factors in making and understanding promises. *Discourse Processes, 10*, 107–126.

Gibson, J. J. (1966). *The senses considered as preceptual systems.* Boston: Houghton Mifflin.

Gibson, J. J. (1971). The information available in pictures. *Viewpoints, 47*, 73–95.

Gifford, S., Murawski, B. J., Kline, N. S., & Sachar, E. J. (1976–1977). An unusual adverse reaction to self-medication with prednisone: A irration crime during a fugue-state. *International Journal of Psychiatry in Medicine, 7*(2), 97–122.

Ginsburg, A. P. (1978). Visual information processing based on spatial constrained by biological data. Doctoral dissertation. Aerospace Medical Research Laboratory, Wright Patterson Air Force Base, Ohio.

Gladue, B. A., Green, R., & Hellman, R. E. (1984). Neuroendocrine response to estrogen and sexual orientation. *Science, 225*, 1496–1499.

Glamzer, F. D. (1976). Determinants of a positive attitude toward retirement. *Journal of Gerontology, 31*(1), 104–107.

Glass, A. J. (1953). Psychotherapy in the combat zone. In *Symposium on stress.* Washington, D.C.: Army Medical Service Graduate School.

Glass, D. (1977). Behavior patterns, stress and coronary disease. Hillside, NJ. Erlbaum.

Glass, D., & Singer, J. (1972). *Urban stress.* New York: Academic Press.

Gleason, J. B., & Weintraub, S. (1978). Input language and the acquisition of communicative competence. In K. Nelson (Ed.), *Children's language* (Vol. 1). New York: Gardner Press.

Glucksberg, S. (1962). The influence of strength of drive on functional fixedness and perceptual recognition. *Journal of Experimental Psychology, 63,* 36–41.

Glucksberg, S. (1984). Commentary: The functional equivalence of common and multiple codes. *Journal of Verbal Learning and Verbal Behavior, 23,* 100–104.

Glucksberg, S., & Danks, J. H. (1975). *Experimental psycholinguistics.* Hillsdale, N.J.: Erlbaum.

Glucksberg, S., Krauss, R. M., & Weisberg, R. (1966). Referential communication in nursery school children. Method and some preliminary findings. *Journal of Experimental Child Psychology, 3,* 333–342.

Glucksberg, S., & Weisberg, R. W. (1966). Verbal behavior and problem solving: Some effects of labelling in a functional fixedness problem. *Journal of Experimental Psychology, 71,* 659–64.

Glueck, B. C., & Stroebel, C. F. (1975). Biofeedback and meditation in the treatment of psychiatric illness. *Comprehensive Psychiatry, 16,* 302–321.

Goddard, H. H. (1917). Mental tests and the immigrant. *Journal of Delinquency, 2,* 243–277,.

Goddard, H. H. (1920). *Human efficiency and levels of intelligence.* Princeton, N.J.: Princeton University Press.

Gold, M. & Petronio, R. J. (1980). Delinquent behavior in adolescence. In J. Adelson (ed.), *Handbook of adolescent psychology.* New York: Wiley. Pp. 495–535.

Goldband, S., Katkin, E. S., & Morrell, M. A. (1979). Personality and cardiovascular disorder: Steps toward demystification. In I. G. Sarason & C. D. Spielberger (Eds.), *Stress and anxiety* (Vol. 6). New York: Wiley.

Goldfarb, W. (1944). Infant-rearing as a factor in foster home placement. *American Journal of Orthopsychiatry, 14,* 162–167.

Goldfarb, W. (1945). Effects of psychological deprivation in infancy and subsequent stimulation. *American Journal of Psychiatry, 102,* 18–33.

Goldfried, M. R., & Davison, G. C. (1976). *Clinical behavior therapy.* New York: Holt, Rinehart & Winston.

Goldhaber, S. (1986). From education: Strategic-systemic therapy undercover. *Journal of Strategic-Systemic Therapy, 5*(1–2) a.46–a.49.

Goldstein, K. (1939). *The organism, a holistic approach to biology derived from pathological data in man.* New York: American Book.

Goode, E. (1969). Marijuana and the politics of reality. *Journal of Health and Social Behavior, 10,* 83–94.

Goodenough, D. R. (1978). Dream recall: History and current status of the field. In A. M. Arkin, J. S. Antrobus, & S. J. Ellman, *The mind in sleep: Psychology and psychophysiology.* New York: Halsted.

Goodwin, D. W., Schulsinger, F., Hermansen, L., Guze, S. B., & Winokur, G. (1973). Alcohol problems in adoptees raised apart from alcoholic biological parents. *Archives of General Psychiatry, 28,* 238–243.

Gordon, E. S. (1960). Nonesterified fatty acids in the blood of obese and lean subjects. *American Journal of Clinical Nutrition, 8,* 704–747.

Gotlib, I. H., & Meltzer, S. J. (1987). Depression and the perception of social skill in dyadic interaction. *Cognitive Therapy & Research, 11,* 41–53.

Gould, R. (1974, March). Adult life stages: Growth toward self-tolerance. *Psychology Today,* pp. 74–78.

Gould, R. L. (1978). *Transformations.* New York: Simon & Schuster.

Gould, S. J. (1981). *The mismeasure of man.* New York: Norton.

Gove, W. R. (1975). *The labelling of deviance: Evaluating a perspective.* New York: Wiley.

Goy, R. W. (1968). Organizing effects of androgen on the behavior of rhesus monkeys. In R. P. Michael (Ed.), *Endocrinology and human behavior.* London: Oxford University Press.

Graf, P., Squire, L. R., & Mandler, G. (1984). The information that amnesiac patients do not forget. *Journal of Experimental Psychology: Learning, Memory, and Cognition, 10,* 164–178.

Granrud, C. E., Yonas, A., & Pettersen, L. (1984). A comparison of monocular and binocular depth perception in 5- and 7-month-old infants. *Journal of Experimental Child Psychology, 38,* 19–32.

Gray, S., & Klaus, R. A. (1970). The early training project: A seventh year report. *Child Development, 41,* 909–924.

Green, D. M., & Swets, J. A. (1966). *Signal detection theory and psychophysics.* New York: Wiley.

Greenbaum, R. R. (1984). A study of range and flexibility of achieving styles in relation to ego development. *Dissertation Abstracts International, 44* (8a). 2415.

Greer, S. (1964). Study of parental loss in neurotics and sociopaths. *Archives of Social Psychiatry, 11,* 177–180.

Gregory, R. L. (1973). *Eye and brain* (2nd ed.). New York: World University Library.

Grice, G. R. (1948). The relation of secondary reinforcement to delayed reward in visual discrimination learning. *Journal of Experimental Psychology, 38,* 1–16.

Griffitt, W., & Veitch, R. (1974). Preacquaintance attitude similarity and attraction revisited: Ten days in a fall-out shelter. *Sociometry, 37,* 163–173.

Grings, W. W., & Dawson, M. E. (1978). *Emotions and bodily responses.* New York: Academic Press.

Guildford, J. P., & Hoepfner, R. (1971). *The analysis of intelligence.* New York: McGraw-Hill.

Guilford, J. P. (1982). Cognitive psychology's ambiguities: Some suggested remedies. *Psychological Review, 89,* 48–59.

Gutmann, D. (1977). The cross-cultural perspective: Notes toward a comparative psychology of aging. In J. E. Birren & K. W. Schaie (Eds.), *Handbook of the psychology of aging.* New York: Van Nostrand Reinhold.

Guzman, A. (1969). Decomposition of a visual scene into three-dimensional bodies. (1969). In A. Grasselli (Ed.), *Automatic interpretation and classification of images.* New York: Academic Press.

Haber, R. N. (1983). The impending demise of the icon: A critique of the concept of iconic storage in visual information processing. *The Behavioral and Brain Sciences, 6,* 1–54.

Hall, E. T. (1966). *The hidden dimension.* New York: Doubleday.

Hall, G. S. (1904). *Adolescence.* New York: Appleton.

Halpin, A. W., & Winer, B. J. (1957). A factorial study of the leader behavior descriptions. In R. R. Stodgill & A. E. Coons (Eds.), *Leader behavior: Its description and measurement.* Columbus: Ohio State University, Bureau of Business Research.

Hamann, J. R. (1956). Panel discussion. American Management Association. *General Management Service,* No. 182, pp. 21–23.

Hamilton, E. W., & Abramson, L. Y. (1983). Cognitive patterns and major depressive disorder: A longitudinal study in hospital setting. *Journal of Abnormal Psychology, 92,* 173–184.

Harlow, H. F. (1949). The formation of learning sets. *Psychological Review, 56,* 51–65.

Harlow, H. F. (1959, July). Love in infant monkeys. *Scientific American Psychologist, 17,* 1–9.

Harlow, H. F. (1971). *Learning to love.* San Francisco: Albion.

Harlow, H. F., Harlow, M. K., & Meyer, D. R. (1950). Learning motivated by a manipulation drive. *Journal of Experimental Psychology, 49,* 228–234.

Harrell, T. W., & Harrell, M. S. (1945). Army General Classification Test scores for civilian occupations. *Educational and Psychological Measurement, 5,* 229–239.

Harter, S. (1978). Effectance motivation reconsidered. *Human Development, 21,* 34–64.

Hartmann, F. (1979). Three spines on a stickleback. *Natural History, 88*(10), 32–35.

Hartshorne, H., & May, M. A. (1928). *Studies in the nature of character: Studies in deceit.* New York: Macmillan.

Hathaway, S. R., & McKinley, J. C. (1951). *The MMPI Manual,* New York: The Psychological Corporation; revised 1967.

Hauri, P. (1977). *The sleep disorders.* Kalamazoo, Mich.: UpJohn.

Hayes, C. (1951). *The ape in our house.* New York: Harper & Row.

Hearnshaw, L. S. (1979). *Cyril Burt: Psychologist.* Ithaca, N.Y.: Cornell University Press.

Hebb, D. O. (1946). On the nature of fear. *Psychological Review, 53,* 259–276.

Heibeck, T. H., & Markman, E. M. (1987). Word learning in children: An examination of fast mapping. *Child Development,* in press.

Heidbreder, E. (1947). The attainment of concepts: III. The problem. *Journal of Psychology, 24,* 93–138.

Heider, F. (1946). Attitudes and cognitive organization. *Journal of Psychology, 21,* 107–112.

Heinicke, C. M. (1973). Parental deprivation in early childhood: A predisposition to later depression? In J. P. Scott & E. C. Senay (Eds.), *Separation and depression: Clinical and research aspects.* Washington, D.C. American Association for the Advancement of Sciences.

Held, R., & White, B. (1959). Sensory deprivation and visual speed: An analysis. *Science, 130,* 860–861.

Helmholtz, H. von. (1962). *Treatise on physiological optics* (J. P. C. Southall, trans.). New York: Dover. (This translation originally published in 1925.)

Helson, H. (1964). *Adaptation-level theory.* New York: Harper & Row.

Helson, R., Mitchell, V., & Moane, G. (1984). Personality and patterns of adherence and nonadherence to the social clock. *Journal of Personality and Social Psychology, 46,* 1079–1097.

Henderson, J. B., Hall, S. M., & Lipton, H. L. (1979). Changing self-destructive behaviors. In G. C. Stone, F. Cohen, & N. E. Adler (Eds.), *Health psychology: A handbook.* San Francisco: Jossey-Bass.

Henry, J. P., & Cassel, J. C. (1969). Psychosocial factors in essential hypertension. *Journal of Epidemiology, 90*(3), 171–200.

Herman, C. P., & Mack, D. (1975). Restrained and unrestrained eating. *Journal of Personality, 43,* 647–660.

Herman, C. P., & Polivy, J. (1975). Anxiety, restraint, and eating behavior. *Journal of Abnormal Psychology, 84,* 666–672.

Herrnstein, R. J. (1973). *IQ in the meritocracy.* Boston: Atlantic Monthly Press.

Herrnstein, R. J., & Hineline, P. N. (1966). Negative reinforcement as shock frequency reduction.

Journal of Experimental Analysis of Behavior, 9, 421–430.

Hersen, M. (1976). Token economies in institutional settings. *Journal of Nervous and Mental Disease, 162,* 206–211.

Hess, E. W. (1959). Two conditions limiting critical age for imprinting. *Journal of Comparative and Physiological Psychology, 52,* 515–518.

Hibscher, J. A., & Herman, C. P. (1977). Obesity, dieting, and the expression of "obese" characteristics. *Journal of Comparative and Physiological Psychology, 91,* 374–380.

Higgins, A. T., & Turnure, J. E. (1984). Distractibility and concentration of attention in children's development. *Child Development, 55,* 1799–1810.

Higgins, E. T., Rholes, W. S., & Jones, C. R. (1977). Category accessibility and impression formation. *Journal of Experimental Social Psychology, 13,* 141–154.

Hilgard, E. R. (1975). Hypnosis. *Annual Review of Psychology, 26,* 19–44.

Hilgard, E. R. (1977). The problem of divided consciousness. A neodissociation interpretation. In W. E. Edmonston, Jr. (Ed.), *Conceptual and investigative approaches to hypnosis and hypnotic phenomena. Annals of the New York Academy of Sciences* (Vol. 296), 48–59.

Hindley, C. B., & Owen, C. F. (1978). The extent of individual changes in I.Q. for ages between 6 months and 17 years, in a British longitudinal sample. *Journal of Child Psychology and Psychiatry, 19,* 329–350.

Hiroto, D. S., & Seligman, M. E. P. (1975). Generality of learned helplessness in man. *Journal of Personality and Social Psychology, 31,* 311–327.

Hochberg, J. (1978). *Perception* (2nd ed.). Englewood Cliffs, N.J.: Prentice-Hall.

Hoebel, B. G. (1971). Feeding: Neural control of intake. In V. E. Hall, A. C. Giese, & R. Sonnenschein (Eds.), *Annual Review of Physiology, 33.*

Hoffman, H. S. (1978). Experimental analysis of imprinting and its behavioral effects. In G. Bower (Ed.), *The psychology of learning and motivation* (Vol. 12). New York: Academic Press.

Hoffman, M. L. (1980). Fostering moral development. In M. Johnson (Ed.), *Toward adolescence: The middle school years, 79th yearbook nsst.* Chicago: University of Chicago Press.

Hohmann, G. W. (1966). Some effects of spinal cord lesions on experienced emotional feelings. *Psychophysiology, 3,* 143–156.

Hokanson, J., DeGood, D. E., Forrest, M., & Britton, J. (1971). Availability of avoidance behaviors in modulating vascular stress responses. *Journal of Personality and Social Psychology, 19,* 60–68.

Holden, C. (1976). Hospices: For the dying, relief from pain and fear. *Science, 193,* 389–391.

Holden, C. (1987). Creativity and the troubled mind. *Psychology Today, 21*(4), 9–10.

Holden, C. (1987). Nimh finds a case of "serious misconduct." *Science, 235,* 1566–1567.

Hollander, E. P. (1958). Conformity, status and idiosyncrasy credit. *Psychological Review, 65,* 117–127.

Hollander, E. P. (1960). Competence and conformity in the acceptance of influence. *Journal of Abnormal and Social Psychology, 61,* 361–365.

Hollander, H. E., & Turner, F. D. (1985). Characteristics of incarcerated delinquents: Relationship between developmental disorders, environmental and family factors, and patterns of offense and recidivism. *Journal of American Academy of Child Psychology, 24,* 221–226.

Holle, M., & Stevens, K. N. (1962). Speech recognition: A model and program for research. *IRE Transactions on Information Theory, IT-8,* 155–159.

Holmes, D. S. (1985). To meditate or not? The answer is rest. *American Psychologist, 40,* 728–731.

Holmes, T. H. (1979). Development and application of a quantitative measure of life change magnitude. In J. E. Barrett (Ed.), *Stress and mental disorder.* New York: Raven.

Holmes, T. H., & Masuda, M. (1974). Life change and illness susceptibility in B. S. Dohrenwend & B. P. Dohrenwend (Eds.), *Stressful life events: Their nature and effects.* New York: Wiley

Holmes, T. H., & Rahe, R. H. (1967). The social readjustment rating scale. *Journal of Psychosomatic Research, 11,* 213–218.

Honsberger, R. W., & Wilson, A. F. (1973). Transcendental meditation in treating asthma. *Respiratory Therapy: The Journal of Inhalation Technology, 3,* 79–80.

Honzik, M. P., McFarlane, J. W., & Allen, L. (1948). The stability of mental test performance between two and eighteen years. *Journal of Experimental Education, 17,* 309–334.

Horn, J. L. (1968). Organization of abilities and the development of intelligence. *Psychological Review, 75,* 242–259.

Horn, J. M., Loehlin, J. C., & Willerman, L. (1979). Intellectual resemblance among adoptive and biological relatives. The Texas Adoption Project. *Behavior Genetics, 9,* 177–208.

Hough, R. L., Fairbank, D. T., & Garcia, A. M. (1976). Problems in the ratio measurement of life stress. *Journal of Health and Social Behavior, 17,* 70–82.

House, J. S. (1981). *Work stress and social support.* Reading, Mass.: Addison-Wesley.

Houston, J. P., & Mednick, S. A. (1963). Creativity and the need for novelty. *Journal of Abnormal and Social Psychology, 66,* 137–141.

Hovland, C. I. (1937). The generalization of conditioned responses: I. The sensory generalization of conditioned responses with varying frequencies of tone. *Journal of General Psychology, 17,* 125–148.

Hovland, C. I., Janis, I. L., & Kelley, H. H. (1953). *Communication and persuasion.* New Haven: Yale University Press.

Hovland, C. I., & Janis, I. L. (1959). *Personality and persuasibility.* New Haven, Conn.: Yale University Press.

Hovland, C. I., Lumsdaine, A. A., & Sheffield, F. D. (1949). *Experiments on mass communication.* Princeton, N.J.: Princeton University Press.

Hovland, C. I., & Mandell, W. (1952). An experimental comparison of conclusion drawing by the communicator and by the audience. *Journal of Abnormal and Social Psychology, 47,* 581–588

Hovland, C. I., & Weiss, W. (1951). The influence of source credibility on communication effectiveness. *Public Opinion Quarterly, 15,* 635–650.

Hsu, L. G. (1986). The treatment of anorexia nervosa. *American Journal of Psychiatry, 143,* 573–581.

Huesmann, L. R. (1982). Television violence and aggressive behavior. In D. Pearl & L. Bouthilet (Eds.), *Television and behavior: Ten years of scientific progress and implications for the 80's.* Washington, D.C.: Superintendent of Documents, U.S. Government Printing Office.

Hughes, J., Smith, T. W., Kosterlitz, H. W., Fothergill, L. A., Morgan, B. A., & Morris, H. R. (1975). Identification of two related pentapeptides from the brain with the potent opiate agonist activity. *Nature, 258,* 577–579.

Hull, C. L. (1943). *Principles of behavior.* New York: Appleton-Century-Crofts.

Hunt, E., & Love, T. (1972). How good can memory be? In A. N. Melton & E. Martin (Eds.), *Coding processes in human memory.* Washington, D.C.: Winston Wiley

Hunt, J. McV. (1965). Intrinsic motivation and its role in psychological development. In D. Levine

(Ed.), *Nebraska Symposium on Motivation, 1965.* Lincoln, Neb.: University of Nebraska Press.

Hunt, M. (1974). *Sexual behavior in the 70s.* Chicago: Playboy.

Hurvich, L. M. (1978). Two decades of opponent processes. In F. W. Billmeyer, Jr. & G. Wyszecki (Eds.), *Color 77.* Bristol, Eng.: Adam Hilger.

Hurvich, L. M., & Jameson, D. (1957). An opponent-process theory of color vision. *Psychological Review, 64,* 384–404.

Hurvich, L. M., & Jameson, D. (1974, February). Opponent process as a model of neural organization. *American Psychologist,* 88–102.

Hyde, J. S. (1979). *Understanding human sexuality.* New York: McGraw-Hill.

Inhelder, B., & Piaget, J. (1958). *The growth of logical thinking from childhood to adolescence.* New York: Basic Books.

Isen, A. M., Shalker, T., Clark, M., & Karp, L. (1978). Affect, accessibility of material in memory, and behavior: A cognitive loop? *Journal of Personality and Social Psychology, 36,* 1–12.

Iverson, L. L. (1979). The chemistry of the brain. *Scientific American, 241*(3), 134–149.

Jacobs, P. A., Branton, M., & Melville, M. M. (1965). Aggressive behavior, mental abnormality, and the XYY male. *Nature, 208,* 1351–1352.

Jacobs, R. C., & Campbell, D. T. (1961). The perpetuation of an arbitrary tradition through several generations of a laboratory microculture. *Journal of Abnormal and Social Psychology, 62,* 649–658.

Jacobsen, E. (1932). The electrophysiology of mental activities. *American Journal of Psychology, 44,* 677–694.

Jacquet, Y. F., & Marks, N. (1976). The C-Fragments of β-lipotropin: An indogenous neuroleptic or antiphychotogen. *Science, 194,* 632–635.

Jakubczak, L. F., & Walters, R. H. (1959). Suggestibility as dependency behavior. *Journal of Abnormal and Social Psychology, 59,* 102–107.

James, W. (1890). *Principles of psychology.* New York: Holt.

Janis, I. L. (1982). *Groupthink* (2nd ed.). Boston: Houghton Mifflin.

Janis, I. L., & Field, P. B. (1959). Sex differences and personality factors related to persuasibility. In I. L. Janis et al. (Eds.), *Personality and persuasibility.* New Haven, Conn.: Yale University Press.

Janoff-Bulman, R. (1979). Characterological versus behavioral self-blame: Inquires into depression and rape. *Journal of Personality and Social Psychology, 37,* 1798–1809.

Janoff-Bulman, R., & Frieze, I. H. (1983). A theoretical perspective for understanding reactions to victimization. *Journal of Social Issues, 39*(2), 1–17.

Jarvella, R. J. (1971). Syntactic processing of connected speech. *Journal of Verbal Learning and Verbal Behavior, 10,* 409–416.

Jeddi, E. (1970). Confort du contact et thermo-regulation comportementale. *Physiology and Behavior, 5,* 1487–1493.

Jemmott, J. B., III, Borysenko, J. Z., Borysenko, M., McClelland, D. C., Chapman, R., Meyer, D., & Benson, H. (1983). Academic stress, power motivation, and decrease in salivary secretory immunoglobulin A secretion rate. *Lancet, 1,* 1400–1402.

Jemmott, J. B., III, & Locke, S. E. (1984). Psychosocial factors, immunologic mediation, and human susceptibility to infectious diseases: How much do we know? *Psychological Bulletin, 95,* 78–108.

Jencks, C. (1972). *Inequality.* New York: Basic Books.

Jensen, A. R. (1969). How much can we boost IQ and scholastic achievement? *Harvard Educational Review, 39,* 1–123.

Jensen, A. R. (1972). Sir Cyril Burt (obituary). *Psychometrika, 37*, 115–117.

Jensen, A. R. (1976, December 9). Heredity and intelligence: Sir Cyril Burt's findings. Letter to the *London Times*, p. 11.

Jensen, A. R. (1980). *Bias in mental testing*. New York: Free Press.

Jensen, A. R. (1982). Level I/Level II: Factors or categories? *Journal of Educational Psychology, 39*, 404–417.

Jessor, R., & Jessor, S. L. (1975). The transition from virginity to non-virginity among youth: A social-psychological study over time. *Developmental Psychology, 11*, 473–484.

Johnson, W. G. (1971). The effect of prior-taste and food visibility on the food-directed instrumental performance of obese individuals. Unpublished doctoral dissertation, Catholic University of America, 1970. Cited in S. Schachter, Some extraordinary facts about obese humans and rats. *American Psychologist, 26*, 129–144.

Johnson-Laird, P. N. (1983). *Mental models*. Cambridge, Mass.: Harvard University Press.

Johnson-Laird, P. N., & Wason, P. C. (1977). A theoretical analysis of insight in a reasoning task. In P. N. Johnson-Laird & P. C. Wason (Eds.), *Thinking: Readings in cognitive science*. Cambridge: Cambridge University Press.

Johnston, L. D., O'Malley, P. M., & Bachman, J. G. (1986). *Drug use among American high school students, college students, and other young adults*. Rockville, Md.: National Institute on Drug Abuse. DHHS Pub. No. ADM 86–1450.

Jonah, B. A., & Grant, B. A. (1985). Long-term effectiveness of selective traffic enforcement programs for increasing seat belt use. *Journal of Applied Psychology, 70*(2), 257–263.

Jones, E. (1957). How to tell your friends from geniuses. *Saturday Review of Literature, 40*, 9–11.

Jones, E. E. (1979). The rocky road from act to dispositions. *American Psychologist, 34*, 107–117.

Jones, E. E., & Berglas, S. (1978). Control of attributions about the self through self-handicapping strategies: The appeal of alcohol and the role of underachievement. *Personality and Social Psychology Bulletin, 4*(2), 200–206.

Jones, E. E., & Davis, K. E. (1965). From acts to dispositions. The attribution process in person perception. In L. Berkowitz (Ed.), *Advances in experimental social psychology* (Vol. 2). New York: Academic Press.

Jones, H. C., & Lovinger, P. W. (1985). *The marijuana question and science's search for an answer*. New York: Dodd, Mead.

Jones, H. E., & Conrad, H. S. (1933). The growth and decline of intelligence: A study of a homogeneous group between the ages of ten and sixty. *Genetic Psychology Monographs, 13*, 223–298.

Jones, M. C. (1958). A study of socialization patterns at the high school level. *Journal of Genetic Psychology, 92*, 87–111.

Jones, M. C., & Bayley, N. (1950). Physical maturing among boys as related to behavior. *Journal of Educational Psychology, 41*, 129–148.

Jones, M. C., & Mussen, P. H. (1958). Self-conceptions, motivations and interpersonal attitudes of early and late maturing girls. *Child Development, 29*, 491–501.

Jourard, S. M. (1968). *Disclosing man to himself*. New York: Van Nostrand.

Juel-Nielsen, N. (1965). Individual and environment: A psychiatric-psychological investigation of monozygous twins reared apart. *Acta psychiatrica et neurologica Scandinavica* (Monograph Supplement, 183).

Just, M. A., & Carpenter, P. A. (1980). A theory of reading: From eye fixations to comprehension. *Psychological Review, 87*(4), 329–354.

Just, M. A., & Carpenter, P. A. (1984). Using eye fixations to study reading comprehension. In D. E. Kieras & M. A. Just (Eds.), *New Methods in Reading Comprehension Research*. Hillsdale, N.J.: Earlbaum Assoc.

Just, M. A., & Carpenter, P. A. (1987). *The psychology of reading and language comprehension*. New York: Allyn and Bacon.

Kahn, E., & Fisher, C. (1976). REM sleep and sexuality in the aged. Presented at the Seventh Annual Scientific Meeting of the Boston Society for Gerontologic Psychiatry.

Kahn, R. L. (1958). Human relations on the shop floor. In E. M. Hugh-Jones (Ed.), *Human relations in modern management*. Amsterdam: North Holland Publishing Co.

Kahneman, D., Slovic, P., & Tversky, A. (Eds.) (1982). *Judgment under uncertainty: Heuristics and biases*. Cambridge, Mass.: Cambridge University Press.

Kahneman, D., & Tversky, A. (1982). The psychology of preferences. *Scientific American, 246*, 160–173.

Kalish, R. A. (1982). *Late adulthood: Perpsectives on human development*. Monterey, Calif.: Brooks/Cole.

Kamin, L. J. (1956). The effects of termination of the CS and avoidance of the US on avoidance learning. *Journal of Comparative and Physiological Psychology, 49*, 420–424.

Kamin, L. J. (1969). Predictability, surprise, attenion, and conditioning. In B. Campbell & R. Church (Eds.). *Punishment and aversive behavior*. New York: Appleton-Century-Crofts.

Kamin, L. J. (1974). *The science and politics of IQ*. Hillsdale, N.J.: Erlbaum.

Kandel, D. (1973). Adolescent marijuana use: Role of parents and peers. *Science, 181*, 1067–1070.

Kanner, A. D., Coyne, J. C., Schaeger, C., & Lazarus, R. S. (1981). Comparison of two models of stress measurement: Daily hassles and uplifts versus major life events. *Journal of Behavioral Medicine, 4*, 1–39.

Kanter, J. F., & Zelnik, M. (1972). Sexual experience of young unmarried women in the United States. *Family Planning Perspectives, 4*(4), 9–18.

Kaplan, H. B. (Ed.) (1983). *Psychosocial stress: Trends in theory and research*. New York: Academic.

Karaz, V., & Perlman, D. (1975). Attribution at the wire: Consistency and outcome finish strong. *Journal of Experimental and Social Psychology, 11*, 470–477.

Kase, S. V., & Cobb, S. (1970). Blood pressure changes in men undergoing job loss: A preliminary report. *Psychosomatic Medicine, 6*, 95–106.

Kassin, S. M., & Wrightsman, L. S. (1980). Prior confessions and mock juror verdicts. *Journal of Applied Social Psychology, 10*, 133–146.

Katz, E., & Lazarsfeld, P. F. (1955). *Personal influence*. Glencoe, Ill.: Free Press.

Kaufman, A. S., & Doppelt, J. E. (1976). Analysis of WISC-R standardization data to terms of the stratification variables. *Child Development, 47*, 165–171.

Keele, S. W., & Summers, J. J. (1976). The structure of motor programs. In G. E. Stelmach (Ed.), *Motor control: Issues and trends*. New York: Academic Press.

Kaufman, L., & Rock, I. (1962). The moon illusion. *Scientific American, 137*, 399–404.

Kavanagh, D. J., & Bower, G. H. (1985). Mood and self-efficacy: Impact of joy and sadness on perceived capabilities. *Cognitive Therapy and Research, 9*, 507–525.

Keenan, J. M., MacWhinney, B., & Mayhew, D.

(1977). Pragmatics in memory: A study of natural conversation. *Journal of Verbal Learning and Verbal Behavior, 16*, 549–560.

Keeney, T. J., Cannizzo, S. R., & Flavell, J. H. (1967). Spontaneous and induced verbal rehearsal in recall tasks. *Child Development, 38*, 953–966.

Keesey, R. E., & Porvley, T. L. (1975). Hypothalamic regulation of body weight. *American Scientist, 63*, 558–565.

Keller, H. (1903). *The story of my life*. New York: Doubleday, Page.

Kelley, H. H. (1952). Two functions of reference groups. In G. E. Sovanson, T. M. Newcomb, & E. L. Hartley (Eds.), *Readings in social psychology* (2nd ed.). New York: Holt, Rinehart & Winston.

Kelley, H. H. (1965). Experimental studies of threats in interpersonal negotiations. *Journal of Conflict Resolution, 9*, 79–105.

Kelley, H. H. (1967). Attribution theory in social psychology. In D. Levine (Ed.), *Nebraska Symposium on Motivation, 15*, 192–238.

Kellogg, W. N., & Kellogg, L. A. (1933). *The ape and the child*. New York: McGraw-Hill.

Kelly, G. A. (1955). *The psychology of personal constructs*. New York: Norton.

Kelley, H. H., & Thibaut, J. (1978). *Interpersonal relations: A theory of interdependence*. New York: Wiley.

Kellman, P. J., & Spelke, E. S. (1983). Perception of partly occluded objects in infancy. *Cognitive Psychology, 15*, 483–542.

Kenniston, K. (1970). Student activism, moral development, and morality. *American Journal of Orthopsychiatry, 40*, 577–592.

Kerckhoff, A., & Davis, K. E. (1962). Value consensus and need complementarity in mate selection. *American Sociological Review, 27*, 295–303.

Keren, G., and Wagenaar, W. A. (1985). On the psychology of playing blackjack: Normative and descriptive considerations with implications for decisions theory. *Journal of Experimental Psychology: General, 114*, 133–158.

Kessler, R. C., & McLeod, J. (1985). Social support and mental health in community samples. Pp. 219–240 in S. Cohen & S. L. Syme (eds.), *Social support and health*. Orlando, FL: Academic Press.

Kessler, R. C., McLeod, J., & Wethington, E. (1985). The costs of caring: A perspective on the relationship between sex and psychological distress. Pp. 491–506 in I. G. Sarason & B. R. Sarason (eds.), *Social support: Theory, research, and applications*. Dordrecht, The Netherlands: Martinus Nighoff.

Kety, S. (1974). Biochemical and neurochemical effects of electroconvulsive shock. In M. Fink, S. Kety, & J. McGraugh (Eds.), *Psychobiology of convulsive therapy*. Washington, D.C.: Winston, 285–294.

Kiang, N. Y. S., Watanabe, T., Thomas, E. C., & Clark, L. F. (1965). *Discharge patterns of single fibers in the cat's auditory nerve*. Cambridge, Mass.: M.I.T. Press.

Kimmel, D. C. (1978). Adult development and aging: A gay perspective. *Journal of Social Issues, 34*, 1113–1130.

Kimmel, D. C., Price, K. F., & Walker, J. W. (1978). Retirement choice and retirement satisfaction. *Journal of Gerontology, 33*(4), 575–585.

Kinchla, R. A. (1969). *An attention operating characteristic in vision*. Technical Report. Department of Psychology, McMaster University, Hamilton Ontario, Canada.

Kinchla, R. A. (1974). Detecting target elements in multi-element arrays: A confusability model. *Perception and Psychophysics, 15*, 149–158.

Kinchla, R. A. Attention in memory. Tech. Rpt. No. 28, Dept. of Psychology, Princeton University, Princeton, N.J.

Kinchla, R. A. (1980). The measurement of attention. In R. Nickerson (Ed.), *Attention and performance: VIII*. Hillsdale, N.J.: Erlbaum.

Kinchla, R. A., & Allan, L. G. (1969). A theory of visual movement perception. *Psychological Review*, 76, 537–558.

Kinchla, R. A., & Wolfe, J. M. (1979). The order of visual processing: "Top-down," "bottom-up," or "middle-out." *Perception and Psychophysics*, 25(3), 225–231.

King, S. H. (1971). Coping mechanisms in adolescents. *Psychiatric Annuals*, 1, 10–46.

Kinsey, A. C., Pomeroy, W. B., & Martin, C. E. (1948). *Sexual behavior in the human male*. Philadelphia: Saunders.

Kinsey, A. C., Pomeroy, W. B., Martin, C. E., & Gebhard, P. H. (1953). *Sexual behavior in the human female*. Philadelphia: Saunders.

Kintsch, W., & Bates, E. (1977). Recognition memory for statements from a classroom lecture, *Journal of Experimental Psychology: Human Learning and Memory*, 3, 150–159.

Kirscht, J. P., & Rosenstock, I. M. (1979). Patients' problems in following recommendations of health experts. In G. C. Stone, F. Cohen, & N. E. Adler (Eds.), *Health psychology: A handbook*. San Francisco: Jossey-Bass.

Klerman, G. L. (1985). The scientific status of neurotic depression. *Psychopathology*, 18, 167–173.

Klima, E. S., & Bellugi, U. (1979). *The signs of language*. Cambridge, Mass.: Harvard University Press.

Knittle, J. L. (1975). Early influences on development of adipose tissue. In G. A. Bray (Ed.), *Obesity in perspective*. Washington, D.C.: U.S. Government Printing Office.

Knittle, J. L., & Hirsch, J. (1968). Effect of early nutrition on the development of rat epididymal fat pads: Cellularity and metabolism. *Journal of Clinical Investigation*, 47, 2091.

Kobasa, S. C. (1979). Stressful life events, personality, and health: An inquiry into hardiness. *Journal of Personality and Social Psychology*, 37, 1–11.

Koestler, A. (1964). *The act of creation*. New York: Macmillan.

Koff, W. C. (1974). Marijuana and sexual activity. *Journal of Sex Research*, 10, 194–204.

Koffka, A. (1935). *The principles of Gestalt psychology*. New York: Harcourt, Brace.

Kohlberg, L. (1963). Development of children's orientation toward a moral order. 1. Sequence in the development of moral thoughts. *Vita Humana*, 6, 11–36.

Kohlberg, L. (1966). A cognitive-developmental analysis of children's sex-role concepts and attitudes. In E. E. Maccoby (Ed.), *The development of sex differences*. Palo Alto, Calif.: Standard University Press.

Kohlberg, L. (1969). Stage and sequence: The cognitive developmental approach to socialization. In D. A. Goslin (Eds.), *Handbook of socialization theory of research*. Chicago: Rand McNally, Pp. 347–480.

Kohlberg, L. (1971). From is to ought: How to commit the naturalistic fallacy and get away with it in the study of moral development. In T. Mischel (Ed.), *Cognitive development and genetic epistemology*. New York: Academic Press.

Kohlberg, L. (1976). Moral stage and moralization: The cognitive-developmental approach. In T. Lickona (Ed.), *Moral development and behavior: Theory, research, and social issues*. New York: Holt, Rinehart & Winston.

Kohlberg, L. (1978). Revisions in the theory and practice of moral development. *New Directions for Child Development*, 2, 83–88.

Kohlberg, L. (1981). *The philosophy of moral development*. New York: Harper & Row.

Kohlberg, L., & Kramer, R. B. (1969). Continuities and discontinuities in childhood and adult moral development. *Human Development*, 12, 93–120.

Kohler, W. (1925), *The mentality of apes*. New York: Harcourt Brace.

Kohler, W. (1940). *Dynamics in psychology*. New York: Liveright.

Kolata, C. (1982). Food affects human behavior. *Science*, 218, 1209–1210.

Kolb, L. C. (1973). *Modern clinical psychiatry*, 8th ed. Philadelphia: W. B. Saunders.

Koluchova, J. (1972). Severe deprivation in twins: A case study. *Journal of Child Psychology and Psychiatry*, 13, 107–114.

Konečni, V. J., & Doob, A. N. (1972). Catharsis through displacement of aggression. *Journal of Personality and Social Psychology*, 23, 379–387.

Kosslyn, S. M. (1980). *Image and mind*. Cambridge, Mass.: Harvard University Press.

Kosslyn, S. M., Ball, T. M., & Reiser, B. J. (1978). Visual images preserve metric spatial information: Evidence from studies of image scanning. *Journal of Experimental Psychology: Human Perception and Performance*, 4, 47–60.

Kotin, J., Wilbert, D. E., Verburg, D., & Seldinger, S. M. (1976). Thioridazine and sexual dysfunction. *American Journal of Psychiatry*, 133, 82–85.

Koyama, T., Lowy, M. T., & Meltzer, H. Y. (1987). 5-Hydroxytryptophan-induced cortisol response and CSF 5-HIAA in depressed patients. *American Journal of Psychiatry*, 144, 334–337.

Krauss, R. M., & Glucksberg, S. (1977). Social and nonsocial speech. *Scientific American*, 236, 100–105.

Kreutzer, M. A., Leonard, C., & Flavell, J. H. (1975). An interview study of children's knowledge about memory. *Monographs of the Society for Research in Child Development*, 40, (1, Serial No. 159).

Kruglanski, A. W. (1975). The endogenous—exogenous partition in attribution theory. *Psychological Review*, 82, 387–406.

Kruuk, H. (1972). *The spotted hyena: A study of predation and social behavior*. Chicago: University of Chicago Press.

Kübler-Ross, E. (1969). *On death and dying*. New York: Macmillan.

Kübler-Ross, E. (1974). *Questions and answers on death and dying*. New York: Macmillan.

Kuenne, M. R. (1946). Experimental investigation of the relation of language to transportation behavior in young children. *Journal of Experimental Psychology*, 36, 471–490.

Kuhl, J., & Blankenship, V. (1979). Behavioral change in a constant environment: Shift to more difficult tasks with constant probability of success. *Journal of Personality and Social Psychology*, 37, 551–563.

Kuhlman, D. M., & Marshello, A. F. (1975). Individual differences in game motivation as moderators of preprogrammed strategy effects in prisoner's dilemma. *Journal of Personality and Social Psychology*, 32, 992–931.

Kuhn, D., Nash, S. C., & Brucken, L. (1978). Sex role concepts of two- and three-year-olds. *Child Development*, 49, 445–451.

Kunda, Z. (in press). Motivated inference: Self-serving generation and evaluation to causal theories. *Journal of Personality and Social Psychology*.

Kunda, Z., & Schwartz, S. H. (1983). Undermining intrinsic moral activation: External reward and self-presentation. *Journal of Personality and social Psychology*, 45, 763–771.

Lacey, J. I. (1967). Somatic response patterning and stress: Some revisions of activation theory. In M. Appley & R. Trumbell (Eds.), *Psychological stress*. New York: McGraw-Hill.

Lacey, J. I., & Lacey, B. C. (1958). Verification and extension of the principle of autonomic response-stereotypy. *American Journal of Psychology*, 71, 50–73.

Laing, R. D. (1964). Is schizophrenia a disease? *International Journal of Social Psychiatry*, 10, 184–193.

Laird, J. D. (1974). Self-attribution of emotion: The effects of expressive behavior on the quality of emotional experience. *Journal of Personality and Social Psychology*, 29, 475–486.

Lamb, M. E. (1973). The effects of maternal deprivation on the development of the concepts of object and person. *Journal of Behavioral Science*, 1, 355–364.

Lamb, M. E. (1976). Twelve-month-olds and their parents: Interaction in a laboratory playroom. *Development Psychology*, 12, 237–244.

Lamb, M. E. (1977). Father-infant and mother-infant interaction in the first year of life. *Child Development*, 48, 167–181.

Lamb, M. E., Frodi, A. M., Hwang, C., Frodi, M., & Steinberg, J. (1982). Mother- and father-infant interaction involving play and holding in traditional and nontraditional Swedish families. *Developmental Psychology*, 18, 215–221.

Lamm, H., & Sauer, C. (1974). Discussion-induced shift toward higher demands in negotiation. *European Journal of Social Psychology*, 4, 85–88.

Landauer, T. K., & Whiting, J. W. M. (1964). Infantile stimulation and adult stature of human males. *American Anthropologist*, 66, 1007–1028.

Langer, E., Janis, I. L., & Wolfer, J. A. (1975). Reduction of psychological stress in surgical patients. *Journal of Experimental Social Psychology*, 11, 155–165.

Langer, E., & Rodin, J. (1976). The effects of choice and enhanced personal responsibility for the aged: A field experiment in an institutional setting. *Journal of Personality and Social Psychology*, 34, 191–198.

Langer, E. J., Taylor, S. E., Fiske, S., & Chanowitz, B. (1976). Stigma, staring, and discomfort: A novel stimulus hypothesis. *Journal of Experimental Social Psychology*, 12, 451–463.

Lanzetta, J. T., Cartwright-Smith, J., & Kleck, R. E. (1976). Effects of non-verbal dissimulation on emotional experience and autonomic arousal. *Journal of Personality and Social Psychology*, 33, 354–370.

Lanzetta, J. T., & Orr, S. P. (1986). Influence of facial expressions on the classical conditioning of fear. *Journal of Personality and Social Psychology*, 39, 1081–1087.

LaPiere, R. T. (1934). Attitudes and actions. *Social Forces*, 13, 230–237.

Larkin, J. H., McDermott, J., Simon, D. P., & Simon, H. A. (1980). Expert and novice performance in solving physics problems. *Science*, 208, 1335–1342.

LaRossa, R. (1983). The transition to parenthood and the social reality of time. *Journal of Marriage and the Family*, 45, 579–589.

LaRossa, R., & LaRossa, M. M. (1981). *Transition to parenthood: How infants change families*. Beverly Hills, Cal.: Sage Publications.

Lashley, K. S. (1950). In search of the engram. Symposium Soc. Experimental Biology, 4, 454–482.

Latané, B. (1981). The psychology of social impact. *American Psychologist*, 36, 343–356.

Latané, B., & Darley, J. M. (1968). Group inhibition of bystander intervention in emergencies. *Journal of Personality and Social Psychology*, 10, 215–221.

Latané, B., & Darley, J. M. (1970). *The unresponsive bystander: Why doesn't he help?* Englewood Cliffs, NJ: Prentice-Hall.

Latané, B., & Harkins, S. (1976). Cross-modality matches suggest anticipated stage fright a multiplicative power function of audience size and status. *Perception & Psychophysics, 20,* 482–488.

Latané, B., Williams, K., & Harkins, S. (1979). Many hands make light the work: The causes and consequences of social loafing. *Journal of Personality and Social Psychology, 37,* 822–832.

Lauer, J., & Lauer, R. (1985). Marriages made to last. *Psychology Today, 19*(No. 6): 22–26.

Layzer, D. (1974). Heritability analyses of IQ: Science or numerology? *Science, 183,* 1259–1266.

Lazarus, A. (1971). *Behavior therapy and beyond.* New York: McGraw-Hill.

Lazarus, R. S. (1977). Psychological stress and coping in adaptation and illness. In A. J. Lipowski, Dr. R. Lippsitt, & P. C. Whybrow (Eds.), *Psychosomatic medicine: Current trends and clinical applications.* New York: Oxford University Press.

Lazarus, R. S., & Alfert, E. (1964). The short-circuiting of threat. *Journal of Abnormal and Social Psychology, 69,* 195–205.

Lazarus, R. S., & Folkman. S. (1984). *Stress, appraisal, and coping.* New York: Springer Publishing.

Lazarus, R. S., Kanner, A. D., & Folkman, S. (1980). Emotions: A cognitive-phenomenological anlysis. In R. Plutchik & H. Kellerman (Eds.), *Emotion: Theory, research, and experience* (Vol. 1). New York: Academic Press.

Lazarus, R. S., & Launier, R. (1978). Stress-related transactions between person and environment. In L. A. Pervin & M. Lewis (Eds.), *Perspectives in interactional psychology. New York: Plenum.*

Lazarus, R. S., Opton, E. M., Nomikos, M. S., & Rankin, N. O. (1965). The principle of short-circuiting threat: Further evidence. *Journal of Personality, 33,* 622–635.

Lazarus, R. S., Speisman, J. C., Mordkoff, A. M., & Davison, L. A. (1962). A laboratory study of psychological stress produced by a motion picture film. *Psychological Monographs, 76*(34, Whole No. 553).

Leahy, A. (1935). Nature-nurture and intelligence. *Genetic Psychology Monographs, 17,* 241–306.

Leask, J., Haber, R. N., & Haber, R. B. (1969). *Eidetic imagery in children, II: Longitudinal and experimental results. Psychonomic Monograph Supplements, 3,* 25–48.

Leavitt, H. J. (1951). Some effects of certain communication patterns on group performance. *Journal of Abnormal and Social Psychology, 46,* 38–50.

Lee, E. S. (1951). Negro intelligence and selective migration: A Philadelphia test of the Klineberg hypothesis. *American Sociological Review, 16,* 227–233.

Lefcourt, H. M. (1983). *Research with the locus of control construct. Volume 2: Developments and social problems.* New York: Academic Press.

Lehrman, D. S. (1964, November). The reproductive behavior of ring doves. *Scientific American, 211*(5), 48–54.

Lenneberg, E. (1967). *Biological foundations of language.* New York: Wiley.

Leon, G. R. (1977). *Case histories of deviant behavior, an interactional perspective* (2nd ed). Boston: Allyn & Bacon.

Lepper, M. R., Greene, D., & Nisbett, R. E. (1973). Undermining children's intrinsic interest with extrinsic rewards: A test of the "overjustification hypothesis." *Journal of Personality and Social Psychology, 28,* 129–137.

Lerner, M. J. (1980). *The belief in a just world.* New York: Plenum.

Lerner, M. J., Miller, D. T., & Holmes, J. G. (1975). Deserving versus justice: A contemporary dilemma. In L. Berkowitz & E. Walster (Eds.), *Advances of*

experimental social psychology (Vol. 12). New York: Academic Press.

Lerer, B. (1985). Alternative therapies for bi-polar disorder. *Journal of Clinical Psychiatry, 46*(B), 309–316.

Lerer, B. (1985). Alternative therapies for bi-polar disorder. *Journal of Clinical Psychiatry, 64,* 309–316.

Levi, L. (1965). The urinary output of adrenalin and nonadrenalin during pleasant and unpleasant emotional states: A preliminary report. *Psychosomatic Medicine, 27,* 80–85.

Levinger, G. (1974). A three-level approach to attraction: Toward an understanding of pair relatedness. In T. L. Huston (Ed.), *Foundations of interpersonal attraction.* New York: Academic Press. Pp. 100–120.

Levinger, G., & Snoek, J. D. (1972). *Attraction in relationships: A new look at interpersonal attraction.* Morristown, N.J.: General Learning Press.

Levinson, D. J. (1978). *The seasons of a man's life.* New York: Ballantine.

Levinson, D. J., Darrow, C. N., Klein, E. G., Levinson, M. H., & McKee, B. (1978). *The seasons of a man's life.* New York: Knopf.

Levinson, D. M., et al. (1978). Assessment of the contact eye cover as an effective method of restricting visual input. *Behavioral Research Methods and Instrumentation, 10,* 376–388.

Levin, I., Wilkening, F., & Dembo, Y. (1984). Development of time quantification: Integration and nonintegration of beginnings and endings in comparative durations. *Child Development, 54,* 2160–2172.

Levy, J., Trevarthen, C., & Sperry, R. W. (1971). Perception of bilateral chimeric figures following hemispheric disconnection. *Brain, 95,* 68.

Levy, J., Trevarthian, C., & Sperry, R. W. (1972). Perception of bilateral chimeric figures following hemispheric deconnexion. *Brain, 95,* 61–78.

Levy, J. V., & King, J. A. (1953). The effects of testosterone propionate on fighting behavior in young male C57 BL/10 mice. *Anat. Record, 117,* 562–563.

Lewin, K. (1931). Environmental forces in child behavior and development. In C. Murchison (Ed.), *A handbook of child psychology.* Worcester, Mass.: Clark University Press.

Lewin, K. (1951). *Field theory in the social sciences.* New York: Harper & Brothers.

Lewinsohn, P. H. (1974). A behavioral approach to depression. In R. J. Friedman & M. M. Katz (Eds.), *The psychology of depression: Contemporary theory and research.* Washington, D.C.: Winston-Wiley.

Liberman, A. M., & Studdert-Kennedy, M. (1978). Phonetic perception. In R. Held, H. W. Leibowitz, & H. L. Tueber (Eds.), *Handbook of sensory physiology* (Vol. 8). Berlin: Springer-Verlag.

Liddell, H. (1950). Some specific factors that modify tolerance for environmental stress. In H. G. Wolff, S. G. Wolff, & C. C. Hare (Eds.), *Life stress and bodily disease.* Baltimore: Williams and Wilkins.

Liebert, R. M., & Baron, R. A. (1972). Some immediate effects of televised violence on children's behavior. *Developmental Psychology, 6,* 469–475.

Liebert, R. M., Neale, J. M., & Davidson, E. S. (1973). *The early window: Effects of television on children and youth.* New York: Pergamon Press.

Lifton, R. J. (1968). *Death in life: Survivors of Hiroshima.* New York: Random House.

Lindsay, P. H., & Norman, D. A. *Human information processing: An introduction to psychology.* New York. Academic Press, 1972.

Lindsay, R. C., & Holden, R. R. (1987). The introductory psychology subject pool in Candian universities. *Canadian Psychology, 28,* 45–52.

Linn, R. L. (1982). Ability testing: Individual differences, prediction, and differential prediction. In

A. Wigdor and W. Gardner (eds.), *Ability testing: Uses, consequences and controveries.* Vol. 2. Washington, D.C.: National Academy Press.

Livson, N., & Peshkin, H. (1980). Perspectives on adolescence from longitudinal research. In J. Adelson (Ed.), *Handbook of adolescent psychology.* New York: Wiley.

Lloyd, M. A. (1985). Adolescence. New York: Harper & Row.

Locke, J. (1690). An essay concerning human understanding. London: Basset.

Loeb, G. (1985). The functional replacement of the ear. *Scientific American, 252*(No. 2):104–111.

Loehlin, J. C., & Nichols, R. C. (1976). *Heredity, environment and personality.* Austin, Tex.: University of Texas Press.

Loew, C. A. (1967). Acquisition of hostile attitude and its relationship to aggressive behavior. *Journal of Personality and Social Psychology, 5,* 335–341.

Loftus, E. F. (1979). *Eyewitness testimony.* Cambridge, Mass.: Harvard University Press.

Lopata, H. Z. (1973). *Widowhood in an American city.* Cambridge, Mass.: Schenkman.

Lopata, H. (1975). Widowhood: Societal factors in life-span disruptions and alternatives. In N. Datan and L. H. Ginsberg (eds.), *Life-span developmental psychology: Normative life crises.* New York: Academic Press.

Lo Piccolo, J., & Lo Piccolo, L. (1978). *Handbook of sex therapy.* New York: Plenum.

Lord, C. G., Lepper, M. R., & Mackie, D. (1984). Attitude prototypes as determinants of attitude-behavior consistency. *Journal of Personality and Social Psychology, 46,* 1254–1266.

Lord, C. G., Ross, L., & Lepper, M. R. (1979). Biased assimilation and attitude polarization: The effects of prior theories on subsequently considered evidence. *Journal of Personality and Social Psychology, 37,* 2098–2109.

Lorenz, K. Z. (1937). The companion in the bird's world. *Auk, 54,* 245–273.

Lorenz, K. Z. (1966). *On agression.* New York: Harcourt, Brace and World.

Lott, A. J., & Lott, B. E. (1968). A learning theory approach to interpersonal attitudes. In A. G. Greenwald, T. C. Brock, & T. Ostrom (Eds.), *Psychological foundations of attitudes.* New York: Academic Press.

Lott, A. J., & Lott, B. E. (1974). The role of reward in the formation of positive interpersonal attitudes. In T. L. Huston (Ed.), *Foundations of interpersonal attraction.* New York: Academic Press.

Lovaas, O. I. (1961). Effect of exposure to symbolic aggression on aggressive behavior. *Child Development, 32,* 37–44.

Lovaas, O. I. (1977). *The autistic child.* New York: Halsted.

Luborsky, L., Singer, B., & Luborsky, L. (1975). Comparative studies of psychotherapies: Is it true that "Everyone has won and all must have prizes"? *Archives of General Psychiatry, 32,* 995–1008.

Luborsky, L., & Spence, D. P. (1971). Quantitative research on psychoanalytic therapy. In A. E. Bergin & S. L. Garfield (Eds.), *Handbook of psychotherapy and behavior changes: An empirical analysis.* New York: Wiley.

Luce, G. G., & Segal, J. (1966). *Sleep.* New York: Coward, McCann & Geoghegan.

Luchins, A. J. (1942). Mechanization in problem solving: The effect of *Einstellung. Psychological Monographs, 54.* 6(Whole No. 248).

Luria, A. R. (1959). Development of the directive function of speech in early childhood. *Word, 15,* 341–352.

Luria, A. R. (1968). *The mind of a mnemonist.* New York: Basic Books. (Originally published in 1920.)

Lyons, E. (1983). Demographic correlates of land-

scaping preference. *Environment and Behavior*, *15*, 487–511.

Maccoby, E. E., & Jacklin, C. N. (1974). *The psychology of sex differences*. Palo Alto, Calif.: Stanford University Press.

Mackie, D., & Cooper, J. (1984). Attitude polarization: Effects of group membership. *Journal of Personality and Social Psychology*, *46*, 575–585.

MacKinnon, D. W. (1965). Personality and the realization of creative potential. *American Psychologist*, *20*, 273–281.

MacMahon, B. (1973). *Age at menarche, United States* (Vital and Health Statistics, Series 11, No. 133, DHEW Publication No. [HRA] 74–1615). Washington, D.C.: U.S. Government Printing Office.

Macnamara, J. (1972). Cognitive basis of language learning in infants. *Psychological Review*, *79*, 1–13.

Madden, J., Akil, H., Patrick, R. L., & Barchas, J. D. (1977). Stress induced parallel changes in central opioid levels and pain responsiveness in the rat. *Nature*, *265*, 358–360.

Madrozo, I., Drucke-Colin, R., Diaz, V. et al. (1987). Open microsurgical autograft of adrenal medulla to the right caudate nucleus in two patients with inalterable Parkinson's disease. *The New England Journal of Medicine*, *316*, 831–839.

Magnusson, D., & Endler, N. S. (1977). Interactional psychology: Present status and future prospects. In D. Magnusson & N. S. Endler (Eds.), Personality at the crossroads: Current issues in interactional psychology. Hillsdale, N.J.: Erlbaum.

Maher, B. A. (1970). Delusional thinking and cognitive disorder. Paper presented at annual meeting of the American Psychological Association.

Mahl, G. F. (1952). Relationship between acute and chronic fear and the gastric acidity and blood sugar levels in *macaca mulatta* monkeys. *Psychosomatic Medicine*, *14*, 182–210.

Malamuth, N. M., & Check, J. V. P. (1981). The effects of mass media exposure on acceptance of violence against women: A field experiment. *Journal of Research in Personality*, *15*, 436–446.

Malamuth, N. M., & Spinner, B. (1980). A longitudinal content analysis of sexual violence in the best-selling erotic magazines. *The Journal of Sex Research*, *16*, 226–237.

Malina, R. M. (1979). Secular changes in size and maturity: Causes and effects. *Monographs of the Society of Research in Child Development*, *44*(3–4, Serial No. 179), 59–120.

Mandler, G. (1962). Emotions. In T. M. Newcomb (Ed.), *New directions in psychology*. New York: Holt, Rinehart & Winston.

Manfredi, M., Bini, G., Cruccu, G., Accormeno, M., Beradelli, A., & Medolago, L. (1981). Congenital absence of pain. *Archives of Neurology*, *38*, 507–511.

Maniscalco, C. I., Doherty, N. E., & Ullman, D. G. (1980). Assessing discrimination: An application of social judgment technology. *Journal of Applied Psychology*, *65*, 284–288.

Markus, H. (1977). Self-schemata and processing information about the self. *Journal of Personality and Social Psychology*, *35*, 63–78.

Markus, H., & Smith, J. (1981). The influence of self-schemas on the perceptio of others. In N. Cantor & J. Kihlstrom (Eds.), Personality, cognition and social interaction (pp. 233–262). Hillsdale, N.J.: Erlbaum.

Marr, D. (1982). Vision: A computational investigation into the human representation and processing of visual information. San Francisco: Freeman.

Marshall, D. S. (1971). Sexual behavior in Mangaia. In D. S. Marshall & R. G. Suggs (Eds.), *Human sexual behavior*. Englewood Cliffs, N.J.: Prentice-Hall.

Marshall, W. A., & Tanner, J. M. (1969). Variations in pattern of pubertal changes in girls. *Archives of Disease in Childhood*, *44*, 291–303.

Marshall, W. A., & Tanner, J. M. (1970). Variations in the pattern of pubertal changes in boys. *Archives of Diseases in Childhood*, *45*, 13–23.

Marx, J. (1985). Anxiety peptide found in brain. *Science*, *227*, 934.

Marx, R. D. (1986). Improving management development through relapse prevention strategies. Special issue: Management development for productivity. *Journal of Management Development*, *5*(2), 27–40.

Maslach, C. (1979). The emotional consequences of arousal without reason. In C. Izard, *Emotions in personality and psychopathology*. New York: Plenum.

Maslach, C. (1982). Burnout: The cost of caring. Englewood Cliffs, N.J.: Prentice-Hall.

Maslow, A. H. (1954). *Motivation and personality*. New York: Harper.

Maslow, A. H. (1967). Neurosis as a failure of personal growth. *Humanitas*, *3*, 153–170.

Maslow, A. H. (1970). *Motivation and personality* (2nd ed.). New York: Harper & Row.

Mason, J. W. (1971). A re-evaluation of the concept of "non-specificity" in stress theory. *Journal of Psychiatric Research*, *8*, 323–333.

Massaro, A. J. (1970). Retroactive interference in short-term recognition memory for pitch. *Journal of Experimental Psychology*, *83*, 32–39.

Masters, W. H., & Johnson, V. E. (1966). *Human sexual response*. Boston: Little, Brown.

Masters, W. H., & Johnson, V. E. (1970). *Human sexual inadequacy*. Boston: Little, Brown.

Matarazzo, J. D. (1980). Behavioral health and behavioral medicine: Frontiers for a new health psychology. *Psychologist*, 807–817.

Matthews, K. A. (1984). Assessment of type A, anger, and hostility in epidemiological studies of cardiovascular disease. In A. Ostfeld & E. Eaker (Eds.), *Measuring psychosocial variables in epidemiological studies of cardiovascular disease*. Bethesda, Md.: NIH.

Max, L. W. (1937). An experimental study of the motor theory of consciousness. IV. Action curved responses in the deaf during awakening, kinaesthetic imagery and abstract thinking. *Journal of Comparative Psychology*, *24*, 301–334.

May, P. R. A. (1968). *Treatments of schizophrenia: A comparative study of five treatment methods*. New York: Science House.

Mayer, D. J. (1984). Analgesia produced by electrical stimulation of the brain. *Progress in Neuro-Psychopharmacology & Biological Psychiatry*, *8*, 557–564.

Mayer, J. (1953). Genetic, traumatic and environmental factors in the etiology of obesity. *Physiological Reviews*, *33*, 472–508.

Mayer, J. (1955). Regulation of energy intake and the body weight: The glucostatic theory and the lipostatic hypothesis. *Annals of the New York Academy of Science*, *63*, 15–43.

McAdams, D. P. (1980). A thematic coding system for the intimacy motive. *Journal of Research in Personality*, *14*, 413–432.

McArthur, L. A. (1972). The how and what of why: Some determinants and consequences of causal attribution. *Journal of Personality and Social Psychology*, *22*, 171–193.

McBurney, D. H., & Collins, V. B. (1977). *Introduction to Sensation and Perception*, Englewood Cliffs, N.J.: Prentice-Hall.

McCarley, R. W. (1978, December). Where dreams come from: A new theory. *Psychology Today*.

McClelland, D. C. (1958). Risk-taking in children with high and low need for achievement. In J. W.

Atkinson (Ed.), *Motives in fantasy, action, and society*. Princeton, N.J.: Van Nostrand.

McClelland, D. C. (1985). *Human motivation*. Glenview, Ill.: Scott, Foresman.

McClelland, D. C. (1986). Some reflections on the two psychologies of love. *Journal of Personality*, *54*, 334–353.

McClelland, D. C., & Pilon, D. A. (1983). Sources of adult motives in patterns of parent behavior in early childhood. *Journal of Personality and Social Psychology*, *44*, 564–574.

McClelland, J. L., & Rumelhart, D. E. (1981). An interactive model of context effects in letter perception. *Psych Review 88*, 375–407.

McClelland, K. (1982). Adolescent subculture in the schools. In F. Field, A. Huston, H. Quay, L. Troll, & G. Finley (Eds.), *Review of human development*. New York: Wiley.

McClelland, L., & Cook, S. W. (1980). Promoting energy conservation in mastermetered apartments through group financial incentives. *Journal of Applied Social Psychology*, *10*, 20–31.

McCloskey, M. (1983). Naive theories of motion. In D. Gentner & A. L. Stevens (Eds.), *Mental models*. Hillsdale, N.J.: Erlbaum.

McCloskey, M., Caramazza, A., & Green, B. (1980). Curvilinear motion in the absence of external forces: Naive beliefs about the motions of objects. *Science*, *210*, 1139–1141.

McConkie, G. W., Zola, D., Blarrehord, H. E., & Wolverton, G. S. (1982). *Perceiving works during reading: Lack of facilitation from prior peripheral exposure*. (Technical Report) Champaign, Ill.: University of Illinois.

McFarland, R. A. (1981). *Physiological psychology*. Palo Alto, Cal.: Mayfield.

McGregor, D. M. (1960). *The human side of enterprise*. New York: McGraw-Hill.

McIntyre, M. E., Silverman, F. H., & Trotler, W. D. (1974). Transcendental meditation and stuttering: A preliminary report. *Perceptual and Motor Skills*, *39*, 294.

McLaughlin, B. (1978). *Second-language acquisition in childhood*. Hillsdale, N.J.: Erlbaum.

McNemar, Q. (1942). *The revision of the Stanford-Binet scale: An analysis of the standardization data*. Boston: Houghton Mifflin.

Mead, M. (1928). *Coming of age in Samoa*. Chicago: University of Chicago Press.

Mead, M. (1939). *From the South Seas: Studies of adolescence and sex in primitive societies*. New York: Morrow.

Mednick, S. A. (1962). The associative basis of the creative process. *Psychological Review*, *69*, 220–232.

Meer, J. (1985). Turbulent teens: The stress factors. *Psychology Today*, *19*(5), 15–16.

Meltzoff, A. N., & Moore, M. K. (1983). Newborn infants imitate adult facial gestures. *Child Development*, *54*, 702–709.

Merbaum, M., & Hefez, A. (1976). "Some personality characteristics of soldiers exposed to extreme war stress." *Journal of Consulting and Clinical Psychology*, *44*, 1, 1–6.

Merriam-Webster. (1973). *Webster's New Collegiate Dictionary*. Springfield, Mass.: Merriam.

Messinger, J. C. (1971). Sex and repression in an Irish folk community. In D. S. Marshall & R. G. Suggs (Eds.), *Human sexual behavior*. Englewood Cliffs, N.J.: Prentice-Hall.

Metalsky, G. I., Abramson, L. Y., Seligman, M. E. P., Semmel, A., & Peterson, C. (1982). Attributional styles and life events in the classroom: Vulnerability and invulnerability to depressive mood reactions. *Journal of Personality and Social Psychology*, *43*, 612–617.

Meyer, D. E., & Schvaneveldt, R. W. (1971). Facili-

tation in recognizing pairs of words: Evidence of a dependence between retrieval operations. *Journal of Experimental Psychology, 90,* 227–234.

Midlarsky, E., Bryan, J. H., & Brickman, P. (1973). Aversive approval: Interactive effects of modeling and reinforcement on altruistic behavior. *Child Development, 44,* 321–328.

Milgram, S. (1963). Behavioral study of obedience. *Journal of Abnormal and Social Psychology, 67,* 371–378.

Milgram, S. (1965). Some conditions of obedience and disobedience to authority. *Human Relations, 18,* 57–76.

Milgram, S. (1970). The experience of living in cities: Adaptations to urban overload create characteristic qualities of city life that can be measured. *Science, 167,* 1461–1468.

Miller, D., & Porter, C. (1983). Self-blame in victims of violence. *Journal of Social Issues, 39,* 139–152.

Miller, F. T., Bentz, W. K., Aponte, J. F., & Brogan, D. R. (1974). Perception of life crisis events: A comparative study of rural and urban samples. In B. S. Dohrenwend & B. P. Dohrenwend (Eds.), *Stressful life events: Their nature and effects.* New York: Wiley.

Miller, G. A. (1956). The magical number seven plus or minus two: Some limits on our capacity for processing information. *Psychological Review, 63,* 81–97.

Miller, G. A. (1981). *Language and speech.* San Francisco: Freeman.

Miller, G. A., & Buckhout, R. (1973). *Psychology: The science of mental life.* New York: Harper & Row.

Miller, G. A., & Cantor, N. (1982). Review of R. Nisbett and L. Ross, *Human inference: Strategies and shortcomings of social judgment. Social Cognition, 1,* 83–93.

Miller, G. A., Galanter, E., & Pribram, K. H. (1960). *Plans and the structure of behavior.* New York: Holt, Rinehart & Winston.

Miller, G. A., & Isard, S. (1963). Some perceptual consequences of linguistic rules. *Journal of Verbal Learning and Verbal Behavior, 2,* 217–228.

Miller, J. (1983). *States of mind.* New York: Pantheon.

Miller, N. E. (1944). Experimental studies of conflict. In J. McV. Hunt (Ed.), *Personality and the behavior disorders.* New York: Ronald Press.

Miller, N. E. (1948). Studies of fear as an acquirable drive: I. Fear as motivation and fear-reduction as reinforcement in the learning of new responses. *Journal of Experimental Psychology, 38,* 89–101.

Miller, N. E., Bailey, C. J., & Stevenson, J. A. F. (1950). Decreased "hunger" but increased food intake resulting from hypothalamic lesions. *Science, 112,* 256–259.

Miller, N. E., & Brucker, B. S. (1979). A learned visceral response apparently independent of skeletal ones in patients paralyzed by spinal lesions. In N. Birbaumer & H. D. Kimmel (Eds.), *Biofeedback and self-regulation.* Hillsdale, N.J.: Erlbaum.

Miller, N. E., & Kessen, M. L. (1952). Reward effects of food via stomach fistula compared with those of food via mouth. *Journal of Comparative and Physiological Psychology, 45,* 555–564.

Miller, P. H., & Weiss, M. G. (1982). Children's and adults' knowledge about what variables affect selective attention. *Child Development, 53,* 5434–5449.

Miller, W. R., & Seligman, M. E. P. (1975). Depression and learned helplessness in man. *Journal of Abnormal Psychology, 84,* 228–238.

Milner, B. (1970). Memory and the medial temporal regions of the brain. In K. H. Pribram & D. E. Broadbent (Eds.), *Biology of memory.* New York: Academic Press. Pp. 29–50.

Minuchin, S., & Fishman, H. C. (1981). *Family*

therapy techniques. Cambridge, Mass.: Harvard University Press.

Mischel, W. (1968). *Personality and assessment.* New York: Wiley.

Mischel, W. (1976). *Introduction to personality* (2nd ed.). New York: Holt, Rinehart & Winston.

Mischel, W. (1981). Personality and cognition: Something borrowed, something new? In N. Cantor & J. Kihlstrom (Eds.), *Personality, cognition and social interaction.* Hillsdale, N.J.: Erlbaum.

Mischel, W. (1985). Assessment from a cognitive social learning perspective. *Evaluacion Psychologica, 1*(1–2), 33–57.

Mischel, W. (1985). Delay of gratification as process and as person variable in development. In D. Magnusson & V. P. Allen (Eds.), *Interactions of human development.* New York: Academic Press.

Mischel, W., & Patterson, D. J. (1978). Effective plans for self-control in children. In W. A. Collins (Ed.), *Minnesota symposia on child psychology* (Vol. 11). Hillsdale, N.J.: Erlbaum.

Mischel, W., & Peake, P. K. (1983). Some facets of consistency: Replies to Epstein, Funder, and Bem. *Psychological Review, 90,* 394–402.

Mishkin, M. (1978). Memory in monkeys severely impaired by combined but not separate removal of amygdala and hippocampus. *Nature, 273,* 297–298.

Miskiman, D. E. (1979). An evaluation of a community outreach program. *American Journal of Community Psychology, 7,* 71–77.

Mitchell, G. D. (1968). Attachment differences in male and female infant monkeys. *Child Development, 39,* 611–620.

Mohler, H., & Okada, T. (1977). Bezodiazepine receptor: Demonstration in the central nervous system. *Science, 198,* 849–851.

Molfese, D. L., & Molfese, V. J. (1980). Cortical responses of preterm infants to phonetic and nonphonetic speech stimuli. *Developmental Psychology, 6,* 574–581.

Money, J. (1970). Sexual dimorphism and homosexual gender identity. *Psychological Bulletin, 74,* 425–440.

Money, J., & Ehrhardt, A. A. (1972). *Man and woman, boy and girl.* Baltimore: Johns Hopkins University Press.

Montgomery, M. F. (1931). The role of the salivary glands in the thirst mechanism. *American Journal of Physiology, 96,* 221–227.

Moore, J. E., & Chaney, E. F. (1985). Outpatient treatment of chronic pain: Effects of spouse involvement. *Journal of Consulting and Clinical Psychology, 53,* 326–334.

Moore, J., Strube, M. J., & Lacks. P. (1984). Learned helplessness: A function of attribution style and comparative performance information. *Personality and Social Psychology Bulletin, 10,* 526–535.

Morgan, C. T., & Morgan, J. D. (1940). Studies in hunger: II. The relation of gastric denervation and dietary sugar to the effect of insulin upon food-intake in the rat. *Journal of Genetic Psychology, 57,* 153–163.

Morris, D., Collett, P., Marsh, P., & O'Shaughnessy, M. (1979). *Gestures.* New York: Stein & Day.

Morris, T., Greer, S., Pettingale, K. W., & Watson, M, (1981). Patterns of expression of anger and their psychological correlates in women with breast cancer. *Journal of Psychosomatic Research 25,* 111–117.

Morrison, A. (1983, April). A window on the sleeping brain. *Scientific American,* pp. 94–102.

Morse, D. R. (1977). An exploratory study of the use of meditation alone and in combination with hypnosis in clinical dentistry. *Journal of the Ameri-*

can Society of psychosomatic Dental Medicine, 24(4), 113.

Morse, J. J., & Lorsch, J. W. (1970), May-June). Beyond theory Y. *Harvard Business Review,* pp. 61–68.

Moruzzi, G., & Magoun, H. W. (1949). Brain stem and reticular formation and activation of the EEG. *Electroencephalography and Clinical Neurophysiology, 1,* 455–473.

Moscovitch, M. (1981). Right-hemisphere language. *Topics in Language Disorders, 1,* 41–62.

Mosher, D. L. (1973). Sex differences, sex experience, sex guilt, and explicitly sexual films. *Journal of Social Issues, 29,* 95–112.

Moshman, D., & Neimark, E. (1982). Four aspects of adolescent cognitive development. In T. Field, A. Huston, H. Quay, L. Troll, & G. Finley (Eds.), *Review of human development.* New York: Wiley.

Mosteller, F., Rourke, R. E. K., & Thomas, G. B., Jr. (1973). *Probability with statistical applications.* Reading, Mass.: Addison-Wesley.

Mowrer, O. H. (1939). A stimulus-response analysis of anxiety and its role as a reinforcing agent. *Psychological Review, 46,* 553–565.

Mowrer, O. H. (1947). On the dual nature of learning—a reinterpretation of "conditioning" and "problem solving." *Harvard Educational Review, 17,* 102–148.

Mowrer, O. H. & Mowrer, W. M. (1938). Enuresis—a method for its study and treatment. *American Journal of Orthopsychiatry, 8,* 436–459.

Moyer, K. E. (1971). The physiology of aggression and the implications for aggression control. In J. L. Singer (Ed.), *The control of aggression and violence: Cognitive and physiological factors,* New York: Academic Press.

Moyer, K. E. (1976). Kinds of aggerssion and their physiological basis. In K. E. Moyer (Ed.), *Physiology of aggression and implications for control.* New York: Raven Press.

Mueller, D., Edwards, D. W., & Yarvis, R. M. (1977). Stressful life events and psychiatric symptomatology: Change or undesirability? *Journal of Health and Social Behavior, 18,* 307–316.

Muir, D., & Field, J. (1979). Newborn infants orient to sounds. *Child Development, 50,* 431–436.

Müller, G. E., & Pilzecker, A. (1900). Experimentelle Beiträge zur Lehre von Gedächtnis. Zeitschrift für Psychologie (Supplement no. 1).

Mumford, E., Schlesinger, H. J., & Glass, G. V. (1982). The effects of psychological intervention on recovery from surgery and heart attacks: An analysis of the literature. *American Journal of Public Health, 72*(2), 141–151.

Munroe, R. L., & Munroe, R. H. (1975). *Cross-cultural human development.* Monterey, Calif.: Brooks/Cole.

Munsinger, H., & Kessen, W. (1964). Uncertainty, structure, and preference. *Psychological Monographs, 78*(Whole No. 586), 1–24.

Munsinger, H., Kessen, W., & Kessen, M. L. (1964). Age and uncertainty: Developmental variation in preference for variability. *Journal of Experimental Child Psychology, 1,* 1–15.

Murdock, G. P. (1965). *Culture and society.* Pittsburgh, Penn.: University of Pittsburgh Press.

Murich, G. (1973). *Visual and auditory perception.* New York: Bobbs-Merrill.

Murphy, G. L., & Medin, D. L. (1985). The role of theories in conceptual coherence. *Psychological Review, 92,* 289–316.

Murray, D. M., Luepker, R. V., Johnson, C. A., & Mittelmark, M. B. (1984). The prevention of cigarette smoking in children: A comparison of four strategies. *Journal of Applied Social Psychology, 14,* 3, 274–288.

Murray, H. A. (1938). *Exploration in personality*. New York: Oxford University Press.

Murray, H. A. (1943). *Thematic Apperception Test manual*. Cambridge, Mass.: Harvard University Press.

Murstein, B. I. (1976). *Who will marry whom*. New York: Springer.

Muss, R. (1975). *Theories of adolescence* (3rd ed.). New York: Random House.

Mussen, P. H., & Jones, M. C. (1957). Self-conceptions, motivations and interpersonal attitudes of late and early maturing boys. *Child Development*, 28, 243–256.

Myers, J. L. (1979). *Fundamentals of experimental design* (3rd ed.). Boston: Allyn & Bacon.

Nachman, G. (1979). The menopause that refreshes. In P. I. Rose (Ed.), *Socialization and the life cycle*. New York: St. Martin's Press.

Naranjo, C. (1970). Present-centeredness. In J. Fagan & L. Shepherd, (Eds.), Gestalt Therapy Now: Theory techniques applications. Palo Alto, Calif.: Science and Behavior Books.

Natelson, B. (1977). The "executive" monkey revisited. In F. P. Brooks & P. W. Evens (Eds.), *Nerves and the gut*. Philadelphia: C. B. Slack.

Nathanson, C. A., & Lorenz, G. (1982). Women and health: The social dimensions of biomedical data. In J. Z. Giele (Ed.), *Women in the middle years*. New York: Wiley.

National Academy of Sciences. (1983). *Identifying and estimating the genetic impact of chemcial mutagens*. Washington, D.C.: National Academy Press.

National Center for Health Statistics (1983, March), Births, marriages, divorces, and deaths, United States. *Monthly Vital Statistics Report*. Vol. 31, No. 12. DHHS Pub. No. (PHS) 83–1120. Public Health Service, Hyattsville, Md.

Natsoulas, T. (1983). Addendum to "consciousness." *American Psychologist*, 38, 121–122.

Nauta, W. J. H., & Feirtag, M. (1979). The organization of the brain. *Scientific American*, 241(3), 88–111.

Navon, D. (1977). Forest before trees: The precedence of global features in visual perception. *Cognitive Psychology*, 9, 353–383.

Neimark, E. D. (1975). Intellectual development during adolescence. In F. D. Horowitz (Ed.), *Review of child development research* (Vol. 1). Chicago: University of Chicago Press.

Neisser, U. (1967). *Cognitive psychology*. Englewood Cliffs, N. J.: Prentice-Hall.

Neisser, U. (1976). *Cognition and reality: Principles and implications of cognitive psychology*. San Francisco: Freeman.

Nelson, K. (1973). Structure and strategy in learning to talk. *Monographs of the Society for Research in Child Development*, 38(1–2, Serial No. 149).

Nelson, R. E. (1977). Irrational beliefs in depression. *Journal of consulting and Clinical Psychology*, 45, 1190–1191.

Nemeth, C. (1972). A critical analysis of research utilizing the prisoner's dilemma paradigm for the study of bargaining. In L. Berkowitz (Ed.), *Advances in experimental social psychology* (Vol. 6). New York: Academic Press.

Nemiah, J. (1975). Hysterical neurosis, dissociative type. In A. Freedman, H. Kaplan, & B. Sadlock (Eds.), *Comprehensive textbook of psychiatry* (2nd ed.) (Vol 1). Baltimore: Williams & Wilkins.

Nerem, R., Levesque, M. J., & Cornhill, J. F. (1980). Social environment as a factor in diet-induced arteriosclerosis. *Science*, 208, 1475–1476.

Neugarten, B. L. (1968). The awareness of middle age. In B. L. Neugarten (Ed.), *Middle age and aging*. Chicago: The University of Chicago Press.

Neugarten, B. L., & Gutman, D. L. (1968). Age-sex roles and personality in middle age: A thematic apperception study. In B. L. Neugarten (Ed.), *Middle age and aging*. Chicago: University of Chicago Press.

Neugarten, B. L., Wood, V., Kraines, R. J., & Loomis, B. (1963). Women's attitudes toward the menopause. *Vita Humana*, 6, 140–151.

Newcomb, T. (1953). An approach to the study of communicative acts. *Psychological Review*, 60, 393–404.

Newcomb, T. (1956). The prediction of interpersonal attraction. *American Psychologist*, 11, 575–586.

Newcomb, T. M. (1971). Dyadic balance as a source of clues about interpersonal attraction. In B. I. Murstein (Ed.), *Theories of attraction and love*. New York: Springer.

Newell, A. (1973). You can't play 20 questions with nature and win. In W. G. Chase (Ed.), *Visual information processing*. New York: Academic Press.

Newman, H. H., Freeman, F. N., & Holzinger, K. J. (1937). *Twins: A study of heredity and environment*. Chicago: University of Chicago Press.

Newmark, C. S., Frerking, R. A., Cook, L., & Newmark, L. (1973). Endorsement of Ellis' irrational beliefs as a function of psychopathology. *Journal of Clinical Psychology*, 29, 300–302.

Newton, N. A., Lazarus, L. W., & Weinberg, J. (1984). Aging: Biopsychosocial perspectives. In S. Offer & M. Sabshin (Eds.), *Normality and the life cycle*. New York: Basic Books.

NIMH. (1969). *The mental health of urban America*. Washington, D.C.: U.S. Government Printing Office.

NIMH. (1975). Report of research task force: Research in the service of mental health. Rockville, Md.: DHEW Pub. 75–236.

NIMH. (1976). *Emergency services in psychiatric facilities*. Washington, D.C.: U.S. Government Printing Office.

NIMH. (1978, March). Changes in the age, sex, and diagnostic composition of the resident population of state and county mental hospitals (statistical note #146). Washington, D.C.: U.S. Government Printing Office.

Nisbett, R. E. (1972). Hunger, obesity, and the ventromedial hypothalamus. *Psychological Review*, 79, 433–453.

Nisbett, R. E., Caputo, C., Legant, P., & Maracek, J. (1973). Behavior as seen by the actor and as seen by the observer. *Journal of Personality and Social Psychology*, 27, 154–164.

Nisbett, R. E., & Ross, L. (1980). *Human inference: Strategies and shortcomings*. Englewood Cliffs, N.J.: Prentice-Hall.

Nisbett, R. E., & Wilson, T. D. (1977). Telling more than we can know: Verbal reports on mental processes. *Psychological Review*, 84, 231–259.

Norman, D. A. (1979). *Memory and attention*, (3rd ed.). New York: Wiley.

Norman, D. A. & Bobrow, D. G. (1975). On data-limited and resource-limited processes. *Cognitive Psychology*, 7, 44–64.

Norman, D. A. & Rumelhart, D. E. (1975). *Explorations in cognition*. San Francisco: Freeman.

Norton, A. J. (1983). Family life cycle 1980. *Journal of Marriage and the Family*, 45, 267–275.

Novak, D., & Lerner, M. (1968). Rejection as a consequence of perceived similarity. *Journal of Personality and Social Psychology*, 9, 147–152.

Novak, M. A., & Harlow, H. F. (1975). Social recovery of monkeys isolated for the first year of life: I. Rehabilitation and therapy. *Developmental Psychology*, 11, 564–565.

Nowak, C. A. (1977). Does youthfulness equal attractiveness? In L. E. Troll, J. Israel, & K. Israel (Eds.), *Looking ahead: A woman's guide to the problems and joys of growing older*. Englewood Cliffs, N.J.: Prentice-Hall.

Nuckolls, K. B., Cassel, J., & Kaplan, B. H. (1972). Psychosocial assets, life crisis, and the prognosis of pregnancy. *American Journal of Epidemiology*, 95, 431–441.

Offer, D. (1969). *The psychological world of the teenager: A study of normal adolescent boys*. New York: Basic Books.

Offer, D., Marcus, D., & Offer, J. L. (1970). A longitudinal study of normal adolescent boys. *American Journal of Psychiatry*, 126, 917–924.

Offer, D., & Offer, J. (1974). Normal adolescent males; The high school and college years. *Journal of the American College Health Association*, 22, 209–215.

Offer, D., & Sabshin, M. (1984a). Adolescence: Empirical perspectives. In D. Offer & M. Sabshin (Eds.), Normality and the life cycle. New York: Basic Books.

Ohman, A., Erixon, G., & Lofberg, I. (1975). Phobias and preparedness: Phobic versus neutral pictures as conditional stimuli for human autonomic responses. *Journal of Abnormal Psychology*, 84, 41–45.

Ohman, A., & Dimberg, U. (1978). Facial expressions as conditioned stimuli for electrodermal responses: A case of "preparedness"? *Journal of Personality and Social Psychology*, 36, 1251–1258.

Ojemann, G., & Mateer, C. (1979). Human language cortex: Localization of memory, syntax, and sequential motor-phoneme identification systems. *Science*, 205, 1401–1403.

Olds, J. (1956). Pleasure centers in the brain, *Scientific American*, 195, 105–116.

Olds, J., & Milner, P. (1954). Positive reinforcement produced by electrical stimulation of septal area and other regions of rat brain. *Journal of Comparative and Physiological Psychology*, 47, 419–427.

O'Leary, V., & Hammock, B. (1975). Sex-role orientation and achievement context as determinants of the motive to avoid success. *Sex Roles*, 1, 225–234.

Oller, D. K., & Warren, I. (1976). On the nature of phonological capacity. *Lingua*, 39, 183–199.

Olton, D. S. (1979). Mazes, maps, and memory. *American Psychologist*, 34, 583–596.

Olton, D. S., & Samuelson, R. J. (1976). Remembrance of places passed: Spatial memory in rats. *Journal of Experimental Psychology: Animal Behavior Processes*, 2, 97–116.

Orne, M. T. (1977). The construct of hypnosis: Implications of definition for research and practice. In W. E. Edmonston, Jr. (Ed.), *Conceptual and invertigative approaches to hypnosis and hypnotic phenomena*. Annals of the New York Academy of Sciences (Vol. 296), 14–33.

Orne, M. T., Sheehan, P. W., & Evans, F. J. (1968). Occurrence of posthypnotic behavior outside the experimental setting. *Journal of Personality and Social Psychology*, 9, 189–196.

Ornstein, R. E. (1977). The psychology of consciousness (2nd ed.). New York: Harcourt Brace Jovanovich.

Ortony, A., Schallert, D. L., Reynolds, R. E., & Antos, S. J. (1978). Interpreting metaphors and idioms: Some effects of context on comprehension. *Journal of Verbal Learning and Verbal Behavior*, 17, 465–477.

Osgood, C. E., Suci, G. J., & Tannenbaum, P. H. (1957). *The measurement of meaning*. Urbana, Ill.: University of Illinois Press.

Ouchi, W. G., & Jaeger, A. M. (1978). Social structure and organizational type. In W. W. Meyer et al. (Eds.), *Environments and organizations*. San Francisco: Jossey-Bass.

Owen, D. R. (1972). The 47, XYY male: A review. *Psychological Bulletin*, 78, 209–233.

Paivio, A. (1971). *Imagery and verbal processes*. New York: Holt, Rinehart & Winston.

Paivio, A. (1978). Comparisons of mental clocks. *Journal of Experimental Psychology: Human Perception and Performance, 4,* 61–71.

Pallak, M. S., & Pittman, T. S. (1972). General motivational effects of dissonance arousal. *Journal of Personality and Social Psychology, 21,* 349–358.

Palmore, E., & Luikart, C. (1972). Health and social factors related to life satisfaction. *Journal of Health and Social Behavior, 13,* 68–80.

Palumbo, S. R. (1978). *Dreaming and memory: A new information-processing model.* New York: Basic Books.

Panksepp, J. (1973). Reanalysis of feeding patterns in the rat. *Journal of Comparative and Physiological Psychology, 82,* 78–94.

Papalia, D. E., & Olds, S. W. (1986). Human Development. New York: McGraw-Hill.

Parke, R. D., Berkowitz, L., Leyens, J. R., & Sebastian, R. (1975). The effects of repeated exposure to movie violence on aggressive behavior in juvenile delinquent boys: Field experimental studies. In L. Berkowitz (Ed.), *Advances in experimental social psychology* (Vol. 8). New York: Academic Press.

Parke, R. D., Berkowitz, L., Leyens, J. R., West, S. G., & Sebastian, R. J. (1977). Some effects of violent and nonviolent movies on the behavior of juvenile delinquents. In L. Berkowitz (Ed.), *Advances in experimental social psychology.* New York: Academic Press.

Parker, G., & Lipscombe, P. (1979). Parental overprotection and asthma. *Journal of Psychosomatic Research, 23,* 295–300.

Partridge, G. (1930). Current conceptions of the psychosomatic personality. *American Journal of Psychiatry, 87,* 53–99.

Patel, C. H. (1973). Yoga and biofeedback in the management of hypertension. *Lancet, 2,* 1053–1055.

Patel, C. H. (1975). Twelvemonth follow-up of yoga and biofeedback in the management of hypertension. *Lancet, 1,* 62–64.

Paul, G. & Lentz, R. (1977). *Psychosocial Treatment of Chronic Mental Patients: Milieu vs Social learning programs.* Cambridge, MA: Harvard University Press.

Paulus, P. R., et al. (1976). Density does effect task performance. *Journal of Personality and Social Psychology, 34,* 248–253.

Paulus, P. B., & Murdoch, P. (1971). Anticipated evaluation and audience presence in the enhancement of dominant responses. *Journal of Experimental Social Psychology, 7,* 280–291.

Pavlov, I. P. (1927). *Conditioned reflexes* (G. V. Anrep, trans.) London: Oxford University Press.

Paykel, E. S. (1973). Life events and acute depression. In J. P. Scott & E. C. Senay (Eds.), *Separation and depression,* (pp. 215–236). Washington: American Association for the Advancement of Science.

Pearlin, L. I., & Schooler, C. (1978). The structure of coping. *Journal of Health and Social Behavior, 19,* 2–21.

Peck, R. C. (1968). Psychological developments in the second half of life. In B. L. Neugarten (Ed.), *Middle age and aging.* Chicago: The University of Chicago Press.

Pedersen, F. A., & Bell, R. Q. (1970). Sex differences in preschool children without histories of complications of pregnancy and delivery. *Developmental Psychology, 3,* 10–15.

Pedersen, L. L., Scrimgeour, W. G., & Lefcoe, N. M. (1979). Variables of hypnosis which are related to success in a smoking withdrawal program. *International Journal of Clinical and Experimental Hypnosis, 27,* 14–20.

Penfield, W., & Jasper, H. (1954). *Epilepsy and the functional anatomy of the human brain.* Boston: Little, Brown, & Co.

Pennebaker, J. W. (1985). Traumatic experience and psychosomatic disease: Exploring the roles of behavioral inhibition, obsession, and confiding. *Canadian Psychology, 26*(2), 82–95.

Pennebaker, J. W., & Skelton, J. A. (1978). Psychological parameters of physical symptoms. *Personality and Social Psychology Bulletin, 4,* 524–540.

Perls, F. S. (1969). *Gestalt therapy verbatim.* Lafayette, Calif.: Real People Press.

Perls, F. S. (1970). Four lectures. In J. Fagan & I. L. Shepherd (Eds.), *Gestalt therapy now: Therapy, techniques, applications.* Palo Alto, Calif.: Science Behavior Books.

Perry, C. (1977). Variables influencing the posthypnotic persistence of an uncancelled hypnotic suggestion. In W. E. Edmonston, Jr. (Ed.), *Conceptual and investigative approaches to hypnosis and hypnotic phenomena. Annals of The New York Academy of Science* (Vol. 296), 264–273.

Pert, C. B., Kuhar, M. J., & Snyder, S. H. (1976). Autoradiographic localization of opiate receptor in rat brain. *National Academy of Science (USA): Proceedings, 73,* 3729–3733.

Pert, C. B., & Snyder, S. H. (1970). Opiate receptors: Demonstration in nervous tissue. *Science, 179,* 1011–1014.

Pert, C. B., & Snyder, S. H. (1973). Opiate receptor: Demonstration in the nervous tissue. *Science, 179,* 1011–1014.

Pervin, L. (1985). Current controversies, issues and directions. In M. Rosenzweig and L. Porter (Eds.), *Annual Review of Psychology, 36,* 1985 Annual Review Time, Palo Alto.

Peterson, A. C. & Taylor, B. (1980). The biological approach to adolescence. In J. Adelson (Ed.), *Handbook of adolescent psychology.* New York: Wiley.

Peterson, C., & Seligman, M. E. P. (1984). Causal explanations as a risk factor for depression: Theory and evidence. *Psychological Review, 91,* 347–374.

Peterson, L. R., & Peterson, M. J. (1959). Short-term retention of individual items. *Journal of Experimental Psychology, 58,* 193–198.

Pfeiffer, E., Verwoordt, A., & Davis, G. C. (1974). Sexual behavior in middle life. In E. Palmore (Ed.), *Normal aging II: Reports from the Duke longitudinal studies, 1970–1973.* Durham, N.C.: Duke University Press.

Phares, E. J. (1979). *Clinical psychology: Concepts, methods, and profession.* Chicago: Dorsey.

Phoenix, C. H. (1974). Prenatal testosterone in the nonhuman primate and its consequences for behavior. In R. C. Friedman, R. M. Richart, & K. L. VandeWiele (Eds.), *Sex differences in behavior.* New York: Wiley.

Piaget, J. (1932). *The moral judgment of the child.* New York: Harcourt, Brace.

Piaget, J. (1954). *The construction of reality in the child.* (M. Cook, trans.). New York: Basic Books.

Piaget, J. (1960). *The child's conception of the world.* Totowa, N.J.: Littlefield, Adams.

Piaget, J. (1972) Intellectual evolution from adolescence to adulthood. *Human Development, 15,* 1–12.

Piaget, J., & Inhelder, B. (1968). *The psychology of the child.* New York: Basic Books.

Piliavin, J. A., Callero, P. L., & Evans, D. E. (1982). Addiction?: Opponent-process theory and habitual blood donation. *Journal of Personality and Social Psychology, 43,* 1200–1213.

Pineo, P. C. (1961). Disenchantment in the later years of marriage. *Marriage and Family Living, 23,* 3–11.

Pinker, S. (1984). *Language learnability and language development.* Cambridge, Mass.: Harvard University Press.

Pirke, K., & Ploog, D. (Eds.) (1984). *The psychobiology of anorexia nervosa.* Berlin: Springer-Verlag.

Pi-Sunyer, X., Kissileff, H. R., Thornton, J., & Smith, G. P. (1982). C-terminal octapeptide of cholecystokinin decreases in food intake in obese men. *Physiology and Behavior, 29,* 627–630.

Pittman, N. L., & Pittman, T. S. (1979). Effects of amount of helplessness training and internal-external locus of control on mood and performance. *Journal of Personality and Social Psychology, 37,* 39–47.

Pittman, T. S. (1975). Attribution of arousal as a mediator in dissonance reduction. *Journal of Experimental Social Psychology, 11,* 53–63.

Pittman, T. S. (1982). Intrinsic and extrinsic motivational orientations toward others. Meeting of the American Psychological Assoiation, Washington, D.C.

Pittman, T. S., Boggiano, A. K., & Ruble, D. N. (1982). Intrinsic and extrinsic motivational orientations; Interactive effects of reward, competence feedback, and task complexity. In J. Levine & M. Wang (Eds.), *Teacher and student perceptions: Implications for learning.* Hillsdale, N.J.: Erlbaum.

Pittman, T. S., Emery, J., & Boggiano, A. K. (1982). Intrinsic and extrinsic motivational orientation: Reward-induced changes in preference for complexity. *Journal of Personality and Social Psychology, 42,* 789–797.

Pittman, T. S. & Heller, J. F. (1987). Social motivation. In M. Rosenzweig & L. Porter (Eds.), *Annual Review of Psychology, Vol. 38.* Palo Alto, Cal.: Annual Reviews, Inc.

Pliner, P., Blankstein, K. R., & Spigel, I. M. (1979). *Perception of emotion in self and others.* New York: Plenum.

Plomin, R., & DeFries, J. C. (1980). Genetics and intelligence: Recent data. *Intelligence, 4,* 15–24.

Pohl, J. M. & Fuller, S. S. (1980). Perceived choice, social interaction and dimensions of morale of residents in a home for the aged. *Research in Nursing and Health, 3:* 49–54.

Poincare, H. (1929). *The foundations of science* (G. R. Halstead, trans.). New York: The Science Press.

Pollack, I., Rubenstein, H., & Decker, L. (1959). Intelligibility of known and unknown message sets. *Journal of the Acoustical Society of America, 31,* 273–279.

Pollard-Gott, L., McCluskey, M., & Todres, A. (1979). Subjective story structure. *Discourse Processes, 2,* 251–281.

Porteous, J. D. (1977). *Environment and behavior.* Reading, Mass.: Addison-Wesley.

Porter, H. (1939). Studies in the psychology of stuttering: XIV. Stuttering phenomena in relation to size and personnel of audience. *Journal of Speech Disorders, 4,* 323–333.

Porter, R. W., Brady, J. V., Conrad, D., Mason, J. W., Galamobos, R., & Rioch, D. (1958). Some experimental observations on gastrointestinal lesions in behaviorally conditioned monkeys. *Psychosomatic Medicine, 20,* 379–394.

Posner, M. I. (1969). Abstraction and the process of recognition. In G. H. Bower & J. T. Spence (Eds.), *The psychology of learning and motivation: Advances in research and theory* (Vol. 3). New York: McGraw-Hill.

Prange, A., Jr., Wilson, I., Lynn, W., Lacoe, B., & Strikeleather, R. (1974). L-tryptophan in mania—contribution to a permissive hypothesis of affective disorders. *Archives of General Psychiatry, 30,* 56–62.

Premack, D. (1965). Reinforcement theory. In D. Levine (Ed.). *Nebraska symposium on motivation.* Lincoln: University of Nebraska Press.

Premack, D. (1976). *Intelligence in ape and man.* Hillsdale, N.J.: Erlbaum.

Premack, D. (1985). Gavagai! The future of the animal language controversy. Cambridge, Mass.: MIT Press.

Pressley, M., Levin, J. R., & Delaney, H. D. The mnemonic keyword method. *Review of Educational Research, 52,* 61–91.

Prinzmetal, W., Treiman, R., & Rho, S. (1986). How to see a reading unit. *Journal of Memory and Language, 25,* 461–475.

Provence, S., & Lipton, R. C. (1962). *Infants in institutions.* New York: International Universities Press.

Pruitt, D. G. (1971). Choice shifts in group discussion: An introductory review. *Journal of Personality and Social Psychology, 20,* 339–360.

Pruitt, D. G. (1971). Conclusions: Toward an understanding of choice shifts in group dissenssion. *Journal of Personality and Social Psychology, 20,* 495–510.

Pruitt, D. G. (1975). Power and bargaining. In B. Seidenberg & A. Swadowsky (Eds.), *Social psychology: An introduction.* New York: Free Press.

Pruitt, D. G. (1976). Conclusions: Toward an understanding of choice shifts in group discussion. *Journal of Personality and Social Psychology, 20,* 495–510.

Putnam, F. (1982 October). Traces of Eve's faces. *Psychology Today, 16,* p. 88.

Rabbitt, P. M. (1982). Breakdown of control processes in old age. In T. Field, A. Huston, H. Quay, L. Troll, & G. Finnley (Eds.), *Review of human development.* New York: Wiley.

Rachlin, H. (1976). *Introduction to modern behaviorism* (2nd ed.). San Francisco: Freeman.

Rachman, S. (1966). Sexual fetishism: An experimental analogue. *Psychological Record, 16,* 293–296.

Radloff, L. (1975). Sex differences in depression: The effects of occupation and marital status. *Sex Roles, 1,* 249–281.

Ragozin, A. S. (1980). Attachment behavior of daycare children: Naturalistic and laboratory observation. *Child Development, 51,* 409–415.

Rahe, R., Romo, M., Bennett, L., & Siltanen, P. (1974). Recent life changes, myocardial infarction, and abrupt coronary death: Studies in Helsinki. *Archives of Internal Medicine, 133,* 221–228.

Raines, H. (1979, December 23). Marijuana from many sources softening cancer chemotherapy. *New York Times.*

Rao, D. C., Morton, N. E., Lalouel, J. M., & Lew, R. (1982). Path analysis under generalized assortative mating. II. American I.Q. *Genetical Research, 39,* 187–198.

Raphael, B. (1976). *The thinking computer: Mind inside matter.* San Francisco: Freeman.

Rappaport, A. (1973). *Experimental games and their uses in psychology.* Morristown, N.J.: Social Learning Press.

Rapaport, D. (1946). *Diagnostic psychological testing.* Vol. 1. Chicago: Year Book Publishers.

Raven, J. C. (1947). *Progressive matrices.* London: Lewis.

Ray, O. S. (1983). Durgs, society, and human behavior (3rd ed.). St. Louis: Mosby.

Raynor, J. O., & Entin, E. E. (1982). Future orientation and achievement motivation. In J. O. Raynor & E. E. Entine (Eds.), *Motivation, career striving, and aging.* New York: Hemisphere.

Reder, L. M., Wible, C., & Martin, J. (1986). Differential memory changes with age: Exact retrieval versus plausible inference. *Journal of Experimental Psychology: Learning, Memory, and Cognition, 12,* 72–81.

Rees, L. (1963). The significance of parental attitudes in childhood asthma. *Journal of Psychosomatic Research, 7,* 181–190.

Regan, D. T., & Fazio, R. H. (1977). On the consistency between attitudes and behavior: Look to the method of attitude formation. *Journal of Experimental Social Psychology, 13,* 38–45.

Regan, D. T., Strauss, E., & Fazio, R. H. (1974). Liking and the attribution process. *Journal of Experimental Social Psychology, 10,* 385–397.

Reich, P. A. (1986). Language development. Englewood Cliffs, N.J.: Prentice-Hall.

Rescorla, R. A. (1967a). Inhibition of delay in Pavlovian fear conditioning. *Journal of Comparative and Physiological Psychology, 64,* 114–120.

Rescorla, R. A. (1967b). Pavlovian conditioning and its proper control procedures. *Psychological Review, 74,* 71–80.

Rescorla, R. A. (1969). Conditioned inhibition of fear resulting from negative CS-US contingencies. *Journal of Comparative and Physiological Psychology, 67,* 504–509.

Rescorla, R. A. (1972). Informational variables in Pavlovian conditioning. In Bower, G. H. (Ed.), *Psychology of learning and motivation, 6,* New York: Academic Press.

Rescorla, R. A., & Wagner, A. R. (1972). A theory of Pavlovian conditioning: Variations in the effectiveness of reinforcement and nonreinforcement. In A. H. Black & W. F. Prokasy (Eds.), *Classical conditioning II: Current research and theory.* New York: Appleton-Century-Crofts.

Revoile, S., Pickett, J. M., Holden, P. L. D., Talkin, D., et al. (1987). Burst and transition cues to voicing perception for spoken initial stops by impaired- and normal-hearing listeners. *Journal of Speech & Hearing Research, 30,* 3–12.

Reynolds, G. S. (1975). *A primer of operant conditioning* (rev. ed.). Glenview, Ill.: Scott Foresman.

Rheingold, H. L., & Adams, J. L. (1980). the significance of speech to newborns. *Developmental psychology, 6,* 397–403.

Rhodewalt, F. (1979). The coronary-prone behavior pattern, psychological reactance, and the self-attributor. Unpublished doctoral dissertation, Princeton University.

Rice, J., Cloninger, C. R., & Reich, T. (1980). Analysis of behavioral traits in the presence of cultural transmission and assortative mating: Applications to I.Q. and SES. *Behavior Genetics, 10,* 73–92.

Rife, D. C. (1940). Handedness, with special reference to twins. *Genetics, 25,* 178–186.

Riley, J., & Foner, A. (1968). *Aging and society, Vol. I: An inventory of research findings.* New York: Russell Sage.

Rimland, B. (1964). *Infantile autism.* New York: Appleton-Century-Crofts.

Rimm, D. C., & Masters, J. C. (1979). *Behavior therapy: Techniques and empirical findings* (2nd ed.). New York: Academic Press.

Riskind, J. H. (1984). They tough to conquer: Guiding and self-regulatory functions of physical posture after success and failure. *JPSP, 47,* 479–493.

Riskind, J. H., & Gotay, C. C. (1982). Physical posture: Could it have regulatory or feedback effects on motivation and emotion? *Motivation and Emotion, 6,* 273–298.

Rist, R. (1970). Student social class and teacher expectations: The self-fulfilling prophecy in ghetto education. *Harvard Educational Review, 40,* 411–451.

Robbins, P. (1978). *Successful midlife career change.* New York: AMACON.

Robbins, S. P. (1974). *Managing organizational conflict: A nontraditional approach.* Englewood Cliffs, N.J.: Prentice-Hall.

Roberts, C. L., Marx, M. H., & Collier, G. (1958). Light onset and light offset as reinforcers for the albino rat. *Journal of Comparative and Physiological Psychology, 51,* 575–579.

Roberts, L. E. (1979). Operant conditioning of autonomic responses. One perspective on the curare experiments. In G. E. Schwartz & D. Shapiro (Eds.), *Consciousness and self-regulation: Advances in research* (Vol. 2). New York: Plenum.

Roberts, W. A., & Van Veldhuizen, N. (1985). Spatial memory in pigeons on the radical maze. *Journal of Experimental Psychology: Animal Behavior Processes, 2,* 24–260.

Robey, D. (1974). Task design, work values, and work response: An experimental test. *Organizational Behavior and Human Performance, 12,* 264–273.

Robin, J., & Langer, E. (1977). Long-term effects of control-relevant intervention with the institutionalized aged. *Journal of Personality and Social Psychology, 35,* 897–902.

Robins, L. N. (1974). A follow-up study of Vietnam veterans' drug use. *Journal of Drug Issues, 4,* 61–63.

Robins, N. L. (1966). *Deviant children grow up.* Baltimore: Williams & Wilkins.

Robinson, L. B., & Hastie, R. (1985). Revision of beliefs when a hypothesis is eliminated from consideration. *Journal of Experimental Psychology: Human Perception and Performance, 11,* 443–456.

Rock, I. (1975). *An introduction to perception.* New York: Macmillan.

Rodgers, D. L., & Jones, A. (1980). Information-seeking behavior in the tactile modality. *Perceptual and Motor Skills, 50,* 1179–1191.

Rodin, J. (1981). Current status of the internal-external hypothesis of obesity: What went wrong? *American Psychologist, 36,* 361–372.

Rodin, J., & Langer, E. (1977). Long-term effects of a control-relevant intervention with the institutionalized aged. *Journal of Personality and Social Psychology, 35,* 897–902.

Roethlisberger, F. J., & Dickson, W. J. (1939). *Management and the worker.* Cambridge, Mass.: Harvard University Press.

Roffwarg, H. P., Muzio, J. N., & Dement, W. C. (1966). Ontogenetic development of the human sleep-dream cycle. *Science, 152,* 604–619.

Roffwarg, H. P., Herman, J. H., Bowe-Anders, C., & Tauber, E. S. (1978). The effects of sustained alterations of waking visual input on dream content. In A. M. Arkin, J. S. Antrobus, and S. J. Ellman (Eds.), *The mind in sleep: Psychology and psychobiology.* Hillsdale, N.J.: Erlbaum.

Rogers, C. R. (1951). *Client-centered therapy.* Boston: Houghton Mifflin.

Rogers, C. R. (1960). *On becoming a person: A therapist's view of psychotherapy.* Boston: Houghton Mifflin.

Rogers, C. R. (1961). *On becoming a person.* Boston: Houghton Mifflin.

Rogers, C. R. (1970). *Client-centered therapy.* (2nd ed.) Boston: Houghton Mifflin.

Rokeach, M. (1968). *Beliefs, attitudes, and values.* San Francisco: Jossey-Bass.

Rokeach, M., & Kliejunas, P. (1972). Behavior as a function of attitude-toward-object and attitude-toward situation. *Journal of Personality and Social Psychology, 22,* 194–201.

Rollins, B. C., & Feldman, H. (1970). Marital satisfaction over the family life cycle. *Journal of Marriage and the Family, 32*(1), 20–28.

Ropartz, P. (1968). The relation between olfactory stimulation and aggressive behavior in mice. *Animal behavior, 16,* 97–100.

Rosch, E. (1977). Human categorization. In N. Warren (Ed.), *Advances in cross-cultural psychology* (Vol. 1). London: Academic Press.

Rosch, E. (1978). Principles of categorization. In E. Rosch & B. B. Lloyd (Eds.), *Cognition and categorization,* Hillsdale, N.J.: Erlbaum.

Rosch, E., & Lloyd B. B. (Eds.) (1978). *Cognition and categorization.* Hillsdale, N.J.: Erlbaum.

Rose, A. M. (1968). A current theoretical issue in social gerontology. In B. L. Neugarten (Ed.), *Middle age and aging.* Chicago: The University of Chicago Press.

Rose, S. (1975). *The conscious brain.* New York: Knopf.

Rosen, B. C., & D'Andrade, R. (1959). The psychosocial origins of achievement motivation. *Sociometry, 22,* 188–218.

Rosenberg, E. J., & Dohrenwend, B. S. (1975). Effects of experience and ethnicity on ratings of life events as stressors. *Journal of Health and Social Behavior, 16,* 127–129.

Rosenberg, M. J. (1960). Cognitive reorganization in response to hypnotic reversals of attitudinal affect. *Journal of Personality, 28,* 39–63.

Rosenberg, M. S. (1987). Psychopharmicological intervention with young hyperactive children. *Topics in Early Childhood Special Education, 6*(4), 62–74.

Rosenblum, L. A. (1977). The development of social behavior in the rhesus monkey. Unpublished Ph.D. dissertation, U. of Wisconsin, 1961. Cited in D. P. Kimble, *Psychology as a biological science.* Santa Monica, Calif.: Goodyear.

Rosenhan, D. L. (1970). The natural socialization of altruistic autonomy. In J. Macaulay & L. Berkowitz (Eds.), *Altruism and helping behavior.* New York: Academic Press.

Rosenman, R. H., Brand, R. J., Jenkins, C. D., Friedman, M., Straus, R., & Wurm, M. (1975). Coronary heart disease in the Western Collaborative Group Study: Final follow-up experience of 8½ years. *Journal of the American Medical Association, 233,* 872–877.

Rosenthal, R. (1967). Covert communication in the psychological experiment. *Psychological Bulletin, 67,* 356–367.

Rosenzweig, M. R. (1966). Environmental complexity, cerebral change and behavior. *American Psychologist, 21,* 321–332.

Ross, L. (1977). The intuitive psychologist and his short-comings: Distortions in the attribution process. In L. Berkowitz (Ed.), *Advances in experimental social psychology* (Vol. 10). New York: Academic Press.

Ross, L., Greene, D., & House, P. (1977). The "false consensus effect": An egocentric bias in social perception and attribution processes. *Journal of Experimental Social Psychology, 13,* 279–301.

Ross, L., Rodin, J., & Zimbardo, P. (1969). Toward an attribution therapy: The reduction of fear through induced cognitive-emotional misattribution. *Journal of Personality and Social Psychology, 12,* 279–288.

Ross, M., & Sicoly, F. (1979). Egocentric biases in availability and attribution. *Journal of Personality and Social Psychology, 37,* 322–337.

Roth, S., & Kubal, L. (1975). The effects of noncontingent reinforcement on tasks of differing importance: Facilitation and learned helplessness. *Journal of Personality and Social Psychology, 32,* 680–691.

Rotter, J. B. (1966). Generalized expectancies for internal versus external control of reinforcement. Psychological Monographs, Vol. 80, no. 1.

Rozin, P., & Kalat, J. (1971). Specific hungers and poison avoidance as adoptive specializations of learning. *Psychological Review, 78,* 459–486.

Rozin, P., & Mayer, J. (1961). Thermal reinforcement and thermoregulatory behavior in the goldfish, *Carassius auratus. Science, 134,* 942–943.

Rubin, D. (1977). Very long term memory for prose and verse. *Journal of Verbal Learning and Verbal Behavior, 16,* 611–621.

Rubin, Z. (1973). *Liking and loving: An invitation to social psychology.* New York: Holt, Rinehart & Winston.

Rubin, Z. (1974). From liking to loving, Patterns of attractions in dating relationships. In T. L. Huston (Ed.), *Foundations of interpersonal attraction.* New York: Academic Press.

Rubin, Z., & McNeil, M. (1977). *The psychology of being human,* 2nd ed. New York: Harper and Row.

Ruble, D. N., & Feldman, N. S. (1976). Order of consensus, distinctiveness, and consistency information and causal attributions. *Journal of Personality and Social Psychology, 34,* 930–937.

Ruble, D. N., Parsons, J. E., & Ross, J. (1976). Self-evaluative responses of children in an achievement setting. *Child Development, 47,* 990–997.

Ruff, H. A., & Birch, H. G. (1974). Infant visual fixation: The effects of concentricity, curvilinearity, and number of directions. *Journal of Experimental Child Psychology, 17,* 460–473.

Rumbaugh, D. M. (1977). *Language learning by a chimpanzee: The LANA project.* New York: Academic Press.

Rumbaugh, D. M., Savage-Rumbaugh, E. S., & Gill, T. V. (1979). The chimpanzee as an animal model in language research. In R. L. Schiefelbusch & J. H. Hollis (Eds.), *Language intervention from ape to child.* Baltimore, Md.: University Park Press.

Rumelhart, D. E. (1977). Understanding and summarizing brief stories. In D. Lolberge & J. Samuels (Eds.), *Basic processes in reading: Perception and comprehension.* Hillsdale, N.J.: Erlbaum.

Rumelhart, D. E., Hinton, G. E., & Williams, R. J. (1986). Learning internal representations by error propagation. In D. E. Rumelhart & J. L. McClelland (Eds.), Parallel distributed processing: Explorations in the neurostructure of cognition. Cambridge, Mass.: M.I.T.

Rumelhart, D. E., & McClelland, J. L. (Eds.) (1986). Parallel Distributed Processing: Explorations in the neurostructure of cognition. Cambridge, Mass.: M.I.T.

Runck, B. (1980). *Biofeedback—issues in treatment assessment.* Rockville, Md.: National Institute of Mental Health.

Rundus, D. (1971). Analysis of rehearsal processes in free recall. *Journal of Experimental Psychology, 89,* 63–77.

Rush, A. J., Beck, A. T., Kovacs, M., & Hollon, S. (1977). Comparative efficacy of cognitive therapy and pharmacotherapy in the treatment of depressed outpatients. *Cognitive Therapy and Research, 1,* 17–37.

Russell, J. A., & Bullock, M. (1986). Fuzzy concepts and the perception of emotion in facial expressions. *Social Cognition, 4,* 309–341.

Ryle, G. (1949). *The concept of mind.* London: Hutchinson.

Saarinen, T. F. (1969). *Perception of the environment.* Resource Paper no. 5. Association of American Geographers.

Sachs, J. S. (1967). Recognition memory for syntactic and semantic aspects of connected discourse. *Perception and Psychophysics, 2,* 437–442.

Sackeim, H. (1985). The case for E.C.T. *Psychology Today 19,* (6), 36–40.

Sackheim, J. A. (1987, June). The case for ECT. *Psychology Today,* pp. 36–40.

Sacks, O. (1986). *The man who mistook his wife for a hat: and other clinical tales.* New York: Harper and Row.

Saegert, S., Swap, W., & Zajonc, R. B. (1973). Exposure, context, and interpersonal attraction. *Journal of Personality and Social Psychology, 25,* 234–242.

Sahlins, M. (1976). The use and abuse of biology: An anthropological critique of sociobiology. Ann Arbor, MI: The University of Michigan Press.

Sakurai, M. M. (1975). Small group cohesiveness and detrimental conformity. *Sociometry, 38,* 340–357.

Salapatek, P. (1975). Pattern perception in early infancy. In L. B. Cohen & P. Salapetek (Eds.), *Infant perception: From sensation to cognition* (Vol. 1): *Basic visual processes.* New York: Academic Press.

Salapatek, P., Bechtold, A. G., & Bushnell, E. W. (1976). Infant visual acuity as a function of viewing distance. *Child Development, 47,* 860–863.

Salapatek, P., & Kessen, W. (1966). Visual scanning of triangles by the human newborn. *Journal of Experimental Child Psychology, 3,* 155–167.

Samuda, R. J. (1975). *Psychological testing of American minorities: Issues and consequences.* New York: Dodd, Mead.

Sanders, G. S. (1981). Driven by distraction: An integrative review of social facilitation theory and research. *Journal of Experimental Social Psychology, 17,* 227–251.

Sapir, E. (1958). Language and environment. In D. G. Mandelbaum (Ed.), *Selected writings of Edward Sapir in language, culture and personality.* Berkeley: University of California Press. (Originally published, 1912.)

Sapolsky, B. S., & Zillman, D. (1981). The effect of soft-core and hard-core erotica on provoked and unprovoked hostile behavior. *Journal of Sex Research, 17,* 319–343.

Sarason, I. G., Johnson, J. H., & Siegel, J. M. (1978). Assessing the impact of life changes: Development of the life experiences survey. *Journal of Consulting and Clinical Psychology, 46,* 932–946.

Sarbin, T. R. (1962). Attempts to understand hypnotic phenomena. In L. Postman, *Psychology in the making.* New York: Knopf. Pp. 745–784.

Sarbin, T. R., & Coe, W. C. (1972). *Hypnosis: A social psychological analysis of influence communication.* New York: Holt, Rinehart & Winston.

Sargent, S. S., & Stafford, K. R. (1965). *Basic teachings of the great psychologists.* Garden City, N.Y.: Doubleday.

Sarnoff, I., & Zimbardo, P. G. (1961). Anxiety, fear, and social affiliation. *Journal of Abnormal and Social Psychology, 62,* 356–363.

Satinoff, E. (1974). Neural integration of thermoregulatory responses. In L. V. DiCara (Ed.), *Limbic and autonomic nervous system: Advances in research.* New York: Plenum.

Satinoff, E., & Henderson, R. (1977). Thermoregulatory behavior. In W. K. Honig & J. E. R. Staddon (Eds.), *Handbook of operant behavior.* Englewood Cliffs, N.J.: Prentice-Hall.

Savage-Rumbaugh, S., McDonald, K., Sevcik, R. A., Hopkins, W. D., & Rubert, E. (1986). Spontaneous symbol acquisition and communicative use by pygmy chimpanzees (Pan paniscus). *Journal of Experimental Psychology, 115,* 211–235.

Savage-Rumbaugh, E. S., Pate, J. L., Lawson, J., Smith, T. S., & Rosenbaum, S. (1983). Can a chimpanzee make a statement? *Journal of Experimental Psychology: General, 112,* 457–492.

Savage-Rumbaugh, E. S., Rumbaugh, D. M., Smith, S. T., & Lawson, J. (1980). Reference: The linguistic essential. *Science, 210,* 992–925.

Scarr, S., & Hall, E. (1984, May). What's a parent to do? *Psychology Today,* pp. 58–63.

Scarr, S., & Weinberg, R. A. (1976). IQ test performance of black children adopted by white females. *American Psychologist, 31,* 726–739.

Scarr, S., & Weinberg, R. A. (1977). Intellectual

similarities within families of both adopted and biological children. *Intelligence, 1,* 170–191.

Schachter, D. L., & Graf, P. (1986). Effects of elaborative processing on implicit and explicit memory for new associations. *Journal of Experimental Psychology: Learning, Memory, & Cog 12,* 432–444.

Schachter, S. (1951). Deviation, rejection, and communication. *Journal of Abnormal and Social Psychology, 46,* 190–207.

Schachter, S. (1959). *The psychology of affiliation: Experimental studies of the sources of gregariousness.* Stanford, Calif.: Stanford University Press.

Schachter, S. (1971). Some extraordinary facts about obese humans and rats. *American Psychologist, 26,* 129–144.

Schachter, S. (1982). Recidivism and self-cure of smoking and obesity. *American Psychologist, 37,* 436–444.

Schachter, S., & Singer, J. E. (1962). Cognitive, social, and physiological determinants of emotional state. *Psychological Review, 69,* 379–399.

Schaefer, E. S., & Bayley, N. (1963). Maternal behavior, child behavior, and their intercorrelations from infancy through adolescence. *Monographs of the Society for Research in Child Development, 28*(3, Serial No. 87).

Schaefer, H. H., & Martin, P. L. (1969). *Behavior therapy.* New York: McGraw-Hill.

Schafer, R. B., & Keith, P. M. (1981). Equity in marital role across the family life cycle. *Journal of Marriage and the Family, 43,* 359–367.

Schaffer, H. R., & Emerson, P. E. (1964a). The development of social attachments in infancy. *Monographs of the Society for Research in Child Development, 29*(3, Serial No. 94).

Schaffer, H. R., & Emerson, P. E. (1964b). Patterns of response to physical contact in early human development. *Journal of Child Psychology and Psychiatry, 5,* 1–13.

Schaie, K. W. (1979). The primary mental abilities in adulthood: An exploration of psychometric intelligence. In P. B. Balters and O. G. Brim, Jr. (Eds.), *Life-span development and behavior.* Vol. 2. New York: Academic Press.

Schaie, K. W., Labouvie, G., & Buech, B. V. (1973). Generational and cohort-specific differences in adult cognitive functioning: A fourteen-year study of independent samples. *Developmental Psychology, 9,* 151–166.

Schaie, K. W., & Willis, S. L. (1986). *Adult development and againg* (2nd ed.) Boston: Little, Brown.

Schank, R., & Abelson, R. (1976). *Scripts, plans, goals, and understanding.* Hillsdale, N.J.: Erlbaum.

Schank, R., & Abelson, R. (1977). *Scripts, plans, goals, and understanding.* Hillsdale, N.J.: Erlbaum.

Schank, R., & Birnbaum, L. (1984, March). Memory, meaning, and syntax. In T. G. Bever, J. M. Carroll, & L. A. Miller (Eds.), *Talking minds* (pp. 209–251). Cambridge, Mass.: MIT Press.

Scheier, M. F., Fenigstein, A., & Buss, A. (1974). Self-awareness and physical aggression. *Journal of Experimental Social Psychology, 10,* 264–273.

Schein, E. H. (1980). *Organizational psychology.* Englewood Cliffs, N.J.: Prentice-Hall.

Schelling, T. C. (1960). *The strategy of conflict.* Cambridge, Mass.: Harvard University Press.

Scherer, K. R. (1984). Emotion as a multicomponent process: A model and some cross-cultural data. In P. Shaver (Ed.), *Review of Personality and Social Psychology* (Vol. 5). Beverly Hills, Cal.: Sage.

Schiff, M., Duyme, M., Dumaret, A., & Tomkiewicz, S. (1982). How much *could* we boost scholastic achievement and I.Q. scores? A direct answer from a French adoption study. *Cognition, 12,* 165–196.

Schiff, W. (1980). *Perception: An applied approach.* Boston: Houghton Mifflin.

Schildkraut, J. (1965). The catecholamine hypothesis of affective disorders: A review of supporting evidence. *American Journal of Psychiatry, 122,* 509–522.

Schill, T., & Chapin, J. (1972). Sex guilt and males' preference for reading erotic literature. *Journal of Consulting and Clinical Psychology, 39,* 516.

Schleifer, S. J., Keller, S. E., McKegney, F. P., & Stein, M. (1979). The influence of stress and other psychosocial factors on human immunity. Paper presented at the 36th Annual Meeting of the Psychosomatic Society, Dallas, TX.

Schlossberg, N. K. (1984a). Exploring the adult years. In A. M. Rogers and C. J. Scheirer (eds.), *The G. Stanley Hall lecture series,* vol. 4. Washington, D.C.: American Psychological Association.

Schmale, A. H., & Iker, H. (1971). Hopelessness as a predictor of cervical cancer. *Social Science and Medicine, 5,* 95–100.

Schmidt, D. E., & Keating, J. P. (1979). Human crowding and personal control: An integration of the research. *Psychological Bulletin, 86,* 680–700.

Schmidt, G., & Sigush, V. (1970). Sex differences in responses to psychosexual stimulation by film and slides. *Journal of Sex Research, 6,* 268–283.

Schmidt, G., Sigush, V., & Meyberg, V. (1969). Psychosexual stimulation in men: Emotional reactions, changes of sex behavior, and measures of conservative attitudes. *Journal of Sex Research, 5,* 199–217.

Schmidt, H. O., & Fonda, C. (1956). The reliability of psychiatric diagnosis. *Journal of Abnormal and Social Psychology, 52,* 262–267.

Schneider, D. J. (1973). Implicit personality theory: A review. *Psychological Bulletin, 79,* 294–309.

Schneider, W., & Shiffrin, R. M. (1977). Controlled and automatic human information processing. I. Detection, search, and attention. *Psychological Review, 84,* 1–66.

Schneider-Rosen, K., Braunwald, K. G., Carlson, V., & Cicchetti, D. (1985). Current perspectives in attachment theory: Illustration from the study of maltreated infants. In I. Bretherton & E. Waters (Eds.). Growing points of attachment theory and research. Monographs of the Society for Research in Child Development, 50*(1–2) Serial No. 209.

Schofield, W. (1964). *Psychotherapy: The purchase of friendship.* Englewood Cliffs, N.J.: Prentice Hall.

Schrank, R. (1978). *Ten thousand working days.* Cambridge Mass.: MIT Press.

Schreiber, F. R. (1974). *Sybil.* New York: Warner.

Schulsinger, F. (1972). Psychopathology: Heredity and environment. *International Journal of Mental Health, 1,* 190–206.

Schutz, R., & Hanusa, B. (1978). Long-term effects of control and predictability-enhancing interventions: Findings and ethical issues. *Journal of Personality and Social Psychology, 36,* 1194–1201.

Schultz, T. R. (1980). Development of the concept of intention. In W. A. Collins (Ed.), Minnesota symposia on child psychology (Vol. 13). Hillsdale, N.J.: Erlbaum.

Schwartz, B. (1978). *Psychology of learning and behavior.* New York: Norton.

Schwartz, B. (1984). *Psychology of learning and behavior* (2nd ed.). New York: Norton.

Schwartz, G. E. (1977). Psychosomatic disorders and biofeedback: A psychobiological model of disregulation. In J. D. Maser & M. E. P. Seligman (Eds.), *Psychopathology: Experimental models.* San Francisco: Freeman.

Schwartz, M. (1978). *Physiological psychology.* Englewood Cliffs, N.J.: Prentice-Hall.

Schwartz, M. D., & Errera, P. (1963). Psychiatric care in a general hospital emergency room. *Archives of General Psychiatry, 9,* 113–121.

Schwartz, R., & Schwartz, L. (1980). *Becoming a couple.* Englewood Cliffs, N.J.: Prentice-Hall.

Scoville, W. B., & Milner, B. (1957). Loss of recent memory after bilateral hippocampal lesions. *Journal of Neurology, Neurosurgery, and Psychiatry, 20,* 11–21.

Scribner, S., & Cole, M. (1981). *The psychology of literacy.* Cambridge, Mass.: Harvard University Press.

Seagert, S. C., Swap, W., & Zajone, R. B. (1973). Exposure, context, and interpersonal attraction. *Journal of Personality and Social Psychology, 25,* 234–242.

Seagraves, R. T. (1977). Pharmacological agents causing sexual dysfunction. *Journal of Sex and Marital Therapy, 13,* 157–176.

Searle, J. (1979). *Expression and meaning: Studies in the theory of speech acts.* Cambridge: Cambridge University Press.

Sears, R. R., Maccoby, E. E., & Levin, H. (1957). *Patterns of child rearing.* New York: Harper & Row.

Seelig, K. (1954). *Albert Einstein.* Zurich: Europe Verlag.

Segal, M. W. (1974). Alphabet and attraction: An unobtrusive measure of the effect of propinquity in a field setting. *Journal of Personality and Social Psychology, 30,* 654–657.

Segal, S. J., & Fusella, V. (1970). Influence of imaged pictures and sounds in detection of visual and auditory signals. *Journal of Experimental Psychology, 83,* 458–474.

Segovia-Riguelma, N., Varela, A., & Mardones, J. (1971). Appetite for alcohol. In Y. Israel & J. Mardones (Eds.), *Biological basis of alcoholism.* New York: Wiley.

Sejnowski, T. J., & Rosenberg, C. R. (1986). NETtalk: A parallel network that learns to read aloud. *The John Hopkins E. E. and C. S. Tech. Rpt.* JHU/EECS-86/01.

Selfridge, O. G. (1959). Pandemonium: A paradigm for learning. In D. V. Blake & A. M. Uttley (Eds.), *Proceedings of the symposium on the mechanisation of thought processes.* London: Her Majesty's Stationery Office.

Seligman, C., Finegan, J. E., Hazlewood, J. D., & Wilkinson, M. (1985). Manipulating attributions for profit: A field test of the effects of attributions on behavior. *Social Cognition, 3,* 313–321.

Seligman, C., Fazio, R. H., & Zanna, M. P. (1980). Effects of salience of extrinsic rewards on liking and loving. *Journal of Personality and Social Psychology, 38,* 453–460.

Seligman, M. E. P. (1968). Chronic fear produced by unpredictable electric shock. *Journal of Comparative and Physiological Psychology, 66,* 402–411.

Seligman, M. E. P. (1971). Phobias and preparedness. *Behavior Therapy, 2,* 307–320.

Seligman, M. E. P. (1972). Phobias and preparedness. In M. E. P. Seligman & J. L. Hager (Eds.). *Biological boundaries of learning.* New York: Appleton-Century-Crofts.

Seligman, M. E. P. (1974). Depression and learned helplessness. In R. J. Friedman & M. M. Katz (Eds.), *The psychology of depression: Contemporary theory and research.* Washington, D.C.: Winston-Wiley.

Seligman, M. E. P. (1975). *Helplessness: On depression, development, and death.* San Francisco: Freeman.

Seligman, M. E. P., Abramson, L. Y., Semmel, A., & von Baeyer, C. (1979). Depressive attributional style. *Journal of Abnormal Psychology, 88,* 242–247.

Seligman, M. E. P., & Hager, J. L. (1972). *Biological boundaries of learning.* New York: Appleton-Century-Crofts.

Seligman, M. E. P., & Maier, S. F. (1967). Failure

to escape traumatic shock. *Journal of Experimental Psychology, 74,* 1–9.

Selman, R. L. (1980). *The growth of interpersonal understanding.* New York: Academic Press.

Seltzer, V. C. (1982). *Adolescent social development: Dynamic functional interaction.* Lexington, MA: Heath.

Selye, H. (1956). *The stress of life.* New York: McGraw-Hill.

Selye, H. (1976). *The stress of life* (2nd ed.). New York: McGraw-Hill.

Selye, H. (1980). *Selye's guide to stress research* (Vol. 1). New York: Van Nostrand Reinhold.

Sem-Jacobsen, C. W., & Torkildsen, A. (1960). Depth recording and electrical stimulation in the human brain. In E. R. Ramey & D. S. O'Doherty (Eds.), *Electrical studies on the anesthetized brain.* New York: Hoeber. Pp. 275–290.

Serbin, L. A., & O'Leary, K. E. (1975). How nursery schools teach girls to shut up. *Psychology Today, 9,* 57–58, 102–103.

Severne, L. (1982). Psychosocial aspects of the menopause. In A. M. Voda, M. Dinnerstein, & S. R. O'Donnell (Eds.), *Changing perspectives on menopause.* Austin, TX: University of Texas Press.

Seymour, T. S. (1977). Effectiveness of marriage encounter couple participation on improving qualitative aspects of marital relationships. *Dissertation Abstracts International, 21*(3), 441–446.

Shaffer, D. R. (1979). *Social and personality development.* Monterey, Calif.: Brooks/Cole.

Shafii, M., Lavely, R. A., & Jaffe, R. D. (1974). Meditation and marijuana. *American Journal of Psychiatry, 131,* 60–63.

Shafii, M., Lavely, R. A., & Jaffe, R. D. (1975). Meditation and the prevention of alcohol abuse. *American Journal of Psychiatry, 132,* 942–945.

Shatz, M. (1978). On the development of communicative understanding: An early strategy for interpreting and responding to messages. *Cognitive Psychology, 10,* 271–301.

Shatz, M. (1978). The relationship between cognitive processes and the development of communication skill. In C. B. Keasey (Ed.), *Nebraska Symposium on Motivation* (Vol. 26). Lincoln, Neb.: University of Nebraska Press.

Shatz, M., & Gelman, R. (1973). The development of communication skills: Modification in the speech of young children as a function of listener. *Monographs of the Society for Research in Child Development, 38*(5, Whole No. 152).

Shaw, D. M. (1966). Mineral metabolism, mania, and melancholia. *British Medical Journal, 2,* 262–267.

Shaw, G. B. (1985). *Collected letters, 1911–1925.* New York: Viking.

Shaw, M. E. (1954). Some effects of unequal distribution of information upon group performance in various communication nets. *Journal of Abnormal and Social Psychology, 49,* 547–553.

Shaw, R., & Bransford, J. (1977). Approaches to the problem of knowledge. In R. Shaw & J. Bransford (Eds.), *Perceiving, acting, and knowing.* Hillsdale, N.J.: Erlbaum.

Sheldon, W. H. (1942). *The varieties of temperament: A psychology of constitutional differences.* New York: Harper.

Sheehy, G. (1977). *Passages.* New York: Bantam.

Shepard, R. N., & Cooper, L. A. (1982). *Mental images and their transformations.* Cambridge, Mass.: MIT Press.

Shepard, R. N., & Metzler, J. (1971). Mental rotation of three-dimensional objects. *Science, 171,* 701–703.

Sheppard, H. L. (1976). Work and retirement. In R. H. Binstock & E. Shanas (Eds.), *Handbook of aging and the social sciences.* New York: Van Nostrand Reinhold.

Sherif, M. (1936). *The psychology of group norms.* New York: Harper & Row.

Sherif, M., Harvey, D. J., White, B. J., Hood, W. E., & Sherif, C. (1961). *Intergroup conflict and cooperation: The Robber's cave experiment.* Norman: University of Oklahoma Press.

Sherif, M., & Sherif, C. W. (1948/1956). *An outline of social psychology* (rev. ed.). New York: Harper & Row.

Sherrick, C. E., & Cholewiak, R. (1986). Cutaneous sensitivity. In Boff, A., Kaufman, L., & Thomas, J. (Eds.), *Handbook of perception and human performance,* Vol. 1. New York: Wiley.

Shields, J. (1962). *Monozygotic twins brought up apart and brought up together.* London: Oxford University Press.

Shiffrin, R. M. (1985). Attention. In R. C. Atkinson, R. J. Herrnstein, G. Lindzey, & R. D. Luce (Eds.), *Stevens' Handbook of Experimental Psychology,* 2nd edition. New York: John Wiley and Sons, Inc.

Shirley, M. M. (1931). *The first two years: A study of twenty-five babies: Postural and locomotor development.* Minneapolis, Minn.: University of Minnesota Press.

Shneidman, E. S. (1973). *Deaths of man.* New York: New York Times Book Co.

Shomer, R. W., Davis, A., & Kelley, H. H. (1966). Threats and the development of coordination: Further studies of the Deutsch and Krauss trucking game. *Journal of Personality and Social Psychology, 4,* 119–126.

Sidman, M. (1953). Two temporal parameters of the maintenance of avoidance behavior by the white rat. *Journal of Comparative and Physiological Psychology, 46,* 253–261.

Siegel, S. (1976). Morphine analgesic tolerance: Its situation specificity supports a Pavlovian conditioning model. *Science, 193,* 323–325.

Siegal, S., Hinson, R. E., Frank, M. D., & McCully, J. (1982). Heroin "overdose" death: The contribution of drug-associated environmental cues. *Science, 216,* 436–437.

Sigall, H., & Aronson, F. (1969). Liking for an evaluator as a function of her physical attractiveness and nature of the evaluations. *Journal of Experimental Social Psychology, 5,* 93–100.

Sigall, H., & Ostrove, N. (1975). Beautiful but dangerous: Effects of offender attractiveness and nature of the crime on juridic judgment. *Journal of Personality and Social Psychology, 31,* 410–414.

Silver, R. L., & Wortman, C. B. (1980). Coping with undesirable life events. In J. Garber & M. E. P. Seligman (Eds.), *Human helplessness: Theory and applications.* New York: Academic Press.

Simon, H. A. (1978). Information-processing theory of human problem solving. In W. K. Estes (Ed.), *Handbook of learning and cognitive processing.* Hillsdale, N.J.: Erlbaum.

Simon, M. L. (1977). Application of a new model of peer group influence to naturally existing adolescent friendship groups. *Child Development, 48,* 270–274.

Simpson, E. L. (1974). Moral development research: A case of scientific bias. *Human Development, 17,* 81–106.

Sinclair-de Zwart, H. (1973). Language acquisition and cognitive development. In T. E. Moore (Ed.), *Cognitive development and the acquisition of language.* New York: Academic Press.

Sizemore, C. C., & Pittillo, E. S. (1977). *I'm eve.* Garden City, N.Y.: Doubleday.

Skinner, B. F. (1948). "Superstition" in the pigeon. *Journal of Experimental Psychology, 38,* 168–172.

Skinner, B. F. (1953). *Science and human behavior.* New York: Macmillan.

Skinner, B. F. (1957). *Verbal behavior.* Englewood Cliffs, N.J.: Prentice-Hall.

Skinner, B. F. (1971). *Beyond freedom and dignity.* New York: Knopf.

Skipper, J. K., & Leonard, R. (Eds.). (1965). *Social interactions and patient care.* Philadelphia: J. B. Lippincott.

Sklar, J., & Berkov, B. (1975). The American birth rate: Evidences of coming rise. *Science, 189,* 693–700.

Sklar, L. S., & Anisman, H. (1981). Stress and cancer. *Psychological Bulletin, 89,* 369–406.

Skodak, M., & Skeels, H. (1949). A final follow-up study of one hundred adopted children. *Journal of Genetic Psychology, 75,* 85–125.

Skolnick, A. (1981). Married lives: Longitudinal perspectives on marriage. In D. E. Eichon, J. A. Clausen, N. Haan, M. P. Honzik, & P. H. Mussen (Eds.), *Past and present in middle life.* New York: Academic Press.

Slobin, D. I. (1971). *Psycholinguistics.* Glenview, Ill.: Scott, Foresman.

Smith, E. E., & Medin, D. L. (1981). *Categories and concepts.* Cambridge, Mass.: Harvard University Press.

Smith, E. E., Medin, D. L., & Rips, L. J. (1984). Approach to concepts: Comments on Rey's "Concepts and stereotypes." *Cognition, 17,* 265–274.

Smith, F. (1970). *Understanding reading.* New York: Holt, Rinehart & Winston.

Smith, G. P., & Epstein, A. N. (1969). Increased feeding in response to decreased glucose utilization in the rat and monkey. *American Journal of Physiology, 217,* 1083–1087.

Smith, M. C. (1978). Cognizing the behavior stream. *Child Development, 48,* 736–743.

Smith, M. E. (1926). An investigation of the development of the sentence and the extent of vocabulary in young children. *University of Iowa Studies in Child Welfare, 3,* No. 5.

Smith, M. L., & Glass, B. V. (1977). Meta-analysis of psychotherapy outcome studies. *American Psychologist, 32,* 752–760.

Smith, S. M., Brown, H. O., Toman, J. E. P., & Goodman, L. S. (1947). The lack of cerebral effects of d-tubercuraine. *Anesthesiology, 8,* 1–14.

Snodgrass, J. G. (1984). Concepts and their surface representations. *Journal of Verbal Learning and Verbal Behavior, 23,* 3–22.

Snow, C. E. (1972). Mother's speech to children learning language. *Child Development, 43,* 549–565.

Snow, C. E., & Hoefnagel-Höhle, M. (1978). The critical period for learning acquisition: Evidence from second-language learning. *Child Development,* pp. 1114–1128.

Snyder, J. (1977). Reinforcement and analyses of interaction in problem and nonproblem families. *Journal of Abnormal Psychology, 86,* 528–535.

Snyder, M. (1981). On the influence of individuals on situations. In N. Cantor & J. Kihlstrom (Eds.), *Personality, cognition and social interaction.* Hillsdale, N.J.: Erlbaum.

Snyder, M., & Swann, W. B., Jr. (1978). Behavioral confirmation in social interaction: From social perception to social reality. *Journal of Experimental Social Psychology, 14,* 148–162.

Snyder, M., & Swann, W. B., Jr. (1978b). Hypothesis-testing processes in social interaction. *Journal of Personality and Social Psychology, 36,* 1202–1212.

Snyder, M., Tanke, E. D. (1976). Behavior and attitude: Some people are more consistent than others. *Journal of Personality, 44,* 501–517.

Snyder, M., Tanke, E. D., & Berscheid, E. (1977). Social perception and interpersonal behavior. On the self-fulfilling nature of social stereotypes. *Journal of personality and Social Psychology, 35,* 656–666.

Snyder, S. H. (1981). Opiate and benzodiazepine receptors. *Psychosomatics, 22*(11), 986–989.

Sohlins, M. (1976). *The use and abuse of biology: An anthropological critique of sociobiology.* Ann Arbor, Mich.: University of Michigan Press.

Solomon, R. L. (1980). The opponent-process theory of acquired motivation: the costs of pleasure and the benefits of pain. *American Psychologist, 35,* 691–712.

Solomon, R. L., & Corbit, J. D. (1973). An opponent-process theory of motivation: II. Cigarette addiction. *Journal of Abnormal Psychology, 81,* 158–171.

Solomon, R. L., & Corbit, J. D. (1974). An opponent-process theory of motivation. I. Temporal dynamics of affect. *Psychological Review,* 119–145.

Solomon, R. L., Kamin, L. J., & Wynne, L. C. (1953). Traumatic avoidance learning: The outcomes of several extinction procedures with dogs. *Journal of Abnormal and Social Psychology, 48,* 291–302.

Sommer, R. (1974). *Tight spaces.* Englewood Cliffs, N.J.: Prentice-Hall.

Sophian, C., & Stigler, J. W. (1981). Does recognition memory improve with age? *Journal of Experimental Child Psychology, 32,* 343–353.

Sorenson, R. C. (1973). *Adolescent sexuality in contemporary America; Personal values and sexual behavior ages 13–14.* New York: Abrams.

Sorrentino, R. M., & Boutillier, R. G. (1975). The effect of quantity and quality of verbal interaction on ratings of leadership ability. *Journal of Experimental Social Psychology. 11,* 403–411.

Spances, G., & Castro, R. (1979). Adjustment to separation and divorce: A qualitative analysis. In G. Levinger and O. Moles (Eds.), *Divorce and separation: Context, causes and consequences.* New York: Basic Books.

Spanos, N. P., Weekes, J. R., & Bertrand, L. D. (1985). Multiple personality: A social psychological perspective. *Journal of Abnormal Psychology, 94,* 362–76.

Spearman, C. (1923). *The nature of "intelligence" and the principles of cognition.* London: Macmillan.

Speece, M. W., & Brent, S. B. (1984). Children's understanding of death: A review of three components of a death concept. *Child Development, 55,* 1671–1686.

Speer, J. R. (1984). Two practical strategies young children use to interpret vague instructions. *Child Development, 55,* 1811–1819.

Speisman, J. C., Lazarus, R. S., Mordkoff, A. M., & Davison, L. A. (1964). The experimental reduction of stress based on ego-defense theory. *Journal of Abnormal and Social Psychology, 68,* 367–380.

Spelke, E. S., & Cortelyou, A. (1981). Perceptual aspects of social knowing: Looking and listening in infancy. In M. E. Lamb & L. R. Sherrod (Eds.), *Infant social cognition: Empirical and theoretical considerations.* Hillsdale, N.J.: Erlbaum.

Spence, J. T., & Spence, K. W. (1966). The motivational components of manifest anxiety: Drive and drive stimuli. In C. D. Spielberger (Ed.), *Anxiety and behavior.* New York: Academic Press.

Spence, K. W., Farber, I. E., & McFann, H. H. (1956). The relation of anxiety (drive) level to performance in competitional paired-associates learning. *Journal of Experimental Social Psychology, 52,* 296–305.

Sperling, G. (1960). The information available in brief visual presentations. *Psychological Monographs, 74*(11, Whole No. 498).

Sperry, R. W. (1964). The great cerebral commissure. *Scientific American, 210*(1), 42–52.

Sperry, R. W., & Hibberd, E. (1968). In G. E. W. Wolstenholme & M. O'Connor (Eds.), *Growth of the nervous system.* London: Churchill.

Spiegel, D., Bloom, J. R., & Yalom, I. (1981). Group support for patients with metastatic cancer. *Archives of General Psychiatry 38,* 527–533.

Spiegel, H. (1970). A single-treatment method to stop smoking using ancillary self-hypnosis. *International Journal of Clinical Hypnosis, 18,* 235–250.

Spitz, R. A. (1945). Hospitalism: An inquiry into the genesis of psychiatric conditions in early childhood. In R. S. Eissler et al. (Eds.), *The psychoanalytic study of the child* (Vol. 1). New York: International Universities Press.

Spitz, R. A. (1946). Hospitalism: A follow-up report. In R. S. Eissler et al. (Eds.), *Psychoanalytic study of the child* (Vol. 2). New York: International Universities Press.

Spitz, R. A., & Wolf, K. M. (1946). Anaclitic depression. *Psychoanalytic study of the child, 2,* 313–342.

Spitzer, L., & Rodin, J. (1981). Human eating behavior: A critical review of studies in normal weight and overweight individuals. *Appetite, 2,* 293–329.

Spitzer, R. L., & Fleiss, J. L. (1974). An analysis of the reliability of psychiatric diagnosis. *British Journal of Psychiatry, 125,* 341–347.

Spitzer, R. L., Forman, J. B. W., & Nee, J. (1979). DSM-III field trials: 1. Initial interrater diagnostic reliability. *American Journal of Psychiatry, 136,* 815–817.

Spooner, A., & Kellogg, W. N. (1947). The backward conditioning curve. *American Journal of psychology, 60,* 321–334.

Springer, S. P., & Deutsch, G. (1985). *Left brain, right brain* (rev. ed.). San Francisco: Freeman 49, 59.

Squire, L. R., Cohen, N. J., & Wadel, L. (1984). The medical temporal region and memory consolidations: A new hypothesis. In Weingartner, H. & Parker, E. (Eds.), *Memory Consolidation,* Hillsdale, N.J.: Erlbaum.

Squire, L. R., Cohen, N. J., & Zonzounis, J. A. (1984). Preserved memory in retrograde amnesia: Spacing of a recently acquired skill. *Neuropsychologia, 22,* 145–152.

Squires, R. R., & Braestrup, C. (1977). Bezodiazepine receptors in rat brain. *Nature, 266,* 732–734.

Sroufe, L. A., Fox, N. E., & Pancake, V. R. (1983). Attachment and dependency in developmental perspective. *Child Development, 54,* 1615–1627.

Staats, C. K., & Staats, W. W. (1957). Meaning established by classical conditioning. *Journal of Experimental Psychology, 54,* 74–80.

Stafford-Clark, D., & Smith, A. C. (1978). *Psychiatry for students* (5th ed.). London: Allen & Unwin.

Stampfl, T. G., & Levis, D. J. (1967). Phobic patients: Treatment with the learning theory approach of implosive therapy. *Voices: The Art and Science of Psychotherapy, 3,* 23–27.

Standing, L., Conezio, J., & Haber, R. N. (1970). Perception and memory for pictures: Single-trail learning of 2560 visual stimuli, *Psychonomic Science, 19,* 73–74.

Stark, L. (1981). Reading: What needs to be assessed? *Topics in Language Disorders, 1,* 87–94.

Stefanko, M. (1984). Trends in adolescent research. *Adolescence, 19,* 1–14.

Stein, A. H., & Friedrich, L. K. (1972). Television content and young children's behavior. In J. P. Murray, E. A. Rubenstein, & G. S. Comstock (Eds.), *Television and social behavior, Vol. 2: Television and social learning.* Washington, D.C.: U.S. Government Printing Office.

Stern, G. G. (1970). *People in context.* New York: Wiley.

Stern, J. A., Brown, M., Ulett, G. A., & Sletten, I. (1977). A comparison of hypnosis, acupuncture, morphine, valium, aspirin, and placebo in the management of experimentally induced pain. In W. E. Edmonston, Jr. (Ed.), *Conceptual and investi-*

gative approaches to hypnosis and hypnotic phenomena. Annals of The New York Academy of Sciences (Vol. 296), 175–193.

Stern, R. S., & Cobb, J. P. (1978). Phenomenology of obsessive-compulsive neurosis. *British Journal of Psychiatry, 132,* 233–234.

Sternbach, R. A. (1966). *Principles of psychophysiology.* New York: Academic Press.

Sternberg, R. J. (1985). *Beyond IQ: A triarchic theory of human intelligence.* Cambridge: Cambridge University Press.

Sternberg, R. J., Conway, B. E., Ketron, J. L., and Bernstein, M. (1981). People's conceptions of intelligence. *Journal of Personality and Social Psychology, 41,* 37–55.

Sternberg, S. (1966). High-speed scanning in human memory. *Science, 53,* 421–457.

Stevens, K. N., & House, A. S (1972). Speech perception. In J. V. Tobias (Ed.), *Foundations of modern auditory theory* (Vol. 2). New York: Academic Press.

Stevens, S. S. (1956). The direct estimate of sensory magnitudes—loudness. *American Journal of Psychology, 69,* 1–25.

Stevens, S. S. (1957). On the psychophysical law. *Psychological Review, 64,* 153–181.

Stinett, N., Carter, L. M., & Montgomery, J. E. (1972). Older persons' perceptions of their marriages. *Journal of Marriage and the Family, 34,* 665–670.

Stodgill, R. M. (1948). Personal factors associated with leadership. *Journal of Psychology, 25,* 35–71.

Stodgill, R. M. (1974). *Handbook of leadership.* New York: Free Press.

Stokols, D. (1972). On the distinction between density and crowding: Some implications for future research. *Psychological Review, 79,* 275–278.

Stokols, D., Novaco, R. W., Stokols, J., & Campbell, J. (1978). Traffic congestion, type A behavior and stress. *Journal of Applied Psychology, 63,* 467–480.

Stone, A. A., & Neale, J. M. (1984). New measure of daily coping: Development and preliminary results. *Journal of Personality and Social Psychology 46,* 4, 892–906.

Stone, G. C., Cohen, F., & Adler, N. E. (1979). *Health psychology.* San Francisco: Jossey-Bass.

Stone, L. J., Smith, H. T., & Murphy, L. B. (Eds.). (1973). *The competent infant: Research and commentary.* New York: Basic Books.

Stoner, J. (1961). A comparison of individual and group decisions, including risk. Unpublished master's thesis, MIT.

Storms, M. D. (1973). Videotape and the attribution process: Reversing actors' and observers' points of view. *Journal of Personality and Social Psychology, 27,* 165–175.

Stratton, G. M. (1896) Some preliminary experiments on vision without inversion of the retinal image. *Psychological Review, 3,* 611–617.

Streeter, L. A. (1976). Language perception of two-month-old infants shows effects of both innate mechanisms and experience. *Nature, 259,* 39–41.

Streib, G. F., & Schneider, C. J. (1971). *Retirement in American society.* Ithaca, N.Y.: Cornell University Press.

Stricker, E. M., Rowland, N., Saller, C. F., and Friedman, M. I. (1977). Homeostasis during hypoglycemia: Central control of adrenal secretion and peripheral control of feeding. *Science, 196.*

Stroebe, M. S., & Stroebe, W. (1983). Who suffers more? Sex differences in health risks of the widowed. *Psychological Bulletin 93,* 2, 279–301.

Stromberg, C. D., & Stone, A. A. (1983). Statute: A model state law on civil commitment of the men-

tally ill. *Harvard Journal of Legislation, 20,* 275–396.

Stromeyer, C. F., & Psotka, J. (1973). The detailed texture of eidetic images. *Nature, 225,* 346–349.

Stroop, J. R. (1935). Studies of interference in serial verbal reactions. *Journal of Experimental Psychology, 18,* 643–662.

Stunkard, A. J. (1983). *Obesity.* Philadelphia: Saunders.

Suedfeld, P. (1980). *Restricted environmental stimulation: Research and clinical applications.* New York: Wiley.

Sugarman, S. (1982). Developmental change in early representational intelligence: Evidence from spatial classification strategies and related verbal expressions. *Cognitive Psychology, 14,* 410–449.

Sugarman, S. (1983). *Children's early thought: Development in classification.* Cambridge: Cambridge University Press.

Suls, J., & Miller, R. J. (Eds.). (1977). *Social comparison processes: Theoretical and empirical perspectives.* Washington, D.C.: Hempishere/Halsted.

Suomi, S. J. (1977). Development of attachment and other behaviors in rhesus monkeys. In T. Alloway, P. Pliner, & L. Krames (Eds.), *Advances in the study of communication and affect* (Vol. 3): *Attachment behavior.* New York: Plenum.

Suomi, S. J., & Harlow, H. F. (1972). Social rehabilitation of isolate-reared monkeys. *Developmental Psychology, 6,* 487–496.

Szasz, T. (1960). The myth of mental illness. *American Psychologist, 15,* 113–118.

Szinovacz, M. E. (1982). Economic resources, wife's skepticism, and marital violence. *International Journal of Family Psychiatry, 3,* 419–437.

Tagiuri, R., Blake, R., & Bruner, J. (1953). Some determinants of the perception of positive and negative feelings in others. *Journal of Abnormal and Social Psychology, 48,* 585–592.

Tajfel, H., Billig, M. G., Bundy, R. P., & Flament, C. (1971). Social categorization and intergroup behavior. *European Journal of Social Psychology, 1,* 149–178.

Tajfel, H., & Turner, J. (1979). An integrative theory of intergroup conflict. In W. Auston & S. Worchel (Eds.), *The social psychology of intergroup relations.* Monterey, Cal.: Brooks/Cole.

Talbert, G. B. (1977). Aging of the reproductive system. In C. E. Finch & L. Hayflick (Eds.), *Handbook of the biology of aging.* New York: Van Nostrand Reinhold.

Tamir, L. M. (1982). *Men in their forties: The transition to middle age.* New York: Springer Publishing Co.

Tanner, J. M. (1962). *Growth at adolescence.* Philadelphia: Davis.

Tanner, J. M. (1970). Physical growth. In P. H. Mussen (Ed.), *Carmichael's manual of child psychology* (Vol. 2) (3rd ed.). New York: Wiley.

Tanner, J. M., Whitehouse, R. H., & Takaishi, M. (1966). Standards from birth to maturity for height, weight, height velocity, and weight velocity; British children 1965. *Archives of Diseases in Childhood, 41,* 454–471.

Tarshis, B. (1979). *The "average American" book.* New York: Atheneum/SMI.

Tausig, M. (1982). Measuring life events. *Journal of Health and Social Behavior, 23,* 52–64.

Tavris, C. (1982, May 2). Women and men and morality. (Review of *In a different voice: Psychological theory and women's development* by C. Gilligan). *New York Times Book Review.*

Taylor, S., & Metlee, D. (1971). When similarity breeds contempt. *Journal of Personality and Social Psychology, 20,* 75–81.

Taylor, S. E. (1978). A developing role for social psychology in medicine and medical practice. *Personality and Social Psychology Bulletin, 4,* 515–523.

Taylor, S. E., & Fiske, S. T. (1975). Point of view and perceptions of causality. *Journal of Personality and Social Psychology, 32,* 439–445.

Taylor, S. P., & Pisano, R. (1971). Physical aggression as a function of frustration and physical attack. *Journal of Social Psychology, 84,* 261–267.

Teghtsoonian, R. (1971). On the exponent in Stevens' Law and the constant in Ekman's Law. *Psychological Review, 78,* 71–80.

Teitelbaum, P. (1957). Random and food-directed activity in hyperphagic and normal rats. *Journal of Comparative and Physiological Psychology, 50,* 486–490.

Teitelbaum, P. (1961). Disturbances in feeding and drinking behavior after hypothalamic lesions. In M. R. Jones (Ed.), *Nebraska Symposium on Motivation.* Lincoln, Neb.: University of Nebraska Press.

Teitelbaum, P., & Epstein, A. N. (1962). The lateral hypothalamic syndrome: Recovery of feeding and drinking after lateral hypothalamic lesions. *Psychological Review, 69,* 74–90.

Teller, D. Y. (1981). Color vision in infants. In R. N. Aslin, J. R. Alberts, & M. R. Peterson (Eds.), *Development of perception* (Vol. 2): *The visual system.* New York: Academic Press.

Tennen, H., & Ellir, S. (1977). Attributional components of learned helplessness and facilitation. *Journal of Personality and Social Psychology, 35,* 265–271.

Terman, L. M. (1916). *The measurement of intelligence.* Boston: Houghton Mifflin.

Terman, L. M. (1917). Feeble-minded children in the public schools of California. *School and Society, 5,* 161–165.

Terman, L. M. (1925). *Mental and physical traits of a thousand gifted children. Genetic studies of genius.* (Vol. 1). Stanford, Calif.: Stanford University Press.

Terman, L. M. (1954). Scientists and nonscientists in a group of 800 gifted men. *Psychological Monographs, 68*(7), 1–44.

Terman, L. M., & Merrill, M. A. (1937). *Measuring intelligence: A guide to the administration of the new revised Stanford-Binet tests of intelligence.* Boston: Houghton Mifflin.

Terrace, H. S. (1979). *Nim.* New York: Knopf.

Terrace, H. S., Petitto, L. A., Sanders, R. J., & Bever, T. G. (1979). Can an ape create a sentence? *Science, 206,* 891–901.

Thibaut, J. W., & Kelley, H. H. (1959). *The social psychology of groups.* New York: Wiley.

Thibaut, J. W., & Riecken, H. W. (1955). Some determinants and consequences of the perception of social causality. *Journal of Personality, 24,* 113–133.

Thigpen, C. H., & Cleckley, H. (1954). *The three faces of Eve.* Kingsport, Tenn: Kingsport Press.

Thoits, P. (1981). Undesirable life events and psychophysiological distress: A problem of operational confounding. *American Sociological Review, 46,* 97–109.

Thomas, A., Chess, S., & Birch, H. G. (1970). The origin of personality. *Scientific American, 223,* 102–109.

Thomas, K. W. (1977). Toward multidimensional values in teaching: The example of conflict behaviors. *Academy of Management Review, 2.*

Thomas, M. Horton, R., Lippincott, E., & Drabman, R. (1977). Desensitization to portrayals of real-life aggression as a function of exposure to television violence. *Journal of Personality and Social Psychology, 35,* 450–458.

Thompson, D. A., & Campbell, R. G. (1977). Hunger in humans induced by 2-deoxy-D-glucose: Glucoprivic control of taste preference and food intake. *Science, 198,* 1065–1068.

Thompson, J. K., Jarvie, G. J., Cakey, B. B., & Cureton, K. J. (1982). Exercise and obesity: Etiology, physiology, and intervention. *Psychological Bulletin, 91,* 55–79.

Thompson, S. C. (1981). Will it hurt if I can control it? A complex answer to a simple question. *Psychological Bulletin, 90,* 89–101.

Thompson, S. K. (1975). Gender labels and early sex role development. *Child Development, 46,* 339–347.

Thompson, W. R., & Heron, W. (1954). The effects of restricting early experience on the problem-solving capacity of dogs. *Canadian Journal of Psychology, 8,* 17–31.

Thorndike, E. L. (1911). *Animal intelligence.* New York: Macmillan.

Thorndike, E. L. (1924). The measurement of intelligence. I: The present status. *Psychological Review, 31,* 219–252.

Thorp, G., & Burns, L. (1983). *The agoraphobic syndrome.* New York: Wiley.

Thorson, G., Hochhaus, L., & Stanners, R. F. (1976). Temporal changes in visual and acoustic codes in a letter-watching task. *Perception and Psychophysics, 19*(4), 346–348.

Thurnher, M. (1976). Midlife marriage: Sex differences in evaluation and perspectives. *International Journal of Aging and Human Development, 7*(2), 129–135.

Thurnher, M., Spence, D., & Fiske, M. (1974). Value confluence and behavioral conflict in intergenerational relations. *Journal of Marriage and the Family, 36,* 308–319.

Thurstone, L. L. (1938). Primary mental abilities. *Psychometrika Monographs,* No. 1.

Thurstone, L. L., & Thurstone, T. G. (1962). *Tests of primary mental abilities* (rev. ed.). Chicago: Science Research Associates.

Tinbergen, N. (1951). *The study of instinct.* Oxford: Clarendon Press.

Tizard, B., & Hodges, J. (1978). The effect of early institutional rearing on the development of eight-year-old children. *Journal of Child Psychology and Psychiatry, 19,* 99–118.

Tolman, E. C., & Honzik, C. H. (1930). Introduction and removal of reward, and maze performance in rats. *University of California Publications in Psychology, 4,* 257–275.

Tolman, F. C. (1948). Cognitive maps in rats and men. *Psychological Reviews, 55,* 189–208.

Tolman, J. & King, J. A. (1956). The effects of testosterone propionate on aggression in male and female C57 BL/10 mice. *British Journal of Animal Behavior, 4,* 147–149.

Treisman, A. (1987). Properties, parts and objects. In Boff, K., Kaufman, L., & Thomas, J. (Eds.), *Handbook of perception and human performance,* Vol. 2. New York: Wiley.

Treisman, A. M. (1964). Selective attention in man. *British Medical Bulletin, 20,* 12–16.

Triplett, N. (1897). The dynamogenic factors in pacemaking and competition. *American Journal of Psychology, 9,* 507–533.

Trulson, M. E., Ross, C. A., & Jacobs, B. L. (1977). Lack of tolerance to the depression of raphe unit activity by lysergic acid diethylamide. *Neuropsychopharmacology, 16,* 771–774.

Tryon, R. C. (1942). Individual differences. In F. A. Moss (Ed.), *Comparative psychology.* Englewood Cliffs, N.J.: Prentice-Hall. Pp. 330–365.

Tseng, L. F., Loh, H. H., & Li, C. H. (1976). β-endorphin as a potent analgesic by intravenous injection. *Nature, 263,* 239–240.

Tuddenham, R. D. Blumenkrantz, J., & Wiklin, W. R. (1968). Age changes on AGCT: A longitudinal

study of average adults. *Journal of Consulting and Clinical Psychology, 32,* 659–663.

Tulving, E. (1972). Episodic and semantic memory. In E. Tulving & W. Donaldson (Eds.), *Organization of memory.* New York: Academic Press.

Tulving, E. (1978). Relation between encoding specificity and levels of processing. In L. S. Cermak & F. I. M. Craik (Eds.), *Levels of processing and human memory.* Hillsdale, N.J.: Erlbaum.

Tulving, E., & Watkins, M. J. (1973). Continuity between recall and recognition. *American Journal of Psychology, 86,* 739–748.

Tumner, W. E. (1985). The acquisition of the sentient-nonsentient distinction and its relationship to causal reasoning and social cognition. *Child Development, 56,* 989–1000.

Turiel, E. (1974). Conflict and transition in adolescent moral development. *Child Development, 45,* 14–29.

Turing, A. M. (1950). Computing machinery and intelligence. *Mind, 59,* 433–450.

Turnbull, C. (1962). *The forest people.* New York: Simon & Schuster.

Turvey, M. T., & Shaw, R. E. (1978). Memory (or, knowing) as a matter of specification not representation: Notes towards a different class of machines. In L. S. Cermak & F. I. M. Craik (Eds.), *Levels of processing and human memory.* Hillsdale, N.J.: Erlbaum.

Turvey, M. T. & Shaw, R. E. (1979). The primacy of percieving: An ecological reformulaton of perception for understanding memory. In L. G. Nilsson (Ed.) *Perspectives on Memory Research.* Hillsdale, N.J.: Erlbaum.

Tversky, A., & Kahneman, D. (1974). Judgment under uncertainty: Heuristics and biases. *Science, 185,* 1124–1131.

Tyler, R. S., Preece, J. P., Lansing, C. R., Otto, S. R., & Ganty, B. J. (1986). Previous experience as an emfounding factor in comparing cochlear-implant processing schemes. *Journal of Speech and Hearing Research. 29,* 282–287.

Udry, J. R. (1974). *The social context of marriage.* Philadelphia: Lippincott.

Ullman, L., & Krasner, L. (1975). *A psychological approach to abnormal behavior* (2nd ed.). Englewood Cliffs, N.J.: Prentice-Hall.

U.S. Bureau of Census (1982). *Statistical abstract of the United States.* 1982–83 (103rd ed.). Washington, D.C.: U.S. Government Printing Office.

U.S. Department of Health and Human Services. (1980). *Project sleep: the national program on insomnia and sleep disorders.* Public Health Service: Rockville, Maryland.

U.S. Department of Health and Human Services. (1984). *Naltrexone: Its clinical utility.* Public Health Service: Rockville, Maryland.

U.S. Census Bureau. Demographic aspects of aging and the older population in the United States. Current Population Reports, Series P-23, No. 100, National Center for Health Statistics. Washington, D.C.: U.S. Government Printing Office.

U.S. Public Health Service (1974). Current estimates from the health interview survey: United States. Vital and Health Statistics, Series 10, No. 100, National Center for Health Statistics. Washington, D.C.: U.S. Government Printing Office.

Utech, D. A., & Horing, K. L. (1969). Parents and peers as competing influences in the decisions of children of differing ages. *Journal of Social Psychology, 78,* 267–274.

Valenstein, E., Riss, W., & Young, W. C. (1955). Experiential and genetic factors in the organization of sexual behavior in male guinea pigs. *Journal of Comparative and Physiological Psychology, 48,* 397–403.

Valenstein, E. S. (1973). *Brain control: A critical examination of brain stimulation and psychosurgery.* New York: Wiley.

Van Praag, H., Korf, J., & Schut, D. (1973). Cerebral monoamines and depression: An investigation with the probenecid technique. *Archives of General Psychiatry, 28,* 827–831.

Vernon, J. A., McGill, T. E., Gulick, W. L., & Candland, D. R. (1959). Effect of sensory deprivation on some perceptual and motor skills. *Perceptual and Motor Skills, 9,* 91–97.

Veroff, J., Wilcox, S., & Atkinson, J. W. (1953). The achievement motive in high school and college-age women. *Journal of Abnormal and Social Psychology, 48,* 102–119.

Verplanck, W. S. (1955). The control of the content of conversation: Reinforcement of statements of opinion. *Journal of Abnormal and Social Psychology, 51,* 668–676.

Vinokur, A. (1971). Effects of group processes upon individual and group decisions involving risk. *Dissertation Abstracts International* (Vol. 31) (12-A), 6721–6722.

Vinokur, A., & Selzer, M. L. (1975). Desirable versus undesirable life events: Their relationship to stress and mental distress. *Journal of Personality and Social Psychology, 32,* 329–337.

Vogel, G. W. (1978). Sleep-onset mentation. In A. M. Arkin, J. S. Antrobus, & S. J. Ellman (Eds.), *The mind in sleep psychology and psychobiology.* Hillsdale, N.J.: Erlbaum. Pp. 97–112.

Volicer, B. J., & Volicer, L. (1978). Cardiovascular changes associated with stress during hospitalization. *Journal of Psychosomatic Research, 22,* 159–168.

Volicer, B. J., & Volicer, L. (1978). Cardiovascular changes associated with stress during hospitalization. *Journal of Psychosomatic Research, 22,* 159–168.

von Frisch, K. (1967). Honeybees: Do they use direction and distance information provided by their dances? *Science, 158,* 1072–1076.

von Hofsten, C., & Fazel-Zandy, S. (1984). Development of visually guided hand orientation in reaching. *Journal of Experimental Child Psychology, 38,* 208–219.

Wadden, T. A., & Anderton, C. H. (1982). The clinical use of hypnosis. *Psychological Bulletin, 91-2,* 215–243.

Wagner, A. R., & Rescorla, R. A. (1972). Inhibition in Pavlovian conditioning. Application of a theory. In R. A. Boakes & M. S. Halliday (Eds.), *Inhibition and learning.* London: Academic Press.

Wagner, H. L., MacDonald, C. J. & Manstead, A. S. R. (1986). Communication of individual emotions by spontaneous facial expressions. *Journal of Personality and Social Psychology, 50,* 737–743.

Wahba, M. A., & Bridwell, L. G. (1976). Maslow reconsidered: A review of research on the need hierarchy theory. *Organizational Behavior and Human Performance, 15,* 212–240.

Wald, G., & Brown, P. K. (1965). Human color vision and color blindness. *Cold Spring Harbor Symposia on Quantitative Biology, 30,* 345–359.

Walk, R. (1966). The development of depth perception in animals and human infants. *Monographs of the Society for Research in Child Development, 31,* (Whole No. 5).

Walk, R., & Gibson, E. (1961). A comparative and analytic study of visual depth perception. *Psychological Monographs, 75* (15, Whole No. 519).

Walker, A. S. (1982) Intermodal perception of expressive behaviors by human infants. *Journal of Experimental Child Psychology, 33,* 514–535.

Walker, B. B., & Sandman, C. A. (1981). Disregulation of the gastrointestinal system. In S. N. Haynes & L. Gannon (Eds.), *Psychosomatic disorders.* New York: Praeger.

Walker, E. (1978). *Explorations in the Biology of Language.* Montgomery, Vt.: Bradford Books.

Walker, T. G., & Main, E. C. (1973). Choiceshifts in political decision making: Federal judges and civil liberties cases. *Journal of Applied Social Psychology, 2,* 29–38.

Walker-Andrews, A. S., Lennon, E. M. (1985). Auditory visual perception of changing distance by human infants. *Child Development, 56,* 544–548.

Wallace, D. H., & Wehmer, G. (1972). Evaluation of visual erotica by sexual liberals and conservatives. *Journal of Sex Research, 8,* 147–153.

Wallace, M., Kogan, N., & Bern, D. (1962). Group influence on individual risk taking. *Journal of Abnormal and Social Psychology, 65,* 75–86.

Wallis, C., (1984, June 11). Unlocking pain's secrets. *Time,* 58–66.

Walster, E., Aronson, V., Abrahams, D., & Rottman, L. (1966). Importance of physical attractiveness in dating behavior. *Journal of Personality and Social Psychology, 4,* 508–516.

Walters, H. F., & Malmud, P. (1975, March 10). "Drop that gun, Captain Video." *Newsweek, 85* (10), 81–92.

Walters, R. H., & Llewellyn Thomas, E. (1963). Enhancement of punitiveness by visual and audiovisual displays. *Canadian Journal of Psychology, 16,* 244–255.

Walton, R. E., & Dutton, J. M. (1969). Management of interdepartmental conflict: Model and review. *Administrative Science Quarterly, 14,* 522–542.

Wanner, E., & Gleitman, L. R. (1982). *Language acquisition: The state of the art.* Cambridge: Cambridge University Press.

Ward, C. H., Beck, A. T., Mendelson, M., Mock, J. E., & Erbaugh, T. K. (1962). The psychiatric nomenclature: Reasons for diagnostic disagreement. *Archives of General Psychiatry, 7,* 198–205.

Ward, C. O., Zanna, M. P., & Cooper, J. (1974). The nonverbal mediation of self-fulfilling prophecies in interracial interaction. *Journal of Experimental Social Psychology, 10,* 109–120.

Ward, R. A. (1979). *The aging experience.* New York: Lippincott.

Warden, C. J. (1931). *Animal motivation: Experimental studies on the albino rat.* New York: Columbia University Press.

Warner, L. G., & DeFleur, M. L. (1969). Attitude as an interactional concept: Social constraint and social distance as intervening variables between attitudes and action. *American Sociological Review, 34,* 153–169.

Washburn, S. (1978). Animal behavior and social anthropology. *society, 15–6,* 35–41.

Wasman, M., & Flynn, J. P. (1962). Directed attack elicited from hypothalamus. *Archives of Neurology, 6,* 220–227.

Wason, P. C., & Johnson-Laird, P. N. (1972). *Psychology of reasoning: Structure and content.* London: Batsford.

Waters, E., Wippman, J., & Sroufe, L. A. (1979). Attachment, positive affect, and competence in the peer group: Two studies in construct validation. *Child Development, 50,* 821–829.

Watkins, L. R., & Mayer, D. J. (1982). Organization of opiate and non-opiate pain control systems. *Science, 216,* 1185–1192.

Watson, A. B. (1986). Temporal sensitivity. In Boff, A., Kaufman, L., & Thomas, J. (Eds.), *Handbook of perception and human performance,* Vol. 1. New York: Wiley.

Watson, J. B. (1919). *Psychology from the standpoint of a behaviorist.* Philadelphia: Lippincott.

Watson, J. B. (1925). *Behaviorism.* New York: Norton.

Watson, J. B., & Rayner, R. (1920). Conditioned emotional reactions. *Journal of Experimental Psychology, 3,* 1–14.

Watson, R. I. (1968). *The great psychologists: Aristotle to Freud.* Philadelphia: Lippincott.

Webb, W., & Bonnet, M. H. (1979). Sleep and dreams, In M. E. Mayer (Ed.), Foundations of contemporary psychology. New York: Oxford University Press.

Webb, W. B. (1975). *Sleep: The gentle tyrant.* Englewood Cliffs, N.J.: Prentice Hall.

Webb, W. B., & Cartwright, R. D. (1978). Sleep and dreams. *Annual Review of Psychology,* 29.

Weigman, A. D. (1972). *On dying and denying.* New York: Behavioral Publications.

Weiner, B. (1974). *Achievement motivation and attribution theory.* Morristown, N.J.: General Learning Press.

Weiner, B., Frieze, I., Kukla, A., Reed, L., Rest, S., & Rosenbaum, R. M. (1971). Perceiving the causes of success and failure. In E. E. Jones et al. (Eds.), *Attribution: Perceiving the causes of behavior.* Morristown, N.J.: General Learning Press.

Weiner, H. (1977). *Psychobiology and human disease.* New York: Elsevier.

Weiner, R. D. (1984). Does electroconvulsive therapy cause brain damage? *Behavioral and Brain Sciences,* 7, 1–53.

Weisberg, R. (1980). *Memory, thought and behavior.* New York: Oxford University Press.

Weisberg, R., DiCamillo, M., & Phillips, D. (1978). Transferring old associations to new situations: A nonautomatic process. *Journal of Verbal Learning and Verbal Behavior,* 17, 219–228.

Weiss, J. M. (1977). Ulcers. In J. Maser & M. E. P. Seligman (Eds.), *Psychopathology: Experimental models.* San Francisco: Freeman.

Weissman, M. M., Klerman, G. L., & Paykel, E. S. (1971). Clinical evaluation of hostility in depression. *American Journal of Psychiatry,* 128, 261–266.

Weissman, M. M., & Meyers, J. K. (1978). Affective disorders in a U.S. urban community. *Archives of General Psychiatry,* 35, 1304–1310.

Weizenbaum, J. (1965). ELIZA—A computer program for the study of natural language communication between man and machine. *Communications of the Association for Computing Machinery,* 9, 36–45.

Welkowitz, J., Ewen, R. B., & Cohen, J. (1977). *Introductory statistics for the behavioral sciences.* New York: Academic Press.

Welsh, G. S., & Dahlstrom, W. G. (Eds.). (1965). *Basic readings on the MMPI in psychology and medicine.* Minneapolis: University of Minnesota Press.

Wertheimer, M. (1945/1959). *Productive thinking.* New York: Harper.

Wetherell, M., & Turner, J. C. (1979). Group polarization and social identification: A theoretical review. Paper presented at the annual conference of the Social Psychology Section of the British Psychological Society, University of Kent, England.

Wever, E. G., & Bray, C. W. (1937). The perception of low tones and the resonance-volley theory. *Journal of Psychology,* 3, 101–114.

Wexley, K. N., & Yukl, G. A. (1977). *Organizational behavior and personnel psychology.* Homewood, Ill.: Irwin.

White, L. K. (1983). Determinants of spousal interaction: Marital structure on marital happiness. *Journal of Marriage and the Family,* 45, 511–519.

White, R. W. (1959). Motivation reconsidered: The concept of competence. *Psychological Review,* 66, 297–333.

Whiting, B. B., & Whiting, J. W. M. (1975). *Children of six cultures.* Cambridge, Mass.: Harvard University Press.

Whiting, J. W. M., Kluckholm, R. C., & Anthony, A. (1958). The function of male initiation ceremonies at puberty. In E. Maccoby, T. M. Newcomb, & E. L. Hartley (Eds.), *Readings in social psychology.* New York: Holt, Rinehart & Winston.

Whiting, J. W., Landauer, T. K., & Jones, T. M. (1968), Infantile immunization and adult stature. *Child Development,* 39, 58–67.

Whorf, B. L. (1940). Science and linguistics. *Technology Review* (MIT), pp. 229–231, 242–248.

Whorf, B. L. (1956a). Languages and logic. In J. B. Carroll (Ed.), *Languages, thought and reality: Selected writings of Benjamin Lee Whorf.* Cambridge, Mass.: MIT Press.

Whorf, B. L. (1956b). Science and linguistics. In J. B. Carroll (Ed.), *Language, thought and reality: Selected writings of Benjamin Lee Whorf.* Cambridge, Mass.: MIT Press.

Wichman, H. (1970). Effects of isolation and communication on cooperation in a two-person game. *Journal of Personality and Social Psychology,* 16, 114–120.

Wickens, D. D. (1972). Characteristics of word encoding. In A. W. Melton & E. Martin (Eds.), *Coding processes in human memory.* Washington, D.C.: Winston.

Wicker, A. (1969). Attitudes versus actions: The relationship of verbal and overt behavioral responses to attitude objects. *The Journal of Social Issues,* 25, 1–78.

Wicklund, R. A., & Brehm, J. W. (1976). *Perspectives on cognitive dissonance.* Hillsdale, N.J.: Erlbaum.

Wicklund, R. A., Cooper, J., & Linden, D. E. (1967). Effects of expected effort on attitude change prior to exposure. *Journal of Experimental Social Psychology,* 3, 416–428.

Wiesel, T. N., & Hubel, D. H. (1963). Single-cell responses in striate cortex of kittens deprived of vision in one eye. *Journal of Neurophysiology,* 26, 1003–1017.

Wilcoxon, H. C., Dragoin, W. B., & Kral, P. A. (1971) Illness induced aversions in rat and quail: Relative salience of visual and gustatory cues. *Science,* 171, 826–828.

Wilder, D. A., & Allen, V. L. (1978). Group membership and preference for information about others. *Personality and Social Psychology Bulletin,* 4, 106–110.

Willerman, L. (1979). *The psychology of individual and group differences.* San Francisco: Freeman.

Willerman, L., Naylor, A. F., & Myrianthopoulos, N. C. (1974). Intellectual development of children from interracial matings: Performance in infancy and at four years. *Behavior Genetics,* 4, 83–90.

Williams, R. J. (1959). Biochemical individuality and cellular nutrition: Prime factors in alcoholism. *Quarterly Journal of Studies on Alcohol,* 20, 452–463.

Willis, S. L. (1985). Towards an educational psychology of the older adult learner; Intellectual and cognitive bases. In J. E. Birren and K. W. Shaie (eds.), *Handbook of the psychology of aging* (2nd ed.). New York: Van Nostrand Reinhold.

Wilson, E. O. (1971). *The insect societies.* Cambridge, Mass.: The Belknap Press of Harvard University Press.

Wilson, E. O. (1974). *Introduction to ecology, evolution and population biology* (Readings from Scientific American). San Francisco: Freeman.

Wilson, E. O. (1975a, October 12). Human decency in animals. *The New York Times Magazine.*

Wilson, E. O. (1975b). *Sociobiology: The new synthesis.* Cambridge, Mass.: Harvard University Press.

Wilson, G., & O'Leary K. (1980). *Principles of Behavior Therapy,* Englewood Cliffs, N.J.: Prentice-Hall.

Wilson, G. T. (1978). Methodological considerations in treatment outcome research on obesity. *Journal of Consulting and Clinical Psychology,* 46, 687–702.

Wilson, G. T., & Franks, C. (Eds.) (1982). *Contemporary behavior therapy: Conceptual and empirical foundations.* New York: Guilford Press.

Wilson, G. T., & Lawson, D. M. (1976). Effects of alcohol on sexual arousal in women. *Journal of Abnormal Psychology,* 85, 487–497.

Wilson, G. T., & Lawson, D. M. (1976). Expectancies, alcohol, and sexual arousal for male social drinkers. *Journal of Abnormal Psychology,* 85, 587–594.

Wilson, J. A., & Glick, B. (1970). Ontogeny of mating behavior in the chicken. *American Journal of Physiology,* 218, 951–955.

Wilson, M. S., & Meyer, E. (1962). Diagnostic consistency in a psychiatric liaison service. *American Journal of Psychiatry,* 119, 207–209.

Winston, P. H. (1975). *The psychology of computer vision.* New York: McGraw-Hill.

Winston, P. H. (1977). *Artificial intelligence.* Reading, Mass.: Addison-Wesley.

Winston, P. H. Learning structural descriptions from examples. *Report MAC TR-76,* M.I.T., 1970.

Winterbottom, M. R. (1953). The relation of childhood training in independence to achievement motivation. Unpublished doctoral dissertation, University of Michigan.

Wissler, C. (1901). *The correlation of mental and physical tests.* New York: Columbia University Press.

Wittgenstein, L. (1953). *Philosophical investigations.* New York: Macmillan.

Wolberg, L. R. (1977). *The technique of psychotherapy* (3rd ed.). New York: Grune & Stratton.

Wolff, E. (no date). *Practical hypnotism.* New York: Louis Tannen.

Wolpe, J. (1958). *Psychotherapy by reciprocal inhibition.* Stanford, Calif.: Stanford University Press.

Woodruff, R. A., Goodwin, D. W., & Guze, S. B. (1974). *Psychiatric diagnosis.* New York: Oxford University Press.

Woods, P. J. (Ed.). (1976). *Career opportunities for psychologists.* Washington, D.C.: American Psychological Association.

Woodworth, R. S. (1918). *Dynamic psychology.* New York: Columbia University Press.

Woodworth, R. S. (1958). *Dynamics of behavior.* New York: Holt, Rinehart & Winston.

Woolfolk, R. L., Carr-Kaffashan, K., Lehrer, P. M., et al (1976). Meditation training as a treatment for insomnia. *Behavior Therapy,* 7, 359–365.

Woolfolk, R. L., & Richardson, F. C. (1984). Behavior therapy and the ideology of modernity. *American Psychology,* 39, 777–786.

Worchel, S., & Yohai, S. M. L. (1979). The role of attribution in the experience of crowding. *Journal of Experimental Social Psychology,* 15, 91–104.

Word, C. H., Zanna, M. P., & Cooper, J. (1974). The nonverbal mediation of self-fulfilling prophecies in intersocial interaction. *Journal of Experimental Social Psychology,* 10, 109–120.

Wortman, C. B., & Conway, T. L. (1985). The role of social support in adaptation and recovery from physical illness. Pp. 281–302 in S. Cohen & S. L. Syme (eds.), *Social Support and Health.* Orlando, FL: Academic Press.

Wortman, C., Panciera, L., Shusterman, L., & Hibscher, J. (1976). Attributions of causality and reactions to uncontrollable outcomes. *Journal of Experimental Social Psychology,* 12, 301–306.

Wren, C. (July 9, 1985). Precise Eskimo dialect threatened with extinction. *New York Times,* p. C1.

Wrightsman, L. S. (1960). Effects of waiting with others on changes in level of felt anxiety. *Journal of Abnormal and Social Psychology,* 61, 216–222.

Wuerthele, S. M., Freed, W. J., Olson, L., Morihisa, J., Spoor, L., Wyatt, R. J., & Hoffer, B. J.

(1981). Effect of dopamine agonists and antagonists on the electrical activity of substantia nigra neurons transplanted into the lateral ventrical of the rat. *Experimental Brain Research, 44*, 1–10.

Wyatt, R. J., & Freed, W. J. (1983). Central nervous system grafting. *Neurosurgery*.

Wyer, R., & Goldberg, L. (1970). A probabilistic analysis of the relationships among beliefs and attitudes. *Psychological Review, 77*, 100–120.

Wyld, H. C. (1931). The superiority of received standard English. *Society for Pure English, Tract XXXVII*, 603–617.

Yarbus, A. L. (1967). *Eye movements and vision.* New York: Plenum.

Yarrow, L. J., Rubenstein, J. L., & Pedersen, F. A. (1975). *Infant and environment: Early cognitive and motivational development.* New York: Wiley.

Yerkes, R. M. (Ed.). (1921). Psychological examining in the United States Army. Washington, D.C.: *Memoirs of the National Academy of Sciences* (No. 15).

Yerkes, R. M., & Foster, J. C. (1923). *A point scale for measuring mental ability.* Baltimore, Md.: Warwick and York.

Young, W. C., Goy, R. W., & Phoenix, C. H. (1964). Hormones and sexual behavior. *Science, 143*, 212–218.

Young, W. S., III, & Kuhar, M. J. (1980). Radiohistochemical localization of benzodiazepine receptors in rat brain. *Journal of Pharmocological Experimental Therapy, 212*, 337–346.

Zajonc, R. B. (1965). Social facilitation. *Science, 149*, 269–274.

Zajonc, R. B. (1968). Attitudinal effects of mere exposure. *Journal of Personality and Social Psychology, Monograph Supplement, 9*, 1–27.

Zajonc, R. B., Heingartner, A., & Herman, E. M. (1969). Social enhancement and impairment of performance in the cockroach. *Journal of Personality and Social Psychology, 13*, 83–92.

Zajonc, R. B., & Sales, S. M. (1966). Social facilitation of dominant and subordinate responses. *Journal of Experimental Social Psychology, 2*, 160–168.

Zajonc, R. B., Wolosin, R. J. Wolosin, M., & Sherman, S. J. (1968). Individual and group risk taking in a two-choice situation. *Journal of Experimental Social Psychology, 4*, 89–106.

Zanna, M. P., & Cooper, J. (1974). Dissonance and the pill: An attribution approach to studying the arousal properties of dissonance. *Journal of Personality and Social Psychology, 29*, 703–709.

Zanna, M. P., Olson, J. M., & Fazio, R. H. (1980). Attitude-behavior consistency: An individual difference perspective. *Journal of Personality and Social Psychology, 38*, 432–440.

Zelazo, P., Kotelchuck, M., Barber, L., & David, J. (1977, March). The experimental facilitation of attachment behaviors. Papers presented at the Society for Research in Child Development meeting, New Orleans.

Zellner, M. (1970). Self-esteem, reception and influenceability. *Journal of Personality and Social Psychology, 15*, 87–93.

Zelnik, M., & Kanter, J. F. (1972). The probability of premarital intercourse. *Social Science Research, 1*, 335–341.

Zhang, G., & Simon, H. A. (1985). STM capacity for Chinese words and idioms: Chunking and acoustical loop hypothesis. *Memory and Cognition, 13*, 193–201.

Zigler, E., & Berman, W. (1983). Discerning the future of early childhood intervention. *American Psychologist, 38*, 894–906.

Zillman, D. (1978). *Hostility and aggression.* Hillsdale, N.J.: Erlbaum.

Zillman, D. (1971). Excitation transfer in communication-mediated aggressive behavior. *Journal of Experimental Social Psychology, 7*, 419–434.

Zillman, D., & Cantor, J. R. (1976). Effects of timing of information about mitigating circumstances on emotional responses to provocation and retaliatory behavior. *Journal of Experimental Social Psychology, 12*, 38–55.

Zimbardo, P. G. (1958). The efforts of early avoidance training and rearing conditions upon the sexual behavior of the male rat. *Journal of Comparative and Physiological Psychology, 51*, 764–769.

Zimbardo, P. G. (1965). The effect of effort and improvisation on self-persuasion produced by role playing. *Journal of Experimental Social Psychology, 1*, 103–120.

Zimbardo, P. G. (1970). The human choice: Individuation, reason, and order versus deindividuation, impulse, and chaos. In W. Arnold & D. Levine (Eds.), *Nebraska Symposium on Motivation, 1969.* Lincoln, Neb.: University of Nebraska Press.

Zimbardo, P. G. (1977). *Shyness: What it is, what to do about it.* Reading, Mass.: Addison-Wesley.

Zimbardo, P. G., Weisenberg, M., Firestone, I., & Levy, B. (1965). Communicator effectiveness in producing public conformity and private attitude change. *Journal of Personality, 33*, 233–255.

Zimmerman, D. W. (1957). Durable secondary reinforcement: Method and theory. *Psychological Review, 64*, 373–383.

Zuckerman, M. (1979). Sensation seeking and risk taking. In C. Izard, *Emotions in personality and psychopathology.* New York: Plenum.

Zuckerman, M., & Wheeler, L. (1975). To dispel fantasies about the fantasy-based measure of fear of success. *Psychological Bulletin, 82*, 932–946.

Index

Subject Index

About the Authors

John Darley is a professor of psychology at Princeton University. He received his B.A. from Swarthmore College and his M.A. and Ph.D. degrees from the Department of Social Relations at Harvard University where he worked with Elliot Aronson. Before coming to Princeton University he taught for four years in the graduate program of the Washington Square unit of New York University. His own research is in social psychology, and over the years has included work on bystander responses to emergencies, the dynamics of self-fulfilling prophecies, and stereotyping and prejudice. John Darley recently co-authored the chapter on environmental psychology in the *Handbook of Social Psychology*.

Sam Glucksberg was born in Montreal, Canada, and moved to New York City, where he attended The Bronx High School of Science, City College of New York, and, finally, New York University, where he received his Ph.D. in experimental psychology in 1960. He then spent three years in the army with the Human Engineering Laboratories at Aberdeen Proving Ground Maryland, where he worked on basic human engineering research problems. He joined the faculty of Princeton University in 1963, where he has been ever since. He has served as chairman of the psychology department, as chair of an NIMH research review committee, and as consulting editor on numerous journals, including *American Scientist, Cognitive Psychology,* and *Developmental Psychology Journal of Experimental Psychology: Learning, Memory and Cognition*. He is now editor of the *Journal of Experimental Psychology: General*. His research focuses on cognitive processes, with emphasis on language and thought processes.

Ron Kinchla has been a professor of psychology at Princeton since 1969. He received his B.A. and Ph.D degrees from the University of California, Los Angeles, followed by postdoctoral research on human perception at Stanford University and the NASA Ames Research Center. Before coming to Princeton he taught at New York University in Greenwich Village and McMaster University in Ontario, Canada. He has published numerous research articles and book chapters on visual and auditory perception, attention, and mathematical psychology. He has been a reviewer or consulting editor on a number of journals including *Perception and Psychophysics, The Journal of Mathematical Psychology, The Journal of Experimental Psychology,* and *Psychological Review*. He has also been a member of The Advisory Committee of the International Society for Studies of Attention and Performance. He is presently Director of Graduate Studies in the Psychology Department at Princeton and is working on a book relating the study of perception and memory.

ALFRED HITCHCOCK

*a guide to references
and resources*

A
Reference
Publication
in
Film

Ronald Gottesman
Editor

ALFRED HITCHCOCK

*a guide to references
and resources*

JANE E. SLOAN

G.K. HALL & CO.
New York

Maxwell Macmillan Canada
Toronto

Maxwell Macmillan International
New York Oxford Singapore Sydney

G.K. Hall & Co.
Macmillan Publishing Company
866 Third Avenue
New York, NY 10022

Maxwell Macmillan Canada, Inc.
1200 Eglinton Avenue East
Suite 200
Don Mills, Ontario M3C 3N1

Macmillan Publishing Company is part of the Maxwell Communication Group of Companies.

Library of Congress Catalog Card Number: 92-15103

Printed in the United States of America

printing number
1 2 3 4 5 6 7 8 9 10

Library of Congress Cataloging-in-Publication Data
Sloan, Jane
    Alfred Hitchcock : a guide to references and resources / Jane E.
    Sloan.
        p.   cm. — (A Reference publication in film)
    Includes bibliographical references and indexes.
    ISBN 0-8161-9057-7 (alk. paper)
    1. Hitchcock, Alfred, 1899– —Criticism and interpretation.
    2. Hitchcock, Alfred, 1899– —Bibliography. I. Title.
    II. Series.
    PN1998.3.H58S57   1992
    791.43′0233′092—dc20   92-15103
                                                                        CIP

The paper used in this publication meets the minimum requirements of American National Standard for Information Sciences—Permanence of Paper for Printed Library Materials. ANSI Z39.48-1984. ⊚™

For my parents, Maxine and Harold Sloan

CONTENTS

PREFACE

This compilation is intended to provide a guide to published information on the films of Alfred Hitchcock. Because Hitchcock was so prolific and his work has attracted a large amount of critical literature, several exclusions have been made.

Chapter III, the "Filmography," includes largely those *credits* listed on the films themselves. Added information, like full names where initials were used, is placed in brackets. Names listed in other filmographies are placed in a note, but in general I have made no attempt to indicate the many uncredited people who worked on these films. The **synopses** are scene-by-scene descriptions; every change of place is recorded. Other aspects of the mise-en-scène—framing, sound, dialogue,and so on—are indicated occasionally according to their relative weight in the production. If a scene includes a lengthy speech, for instance, some of that speech will be quoted. Hitchcock's appearance in a film is denoted by a super-script[H]and described in a note at the end of the entry. For the U.S. and some of the British titles, commercially available video versions were used to produce the synopses. The 35mm prints at the British Film Institute's National Film Archives were used for the synopses of some of the silent and early sound films as well as the two propaganda films done for the Ministry of Information.

Films on which Hitchcock worked in a nondirectorial capacity or that he directed for television are lised in chapter VI, "Other Film Credits." This chapter includes only television episodes that Hitchcock directed; it does not include the other episodes that were part of the series, or the publishing spinoffs like *Alfred Hitchcock's Mystery Magazine.*

Chapter IV, the "Annotated Bibliography," includes citations for most of the substantial critical commentary in English, French, and Italian through the end of 1990, as well as monographs in several other languages. A sampling of contemporary reviews and news reports, generally from major news weeklies, is included, though the bulk of this type of journalism is listed in chapter V, "Supplemental Bibliographic Citations." Some citations in languages other than English that were not inspected but could be determined to be concerned with a single film are also included in this chapter. Following are the general categories of material excluded from both listings: encyclopedia entries and general histo-ries; newspaper and magazine reviews available in anthologies and compilations, such as *Variety Film Reviews*; promotional pieces commonly planted in weeklies like *Collier's* and *Life* (many of these are listed in Wulff, entry 703); most news reports and announcements, especially after 1971, when *Film Literature Index* began; and most interviews and biographies of associates like Ingrid Bergman, Grace Kelly, and Michael Balcon. Those items that were not inspected, and therefore not annotated, are marked with an asterisk immediately preceding the entry number.

The research was conducted at the University of Southern California Libraries, Rutgers University Libraries, New York Public Library, Princeton University Library, and the British Film Institute Library. Thanks go to the Professional Development Committee of USC Libraries and the National Endow-ment for the Humanities for grant funds that enabled me to obtain word-

processing support and to travel to the United Kingdom and to Rutgers University for a short research leave in 1991.

Many people contributed to this project during the four years it took to bring to completion. First, I would like to thank Julia Johnson, who helped to build the basic bibliographic database with me in 1988; she also contributed the Los Angeles sections of the chapter on archives and provided significant conceptual advice regarding the general organization of this project and its automation on ProCite. Thanks also to Christopher Dougherty, who read and annotated the material in Italian, Belinda Redden, who summarized a portion of the material in French, Siân Murray, who provided a home away from home, and Jan Schmidt, who did lots of word processing while providing her special kind of lightening effect. Thanks also to Dana Polan for commenting on the introductory material, and to Patterson Lamb for her especially thorough copy editing. Very special thanks to the editor of this series, Ronald Gottesman, who provided me with an exciting opportunity and offered excellent advice at crucial times.

I would also like to thank the staff, particularly Phyllis Palfy, of Douglass Library at Rutgers who supported and indulged me with exceptional good humor during the seemingly endless final year of this project. I am enormously indebted to the Douglass librarians for their granting of that most important type of help, time: Rebecca Gardner, Lill Maman, Thelma Tate, and Françoise Puniello. Finally, I want to thank Dosier Hammond, for his daily support, and contributions too numerous to list.

ALFRED HITCHCOCK

*a guide to references
and resources*

I

BIOGRAPHICAL BACKGROUND

The facts of Alfred Hitchcock's personal life are only minimally documented. Both book-length biographers, Donald Spoto and John Russell Taylor, lament the lack of letters and other testimony and proceed from the premise that the films represent the life.[1] Taylor goes so far as to say that there is no Hitchcock outside his films. While Spoto's biography is not "authorized" like Taylor's, both men have difficulty describing this enormously complex, secretive, and influential personality, who lived virtually his entire adult life in the public eye, yet apparently had no close friends other than his wife, Alma Reville Hitchcock, and his daughter, Patricia. Spoto, on the basis of a range of testimony concerning Hitchcock's cruel practical jokes, immoderate drinking, and other neurotic behavior, concludes that his personality was somehow aberrant, as pathological perhaps as the personalities of some of the characters in the films. Unless otherwise noted, the facts related here are taken from the Spoto and Taylor biographies.

Born August 13, 1899, Alfred Joseph Hitchcock was the third and last child of William and Emma Hitchcock, Cockney Catholics who had moved to the Leytonstone District near London in order to expand their grocery. The hard-working family moved twice more, and throughout Hitchcock's youth, his older siblings were away attending school, a situation that contributed to his development as a loner. His isolation is explained by several factors: a sensitive artistic nature, his weight problem, his minority status as a Catholic, and a typical lower-middle-class upbringing that supported him well economically but was otherwise repressive.

While Hitchcock's father is frequently described as "strict," there is not much evidence that his discipline was any more severe than that normally applied by

working- or lower-middle-class parents who aspire to improve opportunities for their children. On the other hand, Hitchcock's main public association with his father, which is a story of his being placed at a young age in the local jail in order to be taught a lesson, definitely indicates some harshness. Patricia Ferrara, through an analysis of the elements of the many versions of this well-known story—Hitchcock's age, the nature of the infraction, the length of the punishment—shows that it has always been presented by Hitchcock as "personal myth," that is, used not to explain his family background but to illustrate his filmic ideas about fear, suspense, and the law.[2] Some versions of the story are even accompanied by the information that Hitchcock "made it up."

In any case, an apparently extremely close relationship with his mother, with whom he lived alone from the age of fifteen after the death of his father, provided him with special confidence and high self-esteem. Much later, at the time of *Stage Fright* in 1950, he would describe the mother in the film, a grey figure of unpredictable but sweet response and bourgeois social pretensions and prejudices, as like his own.

Until 1913 Hitchcock attended a variety of Catholic schools, including Saint Ignatius, a Jesuit institution. Spoto tells of Hitchcock arrogantly playing cruel and reckless practical jokes in school, resulting in his nickname, "Cocky." The influence of the Catholic aspect of his youth is unclear. It is not unusual for Catholics to approach dogma with a free spirit, and such facts that are presented to prove Hitchcock's piety, such as Alma Reville's conversion to Catholicism before their marriage, do not necessarily support the conclusion that Hitchcock or his family were "strict Catholics." In any case, Hitchcock throughout his life indicated that his love of his work was far greater than any moral or religious influence. Emmanuel Decaux argues that Catholicism in Hitchcock's work is more of a popular theme than a religious underpinning. She emphasizes the minority status of Catholics in Great Britain to suggest that the importance of Hitchcock's religious upbringing is in its placement of him as a "marginal," making him sensitive to being "in" or "out."[3] Hitchcock himself indicated that what he learned most from the Jesuits was organization and control as well as how "to be realistic."[4]

A far more lasting influence on him was the death of his father on December 12, 1914, when he was barely fifteen years old, an event that was at the least economically devastating. Because of his father's illness, Hitchcock had already left school and was helping out with the family business. He had many solitary diversions: maps, wall charts, travel schedules, cinema, theater, books, and the popular boys' literature of the time, some of which, like the novels of John Buchan, he would later adapt into films. He also attended evening classes in navigation, mechanics, and draftsmanship at the University of London evening school.

In early 1915, he began working at the Henley Telegraph Company as a clerk while he continued with night classes in art history, economics, political science, and drawing, especially illustration. His talent was noted and he was transferred to the advertising department. At this time he began buying issues of technical and trade film magazines; he also read the work of Edgar Allan Poe, which made an enormous emotional impression on him.[5] By 1917, he had taken an Army medical exam and been excused from service for reasons that are unclear, enlisting instead in the volunteer corps of the Royal Engineers, a circumstance that no doubt further isolated him as different. But he remained with Henley's

and seems to have eagerly taken advantage of whatever opportunities they could offer him. His short story, "Gas," was printed in the first issue of the company's staff magazine.[6]

In early 1920, he took some sample work to Famous Players-Lasky, a U.S. firm that had opened a branch in London, and was hired part-time to draw title designs. "It never occurred to me to go and offer my services to a British company," he said later, but the United States inspired him; "I did regard their movie making as truly professional and very much in advance." [7] He continued to work at Henley's until late in the year when the first films for which he did titles were successful enough for him to be employed full-time with Famous Players-Lasky. During the next couple of years, he designed drawings and lettering styles for all their films, also working on sets, costumes, props, and scripts; he was to all accounts a cheerful, willing, and extremely talented worker. During this time he met Alma Reville, who was near his age but who had been working in films for several years before him; she was already writing and editing.

By the end of 1922 he was assigned the direction of a two-reel short, *Number 13*, but the project was aborted due to the deteriorating financial condition of Famous Players-Lasky. The ailing company began to rent out its studio at Islington to independent producers, in particular Michael Balcon and Victor Saville, who set up Gainsborough Pictures.

In the summer of 1923 Balcon and Saville produced, and Graham Cutts directed, *Woman to Woman*, with Hitchcock working on sets, script, and whatever else needed to be done. The film was unusual in that it was a huge success in the U.S. market because it was well made and, more important, had an American (U.S.) star. Tom Ryall explains in detail the extent to which the British film industry was floundering at this time, a crisis that reached its nadir in 1925, when national debate led to the quota laws of 1927.[8] A few years later, a press kit for another film describes Hitchcock during the summer of 1923 as a man who spent "his spare cash on entertaining pressmen to drinks. He had a theory, youthful though he was, that the way to fame was via the newspapers and was a rabid publicity seeker." [9] In late 1923, Hitchcock asked Alma Reville to marry him, a move he later said he put off until he had achieved a position securely superior to hers.

So Hitchcock not only impressed people with his hard work and talent, but also made sure that anyone who might be in a position to help him knew about him. More important during this period, as in fact throughout his life, he continued to build his expertise in filmmaking through spectacular energy and ambition. His set design work on *The Passionate Adventure* in 1924, for instance, involved the design and building of a "complete stretch of canal with houses beside it, all on a 90-foot stage." [10]

Subsequent work with Cutts (which sent Hitchcock to the Ufa Studios in Germany where he was able to observe F. W. Murnau on the set of *The Last Laugh*) produced a situation of jealous competitiveness between Hitchcock and the British director. On assigning Hitchcock his first directorial position in 1925 on *The Pleasure Garden* (and then, because he was pleased with that effort, *The Mountain Eagle*), Balcon wrote later, "I had to arrange to have these two subjects made in Germany, at least as far as Hitchcock is concerned, because of the resistance [in England] to his becoming a director. At that time, we were very much dependent on distributors' support and it was hard to convince them that new people were any good." [11]

In March of 1926 the press screening of *The Pleasure Garden* produced a rave in the *Bioscope,* but C. M. Woolf, who headed the distribution company, found the film too sophisticated and persuaded Balcon to shelve it on the grounds that it might confuse the audience and endanger other bookings. Balcon nonetheless continued to support Hitchcock and the next month gave him *The Lodger* to direct; it too, along with *The Mountain Eagle,* was shelved by Woolf for being "too highbrow" and arty. Balcon was embarrassed financially and brought in Ivor Montagu, a leading figure of what Ryall calls Great Britain's "minority film culture," to suggest changes in *The Lodger.*

Ryall offers an extensive picture of this "minority film culture," in which many people Hitchcock knew participated, and its promotion of "art" cinema through the London Film Society, and later, journals like *Close Up.*[12] Art cinema for this intellectual group was not generally perceived to be made in Great Britain; Soviet, German, French, and even American films were considered much more interesting. Nonetheless, there appears to have been something of a "cause" surrounding Hitchcock's talent and its squelching by C. M. Woolf. In March of 1926, when Hitchcock's pictures had been seen only at previews, Cedric Belfrage, in an article oddly titled "Alfred the Great," declared the films to be "almost perfect in their technical and artistic production" and Hitchcock to be an "unassuming and delightful personality." [13]

Hitchcock later described the painful evening when he and Alma waited for the verdict on the streamlined version of *The Lodger,* knowing that it was unlikely he would ever direct another film if none of these first three had a commercial run. Fortunately, Balcon convinced Woolf to release the film in September 1926, and its huge success allowed the first two films to be released as well. "There you see the thin red line between failure and success," Hitchcock commented.[14]

Shortly thereafter, on December 2, 1926, Alfred Hitchcock and Alma Reville were married. She continued to script and edit other projects but was usually involved with Hitchcock's as well; these included *Downhill, Easy Virtue,* and especially *The Ring,* the next picture for which she was credited after *The Lodger.* She was generally seen to have a keen sense of people and business as well as a large talent that some thought would result in an independent directorial career; but after 1929, she worked solely on his projects and later said that she was never very ambitious. By the end of 1927, *The Ring,* which was the first picture Hitchcock made under a new contract with British International as "the highest paid director in England," was lauded as "the most magnificent British film ever made." [15] At Christmas 1927 Hitchcock designed and sent to his friends the first version of his famous caricature profile, drawn on a wooden puzzle.

Easy Virtue, made before *The Ring,* showed in its main theme Hitchcock's acute consciousness of the difficulties of the media image he was so avidly pursuing. By 1928, the conflicting elements of this image—artist? entertainer?— which had already nearly cost him his career, were being played out in the press over his other films. *The Ring* was sarcastically dismissed in *Close Up* as the overpraised best of the worst, and Rachel Low summed up Hitchcock's dilemma of the time: "Had Hitchcock been German, Russian, or French, had he even presented himself as a more Bohemian figure, he would almost certainly have been taken more seriously." [16] Ryall describes the other side of the bind: "Hitchcock was developing an artistic reputation during this period and an identity as a film maker which was at odds with the expectation of business

figures in the industry like Woolf." [17] On the one side, he was too artful to be commerical; on the other, his art was mere pretension, not deep enough to be truly "art."

Hitchcock, however, as an intelligent product of the working class, would always be first concerned about earning a living; if he could say what he wanted, so much the better, but if he could not, well, that was more than understandable. Nonetheless, he displayed an outspoken idealism concerning excellence in film-making, and throughout his British career, he never hesitated to proclaim publicly his ideas in this area, which were frequently critical of the established ways of production. In a letter to the *London Evening News* in 1927, he admonished the British film industry to learn better "the nouns and verbs" of their trade just like a "great novelist," and defended the artistic mission of the film director in creating mood and tempo.[18]

On July 7, 1928, the Hitchcocks' daughter, Patricia, was born, but the business year brought only commercial disappointments. Though *The Farmer's Wife* was a successful and witty play adaptation and *The Manxman* an extremely moving melodrama, *Champagne* was a frothy star vehicle for Betty Balfour, and none of the three made a distinctive impact. Later, he wrote of his "bitter disappointment" that *Blackmail* was to be shot silent, though he planned ahead for eventual reversal of this decision by the producers, and, indeed, ended up reshooting the film with sound.[19] In June of 1929, the "talkie" version of *Blackmail* was screened to much excitement and immediate international recognition; it contains Hitchcock's first clearly recognizable personal appearance. By 1930, he had formed a publicity company, Hitchcock Baker Productions, Limited, for the purpose of "advertising to the press the newsworthiness" of himself.[20]

The next year *Murder!* was also very well received. John Grierson, another leader of Great Britain's "minority film culture," in this case the documentary movement, described Hitchcock around this time as "the best director . . . of unimportant films." [21] It is interesting to note that Grierson and the other film people with whom Hitchcock was friendly—Montagu, Balcon, other members of the London Film Society and critics for *Close Up*—were university-educated men. Hitchcock appears to have been the only Cockney at these high levels in what was by 1930 a growing but still relatively small film culture. In 1932, after seeing *Rich and Strange,* Grierson assessed Hitchcock's "weaknesses" as those of a "provincial, a true-born Londoner [who] knows people but not things, situations, but not events." [22] Further, he suggested that Hitchcock had been sent off in the wrong direction by the "highbrows."

During this period, Hitchcock first publicly expressed his ideas on the importance of women characters, who "must be fashioned to please women rather than men, for the reason that women form ¾ of the average cinema audience. . . . Most women are idealists and want to see ideals personified in heroines." [23] His own idealism—and diligence in seeking out whatever marketing information about the audience was available at the time—is apparent. This kind of practical pronouncement continued to be issued in the industry press under his name, resulting in articles like "Are Stars Necessary?" in which he explained that stars were a gift to the audience, who had "little enough glamour in their drab business world." [24]

As the top director at British International in the early 1930s, Hitchcock was handed the prestige theater projects of the day: *The Skin Game* and *Juno and the Paycock.* These were handled in interesting ways but were disparaged by the

"art" cinema intellectuals, while not having exceptional appeal to the movie-going public, either. During 1932, *Rich and Strange,* from his and Alma Reville's own idea and script, was received poorly, and *Number Seventeen* gave the impression of being a throwaway. Indeed, Rodney Acklund, who worked on the script with Hitchcock, described it as a juvenile parody meant to provoke the ire of stuffy studio executives. According to Spoto, Hitchcock was depressed during this period. Later he told Truffaut, "I don't ever remember saying to myself, 'you're finished, you're at your lowest ebb.' Yet, outwardly, to other people, I believe I was. . . . *Number Seventeen* represented a careless approach to my work. There was no careful analysis of what I was doing." [25]

In 1933, Hitchcock signed a short-term contract with Alexander Korda, but Korda was unable to supply financing for any project, which eventually freed Hitchcock to go with the independent producer, Tom Arnold, and film *Waltzes from Vienna.* Hitchcock's unconventional approach to the musical resulted in a film of distinctive charm, but he was nonetheless reportedly bored and unhappy with the project. Michael Balcon once again rescued him with an offer to produce *The Man Who Knew Too Much,* a project Hitchcock had purchased from British International Pictures and then sold to Balcon for double the price Hitchcock had paid.

In December 1934, *The Man Who Knew Too Much* opened to plaudits, though C. M. Woolf had first announced he would have the film reshot and then released it on the second half of a double bill. It was the final episode in the struggle between Woolf and Hitchcock, however, as the enormous success of the film assured that Hitchcock's security would never again be threatened.

The "thriller cycle"—*The Man Who Knew Too Much, The 39 Steps, Secret Agent, Young and Innocent,* and *The Lady Vanishes*—that filled the decade of the 1930s ended Hitchcock's reputation as a "critic's director" in Great Britain, while bringing him cult fame in New York City. The thrillers also showcased his marked ability to portray contemporary times and issues—in this case, the political turmoil of the 1930s. During this extremely successful period of working with Ivor Montagu and Michael Balcon at Gaumont, and then with Edward Black at Gainsborough after Gaumont was sold and its producers fired, Hitchcock continued to place his ideas about filmmaking before the public.

In his self-appointed position as educator of the masses, he wrote many articles for the fan and trade weeklies. Some related the circumstances of his own career, such as "My Screen Memories"; others were more theoretical, such as "If I Were Head of a Production Company." In the latter he complained that American films "lack what we call soul," while British films, by contrast, are a "product of individuality." [26] "Why Thrillers Thrive" discussed subjective camera viewpoints versus spectatorship in the live theater, and "More Cabbages, Fewer Kings" lamented that English producers appeared to be interested only in the rich and the poor.[27] This piece recommended the production of more film stories about the middle class, where "manners and ways [flow] easily, speech [is] unaffected, emotions more free, and instinct sharper." The diligence paid off; by 1937, when Hitchcock first visited New York, autograph-seeking fans greeted him outside a movie theater.

Around this time, he began to negotiate with several different U.S. studios and producers. Professionally, he had never made a secret of his frustration with the lack of qualified technical personnel in England and had always openly admired American methods, if not the message of the films. After signing in the

middle of 1938 with David O. Selznick, Hitchcock returned to England to complete his final British production, *Jamaica Inn,* for Charles Laughton. Leonard Leff indicates that the Selznick contract left more than the usual freedom for Hitchcock but paled in terms of remuneration next to the salaries of the most famous U.S. directors of the time. Hitchcock had first to prove that he could work fast and make large profits in the new atmosphere, no matter what amount of resentment he might have over the exploitation of his talents. Having been the "highest paid" in Great Britain, Hitchcock was sensitive in this area, and Selznick's persistent loanouts of him at twice or more the salary he was paying him, which began immediately after *Rebecca* in late 1939, exacerbated his annoyance.

After arriving in the United States in March 1939, Hitchcock began work at Selznick International Pictures in Los Angeles, according to Spoto, appearing at his small office usually with Alma. In June, Selznick rejected "the entire composition" of the treatment for *Rebecca* that Hitchcock had prepared. The Selznick-Hitchcock relationship, which lasted through several renegotiated contracts until 1947, would always be marked by this type of creative power struggle. For these reasons—money and creative freedom—Hitchcock began to seek more independent ways of production soon after his arrival in the United States.

By his own and others' accounts, Hitchcock survived the battles with Selznick by devious rather than confrontational means. This description of his personal style became a repetitive aspect of his interviews and can be related to a major theme of the films—neutrality, a sophisticated, distanced, kindly tolerance of the vagaries of human nature. Patricia Ferrara argues that "the public persona of macabre, straight-faced joker that he cultivated . . . [emphasized] the obviously false distance between himself and his films." [28] She argues, as others like Jean Douchet do more elaborately, that the aesthetic distance of the films is commercially effective, as well as critically interesting, because it is a passionate resolution of the conflict between the commercialism that assured the continuation of his career and the personal satisfaction he derived from making films exactly as he pleased. This tension led to the sympathetic movement from character to character that is a marked feature of the films and which remains in stark contrast to his treatment of people in real life, behavior that was to all accounts considerably more rigid and demanding. Said Hitchcock himself, "I dislike conflict. But I won't sacrifice my principles. I draw the line at my work. I loathe people who give less than their full effort . . . that's deceit. I cut such people off." [29]

The struggle with Selznick made Hitchcock tougher. While he generally acceded to Selznick at the script stage, he became crafty about avoiding the producer's interference in areas like shooting where Selznick was less knowledgeable. *Rebecca,* originally budgeted at $950,000, eventually cost $1,000,000; it was, however, a huge success and won for Selznick an Academy Award for best picture.

By the end of 1939, Hitchcock was working with independent producer Walter Wanger on *Foreign Correspondent,* a film that further satisifed his ambition by providing him with another budget significantly larger than the ones that had been available to him in Great Britain. Costing $1,500,000, it included sets of a square in Amsterdam that required drainage for a rain scene, "a strip of Dutch countryside with windmills, several parts of London, and a large plane, interior and exterior, the latter requiring the use of a giant studio tank for the spectacular air crash sequence." [30] The film was another success, noted in the

press to be much more of a "Hitchcock film" than *Rebecca* and admired for its propagandistic value in encouraging the United States to enter the war, a message that was of primary concern to Wanger.

The next year, with Europe in the middle of war, Hitchcock returned to England to try to persuade his mother to move to the United States; she refused, however, and he quickly returned to work on the script of *Suspicion* for RKO.

In the latter part of 1940, Michael Balcon publicly accused Hitchcock of preferring to stay in Hollywood rather than return to Great Britain for the war effort. Hitchcock replied in a New York newspaper: "By what authority does this man take this attitude? . . . The British government has only to call on me for my services. The manner in which I am helping my country is not Mr. Balcon's business." [31] Several years later he would provide such services, but for now he continued to work on his third production that year, again for RKO: *Mr. and Mrs. Smith. Suspicion* was filmed in the first half of 1941, and *Saboteur* for Frank Lloyd at Universal followed quickly thereafter.

In August 1942, his mother died at the age of 79; a few months later his brother, William, also died. In early 1943 Hitchcock, weighing just under 300 pounds, went on a well-publicized diet and lost one-third of his weight.

At the end of 1943, after completing *Shadow of a Doubt* and *Lifeboat* for Twentieth Century-Fox, Hitchcock returned to England at the request of his friend, Sidney Bernstein, then head of the film division of the British Ministry of Information. There, he directed *Bon Voyage* and *Aventure Malgache* for the M.O.I. in French with an exiled French theater troupe, the Molière Players.

Upon his return *Lifeboat* was released to a "storm of controversy" over its supposed "elevation of the Nazi superman" in the character of Willie. This protest, along with the weak propagandistic qualities of the two shorts he had made (neither was widely distributed) illustrate the paradoxical aspects of Hitchcock's essentially apolitical nature. On the one hand is his limited ability to assert distinctly any particular ideology, even the most commonly felt one of the time; on the other is his appealing knack for and glee in offending the powers that be. Sam Simone's characterization of Hitchcock as an "activist" during the 1940s is unusual in this regard as it belies most of the evidence regarding Hitchcock's interest in embracing an ideological agenda.[32] It seems more likely that Hitchcock had a natural curiosity about the nature of current events, and illustrating them was merely another way of relating to the people, assuring their attendance at his films. As many have pointed out, a significant part of Hitchcock's popularity was his talent for reflecting the contemporary society in which each of his films was made, despite shaky ideological underpinning. In fact, Hitchcock's films repeatedly showed that the reflection need not be realistic in order to be effective. *Frenzy,* for instance, was criticized for its old-fashioned view of mercantile London, yet its treatment of criminal sexual behavior was very up-to-date.

In subsequent years, between 1945 and 1947, Hitchcock made *Spellbound* and *The Paradine Case* with Selznick, and *Notorious* for RKO. Throughout this period, he flew several times to England to meet with Sidney Bernstein over a possible partnership, which came to fruition in April of 1946 under the name Transatlantic Pictures.

After mining Hollywood studios for all the support they could provide, Hitchcock, as his own producer at the end of the decade, began a new stage of radical technical innovations and ever more concentrated methods of control. Transatlantic Pictures' first production, and Hitchcock's first color film, *Rope,* was

rigorously designed around ten-minute takes. The shooting in Los Angeles was to all accounts frustrating for the actors, who were blocked into long, complex camera movements involving furniture and walls being rolled in and out of their path. *Under Capricorn,* an even more elaborate mixture of long takes, bold technicolor, and difficult behavior for the actors, was a greater trial. Hitchcock himself assessed his actions in producing it as "stupid and juvenile," probably because the film cost $2,500,000 and was a financial failure that brought about the end of Transatlantic Pictures.

Under Capricorn, however, sparked a reevaluation of Hitchcock in France; Alexandre Astruc equated the film with the British cinema's greatest theme of "the mystery of the human personality." [33] John Belton considers *Under Capricorn* important in preparing Hitchcock for his next decade of extraordinary productivity and effectiveness.[34] At this point also, the pattern of Hitchcock's career became set: the extremely successful entertainments, primarily of the thriller genre, interspersed with the more somber melodramas, which provoked a varied response. By now his income and his independence as a producer were not only secure but were also accompanied by growing international fame. As Ado Kyrou put it in a typical anti-Hitchcock diatribe, the director has the freedom and prestige to make a great film, "but we await it with little hope." [35]

After he had moved to the United States, Hitchcock ended the idealistic public pronouncements in which he had occasionally indulged in Great Britain, even, in 1947, sarcastically noting (or perhaps, ghost-noting) that he no longer worried about what would happen to the "heroine" as he was now "hardened, and emotionally muscle-bound." [36] In interviews he gave in 1938 Hitchcock mentioned his desire to make films of "sociological interest," perhaps an anti-capital punishment film or a film about the general strike of 1926; but he also indicated that these were precisely what the British censor would not allow him to make. His comments probably reveal more about his sensitivity to restriction than his desire to express any particular ideas.[37] By 1952, after twelve years in the technically and politically less restricted environment of the United States as well as several years of independent producing, his view was much more pragmatic: "I would say it is harder to make a film that has both integrity and wide audience appeal than it is to make one that merely satisfies one's own artistic conscience." [38]

To the social isolation to which he had always been susceptible in England was now added cultural isolation; several critics, Alexander Doty at length, describe the transition period of the 1940s as a deepening and darkening of the vision. [39] During this period Hitchcock became fanatically attached to the trappings of English culture, and the change of country clearly solidified his disinclination to be assimilated into any group beyond his immediate family. Many have remarked that in the United States his identity became subsumed into his public image. Chabrol and Rohmer theorized that Hitchcock began as early as the production of *Sabotage* (1936) deliberately to create "a second personality that completely corresponded with the idea that others had of him." [40]

Changing approaches to talent in the studios allowed him to be one of the first to take advantage of newer, freer contracts. In January of 1949, he signed with Jack Warner to produce and direct four pictures over a six-and-a-half-year period for a total of $999,000: *Stage Fright, Strangers on a Train, I Confess,* and *Dial M for Murder.*

He next contracted an unusual arrangement with Paramount Pictures that

allowed the rights of the films he made for them eventually to lapse to him: *Rear Window, To Catch a Thief, The Trouble with Harry, The Man Who Knew Too Much,* and *Vertigo.*

By 1955, he had signed over the use of his name to Richard E. Decker, who published the *Alfred Hitchcock Mystery Magazine* with ghostwritten introductions. Most spectacularly, he had signed with CBS and Bristol-Meyers for a network television show, "Alfred Hitchcock Presents," at $129,000 per episode, to be produced by his own company, Shamley Productions. In 1955, he also arranged with Vera Miles the first of a series of contracts with actresses who were signed to work exclusively on his productions. The same year, while shooting *To Catch a Thief* in France, he met François Truffaut and Claude Chabrol. The films of this period, especially *Rear Window* and *Vertigo* (the latter was not commercially well received) were uniquely recognized by French critics as important art.

Hitchcock's critical reputation had now come completely full circle. A cover story for *Newsweek* magazine pronounced him a "bona fide celebrity" because of his appearances on television, and capsulized his British films as "art-house." [41] Between the years 1955 and 1960, he directed twenty episodes for the television series at the same time he was completing five feature films. By the end of 1959, after *North by Northwest* had delivered the planned-for blockbuster success, he was at a peak of international fame few directors have experienced. Characteristically, after a couple of extremely expensive aborted projects on the same level of *North by Northwest,* he pragmatically decided in 1960 to turn away from the formula.

Instead, Hitchcock turned to *Psycho* and the expressed intent of "shocking" his audience, though he first had to contend with producers and colleagues appalled enough at the thought of the project to refuse to be associated with it. Stephen Rebello speculates that the extreme change in production values that *Psycho* represents was a result of this lack of support as well as other frustrations—with star salaries, with aborted projects, and with the success of *Les Diaboliques,* which had provided its French director, Henri-Georges Clouzot, with an international reputation as a suspense director that rivaled Hitchcock's own. Rebello compares the gritty black and white *Les Diaboliques* to *Psycho,* most convincingly in their similar advertising campaigns, both of which pleaded with the audience not to reveal the film's ending. [42] In any case, what many saw to be a great risk, even at the extremely low cost of $800,000, turned out to be an even greater height for Hitchcock's commercial career, inspiring a promotional tour of openings around the world in mid-1960 that included Japan and China.

Critically, *Psycho* enjoyed a belated but astounding success, encouraging Hitchcock to exercise his power openly at even broader levels. According to Robert E. Kapsis, the development of *The Birds* revealed Hitchcock to be expressly conscious of his new found "art" audience; he argued for certain points in the script with reasoning such as "We are going to run into all kinds of critiques from the highbrows." Hitchcock not only tailored the film to appeal to this group but also launched a "propaganda campaign [to] transform his image" into that of a serious director of film art. To enhance this image he mailed out with publicity for *The Birds* the monograph by Peter Bogdanovich, which validated as great art a Hitchcock retrospective at the Museum of Modern Art, and a "solicited tribute" from François Truffaut, with whom he was also about to embark on their famous series of interviews." [43]

The Truffaut interviews of 1962 show Hitchcock generally agreeable to

Truffaut's prior judgments and eager to share his technical knowledge but also occasionally non-plussed at Truffaut's opinions. When Truffaut insisted that the films, in their treatment of "metaphysical anxieties" such as fear, sex and death, avoided more "daytime" anxieties such as unemployment, poverty, or "everyday love conflicts between men and women," Hitchcock objected, "Isn't the main thing that they be connected with life?" [44] Kapsis argues that Hitchcock's cooperation with Bogdanovich and Truffaut not only solidified his own critical reputation but also affected the reputation of the thriller genre and heightened critical consciousnes of film aethestics in general. [45]

The rest of the decade saw the beginning of what is considered to be the director's decline, with *Marnie, Torn Curtain,* and *Topaz,* though the first has already been significantly reevaluated through feminist criticism. Michael Walker relates the more lumbering qualities of the latter two and their persistent theme of betrayal to the melancholia of the director's "old age." [46]

After these commercial embarrassments (*Topaz* went through three different filmed endings) Hitchcock rebounded in 1972 with *Frenzy,* largely seen to be a successful return to formulaic horror, though hardly formulaic in its brutality.

The next year he had a heart pacemaker implanted, and two years later, he completed his final film, *Family Plot.* His perennial youthful spirit and rebellious attitude is well illustrated by an anecdote from the set of that film. Knowing that Hitchcock owned a sizable amount of MCA stock, Bruce Dern, one of the stars, suggested that they paint the garage door in the film with graffiti of the *Jaws* logo, an MCA-financed hit. Hitchcock replied, "No, Bruce, I know what we should write—Fuck MCA!" [47]

Awards and honors flowed during this period: the Irving G. Thalberg Memorial Award, given by the Association of Cinemotographers, Television and Allied Technicians at the Academy Award ceremonies; honorary degrees from the University of California at Santa Cruz and Columbia University; and a spectacular gala sponsored by the Film Society of Lincoln Center in 1979.

Though Hitchcock, at the age of 79, began work on another film, David Freeman related a sad story of his senility while working with him on this last project, *The Short Night.* [48] In May of 1979, he finally closed up his offices at Universal Studios, and on April 29, 1980, he died in Los Angeles.

Notes

1. Donald Spoto, *The Dark Side of Genius: The Life of Alfred Hitchcock* (New York: Ballantine, 1983) (paperback edition of entry 702); John Russell Taylor, *Hitch: The Life and Work of Alfred Hitchcock* (Boston: Faber & Faber, 1978). (entry 499)

2. Patricia Ferrara, "The discontented bourgeois: Bourgeois morality and the interplay of light and dark strains in Hitchcock's films," *New Orleans Review* 14, no. 1 (Winter 1987):79–87. (entry 814)

3. Emmanuel Decaux, "L'ennemi intèrieur," *Cinématographe,* no. 59 (July-August 1980):24–12. (entry 558)

4. Catherine De La Roche, "Conversation with Hitchcock," *Sight and Sound* 25, no. 3 (Winter 1955):157–158. (entry 227)

5. Alfred Hitchcock, "Pourquoi j'ai peur la nuit," *Arts,* no. 777 (June 1, 1960):1, 7. (entry 281)

6. Alfred Hitchcock "Gas," *The Henley* 1, No. 1 (1919). (entry 58)

7. François Truffaut, with the collaboration of Helen G. Scott, *Hitchcock*, rev. ed. (New York: Simon & Schuster, 1983), p. 125. (entry 338)

8. Tom Ryall, *Alfred Hitchcock and the British Cinema* (London/Urbana: Croom Helm/ University of Illinois Press, 1986), pp. 40–45. (entry 775)

9. Press release for the sound version of *Woman to Woman,* 1930, in the British Film Institute clipping file under that title.

10. Taylor, *Hitch,* p. 54.

11. Peter Noble, *An Index to the Creative Work of Alfred Hitchcock,* Special Supplement to *Sight and Sound,* Index Series, 18 (London: British Film Institute, 1949), p.15. (entry 192)

12. Ryall, *Alfred Hitchcock and the British Cinema,* p. 7–23.

13. Cedric Belfrage, "Alfred the Great," *Picturegoer* 11, no. 63 (March 1926):60. (entry 61)

14. George Angell, "The time of my life," *BBC Home Service* (recorded July 30, 1966):Tape no. TLO 634/725. (entry 324)

15. "The Ring," *Bioscope* (October 6, 1927):43. (entry 68)

16. Rachel Low, *The History of British Film: 1918–1929* (London: Allen and Unwin, 1971), p. 307.

17. Ryall, *Alfred Hitchcock and the British Cinema,* p. 88.

18. Spoto, *Dark Side of Genius,* pp. 113–114.

19. Alfred Hitchcock with John K. Newnham, "My screen memories: The story of *Blackmail,*" *Film Weekly* (May 9, 1936):7. (entry 110)

20. Spoto, *Dark Side of Genius,* p. 138.

21. John Grierson, "[Review of *Murder!*]," in *Grierson on Documentary,* edited and compiled by Forsyth Hardy (New York: Harcourt, Brace, 1947), p. 71. (entry 175)

22. John Grierson, "The Hitch in Hitchcock," *Everyman* (December 24, 1931):722. (entry 89)

23. Alfred Hitchcock, "How I choose my heroines," in *Who's Who in Filmland,* 3rd ed., edited by Langford Reed and Hetty Spiers (London: Chapman & Hall, 1931), pp. xxi–xxiii. (entry 91)

24. Alfred Hitchcock, "Are stars necessary?" *Picturegoer* (December 16, 1933):13. (entry 93)

25. Truffaut, *Hitchcock,* p. 85.

26. Alfred Hitchcock, "If I were head of a production company," *Picturegoer* (January 26, 1935):15. (entry 100)

27. Alfred Hitchcock, "Why thrillers thrive," *Picturegoer* (January 18, 1936): 15; Alfred Hitchcock, "More cabbages, fewer kings; a believer in the little man," *Kine Weekly* (January 14, 1937):30. (entry 115)

28. Ferrara, "The discontented bourgeois," p. 81.

29. Stephen Rebello, *Alfred Hitchcock and the Making of Psycho.* (New York: Dembner, 1990), p. 87. (entry 861)

30. Taylor, *Hitch,* p. 167.

31. Spoto, *Dark Side of Genius,* p. 245.

32. Sam P. Simone, *Hitchcock as Activist* (Ann Arbor, Mich.: UMI Research Press, 1985). (entry 755)

33. Alexandre Astruc, "Au-dessous de volcan," *Cahiers du Cinéma* 1, no. 1 (April 1951):29. (entry 201)

34. John Belton, "Alfred Hitchcock's *Under Capricorn*: Montage entranced by *mise-en-scène,*" *Quarterly Review of Film Studies* 6, no. 4 (1981):365–383. (entry 605)

35. Ado Kyrou, "Mais qui a lancé Alfred? Ou le mythe de Hitchcock," *Lettres Nouvelles* 47 (1957):421. (entry 251)

36. Alfred Hitchcock, "The film thriller," In *Film Review, 1946–47,* edited by F. Maurice Speed (London: MacDonald, 1947), pp. 22–23. (entry 176)

37. Leslie Perkoff, "The censor and Sydney Street," *World Film News* (London) 2, no. 12 (March 1938):4–5.(entry 128); J. Danvers Williams, "The censor wouldn't pass it," *Film Weekly* (November 5, 1938):6–7. (entry 129)

38. Gerald Pratley, "Alfred Hitchcock's working credo," *Films In Review* 3, no. 10 (December 1952):503. (entry 208)

39. Alexander Michael Doty, "Alfred Hitchcock's films of the 1940's: The emergence of personal style and theme within the American studio system" (Ph.D. diss., University of Illinois, 1984). (entry 717)

40. Eric Rohmer and Claude Chabrol, *Hitchcock,* Classiques du Cinéma, 6 (Paris: Universitaires, 1957), p. 47. (entry 246)

41. "Alfred Hitchcock—director, TV or movies, suspense is golden," *Newsweek* 47 (June 11, 1956):105–108. (entry 233)

42. Rebello, *Alfred Hitchcock,* pp. 15–23.

43. Robert E. Kapsis, "Hollywood filmmaking and reputation building: Hitchcock's *The Birds,*" *Journal of Popular Film & Television* 15, no. 1 (Spring 1987):5–14. (entry 823)

44. Truffaut, *Hitchcock,* p. 241.

45. Robert E. Kapsis, "Alfred Hitchcock: Auteur or hack?" *Cineaste* 14, no. 3 (1986):30–35. (entry 790)

46. Michael Walker, "The old age of Alfred Hitchcock," *Movie,* no. 18 (Winter 1970):10–13. (entry 371)

47. Joseph McBride, "Buts and rebuts—Hitchcock: A defense and an update," *Film Comment* 15, no. 3 (May–June 1979):70. (entry 525)

48. David Freeman, *The Last Days of Alfred Hitchcock* (London/Woodstock, N.Y.: Pavilion-Michael Joseph/Overlook, 1984). (entry 718)

Obituaries

"Alfred Hitchcock." *Newsweek* 96 (December 29, 1980):52.

Canby, Vincent. "Film maker transformed commonplace into exotic." *New York Times* 129, no. 1 (April 30, 1980): Section D, p. 23.

Cottom, J. von. *Cinè Revue* 60 (May 8, 1980):38–39.

Flint, Peter B. "Alfred Hitchcock dies; a master of suspense." *New York Times* 129 (April 30, 1980):Section A, p. 1, col. 1.

Granum, B. "Filmen var hele hans verden." *Film & Kino* 152, no. 4 (1980).

"Hundreds at funeral for Hitchcock include set workers and stars." *New York Times* 129, no. 234 (May 3, 1980):2–6.

Kosmorama 26, no. 148 (September 1980):124–125.

Lehman, Ernest. "Hitch." *American Film* 5,no. 9 (July–August 1980): 18.

Linck, D. "Hitchcock leaves legacy of art and showmanship." *Boxoffice* 116 (May 5, 1980):1.

Maslin, Janet. "Hitchcock: The master puts on immortality." *New York Times* 129 (May 4,1980):Section 4, p. 9, col. 1.

Miller, A. I. "Master of suspense." *Film News* (Winter 1979–1980):36–37.

Miller, Mark Crispin. "In memoriam—A. H. (1899–1980)." *New Republic* 183 (July 26, 1980):27–31.

"La mise en scène." *Positif,* no. 234 (September 1980):2–6.

Revue du Cinéma/Image et Son, no. 351 (June 1980):8–9.

Sarris, A[ndrew]. "The man who knew so much." *Village Voice* 25 (May 12, 1980):49–50.

Schickel, R[ichard]. *Time* 115 (May 12, 1980):74–75.

Skoop 16 (May–June 1980):3.

Skytte, A. "Hitchcock 1899–1980." *Kosmorama* 26, no. 148 (September 1980): 124–125.

S[auvaget], D. "Hitch n'a plus la mort aux trousses." *Revue du Cinéma/Image et Son,* no. 51 (June 1980):8–9.

Time 115 (May 12, 1980):74–75.

Variety 298 (April 30, 1980):198.

Variety 299 (May 7, 1980):6.

Wiener, R. "Hollywood bids goodbye to Sir Alfred." *Boxoffice* 116 (May 12, 1980):1.

II

CRITICAL SURVEY

From the beginning of his career, Alfred Hitchcock experienced the misunderstanding that often plagues those artists who work within the commercial forms of popular culture. In fact, the first three films that he directed were thought too sophisticated for a general audience and withheld from distribution. Later, a similar confusion—deep artist? superficial manipulator?—defined the parameters of critical debate about the films he directed, and still characterizes the field of commentary in the general press, where the question of whether to take the films seriously continues to inhibit critical understanding of this most popular of film directors. Although we are all continually exposed to its influence, popular culture as an object of study often requires a defense. The review of the critical literature that follows summarizes some of the early journalistic work on Hitchcock but focuses primarily on the academic criticism that has attended these films since the 1950s, and which has, in a sense, furthered the aura of "progressivism" that was historically attached to Hitchcock's first British films by their defenders.

AUTEUR CRITICISM

Until 1965, when Robin Wood published a book titled *Hitchcock's Films*, thereby answering his own question about whether or not we should take Hitchcock seriously, Hitchcock had been the object of deliberate study mostly in languages other than English.[1] In his work, Wood delineated the use of identification techniques (methods by which the viewer of a film is encouraged to empathize with a character or the filmmaker) in Hitchcock's American films, and saw in

them a "therapeutic theme" whereby the audience is induced to experience a quandary and gain understanding from it; he insisted on their moral clarity. The next year Peter Wollen, writing as Lee Russell, reviewed the work of Wood and the French critics that preceded him and called for the "important task of popularization" of the critical debate surrounding Hitchcock."[2] Since then, the academic debate has produced numerous, dense analyses, some of which effectively lay bare the fascinating quality of the films, but Wollen's ideal of "popularization" still lags significantly behind.

The questions surrounding serious attention to film and its foremost genre, *melodrama,* parallel this critical history, just as Hitchcock's career can be said to parallel film history. In discussing Hitchcock's films, Edward Buscombe explains the lack of fit between melodrama and the tenets of the "Great Tradition'" in English literary criticism, which judged the genre too popular, too crude, too fanciful, and too unrealistic.[3] Further, he criticizes Robin Wood (and, by extension, *auteur* criticism) for his emphasis on the films' characters at the expense of the genre elements. Wood's approach was nonetheless far-reaching in its articulation of both identification techniques and suspense techniques, and especially in its assessment of Hitchcock's "essential subject matter" as *male/female relationships.* As many have pointed out, melodrama, especially in its coinciding with romance, is closely associated with fiction for women, a factor, as was detailed in the biographical section, of which Hitchcock himself was very much aware.

The classic theme of *appearance and reality,* which is pervasive in both the popular commentary and the academic criticism, received its full career explication in Donald Spoto's *The Art of Alfred Hitchcock.*[4] Tania Modleski, working from more complex theoretical constructs than these *auteur* critics, effectively combines the major themes of male/female relationships (the formation of the couple) and appearance and reality in analyses of the world of illusion and false or mixed identity created by Hitchcock's "theatrical space." She argues that Hitchcock's world of appearances is fascinating but also "dreadful to men" because it is suggestive of femininity as well as bisexuality.[5] Certainly Hitchcock's interest in unconventional sexual expression and/or the naturalized "perversions" of conventional sexual expression is evident in all his films.

Between the work of Wood, which valorized Hitchcock as a moralist in the tradition of nineteenth-century novelists, and that of Spoto, who eventually assessed him as a moral cynic, an *auteur* debate flares—one which actually began in France in the early 1950s. On the one hand, Hitchcock is judged a director of "contentless virtuosity" whose American films, through their increased reliance on Hollywood superficiality have failed to live up to the potential of the more "realistic" British films. On the other hand, he is seen as an artist of the deepest moral concerns with a desire to have his audience experience catharsis through his mastery of identification techniques and suspense, a mastery most clearly evident in the American films.[6]

In his systematic, historically detailed account of the films, Raymond Durgnat argues that Hitchcock's films are no more morally complex than their contemporaneous genre counterparts. Seeking to maintain a middle course between the superficial and the deep debate, Durgnat suggests that all the films are carefully and intelligently constructed, but that their content rarely presents a "coherent world-view." [7]

Sometimes these opposing views are explained by further appeals to great-

ness, as in the notion that the intense subjectivity of great work provokes equally subjective response; but more frequently, the discrepancy in valuation is blamed on *suspense* and the suspense genre. Wood laments Hitchcock's own refusal to take himself seriously, with his constant talk of MacGuffins (the excuse for the pursuit), his crude humor, and insistent technical focus. Jean François Tarnowski blames critics who have been conformists in the face of Hitchcock's complexity and nicknamed him the "Master of Suspense."[8] Sam Simone, for instance, uses this phrase interchangeably with and almost as much as Hitchcock's own name; the notion is also the wellspring of Hitchcock's unusually persistent presence in the general press.[9] While the creation of suspense is usually noted to be one of Hitchcock's major concerns, along with male/female relationships and appearance and reality, it was not until the debate moved out of traditional *auteur* criticism and was taken up by those who practiced structural, semiotic, and psychoanalytic methodologies that the intimate relationship between the major technique and the major themes was made clear.

Hitchcock has always stated that his mining of the suspense genre was commercially motivated. Although he was a thorough professional who showed a creative interest in virtually all aspects of filmmaking, critics have repeatedly demonstrated that Hitchcock's most intense evocation of suspense was the suspense of relations with the "other," the elemental fear of rejection or loss. When developing a literary property in the 1940s, he emphatically stated that he must "introduce a heroine, for without one, there's no film."[10] Many of the writers who compare the films to the literary source material illustrate the consistent application of this rule.

Hitchcock's interest in self and other, however, goes beyond male/female relationships, for many of Hitchcock's "others" are of the same sex, a situation, like most of the heterosexual relationships, that inevitably leads to betrayal or unhappiness, but unlike them is never granted the *deus ex machina* of the happy ending. The first silent British films show this interest in the relations of self and other most pointedly. Kirk Bond discusses the early films and their reliance on the subtle details of character to illustrate dominance and submission. In *The Pleasure Garden*, Hitchcock's first film, Patsy, a spirited chorus dancer, is not quite equal in assertiveness to her new friend, Jill, and suffers at the loss of the friendship when she tries to impose her own conventional morality on the more ambitious woman. *The Ring, Downhill, The Farmer's Wife,* and *Champagne* all focus on the typical aspects of characters—particularly those derived from class and sex—and the limitations those typical aspects present in achieving happiness. Bond describes the strength of these early films as "imaginative quiet" and pronounces them superior to the "overdone gothic romances" of the U.S. period.[11]

While the British films of the 1920s and early 1930s enjoyed varying degrees of success with the public, Tom Ryall explains that the most sophisticated British critics of the period were interested in flashier, more visibly artful fare, such as the films being imported from the Soviet Union, Germany, France, and even Hollywood.[12] The critics at *Close Up* and influential personages like John Grierson ignored or rejected Hitchcock's films as unoriginal and pretentious, or, in the case of *Blackmail*, overrated.[13] In fact, few British films of the time were distributed outside the country, so that while Hitchcock was the "highest paid" director in Great Britain, he was frustrated in his larger ambition to reach an international audience. Although prestigious projects like *Juno and the Paycock* by Sean O'Casey and *The Skin Game* by John Galsworthy were adapted into

powerful and faithful versions of the plays, their restraint and intelligence meant they lacked the graphic qualities that in Britain at the time might have marked them as cinematic art.

Consequently, in 1933, after what many termed the "comeback" success of *The Man Who Knew Too Much*, Hitchcock devoted himself to the development of his own audience via the sure success of the suspense formula. The films of the "thriller cycle" of the 1930s—*The 39 Steps, Secret Agent, Sabotage, Young and Innocent*, and *The Lady Vanishes*—were distributed around the world and in 1938 Hitchcock moved his operations to the United States, where he periodically returned to melodrama, but always at the risk of frustrating the expectations of his audience. During this period of great ambition and commercial success, virtually no serious study attended the films.

By 1949, Lindsay Anderson, writing in *Sequence,* codified Hitchcock's position as a master technician of superficial gloss, a director whose "unglamorized" British films revealed the ingenious combination of sound and visual effects that made up the "Hitchcock touch," but who did not have the depth to withstand the enlargement his style had undergone in Hollywood.[14] Longer essays began to appear in the general press as well as film literature, and Anderson's approach, the preference for the British films over the American, dominated English language criticism for the ensuing decade.

But in France in 1951, Alexandre Astruc wrote an article in the first issue of *Cahiers du Cinéma* about a film from the American period, *Under Capricorn,* extolling its intelligent and restrained treatment of the melodramatic plot, and positing the "mystery of the human personality" as the fundamental theme of English cinema.[15] In the second issue of the journal, Jean-Luc Godard reviewed *Strangers on a Train* and pronounced Hitchcock one of the greatest directors of cinema.[16] Toward the end of the same year, Maurice Schèrer (who also wrote under the name of Eric Rohmer) grouped *Under Capricorn* with *Stromboli* and *The River* as the first truly modern films, because of their increased interest in human social interaction and the material things and events that reveal it.[17] Schérer was one of the first to relate Hitchcock's films to the development of cinema in general and its unique capability to continue the trend of the nineteenth-century novel to reveal in characters the classical oppositions of societal/natural, material/spiritual, and desire/grace.

André Bazin, who had asserted the opposing viewpoint in France since the late 1940s, continued to insist that Hitchcock's films revealed more interest in technical than human themes.[18] In 1954, *Cahiers du Cinéma* devoted a special issue to Hitchcock (who filmed *To Catch a Thief* in France that year) that included interviews with Hitchcock by Bazin, and jointly by Claude Chabrol and François Truffaut. These interviews attempted to discover Hitchcock's position in the debate about possible moral depth in the films.[19] Please tell us, they said, are your films serious or not? Pressed about God, morality, and the devil, Hitchcock remained mum and wide-eyed, referring to his responsibility to satisfy his audience and make money for his producers. Bazin and he had a particularly interesting exchange when Hitchcock agreed that the American films might be weaker because they are made for women, who have "sentimental" taste. But Hitchcock, typically, was being not only amenable, but contradictory. From his earliest silent days, when he had assessed women to be the statistically larger part of his audience, he had made films for them.

In 1957, Rohmer and Chabrol published the first book-length study of

Hitchcock's films, which was translated into English some twenty years later. Their version of the "Hitchcock touch" includes the technical skills that Lindsay Anderson admired, but it also involves the theme of intertwined innocence and guilt, and an obsession with Christian iconography, the last a factor that has been largely received rather than investigated by critics who followed. Their study also presented several strands that have been persistently explored in the development of critical understanding of the films. They emphasized Hitchcock's creative authorship via his assimilation of commercial demands and studio practice into his own creative will. They were the first to assert Hitchcock's chronic vulnerability to critical misunderstanding that began with the thrills of *The Lodger,* the mere production of which signaled superficiality to some, and blocked acceptance of his subsequently more restrained and straightforward work. They also pinpointed the 1930s as a time when Hitchcock, in defense, "created a second personality that completely corresponded with the idea others had of him." Their thematic continuum presented schizophrenia, fascination, amoralism, and domination at one end, and knowledge, self, unity, acceptance, confession, and communion at the other, but their deepest understanding was formal. In Hitchcock's work, they concluded, "form does not embellish content; it creates it." Although they acknowledged the presence of misogyny and homophobia, they may have inhibited further exploration by pronouncing this aspect of the films unimportant to critical study: critical consideration "may close more doors than it opens." [20]

In the early 1960s, this debate moved out of France, though monographs were published in German and Dutch before they were in English. In the United Kingdom, Ian Cameron and other critics at the journal *Movie* analyzed the mechanisms of suspense and the careful buildup of it through curiosity, suspicion, apprehension, and worry in the spectator. They related the characters' vulnerability to crisis to the preoccupations of the male characters with issues of dominance, and similarly related the success or failure of the characters' attempts to dominate to the satisfactory resolution of the film.[21]

During this same period, through his films and regular exposure in the press, Hitchcock was mining the expression of fear in the cinema, calling it "my special field, [which I have split] into two categories—terror and suspense . . . terror is induced by surprise, suspense by forewarning." [22] He repeatedly avowed his intention to forewarn the spectator so rigorously that the only thoughts possible were those concerning what would happen to the characters. Though he also insisted that he specialized in suspense for commercial reasons, his enthusiasm for its mechanisms belied this. Persistently and pedantically, he emphasized point of view and the creation of emotional involvement in the spectator through identification with the character. On the other hand, he seldom discussed endings; apparently, he learned to forego aesthetic interest in them, for commercial and other reasons: "I've usually encountered a firm insistence from the front offices . . . that I attach a satisfactory ending; [otherwise, one commits] the unforgivable Hollywood sin called 'being downbeat.' " [23]

This early critical discussion of suspense that focused on Hitchcock's smooth "mastery" of its mechanisms contributed greatly to the assessment of his work as all artifice/no meaning. Commercial success, manipulation of the audience, illogical character development solidified by nonsensical "happy" endings all pointed to lack of depth. Beginning with the writing of Peter Wollen, who stated about Hitchcock in 1969, that the rhetoric of the "master-technician [is] none

other than the rhetoric of the unconscious," later criticism would move away from this focus on the author's conscious intent as the source of meaning.[24] About the same time, the work of Raymond Bellour would push even further toward a perspective of the author as one part of the larger conscious and unconscious structuring of the production of meaning.

In this way the equating of suspense mechanisms with superficial content passed, at least in the academic film literature. Its *auteur* counterpart, the equation of formal intricacy with philosophical meaning, became reformulated in a significantly expanded debate about cultural codes, narrative systems, authorship and spectatorship, and sexual difference. Ideas concerning the double, structural polarities and patterns, and the processes of spectator identification, as well as the unfailing focus of the films themselves on the vagaries of human relationships, all contributed to the development of a large body of Hitchcockian criticism, and to the regular insertion of the films as a central example in a larger theoretical debate about the nature of cinema itself.

STRUCTURAL CRITICISM

"Clarify, clarify, clarify," said Hitchcock, "you can't have blurred thinking in suspense."[25] Hitchcock's exertion of control at the preproduction stage, through greatly detailed scripts and storyboards, was a main factor in his initial success in silent pictures as well as in his mastery of suspense technique.

Countering Hitchcock himself, Robin Wood and other *auteur* critics originally contended that suspense belongs more to the method of the films than to their themes and meaning. The structuralist critics of the 1970s, however, avoided this assertion, and proceeded to lay out a large amount of the territory that is now known as Hitchcock's formal system through thematic oppositions that placed the individual character in relation to the world. This effort began with Peter Wollen, who effectively argued that the "first priority" in reading Hitchcock's films was to understand the structures, which he stated revolve around the manhunt/pursuit and spying/gazing.[26] Quickly, he sketched in the boundaries of the study, suggesting a "psychology-semiology" of gazing, watching, and observing, and emphasizing the importance of Freudian constructs such as scoptophilia, voyeurism, and narcissism. In a complementary synthesis, Sylvia Lawson described the "deliberate artificiality and bland control" with which all aesthetic elements are treated in Hitchcock's films. She contended that this control creates a symbol system in which expressivity accrues to everything on the screen, including the smallest detail, thereby forcing the viewer toward an intellectual appreciation of the material.[27]

The same year, 1969, Raymond Bellour published two essays, one on *Marnie* that focused on the structuring of the look and the "double game" of multiple points of view, and the other on the boat sequence in *The Birds*.[28] The latter analysis listed certain filmic codes shot by shot: camera movement, framing distance, and who (of the characters) is looking or being looked at. Analysis of these charts led Bellour to an understanding of the controlling male gaze (or look) as a basic formulation of classical narrative film, and the representation of the male's identity through control of the image of the female body, a condition that provoked her punishment. I will return later to this psychoanalytic aspect of Bellour's approach that emphasized the relation of formal system to meaning in more extensive ways than mainstream structuralists.

Hitchcock himself always contended that the purpose of formal control, the purpose of cinema even, was the creation of emotion in the spectator through identification. An audience pays to be excited, and Hitchcock's struggle with the censors in both Britain and the United States as well as his persistent popularity attests to his devotion to exciting his audience. As a student of psychology, he appreciated the importance of the question of who authorizes the looks with which the audience identifies, especially the importance of the sex of the linked characters, as his undersanding at the least included the conventional psychological identification of a child with the parent of the same sex.

Pascal Bonitzer shows how this authorization is focused on control of the look, that is, the arrangement of glances or gazes from a character or the camera toward objects or other characters, as understood by the spectator, who is also· looking. Bonitzer asserts that, since D. W. Griffith, the very nature of cinema— the combining through editing of subject, object, and separate parallel actions— has involved suspense. He describes Hitchcock as the filmmaker who "has drawn the most logical conclusions . . . from this revolution in the process of meaning production." Unlike Griffith, Hitchcock does not rely primarily on chase sequences to produce suspense but more frequently on the slowing down of time, an emphasis on the choice of framing and angle that may be as subtle, according to Bonitzer, as "that moment when the look in the camera becomes the slightest bit too interested." This infusion of awareness is usually more precisely marked, as when the camera offers the spectator a piece of information that the character does not have (according to Hitchcock, the very definition of suspense); this gives the images "a past and a future" and all actions that follow, a double meaning.[29]

Around the same time, Jean Narboni codified facial expressions as another basic aspect of this suspense film form. He discerned in them a "meteorology of suspicion," where suspicion is continually revived through a forced emphasis on the "micro-changes" of facial expressions. As a consequence, the spectator's attention is never satisfied with an understanding of "reality" because it is continually confronted with a different character's or the director's subjectivity.[30] Several years later, Marian Keane expanded on a notion of "photogenesis" to illustrate the extremely important collaborative aspect, aside from their roles, of actors, especially star actors, in Hitchcock's films.[31]

In 1971, Michel Estève edited a volume for *Études Cinématographiques* that included several descriptions of production codes and symbols in Hitchcock's films and a formal analysis of doubling as it relates to the structure of the unconscious.[32] In the same volume Philippe Parrain outlined the components of Hitchcock's formal rigor; among them are (1) characters marked with a "certain frigidity that abstracts them from their surroundings and makes them clearly delineated entities, ready to obey"; (2) movement toward the ending via polarized tensions; (3) movement created through the use of modes of transportation; (4) narrative structure based on the law of return, the boomerang, and the circle; and (5) concentration of the mechanics of cause and effect with rapid movement between the two.[32] Michel Serceau analyzed the couple and love themes as they support Hitchcock's ability to appeal to the spectator's complacent inclinations while actually unsettling them. He described a series of oppositional relationships formed by the degradation of love versus Christian love and seeing-observing-fantasizing (passivity) versus knowing-working-struggling (activity), attributing these to the female and male roles. In terms opposite those of Bellour's analyses, he generalized about the passivity of the Hitchcock male, trapped by the tempting

female, caught up in passion and unable to see the truth.[34] In fact, this approach is closest to Hitchcock's own, which was frequently expressed in the traditional terms that equate sexuality outside marriage with degradation.[35]

Focus on Hitchcock, edited by Albert LaValley in 1972, an early compilation of reprinted articles, also brought structural criticism to the fore, mentioning the importance of fairy tale and genre as well as psychoanalytic concepts like voyeurism. It included a shot analysis of the cornfield sequence in *North by Northwest* and an essay on the formal patterning of doubles, though it was primarily oriented toward *auteur* theory and morally assessed Hitchcock's world-view as close to "nihilism."[36]

Structural criticism was also prominent in Italy, where Fabio Carlini published a monograph in 1974 that began with an alphabetical listing and explication of terms deemed essential to understanding Hitchcock, including collaborators, source material, film history, critical response, theories of acting, phobias, neuroses, philosophical and political subjects, and material objects. He then argued for study of the films through these objects, obsessions, and biographical elements, and emphasized the psychoanalytic richness of the style.[37]

Meanwhile, Wollen, using the ideas of the Russian formalist Vladimir Propp, published a lengthy "morphological" analysis of *North by Northwest,* proposing a relation between contemporary mass culture and folk tales. This method, which examined the plot formations around pairs—interdiction and violation, reconnaissance and receipt of information, and trickery and submission—proved fruitful for other critics, such as Richard Abel, who wrote an analysis of *Notorious.* Wollen's approach however, has been criticized by David Bordwell as "distorted."[38]

The concept of the double is the central motif of a large amount of the criticism, effectively linking *auteur*-humanist and newer methods. Barbara Bannon describes the wide application of doubling in psychology, film, literature, and the films of Hitchcock. She distinguishes between overt doubles and latent, or structural, ones, which in the broadest instance involve the paralleling and reversing of scenes.[39] These are the elements that fascinated Hitchcock: patterning, repetition, and pairing. Critics like Bannon see in doubling his obsession with objectivity and critical distance—the evenhanded approach of the sophisticate—as well as his willingness to let the pattern go, to risk chaos. As Thomas Hemmeter points out, there is a "tense dialectic" within the films between subjective suspense techniques on the one side, and alienation techniques and abstract patterns on the other.[40]

François Regnault, like Jean Douchet before him, suggests that the patterning principle chosen by Hitchcock for each film—lines, spirals, broken lines, grids, or circles—becomes autonomous from the film, in the process communicating a metaphor for cinema in general, which allows the spectator to identify with the point of view of the director. Alongside this principle, he finds the "distinctly Hitchcockian" use of place, which puts the plots on a continuum: running a course from place to place at one end (the spy thrillers), and being appointed a residence at the other (the one-set films). Two combinations fall in between, involving a "pilgrimage to origins" (*Shadow of a Doubt, Psycho, Marnie,* etc.), and the spiral inversion of both place and movement (*Downhill, Blackmail, Vertigo,* etc.).[41]

Hitchcock's films as a "metaphor for cinema" is a concept that appears regularly in the literature and begins with the director's own references to "pure cinema" and *Rear Window* as a prime example of it. In discussing that film with

Hitchcock when it was first made, André Bazin concluded that Hitchcock's primary interest in the "means" of telling its story may in fact be another word for "theme"; Jean Douchet saw *Rear Window* as a lesson in cinema for the audience.[42] These ideas have been fruitfully expanded many times since, most recently by John Belton, who analyzes *Rear Window* in relation to its amalgam of "theatrical and cinematic modes of narration," that is, its extremely refined use of space conventions to speak a variety of "psychologies."[43]

It is this depth of design that seems to be the strongest attraction of Hitchcock's films for critics, and it also seems to be the main factor in the works of the Hitchcock canon that are most frequently written about, including *Psycho, Rear Window, Vertigo,* and, at the second tier, *The Birds, Blackmail,* and *North by Northwest.* While sociological interest is also important here, especially in explaining the prominence of *Psycho,* at least one of these films (*North by Northwest*) is not usually discussed in terms of its sociological import, while all are known for their formal design. Feminist critics object to the development of the canon on the basis of the standards of "pure cinema." Patricia Ferrara, for instance, analyzes *Rear Window,* not as a mere "essay on film viewing" but as a much broader expression of the differences in the way people see and the need to accommodate others' vision.[44] Virginia Wright Wexman discusses *Vertigo*'s privileged status among intellectuals and film scholars as "pure cinema," and wonders about the appeal of stars and scenery.[45]

In a lengthy study of five of the films, William Rothman takes this accumulation of well-charted ambiguities and double meanings one step further and defines the camera itself as "fundamentally ambiguous" by its representation of the audience's passivity alongside the authorial voice. However, Rothman's extremely detailed shot-by-shot analyses reveal familiar philosophical dichotomies and conundrums (and some not so familiar, like the relationship between murder and marriage); and he is most intent on proving the films' ability to support sustained reflection and "high-minded analysis," once again, on illustrating the "seriousness" of the films and valorizing Hitchcock as a "great" artist.[46]

Other formal studies have effectively concentrated on a single aspect of the *mise-en-scène*—such as acting, cinematography, or sound. While Hitchcock occasionally spoke of contributions by collaborators, it was usually in terms of what he expected from them and whether he got it, rarely in recognition. He could, in fact, be extremely harsh in his judgment about even those with whom he had enjoyed long positive working relationships. Those articles that are written by colleagues and discuss his films generally do so from the vantage point of an enthusiastic creative person glad for the challenge of working with such a knowledgeable director. Aside from these testimonies, there is very little in the literature that attempts to sort out the varied roles that collaborators played, with the exception of efforts such as Lenoard Leff's on Hitchcock and David Selznick, or James Naremore's and Andrew Britton's on Cary Grant.[47] Elizabeth Weis documents the career-long sophistication in the application of sound, including music and effects, but attributes all the ideas and execution personally to Hitchcock. She argues that Hitchcock's early experiments with sound (*Blackmail* remains a classic textbook example of innovation), which were expressionist, developed into a more classical style tied to the realistic context of the narrative.[48]

Studies like Weis's in some ways flesh out Lawson's and Wollen's structural outlines of Hitchcock's gift for commanding the details of a wide array of aesthetic, cultural, political, and social associations, and inserting them at many

different levels to create a complex understanding. But they shed less light on the way the processes of the film industry, or the contributions of collaborators, for instance, contributed to that complexity.

Synthesizing the critical opinion in 1982, Noël Simsolo described Hitchcock as one of the few directors interested in the commercial aspects of the industry, who, as a consequence, tapped into the "unconscious" of his audience. He further comments on the films' focus on the couple, and understands this theme as an obsession with the "animal function" of humans and the powerlessness of men to gain knowledge and mastery.[49] This powerlessness, this passivity, which expresses itself in the depiction of perverted erotic activities, such as voyeurism, narcissism, and fetishism, also prompted a debate concerning the social meaning of the films and their assertion of, or lack of, normative values.

SOCIAL AND POLITICAL HITCHCOCK

The double is also the cause and effect of Hitchcock's political orientation. In no way a political active person, Hitchcock's interest in polarities led naturally to an interest in social and political issues for which the most supreme and subtle model is interpersonal conflict. He consistently approached these issues from an imaginative, classically conservative point of view that focused on individual free expression, what Graham Greene called "the human factor." In Hitchcock's films, the conflict of the individual with society (including political institutions) is influenced primarily by the strengths and weaknesses of the human personalities involved, regardless of the larger mission in which they participate. As a result, his propaganda films made with the French Resistance, *Aventure Malgache* and *Bon Voyage,* are stunningly ineffective in their supposed purpose. The first concerns a free-French lawyer who succeeds only by being less hypocritical for a better cause than his enemy, and the second is about an escaped British prisoner of war who, preoccupied by the lack of food and shelter, is easily manipulated by his beloved fascist companion.

Likewise, the conflict of individuals in the silent films is always a result of the restrictions of class and sex. The working-class heroines of *The Pleasure Garden,* carefully defined in relation to the men (in the audience, as boss, as friends and husbands), are narratively contrasted in their handling of their demeaning position. Patsy is naively manipulated into marriage by a man who cannot support her, and suffers near-death at his sadistic hands, while Jill manipulates to obtain the best offer (from a prince) and suffers only Patsy's disapproval. *The Lodger* can also be seen as the story of the difficulties of the working-class Daisy in obtaining a suitable mate. Rothman describes Daisy as "a golden girl" living beneath her station, destined (waiting) to be attached to the wealthy lodger, but the film clearly shows her less romantic understanding of her position by her encouraging the lodger's competition, the detective, until the very end. *The Manxman, The Skin Game, Marnie,* and in varying degrees many of the other films are about the effect of class on romantic attachments and marital decisions. *The Farmer's Wife* is particularly poignant in its depiction of a smart and beautiful servant who graciously accepts the hand of the slightly humbled widower whom three of the propertied women in the neighborhood have refused. O. B. Hardison discusses the strong class identity of many of the protagonists of the British films and carefully points out the variance in what that identity

communicates. For instance, Sir John, of *Murder!*, represents the upper class as *noblesse oblige*, a source of deliverance for the wrongly accused woman, while the leader of *The 39 Steps* represents the evil of the extremely wealthy, who must be destroyed by the middle-class hero.[50]

While Hitchcock continued to the end of his career to sketch character with the symbols of class status, his acuteness in this regard fell out of step in the more mutating environment of the United States and the changing sexual mores of the postwar period. For instance, he claimed that the "idea" of *The Paradine Case* and *Under Capricorn* was the same, the central love affair as a study in "degradation"—in the first film, a lawyer who "gives up an elegant wife for a woman who can take any man, even a groom (servant)," and in the second film, a woman of property who marries a servant.[51] This assertion, however, is belied by the more essential differences between the two films. The first is a story about a man whose pride and confidence blind him, while the second is a story about a woman victimized by her family. As well, and typically, the provoking characters in each film are empowered and humanized sufficiently to make the simple concept (degradation) that Hitchcock continues to associate with the films totally disappear. In fact, it is their reference to sex differences, not class differences, that allows these films to have the same "idea."

John Smith describes the British films as revealing a dialectical struggle of the claims of social propriety over those of the instincts, a struggle that is played out in a narrative interest in order and disorder. He argues that the commitment of the character to individualism forces the "endurance" of disorder, cruelty, evil, and perhaps madness, but generally ends in a "balanced acknowledgment of social reality," a mature acceptance of "impersonal forces." Hitchcock's political position is thus defined as conservative individualism. In reasoning typical of much Hitchcock criticism, Smith focuses (in a discussion of *The Farmer's Wife*) on the farmer's triumph in accepting what he has—after all, he has found the "perfect wife" in his servant—rather than the servant's triumph in gaining an economic foothold in exchange for her continued "endurance." Nonetheless, Smith's is an argument of considerable subtlety, which suggests that Hitchcock's own commitment to a commercial style parallels his thematic interest in the submission of individual character to impersonal forces for the purpose of gaining success and happiness in the world.[52]

In a similar vein, other critics have pointed out that one of Hitchcock's strengths is his disinclination to associate a clear identity with any social institutions, especially law enforcement. Ed Buscombe argues that Hitchcock, like Charles Dickens, used his "own personal feelings about the law to prevent the audience from assuming an identity between the forces of law and the forces of good."[53] In other words, representatives of law and government are as blandly unpredictable as other humans. From the time of *The Lodger* (in which the detective, in the grip of jealousy, convinces himself that the lodger is the muderer), Hitchcock carefully documents their vulnerability to the weakening effects of desire and fantasy.

In discussing *Topaz*, intended to be a pro-West Cold War film, Michael Walker points out that it is actually directed so that the political viewpoint is canceled by sympathy for the characters, who experience betrayal at every turn, and reveal a "universal sense of suffering and loss."[54] Kirsten Witte chronicles the reception of Hitchcock's films in Germany, where he has always been known as a political filmmaker, with first an anti-fascist and anti-German bias, and

later, in the 1960s, an anti-communist bias. Witte, however, finds the films of the 1930s and 1940s not at all biased but a reflection of the prevailing "complex of fear, an exceptional document of the real suffering in Europe, an expression of political persecution."[55] Ina Rae Hark examines the role of "citizen-amateur" in the British thrillers, its literary antecedents and historical context. She draws an analogy between the "ill-behaved spectators" in the many theater scenes in the films and the actual spectators of a Hitchcock film, and concludes that Hitchcock encouraged the viewers of his films to mentally "disrupt [his own directorial] performances designed to lull them into complacent reliance on authority."[56]

Thus this conservatism is tied to responsibility and to narratives that illustrate the consequences of complacency, or irresponsibility. Andrew Sarris first expounded the centrality of this theme after Hitchcock himself had repeatedly described complacency as the central theme of *The Birds* while promoting the film in 1963. "Hitchcock's repeated invasions of everyday life with the most outrageous melodramatic devices have shaken the foundations of the facile humanism that insists that people are good, and only the systems evil. . . . He insists upon a moral reckoning for his characters and for his audience."[57]

This expounding of the relation of the individual to society (and its institutions) has its most persistent evocation in the depiction of sex roles. Michel Serceau argues that Hitchcock's understanding of sexual politics—the tempting woman, the trapped man—allow him to generalize about men's passivity and complacent desire to enjoy only the material things offered them. The protagonist's superficiality means that "physical love is never based on or motivated by an understanding between two beings; it occurs . . . in this void, which points out the danger."[58] Robin Wood analyzed *Shadow of a Doubt* as it reveals the structural tensions and contradictory myths of American capitalist ideology. After listing the economic issues surrounding the depiction of home, workplace, opportunity, and income, he develops a similar idea of the Ideal Male ("potent adventurer," unattached man of action) and Ideal Female (supportive mother, devoted wife), contrasted with their "shadows," the dull husband/father and the erotic woman/betrayer.[59] Hitchcock's belief in and fascination with the construction of, as Wood puts it, the "Ideal Couple of quite staggering incompatibility," is evident, as is his fascination with the shadow types.

James B. McLaughlin examines the characters in *Shadow of a Doubt* and relates the theme of the family to the theme of disgust, where the doubles mock "all bourgeois conceptions of the individual as a single solitary self." Through Charlie's transformation from an independent woman (shadow type) to a supportive wife, he theorizes the family as both threatening and a trap.[60] Diane Carson analyzes the lead and supporting roles in the same film to illustrate further the dependency of all the characters' identities on sex roles and the unhappiness that arises from it, especially for the women. With brief references to other films, she concludes that Hitchcock's women characters live in "the nightmare world of patriarchal rule," where neither marriage nor independence is an escape.[61]

Social and political Hitchcock is then very much patriarchal Hitchcock, revealing at the broadest level a fatherly interest in the characters and their circumstances, a tolerant urge to accept and protect them, along with a moral urge to correct them and thereby instruct the audience. Alongside this is the expected upset and confusion over the place of sexuality in what is conceived to be a god-like role; the image of the patriarch is tarnished by the guilt generated by

"base" instincts. Rohmer and Chabrol discuss the *libido sciendi*, or lust for knowledge, that drives many of the characters as well as the director, and Noël Simsolo assesses the director as a man who "esteemed himself" above all others and desired to create as an equal of God.[62]

PSYCHOANALYTIC CRITICISM

The complexity and depth of Hitchcock's work have made it attractive to psychoanalytic-semiotic criticism. In summarizing what can only be described as extremely challenging material, I would first like to quote Janet Bergstrom's assertion about the work of Raymond Bellour, that "it is impossible to reduce these studies to schematic arguments or information."[63] This caveat applies to some of the literature I have already discussed and most of what follows in this critical survey. Second, the psychoanalytic concepts referred to in these summaries, especially the ones from Jacques Lacan, are sometimes interpreted by each author for his or her own critical purposes. To illustrate, Bellour's analysis of *North by Northwest* (summarized below) is titled "*Le blocage symbolique*." This title is interpreted by Bill Nichols as an aspect of the spectator, who is "pinned down" by illusionist strategies of cinema, unable to exit the fantasy world of what "I" might be and enter the symbolic world with the ability to pursue a relationship based on a solid identity. Leland Poague and Marshall Deutelbaum, on the other hand, define "*le blocage symbolique*" as closure of the narrative, the displacement of the (now-dead) father by the son, and the maturing into the symbolic of the story character.[64] While it may be possible to reconcile these two usages of the term, it clearly cannot be done in the space available here. As the terms are in any case philosophically (and freely) applied, I link them together with only the most general attempt to make them consistent.

One of the many directions in which Hitchcock's own lust for knowledge sent him was on a quest for an understanding of human psychology. After all, he not only had to reliably predict audience attendance, which he thought depended on his ability to create "believable" characters, he also had to direct large teams of collaborators and support workers in his vision, which required him to get their cooperation. Kenneth MacPherson wrote an article in 1929 that undoubtedly encouraged Hitchcock's native interest in the relationship of character psychology to the technical apparatus with which he worked. MacPherson lauded *Blackmail* for its "comprehension of the relationship of techniques" and contribution to a "sight-sound aesthetic." He recommended that all filmmakers explore action and its source, "the interacting of conscious and unconscious. [The highest form of film is] the film of imagery and action, psychology and physiology, or better still, psychology through physiology."[65]

Hitchcock's films consistently reveal a belief, as Victor Burgin has summarized in relation to them, that "unconscious wishes and forces are as immutable a force in our lives as any material circumstance.... [They are marked] by stability, coherence, and constancy of [effect] upon perceptions and actions of the subject." But, as Burgin continues, aside from this knowledge, and absent from Hitchcock's work, is the fact that "psychoanalysis recognizes no such possible state of unambiguous and self-possessed lucidity in which the external world is seen for and known as simply what it is."[66]

Hitchcock's lifelong respect for psychology as an aid to understanding human

nature became a movie theme in *Spellbound,* a film that, according to Alexander Doty, "summarized and integrated all previous cinematic lore on Freud and psychiatry." Doty suggests that Hitchcock and the screenwriter, Ben Hecht, simplified the material in an "earnest" effort to communicate psychoanalytic principles to the audience.[67] Andrew Britton points out that the vocabulary of the opening titles "suggests that the attainment of normality (reason) is like the entry to a state of grace, and that psychoanalysis is analogous to exorcism."[68] At the level of narrative, psychoanalysis is in this way shown to be Hitchcock's faith, his religion. Garry Leonard argues that Hitchcock understood these principles to be outside himself, insisting on the "self-possessed lucidity" of the director as "the representative of the patriarchal order, and the myth of the coherent self," and Raymond Bellour, when discussing the prevalence of the mask in Hitchcock's films, describes its appearance in *Marnie as psychoanalysis.*[69]

The attribution of a character's action to unconscious motive is evidenced in virtually all the films; to the extent Hitchcock used mental disorder as a theme (amnesia in *Spellbound,* nervous breakdown in *The Wrong Man,* voyeurism in *Rear Window*) there is critical commentary. However, the first extensive Freudian interpretation of Hitchcock is Jean Douchet's *Alfred Hitchcock,* published in 1967. Unlike Robin Wood, Douchet did not put aside suspense as method secondary to meaning; instead, he presented it as having many clearly differentiated manifestations: "esoteric suspense," "aesthetic suspense," and "the suspense of creation." With this critical construct, Douchet connects Hitchcock's method as well as his personality—in particular the persistent vitality of his intellectual approach to filmmaking—to his success and the depth of meaning in his films. For Douchet, Hitchcock is constantly meditating on the "powerful hold of impotence, the sole source of suspense." Even in those like Norman Bates, who hold the power of life and death over other characters, weakness must be uncovered because the feeling of weakness is the source of the neurotic or psychotic action.[70]

According to Douchet, Hitchcock himself attempts to overcome weakness by his position as a film director, an on-the-set "all-powerful Father." As I indicated in the biographical section, Hitchcock's ambition was to affect as large an audience as possible and he carefully measured his career to that end. Douchet argues that Hitchcock, beginning in the 1950s, attempted to empower the spectator through "cinematic lessons" as a new way to hold the more sophisticated modern audience. The focus on the distance between spectator and spectacle in *Rear Window,* resulting in the film's internally articulated relation to voyeuristic pleasure, is one example.[71] Likewise, the graphic emphases of *North by Northwest* create in the spectator an awareness of the construction of the story, while *Vertigo,* generally considered the most personal of Hitchcock's films, shows the limits of the "fetishistic director" in its elaboration of the horrible consequences he fears from his own compulsive behavior. In an unusual interpretation of *Family Plot,* Douchet describes the film as the final step in the director's efforts to "mobilize the intellectual world of the public" by leading them to an awareness of the story as story, and so prove himself a good Father. Ironically, it is a very smart stereotypical female character—the alternately demanding and hysterically dependent Madame Blanche—who "parodies the master" with her crystal ball and indulgently winks at the audience in the final shot of the film, signaling the cover of her good detective work with superstition.[72]

Alongside the study of the aesthetic appearance of Freudian ideas about

scoptophilia—voyeurism, fetishism, as well as more psychotic behavior—is the originally structural study of narrative as Oedipal transformation. Peter Wollen calls it the "hybrid plot" and describes the distinctive relationship of the Oedipal story to Hitchcock's films in the similar identity of the investigator and the criminal. While the plots are otherwise not alike, they are related through similar "mechanisms of transformation" that concern what Freud called the "family romance," the fantasy of belonging to an imaginary family that is different from one's own, the fairy tale "family of the princess."[73]

In 1974, Raymond Bellour proved Douchet's notion of the obsessive graphic patterning of *North by Northwest* and combined it with Wollen's ideas about fairy tale structure in his own obsessive 115-page analysis of the Hitchcockian dialectic, defined as the Oedipal trajectory of the hero through an identity crisis and into a bourgeois marriage, or socially sanctioned sexual relationship.[74] As Janet Bergstrom, after Bellour, puts it, the end of the film "underscore[s] emphatically the positive resolution of sexuality as a *problem.*"[75] Though a reading of Bellour's essays offers a plethora of approaches to the films he discusses, his work is typically summarized as focused on the controlling mechanisms of the male gaze in classical narrative cinema, exemplified by the films of Hitchcock, in which is presented a tale of the successful formation of the couple, a movement of the male character through the immaturity of perverted forms of sexuality toward a happier, conventional heterosexual relationship.

The ways in which Hitchcock's films contradict this collapsed argument have been analyzed from several different angles. In a psychoanalytic reading of *Notorious,* Michael Renov analyzes the processes of identification, especially around the paired activities of knowledge and sight, and the splitting of the male function between Alex and "Dev." He concludes that "Alicia is made to pay the price of female transgression against the male value system through the spectator's identification with [Alex] at the film's conclusion." In other words, the happy heterosexual relationship is marred by its consummation at the expense of someone else.[76] Other writers reach similar conclusions, illustrating the consequences for audience identification of Devlin's manipulations, Alicia's near-death, and Alex's presumed death, to the extent these events put into question the notion of the couple's living happily ever after.

In a similar vein Andrew Britton explicates the "ideological projects" of *Spellbound,* the validation of psychoanalysis as truth leading to normality, and the transformation of a professional woman into a "real" woman—wife. Focusing on sexual imagery and parental and sex roles, he concludes that these projects are on the surface of the film, subverted by the repressed meanings, which blur the "normal and the abnormal [and indicate] insoluble conflicts in the main sexual relationship."[77] Some of this "subversion," which exists in the enunciation—in the telling of the story, not necessarily in the story itself—is a persistent aspect of the criticism, and has been shown to be consciously imposed. Hitchcock, for instance, told an interviewer that he had to threaten the eleven-year-old Nova Pilbeam in order to get her to recoil from her movie parents in the last shot of *The Man Who Knew Too Much* (1934); the young actress did not understand this nonresolute aspect of the resolution of the film. Though she is saved by her parents, the audience is not allowed to forget that she has suffered by their negligence and will continue to suffer.[78]

In other words, Hitchcock's reworking of the Oedipal fantasy—the "myth of the coherent self"—at the narrative level is consistently undercut by his focus on

the impotence of the characters. Feminist critics, particularly Tania Modleski, emphasize this aspect especially for the women characters, who are at the very least psychically trapped and frequently physically abused. Robin Wood says it is a "basic principle" of Hitchcock's identification practice to associate the audience with whoever is being threatened. It is this aspect, one of the most noted examples of which is Norman Bates's vulnerability, that accounts for Hitchcock's reputation for realism, as well as some of the charges of "immorality." Like most critics, Wood describes *Psycho* as "one of the key works of our age" in its articulation of the dominance of the past over the present and the persistence of parent-child relationships; others see it as profoundly shocking, the first of a still-growing list of offensive horror films that depict the victimization of women. Aside from the issues raised in these statements by the uneasy relationship of morality and aesthetics, it is these kinds of ideas that lead some critics, like Raymond Bellour, to step away from frequently voiced critical concerns such as the normality or abnormality of the characters, suggesting that everyone identifies to some extent with the neurotic space of the films.

In an analysis of *The Birds,* Bill Nichols cautions against a "reductionism that describes virtually all social phenomena in terms of the re-enactment of the childhood scenario." Nonetheless, he finds the film "regressive" in its punishing of Melanie as the other, who has dared to "infiltrate" the Brenner family. It is not only her narrative functioning that makes her vulnerable; it is also, at the level of enunciation, her show of power to the audience. Nichols is one of many who sees the character of Melanie as the culmination of a long line of women in Hitchcock's films who are viciously punished for daring a commanding look, being a better intelligence gatherer, or, as Nichols theorizes, attempting to replace the mother.[79] In fact, in *The Birds,* it is that moment in the boat when Melanie consciously transforms her look into one of sweet innocence (disguising her guile) that the first bird attacks her.

FEMINIST CRITICISM

In their emphasis on family relationships and sexual development, psychoanalytic analyses opened many new approaches to the traditional Hitchcockian theme of male/female relationships. Early French critics skipped over the aspect of violence to women in the films, preferring to speak of "man's passivity" and lust for knowledge, and assuming the protagonist's goal of obtaining a "beautiful woman" to be a legitimate and uncomplicated one. English critics followed in step, and not until very recently have these assumptions been consistently challenged. Because the work summarized here is limited to commentary on Hitchcock, only pieces of a much larger debate in feminist film theory will be evident.

Readings of Hitchcock films that reflect a "male" understanding of what is on the screen are the majority; frequently they are supported by quotations from (appeals to the authority of) Hitchcock himself. Tania Modleski illustrates well the difference between Hitchcock's precis of *Blackmail,* centered on the detective's conflict between love and duty, and the film itself, which is centered on the conflict of the woman; she also points out the euphemisms (like "seduction") and jokes male critics use to describe the attempted rape in the film.[80] Critical treatment of the contrasted characters of Midge and Madeleine/Judy in *Vertigo* is also revealing in this regard. Most critics adopt an understanding of these two

characters based on the stereotypical Ideal Female coding of the film. At the extreme, this results in a view of Scottie on a "spiritual" quest, thwarted by Judy's "destructive" refusal to be Madeleine, and misunderstood by Midge, who represents a "cruel debasement of feminine values."[81] Feminist critics, on the other hand, are more likely to point out the film's centering of Midge's stability, her courage in attempting to laugh Scottie out of his obsession, and her caring for him in the sanitarium. As Karen Hollinger points out, these scenes "graphically illustrate the incompatibility of male desire with female individuality, independence, and imagination as expressed in the character of Midge."[82]

In 1975 Laura Mulvey published an influential analysis concerned with the relationship of the development of sexual difference to film form, arguing that classical narrative cinema is determined by a male visual system. She theorized that Hitchcock's films, and by extension, all Hollywood classical narrative films, consistently illustrate two "avenues of escape"—types of scoptophilia—from the castration anxiety that the female form evokes through its "lack" or representation of castration. These are voyeurism, an obsessional investigating of the form through the framing of the look, and fetishism, the building up of the beauty of the object. *Rear Window* and *Vertigo,* respectively, represent these problems of the protagonist as he unconsciously grapples with the tensions and contradictions surrounding issues of identity that these avenues of escape do not entirely smooth over.[83] Jacqueline Rose adds to this an idea of paranoia as the "aggressive corollary of the narcissistic structure" that the above construct assumes cinematic form to be. Analyzing *The Birds,* she argues that the male is actually dependent on the female, acquiring his identity only through the woman and her representation of castration. The woman is defined as transgression, made to be "both the cause and effect of the aggressivity which drives the narrative" to its resolution.[84]

While neither of these critics presents the male system attributed to Hitchcock quite as monolithically as is generally assumed (Mulvey asserts that the gaze of Hitchcock's camera is "uneasy"), Sandy Flitterman is one of the first feminist critics to suggest that Hitchcock's films may in some way admit power to the female characters. In explicating the work of Bellour on *Marnie,* which theorizes Hitchcock, "the enunciator," a man of "pure image-power, the camera-wish, of which the object choice is here the woman," Flitterman focuses on his analysis of the first appearance of Marnie's face, when she washes the dye from her hair and looks into the camera. She asserts that Marnie, by changing her own identity, "constitutes herself as an image of desire." Knowing she/it is objectified, she consciously offers herself to the viewer as an image.[85]

Building on these ideas, Bellour in 1979 analyzed *Psycho* as an exceptionally clear version of the Hitchcockian system, a film that announces in itself "the mechanisms that govern its operation," mechanisms provoked by problems of sexual difference and identity. He concludes with a conception of Hitchcock as an artist who reflects, perhaps unconsciously, on the "inevitable relationship" in our society between neurosis, here represented by theft, and psychosis, represented by murder. In *Psycho,* the "woman, the subject of neurosis, becomes the object of psychosis of which the man is the subject." Bellour outlined further tenets of the Hitchcockian system. First, that the woman characters *do* kill, but only in response to being the object of a psychotic attack, such as in *Blackmail* or *Dial M for Murder.* Second, that women characters manifest psychotic tendencies only to the extent their male-hero-counterpart has suffered a loss of identity, as in *The Wrong Man* and *Under Capricorn.* Finally, that male characters may be the

subject of neurosis, but if they are, it is always overshadowed by a psychosis (ritual testing) that allows the neurosis to be resolved by action, as in *North by Northwest*.[86]

The relationship between the formation of the heterosexual couple and violence to women begins at this point to take clearer form. At the end of the previous section, the concept of the narrative "punishment" of the woman was noted, punishment that frequently results in the literal obliteration of her look. The unfocused staring off of a character signaling depression or trauma is a staple of Hitchcockian expression, occurring in a minor fashion in almost every film: Larita in *Easy Virtue*, Johnnie in *Juno and the Paycock*, Eliza in *Secret Agent*. Certain films, however, are narratively centered on such trauma. The first such victim in Hitchcock's films is the character played by Ivor Novello in *Downhill*, a youth victimized by his own upper-class mentality, who stumbles home in the last scene through an expressionist blur. The next male victim appears thirty years later—Scottie in *Vertigo*. In between and after are women: Alice in *Blackmail*, Diana in *Murder!*, Alicia in *Notorious*, Melanie in *The Birds*. More extreme are the murdered women of *Psycho* and *Frenzy*, their end confirmed by a dead stare. Jeanne Thomas Allen, in an analysis of *Frenzy*, takes the end view of Hitchcock as a misogynist, arguing that the film is centered on the victimization of women and negates the importance of women's welfare. She concludes that Hitchcock metaphoricizes "women's victimization into a human universal" and manipulates the spectator into identification with male aggression.[87]

Susan Lurie, in a move away from this notion of woman as lack, symbol of castration, inevitable powerless victim, assesses the depiction of physical punishment in light of the character of Melanie in *The Birds* as a symbolic "powerful castrated penis." She analyzes the film and its metaphors, particularly cages, as it expresses the male need to contain "the lovely young woman" who has successfully advanced on Bodega Bay, by the "positioning of the desired woman in the place of a helpless child," that is, by punishing her desire and capacity.[88]

Barbara Klinger and Tania Modleski subsequently published articles in 1982 that further questioned the use of Hitchcock's films as exemplary of the visual system of classical narrative cinema. Modleski theorizes the narrativization of a female Oedipal trajectory in *Rebecca*, its many difficulties, and disconcerting resolution. She illustrates the film's obsession with getting rid of the memory of *Rebecca*, the "perfect wife" who in fact scorned her husband, so that the unnamed second wife may evolve into a confident and true "perfect wife."[89] Klinger addresses the notion of symmetry in *Psycho* and the formal requirement of an end that replies to the beginning. She shows that the terms of problematic sexual difference expressed in the beginning (Marion as erotic object, without her clothes, in a sexual liaison outside the law) are in the end repressed, displaced by a focus on the mother, who in the end, in an "erasure of difference," possesses a phallus.[90]

Modleski's 1988 monograph, *The Women Who Knew Too Much*, directly counters the view of women in these films as passive objects of male voyeurism and women spectators as masochistic. She argues that Hitchcock's films reveal a "strong fascination and identification with femininity" that makes them deeply ambivalent toward women and "resistant to patriarchal assimilation" while expressing an intertwining of misogyny and sympathy for women. Focusing on the concept of female bisexuality and the consequent "double desire" of the female spectator who is likely to identify with both the female and the male characters,

she asserts that Hitchcock's identification with femininity is shared by the male spectator, who is made frightfully aware of his own potential bisexuality, and therefore requires the violence toward women that marks the films. Analyzing several of the films, she effectively ties bisexuality to power relations and their playing out in Hitchcock's films, where the male subject is fascinated and then threatened by bisexuality, and the woman "pays for this ambivalence—often with her life itself."[91]

Most recent academic articles on Hitchcock are informed by an awareness of, if not a reliance on, feminist critical principles; it is the formal rigor of the films and emphasis on the processes of identification that have made his work so fertile for analysis of sexual difference. One of the most recent instances is an essay by D. A. Miller on homosexuality and *Rope* that illustrates the obsession of technique (the ten-minute take) with the "non-obsession" of homosexuality, so that "technique acquires all the transgressive fascination [Hitchcock and his critics have always claimed the long takes did not work] of homosexuality, while homosexuality is consigned to the status of a dry technical detail."[92]

This continuing investigation of difference has also led to a broadening of the study to include other social issues such as class. Michele Piso, for instance, discerns class antagonism between the two main characters of *Marnie,* a power relationship between a domineering man of wealth and a rebellious woman of poverty, that necessarily takes the plot toward the conservative conclusion of the woman's maturation and acceptance of the man's superior knowledge. Piso shows that despite the "happy" end, even within the film's own terms, the central relationship remains clearly one of subjugation.[93]

HITCHCOCK AND FILM HISTORY

Other recent work on Hitchcock is concerned with his relation to film history and the different film cultures (of place, of time) in which he worked, as well as the broader social environment in which the films participate. Most of the studies discussed above, while covering the internal aesthetics and moral viewpoint of the films, have revealed little about, for instance, their popularity. Maurice Yacowar, whose *Hitchcock's British Films* is the lone comprehensive *auteur* study of the British period, comments that *The Pleasure Garden* reveals "the moral rigor ... of a director fresh from the working class."[94] Why this is so or what relevance it might have is not investigated.

Patricia Ferrara, opposing standard critical assumption, deemphasizes Hitchcock's Catholic upbringing and emphasizes the British middle-class aspect of his youth, which she sees expressed in the "bourgeois" fears of breaking the law or offending social morality. She posits a "neutral attitude," not dogma, to be the crux of Hitchcock's films and relates this to the critical accusations of a lack of substance, which she interprets as a lack of "political ideology ... a severe disinclination to take sides." Finally, she examines the theme of conventional-unconventional as a continuum, concluding that the dark side of the films internalizes social rigidities while the light side shows characters who escape such a rigidity, and that both are the serious reflection of a man who was not sure where he fit in conventional society.[95]

Tom Ryall's work, *Alfred Hitchcock and the British Cinema,* is the most detailed and extensive in the area of cultural history, a contextual synthesis that

reveals a great amount about Hitchcockian influences and sources. Opposed to *auteur* criticism, Ryall describes in fascinating and complex detail the "norms and conventions of film making" in the 1920s and 1930s, effectively intertwining British film culture and national cinema with the rise of Hitchcock. In addition to the historical descriptions referred to in the "Biographical Background" of this work, Ryall also devotes chapters to Hitchcock and the thriller genre and Hitchcock's relation to classical narrative cinema. He defines the thriller genre that influenced Hitchcock as primarily literary and shows that the varying literary sources of the films explain the differences in philosophy among them. He also asserts that romance, in the sense of male/female relations, is the uniquely Hitchcockian addition to the thriller genre, arguing that the heterosexual couple is placed in the position of the hero.[96] Both of these points are reinforced by other writers in the critical literature, such as Stuart McDougal on *The 39 Steps* or James Goodwin on *Sabotage*.[97]

While the literary influences have been thus documented, the film influences remain more elusive. Genre criticism is dominated by a wide range of popular, impressionistic critical works—on the thriller, spy films, mysteries—most of which contain commentary on the films of Hitchcock as a successful example. Nonetheless, there is no acceptance of precisely what elements compose a film genre, though it is generally agreed that categories used are too large or insufficiently defined as to time period. In discussing Hitchcock's films, Durgnat suggests many comparisons to contemporaneous British and American formula films, but none are detailed; most other genre discussions are structural compcomparisons of two films, such as Ricarda Strobel's book-length comparison of *Lifeboat* and *The Stranger* as melodrama and propaganda, or Robin Wood on *Shadow of a Doubt* and *It's a Wonderful Life*.[98]

Ed Gallefant defines a new genre called "the paranoid couple's film," which combines melodrama, in assigning fantasy to the woman, and realism/horror, in assigning purpose to the man. But, he argues in an analysis of *Rebecca,* the combination results in a turnaround, for "the fantasy life of the man is as important as that of the woman" and even guides the woman toward "realistic" behavior intended to fulfill the man's fantasy.[99]

The generic conventions of realism, fantasy, and the woman's film are in this way intertwined, and a look back at the films and the criticism reinforces Gallefant's point. The collapse of the man's fantasy results in the dreaded "downbeat" ending, as well as commercial weakness, in *The Manxman, The Skin Game, Jamaica Inn, The Paradine Case,* and *Vertigo.* In some of the other more popular films, the fantasies are combined into the man's fantasy of a "perfect wife." Mary Ann Doane describes the woman's film as an attempt to constitute itself as the "mirror image of dominant cinema," centering instead on a female protagonist while remaining ideologically compatible. The "aggressivity of the look," which many critics argue results in punishment for the woman, is alternatively transformed into the "narrativised paranoia" surrounding woman's desire to replicate an image that attracts the male gaze.[100] *Suspicion* and *Rebecca* are the exemplary films here, both made at the height of the popularity of the woman's film formula. Michele Duckert discusses them as cautionary tales not only to the woman but also to the man, whose lack of integrity is revealed. Following this logic, the films also become exercises in compromise, where the powerful woman does not resist enough, but stays for the sake of companionship and a future in society.[101]

But it is the horror film, and its prime representative *Psycho*, that has been most clearly revealed within the study of genre. In one of several structural analyses of the slasher film, Carol J. Clover argues in support of Wood's definition of the horror film as the "byproduct of cultural crisis and disintegration . . . the most important of all American film genres and perhaps the most progressive, even in its overt nihilism," and of Modleski's definition of the slasher film as a genre that "does not promote harmony or specious good, does not ply the mechanisms of identification, narrative continuity, and closure to provide pleasure in constituting dominant ideology." Clover then distinguishes between the more modern (post-Hitchcock) interest of the genre in the fantasy of role reversal and the "higher forms of horror" like *Psycho* where "femininity is more conventionally elaborated and inexorably punished in an emphatically masculine environment."[102]

In another chapter of his book Ryall traces Hitchcock's career as it coincides with the development of classical narrative cinema. Filling out the work by Bonitzer on the look that was discussed earlier in this essay, Ryall concludes that Hitchcock balanced the features of the classical norm (which in any case was his major influence) with more open, documentary-like "loose ends."[103]

William Fisher describes the resultant flexibility of Hitchcock's work in fulfilling the "masterpiece requirements of auteurist values" as well as providing a textbook illustration of psychoanalytic-semiotic principles, and argues that the work provides a basis of shared understanding that defies the "sclerotic character" of the term *classical narrative cinema*.[104] Taking up Harold Bloom's idea of "strong poets" who take and use their own readings of the language and images of their predecessors in their work, Fisher posits such "intertextuality" as the basis of Brian DePalma's work as it relates to Hitchcock's. He argues that DePalma uses the shared cinematic experience with the audience that Hitchcock's work has supplied in order to render a "formal reinvention of the received moments" but for more progressive ends. Mark Van Doren wrote similarly of Hitchcock in 1937, that "a live wire seems to run backward from any of his films to all the best films one can remember, connecting them with it in a conspiracy to shock us into a special state of consciousness with respect to the art."[105]

These areas of genre criticism and classical narrative are further complicated by the fact that in the films of Hitchcock genre, plot, and character conventions are freely mixed, just as identification and technical methods are. Robin Wood, and later, John Belton, describes Hitchcock's formal appropriation of both Expressionist and constructivist techniques, which arose out of opposing ideologies. Wood concludes, much like Ferrara above, that Hitchcock's films arrive at a nonideological synthesis of them, or as Wood says, a "perversion" of both for the purpose of creating "bourgeois entertainment."[106]

Just as Hitchcock freely mixed, so do his critics, frequently arriving at contradictory conclusions. Equating melodrama with essential cinematic form, Michael Pressler analyzes the two versions of *Strangers on a Train* and concludes that the "rapid motion and mounting tension— the rigors of melodramatic form," preclude the more subtle psychoanalytical approach of the book because such changes effectively satisfy audience expectation of the hero's upright moral character.[107] Ronald Christ, however, argues in discussing the same film that any such search for meaning (either psychoanalytic or ethical) *"reduces* the quality of perception" of the film, which, in its purity of form, has actually freed us "from the obligation to moralize and psychologize."[108]

Fredric Jameson, in a critique of Rothman's *The Murderous Gaze* that might apply as well to the above two critics, discusses the theoretical pitfalls attending Rothman's lack of a historical understanding of genre, and concludes that his readings reveal a type of idealism that transforms "a formal structure or feature into a type of content."[109] As this is the single most common conclusion concerning Hitchcock's work—that form creates content—Jameson is in effect questioning a large amount of the criticism. Following his logic, the majority of criticism on the films of Hitchcock, beginning with Chabrol and Rohmer and culminating in the work of Rothman and Lesley Brill, exhibits in itself the very weakness it denies in the films, that is, an emphasis on the ordering of the formal surface resulting in arbitrary meaning, or "no" meaning.

The work of Lesley Brill, whose understanding of the meaning of Hitchcock's films is very much at odds with the majority of Hitchcockian criticism, is most relevant here. Brill, who in analyzing the formal elements makes few references to anything outside the films, sees them as "a romantic vision of innocence and immortality," "happy fairy tales," which through the *integration* of past and present, and true and false love, lead to the "recovery of innocence in wedded bliss."[110]

Looking at the criticism on Hitchcock, especially monographs like Rothman's and Brill's, it is difficult to appreciate David Bordwell's assertion in *Making Meaning* that film critics of the last twenty years pay "scarcely any attention to form and style." When Bordwell reviews the critical history of *Psycho* in his book, he concludes that the seven works he analyzes (from Douchet in 1960 through Poague in 1986) "display a high degree of consensus" due to their "tacit dependence upon norms of comprehension[:] genre conventions, beginnings and endings, character actions, decisive twists in the plot, key props." But in order to clear the way for this consensus, he must first equalize the differing interpretations. Summing up the work of Raymond Bellour, for instance, he concludes, for "the film critic as social critic, criticism [is] an assault on dominant ideology . . . [which] may excite the emotions of a reader who hopes to participate in the dismantling of oppressive political structures." Social criticism is then one of many methods, all dependent on the same "norms of comprehension," and therefore allowing merely differing interpretations of, to his mind, equal merit.[111]

But as I indicated in the section on feminist criticism, it is these "norms of comprehension" that are frequently for feminist critics the more important point of contention. In her essay on *Blackmail*, Modleski quotes various critics' descriptions of the rape scene: "violent love," "fairly violent pass," "seduction," "forcibly embraced," and also points out the common critical presumption of Alice's guilt in murdering her attacker. She then disputes such "obvious" understanding, and quotes Catherine MacKinnon on the importance in legal interpretation of "whose meaning wins." Whether the act is a rape or a seduction is not merely an interpretive difference but has consequences—Alice's guilt or innocence. In Hitchcock's typically evenhanded design, the film itself seems to be aware of these differing interpretations, though also, just as typically, it displays little interest in "whose meaning wins."[112]

Ryall quotes an assessment by Thomas Elsaesser which concludes that Hitchcock displayed "a far more explicitly intellectual analytic approach" to filmmaking than classical norms required.[113] It is this insight that perhaps provides the most significant clue to the enduring fascination Hitchcock's films hold for such a wide range of viewers. That he developed an opinion on and some

expertise in virtually every detail of filmmaking during his fifty years in the business is significant. How he did this—the question of his collaborative style—has not been sufficiently investigated. His biographers document his persistent attraction to strong creative talent, his pride in working with well-known writers, for instance, and his bitterness when he had to settle for talent he considered second-rate. One of the themes of the Truffaut interviews is the placing of blame for failings in the films on the compromise use of the "wrong" writer or actor. This attraction to free-thinking talent, which to some extent became associated for Hitchcock with youthful talent, never really faded and is largely undocumented. His disinclination to express gratitude, for example, hides his career-long dependency on others for both stories and dialogue. But the fact that he denied the input of others is not as significant as that he consistently used their ideas. From what little is known about Alma Reville Hitchcock we can deduce that Hitchcock never worked from a single mind. And that acknowledgment hardly begins to consider the many other enduring creative relationships he had. Two cinematographers, Robert Burks and Jack Cox, for instance, shot twenty-three of the films.

In this light the historical understanding of genre that many note as missing from film criticism becomes even more of a gap in Hitchcockian criticism because Hitchcock's primary method was in fact "formal reinvention"—of literary work, of other films, of stories in the newspapers, of others' ideas, of his own ideas; his favored analogy for film directing was music conducting. As Jean Narboni concluded, in Hitchcock, there are "many signs, no facts."[114] Far from the lonely romantic artist, he appears to have been more of a sponge, eager to adapt the point of view that would sell, and open to any idea that seemed good, insistent only that it fit his design.

Notes

1. Robin Wood, *Hitchcock's Films Revisited* (New York: Columbia University Press, 1989). (entry 852, includes reprint of 1965 work, entry 355)

2. Lee Russell [Peter Wollen], "Alfred Hitchcock," *New Left Review*, no. 35 (January–February 1966):89–92. (entry 334)

3. Edward Buscombe, "Dickens and Hitchcock," *Screen* 11, no. 4–5 (August–September 1970):97–114. (entry 365)

4. Donald Spoto, *The Art of Alfred Hitchcock: Fifty Years of His Motion Pictures* (New York: Hopkinson & Blake, 1976). (entry 445)

5. Tania Modleski, *The Women Who Knew Too Much: Hitchcock and Feminist Theory* (New York: Methuen, 1988). (entry 833)

6. Charles Thomas Samuels, "Hitchcock," *American Scholar* 39, no. 2 (Spring 1970):295–304; Lindsay Anderson, "Alfred Hitchcock," *Sequence* (London Film Club), no. 9 (Autumn 1949):113–124; William S. Pechter, "The director vanishes," *Moviegoer*, no. 2 (Summer 1964):37–50. (entries 370, 187, 314) Examples of the opposite viewpoint are Wood, *Hitchcock's Films Revisited*, and Peter Bogdanovich, *The Cinema of Alfred Hitchcock* (New York: Museum of Modern Art Film Library, 1963). (entry 295)

7. Raymond Durgnat, *The Strange Case of Alfred Hitchcock* (Cambridge, Mass.: MIT Press, 1974). (entry 363)

8. Jean François Tarnowski, "De quelques problèmes de mise en scène (propos de *Frenzy* d'Alfred Hitchcock)," *Positif*, no. 158 (April 1974):46–60. (entry 425)

9. Sam P. Simone, *Hitchcock as Activist* (Ann Arbor, Mich.: University of Michigan Research Press, 1985). (entry 755)

10. Charles Bitsch and François Truffaut, "Rencontre avec Alfred Hitchcock," *Cahiers du Cinéma* 11, no. 62 (August–September 1956), p. 5. (entry 234)

11. Kirk Bond, "The other Alfred Hitchcock," *Film Culture*, no. 41 (Summer 1966):30–35. (entry 326)

12. Tom Ryall, *Alfred Hitchcock and the British Cinema* (Urbana: University of Illinois Press, 1986), pp. 7–18. (entry 775)

13. John Grierson, "The Hitch in Hitchcock," *Everyman* (December 24, 1931):722; Robert Herring, "The latest British masterpiece," *Close Up* 2, no. 1 (January 1928):32–38. (entries 89 and 71)

14. Anderson, "Alfred Hitchcock," *passim.*

15. Alexandre Astruc, "Au-dessous de volcan," *Cahiers du Cinéma* 1, no. 1 (April 1951):29. (entry 201)

16. Hans Lucas [Jean-Luc Godard], "Suprématie du sujet," *Cahiers du Cinéma* 2, no. 10 (1952):59–61. (entry 207)

17. Maurice Schèrer [Eric Rohmer], "De trois films et d'une certaine école," *Cahiers du Cinéma* 5, no. 26 (August–September 1953):18–25. (entry 212)

18. André Bazin, "Faut-il croire en Hitchcock?" *l'Observateur*, no. 88 (January 17, 1952), p. 23. (entry 205)

19. Claude Chabrol, "Histoire d'une interview," *Cahiers du Cinéma* 7, no. 39 (October 1954):39–44; André Bazin, "Hitchcock contre Hitchcock," *Cahiers du Cinéma* 7, no. 39 (October 1954):25–32. (entries 216 and 215)

20. Eric Rohmer and Claude Chabrol, *Hitchcock: The First Forty-Four Films* (New York: Ungar, 1979), p. 91. (entry 246)

21. Ian Cameron, "Hitchcock and the mechanisms of suspense," *Movie*, no. 3 (October 1962):4–7; "Hitchcock: Suspense and meaning," *Movie*, no. 6 (January 1963):8–12; with Richard Jeffery, "The universal Hitchcock," *Movie*, no. 12 (Spring 1965):21–24. (entries 292, 298, 319)

22. Alfred Hitchcock, "Enjoyment of fear," *Good Housekeeping* 128 (February 1949), p. 39. (entry 189)

23. Pete Martin, "I call on Alfred Hitchcock," *Saturday Evening Post* 230, no. 4 (July 27, 1957), p. 73. (entry 252) Another factor in Hitchcock's success in suspense was his understanding of human nature as contradictory. Hinting to one interviewer his intent to educate, he related his planting of what he called "icebox talk scenes," which are scenes that strike the audience as curious and provoke discussion over leftovers after the movie. Discussed in an article by Louis Phillips, "*Vertigo:* After such knowledge, what forgiveness?" *Armchair Detective* 17, no. 2 (Spring 1984):188–191. (entry 742)

24. Peter Wollen, "Hitchcock's vision," *Cinema* (Cambridge), no. 3 (June 1969):2–4. (entry 362)

25. Bogdanovich, *The Cinema of Alfred Hitchcock*, pp. 40, 43.

26. Wollen, "Hitchcock's vision," p. 4.

27. Sylvia Lawson, "The Pierce/ Wollen code signs: Functions and values," *Australian Journal of Screen Theory*, no. 3 (1977):47–65. (entry 486)

28. Raymond Bellour, "*Marnie:* Une Lecture," *Revue d'Esthètique*, no. 20 (1969):169–179; "*Les Oiseaux:* Analyse d'une sequence," *Cahiers du Cinéma* 216 (October 1969):24–38. (entries 353, 354)

29. Pascal Bonitzer, "It's only a film/ou la face du néant," *Framework*, no. 14 (Spring 1981):22–24. (entry 608)

30. Jean Narboni, "Visages d'Hitchcock," in *Alfred Hitchcock* (Paris: l'Etoile, 1980), pp. 30–38. (entry 537)

31. Marian E. Keane, "A closer look at scopophilia: Mulvey, Hitchcock and *Vertigo,*" in *A Hitchcock Reader,* edited by Marshall Deutelbaum and Leland Poague (Ames: Iowa State University Press, 1986), pp. 231–248. (entry 791)

32. *Alfred Hitchcock,* edited by Michel Estève (Paris: Minard, 1971). (entry 373)

33. Philippe Parrain, "La construction dramatique et les lois du mouvement," in *Alfred Hitchcock,* edited by Michel Estève (Paris: Minard, 1971), pp. 5–27. (entry 381)

34. Michel Serceau, "Les récits d'espionnage et le chemin de la connaissance," in *Alfred Hitchcock,* edited by Michel Estève (Paris: Minard, 1971), pp. 56–76. (entry 696)

35. Truffaut, *Hitchcock* pp. 173, 187.

36. *Focus on Hitchcock,* edited by Albert J. LaValley (Englewood Cliffs, N.J.: Prentice-Hall, 1972). (entry 386)

37. Fabio Carlini, *Alfred Hitchcock,* Il Castoro Cinema, 5 (Firenze: La Nuova Italia, 1974). (entry 411)

38. Peter Wollen, "*North by Northwest:* A morphological analysis," *Film Form* (Newcastle upon Tyne) 1, no. 1 (1976):19–34: Richard Abel, "*Notorious:* Perversion par excellence," *Wide Angle* 1, no. 1 (1979):66–71; David Bordwell, "ApProppriations and imPropprieties: Problems in the morphology of film narrative," *Cinema Journal* 27, no. 3 (Spring 1988):5–20. (entries 472, 515, 836)

39. Barbara M. Bannon, "Double, double: Toil and trouble," *Literature/Film Quarterly* 13, no. 1 (Winter 1985):56–65. (entry 758)

40. Thomas Martin Hemmeter, "Hitchcock the stylist" (Ph.D. diss., Case Western Reserve University, 1980.) (entry 535)

41. François Regnault, "Système formel d'Hitchcock (Fascicule de résultats)," in *Alfred Hitchcock,* edited by Jean Narboni (Paris; L'Etoile, 1980), pp. 20–29 (entry 584)

42. Bazin, "Hitchcock contre Hitchcock"; Jean Douchet, *Alfred Hitchcock* (Paris: Herne, 1967), p. 240. (entry 337)

43. John Belton, "The space of *Rear Window,*" *M.L.N.* 103, no. 5 (December 1988):1121–1138. (entry 834)

44. Patricia Ferrara, "Through Hitchcock's *Rear Window* again," *New Orleans Review* 12, no. 3 (1985):21–30. (entry 762)

45. Virginia Wright Wexman, "The critic as consumer: Film study in the university, *Vertigo* and the film canon," *Film Quarterly* 39, no. 3 (Spring 1986):32–41. (entry 807)

46. William Rothman, *Hitchcock—The Murderous Gaze* (Cambridge, Mass.: Harvard University Press, 1982). (entry 679)

47. Leonard J. Leff, *Hitchcock and Selznick* (New York: Weidenfeld & Nicholson, 1987); Andrew Britton, "Cary Grant: Comedy and male desire," *CineAction!,* no. 7 (December 1986):36–51; James Naremore, "Star performances: Cary Grant in *North by Northwest;* Film as performance text: *Rear Window,*" in *Acting in the Cinema* (Berkeley: University of California Press 1988), pp. 213–238, 239–261. (entries 818, 780, 846)

48. Elizabeth Weis, *The Silent Scream: Alfred Hitchcock's Sound Track* (Rutherford, N.J.: Fairleigh Dickinson University Press, 1982). (entry 681)

49. Noël Simsolo, "Alfred Hitchcock (1899–1980)," *L'Avant-Scène du Cinéma,* Anthologie du cinéma, no. 110 (December 1/15 1982):305–336. (entry 697)

50. O. B. Hardison, "The rhetoric of Hitchcock's thrillers," in *Man and the Movies* (Baton Rouge: Louisiana State University Press, 1967), pp. 137–152. (entry 341)

51. Truffaut, *Hitchcock* pp. 173, 187.

52. John M. Smith, "Conservative individualism: A selection of English Hitchcock," *Screen* 13, no. 3 (Autumn 1972):51–70. (entry 403)

53. Buscombe, "Dickens and Hitchcock," p. 98.

54. Michael Walker, "The old age of Alfred Hitchcock," *Movie*, no. 18 (Winter 1970):10–13. (entry 371)

55. Kirsten Witte, "Hitchcock in Germania," in *Alfred Hitchcock: La Critica, il Pubblico, le Fonti Letterarie*, edited by Roberto Salvadori (Firenze: La Casa Usher, 1981), pp. 73–75. (entry 674)

56. Ina Rae Hark, "Keeping your amateur standing: Audience participation and good citizenship in Hitchcock's political films," *Cinema Journal* 29, no. 2 (Winter 1990):8–22. (entry 863)

57. Andrew Sarris, "Pantheon directors: Alfred Hitchcock," in *The American Cinema: Directors and Directions 1929–1968* (New York: Dutton, 1968), p. 60. (entry 350)

58. Serceau, "Les récits d'espionnage," p. 56.

59. Robin Wood, "Ideology, genre, *auteur*," *Film Comment* 13, no. 1 (January–February 1977):46–51. (entry 495)

60. James B. McLaughlin, "All in the family: Alfred Hitchcock's *Shadow of a Doubt*," *Wide Angle* 4, no. 1 (1980):12–19. (entry 576)

61. Diane Carson, "The nightmare world of Hitchcock's women," in *The Kingdom of Dreams in Literature and Film* (Tallahassee: Florida State University, 1986), pp. 11–20. (entry 784)

62. Simsolo, "Alfred Hitchcock," p. 336.

63. Janet Bergstrom, "Enunciation and sexual difference (part 1)," *Camera Obscura*, no. 3–4 (Summer 1979):38. (entry 518)

64. Bill Nichols, "Birds: At the window," *Film Reader*, no. 4 (1980):166 (entry 581) Leland Poague and Marshall Deutelbaum, "Hitchcock and film theory: A *Psycho* dossier," in *A Hitchcock Reader* (Ames: Iowa State Press, 1986), p. 308. (entry 771)

65. Kenneth Macpherson, "As is," *Close Up* 5 (December 1929):54. (entry 78)

66. Victor Burgin, "Diderot, Barthes, *Vertigo*," in *Formations of Fantasy*, edited by Victor Burgin, Donald James and Cora Kaplan (London: Methuen, 1986), p. 105. (entry 783)

67. Alexander Michael Doty, "Alfred Hitchcock's films of the 1940's: The emergence of personal style and theme within the American studio system" (Urbana: University of Illinois Press, 1984). (entry 717)

68. Andrew Britton, "Hitchcock's *Spellbound*: Text and counter-text," *CineAction!*, no 3–4 (Winter 1986):72. (entry 781)

69. Garry M. Leonard, "A fall from grace: The fragmentation of masculine subjectivity and the impossibility of femininity in Hitchcock's *Vertigo*," *American Imago* 47, 3–4 (Fall–Winter 1990):271–291; (entry 864) John Fletcher, "Versions of masquerade," *Screen 29*, no. 3 (Summer 1988):43–70, explains in more detail the concept of the mask. (entry 839)

70. Jean Douchet, *Alfred Hitchcock*, Collection L'Herne Cinema, 1 (Paris: L'Herne, 1985). (revised version of entry 337)

71. Modleski, *The Women Who Knew Too Much* (pp. 41–42), also suggests that "one of Hitchcock's main interests for feminism lies in the way his films show the desire for distance itself to be bound up with the male's insistence on his difference from woman."

72. Douchet, *Alfred Hitchcock*, pp. 239–262.

73. Peter Wollen, "Hitchcock: Hybrid plots in *Psycho*," *Framework*, no. 13 (Autumn 1980):14–16. (entry 598)

74. Raymond Bellour, "Le blocage symbolique," *Communications*, no. 23 (1975):235–350. (entry 431)

75. Bergstrom, "Enunciation and sexual difference," p. 51.

76. Michael Renov, "From identification to ideology: The male system of Hitchcock's *Notorious*," *Wide Angle* 4, no. 1 (1980):30–37. (entry 585)

77. Britton, "Hitchcock's *Spellbound,*" *passim.*

78. Andy Warhol, "Hitchcock," *Andy Warhol's Interview* 4 (September 1974):8. (entry 426)

79. Nichols, "Birds," *passim.*

80. Modleski, *The Women Who Knew Too Much,* pp. 28–29.

81. Walter Poznar, "Orpheus descending: Love in *Vertigo,*" *Literature/Film Quarterly* 17, no. 1 (1989):58–65. (entry 856)

82. Karen Hollinger, "The look, narrativity, and the female spectator in *Vertigo,*" *Journal of Film and Video* 39, no. 4 (Fall 1987):24. (entry 822)

83. Laura Mulvey, "Visual pleasure and narrative cinema," *Screen* 16, no. 3 (Autumn 1975):31–39. (entry 439)

84. Jacqueline Rose, "Paranoia and the film system," *Screen* 17, no. 4 (Winter 1977):85–104. (entry 489)

85. Sandy Flitterman, "Woman, desire, and the look: Feminism and the enunciative," *Cine-tracts* 2, no. 1 (Fall 1978):63–68. (entry 815)

86. R[aymond] Bellour, "Psychosis, neurosis, perversion," *Camera Obscura,* no. 3–4 (Summer 1979):104–134. (entry 516)

87. Jeanne Thomas Allen, "The representation of violence to women: Hitchcock's *Frenzy,*" *Film Quarterly* 38, no. 3 (Spring 1985):30–38. (entry 757)

88. Susan Lurie, "The construction of the 'castrated woman' in psychoanalysis and cinema," *Discourse,* no. 4 (Winter 1981):52–74. (entry 652)

89. Tania Modleski, "Never to be thirty-six years old: *Rebecca* as a female oedipal drama," *Wide Angle* 5, no. 1 (1982):34–41. (entry 693)

90. Barbara Klinger, "*Psycho*: The institutionalization of female sexuality," *Wide Angle* 5, no. 1 (1982):49–55. (entry 690)

91. Modleski, *The Women Who Knew Too Much, passim.*

92. D. A. Miller, "Anal *Rope,*" *Representations,* no. 32 (Fall 1990):114–133. (entry 685)

93. Michele Piso, "Alfred Hitchcock: For loss of the world," (Ph.D. diss., University of Oregon, 1986). (entry 774)

94. Maurice Yacowar, *Hitchcock's British films* (Hamden, Conn.: Archon Books, 1977), p. 20. (entry 477)

95. Patricia Ferrara, "The discontented bourgeois: Bourgeois morality and the interplay of light and dark strains in Hitchcock's films," *New Orleans Review* 14, no. 1 (Winter 1987):79–87. (entry 814)

96. Ryall, *Alfred Hitchcock and the British Cinema,* pp. 115–140.

97. Stuart Y. McDougal, "Mirth, sexuality and suspense: Alfred Hitchcock's adaptation of *Thirty-Nine Steps,*" *Literature/Film Quarterly* 3, no. 3 (Summer 1975):232–239; James Goodwin, "Conrad and Hitchcock: Secret sharers." In *The English Novel and the Movies,* edited by Michael Klein and Gillian Parker (New York: Ungar, 1981), pp. 218–227. (entries 437 and 643)

98. Ricarda Strobel, *Propagandafilm und Melodrama: Untersuchungen zu Alfred Hitchcocks* Lifeboat *und Orson Welles* The Stranger (Rottenburg-Oberndorf: Faulstich, 1984) (entry 721); Wood, "Ideology, genre, *auteur,*" *passim.*

99. Ed Gallafent, "Black satin—fantasy, murder and the couple in *Gaslight* and *Rebecca,*" *Screen* 29, no. 3 (Summer 1988):84–103. (entry 840)

100. Mary Ann Doane, "*Caught* and *Rebecca*: The inscription of femininity as absence," *Enclitic* 5–6, no. 1–2 (1981):75–89. (entry 631)

101. Michele Duckert, "Original sins and classical narratives: Hitchcock through Foucault," in *Proceedings of the Purdue University Seventh Annual Conference on Film*

(West Lafayette, Ind.: Department of English, Purdue University, 1983), pp. 295–300. (entry 709)

102. Carol J. Clover, "Herbody, himself: Gender in the slasher film," *Representations,* no. 20 (Fall 1987):5–89 (entry 813)

103. Ryall, *Alfred Hitchcock and the British Cinema,* pp. 141–167.

104. William Fisher, "Re: Writing: Film history: From Hitchcock to DePalma," *Persistence of Vision,* no. 1 (Summer 1984):13–22. (entry 731)

105. Mark Van Doren, "Alfred Hitchcock," *Nation* 144 (March 13 1937):305–306. (entry 117)

106. Wood, *Hitchcock's Films Revisited;* John Belton, "Dexterity in a void: The formalist esthetics of Alfred Hitchcock," *Cineaste* 10, no. 3 (Summer 1980):9–13. (entry 544)

107. Michael Pressler, "Hitchcock and the melodramatic pattern," *Chicago Review* 35, no. 3 (Spring 1986):4–16. (entry 804)

108. Ronald Christ, *"Strangers on a Train:* The pattern of encounter," in *Focus on Hitchcock,* edited by Albert J. LaValley (Englewood Cliffs, N.J.: Prentice-Hall, 1972), pp. 104–110. (entry 389)

109. Fredric Jameson, "Reading Hitchcock," *October,* no. 23 (Winter 1982):15–42. (entry 689)

110. Lesley Brill, *Romance and Irony in Hitchcock's Films* (Princeton, N.J.: Princeton University Press, 1988). (entry 830)

111. David Bordwell, "Rhetoric in action: Seven models of *Psycho,*" in *Making Meaning* (Cambridge, Mass.: Harvard University Press, 1989, p. 260. (entry 853)

112. Modleski, *The Women Who Knew Too Much* p. 22.

113. Ryall, *Alfred Hitchcock and the British Cinema,* p. 165.

114. Narboni, "Visages d'Hitchcock," p. 38.

III

FILMOGRAPHY

1 *The Pleasure Garden* (1926)

Director	Alfred J. Hitchcock
Continuity and Assistant Director	Alma Reville
Producer	Michael Balcon*
Production Company	Emelka G. B. A.*
Screenplay	Eliot Stannard, based on the novel by Oliver Sandys
Photography	Baron [Gaetano] Ventimiglia
Cast	Virginia Valli (Patsy Brand), Carmelita Geraghty (Jill Cheyne), Miles Mander (Levet), John Stuart (Hugh Fielding), Nita Naldi (the native), K. Martini (the patron), Florence Helminger (the patron's wife), George Snell (Oscar Hamilton), C. Falkenburg (Prince Ivan)
Filmed	at Emelka Studios, Munich
Running Time	approximately 85 minutes
Distributor	Wardour & F., Aymon Independent (U.S.)
Release Date	March 1926†

Other titles: *Irregarten der Leidenschaft, Le Jardin d'Agrément*)

Synopsis

Next to the credits, a jazz dancer gyrates energetically in a spotlight in the corner of the screen.

Costumed dancers move quickly down a circular stairway to the stage, where they form a line, kicking high. Gaping men in formal wear sit in the audience, some bouncing with the music, others ogling and sweating. One picks up binoculars and views the row of legs. Finding Patsy Brand, he moves the glass up to her smiling face and wets his lips in anticipation. Noticing him, Patsy frowns. The man gets up, bumping into another customer on his way to ask who she is.

Title: "Oscar Hamilton, manager of the Pleasure Garden Theater." Oscar, in his top hat, smokes in front of the backstage "No Smoking" sign. The man from the audience approaches him and comments, "Your chorus is certainly most tempting." Oscar calls Patsy over and the man wrings his hands while he waits. Left alone with her, he says, "I've fallen in love with that charming kiss curl of yours." She snaps off the fake blond hair with a laugh and gives it to him. Disgusted, he humorlessly returns it to her. She walks off.

A poster for the Pleasure Garden decorates the brick wall outside the stage door; a car sits nearby. A brunette woman wearing a cloche and dark coat hesitates before the theater door where two shabbily dressed men linger. A spotlight illuminates her purse in close-up and they spy it knowingly. As she turns, one removes the contents from the purse.

Inside, the woman, Jill Cheyne, inquires at the stage manager's cubicle, her face reflected in the window that surrounds him. She offers a letter of introduction for the manager, then is startled to discover that all her money and the letter are gone. Leaning through the opening, she pleads with the man to let her through, but he frowns.

In their plain dressing room, with partitioned makeup mirrors and tables lining one wall, the women banter while they busily dress.

Out at the stage door, Jill clutches her breast, while two suited men notice her difficulty and approach her. Patsy, now her natural brunette self, dressed in a dark suit and neat white collar and tie, rounds the corner. Angry, she strides quickly over and pushes the men away from Jill, who tells her story: ". . . and now I can't pay for my cab, and I've nowhere to sleep even!" The men guffaw at her plight, and Patsy smiles a little herself, but she suggests that Jill stay with her that night and see Oscar in the morning. Jill hesitates, but then goes along with the cheerful Patsy, throwing a coy smile at the men as they leave. The two women giggle on their way out.

At home, Patsy turns on the light to discover her dog has ripped apart some clothing. The front room of her flat is medium sized, a round table with flowers in the center and a fireplace and chairs on the right. The landlady and her husband carry in Jill's huge trunk, and the landlady takes the opportunity to complain.

Back in their own apartment, the landlady glares at her husband as she follows him into their sitting room.

In Patsy's bedroom, Jill removes the dog from the bed, then takes a framed photograph of her fiance from her case. Patsy carefully inspects the close-up of the unsmiling profile, and Jill yawns. They undress on opposite sides of the room, laughing as Jill tells her story: ". . . So I wasn't going to spend all my life being companion to a sick old lady in the country." Patsy notices Jill casually throwing her clothes on her bench, then decides to throw hers on Jill's nearby trunk. The

clothes land in their respective resting places in the same shot, as Jill continues, ". . . and on reaching London, I went straight to Mr. Hamilton before bothering about a hotel!" With her leg gaily in the air, Patsy flings off her stocking, "Did you think he'd be waiting on the mat with a contract?" "I'm sure he'd have given me a part if I hadn't lost that letter of introduction," replies Jill. Now standing in her modish pajamas, Patsy points her hair brush at Jill, "It's lucky for you, O Village Maiden, that you fell into the poor but honest hands of Patsy Brand." Jill frowns, then skips around and angrily removes the dog's bone from the big brass bed. She then drops to the floor in prayer, while Patsy indulgently observes her. The dog comes over to lick Jill's upturned feet and she kicks him away. Jumping into bed, she fluffs up the lone pillow for herself, while Patsy puts her head on the edge of it.

Close-up of bulletin: CALL—Passion Flowers—entire company to be on stage for full rehearsal tomorrow, Wednesday, June 5th, 11 A.M. sharp.

Jill nervously sits on a wicker trunk near the stage door. Patsy signals her to come in. A long shot shows the stage full of activity. Backstage, Patsy tries to interest the stage manager in Jill, but he angrily dismisses her. As some other male observers and Oscar Hamilton file into the audience, Jill puffs herself up with determination. After the rehearsal begins, Oscar angrily crosses the plank over the orchestra pit and berates the lead actress. Jill boldly approaches him and tells him she "can dance much better than that." Pursing her lips, she mentions she has never before been on a stage. Intrigued, Oscar stops the proceedings and announces that "a great genius, who has never been on the stage, has called to teach us our business." Everyone except Patsy laughs heartily as Jill assures the conductor she can dance equally well to any tune. A close-up shows Patsy's alarm, but the dance looks good and Oscar offers Jill five pounds a week, to which she counters with a demand for twenty, and he agrees.

Title: "What every chorus girl knows." Close-up of stockings being washed in a bowl. The landlady lets Hugh, Jill's "fiasco," into Patsy's empty front room. Glancing at a picture of Patsy on the mantel, he looks down at her dog and then plays on the floor with him. Patsy, back in the bedroom, hurriedly removes her other stocking and jumps through the curtain between the parlor and the bedroom, tumbling over Hugh. Sitting on the floor together, laughing, they try to tidy themselves. Finally, they rise and Patsy tells him Jill has gone for a costume fitting.

Jill, dressed in a stiffened fairylike costume with a helmet hat, walks down a runway in a show room. The long-haired male costumer leaves Oscar on the couch and fusses over her.

At home, Hugh and Patsy sit down to tea.

At the showroom, Jill sits coyly next to Oscar in front of a small tea table. "You shouldn't talk to me like that . . . until I'm in a flat of my own," she says.

At the table, Hugh looks around nervously and announces, "After two years in the East, I'll be rich enough to come home and marry . . . and Jill's promised to wait for me, bless her!" A mustached friend of Hugh's named Levet arrives and smiles nervously, glancing at Patsy, who smiles at him. "Mr. Levet follows me to the East in a couple of months and will be my only friend out there," says Hugh. The three stand and talk. "And for two years, Miss Brand, we shall be removed from everything that makes life worth living," laments Levet. Hugh sighs as he leans on the mantel, then brightens when Jill enters. He embraces her, and she turns her cheek for a kiss. Levet and Patsy are framed on the other side of the

room, looking off. "Love is a wonderful thing," comments Levet to Patsy's back; she turns thoughtfully toward him.

A picture of Jill on a program. Hugh, sitting with Levet in the audience, excitedly announces that she is next! Levet remains somber as Jill oohs and aahs through a jazz number. A goateed Prince Ivan sits sternly in a side balcony. Levet sits up when he sees the smiling Patsy in the chorus line.

Hands raise champagne in a toast to Jill. Patsy, Levet, and Hugh sit with her at a table. "Here's wishing Jill something greater than fame—happiness!" The stage curtain that decorates this title is pulled slightly askew, leaving a dark hole. A couple dances exuberantly behind the group, who are seated in a very large restaurant. Prince Ivan walks down the open central stairway and Oscar takes him over to congratulate Jill. He smoothly kisses her hand, then with fingers to his lips, announces, "I shall often give myself the pleasure of seeing you dance." Hugh sulks disconcertedly as Levet takes Jill off to dance. "Don't worry," says Patsy, "I'll guard her against every danger whilst you're away." The jazz band of saxophones and banjos blares away as Levet and Patsy now dance. "Poor Hugh seems scared that some Pleasure Garden libertine may take his tender flower," they lament.

Title over a drawing of the sea: "Hugh reaches his destination determined to succeed for Jill's sake." Palm trees and rounded archways decorate the unnamed town of the "East." Hugh, in helmet and khakis, rides through on a donkey. A robed woman pokes at his donkey and begs change. He meets an Englishman, but his "thoughts are only of Jill."

Patsy sits morosely on her bed reading a letter from Jill: "I am so sorry to leave you so soon but . . . you will realize that I couldn't stay in cheap lodgings as I am nearly a star."

Title: "From day to day, Patsy's promise to guard Jill becomes increasingly difficult." Patsy comes around the corner near the stage door, and, seeing Prince Ivan, decides to go back up and warn Jill. In her elegant new dressing room, wrapped in a fur-collared robe, Jill coldly greets Patsy. "A fine price your prince is paying," frowns Patsy, waving her hand dramatically at his photo on a table nearby. "You either break with him or with me," she yells, sticking her chin in the air and haughtily pulling at Jill's pearls and fine outfit. Jill stalks out.

At the stage door, Patsy catches up to Jill, "If you can't think of me, think of Hugh," she says, but Jill only glares at her. Sweetening her expression, she turns to Ivan, "It appears that my acquaintance in the chorus line does not approve of you!" They laugh.

Patsy, spotlighted outside on the sidewalk, kicks the dust in front of her. Levet surprises her from behind. "I'm so worried. I can't stop Jill from fooling about with that Prince fellow," complains Patsy. Levet, dapper in a suit and striped tie, tells her she is "well rid of her," and takes her away.

At a fancy restaurant, three waiters hover around Prince Ivan and Jill.

At her apartment, Patsy and Levet enter and the dog growls from under the table. "Funny, he never growled at Hugh," mentions Jill. "Your dog had no reason to be jealous of Hugh," says Levet; he moves toward her, holding out his hands. She stiffens. He starts to kiss her but the landlady interrupts them.

At the restaurant, Prince Ivan makes a similar move toward Jill, who pushes his hand from her arm. Two cigar-chomping men at a nearby table laugh and comment, "Cunning little minx! She'll fool him into marrying her—mark my words!"

Levet rushes across the room toward Patsy, "I'm as lonely as you are!" He kisses her determinedly and she submits. The dog growls. "I don't go back to the East for a month. Darling, take pity on me!" He looks past her imploringly, and she hugs him. "I hardly know you, yet it seems I could marry you anytime you ask," she says. A close-up of Levet as he smiles, then kisses her and moves away toward the fireplace. "It wouldn't be fair to you . . . my business is unsettled . . . I couldn't even afford to make you an allowance," he says, peering at his nails. Walking over to him, Patsy exclaims, "Don't talk of money! I'd go on earning my own living . . . until the time came when you could send for me." They kiss, her dark hair filling the screen.

In her salon, Jill lounges with a cigarette holder, while the Prince stands behind her. Holding his hands around her neck, she leans back toward him. Suddenly he moves over to kiss her arm and she bangs the cigarette into his forehead. As he jumps back to soothe himself, she stands in the large elegant room and offers him his hat and cane.

Title: "Patsy's wedding day." A joyous Levet arrives at her flat, but Patsy is disturbed by her dog's howling.

A title describes their honeymoon journey by train to Lake Como, moonlight over the water. Patsy and Levet sit near the lake, lattice-work framing the terrace, a vista of water and cypress trees in the background. At the table, Patsy picks up a rose and Levet ardently kisses her hand, crushing it. She looks down, saddened. Night falls as they walk through formal gardens, and Patsy goes back to their room, where the maids offer her fruit. Outside, Levet waits, smoking.

Title over clouds and a moon: "Awake! for morning in the bowel of night, has flung the stone that puts the stars to flight." Patsy sleeps. Levet, dressed, watches as the maid brings in tea. Patsy wakes suddenly and they kiss.

Patsy stands in a square in front of statue of the Sacred Heart. Levet, lying nearby in the grass under a tree, sneers at her. She comes over and tells him she has been praying for their happiness. He yawns, then huddles close to her.

In a stone alleyway, Patsy tends to a mother and her small children. Levet calls her away, "I wish you'd not be so sloppy and sentimental with the filthy brats." She appeals and he throws a flower in a nearby canal. "That was the rose I gave you," she says, but he just laughs.

Title: "A golden smile but a heart of lead." Standing in a crowd of people on the dock, Patsy waves good-bye to Levet high up on a ship. He seats himself on a deck chair and begins reading the newspaper while she stands still waving. A close-up focuses on her waving arm, dissolving into a similar close-up of a bare arm decorated with a bauble, waving on the other side of the frame. A long-haired dark woman in a sarong stands at the top of some village stairs and rushes down to greet Levet, who is dressed in a white suit and riding a horse.

In a thatched cottage by the sea, Levet grabs the woman and kisses her, then sits down for a pipe and a drink. Hugh arrives, finding the woman draped over Levet's lap. Asking for news of Jill, Levet replies he never saw her after Hugh left.

Title: "Still a girl of the chorus at the Pleasure Garden, Patsy awaits news of her husband."

Levet picks up some mail and stuffs it in his pocket. Going through his own mail, Hugh finds a picture of Prince Ivan and Jill in a newspaper and crumples it in anger. "Why worry?" says Levet, preening in the sun, "There are as good fish in the sea as ever come out of it!"

At home, Patsy excitedly opens a letter from Levet, "I'm so sorry I have not written . . . been down with fever. This is an unhealthy spot for Europeans . . ." Stricken, Patsy leaps up and announces that she must go to him, "He hasn't anyone to nurse him!"

A title over the sea: "Planning a pleasant surprise for her husband, Patsy does not cable her coming." Patsy walks off the boat in a dramatic black and white outfit.

Levet, drunk, staggers around his hut. Patsy enters, and at first laughs at the scene, then turns serious. Levet orders out the other woman, who cringes in fear. He grabs her by the hair, and Patsy glares at him, "Do you think I'd stay here now and rob that child of her HOME? You . . . BEAST!" She races out, but Levet follows her and grapples with her near the beach, reminding her that she is his wife, and she is going to stay! Patsy gets away from him and rushes into the arms of the Englishman who escorted her there, demanding that he help her get away. The man stares Levet back into the bungalow. "There's another white chap down with fever—help me nurse him until the next boat," says the guide.

Inside the hut, the woman grovels at Levet's feet; he kicks her out.

On the porch of another hut, Patsy finds Hugh lying delirious under some netting.

Levet watches the other woman walk into the sea and runs after her. When she is neck high in water, he catches up to her and she turns gratefully to him, but he pushes her under the water.

Hugh rises, thinking that Jill is by him, then passes out.

Levet, dressed in a filthy shirt made of netting, staggers around.

Hugh asks for a kiss, and suddenly recognizes Patsy. Levet staggers toward them, demanding Patsy back "because she's my wife!" He threatens to make "pulp" of Hugh, and Patsy agrees to "humor him and go." Holding up Hugh's head, she promises him she will return.

Levet meanders after Patsy back to the hut, where she lights a candle. In its flame, he sees an apparition of the other woman. Rising hysterically, he cries out "My wife's here now. You're not wanted!" and falls onto Patsy's breast. Disgusted, she removes herself to an inner room and closes a lattice door between them. He cries out, "The sword! that's it. . . . She'll haunt me until I've killed you!" Taking a long curved sword from the wall, he attacks her through the door until she jumps away from it, and he breaks through. She cringes among a heap of rugs until a gun appears on the edge of the frame and someone shoots him. Muttering, Levet turns, then keels over.

The guide tells Patsy that Hugh warned him of Levet's condition. Outside, two native men have carried Hugh on a stretcher over to the hut; he rises to his feet and holds her. "But *you* saved *my* life . . . it is only a debt repaid," he assures her. Sad, she holds his hand, "We've both suffered . . . what have either of us got to live for now?" Responds Hugh, "We have one of the greatest things of life . . . youth!"

Notes. * Most filmographies credit Erich Pommer as producer, Gainsborough as the production company, and C. Wilfred Arnold as art director. † This was a press screening. The actual commercial run did not begin until January 1927, as the film was shelved by C. M. Woolf, the head of Wardour & F. (Spoto entry 702, p. 92)

2   *The Mountain Eagle* (1926)

Director	Alfred Hitchcock
Producer	Michael Balcon
Production Company	Gainsborough-Emelka G. B. A.
Screenplay	Eliot Stannard*
Photography	Baron Gaetano Ventimiglia
Cast	Bernard Goetzke (Pettigrew) Nita Naldi (Beatrice), Malcolm Keen (Fear O'God), John Hamilton (Pettigrew's son)
Filmed	at Emelka Studios, Munich, and in the Austrian Tyrol
Running Time	approximately 89 minutes
Distributor	Wardour & F.
Release Date	October 1926

Other titles: *Der Bergadler, Fear O' God* (U.S.), *L'Aigle de la Montagne*

Synopsis

This is a lost film. The most detailed synopsis, which follows, was found in Noble (entry 192).

"Beatrice, a school teacher in a small mountain village (set in Kentucky) incurs the enmity of Pettigrew, local justice of the peace and owner of the village store, because he believes that she encourages the attentions of his [disabled] son Edward, who takes evening classes. At first antagonistic toward her, Pettigrew later becomes enamored of her. When she rebuffs him, he is furious and proclaims her wanton. The angered villagers drive her to the hills, but she is saved from their fury by Fear O'God, a mysterious stranger who lives a solitary life in a mountain cabin to which he takes her. To stop any scandal Fear O'God takes Beatrice to Pettigrew and makes him marry them, telling her he will give her a divorce whenever she wants it. She is, however, content. Pettigrew is vastly angry with this turn of events, and begins a feud. When his son suddenly disappears from the village he has Fear O'God arrested for his murder, and in spite of no body being found Fear O'God, the hermit, is tried, found guilty, and imprisoned. After a year in jail, he escapes and seeks shelter in the mountains with his wife and baby. When the child becomes ill, Fear O'God goes to the village for a doctor. He meets Pettigrew and a fight occurs, but the sudden return of Pettigrew's son puts everything in order and all ends happily."

Note. *John Russell Taylor (entry 499) credits Charles Lapworth with the story.

3   *The Lodger, A Story of the London Fog* (1926)

Director	Alfred Hitchcock
Assistant Director	Alma Reville
Producer	Michael Balcon
Production Company	Gainsborough
Screenplay	Eliot Stannard, based on the novel by Marie Adelaide Belloc-Lowndes

Photography	Baron [Gaetano] Ventimiglia
Editing and Titles	Ivor Montagu
Inter-Titles Design	E. McKnight Kauffer
Art Direction	C. Wilfred Arnold, Bertram Evans
Cast	Ivor Novello (the Lodger), Malcolm Keen (Joe Betts), June (Daisy Bunting), Arthur Chesney (Mr. Bunting), Marie Ault (Mrs. Bunting)
Filmed	at Islington Studios, London
Running Time	approximately 100 minutes
Distributor	Wardour & F., Amer-anglo Corp. (U.S.)
Release Date	September 1926

Other titles: *The Lodger, The Case of Jonathan Drew* (U.S.), *Les Cheveux d'Or, Il Pensionante, Le Locataire*

Synopsis

A black V closes over a figure chiseled in black on the white background, and the credits appear on the now-black background. When they are finished, the V opens again to reveal the figure, angled across the screen.

Close-up: a woman screams in the night. A neon sign blinks: To-Night. Golden Curls. The camera sits at a low angle next to a woman's body sprawled in the street, street lamps converging in the distance behind. Another woman talks to the police, while a reporter jots down her words and a group of bystanders gawk. A note is found on the body from the Avenger, the signature inside a triangle. The investigation continues at a serving counter, where steaming cups are handed down. The reporter calls from a telephone booth. The witness describes the murderer, a man with a scarf pulled up over the lower half of his face. A man standing nearby imitates the description and she gasps, pointing in horror.

Editors group around the wire in the newsroom and avidly scan the fresh copy.[H] The presses roll. Roped stacks of newspaper are thrown onto the trucks and driven to the streets. The headlines scream: "Murder! The Avenger! Another fair-haired woman dead." People rush to buy papers as the news is flashed on a neon bulletin board and announced on the radio. Close-ups of angry and fearful faces fade into one another. To-Night. Golden Curls.

After a performance, happy chorus dancers in huge curly blond wigs crowd into a dressing room to hear the news; a blond thoughtfully strokes her hair, and a friend jokes with the group, covering his face with a cloth.

A triangle decorates a title: "Daisy." The blond Daisy Bunting, white fur billowing around her, models fashions in an elegant showroom. The news is announced in her dressing room. "No more peroxide," says one and another sticks some dark curls under her hat announcing "Safety-first!"

Out on the sidewalk, Mr. Bunting buys a newspaper and steps down into his home, where Mrs. Bunting rolls some dough in the below-street-level kitchen and chats with Joe Betts, a detective friend of Daisy's. He reads to Joe about the seventh successive Tuesday murder of a blond woman and teases him about his force being ineffective. Daisy arrives home and Joe teases her, "I'm keen on golden hair myself, just as the Avenger is." Daisy laughs, but turns away. Only momentarily put off, he cuts out a couple of hearts from the dough and pushes

them toward her. She picks up one and throws it back near him; he tears it in two, and throws it back toward her. Mrs. Bunting enjoys the "courtship," but her husband throws a less amused glance her way. A wall lamp flickers out at the same time a shadow approaches their front door. After the parents leave, Joe grabs Daisy and abruptly kisses her.

In the hallway outside the kitchen door, Mr. Bunting steps up onto a chair to reach the electric meter, while Mrs. Bunting opens the front hall door to a wild-eyed man in a black cape, surrounded by fog, a muffler wrapped around his neck and face. She grimaces, but lets him in. Slowly he reveals his face and asks about the room to let. Hidden at the rear of the stairway, Mr. Bunting suddenly falls from the chair and lands on his back. The man starts at the noise, appearing very somber. Mrs. Bunting walks back to see her daughter laughing heartily at her father, who is unable to rise from his position, then returns to show the room.

Upstairs in the large, two-room suite, the lodger looks ominously around the walls at the portraits of fair-haired women, the last one a picture of a woman tied to a tree. Wide-eyed, he walks over, hand to his breast, and stares. Moving to the window for air, he sees on the street a hawker with a sandwich board announcing the murders, and he throws back his head and winces. Mrs. Bunting points out the adjoining bedroom and he wearily sits down, facing away from her, and throws some bills on the table for a month's rent. She protests, but he shivers in disgust and demands "Nothing more, please, just some bread and butter and milk." He is left alone, staring out, then carefully picks up his black satchel and hides it in a cabinet.

Downstairs, Mr. Bunting entertains his daughter and Joe with tricks, as Mrs. Bunting returns to the Lodger's room and finds him turning the portraits to the wall. "I'm afraid I don't like these pictures," he complains, so she calls Daisy, who enters laughing, thinking the portrait problem humorous. The Lodger turns from his head-holding stance at the fireplace to glare at her as she and her mother remove the pictures. He softens and apologizes, "They got on my nerves," but Mrs. Bunting frowns.

Downstairs, Joe and Daisy are kissing in the parlor when Mrs. Bunting returns with the last picture. Ever joking, Joe comments that he is glad the Lodger is not "keen on the girls," and Daisy disconcertedly looks away. Joe jokes and pokes her until she jumps, when suddenly all three hear the Lodger pacing. As they gape up at the ceiling, he appears as they imagine him from beneath, walking above them, only the chandelier in between.

Next morning, Daisy takes breakfast to the Lodger. Dressed in a suit, he sits at the table reading the paper. He seems more relaxed and smiles at her, animatedly illustrating a point by jabbing a butter knife in the air. Briefly, he teases her by blocking her way in front of the door, then graciously opens it for her and returns to his newspaper. She slowly moves down the stairs and kisses her mother good-bye in the kitchen.

Title over a geometric sunburst design: "One evening, a few days later, the Lodger made himself agreeable." The Lodger, in an elegant smoking jacket, and Daisy, in a slinky dress with pearls, play chess and flirt in front of the fireplace in his room. "Be careful, I'll get you yet," he warns. She drops a chess piece on the floor and as she reaches to pick it up, he leans over with her, but picks up the fireplace poker and stares at her.

Meanwhile, Joe appears in the kitchen window and enters to find Mrs. Bunting trying to tie her husband's black tie, jerking him back to position when he tries to say hello.

Upstairs, the Lodger pokes the fire alive.

"Great news," Joe announces, "they've put me on the Avenger case." Mrs. Bunting leaves as Mr. Bunting explains that he is an extra waiter for a dinner party that night.

Meanwhile Daisy and the Lodger are alternately bowing their heads over the game and peering at each other, their heads only a chess board apart. "Beautiful golden curls," mutters the Lodger, starting to touch her. The camera moves to a long shot as Daisy starts and the two sit back in their chairs. Mrs. Bunting enters and Daisy leaves to go meet Joe. Mrs. Bunting stays to poke the fire as the Lodger stands by, his eyes darting. Noticing some coins on the mantel, Mrs. Bunting tells him he should lock up his money; "It's tempting Providence." "Providence is concerned with sterner things than money," he stiffly replies.

Downstairs, Joe banters with Mr. Bunting, showing him some brand new handcuffs "for the Avenger." Mr. Bunting declares he will be gone most of the night. Daisy appears smiling, and Joe announces that when he has put a rope around the Avenger's neck, he will "put a ring around Daisy's finger." Daisy turns away and frowns. Mr. Bunting leaves and Joe grabs Daisy's hand, but she steps away, then laughingly rushes up the stairs while he chases her, playfully putting the handcuffs on her at the landing. Suddenly losing her smile, she screams out in anger. Mrs. Bunting and the Lodger hear her and run to the top of the stairs where the Lodger impassively observes the couple as they tussle and Daisy pleads to have the cuffs removed. Mrs. Bunting walks down and escorts Daisy away, leaving Joe scratching his head, while the Lodger, still unobserved by them, turns away in satisfaction.

Joe follows Daisy and her mother into the parlor and makes apologies, which Daisy, who pouts at first, finally accepts. They kiss for a moment, then she suddenly runs off upstairs, leaving Joe again scratching his head. He closes the door and consults with Mrs. Bunting, both facing the camera. "Does this lodger of yours mean any harm to Daisy?" "Don't be silly," Mrs. Bunting laughs, "he's not that sort." Joe agrees, "Even if he is a bit queer, he's a gentleman."

Later that night after the show, the dancers finish dressing and file out. Outside, a brunette woman drives off in a chauffeured automobile with a man in evening dress, revealing a more modestly dressed man waiting on the sidewalk for a blond woman, who eventually emerges and greets him with a kiss.

Meanwhile, police file through the streets, and the Lodger emerges from his room enshrouded in his scarf. Hearing him, Mrs. Bunting sits up in bed alarmed; expressionistic shadows fill the wall behind her. The camera views his exit from above, his hand sliding down the banister. She rises to see him cross the street outside.

Outside a large spired building, the blond woman stomps her foot, and she and her boyfriend part ways. She stops near a street lamp to fix her shoe, then suddenly turns to look up in terror and screams. A woman, sleeping on a stoop with her child, slowly wakes, a cat jumps out of a garbage can, and a policeman turns his head. A dark figure walks quickly away from the camera. A crowd gathers around the woman and the Avenger's card is uncovered.

At home, Mrs. Bunting wakes, the camera viewing her from above as she goes slowly downstairs and into the Lodger's room to investigate. She finds the locked cabinet door just as the Lodger returns.

Next morning, Daisy finishes the Lodger's tray, while her parents both yawn. Her father jumps up from his chair at the news in the paper: "There's been another one last night—just around the corner." Mrs. Bunting, suddenly

faint, grabs the counter, then leans over his shoulder to read. Joe appears coming down the stairs outside the kitchen and walks in, upset, pulling on his suspenders. His eyes are cased in dark circles as he sits at the table; "The way that fiend did her in . . ." Mrs. Bunting, standing behind him, clutches her breast. Suddenly Daisy screams upstairs and Joe runs up, Mr. and Mrs. Bunting following.

Joe barges into the Lodger's room to find Daisy in the man's arms and them both laughing. They do not part as he approaches and pulls Daisy away, demanding to know what he is doing with her. Mrs. Bunting arrives to console Daisy, but Daisy pulls away and retorts, "I was silly enough to be scared by a mouse." "That's no excuse for you to take hold of her," shouts Joe and the three continue to argue as Daisy kneels on the floor cleaning up the spillage. The Lodger walks to his door and commands Joe out of his room. Joe first insists on taking Daisy with him; she follows, but apologizes to the Lodger on her way out as her mother watches, wide-eyed. Swiftly closing the door behind the pair and blocking her way out, he warns his landlady, "If I am disturbed like this again, I shall have to go elsewhere."

Downstairs Daisy and Joe argue. "Sorry I lost my temper, but there's something about him I can't stand," pleads Joe to her back. On her way down, Mrs. Bunting listens at the door and smiles as they kiss and make up.

Later, Mrs. Bunting tells her husband that the Lodger went out late the night before, "and half-an-hour later he came creeping back as if he didn't want to be heard." Mr. Bunting pokes her in the shoulder in disbelief and goes back to his paper. She stares out, then at the portraits that line the room, and leans over to him, "You don't think that he . . ." Mr. Bunting wonders now. "Anyway, Daisy mustn't be left alone with him again, understand?" and he agrees. They both stare up at the ceiling chandelier.

The Lodger sits in the audience at Daisy's modeling session. A title announces Daisy who walks out in a slinky, shiny dress, smiling at him. He signals an attendant.

At headquarters, Joe talks with a group of detectives. "If one makes a plan of the murders, one can see they have been moving steadily in a certain direction." The men nod and Joe brings out a map showing where the next murder will be. The marks of the crime scenes are filling in a triangle on the map.

That evening, Daisy enters the parlor where her mother embroiders and her father fixes a clock. She opens a box on the table and excitedly pulls out the dress she modeled that afternoon, telling her parents that the Lodger had seen her in it, "but I never dreamed he was going to buy it for me." Her mother is appalled and Mr. Bunting agitatedly boxes up the dress and takes it upstairs. Hesitating, he enters the Lodger's room and sets the box in front of him on the table. Hurt, the Lodger appeals but Mr. Bunting insists his daughter cannot accept presents from strangers. The Lodger broods and looks away. On his way down the stairway, Mr. Bunting talks excitedly to his wife. Upstairs, the Lodger's hand limply falls to his lap. He stands, dejected, then looks at the door with resolve.

Title decorated with expressionist geometric design: "That same evening." Daisy undresses and runs a steamy bath. At his table, the Lodger smokes and mulls over a city map with the same triangle that the police have marked. Going to the window, he lets the drape fall back on the rain outside, then turns, hearing Daisy singing in her bath. In the hallway, he tries the bathroom door, but it is locked so he knocks. Daisy wraps herself in a towel and goes to the door. "You're not angry with me about that dress?" he calls to her on the other side. She laughs

when he worriedly mentions that her father does not want them to go out together. Title: "But Daisy didn't worry."

Later, Mrs. Bunting cleans up the Lodger's table while he goes out and meets Daisy at the bottom of the stairs. Mrs. Bunting overhears and runs through the house calling for her daughter. Mr. Bunting finds her at the bottom of the stairs and she falls on him, "I let her go out with the Lodger . . . and it's Tuesday night!"

Daisy and the Lodger sit down on a bench on a dark street, a lamp behind them. He takes her hand and they start to kiss just as Joe rounds a corner and demands the Lodger let her go. The Lodger slowly rises and Joe leans into him, but Daisy jumps up between them and shouts at Joe, "I'm sick and tired of your interference; I never want to see you again." Sickened, Joe does not give up, but Daisy asks the Lodger to take her home, and Joe is left desolate on the bench, head in hands. He looks up, then down again at a footprint in the ground. A montage of what he knows about the Lodger—the paintings, his embrace with Daisy, and his pacing—is superimposed on the footprint. Joe rises with new vigor.

At home, Mr. Bunting helps his wife take a drink, as Daisy and the Lodger walk up the stairs. They go into his room and he turns her toward him. She bows her head and he closes his eyes, his chin on her hair. They talk and laugh and a close-up moves into his face, now very serious, and an extreme close-up of his lips. They kiss. Mr. and Mrs. Bunting sit in the kitchen despondent. Upstairs on the couch, the Lodger pushes Daisy away, and she pleads with him to return to her.

Meanwhile her parents go to the front door to greet Joe and his men, who want a word with the Lodger. Upstairs, Joe barges in on a kiss and says he has a warrant to search the room. Joe demands the key to the cabinet and they find the satchel with a gun in it and the map of the Avenger murders along with some news clippings. The Lodger, leaning dejectedly on the table, claims his sister was the first victim. Daisy looks gratefully upward, but Joe insists on making an arrest. The Lodger tries to collar him, but Joe's men overpower him and lead him handcuffed downstairs, where the Buntings huddle together in horror. "Meet me by the lamp," the Lodger tells Daisy, then runs out the door. Mrs. Bunting faints, and the police set out for the chase, while Daisy stands petrified, holding the Lodger's coat.

On the bench under the street lamp, the Lodger waits, dejected and cold, still handcuffed. He curls up on top of the bench, dozing until Daisy finds him, and he tells her the story of his sister.

The Lodger and his sister dance at her coming-out ball; the camera moves through a window to observe the scene. Suddenly, a gloved hand flicks the lights out. When the lights are turned on again, the crowd surrounds her dead body.

The Lodger explains that his mother died from the shock.

He sits on his mother's white-lace bed and at her request swears he will not rest until the Avenger is brought to justice.

Daisy is sympathetic as he laments that now he will miss his chance. She wraps him in his coat and walks him to a pub for some brandy. Inside, curious onlookers stare as she holds the glass for him to drink. They leave just before Joe and his men arrive. The onlookers are excited to hear Joe announce on the telephone to his chief that the fugitive is handcuffed and nearby, but after they have run off to give chase, he is told that the real Avenger has just been taken "red-handed."

Outside, Daisy, and the Lodger split up as the crowd chases after him. "Quickly, before they tear him to pieces," yells Joe to his men. The crowd, now

grown large, races after the Lodger. He catches his handcuffs on a railing and hangs dangling above another street below. The crowd converges on both sides and beat on him until blood appears at his mouth.[H] Joe and his two men push through the crowd. Finally they extricate him just as the evening paper announces the Avenger's arrest. Daisy kisses the collapsed, but still conscious, Lodger.

In a bright white hospital room, a doctor stands over the Lodger's bed and speaks to Daisy, seated on the other side. "He has suffered a severe nervous strain, but his youth and vigor will pull him through." With great effort, the Lodger pulls his hand out from under the cover to find hers.

Title: "All stories have an end." The Lodger walks down a staircase in his lavish home to greet Daisy and the Buntings, who are agape at the luxury. Daisy stands with him as her mother offers the toothbrush he left behind. Mr. Bunting suggests he and his wife go to the fireplace and make themselves at home, as the Lodger and Daisy walk off. The camera moves in as they kiss in front of a large window, city lights in the distance, and the sign still blinking: "To-Night. Golden Curls."

Note.[H] Hitchcock does two bits, as a man in the newsroom and as an onlooker during the Lodger's beating at the hands of the crowd.

Remakes: *The Lodger* (U.S., 1944), directed by John Brahm, and *Man in the Attic* (U.S., 1953) directed by Hugo Fregnese.

4 *Downhill* (1927)

Director	Alfred Hitchcock
Assistant Director	Frank Mills
Producer	Michael Balcon
Production Company	Gainsborough
Screenplay	Eliot Stannard, based on a play by Ivor Novello and Constance Collier (under the pseudonym David LeStrange)
Photography	Claude McDonnell
Art Direction	Bert Evans
Editing	Lionel Rich*
Cast	Ivor Novello (Roddy Berwick), Robin Irvine (Tim Wakeley), Isabel Jeans (Julia), Ian Hunter (the Man, Archie), Norman McKinnel (Sir Thomas Berwick), Annette Benson (Mabel), Sybil Rhoda (Sybil Wakeley), Lillian Braithwaite (Lady Berwick), Violet Farebrother (the poet), Ben Webster (Dr. Dawson), Hannah Jones (the dressmaker), Jerrold Robertshaw (Rev. Henry Wakeley), Barbara Gott (Mrs. Michet), Alfred Goddard (the Swede), J. Nelson (Hibbert)
Filmed	at Islington Studios, London
Running Time	approximately 105 minutes

Distributor   Wardour & F., World Wide Dist.
                                               (U.S.)
Release Date   May 1927
Other titles: *When Boys Leave Home* (U.S.), *La Pente*

Synopsis

Titles: "A tale of two schoolboys who made a pact of loyalty" and "The World of Youth."

A young man blows on a whistle. A crowd cheers. Roddy Berwick, a handsome, dark-haired boy, grabs the football during a tackle. The scene widens to include the field and the large crowd of onlookers. Children squabble, but the crowd is having a good time. The hero of the game, Roddy, smiles broadly, then frowns slightly as the crowd rushes at him and picks him up on its shoulders. The crowd filters over into the soft-lit, ivy-covered gothic walls of the school halls.

In the kitchen, Mabel, a dark-haired, gay servant, writes a note: "I'll be in the Bunne Shoppe after 6 P.M. Do come."

The families and the boy students in their striped caps mingle in the corridors. Tim Wakely stops by a bulletin board with his father, Reverend Wakely, who points to a notice about the Roynford Scholarship. "Tim, if you can get that, I can afford to send you to Oxford." His younger brothers chase each other and fight in the bare stairwell. Their sister, Sybil, follows to watch over them, and runs into Roddy, who is standing half-naked in the washroom with the door propped open. He starts at the sight of her, quickly grabs a towel, and covers himself.

Startled, she walks back down to join her family at the bulletin board. They proceed into a large dining hall where tables are stretched out in rows.

Mabel sticks her note in Tim's hand and purses her lips at him. The hundred or so people rise in their places to say grace, and Roddy just makes it to the entrance in time to bow his head. Mabel pauses near him and steps on his toe, forcing him to smile, but his stern father frowns at them from across the room. A title quotes part of the Latin prayer. At the table, Tim reads the note from Mabel, who flirts with him as she serves cake and coffee. Roddy, now in a striped tie too, sits next to Sybil and across from his father. A close-up shows a young boy shooting food out of his straw, first at Mabel, then into one of the gentlemen's cups; everyone looks up for the source of this traveling matter. It's 5:20 P.M.

The clock in the tower shows 6:05 P.M. A close-up of the rendezvous note dissolves into Ye Olde Bunne Shoppe. Mabel waits in the doorway, then quickly primps herself when she sees the boys on the sidewalk.

Inside the store is crowded with a few tables and a large candy counter. Tim and Roddy walk with Mabel through the beaded curtain into the back room. She puts on a record and starts to shimmy, pursing her lips at the boys and singing along. She and Roddy dance, while Tim taps his fingers and bounces along with the music. The couple dances through another beaded curtain into a darkened room and Tim cranes his neck, trying to keep them in sight; inside, light through the blinds crosses over them. Some children enter to buy candy and Mabel rushes out front to help them. Roddy disdainfully picks one of her hairs off his coat, then mocks Tim's attachment to her, holding his hand over his heart. She returns, dancing again, though the men are quiet on either side of the room. Tim finally decides to take Mabel in his arms, but he is not as smooth a dancer as Roddy and

steps on her toe. She impatiently pushes him away, preferring to flirt with Roddy, but he is no longer interested. She returns to Tim and he dances her through the beaded curtain.

Out front, a dirt-spotted urchin enters and Roddy goes out to help him, making fun of the grimy half-penny he proffers. Roddy puts on a lampshade hat, and finally trades the half-penny for a large box of fancy candy. Continuing to be slapdash, he rings up £1 for the sale. Returning to the back, he notices Tim and Mabel passionately kissing, the beads clinging to them; then a crowd of urchins appears behind him holding out their hands. Mabel appears and shooshes them away. She and Roddy argue as he explains at length about the sale, then gives her some bills to make up for it. When they leave, Mabel leans over to kiss Roddy, but he laughs in her face. She immediately becomes angry, and Tim, embarrassed and sullen, gives her a quick peck.

A large hall with a dais. Roddy has been appointed Captain of the School; a new striped hat and insignia go with the honor.

Close-up of the hat, sitting on top of a box from the Bunne Shoppe. Tim studies in his room, graced with curved, leaded glass windows, and suddenly throws the Bunne Shoppe box to the floor in disgust. Roddy sarcastically picks it up with his foot and replaces it on the table. Their valet enters and announces the headmaster wants to see them both. "Me!?" cries Tim.

They follow the servant down a vast corridor into a huge, sparely furnished room, gothic windows on one side, the master behind his desk at the far wall. Unnoticed by them, Mabel sits near the door; the camera moves with them as they walk the long way to the desk. "You can no doubt guess why I have sent for you," announces the headmaster. Mabel swells menacingly in her chair. She drops her purse, and Roddy turns, then Tim. Roddy gulps. "The girl has brought a most serious charge"; the boys stare as Mabel angrily narrows her eyes and shouts until the headmaster quiets her. "Which boy is it?" demands the head-master. Mabel sneers as she rises and the camera now moves with her as she walks toward the two boys; pausing in the middle of them, she points at Roddy, who bursts out laughing.

Tim is dismissed, and he walks out hunched over. Mabel turns to Roddy and flings her pearls at him in disgust. A close-up shows the bitterness of her face; superimposed over her is the payment Roddy made for the candy at the Bunne Shoppe, and the sign, saying closed Wednesdays. She shouts, "He's rolling in money—He's got to see me through it!" The headmaster sends her into the next room, and the two men sit, facing one another as he asks, "Have you nothing to say?" Told he can remain one more night at school, Roddy wonders, pouting slightly, "Won't I be able to play for the Old Boys, Sir?"

The long hall back. Train schedules. Tim is seen in the light of their dorm window as Roddy packs his bags and sneers. "I couldn't speak, Roddy, my scholarship . . ." pleads Tim, and Roddy nods. "You needn't be afraid. I won't sneak," he says.

Going down the stairway, Roddy pauses near the bulletin board. Tim starts after him, then halts. The large school courtyard is empty when Roddy, in extreme long shot from above, crosses it.

Neon lights of the city. Roddy enters his home, a huge stone mansion with marble stairs and banister. He greets his mother, then collapses in a chair in the sunken, columned, living room. He hears his father arrive with another formally attired gentleman, and jumps up belatedly after they walk by him into the room. "I've heard great things about you," congratulates the other man, as Father in the

foreground mixes a drink, and starts at the sight of the calendar, realizing his son is home early.

After the guest is gone, Roddy begins, "That waitress . . ." but his father is furious, "Expelled!" Roddy swears he did nothing, but his father calls him a LIAR! After Roddy walks out disgusted, his mother pleads for him, but his father chains the door. Roddy enters the Underground and proceeds down one of the steep escalators.

Titles: "So the pact was kept—at a price" and "The World of Make-Believe."

Close-up of Roddy serving espresso to a couple at a café table, the man vigorously eating, the woman staring off languorously. Roddy pockets something from the table after they rise to leave. The scene widens into a stage musical, bathing beauties kicking in the front row, Roddy, in his apron several rows back, singing in the chorus.

In a dressing room, Roddy sulks.

In his dressing room, the star actor, Archie, commands his servant, and blows smoke.

The shot is matched by one of the star actress, Julia, in her room, as she smokes, primps in her mirror, and squirts perfume at a portrait of her leading man. Roddy enters and she playfully leans back to look at him upside down. Accepting the cigarette case she "forgot," she flirts with him, flipping her pearls, and shivering at the rain outside. She comments on his lack of an overcoat, but he insists he never wears one. Archie appears carrying his huge fur coat and installs himself unnoticed in a stuffed chair on the other side of the room. The two continue their flirtation as Julia accuses Roddy of "falling in love" with her. Finally Roddy discovers they are not alone when Archie sneezes and squirts some seltzer into a drink.

Outside in the rain, the three take a taxi together. The camera follows along, positioned on the outside, sheets of rain covering the vehicle; Archie sits in the dark while Julia, brightly lit, and Roddy, across, flirt.

Roddy rides the bus home.

His shadow fills the narrow stairwell of his apartment building as he walks up to his dingy room at the top. Opening his mail, he finds he has inherited £30,000.

Later, he enters Julia's dressing room in a new suit of evening clothes. Nervously, he smiles at her, again failing to notice Archie sitting with his back turned on the other side of the room. He shows her the letter and she points to the smoke rising out of Archie's chair. Feeling clever, he writes "Supper?" on her hand mirror. Archie engages Roddy in talk and then hands him a sheaf of bills, "They're yours, regard them as an entrance fee." Nonplussed, but smitten, Roddy stands back as Julia and Archie glare at one another. Roddy and Julia leave. The cheery maid helps Archie with his huge fur coat, but he flicks his cigar ash in her outstretched hand.

Once again, the three take a cab together, but Julia sits next to Roddy this time. A close-up from above shows Julia and Archie rubbing knees.

News item: Famous actress weds. Archie leaves the reception with an *au revoir*, while Roddy, enraptured, smiles at his bride.

Light glows over a mound of feathers draped over Julia's back. She and Roddy kiss, but she moves over to the dressing table to fix her hair and he rises in frustration, walking over to sulk by the large, curved closet doors.

Another day, Julia receives Archie in their elegant city apartment. He

advises her to send her jewels to her own bank before the crash comes. Suddenly they hear Roddy arrive, and Archie hides in the closet. Julia walks into the parlor to greet Roddy while he is mulling over a stack of overdue bills. Angry, he shows her one informing him of his overdrawn bank account. He sits down at the secretary, and she pleads with him, then he accidentally places his hand on Archie's top hat. Roddy rages into the bedroom, stares at the closet door, and peeks into the right-hand one, just as Archie sneezes while attempting to sneak out of the left-hand door. They struggle, and Julia grabs a large vase from a stand in order to protect it, as the men move into the parlor punching one another. Finally, Archie lands on the floor near a stuffed animal. "Get out! Both of you!" yells Roddy. "You made the flat over to me, so you can get out yourself!" Julia reminds him. He laughs pitifully.

In the apartment elevator, he descends several flights.

Title: "The world of lost illusion."

Neon signs light up a Paris Music Hall. By day, it is a grubby, empty street.

A crowd swirls around a dance floor. A title introduces "Madame, La Patronne, expert in human nature," a large, sequined, wily looking woman. As Roddy dances, she advises a customer that he is a "nice, English boy, cheap at 50 francs a dance." Roddy also attracts the attention of another older woman, who is muscular and large-featured (in the credits named "the poet") and raptly stares at him. Between dances, Roddy obtains a tip from a man whose partner he has entertained, but La Patronne grabs it out of his hands, reminding him that he now owes her forty-five francs. Roddy shrugs. La Patronne sits down with the large woman, and they discuss Roddy's price.

The woman is nervous as Roddy approaches and sits down with her. "How did you come to this—poor boy," she smiles. He tells her his story. Later, he continues, ". . . and then I married—that was the worst part." The crowd has thinned considerably as the band packs up, and he catches himself, wondering why he is telling her all this. But the woman is still wide-eyed, enraptured. "You seem different, somehow, among all this artificiality," he says peering at her. She breathes deeply.

Over at another table, a man passes out, and someone rushes to open the curtains and large windows. Air, and the bright light of day, floods into the hall, making people blink. Roddy starts, and the camera circles the room with him, coldly taking in the smeared makeup and groggy faces of the twenty or so customers scattered around the hall. He lights on the yearning face of his companion. "Come with me," she mouths. But he stands and turns away and she goes off in the other direction. At another table, La Patronne counts her money as Roddy strides to the door and says good-bye.

Outside, the double doors of the hall, twice his size, dwarf him.

Title: "Downhill, till what was left of him was thrown to rats at Marseilles dockside."

A kerchiefed woman, or perhaps a man in blackface, and two younger men, one black, one white, sit around a table in a shack. "Best take him back to London," says one, thinking there might be some money in it. Off in a side room, Roddy lies on a bed of rags, raving, "You've got to take me back, Father!" Hearing him, the three enter and excitedly discuss their charge, "He's dotty—seeing things!" They drag him into the kitchen and feed him some soup. Roddy offers them the few coins he has left, then they search him and find a letter to Tim Wakely: "I'm done for, dead and buried, but I've kept my promise." The men argue

about what to do with him, but finally drag him up and out, down a nearby plank to a ship. Leaning on them, he staggers along, as they help him down into a lower cabin and place him in an upper bunk.

Still delirious, he sees beneath him one of the sailors, who turns around and becomes his scowling father. In his fever Roddy sees Julia, Archie, La Patronne, the woman from the dance hall, and Mabel all leaning around a table and arguing over his money, pointing and laughing at him. The ship's engines roll. Roddy's mind turns into a whirring record as the women from his past make kissing lips at him. He wakes, startled, crying, "No! No!," but Ye Olde Bunne Shoppe closes in on him, and he falls back asleep. Outside the portal is the sea.

Title: "Five days and nights in a world of delirium."

Roddy awakens with a start. Outside, a policeman turns toward him, showing the face of his scowling father. Roddy gets down and walks out into the bright light of the dock. A series of dissolves create a montage around him of the industry near the dock, the neighborhoods, and downtown lights of the city. Title: "Blind instinct led him home."

Roddy stands at his columned, double front door. He hesitates, then rings the bell. The butler, very happy to see him, pulls him inside. His parents are out, so he collapses with relief into the stuffed chair still larger than he is, by the fireplace in the parlor. Hearing a key in the door, he cringes, then waits while his father walks past him into the room. Standing behind his father, who is in the foreground, Roddy stammers, "F-f-father!" Father turns aghast, "I've been searching for you to ask your pardon. . . . Can you forgive me?" Roddy grins, as his mother, walking down the marble stairs behind, brightens at the sight of him. They all hug.

On the field at the Old Boys Match, Roddy, in his striped cap, grabs the ball.

Note. *Some filmographies credit Ivor Montagu with film editing.

5   *Easy Virtue* (1927)

Director	Alfred Hitchcock
Assistant Director	Frank Mills
Producers	Michael Balcon, C. M. Woolf
Production Company	Gainsborough Pictures
Screenplay	Eliot Stannard, based on the play by Noel Coward
Photography	Claude McDonnell
Editing	Ivor Montagu
Art Direction	Clifford Pember
Cast	Isabel Jeans (Larita Filton), Franklin Dyall (her husband), Eric Bransby Williams (Claude Robson, the co-respondent), Ian Hunter (plaintiff's counsel), Robin Irvine (John Whittaker), Violet Farebrother (Mrs. Whittaker), Frank Elliott (Mr. Whittaker), Darcia Deane (his older sister), Dorothy Boyd (his younger sister), Enid Stamp Taylor (Sarah)

Filmed	at Islington Studios, London
Running Time	approximately 105 minutes
Distributor	Wardour and F., World Wide Dist. (U.S.)
Release Date	August 1927

Other titles: *Le Passé Ne Meurt Pas, Vertù Facile*

Synopsis

A title is shown at the end of the credits which appear over the silhouette of a camera: "Virtue is its own reward they say, but 'easy virtue' is society's reward for a slandered reputation."

A document announces the divorce proceedings of *Filton vs. Filton and Robson.*

The top of a rug-type white wig, sewn down the middle. The judge raises his head from the bench, looks through his monocle at the audience, finds the speaker (the plaintiff's counsel), yawns, and lowers his glass. Through the blur, he hears Mrs. Larita Filton, a young blond woman, speaking and raises his glass to view her. The questioning continues: "Do you wish the jury to believe that the co-respondent never kissed you?" She shakes her head and hand, no, then stops, realizing her admission, and stares at her hand in the air. The crowd becomes agitated and the judge silences them. The counsel asks her to repeat her statement about a decanter he holds in his hands.

A close-up of the decanter leads to a flashback of the scene being described. Mr. Filton, dressed in a business suit, pours a drink from the decanter as the scene widens to show the artist painting a portrait of the defendant, who sits lavishly robed in an elegant chair. She glances sideways at her husband gulping another drink, then raises her hand to stop him from pouring another one, but he goes ahead, and she remains impassive as he angrily leans toward her.

A close-up of his scowling face brings the action back to the courtroom, as Mr. Filton suddenly rises and shouts above the voice of his counsel, who tries to silence him. She continues to defend herself calmly, "And so, for three days, I was unable to sit for my portrait . . ." One of the jurors writes the next question on a notepad: "Was the maid always present when Larita disrobed?"

Back to the scene in the studio, Larita finishes dressing with the help of her maid, then walks out into the main room and assumes her pose. The artist brightens the light around her, adjusts her gown, touches her hand. "That hurts, Claude; he bruised by wrist after he'd been drinking." "I promise you he'll never get another drink here," the artists swears.

The decanter once again becomes the focus in the courtroom. "Do you suggest that your husband is a habitual drunkard?" Larita looks sadly at the jurors and nods yes. The juror adds to her pad: the artist and the woman he pitied, alone together . . . pity is akin to love. Bored, the judge interrupts to ask if so many details are necessary! Larita and the opposing counsel are now juxtaposed in complementary close-ups as they speak, back and forth, question and answer. The jury's attention moves from one to the other, and someone methodically swings a chain, then a clock pendulum ticks.

The counsel presents a letter from the artist: Darling, why suffer that foul brute when you know I'd give everything I have in the world to make you happy. Claude.

Larita sits reading it in the studio as Claude walks over to her, but she greets him skeptically. He pleads with her, but she resists his attentions, though they are close together, almost touching. Suddenly her husband appears in the doorway. They wait in shock, the artist wide-eyed in the foreground, Larita staring out from behind his shoulder, as Mr. Filton laughs hysterically, then approaches them. He circles toward Claude; Larita tries to stop him, but he angrily pulls away from her. Claude runs to a desk drawer, pulls out a gun, and shoots Mr. Filton, who runs toward Claude and furiously beats him, then collapses. Claude is aghast, still holding the gun. Larita is despondent; she picks up her husband and he wakes, then looks down and picks up the fallen letter.

Holding up the letter, the prosecution continues its attack. "Didn't the co-respondent already leave you everything in his will?" "Yes, but . . ." The juror notes in her pad: nearly £2,000 a year.

The jury sits around a table and debates the case: "An attractive wife with a drunken husband; she is left alone with the man who loves her AND the co-respondent left all his money to another man's wife! The evidence seems conclusive."

The verdict is announced over the image of a camera; the jury files into the courtroom. Larita Filton is found guilty of misconduct with the "late Claude Robson." The audience files out of the room.

Larita walks out the front door and hides her face from the large group of reporters and photographers. A title announces her escape to a vacation in the Mediterranean.

At her hotel, she starts to sign the register, then stops. A camera looms in her imagination and she signs a false name.

Title: "She could hide her scarred heart, but not her magnetic charm. . . . Soon came attentions which she most desired to avoid." At the hotel desk, her identity and notoriety is commented upon.

Lounging near the tennis courts, she is hit by a ball. The perpetrator, John Whittaker, walks over to apologize. While gazing into her bruised eye, he becomes enamored.

They walk into the hotel; people stare. They relax on a terrace overlooking the sea and flirt. An attendant dabs something on Larita's eyes. John gets up to make drinks, begins to shake the mixture, then stops, pensive; she laughs, and he resumes his task, smiling. Sitting down with her, he sees a card with some flowers "from the Duc . . . with undying admiration." He kisses her hand; she flutters her eyes.

The next morning John brings flowers to her room; Larita averts her eyes from his gaze. She sits back, raises her arms high, then spurns him when he approaches. Finally they kiss.

Title: "Larita found something reassuring in John's devotion. It was like a cool breeze sweeping away the ugly memories of the past."

They ride in a horse-drawn buggy along the shore. She enjoys the scenery, pointing at the lovely spots, but he can't see anything but her. She is distressed to hear of his love. "Don't you want to know about me?" He insists his love is enough. And so, she is charmed, and sits back to enjoy the view. He leans around, trying to get her attention, but she remains looking out. "We could marry, go live with my people." Their driver dozes off at the top of the hill, and a car stuck behind them honks its horn. They decide to get down and walk.

Title: "As the evening wore on, so John's patience wore out, until . . ."

A switchboard operator reads on the job until something on the lines begins to interest her. She listens with rapt attention, oohs and ahs, first charmed, then anxious, and is finally happily relieved of the suspense in the conversation.

John's and Larita's luggage is packed and sent. The train arrives, and the happy couple take off in a car through featureless countryside to John's home.

They arrive at a huge mansion made of large timber. John's father graciously greets the new bride at the door. A younger sister smiles, "I thought you'd be dark and foreign looking." A frowning Mrs. Whittaker appears at the top of the stairs. Greeting Larita, she says, "I trust you won't be bored with our simple life."

Mrs. Whittaker informs John that Sarah is dining with them; he looks sick. His younger sister mimics Larita as the older sister takes the newcomer to her room and explains to her that Mrs. Whittaker always expected Sarah to marry John. John and Larita dress for dinner; they talk and hug until the dinner gong is struck and John leaves. The younger sister goes upstairs to fetch Larita, who is still at her dressing table, primping and smoking. The girl is awed by the display of cosmetics.

They go down to the living room and Sarah warmly greets Larita, who continues to smoke.

At the dining table, Mrs. Whittaker wonders if she and Larita have mutual friends. No, says Larita, still smoking. Dinner over, the group disperses.

Mr. Whittaker and John share after-dinner drinks in the next room; John's father admits he finds Larita "fascinating." Mrs. Whittaker enters and confronts her son: "What do you know of this woman? Where does she come from? Who is she?" Mr. Whittaker defends her and John pleads for kindness.

Mr. Whittaker serves drinks in the living room. Glum, John walks in and plops down on the couch. Larita drinks, then says she is tired and goes to bed. John sits back to talk with Sarah.

Larita enters the room upstairs, tells the maid to leave, and sits on the bed, staring out.

Title: "During the days that followed, Mrs. Whittaker made Larita's life a burden to her—in private. But she was all smiles and sweetness with her—in public."

At a polo match, the family sits on the sidelines. Larita notices her ex-husband's counsel and tries to avoid him. Elsewhere, the barrister greets her new husband, and they chat for a while. The women leave. As they are driving out, John waves good-bye to the man. Larita peeks from the back of the car to see who it is, then shrinks to see it is the barrister, who recognizes her.

The Whittaker women send invitations to a dance at their home. Larita offers to help write them, but Mrs. Whittaker dismisses her, and she wanders outside.

The barrister drives up with his wife. They meet Larita, who drifts back into the house, despondent. A camera sits on a table near her and, horrified at the sight of it, she throws a book at it.

Later, Larita sleeps alone, wakes, and screams. John rushes in. "John, I'm miserable, this place is getting on my nerves. Let's go back to the south of France." "But why can't you be happy here?" "Because your family is teaching you to hate me," she replies.

Another day, Larita sits in a lawn chair reading. On the other side of a bush, Sarah tells John, "You're neglecting Larita. It's not fair to her." He admits, "It's all been a terrible mistake. My mother has shown me that." Larita, despondent, gets up and walks off.

John's little sister finds a magazine picture of them all at the polo match, including the divorce counsel. She shows it to Mrs. Whittaker, who lights up: "The Filton divorce!"

In the study, Mr. Whittaker tries to console Larita. Mrs. Whittaker and her daughter discover more pictures of Larita and enter the study armed with them. Larita remains stoic and proud under the attack. "She was concealing a secret!" they cry. Mr. Whittaker defends her, "Larita's past life is no affair of ours." Larita smokes defiantly. Outside, Sarah tells John that no matter what has happened, he must stand by Larita. Larita watches him as he becomes choked at the news and looks away from her, dejected and embarrassed. Mrs. Whittaker continues, "Even though he said no explanations were necessary, you should have told me! It will disgrace us." Larita insists the scandal affected only her. Mrs. Whittaker says, "In our world, we do not understand this code of easy virtue." "In your world, you understand very little of anything," retorts Larita. A servant wanders into the room from the garden, wondering what kind of lantern they want for the party. Mrs. Whittaker glares at him; Larita smiles and indicates a preference. One of the sisters takes him by the arm and leads him out of the room; the other sister is told to follow. Mr. Whittaker tries to smooth over the situation but is forced to give up. Larita sadly looks over at John, then at the rest. "Now that you've exhausted your venom, I shall retire." Mrs. Whittaker indicates she hopes she has the decency to stay in her room during the party as well. Larita laughs and exits. In the next room, Mr. Whittaker consoles her, "It will be O.K., if he really loves you."

That evening at the dining table, John hangs his head. Mrs. Whittaker later announces that they'll prevent a scandal by behaving as usual; John objects to the arrangements, but finally agrees.

The musicians arrive. Mrs. Whittaker chides Sarah about acting as a peacemaker, but Sarah says she feels sorry for John and Larita. The guests arrive.

Upstairs, a servant cuts the bodice netting from the gown Larita is wearing to make it more revealing.

More guests arrive; they inquire about the new bride, but Mrs. Whittaker explains that she has a headache tonight. The crowd grows and John's sister tries to pull him out of his depression. They dance; the floor is now full of couples. Suddenly at the top of the stairs, Larita appears, glowing in feathers and beads and a big smile. All eyes move to her. John, sitting on the stairs beneath her, doesn't notice her until she forces him to turn; then he is dumbstruck. She continues her walk toward Mrs. Whittaker, who alludes to her headache. Larita smiles and says she hasn't any headache, then goes over to greet the divorce counselor. "You sent them spying," she says. No, he protests. They dance, moving out to a side room, where they sit and talk. Larita is distraught, angry with herself for being a coward and marrying John. She asks the lawyer about the possibility of a divorce if she left the suit undefended.

The maid packs her clothes. Larita tells Sarah she is leaving tonight; they kiss.

A legal notice announces *Whittaker vs. Whittaker and Unknown.* The same wig introduces the same judge. Larita watches from the balcony, but a reporter recognizes her. After it is over, she is approached outside by a group of photographers. "Shoot," she says, sticking her chin out defiantly, "there's nothing left to kill."

6 *The Ring* (1927)

Director	Alfred Hitchcock
Assistant Director	Frank Mills
Producer	John Maxwell
Production Company	British International Pictures
Screenplay	Alfred Hitchcock, from his story*
Photography	John J. Cox
Art Direction	C. W. Arnold
Cast	Carl Brisson (Jack Sanders), Lillian Hall-Davies (Nelly), Ian Hunter (Bob Corby), Harry Terry (Showman), Gordon Harker (the trainer), Billy Wells (a boxer), Forrester Harvey (James Ware, the promoter)*
Filmed	at Elstree Studios, London
Running Time	approximately 110 minutes
Distributor	Wardour & F.
Release Date	October 1927

Other titles: *Le Masque De Cuir, Le Ring, La Piste, L'Arène, Vinci Per Me*

Synopsis

Drums beat. The fairgrounds are lively with laughing crowds and whirling rides. The camera swings deliriously back and forth with a young girl on a swing. Close-ups show the barkers' mouths shouting their wares. At one booth, the contest involves dumping a black man into a tank of water by throwing a ball at a lever that collapses his chair. Children throw eggs at one of these men as well; a policeman laughs at their new variation on the game.

The Showman on a stage tries to get volunteers to go up against "one-round" Jack. Nelly, a dark-haired woman, sells tickets from a counter on the ground near the entrance to the large tent behind them. Pulling open a flap behind her, she can see the ring far over in the center of the tent. A man emerges from the tent with a sore jaw. Outside, Jack is lackadaisically introduced by his trainer with a sign that takes some time to get righted. Nelly, who chews gum with abandon, flirts with a tall man in a bow tie, who eventually walks over to talk with her. "A friend of yours?" he asks, peering up at Jack. "A very good friend," she replies. She winks and invites him to be a contestant; meanwhile the Showman has rounded up a sailor and a burly man pushed to the front by his wife. Up on the stage now with the barker, Jack watches Nelly flirt with the stranger, then cheerfully interrupts them with a challenge. Nelly, breathing hard, says "He doesn't think he can stay a round, Jack." The stranger puts down his money.

Inside the smoke-filled tent the show begins. The sailor falls against the ropes, winded and staggering from the blow. One man imagines Jack as all his opponents, the images whirling around his face. While another contestant heads for the exit, the burly man's wife pushes him into the ring where he trips and falls, down for the count. Now, the elegantly dressed stranger takes off his coat, and the trainer puts it on a hanger. Jack sits back proudly in his corner. The bell rings, but it is a more even match this time.

Peeking in from outside, Nelly seems alarmed and calls to the Showman. But

he starts bringing in customers for a "real" fight, and they sell more tickets. The camera views the fight from the back of the crowd, until Jack is counted out. At the ticket booth, Nelly is downcast. The rest of the team huddles around Jack.

Outside, the winner is dressed and again flirting with Nelly; the promoter joins them. "We heard he was good and now we know." Nelly is miffed, "We were hoping to get married, but now you've lost him his job!" The promoter hands her a card scribbled with a note: "Don't fix any other job until I have seen you tonight." On the other side is a business card: James Ware, manager for Bob Corby, famous fighter. Nelly brightens at the name, sweetly smiling at Bob.

The day fades into night at the fairground and the booths start to come down; Jack begins to wash up in front of a mirror. Nelly comes to check out his hurt eye and clean it for him. Suddenly seeing Bob and James enter the tent, she stands mesmerized, wiping the towel down Jack's face. He pushes her away as the two men approach. Nelly, breathing hard, introduces them, and shows Jack the card they gave her. Jack and the promoter walk off, leaving Nelly and Bob eyeing one another and laughing. Jack's trainer and his team glare at them from the other side of the tent.

Outside, Nelly and Bob walk through the fairground, past a large gypsy woman who runs into her trailer to spy on them. Bob hands Nelly a bracelet, "a present for you from the money I won." On the other side of the trailer, Jack and the promoter talk. "If you win the trial fight you can be Bob's sparring partner." Their handshake on the deal dissolves into a shot of Bob putting the snake bracelet on Nelly's arm and then up over her elbow. She looks knowing, happy, and kisses him lightly; he grabs and kisses her passionately. She becomes nervous and they walk off together to join Jack, who excitedly greets her. She slips off the bracelet and hides it under her hand, ignoring the proffered handshake from Bob. They all walk off and she runs to the gypsy's trailer and demands her fortune, sitting excitedly on top of the table as the cards are laid. The pipe-smoking gypsy tells her a "tall, rich, man" is in her life. Jack appears in the doorway, dampening her enthusiasm only slightly, and she again hides the bracelet as he exclaims "King of Diamonds. That's me! I'm going to make real money now!"

The next day, Jack washes outside in a pond; Nelly kneels by him and they are reflected in the water, happy together. Her bracelet falls off and he gallantly retrieves it. "He bought the bangle because he didn't like taking the money he won . . . so it was really you who gave it to me," she explains. "Then I give it to you like this," he says, placing it over her ring finger. "If I win the trial fight, we'll get married tomorrow." She nods her head enthusiastically, then thoughtfully stares out, holding on to her bracelet.

Title: "The Day of Jack's Flight." At the ticket counter, Nelly worries, listlessly giving out tickets. She breathes heavily, worried, imagining Jack being beaten. A crowd surrounds her, then a boy materializes out of it with a telegram: "Have won. Will see you in church tomorrow. All arranged."

At the church, the guests arrive. The deacon bites his nails at the odd behavior of the guests, among them Siamese twins. Nelly warily walks up the aisle with the Showman; the boisterous group talks loudly across the aisle of the church as the deacon widens his eyes in annoyance. The participants group at the front for the ceremony, though Nelly has to push the trainer out of her spot next to Jack. The vows are read with some suspense, as Nelly looks up at Jack, alternately sweet and aware, and Bob yawns. The trainer is finally forced out of a daydream and produces the ring, after first handing over a button just popped

from his coat. Jack puts the ring on Nelly's hand, and the bracelet falls down her arm to rest in front of it.

At the outdoor reception, a horseshoe falls off the wall and the gypsy woman carries it over to Bob, wishing him "better luck next time." The group, seated at a long, white-clothed table, finds this hilarious. Everyone drinks and eats with abandon, especially the trainer, who drains a mug of beer in one gulp. Bob rises to say that the "prize at the booth should have been this charming bride . . . but now that he's my sparring partner, I shall take my revenge." Across the table, Jack rises proudly, "I will always be ready to fight for my wife against any man." They spar for a time, until, from the viewpoint of the trainer, the focus blurs and they recede into a drunken haze.

At training, the two men spar. Nelly watches soberly from ringside, her eyes falling on Bob. After they break, she catches his eye, and he puts his hand on her arm. A bystander asks to be introduced to her "husband." On the other side of the ring, Jack stiffens at this, then jumps over in a rage, holding clenched fists behind his back. The trainer calmly walks over and breaks up the action, directing Jack to a punching bag, where he imagines Bob's face. But the punching bag spins off its hook and Jack stomps out, slamming the door behind him.

Later he is dressed in a suit and reappears through the door only to find Nelly and Bob still talking and laughing. "Wait for me outside," he commands her. She stiffens, but goes, and Bob remains uninvolved, "Anything wrong?" he asks. "No, just go easy, that's all," says Jack.

In an office, the promoter and Jack talk at the desk. "It seems as though I will have to fight for my wife after all," says Jack. The promoter laughingly points to Bob's name in much larger size type than Jack's on a poster on the wall.

Somewhere out in the city, a similar poster advertisement for a series of fights is plastered on the side of a building, a fence and sidewalk beneath it. As people walk by and the seasons pass, Jack's name appears in larger and larger type, closer and closer to the top.

In a room at his home, Jack, now in a tuxedo, listens to the promoter, "If you win this fight with the nigger, you'll be in the running for the championship." Jack glances into a mirror, where he can see his wife in the next room seated on the arm of a chair next to Bob Corby.

A drunken woman falls onto Bob and Nelly, and they laughingly push her onto the floor. It's a wild party, with a pair of frenzied woman dancers dominating the living room floor. Bob whispers in Nelly's ear, "Next time we go out, I'll take you to see their show." She brightens, excited, then her smile fades, as she too can see her husband, reflected in the mirror, still talking business in the next room. The dancing girls collapse and are fed more champagne; everybody is up dancing now. Nelly and Bob stay close in the corner.

Back in the office, Jack is told he is to start training tomorrow: "It's not necessary for you to bring your wife, she can stay here." Jack is unable to get the mirror image from his mind; it pushes out his manager's talk. Suddenly everything becomes distorted, the dancers, the piano player's fingers; through the superimpositions Jack sees Nelly and Bob kiss. He hysterically jumps up and interrupts the party. The celebrants freeze and stare at him. He apologizes and returns to the office, pacing. "I'd be training for a divorce if I left her here!" "I thought you said you'd fight for her!" sneers the promoter. Jack peers at the floor, chastened. "She's all right, really, the trouble is, he's a champion and you're not—yet."

Entering his living room he finds it trashed and everyone gone except Nelly, who romantically plays the piano; Jack walks over to put his hands on her shoulder and finds Bob's picture staring at the two of them.

A montage of fights, training, and wins. In his dressing room Jack is ecstatic among a crowd of well-wishers; the trainer wipes him down. His buddies from the fairground enter to congratulate him, and they relive the fight, all of them laughing and gay. "Now I'd like to see you lick that bloke who knocked you out at the fair," says one. Jack's look darkens for a moment, then one of the men asks after "the old woman." Jack's trainer clenches his teeth, then throws a towel over Jack's head and starts wiping. Jack emerges calm, "She's anxiously awaiting to hear the results of the fight . . . you boys must come home with me and celebrate!"

Outside a large crowd greets the champion as he leaves in a chauffeured car.

At home, Jack has his friends wait while he looks for Nelly, but finally has to admit she is not there. The four men tentatively inspect the plush furniture in the living room and end up squished together on the couch. Jack brings champagne in on a tray and pours six glasses. He hears the elevator, thinking it might be Nelly, and announces they will wait until she arrives, but the elevator passes his floor. The champagne goes flat as they wait, sitting around morosely, some sleeping, Jack gazing out the window on the city lights. Jack is apologetic but unable to cheer up, and the trainer points out Bob Corby's picture on the piano to the others, signaling thumbs down. The men decide to leave. Jack sits, despondent, then paces the room, staring out the window again. He looks down to see Nelly emerge from a car, then lean over into the back seat for a last good-bye. His eyes narrow; the picture of Bob falls over. She enters, lively in a striped chinchilla coat and feathery evening dress; he is silent, able only to stare at her. "What are you standing there for, can't you speak, did you lose, then?" Noticing the champagne, she gathers that he won, but he is still too angry to speak. Annoyed, she walks over to right the photo of Bob, then he yanks it out of her hand and smashes it on top of the champagne glasses. Picking it up, she insists it is hers, and he yanks part of her blouse off, and then the bracelet. She locks herself in another room. "I wish I'd gone on to another club with Bob!" she screams.

Jack goes out to a club, receiving congratulations as he walks through. A woman asks him to dance and he obliges, then bumps into Bob on the dance floor. At the end of the dance, he abandons his partner to confront Bob at his table. "We must celebrate your win," offers Bob. Jack just stares at him, then pours the proffered champagne over the side of the table. Angered, Bob quickly rises, throwing over the table, but Jack punches him to the floor. "He can try to reverse this inside the ring if he likes," he tells the promoter as he walks out.

At home, he finds Bob's photo placed on the mantel and a note from Nelly: "I have gone to people who know how to treat me properly."

Crowds pass by the Corby versus Sanders fight poster. The fight is in a very large stadium, with people streaming through many passages. Jack's trainer notices Nelly arrive. "We mustn't let him know she's here." She goes in to see Bob. She seems tentative, wishes him well and leaves.

In his dressing room, Jack wakes from his nap. "It's funny, I dreamt she was here tonight." The contenders file into the ring. Nelly waves to Bob from ringside. Men dust the stage, the ringmaster announces the referee, Mr. Eugene Corri. Several rounds go by, then the fight becomes more heated, the fighters face to face. In a clinch, Jack suddenly sees Nelly in the crowd. His concentration is lost

and he is knocked out. Back in his corner everything is in a flurry while his team tries to revive him. They're up for the next round, but Jack gets knocked down again, rising just in time, and reeling back to his corner. Nelly is now upset, crying. The men begin another round, both more tired now, their teams feverishly working over them between rounds. The trainer, scared, looks up as Nelly approaches Jack's corner. "Jack, I'm with you, I'm in your corner," she says, smiling at him. He smiles, and new vigor takes over him. Next round, he knocks Bob out. The lovers reunite; Bob nods at her from the other side of the ring, and she takes off his bracelet.

Later, in Bob's dressing room, one of his team walks in with the bracelet, "Look what I found at the ringside, Guv'nor." Bob throws it back at him and smugly returns to tying his tie.

Note. *Most filmographies indicate Alma Reville also worked on the script. Gifford, in *A Catalog of British Films*, adds to the cast Clare Greet (Gypsy), and Charles Farrell.

7 *The Manxman* (1928)

Director	Alfred Hitchcock
Assistant Director	Frank Mills
Production Company	British International Pictures*
Screenplay	Eliot Stannard, based on the novel by Sir Hall Caine
Photography	Jack Cox
Editing	Emile de Ruelle
Art Direction	W. Arnold
Cast	Carl Brisson (Pete Quilliam), Malcolm Keen (Philip Christian), Anny Ondra (Kate Cregeen), Randle Ayrton (Mr. Cregeen), Clare Greet (Mrs. Cregeen)
Filmed	at Elstree Studios, London, and on the Cornwall coast
Running Time	approximately 100 minutes
Release Date	January 1928

Other title: *L'Isola Del Peccato*

Synopsis

Waves roll onto a large rock on the coast, and the credits appear over the scene. Title: "What shall it profit a man if he gain the whole world and lose his own soul?"

The camera pans from a close-up of a Catherine wheel to reveal the harbor and fishing boats moving into it. Peter Quilliam, a fisherman, is happy to see the village and waves excitedly at his suited friend, Philip, who waits on the dock. While Peter throws large fish from the boat, he chats gaily with Philip, a lawyer. Title: "They met as boys and grew up as brothers." Philip shows Pete a petition to stop "encroachment on fishing grounds." Title: "Still the staunchest friends, they fought side by side for the cause of the lowly fisherfolk."

Pete and Philip lead the rest of the men in a large winding file over the dock and up to the nearby Old Caesar's Inn.

Inside, Pete and Philip both stop to smile a greeting at the blond Kate Cregeen, then walk toward her together, each holding out a hand. She excitedly takes one hand in each of hers and smiles back and forth, then lights on Philip alluringly, "It's just like you, Mr. Christian, to help our men." "I'd do anything for Pete, his friends are mine," replies Philip, as Pete looks devotedly at Kate. The scene widens to include the other men filling the pub to standing-room only; Philip strides into their midst to assure them that he "will take it to the governor" if necessary. As he speaks, he spies Pete at the edge of the crowd, flirtatiously flipping Kate's hair. The pair stand highlighted in long shot, surrounded by the heads of the crowd. Hesitating at this distraction, Philip decides to call Pete over. Pete laughingly shouts back, then turns again toward Kate, but Philip, frowning, insists on his demand. Pete finally walks over, the first to sign the petition, then quickly sidles down the edge of the bar back to Kate; the rest of the men pass the pen until the paper is full of signatures. Philip excitedly shows the long list to Pete, who is still talking with Kate.

The beam from the lighthouse methodically breaks the night over the sailboats. The tavern is empty. Pete, leaning on the bar, watches Kate through the square panes of the window between the bar and her family's parlor. Suddenly he announces to Philip, "Now's as good a time as any to ask old Caesar about me and Kate." Philip's face clouds, but he agrees, then bows his head to his paper on the table where he sits. Pete moves slowly to the doorway and stares at Caesar, who rises menacingly from his chair, a frowning close-up superimposed on him. Frightened, Pete staggers backward into Philip, who laughs and encourages him. Pete gets an idea: "You speak for me—you've got a way of making things sound better." Philip frowns, then rises with Pete's excitement. As the lighthouse beam moves around outside the window, he finally agrees to help. The camera moves with Philip as he strides through the door, then sits in front of the window and observes Kate and her father rise at the sight of him. Ceaser sends Kate out, and as she stops near the door, Pete signals excitedly to her, but she insists that she must go upstairs. Pausing on the landing, she looks down at him still gesturing for her to return, but she continues up the stairs. Pete frowns and looks over through the window at Caesar, who is showing something in the newspaper to Philip as they talk. Mrs. Cregeen, who sews nearby, begins to listen in earnest. Caesar slowly folds up the newspaper and concentrates on what Philip is saying, then loses his smile and turns sternly toward Pete when Philip points outside. Philip denies his own interest and points again at Pete. The Cregeens peer through the window at the expectant figure. Caesar pushes Philip aside and strides into the bar and opens the outside door. He stalks into a close-up toward Pete, who backs away as they face one another. "How dare you mention my daughter's name, you penniless lout!" Pete is defiant as Caesar turns away, "I'll make you take that back one day!" Caesar walks back into his parlor, and Philip walks over to put his hand on Pete's shoulder. Pete smiles resignedly and they walk out.

Outside, they sit in the beam of the lighthouse and Pete swears, "I'll show him. I'll go abroad to Africa. I'll work my passage. I'll come back rich." Philip rears his head in anticipation of this, then sulks again when Pete suggests they go tell Kate.

They walk around the tavern and Pete tosses pebbles at Kate's second-story

window. She opens it and smiles down at them, first putting her hands in front of her nightgown, then grabbing a shawl. Pete tries to climb up and she teases him, flicking at his hand. Inside her bedroom, she turns away from the window and primps her hair and giggles until Pete suddenly appears leaning on the window sill. Outside, Philip holds Pete up on his shoulders. Inside, Pete pleads with Kate to wait for him. She laughs heartily, nodding yes, then no, his expression following her back and forth. "Aw, Kate—hold your capers—be serious for a while," he pleads. She pauses and sighs. Outside, Philip listens. Finally, she agrees, "I promise." Preening toward him, she kisses him lightly, then abruptly pulls down the blind in front of him. Turning her back on the window, she laughs and giggles in excitement, then looks out a side window panel to see Pete ask Philip to take care of her while he is gone. As they walk off, Pete hugging Philip, she has second thoughts, and flips up the blind, but hesitates to call out. Turning back, the light flashing behind her, she becomes increasingly distraught.

Title: "From the Isle of Man to Liverpool, then on to foreign ports." Philip waves good-bye to Pete on the huge steamer.

The camera frames the pages in Kate's diary turning: "Pete sailed; Mr. Christian called; ~~Mr. Chr~~ Philip took me for a walk; Phil met me by the brook."

In the countryside mottled with sunlight, Kate runs ahead by the brook, and Philip obligingly follows and takes her hands under a tree. She hugs him.

Title: "The home of Philip Christian, cradle to a line of deemsters (a judge on the Isle of Man)."

Low lights glow in the large, dark living room where Philip's aunt sits on a couch near the tall fireplace, embroidering. "You were seen with that publican's daughter again today," she complains. Smoking, Philip turns to sit near a huge vase of flowers on a bureau nearby, explaining that he promised Pete he would take care of her. "It's not fair to the girl—it's not fair to yourself," she insists, "Your father married beneath him—let his ruined career be a warning to you! I've devoted my life to fitting you for the day when you become deemster." He stiffens at this and strides out.

Later, he walks near the tavern, and enters to find the men staring at him, "Pete's dead! Killed in South Africa!" Through the crowd, on the other side of the doorway, Kate stands in her parlor, her back turned. Caesar says to Philip, "Maybe I was wrong about Pete and Kate. She hasn't spoken a word . . ." Philip walks in to her, but she does not move. Finally, she turns, clear-eyed, "Philip, we're free." His face darkens as she pleads, "Don't you see what this means?" He bows his head at her appeal, then abruptly kisses her hands. She moves back in ecstasy, then, noticing the men in the bar, hides her face from them.

Pete smiles broadly. Inside an office, he writes a letter to Philip, as half-dressed workers carrying huge bundles on their shoulders file by behind him outside. He has "made money," and is coming home, but wants to surprise Kate.

Kate and Philip stand outside an old watermill. She takes him into the attic area to show him the room-high gear workings, then suddenly turns very serious, and moves toward him. They kiss passionately. The gears turn; darkness falls.

On the ship, Pete, now wearing a suit, fingers a ring. He debarks, and sends a telegram to Philip.

Kate opens a note—"meet me usual place." She primps and rushes out of her bedroom, slowing down on her way past the customers, then gaily tossing her purse once outside. She climbs a hill and heads down to the rocky beach, spying Philip through the hole in a huge rock formation. She runs to him and they kiss,

but he has something on his mind. A ship approaches the harbor in the distance, and he pulls out the telegram. She is aghast, nearly fainting. "I'm glad Pete's alive, but it makes no difference. I don't love him," she insists. "You promised yourself to him," admonishes Philip. "I promised myself to him, but I've given myself to you," she responds. Philip turns toward the sea, "I can't go on, Kate. Pete trusted us and he is coming home with faith in our loyalty. . . . If he ever knew we had been false to him, it would break his heart. We must think of his happiness." She hangs on him, pleading. "Pete must never know," says Philip as he kisses her and the ship steams into the harbor.

Kate and Philip move toward the tavern. "You go. I can't face him," she says, hanging back at the door. Philip sees Pete inside greeting his friends. Pete turns ecstatically to him and hugs him, then sees Kate outside and moves toward her. She smiles, briefly glancing at Philip's bowed back, then steps gingerly into Pete's arms. Philip glares as they walk into the parlor and are warmly greeted by her parents. Still tentative, Kate calls for Philip to join them. Pete proudly asks the Cregeens if he "can tell Kate" her parents have agreed to their marrying. Everyone congratulates the two as Kate walks away from the group into a close-up, her expression revealing complete despondency. Still standing by the fireplace, her back to the others, she becomes cheerful again when Pete walks over and hugs her. He appoints Philip best man, and as Philip falteringly agrees, Kate faints in Pete's arms. He sends her upstairs with her mother, commenting that the surprise of seeing him again must have been "too much for her."

Upstairs in Kate's bedroom, Mrs. Cregeen tries to soothe her daughter, but Kate sends her away.

Kate sits sadly at her window. A series of dissolves shows a wedding veil placed on her bowed, unsmiling head, and a ring placed on her finger.

The bridal party crosses the millpond and enters the attic of the same water mill where Philip and Kate first kissed. The reception table is set in front of the gear workings. Several tiers of white cake sit between Pete and Kate, and an image of Philip becomes superimposed on top of them. Later, as the bride cuts the cake, the group stands around her. Caesar pontificates at length, "Marriage be a mighty reverent thing . . . all manner of punishment comes to them that's false to its sacred vows . . ." Kate turns sadly away and Philip winces, as Caesar walks back to the gears to illustrate, "See, the mills of God grind slowly." Pete sits patiently with his chin in his hand, until he sees a couple of women at the end of the table beginning to doze off. "Hey, Caesar, this is not a funeral, it's a wedding!" he grins, and Kate laughs until she sees Philip, who is not cheered. The gears turn.

Philip leads Kate and the rest of the party to their new home, a cottage with a large center room and a fireplace. Kate turns away from the congratulations for some fresh night air at the front door. Pete goes out to kiss her and bring her back in for a toast around the table. The party leaves and Mrs. Cregeen gets the last hug and kiss. Pete closes the door, and Kate's eyes widen. She runs to the window one last time, then goes to sit by the fire alone, her shawl pulled over her hunched back. He kneels in front of her, and lays his head in her lap. She hesitatingly puts her hand on his head and they kiss, but she looks askance, and rises when he passionately kisses her hand.

Title: "A trusting joyous husband, an adored, unhappy wife, whose secret misery brought death into her soul."

News item: Philip Christian returns from holiday, may be appointed deemster. Kate happily reads this news to Pete one morning. She serves breakfast for

them; he takes up the tray of dishes when they're finished. They seem happy, and kiss good-bye when he goes off down the hill to the dock. Inside, Kate quickly writes a note to Philip, "Thank Providence you're back. I must see you before the fishing fleet returns." She waits by the window until Philip enters, then takes his hand and pleads, "You've got to take me away!" Shocked, he watches as she falls into a chair and announces, "I can't keep my secret any longer." Facing the camera in close-up, she swallows hard and tells him she is pregnant. Pulling at his hair, he wonders why she did not tell him this before; "It would have made all the difference." "You kept away from me. You thought more of your future than of mine," she retorts, wringing her hands. He becomes angry and pulls at her collapsed figure. She moves to a chair on the other side of the room and insists they tell Pete everything. "No! Not now! Think of the shame!" cries Philip.

Pete starts home along the shore.

Kate and Philip stand side by side arguing, as Pete approaches the cottage. Seeing a man's back through the window, he frowns, and bursts in, becoming happy to see it is Philip. But Kate persists in her plan and takes Pete's hands, telling him she is pregnant. He is ecstatic, kisses her forehead, and hugs her with great enthusiasm. Outside, Philip waits, then reenters with bowed head for the news. He and Kate face the camera, staring out, as Pete stands jubilantly behind and between them, raising his arms in triumph.

Later, a top hat and gloves adorn the table in the middle of the cottage. Pete and Philip play checkers, waiting for news from upstairs. Pete becomes increasingly anguished; hearing screams, he collapses on his knees into a chair, while Philip stands by stoically. The doctor comes down, rolling up his sleeves and wondering who the father is. Philip hesitates, then points down at Pete who peeks over the chair, finally rising with the good news. Pete dances around the room, hugs Philip, and races upstairs.

Later, Kate solemnly rocks the baby near the fireplace as Pete stands behind her.

A poster announces that Philip is to be made deemster. He greets his admirers, including Pete, from a stately stone balcony. Turning back into his book-lined, paneled office, he is shocked to receive Kate as a visitor. She sits, wringing her hands. "I've left him, Philip; I cannot live this life of deceit any longer." "But what are you going to do?" he asks, and she looks up at him and stutters. "I want to be with you, do take me." Appalled, Philip spreads his arms, then turns away. She rises to meet him, wondering if she cannot stay in the office, "I wouldn't be any trouble." He turns away again, and she leans on his shoulder.

Returning home, Pete smiles hello to his baby. Finding the place empty, he rushes outside, then notices the cheese set out for one, and a note in Kate's place. "I am going away. Before I married you, I loved another man. I love him still." He shakes and cries and shares his grief with the baby in the cradle.

Pete darns a sock outside his front door and explains to the neighbors that Kate has gone on a holiday. Later, he tells the same story to the men in the tavern.

Visiting Philip in his office, he bows his head and tells the truth. Kate stands behind a doorway and listens. "Help me to find her," he pleads, then explains that he must get back to his baby. Kate raises her eyes mournfully at the mention of the child.

Back at the cottage, Caesar finds the note Kate left and glowers at Pete, who proudly picks up the baby, glad that he still has her.

In his darkened office, Philip finishes some paperwork as Kate emerges from

her hiding place. He stares, and she becomes more nervous, then angry, "You must choose between your career and me." He urges her to be patient, asking for "time to think." She announces that she is going to go get their baby: "the last thing I have in the world." He moves to stop her, but the telephone rings and he lets go; after all, tomorrow is the "greatest day" of his life; he will become deemster.

Kate peeks in the window of her home, then slowly pushes the door open. Pete walks toward her, but she is petrified, staring out, and starting at the slightest noise. He pours tea at the new, black-covered table; she announces she has only come for the baby. He refuses, blocking her way to the cradle. She becomes hysterical, then angry and blurts out the truth. "It's a lie!" he cries and takes the baby upstairs. Kate follows, determined, but the door is locked. Her hands scrape at the door, and she gives up, wild-eyed, and staggers back down the stairs. She walks into the night and down the streets of the town to the dock near the lighthouse. She jumps into the water.

Philip, wigged and serious, presides in court. The room is filled with activity, and the judge is first asked to dispose of a "minor" case of attempted suicide and a prisoner who "refuses her name." Saved by a passing policeman, Kate enters, sheathed nunlike in black, her face hidden. Philip calmly asks if there is nobody who will answer for her; as she looks up, he jumps back, his eyes darting from side to side. She puts her finger to her mouth, and Pete enters to speak for her. Philip discharges her to return to her husband. Pete is grateful, but Kate calmly announces she will not return. Her mother stands next to her, and her father sits nearby, glaring at Philip. Pete explains about the other man, and Philip sits back. Caesar looks back and forth from Pete to Philip to Kate, until he finally rises, shaking and pointing, "There, before you is her betrayer, the deemster himself!" The police restrain him as Pete stares, dumbfounded, "Can't you see, Pete, can't you see?" cries Caesar.

Philip solemnly stands and speaks the truth, "I stand before you a man who has broken faith with his best friend and taken away a woman's honor . . ." Finally hanging his head he resigns, "so that I may devote myself to righting the wrong I have done." He removes his wig; Pete glares, and grabs him by the neck as he steps down. Kate interferes, "Pete, we too have suffered," and all bow their heads.

Neighbors crowd around the front window of Pete's cottage as he kisses his baby good-bye. Outside, the crowd taunts Philip and Kate as they walk away with the child.

Pete stands on his boat, gauntly staring out over the fleet, as he and the other fishermen sail out of the harbor.

Note. *Most filmographies credit John Maxwell as producer.

8   *The Farmer's Wife* (1928)

Director	Alfred Hitchcock
Assistant Director	Frank Mills
Production Company	British International Pictures
Screenplay	Alfred Hitchcock, Eliot Stannard, based on the play by Eden Phillpotts
Photography	John J. Cox

Art Direction	C. Wilfred Arnold
Cast	Jameson Thomas (Samuel [Sam] Sweetland), Lillian Hall-Davies (Araminta ['Minta] Dench), Gordon Harker (Churdles Ash), Maud Gill (Thirza Tapper), Louise Pounds (Louise Windeatt), Olga Slade (Mary Hearn), Antonia Brough (Susan), Ruth Maitland (Mercy Bassett), Hayward Watts, Gibb McLaughlin
Filmed	at Elstree Studios, London
Running Time	approximately 100 minutes
Distributor	Wardour & F.
Release Date	March 1928
Other title: *Laquelle Des Trois*	

Synopsis

Sheep graze in the meadows of the Welsh countryside. Samuel Sweetland, a slightly greying but substantial-appearing man, stares somberly out of the upstairs window of his large, big-beamed, farmhouse. His two spaniels trot in the front door and lay their heads on the top step near the bedroom door. Churdles Ash, his handyman, comes slowly down the stairs past them, puts on his hat, and goes outside. Sam shakes his head back and forth when Churdles turns to look up at him. Inside the bedroom, his wife, tended by their maid, the dark-haired Araminta, raises her head slightly to whisper to her "Don't forget to air your master's pants," and then dies.

Long underwear dries by the fireplace, on a hedge, on the line. A clean dry pair is placed carefully on a big bed. Sam excitedly enters the bedroom. Downstairs in the kitchen, 'Minta directs the attendants in preparing the food, then goes to check on the bride, Sam's daughter. Back upstairs, she helps an agitated Sam with his tie, then outside she helps Churdles decorate the carriage. He makes a disparaging comment about marriage, but she sweetly objects. "There's something magical about the married state. It have a beautiful side."

Inside the large main room, the bride and attendants are ready. Sam pauses to talk quietly with his daughter until 'Minta, watching at the front door, reminds them the others are waiting.

Back in the kitchen, the crew prepares for the reception. 'Minta puts out a roast to turn in the fireplace, while Churdles rails against women. Later, when the meat is nearly done, he snatches a bit from the drippings when 'Minta is not looking. The church bells ring and 'Minta rushes out to greet the bride and groom. A dozen other guests arrive and, with Churdles, crowd around the white-clothed table. Louisa Windeatt, a stout, dark-suited widow, Thirza Tapper, a curly haired, frail woman, and Mary Hearn, the plump, smiling postmistress are all present. They say grace and eat; Sam's daughter looks sadly over at the downcast Sam, but he brightens up. A goateed white-haired gentleman at the head of the table, speaks: "There be many here wishful of a partner . . ." Sam looks over at the empty chair by the fireplace. Their dinner complete, the party rises to socialize in groups around the room. Thirza reminds Sam about her party on Thursday and

asks if Mr. Ash would be able to announce her guests; she has "some livery" for him. Churdles stands behind her and frantically signals "no" to his Master, but Sam scratches his head and obliges.

'Minta excitedly hands out little presents to the women, and the bride comes down from upstairs ready to leave. 'Minta takes the groom for a talk while Sam says good-bye to his daughter. The couple drive off in a carriage, and the rest of the guests gradually depart as Sam warmly bids them, especially the women, good-bye, and then is left brooding on his stoop.

Inside, 'Minta brings down his old jacket as he stands still brooding in front of the fireplace, picking confetti off his jacket. He glances up at his wedding picture, and again at the empty chair. He walks to the mirror and pulls at his mustache, inspecting his face and primping himself. Suddenly he calls 'Minta and announces, "I must take time by the forelock, else I'll be a lonely man soon. . . . There's a female or two be floating around my mind like a Sunday dinner. . . . Get a pencil." 'Minta looks at him wonderingly, but sits down at the table with pencil and paper. He sits by the fireplace and imagines Louisa Windeatt sitting in the chair opposite. 'Minta frowns at her name. "Her back view's not a day over thirty," offers Sam. "But you have to live with her front view," reasons 'Minta, though she writes down the name. She then suggests Thirza Tapper, and Sam agrees, imagining her in the chair. Next he suggests Mary Hearn, and 'Minta energetically frowns, "A woman that's a pillow at thirty is often a feather bed at forty." But her name is added, and Mercy Bassett from the Royal Oak Inn is thrown in for good measure. "It's almost indecent to see 'em all on one bit of paper," says Sam.

Sam's shoes are shined, his hair his slicked back, and a new plaid jacket covers his checkered vest. "No need to wish me luck . . . she'll come like a lamb to slaughter," he brags to 'Minta on his way out the door.

He winds his way through the countryside on his black and white horse, and runs into Louisa on the trail. At her front door, he surveys her property and grandly greets her handymen working near the stables, who stare at him blankly. Inside, she asks what brings him up her "hill," and he slyly says he is out to "pick up a fat hen." She offers a drink, but he demands they wait and mentions marriage, to which she wonders if the hen is for the wedding breakfast. Quickly, he moves ahead, "You're the first to know your good luck. . . . I am a man that little children can lead, but a regiment of horses couldn't drive. . . . Yes is a short word." "But there's a shorter," she replies, looking at him seriously, for she knows, she says, she is "too independent" for him. He assures her she would "only feel the velvet glove" and never know he was breaking her in, but she is firm, even laughs. Furious, he picks up his stick and goes to the door, "You haven't treated me in a ladylike spirit over this job . . . so don't go changing your mind. You've brought your doom on yourself." Laughing, she offers him one for the road, but he races away, barking at the handymen for his horse on the way out.

Back home, he stalks in, wakes up the dozing Churdles, and yells at him and 'Minta, "Don't let that Louisa Windeatt in this house again!" He pulls out the list and crosses off her name.

A note from Thirza reminds him that her party starts at "four o'clock *punctual.*"

Inside Thurza's kitchen, her maid, 'Minta, and Churdles busily prepare the food. Upstairs, Thirza creams her face. It's 3:25. Everyone is startled to hear the doorbell. The maid opens the door to find Sam; shocked, she reminds him the party

has not yet started, but he insists she tell Thirza he is there. Thirza is soaking her feet and this announcement sends her into a tizzy. Sam sits directly at the bottom of the staircase, and Thirza peeks out the bathroom door at him, realizing she has to negotiate the landing in order to get to the bedroom door and her clothes. She tries a couple of times, but is forced to retreat into the bathroom. Finally, she lunges, getting her robe caught in the door and making a ruckus, while Sam greets her cheerfully from below. He hides a gift basket behind him, not even letting 'Minta take it from him, and paces back and forth. Finally, Thirza comes down the stairs uncontrollably fluttering her eyelids. She takes him into the parlor, where he knocks over the centerpiece with his basket; she runs back to the kitchen with it, returning with some dishes of food. Sitting on the piano bench, he jumps up when she returns and knocks over the bric-a-brac on top. Thirza's whole body is now fluttering. Finally, he yells at her to stop, which, startled and wide-eyed, she does. Smiling broadly, he begins, "Some men like a bit of fat on a female . . ." The maid interrupts, and Thirza returns to setting her table. Sam erupts, "Hang it, Thirza, I'm asking you to marry me!" Thirza drops into a chair, unable to control herself. On his knees, he continues, "I'm a man a little child can lead, but a regiment of soldiers couldn't drive." Calm now, she stands and bids him rise, "You are the first man to accept my sex challenge . . . but I shall never seek the shelter of a man's arms, not even yours." The maid appears with the melting ices that were mistakenly put near the fire. Thirza falls apart again, and Churdles, disgusted at his master's humiliation, tries to get Sam to keep quiet. Then Churdles decides to shame Thirza, complaining mightily to her about the pants from the livery, which are inches too big. She takes him into the hallway, and sheepishly digs the matching, but torn, jacket out of a dustbin under the stairs and gives it to him. He sits on the stairs, trying to tie his shoes with some string, until she returns to sew up his sleeve. He glares at her and she turns away.

The doorbell rings and the party begins. As each invited guest arrives, Churdles steps down into the small parlor, closes the door on the guest, and churlishly makes an announcement; then he opens the door, and lets another guest in from the hallway. About twenty people arrive in comic fashion, including the man with the goatee, who laughs at Churdles's livery, then inspects the table, nose to the food, and pronounces it "as perfect as a railway refreshment room."

Outside, Sam paces until he sees Mary Hearn arrive, then waves gaily at her and quickly checks his list. Hands in pockets, he pumps himself up and strides into the parlor, first glaring at Thirza and Louisa, then making a seat for himself next to Mary by pushing another guest aside. The parson arrives with his disabled wife who is in a three-wheeled chair with a large rotating handle, and there's much commotion about fitting it through the door and into the room. Lined around the room in rows, the crowd eats and drinks, while Thirza looks worried. Churdles attempts to eject the glee singers, who have walked in without knocking, but soon they are set up in the garden, and Thirza directs the guests outside to hear the entertainment. Sam confidently leers at 'Minta on his way out the door. Churdles relaxes with some coffee and the women clean up the table until Thirza grandly comes to the garden door and demands "Fruit in the garden."

Outside, 'Minta offers plums to Sam and Mary, who takes two. He frowns and tries to get her to go back inside, but she frowns back. Finally, he goes to the door and commands her; she resists, then unhappily relents. He closes the door after her, and while she stares he comes to the point. "That's funny, a fortune-teller told me I'd be married within the year," she says. "I bet I can tell you who it is,"

he challenges, and takes her over to the mirror. Her face contorts, "*You!* At your age!" He comments on *her* age. "Full-blown and a bit over." She falls onto the couch, dumbstruck to hear him cry, "You're too fond of dressing your mutton lamb fashion!" "Is this a nightmare!" she screams, waving her arms. He continues to berate her. Thirza and the guests appear at the door, then fill the room with cries of "What's Sammy doing?" Mary remains hysterical; nothing calms her. Finally, Thirza moves away from the crowd, flapping her arms; backing into Churdles, she faints on him and he loses his pants. Now the maid is jumping up and down next to Mary's flailing legs.

'Minta and Sam sit by the fire. "I shan't finish the list," he says. She tries to soothe him, but he insists, "Mary Bassett will be just like the rest." Churdles arrives pouting and sullen. Sam walks out, but overhears Churdles say, "I'm ashamed of Samuel Sweetland, offering himself at sale prices all round the country." Sam stops in his tracks, then walks back and barks, "Get my horse saddled! And my other coat!" 'Minta runs upstairs.

A close-up shows 'Minta as she wistfully waves good-bye, gulps, and goes unhappily inside the house. She walks over to the chair and rubs it, finally sitting down and staring longingly across at the other chair.

Sam gallops to the Royal Oak Inn where a large party is about to begin a hunt. Louisa, Thirza, and Mary are all there. He sits warily on his horse for a while, then boldly reigns in at the tavern. Inside, the crowd of men are having a good time, and the man with the goatee buttonholes him. Mercy waves a spirited hello from behind the bar, and Sam walks over to flirt with her. The other customers call for service, but Mercy continues talking to Sam. Outside, the riders go out with a swarm of foxhounds leading the way.

At the post office, Thirza is still angry that Mary ruined her party and Mary tells her she's a "pinnicking little grey rat," to which Thirza retorts that she could have married that fine man Samuel Sweetland.

Sam returns to find his servants still discussing his romantic excursions. They both look fearfully up at him, but he smiles. 'Minta backs away and Churdles mopes off. As 'Minta nervously fingers the chair, Sam suddenly changes and bows his head, " 'Tis all over . . . the whole power of the female sex be drawn against me. They've taken my self-respect." She admonishes him, "I won't hear a strong sensible man talk like that." He moves over to his chair and imagines the women in turn sitting across from him: Louisa laughing, Thirza sniffling, Mary hysterical, and Mercy yelling and shaking her fists at him. Then 'Minta sits down in the chair and suddenly he changes. He rises and swaggers away, while 'Minta mulls over his problem. She suggests another name, then he writes her name at the top of the list and hands it to her. She is moved, then questions him. "Don't think you'll make me angry by saying no. I been tamed to hearing no. . . . I'm offering myself humble as a worm . . . a little child can lead me." He convinces her he is sure, and she says she would "be proud to enter in." He asks her to put on the party dress his wife gave her. Churdles pulls her into the kitchen and she tells him the news. He is wide-eyed, "The next best thing to no wife, is a good one. . . . Don't forget to tell him I'm cruel underpaid." Sam commands her upstairs, grinning. Thirza and Mary arrive, saying Mary's changed her mind. The man with the goatee arrives and suggests another candidate. Sam brings out a bottle, and 'Minta, radiant in the bright dress, joins them. The others drink as she fetches down his old coat and puts it on him.

Note. *Most filmographies credit John Maxwell as producer and Alfred Booth as editor.

9   *Champagne* (1928)

Director	Alfred Hitchcock
Assistant Director	Frank Mills
Production Company	British International Pictures*
Screenplay	Eliot Stannard, Alfred Hitchcock (adaptation), based on an original story by Walter C. Mycroft
Photography	John J. Cox
Art Direction	C. W. Arnold
Cast	Betty Balfour (the Girl), Gordon Harker (the Father), Theo von Alten (the Man), Marcel Vibert (Maitre d'Hotel), Jean Bradin (the Boy), Jack Trevor†
Filmed	at Elstree Studios, London
Running Time	approximately 104 minutes
Distributor	Wardour & F.
Release Date	August 1928

Other titles: *A l'Américaine, Tabarin Di Lusso*

Synopsis

The Father, his cheek twitching and a big cigar in his mouth, rips through a stack of newspapers. "Wall Street magnate defied by headstrong heiress daughter . . . makes flight to join lover on Atlantic liner" shrieks one headline.

The wired head of a champagne bottle fills the screen. Champagne flows into a crystal ball-like view of the gay life on an ocean liner, a crowd of twirling dancers. Finishing off the glass of champagne, the Man, marked by a pencil-thin mustache, raises his eyebrow ominously. News passes quickly through the crowd, which runs up the gilt and wrought-iron staircases to the decks to watch the captain direct a group of seamen, who scramble to launch a lifeboat and paddle out to the rescue of a fallen plane.

The blond Girl appears at the door of the plane, smudge-faced and bright eyed. "You'd better hurry, Miss, before she sinks," warns a rescuer, but the Girl disappears back into the plane and hands out her several bags of luggage. Blowing a good-bye kiss to her plane, she eyes a line of tuxedoed men on one of the decks and decides to take off her flying gear before she embarks. On the boat, she gawks at all the fancily dressed passengers, and they gawk back at her. She responds, "Oh dear no, I just wanted to catch this boat," to a query from a taken-aback crewman. Standing nearby, the Man now raises his eyebrow leeringly at her. The Boy is in the crowd too, but he and the Girl refrain from recognizing one another.

A cabin is quickly found for her; the Man loiters in the corridor near it until the Boy arrives. Inside, the Girl has cleaned up and greets the Boy excitedly. He picks her up, they kiss and become serious for a moment, but she is unable to hold back her laughter. "Wouldn't I love to see dear Daddy's face when he hears I've run away with you after all, and lost his aeroplane besides."

Back in New York, Daddy furiously pushes papers off his desk and slams his hand down on a row of buttons. A file of secretaries hurries in so he can scream and yell at them.

Title: "Introductions aboard ship are easily arranged." The Man leers at the Girl as she is introduced to a group of eager young men, including the Boy. She and he move off excitedly on their own, racing through the corridors together to the elevator. The Man finds the Girl alone after her boyfriend has left to retrieve some coats for a trip out onto the windy deck. The Boy returns, frowning and displeased.

Out on the deck, they kiss, and he gives her a ring, which fits her thumb.

Title: "Cupid at the prow, but Neptune at the helm." A dinner menu, a food buffet, and an empty dining room rock back and forth with the ship. The Girl staggers down the stairway to get a table. The Man is also alone and she joins him, but looking at his food ruins her appetite. The Boy, seasick, staggers down the stairs, but becomes faint at the sight of a pig's head on the buffet and his girlfriend sitting with the Man. He decides to retreat. A uniformed boy deftly winds his way down the swaying stairs to deliver telegrams to the Girl and Man. "Does life mean nothing to you that you risk it for that cad?" rails her Daddy in print. She laughs, but the Man stares sternly at her and she becomes serious thinking of her father.

Back in the cabin, the Boy lies down with a towel over his head. The Girl arrives, still gay and standing, swaying back and forth as she talks to him. The telegram makes him sit up, very angry, but she is unperturbed. "I've arranged for the Captain to marry us!" she announces. "*You've* arranged—don't I arrange anything? . . . You think your money entitles you to do all the arranging." "My money enabled me to fly halfway across the Atlantic to join you," she retorts. "And your father thinks his money enables him to insult me by wireless!" Her mood changing, she hands back his ring. They both fall down before he can grasp it, and he gropes on the floor for it. "You'll not spoil my trip. I'll have a good time in Paris in spite of your ideas," she says and stomps out. Moments later, he opens the door and she is still standing there, but sticks her chin out and stalks off.

Title: "Paris—revelry—and at last the longed for arrival." The Boy is let into the Girl's hotel vestibule by a servant. He hears the sounds of a party inside and starts to leave, but the Girl appears. "You've neglected me for a whole week . . . come on in. I've met some lively people—invented a new cocktail—and bought a lot of snappy gowns." She drags him into her living room full of party people. The Man is there; he and the Boy exchange significant glances.

The Girl disappears into her dressing room full of servants and boxes from stores. The attendants, all in black, help her into a flashy dress with netting and jewels and a large stiff collar. One stares longingly at her outfit, and the Girl is forced to look up and down her servant's plain dress. Becoming sober, then bright again, she gives the girl a garment, then walks out for her grand entrance.

The women ohh and ahh over the outfit, while the men mill around talking, and the Boy and Man glare at one another. The Girl walks over to the Boy and the Man, demanding their comments. The Boy snips, "I've always understood simplicity was the key to good taste." She frowns, then smiles, "If I've offended your good taste then I must try to make amends." She exits, slamming the double doors behind her.

Shortly, she returns in one of her servant's black dresses, her head shrouded in a babushka; melodramatically saddened, she glides sarcastically toward her boyfriend, then laughs. He rips the scarf off and offers it to her. She turns to the Man, "Which do you think is the most charming creation," she asks. "The wearer, undoubtedly," he obliges. She nods in triumph.

The doorbell rings. It's Daddy. She greets him with a huge smile, and he puckers up to the camera. "Betty, I've something serious to say to you alone," he tells her, she takes him into her dressing room. "That dress suits you better than you know," he says, "I followed you . . . the market broke, and I've just learned that we're ruined." The room spins around her, but she laughs. She imagines her friends in the next room laughing at her, then enters to join them, and smilingly bids them good-bye. Only the Boy is left. "We lost all our money; I suppose you're happy now," she moans to him, nervously fingering her face. She runs to hug her father, and the Boy wanders out. "Just as I thought," says the Father. The Girl seizes her jewelry box, and says she will sell everything in it.

Another day, in a scene shot in close-ups from the waist down, the Girl walks the street carrying the jewelry box. A man follows, grabs it from her, and flees. She hesitates, then runs back.

In their new, considerably more modest, hotel room, the Father is still in bed when she returns and is angry to hear of the theft. He rises and begins doing some knee bends, while she is defensive: "I didn't find fault with you and you lost millions." Unperturbed, he begins doing push-ups next to the bed while she tries to turn over the mattress, even though he is right next to it. It falls on him, but he gets up and goes on his way, leaving her to push at it.

The striped mattress that fills the screen is replaced with a fluttering checked tablecloth. The Girl proceeds to set the table for lunch. The Father returns, dressed in a suit, and starts to hug her but she moves quickly away. Noticing the gesture, which he tries to hide by picking at his fingernails, she moves over to hug him. Seated now, he spurns the first plate she offers and takes a knife to some very hard rolls she baked herself. She imagines the Man and the Boy, then becomes somber and "not very hungry." The Father rises and leaves. She cries, staring down at their frugal meal, and the unappealing plate dissolves into fancier fare.

The plate is Daddy's; he is out having lunch at an expensive restaurant, several formally dressed waiters hovering over him.

Another day, she is again attempting to bake, throwing flour all over the room as well as herself. She alternately beats the dough with the roller and pours water on it. The Boy knocks on the door and she is ecstatic to see him. They laugh and kiss and he looks around the modest room. "Now I've found you I'm going to take you out of this wretched place." "Do you think I'd leave Daddy now!" she protests. "I'd even take care of your father," he responds. "Very kind of you—but you needn't bother. You seem to forget there's such a thing as pride." "You can't live on pride," he says, turning around and showing flour handprints on his back. The Girl starts after him, but stops, and returns sadly to her table to uncover with her roving finger the newspaper under the flour: a picture of a cruise ship, and then a want ad for girls with good teeth. She brightens with a new idea.

On board a cruise ship, the crowd dances in the ballroom, but the scene freezes into an ad in a shop window. The Girl walks down the street into a modeling agency and shows her teeth. "We're only interested in legs," is the reply from the man behind a big desk strewn with photos of women. "It doesn't matter to me as long as you give me a job," she insists. Another man walks up behind her and surreptitiously lifts her skirt with his foot, eyeing her legs. He whispers to the man behind the desk, and she is given a letter of introduction to a cabaret.

She walks into the still-quiet cabaret, which consists of a large, square, center area and a surrounding mezzanine. The woman who takes her to the boss

shrinks to find him eating in the dining room, shouting at the waiters. "I wouldn't go near him just now, dearie," she says, but the Girl gamely walks up to him, and he stops yelling and starts rubbing his hands at the sight of her until he finds out who she is. Then he resumes shouting—at her. "How dare you interrupt my dinner! I'm the maître d'hôtel!" he shrieks, throwing his hands in the air. "I'm sorry, I thought you were a gentleman" she says. An attendant walks her out of the plush dining room; the Girl takes a longer look at a couple she saw embracing when she walked in. Later, she returns smiling in a feather-and-spangle outfit, and the boss, still yelling at her, gives her a tray of flowers "for gentlemen in evening dress only."

The night begins. Food is slopped around in the kitchen from the floor to a diner's plate, and the place fills up with dancers. Suddenly, the boss looks up on the balcony to see the Girl giving flowers to the formally attired musicians; he storms up and pulls her away. She settles down at the bar, enjoying watching the bartender make drinks and the silly patrons gyrate. Suddenly, she sees the Man across the room, and tries to hide from him, but he finds her and stares wonderingly at her tray of flowers. He comments that their meeting is "strange," and she sadly agrees: "I used to pay to come to places like this; now they pay me." He demands another table and they are seated in the middle of the crowded dance floor. The boss comes by, pleased at her catch, but he pinches her on the arm as he moves on. The floor is very crowded now, and the couple sits uncomfortably. "Don't you realize that anything could happen to you in a place like this?" warns the Man. They rise, but on the way out he cajoles her into sitting at an empty table in a dark corner and forces himself on her. She runs screaming into the ballroom.

Suddenly she is back with him at the table on the dance floor. The Boy appears; she waves excitedly at him and he joins them. The Man writes out a note and leaves. The note says, "Always your good friend if you are in need." She explains to the Boy that she is one of the flower girls. They look over at another flower girl flirting with customers and both frown. One of the dancing girls floats by, "For a beginner, you sure know how to pick 'em, kid." A couple of women dance by and the Girl enjoys joshing with them. The Boy glares at her, but she raises her chin in pride. The boss starts glaring at her too, and she breaks into a sit-down dance. The Boy pours more champagne, still glaring. He grabs her wrists, "It's bad enough to find you here, worse to find you enjoying it." They start to leave, but the boss won't let her go out. She breaks away, then decides to let the Boy go.

Later, the Boy returns with the Father who reproaches her on the stairs, "How dare you, a daughter of mine, disgrace yourself like this." "But I was only trying to help you," she pleads. He hands her a newspaper clipping headlining his ire and his promise to teach her a lesson "she'll never forget." She's happy to find their poverty a hoax but angrily berates him: "You fooled me! humiliated me! behaved like the worst of men. . . . I hate you both!" She runs upstairs. An acrobatic act takes over the floor and the scene fades out.

Gripping the card from the Man, she rings his doorbell. "You at this strange hour!" he says, but agrees to take her with him to America.

They take the train to the coast, while the Boy drives.

The Man lets her into a compartment for two, then locks her in. She tries to leave and becomes desperate, until suddenly the Boy arrives. She hits him on the head when he comes through the door, thinking he is the Man. She explains, and they hide and wait in the bathroom. The Man arrives with the Father, who

reveals he and the Man are old friends. Daddy had instructed him by telegram to "prevent her elopement on all counts." The Boy appears and tries to strangle the Man, but Father forces a handshake. "I'll arrange for the Captain to marry us," announces the Boy. "*You'll* arrange!" challenges the Girl. The happy couple is reflected in a champagne glass.

Notes. *Most filmographies credit John Maxwell as producer. †Gifford, in *A Catalog of British Films*, adds to the cast Clifford Heatherly (the manager), Claude Hulbert, and Balliol and Merton (the dancers).

10   *Blackmail* (1929)

Director	Alfred Hitchcock
Assistant Director	Frank Mills
Production Company	British International Pictures*
Screenplay	Benn [W.] Levy (dialogue), Alfred Hitchcock (adaptation), based on a play by Charles Bennett
Photography	Jack [John J.] Cox
Camera Assistants	Michael Powell, Derick Williams, Ronald Neame
Editing	Emile de Ruelle
Set Direction	Norman Arnold, C. W[ilfred] Arnold
Sound	R. R. Jeffrey (post-synchronization of dialogue)
Music	Campbell and Connelly, Henry Stafford (score), Hubert Bath (arrangements), performed by the British Symphony Orchestra, conducted by John Reynders
Cast	Anny Ondra (Alice White), Cyril Ritchard (Crewe), John Longden (Frank Webber), Sara Allgood (Mrs. White), Charles Paton (Mr. White), Donald Calthrop (Tracy), Hannah Jones (the Landlady), Harvey Braban (the Chief Inspector),† Phyllis Monkman (the Servant), Ex-Detective Sergeant Bishop (the Detective Sergeant)
Filmed	at Elstree Studios, London
Running Time	approximately 80 minutes
Distributor	Wardour & F.
Release Date	June 1929

Other titles: *Erpressung, Chantage*

Synopsis

The credits appear on black, accompanied by chase music that continues over the first scene. A hub cap spins. Police take a call from a radio in the back of the paddy wagon; as it quickly spins around, they jump out the back and run into a

courtyard—children playing, clothes hanging above on a line. Pushing aside a woman at the entry, two policemen mount the narrow stairs to find a man smoking and reading a newspaper in bed; he spies them in a mirror as they pause in the doorway, light streaming over them through the slats in the blinds. The man reaches for his gun from behind the paper, but the detectives are ready and pounce on him.

Outside, the crowd hovers around as the policemen put the man in the back of the truck.

At New Scotland Yard, the man is taken down large halls to a chief investigator's office and interrogated as his two captors stand by and watch. Initially he is given coffee and cigarettes; time passes as the ash tray fills up. An identification parade is put together, and a witness walks by the suspects. Finally, the man is charged, fingerprinted, and walked to a large cell.

The camera tracks behind the two detectives on their way back from the cell, and their chatting about the day is the first dialogue. They enter a washroom full of men and an indistinct atmosphere of talking and good cheer. They exit down the corridor to the lobby where Alice, a blond woman in a cloche and fur-collared coat, turns her cheek to one of the men, Frank, for a kiss. After his partner is gone, she complains to him that she has been waiting half an hour, and Frank rolls his eyes to the side. The police officer at the door whispers a joke to Alice, who giggles and throws her head back as Frank, not privy to the joke, follows her out the door.

In the street full of people and traffic, Frank peers into her face and she turns away, but she finally relents and giggles.

On the Underground, they sit across from one another near a high-spirited child, who pokes at the passengers.

Up a grand staircase, people streaming everywhere, they enter a large city restaurant. Managing to grab a table in front of a center pillar, they immediately start bickering about Frank's being late. "You expect the entire machinery of Scotland Yard to be held up for you?" he protests, then teases her about the hole in her glove. As he tries in vain to flag a waitress, Alice hesitates about going with him to a movie. After she checks a note in her bag about a 6:30 appointment, and notices the time is 6:50, she agrees to go. Suddenly her face lights up and a man approaches, smiling at her. She nods him away and tells Frank she is not going to the movie. Fed up, he quickly pays the bill and stomps out into the entryway, where he paces for a few moments, thinking. Just as his face softens, Alice emerges in the smiling company of the strange man. Chagrined, Frank stares, but she does not notice him as they pass.

Outside a columned, narrow apartment house, a man paces, then skips away when he sees Alice and her new friend, Crewe, an artist. As they chat about being neighbors, Crewe invites her up to see his studio. She demurs, but he accuses her of being frightened. She refuses, saying it is too late, but he persists, insisting that she is frightened. "It takes more than a man to frighten me," she says, then relents when he pleads for her to trust him and sweetly asks to call her Alice. A close-up reveals that the other man is listening; he jumps out and asks to speak with Crewe as they move to enter.

Inside, a low shot reveals a steep stairway. Crewe takes his mail and mulls over one piece, then sends Alice up the stairs while he speaks with the landlady about a certain caller. Returning to the stairs, now viewed with the wall cut away, the couple walks up the four-and-a-half flights to the top.

Alice is impressed with the lovely room, peering first outside at the policeman walking his beat, then giggling at a painting of a jester guffawing and pointing at the viewer. Crewe lights a fire and she picks up a brush and makes a simple face on an empty canvas, to which Crewe adds an outline of a nude body while holding her hand with the brush in it. She signs it, and laughs, "Oh, you are so awful!"

He brings out some drinks and she admires a fluffy costume dress which he encourages her to put on. She hesitates, saying she must go home, but he coolly turns away to play the piano, mentioning that he had wanted to sketch her in the dress. Finally, she decides to try it on and walks on the other side of a screen next to the piano; unable to contain himself, he gleefully strides to the other side of the room, then returns to play some more. As she undresses behind the screen on the right, he sits on the left, playing a "song about you, my dear." She emerges in the middle of the song and he leans around to view her legs. After the song, she jumps into the middle of the room and kicks up her heels to show off the costume; he moves over to "make it quite right," pulling down the straps over her shoulder. She blanches slightly, but stands proudly, until he roughly pushes his fingers through her hair and kisses her. Quickly, she struggles and frees herself. Still for a moment, she regains her composure, and facing the camera, finally murmurs that she must be going, and heads for the screen. He stands aside at first, but spins around in frustration after she has gone behind the screen; with a spark in his eye, he grabs her dress from where it hangs over the screen, then merrily starts in again at the piano. Noticing the dress gone, she panics, but sweetly begs him for it back, "Please!" He throws it over to the other side of the room, bangs on the piano with a flourish, then jumps up and pulls her out, saying firmly, "Don't be silly, Alice." She screams as the camera cuts outside to the cop walking his beat. "Let me go!"

Inside, their struggle is shadowed on the wall as he forces her onto the curtained bed; the camera moves from the wall to the curtain. Her hand is seen frantically groping outside the curtain; shapes move inside it. She screams. She finds a knife by the bedside and brings it in. Eventually, the motion subsides, and Crewe's lifeless hand drops out from behind the curtain of the bed.

Alice emerges wild-eyed; stupefied, she stiffly sets the knife on the table. Zombielike, her arms outstretched, she shivers with the cold and becomes more aware. Peering out the window, she pulls her dress from the jester painting, then rips at the image with her fingers. The scene widens to include the whole room as she quickly moves behind the screen, dresses, and leaves, returning to paint over her signature on the canvas and turn out the lights.

In the hallway, a high angle reveals the deep spiral of the stairs beneath her as she tiptoes down in broad, deliberate steps, then out the door.

Still in shock, Alice wanders the street, passers-by moving quickly around her; a policeman's outstretched hand brings to mind the victim's hand sticking out from the curtain. She pushes her way through a theater crowd and the neon lights of the city blaze at her; a shaking cocktail sign turns into a thrusting knife. Dawn arrives in a large public square and she still paces, ashen, the image of Crewe's hand appearing over and over. She notices a person sleeping in the street, his lifeless hand outstretched, and screams.

The scream turns into the scream of the landlady who has discovered Crewe's body back at the loft. The police have trouble hearing her report over the telephone.

Frank appears at the door of the loft to join two of his colleagues and is

directed to inspect the room. Whistling, he flips up the tear in the jester painting, and flicks the material of the costume. Suddenly, he finds a glove and starts to announce it as a clue, but as he turns triumphantly toward his two colleagues murmuring over the body in the bed, the camera moves quickly with his turning into a close-up of Crewe's face. Recognizing the man and suddenly realizing he holds Alice's glove, Frank turns slowly back, and meditates over it. Then he stares into the camera, which cuts to the joker, then moves in to his hand, which folds and covers the glove, somber music in the background.

Alice sneaks into her home, runs upstairs, and jumps into bed as her mother arrives with coffee and news of the murder around the corner. The birds start singing when Mrs. White undrapes their cage near the window. Alone again, Alice rises, still dressed, the camera taking in a picture of Frank on the wall in his bobby uniform. Sitting at her dresser mirror, she stares for a moment at herself, then busily starts to powder her face, dropping the top of the jar at the sight of Frank's picture. Recovering, she grabs a new dress and changes clothes, and the camera moves into a close-up of her legs as she changes her stockings.

Appearing at the top of the stairs, Alice steps down carefully, then pats herself into normal composure and enters the tobacco shop that her parents keep on the ground level of their home. She goes to the phone booth inside but hesitates over the POLICE listing in the phone book.

As Alice sits down to breakfast with her parents, a customer stands in the doorway between the shop and their parlor/dining area and gossips about the murder. Dressed in stylish wide stripes, she insists there is "something British" about a "good clean whack with a brick," but a knife! "No matter what the provocation," she herself could never use a knife. The camera pans over to Alice, whose eyes begin to dart uncontrollably as the word *knife* echoes in her head. Her father asks her to cut some bread, and she shakily tries to oblige, but the word *knife* shouts out at her and she throws the knife into the air. The camera takes in the whole room as her father rises to caution her, "You might have cut somebody with that!" The shop bell rings.

Alice moves out from behind the counter to greet Frank. Her parents eagerly rise and join the couple, wondering about the murder. Bowing his head, Frank admits he has been put on the case. Finally, he invites Alice into the telephone booth; the man from outside Crewe's apartment the night before appears through the window pacing the sidewalk outside. Frank asks about last night, but Alice stares vacantly away until he produces the glove, then nods her head, yes. They are interrupted by the man from outside, who, with a smirk, asks to use the telephone—to call Scotland Yard—then changes his mind. Instead, he demands the best cigar in the shop from Mr. White. Frank and a nervous Alice stand nearby until the man walks over to them and reveals that he has Alice's other glove. He then returns to the counter to hum and cough over the final selection of his cigar. Lighting it from a lighter stand on the counter, he loudly asks Frank to pay for it, and Alice moves back behind the counter to relieve her father. Draping himself over the counter, and sarcastically announcing that he has no interest in blackmail, he flicks off Frank's attempt to manhandle him. The scene widens as customers come in and out of the shop and the morning traffic rushes by outside. Frank paces the store, then demands to know what the man wants. Casually, the man suggests breakfast.

The three enter the back room, startling Alice's parents with the intrusion. Alice and her mother walk toward the camera, and Alice reassures her that the

man, Tracy, is an "important friend." Tracy makes himself comfortable in Mr. White's stuffed chair as Frank stands by wringing his hands.

Crewe's joker painting fills the screen as it is being moved about by the police. At Scotland Yard, detectives question the landlady about Tracy, whom she describes as "mousy," adding a mimic of his smirk. A montage of flip books containing mug shots ends in a picture of him. Rubbing his hands with pleasure, the head detective directs his men to pick up Tracy.

Back at the dining table, still in Mr. White's stuffed chair, Tracy sits and whistles over his breakfast. A brooding Frank smokes next to him. In the hall, Mrs. White admonishes Alice about Tracy, and Alice returns just as Frank is called to the telephone in the shop. Frank is surprised by something he hears, and stalks quickly back into the parlor. He faces Alice and Tracy with new determination and commands Alice to lock the hall door. Tracy rises in front of the window as Frank faces him with news that the police are seeking to arrest him for the murder. Alice cries out, but Frank tells her to be quiet and she obediently sits in front of the table facing the camera, her back to the two men behind her. Tracy leans against the table and, next to him, Frank sits on it, crossing his legs confidently as they discuss the options. The camera moves to a close up of a frightened Alice, as Tracy objects, "It's my word against hers." She rises to tell Frank he "can't do this," but Frank persists. Tracy demands to know why Frank won't "let her speak," warning Frank that he is "playing with fire," but Frank remains stolid, calmly smoking in the foreground. He finally turns toward the room again as the shop bell rings and the three square off: Frank, clenching his jaw; Alice, eyes lowered; and Tracy, defiant, then wily. As the detectives enter behind Frank, Tracy leaps forward and the sound of breaking glass is heard. He leads a chase through the broken window, and up and over the next building.

Wheels turn, radios signal, police cars and paddy wagons take to the street in pursuit.

Alice stares out from behind a desk under a sunny window at home, and wrings her hands.

Tracy's taxi stops in front of the upraised hand of a traffic cop and he nervously jumps out and walks along a fence near the British Museum. Seeing his pursuers gather around him, he runs up the vast steps, pauses to drink from a fountain among the huge columns, and enters. Inside, he walks through the halls full of antiquities, as more police gather outside and Alice sits at home, still stationary. The music trips lightly around the action, then intensifies as the police begin to run. Suddenly Tracy appears, lowering himself by rope from one hall down to another, past a huge Egyptian stone face. He enters the reading room of the library, a spiral of desks with tables arranged like spokes, then he runs through a mazelike stack area and up a ladder through a hatch in the roof.

A long shot shows him running up the side of the huge dome, yelling at Frank and his colleagues close behind, "It's him you want. Ask him!" Suddenly he falls through the dome's center window.

At the sound of the breaking glass, Alice completes her note, "I am going to give myself up—I cannot bear the thought of that man being accused of something I have done." She rises into the sunlight, raises her eyes upward.

At Scotland Yard, Alice greets the friendly policeman at the door and fills out a form to see the Chief Inspector, Walls, about the Chelsea murder. As she waits, she watches the traffic go by outside. Taken down the windowed corridor, she waits again, brooding, but is finally let in to see Walls. Frank is also there and,

as she falters in speaking, he wonders aloud if this is necessary, now that "everything is cleared up." Walls objects, "Yes, let's hear what she has to say!" But the telephone rings, and he instead instructs Frank to "deal with the young lady." Frank and Alice step outside and he quietly asks her why she came. "I did it," she replies. Pausing, staring out, he finally replies, "I know." But she persists, "you don't know . . . I was defending myself . . . I didn't know what I was doing!" They walk down the corridor arm in arm, separating before going into the entry hall.

In the lobby, the policeman teases Frank about Alice coming to tell them who did it. "Watch out, you'll be losing your job," he laughs, and Frank and Alice laugh too as the camera moves to Alice standing in the middle. She stops wide-eyed at the sight of Crewe's joker painting, laughing and pointing, being carried with her own drawing behind it. The two pieces of evidence are transported through the lobby doors and down the corridor as the men continue laughing.

Notes. * Most filmographies credit John Maxwell as producer. † According to Gifford, *A Catalog of British Films,* Sam Livesay appears in the silent version as the Chief Inspector. The voice of Joan Barry was used in dubbing the role played by Anny Ondra. The song, "Miss Up-to-Date," was written by Billy Mayer and Frank Eyton for the stage play *Love Lies* in which Cyril Ritchard appeared in 1929. ᴴHitchcock appears as passenger on Underground who pokes at the pesky child.

11   *Juno and the Paycock* (1929)

Director	Alfred Hitchcock
Assistant Director	Frank Mills
Production Company	British International Pictures*
Screenplay	Alma Reville, Alfred Hitchcock (adaptation), based on the play by Sean O'Casey
Photography	J[ohn] J. Cox
Editing	Emil de Ruelle
Art Direction	J. Marchant
Sound	C. Thornton
Cast	Sara Allgood (Juno Boyle), Edward Chapman (Captain Boyle), John Laurie (Johnny Boyle), Marie O'Neill (Maisie Madigan), Sidney Morgan (Joxer Daly), John Longden (Charles Bentham), Denis Wyndham (the Mobilizer), Kathleen O'Regan (Mary Boyle), Barry Fitzgerald (the Orator), Dave Morris (Jerry Devine), Fred Schwartz (Mr. Kelly)
Filmed	at Elstree Studios, London, in R.C.A. Photophone
Running Time	approximately 85 minutes
Distributor	Wardour & F., British International Pictures (U.S.)
Release Date	June 1929

Other titles: *The Shame of Mary Boyle* (U.S.), *Giuone e Il Pavone*

Synopsis

March music over the titles ends as the "orator," swathed in a plaid scarf, stands above a crowd of poorly dressed men. "Fellow countrymen! Courageously we have struggled for nation, salvation, and Ireland. . . . When we have taught together and fought together we have always won." The camera moves up over the street sign into a long shot of the crowd, the cross traffic behind. "When we have been divided in thought and opposite in action, we have always lost. . . . We must strive for a wide-awake Ireland. . . . We must skate between those who want us to kill one another." The orator is machine-gunned from a nearby building window. The crowd scatters, many escaping into the nearby Foley's Bar.

Inside the pub, two men, Captain Jack Boyle, a stocky, proud fellow, and Joxer, his gawky, string-bean friend, dust off in front of the bar. They explain what happened to Maisie Madigan, a blond, friendly woman in a black cape. She tells them more news: the young Tancred boy was gunned down the night before and left for dead near a "babblin' brook." Someone in the neighborhood informed on him, and the Republicans are raging, determined to get the informer. Joxer cautions that "the Republicans and the Free Staters must be cooled down or we'll be spending the rest of our lives dodgin' bullets." Jack appeals to Joxer for a beer, but Joxer pulls out his empty pockets. Maisie finally offers to stand them a drink, and they quickly tip their hats and leave when the time comes to return the favor.

Out on the sidewalk, Jack assures Joxer that his wife, Juno, is out and invites him home for a "cup o' tea." The camera moves up over the small ornamented doorway of their apartment building to an open window where Juno, a large, tired, but dignified woman, closes it. She tiptoes across the center room, a fireplace and bedroom door at the right, a table in the middle, and the front door and an alcove with a bed in it on the far wall; here and there the plaster is peeled down to the inner wall. Hearing the men coming up the stairs, she hides behind the front door and mumbles, "It's not for a job he's prayin'." The men pass by her to the fireplace where Joxer sympathizes with Jack for being attached to a "grouchy" woman. Joxer quickly moves to leave when they notice Juno, arms akimbo, standing behind them, but Jack stops him near the door and engages him in a long conversation about a friend, "a darlin' man" according to Joxer, who has offered them work. Jack extols the wonderful opportunity of the offer, and in a final flourish, suggests they bring their shovels along for the interview, "so as to be prepared for any eventuality." Joxer is reminded of an appropriate "darlin' " proverb, but Juno loses her patience and walks over and pushes him out the door. Jack is left holding his shovel as Juno rages behind him, "Shovel! You do more work with a knife and fork than a shovel!" Jowl tensed and chin out, he laments being treated so poorly—"I be better off dead"—and proudly refuses her offer of breakfast.

Mentioning that he just missed Jack at the bar, Jerry Devine, a young man in a suit, walks in with the offer of another job for Jack. Jack leans over, his leg suddenly in great pain. "Won't be long till it travels to the other one," snips Juno. Jack limps off into the bedroom, and Jerry and Juno laugh. Johnny, the Boyles' grown son, who has lost an arm, mopes in the background near the fireplace. Jerry looks worried and suddenly moves close to Juno to ask after Mary, Juno's grown daughter. He informs her that he saw Mary last night with a "slick dude with a walking stick." Juno tells him Mary can take care of herself and walks out the door. Jack returns and complains at length to Jerry about the "nice turn. . . .

It's a curious way to reward Johnny by makin' his poor father work." "Dry up," says Jerry and walks out.

The camera views the fireplace straight on, a wash line with some clothes in front of it and a kettle inside. Jack trips over his son, who was seated in front of the fire but now gets up and leaves. Spying something in the cupboard on the far wall, Jack paces in front of it for a time, then dips down to grab a frying pan and some sausages and sets them on the fire. Hearing footsteps, he grabs the pan and throws it under the bed in the alcove. The footsteps belong to a sewing machine salesman whom Jack quickly dismisses. Just as Jack puts the pan back in place, Joxer appears, and then Johnny, who hysterically demands to know who's pounding on the downstairs door. Joxer refuses to go near the window, and Jack comically strides over, then drops to the floor and peeks out. "A man in a trench coat" who is going away, says Jack, and Johnny morosely turns back into the bedroom.

The men sit down to eat; Jack takes the sausage and pours the grease out for Joxer. Joxer mentions that the job is good news, but the Captain is disgusted, thinking of his leg pains. They yearn after their seafaring days: "What is the stars?" they wonder, "What is the moon?" Juno's footsteps interrupt their musings and Joxer jumps out the window to the fire escape to hide. Jack picks up the food in the tablecloth and throws it into the cupboard, falling on his back in the process.

Wearing a trim hat, Juno comes in and commands him to put on a shirt and tie because Mary is bringing up a guest with a big surprise. Noticing the floor is wet, she traces it to the loaded tablecloth; some of the dishes fall out in front of her and break. "Joxer was here," she laments, and pushes the lot back inside. Quickly, she puts out a clean tablecloth. Mary, dark-haired and fashionably dressed, enters and sits down with the ill-at-ease Charles Bentham, a young, snappily dressed law clerk. They hear her father ranting in the next room. Juno calls out to Johnny, "whose arm was blown off in the fightin'." "I'd do it again," snorts Johnny. Finally, Jack enters and Charles announces an inheritance from one of Jack's relatives. Johnny, always seated by the fireplace in the background, mumbles gratefully that they can go someplace where they are not known, and everyone is happy they needn't worry any more about Jack's getting a job. Charles and Jack shake hands; Charles immediately wipes his hands on his jacket. Juno, Charles, and Mary stand as Jack commands a time of mourning for their uncle who left them the legacy. Pompously grabbing his low-slung belt and sticking his chin out, he intones that unfortunately, everyone must die, "you Juno, today, and me, maybe tomorrow.... God save Ireland.... Juno, I'm done with Joxer, he's nothin' but a prognosticator and a procrastinator." At this, Joxer jumps in from the fire escape where he has been hiding and complains of the insult. Jack winces, but Juno points to the door, and Jack backs her up, leaning threateningly into Joxer. That done, Jack rejoins the group, but the camera moves in to a close-up of Johnny's brooding face. He looks up, wide-eyed, toward the window. Rain pours outside in the sunlight of the open window, the iron grating of the fire escape beyond. A burst of machine-gun fire is heard.

Close-up of a gramophone speaker. The camera moves out from a shop counter to show Mary picking at her fingernails as Juno purchases the machine and some records on credit—the £2000 arrives next week. Mary wonders if they are not getting into too much debt, but Juno hushes her with a pat. They walk down the street loaded with packages.

Arriving home, they find Jack with his feet up on a new settee. Johnny sits by the fire brooding in his usual position on a straight-back chair; Juno got the gramophone for him, but he refuses to be cheered by it. Juno is happy to have Charles arrive, but Jack sneers and throws the man's hat and cane on the bed. Charles sits primly on one of the straight-backed chairs as Mary and Juno serve cake and tea, a ceremony that Juno carefully directs so that Jack, lying again on the settee, receives the smallest piece. The camera frames the group seated around the room in a tableau: tea table on the left, and Johnny in the background staring at the floor. Their polite chat turns intellectual as Charles warms to the subject of theosophy, explaining that it is concerned with "man's sympathy with his spirit." Jack proclaims that people have no interest in religion and know more about Tom Mix and Chaplin than Peter and Paul, and Juno wonders about ghosts. The camera moves into a close-up of Johnny as Charles observes that "ghosts are seen by persons of a certain nature, they say that sensational actions, such as the killing of a person, demand great energy and that energy lingers in the place where the action occurred." Johnny turns from the floor to glare at him, then suddenly rises in anger, "Isn't there something better to talk about than killing people!" and staggers back into the bedroom. Charles apologizes, but Johnny runs back into the room, screaming that he has seen a ghost, Robbie Tancred out by the statue, "bleedin' and lookin' up at me." Juno puts him on the bed in the alcove and demands a drink to calm him as he pleads with her to go look. Afraid, she hesitates, commanding Jack to go, who commands Mary to go, who is rescued by Charles, who walks back into the bedroom and proclaims it is only a light by the statue in the square.

Maisie and Joxer join the party, and Maisie extols Mary's beauty until Charles becomes visibly embarrassed. The newcomers congratulate and flatter until everyone has their eyes raised to the ceiling in boredom. Jack calls for a song, and Juno and Mary stand in front of the fireplace, and perform an Irish folk song in sweet soprano voices. The rest clap heartily, then Juno insists that Maisie sing; in a whiskey voice, she leads them in a rousing version of a more ribald song, then starts to bore them about what her voice used to be, until Jack interrupts and asks Joxer to sing. Joxer closes his eyes and caterwauls, then forgets the words. "I 'ate to see a fellah try to do what they're not able to do," moans Jack.

Johnny sits up in bed now as Mrs. Tancred can be heard in the hallway on her way down the stairs to her son's funeral. Juno goes out to invite her in for tea, but the woman wails, "Ah, what's the pains I suffered bringin' him into the world to the pains I'm suffering now carrying him out of the world to his grave!" Juno and the other women stand in the stairwell, holding her and grieving. Inside, Johnny gets up from the bed in the alcove and runs into the back bedroom. The men pout and have a drink of beer. They relate that Johnny and the dead boy used to be together all the time, but Jack is unsympathetic. After all, death is the fate of a soldier, and Juno, on her return, also turns punitive: "She let the Die-Hards make an open house of the place!" Maisie suggests another song, but Mary and Charles decide to leave; the group turns toward the gramophone and a rousing version of "If you're Irish, come into the parlor, there's a welcome mat for you." Johnny gulps in agony and tells them to stop; outside the funeral procession is passing, singing a different tune. The camera stays on Johnny's desperate face as the rest run to the window to watch, then go outside as Joxer has pronounced it a "darlin' funeral."

Johnny stares mournfully at the statue of Mary and Jesus on the mantel. A

man's voice interrupts his reverie, wondering why he is not at the funeral. All
that can be seen of the man, who wears a trench coat, is his hand in his pocket
as he leans into Johnny's shoulder. Johnny refuses to go to a "meeting," and the
man reminds him about his oath. Looking up at him, Johnny pathetically
appeals, "Haven't I done enough for Ireland?" "No one's done enough," says the
man, leaving Johnny to sink horrified back into his chair. Wide-eyed, he stares
out through the window into the sunlight and rain. Machine-gun fire rings out.

A contemplative Jack emerges from the solicitor's office and walks down the
stairs, the happy voices of his family ringing in his ears. A hand paints over
Charles Bentham's name on the office door.

Ear to mouth, Joxer and Mr. Kelly, a tailor who has made a custom suit on
credit for Jack, whisper back and forth about the Boyles' financial situation,
rumor being that the inheritance is not coming through. "Why, who would leave
anything to that old bummer Boyle!" says Joxer. They quiet when they notice
Mary and Juno walking down the street toward them. Juno tells them Jack is at
home, nursing the pains in his legs. Kelly decides to go retrieve his suit, and
Joxer follows.

Upstairs in the Boyles' flat, Kelly strides in toward the bedroom where Jack
is lying on the bed, and demands his £7, finally just grabbing the suit. "Go ahead,
step in a pillow slip!" he advises the irate Jack. Joxer agrees as he steals a beer
from the front room table: "He who goes a borrowin', goes a sorrowin'." Jack runs
into the stairwell after Kelly and instead finds Joxer, who moans in sympathy
over his lost stout. An angry Maisie appears, demanding the £3 Jack owes her.
She decides to take the gramophone and pawn it; she and Jack struggle briefly
over it. "I'll pull some of those gorgeous feathers out of your tail!" she screams at
him.

Joxer and Jack then go nose to nose over Joxer's insinuations that the
inheritance has dried up, until Jack drives him up the stairs in anger and Juno
drags herself up from the street, wringing her hands. Worried, she sits at the
table, while Johnny takes up his chair near the fireplace. She commands her
husband to sit down and indirectly tells him their daughter is pregnant.
Elsewhere, a close-up shows Mary, her sad head bowed. Jack commands that
Charles must marry her, but, hearing that the culprit has left Ireland, he easily
switches gears and threatens Mary with banishment. Juno firmly tells him he
had better not touch her; after all, she has always taken care of herself, as his
"fatherly care never troubled her." Refusing to be moved, Jack struts, hands in
his belt. "If Mary goes, I go with her," says Juno. Johnny cries out in defense of
his father, "She's disgraced us!" Finally, Juno suggests that they all just leave,
and Jack tells her the other bad news: Charles misread the will and the cousins
are appearing from everywhere, even Australia. The inheritance has gone to the
lawyers. Downcast, Juno moves into the foreground, weak voiced and desperate.
"Isn't there even one middlin' honest man left in the world?" she cries at the
ceiling. Jack decides to go get a beer and walks into the hallway calling for Joxer,
who responds, "I'm only waitin' for the word, and I'll be with you like a bird."

Out on the sidewalk, the men pass Mary standing near the iron fence, she
walks slowly by some children playing and goes inside. In the downstairs entry
hall, she is stopped by Jerry, who eagerly asks her to marry him. When she
alludes to her condition, he balks, "Oh, I didn't know you'd sunk that low," and
apologizes for troubling her. "Your humanity is just as narrow as the others'," she
groans; left alone, she stares out, resting her stricken face in her palm. Workmen

carry the Boyles' new furniture past her out the door; and Juno runs down the stairs after them. She and Mary go to get Jack in hopes that he can stop them. On the way out, they pass two men in trench coats who mash their cigarettes on the sidewalk before entering.

Upstairs, the men confront Johnny with handguns raised. They send the furniture men, arms upraised, into the foreground, and drag him out, accompanied by his screams of "Hail Mary!," down the stairs and into a car. The scene dissolves into a close-up of the statue of Mary and Jesus over the sound of machine-gun fire.

Juno and Mary, who clutches Juno's shoulders, stand in their empty apartment. The camera moves to a close-up of Juno, who moans, "If anything happened to Johnny, I'd lose my mind." They cringe at the sound of a soft knock on the door. Maisie appears dramatically before them, "May God be with you this night!" Down on the street, two policemen wait. "Johnny!" cries out Juno, then turns to comfort her daughter, "Hush darlin', you'll soon have your own troubles to bear." Mary walks into a long shot in front of the fireplace and cries out, "It's true, there isn't a God. He wouldn't let these things happen!" Juno hushes her, "What can God do against the stupidity of man? We'll go and we'll come back here no more. Let your father forage for himself." Mary laments that her child won't have a father, and Juno embraces her, "Sure, it'll have better, it'll have two mothers!" Juno then sends Mary off, in order to face the ordeal of identifying Johnny's body herself.

Regretting her lack of sympathy for Mrs. Tancred, Juno paces alone in the room for a time, repeating to herself the other woman's cry of grief, "What's the pain I suffered bringin' you into the world to the pain I suffer now takin' ya' out to your grave!" She walks over to the statue on the fireplace to complain to the Virgin, "Where were ya' when my darlin' son was riddled with bullets?" The camera moves back into a long shot of the room as Juno turns toward it and walks into the center, her arms raised high, "Take away this murderous hate and give us thine own eternal love!" She walks out the door, leaving the room empty.

Note: * Most filmographies credit John Maxwell as producer.

12 *Elstree Calling* (1930)

Director	Adrian Brunel
Director of "Sketches"	Alfred Hitchcock
Production Company	British International Pictures, Ltd.
Screenplay	Val Valentine
Photography	Claude Friese-Greene
Editing	A. C. Hammond, under the supervision of Emile de Ruelle
Sound	Alec Murray
Music	Reg Casson, Vivian Ellis, Chick Endor, Ivor Novello, Jack Strachey. Lyrics: Douglas Furber, Rowland Leigh, Donovan Parsons. Conductors: Teddy Brown, Sydney Baynes, John Reynders
Production Manager	J. Sloan

Cast	Cicely Courtneidge, Jack Hulbert, Tommy Handley, Lily Morris, Helen Burnell, the Berkoffs, Bobby Comber, Lawrence Green, Ivor McLaren, Anna May Wong, Jameson Thomas, John Longden, Donald Calthrop, Will Fyffe, Gordon Harker, Hannah Jones
Filmed	at Elstree Studios, London, in R.C.A. Photophone
Distributor	Wardour Film, Ltd.
Length	7617 feet
Release Date	February 1930

Synopsis

Hitchcock directed the bridging segments of this all-star British musical revue. These six segments, which total no more than five minutes of screen time, involve the actor Gordon Harker playing a crotchety old man who is trying to tune in the revue on his new (homemade?) television set.

1: The man stands in his handyman's room which is strewn with wires, some leading into and out of the picture tube, which stands up on a shelf over the center table. He manages to tune in Tommy Handley introducing the show.

2: The television blips off. His wife, played by Hannah Jones, and a neighbor friend advise as he fiddles with the machine; he accuses her of letting the children into the room when he finds a toy model on the television stand.

3: As the man beats on the television set with a hammer, his neighbor sits in his comfortable living room where the show is coming in perfectly. The neighbor pops over to announce the next act.

4: The man bends down in a mass of wire, and his wife hands him a tool that burns him. The neighbor pops in again.

5: Wife and neighbor kibbitz, as the man still struggles with the inoperative tube.

6: The man tunes in the sound and picture just in time to hear Tommy Handley say "Goodnight."

13　*Murder!* (1930)

Director	Alfred Hitchcock
Assistant Director	Frank Mills
Producer	John Maxwell
Production Company	British International Pictures
Screenplay	Alma Reville, Alfred Hitchcock (adaptation), Walter Mycroft (adaptation), based on the play and novel *Enter Sir John,* by Clemence Dane and Helen Simpson
Photography	J[ohn] J. Cox
Editing	Emile de Ruelle, Rene Marrison

Art Direction	J[ohn] F. Mead
Sound	Cecil V. Thornton
Music	John Reynders
Cast	Herbert Marshall (Sir John), Norah Baring (Diana Baring), Edward Chapman (Ted Markham), Phyllis Konstam (Doucie Markham), Esme Percy (Handel Fane), Miles Mander (Gordon Druce), Donald Calthrop (Ion Stewart), Amy Brandon-Thomas (lawyer for Diana Baring), Esme V. Chaplin (Prosecutor), Joynson Powell (the Judge), Marie Wright (Mrs. Mitcham), Hannah Jones (Mrs. Didsome), S. J. Warmington (Bennett), R. E. Jeffrey (Jury Foreman), and Members of the Jury: William Fazan, Alan Stainer, Clare Greet, Kenneth Kove, Guy Pelham Boulton, Violet Farebrother, Drusilla Wills, Robert Easton, George Smythson, Ross Jefferson, Picton Roxborough
Filmed	at Elstree Studios, London, in R.C.A. Photophone
Running Time	approximately 100 minutes
Distributor	Wardour Films, Ltd., British International Pictures (U.S.)
Release Date	October 1930

Other titles: *Meutre, Omicidio!*

Synopsis

Credits appear on black, Beethoven's Fifth Symphony on the soundtrack.

A clock chimes 1:30. A scream, followed by a dog's barking and heavy knocking sounds waken the neighborhood. The camera passes by a series of windows as the occupants open them. Inside the last, the Markhams, blond and cheery Doucie, and Ted, who grabs his false teeth, dress hurriedly after noticing that a crowd, as well as the police, are outside the house where Diana Baring is staying. Doucie runs up the sidewalk and pushes through the bystanders at the door.

Inside, a policeman stands aghast; the camera moves to the seated, hunched Diana, who stares out as if in a trance, a bloody poker beneath her dangling hand, and the body of Edna Druce in front of her before the fireplace. The policeman summons the inspector, who begins to ask questions. Ted Markham, already up front, explains they are all part of the theater troupe and he is the stage manager; Doucie interrupts. The victim's husband, Gordon Druce, falls to the floor next to Diana, babbling, "You always hated Edna, thought yourself too good for her." Diana stares into space, unable to move, speechless. Someone asks for brandy for Gordon; Diana tells them where to find a flask, but it's empty.

Offering to help the landlady make tea, Doucie follows her back and forth several times from the table in the dining room to the stove in a back room, and they gossip about Edna and Diana. According to Doucie, the two were enemies, but Edna suddenly made peace just the night before. Diana was puzzled but asked her to supper anyway. The landlady doesn't believe Diana could have done the murder and neither does Doucie, who "can't help but think" Edna had some reason for getting Diana alone. They return to the front room with the tea just as the police are taking Diana to the station.

A clock chimes 6:05. A crowd gathers at the theater box office where a sign announces that Diana and Edna will be replaced by understudies.

The stage curtain rises along with the cover of the peephole in Diana's cell. She stares, hunched, into the camera. She turns away, preening as she imagines the laughter and applause of her audience, then winces as she hears the announcement of the understudy.

Backstage at the performance, the police speak with Ted and try to interview the troupe between cues, sound effect interruptions, and exits and entrances. The first actor says, yes, Edna and Diana left together last night, very unusual, and Handel Fane saw them too. Handel Fane walks up to confirm this; introduced as "100 percent he-woman," he is in drag. He says that after seeing them he went to his room with Ion Stuart, another actor, who now glares at them from the set door, while Ted explains that Ion and Edna were friends. Doucie, costumed in a riding outfit, makes her entrance while Ion and Handel change costumes—Ion, from a police uniform to a dress; Handel, from a dress to a uniform. Handel wonders aloud about poor Diana in jail and complains that blood always makes him feel sick.

A title announces "*Rex v. Diana Baring*." She continues to appear very grave, but proud. The jury are shown one by one as the charge is read; throughout the proceedings their attention follows the action in unison. The prosecution addresses them about the equality of men and women and the necessity for dispassion as they weigh the testimony. Diana, in fur collar and cloche, testifies that she remembers a final moment when Edna inexplicably looked at her in fear and shock saying, "How dare you!," but nothing after that. "I just don't remember!" she cries. The defense, argued by a woman, rests its case on the truthfulness of Edna's testimony and the confidence that her behavior shows "sheer innocence." The judge tells the jury that "truth can be stranger than fiction," and quotes the prosecution to the effect that "neither beauty nor youth can mitigate the crime of murder."

In the jury room, the foreman goes over the "broad facts": the women quarreled, Diana won't give the name of the man they were quarreling about, and she was caught red-handed. Further, the defense doesn't deny Diana killed Edna, but contends it was done under "some kind of fit." Ballots are collected, with three jurors writing "not guilty" and two undecided. The first undecided juror complains at length about the injustice of the system but supposes Diana to be guilty anyway. The second juror is vague and easily persuaded by the foreman to write "guilty." The first juror to vote not guilty, Mrs. Ward, explains in an erudite manner that Diana is a "victim of circumstances," suffering from mental anguish and therefore not responsible for her actions. She is persuaded in the other direction when another juror protests that the crime might be repeated. The second not guilty voter, Mr. Daniels, says he just can't believe someone like her could murder, but changes his mind under the burden of explanation and finds her guilty, "I suppose."

The last to vote Diana not guilty, Sir John, suffers greatly through his explanation, being only a "poor actor" trying to "apply the technique of my art to a problem of real life." The foreman tries to move him along, saying "time is money," but Sir John is convinced Diana is telling the truth. He is impressed by her behavior and sure that his "reasoning is deeper than Daniels's." Some of the jurors rise and gather around him; they all try to sway him by repeating the testimony of the rest of the troupe, who said the two were sworn enemies and Diana had been rough to Edna once, proving "her violent nature." They also repeat the proof of the crime scene, remind him of the testimony of the policeman who said she was drunk, and of Ted Markham, who found the empty brandy flask. Sir John objects that these things were not borne out by Handel Fane, but someone cuts in that "he was obviously in love with her."

All the jurors are now crowding around Sir John. They become an aggressive circle, throwing out evidence and demanding "an answer to that, Sir John." Eventually, they are chanting "Any answer? Any answer to that?!" and he reluctantly agrees to a guilty verdict. They file out.

A clerk comes in to tidy the room while the verdict can be heard being read outside, a sentence of death. "It's absurd, I tell you," pleads Diana.

At Sir John's apartment in Berkeley Square, the well-appointed rooms are quiet. Sir John shaves in the bathroom; his attendant brings in a radio. Over the din, he asks the servant to ring up his manager Mr. Bennett and request the details of the last three nights' take. As he studies his face in the mirror and the radio plays the overture to *Tristan and Isolde,* we hear his thoughts; "amusing . . . the way she stood up to everybody . . . very attractive. . . . That's what harmed her. . . . Who drank the brandy? Why didn't I force that point? The girl says she didn't drink it . . . easy to figure these things out afterward . . . but I'm glad I brought it up . . . that's the whole thing, whoever drank the brandy!" Mr. Bennett is announced.

In his living room, Sir John morosely greets Bennett, who sympathizes, saying it must have been awful for him as a member of the jury. Sir John instructs him to put in his understudy for the night and to get hold of Diana's touring company, in particular the stage manager. Bennett, surprised, asks if the trial isn't over, but Sir John replies no, and muses to himself about why he "sent away" Diana.

A classified ad indicates the Markhams are looking for work. In a living room, their daughter stumbles through a piano piece while an older woman views them suspiciously. "She won't let us stay here much longer," muses Doucie. Suddenly a summons appears from Sir John. They hurriedly primp for the noon appointment.

At Sir John's large office, Ted walks across the carpet, which is shown by the camera to feel pillow-like under his feet. He greets Sir John, who philosophizes about artists "who use life to create art, and art to criticize life." The latter he terms a duty that is sometimes forgotten in pursuit of the former. He mentions the trial briefly, then continues to circle, offering Ted a job with a Christmas tour. Ted talks Sir John into hiring his wife, too. Sir John sends downstairs for Doucie, then returns to the matter of the trial. Ted is startled; "You think she's innocent!" "She was assumed guilty because she didn't deny it," says Sir John. Doucie arrives and is quickly brought into the plan to approach the murder from another angle so "we should be able to arrive at a different result." They begin to go over the events, the Markhams having volunteered to work with Sir John for a couple of days.

The rooming house near the scene of the crime: Sir John and the Markhams lean out the window from which Ted and Doucie had looked after the scream and had noticed a policeman who later disappeared.

They go down to the murder scene where the victim's husband has also returned to harangue. They go inside and tour the rooms, noticing a back window leading to the dressing rooms of the theater. The landlady insists she heard only women arguing, but Sir John tricks her into questioning herself by mimicking a high-pitched voice from the other room. They inspect Diana's room, where Sir John finds a picture of himself, and pauses before it.

Briefly, they discuss their strategy on the sidewalk outside,[H] and decide to return to the theater where an attendant gives them a cigarette case left behind, and takes them upstairs to see Handel and Ion's room. In it is a window facing the private houses around the corner, and a broken wash basin. As they walk down the street to the rooming house, Sir John wonders if he shouldn't stay at the Red Lion instead, imagining a steaming hot meal, but Ted reminds him that they are there to gather evidence.

In the morning, Sir John is wakened by a screaming baby and the proprietor with her four other children, who jump on the bed while Sir John listens to the woman tell of finding a uniform. She spoke to Handel about it; he said it was Ion Stewart's. Ted arrives, and the family exits. He pulls out the cigarette case with the news that it belongs to Stewart, "and there's a blood stain on it!" Sir John decides he must find the name that Diana withheld.

The screen shows Sir John's permit to visit prison. He is ushered into a stark room with a long table, over which the camera pans from one empty chair to the other. Diana arrives, extremely polite and surprised. He explains his guilt: "If I hadn't sent you away on tour. . . ." "I knew someone would try to get me out," she replies, but expresses great despair. There must be grounds for appeal, he says, and asks her to tell him the name of the man she and Edna were discussing before the murder. "He has no connection with the case," she says; "she tried to say poisonous things about him, but I stuck my fingers in my ears!" "You're shielding him, because you're in love with him!" provokes Sir John. "But that's impossible, the man's a half-caste . . ." she gasps. Struggling to understand, Sir John mutters, "Black blood!" and spins the cigarette case towards her. She matter-of-factly says that it belongs to Handel Fane, not Stewart. Their time is up; they stand and face each other. Sir John passionately asks about the photo of himself in her room. She replies, ". . . one has one's heroes." After she is gone, he calls after her, "I'll find Fane!"

The screen shows a montage of a weather vane and a high-angle long shot of Diana pacing in her cell as the shadow of the gallows rises. Snatches of Sir John's search for Handel can be heard on the soundtrack; no one knows where he is, but finally he is discovered working as a trapeze artist.

At the circus, Ted and Sir John watch Handel, costumed as a woman, swing in the air. Sir John alludes to *Hamlet,* Act III, Scene 2, which Ted knows well, and tells him they will proceed on that basis.

At Sir John's office, Handel enters prepared to read for a part and is told the script, "the inner story of the Baring case," is not yet entirely written, but "perhaps he can help." Handel turns away in fear but manages to stand his ground, and even asks for a poker for a prop. Coming upon an empty page, he tells Sir John that he's not good at writing, but he'll be glad to read again when the script is finished.

At the circus, Sir John approaches Handel in his dressing room but is put off until after the show.

Handel enters the huge tent in a long cape and feathers. His trapeze act becomes a montage of his breakdown under the imagined stares of Diana and Sir John. Resting on his perch, he stops the music, forms a noose from the rope, and falls into it. Down on the floor, Sir John reads a note from Handel, in which he completes the murder scenario, and explains that the victim was about "to reveal his deepest secret to the woman he dared to love."

Diana walks from prison to meet Sir John; in the car, they hug as he offers her a part in his next play.

In an elegant living room, they warmly greet one another as servants stand by; the camera moves out to reveal a stage set.

Notes. *Mary* is a German version.[H] Hitchcock does bit as passer-by.

14   *Mary* (1931)

Director	Alfred Hitchcock
Assistant Director	Frank Mills
Producer	John Maxwell
Production Company	British International Pictures
Screenplay	Alma Reville, Herbert Juttke, Dr. Georg C. Klaren, based on the play *Enter Sir John* by Clemence Dane and Helen Simpson
Photography	Jack Cox
Editing	Emile de Ruelle, René Marrison
Art Direction	John Mead
Music	John Reynders
Cast	Walter Abel, Olga Tschechowa, Paul Graetz, Lotte Stein, Ekkehard Arendt, Jack Mylong-Münz, Louis Ralph, Hermine Sterler, Fritz Alberti, Hertha von Walter, Else Schünzel, Julius Brandt, Rudolph Meihardt-Jünger, Fritz Großmann, Lucie Euler, Harry Hardt, Eugen Burg, Heinrich Gotho
Filmed	at Elstree Studios, London
Distributor	Wardour & F.
Release Date	None found

Other title: *Sir John greift ein!*

Note. German version of *Murder!* (1930) shot simultaneously with same technical personnel.

15   *The Skin Game* (1931)

Director	Alfred Hitchcock
Assistant Director	Frank Mills
Producer	John Maxwell

Production Company	British International Pictures
Screenplay	Alma Reville, Alfred Hitchcock (adaptation), based on the play by John Galsworthy
Photography	J[ohn] J. Cox
Camera Operator	Charles Martin
Editing	R[ene] Marrison, A. Gobett
Art Direction	J. B. Maxwell
Sound	Alec Murray
Cast	Edmund Gwenn (Mr. Hornblower), Jill Esmond (Jill Hillcrist), John Longden (Charles Hornblower), C. V. France (Mr. Hillcrist), Helen Haye (Mrs. Hillcrist), Dora Gregory (Mrs. Jackman), Phyllis Konstam (Chloe Hornblower), Edward Chapman (Dawker), Frank Lawton (Rolf Hornblower), Herbert Ross (Mrs. Jackman), Ronald Frankau (Auctioneer), R. E. Jeffrey (first stranger), George Bancroft (second stranger)
Filmed	at Elstree Studios, London, in R.C.A. Photophone
Running Time	approximately 89 minutes
Distributor	Wardour & F., British International Pictures (U.S.)
Release Date	June 1931

Other titles: *Bis auf's Messer, Fiamma d'Amore*

Synopsis

Bucolic music sets the scene as three men walk toward a sprawling tree at the edge of a meadow, take off their jackets, and bring out a huge saw.

Rolf Hornblower, in his open car, meets Jill Hillcrist, on horseback, coming toward him on the road. They stop to chat, he sitting up on the back of the car seat, she leaning down on her horse's neck. Chomping on an apple, she asks him why they are having the trees cut down near Long Meadow, and he explains that his father is going to build more cottages. Displeased, she reminds him that her family has "been here since Elizabeth," and he retorts, "You call it spoiling, we call it progress." He accuses her of having the same "attitude" as her people and wonders why her mother has not called on his sister-in-law; Jill agrees that the neglect is not nice of her. But she still doesn't like his "pushy" father, while Rolf insists his father is "just as human" as hers. "But you won't let it come between us," he pleads. "I don't know," she responds, and moves on.

Long shots show her riding home through a lane lined with tall trees forming an arch over it, and him puttering up to his father's mansion, newly planted with young trees.

At Hornblower Potteries, there's a traffic jam, goats bleating, dogs barking, and men shouting.

Outside a thatched cottage, the camera moves in toward a chauffeur, who patiently paces back and forth in front of the door, his head bowed. An argument can be heard inside as Mr. Hornblower informs the tenants, Mr. and Mrs. Jackman, that he intends to evict them. Angered at their resistance, he threatens them: "Take care you're not late, or your things will be put out in the rain!" Sarcastically wondering if their "fine friend," Mr. Hillcrist, can protect them, he backsteps out the door just in front of Mr. Jackman, who thrusts his chin out at him.

The Jackmans visit Mr. Hillcrist, a white-haired country squire, at his large Tudor mansion, all the walls paneled in dark wood. Mr. Hillcrist had sold the property to Mr. Hornblower on the condition the tenants would not be moved. Mr. Jackman mentions that Hornblower is interested in the Centre property, which adjoins Hillcrist's, and Hillcrist wanders off toward the leaded windows that face his garden to gaze at the vista, as Mrs. Jackman reminds him his "father owned it, and his father before him." Ignoring Mrs. Jackman's chatter, Hillcrist imagines the vista filled with smokestacks and clanging machinery. He turns back to them and bids them good morning, telling them to "leave it" to him.

He finds Mrs. Hillcrist and the family adviser, Dawker, in the study tending to a show dog, and tells them the news. Mrs. Hillcrist is grim faced. None of them believe the Centre has really been sold, and Mr. Hillcrist suggests he'll confront Hornblower when he visits that day. Dawker warns him, "You'll make him all the keener . . . better get him first, ape his methods!" Mrs. Hillcrist firmly sends Dawker off to see Mrs. Mullins, who owns the Centre.

As Mr. and Mrs. Hillcrist enter their large hallway, Mr. Hornblower arrives with cheerful greetings to which they remain silent. They take him into the great hall and he teases Hillcrist about his gout, mentioning that he himself has "only his own drinking to answer for" and is "lucky to have no past, just the future." Mr. Hillcrist complains about his treatment of the Jackmans, but Hornblower, changing tone, sincerely tells him he didn't realize he would need the cottages when he bought them, thinking he could obtain some other land to use for his work, which is "important work, you know." Mr. Hillcrist protests that the Jackmans are important too, and Hornblower suggests he build them a cottage himself; "You've certainly got the space!"

Realizing the gulf between them, Hornblower stands and tries to explain, "Look, you've not had an occasion to understand men like me. I've got the guts, I've got the money, and I'm not going to sit on it. I'm going ahead because I believe in myself. . . . I've no use for sentiment . . . 40 Jackmans don't mean a little finger to me." Mr. Hillcrist rises at this, but Hornblower continues, and begins to wonder if there is room for the "two of us" and their competing visions in the village. Mrs. Hillcrist inquires when he is leaving, but her husband changes the subject to the question of chimneys in the Centre. "You'll utterly ruin the house we've had for generations and our pleasure here . . . it's a skin game." Hornblower wonders at the "nice expression," but calls them both "an obstruction . . . and anything in my path stays there only on my terms . . . chimneys in the Centre!" Mr. Hillcrist responds that his plans are not very "neighborly." To this Hornblower finally angers, wondering what "neighborly" means, and addresses Mrs. Hillcrist, "I may not have a wife, but I've a daughter-in-law . . . have you called on her?" Mrs. Hillcrist smirks and looks away. "No, I'm new," he continues, "and you're an old family, and you don't like that. You think I'm a pushy man. I go to chapel and you don't like that. I make things and sell them and you don't like

that. I buy land and you don't like that, it threatens the view from your windows! Well, I don't like you. . . . You've had things your own way too long." Mr. Hillcrist ventures that this is a "declaration of war," but Hornblower suggests an alternative, "I'm going to make this a prosperous place. . . . You take me on as a neighbor, and I'll manage without chimneys in the Centre." But Mr. Hillcrist turns away from his outstretched hand, "Your ways are not mine." "Now you'll learn some things," cries Hornblower, and reminds them that he owns land on virtually all sides of their property.

Jill enters from the garden, commenting that Hornblower is "not very sporting" and adds her pleas for the Jackmans. "They don't matter, compared to the schemes I've got for bettering this neighborhood," retorts Hornblower; "I'll answer to God, not you." Jill, insouciantly throwing her glove in the air, pities God, and Hornblower looks around at her mother, shocked at the blasphemy. Mr. Hillcrist asks his daughter to "kindly not talk" and bids Hornblower good day.

Dawker enters the main room to tell the Hillcrists that the owner is going to put up the Centre at auction. He asks to see Mrs. Hillcrist alone, and Jill and her father are left together. She complains about Dawker, "He's so common." "We can't all be uncommon," replies her father. But Jill is concerned about her mother and Dawker scheming—"Mother's fearfully bitter when she gets her knife in"—to make her father do something he "doesn't approve of." "I was just beginning to enjoy myself," she complains, and now everything will be "horrible" with her mother in a "mood." Her father asks her if there is anything between her and Rolf, and she replies no. "I love being friends, but now we're all going to wallow," she laments. Standing at the open doors, her father rhapsodizes about their property: "There is nothing so good and so beautiful."

The vista dissolves into a photograph of land on a poster for the Centre auction. Hornblower's hearty laugh punctuates the change as the camera backs down the narrow street, past him standing with some local men, and then groups of tradespeople and wagons. Charles, Rolf, and Chloe Hornblower, Charles's dark-haired beautiful wife, pull up in their big car, followed by the Hillcrists. Charles goes off to greet his father, and Chloe asks Rolf to leave her so that she will be alone when the Hillcrists pass. Chloe smiles at them, but Mrs. Hillcrist walks by with her chin in the air, and the other two follow. "I'll make her pay," vows Mr. Hornblower when he walks up afterward.

Inside the nearby meeting hall, Mrs. Hillcrist sits by the wall. Chloe boldly sits next to her, and asks nervously why she snubs her. "I'm not aware I've acted at all," says Mrs. Hillcrist, then wonders why Chloe does not stop her father-in-law from his schemes. Chloe claims she has tried. "I suppose such men pay no attention to what women say," says Mrs. Hillcrist, and dismisses her. Jill sits down then, coyly smiling and ignoring Rolf, who blindly sits next to her until he notices the unsmiling Mrs. Hillcrist on his other side. Dawker then takes up the empty space, but Mrs. Hillcrist quickly tells him to rise for their discussion, which involves Mr. Hillcrist blowing his nose as a signal during the auction. Down the bench, Chloe suddenly notices Dawker with a stranger in a leather coat and gasps. She faints under her black veil, and the camera moves in on her eyes as the faces of various men appear to her.

The auctioneer begins, "A unique property . . . an A1 chance for an A1 audience . . . 200 acres of grazing and corn land between the Duke's and Squire Hillcrist's . . . and no tenants to hold you up!" Bidding begins at £2000. With the

auctioneer, the camera spins over the crowd to find the first bidder, then follows it back and forth between Dawker and Hornblower. "How we regret it, if we don't get the finest spot in the country," encourages the auctioneer as the bidding lags at £5,800. Mr. Hillcrist blows his nose to tell Dawker to go over £6000, but whispers to his wife that he does not know how they will cover more than £7000. Over his wife's objections, he blows again and stops Dawker bidding, but then decides to bid himself. He and Hornblower battle to £9000 until someone in the back of the room ends the bidding at £9500.

Outside, Chloe faints on a bench when Dawker walks by her. The Hillcrists get in their car; when it stops at the light, Hornblower steps into their sedan and informs them the winning bid was his, and he had to pay too much because of Mr. Hillcrist's "obstinacy." "A trick," bleats Mr. Hillcrist. "Your agent bid at the beginning, mine at the end—what's the trick in that?" replies Hornblower; besides his "dander's up" over their snubbing his daughter-in-law. "I'm going on with as little consideration, as if you were a family of black beetles!" Mrs Hillcrist steps from the car after Hornblower to have a talk with Dawker, then Mr. Hillcrist walks off with Dawker to learn the secret. Returning with Dawker and the strangers, Mr. Hillcrist is disinclined to be involved in the spread of the information. His wife reassures him, "It won't be spoken of if Hornblower is wise." But Mr. Hornblower is angry, "It's repugnant! I won't have it." They glare at one another as the others watch.

Hornblower stands on his staircase reading a letter from Mrs. Hillcrist: "I have something of the utmost importance to tell you . . . the matter is so bitterly vital to the happiness of all your family." He calls out for Chloe. She hides from him and instead goes with Rolf into the dining room, where he tells her Dawker is waiting by the garage. "Don't say anything to Charlie," she pleads. Their father comes in and sweetly asks her to tell him the truth.

Chloe goes out to meet Dawker; they stand illuminated above by an outdoor light. "You call this cricket," she says. "No, I call it business . . . you're small fry, I've got to use you," he responds. She offers him all the money she has, but he is not interested. Charles yells out for her.

Back in their suite, Charles tries to cheer her up, and she tells him she is pregnant. He castigates the "confounded stuck-up woman" who stands in their way; "as long as she's here, we can't take our proper place."

In the Hillcrist's garden, Rolf tries to talk with Jill, while she plays catch with one of her dogs. "You can't fight and not feel bitter," she says. He comments on her mother's snobbish manners. "She may not be in your class, Jill." But Jill starts whistling, finally singing, "Should auld acquaintance be forgot . . ."

Mrs. Hillcrist meets Dawker in her hallway with the strangers, who have a clipping from the "actual case." She indicates she has not told Mr. Hillcrist of their plan and they decide to put the two men in the study until they need them. Hornblower arrives very angry, demanding to know what she and her "bull terrier" are up to. As he stands close to her face, she informs him that his daughter-in-law was employed as the "other woman" in divorce cases, at £20 a case. He bellows it is a lie, and brings Chloe in, who nervously denies it. The stranger in the leather coat walks out to "refresh her memory." Defiantly, she denies knowing him. Suddenly the other stranger appears, and the camera pulls away from Chloe, isolating her figure in the large room, and then her father-in-law with her. It moves back in to her as she cries out, "Don't tell Charlie!" Broken,

Hornblower approaches Mrs. Hillcrist, "What do you want for this secret?" She demands that he sell the property back to them for considerably less than he paid and Dawker brings out the papers. Hornblower makes them swear on the Bible, repeating after him, they they will never tell anyone.

Her chauffeur lets Chloe off at Hillcrist's front door, and she goes around to the side, dwarfed by three stories of bay windows. She listens to Jill and Mr. Hillcrist discuss her reputation, then cries out in pain; Jill hears her and kindly invites her in. Shaking, she sits with them and tells them of her difficulties, her father going bankrupt, and what a wonderful relief Charles was, and how afraid she is of him. Jill is very sympathetic, and Chloe convinces them to lie to Charles. "What gets in the wind, never gets out, just blows home," she intones. Suddenly, Charles is heard in the hallway, and Chloe hides behind the curtains. He stomps in and Mr. Hillcrist indicates that he had heard of some kind of financial misdealing, but really did not believe it. Charles accuses him of lying and insists that Chloe has been there and talked them into it. Chloe's hand grips the curtain, then drops and disappears. Charles continues to rave until Jill opens the drapes, then he runs out.

In the hallway, Mrs. Hillcrist, dressed in a long gown with a train, instructs a servant to tell the Jackmans to return to their home. Dawker arrives to tell her that Charles goaded him into revealing the secret. Suddenly Hornblower strides in, booming "Give me that deed!"

Outside in the garden, Dawker and Hornblower can be seen through the open doors of the great hall, fist-fighting. In the foreground, the others remove Chloe's body from the pool. Charles carries her dripping body into the great hall. Hornblower rails at Mr. Hillcrist, who apologizes. "Hypocrite," sneers Hornblower. Mr. Hillcrist walks solemnly to a chair, and his wife follows, speechless, raising her hand, then just standing by him. The Jackmans arrive to say thank you, but the couple is too stunned to respond. "I'd forgotten their existence," muses Mr. Hillcrist.

Rolf and Jill stand outside by the open garden doorway. Their hands reach for each other, as she peers in at her parents. Her father ruminates, "When we began this fight we had clean hands. Are they clean now? What's gentility worth if it can't stand fire?"

Out in Long Meadow, the big tree falls.

16 *Number Seventeen* (1932)

Director	Alfred Hitchcock
Assistant Director	Frank Mills
Producer	Leon M. Lion*
Production Company	British International Pictures, Ltd.
Screenplay	Alma Reville, Alfred Hitchcock, Rodney Ackland, based on the play by J. Jefferson Farjeon
Photography	John C. Cox, Bryan Langley
Editing	A. C. Hammond
Art Direction	Wilfred Arnold
Sound	A. D. Valentine
Music	A. Hallis

Cast   Leon M. Lion (Ben), Anne Grey
                                         (Nora Brant), John Stuart (Detective
                                         Barton), Donald Calthrop (Brant),
                                         Barry Jones (Henry Doyle), Garry
                                         Marsh (Shelldrake), Anne Casson
                                         (Rose Ackroyd), Henry Caine (Mr.
                                         Ackroyd), Herbert Langley (Guard)
Filmed   at Elstree Studios, London
Running Time   approximately 65 minutes
Distributor   Wardour Films, Ltd.
Release Date   July, 1932
Other titles: *Nummer siebzehn, Numéro 17*

Synopsis

Credits appear on a grey background over somber music.

A spindly bush rocks in the wind, its leaves falling to the sidewalk below. Dramatic, vaguely Eastern music accompanies the camera as it follows along the walk full of blowing leaves and finds a rolling hat, which settles in front of an open gate. A suited man picks up the hat and brushes off the dirt, then notices the For Sale sign on the Mediterranean-style building. He walks up to the front door, which opens in front of him, then cautiously enters the large, empty central hall. He approaches the curving central stairway, staring up over the railing at the two open stories; someone holding a candle at the top disappears into a doorway. A close-up shows a lifeless hand sticking out through the banister.

Arriving at the top, he meets a rumpled, unshaven man near the corpse. They both discover the body at the same moment and open their mouths in fright, while a train screeches through the frame. The inhabitant, Ben, skids down the stairs on his rear end while the man, an undercover detective named Barton, runs down at first to help him, then to accuse him. Ben insists he killed no one; he was just looking for a place to sleep, as he is a merchant marine who has lost his ship. Taking charge, Barton coaxes Ben back up the stairs. He questions him while Ben mumbles about the shadowy hall. With a sarcastic expression on his face, Ben searches his own pockets for the murder weapon. A close-up shows a picture of Ben's daughter, whom Barton comments to be a "jolly little kid." "She was," replies Ben.

As they talk, elsewhere a hand reaches for a doorknob. The wind whistles through the hallway, and the two men hear the front door slam. Barton walks down to investigate while Ben gapes in horror, but then takes courage and decides to jump over the body and do some investigating himself. He discovers some handcuffs on the body and a gun. After playing with the gun (peering down the barrel and wondering "if it's loaded"), he pockets it. Noticing a looming shadow on the wall, he eventually figures out it is his own after playing with it.

Barton returns, picks up the handcuffs, and queries Ben, who claims he's never seen handcuffs. "I was brought up a Baptist," grins Ben. "It pays for an innocent man to play it straight," cautions Barton. Ben objects, "This is a bobby's job—you're just messin' about." Barton, who does not reveal his identity until the end, argues with Ben until they both hear something above them. They see a shadow cross the wall and follow it. Plaster drops from the ceiling, and a woman

crashes down on top of them, unconscious. After they give her a drink, she wakes up fighting, screaming, "Let me go! Daddy!" Barton restrains her and she eventually calms. Frightened, she asks them to go on the roof and see if anyone is around, and Barton orders Ben to the task. The woman, named Rose, starts smiling, chatting more amiably with Barton, who discovers she and her father live next door. She shows him a calling card, explaining she went to the roof to give her father a telegram. Suddenly Ben joins them again and the woman smiles at his complaints. At Barton's insistence she takes the telegram out of her pocket: "Have traded the Suffolk necklace to Shelldrake—Expect him to make getaway tonight—Watch No. 17—Will arrive later—Barton." The monogrammed card reveals something is going to happen after midnight.

Barton looks at his watch and decides they must move. Suddenly, clocks chime, the doorbell rings, and Ben panics; they all gasp. Barton tiptoes down the staircase, and Ben pulls out his gun. Rose balks at the sight of it, but she and Ben slowly follow. Suddenly, Ben looks down and exclaims, "It's gone!" The camera moves down to the empty floor where the body once lay.

Downstairs, Barton sets down his candle in the large center hall and waits. A gloved hand reaches in through the mail slot and flashes a monogrammed card like the one Rose had. Barton hesitates for a moment, then opens the door. The camera moves into the dark face of Brant, then Barton, then Brant's companion, Nora. Barton and Brant check their watches, their shadows meeting on the door between them, but Brant steps right in anyway, asserting that the agent said they could see the house. As the door closes, another man, Henry, puts his foot in it, then cheerily invites himself in calling Brant "Uncle," and saluting Nora, who greets him blankly. Turning away, Brant checks the room while Nora turns somber, staring first at their "nephew" Henry, then back at Barton. Barton, holding his candle again, leads them upstairs, where Rose watches and Ben taunts, "Come on up, they won't find no bloomin' body up here!" He continues to rail, telling them the events of the evening and waving the gun in the air. Brant pulls out his own gun, then Henry grabs Ben and starts wrestling with him until the gun goes off, shooting Barton in the hand. Barton falters, and Nora, who can neither hear nor speak, helps him to bandage his hand.

Brant pushes Barton into one of the empty rooms with Ben and Rose, while Henry searches him and Nora looks on, pained. Henry searches Ben, who talks sarcastically to him, then Rose, where he finds the monogrammed card and telegram. Nora signals Brant who walks over and demands the telegram, then queries Rose, who tells him to mind his own business. Henry walks into the hallway and discovers the handcuffs. Back in the room Brant persists with Rose. "Mightn't your father have some secrets he is keeping from you?" "If you ask me any more questions I'll spit in your eye," she replies. Ben slaps her on the rear in support, and she slaps him back.

Brant hands the gun to Nora out in the hallway, while Henry hides the handcuffs from Brant. A train rumbles by, its shadows falling on the walls of the hall as Henry and Brant lean on the railing and talk, exchanging cards and names. The wind blows some debris in and the distraction allows Ben to attempt an escape. Silhouetted in the doorway, he, Brant, and Henry struggle, then Ben runs out with the two of them in close pursuit. They grab him and force him back up the stairs, then lock him in a bathroom.

Inside the bathroom, another mustached man, Shelldrake, grabs Ben by the neck and slaps him to the floor. Pretending to be unconscious, Ben spies

Shelldrake take the diamond necklace from inside the water tank of the toilet. As he leans down by Ben to listen at the keyhole, Ben takes the necklace out of Shelldrake's pocket.

In the hallway, Brant and Henry continue to talk. "Shelldrake has hidden the jewels too well—probably in this house." Detective Barton is also a consideration; "If he turns up we'll be finished." They wonder if they can make Shelldrake divide the proceeds somehow. Suddenly they look down to find a man slowly climbing the stairs. It's the bloodied "corpse," Rose's father, Ackroyd, who calmly approaches them and asks for their cards, wondering if they are both from the train. They decide they had "better be getting down," and tie Rose, who winks secretly at her father, and Barton to the railing. "Through there, to the train," indicates Ackroyd to Brant, Henry and Nora then quickly locks them inside a room. Before Ackroyd unties the other two, Rose tells him to go get Ben from the bathroom, where he's been dumped in the bathtub.

When Ackroyd enters, Shelldrake jumps out fighting. They fist-fight at length, as Rose and Barton, still handcuffed to the banister, watch. Ben finally gets out of the tub and picks up a stick. The men circle in front of him as he tries to aim at Shelldrake, but misses and hits Ackroyd instead. Shelldrake pulls a gun on Ben and puts him back in the bathroom along with Ackroyd, then lets the others out of their room. "You're a fine bunch. I've a good mind to wash my hands of the lot of you," he complains, as he directs them down to the train. Brant tells Shelldrake to go down to the cellar first, and Nora whispers to Barton and Rose on her way out that she will be back. "She spoke!" marvels Rose.

Rose and Barton are left to struggle with their bindings; "It's like the pictures, isn't it," she comments. Suddenly the railing gives way and they fall over, suspended by their handcuffs over the downstairs hall. Rose faints at this, then faints again at the sight of the floor far below. Nora returns from the other stairwell and helps them down, just as the railing completely breaks off. They let Ben out of the bathroom and he comes out fighting and knocks down Rose, who returns his punch. Her father is still on the floor of the bathroom, badly hurt.

Barton and Ben leave Rose with her father and go down the narrow circular stairway to the cellar, where the group waits, unaware of them in the next room.

Nora announces to Brant's group that she is not going with them, but she knows too much to be left behind. As Ben and Barton pound on the door, they push her down the stairs that lead to a large train bed below, and lock the trapdoor behind them. A moment later, Ben and Barton break into the room and kneel to struggle with the trapdoor.

Shelldrake, Henry, Brant, and Nora head for the train; meanwhile, as Ben continues to struggle with the door, Barton notices an advertisement on the wall for the ferry train. Ben and Barton finally get the trap door open and climb down to follow Shelldrake's group. They run to get on as the train starts up, but Barton is knocked off. Ben finds himself in a freight car full of wine.

Shelldrake has noticed that one of the train guards has seen them and leads Brant and Henry inching along the side of the train to the back. They knock the guard out and tie him up.

Barton telephones the police, while Ben gets high on wine and admires the necklace he took from Shelldrake. The train speeds along as Ben decides to venture out of his car, and Barton waits in an empty street. Suddenly Barton remembers he has a gun and hijacks a bus.

Ben bumbles along to a boxcar where Nora waits.

Back at the end of the train, Brant asks Shelldrake about the diamonds and suggests a split.

The bus that Barton has commandeered races along, jostling the passengers.

Brant pulls a gun on Shelldrake, who accuses Henry of being Detective Barton. Shelldrake discovers he no longer has the necklace and turns on Brant, screaming he "got that rotten deaf and dumb girl" to take it from him. They struggle and Henry remembers Nora's purse and decides to jump back to retrieve it. The other two follow. Back in the boxcar, Henry demands the necklace from Nora, then starts to search her. Ben tries to protect her by offering the necklace, but just as he is about to pull it out, the others arrive and all scramble for the diamonds as the car careens. It appears that Henry grabs the necklace, and he then races out, slamming the boxcar doors behind him. He hides between a couple of gondola cars, while the others jump over him, then he starts back the other way.

The passengers on Barton's bus are now standing up, complaining about its speed.

The train races along a track parallel to the path of the bus on the road. [All the long shots depicting the ensuing chase scene and wreckage are obviously pictures of a model set.] Henry returns to the boxcar and looks through the straw for the necklace, then turns on Nora and pulls out the handcuffs.

Up near the engine car, Shelldrake and Brant, stymied in their search for Henry, are suddenly spied by one of the engineers. From atop the boxcar behind, they shoot the stoker and he falls off the train. They jump into the engine car, and the engineer faints at their feet.

The people on the bus are now screaming as it roars by a sign, "Stop here for Dainty Teas."

The train speeds along as the men fail to revive the engineer, then struggle with the engine controls; desperate, they pull every lever. The train and bus speed along side by side, finally one going over, and the other under, a bridge. Twice the camera moves to a close-up of the terrified Shelldrake and Brant.

Slowly, the train ferry pulls into port and locks. Horns blow and the ferry men try to flag down the train. Just as the bus arrives, the out-of-control train barrels onto the ferry, eventually stopped by its own wreckage. The ferry's ropes break and it moves out into the water, dragging the train with it. Nora is still handcuffed inside the boxcar half in the water, half out. Seeing her, Barton strips off his coat and jumps in the water. A crowd stands on shore, watching as he swims into the train and brings her out of the car. Ben flails around, holding on to another sinking car nearby.

Inside a station room, the group dries off. Henry, posing as Barton, laments that the others learned who he is, and though he does not have the necklace, at least he has Nora. But Barton confronts him, "You're Doyle. The necklace would draw Shelldrake and Shelldrake would draw you, Henry Doyle. The comic part of it is, I'm Barton." He shows Henry the door where the police wait to take him away. "You! a detective! and making me do all the work," moans Ben. Barton turns back with Nora, and directs her to come and have breakfast with him. Relieved, she laughs. Ben offers a wedding present in exchange for a lift; with a grin, he opens his blanket wide, revealing his long underwear and the necklace around his neck.

Note. * Most filmographies credit John Maxwell as the producer.

17   *Rich and Strange* (1932)

Director	Alfred Hitchcock
Assistant Director	Frank Mills
Producer	John Maxwell
Production Company	British International Pictures
Screenplay	Alma Reville, Val Valentine (additional dialogue), Alfred Hitchcock (adaptation), based on a theme by Dale Collins
Photography	John Cox, Charles Martin
Editing	Rene Marrison, Winifred Cooper
Art Direction	C. Wilfred Arnold
Sound	Alec Murray
Music	Hal Dolphe (composition), John Reynders (direction)
Cast	Henry Kendall (Fred Hill), Joan Barry (Emily Hill) Percy Marmont (Commander Gordon), Betty Amann (the Princess), Elsie Randolph (Elsie)
Filmed	at Elstree Studios, London
Running Time	approximately 87 minutes
Distributor	Wardour & F.
Release Date	March 1932

Other titles: *East of Shanghai* (U.S.), *Endlich sind wir reich, A l'Est de Shangai*

Synopsis

Credits appear in a bright white script on a grey background.

Close-up of a hand moving a pencil down an accounting ledger. The camera moves up over rows of employees behind partitioned desks, then over to the locker area where the men are beginning to file out in their bowlers and overcoats. Bustling music combines with the chatter of the crowd as the women walk past file cabinets, meeting the men at the stairwell and filing out with them into the rain. At the threshold, they stop in pairs to the rhythmic sound of opening umbrellas. One man, Fred, pauses, grimacing: he cannot get his umbrella open. After a while, the umbrella still closed, he moves into the street.

The crowd pushes into the Underground, filling escalators and platforms. An older woman holds up a group before a train door; suddenly they burst past her. Fred is carried along into the car. As it moves, he loses his balance and accidentally catches the pom pom from a woman's hat, ungraciously returning it. Fred's distaste at his surroundings intensifies; he stares at the crass advertising of luxury items and then at a boy standing and eating a sandwich. Trying to read a newspaper, he accidentally knocks a neighbor in the face. His paper falls apart, and he fusses with it at length, finding an ad: "Are you satisfied with your personal circumstances?" Daydreaming, he again smashes into the woman's hat.

Night on a newly developed street of townhouses. Fred walks home, triumphant music accompanying his final try—and success—in opening his umbrella, just as he turns into his doorway. The music calms to sweet violins.

Inside their small front room, his wife, Emily, a smiling blond woman, sews at the table and exclaims that he will like the dress when it is done. She suggests they go out to the pictures, but he morosely cries, "Damn the pictures! I want some life!" She offers him liver pills and protests that she is happy, but he turns on her, "That's just it, the good little women like you don't want enough!" She appeals, but he falls sullenly back into a rattan chair and stares longingly at a painting of a ship. Food sits on the table in the foreground, along with their black cat. Fred angrily throws something at the cat. Suddenly their landlady, Mrs. Porter, brings them a telegram. "Dear Nephew: You say you want to enjoy LIFE. . . . See my solicitors and they will fix you up with the money to experience all the life you want by traveling everywhere." Emily reads, rising from her chair, the words MONEY TO EXPERIENCE ALL THE LIFE YOU WANT BY TRAVELING passing in front of her eyes. Fred throws her material disdainfully on the floor; "Now you'll have some real clothes!" But Emily frowns and retrieves it. The pot boils over on the stove.

Title: "Doth suffer a sea change into something rich and strange." *The Tempest.*

Waiting in the train station, Fred, sporting a cigarette holder, and Emily experience a moment of anxiety as his former associates file through the station on their way to work.

Title: "To get to Paris you must cross the channel." After boarding the ferry, Emily and Fred stand at the railing, smiling at the day. Later, Fred tries to take a photo of her on deck, but cannot keep her in the picture because of the motion. Feeling sick, he decides to get some magazines, even though she already carries an armful.

Title: "To get to the Folies Bergere, you have to cross Paris." A swiftly edited montage of the sights of Paris is intercut with fast motion reaction shots of Fred and Emily.

Inside a large theater, Fred now chews on a cigar stub, and Emily takes off her shoes and rubs her feet together. She is momentarily embarrassed at the nudity on stage and glances briefly down at her own fashionably skimpy outfit. A montage skips through the many acts to which the enthusiastic crowd is treated, including a black banjo player and several finales of kicking dancers. The lights go up.

At a dingy, after-hours jazz bar, Emily is pinched by a stranger and insists she and Fred leave. They proceed to a late-night café, where another couple is having a raucous time, and the bartender, with a flourish, provides them with large drinks.

Title: "And to get to your room, you have to cross the lounge." A long, narrow, art deco lounge looms in front of the couple as they drunkenly tiptoe across, then stiffly wait by the elevator, where Fred corrects the time on his watch by the floor indicator.

In their room, Emily's smile has turned vacant. Fred presents her with a new nightgown; the camera moves into her midsection as she holds it up, then dissolves into a shot of her wearing it. Later they attempt to step into bed, but Fred finds it easier to copy Emily, who has dropped to the floor in prayer.

Title: "Marseilles, the big ship bound for the Far East." Foreboding music accompanies the passengers as they file up the plank to the ship. Fred winces at the feel of the deck and announces he is retiring to their cabin. Commander

Gordon, an elegantly dressed man in a white suit, bumps into Emily, and Miss Gossett, a cheery, dark-haired woman with glasses, inserts herself between them. The ship moves out into a stormy sea.

That night, Emily, in a revealing evening gown, stands alone at the railing. Gordon, now smoking a pipe and dressed in a tuxedo, joins her and asks after her sick husband. Six young women run across the deck and try to pull him away, but he refuses, commenting that "bright young people make me feel old."

In their cabin, Fred rolls his eyes in agony. A steward brings in a dinner menu, but just the names of the dishes make him feel faint.

Over the white-capped Mediterranean, social activities abound: pool, indoor poker, swimming. Bells clang and the engines hum. Fred remains sick.

One day, Emily and Gordon sit at a table on the deck and he shows her photos of himself on a tropical veranda. One of the photos has an empty chair, and she draws a cartoon of herself in it. "You're delicious," he smiles. "You're laughing at me," she says, but he insists on her charms. "You're just a man and not my husband," she rationalizes. "If you get bored, you can just get up and leave. . . . Have you ever been in love, Mr. Gordon? Well, I love Fred and he loves me, but when I talk to him, I'm afraid of saying something foolish. He's very clever. And I'm not." Gordon laughs and she goes on, "Love is dangerous business. It doesn't make people brave, it makes them timid, frightened when they're happy and sadder when they're sad. . . . I haven't made myself clear, love is a wonderful thing." Gordon protests, "Are you trying to pull my leg?" Seeing her incomprehension, he apologizes. Some other guests approach them, presuming Emily to be "Mrs. Gordon."

After dinner, Fred is still sick, and Emily and Gordon sit at a café table in dinner clothes. Miss Gossett sits down between them, but they quickly leave her to her solitaire game.

Sunset on the deck; Emily, in an elegant, long white dress with a train, and Gordon stroll. The camera frames their legs as they walk over the ships' ropes, and the music fades into the sounds of the waves and a lone accordion coming out of the poker room. They go up some narrow stairs to an isolated end of the ship where they kiss. She is startled and demands they go back. They retreat over the same path, the camera following in the same manner, as the accordion sours and the game breaks out into a fight. Solemnly, they walk the deck, heads bowed until they run into the lively Miss Gossett, who teases them about Fred getting well and Gordon "fading into the background." Emily leaves Gordon on the deck, smoking a cigarette.

In their cabin, Fred complains in his sleep, "Steak and kidney pie again!?" as Emily stands over him.

Another day, Fred, with a bright, cleaned-up expression, faces the sunny deck, and sickens, but bravely moves on. A dark-haired princess flirts with him when the ball from her game accidentally hits him.

At Port Said, the ship drops anchor. Excited passengers look out over the rug vendors, who show their wares from small boats. Fred chastises Emily for looking like a tourist because she carries her camera. The Princess, in a fashionable veil, joins them at the railing as they all view the city of rounded domes. Fred eagerly goes off with her, and Gordon joins Emily as they all debark.

The foursome ride through the city in an open, horse-drawn carriage. In the narrow lane of the market area, they walk by the busy stalls of the rug

merchants, where Miss Gossett stolidly tromps on a rug she is considering purchasing. Emily turns in the street and notices Fred holding the Princess's arm; Gordon joins Emily, but she remains sad.

At the Suez Canal, the huge ship is seen passing in the distance by a group of Arabs, who sit under palm trees.

It's carnival time; everyone is in costume. Emily is in a nurse's outfit, Gordon is in a black cape. Fred, dressed as a turbaned prince, accompanies the Princess on a stroll. "Our little twin beds, no?" smiles the Princess as they stop near some deck chairs in an isolated area. Sitting down, Fred looks around nervously, then takes her hand. Fumbling with her veil, he tries to kiss her, then finally removes it, kissing her and clenching his fist at the side of his body. They rise, kiss again, then separate; the Princess commands him—later—to cabin no. 19.

On deck, Miss Gossett embraces Fred and takes him on to the dance floor for a contest. They comically sway back and forth and he jolts her with an occasional quick move. Abandoning her, he races down the hall to Room 18 and strides in to a scream, then out and into Room 19.

On the deck, Emily and Gordon kiss passionately. Drunken, they become upset, and he hangs his head. They come across Fred and the Princess in a lounge area, where the four blandly drink together, Fred and Emily facing the camera, not talking, though Emily is always glancing over at him. Miss Gossett falls asleep on a nearby chair.

Title: "Colombo—but to Emily it was people—not places—that matter now." Discovering her husband has gone ashore with the Princess, Emily greets Gordon on the empty deck; he offers to accompany her.

They ride in a carriage through town; Fred and the Princess ride down another street in another carriage. The Princess wonders if Fred has no regrets, and he boringly replies no, "She is fond of me, in her own way. We were fine in our little home until we took this trip. But how can I be expected to love Emily when I love you? . . . Of course, once you've had champagne, how can you settle for water?" The Princess reassures him, "Well, maybe she'll find someone of her own level." Inexplicably, the two carriages suddenly become stuck together, and Emily and Fred fume.

On the last night of the voyage, the strains of "Auld Lang Syne" can be heard as Emily and Gordon, in evening clothes, stand at the railing. Their faces cloud as he shows Emily the photo on which she had drawn the cartoon; "You are going to let me take care of you, aren't you?"

Meanwhile, Fred and the Princess stand in front of the windows of the ballroom. Fred rhapsodizes, "After tomorrow, we will always be together," but the Princess informs him that she must debark alone. Quieting his guilt, she tells him, "If a woman can't hold her man, there's no reason why he should take the blame." The crowd inside cheers.

In Singapore, Emily's luggage is marked care of Commander Gordon, Kuala Lumpur. They ride together in a carriage and Gordon bitterly tells her how much he resented her "kowtowing" to her baby of a husband. Relieved, he gloats that she is no longer Fred's wife. Staring at the road speeding under them, she becomes increasingly upset to hear that the Princess is merely "a common adventuress," and she wonders what will happen to poor Fred. "I don't know and I don't care," says Gordon. Emily orders the driver to stop.

Title: "The love nest." A large ceiling fan graces the comfortable hotel room where Fred shaves in the back and Emily walks in on the Princess, who hisses

into Emily's ear, and leaves, muttering in passing that she was a fool to leave Gordon. Emily tries to reason with Fred but he becomes infuriated as she explains the extent of her affair with Gordon and how he enabled her to see Fred more clearly; "He said you were a sham, nothing but a bluff." "Well, why didn't you go with him?" cries Fred. "Because without me you'd be lost. Is that wrong? . . . She's not a princess. . . . You were the only one on board ———." Fred suddenly grabs Emily and throws her hard on the bed, then leaves.

In long shot, palm trees outside the window, Emily rises from the bed, dries her tears and reads a letter from Gordon. "Knowing you, I accept your verdict. . . . I love you, Emily, so much that I can't write anymore." She cries, the page blurring in front of her. Suddenly Fred returns with his own news, "She thanks me for my company and says her father kept a cleaning shop in Berlin! She's a swine! . . . I tell you, I'll strangle you if you say I told you so!" A cleaning man starts through the door, but Fred throws things at him until he backs out. Continuing to rant, he reveals that all their money and their return tickets are gone.

Brown's Steamers. Fred and Emily lie in a plain dark room. Suddenly water floods into the baggage room, and something falls on Fred's head. Screams fill the air while Emily nurses him awake. He panics and they both look up to see the water rising over their portal. Unable to open their door, they finally sit and wait, hugging one another, and swearing their love. The light fades and water seeps under the door.

A bright light outside wakes them. They laugh hysterically, then crawl out the portal window to find the ship upended and deserted. Still in their night clothes, they walk the foggy deck, as water flows into their open portal window. They put on some uniforms from a storeroom, and pick up a stray cat. Blanching at the sight of a dead passenger sprawled in their path, they stumble into the bar for a drink, and Emily balks at using the "gentlemen's room." "No sense in being suburban," smirks Fred. Suddenly there is another crash and the ship is overrun by Chinese pirates. Emily and Fred climb down into their boat as a pregnant woman, arms akimbo, sternly watches. The men scramble back onto the boat as it begins to sink rapidly. One of them catches his ankle in the ship's ropes, and the others watch impassively as he goes down with it.

Later, the woman brings them bowls of food, which they eat voraciously with their fingers, Fred contemptuously throwing away the chopsticks. The others watch, and the couple wave back, until one of the men puts the stray cat's skin up to dry on the wall of the boat's cabin. Sickened, Fred and Emily quickly rise and lean over the side.

Another day, they wait, an island in the distance. A baby cries and Emily becomes ecstatic at the birth, but cries when Fred squelches her urge to "go help." "They don't want us. These dumb Chinese be like rabbits. . . . Gosh, it is ugly," he sneers, looking at the baby. Emily becomes more upset when the men pour water over the child, and Fred softens watching one of the men gently holding it: "I bet that chap's the father—see how proud he is."

The neon lights of London. Announcing a nice steak and kidney pie for dinner, the landlady lets them into their home, where the cat sits on the table, and Fred throws him off. They sicken at the thought of their other cat, but eventually kiss and move toward the door to enjoy the air. When Fred wonders if they can get a pram down the walk, Emily objects, insisting that she wants a bigger house. They argue beyond the fade-out.

18 *Waltzes from Vienna* (1933)

Director	Alfred Hitchcock
Assistant Director	Richard Beville
Producer	Tom Arnold
Production Company	A Tom Arnold Production*
Screenplay	Alma Reville, Guy Bolton, based on the play by Dr. A. M. Willner, Heinz Reichert, and Ernst Marischka
Photography	Glen McWilliams
Editing	Charles Frend
Art Direction	Alfred Junge, Oscar Werndorff
Set Direction	Peter Proud
Sound	Alfred Birch
Music	Johann Strauss, Senior and Junior, Hubert Bath (adaptation, based on the arrangements of Julius Bittner and E. W. Korngold), Louis Levy (direction)
Production Manager	Henry Sherek
Cast	Jessie Matthews (Rasi), Esmond Knight (Schani Strauss), Frank Vosper (the Count), Edmund Gwenn (Johann Strauss, Senior), Fay Compton (the Countess), Robert Hale (Ebezedar), Hindle Edgar (Leopold), Marcus Barron (Drexler), Charles Heslop (the Valet), Sybil Grove (Mme. Fouchet), Bill Shine, Jr. (Carl), B. M. Lewis (Domeyer), Cyril Smith (Secretary), Betty Huntley Wright (Lady's Maid), Bertram Dench (Engine Driver)
Filmed	at Lime Grove Studios, London, in British Acoustic Film
Running Time	approximately 80 minutes
Distributor	G.F.D.
Release Date	1933

Other titles: *Strauss's Great Waltz* (U.S.), *The Great Waltz*

Synopsis

Close-up of a blaring pneumatic horn. The camera moves out to reveal a Vienna Fire Brigade truck whizzing through the city streets, the horn honking into the ear of the driver, who asks a man in a baker's cap behind him just where the fire is. Finally, he understands: "Ebezedar's Café!"

At the café on a crowded square, swirls of light smoke move around inside as the waiters hurriedly carry out the tables and reseat the customers on the sidewalk. Ebezedar holds a couple of table vases for future placement. Ridding himself of them, he retrieves a three-tiered wedding cake from a child about the same size as the cake, and ends up dropping it himself. The horse-drawn fire truck

eventually breaks through the crowd and the baker jumps out to ask Ebezedar where Rasi is. "Your daughter!" exclaims the exasperated young man. "Why, she's upstairs having a music lesson," says Ebezedar.

Above the café, Rasi, a pretty young woman with brunette curls, sings "With all my heart," as Schani Strauss plays the piano and joins in.

Across the street in the back of the corner dress shop, a group of women in their underclothes stand at the window, the drapes pulled up in front of them, listening adoringly to the song. The blond and beautiful Countess pokes her head in from the shop, and, in close-up, wonders who the handsome gentleman across the street is.

In the music room, Schani reminds Rasi that he dedicates all his songs to her; after all, he wants to be her husband. She wonders how to get them published.

Outside the firemen pump out a few spurts of water, until the first big burst soaks Ebezedar. The baker climbs a ladder to the music room window and finds Schani and Rasi hugging. Unperturbed, he climbs in announcing that he has come to rescue her. Rasi, only now aware that the house is on fire, flippantly wonders if he wants her to swoon. Schani objects, but Rasi insists they not fight, suggesting instead they all walk down together. But the baker claims she must be rescued and picks her up and starts for the window. Schani pulls him around so that Rasi's legs end up in his arms and the two men tug over her, her long ruffled dress adding to the confusion. "She's not your property!" screams the baker; "She's going to be!" cries Schani, as they drop her on the floor. After the baker picks her up again, Rasi discourages Schani from pursuing the matter and allows herself to go out the window with the baker. Outside the window, the crowd watches as the baker misses the ladder with his exploring foot. "I'd be a lot safer if you'd let me climb down myself," yells Rasi, grabbing at his shirt. Her skirt gets caught half-way down and she ends up in her underclothes, the baker grinning at his triumph, while the crowd laughs at the sight of the two, still unaware of Rasi's predicament.

Suddenly looking down, Rasi scurries around, and ends up across the street in the dress shop. "Get me a skirt, please!" she appeals, but the shop owner, ornamented with a huge bonnet, merely chastises her for her indecent appearance. Viewing the Countess seated nearby, Rasi refuses to be penitent, and instead smugly mumbles something about how "particular great ladies are."

Outside, someone announces the fire is spreading, but it is only the fire chief's pipe; he announces the fire is out. Ebezedar serves canapes to all as the band plays on.

Schani carries Rasi's skirt into a back alley and impulsively steps into the back room of the dress shop, where the women scream in pleasure at the sight of him. He drops the skirt and is shooed into the showroom, where the Countess stares him down. Hearing the fire is out, she claims it is a pity, for there is not enough fire in the world—"I mean like the kind of fire you put into your music." He stands before her in his waistcoat and ruffles, trapped and embarrassed. She has him pull up a chair and he warily peers up at her and responds to her questions. He tells her his father is Johann Strauss—"He's a great man, but a little peculiar"—and, more dejectedly, how he, Schani, plays second fiddle in his father's orchestra while his two brothers study music in Berlin. "Like all great men, he has a fear of youth knocking at the door," she says soothingly. "My father needn't worry about his reputation!" cries Schani. The Countess looks toward the camera and wonders. She suggests that Schani set some of her verses to music

and indicates she has friends that might make it possible for his father's orchestra to play them, but he is positive his father would never play any of his music. Rasi enters the shop and thanks him for bringing over her skirt. He falteringly introduces her to the Countess Helga von Stahl, but Rasi merely sticks out her chin in displeasure. Halted, the Countess turns toward the camera in mock surprise, then warmly bids Schani good-bye as the pair leave. The shop owner enters, claps her hands, and the models step in as the band starts up a march.

Outside, the band surrounds Rasi, who stands furtively looking back at the shop.

A clock chimes and a light comes up over some very large double doors. A coterie of servants comes through with a tub and towels for the Countess's bath. In the Prince's bedroom, he fitfully dreams of being in a duel, as the Countess watches him and smiles. Hearing "his honor satisfied," the Countess moves on to her bath as the camera cuts to a long shot of their huge bedroom, the canopied bed dwarfed by the elaborately scrolled and draped architecture. Another half-dozen servants enter with the Prince's bath, as he lights a cigar. Finding the Countess's verses, he becomes jealous and stands at her bathroom door and complains. But she reassures him and he retreats opposite to his own bathroom.

The camera remains between the doors of the two off-screen bathrooms as the Prince demands to know what the Countess is saying now. The head maid comes out to meet the valet; as they kiss in their formal black and white outfits, they relate the messages of the royal pair to each other. Finally, her ladyship wants to know the color of the Danube; dirty brown, they jokingly whisper. But the toweled Prince appears and breaks up the idyll.

Now in their opposite dressing rooms, the Countess is struck by her maid's suggestion of a blue outfit: "Blue! That's it!" Meanwhile the Prince decides that Strauss must put his wife's verses to music. "The great Strauss?" wonders the valet, as the Countess whispers that she will see only Schani that afternoon.

At Staatstheatre, Johann Strauss leads his orchestra from a stand in a low-ceilinged pit. He takes offense at Schani's aside that the waltz should "progress" from the success of the famous Lorelei. Removing the music stand from between them, Johann dares Schani to play a better waltz. Schani does a brief introduction at the piano but quits in frustration. His father accuses him of "aborted improvisations," and Schani leaves, saying he will not be back. The Prince's valet enters while Johann is still very flustered by his son's action. Looking over the verse the Prince wants put to music, Johann rails about its stupidity. "What a fool! In Germany, they worship titles; here in Vienna, artists are superior."

In the Countess's sparely furnished but large and bright music room, Schani hesitates while playing her carved grand piano, complaining that he has lost his confidence. She encourages him and they sing a short duet about the sun in the sky. Elsewhere, curled up on a bench on a moonlit veranda, Rasi sings one of the verses. "Now I can write your song," exclaims Schani.

Out in the hallway, the Prince meets the valet at the bottom of the carved marble stairs adorned with life-sized cupids. Taken aback to hear the Countess is with a young man, he becomes even more angry that Johann Strauss rejected her verses and bats the valet all the way up the stairs.

The Countess and Schani look askance at the disturbance and she demands he play something as the Prince now flips the valet down the stairs to the

accompaniment of a glissando. Joining them in the music room, the Prince is pleased to hear the name Strauss will appear over the Countess's verses after all.

Next morning, Schani stalks down the street and into Ebezedar's café, where several women are on their hands and knees cleaning the floor. Rasi greets him from behind the counter and demands a kiss, as she has told her father they are in love. They discuss his financial potential, and she invites him into the family business. He shows her the commission from the Countess; she frowns, but recalls a tune of his that might fit. Da-da-da-da! Da-dat! Da-dat! They cry out in glee and kiss, until her father sternly interrupts: "Your mother didn't allow me to kiss her until we were married six months!" "Now I know why you were fifty years old when you had me!" retorts Rasi. But the news that Schani is interested in taking over the bakery delights Ebezedar, and he takes him downstairs to the cellar to show him the bins and different types of bread. As one of the helpers methodically throws sticks of French bread across the room into another man's apron, the rhythm allows Schani a better grasp of his budding tune, the phrases bubbling out of him as he continues Ebezedar's proud tour. "A silly song!" cries Ebezedar, offended by Schani's interruptions. But Schani cannot stop; inspired by a sputtering, revolving dough machine, he races up the stairs in triumph, leaps over the cleaning woman, and grabs Rasi, who primly tells him he cannot sing there. What does the shop matter, he grumbles, but she insists it matters as much as his songs. Discouraged, he announces he is going to visit the "man" who wrote the verses.

In the Countess's music room, Schani begins to play "The Blue Danube" waltz, and the Countess kisses him. He is taken aback, but insists he does not mind, then plays some more, her diamond-ringed hand on his shoulder. The scene dissolves into the same close-up of his face, showing Rasi's ringless hand on his shoulder, as she says she especially wants this piece dedicated to her. He frowns, but she hands him a pen and he fitfully signs. His signature dissolves into another dedication—to the Countess, who takes the music, rolls it up under her arm, and walks off in her huge military-inspired feathered hat. The scrolled music also appears under Rasi's arm as she places it lovingly at her grand piano.

In his studio at Music Verlag, a large spare hall with only a piano and a few chairs, Anton Drexler schemes with the Countess, dressed in a cascade of white ruffles and extra blond curls, to have the elder Strauss's orchestra play Schani's music.

Nearby in a very large bright hall Strauss's orchestra sits on a grandstand, while Johann leads the musicians in a march. Rasi pauses in the over-sized doorway, trying to get the conductor's attention. Outside, Schani arrives to join Drexler and the Countess. Inside, Johann, very annoyed at the intrusion, stops. He and Rasi argue about Schani's music—"rubbish"—and he accuses her of being Schani's messenger. Frustrated, she grabs his music from the stand and throws it in the air, to which he calmly turns his back and starts up the orchestra.

Accompanied by a drumroll, Rasi, in tears, runs out and down the large corridor toward the camera and into a close-up. Suddenly she stops, wide-eyed, hearing Schani and the Countess singing "The Blue Danube." "My song!" she cries. Calming herself, she pauses at the door, then strides into Drexler's studio and offers the Countess her copy of the music, so she "won't have to look over

Schani's shoulder." The two women notice the discrepancy in the dedications, and Schani weakly tries to explain to them as they stand on either side of him. The Countess proudly gives up her dedication, sarcastically referring to "your little friend," and the camera follows Rasi as she stomps out and bangs the door. Schani follows. The Countess moans to Drexler about what a fool Schani is, but plays "The Blue Danube" for him "one last time."

Down the street lined with artificial trees, Schani races after Rasi and stops her, swearing he will give up his ambition. They kiss. "I love you so much," she whispers.

The Countess finishes the piece and Drexler declares the song "has to live!"

Later at Ebezedar's café, Rasi receives a note for Schani from the Countess and insults the messenger. Schani, wanly smiling, rounds the counter carrying a box of sweets on his head. They argue bitterly about the Countess's invitation to the St. Stephen's Festival. With clenched mouth, Rasi tells him she will never again speak to him if he goes. "I won't be dictated to," Schani says, but she defiantly insists she is only "warning" him. "Go back to it—go back to her!" Dejected, he walks off and the few customers stare. Ebezedar walks up muttering that Schani will never make a baker, but thankfully they have a contract for the St. Stephen's Festival!

The Countess, her face framed in a huge organdy collar, pours tea for Drexler in front of the French windows of her breakfast room. The camera moves out to reveal the Prince snoring in the next room on a couch, a lace hanky over his face. The camera moves farther out as the pair buzz about their plan.

In Johann's more old-fashioned dressing room full of dark furniture, he prepares for the concert at St. Stephen's: "All the critics will be there!" Drexler arrives and invites him to the Prince's home, but Johann insists he does not have the time to go until Drexler sets back Johann's pocket watch, and mentions that the Prince may be thinking of bestowing an honor on Strauss.

At the Prince's, there is a large party, and Johann is ushered upstairs for a private audience. The Countess, now covered in ruffles and spangles, compliments Drexler on his good work.

At the festival, the camera pans around the yard full of white tables and parasols, and a laughing, gay crowd. A columned, white bandstand rises above them at one end. Rasi wipes beer mugs behind a counter and the Countess steps from her carriage in front of the white lattice archway. The organizer of the festival scurries around wondering why the maestro is late.

The Prince takes Johann into a large hall where couples are waltzing, and introduces him. After grandly bowing to the group, Johann declines to play, not having the time, but gives in when told the requestor has great influence with the Emperor.

Back at the festival, a smiling Schani appears, dressed in his best waistcoat and ruffles. Rasi huffs at the sight of the Countess and drops a load of dishes she is carrying. Schani appears at her feet to help her and smilingly assures her that he is not with the Countess. He grabs a baker's hat, and finally she laughs. "I love you so much," she cries. He laughs, "You always say that after we've quarreled." Ebezedar walks around the food table to them and demands Schani make up his mind once and for all: "Confectioner or musician!" Rasi assures her father that Schani has chosen her and sends him off to work, smoothing down his ruffles as he hesitates, frowning.

The orchestra is assembled and waiting, some of them mumbling about an

arrangement of "The Blue Danube" waltz that sits on all their music stands. "Can't imagine playing that!" The crowd becomes impatient.

Johann struggles through the "Lorelei Waltz" at the piano, sneaking glances at his watch while he plays.

At the festival, the camera pans around a nervous Countess standing with Drexler in the middle of the crowd. She calls over Schani, who tries to move quickly away saying he has serving duties, but she insists this is his chance to conduct. "You mean my father's consented?" he asks. Avoiding his eyes, she answers yes. Behind the beer tables at the edge of the crowd, Rasi spots them and becomes angry. The audience bangs on their tables and Schani is introduced. He takes off his white hat and Rasi runs to stop him, but the Countess stops her. Furious, Rasi tells the Countess she can have him.

The quiet violin overture begins. The camera pans around the orchestra and its instruments, and then the first section begins. The crowd becomes attentive. At the second section, a woman in the front of the crowd looks up at her partner and asks him to dance. They spin out, followed by others. Rasi sits at the counter, her face buried in her hands. At the entrance, Johann arrives, his face stricken, hurt. At the end of the piece, the crowd stands to cheer. Johann winds his way up to watch his son jump down to greet Rasi, who snootily congratulates him. Johann walks over and accuses her of masterminding the incident. The organizer wants Schani to play again, but Johann objects, "They're calling for me!" No, says the organizer, *you* were late. Bitter, Johann complains, "The late Strauss and his illustrious son! Fickle, brainless idiots!" Schani tries to apologize, then goes looking for Rasi and is told she has gone home. He leaves and the Countess follows.

Followed by his entourage, the Prince arrives, bragging of the success of "the Blue Danube" waltz, which he helped to write. Johann confronts him with his trick and taunts him with the news that the Countess has now made a fool of him; she is with Schani "talking art!" The Prince stutters, demanding to know where the Countess is. After throwing the baker into a pile of dishes, he finally gets Schani's address.

Chase music accompanies his carriage to the plain back stairs of Schani's apartment. Inside, the Countess asks Schani's forgiveness and wonders if it's over with Rasi. Rasi runs silently through the streets. Schani stands, and the Countess rearranges herself closer to him, then pulls him down to her on the settee. "You'll never be the same again," she mutters as he kisses her. They hear a commotion outside and the Countess hides in the bedroom. Outside, someone suggests a duel, but the Prince demurs and begins a fist-fight instead. Rasi arrives during the struggle and enters the bedroom from the long balcony, letting the Countess out down a ladder. Hearing her friends singing "The Blue Danube" waltz, the Prince inadvertently frightens them with a chair raised high. Backing into the room, he sees Rasi come out of the bedroom and apologizes as the Countess innocently walks up the front stairs and greets him.

Schani and Rasi are left to make up. "All that happened tonight meant nothing to me because I thought I'd lost you," says Schani.

Johann wanders through the empty festival tables, and a child comes up to him and asks for his autograph. As an afterthought, He adds "senior" to his signature. The lights go down on the bandstand.

Note. * Most filmographies list Gaumont British as a production company.

19   *The Man Who Knew Too Much* (1934)

Director	Alfred Hitchcock
Associate Producer	Ivor Montagu*
Production Company	Gaumont British Picture Corporation, Ltd.
Screenplay	A. R. Rawlinson, Edwin Greenwood, Emyln Williams (additional dialogue), based on an original subject by D. B. Wyndham Lewis and Charles Bennett
Photography	Curt Courant
Editing	H. St. C. Steward
Art Direction	Alfred Junge
Sound	F. McNally
Music	Arthur Benjamin, Louis Levy (direction)
Production Manager	Richard Beville
Cast	Leslie Banks (Bob Lawrence), Peter Lorre (Abbott), Edna Best (Jill Lawrence), Nova Pilbeam (Betty Lawrence), Frank Vosper (Ramon), Hugh Wakefield (Clive), Pierre Fresnay (Louis Bernard), Cicely Oates (Nurse Agnes), D. A. Clarke Smith (Inspector Binstead), George Curzon (Gibson)
Filmed	at Lime Grove Studios, London
Running Time	approximately 85 minutes
Distributor	General Film Distributors, Ltd.
Release Date	December 1934

Other titles: *Der Mann, der zuviel wuβte, L'Homme Qui En Savait Trop, L'Uomo Che Sapeva Troppo*

Synopsis

Credits appear over some travel brochures and then mountain scenes, accompanied by dramatic music.

St. Moritz. A long ski jump flanked by trees. A crowd standing at the bottom cheers on a skier, when suddenly a dog jumps out of the arms of its adolescent owner, Betty, and runs in front of the skier's path. Louis Bernard, the skier, aborts his jump and rolls over into the crowd. No one is hurt, though Louis and a bystander named Abbott exchange cryptic glances as they good-naturedly brush the snow off themselves. Bob Lawrence, Betty's father, and Louis and Betty chat afterwards about getting together for dinner on Louis's last day in St. Moritz, and about Jill, Betty's mother, who is elsewhere participating in a skeet-shooting match.

In another snow-covered outdoor setting, Ramon, a slickly "brilliantined" vacationer, and Jill shake hands before their skeet match. Ramon flatters her beauty but she dismisses his talk for the business at hand. Lawrence and Betty join the crowd, and Betty interrupts her mother, who is jokingly impatient with her, preferring to concentrate on shooting. Abbott pushes a chiming watch at Betty, who offendedly retorts that she's "not a child," further putting off her

mother's's aim. Ramon wins and Jill takes consolation in pretending to ignore her husband and "the brat."

That evening, the ballroom is crowded with dancers; Louis and Jill dance and make fun of Bob and Betty who sit at a table in the foreground. Bob retorts by tying to Louis's tailcoat a piece of unraveling yarn, which wraps around the other dancers. The joke is just getting attention when suddenly a gun shot pierces a window and hits Louis in the heart. Jill bends over him as he collapses to the floor and whispers his secret, "Tell Bob to take the brush in my room to the British Consulate." He hands her his key.

Bob enters Louis's room to search; the police try the door, but he has left the key on the inside to thwart them. Checking around, he finds a note in the shaving brush in the bathroom: "Wapping. G. Barbor make contact A. Hall March 21st." Bob whisks out a second door and runs into Ramon in the hall, who demands the information from him; but the hotel police also catch up and begin to ask questions, forcing Ramon to back off.

The hotel manager excitedly leads Bob to his office where the police are questioning Jill. Told to wait in an anteroom, Bob is querying a German bellhop in German-accented English about the whereabouts of the British Consulate when a messenger brings him a note warning him to reveal nothing or risk never seeing Betty again. Bob breaks into the office and shows the note to Jill who raises her eyes in pain, then sees double as the detectives demand the note from her. She faints and Bob grabs the note and throws it into the fireplace.

A wide-eyed, extremely terrified Betty rides on a sleigh through the woods with Ramon, who finally removes his hand from her mouth. The Alps dissolve into the neon signs of London.

One night in the sitting room of the Lawrences' elegant apartment, Bob is questioned by Inspector Binstead and his assistants, who wonder why he and Jill returned to London without Betty. He serves them whiskey as they insinuate that they know Betty may have been kidnapped.

In a nearby room, Jill waits despondent and suspicious; "Uncle" Clive, who sits on the floor playing with Betty's electric train set, reassures her that Bob is not going to "spill the beans."

Bob shakes hands with the detectives and sends them out the door, but one of them, Gibson, who is from the Foreign Office, stays behind and confronts Bob with the shaving brush and the news that Louis Bernard worked for them. Jill enters and Gibson explains that Bernard was killed because he uncovered a plot to assassinate a statesman named Roper. The Lawrences refuse to cooperate, insisting that Betty's life must mean more to them than anyone else's. A woman telephones for Bob and reminds him to keep quiet, then puts Betty on the line. The camera moves into a close-up of Jill as she speaks gently with Betty, and Bob impatiently and repeatedly demands that she ask Betty where she is; when Jill finally does ask, Betty is pulled away from the phone. Gibson discovers that the phone call originated in Wapping and orders the district covered with plain-clothes detectives. The Lawrences continue to claim ignorance and Gibson, losing patience, leaves, reminding them that this "is not a good thing to have on your conscience." Bob determines to go to Wapping with Clive, thinking that the police Gibson has sent will endanger Betty.

In Wapping, a river port area, Bob and Clive stand in front of a crudely lit storefront belonging to a dentist named Barbor. They go up the stairs and Clive is ushered into a padded room for a checkup. Clive, moaning in pain, goes back down to the street. Bob goes in next. The dentist searches for the right

instrument as Abbott, announced by his watch chime, passes through to a back room, wondering if "he's arrived yet." Barbor, suspicious, asks Bob details about his boat and discovers that he is lying, then decides to extract a tooth and tries to gas Bob, who reaches for Barbor's throat and easily throws him over into the chair and gases him instead. Hearing someone coming up the stairs, Bob quickly puts on the dentist's white coat and arranges the light so that it shines into the doorway. Ramon enters and meets Abbott, who sports a blond streak in the middle of his hair; they stand nearby and discuss their plans for that night involving Ramon's skills as a marksman, box seat conveniently placed in the theater, and a "hole in the ground somewhere" for the "charming" Miss Lawrence.

After Ramon and Abbott have left, Bob finds Clive down in the street and they follow the pair to the Tabernacle of the Sun Church. Bob and Clive, still nursing his tooth, enter. Inside the congregation sings and Clive and Bob pretend to follow along. Bob (not exactly in tune) sings a warning to Clive who responds in kind, as a woman, Nurse Agnes, gets up to preach. Asking those "not in tune" to submit to a "form of control," she asks Clive directly to volunteer. Clive goes to the front and sits while she hypnotizes him. All those not of the fourth circle are instructed to leave; everyone in the congregation except the gang of three men and two women does so. The older woman stops Bob from exiting by putting a gun in his side as the others lock chains around the doors. Abbott appears. At the mention of Betty being asleep upstairs, Bob starts throwing chairs. Fearing the sound of gunshots in the crowded neighborhood, the others fight back with chairs, as the older woman plays the organ, and Abbott stands aloof, smoking. When Bob grapples with Ramon, he notices a ticket for a concert at Albert Hall that night, and yells out to Clive, who finally wakes after a couple of chairs hit him, and commands him to jump out the window and tell Jill to go to Albert Hall. Caught protecting the window, Bob is finally subdued. Abbott frowns viciously at him and instructs one of the women to get hold of Jill and tell her that if she goes to Albert Hall, Betty is "kaput."

At a phone booth, Clive calls Jill. Inside the church Agnes dials at the same moment, but by the time she gets through Jill has already left.

The gang waits out the afternoon on the second floor living quarters of the church, which are padded and armored. The older woman asks to leave, not wanting a part in this "nasty business," but Abbott assures her continued presence by having one of the men remove her skirt. Agnes joins them, admitting to Abbott that she did not find Jill at home, just as Clive arrives at the front door with a policeman. Abbott and Agnes effectively persuade the policeman that Clive has been drunk and disorderly; the policeman whistles to another officer and they lead Clive away, struggling.

Back in the church, Bob is upset by the news that Abbott has successfully tricked the police, then faces a new tease. Agnes brings in Betty for a "final good-bye"; sobbing, Betty rushes in and buries herself in her father's arms. Abbott plays a record for Ramon of the concert piece to be performed that night, pointing out the cymbal crash that will drown out the gunshot, and reminds him it is time to go to Albert Hall. Betty is dragged out screaming after another death threat.

At Albert hall, the crowd enters. Jill waits outside, noticing the arrival of the dignitary, Roper. Ramon walks up to her and hands her a brooch picturing a skier that she had given Betty in St. Moritz. Jill takes her seat in the back of the hall,

and the music begins. She glances up at Roper, then sees Ramon hiding in the shadows of a balcony box.

Back at the church, the gang listens to the concert on the radio.

Jill notices the curtain move, then sees Inspector Binstead arrive at the hall. Jill's vision blurs as the gun emerges from behind the curtain, and she focuses on her dilemma. The cymbals are raised. She stands and screams a moment before they crash.

Back at the church, Abbott hopes "it went all right for all our sakes."

Roper slumps over in his seat; Jill runs out to the entrance and points out the assassin to some detectives, who follow his car.

At the church, the gang waits. Ramon stiffly walks up the stairs, reassuring them the assassination was successful, but the radio announces that Roper is fine, the shot had only grazed him. Abbott is furious, then turns to Bob, who smiles sarcastically at him. Going to a window, Abbott sees that detectives are waiting down in the street. Pointing out this development to the rest of the gang, he solemnly turns out the lights.

A crowd, including a large contingent of police, gathers across the intersection from the church. One of the policemen is ordered to walk over and knock on the church door and is shot down; several others rush to help him and are gunned down in the street until those still standing retreat. The battle wakes the entire neighborhood, and the streets are cleared of all traffic. A growing crowd is pushed further back behind a police barrier, where a double-decker bus looms over the scene.

Starting at the persistent gunfire while they stand inside a nearby shop, Binstead asks Jill if Betty is in the church, but she admits she knows only that Wapping was mentioned in the note. Two higher government officials in evening dress wind their way through the crowd to consult with Binstead. Rifles are ordered for the police and distributed from the back of a truck. Scaling a series of garden walls, the police take over the building opposite the street, commandeering apartment rooms and placing furnishings in front of the windows for protection. The battle resumes when a window shade is accidentally drawn and another policeman shot. A contingent of detectives and police rush the front door of the church and scatter through the destruction inside. They break down the inside doors with axes, and finally find the armored door to the second floor.

Upstairs, two of the gang are already dead and the fugitives surround a window, shooting, Abbott smoking on the floor, filling the guns with ammunition. Agnes crawls down to get more ammunition. Bob pushes at the locked door of his room; Betty cringes inside another. Bob finally breaks down the bullet-riddled padded door, then crawls outside past the preoccupied Abbott and into Betty's room, just as Agnes is laboring back up the stairs with her load of ammunition. She crawls, pulling the heavy box, to the gunmen. Seeing her, Ramon suddenly announces that he is finished, and she rises to her knees in anger and points a gun at him, demanding that he continue; she is shot in the chest and falls into Abbott's arms. Abbott is momentarily deeply grieved, then, loosening his collar for the first time, takes up a gun at the window himself, coolly shooting a policeman. "Now we'll have to try and use the child," he says to Ramon, as another gunman drops dead. Ramon goes out to get Betty.

Bob and Betty are in the stairwell and he pushes her up to the roof just as Ramon finds them and shoots Bob, who falls down the stairs, wounded in the arm. Outside on the roof, Betty, in her white nightclothes, evades Ramon by going down to the edge of the roof.

Down on the sidewalk, the police realize that the fugitives are no longer shooting as much. Rounding a corner, Jill looks up in horror to see Betty backing across the gutter, the gun-carrying Ramon menacing her a few feet away; the camera pans from Betty's alert face through the black night to Ramon's outstretched hand. Ordered to shoot him, a policeman demurs, as Ramon and Betty are now melded in his sight. Jill grabs the rifle from him, and shoots; Ramon falls from the roof.

Binstead and his men finally break through, finding a mess inside and Bob faint on the stairwell. Hearing the watch chime, they shoot through a door and kill Abbott.

Petrified and sobbing, Betty is let down from the roof by two policemen. Bob and Betty coax the hesitant child into their arms.

Note. * Most filmographies list Michael Balcon as the producer and Peter Proud as Set Director.

Remake: *The Man Who Knew Too Much* (U.S., 1955), directed by Alfred Hitchcock.

20   *The 39 Steps* (1935)

Director	Alfred Hitchcock
Producers	Michael Balcon, Ivor Montagu
Production Company	Gaumont British Picture Corporation, Ltd.
Screenplay	Charles Bennett, Ian Hay (dialogue), based on the novel by John Buchan*
Photography	Bernard Knowles
Editing	Derek N. Twist
Art Direction	Otto Werndorff
Set Direction	Albert Jullion
Sound	A. Birch
Music	Louis Levy
Costumes	J. Strassner, Marianne (wardrobe)
Continuity	Alma Reville
Cast	Robert Donat (Richard Hannay), Madeleine Carroll (Pamela), Lucie Mannheim (Annabella Smith), Godfrey Tearle (Professor Jordan), Peggy Ashcroft (Margaret), John Laurie (John), Helen Haye (Mrs. Jordan), Frank Cellier (the Sheriff), Wylie Watson (Mr. Memory), Peggy Simpson (Maid), Gus McNaughton and Jerry Verno (Travelers)†
Filmed	at Lime Grove Studios, London
Running Time	approximately 81 minutes
Distributor	G.F.D.
Release Date	September 1935

Other titles: *Die neununddreißig Stufen, Les Trente-Neuf Marches, Il Club Dei Trentanove*

Synopsis

Credits appear over a large shadow graphic of the title; chase theme music is heard.

A blinking neon sign advertises a music hall. Richard Hannay, a smartly dressed man, goes in and sits with his back to the camera, as tinny orchestra music introduces a performer named Mr. Memory. The audience is invited to test the performer's brain, and they boisterously throw out questions and smart remarks. Amid the shouting, Richard wants to know the distance between Montreal and Winnipeg, and finally gets the correct, detailed answer. A fight develops in the back bar area; suddenly a gun fills the frame and is shot twice. The crowd panics and runs out the door; the music starts up and Richard is left outside clutching a mysterious woman who asks to go home with him.

The pair hop on a bus to Portland Place,[H] where Richard, a visiting rancher from Canada, has rented a flat. Upstairs the furniture is covered with sheeting; the woman, Anabella Smith, rushes to hide from view as he turns on the lights, then asks him not to answer the phone when it rings because it is probably for her. She insists on retreating to the kitchen where they can pull the blind. There, she tells him that she was the one who fired the gun in the theater; she did it to create a diversion because some men were there who wanted to kill her. As Richard fries haddock for her to eat, she tells him she is a spy who offers her services to the highest bidder; another "brilliant agent" is on the verge of uncovering a British secret, "vital to its air defense," and taking it out of the country. Richard scoffs at her story, but she sends him to the window to see her pursuers in the street, and he returns convinced. They are agents of the 39 Steps "who will stop at nothing" in their mission. Their ruthless and clever chief "can look like a hundred men," but he cannot disguise his finger that has a missing joint. After this intense warning, Anabella asks for a map of Scotland.

That night the wind whips through an open window in the hallway; Anabella bursts into the living room where Richard sleeps on the couch, gasps a warning to him and collapses, knifed in the back. The telephone rings as Richard paces around the apartment. He removes the map of Scotland from her grip and notices a place has been circled, Alt-Na-Shellac. Anabella appears superimposed over the map, and her words return to Richard, "There is a man in Scotland I must visit if anything is to be done."

Richard sneaks down to the lobby of his apartment, notices two men outside waiting, bribes the milkman to give him his white coat and hat, and escapes.

At the train station, he boards the train and waits anxiously, but the train pulls out just seconds ahead of his pursuers, who jump out of a car and run after it.

A woman, who has just discovered Anabella's body, screams along with the screeching train.

Richard sleeps, his head against the window, while two corset salesmen talk business across from him. At Edinburgh, they pick up a newspaper and comment on the murder in the West End flat. Borrowing the paper, Richard finds a picture of himself on the front page. He jumps out and paces up and down the platform. Testing, he queries a policeman who is looking at the paper, but he is not recognized. Back on the train, detectives walk through the aisles and Richard jumps into a compartment where Pamela, a beautiful blond passenger sits. He forces a kiss on her and pleads for protection. The detectives enter to query her

and she points at him. He jumps out the outside door, climbs back into the next compartment, and runs down the corridor just ahead of the detective. Coming to the baggage car and a couple of barking dogs, he disappears. The train has been stopped in the middle of the Forth bridge; the detectives scurry around as Richard stands precariously behind one of the girders. The engineers insist the train must continue its journey, as the radio broadcasts a call for Richard's arrest.

A Scottish hillside. Richard walks along a deserted road, then comes upon a suspicious sheepherder. The man agrees to let Richard spend the night for a fee. Richard mistakes the farmer's wife for his daughter, then enters the small home and talks with her while she fixes supper. Margaret, warmer and sadder than her husband, is from Glasgow. Richard sneaks a look at the newspaper with a front page story about the incident on the bridge; at supper Margaret notices the story and connects it with him. Her husband notices their exchange of glances during his prayer for us "miserable sinners" and walks outside to peek through the window at them as they stand and talk heatedly over the table.

That night Margaret lies awake and her husband watches her rise at the sound of a car horn. She wakes Richard to warn him and her husband follows to accuse them of being lovers. "Go," she says, but Richard insists on explaining himself even as the police shine a spotlight through the window. The farmer takes a bribe from Richard to mislead the police, but cannot resist asking them if there is a reward. Knowing her husband is not trustworthy, Margaret gives Richard her husband's best coat and pushes him out the back door, reassuring him that her husband will only pray over her. She is desolate at his leaving.

Outside, the police see Richard running across a hillside about an eighth of a mile away. Taking up the chase on foot, they come to river rapids. Only slightly ahead now with cars and a plane closing in, Richard sees a sign for Alt-Na-Shellac and runs toward a mansion where he bangs on the front door.

Richard gives the name of Anabella Smith to the maid and waits on the stoop. At the front gate, the police arrive, but by the time they get to the front door Richard is gone and the maid tells them no one has been there for at least half an hour.

Inside, a large cocktail party is in progress and Richard is introduced as "Hammond" to several people, including the Sheriff. Returning to the party, the host, Professor John Jordan, reassures Richard that everything is all right, then takes him to the window to watch the police scurrying around the rapids while the guests have a gay chat about the escaped murderer. Suddenly they all say good-bye and leave.

Left in the large living room alone, Richard waits until the host returns and locks the door. He and Richard discuss Anabella's murder and Richard tells him what he knows about the foreign agent with part of a finger missing. "This one?" says the host, holding up his deformed hand. Luisa, the Professor's wife, announces lunch and the Professor sarcastically wonders what he is going to do with Richard as Richard focuses on the door. Offering a gun, he suggests a convenient suicide, but Richard does not respond and is shot, dropping to the ground.

The sheepherder stands by the coat rack in his house and wonders where his hymnal is; hearing from Margaret that she gave his coat with the hymnal in it to "that man," he reaches out and slaps her.

Richard laughs with the Sheriff as he shows him the hymnal which stopped the bullet fired at him. The Sheriff queries him about his escape and reassures him that he is convinced of his innocence. Some detectives from Scotland Yard arrive and the Sheriff denounces Richard to them as a "murderer" and angrily announces that Professor John is his best friend.

Out in the busy street, a leather-coated man worries that "Richard is inside spilling the beans," when suddenly Richard, still in handcuffs, smashes out the front window of the Sheriff's office. The chase is on. Richard joins in a local parade as the police scurry by, then veers off down a small street and blunders into the back stage of a lecture hall full of people. The main speaker is introduced, a supporter of a local election candidate, and everyone looks at Richard, who rises and announces that he is "delighted and relieved to find" himself at the lectern, where he easily covers his handcuffs. He notices Pamela, the woman from the train, walking toward him down one of the aisles and sees her immediately report him to the authorities. As the hall fills with police, Richard requests topics for discussion—unemployment? the idle rich?—and becomes inspired to give a rousing address about an ideal world where there is no suspicion, no persecution, "a square deal and a sporting chance. . . . Is that the kind of world you want?" The crowd rises to its feet in approval and advances on Richard who backs into the man with the leather coat and is apprehended. Pulling away, he berates Pamela, and pleads with her to report the impending theft of the secret documents. She coldly refuses to help him but is asked by Richard's captors to accompany them to the station and identify him.

In the car, Pamela becomes alarmed when they pass the police station but is informed that they are driving two hours to another station. Passing through the countryside, they move into heavy fog, and when Richard realizes that they are going to the Professor's house, he taunts them about their boss having a finger missing. Stopped by a flock of sheep, the men handcuff Pamela to Richard to immobilize them, but Richard promptly jumps out of the car forcing her along. Escaping through the fog, Richard carries and pulls her, clamping his hand over her mouth when necessary to keep her quiet. They hide under a waterfall. The two men jump around the rocks on top of them, then give up the search.

Later that night, Pamela and Richard struggle along a road; he is still unable to convince her of his innocence and their danger. Desperate, he switches tactics, pretending the pipe in his pocket is a gun and threatening to kill her if she does not obey. Coming across an inn, they manage to sign in for a room, explaining their car broke down. Upstairs in their room, they argue in front of the innkeeper's wife, but she surmises they are simply a quarreling romantic couple. Eventually they eat sandwiches, lying on the bed, and begin to chisel off the handcuffs while Richard repeatedly wonders about the tune he cannot get out of his head. Richard lulls Pamela to sleep with a sarcastic but charming recitation of his life story.

At the mansion, the Professor bids his wife good-bye and sets out on a secret mission.

At the inn, Pamela wakes and manages to squeeze her hand out of the cuff. She walks out on the balcony above the lobby and hears the two men from whom they escaped reporting to the Professor's wife on the telephone. The Professor is on his way to the London Palladium to warn the 39 Steps. Just as they ask the innkeeper about the fugitive couple, the innkeeper's wife interrupts excitedly and

kicks them out for drinking after hours, then cautions her husband not to give away the young couple.

Pamela returns to the room with a softer, more protective look, then goes to sleep on the couch. Next morning, she tells Richard what she learned and he is angry that she did not wake him right away.

In London, Pamela speaks with a detective at Scotland Yard who is still convinced that Richard is a murderer because no information from the Air Ministry is missing. The detectives follow her to the Palladium.

At the Palladium, the show is on. Police wait outside; no one is allowed to leave the theater. Pamela enters a balcony and searches the main floor, all the while followed by detectives. Richard is seated in the middle; he takes up opera glasses and notices the Professor hiding behind a balcony curtain, only his injured hand visible. Pamela joins him with the bad news. Noticing a familiar tune, he remembers the music hall where his plight began. When Mr. Memory is introduced on stage and he sees him nod to the Professor, Richard suddenly realizes that Mr. Memory holds the secrets in his head. The police converge, calling Richard and Pamela from the audience, and starting to lead them out. Richard yells out to Mr. Memory "What are the 39 Steps?" and the performer proceeds rotely to describe the secret organization, then is shot down by the Professor, who leaps from the balcony and is trapped on the stage by police.

Backstage, a wounded Mr. Memory begins to recite the secret documents, commenting on the difficulty of retaining them, then faints, as the crowd closes in and Richard and Pamela join hands.

Notes. *Many filmographies credit Alma Reville as having worked on the script adaptation. †Gifford in *A Catalog of British Films,* adds Hilda Trevelyn (Innkeeper's Wife) and John Turnball (Inspector) to the cast. ┌Hitchcock does a bit as passer-by at the bus stop.

Remakes: *The Thirty-Nine Steps* (U.S. 1958) directed by Ralph Thomas, and (U.S., 1978) directed by Don Sharp.

21   *Secret Agent* (1936)

Director	Alfred Hitchcock
Associate Producer	Ivor Montagu*
Production Company	Gaumont British
Screenplay	Charles Bennett, Ian Hay (dialogue), Jesse Lasky, Jr. (additional dialogue), from the play by Campbell Dixon, adapted from the novel *Ashenden* by W. Somerset Maugham*
Photography	Bernard Knowles
Editing	Charles Frend
Art Direction	O[tto] Werndorff
Set Direction	Albert Jullion
Sound	Philip Dorté
Music	Louis Levy
Costumes	J. Strassner

Continuity	Alma Reville
Cast	Madeleine Carroll (Elsa), John Gielgud (Ashenden), Peter Lorre (the General), Robert Young (Marvin), Percy Marmont (Mr. Caypor), Florence Kahn (Mrs. Caypor), Lilli Palmer, Charles Carson (R)*
Filmed	at Lime Grove Studios, London
Running Time	approximately 83 minutes
Distributor	G.F.D.
Release Date	January 1936

Other titles: *Der Geheimagent, Quatre de l'Espionnage, L'Agente Secreto, Amore e Mistero*

Synopsis

Dramatic music accompanies the credits that appear over Art Deco silhouette graphics of soldiers on a battlefield.

May 10, 1916, 84 Curzon St., W. (London). A group of twenty or so men in dark suits mill around a large hall with a draped casket in the center. As the group files out, one man pauses at the door and talks with the attendant, who explains that the young soldier/novelist died of a chill in his sleep. After the people have left, the one-armed attendant locks himself in the room, casually lights a cigarette with a tall candle, and attempts to take down the empty casket. Fumbling the job, he lets the box fall and glances ruefully up at the large portrait on the wall of a young uniformed soldier; the camera moves quietly into the face on the portrait.

Bombs fall through the night sky of London, crisscrossed by search lights. The camera moves over the rooftops into an office where R goes to the door to greet John Brodie, a pale Englishman who is not happy, but somewhat intrigued, to have discovered an item in the paper reporting his death. R calmly tells him that he is being sent to Switzerland to locate a certain German agent who is leaving for Arabia via Constantinople and thought to be staying at the Hotel Excelsior. The man accepts his new name, Richard Ashenden, as well as the assignment and passports that go with it. The two exit onto the central stairs, where they hear a scream, and then a maid runs into them. Close behind her is Richard's assistant, the curly haired and obsequious General who proudly rattles off his very long Spanish name and scurries after the woman. "Lady killer?" remarks Richard, and R laughs, "Not only ladies." Richard is dismissed and goes outside to a car to begin his journey to Dover.

Later, he walks down a plank and into a Hotel Excelsior taxi, and then through the luxurious lobby to the check-in desk, where he is informed that his wife has already arrived. Hearing that she is *"ravissant,"* he becomes distracted and accidentally steps on a dachshund belonging to Mr. Caypor, another English guest.

Finding Room 234, he enters and discovers the young Robert Marvin, his back to the camera, eating grapes and flirting with Elsa Carrington (also known as Elsa Ashenden) who is in the next room. Slamming the door to announce

himself, Richard gets the attention of Robert and the blond Elsa, who appears wrapped in a towel, her face smeared with cold cream, delighted to see him. Chagrined at this development, suave Robert smiles, "I guess it's time for the triangle to retire from the family circle. Exit baffled."

Left alone, Elsa explains that she was not expecting him so soon. "My dear, no need to play a role now," says Richard dryly. He demands to see her passport and is grudgingly pleased to have her demand to see his. They continue negotiations in the bathroom while she sits at a mirror in the foreground and puts on her "face." When asked, she responds she is pleased with his looks, but he foregoes comment on hers until she has finished applying her makeup. She tells him she is in Switzerland for "excitement, danger, maybe a little . . ." and makes a gun with her hand. She becomes angry when he questions her enthusiasm for killing, but they are interrupted by the General, who walks in referring coyly to the "beautiful woman—lady—girl . . ." and lowering his eyes. He explains he has been through their passports already but is pained to discover that Elsa has been "issued" to Richard by R, and collapses in confusion. Richard kneels by him and reassures him that "she is part of my disguise. She's nothing to me and I'm nothing to her." The General gratefully revives at the thought of the "lady's affections" being free for him. But Elsa is bored at his attention, and Richard urges the General to get to work. He reminds him their first business is to go to a church in Langenthal to meet a contact.

After the General is gone, Elsa rises from her chair to face Richard. Anticipating a compliment on her freshly made-up face, she becomes angry to hear him instead wonder if she is not "a bit fond" of herself. She slaps him on the cheek and he slaps her back. "Well, married life *has* begun," she says, rubbing her face.

A hand moves down a column of chocolate bars to pick out one in the middle. The scene widens to show the clerk in a shop, who hands over the bar to a bearded old gentleman in a suit. Out in the narrow street, the man discards the chocolate and reads a note on the wrapper: "Novelist Brodie reported dead arrived today . . . take steps."

Goat bells sound in the valley of a mountain village. The General and Richard enter Langenthal Church to the sound of a monotonous organ chord. They light three candles and wait on their knees; the General becomes anxious and grabs some more candles, but Richard, anxious himself, calls him a fool. Slowly they approach the slumped organist, whose hand slips off the keyboard when the General touches him and falls back lifeless over the bench. "Strangled!" says Richard, and the General comments with a smile and a kiss to his fingertips, "Nice work, neat, very neat!" They discover a leather button in the man's hand, and Richard peers at it, announcing that the man who owns the button must be the man who killed him as well as the man they are looking for. They hear footsteps coming up the stone path outside and run up into the belfry to hide, carefully spanning the rafters. Looking straight down on the organ, they see a man rush to the body and immediately begin ringing the huge bell next to them. As the villagers go to their doors, Richard yells into the General's earringed ear, "We'll have to stay up here for hours!" and the General turns his mustached thick lips to Richard's ear, "But your wife will wonder what happened to her poor little general!"

Back in town, Robert and Elsa flirt in a horse-drawn carriage. He teases the non-English-speaking driver, who blows him a kiss in response to a request for

cigarettes. Later, he leans over to kiss Elsa, who arches her back to avoid him and threatens to call the police. Suddenly more serious, she allows that she thinks she loves her husband, and Robert takes her hand to stifle his yawn. The coachman returns with two very long pipes for the gentleman and for her.

Richard and the General enter the hotel lobby, and the concierge tells them that Mrs. Ashenden is in the casino; she hands them a telegram that warns them that their man is probably leaving the day after tomorrow and "at all costs must be found. Consult General." The General, impatient to find Elsa, thinks the message silly, but Richard upbraids him for not taking their task seriously. Agreeing that Elsa may have learned something, he agrees to go change for the casino.

The camera follows Robert and Elsa as they walk among the gambling tables. He repeatedly tries to grab her, and each time she shrugs him off. Finally, they stop at a table; he consents to give her one chip after she informs him she hasn't any money of her own. Richard and the General, now in tuxedos, finally appear, and Elsa eagerly greets her husband. After hearing his long name, Robert suggests he call the General "Charlie," and the General scowls. Turning to the roulette table, Richard shows Elsa the button they found and accidentally drops it on the winning number. The croupier announces the button and Robert suggests it belongs to Mr. Caypor, who, looking at his matching coat buttons, agrees. Richard turns solemnly to the General, while the camera moves on to Elsa behind them, whose eyes widen in recognition as well. She starts at the sound of a dog barking, and Mr. Caypor's dachshund scurries in and jumps into Mr. Caypor's arms. The maitre d'hotel rushes over to upbraid Mr. Caypor, and they argue in the background about the dog, as Richard comments to Elsa, "That's our man." "How thrilling!" she replies, staring off, "but he's English . . . he looks so harmless!" Richard and Robert move in to tease the maitre d'hotel about his rules, demanding them in writing. Mr. Caypor enjoys the joke and a friendship begins. Smiling introductions and talk follow, and Mr. Caypor apologizes for his outfit, saying he has been hiking near Langenthal all day. The General moves excitedly to Richard's side to consult with him, and adds in passing, about Robert, "This college boy! No sympatico." Richard impatiently dismisses him.

The group enters the dining hall and joins Mrs. Caypor, a solemn grey-haired woman. Richard and the General hear that Mr. Caypor leaves the day after tomorrow and become more convinced that he is their man. Elsa, smiling, asks Mrs. Caypor a question about England; she dourly replies that she has never been to England and, in fact, this is her first time away from Germany; the women part awkwardly.

As the group settles around the table, Richard and the General start to bicker about their mountain-climbing abilities. Robert tries to calm them as Elsa knowingly observes. "Me as much touchy as I want!" cries the General, as Richard reluctantly agrees to the dare of the mountain climb. Mr. Caypor suggests the Langenthal Alp and expresses regret that he will not be able to guide them himself. Eventually, he suggests they move up the hike to the next day when he is available, and Richard stabs out his cigarette in secret triumph at the offer. Elsa and Richard rise to dance and she excitedly compliments him on his success. Sneering, he instructs her to stay behind with Mrs. Caypor, and when she objects, he lectures her. "It's murder . . . simple murder, and all you can see in it is fun!" Mr. Caypor smilingly waves at Richard from across the room, and he stiffly manages a smile in return.

A funicular crosses the white mountains. Inside the vehicle, Mr. Caypor plays with a small child passenger.

Back at the Caypor's hotel sitting room, Elsa restlessly noses about while Mrs. Caypor knits, admonishing her in response to a question that "we do not talk about the war." They begin their German conversation lesson, and Robert arrives, insinuating himself into their company. Suddenly, the dachshund begins to scurry around and whine.

In close-up profile, Mr. Caypor hikes along the trail and turns jovially to his companions behind, commenting on the appetite they are working up.

At the hotel, the German lesson continues, but the dog is now scratching at the door. The men continue their climb, and Mrs. Caypor comments on the dog's attachment to her husband; "He thinks of him all the time!" Elsa, distracted at this, tries to concentrate on her German.

The camera returns to the introductory close-up of Mr. Caypor as he leads the men up, and the dog's scratching remains on the soundtrack. Richard suddenly has second thoughts and whispers to the General that he wants to give it up and go back. But the General frowns and wonders about his payment for the job. The three decide to leave Richard at the observer hut, while the other two finish the climb.

Elsa, now wide-eyed with concern, stares off at the whimpering dog. Mrs. Caypor picks him up to try to quiet him, but the dog will not be calmed, and Elsa becomes increasingly agitated.

Inside the hut, Richard watches the two men climb a snowy bluff, then looks through a telescope for a close-up view of Mr. Caypor as he turns to laugh with the General behind him. The dog scratches frantically as Richard watches the General raise his hand to push Mr. Caypor over the edge, and screams out, "Watch out, for god's sake!" But when his hand, raised in alarm, has passed over his eyes, only the General is left, a tiny dot on the white cliff. The shadow of a cloud passes over the scene as the dog lets out a wail.

Mrs. Caypor rises in alarm, and Elsa, seeing the woman's grief, buries her head in her hands.

The camera moves from a close-up of a pair of folk-costumed singers across the stage where they are dancing with a troupe, and then across the beer garden audience, to find Elsa, staring morbidly off, and Richard, drinking. He goads her, "My, you're quiet tonight!" Relieved to see the General arrive, he waves him over, but his smile fades as he wonders how the police inquiry went. Elsa stares out from between the men, zombielike. The performers begin a more solemn folk song, based on the monotonal percussive sounds of coins rolling inside bowls, the *taler schwingen*. Elsa stares at the General as he flings a coin in the bodice of the woman next to him. Lowering her eyes in contempt, Elsa moves her dull gaze back to the center. Richard leaves to decode a telegram the General has brought with him while the General turns more seriously to the woman next to him. A close-up of a coin rolling in a bowl is tied to Elsa's stare, and even the General seems affected by the funereal sound as Richard returns and throws the message at them: "You are after wrong man, look elsewhere." Elsa's hand goes up to her forehead, "But the button!" she exclaims, and the button rolls around the bowl superimposed with the coin. The General breaks out into a loud laugh, "The wrong man!" and the song ends. Elsa rises and leaves to the sounds of a more cheerful *Edelweiss*, and Richard follows her onto a river boat.

Seated alone on the back bench, she lets out a torrent of sarcasm about all the

charming people in Switzerland: "I love them all . . . especially the General." Richard implores her to calm herself, but she continues, telling him that she fell in love with him at first sight but is glad now that it is over. Richard's face softens toward her, but he agrees their arrangement must be viewed as a job. "You are paid a salary, I suppose?" "Yes, of course, I'm doing it for money," she snaps, but he counters her insincerity and she cries, "Somehow I don't like murder at close quarters as much as I expected." Both looking in opposite directions, he commiserates, "I don't like it much either." But she confronts him bitterly, "Oh, don't make me laugh!" and turns away again.

Later, on the shore, they stand by a stone fence and talk. He tells her he watched the murder from a telescope and she cries in relief. "Does that make any difference?" he objects. She suggests they give it all up, and he frowns, wondering what she means, but she smiles and they kiss.

A Roman shade pulls up over a sunny window. Richard and Elsa giggle and embrace. She wonders about his resignation, a short note he has written advising R to find another "butcher." But the General drops in on the couple's musings and talks Richard into coming with him to hear some new information. "Don't go!" cries Elsa, and the camera closes in on Richard's face for the response, the General shadowy in the background, as he softly reassures her that he will be back in a few minutes. After they have left, she turns and drops crestfallen into a chair.

The General takes Richard down the hall, jumping back and forth in front of a maid on the way, to a room where they find the woman from the night before eating breakfast from a tray in bed. Her fiance works in a chocolate factory, which happens to be the German information center, and he knows that a message has been received from the man they are looking for. From her bed across the room, she demands 5000 francs for the information. The General leaps over to her and cries out that he has already given her 100 francs, but she remains firm. Richard rings up Elsa to ask her to send his coat down the hall, as he must go out. She reluctantly accepts this and he eagerly explains that they can still catch the night train. Resigned, she hangs up the telephone and picks up his resignation letter; with a pair of scissors, she cuts it into a ribbon.

The chocolate factory. Inside, the General and Richard stand in front of a window overlooking the assembly line. The camera moves through the window to accompany the two men on a tour with a manager. Several of the workers stare ominously at them, and the General notices one slip a note into a box of candy moving along a conveyor belt. The General watches it move over and up a circular stair, then through a hole in the wall, where he sees a pair of hands open the note: "Two English spies here, phone police anonymously."

The German-speaking police excitedly take the call and the operators buzz back to the manager at the factory.

A note from Elsa: "It was nice of you to pretend last night . . . you will be better off without me . . ." The camera passes from the note to her suitcase; light sobbing is heard on the soundtrack as she throws her finery into it.

The General's contact excitedly finds her boyfriend near some noisy chocolate beaters. Gleefully, she holds up five fingers, and he nods. Leaving his post, the young blond man finds the Englishmen and tries to signal them as they stand with the manager, who is plying them with candy. But the General looks out the window and notices the police arriving outside. He feigns illness, and Richard pushes an alarm, sending the several hundred white-uniformed workers rushing

out the corridors and effectively blocking the police at the entrance. Alone, the General and Richard race through rooms filled with spinning conveyor belts, followed by the young informer. He catches up with them in a corridor piled high with tables, and the General turns and knocks him down. He continues to pursue them down some stairs and into another machine room, but manages this time to convince them who he is. They exchange a note and the money and Richard and the General discover that their prey is named Marvin. They have only a moment to be shocked that it is someone they know before a crowd of police come upon them; they run outside and leap into their car.

In the hotel lobby, a distraught Elsa asks the concierge about her trunks and then realizes that she has no idea where to send them. Seeing Robert Marvin, she cheerfully approaches, but he senses that something is odd when she laughs over loud at a funny picture he intended to leave for her. Near tears, she pleads with him to take her to Greece with him. Frowning, and in a hurry himself, he insists it is impossible, but relents.

They rush out just as the concierge takes a telephone call from Richard. Discovering that Elsa and Robert have gone to the station together, Richard brightens, assuming she has figured things out ahead of them. The General kisses his fingertips in celebration of the "first-classest bloodhound of all of us!"

That night at the train station, the General and Richard are stuck with a crowd behind a gate. Suddenly, Richard sees Elsa on the platform and she excitedly comes over to greet him. Finally, the men are let through to be with her and Richard tells her about Robert, who has left her to get cigarettes. She is disbelieving, but follows them to the Constantinople train, where they see him surreptitiously loading his bags. The train begins to pull out and Richard instructs her to wait for him, but she climbs aboard with the men.

Installed in a compartment, Richard starts to instruct her about how to handle the ticket taker, but she firmly announces, "You're not going to kill him." The camera moves into a close-up of the General in the foreground, who turns away from them, disgruntled. Richard and Elsa argue, and Richard insists it is his job; besides, any minute, they will be in enemy territory. She threatens to turn them in just as the train stops to pick up a crowd of soldiers and weapons. Their passports are checked; outside in the distance, three men hang from gallows, silhouetted on the night sky—"spies," a passenger tells them. Elsa stares at the spectacle; suddenly Robert appears. Surprised, he questions her as she stands in the compartment doorway, with Richard and the General hiding behind her on either side and several soldiers crowded onto the rest of the benches. Noticing the soldiers and believing her when she says she is alone, he commands her to follow him and leads her through several cars, stopping for a moment to speak in German with a soldier. As she walks, "Save Ashenden" rings through her ears over the clack of the train wheels. Finally they reach a compartment and he shows her a small gun. Leaning across to her, he says he doesn't trust her. "You're on business, too . . . the lonely neglected wife, and I fell for it!"

Back in the compartment, Richard, impatient, rises to follow.

Reminding her she is in enemy territory, Robert insists on the truth about her friends, but she convinces him that she has always been in love with him. Suddenly, the train is attacked from the air. Robert pushes her to the inside corner of the compartment with a taunt, "Chivalrous German spy protects British lady from British bombs," and abruptly kisses her. Richard and the General

enter. "Very neat," says the General, and brings out his knife, insisting on doing the job himself. But Elsa grabs the handgun and tells them she cares about Robert and they are not going to have this on their conscience. While she and Richard argue, the train derails and all are thrown out.

From afar, Richard views the fiery wreckage. Robert is trapped nearby, and Richard's hands reach out for his neck, then go limp. Elsa crawls over to them, and the General appears from the other side. He walks over to sit near Robert, and sets the gun down in front of him. Robert picks it up and, just before expiring himself, shoots the General, who rises to intone his full name one last time, then falls to the ground. Elsa and Richard embrace.

Armies cross the desert; superimposed over the scene are headlines of the Allied advance into Turkey, and finally, victory. The montage ends with R shaking hands with some military leaders while he looks down at a postcard on his desk. "Home safely, never again, Mr. and Mrs. Ashenden." Heads touching, the couple stare out from the screen together, and smile.

Note. *Most filmographies credit Michael Balcon as producer, and Alma Reville with work on the adaptation of the screenplay. Some add Michel Saint-Denis to the cast.

22   *Sabotage* (1936)

Director	Alfred Hitchcock
Production Company	Gaumont British Picture Corp., Ltd.*
Screenplay	Charles Bennett, Alma Reville (adaptation), Ian Hay (dialogue), Helen Simpson (additional dialogue), from the novel *The Secret Agent* by Joseph Conrad*
Photography	Bernard Knowles
Editing	Charles Frend
Art Direction	O[tto] Werndorff
Set Direction	Albert Jullion
Sound	R. Cameron
Music	Louis Levy
Costumes	J. Strassner, Marianne (wardrobe)
Continuity	Alma Reville
Cast	Sylvia Sydney (Mrs. Verloc), Oscar Homolka (Mr. Verloc), Desmond Tester (Stevie), John Loder (Ted), Joyce Barbour (Renee), Matthew Boulton (Superintendent Talbot), S. J. Warmington (Hollingshead), William Dewhurst (the Professor), Peter Bull, Torin Thatcher, Austin Trevor*
Filmed	at Lime Grove Studios, London
Running Time	approximately 76 minutes
Distributor	G.F.D.
Release Date	December 1936

Other titles: *The Woman Alone* (U.S.), *Agent Secret*

Synopsis

Credits appear over a close-up of a dictionary definition of sabotage, accompanied by ominous theme music.

A bright light bulb fills the screen, then flickers. Blackout in London. Officials find sand in the public works, "Sabotage! Who did it?" A frowning, hatted man walks into a close-up; passengers file calmly out of stuck subway cars, and the people have fun lighting candles and matches.

At the Bijou Cinema theater she and her husband manage, the young dark-haired Mrs. Verloc, dressed in a trim sailor-style dress, handles a crowd of angry filmgoers who demand their money back. "It's Providence!" she pleads, as her neighbor, a young produce man named Ted, taunts her about "robbin' the people." Ominous music accompanies Mr. Verloc, the frowning man from before, as he enters the empty theater. Inside their apartment in back of the theater, he washes his hands; sand settles in the bottom of the sink. He enters his bedroom, smiling ruefully at the light switch that does not work, then lies down and puts a newspaper over his head. Leaving her cashier to argue with the customers, Mrs. Verloc runs upstairs to ask advice from her husband, Carl, who feigns sleep. She queries him about his whereabouts but accepts his reply when he denies having been out, and he advises her to return the ticket money. She meekly objects, contending that he is always complaining that they never cover expenses.

Down on the sidewalk, Ted is now persuasively turning the crowd around to agree with Mrs. Verloc—"It's an act of God . . . defined as any activity actuated by an actual action"—when she arrives and impatiently contradicts him about returning the money. Suddenly the lights return and the city starts up.

Back inside, Mr. Verloc starts when the light goes on, while downstairs the maid leaves, stopping to tell the two women in the ticket booth that Mrs. Verloc's brother, Stevie, is finishing the dinner preparation.

In the kitchen, Stevie, a fair-haired ten year old, catches a rag on his head, and breaks a plate while trying to take the meal off the stove.

Mrs. Verloc and Stevie happily serve dinner to the waiting and sullen Mr. Verloc, who explains that he decided to refund the ticket money just to have quiet and complains about the overdone vegetables. Mrs. Verloc quickly sends Stevie downstairs to get some fresh lettuce, and Ted accompanies him on his return, carrying several varieties for Mrs. Verloc to choose from. Ted mentions in passing that he just observed Mr. Verloc return home, but Mr. Verloc denies it, and Mrs. Verloc backs him up.

Leaving through the theater, Ted finds his boss at the produce stand and asks if he may leave early, then rushes out.

In an office at New Scotland Yard, Ted, an undercover detective, speaks to a superior who advises him about the case.

Another day, Ted chats with Mr. Verloc on the crowded sidewalk, then signals another undercover detective to tail him.

Mr. Verloc meets a friend with a German accent in an aquarium; in front of one of the large tanks, they discuss payment for his activities. The man is unhappy with a report describing the fun Londoners had during the blackout and tells Mr. Verloc he will not be paid until he has earned his money by frightening people. Mr. Verloc objects to injuring anyone, but, needing the money, he agrees to pick up a bomb at a bird shop. Dismissed, the sullen Mr. Verloc stares into a

fish tank and sees a crowded London street corner explode. The detective tailing the by-now totally distracted Mr. Verloc helps him move the exit turnstile in the correct direction.

Ted runs into Mrs. Verloc and Stevie on a busy street and invites them to lunch. Though Mrs. Verloc hesitates, Stevie enthusiastically suggests Simpson's, an expensive popular restaurant, and she smiles and goes along. At the table in the crowded bright restaurant, Mrs. Verloc first tries to order the least expensive item on the menu, then innocently answers Ted's questions about her life, becoming slightly disturbed at his interrogation about her "nice happy family." She assures him they are quiet, average people. Though he has told her he has never been in the restaurant before, the waiter recognizes him; curious, she energetically questions him about his ability to pay, but he jokingly turns on her about *her* "secret activities."

Later, at Scotland Yard, a close-up shows the cash voucher he had intended to submit for the lunch as Ted tears it up, then strides into his boss and informs him Mrs. Verloc knows nothing. "A pretty one?" counters his supervisor, who then wonders about Mr. Verloc, and reads for Ted the other detective's report on the aquarium meeting. The detective, Hollingshead, is now waiting at a bird shop for Mr. Verloc to show up.

The camera moves from a close-up of a Liverpool Road street sign into a bird shop where the owner argues with a customer about a bird that won't sing. He then takes Mr. Verloc into his "other department" and alludes to his wares, time bombs, while his daughter and granddaughter look on. He and Mr. Verloc agree to meet again on Saturday at 1:45 P.M. Mr. Verloc sees a policeman pacing outside and breaks into a sweat, though the policeman moves on.

That evening at home, Mr. Verloc writes a note to someone named Max about a job he has available, while Mrs. Verloc and Stevie discuss their lunch at Simpson's and decide that Ted must be the owner's son. Stevie warms to the subject of all Ted knows about gangsters, and Mr. Verloc slowly raises his head, recognizing danger.

Friday. Mrs. Verloc is in the ticket booth and passes one stranger in to see her husband, then another one. She smiles broadly at Ted, who requests free entry too. Inside the theater, Ted sneaks back to the aisle between the Verloc lodgings and the projection booth and runs into Stevie, who innocently helps Ted sit up on a high windowsill and peek through at Mr. Verloc and his friends. One of them notices Ted's hand on the sill and pulls him tumbling down into the room. Ted quickly exits as Stevie explains their innocence, but one of them recognizes Ted as Detective Sergeant Spencer from Scotland Yard. The men quickly decide to drop the job and scatter. Mr. Verloc goes out to tell his wife that Ted is spying on his friends, not on him, of course; concerned, she offers to speak to Ted, but Mr. Verloc walks over to the produce stand himself. He queries the owner of the grocery, who apologizes for the deception and tells him Ted has left his employ, but that he was probably just suspicious about "funny sorts of films." Returning to the ticket booth, Mr. Verloc is despondent; Mrs. Verloc hands him a note that reads "London must not laugh on Saturday."

Saturday, Lord Mayor's Show Day. Mr. Verloc tries to contact the bird shop owner, but "it's too late to stop him." The package has arrived. Nervously, he takes the package out of the bottom of the cage and finds a note: "birds will sing at 1:45."

Stevie arrives with Ted, and Mrs. Verloc expresses her anger at his spying on them. They talk and Ted tells her Mr. Verloc is a suspected saboteur. She insists her husband is a harmless person, just as Mr. Verloc emerges from the back carrying the bomb. Mr. Verloc turns around, realizing he cannot walk past them; he calls Stevie, who is enjoying whistling with his new bird, and asks him to do the errand, which involves delivering a film canister. Stevie finds other things to do until Mr. Verloc finally loses his temper and yells at him that the film must be at the station by 1:30 P.M. at the latest. On the way out, Stevie chats with Ted and Mrs. Verloc, showing them the film, *Bartholomew the Strangler.* Ted walks back to the apartment to query Mr. Verloc; he apologizes for his deceit, but talks the suspect into writing down an explanation of his activities.

Meanwhile out on the street, Stevie is manipulated by a hawker who brushes his teeth and splashes hair tonic all over his head. Finally freed, he continues his long walk, but is stopped by the Mayor's parade, a long event, which he enjoys despite himself. By the time he is able to cross the street, it is so late he is forced to talk himself onto a bus, as flammable film is not ordinarily allowed on public transportation. Stuck in a traffic jam, Stevie sits next to a woman and her small dog and worriedly peers out the window until 1:45 arrives and the bus explodes.

Back at the Verlocs, Ted and the couple laugh as Mr. Verloc's statement is completed; Ted takes a telephone call and announces that a bus load of people has been blown up on the west side. Mr. Verloc blurts out, "What time?" and Mrs. Verloc is dumbfounded.

At the wreckage, Ted discovers the film canister from *Bartholomew the Strangler.*

Outside in front of the ticket booth, Mrs. Verloc worries about Stevie, then picks up a news item about the *Bartholomew the Strangler* clue found in the bombing wreckage. She faints. Rising, surrounded by a sea of faces, she imagines Stevie among the crowd, then goes to find Mr. Verloc.

Back inside their apartment, Mrs. Verloc sits sideways on a chair, her hand propping up her head. Confidently standing above her, Mr. Verloc apologizes and urges her to think about tomorrow: "Be reasonable ... that swine in the aquarium! It's your Scotland Yard friend! Blame him. I would have carried the thing myself but he was sitting around watching." She stares out, silent. He kneels in front of her, but she rises and walks out. She stops to sit with the theater audience and is briefly amused by a cartoon, then frowns when "Cock Robin" falls from the tree. The maid stops by to advise her that dinner is ready and she returns to serve her husband.

Trying to be resigned, she frowns, then suddenly throws down her serving knife, and hesitates to pick it up again. He complains about the overdone vegetables, and asks, "Couldn't we send downstairs ..." Again she picks up the knife and starts to serve, increasingly disturbed. Aghast at her movement, Mr. Verloc rises and approaches her slowly around the table, but she holds the knife and stabs him when he makes a sudden close move. She cries out "Stevie!" From below, the camera views her as she walks by his fallen feet in the foreground and out of the room.

Later, Mrs. Verloc sits motionless in her hallway; Ted enters. "I'd do anything for you," he tells her. "There's nothing you can do for either of us," she says, staring out helplessly. As he continues to tell of his feelings for her, he

suddenly realizes something is wrong and walks into the apartment to find Mr. Verloc's body. He resists her suggestion to go to the police, then accompanies her out into the street crowded with hawkers and nightlife. She forgets her urge to confess when she grabs by the shoulders a young boy who reminds her of Stevie. Ted pulls her aside and convinces her to run away with him.

Meanwhile at the bird shop, the owner's daughter demands that he retrieve the bird cage before the police find it. The police tail the owner in a radio truck to the Bijou, where they are ordered to arrest him and Mr. Verloc.

Still out on the street, Mrs. Verloc appeals to Ted, "No matter what happens . . ." and they kiss. They notice a police van approaching, and Mrs. Verloc pulls away to rush over and confess to the inspector. Ted tries to quiet her, and the inspector is called away before she is able to speak.

Inside the Verlocs' apartment, the bird shop owner locks himself in after seeing the police. They approach through the theater and confront him on the other side of the locked door, but he threatens to set off a bomb if he is not left alone. The police alert the crowd and evacuate the cinema. Breaking through an inside apartment door, the bird shop owner finds Mr. Verloc's body and pauses at the discovery.

Outside, the inspector questions Mrs. Verloc about her husband's ability to control the bomber. "He's dead!" she cries, at the moment the theater blows up. Ted pulls the sobbing Mrs. Verloc to him and holds her. The inspector wonders aloud if he heard her say "He's dead" before the explosion, but then decides he "can't remember." Ted pushes Mrs. Verloc through the crowd away from the police.

Note. *Most filmographies credit Michael Balcon as Producer and Ivor Montagu as Associate Producer. Some credit E. V. H. Emmett with additional dialogue, and Clare Greet, Sam Wilkinson, Sara Allgood, Martita Hunt, and Pamela Bevan in the cast. Cartoon sequence from *Who Killed Cock Robin*, by "arrangement with and thanks to Walt Disney."

23 *Young and Innocent* (1937)

Director	Alfred Hitchcock
Producer	Edward Black
Production Company	Gainsborough-Gaumont British
Screenplay	Charles Bennett, Edwin Greenwood, Anthony Armstrong, Gerald Savory (dialogue), based on the novel *A Shilling for Candles* by Josephine Tey*
Photography	Bernard Knowles
Editing	Charles Frend
Art Direction	Alfred Junge
Sound	A. O'Donoghue
Music	Louis Levy, Lerner, Goodheart, and Hoffman (song)
Costumes	Marianne
Continuity	Alma Reville

Cast	Derrick de Marney (Robert Fisdall), Nova Pilbeam (Erica Burgoyne), Percy Marmont (Colonel Burgoyne), Edward Rigby (Old Will), Mary Clare (Erica's Aunt), John Longden (Inspector Kent), George Curzon (Guy), Basil Radford (Erica's Uncle), Pamela Carme (Christine), George Merritt (Sergeant Miller), J. H. Roberts (Solicitor), Jerry Verno (Lorry Driver), H. F. Maltby (Police Sergeant), John Miller (Police Constable), Torin Thatcher, Peggy Simpson, Anna Konstam
Filmed	at Lime Grove and Pinewood Studios, London
Running Time	approximately 80 minutes
Distributor	General Film Distributors, Ltd.
Release Date	November 1937

Other titles: *The Girl Was Young* (U.S.), *Jung und unschuldig, Jeune et Innocent*

Synopsis

A diagonal Art Deco graphic appears under the credits, accompanied by the "Drummer Man" music.

The camera frames the full face of an impatient woman as a man yells "Christine!" "Don't shout!" she says and turns away. The scene widens to include the man who walks toward her and calls her a liar. They argue intently about an impending divorce as a thunderstorm rages outside. He is jealous; she has "boys" hanging around. She shrieks "Why don't you listen?" and slaps him; he glares at her, then walks out to a balcony. His eyes twitch uncontrollably as he stares back toward the house with the dark cliffs and stormy sea behind him.

Morning. Sea gulls flutter over the rocks; a body washes up on the beach, along with a cloth raincoat belt. A young man, Robert Fisdall, walks at the top of a cliff, then runs down to the body, the music building with the action. "Christine!" he stares momentarily, then runs off just as two women beach walkers round a rock and see the body. They run over to it, and the music climaxes with the cries of the gulls. They look up to see Robert running off in the distance.

The police and a crowd of bystanders have gathered on the beach. One of the constables asks who found the body first. Robert says "I did." The women say, "We did," and accuse him of running away. "I went off to get help. . . . I was only there a few minutes," he says. A policeman observes that the woman has been dead only a few minutes; Robert looks into the camera as he realizes his predicament.

News headlines relate the violent death of Christine Clay, movie star, and the raincoat belt clue; one states a man has been detained.

Facing the camera, Robert yawns; the detectives yawn too as one of them rises to open the blinds of the interrogation room to the morning light. One of the detectives harasses Robert throughout, and Robert is not very patient. They ask

him if the belt is his. His own coat was stolen from his car in front of a "common shelter named Tom's Hat," he tells them. He was a friend of the victim, but not her lover. They ask him about money; he replies that she paid him for a story he had written three years ago. One of the two detectives writes in his notebook, "she gave me money on former occasions." Robert admits to not being well off and they inform him that she's left 1200 pounds in her will. He faints. A young woman walks in. She has knowledge of first aid and orders one of the detectives to get some brandy. Kneeling on the floor, she holds Robert's head in her lap and slaps him. She asks the detectives if he's guilty; they don't know. He wakes, still groggy, and cuddles closer. Suddenly he notices her and pulls away, standing. She leaves the room. "Who's that?" he asks. "The chief constable's daughter," they respond.

Erica walks into the street and crosses over to interrupt her father and another constable, who are talking about the Scotland Yard case. Eventually, Col. Burgoyne turns to his daughter and teases her about her dog in the car nearby. She walks over to start the car. As she's laboring, Robert is being escorted across the street and teases her in passing. She drives off.

Inside the police station, Briggs, the assigned counsel, chats with Robert at a table. He is a cheery but confused and vacant sort. He bumbles around the evidence, and decides it doesn't look too good, then asks for a down payment of two pounds out of the two pounds three shillings that Robert has in his pocket. A constable arrives at the doorway to announce the hearing, and Briggs asks for a delay because he's misplaced his glasses.

Escorted by the constables, Robert and his counsel walk into the hall and head for the courtroom.

In the courtroom, a wife-abuse case is winding to an end, as the judge admonishes the husband to keep the peace for six months and the wife wonders if she can't have eight in order to get through Christmas. "No," bellows the judge.

In the hallway, the next crowd begins to enter and Robert slips away from his escorts, entering the first door he finds. It's another aisle of the same courtroom. A whisper travels through the room: the prisoner has escaped! Robert sits down and slips on Briggs's very thick glasses. The confusion escalates and most of the crowd exits the room, including Robert. Outside,^H he walks calmly through the crowd of scurrying officers and crosses a street as one of them commandeers Erica's car.

Out in the countryside, the car runs out of gas and the two constables get out to push it. Erica tells them they should leave her with the car and go on. A farmer with a cart full of pigs pulls up and they decide to commandeer it, though the farmer is not pleased and puts them in the back with the pigs. Erica takes off her jacket and starts to push the car on the steering-wheel side. She is puzzled as she notices it is moving with little effort and suddenly Robert pops his head up over the other side. She is stern, but he charms her and continues to push the car.

They pull up to a petrol station; a child is ordered to pump the gas. Erica has no money and Robert pulls out his last shillings to pay. Robert asks the attendant for directions to Tom's Hat and repeats the directions to Erica, who is now in the driver's seat. She objects. He reminds her it is his petrol. They drive off.

They arrive at a deserted mill and she asks him to get out. He sits on the hood, stalling, and proposes that she return after dark and take him to Tom's Hat. Finally he admits that the situation is not funny, but "I can laugh because I'm innocent." She drives off and he enters the mill, watching her leave through the

cobwebbed windows. He sees her meet a police car at the top of the road and blows her a kiss as he watches it pass by.

In the well-appointed dining room of the Burgoynes' home, four boys try the patience of Erica, their sister, who sits at one end of the table, and their father, at the other. They discuss the exciting escape of the day and what the suspect might be doing. Erica is disturbed to hear them discuss how far Robert won't be able to go on the three shillings they know he has; she knows it is spent. He might even starve, says one. Col. Burgoyne is called to the telephone and Erica slips away from the table and goes out.

She drives up to the mill, leaves a sack outside, then changes her mind and takes it in. Accompanied by light romantic music, she climbs up a rickety ladder, uncovers the dozing Robert from a pile of straw, and puts three shillings on his chest. He smiles, "You do think I'm innocent." He picks up the sack of food as she starts down the ladder. Stowing the bread inside his shirt, he blurts out his story: if he can just get to Tom's Hat where his coat was stolen and find the belt with it, he can prove his innocence. She returns to sit down and asks about Christine Clay; he tells how he met her in Hollywood, absent-mindedly throwing a paper from his cheese out the window.

Up on a hill above the mill, two constables notice the paper floating out. Erica's dog barks at them as they approach and the older one orders the younger one to grab it; meanwhile Erica and Robert escape out a side window. The constables finally enter, and stand in front of a lower window; Robert's legs dangle in the air outside it and hit one of the men in the head. The couple scurry to the car and take off, the dog running after. Robert suggests that the dog will catch up, but Erica demands he stop and she scoops up the dog. She lectures Robert about her position and he stops suddenly, agreeing that she must drive back straight away.

Erica drives now and he is the passenger. The fork in the road described in the directions ("left for Tom's Hat") looms ahead. They both worry about which way they will go. They pull up to find the right fork blocked. He's ecstatic as they must go left, and she proudly says she was going to do that anyway.

At Tom's Hat, a plain roadside pub, Erica tells Robert to stay outside. "I might as well see this through now," she says, and goes in to ask about the coat. Inside, a raucous group quiets when they see her. She orders a cup of coffee at the counter and banters with the customers seated at the few tables. She asks about the coat and the man behind the counter starts to tell her about Old Will, the china mender, but is hushed up by the customers. One, however, pipes up to complete the information about the tramp who claims he was given a new coat. Some other customers defend Old Will from having "his name bandied about" and a fight breaks out. Suddenly everyone in the place is punching someone else and Erica is jammed against the counter. She extricates herself and flees out the back door as Robert tries to push his way in the front door to save her. She calls to him from outside and he gets thrown out as he turns around and knocks his head on a post. She dabs his wound at a nearby water fountain and they do a comic bit as the water gushes up every time she pushes his head down. A customer stops by to tell her she can find Old Will at Nobby's in Gilchester. Erica tells Robert she's glad now that she took the left fork, and he tells her good-bye and walks down the road toward Gilchester.

Once again, Erica drives and Robert sits next to her in the car. He tells her she's marvelous but wonders if she's being sensible. She says she can explain to her father if they stop at her aunt's home nearby and call him from there as a

cover. She hands him a broken china cup "for getting in touch with Old Will" but he doesn't think it's worth saving and throws it out the car.

They stop at a large country home, and Erica tells Robert to wait in the car, she will only be a minute. Erica enters her aunt's house in the middle of her cousin's birthday party. She hesitates, but out of politeness lingers for the festivities with the twenty or so children.

Outside, Robert becomes anxious.

Inside, her aunt plans to have Erica help with a game.

Outside, Robert writes a note indicating it's too risky to wait any longer. A car pulls up and Robert turns away, but the man who gets out recognizes Erica's car and insists he come in because it will be a while before she returns from his daughter's party and Robert mustn't stay out there "like a criminal." The uncle mentions that "Erica always brings over a present on Felicity's birthday . . . there would be something radically wrong if she forgot." Robert picks up a stone statue from the stairs on the way in.

In the hallway, the aunt interrupts as Robert approaches Erica and whispers they must leave right away. He explains they came to give Felicity her present and abruptly hands over the stone statue to the surprised hostess, who insists they enter the living room with her. The children crowd excitedly around Erica, and Robert gives a fake name when the aunt asks, piquing her interest. Several times, Erica tries to leave, but circumstances prevent her, and the signals between her and Robert make her aunt increasingly suspicious. Everyone acquires a party hat and her uncle notices the couple's predicament as they once again attempt to leave, but Erica's aunt gives them work to do. In turn, the aunt queries Erica and Robert about his background, and, of course, gets different stories. Erica's uncle, wanting to relieve them of their discomfort, decides that his wife must be the first blind man in a game of bluff. He signals them to leave and they skirt the blind man as she gropes around. Taking off her blindfold, she becomes very angry with her husband for letting the young couple go.

She rushes out and into the study in time to observe them going in the opposite direction from home, then calls her brother, Erica's father, to report the suspicious goings-on.

Col. Burgoyne is shocked and immediately telephones his constables with orders that Erica be stopped at Leaming and asked to telephone him.

Erica and Robert drive and laugh over the party and their good luck. They flirt; he's touched when she calls him Robert.

At Leaming, a constable stops them. Robert looks over at him and is recognized. He pushes the constable away and orders Erica to "step on it." They drive off; she is very upset about what she has done.

Her father receives the news over the telephone. He asks to have her name kept out of it and is told that the policemen are "combing the forest."

Spotlights move around Ashcroft forest.

The camera moves over the industrial section that surrounds the train tracks at Gilchester where Erica and Robert are parked in the track bed. He tries to cheer her up, but she is quiet, sad, and tired, staring out. He suggests she go home, but she says she is going to stick it out. He leaves her asleep in the car.

At Nobby's Lodging House, he gets a bed for the night and asks after Old Will, but Will's bed is empty and Robert is unable to stay awake.

The next morning he rises late and stares at Will's bed, slept in, but empty. The place is full of men milling about, but he can't get an answer about Will. He grabs a cup and breaks it; the owner becomes angry and Will, the "china mender"

is identified. Suddenly Robert remembers Erica outside; he pleads with Will to help him and finally drags the man with him to the car. A commotion develops as the others report the incident. With Will in the back seat, Robert and Erica drive off, slipping just in front of a train that stops the constables from following them.

As they drive, Will is grumpy about being kidnapped, but the dog discovers the missing raincoat underneath Will's other clothes, so he's obliged to help. They stop at the side of the road while Will undresses. He informs them that there was no belt with the coat when he got it and that a man who blinked gave it to him. They hurry back into the car and decide to head for "the old mine workings."

They speed toward the mine to evade their pursuers, who take a wrong turn, but quickly get back on their trail. As they drive into the mine the car slips down a rock slide cave-in. Old Will and Robert jump out of the car quickly enough, but Erica falls down many feet with the car. They finally pull her up, each one holding on to the other. A constable shouts, "There they are!" just as Erica returns to pick up her dog, and she is caught.

At a police station, Erica defends Robert vehemently as "the finest person . . . too kind and gentle" to be guilty. Her father, with a grave expression, enters in the middle of this speech.

At the dining table, her brothers stare at her in silence. Her father summons her into the study and asks if she wants to tell him something. No, she says. He is angry but resigned; feeling responsible for her "criminal offenses" he shows her his resignation letter and sends her to her room.

She goes upstairs, throws herself on her bed, and sobs.

That evening, Old Will waits outside as Robert crawls in Erica's window while she sleeps. She runs to hug him. He tells her he wants to give himself up, that the coat was the end for him. He asks if there was anything in the coat the constables found in the car and she says just some matches from the Grand Hotel. She turns away from him, despondent, then crying. Suddenly, he realizes the matches are meaningful: "I've never been there in my life!" he cries.

At the Grand Hotel, Erica sits in the lobby looking around.

Robert waits outside as Will buys a bowler and suit in a shop. A suspicious constable accosts Will as he walks out of the store in his finery.

Will enters the hotel and greets Erica who thanks him for helping. Constables watch them. The couple walk around and decide to go into the ballroom where about a hundred people are dancing and dining; seated at a back table, they order two cups of tea and wonder how to find their man among so many people. The camera travels from high in the lobby through the windows into the dining room, toward the band—all in blackface and playing "The Drummer Man"—and then into a close-up of the drummer, whose eyes twitch. Erica and Will sit at the table depressed. As people sit down after the end of the song, the drummer recognizes Will as the tramp to whom he gave the coat. Will suggests he and Erica dance; he steps out with exaggerated movements. As they dance, the drummer becomes more and more nervous and abruptly gets up to play the xylophone. The band leader turns around and frowns at him. The drummer then breaks out in a sweat when he notices the constables continuing to watch the scene through the lobby windows. At the end of the song, the bandleader warns him. Seated again at their table, Will and Erica discuss the constables who surround them.

At the break, the drummer walks out back for a cigarette, and notices a group of law officers approach. He rushes into a back room and takes some pills, explaining to another musician that he must have them because the twitch gets on his nerves.

Outside, Col. Burgoyne tells the constables to do whatever they must; "It's all beyond me," he says. Robert suddenly appears next to them and gives himself up.

Inside, the band starts up again. The officials there ask Erica and Will to come out to the lobby. During the first song, the drummer is unable to perform, crashing cymbals and drums indiscriminately. His situation deteriorates as the camera pulls out over the crowd and he finally faints and the music stops. They carry him off the stage.

In the lobby, just as her father is taking Erica out the door, someone calls out for a doctor and Erica pushes through the crowd to help with first aid. As she kneels over the man she notices the twitch and calls over Will, who says, "Yes, that's him." Erica asks the drummer what he did with the belt and he laughs hysterically and confesses that he murdered Christine Clay.

Erica goes out and meets Robert. They see her father and she runs over to kiss him, ending up between the two men, smiling.

Notes. * Most filmographies credit Alma Reville for adaptation. [H]Hitchcock does bit as a photographer outside the courthouse.

24   *The Lady Vanishes* (1938)

Director	Alfred Hitchcock
Producer	Edward Black
Production Company	Gainsborough
Screenplay	Sidney Gilliat, Frank Launder, based on the novel *The Wheel Spins* by Ethel Lina White*
Photography	Jack Cox
Editing	R. E. Dearing
Cutting	Alfred Roome
Set Direction	[Alec] Vetchinsky
Sound	S. Wiles
Music	Louis Levy
Continuity	Alma Reville
Cast	Margaret Lockwood (Iris Henderson), Michael Redgrave (Gilbert), Paul Lukas (Dr. Hartz), Dame May Whitty (Miss Froy), Googie Withers (Blanche), Cecil Parker (Mr. Todhunter), Linden Travers ("Mrs." Todhunter), Mary Clare (Baroness), Naunton Wayne (Caldicott), Basil Radford (Charters), Emile Boreo (Hotel Manager), Sally Stewart (Julie), Philip Leaver (Signor Doppo), Zelma Vas Dias (Signora Doppo), Catherine Lacy (the Nun), Josephine Wilson (Madame Kummer), Charles Oliver (the Officer), Kathleen Tremaine (Anna)

Filmed	at Lime Grove Studios, London, "Full range recording at Islington, London"
Running Time	approximately 97 minutes
Distributor	MGM
Release Date	October 1938

Other titles: *Eine Dame verschwindet, Une Femme Disparaît*

Synopsis

Credits appear over mountain scenery and variations of the secret message theme.

The camera pans from idyllic snowy mountain scenery past a small train station into the window of a hotel lobby filled with people and luggage. A stiff gale blows outside. The quiet is disrupted by an announcement in several languages by the bright-eyed hotel manager that the train will not leave until tomorrow and all must register now if they want to spend the night there. Two Englishmen, Caldicott and Charters, watch as the manager personally attends to three young American women whose rooms he has reserved and whose leader, Iris Henderson, a confident woman with brunette hair, orders champagne and chicken to be brought to their room. The manager returns behind the counter to face the now clamoring crowd; Mr. Todhunter asks for separate rooms for him and his mistress, which annoys her, and the Englishmen are assigned the maid's room, all that is left.

Iris, now partly undressed in knickers and socks, stands on top of the table in the middle of her room and makes fun of her forthcoming marriage. A waiter arrives with the champagne, and, embarrassed, helps her down. Sitting between her friends and sipping champagne, she glumly says, "I've been everywhere and done everything. . . . What is there left for me, but marriage?" In the hallway, the butler is annoyed at the maid's merry assertions in the local tongue, Bandrikanese.

Unpacking in their room, Caldicott and Charters are interrupted by the cheery maid, who comes in to change her clothes, but speaks no English. Miffed, but already dressed formally themselves, they decide to leave her alone and go down to the lobby. Overhearing the manager take a London call for another guest, Caldicott picks up the telephone to inquire about the cricket scores, then hangs up in disgust when the caller does not know. The pair skulk away when they see they have cut off an eagerly awaited call.

In the crowded restaurant they struggle with another couple for a pair of empty seats across from Miss Froy, a smiling grey-haired English governess. The waiter urgently tries to convey something to them in Bandrikanese, but they ignore him and Miss Froy finally explains that the food is gone, then rhapsodizes about the joys of the tiny mountain country as the men sit glumly opposite her, chins in hand.

Upstairs in the hall, Iris says "goodnight, my children" to her friends as Miss Froy comes up the stairs to her room next door. Outside, a man serenades under Miss Froy's balcony. She is just beginning to enjoy the music when a heavy footed folk dance begins above her. Going out into the hall, she finds Iris, also irritated at the noise, who calls the manager and complains about the "musical chairs with elephants."

The manager goes up to the dancers' room to ask them to stop, but the man who leads them with a recorder, an English musicologist named Gilbert, insists that he must continue to record "the ancient music with which your peasant ancestors celebrated every wedding." Told that the occupant downstairs complained, he kicks the manager out.

Over the din of the clomping and stomping, Iris bribes the manager to kick Gilbert out of his room.

The *International Herald Tribune* fills the screen as Caldicott and Charters, seated in bed behind it, complain that it has no cricket scores. The maid returns to put away some of her clothes.

Gilbert enters Iris's pine-paneled room without knocking and readies himself to sleep next to her in bed, calmly lifting her own things from the bedposts to the floor. She starts to call the manager but he warns her he will tell everyone that she invited him. While he fusses in the bathroom, she calls downstairs to the manager and says she has changed her mind about the room upstairs and that there is no need for Gilbert to be evicted from it. Hearing this, Gilbert pauses briefly before her to ask that she have his things sent up as well. After she calls him "contemptible," he sticks his head back through the door and comments that she is a bit of a "stinker too."

Miss Froy stands in her window enjoying the guitar serenade. Someone comes up behind the musician and strangles him, a shadow of his quiet struggle passing over the garden wall; she throws down a coin, assuming the song is over, but is slightly puzzled at the abrupt end.

Next morning, the guests crowd the station platform to board the waiting train. Iris, in her full mink coat, is urged by her friends to break her engagement and stay, but she proudly insists that she doesn't mind leaving, really. Miss Froy approaches them wondering about her missing bag; distracted, she drops her spectacles and walks off. Iris returns them to her just as someone pushes a window box from its perch above them; it bangs Iris on the head. As the train pulls out Miss Froy promises Iris's friends to watch Iris, who faints as she waves good-bye, images of her friends swirling around her.

Later, Iris wakes in her compartment to find the rest of the occupants, the veiled Baroness, and the Doppo family, parents and child, staring at her. Miss Froy suggests some tea, and she and Iris stumble down the corridor of the swaying train, forcing Mr. Todhunter and his mistress to close their shade when Miss Froy falls into their compartment.

Inside their compartment, "Mrs. Todhunter" is again annoyed at her companion's desire to hide, and he makes excuses.

Arriving in the dining car, Iris and Miss Froy introduce themselves to each other, though Miss Froy must trace her name in the condensation on the window because of the noise of the screeching train; she hands the steward her own special tea, Harriman's Herbal Tea, for preparation. Across the aisle, Caldicott and Charters are illustrating a cricket move with cubes of sugar; Miss Froy requests the sugar for her tea and they sullenly gather it up into the bowl and hand it over.

Back in their compartment, Iris easily falls back to sleep as the tracks and overhead wires zoom by. Later the train's whistle screeches and she wakes to find Miss Froy gone. The Baroness informs her there was never an Englishwoman in the compartment, and the others support her story. Iris rises to search the train and, finding the steward, discovers that he thinks she drank her tea alone. The

waiter, who starts to contradict the steward, searches for the bill, and discovers that it says tea for one. Disgusted, Iris continues her search into the other cars and bumps into Gilbert in the smoke-filled second-class car where the passengers dance and sing behind them. They banter insults back and forth for a while, but she tells him her story and he offers to help.

Going back to her compartment, they talk with the newly arrived, suave Dr. Hartz, a brain surgeon, as well as the others. Gilbert queries the Baroness and Signora Doppo in Italian, then asks Iris to describe in detail what Miss Froy looked like. They visit Mr. Todhunter's compartment but he insists that he never saw Miss Froy. In the corridor, Iris spots Caldicott and Charters, who try to avoid her as they are leery of her "scenes"; not wanting to be involved, they assert that they were deep in conversation about cricket and did not notice anything. They become incensed at Iris's dismissal of their excuse and turn away. Dr. Hartz suggests again that Iris's blow on the head may be a factor, that Miss Froy "is merely a subjective image." The train stops and Gilbert continues to help with the search as they check each side of the train for signs of Miss Froy and watch Dr. Hartz's patient, fully wrapped in gauze, put on board in a stretcher.

In the next compartment, the Todhunters argue about whether he will divorce his wife. She accuses him of lying to Iris. He quickly closes the windows and warns her what a scandal would do to him, an aspiring judge.

Pulling out of the station, Gilbert consoles Iris. "Mrs. Todhunter" appears and tells them she saw Miss Froy.

Inside the Todhunters' compartment, she confronts him with what she has done, but he coldly informs her that his wife will never divorce him, no matter what happens.

In the corridor Iris and Gilbert meet Signor Doppo, who tells them Miss Froy has returned. Back in the compartment, they find Madame Kummer, a German woman dressed exactly the same as Miss Froy, who claims she helped Iris onto the train. Dr. Hartz interferes to explain this new development and they take Madame Kummer down the corridor to meet "Mrs. Todhunter," who falters, but agrees that Madame Kummer is the woman she saw before. "They're all lying, but why? Why?" exclaims Iris. Angry, she goes into her compartment and shuts the door on Gilbert. In close-up, she stares in turn at her fellow passengers, seeing Miss Froy in each smug face, then the scowling Madame Kummer frightens her so that she jumps up and goes out into the corridor, where Gilbert waits. Vehemently he tries to convince her to give up and she assents.

Relieved, he invites her to the dining car, and they sit down for some tea. She tells him she is engaged and he is disappointed. He tries to appeal to her with the story of his life, but she becomes contemplative and notices Miss Froy's name still written on the window. Renewed in her determination, she leaps up to appeal to the passengers to have the train stopped. Dr. Hartz and Gilbert restrain her on either side as she becomes hysterical, then breaks away, pulls the emergency cord to stop the train, and faints.

Later, the train is speeding along as Caldicott and Charters relax in their compartment and discuss the strange disappearance of Miss Froy.

In Iris's compartment, Dr. Hartz advises her to rest. She is stubborn but resigned. While Gilbert waits in the corridor, he sees the cook throw some garbage out the window and notices a Harriman's Herbal Tea bag stick to the window for a moment. He goes in and sits down next to Iris and, on a ruse, gets

her to leave with him. Out in the corridor, he admits that she must be right and suggests they search the train. They walk back to the baggage car and find the accoutrements of Signor Doppo's magic show—posters, disguises, and boxes with hidden compartments. Having fun stumbling around, they finally sit and go over the facts of the case, then accidentally discover Miss Froy's spectacles. Signor Doppo appears behind them and demands they give them to him; he and Gilbert struggle. Iris helps by kicking and biting, then knocks Doppo on the head. They lock him in a large box and tie it. The box, however, is a trick one and he disappears from the car. Desperate, they decide to find Dr. Hartz.

Walking by the compartment where Dr. Hartz's patient lies, Iris notices that the nun attendant has on high-heeled shoes and suddenly wonders if the patient might be Miss Froy. They enter and start to unwrap the patient in front of the mute nun, but Dr. Hartz arrives, and, angry at their intrusion, kicks them out. After they leave he berates the nun, who speaks English and is unhappy they have kidnapped an English woman, but she insists she does not know how Iris and Gilbert discovered what she and the doctor had done.

Dr. Hartz meets Iris and Gilbert in the dining car and they tell him of their suspicions. Caldicott and Charters observe, hoping that "she doesn't create another scene." Drinks are served with a knowing glance from the steward as the doctor tries to convince the couple they are being alarmist. They both finish the drinks. Putting the two in the compartment next to his, the doctor reveals his enmity and points a gun at them. Iris passes out and Gilbert feigns to do so after hearing that Miss Froy will be leaving the train in three minutes and then be murdered.

After Dr. Hartz leaves, Gilbert revives Iris. Their door is locked, so he climbs out the window and passes over to the next compartment, where the nun sits with Miss Froy. The nun helps him and says she did not put the drugs in their drinks as instructed. Madame Kummer interrupts them and they tie her up and put her in Miss Froy's place. The doctor returns and they all take up their sleeping positions and hide Miss Froy in a closet. The train stops and Dr. Hartz puts the patient into an ambulance, only to discover that it is Madame Kummer. Silencing her, he walks with determination to the train, then stops some police and speaks to them. Some of the cars are unhitched from the train.

Back in the compartment, Dr. Hartz informs the nun that all must die.

Imagining they are over the border and out of Bandrika, Gilbert goes out into the corridor and opens the door to find theirs is now the last car and the rest of the train is speeding off in the distance. Though Gilbert pressures her for an explanation, Miss Froy insists that she does not know why all this is happening, and they decide to visit the dining car ahead. Caldicott, Charters, and the Todhunters are there, but Gilbert is unable to convince them of their danger. Suddenly the nun, bound and gagged, falls into the car.

The train stops in some woods; leaving his auto entourage in the trees, a Bandrikan policeman boards and apologizes to the passengers. They want to believe him, but Gilbert knocks him out with a chair. Disgusted, Caldicott moans, "Now we must go out and apologize." The steward runs out to inform the police of this development, and another policeman shoots a stoic Caldicott as he stands at the door of the train. The passengers are now convinced of their danger, and the nun is adamant, "Don't let them in. They are murderers." A gun battle ensues and Gilbert wounds several policemen. The Todhunters wrestle over his gun.

Miss Froy pulls Gilbert and Iris aside and tells them she must leave, she is a spy, and asks Gilbert to memorize a tune to pass on to the Foreign Office in case she does not make it through. Let out the window, she runs off into the woods, and Gilbert decides to try to start the train. Mr. Todhunter gives himself up and is shot dead waving a white flag. His mistress becomes hysterical, as there is no more ammunition, and the police start to walk closer to the train. Suddenly, it starts up and pulls away. Both engineers are shot down as the police chase in their cars. Inside the dining car, the Bandrikan policeman wakes up and grabs Gilbert's gun, preventing them from switching the tracks as instructed by Gilbert. The nun sneaks away to accomplish this, but is wounded being pulled back up into the engine as they speed away.

"Jolly good luck," comment the Bandrikans left behind at the border.

In London, the train with Gilbert and Iris enters the station. In their compartment, he is focused on remembering his tune and plays hard to get when she suggests a date but admits Charles, her husband to be, is meeting her at the station.[H] Disembarking, Caldicott and Charters are struck dumb at a sign that their cricket match is canceled, as Iris and Gilbert stand awkwardly waiting for Charles to appear. Iris suddenly jumps into a taxi to hide from Charles and Gilbert follows her; he kisses her and they passionately embrace.

Waiting at the Foreign Office, they discuss their honeymoon. When called to enter, Gilbert is distressed to find he has forgotten the tune, but the sound of a piano playing it inside drifts out to them and they walk in to find Miss Froy behind the piano. She gleefully greets them with open arms, taking their hands from each side of the frame into hers.

Note. * Most filmographies credit Alma Reville for adaptation. [H]Hitchcock does bit as man at the railway station.

Remake: *The Lady Vanishes* (Great Britain, 1979) directed by Anthony Page.

25 *Jamaica Inn* (1939)

Director	Alfred Hitchcock
Producers	Erich Pommer, Charles Laughton
Production Company	Verity Films, Inc*
Screenplay	Sidney Gilliat, Joan Harrison, J. B. Priestley (additional dialogue), from the novel by Daphne Du Maurier
Photography	Harry Stradling, Bernard Knowles
Editing	Robert Hamer
Set Direction	Tom Morahan
Sound	Jack Rogerson
Special Effects	Harry Watt
Music	Eric Fenby, Frederic Lewis (direction)
Costumes	Molly McArthur
Makeup	Ern Westmore
Continuity	Alma Reville
Production Manager	Hugh Perceval

Cast   Maureen O'Hara (Mary), Charles
                                    Laughton (Sir Humphrey Pengallan),
                                    Leslie Banks (Joss Merlyn); Merlyn's
                                    Gang: Robert Newton (Jem
                                    Trehearne), Emlyn Williams (Harry
                                    the Pedlar), Marie Ney (Patience
                                    Merlyn), Wylie Watson (Salvation
                                    Watkins), Morland Graham (Sea
                                    Lawyer Sydney), Edwin Greenwood
                                    (Dandy), Mervyn Johns (Thomas),
                                    Stephen Haggard (the Boy); Pengal-
                                    lan's Household: Horace Hodges (the
                                    Butler), Hay Petrie (the Groom),
                                    Frederick Piper; Pengallan's Tenants:
                                    Herbert Lomas, Clare Greet, William
                                    Devlin; Pengallan's Friends: Basil
                                    Radford, Jeanne de Casalis, George
                                    Curzon, Mabel Terry Lewis, A. Brom-
                                    ley Davenport
Filmed   at Elstree Studios, London
Running Time   approximately 100 minutes
Distributor   Associated British
Release Date   May 1939
Other titles: *Riff-Piraten, La Taverne de la Jamaîque, La Terverna della Gia-
maica*

Synopsis

Credits appear over craggy rocks and the rough-hewn sign of the Jamaica Inn, accompanied by dramatic music.

Close-up of an old document of a prayer asking not that wrecks happen, but when they do, they be "guided to the coast of Cornwall ... for the benefit of the poor inhabitants."

Waves bang huge rocks off the coast. Title: "So ran an old Cornish prayer of the early nineteenth century, but in that lawless corner of England before the British Coastguard Service came into being ... there existed gangs who ... deliberately planned the wrecks, luring ships to their doom ..."

The sign for the Jamaica Inn squeaks on its hinges in the gloomy light of dusk. A man on a horse rides out through the countryside to a lamp swaying in the wind at the edge of a cliff; peering out into the dark sea, his face lights up when he sees a ship among the waves. Fighting against the storm, the crew on board struggles to steer away from the lamp, when suddenly the man on shore covers it up. The ship crashes into the rocks and the survivors leap off onto the rocks and beach. A gang runs to meet them, murdering them in greeting; in close-up, one man's smile fades as he takes in the raised weapon and realizes the true meaning of the wild grin on the face of the stranger he has met. One by one the crew is knifed, strangled, or drowned in the surf and stripped of their valuables. The gang swarms over the ship, opening the hatches and quickly

moving the goods onto horses. Their leader, Joss Merlyn, barks orders over the roar of the sea, commanding them to make sure no one gets away. As they are leaving, a survivor clinging to one of the rocks suddenly cries out. One of the gang, grinning, pulls out his knife and finishes him off. The stormy sky breaks.

A carriage rolls through the evening light of the coast road. Up front, the driver speaks of the bad reputation of the Jamaica Inn. Inside, a dark-haired young woman named Mary inquires of her traveling companions about the Jamaica Inn, and they start in fear. The driver speeds up as they approach the inn and Mary is forced to lean out the window and yell at him to get him to stop; still, she's too late. Berating him for not letting her off at the inn, she is left alone on the windy barren road, her trunk thrown down next to her. She peers up the road at a mansion with large columns framing the front door.

Inside the lavish home of Squire Pengallan, a dinner party is in progress. The camera moves down the table as a guest offers a toast to Sir Humphrey, a large-faced complacent gentleman who presides at the end, eating some fruit from a knife. Seated next to two fawning women, he barks at his patient butler, Chadwyck, and wonders which lake he admires the most. "Lake Windemere," replies Chadwyck, and the conversation turns to beauty, whereupon Sir Humphrey produces a figurine ("But it's not alive," exclaims one of the guests); his horse, "my exquisite Nancy," is then brought into the dining room.

A strange woman is announced. As Sir Humphrey strides into the huge center hall, he gaily calls over his shoulder to one of his guests, "Bet you 200 guineas she's ugly!" With a closer look at Mary he gently asks if she would oblige him by taking off her coat. "Why should I?" she asks. "I've a wager here," he replies, moving to help her, then leaving the coat half on. He compliments her "exquisite shape," and turns back toward the dining room as she stands frowning behind him. "Ringworm, you've won!" he cries and throws a bag of money into the middle of the table, where several of the guests dive for it.

Sir Humphrey turns back to Mary and circles her, "She walks in beauty like the night . . ." He helps her back into her coat. "Thank you, sir, but I didn't come for poetry, but for a horse," she says. "A horse!" he cries, turning, pleased, toward Nancy. Hearing that Mary wants to go to Jamaica Inn, he warns her, but she tells him her only living relative, Aunt Patience, is there and she has come all the way from Ireland to be with her. It is decided that Sir Humphrey will accompany her to the inn. He whispers to Chadwyck to set out some hot brandy and a warming pad for his return. Suddenly Mary becomes uncomfortable as Sir Humphrey turns again to circle her, rudely eyeing her body.

The two ride up to Jamaica Inn in the dark. Taking her trunk from his horse, he offers "any service. . . . Remember I'm Pengallan and this is Pengallanland." She cheerily waves good-bye to him, then frowns when she turns toward the crude door of the inn, hearing odd noises and cackles from inside.

A scowling man greets her knock with a gun in his hand. Informed that she intends to live with them, he treats her even more rudely, and she indignantly threatens to have her uncle turn him out. When he asks leeringly for a kiss, her eyes widen with recognition that he is her uncle. "Correct, entirely correct," the unshaven Joss sneers. Patience, his blond, placid wife appears from behind and Joss finally moves away from the door allowing Mary to enter.

The low-ceilinged center hall is empty, but Patience warmly greets her niece and they hug. The two women talk in close-up, Joss in the background between them. He accuses his wife of inviting Mary to stay, but she eagerly reassures him

she had no such idea. Mary objects, and Patience, noticing Mary is in black, is stricken to learn that Mary's mother, Patience's sister, is dead. Joss turns away disgusted, then returns to bid Patience hurry and retrieve the visitor's trunk. Outside, Mary starts to help Patience, but Joss grabs her "soft" hand and cautions her not to bother herself. Mary jerks her hand away and speaks sharply to him, but Patience cautions her.

Joss moves off into the noisy parlor and commands the group of men there to be quiet. Harry, a young smirking man in a top hat who before had peeked in the door, comments on "the nice piece." The camera moves from one scruffy man to another, mostly dressed in vests and open shirts and high boots, as each comments on the arrival of the woman.

In the kitchen, Patience serves Mary some soup and defends her marriage; looking off, she insists "there's nothing I'd change even if I could."

Back in the parlor, the men sit around a candle on a table; one complains about the take they are getting from the wrecks. Joss challenges him and the man claims he got the idea from Sidney, so Joss jumps around the table and collars Sidney, accusing him of helping the other men who can't read or add. Suddenly, a clean-shaven man, Jem Trehearne, taps Joss on the shoulder. Joss slowly turns and meets his gaze with a glare. Calmly, Jem tells him that he has figured it out. "Reckon by our share of it . . . maybe you're not getting the right price for the stuff. Maybe there's a leak somewhere." Joss strides toward the always whistling Harry, who casually leans against the wall and claims ignorance. So Joss stalks the room, wondering if the leak isn't among them, and asking how long each man has been with him. Jem is by far the newest recruit, having joined the gang only two months earlier; Joss strides to his side with a leer. Realizing that the other men are eyeing him suspiciously, Jem stiffens, but suddenly Patience appears in the doorway. "Clear out!" screams Joss, and walks over with his hand raised to strike her. She pleads, and he accompanies her into the center room.

Hearing that Mary arrived with Sir Humphrey, Joss leads Patience quickly back into the kitchen and the camera follows him as he finds Mary and in a threatening manner asks about her connection with Sir Humphrey. "He was most kind. He knows how to treat a woman," she snippily tells him, and Joss clomps to the stairs, stops to throw her trunk up the steps, then enters a room nearby.

Inside, he apologizes about the meager take, explaining that "there was a full gale down there." The camera moves slowly from him over some fine white material unwound from a bolt and held at the other end by Sir Humphrey. Commanding him to get some scissors, Sir Humphrey grandly reassures Joss that the sailors deserved their fate, the "poor scum"; after all, the only thing that matters "is whatever is perfect of its own kind." Stretching his arms with pride, he extols all the people of Bristol he would give up to "save a beautiful woman a single headache. . . . Something you don't understand . . . because you're neither a philosopher or a gentleman." Poking his finger at Joss's breast, he suddenly changes tone and demands to know if Joss is sure there were no survivors the night before. Joss reassures him about security and wonders at the risk Sir Humphrey has taken to be there tonight. "Everything's a risk," he retorts, and asks, looking away, about Mary and her "fine character." "Oh, leave her to me. I'll manage her just as I manage Patience," says Joss. "I don't see any resemblance to your wife," frowns Sir Humphrey as he inspects some jewelry, but Joss insists that Patience was beautiful when he married her. Sir Humphrey complains again about the take, and Joss tells him the men also complain, wanting more for

themselves. In close-up, an impatient Sir Humphrey demands, "What for? . . . To rot their innards out? . . . I know what to do with money when I have it, that's why I must have it. Understand?"

Hearing shouting downstairs, Joss rushes out to find his men dragging Jem into the center room. Nearby, Patience sends Mary to bed with a tray of food, which she quickly sets down so she can listen intently to the struggle in the next room. The men find too much money in Jem's wallet and start to tie him up. While they hold him, Joss leans into him for an explanation, but he insists Joss is the culprit and insinuates he is not in the shipwrecking scheme alone. At this, Joss grabs a cup and throws it at Jem's head, knocking him out. Harry whistles and readies a rope. Mary, who can clearly hear the discussion, steps carefully to the wall and cleans the smear from a window so she can see them.

Joss stomps up to consult with Sir Humphrey, now hatted and putting on his white gloves, who finds hanging a "trifle formal" but assents. Instructed to continue, the men tussle over who will be allowed to watch, then drag the still-unconscious Jem down to another room. Mary moves over to watch through an opening in the ceiling. Two men carry him while they debate whether to wake him or not, while Harry climbs the stairs to set the rope on a rafter directly under Mary. Wincing, she turns away at the groaning sound. One of the men jumps at the body, and Harry and the others are distracted while pulling him away. Mary searches her room, and, seizing the knife from her tray, rips at the shingles and cuts through the hanging rope, dropping Jem to the ground. She runs downstairs and, while the other men are still fighting with each other, drags the half-conscious Jem into the kitchen and sends him out the door just as Sir Humphrey exits the door above and rides off.

Mary rushes up to her room to find Joss waiting by her bed. Slowly, she closes the door behind her as he leeringly assures her that he could not send her away, such a pretty woman of such fine character. But the men shout for him and he runs out, first to face Patience glaring at him in the hall.

As the men inform Joss that Jem is gone, Patience approaches Mary in her room and warns her to leave this minute. Elsewhere, Joss declares he will kill "that blasted girl." Patience runs downstairs with Mary to send her outside, then silently stands to face Joss's ire.

Outside, Mary pauses and is suddenly pulled up to the roof by Jem's hand. Lying on the roof together, they listen to the men scurry about, their heads right beneath Mary's and Jem's feet on the edge of the low-pitched roof. After it becomes quiet, they jump down into the courtyard and disappear. Joss strides in leading his horse and instructs his men for the hunt. As they disperse, Mary and Jem are revealed lying in front of the courtyard wall.

From below, the camera frames a wrought-iron railing with a large portrait behind it. On the balcony Sir Humphrey, in his dressing gown, greets Chadwyck, who informs him that the butcher needs his bill paid. "Remarkably unattractive occupation . . ." drones Sir Humphrey, but Chadwyck supposes that butchers must live. "Must they?" yawns Sir Humphrey, but finally loses patience, grabs the overdue bills, and flings them over the railing, screaming "You old numbskull!" Chadwyck slinks away. The camera remains on the chagrined Sir Humphrey, then moves to a view of the black and white sunburst pattern on the floor of the central hall below as Chadwyck stoops in the center picking up the bills. A faint sound of galloping horses is heard on the soundtrack as Sir Humphrey walks up to Chadwyck and, in close-up, mutters an apology. "I can't

think what comes over me!" Looking off with a glint in his eye, he intimately wonders what happened to his grandfather, but answers himself: "Went mad, didn't he?"

Seen through an opening in the opulently patterned drapes, Joss knocks at one of the French doors nearby. Sir Humphrey motions him away and sends Chadwyck to bed with a pat on the back. Outside, he finds Joss on a porch and berates him for coming to his home. Hearing of Jem's escape, he calmly continues, "In this little organization you and your fellows are only the carcass; we are the brains right here. . . . If you want any more fat pickings on the shore, just obey orders!"

Waves crash against the coast in bright daylight. Near a rowboat on a small beach surrounded by rock, Mary sleeps in Jem's arms. Waking at the sound of sea gulls, she is startled at the sight of his hand, then rises in alarm and runs into the boat to flee. But he wakes and confronts her in the echoing cave. While they argue about the gang's activities, the boat drifts out to sea. Up on the cliffs above them, Harry and the gang notice the boat and start to file down to the shore. The camera moves in on Mary, who sits sullenly next to an exasperated Jem as he explains they must move before high tide. Lamenting being stuck with a woman, he is forced to admit that she did save his life, and she sarcastically hopes he makes "better use of it in the future." As they banter, a rope wrapped around a book hits Jem on the head, and they jump away to see the gang directly above them surrounding a hole in the rock. One of the gang slips down another rope, but Jem swings the rope and knocks him out. The others become wary, so three of them start down the rope at once. Jem urges Mary to take off her dress and swim with him, but she resists until he threatens to take it off himself. Out in the waves, they hide behind a rock as two of the men row by in a boat, then Jem takes Mary on his back off into the roaring water.

Back at his central hall, Sir Humphrey sits in judgment on a group of debtors, graciously forgiving one whose son is ill but throwing out another who demands his equal rights.

Mary and Jem run near a cliff and spot the squire's house; she excitedly tells him they can get help there. As Sir Humphrey deals more harshly with another man, he suddenly hears Mary and Jem at the door. Walking out to greet Mary and struck by her state of dress, he takes her in by the fire and hears the story of Jamaica Inn. "She saved my life," says Jem humbly. "Extraordinary," blinks Sir Humphrey, widening his eyes in thought. Mary retires with a maid to get some clothes, and Sir Humphrey dismisses the eager Jem to a meal of bread and beer in order to enter a sitting room where two uniformed friends await him. One is a captain who says his boat will pass by tomorrow. Jem interrupts to hand Sir Humphrey a note announcing himself as an "officer of the law," and Sir Humphrey mutters and excuses himself.

Sir Humphrey takes Jem into his study for a brandy and listens to his story. Much worse than smuggling, these wrecks have one thing in common—there are never any survivors, Jem tells him. As they stand behind a buffet table in the foreground, Sir Humphrey quickly downs his drink and sympathizes, shocked at "the most awful thing!" Hearing Jem's conjecture that the gang is receiving inside information, he is more silent. He exits briefly to bid a cheery good-bye to his visitors, then joins Jem again as he sits at a small table. Eating voraciously, Jem turns excitedly to Sir Humphrey, now seated in a stuffed chair across from him: "I'm after bigger fry than just Merlyn!" Sir Humphrey slouches in his chair

as Jem tells him he thinks the informer will be going to the inn tonight to plan another wreck. Rising in collusion, Sir Humphrey slaps Jem on the shoulders and declares they must get there first.

Mary, now dressed in a simple but revealing gown, moves to join the men, but she realizes that they are discussing something sensitive and stops to listen. She overhears their plan to confront her aunt and uncle and the gang, and moves to hide herself behind a column as they emerge from the room. Jem, now elegantly dressed in a double-breasted white uniform, counsels Sir Humphrey about "the girl," regretting that he "couldn't hardly tell her the truth." Boisterously the two men go off to wait among the oversized columns of Squire Pengallan's front portico, only to find that Mary has commandeered their coach.

Back at Jamaica Inn, Mary warns Patience. In close-up, the women face one another, Patience insisting that she will not leave without Joss. Mary defiantly tells her he is a murderer, but Patience responds even more firmly, "He's my husband." The camera moves out as Patience pleads for understanding and Joss appears behind them staggering and demanding to know where Jem is. A knock at the door interrupts them. Joss skulks toward the door with his gun ready and kicks it open to face Jem, and then Sir Humphrey. Joss starts, confused, as Sir Humphrey pushes him back with his own gun, but winks at him as the men join with Mary and Patience. Mary takes the opportunity to lash into Jem, who goes after Patience, but Mary stridently assures him that Patience is innocent, except that "nothing in the world would drive her away from Joss!" Sir Humphrey and Jem take Joss upstairs and Sir Humphrey pauses gallantly to apologize to the women, "Try not to worry; we'll do our best."

Left alone, Patience looks off as Mary urges her to leave Joss, but hears the quiet reply, "People can't help being what they are."

Upstairs, Jem takes charge, pointing out clues and demanding from Joss the key to "the secret room" where Joss meets his secret collaborator. Sir Humphrey disdainfully mentions the "careless" Joss when Jem discovers a scissored bit of the expensive white material from the night before. Noticing a signal outside, he sends Sir Humphrey to check. Jem questions Joss about who plans the wrecks and Joss tells him "Santa Claus." Sir Humphrey returns and sends Jem to fetch the women so he can instruct Joss on their last wreck; after tonight, he will take a vacation in France. Jem locks the women in a room, then returns to discover Sir Humphrey and Joss laughing. Not to be distracted, he sets in again on Joss to persuade him to reveal the identity of his adviser, but Joss peers glumly at the seated Sir Humphrey, who contemplates his nose. Urgently, Jem describes the mastermind, as the camera focuses on a close-up of Sir Humphrey's face: "A man like that would save his own skin first. . . . This man deliberately plans the cold-blooded slaughter of any who survive the wrecks . . . but he remains aloof . . . thinking there's no blood on his hands!"

A commotion develops outside, and Jem runs downstairs, only to be caught by the gang. Joss brings Sir Humphrey down in front of a gun, and Harry announces they will do away with both of them. But Joss pulls Harry aside to whisper that they've more important business—another wreck. Patience is left behind to hold a gun on the roped Jem and Sir Humphrey, while Mary is dragged along with the gang. After they have left, Sir Humphrey calmly rises from his loosened ropes. Jem, aghast, is left tied up, pleading with Patience to let him go.

A gale blows by the rocks at the beach as Joss commands his men.

Back at the inn, Jem describes to Patience the horror of the wreck for which

she will be responsible. Appalled, she runs off to the stairway, insisting she has never known where the wrecks occur. He screams at her hesitant frozen figure, and the camera flashes back and forth between them as he argues that there are many lives at stake, and after all, Joss is only one man, though he offers to let Joss escape.

The gang waits behind a rock at the beach.

Patience stands, knife in hand, next to the turned-over chair from which she has cut the ropes binding Jem. Out on the road, Jem commandeers a coach.

A ship appears in the stormy sea, and Mary slips away from her inattentive guard. The wind and the rain flurry around the men as Mary finds the lamp at the top of the cliff and drags it back. She struggles with the man who has been sent to douse the light, and the lamp ignites a nearby cloth, but she succeeds in knocking the man down. She raises the flaming cloth and the ship turns away. The men on the beach roar with frustration, and one of the gang drags Mary down to them. Harry starts to rip her dress, but she defiantly ties it back together, and Joss pushes her into a cart away from them. The men vociferously object, but Joss jumps on the cart with her and drives away. One of the gang shoots him in the back.

At the Squire's mansion, Sir Humphrey bids good-bye to Chadwyck, and rides off in his carriage.

Mary and the wounded Joss drive into the courtyard of the inn. She and Patience drag Joss inside, but he collapses after warmly hugging Patience. While Patience tries to remove the bullet from Joss's back, she tells Mary that she has discovered who Joss's master is. Just as she is about to pronounce the name, she is shot in the back. Mary screams, and Joss rouses to demand a drink, then dies. Mary screams again, and Sir Humphrey appears in the doorway. Lamenting having to shoot Patience but more annoyed that Mary stopped the wreck, he gags her and ties her wrists behind her back. She becomes very calm, her eyes starkly alert and her lips taut with anger over the gag. He raises a black hood over her head, but her eyes wander sadly, and she drops to Patience on the floor to weep. A close-up shows his hand grab her shoulders and pick her up.

Outside, the gang returns, and Harry stops them as they watch Sir Humphrey and Mary steal away from the inn. "What about Joss?" the others cry, and the gang spreads over the building. Harry is stunned to find the bodies and tells the men to scatter, but soldiers rush the door. Jem collars Harry on the stairs and demands to know where Mary is. "You're not going to like it. She's found another gentleman," sneers Harry, and Jem takes some soldiers with him for the chase.

In a ship cabin, Sir Humphrey ungags the still-sobbing Mary, who drops to her knees. Impatient, he extols her to be strong; "The age of chivalry is gone!" Rising below his nose in the air, she starts at these words and the clack of horse's hooves outside. Through a portal window, they see Jem ride up. She screams and runs out the door with Sir Humphrey close behind. On the crowded deck full of passengers, he holds a gun in one hand and her in the other. Chadwyck arrives at the crowded dock, where soldiers are preparing to shoot, but Mary screams at them to desist, insisting that the Squire is mad. Jem sneaks up on them from behind and startles Sir Humphrey, allowing Mary to escape. Sir Humphrey starts up the rigging, climbing backward, and moves all the way to the top of the mast. At first cocky ("I'll be down before you're up to me!"), he drops his gun, which explodes on the deck, then he becomes disoriented, blinking at the crowd far below. Recovering, he cries out "You can tell your children how the great age ended. Make way for Pengallan!" and jumps into the crowd.

Jem helps a distraught Mary down the plank. They greet Chadwyck in silence, who turns toward the camera, wide-eyed, shaking his head, as Pengallan's voice is heard echoing around him, "Chadwyck, Chadwyck!"

Note. Some filmographies also list Mayflower Pictures as a production company.

26 *Rebecca* (1940)

Director	Alfred Hitchcock
Assistant Director	Edmond Bernoudy
Producer	David O. Selznick
Production Company	David O. Selznick
Screenplay	Robert E. Sherwood, Joan Harrison, Philip MacDonald (adaptation), Michael Hogan (adaptation), based on the novel by Daphne Du Maurier
Photography	George Barnes, A.S.C.
Editing	Hal Kern, James E. Newcom (associate)
Art Direction	Lyle Wheeler
Set Direction	Herbert Bristol, Joseph B. Platt
Sound	Jack Noyes
Special Effects	Jack Cosgrove
Music	Franz Waxman
Production Assistant	Barbara Keon
Cast	Laurence Olivier (Maxim De Winter), Joan Fontaine (X, Mrs. De Winter), George Sanders (Jack Favell), Judith Anderson (Mrs. Danvers), Gladys Cooper, Nigel Bruce (Major Giles Lacey), C. Aubrey Smith, Reginald Denny, Philip Winter, Edward Fielding, Florence Bates (Mrs. Van Hopper), Melville Cooper, Leo G. Carroll (the Doctor), Forrester Harvey, Lumsden Hare, Leonard Carey
Filmed	at Selznick International Studios, Los Angeles
Running Time	approximately 130 minutes
Distributor	United Artists
Release Date	March 1940

Other titles: *Rebekka, Rebecca, la Prima Mogile*

Synopsis

Shots of sun-dappled but dark woods appear under the credits with the romantic theme music.

A moonlit night. "Last night I dreamt I went to Manderly. . . ." The camera pauses at a pair of tall iron gates, then moves up the misty overgrown driveway

until it finds the burnt shell of an enormous mansion. The narrator wistfully describes the house, then begins her story, "In the south of France. . . ."

Waves crash against the rocky coast. The camera moves up to view a dark man, well-dressed in a black suit, standing at the top of a cliff. A close-up shows his foot move toward the edge and suddenly, a blond young woman runs toward him shouting "No! Stop!" He frowns and angrily demands she go away, then leaves himself.

A large hotel in Monte Carlo. In the lobby, X (the young woman, who is never named) sits with Edythe Van Hopper, a large woman who laments the absence of "well-known personalities" at the resort. Noticing Maxim de Winter, the man from the cliffside, nearby, she is elated and loudly introduces herself to her "old friend," who sits down to have coffee with them. X shyly mentions she thinks Monte Carlo is artificial; Maxim seems interested in her but offended by Mrs. Van Hopper, who offers to have her companion unpack his bags for him. He abruptly leaves. The two women start off for their quarters; at the elevator, Mrs. Van Hopper scolds her companion for being too forward in conversation, "Men loathe that sort of thing. . . . I suppose he can't get over his wife's death."

A lunch menu. X walks into the dining room. As she is seated, she knocks over a flower vase. Maxim rises from his table and invites her to come and have lunch with him; Mrs. Van Hopper is sick in bed. She demurs, but he insists and she nervously joins him. She tells him she is Mrs. Van Hopper's paid companion. Her mother has been dead for many years, her father, a painter, died last summer, and then she took this job. "How very rotten for you," he says, and offers to take her for a drive.

The sea. They sit behind a railing; he teases her about taking so long with a sketch, which turns out to be of him. He modestly suggests she concentrate on the scenery and asks her if she has ever been to Cornwall. Yes, she replies, and she has seen Manderly, though "felt stupid" for having to ask what it was. He becomes solemn speaking of his home and she awkwardly tries to divert him with small talk about the warm water and the undertow and drowning. His eyes dart and he turns back, announcing he will take her home now.

The hotel. X enters her suite to hear Mrs. Van Hopper explaining to a nurse that the beautiful Rebecca de Winter drowned in the sea near Manderly. Turning to greet X, she screams, "Hurry up, I want to play some rummy."

That night, X lies in bed, dreaming a chant, "He's a broken man . . . beautiful Rebecca."

The next morning, she bids Mrs. Van Hopper, still sick in bed, good-bye to go play tennis.

At the revolving door, she runs into Maxim, who asks if she's really keen on tennis, and hearing no, offers to take her for a ride.

In the car, she smiles shyly at him.

Returning, she gaily greets Mrs. Van Hopper. Mrs. Van Hopper wonders if De Winter is still in the hotel, for he has not returned her phone calls.

A handwritten note to Maxim: "You naughty man. . . . I promise to keep you from being bored. . . . Edythe Van Hopper."

Maxim and X dance; she is in a dream state. He stares at her and she wakes, then smiles shyly.

Another day, she bids good-bye to Mrs. Van Hopper, who shrilly tells her she will have to stick to her job after this. Alone, Mrs. Van Hopper wonders why her notes to Maxim are not being answered, hating to see him so alone.

The happy couple speed along in the car. She wonders if it would be possible to collect memories in a bottle, "like perfume, it would never get stale." She wants to keep the last few days and he reminds her that "some bottles contain demons." Put down, she starts biting her nails. "Stop biting your nails," he snaps. She asks him why he chose her for his "charity." He stops the car in the middle of the road. Sternly, he tells her nothing "blots out the past" for him as well as her presence, and if she thinks it's charity, she can walk, and, please, do not call him Mr. De Winter. She cries, and he softens.

A thank-you card and roses from Maxim. Suddenly, Mrs. Van Hopper exclaims, "My daughter's engaged to be married . . . we must leave at once." Her companion rushes to telephone Maxim, but he is out until noon.

At noon, they are packed and ready, and go downstairs to a taxi. X leaves Mrs. Van Hopper sitting in the taxi at the curb to search for Maxim, in the lobby, at the restaurant, and finally in his room.

Surprised, he greets her fresh from a shave; faltering, she tells him good-bye. He asks her to marry him and invites her to breakfast. She tells him she is not of his circle, but he confirms that she loves him, then comments that it's a pity she must grow up. "That settled," he instructs her how to pour his coffee. Hearing of Mrs. Van Hopper at the curb, he commands her to his room.

Still waiting in the taxi, Mrs. Van Hopper is delighted to be invited to Maxim's room. She arrives, smoothly ingesting the news of her companion's engagement and offering to act as the bride's mother. Maxim refuses and goes down to get X's luggage, leaving her alone with Mrs. Van Hopper. "So this is what's been happening during my illness! . . . Still waters certainly run deep. . . . You haven't the faintest idea what it means to be a great lady." Finally, X asks her to leave.

A provincial marriage hall; their ceremony over, the couple, in dark suits, race down the stairs past a wedding party in traditional garb. Maxim buys X a huge bouquet of flowers that nearly covers her face.

The iron gates of Manderly. They drive in down the long road in an open car. He tells her she needn't worry, just be herself, and besides, there is a housekeeper. It starts to rain very hard and he gives her a coat to put on her head. "That's it!," he cries, "that's Manderly!"

They enter the great hall, greeted by a staff of over fifteen people, spread out as for a picture. Mrs. Danvers, dark-haired and unsmiling, glides into a close-up in the forefront. X is very nervous and drops her gloves, meeting Mrs. Danvers as they both kneel to pick them up.

The clock strikes 6:00. Mrs. Danvers knocks and enters X's grand bedroom. She informs her that she must have a personal maid, and that the east wing has never been used before, noting that "of course, there's no good view of the sea here." X is apologetic and suggests she will leave all the household arrangements to her. Mrs. Danvers ushers her out and they traverse the long, gloomy, halls livened by the shadows of the rain water trickling outside on the windows. On the way to the stairs, Mrs. Danvers points out the huge doors to the west wing, where Rebecca, the first Mrs. De Winter, slept; the music climaxes as the camera remains on them.

A monogrammed napkin, RW, on X's plate. Formal march music accompanies as the scene widens to show Maxim sitting at one end of the long table and X at the other, many candles in between.

Next day, X opens a large door with a door knob as tall as she. Frank

Crawley, who manages the estate, is seated at the table and wishes her good morning. She suggests that she might be able to help, but Maxim enters boisterously, saying "Oh, no." The two men go off, leaving her with a large buffet of food, and the news that her "blunt" sister-in-law and brother-in-law have invited themselves for lunch. Two butlers enter; she nervously exits and one of them follows her out. Walking into a large hall, she comments, "It's big," and he tells her the public is admitted there once a week. She walks into the library where a cool breeze enters through an open window. The butler follows her to tell her she can find a fire in the morning room unless she would like to have one made here. He watches her flounder until she asks where it is.

R is monogrammed on an array of stationery on the desk where X sits down in the morning room. The telephone rings and she picks it up, but responds that Mrs. De Winter is dead. Mrs. Danvers enters, informing her the caller was probably the gardener wanting instructions. She offers X the lunch menu, indicating that Rebecca was choosy about sauces. X tells her to have whatever Rebecca would have ordered. Alone, X sits, wide-eyed and shrinking. Looking through the address book, she topples a ceramic cherub from the desk; it smashes to the ground and she puts the pieces in the back of the desk drawer and covers them with paper.

Bea and Clive Lacey arrive at the front door. X peeks at them from behind a door as they enter, then, wringing her hands, goes to greet them in the morning room. Clive is just finishing some speculation about her chorus girl background. Bea is very friendly to her assuring her she should have as little as possible to do with Mrs. Danvers, who, "don't you know? . . . simply adored Rebecca." In the foreground, X, distressed, turns away in a close-up profile.

At the lunch table, they discover that X doesn't ride, doesn't rhumba, but "sketches a little." The mention of sailing brings the whole table to silence.

As Bea readies herself to leave, she comments on X's hair, then brushes it off with "I can see from the way you dress you don't care a hoot about clothes." Bea encircles X's shoulders reassuringly, and the camera follows them as they walk to the front door. They bid good-bye, and Bea warmly says she hopes they'll be very happy.

Left alone, Maxim and his wife decide to go for a walk. She asks him what he thinks of her hair; he's more concerned about getting her a raincoat, because you "can't be too careful with children." Jessica, their dog, runs ahead and down to the beach. Maxim doesn't want her to follow the dog, but she insists. The waves are high, and she catches up to Jessica at a beach house where she frightens Ben, a deranged drifter. She enters the house looking for a rope to tie the dog; it is homey but dilapidated, with more R monogrammed towels. Running back up, she is forced to chase after Maxim, who screams at her, "You knew I didn't want you to go there, but you deliberately went. . . . If you had my memories you wouldn't go there." He then says sadly, "We should never have come back to Manderly." He apologizes when she starts to cry and they walk on. She takes a handkerchief out of her pocket and, frowning, notices another monogrammed R. The sea continues to be violent.

Sitting one morning in a window, she gets up determinedly, goes into an office where Frank is working, and offers to help him. She starts talking about Ben and the cottage; Frank becomes a little anxious but tries to answer her questions. He tells her Rebecca "wasn't afraid of anything" but she drowned one night in the sea. X pleads for understanding, lamenting how everyone is always

comparing her with Rebecca; Frank warmly reassures her, "It's very refreshing to find someone like yourself, who is not entirely in tune with Manderly.... You have qualities that are more important ... kindliness, sincerity, and modesty." She is not satisfied and he is forced to admit that Rebecca "was the most beautiful creature [he] ever saw."

Beauty, a fashion magazine; inside an ad for an evening dress with large flowers across the bodice.

X appears in the dress and enters to greet Maxim, who is busy setting up a projector. He starts to smile at her when he notices the dress, but then tells her it's nice for a change. They watch movies from their honeymoon. A butler enters for a moment to say there's trouble between Robert and Mrs. Danvers, who has accused him of stealing a china cupid. X tells Maxim that she broke it and he, exasperated then patient, wonders why she acts so afraid of the servants. Mrs. Danvers enters with the butler and the matter is cleared up, to X's embarrassment. As the pictures again flicker on their faces, she tries to make him understand how difficult it is for her with everyone looking her "up and down as if I were a prize cow.... I suppose that's why you married me.... You knew there wouldn't be any gossip about me." Their faces alternately isolated in the dark by the light from the camera, he frowns; she becomes defensive and apologizes for being rude. He turns on the lights and wonders if he were selfish in marrying her. She protests that they're happy, but he says he knows nothing about happiness. He begins the picture again, and she is left desperate, in close-up, light only on her eyes.

A handwritten note from Maxim explains that he has gone to London for the day and suggests "this holiday from me should be welcome."

X sits in the morning room crying; the camera moves back from her still figure. She turns away when a maid brings her lunch. She goes to the window and notices some activity in the west wing. She walks out into the central hall and hides when she hears voices: "If you leave through the garden door, she won't see you." From behind her, Favel, a dapper young man, surprises her. "Looking for me?" he asks. Mrs. Danvers enters and introduces them. X invites Favel to tea. Mrs. Danvers signals him to decline. Making his leave, he casually announces that he was "Rebecca's favorite cousin." More disturbed now, X goes back into the hall and upstairs, pausing briefly at the landing.

She enters the dark bedroom and opens a drape and a window, letting in the sun. The window bangs on the wall, then Mrs. Danvers appears, wondering why X has never asked to see the room. She opens the rest of the drapes, exposing the room to an expanse of floor-to-ceiling light. She reminisces about Rebecca, her precise habits and luxurious clothes, furs, and lingerie. X allows herself to be seated at Rebecca's dressing table; throughout she is shrunken and immobile with fear. Finally, she tries to leave, stopped at the door by Mrs. Danvers' continuing monologue. She cries, and Mrs. Danvers peers into her face, wondering if Rebecca doesn't come back "to watch you and Mr. De Winter together." She suggests she should stay there and rest, but X escapes as Mrs. Danvers floats off, reminiscing about the sea.

X sits at the desk in the morning room, crying. She picks up the telephone and firmly demands to see Mrs. Danvers immediately. Piling up the mono-grammed stationery, she tells Danvers to "get rid of all these things." When Danvers protests, she tells her she "is Mrs. De Winter now.... I prefer to forget everything that happened this afternoon." Mrs. Danvers is left staring after her as she goes out.

She runs out to the hall to greet Maxim, jumping into his arms. She takes him into the library and pleads with him for permission to host a costume ball.

Later, she sketches a Joan of Arc costume, adding it to a pile near her on the bed. Mrs. Danvers enters and suggests she might find an idea for a costume in the family portrait gallery. In the hall, they stop at a portrait of Lady Caroline De Winter dressed in ruffled white, which Mrs. Danvers describes as Maxim's favorite.

A blustery night. Frank enters in his cap and gown. The large hall is filled with tables and garlands. Bea and Clive arrive, dressed as strongman and woman. Bea goes upstairs to help X, but she says she doesn't want anyone to see her costume.

Inside, X excitedly completes the final primping, then rushes out, smiling and expectant, and calmly goes down the stairs. Their backs turned, Maxim, Bea, and Clive stand at the bottom. Near them in the large-brimmed white hat, she says, "Good evening, Mr. De Winter," and Maxim turns, appalled, angry. "Go and take it off . . . what are you standing there for, didn't you hear what I said!" he brings his hands up to his head in pain. Told the same dress was worn by Rebecca, she turns and races upstairs. Pausing at the portrait, she notices Mrs. Danvers enter the west wing and follows her into Rebecca's bedroom.

"Why do you hate me?" she pleads. "You thought you could be Mrs. De Winter . . . take her things. . . . No one ever got the better of her, never, never." X collapses in tears on the bed, crying "Stop it!" Mrs. Danvers opens a window to the fog and suggests she needs fresh air. X rises and leans near the window next to Mrs. Danvers, who intones, "You've nothing to live for . . . look down there. It's easy, isn't it, why don't you?" The camera closes around their still faces, X staring at the sea, Mrs. Danvers focused on X. Suddenly fireworks light the sky and someone yells, "Shipwreck!" X regains her senses, and turns to go downstairs. Mrs. Danvers is left staring out the window.

A clock shows 2:30 A.M. Out on the foggy beach, rescuers move small boats around and X runs into Ben and asks him if he's seen Maxim. Then she sees Frank, who tells her a diver has found Rebecca's boat. Walking away, she sees a light coming from the beach cottage.

Inside, she finds Maxim, sitting alone, morbidly depressed. "We've lost our little chance at happiness. . . . The thing has happened, the thing I've dreaded. . . . Rebecca has won." He tells her the diver found the boat and Rebecca's body. The year before, he knowingly identified a stranger to be put in the family crypt, even though he knew Rebecca's body was in the boat because he put it there. Asking her if she still loves him, she turns away. "You see, it's too late," he says. No, she protests clutching him, she does love him, but how could they be close when she knew he still loved Rebecca. Startled, as the music swells he cries, "I hated her!" Roaming the room, he tells her about Rebecca, who had everything, "breeding, beauty, and brains," and the sordid story of their marriage and her death. "She was her incapable of love or tenderness. . . . That cliff in Monte Carlo? . . . that's where I found out about her, her black hair blowing in the wind. . . . I wanted to kill her." She promised to play the part of a devoted wife, "but she began to grow careless . . . took a flat in London . . . started bringing her friends down here." He told her not to bring Favel to the cottage and had come down to confront them the night of her death, but she was alone. As he relates their final argument and her taunts about having an heir that would not be his child, the camera pans around the cottage, marking the spots where Rebecca was in the story and returning to

him as he tells of her ending taunt, "Aren't you going kill me?" "I must have struck her . . . then she started toward me . . . stumbled and fell. . . . I realized she was dead." X cries out that it was an accident. He describes taking the body out to the boat and making it sink. She advises him to say he made a mistake about the other body, convinced they can hide the truth. Broken, he insists that Rebecca has won. The telephone rings; the constable wants to speak with him.

A group of men stare down, then, led by Maxim, turn and walk out of a bare room. The constable informs Maxim there must be another inquest.

That night at Manderly, X walks down the central stairs. One of the butlers offers her the evening papers.

She turns politely away into the library, where Maxim stares at the fire. "Promise me you won't lose your temper," she says, asking to accompany him to the inquest the next day. He kisses her forehead, looking at her intently. "It's gone forever, that funny young, lost look I loved. . . . In a few hours, you've grown so much older."

Kerrith Board School: outside a police officer boasts to the crowd of onlookers about one of his arrests. He peeks in on the proceedings on the other side of the door behind him.

Inside, Ben, standing in front of a seated crowd, is questioned. He "knows nothing," and is dismissed. The man who reconditioned Rebecca's boat is questioned next; he points out that the drain valves in the bottom were deliberately opened. The questioner turns to the constable, who responds negatively when asked if the former Mrs. De Winter might have been capable of suicide. Maxim is called for further questioning and asked to elucidate about the holes in the boat; he responds somewhat sarcastically, then impatiently, prompting a direct, "Were relations between you and Mrs. De Winter perfectly happy?" Maxim begins to yell, "I won't stand it any longer," but X, in the front row, falls in a faint to the ground. The group adjourns until after lunch.

Outside, the couple walks to the car for lunch. Maxim leaves X in the back seat with a strong drink. Favel intrudes with a greeting, then opens the car door to speak with her. Maxim appears and asks him to go away, but he invites himself in for lunch, alluding to the holes in the boat and "foul play." They listen, unimpressed, as he helps himself to some meat and produces a note from Rebecca; then he suggests a deal, involving "some advice on how to live comfortably." Frank arrives; Maxim tells him he and Favel are going to discuss some business at the inn and asks that he fetch Colonel Julien immediately.

The inn is crowded; they enter and Maxim asks for a private room. They're ushered into the back, and Colonel Julien, X, and Frank follow them shortly. Maxim announces that Favel has offered to withhold evidence if Maxim can make it worth his while. Favel pushes ahead with his suspicions, showing the note in which Rebecca arranged a meeting with him the night of her death, insisting she did not intend to kill herself. Colonel Julien is respectful, asking him if he has any witnesses. Favel mentions Ben, then prattles on, alluding to Frank's unrequited passion for Rebecca and suggesting he'll have better luck with X. Maxim punches him in the jaw. Favel falls to a chair, warning Maxim about his temper. Colonel Julien asks if Favel has a motive, indicating that the accusations must be pursued. Favel produces Mrs. Danvers and asks her who Rebecca's doctor is. Wanting to shield Rebecca, she is not entirely cooperative, but is forced to admit that "love was a game for her." Crying, startled, at the mention of suicide, then murder, she tells them about Dr. Baker. Favel is triumphant, sure the doctor will

confirm that Rebecca was pregnant with a baby that Maxim knew was not his. The officials decide to visit Dr. Baker, and Mrs. Danvers stands, staring with menace at Maxim and X.

Outside, Maxim puts X into the car, kissing her good-bye. The four men drive through the countryside to see the doctor.

In his office, they sit in a circle. Dr. Baker says he has no patients named De Winter, but, in reading the names of the patients he did have that day, they discover one named "Danvers." They ask him if he knows of a motive for suicide, and he tells them that Rebecca had cancer. Favel turns away, stunned.

Out on the street, the men part after Colonel Julien upbraids Favel about the dangers of bribery and compliments Frank for being such a good friend to Maxim. Left alone, Frank listens to Maxim's realization that Rebecca had wanted him to kill her; he advises him not to think of it anymore.

In a phone booth, Favel tells Mrs. Danvers the news and comments that Maxim and his bride will be able to live happily ever after.[H]

Maxim and Frank drive; Maxim worries that "something is wrong" at Manderly.

At Manderly, Mrs. Danvers carries a lighted candle through a darkened hall. She approaches X, who is sleeping by a fireplace in the dark with one of the dogs.

The car speeds along, then slows, as the two men see a bright glow over the tree tops. They speed again toward the house engulfed in flames.

The front lawn is full of people. Maxim jumps out, looking for X, who calls out to him and tells him that Mrs. Danvers told her "she would rather destroy Manderly than see us happy here." From outside, Mrs. Danvers can be seen through an east wing window.

Inside, beams crash down around Mrs. Danvers and fire engulfs the monogrammed linen on Rebecca's bed.

Note. [H]Hitchcock does bit as man outside phone booth being used by George Sanders.

27   *Foreign Correspondent* (1940)

Director	Alfred Hitchcock
Assistant Director	E[dmond] F. Bernoudy
Producer	Walter Wanger
Production Company	Walter Wanger-United Artists
Screenplay	Charles Bennett, Joan Harrison, James Hilton (dialogue), Robert Benchley (dialogue)
Photography	Rudolph Maté, A.S.C.
Editing	Otto Lovering, Dorothy Spencer
Art Direction	Alexander Golitzen, Richard Irvine (associate)
Set Direction	Julia Heron
Sound	Frank Maher
Special Effects	Paul Eagler, A.S.C., William Cameron Menzies (special production effects)
Music	Alfred Newman
Costumes	I. Magnin & Co.

Cast	Joel McCrea (Johnny Jones/Huntley Haverstock), Laraine Day (Carol Fisher), Herbert Marshall (Stephen Fisher), George Sanders (Scott Ffol-liott), Edmund Gwenn (Rowley), Albert Basserman (Van Meer), Robert Benchley (Stebbins), Harry Davenport, Eduardo Ciannelli, Martin Kosleck, Eddie Conrad, Cranford Kent, Gertrude W. Hoffman, Jane Novak, Joan Brodel-Leslie, Louis Borell, Elly Malyon, E. E. Clive
Filmed	at United Artists Studios, Los Angeles
Running Time	approximately 120 minutes
Distributor	United Artists
Release Date	August 1940

Other titles: *Mord, Correspondant 17, Cet Homme Est un Espoin, Il Prigioniero di Amsterdam*

Synopsis

Credits appear over a turning metal globe, with gay music and then the romantic theme.

Introductory titles: "To those intrepid ones who went across the seas to be the eyes and ears of America . . . to those forthright ones who early saw the clouds of war while many of us at home were seeing rainbows . . . to the Foreign Correspondents . . ."

The camera travels into a window of the modern skyscraper that houses the *New York Morning Globe* newsroom. Mr. Powers, the editor, fumes in his large office, unhappy with the pallid reporting of his staff in Europe. "No more economists!" he shouts, "I want a real reporter!" Johnny Jones, on the verge of being fired for beating up a policeman, is summoned from his desk in the newsroom where he is busy cutting paper designs. After briefly assessing Johnny's meager knowledge of current events, Powers demands that he go to Europe and find out what's going on by contacting Mr. Van Meer, Holland's "strong man." Stephen Fisher, the urbane head of the Universal Peace Party, enters and is introduced to Johnny, who is now officially dubbed Huntley Haverstock, a name Powers thinks has more cachet than John Jones.

A montage covers preparations for Johnny's trip to London on the Queen Mary, starting with shopping with his mother, the purchase of a derby, and a good-bye party in his cabin. The camera moves into a close-up of his suddenly saddened mother, who realizes she must say good-bye, and as the ship leaves, to a grinning boy from the party, who has taken Johnny's derby.

London. Stebbins, the *Globe*'s European correspondent, meets Johnny at the train station; taking him into the bar, he laments his alcoholism over a glass of milk and admits he does not keep up much, just sends back press releases. An invitation, dated August 25, 1939, to have lunch with Van Meer awaits Johnny at his hotel.

Outside his hotel on the way to the lunch,[H] Johnny runs into Van Meer, who

invites him into his cab but evades his questions, preferring to talk of beauty and the birds.

Walking into the reception, Van Meer asks what paper Johnny works for, and Johnny denies he is a reporter. But before they are separated, he manages to get one comment from Van Meer about the war: "I feel old and tired and powerless."

Elsewhere in the hall, Stephen Fisher's daughter, Carol, a bright, dark-haired young woman, contradicts a gentleman who argues that the upcoming war is beyond anyone's control. "A very convenient excuse," she says; "you never hear of circumstances over which we have no control rushing us into peace, do you?" Her father whisks her away, congratulating her on her spunk.

While mingling, Johnny meets Carol; they flirt and he assumes she is doing publicity for this "amateur group." She sarcastically dismisses him, giving him a false name. The crowd assembles at the round tables in the dining room. Stephen Fisher begins the program by announcing that Van Meer has been unable to attend, but his daughter will speak instead. Johnny briefly frowns at this. In her talk, Carol directly confronts Johnny's accusation of amateurism; he sits in the audience grinning stupidly at her. The stack of notes he has sent her by a waiter finally finds its way to her as she speaks, and she loses her train of thought, taken by his open adoration. Unable to think of her next sentence, she flounders, and Johnny tries to save face by prematurely clapping, but no one in the audience follows his lead.

A telegram instructs Johnny to attend a peace conference in Amsterdam. The camera moves over and down into the crowded streets of the city during a downpour: streetcars and autos snaking through, and pedestrians all carrying umbrellas. Johnny, wearing a trenchcoat and no hat, waits at the top of the grand stairs to the hall until the camera finds him. He greets Stephen Fisher, also in attendance, who leaves him abruptly. Spotting Van Meer, Johnny walks down to greet him, but the old man fails to recognize him despite Johnny's repeated reminders. Momentarily speechless, Johnny watches as a photographer steps close to them and shoots Van Meer with a gun camouflaged by his camera. Johnny chases the assassin through the crowd, then down to the street where he hops into the first car he sees and demands they pursue the gunman's escape vehicle. The driver is another journalist, Scott Ffolliott, and his passenger is Carol Fisher.

The chase moves quickly into the countryside, as the assassin shoots back at them and a trail of police cars follows. At a small village crossroads, a resident steps into the road several times, but, faced with the stream of speeding cars, finally gives up and goes home. Suddenly, in the middle of vast fields marked only by a few windmills, the assassin's car disappears. The police move on beyond Johnny, Scott, and Carol, who stand near a windmill and wonder what has happened. Johnny notices the windmill change direction against the wind, then persuades the other two to go and summon the police. A plane lands, and Johnny realizes it has been signaled; he goes into the windmill to investigate and discovers the car that had disappeared, then hears voices.

Inside, the huge gears creak as Johnny observes two men making a payoff. The men from the plane join them and Johnny quickly hides near the top of the stairs and watches them from above. Through a door at the top he finds Van Meer seated in an empty store room. "They want the world to think I've been assassinated to conceal the fact that I am in their hands." Drugged, he is unable

to explain further, only mumbles about birds, then demands a pen and scribbles down something. He is staring out, unaware of the events around him, when the gang from below comes up to get him. Hiding next to a man-sized gear, Johnny watches them; his coat becomes caught in the machinery and he quickly takes it off, retrieving it when it falls out of the bottom. For the second time, Van Meer stares off in Johnny's direction, and the men follow his glance in alarm, but Johnny has already managed to escape from view. Outside, the huge arms of the mill turn next to Johnny, who is on the roof. He precariously reenters through a dormer window and descends the stairs only to find that he is now caught between two groups of the gang: one up with Van Meer, the other down below. Quietly, he manages to flee undetected.

Later, he demands help from a policeman through a schoolgirl interpreter.

At the windmill, a crowd gathers as Johnny leads them to the site only to find no one and no trace of the gang or the car, just one of the gang pretending to be a vagrant. Carol and Scott look disappointed as Johnny vigorously defends his claims; the hobo, noticing his too-clean hands, reaches down to rub dirt into them.

At his room in the Hotel Europe, Johnny types a reassuring telegram to the *Globe*: "biggest story of century, no kidding . . ." A knock at his door brings a detective and a policeman who request his presence at the station. Taking time for a phone call, Johnny finds the line dead, and the camera moves up to a close-up of the cut wires. He asks to take a bath before accompanying the men and watches through the keyhole as the intruders take out their guns. Whistling and turning on the water, Johnny climbs out on the roof behind the hotel's neon sign and over into a room full of people, where Carol Fisher is the hostess. Finding himself in her bedroom and still in his nightclothes, he offends one of her guests. Letting his garters show under his robe, he listens attentively as Carol berates him for making a fool of her in front of the police and breaking into her bedroom. His defense sounds silly to her: "Your childish mind is as out of place in Europe as you are in my bedroom," she fumes, then demands that he go. He makes a heartfelt appeal, hanging his head; then, as he turns to leave, she finally consents to help him.

Water seeps out of Johnny's bathroom, alerting his pursuers who break in the door. The room fills up with investigators, and a valet sent by Johnny surreptitiously walks in and grabs his clothes.

Johnny and Carol peek into his room on their way out; they are noticed by the intruders, but they quickly escape.

Boarding a large ship, Carol and Johnny are unable to get a cabin but successfully evade their pursuers, who just miss the boat. Hooded in blankets, they spend the night on the deck in the cold wind; the mood softens as he tells her his story and then proposes marriage. To his surprise, she accepts, assuring him her father will approve.

In London the next morning, they enter her father's home; a Mr. Krupf is breakfasting with Stephen. Johnny recognizes him as one of the gang and warns Stephen, who loudly requests that Krupf leave his home as he leads him into a sitting room.

When Stephen consults with Krupf in private, however, we discover that Stephen is one of them, but laments his daughter's involvement. "This is close to home. In fact, it is my home. After all, I'm only a politician," he moans, "and politicians aren't usually called upon to do away with their guests." He and Krupf

concoct a scheme to have Johnny hire an assassin friend of theirs, Roley, as a bodyguard.

Returning to his daughter and her friend, Stephen insists that he let Krupf go in order to "keep it quiet" and save Van Meer. Pursuing his plan, he convinces Johnny that he needs to protect himself. Outside at the front door, Roly inspects his hands as he waits to accompany Johnny.

Inside, Carol cries at Johnny's departure; so visibly upset is she that Stephen briefly has second thoughts. Turning away from her toward the camera, he hesitates, but then takes no action to save Johnny.

While Johnny and Roly wait in town for a taxi and discuss their mode of operation, Roley suddenly pushes Johnny into the path of an oncoming truck, then explains that he did it to save him. In the taxi, Roley begins to respond to an imaginary pursuer and recommends giving him the slip. Entering Westminster Cathedral, he leads the always good-natured Johnny to the top of the tower, which is cluttered with repair tools and schoolchildren. The crowds disappear, and Roley backs up a few feet, ready to take a leap at Johnny; from below a body falls through the air and a woman screams.

A newspaper account details the "strange accident." Johnny and Stebbins read it in their small Fleet Street office, and Johnny realizes that Stephen was behind the attempt on his life. Scott strides in with congratulations and new information. He has been suspicious of Stephen since last year; he and Johnny agree to work together as Scott explains that Van Meer signed a treaty with a very important secret clause. He suggests kidnapping Carol to put pressure on Stephen; Johnny resists, but Carol walks into the office and proposes she take him to hide in the country. Johnny feels used but goes along with Scott's plan to get Stephen while Carol is supposedly kidnapped but with him in the country.

Carol drives; Johnny remains depressed.

Scott's messages pile up at Stephen Fisher's house.

At Johnny's room in a country inn, Carol starts to leave, but Johnny asks her to stay for dinner; they kiss. He goes down to the lobby to take a call from Scott, who frantically demands that he keep Carol there the rest of the night. Carol observes Johnny at the registration desk requesting a room for her, then she disappears.

At 10:20 P.M. that night, Stephen finally arrives home and soberly begins to make plans for the family to leave for the United States. Scott consults with him in his study and announces the kidnapping of his daughter, demanding to know where Van Meer is being kept. Krupf calls and asks Stephen to meet him because Van Meer has so far refused to talk. Carol arrives before Scott can get any information. She is unsettled by her father's sudden plans but agrees to accompany him upon hearing that war will be declared the next day; besides, she has been gravely insulted by Johnny's actions. Scott hides outside, hears the address on Charlotte Street when Stephen finally emerges to take a taxi to Van Meer, and sends a message to Johnny to meet him there.

Inside, Carol picks up a call from Krupf, frowning in pain at what she begins to understand.

On seedy, crowded Charlotte Street, a group of female guards send Stephen through to Krupf and Van Meer, who is being tortured with floodlights and loud music. Stephen demands the lights be turned down and holds Van Meer, who is grateful for the solace. As Stephen pumps Van Meer in a friendly way, Scott

barges in, followed shortly by one of the guards pointing a pistol at him. From the shadows, Scott tells Van Meer not to trust Stephen, and the old man is left alone again, in his bed of light. He gains the energy to lecture them, as they stand in the dark surrounding his light: "You will never conquer *them* . . . the little people everywhere . . . lie to them . . . whip them . . . Force them into war, but the beasts like you will devour each other." Stephen motions, and off screen Van Meer cries and moans. The female guard and Scott respond with pained expressions, finally writhing in horror, and the woman turns her back at what they are witnessing.

Down on the street, Johnny notices a fight breaking out upstairs immediately on his arrival. Scott leaps out of the window and falls through an awning, springing to his feet to command his friends to follow him back upstairs. But the gang has escaped by car.

At New Scotland Yard, Scott tries to convince his brother, a detective, to nab Stephen Fisher before he gets on a plane for the United States, but there is not enough evidence.

Scott and Johnny head for the airport. Stebbins is sent to visit Van Meer in a nursing home. On the streets, the declaration of war is announced.

The Fishers sit on the Clipper in the first class cabin. Scott and Johnny are back in the tourist section. The flight crew carries back a message for Scott that is intercepted by Stephen: Van Meer is conscious and has told the whole story; police will meet the plane. Faltering, Steven tells Carol the truth: "I've got to make a forced landing . . . [I'm sorry] for using the tactics of the country I grew up with." Johnny, unable to restrain himself, walks forward to confront Carol, who responds by defending her father. Scott joins them as she indignantly continues, when suddenly their plane is rocked by gunfire. Carol immediately starts to hand out life jackets; another passenger is shot dead as pandemonium takes over and a wing is damaged, shredding to pieces before their eyes while the pilots strain to bring the plane back up.

The plane crashes into the water, sending the crew leaping to the back where everyone else has already fled. People swim through but no one can open the doors, and some drown at the ceiling. Finally a window is smashed open and six people clamber outside, moving over to a wing as the body of the plane sinks. The pilot appears on another piece of wreckage and swims over to join them, but one survivor yells out that if they let him on they will all sink. Stephen decides to sacrifice himself, swimming off into the stormy sea. Scott and Johnny begin to follow, but then let him go. An American ship appears on the horizon.

Safe and dry in the captain's lounge of the ship, Scott and Johnny lament losing their story; they are two days away from New York and the ship's captain, in the name of neutrality, will not let them radio out. Carol enters just in time to hear Johnny defend her father; after all, he "died like a hero." Grateful, she convinces him that he must send out the story anyway. Pretending the call is to Johnny's uncle, they get Powers at the *Globe* on the line just in time to ask him to hold on. Johnny sets the phone down as the captain arrives to angrily accuse them of being journalists; he will not allow anything embarrassing to the United States to be sent out. Johnny agrees with his concerns, but proceeds to tell his story to the captain as a "courtesy," with Scott chiming in with essential asides. Powers is ecstatic at the big news story of Fisher and Van Meer.

A montage of Johnny's front page articles from all over Europe illustrates his continued coverage of the war and his fame as a foreign correspondent.

One day in a London studio, Carol by his side, Johnny speaks into a radio

microphone. Bombs start to fall, and he is advised to stop broadcasting when the lights go out, but he persists, lamenting a "part of the world being blown apart. . . . It's death coming to London. . . . It's too late to do anything here now except stand in the dark . . . but there's still lights in America. . . . Keep those lights burning, cover them with steel, ring them with guns. . . . The lights are all out everywhere, except in America."

Note. ^HHitchcock does a bit as man reading newspaper.

28   *Mr. and Mrs. Smith* (1941)

Director	Alfred Hitchcock
Assistant Director	Dewey Starkey
Executive Producer	Harry E. Edington
Production Company	RKO Radio Pictures, Inc.
Screenplay	Norman Krasna
Photography	Harry Stradling
Editing	William Hamilton
Art Direction	Van Nest Polglase, L. P. Williams (associate)
Set Direction	Darrell Silvera
Sound	John E. Tribby
Special Effects	Vernon L. Walker
Music	Edward Ward
Costumes	Irene
Cast	Carole Lombard (Ann), Robert Montgomery (David), Gene Raymond (Jeff Custer), Jack Carson (Chuck), Philip Merivale (Mr. Custer), Lucile Watson (Mrs. Custer), William Tracy (Sammy), Charles Halton (Mr. Deaver), Esther Dale (Mrs. Krausheimer), Emma Dunn (Martha), Betty Compson (Gertie), Patricia Farr (Gloria), William Edmunds (Proprietor of Lucy's), Adele Pearce (Lily)
Filmed	at RKO Radio Studios, Los Angeles
Running Time	approximately 95 minutes
Distributor	RKO Radio
Release Date	January 1941

Other titles: *Joies Matrimoniales, M. et Mme. Smith, Il Signore e la Signora Smith*

Synopsis

Under the credits, scenes of Park Avenue in New York, with lightly gay, then more romantic music.

Deep inside his apartment, on the floor of his bedroom littered with dirty dishes, David Smith, dressed in his robe, sits playing solitaire. At the sound of a

knock, Ann (Mrs. Smith), still huddled under the covers, opens wide one eye and watches alertly as David brings in the breakfast tray from the maid, who peeks over him at her. Ann feigns sleep as he sets the tray near her, takes his own, and walks away.

In the kitchen, the maid excitedly passes on the news to her colleagues. Someone from David's office phones and is told it has been three days, but they have been known to keep it up for eight. Sammy, a well-dressed young business-man, enters the kitchen; he must get David to sign some papers today. Meekly going to the bedroom door, Sammy gets his signature.

Inside, David pretends to leave and Ann is startled into revealing her wakeful state. They hug and she extols the virtues of their rule: never leave the bedroom after a quarrel until you've made up.

Later as she shaves him, she chats about their wonderful marriage, the trust, the confidence, and the "respect for each other as persons." "Always tell the truth no matter what the consequences," she exclaims, nose in air. At the breakfast table, each attempts to take the blame for their quarrel. Several times she mentions their "rules"; he is less keen on them but always agrees with the face of her reason, which is the structure of their "wonderful relationship." She asks him if he had the chance to do it over again, would he marry her, and he answers (truthfully) no. Letting her feet fall from their resting place on his calves, and stiffening, she replies that she "doesn't want to cling [where she's] not wanted." Anguished at this turn in her mood, he insists the question and answer were hypothetical, and reassures her: "I love you . . . I am used to you . . . you are my little girl. . . . Now can I go to work?" She valiantly covers her emotion and lets him go with a smile.

At his law office, the secretaries stare as he walks in, and his partner admits to jealousy. Mr. Deaver, an official from the town where the Smiths were married, is ushered in and informs David that his marriage, because of a minor techni-cality, is not legal. At the return of his $2 fee, David laughs. Left alone, he gleefully makes a dinner date on the telephone with Ann, noting Miss Ann Krausheimer in his calendar for 6:30.

Mr. Deaver, who happens to know Ann because she grew up in the town in which she was later married, impulsively decides to visit her. He has tea with her and her mother and tells them the news. The women are shocked, especially Mrs. Krausheimer.

Later, Ann expectantly puts on her wedding suit, which won't stay zippered because it is now too tight. But she wears it to dinner anyway, mugging her way through its occasional unzipping. In a romantic mood, she suggests Mama Lucy's, where David first asked her to marry him. Lucy's is now a grimy luncheonette, but they persist, even asking that a table be put outside, but a group of scruffy children gather around them and stare.

Reseated at a table inside, Ann stoically eats the soup while David frowns at it. She asks where they are going next and he says home. Taken aback, she questions him about his day, but he remains mum. She takes a phone call from her mother in the restaurant's kitchen and is forced to admit that David has not yet proposed. Mrs. Krausheimer breaks down in tears, but Ann reassures her. "If worse comes to worse, I'll spend the night with you." She returns to the table with a more set expression, and David offers a secret: "You're a great kid."

At home, David cheerfully presents champagne in a bucket while she moves

around in elegant nightclothes, stunned. Whistling, he puts on his pajamas, and returns to the living room and the loud crash of breaking glass. Furious, she screams at him: "You were going to throw me aside like a squeezed lemon! I've always had suspicions about you!" He insists he was going to tell her later. She kicks him out and throws his clothes in front of him. He is left wide-eyed in the hallway, pounding on the door.

He takes a room at the Beefeaters Club. Wrapped in a white towel, he seeks solace in the steam room and bumps into Chuck Benson, an acquaintance. Poking his finger into his chest, Chuck advises David to ignore the incident and go home the next day as usual.

The next evening, David finds "Miss Krausheimer" not at home and the maid refusing him entrance. He waits in the lobby with his gift until Ann returns from her date with a Mr. Flugel. After briefly staring down Flugel, he goes upstairs and pounds on the door; she quickly throws out a pen that he had left behind.

He returns to the club.

Another day, he pushes himself into her cab and tells her he's tired of her games. She informs him they are not married; angrily, he replies that they will get married. "You had a hard enough time getting me to marry you before and I didn't know you then," she says. He advises her he will not support her anymore and she gets out of the cab and walks into the employees' entrance of a department store.

David enters the store with the crowd of women waiting for the doors to open and finds Ann behind the counter in curtains and draperies. He grabs her and a fracas ensues; the store manager interferes and is disconcerted to learn that Miss Krausheimer is married, as it is the policy of the store not to hire married women. Both Smiths are escorted to see the head of the firm, Mr. Flugel. Dismayed, David pushes Flugel around and both he and Ann are thrown out on the street.

Quarreling on the sidewalk, she tells him that she will not marry him because he is too jealous and temperamental, "always knocking people down." A crowd surrounds them, including a police officer who sends them in different directions.

David's partner comes to visit one morning at the Beefeaters Club as David lackadaisically prepares for work, visibly depressed. Jeff has put off most of David's cases in an attempt to help. He suggests that David "drop in" on Ann that evening, indicating that he might have a plan that will get them together. David eagerly agrees, reassuring Jeff that it was just a "little marital quarrel, nothing at all." Of course, Jeff replies, "you're too fine to do anything shoddy." Looking for words to express his gratitude, David wrings Jeff's hand and comes up with a series of compliments, but their eyes lock when he recalls Jeff as the best fullback Alabama ever had.

That night, David merrily approaches the apartment, but Ann and Jeff greet him with set expressions. Having heard the other side of the story, Jeff has now agreed to act as Ann's lawyer, and, realizing she is available, has asked her for a date. Incensed, David calls off his relationship with Ann and removes the chain from Ann's front door on his way out with Jeff.

At the elevator, the men stand silent, David eyeing Jeff with hostility and insulting his football talent in a parting shot at the front sidewalk.[H]

Later, David returns to the apartment, bribing the elevator man so that Ann will open the door. Unmoved she slams it on his nose.

Holding a bottle of gin, David tries to relax in the steam bath with Chuck, who has recommended the gin for his nosebleed and listens to his problems. Chuck makes a date with Gertrude and her friend Gloria for himself and David, who is skeptical but warms to Gloria's flattery over the telephone. Anxious for revenge, he suggests the Florida Club where he knows Ann and Jeff are going to have dinner.

David winds his way through the crowd at the bustling Florida Club, where Chuck is sitting next to an elegant blond woman, who turns out to be with the party at the next table. Gloria and Gertrude, on the other side, are more curly and cute than elegant, and David immediately starts agitating for the group to leave. Spotting Ann, he pretends to be talking to the beautiful woman on his other side in order to make Ann jealous, but he is eventually forced to turn toward his own party, who are cheerily eating pheasant. Recalling his nosebleed, David jabs himself a few times to get it going again, but Gertrude turns out to be an expert at stopping nosebleeds, and appropriate emergency procedures are forced on him, causing everyone to stare.

On the way home in a cab, an angry Ann suggests to Jeff they go to the fair. Once there, they go up in a parachute ride, which breaks down with them at the top, causing Ann to become hysterical. It rains.

Finally returning to Jeff's apartment, she is impressed with its clean, tasteful appearance, then discovers he doesn't drink, as he relates to her a lecture he once attended on temperance. Concerned because he is wet from the rain, she insists a drink is really medicine and feeds him two full glasses of whiskey, until he stiffens. Finally she decides to go home, allowing him a kiss on the cheek.

Another day, David and a cab driver sit outside Ann's apartment drinking coffee and eating donuts. They have been following her for several days. On this day they follow her to his office.

He runs up, thinking she's looking for him, but finds an irate client instead. In Jeff's office, Ann is visiting with him and his parents, who have stopped by on their way to Lake Placid. David barges in, hinting about his and Ann's intimate relationship. Jeff's stuffy parents become increasingly alarmed as he laments the loss of this woman he has had breakfast with every day for three years. Jeff's parents drag him into a utility closet and lecture him about this "loose woman," while Anne lectures David about his lack of Jeff's "fine qualities." Still sequestered in the closet, Jeff reassures his parents that things are not as they appear.

At a Lake Placid resort, Ann and Jeff are given a cabin half a mile away by sleigh from his parents. Jeff is upset at the isolated and unchaperoned circumstances. Suddenly they see David, covered with snow, keel over outside their room; they carry him inside and put him in the adjoining room he has rented. Ann is very concerned, tenderly interpreting his drunken mumblings, but Jeff sends her away so he can undress him.

Later, David sits calmly in his room smiling, while Ann worries. When she and Jeff visit him, he feigns delirium. Against Jeff's protests, she insists on shaving the poor sick man.

Returning to their suite, Jeff suggests to her that she probably will not be happy without David and asks her to take back her promise to marry him. Returning to check on David, she peeks through the window first and discovers that he has been fooling them. She goes in and throws some water at him and

orders him out of bed. David makes a desperate appeal, but she is angry and tells him she is going to marry Jeff. "I know you; you couldn't have anything to do with that pill of a southern fried chicken," he reasons, finally and poignantly giving up.

Agitated, Ann returns to Jeff and reaffirms her desire to marry him; he offers her fried chicken.

Returning from dinner in the sleigh, Ann worries that David might turn to drinking, then decides he must be made to hate her in order to free himself.

Armed with her idea, she tells Jeff good night, then acts out a boisterous drunken seduction with him in her room, as David listens and frowns on the other side of the wall. She ends with a flourish of frantic cries suggesting coercion. David barges in for the rescue and, finding her alone, collars her instead. She screams for Jeff to help her, and he joins them; but wanting out, he graciously forgives David for manhandling Ann and merely intones that "violence is a sign of lack of character." Offended that Jeff won't "sock" David, Ann questions his masculinity at the top of her voice, just as his parents arrive. David stands by smiling as they forbid Jeff to marry "this woman." Irate, Ann screams, "You forbid *him* to marry *me!*" Turning to Jeff, she cries, "Taking your hat off on an elevator doesn't make a man out of you. You can teach a monkey to do that! And I'll take a monkey anytime to a lump of jelly like you!" But "I'm not taking *you*, either!" she screams at David, and stomps out. Jeff and his parents ride away.

David follows Ann into her room as she is putting on her skis and trips her so that she gets caught in a chair. He calmly undoes his tie as she becomes hysterical and unable to rise. "I'll break every bone in your body!" she cries; at the same time she surreptitiously rebuckles one of the boots when her foot falls out. As she continues to scream, David coolly walks up behind her and she raises her arms toward him. "Oh, David . . ."

Note. ᴴHitchcock does a bit as passer-by.

29 *Suspicion* (1941)

Director	Alfred Hitchcock
Assistant Director	Dewey Starkey
Producer	Harry Edington
Production Company	RKO Radio Pictures, Inc.
Screenplay	Samson Raphaelson, Joan Harrison, Alma Reville, from the novel *Before the Fact* by Francis Iles [Anthony Berkeley]
Photography	Harry Stradling, A.S.C.
Editing	William Hamilton, Carroll Clark (associate)
Art Direction	Van Nest Polglase
Set Direction	Darrell Silvera
Sound	John E. Tribby
Special Effects	Vernon Walker
Music	Franz Waxman
Costumes	Edward Stevenson

Cast   Cary Grant (Johnnie Aysgarth), Joan
                                             Fontaine (Lina McLaidlaw), Sir Ce-
                                             dric Hardwicke (General McLaid-
                                             law), Nigel Bruce (Beaky), Dame
                                             May Whitty (Mrs. McLaidlaw), Isabel
                                             Jeans (Mrs. Newsham), Heather An-
                                             gel (Ethel), Auriol Lee (Isobel Sed-
                                             busk), Reginald Sheffield (Reggie
                                             Wetherby), Leo G. Carroll (Captain
                                             Melbeck)
Filmed   at RKO Radio Studios, Los Angeles
Running Time   approximately 100 minutes
Distributor   RKO Radio
Release Date   September 1941
Other titles: *Verdacht, Soupçons, Il Sospetto*

Synopsis

A line drawing of the countryside appears under the credits, accompanied by the dramatic theme music.

A train whistles in the dark. Johnny Aysgarth apologizes for bumping into Lina McLaidlaw. At the end of a tunnel, daylight illuminates the inside of a train coach, and Johnnie garrulously explains that smoke drove him out of his other compartment. The camera moves over his hush-voiced traveling companion's thick reading glasses, heavy shoes, and book on child psychology, and he settles back. The conductor stops to collect tickets, but Johnnie, surprised to find he has only a third-class one, offhandedly requests the fare difference from Lina, who silently obliges with a postage stamp. Johnnie then closes his eyes to rest, while Lina goes back to her magazine, and finds a picture of Johnnie staring at her from the society pages.

People, horses, and cars mill around the outside of a country estate, readying for a hunt. Johnnie is distracted from his flirting with a group of women by the sight of Lina, who suddenly appears holding down a spirited horse. "Can't be the same girl," he mutters, as the horns sound.

Lina sits in front of the leaded windows of her parents' spacious living room reading a book when some acquaintances stop by to introduce Mr. Aysgarth to her. "Why?" she asks. But Johnnie jokes and charms her into accompanying them to church. When she goes off to change, he finds his picture cut out and used as a bookmark.

As they approach the church, Johnnie intercepts Lina and pushes her to a stop, insisting she take a walk with him instead.

On a nearby knoll, a long shot shows them tussling, and Lina's hat flies off in the struggle. The camera moves in closer to hear them. Johnnie laughs, holding onto her wrists and taunting her about her vigorous defense, "Now what did you think I was trying to do? Kill you?" Looking askance, her countenance firm, she calmly demands to be let go. He continues to tease her and plays with her hair, putting it in a tail atop her head. Throughout she patiently ignores his remarks, only smugly commenting at one point as she faces the camera that she doesn't think she would have any trouble "controlling" him if she had the chance. He

dubs her "monkeyface" when she takes out her mirror to see what he has done to her hair, and then tries one last time to kiss her, but she busies herself with snapping her purse shut.

Walking Lina home, then holding her coat out of reach, Johnnie demands to see her again at 3 P.M. She finally gets away, but as she approaches her front door, she overhears her parents discussing her "spinster" inclinations, which her father defends. "The old maid's a respectable institution. . . . Lina has intellect and a fine solid character." Mortified, she turns away only to find Johnnie inches behind her, a cocky smile on his face. She fiercely kisses him and strides inside.

At lunch, served by a butler and maid, Lina tells her parents about Johnnie; her father comments he has heard Johnnie is wild, cheats at cards or something. Johnnie telephones, and in the background the violins swell as she assents to his canceling of their date; then she returns to the table and proudly faces her father.

Alone, Lina flips through magazines and finds another picture of Johnnie. She furtively telephones him, checks at the post for mail, and returns to the knoll near the church.

The evening of the Hunt Ball, she has a headache and doesn't want to go until a telegram arrives from Johnnie.

Having removed the collar from her frilly evening dress to make it more revealing, Lina's bare back fills the screen, as she nervously looks around the ballroom. On the sidelines, a friend of her father's comments that he barely recognizes her. General McLaidlaw is informed that Johnnie has announced himself at the door as part of his party. Before he can do more than object, Johnny pushes his way through, and Lina, along with several other female guests, warmly greets him. He eagerly spins Lina off onto the dance floor, then quickly out a back door. She laughingly protests, but they drive off in her car.

He stops the car to kiss her and she solemnly professes her love. At first uncomfortable, he then responds, admitting he was afraid of falling in love with her. They stop at her home for a drink.

In the study, he pulls her to him. The camera circles their kiss until Johnnie notices the portrait of her stern father on the wall. Taunting her with her father's disapproval and suspicion of the unhappiness their affair will bring her, he asks her to marry him. Ecstatic, she insists nothing else matters. They both hear the music from the hall and dance around the room.

The next day, Lina comes down the stairs with a suitcase. Wistfully, she goes into the parlor and says good-bye to her parents, pretending to go to the post.

It rains at the registrar of marriages. Stickers from their European tour get slapped on their bags. They return home to a large, bright, and gracious home with a central curved stairway and a maid, Ethel.

Walking in, Lina wonders if they can afford it, but Johnnie puts on a recording of their song and they dance until Ethel brings in a telegram from one of Johnnie's creditors. The waltz music becomes somber. Lina is alarmed to find that Johnnie borrowed £1000 for the honeymoon and has no money of his own; indeed, as he calmly explains, he has "been broke all [his] life." As they talk on the couch, he mentions her inheritance, and she sweetly calls him a child and replies that her income would "never pay for all this." Briefly daunted, he suggests that her father might help, and she reminds him of her parents' coolness toward their union. "Anyway, you wouldn't actually want to live on your wife's allowance," she reasons. Slightly ruffled, he ventures that he will just have to borrow more, but Lina finally tells him, no, he will have to work. Plucked strings

are heard and then he does a double take at the mention of the word "work." "I'm afraid you're a bit of a dreamer. . . . Let's be practical about this," he objects.

A precious gift arrives from her father, two antique chairs, which Johnnie sarcastically accepts—"Shouldn't they be in a museum?" When they speak on the telephone with her father, he also queries Johnnie about his job prospects. Eventually, Johnnie, who "never dreamed he'd need it," produces a letter from Captain Melbeck, a cousin, offering him a job.

Another day, Lina returns from a horse ride to find an old friend of Johnnie's, named Beaky, who mentions that he's just seen Johnnie at the races. He blathers on until Lina, noticing her father's chairs are gone, becomes distressed. At Johnnie's arrival, Beaky tries to cheer her up, "If you want to see Johnnie at his very best, just say something about chairs. . . . He doesn't need more than one second to invent the most howling lie you ever heard." Johnnie obliges, but Lina graciously believes him; the sequence culminates in her quietly rebuking Beaky for implying her husband is a liar. She walks out of the living room between the two embarrassed men who roll their eyes over her head as she stares out blankly from between them.

In town later that weekend, Lina runs into Isobel Sedbusk, a local mystery writer, and accidentally comes across her chairs in a store window. She returns home and solemnly apologizes to Beaky for doing him an "injustice." Guessing her thoughts, Beaky counsels her, "You mustn't be angry at Johnnie. It's a waste of time [besides] that's what makes Johnnie, Johnnie."

Johnnie suddenly appears joyously carrying a load of gift boxes. He demands drinks from Ethel, and passes out some expensive presents—jewelry, fur coat, terrier. Eventually he proudly announces he won a big bet on a horse. Lina, already suspicious of the presents, is crestfallen at this news. The boys try to tease her out of her mood with chin tickling and funny faces and animal noises. Finally, Johnnie pulls out a paid receipt for the chairs and announces they will soon be delivered. Lina breaks down in tears and gratefully hugs him. The drinks arrive and Ethel is grandly presented with a fur stole. Johnnie warns Beaky away from the brandy, but Beaky pours some for himself anyway. They toast Johnnie's self-proclaimed "last bet," but Beaky has a fit, dropping his glass and nearly fainting. Johnnie coldly watches his friend, saying there is nothing to be done, he has seen it before. Beaky recuperates and apologizes.

Another day, Lina emerges from the town bookshop[H] to greet an acquaintance who tells her she saw Johnnie at the races recently. Lina coolly moves away, then nervously heads for Captain Melbeck's office and asks for Johnnie. Told he is not there, she speaks with Captain Melbeck who tactfully informs her that he fired Johnnie for embezzlement six weeks earlier. He has promised not to prosecute now and is expecting replacement of the £2000. Lina falls into a chair at the news.

She returns home with new determination, packs her bags, and sits down to write to Johnnie. The music swells in the background; her face is anguished as she writes that they must never see each other again. As she rises to leave, she rips up the note just as Johnnie appears quietly behind her with a telegram announcing her father's death. She cries in his arms.

In her parents' home, at the executor's reading of the will, Lina and Johnnie learn that their £500 allowance will continue and that they have also been bequeathed her father's portrait. Soured, Johnnie enters the study for a drink and toasts the portrait: "You win, old boy."

Driving back along the coast, Johnnie asks Lina if she has any regrets about marrying him. She turns the question back to him. "Monkeyface, marrying you is

the one thing I've never had any regrets about," he says, then becomes very solemn at the thought of her dying first. She admits that once she tried to stop loving him when she found he had lost his job. He loses his composure and queries her, but she does not reveal that she knows about the embezzlement and he does not tell her. They stop overlooking a spectacular cliff, and Johnnie changes the subject to an idea he has for developing the cliff area.

Later in their living room, Johnnie and Beaky lay out their plans for a resort hotel on the cliff. Lina soberly approaches them, wondering if Beaky, who is going to put up the money, understands the financial complexities surrounding the real estate company, which will be in Johnnie's name. Johnny is called away to the telephone, where he promises Captain Melbeck the money in a couple of weeks, and Lina hints to Beaky that he had better watch his money more carefully. Johnnie overhears and, after sending Beaky off, angrily and coldly berates Lina for interfering in his affairs. She weakly defends her advice to Beaky, but, as he menacingly follows her up the stairs, meekly agrees to his demands for her cooperation.

The next day, Lina is pruning in the garden when Johnnie appears, back to the camera. He moves next to her and announces he is calling off the venture. She wonders about his anger; he reassures her that he loves her but moves quickly away.

That evening, they play a word game. Lina forms DOUBT, then MUDDER becomes MURDER in her hands, as the men discuss one last look at the property. Startled, then wide-eyed at the word before her, Lina envisions Johnnie pushing Beaky off the treacherous cliff, Beaky flying through the sky. She faints to the floor.

Next morning, she awakens, alarmed to notice Johnnie already gone. She rushes out and drives to the cliff. Briefly, she frowns down at the violent sea, then drives home, her countenance deeply sad.

She slowly enters the quiet house, walking toward the living room where Johnnie whistles their favorite song. Peeking in, she sees Beaky; as the waltz music swells up from the record player and the lights go up in the room, Lina crosses swiftly to hug Johnnie warmly. Beaky mentions that he nearly lost his life at the cliff, but Johnnie saved him. Lina is gay now, and the men go off to London, Beaky intending to go on to Paris.

Later, Lina arranges good-bye flowers from Johnnie when two detectives arrive, Police Inspectors Hodgson and Benson. In the study, the camera moves to a close-up of her stricken face as they tell Lina of Beaky's mysterious death in Paris, after drinking large beakers of brandy with an English companion. They prompt her to see them out; the younger detective becomes absorbed in a modern painting in the hall and must be reminded to leave.

Lina returns to the study flexing her hands in consternation and informing her father's portrait that Johnnie did not go to Paris. Ringing up the Hogarth Club in London, she discovers Johnnie left the morning before. She sits in a chair despondently staring out, when Johnnie suddenly appears, talking about how much he loved Beaky. Lina is skeptical and tells him the police were there to see her. As he leans over her, still slumped in the chair, Johnnie queries her closely about what she told them, telling her she should not have said anything about his financial dealings with Beaky. He calls the police and Lina overhears him tell them he stayed at his club the night before. Distracted, Lina notices the mystery book by Isobel Sedbusk that Johnnie had carried in with him.

Later, Lina walks down the lane to Isobel's picket-fenced cottage. They

sit on her couch together, and Lina tentatively asks if accidental murder is really murder. Isabel wonders what Johnnie thinks since the circumstances of Beaky's death were similar to those in a book she had lent Johnnie some time ago.

Lina goes home and searches for the book. The music swells as she finds it in a drawer with a note inside to Melbeck, pleading for time. The insurance company calls about a request from Johnnie and tells her they will reply in next morning's post.

The following day, Lina stands calmly by the bedroom window, waiting for the post to arrive. Johnnie comes in and nervously opens his mail; she watches him hide the official letters in his coat pocket. As he bathes, she runs over to read them, discovering that his request for a loan has been denied; payment can be made only upon her death. Chilled, she stands by the window again; Johnnie comes over to embrace her.

They dine that evening with a group at Isobel's where their conversation over squab is about murder. Isobel pronounces Johnnie incapable of murder and Lina appears slightly relieved.

Later when they arrive home, Johnnie locks the door and turns out the light as Lina nervously asks after their servants, who both have the day off. They walk upstairs in the dark, Lina's evening coat glittering. In the bedroom, Johnnie expresses concern about her chill, and Lina asks him to sleep in another room. Immediately angry, he objects, but stiffly says goodnight, and Lina faints to the floor.

The next day, Johnnie and Isobel are sitting on the bed with Lina when she wakes. They have been watching her all day because her nerves seemed "shot." Johnnie goes to get her a meal, and Isobel tells her that Johnnie has pumped out of her the secret of an undetectable poison. "Is it painful?" asks Lina, staring out into space, and Isobel assures her it is not.

Later, Lina sits up in bed. Downstairs Johnnie casts a sudden long shadow; then, accompanied by dramatic music, he walks slowly up the stairs carrying a glass of milk on a tray. They kiss good night and he leaves. The music swells as she looks after him.

Next morning, the milk is still by her side as Lina packs her bags and Johnnie sarcastically complains about her going to her mother's. He insists on driving her.

They speed along the coast road, Lina becoming increasingly frightened, the music pumping along with the screeching tires. Johnnie makes a quick turn and Lina's door falls open. He turns toward her and puts his hand out over her, and she hysterically pushes him away. The car swerves to a halt and Lina jumps out and runs. Johnnie catches her, shaking her and shouting out his disappointment in her pushing him away, "Lina! You're my wife! . . . Don't worry, I won't run after you again," he finishes, and turns away. Startled, she runs after him, asking about the poison and suggesting that he wanted it for himself. Quickly, he explains that he has decided to face prison instead, and that he was in Liverpool when Beaky died. "If only I'd known," Lina cries, "I was only thinking of myself!" Tearfully, she pleads with him to return home with her. He insists it is not possible. They get into the car. The car makes a U-turn, and Johnnie's arm folds around her.

Note. [H]Hitchcock posts a letter at box in introductory long shot.

Remake: for television, *Suspicion* (American Playhouse, April 4, 1988), directed by Andrew Grieve.

30   *Saboteur* (1942)

Director	Alfred Hitchcock
Assistant Director	Fred Frank
Producer	Frank Lloyd
Associate Producer	Jack H. Skirball
Production Company	A Frank Lloyd Production Inc.-Universal Pictures, Inc.
Screenplay	Peter Viertel, Joan Harrison, Dorothy Parker, based on an original subject by Alfred Hitchcock
Photography	Joseph Valentine
Editing	Otto Ludwig
Art Direction	Jack Otterson, Robert Boyle
Set Direction	R. A. Gausman
Sound	Bernard B. Brown, William Hedgecock (technician)
Music	Frank Skinner, Charles Previn
Continuity	Adele Cannon
Cast	Robert Cummings (Barry Kane), Priscilla Lane (Pat), Otto Kruger (Tobin), Alan Baxter (Freeman), Clem Bevans (Neilson), Norman Lloyd (Fry), Alma Kruger (Mrs. Sutton), Vaughan Glazer (Mr. Miller), Dorothy Peterson (Mrs. Mason), Ian Wolfe (Robert), Frances Carson (Society Woman), Murray Alper (Truck Driver), Kathryn Adams (Young Mother), Pedro de Cordoba (Bones), Billy Curtis (Midget), Anita Le Deaux (Fat Woman), Anita Bolster (Lorelei), Jeanne Romer, Lynn Romer (Siamese Twins)
Filmed	at Universal Studios, Los Angeles
Running Time	approximately 109 minutes
Distributor	Universal
Release Date	April 1942

Other titles: *Saboteure, Cinquième Colonne, Sabotatori, Danger*

Synopsis

Under the credits, the shadow of a man walks toward a defense plant hangar.

Inside, the lunch horn sounds and the massive sliding doors open to let the crowd of workers out to the eating tables. Two young friends, Ken Mason and Barry Kane, bump into an unfriendly stranger who drops some letters and cash. They discover a $100 bill and Barry remembers the name on the letter, Frank Fry, and seeks the man out at one of the long tables to return it, but Fry snarls at him.

The silence of the empty factory gives way to ominous horn music as black smoke seeps into the brightly lit hangar and an alarm sounds. The workers race

inside, and Fry hands Barry an extinguisher, but Ken grabs it from him, exclaiming, "Don't I get to play, too?!" He runs over to the flames and is immediately engulfed himself.

Inside an office, a witness whose hands are swathed in bandages relates that he saw Barry pass the extinguisher to Ken, but did not notice anyone else. Barry is ushered in to tell his story, but chokes up, wide-eyed, at the remembrance of his friend's death.

Outside the office on the stair landing, the workers mill around, and one mention's Ken's mother; Barry suddenly leaves, though he has been told to "stick around."

Mrs. Mason sits grief stricken in her modest living room, when Barry arrives; he then goes to the kitchen to look for some brandy. A nosy neighbor invites him over to get some, while Mrs. Mason opens her front door to a couple of detectives who are looking for Barry, now a suspect. Even more distraught and confused at this news, she sends them away, telling them nothing. Barry returns and she tells him what she has learned; he is incredulous to hear there is no one named Fry at the plant and passionately proclaims his innocence. She asks him to go, and he sneaks out the back door when someone else knocks at the front.

That night, he rides along with an amiably chatting truck driver. Near Springville, Barry suddenly remembers the address on the letter to Fry: Deep Springs Ranch. A policeman stops the truck, and Barry starts to sneak off, but the officer just points out a missing taillight, hearing the bulletin about the fugitive after the truck pulls away.

Next morning, Barry gets off at Deep Springs Ranch. The maid invites him in but does not acknowledge the name Fry. Tobin, the owner, is playing in the large backyard swimming pool with his toddler grandchild, but he warmly greets Barry who blurts out his problem. Tobin cannot remember anyone named Fry. In Tobin's absence, the child hands Barry a letter from Fry in Soda City just as Tobin reappears and jokingly dismisses Barry, now confirmed by a radio report to be a saboteur. Barry persists, though Tobin confidently asserts that no one will ever believe him. When a servant pulls a gun on him, Barry grabs a horse, briefly using the child as a hostage. A posse of cowboys rope him in and take him back to the ranch where he is handed over to the police.

Barry fumes in the backseat of a car with the police, then, battering one of them with his handcuffed fists, he jumps out when the car is stuck behind a stalled truck. In a long shot, he leaps over a bridge into the river far below, hiding among some rocks in the rapids until his truck-driver friend from the night before helps him escape by pointing the detectives in the opposite direction. Triumphant orchestral music accompanies his scamper up the rocky bank.

During a storm, Barry furtively sneaks by the warmly lit windows of a log cabin in the woods. The occupant, Philip Martin, calmly invites him in to dry by the fire. Discovering Philip is blind, Barry stops hiding his handcuffs, but Patricia, the man's young blond niece, arrives, exclaiming about the escaped saboteur in the area. She and her uncle contentiously discuss the fugitive, whom she assumes is guilty, while Philip is more suspicious of the police, arguing, "How could they be heroes if he were harmless?" Aghast, she notices Barry's handcuffs and insists it's their duty to turn him in, but Philip, having heard the handcuffs when Barry arrived, pontificates about Barry's presumed innocence and insists she take him into town to the blacksmith to have the handcuffs removed.

Driving the car, Pat maneuvers Barry into wrapping his arms around the

wheel. Both angry, they argue about his situation, then he pins her to the door and starts steering himself. Stopping at a lonely place on the open road, she stomps off to flag down a car while he holds his handcuffed wrists up to a whirring flywheel on the engine. Finally succeeding in cutting the handcuffs, and breaking the car belt in the process, he grabs her off the road in front of a couple who have stopped to pick her up. He throws her screaming into the car, and the older couple marvel, commenting on how much they must be in love.

Police discover the stalled, abandoned car.

Pat and Barry spend the night in a field, arguing; the air is chilly and Pat leans against him for warmth. A caravan of circus vehicles winds toward them, and Pat runs to cry for help, but Barry subdues her. Then he warns her about snakes and hops on the end of the caravan himself. He insists she help him before giving her a hand up. Surprised at the intrusion, the group of entertainers inside the car gather around. Bones, the human skeleton; Esmerelda, the bearded lady; Tania, the fat lady; a male midget who wants to kick them out; and a pair of Siamese twins debate what to do with them. Bones finds in their predicament "a relationship to the present world situation" and pontificates about democracy, insisting they put the matter to a vote. Esmerelda, her beard in curlers and holding the deciding vote, passionately describes Pat as one of the "good people." The camera moves into a close-up of the wide-eyed Pat, who silently hears herself complimented for "standing by her man." The decision to hide them is made just in time, as the police have stopped the caravan and are searching every truck. When they arrive at their car, the group harasses the police, who flash their light on each of the occupants, including Pat, the "snake charmer." After they're gone, Pat warms to Barry and apologizes, admitting that the trusting circus people shamed her; they sleep.

Next day, Pat and Barry start walking the two miles through the mountainous desert to Soda City, now a ghost town. Inspecting a cobwebbed shack, they suddenly hear a telephone ring. Letting themselves into the adjoining office through an outside window, they find a field telephone and telescope equipment meant to view nearby Hoover Dam. Neilson, a worker, and Freeman, a well-dressed and refined city man in wire-rimmed glasses, arrive after Barry hides Pat in a side room. Becoming hysterical, Barry holds up his photo in the newspaper, convinces them he is on their side, and pleads that they must escort him out of the west. A door slams; the men investigate but find nothing.

Later, Pat, who has assumed Barry has betrayed her, discusses the case with a sheriff before her return to New York City.

Now well dressed and sitting in a sedan with Freeman, Barry views Hoover Dam while Freeman comments on Tobin's "good heart" and his own wonderful children: two small boys, one who likes to break things, the other who has long hair, just as Freeman did when he was a boy.

Later, the other men in the car sing as they ride through the country.

They enter New York City and Freeman becomes anxious because their office phone has been cut off; one of the gang mentions tomorrow's job in Brooklyn. They enter the back room of a drugstore, then an alleyway, and a huge kitchen on their way to an elegant residence where a ball is taking place. Finding Mrs. Sutton, the hostess, in an upstairs room, they listen to her tirade about their jeopardizing her social position. Pat is being held hostage there as well, as the sheriff turned out to be a friend of the "firm." Tobin joins them, reveals that they have all been exposed, and says Barry and Pat must be killed, though their planned operations

will continue. An intruder from the party gives Pat and Barry an opportunity to escape and join the crowd downstairs.

Barry makes some direct appeals to guests but gets cold stares in return as Tobin's men surround the ballroom. In love now, Pat and Barry dance; they decide to let her escape, then kiss passionately. A man rudely cuts in and dances Pat out of the room. Desperate, Barry begins to announce his predicament, but is dissuaded by a gun pointed at him from a balcony. Deciding instead to announce an auction of the hostess's jewelry, he then hands the proceedings over to a nearby gentleman before being led away.

He is taken upstairs to Tobin, who assures him that the "competence of the totalitarian nations is much higher than ours." "You really hate all people," replies Barry, insisting on the strength of the "good people from all countries who will fight for life and truth," until he is knocked out by a servant.

Outside the American Newsreel office, Freeman preps his men about an upcoming job. Inside he visits Pat, who is confined in a top floor of the building, eating her breakfast.

Barry sits shivering in the pantry of Mrs. Sutton's mansion with a can of food. Noticing a fire alarm, he sets it off. The servants scurry through the house.

Out in the street, Barry gawks with the crowd, notices an article about a new ship launching at the Brooklyn Navy Yard, and hops into a cab.

In the Newsreel office, many stories up, Pat writes a note with lipstick for help and throws it out the window. Half-way down, it sticks in a windowsill long enough for the soundtrack to pick up the radio broadcast of the ship launching, then floats down and lands near some cab drivers, who are listening to the same broadcast. They spot her S.O.S. signal high above them.

At the shipyard, Barry demands to see "the guy in charge," then, ignored, runs off to the launch site by himself. He discovers Fry sitting in the back of a Newsreel truck and tackles him. The radio continues to blare the events of the ship launch as they struggle, and Fry manages to reach the button to set off the bomb just as the ship is moving away from the dock. The Newsreel truck speeds out while Fry holds Barry with a gun in his back.

They take him up to the Newsreel office, now full of police summoned by Pat's note. Surprised, Fry and the men race back to the elevator and split up.

Fry enters a large movie theater where a melodrama plays out the gunshot-filled denouement. Police converge on the theater and a shootout ensues, covered by the sound effects of the film. Fry ends up silhouetted on the stage, a smoking gun in his hand. The audience panics as they are told to get out, and one of them is shot by him, but Fry effectively hides himself in the crowd and hops into a cab outside.

At the same instant, Pat and Barry are being escorted from the building by the police when Barry tells Pat to jump into a cab and follow Fry. "It's our only chance!" he yells, as the police lead him away.

En route to the Statue of Liberty ferry, Fry and Pat, in their separate taxis, pass the new ship lying on its side in the water. On the ferry, Pat eyes Fry who eyes her back. On Liberty Island, Pat calls the FBI for help.

Up in the crown of the statue, Pat stands next to Fry and flirts with him, but he insists on catching the next ferry out until she boldly calls him by name. Angered, he turns back to grab her just as the police and Barry arrive. Fry flees the stairwell for the outside of the statue's torch held high above the water. Barry races after him and confronts him with a gun. Fry falls over the side of the railing,

and is left clinging to the hand of the statue as Barry climbs down and holds him up by the sleeve, but the sleeve tears and Fry drops to his death. Barry climbs back up and embraces Pat.

Note. Hitchcock reportedly does bit as man at a newsstand. He is not recognizable in print viewed.

31   *Shadow of a Doubt* (1943)

Director	Alfred Hitchcock
Assistant Director	William Tummell
Producer	Jack H. Skirball
Production Company	Universal-Skirball Productions
Screenplay	Thornton Wilder, Alma Reville, Sally Benson, from an original story by Gordon McDonnell
Photography	Joseph Valentine
Editing	Milton Carruth
Art Direction	John B. Goodman, Robert Boyle (associate)
Set Direction	R. A. Gausman, E. R. Robinson (associate)
Sound	Bernard B. Brown, Robert Pritchard (technician)
Music	Dimitri Tiomkin (score), Charles Previn (director)
Costumes	Adrian, Vera West
Cast	Joseph Cotton (Charles Oakley [Uncle Charlie]), Teresa Wright (Charlie Newton), MacDonald Carey (Jack Graham), Patricia Collinge (Emma Newton), Henry Travers (Joe Newton), Hume Cronyn (Herb Hawkins), Wallace Ford, Charles Bates, Edna May Wonacott, Irving Bacon, Clarence Muse, Janet Shaw, Estelle Jewell
Filmed	at Universal Studios, Los Angeles
Running Time	approximately 108 minutes
Distributor	Universal
Release Date	January 1943

Other titles: *Im Schatten des Zweifels, L'Ombre d'un Doute, L'Ombra del Dubbio*

Synopsis

The "Merry Widow Waltz" plays: dancers in billowing ball gowns waltz, filling the screen as the credits pass.

A cityscape with river bridge. The camera passes over a junkyard to children playing on a working-class city block, then into a window of one of the row houses

with rented rooms. Charles Oakley lies fully dressed on his bed vacantly playing with his cigar, money strewn on the table and floor. The landlady enters to tell him two men called but she didn't let them in per his instructions. He speaks cryptically and tells her to let them in when they return. On leaving, she pulls down the blind, the shadows crossing his face. After she leaves, he sits up, drains a glass, and, rising, suddenly throws it at the sink. He goes to the window, sees the two men standing on the corner and mutters "You've nothing on me." As the music escalates, he goes out, walks directly toward and past them. They follow, but lose him in an abandoned lot. From high above, Charles watches them regroup.

At a telephone in a pool hall, Charles calls in a telegram to Santa Rosa, California: "Will arrive Thursday . . . try and stop me . . . a kiss for little Charlie from her Uncle Charlie, Love, Uncle Charlie."

Santa Rosa, a small town nestled in hills. An officer directs traffic downtown. Nearby is a large clapboard home with bay windows and a wraparound porch. The camera enters a window upstairs where Charlie lies in her bedroom, staring out. The telephone rings.

Downstairs, Ann, around eight years old, reluctantly picks up the phone, still reading her book. Unwilling to look for a pencil, she fails to get the telegram message, saying her mother will call back. Joe, the father, arrives home and assumes the message is about an accident. Ann teases him about the book in his pocket, *Unsolved Crimes*. He goes upstairs to speak with Charlie, who's "been thinking for hours" because her family "has gone to pieces . . . we're in a terrible rut." He tries to console her with his new raise, but she says she's not talking about money, but souls, and laments the condition of her poor mother, who "works like a dog." Emma, her mother, enters and Charlie sits up at the sight of the "horrible hat" she's worn downtown. They both go downstairs and Charlie, still frowning, gets a sudden idea and follows them down the stairs and out to send a telegram to Uncle Charlie. Emma calls about the telegram and is ecstatic to hear her brother is on his way.

Telegraph office. Charlie writes at the counter but the clerk interrupts and gives her the telegram from her uncle to take home. She's ecstatic about the "mental telepathy."

The train. Uncle Charlie hides behind a curtain; he has told the porter he's too sick to see anyone.[H]

Joe and the children, including Roger, five years old or so, drive up to the station as the train pulls in, steam blackening the sky. Uncle Charlie limps off, but recovers quickly when he sees them. Charlie notices and comments how "strange" his appearance is.

At the house, Emma rushes out to meet her brother, who insists she looks more like the Emma of her maiden name. Charlie is ecstatic.

Joe takes Uncle Charlie to Charlie's room where Charlie has insisted her uncle will stay. Uncle Charlie is pleased and throws his hat on the bed, even though Joe has warned him about this superstition.

The dinner table. Uncle Charlie holds forth with a description of a faraway place, then brings out presents, including a mink collar for his sister. Charlie says she doesn't want anything and goes into the kitchen. Uncle Charlie follows her, where she continues to insist she's just happy to have him there. She talks about their secretive natures and special relationship, "like twins." He puts a ring on her finger and she notices the engraving of strange initials inside. He's slightly

taken aback. "The jeweler must have fooled me," and offers to return it, but she insists on keeping it.

The dancers turn round the ballroom.

Charlie starts to hum the waltz. Back at the dinner table, Uncle Charlie talks about putting some money in the bank where Joe works, thirty or forty thousand dollars. Charlie tries to name her tune, wondering where it came from and if music "jumps from head to head." Uncle Charlie becomes nervous, telling her it's "The Blue Danube" waltz, but she frowns and remembers it's the "Merry—" but he knocks over his glass of wine before she can finish her thought.

They move to the living room where Emma gives Uncle Charlie her husband's newspaper. A neighbor, Herb, arrives and he and Joe go out.

On the front porch, the men, both true crime fans, avidly discuss techniques for killing one another.

Inside, Uncle Charlie smokes and reads the newspaper, which fills the screen, then lets it fall to reveal his self-conscious face. He calls Ann over to watch him make a house out of the paper which she politely does. Ann and Roger, and then Charlie are alarmed at the obliteration of their father's paper. Charlie puts it back together, wondering about a couple of missing pages that the camera shows her uncle folding behind his back.

Charlie carries a tray upstairs to Uncle Charlie in his room. As she is leaving she spies the newspaper in his pocket and turns around to tell him that she knows a secret about him, triumphantly grabbing the missing newspaper page and spreading it before him. Heretofore remaining calmly shining his shoes, he rises quickly, walks over to her and wrenches her arms down and the paper away from her, keeping a tight grip on her wrists. She is shocked, but he tells her he was only fooling, and the item was only gossip about a friend.

Outside, the town clock chimes.

In Ann's room, she and Charlie prepare for sleep, turn out the light, and lie down. Charlie hums the "Merry Widow Waltz."

Uncle Charlie sits up in bed, blowing out smoke rings.

Next day, Emma brings Uncle Charlie breakfast in bed. She unpacks his bags and tells him about upcoming events: they're going to be interviewed and photographed as a typical family, and her women's group wants him to give a lecture. He discourages the interview, at one point blurting out that "women are fools," then softening his disapproval, but insisting he has never been photographed and never will be. Charlie produces an old photograph of him as a child and Emma tells of a childhood bicycle accident that nearly killed him.

The two Charlies walk downtown to the bank. Some friends of hers eye his fancy black and white outfit.

At Joe's teller window, Uncle Charlie loudly teases Joe about embezzling. Charlie is disturbed by this, but Joe patiently ushers them into the manager's office to open the account. Uncle Charlie disdains the procedure, until the manager's wife and a friend interrupt. Uncle Charlie flirts with the friend, who lets him know she's a widow. As they exist, he teases Joe about taking his boss's position.

Two men sit in a car in front of the Newtons' home. They spot the two Charlies returning in a taxi. When Charlie walks up to meet the "interviewers," Uncle Charlie brushes by and goes upstairs.

In the living room, the visitors are an hour early; Emma is upset. They try to insist on interviewing Uncle Charlie too, but Charlie tells them perhaps they

should find another family, and they quickly agree to the restriction of excluding him.

Taken to the kitchen, they continue to ask questions, mostly about Uncle Charlie; Emma continues to be miffed at being caught unprepared. Charlie takes Jack Graham and Saunders, the photographer, upstairs where Saunders goes into Charlie's room to photograph it (Uncle Charlie has disappeared) while Charlie tells Jack how much happier she is now and that her uncle is there. She starts to fiddle with her hands, disturbed at his coolness toward her enthusiasm. Emma calls up that she's ready to be photographed just as Uncle Charlie appears at the back stairs. Saunders takes a picture of him, but to Charlie's embarrassment, Uncle Charlie demands the film and Saunders hands it over. They go downstairs and Jack asks to take Charlie out that evening. On the porch, Charlie tells her mother she'll feign illness to break her date with her friend.

From the sidewalk, the camera views Charlie and Jack sitting in the window of a diner talking and laughing. They exit to the street, laughing gaily. Outside a theater, they meet her friend who thought she was sick, and Charlie is embarrassed, but she laughs, flirting with Jack.

The camera rests, then moves out from a close-up of Charlie, anxious and wide-eyed, to show her and Jack sitting on a park bench. "You lied to me . . . you're a detective!" He explains that he's hunting a man, who might be her uncle, and convinces her to "keep her mouth shut."

He drives her home and says good night. Out front, Charlie pauses on the porch, noticing through the window her uncle and mother talking in the front room. Worried, she turns and walks around the house, running into her father and Herb, who tells her Uncle Charlie's been looking for her. She says she would rather just go up the back way. Joe and Herb walk on, talking about poisoned coffee.

Upstairs, Charlie pauses, then decides to enter her own room and searches the waste basket for the newspaper. Back in Ann's room, she tries to find the article, but Ann tells her she can find the whole thing at the library. Charlie says it's only a recipe, but wonders when the library closes (9:00 P.M.), and goes out.

In the hall, she pauses for a moment, then runs down the back stairs and walks quickly downtown. At a crowded intersection, she walks in front of a car and the traffic officer yells at her to get back on the curb. It's 8:55 P.M.; finally the light changes. As she steps out, the officer stops and reprimands her. The piano concerto music culminates as she races up the steps of the library just in time to see the lights go out. She pleads with the librarian, who lectures her, but allows her to find the newspaper. Charlie sits, appalled to find the headline "Where Is the Merry Widow Murderer" over a story about a nationwide search. She takes off the ring her uncle had given her and sees the initials in it are those of a victim. Broken, she rises and walks slowly out, and the dancers and music appear.

The next morning, Uncle Charlie walks in their yard, reading the paper. He looks up at Emma poking her head out of a window and asks about Charlie. She's still sleeping.

That evening, in the sitting room, Emma announces that Charlie has just awakened.

Upstairs, Charlie listens at the top of the stairwell, then goes out the back door. She enters the kitchen and tells her mother that she will finish making dinner. Emma hums the "Merry Widow Waltz" and Charlie tells her she must

stop "humming that tune." Ann enters and announces she wants to sit next to her mother, not Uncle Charlie.

They all sit down to dinner as Joe hands Uncle Charlie the paper, and Charlie prepares herself to face him. She walks in and tells him she's been having nightmares all day about him "on the train . . . running away from something." She rises to clear the dishes, and comments that "we all have to face facts." Ann informs Uncle Charlie that "no one is allowed to read at the table; it isn't polite" and Charlie adds, "We needn't play any games with it tonight." Uncle Charlie opens some wine and they all become gayer as he warms to an intensely felt subject, the rich men of the city who die and leave fortunes to "their silly wives . . . useless women . . . proud of their jewelry but nothing else." The camera moves in to an extreme close-up of his profiled face (from Charlie's viewpoint) and Charlie interrupts, "They're alive! They're human beings!" "Are they?" he responds, turning to look (directly into the camera) at her, but Charlie averts her eyes. Emma hopes Uncle Charlie will not speak like that to her friends. Herb arrives and sits in the corner near Joe. They start to whisper about poisonous mushrooms and drowning in the bathtub—"been done, but it's still good." Suddenly, the camera views the room from above as Charlie jumps up and screams, "Do you always have to talk about killing people?" She stomps out of the house, and Uncle Charlie goes after her.

She races ahead, unaware that he is following until she bumps into the traffic officer at the busy intersection and Uncle Charlie grabs her arm, apologizing to the officer. Moving on, he demands to know what's wrong, but she only tries to escape from him. Finally he pushes her into a bar, the Till Two.

Inside the smoke-filled, noisy place, they sit in a booth. A classmate of Charlie's waits on them, commenting she never thought she'd see Charlie in there. Uncle Charlie questions his niece aggressively ("What did he tell you?!") and, alternately, tries to smooth-talk her into being more sympathetic. She is sick, finally showing him the ring. The waitress arrives and comments that she'd "just die for a piece of jewelry like that." Her uncle snidely lectures Charlie on her ordinary life and she finally walks out.

He follows. On their front walk, he asks her to help him, pleading for a few days, reminding what revealing his past would do to his sister, and even mentioning the electric chair. She sends him in alone, pausing at the doorway to watch him carry Ann upstairs on his back. Despondent, she leans on the porch post, looks to the sky, and cries.

Church services are over and the congregation is leaving. Jack and Saunders wait across the street and call Ann to fetch her sister. Saunders takes Charlie along on the walk home and tells her they've identified Uncle Charlie as one of two suspects. She agrees to tell them when he leaves town, but refuses to offer more information. Jack, previously walking ahead with Ann and another friend, joins them to pressure her more.

The group breaks up in front of the Newton house, and Ann and Charlie meet their uncle on the porch. Below them, Herb and Joe round the corner of the house, discussing the death of the Merry Widow murderer in Maine. Charlie is stupefied, but her uncle exultantly starts up the hall stairs to get ready for dinner. The camera follows his back up the stairs as he stops suddenly and turns slowly, thoughtfully, to see Charlie standing out on the porch looking up at him.

In his room upstairs, Uncle Charlie paces the diagonal frame of the camera, finally letting his cigar drop and his hands form a circle as he contemplates

Charlie who is standing out on the walk. He sees Jack drive up and the pair walk to the back of the house.

Jack announces the investigation is over as they talk near the garage. Charlie is very distracted. Moving inside the garage, he shyly discusses their future, his love for her, and a possible marriage. The garage door slams closed and they struggle to push it open. Outside, Uncle Charlie waits on the lawn and they all say good-bye. Charlie calls after Jack as he drives off, then turns around to face her uncle, who stands on the porch. She walks toward him, then veers off away from him to the back of the house.

Later, on the back porch, Charlie calls out to her mother for additions to the grocery list, then starts down the stairs. She trips and falls midway, and the camera swoops down to show Uncle Charlie peeking through the banister at her. He moves away when Emma comes down to help her, noting that she "could have been killed." Realizing her predicament, Charlie frowns at the broken stair, then up at the second story of the house. Inside, Uncle Charlie pauses at the top of the stairs, listening.

That night, Charlie inspects the staircase with a flashlight. Uncle Charlie appears above on the porch. He tells her he wants to settle down there when Charlie asks when he's leaving. She tells him to go away or "I'll kill you myself."

Another evening, Uncle Charlie leaves the car running inside the garage, removes the key, and closes the door. Back in the house everyone is dressed up to go to the lecture. Uncle Charlie insists that the rest of the family take a taxi, and he and Charlie will drive in the family car. Charlie goes out, but first grabs her mother's wrists and pleads with her to ride with them.

Charlie walks to the garage to find it full of fumes and the key gone from the car. The door closes behind her.

Inside, her uncle returns from upstairs and mentions it's cold, closing a window and turning up the music. Herb suddenly rushes in, saying someone is trapped in the garage. They all run and Charlie collapses to the ground when Uncle Charlie kicks a stick from under the door and opens it. He quickly goes in and turns off the car. Charlie lies stretched out on the grass and he runs to kneel over her, but she looks up and firmly tells him to go away. They all decide to go and leave Charlie as she insists she is all right. The camera pauses on Emma in the backseat of the car, ruminating on Charlie's fall, and "now this."

Charlie rushes inside and makes several unsuccessful calls on the telephone to find Jack. She goes up to Uncle Charlie's room and searches it.

Later, the group returns for the after-lecture party. Uncle Charlie passes champagne and the others, including a clergyman, toast this fine addition to their community. Uncle Charlie raises a glass to Charlie when she appears on the staircase but stops short as the camera moves into a close-up of the ring on her hand; suddenly he announces that he is leaving the next morning. Emma is shaken at this, and he speaks sentimentally to appease her: "I'll miss you . . . and this place of hospitality and kindness and homes." Tears come to Emma's eyes as the embarrassed guests bow their heads, and the camera moves in on a distraught Charlie, who watches her mother lament her present life and the loss of her brother. "We were so close . . . and then I got married. You know how it is. You sort of forget you're you. I'm my husband's wife."

Next morning, friends and family bid Uncle Charlie goodbye at the station. He invites Charlie and the children onto the train with him, then maneuvers to be alone with her in the corridor, grabbing her hands and talking until the train

is moving. She panics and runs between cars, where she is trapped with him and he tries to push her off. They struggle, reversing positions, and he falls into the path of an oncoming train.

A funeral procession. The church. Charlie stands at the front door with Jack as Uncle Charlie is eulogized. "I couldn't have faced it without someone who knew," she says, wondering just how bad the world really is. He tells her it's not so bad; "It just goes crazy sometimes, like your Uncle Charlie."

Note. [H]Hitchcock does bit as man playing cards on train.

Remake: for television, *Shadow of a Doubt* (U.S. 1991), directed by Karen Arthur.

32   *Lifeboat* (1944)

Director	Alfred Hitchcock
Producer	Kenneth MacGowan
Production Company	20th Century-Fox
Screenplay	Jo Swerling, based on an original subject by John Steinbeck
Photography	Glen MacWilliams, A.S.C.
Editing	Dorothy Spencer
Art Direction	James Basevi, Maurice Ransford
Set Direction	Thomas Little, Frank E. Hughes
Sound	Bernard Freericks, Roger Heman
Special Effects	Fred Sersen
Music	Hugo Friedhofer
Costumes	Rene Hubert
Makeup	Guy Pearce
Technical Adviser	Thomas Fitzsimmons, National Maritime Union
Cast	Tallulah Bankhead (Constance [Connie] Porter), William Bendix (Gus Smith), Walter Slezak (Willie), Mary Anderson (Alice), John Hodiak (Kovac), Henry Hull (Charles Rittenhaus), Heather Angel, Hume Cronyn (Stanley Garrett), Canada Lee (Joe)
Filmed	at Twentieth Century-Fox Studios, Los Angeles
Running Time	approximately 96 minutes
Distributor	Twentieth Century-Fox
Release Date	January 1944

Other titles: *Das Rettungsboot, I Prigionieri Dell'Oceano*

Synopsis

Climactic music and an explosion accompany the credits over the smokestack of a ship.

The ship disappears in the tumultuous ocean as cargo and personal belongings float to the surface. Voices cry out in the distance accompanied by peaceful,

dramatic music. Fog takes over as the water calms; a body floats by, face down, and the camera moves out to find the glamorous Constance Porter, a photographer, alone in a lifeboat. A man swims toward her and she takes a few moving picture shots before helping him aboard. Kovac is from the engine room of the ship, where everyone was "slaughtered"; Constance excitedly tells him of all the great shots she has in her camera. Disgusted, he bats a baby bottle away from her lens before she can capture "the perfect touch." "Why don't you wait for the baby to float by!" he shouts. Another survivor calls out and Kovac spills Constance's camera into the water as he hurriedly responds. Angry, but never failing to cross her legs gracefully, Constance berates him as he pulls in Stanley "Sparks" Garrett who, like Kovak, is covered in oil and grime. Quickly, they come across three others floating on some scrap: Alice MacKenzie, a nurse; C. J. "Rit" Rittenhouse, a wealthy businessman; and Gus Smith, a sailor with a badly wounded leg who had changed his name from Schmidt. Alice works to remove the shrapnel from Gus's leg as old friends Rit and Connie trade quips. Someone else calls out, and "Charcoal" Joe Spencer appears, carrying with him Mrs. Iggley and her child, whom the group quietly notices is dead, though no one mentions it. As they are discussing her case, a German, Willie, climbs aboard.

Later, Constance interprets Willie's story; he assures them he was merely a crew member, but Kovac demands he be thrown overboard and accuses Connie of German sympathies when she attempts to defend him. Connie, the only one who is clean, and in fact, perfectly made-up and coiffed, stands in the middle of the bedraggled, exhausted group, calmly smoking and posed, one elbow resting on the other arm at her waist. Rit, a self-described Christian and democrat, recommends at length a peaceful, humanitarian solution. Each in turn tries to respond to the predicament raised by the German: Sparks suggests waiting for proper authority, Alice complains that she does not understand the issue, and Joe opts to "stay out of it." Suddenly Mrs. Iggley realizes her child is dead. They grope for a burial prayer, and Joe dramatically steps into profile in the foreground with the words, "The Lord is my shepherd . . ."

Later, Mrs. Iggley wakes, then becomes hysterical as she remembers where she is and attempts to join her baby in the sea. The others subdue and tie her down.

Next morning, Rit is asleep on watch when Sparks wakes him to discuss their fate—little water or food, a leaky boat, and a broken compass. Suddenly, they notice Mrs. Iggley has pitched herself overboard and floats dead at the end of her rope.

Later, a close-up reveals a compass hidden in the German's hand. Rit disburses supplies and assigns jobs to the others, suggesting they get organized.[H] Some comment on their self-appointed captain, while Kovac and Connie revisit their quarrel about the nature of her work, and Gus reminisces about his girlfriend at home, Rosie. A tattered sail is raised, prompting discussion about their course and who is to lead them. A lengthy discussion ensues, Rit and Connie inclined to trust the German's motives so they can use his expertise, and Willie smilingly reassuring them all that he would, of course, prefer POW status in Bermuda to the lifeboat. Sparks and Gus, the only sailors, are both disinclined to assume leadership, and Kovac finally demands to take charge, as Rit demurs to the others' lack of faith in his abilities and Willie is assessed to be untrustworthy for the position. Constance has addressed him as "Captain" and he has revealed

himself by responding. They decide to go in the opposite direction to the one he suggests, reversing the sail and sending Connie's typewriter into the sea.

Later, Joe plays a pipe as Sparks and Alice, at the helm, speak of his life in the merchant marine. Connie complains about the loss of her possessions as she kneels next to Kovac and Rit, who play cards with a deck Kovac has made from Connie's memo pad. The camera moves with Connie into a close-up of Kovac's chest tattoo, "BM" in a heart. Suddenly Alice rises to help Gus and unbandages his leg, which is now gangrenous. Saying he is a doctor, Willie offers to amputate. Eventually Connie convinces Gus to cooperate, to "trust Rosie" not to reject him as a "gimp." She gives him her brandy, which he guzzles, and then he asks her for a kiss and Joe for some music; they both oblige. Preparations continue as a wind comes up; a close-up shows the group's hands protecting the lighter flame that sterilizes the knife. The men hold Gus down as the sea becomes very rough and the operation proceeds.

Later, the boat is calm as Willie furtively studies his compass, and the subject of their course—whether or not they are headed for Bermuda—comes up. Willie suggests they are not, and Connie believes him, arguing that they need to get Gus to a hospital soon, but Kovac insists that Willie cannot be trusted and is probably sending them toward a German supply ship. The others listen and decide to switch to the German's course, swayed by his assumed superior knowledge. Turning from them, Willie checks his compass.

That night, as Sparks's legs dangle above them, Connie listens to Alice admit she is in love with a married doctor; Connie then feigns sleep, forcing Alice to rise and join Sparks at the helm and finish telling her story to him. Stars dot the sky behind them. Suddenly Sparks recognizes Mars and Venus in the sky and realizes they are headed away from Bermuda.

Next morning, Willie sleeps as the rest discuss his betrayal and set Joe, a reformed pickpocket, on him to steal his "watch." They are all holding their collars up around their necks now, because of a cold wind. They discover the compass and Kovac gets out his knife to execute Willie, but the others object, a storm rising with their tension. Suddenly they are overtaken by waves and Gus is thrown in the water. To their surprise, Willie barks orders at them in English as they work to tie Gus to the mast, and bail out the boat. They are unable to save their water and rations; the sail breaks off and Connie and Kovac prepare to go down together—kissing. Water rushes everywhere.

The torrents dissolve into a long shot of the boat on a calm sea. Willie rows and sings a song in German to Rit's pipe. Under the wreckage, Sparks unties Alice's hair bow and, above, Connie lounges across Kovac's lap. Kovak lectures Willie and the others that they are prisoners of Willie, who sings them "German lullabies" while he takes them to a concentration camp. Willie convinces them that Bermuda is too far away and they must head for the German supply ship. Willie insists that only he need row, and they are too exhausted to object. Gus is delirious from thirst, while Connie pokes her finger through Kovac's paper. She wonders about his other women and about their relationship, softly offering that they're from the same neighborhood; he demands to know the story of her diamond bracelet, then responds to her smooth talk and kisses her, throwing her off with a sneer, "Quit slumming!" They move to the other end to join the rest of the group. Willie offers to fix Connie's bracelet: "He likes you," he advises her about Kovac, "but he hates the bracelet." Alice repeatedly reminds Gus not to

drink from the ocean as the others discuss restaurants, making Connie faint, then hysterical. She blames Rit for the loss of their supplies, then cries out that Willie is made of iron and they are just "hungry flesh and blood!" Rit and Kovac, slowed by their condition and on edge, play poker until Rit has his winning hand blown away by a gust of wind and then irrationally accuses Kovac of cheating. Rain comes, lasting just long enough for them excitedly to hold out the sail and watch some drops dapple it. Despondent, they all peer at the sky as Gus drinks from the ocean.

Later that evening, Willie rows as Gus, stupefied, verbalizes his fantasies and asks Rosie for a drink; the others lie about deep in sleep. Willie surreptitiously takes a drink from a flask; Gus half-comprehends and tries to wake Sparks, but Willie subdues him with encouragement to "go off to Rosie." Willie pushes him overboard; Gus cries out for help, then disappears under the water just as Sparks wakes and alarms the others. The group stands opposite Willie, his eyes in extreme close-up and their consciousness of his enmity and evil becoming complete as they comment on his sweat and good health. Sparks remembers Gus's calling for help and saying something about water. Joe pulls the flask from inside Willie's shirt, and it falls to the floor and breaks open. Willie calmly informs them that he had food and energy tablets too. He laments it is "too bad Schmidt" couldn't wait, as they all will be saved soon, thanks to his foresight. Alice screams and leaps at him, quickly followed by the others, who beat on him with fists and sticks. Joe alone stands aside, pleading with "Miss Alice" to stop when she is momentarily thrown back near him. They push Willie overboard and struggle to break his grip on the edge of the boat; then Rit finishes him off with Gus's shoe.

Later, they sit scattered around the boat, stunned, hanging their heads and silent, except for Rit, who wonders aloud how Willie could do what he did, and what they are going to do now without their "motor." Joe looks up to heaven, Sparks proposes to Alice, and Connie, feisty again, provokes them, "So we're all going to fold up and die just because that ersatz superman is gone." Rit will not be moved; "My only regret [is] I joined a mob." Nonsense, objects Connie, "We weren't a mob when we killed him, we were a mob when we sat around . . . obeying him." Accusing them of being quitters, she shouts, "We not only let the Nazi do our rowing for us, but our thinking!" Her mind wandering over the word "fishes," she offers her bracelet as bait in a new effort at catching some. They all eagerly line up at the side of the boat and throw a line over. Underneath in the water a big one bites. As they start to pull him up, Joe spots a ship, and, in the confusion, they let the fish and bait go. Connie laughs hysterically.

Later, they wait sullenly as a rowboat from the German supply ship approaches, then inexplicably turns back. Shelling begins from an American ship on the horizon, and the German ship starts speeding toward them. Rowing furiously, they finally surrender to the foamy path that surrounds them, crouching in the bottom of the boat as the ship glides by.

Rising afterward, they watch the battle, as torpedoes find their way into the German ship and it goes down. Assured of safety, Joe mentions his wife and family ("Those things happen to everybody you know."). Connie becomes upset about "looking a fright" and grabs her lipstick while Rit offers Kovac $50,000 for poker losses. A pair of hands grip the side of the boat and they pull up a young German sailor, who pulls a gun on them, but is disarmed by Joe. They hold back Rit, who wants to throw him overboard, while the youth wonders why they don't kill him. Philosophical, Kovac marvels at the boy's pessimism: "What do you do

with people like that?" Sparks remembers Mrs. Iggley and her baby, and Gus. The camera moves into a close-up of Connie as she replies to Kovac, "Well, maybe they can answer that."

Note. ᴴHitchcock is man in "Reduco" advertisement in newspaper held by Gus.

33   *Bon Voyage* (1944)

Director	Alfred Hitchcock
Producer	British Ministry of Information
Production Company	Phoenix Films
Screenplay	[J. O. C. Orton, Angus McPhail, based on an original subject by Arthur Calder-Marshall]*
Photography	[Gunther Krampf]*
Set Direction	[Charles Gilbert]*
Cast	John Blythe (Sergeant John Dougall), the Molière Players†
Filmed	at Associated British Studios, Welwyn
Running Time	approximately 35 minutes
Release Date	1944††

Synopsis

Street scenes of London, 1943. Sergeant John Dougall, of the Royal Air Force, has just escaped from Germany and is being questioned about his trip by an officer of the French Deuxième Bureau.

The French officer sits behind a desk in a large government office, a portrait of General De Gaulle behind him on the wall. He apologizes to a British officer about "disturbing him with this business," and then receives John. John, guileless and cooperative, refuses compliments on his escape and credits his Polish companion, Stefan Godovsky, with its success. Wondering if Stefan escaped as well, he expresses sorrow when told he did not, but the officer merely persists with his questioning, to which John responds with his story.

Flashback. Stefan and John crouch near a stone wall with a marker pointing to Rheims. They jump through a large crack to hide; John offers half of his last English cigarette, while Stefan reads their instructions to go to the Café du Commerce in Rheims. Stefan decides to go alone because John's accent is too noticeable.

Later, John jumps out of the hiding place to meet Stefan, who nearly faints. He has hurt his wrist; while John wraps it for him, Stefan relates that he was followed from the café (where no one met him) by a Gestapo agent. He slipped into a nearby cellar, but the agent followed him. Smiling oddly, Stefan admits that he killed him. John suggests they must do something about the body, so the two set off for the cellar.

They enter the cavernous wine cellar through a door on top of a landing and discover the body is gone. Hearing a noise, they crouch behind some casks but are discovered by a man and woman, members of the Resistance, who tell them they followed Stefan before and have already disposed of the body. John proudly tells

them he is a member of the RAF, and he and Stefan are both escaped prisoners of war trying to get to England—also, they are very hungry. "Poor children," comments the woman, and the man gives them directions to a farm, where they will find bicycles, papers, and food in a stable.

Two bicycles await them in the shining, early-morning straw of the stable. They tiptoe up to them; John grabs some bread while Stefan discovers further instructions to go to a hotel. John is amazed at their good luck ("a bed!") and they set off.

Next morning John rests on a white pillow in a darkened room. A blind snaps up letting in bright light as two suited men, introducing themselves as police, demand his papers. He genially tells them he is an Irish mechanic on his way to Rheims and they leave. Stefan sneaks in directly after and excitedly demands to know what he told them. John is lackadaisical, "Oh, I said what I said . . . one of them thought I was from Scotland!" Stefan relaxes and pulls some old, dirty clothes out of one of the dresser drawers, presenting them as the disguise in the next step of their escape. They will catch the 9:42 train and sit in a designated compartment, where John will read a paper, which Stefan will ask to borrow. John will reply that it is Monday's paper and this will be the cue for a Resistance agent to contact them. "Disgusting," frowns John as they put on the dirty clothes.

A crowded (five abreast) train compartment. John at one end reads his newspaper and signals Stefan, who sits across from him between two other passengers. Getting a nod, John says his line and a woman next to Stefan cheerfully responds. The compartment darkens as they go through a tunnel. Suddenly the train stops and the woman opens the outside door and directs the two men to jump out in front of her.

Back in the office, John explains that the conductor as well was a member of the Resistance. As the British officer sits in an easy chair in the back and listens, John continues, somewhat sheepishly, to relate how Jeanne took them to her father's farm, where there was a plane leaving for England with only one seat. He and Stefan tossed for it and he won. "And then we ate!" he adds.

In her kitchen, Jeanne tends Stefan's wound as he leans against the long center table while John sits at the end and eats. She tells John that a car will take him to the plane and Stefan thanks her, then bids good-bye to both. As she picks up John's empty plate, he offers her a cigarette and mentions that he has not smoked since Rheims when Stefan got cigarettes at the Café de Commerce. As she lights his cigarette, she wonders if it was not the Café des Marronniers, but John replies no and tells her the story of Stefan killing the Nazi. She frowns at this, but they are interrupted by the sound of a car outside and he runs upstairs to gather his things to go.

Back in the London office, the French officer indicates he is aware of a letter Stefan gave John and asks him to tell him the name and address of the person for whom it was intended. John replies that he gave his word not to. The officer says that it is his duty, but John disagrees. Standing now, a sandbag bunker outside his window, the officer tells John that Stefan was really a Gestapo agent and that the real Stefan is still a prisoner of war. John is incredulous, insisting that they must be misinformed even though the British officer nods in support of the revelation; John apologizes for his position but takes in his breath and stiffens. The French officer then tells his version of the escape from Rheims.

Flashback to the dark alleyway, where Stefan goes down into the wine cellar and meets a man named Oscar Henberg. Stefan wanted to abandon the project

because the Resistance could identify him at the Café du Commerce, but Oscar insisted that they continue because it was important to help John back to London.

Piano music accompanies the officer's narration of the scene in the Café des Marrionniers, where Stefan sits near the bar and drinks some wine. At a table next to him, Oscar reads a paper. Another suited man, another spy, enters and stands at the bar. Stefan conspicuously rises to light his cigarette from a standing lighter attached to the bar. The couple from the Resistance, seated near the door, observe him also. He leaves, followed by the Nazi, then the couple. Oscar watches from his seat.

In the darkened alley, Stefan waits, then steps into the cellar, where the spy warily meets him at the bottom of the stairs. The man asks for Stefan's papers, all the while holding a gun on him. As he looks away to inspect the documents, Stefan rises up and punches him in the back with his fist. They struggle, the spy's hands at Stefan's throat. The wind whisks debris through the alley outside. The spy staggers up the stairs after Stefan, who now has the gun and shoots him. Grabbing his hurt wrist, Stefan staggers out into the alleyway as the couple, standing in the opposite doorway, observe him.

Back in the office, John earnestly wonders why one spy would kill another, and the officer explains that it was to convince the Resistance that he was the real Stefan. He continues to explain how Stefan duped the man and woman as well as the proprietor of the hotel. John realizes that the two "police" at the hotel must have been fake.

Flashback to the hotel corridor. The two policemen go to Stefan's door where, smirking, he shows them his papers; they immediately bow and tip their hats. "Perfect," he explains at their fortuitous appearance and tells them which train they will be on and where they will sit; then he sends them to John's room. Oscar appears in the corridor as well.

Back at the office, John asks if the Nazis perhaps thought he was one of them, but the officer thinks they were using him for protection. John wonders about Oscar Henberg's fate.

Flashback to the train in the tunnel. Stefan, John, and Jeanne jump out. Oscar gets up to follow but he is set upon by the other passengers in the compartment.

Back in the office, the French officer also tells John that Stefan deliberately lost the toss for the seat because he needed John to deliver his message.

Flashback to the farm as John runs up the stairs to get ready to leave. Jeanne's father comes in and says that there was a spy on the train but that he has been captured; Jeanne thinks this is strange as they usually travel in pairs. John bounds down the stairs and bids Jeanne a warm farewell, hoping to see her again. After the two men have gone, Jeanne rushes to the telephone. Frowning, she dials a number, but a strange hand covers the receiver and Stefan appears next to her as the camera cuts from a gun in her side to an extreme close-up of her stricken face as she listens to the car pull away outside. A shot rings out and the music climaxes over her face as she drops to the ground. Stefan calmly telephones Oscar, at the same time bending over and removing her wristwatch, coolly assessing and pocketing it.

A close-up of Oscar, at the telephone, agreeing to wait for Stefan in Rheims. After he hangs up, the camera moves out to reveal him surrounded by guns and members of the Resistance.

Back at the office, John gives the name and address to the French officer, who

rises to put his hand on John's shoulder. John is distressed at the news of Jeanne's death, remembering aloud that he wanted to see her after the war. The camera moves in to his distraught face as the French officer says that perhaps one day in France, there might be a tomb for the unknown civilian.

Notes. *Translations of titles and dialogue in French are by author. Some filmographies credit Krampf with photography and Gilbert with set direction, but neither name appears in the film; nor does the name of the screenplay author.† The Molière Players are a group of refugee actors from France who had formed a troupe in London. ††Spoto (entry 702) and most filmographies indicate that this film was never released, but Noble (entry 192) states that it and *Aventure Malgache* were both shown throughout France in 1944–1945.

34   *Aventure Malgache* (1944)

Director	Alfred Hitchcock
Producer	British Ministry of Information
Production Company	Phoenix
Photography	[Gunther Krampf]*
Set Direction	[Charles Gilbert]*
Cast	The Molière Players†
Filmed	at Associated British Studios, Welwyn, in R.C.A. Photophone
Running Time	approximately 40 minutes
Release Date	1944††
Other titles: *Malgache Adventure*	

Synopsis

Title: "The whole world has heard of the dramatic events of the Resistance in France, a heroic period in the nation's history. The story we are going to show you is not so well known. It shows that even in the far reaches of the French empire, the same breath animates the people."

Title: "London, 1944. A handful of French actors is reunited, charged by the French military to form a troupe to present theater to the soldiers, civilians, and English people who know and love France. One of the actors plays the part of Jacques Clarus, a lawyer in Madagascar before the war. But listen to his story." (Throughout the narrative, the actors and the characters they play are referred to by the same names.)

June 28, 1940. A poster for the Molière Players on a wall. A uniformed gendarme enters the door nearby. Inside, two other actors are removing their makeup in front of a mirror on the left side of the frame. The gendarme removes his coat and sits down, facing the mirror on the right. He complains that he does not understand his role, but Clarus, the actor behind him, turns to tell him that if he had known his "friend" Michel better, he would understand.

The camera pans over a map of Africa to the island of Madagascar. Michel, in his white uniform as the head of Madagascar's secret service, stands in the center of a plain but formal courtroom. A few people sit behind in the audience, and the judge and other officials are perched above. Clarus, defense attorney, stands face to face with Michel and accuses him of organizing a plot against the defendant for the reward payable to those who uncover fiscal frauds. As he details the money

involved, the exchange between the men becomes heated, and the judge warns Clarus. But Clarus further accuses Michel of having an affair with the defendant's wife. Michel sputters at this, and Clarus calls him a gangster; the judge demands order and adjourns the trial.

Back in the dressing room, Michel, like the others, is now in a dressing gown, and he and Clarus, back to back, turn their heads to talk over their shoulders. Clarus had the evidence to convict Michel but something else interfered.

At a Madagascar café, men are grouped around the tables among the arched pillars listening to Pétain on the radio announce capitulation. The soldiers pound the tables in protest while one man, apparently Clarus (only his back fills the foreground) calms them with suggestions for resistance.

In the General's large bright office, a group of servicemen, represented by Clarus, offer their help. Michel faces away toward the window, then turns to the group and wonders how they will obtain weapons, ammunition, and transport. Clarus objects that all can be arranged if they find the will, but Michel insists that such plans are not realistic. He points out that if they appeal to the British for help, the British will probably take the opportunity to occupy the island. Clarus responds that British occupation is much the lesser slavery compared to occupation by the Germans and the Japanese. But Michel insists they are obliged to remain loyal to Pétain. Finally, the General paces in front of the group and ruminates about loyalty versus rebellion, eventually deciding that they must think more before acting.

Back in the dressing room, the actors discuss Clarus's decision to stay and organize the resistance. A night scene on the beach shows Clarus shaking hands with people carrying suitcases. Clarus describes himself as being "more Vichyist than Vichy themselves," and he asserts that the Governor as well turned a blind eye, lamenting the many escapes that took place but taking no action.

In the Governor's paneled, book-lined office, Michel sits in the foreground, picking at the fingernails of his tight fist. The Governor reads to Clarus, who stands next to him, a stern directive that no French citizen will be allowed to join a foreign army. Clarus remarks sarcastically, "The German army, for example," then matter-of-factly discusses the difficulties of escaping from the island while the Governor listens intently. The Governor demands that Clarus help in combating the growing influence of the Gaullists and both smile as Clarus warmly accedes, then departs. Michel finally turns from his nails to watch Clarus leave, then rises to stand before the Governor. A secretary comes in with a report of more escapes, several officers and families, by ship. Michel suggests that Clarus is behind the business and commands the secretary to have Clarus followed. The Governor accedes to the investigation but sternly warns Michel that the evidence against Clarus must be irrefutable.

The actors wonder about the growing danger of the events.

Clarus goes down the open stairway of a cellar to tell a waiting group of men that their plans are increasingly suspect. Michel is getting closer to their scheme and they must move quickly. The five who were going to escape at the end of the week must go tonight and may not leave the cellar until a truck arrives to pick them up at midnight. Clarus turns away, but one of the young men, Pierre, rises and stops him near the stairs. At first, Clarus refuses the man's request to see his fiancee, then he relents.

Back in the dressing room, Clarus wonders if Pierre ever knew how his last kiss changed their lives.

Walking through the netting of a bedroom to greet Yvonne, Pierre urgently tells her of his plans and Clarus's part in them. She is extremely upset and grabs his elbows as she pleads with him to reflect on the decision; their wedding day is only a few weeks away, after all. Pierre leaves anyway, protesting that he loves her, but it is his life and a free country will be better for both of them. After he has gone, Yvonne sits on her bed wide-eyed and miserable, then focuses on the telephone in the foreground. Finally rousing herself, she picks up the receiver and asks for the secret service.

Back in the dressing room, the actor playing Clarus relates that two hours later Clarus was jailed.

The hall of a prison. Clarus is let into a meeting room to talk with his lawyer, Panisse. They share warm greetings, then sit down at the table across from one another. A uniformed guard stands in the background in the hallway, centered between them. They discuss the charges of conspiracy in the escapes, and Clarus wonders if they have a chance against Michel. Panisse assumes that Clarus has destroyed all possible evidence but also indicates that there are numbers of telegrams already public that could be interpreted against him. Panisse gives Clarus some papers, and Clarus unctuously reminds him he has nothing to write with. Panisse departs, and after the outside door bangs shut, Clarus stands near the guard and swears after the "traitor."

Back in the dressing room, the actor playing Michel talks about Michel's ambition; he rises to light a pipe, the camera now in a wider shot that reveals the dressing room to be larger, with a fireplace in back.

Seated in his plain office lined with file cabinets, Michel discusses the telegrams as a turbaned black man manicures his fingernails. An expert witness who has examined the telegrams stands before him and they argue about the code embedded in them; in anger, the expert finally flings the telegrams down on the desk when Michel pressures him for a particular interpretation. A suited man listening in the background indicates that it has been reported that all copies of La Fontaine's *Fables* have been sold out everywhere in the colony. Michel slaps the papers in determination; La Fontaine must be the key.

In the courtroom, Clarus sits in the foreground, his back to the camera, as Michel, again in his white uniform, stands in the center in front of the tribunal. On the proof of 132 telegrams, he accuses Clarus of being the leader of the resistance community and demands the death penalty. Panisse responds weakly that Clarus admits sending the telegrams and knowing of the escapes, but that he has not recently been involved. Formal sentencing follows: death within 24 hours.

Clarus, in white shorts, paces his cell.

Back in the dressing room, the actors exclaim, "So he's dead!" No, replies Clarus, Pétain himself pardoned him because of his service at Verdun in World War I.

Clarus lies on his cot in his cell, holding a small clock that emits radio signals to his ear.

Back in the dressing room, Clarus explains that Michel never discovered the trick of the clock.

Clarus is brought in to see Michel in his office, which is now graced with a gilt-edged landscape painting. Michel orders his handcuffs removed and offers him a glass of rum and a deal: freedom if Clarus will reveal the location of the secret transmitter; hard labor if he will not. Standing calmly, his head bowed,

Clarus looks up at the end and responds with quiet insults. Michel spits rum in his face, and Clarus stiffens proudly.

In the dressing room, their makeup now complete, the men have removed their gowns and are in the process of putting on their costumes. They discuss Clarus's last hope—that the resistance might act to save him, that the British Navy might arrive, "one chance in a thousand!"

One night, Clarus stands on the top bunk of his cell, excitedly watching out the window and dragging up his turbaned cell mate, who refuses to believe that British ships are nearby.

The actors relate how a freed Clarus persuaded the allies to build a radio transmitter to convince all Madagascar to liberate itself.

In a small room, Clarus sits before a table with a microphone, and announces "Free Madagascar speaking tonight!" Michel morosely listens to his own radio; Clarus, in imploring the people, begins to speak directly to Michel, "You old hypocrite, Vichyist traitor." Clarus ends the broadcast, then tunes into another channel and smiles to hear that the tribunal has once again sentenced the ex-convict Clarus to death for "seditious propaganda and anti-French radio speeches."

Newsreels of May, 1942; British soldiers land and a military parade marches through the streets. The British, however, declare that the French flag should fly over the town hall.

Back in the dressing room, the actors are putting on their hats, but still wondering about Michel. "As soon as he heard of the allied landing . . ."

In his office, Michel picks up a picture of Pétain and a bottle of Vichy water and hides them in a cabinet. He then pulls out a large, gilt-edged portrait of Queen Victoria.

The actors discuss Michel's arrest, and the one who plays him bursts out, "And you want me to play this infamous part?" Clarus appears upset; the third actor tries to calm them, but they look at each other and smile. Music returns as they exit for the performance.

Notes. *In French. Translations of titles and dialogue are by author. Some filmographies credit Krampf with photography and Gilbert with set direction. †The Molière Players were a group of refugee actors who formed a troupe in London. ††According to Spoto (entry 702), both this film and *Bon Voyage* were shot between January 20 and February 25, 1944, and never released, shelved by a "disappointed French distributor." Noble (entry 192), however, states that both were shown throughout France in 1944–1945.

35 *Spellbound* (1945)

Director	Alfred Hitchcock
Assistant Director	Lowell J. Farrell
Producer	David O. Selznick
Production Company	Selznick International
Screenplay	Ben Hecht, Angus MacPhail (adaptation), suggested by *The House of Dr. Edwardes* by Francis Beeding [Hilary St. George Saunders and John Palmer]

Photography	George Barnes
Editing	William H. Ziegler, Hal C. Kern (supervising)
Art Direction	James Basevi, John Ewing (associate)
Set Direction	Emile Kuri
Sound	Richard DeWeese
Special Effects	Jack Cosgrove
Dream Sequence Designs	Salvador Dali
Music	Miklos Rozsa
Production Assistant	Barbara Keon
Psychiatric Adviser	May E. Romm, M.D.
Cast	Ingrid Bergman (Constance Peterson), Gregory Peck (John Ballantine), Rhonda Fleming, Leo G. Carroll (Dr. Murchison), Michael Chekhov (Dr. Brulov), Donald Curtis, John Emery, Jean Acker, Norman Lloyd (Garmes), Steven Gerary, Paul Harvey, Regis Toomey, Art Baker, Erskine Sanford, Victor Kilian, Wallace Ford, Bill Goodwin, Dave Willock, Janet Scott, Addison Richards, George Meader
Filmed	at Selznick International Studios, Los Angeles
Running Time	approximately 110 minutes
Distributor	United Artists
Release Date	October 1945

Other titles: *Ich kämpfe um dich, La Maison du Docteur Edwardes, Io Ti Salverò*

Synopsis

Credits and the eerie love theme appear over a shot of a nearly bare tree silhouetted against a white cloud. Shots of Green Manors, a psychiatric institution, appear under the introductory titles: "The fault is not in our stars . . . but in ourselves."—Shakespeare

"Our story deals with psychoanalysis, the method by which modern science treats the emotional problems of the sane. The analyst seeks only to induce the patient to talk about his hidden problems to open the locked doors of his mind. Once the complexes that have been disturbing the patient are uncovered and interpreted the illness and confusion disappear . . . and the devils of unreason are driven from the human soul."

Four female patients play bridge; one of them, the dark-haired, voluptuous Miss Carmichael, is called into Dr. Constance Peterson's office. Escorted by a nurse named Harry, the patient flirts with and then viciously scratches him. In Constance's well-appointed office, the patient taunts her doctor, finally having a tantrum and throwing a book at her. Harry and Dr. Fleurot enter and Miss Carmichael is taken away.

Dr. Fleurot relaxes in front of the fireplace and starts criticizing Constance,

then moves next to her and accuses her of approaching her problems with an ice pack on her head. "Are you making love to me?" she asks, smiling, but he continues undaunted, expressing his passion for her. She is unimpressed. Dr. Murchison interrupts them to announce the arrival of Dr. Anthony Edwardes, his successor as head of Green Manors, and Dr. Fleurot leaves. Left alone, Dr. Murchison and Constance discuss Dr. Murchison's breakdown the previous year, which has led to his being replaced. Another patient, the timid Mr. Garmes, is brought in for a session.

In the director's even more spacious and elegant quarters, Dr. Murchison introduces Dr. Edwardes to some of the staff.

In the dining room, Constance tells the others at her table that she has read all of Dr. Edwardes's books and thinks very highly of them. Anthony Edwardes walks into a close-up to join them, and he and Constance lock eyes as they are introduced, romantic violins scoring the encounter. The group discusses plans for a new swimming pool and the music turns ominous when Constance starts to indicate the shape of the pool by pressing her fork into the tablecloth. Anthony becomes unsettled, blurting out a sarcastic comment about the "unlimited supply of linen." Constance smooths over this embarrassment with small talk as Anthony furtively takes a knife and blends out the lines.

Dr. Fleurot lies on the couch in Constance's office as they exchange witticisms. Harry interrupts them with a note from Anthony requesting she come immediately to his office.

In Anthony's office, the patient Garmes is telling him that he killed his father. Constance arrives and explains to Garmes that this is only a "misconception" caused by his "guilt complex." Harry takes Garmes away and the two doctors discuss the case in private. Anthony finds the case curious, but Constance reminds him that he has written about such cases many times. He asks her to go out with him for the afternoon; she offers excuses, but he insists. He takes a telephone call and is upset by it, denying he knows the caller and abruptly hanging up.

Constance and Anthony stroll through the countryside. She disparages the poets' effect on people, who "read about love as one thing and experience it as another." She stumbles a couple of times and he helps her up. Flushed, she describes the day as "perfect"; he, behind her in the close-up and looking at her unawares, replies, yes, "perfect."

In the dining room, their empty seats are noted as well as the odd way Anthony is spending his first day on the job. Constance arrives looking disheveled. They tease her about her tardiness, and appearance—Dr. Fleurot even picks leaves from her hair. Refusing to be defensive, she excuses herself from the "nursery."

That night, violins encore the main love theme as Constance lies awake. Putting on her robe, she brushes her hair, then goes out and up the stairs. Finding a light under Anthony's door, she slows and the music swells. Walking past and into the library, she takes down his book *The Labyrinth of the Guilt Complex* and starts back downstairs. Faltering, she turns and opens his door to find him asleep in a chair. He wakes and she mumbles something about discussing his book with him, then admits to her subterfuge. He reassures her, explaining that "something has happened" to them. Increasingly narrow alternating close-ups, culminating with shots of just their eyes, describe the scene as he moves toward her. She closes

her eyes and a series of doors open as they kiss. But the ominous version of the love theme intrudes as he fixates on the stripes in her robe and pushes her away, saying it is something about the dark lines that upsets him. The phone rings and Anthony is informed that Garmes has tried to kill Dr. Fleurot and then himself; the patient is now in surgery.

In the operating room, Anthony and Constance enter dressed in surgical gowns. Anthony becomes hysterical about the lights in the corridor, then collapses.

Sitting nearby while he lies unconscious in bed, Constance watches over him, then compares the autograph in his book to his signature on the note he sent her that day; they are different. He wakes and apologizes contritely. "Who are you?" she asks, and he furrows his brow. "Anthony is dead. I killed him and took his place. I'm someone else. I don't know who." Later, he paces, trying to remember, realizing he has amnesia and may have murder on his conscience. Constance is sympathetic, forging ahead to unravel the mystery. She asks about the telephone call, which was from Anthony's office assistant. He remembers finding a cigarette case in his hotel room with the initials J. B. Finally, she leaves him to sleep, but he remains distraught.

Later, dressed to go out, he writes a note to her: "I cannot involve you . . . I love you . . . I am going to the Empire State Hotel in NY. J. B."

The note is thrust under her door as she paces near her bed.

Elsewhere, Anthony's assistant explains to Dr. Murchison and the police her conviction that the man she spoke with on the phone was not Anthony. They go up to J. B.'s suite to confront him.

The note still sits on the floor near Constance's door. Dr. Murchison enters with the police and they ask her about the "paranoid imposter" who has disappeared, but she offers no information, preoccupied with the letter under their feet. As he leaves, Dr. Murchison offers his condolences, then picks up the note and hands it to her. The music swells with her relief on reading the note.

In the library, her colleagues discuss the case as Constance reads. Dr. Fleurot points out that the most plausible action for the suspect is suicide to "put an end to his pain and nightmare fantasies." Dr. Murchison apologizes to Constance for the rude talk, but she is shaken and decides to retire.

In her suite, she nervously listens to the radio, then suddenly moves with a purpose.

In the Empire State Hotel lobby ᴴ Constance looks around and sits down on a couch. A man sits next to her and flirts. The hotel detective moves him along, then offers to help her. Stringing together his leading questions, she makes up a story of a missing husband, and he volunteers to see if he can locate her man. He returns with a stack of registration cards and she picks out J. B.'s handwriting.

Constance goes to the room, and vows to take care of J. B. until he is cured. "It has nothing to do with love," she says, as he passionately embraces her.

Later, he lies in front of her and she asks him questions. She confirms he is a doctor, and he applies some logic to the news reports of Anthony's death, which state that Anthony was last seen with a patient. He suggests she is "mad . . . to run off with a pair of initials." As she urges him to remember, his mind goes briefly into the past. A bellboy brings up the day's papers and notices that Constance is in a picture on the front page. Closing the door, she realizes they must escape.

They walk cautiously through the lobby, and the camera leaves them to move over to the bellboy, who shows the house detective the newspaper, and then into a close-up of the detective's annoyed face.

At Penn Station Constance urges J. B. to try to remember where he went with Anthony. Petrified at the pressure as she extols him to come up with a destination, he stands wide-eyed in the ticket line. At his turn, he is unable to speak. Finally, he mutters Rome, and Constance supplies Georgia, as he faints on the counter. A policeman offers to help, but Constance whispers urgently to J. B. to pull himself together and insists on pushing him along herself. The camera follows as they walk down to the track, and Constance explains that they are not going to Rome but over to Grand Central Station and on to Rochester so they can evade the police.

At Grand Central, they are happier, and she tells him they are going to visit Dr. Alex Brulov, a doctor, her friend and teacher. They approach the ticket taker, kiss (good-bye—like the many other couples around them), then walk to the train together as the ticket taker frowns in confusion. On the train, she starts grilling him again and he objects, but she insists that he think about Rome and he becomes fixated on the tracks speeding by. He remembers an accident during the war, then berates her for being a "smug woman." She takes it in stride, determined in her mission to cure him.

They arrive at Dr. Brulov's home and are greeted by his housekeeper, who has already placed a couple of other gentlemen to wait in the sitting room. The new arrivals settle in awkwardly as the other two chat about their work as police detectives. Alex arrives and warmly greets Constance. The detectives rise and ask Brulov about Anthony, whom he disparages professionally; impatient with their questions, he asks them to leave. Constance then introduces her new "husband", and Brulov invites them to stay. "Women make the best analysts," he says, "until they fall in love; then they make the best patients."

Upstairs in their room, J. B. wonders if Alex doesn't know more than he appears, but Constance assures him Alex is "always in a dream state socially." They are very much in love and chat about their "honeymoon," though she puts off his kisses and offers to sleep on the couch. Suddenly he fixates on the lines in the chenille bedspread; he becomes petrified and abusive toward her again. She pushes him to remember, beginning to connect the other incidents of white with dark lines. He faints, but she is encouraged at the new information.

Later, she is asleep in the bed and he rises anguished from the couch; he goes into the bathroom where he opens a straight razor and starts to shave. Seeing the hairs of the brush against the soap, he begins to reel, then, staring at Constance, he walks toward her pointing the razor in front of him, but turns and walks slowly downstairs; a close-up of his hand is shown holding the open razor. Alex's voice greets him from across the room. He offers J. B. some crackers and milk and walks by him, the camera again picking up the hand with the razor, the lighted kitchen through the door in the background. Immobile, vacant, J. B. takes the milk; the camera views Alex, still full of soothing chatter, through the bottom of the upturned glass and milk fills the screen.

Next morning, Constance dresses hastily and goes downstairs to find Alex sprawled on a chair. The music escalates as she kneels next to him and pushes him to see if he is alive. He wakes. J. B. is asleep on the couch. Alex asks for the truth, telling her he stayed up the night before, knowing J. B. might be dangerous, and gave him a bromide. Constance insists J. B. is not dangerous, but

Alex shows her the razor. She persists and he becomes impatient, accusing her of "female contradictions." He indicates he will call the police, and she pleads for understanding, but he makes fun of her being in love, "operating on the lowest level of the intellect." "The mind isn't everything," she counters; "the shock of a police investigation might ruin his chances for recovery." She pleads for time, and Alex finally agrees to wait a few days; they hug.

Grateful, she assents to his demand to make coffee, and Alex smacks J. B. a few times to wake him. J. B. groggily pronounces Freud "a lot of hooey," as Alex grumpily explains why they are going to analyze his dreams, "to examine the puzzle and find the truth." Constance enters with the coffee and offers to take notes.

J. B. stares out, and narrates his dream: large eyes circle the screen, then appear painted on curtains; a man cuts the curtain with scissors, and a girl "with hardly anything on" walks around the gambling room kissing everyone. Across a long distorted table, a man in a stocking mask deals a hand of 21 that has blank cards; the proprietor accuses the player of cheating. A sloping roof of a high building: a man with a beard falls off; a man in a mask is hiding on the roof, holding a small wheel. J. B. relates that he ran down the hill with wings chasing him.

Given more coffee in the present, J. B. becomes paranoid at the sight of snow falling outside and children sledding down a hill. Constance remembers Dr. Edwardes's love of skiing, and J. B. drops his coffee cup.

Later, the two doctors interpret the dream as J. B. sits petrified, staring out. Suddenly he remembers Gabriel Valley, and decides himself to call the police, but Constance insists they must go to Gabriel Valley themselves. Meanwhile, at the police station Constance's photograph is received. J. B. is uncomfortable, sure that he killed Anthony, but Constance reassures him that he must be thinking of some other incident from his childhood. He fears that he may kill again, but she prevails, sure in her "faith," and they embrace. Alex sadly turns away, and Constance, seeing him over J. B.'s shoulder, frowns, but shuts her eyes.

In their office, the detectives draw a pair of glasses on Constance's picture and realize who they met in Dr. Brulov's parlor.

On the train, Constance babbles as she and J. B. eat lunch. He panics at the sight of the knife and fork.

Constance and J. B. walk up a slope carrying their skis. He stares at her wide-eyed as she instructs him to put on the skis. They descend, the music driving with them as they speed down together, anxiously eying one another, she slightly ahead. He narrows his eyes as they come to a precipice and she appears frightened. Suddenly he remembers a childhood accident and sees himself as a young boy sliding down a porch banister, forcing his brother, perched at the bottom, to leap and impale himself on an iron fence. Suddenly he grabs Constance and pulls her to the ground with him, hugging her, and crying out, "It was an accident!"

The police report "new evidence" in a telegram.

At a lodge, Constance and J. B., now John Ballantine, stand by the fireplace. He tells the story of meeting Dr. Edwardes and skiing with him when Anthony fell over a cliff. The detectives enter and inform them that they found the body where John said it would be, but there is a bullet in the back. Constance is shocked when they detain John for murder.

Her face is superimposed over jail bars and surrounded by abstract images indicating a trial, then her testimony as she pleads for John's innocence. In close-up, facing the camera, she says good-bye, vowing to free him.

At Green Manors, Alex advises her to give up; the evidence was definite. She becomes hysterical, crying that "it's not over," then thanks him for "straightening things out with Dr. Murchison." Dr. Murchison enters to announce that Alex's car is waiting, then tries to console Constance, indicating that he "knew Anthony only slightly. . . . I never liked him very well." At her door, she pauses, repeating this phrase to herself until it pounds in her head. Taking out her glasses, she retrieves her notes from John's dream, and walks with conviction up to Dr. Murchison's suite.

Entering, she finds him behind his desk. She wants to discuss John Ballantine's dream and he teases her about her loyalty. She explains about the gambling house with blank cards and the eyes on the curtains; pacing the room, he chimes in regularly with interpretations. They hit on the 21 club and Green Mansions as a locale, then conclude the proprietor is in fact Dr. Murchison. He asks if she has told anyone else. She continues reconstructing the murder, suggesting the small wheel represents a revolver that was dropped in the snow. Dr. Murchison brings out a gun from his drawer and points it at her. He has already realized his mistake. She confronts him with the rest of the evidence, then insists that he will not be so stupid as to murder her deliberately, when the other crime had extenuating circumstances and conviction might leave him relatively free. The camera focuses on his hand and gun in the foreground as she rises and circles around to leave him, the gun pointed at her back. He turns it sideways, then toward himself (the camera) and shoots.

The happy couple arrive at the train station, where the same ticket taker they met in an earlier scene stares at them as they kiss, then walk down the platform together; the ticket taker mugs into the camera.

Note. [H]Hitchcock does bit as man walking out of crowded elevator.

36   *Notorious* (1946)

Director	Alfred Hitchcock
Assistant Director	William Dorfman
Producer	Alfred Hitchcock
Production Company	RKO Radio
Screenplay	Ben Hecht, based on a subject by Alfred Hitchcock
Photography	Ted Tetzlaff, A.S.C.
Editing	Theron Warth
Art Direction	Carroll Clark, Albert S. D'Agostino
Set Direction	Darrell Silvera, Claude Carpenter
Sound	John E. Tribby, Terry Kellum
Special Effects	Vernon L. Walker, A.S.C., Paul Eagler, A.S.C.
Music	Roy Webb, F. Bakaleinikoff (director)
Costumes	Edith Head
Production Assistant	Barbara Keon

Cast

Ingrid Bergman (Alicia Huberman), Cary Grant (Devlin), Claude Rains (Alexander Sebastian), Louis Calhern (Paul Prescott), Madame Konstantin (Mme. Sebastian), Reinhold Schunzel (Dr. Anderson), Moroni Olsen (Walter Beardsley), Ivan Triesault (Eric Mathis), Alex Minotis (Joseph), Wally Brown (Mr. Hopkins), Eberhard Krumschmidt (Kupka), Fay Baker (Ethel), Peter von Zerneck, Lenore Ulric, Ramon Nomar, Sir Charles Mendl (Commodore), Ricardo Costa

Filmed   at RKO Radio Studios, Los Angeles
Running Time   approximately 100 minutes
Distributor   RKO Radio
Release Date   July 1946

Other titles: *Berüchtigt, Weißes Gift, Les Enchaînés, Notorious—L'Amante Perduta*

Synopsis

The dramatic theme music accompanies the credits, which appear over a cityscape drawing with a low horizon.

Title: "Miami, Florida. 3:20 P.M. April the Twenty-Fourth, Nineteen Hundred and Forty-Six."

Beginning with a close-up of a hand holding a camera, the camera pans over a group of reporters and photographers, then to the door of the U.S. District Court. One of the group peeks inside the doorway.

Inside, an impenitent John Huberman is found guilty of treason and sentenced to twenty years in prison. The court is adjourned. "Here she comes," the observer says. The audience exits, and the camera moves with Alicia Huberman, a young woman in a black, broad-brimmed hat, who is barraged with questions about her father. As the crowd passes by, a man says to another, "Let us know if she leaves town."

The man paces in front of a middle-class residence.

That night, there's a party inside. Alicia serves a drink to a "party crasher," who sits silent, his back silhouetted to the camera. She banters with the rest of her drunken guests and drinks some more herself as they discuss the police that follow her. Eyeing the stranger, she announces they all must leave.

Later, in quiet, the camera moves around the stranger and the inebriated Alicia sitting together at a table. He is cool; in close-up, she flirts and invites him for a picnic. "It is understood" she will drive. They go out into the breezy night and he notices her bare midriff and puts his scarf around her.

The car drives wildly past some palm trees. A close-up shows his hand ready near the steering wheel. She drunkenly asks if he's scared, then says she's going to go faster "to wipe that grin off your face." A motorcycle policeman stops them and apologizes when Devlin hands over his identification. Alicia realizes he must

be "a cop" and angrily attacks him. He says he's going to drive her home and they struggle; finally he knocks her out and moves into the driver's seat.

The next morning, she wakes, a glass of juice by her head. From afar, Devlin pushes her to drink it. His image first shadowy, then spinning, he approaches her. She is disgusted at the "copper," but he tells her he has a job for her infiltrating some financiers in Brazil. "I'm no stool pigeon," she says, but he persists. She says she's not interested in patriotism, so he pulls out a recording of an argument with her father in which she refuses to work with him and claims to "love this country." She is sobered now but still wants "good times and laughs," and has no interest in being "put in a shooting gallery." A friend interrupts, reminding her of their sailing trip. Devlin puts the question again, and she agrees to go.

The Andes. Alicia sits on the plane. Devlin stands in the back talking to his boss, Paul Prescott, then returns to sit next to Alicia; he tells her that her father committed suicide that morning. Saddened, she speaks of "how nice we once were" and how she doesn't have to hate him or herself anymore. Devlin announces they're coming into Rio and she leans over him to look out the window. He starts, her profile before him in the frame.

A cityscape. A streetcar passes a café where Alicia and Devlin sit outdoors. She refuses a drink and compliments her own sobriety; he dismisses it as a "phase." She teases him about being afraid of falling in love with her, but he remains unflappable and cold. "Why won't you believe in me?" she pleads.

On a hilltop, she taunts him about being in love with "a little drunk" and he grabs her and kisses her.

In his office, Paul announces to his colleagues that Alicia is perfect for the job and that Devlin doesn't know about "the nature of the work" yet.

Devlin and Alicia drive up to her apartment. Inside, he goes out on the balcony over the beach. She follows him out and they kiss while discussing dinner. Still holding on to each other, he walks in to use the telephone. She says it is a "strange love affair" because he doesn't love her. He replies "actions speak louder than words." He learns that Paul wants to see him right away, and, still kissing him, Alicia sends him out the door.

Devlin drives up and carries a bottle of champagne into the office building. Inside, he slaps his hand on a table near the bottle and rises, alarmed, "I don't know if she'll do it! . . . She's not that type of woman!" But then he is told that Alexander Sebastian, the target, knows her and was once in love with her. They agree to proceed. Devlin hesitates, but Paul peremptorily dismisses him and is left pondering Devlin's forgotten champagne.

Devlin enters the apartment. Alicia struggles with a burnt chicken in the kitchen, bubbling over with talk as she goes to meet him on the balcony. Kissing him, she wonders what is the matter. He is cold and they begin to bicker, but then he tells her about the job to "land Sebastian." Moving away, she sits to listen, then wonders whether he defended her honor. He says he's leaving that to her. Finally, she asks if he wants her to take the job, but he remains adamant that it's up to her whether she wants "to back out." She pleads for him "to tell me what you didn't tell them," but "Dev" (as she calls him throughout the film) only demands her answer. Moving away behind a window, she takes a drink and grimly makes her decision to go. Smoking, he joins her, remembering the lost champagne but not where he left it.

Discussing strategy, they drive to their meeting with Alex Sebastian.

On horseback, Alicia, in a fedora and tie, and Devlin, open-shirted, follow

Alex and a companion down a horse trail, then catch up and slowly pass them. She hides under the brim of her hat and Alex does not greet her. Devlin says they'll give him another chance and jabs her horse into a run. Alex immediately takes to the chase and Devlin and the other woman watch from afar as he catches her.

In a café, Devlin waits, smoking.

Alicia waits in a fancy lounge. Alex arrives, they flirt, she says she feels "at home" with him; he speaks of his desire for her. She describes Devlin as a pest and assures him there's nothing between them. Alex picks up the menu and she loses her brightness, becoming thoughtful.

A gift card from Alex. Paul and Devlin stand as Alicia emerges from her bedroom, dressed in white fur and rented jewelry. Paul instructs her how to handle the dinner party at Alex's home; Devlin is silent, his back to the camera.

A limousine brings Alicia to a mansion on the coast. The camera moves over the noise of the party behind closed doors, showing the large central hall and curved stairway, but she is ushered into the library to await Mme. Sebastian, who walks downstairs to greet her. Mme. Sebastian wonders why Alicia did not testify at her father's trial and Alicia smoothly replies her father did not want it. Alex arrives and they walk over to join the other guests.

Alicia is presented one by one to five formally dressed men, who approach her in close-up and kiss her hand. The group files into the dining room, and Alicia, the first to be seated, observes one of the men, Emil, point to a wine bottle with alarm. Alex takes his arm and moves him away, and the camera returns to a close-up of the bottle.

Later, Emil paces outside a closed door. Inside, the camera views from above as the other men discuss his blunder in pointing out the wine bottle; indicating it is not the first mistake, they decide he must be murdered. Emil enters, abjectly apologizing, and is quickly ushered out.

The horse racetrack. Alex and his mother sit near a railing, Alicia's empty seat between them. Alex complains about her coldness to Alicia, but she comments that it would be ridiculous if "both of us grinned at her like idiots."

Elsewhere, Devlin scans the crowd. He finds Alicia and they lean over the railing, facing the camera, conversing in low voices. She gives him some details about Alex's friends, then says he can "add Sebastian's name to [her] list of playmates." He is angered at her "fast work" and bitterly tells her how lucky he is not to have had faith in her. "That's what you wanted, isn't it?" she says, hurt; "if you only had once told me you loved me." He fails to be moved as tears come to her eyes. Alex approaches them through the crowd and she regains her composure. Devlin says good-bye and Alex tells her that he's been watching her and thinks she might be in love with Devlin. She denies it and he slyly says he needs to be convinced.

Paul and his colleagues discuss the famous scientist who lives and works in Alex's home under the name of Dr. Anderson. Devlin stands at the window, his back turned. Alicia's arrival is announced and one of the men states his worry about "a woman of that sort." Devlin turns toward him, angry and sarcastic, "She may be risking her life, but when it comes to being a lady, she doesn't hold a candle to your wife, sir, sitting in Washington playing bridge with three other ladies of great honor and virtue." Paul tells Devlin to "take it easy," and he is forced to apologize as Alicia enters. She sits and tells them that Alex wants to marry her right away. Paul wonders if she is willing to go so far and she quietly

answers yes. Devlin grits his teeth and asks how this happened, does Alex think she is in love with him? "Yes," she replies. The plan agreed upon, Devlin leaves as the rest of the men thank her for handling the operation so "intelligently."

Alex argues with his mother while she sits and sews, the camera near her elbow in the foreground. He tells her the wedding will be next week, and she will be welcome if she chooses to come.

Alicia and Alex arrive home from their honeymoon to a darkened house. Mme. Sebastian has commanded everyone to retire early.

The next day, Alicia directs the servants while she unpacks. She starts to investigate the closets and finds one of them locked.

Behind closed doors, Alex and his colleagues discuss their work. Alicia interrupts to ask for the keys. She and Alex hold hands as they go upstairs so Alex can get the keys from this mother. After he goes into his mother's room, Alicia hears raised voices, then goes to her room until Alex returns with the keys.

A montage shows Alicia, accompanied by Joseph, the butler, as she systematically unlocks all the doors until they arrive at an extreme close-up of the wine cellar lock. Alicia is told that Mr. Sebastian has the key to it. They walk away as the music climaxes and the camera closes in on the lock.

Alicia sits with Devlin on a park bench in the middle of the city and talks. She is tired and doesn't think she can get into the wine cellar. He sarcastically assures her she "can handle it," but finally suggests she have a party and invite him so he can help.

The night of the party at the mansion, Alicia walks out of her room and over to a desk with Alex's key ring on it. While Alex speaks to her from the bathroom, she removes one of the keys and walks away just as he emerges in his bathrobe. He swiftly catches up to her and takes both her hands, in close-up, opening and kissing one. Then, as he moves toward the other, she passionately throws her arm around him, drops the key to the rug behind him, and pushes it out of the way with her foot.

Formally attired guests fill the entry hall as the camera moves from near the chandelier above the curved stairway down to a close-up of Alicia's hand holding the key. She nervously looks around as Alex suggests they go in and join the other guests. Devlin arrives, goes to her across the room, and kisses her hand; she passes him the key. Alex spots them and quickly moves to join them. They greet each other and Alex excuses himself.

Devlin is concerned at Alex's attention. "This is not going to be easy. He's going to watch us like a hawk," he says, hoping that the liquor doesn't run out, an event that would send Alex to the cellar without his key. After another guest takes Devlin away, ^{H} Alicia asks Joseph if there is sufficient champagne and finds there may not be. She interrupts Devlin and takes him to sit on a couch where they laugh while discussing their predicament. She suggests he go out back to the garden and wait for her. Leaving him to join her husband, she socializes while he stops by the bar to notice seven bottles left. Distracted by a large tray of champagne-filled glasses, Alicia excuses herself.

Devlin waits outside and she arrives, letting him in the garden door, then waiting outside while he enters the wine cellar.

Inside, Devlin inspects while upstairs there are five bottles left. He accidentally pushes a bottle from the shelf and it shatters on the floor, spilling black sand/ore. Alicia runs in after the noise, and they take a sample, clean up, and substitute another bottle.

Upstairs, Joseph looks for Alex and pulls him aside to talk.

Downstairs, Devlin finishes brushing away the last specks of sand and they leave the cellar. Alicia spots Alex coming down the stairs and realizes he has seen them. Rushing out the door, Devlin demands that she kiss him; Alex and Joseph stop at the sight. Alex dismisses Joseph and walks outside to confront the lovers. Alicia blames it on Devlin and Devlin assures Alex their affair is over, then leaves. Alex sends Alicia back up to her guests.

Upstairs, Devlin says goodnight to Mme. Sebastian and Alex tells Joseph they can now go down to get the wine. They approach the cellar door and Alex realizes that he does not have the key. He tells Joseph he's changed his mind.

At the end of the party, Alex bids Alicia a warm good night at the bottom of the staircase and apologizes for acting like "a stupid schoolboy."

Later, at his night table, he ponders his key ring and throws it down.

The next morning, he morosely lies in bed, then rises and goes to look at his key ring, now containing the missing key.

Still in his robe, he enters the wine cellar, notices the sink is stained, then fingers a series of labels and finds the misplaced bottle and glass shards.

From above, first his shadow, then he crosses the main hall and goes upstairs to his mother's room where she is still sleeping. He wakes her. "Why are you up so early?" she says, heartened to hear it is a problem with Alicia. "I am married to an American agent," he says, and she thoughtfully picks up a cigarette. As Alicia sleeps, Mme. Sebastian reassures the nearly hysterical Alex, who is worried about what his colleagues will do to him, that they will never believe it. "You are protected by the enormity of your stupidity," she says, and outlines a plan for the illness and slow death of Alicia.

On a bright morning, Alex encourages Alicia to drink her coffee.

Later, speaking with Paul in his office, Alicia complains of the light and a headache. He informs her they are looking for uranium and that Devlin has asked for a transfer to Spain.

Another empty coffee cup, as Alicia and Alex start off for a walk, and she becomes dizzy.

At the park, she walks to meet Devlin on the bench. He tells her she looks sick; she says it's a hangover. Despondent, she tries to get him to tell her he is leaving, but he does not mention it. She returns the scarf he lent her when they first met in Miami, and says good-bye.

In the Sebastian's living room, Dr. Anderson tells Alicia she looks awful and advises her to go to a doctor. She is not interested, but he continues to be solicitous and she becomes suspicious when Alex several times tries to get him away from the subject. When Anderson mistakenly picks up her coffee cup and both Sebastians leap to tell him it belongs to Alicia, the camera moves from a close-up of the cup, to Alicia, then zooms into Mme. Sebastian staring, and then Alex calmly reading. Distraught, Alicia rises from her chair in pain and says she is going to bed. Her senses become distorted as Alex and his mother turn into wavering silhouettes offering to help her. She turns from them only to be faced with shadows on the door, and then the huge wavering stairway in the hall. From above, she falls, then Joseph and Dr. Anderson help her up the stairs, but she becomes hysterical at the sight of Alex. Alex commands the phone be disconnected.

Devlin waits on the bench. Alicia lies in bed. Mme Sebastian sews. Night falls, and Devlin still waits.

While Paul lies in bed, eating, Devlin tells him he is suspicious and is going to pay a call on the Sebastians.

He drives up to the mansion. Speaking with Joseph he discovers that Alicia is very ill. In a meeting, Alex hears stories from his colleagues about their being followed. Eric, who has always been presented as the most stern, eyes Alex suspiciously; Joseph interrupts to announce Devlin.

Sitting in the entry hall, Devlin decides to go upstairs on his own, the music rising with him. He enters Alicia's room, where she lies barely awake. Moving close to her, he whispers in her ear, asking what is wrong with her; she tells him they are poisoning her, and that they killed Emil. They kiss and he tells her he loves her and apologizes for being afraid and acting badly. Pulling her up, he drapes her mink coat around her, but she tells him she's been given sleeping pills and can barely walk. Slowly they approach the stairs, Alicia nearly lifeless, leaning on Devlin's shoulder.

Mme. Sebastian and Alex meet them at the top of the stairs. His associates watch as the group descends, close-ups of Devlin and Alex alternating as Devlin tells Alex he had better play along. Mme. Sebastian encourages Alex to help, but he defiantly whispers he is not afraid to die and only then latches on to Alicia to help support her. Devlin continues to whisper what he knows, bribing them. Alex, Devlin, and Alicia move out the door and down the walk toward Devlin's car as the rest watch from the doorway. Devlin quickly hops in over Alicia and locks the car door, as Alex pleads that they must take him with them because "they" are watching him. "No room," says Devlin, and Alicia smiles gratefully.

Alex is left frowning in close-up, while Eric calls to him. Resigned, he slowly walks into the house and the door closes behind him.

Note. [H] Hitchcock does bit as man drinking champagne.

37   *The Paradine Case* (1947)

Director	Alfred Hitchcock
Assistant Director	Lowell J. Farrell
Producer	David O. Selznick
Production Company	Selznick International-Vanguard Films, Inc.
Screenplay	David O. Selznick, Alma Reville (adaption), from the novel by Robert Hichens
Photography	Lee Garmes, A.S.C.
Editing	Hal C. Kern, John Faure (associate)
Production Design	J. McMillan Johnson
Art Direction	Thomas Morahan
Set Direction	Joseph B. Platt (interiors), Emile Kuri
Sound	James G. Stewart (director), Richard Van Hessen
Special Effects	Clarence Slifer
Music	Franz Waxman
Costumes	Travis Banton
Hairstyles	Larry Germain

Scenario Assistant	Lydia Schiller
Unit Manager	Fred Ahern
Cast	Gregory Peck (Anthony [Tony] Keane), Ann Todd (Gay Keane), Charles Laughton (Judge Horfield), Charles Coburn (Simon Flaquer), Ethel Barrymore (Sophie Horfield), Louis Jourdan (Andre Latour), [Alida] Valli (Mrs. Paradine), Joan Tetzel, Leo G. Carroll (Sir Joseph Farrell), Isobel Elsom
Filmed	at Selznick International Studios, Los Angeles
Running Time	approximately 132 minutes
Distributor	Selznick Releasing Organization, Inc.
Release Date	December 1947

Other titles: *Der Fall Paradin, Le Procès Paradine, Il Caso Paradine*

Synopsis

Credits appear over a still of an elaborately carved judicial bench, accompanied by the romantic theme music.

London: the recent past. The camera passes over a block of elegant townhouses and up to a door.

Inside, piano music is heard as a butler brings a cocktail into the large sitting room and announces dinner. At the grand piano, Mrs. Paradine, young and dark-haired, drinks, staring at a life-sized painting of a uniformed gentleman. The butler interrupts her reverie, announcing Inspector Ambrose. She glances in the mirror as they enter to announce her arrest. Her rights and the charge—poisoning her husband—are read to her as the camera frames her calm face.

They drive to the police station. In a waiting area, she chats with Sir Simon, a portly older gentleman-barrister, who assures her everything will be all right and instructs her to say "no reply" after the charge is formally read.

Facing a man behind a desk, she responds as directed.

Afterward in the hall, Sir Simon tells her Anthony Keane will be her counsel.

Later, she stands in prison robes as her hair is undone. Escorted down a corridor of cells she is led into one and the door is slammed behind her.

It rains outside the door of another fashionable townhouse. Tony Keane, dark, young, and handsome, arrives home, greeted warmly by his blond wife, Gay. They go up the winding staircase to their room for a shower and a drink, discussing his day and the new Paradine case. Gay says "nice people don't murder other nice people" and he says she's "full of delusions." She grabs his wet head and covers it completely with a towel, rubbing fiercely and flattering him about his superiority. He grabs her; they kiss.

Sir Simon escorts Tony to the prison. In a waiting room, they meet Mrs. Paradine. Tony reassures her that he knows "what she's been thinking"; she is silent. They sit and discuss strategy: how she gladly devoted herself to her husband Dickie, a blind man who, Tony implies, never understood her sacrifice because he never saw her beauty.

A busy London street. In the sitting room in Sir Simon's home, his daughter,

Judy, fixes his black tie. "So you think Tony was taken with her," she says, making fun of him "riding to the rescue."

A formal dinner party. The host, a fat and surly judge, casually insults his grey-haired, idealistic wife at the other end of the table. She timidly hesitates and they finally all rise, the ladies leaving the men to their cigars and brandy while the hostess apologizes, "This is so antiquated, but he likes it." The three men sit again; Sir Simon and the judge compliment Tony on his courtroom successes but are critical of his emotional approach.

Meanwhile, the judge's wife sympathizes with Gay about the difficulty of murder trials. Impatient, Judy fetches the men and as they enter, the judge focuses on a close-up of Gay's bare shoulder. Sitting next to her, he tells her she looks "appetizing," and he takes her hand. She finally rises and walks away, commenting that his wife has good taste "in some things." He yawns.

When they return home, Tony heads for the library. Gay pleads with him to come upstairs, then follows him. He complains of his caseload and comments that Mrs. Paradine is "strangely attractive." Teasing, she reminds him of their forgotten anniversary trip. He apologizes, promising they'll go to "colorful" Italy. Thinking this has something to do with Mrs. Paradine, she accuses him of being transparent, but they kiss and he follows her upstairs.

Prison. It rains. Mrs. Paradine and Tony face one another; the camera observes from the vantage point of the guard outside. Inside, Tony winds up the session, standing, then suggesting they talk about her past. She declines, saying it's of no importance, but he pleads for her cooperation. Somber music rises with the antagonisms of the discussion, as she talks of running away with her first lover at the age of sixteen. Tony flinches and tries to make excuses for her, but she persists sarcastically with her revelations.

Night. A bell clock tower chimes 1 A.M. Inside Tony's study, he and Sir Simon discuss the possibility of proving suicide. Tony suggests the valet, Latour, is involved. Sir Simon tells him to forget it and becomes impatient, reminding him that they cannot "hurl other names into the case. . . . We must answer the Crown on Mrs. Paradine." Tony passionately rises to defend her as "too fine a woman . . . a noble self-sacrificing woman any man would be proud of." Decorative bars that form part of the wall separate him from Gay, who, hearing, hesitates for a moment outside. Finally noticing her when she enters, Tony becomes embarrassed. Sir Simon requests a strong drink and the camera moves to his concerned countenance.

Day. Prison. Tony and Mrs. Paradine talk about Latour; she lets slip his first name, Andre. Anthony is shocked and she informs him that she is not "trained" in "his" snobberies. Things become tense as he persists in implicating Latour, and she puts him on the defensive, wondering what happened to "her defender."

Sir Simon and Judy play chess in their home. They discuss the case, mostly Tony's state of mind. Finally, Sir Simon tires of the speculation and accuses her of having an "unfeminine interest in things." She furrows her brow and asks whether Tony is infatuated with Mrs. Paradine. Warming to her theory, she excitedly goes over to her father, speculating that Latour and Mrs. Paradine had an affair and Tony has found out and is jealous. Her father pushes her away, and she throws herself on the couch, persisting in discussing the "possible betrayal of Gay . . . men are such horrible beasts." Finally Sir Simon admits Mrs. Paradine is "fascinating. . . . I'm an old ruin, but she certainly brings my pulse up."

Tony arrives home late and notices a light under the bedroom door. Guiltily, he enters to find Gay removing her makeup. He tells her he must go up to the

Lake Country to see the Paradine mansion and indicates he prefer she stay at home, "warm, cozy, and protected." She alludes to his infatuation, and over-wrought, he suddenly decides to give up the case. But she hugs him and convinces him he must go on, even thanking him for "being so good." Sensing danger, he still wants to quit and is chagrined at her continuing insistence. He tries to kiss her, but she turns away, and he forlornly walks to the bathroom. She pulls down the covers on their bed, lethargically staring out over it.

Lake District. A train pulls in and Tony walks into the station hotel. [H] The innkeeper gossips with him about the Paradines; Tony says he's interested in renting the house.

A driver takes him by pony and cart up to the Paradine mansion, as the music swells pompously at their arrival. Latour opens the door and greets him by name but immediately disappears. Another servant takes him around the rooms and leaves him in Mrs. Paradine's very large bedroom, a huge oval portrait of her embedded in the headboard of the bed. He lingers over everything, the clothes, the piano, but mostly the portrait. He hears laughter, opens the window, and asks Latour to take him around the gardens. When he arrives downstairs, Latour has vanished.

In his sitting room at the rustic hotel, a high wind moves Tony to tighten the window shutter. Someone knocks and he opens the door curtain to see Latour. He lets him in and very aggressively questions him about his "former mistress." Latour takes issue with this, insisting he "would never serve a woman." Latour tells Tony he is "on the wrong side ... she's bad to the bone." Tony loses his patience and orders him out: "I don't want any dirty, lying sneaks in my room!"

His train arrives in London. Tony takes a taxi to the prison.

At the prison, Mrs. Paradine greets him: "I'd thought you'd forgotten me." He asks her why Latour hates her. They argue and he confronts her about a possible affair. She walks away, offended. He mentions his "personal feelings" and she haughtily tells her life is more important. He apologizes and she turns back and takes his hands as he begs forgiveness.

At a restaurant table near a bright window, Judy and Gay face one another. Gay defends her tolerance of Tony; "After all, I don't own him, I just love him."

A photograph in the newspaper shows Tony leaving the prison that day. Gay tucks it away in the couch as Tony enters for tea. They discuss his journey, and he accuses her of hoping he will lose the case. She quietly objects and explains at length that she wants Mrs. Paradine to live so there will be an end to Tony's being "mixed up." She leaves him in the room, staring out.

The courthouse, emblazoned outside with the motto, "Defend the children of the poor, punish the wrongdoer." Mrs. Paradine is called from her holding room and escorted down a hall and up the stairs leading to the center of the large, packed courtroom. There is a murmur as she appears, looking around at the many spectators, and down at Tony, who avoids her. The charge is read.

On the telephone, Judy talks Gay into attending the trial. They enter a courtroom balcony; Gay stares down as the camera moves into a close-up of Mrs. Paradine, then around the audience to the prosecutor.

Sir Joseph, the prosecutor, narrates the events of the night and speaks of the tragedy of Col. Paradine's life, dramatizing Mrs. Paradine as a woman full of resentment, though outwardly "no ordinary woman. She had patience. She could wait." Tony questions the butler, intimidating him and confusing the importance of a glass of burgundy. He replies sarcastically when the judge sets the record straight. Latour is called, and the camera follows him as he circles behind Mrs.

Paradine and walks up to the box. Tony grips the railing. The prosecution leads Latour to speak of his long and close relationship with Col. Paradine, who was the "finest man" he knew.

A London cityscape. In their sitting room, the judge reads and drinks while his wife wrings her hands. In her cell, Mrs. Paradine worries. At their home, Gay lies awake and Tony walks in to look at her.

Next day in the courtroom, Latour continues his testimony. He describes a fight he and Col. Paradine had the night of his death, when his master had accused him of betraying him and ordered him to leave. Tony then begins his questioning, first asking Latour about a woman who had jilted him many years ago in Quebec. Then he wonders if Latour is aware of the 3500 pounds he has been left in Col. Paradine's will and emotionally accuses Latour of lying to the court. The witness is now very nervous, and Tony, increasingly arrogant, sensing triumph, continues to go over details of the fatal night, and then asks about a time when Latour was forced to poison a sick dog. Latour breaks down, screaming that he didn't do it. The judge carefully explains that he need not defend himself against accusations with which he has not been charged. They adjourn. Latour wipes sweat from his brow.

On the way out of the balcony, Judy and Gay comment, "horrible . . . he's torn him to pieces."

Tony strides purposefully out of the courtroom and into the defendant's cell. She immediately accuses him of not "keeping faith. . . . I will not forgive you for this." He is dumbfounded, saying "I've exhausted myself. . . . I was idiot enough to fall in love with you." "You will save me, but not at his expense," she commands, but Tony insists that his strategy will remain, and when the time comes she can answer as she pleases.

In court the next day, Tony rises in close-up to continue his questioning of Latour. He wonders why the valet stayed on after the death, despite the discharge, and then accuses of him of washing the poisoned wineglass. Mrs. Paradine sits emotionless. Latour denies washing the glass, but Tony persists, reminding him of the penalty for perjury. He attacks anew with accusations of a love affair with Mrs. Paradine. As their voices rise, the camera shows the men in a series of close-ups; Mrs. Paradine turns her head and clenches her jaw. Latour finally admits there was an affair, but he kept it secret because he did not want to hurt the dead man's name. He attempts to continue his story ("I hated every moment with her"), but Tony interrupts to silence him. The judge blames Tony for the "over-emotional atmosphere" in court, but Tony, undaunted, suggests that charges of perjury and murder be drawn. "You seem anxious to usurp the duties of the judge," the judge admonishes. Tony is taken aback, as the prosecution rises to clarify the existence of the adulterous relationship. Shamed, Latour explains, "I tried not to, but . . ." Mrs. Paradine is frozen. Dismissed, the camera circles with Latour as he walks out and glances back several times. His steps sound in the quiet courtroom.

Tony rises, explaining that his client is friendless and alone, but secure in a country with a passion for justice. He announces he has decided to call no witnesses other than the prisoner, confident she is not guilty. Mrs. Paradine walks through the courtroom into the witness box and insists she would rather stand than sit. She talks of her background, then the night of her husband's death. She had complained to her husband of Latour's familiar manner and asked him to have the valet find another situation. Tony pushes her to try to implicate Latour otherwise. The judge is forced to interfere and warns Tony not to "bandy

words" with him. Tony pushes her about the details of the aftermath of the poisoning, trying to make her say that only Latour was in a position to have washed the glass. Finally, she admits that she did it. Tony asks for an adjournment because of the new evidence.

At home, he enters just as Judy walks down the stairs. She tells him she and Gay were in court that day. He dismisses her sarcastically, but she follows him into the library, where they quarrel. She asks why he is hammering at the witnesses; he explains that he wants to get at Latour's motive. She wonders about Tony's motive and stalks out, warning him that he is going to ruin his career and lose the case.

The Courthouse. In the courtroom, Tony stands and announces that he has completed his case. Sir Joseph begins to question the witness, wondering why she had not complained about Latour's attentions before that night, and wondering if she "were not madly in love with him." A policeman enters and whispers in Sir Joseph's ear. He announces that Latour has just committed suicide. The judge and lawyer decide the trial will continue regardless; Mrs. Paradine is despondent, distracted, not hearing the questions. Finally, she speaks: "The man I love is dead. . . . Andre wouldn't help me. . . . he knew I killed the blind man." Tony slumps in his chair. Turning to him, Mrs. Paradine chastises him: "The only comfort I have is the hatred and contempt I feel for you." In close-up, Tony hangs his head, then rises to speak, breathing hard and faltering. "My Lord, I've done my best. . . . More than ever I am conscious of my shortcomings. . . . Do not confuse my incompetence with the issues of this trial." He wipes the sweat from his brow, and, unable to continue, turns the case over to his colleague and exits. A long shot from above shows his walk through the crowd, only his steps audible in the hush.

The judge and his wife sit at either end of their dinner table. She pleads for this "woman who's sinned." Angry, he says he is tired of her silly pity, but she persists. Suddenly he announces Mrs. Paradine will be hanged. His wife leaves the room, distraught; he remains seated, picking his teeth.

A high-rise office, with a cityscape outside the glass walls. Sir Simon suggests to Tony that he telephone Gay, gently consoling him not to despair. Judy calls for her father and whispers in his ear. Sir Simon leaves, and Gay enters the room. She asks Tony to have breakfast with her, but he refuses and begins to leave. She tells him she was proud of him yesterday, but he can only meet her eyes with a little-boy look of shame. "The most important moment is now," she concludes, reassuring him about his worth and her love for him. "There you go again," he says as they hug, "all your fancy ideas about me."

Note. [H] Hitchcock does bit as man with cello at station.

38 *Rope* (1948)

Director	Alfred Hitchcock
Assistant Director	Lowell J. Farrell
Producers	Alfred Hitchcock, Sidney Bernstein
Production Company	Transatlantic Pictures
Screenplay	Arthur Laurents, Hume Cronyn (adaptation), from the play by Patrick Hamilton

Photography	Joseph Valentine, A.S.C., William V. Skall, A.S.C.
Technicolor Director	Natalie Kalmus, Robert Browe (associate)
Camera Operators	Edward Fitzgerald, Paul G. Hill, Richard Emmons, Morris Rosen
Lighting Technician	Jim Potevin
Editing	William Ziegler
Art Direction	Perry Ferguson
Set Decoration	Emile Kuri, Howard Bristol
Sound	Al Riggs
Music	Leo F. Forbstein, based on Francis Poulenc's *Perpetual Movement No. 1*
Radio Sequence	The Three Suns
Costumes	Adrian
Makeup	Perc Westmore
Production Manager	Fred Ahern
Cast	James Stewart (Rupert Cadell), John Dall (Brandon), Farley Granger (Phillip), Joan Chandler (Janet), Sir Cedric Hardwicke (Mr. Kentley), Constance Collier (Mrs. Atwater), Edith Evanson (Mrs. Wilson), Douglas Dick (Kenneth), Dick Hogan (David Kentley)
Filmed	at Warner Bros. Studios, Los Angeles, in Technicolor
Running Time	approximately 80 minutes
Distributor	Warner Bros.
Release Date	August 1948

Other titles: *Cocktail für eine Leiche, La Corde, Nodo Alla Gola, Cocktail Per un Cadavere*

Synopsis

Light music accompanies the credits, which appear over a sharply angled shot from a roof of a quiet, uptown residential street.

The camera moves back over the roof to a curtained window. A scream. Inside David Kentley's head drops, Brandon on one side holding him and Phillip on the other side grasping a rope at his neck. Brandon checks the victim's heart as Phillip lets the rope slacken. Brandon catches David and commands Phillip to open the chest in front of them. After they put in the body, Phillip sits on the chest, breathing hard. Brandon turns on a light, but Phillip protests, "Not just yet, let's stay this way for a minute." Brandon impatiently lights a cigarette, remarking they don't have much time. He walks back and opens the curtains over their grand penthouse window that spans the room, revealing the skyscrapers beyond. "The Davids of this world merely occupy space, which was why he was the perfect victim for the perfect murder," intones Brandon; "he was a Harvard undergraduate." Phillip tries the lock on the chest and complains that it does not work. Worried about what they have done, he wishes it had been someone else,

"you, perhaps," looking at Brandon, then hesitating. "I'm only kidding. I can't take it, so I'm turning on you." Tight-lipped, close by, Brandon peers at him: "Rather foolish, isn't it?"

The camera follows Brandon through the entrance hall to the dining room as he goes into the kitchen to get some champagne. Returning to Phillip, who stands by the swinging doorway to the kitchen, he joyously proclaims that "the power to kill can be just as satisfying as the power to create. . . . Do you realize that we've actually done it?" Phillip finally grabs the bottle from him and pops the cork himself. Calm now, he asks Brandon how he felt. Brandon responds, "Not much of anything . . . until his body went limp, then I felt exhilarated. How did you feel?" But Phillip changes the subject and the camera moves to the large centerpiece of white flowers on the dining room table set with silver and candles. "You don't think the party's a mistake, do you?" "Of course not," cries Brandon, "it's the signature of the artist!" He comments on the boring nature of some of the guests but thinks it will be interesting to watch Janet, who has "banked everything on hooking David," relate to Kenneth, a former flame.

Brandon suddenly grabs one candelabra and commands Phillip to follow him with the other one out to the chest in the living room, announcing they will set dinner on the chest. Phillip becomes upset about how they will explain this strange arrangement, but Brandon quickly decides they will set up the first editions for Mr. Kentley on the dining room table, where there is "more room." Bending to pick up some books near the chest, Phillip notices the rope hanging out the side and sickens. "Brandon!" he squeals, unable to move, and Brandon comes over, yanks it out, and lectures him as they cart the books back. "The only crime we can commit is a mistake. Being weak is a mistake." Phillip slams the books down on the dining room table and angrily replies, "Because it's human?" "Yes," says Brandon. The doorbell rings.

It's Mrs. Wilson, their talkative maid, who immediately complains about their unsetting her table. Moving into the living room, Phillip becomes upset to notice Brandon is still casually holding on to the rope. Brandon insouciantly swings it, pronouncing it an ordinary household item, and walks to the kitchen (which the camera always observes from the dining room) and places it in a drawer between swings of the door. As he and Mrs. Wilson chat, Phillip, not happy to overhear that Rupert Cadell has been invited, quickly picks up a bowl and stalks off. Brandon pursues him to assure him that Rupert is the most important guest, the one who will appreciate their deed from "our angle"; in fact, he even almost invited Rupert to partake in the crime but decided he was to "fastidious." Phillip is sullen. Mrs. Wilson walks in to whisper to him to eat well, especially the paté, because he's too thin.

Phillip tries the lock again as the first guest arrives; it is Kenneth, who is "surprised to be invited" because he hasn't seen them in a while. Brandon brags that he wangled a debut for Phillip, who is a pianist, and they discuss the other guests. Kenneth is perturbed to discover Janet has been invited, wondering if Brandon didn't know that he and she were "all washed up," but Brandon soothes him; "I think your chances are better with her than you think."

An elegantly dressed Janet arrives, smiles, hugs, and kisses the "darlings," until she sees Kenneth. "You dirty dog," she mutters under her breath at Brandon, then takes him into the hall to berate him about his manners. "You know I'm practically engaged to his best friend," she hisses, and Brandon pouts, claiming it's hard to keep up with her romances—first him (Brandon), then

Kenneth, then David. "Why the switch, anyway?" he asks brightly. She responds that David is nicer, and Brandon asserts that he is richer, whereupon Janet moves indignantly back into the living room.

Grouped around the piano, the four discuss Rupert, the boys' former house-master from prep school. One points out that Brandon "sat at the master's feet," and they discuss Rupert's theories about murder being a crime for most men but a privilege for the few.

Mr. Kentley arrives with Mrs. Atwater, his sister-in-law. She and Mrs. Wilson begin to chat, but Brandon swiftly interrupts them and takes Mrs. Atwater into the living room. "David!" she cries, looking at Kenneth. Phillip's glass breaks in his hand and he quietly moves behind the group to the cocktail table in the center of the room. There follows much hubbub concerning the physical resemblance of Kenneth and David and exactly where David is, as Brandon says he expected him with his family. Janet leaves for the bedroom to telephone Mrs. Kentley, and Brandon sends Kenneth after her with a glass of champagne.

At the piano, Mrs. Atwater reads Phillip's palm, and he becomes momentarily paralyzed, staring down at his upturned hands. He moves over and begins playing. The scene widens and moves left to include the newly arrived Rupert, who moves smoothly around the room and greets everyone with a sarcastic witticism. Brandon stutters while explaining the reason for the champagne. "You always did stutter when you were excited," says Rupert before he walks forward with Mrs. Wilson to the chest of food.

After she has gone, he dryly says to himself, "I may marry her." Mrs. Atwater and Janet join him and converse in superlatives about movies whose titles they cannot remember and film stars whose names they know well. Rupert engages the subject sarcastically until Mrs. Atwater becomes uncomfortable and Mrs. Wilson pushes in to warn Janet away from the paté: "Calories, dear."

The group around the chest changes as people fill their plates until Janet is left alone with Phillip who is nervously explaining why he does not eat chicken. The group then rearranges itself around the large room. Brandon picks up the conversation about Phillip's dislike by telling a story about Phillip killing some chickens and Phillip abruptly yells out, "That's a lie!" The camera cuts to a close-up of Rupert, who thoughtfully listens and watches the exchange off screen as Phillip insists that he "never strangled any chickens." As the tension breaks, Rupert mutters to them, "In another minute you would have strangled each other."

Rupert takes some more champagne from the table and sits down next to Mrs. Atwater in front of the window. The group begins to discuss his theories and the crowding problems murder would solve—no more standing in line, and so on. Rupert and Mrs. Atwater fill the frame; she doesn't quite understand, and, as the camera moves right toward Mr. Kentley and Brandon, Rupert explains that committing murder is only for superior beings. Brandon chimes in about the inferiority of the victims, "whose lives are unimportant anyway!" Rupert contin-ues dryly, "I don't believe in open season. . . . I'd prefer cut-a-throat week." Mr. Kentley frowns, protesting that he cannot appreciate such morbid humor. Rupert insists he is serious and Brandon avidly takes up their position with Mr. Kentley, who still believes they are pulling his leg; Brandon earnestly points out that he and Phillip and maybe Rupert are some of the privileged. "I'm sorry, Kenneth, you're out," says Rupert. Mr. Kentley brings up Nietzsche and Hitler, and

Brandon cries that he would naturally "hang all incompetents and fools." Mr. Kentley angrily says he will hear no more of his "contempt for humanity," and Brandon sarcastically calls this hypocrisy, bringing up Rupert's name for support. The camera moves back to Rupert, but he now separates himself from the subject of the conversation. Mr. Kentley rises, hanging his head sadly, and Rupert suggests they go in to view the first editions. Mr. Kentley brightens and heads for the bedroom to telephone his wife. Rupert follows Brandon and stops him by the piano, "You were pushing your point rather hard. You're not planning to do away with a few inferiors . . ."

Kenneth and Janet are left alone in the living room to compare stories; Kenneth repeats Brandon's remark that indicated to him that David was "out of the running," and they realize that Brandon has lied to both of them. They turn and Janet calls Brandon, who claims he did not mean what he said to Kenneth, but she accuses him of deliberately not inviting David. "He's never this late!" In the background, Rupert listens as Brandon dismisses their concerns in a sarcastic manner.

After they have stalked out, Rupert wonders if "something's gone wrong" and mentions he misses David. Brandon walks away and leaves Rupert to offer one of his plates of ice cream to Mrs. Wilson. "My, it's peculiar party," she whispers, and tells Rupert the whole day was strange. "They both must have gotten up on the wrong side of the bed," she says, relating how Brandon made her rush through the preparations in the morning and then had her take the whole afternoon for shopping. Still standing near the chest in front of a large painting of gray hooded figures, she tells him Brandon and Phillip were quarreling when she returned, and for some reason had moved the food onto the chest. As the camera moves away and her talk dissolves into murmurs, Phillip appears. Noticing her gesturing at the chest, he turns wide-eyed in fear toward the camera and back toward Brandon, then decides to face her. "Mrs. Wilson, please serve the guests, don't lecture," he says and turns away. Rupert sighs, puts down his dessert, and walks over to the piano where Phillip is now playing.

"I seem to be the only one having a good time. . . . What's going on, Phillip?" Phillip curtly asks him to turn off the lamp he has just turned on. Rupert persists as faint sirens join the minor-key chords of the piece Phillips plays. Phillip angrily stops playing, but Rupert commands him to continue and brings him a drink. He sets the metronome going, then asks where David is and wonders what Brandon is doing with Kenneth and Janet. Phillip breaks out into a relieved laugh, and Rupert smiles, "Am I so far off as that?" Phillip loudly proclaims that nothing is going on. Rupert indicates that is the second time Phillip has lied tonight, and reminds him that he knows he is adept at strangling chickens, whereupon Phillip becomes loudly defensive. Turning away, he is aghast to see Mr. Kentley enter the room carrying a pile of first editions tied up in the rope. Jumping up, he stiffens, and Rupert leans into him, "You don't want Mr. Kentley to have the books?" "No! I just think that's a clumsy way of tying them up." Rupert turns to stare at the bundle now on a chair, then back at Phillip, who goes over to get a drink. Brandon meets him at the table and warns him. "Don't you ever again tell me what to do," mutters Phillip under his breath. Rupert walks between them, "There's something upsetting both of you a great deal," he says.

Mrs. Wilson announces a call from Mrs. Kentley and the whole group (off camera) takes up the subject of David as the camera shows the chest in the foreground, the hall and dining room beyond, and Mrs. Wilson busying herself

back and forth, cleaning off the chest and bringing in a handful of books on each return. Rupert pushes ahead the query about David's whereabouts, and the conversation takes a turn when the hosts deny having spoken to David recently, but Mr. Kentley says he heard David talking to Phillip. Phillip claims he'd forgotten, and Rupert moves over by the chest to help Mrs. Wilson. Just as she starts to open it, Brandon swiftly moves over and firmly puts his hands on the chest, commanding Mrs. Wilson to wait until tomorrow to replace the books. Rupert looks at him wonderingly and Mrs. Atwater walks in to announce that Mrs. Kentley has not heard from David and wants Mr. Kentley to call the police. Mr. Kentley reassures her, but Phillip's mouth drops open as Rupert watches him. The group decides to leave, and Janet invites Kenneth to come with them.

In the hall, the camera turns away from the departing guests toward the far end of the living room as Rupert moves toward Phillip's back, then hesitates, frowning, and strides into the hall to get his hat. But the hat is too small and has the initials DK written in it. He walks out quietly, and Brandon closes the door on him and leans against it with a shudder. Taking a cigarette, he gaily walks into the living room and grandly gestures in front of the windows, "This party really deserves to go down in history!" Phillip is not so happy, pointing out Rupert's "prying and snooping." They argue, then Phillip becomes frightened they will get caught.

A door shuts, and they move into the hall to say good night to Mrs. Wilson. Brandon orders his car on a telephone in the hall, then goes to the chest and starts to open it. Uncomfortable, he suggests they draw the curtains. As they stand at the side windows, the telephone rings and they freeze. Phillip is disheveled and desperate now as Brandon commands him to the phone and hurriedly replaces the books on the chest. Phillip sets down the receiver with a thud and stumbles forward, crying, "It's Rupert! He forgot his cigarette case!" Brandon commands him back to the phone and they argue until Brandon stiffly walks over to it himself. Phillip is ashen, collapsed in a chair, and Brandon insists that they are not going to get caught. Brandon finds a handgun and puts it in his pocket.

Rupert arrives and surreptitiously sets down his cigarette case behind the books on the chest, mentioning that he must have "wanted to come." Phillip aggressively cries out, "Why?" Rupert takes a drink from Brandon and points at the chest, then turns toward it, floundering, and decides to "find" his case. He sits in the wing chair and the two men hover over him, waiting. He stalls, fishing with talk about the "strange" party and David. He finally stands and Brandon challenges him to imagine how he would "get rid of David." The camera roams the room with Rupert's glances as he puffs on a cigarette and relates a possible scenario. As he approaches the idea of putting the body in the chest, he notices the bulge in Brandon's pocket and decides to hypothesize taking the body directly out the door. But Brandon challenges him, reminding him that it is "broad daylight." Rupert looks askance, thinking, until Phillip throws his glass down and sneers, "cat and mouse!" Rupert confronts Brandon about the gun, which Brandon gleefully throws on the piano, claiming it was for the country. The air is cleared until Rupert calmly takes the rope out of his pocket, and the two men stand open-mouthed. Phillip jumps for the gun, shouting that he would just as soon kill Brandon, but Rupert grabs him and they struggle over it until it goes off. Rupert seizes the gun, then moves toward the chest and raises the lid. Stricken, he turns toward Brandon, who eagerly explains, sure that Rupert "will understand. . . .

We've always said, you and I, that moral concepts of right and wrong don't hold for the intellectually superior." The camera moves around to a close-up of a thoughtful Rupert, stunned at his words from earlier in the evening coming back to him, then Brandon finishes, "Don't you see. . . . He [Phillip] and I have done what you and I talked about!"

After a moment, Rupert rises out of his slump and lectures them, "This world and the people in it have always been dark and incomprehensible to me . . . but you've given my words a meaning that I never dreamed of! You've tried to twist my words into a cold logical excuse for your ugly murder! Well, they were never that. . . . There must be something deep inside of you from the very start that let you do this thing, but there's always been something deep inside of me that would never let me do it. . . . By what right did you dare say there's a superior few to which you belong?" Rupert circles Brandon, who stands in the foreground in close-up, stunned at Rupert's change of attitude. But Rupert is just beginning to warm to his backstepping, crying out, "You've murdered! You've strangled the life out of another human being who's lived and loved as you never could! You're gonna die, Brandon, both of you!" Opening a window, he shoots the gun in the air three times; the camera moves away from a close-up of his hand with the gun to widen the scene as a commotion rises from the street. "They're coming," says Phillip, who sits at the piano, as Rupert, his back to the camera, plops down in a chair next to the chest in the foreground, and Brandon pours a last drink.

Note. ᴴ Hitchcock does bit as man crossing street, after titles.

39   *Under Capricorn* (1949)

Director	Alfred Hitchcock
Assistant Director	C. Foster Kemp
Producers	Alfred Hitchcock, Sidney Bernstein
Production Company	Transatlantic Pictures
Screenplay	James Bridie, Hume Cronyn (adaptation), based on the novel by Helen Simpson
Photography	Jack Cardiff
Camera Operators	Paul Beeson, Ian Craig, David MacNeilly, Jack Haste
Technicolor Director	Natalie Kalmus, Joan Bridge (associate)
Editing	A. S. Bates
Production Design	Thomas Morahan
Set Dresser	Philip Stockford
Sound	Peter Handford
Music	Richard Addinsell, Louis Levy (director)
Costumes	Roger Furse
Makeup	Charles Parker
Continuity	Peggy Singer
Production Manager	Fred Ahern
Unit Manager	John Palmer

Cast   Ingrid Bergman (Henrietta [Hattie]
                                        Flusky), Joseph Cotton (Sam Flusky),
                                        Michael Wilding (Charles Adare),
                                        Margaret Leighton (Milly), Jack Wat-
                                        ling (Winter), Cecil Parker (Gover-
                                        nor), Denis O'Dea (Corrigan), Olive
                                        Sloan (Sal), Maureen Delaney (Flo),
                                        Julia Lang, Betty McDermot, Bill
                                        Shine, John Ruddock (Mr. Potter), Rod-
                                        erick Lovell, Ronald Adam (Mr.
                                        Riggs), G. H. Mulcaster (Dr. McAllis-
                                        ter), Victor Lucas, Francis De Wolff
                                        (Major Wilkins)
Filmed   at MGM British Studios, Elstree, Lon-
                                        don, in Western Electric Recording
Running Time   approximately 118 minutes
Distributor   Warner Bros.
Release Date   September 1949
Other titles: *Sklavin des Herzens, Les Amants du Capricorne, Il Peccato di Lady
Considine, Sotto il Capricorno*

Synopsis

Credits appear over a blue and brown relief map of Australia, along with the Irish
theme music.

Bird's-eye view of the settlement by the bay circa 1770, which became
Sydney, capital of New South Wales, Australia. Scene dissolves into the bustling
port sixty years later, still growing "on the edge of three million square miles of
unknown land. The colony exported war materials, and imported material even
rawer—prisoners, many unjustly convicted." Under a bright blue sky, prisoners
file off a boat.

In 1831, a new governor has been sent to the colony, and a welcome banner
is spread across the large center of the military fort, which teems with red-
uniformed soldiers and a marching band. The Governor speaks to his new
constituents as his second cousin, the Honorable Charles Adare, stands in the
crowd. Charles, elegantly dressed in light blue, is approached by Cedric Potter,
the manager of the local bank.

Next day, Charles visits the bank, but Mr. Potter is unhappy to learn that the
young man has no work experience. While they are conferring in his glass-
partitioned office, Sam Flusky is announced. The two men stand at the window
looking out on the patrons in the lobby and Charles wonders about the name
Flusky; the manager explains that the man is a "financial genius [who] works
like a galley slave." Charles jovially spins around and laments that Mr. Potter
cannot tell him how to get rich. "Only by hard work," admits Mr. Potter, and
Charles's face falls. Brightening, he says he will approach Flusky, but Mr. Potter
bridles at his curiosity about him, saying that they do not talk about the past of
their successful men in Australia. Eventually the unsmiling Sam is invited in for
an introduction. Learning that Charles is from Ireland, he offers to help him, and
Mr. Potter pulls Charles aside and warns him not to go to Sam's house if invited.

Sam and Charles walk from the bank into the bright daylight and the camera follows as they walk down the sidewalk past the jail. Sam suggests he lend Charles money for some land, which he will immediately repurchase, as he has met his own limit for land grants. Opening a large shutter door, Sam invites Charles into the land grant office to fill out an application.

Inside, the manager offers Sam the services of a prisoner named Winter. Sam inspects the boy's mouth and complains about his "chicken-like" arms, but he takes him.

Outside on the boardwalk again, Sam is furtively approached by a man selling a shrunken head, and he pushes the man to the ground, spilling out his wares. The man calls him a murderer, and Sam blanches, but then quietly turns and ask Charles to dinner the next evening. Charles demurs, but accepts without objection after Sam hands him £100.

Charles rides in an open carriage toward the huge, columned mansion of the Governor. He strides into the massive central hall and upstairs where the camera follows him down another hall through a series of doors into the Governor's bathroom. The Governor sits in a small tub dictating to his secretary. Charles takes a drink and tells him about Sam Flusky. The Governor cautions him to "work harder" this time, and Charles passively assents. Hearing Sam is an ex-convict, the Governor orders Charles to stay away from him.

The next evening, under a deep blue sky, Charles is let off far in front of the Minyago Yugilla, a rounded Spanish-type mansion with a portico and verandas. Romantic music accompanies his walk to the front door; he continues down the veranda and peeks through the open French doors. He watches Sam sternly instruct his maid, Millie, and Winter on the "nob" dinner. A fight breaks out among the cooks in the kitchen as one tries to strangle another. Millie, a dark-haired, stern woman, breaks the fight up by beating the cooks with a stick. In his blue velvet waistcoat, Charles finally steps inside and introduces himself, putting forth an excuse about the doorbell not working, just as it clangs.

Sam is glad to see him, and the camera swiftly follows the two men through the elegantly blue-draped dining room to the center hall, where they greet two men who both apologize for the absence of their wives. As the red-haired minister thanks Sam for his gift of the baptismal font, more guests arrive, all with apologies for their wives. Charles makes a crack about the coincidence, and playfully discusses Sydney "society—is there any?" with a gentleman who picks his teeth. The commandant of the prison complains about the "pig-sty" conditions there, and finally the last guest arrives as Sam strides into the group, frowning, with some gruff introductions. He calls after Millie and walks with her into the dining room; he tells her not to let his wife come down. Turning, he announces dinner to the gentlemen: "We may as well get it over with."

The men sit at the table, three on either side of Sam, the other half of the table empty. Just as the minister finishes grace, there is sudden silence, and Sam turns slowly in his chair. Bare feet under a long blue dress walk into the doorway behind him, and his wife, Henrietta, puts her hands on his shoulders; her face still off camera, she requests the gentlemen to "be seated." The camera moves up to her pale face, her brown hair in ringlets, and follows her to the other end of the table, where Charles helps her to sit down and then sits attentively next to her. Quavering, extremely drunk, she remembers him as a child and recalls their families in Ireland, making bitter reference to herself and Sam, whom she glances at down the table. Finally, she admits to not being well; Charles helps her to the

curving stairway in the hall, where she thanks him and grabs the "good old balustrade."

Once upstairs, she cries out after "Charlie" and Sam tells him to go. Charles runs up the stairs to find her quivering next to her doorway, afraid of something on the bed. He walks into the blue bedroom with his gun, shrugs, then decides to shoot a bullet into the fireplace. Reassured, she sidles back into the room past him.

Thoughtfully walking downstairs, Charles comments about the rats upstairs. "Pink rats," remarks the doctor, but Charles retorts, "The color is immaterial. There are rats in New South Wales." The camera moves in to a blue-suffused close-up of the brooding Sam.

Outside, Sam and Charles turn the corner of the veranda, talking. Sam speaks of Hattie's courage as a youth. "She'd go at a fence like it had the Kingdom of Heaven on the other side.... I would no more have thought of making love to her than if she were a blessed angel. There was bound to be trouble." Sadly, he relates their affair—he was the family's groom—and the trouble that got him sent to prison for seven years. She followed him to Australia and they married, but they "were changed people.... She missed her own sort." As they walk among the vines, the camera moves up to find Hattie slightly delirious, leaning on the wrought-iron balcony in the breeze. Underneath her, Sam tells Charles he was hoping the wives would come that night to meet the Governor's cousin, and Hattie might have some society. He thanks him for "treating her right," and Charles apologizes for not doing enough. As they pass the open front doors, Hattie screams, and Sam says that Millie will take care of her. Charles offers his help, and Sam brightens; "Maybe there's hope after all—riding, clothes, old times—yes sir, I think she took a fancy to you." The camera moves up over the portico to find Millie pouring a drink for Hattie, who moans off screen.

Charles, back to the camera, sits on the desk centered in his cousin's large bright office. The Governor berates him for going to Sam Flusky's home. Charles retorts that Richard Corrigan, the Attorney General who is in the room, was also present, but the Governor refuses to be diverted and objects to the application Charles has made for land. Ruefully, Charles explains that he is going to try sheep farming. But the plot is in the center of the city, and the Governor bursts out in anger. He threatens to kick Charles out of his house if the document is not torn up, but Charles thinks he can be accommodated at Minyago Yugilla. Corrigan relates the tale of Sam Flusky, who was convicted of murdering his wife's brother and "still has a reputation for violence," but Charles bristles at his interference and makes up his mind to proceed with his plan. Handing his cousin a pen, he commands him to sign, and the Governor grimly accedes.

Surrounded by the pink and blue of the day-lit veranda, Hattie, swathed in a lace shawl, sits morbidly while Charles leans on the lattice and chews on some grass. She thanks him for his kindness the night of "that dreadful party," and he tells her she was "extremely drunk." She is taken with his frankness and he moves to kneel by her, suggesting she needs help. But it is too late, she says, she is "no good." He tries to convince her to take over the running of her house, but she impatiently insists Millie does all that. He jumps up and puts his coat behind the glass door so she can see her face in it; he convinces her that she will look in a mirror every day and it will tell her "to beat back the shadows." Inside, Millie approaches, and Charles shudders, saying he feels like someone passed over his

grave. "It's only Millie," says Hattie, "she's a wonderful woman," but Charles laughs at this. Sam appears behind them and takes Hattie's shoulders, but she rises and leaves them. He picks up some embroidery and mutters gratefully, "So you got her working on this again!"

Another day, Charles rips wrapping paper off a new mirror to reveal a close-up of Hattie in a flower-bedecked bonnet. Shyly, she smiles, and he kisses her on the neck. Weakly, she objects, but he insists his actions are "respectful," and kisses her again on the cheek. "The first work of art I've ever done, and it's wonderfully beautiful!" he beams. The camera moves away from them over to Millie who stands in the doorway of the hall and eavesdrops as he criticizes Hattie for allowing Millie to have the keys to the house, insisting that carrying them will give Hattie confidence. He challenges her with the task of entering the kitchen, then sets the task to a tune. Laughing, she goes off on his arm, and Millie steps away to avoid being noticed.

As Charles sends Hattie off into the kitchen, Millie stomps upstairs into Hattie's bedroom and gathers up her liquor bottles in a sheet and commands Winter to carry them. Foreboding music climaxes as Millie opens the kitchen door to find Hattie hesitating in the middle of the room, the three maids grouped around her. Hattie complains that they are not responding to her, and Millie says they are an ignorant lot and she will take care of them, but Hattie firmly tells her no, that from now on she wants to be consulted about everything and will give instructions to Millie every day. She demands the key to the linen closet, but Millie nods her head at Winter, who spills the sheet full of bottles on the table. The maids loudly guffaw, and Hattie moves out of the room, the camera following her as she cups her mouth and runs through the dining room and hall upstairs to her room.

A close-up of the dining table set with dessert fruit, one of the three places unused. The camera moves away to the veranda where Sam complains to Charles that Hattie, who has locked herself into her room, spends more time with Charles than she does with him. They argue, and Charles suggests Millie might be to blame, but Sam becomes angry at the suggestion. Charles determines to do something and runs upstairs and pounds on her bedroom door. The camera stays outside with Sam, who watches, then turns away to puff on his cigarette when Charles returns with no reply. Undaunted, Charles climbs the terrace wall up to Hattie's room and sits by her unconscious figure on the bed.

She wakes at his touch and moans about how useless she is. Ashen, disheveled, she rises to her feet at his insistence that she "must never give way." In tears, she collapses on his chest, and he passionately proclaims that he has never before been serious about anything, and kisses her. Still incoherent, she frowns, but then struggles to think. She looks him in the eyes and tells him how she "couldn't take control in the kitchen. Millie was right." He soothes her with reminiscences of Ireland and pulls the bell for Millie to come and put her to bed. Millie arrives, but refuses to help when Charles opens the door, telling him it is "his job." At first offended, Charles quickly adapts to the notion, and the romantic music swells as he smilingly walks back to the bed and kisses Hattie good night. He then walks to the open doors of the balcony and sees Sam down on the lawn, smoking, looking up at him.

A close-up of Millie as she complains to the brooding Sam about "interference in the kitchen." Winter stands nearby, and Charles enters from the garden and

challenges her story; Sam becomes annoyed at the bickering and, on hearing about the bottles, dismisses Millie and Winter. Alone now, Charles assures Sam he is better off without Millie, but Sam questions Charles's behavior as well. Charles piously assures him of the worth of his word, but Sam gloomily wonders about "ladies and gents" and suggests that he and Millie, being servants, might see things differently. But Charles insists on the "hope" he offers and the men shake hands.

Later, Sam sends Millie off in a carriage. Watching from her balcony, Hattie becomes alarmed and rushes downstairs. Sam gruffly sends Winter into the kitchen to deal with "those women," and Hattie hysterically bemoans the loss of Millie until Charles cheerily joins them, insisting "it's a perfect day!" Chastened by his pep talk, Hattie goes into the kitchen herself after Winter fearfully rushes out.

The camera follows her as she enters and the chatter stops. She takes the strap from the mantel and puts it in the fire. Breathlessly, she tells the women that there will be no more beating, but she will not tolerate noise, fighting, or stealing and will send them back to prison if they do not obey her. Hearing Charles's whistle from outside, she gains courage and queries them about cooking breakfast, deciding on a contest—each will make a separate dish and whoever makes the best will be the cook. The women eagerly start squabbling over the pans.

Waiting in the dining room, a frowning Hattie rings the bell as Sam and Charles flank her at the table. The plates are delivered and the camera pans from the sneering Charles, to a stunned Hattie, and to Sam, happily forking up his eggs. The other servings are charred and raw. Not down for long, Charles produces an engraved invitation to the Fluskys for an Irish Society Ball at the Government House. Sam and Hattie both take offense at the "joke," but Charles convinces them that Hattie should go and she smilingly asks Sam to go with her, but he refuses. Sam is pleased, though, and rising in anticipation of the event, attaches the house keys to Hattie's waist, suggesting that he will buy her a new dress. Charles blanches at the exchange and interrupts to suggest that he go along for the shopping or, "better yet, just send Hattie and me!" Sam quickly steps away, admitting he would be better at buying harnesses. Charles gaily changes the subject to a letter for his sister and takes dictation from Hattie. As she moves to his side and warmly thanks him for being "our guest," the camera moves away from them, around the table to Sam's empty chair and over the dining room to find Sam in the center hall walking slowly away.

Blue night surrounds Minyago Yugilla. Inside the hall, Sam hides some jewelry in his hands behind his back as he and Charles wait for Hattie to come down. She floats down the stairway in a white satin empire dress, wondering how she looks. Sam says "all right," and Charles sarcastically chastises his understatement. Sam wonders if a necklace of rubies would help, but Charles objects that she will "look like a Christmas tree," and Sam quickly gathers up the stones and hides them in his back pocket.

Left in silence after their carriage is gone, Sam walks into a close-up profile, and then Millie's voice sounds. She has a new position, but asks to stay the night; her box will be picked up in the morning. She begins to prattle about how beautiful Hattie looked in the dress everyone knows Charles picked out, and Sam quietly paces around the hall, turning to her as she warms to her subject. "They're

gentry. They don't have the same rules as us. They take everything for granted," she says. Pouting, he brushes by her, and she is left in close-up making repeated allusions to an affair between Charles and Hattie until the camera moves to a close-up of Sam as her fading words echo in his ears.

When Hattie and Charles arrive at the ball, Charles is told they are not on the list, but he tells the attendant he is incompetent and throws down his invitation before following Hattie into the ballroom. Shocked, the men at the entry compare the handwriting and decide it has been forged.

Hattie is immediately asked to dance, and the camera pans from a self-satisfied Charles on the sidelines, over the whispering crowd, who all notice the beautiful strange woman, to the Governor in his bright-red uniform, who points at her. An attendant shows him Charles's phony invitation, and Charles strides over to the Governor's side with a smirk. Facing the camera and the dance floor, they argue, and Charles calls his cousin "an old woman" who listens to gossip. The Governor demands that he leave, but suddenly his eyes light up as Hattie moves toward them. The Governor is charmed and invites her to supper, but Charles contradicts him, telling Hattie he has been ordered to take her home. Embarrassed, the Governor insists they stay, and takes Hattie off on his arm.

Charles turns toward the entrance and sees Sam striding through the crowd, the attendants hustling after him. Frowning, Charles recovers himself with a big smile and greets Sam, trying to sway him from "spoiling Hattie's success," reminding him that he is not dressed for a ball. "Spoil it! I don't want anything more from you," mutters Sam, pulling his arm out of Charles's grip and moving toward Hattie. He interrupts her and the Governor just as she is relating how much her husband loves horses. Noticing him, she turns pale and stops mid-sentence. Sam pauses, his teeth clenched, and Hattie tries to resume but he interrupts, saying she was telling the Governor that he was brought up in a stable. Hattie bravely continues but Sam will not allow her politeness, angrily telling the Governor that "she married beneath her." "No doubt," replies the Governor, and Sam throws some coins on the floor, crying out that they are for his wife's supper—and Charles's too. "He hasn't got a penny that I didn't give him," says Sam, turning toward Hattie, who is shaken but pulls herself erect. The camera moves in front of her as she walks out, head held high, and the argument, which continues, fades out behind her.

A blue-suffused long shot of the mansion. Inside the stark, draped dining room, Hattie sits and complains about Sam to Charles. He stands in the foreground, harshly condemning Sam's jealousy of her superiority and commanding her to return to Ireland. But she comes around the table to face him, calmly explaining, "Sam is part of me and I am part of Sam forever and ever. It was long ago when I learned that . . . nothing can change it." She turns away, rhapsodizing about their daylong horse rides and the trust her father placed in Sam, who always rode respectfully behind her. Delicate violin music and the camera follow her as she circles the room and relates how she felt his love, though they never spoke. Charles hangs his head. The story is romantically detailed, a full remembrance; she offered "to save" Sam and they eloped to Scotland. Feverishly she relates how her brother Dermot showed up the next day with a pistol. "He was a hard rider, that was the only good thing about him." He leveled the pistol at her, but Sam jumped in front of her and she picked up Sam's pistol and killed Dermot.

"He had a surprised look in his eye," she says, and she was sent home, delirious for several weeks. Sobbing that Sam took the blame, Hattie staggers to the fireplace mantel: Sam wrote her from the convict ship and commanded her never to reveal the truth. Hysterically, she recalls the years she spent in seedy poverty after following Sam to Australia. "Even now I sometimes long to go down, down, down to where nothing can hurt me anymore." Charles jumps up to hug her from behind and again urge her to leave Sam. Sam appears in the hallway and angrily commands Charles out.

After Charles leaves on Sam's mare, Hattie berates Sam for acting like "a madman," insisting she does not understand him, but he calls her "trash." Charles's steps interrupt them; the horse broke her leg. Sam retrieves a gun and goes out to shoot her as Hattie and Charles wait in the house. Sam returns to face Charles: "You bloody murdering gentleman!" They struggle until the pistol goes off and Charles falls.

Next morning Millie serves coffee to Sam as he waits anxiously on the veranda. Winter returns with news that Hattie will stay at the hospital, then wonders if Millie is going to stay. Sam glumly looks away.

At the hospital, Hattie is refused entrance to Charles's room where the Governor and the Attorney General stand over him and demand a statement. But Charles demurs, and the doctor sends them out.

In the corridor, the Governor talks sternly with Hattie and insists that Sam's second offense will be dealt with harshly. But Hattie sits on a bench to steady herself and admits her own guilt. Moved, the Governor joins her, warning her of the seriousness of her "story," but she calmly insists on the truth.

Later, Hattie joins Sam in their living room. He smokes and sits in a tall chair as she collapses, sobbing, in the chair opposite. She will be returned to Ireland for a trial. But Sam swiftly walks away, disparaging the machinations that have resulted in her and Charles returning to Ireland together. "And what do I do? Sit here and mind the house!" he cries. Shocked, she objects, claiming that she did it for him, but Sam's anger only grows and he stomps out. Crying, Hattie chases after him, and Millie suddenly appears between them in the hallway, her arms open, ready to hold and soothe the grateful Hattie.

At the Governor's mansion, Charles recuperates, his arm in a sling. The Governor enters to tell him that he cannot go back on the same ship as Hattie and then relates the confession. Surprised, Charles asks how she is and is told that she has gone back to "her old habits."

A thunderstorm at the mansion. Inside, Millie greets Sam in the living room, and asks to sit across from him near the fireplace. Smugly taking up her darning, she shows him the "strong stuff" that the doctor recommended for Hattie and comments how peaceful things will be without her. But Sam says he is selling the house and going back with her. Millie pleads with him to stay, and when Hattie's cries interrupt them, she tells him to leave Hattie to her, but he angrily tells her to do as she is told.

Upstairs Hattie fearfully wanders the room and asks Sam to sit with her by the window, insisting there is something in the bed "grinning" at her. He walks over and puts her to bed, insisting it is all in her head. Thunder strikes as he leaves her alone and she immediately rises in desperation, circles the bed, and suddenly pulls the sheet away. The camera jumps to a closeup of a leering, shrunken head, and Hattie faints to the floor.

Later, she sleeps propped up on the edge of the bed as Millie's hands lift the head and put it in a box. Hattie's eyes dart open and she watches Millie fill her brandy glass, then pour the entire bottle of medicine in it. Her eyes widen in horror as Millie, soothing her in a distant voice, brings her the drink. Hattie cries out for Sam, and then tells him about the medicine and the head—both of which he finds and seizes. He leans angrily into Millie, who pleads, "You drove me to it. How could I let you go!" The three argue their sides: Sam finally begins to understand, and Hattie forthrightly blames Millie. But Millie stands her ground, finally proclaiming, "I'm not good enough for you. I'm only good enough to work for you and slave for you . . ." Sam laughs at her and she finally staggers down the hall stairs, just as the Attorney General arrives.

The officials ask for Sam's corroboration of Hattie's story, but Sam refuses to cooperate. Corrigan reminds him that he may be prosecuted for the assault on Charles.

After they are gone, Sam meets Hattie on the stairs. Increasingly calm, he holds an arm out to her, "You were determined to risk your neck for me!" They embrace. "Sacrifice! All along we've sacrificed ourselves for each other. There must be an end. . . . Why must they go on and on and on," cries Sam. Arm in arm, they retire upstairs.

The next morning soldiers take away Sam, and Hattie announces that she will go too.

Close-up of Hattie in her pink bonnet as she appeals to the Governor in his office. He insists that Charles's statement concerning the shooting is not necessary, but Charles interrupts them. Hattie pleads with him to tell the truth, and he turns stoically away, hesitating, as the Governor insists that everyone knows what happened. The camera moves into a close-up of Charles as he finally speaks and dramatically tells the story of Sam's anger and the lame horse, eventually making light of the shooting—clearly it was an accident. Hattie, seated nearby, takes Charles's hand and kisses it. The Governor commands Sam's freedom and asks Hattie to leave. "I'm too busy to entertain ladies," he says ruefully as Hattie backs out of the room.

Another day, Charles says good-bye to Sam and Hattie on the dock. He walks down to the boat with Winter, who wonders why he is leaving, but Charles tells him that the country is "not quite big enough!"

40 *Stage Fright* (1949)

Director	Alfred Hitchcock
Producers	Alfred Hitchcock, Fred Aherne
Production Company	Warner Bros.-First National
Screenplay	Whitfield Cook, Alma Reville (adaptation), based on a novel by Selwyn Jepson*
Photography	Wilkie Cooper
Editing	E[dward] B. Jarvis
Set Direction	Terence Verity, Jr.
Sound	Harold King
Music	Leighton Lucas, Louis Levy (director)
Makeup	Colin Garde

Production Manager	Fred Ahern
Cast	Marlene Dietrich (Charlotte Inwood), Jane Wyman (Eve Gill), Michael Wilding (Wilfred "Ordinary" Smith), Richard Todd (Jonathan Cooper), Alistair Sim (Commodore Gill), Sybil Thorndike (Mrs. Gill), Kay Walsh (Nellie Goode), Miles Malleson (Mr. Fortesque), Hector MacGregor (Freddie Williams), Joyce Grenfell ("Lovely Ducks"), André Morell (Inspector Byard), Patricia Hitchcock (Chubby Banister), Ballard Berkeley (Sergeant Mellish)
Filmed	at Elstree Studios, London
Running Time	approximately 110 minutes
Distributor	Warner Bros.
Release Date	February 1950

Other titles: *Die rote Lola, Le Grand Alibi, Paura in Palcoscenico*

Synopsis

Under the credits, a baroquely decorated theater safety curtain rises over the live action of the first scene, the chase music ending with the last name.

In extreme long shot, a car speeds down a London Avenue near St. Paul's Church. "Any sign of the police?" asks Jonathan, as Eve drives out of town toward her father's boat. "It's Charlotte Inwood. . . . I had to help her." A flashback continues his story.

The doorbell rings in Jonathan's apartment and he walks downstairs to greet Charlotte, whose dress is stained with blood. She breathlessly tells him she didn't mean to kill her husband, but they had a quarrel over her relationship with Jonathan. Shaking, she claims she "can't go on," but he persuades her to continue as if nothing has happened, and then offers to return to her apartment and retrieve a new dress for her. Shrinking from her ready agreement, he hesitates, thinking of the risk, then bravely goes out the door when she reminds him that she thought he loved her.

There's carnival music in Charlotte's neighborhood, as Jonathan, wearing gloves, enters her apartment and cautiously goes up the wide curving stairs into her bedroom. The body lies in front of the closet, but he manages to get in and find the dress, then goes into the office to break some glass in the door and dishevel things on the desk. As he pauses over a picture of Charlotte and himself, first in her male chorus line, a woman screams and he looks over into the bedroom to see Nellie, the maid, looking at him. He runs out.

Back at Jonathan's apartment, Charlotte dresses. They reassure one and other of their love, and she leaves after he assures her he will get rid of the blood-stained dress. Hesitating to put the dress in the fireplace, he lays it aside and imagines Nellie telling the police as the phone rings. He stares at the phone until it stops ringing, then dials and asks for Eve Gill, only to find that she is rehearsing at the Royal Academy of Dramatic Art. He answers his door buzzer,

politely greets the police, then quickly locks the door between him and them and
jumps into his car. It falters at the start and the detectives pound at the windows
until he finally pulls away.

At the Royal Academy of Dramatic Arts, police pull up next to Jonathan's
car; he is inside trying to get Eve's attention while she is rehearsing on stage. He
grabs a large feathered hat and throws himself at her in a stage move just at the
moment the police peek into the auditorium. He whispers his plight and Eve tells
him the police are gone. After a reprimand from her director, she leaves with
Jonathan.

Back in the car, his story complete to the present, Jonathan wonders if Eve
hates him, and he is pleased to hear her reassurance that they're "old friends,"
though she wonders if she should take lessons in "second fiddle."

At her father's home by the sea, Eve motions Jonathan out toward the boat,
but Commodore Gill commands them inside, where it is warm.

Later, as Jonathan sleeps on the spartan bench and Commodore Gill plays
his accordion, Eve tells him the story. He wonders aloud about his reputation,
teasing her about her tendency toward "dramatic situations." He notices the
blood has been deliberately smeared on the dress and suggests they call the
police. Alarmed by this news, Eve wakes up Jonathan, who flies into a rage at the
revelation, throws the dress in the fireplace, and accuses Eve of being jealous. Her
father politely requests better manners from Jonathan, who quickly apologizes
and pleads that he must get some sleep.

Eve and her father go out for a walk by the sea. They ponder how to bring
Charlotte to confess now that the evidence is gone and Eve says she'll confront
her, "one woman to another." "An impressive situation at any time," intones her
father, but agrees to be drawn into the plot anyway. He argues the scheme is
dangerous and reminds Eve that she is guilty of concealing a fugitive and could
end up in prison, "meditating on the folly of transmuting melodrama into real
life." She insists Jonathan means too much to her not to help him.

Next morning, Commodore Gill sleeps in a downstairs alcove curled up with
his accordion, and Eve slips out to find a warning note from him on the seat of her
car. In London, she rounds a corner near Charlotte Inwood's apartment and finds
a crowd gathered outside. She telephones her father from a nearby booth and he
sarcastically encourages her to return. Some detectives emerge from the building
and Eve follows one into a pub across the street, transforming herself into a
grieved woman before stepping inside. She mournfully asks for a small brandy
and then sits sadly at a table by herself. The detective, finding her attractive,
eventually joins her. She claims to be upset by the murder. Twice she slips and
alludes to knowing his occupation and he momentarily frowns, but her pleasant
chatter makes him smile again. She insists on gossiping about the murder and he
discourages her, until Charlotte's maid, Nellie, enters and loudly starts telling
everyone about the murder and her awful experiences with the police. Having
had enough, Inspector Smith asks Eve if he can see her home.

Outside her house, he flirts with her, introducing himself as Smith. "Just
Ordinary Smith?" she smiles, and he shows a calling card with Wilfred O. on it.
She agrees to have him over for tea the next day.

Back in the now very crowded pub, Eve, pretending to be a reporter, talks to
Nellie and bribes her to pass her off as her cousin, a substitute for Nellie because
she is sick.

At home, Eve pulls her hair back primly and adds a lit cigarette and

thick-lensed glasses for her new job. She goes outside and rings the bell to test her disguise, but her mother recognizes her instantly.

Now looking merely plain, Eve, using the name Doris Tinsdale, approaches Charlotte's apartment for her first day of work. ^H Inspector Smith follows shortly behind her, but she runs up the stairs and barges into Charlotte's sitting room before he can see her. The camera slowly tracks "Doris" around a corner to find Charlotte being fitted for her mourning clothes, wondering out loud if she should "go on tonight" and requesting a little more décolletage. When the inspector is announced, "Doris" is sent into the next room for the purpose of listening and interrupting when Charlotte signals. Smith and a colleague briefly question Charlotte about Jonathan, then leave, followed down the stairs by the dismissed "Doris." Afterward, Charlotte and Freddie Williams, her producer, embrace; he reassures her that the truth "would break her" and he will not allow it.

Later, in the cozy parlor of Eve's home, Inspector Smith chats with Mrs. Gill over tea as Eve sneaks by them to go change her clothes. Her father joins the tea drinkers, then Eve bursts in with apologies, saying she must return to the theater immediately. She and her father exchange a few words about "poor old Johnny," and Eve anxiously insists that Wilfred, whom she has now dubbed "Ordinary," play a piece on the piano. Acquiescing, he listens curiously to Eve's father continue his talk of Jonathan's strange actions until Eve is compelled to tell him that Ordinary is an inspector on the Inwood case. Ordinary calmly asks how she knows that, and Eve smilingly responds that she saw his picture in the paper. He begins to play a romantic piece, and for a moment they all drift, composed in a tableau facing the camera, until the clock chimes and Eve rushes out, whispering in her father's ear that he must meet her at the theater, and in a normal tone, insisting that Ordinary stay. In turn, Ordinary demands she call him the next morning.

At the theater, Charlotte Inwood walks through a musical number surrounded by tuxedoed gentlemen. Standing in the wings Eve tries to convince her father of the wisdom of her scheme, then races off to attend to Charlotte at the break and pump her unsuccessfully about the murder. Passing by her father on her way back to the stage, she urges him to find Jonathan. Charlotte sings "I'm the Laziest Girl in Town," on and off a divan, while Eve anxiously watches. Suddenly Jonathan appears in front of the stage, then enters the wings where Eve spots him. After the number, he heads for the dressing room and Eve boldly warns Charlotte away from "a man in the room." "You're an imbecile," snorts Charlotte glancing backwards, "I'll change myself, you needn't come up." Eve follows and listens at the door.

Inside Charlotte wonders how she can "repay" Jonathan, as the camera moves in to his confused and surprised expression. She glibly tells him he was foolish to come and his best bet is South America where she may join him "for a week or two" when the show is over. "A week or two!" Jonathan protests, then his expression hardens. Understanding now, he taunts her with the dress, which she is appalled to hear has not been destroyed. Triumphant, he declares that *he* will decide how long the show will run. Charlotte gets a curtain call; on her way to the stage Detective Loomis tells her Jonathan is in the building and they are going to search her dressing room. Eve takes the detective upstairs, loudly proclaiming their arrival to warn Jonathan. He hides in the bathroom, and as the inspector attempts a search, Eve faints, then clutches him to her, completely commanding his attention.

That night, Commodore Gill walks Eve home and she concocts a scheme to

take Inspector Smith to a garden party the next day in hopes of convincing him of Charlotte's guilt.

At home, Mrs. Gill is chatting with Jonathan, who has requested shelter for the night. Mrs. Gill is taken aback at this and Commodore Gill tells her the truth, but she refuses to believe him and perversely agrees to harbor Jonathan. Back in the parlor, Jonathan further pleads with Eve and complains that Charlotte has betrayed him. They embrace, but Eve hears Ordinary Smith at the piano.

Next day, Ordinary meets Eve at a taxi stand. On the way to the garden party, he tells her they are searching for Doris Tinsdale, yesterday's incident clearly having annoyed him. He compliments her beauty, but she persistently returns to the murder case, wondering this and that. As they look into each other's eyes, romantic music behind, she points out at length Charlotte's "cold calculating actions" while he indulgently explains them away, increasingly concerned with gazing at her. The camera draws closer to them as they draw closer to one another until she, sounding less and less convincing, almost forgets her goal, and he, drained, agrees completely with her. They kiss.

A sea of umbrellas at the garden party parts to reveal a tough-looking Nellie under one of them. Startled at the sight of her, Eve insists that Ordinary amuse himself and sends him off to another tent with a couple of her friends.

Outside Eve gives £5 to Nellie, who has discovered her ruse, and promises to give her twenty more in half an hour to buy her silence. Eve telephones her father from one of the tents and asks him to bring some cash quickly. Outside again, she runs into Freddie Williams. Adopting her guise as "Doris", she goes with him to see Charlotte, who sets her to work.

At an ice cream table, Charlotte's friends, Chubby Banister and Valerie Maynard, let it slip to Ordinary that Charlotte has not been to rehearsal in days.

Nellie waits threateningly outside Charlotte's tent until Commodore Gill arrives and "Doris" signals their relationship to them. He hands over the £20 and a cutting remark, as Eve escapes from Charlotte and rushes out to explain to him the day's events and her presence in Charlotte's tent. "If there's one thing I hate, it's saying I told you so," says the Commander. Desperate, Eve says she is going to find Ordinary and tell him the truth. Her father asks if she succeeded in convincing the inspector of Charlotte's guilt, but Eve fades away, disconcerted. "I see, some more important topic arose in the conversation," he says, "You're not, by any chance, thinking of changing horses in midstream?" Innocently, Eve admits so and he wonders aloud at the bad timing, as Jonathan is hiding in their house. Ordinary Smith arrives and Commodore Gill skulks away to mull over the new developments. He catches sight of a kewpie doll and calls Eve over with instructions to get Smith up front for Charlotte's show. Ordinary doesn't remember promising to take Eve to hear Charlotte sing but melts agreeably at the memory of the scene in the taxi.

Commodore Gill tries to barter the doll from the game booth, but, lacking the cash, is forced to shoot for it. Trying to claim for his own another shootist's hit, he at first fails, then finally finds a short man to intimidate into giving up his hit. Grasping the finally won doll, he cuts himself and smears blood on the front of the dress then finds a Boy Scout and instructs him to carry the doll up to Charlotte. Slowly walking the aisle and climbing the steps to the stage, the boy holds up the doll until Charlotte falters and stops singing. Freddie orders "Miss Tinsdale" from the audience to the stage and Eve obliges. She looks apologetically at Ordinary, who completes the connection.

At home, Commodore Gill and Eve explain their predicament to Jonathan,

who wonders if he should give himself up. Mrs. Gill enters and announces Inspector Smith downstairs.

Down in the parlor, Ordinary angrily confronts Eve, while she confidently tries to explain. Depressed, he offers to help her, and she tries to convince him she has fallen in love with him. Her parents come in bringing drinks and Mrs. Gill leaves to tend to "Mr. Robinson." Smith wonders angrily "what sort of a father" the Commodore is, and the Commodore, refusing to be put on the defensive, calmly replies, "unique." Throwing out a new idea, he relates Nellie Goode's blackmail scheme and suggests that "Doris" should try to blackmail Charlotte while the inspector listens. Discovering there is no blood-stained dress, Smith leaves in disgust, recommending that "Doris" return to the theater.

At a phone booth, Smith posts some men at the theater, then calls Mrs. Gill, and asks for "Mr. Robinson."

A microphone feeding into loudspeakers in the auditorium is installed in a prop room near the stage. Commodore Gill and Smith wait there together. "Doris" helps Charlotte get ready to leave, then demands a private audience with her in the prop room, where she tries to blackmail her; instead she is told that Jonathan killed Charlotte's husband, and though it was in her presence, Charlotte had nothing to do with it. The conversation booms to the men in the empty auditorium as Eve drops her guise and confronts Charlotte more aggressively, but Charlotte insists on her innocence. Smith moves to end the confrontation, meeting Eve as she exits despondent and crying. In the front row, her father gently claps for her. Jonathan suddenly appears surrounded by detectives and when Eve cries out, he makes a break and runs down the stairs. The detectives and Eve follow, but she finds him first and guides him farther down and away.

In the wings, Charlotte sits in the company of a detective. Seeing the microphone, she understands and wearily begins to tell the rest of her story, comparing her husband to a dog to whom she had given all her love but who had rejected it. A close-up from above shows smoke swirling around her bitter face.

Nearby Inspector Smith hangs up the telephone and informs Commodore Gill that Jonathan has killed before and Eve is in very great danger.

Deep down in a storage room of the theater, Eve and Jonathan hide in a carnival vehicle, bits of light illuminating their eyes. Outside, they can hear her father calling for her to come away because Jonathan is dangerous. Jonathan, wild-eyed and sweating, tells Eve the truth, pleading for understanding of his impulsive behavior. Turning toward her, he realizes that he might be in a better position to plead insanity if he murdered her "for no reason whatever." He raises his hands, warming to the notion, but Eve raises hers in alertness and succeeds in convincing him that it is time to try to escape. As they tiptoe out, she suddenly slams a door behind him, locks it between them, and screams out for help.

Jonathan surfaces in the orchestra pit, fully visible to the detectives scurrying around the auditorium who race to surround him. Frantic, Jonathan slips near the edge of the stage, becomes caught under the dropping metal curtain, and is killed.

Eve is consoled by Ordinary, who puts his arm around her and walks her away.

Notes. *Some filmographies indicate the script is based on the stories "Man Running" and "Outrun the Constable" by the same author. † Hitchcock does bit as passer-by, who stares at Eve on the sidewalk.

41   *Strangers on a Train* (1951)

Director	Alfred Hitchcock
Producer	Alfred Hitchcock
Production Company	Warner Bros.
Screenplay	Raymond Chandler, Czenzi Ormonde, Whitfield Cook (adaptation), from the novel by Patricia Highsmith
Photography	Robert Burks, A.S.C.
Editing	William Ziegler
Art Direction	Edward S. Haworth
Set Direction	George James Hopkins
Sound	Dolph Thomas
Special Effects	H. F. Koenekamp, A.S.C.
Music	Dimitri Tiomkin (composer), Ray Heindorf (director)
Costumes	Leah Rhodes
Production Associate	Barbara Keon
Cast	Farley Granger (Guy Haines), Robert Walker (Bruno Anthony), Ruth Roman (Anne Morton), Leo G. Carroll (Senator Morton), Patricia Hitchcock (Barbara Morton), Laura Elliot (Miriam Haines), Marion Lorne (Mrs. Anthony), Jonathan Hale, Howard St. John, John Brown, Norma Varden, Robert Gist, John Doucette
Filmed	at Warner Bros. Studios, Los Angeles
Running Time	approximately 100 minutes
Distributor	Warner Bros.
Release Date	June 1951

Other titles: *Verschwörung im Nordexpreß, L'Inconnu du Nord-Express, L'Altro Uomo, Delitto per Delitto*

Synopsis

Credits appear over the large, gracefully roofed turnaround of a train station.

A taxi pulls into the driveway, the camera centered low at the curb. A man in two-toned black and white shoes emerges and takes his bag from the driver. Another taxi drives up and a man in plain dark shoes emerges, following the same path into the station and onto the train. The two pairs of legs enter the lounge car and sit across from one another, one foot knocking the other across the way, and the owner making excuses.

Looking up, Bruno, one of the dark-haired young men, says, "Aren't you Guy Haines, the tennis player?" and moves over next to him. Guy smiles slightly in response, but Bruno forces the conversation, wondering that "it must be exciting to be so important." Guy gives Bruno his cigarette lighter to use and turns slightly sullen when Bruno guesses the lighter is from his famous girlfriend, Anne Morton, the daughter of a senator, and then is offended when Bruno goes on to guess that Guy is probably anxious to get rid of his wife so that he can marry her. Bruno quickly apologizes, then insists Guy have lunch in his compartment.

In Bruno's compartment, he tells Guy he hates his father and wants to kill him. Guy laughs, but becomes upset when Bruno returns, in his familiar way, to chatting about Guy's wife and girlfriend. Sitting up, Bruno broaches the subject of the perfect murder. Guy is calm and smiling again, responding, "I may be old-fashioned, but I thought murder was against the law." Bruno bangs the table, shouting, "What is a life or two . . . some people are better off dead!" He warms to the subject as Guy rises to get off the train, brushing aside Guy's protests, he explains his idea to swap murders: "your wife, my father, crisscross!" When Bruno asks Guy what he thinks of his theories, Guy humors him, "Sure, they're O.K.," he says on his way out. Bruno picks up the lighter Guy has left behind, and, lying back, mutters "crisscross."

Guy gets off the train at Metcalf and leaves his bags with a friendly attendant. ^H He starts off into the town and looks in the shop window of a music store.

Inside, he approaches the counter where his wife Miriam, an unpleasant woman in thick glasses, is working; she compliments him on the tan he's getting playing with his "rich friends." He asks when they meet with her lawyer, but she wonders if he might not be jealous since he didn't agree to the divorce right away. She motions him into a sound booth so they won't be overheard. He hands her some money for the divorce, but she tells him she's not going to go through with it. They argue; she's pregnant by another man and says she is going to Washington to live with him. He leaps at her, but she coolly tells him to keep his voice down. She threatens him with a lawsuit and he grabs her, causing the rest of the people in the shop to turn and look. A man opens the door on their struggle and Guy walks out, with Miriam shouting and running after him.

In a phone booth, Guy tells Anne that Miriam is refusing the divorce. "You sound so savage," she says, and he tells her twice he'd like to break Miriam's neck, finally shouting over the noise of the trains that he'd like to "strangle her."

Bruno flexes his hands as the camera moves out to show him and his mother, who is filing his nails. She giggles over her "naughty boy" and reminds him to shave before his father gets home. He slams the table in protest; to soothe him she takes him over to the other side of the large sitting room to see her painting. She is disconcerted as he laughs uncontrollably at the swirling gargoyle figure which he says looks like his father. The butler announces Bruno's call to Southampton is ready, just as his father walks in. Bruno brushes by him to the phone, and his parents begin to argue in the background. Bruno asks Guy, who is in a gym locker-room, if he is going to get the divorce. He becomes sympathetic hearing of the betrayal, then Guy abruptly hangs up. Bruno hears his father arguing with his mother about "restraints" for his dangerous son.

The train pulls into Metcalf and Bruno gets off and walks purposefully to a telephone booth.

That night, sitting at a bus stop, he watches as Miriam emerges from her home accompanied by two men. Laughing, they run across the street to catch the bus. Bruno follows. They all get off at an amusement park. Miriam notices Bruno watching them as they buy ice cream. Walking on, Bruno bursts a small boy's balloon when the boy pesters him with a play gun. At a strongman contest, Miriam turns to look for Bruno and finds him unexpectedly close behind her. He strides up after her boyfriends have finished and tops the machine. At the merry-go-round, he gets on a horse behind her, and she turns to flirt with him as they all sing along with the calliope on "The Band Played On."

At the tunnel of love, Bruno follows them in a separate boat, munching on

popcorn, and she playfully screams in the tunnel when one of the men tries to kiss her. Debarking across at a dark island, the three continue their chase game. Miriam, suddenly alone in a close-up, turns to face Bruno. Snapping the lighter in her face and confirming her name, he immediately grabs her by the neck, causing her glasses to fall. The calliope music from the merry-go-round continues in the background; the scene is reflected in her glasses and he slowly forces her to the ground, strangling her as her friends continue to call her name, looking for her. Bruno steps quickly to his boat and shoves off, just as the men shout that they've found her: "She's fainted!" then, "She's dead!" Their shouts attract a crowd at the gate of the ride. Bruno steps off his boat and strides through, but the attendant in charge of the ride notices him. On his way out of the park, Bruno stops to help a blind man cross the street.

Sitting on the lounge car of a train, Guy chats with a drunken professor, who lapses into singing.

That evening, a taxi pulls up to an apartment house. Guy runs up the steps to his door, but turns when he hears Bruno eerily call him from across the street. He goes to meet him behind a tall iron fence which shadows them in the streetlights. Bruno shows him Miriam's glasses and informs him "it was all over in no time." Guy threatens to go to the police, but falls speechless as Bruno tells him they'll both be arrested if he goes to the police, because, after all, Guy has the motive for the murder. The phone rings in Guy's apartment, but Guy stands, transfixed. The police drive up and ring his bell, and he moves back, hiding with Bruno. "You've got me acting like a criminal, you crazy fool!" Bruno becomes angry at this, but recovers to discuss his father's murder. Guy walks away, and Bruno follows him up the steps, trying to soothe him, "You're not yourself, you're tired." But Guy angrily shouts that he never wants to see him again, and Bruno gives up for the moment.

Inside his apartment, Guy picks up the telephone and tells Anne, who is upset, that he will be over right away.

She opens the door to him and they embrace and kiss passionately. "You're trembling," he says. "I wonder if you know how much I love you," she says, then solemnly ushers him into the elegant living room to see her father. Senator Morton stands stiffly, but Babs, Anne's teenage sister, runs to embrace Guy, saying something terrible has happened. They break the news and Anne haltingly says, "It's not as though anyone could say you had anything to do with it." A close-up of Anne from above shows her blank stare as she quietly says, "She was strangled." Guy wants to keep them out of it, but the senator advises him not to lose any sleep over accusations and to call the police. Babs and her father say good night and Anne moves to embrace Guy; she reminds him of what he said to her over the telephone. She stops him with a kiss on the word strangle. He is visibly nervous and opens his eyes when they kiss again.

Guy enters a police office and asks for Captain Turley. On edge, he waits, then is relieved to notice the professor from the train. He is taken in to see the captain, who calls in the professor, but the man has forgotten Guy. Depressed at first, Guy brightens as he suggests that the important thing is that he named someone on the train and the police found him.

In the Morton living room, Guy tells them about the professor and the police theory that he still could have boarded the train after Miriam's murder. He shows them his guard, Leslie Hennessey, standing in front of the house. They are all concerned that he has no alibi. The butler comes in carrying a telephone, and Guy

takes the call there. Quiet eerie music begins on the soundtrack when Bruno says hello, and Guy hangs up, startled at the intrusion, while everyone else stands behind him, quieted by his odd behavior.

Hennessey and Guy stride around the Lincoln Memorial talking tennis. Guy expresses his desire to go into politics, then suddenly notices Bruno looming far away up on the steps of the memorial. Guy suggests they get a taxi, and they circle back by Bruno, who still stares at them.

Guy comes out of his bedroom in his robe and notices a note on the floor. He picks it up and opens it: "We must get together and make plans. My father will be going away soon. Call me. B." Guy crushes and burns it.

Anne and Guy stroll in a museum, commenting on the little time they have together. Bruno calls Guy over and anxiously tells him his father is leaving next week; Guy hisses at him to stay away. Anne stares at Bruno's signature tie clip, then Guy returns and tells her he's only a fan.

At the Mortons, a secretary hands Guy a piece of registered mail. It's a letter from Bruno with a floor plan of his home and a key.

At a tennis match, Guy walks onto the court and notices Bruno in the audience, the only one not following the volleys back and forth.

Later, Guy runs up to the café area to find Bruno socializing with Anne and some friends. The eerie music begins again when Anne notices the same tie clip and becomes suspicious. Babs comes up and distracts Guy with a ghoulish anecdote, then asks who the attractive man is. She moves over to the table and when introduced, Bruno stares at her sullenly, seeing a likeness to Miriam that is reinforced by a reprise of the calliope music. Anne also notices the awkward moment that makes Babs's gracious smile fade.

Guy unwraps a gun from its brown paper wrapping. His door buzzes and he quickly sets the gun inside a drawer. Hennessey comes in and they chat while Guy finishes putting on his tuxedo.

Anne nervously looks around at a formal party. Guy stands fiddling absent-mindedly with his glass when Babs appears and cheers him up. Anne spots Bruno standing in the doorway. Seeing Guy, Bruno rushes over holding out his hand, which Guy refuses. Turning, Bruno sees Anne and walks swiftly to greet her. She introduces him to her father. Bruno warmly shakes the senator's hand and tells him of his idea for "harnessing the life force," and other strange notions, then moves away. The senator is dumbfounded, asks who invited him, and wonders at his "unusual personality." Babs becomes alarmed at the sight of Bruno and follows to watch as he talks with a guest about murder. Attracting attention, he warms particularly to a couple of laughing older women and sits across from them. As he attempts a demonstration of strangulation on one of them, the camera moves into a close-up of Babs watching from behind; Bruno fixates on her, once again hearing the calliope music, and nearly strangles the woman, who starts to sob. Her friend calls for help and Bruno faints to the floor. As some guests carry Bruno into the library, the camera remains on Babs who hunches her body in fear.

Alone in the library with Bruno, Guy angrily calls him a "mad, crazy maniac" and punches him back down when he wakes up, then straightens his tie and leads him out the door. Aghast, Babs watches them leave, then meets Anne by the stairs and tells her "he was strangling me . . . he went into a trance . . . it was horrible." She takes off her glasses and Anne looks down at a close-up of them as "The Band Played On" is briefly reprised on the soundtrack.

Outside the front door, Anne meets Guy, who has just put Bruno in a cab.

Confronting him, she asks what Miriam looked like, did she wear glasses? "How did you get him to do it?" she says, and Guy tells her the story, finishing with, "and now the lunatic wants me to kill his father." "Why didn't you go to the police?" she asks. "And have them say what you just said?" he replies, "Bruno would just say we planned it together." She notices Hennessey watching from across the street, and he tells her he didn't want to drag anyone else into it. "Look, now you're acting guilty, too!" They go inside.

Out on the sidewalk, Hennessey tells his replacement, Hammond, that "something funny is going on."

From his room, Guy telephones Bruno and tells him he will kill his father that night. He instructs Bruno to get out of the house and not come back until the next day. He then takes the gun out of the drawer, and slips out down the back fire escape.

He crosses the vast lawn in front of Bruno's home and lets himself in the front door of the dark house. Inside, he puts a flashlight on the map, then starts upstairs, meeting a large dog that growls, then becomes docile and licks his hand. Upstairs, he opens the door to the father's room and, seeing the figure in the bed, calls out "Mr. Anthony . . . I need to talk with you about your son." Bruno, the figure in the bed, switches on the light, commenting that he wondered about the "sudden decision." Guy says he has no intention of going through with the murder and hands over the key and the gun. He pleads with Bruno to get help for his sickness, then turns his back and walks out as Bruno sits on the bed pointing the gun at him. He goes out and down the stairs with Bruno following him. Guy watches warily but Bruno tells him not to worry, he doesn't want to wake his mother.

Hennessey and Hammond discuss Guy's disappearance. Hammond wants to take Guy in when they find him, but Hennessey reminds him that there is no evidence to connect him to the scene of the crime.

At Bruno's home, Anne, primly dressed in suit and hat, speaks with his mother about the murder. Mrs. Anthony avoids responding to the accusation, but giggles nervously about Bruno's escapades, suggesting that it's probably just another practical joke. She leaves her puzzled guest, and Bruno stops by in his dressing gown, telling Anne he is very upset with Guy. She winces as he sits behind her on the arm of the couch and tells her how Guy asked him to go with him to pick up his lighter from the scene of the crime. Tears fall down her cheeks as he walks out, teasing her with a little wave good-bye.

Crowds pour into the tennis stadium. Inside at a café table, Anne sits with Guy and tells him what Bruno said about the lighter. She tells him he should go to Metcalf right away, but he wonders about making Hennessey suspicious. They plan to have her cover for him while he escapes after the game.

Hennessey and Hammond stand outside the stadium and discuss when to pick up Guy.

Guy returns to the court as Anne sits next to Babs in the stands and tells her of her part in the plan.

The game starts. Guy plays hard, his eye on the clock. In Washington, Bruno enters a cab and heads for Union Station. Back at the game, it is noted that Guy has abandoned his "usual watch and wait strategy." On the train Bruno gives a passenger a light with matches, hiding the lighter. Guy is on his way to a straight-set win; in the stands, Anne tells Babs to get ready. Complaining that she wished she knew "what it was all about," Babs gets up to do her errand.

The game continues. Babs puts Guy's pants in the back of a waiting taxi. Guy's opponent starts to make headway in the match, then wins the third set, as Guy, frustrated, gulps a glass of water.

Bruno leaves the train fondling the lighter, then accidentally drops it in a grated drain. The tennis match has turned into a "dogfight." Bruno tries to enlist the help of a uniformed man to get the lighter out of the drain; a group of bystanders assembles around the grate, agreeing that the lighter is gone. Guy continues to play. Bruno sticks his hand down the grate and manages to pick up the lighter with his fingertips, but drops it farther down the hole. The match continues with just one point between Guy and a win. Bruno forces his arm farther down the grate as the game continues. He sweats, his hand an inch above the lighter lying on some leaves. The game continues and Bruno touches the lighter again, finally getting a good grip on it, pulling it up, then quickly running off.

Guy wins the match and runs over to Anne, who tells him the taxi is waiting. Babs distracts Hennessey by dropping her open compact and powder on him. Hammond spots Guy rushing through the crowd and Hennessey pushes Babs to the ground to get her away from him. The two detectives see Guy get into a cab, then commandeer a limousine with an older woman in it who's excited at the prospect of a chase. Guy gets out at Penn Station and the two follow him down stairs to a ticket window. Standing back, they wait until he buys a ticket, then find out from the agent he is going to Metcalf. They decide to let the men there handle it.

From very high, the camera shows Bruno entering the amusement park. He stops at a soda fountain and asks what time it gets dark.

Guy sits in the lounge car and watches a couple of strangers meet when one hits the other with his foot. Guy turns uncomfortably away.

Bruno loiters near a soda concession and the attendant mentions the good business they are doing since the murder. "I don't think that's a nice way to make money," snarls Bruno, then gazes impatiently at the sun.

On the train, Guy also notices the sun going down.

The train pulls into Metcalf. Guy gets off and gets into a cab; a nearby detective reports to a waiting police car that he's headed for the amusement park.

At the park, Bruno eyes the tunnel of love, then walks past the merry-go-round to stand in the long line.

Guy sits in the taxi, his teeth clenched.

Police arrive at the front gate of the park and disperse. Guy arrives, notices a police car, but pushes ahead; the police spot him and orders go out for all to follow. Bruno waits in line; the police arrive and warn the attendant, who had noticed Bruno the night of the murder, to be on the lookout. Guy walks nervously through the grounds, constantly looking over his shoulder. Bruno hides his face under the shadow of his hat, but a light glares over him momentarily; the attendant notices him and walks over to tell the police. Bruno sees him and moves away from the ride. Turning, he sees another policeman, then Guy. Guy yells out his name and Bruno hops on the merry-go-round, Guy quickly after him. The police bring out their guns and accidentally shoot the driver of the ride, who falls on the controls sending it into high gear. Two detectives try to jump on but are thrown back onto the ground by the speeding motion. Moving to the edge of the platform, Bruno sees only a blur. Guy comes up behind him and demands the lighter. They struggle around an outside pole as the other passengers scream.

The detectives gather around as the attendant points at the two men fighting: "That's the one." "Of course, we know that," Captain Turley says. Bruno and Guy fist-fight as an older man volunteers to stop the carousel. He begins to crawl under it toward the controls in the center. Bruno pushes at Guy who hangs on to one of the ponies as a woman screams in fear for her little boy. The boy is having fun riding up and down as the fight moves near him, and the man underneath continues his crawl. The boy starts beating on Bruno too, and Bruno turns and pushes him off his perch. As the boy rolls toward the edge of the platform, Guy leaps down and picks him up and puts him on a bench. Bruno grabs Guy from behind and they fall to the floor, the screams intensifying as Bruno struggles to place Guy's head under a pony's moving hoof. Guy squirms out, holding onto a pole and lying on the floor. Bruno hits with his feet at Guy's hands. The man underneath wipes his brow. Bruno stomps hard on Guy's knuckles. The man rises in the inside and pulls back the controls, stripping the gears and destroying the carousel. Ponies fly loose and the wreck spins off kilter and finally comes to a dusty halt.

The screaming crowd pushes toward the wreckage. Turley is next to Guy. Hammond rushes over with the attendant who says it's not Guy they want but the man he was fighting. Turley is disbelieving and asks Guy for the story. He tells them Bruno has his lighter and was going to plant it at the scene of the crime; they find Bruno, trapped in the wreckage, barely able to whisper. "Hello, Guy," says Bruno sweetly. Guy introduces the chief of police to him, and Bruno calmly denies he has the lighter. But he dies and his hand relaxes uncovering the evidence.

Guy telephones Anne. She tells her family Guy will be back the next day and they are all jubilant.

Another day, Anne and Guy sit in the lounge car of the train. A clergyman sitting across the way recognizes Guy who briefly smiles, but then gets up with Anne and rushes away.

Note. [H] Hitchcock does bit as man boarding train with cello.

Remake: *Once You Kiss a Stranger* (U.S., 1970), directed by Robert Sparr.

42   *I Confess* (1953)

Director	Alfred Hitchcock
Assistant Director	Don Page
Producer	Alfred Hitchcock
Production Company	Warner Bros.-First National
Screenplay	George Tabori, William Archibald, from a play *Nos Deux Consciences* by Paul Anthelme
Photography	Robert Burks, A.S.C.
Editing	Rudi Fehr, A.C.E.
Art Direction	Edward S. Haworth
Set Direction	George James Hopkins
Sound	Oliver S. Garretson
Music	Dimitri Tiomkin (composer and conductor), Ray Heindorf (direction)
Costumes	Orry-Kelly
Makeup	Gordon Bau

Production Supervisor	Sherry Shourds
Production Associate	Barbara Keon
Technical Adviser	Father Paul La Couline
Cast	Montgomery Clift (Michael Logan), Anne Baxter (Ruth Grandfort), Karl Malden (Inspector Larrue), Brian Aherne (Willy Robertson), O. E. Hasse (Otto Keller), Roger Dann, Dolly Haas, Charles Andre, Judson Pratt, Ovila Legare, Gilles Pelletier (Father Benoit)
Filmed	at Warner Bros. Studios, Los Angeles, and in Quebec
Running Time	approximately 95 minutes
Distributor	Warner Bros.
Release Date	February 1953

Other titles: *Ich beichte, La Loi du Silence, Io Confesso*

Synopsis

A night sky over the river silhouettes Quebec. As the credits appear, the camera moves up to the spires and the sky, accompanied by the young-love theme music.

A series of Quebec streets ^H and one-way signs come to an end as the camera moves into the window of an office where a man is sprawled dead on the floor. A bead curtain jangles from recent activity.

Outside, a cleric steps swiftly down the sidewalk; a couple of young girls walk behind. Down another street, alone now, the man takes off his robe and carries it.

Father Michael Logan, a dark-haired, intense man, looks out the window of his room and notices the man enter the church next door.

Father Logan rounds the altar of the church looking out into the dark of the pews. Moving over to the votive lights and picking up one, he walks down the middle aisle and finds Otto Keller. "What are you doing here so late at night?" he softly asks. Otto is distraught and thanks him for giving him and his wife, German refugees, work at the rectory and a home, "even friendship. You will hate me now," he says. Father Logan says he doesn't hate anyone, and Otto, gaining resolve, says he want to make a confession.

They enter the confessional and Otto tells him he has killed Mr. Villette. Streaked in shadow, Father Logan moves his hand in agitation. Otto says he went there to steal, but Villette interrupted him.

Later, in his own quarters, Otto continues telling the story to his wife, Alma. "I didn't mean to kill him. It was an accident . . . $2,000 . . . Father Logan told me I must give it back . . . but I can't," pleading, he looks at her, their heads almost touching. She tells him Father Logan will tell the police whether he does or not. His eyes become more alert as he realizes that Father Logan cannot tell what he heard in the confessional. Rising and gripping Alma violently, he insists that "no one knows."

The next morning, outside the front stairs of the rectory, Alma asks Otto if he is going to the police, but he calmly replies he is going, as usual, to tend Mr. Villette's garden. She shudders, then stares after him.

He walks by the church, pausing to notice the worshipers leaving mass.

Inside the vestibule, Father Logan disrobes, attended by his altar boy. He goes into the rectory through the connecting passage, where Alma, carrying a tray, shrinks when she sees him. He stops to look at a half-painted room strewn with sheeting; joining him, Father Milet, his superior, wonders how long it will take to finish and if he knows of any paints that do not smell.

In the paneled dining room, they sit at the table and pray. Father Benoit, the youngest priest, flops his bicycle in the hall and joins them as Alma serves breakfast. When Benoit asks to have Otto mend his bicycle, Alma says her husband has gone to tend Villette's garden; she stares at Father Logan's back as she lies. Father Milet sermonizes about tending to one's own possessions and Father Logan suddenly rises and excuses himself, causing the others to stare after him.

Forceful orchestral music accompanies Father Logan as he walks purposefully down the streets, coming to a crowd surrounding Villette's home. He walks through and stops at the barrier; one of the guards recognizes him and tells him of the murder. Pushing on to the front door, he tells the guard he had an appointment with Villette and offers to help.

Taken into the house, he meets Inspector Larrue, Otto lurking behind him in the hall. Larrue says he would prefer to speak with him later. Father Logan pauses, framed momentarily in the doorway on his way out. One of the detectives brings Larrue a strongbox of money, suggesting the motive was not robbery. Larrue queries Otto, who tells of his great fear, "a man without a country," in finding the body. Larrue becomes distracted noticing Father Logan outside pacing the sidewalk in front of the crowd. Dismissing Otto, he watches until Father Logan is greeted by a woman emerging from the crowd.

Outside, Father Logan grabs the blond woman's hand and tells her Villette's been murdered. "We're free," she says, as they move away into the crowd.

Larrue watches, thoughtful.

A large courthouse. Ruth Grandfort, the woman who had just met Father Logan outside Villette's house, parks her car in front. She asks a guard if her husband, Pierre Grandfort, is in the chamber. She enters during a debate about equal salary for female schoolteachers. One of the legislators argues that such a move "would bring disaster to the whole economy," but "not the economy of female schoolteachers," retorts Pierre. They adjourn, and Ruth asks Pierre to take her to lunch; he expresses happiness that she is not depressed.

Father Benoit carries his bike down the stairway of the rectory, greeting Otto on the way up. Inside, Otto finds Father Logan on a ladder painting the room while Father Milet offers advice. Milet asks after Villette, and Otto tells him the news. "I discovered the body," he says innocently, eyeing Father Logan, who has his back turned to him. After Milet leaves, Otto appeals to Father Logan, coming close to him from behind. Otto needs better advice because he can't turn himself in; "they would hang me." Father Logan turns, saying there's nothing he can add to what he said. "You're so cold . . . it's easy for you to be good," Otto says. Alma nervously interrupts and Father Logan goes back to his painting.

The mustachioed Crown prosecutor, Willie Robertson, plays with some forks and a glass of wine in his office. He makes fun of Inspector Larrue, who brings in a couple of schoolgirl witnesses. They tell the men they saw a priest leaving Villette's house the night before. Robertson doubts a priest could be involved, but

Larrue indicates he has suspicions and asks an aide to find out which priests in the area were out the night before.

Horns punctuate a montage of spires and rectories with priests in them shaking their heads "no." Milet speaks to a detective, who waits for Father Logan and asks him to come down to the station.

Observing this, Otto goes into the vestibule where the crucifix and candles loom in the foreground and tells Alma not to wash the cassock.

At the station one evening, Larrue questions Father Logan, who sits across the desk from him. Reviewing his heroic war record, Father Logan admits he "survived," and Larrue wonders if he's "given to understatement." He asks about Villette's appointment and the woman he met out front. Father Logan seems evasive, unable to offer information, saying the inspector will have to take his word that his actions and reasons are not relevant. Finally, Larrue tells him a priest was seen leaving the house at the time of the murder. Pressed to respond, Father Logan says, "What would you want me to say?" then suggests that it is too little evidence. But Father Logan is the only priest who cannot account for his whereabouts. He was walking with someone, but cannot say whom. Larrue angrily bids him good night, then walks back to his desk. He picks up the telephone and demands to have Robertson contacted right away.

Willie Robertson is at a party in an elegant home juggling a glass of liquid on his head. Ruth Grandfort, the hostess, goes to the telephone in the study, but Robertson catches up and answers. He is worried by what he hears, and turns to his hosts to tell them Father Logan is suspected in the Villette murder. Ruth is stunned and stares toward the camera, her back to the men. Robertson says good night and Pierre turns sympathetically to Ruth, but she pushes by him, saying, "We have guests."

Later, picking up the dirty glasses in the living room, Ruth says good night to the maid. Pierre enters and tells her not to worry about Father Logan, it's too ridiculous. She loses her temper. "I've never been in love with you," she says, "I've never pretended." He leaves, hoping Father Logan is in trouble. She breaks into tears, then walks into the study to the telephone. Sitting hidden in a large wing chair, back to the camera, she dials and Alma tells her Father Logan is asleep, but he appears on the stairs and comes to the wall telephone. She tells him she must see him and he agrees to meet her at the ferry.

The next morning Father Logan walks out of the rectory and a car follows him.

The ferry starts out. Ruth searches the deck, then sees Father Logan standing by the railing. He walks over to her, saying they shouldn't be seen together. She tells him he is being suspected and that she must tell the police she was with him that night. He tells her to think of her husband. "Think of Pierre? Think of him before I think of you? I've never been able to do that," she says passionately. He is alarmed at her declaration of love for him, knowing that she has been married to Grandfort for seven years. Suddenly she suggests that he is also in love with her. He tries to correct her in a circumspect way, "I chose to be what I am. . . . I want you to see things as they are and not go on hurting yourself." She turns her back on him, refusing his "pity."

In Larrue's office, a detective tells Larrue what he observed on the ferry. Willie smokes nervously, hearing that Mrs. Grandfort, his friend, is involved. Larrue grandly assures him that he will apologize, if necessary, and pushes him to call Ruth. At the other end of the telephone in her home, Ruth hangs up and

tells Pierre that Willie wants to see her immediately. She explains that she knows Father Logan did not kill Villette because he was with her at the time. Pierre offers to go with her.

Willie and Larrue wait, as Ruth and Pierre enter. Father Logan has also been summoned and enters. As Larrue questions Ruth, who is at first evasive, the camera moves occasionally to Father Logan. She tells of their series of appointments, including a drive the night of the murder until 11:00 P.M., and Villette's attempt to blackmail her. Father Logan interrupts, wondering if it is necessary for Larrue to be so personal in his questions, but Larrue impatiently continues. Ruth says Father Logan "couldn't advise her to tell her husband about the blackmail," at which point Robert and Larrue exchange raised eyebrows. Larrue pushes on, uncovering the fact that Ruth had not seen Father Logan, "an old friend," for many years until recently. Pierre argues with Larrue about the aggressiveness of the questions, and Father Logan tells Ruth she does not have to answer when asked why she was being blackmailed. She begins softly to cry, wondering herself about the inspector's insensitive questioning, but Larrue is angry and frustrated at the evasions. The others express concern for her, but she begins to tell the story of her young love for Michael, now Father Logan.

A love theme sung by a soprano dominates the flashback scenes that Ruth narrates detailing her ecstatic passion and Michael's kindly distance. She greets him near the circular stairs of her flat; they kiss. She watches him march in the street, hating him for being one of the first to enlist in the war. She clings to him at a dance the night before he leaves, then cries bitterly, facing the camera.

Back at the office, Pierre hangs his head, then looks sympathetically at her. "I had to wait for him," she says.

Standing in the rain at the top of her stairs, she mournfully watches the passers-by.

She began working for Pierre in his office and Michael stopped writing. In the detective's office, she falters. Larrue tells her she need not continue. "Pierre was always so brilliant," she says; "he realized I was unhappy."

She and Pierre laugh together across his desk. They receive their wedding guests, their backs to the camera; in the line is Villette; it is their first meeting.

She thought she was over her feelings for Michael. Back at the office, she says she was aware when the men were coming home from the war, however, and went to meet Michael's ship.

She stands in the crowd at the dock. Michael pushes through to meet her and they hug, though he's surprised to see her. They meet the next day, and spend it sitting on a country hillside as he talks animatedly of his experiences. She kisses him and he is slightly taken aback. A violent storm suddenly appears and they run across the field to a house; it's closed and they take refuge in a nearby gazebo.

They had missed the last ferry, however, and there was no way she could contact her husband. Ruth is clear-eyed now, telling her story.

The next morning, the couple wake in the sunlight. Villette, who owns the property, walks over to meet Michael and makes insinuations that prompt Michael to punch him. Villette then sneeringly recognizes "Mme. Grandfort" and Michael looks back at her; Ruth had not told him of her marriage.

The group in the office listen to her as she says she did not see Michael again for five years, nor Villette until the day Michael was ordained.

In a cathedral, Ruth watches the ceremony, then notices Villette, who

appears later at a restaurant, and at another time, approaches her in a balcony at Parliament. "I tried to ignore him," she narrates, as she is shown surreptitiously speaking on the telephone at home. Villette greets her on the sidewalk with an ultimatum.

She decided it was time to call Father Logan. The day before the murder, they walked along the water; Father Logan became angry and they decided to meet the next morning at Villette's house. She drives up the next morning and pushes through the crowd. From above, a different viewpoint is presented of their meeting on the sidewalk. "I couldn't believe it. . . . I was free," she says.

Pierre requests permission for them to leave; Ruth asks Willie if Father Logan has his alibi; yes, he replies. Father Logan says good night as well. Alone, Larrue shows Willie the autopsy report showing that Villette could not have died before 11:30 P.M.

Ruth sleeps; Pierre enters to tell her Willie is on his way over as her statement did not provide an alibi. Rising and opening the window to the morning sun, she wonders why Larrue allowed her to speak when her statement wasn't necessary. But Father Logan is to be charged with the murder and her statement provided his motive. "I should have lied," she says bitterly; "they'll twist what I said. . . . I've destroyed him . . . and what have I done to you." She hangs her head.

Sitting in a pew at the church, Ruth anxiously asks Father Logan what they might do, insisting there can be no trial. "Nothing," he says, returning to the confessional to meet a little boy. She stares out, then kneels in the aisle and turns. At the door, she runs into Otto Keller, entering with a large bouquet of flowers.

Otto walks up the center aisle to the altar and turns to see Father Logan approaching. Father Logan brushes by him and Otto whispers after him, "You've told them about me, Father?" Father Logan tells him he, Father Logan, is going to be arrested, but Otto follows him, pestering, then threatening him. "You think I am easy to frighten after what I've done? . . . Maybe they will hang you instead of me . . . perhaps you will tell them?" Father Logan ignores him until Otto moves around to block him, then he stares at Otto blankly. Otto watches as he goes out the front door of the rectory. Alma watches as Otto turns and goes up the stairs to their attic apartment, getting a gun out of a desk. "He is afraid; he thinks he can tell the police," he says.

Father Logan crosses the intersection away from the church. A detective comes to the rectory door and asks for him. Otto tells him, in the presence of a puzzled Father Milet, that he saw Father Logan leave and that he seemed frightened and would not speak to him.

From a telephone booth, the detective calls Larrue to say Father Logan is gone.

Father Logan walks through a commercial section, stopping to look at a shop window picture of a man in handcuffs. Elsewhere, a group of detectives walks purposefully through town and into a car. Father Logan stares at the sidewalk, and the detectives stop a strange man in a cassock. Overcome, Father Logan puts his hand to his face, leans against a stone post, and goes up the stairs into a church, staring at the altar.

Alma serves lunch to Father Benoit as Father Milet stares out the window.

Father Logan enters Larrue's office.

At the trial, a detective testifies that the cassock in evidence belongs to

Father Logan. Alma sits in the audience. Dr. Bonnard testifies that the stains on the cassock are human blood; Alma lowers her eyes. Otto testifies he spoke to Father Logan the night of the murder, revising the events so that his and Father Logan's actions are reversed. Father Logan stares, disbelieving, clutching himself. Alma sighs miserably at the artful fabrication.

Ruth testifies and becomes angry at Willie's prosecutorial questioning. She admits she was in love with Father Logan at the time of the murder, but vehemently denies a continuing love affair. Father Logan testifies that he cannot say who might have put the cassock into his trunk. His calm testimony relates the earlier incident at the gazebo. Willie pursues the incident as a violent precursor to the murder. "I am not capable of murder," says Father Logan. Then, when grilled about resorting to physical violence, he yells, "No, I would not!" His words ring forcefully through the courtroom, causing the crowd to murmur. Willie continues with the events of that night. Father Logan agrees to the time, but says simply that the rest of Otto's testimony is not true though he cannot say what did happen, allowing Willie to advance a forceful picture of his guilt.

The jury is instructed by the judge not to judge Father Logan's relationship with Mme. Grandfort, and withdraws. Father Logan stares out, then turns away with his guards.

In the jury room, a juror paces and smokes, asserting his belief that Father Logan and Ruth had an affair beyond what they admit.

Back in the courtroom, Father Logan is brought in, then the jury. They pronounce him not guilty because of insufficient evidence, though they attach "grave suspicion to the accused." Father Logan sighs heavily; observers murmur nervously, and Larrue leans over to Willie, saying, "Why couldn't they have said not guilty simply and leave it at that?" The judge discharges Father Logan, announcing his own disagreement with the jury. The audience rises, and Father Logan steps down to hisses and walks out to a cry of "Take off that collar!"

He walks alone down the curving stairs lined with people staring at him and goes out into daylight to face a large crowd, stares, and taunts. Walking forward, the police close arms around him in an attempt to protect him from the pushing crowd.

Pierre enters Willie's office. "Are you satisfied?" he asks, but Willie claims not to have enjoyed it.

Outside, Otto and Alma watch as the crowd pushes Father Logan into a car window, breaking it. Alma is open-mouthed and shaking. She breaks away from Otto and walks through the crowd up the police, saying, "He's innocent," then turns and points to her husband. Otto brings out a gun and shoots her. The crowd panics as the police chase Otto, and Alma is laid on the running board of the car, Father Logan holding her as Milet and Larrue lean over her. She is unable to speak clearly and Larrue demands to know what she is murmuring. "She says forgive me," says Father Logan. Alma closes her eyes. Larrue stands, directing his men not to shoot Otto. Father Logan joins him and they walk, Larrue irritated, wanting to know about Otto. "Let me talk to him," says Father Logan. They lead a crowd into the large Chateau Frontenac hotel, where all the entrances have been closed. Detectives are dispersed throughout; screams in the laundry, then a shooting victim in the kitchen point the way to Otto.

In the lobby, Larrue is informed of the shooting by telephone. Turning, he asks Father Logan if he is protecting him, but Father Logan continues to be impassive.

Running through an empty lounge, detectives find Otto in a large empty auditorium. A crowd of detectives, Larrue, Pierre, and Milet assemble outside. Larrue demands he give up, but Otto is hostile, threatening to do more harm. At the mention of Villette, Otto sarcastically shouts, "So the priest talked . . . my only friend, Father Logan . . . how kindly he hears my confession . . . that's all it takes to make him talk, a little shame, a little violence," he laughs. Father Logan winces; the others stare at the revelation. Ruth smiles and turns to Pierre and asks him to take her home.

A detective shoots Otto in the shoulder and Father Logan walks purposefully forward, crossing the large floor to confront Otto, who is leaning against the stage. "You won't shoot me," says Father Logan. "Why not," says Otto, "because you call me in such a friendly way, like Alma. . . . I loved her." Intransigent, Otto blames her death on the priest, saying they are both alone. "I'm not alone," says Father Logan, but Otto mocks him for having no friends and raises the gun. The camera watches from behind as a detective shoots Otto again and Father Logan catches him as he falls. "Father forgive me," says Otto, and the camera moves to a close-up of Father Logan who repeats the last rites.

Note. ᴴ Hitchcock does bit as man crossing top of flight of steps.

43   *Dial M for Murder* (1954)

Director	Alfred Hitchcock
Assistant Director	Mel Dellar
Producer	Alfred Hitchcock
Production Company	Warner Bros.-First National
Screenplay	Frederick Knott, from his play
Photography	Robert Burks, A.S.C.
Editing	Rudi Fehr, A.C.E.
Art Direction	Edward Carrere
Set Direction	George James Hopkins
Sound	Oliver S. Garretson
Music	Dimitri Tiomkin
Costumes	Moss Mabry
Makeup	Gordon Bau
Cast	Ray Milland (Tony Wendice), Grace Kelly (Margot Wendice), Robert Cummings (Mark Halliday), John Williams (Chief Inspector Hubbard), Anthony Dawson (Captain Lesgate/ Swann), Leo Britt, Patrick Allen, George Leigh, George Alderson, Robin Hughes
Filmed	at Warner Bros. Studios, Los Angeles, in Warnercolor
Running Time	approximately 123 minutes
Distributor	Warner Bros.
Release Date	April 1954

Other titles: *Bei Anruf Mord, Le Crime Était Presque Parfait, Il Delitto Prefetto*

Synopsis

Credits appear over close-ups of a telephone and its dial, a red letter "M," accompanied by the romantic theme music.

A policeman patrols a London street of elegant townhouses.

Inside one of them, Margot, a blond in white wool, and Tony Wendice, in a dark brown business suit, kiss; she returns to reading the newspaper; he sits down across from her at the breakfast table in the center of their sitting room. She peeks at her husband, then at an announcement of the Queen Mary's arrival that day, carrying the American writer Mark Halliday.

At the dock, Mark, a young man dressed in tweed, walks off the ship.

Margot and Mark kiss. Dressed in a bright-red lace evening gown, she moves away, walking around her well-appointed living room which has a large fireplace at one end and the velvet curtains of the garden doors at the other. She makes him a drink and tells him she hasn't told Tony about them yet. Mark is understanding and relaxed; she explains that Tony has given up tennis for a job and is a changed person. Furthermore, though she burned all of Mark's letters but one, that one was stolen from her purse in Victoria Station. Sitting by the fireplace across from him, she tells him she received a blackmail note from the thief. Mark excitedly asks to see it, and she goes into her bedroom and brings it out to him. He grabs it anxiously and looks at the block-printed note. He is distressed to hear she has paid money and does not want anything revealed. Then he wonders why she didn't burn the one letter; softening in response, she kisses him and they hear Tony entering the outside door.

Their shadows part at the front door as Tony enters to greet the two now standing at opposite sides of the room. He asks to be excused from their theater date but invites Mark to a stag party the next evening, brushing over his objections. Margot and Mark leave and Tony gaily yells after them to sell the extra ticket.

Left alone, Tony appears thoughtful; he closes the drapes and makes a phone call, inviting a Captain Lesgate to come over and discuss the purchase of his car. He sets out a new pair of gloves and a cane. Lesgate, a mustached, thin man in a trenchcoat and checked jacket arrives. They recognize each other, Tony eventually remembering a different name—Swann. Lesgate/Swann is suspicious, but sits down on the couch in front of the fireplace to have a drink. Tony shows him a picture of a reunion dinner ᴴ and reminds him of some stolen ticket money from student days. They banter about the car and the convenience of owning capital, then Tony relates the story of his marriage. His wife has money, but he quit tennis because she had an affair and almost left him the year before. He remembers being "so scared" at the thought of living without her money that he considered killing her lover, then decided it would be better to kill her. Swann is attentive as Tony goes on to tell of her letters that followed after Mark left London and the one that Margot always carried with her. Tony finally stole it because it "became an obsession." Showing the letter, he lets it drop from his wallet and Swann picks it up. Eventually the correspondence stopped and "we lived happily ever after."

Still sitting in a chair opposite Swann, Tony then switches the conversation to what he has found out about Swann, including his prison term. Swann rises to leave, but Tony, resting his chin on his cane, slyly asks if Swann doesn't want to know why Tony asked to see him. Tony abandons his cane and begins to move

around the room, wiping the objects that Swann has touched. He tells Swann he realized he needed an alibi, and also, without money it would be hard to find someone else to murder Margot. So he has been following Swann for a year, to the dog races, through his courtships, hoping to catch him in something illegal. Interrupting himself, he asks Swann to put on gloves if he wants to touch anything else. Still moving around the room, Tony continues his snide discourse through Swann's several name changes, failure to pay rent, and affair with the deceased Miss Wallace. Swann suggests he will go to the nearest police station and tell them he is being blackmailed, but Tony, calmly sitting now, insists "it will be a straight case of your word against mine." He will say he bought the letter from Swann, who was blackmailing him. Rising and moving behind Swann, who sits facing the camera, concentrating, Tony explains that he has had time to think things through "and is sure Swann will agree . . . for the same reason a donkey with a stick behind him and a carrot in front always goes forward." He offers Swann £1000 to murder his wife and reminds him of poor Miss Wallace's poisoning.

Near an understanding, they both stand now as Tony explains the plan, walks to the desk in front of the doors, and flings £100 across the room at Swann. Swann wonders about tracing the money and asks to see Tony's bank statement. Joining Tony behind the desk, he jumps when Tony insists that the murder must take place the next night when he and Mark will go to the stag party and leave Margot by herself. At 10:57 P.M., Swann will enter, using a key left under the hall stair carpet. Tony will call home, bringing Margot out to the phone; Tony will wait until she has been killed, then immediately call his boss and return to the party. Swann will make it look like a robbery, and the garden door will be left open to explain his entry. Swann brings up more details, but Tony has an answer for all. Wiping more prints off the furniture, Tony explains he will take her key from her purse and hide it, keeping his own so he can let himself and Mark in later for a nightcap. The telephone rings; Swann puts on the gloves and continues to case the apartment while Tony speaks on the telephone with his wife, who asks him to join her. Finished, Swann walks over to the chair and picks up the £100 as a loud chord of foreboding is heard on the soundtrack, and Tony regally looks on.

The next evening, the camera moves by the silent telephone, then over to Tony, who daydreams and stirs a pitcher of martinis. Sitting on the couch together, Margot shows Mark clippings from Tony's career. Tony wonders when she is going to finish pasting the clippings, and the group starts discussing a detective story collaboration, the "perfect murder." Rising to go, Tony notices the door lock and asks Margot if she has his key, feigning loss. She goes into the bedroom to get her bag and tells him she doesn't have it. When he asks to borrow hers, she pouts and says she may go out to a movie. Calmly ingesting this information, he tries to convince her to stay home. "You know how I hate to do nothing," she protests, flinging herself over the arm of the couch, and he suggests she "do the clippings." As she more vigorously protests this idea, he threatens her, saying he and Mark will just have to stay home, then. She pleads with him not to be so childish, then relents. Mark goes out to get a taxi while Tony helps her with the paste and scissors, eyeing her handbag. He asks to borrow some change and picks it up, but she immediately strides over, demanding that he stay away from her pocketbook. He hides it behind his back, and she surrounds him with her arms reaching for it. They laughingly struggle as he deftly removes the key from

the bag. Mark returns to get Tony, but Tony stops at the door, still holding the key. He knows he must somehow put it under the stair carpet for Swann. Margot pushes him to go and they all say good night. After she has closed the door, Tony returns and calls after her, leaning on the stairs to give her a last minute instruction. He kisses her warmly, and she looks at him very seriously. A close-up shows the key is under the stair carpet.

In the darkness, Swann walks toward the apartment; his watch says 10:53. He enters the hallway, finds the key, and enters the apartment. Margot is asleep. He crosses the darkened living room and hides behind the drapes, winding a white scarf around his hands. It's 10:58.

At the black-tie party in a restaurant, Mark and Tony look bored at the conversation around the dinner table. Tony, impatient, checks his watch. It reads 10:40.

Swann waits at the window, staring at the silent phone.

Tony again checks his watch, and realizes it has stopped. As smoke swirls around them, he anxiously asks the other men what time it is and discovers it's 11:07. Rising, he announces he is going to call his boss.

Swann starts to leave the apartment. Tony finds the phone booth in the lobby occupied and waits; as the music rises to a climax he is finally able to dial. Swann is just stepping out the front door when the phone rings and he notices the light go on in the bedroom. Margot in a revealing long nightgown, walks to pick up the phone, but no one replies. Ominous music begins on the soundtrack as she frowns and says hello four times. Tony, silent, frowns at the other end. Finally, she puts down the receiver and Swann throws the white scarf around her neck, as orchestral music surges. They struggle violently, breaking glass; Tony winces at Margot's groans and gasps heard through the telephone. Thrown back on the desk, Margot gropes toward the camera, finds the scissors, and jabs them into Swann's back. He pulls back sharply, then stands and falls on his back as she watches. She pulls herself up on the desk and asks into the telephone for the police. Tony clicks through some money, and says hello. Distraught, she pleads with him to come right away. He tells her not to do or touch anything. She walks out the garden door, clutching her throat and sobbing. Turning back inside, she sees the body and shudders.

Tony goes back into the dining room and tells Mark that Margot is not feeling well and insists that he stay there. Later, he sits in a taxi, thinking.

Tony enters the apartment, and Margot runs to him. He holds her, clutching the key, and again eyeing her handbag. Letting her go, he kneels down by the body, feeling in Swann's pocket. He turns and stands to watch her looking through her pocketbook, but she finds the aspirin she needs and walks to the bathroom to take it. Taking the key from Swann's pocket, he puts it in her purse just as she returns, calm for the first time. Putting a blanket on the body, he asks if she has called the police. Taken aback, she says no, has he forgotten he told her not to? He calls as she watches, describing the death as an accident, but evading the question when the officer mentions murder. Promising the police not to touch anything, he hangs up and tells Margot she must go to bed; he "will tell them everything they need to know." Rushing her into the bedroom, he blanches when she wants to know why he telephoned her. Recovering, he says he will tell her about that later, then quickly moves on to ask her what the man strangled her with. Closing the door on her, he searches the room, finds the scarf outside on the veranda, and burns it.

In the bedroom, Margot slumps on the edge of her bed, immobilized, and staring out.

Taking a pair of stockings out of her sewing bag, Tony drops one on the veranda outside and hides the other under the desk pad, then puts the blackmail letter in Swann's breast pocket. Sitting by the fire, he takes out a cigarette.

Seen from above, the room is now full of detectives gathering evidence. Tony brings out a tray of tea as the camera moves down and in to show him pushing the desk pad over to make room for it. One of the detectives immediately notices the now-uncovered other stocking.

Outside the next morning, there's a crowd of onlookers.

Inside, Tony stands by the desk, then walks over to check the fireplace. Turning, he meets Margot walking out of the bedroom and tells her the detectives wanted to know why she didn't phone them earlier. Slightly affronted, she reminds him that he was on the telephone and distinctly told her not to speak with anyone. He interrupts, telling her to say she assumed he would call, and suggesting there might be too many questions otherwise.

The doorbell buzzes and an Inspector Hubbard enters and introduces himself. As he looks around, Tony tries to put him off. When Hubbard asks Margot a question, he answers for her, explaining how distraught she is. Hubbard sits down across from Margot and traps her into contradicting herself about whether she had seen the victim before. Again, Tony intercedes to clarify. Tony then identifies the victim as Swann, whom he last saw at Victoria Station about six months ago. Margot rises to tell her version of events, where she stood to answer the telephone, why the scissors were there. Tony energetically intervenes again to assure the inspector that the garden door was locked. Asked why she didn't call the police, Margot hesitates as Tony circles behind the inspector and peers over his shoulder at her, but she tells Tony's version of the story. When asked why she didn't call a doctor, she becomes upset, insisting she knew the man was dead, but the inspector seems increasingly suspicious. Moving on, he turns to the matter of the key, saying he's sure the victim entered through the front door. Tony suggests the key might have been copied when her handbag was stolen at Victoria Station. Hubbard's interest is piqued as he queries her about the theft incident. At first evasive, then wide-eyed and unblinking, she tells him nothing was missing except money. Suddenly leaping over the notion of a stolen key being used, Hubbard tells them in any case there was no key found on the dead man's body.

Hubbard asks them to visit his office to make an official statement. As he is about to leave, Mark rings the door buzzer and Hubbard questions him about the time of the telephone call. Margot turns to Tony and asks again her earlier questions about why he telephoned her, but Hubbard impatiently interrupts, preferring his own line of questioning. Tony then explains that he did not have his boss's number and called Margot to get it. "You mean you hauled me out of bed just to get his number?" she complains. Hubbard asks Mark to write down his name and number for him, then instructs Tony to go out and check the gate while Margot goes into the bedroom. In their absence, Hubbard asks Mark how much Tony knows about him and Margot and tells him his letter was found in the dead man's pocket. Margot reappears and the inspector asks again about the stolen letter. Again, she claims ignorance, but Mark contradicts her, then eagerly shows the blackmail letters to Hubbard. Hubbard warns Margot that from now on, anything she says may be used as evidence. Alarmed, she stands silent. Tony

enters as Hubbard explains there is no sign of burglary, only blackmail. Going over the conflicting evidence about entry, Margot adamantly insists only two keys exist, but Hubbard says she could have let Swann in the door herself and could even have caused her bruises with her own stocking. Unable to respond, she moves over to her sewing basket, imploring, "Tony, there *was* a pair of stockings here." Tony feigns anger, blames the police for planting evidence, and rushes to call a lawyer friend, telling him that the police are suggesting Margot killed Swann intentionally. Listening, Hubbard shakes his head. The group leaves for the nearby station.

A plain canvas background behind her, Margot appears facing the camera in close-up. Accused, she shakes her head no to a sound montage of evidence, ominous orchestral music punctuating it. The frame suffused with red, she is found guilty. A judge appears in the same composition, a black triangle placed on his head, he pronounces her sentenced to death.

Mark rides in a taxi toward the Wendices's apartment. He notices Tony entering the building.

Inside Tony takes a briefcase into the bedroom and quickly covers it when the door buzzer sounds. Mark enters, staring at the newly installed bed in the middle of the living room. The execution is tomorrow. He excitedly presents a last-minute plan to save Margot. The scenario has Tony going to the inspector with a new story implicating Tony himself: he hid the key "somewhere in the stairway," planned the murder, stole the handbag, and planted the blackmail letter. "But why should I want anyone to kill Margot?" Tony reasonably pleads. Sympathetic, choking, Mark says, "I know Tony, that's tough for us to see because we both love her . . ." Mark insists that it's worth a try; after all, the most Tony would risk would be "a few years in prison." Tony grimly thanks him for his concern. Tensions heighten as Tony points out that it was Margot's association with Mark that lost her the sympathy of the jury. Trying to smooth over that comment, Tony returns to the plot, protesting that it could not possibly be convincing, but Mark expresses great faith in Tony's ability to convince the police.

The door buzzer sounds and Tony opens it to Inspector Hubbard; Mark hides in the bedroom. The inspector is inquiring about a recent robbery and wants to know where Tony has obtained the large sums of cash he has been spending recently. In the bedroom, Mark sits down on top of Tony's briefcase. Having a smoke, Hubbard takes a key out of his pocket and pretends to have found it on the rug. Asking if it is Tony's, Tony quickly confirms that he has his own; Hubbard tries the front door but it does not work. He returns to the question of the large payments, while Mark, intently listening in the bedroom, moves the briefcase he has been sitting on. Tony explains that he has been winning at dog racing, but, of course, he's embarrassed to admit going to the races while his wife is under a death sentence. Hubbard leaves, but stops at the open door, wondering about a small blue attaché case; Tony replies that he thinks it's been stolen, a response that brings Hubbard back inside the living room.

In the bedroom, Mark grabs the same case and pries it open, finding bundles of cash. As Hubbard starts to leave again, Mark calls to him and brings them both to the bedroom to see the money—over £500. Mark theorizes that this was the money meant to pay Swann. Tony stands calmly, leaning against the doorway, then walks over and sits on the bed, sarcastically relating Mark's imagined account of Swann's death. Hubbard listens impassively as Mark energetically

takes over from the lackadaisical Tony, rushing to the front door to explain about the key. Hubbard counters him as to how Tony got in later that night if he had given his key to Swann, and Tony confidently sits, waiting. Hubbard interrupts, saying all he really wants to know is where Tony got the money; turning, he goes round to the desk, to take out Tony's bank book. Mark leaps over to his side and they grapple with the book, Mark pointing out the regular withdrawals and saying Tony could have saved the money over time.

Violins again begin to accompany the drama as Tony, sitting across the room near the fireplace, tells a story of finding the hysterical Margot after the killing and her giving him the money she had collected to pay off Swann. Hubbard agrees the story is plausible, and Marks storms out, telling Tony that Margot might change her will when she hears this story. Tony looks slightly alarmed, and Hubbard tries to reassure him. Getting Tony out of the room on a ruse, he switches their trench coats. On his way out, he asks Tony to come to the police station and collect Margot's things. Tony closes the door and takes a large drink, then picks up his coat and leaves. From the upstairs hall landing, Hubbard watches him go.

Outside, Mark jumps behind a bush when he sees Tony emerging. In the hallway, Hubbard takes Tony's key out of the trench coat, and lets himself back into the apartment. Inside, he uses a flashlight to call the sergeant and "start the ball rolling." Mark knocks, calling to him, and Hubbard sighs and lets him in, telling him firmly to keep quiet. Looking out the window, Hubbard watches as Margot is let out of a car, walks in, tries her key, then goes back out to the detectives. Mark wonders what is going on and Hubbard exclaims his annoyance at the "gifted amateur." Opening the drapes, they wait until Margot appears at the garden door. She comes in and Hubbard questions her about her key and shows her the attaché case, which she does not recognize. Confused, she wonders why she couldn't get the door open and where Tony is. Hubbard finally explains they suspect Tony contracted with Swann to kill her. She sits, "unable to feel anything," admitting that she never suspected him herself. Hubbard explains he took the key from her handbag in order to secretly check Tony's bank statement, then discovered that it did not fit her door.

They get a signal that Tony is arriving. Through the front bedroom window, Hubbard watches Tony search for his key, then turn around and leave. Hubbard returns to telephone headquarters and make sure the handbag has been returned to the station. He then shows them the key under the stair carpet and explains that he had to find out if Margot had known it was there. She is shocked, realizing the import of her ignorance. Tony enters the hallway again, tries the key, and walks away. Stopping on the outside stairs, he stares at the key, while Hubbard peeks out the window at him and imagines what he is thinking. "He's remembered!" he says, as Tony returns, takes the key out from under the carpet, frowns, then opens the door. As the lights go on in the dark apartment, he turns and faces the group; Margot averts her eyes. Quickly turning, he opens the door to escape, only to find a detective waiting. Turning back, he calmly pours himself a drink, congratulates the inspector, and offers to serve them all a drink as well. Hubbard dials the telephone and ruminates while thoughtfully brushing his mustache with a pen.

Note. [H] Hitchcock appears as man in school reunion dinner photograph.

44   *Rear Window* (1954)

Director	Alfred Hitchcock
Assistant Director	Herbert Coleman
Producer	Alfred Hitchcock
Production Company	Paramount-Patron, Inc.
Screenplay	John Michael Hayes, based on the short story by Cornell Woolrich
Photography	Robert Burks, A.S.C.
Editing	George Tomasini, A.C.E.
Art Direction	Hal Pereira, Joseph MacMillan Johnson
Set Direction	Sam Comer, Ray Moyer
Sound	Harry Lindgren, John Cape
Special Effects	John P. Fulton, A.S.C.
Music	Franz Waxman
Costumes	Edith Head
Technical Adviser	Bob Landry
Cast	James Stewart (L. B. Jeffries), Grace Kelly (Lisa Fremont), Wendell Corey (Tom Doyle), Thelma Ritter (Stella), Raymond Burr (Lars Thorwald), Judith Evelyn, Ross Bagdasarian, Georgine Darcy, Jesslyn Fax, Rand Harper, Irene Winston, Havis Davenport, Sara Berner, Frank Cady
Filmed	Paramount Studios, Los Angeles, in Technicolor
Running Time	approximately 112 minutes
Release Date	July 1954

Other titles: *Das Fenster zum Hof, Fenêtre Sur Cour, La Finestra Sul Cortile*

Synopsis

Under the credits accompanied by jazz music, the blinds go up over the four open windows of a small Manhattan apartment. The camera moves through the window to view the buildings that surround the courtyard: many stories on the right, four stories right across, and two directly across, with a gangway to the opposite street between that and many stories on the left. The camera moves back into the apartment to a close-up of L. B. Jeffries sleeping, sweat dripping down his face. The temperature gauge reads 94 degrees. The camera moves to the loft next door where the occupant shaves, then turns the dial on the radio as it blares: "Men . . . when you wake up in the morning, do you feel tired and run down?" The camera moves to the left where a couple sleeping on the fire escape rise at the sound of their alarm. Next door, a blond young woman kicks high in skimpy underclothes, the pigeons cooing as she dresses for the day. Back in Jeffries's apartment, the camera moves back to reveal him lying in a wheelchair with a cast on his leg, and then goes around the room full of photographs that reveal his occupation.

Later, Jeffries shaves, facing out the window. His editor calls to check on his leg. We learn he tried to take a shot in front of a race car; the cast comes off in a

week. They talk about another missed assignment as Jeffries gazes at the dancer across the way energetically practicing a routine as she eats her breakfast. He glances at the woman beneath her, then at the pianist in the loft to the right. Pleading with his editor to get him out of his boredom and give him an assignment, he fixes on a heavyset man entering the opposite apartment and greeting his wife, who is sick in bed. Jeffries laments the man's married and pedestrian future, coming home to a nagging wife. His editor retorts with the information that "wives don't nag anymore, they discuss," but Jeffries is not swayed: "In the high-rent district, they discuss; in my neighborhood, they still nag." Still sour, Jeff says good-bye and reaches for a stick to push down into his cast to scratch an itchy place. Relieved, he sees the husband go down to his garden to cut some flowers. The woman on the left leans over the fence to advise him to not water so much, and the man tells her to shut up.

Jeffries's nurse, Stella, enters and warns him of the dangers of being a peeping Tom. "What people oughta do is get outside their own house and look inside sometime," she says, chatting away as she makes up a bed and sets him face down on it for a massage. Taking up her theme, he "smells trouble" himself coming from his girlfriend, Lisa Fremont, who is "too perfect . . . too beautiful, too sophisticated . . . too everything but what I want. . . . I need a woman who is willing to go anywhere and do anything and love it," he says, moving back into his wheelchair. Stella is skeptical, telling him he thinks too much. Looking around at his neighbors, Jeff sees a groom carry his bride over the threshold of their room. He averts his eyes; "Window shopper," says Stella, surprising him from behind.

That evening, the courtyard bustles, a soprano practices, and Jeff dozes. Close-up, the blond "cover girl," Lisa approaches him. Looking into his opening eyes, she kisses him. "Who are you," he asks, and she moves around the room turning on three lights while pronouncing her three names, Lisa-Carol-Fremont. "The same Lisa Fremont who never wears the same dress twice?" he says unpleasantly, as she shows off an $1100 "steal." She picks up a cigarette box ("It's so cracked . . . ornate and gaudy") and tells him she is sending him a plain silver one "with just your initials" on it. Softly, he wonders about her spending "her hard-earned money" and she suddenly announces dinner from Twenty-One. Opening the door, she ushers in a uniformed waiter carrying an ice bucket and food containers.

Over the wine, she details her busy day, appointments with wealthy notables, fashion showings, and even time to plant some publicity for him. She ventures that someday he might want to open a studio in Manhattan, and when he objects, pushes him to "come home." She wants him to do fashion portraits; he prefers the news in Pakistan. Finally he loses all patience: "Let's stop talking nonsense, shall we?" Hurt, she goes into the kitchen to get dinner.

His eyes drift out the window; he notices "Miss Lonelyhearts" across the way, setting her table for two and putting out a bottle of wine. His interest piqued, he notices her mimic an entrance, then the presence of a guest, and a toast, as a baritone sings "To See You Is to Love You." She buries her head in her hands in despair as Lisa comes out of the kitchen. "You'll never have to worry about that," he says, looking toward the lonely woman. She retorts that he can't see her apartment from there, but, persisting, he insists that Lisa is more like "Miss Torso," the dancer, who is now serving drinks to three men. They both watch, offering conflicting interpretations: the Queen Bee and her drones, or, alternately,

a poor woman dealing with wolves. Lisa walks away and Jeff glances warily at the closed shade of the newlyweds, then goes back to the sick wife in bed; her husband brings in a tray and an argument ensues between them. The man walks back into the living room to speak on the telephone, but she rises from her bed to listen and mock him. The composer plays the piano ^H and Lisa returns with the tray of food, commenting on the beauty of the song; Jeff bitterly comments about the dinner, "perfect as always."

Later, Lisa lies back as Jeff sits before her. In the midst of argument over whether they can live with each other, she interrupts him several times until he finally asks her to "shut up for a minute." She accuses him of being rude, repeating the gist of her argument that "anybody can live anywhere" until he shouts "Shut up!" He offers his own argument, consisting of a litany of jungle and high-altitude hardships, the conditions of his employment as a professional photographer. Finally, rising from the couch, she concludes, "You won't stay here and I can't go with you." Saddened, she readies herself to go, wondering if there's any way, because, after all, she is in love with him, but he says no and she says good-bye. Suddenly worried, he asks her why she's not saying good night and if they couldn't just "keep things status quo." No, she says, but when he pleads, she gives in and says he will see her the next night.

Momentarily thoughtful, Jeff turns toward the quiet, darkened courtyard just in time to hear a scream and the sound of breaking glass.

Later, thunder rolls over the dozing Jeffries, and a record player starts up along with the rain. The couple sleeping on the fire escape comically rush inside. Jeff notices the salesman-husband leave his apartment with his sample case. It's 2 A.M. At 2:35, the man returns; a light glares on Jeff from the composer's studio as he staggers in drunk. The salesman exits again with his sample case. Jeff looks over to the gangway as the man reappears on the sidewalk.

Later, Jeff shakes himself from a daze as Miss Torso enters her apartment, pushing her door closed on an insistent date. The salesman returns again carrying the sample case. Jeff dozes off.

The next morning, Jeff still sleeps as the salesman leaves his apartment with a woman.

Later, the whole courtyard is awake: the woman sculptor down left works on a piece, the dancer works out, the woman up right lets her dog down into the salesman's garden in a basket on a pulley, and Stella gives Jeff a massage. She lets him know she can tell he has been sitting up all night. He tells her he saw the salesman carry out his case several times during the night. She engages in this tale and he turns excitedly when she tells him the shades are up now in the man's apartment. The salesman stares out his window and Jeff tells Stella to back up out of the light. Stella says good-bye and he asks her to hand him his binoculars on her way out. "Trouble," she says, "I can smell it."

Using the binoculars, Jeff watches the man refill his sample case with items, then, suddenly self-conscious in the light, Jeff moves back but takes up the binoculars again. Not finding them sufficient, he pulls a camera and large lens out of a cabinet near him. Children play and scream, the composer plays. Viewing the salesman's kitchen, Jeff sees the man wrap a large saw and a butcher knife in newspaper. Jeff looks sideways, wide-eyed.

Later, it's 80 degrees; the composer cleans his apartment, trying the odd chord, and the other residents go about their business. Jeff and Lisa kiss. She continues to kiss him as he tells her about the previous night's events. The man

has not been in his wife's bedroom and Jeff thinks there is "something very wrong." Her kisses ignored, Lisa rises and goes to smoke a cigarette on the couch. "That would be a terrible job to tackle," Jeff dreamily continues; "how would you cut up a human body?" Lisa sits up and turns on another light. "You're beginning to scare me a little." "Shhh!!" snaps Jeff, absorbed in the window, "he's coming back." The salesman enters his apartment carrying a rope and walks into the shaded bedroom. Lisa suddenly gets up, pulls Jeff's chair around, and takes away his binoculars. "It's diseased," she tells him, but he indignantly defends his innocent curiosity; after all, the man's wife is an invalid, and Jeff is concerned about her. They argue spiritedly about the case, she trying to convince him he is just "wildly speculating," he pointing out the clues and latching on to her first use of the word "murder." She says there is probably something more sinister going on behind "those blinds," pointing to the newlywed's room, and he replies, "No comment." Suddenly Lisa rises to stare out the window, and Jeff swings his chair around to look. The salesman is tying up a large crate in front of the rolled-up mattress in the bedroom. Lisa is now a convert. "Tell me everything . . . and what you think it means."

Later, Jeff sits with his hand on the telephone. Lisa calls to tell him the name and address of the man, Lars Thorwald.

Next morning, Jeff talks a detective friend into coming over as Stella serves him his breakfast. Excited, Stella wonders if he has called the police, and piques his curiosity with chatter about the dismemberment. Jeff checks around, then sees Thorwald giving the crate to some delivery men. Stella runs out to get the name off the freight truck. Jeff sees her through the gangway, shaking her head no as the truck speeds away.

Tom Doyle, Jeff's friend, looks out the binoculars at Thorwald's apartment. He is skeptical, insisting that there is probably a simple explanation for the events. Leaving, he agrees to "poke into it a little" on his own. Jeff turns back to the window to see Thorwald walk into his garden and gently push the neighbor's digging dog on his way.

That night, Tom tells Jeff he has found out that Thorwald and his wife left the apartment the previous morning at 6 A.M. to go to the railroad station. He put her on a train to the country, and Tom assures him there are witnesses. Jeff remains unconvinced and demands that Tom go over and search Thorwald's apartment. Stridently, Jeff pursues this idea, while Tom reminds him of the Bill of Rights. Finally, he tries to make fun of Jeff, who becomes abusive. "One thing I don't need is heckling," says Tom on his way out. He further informs Jeff of a postcard he noticed in Thorwald's mailbox from his wife, telling him she arrived safely. Tom gone, Jeff reaches to scratch another itch.

That night, Jeff eats a sandwich as the dog is lowered down the pulley and Miss Lonelyhearts primps and drinks. While he watches through his lens, the composer receives some guests and Miss Torso practices with a partner. Jeff follows Miss Lonelyhearts as she goes out and enters a restaurant across the street. Suddenly Thorwald enters the frame carrying a laundry box. Going up to his apartment, he starts packing a suitcase. Jeff excitedly calls to get Tom over because Thorwald is leaving. Sitting in his living room, Thorwald talks on the telephone while he goes through the contents of his wife's handbag. More guests arrive at the composer's home.

Lisa enters the darkened room as Jeff peers out the window; he excitedly tells her what Thorwald has been doing, that he seemed worried about his wife's rings

and jewelry in the handbag. Lisa, walking around the room, tells him she's had a difficult time keeping her mind on her work that day and questions Mrs. Thorwald leaving her "favorite handbag" and jewelry behind. Jeff counters some of her points but is obviously pleased to have her mind on the mystery. Sitting on his lap and kissing him, she tells him that she is going to spend the night. Raising his eyebrows, he offers some spurious objections, and she gets up and returns with her "suitcase," a small bag stuffed with fluffy things. The composer plays for his guests, and Lisa moves in his direction, taken by the melody. Lying down on the couch in front of Jeff, she wishes she were more creative and he teases her about her knack for trouble. She is gracious and tolerant as he digs into her about the girl who always helps out but never gets married. Rising, she goes into the kitchen to make coffee. He notices, again, the newlywed's shade go up and the groom lean out the window for a smoke, only to have his wife call out after him.

Tom Doyle enters solemnly, takes a drink, and notices Lisa's overnight kit. He looks around the courtyard dominated by the party's noise and asks what else Jeffries has on Thorwald. Lisa enters with some brandy, and the men exchange glances as Jeff introduces her and Tom again notices the lingerie. She announces they think Thorwald is guilty. The telephone rings for Tom. After the call, they tell him Thorwald has his wife's jewelry wrapped in his clothes. Walking into a close-up, Tom announces that "Lars Thorwald is no more a murderer than I am"; forcefully, he insists their "logic is backward." Lisa, insistent, argues that Mrs. Thorwald would not have left without her jewelry, but Tom disdainfully tells her "that female intuition stuff . . . is still a fairy tale." Jeff moves away from them as they discuss the trunk, which Tom has found to contain only clothes. Staring, pointedly comparing the lingerie clue in the room to the clues Jeff and Lisa have presented about Thorwald's apartment, Tom angers Jeff, who spins around and toward the window. Lisa clarifies with Tom that he is "through with the case." She walks over to Jeff and stands by him, silent. The coldness forces Tom to say good night; they do not respond as he advises Jeff to consult the yellow pages if he needs any more help. With Tom at the door, Jeff rouses himself to turn and sweetly ask who the trunk was addressed to, earnestly suggesting they should wait and see if it arrives. Tom informs him that the telephone call a few minutes ago was the police confirming the trunk had been picked up.

The party guests next door are now singing a reveler's rendition of "Mona Lisa." Across the way, Miss Lonelyhearts brings home a male guest. He kisses her and pushes her down to the couch. Angry, she pushes him out of the apartment. Lisa and Jeff are not cheered by this sight; Jeff begins thoughtfully, "Much as I hate to give Doyle credit . . . I wonder if it's ethical to watch a man with a long-focus lens." Lisa walks away, saying she is "not much on rear window ethics." She wonders about their state of despair; why aren't they happy there has been no murder? Crossing back from the fireplace, she leans over the back of his chair to kiss him on the neck. They wonder about "love thy neighbor" and Lisa goes over to let down the blinds. "Show's over for tonight," she says and walks into the next room with her bulging case.

Later, she poses at the door in her elegant nightgown when someone screams. Lisa quickly raises a blind and everyone in the courtyard moves to their windows. The dog lies dead in Thorwald's garden. The owner cries out from her fire escape as the body is drawn up on the pulley; sobbing, she yells about a neighborhood where nobody "cares if anybody lives or dies!" After the outburst, everyone goes back inside. Jeff is back on the track, telling Lisa that only one person stayed

inside when the dog was discovered. Across the way, in Thorwald's darkened apartment, a cigarette glows.

The next day, Stella, Lisa, and Jeff watch as Thorwald scrubs his walls. Jeff gets an idea. Taking out a slide photograph of the garden, he shows that some flowers in the garden were taller earlier than they are now; he is sure that something is buried there. Seized with another idea, he demands a pencil. From above, the women watch as he prints in large letters a note to Thorwald: WHAT HAVE YOU DONE WITH HER?

Later, Lisa stands in the gangway signaling Jeff, who watches through his lens. She enters Thorwald's apartment building, goes upstairs to the corridor, sticks the note under his door, then runs back. Thorwald sees it immediately and opens the door to look out. Closing the door, he reads the note in the kitchen, then rushes out to the corridor again. Lisa runs down the first floor corridor to the courtyard to hide from him. He checks the corridor balcony, then returns to his apartment and continues packing his things. Stella asks to look through the lens and notices Miss Lonelyhearts laying out some pills. Lisa returns, breathless, and staring out the window, she sees Thorwald looking in the handbag. Stella and Lisa decide to go down and find out what is buried in the garden. Jeff tries to discourage them, then thinks of a scheme to get Thorwald out of the apartment. Moving back into the kitchen corridor, he telephones Thorwald, who stands watching the telephone and lets it ring. When he finally picks it up, Jeff asks if he got his note and tells him to meet him at the Albert Bar. Thorwald pleads ignorance, but when Jeff presses him, he agrees, then puts on his hat and leaves his apartment. The two women rush out and Jeff tells them he'll signal Thorwald's return with a flashbulb. Wheeling over to his bag, he gets one ready.

Downstairs in the courtyard, Stella carries a shovel as both women climb over the garden wall. Stella starts to dig.

In the dark, Jeff telephones Tom and leaves an urgent message with the baby-sitter. The composer plays with a horn group. Jeff focuses on the hole Stella is digging; there's nothing. Lisa suddenly climbs the fire escape and jumps over it to enter Thorwald's apartment through an open window. Jeff is beside himself with anxiety as she rushes into the bedroom and picks up the handbag. She shows him it's empty. Stella enters, saying Lisa wants them to telephone Thorwald's apartment when they see him coming. Jeff starts to call immediately, but Stella becomes concerned that Miss Lonelyhearts is readying to take a lethal dose of pills, so he calls the police instead. Meanwhile, Miss Lonelyhearts stops to listen to the composer's music and Thorwald appears in his corridor, just as Lisa is moving toward the kitchen. Hearing him approach, she runs back to hide as he enters. Jeff gets through to the police and tells them there is an assault at Thorwald's apartment.

Walking back to the bedroom, Thorwald notices that the handbag is in a different place. Turning, he starts moving slowly forward; Lisa appears backing away from him into the living room, animatedly talking to him. He grabs her by the wrist and shoves her into a chair; she starts to leap for the door again, but he grabs her. Stella stands by Jeff, who watches in misery as Lisa starts screaming "Jeff!" The struggle continues as Thorwald turns out the light and Jeff writhes in distress.

The police appear in the corridor and Thorwald goes to answer the door. He lets them in and Lisa speaks with them, her back to the window. Putting her hands behind her, she signals Jeff, showing off a ring on her finger; Thorwald

notices the action and looks directly into the lens. Jeff excitedly backs away, commanding Stella to turn out the light. The police take Lisa away.

Jeff and Stella collect their available cash to bail Lisa out of jail, and Stella takes the money and leaves. Thorwald leaves his apartment, glancing over toward Jeff. Tom Doyle calls and Jeff stridently whispers the latest developments: the dead dog, Lisa's capture of the wedding ring, her arrest, and a series of other explanations he has thought of for old clues. Anxiously hanging up the phone, he looks out and notices Thorwald's dark apartment. The phone rings again and Jeff unthinkingly assumes it is Tom calling again and blurts out that he thinks Thorwald's left; the noise of the line clicking off makes him realize his mistake. He sits, glancing around warily. Suddenly he is frightened by a loud thump. Watching the light crack under his door, he slowly turns toward it. Heavy footsteps sound closer, as Jeff tries to reach the door (there is a step up to it), and the hall light is turned off. Jeff readies himself with a flashbulb and pushes his chair to the back of the room so that he is silhouetted by the window. Thorwald enters, calmly asking what Jeff wants from him. Jeff does not respond until he asks for the ring back, then Jeff tells him the police already have it. Thorwald moves toward him and Jeff, anxiously looking behind him out the window, pops a flashbulb in Thorwald's face, temporarily blinding him, then popping another and another each time the man recuperates and begins to move forward. Finally, he sees Lisa and Tom entering Thorwald's building and yells at them. Thorwald dives at his throat. They struggle and Thorwald dumps Jeff out onto the bed, then manages to get him out the window. Jeff hangs from his hands outside as people scurry toward the action. The police grab Thorwald from behind and we watch Jeff fall to the ground. Below, his landing is buffered by a couple of detectives.

Tom runs over to Lisa, who holds Jeff's head in her lap. The police yell down that Thorwald is ready "to take them on a tour of the East River." Stella asks about the flower bed, and Thorwald has already told them he removed whatever he had buried there.

The temperature is down to 72 degrees; Miss Lonelyhearts is visiting the composer, who plays his record for her. The Thorwald apartment is being repainted, and the fire escape couple have a new dog. Miss Torso greets her very ordinary appearing Army boyfriend, the sculptor sleeps, and the newlyweds quarrel. Jeff dozes away, now encased in two leg casts, and Lisa, seeing that he is asleep, substitutes *Harper's Bazaar* for his Himalayan adventure book.

Note. [H] Hitchcock does bit as man winding clock in the composer's apartment.

45   *To Catch a Thief* (1954)

Director	Alfred Hitchcock
2nd Unit Director	Herbert Coleman
Assistant Director	David McCauley
Producer	Alfred Hitchcock
Production Company	Paramount Pictures Corporation
Screenplay	John Michael Hayes, based on a novel by David Dodge
Photography	Robert Burks, A.S.C., Wallace Kelley, A.S.C.
Technicolor Consultant	Richard Mueller

Special Effects	John P. Fulton, A.S.C., Edouart Farciot, A.S.C.
Editing	George Tomasini
Art Direction	Hal Pereira, Joseph MacMillan Johnson
Set Direction	Sam Comer, Arthur Crams
Sound	Harold Lewis, John Cope
Music	Lyn Murray
Costumes	Edith Head
Makeup	Wally Westmore
Dialogue Coach	Elsie Foulstone
Cast	Cary Grant (John Robie), Grace Kelly (Francie Stevens), Charles Vanel, Jessie Royce Landis (Jessie Stevens), Brigitte Auber, John Williams, Georgette Anys, Jean Martinelli, Gerard Buhr, René Blancard, Roland Lesaffre
Filmed	in VistaVision and Technicolor in the south of France
Running Time	approximately 97 minutes
Release Date	July 1955

Other titles: *Über den Dächern von Nizza, La Main au Collet, Caccia al Ladro*

Synopsis

Under the credits, with romantic theme music, a travel agency shop window advertises the idyllic beaches of France.

A woman swathed in face cream screams, "My jewels!" and runs crying for help to her balcony overlooking the Mediterranean.

Night. A black cat crosses a pitched slate roof. Inside, a black-gloved hand picks up some diamonds. The cat crosses back over the roof. The next morning, a scream comes from another high-rise hotel on the beach.

At the police station, Lepic, the head detective, lectures and disperses his force. A black car drives off down the coast road.

At a villa overlooking the sea, a maid dusts. A black cat rests on the couch near a newspaper report of the work of the renowned but reformed "cat burglar," John Robie. Outside, John cuts roses in his garden. Hearing screeching tires coming up the road, he throws down his pincers and runs up the stairs and to his bedroom. He rushes to the window in time to see a black car carrying five detectives pull into the driveway. Two come to his door; the others are stationed around the grounds. As he takes out a rifle, Germaine, the maid, calls him downstairs. He goes down to greet the men, who ask him to accompany them to Nice for questioning. John asks to put on something more formal and goes up to the bedroom, locking the door behind him. A gunshot rings out, bringing all the detectives up to the door to break it down. Gaining entry, they hear the roar of John's car racing away. The five men run out and into their own car, chasing Robie down the spectacularly scenic road, past sea cliffs and through mountainside villages to the accompaniment of gay music. At one point, the detectives stop

their vehicle to get out and look around, then see John's car come from behind and pass them. Taking up the chase again, both cars are stopped by a herd of pigs on the road, but an excited French woman, not John Robie, is driving the other car.

Meanwhile, John stands in the middle of the road and signals an approaching bus to stop. He gets on and watches out the back window as the detectives pass by in the other direction.^{H}

John gets off the bus at a coastal town and walks down stone steps into an elegant seaside restaurant where several waiters suspiciously eye him. As he peers through the window of the kitchen, the cooks stare at him with hostility and one throws an egg at the pane in front of his face. Smiling with resignation, John turns to greet the owner, M. Bertane. He tells Bertane he had nothing to do with the robberies, though he knows everyone there thinks that he did. Everyone who works in the restaurant was in prison with John, then were rehabilitated via service in the French Resistance during the war and afterward paroled to work in the restaurant. They feel John has let them down, jeopardizing their freedom. After Bertane is called away by a phone call, John enters the kitchen where he is confronted by a man wielding a broken plate. John takes up a wine bottle and throws it underhand to him. The worker drops the plate and catches the bottle as Bertane quiets the group and brings John back into his office. As the camera views Bertane from below and John from above, the men sit and talk about the coincidental crime wave and the uncanny similarity of the burglar's mode to John's. John decides to try to catch the thief himself. Bertane gives him the business card of a man who is interested in people who own jewels. Suddenly, the police arrive and John is rushed out the back way. A detective walks into the kitchen demanding to know if the workers have seen M. Robie, but no one replies.

Downstairs in the wine cellar, John is given over by the maitre d' to Danielle, a young blond woman, who will drive him by boat to Cannes. She teasingly calls him "cat" but he anxiously tells her his name is John.

Upstairs, one of the detectives notices the boat heading out and they run from the restaurant to a telephone booth.

The small boat speeds up the coast. Danielle banters with John, first about marrying her, then about his "expensive villa" and easy life contrasted with the hard work the rest of them do. He protests that he too works hard raising grapes and flowers; she adds "and rubies and diamonds." He stops the motor in order to lecture her about bad manners while she, unperturbed, tries to talk him into going to South America with her. A police plane flies near them and John hides in the cabin as she starts the boat again. He changes into swim trunks and they speed on to Cannes.

Floating in the water at the beach, John watches the police fly away, then walks up and lies on the sand. A boy approaches him with news he is wanted on the telephone. A woman in turban and sunglasses lying on the beach stares after him.

On the beach telephone, John listens to Bertane tell him that the man who wants to know about the jewels will meet him at the flower market. In the foreground, a man doing pull-ups strains to overhear.

At the edge of the flower market, John stands tossing a coin, and H. H. Huston from Lloyd's of London introduces himself. They banter about insurance, which John relates to gambling, and their unorthodox coming together. John wants a list of Huston's most bejeweled clients in exchange for a possible return on some of Lloyd's losses. Huston is worried about the risk but decides he is willing to deal—on "an unofficial basis." Noticing several detectives watching

them from a car, John takes Huston walking through the market; they speed up as the detectives chase them, then John knocks over a large basket of flowers and hides in the spill. The detectives jump in after him and he almost escapes, except for the interference of the elderly woman whose flowers he has ruined. She corners him near a tree until the police arrive and lead him away.

Back at his home, John and Huston sit on a wall overlooking the valley and click glasses, then walk to the veranda, where Germaine serves lunch. John is out on "provisional liberty based on insufficient evidence" for ten days; he is anxious to have the list. Over lunch, he tells about his past, the seventy-two people he killed in the war, his natural move from trapeze artist to burglary, where he acquired the "extraordinary taste" that Huston now compliments him for. "But I only stole from people who wouldn't go hungry," he says, denying a Robin Hood ethic as he has always kept the proceeds for himself. Rising, John concludes, "I was an out-and-out thief . . . like you." He lectures Huston about taking ashtrays from hotel rooms and cheating on his expense account, then explains his anger. "You don't have to spend every day of your life proving your honesty, but I do . . . [give me] the list." Huston tells him that he has informed the police about their plan; finally handing John the list, he expresses concern about his success, but John ignores him now. He decides to start with Mrs. Stevens and her daughter, and Huston remarks that he is having dinner with them the next evening.

At dinner in the hotel, Huston counsels Mrs. Stevens to put her jewelry in the hotel safe, but she is a red-haired, feisty Texas sort, who didn't buy these things for her "old age." Rising to leave, Mrs. Stevens notices John Robie from afar and embarrasses her reserved and very blond daughter, Francie, by remarking that she wouldn't mind buying *that* for her. Walking out of the restaurant and through the lobby, they overhear John telling a salesman that he is from Portland, Oregon.

At the roulette table, John watches tentatively at one end of the table while Mrs. Stevens boisterously bets at the other. Noticing the deep cleavage on the woman sitting next to him, he drops a chip down her front. Gasping at first, the woman decides to ignore the incident, as John, flustered, tries to explain to the woman that it was a 10,000 franc chip. Finally, the woman hands him some of her chips, and he comments that he will trust her too and not count them. Mrs. Stevens visibly enjoys this encounter and her eyes meet John's over a good laugh.

Later, the Stevens, Huston, and John, now known as Conrad Burns, surround a table as Mrs. Stevens tells stories of her dead husband and their oil ranch while the others sit poker-faced; Francie suggests they not bore Mr. Burns, but her mother ignores her. Finally, Mrs. Stevens ("please call me Jessie") asks Mr. Burns why he hasn't made a pass at her daughter, and John replies that she seems nice, quietly attractive. Yes, Jessie says, "too nice; sorry I sent her to finishing school. I think they finished her there." Francie rises and they all get up to go.

John escorts the woman to their room, first Jessie, then Francie, who opens her door, turns to him and, looking into his eyes, firmly kisses him, then quickly closes the door. John hesitates, then turns to show a bemused smile. He walks back down the hall and out onto the terrace. Noticing a man loitering down on the corner, he pulls back.

Next morning in the Stevens's sitting room, John and Jessie hear the story of the night's burglary from Huston. Eyeing John warily, Huston implores Jessie to put away her jewels, but she taunts him about the "bet" his company accepted.

Francie enters and tells John she "summoned him" for a swim. Huston remains nervous and tries to arrange a meeting with John, but John avoids him, saying he is going to investigate some villas he might rent.

John paces the lobby holding his swim towel. He turns to see Francie in a fashionable black and white outfit with a very large sun hat. She calmly ignores his discomfort, which increases as everyone who passes stares at her. At the desk, John is handed a note: "Robie, you've already used up 8 of your lives . . ."

At the beach full of umbrellas, John and Francie talk. Danielle waves to him, then swims out to a raft. John swims out to meet her and they talk, he in the water holding on to the raft and she lying on the raft. She tries to warn him away with rumors that the men from the restaurant want him dead. He again refuses her invitation to accompany her to South America, then sees Francie swimming out to meet them. Moving into the water, Danielle introduces herself, indicating that she and John just met. As Francie treads water, the women trade insults and John attempts to smooth things over. Finally, Francie moves away and John follows her after a momentary struggle with Danielle.

John exits his dressing room and notices a wet fingerprint on the list in his breast pocket. A detective follows him as he walks from the beach to the Carlton Hotel. Seeing Francie waiting on the steps of the hotel, John starts to turn, but then decides to face her. She asks if he has time for her now; he suggests cocktails at 6 P.M. She has already readied a car and a lunch to take him to see the villas. He protests that picking out a villa is a personal thing, but she persists and he, after noticing the detective, agrees to go with her.

Two detectives get ready to follow them in their car.

Francie drives up a mountain road and opens the conversation by asking him what he thought of her kiss. He is not impressed, calling her a "rich, headstrong girl . . . a jackpot of admirable traits. . . . Not only did I enjoy that kiss, I was awed by the efficiency behind it." He frowns, but she is unperturbed, taking it all as a compliment. He accuses her of being in Europe to buy a husband, but she says the man she wants doesn't have a price. "Well," he says, "that eliminates me."

The detectives behind them stop and walk up to the gate John and Francie have already driven through. Parked inside, the couple walk the grounds; he studies the roofs, she becomes a little defensive as their conversation continues in the same vein. Watching Bertane come down the stairs and cross their path, John tells her she is insecure and needs some time at Niagara Falls with a good man, though he himself does not have "the time or the inclination."

Outside the villa gate, the detectives are kicking a ball around, then rush to their car when they see the couple drive off. Noticing the police car behind them, John wonders why they're dawdling. Francie picks up speed, screeching around the cliff-edged curves; John becomes tense, knitting his brow and flexing his hands over his knees. Thoroughly enjoying herself, Francie misses a bus rounding a corner and stops just short of an elderly woman carrying laundry at a village crossing. The detectives are close behind until they swerve to avoid a chicken and crash into a stone wall. John hears the crash and tells Francie she can slow down, but she is not going to "let them catch us." He pretends ignorance, but she lets on that she knows he is John Robie.

They pull into a picnic area overlooking a town on a bay. John gets the picnic basket out of the trunk, then sits down on the floorboard at the open passenger door. He casually insists he is Conrad Burns, but Francie happily explains that she read about him in Paris and saw him walk out of the water before he

registered at the hotel; besides, he's always looking at her mother, not at her. "The cat has a new kitten," she smiles as she presents a scheme to help him rob the villa they just left, where there is a famous jewel cache. Grabbing her wrist, he firmly denies involvement, but she knows the villa is not for rent. As she admires his "strong grip," he pulls her down to the basket and kisses her. Francie commands him to her room for dinner that night; he refuses, saying he has a date, but she threatens him with exposure and he relents.

From the telephone in his room, John speaks with Bertane, whose men are serving the party next week at the villa. John tells him he heard his old cohorts want him dead, but Bertane denies it.

In Francie's room, the fireworks can be seen in the night sky beyond the French doors. She turns out the lights and faces John standing on the other side of the window. She teases him about the diamonds she wears with her white strapless gown. Her face in shadow, she paints an elaborate picture of a thwarted theft, wondering how he would handle it. He fails to rise to the bait and she switches to her scheme to rob the villa. Walking away from him to sit on the couch, she tells him she will get him an invitation to the gala and they will do the job together. "Give up John . . . admit who you are," she says seductively. He sits next to her; the fireworks explode more frequently. She kisses his hand and places it on her necklace; he calls it a crazy offer. They kiss as the music and the fireworks peak.

Afterward, she is asleep on the couch while he goes out on a balcony.

Later, he sits alone in his room and Francie bursts in demanding the return of her mother's jewels. He denies any knowledge, but she is distraught and they struggle as he exits, leaving her there to search.

Entering Jessie's room, John tells her Francie is searching his room, then asks to look around her suite. Walking through the rooms, he tells Jessie his real identity and she pronounces it a "wonderful surprise." Trying to size up this new development, she calmly sits down and watches him inspect the scene. Francie enters and tells her mother not to talk to John. She announces she has called the police and presents the list of jewel owners she found in John's room. Unconvinced, Jessie wonders what John is doing there now if he is guilty. "Returning to the scene of the crime," says Francie confidently. "Since when is love a crime," says her mother, as John, nonplussed, stands between them. Jessie compares him favorably to Francie's swindler father and John graciously thanks her. Francie walks out to open the front door to the police; returning, she finds John gone and Jessie claiming ignorance.

Out on the roof, John crouches in the dark, then slips away.

Pacing in circles around a couch, Francie and Jessie trade barbs. Jessie is most upset, arguing that a man is innocent until proven guilty and threatening to "pound some sense" into her daughter.

The crime wave is again big news—at a press conference, at the restaurant, and at the beach, crowds gather to discuss it.

A lone man sits on a wharf fishing. Walking up behind him, Huston discovers John, disguised in a vest and sunglasses, who tells him he has an idea to catch the burglar at the Silver's villa but needs the help of the police. John shows a note warning him to stay away, and Huston agrees to ask Lepic to have some men at the villa that night.

Later that evening, it is quiet outside a villa; a breeze rustles the bushes in the shadows. Suddenly, someone shouts "M. Robie!" and John appears in close-up,

being strangled from behind. A large wrench is raised in silhouette, sending a man over the cliff edge nearby and into the sea.

The Stevens walk by a newsstand and Francie buys a paper pronouncing the "cat" dead.

In Lepic's office, Huston asks if he is sure Froussart, Danielle's father, was the "cat." Lepic is evasive. John enters to tell them Froussart had a wooden leg, and, furthermore, he knows who the cat is and will catch him. Lepic angrily reminds him that he is free because of his assertion that Froussart was the criminal. John stalks out.

At Froussart's burial site, a large crowd pays respects. John looks around; Danielle glares at him. Bertane comes over to stand near him; he advises him to marry Francie and return to the United States. John says they can discuss it more this weekend at the costume ball. Danielle bursts out in French, nearly spitting her contempt at John, calling him a thief and a murderer; "It's because of you he is dead." John, clenching his teeth, slaps her and turns to go, pushing at the crowd of men that surrounds him.

Outside, he sits near the wall of the cemetery staring at the ground. Francie calls him from her car. Hesitating, he walks over and tells her Froussart is not the "cat." She offers to help, but he prefers their "mutual disregard" and attempts to leave. She grabs his arm and announces that she is in love with him. Stunned, he replies, "That's a ridiculous thing to say . . . to you words are just playthings." She pouts at his put-down, and he agrees to take her to the Sanford gala, promising her a "real live burglary in action."

Night. The rooftops of the Sanford villa. Inside, a soothing orchestra plays and the party guests mill around in their eighteenth-century costumes. They create a long aisle for the new arrivals to walk through so everyone can admire the costumes and spectacular jewelry. There's much clapping and bowing. Outside at tents and tables, Bertane oversees teams of workers on the food. Inside, Francie and Jessie enter: one in gold and one in black and silver, with a blackened face walking behind them carrying an umbrella—John. John points out Lepic to the women and walks over near him. Jessie calls John by name, asking him to fetch something for her and alerting Lepic to his disguise. Lepic goes around to his men whispering the news. After John returns, Francie and he dance. Time passes, as the music moves into a samba, then, as the crowd shrinks, a slow waltz. John and Francie are the only ones still dancing when the orchestra leader abruptly cuts off the music. The couple walks quietly away as a group of detectives gather in the empty ballroom to watch. Walking up to a room, Francie takes John in with her. A detective goes out on a balcony. Inside, Huston takes off the mask John wore before.

Out on the roof, John views the end of the party below as a costumed couple climb into a car and drive away. Lepic checks the time with his crew. The lights go out in the house; a black gloved hand picks up some jewelry from a dresser. John moves from his perch and, accompanied by a warning chord of music, suddenly hears a noise. The music accentuates his awareness as he turns and watches a black-clad figure walk the roof. Crossing, he rushes to follow. On the ground, the police hear a crash. John chases the figure, then grabs and unmasks Danielle. Outraged, he cries, "I knew it was you!" On the ground, the police shout "Come down, Robie," and glare a spotlight on the roof. Danielle slips away and John is left alone in the light. Francie and Huston run out of their room as Lepic

threatens to shoot if John doesn't come down. The shots start immediately and suddenly Danielle is hanging from a gutter, but she manages to climb back on the roof. Francie runs over to Lepic to tell him he has the wrong person, but Lepic is unconvinced. John sees Danielle climb up on the other side and starts out after her. She descends carefully, coming to a steep wall, then jumps to the next roof; but she trips and is left hanging again from the gutter. John holds on to her hands and forces her to tell the group on the ground that she was working for her father—and Bertane. Francie is near to fainting, holding on to Huston.

From the air, a car chase, squealing tires. John walks out on his veranda. Francie quickly follows, still in her gold gown. Admonishing him for running away, she claims she wants a proper thanks and good-bye. He agrees; as she extends her hand, he pulls her toward him and kisses her. Opening her eyes on his embrace, she looks around the veranda, commenting that "mother will love it up here." He eyes her sideways.

Note. [H]Hitchcock does bit as man sitting next to John Robie at the back of bus.

46 *The Trouble with Harry* (1954)

Director	Alfred Hitchcock
Assistant Director	Howard Joslin
Producer	Alfred Hitchcock
Associate Producer	Herbert Coleman
Production Company	Paramount-Alfred Hitchcock Productions
Screenplay	John Michael Hayes, based on the novel by John Trevor Story
Photography	Robert Burks, A.S.C.
Technicolor Consultant	Richard Mueller
Editing	Alma Macrorie, A.C.E.
Art Direction	John Goodman, Hal Pereira
Set Direction	Sam Comer, Emile Kuri
Sound	Harold Lewis, Winston Leverett
Special Effects	John P. Fulton
Music	Bernard Herrmann
Costumes	Edith Head
Cast	Edmund Gwenn (Captain Wiles), John Forsythe (Sam Marlowe), Shirley MacLaine (Jennifer Rogers), Mildred Natwick (Miss Gravely), Mildred Dunnock (Mrs. Wiggs), Jerry Mathers (Arnie), Royal Dano, Parker Fennelly, Barry Macollum, Dwight Marfield
Filmed	in VistaVision and Technicolor
Distributor	Paramount
Release Date	October 1955

Other titles: *Immer Ärger mit Harry, Mais Qui a Tué Harry, La Congiura Degli Innocenti*

Synopsis

Credits appear accompanied by the theme music as the camera pans over a child's drawing of the outdoors, ending with Harry lying on the ground.

A spired church and bandstand grace the countryside in the bright Vermont fall. Arnie, a small boy, plays with his gun in the woods; hearing real gunshots, he becomes frightened and drops to the ground, then hears voices and a thud. The perky horn music turns into blares as he walks out into the clearing and discovers a man's body; then Arnie scurries away into the background of a close-up of the man's upturned shoe soles.

Elsewhere in the woods, light romantic music accompanies the Captain, an elderly sweet-faced man, as he sits on a stump and philosophizes to himself. His hunting done for the day, he has satisfied his "primitive nature," though not sure he's gotten any rabbits. Walking off, he picks up a beer can shot through with holes, then a "No hunting" sign; then he comes upon the corpse and naturally assumes he fired the fatal shot. Reprimanding the corpse for being where he doesn't belong, he searches the body and finds an envelope in the vest pocket with a name, Harry Warp.

The Captain starts to drag Harry by his feet, when Miss Gravely, a grey-haired, prim woman, appears over the rise and matter-of-factly asks what the trouble is. "An unavoidable accident," the Captain replies. He tells her he is going to hide the body, and grabbing her by the elbow, pleads with her to "chase it out of her mind"; he thought it "was a rabbit or something . . . and committed a human error." Embarrassed at his hold on her, Miss Gravely sympathizes with him. He flatters her "warmth and understanding" and she invites him over for blueberry muffins and, perhaps, some elderberry wine. They shake hands as she steps over the body to proceed on her way.

The Captain returns to picking up Harry's feet, but is forced to run and hide behind a bush when he hears Arnie leading his mother, young red-haired Jennifer Rogers, up to the clearing. Jennifer immediately recognizes Harry and thanks Providence for the last of him. She tells Arnie to forget he ever saw the body and takes him back home for some lemonade.

Coming out from his hiding place after they have left, the Captain jumps back again when he sees another stroller coming over the rise and mumbles that there wouldn't be more people if he had sold tickets. Avidly reading a book, Dr. Greenborough trips over Harry's feet, fishes around for his fallen glasses, then goes back to his book and walks on without noticing the dead man. After the doctor has left, a hobo appears coming from the other way; he kicks Harry a few times, then sits in between his feet and steals his shoes. Clicking his new shoes in happiness, he toddles off.

A covered bridge is tucked away among the colorful foliage of the soft hills. A man sings "Flaggin' the Trains to Tuscaloosa" as Jennifer comes out on her porch to enjoy the air. The Captain sleeps near where Harry lies: the soles of his upturned feet again fill the screen, now in red-tipped sport socks.

Down near the road, Mrs. Wiggs, the local merchant, arranges her wares on her outdoor stand. Sam Marlow, a young artist, walks up with one of his paintings. "Wiggsy, you haven't sold one yet!" he says, wondering how he's going to eat. Over in the garage, Calvin Wiggs, Mrs. Wiggs's son and the local part-time deputy sheriff, succeeds in getting his antique jalopy going. Meanwhile back at the stand, Sam buys a half a pack of cigarettes while Mrs. Wiggs admires his

paintings and informs him Mrs. Rogers likes them too. Sam gives her his shopping list and she walks back inside the "emporium" to work. Following her, Sam walks by Calvin sitting in his rumbling car. Calvin asks him if he has heard any shooting but Sam replies no. As Calvin putters away, an elderly man in a chauffeur-driven car drives up to the stand and gets out to peer at the paintings.

Inside the store, Mrs. Wiggs cuts bacon for Sam as Miss Gravely enters and oohs and aahs over Sam's paintings, which surround the inside of the store as well. Sam tries to make a deal with Mrs. Wiggs to pay his bill, but she interrupts him, nodding her head toward Miss Gravely. Sam follows her gaze and turns to observe Miss Gravely standing transfixed in front of a large cup and saucer she holds in her hand. Noticing their attention, Miss Gravely asks Sam to try it, to put his fingers through the handle. He patiently holds it up in the air while she inspects the fit of his finger. She decides to buy it, so Sam queries her about the importance of the finger size and she tells him she is having a man visit her that afternoon. Mrs. Wiggs mentions the "near-sighted cider customer" outside,^H but Sam is excitedly focused on the thought of bringing out Miss Gravely's inner qualities, "the true Miss Gravely, sensitive, young in feeling. . . . I can do it!" Mrs. Wiggs starts out the door to attend to the customer, but Sam commands her to find some powder and lipstick. He runs outside to get the scissors from the stand as Mrs. Wiggs smiles patiently at the sight of the excited Miss Gravely.

Outside, Sam is so engrossed in his mission that he doesn't notice the wealthy man inspecting his paintings and interrupts the man's query to run back into the store with the scissors.

Inside, Miss Gravely sits on the counter, a towel draped around her shoulders. Mrs. Wiggs stands behind cutting her hair and Sam, his arms akimbo, advises in front. Calvin drives up. Miss Gravely anxiously asks if he is alone and is relieved to hear that he has not arrested the Captain.

Sam carries a drawing pad by the clearing and, noticing the vista, sits down on a log and starts to sketch. Suddenly realizing the unharmonious presence of Harry's socks in his drawing, he gets up and strides over to ask him to "get out of his picture." Peering down at the body, he suddenly realizes that Harry is dead. He rushes away, then stops and returns, having decided to sketch Harry's face. Nearby, the bleary-eyed Captain wakes up. Seeing Sam, he mumbles, "Next thing, they'll be televising the whole thing!" Coming out from his hiding place, he approaches Sam from behind. Turning, still hunched down, Sam notices the Captain's gun and asks if Harry is *his* "body." Affronted, the Captain retorts that, after all, it could have happened to him, and Sam suggests they "straighten the thing out." The Captain relates the story of his day, beginning with the awful sight of a drunken robin as Sam continues his large sketch of Harry.

Later, satisfied with the Captain's story, Sam finishes his work and comments that "it stands to reason, they can't touch you for it." "Nothing these days stands to reason," replies the Captain. But Sam devises an elaborate rationalization: it's "destiny . . . divine will . . . your conscience is quite clear." "I haven't got a conscience," says the Captain; "it's the police I'm worried about." He tries to make a case for burying the body and having done with it, but Sam points out that one of the people who has already seen Harry might start to care. "I can't wait for people to start caring whenever they feel like it. I don't want a little accident to turn into a career," complains the Captain. Sam wonders about the woman who knew the victim's name; when he discovers it was Jennifer Rogers, he abandons his sketch and walks over to a fallen tree limb to have a smoke. He tells the

Captain he should mail Harry back to the address on the envelope in the victim's pocket. Reminded that Calvin is in charge of the mail, Sam suggests they find out if Jennifer intends to report the body. It is now noon and the Captain remarks that he must get ready for his date with Miss Gravely. Sam teases him about being the first to "cross the threshold." They decide to hide the body before they leave and each grab a foot, but they stop dead upon seeing a man enter the clearing. Running behind the tree, they watch Dr. Greenborough, still reading his book, trip over the corpse once again and beg Harry's pardon. After he's left, Sam and the Captain pull Harry behind the fallen log.

The Captain approaches Wiggs Emporium and notices Calvin leaning into the driver's window of a state police car; ominous horns interrupt the cheery piccolo as the captain walks by hiding his gun.

Later, Sam winds his way through the countryside to Jennifer Rogers's home. She waits on the porch and he greets her with flowery compliments on her beauty and asserts that he would like to paint her in the nude. Unimpressed, Jennifer tells him to sit on the porch while she brings him some lemonade. She bumps into Arnie in the doorway, who shows off the stiffened, dead rabbit he found in the woods. Crouching to the porch floor, Sam shows them his frog. It leaps around a bit until they get it back into the bag and Sam and Arnie decide to trade playthings. Jennifer goes inside while they sit on the porch bench together and trade nonsense until she returns with a pitcher of lemonade. Arnie asks Sam for his rabbit back, explaining it might come in handy for another trade, then heads off to play.

Sam sits down with Jennifer and asks her who the man up on the path is. Jennifer, frowning at the taste of the lemonade, tells him Harry was her husband, though not Arnie's father. She blandly asserts that "he was too good to live." When Sam rises and tells her they had hoped she would know what to do with him, she recommends they "stuff him." Sam wonders why she cared so little about Harry and they sit on the banister together as she begins her story.

Her first husband, Harry's brother, Robert, was killed and "little Arnie was on the way." In order to help her out, Harry "the saint . . . Harry the good" offered to marry her. But on her second wedding night, she learned the truth about him. Jumping off the banister, she falters at revealing the "intimate details" of that night, Sam being a stranger and all, but Sam assures her he is not bored and convinces her to continue. So she does. That night, after she had gone to a lot of trouble to work up "an enthusiasm" for Harry, whom she did not love, he never came home. The next day, he called to tell her his horoscope advised him to not start any new projects. She found this unacceptable in a husband ("Suppose I wanted him to do the dishes . . . and his horoscope didn't let him?") so she moved away and changed her name. Then this morning, he appeared at her door, finally lonely for his wife, and she knocked him "silly" with a milk bottle. He staggered off up the path, swearing he was going to drag his wife home if it killed him.

A vista of the golden hills introduces the Captain on his way to Miss Gravely's home. She waits on her porch for him, dressed, like Jennifer Rogers, in bright blue. Arnie traipses through the countryside carrying his dead rabbit. On her porch, Miss Gravely and the Captain sit across from each other, eating muffins at a table laid with white linen and china. She says she picked the blueberries herself up near where Harry lies. Responding to the Captain's compliment on the "man-sized cup," she tells him it's been in the family for years. Arnie steps up to the porch with his dead rabbit and trades it for a couple of muffins. Miss Gravely returns to the question of Harry, suggesting that the

Captain could avoid a lot of digging by throwing Harry off the pier, but he convinces her Harry should be buried.

Sam and the Captain walk up the path to the clearing with shovels slung over their shoulders. They poke around for a soft and comfortable resting place for Harry. Sam starts to dig while the Captain wipes his brow. At the sound of Calvin Wiggs's jalopy, the Captain starts to dig as well.

Later, some five feet down in the ground, they decide to quit and "pop him in." The hole filled up, they hear Calvin's car again, and wonder if he is looking for Harry. Smoothing over the ground, they discuss their midday: Jennifer, Arnie, the rabbit the Captain shot, Miss Gravely, and the new cup and saucer. The Captain's eyes glisten at the news of Miss Gravely's makeover and "love" is mentioned. Finished, they sit on the log for a smoke. The Captain counts his day's bullets, the "No Shooting" sign, the beer can, and the rabbit. Suddenly realizing that he couldn't have shot Harry because he only had three bullets, he takes up the shovel and starts to dig. Sam is less inclined to go to this trouble. "You'll have much more of a job explaining away a body that you didn't kill and buried, than a body you accidentally killed and buried," he argues. But the Captain convinces him that he must help dig him out of this mess.

Later, Sam lies on the ground to inspect Harry below. He pronounces the wound to be not from a bullet, but from a "blow from a blunt instrument. . . . I think we're tangled up in a murder." The Captain suggests Jennifer might be suspected, and Sam argues for covering up Harry again, but the Captain says he is not "burying someone else's bad habits." Sam then suggests that Miss Gravely might be the culprit, but the Captain laughs, saying Sam knows nothing about etiquette, and, hence, nothing about Miss Gravely. Finally, they put the dirt back over Harry.

At the Captain's lake cottage, he and Miss Gravely walk up the pier. Inside, the romantic music suddenly pauses and the Captain halts his ebullient description of his sea-motif-decorated abode at the sight of his long underwear hanging near the stove. Ripping it down, he changes the subject to Miss Gravely's fine human qualities. Sitting in a chair near the door, she attempts to contradict these compliments by explaining her motive for the invitation to muffins; leaning against a masthead of a full female figure in a red dress, he interrupts, objecting that he understands already, but finally she manages to tell him that she invited him over because she was "grateful to him for burying [her] body." Startled, he moves toward her as she explains that she hit Harry over the head with the heel of her hiking shoe. Harry had pulled her into the bushes, raving that she was his wife. They struggled and she hit him. "I don't think I've ever been so annoyed," she complains. "So Mrs. Rogers knocked him silly and you finished him off," concludes the Captain. Still feeling guilty, Miss Gravely laments that she had thought it so convenient that the Captain thought *he* had shot Harry. "Only natural," the Captain sympathetically replies, but she insists she feels "under an obligation." "Forget it," he says, and sits down again, but jumps up at the mention of bringing in the authorities. She thinks things can be explained now, but the Captain strains to convince her that it would be best to let Harry lie. She protests that it's *her* body and she "should have the say so." Getting up to leave, she tells him to get a spade, and after they have dug up Harry, she'll make him some hot chocolate. The Captain objects, but he puts on his hat and follows her out.

Later, dirt comes flying out of Harry's grave as the Captain sits nearby and smokes his pipe.

Sam paces in Jennifer's country-patterned living room. She enters with a tray of coffee and hands him a cup, then plops down on the couch as he remains standing behind her. They agree they feel comfortable with each other, then, frowning, she turns to say she is uncomfortable about one thing, though—Harry.

A knock at the door brings in a grimy Miss Gravely and the Captain. Exhausted, Miss Gravely sits down in the rocker and tells them she killed Harry, and she and the Captain are on their way to tell Calvin. "You haven't dug him up again?" cries Sam, as a nearby closet door swings open and Jennifer gets up and closes it. Sam tries to convince Miss Gravely that a murder case would mean "indecent" prying, but she's made up her mind. Meanwhile, the Captain has decided to bring in his shovel and sits down next to Jennifer on the couch. Miss Gravely explains that she only stopped by to get Jennifer's thoughts on the matter since she's so closely connected. Jennifer replies that she doesn't know why they are so worried, but as long as they have already dug up Harry, she doesn't care what they do. "So I have a free hand," prompts Miss Gravely. "Free as a bird," replies Jennifer.

Jennifer stands now and pours coffee for the Captain. Sam walks over by Miss Gravely and reminds Jennifer that this means all the details of her marriage will be public property. His line of reasoning convinces the group to bury Harry again. As they leave, Jennifer says she has never been to a homemade funeral before and the Captain, still on the couch, discouragingly says this is his third. The closet door swings open again.

Dark has fallen; the group stands around the grave throwing leaves on top of it. Silhouetted, they hear trumpets on their way down the lane, and then someone yelling. It's Mrs. Wiggs, running in her nightgown and cap to tell Sam that a millionaire wants to buy all his paintings.

Standing around the stove in Wiggs Emporium, the millionaire, accompanied by an art critic, says the paintings are "works of genius." Sam refuses to sell, but the Captain tells him not to be foolish. So Sam turns to Jennifer and asks what she wants, and she replies, "fresh strawberries." Then Sam goes around the room asking each of his friends what they would like to have, as the millionaire writes out a list: a chemical set, a cash register, a hope chest, a hunting outfit, and a whispered request from Sam. Sam says he'll have more paintings for him next month, and the buyer leaves.

Sam leans over to face Jennifer and ask if he did the right thing. He tells her he loves her and wants to marry her. She hugs her knees and pouts. Having just gotten her freedom, she wants some time to think. Calvin arrives carrying Harry's shoes, and his mother tells him the news. The group says good-bye as Calvin goes to the telephone to call the state police about the shoes; while he is waiting on the line, he notices Sam's sketch of Harry, commenting that it matches the hobo's description of the dead man.

Later that night the foursome approach Jennifer's house; pausing outside the open door, the two men discuss the new development. Sam is reassuring, unable to imagine that Calvin can trace the shoes back to them, but the Captain worries about being psychologically worn down by modern police techniques.

Entering the living room, Sam finds Jennifer ready to announce that she will marry him. The Captain, sitting on the arm of the couch across from Miss Gravely in the rocker, interrupts with a warning: "Marriage is a comfortable way to spend the winter," he says, "but right now we should be working on some good story to satisfy the state police." Sam and Jennifer kiss anyway, and the other couple rise

to congratulate them. "Hold it!" cries Sam, walking into the center of the room, "Jennifer can't be married until she proves that Harry is dead." "Please don't ask me to dig up Harry again!" pleads the Captain. Jennifer generously argues that they must protect Miss Gravely, but Miss Gravely insists that Harry must be uncovered.

The two women sit on the log near the gravesite while the men dig. Jennifer wonders if they can't pin the body on someone else, but since she and Sam are the ones with the motive, the group decides to stick with the truth. Standing around the newly dug-up Harry, they debate whether to clean him up. Suddenly they hear a voice nearby and rush to hide behind the log. Dr. Greenborough again approaches, now reciting poetry, as it is too dark to read. This time he notices Harry. The group comes out of hiding and asks his opinion about the cause of death. They decide to meet the doctor later at Jennifer's house where there's some light.

The men carry the body back across the clearing.

Inside her house, Jennifer irons, Sam brushes off Harry's suit, Miss Gravely hangs out Harry's shirt to dry, and the Captain dozes. The closet door swings open again. Calvin arrives and Jennifer tries to keep him on the front stoop, but he pushes by her. In the living room, the Captain and Miss Gravely sit playing cards and Sam leans against the closet door. Calvin questions Sam about the sketch of Harry, but Sam explains that he drew it from his subconscious. Looking frightened, the Captain throws down his cards and says he must go home. Calvin doesn't believe Sam's story, so Sam takes the sketch and alters it, offering in explanation a lecture about the subtleties of art. Calvin, angry at his evidence being destroyed, swears he'll get to the bottom of the mystery. Sam moves away from the door and the drying rack falls out of the closet just as Arnie opens the hall door and asks why "he's in the bathtub." Behind Arnie, Harry's feet stick out over the edge of the tub. Sam alludes to the frog, and Jennifer whisks Arnie back to bed and closes the hall door. Arnie quickly reappears and she shuts the door on him again.

Dr. Greenborough walks in the front door, wondering where "he" is. After some moments of silence, Jennifer replies "he" is in the bathroom playing with his frog. Sam takes the doctor into the hallway, and Jennifer explains to Calvin that Arnie is sick. Then a fog horn blares outside and Calvin leaves. Miss Gravely collapses on the couch. Sam closes the hall door again, indicating that the doctor wants to be alone. The Captain returns and Miss Gravely asks if he has gotten over his fright, but the Captain adamantly denies that he was ever frightened. Faced with the others staring at him incredulously, he changes the subject; in a boyish appeal to Miss Gravely, he admits his exaggerations of bravery and tells her that, in fact, he was only a tugboat captain on the East River. Flattered, she reassures him that he must have been the "handsomest tugboat captain." Gleefully he pulls out Harry's shoes, which he stole from Calvin's car.

Dr. Greenborough emerges from the hall to tell the group that Harry died of a seizure and wonders why they've stored him in the bathtub. Jennifer relates to him the events of the day. Warming to her subject, she sits in the rocker and elaborates about the decisions they made about how to deal with Harry. The doctor becomes confused; she appeals to him not to tell anyone and he stumbles out the door, glad to be done with them. "He's kinda strange, isn't he?" remarks Jennifer. The group returns to work cleaning Harry's clothes, and Jennifer suggests they have Arnie discover the body again.

Next morning, the group hides behind the log near the clearing as Arnie, carrying his gun, approaches Harry. To their consternation, Arnie hesitates, then finally turns and runs. The four start to leave, but the Captain wants to know what Sam asked the millionaire for—they whisper it around and giggle: a double bed!

Note. ^HHitchcock reportedly does bit as man walking past roadside stand. The lone passer-by (in this scene) is not clearly recognizable.

47   *The Man Who Knew Too Much* (1955)

Director	Alfred Hitchcock
Assistant Director	Howard Joslin
Producer	Alfred Hitchcock
Associate Producer	Herbert Coleman
Production Company	Paramount-FilWite Productions
Screenplay	John Michael Hayes, based on a story by Charles Bennett and D. B. Wyndham-Lewis*
Photography	Robert Burks
Technicolor Consultant	Richard Mueller
Technical Advisers	Constance Willis, Abdelhaq Ghraibi
Editing	George Tomasini
Art Direction	Hal Pereira, Henry Bumstead
Set Direction	Sam Comer, Arthur Krams
Sound	Paul Franz, Gene Garvin
Special Effects	John P. Fulton, Edouart Fargiot
Music	Bernard Herrmann (score), "Storm Cloud Cantata" by Arthur Benjamin and D. B. Wyndham-Lewis. Performed by the London Symphony Orchestra, conducted by Bernard Herrmann, with the Covent Garden Chorus and Barbara Howitt, soloist.
Songs	"Whatever Will Be" and "We'll Love Again," Jay Livingston and Ray Evans
Costumes	Edith Head
Makeup	Wally Westmore
Cast	James Stewart (Dr. Ben McKenna), Doris Day (Jo McKenna), Daniel Gelin (Louis Bernard), Brenda De Banzie (Mrs. Drayton), Bernard Miles (Mr. Drayton), Ralph Truman, Mogens Wieth, Christopher Olsen, Hilary Brooke, Carolyn Jones, Alan Mowbray, Richard Wattis, Alix Talton, Reggie Nalder (the Assassin), Noel Willman, Yves Brainville
Filmed	in VistaVision and Technicolor, in London and Morocco

Running Time	approximately 120 minutes
Distributor	Paramount
Release Date	May 1956

Other titles: *Der Mann, der zuviel wußte, L'Homme Qui en Savait Trop, L'Uomo Che Sapeva Troppo*

Synopsis

Credits appear over the climactic orchestral music sequence. The camera moves into a close-up of the cymbals as they crash and a title appears: "A single crash of cymbals and how it rocked the lives of an American family."

In the back of a bus to Marrakesh sit the McKenna family: Jo, Ben, and Hank, their son, around ten years old. Hank gets bored with the desert scenery and walks around; the bus lurches, and he accidentally rips the veil off the face of a female passenger. An angry exchange ensues between the woman's male companion and the McKennas, Hank still holding the veil. It is mediated and ended by one Louis Bernard, at ease in both the necessary languages. The McKennas and Louis converse for the duration of the trip; Louis queries Ben, the father and a doctor, who answers openly about their background; Jo queries Louis in return, who answers evasively.

Honking its way, the bus enters the city walls and snakes through the crowd.

They disembark and ask Louis to share a taxi to the hotel. He says he has business. Jo asks what business, but he ignores her, instead offering to meet them for a drink in their room and take them to dinner.

As they climb into their open taxi-wagon, Jo observes Louis talking to the Arab who had shouted at Hank over the veil incident. She expresses suspicion: "You know nothing about him, but he knows everything about you." "I have nothing to hide," says Ben, finally teasing her out of her train of thought by accusing her of being jealous because Louis did not speak more to her.

Their carriage glides out of the bustle of town and into an area of quiet, clean streets to their hotel. "Well," she says as they step down, "this eases the pain."

At the door of the hotel, they pass a couple; the woman glances at Jo, who whispers to Ben, "We're being watched." Ben is impatient, but the camera shows the woman is watching.

That night. In their hotel room, Louis drinks, Ben finishes dressing, and Jo and Hank sing a duet, "Whatever Will Be," as she puts him to bed. Louis offers to make Jo a drink and asks her if she has been on the London stage; annoyed, she tells him she has been on the New York, London, and Paris stage and queries him about what business he's in. Finally, he says he would rather talk about the stage. Someone knocks at the door and Ben opens to a stranger who looks in and notices everyone, then excuses himself, saying he is looking for some other people. After he is gone, Louis asks to use the telephone, gives instructions in French to the person at the other end, and suddenly and apologetically departs.

At a Moroccan restaurant with a black and white checkered floor, Ben clowns over the awkwardness of his tall frame at the traditional low table. A man peers at them from a table behind, and Jo again expresses suspicion. Ben complains, "Would you stop imagining things!" Then the couple turn around and introduce themselves as fans: "You're Jo Conway, the singer, aren't you? Will you continue your career?" Jo and Ben reveal some disagreement over her career (New York)

versus his (Indianapolis). Polite conversation continues as they eat dinner together, with much attention paid to Ben's difficulties eating without utensils. Louis suddenly appears; Jo is miffed, but Ben makes excuses for him, and their conflicting perceptions are aggravated. They argue, and Ben finally decides to "go get Louis," but Jo pulls him back. He yanks his arm away from her grip, and the English couple divert him by inviting them to the market tomorrow. Ben is finally so frustrated that he grabs the food with two hands, horrifying the waiter. Louis sits at a table on the other side of the room with a woman, who whispers in French, "Is that the couple we're looking for?"

The crowded marketplace is full of entertainers and gymnasts.[H] Hank is with the English couple, the Draytons, while Joe and Ben stroll and joke about his patients' maladies and the fun the McKennas have spending the fees. "Hey, I'm wearing Johnny Miller's appendix," she smiles, then wonders when they are going to have another child. Suddenly, there is a disturbance—a police chase from the center through the side streets. As the fleeing men complete a circle back to the marketplace, one of them is stabbed in the back. Ben looks up to see the disguised, stricken Louis Bernard approaching, appealing to him for help. Ben leans toward him, and as their faces fill the screen, Louis whispers his secret: a statesman is to be assassinated in London soon; tell police to try Ambrose Chapel. He dies; Ben moves away and pulls out a pen and paper to write down the message. The police ask the McKennas to accompany them to the station; Mrs. Drayton offers to take Hank home with her.

Mr. Drayton counsels Ben outside the police office: "A cynical lot, these French. . . . Are you going to show them what you wrote?"

In the detective's office, Ben's relationship to Louis is questioned; Louis was an FBI agent. The detective is not tactful, and Ben becomes very angry, yelling that he didn't come here for a "grilling." In the middle of the session, he goes to take a telephone call in another room, and the camera moves into a close-up of the receiver. Then, shown from above, the caller is seen in an elegant Moroccan decor. He advises Ben to say nothing as they have kidnapped his son. Commanding Mr. Drayton to confirm that his son is at the hotel, he returns to the interrogation, dismisses the call as nothing, and signs a statement.

Jo and Ben ride back in a carriage and argue about what to do. She doesn't understand why he didn't show the message to the police. "Let's not get any more involved," she says.

At the door to the hotel, Ben finds that Mr. Drayton has checked out.

Back in their room, Jo starts to call Mrs. Drayton so Hank can return, but Ben stops her. When she asks why, he snaps, "Because I asked you to." They argue; he wants her to take some sleeping pills; she wants to know what's going on. Finally he bribes her, saying the price of information is the pills. Just as she is ready to fall asleep from the pills, he tells her what he knows about Louis and the Draytons, and that their son has been kidnapped. She's angry, crying and hysterical at the news and at having been given sedatives; "How could you!" As she pummels his chest, the camera views from below the bed where he forces her to lie down.

Night falls. He packs; she drowses, then watches him. He tells her the Draytons are gone and he can't bring the police in, so they will go to London and look for "this fella Ambrose Chapell." She stares into space, then finally rouses herself to hold him.

Airport. They deplane to the screeching of her fans; one in thick glasses is

singled out. Inspector Buchanan from Scotland Yard escorts them as the woman in the glasses makes a telephone call.

At the airport police office, Buchanan tells them he's sorry about Hank, but he knows that Louis trusted Ben with information and Hank was taken so that Ben would keep his mouth shut. Ben denies it. Buchanan criticizes them for not being cooperative and he and Jo become divided, as she thinks the police should be told. They argue and she counters his control: "You act as though you're the only one who's concerned about him." Mrs. Drayton calls in the middle of the talk and allows Hank to speak to his mother over the phone. From above, the camera moves in on the conversation as Jo tearfully speaks, then Ben grabs the phone, just as an airplane zooms overhead and the receiver clicks off. Reentering the room as the couple hold one another, Buchanan hopes they will change their mind.

A London hotel room full of flowers. Ben grabs the phone book and finds an Ambrose Chapell listed. Some of Jo's friends arrive to meet her husband, who exits hurriedly after brief introductions.

Ben takes a taxi to the address and walks down a lonely street, then into the long interior brick corridor that leads to the Ambrose Chappell taxidermy shop. Inside the shop full of exotic animal skins, there ensues a long scene of confused conversation, forcing Chappell to call the police and culminating in a fist-fight between the employees, who are protecting their employer and his wares, and Ben, who is belligerent and assumed to be crazy. Ben finally understands he is in the wrong place and escapes.

Back at the hotel room, Jo hits on the notion of Ambrose Chapel as a place when one of her friends mentions that Ben has gone to see somebody named Church. She finds an address and rushes out, asking them to explain to Ben where she has gone when he returns.

Ambrose Chapel. Jo gazes at the stark building, sighs, and goes down the street to a telephone booth to call Ben.

Back at the hotel room Ben arrives, takes the call, and immediately leaves again to go after her. Their friends stay behind, shaking their heads in confusion.

Inside the empty chapel, Mrs. Drayton prepares for the service. She walks upstairs to visit Hank, who plays checkers with Edna, the woman with the thick glasses from the airport. Mrs. Drayton then checks a room across the hall, where the stranger who mistakenly knocked on the McKenna's hotel room door in Marrakesh adjusts his tuxedo and his shoulder holster. He accepts two tickets for a concert at Albert Hall from Mr. Drayton and they go over the assassination plot, rehearsing with a phonograph the point in the music where the gunshot will be strategically placed. There are expressions of distrust between the two, and the assassin goes out the back door.

In front of the chapel, Ben joins Jo and they decide to "take a crack at this alone." They join the congregation of about sixty people inside and sing along with the hymns. While moving down the aisle, Mrs. Drayton notices them and signals to her husband, who begins a sermon on adversity. Ben tells Jo to go out and call Buchanan; she exits. Mr. Drayton cuts the sermon short, and dismisses the congregation with instructions to go home and meditate; the doors are locked and only Ben is left in the chapel. He and Mr. Drayton discuss the whereabouts of Hank. Finally Ben yells and Hank yells back. Ben runs for the stairs where the voice came from, but a struggle ensues and he is knocked out by a couple of thugs.

Outside, Jo is at the phone booth, arguing with a detective; finally she

convinces him to find Buchanan, who is attending the concert at Albert Hall. She returns to the chapel and is shocked to find the doors locked. The police arrive; she suggests they force the door open. "I'm sorry, Madam, that takes a search warrant," she is told. Inside Ben has passed out at the bottom of the altar. As he wakes, the police and Jo decide to leave, as there is "no sign of life." Jo gives up on the police, but asks them to take her to Albert Hall, then settles for the offer of a taxi stand.

In the back of the church, the Draytons, Hank, Edna, and the thugs slip out and leave by car. Ben is left trying all the doors.

The rear entrance of an embassy. The Draytons' car pulls up in the driveway. A man greets them at the door and tells them to wait until he clears the kitchen. In the bustling kitchen, he whispers to the maitre d' who orders everyone outside. The workers crowd in the hallway muttering, "There's always something funny going on at this embassy." One of the workers is shown to be particularly attentive to the activity inside.

At Ambrose Chapel, a crowd is gathering in the street in response to its wildly clanging bell. Inside, Ben is pulling himself up the bell rope through the tower in order to escape. From above, the camera shows him climbing out and down the roof.

At Albert Hall, Jo hurries in the front door. Inside, she searches the crowd for the manager and notices the assassin, who walks toward her into a close-up, smiling, "You have a very nice little boy. His safety will depend upon you tonight." A prime minister is whispered to be in the crowd, and Jo begins to put together the plot. She sees Buchanan, but, uncertain, avoids him. At a balcony door, amid deafening clapping as the orchestra rises, she sees the assassin in a box.

The music begins. A montage follows the music: the conductor, the orchestra, the very large choir, the cymbals, and Jo becoming increasingly upset as she watches the assassin prepare. After a lengthy introduction, the soprano and the choir begin to sing and the assassin pulls the opera glasses from his assistant in order to have a better view of the prime minister. Jo stands uncertain, tormented. The assassin's assistant follows the music score in her lap, then rises and leaves the box, followed by the assassin.

In the lobby, Ben arrives; as before, we can hear only the sound of the huge orchestra and choir. He meets Jo, who tells him the story in gestures. He runs out and up to the balcony, stopping an officer to alert him. Downstairs, Jo anxiously searches the hall. The cymbals player rises from his seat; the assassin pulls his gun from behind a curtain. Ben is still trying to get help when Joe notices movement behind a curtain. As the chorus swells, a close-up shows the gun sneak from behind the curtain. Ben is now frantically trying balcony doors, many of which are locked. In close-up, the gun turns toward the prime minister's chest, and Jo loudly screams, just a moment before the cymbals crash and the prime minister grabs his arm. Simultaneously, Ben falls into the right box and grapples with the assassin, who steps on the ledge and careens over the box to the main floor. Jo explains to police, "He was ready to kill him and I realized I had to scream." They meet Ben, and then the prime minister in the lobby, who thanks them and offers to thank them properly later. They confer with Buchanan, who upbraids them. "So you knew the time and place all along!"

At the embassy, the Draytons are ushered in to see their leader in his plush office with a large portrait of the prime minister behind him. They argue over the failed assassination. "You've muddled everything. Don't you realize American

people don't like to have their children stolen?" Because the child knows too much, it is decided he must be "removed." Mrs. Drayton cries, "Oh, no!"

Back at the detective's office, Ben winds up his explanation to Buchanan. A telephone call reveals the Draytons are at the embassy, but Buchanan claims there is nothing to be done. "I'm not responsible for the complications of international law," he tells them. So Ben decides they should request a final audience with the prime minister, who is attending a party at the embassy that night.

In a taxi, he explains the plan to Jo.

At the party, the prime minister introduces Jo, who will supply "a tranquil coda to a dramatic evening." She sings "Que Sera Sera" very loudly so that it rings up the stairs and through the building. Upstairs, Hank awakens, "It's my mother singing!" Mrs. Drayton instructs him to whistle back.

Downstairs, Ben manages to duck out of the audience and up the stairs.

In the basement, Mr. Drayton tells a couple of thugs to wait and starts up the stairs himself.

Distraught, Mrs. Drayton tries the window and finds it locked, then walks over to hold Hank. She cries out when the door knob turns, but it is Ben, who hesitates, wondering about her, when suddenly a gun appears at the boy's head. Mr. Drayton says the three of them will go down together and out to the nearest taxi stand. The camera moves with them, and halfway down, Ben grabs Hank and kicks Mr. Drayton down the stairs, where he accidentally shoots himself. Hank runs to find his mother, who was finishing up her second song when the commotion stopped the concert.

Back at the hotel room, the group of friends is sleeping, waiting for the return of their hosts. They finally arrive and Ben apologetically says they had to pick up Hank.

Note. * Angus McPhail is reported to have worked on the script. [H]Hitchcock does bit as man in crowd at the market watching acrobats.

48 *The Wrong Man* (1956)

Director	Alfred Hitchcock
Assistant Director	David J. McCauley
Producer	Alfred Hitchcock
Associate Producer	Herbert Coleman
Production Company	Warner Bros.
Screenplay	Maxwell Anderson, Angus McPhail, based on "The True Story of Christopher Emmanuel Balestrero" by Maxwell Anderson
Photography	Robert Burks, A.S.C.
Editing	George Tomasini, A.C.E.
Set Direction	William L. Kuehl
Sound	Earl Crain, Sr.
Music	Bernard Herrmann
Makeup	Gordon Bau, S.M.A.
Technical Advisers	Frank D. O'Connor, District Attorney, New York; George Groves, Sergeant NYPD.

Cast	Henry Fonda (Christopher Emmanuel [Manny] Balestrero), Vera Miles (Rose Balestrero), Anthony Quayle (Frank O'Connor), Harold J. Stone, Charles Cooper, John Heldabrand, Esther Miniciotti (Mrs. Balestrero), Doreen Lang, Laurinda Barrett, Richard Robbins, Norma Connolly, Nehemiah Persoff, Lola D'Annunzio, Kippy Campbell, Robert Essen, Dayton Lummis, Peggy Webber
Filmed	in New York City
Running Time	approximately 105 minutes
Distributor	Warner Bros.–First National
Release Date	December 1956

Other titles: *Der Falsche Mann, Le Faux Coupable, Il Ladro*

Synopsis

Before the credits appear, Alfred Hitchcock stands spotlighted in extreme long shot, a tall shadow behind him; he introduces the story as true, unlike anything he has ever done before, but similar in theme.

Over a scene at the Stork Club with a jazz orchestra playing music of various moods, a title introduces January 14, 1953, a day in the life of Christopher Emmanuel Balestrero that he will never forget.

During the credits, the crowd dances, then thins as the evening wanes and the orchestra stops.

Manny goes home on the subway, reads the paper, and checks the racing sheet and an ad for a new car. He stops in a shop for a cup of coffee, where he sits at a booth and marks the form.

In the shadow of the elevated train tracks, he walks down a street of row houses to his front door. Picking up the milk bottles from the stoop, he goes in and checks on his two sleeping boys. In the bedroom, his wife, Rose, is awake with a toothache and the news that it will cost $300 to have her wisdom teeth removed. He kisses her as she wonders how they will pay for it and complains about the installment plan always keeping them broke. He chats with her while he undresses, then warmly hugs her and reassures her how lucky they are to be in love and have their children. After she has dozed off, he turns thoughtful; in close-up for a moment, he stares at the racing form, then kisses her on the neck.

The next day, Rose is washing the dishes when Manny announces that he thinks there is enough money in her life insurance policy to pay the dentist. Their boys begin to quarrel up in the front room; Manny calmly breaks up the argument and soothes them with promises of piano lessons. The phone rings; Manny's mother wants him to stop by because "Pop" doesn't feel well. Hanging up, Manny announces that he's going down to the insurance company, then to see his parents; he will be back by 5:30.

Manny takes the subway to the insurance office. Inside, he hesitantly approaches the teller window, waiting for the clerk to be free. The clerk stares nervously at him. As he approaches and puts his hand in his breast pocket, she

holds her breath. He brings out the policy and asks how much he can borrow on it. She asks if he would mind waiting; turning, she closes her eyes in horror and walks back to consult with her supervisor. She thinks Manny is the man who robbed them, and the two women move over to the next desk where the robbery victim sits; all three pretend to look at the policy while they discuss the situation. The victim is afraid even to look at Manny, but the others talk her into glancing at him; Manny stands innocently in profile, as, quaking, the victim firmly pronounces him to be the thief. The clerk returns to tell Manny his wife must come in to sign for the money. Manny leaves. The clerk turns back to comfort her friend as another worker agrees that it looks like the same man.

Manny kisses his mother good-bye on her porch.

At the insurance office, detectives tell the women to wait at home until they bring in Manny.

At home, Rose rolls some dough in the kitchen and reminds her boys that their dad is always on time. The phone rings and a man asks Robert when Manny will be home.

Manny gets off the bus and walks up to his house. Two detectives are waiting outside to intercept him. They take him by the arm and ask him to come to the precinct station with them. He motions backward and asks to tell his wife, but they place him in the backseat of their car.

The jazz score drifts along as Manny silently and slowly looks around, jammed between the two detectives in the back seat.

The group enters the station and walks down the hall to an interrogation room. The detectives sit Manny at a table and inform him that he fits the description of a holdup man; Manny protests that he is completely innocent. The older detective, sitting across from him, calmly explains that "an innocent man has nothing to worry about." He asks Manny to "help them out" by visiting a couple of stores with them.

In the car, Manny glumly informs them he plays bass at the Stork Club and does not drink. The car stops at a liquor store and the detective instructs him to go in. Manny asks if that won't look funny, but the detective reassures him. With a very serious expression, Manny walks in and out as the man behind the counter stares at him. They drive off; the detectives are quiet. One asks if Manny's wife ever accompanies him to the Stork Club, and Manny blankly responds that it's too expensive. They stop at a delicatessen. Manny walks by the man and woman helping a customer at the counter. On his way out the woman is friendly until her employer interrupts to point out that Manny is accused. She frowns; they stare at Manny who looks blankly back.

Back home, Rose talks on the telephone in the hallway to her mother-in-law.

At the precinct station, Manny sits across from the younger detective as the older one paces, questioning him about his visits to the insurance office, his finances, and his gambling habits. Manny explains that he needs money for the dentist, but falters over the gambling, then denies he plays the horses. Leaning over the table, the detective pressures him about how much he has borrowed and how much he owes. Manny calmly responds, then suddenly blurts out, "What is this? Am I being accused of something?" The detective patiently explains the charges made by the women at the insurance company, then tells Manny that he can help himself by cooperating and printing the words of the robbery note so they can compare handwriting. "An innocent man has nothing to fear, remember that," he reassures Manny, who writes the note. There is a rough similarity in the

printing and Manny is asked to print again: "Give me the money ..." The detective counsels Manny that it looks bad; he made the same spelling error as the holdup man. Pointing his finger at Manny, the detective stands and asks if the witnesses are ready.

At home, Rose hangs up the phone, wondering if Manny might be trying to call her.

The detective motions Manny into an informal lineup in a room. The two secretaries view the six men in the room from across the hall through the shadow of two open doorways. They are asked to count and stop at the one they recognize; both identify Manny, who stands in the middle. He closes his eyes. The women emerge from the shadows and the other men disperse. The older detective commands Manny to follow him while the younger detective shows Manny's file to a third detective. This one confronts Manny with the evidence, advising him to confess. Manny protests that he is just trying to tell the truth, but the man informs him that he must come up with a better story. Told to relax, Manny is then fingerprinted under a glaring light.

Manny is escorted to the precinct desk, where a lieutenant books him for the robbery of $71.00 from the Associated Life Insurance Company. Allowed to keep his rosary beads and facing a hallway with bars at the end of it, Manny wonders if he can now call his wife and is told that "it's been taken care of."

At Manny's home, Gene Conforte, Manny's brother-in-law speaks with the police. Rose, Manny's mother, and his sister surround Gene as he hangs up the telephone and announces Manny's arrest. His mother wonders if Gene heard right, which exasperates him, while the rest mutter that it can't be true.

Manny paces his cell, knocks against the bars, and flexes his hands as the camera moves up to his frustrated countenance. His eyes close as the music and camera escalate in a stir around him.

Next morning, Manny is driven in a truck to a courthouse where a crowd views a lineup on a stage in a large auditorium. Manny waits sullenly behind the lighted staging area until he is ushered in front of the microphone while the charge is read.

The police truck takes Manny to another building; he is taken in the back door to a courtroom where his family sits in the audience. Bearded, haggard, he shakes his head "no" when he meets Rose's eyes. A lawyer joins him in front of the judge, pleads not guilty, and requests a lesser bail amount because of Manny's job and family, but the judge denies it. Pushed out into a stark corridor, Manny comments, "I guess I didn't know what happened."

Manny is handcuffed and taken to the truck again; he sits stupefied, staring out at his clamped wrist and the circle of prisoners' feet on the truck floor. He is led into another back door, the handcuffs are removed, and Manny is checked in at another counter. Inside a large cell, Manny undresses amid much hubbub and shouting. Carrying his bedding and clothes, he is led up a flight of stairs to an enclosed cell. The door clangs shut and he hears his name echoing down the hall. Just as he turns, the door is opened and the payment of his bail is announced.

Rose meets Manny coming out of the Queens Prison. They hug. "You'll never know how much I needed you," says Manny, starting to faint.

On their front stoop, Manny stares at the curb where the police car stood. Inside he hugs his mother, then immediately goes to lie down. Bob, his oldest boy, comes in and they talk about what happened. "You're the best dad," he tells Manny, and hugs him.

On the back porch, elevated trains rumbling nearby, Rose tells Manny's mother that the lawyer in felony court recommended another lawyer, Frank O'Connor; she worries about not knowing what to say to him. Rose telephones Frank O'Connor and gets his wife; near tears, she admits that she would rather talk with her and tells her the story.

Manny and Rose take the subway to the lawyer's office. Rose eagerly asserts Manny's innocence, but Frank asks first for Manny's story and the secretary comes in to take down his statement as the shadows of the elevated train move over the dictation pad. Later, when Manny is finished, Frank says he will take the case, but warns them that he is not an experienced criminal lawyer and they might be at a disadvantage. Manny assures him that trust is all that is necessary; after all, there is the problem of payment for which Frank has agreed to wait. Frank asks them to dig carefully for an alibi for the two dates in question; Rose begins to discuss possibilities, and Manny finally pushes her along saying, "We can't keep Mr. O'Connor any longer."

A country inn covered in snow. Inside the empty dining room, the proprietors speak with Rose and Manny about their four-day stay there the previous summer. It was crowded, but the woman remembers it was raining because it was her birthday. His memory jogged by this clue, Manny walks out and across to another building. Stopping on the porch, he tells the others that he and Rose played cards all that day with another couple whose names he doesn't remember. They put together some clues and find the names in the register.

That night they visit an apartment building under the shadow of a large bridge. Going up the stairs they hear the raucous giggling of two young girls who inform them that the tenant, Lamark, died and his wife moved. At another dilapidated building by a port, they buzz Mr. Molinari's door. A Spanish-speaking woman downstairs tells Manny that Molinari is dead. Rose breaks into tears and then giggles at this news; Manny stares at her.

Later, as Manny prepares for work, Rose, still in her coat, blames their predicament on herself, her wisdom teeth, her inability to economize. "I let you down. . . . I haven't been a good wife," she says. Concerned, turning toward her, Manny softly tells her she is "just talking nonsense."

At the Stork Club, Manny stares at the floor while he plays.

In Frank O'Connor's office, Manny talks; Rose is wide-eyed and silent. She stares out and finally rouses herself to answer a question. Both Manny and Frank notice her strange behavior; Frank tries to focus on the other robbery date, when Manny had a swollen jaw that would have made him recognizable. Rising, Frank walks behind the couple and looks down at Rose, who hangs her head, anxiously gripping the inside of her elbow. Manny rises to leave and the two men stare back at her, still sitting, unaware of them. Manny calls to her and she rises; Frank smiles, telling her they are "going to win this case." She murmurs good-bye and walks out. Frank whispers to Manny that she should see a doctor.

Later that night, Manny leaves the Stork Club and arrives home. Opening the door in his bedroom he finds Rose sitting up in the chair, the bed still made. He tells her he is worried, she doesn't sleep, doesn't eat; she should see a doctor. "There's nothing wrong with me . . . we can't pay for things now," she frowns. Sitting down across from her on the bed, he tells her it seems as though she no longer cares what happens to him. "Don't you see, it doesn't do any good to care. . . . No matter what you do they've got it fixed so that it goes against you," she says solemnly; "we're not going to play into their hands. . . . You're not going

out . . . the boys aren't going to school. . . . I've thought it all over; we're going to lock the doors and stay in the house." Mildly, Manny agrees, then wonders if the boys shouldn't go stay with his mother. Rose becomes angry and rises to lean over him, "You think I'm crazy. . . . How do I know you're not guilty!" Shocked, he tries to calm her and walks over to close the door. She continues to rave: "You went to the loan company to borrow money for a vacation. . . . I told you not to, I told you they'd pile up . . . and then they reached in from the outside and they put this last thing on us . . ." He suggests she see a doctor and reaches for her, but she backs away, then picks up a hair brush and hits him on the forehead. Shocked at herself, she grabs and hugs him, then returns to the chair. "It's true, Manny . . . there is something wrong with me."

Later one day, Manny looks out a city office window, then over at a closed door. Inside the darkened room on the other side, Rose sits under a light and a doctor paces behind her, trying to counter her paranoid logic with facts. "I let them down . . . they want to punish me . . . they knew he wasn't guilty, I was guilty . . . it's useless," she says. The doctor strides out of his office and across the anteroom to speak with Manny. "Is it her mind?" Manny softly asks. The doctor describes the pattern of the illness: she is now in an "eclipse . . . buried under a landslide of fear and guilt." He recommends she be institutionalized and Manny's teeth clench. "I want her to have the best," he says.

Manny lets Rose out of the car; she stands, staring vacantly off and they walk up the steps of an older building. Inside the hallway, they are greeted by two nurses; one tells Manny it would be best to say good-bye here. From behind, we see Rose eerily turn her head to respond to Manny's good-bye. She walks up the winding central staircase as Manny watches, quietly calling after her but receiving no response. He turns and walks out, standing momentarily on the porch.

Manny rises in court to hear his indictment; during the prosecutor's introduction, he sits holding his rosary beads. The prosecutor says the detectives will testify that Manny told them he needed money to pay off bookies. This startles Manny and he shakes his head "no" to Frank. Frank then explains to the jury that they must decide from the testimony of the witnesses, and sets forth a theory of mistaken identification.

Mrs. James, one of the insurance company clerks, testifies; she is asked to and, after balking, walks down from the stand and places her hand on Manny's shoulder to identify him. The cross from Manny's rosary hangs down from his hands as he hunches over and listens. Another of the secretaries testifies and identifies Manny. Later, Frank questions the third insurance company secretary, Miss Willis, about the lineup. The judge plays with his pen. As Manny looks nervously around the room, no one seems to be paying attention: the prosecutor laughs at a colleague's whispered comment, Manny's sister-in-law puts on lipstick, many others whisper during Frank's labored, tentative questioning. Finally a juror rises to ask the judge if they "must" listen to all this. Frank approaches the prosecutor and then asks to speak to the judge. The three men talk near the bench; Frank returns to the front and requests a mistrial be declared. The judge assents. Walking back to sit down next to Manny, Frank whispers that it had to be done; they must start all over again. "Can you take it, Manny?" "I can try," sighs Manny, staring off.

At his home, Manny goes into the kitchen and sits down across from his mother, who is sewing. "I've been such an idiot; you'd all be better off without me," he says, putting his forehead in his hands. Near tears, she tries to console

him and asks if he has prayed. Yes, he responds calmly, then becomes angry at the thought of the real culprit out there somewhere. He rises impatiently, saying he has to go to work, and leaves his mother crying.

In his bedroom, Manny stares, mouthing a prayer at a picture of the Sacred Heart. Double-exposed over his stricken look reflected in the glass, another man walks up a street, his face almost identical with Manny's.

The man, having the same chiseled facial structure as Manny, goes into a small store and asks the woman behind the counter for a pound of ham. She turns to get it and he walks around behind the counter and points a gun at her. She picks up a knife and stamps her foot twice. Her husband comes out of the back and wrestles the man down as he cries for mercy, saying he has children at home. The woman calls the police.

At the station, a policeman takes the man in the front door, just as one of the detectives who had interrogated Manny walks out. The detective stops on the sidewalk out front, then turns and goes back inside.

At the Stork Club, the manager walks over to the stage and tells Manny they want him at the 110th precinct.

At the station, Miss Willis is down the hall making another positive identification. She and one of the other secretaries from the insurance company emerge and walk down the hall toward Manny. They stop in confusion, looking at him, then continue, one bowing her head, unable to look him in the eye, the other shaking her head at him, then both run out. The detective approaches Manny, who smiles at him. The suspect walks toward them until he and Manny face one another. "Do you realize what you have done to my wife?" says Manny.

Manny takes a cab out to the home where Rose is staying. Waiting on the porch, he checks the news story of his case. He and a nurse briskly walk down the hall to Rose's room, where she stands by the window clutching herself. He walks over and tells her the news, but she is unable to respond to it or his hug. The nurse suggests he tell her again, and he sits down before her. She stares suspiciously down at him as he tells her they have friends. "It's all over." "That's fine for you," she says despondently, "nothing can help me . . . you can go now." She stands by the curtain and rubs her arms. He persists but the nurse interrupts. Manny is shocked; he was "hoping for a miracle." "They happen sometimes, but it takes time," says the nurse; "she's not listening now."

Title over a palm tree-lined Florida street: "Two years later, Rose Balestrero walked out of the sanitarium—completely cured. Today she lives happily in Florida with Manny and the two boys . . . and what happened seems like a nightmare to them, but it did happen. . . ."

Title: "Final thanks to Sherman Billingsly for permitting scenes of the Stork Club."

49 *Vertigo* (1957)

Director	Alfred Hitchcock
Assistant Director	Daniel McCauley
Producers	Alfred Hitchcock, Herbert Coleman (associate)
Production Company	Paramount-Alfred Hitchcock Productions

Screenplay	Alec Coppel, Samuel Taylor, based on the novel *D'Entre Les Morts* by Pierre Boileau and Thomas Narcejac
Photography	Robert Burks, A.S.C.
Editing	George Tomasini, A.C.E.
Special Effects	John P. Fulton, A.S.C.
Process Photography	Farciot Edouart, A.S.C., Wallace Kelley, A.S.C.
Technicolor Consultant	Richard Mueller
Art Direction	Hal Pereira, Henry Bumstead
Set Direction	Sam Comer, Frank McKelvy
Sound	Harold Lewis, Winston Leverett
Special Effects	John Ferren
Titles	Saul Bass
Music	Bernard Herrmann
Costumes	Edith Head
Makeup	Wally Westmore, S.M.A.
Hairstyles	Nellie Manley, C.M.S.
Cast	James Stewart (Scottie Ferguson), Kim Novak (Madeleine Elster/Judy Barton), Barbara Bel Geddes (Midge Wood), Tom Helmore (Gavin Elster), Konstantin Shayns, Henry Jones (Coroner), Raymond Bailey, Ellen Corby (McKittrick Manager), Lee Patrick
Filmed	at Paramount Studios, Los Angeles, in Technicolor
Distributor	Paramount
Release Date	May 1958

Other titles: *Aus dem Reich der Toten, Sueurs Froides, La Donna Che Visse due Volte*

Synopsis

Under the titles, an extreme close-up of a woman's lips, then her frightened eyes, which dart, and a close-up of one eye, which flushes red. Eerie theme music accompanies as the image is replaced by a spiral animation design.

Close-up: with a clank, a hand reaches up and grasps a railing that cuts through the middle of the dark screen. The scene widens to show a fugitive leading a chase across the roofs of San Francisco with a policeman, and the suited John (Scottie) Ferguson following. The trio jump a gap onto a high-pitched roof, but Scottie trips and is left hanging from a creaking gutter. The policeman turns back to offer his hand, but Scottie is frozen in fear at the sight of the ground many flights below, and is unable to respond. In an attempt to reach closer toward him, the policeman careens over Scottie and falls. Scottie remains hanging, terrified.

Midge Wood, a blond woman with glasses, designs lingerie at a drafting table in her hillside apartment, San Francisco spread out in front of her picture windows. Scottie (she calls him Johnny) slouches on the couch and chats with her

about his recovery and their relationship. The camera sits close above Midge during this exchange as she concentrates on her work, and it is revealed that they were briefly engaged in college days, though she broke it off. He teases her about still being "available Ferguson." They discuss his newly diagnosed acrophobia, which he feels has left him unfit for police work. He mentions an old college acquaintance, Gavin Elster, who has left him a message after many years' absence.

Scottie suddenly decides to experiment with his illness by stepping on a stool, theorizing that he can cure himself by gradually getting used to heights: "I look up, I look down." Midge enthusiastically provides a stepladder, but as he approaches the last step and looks out her window at the steep drop, he breaks out into a sweat, violins sharply quivering, and faints into Midge's arms.

Scottie visits Gavin Elster, an elegantly dressed man, at his large Mission District shipyard office, ^H huge cranes pictured through a massive window behind him. Gavin has married into the business. They chat about the changing city and their lives. Finally, Scottie asks Gavin why he called and Gavin explains that he thinks his wife is possessed by someone from the past; he wants Scottie to follow her. Scottie scoffingly suggests a doctor, then softens and offers the services of a detective agency. But Gavin insists that only Scottie will do, and suggests that he "can see" his wife that night at Ernie's Restaurant.

Scottie sits at the bar at Ernie's, a darkened restaurant with white table-cloths. The music swells as the camera crosses the crowded dining room and finds Gavin and his blond wife, who rise to leave. Madeleine, elegant and calm, walks into a close-up near Scottie as he nervously eyes her.

Scottie reads the newspaper in his car while he waits outside the Elsters' high-rise apartment. Madeleine emerges and drives away in her Rolls Royce. He follows her, turning several corners, finally into an alley, where she goes into a back door. He walks into the grimy back room after her, then peeks farther into a bright flower shop, where she buys a hand corsage.

Next, she stops at Mission Dolores. He walks through the dark church, then finds her in the backyard cemetery standing at the grave of Carlotta Valdez, 1831–1857. She goes then to the Palace of the Legion of Honor, where she sits in front of a portrait, and he notices the similarities between her and the painting, the swirl of her hair and the corsage. An attendant tells him it is a portrait of Carlotta Valdez.

Finally, he follows her to the old McKittrick Hotel. He sees her in a second-floor window, but when he goes in to the dark, paneled central hall and queries the attendant, she insists that Miss Valdez has not been there today and shows him her empty room to prove it. Looking down at the street, he sees that her car is gone; later he finds it parked in front of her apartment building.

Scottie visits Midge and asks her to recommend an authority on San Francisco history. Quickly grabbing her coat, she takes him to Pop Liebel at the Argosy Book Shop, who tells them about the "beautiful, sad Carlotta." A wealthy man built the house that is now the McKittrick Hotel for her, taking their child and banishing her there when he tired of her. Later, she went mad and killed herself. On their way out, Midge cheerfully demands Scottie's story in exchange for the information.

Later in the car, he still refuses to tell Midge what is on his mind, but she guesses that it has to do with Gavin, even that Carlotta has returned to take

possession of his wife. She scoffs at this notion and Scottie is forced to admit that Madeleine is pretty. After she has gone, he opens a book with a reproduction of the portrait; Madeleine's profile is superimposed over it.

Scottie meets Gavin at a luxurious club for a drink. He points out that the tragic story of Carlotta Valdez explains Madeleine's imbalance, but Gavin blandly explains that the story of Carlotta, Madeleine's great-grandmother, has been kept from her; unsatisfied with Scottie's explanations, he demands more information.

Another day, Scottie follows Madeleine to the Palace of the Legion of Honor, horns announcing its looming presence, and he watches her sit in front of the portrait. Next, the two cars enter the road that traverses the Presidio woods and drive down to the water's edge under the Golden Gate Bridge. Scottie gets out as Madeleine disappears under the bridge; then he watches her throw petals from her corsage into the water. She calmly jumps into the water, and the music swirls as Scottie runs to leap in after her. He carries her back to her car, where he breathlessly looks into her unconscious face and calls her name.

Back at his apartment, the camera moves from Scottie making a fire, around the room to the kitchen, where Madeleine's clothes hang on a line, then to the bedroom where she sleeps, muttering in her dreams. She wakes when he walks in to answer the telephone, and he hands her his maroon robe. She emerges from the bedroom to sit on the floor by the fire and he questions her about where she was during the day. She claims to have never been inside the Palace of the Legion of Honor, thanks him mildly for helping, and compliments him for his directness. As they talk, she becomes thoughtful, commenting that "living alone is wrong," and then, looking directly at him, says, "I'm married, you know." He remains still, then eagerly sits forward and asks if this has ever happened to her before; she laughingly replies no. Gavin calls and Madeleine leaves while Scottie is speaking with him. Outside, Midge drives up just in time to watch Madeleine get into her car. She comments ruefully, "Was it a ghost? Was it fun?" She drives away when Scottie comes to the door.

Next day, Scottie waits for Madeleine outside her apartment, then follows her in circles around the city; up and down hills, finally to his own apartment where she goes up to the mailbox with a thank-you note. He gets out and greets her; she apologizes for the day before and he says, faltering, that he "enjoyed it." She says good-bye and he asks to accompany her on her "wanderings."

They head up the coast in her car, then stop and walk in a dark redwood forest, which dwarfs them. "I don't like [the trees]," she says, "knowing I have to die." A close-up of a display that consists of a cross-section of an old tree shows its thousand years of history; she marks out the centimeter of her life among the rings, then disappears. Finding her, Scottie questions her about what she remembers and where she goes, until she becomes distraught and pleads with him not to ask her such questions.

Later she walks toward an ocean cliff, and he follows and tells her he is responsible for her now because he saved her life. She claims not to know what is happening to her, and describes a dream consisting of long corridors, rooms, an open grave waiting for her, and a bell tower with a garden below. "If I'm mad, that would explain it," she says, and starts running down the rocks to the sea. He catches up to her and they embrace and kiss as she pleads with him to stay with her. The full orchestra climaxes on a fade to black.

Midge, in a red sweater, busily paints in her studio. Scottie visits. She has not

seen him much lately and he suspiciously queries her about her motives in inviting him over. He smugly insists he has merely been "wandering," and congratulates her for beginning to paint again. "I always thought you were wasting your time in the underwear department." She shows him her portrait of herself as Carlotta Valdez. Solemnly, he shakes his head, "It's not funny, Midge," he says and leaves. She is tortured by this turn of events and, pulling at her hair, bitterly accuses herself of being stupid.

Scottie walks down a street in the dark blue night. Later, in his apartment, he dozes. Madeleine rings his doorbell at dawn, a sharp violin accenting her silhouette at the door; she says she had "the dream" again about the bell tower in an old Spanish village, and the music turns to a habañera theme. Scottie recognizes her detailed description of the mission at San Juan Batista, and cries out "Something to work on!" He tells her they will go there at noon.

They drive down the long winding road through tall trees.

At the mission, the camera moves over the courtyard to find Scottie in a dark stable, and Madeleine, depressed, sitting in a carriage. Scottie tries to prompt her memory of when she had been here before. Drumming on a wooden horse that is part of the exhibit, he assures her "there's an answer for everything!" She mumbles about school days, but remains depressed. They kiss and express love for one another. "But it's too late," she says, "there's something I must do. . . . It wasn't supposed to happen this way." Crying, she pushes him away and starts across the courtyard, and he catches up to her on the grass and holds her tightly. They struggle, but she insists on going into the church alone, "You believe I love you? . . . then if you lose me, you'll know I loved you." He loosens his grip, and she quickly runs. Glancing up at the bell tower, Scottie decides to chase up the stairs after her, but slows down, experiencing vertigo at every turn, the camera from above accentuating the depth of the crude wooden stairwell. Suddenly he hears a scream and watches her fall by the window in front of him. Sweating, he starts back down the stairs. From above the church, the police can be seen climbing a ladder to her body on the roof, while Scottie's small figure moves out the ground-level door.

The police converge on the Mission for a hearing. A judge describes the suicide, snidely referring to Scottie's "lack of initiative" in not saving Madeleine and his "strange behavior" in disappearing from the scene of the death. "Either he suffered a blackout as he claimed or he could not face the tragic result of his own weakness and ran away," states the judge in finding a verdict of suicide. Gavin apologizes to Scottie for the harshness of the judge and tells him that he is moving away. Unable to reply, Scottie refuses to shake Gavin's hand.

Scottie visits Madeleine's grave. At home, asleep in bed, he has nightmares of suffused colors and wind, appearing in a montage of swirling special effects and animation—the nosegay, the cemetery, the open grave, and the fall into the roof—all tormenting him until, in the middle of the fall, he suddenly wakes and sits up petrified.

Midge brings a Mozart record to Scottie, who is now in a psychiatric institution. She suggests it will "sweep the cobwebs" away, but he sits silent and impassive as she tries to cheer him. "Try, please," she says, hugging him, "you're not lost, mother's here." Her time up, Midge goes down the hall and tells a doctor that Scottie was in love with Madeleine and still is. "I don't think Mozart is going to help at all," she laments. Beginning to cry, she turns away, and the camera remains stationary as she walks away from it down the empty hall.

Later, the camera pans over a bright San Francisco day and finds Scottie standing in front of the Elsters' former apartment building, anxiously asking one of the tenants where she obtained Madeleine's Rolls Royce.

He goes into Ernie's bar and stares at a blond woman who reminds him of Madeleine. He stops at the Palace of the Legion of Honor and stares at a nosegay in a downtown shop window. Noticing a dark-haired woman in a tight sweater dress who looks like Madeleine, he follows her up to her room in the drab Empire Hotel.

He tells her he just wants to ask her some questions, but she angrily accuses him of trying to pick her up. He persists and finds out that her name is Judy Barton. Taking pity on him, she apologizes for yelling, and he asks her out to dinner. She agrees when he assures her it is not just because she reminds him of Madeleine.

After he is gone, Judy leans on her desk and, in close-up, turns toward the camera. Grimacing, she remembers the day at the Mission. We see a flashback of her (as Madeleine) running up the stairs, then Gavin Elster throwing his wife from the tower just as Judy appears at the top; immediately he grabs Judy and covers her mouth. Back in her room, Judy closes her eyes in grief, then takes her suitcase and starts to pack. Going to the desk, she begins a letter to Scottie, explaining Gavin's plot and the mistake she made in falling in love with Scottie. Wishing she had the nerve to stay and make him love her again, she suddenly rises with new resolve and puts away her suitcase.

At Ernie's, Scottie and Judy are dining when an elegant woman suited like Madeleine walks into the restaurant and distracts him. In contrast, Judy is dressed in figure-revealing purple. Later, as Scottie says good night to Judy at her door, he asks to see her the next day, then adds that he wants to take care of her. At first, she refuses, her profile silhouetted in the moonlight, but he persists, and she relents.

Next morning, they walk around the grounds of the Palace of the Legion of Honor. That evening, they dance. Another day, he buys her flowers, then offers to buy her clothes. She demurs, but he takes her into an expensive salon, where a model shows them a suit. Scottie anxiously says it is not what he wants, and describes to the saleswoman the grey suit Madeleine wore. Distressed at his obvious intentions, Judy protests that she likes what she just saw. He calmly replies that he just wants her to look nice. Embarrassed and angry, she jumps up and asks to leave; as they stand in front of a mirror, he pleads with her to make him happy: "It can't mean anything to you!" "I want to get out of here!" she hisses, just as the saleswoman arrives with the grey suit. Scottie persists. Later, she tries on shoes and he dictates the color to the clerk.

Back in her hotel room, she sits sadly at the desk, still unhappy at his scheme, and he offers her a drink. She says she would like to go away but admits she cannot, then agrees to wear the clothes, pleading with him to "just like me." As she speaks, he focuses on her hair, and the romantic music begins; wincing, she cries out, "Oh no! . . . if I change the color of my hair, will you love me?" They kiss and he moves her over by the fire.

At a beauty salon, Scottie discusses the correct hair color with the beautician; Judy's nails and makeup are also redone.

Scottie waits in her room, then stands at the door as she silently returns. He criticizes her hair. "It should be pinned back off your face, I told them that." She protests, but finally walks into the bathroom to fix it. Anxious, he waits. She

appears at the door, first ghostlike, then slowly walks toward him looking now exactly like Madeleine. He kisses her passionately, then imagines himself in the stable at the Mission. The camera circles around them as the music reaches a climax.

Later, he sits, relaxed and joking in her room as she dresses for dinner. She is cheerful now, then puts on a necklace that he recognizes from the portrait of Carlotta. Stiffening with realization, he suggests they drive down the peninsula for dinner.

As they drive, he is silent and, looking up at the trees, she realizes something is amiss. By the time they arrive at the mission, it is dusk and she is frightened. "I need you to be Madeleine for a while," he says, "then we'll both be free."

"I'm scared," she says, as he holds her firmly by the arms and begins to recreate the death scene. "I don't want to go in there," she cries, but he forces her into the church, telling her she is his "second chance." He pushes her up the stairs, but his vertigo affects him as he follows behind. Midway, at the opening where he was stopped by the sight of Madeleine's fall, Scottie tells Judy that he knows the truth because he recognized the necklace. She starts to back down the stairs and they struggle as he demands to know about the plot, and now drags her. "You were the copy, you were the counterfeit!" he yells. "I wanted to stop it!" she cries, but he is furious, in a sweat. "He made you over too, but better! . . . Not only the clothes and the hair, but the looks and the manner and the words!" he shouts, pushing her closer to the open window. He drags her up screaming, then stops suddenly as he realizes his vertigo is gone. Confident now, he drags her all the way to the top, her feet bumping on the stairs, all the while questioning her about his betrayal. Cringing in a corner of the tower, she continues to insist that she loves him and moves toward him; finally he softens, and they embrace and kiss. A nun, at first hidden in shadow, emerges from the stairs and frightens Judy so that she backs away and falls screaming through the window. The nun rings the bell, and Scottie walks out on the ledge, stunned, staring down.

Note. [H]Hitchcock does bit as passer-by on sidewalk carrying a horn case.

50   *North by Northwest* (1959)

Director	Alfred Hitchcock
Assistant Director	Robert Sounder
Producer	Alfred Hitchcock
Associate Producer	Herbert Coleman
Production Company	Metro-Goldwyn-Mayer
Screenplay	Ernest Lehman
Photography	Robert Burks, A.S.C.
Color Consultant	Charles K. Hagedorn
Editing	George Tomasini, A.C.E.
Titles	Saul Bass
Production Design	Robert Boyle
Art Direction	William A. Horning, Merrill Pye
Set Direction	Henry Grace, Frank McKelvey
Sound	Frank Milton
Special Effects	Arnold Gillespie, Lee LeBlanc
Music	Bernard Herrmann

Cast	Cary Grant (Roger Thornhill), Eva Marie Saint (Eve Kendall), James Mason (Phillip Vandamm), Jessie Royce Landis (Clara Thornhill), Leo G. Carroll (the Professor), Philip Ober, Martin Landau, Adam Williams, Robert Ellenstein, Josephine Hutchinson, Edward Platt, Ken Lynch, Doreen Lang, Les Tremayne, Philip Coolidge, Edward Binns, Pat McVey, Nora Marlowe, Ned Glass, Malcolm Atterbury
Filmed	at MGM Studios, Los Angeles, New York, and South Dakota
Running Time	approximately 136 minutes
Release Date	July 1959

Other titles: *Der unsichtbare Dritte, Das Erbe des Grauens, La Mort Aux Trousses, Intrigo Internazionale*

Synopsis

The credits, accompanied by the chase theme music, slice across a glass building that diagonally fills the screen.

Roger Thornhill, advertising executive, cheerily dictates a business memo to his secretary as he leads her out of their modern Manhattan office building.[H] He rudely grabs a cab from another customer and on the way to the Plaza Hotel continues his litany of instructions, including directions to send candy to an ex-wife and to telephone his mother to remind her of their date that evening.

At the Plaza, he meets several business associates in a bar, but quickly excuses himself, explaining that the instructions he gave his secretary to contact his mother won't do; he must send a telegram. As he walks back into the lobby, two men accost him and force him into their car.

Seated between them in the back seat of a car, he tries to provoke them with sarcastic comments, but they are silent. He makes a jump for the door, but it is locked.

They enter the grounds of a Glen Cove estate, a large mansion with stone columns, where Roger is escorted into the library and locked in. The distinguished Lester Townsend enters; the camera pans each man in turn as he and Roger circle the room eyeing one another. Lester notes that Roger is "more polished than the others" and accuses him of being George Kaplan, an agent who moves from hotel to hotel and city to city. Finally, he demands Roger's "cooperation." Dumbfounded by the events, Roger is pugnacious, and Lester hints that he might not survive the evening. Giving up his quest for whatever Kaplan knows, Lester calls in his thugs and leaves. One named Leonard offers Roger a drink. Told he must drink, Roger leaps for the door, but the thugs force him down to the couch and pour him a glass full of bourbon in front of his alarmed eyes.

On a dark cliff road, accompanied by strains of the film's chase music, they drag the besotted Roger into the driver's seat of a car and push him over the edge. But he wakes at the sight of the ocean below, takes control, and careens off down the highway. The thugs chase after him until a police car takes up the chase as well and rear-ends Roger's car.

Raving, Roger is taken into custody at the Glen Cove jail where he lounges over the front-row seats of the courtroom. The police discover that he was in a stolen car and take him to a phone to call his lawyer. He calls his mother, insisting in a slurred voice that he has not been drinking. A doctor interviews him and pronounces him intoxicated. Next morning, he and his lawyer stand before a judge and tell the story; the judge decides to have it investigated.

At the Townsend mansion, Roger, his mother, and a group of detectives are ushered into the library where the liquor stains have been removed from the couch and the liquor from the cabinet. Roger is puzzled, then aghast when Mrs. Townsend, whom he saw only briefly, enters and acts as though he were an old friend who drank too much at a dinner party the night before. "What a performance!" he cries. She informs them that Lester Townsend is at the United Nations addressing the General Assembly. Roger's mother is increasingly sarcastic about his claims, and the detectives are satisfied with the answers they get to their questions. Roger is angry, but beaten. "Pay the two dollars," advises his mother. As they leave, one of the thugs prunes some bushes nearby.

Roger and his mother go to the Plaza Hotel; he bribes her with cash to ask for the key to Kaplan's room, which they discover has not been used. The maid mistakes Roger for Kaplan and he wonders if he might look like the man; during his search he finds a photograph of Lester Townsend and discovers that neither the maid nor the valet has ever seen Kaplan. One of the men from the night before telephones from the lobby. Roger and his mother run out, but the thugs join them in a crowded elevator and mother loudly teases them about trying to kill her son. Everyone laughs except Roger, who insists on escorting the women off the elevator first, then runs for the cab stand outside.

The driver takes Roger to the United Nations building. In a large bright waiting area, Roger announces himself to the woman holding the intercom as George Kaplan. Outside the hall, one of the thugs puts on some leather gloves. Roger meets Lester, but he is a different man; this Lester assures him his wife is dead and his house in the country is empty. As Roger brings out the photo he has of the other Townsend, Lester is knifed in the back to the sound of ominous horns and strings. He falls on Roger, who pulls the knife out of Lester's body and is photographed holding it high. Realizing his blunder, Roger runs out and into another cab.

In a conference room, graced with maps of the world and a view of the Capitol, a group led by a man called "Professor" discusses Roger's case as described on the front page of the newspapers. They know George Kaplan; he is a fictional character they created as a decoy, and they are concerned that he has now "come alive." Mrs. Finley, the lone woman in the group, wonders if they are being "callous" in ignoring Thornhill's plight. But the Professor persuasively argues that they must ignore him in order to protect their own agent. "Good-bye, Mr. Thornhill, wherever you are," intones Mrs. Finley, as the camera peers down on the group from above.

At Grand Central Station, police and detectives excitedly search for Roger, who sits in a phone booth talking to his mother. Putting on sunglasses at the sight of a headline advertising the manhunt, Roger gruffly tries to buy a ticket; the ticket seller turns away to call the police, then looks back to find Roger gone. Roger bluffs his way through the ticket gate and on to the train, then bumps into a blond woman in a corridor, who misleads the police for him. Hiding in the toilet, he evades the ticket takers, then goes to the dining car, and romantic music accompanies him as he is seated across from the same woman. Eve Kendall knows

all about Roger; she holds his hand and blows out a match he lights for her cigarette, then invites him to hide in her drawing room. Eve notices the train has stopped so that several detectives can board, and she warns Roger.

Later, he hides in the closed upper bunk of her compartment as the detectives stop at her door to question her. After, Roger and Eve kiss at length while discussing their situation; they are falling in love.

Afterward, she sends a message to VanDamm, the man who posed as Lester Townsend and who is seated in another sleeping car room with Leonard. "What do I do with him in the morning?" she writes.

The next day, Eve gets off in Chicago and Roger, dressed in a Red Cap uniform as a porter, carries her bags; they are stopped by the train detectives but not suspected. Eve volunteers to call Kaplan while Roger changes clothes.

Meanwhile, the chase music begins as the Red Cap in his underwear alerts the police; detectives race through Union Station grabbing Red Caps, while Roger shaves in the restroom. Leonard and Eve talk to each other from opposite ends of a phone booth block. She finds Roger and gives him instructions from Kaplan to meet him at a prairie bus stop about one-and-one-half hours from Chicago. Roger notices her discomfort and wonders when he will see her again, but she urges him to go.

A bus stops at a barren crossroads, just fields and sky. Roger disembarks and waits. An occasional car speeds by, and a truck showers him with road dust. A man comes to wait on the other side for a bus and mentions that a plane is "dustin' crops where there ain't no crops." After Roger is alone again, the plane comes around and dives at him, forcing him to sprawl on the ground, then rains gunshots on him. Watching the plane circle and return, he tries to flag down a car, then starts running toward a dried cornfield. The plane dumps a load of pesticide on the field, flushing him out. He runs out in front of a semi trailer, waves until it stops, and falls under the bumper. The plane crashes into the truck's gas tank and he and the drivers run as it blows up. When passengers in a pickup truck stop to gape, Roger jumps into their truck and speeds away.

Later, the police find the abandoned truck on a Chicago street. Roger wipes the dust off his suit and enters the Ambassador Hotel. He discovers that Kaplan checked out that morning *before* Eve claimed to have received the message. Suddenly, he notices Eve, dressed in a red gown, crossing the lobby; he follows her to her room. She runs and hugs him; he clenches his teeth and holds his hands away from her, demanding a drink. He coyly tries to get her to confess but she coolly avoids his questions. She takes down an address for a meeting from a telephone call, but he insists he is not letting her out of his sight. Calmly, she tells him to leave her—"Last night was last night"—pleads with him even, then relents and agrees to have dinner with him if he gets his suit cleaned. As they negotiate, he reproves her for trying to tease him: "You're wicked, up to no good. . . . Ever kill anyone?" He pretends to shower as he watches her sneak out, then picks up the address of her destination from an impression left on the notepad.

At the chic North Michigan address, Roger finds a crowded art auction taking place. Inside, VanDamm stands in the front row; Eve is seated by him and he lovingly fingers her neck. Leonard sits nearby. Roger walks up the middle aisle and confronts them; hearing Roger was in her hotel room, VanDamm conspicuously removes his hand from Eve's shoulder and stares down at her. Roger sarcastically describes Eve's betrayal as VanDamm continues to bid in the

auction. Eve jumps up in anger as the volume of the conversation escalates. Leonard and the other thugs appear at the exits; the Professor is also in the audience observing the altercation. Roger finally threatens them with giving himself up to the police and stalks away, leaving Eve with tear-filled eyes. At every exit, Roger runs into VanDamm's men. He decides to sit down and is disconcerted to watch Eve and VanDamm leave. He starts to bid erratically and otherwise disrupt the proceedings, deliberately provoking a fight that gets him arrested but away from VanDamm's thugs. The Professor makes a phone call in the lobby.

In the police car, Roger identifies himself as the United Nations killer and demands to be taken to headquarters. The police are instructed by phone to take him to the airport, to which he vociferously objects.

At the terminal, they are met by the Professor who escorts Roger alone. As they walk to the plane, the Professor identifies himself as a government agent laboring in the Cold War: "CIA, FBI . . . we're all in the same alphabet soup." Furthermore, he tells him they are going to Rapid City, South Dakota, that Kaplan does not exist, that Eve is VanDamm's mistress, and various other things that are covered by the noise of airplanes on the field. Roger is angry and insists he will no longer be a decoy. But the Professor explains that Eve is the agent they must protect and she is in grave danger because of him. Roger is horrified.

The Professor sits under a blue sky on a viewing deck of a park building, as Roger looks through a telescope at Mt. Rushmore nearby. VanDamm is expected to leave the country that night, and they must restore Eve to his "good graces." VanDamm and Eve drive up.

Roger gets a cup of coffee inside the cafeteria and demands to speak to VanDamm alone when his party enters. He offers to let VanDamm leave the country free in exchange for Eve. VanDamm demurs, then Eve interrupts them; a scuffle ensues as Roger grabs Eve and she pulls out a handgun and shoots him. She runs out and drives off by herself as VanDamm and Leonard watch the disturbance with the crowd. The Professor shakes his head over Roger's body, then attends him in the ambulance.

Later, in a pine forest, the ambulance pulls up and Roger jumps out unharmed. He has been taken there momentarily to meet Eve. They apologize, make explanations, then kiss good-bye. Roger then learns from the Professor that Eve is going with VanDamm that night, and becomes very angry. "I don't like the games you play, Professor. . . . Perhaps you ought to start learning how to lose a few cold wars!" "I'm afraid we're already doing that," laments the Professor. Agitated, Eve rushes to her car and speeds away as the Professor's driver punches Roger to the ground.

Roger paces in his locked hospital room, listening to a report of his death. The Professor visits, bringing new clothes. Eve and VanDamm are leaving in an hour. After the Professor is gone, Roger goes out to the window ledge and over to the next room. He takes a cab to VanDamm's house.

Roger approaches the spectacular, mostly glass home from below and walks under the cantilevered main rooms. Lights blink outlining the airstrip on the other side. Climbing up the beams, he peeks inside over the floor boards and hears VanDamm and Eve reassuring one another. After she has gone upstairs, Leonard alerts VanDamm to Eve's betrayal by shooting some blanks from her gun at him. VanDamm punches Leonard into a chair, but then indicates he will dump Eve out of the plane over the ocean.

Roger climbs the wall up to Eve's balcony just as she returns downstairs. He

scribbles a warning note on a packet of his monogrammed matches and drops it down to the living room near where she is seated. She gets the message and makes an excuse to go upstairs even though the plane is waiting; Roger warns her, telling her he will steal a car and pick her up outside.

The housekeeper is left behind as the others go out; she notices Roger's reflection in the television set and puts a gun on him.

VanDamm, Leonard, and Eve walk nervously to the plane as Eve anxiously turns back expecting Roger to appear. Finally, gun shots ring out and Roger drives up; she grabs the microfilm/statue from VanDamm and jumps into the car. Unable to open the driveway gate, they are forced to abandon the car and start running through the woods. As they come to the top of Mt. Rushmore, the rounded rocks loom in front of them, but VanDamm's men are close behind; Roger and Eve start down. The others follow different paths down the sculpted rocks; one of them corners Roger and Eve at one point and Roger throws him over. Eve gets caught holding on to a thin ledge and Roger tries to grasp her and pull her up. He appeals to Leonard for help, but Leonard crushes Roger's hand with his foot. A shot rings out and Leonard drops the newly retrieved microfilm and falls to his death. The Professor and a contingent of police watch from the top of the monument. Roger continues to struggle to help Eve back up onto the ledge. Their faces in close-up, she suddenly becomes "Mrs. Thornhill" and Roger pulls her up to the top bunk of a rail car sleeping room.

The train races into a tunnel.

Note. ᴴHitchcock does bit as man who misses bus.

51 *Psycho* (1960)

Director	Alfred Hitchcock
Assistant Director	Hilton A. Green
Producer	Alfred Hitchcock
Production Company	Paramount-Shamley Productions
Screenplay	Joseph Stefano, based on the novel by Robert Bloch
Photography	John L. Russell
Editing	George Tomasini
Art Direction	Joseph Hurley, Robert Clatworthy
Sound	George Milo
Special Effects	Clarence Champagne
Titles	Saul Bass
Music	Bernard Herrmann
Costumes	Helen Colvig
Cast	Anthony Perkins (Norman Bates), Janet Leigh (Marion Crane), Vera Miles (Lila Crane), John Gavin (Sam Loomis), Martin Balsam (Milton Arbogast), John McIntire (Sheriff Chambers), Lurene Tuttle (Mrs. Chambers), Simon Oakland, Frank Albertson, Patricia Hitchcock (Caroline), Vaughn Taylor, Mort Mills, John Anderson

Filmed   at Revue Studios, Los Angeles
Running Time   approximately 110 minutes
Distributor   Paramount
Release Date   June 1960
Other titles: *Psychose, Psyco*

Synopsis

The driving theme music plays under the credits, which are inserted and broken
down by streaking black and white lines.

Phoenix, Arizona, cityscape. Friday, December 11, 2:43 P.M. The camera
moves into a stark high-rise hotel window. Marion, half undressed, lies on the
bed. Sam, also shirtless, leans over to kiss her; they embrace, then discuss their
relationship as they finish dressing. She wants to marry, have "respectability";
with an ex-wife and a struggling business, he thinks he can't afford it. She
suggests an end to their relationship as it is and leaves when he teases her about
it. They are both frustrated, but in love.

At the storefront realty office where she works,[H] Marion, a trim blond
woman, enters, anxious about being late, but the other secretary informs her
their boss is not yet back himself. Marion's co-worker offers her some tranquilizers
for the headache Marion has complained about. Her boss, Mr. Lowery, arrives
shortly with a customer, Mr. Cassidy, who is sweaty from drink and the heat. Mr.
Cassidy sits on Marion's desk and flirts with her, waving $40,000 in cash that he
plans to put down on a house for his daughter's wedding present. After the boss
finally cajoles him into the inner office, Lowery pauses near Marion and whispers
to her to go to the bank and put it in a safe deposit box right away. After finishing
up some paperwork and letting her co-worker admire the money, she goes into the
office and asks to go straight home after the bank because of her headache.

The camera moves from Marion, now in black underwear, to a close-up of the
money in a bulging white envelope. In her small square bedroom, she finishes
dressing; her suitcase is already full. Worried, she stares at the money, then
shoves it into her purse.

Driving, she waits at a stoplight, hearing Sam's surprise when he sees her in
Fairvale. Her boss passes by the pedestrian walk in front of her; they smile a
greeting at one another, then he furrows his brow. Marion is unnerved, and the
jarring music begins. Night falls. She continues to drive, blinking her eyes.

Next morning her car is parked at the side of a road beneath some bare hills.
A policeman pulls up behind her, then knocks on her window to wake her as she
lies across the front seat. He suggests she would be safer in a motel. She's visibly
nervous and short with him; finally he asks for her license. The camera watches
from a low angle on the front seat while she surreptitiously turns her back to the
policeman, who leans into the window behind her, and she carefully digs through
her purse for the license, hiding the money as she looks. She drives off and the
music continues. She watches as he follows her then finally turns away.

Passing through a town, she pulls into a used car lot. She buys a newspaper
from a vending machine and notices the same policeman watching her from
across the street. She hurries the car salesman ("first time I ever had a customer
rush me"), and agrees to $700 plus the trade-in for a new car. She goes into the
restroom to take the money and title out of her bag. The policeman crosses over

just as she is hurriedly getting into the car to drive off. The mechanic calls after her to stop; she's forgotten her luggage. Dumbfounded, the three men watch her drive off.

In the car, she bites her lip, imagining what the three men are saying about her. Dark falls again. Worried, she imagines the scene at her office on Monday, her boss getting wise, but she smiles in satisfaction at Cassidy's indignation. A heavy rain begins to fall and the bright lights of the oncoming cars make her blink; eventually the traffic subsides and the road is dark. She searches the roadside until finally the Bates Motel sign appears.

Rain pounds down as she gets out of her car and looks into the tiny, unattended motel office. She peers around the corner at an old, grey, Victorian house at the top of a rise and sees a woman passing in front of the window. Marion reenters the car and honks the horn a few times. Norman Bates comes bounding down the hill, smiling.

Inside the office, she signs in as Marie Samuels, from Los Angeles. Norman fingers the room keys and finally decides on Room 1; he is very friendly and makes jokes. He shows her the room; unable to say "bathroom," he points. Finally leaving, he shyly invites her to have dinner with him. After he's gone, she looks around for a place to hide the money, finally deciding to wrap it up in her newspaper. Through the window, she hears him arguing with his mother, who is disgusted with him for inviting a woman up to the house.

Marion waits at the front door for him as he walks down the hill with a tray. "I've caused you some trouble," she says, and invites him into her room. He stiffens and says the parlor behind the office is warmer. She pauses at the door of the room filled with stuffed birds, then graciously sits down. He stutters more now, and talks about his hobby: "Only birds look well stuffed because they're kinda passive. . . . It's an uncommon hobby, not expensive." She asks about friends; he says "friends make him nervous." She is saddened. "What are you running away from?" he asks, but she frowns, so he changes the subject. He sympathetically tells the story of his mother and her hard life: losing her husband, building the motel, then losing her lover. "A son is a poor substitute for a lover," he says. But, he hates "what she's become—the illness." Marion suggests putting her "someplace," and he angrily retorts, "Why, she's as harmless as one of those stuffed birds!" He relaxes and smiles, "We all go a little mad sometimes; haven't you?" Sometime after telling him her real name, she readies to leave, saying she has a long drive back to Phoenix the next day. He watches her go, then turns back to check the register, smirking at the false name.

Walking back into the parlor, he listens at the wall, then takes a picture off its hook and stares through a hole chipped out of the board. A close-up shows his profiled eye watching as she puts a robe over her underclothes. He replaces the picture with new determination in his eyes, then walks out and up to the house.

At the house, he starts up the elaborately carved stairs but stops and pauses, then goes and sits hunched over at the table in the kitchen.

Marion sits at the desk in her room, subtracting the money she's spent from what she stole. She rips up the paper and, thinking, finally puts it in the toilet and flushes. She closes the bathroom door, steps into the shower and turns on the water. Seconds later, the music starts up and a grey figure in a robe appears, pushes away the shower curtain, and stabs at her with a very large knife. Slowly she collapses against the tiles after the grey-haired woman who attacked her has left; a close-up shows her hand as it grabs the shower curtain and rips it down

with her as she collapses over the edge of the tub. Blood flows down the drain. The camera moves from a close-up of the drain to her eye, open but lifeless, to the tile floor, out of the bathroom, over the newspaper in the bedroom, and out to view the house.

From the house, there are cries of "Mother! Oh, god! Blood!" Norman runs down the hill and into the scene of the crime. He cups his hand to his mouth, turning away nauseated. He closes the window, sits shaking on a chair, then leaves the room, closing the door behind her. He goes into the office, turns out the lights, and returns with a pail and mop.

He walks into the bathroom, turns off the water, and lays the shower curtain out on the floor of the bedroom. He drags Marion out onto the plastic, looks around the bathroom, washes his bloody hands, then rinses the sink. He swabs down the bathtub and floor with the mop, then takes a towel and wipes everything dry. He tiptoes around her body on his way out to her car. He backs up the car so the trunk is near the door, then returns to wrap the body in the plastic and puts it inside the trunk. Returning to the room, he clears out the rest of her things and turns out the lights. Someone drives by, frightening him, but he returns again to check the room; this time he notices the newspaper and picks it up and throws it in the trunk.

It's daylight, and he drives the car into a marshy area. Getting out, he pushes the car into a pond and watches as it sinks. It pauses with the top still visible and he looks around nervously, then it finally disappears.

Sam Loomis Hardware letterhead. Sam writes to his dear "right-as-always-Marion," asking her to marry him. The camera moves out from the cramped back room, where he sits at a desk, into the store area past a clerk trying to help a customer choose the proper insecticide, one that's "painless." At the front door, a blond woman enters and asks for Sam; she introduces herself as Lila, Marion's sister. They've just begun to discuss Marion's disappearance when a private investigator, Arbogast, enters, and suggests they work together. Sam finds out about the $40,000 and Arbogast says he is sure Marion will come looking for her boyfriend. He leaves.

A montage of hotels and motels shows Arbogast querying the various managers. As the sun begins to go down, he sees the Bates Motel and pulls up.

Showing him a picture, Arbogast tells Norman he's looking for a missing person; Norman takes him into the office and tells him he hasn't seen anyone in two weeks. Arbogast becomes curious at Norman's halting replies and asks to see the register. Finding the matching signature, Arbogast pressures Norman, who leans awkwardly over the book, peering at it. Stuttering now, he finally remembers Marion, explaining that she came late and left early and made no phone calls. Arbogast asks if he spent the night with her and Norman is forced to admit to the sandwich in the parlor. Getting angry, Norman pleads that he has work to do, and they walk out onto the porch; but Arbogast hesitates; there's "something missing." Norman invites him to follow while he changes the beds, but Arbogast takes the opportunity to poke around; he notices the eerie house and asks if anyone is home. Norman says no, but Arbogast says there's someone in the window, and Norman explains that it is only his invalid mother. Arbogast suggests that Norman might be hiding Marion there, taken in by her enough to lie. Norman becomes angry; "I'm not a fool . . . and even if I was, she didn't fool my mother!" Arbogast wants to talk to the mother and they argue, but finally Norman insists that he leave.

At a phone booth by the road, Arbogast calls Lila and explains what he found at the Bates Motel. He says he is going to return to the motel to try to talk with the mother and tells her he will see her in about an hour.

Outside the motel, Norman walks down the long L-shaped walkway in front of the rooms and disappears. Arbogast drives up and goes into the office, then the parlor. Momentarily transfixed by the stuffed birds, he inspects the desk; then he walks out and around toward the house.

He enters the front door, stands for a moment in the hallway, then starts up the stairs toward the camera. A crack of light appears on the floor as a door opens. The screeching music starts, and from overhead, the camera shows the woman stomp out of the room to the right at the top of the stairs, knife raised high in her hand. Arbogast, just reaching the top is surprised and slashed, tumbling backward down the steps.

Sam and Lila wait in the hardware store; it's been three hours since they've heard from Arbogast. Lila wants to go out to the motel; Sam finally relents, but insists on going himself.

Norman stands near the pond again, watching. At the motel, Sam calls out for Arbogast. Norman, incredulous, hears the faint cries.

Back at the hardware store, Sam returns with no new information, only that he saw the sick old lady in the window, but she was unable to answer the door. They decide to alert the sheriff.

Inside his house, the sheriff walks down the stairs in a robe. He and his wife know Norman lives "like a hermit." The couple convince him to call Norman and ask about Arbogast, though the sheriff is dubious of any wrongdoing. Norman politely answers; yes, Arbogast was there and then left. As Sam and Lila continue to talk of the mother, the sheriff tells them about the famous murder-suicide of Mrs. Bates and her lover; Norman discovered them in bed together, dead. Sam persists, saying he saw the woman in the window.

His hand still on the telephone, Norman decides on his course of action. He moves with determination, out of his office, up to the house, and up the stairs. From overhead in the hallway, we hear him tell his mother she must stay in the fruit cellar for a while. She refuses vehemently. They argue. Finally, he carries her out and down the stairs.

At church, Lila and Sam meet the sheriff and his wife. They have already been out to the Bates Motel and assure the young couple that Norman is alone there.

Afterward in the car, Lila and Sam decide they must go to the motel themselves. He wonders what to do and she replies firmly that they will register as man and wife and search the place.

They arrive nervous, with no baggage. Inside the office, Sam awkwardly insists on signing the register, for "business" reasons. Norman is not his joking self and puts them in Room 10 near the end.

Inside their room, Lila is sure that something happened there and they must search. She convinces Sam by telling him how much she trusted Arbogast.

They go out down the walkway; Norman is not around, so they enter Room 1 and search it. In the bathroom, Sam notices the shower curtain is gone, then Lila finds some paper stuck to the toilet. Noticing the figures match the stolen money, she's encouraged. They agree to split up; Sam will watch Norman while Lila goes into the house to question the mother. When Lila disappears from the walkway, Norman suddenly appears and surprises Sam. Sam says Lila is sleeping and he's in the mood to talk.

Lila walks up the hill toward the house, the camera tracking with her. Inside, she searches the hallway.

In the office, the men talk about lonely people; the atmosphere is very strained as Sam is aggressive and Norman is suspicious.

Back at the house, Lila enters the room at the top of the stairs. It is an old-fashioned, very stuffy woman's bedroom. She looks through the closet, starts at her reflection in the mirror, then fingers the deep impression in the lumpy bed.

In the office, Norman tells of his happy childhood, but Sam doubts his contentment.

Lila enters Norman's room, a child's room, full of toys and stuffed animals, with a recording of Beethoven's *Eroica* Symphony on the turntable.

Sam speculates about Norman's desire to get away from the dilapidated motel and begin a more profitable business. "Where are you going to get the money?" he asks. Norman suddenly wonders where Lila is. He turns to leave and they struggle; he knocks Sam out and races up the hill.

Coming down the stairs, Lila sees Norman through the front door window. She runs around and hides on the basement stairs, then notices the finished door and decides to continue her search. She tiptoes down and opens the door to find a seated figure in the middle of a back room. She puts her hand out, calling Mrs. Bates, and the figure turns, a dressed up, bewigged skeleton. She screams just as the screeching music starts and the grey-haired woman enters, grimacing, knife held high. Just as suddenly, Sam appears behind and grabs the attacker, whose wig and clothes fall off, revealing Norman. The cadaver laughs.

A crowd mills around outside the courthouse. Inside, the psychiatrist rises and stands in the middle of the room: "You see, the mother had taken over. . . . Norman only half existed. . . . Did he kill? Yes and no. . . . Norman murdered his mother and her lover. She was clinging and demanding. Matricide is unbearable so he had to erase it. . . . Since he was jealous of her, he assumed she was as jealous of him, so when he felt attracted to someone, his mother went berserk. And now the mother has taken over completely." An officer interrupts to ask if he can take Norman a blanket.

Walking down the hall with the blanket, he hands it into a room; the mother's voice politely says, "Thank you."

Norman sits in the center of the stark white room. He "regrets having to tell on Norman." He frowns, staring at a fly on his hand. "Why, I wouldn't even harm a fly," he says proudly.

The car is dredged up from the pond.

Note. [H]Hitchcock does bit as man wearing a Texan hat outside realty office.

52   *The Birds* (1963)

Director	Alfred Hitchcock
Assistant Director	James H. Brown
Producer	Alfred Hitchcock
Production Company	Universal–Alfred Hitchcock Productions
Screenplay	Evan Hunter, from the short story by Daphne Du Maurier
Photography	Robert Burks, A.S.C.
Editing	George Tomasini, A.C.E.

Art Direction	Robert Boyle
Set Direction	George Milo
Sound	Waldon O. Watson, William Russell
Special Effects	Lawrence A. Hampton, Ub Iwerks, A.S.C., Albert Whitlock
Titles	James S. Pollak
Music	Remi Gassmann, Oskar Sala, Bernard Herrmann (consultant)
Costumes	Edith Head
Makeup	Howard Smit, S.M.A.
Bird Trainer	Ray Berwick
Production Assistant	Peggy Robertson
Production Manager	Norman Deming
Cast	Tippi Hedren (Melanie Daniels), Rod Taylor (Mitch Brenner), Jessica Tandy (Lydia Brenner), Suzanne Pleshette (Annie Hayworth), Veronica Cartwright (Cathy Brenner), Ethel Griffies, Charles McGraw, Ruth McDevitt, Malcolm Atterbury, Lonny Chapman, Elizabeth Wilson, Joe Mantell, Doodles Weaver, John McGovern, Karl Swenson, Richard Deacon, Doreen Lang, William Quinn
Filmed	at Universal Studios, Los Angeles, and northern California
Running Time	approximately 120 minutes
Distributor	Universal
Release Date	March 1963

Other titles: *Die Vögel, Les Oiseaux, Gli Uccelli*

Synopsis

Bird cries sound, and silhouetted birds on a white background dart through the screen, breaking down the credits as they appear.

Downtown San Francisco. On her way into a pet shop,[H] blond, elegantly suited Melanie Daniels notices a large number of gulls dotting the sky. Inside, where all kinds of birds are screeching, she discovers the shop does not yet have the mynah bird she ordered, and she instructs the shopkeeper to deliver it when it arrives. Mitch Brenner bounds up the steps while she's writing down her address and mistakes her for a sales clerk. She obligingly walks him around the store looking for lovebirds. Their arch exchange is an even match, until he throws her by demanding to "see" a bird in his hand; she attempts to oblige him, only to have the bird fly off around the store. The saleswoman and Melanie raise their hands helplessly until the bird lands on an ashtray and Mitch captures it in his hat. He then sarcastically calls the bird by Melanie's name and reminds her that he was on the wrong side of one of her expensive practical jokes. She is piqued at his effrontery, and chases after him to memorize his license plate. Imperiously using the pet shop telephone, she calls a friend at the *Daily News* where her father is an executive and sweetly manipulates him ("Charlie, would *I* pressure

you?") into calling the Department of Motor Vehicles to learn the identity of the man at the pet shop. She then orders a pair of lovebirds and leaves.

Later, dressed in a full-length beige mink coat, Melanie enters a building carrying a cage of lovebirds and takes the elevator up to Mitch's apartment. Eyed by a neighbor, she sets the cage in front of Mitch's door with a card, but is informed by the neighbor that Mitch has gone for the weekend to Bodega Bay, sixty miles north.

Looking placidly confident, Melanie floors the pedal of her convertible sports car on the way up the Pacific coast road, the tires screeching and the lovebirds bending into the turns.

In Bodega Bay, she stops at the general store and asks where Mitch lives. Discovering there is only one road around the bay to his house, she decides to rent an outboard motor boat so she can "surprise" him. Failing to get Mitch's sister's "exact name," she is directed to Annie Hayworth's house for the information.

Up the road, a disheveled Annie comes out of her back garden, shares her cigarettes, and asks a few questions of her own. Their chat is easygoing, but full of innuendo about each one's relationship with Mitch. Moving on, Melanie drives out to the dock to pick up her boat.

Still in her mink, speeding across the lake, Melanie gets close enough to see that Mitch is alone in the barn. Cutting the motor, she paddles into the dock and sneaks up and into the house, the camera moving forward with her as she watches out for Mitch. She leaves the cage in the living room, and sneaks out and into the boat. After paddling out a while, she waits for Mitch to emerge and watches him go into the house, then hastily run back out and peer down the road. Turning, he sees her boat, then runs back in for his binoculars and watches her in close-up as she starts the boat. Melanie smugly watches him jump into his truck and race around the bay, appearing on the dock just before her arrival. Seeing him nonchalantly leaning on a post, she clears the smile from her face and cocks her head in a sweetly open expression. At the same moment a gull swoops down and pokes her in the head, destroying her pose, and bloodying her head and glove.

The blood runs down her forehead as they walk to a café bar, where the owner supplies her with some peroxide to clean the wound. She and Mitch sit in a booth together while Melanie tells Mitch that she was coming to Bodega Bay this weekend to see her friend, Annie Hayworth. Mitch is skeptical, but when his mother arrives, he tells her that he has invited Melanie for dinner. "Maybe," Melanie replies. Mrs. Brenner, a grey-haired woman with the same French-twist hairstyle as Melanie, is cool, raising her eyebrows at the situation. She looks at Melanie's head and Melanie sweetly explains that a gull hit her.

Later, at Annie's house, Melanie asks if she can rent her spare room for a night. Annie wryly smiles and agrees.

Melanie arrives at the Brenners' door as the family walks in from the barn. Cathy, Mitch's preteen sister, greets Melanie with a hug, exclaiming that the lovebirds were just what she wanted. Lydia is more reserved, concerned about the poor feed she just purchased that her chickens will not eat. Inside, she walks quickly into the foreground to telephone a complaint to the man who sold her the feed; he convinces her that her chickens might be sick.

After dinner, Melanie plays a piece by Debussy on the piano while Cathy stands nearby and talks with her about the "hoods" her brother, who is a lawyer, defends. She pleads with Melanie to come to her surprise birthday party the next day.

Meanwhile, in the kitchen as they clean up, Lydia questions Mitch about

Melanie. She mentions seeing Melanie's name in the news several times, including an item about her jumping naked into a fountain in Rome. Mitch firmly tells her he can handle Melanie on his own, *and* he knows "exactly" what he wants.

Later, he walks Melanie to her car and confronts her with the fountain story, criticizing her activity and motives. She admits she did not know Annie and lied. But he refuses to acknowledge her sincerity and she finally zooms off, angry at his stubbornness. After she leaves, Mitch looks over to see flocks of birds lined up on the telephone lines near the house.

In her modest bungalow, Annie is curled up in her robe and pajamas when Melanie arrives home for the night. Annie offers brandy and they exchange jaded observations about Mitch and Bodega Bay. Annie relates the story of her romance with Mitch that lapsed when she met Lydia, who, she insists, "is not jealous and possessive" but "afraid of being abandoned." Melanie listens sympathetically to Annie, who moves restlessly around the room, sitting, then standing; Annie tells her she moved to Bodega Bay because she does not want to lose Mitch's friendship "ever." Mitch telephones for Melanie and pleads with her to come to Cathy's party, while Annie sits in a chair nearby, smoking, staring away. Afterward, Melanie questions Annie about whether she should go, and Annie sincerely encourages her to do what she wants. A thud sounds at the front door and they open it to find a dead gull on the stoop. "Must have lost its way in the dark," says Annie. "But there's a full moon!" responds Melanie.

The next day, Mitch and Melanie walk up a sand dune away from the lawn and the children at play. He pours martinis from a pitcher he carries, and she demurs, saying she must drive back soon. He pressures her to stay for dinner, and she relates her busy schedule of volunteer work and classes, moving to an emotional description of her "lost" summer in Rome and the mother who "ditched" her. Tearfully turning away, she straightens up and decides to return to the party to help. Down on the lawn, both Annie and Lydia anxiously observe the couple returning from their walk. A gull swoops down and touches Cathy, the "blindman" in a game of blindman's bluff, and suddenly many gulls swoop over and peck at the children. Melanie and Mitch throw down their glasses and run to help Annie pick up Cathy from the ground. The other children run this way and that as the adults try to corral them into the house; two of the children lie on the ground helplessly flailing their arms as birds flap at their necks. After the attack has subsided, they all stare at the sky, and Melanie tells Mitch of the third incident last night at Annie's. He urges her to stay for dinner so he will "feel more comfortable" about her safety.

That evening, as they sit in the living room eating their dinner from plates in their laps, Melanie notices a sparrow perched on the floor near the fireplace. The camera watches her closely from above as she assumes a pose of great concentration and calmly calls Mitch. Suddenly the fireplace opening explodes with the intrusion of hundreds of sparrows. Mitch opens a door and tries to bat them out as Melanie and Cathy huddle on the couch and Lydia stands apart covering her eyes and beating at the birds. Finally, Mitch throws a table over the opening of the fireplace and Melanie leads Cathy and Lydia into the next room.

Later, the sheriff stands in the living room with them. He is skeptical about their being "attacked," though he is unable to explain the incident. Melanie watches Lydia nervously go through the rubble and pick out pieces of broken porcelain. Finally Melanie announces she will take Cathy to bed and spend the

night. Lydia, startled at this news, is left in the foreground staring out into space as the others leave the room.

Next morning, Mitch is outside and Melanie is putting on her makeup when Lydia and Cathy drive off in the truck.

Later, Lydia arrives alone at her friend Dan Fawcett's farm and walks through his unlocked kitchen door when he does not answer her call. Alarmed at the sight of a row of broken cups, she moves down the hall to his bedroom, where the damage is complete. Dan's lifeless and bloody body sits sprawled in a corner, the eyes plucked out. She runs down the hall, mouth open, unable to utter a sound. Running outside, she meets Dan's handyman, George, but can only gape wide-eyed at him. She hops into her truck and drives off, leaving a trail of dust. She pulls up in front of Mitch and Melanie at the house and falls out of the car, crying; Mitch runs to her but she pushes past them both and escapes into the house.

As Melanie makes tea in the kitchen, Mitch asks permission to go meet the sheriff. They kiss lightly, urging one another to be careful, and Melanie pauses to smile to herself after he leaves. She takes the tea tray into Lydia's bedroom and Lydia suspiciously wonders where Mitch is. She asks Melanie if she seems foolish to her and Melanie sincerely replies no. Lydia then gives in completely to her feelings of powerlessness and talks at length about her fears, the large window in Cathy's school, and how badly she still misses Frank, her husband. She pleads with Melanie to stay with her and breaks down crying at the thought that she might be left alone. Finally, Melanie offers to go check on Cathy at school, and a grateful Lydia thanks her.

Pulling up to the Bodega Bay School, where the children are singing a song, Melanie goes inside and signals Annie, who teaches there. Back outside, she sits on a bench near a fence where the sing-song of the children is still audible. A crow lands on the jungle gym behind her as she smokes, and each time the camera cuts from her to include the scene behind her, more birds settle in. Finally, she notices one flying above and watches it until it lands, joining the flock of several hundred now behind her. Turning, she stands gaping, then walks swiftly back into the schoolhouse and warns Annie. Annie directs the children to enact a fire drill, and after some complaining, they file out. Outside the birds are perched tightly together, then fly off suddenly at the sound of the children running. The children head down the hill with the birds at their necks. One of the children falls and calls after Cathy for help; Melanie puts Cathy and her friend into a nearby car and starts honking the horn. Finally, the birds go away.

Later, Melanie speaks with her father on the telephone in the café. The patrons are intrigued with her conversation about the bird attack at the school, and wonder whether the birds were crows or blackbirds. Mrs. Bundy, a tweed-dressed self-described ornithologist, tells Melanie that birds are not aggressive. "They bring beauty into the world. . . . It is mankind, rather, who insists upon making it difficult for life to exist." Mr. Carter, the bartender, defends Melanie's story. Another man at the end of the bar, quoting Ezekiel, pronounces the end of the world; then a boat owner says that gulls attacked one of his boats. Mrs. Bundy persists in her argument that birds couldn't possibly "start a war," and then a businessman arrives and recommends they get guns and shoot them all. A woman, who has become increasingly fearful and unable to enjoy lunch with her two children, becomes hysterical. Mitch finally arrives with the sheriff, who downplays the enemy bird theory, suggesting that the birds entered Dan Fawcett's home after he was murdered. Mitch tries to convince a reluctant

Sebastian, the boat owner, to do something, when Melanie notices that gulls are attacking a garage attendant outside.

The men run out while Melanie and the others collect around a high window. The stricken man has dropped a still-flowing pump, and gas runs across the street, puddling around a man who starts to light a cigar. Melanie flings open the window and everyone yells at him, but too late. Several cars explode. High in the sky, gulls swoosh around the fire below, gathering for a descent. Everyone rushes out of the café and Melanie runs for shelter in a telephone booth. Birds beat against the sides as she knocks around helplessly inside it; outside, the chaos escalates. A man being attacked while driving a car plows into the fire wreckage; firemen arrive, are attacked themselves, and lose control of a water hose. A bleeding man falls against the phone booth, and Melanie hysterically holds up her hands as the birds start to splatter holes in the glass. Finally, Mitch pushes open the booth door and pulls Melanie out and into the now-empty café. Slowly, they round a corner in the back of the restaurant and find a group of women and children huddled there. The woman with the two children rises and hysterically accosts Melanie, saying, in close-up, that she heard it all started when Melanie arrived in town and accuses her of being evil. A tight-lipped Melanie slaps her in the face and turns away as Mitch puts his arms around her. The bartender races in, announcing the birds are gone.

Mitch and Melanie start up the road to Annie's house to get Cathy. The crows still cover the schoolhouse and they find Annie's body splayed out over her front steps. A tearful Cathy pokes her head out through a curtain. Mitch angrily picks up a rock, but Melanie, holding Cathy, screams at him to let it go. He puts his coat over Annie and Melanie pleads with him not to leave Annie there, so he carries her body into the house. They slowly walk down the road in front of the watching birds and get into Melanie's car. As they drive, Cathy tearfully relates how Annie died saving her.

Boards cover the windows of Mitch's house as he stands on a ladder and finishes the job. Inside, Lydia is excited to get some news on the radio, but only discovers that the outside world does not know how serious their danger is. Mitch pushes on with his plans, but Lydia becomes hysterical, questioning his actions and screaming that things would be better if his father were there. Nonplussed, Mitch tells her to make some coffee.

That night, the women huddle in the living room as Mitch finishes boarding up the inside of the house. The lovebirds sit peacefully in their cage in the kitchen. Later, each of the group sits alone, except for Melanie, who holds Cathy on the couch. A screeching din begins outside, sending Lydia into hysterics as Mitch throws more logs on the fire. Cathy runs to her mother and Melanie cringes on the couch at a large crash, while Mitch goes to fight with an intruding gull. Bloodied, he picks up his terrified mother and sister and sets them on the couch. Meanwhile the birds have almost pecked through the back door, so he nails some furniture to it. The lights go out. The pecking subsides. In long shot, the three adults stand mesmerized and separate from one another, looking up at the ceiling.

Later they rest—Mitch, Lydia, and Cathy asleep, Melanie wide-eyed. She hears a flutter and rises to investigate. Carrying a flashlight, she heads upstairs and discovers a hole in the roof of one of the bedrooms. Suddenly the birds swoop down and overpower her and she slowly collapses, wounded, in front of the closed door. Mitch pushes the door in on her and manages to pull her out

and bring her downstairs. Pecked everywhere, she wakes on the couch, flailing, unable to get away from her terror. Her eyes remain lifeless. Despite Lydia's fears, Mitch insists they take her to a hospital.

It is now daylight, and Mitch goes outside among the masses of crows and gulls that cover and surround his house. He gingerly steps through them; two peck at him, but the hordes remain calm. In the garage, he breathes a sigh and gets into Melanie's car. A radio program tells him that most of the people have left Bodega Bay and roadblocks are set up. He slowly drives the car up to his front door and reenters the house. The women are dressed to go, Melanie back in her mink, her head bandaged, still expressionless. At the sight of the birds outside the front door, she cries out "No!" but the others move her along. Cathy asks to bring the lovebirds; "They haven't harmed anyone!" Mitch says she may. Inside the car, Lydia holds Melanie, who looks up gratefully at her. They drive off through the thousands of screeching and fluttering birds.

Note. ᴴHitchcock does bit as man who walks into pet shop with two terriers.

53 *Marnie* (1964)

Director	Alfred Hitchcock
Assistant Director	James H. Brown
Producer	Alfred Hitchcock
Production Company	Universal-Geoffrey Stanley, Inc.
Screenplay	Jay Presson Allen, from the novel by Winston Graham
Photography	Robert Burks, A.S.C.
Camera Operator	Leonard South
Editing	George Tomasini, A.C.E.
Art Direction	Robert Boyle, George Milo
Sound	Waldon O. Watson, William Russell
Special Effects	Albert Whitlock
Music	Bernard Herrmann
Costumes	Edith Head, Vincent Dee, Rita Tiggs, James Linn
Makeup	Jack Barron, Howard Smit, Robert Dawn
Hair	Alexandre of Paris, Virginia Darcy
Production Assistant	Peggy Robertson
Script Supervisor	Louise Thurman
Unit Manager	Hilton A. Green
Cast	Tippi Hedren (Marnie Edgar), Sean Connery (Mark Rutland), Diane Baker (Lil), Louise Latham (Bernice Edgar), Martin Gabel (Sidney Strutt), Bob Sweeney (Cousin Bob), Alan Napier (Mr. Rutland), Mariette Hartley (Secretary), Edith Evanson, Milton Selzer, Henry Beckman, S. John Launer, Meg Wyllie, Bruce Dern
Filmed	at Universal Studios, Los Angeles

Running Time   approximately 120 minutes
Distributor   Universal
Release Date   June 1964
Other title: *Pas de Printemps Pour Marnie*

Synopsis

The credits appear on large sheets with a scroll border; they are turned, accompanied by the theme music.

A large yellow handbag is firmly carried under an arm. The woman holding it walks away from the camera down a train platform.

"Robbed!" exclaims a businessman. The scene widens to include the man's office and the two detectives questioning him. Marion Holland was her name and, yes, he can describe her perfectly. As he does so, his secretary discreetly lowers her eyes, then reminds him that he hired the thief without references. An important client, Mark Rutland, interrupts the proceedings, and the business-man, Strutt, elaborates to him about the woman, who was so efficient, so nice, and "always pulling her skirt down over her legs as if she were hiding some treasure."

Marnie walks down a hotel corridor, enters a room, packs a bag with newly purchased clothes, and distributes the money from the bag on top of them. She exchanges her social security card with one in the name of Margaret Edgar that she pulls from a hidden supply. She rinses her black hair in the sink, and raises her face to the camera for the first time, a blond.

In a station, she carries two large suitcases to a locker area, places one in a locker, and throws the key down a grate.

A courtesy cab drives up to the Red Fox Tavern and lets Marnie off. Inside she is a familiar guest, eager for a ride to Garrett's stables.

Arriving at the stables in a riding outfit, she gets on her horse, Forio, and rides off into the woods.

A street of row houses at the edge of a port is shown; a large ship looms over the block and girls sing and play on the sidewalk. Marnie drives up in a cab. A girl of eight or so answers the door of her mother's home, and Marnie is annoyed. Entering the small front room, she greets her mother, who uses a cane. They hug as Marnie stiffens at the sight of a vase of red gladiolus, the color of which suffuses the shot. She abruptly exchanges them with the chrysanthemums she has brought, complaining that she can't stand gladiolus and commanding the girl, Jessie, to get rid of them. Her mother disapproves of her lightened hair and chastises Marnie, who has offended her by quoting the Bible in defense of spending money. Marnie tries to rest on the floor at her mother's knees, but her mother complains of her leg and asks Marnie to move; then she takes Jessie on her lap to brush her hair. The conversation is sprinkled with talk of Mr. Pemberton, the millionaire Marnie works for, the raises he has given her, and men in general. After giving her mother a mink scarf, Marnie assures her, "We don't need men, we can do very well for ourselves." Mrs. Edgar is proud of Marnie for being too smart to get "mixed up with men."

While pouring the syrup for Jessie's pecan pie in the kitchen, her mother mentions that she might ask Jessie, whom she now baby-sits, and Jessie's mother to move in with her. She warns Marnie not to be so jealous of the child and Marnie quietly pleads, "Why don't you love me, mama? . . . You've never given me half

the love you give Jessie." When her mother moves away, she becomes more strident, "When I think of the things I've done to make you love me!... What are you thinking... that I'm Pemberton's girl?... Is that why you won't let me touch you?" Mrs. Edgar slaps Marnie hard; pecans fly. Marnie stares ahead, apologizing as if a different person; then she goes upstairs to rest.

Later, in the bedroom, the shadepull taps on the window as Marnie dreams, and red washes over the screen. "No, mama, I don't want to..." she murmurs. Her mother appears at the door, "Wake up for supper, Marnie." Marnie opens her eyes: "It's that old dream... you come to the door and the cold starts." Mrs. Edgar turns down the stairs; the camera watches her shadow disappear.

The Philadelphia train station. Marnie is now auburn haired. She fingers down the want ads, stopping at one for the Rutland Company.

In a large office with many desks and partitions, she waits in a reception area. Mark Rutland walks by, notices her, and enters his manager's office just as another job candidate is leaving. Closing the door, the manager informs Rutland the candidate is ideal, then almost immediately the door opens and he calls in Marnie. She is now the recently widowed Mary Taylor, inexperienced but articulate; as they discuss references, Mark has a moment of recognition. She is hired over the manager's objections. As they move into the outer area, a young dark-haired woman, Lil, arrives to have lunch with Mark and to cash a check. Marnie has time to observe the location of keys as well as the opening of the safe. The secretary, Susan, tells her Rutland's wife is dead and Lil is his sister-in-law.

Marnie types in the reception area; she looks through the doorway as the secretary opens the safe inside the office. She continues to work as the others go to coffee. Spilling red ink on her blouse, she gasps violently and runs to the restroom. Mark sees her panic and, thinking she's been hurt, sends Susan in after her, but Marnie is disdainful at the attention: "Good heavens, what a lot of excitement over nothing."

During the day, Susan is talkative and trusting; Marnie discovers the combination to the safe is written inside her locked desk drawer. At one point, the manager tells Marnie that Mark has requested she work overtime on Saturday with him. She readily agrees.

She enters the empty building on a stormy day. Mark calls her into his luxurious office full of pre-Columbian art. They banter for a while as he tells her he is trained as a zoologist in instinctual behavior and she wonders how lady animals figure in his work. A bolt of lightning frightens her so much that she jumps up and cringes near the door. Mark walks over to hold her, but she cannot move. "Get rid of the colors," she says, closing her eyes against the imagined red. Suddenly a tree branch crashes through the window, destroying a display cabinet. He holds her; his kiss fills the screen. He asks about the colors, but she denies being frightened of anything but thunder and lightning. They leave.

In his car, the rain continues and she expresses sympathy about his smashed cabinet. He brushes off her concern but asks her to the races next Saturday.

At the Atlantic City racecourse, they sit at a white-clothed table near the railing. Marnie is clearly an expert on the horses. Mark gets up to make a bet and a man who has recognized her approaches. She denies ever having met him, but he continues to watch and follows them as Mark actively fends him off. They take a trip to the paddock, but large red dots on one of the jockey's shirts make her stiffen. Seated again, Mark questions her about her childhood and beliefs; at one point she bitterly says, "I don't believe in anything."

Another weekend they drive through the countryside, and Mark announces they are going to his house to meet his father.

They arrive at the portico of a colonial mansion and enter. Mark's taller, distinguished father greets them warmly at the bottom of a grand circular stairway.

In a sitting room, where Lil has been lounging, tea is ready on a silver tray. In open jealousy, Lil declines to pour, claiming an injured wrist. They discuss horses and Mark takes "Mary" out to the stables.

In the stables, they kiss, and he invites her back the next weekend to have her pick of the horses.

Rutland Company offices. At the end of the day, Marnie walks into the restroom and hides in a stall. Finally, the voices die down and she emerges carefully in the silence. Taking the key from her purse, she opens the desk drawer, memorizes the combination, props the door open to the office, and opens the safe. A long shot from the floor showing the office on the right and the aisle and desks on the left, reveals a cleaning woman beginning to swab down the floors, working her way toward the exit as Marnie, on the other side of the wall, finishes stuffing her bag. Marnie hears her and takes off her shoes, putting them in her pockets. One of them falls as she tiptoes toward the stairs, but the woman doesn't notice. As Marnie exits, a janitor crosses her trail and taps the cleaning woman on the back, talking loudly to her, confirming she is hard of hearing.

Marnie rides through the countryside on Forio. Rutland appears and confronts her about the theft, seating himself on the horse while she walks back.

At her hotel, she packs while they argue. She claims the theft was only a one-time impulse and makes up stories about her background. He challenges her on the details and she becomes more elaborate in her lies.

As he drives, they continue to argue; he tries to get the story straight while she concocts a tale of her dead family and some insurance money. Finally, he tells her he knows about the Strutt case; she is incensed: "You've been trying to trap me!" He goes on, wondering to what degree she is a thief and a liar. Her defiance is occasionally clothed in a strategy of regretful vulnerability, but she continues to lie.

They stop at a restaurant and are seated in a booth. He continues to question her about her past. At one point she blurts out a litany of relationships she has not had: "no lovers, no steadies, no beaus, no gentlemen callers, nothing!" Then he tells her of his plan: she will return to Rutland's, because he has already replaced the money, and act as though all is normal.

In the car, she repeats that she was never interested in men, then corrects herself, "until you." He claims not to be taken in, but nevertheless informs her of his intention to marry her "before the week is out." She is very angry and tells him he's crazy. "You know what I am ... a thief and a liar. ... If you love me, you'll let me go. ... I'm not like other people ... I'm just something you've caught." He agrees, but insists that he loves her; besides, "It's either me or the police, old girl." She chafes under his demands and he reminds her to behave herself for a week, "then you can take legal possession."

At the house, their marriage ceremony ends. A small group stands at the entry to send them off on their honeymoon cruise. After they've gone, Mark's banker-cousin indignantly discusses with Lil the large amounts of money Mark has spent in the last week—over $70,000, including a $42,000 engagement ring.

Later, upstairs, Lil goes through Mark's desk and finds a list that includes a note to "pay off Strutt."

A cruise ship. Mark complains because Marnie has spent forty-seven minutes in the bathroom; she emerges in a high-necked white gown. He tries to kiss her, but she rushes away, adamantly resisting him now, saying she "cannot bear to be handled." They argue and he tells her she needs a psychiatrist. "Men!" she says, "say no to one of them and bingo! you're a candidate for a funny farm." She refuses to respond to his attempts to help her and he finally suggests that they "try to be kind to one another." He gives his word that he will not touch her.

In a series of dining scenes, he talks at her about different things, and she, looking beautiful and polite, responds not at all or, when pressed, sarcastically.

Back in their suite, he peers at her over a book. He refers to the difficulties he has trying to find a subject in which she is interested. Angry, she wonders how long he is going to persist in this facade and slams the door on him. He rises in anger, barges into her room, and rips her gown off. She stares out stupefied, and he apologizes. He puts his robe over her, then kisses her. She is motionless; a close-up of her blank face shows her descending to the bed with his face over her. Her eye stares coldly out over his shoulder. The music escalates as the camera moves to the porthole.

The next morning, he wakes to see her empty bed and races out of the room down deserted gangways looking for her. He finds her face down in a swimming pool, jumps in, and pulls her out. She revives. Angry, he asks her why she didn't throw herself in the ocean. She quips she only wanted to kill herself, not feed the sharks.

Back home, they greet Lil and Mr. Rutland.

Upstairs, Marnie looks around their rooms and Mark begins to explain the routine of their domestic facade. She calmly closes the door in his face.

The next morning, he continues instructing her as she sees him off. She asks him for money. They talk outside the front door as Lil listens from a second-floor window. Mark tells Marnie he's paid off Strutt and she calls him a fool. "But they don't send you to jail for being a fool," he replies.

Back in the house, Marnie closes herself in the library to telephone her mother. Lil eavesdrops from the hallway as Marnie says she's been sick and will visit Baltimore as soon as she can.

Later, Mark brings Marnie's horse Forio to the front door. She is ecstatic and rides off bareback and in her stocking feet. Mark and Lil stand together as she goes off, and Lil offers to help him. She tells Mark about Marnie's mother in Baltimore. He is sad.

Another day, Mark arrives home to discover that Marnie has gone to the hunt country with Mr. Rutland. Mark goes upstairs to take a phone call.

In his study, he speaks over the telephone with a detective who has found Bernice Edgar. "She killed him! What happened to the five-year-old child? . . . Find out!"

Marnie sleeps in a dream set of impoverished furnishings, occasionally bathed in a red glow. Someone knocks on the window: "Don't hurt my mama. . . . It's cold." The camera pans around the wall to find her elegant Rutland bedroom. Trying to make sense of her ravings, Mark approaches. Suddenly she wakes and shrinks before him, yelling "Don't!" Lil enters swiftly to comfort her, then teases Mark when Marnie says she's cold. "That's supposed to be your department, isn't it?" As she's taking her leave, Lil notices in their sitting room the book Mark is reading: *Sexual Aberrations of the Criminal Female.*

Back in Marnie's room, Mark questions her about the pills she's been taking. He sits by her and insists on discussing the dream. Finally, she realizes what he

is doing: "You Freud, me Jane?" Unfazed, he suggests books for her to read. "I don't need to read that much to know that women are stupid and feeble and men are filthy pigs!" she blurts out. He persists. "Why can't you leave me alone!" she says. "Because I think you're sick, old dear," he replies. "I'm sick! Take a look at yourself, old dear . . . talk about a dream world." He persists and she suggests she free associate while he "plays doctor." She responds spiritedly to his leads: water, air, death, white, red. At first clever and distant, she finally breaks down thinking of red. He moves over to hold her, and she sobs into his chest, crying out for "somebody" to help her.

The central hall of the house fills up with people in evening clothes. Guests arrive, and then Strutt, who thanks Lil for the invitation. Mark and Marnie are gay until she sees Strutt; Mark insists they'll succeed in bluffing their way through, but Marnie is terrified. Strutt recognizes her, but she denies they've ever met.

In her bedroom Mark yells at her. She's already packed, "dressed up like a cat burglar," and ready to flee. They argue and she informs him an investigation might lead to her incrimination in "other, similar, jobs." A close-up shows his eyes widen at this. He demands the truth and lays out two elaborate alternatives: they can give her up and hire a lawyer and a psychiatrist, or they can go secretly to the victims and try to make amends. He will try to deal with Strutt tomorrow while Marnie rides in the hunt. Finally, he tells her "tonight the door will stay open."

The hunt begins, dozens of riders jumping fence and stream. They stop to watch as the pack of dogs goes after a catch. Marnie is offended at the violence and fixes in fear on the red jacket of one of the riders, suddenly moving Forio away from the crowd. Lil observes and follows her. Marnie races cross country, losing her hat and breaking branches in her flight, with Lil in the distance. She sees a high wall ahead and, concerned, tries to rein in the horse. But it is too late and they careen over the wall, both falling to the ground. Marnie stands; Forio cannot get up. Marnie is hysterical at his injury, runs to a nearby cabin, and demands a gun. The occupant hesitates, and Marnie tries to force her into complying. Lil arrives and they both try to calm Marnie, but she insists on having the gun. Lil and Marnie struggle over the weapon, and finally Marnie grasps it and shoots Forio. "There, now," she says distantly with a fond, slight smile on her face.

Back at the house, Rutland tries to suggest to Strutt that it would be best for both of them to handle this in confidence. Strutt is not convinced, scorning such a "fashionable attitude."

Marnie enters the front door still holding the gun, pauses to hear their voices from the hall, and runs upstairs. She takes the keys to the Rutland offices from Mark's desk and walks down the stairs and out.

Mark receives a call about the accident and excuses himself to Strutt.

Marnie lays the gun on a table near the safe. She approaches thoughtfully, grimly smiling. After opening the door, she reaches for the money, but suddenly can't force herself to reach far enough. She grimaces and gasps for air as the music escalates. Mark approaches her from behind. "I'll take you home . . . you're just exhausted," he says, and grabs the gun just as she leaps for it. She turns back to the money in the safe. He encourages her to take it because it's hers; they struggle and he releases her violently. "Now we will go to Baltimore and see your mother," he says.

They drive in the rain. "If you tell my mother about me, I'll kill you," says Marnie.

They drive up to her mother's door in a thunderstorm. Mark forces Marnie out of the car, throwing his coat over her. As they enter, she falls onto the stairway. He rushes in, closing the drapes over the lightning. He introduces himself to the annoyed Mrs. Edgar as Marnie's husband, saying Marnie needs help, needs to hear the truth from her mother about "what happened that night." He says Marnie can't "stand to have a man touch her," and Mrs. Edgar proudly says Marnie is "lucky to feel that way." But he has read the records, and knows that Mrs. Edgar "made her living from the touch of men." Mrs. Edgar becomes furious and beats at him to get out of her house. Collapsed on the staircase, Marnie has become her little girl-self: "You let my mama go." Mark taps on the wall, prompting her, "Who am I, Marnie?" "You're one of the men in the white suits . . . mama comes and gets me out of bed." Marnie stares at the couch.

The image of a similar living room appears. A sailor waits while the young and blond Bernice Edgar wakes her young daughter and puts her to sleep on the couch with a blanket and a kiss. Thunder makes the child scream and the sailor comes out of the back room to comfort her, leaning over her head.

At Mark's prompting Marnie cries, "I don't like him! He smells funny. I want my mama!"

Back to the scene, the sailor pets Marnie on the head, then kisses her neck. Bernice runs out from the bedroom yelling at him to get away and beating him.

Marnie's mother sadly watches her as Marnie sits in a trance on the staircase: "Make him go, mama."

Bernice beats furiously on the sailor and they struggle.

Mark interferes again with a question and Marnie answers, "He hit my mama!"

Bernice grabs a fire iron and beats the sailor; they fall, she is trapped under him, crying out, "My leg!" She calls for Marnie to help and the child picks up the fallen poker and beats the sailor over the head.

On the stairwell, a terrified Marnie screams, "I hit him with a stick!"

At the scene, the women are aghast at the bloodied man; they scream. Red washes over the screen.

Mark picks Marnie up from the stairs and sets her down in a chair across from her mother. Mrs. Edgar finally speaks. She thought Marnie's losing her memory of that night was a sign of forgiveness and a second chance to make things right for her. She told the police she did it in self-defense and never told anyone the truth. "I was so young . . . never had anything of my own," she says, as she tells the story of Marnie's conception, of trading her self for a basketball sweater at age fifteen. Later, after the "accident" she vowed she would bring up "Marnie different from me . . . decent." "Decent!" says Marnie, "I'm a cheat, a liar, and a thief, but I am decent." Mark intercedes, "If a child can't get love . . . it takes what it can get." Marnie leans on her mother's lap; the older woman starts to stroke her daughter, but then she reminds her she's "aching her leg." Totally broken, Marnie asks Mark if she will go to jail. "Not after what I have to tell them," he says putting an arm around her. They say good-bye to Mrs. Edgar, who vacantly smiles.

They exit on to the street where the children sing a rhyme: ". . . call for the doctor, call for the nurse, call for the lady with the alligator purse."

Note. [H]Hitchcock does bit as man in hotel corridor.

54   *Torn Curtain* (1966)

Director	Alfred Hitchcock
Assistant Director	Donald Baer
Producer	Alfred Hitchcock
Production Company	Universal
Screenplay	Brian Moore
Photography	John F. Warren, A.S.C.
Camera Operator	Leonard South
Editing	Bud Hoffman
Production Design	Hein Heckroth
Art Direction	Frank Arrigo
Set Direction	George Milo
Sound	Waldon O. Watson, William Russell
Special Effects	Albert Whitlock
Music	John Addison
Costumes	Edith Head, Grady Hunt
Hair	Hal Saunders, Lorraine Roberson
Makeup	Jack Barron
Script Supervisor	Lois Thurman
Unit Production Manager	Jack Corrick
Production Assistant	Peggy Robertson
Cast	Paul Newman (Michael Anderson), Julie Andrews (Sarah Sherman), Lila Kedrova (Countess Kuchinska), Wolfgang Kieling (Hermann Gromek), Hansjoerg Felmy (Heinrich Gerhardt), Tamara Toumanova (Ballerina), Ludwig Donath (Professor Lindt), Günter Strack (Professor Karl Manfred), David Opatoshu, Mort Mills (Farmer), Gisela Fischer (Dr. Koska), Carolyn Conwell (Farmer's Wife), Arthur Gould-Porter, Gloria Gorvin
Filmed	at Universal Studios in Technicolor
Running Time	approximately 120 minutes
Distributor	Universal
Release Date	July 1966

Other titles: *Der zerrissene Vorhang, Le Rideau Déchiré, Il Sipario Strappato*

Synopsis

Under the credits and the theme music, a diffuse red light on the left, and, on the right, vague superimpositions of the various characters, their faces in varying states of emotion.

Osterfjord, Norway. A ship moves on the fjord, flanked by steep mountains. The deck is empty because of very cold weather; Professor Karl Manfred asks one of the crew about the heat.

Passengers bundled in coats and hats surround a dinner table. Their badges show they are mostly from American universities. Karl, an always serious man, enters the dining room and looks at an empty table.

Dr. Sarah Sherman and Professor Michael Armstrong are warm beneath their bright bed covers and coats. Light romantic music is heard as they kiss and discuss their life and future marriage. Michael is sarcastic about this "serious congress of physicists." Their faces fill the screen as they continue to kiss and Sarah reminds him of their agreement: "You weren't going to blast off about Washington and I wasn't going to ask you again why you didn't want me to go along on this trip." A porter brings a radiogram to the door; Michael reads it but returns it, saying it's not for him.

Later, at the communications room, he asks to see the radiogram again, and runs into Karl, who asks him where Miss Sherman is, as they had a lunch date. After he is alone again, Michael responds to the message, giving his Copenhagen address.

Copenhagen. A large hotel lobby.^{H} Michael is in the shower in his room and Sarah enters, asking if she can unpack for him. At his negative reply, she sighs and lies on the bed, then picks up the ringing telephone. It's some bookstore, she calls to him, but the connection is broken. She wonders about their schedule today. He tells her to "take a stroll" until time for their lunch with Professor Engstrom. She's slightly deflated, but the phone rings again and she takes the address and tells Michael she's going to pick up his book for him. "No, wait!" he cries, running out of the bathroom, but she's gone.

In the lobby, she greets Karl, who reminds her that she forgot their lunch date, but she seems not to care.

Outside, she asks for directions to the bookstore and once again Karl appears behind her and offers to escort her. As they walk down the sidewalk, he queries her about Michael and she tells him they're engaged, news that surprises him.

At the bookstore, the proprietor wonders why Professor Armstrong did not come himself, but he takes Sarah into the back and gives her the book covered in brown paper. Glancing meaningfully at Karl, who peeks around the corner of a bookcase at them, he cautions her to take good care of it. As Sarah and Karl leave, the bookstore assistant asks her employer just who Professor Armstrong is; he replies, "Pray for him."

Sarah carries the book into the lobby, then hands it to Michael, who is with Professor Engstrom. She dismisses Karl, just before a travel agent calls Michael to his counter. While she is talking with Engstrom, Sarah watches Michael surreptitiously put a ticket folder into his suit pocket. When he returns, he announces to Engstrom that he has promised Miss Sherman to have lunch with her, then walks off, saying he wants to leave the book with the concierge. Puzzled, they watch as he enters the restroom.

Michael carefully locks himself in a stall, unwraps the book, and sets it on the water tank. He follows the directions on the title page to interpret a series of underscored letters and a circled π sign. Taking some toilet paper, he decodes "contact π in case . . ."

A fancy restaurant. Sarah and Michael sit outside. "Well, Michael, will you tell me before we eat or after?" Sarah asks. He claims ignorance until she asks about the tickets. He tells her he has to go to Stockholm, and the occasion is much more important than his speech tonight. Unsatisfied, she continues to ask

questions, which he evades. Avoiding her eyes, he admits he may not be back in time for their wedding; finally, he refuses to discuss it anymore, preferring to read at the table. Sarah gets up and leaves, and he glares after her.

Walking into the lobby, she goes directly to the travel counter and asks for the next flight back to New York. On a second thought, she asks when Professor Armstrong's plane leaves for Stockholm and is told that he's going to East Berlin. "But that's behind the Iron Curtain!" says Sarah, alarmed.

In the plane, Michael sits with his hand to his chin; worried, he furtively glances around. The camera moves to Karl next to him, then continues back down the aisle where it turns to view Sarah from above. Up ahead, Michael turns to ask a question and notices her. He rises and stalks back to lean over her. "What in hell's name are you doing here? . . . Stay away from me. . . . When this plane lands you take the next one out of here . . . go home!" She silently accepts his abuse as others on the plane stare; near tears, she bows her head at his retreating back and the screen suffuses red over the fadeout on her.

As the passengers disembark, she notices Karl, who queries Michael about her. Michael insists she knows nothing. They go down the ramp following a ballerina who imagines the press is there waiting for her. A close-up shows Sarah staring intently from the top of the ramp as Michael walks down from the plane to become the center of the press's attention, and she hears the announcement that he "has decided to live and work for peace in the people's democracies." Karl returns to escort her down.

In the terminal, Karl asks Sarah to wait in the hall.

Michael enters an office where a group of men greet him. Heinrich Gerhardt, chief of state security, introduces himself, then Mr. Gromek, Michael's "personal guide." Karl enters and reminds them about Sarah. Gromek, dressed in black leather and carrying a poorly functioning lighter, begins to talk about New York but is signaled to be quiet. They discuss the "excess baggage" and express surprise as to what Michael expected Sarah to do. He is vague, and they all lament the nature of women and ask her in. Michael broods as she enters and is introduced, then looks over at her sitting isolated on the leather couch. She is asked if she wants to join him in living there, but it is decided the question can wait until tomorrow. They all exit to the press conference waiting outside.

There is much applause as Michael steps to the center and reads his statement. At the edge of the crowd, Sarah listens, frowning. "There are people in high places who do not want to see atomic war abolished, and because of that a project I was working on for six years was canceled by my government . . . that was more important than considerations of loyalty to one country." Looking at Sarah through the crowd, he falters, but commits to abolishing the terror of nuclear warfare. Shielded from the photographers, Sarah and Michael are taken away.

Driving with Gromek, Michael wonders about all the foreign press. Sarah sits in the middle, silent.

They pull up to the Hotel Berlin and are greeted by another flurry of press people.

In the hallway, Michael crosses and enters Sarah's room. "Now you know," he says. In long shot, the large room separates them; she stares out the window as he, hanging his head, paces the floor. "You must have been planning this

for months," she reasons, then pleads with him to take her home. Karl enters, asking them to dinner. Sarah declines, not hungry, and the men leave together.

The next day, Sarah sleeps. Karl enters, handing her a note left under the door. She opens it: "Gone for a walk. Go home! Michael."

Downstairs, the camera views Michael from above as he exits the elevator; several women on their hands and knees scrub the lobby floor and the camera circles over them to a close-up of Gromek in a chair. Running, Michael catches a bus outside, and Gromek follows on his motorcycle.

Noticing Gromek, Michael gets off at the Muzeen zu Berlin, where he approaches the entrance through the huge columns.

From above, we see him swiftly cross the elaborate geometric floor. He walks through a maze of empty, narrow galleries, pausing several times to listen to the echoing footsteps that follow him. He walks faster, then comes upon a door to the outside.

Out on the street, he picks up a taxi, which takes him to a farm in the countryside. A woman answers the door and he scrapes with his shoe the sign π in the dirt for her to see. She points to a man out tilling the field.

Michael starts across the field, and the man stops his machine, getting down to greet him. "How does it feel to be a defector? . . . You put on a great act," he says. The farmer takes him for a ride; as they talk, Michael explains that he devised his defection in order to "pick the brain" of a scientist who has a solution for his stalled experiment. He gets the name of another agent in Leipzig who will help him and Sarah escape the country when his mission is complete.

After he waves good-bye, Michael notices Gromek and hurries frantically into the house wondering if there's a back way out. Gromek enters and Michael explains that the woman is a relative. Cracking gum, Gromek opens the door and asks Michael about the π sign in the ground. Michael claims ignorance, but Gromek pokes him in the stomach a couple of times, then screams at him, "A dirty little two-bit organization for spying and escaping. . . . Can't you do better than that?" Michael and the woman stare as he berates them and starts to telephone his office. Suddenly, as he fiddles with his malfunctioning lighter, the woman throws a jar of milk at him, briefly stunning him. He stalks over to her, taking out his gun, but Michael grabs him from behind and the gun drops on the counter. They struggle as the woman reaches for the gun, but, noticing the taxi driver waiting outside, she picks up a butcher knife instead. Gasping for breath under Michael's hold, Gromek makes fun of her. Then, she stabs him in the neck and the handle of the knife breaks off, leaving the blade in him. He continues to struggle as she searches for another weapon. She picks up a shovel and bangs him on the knees; he falls. They stare, incredulous, as he rises slowly from the floor and leaps to open the window. As they both slam the window shut, Gromek grabs Michael by the neck and the struggle continues until the woman turns the gas on in the oven. Grimacing, she helps pull at Gromek's hands, while they slowly inch him along the floor toward the oven and stick his head inside. Seen from above, his hands finally drop from Michael's neck and Michael and the woman lean exhausted on the stove, then finally rise from the floor.

Michael is stupefied, unable to move, and the woman admonishes him in German, washing his bloody hand, and gesturing with the shovel that she will take care of the body and the motorcycle outside. He goes out to meet the waiting

driver and she brushes out the π sign. Michael glances back with a worried look as the cab drives off.

Michael walks purposefully up the sidewalk to his hotel. At the door a man tells him the head of security wants to see him, and he puts Michael in the back of a car.

Michael is ushered into the office where Karl, Sarah, and Chief Gerhardt are waiting to tell him that Sarah has agreed to stay with him. She is the only one sitting as they drink to celebrate and agree that the couple will leave immediately for Leipzig. Gerhardt receives a message that Gromek has been "lost."

Leipzig. In a corridor at Karl Marx University, Michael and Sarah are introduced to a group of professors as well as a new security guard. Karl is seen in close-up, pondering the news of Gromek's disappearance.

The group walks down the stairs of the new physics building and someone trips Michael at the landing, making him slide, face forward, down the stairs.

A pinpoint light shines into Michael's eye. The doctor tells him she tripped him because she is Koska, his contact. As she examines him in her office she tells him they must hurry because of Gromek and outlines the plan to get him and Sarah out of the country. She also prepares him with information about Lindt, the professor Michael is looking for. She is skeptical about his getting the information quickly, but Michael says he's depending on Lindt's curiosity. Still, she reflects, "it will be a long business," and indicates that she doesn't want to see him again until he is ready to leave.

Back in East Berlin, the taxi driver notices a picture of Hermann Gromek in the newspaper. He hurries to see the chief of security where, in a brief flashback, he tells the story of seeing Gromek go into the farmhouse. Gerhardt immediately gets on the telephone.

Meanwhile, at Karl Marx University in Leipzig, Michael is escorted by Karl into a tiered classroom and is presented to five professors, one sitting alone near the top of the room. Seated at a front desk, Michael begins to speak when Haupt, his new security guard, interrupts with whispers to the professors and Karl. One of them asks Michael if he visited a farm near Berlin. Michael admits to visiting a relative, but denies that he saw Gromek there. The group is told they cannot speak with him until security clears the matter. Michael protests and demands to know where Professor Lindt is. The lone man at the top announces himself as Lindt and impatiently demands his briefing whether security assents or not. Lindt, goateed and cantankerous, decides that Sarah, who is not in trouble, can tell him what she knows of the "Gamma 5 experiments." Michael remains impassive as she enters and is seated. Offended by the questions asked, she is puzzled and looks to Michael. Karl tells her she must cooperate, but she angrily insists she has nothing to say and glares at Michael, "You tell them! ... You're the one who sold out!" She stalks out and Lindt insists someone "do something."

Rounding the corner of a walled garden outside, Karl tries to influence Sarah. Michael follows, then asks to speak with her alone, though she angrily says she wants out. They walk up a short rise and Karl watches from below as Michael gesticulates and the city traffic noise covers their conversation. The music suddenly softens as Sarah starts to turn toward Michael; then in close-up the camera moves around her now-understanding face. He finishes explaining, then pulls her behind a bush for a long kiss and embrace.

At the Berlin farmhouse, soldiers stand guard as Gerhardt and his men search the now-abandoned structure; Gerhardt seizes the torn telephone cord.

In Leipzig, a trio plays dinner music in a crowded hall of dancers and drinkers. Sarah, in a white dress, and Michael sit with Karl at a table. Sarah waves at Professor Lindt at another table; Dr. Koska appears and Michael walks over to ask her to dance.

As they dance, he tells her of the day's events. She says they must get out immediately and he hesitates, throwing a glance at Lindt. She tells him to be in her office with Sarah at 10 A.M. the next morning. Koska leaves, and Sarah dances with Lindt.

Lindt joins them for a drink. He is tipsy, singing along with a Viennese waltz. Sarah asks Karl to dance; Karl does not want to leave, but Lindt urges him to go. At the first question about Gamma, Lindt laughs and says he never discusses his work while having fun, but Michael piques his interest and Lindt tells him to meet him the next day for a shave at 9:30 A.M.

At the farmhouse in Berlin, the police dig up the buried motorcycle.

The next morning, Sarah and the doctor wait in her office; it's 10:10 A.M. Koska gets a telephone call saying Gromek's body has been found. They notice security guards entering the building.

Michael teases the professor with clues as they wander down the hall and into Lindt's workroom. Michael begins writing equations on the blackboard, but Lindt, impatiently smoking a cigar, finishes them for him. Michael starts to write anew, but Lindt complains he "has very little to offer." Michael blusters on and they start to argue. Finally, Lindt is so irritated he starts to write himself. An announcement about Michael and Sarah comes over the loudspeaker. Lindt ignores it and Michael goads him into revealing the whole formula. "It's brilliant," he says, and Lindt suddenly realizes his blunder when the loudspeaker announces that all students are to look for Professor Armstrong. Lindt demands that Michael not leave the room, but Michael walks out.

Outside, the halls and stairwells are buzzing with students and security police. Michael deftly makes his way upstairs.

Entering the doctor's office, he makes the women wait as he writes something down, then all three run down the back staircase and out to some waiting bicycles.

They ride down the sidewalk and across an intersection to a warehouse where they are whisked inside. Dr. Koska bids them good-bye, reminding them to make contact in Berlin by 7:00 P.M.

Inside, they board a bus already full of passengers; their escort, a grey-haired man named Jacoby, seats them in back. Someone puts a babushka on Sarah and an overcoat on Michael. They begin their journey and Jacoby informs them that the bus is a cover, though they take the same route as the official bus. Motorcycle police move near them and one woman complains bitterly that these wanted Americans are endangering their operation. They run into a roadblock and a policeman boards the bus to search. As he approaches the back, Jacoby offers a cigarette across the aisle, just covering Michael's face, and the policeman turns back, satisfied. They pass up a regular passenger, now eight minutes instead of ten minutes ahead of the regular bus. Jacoby spots the regular bus behind them on a mountain road.

Next they are stopped by some army deserter bandits, who are, in turn, interrupted by the police and chased away. The police decide to escort the bus to its destination. Michael suggests they debark, as their leaving will make the bus safer for the other passengers, but Jacoby insists they stay. He is more worried

because their bus will now have to act like a regular bus and lose more time. The complaining woman demands to get off and, after a struggle, the bus stops to let her go. Jacoby starts to give Michael the name of his contact in Friedrichstrasse, but there is another disturbance as the bus stops for an old woman with a large shopping cart, and three passengers must help her embark. The regular bus is now close and just as the police escort notices it, they enter the outskirts of Berlin. There is mounting anxiety, but by then they are among streetcars and buildings. Michael and Sarah get off as the police stop both buses, first questioning the driver of the second bus. Suddenly, the first bus is emptied and a policeman machine-guns the street after the fleeing passengers.

Michael and Sarah walk down a busy street, trying to remember what they didn't write down, "something strasse" and Albert. Sarah stops to ask the location of the post office and they are spotted by a red-haired woman with a French accent and a leopard-skin hat, who introduces herself as the Countess Kuchinska, giggles, and insists they accompany her for coffee. They hesitate but she has recognized them and so they must go.

They sit down in a nearby coffee shop, and the Countess reassures them they are quite safe. Chattering away, she finally breaks down, telling them of her deep desire to emigrate to the United States and pleads with them to be her sponsor. Sarah takes pity on the sobbing woman who brightens with gratefulness and takes the pair to the post office.

They enter the large, modern building and the Countess goes directly to the counter, ahead of the line, pleading special need to the waiting patrons. Several men come in and out of the back room and she assiduously questions each one about Albert. A uniformed man waiting in line recognizes Michael and walks out. Finally, Albert appears, asks them to wait, then returns and passes them an address just as the police appear. They run away from the uproar and down the back stairs. The Countess tackles the first armed soldier on the stairs and topples him and herself. Left sitting on the stairs, she cries out, "My sponsor!"

Outside Michael and Sarah walk briskly. On the street near their contact's office, the police are rounding up some men and putting them into a van. Michael and Sarah turn to leave, but the farmer who Michael met in Berlin and another man appear. The four walk down the sidewalk and stop in front of a shop window with television sets in it. Facing the window, Michael compliments the organization and they discover no one has yet been hurt. The fourth man explains the plan for their escape in the costume trunks of a ballet company sailing for Sweden. They are given tickets to the ballet and a payment for Hugo, a stage worker who will help them. As the group parts, Michael appears on the television screens.

At the ballet, the ballerina is the same woman from the Berlin plane ride; she recognizes Michael sitting in the audience as she executes a series of stop-motion turns. At her exit, she rushes offstage and takes the manager to a peephole to show him. Her eye fills the screen while the manager runs to the telephone. Michael and Sarah sit unaware, watching the rest of the dance, as police appear at each of the exits. Sarah first notices a policeman in the orchestra pit, then they see police everywhere. Gerhardt appears in the back and walks down the aisle. Uneasy, trapped, the pair sit. Michael, focusing on the paper fire on stage, suddenly leaps up and yells "Fire!" The audience jumps to its feet, and Gerhardt forces his way toward the couple, who become separated in

the panicked crowd. Sarah grabs on to a wall and calls Michael over. They move against the crowd to a red door where Hugo had stood before and signaled them. They knock and he quickly takes them to the waiting wicker trunks and locks them in.

The next day on the ship, Hugo smokes his pipe near his charges. They anchor in Sweden and the ballerina watches carefully as the trunks are lifted by a crane. She notices Hugo wish the trunk "good luck" and begins screaming to have their landing stopped. The ship captain commands that the trunks be shot down and the trunks fall, piles of costumes falling out. The camera moves to the other side of the ship, where two empty trunks sit.

Michael, Sarah, and Hugo swim to the dock and are greeted by Swedish military.

Elsewhere, a photographer rushes down to the ship to find Dr. Armstrong but runs into the ballerina instead; he refuses her offer to be a substitute subject for his photograph. Inside, he queries the guard, then climbs onto a box to peer into a window and spy on Michael and Sarah, sitting by a stove. He knocks on the glass to ask for a picture, but Michael responds by pulling their blanket over their heads.

Note. [H]Hitchcock does bit as man holding baby in hotel lobby.

55   *Topaz* (1969)

Director	Alfred Hitchcock
Assistant Directors	Douglas Green, James Westman
Producer	Alfred Hitchcock
Associate Producer	Herbert Coleman
Production Company	Universal
Screenplay	Samuel Taylor, based on the novel by Leon Uris
Photography	Jack Hildyard, B.S.C., Hal Mohr, A.S.C. (consultant)
Camera Operator	William Dodds
Editing	William Ziegler, A.C.E.
Production Design	Henry Bumstead
Set Decoration	John Austin
Sound	Waldon O. Watson, Robert R. Bertrano
Special Effects	Albert Whitlock
Music	Maurice Jarre
Costumes	Edith Head, Peter Saldutti (supervisor), fashioned by Pierre Balmain
Hair	Larry Germain, Nellie Manly
Makeup	Bud Westmore, Leonard Engelman
Script Supervisor	Trudy Von Trotha
Unit Production Manager	Wallace Worsley
Production Assistant	Peggy Robertson
Technical Advisers	J. P. Mathieu (Cuban), Odette Ferry (French)

Cast   Frederick Stafford (Andre
                                  Devereaux), John Forsythe (Michael
                                  Nordstrom), Dany Robin (Nicole
                                  Devereaux), John Verson (Rico
                                  Parra), Karin Dor (Juanita de Cor-
                                  doba), Michel Piccoli (Jacques Gran-
                                  ville), Philippe Noiret (Henri Jarre),
                                  Claude Jade (Michele Picard), Michel
                                  Subor (Francois Picard), Roscoe Lee
                                  Browne (Philippe DuBois), Per-Axel
                                  Arosenius (Boris Kusenov), Edmon
                                  Ryan, Sonya Kolthoff
Filmed   at Universal Studios in Technicolor
Running Time   approximately 126 minutes
Distributor   Universal
Release Date   December 1969
Other titles: *Topas, L'Étau*

Synopsis

Marching band music accompanies the credits and an introductory title, which appears over a military parade in Moscow's Red Square: "Somewhere in this crowd is a high-ranking Russian official who disagrees with his government's display of force . . . soon his conscience will force him to attempt to escape . . ."

1962, Copenhagen: the military music is sustained over the beginning of this scene. At the Soviet Embassy, Mr. and Mrs. Boris Kusenov and their adult daughter, Tamara, grimly leave the fenced compound. They are followed by a man and another couple, who lose them in a large square where the sounds of traffic and crowds now prevail. The Kusenovs enter a ceramics factory and join a public tour, which shows the delicate operations involved in the manufacture of figurines. Boris looks furtively outside, then Tamara eyes one of their pursuers in the tour crowd. She holds him in a showroom until the tour moves on; silence falls on a close-up of a figurine of a kissing couple as she deliberately breaks it, then maneuvers herself into a private room to make a telephone call.

At the United States Embassy, Michael Nordstrom takes the call and directs Tamara to Den Permanente, a large department store.

Outside Den Permanente, Nordstrom waits while the preoccupied Kusenovs shop inside the huge crowded store. Suddenly the closing bell rings and the group runs for a waiting car as agents block the way of their pursuers. The escape almost fails as Tamara collides with a bicyclist on the way to the car.

Later, in darkness, they board a waiting plane and Boris upbraids Michael for the "clumsy" escape.

They arrive safely in Washington, but the Kusenovs remain unsmiling on their automobile ride through the city; only Tamara is impressed by the buildings. They debark at their new home, a large colonial mansion full of servants.

At the French Embassy, Rene D'Arcy, Andre Devereaux's superior, and a general await Andre, complaining of his "lack of respect." They tell him the news of the defection and he immediately wonders how his government found out so quickly. Darcy dismisses his concern, but Andre stalks out.

At the Kusenov home, Tamara plays the piano while a group of agents grill

Boris under microphones in the dining room. He is grudgingly cooperative. Michael rises from his chair in anger to lean over Boris as the questions touch on Topaz. A message from Andre Devereaux requesting a dinner meeting makes him suspicious.

In Andre Devereaux's townhouse, his blond wife, Nicole, becomes upset with him; homesick for Paris, she questions Andre's partiality for the American side in the Cold War and finally cries out that he may be killed. He frowns.

Later, after dinner, Nicole complains again in front of Michael about the "spy" business. After she has gone, Michael shares the secret of Kusenov's defection with Andre.

Next day, the agents grill Kusenov about Cuba and he, though openly sarcastic in his answers, leads to them to Rico Parra, who carries with him a secret trade pact with the Soviets, and his secretary, Luis Uribe, who can be "bought," but not by Americans, as he hates them. Kusenov arrogantly taunts the Americans, wondering what they will "do with the information" now that he has given it to them.

Andre and Nicole greet their daughter, Michele, and son-in-law, Francois Picard, at an airport terminal in New York.ᴴ

They arrive at their rooms at the St. Regis and find Michael Nordstrom waiting for them. Nicole greets him coldly. Left alone, Andre lets Michael know he is unhappy at the intrusion but agrees to help him contact Uribe and obtain the document; "A quick trip to Harlem is all I ask," Michael tells him. Andre calls in Francois, who is a journalist/artist covering the United Nations, and he gives them a sketch of Uribe. Michael hands a packet of money to Andre in the hotel corridor as they leave.

Later, Andre enters the Martinique Floral Shop in Harlem. He and the owner, Philippe DuBois, enter a glassed-in cooler to discuss the job. They walk around the corner to the Hotel Theresa where a crowd is gathered outside waiting for a glimpse of the Cuban delegation. From across the street where Andre stands, only the traffic noise can be heard, as Philippe enters the hotel, shows his phony press card, then bumps into Uribe in the lobby and talks to him. Uribe takes offense and tries to move away from him down the street, but Philippe says something that changes his mind; Uribe returns to the hotel alone as Philippe signals five fingers over to Andre.

Meanwhile back at the hotel lounge, Nicole, seated with her daughter and son-in-law, drinks in silence.

At the Hotel Theresa, Philippe takes the elevator up to a corridor teeming with activity and explains to Cuban security that he has an appointment with Uribe. Passing by an altercation in the hall over Rico Parra's heavily guarded seclusion, Philippe is taken by Uribe into a bathroom, where Philippe insists he will interview Parra so Uribe will have an opportunity to remove the red case that holds the document. Moving down the hall, Philippe accidentally gains contact with Parra in the corridor. Cleverly, he convinces Parra that he is not an ordinary American but a comrade from *Ebony* magazine who wants some pictures of Parra waving to "his" people outside. Parra agrees and Uribe grabs the suitcase while they are out on the balcony. Philippe waves good-bye at the elevator, then reenters from the stairwell into Uribe's room at the end of the hall.

Down the hall, Parra pulls a paper out from under a half-eaten hamburger, hands it to his secretary, takes a drink, then notices the red briefcase is missing. Quickly discovering Uribe has taken it, he starts down the corridor with his

guard, Hernandez, where they break down Uribe's door and catch the men in the act of photographing the documents, which are displayed on the bed. Philippe jumps out of the window and Parra shoots after him, but Philippe lands safely on an awning, jumps down to the sidewalk, and runs through the crowd. Shots and screams ring out as the Cubans pursue Philippe, who pushes Andre down on the sidewalk and transfers the camera to his hand. The burly, red-haired Hernandez helps Andre up.

Back at their home in Washington, Andre readies to leave for Cuba as Nicole stands in the bedroom doorway and pleads with him not to go. He explains that the papers they photographed frightened him and he must find out for himself what the Russians are doing there. Turning quiet, Nicole asks him about Juanita de Cordoba. Andre emerges slowly from the closet and demands she never speak that name again, as Juanita is a member of the underground. Nicole persists and he finally refuses to discuss it anymore. Taking up his suitcases, he asks her to accompany him downstairs and kisses her good-bye on the cheek. Moving briefly away from the hallway, he returns to find her shadow already disappearing in silence at the top of the stairs.

On the plane, Andre reads the paper; an ominously jarring chord accompanies the close-up of a headline of the current crisis over Soviet military development in Cuba.

Andre is driven in a limousine to the peaceful, luxurious estate where the beautiful, dark-haired Juanita de Cordoba lives. She and Rico Parra appear at the front door, his arm around her. Andre greets them, handing Juanita a gift, as he and Parra engage in sardonic conversation about the "routine" events of the last twenty-four hours in Washington and New York. Rico drives off in his jeep. Now behind her front door, Juanita and Andre kiss. Concerned, she reminds him that this is a bad time, "security is tight." Taunting her about her relationship with Rico, she asks after his wife, and he laughs, kissing her again. Disconcerted, Juanita pulls away, wondering why the French care what the Russians do in Cuba. In response to his persistent questioning, she tells him most of her people are in hiding, but of course she will try. The camera centers on a tight close-up of her softening face as she asks him to stay with her for a few days.

Later, over a drink in her bedroom, he brings out some electronic gadgets and cameras that were hidden in her present, then queries her about the various operations in which he is interested. The gift box actually does hold a present for her, but he quickly moves on to a demonstration of a Geiger counter until she finally pulls him to the bed.

Next morning, they gaily cross her huge, tiled entry hall and she sends him off. In the kitchen, she completes plans with her servants, Thomas and Dolores, and also Mr. and Mrs. Mendoza, for their scheme to photograph the Russian encampments under the guise of a picnic.

On a hill overlooking a busy military port, the Mendozas lie taking photographs, their picnic lunch behind them.

Down below, a soldier on lookout notices a gull carrying a piece of bread, then, curious, looks up to notice the Mendozas scurrying the birds from their site. Soldiers race up the hill and shoot after the fleeing spies. Returning to their jeep to give chase, the soldiers discover the Mendozas pretending to be stalled on the road near a bridge; but one of them notices that Mrs. Mendoza is wounded, and they are promptly arrested and driven off. The road is silent for a few moments until a man on horseback arrives and removes the camera from the hollow bridge railing.

In Havana, Dolores enters and exits a poultry market, then returns home to the Cordoba kitchen where she removes the camera from inside a chicken. Thomas then takes it back into a concealed darkroom behind the pantry.

At a large party rally, Rico, Juanita, and Hernandez stand in the crowd. Hernandez is startled by the sight of Andre, whom he remembers from the street outside the Hotel Theresa in Harlem. He walks over to warn Rico, who grimly returns to Juanita's side.

Later that evening, Rico walks into Juanita's home while she and Andre are having dinner. He describes Uribe's betrayal and accuses Andre of having been there, but Andre insists it was a coincidence. Angry, Rico warns Andre that only Juanita protects him from death, as she is an honored widow of a hero of the revolution. He warns him to leave immediately and that he will certainly be searched on his way out of the country. Juanita angrily interrupts, insisting that Andre will stay with her as long as he likes and asks Rico to go. He relents, but reminds Andre that he must leave Cuba the next morning.

Later, Juanita smokes in her bedroom as Andre prepares to leave. Thomas arrives with articles with hiding places, including a razor kit. Andre and Juanita have a tense, tearful farewell. She is left alone and despondent in the foreground, her back to him as he walks out the door.

Mr. Mendoza lies tortured on the lap of his battered wife, who sits on a bench in a large bare room. Rico arrives to learn who they were working for, and the henchman insists that he ask Mrs. Mendoza himself. She is stunned, gaping, and is unable to speak audibly. Rico leans over to put his ear near her bloody mouth and in close-up she breathes Juanita's name. Rico's hands spread out as he rises, his jaw flexing.

Troops arrive at Juanita's home; she fights with them, pushing one down the stairs, but quiets when Rico calmly directs her to come down. He confronts her, still hoping she is innocent, but the other men discover the darkroom and photographic equipment. Quickly they call the airport to alert the troops there to the fake razor kit Andre is carrying. Parra grabs Juanita's hand, explaining that he did not want to believe, but now he must. Taking her other hand to his chest, he holds her tightly as the camera moves around them and he laments her fate—the torture her body will endure—then shoots her in the back. Her head falls back, eyes wide open. Seen now from above, she falls to the checkered tile floor, her long dark dress billowing out in a circle around her. The airport calls to say they have had to let Andre go as they found nothing. Moments later, Andre calls and is told Juanita is dead.

On the plane, Andre stares out, sighs, moves his hand over to his briefcase and pulls out the book Juanita had given him as a gift before he left. Fingering the cover that inside is marked "With all my love October 1962," he realizes something is hidden in it and goes to the restroom to lift up the lining and find the microfilm.

At his home in Washington, Andre, with Michael, pushes the door open in front of a pile of mail. Michael asks if Nicole has gone away and Andre flounders with excuses, then insists Michael come in for a drink. Rene D'Arcy drops by and he and Andre retire to the study to talk. "You left quite a few complications behind," warns D'Arcy, telling Andre he must return to Paris immediately. Hearing the news of Andre's recall, Michael asks Andre to listen to Kusenov's information about leaks in Paris before returning there.

Boris Kusenov pours his visitors tea, then sits back with a cigar to explain

Topaz, a code name for a group of French officials who work for the Soviet Union. Andre is taken aback, and Boris advises him not to go home, saying he would be well taken care of right here. Michael threatens Andre with potential war, and Andre doubts his ability to control the situation in Paris.

In a small restaurant in Paris, Andre meets with a group of intelligence officials, including Henri Jarre, who was implicated by Kusenov. He has convened the group to ask for advice before he faces the Board of Inquiry. Andre insists he cannot reveal the Cuban information because there are leaks in the government. The men are uncomfortable as he tells them about Topaz. Suddenly Henri announces that Boris Kusenov has been dead for a year; the others stare at Andre reproachfully, and Andre is confused.

Later, Henri takes a taxi to meet his superior, Jacques Granville, at his home. Jacques tells him he was foolish to lie about Kusenov and Henri suggests that Andre should be faced with the "final solution," a notion that Jacques dismisses. In the street on his way out, Henri walks by Nicole, who goes to Jacques's home and greets him with a kiss, telling him that she is a "free woman."

Francois Picard winds his way up the elegant stairs of Henri's apartment to interview him. Francois sketches while he asks a defensive Henri questions about his access to "confidential files." Confronted with his lie about Kusenov, Henri falls silent. Discovering that Francois has been sent by Andre, Henri asks to speak directly with Andre. Two men enter the apartment while Francois is on the telephone, and he and Andre are cut off.

Sensing something is wrong when no one answers his return call, Andre and Michele race over to Henri's apartment and find him dead, having fallen from the window of his upstairs apartment onto the top of a car hood, and the apartment empty.

Andre and Michele find Nicole at home, then Francois enters, wounded. During the conversation, he opens his notebook to show his sketch of Henri; Nicole recognizes him and rises in consternation. Francois relates that he overheard a telephone number while he was knocked out on the floor and Nicole tearfully identifies it as the number for Jacques Granville's home. Andre is stricken, his eyes falling on an old picture of the three of them—Andre, Nicole, and Jacques—together.

Later Andre greets Michael at the airport with the news of Jacques's spy identity.

A group of twenty or so French and American diplomats enter a large, elegant, eighteenth-century meeting room. Michael points out Jacques to one of his French colleagues as the camera moves out to view the group from above. Negotiations begin as Michael walks back and forth between the French and American groupings until one of them apologetically asks Jacques to leave. His face tenses and he turns his back.

Outside Jacques's home, his front door closes and a gunshot is heard inside.

Headlines proclaim the Cuban missile crisis over as the bodies of the Mendozas, Henri Jarre, and Juanita De Cordoba are superimposed over Andre, once again seated on a plane. The newspaper is discarded on a bench near the Arc de Triomphe.

Note. ᴴHitchcock does bit as man getting out of wheelchair to greet someone at airport.

56 *Frenzy* (1972)

Director	Alfred Hitchcock
Assistant Director	Colin M. Brewer
Producer	Alfred Hitchcock
Associate Producer	William Hill
Production Company	Universal
Screenplay	Anthony Shaffer, based on the novel *Goodbye Piccadilly, Farewell Leicester Square* by Arthur La Bern
Photography	Gil Taylor, B.S.C.
Camera Operator	Paul Wilson
Editing	John Jympson
Production Design	Syd Cain
Art Direction	Bob Laing
Set Design	Simon Wakefield
Sound	Gordon K. McCallum
Sound Editor	Rusty Coppleman
Special Effects	Albert Whitlock
Music	Ron Goodwin
Makeup	Harry Frampton
Hairdresser	Pat McDermott
Production Assistant	Peggy Robertson
Production Manager	Brian Burgess
Continuity	Angela Martelli
Casting	Sally Nicholl
Cast	Jon Finch (Richard Blaney), Barry Foster (Robert Rusk), Barbara Leigh-Hunt (Brenda Blaney), Anna Massey (Babs Milligan), Alec McCowen (Chief Inspector Oxford), Vivien Merchant (Mrs. Oxford), Billie Whitelaw (Hetty Porter), Clive Swift (Johnny Porter), Bernard Cribbins (Felix Forsythe), Elsie Randolph, Michael Bates (Sergeant Spearman), Jean Marsh, Madge Ryan, John Boxer, George Tovey, Jimmy Gardner, Noel Johnson, Gerald Sim
Filmed	at Pinewood Studios, London
Running Time	approximately 115 minutes
Distributor	Universal
Release Date	May 1972

Synopsis

Under the credits an aerial excursion of London, accompanied by a royal theme.

Cruising the Thames, the camera moves toward a sidewalk next to the river where a politician promises his audience that pollution will soon be gone from the

water.^H Someone notices a body float toward them and everyone's attention is diverted toward the river. "Another necktie murder!" The word moves quickly as the woman victim drifts ashore with only a tie on her body.

In his room at the Globe Pub, Richard Blaney ties his tie in the mirror and goes downstairs to the bar. He takes a drink and says good morning to his boss, Forsythe, who fires him for stealing liquor, though Dick protests he always pays. Babs Milligan, a barmaid, appears and defends Dick's honesty, but Dick quickly gives it up and leaves in a huff, turning in his salary advance out of spite. Babs follows him out to the street to see if he is all right and he seems calmer. She returns to work as he strides down the street through Covent Garden and into a produce warehouse to see his friend, the blond Bob Rusk. Bob offers to lend him money, which Dick refuses, then gives him a box of grapes and a tip on a long shot at the track. Dick disappears when a policeman starts to discuss the necktie murders with Bob.

Moving on to a busy pub, Dick has a brandy while two lawyers discuss the difficulties of psychopathic murderers and their value for the tourist trade. Dick belligerently demands more brandy in his second order, then moves on.

Bob sticks his head out of his upstairs flat to greet Dick, who is down on the sidewalk. He congratulates him with the news that the long shot came in. His blond head peeking over the red flowers in his window boxes, he also introduces his red-haired mother to Dick, who is visibly disconcerted. Away from them, he squashes the grapes in anger: "Twenty to one! Bloody hell!" He rounds a corner and walks up some stairs to his former wife's office, a matchmaking service. Her secretary bids some satisfied customers good-bye, then haltingly lets the belligerent Dick in to see his ex-wife. Brenda is sympathetic and patient with him, even though he insults her as he complains of his lost job and missed bet. She invites him to dinner at her club.

At dinner, he thanks her for a nice evening but continues to dwell on his bad luck. His anger boils over suddenly as he vociferously resents her success. "If you can't make love, sell it!" he booms, causing other diners to turn their heads. She lowers her eyes but remains kind and patient. He crushes a glass in his hand and finally calms down and apologizes.

At her door, he talks her into letting him come up to her flat.

Later, he sleeps at the Salvation Army while the man next to him picks his pocket; waking, Dick angrily demands back what the thief took. Amazed, he realizes that Brenda must have slipped him the twenty pounds the man had taken.

Next day, Bob Rusk barges in on Brenda in her office while she is powdering her nose. She coldly greets him as Mr. Robinson, reminding him that her agency is not able to help someone with his tastes; in any case, he should return and make an appointment with her secretary. Suspicious, she wonders how he got by her secretary and he flatly tells her he waited until he saw the secretary leave. He slams the file drawers a bit and argues with her as she attempts to avoid his attentions. Finally, he insists that only she can help him because he likes her, she's his "type." Realizing she is in danger, she attempts to excuse herself to make a phone call. He slams down the receiver in front of her, then grabs an apple and starts eating it while seated on her desk. He invites her to lunch and she agrees after hesitating, then rises to go, but he slams her against the wall and pins her arms back. She warns him that her secretary will appear any moment, but he tells her he has locked the outer door behind him. She tries to talk herself away

from him, but he wrenches her arms until she falls into a chair. She pulls up both her legs, forcefully shoves him away, and runs for the door. He catches her ankle and pounds her to the floor, then throws her on the chair, and falls on her, kissing her. She offers him money and pleads to answer the phone which is ringing, but he again refuses to be distracted. "I like you to struggle," he tells her and rips off her dress and brassiere. She is motionless, neck bent and praying, as he rapes her to a chant of "Lovely!" Spent, he turns dissatisfied and scowls at her. Relieved, assuming it's over, she watches in horror as he quickly undoes his tie and wraps it around her neck, choking off her scream. She struggles until her hands drop from the tie and her eyes are motionless. Finally, he sweats, panting, and moves away from her sprawled body to finish eating his apple. Taking money from her purse, he picks his teeth and walks out into the street.

Dick appears from the other direction, but finds the office door locked and leaves just as Brenda's secretary arrives back from lunch. The camera waits outside in silence until she screams.

Dick calls the Globe from a pay phone looking for Babs, who wrests the phone from an angry Forsythe. She agrees to bring his things from his room there and meet him later.

In Brenda's office, the police speak with Miss Barling, the secretary, who has told them she saw Dick—"That beast!"—and proceeds to relate to them his violent encounter with Brenda the day before. Inspector Oxford is impressed with the precision of her testimony. They note money missing from Brenda's handbag.

Dick greets Babs in a cab and takes her to the Coburg Hotel, where he signs in as Mr. and Mrs. Oscar Wilde over Babs's objections. The proprietress watches him warily and demands the money for the room up front.

Upstairs, Dick arrogantly hands over his clothes to the porter for cleaning. Early the next morning, Babs gets up and sees a paper announcing Brenda's murder. Downstairs, the porter recognizes Dick from a description of his coat in the paper and calls the police, who arrive shortly, only to find Dick and Babs gone.

Sitting on a park bench, Dick passionately tries to convince Babs of his innocence. She eventually gives up her doubts and they hug, then kiss. He refuses to turn himself in. Suddenly an old friend of his from the RAF, Johnny Porter, notices Dick and invites him and Babs up to his high-rise apartment nearby. The camera zooms up to find Johnny's wife, Heddy, looking down at them from the window of the apartment, where she moves back and paces.

Up in the apartment, Johnny introduces his guests, but Heddy immediately rips into Dick for murdering his wife, reminding him of the divorce petition that described his "physical and mental cruelty." Arms imperiously spread across the back of the couch, she refuses to be swayed and is furious with Johnny for offering to harbor a criminal. Finally, she rises and announces that she is "going shopping." Undaunted, Johnny offers Babs and Dick jobs in his new Paris pub, and Babs agrees to meet Dick next morning at Victoria Station.

At New Scotland Yard, Inspector Oxford shovels down a sausage and potatoes lunch while Sergeant Spearman watches closely. Oxford explains that his wife is taking a course in continental gourmet cooking, and he never gets enough to eat. The lab report has identified Brenda Blaney's face powder on the pound note Dick used at the Coburg Hotel. That finishes the case, and the inspector lectures the sergeant that these types are impotent sadists and refers him to Blaney's divorce petition for a description of sadism. Forsythe telephones to tell the police that Dick used to work for him and has gone off with Babs.

Returning to the Globe, Bob stands at the bar with a friend. Babs rushes in late for her shift and she and Forsythe have a screaming match over Dick. She races out into the street and stops, thinking hard in a frozen, silent close-up. Bob's voice greets her from behind and he offers her a place to stay. Taking her through the produce warehouse, he pumps her about Dick on the way to his flat, and assures her that he is going away for the day she will be there. They walk together up the stairs to his apartment and he closes the door as he tells her that she is his "type of woman." The camera travels silently back down the stairs and through the corridor, where the sound of traffic intrudes, and into the street below, full of people and business.

That evening, the inspector arrives home to his cheerful wife and a "soupe de poisson." Frowning at the food, he tells her of the evidence piled up against Dick while he surreptitiously returns his soup to the pot. He is worried that they may not find Dick before his "appetite is whetted again."

Meanwhile, outside his apartment, Bob wheels down a hand truck with Babs's body in a sack. Dressed in his market apron, he takes her to a truck full of other sacks, laboriously lifts her in, then returns to his flat. Tired, he flops on the couch and drinks and eats a bit. Jumping up to view the truck from his window, he suddenly realizes his stick pin is gone and frantically races around the room looking for it, searching through Babs's clothes that he has hidden in his dresser. Rising, he recalls the murder scene, and Babs clutching his breast and the pin.

He runs out to the truck and climbs aboard, leaving the back door open, just as the driver starts the engine and moves out. He continues to struggle with the bag stuffed with potatoes and the body until he finds Babs's legs, her foot slapping him in the face a couple of times. Sticking his head in the sack, he swears at the corpse, just as the truck lurches and spills out a couple of bags of potatoes. The driver stops and comes around to close the back door, but Bob successfully hides himself. Back to work as the truck moves again, Bob finally discovers his pin stuck in Babs's hand and is forced to break her fingers open in order to retrieve it. The truck stops again at a diner and Bob falls out and hides in the restroom until the driver leaves, his back door once again open.

Later, the police watch as Babs's body is now visible in the rear of the truck. When the truck screeches to a halt, she falls out and lies on the road between it and the police car.

Heddy races into a room where Dick is sleeping and hysterically demands that he wake up, accusing him of killing Babs. "Get out!" she screams; "I'd call the police myself if I knew how to do it without getting involved." Johnny explains that Dick could not have done it; the radio said Babs was killed right after she left them the day before and Dick was there with him until he went to bed. Pacing, Dick is silent as Heddy and Johnny quarrel over Johnny's suggestion that they go immediately to the police and provide Dick with an alibi. Swayed by her argument that they will be arrested as accessories to the earlier murder, Johnny reluctantly changes his mind. Angry, Dick shouts at them both and leaves in a huff.

At the produce market, Forsythe and Bob talk about the case. Turning, Bob finds Dick hiding behind some crates. He proclaims his innocence and Bob sympathizes and sends him back to his apartment by the long route. Bob runs up his stairs carrying Dick's bag, and Dick follows shortly after. Inside, Bob stands in front of a wall between his two portraits of dark-haired women and welcomes Dick, who is very grateful, then leaves him. Taking a drink, Dick is quickly

surprised by the police who burst in and arrest him. Outside, a policeman thanks Bob for his help.

The inspector arrives at the police station to query Dick, who is surrounded by plainclothesmen. Opening his bag, they find Babs's clothes and Dick springs to his feet: "Rusk! It's Rusk!"

In a courtroom, a jury returns a guilty verdict: life imprisonment. Dick is dragged out screaming, "Rusk I'll kill you!" and thrown into a solitary cell.

Back in the courtroom, the inspector is left alone, Dick's words ringing in his ears.

Another day, the inspector takes a photographer by the market to get a picture of Bob Rusk.

Later, he listens to Brenda Blaney's secretary relate her experiences with "Mr. Robinson." "Men like this leave no stone unturned in their search for disgusting gratifications," she explains.

At the prison, Dick throws himself down a flight of stairs and is taken by ambulance to a hospital.

At home, over his pig's-foot dinner, the inspector is assured by his wife that he is now on the right track. He is expecting proof of Bob's guilt soon. He explains that Rusk must have traveled in the truck with Babs's corpse. Choking on his food while his wife thoughtfully munches on bread sticks, he indicates that he expects to trace Bob to the truck stop. Spitting out a chunk of foot, he rises to answer the door. Sergeant Spearman has found a woman at the diner who can identify Rusk and has even given the sergeant a brush she lent Bob to get the potato dust off his suit. "Poor Mr. Blaney, we must have him over for a really good dinner," laments Mrs. Oxford.

That night at the hospital, the inmates wait for their guard to fall asleep from pills. Dick puts on a white coat and walks out while the others tend to the fallen guard. Outside, he picks up a crowbar and hot-wires a car.

At home, the inspector receives the news and rushes out.

At Bob's flat, Dick advances with the crowbar up the dark stairs and opens the door. He walks over to the form on the bed and beats it until a woman's arm falls out, and he uncovers a strangled corpse. The inspector suddenly enters and stares at Dick, who protests "No!" Hearing noise in the stairwell, the inspector quickly motions him silent and hides behind the door. Bob enters, dragging a large wardrobe behind him, then is left stupefied as the inspector calmly confronts him: "Mr. Rusk, you're not wearing your tie." The camera rests viewing the top of the old wooden wardrobe.

Note. [H]Hitchcock does bit as man in crowd listening to opening speech.

57   *Family Plot* (1976)

Director	Alfred Hitchcock
Assistant Directors	Howard G. Kazanjian, Wayne A. Farlow
Producer	Alfred Hitchcock
Production Company	Universal
Screenplay	Ernest Lehman, based on the novel *The Rainbird Pattern* by Victor Canning

Photography	Leonard South
Editing	J. Terry Williams
Art Direction	Henry Bumstead
Sound	James W. Payne, James Alexander, Robert L. Hoyt
Special Effects	Albert Whitlock
Music	John Williams
Costumes	Edith Head
Makeup	Jack Barron
Production Assistant	Peggy Robertson
Production Illustrator	Thomas J. Wright
Production Manager	Ernest B. Wehmeyer
Script Supervisor	Lois Thurman
Cast	Karen Black (Fran), Bruce Dern (George Lumley), Barbara Harris (Blanche Tyler), William Devane (Arthur Adamson), Ed Lauter (Joseph Maloney), Cathleen Nesbitt (Julia Rainbird), Katherine Helmond (Mrs. Maloney), Warren J. Kemmerling (Grandison), Edith Atwater (Mrs. Clay), William Prince (Bishop Wood), Nicolas Colasanto (Constantine), Marge Redmond (Vera Hannagan), John Lehne (Andy Bush), Charles Tyner (Wheeler), Alexander Lockwood (Parson), Martin West (Sanger)
Filmed	at Universal Studios, Los Angeles, and San Francisco, in Technicolor
Running Time	approximately 120 minutes
Distributor	Universal
Release Date	March 1976

Other titles: *Familiengrab, Complot de Famille, Complotto di Famiglia*

Synopsis

Under the credits, a close-up of a crystal ball is accompanied by the eerie soprano theme music. The face of "Madame" Blanche, a young psychic, appears reflected in the ball: "Someone is here. . . . I feel a holding back. What's the trouble, Henry?"

The plush, red-velvet room in which she sits becomes apparent, as her voice suddenly changes to a deep baritone, "Too many memories, too much pain, too much sor—row." The camera circles the ornate seating area to find Julia Rainbird, a white-haired woman in a heavy lace shawl, who eagerly suggests the voice must be her sister Harriet. Blanche pleads for peace for her client, who is amazed that Blanche knows about her "troubled sleep." "No love or kindness for Harriet," says Blanche matter-of-factly, but her client remains firm; she knows what to do and does not need Harriet goading her in her dreams. From her

"trance," Blanche peeks at Julia between her fingers that cover her face. Finally she appears to come out of it, claiming not to remember any of the details, "only the gist." Julia demands the "gist" and Blanche confidently relates that Julia took Harriet's illegitimate child away from her and now, out of guilt, wants to bring her "only heir" back into the family to gain his rightful fortune. "Don't think I'm a prude," says Julia, "but I still want it kept a secret." She offers Blanche $10,000 to find the man. Blanche is startled at this figure, but she quickly lowers her eyes and indicates that the money would, of course, go to charity. They walk into the oriental-carpeted, very red central hall and Blanche leaves.

Outside the mansion, Blanche gets into a red taxi. Sitting in the back-seat, she complains that "Henry is murder on her throat," speaking intimately with the driver, a young man named George. They argue, and he occasionally turns all the way around to effect a retort. He claims he learned from the druggist about all the sleeping pills Julia Rainbird was taking, and Blanche claims he forgot to tell her, since she and Henry (her contact with the spirit world) did all the work. "You're as psychic as a dry salami," he maintains, and she calmly tells him he is just jealous of Henry. Finally, she tells him the news about the "ten big ones," and he brightens at the thought of all they could do with so much money. "We could get married," she beams, but he sours at the suggestion. He becomes more annoyed when he hears that in order to get the money they have to find a man whose name and whereabouts no one knows. Blanche cautions him about fretting; after all, "as an actor, you should know fretting will ruin a performance." Exasperated, he flings back a remark about a "standing ovation," then brakes suddenly when he sees a tall blond woman in a black coat, hat, and sunglasses step off the sidewalk and walk in front of the car.

A mysterious comic twang in the soundtrack accompanies the woman as the camera follows her to a field office, where a uniformed guard escorts her farther into a bright office building. She enters, pointing a gun at the businessmen inside. "As long as you have Victor Constantine, there is nothing we can do, so put that gun away," cautions one. They place a small bag on the counter between them and her black-gloved hand takes a huge glittering diamond out of it. In close-up, she weighs it on a nearby scale, then hands them a note when asked about Mr. Constantine. Outside, a bass drum marks their walk to a nearby helicopter; she gets in with the waiting pilot and points to the compass. Still having not spoken a word, but shooting the gun once in response to the pilot's claim it is not loaded, she directs the pilot to land on a golf course, where she walks into the dark bushes and shows the diamond to a waiting man. The crickets chirp for a few moments and the pilot eventually runs after her and discovers the unconscious Mr. Constantine.

The woman, Fran, and her husband, Arthur Adamson, are already in their car and driving away. She complains about "the damn six-inch heels" while she is taking off her blond wig; he says that he needs the tall blond woman one more time, and she blanches. They corner a city block and move into their garage, which has a large automatic door. Inside, they step up and over into the boiler room, where they uncover a lock hidden in a brick wall and enter a concealed cell to clean up after Constantine. As Fran takes the sheets off the bed, she insists that Arthur empty the chemical toilet right away. "Bitch!" he mutters. They continue upstairs into their elegant townhouse, past a large crystal chandelier. Fran is somewhat sickened by their escapade but turns lovingly toward him as

they go up the central stairway arm in arm. The camera remains on the chandelier, then moves into a close-up of the diamond Arthur has hidden there. The light goes out.

In a large bright office, a blustery Mr. Constantine paces behind his desk and rages at the FBI detectives arranged around him. They query him about his confinement, and he replies sarcastically because he remembers only a disembodied voice; he saw no one.

A Rolls Royce and a chauffeur sit outside Blanche's small California bungalow. George drives up in his cab and enters the kitchen. He peeks through the beaded curtain into the living room where Blanche sits in a trance across from a client. He sets a wind chime in motion to gain her attention. The camera zooms into her eye as she peeks out at him, and he frantically motions her into the kitchen. She imagines Henry beckoning her and moves dramatically around the room and through the beads, where she snaps into consciousness and demands to know what George wants. He demands her car keys, and, between howls and cries from Henry, she discovers that he has found a lead to the identity of the man they are seeking. George has located the Rainbird chauffeur's daughter.

A large, glittery department store. Over a counter, George queries Mrs. Hannagan, the daughter, telling her he is a lawyer, and her recollections might be worth something to him. She cheerfully tells him all she can remember about her father's friend, Harry Shoebridge, and especially about one strange night, then informs him the Shoebridges died in a fire. The boss stalks over and commands Mrs. Hannagan back to work. Mrs. Hannagan whispers about payment, but George interrupts with one more question and finds out that their son, Eddie Shoebridge, is dead.

George drives into an old cemetery with a small utility shack. The camera tracks with him as he takes out his pipe and walks around the grounds, literally stumbling on the graves. From a low angle, dirt flies out of the ground beyond George; ominous piano music accompanies the caretaker who climbs out of the grave he is digging and approaches George to help him. George comments that the stone for Eddie is much newer than the other stones, though all the Shoebridge family died in 1950, and the caretaker smiles cryptically at him. George pokes around a close-up of the bottom of the stone.

Rock music blares over a close-up of a headstone and the large chiseled letters DIED. From across the outdoor work area, the owner asks the young worker who is carving the stone to turn down the radio, then he takes George into his office, where he confirms that Eddie's headstone was purchased in 1965 by a slightly bald fellow who paid cash and picked it up.

At the Registrar of Births and Deaths,[H] there is no death certificate for Eddie, just an application signed by Joseph B. Maloney that was denied.

Near some bare hills, George sits in Blanche's white Mustang across the highway from the Maloney gas station, and Maloney and his wife notice him. He U-turns into the station and gets out to stretch and fool with his Sherlock Holmes-type pipe. Maloney nervously moves around him in close-up. George (still presenting himself as McBride, a lawyer) offers him money for information about Eddie, then confronts him with his information about the headstone and death certificate. Maloney becomes angry and takes down George's license plate number when he leaves.

A small, but elegant, jewelry store. Arthur Adamson, the proprietor, registers displeasure when a dressed-up Maloney enters. He takes him into his paneled

office, and Maloney relates the story, including Blanche Tyler's address. Maloney is anxious, as he helped Eddie (now Arthur Adamson) murder his parents in the house fire—"the perfect murder," grins Arthur. Arthur's assistant announces that the police are waiting outside. "Jesus Christ, Eddie!" swears Maloney, but Arthur patiently tells him to wait.

In the store, two detectives routinely query Arthur about the diamond that was used as ransom for the kidnapped Mr. Constantine, wondering if he has seen anything suspicious.

Arthur returns to his office to find Maloney gone, the window open, and the note with Blanche's address.

That night, Fran, in white bell-bottom trousers, cases Blanche's bungalow. She returns to the car where Arthur waits; they watch from across the street as George's cab pulls up and Blanche and he carry in some groceries. George and Blanche argue on her front stoop; she insists he stay, but he wants to go home because he is "too pooped to pop," and she screams that he is "useless" to her. Eddie and the money are mentioned before George leaves, and he insists everything can wait until Sunday, his day off. In the car, Arthur capsulizes what he knows, but Fran does not appear to know that he is also Eddie Shoebridge.

At the Rainbird home, Julia, in heavy white lace and satin, and Blanche, in a trance, sit at either end of her couch. Blanche agonizes over the chauffeur's driving so fast, and then speaks of a fire before she says good-bye to Henry and snaps her head alert. Julia now remembers that the chauffeur wrote from his deathbed to say that the parson promised to keep in touch with the child.

Later in the cab, George is annoyed that there is still no money in sight; Blanche leans on the backseat and tells him about the parson, who is now Bishop Wood at St. Anselm's.

From above, the camera watches George's small figure as he walks up the many broad steps to the huge stone Gothic cathedral. Inside, he inquires of a priest how he might make a date with the Bishop and is told to wait until after the service. Up front, Fran, disguised in grey hair and a bun, walks in front of the Bishop and faints. Arthur, dressed in clerical robes, swiftly enters the frame and sticks a needle into the Bishop, who is leaning over Fran. A close-up shows the Bishop's head as it arches backward and he faints. Close-ups show Fran's alert eyes open and her feet quickly moving. The pair's gloved hands take hold of the Bishop and quickly usher him out as the large congregation stands dumbfounded.

In the car, Blanche and Arthur take off their disguises, and Blanche asks about "the man with the pipe" whom she noticed in the crowd. Arthur tells her Joe Maloney is "itching" for that job, but they still wonder how George knew, and decide that Blanche must "go" with him. Fran balks at being involved in a murder, but Arthur insists that "that's what's exciting—we move as one, nothing held back." She stares off to the accompaniment of driving organ music.

At Blanche's home, George, in an apron, cooks hamburgers for them. She complains about his "gross negligence" in losing the Bishop. "I suppose Henry and I are going to exhaust ourselves doing *your* work for you." "What do you mean, *my* work? My work is driving a cab!" cries George, between bites of his hamburger. The telephone rings and Joe Maloney offers to help them in their quest, for a fee. They agree to meet him at Abe and Mable's Café, wondering because the proposal smells "fishy." Blanche demands another hamburger, but George refuses, and they quickly leave.

As they drive over the mountain road, Blanche is glum, and the camera pans

to stop behind an old green car on the roadside. Momentarily, Joe Maloney pops up from his hiding place on the seat.

Inside Abe and Mabel's Café on the roadside, Blanche and George sullenly sit down and order beers. Outside, Joe arrives, and bass drums sound as he looks at their car. Blanche and George wait as a series of other customers come in. Outside, Joe wipes his hand on a rag. After two more beers, Blanche rises and says, "He's not coming."

They pull the white Mustang onto the road and the camera moves into a close-up of leaking brake fluid underneath. They swerve around a few corners and Blanche wonders what the big hurry is. George admits the accelerator is stuck and she grabs onto him, moaning that her "hamburger is coming up." The brakes are gone too, and they reel down the road, George doing his best to avoid the cliff on their left as well as the oncoming cars and motorcycles. Blanche hysterically hangs on to him, sometimes getting her feet in his face, sometimes tightly pulling on his tie. Finally, he drives off the road into a ditch and the car comes to a stop on its side. Blanche steps on his head in order to crawl out the top, and he falls out the bottom, but both are all right. Blanche hits him until he yells out that it was Maloney, then she finally apologizes as they limp off down the road to mellow romantic music. Suddenly, Maloney's green car appears at the end of a cliff, and Joe pulls up to offer them a ride, which they refuse. From above them, we see the car turn around as chase music begins on the lonely open road and Joe speeds at them. They run; then another car full of young people appears, and Joe, veering away from it, falls over the edge of the cliff. The teenagers run away, and Blanche and George walk to the edge to see the fireball down below.

In the jewelry shop, Fran, glamorously dressed and hatted, enters and asks about a bracelet. She sits down at the counter with Arthur to buy pearls and tells him of the new jewel they have been offered in exchange for the Bishop. Then she shows him a news account of Joe's death, and Arthur laughs. She frowns, then he turns bitter and angry, calling Joe "that incompetent!" He informs her they will do the job themselves. Wide-eyed at this, she says she "can't." But he coyly reminds her they "share and share alike." "Stop it!" she hisses, then knocks over her chair as she hurries out.

At the cemetery, a large crowd mourns Joe Maloney. Standing apart, George fiddles with his pipe. Suddenly Mrs. Maloney recognizes George, and, upset, breaks away from the crowd. The camera views from above the paths of the unkempt cemetery as Mrs. Maloney flees and George follows her, finally catching up. She pushes at him and he threatens to call the police. Bitter, she tells him about Arthur Adamson, who is Eddie Shoebridge.

In Blanche's kitchen, George argues with his boss on the telephone about having the night off. Blanche complains that he "didn't put up much of a fight," but he insists he must keep his job. He instructs her to go through the phone book and find the Arthur Adamson who is around forty years old and trembles at the name Shoebridge.

A montage is shown of Blanche in a long skirt and sweater as she visits a number of shops and houses marked A. Adamson. Finally, she comes to the jewelry store and the assistant takes her in to write a note to Arthur, but she wheedles for and gets his home address. On her way to Arthur's home, she stops by a hotel and leaves a message for George with the doorman.

In her bedroom, Fran dresses and Arthur puts a gun in her purse. They go to the basement, then speak through the microphone to the Bishop, instructing him

to sit with his back to them before they come in. On entering his cell, they inject him with a blackout drug. Their front doorbell rings and Fran is appalled to go to the peephole and see Blanche. "It's her!" she cries, but Arthur tells her to ignore the intrusion; they have a rendezvous in a half-hour and must hurry. Meanwhile, Blanche decides to leave a note on the door, then walks down their front stairs. Inside the garage, the door opens just as Blanche is walking by to her car. She cheerily greets them and tweaks Arthur's cheek as she mentions the name Shoebridge. He becomes angry as she tries to explain about the Rainbird fortune, then cheers up when he understands. Suddenly Fran, who has noticed the Bishop's red cloak hanging out the bottom of the car door, circles around behind them and tries to push it back in, but instead the Bishop's head falls out the door. Blanche gasps and runs for the garage door, but it closes in front of her and she drops to her knees, arms stretched over her head as the door comes down. She backs away swearing that no one knows she is there, but Arthur steps over and slugs her to the ground. Arthur suggests she "needs a rest" and Fran vehemently shakes her head no until he hisses at her, "Will you do as I say!" The needle is raised; he and Blanche struggle until he stabs her and she cries out and falls. He carries her into the hidden compartment behind the brick wall.

Later, in the car, Arthur holds up a large diamond, and announces it is time for "Madame Blanche."

George gets out of his cab and notices Blanche's Mustang near the garage. He crosses the busy street in front of the house's elaborate double stairs and finds her note at the top, then the keys in the car. He tries the garage door, then notices paint spilling out from inside. Elsewhere, Arthur and Fran drive in silence. Around the side of the house, George finds a low basement window, undoes the lock, and climbs in. He walks along the brick wall, then upstairs, and down into the garage where he finds Blanche's purse splattered with blood. He continues his search up the central stairs in the hall full of antiques, then hears Arthur and Fran come in arguing. "It's my stomach; murder doesn't agree with it," says Fran. Inside the kitchen, he sees their feet go by as she refuses to cooperate. He takes his shoes off and tiptoes down the stairs by them.

Near the brick wall, he waits in the shadows and watches Arthur open the hidden door and check to see that Blanche is still unconscious. Arthur returns, leaving the door open, and Blanche lets George know she is awake. Fran, sulking, goes with Arthur to the cellar to wake Blanche, who rises suddenly, yelling and screaming; she bolts out the door and locks them in. "You faked that one beautifully," says George, smiling. "You're still the champion!" They move around the house, wondering if they can find the diamond. Psychic music takes Blanche upstairs, becoming louder and louder until she turns her gloved hand and points at the diamond in the chandelier. "Blanche, you *are* psychic!" cries George. "I am," she says blankly, coming out of her trance. He telephones the police from the study, and she sits on the stairs, turns to the camera, and winks.

Note. [H]Hitchcock does bit as silhouette behind office window.

IV

ANNOTATED BIBLIOGRAPHY OF WRITINGS
BY AND ABOUT HITCHCOCK

An asterisk preceding the entry number denotes that the publication was not actually inspected.

1919
Articles and Shorter Writings

*58   HITCHCOCK, ALFRED.   "Gas." *The Henley* 1, no. 1.
A short story (less than one page) of the horrific flight of a woman through the black streets of Montmartre into the arms of a gang of thieves and murderers. The scare turns out to be a trip to the dentist. *The Henley* was the in-house social magazine of a company where Hitchcock worked.
Reprinted in *Sight and Sound* 39 (1969–1970), and in entries 499 and 702.

1924
Articles and Shorter Writings

*59   "*Woman to woman.*" In *Representative Photoplays,* by Scott O'Dell. Hollywood, Calif.: Palmer Institute of Authorship, pp. 133–137.
Cited in *New Film Index* (New York: Dutton, 1975). "Full synopsis and

1926

scenario analysis." Hitchcock was scriptwriter and art director on this film, which was successful enough to be distributed in the United States.

1926
Articles and Shorter Writings

60   BARRY, IRIS. *Let's Go to the Movies.* London: Chatto & Windus, pp. 235–236.

A paragraph under the heading, "a note on some clever young men," and a still from *The Lodger,* "a brilliant English film." "*The Pleasure Garden* . . . had an adult air, was often gracious to the eyes. His second, *The Lodger,* was a positive shock so unlike anything else it proved . . . excellent, stimulating, evocative of the imagination."

61   BELFRAGE, CEDRIC. "Alfred the Great." *The Picturegoer 11,* no. 63 (March):60.

Describes the career of Hitchcock, who "achieved his aim purely by his own industry and enterprise." Left penniless at fifteen by the death of his father, he took a job as a clerk, and then moved to Famous Players-Lasky, where there is "no doubt" his work on *Woman to Woman* was significant in its success. The work that followed soon established him as a "first rate art director and man of ideas." At the age of twenty-six, he had produced two films, *The Pleasure Garden* and *The Mountain Eagle,* which "all who have seen declare to be almost perfect in their technical and artistic production." "An unassuming and delightful personality, Hitchcock has been . . . able to take far more complete control of his productions than the average director of four times the experience. The fact is that he has crammed 20 years of experience into 5 years of practice, while his youth is a tremendous asset towards freshness of treatment."

62   *"The Lodger." Bioscope* (September 16):39.

Review: "A mystery drama, which through imagination and skill of director holds the interest in remarkable degree. . . . It is possible that this film is the finest British production ever made. Hitchcock has avoided the sins of commission and omission so common not only in British films, but in those of other countries. . . . The tempo of the whole has seldom been equalled."

63   *"The Mountain Eagle." Bioscope* (October 7):47–48.

Review: "Artistic merit should compensate for weakness of story. . . . The producer, Alfred Hitchcock, has not been well served by his author, and in spite of skillful and at times brilliant direction, the story has an air of unreality. . . . Beautiful pictures of mountain scenery in summer and winter, and picturesque timber interiors are shown with unusually artistic lighting effects and excellent photography. Locale is not indicated, though the village is obviously continental."

64   *"The Pleasure Garden." Bioscope* (March 25):40.
Review: "Powerful and interesting story, well adapted, with masterly production, all combine to make this film of outstanding merit . . . a credit to a British Studio."

1927
Articles and Shorter Writings

65   *"Downhill." Bioscope* (May 26):43.
Review: "Study of the degeneracy of a weak character and his ultimate recovery. . . . Adaptation of play is provided with an ending to suit popular taste. . . . It is more by the brilliant treatment of the director and the excellent work of the artists that this film is likely to appeal. . . . Various settings show originality and in every instance add to the effect."

66   *"Easy Virtue." Bioscope* (September 1): 67.
Review: "Selling angle: the established reputation of the author, Noel Coward, and Alfred Hitchcock, the producer [who] has done the best possible for a subject which does not lend itself readily to the screen." Further criticizes the unbelievability of the plot.

*67   HITCHCOCK, ALFRED.   "The Americans: A letter." *London Evening News* (November 16).
Cited in entry 702. Letter calling for "more intelligent treatment of film stories," like the Americans who "have learnt to put the nouns, verbs, and adjetives of the film language together."

68   *"The Ring." Bioscope* (October 6):43.
Review: "The most magnificent British film ever made. . . . Alfred Hitchcock has proved [it is not necessary] to pay fabulous prices for film rights of works which were not intended [for the screen]. . . . He has written a simple story of everyday life with a view to its expression in pictorial form, and produced with genuine sincerity."

1928
Articles and Shorter Writings

69   *"Champagne." Bioscope* (August 28):39.
Review of this Betty Balfour star vehicle: "The beginning, ending, and intermediate part of the entire film . . . shows every phase of her talent. Efficient, but may not arouse enthusiasm."

1929

70   *"The Farmer's Wife." Bioscope* (March 8):75.
Review: "Hitchcock has succeeded in conveying the Devonshire atmosphere. . . . At times he is rather led away by his tendency to fantastic angles of photography, but he has many happy inspirations . . . which greatly strengthen the theme of the story."

71   HERRING, ROBERT.   "The latest British masterpiece." *Close Up* 2, no. 1 (January):32–38.
Diatribe on *The Ring,* a film to which the author claims the word "masterpiece" has been too hastily applied by the British press. Charges the film has no originality, an actress of "hard efficiency and no charm," and "pretentious" visualizations of facts that might have been communicated more quickly with a title.

1929
Articles and Shorter Writings

72   BETTS, ERNEST.   "Ordeal by talkie." *Saturday Review* 148 (July 6):7–8.
Overview of early sound films that emphasizes *Blackmail,* which "has many touches of art; it's spell is complete. For as the right balance has been maintained between the rhythmic values, hastening and retarding the traffic of the story, so also has a sensitive touch controlled the sound."

73   *"Blackmail." Bioscope* (June 26):31.
Review: "Masterly production . . . breaks away from a tradition and deals of matters which are of a general, rather than a parochial appeal." Proves the talking picture "affords opportunities to British producers which cannot be equalled in any other country."

74   "Britain's first talking film." *New York Times* (October 13):Section 9, p. 6, col. 3.
Review of *Blackmail:* "Fairly smooth example of audible screen story-telling . . . characters don't ring true."

75   B[LAKESON], O[SWELL].   "One swallow." *Close Up* 5, no. 3 (September):244–245.
Complaint that the British cinema's latest triumph, *Blackmail,* is being blown out of proportion. The author admits there are "nice" things in the film, but laments, "If only we could all go ahead and forget that we had made one fair film."

76   CASTLE, HUGH.   "Elstree's first talkie." *Close Up* 5, no. 2 (August):131–135.
Sarcastic review of *Blackmail.* "A fortnight had elapsed without us having a 'greatest ever,' and the event was about ten days overdue." Castle allows that

Hitchcock "has made a good job of it" and assesses the film as a "comeback" after *Champagne* and *The Manxman*. Criticizes it for bowing to the "almighty German technique" and for having "an inconsequential theme," but finds the Cockney humor "fascinating."

77   HALL, MORDAUNT. "Isle of Man scenes." *New York Times* (December 17):28.
Review of *The Manxman*: "Enchanting scenes . . . as beautiful as anything that one would hope to behold on the screen. Hall also lauds interiors, "evidently faithful reproductions." He is less keen on the acting, which is merely acceptable, but compliments Hitchcock's "restraint."

78   MacPHERSON, KENNETH. "As is." *Close Up* 5 (December):447–454.
Essay on the dangers of theoretically constructed cinema, a result of Soviet "montage consciousness." "Build cinema as vision, your own vision, and you will build something worth while," extols Macpherson. *Blackmail* is presented as an example of the use of sound symbolism, the shop bell becoming a physical manifestation of danger. The author recommends the filmmaker explore action and its source—"the interacting of conscious and unconscious. . . . The highest form is . . . the film of imagery and action, psychology and physiology, or better still, psychology through physiology."

79   ———. "As is." *Close Up* 5, no. 4 (October):257–263.
"Those who have mentioned *Blackmail* in *Close Up* have left much to say about it. . . . [It] is the first sign of a comprehension of the relationship of techniques." While MacPherson does not like certain of the scenes, he gives many examples of the successful orchestration of sound for the purpose of calling for a critical construction of a "sound-sight aesthetic."

80   *"The Manxman." Bioscope* (January 23):38.
Review: "Cleverly directed, finely played human interest story. . . . Only a skillful director could have devised from a story of this kind a picture of such remarkable power and interest. The unflinching realism and masterly manner [make the spectator] oblivious to the drabness of the story."

81   MARSHALL, ERNEST. "Good and bad points of *Blackmail*, Britain's first talking picture." *New York Times* (August 11):Section 8, p. 5.
Thinks *Blackmail* has been overpraised, though grants it is artistic and speaks at length of Hitchcock's mastery of the microphone. But Marshall says the film is at times repugnant, lacking in humor, and "you are never carried away; you know throughout that it is a world of unreality."

1930

82   "Talkie development." *New York Times* (August 14):22.
Discusses the defects of talkies and suggests that the technique of *Blackmail* points the way for "artists in the talkies."

1930
Articles and Shorter Writings

83   B[LAKESTON], O[SWELL]. "Advance monologue." *Close Up* 7, no. 2 (August):146–147.
Interview: "The talkies have given most of us a past about which we need to be ashamed. Why, we used to bore a hole in an actor's head and superimpose tiny images representing his thought! Sound has done away with such clumsiness," deadpans Hitchcock. Hitchcock also comments on the ending he planned for *Blackmail* that was deemed uncommercial "according to the disciples of the happy end," Russian quick cutting (too expensive), and the "worthwhile compromises" he is making with *Murder!*

84   CASTLE, HUGH. "Attitude and interlude, or contemporary cinema architecture in the light of Bunyan's *Pilgrim's Progress*." *Close Up* 7, no. 3 (September):185–189.
Murder! is compared positively to other current releases. Hitchcock "is the one man in this country who can think cinema." Castle is particularly taken with the "speech montage" of the jury scene. In general, Hitchcock is a man of ideas, though some are "flung off, used to serve a purpose and then forgotten." Unfortunately the film "gets dangerously near the highbrow. . . . Its literary link is too strongly noticeable. . . . [There is a problem] as to whether Hitchcock's attitude is compatible with the filmgoers'."

85   "Juno and some others." *New York Times* (July 16):Section 8, p. 3, col. 6.
Review of *Juno and the Paycock:* "Good acting and dialogue, a faithful, restrained, intelligent adaptation of a fine play."

86   SIMPSON, CELIA. *"Juno and the Paycock."* *Spectator* 144 (March 8):363.
Review: The first half sags, not entirely keeping the viewer's attention, but the last half is "completely successful." Stimpson especially likes the actors and notes the best thing about the production is that the play has been immortalized.

87   ———. *"Murder!" Spectator* 145 (October 11):489.
Negative review: A bad story, "which necessitates its being told in words rather than actions. The result is 'imitation theatre,' and while there are many amusing shots, none of the characters has "any resemblance to real people."

1931
Articles and Shorter Writings

88   BAKSKY, ALEXANDER. "Films: Love and sex." *The Nation* 133 (July 8):47–48.
Very short notice of *The Skin Game:* "The utter triteness of the Hollywood love formula is brought home by the unexpected impression of freshness and significance produced by an ordinary and not over-profound film like *The Skin Game.* . . . If only for that it is worth seeing."

89   GRIERSON, JOHN. "The Hitch in Hitchcock." *Everyman* (December 24):722.
Rich and Strange, which is set outside Britain, allows Grierson to "see clearly" Hitchcock's weaknesses. The film shows he is provincial, "a true-born Londoner [who] knows people but not things, situations and episodes, but not events. His sense of space, time, and the other elements of barbarian religion is almost nil." Grierson concludes that Hitchcock concentrates too much on detail, in the process destroying his characters; he also has been sent "off in the wrong direction" by the "highbrows." Reprinted, entry 175.

90   HALL, MORDAUNT. "A British film." *New York Times* (June 28):Sec. 8, p. 3, col. 4.
Negative review of *The Skin Game:* "Hardly a feather in the cap of its director. . . . The voices are poorly recorded and [the performances] emphatically mediocre."

91   HITCHCOCK, ALFRED. "How I choose my heroines." In *Who's Who in Filmland,* edited by Langford Reed and Hetty Spiers. London: Chapman & Hall, pp. xxi–xxiii.
Introductory essay to this dictionary of film personalities. "The chief point I keep in mind when selecting my heroine is that she must be fashioned to please women rather than men, for the reason that women form 3/4 of the average cinema audience." Hitchcock contends that popular stars have "no sex appeal as the phrase is used in the jargon of today," but owe their success to "natural talent and charm" and roles that "appeal to the best in human nature." He goes on to say that most women are idealists and want to see ideal personified in heroines. A "good heroine has vitality" in looks as well as voice, and "real beauty and real youth," as the camera is too close to disguise anything else. Finally, a "heroine must be sensitive to direction . . . the kind of girl I can mold into the heroine of my imagination."
Translated into French (entry 537).

92   LEJEUNE, C[AROLINE] A[LICE]. In *Cinema.* London: Maclehose, pp. 10–13.
In initial essay justifying the omission of the British cinema from the book, Hitchcock is described as "the most ingenious" of filmmakers who lags behind

Anthony Asquith in "fervency and conviction of thought." He is a shrewd craftsman unhampered by tradition, but lacking in "human understanding."

1933
Articles and Shorter Writings

93   HITCHCOCK, ALFRED. "Are stars necessary?" *The Picturegoer* (December 16):13.

Explains the star system and defends its legitimacy. "It is all really a question of supply and demand. . . . There is very good psychological reason for star worship; it fills some inherent need of which I see no reason why the public should be deprived. . . . After all, is not sheer artistic emotion something to be proud of and not ashamed? There is little enough glamour in the drab business world of many of the audience; why then should they be blamed for wanting it in their relaxation?"

94   WATTS, STEPHEN. "Alfred Hitchcock on music in films." *Cinema Quarterly* (Edinburgh) 2, no. 2 (Winter):80–83.

Interview at the time of *Waltzes from Vienna,* a picture Hitchcock was attracted to as an opportunity to try new ideas concerning the relation of music to film. Hitchcock says music in the talkies has become merely slow music for love scenes, but "conventional soft music is the basis of the right idea—expressing the mood of the scene." He indicates he has not made up his mind about its place in dialogue yet, but he is sure that "film music and cutting have a great deal in common—to create the tempo and mood of a scene. . . . The basis of the cinema's appeal is emotional. Music's appeal is to a great extent emotional too. To neglect music is to surrender a chance for progress in filmmaking."

1934
Articles and Shorter Writings

95   DAVY, CHARLES. *"The Man Who Knew Too Much." Spectator* 153 (December 14):924.

Review: "Most of the film is pitched in an oddly subdued key, perhaps because Hitchcock wants to make melodrama seem more realistic by depriving it of rhetoric." Good performances, exciting climax, "but I prefer more meat."

96   ———. *"Waltzes from Vienna." Spectator* 152 (March 9):370.

Negative review: "The recent revival in British pictures has passed [Hitchcock] by . . . slender stuff, many skillful touches, but the story tends to be weak and artificial, largely [because of] the ridiculous tantrums of Johann's feather-witted sweetheart. Gwenn walks off with acting honors."

97   LEJEUNE, C[AROLINE] A.   "Man who knows enough: The new Hitch-
      cock film." *Observer* (December 2):35.
   Claims Hitchcock's reputation as a critic's director has hindered him; the
intellectual subtleties aren't there. *The Man Who Knew Too Much,* however, is a
welcome move toward audience excitement.

98   ———.   "The pictures; directors wanted." *Observer* (March 4):(from
      British Film Institute Library clipping file).
   Written after the appearance of *Waltzes from Vienna,* which shows Hitchcock
"should take his share of the week-in week-out drove of British production. . . . No
one can produce as efficient a script as Hitch. . . . Every scene is annotated with
a line drawing beforehand."

1935
Articles and Shorter Writings

99   FERGUSON, OTIS.   "Mostly clinical." *New Republic* 82 (May 1):341.
   Negative review of *The Man Who Knew Too Much:* Ferguson says film is
characterized by a lack of imagination and has been over-directed in "arch
clumps" that throw everything out of key. Reprinted in *The Film Criticism of Otis
Ferguson* (Philadelphia: Temple University, 1971).

100   HITCHCOCK, ALFRED.   "If I were head of a production company." *The
       Picturegoer* (January 26):15.
   Opens with a remark that he will confine himself to his own experiences;
even so, his "ideal conditions might cost a lot of money." First, plenty of physical
space to build permanent sets and provide plenty of "mental elbow-room." The
American school keeps directors at too much distance before the first day's
shooting. Consequently, Hollywood films are slick, smart, efficient, but lack what
"we call soul." British films, on the other hand, "adhere to a product of
individuality." Therefore, "I would seek out men who are capable of taking charge
of a whole film" and personnel able to "think pictorially." On stars: prefers "the
American plan of flinging them on to the screen as often as possible . . . then
gradually withdrawing them," in order to create demand. Projects that are
otherwise unattractive can be camouflaged with a star. On marketing: film is the
only business "where retailer gauges public taste," so he would alter this by
having investigators report to him on trends for his company. This way he "would
have my fingers on the public pulse, find out what was wanted, and make my
plans accordingly."

101   LORENTZ, PARE.   *"The 39 Steps." McCall's* 12 (September):17.
   Positive review: "well-played, skillfully directed, beautifully photographed.
The real virtue is in the neat story design." Reprinted in *Lorentz on Film* (New
York: Hopkinson & Blake, 1975).

1936

102 ———. *"The Man Who Knew Too Much." Time* 25 (April 8):25–26.
Review: "Cannot be pigeon-holed as a feeble foreign imitation . . . a sense of reality grows on the audience . . . told in abbreviated sequences which gather speed."

103 SENNWALD, ANDRE. *"The 39 Steps." New York Times* (September 14):8.
One of the "most original, literate, entertaining" melodramas of 1935. Reprinted in *American Film Criticism* (New York: Liveright, 1972).

104 ———. *"The 39 Steps:* An appreciation of the new Hitchcock film, with a word on censorship." *New York Times* (September 22):Section 10, p. 5.
Argues that *The 39 Steps* is superior to *The Man Who Knew Too Much.* Discussion of the Hays morality code indicates that the censors removed "damn" two times from the soundtrack of the former film.

105 ———. *"Strauss's Great Waltz." New York Times* (April 8):23.
Review of *Waltzes from Vienna,* released in New York three years after its British premiere: "Discreet and sober little romance . . . telling about the great rivalry between the father and son."

1936
Articles and Shorter Writings

106 FERGUSON, OTIS. "Wings over nothing." *New Republic* 87 (June 24):205.
Positive review of *The Secret Agent,* though its plot, as usual, is "full of holes." Ferguson emphasizes the fine acting and use of character effects, "neither exploiting or restricting." He describes the two set pieces of the mountain death and the folk festival aftermath, and notes the unequaled use of sound, claiming Hitchcock has no rivals in matters of treatment. Reprinted in *The Film Criticism of Otis Ferguson* (Philadelphia: Temple University, 1971).

107 "Hitchcock vs. the censor." *Film Weekly* (May 16):3.
Editorial complaining that Hitchcock should not have spoken in public about the role of the censor's office in the production of *The Secret Agent,* as the film public may feel cheated by its interference. Nonetheless, "our sympathies are with Hitchcock . . . as the censor's code is stupidly inflexible . . . and makes no allowance for artistic license."

*108 HITCHCOCK, ALFRED. "Close your eyes and visualize." *Stage* 13 (July):52–53.
Cited in entry 703.

109 ———. "Why thrillers thrive." *The Picturegoer* (January 18):15.

Human beings need thrills, "or we grow sluggish and jellified; but our civilization has so screened and sheltered us that it isn't practicable to experience sufficient thrills first-hand. So we have to experience them artificially, and the screen is the best medium for this." Hitchcock explains audience participation in cinema (via subjective camera viewpoints) versus spectatorship in theater with two examples: the view in a film from the pilot's seat during a crash—in *Hell's Angels,* and phony columns falling from a stage onto an audience, then stopping just in time. Both provide a thrill but the cinema is "safer" and more pleasing to the public, who remain secure in their "subconscious." Cinematic scenes of danger "are highly beneficial for indigestion, gout, rheumatism, sciatica, and premature middle age." Contrasts the thriller with the "horror" film, which, "to supply the desired emotional jolt, exploits sadism, perversion, bestiality, and deformity." These films attract "a neurotic section of the public . . . and are successful in direct ratio to their power to create unnatural excitement. As a matter of fact, they are bound to fail, because the public is, as a rule, healthy-minded." He concludes that the horror film will die while the thriller thrives.

110 ———, with John K. Newnham. "My screen memories." *Film Weekly* (May 2, 9, 16, 23, 30):16–18, 7, 28–29, 28–29, 27.

Five-part series: The introduction describes Hitchcock as the first "big money director in the country, who has again and again set the pace in ideas and techniques." Part I: "I begin with a nightmare." Hitchcock details the "trials and tribulations" of making *The Pleasure Garden,* Miles Mander's lost makeup box, the confiscated film stock, stolen expense money, extras who thought the project "a huge joke," and Alma Reville's difficulties with Virginia Valli, the star of the film. He also relates his successful extortion of cash from Valli through her friend, though he left to his wife all "the dirty work . . . as women can do these things more discreetly than men."

Part II: "The story beind *Blackmail.*" Relates his "bitter disappointment" when he was told *Blackmail* was to be a silent. He was certain the producers would change their minds and so he imagined while he was making it that he would be asked to add dialogue or remake it as a talkie. This allowed him to "improve on his original ideas." He also discusses the excellent actors, Donald Calthrop and Sara Allgood, as well as Herbert Marshall in *Murder!*

Part III: "My strangest year." Relates his year on contract with Alexander Korda, when he did not make a single picture. Hitchcock also comments on his "ruthless" methods of adapting stories and remarks on films made during the years 1932 to 1935.

Part IV: "Making *The 39 Steps.*" Relates his work on the film, which began two years before it went into production, and his "rough handling" of Madeleine Carroll, which was done for the purpose of making her "more natural."

Part V: "My spies." Relates the difficulties of working with two separate stories on *The Secret Agent;* also compliments the many stars he worked with on it, such as Robert Young, Percy Marmont, and others.

111 *"The Secret Agent." Time* 27 (June 15):56–57.

"Ashenden belongs to the modern school of sleuths whose flexibility makes them plausible . . . 1st rate example of [Hitchcock's] knack of achieving speed by

never hurrying. . . . Most irritating flaw is old-fashioned tag shot." Especially impressed with Gielgud's performance.

112   VAN DOREN, MARK.   "Films." *The Nation* 142 (February 12):203.
   Among general discussion of movies and morals and the value of exciting entertainment, a comment on *The 39 Steps:* "If such a film is shallow I do not mind. . . . Popular devices . . . are the profoundest, as Euripides and Shakespeare knew."

1937
Articles and Shorter Writings

113   "Falstaff in Manhattan: Alfred Hitchcock tests our kitchens and our tastes in melodrama." *New York Times* (September 5):New York Public Library clipping file).
   Describes "the Hitchcock touch," its expansiveness, thoroughness, and focus on story. Author comments on the censoring of *The Man Who Knew Too Much,* prizefights, Twenty-One's iceboxes, and London slang.

114   HITCHCOCK, ALFRED.   "Direction." In *Footnotes to the Film,* edited by Charles Davy. London: Lovat Dickson & Thompson, pp. 3–15.
   "Many people think a film director does all his work in the studio, drilling the actors, making them do what he wants. . . . That is not at all true of my own methods," begins Hitchcock. Hitchcock then proceeds to describe his own approach to a film, which usually begins with a "vague pattern" and a "standard plot." After that comes the need to make changes "for commercial reasons." He writes further about settings, the difficulties of "getting players to adapt themselves to film techniques," and his breaking up of a scene into "bits . . . the screen ought to speak its own language, freshly coined." He also comments on ways to supply emphasis— mostly with the camera as opposed to the actor—and on his avoidance of "obvious camera devices." "I have become more commercially-minded; afraid that anything at all subtle may be missed," he complains. He concludes with a prediction of the "decline of the individual comedian [because] public taste is turning to like comedy and drama all mixed up," and a plea for his own independence. "The art of directing for the commercial market is to know just how far you can go. In many ways I am freer now to do what I want to do than I was a few years ago. I hope in time to have more freedom still—if audiences will give it to me."
   Reprinted in entry 386, and Richard MacCann, *Film: A Montage of Theories* (New York: Dutton, 1966). Abridged version, "My own methods," in *Sight and Sound,* 6, no. 22 (Summer, 1937). Translated into French *Positif,* no. 234 (September 1980), Italian (entry 566), and German (entry 288).

115   ——.   "More cabbages, fewer kings; a believer in the little man." *Kine Weekly* (January 14):30.
   Extols a cartoon in *The Daily Express* titled "The Little Man" and its deserved popularity because the "little bowler-hatted individual reflects the only

genuine life and drama that exist in this country." "The middle classes are the essence of England," but English producers are interested only in the rich and the poor, so the people of the world think the English "live only in cottages or cocktail cabinets. Forgotten are the men who leap into the buses and the girls who pack into the tube. Here are manners and ways flowing easily, speech unaffected, emotions more free, instinct sharper. . . . The higher you run your fingers up the British social scale, the quicker the drama dies, the veneer of civilization is so thick among the rich that individual qualities are killed." Hitchcock concludes with an appeal to producers: "I am fighting against a hard enemy, the film of chromium plating, dress-shirts, cocktails, and Oxford accents, which is continually made with the idea that is how the English live."

116 ———. "Search for the sun: Director Hitchcock lists that and a few other things as his chief trials." *New York Times* (February 7):(New York Public Library clipping file).
Hitchcock writes to dispel the "illusion" of studio life as "unparalleled luxury and little work." He describes a cold London set location out in a field and the misery of waiting for the rain to stop before work can continue.

117 VAN DOREN, MARK. "Alfred Hitchcock." *Nation* 144 (March 13):305–306.
Review of *The Woman Alone (Sabotage)* in which Hitchcock proves once again that "he is the best film director now flourishing." The superlatives continue: brilliant, virtuoso, "nothing but detail and all of it good." Hitchcock "knows exactly what a movie should be and do; so exactly, in fact, that a live wire seems to run backward from any of his films to all the best films one can remember, connecting them with it in a conspiracy to shock us into a special state of consciousness with respect to the art."

118 *"The Woman Alone." Time* 29 (January 18):26.
Review of *Sabotage,* "which lacks the top-notch quality of other films from same producers."

1938
Articles and Shorter Writings

119 CREELMAN, EILEEN. "Picture plays and players: Alfred Hitchcock, English director, to take a look at Hollywood." *New York Sun* (June 15):(New York Public Library clipping file).
Alfred Hitchcock stopping over in New York, eating, dieting, promoting *The Lady Vanishes,* and talking about being a perfectionist and the need for better acting.

1938

120   FERGUSON, OTIS. "War and other places." *New Republic* 96 (October 19):107–108.
Review of *The Lady Vanishes,* a "typical work of genius," put to use "where it will do the least harm to the most effect." Ferguson emphasizes Hitchcock's technical skill, which shows where "the true beauty" of film is. Reprinted in *The Film Criticism of Otis Ferguson* (Philadelphia: Temple University, 1971).

121   *"The Girl Was Young." Time* 31 (February 14):32–33.
Review of *Young and Innocent:* "A melodramatic hodge-podge that lacks the vivid outlines and clear characteristics of previous Hitchcock films. Authentic is the early planting of the twitching eye clue, the rest is boring."

*122   GOODMAN, E. "Mysterious Mr. Hitchcock." *Cinema Progress* (Los Angeles) 3, no. 2:9.
Cited in entry 703.

123   "Hitchcock for Hollywood." *Film Weekly* (July 16):3.
Editorial suggesting that experience of Hollywood's mass methods of production will do Hitchcock good, for while he is Britain's most individualistic director, he has been "unchallenged and allowed to make his pictures exactly as he pleases." Readers complain he "estranges their sympathies" and so has become "wayward and willful," but writer is sure Hitchcock will return as he is "essentially British."

124   HITCHCOCK, ALFRED. "Crime doesn't pay." *Film Weekly* (April 30):9.
Article on screen heavies, who Hitchcock thinks are able to have a long career only if they develop into other kinds of roles. Because they do not get audience sympathy, they can acquire a following only by doing dramatic roles. Discusses many actors and Peter Lorre in particular.

125   ———. "A director's problems." *Living Age* 354 (April):172–174.
Comments on the frustrations of making a film, particularly the costliness of the effort. "It takes a lot of brains and a lot of money to make even a bad picture" thus, the big business aspects have "pretty well gone a long way to destroying it as an art." Describes the creation and motivation of the stabbing murder scene in *Sabotage.* On producers: their job is to criticize, to "watch the film from the point of view of the audience." On writers: "the producer of the future is the writer. . . . The control of the film should come from its original creator." Discusses English versus American films—which have an important "international" outlook, an entertaining fast pace, and happy versus natural endings, which are "fatal from a commercial point of view." But the biggest problem of all is the cinema's universal appeal, which encourages an "appeal to everyone. . . . The moment [filmmakers] become imaginative, they begin to segregate their audience" and lessen the chance of financial success.

126 *"The Lady Vanishes." Time* 32 (November 21):53.
Review: "The ingredients of a Hitchcock picture rarely vary much. . . . Before it goes before the camera, it has been written four times . . . finally by Hitchcock and his wife Alma." Reviewer finds the films sometimes too intricately built to appeal to the "masses."

127 MALONEY, RUSSELL. "Alfred Joseph Hitchcock." *New Yorker* 14 (September 10):28–32.
Portrait-interview: Primarily focused on working methods rather than critical assessments, with some anecdotes from the early days.

128 PERKOFF, LESLIE. "The censor and Sydney Street." *World Film News* (London) 2, no. 12 (March):4–5.
Report of conversations with Hitchcock, who laments the lack of qualified technical personnel in English studios, wondering if London is "too distracting" and noting that much English talent ends up in Hollywood. Hitchcock also comments on documentary films ("I would like to make them"), stars, the importance of local idioms, and his desire to make an anti–capital punishment film, were it not for the British censor.

129 WILLIAMS, J. DANVERS. "The censor wouldn't pass it." *Film Weekly* (November 5):6–7.
Interview: Hitchcock discusses his desire to make films of sociological interest, his "desire to generate excitement in other people," and the censor's blocking of his portrayal of the police in *The Man Who Knew Too Much* and in an unmade film about the general strike of 1926.

1939
Articles and Shorter Writings

130 CHURCHILL, DOUGLAS W. "Water over the Hollywood dam: Alfred Hitchcock and Mr. Breen come to grips." *New York Times* (October 1):Section 9, p. 3.
Discussion of Hays Office production codes in the United States and *Rebecca*.

131 FERGUSON, OTIS. *"Jamaica Inn." New Republic* (September 6):390.
Review of *Jamaica Inn,* which has defects but is "full of honest picture skill." Author is especially impressed with Laughton's performance, the fine tone, the inn, the coaches and night roads, and the "English types" that Hitchcock knows so well. Reprinted in *The Film Criticism of Otis Ferguson* (Philadelphia: Temple University, 1971).

1940

132   HELLMANN, GEOFFREY T.   "Alfred Hitchcock: England's best and biggest director goes to Hollywood." *Life* (November 29):33–43.
Lengthy portrait of the director at home and at work, his "professional economy [vs.] heedless extravagance in personal affairs," his "travel mania," and other eccentric habits. Includes series of posed at-home portraits.

133   HITCHCOCK, ALFRED.   "My ten favorite pictures." *New York Sun* (March 15):(New York Public Library clipping file).
Saturday Night, The Isle of Lost Ships, Scaramouche, Forbidden Fruit, Sentimental Tommy, The Enchanted Cottage, Variety, The Last Command, I Am a Fugitive from a Chain Gang, and *The Gold Rush.*

134   HOELLERING, FRANZ.   "Films." *Nation* 148 (January 7):44.
Positive review of *The Lady Vanishes:* "Precise and without pretensions. . . . A whole arsenal of old tricks is employed, but with authority and irony."

135   *"Jamaica Inn." Time* 34 (October 30):49.
Review: "No Hitchcock, but an authentic Laughton. Scarcely a shot in the whole picture revealed the famed British director's old mastery of cunning camera."

1940
Articles and Shorter Writings

136   FERGUSON, OTIS.   "Hitchcock in Hollywood." *New Republic* 103 (September 16):385–386.
Review of *Foreign Correspondent,* a return for Hitchcock to his true ground— action and suspense, humor and entertainment. Contains "ham elements," but overall, the fascination is in the technical detail, accumulated "like a Dutch painter." Reprinted in *The Film Criticism of Otis Ferguson* (Philadelphia: Temple University, 1971).

137   ——.   "Slight cases of marriage." *New Republic* 102 (April 8):474–475.
Review of *Rebecca,* a film of "wispy and overwrought femininity" that takes advantage of Hitchcock's sense of mystery and timing too late, [the director being] a man of more talent than taste." Reprinted in *The Film Criticism of Otis Ferguson* (Philadelphia: Temple University, 1971).

138   *"Foreign Correspondent." Time* 36 (September 2):31.
Review: "Easily one of the year's finest pictures. [The real] reporter in [the film] is Hitchcock's camera." Some production history.

139 HARTUNG, PHILIP T. "Hitch bites dog." *Commonweal* 32, no. 19 (August 30):390–391.

Positive review of *Foreign Correspondent,* directed in Hitchcock's "usual brilliant style."

140 ———. "Jane Eyre again." *Commonweal* 31, no. 25 (April 12):534.

Positive review of *Rebecca,* "an intelligent cinematization of a love story," which captures "the thrilling feeling of expectancy, suspense, and remembrances."

141 MOSHER, JOHN. "From *Rebecca* to Ellie May." *New Yorker* 16 (March 30):63.

Positive review of *Rebecca,* "a rich, ripe film" limited only by the material, though it manages to be "more stirring than the novel."

142 *"Rebecca." Time* 35 (April 15):96, 98.

Raves for film and a star portrait of Joan Fontaine. Hitchcock "does it all his way. . . . Most exciting scenes come from handicap of wordy book."

143 WANGER, WALTER. "Hitchcock—Hollywood genius: A profile of the great English director by one of America's outstanding producers." *Current History* 52 (December 24):13–14.

Profile promotion of Hitchcock as an "institution" by the producer of his current film, *Foreign Correspondent.* Wagner is enthusiastic about Hitchcock, who is always on time, always reasonable, always sure-footed, and never self-satisfied or over-confident.

1941
Articles and Shorter Writings

144 FERGUSON, OTIS. "Not all to the good." *New Republic* 104 (March 3):306.

Review of *Mr. and Mrs. Smith,* "a story arch enough to be annoying." Wishes Hitchcock would stick to what he does best, that is, incidental rather than central comedy. Reprinted in *The Film Criticism of Otis Ferguson* (Philadelphia: Temple University, 1971).

145 ———. *"Suspicion." New Republic* 105 (November 10):622.

The film is a "sordid" story about "less admirable characters"; unfortunately, the Cary Grant character is so irresistible that the focus falls on Joan Fontaine, who becomes "a pretty negative type." Hitchcock appears to be "thinking more of his box office than his story logic and picture effect." Reprinted in *The Film Criticism of Otis Ferguson* (Philadelphia: Temple, 1971).

1942

146   HARTUNG, PHILIP T.   "Strange heroes." *Commonweal* 35, no. 7 (December 5):1979–1980.
Positive review of *Suspicion*, "as strangely different a film as has ever been made in this country," though the ending is unsatisfactory.

*147   JACOBS, LEWIS.   "Film directors at work: I. Alfred Hitchcock; II. Frank Capra." *Theatre Arts* 25 (March):225–232.
Cited in *New Film Index* (New York: Dutton, 1975).

148   MOSHER, JOHN.   "Ellie May and her set." *New Yorker* 17 (March 1):53.
Review of *Mr. and Mrs. Smith:* "As commonplace a film as one may find anywhere."

149   *"Mr. and Mrs. Smith." Time* (February 17):94.
Review: "Will be a shock to film followers who think that the roly-poly [director] can do no wrong . . . a sly, exasperating chase."

150   *"Suspicion." Time* 38 (November 17):92.
Review: "Good up to the last few minutes [then] falls apart. . . . Thanks to Hitchcock's tricks (letting camera pause disturbingly on people's faces) the film has a texture which can almost be touched."

1942
Articles and Shorter Writings

151   "Hitchcock brews thrillers here." *House and Garden* (August):34–35.
Photographs of Hitchcock's Hollywood home.

152   RYE, P. H.   "Films." *Nation* 154 (May 23):609.
Negative review of *Saboteur:* "Wild without being exciting."

153   *"Saboteur." Time* 39 (May 11):87–88.
Review: "Ingredients are not uncommon, but the master . . . deals them out in a sinister manner that makes them appear so." Reviewer admires understated characters and political intent.

154   "Shadowing Mr. Hitchcock's shadow." *New York Times* (November 1): Section 8, p. 4.
Discussion of shooting locations in New Jersey, Manhattan, and Santa Rosa, California, for *Shadow of a Doubt*. Author describes the set of the Santa Rosa house, and the $5,000 government-set limit on fees for it.

1943
Articles and Shorter Writings

155   HITCHCOCK, ALFRED. "Speaking of pictures." *Life,* December 27 (15):12–13.
Photo-essay: Hitchcock reduces as house plant expands.

*156   JOHNSTON, ALVA. "300-pound prophet comes to Hollywood: Alfred Hitchcock." *September* 215 (May 22):12–13.
Cited in *New Film Index* (New York: Dutton, 1975). "Hitchcock has transformed thrillers into high screen art."

157   L[ARDNER], D[AVID]. "Outline for a monograph." *New Yorker* 18 (January 16):42.
Review of *Shadow of a Doubt:* Notes exceptional similarities in styles of Hitchcock and Orson Welles. Suspense is sustained all right, but acting is of variable quality.

*158   ――――. "The man who weighed too much." *Cue* 12, no. 51 (December 18):10.
Cited in entry 703.

159   *"Shadow of a Doubt." Time* 41 (January 18):98.
Similar to but much better than *Suspicion,* picture "hits few false notes." Author especially admires Wright's performance.

*160   SHERWOOD, ROBERT, and JOAN HARRISON. *"Rebecca."* In *Twenty Best Film Plays,* edited by John Gassner and Dudley Nichols. New York: Crown, pp. 233–292.
Cited in entry 703. Script.

1944
Articles and Shorter Writings

161   AGEE, JAMES. "Films." *Nation* 158 (January 22):108.
Review of *Lifeboat* emphasizing Agee's disappointment. Perhaps Hitchcock has become so "engrossed in the solution of pure problems of technique that he has lost some of his sensitiveness to the purely human aspects." Agee suggests he may have been dominated by Steinbeck. Reprinted in *Agee on Film,* vol. 1 (Boston: Beacon, 1958).

1945

162   CROWTHER, BOSLEY. "On writing for the screen." *New York Times* (February 6):Section 2, p. 3.
Discusses John Steinbeck's credit on *Lifeboat* and a rumor that the author was agitated by what appears on screen. Crowther cites differences between story lines of the novel and the film, and suggests that writers need legal/contractual rights.

163
    MacGOWAN, KENNETH. "The producer explains." *New York Times* (January 23):11.
Letter to the editor regarding critic's review of *Lifeboat,* which described the people of democracy as "craven," while MacGowan, the producer, saw them as heroic.

1945
Articles and Shorter Writings

164   AGEE, JAMES. "Films." *Nation* 161 (November 10):506.
Tepid review of *Spellbound,* which uses "practically none of the movie possibilities of a psychoanalytic story. . . . Impossible to disidentify [Peck and Bergman] from illustrations in a slick-paper magazine serial."

165   CASIRAGHI, UGO. "Hitchcock e Forst: Due interpretazioni di Ribecca." In his *Umanità di Stroheim e altri saggi.* Biblioteca Cinematografica; Prima Serie: Saggi Critici, 1. Milano: Poligono.
A comparison of Hitchcock's *Rebecca and Serenade,* a film directed by Willy Forst. Though author considers *Rebecca* Hitchcock's best film to date, it is not as satisfying as the superior "plastic" experience of *Serenade,* which also has a more developed psychological treatment. Blame is placed on the "lightweight" Du Maurier novel, which poorly serves Hitchcock's "obvious mastery."

166   CROWTHER, BOSLEY. "Hitchcock marches on." *New York Times* (November 11):Section 2, p. 2.
Assesses Hitchcock's work in the United States as not in the same "league" as the British thrillers. *Spellbound* is the first to achieve their excellence and is, in fact, "the most mature" of Hitchcock's melodramas, evidence of "emotional development [and] the ultimate refinement of his art."

167   *"Spellbound." Time* 46 (November 5):98.
Review: "Makes the mistake of trying to give the audience a lesson in psychiatry. . . . Good entertainment, but it does not tingle with Hitchcock's usual sustained suspense." Reviewer especially admires secondary character bits.

1946
Articles and Shorter Writings

168   AGATE, JAMES. "Bravo the British." In *Around Cinemas*. London: Home & Van Thal, pp. 59–61.
Reprint from *The Tatler,* March 5, 1930: A rave review of *Juno and the Paycock,* describing it as "very nearly a masterpiece, which completely justifies the talkies." Also reviews of *Suspicion* and *Jamaica Inn.*

169   AGEE, JAMES. *"Notorious." Nation* 163 (August 17):195.
Review: "Hitchcock has always been as good at domestic psychology as at the thriller." Agee compliments the performances and the film as having "a cool kind of insight and control which suggests a good French novelist."

170   BARBER, JOHN. "Hitchcockney from Hollywood: The old master comes back and tells all." *Leader Magazine* (May 25):18–19.
Profile-interview: Comments on Hitchcock's work habits, *Spellbound,* and audience marketing. Audiences "are entitled to demand everything be presented plain and clear. That's not to say stories must be simple. But they must be simple in the telling."

171   FEARING, FRANKLIN. "The screen discovers psychiatry." *Hollywood Quarterly* 1, no. 2 (January):154–159.
Finds the attempt to explain psychopathology in *Spellbound* weak, especially as the sex life of the patient is not explored at all. The material "is not organically related to the total situation in a manner to illuminate and interpret human character. . . . Rather it is exploited for its spectacular and bizarre" aspects.

172   MCNULTY, FRANK. "A Hitchcock brew and a Franken milk shake." *New Yorker* 22 (August 24):42.
Positive review of *Notorious:* "Excellent melodrama made with superb slickness." McNulty especially admires script.

173   *"Notorious." Time* 48 (August 19):98, 100.
Review: "Top drawer thriller. . . . Thriller expert takes his time about uncorking his thrills." Author expresses concern about ineptness of U.S. agents.

1947
Articles and Shorter Writings

174   "Alfred Hitchcock builds a movie; his eloquent hands create drama just as those of a symphonic conductor create fine music." *Cue* 16, no. 44 (November 1):11.

1948

Short publicity quotes on *The Paradine Case,* including one on his preference for "negative acting."

175   GRIERSON, JOHN. "[Two reviews]." In *Grierson on Documentary,* edited and compiled by Forsyth Hardy. New York: Harcourt, Brace, pp. 71–74.
Reprint of review of *Murder!* (*Clarion,* October 1930): Describes Hitchcock as "the best director [and] the slickest craftsman . . . of unimportant films. . . . Not one has outlasted a couple of twelvemonths." Grierson points out Hitchcock's observation of class differences and his varied use of sound, but concludes that "the excellences are incidental excellences." Also reprint of entry 89. Both reprinted in Daniel Talbot, *Film: An Anthology* (Berkeley: University of California, 1959).

176   HITCHCOCK, ALFRED. "The film thriller." In *Film Review,* 1946–1947, edited by F. Maurice Speed. London: MacDonald, pp. 22–23.
Hitchcock, described in the introduction as "chubby," writes about suspense, a word that "bores" him because of its hackneyed overuse. He prefers "seat-clingers." Admits he too worried about what would happen to the heroine until he became "hardened, and emotionally muscle-bound."

177   LIGHTMAN, HERB A. "Cameraman's director." *American Cinematographer* 28, no. 4:124–125, 151.
Article and interview that emphasizes Hitchcock's reputation behind the camera as "the personification of calm . . . and an especially cooperative co-worker." Lightman summarizes the career, the habit of thorough preparation, "cutting in the camera," and his "revolutionary" approach to photography.

178   MOSDELL, D. *"Notorious." Canadian Forum* 26, no. 314 (March):280.
Negative review finding the film lacking in pace, humor, and excitement.

1948
Articles and Shorter Writings

*179   "Bright star meets top director." *Cue* 17, no. 41 (October 9):17.
Cited in entry 703.

180   CROWTHER, BOSLEY. "A lesson in cinema, further comment on the method used in *Rope.*" *New York Times* (September 5):Section 2, p. 1.
Discussion of *Rope,* and how it was shot with only one set and seemingly continuous action. Crowther claims that Hitchcock in *Rope* has not made use of modern filmmaking techniques; whether he is doing it to save money or to "challenge ingenuity," it is a step backward.

181   HITCHCOCK, ALFRED.   "Production methods compared." *Cine-tech-
nician* 14, no. 75 (November–December):170–174.

The "first rule" of direction is flexibility, writes Hitchcock, as every filming is
a problem and there is no such thing as a "mass solution." "A quick way to
unemployment in the film industry is to have fixed ideas and to be unwilling to
change them." Hitchcock explains that he does not give a "slice of life, because
people can get all the slices of life they want out on the pavement in front of the
cinema and they don't have to pay for them." But the story must not be fantasy,
either.

After the director acquires a good story, the characters and plot are carefully
developed and the shooting script is edited before shooting. If this is not done, the
editorial problems, such as unidentified locations and lapses of time, are handled
afterward in uninteresting ways. But the most glaring omission in a conventional
script is the camera movements. Finally, the director tries to shoot in sequence so
that the audience point of view can be better handled, and the actors have an
easier time with motivation.

First paper of the combined A.C.T.–B.K.S. 1948–1949 lecture season, read
Wednesday, September 22, 1948. Reprinted, "Production methods compared," in
American Cinematographer, 30, no. 5 (1949).

182   McCARTEN, JOHN.   "Murder by Selznick." *New Yorker* 23 (January
10):77–78.

Blames failure of *The Paradine Case* on Selznick's "soapy dialogue," but
performers don't help either; "boring."

183   MOSDELL, D.   *"Rope." Canadian Forum* 28, no. 335 (December):207.

Positive review, admiring of the distance, intelligence, and restraint of the
film.

184   *"The Paradine Case." Time* (January 12):54, 56.

Film has "high polish and intelligence ... but only an inspired talent for
drama and characterization could have saved it from obvious artificiality. No
such talent is in evidence. [Characters] are lifeless participants in a rigid,
theatrical dance."

*185   PARSONS, LOUELLA O.   *"Cosmopolitan's* citation for the best direction
of the month." *Cosmopolitan* 125 (October):12.

Cited in *Dramatic Index,* 1948.

186   YATES, VIRGINIA.   *"Rope* sets a precedent." *American Cinematographer* 29, no. 7:230–231, 246.

Production details of *Rope,* including interview with Joe Valentine, who
discusses conferences, shooting, and especially, lighting difficulties.

Articles and Shorter Writings

187   ANDERSON, LINDSAY. "Alfred Hitchcock." *Sequence* (London Film Club), no. 9 (Autumn):113–124.

Discussion of Hitchcock's career through 1949, pointing out his most congenial subject—suspense and horror among humdrum surroundings. Also discusses the authentic "unglamorized" locales and characters in the British films as well as the "Hitchcock touch"—the ingenious combination of sound and visual effects.

After neatly summarizing these positive creative qualities of the British films, Anderson argues that Hitchcock's move to the United States has not been successful, probably because Selznick embodies the worst in Hollywood: size for its own sake, stars for their own sake, glossy photography, high-toned settings, and lush musical scores. The American films lack conviction: *Suspicion* is a "failure" with a "pure Burbank" British background; *Foreign Correspondent* has "a diffuse and vexatious story;" and *Saboteur* "has the over-emphasis of parody." Only *Shadow of a Doubt* brings back the "realism." From 1945 on the quality most visible is neither excitement nor entertainment, but "technical virtuosity." The tendency to overplay, to inflate, "swells to an obsession" in *Notorious,* along with *The Paradine Case* and *Rope,* the "worst of his career." Particularly offended by the "fake intimacy" of the kissing scene in *Notorious,* Anderson indicates these failures are as much from a lack of writers in America as from a need to compromise for commercial reasons. He concludes that the later "films lack the wholeness of their predecessors," and, while Hitchcock "has never been a serious director," the enlargement his style has undergone in Hollywood has been accompanied by "no equivalent deepening of sensibility of subject matter. . . . [His] attitude towards his characters (and his audience) would seem to have hardened into one of settled contempt."

188   CARDIFF, JACK. "The problems of lighting and photographing *Under Capricorn.*" *American Cinematographer* 30, no. 10 (October):358–359, 382.

The difficulties of shooting *Under Capricorn,* which was done with the same ten-minute-take technique as *Rope.* Details in particular on the pieced-together furniture and the lighting.

189   HITCHCOCK, ALFRED. "Enjoyment of fear." *Good Housekeeping* 128 (February):39, 241–242.

Hitchcock considers fear to be a good thing that many people "pay huge sums of money to experience," mostly in sports. But people also seek it vicariously, in theater and cinema, where they can experience the worst fears without paying the price. "Fear in the cinema is my special field, and I have [split it] into two broad categories—terror and suspense. . . . Terror is induced by surprise, suspense by forewarning." Concludes with discussion of the "invisible cloak" that must protect from harm those characters with whom the audience has identified, and relates the anecdote about *Sabotage* in which he defied the convention.

190 KANE, LAWRENCE. "Shadow world of Alfred Hitchcock." *Theatre Arts* 33 (May):32–40.
Written in the wake of *Rope,* a "mouse of a picture," following "mountainous labors." Kane describes the technical ingenuity evident in Hitchcock's career and concludes that his gift is "essentially a minor one."

191 MCCARTEN, JOHN. "The sun is Alfred's undoing." *New Yorker* 25 (September 10):62.
Under Capricorn is not even up to Hitchcock's "West coast" standard, which is inconsequential next to the British. . . . Looks as if photographed in a bathysphere; insults "Australian, Irish, and the average intelligence."

192 NOBLE, PETER. "An index to the creative work of Alfred Hitchcock." *Special Supplement to Sight and Sound, Index Series,* 18. London: British Film Institute, 42 pp.
Detailed filmography with credits, synopses, excerpts from contemporary reviews, and comments by Noble, including personal correspondence with some key participants. Reprinted (New York: Gordon, 1980).

193 SHERIDAN, BART. "Three and a half minute take . . ." *American Cinematographer* 29, no. 9:305–306, 314.
Detailed description, including frame enlargements, of the parlor scene in *The Paradine Case,* a long take, using an innovative (at the time) "all angle" camera dolly.

194 THEROND, R. M., AND J. C. TACCHELA. "Hitchcock se confie." *Ecran Français* (January 25):3–4.
Article with many quotations from interviews concerning the films. The authors are particularly interested in the new technical approach exemplified in *Rope.*

195 *"Under Capricorn." Time* 54 (September 26):99–100.
"At best, a florid, historical romance." Especially critical of heroine—"a fratricide, a moral coward, and a tosspot."

1950
Articles and Shorter Writings

196 BRADY, DAVID. "Core of the movie—the chase: Physical or psychological, it is the substance of drama from *Hamlet* to boy pursues girl, says Mr. Hitchcock." *New York Times Magazine* (October 29):22–23.
Interview: Hitchcock discusses the chase, his own approach, and favorite other instances including *Birth of a Nation* and *Bicycle Thief.*

1951

197   HARCOURT-SMITH, SIMON.   *"Stage Fright* and Hitchcock." *Sight and Sound* 19, no. 5 (July):207–208.

Hitchcock "luxuriates" in the dream world of Anglo-Saxon cinema, a "world of glorified adolescence . . . where adultery can [never] end in happiness and scenes of advanced sadism apparently do nobody any harm." Now that he is little more than a "purveyor of fashionable entertainment," *Stage Fright* gives the impression of Hitchcock's boredom with "second-rate" material.

198   McCARTEN, JOHN. "Action in the South Pacific." *New Yorker* 25 (March 4):85.

Short notice on *Stage Fright,* a "rambling, disappointing" effort.

199   *"Stage Fright." Time* 55 (March 13):94, 96, 98.

A fine film that does not compete well with Hitchcock's "overpowering reputation." Virtues are not in the humor, or the suspense, but in the performances.

200   TURNER, JOHN B.   "On suspense and other film matters." *Films in Review* 1, no. 3 (April):21–22, 47.

Interview at the release of *Stage Fright.* Turner discusses with Hitchcock his influences, the difference between working in the United States and England (England "has more historic local color"), and his preference for "ordinary everyday" characters, people he "knows."

1951
Articles and Shorter Writings

201   ASTRUC, ALEXANDRE.   "Au-dessous de volcan." *Cahiers du Cinéma* 1, no. 1 (April):29–33.

Essay contrasting the performances of Ingrid Bergman in *Stromboli* (1950) and *Under Capricorn.* Positing the "mystery of the human personality" as the fundamental theme of English cinema, *Under Capricorn* is extolled for its restrained style and emphasis on the silence and dislocation of its main character.

202   FARBER, MANNY.   "Films." *Nation* 173 (July 28):77–78.

Negative review of *Strangers on a Train:* "fun to watch if you check your intelligence at the box office. . . . [Hitchcock] has gone farther on fewer brains than any director since Griffith, cleverly masking his . . . underlying petty and pointless sadism with a honey-smooth patina of sophistication, irony and general glitter."

203   McCARTEN, JOHN.   "Hitchcock serving." *New Yorker* 27 (July 14):61.

Negative review of *Strangers on a Train,* which McCarten says has a shaky plot and foolish theme; however, "though the shots are familiar, there's nothing boring about them."

204   *"Strangers on a Train." Time* 58 (July 16):90–91.
Review: "Implausible, but intriguing and great fun to ride. . . . [Hitchcock] seems most interested in teasing, tricking, and dazzling [the audience] with the masterful touch of the cinematic show off."

1952
Articles and Shorter Writings

205   BAZIN, ANDRÉ. "Faut-il croire en Hitchcock?" *l'Observateur,* no. 88 (January 17):23–24.
Argues that Hitchcock persists in showing more interest in technical effects than in human themes. Bazin expresses "second thoughts" about this viewpoint because of Hitchcock's special ability to write "everything and everywhere." Nonetheless, Hitchcock has failed to understand the movement "toward essentials" and away from "cinema." Bazin is particularly offended at the director's use of parallel editing (saying it became overused long ago) in *Strangers on a Train.* On the meaning of Hitchcock's regular appearances in his films: "At times, this wonderful mechanism grates on one's ears. Through the . . . reassuring sadism of American films, Hitchcock sometimes makes you hear over the victim's screams of fright, the true cry of joy that does not deceive you—his own."
Reprinted, entry 430. Translated into English, entry 684.

206   BLACK, HILDA. "The photography is important to Hitchcock." *American Cinematographer* 33, no. 12 (December):524–525, 546–547, 549.
Article on the filming of *I Confess* and an interview with Robert Burks, the cinematographer. It includes many details concerning sets (mostly on location), lighting (mostly from the floor), makeup (most actors wore none), and the many official, authentic church settings.

207   LUCAS, HANS [JEAN-LUC GODARD]. "Suprématie du sujet." *Cahiers du Cinéma* 2, no. 10:59–61.
Poetic discourse on *Strangers on a Train* and Hitchcock's films in general, containing an understanding of "cinema as the art of contrast" and an appreciation of "the innate sense of comedy possessed by the great filmmakers," including Hitchcock.
Reprinted in *Jean-Luc Godard par Jean-Luc Godard* (Paris: Belford, 1968) and translated into English in *Godard on Godard* (London: Grove, 1972). Translated into German, entry 288.

208   PRATLEY, GERALD. "Alfred Hitchcock's working credo." *Films in Review* 3, no. 10 (December):500–503.
Interview for the Canadian Broadcasting Company while Hitchcock was shooting *I Confess* in Quebec. Lengthy discussion of compromise in filmmaking, responsibility to the producer, and secondarily, responsibility to one's own ideas.

1953

"I would say it is harder to make a film that has both integrity and wide audience appeal than it is to make one that merely satisfies one's own artistic conscience."

1953
Articles and Shorter Writings

209   FARBER, MANNY.   "Films." *Nation* 176 (April 11):314.
Excepting the sensitive performance of Montgomery Clift, Farber considers *I Confess* a "problemless piece of stagecraft"; says Hitchcock "has negated the realism to settle for the effects."

210   *"I Confess." Time* 61 (March 2):92.
Review: "Develops in straightforward fashion with few surprises or plot twists. . . . Fair-to-middling [Hitchcock] unlike his best movies, it is often verbal instead of visual."

211   McCARTEN, JOHN.   "Meandering with Alfred." *New Yorker* 29 (April 4):82–83.
Negative review of *I Confess,* which critic considers slow and windy— "neither a suspense or entertainment." McCarten describes Hitchcock's use of "prolix scripts" as the main change in this "new-day product."

212   SCHÉRER, MAURICE [ERIC ROHMER].   "De trois films et d'une certaine école." *Cahiers du Cinéma* 5, no. 26 (August–September):18–25.
A call for more modern filmmaking, as exemplified in *The River* (1950), *Stromboli* (1950), and *Under Capricorn,* all marked by an increased interest in human social interaction and the material things and events that reveal it. Shérer refers to art and literary history, particularly the development of the nineteenth-century novel, to argue that cinema (particularly the cinema of Hitchcock) is uniquely capable of continuing the ambitions of this history—that is, of revealing the two orders expressed by the oppositions of natural/free, material/spiritual, and desire/heroism. It is the privilege of cinematic art to translate these classical oppositions most directly through the intermediary of the sign.

1954
Articles and Shorter Writings

213   ACKLAND, RODNEY, and ELSPETH GRANT.   "Borstal days with Hitchcock." In their *The Celluloid Mistress or The Custard Pie of Dr. Caligari.* London: Wingate, pp. 24–40.
Reminiscences of a screenwriter at British International Pictures who was assigned to work on *Number Seventeen.* Describes several practical jokes and

Ackland's work with Hitchcock in Hitchcock's home. Because both had wanted to develop a different property, they "got back" at the studio by making the film a send-up, with a heroine who was literally dumb and a final chase scene that was deliberately preposterous.

214   BAUDROT, SYLVETTE. "Hitch, au jour le jour." *Cahiers du Cinéma* 7, no. 39 (October):14–17.
   Diary entries of Baudrot, who did script continuity on *To Catch a Thief*. Anecdotes concerning the shoot, a decision to switch a scene from location to the studio, and Hitchcock's culinary interests. Translated into German, entry 288.

215   BAZIN, ANDRÉ. "Hitchcock contre Hitchcock." *Cahiers du Cinéma* 7, no. 39 (October):25–32.
   Bazin spent two hours interviewing Hitchcock during the filming of *To Catch a Thief* with the intent of getting him to adimit that his films have serious (moral) intent. Hitchcock first reasserts his primary interest, not so much in the stories "as in the means of telling them." There follows an account of *Rear Window* and its technical improvisations, until Bazin suggests that "means" may in fact be another word for "theme." Hitchcock inexplicably replies that he does have a certain interest in the relation between drama and comedy, leading both men to agree that the English films are more "Hitchcockian" because America is lacking in color, and, besides, American films are made for women, who have "sentimental" taste. Hitchcock then refers to his "weakness," which is his sense of responsibility for the producer's money. Bazin suggests a further British/American distinction in that the pursuit of technical means is more enthusiastically supported in Hollywood, but Hitchcock replies that this only gets in his way as he tries to achieve a "quality of imperfection," which Bazin interprets as the British/male/humor part of the films.
   Reprinted, entries 430 and 537. Translated into English, entries 386 and 684. Translated into German, entry 288.

216   CHABROL, CLAUDE. "Histoire d'une interview." *Cahiers du Cinéma* 7, no. 39 (October):39–44.
   Account of a press interview in Hitchcock's Paris hotel room, attended by Chabrol with François Truffaut. The piece largely concerns Chabrol's frustration with the limited response to questions such as "Do you believe in the devil?" and Hitchcock's habit of supplying anecdotal responses to philosophical questions. After the group has been dismissed, the pair decide to return with one last question about the "search for God," which Hitchcock hears as "search for good"; yes, he replies, there is a search for good in his films.
   Translated into German, entry 288.

217   *"Dial M for Murder." Time* 63 (May 24):102.
   Positive review: 3-D "brings alive the theater's intimacy and depth of movement." The review presents a star portrait of Grace Kelly, who is "required to do no more than look beautiful and vulnerable."

1954

218   DOMARCHI, JEAN. "Le chef-d'oeuvre inconnu." *Cahiers du Cinéma* 7, no. 39 (October):33–38.

Analysis of *Under Capricorn,* an unacknowledged masterpiece in its illustration of the "eternal theme of freedom." Domarchi declares the film part of the great modernist tradition of *Finnegans Wake* and *Light in August,* that is, a work of complexity, best appreciated within the context of Hitchcock's work as a whole.

219   GAVIN, ARTHUR. *"Rear Window." American Cinematographer* 35, no. 2 (February):76–78, 97.

Article on the cinematography, including an interview with Robert Burks. Gavin is primarily concerned with the difficulties of shooting everything from Stewart's point of view. He also discusses the "pre-lighting" phase, a ten-day stretch when every apartment on the set was lit for day and for night, then controlled throughout the shooting by separate switches.

220   HITCHCOCK, ALFRED. "Préface." *Cahiers du Cinéma* 7:11–13.

Translation of a preface for a collection of detective short stories. "The detective story is distinguished among fiction genres by its insistence on the normal," begins Hitchcock, who goes on to discuss the formal intrusion (motion on stagnancy, color on dullness) of crime into the otherwise predictable landscape. He describes the great detectives as having "cinematographic perception" and great sensitivity to the details—aural, verbal, visual—of a scene.

221   McCARTEN, JOHN. "Hitchcock confined again." *New Yorker* 30 (August 7):50–51.

Review of *Rear Window*: "Another example of [Hitchcock's] footless ambition to make a movie that stands absolutely still." The movie is foolish and implausible, though Grace Kelly's performance makes it tolerable.

222   "The new pictures." *Time* 64 (August 2):72–73.

Review of *Rear Window*: "Possibly the second most entertaining picture (after *The 39 Steps*) ever made by Alfred Hitchcock." Author admires the "trick" structure and the performances, but disparages the "lapses of taste."

223   SCHÉRER, MAURICE [ERIC ROHMER]. "A qui la faute?" *Cahiers du Cinéma* 7, no. 39 (October):6–10.

Introductory essay to special issue devoted to Hitchcock that asserts the importance of the essays that are included. Schérer assesses Hitchcock as a formalist but thinks the complex resources of the cinema demand such an approach. Though the different pieces may appear superficial or unrealistic, they in fact consistently shed light on the nature of the struggle between human beings, "the ascendancy of one conscience over another, of one soul over another soul."

Reprinted, entry 537.

1955
Articles and Shorter Writings

224 BUCHWALD, ART. "Hitchcock steps off the deadly trains." *New York Herald Tribune* (January 16):Section 4, p. 4.
Interview from St. Moritz. Hitchcock comments on trains, mysteries, and his latest film, *The Trouble with Harry.*

225 CHABROL, CLAUDE. "Les choses sérious." *Cahiers du Cinéma* 8, no. 46 (April):41–43.
Rear Window is presented as proof to the skeptics who doubt the serious nature of Hitchcock's films. Chabrol discerns three themes: the romantic plot, the murder plot, and, something more complex, having to do with the interaction of the courtyard and its inhabitants. He focuses specifically on the death of the dog as a turning point that "crystallizes" the themes.
Translated into English in *Cahiers du Cinéma, the 1950s,* edited by Jim Hillier (Cambridge: Harvard Unviersity Press, 1985).

226 CHABROL, CLAUDE, and FRANÇOIS TRUFFAUT. "Rencontre avec Hitchcock." *Arts,* no. 502 (February 9):5.
Interview: Comments on *I Confess,* production methods, and Hitchcock's preference for the American films ("with a little bit of British humor" in them) over the British.

227 DE LA ROCHE, CATHERINE. "Conversation with Hitchcock." *Sight and Sound* 25, no. 3 (Winter):157–158.
Interview: Discusses melodrama, the combination of realism and fantasy, and the difference of opinion between Hitchcock and certain critics about the existence of metaphysical elements in his work. Much discussion of the production of *To Catch a Thief.*

228 HATCH, ROBERT. "Films." *Nation* 181 (August 20):162.
Negative review of *To Catch a Thief,* lamenting the decline of Hitchcock and the loss of his "British detective fiction" charm.

229 McCARTEN, JOHN. *"To Catch a Thief." New Yorker* 31 (August 13):48–49.
Negative review of an absurd, silly, film: "Grace Kelly does not, presumably, try to act."

230 SARRIS, ANDREW GEORGE. "The trouble with Hitchcock." *Film Culture* 1, no. 5–6 (Winter):31.
Review of *To Catch a Thief* and *The Trouble with Harry* agreeing with John Grierson's assessment (entry 89) that Hitchcock reaches for the "smart" detail

and destroys his characters in the process. John Hayes's "overall comic conceptions, like Hitchcock's, sag badly in the playing." Sarris says the films are parodies, filled with tricks, twists, and gimmicks, which render them minor.

231   *"The Trouble with Harry." Time* 66 (November 7):114, 116.
Review: Harry "is ghouled for more giggles than he is really worth. . . . The comic pace gets so slow, the moviegoer realizes he is, after all, at a funeral."

232   TRUFFAUT, FRANÇOIS, and CLAUDE CHABROL. "Entretien avec Alfred Hitchcock." *Cahiers du Cinéma* 8, no. 44 (February):19–31.
Interview: Hitchcock discusses the shooting of *The Trouble with Harry,* his opinions on various films, and his approach: "It is the manner of treating things which interests me." In answer to a suggestion that "all your films seem to us to have a nearly metaphysical order," he replies, "Oh, that is me. That is my soul getting into the subject. That belongs to me." Further, the Hitchcock film is not a matter of purely technical changes, but a "change that the characters undergo."

1956
Articles and Shorter Writings

233   "Alfred Hitchcock—director, TV or movies, suspense is golden." *Newsweek* 47 (June 11):105–108.
Cover story about Hitchcock's now "bona fide celebrity," a result of his appearances on his television show. The article capsulizes his British career as "art-house" and emphasizes the international aspects of the films, with a full-page map of set locations.

234   BITSCH, CHARLES, and FRANCQIS TRUFFAUT. "Rencontre avec Alfred Hitchcock." *Cahiers du Cinéma* 11, no. 62 (August–September):1–5.
Interview: Discusses *Shadow of a Doubt,* his favorite American film, and *The Wrong Man* as a turning point in his understanding of directing. The article describes the latter film in detail and his approach to it.
Translated into German, entry 288.

235   DEMONSABLON, P[HILIPPE]. "Lexique mythologique pour l'oeuvre de Hitchcock." *Cahiers du Cinéma* 11, no. 62:18–29, 54–55.
Alphabetical listing of recurring things (rings, cats, etc.) and events (falls, shadows, etc.) and the circumstances of their appearance in the range of Hitchcock films. Translated into German, entry 288, and into Portuguese, entry 676.

236 GODARD, JEAN-LUC. "Le chemin des écoliers." *Cahiers du Cinéma* 11, no. 64 (November):40–42.
Review of *The Man Who Knew Too Much* (1955), the most unlikely but also the most realistic of Hitchcock's films because of its depth and documentary character. "This film said to be made by a misogynous director has as its mainspring . . . feminine intuition."
Reprinted in *Jean-Luc Godard par Jean-Luc Godard* (Paris: Belfond, 1968) and translated into English, *Godard on Godard* (London: Grove, 1972).

237 HATCH, ROBERT. "Theatre and films." *Nation* 182 (June 9):498.
Negative review of *The Man Who Knew Too Much* (1955), a slack, "assertively unreal" picture with an obtuse hero and slick Hollywood varnish.

238 HAVEMANN, ERNEST. "We present Alfred Hitchcock." *Theatre Arts* 40, no. 9 (September):27–28, 91–92.
Discussion of Hitchcock's technique and the MacGuffin. Reprinted in *Readers Digest* 69, no. 9 (1956):165–168.

239 "Hitchcock anglais." *Cahiers du Cinéma* 11, no. 62 (August–September): 8–16.
Synopses of the British films through 1938.

*240 "Hitchcock Speaking." *Cosmopolitan* 141 (October):66–67.
Cited in *New Film Index* (New York: Dutton, 1975). "Interview in which he discusses television, scripts, Hollywood."

241 HITCHCOCK, ALFRED. "The woman who knows too much." *McCall's* 83 (March):12, 14.
Humorous relating of his courtship and marriage to Alma Reville.

242 "*The Man Who Knew Too Much.*" *Time* 67 (May 21):114, 116, 119.
Review: Too much Technicolor indulgence, a "normal family" in the "eternal grime of Marrakech." Very critical of the music, which is unfortunately "put up front."

243 McCARTEN, JOHN. "Hitchcock inflated." *New Yorker* 32 (May 26):119–120.
Negative review of *The Man Who Knew Too Much* (1955), which does not

1957

have "the agility of its predecessor." Hitchcock "has agreed to the notion that an American family without wit or enterprise is worth wasting two hours on."

*244   NASH, OGDEN. "What every Christmas turkey should know: How to harass a Hitchcock." *House and Garden* 106:42–43.
     Cited in entry 703. "Poem."

245   ROSS, DON. "Alfred Hitchcock, a very crafty fellow." *New York Herald Tribune* (March 2):Section 2, p. 8.
     Interview about *The Wrong Man:* Hitchcock primarily discusses the details of the Balestrero case.

1957
Books

246   ROHMER, ERIC, and CLAUDE CHABROL. *Hitchcock. Classiques du Cinéma,* vol. 6. Paris: Universitaires, 181 pp.
     The first bio-critical account, which ends with a critique of *The Wrong Man.* The authors work through the material chronologically, beginning with *The Lodger,* where they discern "The Hitchcock touch": innocence suggesting guilt, handcuffs, an "obsession" with Christian iconography, and superior technical skills. *Downhill* is the first "itinerary" film but with the impressive detail of *The Ring,* the director becomes an accomplished auteur.
     The lack of public acceptance of that film, as well as the "Griffithian" straightforwardness of *The Manxman,* illustrates his chronic vulnerability to critical misunderstanding. These films disappointed those looking for the thrills of *The Lodger,* thrills that were already "being interpreted as a sign of superficiality." The two films also introduce the major theme of adultery played out within a romantic triangle.
     Blackmail is the first example of a film with a balance of "commercial elements and creative will." It emphasizes and introduces two important themes: the documenting of a woman's suffering and the transfer of guilt. With *Rich and Strange,* a key film for the authors, the auteur's position clearly becomes one of contempt, which "hides the bitterness of the moralist [though] the least surge of feeling on the part of the characters is enough to transform Hitchcock's contempt to affection."
     Sabotage is another key film, as the classic Conrad novel was freely and brilliantly adapted for the purposes of personal prestige. During this time, Hitchcock "created a second personality that completely corresponded with the idea others had of him [though he was] aware the result would be academic and cold." With *Rebecca,* the Hitchcock touch becomes a true world view, and "spontaneity submits to a system." The two extremes of Hitchcock's thematic concerns become clear: schizophrenia, fascination, amoralism, and domination at one end; knowledge, self, unity, acceptance, confession, and communion at the other.
     Throughout the study, which comprises a significant amount of the opinion concerning Hitchcock's work that subsequently became standard (for instance, doubling in *Shadow of a Doubt*), Chabrol and Rohmer emphasize the director's distanced interest in human nature (his refusal to judge), the persistence of Catholic correlations (psychoanalysis is the "medical equivalent of confession"),

the theme of shared guilt, and the contradictions and influence on his work of his critical reputation. While they posit the presence of homophobia and misogyny in the films, they also gloss over the importance of these for study ("It may close more doors than it opens"), stating, among other things, that "Hitchcock's condemnation of homosexuality is justly based on the impossibility of true homosexual love." Finally, the study is well sprinkled with descriptions of favored technical moments, leading to the authors' concluding assertion that Hitchcock is "one of the greatest inventors of form. . . . In Hitchcock's work, form does not embellish content, it creates it."

Translated into English by Stanley Hochman, *Hitchcock: The First Forty-Four Films* (New York: Ungar, 1979).

Reviews: Decaux, E. *Cinématographe* 56, no. 59 (July–August 1980).

"*Hitchcock: The first forty-four films.*" *Films in Review* 30 (October 1979):493.

Rubenstein, Lenny. *Cineaste* 9, no. 4 (1979):57.

Truffaut, François. "Réalisateur de 45 films en 34 ans: Hitchcock est le plus grand 'inventeur de formes' de l'époque." *Arts,* no. 647 (December 10, 1957):7.

Articles and Shorter Writings

247   FOSTER, FREDERICK.   "Hitch didn't want it arty." *American Cinematographer* (February):84–85, 112–114.

Report of shooting of *The Wrong Man,* including interview with cinematographer Robert Burks, who discusses in detail the use of a new, very small lighting unit, particularly compact and portable, used inside locations as well as to light whole streets.

248   GODARD, JEAN-LUC.   "Le cinéma et son double." *Cahiers du Cinéma* 12, no. 72 (June):35–42.

Lengthy review of *The Wrong Man,* a film about chance, the "twists of destiny," a lesson in mise-en-scène without a wasted shot. Godard discusses the "transference of innocence" as a result of Rose's naivete and the "most subtle emotions," which provoke her guilt and her madness.

Reprinted in *Jean-Luc Godard par Jean-Luc Godard* (Paris: Belfond, 1968). Translated into English in *Godard on Godard* (London: Grove, 1972) and into German in *Godard/Kritiker* (Munich: Hanser, 1971).

249   HATCH, ROBERT.   "Theatre and movies." *Nation* 184 (January 5):27.

Positive review of *The Wrong Man,* an engrossing film though material could have been handled more factually.

250   HITCHCOCK, ALFRED.   "Murder—with English on it: What makes high crime as practiced on the tight little island so special? An old hand at murder at second hand explains its ghostly glamour." *New York Times Magazine* (March 3):17, 42.

Attempts to explain English "contributions to the literature of crime." First, English crimes are "intrinsically more dramatic," and, because they occur less

1958

often, "more is made of them." Also, there are basic sociological differences, such as little space to dispose of bodies, requiring ingenuity, and many people living closely together, a homogeneous people, lacking in "hot-blood" and known for their reserve leading to "more bizarre manifestation."

251   KYROU, ADO. "Mais qui a lancé Alfred? Ou le mythe de Hitchcock." *Lettres Nouvelles* 47:412–421.
    Diatribe concerned with the crude special effects of Hitchcock's work, which Kyrou thinks are poorly integrated into the meaning of the films. Kyrou concludes that Hitchcock should be put in his place as a mediocre director, though he has enough freedom and prestige to do exactly what he wants and make a great film, "but we await it with little hope."

252   MARTIN, PETE. "I call on Alfred Hitchcock." *Saturday Evening Post* 230, no. 4 (July 27):36–37, 71–73.
    Interview: Comments on his recent operations, his nonobsequious approach to television sponsors, gallows (typically British) humor, television versus motion pictures, and his mystery story series.

253   McCARTEN, JOHN. "Hitchcock, documentary style." *New Yorker* 32 (January 5):61–62.
    The Wrong Man is "coldly factual," unbelievable and boring, mostly because the Henry Fonda character is so "simple-minded."

254   *"The Wrong Man." Time* 69 (January 14):52, 54.
    Review: "The dramatic heart tugs and near tragedy" of the original story "have been dissipated." The reviewer criticizes the "completely literal rendering" that misses "the truth."

1958
Articles and Shorter Writings

255   CROWTHER, BOSLEY. "Thrills and such: Mr. Hitchcock is out to match M. Clouzot." *New York Times* (June 1):Section 2, p. 1.
    Comparison of Henri-Georges Clouzot's film *Diabolique* and *Vertigo*.

256   HATCH, ROBERT. *"Vertigo." Nation* 186 (June 14):55.
    Tepid review of *Vertigo,* which Hatch found "a little too difficult," but "the last word in whodunit sophistication."

257   McCARTEN, JOHN. *"Vertigo." New Yorker* 34 (June 7):65.
    Film makes author "slightly carsick"; Hitchcock "has never before indulged in such farfetched nonsense."

*258 PATALAS, ENNO. "Alfred Hitchcock—Melodramatiker oder Metaphysiker?" *Kirche und Film* 11, no. 3 (September):5–8.
Cited in *Bibliographie der deutschen Zeitschriftenliteratur, 1958.*

259 *"Vertigo." Time* 71 (June 16):97–98.
Review: "Another Hitchcock and bull story, in which the mystery is not so much who done it, but who cares."

1959
Articles and Shorter Writings

260 AGEL, HENRI. "Alfred Hitchcock." *Etudes* (Paris), no. 300, 388–393.
Argues from a Christian viewpoint that while Hitchcock is hardly a "spiritual auteur," he should not be reduced to a mere master of suspense, and his detractors show stubbornness in refusing him his due. Agel concludes that Hitchcock "imposes a construction as harmoniously austere as that of the great Christian works . . . [which concern themselves with] the relativity of all things human."

261 BITSCH, CHARLES. "Alfred Hitchcock entre trois films." *Cahiers du Cinéma* 16, no. 92 (February):24–26.
Reporting of a press conference interview. Hitchcock comments on *Vertigo,* French films, and the circles around Jeanne Moreau's eyes ("unthinkable in America"); also makes lengthy comments on television producing.

262 BREAN, HERBERT. "Master of suspense explains his art." *Life* 47 (July 13):72–73.
Interview: Hitchcock comments on weakness of other genres—horror, detective, spy, gangster—and extols suspense and the laughter that relieves it. He also comments on the soon-to-be-released *North by Northwest.*

263 DOMARCHI, JEAN, and JEAN DOUCHET. "Entretien avec Alfred Hitchcock." *Cahiers du Cinéma* 17, no. 102 (December):17–29.
Interview: Hitchcock contrasts *Vertigo,* "a film approaching necrophilia," with *North by Northwest,* which has a lighter spirit and is more an amusing diversion. He also comments on *Saboteur, Secret Agent,* the chase film, the two-dimensional world of cinema—horizontal and vertical—and his disdain for logic ("imagination is more important"); also the use of the zoom and his next project, *Psycho.*

264 DOUCHET, JEAN. "Le troisième clé d'Hitchcock." *Cahiers du Cinéma* 17, no. 99, no. 102 (September, October):44–50; 30–37.
Part I examines suspense as the main "motor" of the Hitchcockian system, which is essentially one of conflict, of literal light and shadow that turns metaphysical, positive and negative, male and female. This struggle is played out

over three realms: the body, the soul, and the spirit. The body is usually deprived or constrained in some way by the plot, thereby forcing the issue of the struggle. The laws of the struggle are those of the occult (the hidden or unexplainable), of logic, and of psychology. Examines the importance of the design of the credit sequences (for example, *Vertigo, I Confess,* and *The Wrong Man*) in indicating the design that the struggle will follow.

Part II refers to the work of Chabrol and Rohmer (entry 246) and its exclusive focus on the laws of logic and psychology, really only the first stage of understanding the films. Illustrates the importance of the physical world in the films and how the unexplainable elements of the plots (for example, Charlie's initial communication with her far-away Uncle Charlie in *Shadow of a Doubt*) allow the intrusion of the world of desire. The result of this intrusion is usually "nightmare and terror." Inversion is shown to be one of the main principles by which the action moves, the indifference of the characters allowing it to occur or to sneak up on them.

The third part of this series is translated into English, entry 787. The ideas are more extensively worked out in book form, entry 337.

265   HENDRICK, KIMMIS. "Film France honors 'the Hitchcock touch'." *Christian Science Monitor* (September 20):(from New York Public Library clipping file).
Account of the "officier dans l'Ordre des Arts et des Lettres" given to Hitchcock.

266   "Hitchcock on sales department psychology: If it's a hardsell, they take it easy." *Variety* (June 17):(from New York Public Library clipping file).
Complaints about the sales help he does not get from the studios, and comments on block booking and *North by Northwest.*

267   HITCHCOCK, ALFRED. "Alfred Hitchcock and his fan mail." *New York Herald Tribune* (January 6):Section 2, p. 14.
Guest column written (or ghost-written) for a "jailed friend," Marie Torre. Hitchcock writes about his hobby, which is reading other people's mail in addition to his own fan mail.

268   ———. "Alfred Hitchcock talking." *Films and Filming* 5, no. 10 (July):7.
Observations during the filming of *North by Northwest.*

269   LEJEUNE, C. A. "Packaged thrills." *Observer* (October 18):(from New York Public Library clipping file).
Review of *North by Northwest,* which is seen to have sophisticated acting but only one scene worth talking about (at the bus stop); all the rest could be had for the price of a glossy, color-plated magazine, "which this much resembles."

270   MERRICK, JAMES W. "Hitchcock regimen for a Psycho." *New York Times* (December 27):Section 2, p. 7.
Hitchcock begins filming *Psycho,* an Inner Sanctum Mystery by Richard Bloch. He is rumored to have bought up all copies of the book, and secrecy surrounds the title of picture.

271   MOULLET, LUC. "Hitchcock: La nouvelle vague c'est moi!" *Arts,* no. 745:7.
Interview: Comments on *North by Northwest* and *Saboteur,* Robert Burks, and the upcoming *Psycho.*

272   *"North by Northwest." Time* 74 (August 17):78–79.
Review: "Wears its implausibilities lightly." The film is characterized as being highly enjoyable, but full of "further extremes."

273   PETT, JOHN. "Improving on the formula." *Films and Filming* 6, no. 3 (December):9–10, 32.
Second of two parts, see next entry. Continuing film-by-film commentary beginning with *Secret Agent.* British thrillers are assessed positively, but the American films after *Foreign Correspondent* show infection by "Hollywood slickness." By 1945, a "distinct change" is evident—slower pace, more expensive and opulent settings, and less effective editing. Only *Strangers on a Train, The Trouble with Harry,* and *The Wrong Man* emerge as successes from this "glossy period [which] paralysed Hitchcock's creativeness."

274   ———. "A master of suspense." *Films and Filming* 6, no. 2 (November):9–10, 33–34.
First of two parts. With the exception of *The Lodger* and *The Ring,* all the silent films are dismissed as having little "to interest us today." Likewise, *Juno and the Paycock*'s effect is made "because of the performances and the play itself, rather than for any cinematic technique." Plot analysis reveals the films beginning with *The Man Who Knew Too Much* (1934) as Hitchcock "at his best." Pett relates the strengths of the British thrillers to the changing values of the time, suggesting "it is possible these films could only have been made as a natural development of the violent undertones of the thirties."

1960
Books

275   AMENGUAL, BARTHEMY, and RAYMOND BORDE. *Alfred Hitchcock.* Premier Plan, 7. Lyon: Serdoc, 41 pp.
Two separate essays. The first, by Borde, discusses Hitchcock's conservatism, the creation of social environment in the films, and his extremely judicious career, which provided him with great confidence in visual imagery. Borde

1960

reviews most of the criticism and interviews up to 1960 and concludes that the films are "technique in the void," finding Chabrol and Rohmer's suggestion of a moral center "a delirium of interpretation." The second essay is a shorter version of another piece by Amengual (entry 374).

*276   BIANCHI, PETRO, and CLAUDIO G. FAVA. *Personale di Alfred Hitchcock. Quaderni del Cineforum,* 1. Genova: Uffizio Mezzi Audiovisi del Columbianum.
Cited in entry 703.

Articles and Shorter Writings

277   CALLENBACH, ERNEST. *"Psycho." Film Quarterly* 14, no. 1 (Fall):47–49.
Positive review of this seemingly trivial but very serious film.

278   GUILD, HAZEL. "Films lost action when sound track came in, asserts Alfred Hitchcock." *Variety* (October 26):New York Public Library clipping file.
Comments from Hitchcock on sound, and television in Germany, where he was traveling to promote *Psycho.*

279   HATCH, ROBERT. "Films." *Nation* 191 (July 2):18–19.
Negative review of *Psycho,* by which Hatch is "offended and disgusted."

280   HITCHCOCK, ALFRED. "My recipe for murder: Pictures by Eugene Cook." *Coronet* 48 (September):49–61.
Titillating pictures (publicity shots for *Psycho*) and commentary: "Here, instead of her dictation pad, she is reaching for the bare back of John Gavin." Concerning "the culprit and the witness . . . which is which, that is the question."

281   ———. "Pourquoi j'ai peur la nuit." *Arts,* no. 777 (June 1):1, 7.
Preface from a French edition of the suspense stories (*Histoires abominables de Hitchcock,* Paris: Laffont). Comments on his own fears, his introduction to Edgar Allan Poe at sixteen years of age, the impression Poe's "sad life" made on him, his own resemblance to Poe, surrealism, and the importance of identification in suspense.

282   KAPLAN, NELLY. "Alfred Hitchcock: Je suis une légende." *Lettres Française* 847 (October 27):7.
Interview in Paris: Comments on the international popularity of *Psycho,* problems of satisfying the audience, and views on women.

283   MARDORE, MICHEL. "Hitch au miroir." *Positif,* no. 32; no. 33 (February, April):35–39; 32–39.
Anti-Hitchcock diatribe, which focuses on the author's assessment of the weaknesses of other French critics' opinions. The writings of Maurice Schérer, for instance, are characterized as exhibiting "mental fatigue."

284   McCARTEN, JOHN. "Merriment to murder." *New Yorker* 36 (June 25):70.
Negative review of *Psycho,* "rather heavy-handed."

285   WOOD, ROBIN. "Psychoanalyse de *Psycho.*" *Cahiers du Cinéma* 19, no. 113 (November):1–6.
Analysis of film as the battle of "normal" Marion, who seeks freedom, and "mad" Norman, a bird of prey who destroys freedom.

1961
Articles and Shorter Writings

286   HITCHCOCK, ALFRED. "Violence: An ever-handy reference manual to the selection, dispatchment and disposal, with taste, of a likely victim." *Esquire* 56 (July):107–112.
Series of posed photographs of Hitchcock with models and satirical captions.

287   KUHLBRODT, DIETRICH. "Porträt Alfred Hitchcock." *Filmkritik* 5, no. 9:428–432.
Stills, filmography, short overview of work.

1962
Books

288   *Alfred Hitchcock: Eine Bildchronik.* Edited by H[ans] P[eter] Manz. Zürich: Sancoussi, 98 pp.
Collection of essays, including an introductory portrait by Manz and translations of interviews by Godard (entry 207), Baudrot (entry 214), Bazin (entry 215), Truffaut/Bitsch (entry 234), and Demonsablon (entry 235). Also undated radio interview done at Paramount-Starkfilm in Zurich, titled "Alfred Hitchcock in Sankt Moritz."

*289   SIERENS, FRANS. *Alfred Hitchcock.* Zwarte Beertje, 688. Utrecht: Bruna & Zoon, 192 pp.
Cited in entry 703. In Dutch.

Articles and Shorter Writings

290   ALLOMBERT, GUY. "Alfred Hitchcock: Si je devenais amateur je tournerais une vie de merlan!" *Cinema Pratique* 38 (February 2):2–5.
    Interview: All questions concern amateur filmmaking, in which Hitchcock has little interest. Most replies focus on documentary or home movies.

291   ALPERT, HOLLIS. "Hitchcock as humorist." In *The Dreams and the Dreamers.* New York: Macmillan, pp. 168–177.
    Hollis maintains that Hitchcock has not won a directorial Academy Award because he is not "serious" enough. In fact, it is impossible for him to be serious; he is at his best with the light suspense material for which he is justifiably famous. "Search for depths in Hitchcock, and you will find only clues to his own personality."

292   CAMERON, IAN. "Hitchcock and the mechanisms of suspense." *Movie*, no. 3 (October):4–7.
    Description of the Hitchcock method as executed in *The Man Who Knew Too Much* (1955): the careful buildup via curiosity, suspicion, apprehension, and worry. The scene of Ben's drugging of Jill is used to illustrate this suspense method as applied to intimate relations ("When is Jill going to break down?"), a scene that puts the audience in the position of being uncomfortable with everything that follows.
    First of two parts, see entry 298. Reprinted in *Movie Reader* (New York: Praeger, 1972).

293   HIGHAM, CHARLES. "Hitchcock's world." *Film Quarterly* 16, no. 2 (Winter):3–16.
    Brief opinions on all the films and Hitchcock's worldview: one of "heartless artificiality." The mechanics of creating terror and amusement are all Hitchcock understands; "the portrayal of physical or intellectual passion is beyond him. . . . He scrawls his signature on the world's lavatory walls without restraint."

294   "Hitchcock on style." *Cinema* (Beverly Hills) 1, no. 5 (August–September):4–8, 34–35.
    Interview: Hitchcock discusses his own production design work, most recently on *North by Northwest,* and his concept of action. Primarily explications of different specific shots from *Psycho,* the upcoming *The Birds,* and *Rear Window.* Includes two pages of production drawings from *The Birds.*

1963
Books

295   BOGDANOVICH, PETER.   *The Cinema of Alfred Hitchcock.* New York: Museum of Modern Art Film Library, 48 pp.

Brief introduction and filmography interspersed with interviews done over several days in February 1963. The author includes comments from Hitchcock on "pure cinema," actors, and working methods. Hitchcock offers some different insights in these interviews than those offered in Truffaut's much longer interview cycle done six months later. Bogdanovich strongly asserts the idea that the American films are in every way "more artful and serious" than the British films and blames critics for the failure of the more serious films like *I Confess.* He discusses the change in Hitchcock's scripting methods between Britain and the United States. Small excerpt reprinted in entry 386.

Articles and Shorter Writings

296   BELZ, CARL.   *"The Birds." Film Culture,* no. 31 (Winter):51–53.

Following a short overview of surrealism, *The Birds* is fit into the tradition because of its conventional setting and ambiguous events and characters.

297   BOGDANOVICH, PETER.   *"The Birds." Film Culture* 28 (Spring):69–70.

Coincident with a major Hitchcock retrospective at the Museum of Modern Art and Bogdanovich's accompanying monograph (entry 295); author finds the film "indescribable" and pleads for recognition of Hitchcock as "consummate artist."

298   CAMERON, IAN.   "Hitchcock: Suspense and meaning." *Movie,* no. 6 (January):8–12.

Essay on themes in *The Man Who Knew Too Much* (1955) that emphasizes linkages—in song, color, composition—and repetition in event and set elements. Cameron argues that the "whole film is an interruption in the lives of a family." He concludes that the film exposes the ways the family is vulnerable: through their son, their dissatisfaction, and most importantly, through the husband's desire to dominate the wife.

Second of two parts, see entry 292. Reprinted in *Movie Reader* (New York: Praeger, 1972).

299   CAMERON, IAN, and V. F. PERKINS.   "Hitchcock." *Movie,* no. 6 (January):4–6.

Interview primarily on *The Birds* and *Psycho.* On music: "When you put music to film it's really sound, it isn't music per se. I mean there's an abstract approach." Hitchcock discusses thematic relationships—Melanie first referred to

1963

in a "gilded cage" and later attacked in a cage—which provoke the interviewers to comment that he expects "quite a lot" of his audience. "For those who want it," he replies, "I don't think films should be looked at once." He also discusses play adaptation, working with writers and stars ("They don't help a picture anymore"), and global audiences.

300   CURTIS, JEAN-LOUIS. "La pature de ces oiseaux." *Nouvelle Revue Française* 11, no. 131 (November):898–901.
    The Birds reviewed in the context of contemporary fears of the end of the world and the sinister potential of animals, crowding, and silence.

301   FALLACI, ORIANA. "Alfred Hitchcock: Mr. Chastity." In *The Egotists: Sixteen Surprising Interviews.* Chicago: Regnery, pp. 239–256.
    Interview: Fallaci complains she has already read the anecotes about pleasing the audience, morality, sex, women, his own fears, suspense, and actors with which Hitchcock obliged her. When she provokes him with a hypothetical question, however, he does leave her with some unusual parting words, reminding her that she, not he, is "the one who's in a dramatic situation . . . because you have to write an article about me, and you don't know anything about me."

302   HOUSTON, PENELOPE. "The figure in the carpet." *Sight and Sound* 32 (Autumn):159–165.
    Career assessment in light of the current conflicting critical opinions of Hitchcock as an artist of elaborate metaphysical themes, and Hitchcock as superficial entertainer. Houston wonders what really interests the director, and concludes not character, not professional crime, not the soul, but the "twists and turns of the mind." The "figures in the carpet" are concrete and "stand in the way of abstractions, metaphysical or otherwise."

303   KAUFFMAN, STANLEY. "The fat boy." *New Republic* 148 (April 13):34–35.
    Review of *The Birds* that castigates Hitchcock in general: "a successful cynic . . . [who has] dallied rather than dealt with political affairs, social relations, psychological problems." *The Birds* is seen as lacking even slick magazine sophistication and has stupid dialogue and tired direction. Reprinted in Kauffman, *A World on Film* (New York: Harper & Row, 1966).

304   MacDONALD, DWIGHT. "Mostly on bird watching." *Esquire* 60 (October):36.
    The Birds described as "a negative print": the color is fake and the characters are idiotic. Author uses the film as an example of the absurdity of Andrew Sarris's ranking of "Pantheon directors." Reprinted in *A Library of Film Criticism* (New York: Ungar, 1974) and in *Dwight MacDonald on the Movies* (Englewood Cliffs, N.J.: Prentice-Hall, 1964).

305   MAYERSBERG, PAUL. "The beak and the eye." *The Listener and BBC Television Review* 70, no. 1798 (September 12):378–380.

Essay review emphasizing thematic coherence in *The Birds:* the uselessness of tragedy borne by complacency and Hitchcock's ability to pass this sense of responsibility on to the spectator. Reprinted in *Film as Film,* edited by Joy Boyum and Adrienne Scott (Boston: Allyn & Bacon, 1971).

306   PERKINS, V. F. *"Rope."* Movie, no. 7 (February):11–13.

Essay on the technique of *Rope* as it illuminates the emotions and styles of the characters. Perkins explicates a triangle motif among Rupert (the planner), Brandon (the administrator), and Philip (the executor). He concludes that the film "makes us feel the power of evil . . . where simple facts cease to provide significant explanation." Reprinted in *Movie Reader* (New York: Praeger, 1972).

307   RHODE, ERIC. "Hitchcock's Art." *Encounter* 21, no. 4 (October):39–44.

Review of *The Birds* set in the context of Hitchcock's vaunted reputation among the tradition-exploding French new wave. Rhode is skeptical of their attribution of philosophical intention but decides that Hitchcock's "infectious enthusiasm" makes all his films special. "In *The Birds,* and most movingly, he is able on at least three occasions to catch our breath at the sheer delight of his filmmaking. It is remarkable how Hitchcock has worked for 40 years within the industry and yet been able to succeed on his own terms; how his exuberance and inventiveness have grown rather than diminished."

308   SHAYON, ROBERT LEWIS. "Screens and dreams." *Saturday Review* 46 (April 20):44.

Report of luncheon where Hitchcock discussed a vision of a future "mass entertainment" in which the audience would be "hypnotized participants in dramatic action." Also includes comments from Hitchcock on television versus motion pictures.

309   TABÉS, RENÉ. "Entretien avec Alfred Hitchcock." *La Technique Cinématographique* 239:58.

Press conference in Paris for *The Birds.* Hitchcock comments on the production and the film's themes, François Truffaut and *Jules and Jim,* a "film not entirely satisfying in form."

1964
Books

*310   DEMONSABLON, PHILIPPE. *Alfred Hitchcock. Collection Cinéma d'Aujourd'hui.* Paris.

Cited in Manz, *Internationale Filmbibliographie,* 1952–1962. "Presentation par Ph.D: Choix de textes et Propos de A. H. Extraits de découpages et scénarios, témoignages, filmographie, etc."

1964

Articles and Shorter Writings

*311   EVERSCHOR, FRANZ. "Cocktail für eine Leiche: The rope." In *Film-analysen, 2: Hrsg. v. Franz Everschor.* Düsseldorf: Altenberg, pp. 25–58. Cited in entry 703. On *Rope.*

312   "Film clips." *Sight and Sound* 33 (Autumn):204.
Hitchcock's story about the development of the script with Ben Hecht, and the uranium MacGuffin in *Notorious.*

313   LEDUC, JACQUES.   "Hitchcock, féminin pluriel." *Objectif* 64, no. 27 (April–May):17–21.
Description of the "Hitchcock woman"—graceful, beautiful, and giving of all her heart to the project at hand. Her presence pleases the intelligence before it pleases the heart. The Hitchcock woman is the pivot of all his ideas of guilt and innocence and confession, and so represents the most "troubling paradox" in his work, the ambiguity of form and content.

314   PECHTER, WILLIAM S.   "The director vanishes." *Moviegoer,* no. 2 (Summer):37–50.
Impressionistic overview, primarily focused on the American films of the 1950s and 1960s, which Pechter judges are not of the same quality as the British films. Hitchcock has lost "contact with his audience," and his identity has "disappeared into his public image." *North by Northwest* is the "most thorough-going exercise in self-contempt in the history of the cinema," *Vertigo* "actually means nothing," and so on.

315   TRUFFAUT, FRANÇOIS.   "Skeleton keys." *Film Culture,* no. 32 (Spring):63–67.
Overview of the American films. Truffaut takes issue with André Bazin's suggestion (entry 215) that Hitchcock is unaware of some of the meaning in his films. He argues that Hitchcock is more aware than other film "geniuses" but "less great than they because of the total absence in his works of that which Gide called 'the share of God.'" Provides examples from all the films, especially *Shadow of a Doubt,* to illustrate the themes of identity, the double, couples, and domination.
Reprinted in *Cahiers du Cinéma in English,* no. 2 (1966). Translation of "Un trousseau de fausses clés" in *Cahiers du Cinéma* 7, no. 39 (October 1954).

316   WEAVER, JOHN D.   "The man behind the body." *Holiday* 36 (September):85–86, 88–90.
Description of Hitchcock's typical day, emphasizing his need for routine, quiet, and order.

1965
Books

317   PERRY, GEORGE. *The Films of Alfred Hitchcock*. New York/London: Dutton/Studio Vista, 160 pp.
Popular, chronological overview, heavily illustrated.

318   WOOD, ROBIN. *Hitchcock's Films*. London/New York: Tantivy Press in association with Zwemmer/Barnes, 93 pp.
Analysis of the work through *Marnie* that focuses specific chapters on selected American films. Wood argues that the chief obstacle to appreciating the films is Hitchcock's own attitude toward them, which discounts before the fact the reasons Wood puts forth for taking Hitchcock "seriously": unity across the films, thematic depth similar to that of Shakespeare, and the essentially disturbing quality of the films.
Wood delineates the use of identification techniques, or what Hitchcock calls "pure cinema," which make the audience not only see but experience. The creation of suspense, one of the major methods of identification, opens up the main themes. Wood identifies these as the "therapeutic theme," whereby the audience as well as the character experiences the quandary that induces the therapy, and the theme of man-woman relationships, never merely "arbitrary love interest, but essential subject matter." These themes are supported by a "complex and disconcerting moral sense in which good and evil are seen to be so interwoven as to be virtually inseparable," as well as Hitchcock's "ability to make us aware . . . of the impurity of our own desires."
Plot and character analysis of *Strangers on a Train* focuses on Guy, his shared guilt, search for identity, and indulgence of his weaknesses. Humor in the film is judged a manifestation of "artistic impersonality." *Rear Window* is "the first masterpiece" and an attempt to "imprison" the audience within "a single consciousness." *Vertigo* is "one of the 4 or 5 great masterpieces of the cinema" that "shows the cinema can be treated with respect equal to other art forms." Formal analysis of its visual elements illustrates that it is organized entirely around its themes. *North by Northwest* is "immensely superior" to the British thrillers it resembles. *Psycho* is about the "dominance of the past over the present," the persistence of parent-child relationships, and "one of the key works of our age." A sequential story analysis of *The Birds* reveals its "organic" circular forms in support of the themes. *Marnie* continues the exploration of the past and presents a case study of conquering the past through memory, Marnie being "a curable Norman." Helping to cure her is Mark, a new Hitchcockian hero—a strong man who is free of the past.
Second edition was slightly revised with the addition of a chapter on *Torn Curtain* (London/New York: Zwemmer/Barnes, 1969).
Review: Weiskind, Ron. *Mise-en-Scene,* no. 1 (1976):7.
Also printed in large format (New York: Castle, 1969). Chapter on *Strangers on a Train* reprinted in entry 771. Third edition, entry 476. Completely revised, entry 852. Translated into Spanish (Mexico: Era, 1968).

1966

Articles and Shorter Writings

319   CAMERON, IAN, and RICHARD JEFFERY. "The universal Hitchcock." *Movie*, no. 12 (Spring):21–24.
The Birds and *Marnie* are stories of the obliteration of the "internal threat" to the self. Formal analysis explicates Hitchcock's ability to attack and affect the audience by associating it with the characters' conflicts. Mitch, and even more, Mark, are presented as new, stronger identification figures who get a "grip" on their dream world and help the other characters. Reprinted in entry 771 and in *Movie Reader* (New York: Praeger, 1972).

320   HITCHCOCK, ALFRED. "Foreward." In *The Filmgoer's Companion*, edited by Leslie Halliwell. London: MacGibbon and Kee, p. 7.
Formal congratulations to this "much-needed enterprise," a dictionary of films and personalities.

*321   MONTY, IB. "Hitchcock i 30'erne." *Kosmorama* 74:138–149.
Cited in *Filmlitteraturen i Danmark 1964–1973* (Danmards Bibliotekssole, 1975).

1966
Books

*322   KOCH, VLADIMIR. *Alfred Hitchcock.* Jugoslovanska Kinoteka, 7. Ljubljane: Jugoslovanska Kinoteka, 108 pp.
Cited in entry 703. In Serbo-Croatian.

Articles and Shorter Writings

323   "Alfred Hitchcock and the dying art." *Film* (BFFS), no. 46 (Summer):9–15.
Interview with Hitchcock recorded during a visit to the Cambridge Film Society. Hitchcock comments on sound and silent film, his independence, actors and stars ("always a compromise"), audiences, television, *Shadow of a Doubt*, *Vertigo*, and *Torn Curtain*. Reprinted in *Film*, no. 79 (1979).

324   ANGELL, GEORGE. "The time of my life." *BBC Home Service*, July 30 (recorded):Tape no. TLO 634/725.
Transcript of a fifty-minute interview with Hitchcock for a BBC program aired August 28, 1966. He discusses the "tremendous influence" of *The Last Laugh* on him and the story of *The Lodger*, which was shelved for two months— "there you see the thin line between failure and success." Other details cover the

advent of sound, the "cycles" of his career, blond leading actresses, the famous writers he knows, actors, and renditions of many well-known anecdotes.

*325   BODELSEN, ANDERS. "De Skyldige uskyldige." *Vindrosen* 2: 88–97.
Cited in *Filmlitteraturen i Danmark 1964–1973* (Danmards Bibliotekssole, 1975).

326   BOND, KIRK. "The other Alfred Hitchcock." *Film Culture,* no. 41 (Summer):30–35.
Argues that the pre-1934 films are superior to later Hitchcock, being a combination of the qualities of Griffith and Stroheim, subtle to a fault. Bond discusses closely *The Pleasure Garden, The Ring, The Farmer's Wife,* and *Rich and Strange,* concluding that Hitchcock's films lost their "imaginative quiet" as he moved toward the overdone gothic romances.

327   CHABROL, CLAUDE. "Hitchcock confronts evil." *Cahiers du Cinéma in English,* no. 2:67–71.
Traces the theme of evil, which the greater resources of the cinema have allowed Hitchcock to explore with more success than "Balzac, Dostoevsky, and Bernanos." At one extreme, evil is broadly considered "the unhappiness of beings" caused by an inability of the characters "to accept not one's destiny, but one's personality." The responsibility this "exorcism and principal condition of man's final triumph" implies is refused by those characters who "have given up," who refuse to confess and accept guilt. Chabrol concludes that "Hitchcock conserves in all his characters their deep-seated ambiguity. There is not one for whom he does not feel some affection." Translation from the French, *Cahiers du Cinéma* 7, no. 39 (October 1954).

328   CRAWLEY, BUDGE, FLETCHER MARKLE, and GERALD PRATLEY. "Hitch: I wish I didn't have to shoot the picture." *Take One* 1, no. 1:14–17.
Hitchcock discusses the challenge of avoiding cliché–especially with today's sophisticated audience, improvisation, preplanning, the handling of sex and color in *Torn Curtain,* and his method of working with a writer, who "becomes part maker of the picture." Reprinted, entry 386.

*329   FARBER, HELMUT. "Theorie und Praxis: Versuch über Hitchcock." *Filmkritik* 8, no. 8:463–474.
Cited in entry 703.

330   HITCHCOCK, ALFRED. "Film directors on film." *Arts in Society* 4, no. 1:65–68.
Hitchcock responded to the editor's query with "an edited copy of an article he wrote for *Encyclopedia Britannica* on the motion picture." The essay on style capsulizes differing national and directorial styles, lamenting the introduction of

1966

dialogue and "the loss of the art of reproducing life entirely in pictures." Compares directing to music conducting and emphasizes the importance of the face of the actor, concluding that the "chief requisite for a good screen actor is to do nothing well."

331 ———. "The real me (the thin one)." *Daily Express* (August 9):(from British Film Institute clipping file).
Text of a luncheon speech to celebrate his fiftieth film, *Torn Curtain*. Includes anecdotes concerning his girth, actors, and television.

*332 ———. "Redigeret af Mortem Piil og Jørgen Stegelmann." *Kosmorama* 77:50–54.
Cited in *Filmlitteraturen i Danmark 1964–1973* (Danmards Bibliotekssole, 1975).

333 LORING, CHARLES. "Filming *Torn Curtain* by reflected light." *American Cinematographer* (October):680–683, 706, 707.
Details of locations and shooting, done entirely in southern California. Loring emphasizes the innovative use of large-size reflectors, particulars of each setup, and Hitchcock's inclination toward "selective" soft focus for a "more realistic effect."

334 RUSSELL, LEE [PETER WOLLEN]. "Alfred Hitchcock." *New Left Review,* no. 35 (January-February):89–92.
Overview intended to begin the "important task of popularization" of the critical debate over Hitchcock. Russell makes reference to the literature (Rohmer and Chabrol, Douchet, and Wood) and reprises the major themes: (1) common and exchanged guilt; (2) chaos underlying order; (3) temptation, obsession, fascination, and vertigo; (4) uncertain identity and the search for identity; and (5) the mother.

335 SARRIS, ANDREW. *"Torn Curtain." Village Voice* 11 (September 1):19.
Positive review, admiring film's commentary on Americans of the 1960s. "Newman is the organization man par excellence, and Andrews is the perfect company wife—smug, superior."

336 SONBERT, WARREN "The other Alfred Hitchcock: Master of morality." *Film Culture,* no. 41 (Summer):35–38.
Case made for Hitchcock as "America's finest director," who is "cynical yet moralistic . . . and exploits the materialism and pettiness" of his audience. Sonbert describes the subjective camera as "another personality" in the films, a brilliant technique that assures identification and allows an "immense contempt" to erupt from Hitchcock's major works.

1967
Books

337 DOUCHET, JEAN. *Alfred Hitchcock.* Collection L'Herne Cinéma, vol.
1. Paris: Herne, 168 pp.

A theory categorizing the several qualities of "suspense" in the Hitchcockian concept. The final chapter is rewritten in the 1985 edition, titled *Hitchcock,* to include the themes of *Frenzy* and *Family Plot.*

"Esoteric suspense" occurs at several levels: first, the "occult" or hidden level, which involves "the battle of shadow and light," the internal logic of the piece, and the "throes" of the struggle between the conscious and the unconscious; second, the logical, which involves cause and effect (in the plot), and the logic of psychology; third, the quotidian, which involves the classic aspects of suspense, particularly of a character caught between two menacing forces. "Aesthetic suspense" is Hitchcock's "unique subject and the object of his work, the anxiety which fertilizes the imagination and the imagination which feeds the anxiety."

Using detailed analyses of *Psycho* and *North by Northwest,* Douchet presents Hitchcock as an artist who addresses all possible givens in the construction of his films, "from pure sensation to pure intelligence," with the sole object of communication—of making the film that the audience sees, the film that he sees. By making the audience identify so intensely, he insists they respond emotionally to the suspense imposed by him.

Finally, "the suspense of creation" is a philosophical underpinning of the other types of suspense, which involves a concept of the individual's escape from "the powerful hold of impotence, the sole source of suspense, [which] demands an utmost will to power." In the case of Hitchcock, this leap is made via his position as film director, and resident "all-powerful Father." Through his own "will to power" as a filmmaker, he supplements the "weak will" of his characters, who are typically unable to stop from holding out for the "vegetative life," of aspiring to return to the womb. In this way Hitchcock is able to express the anxiety both of the hero, who takes recourse in the closed authority of the Father (and directorial deus ex machina), and of the Father (director), who, "in order to deny the weakness of his own nature, accords no one any rights, and imposes only his own duties."

Douchet concludes with a historically inflected assessment describing *Rear Window* as a turning away from the moral type of suspense of the previous films, based on a Victorian era fear of scandal, toward a more American suspense, based on the consumer society's spirit of conquest and desire always to have more. Prior to this, the peak of Hitchcock's production was *Shadow of a Doubt,* which conformed best to the realist criteria of the nineteenth-century novel. This progression is reflected as well in Hitchcock's conscious handing over of aesthetic power to the spectator in *Rear Window,* which presents a "cinematic lesson" to the audience by showing the process of the cinematic spectacle and the distance between the spectacle and the spectator, the main requirement of the voyeur. Likewise, *North by Northwest,* in its graphic emphasis on movement and angles, gives another lesson in the construction of the story, while *Vertigo* shows the limits of the "fetishistic director," the failure of that moment when he is "subjugated to a shot that escapes him, which he cannot control."

Subsequently, this confronting of the voyeuristic distance, this "mobilizing of

the intellectual world of the public," which leads into an awareness of the story as story, becomes the very subject of the films through *Frenzy*. The "pattern of exposed behavior" continues up until the final turning point of *Family Plot*, where Madame Blanche "parodies the master" with her crystal ball and reveals the converging point of fears and desires. The classic schema of relay race-distance-stage (*North by Northwest*) meets the classic schema of projection booth-distance-screen (*Rear Window*) in the "concretization of Hitchcock's final thoughts."

Excerpted in *Cahiers du Cinéma*, no. 163 (February, 1965). Reprinted and partly revised in 1985 as *Hitchcock* (Paris: Herne). Earlier versions, entry 264, entry 787.

Reviews: LeGuay, P. "*Alfred Hitchcock*, de Jean Douchet." *Cinématographe*, no. 59 (July–August 1980):56.

Patar, B. "Hitchcock." *24 Images* 9, no. 28–30 (Autumn 1986).

Philippon, Alain. "Les arcanes de la création." *Cahiers du Cinéma*, no. 381:Journal no. 60 (March 1986):xiv–xv.

338   TRUFFAUT, FRANÇOIS, with the collaboration of Helen G. Scott. *Hitchcock*. New York/London: Simon & Schuster/Secker & Warburg (1968), 256 pp.

Originally published as *Le cinéma selon Hitchcock* (Paris: Laffont, 1966). A basic primary source, comprising fifty hours of interviews and quoted by nearly everyone who writes on Hitchcock. Not all, but most of the anecdotes and opinions expressed by Hitchcock in the other interviews included in the present bibliographic listing either originated or are reprised here. The questioning proceeds through each film in chronological order and addresses "the circumstances attending the inception of each picture, the preparation and structure of the screenplays, directorial problems, and Hitchcock's own assessment of the commercial and artistic results."

In the introduction, Truffaut finds Hitchcock a "fearful person" bent on protecting himself from the people around him. "To stay with his audience, Hitchcock set out to win it over by reawakening all the strong emotions of childhood." He argues that Hitchcock is "the most complete filmmaker of all, an all-round specialist, who excels at every image, each shot, and every scene." He describes him as a voyeur (not an exhibitionist) who contemplates life and has one passion, cinema. As an "artist of anxiety," his work is "not necessarily exalting [but] invariably enriches us, if only through the terrifying lucidity with which it denounces man's desecrations of beauty and purity." Ultimately, he "helps us to understand ourselves." Along with Douchet, Truffaut was one of the first to point out the importance of the technical aspects of suspense, defining it as "the spectacle itself" and not a mere variant.

The third revised edition includes critical comment on the films released after the first edition, of which Truffaut has a generally low opinion, bolstered by his sense that Hitchcock himself was not "satisfied" with any of his films after *Psycho*. From their correspondence and occasional meetings of the period, Truffaut draws a picture of a depressed man in artistic decline. Entry 750 is a version of this final essay.

Excerpts from the French in *Cahiers du Cinéma* 25, no. 147 (September 1963). Translated into German (Munich: Hanser, 1973) and serialized in *Film und Ton* (1974–1976). Translated into Chinese (Chiu-luns: Wen i shu wu, 1972) and Danish (Copenhagen: Rhodes, 1973).

Reviews: entry 346.

Weiskind, Ron. *Mise-en-Scene,* no. 1 (1976):7.

Baumbach, J. *Commonweal* 87 (March 1, 1968):658–659.

Leavitt, J. *Nation* 206 (March 4, 1968):313–314.

Second edition with same title (Paris: Filméditions, 1975 and London: Granada, 1978).

Review: Decaux, E. *Cinématographe* 56, no. 59 (July–August 1980).

Third edition, titled *Hitchcock* (Paris: Ramsay, 1983) and (New York: Simon & Schuster, 1984; London: Paladin, 1986). Shorter version of the new preface in *American Film,* no. 5 (March 1979).

Reviews:

Brdeckove, T. "Folmova literatura: Rozhovory Hitchcock—Truffaut." *Film a Doba* 34 (September 1988):530.

Historical Journal of Film, Radio and Television 6, no. 1 (1986):127–128.

Lopate, Phillip. *New York Times Book Review* (December 30, 1984):9.

Taylor, J[ohn] R[ussell]. "Film books." *Films & Filming,* no. 375 (December 1985):26–27.

Articles and Shorter Writings

339   COURNOT, MICHEL. "L'empire d'Alfred; c'est le génie de Hitchcock qui a fait prendre la farce au sérieux. Mais depuis . . ." *Nouvel Observateur* 152 (October 11):48–49.

On viewing *Vertigo* for the fifth time, the writer ponders the overestimation of Hitchcock's reputation, advancing the notion of the "hypnotized" spectator, who is led "to spiritually valorize sensations which are, in reality, merely sensory." Further, he finds this veneration of technique in critics disturbing.

340   DURGNAT, RAYMOND. "Inside Norman Bates." In *Films and Feelings.* London: Faber & Faber, pp. 209–222.

Essay that emphasizes the "erotic" and psychological aspects of the relationships between Norman and Marion, and Norman and his mother. The characters are presented as both visually and emotionally isolated, yet "convincingly real." *Psycho,* "in its powerful vagueness, works on the spectator not unlike music." Durgnat asserts that the psychologist's purpose is to vindicate "Mom," rationally explaining Norman's control of her image, after which Norman's final turn, "cackling to himself in Mummy's mummy's voice," is the emotional reinforcement. "Mom has just killed Norman and disguised himself as him." Reprinted, entry 386; also Braudy and Dickstein, *Great Film Directors: A Critical Anthology* (New York: Oxford University Press, 1978).

341   HARDISON, O. B. "The rhetoric of Hitchcock's thrillers." In *Man and the Movies,* edited by W. R. Robinson. Baton Rouge: Louisiana State University Press, pp. 137–152.

Overall assessment that distinguishes between a work of art, which "we study aesthetically," and a work of rhetoric, which is shaped by its audience

1968

according to formula and which is a branch of sociology. "Professional entertainment" and Hitchcock, who has perfected the formulas, are part of the latter. After a review of Hitchcock's career and a defining of the thriller (alien setting, victim hero supported by providence), Hardison examines the class theme and concludes that Hitchcock produces dreams that work for a culture that has difficulty distinguishing the "elect from the reprobate."

342   LIGHTMAN, HERB A.   "Hitchcock talks about lights, camera, action." *American Cinematographer* 48, no. 5 (May):332–335.

Hitchcock discusses cinematography in general, lighting, focus, image size, location shots, and other technical matters, mostly in relation to *Torn Curtain,* but also *North by Northwest.*

*343   NARBONI, JEAN.   "La machine infernale." *Cahiers du Cinéma,* no. 186.

Cited in entry 703. Translated in *Cahiers du Cinéma in English,* no. 10 (1966).

344   THOMSON, DAVID.   "Moralist: Hitchcock." In *Movie Man.* London/New York: Secker & Warburg/Stein & Day, 149–155.

Asserts that the "essential" of a Hitchcock film is the "awareness the director has of his spectator," which results in claustrophobic filmmaking concerned with issues of freedom. Reprinted in Braudy and Dickstein, *Great Film Directors: A Critical Anthology* (New York: Oxford University Press, 1978). Translated into Italian, entry 513.

1968
Books

*345   UPPSALA STUDENTERS FILMSTUDIO.   *Alfred Hitchcock.* Uppsala: Selbstverlag.

Cited in entry 703: "Collection of periodical material on Hitchcock." In Swedish.

Articles and Shorter Writings

346   BRAUDY, LEO.   "Hitchcock, Truffaut, and the irresponsible audience." *Film Quarterly* 21, no. 4 (Summer):21–27.

Discussion of Truffaut's interviewing method in entry 338. Braudy is critical of Truffaut's "lack of interest in the psychological dimensions of Hitchcock's films," finding him arrogant and adulatory at the same time. Overly engrossed with workmanship and technical detail, Truffaut fails to query Hitchcock about more complex themes, which makes him "blind to the area where technique and theme coincide in the study of voyeurism." Includes analysis of *Psycho* and the cycle of identification and guilt it presents. Reprinted, entry 386.

347   HITCHCOCK, ALFRED.   "It's a bird, it's a plane. it's *The Birds.*" *Take One* 1, no. 10:6–7.
Essay on special effects, traveling mats, and the specific technical development of several shots in *The Birds.*

348   ———.   *"Rear Window." Take One* 2, no. 2:18–20.
Partial transcription of remarks made by Hitchcock on the occasion of a special showing of *Rear Window* at the Academy of Motion Picture Arts and Sciences. Anecdotes concerning his career, montage, the MacGuffin, copy-cat crimes after *Psycho,* and the special intricacies of *Rear Window* are related. Concludes with a discussion of violence: "Go right back to a 3 month old baby . . . the mother says Boo! . . . That's how fear is born. Later, the child grows up and goes on a swing and becomes violent to itself . . . higher and higher [then] over the top. . . . So there's nothing new in it. We've always had violence—it's communication." Reprinted in entry 386. Translated in Italian, entry 566.

349   NEVINS, FRANCIS M., JR.   *"Vertigo* re-viewed." *Journal of Popular Culture* 2, no. 2 (Fall):321–331.
Plot explication of the film, emphasizing the opposition of the two female characters, Midge and Madeleine/Judy, as well as the more muddled but also opposing personas of Madeleine and Judy. Nevins posits the theological notion of a "spiritual sickness" involved in an aversion to humanity and ordinary life and an attraction of the nonhuman dream world.

350   SARRIS, ANDREW.   "Pantheon directors: Alfred Hitchcock." In *The American Cinema: Directors and Directions 1929–1968.* New York: Dutton, pp. 56–60.
Explicates the major theme of complacency, relating it to the sagging fortunes of Hitchcock's reputation, "which has suffered from the fact that he has given audiences more pleasure than is permissible for serious cinema. . . . Hitchcock's repeated invasions of everyday life with the most outrageous melodramatic devices have shaken the foundations of the facile humanism that insists that people are good, and only the systems evil. . . . He insists upon a moral reckoning for his characters and for his audience." Reprinted, entry 386.

351   THOMAS, BOB.   "A talk with Alfred Hitchcock." *Action* 3, no. 3 (May–June):8–10.
"I'm American trained," begins Hitchcock. Discusses his early career, the role of background in a story, screenwriters, and suspense. Reprinted in *Making Films in New York* 2 (August, 1968), and *Directors in Action: Selections from Action* (Indianapolis: Bobbs-Merrill, 1973).

1969
Books

352   SIMSOLO, NOËL. *Alfred Hitchcock.* Paris: Seghers, 189 pp.
Chronological commentary on each of the films, comprising some production history, brief critical assessments, and short excerpts from other critical texts and interviews. Filmography, bibliography.

Articles and Shorter Writings

353   BELLOUR, RAYMOND. *"Marnie: Une lecture." Revue d'Esthétique,* no. 20:169–179.
Within a larger discussion of Hitchcock techniques, including the structuring of "the look" and the "double game" of multiple points of view and shifting positions, an analysis of *Marnie* that attends to the formal aspects of the film as well as Hitchcock's attitudes reflected in it. Bellour discusses the concept of the mask, which runs throughout Hitchcock's work, and in *Marnie* "is psychoanalysis." He assesses *Marnie* as "a story of love prey to the game of appearance and identity."

354   ———. *"Les Oiseaux: Analyse d'une séquence." Cahiers du Cinéma,* no. 216 (October):24–38.
Detailed analysis of the boat sequence in *The Birds,* based on a shot listing that indicates camera movement (or not), distance in the shot, and who is looking or being looked at. The sequence is defined as having two centers, the first organized around Melanie as she crosses to the house and the second organized around Mitch as he follows by truck as she returns. Various symmetries and oppositions are detailed. The functioning of the birds and the position of the male characters, as well as the *auteur* (Hitchcock) are discussed.
Critiqued in "Alternation, segmentation, hypnosis," by Janet Bergstrom, in *Camera Obscura,* no. 3–4 (1979) and entry 518. Reprinted in Bellour's *L'analyse du film* (Paris: Albatros, 1979). There is a mimeographed English translation from the British Film Institute, Education Advisory Board (date unknown).

355   BORDWELL, DAVID. "Alfred Hitchcock's *Notorious." Film Heritage* 4, no. 3 (Spring):6–10, 22.
Analysis of the "rigorous purity" of point of view in the film, particularly as structured by "glances."

356   HERRMANN, BERNARD. *Portrait of Hitch* [score]. Borough Green, Sevenoaks, Kent: Fairfield.
Musical portrait of Hitchcock derived from tunes written for *The Trouble with Harry.* Recorded by the London Philharmonic Orchestra, "Music from the Great Movie Thrillers," Decca PFS 4173.

1969

357   HIGHAM, CHARLES, and JOEL GREENBERG.   "Alfred Hitchcock." In
      The Celluloid Muse: Hollywood Directors Speak. London: Angus & Rob-
      ertson, pp. 86–103.
      Interview: Comments on Selznick, *Rebecca, Foreign Correspondent,* the
concept of "keeping inside the action," how to dramatize settings, the compromise
ending of *Suspicion,* and the casting mistakes of *The Paradine Case.* Also
remarks on *Saboteur, Shadow of a Doubt, Lifeboat, Notorious, Strangers on a
Train, I Confess, Vertigo, Rear Window, Psycho,* and extensive technical discussion of *The Birds.* Comments on his pet projects—*Mary Rose* and a day in the life
of a big city.

358   HOUSTON, PENELOPE.   "Hitch on *Topaz.*" *Sight and Sound* 39, no. 1
      (Winter):16.
      Reported conversation with Hitchcock on the three different endings of
Topaz, all of which were shot: first, a duel in a football field; second, Devereax and
Granville heading in two different directions at an airport; and third, Granville's
suicide.

359   MILLAR, GAVIN.   "Hitchcock versus Truffaut." *Sight and Sound* 38, no.
      2 (Spring):82–88.
      Discussion of the Truffaut interviews (entry 338), seen as "idolatory and
accepting," and career assessment of Hitchcock as a "simplifier . . . [who makes
films] of unitary ideas, rising directly but perhaps unconsciously from his own
needs rather than thoughts."

360   SARRIS, ANDREW.   "Alfred Hitchcock." In *Interviews with Film Direc-
      tors.* New York: Avon, pp. 241–252.
      Comments on *The Birds,* its theme of complacency, the "feminine nature" of
Norman Bates, *North by Northwest, Psycho,* and the process of script development.

361   UNGARI, ENZO.   "Introduzione all'arcipelago Hitchcock." *Cinema e
      Film* 4, no. 10:7–50.
      Film-by-film survey of Hitchcock's career.

362   WOLLEN, PETER.   "Hitchcock's vision." *Cinema* (Cambridge), no. 3
      (June):2–4.
      Argues that the "first priority" in reading Hitchcock is to understand the
structures, which he sees as revolving around "the manhunt/pursuit and spying/
gazing." Suggests a "psychology-semiology" of gazing, watching, and observing,
and emphasizes the importance of Freudian constructs, such as scoptophilia,
voyeurism, and narcissism. Wollen concludes that the rhetoric of the "master-
technician" is "none other than the rhetoric of the unconscious."

1970
Books

363   DURGNAT, RAYMOND. "The strange case of Alfred Hitchcock, parts I–X." *Films and Filming* 16; 17, nos. 5–12; nos. 1–2 (February–November):various pagings.

Slightly expanded and rewritten version published in 1974, *The Strange Case of Alfred Hitchcock or the Plain Man's Hitchcock* (Cambridge: MIT Press).

Durgnat systematically moves through a chronological outline of the biographical material and artistic product. The first three parts are given to varied organizational schemes and the assessments of other critics. Other than the British and American periods, he distinguishes eleven "producer periods": (1) the initial years of 1921–1922 at Famous Players-Lasky, (2) the scenarist years of 1922–1925, (3) the Michael Balcon years of 1925–1927, (4) the John Maxwell/BIP years of 1927–1933, (5) the Gaumont British years of 1937–1938 (Ivor Montagu and Balcon), (6) the Gainsborough-Edward Black years of 1937–1938, (7) the Selznick years of 1940–1947, (8) Transatlantic Pictures, 1948–1949, (9) Warners, 1950–1954, (10) Paramount, 1954–1956, and (11) Universal, 1963 to the present. Durgnat then lists films under genres and themes: romantic novelettes, dramatic realism, the thriller, wish-fulfillment high life, picaresque pursuits, the twining of innocence and guilt, heroes and villains, and "aesthetic interests." The last two lead into a discussion of early British and French critics and their preference for the British films, and to reevaluations of Rohmer and Chabrol (entry 246), concerned with moral preoccupations, and Cameron and Perkins (entries 292, 298, and 306), concerned with audience manipulation.

Durgnat speaks against the assumption of moral patterns unique to Hitchcock and argues that the genres in which he worked already involved similar moral schemata, which can also be found in many non-Hitchcock films. While some films have unique and powerful insight (especially *Psycho*), in general he finds Hitchcock's "sinister universe" superficial. He compares Hitchcock's films to those of Michelangelo Antonioni and finds that Hitchcock's flow away from the latter's "sea of spiritual understanding" toward a sea of "escapist nonsense." Even so, seeking to maintain a middle course between those who see Hitchcock as "master of nothing" and those who see a "profound and salutary moralist," Durgnat contends that even the lesser films are as carefully constructed and intelligent as the greater ones, the difference lying in the "content which is structured." He explains the Hitchcockian philosophy as a "balance of religiously practiced absurdity and a worldly but prudential order"—in the end, "a mixture of contrarities . . . paranoid themes and picaresque genres, which rarely become a coherent world-view."

Assessments and descriptions of each film generally follow the introductory remarks and include many insightful details concerning thematic relationships and comparisons to other British and American films. Durgnat also offers comparative analyses of alternative scenarios.

Reviews (of 1974 book): Belton, John. *Filmmakers Newsletter* (April 1977):55.

Cinema Papers 2 (November–December 1975):279.

Filmmakers Newsletter 10 (April 1977):55–56.

Jameson, Richard T. "Book marks." *Film Comment* 11, no. 6 (November–December 1975):60–61.

Millimeter 4 (November 1976):58.

Movietone News, no. 44 (September 29, 1975):23–24.

New York Times 124 (April 13, 1975):section 7, p. 22.

Paul, W. "Mr. Hitchcock, Mr. Durgnat, and Mr. Bates." *Thousand Eyes* 2 (January 1977):8–9.

Rothman, William. *University Film Study Center Newsletter* 5, no. 4 (April 1975):4.

Screen 16, no. 2 (1975):120–124.

Thomas, Paul. *Film Quarterly* 30, no. 3 (Spring 1977):57–62.

Thousand Eyes Magazine 2 (November 1976):10.

Times Literary Supplement, no. 3786 (September 27, 1974):1035.

Articles and Shorter Writings

364   BELTON, JOHN.   "[Reply to Samuels' Article on Hitchcock]." *American Scholar* 39, no. 4 (Autumn):728–731.

Letter response to entry 370 focusing on Samuels' distinction between form and content, arguing that the work is a union of the two and that unity is "an integral part of [Hitchcock's] greatness." Belton uses *I Confess* to illustrate Hitchcock's concern with moral problems. Samuels counters with a rebuttal.

365   BUSCOMBE, EDWARD.   "Dickens and Hitchcock." *Screen* 11, no. 4–5 (August–September):97–114.

Compares Charles Dickens and Hitchcock, who both became very successful in a society "where artists were alienated" but never felt constrained by commercial intent. Both were showmen and neither had an interest in discussing the content of their work. They shared similar working methods and a similar sense of humor, and though they were very interested in creating realistic detail, neither was the least interested in being "realistic." Complexity is added to their work by "their own personal feeling about the law [which] prevents the audience from assuming an identity between the forces of law and the forces of good." Also includes discussion of the status of melodrama within the "great tradition" of F. R. Leavis, and Robin Wood's emphasis on the characters at the expense of the plots for the purpose of bringing Hitchcock "in" to the "great tradition," even though Dickens is already "out."

366   CORLISS, RICHARD.   *"Topaz." Film Quarterly* 23, no. 3:41–44.

Negative review of "slick, manipulative, and lifeless" film, marked by unevenness—an anthology of Hitchcock's insights and excesses.

367   LOVELL, ALAN.   "The common pursuit of true judgement." *Screen* 11, no. 4–5 (August–September):76–88.

Response to Robin Wood's complaints in *Screen* about critics and film criticism lacking in "force and complexity." Lovell objects to Wood's (denied) interest in only "great artists and great work," arguing that his work on

1970

Hitchcock is clearly an effort of prior evaluation. Regarding Hitchcock, Lovell disputes Wood's assertion that "direct moral judgement" is presented in the films, using an example from *North by Northwest,* where Roger Thornhill cheats some pedestrians out of a taxi. To Wood, this shows the character's "irresponsible and inconsiderate" nature, while Lovell interprets it as a demonstration of the character's "ability for quick improvisation and witty rationalization." While not concerned with a detailed reading, Lovell seeks to place Hitchcock's work within the conventions of "stylized comedy" for the purpose of pointing out that there are many different modes other than moral realism for approaching Hitchcock's work.

368   MOGG, KEN. "Hitchcock and the Mogg synthesizer." *Melbourne Film Bulletin,* no. 14 (October):2–22.

Interview on *Topaz* with Ken Mogg, a film writer who has extensive knowledge of the detail of the scenes and characters in the film, especially as they relate to current political events.

369   MUNDY, ROBERT. "Another look at Hitchcock." *Cinema* (Cambridge), no. 6–7 (August):10–12.

Defense of *Topaz* and *Torn Curtain* as densely and deliberately stilted explications of betrayal on all levels. Mundy includes a review of critical literature and suggestions of a metaphysics explicated by, for example, water images.

370   SAMUELS, CHARLES THOMAS. "Hitchcock." *American Scholar* 39, no. 2 (Spring):295–304.

Diatribe seeking to rectify critics' views of Hitchcock as a "moralist" when he really "poses moral problems only to evade them." Hitchcock is "discomfited by intellectuals," whimsically follows political trends, and is an "indifferent technician." His secret is "the absence of meaning, the absolute identification of meaning with effect." Analysis of *The 39 Steps, The Lady Vanishes,* and *North by Northwest* follows to illustrate this "contentless virtuosity" that revels in pure form and neutralizes morality. Discussion of *Shadow of a Doubt* and *Strangers on a Train* illustrates his assumption that "everyone is latently a killer."

371   WALKER, MICHAEL. "The old age of Alfred Hitchcock." *Movie,* no. 18 (Winter):10–13.

Analysis of characters and themes in *Topaz,* written as a pro-West Cold War film but directed so that the political viewpoint is canceled by sympathy for the characters and a "universal sense of suffering and loss." Walker discusses the rounds of betrayals and exploitations among the characters, mirror images, and recurring triangles. He concludes that the film is one of the artist's "old age" in its "slow, deepening sense of melancholy."

1971
Books

372   BRUNETTA, GIAN PIERO.   *Alfred Hitchcock o l'universo della relativita.*
       Problemi e Protagonisti dello Spettacolo, 1. Citadella: Delta Tre, 125 pp.
Dense presentation of the major themes, synthesizing the work of other
critics and theorists. First, the "Truffaut" Hitchcock is described, emphasizing the
completeness of the career and Hitchcock's interest in all aspects of filmmaking.
A discussion of the influences of German Expressionism, *kammerspiel,* and
surrealism is followed by analysis of Hitchcock's particular vision, his sense of
observation, and interest in the interaction of decor and action. The male
characters are common men, "fragile on the psychological and sentimental level,"
while the female characters are symbolic.
    The book also has chapters on the couple, and space and time, where
Rossellini's and Welles's more naturalistic use of space is compared to Hitchcock's
abstractions. Chapters titled "The Semantic Axis" and "Gaze of Hitchcock"
analyze the process of signification, with particular reference to Bellour's analysis
of *The Birds* (entry 354). Brunetta concludes with a chapter on the development
of the story and the dialectic Hitchcock creates between the story and the
language of telling it.

373   *Alfred Hitchcock,* edited by Michel Estève. Études Cinématographiques,
       84–87. Paris: Minard, 173 pp.
    Anthology: Includes bibliographic essay by René Prédal. See entries this year
under Amengual, Magny, Parrain, Pinel, Prédal, Rocher, Serceau, and Sorel.

Articles and Shorter Writings

374   AMENGUAL, BARTHELMY.   "A propos de *Vertigo* ou Hitchcock contre
       Tristan." In *Alfred Hitchcock,* edited by Michel Estève. *Études Cinémato-*
       graphiques, 84–87. Paris: Minard, pp. 37–55.
    Philosophical analysis of *Vertigo* in its relation to the myths of Tristan. The
author discusses types and doubles and is particularly concerned with shot
composition. Longer version of earlier essay (entry 275).

375   BELLOUR, RAYMOND.   "Ce que savait Hitchcock." In *Le Livre des*
       Autres. Paris: l'Herne, pp. 87–95.
    An appreciation of Truffaut's interview with Hitchcock as a systematic un-
dertaking of great subtlety and depth. Reprinted in *Cahiers du cinéma,* no. 190,
1967.

376   GILLIATT, PENELOPE.   "The London Hitch." *New Yorker* 47 (Septem-
       ber 11):91–93.
    Portrait developed after a retrospective of the films and a trip to Hitchcock's
home in Bel Air. The author describes Hitchcock as "dedicated to clarity." His

1971

cynicism appears to be the cover for a pessimistic and vulnerable temperament, which has made him "the calligrapher of off-center worry." She places the English films above the American, which "were sometimes dogged by sentimentality and an unattractive cynicism."

*377   HIRSCH, PETER. "Spiner under ny synsvinkel: En redegørelse for Alfred Hitchcocks to seneste film Bag jerntæppet og *Topaz* i relation til hinanden og til mesterens tidligere film." *Sunset Boulevard* 2:3–8.
Cited in *Filmlitteraturen i Danmark 1964–1973* (Danmards Bibliotekssole, 1975).

378   JULIA, JACQUES. "Le monde d'Hitchcock." *Cinéma* 71, no. 160:69–75.
Formal and thematic analysis of the series of oppositions and symmetries that make up Hitchcock's work: doubles, opposites, ambivalences, and so on. Julia argues that Hitchcock is able to express the structure of the unconscious through these complex expressions.

379   MAGNY, JOËL, and STÉPHANE SOREL. "Notes pour une relecture de Hitchcock." In *Alfred Hitchcock,* edited by Michel Estève. *Études Cinématographiques,* 84–87. Paris: Minard, pp. 77–84.
A reading of Hitchcock's films that identifies the following codes: the production codes that produce the informational and connotative levels (while not unique to Hitchcock, they are especially rich in detail in his films), the narrative symbols that produce themes, and the "Hitchcockian" symbols—the personal themes—which the author sees as admirably explicated by Jean Douchet (entry 337).

380   MAMBER, STEPHEN. "The television films of Alfred Hitchcock." *Cinema* (Beverly Hills) 7, no. 1:2–7.
Discussion on the visual points of each television film and the relationship of these productions to the feature films.

381   PARRAIN, PHILIPPE. "La construction dramatique et les lois du mouvement." In *Alfred Hitchcock,* edited by Michel Estève. *Études Cinématographiques,* 84–87. Paris: Minard, pp. 5–27.
Extensive, detailed essay analyzing Hitchcock's stated goal of completely directing the thoughts of the spectator and thereby holding absolute attention. Parrain outlines the formal rigor necessary to attain such an aim: (1) characters marked with a "certain frigidity that abstracts them from their surroundings and makes them clearly delineated entities, ready to obey"; (2) concentrated focus on movement toward the ending through use of polarities (tensions); (3) movement and interest created through the use of modes of transportation; (4) narrative use of the law of return, the boomerang, and the circle; (5) concentration on the mechanics of cause and effect and rapid movement between the two; (6) escalation of the action; (7) use of the logic of excess; (8) the creation of a confluence of motion, "clockwork precision, frozen precision."

382   PECHTER, WILLIAM S. "The director vanishes." In *Twenty-Four Times a Second: Films and Filmmakers*. New York: Harper & Row, pp. 175–194.

Assessment of Hitchcock's career, finding the American films less successful than the British, Hitchcock having "lost contact" with his audience. His strength returns in the "profoundly frightening" *Psycho,* however, and Pechter concludes that the director produces "art, but not works of art."

383   PRÉDAL, RENÉ. "Le peur et les multiples visages du destin ou de quelques aspects de la thématique hitchcockienne." In *Alfred Hitchcock,* edited by Michel Estève. *Études Cinématographiques,* 84–87. Paris: Minard, pp. 85–140.

Analysis making specific reference to most of the films while illustrating Hitchcock's use of the voyeur, suspense, the mirror (double), the transference (of guilt), the false lead, and the confluence of innocence and guilt. Prédal offers extensive comment on the literary sources as well. Concludes with a structural discussion of the Christian themes: the will (toward good and evil), flight and destiny, and the expiation of guilt.

384   ROCHER, DANIEL. "*Strangers on a train* ou l'insolite est quotidien." In *Alfred Hitchcock,* edited by Michel Estève. *Études Cinématographiques,* 84–87. Paris: Minard, pp. 28–36.

Primarily a discussion of Hitchcock's creation of fear within the depiction of everyday life. Lacking expressionistic or fantastic elements, *Strangers on a Train* is the epitome of this technique.

385   SERCEAU, MICHEL. "Les récits d'espionnage et le chemin de la connaissance." In *Alfred Hitchcock,* edited by Michel Estève. *Études Cinématographiques, 84–87. Paris: Minard, pp. 56–76.*

Analysis of the couple and love themes in the films, especially *The Paradine Case, Rear Window,* and *Notorious,* as they relate to Hitchcock's ability to appeal to the spectator's complacent inclinations while actually unsettling them. Serceau describes oppositional relationships formed by the degradation of love (as in physical attraction) versus Christian love, and seeing-observing-fantasizing (passivity) versus knowing-working-struggling (activity). These poles are then attributed to the male and female roles that create a typical scenario: the woman tempts and the man becomes trapped, and then frightened to death (i.e., makes a big mistake, which he blames on her) because his desire to possess her physically precludes an understanding that would allow him to know her spiritually. This dilemma allows Hitchcock to generalize about the passivity of the male, caught up in passion and unable to see the truth—for example, Devlin's refusal to properly weigh his relationship with Alicia, insisting on blaming her for her deterioration and consequently missing the first signs of poisoning.

1972
Books

386   *Focus on Hitchcock,* edited by Albert J. LaValley. Englewood Cliffs, N.J.: Prentice-Hall, 186 pp.

Anthology: Introduction includes a review of the literature and emphasizes the "intermeshing of themes," assessing *Notorious* as the point where the mixture in the films become "most disquieting." LaValley touches upon many other critical approaches, such as the fairy tale, genre, and voyeurism, and concludes that "Hitchcock's viewpoint seems to me to be close to nihilism." Another essay by LaValley is a shot-by-shot analysis of the cornfield chase sequence in *North by Northwest,* which uses storyboard drawings of each shot.

Includes essay by Christ, see entry this year. Also reprints of Crawley (entry 328), Bogdanovich (entry 295), Hitchcock on direction (entry 125) and on *Rear Window* (entry 348), Anderson (entry 187), translation of Bazin (entry 215), introduction to Wood (entry 318), part three of Durgnat (entry 363), Agee (entry 169), translation of Rohmer and Chabrol on *The Wrong Man* (entry 246), Braudy (entry 346), Sarris (entry 350), and Durgnat (entry 340). Also reprinted reviews by Pauline Kael and John Crosby, and excerpts from *Raymond Chandler Speaking* (Boston: Houghton Mifflin, 1962).

Review: Schuth, H. Wayne. "Review of *Focus on Hitchcock.*" *Cinema Journal* 12, no. 1 (Fall 1972):69–70.

387   LEHMAN, ERNEST.   *North by Northwest.* New York: Viking, 148 pp.

The shooting script, shot by shot, with footnotes indicating the minor differences between the script and the film.

Review: *"North by Northwest." Interview,* no. 33 (June 1973):42.

Articles and Shorter Writings

388   AMERICAN FILM INSTITUTE.   "University Advisory Committee Seminar." *Dialogue on Film* 2, no. 1:3–23.

Round table discussion on film education with Charlton Heston as convenor, directors Robert Wise, George Stevens, George Seaton, Hitchcock, and others. Hitchcock, somewhat contentiously, argues the wisdom of complete preplanning and delivers standard description of his own early film education.

389   CHRIST, RONALD.   *"Strangers on a Train:* The pattern of encounter." In *Focus on Hitchcock,* edited by Albert J. LaValley. Englewood Cliffs, N.J.: Prentice-Hall, pp. 104–110.

Essay on the formal patterning of doubles and the crisscross theme in the film, arguing that aesthetic play and not the psychological double is Hitchcock's true interest.

390 GOUGH-YATES, K. "Private madness and public lunacy." *Films and Filming* 18, no. 5 (February):26–30.
Psycho, Peeping Tom, and *Lilith* are discussed as part of a group of films "where the hero is seemingly mad and yet incorporates social sickness and obsessions." Author argues that the insane characters are "an amalgam of all the perversions and monstrosities of other people."

391 GOW, GORDON. *"Frenzy." Films and Filming* 18, no. 10 (July):58–59.
Negative review of the film describing it as plodding and exploitative melodrama. Gow is particularly disappointed that the leading man is not strongly established.

392 GREENE, GRAHAM. [Reviews]. In *Graham Greene on film; collected film criticism 1935–1940.* New York: Simon & Schuster, various paging.
Greene is not impressed with Hitchcock's work and at once apologizes for his "prejudices" and defends his assessments in the introduction to this collection of reprints. In *Secret Agent,* Hitchcock shows that "as a producer he has no sense of continuity and as a writer he has no sense of life." *Sabotage* is described as "convincingly realistic" and well acted, but *Jamaica Inn* is "unsatisfactory . . . a girl's dream of violent manhood."
Reprints of reviews from the *Spectator* (May 15, 1936; December 11, 1936; March 19, 1939).

393 HAAKMAN, ANTON. "Vallen met Hitchcock (of Hitchcock laten vallen?)." *Skoop* 8, no. 4:24–39.
Study of Hitchcock's work and relation to *Frenzy,* the nature of suspense, and so on. In Dutch.

*394 HENSTELL, BRUCE. *Alfred Hitchcock.* Washington, D.C.: American Film Institute, 27 pp.
Cited in entry 703.

395 JOHNSON, ALBERT. *"Frenzy." Film Quarterly* 26, no. 1 (Fall):58–60.
Review outlining the standard critical reaction of the time: *Frenzy* as a "return to the realm Hitchcock commanded so long," after his post-*Psycho* decline. The characters and setting are, once again, "real."

396 KAPLAN, GEORGE [ROBIN WOOD]. "Alfred Hitchcock: Lost in the wood." *Film Comment* 8, no. 4 (November–December):46–53.
Critical commentary of Wood's own previous view of Hitchcock, entry 318. Kaplan objects to the positing of a "therapeutic" theme in the films, contending that Hitchcock's fascination is with the abnormal characters, not the normal ones. Kaplan also argues the preeminence in the films of heterosexual relations characterized by romantic passion rather than a real sense of possibility. He

argues further that Hitchcock's control of image and editing leads to aesthetic limitations because (1) audiences can be maneuvered into indentifying with generalized behavior; (2) only limited range of behavior is useful under such circumstances; and (3) apart from these obsessive-compulsive states, only "nondescript ciphers" are possible. Kaplan criticizes Wood, who applies "serious standards," for avoiding a clear statement that Hitchcock is the equal of Shakespeare, because if he did, he would be forced to reevaluate and admit Hitchcock's inferiority. The potato sack scene in *Frenzy* "sums up everything in Hitchcock that is most morally suspect." Ultimately, the author finds Hitchcock weak as an artist because of his lack of interest in "normal life" and insistence on using obtrusively artificial effects, as "everyone" finds them "distracting and alienating."

397   KINDER, MARSHA, and BEVERLE HOUSTON. *"Blackmail."* In *Close-up: A Critical perspective on film.* New York: Harcourt, Brace, Jovanovich, pp. 52–58.
Analysis of *Blackmail* as a textbook example of sound, focusing on its expression of the inadequacy of all forms—verbal and visual—of communication.

398   NOGUEIRA, RUI, and NICOLETTA ZALAFFI. "Hitch, Hitch, Hitch Hourra! Alfred Hitchcock interviewé." *Ecran* (July–August):2–8.
Interview: On himself as an "auteur": "I don't possess such vanity. If I made films for myself they would be much different than those you see. They would be more dramatic, perhaps without humor, more realistic. I specialize in suspense for strictly commercial reasons." Hitchcock also comments on his preference of "filmmaker" to "director," and relates anecdotes about critics, Paul Newman, Kim Novak, the story of the compromise end for *Topaz,* his use of documentary footage from the Cuban revolution, and the characters in *Frenzy.*

399   NOLAN, JACK EDMUND. "Hitchcock's TV films." In *Focus on Hitchcock,* edited by Albert J. LaValley. Englewood Cliffs, N.J.: Prentice-Hall, pp. 140–142.
Listing and short plot synopses of the twenty television films. Reprint of article in *Film Fan Monthly* (June 1968).

400   PERCHERON, DANIEL. "Arrêts sur l'image." *Communications* 19: 195–200.
Comparison of the suspense mechanisms of *North by Northwest* and *Rosemary's Baby,* the classical scheme of the former being "perverted" in the latter.

401   SAMUELS, CHARLES THOMAS. "Alfred Hitchcock." In *Encountering Directors: Interviews.* New York: Capricorn, pp. 231–250.
Samuels has omitted much of the interview, which he found to be confined and repetitive. The comments remaining address screen size, directing as conducting, Hitchcock's working methods, a denial of "brutality" in *Psycho,* and

clichés of location shooting. Samuels pushes Hitchcock on many points and succeeds in provoking some new information.

402   SKOLLER, DONALD. "Aspects of cinematic consciousness: Suspense and presence/dis-illusion/unified perceptual response." *Film Comment* 8, no. 3 (September–October):41–51.
In the context of "structural film and its relation to the problems of illusionism," Skoller compares *Vertigo, Last Year at Marienbad,* and *Wavelength.* Each is a different "exercise in the reduction of an illusion."

403   SMITH, JOHN M. "Conservative individualism: A selection of English Hitchcock." *Screen* 13, no. 3 (Autumn):51–70.
Detailed analyses of the early films, most of which have protagonists who are "victims of themselves." The narratives embody a dialectic between the claims of the instincts and those of social proprieties, generally resolved in a "submission" of character and event to "a common level of being."
,   Smith begins with a comparison to the work of Joseph Conrad, who maintained "impersonal control and unity" in his novels, a feat more difficult in filmmaking, though Hitchcock succeeds more than most. Both, however, are persistently interested in the "relative maneuvering of order and disorder," which is defined as the question of individualism. Hitchcock explicates this theme in many ways: performer versus audience, woman versus man, subject versus the nation. The commitment of the character to individualism forces the "endurance" of disorder, cruelty, evil, and perhaps madness, but it generally ends in a "balanced acknowledgement of social reality," a maturing and acceptance of "impersonal forces."
Finally, *Young and Innocent,* with its "solid" heroine, absolutely respectful of the social order, is the "simplest demonstration that [Hitchcock's] individualism is conservative." In the other films, which are more concerned with evil and disorder, this quality is "integrated into the final unities. . . . The characters have to live with the knowledge that they have acquired, of what they themselves are." Also discusses *The Lodger, The Farmer's Wife, The Pleasure Garden, The Man Who Knew Too Much* (1934), and *The 39 Steps.*

1973
Books

404   NAREMORE, JAMES. *Filmguide to* Psycho. *Indiana University Press Filmguide Series,* 4. Bloomington: Indiana University Press, 87 pp.
An introduction to the director's work emphasizes his repression, timidity, and superior organization, concluding that the films are not "mere thrillers" but take place in a "region of the mind." There follows a history of the production of *Psycho* and a lengthy scene-by-scene analysis of all filmic elements. The final critique assesses Hitchcock as primarily a craftsman and formalist, asserting that his "themes can be found in every suspense story." The most original part of the essay discusses the social environment in which the film was produced and received.

Articles and Shorter Writings

405   APPEL, ALFRED, JR.   "The eye of knowledge: Voyeuristic games in film and literature." *Film Comment* 9, no. 3 (May–June):20–26.

Discussion of *Rear Window, Vertigo,* and *Frenzy* within an essay on the major themes of the fiction of Vladimir Nabokov. In the work of both, "the mirrors of possibility" create suspense, which the artist provokes, providing insight into "the limitation of language, the nature of love and loss, and the deathly cul-de-sac of nostalgia."

406   BRODY, ALAN.   "The gift of realism: Hitchcock and Pinter." *Journal of Modern Literature* 3, no. 2 (April):149–172.

Historical account of the audiences and formal relationships of film and theater is followed by a detailed analysis of *Shadow of a Doubt* and Harold Pinter's *The Birthday Party.* Brody discusses "transformative" developments—in characters and things, the process of exposure and recognition, and the handling of time and timing in presenting an argument concerning the development of realism in both arts. "Film . . . had taken the gift of realism from the stage, [which] gave the theater a chance to redefine itself."

407   POAGUE, LELAND A.   "The detective in Hitchcock's *Frenzy*: His ancestors and significance." *Journal of Popular Film* 2, no. 1 (Winter):47–58.

Analyzes *Frenzy* in relation to its "thematic point . . . that people are unified in their common humanity and propensity for evil . . . but different in that some act out their evil" and some do not. Poague puts Inspector Oxford at the moral center of the film and compares him to the inspectors in *Stage Fright, Sabotage,* and *Dial M for Murder.* He also compares Mrs. Oxford to the Constance Peterson character in *Spellbound.*

408   SGAMMATO, JOSEPH.   "The discreet qualms of the bourgeoisie: Hitchcock's *Frenzy.*" *Sight and Sound* 42, no. 3 (Summer):134–137.

Analysis of the film and assessment of the work in general, which "cinematizes that part of all of us which prefers hell to heaven" and is indicative of the "fluctuating rhythm of the middle-class imagination." While asserting the notion that Hitchcock has "nothing to say," author finds the "union of two sets of eyes, director's and spectator's, a mystery . . . which leads one fumbling blindly after the roots of film itself."

409   THOMAS, BOB.   "Alfred Hitchcock: The German years." *Action* 8, no. 1 (January –February):23–25.

Interview: Anecdotes from throughout the career, not just the German period, with specific comments about *The Last Laugh,* the difficulties of the German version of *Murder!,* and the German emphasis on the visual, which

Hitchcock thinks made the Germans more successful in Hollywood than the British.

*410   TORP PEDERSEN, BO. "Livets muligheder, Alfred Hitchcock." *Spotlight* 4:165–172.
Cited in *Filmlitteraturen i Danmark 1964–1973* (Danmards Biblioteksson, 1975).

1974
Books

411   CARLINI, FABIO. *Alfred Hitchcock. Il Castoro Cinema,* 5. Firenze: La Nuova Italia, 116 pp.
Auteurist study beginning with "A small Hitchcock lexicon," which lists terms essential to the understanding of Hitchcock's style and themes. The lexicon includes background information on the collaborators, sources, pertinent film history, critical response, theories of acting, relevant phobias, and neuroses as well as philosophical, political, and psychoanalytical subjects. Each term, beginning with *Adaptation, Ambience, America,* through *Telephone, Traveling, Voyeur,* is illustrated with a direct quote culled from conversations with Hitchcock over the years.
A critical essay follows, discussing the "new criticism" and the "closed system" of images and locales. Combines a mixture of the popular and sensational aspects of Hitchcock alongside the more critical, with an emphasis on the psychoanalytical richness of his style. Carlini argues for a structural Hitchcock, with effects traced through objects, obsessions, and biographical elements, ending with an insightful reflection on Hitchcock's own personal history. Hitchcock is allowed to float here as an "open text"; his universe is not so much defined as refined, and he is seen as having achieved a certain mastery of ambiguity: "having perfected the awareness of the characteristic illusion of the cinema and its impossibility . . . [Hitchcock] signifies a continual underlining of the phantasmic nature of the imagination." He invents "stories which make no pretense to verisimilitude . . . [but] confound, entertain, and introduce the spectator into a labyrinthine game that hides behind its apparent uselessness the risks involved in every dramatic encounter." Includes complete filmography.

412   CUENCA, CARLOS F[ERNANDEZ]. *El Cine Britanico de Alfred Hitchcock. Libros de Bolsillo.* Madrid: Nacional, 173 pp.
Detailed filmography (through *Jamaica Inn*) and synopses. Introduction and critical histories of the silent and sound periods.

*413   SKWARA, JANUSZ. *Hitchcock. Kleinformat,* 16. Warszawa: Wyd. Artyst i Film, 140 pp.
Cited in entry 703. In Polish.

1974

Articles and Shorter Writings

414   BUCKLEY, MICHAEL.   "Alfred Hitchcock." *Films in Review* 25 (June—July):380–381.
Account of Lincoln Center Gala, detailed list of attenders, and so on.

415   GARDNER, P.   "Hitchcock skill for mood and imagery are recalled at gala benefit tribute." *New York Times* 123 (April 30):46, 48.
Report of gala at Avery Fisher Hall, where the Lincoln Center Film Society saluted Hitchcock, followed by comments from stars attending.

416   "Hitchcock: Mr. Hitchcock's address to the Film Society of Lincoln Center, New York on the 29th of April, 1974." *Film Comment* 10, no. 4 (July–August):34–35.
Text of 300-word address and stills of 15 appearances in his films.

417   HUMBERT, MICHAEL, and DANIEL DELOSNE.   *"L'inconnu du nord-express." Revue du Cinéma/Image et Son,* no. 286 (August):87–92.
Lengthy synopsis, overview of critical opinion on *Strangers on a Train.*

418   JENSEN, PAUL.   "Raymond Chandler: The world you live in." *Film Comment* 10, no. 6 (November–December):25–26.
Brief discussion of Chandler's relationship with Hitchcock on *Strangers on a Train.*

419   PAUL, W.   "Hitchcock gala: A drowning man with dry feet." *Village Voice* 19 (May 9):86.
Account of the ceremony honoring Hitchcock at Lincoln Center.

420   PHILLIPS, GENE D.   "A Hitchcock hurrah." *America* 130, no. 17 (May 4):340–341.
Generic overview of Hitchcock's career on the occasion of the Lincoln Center celebration: "Each of us is, as Hitchcock suggests, a fascinating bundle of paradoxes."

421   RINGEL, HARRY.   *"Blackmail:* The opening of Hitchcock's surrealist eye." *Film Heritage* 9, no. 2 (Winter):17–23.
Description of surrealist themes and techniques in the films: the noting of "non-action," gesture as a state of mind, and the personalization of the character's environment. Also comments on Expressionist influences as well as influence of Joseph Von Sternberg and Carl Dreyer.

422 ROUD, RICHARD. "In broad daylight." *Film Comment* 10, no. 4 (July–August):36.
Reprinted from the program of the Lincoln Center tribute. Roud focuses on Hitchcock's plots as forays into self-knowledge, the ordinary person confronted with the extraordinary event, and so on.

423 SARRIS, ANDREW. "Alfred Hitchcock, prankster of paradox." *Film Comment* 10, no. 2 (March–April):8–9.
Response to negative contemporary criticism. Sarris claims it is a mistake to locate Hitchcock's films in any particular genre, and, while some are failures, they all age better than they appear.

424 STEINER, FRED. "Herrmann's black-and-white music for Hitchcock's *Psycho*, Parts I, II." *Filmmusic Notebook* 1 (Fall; Winter):28–36; 26–45.
Description of the composition and its pointed upholding of Hitchcock's "out of the ordinary" concept, which "sets it apart from any other score produced up to that time." Steiner discusses the difficulties of using only strings, which deprived the composer of most traditional suspense music formulas. Herrmann described it as a "black and white orchestra" to go with black and white film, for strings, while having only one tone color, have a wide range of other attributes. Herrmann's general style is characterized as an avoidance of tunes and melodies for the purpose of short "musical modules" that can be used like building blocks. Part II provides a detailed analysis of selected sequences involving technical description of musical motives such as the water, the stairs, and the murder. Some reproductions of the score.

425 TARNOWSKI, JEAN FRANÇOIS. "De quelques problèmes de mise en scène (à propos de *Frenzy* d'Alfred Hitchcock)." *Positif,* no. 158 (April):46–60.
Introductory remarks include review of Hitchcock criticism, which author thinks has impeded more intelligent appreciation by its conformity and focus on the suspense category. Analysis of *Frenzy* is presented "to bring to light a theory of cinema which reveals the work of the filmmaker in a concrete way." Tarnowski assesses the mise-en-scène, which he sees as devoted to clichés, as an open question, then examines point of view and dramatic duration as related aspects. He concludes the film is not a mystery or "closed language system," but rather reveals a diversity of problems in its very unity, and thus effects a kind of "open" cinema. Jean Mitry, in *Positif,* no. 173 (September, 1975), begins a debate over some of the theoretical questions raised, to which Tarnowski responds at length in a later issue, *Positif,* no. 188 (1976).

426 WARHOL, ANDY. "Hitchcock." *Andy Warhol's Interview* 4 (September):5–9.
"Redacted by Pat Hackett." Many attempts to make the interview more personal ("Do you know so-and-so?") are quickly passed over. Comments on murder, England, his family, his signature, the atom bomb, Greta Garbo, and sex.

1975
Books

*427   *Omaggio a Alfred Hitchcock: Antologia Critica,* edited by Movie Club di
Torino. *Quaderni di Documentazione,* October. Torino: Centro studi
cinematografici di Torino.
Cited in entry 703. Critical anthology.

428   PERRY, GEORGE. *Hitchcock.* New York/London: Doubleday/
Macmillan, 126 pp.
Popular, chronological overviews, illustrated, some in color.

Articles and Shorter Writings

429   ANDEREGG, MICHAEL A. "Conrad and Hitchcock: *The Secret Agent*
inspires *Sabotage.*" *Literature/Film Quarterly* 3, no. 3 (Summer):215–225.
Detailed comparison of Joseph Conrad's novel and the film. The author
argues that adaptation involves more than faithfulness to broad elements of plot
and theme. He discusses the similar approaches in both works to creating the
atmosphere of London, the "blow-up" in the film of certain minor details of the
novel, and the "nearly parallel statements . . . [revealing] a claustrophobic world
of limited options and stunted emotions."

430   BAZIN, ANDRÉ. "Alfred Hitchcock." In *Le Cinéma de la cruauté.* Paris:
Flammarion, pp. 121–199.
Reprints of three essays, entry 205, entry 215, and "Panoramique sur
Hitchcock," from *Ecran Français,* January 23 (1950). The last asserts a kind of
"swindle" because Bazin thinks that Hitchcock's true period of creativity ended in
1943 with *Shadow of a Doubt.* While the director continues to be formally
inventive, it is at the service of the most traditional of filmic ideas, and his work
as a result in no way equals that of Orson Welles or William Wyler.
Also reviews, translated into English and summarized in entry 684, of *Shadow
of a Doubt,* from *Ecran Français,* October 3 (1945); *Suspicion,* from *Ecran Français,*
October 29 (1946); *Notorious,* from *Ecran Français,* March 16 (1948); *The Lady
Vanishes,* from *L'Observateur,* April 10 (1952); *Dial M for Murder,* from *Radio,
Cinéma, Télévision,* February 13 (1955); *To Catch a Thief,* from *France Observa-
teur,* December 19 (1955); *Lifeboat,* from *France Observateur,* June 14 (1956); and
The Man Who Knew Too Much (1955), from *France Observateur,* October 18 (1956).
Reviews: LeGuay, P. "Alfred Hitchcock, par André Bazin." *Cinématographe,*
no. 59 (July–August 1980):57.
"*Le cinéma de la cruauté.*" *Cinéma* 76 (1976).

431   BELLOUR, RAYMOND. "Le blocage symbolique." *Communications,*
no. 23:235–350.
North by Northwest as an illustration of the Hitchcockian dialectic, here
defined as the Oedipal trajectory of the hero through an identity crisis and into

the arms of a "good" woman. The narrative is separated into three movements: from the introduction of Roger to the slaying (of the symbolic father) at the United Nations, from his encounter with Eve on the train through the cornfield disaster, and finally, from the reconciliation with her in the woods to the marriage. Support for this structure is then detailed in most aspects of the plot, dialogue, the male characters, and costumes. Over half the essay is an even more detailed analysis of segment 14, the cornfield sequence, which includes a representative frame from each shot and several descriptive charts indicating shot-reverse shot sequences, their changing point of view (alternation), and who is looking or being looked at. Means of transportation are charted and the involvement of the characters, particularly Roger—who becomes a "symbolic phallus"—with the range of buses, cars, and taxis is examined at length in its symbolic and literal evocation of the Oedipal journey.

Reprinted in author's *L'Analyse du Film* (Paris: Albatros, 1979). Critiqued in "Alternation, segmentation, hypnosis: Interview with Raymond Bellour," by Janet Bergstrom, *Camera Obscura,* no. 3–4 (1979), "Bookkeeping on an analyst's couch: A French critic's approach to Hitchcock," by D. Bombyk, *Take One* 5, no. 2 (May 1976), and entry 518.

432   B[ROWN], R[OYAL] S. *"Spellbound:* Classic film scores of Miklós Rózsa." *High Fidelity* and *Musical America* 25 (July):97–98.
Technical description of the score as conducted by Charles Gerhardt (RCA Red Seal ARL1-9011) in a "heavy handed interpretation emphasizing the romantic side"; also the "far superior" issue of the original Warner Bros. tape conducted by Ray Heindorf, Stanyan SRQ 4021.

433   DERVIN, DANIEL. "The primal scene and the technology of perception in theater and film: A historical perspective with a look at *Potemkin* and *Psycho." Psychoanalytic Review* 62, no. 2 (Summer):269–304.
Within a larger essay, an analysis of *Psycho,* in particular the shower scene, as an instance of a reenactment of the "primal scene," the shower being the male partner, and the transvestite/murderer, "the destructive potential come to be in the witness."

434   EVERSON, WILLIAM K. "Rediscovery." *Films in Review* 26, no. 5 (May):293–296, 299.
Detailed historical discussion of *Easy Virtue,* the circumstances of its adaptation, production, and distribution.

435   FRAYNE, JOHN P. *"North by Northwest." Journal of Aesthetic Education* 9, no. 2 (April):77–95.
Study guide for the film. Includes overview of standard critical approaches, emphasizing the French critics, biographical and interview material as it relates to themes, a "sequence outline, and study questions."

1975

*436   JAHNKE, ECKART.   "Hitchcocks Kino." *Prisma* 6:221–238.
    Cited in entry 703.

437   McDOUGAL, STUART Y.   "Mirth, sexuality and suspense: Alfred
    Hitchcock's adaptation of *The 39 Steps.*" *Literature/Film Quarterly* 3, no.
    3 (Summer):232–239.
    Comparison of John Buchan's novel to the film. McDougal argues that
Hitchcock "transformed" the mystery into a quickly paced work of suspense by
altering the structure and simplifying the plot; he also made it into "an
exploration of male-female relationships." He discusses the topography as an
integral part of the story as well as couples and families.

438   MEYER, ANDREW.   "The plot thickens." *Film Comment* 11, no. 5
    (September–October):21–23.
    Description of a day on the set of *Family Plot* with details of the shooting and
quotes from Barbara Harris, Bruce Dern, Karen Black, and William Devane.

439   MULVEY, LAURA.   "Visual pleasure and narrative cinema." *Screen* 16,
    no. 3 (Autumn):31–39.
    An influential feminist theoretical analysis concerned with the relation of film
form to the development of sexual difference. Looking, as it controls the flow of the
narrative, is posited as the expression of an "active-passive heterosexual division
of labor," where the male movie star is a natural "figure in a landscape," mover of
the story, whole powerful ego, and the female movie star is a passive, isolated,
frequently objectified icon. But the female figure in psychoanalytic terms also
represents castration and therefore evokes the same anxiety in men that the
containing of the figure in the frame of the camera is paradoxically intended to
control. Hitchcock's films consistently illustrate both avenues of escape (scopophilia) from this anxiety: obsession with the form in an increased attempt to
control it (voyeurism) and the fetishizing of the form, breaking up or building up
the beauty of the object, "making it something satisfying in itself." *Vertigo* and *Rear
Window* are put forth as representative of the male point of view as the protagonist
unconsciously grapples with the tensions and contradictions surrounding issues of
identity that these avenues of escape do not entirely smooth over. Reprinted in
Movies and Methods, vol. 2, edited by Bill Nichols (Berkeley: University of California Press, 1985).

440   ROTHMAN, WILLIAM.   "Alfred Hitchcock's *Notorious.*" *Georgia Review*
    29, no. 4 (Winter):884–927.
    Describes the film as a "paradigm of highly complex narrative, wedded to a
rigorously composed cinematic form." Detailed analysis, presented scene by
scene, includes descriptions of shots and edits as well as quoted dialogue.
Rothman concludes that the film was freely created and asserts that the free
actions of its characters lead to "a profound paradox." Just as Alicia wants Devlin
to see her actions as reactions to his "expectations and desires," so also Hitchcock
wants to please the viewer. But the film shows and Devlin knows that "her

passivity is an act," and the viewer is called to "acknowledge oneness with the figure [the director] whose nature compels him to renounce the possibility of ever entering into such a relationship."

441   SCHICKEL, RICHARD.   "Alfred Hitchcock." In *The Men Who Make the Movies; Interviews*. New York: Atheneum, pp. 271–303.
Portrait of the director as a timid embodiment of all "our" fears, including, most persistently, being wrongly accused. A thorough review of most of the comments and attitudes expressed in his U.S. period follows in the form of a first-person narrative. Hitchcock comments on the psychological problems of his childhood, his ideas of degradation and punishment, evil as "complete disorder," the spreading of evil in modern times, murder, the art of film adaptation, pure cinema as the manipulation of point of view, dialogue, MacGuffins, suspense versus mystery, and his literary influences.
Reviews: *"The Men Who Make the Movies." Variety* 278 (May 7, 1975):130. *"The Men Who Make the Movies." New York Review of Books* 23 (April 15, 1976):33–35.
"The Men Who Make the Movies." New Statesman 93 (February 25, 1977):261.
"The Men Who Make the Movies." Audience 7 (June 1975):9.

442   SIMPER, DELOY.   "Poe, Hitchcock, and the well-wrought effect." *Literature/Film Quarterly* 3, no. 3 (Summer):226–231.
Comparison of Edgar Allan Poe and Hitchcock, both of whom were popular, emulated by French critics, and held up as masters of suspense and horror. Using an essay by Poe on composition and interviews with Hitchcock, Simper puts forth a short analysis of *The Birds* to illustrate its conscious and planned artistry, similar in calculation to "The Raven."

443   STRICK, PHILIP.   "Hitchcock in the balance." *The Listener* 93, no. 2408 (May 29):707–708.
Argues against Hitchcock's currently low reputation (occasioned by a BBC retrospective); claims Hitchcock is a master of manipulation, able not only to shock but also to communicate identification and recognition.

1976
Books

444   HARRIS, ROBERT A., and MICHAEL S. LASKY.   *The Films of Alfred Hitchcock*. Secaucus, N.J.: Citadel, 256 pp.
Fans' description of the films presented in chronological order. Many photographs, though actors are sometimes misidentified, especially those from British films.
Translated into German (Munich: Goldman, 1979), French (Paris: Veyrier, 1980), and Italian (entry 678).

1976

445   SPOTO, DONALD. *The Art of Alfred Hitchcock: Fifty Years of His Motion Pictures.* New York: Hopkinson & Blake, 525 pp.

Chronological thematic, visual, and character analysis. One chapter on the early films, then chapters on each of the films beginning with *The 39 Steps.* Spoto examines the primary theme of appearance and reality through explication of plot elements that reverse the expected, and the plot framework of pursuit. Other major themes are the power of the dead over the living and the fragility of the ordered world. By far the longest chapter is given to *Vertigo* and its most complete treatment of all the major themes. Throughout, symbols and metaphors are examined, such as birds, eyes, water, memory, journeys, art, and dreams. Particular focus is placed on the details of mise-en-scène, sets, costumes, music. After *Shadow of a Doubt,* the author describes a predominant tone of "moral cynicism."

Reviews: *"The Art of Alfred Hitchcock." Filmmakers Newsletter* 10 (April 1977):55–56.

"The Art of Alfred Hitchcock." Movie Maker 12 (July 1978):593.

"The Art of Alfred Hitchcock." Skoop 14 (August–September 1978):34.

"The Art of Alfred Hitchcock." Cinéma 77, no. 224–225 (August–September 1977):220–221.

"The Art of Alfred Hitchcock." Thousand Eyes Magazine 2 (November 1976):10.

"The Art of Alfred Hitchcock." Millimeter 4 (November 1976):58.

"The Art of Alfred Hitchcock." Films and Filming 24 (March 9, 1978):9.

"The Art of Alfred Hitchcock." Quarterly Review of Film Studies 4, no. 2 (1979):257–265.

"The Art of Alfred Hitchcock." University Film Study Newsletter 7, no. 3 (1977):12–13.

"The Art of Alfred Hitchcock." Sight and Sound 46, no. 2 (1977):130.

"The Art of Alfred Hitchcock." Focus on Film, no. 28 (1977):50.

Counts, Kyle B. *Cinefantastique* 6, no. 2 (Fall 1977):37.

Kindem, Gorham. *"The Art of Alfred Hitchcock." Cinema Journal* 17, no. 1 (Winter 1977):49–51.

Thomas, Paul. *"The Art of Alfred Hitchcock." Film Quarterly* 30, no. 3 (Spring 1977):57–62.

Articles and Shorter Writings

446   "Alfred Hitchcock: A friendly salute." *Take One* 5, no. 2:6–50.

Anthology of material including short interviews or correspondence with Ingrid Bergman, Cary Grant, James Stewart, and Philip Halsmann, portrait photographer.

Introductory essay by James Monaco sees Hitchcock as underrated, not well served even by his own public persona. He is "the existential poet of the cinema par excellence . . . whose hunted men and women suffer for us all." The author suggests the Rohmer-Chabrol (entry 246) "system of exchanges, transferences, reversals of guilt and responsibility" can be put forth in support of a "dramatic system" as well as a religious one, which in Hitchcock lacks the crucial "higher authority." The author suggests he invokes a "political response" with his explication of power relationships. He describes the visual style, camera techniques, clichés, signs, types, and all kinds of "unrealistic" created shots.

Also includes short essays by Maurice Yacowar on the early British films and John Russell Taylor on visual style; also portraits by Mike Hodges and Truffaut, portraits of Alma Hitchcock by Taylor and Bernard Herrmann by Brian De Palma as well as a review of *Family Plot,* filmography, and bibliography.

*447   BOOST, C. "Take One entleedt Hitchcock; de ontdekker van de funda-mentale logica in de film." *Skoop* 12, no. 7:21–25.
Cited in entry 703. In Dutch.

448   BORDONARO, PETER. *"Dial M for Murder*: A Play by Frederick Knott/a film by Alfred Hitchcock." *Sight and Sound* 45, no. 3 (Summer):175–179.
Detailed comparison of the play script with the film, examining the setting and the subtle shifts in dialogue that make each of the characters more complex and ambiguous, and the extension of the murder into a set-piece, which generally makes the film a more sophisticated suspense creation.

449   BROWN, ROYAL S. "Bernard Herrmann and the subliminal pulse of violence." *High Fidelity and Musical America* 26 (March):75–76.
Technical description of the complete original score of *Psycho,* conducted by Bernard Herrmann in its first release, from the National Philharmonic Orchestra, Unicorn, RHS 336. "One is struck by the thorough appropriateness of the music to the film."

450   COCKS, JAY. "Grave error." *Time* 107 (April 26):45, 48.
Review of *Family Plot:* "Out of respect for Hitchcock, should be considered as fleetingly as possible . . . vulgar, lifeless, and maladroit." The wink at the end is a sign of "directorial desperation."

*451   DUYNSLAEGHER, P. "Alfred Hitchcock." *Film en Télévisie,* nos. 230–231; 232; 233 (July–August; September; October):16–19; 32–35; 26–29.
Cited in *Film Literature Index,* 1976.

452   DYNIA, PHILIP. "Alfred Hitchcock and the ghost of Thomas Hobbes." *Cinema Journal* 15, no. 2 (Spring):27–41.
Description of *The Man Who Knew Too Much, The 39 Steps, The Secret Agent, Sabotage, The Lady Vanishes, Foreign Correspondent, Saboteur, Lifeboat, Notorious, Torn Curtain,* and *Topaz* culminating in a brief analysis of Hitchcock's "political philosophy" as both Hobbesian—emphasizing human anxieties and fear of death—and non-Hobbesian—revealing lack of faith in government. From this "lunatic dichotomy" Dynia concludes that Hitchcock's political message is that "we must recognize the limits of state imposed orders."

1976

453   FISHER, RICHARD. "Hitchcock and Welles: Tormented wives and
        other matters." *Thousand Eyes Magazine,* no. 10 (May):6–7.
   Comparison of the visual compositions of *Citizen Kane* and *Rebecca.* (*Rebecca*
had premiered four months prior to the beginning of shooting for *Citizen Kane*).
The year before, Welles had produced a radio version of *Rebecca,* to which
Selznick had recommended Hitchcock listen.

454   FISHER, RICHARD. "Hitchcock's figure on the staircase." *Thousand
        Eyes Magazine,* no. 12 (July–August):3–4.
   Discussion of the use of staircases, primarily as they relate to plots, with
extended analysis of "the battle on the stairway" in *Shadow of a Doubt.*

455   GILLIATT, PENELOPE. "Hitch." *New Yorker* 52 (April 19):102–104.
   Positive review of *Family Plot:* "Hitchcock has never made a strategically
wittier film, or a fonder. . . . Only a very practiced poet of suspense could slacken
the fear without seeming to cheat." Reprinted in *Three Quarter Face* (New York:
Coward, McCann, 1980).

456   GREENSPUN, ROGER. "Plots and patterns." *Film Comment* 12, no. 3
        (May–June):20–22.
   Family Plot as a "couples movie." It is one of the "great normative visions. . . .
Men and women still have the option of loving one another and living together in
sanity." In total, the film is seen as exceptionally benevolent, never missing
"prospects for casual good-feeling."

457   HODENFIELD, CHRIS. "Muuuurder by the babbling brook." *Rolling
        Stone,* no. 218 (July 29):38–43, 56.
   Series of interviews and portrait at the time of *Family Plot.* The author
begins with an anecdote about a turn of the century theater trick and includes
comments on the limitations of Hitchcock's imitators, Catholicism, directing.

458   LAMBERT, GAVIN. "Hitchcock and the art of suspense." *American
        Film* 1, no. 4; no. 5 (January–February; March):16–23; 60–67.
   Evenhanded general discussion of Hitchcock's career integrating early biographical anecdotes with a synthesis of critical thinking. Lambert speculates that
the director's Jesuit background helped him to appreciate the control good
organization can attain. He concludes that the "poetic intensity" and impartiality
of the films is a result of Hitchcock's allegiance to "pure cinema" and a love of
making films that is "stronger than his love of morality."

459   MACKLIN, F. ANTHONY. "It's the manner of telling: An interview
        with Alfred Hitchcock." *Film Heritage* 11, no. 3 (Spring):11–22.
   Comments primarily on *Family Plot;* also on happiness in marriage, and
Frenzy.

460 MacSHANE, FRANK. "Stranger in a studio: Raymond Chandler and Hollywood part two." *American Film* 1, no. 7 (May):54–60.
The relationship of Raymond Chandler and Hitchcock on *Strangers on a Train* was unsatisfactory to both. Chandler found Hitchcock interfering and, toward the end, insufficiently communicative; as his script was entirely rewritten by Czenzi Ormonde, the experience was quite bitter for Chandler. Excerpted from *The Life of Raymond Chandler*.

461 McBRIDE, JOSEPH. "Mr. and Mrs. Hitchcock." *Sight and Sound* 45, no. 4 (Autumn):224–225.
Conversation with Alma Reville concerning her role as critic, and observations on the couple's interactions. She is independent, with "peppery" opinions, their ideas about filmmaking are identical, they often complete each other's sentences, and so on.

462 McCARTHY, MARY. "Mary McCarthy goes to the movies." *Film Comment* 12, no. 1 (January–February):34.
Short analysis of *Lifeboat* as an allegory of the heart and the head, and a bow to the theory of the superhuman.

463 McKEGNY, MICHAEL. "The disordered world—Hitchcock's *Topaz.*" *Cinemabook* 1, no. 1 (Spring):4–9.
Assessment of *Topaz* as "one of Hitchcock's most stylistically subdued works," lacking the moral normative values that Hitchcock has always adhered to. Nonetheless, "its compassionate awareness of physical and mental suffering . . . makes it one of his most rewarding"; also offers a sober look at modern international affairs and the intimacy they shun.

464 MILLER, GABRIEL. "Hitchcock's wasteland vision: An examination of *Frenzy.*" *Film Heritage* 11, no. 3 (Spring):1–10.
Plot and character analysis of *Frenzy* as a portrait of "total decay."

465 MORSEBERGER, ROBERT E. "Adrift in Steinbeck's *Lifeboat.*" *Literature/Film Quarterly* 4, no. 4 (Fall):325–338.
Describes the film as an "uneven conglomeration of Hitchcock suspense, Steinbeck philosophy, and Swerling situation and dialogue. Morseberger discusses contemporary criticism of the Nazi character as too strong and the story as unrealistic. Comparing the film to the original film treatment by Steinbeck, Morseberger argues that while not as "exciting," this original version is more politically aware and substantive.

1976

466   PECHTER, WILLIAM S. "Hitchcock in retrospect." *Commentary* 62, no. 5 (November):75–78.
Reflections on *Family Plot* and Hitchcock's body of "work, not rich in richly imagined characters," but stuck in a child's world, where sex is a "dirty adult secret." Pechter finds that the persistence of themes makes the later films more interesting but less enjoyable. They demonstrate "he knows what he is doing" but we "learn nothing," because the plot just lies there, "slack, tensionless, stillborn."

467   ROSENBAUM, JONATHAN. "Journals." *Film Comment* 12, no. 4 (July–August):2–3.
Hitchcock "devotes his energy to showing us how a thriller works" in *Family Plot*. It's about his own "sexy forms of duplicity and deception . . . sound and image."

468   ROSS, T. J. "Aspects of Hitchcock." *December* 18, no. 2/3: 75–91.
Discussion centered on *Frenzy* of Hitchcock's "distinctive world" and character types, consisting of settings with "an impression of narrowed horizons" charged with "violent intensities." Ross describes the "double nature" of the villains and the protagonists as well as the couples, especially as they relate on the continuum of sadomasochism, and mother-child—the women being parental figures and the men, boy-children (who are, nonetheless, victimizers of women).

469   SCHEIB, RONNIE. "Charlie's uncle: Ronnie Scheib on *Shadow of a Doubt*." *Film Comment* 12, no. 26 (March–April):55–62.
Florid exposition of themes in the film. Class and sex roles are linked: "the discovery of the phallus coincides with the discovery of the lower classes," along with sexual, economic, and political forces: "there is in Hitchcock no Langian handshake by which conflict of interest is resolved in the promise of a liberal compromise." Ultimately, "the film is a series of deaths."

470   SCHENKER, SUSAN. "Plotting the Hitchcock family." *Take One* 5, no. 2:47.
List of crews and cast according to the number of times each has worked with Hitchcock. Translated into Portuguese, entry 676.

471   SILVIR, ALAIN J. "The fragments of the mirror: The use of landscape in Hitchcock." *Wide Angle* 1, no. 3:52–61.
Analyzes Hitchcock's use of landscape in various senses, as physical screen space and metaphor or synecdoche. The terms *monumental landscape, transcendent landscape,* and *cityscape* are employed in structural analysis of *Vertigo*, with examples from many other films. Includes diagrams and photographs.

472   WOLLEN, PETER. *"North by Northwest:* A morphological analysis." *Film Form* (Newcastle upon Tyne) 1, no. 1:9–34.

After Vladimir Propp, an "attempt" to generalize concerning the relevance of morphological analyses for cinema, proposing a relation of contemporary mass culture to folk tales. Wollen examines the film's structure surrounding the pairs: interdiction and violation, reconnaissance and receipt of information, and trickery and submission. He concludes that the basic fairy tale structure is present, though reformulation for cinema is necessary.

Reprinted in *Readings and Writings* (London: Verso, 1982).

473   YACOWAR, MAURICE.   "Hitchcock: The best of the earliest." *Take One* 5, no. 2:42–45.

Short critical summaries of the British films, all showing "Hitchcock at work. We have the familiar leg shots, witty undressing . . . comic fights, and vision of man leading a precarious life."

1977
Books

474   *Alfred Hitchcock.* [Mexico]: Filmoteca Nacional de España, 181 pp.

Detailed filmography with comments, translated excerpts, and other supporting material, including reproduction of some production storyboards from *Family Plot.*

*475   BERNARDONI, MASSIMO, and HARTWIG KEMMERER. *Alfred Hitchcock.* Hildesheim: Hildesheimer Volkshochschule.

Cited in entry 703.

476   WOOD, ROBIN. *Hitchcock's Films.* London/New York: Zwemmer/ Barnes, 174 pp.

The third edition of entry 318 adds a chapter titled "Retrospective." In an attempt to define Hitchcock's art more precisely, Wood discusses the formal influences of Expressionism, realism, Soviet montage, and the "set pieces of pure cinema," a result of an intense method of preplanning. Formal aspects are even more intensely related to content: "the desire to control, the terror of losing control . . . describe Hitchcock's conscious relationship to technique and to audiences, but also the thematic center of the films." Wood now sees limitations in the films, which only a few transcend. First, the equivocal relationship between the artist and the entertainer, which results in films that work up to a point, then collapse under sudden simplification. Second, the weakness of the "normative impulse," which establishes "bourgeois normality as empty and unsatisfying: and everything beyond it as terrifying."

Chapter on *Strangers on a Train* reprinted, entry 771.

Reviews: entry 599.

Rubenstein, Lenny. *Cineaste* 9, no. 4 (1979):57.

1977

477   YACOWAR, MAURICE. *Hitchcock's British Films*. Hamden, Conn.:
Archon Books, 314 pp.

Chronological thematic, visual, and character analysis of the British films. In
general, Yacowar shows a precise familiarity with the early films that allows him
to counter effectively the misconceptions of critics' work on *Murder!* and the other
thrillers as well as to present appreciations of the lesser-known films. While class
and sex differences are presented as major themes, they are generally naturalized
in the descriptions rather than explicated.

The Pleasure Garden is shown to have "the moral rigor . . . of a director fresh
from the working class" as well as the irony of the "Hitchcock touch"—for
example, in the contrasting of the Pleasure Garden music hall as "a false image
of the jungle" with that of the true jungle, "the East." The long and middle shots
that characterize this film are contrasted with the close-up, restricted framing of
The Lodger. Throughout, visual motifs are detailed—circles, arcs, triangles, Xs,
abstracted staircases—and compared to their presence in the more well-known
American films. With the evidence of these visual signs and the well-documented
instances of subtle character portrayal, Yacowar argues that Hitchcock was, from
the very beginning, clearly devising "more than entertainment." The films were
"moral tests for his audiences—and often traps."

Examines *Downhill* as "Hitchcock's first pessimistic whole." The values and
upper-class assumptions that belong to the main character are shown to be
insubstantial. The film's relation to the themes of *Vertigo* indicate its importance
as a reflection of Hitchcock's personality. *Easy Virtue* is the first full-blown
instance of the theme of public versus private, while *The Ring* is a study in the
contrast between "partial and total commitment." "From *Champagne* through
The Manxman to *Blackmail* one can define a movement in Hitchcock's mind away
from an unquestioning adherence to conventional tenets and towards the anar-
chic, subversive spirit for which he is known."

Comment on *Rich and Strange* focuses on Fred's "exposure" as an incompetent and the film's consequent anticipation of "the unexamined selfishness that
comes to characterize the later Hitchcock heroes." *Waltzes from Vienna,* along
with *The Skin Game,* illustrate "the passage of power from the stiff traditional old
way to the flexible and cunning new." The former film is also the first film in
which the "women are so clearly superior to the men."

Other thematic aspects are discussed throughout: the confused conception of
hero and heroic, the emphasis on psychological over physical reality, the harsh
father figures, the acknowledgement of the limitations of subjective judgment,
and the "dramatic appeal of the insecure." Technique is argued to be the center of
meaning. A concluding essay, "Hitchcock's Imagery and Art," referring to all the
British and the American films, along with an appendix on the personal
appearances, presents Hitchcock as an "irrepressible ironist" and poetic realist
"engaged with the moral and perceptual nature of man."

The final chapter is reprinted in entry 771.

Reviews:

"Hitchcock's British Films." Bianco e Nero 39 (January–February 1978):137.

"Hitchcock's British Films." Take One 6, no. 6 (1978):53–54.

Mayne, Richard. "Chilling the spine." *Times Literary Supplement,* no. 3932
(July 22, 1977):884.

Rothman, W. "How much did Hitchcock know?" *Quarterly Review of Film
Studies* 5, no. 3 (1980):381–392.

Rubenstein, Lenny. *Cineaste* 9, no. 4 (1979):57.

Articles and Shorter Writings

478   BELLOUR, RAYMOND.   "Hitchcock, the Enunciator." *Camera Obscura,*
   no. 2 (Fall):66–91.
Theoretical analysis using the beginning sequences of *Marnie* to illustrate
the inscription in the film of the woman's body as the image of sexuality and the
male spectator's desire, which both creates and is aroused by the image (voyeurism). Bellour also discusses in general the nature of viewing pleasure. He
presents a theory of the camera as Hitchcock, the enunciator, "the first among all
his doubles . . . as pure image-power—the camera-wish, of which the object choice
is here the woman." Both Hitchcock's appearances and the credit sequences of
other films are presented as evidence of this system of pleasure derived from a
fantasy made up of images.
   Translation of "Enoncer" in author's *L'analyse du film* (Paris: Albatros,
1979). Critiqued in "Alternation, segmentation, hypnosis; interview with Raymond Bellour," by Janet Bergstrom, in *Camera Obscura,* no. 3–4 (1979) and
entries 505 and 518.

479   BONITZER, PASCAL.   "Voici: La notion de plan et le sujet du cinéma."
   Cahiers du Cinéma, no. 273:10–16.
Theoretical essay, after Christian Metz and Jean Mitry, on screen space as
described through a taxonomy of the shot. Bonitzer posits Hitchcock's "genius" as
resting on his emphasis on point of view as a productive force equal to montage,
not merely a secondary element of it.

480   CARRÈRE, EMMANUEL.   "La somnambule et le magnétisur (quelques
   images de rêve dans le cinéma fantastique)." *Positif,* no. 193 (May):48–52.
General discussion of dreams and opposing approaches to dream: psychoanalytic, where all is individual, and German romanticism, where nature, other,
and larger realities interact with the individual reality. In cinema, the first is
expressed when dream elements are easily explained—*Marnie* is the "masterpiece" of the genre. The second is the "true fantastic," where dream elements
bleed into the exterior life of the character and create destiny: the prime example
is *Vertigo,* not only because of its dream themes, but because of the place accorded
dreams in the narrative.

481   "Civic group objects to Hitchcock series." *Boxoffice,* 110 (March 7):E–7.
   Report of a protest by religious group over a Hitchcock series in a Philadelphia library.

482   DAHAN, LUCIEN.   "Le gros plan: Figure de style et évidence." *Cinématographe,* no. 25 (March):2–6.
Wide-ranging discussion of the use of the close-up and the varied methods for
achieving the effect of a close-up, with several examples from Hitchcock films.

1977

483   GILMAN, RICHARD. "Cult and puffery." *American Film* 2, no. 4 (February):74–75.
Under the guise of a book review, Gilman disparages Hitchcock's overblown reputation. He claims Hitchcock is neither a great nor bold film artist because of "his conception of the audience as a malleable and . . . naive set of witnesses" and because of "his refusal to take real chances."

*484   HERRMANN, BERNARD. "The contemporary use of music in film: *Citizen Kane, Psycho, Fahrenheit 451.*" *University Film Study Newsletter* 7, no. 3:5–10.
Cited in *Film Literature Index,* 1977.

485   HITCHCOCK, ALFRED. "Foreword." In *The Flicks or Whatever Became of Andy Hardy?* by Charles Champlin. Pasadena, Calif.: Ward Ritchie Press, pp. iv–v.
A portrait of Hitchcock's media relationship to Champlin, "one of the least terrifying of critics."

486   LAWSON, SYLVIA. "The Pierce/Wollen code signs: Functions and values." *Australian Journal of Screen Theory,* no. 3: 47–65.
In a larger essay on the working of signs and symbols in the history of film, Lawson places Hitchcock "in a place by himself" due to his deliberate and prolific use of symbolism. Using the terminology of C. S. Pierce, she finds his planting of symbolism in the subordinate detail (the index) unusual, and concludes that the traditional "gap between the icon and the index" in his films is comparatively small. This balance means, therefore, that everything on the screen takes on visible importance; the settings, the furnishings—all carry equal weight with the characters.

487   LEGRAND, GÉRARD. "Sur trois rééditions de films à costumes." *Positif,* no. 193 (May):34–41.
Comparison of three costume dramas: *Jamaica Inn, Forever Amber,* and *Cleopatra.* Legrand emphasizes their status as women's pictures.

488   MONTAGU, IVOR. "Michael Balcon, 1896–1977: Islington and the Bush." *Sight and Sound* 47, no. 2 (Winter):9–11.
Anecdotes from working days with Michael Balcon; also short tribute by Hitchcock: "Mick Balcon gave me my first job as an assistant director, also my first job as screenplay writer and afterwards art director. Such faith in me at the beginning of my career demands the greatest gratitude to his memory."

489   ROSE, JACQUELINE.   "Paranoia and the film system." *Screen* 17, no. 4
(Winter):85–104.
Theoretical discourse that uses *The Birds,* along with the ideas of Freud and
Jacques Lacan, to explore paranoia as the "aggressive corollary of the narcissistic
structure," hence related to the structure of cinema itself. Sharply original
character analysis, based primarily on dialogue, is arranged to argue that the
male acquires his proper identity through the woman. The woman is defined by
the narrative as transgression and is "both the cause and effect of the aggressivity
which drives the narrative" to its resolution.

*490   SPOTO, DANIEL.   "Hitchcock the designer." *Print* 31 (July–August):
37–43.
Cited in *Film Literature Index,* 1977.

491   TAYLOR, JOHN RUSSELL.   "Surviving: Alfred Hitchcock." *Sight and
Sound* 46, no. 3 (Summer):174–175.
Interview at Universal Studios. Hitchcock discusses *The Short Night,* his
regrets—not being a criminal lawyer, not completing one of his favorite scripts,
Mary Rose—and his style of survival—not tough or confrontational, but devious.

492   THOMPSON, KRISTIN.   "The duplicitous text: An analysis of Stage
Fright." *Film Reader* 2:52–64.
Neoformalist analysis based on ideas of the Russian formalists, particularly
of the fabula-syuzhet construct, which distinguishes between the "structured set
of causal events we see and hear" (syuzhet) and the mental reconstruction of
events in chronological order (fabula, a "viewing skill"). The focus of the essay is
the "lying" flashback in the film, which is seen to provide a "challenge" for the
viewer in its "extremely and overtly duplicitous structures." Thompson examines
theatrical imagery in support of the argument. Reprinted in *Breaking the Glass
Armor* (Princeton: Princeton University Press, 1988).

*493   VIAN, WALT.   "Versuch über Alfred Hitchcock." *Filmbulletin* 101:5–21.
Cited in entry 703.

*494   ———.   "Vertrauen und Mißtrauen in Hitchcock-Filmen." *Zoom,* no.
9:10–12.
Cited in entry 703. Uses examples from *The 39 Steps, North by Northwest,
Saboteur, Spellbound, Torn Curtain, To Catch a Thief.*

495   WOOD, ROBIN.   "Ideology, genre, auteur." *Film Comment* 13, no. 1
(January–February):46–51.
Structural-semiotic discussion of *Shadow of a Doubt* and *It's a Wonderful
Life.* Wood argues that both share the same "basic ideological tension" in the
opposition between city and small town, though the "bitter taste" of the Hitchcock
film contrasts with the more pleasant associations of the Frank Capra film.

1978
Books

496   ANDERS-KINDEM, GORHAM. "Toward a semiotic theory of visual communication in the cinema: A reappraisal of semiotic theories from a cinematic perspective and a semiotic analysis of color signs and communication in the color films of Alfred Hitchcock." Ph.D. Thesis. Evanston, Ill.: Northwestern University, 279 pp.

Reviews the literature concerning the theories of Ferdinand de Saussure, Charles K. Pierce, Umberto Eco, Christian Metz, and Peter Wollen. Using a listing of color signs by number and narrative unit, the author puts forth an interpretation of color in relation to characters, settings, and times, and concludes with more general speculations about repetitive color patterns in the films. Includes tables.

*497   TARNOWSKI, JEAN FRANÇOIS. *Hitchcock—Frenesi—Psicosis*. Valencia: Torres, 120 pp.

Cited in entry 703. In Spanish.

*498   TAST, BRIGITTE, and HANS-JURGEN TAST. *Alfred Hitchcock. Kulleraugen-Materialsammlung*, 1. Hildesheim: Selbstvlg, 32 pp.

Cited in entry 703.

499   TAYLOR, JOHN RUSSELL. *Hitch: The Life and Work of Alfred Hitchcock*. London/Boston: Faber & Faber, 320 pp.

Biography written from interviews and correspondence with many associates as well as Hitchcock and his family, though few of the references are specifically traced. The lack of prior personal documentation, even of the production of the British films, is noted. Taylor chronicles the "exemplary, conservative private life," the dedicated professionalism, and the "artistic enigma." He describes Hitchcock as a man who perfected himself as a "machine for making movies" and suggests that "there is no real Alfred Hitchcock outside his movies." The director's fears and consequent vulnerability made him "stern" in creating a "safe world" for himself in his films. Taylor focuses on anecdotal descriptions of the productions, most of which are subsumed in Spoto's later biography, entry 702.

Translated into German (Munich: Hanser, 1980).

Reviews: Berg, C. "Hitch." *Journal of Popular Film* 8, no. 1 (1980):56–57.

French, Philip. *Observer* (October 8, 1978):31.

"Hitch: The Life and Times of Alfred Hitchcock." *Film en Télévisie*, no. 260 (January 1979):37.

"Hitch: The Life and Times of Alfred Hitchcock." *Penthouse* 10 (February 1979):48.

"Hitch: The Life and Times of Alfred Hitchcock." *Focus on Film* 25 (April 1979):46.

"Hitch: The Life and Times of Alfred Hitchcock." *Cinema Papers*, no. 21 (May–June 1979):389.

"Hitch: The Life and Times of Alfred Hitchcock." *Films and Filming* 25 (April 1979):46.

"Hitch: The Life and Times of Alfred Hitchcock." *Skrien,* no. 80 (November 1978):34–35.

"Hitch: The Life and Times of Alfred Hitchcock." *Skoop* 14 (November 1978):48–49.

"Hitch: The Life and Times of Alfred Hitchcock." *New York Times* 127 (November 9, 1978): Section 7, p. 11.

"Hitch: The Life and Times of Alfred Hitchcock." *New Statesman* 96 (October 13, 1978):477.

"Hitch: The Life and Times of Alfred Hitchcock." *New York Times* 127 (November 28, 1978):Section C, p. 11.

"Hitch: The Life and Times of Alfred Hitchcock." *Filmkunst,* no. 81 (1978):12.

Mayne, Richard. "Appointment with fear." *Times Literary Supplement,* no. 3993 (October 13, 1978):1138.

Noble, Donald R. "Hitch: The Life and Times of Alfred Hitchcock." *Southern Humanities Review* 15, no. 3 (1981):272–275.

Rothman, W. "How much did Hitchcock know?" *Quarterly Review of Film Studies* 5, no. 3 (1980):381–392.

Rubenstein, Lenny. *Cineaste* 9, no. 4 (1979):57.

Thomas, Paul. "Hitch: The Life and Times of Alfred Hitchcock." *Film Quarterly* 33, no. 2 (Winter 1979–1980):60–61.

Turan, Kenneth. "Nothing too personal." *American Film* 4, no. 3 (December–January 1979):72–74.

500   ALLOMBERT, GUY. "Cet anglais méconnu, Alfred Hitchcock: 1925–1939: Entre frisson et sourire." *Revue du Cinéma/Image et Son,* no. 326 (March):43–54.

Short synopses and commentary on ten of the English films, at the time largely unknown in France.

501   B[ROWN] R[OYAL] S. "Herrmann and Hitch." *High Fidelity and Musical America* 28 (April):80–81.

Musical and historical commentary on the reissue of the *Vertigo* soundtrack, conducted by Muir Mathieson (Mercury SRI 75117); also the "rescue" of the unused *Torn Curtain* score by Bernard Herrmann, conducted by Elmer Bernstein, Film Music Collection 10.

502   CABRERA INFANTE, GUILLERMO. "El bacilo de Hitchcock." In *Arcadia Todas las Noches.* Barcelona: Seix Barral, S. A., pp. 59–84.

Critical overview. Cabrera Infante also reviewed many of Hitchcock's films individually as a working film critic.

503   CAMP, JOCELYN. "John Buchan and Alfred Hitchcock." *Literature/Film Quarterly* 6, no. 3 (Summer):230–240.

Comparison of the novel *The 39 Steps* to the film *The 39 Steps* and to *North by Northwest.* Camp argues that *North by Northwest* is "closer to Buchan's novel"

than the earlier film. Plot elements, especially the airplane scene, and themes, particularly theater/acting metaphors are given in support of the argument.

504   FELL, JOHN L.   "Structuring charts and patterns in film." *Quarterly Review of Film Studies* 3, no. 3 (Summer):371–388.

Within a larger essay on the use of diagrams and other abstract visual plans in structural analysis, sketches from *Family Plot* are used as an example of a preproduction design intended to control semiotic patterns.

505   FLITTERMAN, SANDY.   "Woman, desire, and the look: Feminism and the enunciative." *Cine-tracts* 2, no. 1 (Fall):63–68.

Explication of Raymond Bellour's analysis of *Marnie* (entry 478). Flitterman reviews the psychoanalytic and semiotic concepts that define classical narrative cinema as a "repository of male fantasy" (the enunciator, the look, scoptophilia, etc.). The author suggests that the most important point of Bellour's work for feminist criticism is his analysis of the first appearance of Marnie's face, when she washes the dye from her hair. By changing her own identity, "she continues herself as an image of desire, desired *because* she is an image, and offers this to the viewer."

Reprinted in *Theories of Authorship; a Reader,* edited by John Caughie (London: Routledge & Kegan Paul, 1981), pp. 242–250.

506   FOLEY, JACK.   "Doubleness in Hitchcock: Seeing *Family Plot.*" *Bright Lights* 2, no. 3:15–28.

Film as an anthology of Hitchcock motifs. Foley examines doubles, the pairing of guilt and innocence, performers and audience, sex, strong mothers, and, especially, the religious references.

507   HAMMOND, J.   "Hitchcock's violence: A fan's notes." *Journal of Popular Film and Television* 6, no. 3:239.

Poem about the murder of Babs in *Frenzy.*

508   HYDE, THOMAS.   "The moral universe of Hitchcock's *Spellbound.*" *Cinemonkey* 4, no. 15:30–34.

Thematic and character analysis focusing particularly on the character of Constance Peterson and Ingrid Bergman's performance in the role. Hyde argues that she illustrates "the inadequacy of intellectual analysis" divorced from compassion. He examines specific events in order to illustrate the presence in the film of "the deception of appearances, the untrustworthiness of authority, the nature of guilt and sin, and the moral responsibility of human involvement." Reprinted in entry 771.

509   TRUFFAUT, FRANÇOIS.   "Alfred Hitchcock." In *The Films of My Life,* translated by Leonard Mayhew. New York: Simon & Schuster, pp. 77–89.

Contemporary film reviews from *Arts* (1955), *Cahiers du Cinéma* (1955), and other sources through 1973. *Rear Window,* concerned with the theme of marriage,

is also about "the impossibility of happiness: and a brilliant parable of the filming of the world with its own director and camera." Hitchcock "is the man we love to hate us." *To Catch a Thief* dispenses with the psychological (connections, exposition, climax) and, though minor, is precise within the image. *The Wrong Man* is compared to Robert Bresson's *A Man Escaped* and judged Hitchcock's best film. *The Birds* must be respected for its unique premise and perfect execution. *Frenzy* is admired for its four women characters, which add "new realism" to Hitchcock's work.

Translated from the French (Paris: Flammarion, 1975). Translated into German (Munich: Hanser, 1976).

510   WEIS, ELIZABETH. "The sound of one wing flapping." *Film Comment* 14, no. 5 (September–October):42–48.

On Hitchcock's aural style, typically resourceful and having several shifts throughout his career. At first, experimental and expressionistic, it later became realistic and classical. "Aural intrusion," the experience of sound as "realistic" intrusion on a more subjective scene, is dominant in *The Birds,* where flapping wings, tapping beaks, and cries are the norm. Next to such din, silence also gains an ability to carry meaning.

*511   WERNER, G. "Nu bygger man filmen utifran Askadaren." *Chaplin* 20, no. 1 [no. 154]:5–12.

Cited in *Film Literature Index, 1978.*

1979
Books

512   FISCHER, ROBERT. *Regie Alfred Hitchcock: Eine Bilddokumentation seiner Kunst.* Schondorf, Ammersee: Programm Roloff & Seeßlen, 96 pp.

Filmography in oversize format, over half illustrations. Detailed synopses of later films.

513   *Una rosa è una rosa è una rosa; il cinema secondo Alfredo Hitchcock.* Giuliana Callegari and Nuccio Lodato, editors. Vedere è un modo di pensare: quaderno di documentazione, 15. Pavia: Centro Stampa dell'Amministrazione provinciale, 137 pp.

Includes a translation of an article on motion pictures written by Hitchcock for the *Encyclopedia Britannica* ("Motion pictures III: Film production," 1968, v.15, pp. 907–911). Also translations of Anderson (entry 187), Thomson (entry 344), and other essays by Adriano Apra, Fernaldo di Giammatteo, Enzo Ungari, Diego Cassini, and Giacci (entry 562).

514   VON BAGH, PETER. *Hitchcock: Merkintöjä Alfred Hitchcockin elokuvasta Vertigo.* Helsinki: Suomen Elokuvasäätiö, 155 pp.

Critical overview. In Finnish.

Articles and Shorter Writings

515 ABEL, RICHARD. *"Notorious:* Perversion par excellence." *Wide Angle* 1, no. 1:66–71.

After Vladimir Propp, an analysis of *Notorious* as a perversion of a fairy tale narrative. Abel argues that the tasks and roles of the hero, heroine, dispatcher, and villain are switched and confused. The hero, for instance, is "reduced" to being a "helper." Roles are discussed as parental and child figures, with "the ritual of couple formation" pushing the story ahead "at the expense of the family." Finally, the traditional structure reasserts itself, though the villain fulfills the dispatcher's role of reuniting the couple (in attempting to save himself, Sebastian helps the escape). This contradiction "rubs—we have become the agents of death for the character whose action has fulfilled what we so desired—the reunion of hero and heroine." Reprinted, entry 771.

516 BELLOUR, RAYMOND. "Psychosis, neurosis, perversion." *Camera Obscura,* no. 3–4 (Summer):104–134.

Analyzes *Psycho* as an exceptionally clear version of the Hitchcockian system, announcing in itself "the mechanisms that govern its operation," all provoked by sexual difference. Plot analysis provides evidence: the unconventional distribution of information among the characters and the replacement of the woman's story by the man's story, effected by the "perversion" of murdering Marion. This is combined with a conception of Hitchcock as an artist who reflects, perhaps unconsciously, on the "inevitable relationship" in our society between neurosis and psychosis, here represented by theft and murder. In *Psycho,* the "woman, the subject of neurosis, becomes the object of psychosis of which the man is the subject."

Further tenets of the Hitchcockian system: that women *do* kill, but only in response to being the object of a psychotic attack (*Blackmail, Dial M for Murder,* etc.); that women manifest psychotic tendencies only to the extent their male-hero-counterpart has suffered a loss of identity; and that men are usually the subject of neurosis, but in that case, it is always overshadowed by a psychosis (ritual testing) that allows the neurosis to be resolved by action. Finally, Bellour explains how perversion and psychosis are related and distinct from neurosis and how *Psycho* depends on perversion (voyeurism, fetishism) in order to function.

Reprinted in entry 771. Translated from the French, *L'analyse du film* (Paris: Albatros, 1979). Critiqued in "Alternation, segmentation, hypnosis; interview with Raymond Bellour" by Janet Bergstrom, *Camera Obscura,* no. 3–4 (1979) and entry 518.

517 BELTON, JOHN. "The main event: Hitchcock in Britain." *Thousand Eyes Magazine* 2, no. 2:5–9.

Short criticism on twenty of the British films, from *The Pleasure Garden* to *Stage Fright.* Belton makes reference to sources, influences, both contemporary and historical, and visual motifs. Reprinted in Belton's *Cinema Stylists* (Metuchen: Scarecrow, 1983).

518   BERGSTROM, JANET. "Enunciation and sexual difference (part 1)."
       Camera Obscura, no. 3–4 (Summer):32–69.
An introduction to the textual analysis of Raymond Bellour. Detailed
explication provides a conceptual context and definitions for his work on Hitchcock and other directors. Bergstrom describes the essays as an "attempt to come
to terms with the fascination" of watching a classical film that arises from the
seamless, formal structures that demand that the viewer repress all knowledge of
the unreality of what he or she sees. The author reworks the analysis of the boat
sequence in *The Birds* (entry 354) and discusses point of view, identification,
mirroring operations, the tying of the formal structures to sexual difference, and
the importance of Hitchcock's popularity.

*519   BIKACSY, G. "Alfred Hitchcock." *Filmkultura* 15, no. 5 (September–
       October):58–72.
Cited in *Film Literature Index,* 1979: on *Psycho* and *The Birds.*

520   C[UEL] F[RANÇOIS]. "De *Rebecca* à personne." *Cinématographe,* no. 46
       (April):53–54.
Thoughts on the relationship of Marguerite Duras's *Le navire/Night* to
Rebecca: actors without characters, characters without names, flashback without
return, mystification, lies, and "feminine text."

521   HABERMAN, CLYDE, and ALBIN KREBS. ". . . and Hitchcock is 80."
       New York Times 128 (August 13):Section B, p. 4, col. 6.
"Notes on People" section. Alfred Hitchcock is 80 and ailing with arthritis,
working on the script for his fifty-fourth picture, *The Short Night.* Says Hitchcock, "There is a saying that all pictures are exciting except the one you're
working on. That's true in this case."

522   "The Hitchcock moment." *American Film* 4, no. 5 (March):26–27.
Pictorial essay of tense moments.

523   KINDEM, GORHAM A. "Pierce's semiotic phenomenalism and film."
       Quarterly Review of Film Studies 4, no. 1 (Winter):61–69.
The first seven minutes of *To Catch a Thief* (through Robie's escape on the
bus) is used as an illustration of the Piercian sets of icon-index-symbol and
metaphor-metonym-copy/double, where relations among the first three produce
"mixtures" of the second three. Includes chart.

524   LUBIN, DAVID. "Buts and rebuts: Hitchcock: A defense and an update."
       Film Comment 15, no. 3 (May–June):66–68.
Response to an article by David Thomson (entry 528), terming it a conventional "high-toned" form/content diatribe. Lubin goes on to illustrate Hitchcock's

1979

mastery of content as well as form and Thomson's reductive confusion of the process of creating art with the process of living.

525   McBRIDE, JOSEPH. "Buts and rebuts—Hitchcock: A Defense and an update." *Film Comment* 15, no. 3 (May–June):69–70.
Description of the circumstances surrounding the American Film Institute tribute to Hitchcock, his infirmity, the production itself, and his current project, *The Short Night.*

526   McCONNELL, FRANK. "The world of melodrama." In *Story Telling and Mythmaking: Images from Film and Literature.* New York: Oxford University, pp. 169–178.
Puts forth Hitchcock's ideas as resembling those of Henry James in showing "the painfulness and the terror of [an] ultimately optimistic vision." McConnell uses *North by Northwest* to illustrate the thematic concepts of the ordinary as "optimal," the loss of innocence, and the reconciliation of "the closed room of the psyche and the open, agoraphobic hell which is other people." He finds in *Sabotage* a contrasting antipathy with the more pessimistic philosophy of Joseph Conrad, which substantiates "the fundamental benevolence—however complex —of Hitchcock's vision of society."

527   SARRIS, ANDREW. "The Hitchcock heritage." *Village Voice* 24 (April 2):45–46.
General discussion of the range of popular critics' treatment of Hitchcock's films.

528   THOMSON, DAVID. "The big Hitch: Is the director a prisoner of his own virtuosity?" *Film Comment* 15, no. 2 (March–April):26–29.
Hitchcock's work is not the achievement it should be but is, rather, mere technique. It lacks wisdom, depth, and humanity. His "sensibility is one of voluntary and neurotic enslavement," incorporating clichéd characters, exploited violence, and the endorsement of frightened passivity and complacency and, perhaps, evil.

529   VAN WERT, WILLIAM. "Composition psychoanalysis: Circles and straight lines in *Spellbound.*" *Film Criticism* 3, no. 3 (Spring):41–47.
Analysis of visual motifs, circles, lines, mirrors, glasses, as they relate to the psychoanalytic and dream themes of the film.

*530   VERSTAPPEN, W. "Analyse op de montagetafel *Notorious:* Een spionageverhaal over erotiek." *Skoop* 15, no. 3 (April):23–33.
Cited in *Film Literature Index,* 1979. "Includes shot analysis."

531 VILLIEN, BRUNO. "Hitchcock et ses masques." *Cinématographe,* no. 50 (September):30–31.
Listing and description of Hitchcock's appearances in the films.

532 WILSON, GEORGE M. "The maddest MacGuffin: Some notes on *North by Northwest.*" *MLN* 94, no. 5 (December):1159–1172.
Essay on the appearance and reality theme in *North by Northwest,* especially as it is expressed through theatrical references, sets, props, going to and acting in productions.

1980
Books

533 CARREÑO, JOSÉ MARIA. *Alfred Hitchcock. Directores de Cine,* no. 3. Madrid: JC, 155 pp.
Overview of the work.

534 COREY, DAVID. "Fearful symmetries: The contest of authority in the Hitchcock narrative." Ph.D. Thesis. New York: New York University, 289 pp.
"Concerned with the particular functions that symmetry and doubles play in the films," which are in general used to reflect order or chaos. Corey reviews the early films, particularly *The Lodger, Blackmail,* and *Murder!,* for signs of the major theme, defined as characters whose psychological conflicts are reflected in the "details of the narrative as well as the formal symmetries." He reviews the transition to Hollywood, then puts forth detailed formal analyses of *Shadow of a Doubt, Notorious,* and *Strangers on a Train.* These films are shown to be important as a "reflexive source of commentary on the issue of symmetry."

535 HEMMETER, THOMAS MARTIN. "Hitchcock the Stylist." Ph.D. Thesis. Cleveland: Case Western Reserve University, 468 pp.
Analysis of the Hitchcock style, which Hemmeter places in the modern tradition of romantic irony, where "fictional worlds present no absolute center of values." Within the films, there is a "tense dialectic" between subjective suspense techniques on the one hand, and alienation techniques and abstract patterns on the other. Shots and angles, mise-en-scène, lighting, editing, and camera and actor movement are analyzed in separate chapters. Each area is broken down and categorized in different ways that illustrate the critical dichotomy, such as distance in shots—human and inhuman—angles in "interpersonal" (point of view) shots and impersonal shots, lighting that engages or disengages the audience, and so on. The author concludes that the viewer ends up adopting "a tense double perspective" similar to Hitchcock's own "anxious world view."

1980

*536   *Hitchcock, la Dimensione Nascosta: Materialie de Studio e di Intervento Cinematografici. Collection Cinema e Cinema.* Venezia: Marsilio, 192 pp.
Cited in entry 703.

537   *Alfred Hitchcock,* edited by Jean Narboni. Paris: l'Etoile/Cahiers du Cinéma, 108 pp.
Collection of articles with introductory essay by Narboni titled "Visages d'Hitchcock," which describes Hitchcock's method. Narboni emphasizes the imposed limits of the "inflexible discipline" that composes the shots via storyboards; the face, in the sense of appearances and expressions, is all that matters. He codifies facial expressions according to sex: sad, terrified, shamed for the women, and urgent, thoughtful, alert for the men, and sums up, "many signs, no facts."
The book includes a reproduction of the entire issue of *Cahiers du Cinéma* (October 1954): see entries that year under Bazin, Chabrol, Domarchi, Hitchcock, Schérer, and Truffaut. Also includes articles by Ferry (see entry this year) and Bonitzer (entry 608), as well as a quotation from a short story by Henry James titled "The Beast in the Jungle" that Truffaut has chosen as "the best portrait of Hitchcock." This quotation describes a man who considers himself the "most disinterested" of men, who hides his burden of "perpetual suspense" with a calm exterior, and who demands from others "no allowance" and only gives to those who ask. Others are discouraged from looking into this hidden aspect of him, the aspect of the "haunted man." Also translations of Hitchcock's videotaped acceptance speech of the American Film Institute's Life Achievement Award, in March 1979, and entry 91.

538   ROSETTI, RICCARDO. *Tutti i Film Hitchcock.* Milano/Roma: Savell, 175 pp.
Catalog of the thirtieth Mostra della Rassegna dei Film di Hitchcock; includes survey of work.

Articles and Shorter Writings

*539   ADAM, GERHARD. "Kurze Filmanalyse von Alfred Hitchcocks 39 Stufen (*The 39 Steps*)." In *Filmanalyse: Grundlagen, Methoden, Didaktik,* edited by Alphons Silbermann, Michael Schaaf, and Gerhard Adam. München: Oldenbourg, pp. 141–166.
Cited in entry 703.

540   ANSEN, DAVID. "Minister of fear." *Newsweek* 95 (May 12):87–88.
Obituary: "Hollywood brought out Hitchcock's paranoid romanticism and its undertones of sexual guilt, misogyny and morbid obsession. The films have already passed the test of time."

541   ARISTARCO, G.   "Il 30 aprile piu de 5 maggio." *Cinema Nuovo* 29, no. 266 (August):7–9.
Obituary: Discourse on the significance of the death of Hitchcock in light of current events and international politics (the invasion of Iran by Iraq) and the positioning of both events by the Italian press.

*542   ARNOLD, FRANK.   "Die dunklen Träume eines furchtsamen Mannes." *Zoom*, no. 10:2–6.
Cited in entry 703.

543   ARNOLD, GARY.   "The enduring image of Alfred Hitchcock." *Washington Post* (May 4):Section H, pp. 1, 8–9.
Obituary: Discusses Hitchcock's restrictive methods, his notion of "pleasurable fear," and disconcerting "jolts." The author thinks it unlikely that his influence or popularity will fade.

544   BELTON, JOHN.   "Dexterity in a void: The formalist esthetics of Alfred Hitchcock." *Cineaste* 10, no. 3 (Summer):9–13.
Marxist analysis describing Hitchcock's films as a synthesis of expressionist and constructivist aesthetics. While these are both formalist, they suggest opposing ideologies. This conclusion leads to an assessment of Hitchcock as a "decadent progressive, a formalist whose interest in the cinema is purely formal and non-ideological." Reprinted in *Cinema Stylists* (Metuchen: Scarecrow, 1983).

545   BELTON, JOHN, and LYLE TECTOR.   "The bionic eye: The aesthetics of the zoom." *Film Comment* 16, no. 5 (September–October):11–18.
History of the zoom lens, describing "the most celebrated" use in *Vertigo,* where it was first devised for the falling/climbing scenes. In that film, the effect is actually a combination of zooming in and tracking out, a technique that creates a distinct deforming of screen space.

*546   BELTRAME, G.   "Bio-filmografia di Alfred Hitchcock." *Cineforum,* no. 197 (September):585–591.
Cited in *Film Literature Index,* 1980.

547   BENHAMOU, ANNE-FRANÇOISE.   "La belle échappée." *Cinématographe,* no. 59 (July–August):40–44.
Discussion of female characters and their position in Hitchcock's unconventional structuring of the couple: efficient women and passive men. The author examines the fiction as a "trap" and the shot as a cage.

1980

*548   BLIERSBACH, GERHARD. "Hitchcocks Thriller: Gelungene Träume?"
Psychologie Heute 7, no. 10:64–73.
Cited in entry 703. On *North by Northwest, Psycho,* and *The Birds.*

*549   BLUMENBERG, HANS C. "Archipel Hitchcock: Über die dunklen
Phantasien eines kleinen fetten Mannes." In *Kinozeit; Aufsätze und
Kritiken zum modernen Film, 1976–1980.* Frankfurt: Fischer Taschen-
buch, pp. 218–224.
Cited in entry 703.

*550   BOLLE, J. "Hitchcock." *Andere Sinema,* no. 17 (March):24–29.
Cited in *Film Literature Index,* 1980. In Dutch.

551   "Les bonheurs d'Alfred H." *Séquences* 101 (July):24–28.
A series of short essays by *Séquence* editors on their favorite Hitchcock films.

552   BONNET, JEAN-CLAUDE. "Un génie allègre." *Cinématographe,* no.
59 (July–August):27–28.
Argues that Hitchcock's comedies and comic moments are equal to his more
serious themes. Bonnet supports his claim by examining examples of the
undermining of the stories and ironic detail.

553   BROWN, ROYAL S. "Hitchcock's *Spellbound:* Jung versus Freud."
Film/Psychology Review 4, no. 1 (Winter–Spring):35–58.
Detailed analysis, including music, of *Spellbound,* which attempts to prove it
is "consciously Freudian and unconsciously Jungian." Brown offers as evidence
the complex role of Constance, a "heroic, mythical" role played against convention
by a woman. The story takes Constance through a "process of individuation,"
freeing herself of "identification with a consciousness-oriented persona." The
author concludes that she attains the strength to overcome "the forces that keep
John Ballantine in prison."

554   CANBY, VINCENT. "Alfred Hitchcock was the poet of civilized suspense." *New York Times* 129 (May 11):Section 2, p. 1, col. 4.
Reminiscence of Alfred Hitchcock's career and personality. It ends with long
quote from Truffaut's book.

555 CARCASSÓNNE, PHILIPPE. "L'ordre et l'insécurité du monde." *Cinématographe*, no. 59 (July–August):13–16.
Overview of the use of back-projection techniques, the development of the technique through Hitchcock's career, and technical and thematic considerations.

556 COUNTS, KYLE B. "The making of Alfred Hitchcock's *The Birds.*" *Cinefantastique* 10, no. 2:14–35.
Lengthy discussion of the special effects for *The Birds* and the production in general. Counts includes interviews with Evan Hunter on script changes ("it wasn't what I had written"); Ron Berwick, who trapped and trained the birds; Tippi Hedren; Ub Iwerks; Bud Hoffman, assistant editor; Howard Smit; and Robert Boyle. The article is illustrated with storyboards that are compared with film, and shows details of Hunter's final scene, dropped from the film.

557 DAHAN, LUCIEN. "Où allons-nous." *Cinématographe*, no. 59 (July–August):29–31.
General overview of suspense techniques comparing them to a "voyage," which may be invoked by a moral itinerary as well as physical movement, and putting forth a concept of creation (sex) as guilt and creators as procurers.

558 DECAUX, EMMANUEL. "L'ennemi intérieur." *Cinématographe*, no. 59 (July–August):24–26.
An appreciation of the contribution of Hitchcock's Catholic upbringing to his "marginality" and sensitivity to being "in" or "out." Decaux argues against the critical assumption that Catholic dogma inflects the films and suggests instead Catholicism in his work became a popular theme. She concludes that Hitchcock "respects differences" and has created an "eclectic normality. He is a marginal saved by his conformity."

559 EBERT, JÜRGEN. *"Vertigo:* The secret of the tower." *Framework*, no. 13 (Autumn):17–18.
Structural analysis of the narrative elements of the film—"a piece of detective fiction and the story of a therapy"—intended to reveal psychoanalytic themes. Ebert emphasizes the tower and the splitting of the story into two parts, offering two "always possible" readings: (1) a rich man kills his wife and another man discovers the woman he loves is the murderer's accomplice, and (2) a man is in love with a dead woman, or the story of a fetishist. Translation by Barri Ellis-Jones from the German in *Filmkritik,* 24, no. 6 (1980).

560 FERRY, ODETTE. "Hitchcock, mon ami." In *Alfred Hitchcock,* edited by Jean Narboni. Paris: l'Etoile/Cahiers du Cinéma, pp. 49–54.
Lengthy reminiscence by the head of publicity at Paramount, recounting Hitchcock's practical jokes and his warmth and simplicity. Ferry relates that he indicated to her that the story of his father's putting him in a cell when he was

five years old was "probably made up." Also includes anecdotes of his family life and final years.

561   GABBARD, GLEN O., and KRIN GABBARD.   "From *Psycho* to *Dressed to Kill:* The decline and fall of the psychiatrist in the movies." *Film-Psychology Review* 4, no. 2 (Summer–Fall):157–167.
        Psycho used briefly to mark the change in attitude that led to a lack of respect for psychiatry as portrayed in motion pictures culminating in the 1980 *Dressed to Kill.*

562   GIACCI, VITTORIO.   "Alfred Hitchcock: Allegory of ambiguous sexuality." *Wide Angle* 4, no. 1:4–11.
        Describes the Hitchcockian universe as one of Christian morality and guilt expounded in oneiric language. Examines the varieties of ambiguous sexuality: homosexuality, fetishism, narcissism, frigidity, and voyeurism. The author concludes that impotence, a "crime against the moral duty of procreation," attracts Hitchcock the most.
        Translation by Michèle S. de Cruz-Sáenz of an essay in *Filmcritica*, 30, no. 293 (February 1979). Reprinted, entry 512.

563   LE GUAY, PHILIPPE.   "Dossier: Gros plan sur Hitchcock." *Cinématographe,* no. 59 (July–August):45–47.
        Examination of the use of close-ups, their structural, metaphorical, and general aesthetic use.

564   HARMETZ, ALJEAN.   "Five Hitchcock films may surface." *New York Times* 129 (July 9):Section C, p. 15, col. 1.
        It is highly unusual for rights to a studio-financed film (in this case, Paramount) ever to revert to a director, which all these did eight years after release.

565   "Hitchcocks (*Vertigo*)." *Filmkritik* 24, no. 6:244–284.
        Casebook on *Vertigo* containing essays by Hartmut Bitomsky, Harun Farocki, and Jürgen Ebert. Also translation into German of interview with Godard (entry 579) and selected reviews. Includes detailed analysis of the beginning sequence and over fifty frame enlargements.

566   "[Hitchcock]." *Cult Movie; Bimestrale di cultura e politica cinematografica* 1, no. 1 (December):3–37.
        Special issue includes "Hitch in Italia: Biblioteca Borges and Circo Barnum," by Enzo Ungari; "Hitch e il giallo; Quando Raymond Chandler uccise Patricia Highsmith," by Buono di Oreste; "Godard parla di Hitchcock: Il trionfo del montaggio," translation of entry 579; "Hitchcock on Hitchcock; Il periodo inglese (1922–1939)," translation of entry 114; "*La finestra sul cortile* e il periodo

americano," translation of entry 348; filmography, biographical chronology, and bibliography.

567 HURLEY, NEIL. "Hitchcock's fearful persuasion." *New Orleans Review* 7, no. 2:190–193.
Discussion of Hitchcock's education in classical rhetoric and his application of those intellectual principles to filmmaking through a concentration on the spectator's point of view.

568 KEANE, MARIAN. "The designs of authorship: An essay on *North by Northwest.*" *Wide Angle* 4, no. 1:44–52.
Analysis of film as a romantic comedy of remarriage, and Hitchcock's "farewell" to successful conventional Hollywood films. The author examines the theater/performance themes, particularly the Shakespearean elements, parts of which present "threats" to Hitchcock's authorship.

569 KERBEL, MICHAEL. "3-D or not 3-D." *Film Comment* 16, no. 6 (November–December):11–20.
History of 3-D, including an analysis of *Dial M for Murder,* which describes the relative subtlety and integrated use of it by Hitchcock.

*570 KORMANOV, A. "Alfred Khichok." *Kinoizkustvo* 35 (November): 63–74.
Cited in *Film Literature Index,* 1980. "Biography, filmography." In Russian.

571 LEGRAND, GÉRARD. "Petit diptyque pour Sir Alfred." *Positif,* no. 234 (September):7–14.
Overview of a "singular" career, the later films a unique combination of "visual rhymes and psychoanalytic figures." Legrand argues that this style is the culmination of a certain fusion of ingredients present in all the films from the beginning: realism, stylization, expressionism, the double, and homosexuality.

572 LINDERMAN, DEBORAH. "The screen in Hitchcock's *Blackmail.*" *Wide Angle* 4, no. 1:20–28.
Semiotic reading of "a grand syntagm from the second movement" of the film, the scene of the "attempted ravishment." Along with an enumeration of the events, symbols are discussed, especially the varied screens, the jester painting, the empty canvas on which Alice draws, the folding screen, and the drapes that screen the bed. The author also analyzes Alice's "oscillating" speech and presentation as an indecisive woman. Linderman concludes that the film "perpetuates with great wit an intertextual ethos of repression of the feminine by raising the sophistication of its own level of desire."

GNY, JOËL. "Mais qui a tué Hitchcock?" *Cinéma 80,* no. 258
ne):42–46.
ation on the history of Hitchcock's critical reputation, the adoration of
ιπε *ιvouvelle Vague,* the sarcasm of the anticritics, and the current popular
assessment of Hitchcock as a master technician of wonderful entertainments that
say nothing. Seeing this as an outgrowth of outmoded humanist criticism, Magny
assesses Hitchcock as a modern artist with a pointed social critique who has yet
to be fully analyzed.

574 MARTINI, E. "The trouble with Alfred." *Cineforum,* no. 197 (September):579–585.
Description of the films, their major themes and concerns.

575 MAURELLI, E. "Hitchcock, il testo, il cinema classico." *Cineforum,* no.
197 (September):573–579.
"Hitchcock, text, classical cinema": discusses the "textual strategy" that
Raymond Bellour found in the cinema of Hitchcock. Notions of the play of the
subject and spectator pleasure are emphasized.

576 McLAUGHLIN, JAMES B. "All in the family: Alfred Hitchcock's
Shadow of a Doubt." Wide Angle 4, no. 1:12–19.
Examines the theme of the family, emphasizing the many doubles, Charlie's
stepping over the boundaries of proper femininity, her desire to be a "merry
widow," and the family as "a source of endless provocation." The author also
compares Uncle Charlie to Dracula. Reprinted, entry 771.

577 MONTAGU, IVOR. "Working with Hitchcock." *Sight and Sound* 49
(Summer):189–193.
Detailed reminiscences of Montagu's work with Hitchcock: saving *The
Lodger,* as associate producer on the British spy thriller cycle, and their final
conflict over *Sabotage.* Montagu relates working methods and comments on
Hitchcock's psychopathology—to him, benign.

578 "More than a MacGuffin." *America* 142, no. 19 (May 17):411–412.
Obituary: "Alfred Hitchcock certainly knew this planet's anxieties and fears
for its future. He identified too those vague unspecified fears that plague the
ordinary man, as well as the intellectual. . . . By an odd, almost paradoxical trust
in humanity, he never adopted the cynic's posture by allowing his characters to
become overwhelmed by their fears and anxieties. Rather they faced the evil in
their world with spirit and style."

579 "La mort de Alfred Hitchcock." *Libération,* no. 1935 (May 2):12–13.
Lengthy interview with Jean-Luc Godard on the importance of Hitchcock.
The author comments on the meaning and unique commercial success of his work

and the exceptional control he exerted. "He solved filmic problems that many other filmmakers were unable to solve."
Translated into Italian, entry 566, and German, entry 565.

580   M[ARTY], A[LAIN]. *"L'inconnu du Nord-Express* et le MacCarthisme."
Revue du Cinéma/Image et Son, no. 352 (July–August):117–125.
Argues that *Strangers on a Train* is a reflection of the 1950s American sociopolitical mentality. The author emphasizes psychoanalytic interpretations of the codes in arguing that the project of the film is to support the perpetuation of the American "ruling class" of which both Guy, via his upward mobility, and Bruno, via his birth, are a part. He discusses sexual roles, locations (public places and functions), and the aspect of suspicion in the American mentality during this period when its institutions were seen to be having difficulty maintaining stability and needed "cleaning up."

581   NICHOLS, BILL. *"The Birds:* At the window." *Film Reader,* no. 4:120–144.
Within a larger discussion of psychoanalytic theory, extensive analysis of the film, including over twenty pages of frame enlargements and attached commentary, using a concept of "at the window" (the screen) where viewer, character, and camera coincide. Nichols illustrates the "regressive" nature of the film in its punishing of Melanie as the Other, who has "infiltrated" the Brenner family. He concludes, however, that we must guard against a "reductionism that describes virtually all social phenomena in terms of the re-enactment of the childhood scenario." *The Birds* is not so simply personal, for the assault on Melanie is not only a result of transgression but also of the social practice that surrounds her. The film's sexism is confirmed on both levels.
Reprinted in Nichols's *Ideology and the Image; Social Representation in the Cinema* (Bloomington: Indiana University Press, 1981).

*582   OLIVA, L. "Muz, kter'y vedel prilis mnoho." *Film a Doba* 26 (December):695–703.
Cited in entry 703. "Study of Hitchcock's style, film language and personality." In Czechoslovakian.

583   RANVAUD, DON. *"Rebecca." Framework,* no. 13 (Autumn):19–24.
Structural analysis of the film as a combination of the fairy tale, the mystery, and the traditional detective story. Ranvaud discusses these three as successive as well as overlapping parts. He also comments on flowers as a metaphor, the relation of the film to the book, costuming, and issues of names and naming.

584   REGNAULT, FRANÇOIS. "Système formel d'Hitchcock (Fascicule de résultats)." In *Alfred Hitchcock,* edited by Jean Narboni. *Cahiers du Cinéma,* Hors Serie, 8. Paris: l'Etoile, pp. 20–29.

1980

Formal description of the entire body of work, involving two "principles": (1) Each film is organized around a pattern, such as straight lines, spirals, broken lines, or graph. This pattern becomes a metaphor for the content and allows the spectator to identify with the point of view of the hero. The spectator is "fascinated" by the form. (2) This formal pattern tends to become autonomous from the film, asserting a "metaphor for cinema in general" and allowing the spectator to identify with the point of view of the director, even to "direct" the film from the audience.

Alongside these principles runs the polarity that marks the work as distinctly Hitchcockian: the opposition between "running a course" from place to place and being "appointed a residence." This polarity has four variations: the two extremes, and two combinations, involving a "pilgrimage to origins" and the spiral inversion of both place and movement.

585   RENOV, MICHAEL.   "From identification to ideology: The male system of Hitchcock's *Notorious.*" *Wide Angle* 4, no. 1:30–37.

Psychoanalytic reading focusing on sexual difference and intended to be "an attempt to comprehend the multivalence of spectatorship and the complex processes of identification in a single classical film." Renov examines "the paired activities of knowledge and sight" and "the splitting of the male function" among the characters, though Alex and "Dev" are most specifically related as the Good and the Bad Law. He concludes, among other reasoning, that "Alicia is made to pay the price of female transgression against the male value system through the spectator's identification with Sebastian at the film's conclusion."

586   SALITT, DANIEL.   "Point of view and intrarealism in Hitchcock." *Wide Angle* 4, no. 1:38–43.

Discussion of point of view throughout the films. Salitt shows that point-of-view shots are not always used for the purpose of creating subjective psychological identification. He suggests other "intrarealistic" narrative strategies, such as changes in proximity of the character to the camera and objects as signifiers of more general concepts.

587   "A sorcerer vanishes." *New York Times* 129 (May 1):Section A, p. 30, col. 1.

A short piece on the opinion page on Hitchcock at the time of his death: "A key to his art was his uncanny ability to tease horror out of the commonplace."

588   TÉCHINÉ, ANDRÉ.   "Le maître des égarements." *Cinématographe*, no. 59 (July–August):32–34.

Impressions from a noted French director of the "crisis of perception" that the films detail.

589 TELOTTE, J. P. "Faith and idolatry in the horror film." *Literature/Film Quarterly* 8, no. 3:143–155.

A phenomenological analysis of the genre of the horror film, positing the preeminence of audience participation in its evocation of "otherness" and its tendency to reveal the dangers of idolatry, which is defined as an avoidance of human concerns and individual responsibility for the group. *Psycho,* and its eye imagery in particular, is discussed in this context as a "realistic" horror film, which emphasizes "the necessity of our participation in the world."

590 *"Les thirty nine marchés:* Découpage intégral après montage et dialogue in extenso." *L'Avant-Scène du Cinéma,* no. 249 (June 1):11–47.

Shot transcription and translated dialogue. Many frame enlargements.

*591 TIRNANIC, B. "Hitchcock ati ptic posmekljinec." *Ekran* 5, no. 5–6:54–60.

Cited in *Film Literature Index,* 1980. In Serbo-Croatian.

592 TOBACK, JAMES. "The great filmmakers—and Hitchcock." *Rolling Stone,* no. 333 (December 25):37–40, 56.

Portrait-assessment of Hitchcock as not quite a "master," defined as an artist who communicates "an obsessive, visionary intuition of death." Hitchcock "teases, flirts with, approaches, but never achieves" this definition. For him, "death is merely a device." Therefore, he is unable to confront it and merely "assuages the fears." Especially emphasizes Hitchcock's desire to please and his repressed characters, concluding that his most visible theme is control.

593 TONNERRE, JÉRÔME. "44 noms pour mémoire." *Cinématographe,* no. 59 (July–August):6–12.

Listing and brief histories of Hitchcock's collaborators: "the family brain-trust," screen writers, novelists, producers, cinematographers, musicians, and others.

594 TURNER, DENNIS. "Hitchcock: Moral *Frenzy* in the declining years." *Film/Psychology Review* 4, no. 1 (Winter–Spring):56–69.

Detailed "linear" analysis that seeks to rescue *Frenzy* from the "evolutionary" model, whereby Hitchcock's later work is typed as self-conscious and repetitive and therefore false. The analysis describes ways in which the viewer is challenged to participate in its production, via the film's "self-reflectiveness."

595 TWADDLE, EDWARD. "Une journée avec Alfred Hitchcock." *Cinématographe,* no. 59 (July–August):54–55.

A day in the Hitchcocks' Bel Air home, then to Universal Studios. Mostly details of personal life. Translated from an uncited British newspaper.

1981

596   VEILLON, OLIVER-RENÉ.   "L'image dans le tapis." *Cinématographe,*
      no. 59 (July–August):17–20.
Investigates the role of certain visual details in several of the films: books,
paintings, portraits, photographs, letters, sight/blindness, and their subjection to
point of view.

597   WEIS, ELIZABETH.   "Music and murder: The association of source
      music with order in Hitchcock." In *Ideas of Order in Literature and Film.*
      Florida State University Conference on Literature and Film, 4. Tallahas-
      see: University Presses of Florida, pp. 73–83.
Series of examples from many of the films that illustrates Hitchcock's use of
music as ironic counterpoint. The author shows that many of the compositions
suggest associations concerning class or social condition that present an opposing
order to the order the characters seek to manifest or recoup.

598   WOLLEN, PETER.   "Hitchcock: Hybrid plots in *Psycho.*" *Framework,*
      no. 13 (Autumn):14–16.
After the ideas of Vladimir Propp, analysis of the similar fairy tale structures
of *North by Northwest, Psycho,* and *Marnie* that finds "a series of transformations
and redistributions of roles reminiscent of those described in an essay by Freud
titled 'A Child Is Being Beaten.' The "hybrid plot" is related to the story of
Oedipus through a common feature, the like identity of the investigator and the
criminal, and also the common "mechanisms of transformation," which concern
what Freud called the "family romance." Wollen concludes that when Hitchcock
"foregrounds psychoanalytic secrets rather than microfilms or money" the story
becomes "a tale of the uncanny. . . . This [is] because it centers not on the kind of
lack which Propp described . . . but on a symbolic lack which cannot be liquidated,
so that instead of the liquidation of the lack, we get the liquidation of the
Princess." Translated into Italian, entry 600.

599   YACOWAR, MAURICE.   "Where's the Hitch?" *The Canadian Review of
      American Studies* 11, no. 2 (Fall):223–232.
Review essay of Wood's *Hitchcock Films* (entry 476), third edition. Yacowar
objects to the new "ideological" approach and defends Hitchcock's work against
the criticism, suggesting it displays insufficient understanding of Hitchcock's
Catholic consciousness, as Chabrol and Rohmer have shown.

1981
Books

600   *Per Alfred Hitchcock,* edited by Edoardo Bruno. *Fotogramma,* 1. Monte-
      pulciano: Grifo, 239 pp.
Anthology of papers presented at a 1980 Rome conference titled "Aprile
Hitchcock." Introductory essay by Bruno, titled "False Openings," attributes
Hitchcock's critical appeal to his "simulated" telling of a story whereby the story

masks something else. The "structural narrative of the film is in fact simply the race to cover as quickly as possible a fiction that *pretends* to narrate, while at the same moment it negates the conflux of narrative themes which preceded."

See other entries this year by Barr, Bellour, Buscema, Beylie, Borgna, Combs, Contenti, La Polla, Maurelli, Menna, Morandini, Narboni, Ranvaud, Rosetti, Salina, Spoto, Tiso, and Turroni. Includes translations of Bonitzer (entry 608), Wollen (entry 598), and Simsolo (entry 668) as well as translations of papers by Thomas Elsaesser, Jean Narboni, and a transcript of a discussion with Ernest Lehman, Tippi Hedren, Farley Granger, and Peggy Robertson.

*601   HALEY, MICHAEL.   *The Alfred Hitchcock Album.* Englewood Cliffs, N.J.: Prentice-Hall, 177 pp.
Cited in entry 703.

602   SALVADORI, ROBERTO.   *Alfred Hitchcock: La Critica, il Pubblico, le Fonti Letterarie. Saggi,* 10. Firenze: La Casa Usher, 141 pp.
A collection of articles presented at or written to be issued as the Proceedings of the "Convegno Internazionale di Studi, Premio Fiesole ai Maestri del Cinema." During the winter of 1978–1979, this prize was awarded to Alfred Hitchcock, as he was considered the most critically discussed, intricate, and rewarding of film directors. Salvadori's contribution, titled "Finalmente Hitchcock . . . ," indicates the intentions of the proceedings: to show the director's popular appeal and to indicate the international character and methodological richness of the criticism. See entries this year by Brunetta, Caldiron, Legrand, Villien, and Witte.

Articles and Shorter Writings

603   BARR, CHARLES.   "Le strutture ipnagogiche: Il periodo inglese in Hitchcock." In *Per Alfred Hitchcock,* edited by Edoardo Bruno. *Fotogramma,* 1. Montepulciano: Grifo, pp. 17–23.
Discusses films prior to 1940, especially *The Manxman,* and the early "original structure," which the author defines as a particular psychological effect occasioned by the spectator's identification with the actual image on the screen as well as the protagonist.

604   BELLOUR, RAYMOND.   "Sulla scelta d'oggetto." In *Per Alfred Hitchcock,* edited by Edoardo Bruno. *Fotogramma,* 1. Montepulciano: Grifo, pp. 24–30.
Psychoanalytic analysis of *Shadow of a Doubt* and *North by Northwest* as a symbolic resolution of an imaginary fantasy, that of the hero presented as a masculine *object.*

1981

605   BELTON, JOHN. "Alfred Hitchcock's *Under Capricorn:* Montage entranced by mise-en-scène." *Quarterly Review of Film Studies* 6, no. 4:365–383.

Analysis of the long takes in the film as "the groundwork for a new aesthetic." Detailed descriptions of the long-take sections show their thematic concerns and relation to later productions. These involve the fragmentation and elaboration of a unified space, uninterrupted attention [to any of several elements], and an unconventionally created "montage," which is consequently "stripped of its cathartic energy." These concerns also contribute to the characters' being understood increasingly in terms of their settings and to Hitchcock's development as an actor's director. Reprinted in Belton's *Cinema Stylists* (Metuchen: Scarecrow, 1983).

606   BERTOLINA, G. C. "Bernard Herrmann e il 'black and white sound.' " *Filmcritica* 32, no. 315 (June):289–296.

Description of Bernard Herrmann's working relationship with Hitchcock; analysis of a musical sequence from *Psycho,* which Herrmann considered his best opportunity for innovation.

607   BÉYLIE, CLAUDE. "Alfred Hitchcock e la tradizione grassa." In *Per Alfred Hitchcock,* edited by Edoardo Bruno. *Fotogramma,* 1. Montepulciano: Grifo, pp. 31–40.

With Hitchcock's rotund physique in mind, the author emphasizes the "bon vivant" side of the Hitchcock genius—"good wines, food, and women." In the film work itself, he finds a dialectic between excess and temperance, cruelty and innocence, and suggests that Hitchcock made his worst films while on a diet. Hitchcock, in his predilection for the good things of life, achieves a perfect semiological balance between desire and its "(dis)contents."

608   BONITZER, PASCAL. "It's only a film/ou la face du néant." *Framework,* no. 14 (Spring):22–24.

Review of the historical development of the look beginning in the silent era, its relation to montage and suspense, and the resultant introduction of conflict or violence into the "very nature of film." Hitchcock is the filmmaker who "has drawn the most logical conclusions . . . from this revolution in the process of meaning-production." Following a discussion of crime and innocence, the principle of Hitchcock's cinema is argued to be the a priori positing of death and crime in the fiction. Unlike Griffith, Hitchcock does not rely strictly on chase sequences to produce suspense; more frequently he uses the slowing down of time and an emphasis on the choice of framing and angle that can be as subtle as "that moment when the look in the camera becomes the slightest bit too interested." The use of these techniques "splits the impression of reality by the introduction of inverted reality"; it gives all actions a double meaning and most of the images a "past and a future"—the conditions of suspense.

Translation of "Le suspense hitchcockien" in author's *Le champ aveugle; Essais sur le cinéma* (Paris: Gallimard, 1982). Translated into Italian, "It's only a film o la facciata di nulla" in *Filmcritica,* no. 311 (January 1981) and in entry 600.

609 BORGNA, GIANNI. "La morale e l'amore." In *Per Alfred Hitchcock,* edited by Edoardo Bruno. *Fotogramma,* 1. Montepulciano: Grifo, pp. 50–52.

Short explanation of the basic motivation in Hitchcock's narrative structure: the increasing tension between eros and thanatos, which allows the spectator to be constructed in the same process as the protagonists. Although the themes of the narrative are at times petty and narrow, wider significance arises from the charged banality of where they are placed.

610 BRION, PATRICK. "Les films de télévision d'Alfred Hitchcock." *Caméra/Stylo,* no. 2 (November):64–80.

Detailed listing, credits, and synopses.

611 BRUNETTA, GIANPIERO. "I processi di identificazione in Hitchcock." In *Alfred Hitchcock: La Critica, il Pubblico, le Fonti Letterarie,* edited by Roberto Salvadori. *Saggi,* 10; Firenze: La Casa Usher, pp. 95–102.

Traces the classic themes and concerns in the films. Brunetta discusses the French critics of the 1950s and their placing of Hitchcock as one of the "pillars" of the *politique des auteurs,* Bellour's analyses, and the theories of Christian Metz in regard to *Lifeboat, Strangers on a Train,* and *Saboteur.* Finally, he emphasizes the importance of Catholic themes for Hitchcock.

612 BRUNO, EDOARDO. *"Shadow of a Doubt." Filmcritica* 32, no. 311 (January):37.

The two Charlies contrasted: one dreams, the other manipulates the real; one desires, the other plays the victim. The fiction of relations is linked with the fiction of intentions, and they are the two faces of representation and fiction.

613 ———. *"Mr. and Mrs. Smith." Filmcritica* 32, no. 311 (January):57–59.

Film consists of "alternating objective and subjective shots," which revive the image and construct a "double reading" that takes to pieces the genre of comedy.

614 BUFFA, M. *"To Catch a Thief." Filmcritica* 32, no. 311 (January):47–48.

Film is unfavorably compared with *Notorious:* "the more Hitchcock plays with ambiguity, the more he seems to empty his characters of all subject. . . . The characters become simulacri, sarcophagi for the audience, who live via the screen the subjectivity of the director."

615 BUSCEMA, MASSIMO. *"I Confess." Filmcritica* 32, no. 311 (January): 44–45.

Psychoanalytic description of this "fable" pressed between two "murky transparencies," the confession of a secret nightmare and the nightmare of an inverted dream (the real).

1981

616 ———. *"Marnie." Filmcritica* 32, no. 311 (January):52–53.
Psychoanalytical discussion of the character *Marnie,* who "kills her secret" to regain her honor.

617 ———. "Vedere, far vedere, nascondere." In *Per Alfred Hitchcock,* edited by Edoardo Bruno. *Fotogramma,* 1. Montepulciano: Grifo, pp. 53–62.
"To See, To Show, To Hide": An analysis of *The Lodger,* its enunciation and narrative, after the theories of A. J. Greimas in *Structural Semantics and Sense,* which involve the interaction of semiotic constrictions.

618 CALDIRON, ORIO. "La biblioteca di Babele e il perfido Alfredo." In *Alfred Hitchcock: La Critica, il Pubblico, le Fonti Letterarie,* edited by Roberto Salvadori. *Saggi,* 10; Firenze: La Casa Usher, pp. 103–114.
Well-researched article on the literary sources of the films. Caldiron discusses the English tradition in detective fiction, the thriller, and light adventure genres as well as the novel-as-game-as-moral tale. He emphasizes Hitchcock's early debt to Joseph Conrad, Eden Philpotts, and John Buchan, and traces his interest in the detective story to a mass phenomenon. Hitchcock early understood the possibilities of the subtle psychology in these genres when placed with the cinema as a mass art form. The progression from early moralistic tales told as spy stories to adventure-thrillers parallels the evolution of the Hitchcock aesthetic of suspense and surprise. It is orchestrated here with reference to G. K. Chesterton, Raymond Chandler, and the literary merits of great writers who also write detective fiction, some of whom have collaborated with Hitchcock. Hitchcock's own use of the thriller suspense genre as a gimmick is placed next to his creation of a body of work comprising subtle satire and serious drama. His distance from the material is noted: "I read a story once; if I like the basic idea, I forget the book completely and make a movie."

619 CARLO, S. *"Spellbound." Filmcritica* 32, no. 311 (January):38–39.
The film "explains the identification of the cinematic with the psychoanalytic. . . . Even the demonstration of the growing love between the couple is, in its essence, a psychoanalytic process." Hitchcock identifies with the institutions and increases the association of love with illness disguised under the exchange of reason, marriage, and discussion. Finally, the film is about the scandal of "revelation" and the curative powers of the cinema.

620 ———. *"Blackmail." Filmcritica* 32, no. 311 (January):29–30.
Another case of "feminine dissatisfaction: a trajectory over a feeble attempt at liberation, a voyage through the psyche, a constant rotation that is the motor of existence. . . . The society is immutable in its guarantee of stratification only for the privileged. For this reason Hitchcock cannot adore the stillness [and finds it] better to improvise explosions and trace them to the forces responsible for law and order, who under the guise of protecting the innocent, investigate them."

621 ———. *"Rear Window." Filmcritica* 32, no. 311 (January):44–46.
Freudian interpretation of the film, including all the versions of the film's statements on voyeurism and spectatorship. Descriptions of various scenes explicate these sexual/castration themes leading to Hitchcock's masculine orientation.

622 CAVELL, STANLEY. *"North by Northwest." Critical Inquiry* 7, no. 4 (Summer):761–776.
Develops a wide-ranging essay on the film as a "comedy of remarriage." Cavell discusses the 1930s formation of the Hitchcock genre of thriller/romance, which came to act as a theme—particularly as developed by Cary Grant. He also comments on the mythic role of the woman and the film as it compares to *Hamlet*. The author concludes that the intent is to legitimize marriage and happiness, though it invests in the man the traditional role of education, requiring the creation of a "new woman" willing to be educated.
Reprinted in Cavell's *Themes Out of School* (San Francisco: North Point, 1984). Later version printed in entry 771.

623 COMBS, RICHARD. "Il cinema di Hitchcock: Spie e spettacolo. In *Per Alfred Hitchcock,* edited by Edoardo Bruno. *Fotogramma,* 1. Montepulciano: Grifo, pp. 63–70.
Analyzes *Torn Curtain* and *Sabotage* as they relate to the experience of watching a Hitchcock film as "being present at a performance, which constitutes one of the subtleties [Hitchcock] intends." Within this theatricality of the psychological, the cinema of Hitchcock anchors its "game with the public."

624 CONTENTI, FULVIO. *"Rebecca." Filmcritica* 32, no. 311 (January): 35–36.
Discusses the "structure of blockage" that figures prominently in the film: one moment can suddenly explode without reason, throwing into uncertainty the logic of the story's flow.

625 ———. *"Dial M for Murder." Filmcritica* 32, no. 311 (January):45.
Described as a film on mechanisms, on paranoia, and the occult aspect of an appearance. The almost glacial behavior of Tony Wendice introduces a total adhesion of dissimulation, a character who is an intermediary between illusion and an external world. His methodical mentality and ability to judge his victims is the measure of a split personality, of a thinking that operates in two worlds simultaneously.

626 ———. *"The Wrong Man." Filmcritica* 32, no. 311 (January):49–50.
A Lacanian interpretation finding that the rationality of the structure of logic kills the man and leads him to nihilism and pure fear before returning him to "the mirror stage" (the "right" man is discovered in a mirror superimposition), where it is possible again to flee into the imaginary.

1981

627 ——. "L'uso degli archetipi narrativi in Hitchcock." In *Per Alfred Hitchcock,* edited by Edoardo Bruno. *Fotogramma,* 1. Montepulciano: Grifo, pp. 71–74.

"The Use of Archetypes in Hitchcock." Analysis focusing on fear, the game, fetishes, dreams, and secrets, all of which interact with the "fabric of the trauma."

628 ——. "*Young and Innocent." Filmcritica* 32, no. 311 (January):34.

As with Lewis Carroll's Alice, the heroine leaves behind her own universe to enter an elusive world created entirely of childish traps and games. The subtle characterization covers up the caricatured nature of the lead and her boyfriend.

629 CRAWFORD, LARRY. *"Psycho-*analysis: A textual perspective for film study." In *The Paradigm Exchange,* University of Minnesota Faculty and Students in Colloquium, 1980–1981, edited by René Jara and others. Minneapolis, Minn.: University of Minnesota College of Liberal Arts, pp. 77–84.

Textual analysis of the Bakersfield car lot scene in *Psycho,* its "rhyming patterns, repetition, and palindromic construction." Crawford also comments on a range of scopic objects—newspaper, money, etc.—and the ideological significance of ropes. Another version, *Enclitic,* no. 1–2 (1981), lists tables of subsegments and textual codes.

630 DICKSTEIN, MORRIS. "Beyond good and evil: The morality of thrillers." *American Film* 6, no. 9 (July–August):49–52, 67–69.

Traces the origins of the current thriller genre, naming John Buchan's *The 39 Steps* its "grandfather." Dickstein emphasizes the work of Buchan and Graham Greene, with frequent references to Hitchcock's version of *The 39 Steps* and *North by Northwest.*

631 DOANE, MARY ANN. *"Caught* and *Rebecca:* The inscription of femininity as absence." *Enclitic* 5–6, no. 1–2:75–89.

Feminist analysis of films as "women's film" intended "in some way to trace female subjectivity and desire." Doane emphasizes two scenes in *Rebecca*—the projection of the home movies, and Maxim's relating of Rebecca's last evening— where the camera follows the space of the tale, forcing the viewer to associate with the male version of events. She argues that the film "disarticulates" the technical apparatus by including it as a prop and a presence in its own right, thereby creating not only a "paranoid text" but a "limit-text," which reveals its own contradictions.

632 "Douchet décortique De Palma." *Cahiers du Cinéma,* no. 326 (July–August):iv–v.

Discussion among Serge Daney, Pascal Bonitzer, and Jean Douchet about the relative merits of the films of Brian De Palma and their relationship to the work of Hitchcock.

633   DURANÇON, JEAN. "Alfred Hitchcock." *Caméra Stylo,* no. 2 (November):1–160.
Special issue consisting of a series of short impressionistic pieces on particular visual and poetic elements throughout the work as well as individual films. See other entries this year under Hussenot-Desonges, Helmstein, Noguez, Peeters, Rabant, and Simsolo. Also includes translation of entry by Jean-André Fieschi in *Cinema: A Critical Dictionary,* edited by Richard Roud.

634   FERZETTI, F. *"The Lady Vanishes." Filmcritica* 32, no. 311 (January): 34–35.
"The mysterious goodness of Miss Froy (so unlike the terrible phallic mothers) seems incomprehensible in the conflicted universe of Hitchcock." The film is the most distant from his obsessions, and, yet, incarnates them completely onto an inoffensive plane of joking and frivolity.

635   ———. *"The Ring." Filmcritica* 32, no. 311 (January):26–27.
An interpretation of the film after the ideas of Ernst Cassirer on antiquity and linguistics in his *Philosophy of Symbolic Forms.*

636   GHEZZI, E. *"The Birds." Filmcritica* 32, no. 311 (January):51–52.
In *The Birds,* the "master of suspense" rejects his own tradition and instead "closes with an opening." It is the first modern catastrophe film, the "truest of millinerian films."

637   ———. *"Lifeboat." Filmcritica* 32, no. 311 (January):37–38.
Hitchcock here explores "the natural space of the cinema": the essential abstraction, intensification, and duality of time and waiting, alongside the natural elements.

638   ———. *"The Man Who Knew Too Much." Filmcritica* 32, no. 311 (January):48–49.
Comparison of the two versions of the film, especially the treatment of the major themes.

639   ———. *"North by Northwest." Filmcritica* 32, no. 311 (January):50–51.
Poetic description of film as a "whole" verisimilitude "filled with holes." We find them everywhere but especially in the more logical conjunctions.

640   ———. *"Torn Curtain." Filmcritica* 32, no. 311 (January):53–54.
Title is translated as "the Torn Stage Curtain or the Torn Iron Curtain." In any case, the film gives lie to Hitchcock's apolitical stance, since his intention is unabashedly anticommunist. Though the film is unsuccessful, it is still worthy of analysis: "The social—in this case East Germany—seems hardly to exist, conse-

1981

quently, the political drains away." Political difference is blotted out in favor of the pure space of the imaginary where the detective story becomes "universal, crosses all borders."

641   ———. *"The Trouble with Harry." Filmcritica* 32, no. 311 (January):48.
Compares film with *North by Northwest,* with an emphasis on the theatricality of the filmed scenes; ultimately it is an "external Hitchcockian game" that cancels out its author.

642   GIACCI, V[ITTORIO]. *"Vertigo." Filmcritica* 32, no. 311 (January): 32–35.
The film is interpreted as a metaphor for cinema. Giacci posits a "mental commotion" in Hitchcock, as the director involves himself with rethinking his ideas and is openly interested in pure creation and its pleasures.

643   GOODWIN, JAMES. "Conrad and Hitchcock: Secret sharers." In *The English Novel and the Movies,* edited by Michael Klein and Gillian Parker. New York: Ungar, pp. 218–227.
Comparison of the two authors' approaches, "similar in theme and narrative technique." Goodwin discusses *Sabotage,* a version of *Secret Agent,* and Hitchcock's setting aside of Conrad's interest in political groups and alternate emphasis on the Verloc household. He finds in the film parallels between cinema and anarchism, and police and criminals.

644   GUÉRIF, FRANÇOIS. "Patricia Highsmith et le cinéma." *L'Avant-Scène du Cinéma,* no. 261 (February 1):53–54.
Short interview with Highsmith and discussion of the adaptation of *Strangers on a Train.*

645   HARTMAN, GEOFFREY H. "Plenty of nothing: Hitchcock's *North by Northwest." Yale Review* 71, no. 1 (Autumn):13–27.
Description of *North by Northwest* in the context of the control exerted by "Mother Hitchcock," concluding that through his manipulation, "we become Romans at the circus." Hartman assumes the view of Hitchcock as an entertainer without substance or moral depth: "High in Hitchcock is an angle from which to shoot. . . . What is there to understand? There is fascination rather than understanding." He posits Hitchcock as the epitome of modern media, which has deprived humanity of "authentic privacy" and "self-realization." Reprinted in Hartman's *Easy Pieces* (New York: Columbia University Press, 1985).

646   HELMSTEIN, LARS. "La rêve de l'autre." *Caméra/Stylo* 2 (November): 148–151.
Poetic essay on dream and reality, with examples from a range of the films.

647   HUSSENOT-DESONGES, ALAIN. "Le malin génie." *Caméra/Stylo* 2
      (November):135–140.
      Reflections on René Descartes in that his principles have been interiorized by
Hitchcock: "from methodical suspicion to permanent doubt."

648   KAMINSKY, STUART M. *"Dressed to Kill." Armchair Detective* 14, no.
      1:14–16.
      Comparison of *Psycho* with *Dressed to Kill,* arguing that the latter's director,
Brian de Palma, is not simply continuing the tradition of Hitchcock but making
manifest the sexual motivations that Hitchcock left latent.

649   KUYPER, ERIC DE. "Hitchcock of: Hoe men een boog spant." *Skrien,*
      no. 108–109 (Summer):74–79.
      Overview of the films, the nature of suspense, and other elements. In Dutch.

650   LAPOLLA, FRANCO. "Hitchcock e la morte, ovvero: I pericoli del
      proprio letto." In *Per Alfred Hitchcock,* edited by Edoardo Bruno. *Foto-
      gramma,* 1. Montepulciano: Grifo, pp. 155–162.
      An account of the appearance and concise form of death, its objects, and
prefigurations in the films. *The Wrong Man,* which the author sees as a model of
the world "Hitchcock likes best," is analyzed in depth.

651   LEGRAND, GÉRARD. "La fortuna di Hitchcock in Francia dal 1950:
      Scoperta progressiva di una regia." In *Alfred Hitchcock: La Critica, il
      Pubblico, le Fonti Letterarie,* edited by Roberto Salvadori. *Saggi,* 10.
      Firenze: La Casa Usher, pp. 61–72.
      "The Success of Hitchcock in France after 1950" describes in detail the
history of French interest in Hitchcock, beginning with Bazin's descriptions of
Hitchcock's use of suspense to create a disequilibrium in the spectator. Legrand
assesses the *Cahiers du Cinéma* literature of Rohmer, Chabrol, Douchet, and
Truffaut, and emphasizes Sadoul's opinion that *Shadow of a Doubt* shows more
technical virtuosity than *Citizen Kane.* Throughout the 1950s, *Cahiers du Cinéma*
devoted almost six full issues to the work of Hitchcock, and Legrand credits the
French with discovering a universal artist. This interest continued into the
1960s; Legrand now finds the earlier writings misleading in their emphasis on
theme over construction and pronounces such construction of the film language
the sole object of Hitchcock's directorial style.

652   LURIE, SUSAN. "The construction of the 'castrated woman' in psycho-
      analysis and cinema." *Discourse,* no. 4 (Winter):52–74.
      Within a larger discussion of the symbolic "powerful castrated penis," an
account of the construction of the "castrated woman" in *The Birds.* Lurie analyzes
the film as it expresses the male need to contain "the young lovely woman" via the
"exorcism of the mother, the positioning of the desired woman in the place of a
helpless child, the punishing of female desire and capacity, and . . . the literal
inscription of castration on the female image with wounds, mutilation, and even

killing." The character of Mitch is tied to the birds as well as to the "desire of the camera," and the metaphor of cages, both literal and cinematic, is extensively analyzed.

653   MASSIMI, G. *"Strangers on a Train." Filmcritica* 32, no. 311 (January):43–44.
The characterizations of Guy and Bruno appear at first to represent two distinct narrative mechanisms: seduction, involving a forced contract of trust and exchange, and a drama of passion and revenge. These distinctions disappear as the two begin to share characteristics: Guy, appearing to have craven motives, and Bruno, revealing an odd sense of loyalty. A mythological interpretation is substituted, emphasizing the dual/twin nature of this "Gemini hero": Bruno, marked by an intense will to live, and Guy, refusing, reversing the contract, and finally, destroying Bruno.

654   MAURELLI, GUIDO. *"Suspicion." Filmcritica* 32, no. 311 (January): 36–37.
An analysis of the system of enunciation in the film, including the mechanism of the observer model, the announcing subject, and the "authorization" and "constriction" of the narrative.

655   ————. "I mondi sospetti dello sguardo." In *Per Alfred Hitchcock,* edited by Edoardo Bruno. *Fotogramma,* 1. Montepulciano: Grifo, pp. 141–147.
Detailed semiotic analysis of *Suspicion* regarding the film as a perfect "closed" text: "To leave [the text] is an illusion; the suspicion continues after and further than the film."

656   MENNA, FILIBERTO. "Trompe-l'oeil: 10 paragrafi per Hitchcock." In *Per Alfred Hitchcock,* edited by Edoardo Bruno. *Fotogramma,* 1. Montepulciano: Grifo, pp. 148–150.
In manifesto style, Menna outlines a theory of fiction for Hitchcock's films. It involves a method of simulation that remains rooted in material reality, an artificial rhetoric that Hitchcock perverts into a cutting away of sign from referent. Types of "artificial rhetoric" are repetition, the displacement of the process of identification, and the shifting of point of view. "Hitchcock knows well that verisimilitude is not the fruit of a simple operation. Rather it is the point of arrival of a sophisticated and complex process, of a mechanism of representation that makes itself one with the spectator's expectation, so that not only the real must be feigned, but feigned so that it is grasped by a certain social group and at a determined moment."

657   MORANDINI, MORANDO. "Confessioni di un critico hitchcockiano a scoppio ritardato." In *Per Alfred Hitchcock,* edited by Edoardo Bruno. *Fotogramma,* 1. Montepulciano: Grifo, pp. 151–154.
Personal reflections on Hitchcock from one of Italy's foremost film reviewers, who describes the "master of suspense" with journalistic references particular to

the Italian movie-going public. Morandini traces the presence of Hitchcock from the end of the war in Italy up until the present.

*658   NARBONI, J[EAN]. "Hitchcock l'egiziano." *Filmcritica* 32, no. 311 (January):17–23.
Cited in *Film Literature Index,* 1981.

659   PAGANELLI, M. *"Notorious." Filmcritica* 32, no. 311 (January):39–40.
"Eroticism and sex are confused in the film . . . because the bodies are separated, and suspense becomes a desire for a solution." The solution appears when the bodies are brought together, when they finally "move in a common direction."

660   PEETERS, BENOIT. "Promenade à travers le discours Hitchcockien." *Caméra/Stylo* no. 2 (November):87–97.
Reviews the criticism and interviews as they relate to Hitchcock's theory of filmmaking. Peeters describes the contradictions that make up this theory: a conscious, extremely local and detailed use of stereotype versus a horror of cinematic cliché, an interest in psychology as expressed through cinematic (visual) means, and a flaunting of an intellectual base, even a paradoxical and complete indifference to content.

661   RABANT, CLAUDE. "Hasard/désir." *Caméra/Stylo* no. 2 (November): 141–147.
Structural-semiotic analysis of *The Wrong Man* as a "misreading," a product of a "signifying machine" that is a "semblance of signs." Rabant argues that there is no direct sign of the guilty one, only crimes.

662   RANVAUD, DONALD. "Il ritorno di *Rebecca.*" In *Per Alfred Hitchcock,* edited by Edoardo Bruno. *Fotogramma,* 1. Montepulciano: Grifo, pp. 163–177.
Semiotic analysis of the "compulsion to repeat" thesis of orthodox Freudian psychoanalysis as it appears in *Rebecca.* One scene, when the lovers first explain themselves to one another in Monte Carlo, is discussed in detail using Vladimir Propp's notion of the "stolen princess."

663   RATTI, T., and S. CARLO. *"Under Capricorn." Filmcritica* 32, no. 311 (January):41–43.
Detailed analysis describing the film as a "search for characters along a trauma-itinerary," a pretext for the exploration of resignation, which Hitchcock likes "even less" than original sin.

664   ROSETTI, RICCARDO. *"Rope." Filmcritica* 32, no. 311 (January):41.
Because Hitchcock is "afraid" of the theater, he puts something more coincidental into effect, linking everything in the film with an "invisible thread,"

discovered by the audience the same way the threads that move the clouds (in the background) are discovered.

665 ———. *"Champagne." Filmcritica*, no. 311 (January):27–28.

Film "recounts a turbulent urban story in the manner of Griffith, has the reasoned sumptuousness of Lubitsch, and confirms that Hitchcock's cinema is a magnifying glass of sorts, playful and perverse."

666 ———. "Il rilievo commune." In *Per Alfred Hitchcock*, edited by Edoardo Bruno. *Fotogramma*, 1. Montepulciano: Grifo, pp. 178–180.

"The common event" refers to the use of place, public and crowded, in many Hitchcock films. It involves a scene of invention, where the plot suddenly erupts, or unfolds an interesting event in a banal or common place. *Secret Agent, The Man Who Knew Too Much* (1934), and *Foreign Correspondent* are discussed in light of their "odd" country settings—Switzerland and Holland.

667 SALINA, FRANCESCO. "Mystery tales e mystery tools: Appunti per una bi-logical filmica." In *Per Alfred Hitchcock*, edited by Edoardo Bruno. *Fotogramma*, 1. Montepulciano: Grifo, pp. 181–184.

Essay on the structure of the films as it works on the unconscious. Taking from the work of I. Matte Blanco in *The Unconscious as Infinite Sets*, Salina finds a kind of "metapsychological research" going on in the narratives. This is made effective through a system of symmetry and formal principles that correspond to a deep structure of the spectator's unconscious.

668 SIMSOLO, NOËL. "Le secret et l'enfant." *Caméra/Stylo* no. 2 (November):16–19.

Extensive ruminations on the subject of fear as it relates to notions of the secret and the child. The child and the couple form a fear construct, its presence indicating a "carnal creation" and its absence meaning sexuality is not sanctioned. Simsolo examines related themes of traveling as displacement, attraction, loneliness, and transfer. He concludes that Hitchcock was always "searching to kill God, as if God were the guilty one, the first creator, the one who procures for the creators to come.... Only he who has no secrets to sell is protected by God."

Translated into Italian in entry 600.

669 SPOTO, DONALD. "Lo sguardo interiore." In *Per Alfred Hitchcock*, edited by Edoardo Bruno. *Fotogramma*, 1. Montepulciano: Grifo, pp. 191–198.

"The interior gaze": the "classic" themes and preoccupations are explored with reference to classical artists, such as Mozart, Sophocles, and others. Emphasizing the tragic themes, Spoto considers Hitchcock the last great cineaste because of his attention to human fragility and imperfection, which the films in their complexity best analyze.

670   S[NOOK], P. A.   "Theater and film." *High Fidelity and Musical America*
31 (February):80.
Technical description of this superior version of the score by Bernard
Herrmann of *North by Northwest,* where he "confines himself, like a musical
jeweler, to small-scaled, detailed reworking of his basic materials." Conducted by
Laurie Johnson, Starlog/Varèse Sarabande, 95001.

671   TISO, CIRIACO.   "Cinema del nodo: Fatture e scioglimento." In *Per
Alfred Hitchcock,* edited by Edoardo Bruno. *Fotogramma,* 1. Montepulciano: Grifo, pp. 199–210.
"The Cinema of Knots: Making and Undoing": a lengthy essay on the
symbolism of knots in the films, here defined as "points of contact," such as figure
and body, plot and intrigue, suspense and suspicion. Ultimately, the author sees
"a sort of large knot, with two sides that one can live in one's own life. . . . This
knot develops in the narrative as well as in two versions: that of the subject who
lives his or her own [part, and that of] the subject thrown into the world,
continually redirected towards the story."

672   TURRONI, GUISEPPE.   "Dietrod'un intervista." In *Per Alfred Hitchcock,* edited by Edoardo Bruno. *Fotogramma,* 1. Montepulciano: Grifo, pp.
211–214.
Personal recollection of a meeting with Hitchcock in Italy in 1972. Turroni
discusses the personality, myth, and legend of the director, and how they match
many themes in the films. He argues for an "ambiguous" reading of the work,
drawing comparisons with Flaubert and Buñuel, two other masters of ambiguity.
The major theme of fear is related to received ideas and the destruction of them,
directly part of Hitchcock's "fear of having or committing stupid ideas—Hitchcock
has always refuted any notion of 'Idea.' In fact, he is petrified of them, placing
them in dreams and nightmares of facts, and thus, totally verifying his irony."

673   VILLIEN, BRUNO.   "Due ipotesi di letture critiche." In *Alfred Hitchcock: La Critica, il Pubblico, le Fonti Letterarie,* edited by Roberto
Salvadori. *Saggi,* 10. Firenze: La Casa Usher, pp. 87–91.
Descriptions of *Juno and the Paycock* and *Elstree Calling,* which emphasizes
their humor and satire as traits that manifest themselves throughout Hitchcock's
career. Noted particularly is the parody of the future of television in *Elstree
Calling,* made in 1930.

674   WITTE, KIRSTEN.   "Hitchcock in Germania." In *Alfred Hitchcock: La
Critica, il Pubblico, le Fonti Letterarie,* edited by Roberto Salvadori. *Saggi,*
10. Firenze: La Casa Usher, pp. 73–75.
Traces the presence of Hitchcock in Germany before and after World War II,
his use of refugees as actors during the 1930s, and the antifascist message of some
of his films. Witte describes the reaction of Goebbels and official Nazi propaganda
to these films and the lingering anti-Hitchcock bias evident in the postwar critical
reception. During the 1960s, the journals *Filmkritik* and *Film* put forth a case for

a "new Hitchcock" that examined his aesthetic value alongside the political. Ironically, Hitchcock is viewed as a political filmmaker, with a certain anti-German bias; this view crosses over to the antibourgeois criticism of progressive critics who find in *Torn Curtain* and *Topaz* a knee-jerk anticommunism of the most primitive kind.

Witte assesses these attitudes in a scholarly examination, finding that the films of the first period (through the early 1940s) were not only a reflection of the prevailing "complex of fear, but an exceptional document of the real story of suffering in Europe, an expression of political persecution." Witte discusses the roles Germans played (Peter Lorre in *The Man Who Knew Too Much* [1934] and Walter Slezak in *Lifeboat*) and shows how these films are seen to be critical of totalitarian Germany, suggesting a national trait, a weakness for violence and subterfuge. In fact, *Notorious, Foreign Correspondent,* and *Lifeboat* were banned from Germany and did not appear in complete prints until the late 1970s, after they were promoted by *Filmkritik* and legitimized by the "Wenders effect" of the film, *An American Friend.* This rehabilitation of Hitchcock's films was based on the notion that his influence could produce nonideological films of the highest artistic merit, but once again, and for different reasons, he is now condemned for being "immoral."

Translation of "Hitchcock in Deutschland" in *Medium* (July 1980).

675   ZITA, JACQUELYN.   "Dark passages—a feminist analysis of *Psycho.*" In *The Paradigm Exchange,* University of Minnesota Faculty and Students in Colloquium, edited by René Jara and others. Minneapolis, Minn.: University of Minnesota College of Liberal Arts, pp. 82–90.

Response to Crawford's analysis of *Psycho* (entry 629). Zita discusses Marion's (the character) "pursuit of anonymity" that renders her the "stereotype of woman as victim" and allows her to be brutalized as an Everywoman. She also comments on the "scopic containment of her body" and the "matricentric" fantasy of her desire for marriage, respectability, and motherhood.

1982
Books

676   *Alfred Hitchcock.* Lisbon: Cinemateca Portuguesa, 222 pp.

Anthology of critical literature, with an introduction by João Bènard da Costa, and other original essays by Luis Noronha de Casta and Jorge Alves da Silva. Translations of Demonsablon (entry 235), Bonitzer (entry 608), Schenker (entry 470), and part of Yacowar (entry 477). Well illustrated. In Portuguese.

677   ARAUJO, INACIO.   *Alfred Hitchcock: O mestro do medo.* Sao Paulo: Brasiliense, 103 pp.

Historical overview of the films, bibliographic essay, and filmography. In Portuguese.

1982

678 BRUZZONE, NATALINO, ROBERT A. HARRIS, MICHAEL S. LASKY
and VALERIO CAPRA. *I Film di Alfred Hitchcock*. Effetto Cinema, 3–4.
Roma: Gremese, 295 pp.
Translation into Italian of entry 444. This edition has additional bibliographic and filmographic material as well as an introductory essay by Bruzzone
and Capra.

679 ROTHMAN, WILLIAM. *Hitchcock—the Murderous Gaze*. Cambridge,
Mass.: Harvard University Press, 371 pp.
Detailed formal explication of five films based on an idea of the camera as
"fundamentally ambiguous" in its expression of both the audience's passivity and
the authorial voice—in the case of Hitchcock, a doubly enigmatic one.
The Lodger is analyzed in detailed shot groupings as a "thesis" film
embodying many of the major themes: the tragic consequences of allowing
wishes to guide judgment, the drama of a girl's coming of age, and the combining
of the protagonist and antagonist as a double. Continuing character and formal
analysis reveals the "philosophical concerns" of *Murder!:* human identity, the
relations of love and desire, murder, dreams, madness, theater, and the nature
of viewing. *The 39 Steps* is analyzed as the first Hitchcock film that "plays" as
well as it "reads," working flawlessly as theater as well as taking theater as its
subject. *Shadow of a Doubt* illustrates the gaining strength of the American
films, the increasing incorporation of extended dialogue scenes, and emphasis
on bold shifts of tone and mood. Analysis of *Psycho* allows the full breadth of
death imagery and meaning, including a notion of the camera that has
"possessed the life" of its subjects and the artist who has given part of his life to
the work.
In a postscript, Rothman stamps Hitchcock's persona most specifically into
his readings, placing them as a personal response and acknowledgment of
Hitchcock's effort and claiming they reveal Hitchcock's "life's blood" in every
frame. The sum is an emotional objection to considering Hitchcock as a mere
master of suspense, and a fervid legitimizing of the films' ability to support
sustained reflection and "high-minded analysis."
A version of the chapter on *Murder!* appeared in *Wide Angle*, 4, no. 1 (1980),
reprinted in entry 771.
Reviews: entry 689
Durgnat, Raymond. "To catch a Hitch: The murderous gaze." *Quarterly
Review of Film Studies* 8, no. 1 (Winter 1983):43–48.
Routt, W. D. *Film Views* 32, no. 131 (Fall 1987):36–38.
Strick P. *Films and Filming,* no. 335 (August 1983):42.
Thomas, Paul. *American Film* (April 1982):72.

680 VILLIEN, BRUNO. *Alfred Hitchcock*. Paris: Colona, 359 pp.
Detailed bio-critical chronology, a chapter for each of the films. Villien traces
the thematic connections among them, often in unusual ways, as when Betty
Balfour, the star of *Champagne,* is put forth as evidence for a theme of
homosexuality. He finds specific examples of voyeurism in virtually all the films,
also in unusual ways, as for example, Daisy's mother as the voyeur in *The Lodger.*

Villien also traces production relationships and particularly focuses on the careers of the actors. He includes many personal interviews and correspondence with actors who relate new biographical anecdotes. Lavishly illustrated in a large format with frame enlargements, set stills, publicity photographs, and other material.

Review: Decaux. *Cinématographe,* 73, no. 114 (December 1985).

681   WEIS, ELIZABETH. *The Silent Scream: Alfred Hitchcock's Sound Track.* Rutherford, N.J.: Fairleigh Dickinson University Press, 188 pp.

Argues Hitchcock's use of sound is not conspicuous but always pointed and thoughtful. It reveals from the beginning an equal weighing of language, music, and sound effects with visual composition. Early experiments with sound in *Blackmail* and *Murder!* introduce characteristic techniques, such as "aural deep focus," overlapping dialogue, interior monologues, "restricted hearing and distortion," and early innovative placing of the speaker in off-screen space. The chapter on *Secret Agent* describes "expressionism at its height" in the death of the organist, the dog's howling, and the use of folk music. *The Man Who Knew Too Much* (1934) is examined as an immediate and complete shift to the classical style where sound grows entirely out of the realistic context of the narrative. The opposition of sound and silence (indicating moral and "emotional paralysis") is explicated.

The next chapter explores the "conjunction of music and murder," including discussion of music as an indicator of class, characters who are amateur and professional musicians, and songs and lyrics, which are used in many films to reveal guilt and innocence. The next chapter explores the "subjective films" of the 1940s and 1950s, particularly *Rear Window,* where "the chief stylistic tactic [is to] show how easily a character—and the viewer for whom he is a surrogate—can misinterpret events according to his own preconceptions." In explaining the "subjective point of view within [the] apparently realistic style" of the film, Weis examines Hitchcock's development of "a unity of sound and a multiplicity of spaces" and the wide range of meaning attached to the song "Lisa." The chapter dealing with aural intrusion and the single-set films is an examination of off-screen sound as it affects on-screen space and characters, a technique particularly evident in *Lifeboat, Rope, Dial M for Murder,* and *Rear Window.* The last two chapters are a detailed analysis of sound in the *Birds* and a discussion of silence and screams, where aspects of the characters, such as garrulousness, reticence, and speechlessness are discussed. Chapter on *The Man Who Knew Too Much,* 1934, reprinted in entry 771.

682   WEST, ANN ADELE. "Comedie Noire Thrillers of Alfred Hitchcock: Genres, Psychoanalysis, and Woman's Image." Ph.D. Thesis. Berkeley: University of California, 172 pp.

Analysis of *Shadow of a Doubt* and *Psycho* as classic *film noir,* and *Foreign Correspondent* and *North by Northwest* as "comedie noire." West includes discussions of psychoanalytic themes, Hitchcock's widening of genre conventions, doubling in characterization, his "concern about the secret powers of women," wartime anxieties, and color in the films.

Articles and Shorter Writings

683   BAILIN, REBECCA.   "Feminist readership, violence, and *Marnie." Film Reader,* no. 5:24–36.

A reading of the film that makes reference to the sociological literature on violence to women, particularly incest. The discovery of who, at different times, enunciates the story is used to argue that "the film's structures parallel those of society" and the film's layers of ambiguity show that Marnie's illness is social in origin.

684   BAZIN, ANDRÉ.   "Alfred Hitchcock." In *The Cinema of Cruelty: From Buñuel to Hitchcock.* New York: Seaver Books, pp. 101–180.

Translation of entry 430. See that and entries 205 and 215 for summaries of three reprinted essays.

The reprinted reviews show that Bazin is not a "fan" but was persistently pushed by the "new Hitchcock-Hawksian criticism" to keep an open mind. *Shadow of a Doubt,* which later acquires the status of one of the "almost" great works, is initially criticized for its lack of courage in wavering between a standard detective story and a serious study of morals and character. This duality is the first recurring theme of the notices; the second theme is Bazin's amazement at Hitchcock's (sometimes abusive) command of film language. *Suspicion* measures "the boundaries of Hitchcock's talent for expression, a fairly vain talent in its cruel refinement." Bazin is impressed with the "diabolical competence" but judges the writer and director harshly for changing the main character's criminal status. *Lifeboat, The Paradine Case,* and *Rope* are good, but they lack originality, relying on the standard language of the shot-reverse shot, even if arrived at in different ways. *I Confess* "plays on the viewer's nerves, whatever his age, temperament, intelligence, or culture," but Hitchcock works on the nerves and gets to the brain, never the heart. *Rear Window* is the most technically perfect and ingenious film, which "might have gone beyond the level of entertainment to first rate."

At the end of the chronological series, Bazin decides that he really prefers the works of pure entertainment, like *To Catch a Thief* and *The Man Who Knew Too Much* (1955), because Hitchcock's "metaphysics" achieves full rein only when it does not illustrate anything metaphysical in the script." Ultimately, the director "excels at delicate characterization . . . but is less serious than he leads us to believe." Also, reviews of *The Lady Vanishes, Dial M for Murder,* and *The Man Who Knew Too Much* (1955), and translations of entries 205, 215.

Review: *"Le cinéma de la cruauté." Journal of Aesthetics and Art Criticism* 36, no. 2 (1978):231–233.

685   BROWN, ROYAL S.   "Herrmann, Hitchcock, and the music of the irrational." *Cinema Journal* 21, no. 2 (Spring):14–49.

Extensive technical discussion of this collaboration. Defines the "Hitchcock chord" and his characteristic use of persistent downward movement, short phrases for themes, and elimination of melody. Brown also includes an interesting discussion of source versus soundtrack music, the "carry-over" use of themes (in more than one film), and harmonizations.

1982

*686   GALASSO, EUGENIO. "Hitchcock e il suo rapporto con le fonti letter-
arie dei suoi film." *Cristallo* 24, no. 1 (April):101–110.
Cited in MLA (CD-ROM).

687   HORWITZ, MARGARET M. *"The Birds:* A mother's love." *Wide Angle*
5, no. 1:42–48.
Argues that "the heroine is punished by the hero's mother because of the
heroine's desirability to him." Using the psychoanalytic model, the characters are
seen to shift roles within the Oedipal configuration and the birds are seen to
function as "extensions of Lydia's hysterical fear of losing her son."

688   "Ils ont fabriqué *Les oiseaux.*" *Cahiers du Cinéma,* no. 337 (June):36–48.
Round table discussion with five reporters and some of the production team
from *The Birds:* Albert Whitlock (matte painter), Harold Michelson (storyboard
designer), Robert Boyle (production designer), and Richard Edlund, who created
the special effects for *Star Wars.* The article includes extensive comments on the
shoot and the difficulties of following the storyboards and controlling the birds.
Includes photos of mattes and storyboards.

689   JAMESON, FREDRIC. "Reading Hitchcock." *October,* no. 23 (Winter):
15–42.
A review of Rothman (entry 679) arguing (after Christian Metz) that
Rothman has adopted the "cocoon principle," which takes up theoretical discourse
for the purpose of protecting an "adored film." Jameson discusses the absence in
the critique of a historical understanding of genre and Rothman's apparent lack
of awareness not only of the importance of social class but also of the films'
"objective susceptibility to misinterpretation." He goes on to develop his own
ideas concerning the films and their landscapes and expression of daily life.
Returning to Rothman, he focuses on the theoretical problems of reification
(Hitchcock as genius-auteur) and identification (as a solely psychological attachment). Jameson concludes that Rothman's readings are "allegorical," revealing a
type of idealism that transforms "a formal structure or feature into a type of
content." A later version of this essay appears in *Signatures of the Visible* (New
York: Routledge, 1989).

690   KLINGER, BARBARA. *"Psycho:* The institutionalization of female sexuality." *Wide Angle* 5, no. 1:49–55.
Following a review of Raymond Bellour's essay on the film (entry 516), Klinger
answers more completely the question of "how the end replies to the beginning,"
one of the presumed requirements of classical cinema. An explication of the enigma
of the title—who is, what sex is, the psycho?—is followed by an analysis of the
opening shots, shown to rely heavily on the terms of sexual difference: Marion as
"erotic spectacle" and "still life." Subsequently her story is contrasted with her
sister's and Norman's stories, in terms of "the law of the discourse, versus the
unlawful subject." Klinger examines Lila's and Sam's association with the law and
the family (an association denied Marion), and the replacement of Marion's prob-

lematic sexuality with Mrs. Bates's extreme family problems, the only ones "explained" by the psychiatrist. In the end, Marion's body is "transposed into a phallic image—the car withdrawing from the swamp," and the narrative represses her entirely in an "erasure of difference." Reprinted in entry 771.

691   *"L'inconnu du Nord-Express:* Découpage intégral après montage et dialogue in extenso." *L'Avant-Scène du Cinéma,* no. 297–298 (December 1):9–33, 67–85.
   Shot description and dialogue of *Strangers on a Train.* Many frame enlargements.

692   LESSER, WENDY. "Hitchcock and Shakespeare." *The Threepenny Review* 11:17–19.
   Discussion of Shakespeare's *Antony and Cleopatra,* sexual politics, and several of the "romances": *Spellbound, Notorious, Vertigo, North by Northwest,* and *Marnie.* Lesser emphasizes Hitchcock's evenhanded depiction of strengths and weaknesses in characters, and the balance of power between the male and female characters.

693   MODLESKI, TANIA. "Never to be thirty-six years old: *Rebecca* as a female oedipal drama." *Wide Angle* 5, no. 1:34–41.
   Rebecca is analyzed as an example of the female Oedipal trajectory and its difficulties. The insignificance and childishness, even the incompetence of the never-named main female character is shown to be her worth in the male character's (and the others') eyes. She is valued for not having any "distinguishing characteristics," of which *Rebecca* had so many. The film is about her (mostly failed) attempts to match her desire with the man's, a desire that is shown to be an enigma, or at least, difficult to understand. Examination of her extreme efforts to figure him out, her concentration on Rebecca and Mrs. Danvers (the desirable mothers), and the film's persistent referral to Rebecca's absence or "lack" centrally positions Rebecca's challenge to conventional married life and the "patriarchal laws of succession." Modleski concludes that the film portrays a "reign of mothers" against some rather "inept" fathers, and so "is (overly) determined to get rid of Rebecca." Later version, entry 833.

694   PERNOD, PASCAL. "L'échange incomplet." *L'Avant-Scène du Cinéma,* no. 297–298 (December 1):5–7.
   Discusses the symbolic construction of *Strangers on a Train,* the grand principle of which is alternation. Pernod describes examples of doubling, shot-counter-shot, coming and going (Metcalf and Washington), and the mathematical precision with which these themes are approached.

695   PICCARDI, A. "Sequenze: I meccanismi del cinema di Hitchcock." *Cineforum,* no. 213 (April):37–42.
   Description and analysis of the final sequence of *Notorious.* Its relationship to the "cinematic apparatus," the "gaze of the subject," and other psychoanalytical topics is emphasized.

1983

696   SERCEAU, MICHEL.   "Le plaisir et l'ordre ou Hitchcock 'directeur . . . de spectateurs.'" *Revue du Cinéma/Image et Son,* no. 378 (December): 44–56.
Analysis of the genre and archetypal aspects of the police and spy stories, which Serceau judges to be constructed in the same way by Hitchcock as other directors, though Hitchcock has made distinct contributions to the ideological discourse of both. Serceau examines themes of unreality, censure, order, and the fantastic, and assesses Hitchcock's "aesthetic as less cathartic than normal, which pulls out of the formal aspects all of the ideological force."

697   SIMSOLO, NOËL.   "Alfred Hitchcock (1899–1980)." *L'Avant-Scène du Cinéma, Anthologie du Cinéma,* no. 110 (December 1–15):305–336.
Chronological assessment of each film reflecting French critical opinion of the time. Simsolo describes Hitchcock as one of the few directors interested in the commercial aspects of the industry, one who tapped into the unconscious of his public. Obsessed with his own desire to create, Hitchcock is entirely original, according to Simsolo, but in his focus on death, he is pessimistic and contemptuous of human beings. Simsolo discusses the films' focus on the couple and understands this theme as an obsession with the "animal function" and the powerlessness of man to gain knowledge. He concludes that Hitchcock "esteemed himself above and beyond other human beings" and desired to create as an equal of God.

698   TARNOWSKI, JEAN FRANÇOIS.   *"Le crime était presque parfait."* *Positif,* no. 261 (November):66–70.
Upon reissue of *Dial M for Murder,* a discussion of the formal aspects of 3-D and their working in the film.

699   WALKER, M.   "Alfred Hitchcock." *Film Dope,* no. 24 (March):35–39.
Short biography and filmography.

1983
Books

*700   *Hsi-ch U-Kao-Ko Yen Chiu,* edited by Kuo-fu Chen and Liang-i Han. Taipei shih: Chung-hua min ku tien ying shih yeh fa chan chi chin hui tien ying tu shu kuan chu pan pu, min kuo, 217 pp.
Cited in the Research Libraries Information Network (RLIN).

*701   McNAMARA, DONALD DAILEY.   "Alfred Hitchcock's Symbolic Fantasies." Ph.D. Thesis. Columbia: University of Missouri, 342 pp.
Cited in the Research Libraries Information Network (RLIN).

702   SPOTO, DONALD.   *The Dark Side of Genius: The Life of Alfred Hitch-cock.* Boston/New York: Little, Brown/Ballantine, 594 pp.

Extensively researched biography based on news reports, interviews, commentary, criticism—both Spoto's own and his synthesis of other's—and extensive correspondence by the author with a large number of people who knew or worked with Hitchcock. Spoto states in his preface that "the lack of primary sources at first seemed a crippling omission. But . . . it became clear that Hitchcock's films were indeed his notebooks and journals." The author attempts throughout to describe Hitchcock's "inner life," freely mixing speculation on his state of mind with quotations from and interpretations of the films to put forth a view of Hitchcock as a man guided by fear and guilt, "an observer rather than a participant," and, ultimately, "someone from another world, a land where murder was routine and betrayal the typical response of one person to another." He is particularly interested in documenting the director's relationships with the women who starred in his productions or otherwise played a large part in his life. Includes detailed index.

Translated into French (Paris: Albin Michel, 1989) and Portuguese (Barcelona: Ultramar, 1985).

Reviews: entry 800.

Davis, H. "Hitchcock's dark side." *On Film,* No. 12 (Spring 1984): 50–53.

Grenier, Richard. *New York Times Book Review* (March 6, 1983):1.

Lehmann-Haupt, Christopher. *New York Times* (March 15, 1983):23.

Wood, R. *"The dark side of genius: The life of Alfred Hitchcock." Post Script* 4, no. 2 (1985):66–67.

You, D. *"The dark side of genius." Film Échange,* no. 28 (Autumn 1984):99.

703   WULFF, HANS JÜRGEN, and PAUL HEISTERKAMP.   *All about Alfred Hitchcock, Bibliographie.* Münster: MAkS Publikationen, 295 pp.

Comprehensive bibliographic listing including criticism, reviews, interviews, publicity material, mystery books, short stories, and magazines produced under Hitchcock's name, and reviews of books on Hitchcock. Includes most languages and arranged by film title. Very good for German language material and popular American magazines, such as Collier's and Good Housekeeping.

Articles and Shorter Writings

704   BARR, CHARLES.   *"Blackmail:* Silent & sound." *Sight and Sound* 52 (Spring):122–126.

Examination of both versions and their "hybrid" nature. Apparently two negatives for many shots were made originally, while other, later, shots were done only for silent or only for sound. Barr analyzes in detail three sequences—when Crewe removes Alice's dress from the screen, when she returns home at dawn, and the knife breakfast scene. He concludes that the silent version was more oriented toward creative montage while the sound version became theatricalized. The later release of the silent version in theaters not equipped for sound was used at the time by the press to support anti-talkie sentiment.

1983

705   BRILL, LESLEY W. "Hitchcock's *The Lodger." Literature/Film Quarterly* 11, no. 4:257–265.
Examination of the myth of Persephone in *The Lodger,* elements of which are not in the source material but which appear often in later Hitchcock films. Brill comments on the murders as "social entertainment" and examines the social context of class. Daisy is described as a "golden girl" living "below her natural station," making her detective-suitor Joe "beneath her" in class; *The Lodger* is described as a "real gentleman," a superior mate. All of these attributes are shown to be "romantic" elements that Hitchcock added. Reprinted in entry 771.

706   "British shown Hitchcock film on holocaust." *New York Times* 133 (December 25):Section 1, p. 47, col. 3.
Alfred Hitchcock oversaw the organization and editing of a film about the holocaust, which included fifteen minutes of footage found when Allied soldiers liberated Nazi concentration camps. See other, differing, reports, entries 746 and 747.

707   CHASE, CHRIS. "French actor remembers Hitchcock." *New York Times* 132 (January 7):Section C, p. 8, col. 1.
Philippe Noiret, who had a supporting role in *Topaz,* interviewed in New York. Noiret says Alfred Hitchcock liked actors, contrary to American opinion: "I think he didn't like boring actors." French actors are not frightened of Alfred Hitchcock "like everybody else."

708   CRAWFORD, LARRY. "Looking, film, painting: The trickster's in site/in sight/insight." *Wide Angle* 5, no. 3:64–69.
Study of the "staging, focusing, delimiting, and playing out of the look" involving "tricksters": one, in a classical painting of a victimizing card shark, and the other, the "troubling policeman" of the Bakersfield car lot sequence in *Psycho.*

709   DUCKERT, MICHELE. "Original sins and classical narratives: Hitchcock through Foucault." In *Proceedings of the Purdue University Seventh Annual Conference on Film,* edited by Marshall Deutelbaum and Thomas P. Adler. West Lafayette, Indiana: Department of English, Purdue University, 295–300.
Discussion of Michel Foucault's *Discipline and Punish* and its ideas concerning punitive measures as spectacle, the spectacle's effect on the spectator as witness, and the event's relationship to behavior. Duckert examines *Vertigo, The Wrong Man, The Birds,* and *Marnie* in relation to the nature and context of the transgressions and punishments of the main characters.

*710   HOLTHOF, M. "Het is allemaal de schuld van Hitchcock." *Sinema,* no.
       54 (December):4–10.
       Cited in *Film Literature Index,* 1984.

711   LEFF, LEONARD J. "Hitchcock at Metro." *Western Humanities Review*
      37, no. 2:97–124.
      Case study of the production of *North by Northwest,* made by a director
"whose reputation warranted independence" and a studio, MGM, whose "fiscal
precariousness" indicated a need for control. Leff chronicles Hitchcock's interactions with producers and screenwriter Ernest Lehman, problems with the
Production Code Administration, problems with the National Park Service
concerning locations, and the film's publicity campaign and reception. Reprinted
in entry 771.

712   MASLIN, JANET. "James Stewart recalls 'Hitch.'" *New York Times*
      133 (October 9):Section 2, p. 21, col. 1.
      Interview with Stewart. The five Stewart films were out of circulation since
initial release to increase their value. Now re-release launched at New York Film
Festival beginning with *Rear Window.* Stewart remembers that Grace Kelly did
her own stunt work in *Rear Window,* and that the most strenuous film he did was
Rope.

713   MILLER, MARK CRISPIN. "Hitchcock's suspicions and *Suspicion.*"
      MLN 98, no. 5 (December):1143–1186.
      Plot analysis of *Suspicion* as a woman's film dominated by Lina's "dark and
too-familiar consciousness," which invites the audience to "cease watching as
escapists." Lina is interpreted as a woman of "narcissistic dominance" who wants
to command Johnny's "unchanging image," but thwarted, she imagines him as
evil.

714   PASCALL, JEREMY. "Alfred Hitchcock." In *The Cinema Greats.* Mor-
      ristown, N.J.: Silver Burdett, pp. 32–40.
      Children's book with chapters on Laurel and Hardy, John Wayne, Hitchcock,
and Walt Disney.

715   ROTHMAN, WILLIAM. *"North by Northwest:* Hitchcock's monument to
      the Hitchcock film." *North Dakota Quarterly* 51, no. 3 (Summer):11–23.
      Very detailed analysis of *North by Northwest.* Focuses on the creation of Eve
as a fusion of Hitchcock's independent thinking women types, a "new woman" of
real feeling and humanity, illustrated by her bond with the camera that reveals
her "inner life." She is so completely progressive a character that Grant (the
actor) must be redeemed and made human to deserve her. Even his failure to
embrace her after she has sent him off to be murdered in the cornfields is
described as a manifestation of his "resolution to withhold his humanity and even
his charm" from her.

1984

716   STAM, ROBERT, and ROBERTA PEARSON. "Hitchcock's *Rear Window:* Reflexivity and the critique of voyeurism." *Enclitic* 7, no. 1 (Spring): 136–145.

Semiotic analysis of the film as a "cautionary tale for voyeurs and an ode to the cinema." The article is primarily an examination of the character of Jeff and the structures of scopophilia and identification that surround him. The authors compare the characters to the performers and Jeff to the spectator and the director, a voyeur, perhaps even "a serious case of psychosexual pathology." They conclude that the breakdown of his passivity is also a cure. Reprinted in entry 771.

1984
Books

717   DOTY, ALEXANDER MICHAEL. "Alfred Hitchcock's Films of the 1940s: The Emergence of Personal Style and Theme Within the American Studio System." Ph.D. Thesis. Urbana: University of Illinois, 380 pp.

Chapters on various aspects of film culture and history of the 1940s are combined with critical analyses of illustrative films: the American studio system and *Rebecca,* genre and *Mr. and Mrs. Smith,* male-female relationships and *Notorious,* the influence of Freud and *Spellbound,* and the Hitchcockian concept of "pure cinema" and *Suspicion.* These studies are intended to illuminate a period of transition that Doty sees as a deepening and darkening of the director's vision. Especially valuable for production details and description of the historical context of the U.S. film industry.

718   FREEMAN, DAVID. *The Last Days of Alfred Hitchcock.* London/ Woodstock, N.Y.: Pavilion-Michael Joseph/Overlook, 281 pp.

Consists of reminiscences of Freeman's relationship with Hitchcock as screenwriter on the last film on which he worked before he died, mixed with critical speculation on the most popular films. Over half the book is a not quite final draft of *The Short Night* and commentary on the development and logic of the script. Translated into French (Paris: Jade, 1985).

Reviews: "Double takes: *Short Night." Sight and Sound* 54, no. 4 (1985):265– 266.

Dunne, P. "Winter's tales." *American Film* 10, no. 4 (January–February 1985):51–53.

"The Last Days of Alfred Hitchcock." Esquire 97 (April 1982):81.

"The Last Days of Alfred Hitchcock." Historical Journal of Film, Radio and Television, no. 1 (1986):6.

Lomb[ardi], F. *"The Last Days of Alfred Hitchcock." Variety* 317 (January 2, 1985):142.

Lopate, Phillip. *New York Times Book Review* (December 30, 1984):9.

Owen, D. *"The Last Days of Alfred Hitchcock." Film* 11, no. 140 (November 1985).

*719   LAUNDER, FRANK, and SIDNEY GILLIAT. *The Lady Vanishes,* directed by Alfred Hitchcock. London: Lorrimer, 101 pp.
Cited in Research Libraries Information Network (RLIN). Screenplay.

720   PHILIPS, GENE D. *Alfred Hitchcock.* Boston: Twayne, 211 pp.
Chronological overview arranged with a section for each film. The thematic criticism characterizes Hitchcock's work as not "mere suspense" because it is also interested in communication and with creating identification in the audience. Likewise, the work is "more than entertainment . . . presenting sobering thoughts about human nature."
Reviews: Edgerton, G. *Journal of Popular Film & Television* 15, no. 1 (1987):51.
"Film books." *Films and Filming,* no. 400 (January 1988):38–39.

721   STROBEL, RICARDA. *Propagandafilm und Melodrama: Untersuchungen zu Alfred Hitchcocks* Lifeboat *und Orson Welles* The Stranger. Rottenburg-Oberndorf: Wissenschaftler-Verlag Faulstich, 234 pp.
Structural analysis of the relationship of the propaganda film and melodrama genres to *Lifeboat* and *The Stranger.* Strobel includes an overview of the literature and extensive description of the formal construction of each film, focusing on each one's portrayal of characters with ideological attributes, in particular, the "Nazi-within-one's-midst." She concludes with a discussion of the portrayal of suffering to produce effect and the structural consequences of such effects. Includes charts.

Articles and Shorter Writings

*722   ALANEN, A. "Kohti pyorteen silmaa." *Filmihullu,* no. 5: 26–33.
Cited in *Film Literature Index,* 1985. In Finnish.

723   BENTON, ROBERT J. "Film as dream: Alfred Hitchcock's *Rear Window.*" *Psychoanalytic Review* 71, no. 3 (November):483–500.
"A profound, frightening fantasy of castration anxiety, voyeurism, and sadomasochism," here analyzed as a dream. The symbols include the dream space of unhappy couples and unhappy singles, and a libido (Jeff) channeled away from health (Lisa) and toward voyeurism. Benton also discusses the symbols of dismemberment, artists and artistry, and mirrors.

724   CHION, MICHEL. "Le quatrième côté." *Cahiers du Cinéma,* no. 356 (February):4–7.
Discussion of the screen space in *Rear Window,* the "fourth side" of Jeffries's apartment, of whose inhabitants, though they are the closest, we see and hear nothing. Chion comments on the never-entered kitchen and bedroom, and the

organizing point of view, broken only once, when the dog is killed. He concludes that the film is conceived as a play with four sides.

725 ———. "Une logique du sonore." *Le Monde de la Musique* (July):26–31.
Lengthy, admiring piece on Hitchcock's always "logical" use of sound, not so much concerned with the logic of the story but with the significance of the music that presents possibilities. Chion assesses him as an artist who does not work with preconceived notions and who creates forms based on pure idea.

726 COURSODON, JEAN PIERRE. "Le désir attrapé par la corde." *Cinéma 84,* no. 311 (November):25–34.
Subtitled "the pleasure of hell, hell of pleasure (notes on the fetishes of the continuous shot of *Rope*)." Analyzes the film as an "eccentric and aberrant" pure formal exercise. The author reviews critical opinion of the time and discusses rope and knots as a Hitchcockian trope.

727 DANIELS, DON. "P.O.V. a date with Judy: The return of Hitchcock's *Vertigo.*" *Columbia Film Review* 2, nos. 5–6 (January–February):12–15.
Analysis of film as a more conventional protagonist/antagonist narrative struggle. Daniels focuses on the composite character of Madeleine/Judy and Novak's performance.

728 DELVAUX, CLAUDINE. "Propositions pour un système des objets (en gros plan) chez Alfred Hitchcock (1ère partie)." *Revue Belge du Cinéma,* no. 10 (Winter):61–71.
Study of the use of close-ups in *The 39 Steps, Secret Agent,* and *Blackmail.* Delvaux examines their use within each work and also their recurring functions across all the films, emphasizing qualities of roundness and point-ness.

729 DEUTELBAUM, MARSHALL. "Seeing in *Saboteur.*" *Literature/Film Quarterly* 12, no. 1:58–64.
Examination of the theme of appearance and reality in the film. Deutelbaum details events for the purpose of illustrating the film's intent "to encourage its viewers to question their habitual perceptions"; he documents the recurrence of a "spoke-like" pattern as well as the separate features of the Statue of Liberty.

730 FISHER, J. "Victor Hitchcock and Alfred Burgin." *Artforum* 22 (May):39–43.
Comparison of two "rigorous formalists." Victor Burgin's collage-tryptic, titled "The Bridge," includes images from *Vertigo* and photographically considers problems of the look and voyeurism. The two pieces are related through their theoretical concerns and similar meaning.

731 FISHER, WILLIAM. "Re: writing: Film history: From Hitchcock to De Palma." *Persistence of Vision,* no. 1 (Summer):13–22.

Theoretical discussion of the writing of film history using as an example the historical relations between the work of Hitchcock and Brian De Palma. Fisher describes the positions of each filmmaker in terms of the changing theoretical and critical discourses that attempt to represent them. The flexibility of Hitchcock's work in fulfilling the "masterpiece requirements of auteurist values," as well as providing a textbook illustration of psychoanalytic-semiotic principles, is indication of the inadequacy of written discourse about films and an instance of the "sclerotic character" of the term *classical cinema.* Fisher argues that films today are made taking into account the "film history" in which the filmmakers were educated and trained. Combining this and other similar ideas with Harold Bloom's description of "strong poets" who take and use their own readings of the language and images of their predecessors in their own work, Fisher posits such "intertextuality" as the basis of an analysis of De Palma's work as it relates to Hitchcock's. He argues that the "privileged trope" is irony and that De Palma uses Hitchcock's work and its shared cinematic experience with the audience in order to render a "formal reinvention of the received moments," but for very different ends. Fisher concludes that De Palma's work is a distinctive critique of the values of middle-class culture, and a progression from Hitchcock.

732 FUNCK, JEAN. "Fonctions et significations de l'escalier dans le cinéma d'Alfred Hitchcock." *Positif,* no. 286 (December):30–35.

Discussion of the functions and meanings of stairways in the films, emphasizing the mystery at the top, the dangers of the space, Freudian interpretations of going up and down, and the satisfaction and danger of curiosity, desire, and loss.

733 JHIRAD, SUSAN. "Hitchcock's women." *Cineaste* 13, no. 4:30–33.

Admiring discussion of Hitchcock's use of blond women. Jhirad intersperses information from Spoto's biography (entry 702) with interpretation of the films, concluding that the director's pathological view—of the stereotypically cold but perfect blond and the nagging, castrating mother—is "deeply ingrained in the psychology of our culture," and his films allow us to understand it.

734 KEHR, DAVE. "Hitch's riddle." *Film Comment* 20, no. 3 (May–June):9–18.

Essay on the five re-released films addressing Hitchcock's concerns with art and the process of art. *"Rope* [takes] literature as a metaphor; *Rear Window,* photography; *The Trouble with Harry,* painting; *The Man Who Knew Too Much,* music; and *Vertigo,* the cinema." Hitchcock works in the "least respectable medium" in the "least respectable genre," where he hides because he is guilty of being a creator, of taking upon himself the "freedom and power" of the artist.

1984

735   LAUDER, ROBERT E.   "Alfred Hitchcock: A film maker of the conscience." *America* 151, no. 3 (August 11):52–54.
General assessment of Hitchcock's work as disturbing, forcing us to "face
ourselves more honestly."

736   LEGRAND, GÉRARD.   "Hitchcock au quart de siècle, en quatre mouve-
ments." *Positif,* no. 286 (December):36–44.
Structural and thematic overview that emphasizes the closed aspect of the
abyss, as nightmare, as suffocation. Legrand discusses doubling, mirrors, windows, and the complexities of metaphor and metonymy throughout the films. Part
two of an essay begun in *Positif,* no. 281–282 (not seen).

*737   LESNIK, B.   "Druzinska zarota." *Ekran,* no. 7–8:9–22.
Cited in *Film Literature Index,* 1984.

*738   LODATO, N.   "Nessun cadavere, niente delitto." *Cineforum* 24, no. 239
(November):43–52.
Cited in *Film Literature Index,* 1985.

739   NORDON, PIERRE.   "Hollywood reflet d'une société: Esquisse d'examen
diachronique." In *Hollywood: Réflexions sur l'ecran,* edited by Daniel
Royot. Aix-en-Provence: Groupe de Recherche et d'Études Nord-
Americaines, Université de Provence, pp. 129–139.
Freudian social analysis of *Strangers on a Train* and John Ford's *Seven
Women* in the context of the postwar American mentality and its emphasis on
family values. Nordon argues that the weak male characters of the first film are
a result of social values put into question by the "subversive agents" of the
McCarthy era. Further, he theorizes that both films are a reflection of a "double
bind," whereby Americans were "confronted with responsibilities for which their
historical tradition had not prepared them" and were forced to "a painful
revision" involving a return to "matriarchal values, a nourishing mother image
of the fatherland."

*740   OKSA, R.   "Puhtaan elokuvani etsijaet." *Filmihullu,* no. 5:6–13.
Cited in *Film Literature Index,* 1985. In Finnish.

741   PEARY, G[ERALD].   Translated by Oliver Euquem. "Hitch vu par sa
fille." *Positif,* no. 286 (December):27–29.
Interview with Patricia Hitchcock, who comments on her "English-style"
upbringing, her father's reading and listening habits (biographies and classical),
and her mother's artistic collaboration in the films.

742 PHILLIPS, LOUIS. *"Vertigo:* After such knowledge, what forgiveness?" *Armchair Detective* 17, no. 2 (Spring):188–191.
General discussion of the themes of death and the double referring to the contemporary best-seller, *The Search for Bridey Murphy* (1956), and interview quotes from Hitchcock.

743 POLLOCK, DALE. "Hitchcock treasure of the past a revelation." *Los Angeles Times* 103 (November 26):Section 6, col. 1, p. 1.
Account of the donation of Hitchcock's papers to the Academy of Motion Pictures Arts and Sciences Library.

744 PRICE, THEODORE. "Hitchcock and homosexuality: The truth about *The Paradine Case.*" In *Sex and Love in Motion Pictures,* edited by Douglas Radcliff-Umstead. Kent, OH: Romance Language Department, Kent State University, pp. 18–24.
Compares *The Paradine Case* to *Murder!* through parallel character roles. Price argues that the groom/valet character is a homosexual and the "Lady" of the "Lady and the groom" theme is actually the lawyer played by Gregory Peck, who is "degraded" by his love for a prostitute.

*745 SCHICKEL, RICHARD. "Inside Hitchcock: Alfred Hitchcock." Videorecording. MPI, American Cinematheque, 55 min.
Cited in Research Libraries Information Network (RLIN).

746 SILVERMAN, STEPHEN M. "People yearn for Hitchcock movies, says his daughter." *New York Post* (March 5): New York Public Library clipping file.
Interview with Patricia Hitchcock. She indicates that reports of her father working on a film of the German concentration camps are rumors. According to Sidney Bernstein, he merely offered some ideas about others' footage.

747 SUSSEX, ELIZABETH. "The fate of F3080." *Sight and Sound* 53, no. 2 (Spring):92–97.
Detailed history taken from the British Ministry of Information files on an hour-long documentary of the German concentration camps on which Hitchcock advised for several weeks in the summer of 1945. Sidney Bernstein, film adviser to the ministry, initiated and carried through the project, for which Hitchcock suggested the filming of scenes to indicate the geography surrounding the camps.

748 TALLMER, JERRY. "U.S. gets first chance to see the film too horrible for Hitchcock." *New York Post* (June 20):42.
Reports that Hitchcock "made secret trip to London" to view concentration camp footage. Author is unclear on the contribution made by the director but

indicates he made two suggestions: to add maps of the surrounding areas and to include a tracking shot of troops entering the camp. See other report, entry 747.

749   TOLES, GEORGE.   " 'If thine eye offend thee . . .' *Psycho* and the art of infection." *New Literary History* 15, no. 3 (Spring):631–651.

Detailed tracing of the metaphor of the eye through Edgar Allan Poe's "Berenice," George Bataille's *Histoire de l'oeil,* and, most extensively, *Psycho.* The eye's "infected" character arises from the "dissociation of authorial self," which leaves the metaphor unable to grow, "having no public meaning except that of shock."

750   TRUFFAUT, FRANÇOIS.   "Slow fade: The declining years of Alfred Hitchcock." *American Film* 10, no. 2 (November):40–47.

Excerpt from the revised version of Truffaut's book (entry 338) on Hitchcock, including part of a short 1972 interview, excerpts from letters, and other reports. Primarily, Truffaut's personal testimony to Hitchcock's greatness as a director.

1985
Books

751   AKTSOGLOU, BAMPES.   *Alphrent Chitskok* [Alfred Hitchcock]. *Kinematographikoarcheio,* 18. Athens: Aigokeros, 151 pp.

Critical overview, filmography. In Greek.

752   BARBIER, PHILIPPE and JACQUES MOREAU.   *Alfred Hitchcock.* Paris: PAC, 87 [200] pp.

Photo album, brief introduction to the films, and list of credits with synopses.

753   KLOPPENBURG, JOSEF.   *Die dramaturgische Funktion der Musik in den Filmen Alfred Hitchcocks.* Munich: Wilhelm Fink Verlag, 297 pp.

Extensive analysis of the interrelationship of meaning in film and music, using examples from many Hitchcock films. The author discusses the concept of succession—as time series, montage, editing, and matching—the identification of kinds of film music, aspects of film music as functional music, and the dramaturgical determinants of film music. A description of methodological problems opens an extremely detailed analysis of the music for *Spellbound* by Miklós Rózsa. Included is a shot-by-shot listing that charts camera movement, dialogue, and musical notation. The author concludes there is not always a connection between the music and the narrative.

754 McCARTY, JOHN, and BRIAN KELLEHEN. *Alfred Hitchcock Presents.* New York: St. Martins, 337 pp.
Listing by season of all shows in the several series produced by Hitchcock. The book includes minimal credits, synopses, air dates, and occasional "author's notes" indicating awards, gossip, and other information.

755 SIMONE, SAM P. *Hitchcock as Activist.* Ann Arbor, Mich.: UMI Research Press, 203 pp.
Expansion of a doctoral thesis intended to show that Hitchcock actively promoted "democratic" values: "his heroes are mainly protagonists who support democracy, while his villains are the antagonists who support Nazism." A chapter each is devoted to *Foreign Correspondent,* as it relates to isolationism; *Saboteur,* as it relates to the real existence of sabotage and espionage within Allied territory; *Lifeboat,* as a microcosm of Allied difficulties against German unity; and *Notorious,* as it relates to the development of the atom bomb. Simone shows in detail that the films "are filled with incidents that parallel actual events of the World War II era." Throughout the book, he moves between journalistic accounts of the war and counterparts in the films, positing Hitchcock's English sympathies and desire to preserve "our ideal lives" as well as the director's complete mastery of suspense technique. He is less successful in proving that the films "derive their impetus and importance from the political clashes of nations whose conflicts escalated to engulf and reshape the world." He attempts to equate the political ideology of the films with "democratic ideology" and then with the ideology of Hitchcock as well as the United States by the use of broad analogies.
Review: Taylor, J[ohn] R[ussell]. *Films and Filming,* no. 389 (February 1987):46–47.

756 VILLIEN, BRUNO. *Alfred Hitchcock.* Paris: Rivages, 195 pp.
Chronological overview of films and themes, valuable for additional information gathered from interviews with several of the actors. Villien discusses most conventional themes as well as blond and brunette women, and food as a metaphor. Over half the book is a detailed filmography with historical notes about the productions and the careers of the actors.

Articles and Shorter Writings

757 ALLEN, JEANNE THOMAS. "The representation of violence to women: Hitchcock's *Frenzy.*" *Film Quarterly* 38, no. 3 (Spring):30–38.
Argues that *Frenzy* is "centered on the victimization of women, and [projects a viewpoint] in which women's welfare and safety are negated." Following a summary of the attitudes of the contemporary review media, Allen analyzes the scenes of violence in the film, especially the first murder-rape, as to dialogue, lighting, and point of view. She argues that these reveal an objectification of women. "The metaphoricizing of women's victimization into a human universal,"

which denies distinction to women's issues, and the manipulation by Hitchcock of the spectator into identification with male aggression both contribute to a denial of the distinctiveness of women's consciousness.

758   BANNON, BARBARA M. "Double, double: Toil and trouble." *Literature/Film Quarterly* 13, no. 1 (Winter):56–65.
Doubling in psychology, literature, film, and Hitchcock. Bannon distinguishes between overt doubles (*The Wrong Man* and *Vertigo*) and latent doubles. She discusses at length three of these—*Shadow of a Doubt, Strangers on a Train,* and *North by Northwest*—in order to illustrate both the creation of character doubles and the structural reinforcements of the theme by doubling, the "paralleling and reversing of scenes." She concludes that both project a view of the world as morally ambiguous and chaotic.

*759   DOLAR, M. "Dva hitchcockovska objekta." *Ekran* 10, no. 9–10:9–14.
Cited in *Film Literature Index,* 1985. In Serbo-Croatian.

760   DUVAL, BRUNO. "L'effroyable secret du professeur Hitchcock." *Revue du Cinéma/Image et Son,* no. 401 (January):80–86.
Overview emphasizing a concept of the Hitchcockian hero as zero, infinity, the void, and the letter O.

761   DUVAL, BRUNO, and RAYMOND LEFÈVRE. "Alfred Hitchcock." *Revue du Cinéma/Image et Son,* no. 401 (January):71–79.
Discussion of the five re-released films, which are assessed as the "height of cinephiliac pleasure." The authors examine related formal and thematic aspects of *Rope, Rear Window, The Man Who Knew Too Much* (1955), *Vertigo,* and *The Trouble with Harry,* and relates the "seeming contradiction" of Hitchcock's approach, which refuses realism but also discards fantasy. This approach cannot succeed with "gratuitous technical feats" and therefore proves Hitchcock's formal emphasis. The article includes a chart comparing the revenues of the original release with those of the re-release.

762   FERRARA, PATRICIA. "Through Hitchcock's *Rear Window* again." *New Orleans Review* 12, no. 3:21–30.
Argues against the prevailing interpretation of Jeffries as a voyeur and the film as an "essay on film viewing." Ferrara describes Jeff as a man of many positive qualities, actively and consciously involved in the world, and Lisa as the unaware character who undergoes "striking changes." Detailed analysis of the events and all the characters, emphasizing clothes (appearances), and their "hidden abilities" shows *Rear Window* to be a film about the differences in the way people see, and the accommodation of others' vision.

763   FRENCH, PHILIP.   "Alfred Hitchcock: The Film-maker as Englishman and exile." *Sight and Sound* 54, no. 2 (Spring):116–122.
Discussion of Hitchcock's English roots and lifelong predilection for things English. French compares him to Charlie Chaplin; he discusses his personal habits and the image of England and English people in his films.

764   SLOAN, KAY.   "Three Hitchcock heroines: The domestication of violence." *New Orleans Review* 12, no. 4:91–95.
Argues that the three female lead characters of *Blackmail, Shadow of a Doubt,* and *The Birds* present unconventional sex roles played out to the point of danger, and are then saved by the "solace of romantic attachment and family structure."

765   THOMSON, DAVID.   "Salieri, *Psycho.*" *Film Comment* 21 (January–February):70–75.
Comparison of the characters of Salieri in *Amadeus* and Norman in *Psycho.* Both are intelligent, sensitive villains, possibly gay, and "models for Hollywood's sense of itself."

766   TURNER, GEORGE E.   *"Rope*—something different." *American Cinematographer* 66 (February):34–40.
History of the shooting of *Rope,* including discussion of the concept of shooting in real time, backgrounds of key technical personnel, dates of conferences, rehearsals, color and cloud consultants, its smooth completion, and modest cost.

767   WELSH, ALEXANDER.   *George Eliot and Blackmail.* Cambridge, Mass.: Harvard University Press, pp. 3–19.
Blackmail is used as a twentieth-century manifestation of the late nineteenth-century theme of blackmail. The film is not related to George Eliot but to the general social conditions that produced a market for "cultural information."

768   WEYL, DANIEL.   "Réflexion sur la théorie du texte: L'exemple filmique de *L'inconnu de Nord-Express* d'Alfred Hitchcock." *Littérature* 60 (December):109–121.
Structural analysis of *Strangers on a Train* detailing paradigmatic and syntagmatic elements: trains, riding, presidential power, country, prostitution, death, and madness. Concludes that "the text destroys the rationale of the story."

*769   ŽIŽEK, S.   "O Hitchcockovskem travelling in nekaterih z njim povezanih zadevah." *Ekran* 10, no. 9–10:3–8.
Cited in *Film Literature Index,* 1985. In Serbo-Croatian.

1986
Books

770   BROWN, BRYAN. *The Alfred Hitchcock Movie Quiz Book.* New York: Perigree, 176 pp.

Tries "to steer a center course between the profound and the trivial," a result of the author's finding the films "far more complicated" than his "adolescent mind" could ever have imagined. Includes 122 pages of questions such as "Who is Al Magarulian?" and "Why does Elsa demand that Ashenden refrain from killing Marvin?" These are followed by 55 pages of answers. Points, scoring, and extra credit.

771   *A Hitchcock Reader,* edited by Marshall Deutelbaum and Leland Poague. Ames: Iowa State University Press, 355 pp.

Anthology intended to support "beginning as well as advanced" course work on Hitchcock. Five sections, each with an introductory review of the literature, look at various aspects of Hitchcock criticism. The historical periods, Britain, Hollywood, and the "late masterwork period" are placed between two general sections illustrating the broad discussion over Hitchcock as an entertainer or an artist, and Hitchcock's connection with film theory.

An essay by Deutelbaum, "Finding the Right Man in *The Wrong Man,*" surveys prior accounts of the Emmanuel Balestrero case to show the changes and omissions of the Hitchcock version and compares the film to the general approach of postwar Hollywood to fiction films based on fact. The author points out many details, for instance, the prior appearances of the real robber in the film, in arguing that the film embodies the themes of the unrealizable nature of perception, one of the most typical of Hitchcock's work.

Essays by Poague: "Links in a Chain: *Psycho* and Film Classicism" is an alternative reading of *Psycho* displacing the notion of a structuring voyeurism with one of the multiple meanings of classical narrative cinema. Poague examines the theme of money and the twirling, spinning visual patterns. He argues that the audience can and should be distinguished from the characters in the film, as the audience is allowed a glimpse of the "truth . . . the connection between capitalism, sexuality, and death."

"Criticism and/as History: Rereading *Blackmail.*" After the "reception theory" of Hans-Georg Gadamer and Hans Robert Jauss, this is a discussion of "doubleness" in the film as it relates to the world of the film and the perceptions of the audience viewing it, creating "two stories." Poague examines the theme of public and private, concluding that double readings are unavoidable and the critic must be wary of readings that provide "once and for all meaning."

Includes additional original essays by Charles L. P. Silet, Patrice Petro, Marian E. Keane, and Michele Piso, and a translation from the French of Jean Douchet (see entries this year). Also reprints of Yacowar (entry 477), three chapters from Wood (entries 318, 476, and 852), Leff (entry 711), Brill (entry 705), chapter two of Rothman (entry 679), Weis (entry 681), McLaughlin (entry 576), Hyde (entry 508), Abel (entry 515), Stam and Pearson (entry 716), Cavell (entry 622), Cameron and Jeffrey (entry 319), Horwitz (entry 687), Bellour (entry 516), and Klinger (entry 690).

Review: Anderegg, M. A. "*A Hitchcock Reader.*" *North Dakota Quarterly* 55, no. 3 (1987):210–213.

772 FRÜNDT, BODO. *Alfred Hitchcock und seine Filme.* Munich: Wilhelm Heyne, 301 pp.
Popular overview of Hitchcock's films.

773 HUMPHRIES, PATRICK. *The Films of Alfred Hitchcock.* London: Hamlyn/Bison, 192 pp.
Popular, chronological overview of career. Exceptionally well illustrated with many photographs.

*774 PISO, MICHELE. "Alfred Hitchcock: For loss of the world." Ph.D. Thesis. Eugene: University of Oregon, 223 pp.
Cited in *Dissertation Abstracts* (On-Line). Social analysis of the films as "meditations on alienation" in the Marxist sense, "expressions of a disenchanted world in which conformity erases character, calculation diminishes giving, and bureaucracy eliminates mystery."

775 RYALL, TOM. *Alfred Hitchcock and the British Cinema.* London/ Urbana: Croom Helm/University of Illinois Press, 193 pp.
An extensive synthesis of British film culture and history and its influence on the films. Ryall begins with a description of his own critical approach, concerned with the limitations of auteur studies and the importance of the ideological forces of local film culture, institutional frameworks, and broad social context. He documents at length the crucial relationship of the British film industry to its government, which employed state censors from the early 1920s and stepped in to save the failing producers with protection laws in 1927. An art historical description of the experimental 1920s film culture illustrates how, in Britain, it developed as a line of "cultural defence" against the rapid dominance of the commercial Hollywood cinema (by 1926, 95% of the films shown in Britain were American). Coincident with this, talent was siphoned away from the industry into noncommercial documentary filmmaking and the critical pursuit of "the ideal of cinematic perfectionism"—understood as being represented in films produced not in Britain or the United States, but in continental Europe.
Ryall documents Hitchcock's participation in both streams by showing the insecurity of his job in an industry "near extinction" and the intellectual stimulation of the London Film Society and journals such as *Close Up,* which translated work by Eisenstein. By the time of the introduction of the quota laws in 1927, Hitchcock was already famous as a creative person, though hampered by being too "arty" for the financiers and too "British" for the intellectual critics. Ryall then moves to a consideration of the British entertainment film of the 1930s and chronicles such aspects as British International's heavy reliance on stage adaptations, the grip of censorship, which focused on political rather than moral issues, conveying an "extremely paternalistic" attitude toward the British

working-class film audience, and the predominance of the crime/thriller genre, which was inexpensive to produce and had deep cultural roots.

A chapter on Hitchcock and the classic thriller genre details the literary history of the distinctly British genre as well as the relationships between Hitchcock's films and their literary sources, which Ryall argues also explains the differences in philosophy among the films themselves. Romance in its understanding as male-female relations is shown to be the uniquely Hitchcockian addition to the thriller genre; the heterosexual couple is placed in the structural position of hero. A final chapter reviews the many definitions of classical cinema and traces Hitchcock's career, which coincides with the development of classical cinema. Ryall concludes that Hitchcock balanced the features of the norm (which in any case was his major influence) with more open and documentarylike "loose ends"; he quotes Thomas Elsaesser to the effect that Hitchcock displayed "a far more explicitly intellectual analytic approach" to filmmaking than classical norms required.

In conclusion, Ryall effectively brings together the many different strands of his research in an articulation of Hitchcock's "cinematic identity." The director emerges as a "hard-nosed professional," a working-class man in a profession primarily reserved for the university educated, and an artist committed to popular culture. Having illustrated the origins of Hitchcock's most distinctive theme—the "chaos-world" in which sexuality and violence "erupt"—Ryall pronounces him a "marooned figure, too businesslike and commercial to be an 'artist,' yet too 'artistic' to be fitted comfortably into the British entertainment cinema of the time."

Reviews: Alster, L. *"Alfred Hitchcock and the British Cinema." Films and Filming,* no. 388 (January 1987):46.

Gerz. *Variety,* no. 327 (May 6, 1987):618.

Richards, J. *Historical Journal of Film, Radio and Television* 7, no. 3 (1987):341.

Thomas, P. *"Alfred Hitchcock and the British Cinema." Film Quarterly* 41, no. 4 (1988):34–35.

Yacowar, M[aurice]. *Journal of Popular Film & Television* 15, no. 1 (1987):51.

776   SINYARD, NEIL. *The Films of Alfred Hitchcock.* New York: Gallery Books, 159 pp.

Popular chronological treatment, including final chapter titled "Influence and Achievement" listing homages, imitations, and other honors. Well illustrated.

*777   TOMLINSON, DOUG R. "Studies in the Use and Visualization of Film Performance: Alfred Hitchcock, Robert Bresson, Jean Renoir." Ph.D. Thesis. New York: New York University, 535 pp.

Cited in *Dissertation Abstracts* (On-Line). "An examination of the relationship between approaches to the art of performance and directorial strategies for its visualization."

Articles and Shorter Writings

778   ALBANO, L. "Il visibile e il non visibile." *Filmcritica* 37, no. 365–366 (June–July):272–282.

Using the theories of the unconscious of I. Matte Blanco, the role of "creative fantasies" is traced through analyses of *Suspicion, Ugetsu Monogatari, Wild Strawberries,* and *Mirage.* Hitchcock and Ingmar Bergman are seen as prime examples of Freudian wish-fulfillment neuroses via cinematic images.

779   BERENELLINI, M. "Un giorno dell'intelligenza l'adila di Hitchcock." *Cinema Nuovo* 35, no. 299 (January–February):10–11.
Reviews of the five films re-released in 1984: *Vertigo, The Man Who Knew Too Much* (1955), *The Trouble with Harry, Rear Window,* and *Rope.* Themes of domestic and familial situations are discussed along with the comedic elements.

780   BRITTON, ANDREW. "Cary Grant: Comedy and male desire." *CineAction!,* no. 7 (December):36–51.
Hitchcock's films are treated within a larger discussion of Grant's roles, their irresponsible side, their emotional shallowness and distance, and their sexual confidence. The roles with Hitchcock are distinguished from the others "by the absence of the comedy of male chastisement," thus bolstering a more generalized and sinister reinstatement of male authority than the other roles Grant filled.

781   ———. "Hitchcock's *Spellbound:* Text and counter-text." *CineAction!* no. 3–4 (Winter):72–83.
Explication of the film as it relates to its ideological projects—the validation of psychoanalysis as truth and normality and the transformation of a professional woman into a "real" woman (wife). Britton analyzes the film meetings and conversation, sexual imagery (doors, entrances, and exits), books, aging, dreams, and structural oppositions, particularly parental and sex roles. He concludes that the ideological projects are "surface" and subverted by the "repressed meaning."

782   BROWN, ROYAL S. "*Vertigo* as Orphic tragedy." *Literature/Film Quarterly* 14, no. 1:32–43.
Structural analysis delineating the paths of the tragic hero, defined by his rejection of the ordinary in preference for "mythic non-reality," and the artist-hero, who straddles the two poles. Brown compares the novel on which the film is based to the film and to the Greek myth of Orpheus. He examines narrative and thematic structure in developing a view of Scottie, not only as victim but also as an "Apollonian" male presiding over the sacrifice of women.

783   BURGIN, VICTOR. "Diderot, Barthes, *Vertigo.*" In *Formations of Fantasy,* edited by Victor Burgin, James Donald, and Cora Kaplan. London: Methuen, pp. 85–108.
In a wide-ranging discussion of the function of fantasy in the production of meaning and the need for the interdisciplinary study of images, *Vertigo* is used as an illustration. Burgin takes from art history the terms *tableau* and *hieroglyph,* used by both Diderot and Barthes, and develops from them a description of the Lacanian concepts of imaginary, symbolic, and real. *Vertigo* is a drama similar to

that described in an essay by Freud titled "A Special Type of Choice of Object Made by Men." This syndrome of male desire involves the choice of a love-object already attached to another man, an object/woman of ill-repute, a move to rescue the object (from water), and a repetition of the same type of passionate attachment. In an imaginative effort, still images and memories of the film take the author further with his ideas.

784   CARSON, DIANE. "The nightmare world of Hitchcock's women." In *The Kingdom of Dreams in Literature and Film,* edited by Douglas Fowler. Florida State University Conference on Literature and Film, 10. Tallahassee: Florida State University, pp. 11–20.

Discussion of the male and female roles in *Shadow of a Doubt,* particularly the minor ones. Emma, the mother, is shown in her essential dissatisfaction with her home and role as a wife; Joe, the father, is linked with Uncle Charlie via his murder fantasies; Roger, the son, continues the male tradition with his fact-finding; and, over all, the detectives predictably preserve the dominant ideology. With brief references to other films, Carson argues that Hitchcock's women characters live in "the nightmare world of patriarchal rule," where neither marriage nor independence is an escape.

Reprinted in *Michigan Academician,* 18 (Summer):349–356.

785   CASETTI, FRANCESCO. "Antonioni and Hitchcock: Two strategies of narrative investment." *Sub-Stance* 16, no. 51:69–86.

Comparison of *Cronaca di un amore* and *Stage Fright,* which both "turn the activity of the spectator into a theme of reflexivity," though in opposing ways. The formal analysis examines the nature of the flashback in each film and its introduction of the themes of lies and secrets, and competency and judgment, as well as its relation to the participation of the spectator.

786   DANEY, SERGE. *Ciné Journal.* Paris: Cahiers du Cinéma, pp. 115–116; 194–197; 205–207.

Impressionistic description of the kissing scene in *North by Northwest,* the hands of a strangler, the cold sensuality, and the roundabout ways ("the film goes north, the still images go west") that mark the film. Also commentary on *Vertigo,* a film of primary emotion, "the story of a man who passes from acrophobia to necrophilia," and *Rear Window* with its emphasis on voyeurism and the look.

787   DOUCHET, JEAN. "Hitch and his public." In *A Hitchcock Reader,* edited by Marshall Deutelbaum and Leland Poague. Ames: Iowa State University Press, pp. 7–15.

Final part of a three-part series (entry 264), which summarizes a theory of the three realities of "Hitchcock's system": the first is the reality of the everyday world, which Hitchcock carefully records; the second is the world of desire, constituted by forms; and the third is the intellectual world, which navigates between the two other worlds and "allows them to communicate." Douchet points out the insistent presence of vehicles and travel in the films that adds to the

spectator's sensation of being "carried off." Examination of *Psycho* illustrates the intellectual concentration necessary to bring the world of forms "into being"; it also shows the "multiple relations between the three realities," one of which is an element of the occult (or fantastic). Ultimately the "occult" is the broadest rationale of the films' power because it is the element that allows the artist's imagination the greatest scope.

Translation of essay in *Cahiers du Cinéma,* 17, no. 103 (1960). A later version is in book form, entry 337.

788   EVANS, PETER. "What's in a name? *Marnie.*" *Durham University Journal* 79, no. 1 (December):91–98.

Analysis of myths, symbols, and religious themes in *Marnie* as they relate to the interdependence of "artist, work, and spectator." The conclusion, that "the connection between economic and sexual exploitation is nowhere treated with more poignancy and sensitivity," is not clearly borne out by the otherwise interesting discussion of *Marnie* as sea creature/water and Mark as firmly rooted manipulator.

789   "Hitchcock's shower scene: Another view." *Cinefantastique* 16, no. 4–5:64–67.

Media tale of Saul Bass's work on *Psycho.* Interview with Bass, who softens the original controversy that began when he claimed to have directed the shower sequence, though Hitchcock never publicly acknowledged his contribution.

790   KAPSIS, ROBERT E.   "Alfred Hitchcock: Auteur or hack?" *Cineaste* 14, no. 3:30–35.

Extensively researched essay on the creation of Hitchcock's reputation. Includes discussion of Hitchcock's publicity machine, his dealings with François Truffaut, Peter Bogdanovich, and the Museum of Modern Art, showing how these influenced basic changes in film aesthetics and improved the status of both Hitchcock and the thriller genre.

791   KEANE, MARIAN E.   "A closer look at scopophilia: Mulvey, Hitchcock and *Vertigo.*" In *A Hitchcock Reader,* edited by Marshall Deutelbaum and Leland Poague. Ames: Iowa State University Press, pp. 231–248.

After presenting the idea of "photogenesis," concerned with the importance of the actors' personages as the camera's subject, Keane analyzes *Vertigo* in contrast with Mulvey's idea (entry 439) that the film embodies the classic male Oedipal crisis. She argues that the Madeleine/Judy character is centrally aligned with the camera and that Scottie's suffering and cruelty is the "brutal" aspect of "human desire," not "some function of a particular phase of male development." Keane discusses several of the other films and their expression of "sexual ambiguity or ambivalence," concluding that Hitchcock associates his camera with Madeleine/Judy, while Scottie stands in for those viewers who are unable to acknowledge "the film or its maker."

1986

792   LEITCH, THOMAS M.   "Murderous victims in *The Secret Agent* and *Sabotage.*" *Literature/Film Quarterly* 14, no. 1:64–68.

Analysis of "the nature of action" as explicated in *Sabotage* (and Joseph Conrad's *Secret Agent*), in which Hitchcock describes it as the "problematic relation between action and identity." This conception is translated into a "cinematic idea" via various ironic combinations of "destructive power and impotence," that is, "murderous victims," and contrasted with the "compulsiveness" that "renders the murderer powerless to resist his own impulses."

793   ———.   "Narrative as a way of knowing: The example of Alfred Hitchcock." *Centennial Review* 30, no. 3 (Summer):315–330.

Essay on the moral and narrative "imputations" in the films, which are conclusions, deductions, or judgments made by the audience based on the juxtaposition of events and character expressiveness. In these films, imputation is never explicit, for "every interpretation is suspect . . . creating a shifting, kaleidoscope effect." These results serve well Hitchcock's favorite subject: the tension or misunderstanding arising from the disparity between a character's reputation—the way he or she appears as defined by the perceptions of the other characters—and essential identity, which is the way he or she actually is. Examples from many of the films are brought to bear on this thesis, which concludes with an explanation of Hitchcock's fondness for false imputations. "An audience invited . . . to make judgments or identifications which are later shown to be unjustified . . . can themselves serve as the subject of moral analysis [forming] a link between the film and the outside world." Reprinted in *Find the Director and Other Hitchcock Games* (Athens: University of Georgia Press, 1991).

794   MATTHEW-WALKER, ROBERT.   "Hitchcock's little joke." *Films and Filming*, no. 382 (July):26–27.

Attempts to explain Hitchcock's widely quoted remark about *Psycho* being his "little joke": an opening title states the first day of the story is December 20, but a calendar on a wall at the end of the film indicates the date is December 17.

795   McEWEN, DUNCAN.   "Hitchcock: An analytic movie review." *Psychology Review* 74, no. 3:401–409.

Analysis of *The Man Who Knew Too Much* (1955) as an exploration of Hank, the ten-year-old son, and his pre-Oedipal regression. McEwen argues that Hank, though absent most of the film, is a central character because he is so heavily identified with the director. He discusses events from the boy's perspective as they relate to typical fantasies a young boy might have.

796   MILLER, GABRIEL.   "Beyond the frame: Hitchcock, art, and the ideal." *Post Script* 5, no. 2 (Winter):31–46.

Defines a "characteristic concern" of the films as "the protagonist's obsession with idealized images, either represented in art or imagined in the mind's eye."

Close analysis of parts of *The Lodger, Rear Window, Vertigo,* and *The Man Who Knew Too Much* (1955) explicates a notion of "characters visiting the other side of the screen," entering dream visions for the purpose of avoiding engagement with the real world.

797 MONTES-HUIDOBRO, MATIAS. "From Hitchcock to García Márquez: The methodology of suspense." In *Critical Perspectives on Gabriel García Márquez,* edited by Bradley A. Shaw and Nora Vera-Godwin. Lincoln, Neb.: Society of Spanish and Spanish American Studies, pp. 105–123.

Explication of *Chronicle of a Death Foretold,* a novel by García Márquez. The author illustrates the influence of Hitchcock's ideas concerning the creation and sustaining of suspense through character behavior and the manipulation of time and space, by comparing events and techniques in the novel with Hitchcock's theories as revealed in interviews.

798 MURRAY, LYN. "Flashback: Chords and discords." *American Film* 11, no. 8 (June):17–20.

Notes by composer on music for *To Catch a Thief.*

799 PALMER, R. BARTON. "The metafictional Hitchcock: The experience of viewing and the viewing of experience in *Rear Window* and *Psycho.*" *Cinema Journal* 25, no. 2:4–19.

Discusses the self-reflexivity of the thematic elements of the two films, arguing that Hitchcock's later work is "metafictional . . . [tending] to be constructed on the principle of a fundamental and sustained opposition" between the creation of an illusion and the uncovering of it as an illusion. Response from Jeanne T. Allen concerning the difficulties of "mixing critical approaches" in *Cinema Journal* 25, no. 4 (Summer 1988) as well as a reply from Palmer.

800 PEELE, STANTON. "Personality, pathology, and the act of creation: The case of Alfred Hitchcock." *Biography* 9, no. 3 (Summer):202–218.

Critique of Spoto's biography (entry 702) and its assumption that an "artistic view can be reduced to a specific set of psychological or psychopathological elements." Peele refutes much of the specific evidence presented by Spoto in support of his contention that Hitchcock was "mentally ill."

801 PETRO, PATRICE. "Rematerializing the vanishing lady: Feminism, Hitchcock, and interpretation." In *A Hitchcock Reader,* edited by Marshall Deutelbaum and Leland Poague. Ames: Iowa State University Press, pp. 122–134.

After the work of Tania Modleski, *The Lady Vanishes* is analyzed as a female Oedipal narrative. The "maternal register" of the film is defined by Iris and her girlfriends, Miss Froy, and the "obnoxious" quality of male authority. While the

narrative appears "to recuperate female desire and make it submit to male authority," Petro argues that the "points of female resistance remain." She is, however, most concerned with exploring the larger questions of feminist criticism and readership, for which she argues that the text supplies sufficiently fertile ground.

802   PHILLIPS, LOUIS. "The burden the living bear." *Armchair Detective* 19, no. 3:293–298.

Appreciation of *The Trouble with Harry* and its unusual approach: none of the characters feels guilty even when trying to shift blame. Based primarily on a comparison with the original novel, to which it is strikingly similar.

803   PISO, MICHELE. "Mark's *Marnie.*" In *A Hitchcock Reader,* edited by Marshall Deutelbaum and Leland Poague. Ames: Iowa State University Press, pp. 288–304.

Analyzes *Marnie* and the "class antagonism" between the two main characters, with her mother representing not only a private debilitating past but also sexual and social exploitation in general. Piso reviews the changing attitudes toward the poorly received film, examines ideas of commodity and gift exchange, and suggests that Marnie's actions are a sign of her "refusal to submit." Mark, in his demands for submission, is a man "unable to free himself from the constraining ideology of his wealth," reflected in "his arrogant assumption of knowledge." Marnie's breakthrough—her acceptance of Mark's help—is a mixed blessing as it leaves behind her wounded mother and gives her over to a marriage characterized by subjugation.

804   PRESSLER, MICHAEL. "Hitchcock and the melodramatic pattern." *Chicago Review* 35, no. 3 (Spring):4–16.

Analysis of *Strangers on a Train* and melodramatic construction in Hitchcock's films, in which "melodrama is the essential cinematic form." Pressler compares the film with the Patricia Highsmith novel on which the film is based, showing that her essentially psychoanalytical approach is replaced with a focus on "rapid motion and mounting tension—the rigors of melodramatic form." He concludes that the battle in the book between Anne and Bruno with Guy as the prize, becomes, in the film, a battle between Bruno and Guy with Anne as the prize. The whole of the structure is determined to satisfy audience expectation of Guy's upright moral character.

805   REBELLO, STEPHEN. "Hitchcock's tour of the Bates Motel." *Cinefantastique,* no. 4–5:77–80.

History of the publicity and reception of *Psycho,* the trailer and other marketing decisions, response of the critics and the public, awards, and effect on Hitchcock's subsequent relations and career.

806   SILET, CHARLES L. P. "Through a woman's eyes: Sexuality and memory in *The 39 Steps.*" In *A Hitchcock Reader,* edited by Marshall Deutelbaum and Leland Poague. Ames: Iowa State University Press, pp. 109–121.

Examines themes of sexual values and sexual jokes, as well as sexuality in general. Hannay's relationships with each of the women are detailed, especially in the coupling of him with Pamela, which culminates in the "secret of sexual equality."

807 WEXMAN, VIRGINIA WRIGHT. "The critic as consumer: Film study in the university, *Vertigo* and the film canon." *Film Quarterly* 39, no. 3 (Spring):32–41.
Objects to *Vertigo*'s privileged status among intellectuals and film scholars as pure cinema and "essential psychoanalytic truth." Wexman discusses the film as it relates to the historical theories of the Cold War period, which are marked by an uncomfortable consciousness of "otherness," and a commercial production history that emphasizes stars and scenery. After reviewing feminist psychoanalytical criticism, which she assesses as idealized in its lack of a cultural component, Wexman comments in detail on issues of gender, class, and most unusually, race as they are revealed in the film and the circumstances of its making.

808 ZIRNITE, DENNIS. "Hitchcock, on the level: The heights of spatial tension." *Film Criticism* 10, no. 3 (Spring):2–21.
Analysis of a persistent structuring pattern in Hitchcock's work, described as a "dialectical tension through vertical space." It encompasses "the main level," banal, complacent, and marked by socially acceptable human reference points, and "the upper level," the oppressive domain of the malignant force, human destructiveness, and moral instability. Zirnite includes discussion of many of the most famous and complex traveling shots as well as an extended discussion of stairways, especially in *The Lodger, Notorious, Shadow of a Doubt, Rear Window,* and *Psycho.*

809 ŽIŽEK, SLAVOJ. "Hitchcock." *October,* no. 38 (Fall):99–111.
Lacanian analysis of Hitchcockian fantasies concerning death and family relations. In *The Trouble with Harry,* "the gap between the two deaths, the real death, and the symbolic death, the settling of accounts" is emphasized. Harry's death (the death of the father, a blot) is isolated as understatement: "keep cool, Dad's dead, so okay." *The Birds* is placed within the sociology of the 1950s American family, a "tragedy of a son paying for his mother's inordinate focus on him." But the birds are not mere symbols in the drama; they actually play a part in that they block and mask the film's true significance, their function being to make us forget that we are dealing with the triangle of the mother, her son, and the woman he loves. Translation of two chapters of entry 832.

1987
Books

810 LEFF, LEONARD J. *Hitchcock and Selznick.* New York: Weidenfeld & Nicholson, 383 pp.
Popular history of Hitchcock's relationship with David O. Selznick and the films they made together: *Rebecca, Spellbound,* and *The Paradine Case,* as well as

a chapter on *Notorious,* for which Selznick was a silent partner. Leff characterizes Hitchcock as "an analytic filmmaker [who] privileged form over character, irony over romance." Selznick is described as bringing "mood, seamless continuity, and psychological nuance to the director's work." He includes details of contractual arrangements, preproduction and shooting histories, Hitchcock's rise to fame in the U.S. media, and both men's personal lives.

Reviews: Combs, Richard. *"Hitchcock and Selznick." Sight and Sound* 57 (Summer 1988):215.

Harvey, Stephen. *"Hitchcock and Selznick." New York Times Book Review* (January 17, 1988):13.

Lehmann-Haupt, C. "Books of the times." *New York Times,* no. 137 (December 10, 1987):Section C, p. 29.

Liebman, Roy. *"Hitchcock and Selznick." Library Journal* 112 (November 1, 1987):121.

Raphael, Frederic. *"Hitchcock and Selznick." Times Literary Supplement* (London) (September 2, 1988):951.

Spoto, Donald. *"Hitchcock and Selznick." Film Comment* 24 (January–February 1988):78.

Articles and Shorter Writings

811   ABEL, RICHARD. *"Stage Fright:* The knowing performance." *Film Criticism* 11, no. 1–2:5–14.

Analysis of character elements that convey sexual difference. Abel argues that the women characters drive the story, despite the illusions of Johnny's flashback in the beginning and of the takeover of the pursuit in the end by Ordinary Smith and the Commodore. He puts forth Charlotte's backstage story and Eve's insistence on freeing Johnny at the end as evidence of the resistance to male control.

812   ANDEREGG, MICHAEL. "Hitchcock's *The Paradine Case* and filmic unpleasure." *Cinema Journal* 26, no. 4:49–59.

Argues that *The Paradine Case* is a minor "canonical work" and a commercial failure because of its ambiguous text and "unpleasurable" experience. Primarily to blame is the "non-existent male" hero, created by a combination of Gregory Peck's performance and the character as written, and placed alongside the ambiguous, unpredictable construction of the female characters. This construction gives power to the female characters, who are "the ones in the know." Finally, however, the film is only marginally progressive, insisting in the end on the potential recuperation of the ideal male and female figures.

813   CLOVER, CAROL J. "Herbody, himself: Gender in the slasher film." *Representations,* no. 20 (Fall):187–228.

Analysis of the gender elements of the modern horror film, beginning with *Psycho.* Questions of point of view and audience identification—male or female, with male or female characters—are examined and theorized as sometimes

presenting a "cross-gender identification." The influence of Hitchcock's films, particularly *Psycho,* is in their "sexualization of both motive and action," their association of the audience with the victim, and their (old-fashioned) lack of interest in role reversal, which later versions of the genre use to show the traditionally male marks of heroism as female. Clover examines the workings of shock and the structural elements of the genre—the killer, the Terrible Place, weapons, and the Final Girl (not present in *Psycho* and an element that "radically alters" the formula).

814 FERRARA, PATRICIA. "The discontented bourgeois: Bourgeois morality and the interplay of light and dark strains in Hitchcock's films." *New Orleans Review* 14, no. 1 (Winter):79–87.

Argues that the "light side" of Hitchcock's aesthetic is "no more commercial, and no less effective and personally motivated than the dark side." Ferrara examines the themes, techniques, and attitudes present in the 1930s spy thrillers, particularly *The 39 Steps* and *The Lady Vanishes.* She adds an insightful biographical interpretation that de-emphasizes Hitchcock's stern Catholic upbringing and focuses on the bourgeois fear of breaking the law or offending social morality. Ferrara posits a "neutral attitude," not dogma, to be the crux of the films. She relates this to critical accusations of a lack of substance, which she interprets as a lack of "political ideology or social viewpoint . . . a severe disinclination to take sides." Finally, she examines the continuum of conventional-unconventional as a theme and concludes that the dark side internalizes social rigidities while the light side shows characters who escape such rigidity, and that both are a serious reflection of this same central theme.

815 FLITTERMAN-LEWIS, SANDY. "To see and not to be: Female subjectivity and the law in Hitchcock's *Notorious." Literature & Psychology* 33, no. 3–4:1–15.

Extensive analysis of Alicia's look, for "it is she who authorizes the majority of the film's subjective images." The author argues that the "more visual authority she achieves, the more distorted and disturbed her views become," eventually turning hallucinatory (at the discovery of the poison), and, at the end, dazed and stunned, unable to look at all. She concludes that Hitchcock "endows her [Alicia] with enunciative vision precisely in order to negate it. It is Hitchcock's particular claim to assert the patriarchal in modes of organizing subjectivity through vision, to reveal the structure of the Law as all-pervasive."

816 GARDNER, GERALD. "Thrillers." In *The Censorship Papers: Movie Censorship Letters from the Hays Office, 1934–1968.* New York: Dodd, Mead, pp. 84–96.

Journalistic discussion of five Hitchcock films includes brief production history and excerpts from the letters of the Production Code Administration, an office set up by the major Hollywood studios to avoid official government censorship. The letters were sent in response to submitted script drafts and generally requested specific changes. *Rebecca* was criticized for its murdering husband and "sex perversion." *Notorious* was advised to gloss over Alicia's "loose

morals." *Strangers on a Train* was criticized for its "light treatment" of Guy and Miriam's marriage, *Rear Window* for its salty language, and *The Birds* for its gruesomely detailed bird attacks. Also, comments on censorship at the state level and in other countries.

817   GOODKIN, RICHARD E.   "Film and fiction: Hitchcock's *Vertigo* and Proust's vertigo." *MLN* 102, no. 5 (December):1171–1181.

Compares *Vertigo* with Marcel Proust's *In Search of Lost Time*. Goodkin discusses the economic narrative of the film versus the subjective flow of the book, the function of Madeleine (character and cake), and a series of thematic correlatives: time, the past, and the differing qualities of fiction and cinema.

818   GREIG, DONALD.   "The sexual differentiation of the Hitchcock text." *Screen* 28, no. 1:28–47.

On the theoretical constructs of Raymond Bellour. Greig argues against the idea of all texts of classical cinema as a presentation of a strictly male Oedipal trajectory. He reviews recent work on fantasy, Lacan's concept of the symbolic, and sexual difference in the cinema to put forth an idea of the relative autonomy of the spectator. Fantasy allows different ways of identifying with different characters in the films so that the structure of any particular Hitchcock film is changing and not necessarily "gender specific."

819   HALL, KENNETH E.   "Cabrera Infante and the work of Alfred Hitchcock." *World Literature Today* 61, no. 4 (Autumn):598–600.

Examines the essays and reviews on Hitchcock of Guillermo Cabrera Infante as well as references to the director in the novels. Cabrera Infante became interested in the films as a youth in the 1930s, admiring the mystery and game-playing, and relating to the Catholic themes, which he judges became more evident after the French critics made them known to Hitchcock in the 1950s. Now the novelist values Hitchcock for his technical command of film language.

820   HARRIS, THOMAS.   *"Rear Window* and *Blow-Up:* Hitchcock's straightforwardness vs. Antonioni's ambiguity." *Literature/Film Quarterly* 15, no. 1:60–63.

Comparison of the two main characters and themes they evoke: responsibility (of the picture-taker), voyeurism, and sexual fulfillment.

821   HESLING, W.   "Classical cinema and the spectator." *Literature/Film Quarterly* 15, no. 3:181–189.

Psychoanalytic analysis of *Psycho* intended to confirm "the remarks [Christian] Metz has made concerning the way a Hollywood film positions the spectator," that is, that classical cinema is "*discours* disguised as *histoire*." Hesling reviews relevant linguistic theories and concludes that "a film can never be labeled as completely *histoire* or completely *discours*. In fact, *Psycho* "fascinates" the audience, despite "numerous moments where it dislocates the spectator."

822 HOLLINGER, KAREN. "The look, narrativity, and the female spectator in *Vertigo.*" *Journal of Film and Video* 39, no. 4 (Fall):18–27.
Argues against Laura Mulvey's ideas concerning spectator identification. Using analysis of the narrative and the visual system, Hollinger examines spectator identification in the main and supporting characters. This examination leads to an assessment of the film as "ideologically subversive" because it exposes the problems inherent in the notion of Oedipal transformation into femininity as easy and natural.

823 KAPSIS, ROBERT E. "Hollywood filmmaking and reputation building: Hitchcock's *The Birds.*" *Journal of Popular Film and Television* 15, no. 1 (Spring):5–14.
Historical account based on letters and memos from the Hitchcock papers of the development of the script and the publicity for *The Birds.* Kapsis covers communication with Evan Hunter, Hume Cronyn, and Victor Pritchett (on the script) as well as François Truffaut, which shows that Hitchcock was concerned about attracting his new-found "art" audience as well as his "regular customers" to the film: "We are going to run into all kinds of critiques from the highbrows," he warned. The author also analyzes the use of the stars and chronicles the marketing campaign, which shows that Hitchcock "aspired to be a serious artist." He even put forth a "propaganda campaign," distributing the Bogdanovich monograph (entry 295) as well as a "solicited tribute" from Truffaut in order to "transform his image."

824 MODLESKI, TANIA. "Rape versus Mans/laughter: Hitchcock's *Blackmail* and feminist interpretation." *PMLA* 102, no. 3 (May):304–315.
Initial version of essay expanded in entry 833. Modleski argues against general feminist view of Hitchcock's work, which describes the female spectator as cut off from a sympathetic response, limited only to a masochistic or a transvestite role.

825 NEVINS, FRANCIS M., JR. "Fade to black: Part two." *Armchair Detective* 20, no. 2:166–168.
Essay on Cornell Woolrich film adaptations, including a historical description of the development and comparison of the story "Rear Window" and the film. Most of the changes made were not in concepts but in characterization, where Hitchcock added characters and significantly deepened Jeffries.

*826 OLDRINI, G. "Hitchcock, ne mago ne genio." *Cinema Nuovo* 36, no. 306 (March–April):55–59.
Cited in *Film Literature Index,* 1987.

827 PALMER, R. BARTON. "The politics of genre in Welles' *The Stranger.*" *Film Criticism* 11, no. 1–2:31–42.
Examines *The Stranger* and *Shadow of a Doubt* as *film noir,* in particular the love triangle, closure (or lack of it) and disclosure, and "anti-establishment" values.

1988

828   PHILLIPS, GENE D.   "Film criticism versus film maker: Greene's criticism of Hitchcock's films." In *Essays in Graham Greene,* edited by Peter Wolfe. Greenwood, Fla.: Penkevill, pp. 119–126.
Discussion of the criticism, the two authors' sharing of metaphors, and Greene's refusal to allow *Our Man in Havana* to be made by Hitchcock.

829   PHILLIPS, LOUIS.   "Wherein the truth lies; honesty and deception in *North by Northwest.*" *Armchair Detective* 20, no. 3 (Summer):254–259.
Discussion of film as an "exploration of one man's education about the nature of truth and lies." Taking from St. Thomas Aquinas "three degrees of lies": jocose, officious (designed to help a situation), and pernicious (designed to hurt), Phillips finds examples of all three, focusing especially on their playful quality.

1988
Books

830   BRILL, LESLEY.   *The Hitchcock Romance: Love and Irony in Hitchcock's Films.* Princeton, N.J.: Princeton University Press, 296 pp.
Brill's thesis is based on an assessment of Hitchcock's "artistic personality . . . as deeply conventional, thoughtful, and rather soft-hearted." The author uses broad, narrative categories based on the ideas of Northrop Frye, and offers detailed analyses of twenty of the films to support the idea that most of them are romantic—"happy fairy tales . . . in which central lovers live more or less happily ever after." Some are "mixed" romances, however, and all display an element of irony, in which "romantic expectations are raised only to be disappointed."
The most romantic films, *Young and Innocent, To Catch a Thief, North by Northwest,* are characterized by the integration of past and present and the opposition of true and false love. They "counsel against despair" and lead to the "recovery of innocence in wedded bliss."
The ironic films, such as *Rich and Strange, Blackmail* or *Topaz,* "counsel against presumption" and present the "failure of love and belief." Brill frequently discusses downward movement (for example, *I Confess* has a "downward gaze") and camera angles, but is most expansive in character analyses, particularly of the minor characters, whose importance in revealing the doubleness of human nature is emphasized.
A final chapter on *The Trouble with Harry* presents it as the purest example of "the romantic vision of innocence and immortality that informs the greater part of Hitchcock's work."
Reviews: Anderegg, Jeanne. "*The Hitchcock Romance.*" *Wilson Library Bulletin* 63 (March 1989):109.
Coward, David. "*The Hitchcock Romance.*" *Times Literary Supplement* (London) (December 15, 1989): 1387.
Thomas, Paul. "*The Hitchcock Romance.*" *Film Quarterly* 42 (Summer 1989):40.

831   DERRY, CHARLES DENNIS.   *The Suspense Thriller: Films in the Shadow of Alfred Hitchcock.* Jefferson, N.C.: McFarland, 351 pp.

Reworking of a Ph.D. thesis that comprised a detailed defining of the suspense genre considerably wider than the films of Hitchcock. Derry provides a review of the literature concerning both the literary and filmic aspects of the thriller and finds two basic common points: the working of the thriller on the audience and the identification of the audience with the pursued victim. The ideas of Michael Balint and Altan Löker are examined to explore the psychological aspects of content and structure. Several kinds of thrillers are then described, each with its own set of numbered criteria, and lists of exemplary films. Hitchcock figures most prominently in the subsets of "Innocent on the Run," "Psychotraumatic," and "Moral Confrontation," and does not figure at all in the chapters called "Murderous Passion" and "Acquired Identity."

832 DOLAR, MLADEN, RASTKO MOCNIK, JELICA SUMIC-RIHA, and ZDENKO VRDLOUEC. *Tout ce que vous avez toujours savoir sur Lacan sans jamais oser le demander à Hitchcock,* edited by Slovoj Žižek and Mladen Dolar. *Analytica,* no. 53, supplement. Paris: Navarin, 216 pp.

Over thirty brief essays, each of which uses a Hitchcock film to illustrate one of the principles of the psychoanalytic theory of Jacques Lacan. The introduction by the editors describes three groupings of films that reveal Hitchcock's development in psychoanalytic terms.

First is the spy trilogy of 1935–1939, which introduces the continuing themes of bourgeois marriage or a couple thrown together by accident who find union through adversity. Second is the early American films, foreshadowed by *Sabotage,* that revolve around triangles, a woman torn between two men, a "pale negative father or husband," and an attractive but weak/young hero. The third set is the psychopathic murderer films, which depict a male who is dysfunctional because of a maternal problem.

Includes essays on *The 39 Steps, Secret Agent, Young and Innocent, The Lady Vanishes, Jamaica Inn, Rebecca, Foreign Correspondent, Mr. and Mrs. Smith, Suspicion, Saboteur, Shadow of a Doubt, Lifeboat, Spellbound, Notorious, The Paradine Case, Rope, Under Capricorn, Stage Fright, Strangers on a Train, I Confess, Dial M for Murder, Rear Window, To Catch a Thief, The Trouble with Harry, The Man Who Knew Too Much* (1955), *The Wrong Man, Vertigo, North by Northwest, Psycho, The Birds,* and *Marnie.* Some pieces translated into English; see entry 809.

833 MODLESKI, TANIA. *The Women Who Knew Too Much: Hitchcock and Feminist Film Theory.* New York: Methuen, 149 pp.

Begins with a review of psychoanalytic film theory that counters the contentions of Laura Mulvey (entry 439) and others that women in films are passive objects of male voyeurism and therefore have a masochistic relationship as viewers. Modleski argues that Hitchcock's films reveal a "strong fascination and identification with femininity" that makes them deeply ambivalent toward women and "resistant to patriarchal assimilation" while expressing an intertwining of misogyny and sympathy for women. Following a discussion of female bisexuality and the consequent "double desire" of the female spectator, Modleski argues that the "fascination and identification" are shared by the male spectator, who is made frightfully aware of his own potential bisexuality and therefore requires the violence toward women that exists in the films. She then effectively

ties bisexuality to power relations and their playing out in Hitchcock films, where the male subject is at once fascinated and threatened by bisexuality and the woman "pays for this ambivalence—often with her life itself."

"Rape vs. mans/laughter: *Blackmail*." In this, a later version of entry 824, Modleski analyzes the film as a "set-up" of the woman, who comes to occupy the place that "Freud assigned to women in the structure of the obscene joke: the place of the object between two male subjects." Modleski examines the jokes and laughter, the pictures, and various set pieces, which consistently place Alice in the position of a silent object in one corner of a triangle between either two male characters or one male character and the viewer. Her initially easy laughter is contrasted with her predicament in the end, when she is stymied, unable to laugh with the men. Second, Modleski shows that Hitchcock's fleshing out of this basic position allows more than one interpretation, arguing that Hitchcock's obsession with victimized women "often takes the form of a particularly lucid exposé of the predicaments and contradictions of women's existence under patriarchy." Finally, *Blackmail* illustrates the problem of the law's inability to accommodate and weigh the experience of women.

"Male Hysteria and the 'Order of Things': *Murder!*" Analysis of the theatrical and legal motifs illustrates that the world of false appearances—always menacing in Hitchcock's films—is "dreadful to men precisely because it is a feminine and feminizing space." Examination of the many sides of Fane's character, as well as Sir John's ambiguous expressions, illustrates the film's deconstruction of "the oppositions on which it appears to depend."

"The Woman Who Was Known Too Much: *Notorious*." Emphasizes the relationship of Alicia and Devlin, her masochistic behavior (alcohol, sex), which also gives her knowledge and power, and his sadistic behavior, monitoring and controlling her. The author reviews the philosophical work on the relation of "seeing" and "knowing" to one's gendered place in the social order and examines these elements in the film, along with the attendant conflicts of public versus private, political versus personal. Modleski argues that Alicia's suffering is related to her anger and eventually provokes Devlin to admit his own pain in watching her suffer. Devlin, however, has not been poisoned, and the two sufferings cannot be equated. Nonetheless, Alicia and the female spectator who identifies with her are "engaged in an active knowing, and rebellious activity."

"The Master's Dollhouse: *Rear Window*." Argues against the critical consensus of the film as a critique of voyeurism and chronicle of Jeff's sexual maturing. Modleski examines Lisa's superiority and success as a woman (generally put down by critics) both in the world and as visualized in the film and finds that it illustrates the double bind of women "assigned a restricted place in patriarchy" (the fashion world) and then "condemned for occupying it." She points out that Jeff's point of view in fact becomes both his and Lisa's as the film progresses, and she compares Lisa's more empathetic response to the other apartment dwellers with Jeff's response. She concludes that the final shot of this film that "all critics agree is about the power of the male gaze" shows that it is actually very aware of Lisa's view: "While men sleep and dream their dreams of omnipotence . . . women are not . . . imprisoned in their Master's dollhouse."

"Femininity by Design: *Vertigo*." Analyzes the film as a "limit text" of the problems of identification. In commenting on the film's obsession with female clothing, Modleski notes that "critics tend to slight . . . elements of the film which work against the seriousness of the 'love theme' and in this they reveal

themselves to be like Scottie." These elements actually show how "femininity in our culture is largely a male construct, a male design." Since women then occupy, in effect, a blind space, Scottie's attempt to cure Madeleine through his own reality fails. He is "plunged into the feminine world of psychic disintegration, madness, and death." Modleski analyzes the final story developments of Judy's revelations and Scottie's discovery of her betrayal, and concludes that "the enigma of bisexuality" in Hitchcock films is the main problem. The woman's relations to the mother, her "blurred boundaries" between self and other are intimidating to the male, who achieves his identity through a "firm boundary," shown in *Vertigo* to be precarious.

"Rituals of Defilement: *Frenzy.*" Approaches the film as the culmination of Hitchcock's "ambivalence towards femininity." The author examines the expression of it through the "polarity of woman as food vs. woman as poison" and finds a relation to Lévi-Strauss's "common cultural equation of male with devourer and female with devoured." She discusses the threat of the "devouring voracious mother" and the resultant "rituals of defilement" that seek to contain this fear. Modleski argues that the extremity of the film is partially a result of the contemporary political demands of women and the "boundary confusion" of male and female spheres, which makes less secure the male's ability "to ensure separateness from the female." Nevertheless, while violence to women must remain the "center of analysis," other aspects, such as the sympathetic women characters, cannot be ignored, for their "capitulation to male desires and expectations is never complete."

"Afterword: Hitchcock's Daughters." A final look at the theatrical space, which "draws man into a world of illusion and false or mixed identity." Modleski critiques Rothman's (entry 679) rationalization of this theatricality via his self-described "submission [to the] terrifying power" of Hitchcock's camera. She argues that feminist critics must refuse this power and instead "affirm the theatrical 'treacherous' aspects of these 'seductive' texts—those parts which 'know' more than their author."

Also "Woman and the Labyrinth: *Rebecca.*" A later version of entry 693.

Reviews: Conley, Verena Andermatt. *"The Women Who Knew Too Much: Hitchcock and Feminist Theory."* SubStance, no. 59 (1989):122–124.

Harper, S. *Historical Journal of Film, Radio, and Television* 9, no. 2 (1989):214–215.

Taylor, John Russell. *"The Women Who Knew Too Much." Films and Filming* (August 1988):43.

Thomas, Paul. *"The Women Who Knew Too Much." Film Quarterly* 42 (Summer 1989):40–42.

Waring, Nancy. *"The Women Who Knew Too Much." Village Voice* (June 21, 1988):55, 58.

Articles and Shorter Writings

834 BELTON, JOHN. "The space of *Rear Window.*" *MLN* 103, no. 5 (December):1121–1138.

After presenting the generally acknowledged view of *Rear Window* as "pure cinema," Belton elaborates a notion of the film as it "explores the parameters of

1988

theatrical and cinematic modes of narration." The two kinds of space are distinguished in several ways: by the way they are designed and constructed, by their potential for manipulation, and by their "psychologies." Belton discusses the murder mystery as it relates to the love story—the alternation from "story-space to story-space"—the manner in which both are developed through set design, cinematography, and editing, and the relation of Jeff's "psycho-spatial system" to that of the other characters.

835   BENSON, PETER. "Identification and slaughter." *CineAction!*, no. 12 (Spring):12–18.
Within a larger discussion on the psychoanalytic concept of identification, Benson argues that the first part of *Psycho* (to Marion's murder) is not sufficiently described by the scopic narcissistic type of identification defined by Lacan because of the persistence of Marion's character. He describes three different types of ego identification (after Freud) and assigns this part of *Psycho* to the last, where the viewer identifies through a desire to be in a similar situation to Marion's, to duplicate its wish-fulfillment aspects, have an affair, steal money, and so on.

836   BORDWELL, DAVID. "ApProppriations and Impro**pprieties: Problems in the morphology of film narrative." *Cinema Journal* 27, no. 3 (Spring): 5–20.
Argues that Proppian analysis has been misapplied, using a critique of Peter Wollen's study of *North by Northwest* (entry 472) as a prime example. Bordwell contends that aside from their distorted interpretation, Wollen and other critics have not understood the importance of Propp's basic theoretical constraints, suggesting that comparable analysis of film would arise only within the creation of a new morphology—new functions, auxiliaries, tale roles, and moves.

*837   CONFORTI, A. "Ancora sulla soggettivita nel cinema." *Cineforum* 28, no. 272 (March):53–58.
Cited in *Film Literature Index,* 1988.

838   DOUGLAS, J. YELLOWLEES. "American friends and strangers on trains." *Literature/Film Quarterly* 16, no. 3:181–190.
Comparison of Wim Wenders's *American Friend* and *Strangers on a Train,* both adapted from novels by Patricia Highsmith. Douglas explicates the radically different styles—Hitchcock's focusing of all resources on the plot, and Wenders's open narrative, full of unconventional nonplot elements. He concludes that Wenders's film is a critique of the Hollywood thriller, deconstructing the genre for the purpose of asserting autonomy.

839   FLETCHER, JOHN. "Versions of masquerade." *Screen* 29, no. 3 (Summer):43–70.
After Joan Riviere's formulation of the masquerade as "an acting out of the wish to take," and hence a double of femininity as pleasure-in-receiving, Fletcher

discusses *Marnie* and *The Locket* and concludes that here "the scenario of the masquerade generates narratives of the woman as an intransigently desiring and active subject." He examines the look, both female and male, and argues that Marnie's "theft of the paternal phallus" has the effect of magnifying "the culture's ideologies of gender so as to precipitate their difficulties and contradictions" within the melodrama, making the film both "crisis and critique."

840 GALLAFENT, ED. "Black satin—fantasy, murder and the couple in *Gaslight* and *Rebecca*." *Screen* 29, no. 3 (Summer):84–103.

Defines a genre called "the paranoid couple's film," which combines melodrama, in assigning fantasy to the woman, and realism/horror, in assigning purpose to the man. Gallafent argues that the "fantasy life of the man is as important as that of the woman" in these films, which in total comprise "an articulated scenario of male fantasy." He examines in *Rebecca* and *Gaslight* "the couple's exchange of fantasies, their attribution of fantasies to each other, and their fantasies of each other's fantasies." Parts concerned with *Rebecca* include discussion of the Fontaine character's "realistic" behavior versus Maxim's "narcissistic fantasies," the economic exchange involved in marriage, and the concept of the "perfect wife."

841 GLENN, KATHLEEN M. "Martinez de Pisón's 'Alusion al tiempo' and Hitchcock's *Rear Window:* Voyeurism and self-reflexivity." *Monographic Review/Revista Monografica* 4:16–24.

Description of Hitchcock's influence on the De Pisón story (from a collection titled *Alguien te observa en secreto,* 1985). Glenn argues that "the story is more indebted to *Rear Window* than its author is consciously aware of or willing to admit" through presentation of voyeur themes and the story's similar focus on the activities of writing, reading, and interpreting.

842 KAPSIS, ROBERT E. "The historical reception of Hitchcock's *Marnie*." *Journal of Film and Video* 40, no. 3 (Summer):46–63.

Using "reception theory" from the ideas of Wendy Griswald, Kapsis analyzes the negative critical appreciation of *Marnie* when it first appeared, the more positive appreciation by academics a few years later, and the decade-later feminist readings of it. He discusses Hitchcock's conscious move away from story to more character development and his desire to satisfy "intellectual critics." Using the production files from the film and a personal interview with art director Robert Boyle, Kapsis presents an extensive case for Hitchcock's intentional implementation of what were originally assessed as awkward, unsuccessful parts of the film.

843 ———. "Hitchcock in the James Bond era." *Studies in Popular Culture* 11, no. 1:64–79.

Assessment of *Torn Curtain* and *Topaz* grounded in their relation to the film culture of the 1960s, particularly the James Bond cycle. Kapsis shows that Hitchcock reacted to the phenomenon from the time of casting Sean Connery

(new Bond hero) in *Marnie*, and then more directly in the later two spy films. He examines publicity and media reception of the films and concludes that the cycle was a significant constraint on Hitchcock, even contributing to his artistic decline as it provoked him to "timidly" return to prior codified generic elements instead of "bold new conceptions."

844   LEE, SANDER H.   "Escape and commitment in Hitchcock's *Rear Window*." *Post Script* 7, no. 2 (Winter):18–28.

Argues that Hitchcock is primarily concerned with "the ability to successfully establish a romantic link with another person." Lee examines the film's standard plot elements as they relate to moral issues, with the intention of showing Jeffries's preference for "evading the responsibility of introspection and commitment" and the film's chronicling of his facing these fears.

845   MOGG, KEN.   "Out of Hitchcock's filing cabinet." *Filmviews,* no. 135 (Autumn):8–12.

Speculation on ideas that Hitchcock acquired from the theater, casual magazine reading, literature, and other films that he kept in his "filing cabinet" for later use. Especially emphasizes material current in the 1940s.

846   NAREMORE, JAMES.   "Star performances: Cary Grant in *North by Northwest;* Film as performance text: *Rear Window*." In *Acting in the Cinema*. Berkeley: University of California Press, pp. 213–238, 239–261.

Two essays. First is a description of Grant's performance in *North by Northwest,* the "quintessential star vehicle." Naremore sees the star quality—"he could seem both extraordinary and ordinary at the same time"—as particularly suitable to Hitchcock's design. He discusses Grant's clothes, physique, comic takes and pauses, athleticism, accent, and enunciation. He links Grant's celebrity to the themes of the film via dialogue and the creation of George Kaplan, a fake identity. Naremore describes Grant as "more concerned with mechanics than feeling" and credits him with the technical creation of his own character.

The second essay is a discussion of the acting in *Rear Window* as a "virtual compendium of theatrical conventions . . . with an almost comic pleasure in its own technique." Naremore details the three different "tasks" that comprise the film's acting: "thinking" for the camera in close-up, large vivid gestures in long shot, and medium shots of the proscenium stage. He concludes with a description of the technique of all five main characters as well as the bit players and an extended discussion of James Stewart, especially his voice and facial expressiveness regarding fear and pain.

847   PETLEWSKI, PAUL.   "Generic tension in *Psycho*." In *Ambiguities in Literature and Film*, edited by Hans P. Braendlin. Florida State University Conference on Literature and Film, 7. Tallahassee: Florida State University, pp. 50–55.

Psycho as a test of "the limits of genre." Author argues that the film switches from a "realist crime story" to a "classical detective story" and that the switch is

effectively masked by the introduction and continuing use of Gothic horror iconography.

848 SCHMIDT, JOHANN N. "Literary adaptation as pure cinema: Alfred Hitchcock's *Psycho.*" *Anglistik & Englischunterricht* 36:11–24.
Comparison of the novel by Robert Bloch and the film. Schmidt argues that Hitchcock, unlike the novelist, presents a more reflective version of essentially the same events.

*849 THEWELEIT, KLAUS. "Der kleine Hitchcock war oft erschreckt:
Erschreckt er uns deshalb mit seinen Filmen: Zur Lust am Biographischen." In *Jahrbuch,* 1988. Darmstadt: Deutsche Akademie für Sprache und Dichtung, pp. 136–168.
Cited in MLA (CD-ROM).

850 THOMAS, DEBORAH. *"Film noir:* How Hollywood deals with the deviant male." *CineAction!,* no. 13–14 (Summer):18–28.
After extensive structural defining of *film noir* as reflective of the anxieties of the postwar period from the viewpoint of the "white American male," Thomas analyzes *The Man Who Knew Too Much* (1955) as the *"film noir* protagonist ten years further along in his life." The father's status has been eroded "both within the marriage and, compared to *film noir,* within the narrative structure of the film."

851 WOOD, ROBIN. "Symmetry, closure, disruption; the ambiguity of *Blackmail.*" *CineAction!,* 13, no. 15 (Winter):13–25.
Argues that symmetry not only functions to produce closure but also marks difference, in that formal closure "opens up" speculation as to the character's continuation. Wood examines various particular scenes and their relation to the film's main theme: "Life in patriarchal capitalist society as an incessant struggle for domination." He analyzes in detail the manslaughter sequence using a chart of shot descriptions and symmetrical relations as well as explications of the various elements: policeman/jester, the pictures, and the dresses. He concludes that the film's final image of the jester laughs at the "oppressive (dis-)organization of gender and sexuality" in the social order as well as at the characters who remain "trapped within its contradictions." Reprinted in entry 852.

1989
Books

852 WOOD, ROBIN. *Hitchcock's Films Revisited.* New York: Columbia University Press, 395 pp.
Revised edition of entries 318 and 476. The new introduction chronicles Wood's changing views and critical history; it explains his decision not to revise

the original work or develop a newly "coherent" approach to the films as a whole. Instead, several new essays and reprinted journal articles are added.

"Plot formations" analyzes the films as they group under different "stories": of the falsely accused man, the guilty woman, the psychopath, the espionage/ political intrigue, and the marriage theme.

"Norm and Variations" examines *The 39 Steps* and *Young and Innocent* as double chase films, a combination of "picaresque story and espionage plot" that focuses on sex roles, father figures, and class differences.

"Star and Auteur: Hitchcock Films with Bergman" disputes analyses based on "the Look," arguing that such a "model of identification . . . is far too simple." In support, Wood presents a detailed analysis of the career and persona of Ingrid Bergman, suggesting that Hitchcock "understood the complexities and potentialities of the Bergman persona more than any other director" and hence built audience identification around her as well as Cary Grant. The discussion moves on from the problems of identification, as expressed through the long take in *Under Capricorn,* to an analysis of class as well as sex roles in that film, which Wood argues is undervalued.

"Murderous Gays: Hitchcock's Homophobia" is an exploration of Hitchcock's relations with gay actors. The author contends that Hitchcock identified with them as much as he displayed hostility. This ambivalent homophobia is linked to his violence against women. A discussion of gay characters follows, an effort which Wood points out is more difficult than critical opinion generally indicates. Many films are included; the discussion of *Rope* is the longest and focuses on Brandon, a typical Hitchcock identification figure in his "desire-for-power/fear-of-impotence."

"The Men Who Knew Too Much (and the Women Who Knew Much Better)" investigates further the methods of creating identification, suggesting that Hitchcock's films "play on a tension between technically constructed identification and emotional identification." The two versions of *The Man Who Knew Too Much* are contrasted according to their differing attitudes of time and place to the same sexual ideology.

Also includes reprints of entries 318 and 851. Earlier version of the introduction, "Fear of Spying," in *American Film,* 9, no. 2 (November 1983).

Articles and Shorter Writings

853   BORDWELL, DAVID.   "Rhetoric in action: Seven models of *Psycho.*" In *Making Meaning: Inference and Rhetoric in the Interpretation of Cinema.* Cambridge: Harvard University Press, pp. 224–248.

Analysis of selected critical essays on *Psycho*—Douchet (entry 787), Wood (entry 318), Durgnat (entry 340), V. F. Perkins (*Film as Film,* Harmondsworth: Penguin, 1972), Bellour (entry 516), Klinger (entry 690), and Poague (entry 771)—which argues that there are similarities in rhetoric shared among all: chronological accounts of the film, equation of the spectator with critic and reader, and agreement on which points of the film are important. This "consensus" is contrasted with the varying "appeals to theory" that each essay represents.

854 COHEN, KEITH. *"Psycho:* The suppression of female desire (and its return)." In *Reading Narrative: Form, Ethics, Ideology,* edited by James Phelan. Columbus: Ohio State University Press, pp. 147–161.

Examination of the narrative in favor of Marion's desire—vivid, obvious, and assertive. Her death provokes confusion in the spectator, but there is a "faint suggestion" of a possible revival of "female sexual energy" in Norman/mother at the end.

855 KAPSIS, ROBERT E. "Reputation building and the film art world: The case of Alfred Hitchcock." *The Sociological Quarterly* 30 (Spring):15–35.

Reviews sociological theories of reputation building, genre meaning systems, and the concept of the biographical legend. Kapsis chronicles the post-*Psycho* story of Hitchcock's relations with François Truffaut, his media relations during the period of *The Birds* and *Marnie,* and the complete public success, with *Frenzy,* of his "great artist" status.

856 POZNAR, WALTER. "Orpheus descending: Love in *Vertigo.*" *Literature/ Film Quarterly* 17, no. 1:58–65.

Thematic discussion of the film emphasizing "the spiritual meaning" of Scottie's love for Madeleine and "the destructive force [engendered by] Judy's refusal to be Madeleine." Contributing to the defining of the ideal female, the character of Midge "reveals a cruel debasing of feminine values."

857 SERED, JEAN. "The dark side." *Armchair Detective* 22, no. 2; no. 3 (Spring; Summer):116–135; 240–258.

Essay comparing Cornell Woolrich and Hitchcock: similar in age, both Catholic, and both self-trained. Sered suggests they were both influenced by Poe and dominated by their mothers. The author discusses aberrations (jokes, crushes) and addictions to food and alcohol, and *Rear Window* and *Rope.* Part two explores mother-son relationships, misogyny, and Hitchcock's "oddly sympathetic attitude towards rapists." Also has themes of premature burial, the church, and the common suspense themes.

858 STAM, ROBERT. "Hitchcock and Buñuel: Desire and the Law." In *The Cinematic Text: Methods and Approaches,* edited by R. Barton Palmer. Georgia State Literary Studies, 3. New York: AMS Press, pp. 23–46.

Comparison of the two directors, both of the same age, with long careers beginning in the silent era. Stam explicates many themes, especially concerning sex, by comparing individual films, especially *The Birds* and *The Exterminating Angel.* He concludes that the two films display very different political impulses, the latter being a "far more radical critique. . . . While Hitchcock thinks in the psychological singular of the subjectivized monad, Buñuel thinks in the social plural of class. Buñuel's frontal assaults on authority, with their historical trail of scandal and censorship, find but faint echo in the kind of devious undermining performed by Hitchcock."

Reprint from *Studies in Literary Imagination,* 16, no. 1 (1983).

1990

859   TOLES, GEORGE E. "Alfred Hitchcock's *Rear Window* as critical allegory." *boundary 2* 16, no. 2–3 (Winter–Spring):225–246.

Identifies two themes of the "first wave" of comment on the film: a notion of Jeffries as a spectator and the anatomy of spectatorship involving passivity, complicity, and gratification, and the ethics of voyeuristic involvement. Toles then offers three alternative readings termed Marxist, deconstructionist, and feminist, all of which challenge Hitchcock's control and shift responsibility for meaning to the spectator. He concludes that the third major theme of the film is the author's formal control, which need not be granted, for the "overthrow of the 'completed text' as an expression of imaginative freedom is supported by the film text, if only by the demonstrated difficulties of an authoritative interpretation." The final section is a reading based on ideas of "the realm of allegory," the mirror and mirroring dimension, both of which introduce "a potential break or rupture within the otherwise seamless pattern" of our identification with the main character.

Finally, in a plea for "openness," Toles objects to any "critic who conceives the artist either as an oppressor or as a de-personalized transmitter of cultural codes already in place and can only grant imaginative authority to texts as armored in skepticism as the perspectives he or she brings to them."

860   VEST, JAMES M. "Reflections of Ophelia (and of Hamlet) in Alfred Hitchcock's *Vertigo.*" *The Journal of the Midwest Modern Language Association* 22, no. 1 (Spring):1–9.

Analysis of *Hamlet*'s influence on Hitchcock and the parallels in *Vertigo* with the play. Emphasizes the similarities to Ophelia of all the female characters— Midge, Madeleine, and Judy—and compares the water imagery.

1990
Books

861   REBELLO, STEPHEN. *Alfred Hitchcock and the Making of* Psycho. New York: Dembner, 224 pp.

Based on the Hitchcock papers and interviews with Hitchcock and many of his collaborators on the film. Rebello chronicles in journalistic detail the origins of the novel in the Ed Gein murders, the background of the novelist, Robert Bloch, and Hitchcock's deal making. He also traces development of the screenplay, the hiring of the crew and cast, preproduction, shooting, problems with the censors, postproduction, publicity, and the film's effect on Hitchcock's future as well as subsequent Hollywood filmmaking. Partially reprinted in *American Film,* 15 (April, 1990).

Articles and Shorter Writings

862   BEEBE, JOHN. "The *Notorious* postwar psyche." *Journal of Popular Film and Television* 18 (Spring):28–35.

The character of Alicia is analyzed as a reflection of the "mildly depressed" state of Ben Hecht and Hitchcock at the end of the war. Using Jungian theory to

describe the characters, Beebe examines the film as an allegory of the collective guilt of the postwar American mentality.

863   HARK, INA RAE. "Keeping your amateur standing: Audience partici-
pation and good citizenship in Hitchcock's political films." *Cinema Journal* 29, no. 2 (Winter):8–22.
Examination of the ideology of the "citizen-amateur" in Hitchcock's British thrillers. Hark discusses the historical context of the "first political film," *The Man Who Knew Too Much* (1934), and its literary antecedents as well as Hitchcock's relationship (both personal and professional) to the writers. Among Hitchcock's contributions to the genre are an amateur who remains amateur and, more broadly, an analogy between amateurs as "ill-behaved" spectators in the films and the actual spectators at the film. The theoretical positioning of the viewer as a guilty, voyeuristic spectator is related to the passive "bad" citizen. The many scenes in theaters, but particularly those in *The Man Who Knew Too Much* (1934) and *The 39 Steps,* are analyzed in support of the view that Hitchcock related his own cinematic will to that of the fascist dictator; he therefore encouraged the viewers of his films to mentally "disrupt those performances designed to lull them into complacent reliance on authority."

864   LEONARD, GARRY M. "A fall from grace: The fragmentation of masculine subjectivity and the impossibility of femininity in Hitchcock's *Vertigo.*" *American Imago* 47, 3–4 (Fall–Winter):271–291.
Using ideas of Jacques Lacan concerning the construction of masculinity and femininity, Leonard analyzes *Vertigo* as showing Hitchcock's understanding of these concepts as "shifting cultural myths," hence, suspenseful. He examines Scottie as a man in conflict, striving to confirm his masculinity but slipping into feminization; Midge as a refusal of the masquerade and therefore not a "woman"; Judy as too skilled at masquerade and therefore forcing Scottie's incertitude and feminization; and, finally, Gavin Elster as the Father/director (Alfred Hitchcock himself) "the representative of the patriarchal order, and the myth of the coherent self."

865   MILLER, D. A. "Anal *Rope.*" *Representations,* no. 32 (Fall):114–133.
Essay on the confluence of the obsession with technique (the supposed 10-minute take) and the nonobsession with homosexuality so that "technique acquires all the transgressive fascination" (Hitchcock always claimed the long takes did not "work") of homosexuality, while homosexuality is consigned to the "status of a dry technical detail." Examines elements in the film that connote homosexuality and its evoking not only the fear of castration but the "negation of castration."

V

SUPPLEMENTAL BIBLIOGRAPHIC CITATIONS

This listing, arranged chronologically by film title, includes newspaper, magazine, and film journal reviews as well as some reports from set locations and other miscellaneous material. A repesentative sampling of this type of material is also included in Chapter IV, the annotated bibliography.

866   *The Lodger*

Combs, R. *"The Lodger: A Story of the London Fog." Monthly Film Bulletin* (British Film Institute) 43, no. 510 (July 1976): 156:

Gordon H. "Speaker of silents: *The Lodger." Classic Images,* no. 79 (January 1982):42.

Manvell, Roger. *"The Lodger." Sight and Sound* 19, no. 9 (1951): 377–378.

867   *Easy Virtue*

Rosetti, R. *"Easy Virtue." Filmcritica,* no. 311 (January 1981):25–26.

868   *The Ring*

Canhan, Kingsley. *"The Ring." Films and Filming* 15, no. 2 (August 1969): 79–80.

Patterson, G. G. "Eloquent though silent." *Filmograph* 1, no. 4 (1970):31.

Rosenbaum, J. *"The Ring."* *Monthly Film Bulletin* (British Film Institute) 43, no. 510 (July 1974):156–157.

Borges, J. L. "Zwei Filme." *Filmkritik* 24 (September 1980):391–392.

869 *The Farmer's Wife*

Yacowar, M. *"The Farmer's Wife."* *Bright Lights* 2, no. 4 (1979):27–29.

870 *Champagne*

Pedlar, G. "Why a failure?: Hitchcock's *Champagne.*" *Classic Images,* no. 151 (January 1988):54–56.

Rossi, A. *"Champagne."* *Cinema e Film* 10 (1969–1970).

871 *The Manxman*

"The Manxman." *Film Daily* (December 22, 1929):10

Bruno, E. *"The Manxman."* *Filmcritica,* no. 311 (January 1981):28–29.

"Enchanting scenes." *New York Times* (December 22, 1929):Section 8, p. 6.

872 *Blackmail*

"Blackmail." *Film Daily* (October 6, 1929):9.

"Blackmail." *New York Times* (September 15, 1929):Section 9, p. 5.

Brown, G. *"Blackmail."* *Monthly Film Bulletin* (British Film Institute) 42, no. 502 (1975):246–247.

Dangeau, Gilles. "Sur quatre films d'Hitchcock." *Revue du Cinéma/Image et Son,* no. 312 (December 1976):104–110.

Erdin, Josef. *"Blackmail."* *Filmbulletin* 101 (1977):23–24.

Evans, Harry. *"Blackmail."* *Life* 94 (October 18, 1929):28.

Hall, Mordaunt. "Britain's first talking film." *New York Times* (October 7, 1929):Section 9, p. 22, col. 1.

Hellwig, Klaus. *"Blackmail."* *Filmkritik* 12, no. 7 (1968):510, 512.

L[efèvre], R. *"Blackmail."* *Revue du Cinéma/Image et Son,* no. 320–321 (October 1977):35–36.

Marshall, Ernest. *"Blackmail,* a recent British picture wins high praise." *New York Times* (July 14, 1929):Section 9, p. 4.

Rosenbaum, J. *"Blackmail."* *Monthly Film Bulletin* (British Film Institute) 41, no. 489 (October 1974):234.

Simpson, Celia. *"Blackmail."* *Spectator* 143 (August 3, 1929):154.

Smith. *"Blackmail." Bystander* 143 (August 14, 1929).
"A British film." *New York Times* (June 28, 1931):Section 8, p. 3, col. 4.

873   Elstree Calling

Orme, M. *"Elstree Calling." London News,* no. 176 (February 15, 1930):240
———. *"Elstree Calling." Nation* (London) 46 (February 22, 1930):704

874   Juno and the Paycock

"A play of Ireland." *New York Times* (June 30, 1930):22, col. 6.
"Juno and some others." *New York Times* (July 6, 1930):Section 8, p. 3, col. 6.
"Juno and the Paycock." Film Daily (June 29, 1930):11.

875   Number Seventeen

Borde, Raymond and Etienne Chaumeton. "Flashback sur Hitchcock." *Cahiers du Cinéma* 3, no. 17 (November 1952):55–58.
G[arel], A. *"Number Seventeen." Revue du Cinéma/Image et Son,* no. 320–321 (October 1977):195–196.
Rosenbaum, J. *"Number Seventeen." Monthly Film Bulletin* (British Film Institute) 42, no. 499 (August 1975):186–187.

876   Murder!

B[osseno], Ch. *"Murder!" Revue du Cinéma/Image et Son,* no. 320–321 (October 1977):185–186.
Gale, Arthur L. *"Murder!" Movie Makers* 5 (December 1930):803.
Lefèvre, R. "Les premier parlants D'Alfred Hitchcock." *Cinéma* 76, no. 215 (November 1976):120–125.
"Murder!" New York Times (November 2, 1930):Section 8, p. 5.
"Murder!" Film Daily (October 26, 1930):10
"Murder is a mystery film; new British offering is intelligent and entertaining." *New York Times* (October 25, 1930):20.
Purcell, J. M. *"Murder!" Armchair Detective* 10, no. 4 (1977):313.
Rosenbaum, J. *"Murder!" Monthly Film Bulletin* (British Film Institute) 42, no. 498 (July 1975):165.

877   The Skin Game

M. H. "A Galsworthy play." *New York Times* (June 6, 1931):20.
Noble, Peter. *"The Skin Game." Picturegoer* (October 17, 1931).

878   *Rich and Strange*

Beylie, C. "Quatre inédits d'Alfred Hitchcock." *Ecran,* no. 52 (November 1976):44–45.

Combs, R. *"Rich and Strange." Monthly Film Bulletin* (British Film Institute) 42, no. 499 (August 1975):187–188.

Contenti, F. *"Rich and Strange—1932." Filmcritica,* no. 311 (January 1981):31.

L[efèvre], R. *"A l'est de Shanghai." Revue du Cinéma/Image et Son,* no. 320–321 (October 1977):11–12.

"Rich and Strange." Picturegoer (June 11, 1932).

"Rich and Strange." Film Daily (March 27, 1932):22.

Thomas, Kevin. *"Rich and Strange." Los Angeles Times* 103 (July 23, 1984):Section 6, p. 3, col. 3.

879   *Waltzes from Vienna*

Davy, C. *"Waltzes from Vienna." Spectator* 152 (March 9, 1934):370.

"Waltzes from Vienna." Film Daily (April 9, 1935):7

"Waltzes from Vienna." Variety (April 17, 1935):14.

"Waltzes from Vienna." Observer (October 22, 1933).

880   *The Man Who Knew Too Much* (1934)

Erdin, Josef. *"The Man Who Knew Too Much." Filmbulletin* 101 (1977): 27–28.

Hamilton, James Shelley. *"The Man Who Knew Too Much." National Board of Review Magazine* 10 (May 1935):12–13.

McGee, J. "Reel reviewer." *Classic Film Collector,* no. 52 (Fall 1976):36–38.

"The Man Who Knew Too Much." Film Daily (March 22, 1935):7.

"The Man Who Knew Too Much." Hollywood Reporter (March 29, 1935):7.

Norden, Helen Brown. "Hollywood on parade; an English triumph." *Vanity Fair* 44 (May 1935):45.

Sennwald, Andre. *"The Man Who Knew Too Much." New York Times* (March 23, 1935):11.

Sennwald, Andre. "Peter Lorre, poet of the damned; the chilling baby killer of *M* contributes another evil portrait in *The Man Who Knew Too Much." New York Times* (March 31, 1935):Section 11, p. 3.

881   *The 39 Steps*

Auty, M. *Monthly Film Bulletin* (British Film Institute) 45 (December 1978):249.

Baker, Peter. *Films and Filming* 5, no. 7 (1959):23, 25.

Bareges, L. *"Les 39 marches." Ciné Revue* 59 (May 3, 1979):4.

Beylie, C. *Ecran,* no. 18 (September–October 1973):79–80.

Blumenberg, Hans C. *"The 39 Steps." Jugend, Film, Fernsehen* 17 (1973):207.

Borde, Raymond and Etienne Chaumeton. "Flashback sur Hitchcock." *Cahiers du Cinéma* 3, no. 17 (November 1952):55–58.

Bory, Jean-Louis. "Ce cher vieil Alfred." *Nouvel Observateur* (July 2, 1973):53.

Bory, Jean-Louis. *"The 39 Steps."* In *Cinéma, 6: L'obstacle et la gerbe.* Collection, 10/18. Paris: Union Générale d'Editions (1976), pp. 125–129.

Carroll. *"The 39 Steps." Sunday Times* (June 9, 1936).

Chapier, Henri. *"Les trente-neuf marches* d'Alfred Hitchcock: Le marathon de suspense." *Combat* (July 2, 1973).

Elley, D. *"The 39 Steps." Films and Filming* 25, no. 2 (November 1978): 32–33.

Forrest, Mark. "A fine picture." *Saturday Review* (London) 159 (June 22, 1935); 797.

Gillissen, O. *Revue du Cinéma/Image et Son,* no. 23 (1979):310.

Greenfield, P. *"The 39 Steps." Movietone News,* no. 62–63 (December 1979):34, 36, 37.

Houston, Penelope. *"The 39 Steps." Sight and Sound* 28 (1959):94.

Marshall, Ernest. *"The 39 Steps* from London." *New York Times* (July 14, 1935):Section 9, p. 2.

McGlashan, Maude. *"The 39 Steps." Films in Review* 11, no. 7 (1960): 429–430.

Miller, D. *"The 39 Steps." The New Captain George's Whizzbang* 4, no. 1 [no. 17] (1974):10–11.

Moreau, André. *"The 39 Steps." Télérama* (December 13, 1975):59.

"The 39 Steps." Life and Letters To-Day (London) 13 (September 1935):202.

"The 39 Steps." Film Daily (September 14, 1934):7.

"The 39 Steps." Filmkritik 1, no. 5 (1957):79.

"The 39 Steps." Hollywood Reporter (June 29, 1935):7.

"The 39 Steps." Der Spielfilm im ZDF, no. 2 (1979):58.

Waldner, Daniel. *"The 39 Steps." Filmbulletin* 101 (1977):28–32.

Wexler, I. *"The 39 Steps:* A Chekhovian chase film." *Thousand Eyes Magazine* 9 (April 1976):3.

882 *Secret Agent*

B. R. C. *"Secret Agent." New York Times* (June 13, 1936):13.

Cros, J. L. *"Agent secret* quatre del-espionnage." *Revue du Cinéma/Image et Son,* Hors séries, no. 25 (1981):13–14.

Decaux, E. *Cinématographe,* no. 65 (February 1981):53–54.

Nugent, Frank S. "Windfalls in an off week." *New York Times* (June 21, 1936):Section 9, p. 3, col. 1.

Paini, D. *"Agent secret." Cinéma 81,* no. 268 (April 1981):98–99.

"Secret Agent." Film Daily (June 13, 1936):4.

"Secret Agent: A one-armed man, a live corpse, brutality, and murder." *Newsweek* 7 (June 13, 1936):40–41.

Serceau, Daniel. *"Agent secret." Revue du Cinéma/Image et Son,* no. 358 (February 1981):53–55.

Tobin, Yann. "De la vie des poissons rouges." *Positif,* no. 246 (September 1981):67–69.

Werner, G. "Stillbilden." *Chaplin,* no. 6 (no. 177) (1981):23–26.

883   *Sabotage*

Borges, J. L. "Zwei Filme." *Filmkritik* 24 (September 1980):401–402.

Bosseno, C. *"Sabotage." Revue du Cinéma/Image et Son,* Hors séries, no. 26 (1982):296–297.

Chion, Michel. "Une morale d'auteur." *Cahiers du cinéma* no. 333 (March 1982):57–58.

Decaux, E. *"Sabotage." Cinématographe,* no. 75 (February 1982):67–68.

Hull, David Stewart. *"Sabotage." Film Society Review* (January 1966):12.

Nugent, Frank S. *"Sabotage." New York Times* (November 16, 1939):29.

———. *"Sabotage." New York Times* (February 27, 1937):9.

———. *"Sabotage." New York Times* (February 28, 1937):Section 11, p. 5.

P.C. *"Sabotage." Film Society Review* (January 1966):12–13.

"Sabotage." Film Daily (January 9, 1937):4.

"Sabotage." Time 34 (October 10, 1939).

"Sabotage." Der Spielfilm im ZDF, no. 2 (1978):40.

Verbraeken, P. *"Sabotage." Cinéma 82,* no. 279 (March 1982):86–87.

884   *Young and Innocent*

Alion, Y. *"Jeune et innocent." Ekran,* no. 72 (September 15, 1978):60–61.

Allombert, Guy. *"Young and Innocent." Revue du Cinéma/Image et Son,* no. 331 (September 1978):112–114.

Barnes, Howard. *"The Girl Was Young." New York Herald Tribune* (February 13, 1938).

Carrère, Emmanuel. "Innocence protégée." *Positif,* no. 211 (October 1978):62–64.

Cousins, Edmund George. "The British studios: Hitchcock's new thriller." *Picturegoer* (July 3, 1937):8–9.

Dahan, L. *"Young and Innocent." Cinématographe,* no. 40 (1978):83.

Guérif, F. *"Young and Innocent." Revue du Cinéma/Image et Son,* no. 332 (October 1978):162–163.

"The Hitchcock formula." *New York Times* (February 13, 1938):Section 10, p. 4.

Magny, J. "*Young and Innocent.*" *Cinéma* 78, no. 236–237 (August–September 1978):181–182.

Nugent, Frank S. "*Young and Innocent.*" *New York Times* (February 11, 1938):27.

Nugent, Frank S. "*Young and Innocent.*" *New York Times* (February 20, 1938):Section 11, p. 5, col. 1.

Werner, Paul. "*Young and Innocent.*" *Filmbeobachter* 22, no. 326 (1978):10.

"*Young and Innocent.*" *The Cinema* (November 25, 1937).

"*Young and Innocent.*" *Film Daily* (January 19, 1938):6.

"*Young and Innocent.*" *Hollywood Reporter* (December 16, 1937):10.

"*Young and Innocent.*" *Der Spielfilm im ZDF,* no. 2 (1978):42.

885 *The Lady Vanishes*

Albrecht, Gerd. "*The Lady Vanishes.*" *Besonders wertvoll. Langfilme* 15 (1971–1972):38–39.

Beylie, Claude. "*The Lady Vanishes.*" *Ecran* 73 (September–October 1973):79–80.

Hall, Vince. "Cinema." *North American Review* 247, no. 1 (March 1939): 176–177.

Hartung, Philip T. "Vanishing ladies and corpses." *Commonweal* (November 4, 1938):49.

Iampol'skii, M. "Ledi ischezact: Velikobritaniia." *Iskusstvo Kino,* no. 11 (1988):110–112.

"*The Lady Vanishes.*" *Film Daily* (October 5, 1938):6.

"*The Lady Vanishes.*" *Hollywood Reporter* (June 1, 1939):3.

"*The Lady Vanishes.*" *Stage* (Theatre Guild N.Y.) 16 (November; October 1938):57; 34.

"*The Lady Vanishes:* And a British trencherman is again spotlighted." *Newsweek* 12 (October 17, 1938):28–29.

Laffel, J. "*The Lady Vanishes.*" *Film News* 31 (April–May 1974):12.

Mosher, John. "Christmas list." *New Yorker* (December 24, 1938).

Nugent, Frank S. "Alfred Hitchcock presents the Globe with a brilliant melodrama: *The Lady Vanishes.*" *New York Times* (December 26, 1938):29.

Schatzdorfer, Gerhard. "*The Lady Vanishes.*" *Jugend, Film Fernsehen* 16, no. 1 (1972):46.

Stanbrook, Alan. "Great film of the century: *The Lady Vanishes.*" *Films and Filming* 9, no. 10 (1963):43–47.

886 *Jamaica Inn*

Barnes, Howard. "*Jamaica Inn.*" *New York Herald Tribune* (October 15, 1939).

Galway, Peter. *"Jamaica Inn." New Statesman and Nation* (March 13, 1939):736.

"Jamaica Inn." Film Daily (October 12, 1939):5.

"Jamaica Inn." Hollywood Reporter (May 22, 1939):3.

"Jamaica Inn." Life 6 (June 19, 1939):67–68.

Lejeune, C. A. "London snow banks *Jamaica Inn." New York Times* (January 22, 1939):Section 9, p. 4.

Nugent, Frank S. "Laughton obscures Hitchcock in *Jamaica Inn* at the Rivoli." *New York Times* (October 12, 1939):33.

Pulleine, T. *"Jamaica Inn." Monthly Film Bulletin* (British Film Institute) 46, no. 547 (August 1979):186–187.

887   *Rebecca*

Alion, Y. *"Rebecca." Revue du Cinéma/Image et Son,* no. 442 (October 1988):37.

Chabrol, Claude. "Sans tambour ni trompette." *Cahiers du Cinéma* 8, no. 45 (1955):46–47.

Coleman, John. *"Rebecca." New Statesman* 100 (August 8, 1980):24.

Cumbow, R. "Orson Welles has a daughter named *Rebecca." Movietone News,* no. 38 (January 1975):27.

Doniol-Valcroze, Jacques. *"Spellbound-Rebecca-Suspicion." Revue du Cinéma/Image et Son,* N.S. 3, no. 15 (1948):72–77.

Grant, J. "La mariée est en gris." *Cinéma 79,* no. 245 (May 1979):76–78.

Lefèvre, R. *"Rebecca." Revue du Cinéma/Image et Son,* no. 340 (June 1979):130–131.

Legrand, Gérard. "Archéologie et signatures." *Positif,* no. 219 (June 1979):68–69.

Nugent, Frank S. "Splendid film of Du Maurier's *Rebecca* is shown at the Music Hall." *New York Times* (March 29, 1940):25.

"Rebecca." National Board of Review of Motion Pictures (April 1940): 13–14.

"Rebecca." Film Daily (March 26, 1940):6.

"Rebecca." Theatre Arts 24 (May 1940):320.

"Rebecca." Photoplay 54 (May 1940):73.

"Rebecca." Life 8 (January 15, 1940):31–32.

"Rebecca." Theatre Arts 24 (May 1940):320.

"Rebecca is first in film daily poll: Selznick production wins vote of 391 of 596 critics in trade paper survey." *New York Times* (January 14, 1941):17.

"Rebecca: Grim and gripping, film hews to lines of novel." *Newsweek* 8, no. 15 (April 1940):34–35.

Stefancic, M., Jr. *"Rebecca." Ekran* 9, no. 7–8 (1984):4–7.

Weiler, A. A. *"Rebecca* brings home the bacon." *New York Times* (March 3, 1946):Section 2, p. 3.

888 *Foreign Correspondent*

Allen, Devere. "Very foreign correspondence." *Christian Century* 57 (October 16, 1940):1284–1285.

E. L. "The state of the union: The truth about foreign correspondents." *American Mercury* 51 (November 1940):358–360.

"*Foreign Correspondent.*" *Film Daily* (August 29, 1940):6.

"*Foreign Correspondent.*" *Photoplay* 54 (February 1940):44–45.

"*Foreign Correspondent.*" *Theatre Arts* 24 (1940):727.

"It's all in the camera man's day: Diary of a fellow sent out to make a few background shots." *New York Times* (April 28, 1940):Section 9, p. 5.

Kotulla, Theodor. "*Foreign Corresondent.*" *Filmkritik* 6, no. 1 (1962):36–37.

Mosher, John. "Thriller." *New Yorker* 16 (August 31, 1940):43.

"Movie of the week: *Foreign Correspondent,* with fact, fiction, spy hunts and suspense." *Life* 9 (August 26, 1940):42–45.

Sarris, Andrew. "*Foreign Correspondent.*" *Film Comment* 10, no. 3 (May-June 1974):22.

"A scoop in war thrills: A reporter outwits the Nazis in *Foreign Corresondent.*" *Newsweek* 16 (August 26, 1940):49–50.

Zinman, David. "*Foreign Correspondent.*" *New York Times* (July 6, 1975):Section D, p. 9.

889 *Mr. and Mrs. Smith*

Crowther, Bosley. "*Mr. and Mrs. Smith.*" *New York Times* (February 21, 1941):16.

Ebert, Jürgen. "*Mr. and Mrs. Smith.*" *Filmkritik* 14, no. 8 (1970):437–439.

Eder, Klaus. "*Mr. and Mrs. Smith.*" *Fernsehen und Film* 8, no. 8 (1970):43.

Fischer, Robert. "*Mr. and Mrs. Smith.*" *Filmbeobachter,* no. 20 (1978): 290.

Gow, G. *Films and Filming* 23, no. 11 (August 1977):37.

"*Mr. and Mrs. Smith.*" *Film Daily* (January 20, 1941):5.

"*Mr. and Mrs. Smith.*" *Life* 10 (January 27, 1941):53–54.

Pulleine, T. *Monthly Film Bulletin* (British Film Institute) 47, no. 561 (October 1980):200–201.

"Smith family slapstick: Lombard-Montgomery comedy upholds marriage rows." *Newsweek* 17 (February 3, 1941):58.

Thirer, Irene. "*Mister and Mrs. Smith*" *New York Post* (February 21, 1941).

890 *Suspicion*

"Charming touch in murder: Cary Grant and a happy ending highlight Hitchcock thriller." *Newsweek,* 18 (November 17, 1941):55–56.

Collet, Jean. "*Suspicion.*" *Télérama* 746 (December 27, 1964).

Crowther, Bosley. "*Suspicion.*" *New York Times* (November 21, 1941):23.

Crowther, Bosley. *"Suspicion." New York Times* (November 23, 1941):Section 9, p. 5.

Loretz, Niklaus. *"Suspicion." Zoom,* no. 20 (1976):17–19.

Mosher, John. "Freshening up Cary Grant." *New Yorker* 17 (November 22, 1941):82.

"Movie of the week: *Suspicion;* Hitchcock directs a tale of torment." *Life* (December 1, 1941):59–60.

Schérer, Maurice. *"Le soupçon." Cahiers du Cinéma,* 2, no. 12 (1952):63–66.

"Suspicion." Film Daily (September 18, 1941):10.

"Suspicion." Photoplay 20 (December 1941):23.

"Suspicion." Der Spielfilm im ZDF, no. 9 (1979):57.

891 *Saboteur*

Crowther, Bosley. "Hitchcock on the loose." *New York Times* (May 10, 1942):Section 8, p. 3.

Crowther, Bosley. *"Saboteur,* Alfred Hitchcock melodrama, starring Priscilla Lane, Robert Cummings, and Otto Kruger." *New York Times* (May 8, 1942):27.

Farber, Manny. "Blaboteur." *New Republic* 106 (May 18, 1942):669–670.

Hartung, Philip T. "Breathes there a hero." *Commonweal* 36 (May 15, 1942):87–88.

Mosher, John. "Hitchcock on sabotage." *New Yorker* 18 (May 9, 1942):67–68.

Patalas, Enno. *"Saboteur." Filmkritik* 2, no. 15 (1958):115.

"Sabotage with suspense." *Newsweek* 19 (March 4, 1942):54–55.

"Saboteur." Film Daily (April 23, 1942):7.

"Saboteur." Life 12 (May 11, 1942):67–71.

"Saboteur." Theatre Arts 26 (1942):318–319.

Waldner, Daniel. *"Saboteur." Filmbulletin* 101 (1977):35–39.

892 *Lifeboat*

"$5000 production: Hitchcock makes thriller under WPB order on new sets." *Life* 14 (January 25, 1943): 70–73, 75–76, 78.

Auriol, Jean George. *"Lifeboat—Shadow of a Doubt." Revue du Cinéma/ Image et Son,* N.S. 3, no. 15 (1948):64–70.

Crowther, Bosley. "Adrift in *Lifeboat:* The new Hitchcock-Steinbeck drama represents democracy at sea." *New York Times* (January 23, 1944):Section 2, p. 3.

Crowther, Bosley. *"Lifeboat,* a film picturization of ship-wrecked survivors, with Tallulah Bankhead, opens at the Astor Theatre." *New York Times* (January 13, 1944):17.

Farber, Manny. "Among the missing: Hitchcock." *New Republic* 39 (January 24, 1944):116.

Hartung, Philip T. "Water water everywhere." *Commonweal* 39 (January 28, 1944):374–375.

"Hitchcock's hand steers *Lifeboat* safely through film's troubled sea." *Newsweek* 23 (January 17, 1944):66–67.

Lardner, David. "Another country heard from." *New Yorker* 19 (February 5, 1944):65.

Lardner, David. "Shipshape." *New Yorker* (January 15, 1944):56–57.

"Lifeboat." Film Daily (January 12, 1944):29.

"Lifeboat." Cosmopolitan 116 (February 1944):92.

"Lifeboat." Time 43 (January 31, 1944):24–25.

"Lifeboat." Der Spielfilm im ZDF, no. 1 (1978):42.

"Movie of the week: *Lifeboat;* Hitchcock throws eight people and the Nazi who torpedoes them together in an open boat." *Life* 16 (January 31, 1944): 78–83.

Rohmer, Eric. "La nef des fous." *Cahiers du Cinéma* 10, no. 60 (1956):35–37.

Truffaut, François. *"Lifeboat." Arts* (June 6, 1956):5.

893   *Shadow of a Doubt*

Auriol, Jean George. *"Lifeboat—Shadow of a Doubt." Revue du Cinéma/ Image et Son,* N.S. 3, no. 15 (1948):64–70.

"Charlie's uncle." *Newsweek* 21 (January 25, 1943):77–78.

Crowther, Bosley. *"Shadow of a Doubt,* a thriller, with Teresa Wright, Joseph Cotton, at Rivoli." *New York Times* (January 13, 1943):18.

Farber, Manny. "Hitchcock in stride." *New Republic* 108 (February 8, 1943):182.

Hartung, Philip T. "Good week." *Commonweal* 37 (January 29, 1943): 373–374.

Lejeune, C. A. *Chestnuts in Her Lap, 1936–1947.* London: Phoenix House, 1948, pp. 87–89.

Patalas, Enno. "Im Schatten des Zweifels." *Filmkritik* 12, no. 3 (1968): 218–220.

"Shadow of a Doubt." Film Daily (January 8, 1943):5

894   *Spellbound*

Crowther, Bosley, *"Spellbound,* a psychological hit starring Ingrid Bergman and Gregory Peck, opens at Astor–Hitchcock director." *New York Times* (November 2, 1945):22.

Decaux, E. *"La maison du Docteur Edwardes." Cinématographe,* no. 49 (July 1979):59–60.

"The famous Hitchcock movie technique goes into action on *Spellbound." Cue* 14, no. 43 (October 27, 1945):12.

Farber, Manny. "Dream manors." *New Republic* 113 (December 3, 1945):747.

Games, M. "Hitchcock's *Spellbound:* Suspense, cynicism, psychological trauma." *Filament,* no. 3 (1983):20–22.

Hartung, Philip T. *"Spellbound." Commonweal* 43 (November 9, 1945):95.

Lefèvre, R. *"La maison du Docteur Edwardes." Revue du Cinéma/Image et Son,* no. 342 (September 1979):133–134.

Nugent, Frank S. "Mister Hitchcock discovers love." *New York Times* (November 3, 1946):12–13.

"Prizewinner for 1946." *Photoplay* 30 (February 1947):44.

"Research into nightmare." *Newsweek* 26 (November 5, 1945):104.

"Salvador Dali goes to Hollywood." *Theatre Arts,* 28 (February 1945): 176–177.

"Spellbound." Cosmopolitan 118 (March 1945):90.

"Spellbound." Theatre Arts 29 (1945):178.

895   *Notorious*

Arnulf, C. and others. *"Les enchainés." Cinématographe,* no. 54 (January 1980):58–62.

Bonitzer, Pascal. *"Notorious." Cahiers du Cinéma,* no. 309 (March 1980): 51–52.

Crowther, Bosley. "Love conquers all: Mr. Hitchcock's *Notorious* marks his happy surrender to romance." *New York Times* (August 25, 1946):Section 2, p. 1.

Crowther, Bosley. *"Notorious." New York Times* (August 19, 1946):19.

Hartung, Philip T. "Simply thrilling *Notorious." Commonweal* 44 (September 6, 1946):504.

Isaacs, Hermine Rich. *"Notorious." Theatre Arts* 30 (1946):519–520.

Lefèvre, Raymond. *"Les enchainés." Revue du Cinéma/Image et Son,* no. 347 (February 1980):51–52.

Maslin, Janet. "Film view: Ingrid Bergman and the enduring appeal of *Notorious." New York Times* 130 (October 26, 1980):section 2, p. 17, col. 3.

Miller, A. I. *"Notorious." Film News* 37 (Winter 1980):36–37.

Mulvey, Kay. "On location." *Woman's Home Companion* 73 (October 1946):11.

"Notorious." Cosmopolitan 121 (August 1946):68.

"Notorious." Photoplay 29 (October 1946):24.

"Notorious." Newsweek 28 (August 26, 1946):78.

Schérer, Maurice. *"Notorious." Revue du Cinéma/Image et Son,* N.S. 3, no. 15 (1948):70–72.

Vian, Walt R. *"Notorious." Zoom,* no. 3 (1980):17–19.

896   *The Paradine Case*

Audibert, Louis. "Paradine densité et épure." *Cinématographe,* no. 59 (July-August 1980):48–49.

Bruno, E. *"The Paradine Case." Filmcritica* 32, no. 311 (January 1981).

"Come out of the dream world, boys! And take a peek at a memo listing the hurdles in independent film making." *New York Times* (February 23, 1947):Section 2, p. 4.

Crowther, Bosley. *"The Paradine Case."* *New York Times* (January 18, 1948):Section 2, p. 1.

Crowther, Bosley. "Selznick and Hitchcock join forces on *The Paradine Case,* thriller at Music Hall." *New York Times* (January 9, 1948):26.

Ducrot, Oswald. "Après *le procès Paradine,* le cas Hitchcock: Raccords." *Revue du Cinéma/Image et Son,* 1 (1950).

Hartung, Philip T. "My wife, poor wretch." *Commonweal* 47 (January 23, 1948):373–374.

Hatch, Robert. "Love and death." *New Republic* 118 (January 19, 1948):36–37.

"Hitchcock in action." *Theatre Arts* 31 (1947):50.

"In old Bailey." *Newsweek* 31 (January 19, 1948):89.

"Movie of the week: *The Paradine Case;* a good whodunit introduces some new European faces to the U.S. but is not the great drama it pretends to be." *Life* 24 (January 19, 1948):65–66, 68.

Nezmah, B. *"Zadeva Paradine."* *Ekran* 9, no. 7–8 (1984):15–16.

"The Paradine Case." *National Board of Review of Motion Pictures* (January 1948):4.

"The Paradine Case." *Cosmopolitan* 124 (March 1948):13.

"The Paradine Case." *Photoplay* 32 (April 1948):22.

Parsons, Louella O. *"Cosmopolitan's* citation for the best production of the month." *Cosmopolitan* 124 (March 1948):13.

897   *Rope*

Canby, Vincent. "Film view: Hitchcock's *Rope:* A stunt to behold." *New York Times* 133 (June 3, 1984):Section 2, p. 19, col. 1.

Crowther, Bosley. "Where we came in: Murder, other mischief still oppress the screen." *New York Times* (September 29, 1948):Section 2, p. 1.

Durgnat, Raymond. *"Rope* (Re-issue)." *Films and Filming* 9, no. 6 (March 1963):140–142.

Hatch, Robert. "Murder for profit." *New Republic* 119 (September 13, 1948):29–30.

"Movie of the week: *Rope;* Alfred Hitchcock's new thriller is a tense but over-talky story about two boys' lust for murder." *Life* 25 (July 26, 1948):52, 57–58, 60.

Pichel, Irving. "A long rope." *Hollywood Quarterly* 3, no. 4 (1948):416–420.

"Rope." *Time* 52 (September 13, 1948):102, 105–106.

Shales, Tom. *"Rope* with scope: Hitchcock's classic of camera technique." *Washington Post* 107 (August 25, 1984):Section G, p. 1, col. 5.

Stempel, Heinz. *"Rope."* *Filmkritik* 7, no. 9 (1963):438–440.

"Super Hitchcock." *Newsweek* 32 (September 9, 1948):68.

898   *Under Capricorn*

Amiel, V. "Les enlacements, le bleu, la passion." *Positif,* no. 336 (February 1989):70–71.

Anderson, Lindsay. *"Under Capricorn." Sequence,* no. 10 (1950):154–155.

Crowther, Bosley. *"Under Capricorn." New York Times* (September 9, 1949):28.

Hartung, Philip T. *"Under Capricorn." Commonweal* 50 (September 16, 1949):561.

Hatch, Robert. "Hitchcock down under." *New Republic* 121 (September 26, 1949):27–28.

"Under Capricorn." Photoplay 36 (October 1949):23.

"Under Capricorn." Theatre Arts 33 (October 1949):7.

"Under Capricorn." Sight and Sound 18, no. 71 (December 1949):21.

"Under Capricorn." Newsweek 34 (September 9, 1949):80.

"Under Capricorn." Christian Century 66 (October 19, 1949):1246.

899   *Stage Fright*

Astruc, Alexandre. "Alibis et ellipses." *Cahiers du Cinéma* 1, no. 2 (1951): 50–51.

Crowther, Bosley. *"Stage Fright,* new Hitchcock picture made in England, arrives at Music Hall." *New York Times* (February 24, 1950):27.

G. L. *"Stage Fright." Monthly Film Bulletin* (British Film Institute) 17, no. 197 (1950).

Graham, Virginia. *"Stage Fright." Spectator* (June 2, 1950):757.

Hangartner, Michael. *"Stage Fright." Zoom,* no. 15 (1977):12–14.

Hartung, Philip T. "Wild goose pimples." *Commonweal* 51 (March 10, 1950):580, 582.

Haskell, Molly. "Film favorites: Molly Haskell on *Stage Fright." Film Comment* 6, no. 3 (Fall 1970):49–50.

"Hitchcock's revival." *New Republic* 122 (March 6, 1950):22.

Knight, Arthur. "Sea change; *Stage Fright* reviewed." *Films in Review* 1, no. 3 (1950):23–25.

Lejeune, C. A. "The Cocteau party." *Observer* (May 28, 1950).

"Stage Fright." Newsweek 35 (March 13, 1950):35–36.

"Stage Fright." Hollywood Reporter (February 23, 1950).

"Stage Fright." Motion Picture Herald (February 25, 1950).

"Stage Fright." The Times (May 29, 1950):8.

"Stage Fright." Zoom, no. 14 (1977):Rez. 77/204.

Whitebait, William. *"Stage Fright." New Statesman and Nation* 39, no. 1004 (June 3, 1950):631.

900   *Strangers on a Train*

Alpert, Hollis. "Some Hitchcock murder and some Pinza marriage." *Saturday Review* 34 (July 14, 1951):32.

Benchley, Nathaniel. "Off stage." *Theatre Arts* 35 (August 1951):28–29.

Crowther, Bosley. "Dexterity in a void; Mr. Hitchcock juggles in *Strangers on a Train*." *New York Times* (July 8, 1951):Section 2, p. 1.

Crowther, Bosley. "*Strangers on a Train*, another Hitchcock venture, arrives at the Warner Theatre." *New York Times* (July 4, 1951):13.

Fishman, K. "*Strangers on a Train*." *Bright Lights* 1, no. 2 (1975):26–27.

Guernsey, Otis L. "Maestro of melodrama, Hitchcock discusses his newest tricks, including a suspensful tennis match." *New York Herald Tribune* (June 17, 1951).

Hart, Henry. "*Strangers on a Train*." *Films in Review* 2, no. 6 (1951):36–38.

Hartung, Philip T. "Tennis anyone?" *Commonweal* 54 (July 20, 1951): 358–359.

Hatch, Robert. "Melodramatics." *New Republic* 125 (July 16, 1951):22.

Life 31 (July 9, 1951):70–72.

Miller, A. I. "*Strangers on a Train*." *Film News* 37 (Winter 1980):37.

"La presse." *L'Avant-Scène du Cinéma*, no. 297–298 (December 1–15, 1982):86.

"*Strangers on a Train*." *Quaderni* 5, no. 29 (December 1985):28–29.

"*Strangers on a Train*." *Christian Century* 68 (August 8, 1951):927.

"*Strangers on a Train*." *Newsweek* 38 (July 9, 1951):40.

"*Strangers on a Train*." *Der Spielfilm im ZDF*, no. 2 (1979):62.

Thirer, Irene. "*Strangers on a Train*." *Saturday Review* (July 14, 1951).

Winnington, Richard. "*Strangers on a Train*." *Sight and Sound* 21, no. 1 (1951):21–22.

Zipperlen, Helmuth. "*Strangers on a Train*." *Zoom*, no. 7 (1976):23–24.

901   *I Confess*

Crowther, Bosley. "*I Confess*, Hitchcock drama of priest's dilemma starring Clift, opens at Paramount." *New York Times* (March 23, 1953):28.

Fisher, David. "*I Confess*." *Sight and Sound* 23, no. 1 (1953):34.

Hangartner, Michael. "*I Confess*." *Zoom*, no. 15 (1977):13–14.

Hartung, Philip T. "*I Confess*." *Commonweal* 57 (March 6, 1953):550–551.

"*I Confess*." *Monthly Film Bulletin* (British Film Institute) (May 1953):67.

"*I Confess*." *Newsweek* 41 (March 2, 1953):90.

"*I Confess*." *Arts* 418 (July 3, 1953).

"*I Confess*." *Radio, Cinéma, Télévision* 182 (July 12, 1953).

"*I Confess*." *Catholic World* 177 (April 15, 1953):63–64.

"*I Confess*." *Christian Century* 70 (April 15, 1953):463.

"*I Confess*." *Radio, Cinéma, Télévision* 383 (May 19, 1957).

"*I Confess*." *Look* 17 (April 21, 1953):110.

"*I Confess*." *Der Spielfilm im ZDF*, no. 2 (1979):61.

Kass, Robert. "*I Confess*." *Films in Review* 4, no. 3 (March 1953):148, 150.

Knight, Arthur. "The star behind the camera." *Saturday Review* 36 (February 12, 1953):33–34.

Marineau, Jean-Claude. "Hitchcock's Quebec shoot." *Cinema Canada* (March 1985):18.

"A priest with a past." *Theatre Arts* 37, no. 4 (1953):89.

Rivette, Jacques. "L'art de la fugue." *Cahiers du Cinéma* 5, no. 26 (1953): 49–52.

Rosengren, Joan. "The after-effects of a crime." *American Photography* 47 (July 1953):16.

Sadoul, Georges. "A propos de mélodrame." *Lettres Françaises,* no. 472 (July 2, 1953):5.

Walsh, Moira. *"I Confess."* America 88: (March 28, 1953), 717–718.

Yacowar, Maurice. "Hitchcock's *I Confess.*" *Film Heritage* 8, no. 2 (Winter 1973):19–24.

902   *Dial M for Murder*

Chaumeton, Etienne. "Hitchcock presque parfait?" *Cinéma 55* (Paris), no. 4 (March 28, 1955):67–68.

Coleman, Jon. *"Dial M for Murder."* New Statesman 106 (August 5, 1983):30.

Collet, Jean. *"Dial M. for Murder."* Télérama 621 (December 10, 1961).

Combs, R. "In the picture: Hitch in 3D." *Sight and Sound* 50, no. 2 (1981):82.

"Le crime était presque parfait." Amis du Film et de la Télévision, no. 201 (February 1973):42.

Crowther, Bosley. *"Dial M for Murder."* New York Times (May 29, 1954):13.

Dahan, L. "Quatre films anglais d'Hitchcock." *Cinématographe,* no. 23 (January 1977):35–36.

"Dial ham for murder, Hitch is still his own best actor." *Life* 36 (May 24, 1954):126, 129.

"Dial M for Murder." Catholic World 179 (June 1954):222–223.

"Dial M for Murder." France Observateur 248 (February 10, 1955).

Doniol-Valcroze, Jacques. "Double détente." *Cahiers du Cinéma* 8, no. 44 (1955):49–51.

Duarte, F. "Revisao de Hitchcock." *Celuloide* 27, no. 335 (May 1982):14–16.

Harvey, Evelyn. *"Dial M for Murder:* Hollywood's master of murder breaks open his bag of tricks for his first 3-D film." *Collier's Magazine* 133 (June 11, 1954):90–91.

"Hitchcock." *Sight and Sound* 52, no. 1 (1982):32–33.

Hoberman, J. *Artforum* 18 (Summer 1980):79.

Ibert, Serge. *"Dial M for Murder."* Téléciné 46 (1955).

Jamison, Barbara Berch. "3-D spells murder for Alfred Hitchcock." *New York Times* 11 (October 1953):Section 2, p. 5.

Lannes-Lacroutz, M. *Cinématographe,* no. 80 (July–August 1982):59–61.

May, Derwent. *"Dial M for Murder."* Sight and Sound 24, no. 2 (1954):89–90.

Philippon, Alain. "Preparez vos lunettes." *Cahiers du Cinéma,* no. 338 (July-August, 1982):iv.

Rabourdin, D. *"Le crime était presque parfait."* Cinéma 82, no. 283–284 (July-August 1982):101.

Sadoul, Georges. "Opération Hitchcock: *Le crime était presque parfait,* mélodrame de Hitchcock, photographié par Robert Burks." *Lettres Françaises* 555 (February 10, 1955):6.

Sarris, Andrew. "Deep threat." *Village Voice* 25 (March 31, 1980):43.

Sondheim, Steve. *"Dial M for Murder." Films in Review* 5, no. 6 (1954):302–303.

Straub, Jean Marie. *"Dial M for Murder." Radio, Cinéma, Télévision* 268 (March 6, 1955).

Walsh, Moira. *"Dial M for Murder." America* 91 (June 5, 1954):287.

903   *Rear Window*

Arlaud, R. M. "L'antiscope." *Combat* (April 1, 1955).

Baroncelli, Jean de. *"Rear Window." Le Monde* (April 5, 1955).

Bornemann, Ernest. *"Rear Window." Films and Filming* 1, no. 2 (November 1954):18.

Canby, Vincent. *"Rear Window*—still a joy." *New York Times* 133 (October 9, 1983):Section 2, p. 21, col. 1.

Crowther, Bosley. "Mr Hitchcock peeps: A *Rear Window* view seen at the Rivoli." *New York Times* (August 5, 1954):18.

Crowther, Bosley. "A point of view: Hitchcock's *Rear Window* provokes contrast of this and other films." *New York Times* (August 15, 1954):Section 2, p. 1.

Daix, Josette. *"Rear Window." Lettres Françaises* 563 (April 7, 1955).

Delpeut, P. *"Rear Window." Skrien,* no. 110 (September 1981).

Garson, Claude. *"Rear Window." L'Aurore* (April 1, 1955).

Hartung, Philip T. "Look now." *Commonweal* 60 (August 13, 1954):463.

Kuyper, E. de. *"Rear Window." Skrien* (September 1981):11.

M., J. "Courrier des lecteurs." *Cahiers du Cinéma,* no. 50 (1955):56–57.

May, Derwent. *"Rear Window." Sight and Sound* 24, no. 2 (October-December 1954):89–90.

McCarten, John. "Hitchcock confined again." *New Yorker* 30 (August 7, 1954): 50–51.

"Peeping Tom spots a killer." *Life* 37, no. 7 (August 16, 1954):88–90.

Phillips, Louis. "Through a glass darkly: A consideration of Alfred Hitchcock's *Rear Window." Armchair Detective* 18, no. 2 (Spring 1985):190–193.

"Rear Window." Ecran Français 147 (March 1955).

"Rear Window." Catholic World 179 (August 1954):383.

"Rear Window." Time 64 (August 2, 1954):65–67.

"Rear Window." France Observateur 256 (April 7, 1955).

"Rear Window." Newsweek 44 (August 9, 1954):80–81.

"Rear Window." Radio, Cinéma, Télévision 296 (September 18, 1955).

"Rear Window." Saturday Review 37 (August 21, 1954):31.

"Rear Window." Look 18 (September 21, 1954):50–51.

"Rear Window ruling favors Woolrich story rights-holder." *Variety* (January 4, 1989):3.

Rose, Lloyd. "Alfred again." *Atlantic* 252, no. 4 (October 1983):100–102.

Rother, R. "Der maennliche Zuschauer in Hitchcock's *Rear Window* und *Vertigo.*" *Filmwaerts,* no. 8 (September 1989):14–17.

Salachas, Gilbert. *"Rear Window." Téléciné,* no. 48–49 (1955).

Sarris, Andrew. "The critical anatomy of Alfred Hitchcock." *Village Voice* 28 (October 18, 1983):57.

Skytte, A. "Gensyn med Hitchcock." *Kosmorama,* no. 168 (August 1984): 77–82.

Sondheim, Steve. *"Rear Window." Films in Review* 5, no. 8 (1954):427–429.

Verstraten, P. "Close-up: Grace Kelly en James Stewart in *Rear Window.*" *Skrien,* no. 154 (Summer 1987):25.

Yvoire, Jean de. *"Rear Window." Radio, Cinéma, Télévision* 274 (April 17, 1955).

904   *To Catch a Thief*

Baker, Peter. *"To Catch a Thief." Films and Filming* 2, no. 3 (1955):16.

Bazin, André. "Maître l'humor plus que de l'angoisse; Alfred Hitchcock tourne en France avec Cary Grant." *Radio, Cinéma, Télévision* 235 (July 18, 1954).

Bazin, André. *"To Catch a Thief." Radio, Cinéma, Télévision* 312 (January 8, 1956).

"Chase on the Riviera." *Newsweek* 46 (January 8, 1955):57.

Crowther, Bosley. "Cat man out topaz: Grant is ex-burglar in Hitchcock thriller." *New York Times* (August 5, 1955):14.

Ferrini, F. *"To Catch a Thief." Cinema e Film,* no. 10 (1969–1970).

Galbraith, Harrison. *"To Catch a Thief." Films in Review* 6–7 (1955):345–346.

Goute, Jean-Yves. "Mettre en suspense." *Cahiers du Cinéma* 10, no. 55 (1956):32–33.

Houston, Penelope. *"To Catch a Thief." Sight and Sound* 25, no. 3 (Winter 1955–1956):150.

Kass, Robert. *"To Catch a Thief." Catholic World* 181 (September 1955):462.

Loinod, Etienne. *"To Catch a Thief." Cahiers du Cinéma* 9, no. 51 (1955): 12–13.

Murnaghan, Brigid. *"To Catch a Thief." Village Voice* 1, no. 3 (November 9, 1955):6.

Rogow, Lee. "Jack and Grace." *Saturday Review* 38 (August 27, 1955):23.

Sadoul, Georges. *"To Catch a Thief." Lettres Françaises* 600 (December 29, 1955).

Schwartz, Delmore. *"To Catch a Thief." New Republic* 133 (November 28, 1955):21–22.

"To Catch a Thief." Films in Review 6, no. 7 (August–September 1955):346.

"To Catch a Thief." Time 66 (August 15, 1955):58.

"*To Catch a Thief.*" *Ecran Français* 160 (1956).

Walsh, Moira. "*To Catch a Thief.*" *America* 93 (August 6, 1955):460.

905   *The Trouble with Harry*

Arnold, Gary. "*The Trouble with Harry.*" *Washington Post* 107 (May 19, 1984):Section C, p. 7, col. 5.

Crowther, Bosley. "*The Trouble with Harry:* Whimsical film from Hitchcock at Paris." *New York Times* (October 18, 1955):46.

Demonsablon, Philippe. "Tueurs à gags." *Cahiers du Cinéma* 10, no. 58 (1956):40.

Domarchi, Jean. "Humain, trop humain . . ." *Cahiers du Cinéma* 10, no. 58 (1956):38–40.

Hart, Henry. "*The Trouble with Harry.*" *Films in Review* 6, no. 9 (November 1955):465–466.

Hartung, Philip T. "Father, dear father, come home with me now." *Commonweal* 63 (November 11, 1955):142–143.

Houston, Penelope. "*The Trouble with Harry.*" *Sight and Sound* 26, no. 1 (Summer 1956):30–31.

Mannock, P. O. "*The Trouble with Harry.*" *Films and Filming* 2, no. 8 (May 1956):21.

Rivette, Jacques. "Faut-il brûler Harry?" *Cahiers du Cinéma* 10, no. 58 (1956):41.

Rohmer, Eric. "Castigat ridendo." *Cahiers du Cinéma* 10, no. 58 (1956): 36–38.

Sarris, Andrew. "Films in focus: Thoughts on Bresson and Hitchcock." *Village Voice* 29 (April 10, 1984):41.

"*The Trouble with Harry.*" *Ecran Français* 160 (May 1956).

"*The Trouble with Harry.*" *Catholic World* 182 (December 1955):218–219.

"*The Trouble with Harry.*" *Télérama* 623 (March 4, 1962).

"*The Trouble with Harry.*" *Téléciné* 59 (August 7, 1956).

"*The Trouble with Harry.*" *Lettres Françaises* 612 (February 22, 1956).

"*The Trouble with Harry.*" *France Observateur* 306 (March 22, 1956).

"*The Trouble with Harry.*" *Radio, Cinéma, Télévision* 323 (March 25, 1956).

906   *The Man Who Knew Too Much* (1955)

Acot-Mirande, Pierre. "*The Man Who Knew Too Much.*" *Téléciné* 63 (January-February 1957).

Alpert, Hollis. "Thrills and spills." *Saturday Review* 39 (May 26, 1956):25.

Carlini, Fabio. "*The Man Who Knew Too Much.*" *Cinema e Film*, no. 10 (1969–1970).

Crowther, Bosley. "At the old stand: Hitchcock's *The Man Who Knew Too Much* bows." *New York Times* (May 17, 1956):37.

Hartung, Philip T. "A little learning is." *Commonweal* 64 (May 25, 1956):204.

H[oveyda], F[ereydoun]. *"The Man Who Knew Too Much."* *Cahiers du Cinéma* 10, no. 60 (1956):13.

"A hair-raiser in a concert hall: Hitchcock movie sets its suspense to music." *Life* 40, no. 17 (April 23, 1956):95–96.

Houston, Penelope. "A Hitchcock double." *Sight and Sound* 26, no. 1 (1956):30–31.

Huret, Marcel. *"The Man Who Knew Too Much."* *Radio, Cinéma, Télévision* 353 (October 21, 1956).

Kass, Robert. *"The Man Who Knew Too Much."* *Catholic World,* 142 (May 18, 1956).

Magnan, Henry. *"L'homme qui en savait trop*: J'en sais trop sur Hitchcock . . . (am.)." *Lettres Françaises,* no. 640 (October 11, 1956):6.

"The Man Who Knew Too Much." *Ecran Français* 165 (November 1956).

"The Man Who Knew Too Much." *Télérama* 608 (September 10, 1961).

"The Man Who Knew Too Much." *Arts* 588 (October 10, 1956).

"The Man Who Knew Too Much.: This is director Hitchcock's favorite among suspense thrillers." *Look* 20 (May 29, 1956):98–99.

"The Man Who Knew Too Much." *Films in Review* 7, no. 6 (1956):285–286.

Mannock, P. L. *"The Man Who Knew Too Much."* *Films and Filming* 2, no. 10 (1956):23.

"Mystery and master." *Newsweek* 47 (May 28, 1956):106–107.

Walsh, Moira. *"The Man Who Knew Too Much."* *America* 95 (May 26, 1956):231–232.

Whitehall, Richard. *"The Man Who Knew Too Much."* *Films and Filming* 9, no. 1 (1962):39.

907   *The Wrong Man*

Alpert, Hollis. *"The Wrong Man."* *Saturday Review* 40 (January 19, 1957):49.

"Court is turned into a movie set; Hitchcock films noted case of mistaken identity at site of the trial in Queens." *New York Times* (April 9, 1956):21.

Esterow, Milton. "All around the town with *The Wrong Man;* Hitchcock troupe shoots new thriller at surface and underground sites." *New York Times* (April 29, 1956):Section 2, p. 7.

Gay, Ken. *"The Wrong Man."* *Films and Filming* 3, no. 7 (1957):26.

Hartung, Philip T. *"The Wrong Man."* *Commonweal* 65 (January 25, 1957):434.

Houston, Penelope. *"The Wrong Man."* *Sight and Sound* 26, no. 4 (1956–1957):211.

Hume, Veronica. *"The Wrong Man."* *Films in Review* 8, no. 1 (January 1957):33–34.

"Iceberg of chills." *Newsweek* 49 (January 7, 1957):68.

Patalas, Enno. *"The Wrong Man."* *Filmkritik* 1, no. 9 (1957):131–134.

Walsh, Moira. *"The Wrong Man."* *America* 96 (January 5, 1957):399.

Weiler, A. H. "Suspense is dropped in *The Wrong Man.*" *New York Times* (December 24, 1956):8.

"The Wrong Man." Der Spielfilm im ZDF, no. 2 (1979):57.

908 *Vertigo*

Beylie, C. *"Vertigo." Cinématographe,* no. 59 (July-August 1980):49–50.

Bitomsky, H. *"Vertigo." Filmkritik* 24 (June 1980):244–247.

Bitomsky, Hartmut. "Sequenzbeschreibungen; Die Verführung." *Filmkritik* 24, no. 6 (1980):270–272.

Browne, Jeremy. *"Vertigo." Films in Review* 9, no. 6 (June-July 1958):333–335.

"Chill chase of a blonde." *Life* 44 (June 23, 1958):57–58.

Conrad, Derek. *"Vertigo." Films and Filming* 4, no. 12 (September 1958):25.

Crowther, Bosley. *"Vertigo." New York Times* (May 29, 1958):24.

Ebert, J. "Sequenzbeschreibungen." *Filmkritik* 24 (June 1980):261–273.

Enckell, Henrik. "Det orfiska uppdraget i *Vertigo." Kulturtidskriften HORISONT* 34, no. 3 (1987):40–47.

Farocki, H. "Schuss-Gegenschuss: der wichtigste Ausdruck im wertgesetz Film." *Fernseh- und Kino-Technik* 25 (November-December 1981):507–516.

G[rob], N[orbert]. *"Vertigo." Filme* 1, no. 1 (1980):10–11.

Giacci, V. *"Vertigo." Filmcritica* 30, no. 300 (November-December 1979):457.

Hartung, Philip T. "What did you have in mind?" *Commonweal* 68 (June 6, 1958):255–256.

Haskell, Molly. *"Vertigo." Village Voice* 16, no. 23 (June 10, 1971):69–70, 73.

Henreichs, Klaus. "Sequenzbeschreibungen; Das Scharnier." *Filmkritik* 24, no. 6 (1980):272–279.

"The Hitchcock twist." *Newsweek* 51 (June 2, 1958):91.

Houston, Penelope. *"Vertigo." Sight and Sound* 27, no. 6 (Autumn 1958):319.

Keeler, P. "Letters." *Films in Review* 39 (February 1988):126.

Kotulla, Thedor. *"Vertigo." Filmkritik* 3, no. 3 (1959):77–80.

Malmberg, C. J. "Legenden, minnet och begaret: En studie i Hitchcocks *Vertigo." Chaplin* 27, no. 4 (no. 199) (1985):210–218.

Maslin, Janet. *"Vertigo* still gives rise to powerful emotions." *New York Times* 133 (January 15, 1984):Section 2, p. 19, col. 1.

Rohmer, Eric. "L'hélice et l'idée." *Cahiers du Cinéma* no. 357 (March 1984):24–27.

Rohmer, Eric. "L'hélice et l'idée." *Cahiers du Cinéma* 16, no. 93 (1959):48–51.

Sarris, Andrew. *"Vertigo." Village Voice* 9, no. 14 (January 23, 1964):13.

Schupp, Patrick. *"Vertigo." Séquences,* no. 101 (July 1980):25–26.

"Vertigo." Filmkritik 24 (June 1980):242–243.

"Vertigo." Catholic World 187 (August 1958):384.

"Vertigo." Saturday Review 41 (July 7, 1958):25.

Walsh, Moira. *"Vertigo." America* 99 (June 7, 1958):319.

## 909	*North by Northwest*

Alpert, Hollis. "Hitchcock as humorist." *Saturday Review* 42 (July 18, 1959):24.

Baker, Peter. *"North by Northwest." Films and Filming* 5, no. 12 (September 1959):25.

Bérubé, Robert Claude. *"North by Northwest." Séquences,* no. 101 (July 1980):26–27.

Boost, C. "Hitchcock blijft voortbestaan." *Skoop* 16, no. 4 (May–June 1980):52–53.

Bourget, Jean Loup. *"La Mort aux trousses." Positif,* no. 254–255 (May 1982):66–67.

Doherty, J. *"North by Northwest." CinemaScore,* no. 15 (Summer 1987):154.

Fitzpatrick, Ellen. *"North by Northwest." Films in Review* 10, no. 7 (1959):418–419.

Gehler, F. *"Der unsichtbare Dritte." Film & Fernsehen* 13, no. 1 (1985):26–27.

Gillett, John. *"North by Northwest" Sight and Sound* 28 (1959):154–155.

Gow, Gordon. *"North by Northwest" Films and Filming* 21 (October 1974): 50–55.

"Hitchcock's newest nightmare." *Look* 23 (August 18, 1959):90.

Houston, Penelope. *"North by Northwest." Sight and Sound* 28, no. 3–4 (Summer-Autumn 1959):168–169.

HRB "Jäger und Gejagter: Hitchcocks Agenten-Thriller *Der unsichtbare Dritte." Frankfurther Rundschau* (February 7, 1972):15.

Kauffman, Stanley. *"North by Northwest." New Republic* 141 (August 10, 1959):23.

"Latest murder pitch from Hitch." *Life* 47 (July 13, 1959):70–71.

Miller, A. I. *"North by Northwest." Film News* 37 (Winter 1980):37.

"North by Northwest." Skoop 16 (May-June 1980):24–38.

"North by Northwest." Good Housekeeping 149 (August 1959):24.

"North by Northwest." New York Times (August 7, 1959):28.

"North by Northwest." America 101 (August 22, 1959):639–640.

"North by Northwest." Der Spielfilm im ZDF, no. 2 (1979):59.

Patalas, Enno. *"North by Northwest." Filmkritik* 4, no. 1 (1960):13.

Requena, J. G. "En al umbral de lo inverosimil (con la muerte en los talones)." *Contracampo* 23 (September 1981):11–18.

Richardson, A. W. *"North by Northwest." Screen Education Yearbook* (1963):45–47.

Sator, Marc. "Les films a la télévision: *La mort aux trousses." Cahiers du Cinéma* no. 295 (December 1978):54–56.

"Slick, slick, slick." *Newsweek* 54 (July 27, 1959):88.

Vallerand, François. "Musique de films." *Séquences,* no. 104 (April 1981): 61–62.

Verstappen, W. "Analyse op de montagetafel: *North by Northwest* de meest Amusante Hitchcock." *Skoop* 16 (May–June 1980):24–38.

Weiler, A. H. "Suspense on screen: Opposing styles shown in two new pictures." *New York Times* (August 16, 1959):Section 2, p. 1.

910 **Psycho**

Baker, Peter. "*Psycho.*" *Films and Filming* 6, no. 12 (1960):20–21.

Boisset, Yves. "*Psycho.*" *Cinéma 61* (January 1961):52.

Cardulo, Bert. "Some notes on classic films." *University of Windsor Review* 21, no. 2 (1988):82.

Christensen, J. H. "*Psycho.*" *Levende Billeder* 6 (June-July 1980):4–9.

Conover, Shirley. "*Psycho.*" *Films in Review* 11, no. 7 (1960):426–427.

"Contrived spooks." *Newsweek* 55 (June 27, 1960):92.

Crowther, Bosley. "Sudden shocks." *New York Times* (June 17, 1960):37.

Durgnat, Raymond. "*Psycho.*" *Films and Filming* 8, no. 4 (1962):13–15, 41, 46.

Dyer, Peter John. "*Psycho.*" *Sight and Sound* 29, no. 4 (Autumn 1960): 195–196.

Hartung, Philip T. "All that a mother can mean." *Commonweal* 72 (September 9, 1960):469–470.

Kauffman, Stanley. "Several sons, several lovers." *New Republic* 143 (August 29, 1960):21–22.

MacDonald, Dwight. "*Psycho.*" *Esquire* (October 1960).

Patalas, Enno. "*Psycho.*" *Filmkritik* 4, no. 11 (1960):329–331.

Poitras, Huguette. "*Psycho.*" *Séquences,* no. 101 (July 1980):27.

Powell, Dilys. "From Hitchcock with love." *Sunday Times* (August 7, 1960).

"*Psycho.*" *America* 103 (July 9, 1960):443.

"*Psycho.*" *Time* 75 (June 27, 1960):37.

Sarris, Andrew. "Here at the village valium." *Village Voice* 25 (August 13, 1980):41.

———. "*Psycho.*" *Village Voice* 5, no. 42 (August 11, 1960):6.

"Shocker." *New York Times* (June 26, 1960):Section 2, p. 1, col. 6.

Thorpe, B. J. "*Psycho.*" *Cinefantastique* 16, no. 1 (1986):27–28.

Vian, Walt. "*Psycho.*" *Zoom,* no. 16 (1977):26–27.

911 **The Birds**

Arnold, Gary H. "Birds and gulls." *Moviegoer* 1 (Winter 1964):33–34.

Baker, Peter. "Peter Baker among Hitchcock's feathered friends." *Films and Filming* 9, no. 12 (1963):20.

Belie, D. de. "Les étonnants secrets du tournage des *Oiseaux* le célèbre film d'Alfred Hitchcock!" *Ciné Revue* (March 21, 1985):52–53.

"*The Birds.*" *America* 108 (April 20, 1963):589.

Bonneville, Leo. "*The Birds.*" *Séquences,* no. 101 (July 1980):27–28.

Callenbach, Ernest. *"The Birds." Film Quarterly* 16, no. 4 (Summer 1963): 44–46.

Conforti, A. "Sguardo e soggetto in *Gli uccelli* di Alfred Hitchcock." *Cineforum* 28, no. 271 (January-February 1988):45–49.

Crowther, Bosley. "Hitchcock's fine feathered fiends: Director's *The Birds* add horror to innocence: Shocks and thrills in a bizarre tale." *New York Times* (March 29, 1963):5.

Cumbow, Robert C. "Caliban in Bodega Bay." *Movietone News*, no. 41 (May 1975):3–8.

Fenin, George. "The face of '63, no. 2 USA." *Films and Filming* 6, no. 9 (1963):60.

Foote, Sterling de G. *"The Birds." Films in Review* 14, no. 5 (1963):309.

Gill, Brendan. *"The Birds." New Yorker* 39 (April 6, 1963):177.

Gregor, Ulrich. "Im Kino an der Croisette: Spektakulärer Cannes-Auftakt mit Hitchcocks Gruselfilm *Die Vögel." Frankfurter Rundschau* (May 13, 1963):7.

Hamilton, Jack. "Hitchcock's new Grace Kelly: Tippi Hedren." *Look* 26 (December 4, 1962):54–58.

Hartung, Philip T. "They is here." *Commonweal* 78 (April 12, 1963):73–74.

Heintze, Friedrich. *"The Birds." Filmstudio* 43 (May 1964):19–21.

"Hitchcock's monster." *Newsweek* 61 (April 8, 1963):92.

Johnson, Albert. "Echoes from *The Birds." Sight and Sound* 32 (Spring 1963):65–66.

Knight, Arthur. "Of violence and nonviolence." *Saturday Review* 46 (April 6, 1963):39.

Lesnik, B. *"Urocen." Ekran* 9, no. 7–8 (1984):11–12.

Magny, J. *"Les oiseaux." Cinéma 85* 4, no. 332 (December 4, 1985).

Patalas, Enno. *"The Birds." Filmkritik* 7, no. 1 (1963):522–525.

Rudkin, David. "Celluloid apocalypse: Notes on Hitchcock's *The Birds." Cinema* (Cambridge), no. 9 (1971):14.

Sarris, Andrew. *"The Birds." Village Voice* 8, no. 24 (April 4, 1963):15.

"They is here." *Time* 81 (April 5, 1963):61.

Thomas, John. *"The Birds." Film Society Review* 2 (September 1966):13–14.

Truffaut, François. "Ça photo du mois: *The Birds* d'Alfred Hitchcock." *Cahiers du Cinéma* 23, no. 137 (1962):33.

912   *Torn Curtain*

Apra, Adriano. *"Torn Curtain." Cinema e Film* 2 (1967).

Bruno, Edoardo. *"Torn Curtain." Filmcritica* (January-February 1966).

Combs, Richard. *"Torn Curtain." Monthly Film Bulletin* (British Film Institute) 42, no. 499 (1975):187–188.

Comerford, Adelaide. *"Torn Curtain." Films in Review* 17, no. 7 (1966):451.

Comolli, Jean-Louis. "Le rideau soulevé, retombé." *Cahiers du Cinéma* no. 186 (January 1967):36–39.

Comolli, Jean-Louis. *"Torn Curtain." Cahiers du Cinéma in English,* no. 10 (May 1967):51–55.

Erdin, Josef. *"Torn Curtain." Filmbulletin* 101 (1977):39.

Godet, Sylvain. "Angoisse derrière la vitre." *Cahiers du Cinéma* no. 186 (1967):39–42.

Godet, Sylvain. *"Torn Curtain." Cahiers du Cinéma in English,* no. 10 (May 1967):55–56.

Gottlieb, Stephen. *"Torn Curtain." Cahiers du Cinéma in English,* no. 10 (May 1967):59–60.

Gow, Gordon. *"Torn Curtain." Films and Filming* 13, no. 1 (October 1966): 9, 12.

Guérif, François. *"Le rideau déchiré." Lumière du Cinéma* 4 (1977):66–71, 82.

Hodgens, R. M. *"Torn Curtain." Film Quarterly* 20, no. 2 (Winter 1966–1967):63.

Houston, Penelope. *"Torn Curtain." Sight and Sound* 35, no. 4 (Autumn 1966):198.

Huber, Bob. *"Torn Curtain." Take One* 1, no. 1 (September-October 1966): 16–17.

Ladiges, Peter M. *"Torn Curtain." Filmkritik* 10, no. 12 (1966).

M[adsen], A[xel] "Hitchcock vu par son scénariste." *Cahiers du Cinéma* no. 175 (February 1966):14.

Narboni, Jean. *"Torn Curtain." Cahiers du Cinéma in English,* no. 10 (May 1967):51.

Nugent, John. "Interview at the time of production of *Torn Curtain." Newsweek* 67 (January 24, 1966):89.

Sarris, Andrew. *"Torn Curtain." Cahiers du Cinéma in English,* no. 10 (May 1967):58–59.

Steele, R. "Alfred Hitchcock's *Torn Curtain:* Fire and ice." *Filament,* no. 4 (1984):46–47.

Téchiné, Andre. "Les naufragés de l'autocar." *Cahiers du Cinéma* no. 186 (1967):42.

913 *Marnie*

Bogdanovich, Peter. *"Marnie." Cinema* (Beverly Hills) 2, no. 3 (October–November 1964):49.

Dyer, Peter John. *"Marnie." Sight and Sound* 33 (1964):199.

Färber, Helmut. *"Marnie." Filmkritik* 8, no. 11 (1964):589–591.

Johnson, William. *"Marnie." Film Quarterly* 18, no. 1 (Fall 1964):38–42.

Leroux, A. *"Marnie." Séquences,* no. 101 (July 1980):28.

"Marnie." Film Quarterly 18 (Fall 1964):38–42.

"Marnie." New Statesman 68 (July 10, 1964):62.

"Marnie." Spectator (August 14, 1964):213.

Martelli, L. *"Marnie." Filmcritica,* no. 153 (1965).

Sarris, Andrew. *"Marnie." Village Voice* 9, no. 38 (July 9, 1964):12–13.

Vrdlovec, Z. *"Marnie." Ekran* 9, no. 7–8 (1984):19–21.

Wharton, Flavia. *"Marnie." Films in Review* 15, no. 7 (1964):436–438.

Whitehall, Richard. *"Marnie." Films and Filming* 10, no. 1 (1964):23.

914   *Topaz*

Bernstein, Samuel. *"Topaz." Focus,* no. 6 (Spring 1970):26–27.

Bruno, Edoardo. *"Topaz." Filmcritica,* 202 (November-December 1969).

Canby, Vincent. *"Topaz." New York Times* (December 20, 1969):36.

Ebert, Jürgen. "Alfred Hitchcocks *Topas." Filmkritik* 14, no. 1 (1970):31–32.

Gow, Gordon. *"Topaz." Films and Filming* 16, no. 4 (January 1970):39–40.

Mazzocco, Robert. *"Topaz." New York Review of Books* 14, no. 4 (February 25, 1970):27–31.

McBride, Joseph. *"Topaz." Film Heritage* 5, no. 2 (1969):17–23.

Rothschild, Elaine. *"Topaz." Films in Review* 21, no. 2 (February 1970): 119–120.

Sarris, Andrew. "The thriller: *Topaz.*" In *The Primal Screen: Essays on Film and Related Subjects.* (New York: Simon & Schuster, 1973), pp. 183–185.

Schaub, Martin. *"Topaz." Fernsehen und Film* 8, no. 2 (1970):7.

Strick, Philip. *"Topaz." Sight and Sound* 39, no. 1 (Winter 1969–1970):49.

"Topaz." Fernsehen und Film 8, no. 1 (1970):2.

915   *Frenzy*

Amiel, M. "Un contre? . . . Non, un pas pour." *Cinéma* (Paris), no. 168 (July-August 1972):140.

Andrew, Nigel. *"Frenzy." Monthly Film Bulletin* (British Film Institute) 39 (1972):113.

Apon, A. *"Frenzy." Skrien,* no. 31 (November 1972):3–7.

Beylie, C. *"Frenzy* ou la traversée des apparences." *Ecran,* no. 7 (July–August 1972):9–12.

Bühler, W. E. "Alfred Hitchcock's *Frenzy." Filmkritik* 16, no. 12 (December 1972):626–643.

Calendo, J. *"Frenzy." Inter/View,* no. 24 (August 1972):49.

Canby, Vincent. *"Frenzy." New York Times* (June 22, 1972):48.

Cleave, A. "Other people's pictures: *Frenzy." Movie-Maker* 6, no. 8 (1972):546.

Comuzio, E. *"Frenzy." Cineforum* 8, no. 120 (February 1973):189–191.

"Conversations with Cecil: *Frenzy* would have been a whole new ball game." *Today's Filmmaker* 2, no. 3 (1973):33.

Cook, Page. "The sound track." *Films in Review* 23, no. 7 (August–September 1972):423–425.

C[hevassu], F. *"Frenzy." Revue du Cinéma/Image et Son,* no. 262 (June–July 1972):157.

C[orbucci], G. *"Frenzy." Cinema Nuovo,* no. 220 (November-December 1972):462.

Di Leo, F. "L'itinerario del dubbio: Nota su *Frenzy* di Alfred Hitchcock." *Filmcritica* 24 (January–February 1973):31–33.

Goodwin, M. *"Frenzy." Take One* 3, no. 5 (July 1972):16–17.

Hirsch, P. *"Frenzy." Kosmorama* 19, no. 111 (October 1972):10–15.

Hirsch, Peter. "Truffaut—Hitchcock—*Frenzy." Sunset Boulevard* 6 (1972):3–9.

Houston, P. *"Frenzy." Sight and Sound* 16, no. 3 (Summer 1972):166–167.

Johnson, William. "A fine *Frenzy." Film Comment* 8, no. 4 (November–December 1972):54–57.

Mack. *"Frenzy." Variety* 282, no. 7 (March 24, 1976):20.

Maurelli, G. *"Frenzy." Filmcritica* 55, no. 311 (January 1981).

McAsh, Ian. "Technical Hitch." *Films Illustrated* 1, no. 3 (September 1971):22–23.

Millar, Jeff. *"Frenzy." Film Heritage* 11, no. 4 (1976):41–42.

Rignall, J. *"Frenzy." Monogram,* no. 5 (1974):17–18.

Rudolf, F. *"Frenzy." Ekran* 11, no. 106–107 (1973):284–285.

Schupp, P. *"Frenzy." Sequence,* no. 71 (January 1973):38–39.

Thompson, Anne. "Photo by James Hamilton." *Film Comment* 18, no. 2 (March 1982):18.

Trevor, Joan Mac. *"Frenzy." Ciné Revue* 55 (December 4, 1975):42–45.

Willis, D. *"Frenzy." Photon,* no. 27 (1977):8–9.

916 *Family Plot*

"Alfred Hitchcock's *Family Plot." Films and Filming* 22, no. 11 (August 1976):14–15.

Allen, T. "Hitchcock's half-century grin." *America* 134 (April 3, 1976): 290–291.

Auster, Albert. *"Family Plot." Cineaste* 7, no. 3 (Fall 1976):39–40.

Bartholomew, D. *"Family Plot." Film Bulletin* 45 (April 1976):C.

Behar, H. "*Complot de famille." Revue du Cinéma/Image et Son,* no. 308 (September 1976):91–92.

Bodeen, DeWitt. *"Family Plot." Films in Review* 27, no. 5 (May 1976): 313–314.

Burg, Vinzenz B. *"Family Plot." Filmdienst* 32, no. 21 (1979).

Canby, Vincent. "Two exhilarating thrillers, plotted by Hitchcock and Nixon." *New York Times* 125 (April 11, 1976):Section 2, p. 1.

Cappabianca, A. *Filmcritica* 27, no. 267 (September 1976):231–232.

Cargin, P. *"Family Plot." Film* (Surrey) 41 (September 1976):3.

Coleman, J. "Gunning it." *New Statesman* 92 (August 20, 1976):250.

Combs, R. *"Family Plot." Monthly Film Bulletin* (British Film Institute) 43, no. 510 (July 1976):146–147.

Craven, Jenny. *"Family Plot." Films and Filming* 22, no. 11 (August 1976):34.

Crist, Judith. "Bergman and Hitchcock: Faces and plots." *Saturday Review* 3 (May 1, 1976):41.

Davay, P. *"Family Plot." Amis du Film et de la Télévision,* no. 245 (October 1976):20.

Duynslaegher, P. *"Family Plot." Film en Télévisie,* no. 233 (October 1976): 30–33.

Ecjquem, O. "La chasse au MacGuffin." *Positif,* no. 186 (October 1976):72–74.

Engelmeier, P. "Spannung aus dem *Familiengrab:* Alfred Hitchcock's neue Schauerkomoedie." *Film und Ton* 22 (December 1976):64.

Giacci, V. "Alfred Hitchcock: *Complotto di famiglia." Cineforum,* no. 161 (January 1977):42–53.

Grant, J. *"Complot de famille:* Les faux coupables." *Cinéma 76,* no. 212–213 (August–September 1976):255–258.

Greenspun, R. *Penthouse* 7 (August 1976):46–47.

Hatch, Robert. *"Family Plot." Nation* 222 (May 8, 1976):572–573.

Hurley, N. "Inside the Hitchcock vision." *America* 134 (June 12, 1976): 512–514.

"Image verpflichtet: Alfred Hitchcocks neuer Film *Family Plot. Weltwoche* (September 29, 1976):31.

Jacobs, D. "Hitchcock, winking once more." *Thousand Eyes Magazine,* no. 10 (May 1976):10–12.

Jungersen, F. *"Family Plot." Kosmorama* 22, no. 131 (1976):217.

Kauffman, Stanley. "Stanley Kauffman on films." *New Republic* 174 (April 24, 1976):16–17.

Klain, S. *"Family Plot." Independent Film Journal* 77 (April 14, 1976):7.

Laubvogel, Eberhard. *"Family Plot." Filmbeobachter,* no. 1 (1976):6–7.

Lehman, Ernest. "Lehman at large: He who gets Hitched." *American Film* 3, no. 7 (May 1978):8–9, 64.

Mack. *"Family Plot." Variety* 282 (May 25, 1976):20.

MacTrevor, J. *"Family Plot." Ciné Revue* 55 (December 4, 1975):42–45.

Maraval, P. *"Family Plot." Cinématographe,* no. 19 (June 1976):21.

McBride, J. "Alfred Hitchcock fields critics' questions, some pretty silly." *Variety* 282 (March 31, 1976):24.

McBride, J. *"Family Plot." Variety* 282, no. 7 (March 24, 1976):20.

Meyer, A. *"Familiengrab." Medium* 6 (October 1976):30.

Millar, J. *"Family Plot." Film Heritage* 11, no. 4 (1976):41–42.

Mogg, K. *"Family Plot." Cinema Papers,* no. 10 (September-October 1976):172–173.

Rosenbaum, J. *"Family Plot." Sight and Sound* 45, no. 3 (1976):189–190.

Salvat, L. "Alfred Hitchcock on the set of 'Family Plot.' " *Millimeter* 4, no. 1 (January 1976):10–13.

Schupp, P. *"Family Plot." Séquences* 21, no. 85 (July 1976):36–37.

Simon, J. "Movies: Old man out." *New York Magazine* 9 (April 19, 1976): 84–86.

Taylor, John Russell. "Hitchcock's 53rd." *Sight and Sound* 44, no. 4 (Autumn 1975):200–204.

Taylor, John Russell, M. Godwin and Donald Spoto. *"Family Plot." Take One* 5, no. 2 (May 1976):21–22, 24, 27, 29–30.

Tessier, M. *"Complot de famille." Ecran,* no. 50 (September 1976):57–58.

Thompson, K. *"Family Plot." Films Illustrated* 6 (September 1976):6.

Tudor, Andrew. "Visions of Hitchcock." *New Society* (August 26, 1976): 453–454.

Verstappen, W. *"Family Plot." Skoop* 12, no. 7 (1976):26–28.

Vian, Walter. *"Family Plot." Zoom* 19 (1976):13–15.

Viviani, C. *"Family Plot." Positif,* no. 183–184 (July-August 1976):88.

Westerbeck, C. "The screen: Past master." *Commonweal* 103 (May 7, 1976):306–307.

Wood, Michael. "Hitchcock laughs." *New York Review of Books* 23 (January 24, 1976):38–39.

Wood, Robin. "Avoiding the heart of darkness." *London Times Educational Supplement,* no. 3203 (October 22, 1976):70.

Zimmer, J. *"Complot de famille." Revue du Cinéma/Image et Son,* no. 320–321 (October 1977):68–69.

Zimmerman, P., and M. Kasindorf. "Hitchcock's no. 53." *Newsweek* 86 (July 14, 1975):78–80.

VI

OTHER FILM CREDITS AND FILM-RELATED ACTIVITY

This chapter includes Hitchcock's nondirectorial film work and the films he directed for television. While he is credited as the producer on many other episodes of "Alfred Hitchcock Presents," it is generally reported that this was in name only. His filming of the opening and closing segments of the television show apparently represent the largest portion of his participation in episodes that he did not direct.

917 *The Call of Youth* (1920)

Director	Hugh Ford
Production Company	Famous Players-Lasky
Inter-Titles Design	Alfred Hitchcock
Release Date	1920

918 *The Great Day* (1920)

Director	Hugh Ford
Production Company	Famous Players-Lasky
Inter-Titles Design	Alfred Hitchcock
Release Date	1920

919 *Appearances* (1921)

Director	Donald Crisp
Production Company	Famous Players-Lasky
Inter-Titles Design	Alfred Hitchcock
Release Date	1921

920   *Beside the Bonnie Brier Bush* (1921)

Director	Donald Crisp
Production Company	Famous Players-Lasky
Inter-Titles Design	Alfred Hitchcock
Release Date	1921

Other Title: *The Bonnie Brier Bush*

921   *Dangerous Lies* (1921)

Director	Paul Powell
Production Company	Famous Players-Lasky
Inter-Titles Design	Alfred Hitchcock
Release Date	1921

922   *The Mystery Road* (1921)

Director	Paul Powell
Production Company	Famous Players-Lasky
Inter-Titles Design	Alfred Hitchcock
Release Date	1921

923   *The Princess of New York* (1921)

Director	Donald Crisp
Production Company	Famous Players-Lasky
Inter-Titles Design	Alfred Hitchcock
Release Date	1921

924   *The Man from Home* (1922)

Director	George Fitzmaurice
Production Company	Famous Players-Lasky
Inter-Titles Design	Alfred Hitchcock
Release Date	1922

925   *Number 13* (1922)

Director	Alfred Hitchcock
Producer	Alfred Hitchcock
Production Company	Famous Players-Lasky
Screenwriter	Anita Ross
Photography	Rosenthal
Cast	Clare Greet, Ernest Thesiger

Other Title: *Mrs. Peabody*

Note. Uncompleted two-reeler. The film was produced when Famous Players-Lasky was entering financial difficulty, and was never fully funded. According to Peter Noble (entry 192), the title refers to a "tenement flat in a Peabody building."

926 *Perpetua* (1922)

Directors	John S. Robertson, Tom Geraghty
Production Company	Famous Players-Lasky
Inter-Titles Design	Alfred Hitchcock
Release Date	1922

Other Title: *Love's Boomerang* (U.S.)

927 *Spanish Jade* (1922)

Directors	John S. Robertson, Tom Geraghty
Production Company	Famous Players-Lasky
Inter-Titles Design	Alfred Hitchcock
Release Date	1922

928 *Tell Your Children* (1922)

Director	Donald Crisp
Production Company	International Artists (Gaumont)
Inter-Titles Design	Alfred Hitchcock
Release Date	1922

929 *Three Live Ghosts* (1922)

Director	George Fitzmaurice
Production Company	Famous Players-Lasky
Inter-Titles Design	Alfred Hitchcock
Release Date	1922

930 *Always Tell Your Wife* (1922)

Director	Hugh Croise *
Producer	Seymour Hicks
Production Company	Seymour Hicks Productions
Screenwriter	Hugh Croise
Cast	Ellaline Terriss, Stanley Logan, Gertrude McCoy
Release Date	1923

Note. * Hitchcock and producer Seymour Hicks took over the direction of the film when Hugh Croise became ill. Many sources indicate it was completed but some state it was abandoned. The British Film Insitute owns "Part I."

931 *The White Shadow* (1923)

Director	Graham Cutts
Assistant Director	Alfred Hitchcock
Producer	Michael Balcon
Production Company	Balcon-Saville-Freedman
Screenwriters	Michael Morton, Alfred Hitchcock
Editing	Alfred Hitchcock
Set Direction	Alfred Hitchcock

Cast	Betty Compson, Clive Brook, Henry Victor, Daisy Campbell, Olaf Hytten, A. B. Imeson
Filmed	at Islington Studios
Distributor	Wardour & F.
Release Date	1923

Other Title: *White Shadows* (U.S.)

932   *Woman to Woman* (1923)

Director	Graham Cutts
Assistant Director	Alfred Hitchcock
Producer	Michael Balcon
Production Company	Balcon-Saville-Freedman
Screenwriters	Graham Cutts, Alfred Hitchcock
Screenplay	based on the play by Michael Morton
Photography	Claude L. McDonnell
Editing	Alma Reville
Art Direction	Alfred Hitchcock
Cast	Betty Compson, Clive Brook, Josephine Earle, Marie Ault, M. Peter
Filmed	at Islington Studios
Distributor	Wardour & F.
Release Date	1923

933   *The Passionate Adventure* (1924)

Director	Graham Cutts
Assistant Director	Alfred Hitchcock
Producer	Michael Balcon
Production Company	Gainsborough
Screenwriters	Alfred Hitchcock, Michael Morton
Art Direction	Alfred Hitchcock
Cast	Alice Joyce, Clive Brook, Lillian Hall-Davies, Marjorie Daw, Victor McLaglen, Mary Brough, John Hamilton, J. R. Tozer
Filmed	at Islington Studios
Distributor	Gaumont
Release Date	1924

934   *The Prude's Fall* (1924)

Director	Graham Cutts
Assistant Director	Alfred Hitchcock
Producer	Michael Balcon
Production Company	Balcon-Saville-Freedman
Screenwriter	Alfred Hitchcock

Art Direction	Alfred Hitchcock
Cast	Betty Compson
Filmed	at Islington Studios
Distributor	Wardour & F.
Release Date	1924

935   *The Blackguard* (1925)

Director	Graham Cutts
Assistant Director	Alfred Hitchcock
Producer	Michael Balcon
Assistant Producer	Erich Pommer
Production Company	UFA/Gainsborough
Screenwriter	Alfred Hitchcock
Screenplay	based on a novel by Raymond Paton
Art Direction	Alfred Hitchcock
Cast	Walter Rilla, Bernard Goetzke, June Novak, Frank Stanmore, Martin Hertzberg, Rose Valiki
Filmed	at Neubabelsverg (UFA Studios)
Distributor	Wardour & F.
Length	9,400 feet
Release Date	1925

Other Title: *Die Prinzessen und der Geiger*

Note. According to Kirk Bond (entry 326), the sets for this film include an impressively large staircase leading up to a "palace in the sky."

936   *Lord Camber's Ladies* (1932)

Director	Benn W. Levy
Producer	Alfred Hitchcock
Production Company	British International
Screenwriter	Benn W. Levy
Cast	Gertrude Lawrence, Nigel Bruce, Benita Hume, Sir Gerald Du Maurier
Release Date	1933

937   *Men of the Lightship* (1941); *Target for Tonight* (1941)

Directors	David MacDonald; Harry Watt
Production Company	British Ministry of Information
Editing (of U.S. versions)	Alfred Hitchcock
Distributors (U.S.)	20th Century-Fox; Warner Bros.
Release Date	1941

Note. Hitchcock apparently supervised the reediting for the U.S. market of these two British war documentaries. According to M. Walker (entry 699), "*The Hollywood Reporter* of 12/23/40 reports that AH was winding up cutting and dubbing on a film called *Lightship 61*. Evidently, this referred to his preparing a version of *Men of the Lightship* for the U.S. market." Hitchcock's name does not appear on the published credits for either title.

938 *Revenge*

Director	Alfred Hitchcock
Assistant Director	Jack Corrick
Producer	Alfred Hitchcock
Production Company	Shamley Productions
Screenwriter	Francis Cockrell *
Screenplay	based on story by Samuel Blas
Photography	John L. Russell, Jr.
Editing	Richard G. Wray, Edward W. Williams
Art Direction	Martin Obzina
Set Direction	James S. Redd
Music	Stanley Wilson
Costumes	Vincent Dee
Production Assistant	Joan Harrison
Cast	Ralph Meeker, Vera Miles, Frances Bavier, Ray Montgomery, John Gallaudet, Ray Teal, Norman Willis, John Day, Lillian O'Malley, Herbert Lytton
Distributor	CBS
Running Time	25 min.
Air Date	October 2, 1955

Notes. 1st episode of "Alfred Hitchcock Presents." * A. I. Bezzerides is sometimes listed as writer.

939 *Breakdown*

Director	Alfred Hitchcock
Assistant Director	James Hogan
Producer	Alfred Hitchcock
Production Company	Shamley Productions
Screenwriters	Louis Pollock, Francis Cockrell
Screenplay	based on story by Louis Pollock
Photography	John L. Russell, Jr.
Editing	Richard G. Wray, Edward W. Williams
Art Direction	Martin Obzina
Set Direction	James S. Redd
Music	Stanley Wilson
Costumes	Vincent Dee
Production Assistant	Joan Harrison
Cast	Joseph Cotton, Raymond Bailey, Forrest Stanley, Lane Chandler, Harry Shannon, Marvin Press, Murray Alper, James Edwards, Mike Ragan, Jim Weldon, Richard Newton, Aaron Spelling, Harry Landers, Elzie Emanuel, Ralph Peter

Distributor	CBS
Running Time	25 min.
Air Date	November 13, 1955

Note. 7th episode of "Alfred Hitchcock Presents."

940   *The Case of Mr. Pelham*

Director	Alfred Hitchcock
Assistant Director	Jack Corrick
Producer	Alfred Hitchcock
Production Company	Shamley Productions
Screenwriter	Francis Cockrell
Screenplay	based on story by Anthony Armstrong
Photography	John L. Russell, Jr.
Editing	Richard G. Wray, Edward W. Williams
Music	Stanley Wilson
Costumes	Vincent Dee
Production Assistant	Joan Harrison
Cast	Tom Ewell, Raymond Bailey, Kirby Smith, Kay Stewart, John Compton, Jan Arvan, Norman Willis, Tim Graham, Justice Watson, Richard Collier, Diane Brester, Major Sam Harris
Distributor	CBS
Running Time	25 min.
Air Date	December 4, 1955

Note. 10th episode of "Alfred Hitchcock Presents."

941   *Back for Christmas*

Director	Alfred Hitchcock
Assistant Director	Richard Birnie
Producer	Alfred Hitchcock
Production Company	Shamley Productions
Screenwriter	Francis Cockrell
Screenplay	based on story by John Collier
Photography	John L. Russell, Jr.
Editing	Richard G. Wray, Edward W. Williams
Art Direction	Martin Obzina
Set Direction	Ralph Sylos
Music	Stanley Wilson
Costumes	Vincent Dee
Production Assistant	Joan Harrison

Cast	John Williams, Isabel Elsom, A. E. Gould-Porter, Gavin Muir, Katherine Warren, Gerald Hamer, Irene Tedrow, Ross Ford, Theresa Harris, Mollie Glessing, Lily Kembel-Cooper
Distributor	CBS
Running Time	25 min.
Air Date	March 4, 1956

Note. 23rd episode of "Alfred Hitchcock Presents."

942   *Wet Saturday*

Director	Alfred Hitchcock
Assistant Director	Jack Corrick
Producer	Alfred Hitchcock
Production Company	Shamley Productions
Screenwriter	Marian Cockrell
Screenplay	based on story by John Collier
Photography	John L. Russell, Jr.
Editing	Edward W. Williams, Richard G. Wray
Art Direction	Martin Obzina
Set Direction	James S. Redd
Music	Stanley Wilson
Costumes	Vincent Dee
Production Assistant	Joan Harrison
Cast	Sir Cedric Hardwicke, John Williams, Kathryn Givney, Jerry Barclay, Tita Purdom, Irene Lang
Distributor	CBS
Running Time	25 min.
Air Date	September 30, 1956

Note. 40th episode of "Alfred Hitchcock Presents."

943   *Mr. Blanchard's Secret*

Director	Alfred Hitchcock
Assistant Director	Richard Birnie
Producer	Alfred Hitchcock
Production Company	Shamley Productions
Screenwriter	Sarett Rudley
Screenplay	based on story by Emily Neff
Photography	John L. Russell, Jr.
Editing	Richard G. Wray, Edward W. Williams
Art Direction	John Lloyd
Set Direction	James Walters
Music	Stanley Wilson

Costumes	Vincent Dee
Production Assistant	Joan Harrison
Cast	Mary Scott, Robert Horton, Dayton Lummis, Meg Mundy, Eloise Hardt
Distributor	CBS
Running Time	25 min.
Air Date	December 23, 1956

Note. 52nd episode of "Alfred Hitchcock Presents."

944   *One More Mile to Go*

Director	Alfred Hitchcock
Assistant Director	Hilton Green
Producer	Alfred Hitchcock
Production Company	Shamley Productions
Screenwriter	James P. Cavanagh
Screenplay	based on story by F. J. Smith
Photography	John L. Russell, Jr.
Editing	Richard G. Wray, Edward W. Williams
Art Direction	John Lloyd
Set Direction	Ralph Sylos
Music	Stanley Wilson
Costumes	Vincent Dee
Production Assistant	Joan Harrison
Cast	David Wayne, Louise Larrabee, Steve Brodie, Norman Leavitt
Distributor	CBS
Running Time	25 min.
Air Date	April 7, 1957

Note. 67th episode of "Alfred Hitchcock Presents."

945   *Four O'Clock*

Director	Alfred Hitchcock
Assistant Director	Hilton Green
Producer	Alfred Hitchcock
Production Company	Shamley Productions
Screenwriter	Francis Cockrell
Screenplay	based on story by Cornell Woolrich
Photography	John L. Russell, Jr.
Editing	Richard G. Wray, Edward W. Williams
Art Direction	John Lloyd
Set Direction	James S. Redd
Music	Stanley Wilson
Costumes	Vincent Dee
Production Assistant	Joan Harrison

Cast

E. G. Marshall, Nancy Kelly, Richard Long, Tom Pittman, Dean Stanton, Charles Seel, Vernon Rich, Brian Corcoran, David Armstrong, Juney Ellis, Chuck Webster, Jesslyn Fox

Distributor NBC
Running Time 50 min.
Air Date September 30, 1957

Note. 1st episode of "Suspicion."

946   *The Perfect Crime*

Director Alfred Hitchcock
Assistant Director Hilton Green
Producer Joan Harrison
Production Company Shamley Productions
Screenwriter Stirling Silliphant
Screenplay based on story by Ben Ray Redman
Photography John L. Russell, Jr.
Editing Richard G. Wray, Edward W. Williams

Art Direction John Lloyd
Set Direction James S. Redd
Music Stanley Wilson
Costumes Vincent Dee
Cast Vincent Price, James Gregory, John Zaremba, Marianne Stewart, Gavin Gordon, Mark Dana, Charles Webster, Nick Nicholson, Therese Lyon

Distributor CBS
Running Time 25 min.
Air Date October 20, 1957

Note. 81st episode of "Alfred Hitchcock Presents."

947   *Lamb to the Slaughter*

Director Alfred Hitchcock
Assistant Director Hilton Green
Producer Joan Harrison
Production Company Shamley Productions
Screenwriter Roald Dahl
Photography John L. Russell, Jr.
Editing Richard G. Wray, Edward W. Williams

Art Direction John Lloyd
Set Direction James S. Redd
Music Stanley Wilson
Costumes Vincent Dee

Production Assistant	Norman Lloyd
Cast	Barbara Bel Geddes, Harold J. Stone, Allan Lane, Ken Clark, Robert C. Ross, William Keene, Thomas Wild, Otto Waldis
Distributor	CBS
Running Time	25 min.
Air Date	April 13, 1958

Note. 106th episode of "Alfred Hitchcock Presents."

948   *A Dip in the Pool*

Director	Alfred Hitchcock
Assistant Director	Hilton Green
Producer	Joan Harrison
Production Company	Shamley Productions
Screenwriter	Robert C. Dennis, Francis Cockrell
Screenplay	based on story by Roald Dahl
Photography	John F. Warren
Editing	Richard G. Wray, Edward W. Williams
Art Direction	John Lloyd
Set Direction	James S. Redd
Music	Stanley Wilson
Costumes	Vincent Dee
Production Assistant	Norman Lloyd
Cast	Keenan Wynn, Louise Platt, Philip Bourneuf, Fay Wray, Doris Lloyd, Doreen Lang, Ralph Clanton, Owen Cunningham, Barry Harvey, Ashley Cowan, Michael Hadlow, Margaret Curtis, Judith Brian, William Hughes
Distributor	CBS
Running Time	25 min.
Air Date	June 1, 1958

Note. 113th episode of "Alfred Hitchcock Presents."

949   *Poison*

Director	Alfred Hitchcock
Assistant Director	Hilton Green
Producer	Joan Harrison
Production Company	Shamley Productions
Screenwriter	Casey Robinson
Screenplay	based on story by Roald Dahl
Photography	John L. Russell, Jr.
Editing	Richard G. Wray, Edward W. Williams

Art Direction	John Lloyd
Set Direction	James S. Redd
Costumes	Vincent Dee
Production Assistant	Norman Lloyd
Cast	Wendell Corey, James Donald, Arnold Moss, Weaver Levy
Distributor	CBS
Running Time	25 min.
Air Date	October 5, 1958

Note. 118th episode of "Alfred Hitchcock Presents."

950 *Banquo's Chair*

Director	Alfred Hitchcock
Assistant Director	Hilton Green
Producer	Joan Harrison
Production Company	Shamley Productions
Screenwriter	Francis Cockrell
Screenplay	based on story by Rupert Croft-Cooke
Photography	John L. Russell, Jr.
Editing	Richard G. Wray, Edward W. Williams
Art Direction	John Lloyd
Set Direction	George Milo
Music	Frederick Herbert
Costumes	Vincent Dee
Production Assistant	Norman Lloyd
Cast	John Williams, Kenneth Haigh, Reginald Gardiner, Max Adrian, George Pelling, Tom P. Dillon, Hilda Plowright
Distributor	CBS
Running Time	25 min.
Air Date	May 3, 1959

Note. 146th episode of "Alfred Hitchcock Presents."

951 *Arthur*

Director	Alfred Hitchcock
Assistant Director	Hilton Green
Producer	Joan Harrison
Production Company	Shamley Productions
Screenwriter	James P. Cavanagh
Screenplay	based on story by Arthur Williams
Photography	John L. Russell, Jr.
Editing	Richard G. Wray, Edward W. Williams

Art Direction	John Lloyd
Set Direction	James S. Redd
Music	Frederick Herbert
Costumes	Vincent Dee
Production Assistant	Norman Lloyd
Cast	Laurence Harvey, Hazel Court, Robert Douglas, Barry G. Harvey, Patrick MacNee
Distributor	CBS
Running Time	25 min.
Air Date	September 27, 1959

Note. 154th episode of "Alfred Hitchcock Presents."

952   *The Crystal Trench*

Director	Alfred Hitchcock
Assistant Director	Hilton Green
Producer	Joan Harrison
Production Company	Shamley Productions
Screenwriter	Stirling Silliphant
Screenplay	based on story by A. E. W. Mason
Photography	John F. Warren
Editing	Richard G. Wray, Edward W. Williams
Art Direction	John Lloyd
Set Direction	Julia Heron
Music	Frederick Herbert
Costumes	Vincent Dee
Production Assistant	Norman Lloyd
Cast	James Donald, Patricia Owens, Harold O. Dyrenforth, Ben Astar, Oscar Beregi, Werner Klemperer, Frank Holms, Patrick MacNee, Eileen Anderson, Otto Reichow
Distributor	CBS
Running Time	25 min.
Air Date	October 4, 1959

Note. 155th episode of "Alfred Hitchcock Presents."

953   *Incident at a Corner*

Director	Alfred Hitchcock
Assistant Director	Hilton Green
Producer	Joan Harrison
Production Company	Shamley Productions
Screenwriter	Charlotte Armstrong from her novel
Photography	John L. Russell, Jr.

Editing	Richard G. Wray, Edward W. Williams
Art Direction	John Lloyd
Set Direction	George Milo
Music	Frederick Herbert
Production Assistant	Norman Lloyd
Cast	Paul Hartman, Vera Miles, George Peppard, Bob Sweeney, Alice Backes, Charity Grace, Leora Dana, Phil Ober, Warren Berlinger, Leslie Barrett, Mary Ellen Hokanson, Alexander Lockwood, Joe Flynn, Florence MacMichael, Jerry Paris, Joe Sullivan, Jack Albertson, Eve McVeagh, Barbara Beaird, Tyler McVey
Filmed	in Color
Distributor	NBC
Running Time	50 min.
Air Date	April 5, 1960

Note. 27th episode of "Ford Startime."

954   *Mr. Bixby and the Colonel's Coat*

Director	Alfred Hitchcock
Assistant Director	James H. Brown
Producer	Joan Harrison
Production Company	Shamley Productions
Screenwriter	Halsted Wells
Screenplay	based on story by Roald Dahl
Photography	John L. Russell, Jr.
Editing	David J. O'Connell, Edward W. Williams
Art Direction	Martin Obzina
Set Direction	James S. Redd
Music	Frederick Herbert
Costumes	Vincent Dee
Production Assistant	Norman Lloyd
Cast	Audrey Meadows, Les Tremayne, Stephen Chase, Sally Hughes, Madie Horman, Harry Cheshire, Howard Caine, Lillian Culver, Ted Jordan, Bernie Hamilton
Distributor	NBC
Running Time	25 min.
Air Date	September 27, 1960

Note. 191st episode of "Alfred Hitchcock Presents."

955 *The Horse Player*

Director	Alfred Hitchcock
Assistant Director	James H. Brown
Producer	Alfred Hitchcock
Production Company	Shamley Productions
Screenwriter	Henry Slesar from his story
Photography	John L. Russell, Jr.
Editing	David J. O'Connell, Edward W. Williams
Art Direction	Martin Obzina
Set Direction	John McCarthy; Julia Heron
Music	Joseph E. Romero
Costumes	Vincent Dee
Production Assistant	Joan Harrison
Cast	Claude Rains, Ed Gardner, Percy Helton, Kenneth MacKenna, Mike Ragan, William Newell, David Carlile, Ada Murphy, Jackie Carroll, John Yount
Distributor	NBC
Running Time	25 min.
Air Date	March 14, 1961

Note. 212th episode of "Alfred Hitchcock Presents."

956 *Bang! You're Dead*

Director	Alfred Hitchcock
Assistant Director	Wallace Worsely
Producer	Joan Harrison
Production Company	Shamley Productions
Screenwriter	Harold Swanton
Screenplay	based on story by Margery Vosper
Photography	John L. Russell, Jr.
Editing	David J. O'Connell, Edward W. Williams
Art Direction	Martin Obzina
Set Direction	John McCarthy, Julia Heron
Music	Joseph E. Romero
Costumes	Vincent Dee
Production Assistant	Norman Lloyd
Cast	Biff Elliott, Lucy Prentiss, Billy Mumy, Steve Dunne, Kelly Flynn, Dean Moray, Juanita Moore, Karl Lukas, Jeff Parker, Olan Soule, Joy Ellison, Scott Davey, Craig Duncan, Mary Grace Canfield, Thayer Burton, John Zaremba, Marta Kristen

Distributor	NBC
Running Time	25 min.
Air Date	October 17, 1961

Note. 230th episode of "Alfred Hitchcock Presents."

957   *I Saw the Whole Thing*

Director	Alfred Hitchcock
Assistant Director	Ronnie Rondel
Producer	Joan Harrison
Production Company	Shamley Productions
Screenwriter	Henry Slesar
Screenplay	based on story by Henry Cecil
Photography	Benjamin H. Kline
Editing	David J. O'Connell, Edward W. Williams
Art Direction	Martin Obzina
Set Direction	John McCarthy, Julia Heron
Music	Lyn Murray
Costumes	Vincent Dee
Production Assistant	Gordon Hessler
Cast	John Forsythe, Kent Smith, John Fiedler, Philip Ober, William Newell, John Zaremba, Barney Phillips, Willis Bouchey, Rusty Lane, Billy Wells, Robert Karnes, Maurice Manson, Ken Harp, Anthony Jochim
Distributor	NBC
Running Time	50 min.
Air Date	October 11, 1962

Note. 4th episode of "The Alfred Hitchcock Hour."

VII

ARCHIVAL RESOURCES

AUSTRALIA

958   Reference Office
       National Film Lending Collection
       National Library of Australia
       Parkes Place
       Canberra ACT 2600, Australia
Telephone: 06-262-1361
Fees: None
Access policy: Distribution library. Films available to organizations and groups
    for noncommercial use only.
Prints: All prints are 16mm: *The Lodger* (1926), *The Farmer's Wife* (1928), *The
    Manxman* (1928), *Blackmail* (1929), *The 39 Steps* (1935), *Young and
    Innocent* (1937), *The Lady Vanishes* (1938), *Jamaica Inn* (1939), *Foreign
    Correspondent* (1940), *Mr. and Mrs. Smith* (1941), *Suspicion* (1941), *Target
    for Tonight* (1941), *Shadow of a Doubt* (1943), *Strangers on a Train* (1951),
    I Confess (1953), *Dial M for Murder* (1954), *Rear Window* (1954), *The Wrong
    Man* (1956), *Vertigo* (1957), *Psycho* (1960), *The Birds* (1963), *Marnie* (1964)

BRAZIL

959   Cinemateca do Museu de Arte Moderna
       Av. Infante Dom Henrique 85 Caixa Postal 44
       20000 Rio de Janeiro, Brazil

Telephone: (21) 210.2188, ext. 33
Contact: Cosme Alves Netto, Ronald Monteiro
Hours of service: Monday through Friday 1:00 P.M. to 6:00 P.M.
Fees: None
Access policy: Call or write in advance.
Prints: 35mm prints: *Sabotage* (1936), *The Lady Vanishes* (1938). 16mm prints: *Suspicion* (1941), *Strangers on a Train* (1951), *The Man Who Knew Too Much* (1955)
Other material: Stills, pressbooks, clippings on numerous films

CANADA

960   Moving Image and Sound Archives
       National Archives of Canada
       344 Wellington St. Room 1014
       Ottawa, Ontario K1A ON3, Canada
Telephone: 613-996-6890, FAX: 613-995-6575
Contact: Caroline Forcier
Hours of service: 8:45 A.M. to 4:45 P.M. Monday through Friday
Fees: None; stills are reproduced for $8.00
Prints or video: *Blackmail* (1929), *Murder!* (1930), *The Man Who Knew Too Much* (1934), *The 39 Steps* (1935), *Sabotage* (1936), *Saboteur* (1942), *Jamaica Inn* (1939), *Rebecca* (1940), *Notorious* (1946) (plus trailer), *Rope* (1948), *Under Capricorn* (1949), *Strangers on a Train* (1951), *I Confess* (1953), *Dial M for Murder* (1954), *Rear Window* (1954), *To Catch a Thief* (1954), *The Trouble with Harry* (1954), *The Man Who Knew Too Much* (1955), *Psycho* (1960), *The Wrong Man* (1956), *Vertigo* (1957), *The Birds* (1963), *Torn Curtain* (1966), *Topaz* (1969), *Family Plot* (1976)
Other Material: The archives holds stills and clipping file material for most of the films.

961   Cinémathèque Québeçoise
       336 boul. de Maisonneuve Est
       Montréal, Québec, Canada
Telephone: 514-842-9763, FAX: 514-842-1816
Contact: Robert Daudelin, Curator of Film; René Bauclair, Librarian
Hours of service: 9 A.M. to 5 P.M. Monday through Friday; library is also open three evenings.
Fees: None for library or viewing table; unspecified charge for screening rooms
Access policy: In-house use only. Photocopiers available.
Prints: 16mm: *The 39 Steps* (1935), *Rebecca* (1940) in French, *Suspicion* (1941), *The Paradine Case* (1947) in French, *Marnie* (1964) in French
Scripts: *Rebecca* (1940), *Suspicion* (1941), *Notorious* (1946), *Rear Window* (1954), *Frenzy* (1972)
Other materials: Clippings on most of the films

DENMARK

962   Det Danske filmmuseum
      Store Søndervoldstræde K
      1419 Copenhagen, Denmark
Telephone: 31-57-65-00
Hours of service: Monday, Thursday, Friday, 12:00 to 4:00 P.M.; Tuesday, 12:00 to
   9:00 P.M.
Contact: Ib Monty, Director; Dan Nissen, Deputy Curator; Karen Jones, Head of
   Documentation
Fees: None, except for photocopying
Prints: 35mm: *The Lodger* (1926), *Blackmail* (1929), *The Man Who Knew Too
   Much* (1934), *The 39 Steps* (1935), *Sabotage* (1936), *Young and Innocent*
   (1937), *The Lady Vanishes* (1938), *Jamaica Inn* (1939), *Foreign Cor-
   respondent* (1940), *Rebecca* (1940), *Suspicion* (1941), *Spellbound* (1945),
   Notorious (1946), *Rope* (1948), *Dial M for Murder* (1954), *Rear Window*
   (1954), *To Catch a Thief* (1954), *The Trouble with Harry* (1954), *The Man
   Who Knew Too Much* (1955), *Vertigo* (1957), *Psycho* (1960), *The Birds*
   (1963), *Marnie* (1964), *Frenzy* (1972), *Family Plot* (1976)
Scripts: Some postproduction script material for films released in Denmark
Other material: Clipping files on films released in Denmark, containing mainly
   souvenir programs, press material, and newspaper clippings

FRANCE

963   Cinémathèque de Toulouse
      12 rue de Faubourg Bonnefoy
      31500 Toulouse, France
Telephone: 61-48-90-75
Contact: Guy-Claude Rochemont
Hours of service: Monday through Friday, 9:00 A.M. to 12:00 A.M., 1:00 P.M. to 6:00
   P.M.
Fees: None
Prints: There are prints in the archive, but specific inquiry is necessary.
Other material: Clipping files and posters for most of the films

SWEDEN

964   Documentation Department
      Svenska Filminstitutet
      Filmhuset, Box 27126
      102 51 Stockholm, Sweden
Telephone: (46-8) 65-11-00
Contact: Margareta Nordström

Hours of service: Monday through Thursday, 10 A.M. to 9 P.M.; Friday 10 A.M. to 5 P.M.

Access policy: Most collections are open to the public, but stills and posters are available for copying only. Special collections available for advanced academic study; inquire in advance.

Prints: "Holdings of the film archive are confidential."

Scripts: *Blackmail* (1929) dialogue sheets; *Number Seventeen* (1932) cutting continuity; *The 39 Steps* (1935) postproduction script; dialogue sheets; *Secret Agent* (1936) dialogue sheets; *Sabotage* (1936) dialogue sheets; postproduction script; *Young and Innocent* (1937) dialogue sheets; *Jamaica Inn* (1939) dialogue sheets; *Foreign Correspondent* (1940) dialogue sheets; *Rebecca* (1940) dialogue sheets; *Saboteur* (1942) dialogue sheets; *Shadow of a Doubt* (1943) script; *Notorious* (1946) dialogue sheets; cutting continuity; *The Paradine Case* (1947) script; *Rope* (1948) postproduction script; *I Confess.* (1953) postproduction script; *Dial M for Murder* (1954) postproduction script; dialogue sheets; *To Catch a Thief* (1954) script; *Rear Window* (1954) script; *The Trouble with Harry* (1954) dialogue sheets; *Vertigo* (1957) script; *North by Northwest* (1959) postproduction script; *Psycho* (1960) dialogue sheets; *The Birds* (1963) cutting continuity; postproduction script; *Marnie* (1964) cutting continuity; *Torn Curtain* (1966) postproduction script; cutting continuity; *Topaz* (1969) postproduction script; cutting continuity; *Frenzy* (1972) postproduction script; cutting continuity; *Family Plot* (1976) cutting continuity

UNITED KINGDOM

965   Library and Information Services
       British Film Institute
       21 Stephen Street
       London W1P 1PL, U.K.

Telephone: 071-255-1444, FAX: 071-436-7950

Hours of service: 10:30 A.M. to 5:00 P.M. Monday, Tuesday, Thursday, Friday; 1:30 P.M. to 8 P.M. Wednesday

Fees: 5 pounds daily charge, 25 pounds a year; reduced charge for students or members of the BFI

Scripts: *Blackmail* (1929) dialogue sheets; *Murder!* (1930) preproduction dated 5–5–30; *The Man Who Knew Too Much* (1934) shooting script; *The 39 Steps* (1935) shooting script; *Secret Agent* (1936) shooting script; *Sabotage* (1936) shooting script and three treatments; *The Lady Vanishes* (1938) release script; *Foreign Correspondent* (1940) continuity; *Rebecca* (1940) master dialogue continuity; *Mr. and Mrs. Smith* (1941) cutting continuity; *Spellbound* (1945) combined continuity, final shooting dated 9–45 with stills, and final shooting dated 7–45 with stills; *Notorious* (1946) combined continuity; *Stage Fright* (1949) release script; *Psycho* (1960) release dialogue script; *Frenzy* (1972) first revised screenplay dated 6–3–71, screenplay dated 7–21–71, export script dated 3–72

Other material: Large clipping file and book collections

966   National Film Archive
      British Film Institute
      21 Stephen Street
      London W1P 1PL, U.K.
Telephone: 071-255-1444, FAX: 071-436-7950
Contact: Jackie Morris
Hours of service: 9:45 A.M. to 6:00 P.M., Monday through Friday
Fees: 7 pounds per hour for viewing
Access policy: Call or write for appointment
Prints: 35mm: *Always Tell Your Wife,* Part 1 (1922), *The Lodger* (1926), *The Pleasure Garden* (1925), *Downhill* (1927), *Easy Virtue* (1927), *The Ring* (1927), *Champagne* (1928), *The Farmer's Wife* (1928), *The Manxman* (1928), *Blackmail* (1929), *Juno and the Paycock* (1929), *Elstree Calling* (1930), *Murder!* (1930), *Mary* (1931), *The Skin Game* (1931), *Number Seventeen* (1932), *Rich and Strange* (1932), *Waltzes from Vienna* (1933), *The Man Who Knew Too Much* (1934), *The 39 Steps* (1935), *Secret Agent* (1936), *Sabotage* (1936), *Young and Innocent* (1937), *The Lady Vanishes* (1938), *Jamaica Inn* (1939), *Foreign Correspondent* (1940), *Rebecca* (1940), *Saboteur* (1942), *Shadow of a Doubt* (1943), *Aventure Malgache* (1944), *Bon Voyage* (1944), *Lifeboat* (1944), *Spellbound* (1945), *Notorious* (1946), *The Paradine Case* (1947), *Rope* (1948), *Stage Fright* (1949), *Strangers on a Train* (1951), *I Confess* (1953), *Dial M for Murder* (1954), *The Man Who Knew Too Much* (1955), *The Wrong Man* (1956), *Vertigo* (1957), *The Birds* (1963), *Torn Curtain* (1966); 16mm: *Suspicion* (1941)

UNITED STATES
California

967   Library and Film Study Center
      Pacific Film Archive
      University Art Museum
      University of California, Berkeley
      2625 Durant Ave.
      Berkeley, California, U.S.A.
Telephone: 510-642-1437, FAX: 510-642-4889
Contact: Nancy Goldman, Lee Amazonas
Hours of service: 1:00 P.M. to 5:00 P.M. Monday through Friday
Fees: Library open to University Art Museum members and UC students. UAM membership is $35.00 annually, $25.00 for non-UC students. Film screenings available by appointment; fee is $15.00 for members, $25.00 for nonmembers
Prints: 35mm: *Easy Virtue* (1927), *The Paradine Case* (1947); 16mm: *Sabotage* (1936), *The Man Who Knew Too Much* (1955)
Other material: Clipping files are available on most of the films.

968   Archive Research and Study Center
      UCLA Film and Television Archive
      46 Powell Library
      Los Angeles, California 90024-1517, U.S.A.

Telephone: 310-206-5388

Hours of service: 8:30 A.M. to 5:00 P.M., Monday through Friday

Prints or video: *The Lodger* (1926), *Blackmail* (1929), *The Man Who Knew Too Much* (1934), *The 39 Steps* (1935), *Secret Agent* (1936), *Sabotage* (1936), *The Lady Vanishes* (1938), *Jamaica Inn* (1939), *Foreign Correspondent* (1940), *Rebecca* (1940), *Men of the Lightship* (1941) (short), *Mr. and Mrs. Smith* (1941), *Suspicion* (1941), *Target for Tonight* (1941), *Saboteur* (1942), *Shadow of a Doubt* (1943), *Forever and a Day* (1943), *Lifeboat* (1944), *Spellbound* (1945), *Notorious* (1946), *Rope* (1948), *Under Capricorn* (1949), *Strangers on a Train* (1951), *I Confess* (1953), *Dial M for Murder* (1954), *Rear Window* (1954), *To Catch a Thief* (1954), *The Trouble with Harry* (1954), *The Man Who Knew Too Much* (1955), *The Wrong Man* (1956), *Vertigo* (1957), *North by Northwest* (1959), *Psycho* (1960), *The Birds* (1963), *Marnie* (1964), *Topaz* (1969), *Frenzy* (1972)

969   Cinema-Television Library and Archives of Performing Arts
       Doheny Library, Room 206
       University of Southern California
       Los Angeles, California 90089-0182, U.S.A.

Telephone: 213-740-8906; Warner Bros. Archives: 213-748-7747

Contact: Steve Hanson, Head; Ned Comstock, Archives Assistant; Leith Adams, Warner Bros. Archivist

Hours of service: September through April: 8:30 A.M. to 10:00 P.M., Monday through Thursday; 8:30 A.M. to 5:00 P.M. Friday; 9 A.M. to 5 P.M. Saturday; 1 P.M. to 8 P.M. Sunday. May through August, 8:30 A.M. to 5 P.M., Monday through Saturday. Manuscript Room: 9 A.M. to 1 P.M. Monday through Friday; 9 A.M. to 1 P.M. Saturday.

Fees: Duplication facilities, $.10 per page, no copying of scripts. Archival material subject to copyright restrictions. Photographs, $20.

Access policy: Call or write for an appointment. Material should be requested at least two weeks in advance.

Scripts: *The Lady Vanishes* (1938), *Target for Tonight* (1941), *Spellbound* (1945), *Lifeboat* (1944), *Mr. and Mrs. Smith* (1941), *Notorious* (1946), *Stage Fright* (1949), *Strangers on a Train* (1951), *I Confess* (1953), *Dial M for Murder* (1954), *The Wrong Man* (1956), *Vertigo* (1957), *North by Northwest* (1959), *Psycho* (1960), *Family Plot* (1976)

Other Material: The Archives of Performing Arts contains a scrapbook for *Shadow of a Doubt* in the Joseph Cotton Collection, some production information on *Saboteur* and *Shadow of a Doubt* in the Universal Studio Collection, and some production information and correspondence on *Rope, Stage Fright,* and *I Confess* in the Jack L. Warner Collection.

Warner Bros. Archives: An index to the archives is available at the USC Cinema-Television Library (Los Angeles) as well as the Princeton University Library (Princeton, N.J.). Material from the East Coast office (primarily financial and distribution files) is located at Princeton; the files from the West Coast studio are at USC. There are extensive files at USC on *Rope* (1948), *Strangers on a Train* (1951), *The Wrong Man* (1956), *Dial M for Murder* (1954), *I Confess* (1953), and *Stage Fright* (1949). The file for each film consists of a research file (memos from the filmmakers to the research department at Warner Brothers and their responses), daily production

reports, a story file (memos before and during production about the screen-play and its source and all drafts), publicity files (these include pressbooks, news clippings, and press releases from the publicity department), legal files (story rights for most of the films and a separate legal file for the picture and the actors), publicity stills for each film and, for some of the films, set stills as well.

970   Margaret Herrick Library
        Academy of Motion Picture Arts and Sciences
        333 South La Cienega
        Beverly Hills, California 90211, U.S.A.
Telephone: 310-247-3020, 9 A.M. to 5 P.M., Monday through Friday
Contact: Requests regarding the Alfred Hitchcock collection described below should be addressed to the Archivist (for the papers), the Film Archivist (for films), and the Photograph Curator (for photographs) at the above address.
Hours of service: 10 A.M. to 6 P.M. Monday, Tuesday, Thursday, Friday
Fees: None for use of library. Duplication service for published material only. $10.00–$15.00 per photograph
Access policy: Photo identification required for use of library. Special Collections available by appointment only for "a bona fide research need."
Scripts: *Foreign Correspondent* (1940), *House across the Bay* (1940) (also treatment), *Rebecca* (1940), *Mr. and Mrs. Smith* (1941), *Lifeboat* (1944), *Spellbound* (1945), *Rope* (1948), *Rear Window* (1954), *To Catch a Thief* (1954), *The Trouble with Harry* (1954), *The Man Who Knew Too Much* (1955), *North by Northwest* (1959), *Psycho* (1960), *The Birds* (1963), *Marnie* (1964)
Other material: The Alfred Hitchcock Collection was donated to the Academy Foundation by Patricia Hitchcock O'Connell in 1984. It consists primarily of papers, photographs, and films relating to Hitchcock's career as a motion picture producer and director in the United States. For information on the small number of films available, contact the Film Archivist. An inventory to the papers, compiled by Barbara Hall and Valentin Almendarez under the supervision of Samuel A. Gill, Archivist, is available at the Academy Library. There is a separate inventory for the photographs.
The collection includes some publicity clippings, scrapbooks, appointment books, periodicals, books, audio tapes, record albums, awards, and plaques. Among the papers, the bulk of the material is scripts and production files for films produced after 1939. The script material usually consists of the original source material, story notes, synopses, screenplays in various drafts, final or shooting scripts, dialogue continuities, and, in some cases, trailer scripts and novelizations of the produced film. Production files usually consist of produc-tion correspondence, memos, casting records, call sheets, staff and crew lists, financial and legal records, location information, research material, music notes, editing and dubbing notes, and publicity and review clippings. Pro-duction files vary in completeness according to production studio: those for films made at Universal are the most complete, those for films made at Paramount less so. The smallest amount of material is in the files from the British films, Warner Bros, RKO, Selznick, United Artists, and 20th Century-Fox.

There are production files for *The 39 Steps* (1935), *The Lady Vanishes* (1938), *Jamaica Inn* (1939), *Foreign Correspondent* (1940), *Rebecca* (1940), *Men of the Lightship* (1941), *Mr. and Mrs. Smith* (1941), *Target for Tonight* (1941), *Saboteur* (1942), *Lifeboat* (1944), *Spellbound* (1945), *Notorious* (1946), *The Paradine Case* (1947), *Rope* (1948), *Under Capricorn* (1949), *Strangers on a Train* (1951), *I Confess* (1953), *Dial M for Murder* (1954), *Rear Window* (1954), *To Catch a Thief* (1954), *The Trouble with Harry* (1954), *The Man Who Knew Too Much* (1955), *The Wrong Man* (1956), *Vertigo* (1957), *North by Northwest* (1959), *Psycho* (1960), *The Birds* (1963), *Marnie* (1964), *Torn Curtain* (1966), *Topaz* (1969), *Frenzy* (1972), and *Family Plot* (1976). Other special collections contain screenplays, clipping files, and large photograph and book collections.

Scrapbooks usually contain clippings and reviews from both Britain and the United States. There are scrapbooks for *The Lodger* (1926), *Downhill* (1927), *Easy Virtue* (1927), *Blackmail* (1929), *Juno and the Paycock* (1929), *The Lady Vanishes* (1928), *Jamaica Inn* (1939), *Foreign Correspondent* (1940), *Rebecca* (1940), *Mr. and Mrs. Smith* (1941), *Suspicion* (1941), *Lifeboat* (1944), *The Birds* (1963), and *Torn Curtain* (1966).

Another large group of material consists of files relating to projects that were never completed. The largest files are those for projects begun after 1960. There are script and production files for *The Attorney, The Bramble Bush, The Dark Duty, Dr. Jekyll and Mr. Hyde, Flamingo Feather, Food of the Gods, Frenzy, Hamlet, In Another Country, The Knave of Newgate, The Lodger, Mary Deare, Mary Rose, No Bail for the Judge, The Short Night, The Three Hostages,* and *Unknown Man #89.*

The next largest gruop of files contains information on different aspects of Hitchcock's career, such as awards, fan mail, guilds and unions, organizations, personal appearances, and writers. These files also contain information on various people with whom Hitchcock collaborated as well as some personal correspondence.

A small group of files covers Hitchcock's television shows; these files contain information on scripts for the lead-ins, four scripts for produced shows, story material submitted for consideration, and financial information about Shamley Productions. There is little concerning the actual productions or credits.

Other files in the collection include story material and screenplays submitted to Hitchcock's office from the late 1930s to the mid-1960s; copies of Hitchcock's speeches from the 1950s to the 1970s; interview transcripts and correspondence regarding interviews, including an extensive exchange with François Truffaut; correspondence regarding tributes held at the Museum of Modern Art, Cinémathèque Française, the American Film Institute, and other institutions; publicity, including newspaper clippings, magazine articles, and correspondence; appointment books; oversized material that includes sketches of hairstyles for *Vertigo* (1958) and *Marnie* (1964); periodicals, including *Alfred Hitchcock's Mystery Magazine;* books, including collections of short stories using Hitchcock's name; audio tapes of story conferences for films of the 1960s and of Hitchcock's interviews with Truffaut; record albums of theme songs from films, radio spots, and interviews; and awards. The library also has large general files that contain related information.

District of Columbia

971 Motion Picture, Broadcasting and Recorded Sound Division
Library of Congress
Washington, D.C. 20540 U.S.A.
Telephone: 202-707-1000
Hours of service: Monday through Friday, 8:30 A.M. to 4:30 P.M.
Fees: None
Access policy: Students and scholars only
Prints: 35mm: *Family Plot* (1976), *Frenzy* (1972), *The Birds* (1963), *Topaz* (1969), *Torn Curtain* (1966), *Marnie* (1964), *Psycho* (1960), *North by Northwest* (1959), *The Wrong Man* (1956), *To Catch a Thief* (1954), *Dial M for Murder* (1954), *I Confess* (1953), *Strangers on a Train* (1951), *Stage Fright* (1949), *Rope* (1948), *The Paradine Case* (1947), *Notorious* (1946), *Spellbound* (1945), *Lifeboat* (1944), *Shadow of a Doubt* (1943), *Suspicion* (1941), *Mr. and Mrs. Smith* (1941), *Jamaica Inn* (1939), *Sabotage* (1936), *Secret Agent* (1936), *The Man Who Knew Too Much* (1934), *The Lodger* (1926), *Easy Virtue* (1927), *The 39 Steps* (1935)

New York

972 Film Department
International Museum of Photography at George Eastman House
900 East Avenue
Rochester, NY 14607, U.S.A.
Telephone: 716-271-3361, FAX: 716-271-3970
Contact: Dr. Paolo Cherchi Usai
Hours of service: Tuesday through Friday, 10 A.M. to 5 P.M.
Fees: $5 per hour for Steenbeck machines. Screening rooms also available upon request. No charge for research on related material.
Access policy: Reservations should be made at least four weeks in advance.
Prints: All prints are 16mm: *Murder!* (1930), *The Man Who Knew Too Much* (1934), *The 39 Steps* (1935), *Sabotage* (1936), *Young and Innocent* (1937), *Foreign Correspondent* (1940)
Other material: Research is required to cull appropriate stills from the collection of over 4.5 million. Contact Ms. Robin Blair Bolger at the Film Stills Archive for more information.

973 Film Study Center
Museum of Modern Art
11 West 53rd St.
New York, NY 10019, U.S.A.
Telephone: 212-708-9613
Contact: Charles Silver, Director
Hours of service: Call for appointment
Fees: From $12, depending on type of print

Access policy: Open to serious scholars only

Prints: Prints marked (c) are in the Circulating collection. *The Lodger* (1926) (c), *Downhill* (1927), *Blackmail* (1929) (c), *The Man Who Knew Too Much* (1934), *The 39 Steps* (1935), *Sabotage* (1936) (c), *Secret Agent* (1936), *The Lady Vanishes* (1938), *Foreign Correspondent* (1940), *Rebecca* (1940), *Lifeboat* (1944), *Spellbound* (1945), *Notorious* (1946), *The Paradine Case* (1947), *Under Capricorn* (1949) (c), *Vertigo* (1957)

Scripts: *Rear Window* (1954), release dialogue script dated June 21, 1954; *The Man Who Knew Too Much* (1956), final draft screenplay plus revisions dated May 7, 1955; *Vertigo* (1957), screenplay dated September 12, 1957; *North by Northwest* (1959), shooting script dated August 12, 1958

Texas

974   Film, Harry Ransom Humanties Research Center
University of Texas
PO Box 7219
Austin, Texas 87813, U.S.A.

Telephone: 512-471-9119, FAX: 512-471-9646
Contact: Charles Bell
Hours of service: 8:30 A.M. to 4:30 P.M., Monday through Friday
Access policy: Call for appointment
Other material: Papers of David O. Selznick and Ernest Lehman

Utah

975   Manuscript Department, Harold B. Lee Library
Brigham Young University
Provo, Utah 84602, U.S.A.

Telephone: 801-378-6371
Contact: Jim D'Arc
Prints: 16mm prints: *Rope* (1948), *Rear Window* (1954) (in the Jimmy Stewart Collection)

Wisconsin

976   Film and Manuscripts Archive
Wisconsin Center for Film and Theater Research
State Historical Society of Wisconsin
816 State St.
Madison, Wisconsin 53706, U.S.A.

Contact: Maxine Ducey
Hours of service: Under revision at time of publication.
Access policy: Film prints for use on site only

Prints: 16mm: *The Lodger* (1926), *The Man Who Knew Too Much* (1934), *The 39 Steps* (1935), *Young and Innocent* (1937), *The Lady Vanishes* (1938), *Jamaica Inn* (1939), *Mr. and Mrs. Smith* (1941), *Suspicion* (1941), *Strangers on a Train* (1951), *The Wrong Man* (1956)

Scripts: 3 versions of *Strangers on a Train,* all dated 1950

Other material: Stills from and portraits of "most major films and personalities." Trailers for *The Man Who Knew Too Much* (1934) and *Frenzy* (1972)

VIII

16MM FILM DISTRIBUTORS IN THE UNITED STATES

Home video versions of all the American films and many of the British ones are generally available. Check your local video outlet or one of the several videocassette directories. The following is a list of rental films; in some cases 35mm prints, sale prints, or videos are also offered. Several of the titles, in particular some of the silent films that are otherwise not available in the United States, are available in excerpted or condensed versions. Check with the individual distributor.

977   Biograph Entertainment, Ltd.
       300 Phillips Park Rd.
       Mamaroneck, NY 10543
Telephone: 914-381-5570
Films: *Blackmail* (1929), *Easy Virtue* (1927), *Foreign Correspondent* (1940), *The Lady Vanishes* (1938), *The Lodger* (1926), *The Man Who Knew Too Much* (1934), *Murder!* (1930), *Number Seventeen* (1932), *Sabotage* (1936), *Secret Agent* (1936), *The 39 Steps* (1935), *Young and Innocent* (1937)

978   Budget Films
       4590 Santa Monica Blvd.
       Los Angeles, CA 90029
Telephone: 213-660-0187
Films: *Blackmail* (1929), *Easy Virtue* (1927), *Jamaica Inn* (1939), *The Lady Vanishes* (1938), *The Lodger* (1926), *The Man Who Knew Too Much* (1934),

The Manxman (1928), *Murder!* (1930), *Number Seventeen* (1932), *Notorious* (1946), *The Paradine Case* (1947), *Sabotage* (1936), *Secret Agent* (1936), *Spellbound* (1945), *The 39 Steps* (1935), *Under Capricorn* (1949), *Young and Innocent* (1937)

979   Em Gee Film Library
        6924 Canby Ave. Suite 103
        Reseda, CA 91335
Telephone: 818-981-5506
Films: *Blackmail* (1929), *Easy Virtue* (1927), *Foreign Correspondent* (1940), *Jamaica Inn* (1939), *The Lady Vanishes* (1938), *The Lodger* (1926), *The Man Who Knew Too Much* (1934), *The Manxman* (1928), *Murder!* (1930), *Number Seventeen* (1932), *The Ring* (1927), *Sabotage* (1936), *Secret Agent* (1936), *The 39 Steps* (1935), *Young and Innocent* (1937)

980   Films, Incorporated
        5547 N. Ravenswood Ave.
        Chicago, Ill. 60640
Telephone: 800-323-4222
Films: *Easy Virtue* (1927), *The Lady Vanishes* (1938), *Lifeboat* (1944), *The Manxman* (1928), *Mr. and Mrs. Smith* (1941), *Murder!* (1930), *Sabotage* (1936), *Secret Agent* (1936), *Stage Fright* (1949), *Suspicion* (1941), *The 39 Steps* (1935), *To Catch a Thief* (1954)

981   Ivy Films
        725 Providence Rd. Suite 204
        Charlotte, NC 28207
Telephone: 704-333-3991
Films: *Blackmail* (1929), *Dial M for Murder* (1954), *Foreign Correspondent* (1940), *Jamaica Inn* (1939), *The Lady Vanishes* (1938), *The Lodger* (1926), *The Man Who Knew Too Much* (1934), *Murder!* (1930), *Notorious* (1946), *The 39 Steps* (1935)

982   Kit Parker Films
        P.O. Box 16022
        Monterey, CA 93942
Telephone: 800-538-5838
Films: *Blackmail* (1929), *Dial M for Murder* (1954), *Easy Virtue* (1927), *Foreign Correspondent* (1940), *The Lady Vanishes* (1938), *The Lodger* (1926), *The Man Who Knew Too Much* (1934), *The Manxman* (1928), *Murder!* (1930), *Number Seventeen* (1932), *Sabotage* (1936), *Secret Agent* (1936), *The 39 Steps* (1935), *Under Capricorn* (1949), *Young and Innocent* (1937)

983   Museum of Modern Art
       Circulating Film Library
       11 West 53rd St.
       New York, NY 10019
Telephone: 212-708-9530
Films: *Blackmail* (1929), *The Lodger* (1926), *Sabotage* (1936), *Under Capricorn* (1949)

984   Swank Motion Pictures
       201 S. Jefferson Ave.
       St. Louis, MO 63166
Telephone: 800-434-1560
Films: *The Birds* (1963), *Blackmail* (1929), *Dial M for Murder* (1954), *Family Plot* (1976), *The Farmer's Wife* (1928), *Frenzy* (1972), *I Confess* (1953), *The Man Who Knew Too Much* (1934), *The Man Who Knew Too Much* (1955), *Marnie* (1964), *Psycho* (1960), *Rear Window* (1954), *Rich and Strange* (1932), *The Ring* (1927), *Rope* (1948), *Saboteur* (1942), *Shadow of a Doubt* (1943), *Stage Fright* (1949), *Strangers on a Train* (1951), *The Trouble with Harry* (1954), *Topaz* (1969), *Torn Curtain* (1966), *Vertigo* (1957), *The Wrong Man* (1956)

INDEX OF FILMOGRAPHY

Titles, names in credits, and subjects in synopses, indexed by entry number in chapters III and VI.

INDEX OF BIBLIOGRAPHY, ARCHIVES, AND DISTRIBUTORS

Authors and subjects, indexed by entry number in chapters IV, V, VII, and VIII.